THE GROSSET
WEBSTER
DICTIONARY

THE GROSSET
WEBSTER
DICTIONARY

Edited by
**Charles P. Chadsey and Harold Wentworth
with a staff of language experts**

Publishers · GROSSET & DUNLAP · New York
A FILMWAYS COMPANY

ISBN: 0-448-16264-4
Copyright © 1978, 1970, 1966, 1957, 1953, 1951, 1949, 1947
by Grosset & Dunlap, Inc.
Published simultaneously in Canada.
Printed in the United States of America.
(Originally published as *Words: The New Dictionary*)

CONTENTS

EDITORS' NOTES

NOTE ON PRONUNCIATION

THE GROSSET WEBSTER DICTIONARY presents a pronunciation system which eliminates completely the bothersome diacritical marks found in many dictionaries. Each word for which pronunciation is necessary is respelled in the closest approximation to the most common values of English vowels and consonants. The stressed syllable is printed in *italic* type. Thus, for the word **advantageous** the following pronunciation is given:

ad-van-*tay*-jus

Say it aloud and place emphasis on the *tay* syllable. The word pronounces itself.

WHAT THE GROSSET WEBSTER DICTIONARY CONTAINS

In this book, you will find that each entry has the proper or accepted spelling of the word, and perhaps an alternative spelling, with the first spelling preferable. It has the pronunciation of the word and, in addition, divides it into syllables phonetically transcribed by a new and easy system to make correct pronunciation automatic. The part of speech of the word is indicated. Then follow the definitions of the word—the most generally accepted meanings, then those drawn from such various fields as commerce or business, or from law, medicine, or science. And, finally, special attention may be given to less familiar or colloquial and informal uses of the word. In other words, each entry, plus any cross references which the editors of the dictionary believe to be important for your knowledge, study, and use, constitutes a complete and final definition of the word and one upon which you can depend.

Besides the "dictionary habit," you must have the "word habit," the desire to know the definition of a word, to know more about it, and to want to *use* the word. It is unfortunately true that we are not born with words: they are not given to us. We have to *want* more words, to want to use *better* words, and to use them correctly.

First of all, we must become "word conscious," aware of a word that we do not know or are not exactly sure of, when we hear it. In other words, we must learn to hear the words that are new to us. Secondly, we must become equally aware of new words when they appear in our reading—not only aware of them, but also irritated with ourselves that we do not already know the true meaning or definition of the word we have met.

Once we have become "word conscious" and acquired the "dictionary habit," the other steps are routine, though none the less important. We hear or we see a word we do not know and we are uncomfortable until we look it up. However, even the best trained memory can be lazy and prone to slough off the responsibility for looking up a word. As a safeguard it is advisable always to carry a small notebook, or a piece of paper or an envelope on which the new word can be jotted down. At the same time it helps to jot down the *way* it was used, for the use which you heard or saw may actually extend the idea which the word symbolizes in a radically new and yet acceptable direction from that given by your dictionary.

Write the word down. Look it up. Then what? It has been often said, and experience demonstrates that *a word used three times belongs to you forever*. Therefore, study the dictionary definition and information about the word briefly, but thoroughly. Then *use* the word. Use it mentally; feel it on your tongue; savor it. Say it aloud to yourself. Then, though it may appear strange to you at first, use the word deliberately in your conversation or in your writing. There are, of course, abstract words which cannot be used easily in your daily speech or writing. These you should practice aloud until they are at least a part of your latent or understood vocabulary—the portion of your vocabulary that enables you to read and listen with intelligence, though you seldom make use of the words yourself.

As a beginning, try the pronunciation quiz below. The words are all to be found in our daily newspapers, in our weekly magazines, or in the talks of radio commentators. They are all words with which we should be familiar to a degree, certainly words that we should know thoroughly if we have the "word habit" and make frequent use of the dictionary.

Now, use the words you did *not* know as the foundation of your own "dictionary habit." Look them up; learn them; use them frequently. Make them a part of *your* new vocabulary. This will be your first step toward really effective speech and writing.

But this, of course, is just a beginning. Go on from there and pin down *every* word you come across. Then, with the help of this practical, modern dictionary, you can make those words your invaluable tools for the rest of your life.

HOW DO YOU PRONOUNCE THESE WORDS?

Check your pronunciation of these words against the simple respellings used as a pronunciation guide in the dictionary.

1. attache (at-ash-*ay*)
2. bayou (*by*-oo)
3. brougham (*broom*)
4. chimera (kuh-*mihr*-uh)
5. cloisonné (*kloy*-suh-nay)
6. coccyx (*kok*-siks)
7. commandant (kom-un-*dant*)
8. concerto (kun-*chehr*-toh)
9. coupon (*koo*-pon)
10. crescendo (kruh-*shen*-doh)
11. cyclotron (*syke*-luh-tron)
12. daiquiri (*dak*-er-ee)
13. detonate (*det*-uh-nayt)
14. entrepreneur (ahn-truh-pruh-*ner*)
15. flaccid (*flak*-sid)
16. genocide (*jen*-oh-syde)
17. ignoramus (ig-nuh-*ray*-mus)
18. indict (in-*dyte*)
19. intermezzo (in-ter-*met*-soh)
20. irrevocable (ih-*rev*-uh-kuh-b'l)
21. jocose (joh-*kohss*)
22. machination (mak-ih-*nay*-shun)
23. mausoleum (maw-soh-*lee*-um)
24. mischievous (*miss*-chiv-us)
25. obsequious (ob-*see*-kwee-us)
26. often (*awf*-'n)
27. phlegm (*flem*)
28. prelude (*prel*-yood)
29. puerile (*pyoo*-er-il)
30. renaissance (ren-uh-*sahnss*)

HOW WORDS CHANGE

The English language is constantly changing. Over the years, many words already in our vocabulary acquire new meanings, and many new words enter our language annually. The creation of new words is influenced by developments in science, medicine, and technology, as well as by political changes in the world. Many new words that start out as slang become a part of our vocabulary, as do words or expressions used on popular television or radio shows. This section of THE GROSSET WEBSTER DICTIONARY will enable you to understand how rapidly our language is changing—all of the words appearing below entered our language a relatively short time ago.

ab·la·tion (ab-*lay*-shun) *n. Aerospace.* The evaporation, vaporization, or melting of a solid surface, esp. by friction.

abominable snowman. A creature of indefinite size and description reported to inhabit the Himalayas and other remote regions. Also called **yeti.**

a·bort (uh-*bort*) *v.* To terminate or abandon, as a space flight or rocket launching; to fail or go wrong. *n.* The act or process of aborting; a failure.

acid rock *n.* A form of rock 'n' roll music in which sound and lyrics are suggestive of psychedelic experiences or drug-taking.

ac·ro·nym (*ak*-roh-nim) *n.* A word composed of the initial letters or syllables in a phrase or title, as UNRRA for United Nations Relief and Rehabilitation Administration.

advance man. An assistant to a political candidate who makes pre-arrival arrangements for meetings and demonstrations of support for the candidate.

aer·o·dy·nam·ics (air-oh-dy-*nam*-iks) *n.* The branch of physics dealing with the motion of gases, especially air, and the effects of such motion on aerospace vehicles. —**aer·o·dy·nam·ic** *adj.*

aer·o·dyne (*air*-oh-dyn) *n.* Any aircraft that is heavier than air.

aer·o·em·bo·lism (air-oh-*em*-buh-liz-'m) *n.* A severe illness characterized by the formation of nitrogen gas bubbles in the blood and body tissues, caused by a sudden decrease in air pressure. It may affect tunnel workers, divers, and aviators.

aer·o·med·i·cine (air-oh-*med*-ih-sin) *n.* The branch of medicine dealing with the effects of flying within the earth's atmosphere. Also called **aviation medicine.**

aer·o·sol bomb (*air*-uh-sol) A spraying can holding under gas pressure a liquid or emulsion such as a paint, deodorant, etc.

aer·o·space (*air*-oh-spayss) *n.* The earth's atmosphere and the space outside it considered as a single region with respect to the launching and guidance of rockets, missiles, and spacecraft.

aerospace medicine. The branch of medicine dealing with the effects of flying through the earth's atmosphere or in outer space.

afro *n.* A full, bushy way of wearing the hair that is fashioned after an African style.

af·ter·bur·ner *n.* A device that by injecting fuel in a jet engine exhaust produces more thrust.

Age of Aquarius. An era described by astrologers as marking the advent of freedom in all areas of life, the rule of brotherhood on earth, and the conquest of outer space.

airbag. A sturdy plastic bag stored in an automobile dashboard and designed to inflate immediately upon impact to form a protective cushion.

air•foil (*air*-foyl) n. *Aeronautics*. A surface of an aircraft, such as wing, rudder, propeller, designed to produce an intended force in airflow.

air lift. System of transport and supply entirely by airplane, particularly when surface routes are blocked.

air pollution. The contamination of the air by smoke, fuel exhausts, noxious vapors and gases from industrial waste, and by radioactive fallout.

air rights. The right to use the open space above an existing building or other fixed installation, obtained by purchase or lease, as for a landing strip for helicopters, etc.

air•strip n. A level plot of land prepared for the use of airplanes in landing and taking off.

alpha particle. Positively charged nucleus of helium atom. Also called **alpha ray.**

alternative society. A society representing cultural values other than those of the present social order.

American Dream. A catchphrase for the ideal of democracy, equality, and freedom upon which the United States was founded; the American way of life.

an•dros•ter•one (an-*dros*-ter-ohn) n. A male sex hormone.

an•gel n. One who subsidizes an enterprise removed from his customary business interests, esp. a theatrical production.

angry young man. One of group of young British writers, artists, and intellectuals who are vehement in their disapproval of contemporary western civilization.

an•ti•bi•ot•ic (an-tee-by-*ot*-ik) *adj*. Having the power to destroy bacteria in the body; descriptive of drugs, like penicillin, developed from mold.—**an•ti•bi•ot•ic** n.

an•ti•his•ta•mine n. One of a family of drugs which act to neutralize symptoms of the common cold, hay fever, etc.

an•ti•mat•ter (*an*-ti-mat-er) n. *Physics*. Matter having the same appearance and structure as ordinary matter, but with opposite charges in its particles.

an•ti•par•ti•cle (*an*-ti-pahr-ti-k'l) n. *Physics*. Any of a group of elementary particles constituting antimatter. When such particles fuse with regular particles they annihilate one another and release energy.

an•ti•pov•er•ty n. A program designed to combat poverty, particularly such a program sponsored by the government.

a•par•theid (uh-*parr*-tate) n. South African Nationalist party doctrine of segregation of racial groups.

aq•ua•lung (*ak*-wuh-lung) n. A diving apparatus consisting of a compressed-air tank and hose connection worn strapped to the back for breathing underwater with a mouthpiece; scuba.

aq•ua•naut n. A person engaged in underwater exploration and research.

ar•col•o•gy (ar-*kol*-o-gee) n. A completely integrated planned city or environment within a single structure.

area code. A three-digit code number preceding a telephone number which designates one of approximately 150 telephone areas in the U.S. and Canada. It is used in dialing between areas.

art deco. A style of decorative design characterized by ornateness, asymmetry, geometrical forms, and bold colors.

artificial satellite. A satellite of the earth, the sun, the moon, or a planet, placed into orbit by man.

as•ta•tine (*az*-tuh-teen) n. [from Greek *astatos*, unstable] *Chemistry*. The only element of the halogens without stable isotopes or varieties.

as•tro•ga•tion (as-troh-*gay*-shun) n. The science of navigation in space.

as•tro•naut (*as*-truh-nawt) n. A person who is trained to fly or navigate through space.

as•tro•nau•tics (as-truh-*naw*-tiks) n. The science of designing, building, and operating space vehicles.

astronomical unit. The average distance between the sun and the earth, equal to 92,897,000 miles, used to express distances in astronomy.

as•tro•phys•ics (as-troh-*fiz*-iks) n. The branch of astronomy dealing with the physical and chemical properties of heavenly bodies.

atomic age. Period in world development inaugurated by the first public demonstration of atomic energy, August 6, 1945.

atomic diplomacy. Power diplomacy backed by the threat of the atom bomb.

atomic power. Thermal power produced in nuclear reactor or power plant.

atomic waste. Radioactive ash produced by nuclear fission, as in a nucler reactor.

atom smasher. *Colloquial*. A cyclotron.

attaché case. A flat, rigid type of brief case with a hinged cover, for carrying papers, documents, etc.

au•di•o•lin•gual (*aw*-dee-oh-*ling*-wool) *adj*. Involving the use of hearing and speech instead of written or printed material.

au•di•o•phile (*aw*-dee-oh-fyl) n. An enthusiast of high-fidelity sound reproduction.

au•di•o•vis•u•al (*aw*-dee-oh-*viz*-yoo-ul) *adj*. Pertaining to the use of recordings, films, television, etc., as supplementary to books in aiding education.

av•gas (*av*-gass) n. Aviation gasoline, a high-octane variety used in aircraft.

aviation medicine. Aeromedicine.

a•vi•on•ics (ay-vee-*on*-iks) n. The application of electronics to aviation, aeronautics, rocketry, and missilry.

back·lash *n.* A reaction of antagonism to pressure exerted by a group or movement.

back-pack *v.* To carry, as food or equipment, on one's back on a camping trip.

bacterial warfare. A technique of waging war by releasing disease-carrying bacteria in territory occupied by an enemy.

bag *n. U.S. Slang.* One's principal interest or habit.

balance of payments. A monetary surplus or deficit after all transactions (imports, exports, investments, tourist spending, etc.) between one country and another are balanced.

ball.—have a ball *Colloquial.* To have a gay time; enjoy oneself.

ballistic missile. Any missile that utilizes reaction propulsion as a power source. It is normally guided by external or internal means during the first portion of its flight, and then follows a trajectory determined by gravitational and atmospheric drag forces after launch power is cut off.

bar·bi·tu·rate (bahr-bih-*tyoor*-ate)*n.* Derivative of barbituric acid used as a soporific and hypnotic.

bar·i·at·rics (baer i *at* riks)*n.* The medical treatment of overweight people.

beam.—off the beam *Slang.* Wrong; mistaken —**on the beam** *Slang.* Right; correct.

beat *adj. Slang.* Of beatniks or their ways.

beat generation. A post-World War II generation of bohemian artists, writers, intellectuals, and their sympathizers who dissociate themselves from contemporary culture and often affect bizarre habits of dress and personal grooming.

beat-nik (*beet*-nik) *n.* One of the beat generation.

Beautiful People. The wealthy, fashionable people of high society and the arts who set the trends in fashion, beauty and elegance.

belly tank. An extra gasoline tank secured to the underside of an airplane so that it may be dropped when empty.

bet·a·tron (*bet*-uh-tron) *n.* An apparatus for accelerating the speed of electrons to a point where they become known as beta rays. It is used in atomic research and development.

Big Brother. A person or government agency that keeps persons under constant surveillance, as the dictator in George Orwell's novel *1984.*

bi·o·de·grad·a·ble (by-o-dee-*grade*-abul) *Adj.* Able to be decomposed by biological agents, especially bacteria.

bi·o·feed·back *n.* A system of brain wave monitoring which allows a person to attempt to control and maintain particular mental states.

biological warfare. A technique of waging war by releasing disease germs, bacteria, etc., in territory occupied by an enemy.

bi·on·ics (bai-*on*-iks) *n.* The science of applying the formation of various biological structures to problems of engineering in electronics, construction, computer programming, etc.

bi·o·te·lem·e·try. *n.* The monitoring of vital functions of a person or animal and the transmission of the data to a distant point for analysis by electronic instruments.

bi·sex·u·al *ajd.* Sexually attracted to or involved with both sexes.

bit *n. Slang.* An instance of some familiar activity, taken to resemble a stage routine, and applied jocularly or sarcastically to anything.

black body. *Physics.* A body or surface that absorbs all the radiation falling on it.

black box. Any component, usually electronic, that can be readily inserted into, or removed from, a specific place in a larger system without knowledge of its detailed internal structure.

Black Muslim. A member of a religious body of blacks who embrace the teachings of Islam and wish to separate themselves from white western culture.

black nationalism. A movement for identifying all black people as a nation or a group separate from the influence of white people.

Black Panther Party. An organization of black Americans seeking to establish black power in the United States by extreme militancy.

black power. Power of black Americans to establish their rights by collective action.

blast·off *n. Slang.* The launching of a missile or rocket; liftoff.

bleed *v. Photoengraving.* To trim a page so as to cut into engraved or printed material.

bleeding heart. *Slang.* A person who is regarded by others as overly sympathetic, esp. to criminals and juvenile delinquents.

blip *n.* A spot of light or other indicator on a radar screen indicating the relative position of a reflecting object such as a missile in flight.

blitz *n. Football.* The defensive maneuver of rushing the quarterback to upset him or the timing of his play, esp. done by linebackers.

block booking. *Motion Pictures.* Practice of requiring a theater owner to book a complete group (**block**) of pictures in order to show one of the group.

block busting. The practice by unscrupulous real-estate brokers of scaring homeowners into selling their homes for fear that members of a minority group may move into the block and reduce property values.

blous·on (bloo-*zon*) *n. Fashion.* A one-or two-piece dress gathered at the waist and billowed fully above the waist.

body language. The unconscious gestures and postures of the body as a form of communication.

boiler room. *Slang.* A place where shady operators solicit the sale of unlisted and highly speculative securities by telephone.

bone-seek·er *n.* Radioactive element or radiation which lodges in the bones of a body.

boob tube. *Slang.* Television.

book·mo·bile (*book*-moh-beel) *n.* A panel truck that carries books to communities as a service of certain public libraries.

boost·er *n.* Radio transmitter at a distance from source transmitter, used to relay signals to greater distances. Also called **relay station.**

boost·er *n.* An auxiliary engine used in launching a rocket or missile to give it sufficient thrust. It then breaks away or burns off.

booster shot. An inoculation repeated to provide continuing immunization against disease.

borscht circuit. *Colloquial.* Hotels in the Catskills noted for Jewish cuisine and as proving grounds for budding entertainers.

bou·tique (boo-*teek*) *n.* A retail specialty shop for women.

brain drain. The emigration of scientists, scholars, etc. to countries that offer better job opportunities.

brain·wash·ing *n.* Intensive, subtly persuasive indoctrination by which a person is made to renounce cherished beliefs and adopt contrary ones. —**brain·wash** *v.*

braless *adj.* Favoring the discard of brassieres as a symbol of women's liberation.

brass *n.* [from the metal insignia worn by officers] *Military Slang.* Officers, regarded as a class or caste. 'The top brass.'

brink·man·ship *n.* The delicate strategy of pursuing a foreign policy to the very edge of war without actually entering into armed conflict.

brother *n.* Afro-American use: 1. A fellow black; a soul brother. 2. Any black man.

buff *n.* An enthusiast or devotee, as of a certain sport, hobby, or other consuming interest.

bug *v. Slang.* 1. To bother; annoy; irritate. 2. To equip with a hidden microphone or transmitter. *n. Slang.* An enthusiast. A concealed microphone or transmitter.

bull session. *Slang.* Any informal discussion on a wide range of topics, as between students in a dormitory.

bummer *n. U.S. Slang.* 1. A disappointment. 2. A bad experience.

bumper sticker *n.* A sticker bearing a printed slogan for display on an automobile bumper.

bur·gle (*ber*-g'l) *v. Slang.* Burglarize.

burn *n.* 1. *Theater.* A piece of comedy business involving exaggerated portrayal of outrage, impotent anger. 2. *Astronautics.* The firing of a rocket engine.

burn·out *n.* 1. The cessation of fuel combustion in a rocket engine when the fuel is exhausted or its flow is cut off. 2. The point in the trajectory of a rocket at which this occurs.

cabin fever. *Slang.* Nervous tension or eccentricity resulting from confinement or isolation.

call girl. *Slang.* A harlot whose assignations are negotiated by telephone.

cal·u·tron (*kal*-yoo-tron— *n.* [from *Cali*fornia University cyclo*tron*]. An electrical machine for the classification of atoms on the basis of differences in their weights.

camp *n.* Anything so exaggerated, banal, mediocre, or outmoded that it is considered clever or amusing because of its unsophisticated artistic quality. — **campy** *adj.*

camper. A vehicle equipped with a stove, bunks, and often bathroom facilities for travel and camping out.

Cap·com (*kap*-kom) *n.* Acronym for *Capsule Communicator.* The person at a space flight center who communicates with the astronauts during a space flight.

cap·sule *n.* A small, sealed pressurized cabin with a suitable environment for carrying a man or animal on extremely high-altitude flights, orbital space flight, or for use as an emergency escape device.

captive audience. Audience, as in a restaurant, bus, or streetcar, which has no alternative to listening to a broadcast.

car·cin·o·ge·nic·i·ty (kar-sin-o-ji-*nis*-i-tee) *n.* The property or tendency of a substance to produce cancer.

car·di·o·ver·sion (kard-eē-o-*ver*-zhon) *n.* Restoration of normal heartbeat by using electric shock.

car pool. A group of people who pool their automobiles for collective use, in order to conserve gasoline, tires, etc.

car·port. *n* A roofed, open-sided structure attached to the side of a house, used as a shelter for automobiles.

car·ry-all *n.* A motor vehicle similar to a station wagon but higher, with seats along the sides, for transportation and hauling.

cas·sette (ka-*set*) *n* A small cartridge of magnetic-tape reels that can be inserted into a tape recorder for automatic playback and recording.

cathode ray screen. *Television.* Luminescent inner surface of cathode-ray tube used to reproduce television pictures.

cathode-ray tube. *Television.* Vacuum tube in which a grid controls the flow of electrons; kinescope, iconoscope, etc. are cathode-ray tubes.

cell *n. Politics.* A small militant division of large organization.

centerfold *n.* An illustrated center spread that is so long it is folded into a magazine or book, and has to be unfolded to be seen in full.

chain reaction. A series, esp. of nuclear fissions, in which each reaction actuates other reactions with the result that the series is self-sustaining.

chairperson. A person who presides at a meeting.

chan·nel *n.* 1. A wave band having a certain assigned frequency range over which radio or television signals, programs, etc., are transmitted. 2. A television station having such an assigned frequency.

cha·ris·ma (ka-*riz*-ma) *n.* Strong personal appeal or magnetism, especially applied to political candidates.

chem·o·sphere (*kem*-oh-sfeer) *n.* A region of the atmosphere between the stratosphere and the ionosphere, marked by great photo-chemical activity due to the sun's radiation.

Chi·ca·no (chee-*ka*-no) *n.* A person of Mexican birth or descent living in the United States.

chop·per *n. Slang.* A helicopter.

Cin·e·ma·Scope *n.* Trademark of a motion-picture process that uses a special type of lens to project a three-dimensional, panoramic image on a wide, curved screen.

Cin·er·a·ma *n.* Trademark of a process for projection of specially prepared motion-picture films onto a curved screen, giving a tridimensional effect.

clean *adj.* Producing very little radioactive fall-out: said of certain atomic or thermonuclear bombs.

clear air turbulence. A violent disturbance in air currents, caused by rapid changes of temperature associated with the jet stream and characterized by severe updrafts and downdrafts that affect jet aircraft flying at high altitudes. *Abbreviation:* CAT.

clone (klone) *v.* To reproduce or propogate asexually, producing genetically identical organisms. *n.* The offspring so produced.

closed·circuit television. Television transmitted by wire or cable and not broadcast over the air, directed to a select audience, as in a school or theater.

closet homosexual. A person who hides his or her homosexuality.

cloud chamber. *Physics.* A device for detecting charged nuclear particles by the formation of minute droplets along their tracks in a saturated vapor, used for the study of particle behavior.

clo·ver·leaf *n.* A traffic interchange in which the ramps form the pattern of a four-leaf clover.

coffee-table book. An oversized, expensive, and richly illustrated book, usually dealing with a specialized subject and designed for display on a coffee table or the like.

cold war. Hostility and tension between Communist and non-Communist states expressed politically, economically, diplomatically, rather than militarily.

com·bo (*kom*-boh) *n. Slang.* A small jazz band.

comfort station. A public toilet.

command module. The unit or section of a spacecraft which contains the control center and living quarters.

common market. An association of countries as a single economic unit with internal free trade and common external tariffs.

com·mune (*kom*-yune) *n.* A place where anyone can stay for a night, a week, or as long as he wants, living with others like himself and usually sharing work or expenses with other members.

communications gap. The inability to receive or pass on information, because of personal differences, especially between age groups, economic classes, political factions, or cultural groups.

com·pact (*kom*-pakt) *n.* An automobile compactly built by American standards, designed for fuel economy and ease of handling and parking. In full, **compact car.**

com·put·er (kum-*pyoo*-t'r) *n.* Any of various mechanical or electric, esp. electronic, machines for the high-speed solution of complex mathematical problems and the storage and retrieval of data.

computer dating. Match-making by computer programmed to match characteristics of interested men and women according to prescribed types.

condensation trail. A visible trail of water droplets or ice crystals left by an aircraft or missile in flight. Also **vapor trail.**

con·do·min·i·um (kan-da-*min*-ee-em) *n.* An apartment house in which each apartment is bought and owned individually as if it were a house.

con·glom·er·ate (kun-*glom*-uh-rayt) *n.* A business organization formed by the merger of companies producing diverse products or services.

consciousness-raising *n.* A gaining or producing a wider awareness of one's condition, needs, motives, etc. as a means to achieving full potential as a person.

con·sole (*kon*-sohl) *n.* A panel of switches, dials, and indicators used to control the operation of electronic equipment, rockets, guided missiles, etc.

con·sum·er·ism (kon-*sue*-mer-iz-em) *n.* Public demand for greater safety and quality in consumer products; popular opposition to unsafe or defective goods.

contact lens. A lens of clear glass fitted directly over the cornea.

con·trail *n.* Short form of *condensation trail.*

control rod. Rod introduced into nuclear reactor to control chain reaction.

convenience food. Canned, quick-frozen, dehydrated or other prepackaged food that is easy to prepare.

cool *adj. Slang.* 1. Excellent; great; first-rate. 2. Relaxed and sophisticated, as certain styles of modern jazz.

cop out *v. U.S. Slang.* 1. To go back on a commitment; withdraw from involvement. 2. To give up a principle, cause, etc; to compromise.

cop-out. *n.* An act of copping out; retreat; compromise.

cos•mo•naut *(koz-*moh-nawt*) n.* An astronaut.

cos•mo•tron *(koz-*muh-tron*) n.* An apparatus for accelerating the speed of protons to a level of energy that exceeds one billion volts.

count•down *n.* The step-by-step process, beginning before a specified event, of performing designated tasks leading up to the event, with time counted in reverse order from the beginning to the event itself.

coun•ter *n.* Device for detecting presence of nuclear radiation and measuring its intensity. Geiger and Geiger-Mueller (G-M) counters are most commonly used.

counterculture *n.* A group made up of those individuals who have rejected the standards and values of the established society.

crash program. Plan for rushing an important project to completion without regard to expense in manpower or money.

credibility gap. A discrepancy between an individual's public statements and positions and his actual deeds, leading to lack of believability.

cry•o•tron *(kry-*uh-tron*) n.* A tiny electric conductor used instead of a vacuum tube or transistor, as in an electronic computer.

cube (kyoob) *n. Slang.* A cubic inch as a measure of volume of the cylinders in an internal combustion engine.

cy•ber•net•ics (sy-ber-*net*-iks) *n.* The comparative study of the human nervous system and electrical-mechanical communications systems.

cy•borg *(sy-*borg*) n.* A human body or other organism whose functions are taken over in part by various electronic or electro-mechanical devices.

cyc•lo•tron *(syke-*luh-tron*) n.* A high-efficiency radio oscillator developed at the University of California to disintegrate atoms in order to study their internal structure. Research with the cyclotron laid important groundwork for development of the atom bomb.

Da•cron *(day-*kron*) n.* Trademark for a washable, nonwrinkling fabric of synthetic fibers.

da•shi•ki (da-*shee*-kee) *n.* A loose shirtlike pullover garment, originally from Africa, usually shortsleeved and brightly colored.

day-care *adj.* Concerned with the care of preschool children, usually of working mothers, outside their homes.

de•con•tam•i•na•tion (dee-kun-tam-in-*ay*-shun) *n.* Ridding of impurities, esp. of poison gas, or effects of atomic radiation.

de•frost•er *n.* A heating device for melting ice from a part where it impedes the operation of an airplane or automobile.

de•grad•a•ble (de-*grade*-abul) *adj.* Susceptible to chemical decomposition.

delta waves. Large, slow brain waves marking the deepest level of sleep.

de•ox•y•ri•bo•nu•cle•ic acid (dee-*ok*-see-rye-boh-noo-*klee*-ik) *n.* An acid in the genes that is the carrier of genetic information. *Abbreviation:* DNA.

de•seg•re•ga•tion (dee-seg-ruh-*gay*-shun) *n.* The doing away with the practice of segregating whites and blacks, as in schools, housing, and public facilities.

de•struct (dih-*strukt*) *n. Aerospace.* The deliberate destruction of a rocket or missile after launching, esp. as a safety measure.

dé•tente *(day-*tant*) n.* A relaxation of strained relations between nations.

deu•ter•on *(dyoo-*ter-on*) n. Chemistry.* Nucleus of the deuterium atom, consisting of one proton and one neutron.

dig *v. Slang.* To comprehend; to be in rapport with.

dirty *adj.* Producing heavy radioactive fallout: said of certain atomic or thermonuclear bombs.

dis•co•theque (dis-koh-*tek) n.* A dance hall where music is supplied by phonograph records, sometimes by musicians.

dis•solve (dih-*zolv*) *n. Television and Motion Pictures.* A technique by which a picture from one camera suddenly overlaps that of another and gradually replaces it. —**dis•solve** *v.*

DNA. Deoxyribonucleic acid, the main carrier of genetic information in living cells.

dock. *v.* To connect with another orbiting spacecraft. *n.* **docking**

doc•u•men•tar•y (dok-yoo-*men*-tuh-ree) *n.* A motion picture, radio or television program which treats a serious theme factually as well as dramatically.

dol•ly *n.* A low four-wheeled cart for a camera used in motion pictures and television. —*v.* **dolly in** To make a close-up by moving the camera on a dolly toward the subject.

do•sim•e•ter (doh-*sim*-eh-ter) *n.* Instrument to measure radiation dosage.

double helix. Referring to the double helical structure (two strands that coil around each other to form a double spiral or helix) of a molecule of DNA, the carrier of genetic information in the cells.

dou•ble-take *n. Theater.* A piece of comedy business, usually a careless glance followed by a second look, then exaggerated comprehension and surprise.

dou•ble-think (dub-'l think) *n.* The ability to hold and accept two conflicting beliefs at the same time. [coined by George Orwell, English novelist, 1903—1950]

dove. A person who is opposed to war or to a confrontation of force; someone who is willing to negotiate with the enemy instead of making war.

drag chute. A parachute for slowing down the speed of an aircraft, space capsule, etc.

drip-dry *adj.* That can be washed and hung without wringing to dry, and needing little or no ironing, as certain apparel fabrics.

drone (drohn) *n.* An unmanned aircraft piloted by remote control, used for reconnaissance or as a target.

drop-out *n.* A person who withdraws from any segment or institution of established society.

dune buggy. A small, lightweight vehicle designed especially for driving on sand dunes and beaches.

earth sta-tion. A station on earth equipped with electronic apparatus to receive and rebroadcast signals transmitted from outer space.

eco-cide (*eko*-side) *n.* The destruction of the earth's ecology through the uncontrolled use of pollutants.

ecol-o-gy. Any balanced or harmonious system; the branch of science concerned with the interrelationship of organisms and their environments.

egg-head *n. Slang.* An intellectual or a self-styled intellectual, esp. one of liberal political beliefs.

e-kis-tics *n.* The study of communities of people with a view to improving them by extensive planning.

Em-my *n.* An award given by the Academy of Television Arts and Sciences for outstanding achievement in each of the phases of television production.

en-coun-ter group. A group of people taking part in sensitivity training.

en-dan-gered spe-cies. A group of animals threatened with extinction.

en-vi-ron-men-tal art. A form of art that involves the viewer rather than confronting him with a fixed image or object.

earth-shine *n.* The faint illumination of the dark side of the moon by sunlight reflected from the earth's surface.

equal time. 1. Radio or television air time given to a political candidate, party, group, or citizen, to present opposing view to earlier broadcast. 2. An equal opportunity to reply to any charge or opposing view.

escalator clause. A clause in a contract allowing for an increase or decrease in prices, wages, etc. according to change in conditions.

escape velocity. The speed a body must attain to overcome a gravitational field. At the earth's surface it is reckoned at 36,700 feet per second.

Es-tab-lish-ment *n.* 1. The ruling groups or institutions of a country; a nation's power structure. 2. The ruling body of any institution. 3. Conventional society.

ev *v.* Electron volt, unit of energy equal to that gained by a particle of electrical charge accelerated through potential of one volt. *See also* **mev.**

ex-ac-ta (egg-*zakt*-a) *n.* In U.S. horseracing, a method of betting in which the bettor picks the horses to win and to place in the exact order of finish. Also perfecta.

ex-is-ten-tial-ism (eg-ziss-*ten*-sh'l-izm) *n.* Philosophy, current in contemporary French literature, that man can be free only through full consciousness of his illogical position in a meaningless universe.—**ex-is-ten-tial-ist** *n.*

ex-o-bi-ol-o-gy (ek-soh-by-*ol*-uh-jee) *n.* The study of life on planets other than the earth.

ex-o-sphere (*ek*-soh-sfeer) *n.* The outermost layer of the earth's atmosphere, above the ionosphere.

ex-press-way *n.* A divided highway for high-speed travel between distant points.

ex-tra-ter-res-tri-al *n.* A creature from another planet.

ex-ur-ban-ite (eks-*er*-buh-nyte) *n.* A resident of exurbia.

ex-ur-bi-a (eks-er-bee-uh) *n.* A fashionable residential area beyond the suburbs of a city.

fail safe *adj.* 1. Designed to automatically stop or alter an operation in the event of a malfunction. 2. Fool-proof.

fall-out *n.* Radioactive particles in the air or on the ground, resulting from the explosion of an atomic or thermonuclear bomb.

family planning. Regulation or limitation of the size of a family by birth control.

far-out. *adj. U.S. Slang.* Very unconventional; weird.

feed-back *n.* The return to the input of a part of the output of a machine, system, or process. 2. A reciprocal effect of one person or thing upon another.

fem-i-nism. *n.* A doctrine advocating the granting of the same social, political, and economic rights to women as the ones granted to men; also a movement in support of this doctrine and the gaining of such rights. *n., adj.* **feminist.**

fi-ber-glass (*fy*-ber-glas) *n.* 1. A synthetic fiber made of fine, flexible filaments of molten glass, used in insulation, textiles, sporting goods, etc. 2. **Fiberglas** a trademark for this.

fis-sion (*fish*-un) *n.* A splitting apart; specifically the splitting of the nucleus of an atom of an element such as uranium.

fis-sion-a-ble *adj. Physics.* Able to be split or broken up by bombardment with neutrons.

fix *n. Slang.* A narcotic injection, esp. of heroin.

flak . 1. Criticism, censure. 2. A heated argument or quarrel.

flower child. A young teenager carrying a flower as a symbol of love.

flow-sheet *n.* A diagram or chart showing the operations involved in successive stages of an industrial process, computer program, etc.

flying saucer. Any of various phenomena, perhaps illusory, reported as flying through the sky and rumored to be hostile aircraft, space ships, etc.

food stamp. A stamp issued by the U.S. government to recipients of welfare and unemployment benefits with which to purchase food.

For·mi·ca (for-*my*-kuh) *n.* Trademark for a heat-resistant plastic material, used as a table and counter covering, wallboard, paneling, etc.

freak *n. Slang.* 1. Any person who has broken from conventional society. 2. A drug addict. 3. A devotee or enthusiast.

free·way *n.* A divided highway with no intersections at grade level, for high-speed, toll-free travel.

Fre·on (*free*-on) *n.* A trade name for an odorless, colorless gas used in certain mechanical refrigerators.

frisbee (*friz*-bee) *n.* A trade name for a small plastic saucerlike toy that is hurled through the air from one person to another.

front *n.* 1. A powerful movement uniting diverse elements in a struggle for a common goal, esp. political. 2. *Colloquial.* Also **front man.** One who is the nominal head of an organization or movement, giving it prestige or respectability.

Fun City. The nickname for New York City.

funky (*fon*-kee) *adj. Slang.* Fine, excellent. Originally a jazz term meaning earthy, unpretentious.

future shock. A state of stress and disorientation brought on by a quick succession of change in new standards of behavior and values in society.

games·man·ship *n.* The art of winning games or other contests by tricking one's opponent into losing his poise. [coined by Stephen Potter, English author, b. 1900]

game theory. The analysis of situations where a person may win or lose and where strategy is determined by the anticipation of strategy of opposing persons or players.

gan·try (*gan*-tree) *n. Aerospace.* A cranelike structure with platforms at different levels, used to assemble and service large missiles. It is placed over the launching site and rolled away just before firing.

gas *n. U.S. Slang.* Usually **a gas.** A great pleasure; a joy, delight.

Gay Liberation. A U.S. militant movement of homosexuals demanding greater civil rights and protesting discrimination in business, etc.

GCA. Also **ground-controlled approach.** A method, employing radar and radio, for assisting planes to land safely through heavy fog.

Geiger counter (*gy*-ger). [from Hans *Geiger*, German physicist] Device employed to detect the presence of radiation.

gene pool. All the genes contained in the genetic makeup of a particular species.

general semantics. The application of semantic principles to social relations, emphasizing training in the critical use of words and symbols toward the goal of better understanding among persons and societies.

generation gap. The differences in social values,

behaviorial attitudes and personal aspirations between one generation and the next.

genetic code. The biochemical code by which the four bases in the DNA molecule combine to specify the synthesis of particular amino acids and proteins that determine the hereditary characteristics of an organism.

genetic engineering. The scientific alteration of genes or genetic material to produce desirable new traits or to eliminate undesirable ones.

gen·o·cide (*jen*-oh-syde) *n.* [Gr. *genos,* race or clan, & Lat. *caedere,* to kill; coined by R. Lemkin for wording of the official indictment of German war criminals, 1945] 1. The calculated extermination or destruction by invading forces of large sections of the civilian population of occupied territories. 2. The systematic extirpation of racial or religious minority groups by the state.— **gen·o·cid·al** *adj.*

ghost *n. Television.* Obstructive secondary image of transmitted picture resulting from reflection in the receiver kinescope.

gob·ble·dy·gook (*gob*-'l-dee-*gook*) *n. Slang.* Pretentious talk or writing that uses more and longer words than necessary.

go-kart *n.* A small, open, four-wheeled racing car for one person.

gone *adj. Slang.* Hep; okay; the greatest.

goof *v. Slang.* To make a mistake; err; blunder.— **goof off** To shirk work; waste time.

goof·ball *n. Slang.* Any barbiturate taken for its hypnotic or exhilarative effects.

grade labeling. A classification of consumers' goods on a basis of quality.

Great Society. The policies and programs advocated by President Lyndon B. Johnson for the United States.

guided missile. Any projectile or plane which may be guided during flight either by remote-control radio or by built-in mechanism designed to direct it on a predetermined course.

gunboat diplomacy. A policy of using the threat of military intervention to enforce treaties and alliances with other countries.

gu·ru (goo-*roo*) *n.* A spiritual teacher; a leading figure or expert on some field.

hab·i·tat. A marine vessel to house researchers or scientists under water over an extended period of time while they are conducting their work.

hang·up *n. Slang.* 1. A psychological or emotional problem. 2. Any problem or difficulty that causes annoyance or irritation.

hap·pen·ing *n.* A spontaneous or improvised public performance, display, event, often involving the audience.

hard-core *n., adj.* A person considered part of the nucleus of any group who fail to meet society's accepted standards.

hard·hat. A construction worker.

hard sell. *Colloquial.* Aggressive, high-pressure

sales techniques.

has•sle *v. Slang.* To abuse or harass. *n.* a fight or struggle; a heated argument.

have•not *n.* A country or people lacking in economic wealth, technology, etc., esp. as distinguished from the haves (those who have).

hawk. A person who favors war or advocates military solutions in a conflict.

heav•y *n. Theater.* The role of a villain, or the actor playing it.

hel•i•port *(hel-*uh-pawrt) *n.* An airport for helicopters.

high-fi•del•i•ty *n.* The reproduction of sound with a minimum of distortion. Also, **hi-fi.**

hip *adj. Slang.* Aware; informed; hep.—**hip•ster** *n.* An informed person, esp. a jazz enthusiast or beatnik.

hip•pie *(hip-*ee) *n.* A person who breaks from conventional society, espousing complete freedom of expression, typically by wearing unconventional clothes, ungroomed long hair, and maintaining a philosophy of love and fellowship.

ho•log•ra•phy (hoh-*luh*-gra-fee) *n.* A lensless method of photography in which a three-dimensional image is recorded on a photographic plate or film by means of laser light beams. *n.* **hologram,** the reproduction of an image thus formed.

hoot•en•an•ny *(hoot-*'n-an-ee) *n.* A concert of folk music, sometimes for the benefit of a liberal cause. Also **hoot.**

hot *adj.* 1. *Slang.* Liable to be searched for because recently stolen or fraudulently obtained. 2. Dangerous because exposed to or possessing atomic radiation.

hot line. A telephone line or other medium providing immediate communication between two points, esp. in an emergency.

hot-rod *n. Slang.* Old car souped up by its youthful owner and raced against other members of a speed cult.—**hot-rodder** *n.*

hot war. A war involving actual armed conflict, as contrasted with a cold war.

hov•er•craft *n.* An automotive vehicle that travels over land or sea on a cushion of air expelled beneath it.

hu•mid•i•fi•er (hyoo-*mid*-uh-fy-er) *n.* An apparatus for keeping air moist.

hy•dro•foil *(hy-*droh-foil) *n.* 1. A device under a boat that raises the boat above water as its speed increases, thereby eliminating frictional drag and affording a smoother ride. 2. A boat equipped with such a device.

hy•per•son•ic (hy-per-*son*-ik) *adj.* Faster than 2,700 miles per hour.

ICBM. Intercontinental Ballistic Missile, having a range of at least 5,000 miles.

i•con•o•scope (eye-*kon*-oh-skohp) *n. Television.* A vacuum tube with electron gun and photosensitive plate used as a camera pick-up.

identity crisis. The time of disturbance and anxiety when a person is in a self-conscious stage of personality development or adjustment.

im•plo•sion (im-*ploh*-zhun) *n.* A bursting inward, esp. a guided explosion focused inward, as in the atomic bomb.

in *Colloquial. n.* 1. A means of entry or access, esp. to a desirable position or condition. 2. That which is accepted, established, or fashionable.—*adj.* Established or accepted as the best; fashionable.

in•ter•change *n.* A traffic intersection provided with ramps and connecting roads for the separation of traffic.

In•ter•pol *(in-*ter-pohl) *n.* International Criminal Police Commission, an international organization for the suppression of crime.

in•tra•u•ter•ine de•vice (-*yut*-a-rin) A contraceptive loop, coil or ring, placed within the uterus as a barrier to implantation. *Abbreviation:* **IUD.**

i•on•o•sphere (eye-*on*-oh-sfeer) *n.* An outer region of the earth's atmosphere in which radiation from the sun ionizes the atoms and molecules of the atmospheric gases. Its range varies with the seasons and the time of day.

IRBM. Intermediate Range Ballistic Missile, having a range of 300 to 1,500 miles.

iron curtain. Phrase popularized by Winston Churchill to describe the methods (notably censorship of press and radio) employed by the USSR to isolate its inhabitants from the peoples of Western Europe.

i•so•met•rics (eye-soh-*met*-riks) *n.* A system of exercises for strengthening and firming muscles by pitting them against immovable objects at brief, regular intervals.

ja•to *n. Aviation.* Jet-assisted take-off.

jet set. *Colloquial.* A group within fashionable international society whose pursuit of pleasure is world-wide.

jig *n.* Framework for holding parts to be worked or joined in the correct relation.

job action. A protest by workers without undertaking a general strike.

jock. *n. U.S. Slang.* An athlete.

jog•ging. *n.* The exercise of running at a slow, regular pace, often alternately with walking.

ju•do *(joo-*doh) *n.* A scientific system of unarmed hand-to-hand combat based on the Japanese ju-jitsu.

juke box. *Slang.* An automatic coin-operated phonograph for public dancing.

jumbo jet. A jet aircraft with a passenger capacity of about 500 people and a freight capacity of about 200 tons.

junk•ie *n. Slang.* A drug addict.

ka•ra•te (kah-*rah*-tee) *n.* A technique of combat, developed by the Japanese, by which powerful blows with the side of the hand are directed against vulnerable body areas.

key club. A private nightclub that admits members who are given keys.

kib•butz (kih-*boots*) *n.* [pl. **kib•butz•im**] A co-operative farm in Israel, conducted as a communal settlement.

kick *n. Slang.* 1. Spree; binge; enthusiastic sortie. 2. Excessive preoccupation with a single interest.

kin•e•scope (*kin*-eh-skohp) *n. Television.* The receiver cathode-ray tube with fluorescent screen which reproduces transmitted video images.

ki•net•ic (kih-*net*-ik) *adj.* Involving motion or the suggestion of motion produced by mechanical, mobile parts, light effects, colors, optical illusions.

klutz (kluhtz) *n. Slang.* A clumsy, awkward person. *adj.* **klutzy.**

knock *n.* Noise caused by improper firing in an internal combustion engine.

kook *n. Slang.* An eccentric, odd, or peculiar person.—**kook•y** *adj.*

lam *n. Slang.* Sudden flight; escape.—**on the lam** In flight; fleeing; escaping.

la•ser (*lay*-zer) *n. Physics.* [*L*ight *A*mplification by *S*timulated *E*mission of *R*adiation] A device for producing a narrow light beam of a single wavelength.

laugh track. A recording of audience laughter added to a sound track, especially of a previously filmed television show.

launching pad. A place from which something starts; a spring board.

LEM *n.* Acronym for *lunar excursion module.* A lightweight manned spacecraft carried by a larger spacecraft and detached while in lunar orbit so that it may land on the surface of the moon.

life-support system. Any system designed to support the physiological processes essential to life.

lift•off *n. Aerospace.* The initial ascent of a missile or space vehicle from its launch pad.

light show. A display of colored lights in kaleidoscopic patterns usually accompanied by music.

load•ed *adj. Slang.* 1. Well-equipped; well-heeled. 2. Intoxicated, from liquor or dope.

lo•ran (loh-*ran*) [*L*ong *R*ange *N*avigation] A system in which pulsed radio signals from paired transmitters are used to determine position.

loss leader. An article of trade sold below cost to attract customers.

love-in. A gathering of hippies, flower children and the like, for the purpose of celebrating or expressing love.

low profile. A deliberately low-keyed or understated attitude or position.

LP *n.* Trademark for the long-playing phonograph records developed by Columbia Records,

Inc.

lu•nar ro•ver (*loo*-ner *row*-ver) *n.* A vehicle for exploratory travel on the surface of the moon.

ma•chis•mo (mah-*cheese*-moh) *n.* Manly self-assurance; masculine drive, virility.

mac•ro•bi•ot•ics (mak-row-bai-*at*-iks) *n.* A dietary system based on the Zen Buddhist division of the world into the opposite and complementary principles of *yin* and *yang,* in which a balanced diet consists of a five-to-one proportion of yin (organically grown sugar, fruits, grains, vegetables) to yang (meat, eggs, etc.). It is essentially a cleansing diet, physically, mentally and spiritually.

Ma•gic Mark•er. The trade name of a writing implement which consists of a metal tube which holds fast-drying indellible ink and a thick felt tip which transmits the ink onto the writing surface.

mag•ne•to•sphere (mag-*net*-oh-sfeer) *n.* A region of the atmosphere beyond the exosphere, with a continuous band of charged particles trapped by the earth's magnetic field. It includes the Van Allen Radiation Belt.

Ma•ha•ri•shi (mah-ha-*ree*-she) *n.* 1. The title of a Hindu guru or spiritual guide. 2. Any guru or teacher.

main•lin•er *n. Slang.* An addict who injects dope into a principal vein.

male chau•vin•ism (-*show*-vin-niz-em) Excessive masculine pride or exaggerated loyalty to members of the male sex. *n.* **male chauvinist,** a man who regards himself or his sex as superior to women.

ma•ri•na (muh-*ree*-nuh) *n.* A docking area, equipped with supply and repair facilities, for small boats.

ma•ser (*may*-zer) *n. Physics.* [*M*icrowave *A*mplification by *S*timulated *E*mission of *R*adiation] A device for amplifying weak short-wave radio signals without significant distortion by the amplifer itself.

max•i (*mack*-see) *n.* A dress, coat, skirt, etc. reaching to the ankles or just above.

Mc•Lu•han•ism (mak-*loo*-en-iz-em) The ideas and theories of communications specialist Marshall McLuhan, especially his emphasis on the influence of electronic communications and the mass communications media in radically reshaping society.

Med•i•care (med-ih-kehr) *n. U.S.* A voluntary health insurance program for persons 65 or older, administered by the Social Security Administration.

meg•a•ton *n.* A million tons; specifically, the power of 1,000,000 tons of TNT.

memory trace. A chemical change occurring in the brain when new information is absorbed and remembered.

mer•i•toc•racy. A ruling class in society whose members are the most talented or have the highest intellect.

me•so•sphere (*mes*-oh-sfeer) *n.* A region of the atmosphere between the stratosphere and the ionosphere, characterized by a layer of electrified air.

me•te•or•oid (*mee*-tee-uh-roid) *n.* A particle of matter in interplanetary space.

meter maid. An auxiliary policewoman who patrols streets for parking violations.

mev. *n.* A million electron volts.

mi•cro•bi•ol•o•gy (my-kroh-by-*ol*-uh-jee) *n.* Branch of science dealing with microorganisms, esp., bacteria, fungi, yeasts, protozoa and algae; research in this field has led to the discovery of such antibiotics as streptomycin and neomycin.— **mi•cro•bi•ol•o•gist** *n.*

mi•cro•groove (*my*-kroh-groov) *n.* A groove much narrower than that employed on the playing surfaces of the previous (78 r.p.m.) phonograph records, especially that devised for use on long-playing (33 1/3 r.p.m.) records and on high-fidelity (45 r.p.m.) discs.

Middle America. A broad cross-section of the American population conceived as politically middle-of-the-road or moderate, belonging to the middle-income class, and geographically situated mainly in the midwestern states.

mi•di *n.* A garment, usually a dress, coat or skirt, that reaches to the mid-calf.

mind-expanding *adj.* Intensifying and distorting perception; psychedelic.

mi•ni *n.* A short shirt, esp. one the hem of which is four or more inches above the knees.

mis•sil•ry (*mis*-el-ry) *n.* The science of designing, building, launching, and directing missiles and rockets.

mod *adj.* Extremely up-to-date and fashionable.

mod•ule. A unit in an aircraft or spacecraft that has a specific function and is often designed to funtion independently of the main craft as a self-contained, self-supporting unit.

molecular rays. A stream of molecules moving or being forced in a single direction.

mon•i•tor *n.* A receiver or other device used to check radio or television broadcasts, as for quality of transmission, content, etc.

Moog syn•the•sizer (moug *sin*-thah-size-er) An electronic keyboard instrument for generating a large variety of sounds.

moon•rock. A rock sample from the moon.

moon•walk. An exploratory walk on the moon's surface.

Ms. (*miz*) Abbreviated title used instead of Miss or Mrs.

mul•ti•me•dia *adj.* Using a combination of various media, such as tapes, film, records, photographs, and slides, to entertain, teach, communicate, etc.

mutual fund. An investment company that in-

vests the funds of its shareholders in the stocks of other companies.

Na•der•ism (*nay*-der-iz-em) *n.* Consumerism; named after Ralph Nader, the founder of the movement.

naked ape. Human being.

na•palm (*nay*-pahm) *n.* A gasoline preparation of jellylike consistency used in flamethrowers and bombs.

narc *n. U.S. Slang.* Federal narcotics agent.

nar•co•syn•the•sis (nar-koh-*sin*-thuh-siss) *n.* A method of psychiatric treatment through the use of narcotics.

NASA. National Aeronautics and Space Administration, a U.S. government agency in charge of research and development in aeronautics and aerospace technology.

NATO. North Atlantic Treaty Organization, organized (1949) by the United States, United Kingdom, Canada, Iceland and nine Western European nations for mutual defense.

ne•o•plas•ti•cism (nee-oh-*plas*-tih-siz'm) *n.* A style of abstract painting in which straightline designs predominate.—**ne•o•plas•ti•cist** *n.*

New Frontier. The policies and programs advocated by President John F. Kennedy for the United States.

nit•ty-grit•ty *n.* The practicalities or details; the basics.

no-fault *adj. U.S.* Of or relating to a form of automobile insurance by which an accident victim is compensated for damages and/or expenses by his own insurance company, whether the accident was his fault or not.

noise pol•lu•tion. The production of noise by vehicles, jet planes, machinery, etc. viewed as harmful to man and his environment.

nose cone. The front section of an aerospace vehicle designed to carry instruments or astronauts. It is built to withstand high temperatures generated by air friction. Sometimes it separates and becomes the satellite.

nuclear energy. Energy released by nuclear disintegration, esp. by fission.

nuclear reactor. Device for producing controlled chain reaction in fissionable materials.

nu•cle•on (*noo*-klee-on) *n.* Any of the particles composing the atomic nucleus, as the proton, neutron, and neutrino.

nu•cle•on•ics (noo-klee-*on*-iks) *n.* Nuclear physics applied to engineering or technology.

occupational therapy. Treatment of a mental illness or physical deficiency through teaching of occupational skills.

OD. Abbreviation of *overdose* (applied to narcotics taken in excess or to addicts sick or dead from an overdose).

odd•ball *n. Slang.* A peculiar or eccentric person; esp. one who differs from others of his group.

off·beat *adj. Slang.* Strange; unusual; unconventional.

Op-Ed page. *U.S.* A newspaper page, so named because it runs opposite a newspaper's editorial page, featuring articles by columnists and other writers.

open classroom. *U.S.* A classroom situation in which the activities are informal, individualized and centered on open-ended investigation and discussion instead of formal instruction.

open enrollment. *U.S.* A policy of unrestricted admission to a college or university that allows poor, unprepared or otherwise ineligible students to matriculate.

open-heart *adj. Surgery.* An operation performed on the interior of the heart while maintaining circulation by means of a heart-lung machine.

Or·lon *n.* Trademark for a synthetic thread or fabric with many of the characteristics of nylon.

Os·car *n.* 1. An award given by the Motion Picture Academy of Arts and Sciences for outstanding achievement in each of the phases of motion picture production. 2. Any special award or prize.

OTB. Abbreviation of *off-track betting*, a state-licensed system in the U.S. for placing bets away from the track where the horses are running.

out *adj. Colloquial.* No longer accepted as the best; out of date; unfashionable.

outer space. Space beyond the earth's atmosphere or beyond the solar system.

o·ver·kill *n.* The capacity of a military power to destroy many times an enemy or the entire world, by virture of excessive armaments.

o·zon·o·sphere (oh-*zon*-uh-sfeer) *n.* A region in the upper atmosphere having a high concentration of ozone, due to ultraviolet radiation.

pace·mak·er *n. Medical.* An instrument implanted beneath the skin for providing a normal heartbeat by electronic stimulation of the heart muscle, used in certain heart conditions.

pad *n.* 1. A launch pad. 2. *Slang.* A room or apartment.

pan *v. Motion Pictures.* [from *panorama*] To follow action with the camera from one side to the other.

pant·suit *n.* A woman's suit consisting of trousers and matching jacket.

pan·ty·hose (pan-tee-hoz) *n.* A woman's undergarment combining both panties and stockings.

pa·ra·pro·fes·sion·al *n.* An aid or assistant in a professional field who does not have full professional training.

pay·load *n.* 1. The revenue-earning cargo of a transportation carrier. 2. The warhead of a guided missile.

pay·o·la *n. Slang.* Undercover payment for a favor to one who is able to grant it, as to a disk jockey for promoting a record.

Peace Corps. A U.S. government organization consisting of volunteers trained to live in, and give educational and technical assistance to, undeveloped countries.

Peter Principle. Educator Laurence Peter's dictum which holds that employees advance until they are promoted to their level of incompetence.

phase out. To plan and carry out in orderly steps the termination of an enterprise, as in defense production.—**phase-out** *n.*

pick·up *n.* A small, light truck for carrying small loads.

pig *n. U.S. Slang.* A policeman.

pig·gy·back *n.* The transportation of loaded trucks or truck trailers on railroad cars to points near their destination.

pile *n.* Nuclear reactor.

pill *n.* **the pill.** an oral contraceptive in pill form.

pip *n.* Mark on a radarscope indicating the echo of a signal returning from a distant object.

pipe·line *n.* 1. An overland system of pipes for carrying water, oil, or natural gas over long distances. 2. A private or secret channel of information.

pitch *n. Slang.* Angle; approach; appeal. 'What's the pitch?'

plane *v.* To skim along the surface of water.

plas·tic *adj.* Not natural or real; artificial.

plug *Slang. n.* A recommendation to buy something, esp. over radio or television.—*v.* To recommend something in this way.

Po·lar·oid (poh-luh-roid) *n.* Trademark of a light-polarizing substance used in glass to cut down light glare.

pop art. A contemporary movement in painting that uses comic strips, advertisements, and commercial design.

pop-top *adj.* Having a ring attached to a metal tab in the top of a can that can be pulled to open the can.

por·nog·ra·phy (poor-*nog*-ra-fee) *n.* A description or portrayal of any activity regarded as obscene. Also called **porno.**

port·fo·li·o *n.* A list of investments, securities, etc., held by a company or person.

pos·i·tron *n.* A particle with a positive charge having the same numerical mass and charge as an electron; antiparticle of an electron.

POW. Prisoner of war.

pre·school *adj.* Of or pertaining to the years between infancy and age five or six.

pressure group. Any group banded together to exert influence on legislation or policy.

printed circuit. *Electronics.* A conducting circuit which is deposited on an insulated surface.

print-out *n.* Information from a computer prepared in printed form.

programmed instruction. Instruction by means of a sequence of small-unit lessons, to be mastered one at a time at a set rate, as used in certain textbooks, teaching machines, etc.

pros·the·sis (*pross*-theh-sis) *n.* Addition of an artificial limb, eye or tooth to the human body.

proximity fuse. Detonator for a projectile designed to set it off in the vicinity of the target rather than on contact.

psy·che·del·ic (sai-ke-*del*-ik) 1. Chemically altering the psyche as to intensify perception; mind-expanding. 2. Loud, bright, kaleidoscopic.

psy·cho·dra·ma (*sy*-koh-dram-uh) *n.* An improvised playlet in which patients undergoing psychiatric treatment are encouraged to act out situations analogous to those which they fear to face in actuality.

psy·cho·gen·ic (sy-koh-*jen*-ik) *adj. Psychiatry.* Of mental, rather than physical, origin.

psy·cho·ki·ne·sis (sy-koh-kih-*nee*-sis) *n.* The supposed ability to will the behavior of inanimate objects such as cards and dice.

psy·cho·so·mat·ic medicine (sy-koh-soh-mat-ik). The branch of medicine that deals with the mutual influences of body and mind with respect to the treatment of disease.

pulp *n.* A magazine printed on coarse paper, usually containing sensational stories.

pul·sar (*pul*-sahr) *n. Astronomy.* A celestial body of unknown composition characterized by the emission of rapidly pulsating radio signals.

push-but·ton *adj.* Initiated or carried on as if by push buttons, as remote-control war.

push·er *n. Slang.* A seller of dope to addicts.

put-on *n. Slang.* An act, statement, etc. meant to fool; a prank, hoax.

Qi·a·na (kee-*a*-nah) *n.* Trade name of a washable, wrinkle-resistant fabric related to nylon.

quad·ri·phon·ic (kwad-ra-*fon*-ik) *adj.* Of or relating to high-fidelity sound reproduction involving signals transmitted through four different channels.

qua·sar (kway-*zahr*) *n. Astronomy.* One of a class of celestial bodies of unknown composition characterized by an extreme red shift and thus, by inference, the most distant objects visible to man.

quick freezing. Process by which food, esp. meat and vegetables, may be prepared for storage over long periods after simple preparation, by freezing almost instantaneously.

radar screen. Fluorescent screen of the cathode ray tube on which is projected the 'pip' representing the echo of a radar signal returning from a distant object. Also, **radarscope.**

radio astronomy. The study of celestial bodies by means of radio waves emitted by them.

radio telescope A telescope that studies celestial bodies by means of radio waves.

rap *v. U.S. Slang.* To talk openly and sincerely.

rap session *n. U.S. Slang.* A group discussion centering around a specific problem.

ra·to *n. Aviation.* Rocket-assisted take-off.

re·cy·cle *v.* To put wastes, garbage, etc. through a purification cycle and convert to useful products.

red alert. An emergency state of readiness in the face of imminent danger.

re·de·ploy (ree-duh-*ploy*) *v.* To move troops or equipment from one theater of war to another.

re-entry *n.* The return of a spacecraft into the earth's atmosphere after travel to very high altitudes.

re·sid·u·al (ree-*zij*-ewe-el) *n.* A fee received by a performer, writer, etc. for every repetition of a commercial or show in whose production he originally participated.

ret·ro·rock·et (ret-roh-*rok*-it) *n.* An auxiliary rocket in a spacecraft that provides a reverse thrust for deceleration, esp. during re-entry.

ri·bo·some (*rye*-ba-soum) *n.* Any of the complex particles in a cell that carry out the synthesis of proteins and enzymes.

Richter scale. A scale for measuring the force of earthquakes, using number 1 to 10.

right on *U.S. Slang.* An expression used to show full approval or agreement.

rip·off *n. U.S. Slang.* A theft, robbery or exploitation.

ro·bot bomb. A jet-propelled, pilotless plane carrying a large explosive charge.

rock-and-roll *n.* A popular style of song and dance music having a two-beat rhythm, developed from hillbilly patterns, and noted for its repetitious, sentimental tone. Also **rock 'n' roll.**

rock·et·ry (*rok*-it-ree) *n.* The designing, building, and launching of rockets.

roent·gen (*rent*-gen) *n.* Unit of measurement of absorbed radiation. *Abbr:* r.

rog·er (*roj*-er) *Interjection.* [from radio-telephone signal for receipt of a message] Understood! O.K.!

ry·a (*rye*-a) *n.* A colorful, handwoven, deep-pile rug, originally from Scandinavia.

sa·bra (*sah*-bruh) *n.* A person born in Israel. [from the Hebrew word for cactus, signifying outer toughness and inner softness]

scam *n. U.S. Slang.* A dishonest scheme; a swindle.

scan (*skan*) *v. Television.* To convert an image into a series of electrical impulses that may be transmitted like a broadcast. **-scan·ning** *n. Television.* Process by which a moving electron beam translates an image on the mosaic of the iconoscope into parallel horizontal lines read like print from left to right and top to bottom.

scan·ning *n.* A diagnostic method for detecting abnormalities in the body by the use of special photographic instruments that record the movement of an administered radioactive substance as it passes through the organs, body fluids, etc.

schmaltz (shmolts) *n. Slang.* Excessive sentimentality, esp. in music and drama. —**schmaltz·y** *adj.*

schmo (shmoh) *n. Slang.* A person of low intelligence and capabilities, esp. one who is the butt of another's jokes.

Sci·en·tol·o·gy *n.* A system combining religion and psychology which stresses spiritual and physical healing through the adherence of certain tenents founded by L. Ron Hubbard.

sci-fi (sai-fai) *adj.* Of or relating to science fiction.

scrub *v.* To cancel, as the launching of a space vehicle or the firing of a rocket or missile.

scu-ba (*skoo*-buh) *n.* [self-contained underwater breathing apparatus] An aqualung.

Sea·lab *n.* Any of several U.S. Navy underwater vessels designed to serve as habitats for people engaged in underwater research.

SEATO. Southeast Asia Treaty Organization.

see-through *adj.* 1. Transparent 2. Very sheer.

self-destruct *v.* 1. To destroy oneself. 2. To disappear, evaporate.

sen·si·tiv·i·ty train·ing. Training in a group guided by a therapist or leader, in which the members are supposed to gain deeper understanding of their own feelings and those of others in the group.

sex·ism. *n.* Discrimination based on a person's sex; specifically discriminatory attitudes and practices against women in business, politics, art, etc. *n.*, **sexist.**

sexual revolution. The overthrow of traditional sexual inhibitions and taboos, especially those that protect the institution of monogamous marriage.

sfer·ics (*sfehr*-iks) *n.* [from atmo*spherics.*] Branch of meteorology dealing with long-range, electronic detection of atmospheric changes.

sho·ran *n.* (short range navigation) A method by which a ship or aircraft can determine its position by the time taken to send electronic signals to two ground stations and have them relayed back.

shrink *n. U.S. Slang.* Psychiatrist.

shtick *n. U.S. Slang.* A gimmick, act or routine.

sig·nal *n. Radio & TV.* Any transmission of electronic waves, whether carrying a message or not.

Silent Majority. *U.S.* The politically nonvocal section of the population that is believed to constitute the majority of Americans.

silent spring. The death of the spring season resulting from the wanton destruction of nature by toxic chemicals, taken from the title of a book by Rachel Carson.

si·lo (*sy*-loh) *n.* An underground shelter with facilities for housing or launching a missile.

si·mul·cast (*sih*-mul-kast; *sy*-mul-kast) *n. Television.* A program presented simultaneously on AM or FM radio and on television.

sit·com (*sit*-kom) *n. U.S.* From **situation comedy.** A type of radio or television comedy series whose humor arises from the plight of characters forced into ludicrous, often contrived, situations.

sit-in *n.* The occupation of seats in a public place by members of a group hitherto barred by local custom or statute, esp. as a protest against segregation.

skin flick *n. Slang.* A motion pictures showing people in the nude, usually engaging in some sexual act.

sky diving. The sport of jumping from an airplane and performing certain maneuvers before opening the parachute.—**sky diver.**

sky·hook *n.* A large plastic helium-filled balloon equipped with scientific instruments for meteorological or aerospace research.

sky·jack *v.* To hijack an aircraft and fly it to a place other than its original destination.

Sky·lab. 1. A U.S. manned space flight project following the Apollo project, designed to establish a scientific space station or orbiting laboratory near the earth. 2. The earth-orbiting space station established by this project.

sky marshal. A. U.S. federal law-enforcement officer assigned to protect aircraft and passengers from skyjacking.

slick (*slik*) *n. Slang.* A magazine, often smart and sophisticated, printed on coated paper.

slum·lord *n.* The landlord of slum property which he allows to fall into disrepair.

smash *adj. Slang.* Sensational, overwhelmingly successful. 'A smash hit.'

smog *n.* Combination of smoke and fog, forming heavy pall in many modern industrial urban areas and causing respiratory ailments.

snow·mo·bile (*snoh*-moh-*bil*) *n.* An automotive vehicle equipped with skis and a belted track for travel over snow.

soft sell. *Colloquial.* Moderate, low-pressure sales techniques.

so·far *n.* [*sound fixing and ranging*] Underwater sonic system used over distances up to 2000 miles in the location of shipwreck survivors by triangulation of reports from widely separated shore stations of explosions of deep-water bombs dropped by survivors.

so·nar *n.* [*sound navigation and ranging*] A method of detecting and locating stationary or moving objects under water by the use of high-frequency sound waves.

son·ic (*son*-ik) *adj.* Pertaining to the speed of sound.

sonic boom. The sound heard when the shock wave formed in front of an object traveling at supersonic speed reaches the ground.

soul *n.* 1. The quality that arouses emotion, especially as exemplified in black music, art, and other black cultural forms. 2. soul music. *adj.*, arousing a feeling of kinship or sense of mutual interest with another.

soul food. *U.S.* 1. Food typically eaten by blacks, and prepared in the traditional southern black manner. 2. Any ethnic food.

sound *v.*—**sound off** 1. *Slang.* To speak one's mind; complain. 2. *Military.* To identify oneself by name, rank, etc.

sound barrier. A critical speed range approximating the speed of sound in which shock waves produced by an aircraft subject it to drag and other stresses. Also **sonic barrier.**

soup.—soup up *Slang.* To readjust fuel mixture or otherwise modify an engine to obtain maximum speed or output.

space age. The current period in history, characterized by remarkable advances in space technology.

space•craft *n.* Any vehicle designed for travel or exploration in outer space.

space platform. An artificial earth satellite serving as a base for aerospace research or for launching other spacecraft.

space ship. Rocket-powered airship or guided missile designed for traveling outside the earth's atmosphere in interstellar space.

space shoe. A custom-made shoe built to conform to the foot for maximum comfort.

space shuttle. A space vehicle designed to transport men and materials to a space station.

space station. A space platform.

space suit. A pressurized suit worn by an astronaut to provide a normal human environment.

space•walk. The act of moving in space outside a spacecraft.

speed-reading. The practice of reading rapidly by the assimilation of several words, phrases or sentences at a glance.

splash•down *n.* The landing of an aerospace vehicle in the ocean prior to recovery.

split *v. Slang.* 1. To go away; leave. 2. To run off; desert.

spot *adj.* 1. Demanding, or specializing in transactions requiring, immediate cash payment. 2. *Radio & TV.* Originating from a local station.— *n. Radio & TV.* A particular time on a station's broadcasting schedule.

spot announcement. *Radio & TV.* An announcement or commercial made at a certain time, independent of any major program.

spring *v. Slang.* To obtain the release of a person from prison; liberate; free.

sput•nik *(spoot-*nik) *n.* [Russian word for *traveling companion*] A man-made earth satellite put in orbit by the Soviet Union in 1957, the first of its kind in the world.

square *n. Slang.* A person who is not in touch with the latest trends, fashions, or fads.

ster•e•o•phon•ic (ster-ee-oh-*fon*-ik) *adj.* Pertaining to sound reproduction whereby a three-dimensional sound effect is achieved.

ster•e•o•scope *n.* Also **ster•e•o.** Method of projection of a dual-image motion picture which, when seen through special glasses, gives an illusion of depth.

ster•oid *n.* A sex hormone believed responsible for growth after puberty.

stra•to•vi•sion *(strat-*oh-vih-zh'n) *n.* Broadcast of television programs from the stratosphere to secure greater range of transmission.

sub•lim•i•nal (sub-*lim*-uh-n'l) *adj.* Pertaining to images, stimuli, etc., below the threshold of conscious perception.

sub•son•ic *(sub-*sawn-ik) *adj.* Pertaining to speeds less than that of sound; below 700-750 miles per hour.

sub•ur•bi•a (suh-*ber*-bee-uh) *n.* The suburbs or the people who live there.

summit meeting or conference. A meeting between two or more heads of state, as to discuss and resolve international problems.

su•per•son•ic (soo-per-*sawn*-ik) *adj.* Pertaining to speeds above that of sound; more than 750 miles per hour.

super•star *n.* One of the most outstanding figures in a particular field or profession, particularly in the entertainment or sports fields.

sur•real *adj.* Bizarrely fantastic.

sustaining program. *Radio & TV.* A program paid for by the station, having no sponsor.

sweat *n.*—**no sweat** *Slang.* Easy to do or make.

tail•gate *v.* To follow a car too closely.

take-home pay. Net wage after tax and other deductions have been made.

take•out *adj. U.S.* Designating food prepared to be eaten away from the premises.

talk *v.*—**talk down** To direct an aircraft to landing by giving instructions to the pilot, as in occasions of poor visibility.

talk show. A television or radio show in which guest celebrities are interviewed.

tee•ny-bop•per *n. U.S. Slang.* A young teenager who follows the current fashions and fads in clothing, music, etc.

tel•e•gen•ic (tel-eh-*jen*-ik) *adj.* Capable of being photographed to good advantage by television; videogenic.

tel•e•ran *(tel-*uh-ran) *n.* [from *Tele*vision *Radar Air Navigation.*] Radionic device for transmitting pilot charts, plus radar-obtained course and altitude data, via television to planes.

tel•e•thon *n.* [*tele*vision mara*thon*] A television program lasting many hours, usually in solicitation of money for charity.

Tel•ex *n.* Trade name for a communications system of teletype machines serving subscribers.

Tel•star *n.* An artificial satellite for the amplification and relay of telephone and televison signals, making possible a system of global communication.

tes•tos•ter•one (tess-*toss*-ter-ohn) *n.* A male sex hormone, natural or synthetic.

test pattern. *Television.* Design planned for transmission to correct focussing and tuning of the television image.

theater of the absurd. A form of theater that stresses the absurdity of the human condition and the futility of man's attempts to cope with it.

thermal barrier. A range of speed at which the friction heat generated by an aircraft exceeds its capacity to endure it. Also **heat barrier.**

ther·mo·nu·cle·ar (ther-moh-*noo*-klee-er) *adj.* Pertaining to the fusion of atomic nuclei at very high temperature, as in the hydrogen bomb.

thi·a·mine. thi·a·min (*thy*-uh-min) *n.* Vitamin B₁, a complex compound whose absence from the diet causes beriberi.

think tank *n. Colloq.* A group of specialists who consider a subject in all its aspects.

Third World. A collective name for the group of underdeveloped countries, especially of Africa and Asia, that receive aid from both the Communist and non-Communist worlds and therefore cannot be aligned with either.

Three-D. Also **3-D.** A motion picture producing an illusion of depth and audience participation by stereoscopic or depth-illusion (see **Cinerama**) techniques.

thru·way *n.* An express highway; turnpike; expressway; freeway.

tie-dye *v.* To dye clothes or fabrics by tying them tightly into knots before immersing them into dye, so as to produce unusual designs in the tied portions not penetrated by the dye.

tie-in sale. Practice of forcing a buyer to purchase an unwanted article in order to buy what he requires.

To·ny *n.* An annual award for outstanding achievement in the American theater, in honor of Antoinette Perry, American actress (d. 1946).

touch·down *n.* The landing of an aircraft or of a manned or unmanned space vehicle.

trans·sex·u·al *n.* 1. A person whose sex is anatomically uncertain or who is anatomically normal but consideres himself or herself as belonging to the opposite sex. 2. A person who has undergone a sex-change operation.

tran·sis·tor (tran-*zis*-ter) *n.* An electronic device that controls an electron current by the conducting properties of germanium or a like material.

tran·son·ic (tran-*son*-ik) *adj.* Pertaining to speeds at or near the speed of sound.

trip *n. Slang.* 1. An hallucinatory experience. 2. Any stimulating experience. 3. Any obsessive course of action, state of mind, etc. in which one is involved for a time.

tro·po·sphere (*trop*-uh-sfeer) *n.* A region of the atmosphere between the earth and the stratosphere, marked by clouds and air turbulence.

tur·bo·jet *n.* A jet engine in which a gas turbine drives a compressor that supplies air to a burner; the exhaust from combustion provides thrust and drives the turbine.

tur·bo·prop *n.* A jet engine in which the turbine drives a propeller to produce thrust.

tweet·er *n.* A loudspeaker for reproducing high-frequency sounds, as in high-fidelity sound equipment.

UFO Unidentified Flying Object; official designation of so-called flying saucers.

u·fo·log·i·cal (you-fo-*loj*-a-kal) *adj.* Of or relating to the tracking of unidentified flying objects. *n.* **ufologist.**

Ugly American. An American living abroad who presents an unflattering picture of Americans in general, especially by insensitivity to the natives and their culture.

ul·tra·high frequency. A band of wave frequencies between 300 and 3,000 megacycles per second. *Abbreviation:* **UHF.**

ul·tra·son·ic *adj.* 1. Supersonic. 2. Designating speeds between sonic and hypersonic.

un·der·a·chiev·er *n. Education.* A student whose performance does not come up to ability.

under·ground *n.* Any group, organization or movement whose activities are outside the established society or culture.

u·ni·sex (*you*-nee-seks) *adj.* Suitable for both sexes.

unit pricing. The pricing of commodities by the pound, ounce or other standard measure together with the overall price.

up·tight *adj. Slang.* 1. Very uneasy or apprehensive. 2. Nervous, tense. 3. Stiff, formal.

upward mobility. The ability to rise from a lower to a higher economic or social class.

urban renewal. The improvement of a rundown urban area, in coordination with local and state or federal agencies.

very high frequency. A band of wave frequencies between 30 and 300 megacycles. *Abbreviation:* **VHF.**

vid·e·o·gen·ic (vid-ee-oh-*jeh*-ıc) *adj.* Capable of being photographed to good advantage by television; telegenic.

vig·or·ish *n. Slang.* Exorbitant interest, as charged by loan sharks.

vi·nyl (*vy*-nul) *n.* Also **vinyl plastic.** A tough durable plastic used in making floor tiling, wall sheeting, phonograph records, etc.

VIP. *Colloquial.* Very important person.

voice·print *n.* A method of individual identification whereby a graph of the patterns of pitch, etc. in a person's speech is produced on a sound spectrograph.

V/STOL (*vee*-stoul) Acronym for *vertical* or *short takeoff and landing,* a type of aircraft.

walkie-talkie (*wawk*-ee-*tawk*-ee) *n.* A portable radio set containing both transmitter and receiver units.

walk-on *n.* A minor part in a play or movie.

war·head *n.* The detachable chamber in the nose

of a bomb, torpedo, or ballistic missile, that carries the explosive.

water bed. A bed with a mattress consisting of a water-filled vinyl bag and usually equipped with a temperature-control device.

water pulse. Water applied to the teeth in a spurt with a water-spray device to remove particles of food.

way-out *adj. Slang.* Far removed from the ordinary.

weight-watcher *n.* A dieter.

weir•do *U.S. Slang.* An odd or eccentric person.

welfare state. A state that undertakes a broad program of social security.

wet•back *n. Colloquial.* A Mexican laborer who enters the U.S. illegally, as by wading across the Rio Grande.

whirl•y•bird *n. Colloquial.* A helicopter.

who•dun•it (hoo-*dun*-it) *n.* [from *who done it?*] *Slang.* A mystery or detective story, esp. one involving murder.

wind•chill factor. Wind velocity as a factor in determining the cooling effect of moving air on the body.

with-it *adj. Slang.* Fashionable, up-to-date.

wok (wak) *n.* A traditional Chinese cooking pot shaped somewhat like a bowl and used for stir-frying.

Women's Lib. A militant movement of women calling for liberation from sexism and all other forms of male domination.

work•a•hol•ic *n.* A person having an uncontrollable need to work incessantly.

xe•rog•ra•phy (zeh-*rog*-ruh-fee) *n. Printing.* A method of reproducing graphic or printed material by reflecting an image onto photoconductive paper, the image being developed with electrically charged powder which is then fixed by heating.

Xerox (*zir*-aks) **copy.** *n.* A duplicate of graphic material made by the dry photocopying process of a Xerox-brand copier.

yip•pie (*yip*-ee) *n. U.S.* Any of a group of politically active, radical hippies.

youth culture. The values and mores of the generation under thirty as a distinctive culture.

zap *v. Slang.* 1. To shoot, hit. 2. To beat, defeat. 3. To move quickly. *n.* 1. Vitality. 2. A confrontation or attack by opponents.

zero population growth. The condition in which a population ceases to grow and a balance is reached in the average number of births and deaths.

zilch *n. U.S. Slang.* Nothing, nil, zero.

ZIP Code. *U.S. Post Office,* A five-digit code which identifies a delivery unit, according to area, major distribution point, and local post office.

THE GROSSET WEBSTER DICTIONARY

A

a (*uh*; emphatic, *ay*) *Indefinite article.* 1. One. 2. Each.—*n. Music.* The sixth tone of the C-major diatonic scale.

A-1 (*ay*-wun) *adj. Colloquial.* High in quality or rating; first class.

aard·vark (*ard*-vark) *n.* The ant-eating ground-hog of South Africa.

aard·wolf (*ard*-wulf) *n.* Carrion-eating hy-enalike animal na-tive to South Africa.

Aa·ron (*ay*-ron, *ayr*-'n) *n.* A Jewish high priest of the Old Testament.—**Aa·ron·ic**, (ay-*ron*-ik) **Aa·ron·i·cal** *adj.*

AARDVARK (1/22 life size)

a·ba (*ah*-bah) *n.* 1. Rough cloth woven of goat's or camel's hair. 2. Arabian outer gar-ment, usually sleeveless.

a·back *adv. Nautical.* Pressed backward; checked by winds.—**taken aback.** Startled; disconcerted.

ab·a·cus (*ab*-uh-kus) *n.* [*pl.* ab·a·ci, ab·a·cus·es] 1. A frame used in arithmeti-cal computations. 2. *Architecture.* The crown or top of a column.

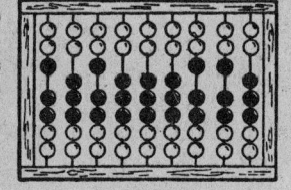

ABACUS

a·baft (uh-*baft*) *prep. Nautical.* Behind; after.—**a·baft** *adv.*

ab·a·lo·ne (ab-uh-*loh*-neh) *n.* An edible shellfish valuable also for the mother-of-pearl lining its shell.

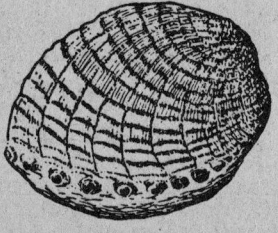

ABALONE

a·ban·don (uh-*ban*-dun) *v.* To desert; forsake; relinquish; release all controls.—*n.* 1. Heartiness; enthusiasm. 2. Re-linquishment; de-sertion.—**-don·er** *n.* **—-don·ment** *n.*

a·ban·doned *adj.* 1. Deserted; forsaken. 2. Un-restrained; profligate.

a·base (uh-*bayss*) *v.* [a·based; a·bas·ing] To lower; degrade.—**a·bas·ed·ly** *adv.*—**a·bas·ed·ness, a·base·ment** *n.*

a·bash (uh-*bash*) *v.* To embarrass; confuse.—**a·bashed** *adj.* Ill-at-ease; embarrassed.

a·bate (uh-*bayt*) *v.* [a·bat·ed; a·bat·ing] 1. To subside; lessen. 2. *Law.* To annul; defeat; put an end to.—**a·bat·a·ble** *adj.*—**a·bat·er** *n.* —**a·bate·ment** *n.*

ab·at·toir (ab-uh-*twahr*) *n.* A slaughterhouse.

ab·ba·cy (*ab*-uh-see) *n.* The office of an abbot.

ab·bé (*ab*-ay) *n.* A priest; abbot.

ab·bess (*ab*-ess) *n.* The head or governess of a nunnery.

ab·bey (*ab*-ee) *n.* 1. A monastery or convent. 2. A church or house attached to a monastery.

ab·bot (*ab*-ut) *n.* The head of a monastery.—**ab·bot·cy** *n.* [*pl.* -cies] The office of an abbot.—**ab·bot·ship** *n.*

ab·bre·vi·ate (uh-*bree*-vee-ayt) *v.* [ab·bre·vi·at·ed; -at·ing] To shorten; abridge.—**ab·bre·vi·a·tion** (uh-bree-vee-*ay*-sh'n) *n.*—**ab·bre·vi·a·tor** *n.*

ab·di·cate (*ab*-dih-kayt) *v.* [ab·di·cat·ed; -cat·ing] 1. To abandon a claim or right, as to a throne. 2. To disinherit. 3. To take leave of.—**ab·di·ca·tion** (ab dih-*kay*-sh'n) *n.*—**ab·di·ca·tive** *adj.*—**ab·di·ca·tor** *n.*

ab·do·men (*ab*-duh-m'n; ab-*doh*-men) *n.* The part of the body between thorax and pelvis.—**ab·dom·i·nal** (ab-*dom*-uh-n'l) *adj.*

ab·duct (ab-*dukt*) *v.* To spirit away; kidnap.—**ab·duc·tion** *n.*—**ab·duc·tor** *n.*

a·beam (uh-*beem*) *adv. Nautical.* Beside; at right angles to the keel.

a·bed *adv.* In bed.

A·bel (*ay*-b'l) *n. Bible.* Adam's son, killed by his jealous brother, Cain.

ab·er·ra·tion (ab-er-*ay*-shun) *n.* 1. Deviation; a wandering off. 2. A disordered state of mind. 3. *Optics.* The deviation of a lens from proper focus.

a·bet (uh-*bet*) *v.* [a·bet·ted; a·bet·ting] To en-courage; help; back.—**a·bet·ment** *n.*—**a·bet·tor, a·bet·ter** *n.*

a·bey·ance (uh-*bay*-uns) *n.* Expectation; con-templation; suspension —**a·bey·ant** *adj.*

ab·hor (ab-*hor*) *v.* [ab·horred; ab·hor·ring]

1. To detest; loathe. 2. To be inconsistent with or contrary to.—**ab·hor·rer** *n.*

ab·hor·rent (ab-*hor*-ent) *adj.* Hateful; detestable; repugnant.—**ab·hor·rence** *n.*

a·bide (uh-*byde*) *v.* [a·bode; a·bid·ing] 1. To reside; stay; remain; continue. 2. To await; be prepared for. 3. *Colloquial.* To tolerate; stand. 'I can't abide her behavior.'—**a·bid·er** *n.*

a·bid·ing *adj.* Continuing; permanent; steadfast.—**a·bid·ing·ly** *adv.*—**a·bid·ing·ness** *n.*

a·bil·i·ty (uh-*bil*-ih-tee) *n.* [*pl.* -ties] Competence; power; skill.

ab·ject (ab-jekt) *adj.* Lowly; mean; despicable.—**ab·ject·ly** *adv.*—**ab·ject·ness** *n.*

ab·jure (ab-*joor*) *v.* [ab·jured; ab·jur·ing] To renounce formally; reject; recant.—**ab·ju·ra·tion** *n.* (ab-joor-*ay*-shun)—**ab·jur·er** *n.*

ab·la·tive (ab-luh-tiv) *n. Grammar.* A case expressing separation or means of accomplishment.—**ab·la·tive** *adj.*

ab·laut (ab-lowt) *n. Philology.* Substitution of one vowel for another in a word root to indicate modification of use or meaning.

a·blaze (uh-*blayz*) *adj.* 1. On fire. 2. Eager; excited.—**a·blaze** *adv.*

a·ble (*ay*-b'l) *adj.* 1. Capable; qualified. 2. Authorized; legally entitled. 3. Talented; competent.—**a·bly** *adv.*

a·ble-bod·ied *adj.* Normally strong; having use of all limbs.—**a·ble·bod·ied·ness** *n.*

able-bodied seaman. *Nautical.* Also **A.B.** A seaman who has passed the Department of Commerce examination for proficiency in seamanship.

ab·lu·tion (ab-*loo*-sh'n) *n.* A washing with water; bath.—**ab·lu·tion·ar·y** *adj.*

ab·ne·gate (ab-nih-gayt) *v.* [ab·ne·gat·ed; -gat·ing] To deny; renounce.—**ab·ne·ga·tion** (ab-nih-*gay*-shun) *n.*—**ab·ne·ga·tor** *n.*

ab·nor·mal (ab-*nor*-m'l) *adj.* Deviating from the usual or standard; irregular.—**ab·nor·mal·ly** *adv.*—**ab·nor·mal·ness** *n.*

ab·nor·mal·i·ty (ab-nor-*mal*-ih-tee) *n.* [*pl.* -ties] Also **ab·nor·mi·ty.** 1. Deviation from standard or normal. 2. Malformation; irregularity; deformity.

a·board *adv.* On or within a ship or train.—**a·board** *prep.*

a·bode (uh-*bohd*) *n.* 1. A residence; habitation. 2. Sojourn; continued stay.

a·bode. *Past tense & past participle* of **abide.**

a·bol·ish (uh-*bol*-ish) *v.* To do away with; revoke; annul.—**a·bol·ish·a·ble** *adj.*—**a·bol·ish·er** *n.*—**a·bol·ish·ment** *n.*

ab·o·li·tion (ab-uh-*lish*-'n) *n.* An annulling; utter destruction.—**ab·o·li·tion·ar·y** *adj.*

ab·o·li·tion·ist (ab-uh-*lish*-un-ist) *n. U.S. History.* One who favored the abolition of slavery prior to and during the Civil War.

a·bom·i·na·ble (uh-*bom*-nuh-b'l) *adj.* Hateful; offensive; annoying; loathsome.—**a·bom·in·a·ble·ness** *n.*—**a·bom·in·a·bly** *adv.*

a·bom·i·nate (uh-*bom*-uh-nayt) *v.* [a·bom·i·nat·ed; -nat·ing] To detest; abhor.

a·bom·i·na·tion (uh-bom-uh-*nay*-sh'n) *n.* 1. Extreme loathing. 2. A detestable act or object; gross vice.

ab·o·rig·i·nal (ab-uh-*rij*-uh-n'l) *adj.* Original; first.—*n.* The earliest inhabitant of a region.—**ab·o·rig·i·nal·ly** *adv.*

ab·o·rig·i·nes (ab-uh-*rij*-uh-neez) *n. pl.* The original inhabitants of a country or area.

a·bort (uh-*bort*) *v.* 1. To give birth before the usual term; miscarry. 2. To produce a miscarriage, esp. illegally.

a·bor·tion (uh-*bor*-shun) *n.* 1. A miscarriage; premature birth. 2. Artificial inducement of a premature birth. 3. A prematurely cast foetus; monster. 4. A plan that fails to be carried out. 5. *Biology.* Absence or underdevelopment of an organ.—**a·bor·tion·ist** *n.* One who illegally induces a miscarriage.—**a·bor·tion·al** *adj.*

a·bor·tive (uh-*bor*-tiv) *adj.* 1. Born prematurely. 2. Imperfectly developed. 3. Failing; producing nothing. 4. *Medicine.* Tending to produce abortion.—**-tive·ly** *adv.*—**-tive·ness** *n.*

a·bound (uh-*bownd*) *v.* To be numerous or copious; teem.—**a·bound·ing** *adj.*—**-ing·ly** *adv.*

a·bout (uh-*bowt*) *prep.* 1. Around; on all sides. 2. Near to. 3. Engaged in; concerned with. 4. Concerning; relating to.—*adv.* 1. Around. 2. Nearly; approximately. 3. Almost begun.

a·bout-face *n.* 1. *Military.* An order to turn half around. 2. A reversal, as of opinion.—*v.* [a·bout-faced; a·bout-fac·ing].

a·bove (uh-*buv*) *prep.* Over; more than; superior to; beyond.—*adv.* Overhead; higher than.—*adj.* 1. Aforesaid, in written matter. 2. Higher.—*n.* 1. Heaven; the overhead. 2. The aforesaid.

a·bove·board *adj.* Open; involving no deception.—**a·bove·board** *adv.*

ab·ra·ca·dab·ra (ab-ruh-kuh-*dab*-ruh) *n.* 1. A supposedly magical word. 2. Meaningless or diverting babble or ritual.

ab·rade (uh-*brayd*) *v.* [ab·rad·ed; ab·rad·ing] To wear down by friction.—**ab·rad·er** *n.*

ab·ra·sion (uh-*bray*-zhun) *n.* 1. A wearing away by friction. 2. Substance worn off. 3. Break in the skin caused by scraping.

ab·ra·sive (uh-*bray*-siv) *n.* An agent which grinds or wears away.—**ab·ra·sive** *adj.*

a·breast (uh-*brest*) *adv.* Side by side; up to a certain level or degree.

a·bridge (uh-*brij*) *v.* [a·bridged; a·bridg·ing] To shorten; curtail; condense; compress.—**a·bridg·a·ble, a·bridge·a·ble** *adj.*—**a·bridg·er** *n.*

a·bridg·ment, a·bridge·ment (uh-*brij*-m'nt) *n.* 1. A reduction; condensation. 2. A book shortened by being more concisely expressed.

a·broad (uh-*brawd*) *adv.* 1. At large; expansively. 2. In a foreign land; beyond the bounds of an enclosure.

ab·ro·gate (ab-ruh-gayt) *v.* [ab·ro·gat·ed; -gat·ing] To repeal; annul; cancel.—**ab·ro·ga·tion** (ab-ruh-*gay*-shun) *n.*—**ab·ro·ga·tive** *adj.*—**ab·ro·ga·tor** *n.*

ab·rupt (uh-*brupt*) *adj.* **1.** Sudden; unexpected. **2.** Steep; broken off. **3.** Unconnected; without adequate transition.—**ab·rupt·ly** *adv.* —**ab·rupt·ness** *n.*

ab·scess (*ab*-sess) *n.* A pus sac or cavity.—**ab·scess** *v.*—**ab·scessed** *adj.*

ab·scis·sa (ab-*sis*-uh) *n. Plane Geometry.* One of two quantities by which a point is located graphically; the horizontal coordinate of a point. In the illustration, the distance BP measured on the line AA' is the abscissa of point P.

ABSCISSA

ab·scond (ab-*skond*) *v.* To decamp; run away to avoid the law.—**ab·scond·er** *n.*

ab·sence (*ab*-s'ns) *n.* **1.** Being away, apart, or wanting; not being here. **2.** Nonexistence. **3.** Inattention; abstraction.—**ab·sent** *adj. & v.* (ab-*sent*)—**ab·sent·ly** *adv.*

ab·sen·tee (ab-s'n-*tee*) *n.* **1.** An owner whose interests are administered by an agent. **2.** Anyone at a distance from his affairs.—**ab·sen·tee** *adj.*—**ab·sen·tee·ism** *n.*

ab·sent-mind·ed *adj.* Forgetful; abstracted. —**ab·sent-mind·ed·ly** *adv.*—**-mind·ed·ness** *n.*

ab·sinthe, ab·sinth (*ab*-sinth, ab-*sinth*) *n.* A cordial of brandy and wormwood.

ab·so·lute (*ab*-suh-loot) *adj.* **1.** Unconditional; unlimited. **2.** Perfect; consummate. **3.** Positive; certain. **4.** *Philosophy.* Existing independently of all variable factors; unchangeable. **5.** [*often cap.*] Divine; beyond human control.—*n. Philosophy.* God, or the ultimate cause of all things.—**ab·so·lute·ly** *adv.*—**ab·so·lute·ness** *n.*

ab·so·lu·tion (ab-suh-*loo*-shun) *n.* **1.** Forgiveness; release from guilt or penalty. **2.** *Theology.* Remission of sins.

ab·so·lut·ism (*ab*-suh-loo-tizm) *n.* Unlimited monarchy; despotism; total control of government by a ruler.—**ab·so·lut·ist** *n. & adj.*

ab·solve (ab-*solv*) *v.* [ab·solved; ab·solv·ing] **1.** To pardon; exonerate; free of guilt or blame. **2.** To acquit; remit. **3.** *Theology.* To grant remission of sins.—**ab·solv·a·ble** *adj.* —**ab·solv·er** *n.*

ab·sorb (ab-*sorb*) *v.* **1.** To soak up; engulf; take in. **2.** To engross; take up completely. —**ab·sorb·a·bil·i·ty** *n.* Capacity to absorb.—**ab·sorb·a·ble** *adj.*—**ab·sorb·er** *n.*

ab·sorbed *adj.* Engrossed; intent; rapt.—**ab·sorb·ed·ly** *adv.*—**ab·sorb·ed·ness** *n.*

ab·sorb·ent *adj.* Able to absorb or take up. —**ab·sorb·ent** *n.*—**ab·sorb·en·cy** *n.*

ab·sorb·ing *adj.* Engrossing; interesting.—**ab·sorb·ing·ly** *adv.*

ab·sorp·tion (ab-*sorp*-sh'n) *n.* **1.** A taking up; encompassing. **2.** Rapt attention or interest. **3.** *Physics.* Retention of molecules or energy by a substance. **4.** *Biology.* Process by which nutritive and other fluids are taken up by organs of plants or animals.—**ab·sorp·tive** *adj.*

—ab·sorp·tive·ness, ab·sorp·tiv·i·ty (ab-sorp-*tiv*-ih-tee) *n.*

ab·stain (ab-*stayn*) *v.* To refrain; deny oneself of.—**ab·stain·er** *n.*

ab·ste·mi·ous (ab-*stee*-mee-us) *adj.* Temperate; avoiding excesses; sparing in diet and drink; moderate.—**-mi·ous·ly** *adv.*—**-mi·ous·ness** *n.*

ab·sten·tion (ab-*sten*-shun) *n.* Self-denial; refusing one's natural desires.—**ab·sten·tious** *adj.*

ab·sti·nence (*ab*-stuh-n'ns) *n.* Nonindulgence; voluntary restraint of desires.—**ab·sti·nent** *adj.* —**ab·sti·nent·ly** *adv.*

ab·stract (ab-*strakt*) *adj.* Not concrete; conceived as independent of a definite object or idea.—*v.* **1.** To extract; separate; withdraw. **2.** To summarize; select from a writing.—*n.* (*ab*-strakt) **1.** A summary of the major points of a treatise. **2.** The essence of anything; epitome.

ab·stract·ed (ab-*strakt*-id) *adj.* **1.** Separated. **2.** Refined; distilled. **3.** Summarized. **4.** Absent-minded; inattentive.—**ab·stract·ed·ly** *adv.* —**ab·stract·ed·ness** *n.*

ab·strac·tion (ab-*strak*-shun) *n.* **1.** Mental process of making generalizations from concrete examples. **2.** An abstract idea or work of art. **3.** Deep mental concentration.

ab·struse (ab-*stroos*) *adj.* **1.** Profound; difficult to understand. **2.** Obscure.—**ab·struse·ly** *adv.*—**ab·struse·ness** *n.*

ab·surd (ub-*serd*) *adj.* Ridiculous; incongruous; inconsistent with common sense or reason. —**ab·surd·ly** *adv.*—**ab·surd·ness** *n.*

ab·surd·i·ty (ub-*serd*-uh-tee) *n.* [*pl.*-ties] **1.** Preposterousness. **2.** A fact or statement that is foolish or unreasonable.

a·bun·dance (uh-*bun*-d'ns) *n.* Plenty; richness; large supply.—**a·bun·dant** *adj.*—**a·bun·dant·ly** *adv.*

a·buse (uh-*byooz*) *v.* [a·bused; a·bus·ing] **1.** To maltreat; do wrong to; injure. **2.** To slander; revile. **3.** To misuse; use for evil.—**a·buse** (uh-*byooss*) *n.*—**a·bus·er** (a-*byooz*-er) *n.*

a·bu·sive (uh-*byoos*-iv) *adj.* Maltreating; offensive; insulting.—**a·bu·sive·ly** *adv.*—**a·bu·sive·ness** *n.*

a·but (uh-*but*) *v.* [a·but·ted; a·but·ting] To adjoin; border.

a·but·ment (uh-*but*-m'nt) *n. Architecture.* A solid structure which supports the end of a bridge or arch.

a·byss (uh-*biss*) *n.* A deep pit; bottomless void.—**a·bys·mal** (ab-*iz*-m'l) *adj.* —**-mal·ly** *adv.*

Ab·ys·sin·i·a (ab-ih-*sin*-ee-uh) Former name of Ethiopia. —**Ab·ys·sin·i·an** *adj. & n.*

ABUTMENT

a·ca·cia (uh-*kay*-shuh) *n.* A group of trees and shrubs of the pea family, native to warm climates.

ac·a·dem·ic (ak-uh-*dem*-ik) *adj.* Also **ac·a·dem·i·cal.** 1. Pertaining to the liberal arts. 2. Pertaining to an academy, college, or university. 3. Theoretical; abstract.—**ac·a·dem·ic** *n.*—**ac·a·dem·i·cal·ly** *adv.*

a·cad·e·my (uh-*kad*-uh-mee) *n.* [*pl.* -mies] 1. A learned society or association. 2. A school or seminary ranking below a college; specialized school. 3. Plato and his philosophical followers.—**ac·a·de·mi·cian** (ak-uh-deh-*mish*-’n) *n.* A member of an academy.

A·ca·di·a (uh-*kay*-dee-uh) *n.* Poetic name of Nova Scotia.—**A·ca·di·an** *adj.* & *n.*

a·can·thus (uh-*kan*-thus) *n.* 1. A Mediterranean herb. 2. *Architecture.* An ornamental work resembling the leaves of the acanthus plant.

ACANTHUS (def. 2)

ac·cede (ak-*seed*) *v.* [ac·ced·ed; ac·ced·ing] 1. To assent; comply; agree. 2. To succeed; inherit.—**ac·ce·dence** *n.*—**ac·ced·er** *n.*

ac·cel·er·ate (ak-*sel*-er-ayt) *v.* [ac·cel·er·at·ed; -at·ing] To increase speed; hasten; bring nearer in time.—**ac·cel·er·a·tion** (ak-sel-uh-*ray*-shun) *n.*—**ac·cel·er·a·tive** *adj.*

ac·cel·er·a·tor (ak-*sel*-er-ay-ter) *n.* 1. An agent for increasing the speed of a chemical reaction. 2. A throttle; lever used to regulate a vehicle’s speed.

ac·cent (*ak*-sent) *n.* 1. Stress placed on a syllable of a word. 2. A mark indicating stress in pronunciation. 3. A peculiar, foreign, or characteristic manner of pronunciation. 4. Quality of expression; inflection. 5. *Music.* Stress placed on certain notes or parts of bars.—*v.* (ak-*sent*) To stress.

ac·cen·tu·ate (ak-*sen*-choo-ayt) *v.* [ac·cen·tu·at·ed; -at·ing] To emphasize; stress.—**ac·cen·tu·a·tion** (ak-sen-choo-*ay*-sh’n) *n.*

ac·cept (ak-*sept*) *v.* 1. To take; receive. 2. To tolerate; take passively. 3. To receive or act upon favorably. 4. To agree to.—**ac·cept·er** *n.*

ac·cept·a·ble (ak-*sep*-tuh-b’l) *adj.* Capable or worthy of being received; welcome; gratifying.—**ac·cept·a·bil·i·ty** (ak-sep-tuh-*bil*-uh-tee), **ac·cept·a·ble·ness** *n.*—**ac·cept·a·bly** *adv.*

ac·cep·tance (ak-*sep*-t’ns) *n.* Also **ac·cep·tan·cy.** 1. Reception; approval; assent to an offer; agreement to terms. 2. A bill of exchange which has been accepted.—**ac·cep·tant** *n.*

ac·cep·ta·tion (ak-sep-*tay*-shun) *n.* The usual, accepted meaning of a word or phrase.

ac·cess (*ak*-ses) *n.* 1. Approach; admittance. 2. An entrance.

ac·ces·si·ble (ak-*ses*-uh-b’l) *adj.* Approachable; attainable; easily reached.—**ac·ces·si·bil·i·ty** (ak-ses-uh-*bil*-uh-tee) *n.*—**ac·ces·si·bly** *adv.*

ac·ces·sion (ak-*sesh*-’n) *n.* 1. Acquiescence; agreement to a proposal. 2. Increase; augmentation. 3. Assumption of a throne or of certain rights and dignities.

ac·ces·so·ry (ak-*ses*-uh-ree) *n.* [*pl.* -ries] 1. An accomplice. 2. An adjunct; concomitant part; appendage. 3. A secondarily contributing factor.—**ac·ces·so·ry, ac·ces·so·ri·al** (ak-seh-*sor*-ee-ul) *adj.*—**ac·ces·so·ri·ly** *adv.*—**ac·ces·so·ri·ness** *n.*

ac·ci·dent (*ak*-sih-dent) *n.* 1. Chance; chance happening; unforeseeable occurrence. 2. A mishap; calamity; casualty.

ac·ci·den·tal (ak-sih-*den*-t’l) *adj.* 1. Occurring by chance; without assignable cause; unintentional. 2. Incidental; not organically required; added on.—**ac·ci·den·tal·ly** *adv.*—**ac·ci·den·tal·ness** *n.*

ac·claim (uh-*klaym*) *v.* 1. To applaud; salute. 2. To proclaim or recognize officially.—*n.* Applause; public recognition; fame.—**ac·claim·er** *n.*

ac·cla·ma·tion (ak-luh-*may*-sh’n) *n.* 1. Demonstration; applause. 2. An oral vote in which individual voices are not counted.—**ac·clam·a·to·ry** (uh-*klam*-uh-tor-ee) *adj.*

ac·cli·mate (uh-*kly*-m’t, *ak*-luh-mayt) *v.* [ac·cli·mat·ed; -mat·ing] To familiarize with a new climate; acclimatize.—**ac·cli·ma·tion** (ak-luh-*may*-shun) *n.*

ac·cli·ma·tize (uh-*kly*-muh-tyz) *v.* [ac·cli·ma·tized; -tiz·ing] To adapt to a change in climate; prepare for different conditions.—**ac·cli·ma·ti·za·tion** (uh-kly-muh-tuh-*zay*-shun) *n.*—**ac·cli·ma·ti·zer** (uh-*kly*-muh-tyz-er) *n.*

ac·cliv·i·ty (uh-*kliv*-uh-tee) *n.* [*pl.* -ties] An upward slope; incline.

ac·co·lade (ak-uh-*layd*) *n.* 1. The ceremony conferring knighthood. 2. An award; statement of high praise.

ac·com·mo·date (uh-*kom*-uh-dayt) *v.* [ac·com·mo·dat·ed; -dat·ing] 1. To fit; make suitable; adapt. 2. To help; do a favor for. 3. To lodge; put up. 4. To reconcile; bring into harmony.

ac·com·mo·dat·ing *adj.* Also **ac·com·mo·da·tive.** Obliging; complying; inclined to do favors.—**ac·com·mo·dat·ing·ly** *adv.*—**ac·com·mo·dat·ing·ness** *n.*

ac·com·mo·da·tion (uh-kom-uh-*day*-sh’n) *n.* 1. Adaptation; adjustment; reconciliation. 2. A convenience. 3. A lodging; place to stay or sleep. 4. A loan of money.

ac·com·pa·ni·ment (uh-*kum*-puh-nee-m’nt) *n.* Music played as background to a solo voice or instrument.—**pa·nist** (uh-*kum*-puhn-ist) *n.*

ac·com·pa·ny (uh-*kum*-puh-nee) *v.* [ac·com·pa·nied; -ny·ing] 1. To go along with; escort. 2. To be associated with. 3. *Music.* To play an accompaniment for.

ac·com·plice (uh-*kom*-plis) *n.* One who contributes to a crime.

ac·com·plish (uh-*kom*-plish) *v.* To carry out; finish completely; achieve.—**ac·com·plish·er** *n.*—**ac·com·plish·ment** *n.*

ac·com·plished (uh-*kom*-plisht) *adj.* 1. Highly

A

skilled; polished. 2. Completed; effected.

ac·cord (uh-*kord*) *n.* 1. Agreement; harmony. 2. Volition. 'He went of his own accord.'—*v.* 1. To grant; concede. 2. To agree.

ac·cord·ance (uh-*kord*-uns) *n.* Agreement; conformity.—**ac·cord·ant** *adj.*—**ac·cord·ant·ly** *adv.*

ac·cord·ing·ly *adv.* 1. Consequently; therefore. 2. Suitably; agreeably.

according to. 1. In accordance with. 2. As alleged by.

ac·cor·di·on (uh-*kor*-dee-un) *n. Music.* A portable keyboard instrument in which the tone is produced by metal reeds vibrated by air from a manually operated bellows. —*adj.* Folded in pleats. 'An accordion bellows.'

ACCORDION

ac·cost (uh-*kost*) *v.* To greet; address first, esp. aggressively.

ac·count (uh-*kownt*) *n.* 1. A reckoning. 2. A record of business transactions. 3. A statement of reasons or causes. 4. Narrative; relating of facts. 5. A statement or vindication of conduct. 6. Esteem; importance. 7. Reason; ground; consideration. 8. Behalf. 'I did it on his account.' 9. Record of a customer's purchases. 10. A customer.—*v.* 1. To deem; consider; judge. 2. To explain; assign reasons. 3. To give a reckoning or statement of particulars. 4. To be responsible.

ac·count·a·ble (uh-*kownt*-uh-b'l) *adj.* 1. Liable; responsible; answerable. 2. Having an assignable reason or cause.—**ac·count·a·bil·i·ty** (uh-kownt-uh-*bil*-uh-tee), **ac·count·a·ble·ness** *n.* —**ac·count·a·bly** *adv.*

ac·count·ant (uh-*kownt*-unt) *n.* A keeper or examiner of financial records.—**ac·count·an·cy** *n.*

ac·count·ing *n.* The science of keeping or auditing business accounts; accountancy.

ac·cout·er, ac·cou·tre (uh-*koot*-er) *v.* To equip; dress, esp. for military service.

ac·cou·ter·ments, ac·cou·tre·ments (uh-*koo*-ter-m'nts) *n. pl.* Trappings; furnishings; military dress and equipment.

ac·cred·it (uh-*kred*-it) *v.* 1. To approve; authorize. 2. To trust; esteem; believe. 3. To send with credentials.

ac·cre·tion (uh-*kree*-shun) *n.* 1. Growth; accrual. 2. An addition to. 3. *Medicine.* The growing together of separate members.—**ac·cre·tive** *adj.*

ac·crue (uh-*kroo*) *v.* [ac·crued; ac·cru·ing] 1. To be added or incurred. 2. To stem from. —**ac·cru·al, ac·crue·ment** *n.*

ac·cu·mu·late (uh-*kyoo*-myuh-layt) *v.* [ac·cu·mu·lat·ed; -lat·ing] To amass; collect; acquire. —**ac·cu·mu·la·ble** *adj.*—**ac·cu·mu·la·tion** (uh-kyoo-myuh-*lay*-sh'n) *n.*—**ac·cu·mu·la·tor** *n.*

ac·cu·mu·la·tive (uh-*kyoo*-myuh-luh-tiv) *adj.*

Tending to pile up or grow; cumulative.—**ac·cu·mu·la·tive·ly** *adv.*—**ac·cu·mu·la·tive·ness** *n.*

ac·cu·ra·cy (*ak*-yoo-ruh-see) *n.* Exactness; precision; correctness.—**ac·cu·rate** *adj.*—**ac·cu·rate·ly** *adv.*—**ac·cu·rate·ness** *n.*

ac·curs·ed (uh-*kerss*-ed; uh-*kerst*) *adj.* 1. Doomed; ruined. 2. Detestable; damnable.—**ac·curs·ed·ly** *adv.*—**ac·curs·ed·ness** *n.*

ac·cu·sa·tion (ak-yoo-*zay*-sh'n) *n.* A charge; statement of offense committed or suspected; indictment.

ac·cu·sa·tive (uh-*kyoo*-zuh-tiv) *n. Grammar.* The case of a substantive used as object of a verb.—**ac·cu·sa·tive** *adj.*—**ac·cu·sa·tive·ly** *adv.*

ac·cuse (uh-*kyooz*) *v.* [ac·cused; ac·cus·ing] To blame; charge with a fault or crime.—**ac·cus·er** *n.*—**ac·cus·ing·ly** *adv.*

ac·cus·tom (uh-*kus*-tum) *v.* To become used or inured; habituate.—**ac·cus·tomed** *adj.*

ace *n.* (*ayss*) 1. A playing card having only one spot. 2. *Aviation.* A fighter pilot credited with downing five or more enemy planes. 3. An expert. 4. *Tennis.* A point won by the serve alone.—*adj.* Excellent; expert.—*v.* [aced; ac·ing] *Tennis.* To score on the serve.

a·cer·bi·ty (uh-*ser*-bih-tee) *n.* 1. Sourness; astringency. 2. Harshness of temper.

ac·et·an·i·lide (ass-ut-*an*-ih-lid) *n.* Also **ac·et·an·i·lid.** A white, crystalline, odorless drug used to reduce pain and fever.

ac·e·tate (*ass*-uh-tayt) *n.* A compound of acetic acid reacted with a base, now widely used as a plastic.—**ac·e·tat·ed** *adj.*

a·ce·tic (uh-*see*-tik) *adj.* Like acetic acid or vinegar; sour.—**acetic acid.** A colorless sour fluid contained in vinegar.

a·cet·y·lene (uh-*set*-uh-leen) *n.* A colorless industrial gas generated from water and calcium carbide and used in welding, lighting, etc. —**acetylene torch.** An instrument for cutting through metals rapidly.

A·chae·an, A·cha·ian (uh-*kee*-un, uh-*kay*-un) *adj.* Relating to ancient Greece or Achaia.—*n.* An ancient Greek.

ache (*ayk*) *v.* [ached; ach·ing] To suffer pain; be distressed.—**ache** *n.*—**ach·ing·ly** *adv.*

Ach·er·on (*ak*-er-on) *n.* The river of woe in Hades.

a·chieve (uh-*cheev*) *v.* [a·chieved; a·chiev·ing] To attain; bring about; finish successfully. —**a·chiev·a·ble** *adj.*—**a·chiev·er** *n.*—**a·chieve·ment** *n.*

A·chil·les (uh-*kil*-eez) *n.* The heroic warrior of Homer's *Iliad.*—**Ach·il·le·an** *adj.*

Achilles' heel. A vulnerable point.

Achilles' tendon. The large muscle from the heel to the calf of the leg.

ach·ro·mat·ic (ak-ruh-*mat*-ik) *adj.* 1. Colorless. 2. *Optics.* Refracting light without decomposing it into component colors.

ac·id (*ass*-id) *n. Chemistry.* Any compound having hydrogen as its electropositive element. —*adj.* Sour; acidlike; corrosive.—**a·cid·ic** (uh-*sid*-ik) *adj.* Having the properties of an acid;

sour.—a·cid·i·ty n. (uh-sid-ih-tee).—ac·id·ly, a·cid·i·cal·ly adv.—ac·id·ness n.

a·cid·o·sis (ass-ih-doh-sis) n. A condition of low alkalinity of the blood.

a·cid·u·late (uh-sid-yoo-layt) v. [a·cid·u·lated; -lat·ing] To make slightly sour.—a·cid·u·lous adj. Slightly sour or acidic.

ack-ack n. Slang. 1. Antiaircraft guns. 2. Flak from antiaircraft shells.—ack-ack adj.

ac·knowl·edge (ak-nol-ij) v. [ac·knowl·edged; -edg·ing] 1. To indicate receipt. 2. Recognize; admit; confess; avow.—ac·knowl·edge·a·ble adj.—-edg·ment, -edge·ment n.

ac·me (ak-mee) n. The zenith; highest point; top.

ac·ne (ak-nee) n. A skin condition marked by pimples, esp. on the face.

ac·o·lyte (ak-uh-lyt) n. 1. Roman Catholic Church. a. Boy who assists in the celebration of the mass. b. Holder of a minor order. 2. An attendant.

ac·o·nite (ak-uh-nyt) n. 1. The plant wolf's-bane or monk's-hood. 2. A drug prepared from the plant.

a·corn (ay-korn) n. The nut of the oak tree.

a·cous·tic (uh-koo-stik). Also a·cous·ti·cal. adj. Pertaining to sound or hearing. —a·cous·ti·cal·ly adv.

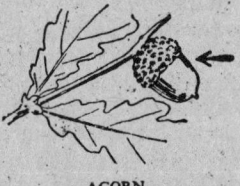

ACORN

a·cous·tics n. sing. 1. The science of sound. 2. [n. pl.] The properties of an auditorium which make it conducive to ready and faithful transmission of sound.

ac·quaint (uh-kwaynt) v. To make known or familiar; inform; communicate.—ac·quaint·ed adj. Knowing; familiar with.

ac·quaint·ance (uh-kwaynt-uns) n. 1. A person slightly known; one neither stranger nor friend. 2. Familiarity; knowledge.—ac·quain·tance·ship n.

ac·qui·esce (ak-wee-es) v. [ac·qui·esced; -esc·ing] To agree; consent; comply.—ac·qui·esc·ing·ly adv.

ac·qui·es·cence n. Assent; concurrence; submission.—ac·qui·es·cent adj.

ac·quire (uh-kwyr) n. [ac·quired; ac·quir·ing]. To gain; obtain; attain.—ac·quir·a·ble adj. —ac·quire·ment n.—ac·quir·er n.

ac·qui·si·tion (ak-wuh-zish'n) n. 1. Obtaining; procuring. 2. A gain; material achievement.

ac·quis·i·tive (uh-kwiz-uh-tiv) adj. Grasping; ambitious to collect personal gains.—ac·quis·i·tive·ly adv.—ac·quis·i·tive·ness n.

ac·quit (uh-kwit) v. [ac·quit·ted; ac·quit·ting] 1. To clear; declare not guilty; absolve. 2. To behave; bear; conduct.—ac·quit·tal n.—ac·quit·ter n.

a·cre (ay-ker) n. A measurement of land. Area: 4,840 sq. yds.—a·cred adj.

a·cre·age (ay-ker-ij) n. Land considered in terms of acres; acres collectively.

ac·rid (ak-rid) adj. Sharp; pungent; bitter. —ac·rid·ly adv.—ac·rid·ness n.

ac·ri·mo·ni·ous (ak-rih-moh-nee-us) adj. Bitter; caustic; biting.—ac·ri·mo·ni·ous·ly adj.—ac·ri·mo·ni·ous·ness n.

ac·ri·mo·ny (ak-ruh-moh-nee) n. Bitterness; malignance; virulence.

ac·ro·bat (ak-ruh-bat) n. Performer of gymnastic feats, as in a circus.

ac·ro·bat·ic (ak-ruh-bat-ik) adj. Gymnastic; pertaining to an acrobat or his feats.—ac·ro·bat·ics n. 1. [sing.] The art of an acrobat. 2. [pl.] The antics or feats of an acrobat.

ac·ro·meg·a·ly (ak-ruh-meg-uh-lee) n. Also ac·ro·meg·a·li·a (ak-roh-meg-ay-lee-uh). Disease characterized by progressive enlargement of the skull, hands, feet, and head.

a·crop·o·lis (uh-krop-uh-lis) n. The citadel of an ancient Greek city, esp. Athens.

a·cross (uh-kross) prep. 1. Over; athwart. 2. To the other side of.—adv. From one side to another; to the other side.

a·cros·tic (uh-kros-tik) n. A verse in which the first letters of the lines, taken in order, spell out words.—a·cros·tic, a·cros·ti·cal adj.—a·cros·ti·cal·ly adv.

act (akt) n. 1. That which is done or being done; action. 2. Performance; entertainment. 3. A major division of a play. 4. A legislative decree or law. 5. Law. A document proving a transaction or contract.—v. 1. To do; exert power; produce results. 2. To behave; comport. 3. To perform as an actor; to play a role.—act·a·bil·i·ty (ak-tuh-bil-uh-tee) n.—act·a·ble adj.

act·ing n. The profession or art of an actor. —adj. Performing a duty temporarily or in place of another. 'Acting vice-president.'

ac·tin·ism (ak-tin-izm) n. 1. The production of chemical changes by light or other radiant energy. 2. The property of radiant energy that effects this reaction.—ac·tin·ic (ak-tin-ik) adj.—ac·tin·i·cal·ly adv.

ac·tin·i·um (ak-tin-ee-um) n. A radioactive element in uranium ore. (Symbol: Ac).

ac·tion (ak-shun) n. 1. Movement; manifested energy. 2. An act; deed; feat. 3. Exertion of force by one element on another; agency. 4. The connected series of events which sustain the plot in a play or other literary work. 5. Law. A claim or legal demand brought before a court. 6. Battle; fight. 7. The working parts of certain mechanisms. 8. [pl.] Comportment; behavior.—ac·tion·a·ble adj. Furnishing ground for a legal action. —ac·tion·a·bly adv.

ac·ti·vate (ak-tih-vayt) v. [ac·ti·vat·ed; -vat·ing] 1. To render chemically active or radioactive; charge with chemical or radioactive energy. 2. To intensify; stimulate.—ac·ti·va·tion (ak-tuh-vay-shun) n.—ac·ti·va·tor n.

ac·tive (ak-tiv) adj. 1. Having movement or

A

energy; lively; busy. 2. Functioning; workable. 3. *Medicine.* Effective; producing a prompt effect. 4. *Grammar.* Expressing action of the subjects; opposed to *passive.* 5. Actually taking part in; working. 'An active member of the party.'—**ac·tive·ly** *adv.* —**ac·tive·ness** *n.*

ac·tiv·i·ty (ak-*tiv*-uh-tee) *n.* [-ties] 1. Movement; vigorousness; agility; briskness. 2. A pursuit; vocation; avocation.

ac·tor (*ak*-ter) *n.* 1. A theatrical performer. 2. A pretender; feigner.—**ac·tress** (*ak*-tris) *n.*

Acts. The fifth book of the New Testament depicting the deeds of Christ's apostles.

ac·tu·al (*ak*-choo-ul) *adj.* Really and objectively existing; present.—**ac·tu·al·ly** *adv.*—**ac·tu·al·ness** *n.*

ac·tu·al·i·ty (ak-choo-*al*-ih-tee) *n.* [*pl.* -ties] 1. Reality; concrete existence. 2. An accomplished fact.

ac·tu·al·ize (*ak*-choo-ul-yz) *v.* [ac·tu·al·ized; -iz·ing] To make real or actual.—**ac·tu·al·i·za·tion** (ak-choo-ul-ih-*zay*-shun) *n.*

ac·tu·ar·y (*ak*-choo-er-ee) *n.* [*pl.* -ies] An insurance specialist; computer of insurance risks or premiums.—**ac·tu·ar·i·al** (ak-choo-*air*-ee-ul) *adj.*—**ac·tu·ar·i·al·ly** *adv.*

ac·tu·ate (*ak*-choo-ayt) *v.* [ac·tu·at·ed; -at·ing] To put into action; motivate; arouse.—**ac·tu·a·tion** (ak-choo-*ay*-shun) *n.*—**ac·tu·a·tor** *n.*

a·cu·men (uh-*kyoo*-m'n) *n.* Keenness of insight or intellect; power of fine discrimination.

a·cute (uh-*kyoot*) *adj.* 1. Sharp; pointed. 2. Penetrating; mentally keen; subtle. 3. *Geometry.* Applying to angles smaller than right angles. 4. *Medicine.* Having severe symptoms; coming soon to a crisis; opposed to *chronic.*—**a·cute·ly** *adv.*—**a·cute·ness** *n.*

acute accent. A diacritical mark (') used, as in French, to indicate stress or the quality of a vowel.

ad *n.* [*pl.* ads] Short for **advertisement.**—*adj.* Short for **advertising.**

A.D. (*ay dee*). *Abbreviation* for **Anno Domini** or year of the Lord, used with dates to indicate time since the birth of Christ.

ad·age (*ad*-ij) *n.* A proverb; old saying.

a·da·gio (uh-*dah*-joh) *adj. Music.* Slow; leisurely; graceful.—*n.* 1. A musical composition in a slow, relaxed tempo. 2. A slow and stately ballet dance performed by two people.

Ad·am (*ad*-um). *Bible.* In the Book of Genesis, the father of the human race.—**A·dam·ic** (uh-*dam*-ik), **A·dam·i·cal** *adj.*—**A·dam·i·cal·ly** *adv.*

Adam's apple. A prominence of the throat caused by the cartilage of the larynx.

ad·a·mant (*ad*-uh-m'nt) *adj.* Hard; strong; impenetrable; unyielding.—**ad·a·mant** *n.*—**ad·a·man·te·an** (ad-uh-man-*tee*-un), **ad·a·man·tine** (ad-uh-*man*-tin) *adj.*

a·dapt (uh-*dapt*) *v.* 1. To adjust; make suitable. 2. *Biology.* To modify to meet changing conditions. 3. To transpose a play or literary work to a different medium of presentation.

—**a·dapt·a·bil·i·ty** (uh-dap-tuh-*bil*-ih-tee) *n.* —**a·dapt·a·ble** *adj.*—**a·dapt·a·bly** *adv.*—**a·dapt·er, a·dapt·or** *n.*

ad·ap·ta·tion (ad-ap-*tay*-sh'n) *n.* 1. Adjustment; rendering fit or suitable; accommodation. 2. *Biology.* A modification for adjusting to changed environment. 3. Revision of a work for a different use. 4. A dramatic or literary work which has been altered for a different mode of presentation.—**ad·ap·ta·tion·al** *adj.*—**ad·ap·ta·tion·al·ly** *adv.*

add *v.* 1. To sum up; total. 2. To augment; attach to; affix. 3. To make additional remarks.—**add·i·ble** *adj.*

ad·dax (*ad*-aks) *n.* A large African antelope having long, spiraled horns.

ad·den·dum (uh-*den*-dum) *n.* [*pl.* ad·den·da] An addition; appendix.

ad·der (*ad*-er) *n.* 1. A family of nonvenomous snakes. 2. The poisonous viper. 3. A person or machine which adds.

ad·dict (uh-*dikt*) *v.* To form a confirmed practice of; be completely possessed by a habit.—*n.* (*ad*-ikt)—**ad·dict·ed** *adj.*—**ad·dict·ed·ness, ad·dic·tion** *n.*

ad·di·tion (uh-*dish*-un) *n.* 1. Adding of sums. 2. Increase; that which is joined or added. —**ad·di·tion·al** *adj.*—**ad·di·tion·al·ly** *adv.*

ad·dle (*ad*-'l) *v.* [ad·dled; ad·dling] To confuse; mix up.—**ad·dled** *adj.* 1. Muddled. 2. Rotten; spoiled.

ad·dress (uh-*dres*) *n.* 1. Directions on mai indicating destination. 2. Official residence; place at which one may be reached. 3. A speech; oration. 4. One's bearing or manner in conversation. 5. [*usually pl.*] Courtship. —*v.* 1. To make a speech; talk to. 2. To direct, as mail. 3. To accost.—**ad·dress·ee** *n.* The person addressed.—**ad·dres·ser, ad·dres·sor** *n.*

ad·duce (uh-*dyoos*) *v.* [ad·duced; ad·duc·ing] To present as proof; quote authority.—**ad·duc·er** *n.*—**ad·duc·i·ble, ad·duce·a·ble** *adj.*

ad·e·noid (*ad*-in-oid) *n.* A swelling of the tissue of the pharynx in the region of the soft palate. —**ad·e·noi·dal** *adj.*

ad·ept (uh-*dept*) *adj.* Skilled; proficient; well-versed.—*n.* (*ad*-ept) An expert.—**a·dept·ly** *adv.* —**a·dept·ness** *n.*

ad·e·quate (*ad*-uh-kwit) *n.* Sufficient; enough; competent; suitable.—**ad·e·qua·cy, ad·e·quate·ness** *n.*—**ad·e·quate·ly** *adv.*

a·der·min (uh-*der*-min) *n.* A B-complex vitamin which promotes growth and healthful skin.

ad·here (ad-*heer*) *v.* [ad·hered; ad·her·ing] 1. To stick fast; become joined. 2. To be devoted; be associated or connected with. —**ad·her·ence** (ad-*hihr*-uns) *n.*

ad·her·ent (ad-*heer*-'nt) *adj.* Sticking; clinging. —*n.* A follower; partisan; supporter.—**ad·her·ent·ly** *adv.*

ad·he·sion (ud-*hee*-zhun; ad-) *n.* 1. A joining or sticking together. 2. *Medicine.* The joining of members normally separate. 3. *Physics.*

The attraction of two dissimilar surfaces in contact.

ad·he·sive (ud-*hee*-siv; ad-) *adj.* Sticky; clinging.—*n.* A self-sticking tape or bandage.—**ad·he·sive·ly** *adv.*—**ad·he·sive·ness** *n.*

a·dieu (uh-*dyoo*) *Interj.* Farewell; good-by.—*n.* [*pl.* a·dieus (uh-*dyooz*), a·dieux (uh-*dyoo*)] A farewell.

ad·i·pose (*ad*-ih-pohs) *adj.* Fat; fatty.—*n.* Fatty tissue.—**-pose·ness, -pos·i·ty** (-*poss*-uh-tee) *n.*

ad·ja·cent (uh-*jay*-s'nt) *adj.* Near; bordering; adjoining.—**ad·ja·cen·cy, ad·ja·cent·ness** *n.*

ad·jec·tive (*aj*-ik-tiv) *n. Grammar.* A word used with a noun to denote qualities, attributes, scope, or relation of the noun.—**ad·jec·ti·val** (aj-ik-*ty*-v'l) *adj.*—**ad·jec·ti·val·ly** *adv.*

ad·join (uh-*join*) *n.* To touch upon; border. —**ad·join·ing** *adj.*

ad·journ (uh-*jern*) *v.* To suspend a meeting or session; postpone; terminate a session.—**ad·journ·ment** *n.*

ad·judge (uh-*juj*) *v.* [ad·judged; ad·judg·ing] 1. To award in a controversy; decide; settle. 2. To pass sentence on.—**ad·judg·ment** *n.*

ad·junct (*aj*-unkt) *n.* A nonessential addition.

ad·jure (uh-*joor*) *v.* [ad·jured; ad·jur·ing] To command or bind by an oath.—**ad·ju·ra·tion** (ad-joor-*ay*-shun) *n.*

ad·just (uh-*just*) *v.* 1. To fit; make suitable; adapt to changed conditions. 2. To settle; resolve differences; rectify. 3. To regulate. 4. To settle an insurance claim.—**ad·just·a·ble** *adj.*—**ad·just·a·bly** *adv.*—**ad·just·er, ad·just·or** *n.* —**ad·just·ment** *n.*

ad·ju·tant (*aj*-uh-tunt) *n. Military.* An officer who assists a commanding officer by handling administrative details.—**ad·ju·tan·cy** *n.*

ad-lib *v.* [ad-libbed; ad-lib·bing] To perform extemporaneously; inject spontaneous variations in a text or score.—**ad-lib** *adj.*

ad·min·is·ter (ad-*min*-us-ter) *v.* 1. To manage; conduct; superintend. 2. To apply; furnish; serve; dispense. 3. To settle (an estate).

ad·min·is·trate (ad-*min*-uh-strayt) *v.* [ad·min·is·trat·ed; -trat·ing] 1. To direct; govern; manage. 2. To look after the estate of a deceased.—**ad·min·is·tra·tor** *n.*

ad·min·is·tra·tion (ad-min-uh-*stray*-shun) *n.* 1. Direction; management; government. 2. The executive functions of government or an organization. 3. The body of officials in a government; the party in power. 4. *Law.* Management of an estate.—**ad·min·is·tra·tive** *adj.*—**ad·min·is·tra·tive·ly** *adv.*

ad·mir·a·ble (*ad*-mer-uh-b'l) *adj.* Praiseworthy; commendable; estimable.—**ad·mir·a·bly** *adv.*

ad·mir·al (*ad*-mer-ul) *n.* The highest rank of naval officer.

ad·mir·al·ty (*ad*-mer-'l-tee) *n.* 1. *British.* The office in charge of naval and maritime affairs. 2. The office or rank of an admiral.

ad·mire (ad-*myr*) *v.* [ad·mired; ad·mir·ing] To regard with pleasure; esteem; approve highly;

praise.—**ad·mir·a·tion** (ad-muh-*ray*-shun) *n.* —**ad·mir·ing·ly** *adv.*

ad·mis·si·ble (ad-*mis*-uh-b'l) *adj.* Capable of being admitted or conceded.—**ad·mis·si·bil·i·ty** (ad-mis-uh-*bil*-ih-tee), **ad·mis·si·ble·ness** *n.* —**ad·mis·si·bly** *adv.*

ad·mis·sion (ad-*mish*-'n) *n.* 1. Right of entrance; access. 2. A price charged for entrance to any entertainment. 3. Acknowledgment; confession; concession.—**ad·mis·sive** *adj.*

ad·mit (ad-*mit*) *v.* [ad·mit·ted; ad·mit·ting] 1. To allow to enter. 2. To acknowledge; confess. 3. To accept an argument as true. 4. To permit; allow; be capable of.—**ad·mit·tance** *n.*—**ad·mit·ted·ly** *adv.*

ad·mix·ture (ad-*miks*-cher) *n.* 1. A mixing; mingling. 2. A tincture; addition.—**ad·mix** *v.*

ad·mon·ish (ad-*mon*-ish) *v.* To warn; caution; advise against; reprove mildly; remind of duty.—**ad·mon·ish·er** *n.*—**ad·mon·ish·ment** *n.*

ad·mo·ni·tion (ad-muh-*nish*-'n) *n.* Caution; serious instruction; rebuke.—**ad·mon·i·to·ry** (ad-*mon*-ih-tor-ee) *adv.*

ad nauseam (ad-*naw*-shee-um, -zee-). To the point of complete satiation; to the point of nausea.

a·do (uh-*doo*) *n.* Trouble; effort; difficulty.

a·do·be (uh-*doh*-bee) *n.* 1. A sun-dried brick. 2. A house of sun-dried brick.—**a·do·be** *adj.*

ad·o·les·cence (ad-uh-*les*-'ns) *n.* Also **ad·o·les·cen·cy.** The period between childhood and adulthood; youth.—**ad·o·les·cent** *n.* A youth. —**ad·o·les·cent** *adj.*

ADOBE

A·don·is (uh-*dohn*-is, -*don*-) *n. Greek Mythology.* 1. A handsome young nobleman beloved of Aphrodite. 2. Any handsome youth. —**A·don·ic** (uh-*don*-ic) *adj.*

a·dopt (uh-*dopt*) *v.* 1. To take or assume as one's own. 2. To take a child into one's home as one's own.—**a·dopt·a·ble** *adj.*—**a·dopt·a·bil·i·ty** (uh-dop-tuh-*bil*-ih-tee) *n.*—**a·dopt·er** *n.*

a·dop·tion (uh-*dop*-shun) *n.* 1. Acceptance or embracing as one's own. 2. Assumption of legal parenthood of another's child.—**a·dop·tive** *adj.*—**a·dop·tive·ly** *adv.*

a·dor·a·ble (uh-*dor*-uh-b'l) *adj.* 1. *Colloquial.* Entrancingly sweet; lovely. 2. Worthy of deepest love or reverence.—**a·dor·a·bil·i·ty** (uh-dor-uh-*bil*-ih-tee), **a·dor·a·ble·ness** *n.*—**a·dor·a·bly** *adv.*

ad·o·ra·tion (ad-uh-*ray*-sh'n) *n.* 1. Profound or idolizing devotion. 2. Homage; worship. 3. *Art.* A representation of the worship of the Magi or shepherds at the manger.—**a·dore** *v.* [a·dored; a·dor·ing] To idolize; revere.

a·dorn (uh-*dorn*) *v.* To embellish; ornament; decorate.—**a·dorn·ment** *n.*

ad·re·nal gland (ad-*ree*-n'l). One of two duct-

A

less glands which secrete adrenalin, located at the upper ends of the kidneys.

ad·ren·al·in, ad·ren·al·ine (ad-*ren*-uh-lin) *n.* An extract or secretion of the adrenal glands, used to constrict blood vessels.

Adriatic Sea (ay-dree-*at*-ik). A narrow sea between Italy and Yugoslavia.—**A·dri·at·ic** *adj.*

a·drift (uh-*drift*) *adj.* Driven or floating unguided.—**a·drift** *adv.*

a·droit (uh-*droyt*) *adj.* Skillful; expert; ingenious.—**a·droit·ly** *adv.*—**a·droit·ness** *n.*

ad·sorp·tion *n. Chemistry.* Adhesion of molecules of gas or liquid to the surface of a body.

ad·u·la·tion (ad-yoo-*lay*-sh'n) *n.* Inordinate and demonstrative praise; flattery.—**ad·u·late** *v.* [ad·u·lat·ed; ad·u·lat·ing].—**ad·u·la·tor** *n.*—**ad·u·la·to·ry** (*ad*-yoo-luh-tor-ee) *adj.*

a·dult (uh-*dult*; *ad*-ult) *n.* A person of legal and physical maturity.—**a·dult** *adj.*

a·dul·ter·ate (uh-*dul*-ter-ayt) *v.* [a·dul·ter·at·ed; -at·ing] To reduce quality or strength; debase; cheapen.—**a·dul·ter·ant** *n. & adj.*—**a·dul·ter·a·tion** (uh-dul-ter-*ay*-shun) *n.*

a·dul·ter·y (uh-*dult*-er-ee) *n.* Act of sexual intercourse with other than one's lawful mate.—**a·dul·ter·er, a·dul·ter·ess** *n.*—**a·dul·ter·ous** *adj.*—**a·dul·ter·ous·ly** *adv.*

ad·um·brate (ad-*um*-brayt) *v.* [ad·um·brat·ed; -brat·ing] 1. To cast a shadow; emerge faintly. 2. To overshadow.—**ad·um·bra·tion** (ad-um-*bray*-shun) *n.*—**ad·um·bra·tive** (uh-*dum*-bruh-tiv) *adj.*—**ad·um·bra·tive·ly** *adv.*

ad·vance *v.* [ad·vanced; ad·vanc·ing] 1. To proceed; to bring or move forward. 2. To increase. 'Butter has advanced twelve cents.' 3. To improve; benefit. 4. To accelerate. 5. To offer; propose; put forth. 6. To furnish on credit; supply or lend in expectation of reimbursement. 7. To progress; promote to a higher position. 8. To set earlier.—**ad·vance** *n. & adj.*—**ad·vanc·er** *n.*—**ad·vance·ment** *n.*

ad·vanced *adj.* 1. In the vanguard of progress in social or scientific development. 2. Ahead in time or place.

ad·van·tage (ad-*van*-tij) *n.* 1. Favorableness; propitiousness. 2. Situation facilitating desired ends; opportunity. 3. Dominance; control; superiority. 4. *Tennis.* Also **ad.** The first of two points scored after deuce.—*v.* [ad·van·taged; -tag·ing]—**ad·van·ta·geous** (ad-van-*tay*-jus) *adj.*—**-geous·ly** *adv.*—**-geous·ness** *n.*

ad·vent (*ad*-vent) 1. Coming; arrival; visitation. 2. [*cap.*] Period of fasting and prayer observed for four weeks before Christmas. 3. [*cap.*] The birth of Christ. 4. [*cap.*] The final coming of Christ.

ad·ven·ti·tious (ad-ven-*tish*-us) *adj.* Accidental; added or acquired by chance.—**ad·ven·ti·tious·ly** *adv.*—**ad·ven·ti·tious·ness** *n.*

ad·ven·ture (ad-*ven*-cher) *n.* 1. A bold, hazardous undertaking. 2. A speculative venture. 3. A noteworthy event or experience. —*v.* [ad·ven·tured; -tur·ing] To risk; venture upon a bold project.

ad·ven·tur·er (ad-*ven*-cher-er) *n.* 1. One who lives by his wits or by imposition. 2. One who takes part in a hazardous or extraordinary undertaking. 3. A speculator.—**ad·ven·tur·ess** *n.*

ad·verb (*ad*-verb) *n. Grammar.* A word which modifies verbs, adjectives, or other adverbs, showing how, when, or where an action occurred.—**ad·ver·bi·al** (ad-*verb*-ee-ul) *adj.*—**ad·ver·bi·al·ly** *adv.*

ad·ver·sar·y (*ad*-ver-ser-ee) *n.* [*pl.* -ies] Opponent; foe; antagonist.—**ad·ver·sar·y** *adj.*

ad·verse (ad-*vers*) *adj.* 1. Opposed; contrary; hostile. 2. Unfortunate; unprosperous; unconducive.—**ad·verse·ly** *adj.*—**ad·verse·ness** *n.*

ad·ver·si·ty (ad-*vers*-ih-tee) *n.* [*pl.* -ties] 1. Trouble; hardship; affliction; distress.

ad·vert (ad-*vert*) *v.* To refer back; turn attention to.—**ad·vert·ence, ad·vert·en·cy** *n.*—**ad·vert·ent** *adj.*—**ad·vert·ent·ly** *adv.*

ad·ver·tise (*ad*-ver-tyz) *v.* [ad·ver·tised; ad·ver·tis·ing] To propagandize for the sale of goods or services; bring to public notice; inform. —**ad·ver·tis·er, ad·ver·tizer** *n.*

ad·ver·tise·ment (ad-*ver*-tiz-ment) *n.* A printed or oral notice of commodities or services for sale; information directed to public attention.

ad·ver·tis·ing *n.* Also **ad·ver·tiz·ing.** Profession of creating public demand for certain commodities by propagandizing for them.

ad·vice (ad-*vyss*) *n.* 1. Counsel; suggestion; recommendation. 2. Information; notice.

ad·vis·a·ble (ad-*vyz*-uh-b'l) *adj.* Prudent; expedient.—**ad·vis·a·bil·i·ty** (ad-vyz-uh-*bil*-ih-tee), **ad·vis·a·ble·ness** *n.*—**ad·vis·a·bly** *adv.*

ad·vise (ad-*vyze*) *v.* [ad·viscd; ad·vis·ing] 1. To counsel; recommend a course of action. 2. To inform; acquaint; make known.—**ad·vis·er, ad·vis·or** *n.*—**ad·vise·ment** *n.*

ad·vis·ed·ly (ad-*vyze*-ed-lee) *adv.* Purposely; deliberately; intentionally.

ad·vi·so·ry (ad-*vy*-zuh-ree) *adj.* Giving or pertaining to advice; able to counsel but not to act directly.

ad·vo·ca·cy (*ad*-vuh-kuh-see) *n.* Intercession; recommendation; support.

ad·vo·cate (*ad*-vuh-kayt) *v.* [ad·vo·cat·ed; -cat·ing] To plead in favor of; support; argue for. —*n.* 1. A defender or supporter of a cause. 2. One who pleads the cause of another; lawyer. —**-ca·tion** (ad-voh-*kay*-shun) *n.*—**-cat·er** *n.*

adz, adze (*adz*) *n.* A tool for chipping the surface of timber. —**adz, adze** *v.*

ADZ, ADZE

Ae·ge·an (uh-*jee*-an) *n.* A sea between Greece and Turkey.—**Ae·ge·an** *adj.*

ae·gis (*ee*-jis) *n.* 1. An armor breastplate. 2. Any protection. 'Under his aegis, we won.'

Ae·ne·as (uh-*nee*-us) *n.* A Trojan hero, the mythical founder of Rome.

Ae·ne·id (uh-*nee*-id) *n.* An epic poem by Virgil celebrating Aeneas and his wanderings.

ae·o·li·an (ee-*oh*-lee-un) *adj.* Pertaining to the wind.

aeolian harp. A stringed instrument tuned so as to produce strains of music when exposed to wind.

AEOLIAN HARP

Ae·o·lus (*ee*-uh-lus) *n. Greek Mythology.* God of the winds.

ae·on, e·on (*ee*-un) *n.* An age; long period of time.—**ae·on·i·an** (ee-*oh*-nee-un), **e·on·i·an** *adj.*

a·er·ate (*ay*-er-ayt) *v.* [a·er·at·ed; -at·ing] To charge with air or any other gas.—**a·er·a·tion** (ay-uh-*ray*-shun) *n.*—**a·er·a·tor** *n.*

a·er·i·al (ay-*eer*-ee-ul) *adj.* 1. Pertaining to the air or atmosphere. 2. Lofty; elevated; rarefied. 3. Ethereally beautiful.—*n.* (*ayr*-ee-'l) A radio antenna.—**a·e·ri·al·ly** *adj.*

a·er·i·al·ist (ay-*eer*-ee-ul-ist, ayr-) *n.* A performer of daring feats in the air; trapeze artist.

a·er·ie (*ay*-er-ee) *n.* Also **ey·rie, ey·ry.** 1. The nest of a bird of prey. 2. A brood of eagles or hawks. 3. A lofty dwelling.

a·er·o·dy·nam·ics (ayr-oh-dy-*nam*-iks) *n. sing.* The science of the physical effects of winds and wind velocities.—**a·er·o·dy·nam·ic** *adj.*

a·er·om·e·ter (ay-er-*om*-uh-ter) *n.* An instrument for determining weight or density of gases.—**a·er·om·e·try** *n.* The science of measuring air.—**a·er·o·met·ric** (ay-er-uh-*met*-rik) *adj.*

a·er·o·nau·tics (ayr-uh-*naw*-tiks) *n.* Science or art of aerial navigation or air travel.—**a·er·o·naut·ic, a·er·o·naut·i·cal** *adj.*—**a·er·o·naut·i·cal·ly** *adv.*

a·er·o·neu·ro·sis (air-oh-noo-*roh*-sis) *n.* [*pl.* -ses] A psychoneurosis occurring among aviators, characterized by nervousness, insomnia, etc.—**a·er·o·neu·rot·ic** (air-oh-noo-*rot*-ik) *adj.*

a·er·o·plane (*air*-uh-playn) *n.* An airplane.

a·er·o·stat *n.* Any lighter-than-air craft.

a·er·y *n. Variant spelling* of **aerie.**

Aes·chy·lus (*es*-kuh-lus) *n.* One of the greatest of ancient Greek writers.

Aes·cu·la·pi·us (es-kyoo-*lay*-pee-us) *n. Greek Mythology.* The god of medicine and healing.—**Aes·cu·la·pian** (es-kyoo-*lay*-pee-un) *adj.*

Ae·sir (*ay*-sir) *n. Mythology.* The major Norse gods.

aes·thete (*es*-theet) *n.* One who makes a cult of beauty.

aes·thet·ic (es-*thet*-ik) *adj.* Also **es·thet·ic, aes·thet·i·cal, es·thet·i·cal.** 1. Pertaining to beauty or the science of beauty. 2. Loving beauty; having cultivated and sensitive taste.—**aes·thet·i·cal·ly, es·thet·i·cal·ly** *adv.*

aes·thet·ics, es·thet·ics *n.* The study of the philosophies and psychology of beauty.—**aes·the·ti·cian, es·the·ti·cian** *n.*

a·far *adv.* Far away; in the distance.

af·fa·ble (*af*-uh-b'l) *adj.* Genial; pleasant; amiable.—**af·fa·bil·i·ty** (af-uh-*bil*-ih-tee), **af·fa·ble·ness** *n.*—**af·fa·bly** *adv.*

af·fair (uh-*fayr*) *n.* 1. Matter; business; concern; situation. 2. [*pl.*] Public management or administration. 3. A love affair, esp. illicit.

af·fect (uh-*fekt*) *v.* 1. To act upon; influence. 2. To pretend; assume or adopt unnaturally or insincerely.—**af·fect·er** *n.*

af·fec·ta·tion (af-ek-*tay*-shun) *n.* False airs; pretense; artificiality of behavior.

af·fect·ed *adj.* Unnatural; artificial.—**af·fect·ed·ly** *adv.*—**af·fect·ed·ness** *n.*

af·fect·ing *adj.* Touching; moving; stirring; pathetic.—**af·fect·ing·ly** *adv.*

af·fec·tion (uh-*fek*-sh'n) *n.* 1. Love; kind feelings; fondness. 2. Aptitude; disposition. 3. A variable circumstance. 4. A characteristic; property. 5. A disorder; disease. 6. *Psychology.* Emotional consciousness.

af·fec·tion·ate (uh-*fek*-shun-it) *adj.* Loving; tender; warm.—**af·fec·tion·ate·ly** *adv.*—**af·fec·tion·ate·ness** *n.*

af·fi·ance (uh-*fy*-uns) *v.* [af·fi·anced; -anc·ing] To become engaged to; promise to marry.—**af·fi·ance** *n.*

af·fi·da·vit (af-uh-*day*-vit) *n.* A written statement or declaration sworn to before an authority.

af·fil·i·ate (uh-*fil*-ee-ayt) *v.* [af·fil·i·at·ed; -at·ing] 1. To join; unite with. 2. To establish paternity or origin.—*n.* A member of an organization; a local labor union which belongs to an international union.—**af·fil·i·a·tion** (uh-fil-ee-*ay*-sh'n) *n.*

af·fin·i·ty (uh-*fin*-uh-tee) *n.* [*pl.* -ties] 1. Attraction; force of attraction. 2. Connection; relationship.

af·firm (uh-*ferm*) *v.* 1. To declare or assert positively. 2. To ratify; confirm.—**af·firm·ant** *adj.*—**af·firm·er** *n.*

af·firm·a·ble (uh-*ferm*-uh-b'l) *adj.* Declarable; assertable; worthy of a solemn declaration.—**af·firm·a·bly** *adv.*

af·fir·ma·tion (af-er-*may*-sh'n) *n.* 1. Confirmation. 2. Declaration; assertion. 3. *Law.* Declaration made in court by a person who declines to take an oath.

af·firm·a·tive (uh-*ferm*-uh-tiv) *adj.* Expressing consent or assent; not negative.—*n.* 1. A word expressing assent. 'Yes.' 2. The side in a debate which maintains the stated proposition or assertion. 3. An assertive statement.—**af·firm·a·tive·ly** *adv.*

af·fix (uh-*fiks*) *v.* To attach to; fasten; add.—*n.* (*af*-iks) A suffix or prefix.

af·fla·tus (uh-*flay*-tus) *n.* Inspiration, esp. poetic.

af·flict (uh-*flikt*) *v.* To distress; try; torment; injure.—**af·flict·er** *n.*—**af·flic·tion** (uh-*flik*-sh'n) *n.*—**af·flic·tive** *adj.*

af·flu·ence (*af*-loo-ens) *n.* 1. An abundant supply; wealth; opulence. 2. A flowing toward; influx.—**af·flu·ent** *n.* A tributary.—**af·flu·ent** *adj.*—**af·flu·ent·ly** *adv.*

af·ford (uh-*ford*) *v.* 1. To be able to buy. 2. To yield; produce; give forth. 3. To be able to endure loss or injury with impunity. —**af·ford·a·ble** *adj.*

af·fray (uh-*fray*) *n.* Brawl; riot; disturbance. —*v.* To frighten.

af·front (uh-*frunt*) *v.* 1. To offend by disrespect; insult; pique. 2. To defy.—**af·front** *n.* —**af·front·ive** *adj.*

af·ghan (*af*-gan) *n.* A heavy blanket or robe of soft wool.—**af·ghan** *adj.*

Af·ghan·i·stan (af-*gan*-ih-stan). A mountainous country of Asia, bounded by Iran, India, and the Soviet Union. Estimated area: 250,000 sq. mi. Capital: Kabul.—**Af·ghan** *adj. & n.*

a·field (uh-*feeld*) *adv.* Astray; off the beaten path; among fields.

a·fire (uh-*fyre*) *adj.* On fire; burning.—**a·fire** *adv.*

a·flame (uh-*flaym*) *adj.* Flaming; burning.

a·float (uh-*floht*) *adj.* Borne along; moving; circulating; unfixed.—**a·float** *adv.*

a·foot (uh-*fut*) *adj.* 1. On foot; walking. 2. In preparation; in action.—**a·foot** *adv.*

a·fore (uh-*for*) *prep. Archaic.* Before in time or place; in front of.—*conjunction.* Before; rather than.—**a·fore** *adv.*

a·fore·said (uh-*for*-sed) *adj.* Previously mentioned.

a·fore·thought (uh-*for*-thawt) *adj.* Premeditated; thought of beforehand.

a·fore·time (uh-*for*-tym) *adv.* Previously; formerly.

a·foul (uh-*fowl*) *adj.* Entangled; in collision. —**a·foul** *adv.*

a·fraid (uh-*frayd*) *adj.* Fearful; frightened.

a·fresh (uh-*fresh*) *adv.* Again; anew.

Af·ri·ca (*af*-rih-kuh). The second largest continent, bounded by the Mediterranean and Red Seas, and the Indian and Atlantic Oceans. —**Af·ri·can** *adj. & n.*

a·front (uh-*frunt*) *adv.* In front of.

aft *adj. Nautical.* After; rear; hind.—**aft** *adv.*

aft·er (*aft*-er) *prep.* 1. Behind; following in place or time. 2. In pursuit of; engaged in. 3. In imitation of. 4. According to the dictates of. 5. Concerning.—*adj.* 1. Later. 2. Farther; behind, esp. toward a ship's stern. —*adv.* Later; afterward.

after-described	after mast	after sails
after-designed	after-mentioned	after-specified
afterglow	after-named	aftertime

aft·er·birth *n.* Placenta and membranous matter discharged from the uterus after a birth.

aft·er·ef·fect *n.* A delayed reaction; effect first felt long after an injury has been incurred.

aft·er·math (*aft*-er-math) *n.* Chaotic or disastrous resulting conditions; consequence.

aft·er·most *adv.* Hindmost; farthest behind.

aft·er·noon *n.* The part of the day between noon and evening.—**af·ter·noon** *adj.*

aft·er·thought *n.* A later reflection; a considera-

tion or action occurring afterward; any appended item.

aft·er·ward *adv.* Also **aft·er·wards.** Later; subsequently.

a·gain (uh-*gen*) *adv.* 1. Once more; a second time. 2. On the other hand. 3. Moreover; besides. 4. In return; in restitution.—*Conjunction.* On the other hand; moreover.

a·gainst (uh-*genst*) *prep.* 1. Opposed to; contrary to. 2. Touching or resting upon. 3. In preparation for. 4. In contrast with.

Ag·a·mem·non (ag-uh-*mem*-non) *n.* A mythical Greek king and hero of the Trojan war.

a·gape *adj.* Open-mouthed.—**a·gape** *adv.*

a·gar-a·gar (*ay*-gahr-*ay*-gahr) *n.* A seaweed gelatin used in cooking and in bacteria culture.

ag·ate (*ag*-it) *n.* 1. A hard translucent stone compounded of chalcedony and other minerals. 2. A child's marble. 3. *Printing.* A size of type.—**ag·ate** *adj.*

a·ga·ve (uh-*gay*-vee) *n.* A family of American desert plants of which the century plant is a common specimen.

age (*ayj*) *n.* 1. The length of time a living organism has existed. 2. The latter part of life; old age. 3. A period; stage; epoch. 4. The present; contemporary time. 5. Maturity; majority. 6. *Psychology.* Individual maturity measured in years of age of a normal person at the equivalent stage of development.—*v.* [aged; ag·ing]—**age·less** *adj.*

a·ged (*ay*-jed) *adj.* Old.—**a·ged·ly** *adv.*—**a·ged·ness** *n.*

a·gen·cy (*ay*-jen-see) *n.* [*pl.* a·gen·cies] 1. An organization which sells a service. 'An employment agency.' 2. Professional action on behalf of another. 3. Action; operation; instrumentality.

a·gen·da (uh-*jen*-duh) *n. pl.* Memoranda; a list of things to be done.

a·gent (*ay*-jent) *n.* 1. One who represents or acts for another. 2. An element producing a certain result. 3. A means; medium. 4. An active power; force. 5. *Colloquial.* A door-to-door salesman.

ag·glom·er·ate (uh-*glom*-er-ayt) *v.* [ag·glom·er·at·ed; -at·ing] To accumulate; collect; amass. —*adj.* Gathered into a mass or heap.—*n.* Also **ag·glom·er·a·tion.**—**ag·glom·er·a·tive** *adj.*

ag·glu·ti·nate (uh-*gloo*-tih-nayt) *v.* [ag·glu·ti·nat·ed; -nat·ing] To stick; glue.—*adj.* (uh-*gloo*-ti-nit) Joined; glued.—**ag·glu·ti·na·tion** (uh-gloo-tih-*nay*-sh'n) *n.* 1. Adhesion; union. 2. *Philology.* The addition of inflectional suffixes to root words, so that both retain their original identities.

ag·gran·dize (uh-*gran*-dyz) *v.* [ag·gran·dized; -diz·ing] To add to; enlarge; extend; promote.—**-dize·ment** (-diz-m'nt) *n.*—**-diz·er** *n.*

ag·gra·vate (*ag*-ruh-vayt) *v.* [ag·gra·vat·ed; -vat·ing] 1. To intensify; make more severe; exaggerate. 2. *Dialectal.* To irritate; provoke. —**ag·gra·vat·ing·ly** *adv.*—**ag·gra·va·tion** (ag-ruh-*vay*-shun) *n.*—**ag·gra·va·tive** *adj.*

A

ag·gre·gate (*ag*-rih-gayt) *v.* [ag·gre·gat·ed; -gat· ing] To collect; amass.—**ag·gre·gate** (*ag*-rih- git) *n. & adj.*

ag·gre·ga·tion (ag-rih-*gay*-shun) *n.* A mass; collection; sum; assemblage.

ag·gres·sion (uh-*gresh*-'n) *n.* Unwarranted at- tack; assault; invasion.

ag·gres·sive (uh-*gres*-iv) *n.* 1. Hostile; quar- relsome; making an unprovoked assault. 2. Ambitious; forceful; enterprising.—**ag· gres·sive·ly** *adv.*—**ag·gres·sive·ness** *n.*

ag·gres·sor (uh-*gres*-er) *n.* Attacker; invader.

ag·grieve (uh-*greev*) *v.* [ag·grieved; ag·griev· ing] 1. To cause pain or sorrow. 2. To de- prive of civil or political rights; oppress.

a·ghast (uh-*gast*) *adj.* Stupefied by amazement or fear.

ag·ile (*aj*-il) *adj.* Nimble; quick; sprightly. —**a·gile·ly** *adv.*—**a·gile·ness** *n.*

a·gil·i·ty (uh-*jil*-ih-tee) *n.* Liveliness; ease and grace of movement; nimbleness.

ag·i·tate (*aj*-ih-tayt) *v.* [ag·i·tat·ed; -tat·ing] 1. To disturb; stir; excite. 2. To rouse to action; foment controversy or revolt.—**ag·i· tat·ed·ly** *adv.*—**ag·i·ta·tion** (aj-ih-*tay*-sh'n) *n.* —**ag·i·ta·tor** *n.*

ag·it·prop *adj. Theater Slang.* Written or per- formed for propaganda or political agitation.

a·glow (uh-*gloh*) *adj.* 1. Glowing; shining. 2. Stimulated; stirred.

ag·nos·tic (ag-*nos*-tik) *adj.* Also **ag·nos·ti·cal.** Doubting the possibility of any knowledge of God.—**ag·nos·tic** *n.*

ag·nos·ti·cism (ag-*nos*-tih-sizm) *n.* Doubt of God's existence and a belief that present phenomena only may be comprehended.

a·go (uh-*goh*) *adv.* In the past; gone by.

a·gog (uh-*gog*) *adj.* Excited; eager.—**a·gog** *adv.*

ag·o·nize (*ag*-uh-nyz) *v.* [ag·o·nized; ag·o·niz· ing] To suffer; torture; distress.—**ag·o·niz· ing·ly** *adv.*

ag·o·ny (*ag*-uh-nee) *n.* [*pl.* ag·o·nies] 1. Pain; anguish; suffering. 2. Extreme emotional state.

a·grar·i·an (uh-*grair*-ee-un) *adj.* 1. Pertaining to land or farming. 2. Favoring agrarianism. —*n.* One who favors agrarianism.

a·grar·i·an·ism (uh-*grair*-ee-un-izm) *n.* Doc- trine and social movement favoring an equita- ble distribution of land among farmers.

a·gree (uh-*gree*) *v.* 1. To be of similar opinion; be in harmony with. 2. To consent; express concurrence. 3. To be consistent with. 4. To resemble; match; correspond. 5. *Grammar.* To correspond in number, case, gender, or person.—**a·greed** *adj.*

a·gree·a·ble (uh-*gree*-uh-b'l) *n.* 1. Pleasant; amiable. 2. Amenable; willing to agree. 3. Suitable; conformable; consistent.—**a·gree· a·ble·ness** *n.*—**a·gree·a·bly** *adv.*

a·gree·ment (uh-*gree*-m'nt) *n.* 1. An oral or written contract; bargain. 2. Harmony; con- formity; coincidence; union. 3. *Grammar.* Conformity of number, gender, case, or form.

ag·ri·cul·ture (*ag*-rih-kul-cher) *n.* Farming; raising of crops or livestock.—**ag·ri·cul·tur·al** *adj.*—**ag·ri·cul·tur·al·ly** *adv.*—**ag·ri·cul·tur·al· ist, ag·ri·cul·tur·ist** *n.*

a·gron·o·my (uh-*gron*-uh-mee) *n.* The science of land-management and crops.—**a·gron·o·mist** *n.*

a·ground (uh-*grownd*) *adj. Nautical.* Stranded; on the shore or ground.—**a·ground** *adv.*

a·gue (*ay*-gyoo) *n.* 1. A type of malarial fever. 2. A paroxysm of shivering.—**a·gu·ish** *adj.* —**a·gu·ish·ly** *adv.*

A·hab (*ay*-hab) *n.* 1. The central, tragic figure of Melville's *Moby Dick.* 2. An ancient king of Israel.

a·head (uh-*hed*) *adv.* Forward; in advance of. —**a·head** *adj.*

a·hoy *interjection. Nautical.* Hello; hail—used to draw attention.

a·i (*ah*-ee) *n.* A three-toed sloth of South Amer- ica.

aid (*ayd*) *n.* Assistance; relief; help.—**aid** *v.* —**aid·er** *n.*

aide (*ayd*) *n.* Assistant to a military or naval officer.

aide-de-camp (*ayd*-duh-*kamp*) *n.* [*pl.* aides-de- camp] *Military.* Assistant to a general or high official.

ai·grette (*ay*-gret) *n.* 1. The egret; feather used as ornament on women's head- gear. 2. A head ornament made of a plume of feathers, a spray of gems, or the like.

ail (*ayl*) *v.* 1. To be ill. 2. To trouble; affect with illness.

ai·ler·on (*ay*-ler-on) *n.* Movable surface at trail- ing edge of an airplane wing which controls sta- bility about its longitud- inal axis.

ail·ment (*ayl*-m'nt) *n.* Sick- ness; disease.

AIGRETTE

aim (*aym*) *n.* 1. Objec- tive; purpose; intention. 2. A directing or pointing at.—*v.* 1. To point at; direct. 2. To strive; aspire.—**aim·er** *n.*

aim·less (*aym*-lis) *adj.* Purposeless; without aim.—**aim·less·ly** *adv.*—**aim·less·ness** *n.*

ain't (*aynt*) *Contraction. Colloquial.* Am not; is not; are not; have not; has not.

air *n.* 1. The mixture of gases, mainly nitrogen and oxygen, forming the atmosphere. 2. A slight breeze. 3. *Music.* A tune; melody. 4. Bearing; appearance. 5. [*pl.*] A haughty or affected manner.—*adj.* Pertaining to avia- tion.—*v.* 1. To ventilate. 2. To display.

air-bound	air-dry	air-slaked
air-blasted	air duct	airspace
air-blown	air-floated	airtight
airborne	airfoil	air twist
air-bred	air-formed	airward
air-chambered	airless	airwayman
air-conveyed	air-locked	air-wise
air-dried	air mail	airwoman
air-driven	air navigation	airworthy

air brake. A pneumatic brake used on railway cars, buses, and trucks.

air·brush *n.* A paint sprayer operated by compressed air.

air castle. A daydream; figment of wishful thinking.

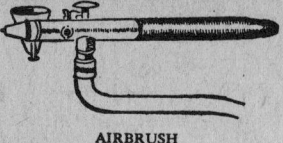

AIRBRUSH

air·con·di·tion *v.* To regulate the temperature or purity of indoor air.—**air·con·di·tion·er** *n.* A machine performing this function.—**air·con·di·tioned** *adj.*

air conditioning. 1. The mechanical regulation of air temperature or purity. 2. The industry which manufactures and services machinery for air conditioning.—**air·con·di·tion·ing** *adj.*

air·craft *n. sing. & pl.* Any airplane or lighter-than-air machine.

aircraft carrier. A large flat-topped battleship serving as a mobile base for war planes.

air·drome *n.* An airport; hangar.

aire·dale *n.* A wiry-haired dog of the terrier family.

air·field *n.* An airport; air base.

air freighter. A large cargo-carrying aircraft.

AIREDALE

air hole. 1. A hole to admit air. 2. A hole in the ice. 3. *Foundry.* A blemish in a casting caused by gas bubbles.

air·i·ly *adv.* Gaily; in a sprightly way.

air·i·ness *n.* Being filled with air; lightness; freshness; blitheness.

air·ing *n.* 1. Exposure to the air or to public view. 2. Exercise in the open air; a walk. 3. *Radio.* A broadcast.

air line. 1. A hose or channel for conducting air. 2. [*one word*] An air transport system or corporation.—**air liner** *n.* A transport plane. —**air-line** *adj.*

air lock. 1. A compression chamber for underwater workers. 2. Displacement of liquid by air in a pumping system.

air·man *n.* [*pl.* air·men] An airplane pilot; one of the crew of a plane.

air map. 1. A projection of the world showing relative distances in plane travel. 2. An aerial navigation chart.

air·minded *adj.* 1. Interested in the development of aviation. 2. Interpreting geography, economics, etc., from the standpoint of air transport.—**air·mind·ed·ness** *n.*

air·plane (*ehr*-playn) *n.* A flying vehicle, heavier than air, driven by a propeller and supported in the air by the action of the airstream across its wings.

air·pocket *n.* A localized area of adverse or treacherous air currents.

air·port *n.* A field with facilities for servicing airplanes.

air·ship *n.* A lighter-than-air craft; blimp or dirigible.

air·sick·ness *n.* Vertigo and nausea produced by the motion of an airplane.—**air·sick** *adj.*

air sleeve. A long cloth cone hung up at an airport to indicate wind direction.

air·tight *adj.* Impermeable to air; hermetically sealed.

air·way *n.* A route or course followed regularly by airplanes.

air·y *adj.* [air·i·er; air·i·est] 1. Pertaining to the atmosphere. 2. Drafty; ventilated. 3. Insubstantial; trifling; empty. 4. Gay; lively. 5. Ethereal; subtle.—**air·i·ly** *adv.*

aisle (*yle*) *n.* A passage-way between seats in an auditorium.—**aisled** *adj.*

a·jar (uh-*jahr*) *adj.* 1. Partly open; neither open nor closed. 2. Jarring; discordant.

A·jax (*ay*-jaks) *n.* A giant Greek hero of the Trojan wars.

a·kim·bo (uh-*kim*-boh) *adj.* With hands on hips and elbows thrust out.

a·kin (uh-*kin*) *adj.* 1. Related by blood. 2. Similar; related in kind.

Al·a·bam·a (al-uh-*bam*-uh). A southern U.S. state, between Georgia and Mississippi. Area: 51,609 sq. mi. Capital: Montgomery.—**Al·a·bam·an** *adj.* & *n.*

al·a·bam·ine (al-uh-*bam*-een) *n.* A rare element of the halogen group. (*Symbol:* Ab).

al·a·bas·ter (*al*-uh-bas-ter) *n.* A near-white, translucent, fine-textured stone much used for sculpture.—**al·a·bas·ter** *adj.*

a·lack (uh-*lak*), **a·lack·a·day** *interjection.* Alas, used to express regret or sorrow.

a·lac·ri·ty (uh-*lak*-rih-tee) *n.* Cheerful willingness; eagerness.—**a·lac·ri·tous** *adj.*

A·lad·din (uh-*lad*-in) *n.* The hero of the *Arabian Nights* tale, "Aladdin and the Magic Lamp."

a·larm (uh-*larm*) *n.* 1. Fear; apprehension; panic. 2. A warning; summons to action, esp. a warning of a fire. 3. A mechanism which rings a signal, as in an alarm clock.—*v.* 1. To arouse; summon to action. 2. To frighten. —**a·larm, a·larm·ing** *adj.*—**a·larm·ing·ly** *adv.*

a·larm·ist *n.* One who arrives at and propagates pessimistic judgments; panicky person.—**a·larm·ist** *n.*

a·lar·um *n. Archaic variant spelling* of **alarm.**

a·las (uh-*las*) *interjection.* An expression of sorrow, pity, apprehension, etc.

A·las·ka (uh-*las*-kuh) A large peninsula of the extreme NW part of North America, an American possession. Area: 586,400 sq. mi. Capital: Juneau.—**A·las·kan** *adj.* & *n.*

Al·ba·ni·a (al-*bay*-nee-uh). A small Balkan nation northwest of Greece. Area: 10,629 sq. mi. Capital: Tirana.—**Al·ban·i·an** *n.* & *adj.*

Al·ban·y (*awl*-buh-nee). The capital of New York state, situated 145 miles north of New York City.

A

al·ba·tross (*al*-buh-tros) *n.* A large sea bird of the petrel family.

al·be·it (awl-*bee*-it) *conj. Archaic.* Although; notwithstanding.

al·bin·ism (*al*-bin-izm) *n.* A pigmentary deficiency in skin and eyes.—**al·bin·is·tic** (al-bin-*iss*-tik) *adj.*

ALBATROSS (1/30 life size)

al·bi·no (al-*by*-noh) *n.* [*pl.* al·bi·nos] Person or animal lacking normal skin pigmentation and eye coloring.—**al·bin·ic** (al-*bin*-ik) *adj.*

Al·bi·on (*al*-bee-un) *n.* An ancient or poetic name for Britain.

al·bum (*al*-bum) *n.* 1. A book for holding photographs, clippings, etc. 2. A volume of envelopes for phonograph records.

al·bu·men (al-*byoo*-min) *n.* The white of an egg.—**al·bu·min·ous,** also **al·bu·min·ose** *adj.*

al·bu·min *n.* A protein substance found in the tissues of plants and animals.—**al·bu·min·ous,** also **al·bu·min·ose** *adj.*

al·cal·de (ahl-*kahl*-day) *n.* A Spanish mayor or judge.

al·che·mist (*al*-kuh-mist) *n.* Student or practitioner of alchemy.—**al·chem·is·tic** (al-kuh-*mis*-tik) *adj.*

al·che·my (*al*-kuh-mee) *n.* Medieval science, forerunner of modern chemistry, which tried to transmute base metals into gold.—**al·chem·ic, al·chem·i·cal** *adj.*—**al·chem·i·cal·ly** *adv.*

al·co·hol (*al*-kuh-hol) *n.* 1. *Chemistry.* An organic compound formed by a hydrocarbon and a hydroxide. 2. Ethyl alcohol, distilled from grain and used in beverages. 3. An alcoholic beverage.

al·co·hol·ic (al-kuh-*hol*-ik) *adj.* Resembling or containing alcohol.—*n.* An habitual drunkard.

al·co·hol·ism *n.* (*al*-kuh-hol-izm) 1. Alcoholic poisoning. 2. Serious addiction to alcohol.

al·cove (*al*-kohv) *n.* A recess; small room partially separated from the main room.

al·der (*awl*-der) *n.* A family of small trees related to the birch.

al·der·man (*awl*-der-m'n) *n.* [*pl.* al·der·men] A municipal administrative official.—**al·der·man·ic** (awl-der-*man*-ik) *adj.*

ale *n.* A malt liquor similar to beer.

a·lert (uh-*lert*) *adj.* 1. Watchful; vigilant. 2. Brisk; quick.—*n.* An alarm or state of watchfulness, esp. when occasioned by the approach of hostile aircraft.—**a·lert·ly** *adv.*—**a·lert·ness** *n.*

Aleutian Islands (uh-*loo*-shun). A chain of islands reaching from Alaska toward Siberia.—**A·leu·tian** *n. & adj.*

Al·ex·an·dri·a (al-ig-*zan*-dree-uh). A seaport and major city of Egypt founded by Alexander the Great.—**Al·ex·an·dri·an** *adj. & n.*

Al·ex·an·drine (-drin) *n.* A line of iambic hexameter.

al·fal·fa (al-*fal*-fuh) *n.* A productive, deep-rooted herb grown for forage, hay, and silage.

al·gae (*al*-jee) *n. pl.* [*sing.* al·ga] A low order of aquatic plants, including seaweeds.—**al·gal** (*al*-g'l) *adj.*

al·ge·bra (*al*-jeh-bruh) *n.* 1. Branch of mathematics which substitutes letters and other symbols for numbers. 2. An algebra book.—**al·ge·bra·ic** (al-jeh-*bray*-ik),-**i·cal** *adj.*—**i·cal·ly** *adv.*—**al·ge·bra·ist** (*al*-juh-bray-ist) *n.*

Al·ge·ri·a (al-*jeer*-ee-uh). A French protectorate on the Mediterranean shore of North Africa.—**Al·ge·ri·an** *adj. & n.*

Al·giers (al-*jeerz*). Seaport and capital city of Algeria, site of a famous casbah.

Al·gon·quin (al-*gong*-kwin) *n.* A large group or family of North American Indian tribes.—**Al·gon·qui·an** *n. & adj.*

Al·ham·bra (al-*ham*-bruh). A beautiful Moorish castle in Granada, Spain.

a·li·as (*ay*-lee-us) *n.* [*pl.* a·li·as·es] An assumed name.—**a·li·as** *adv.*

al·i·bi (*al*-ih-by) *n.* [*pl.* al·i·bis] 1. An excuse. 2. *Law.* A plea or defense of having been elsewhere at the time of the crime.—*adv.* Elsewhere.

al·ien (*ayl*-yen) *n.* A foreign-born non-citizen.—**al·ien** *adj.* Strange; foreign; having nothing in common. 'Beliefs alien to democracy.'

al·ien·ate (*ayl*-yuh-nayt) *v.* [al·ien·at·ed; -at·ing] 1. To estrange; create a breach. 2. To transfer.—**al·ien·a·tion** (ayl-yuh-*nay*-shun) *n.*—**al·ien·at·or** *n.*

a·light *adj.* Lighted up; bright.—*v.* [a·light·ed; a·lit; a·light·ing] 1. To descend; get down. 2. To settle or land upon.—**a·light** *adv.*

a·lign (uh-*lyn*) *v.* 1. To line up; arrange in a straight line. 2. To join or identify oneself, as with a political cause.—**a·lign·er, a·lin·er** *n.*—**a·lign·ment** *n.*

a·like *adj.* Similar; corresponding; identical.—**a·like** *adv.*

al·i·ment (*al*-ih-m'nt) *n.* Food; nutrition.—**al·i·men·tal** *adj.*—**al·i·men·tal·ly** *adv.*

al·i·men·ta·ry (al-ih-*men*-tuh-ree) *adj.* Pertaining to food or nourishment.

al·i·mo·ny (*al*-ih-moh-nee) *n.* [*pl.* -nies] *Law.* An allowance for support by a husband to his divorced or legally separated wife.

a·line *v.* [a·lined; a·lin·ing] *Variant spelling* of align.

a·lit. *Past tense & past participle* of alight.

a·live *adj.* 1. Existing; living, not dead nor inorganic. 2. In force or operation. 3. Lively; cheerful. 4. Susceptible; easily impressed. 5. Thick or covered with moving bodies.

al·ka·li (*al*-kuh-ly) *n.* [*pl.* al·kal·ies, al·ka·lis] A substance basic in its reaction.—**al·ka·li** *adj.*

al·ka·line (*al*-kuh-lyn) *adj.* Like an alkali; not acidic.—**al·ka·lin·i·ty** (al-kuh-*lin*-ih-tee) *n.*—**al·ka·lize** *v.* [al·ka·liz·ed; -liz·ing].

al·ka·loid (*al*-kuh-loid) *n.* An inorganic substance which is alkaline or basic in reaction.—**al·ka·loid, al·ka·loid·al** *adj.*

all (*awl*) *adj.* Every; the whole quantity of.
—*adv.* Completely; altogether.—*n.* Everything; the total.

all-absorbing	all hail	all-possessed
all-aged	all in	all-rounder
all-fired	allover	all-time
all fours	all-overish	all-wise

Al·lah (*al*-uh, *ah*-luh) *n.* The God of the Mohammedans.

all-A·mer·i·can *n.* A collegiate football player selected by a poll of experts as being the best in the country at his position.—**all-A·mer·i·can** *adj.*

all around. Also **all-round, all-around.** 1. Versatile; having many interests and abilities. 2. From every point of view; thorough; complete.

al·lay (uh-*lay*) *v.* 1. To pacify; calm; subdue. 2. To relieve; assuage.—**al·lay·er** *n.*

all clear. A signal indicating the end of an air raid alert.

al·lege (uh-*lej*) *v.* [al·leged; al·leg·ing] 1. To assert; maintain. 2. To offer as an excuse. —**al·le·ga·tion** (al-uh-*gay*-shun) *n.*—**al·lege·a·ble** *adj.*—**al·leg·ed·ly** (uh-*lej*-id-lee) *adv.*—**al·leg·er** *n.*

Al·le·ghe·ny (al-uh-*gay*-nee) *n.* 1. A range of mountains forming part of the northern Appalachians. 2. A large river of Pennsylvania and New York.

al·le·giance (uh-*lee*-j'ns) *n.* 1. The obligation of a citizen to his government. 2. Loyalty; obedience; respect.

al·le·go·ry (*al*-uh-gor-ee, -goh-) *n.* [*pl.* al·le·go·ries] *n.* A literary or art work in which the meaning is conveyed through symbolism.—**al·le·gor·ic, al·le·gor·i·cal** *adj.* Figurative; symbolical.—**al·le·gor·i·cal·ly** *adv.*

al·le·gro (uh-*lay*-groh) *adj. Music.* Brisk; rapid.

al·le·lu·ia, al·le·lu·iah, al·le·lu·ja *Variant spellings* of **hallelujah.**

al·ler·gen (*al*-er-j'n) *n.* Any substance which can evoke allergic manifestations.

al·ler·gy (*al*-er-jee) *n.* [*pl.* al·ler·gies] Hypersensitivity to substances which are harmless to most people.—**al·ler·gic** (uh-*ler*-jik) *adj.*

al·le·vi·ate (uh-*lee*-vee-ayt) *v.* [al·lev·i·at·ed; -at·ing] To lessen; relieve; assuage.—**al·le·vi·a·tion** *n.*—**al·le·vi·a·tive** *adj.* & *n.*—**al·le·vi·a·tor** *n.*—**al·le·vi·a·to·ry** (uh-*lee*-vee-uh-tor-ee) *adj.*

al·ley (*al*-ee) *n.* [*pl.* al·leys] 1. A narrow passage or way; an aisle, as between buildings. 2. A long strip of flooring for bowling.

al·ley·way (*al*-ee-way) *n.* A passageway; alley.

All Fools' Day. April 1, a day devoted to playful deceptions.

All·hal·lows (awl-*hal*-ohz) *n.* Also **All·hal·low·mas.** All Saints' Day, November 1.

al·li·ance (uh-*ly*-uns) *n.* 1. A league or compact between nations or persons. 2. A treaty of friendship or mutual assistance. 3. A marriage; union; relationship.

al·lied (uh-*lyd*). *Past tense & past participle* of **ally.**

Allied Military Government. The army organization charged with setting up government in occupied countries. *Abbreviation*: **A.M.G.**

al·lies. *Plural* of **ally.**

al·li·ga·tor (*al*-uh-gay-ter) *n.* A large, scaly amphibious reptile similar to the crocodile, common to North and South America.

ALLIGATOR (1/60 life size)

al·lit·er·a·tion (uh-lit-er-*ay*-shun) *n.* Repetition of the same beginning sound in several words in close proximity.—**al·lit·er·a·tive** *adj.*—**al·lit·er·a·tive·ly** *adv.*—**al·lit·er·a·tive·ness** *n.*

al·lo·cate (*al*-uh-kayt) *v.* [al·lo·cat·ed; -cat·ing] To assign; allot; set apart.—**al·lo·ca·ble** *adj.* —**al·lo·ca·tion** (al-uh-*kay*-shun) *n.*

al·lop·a·thy (uh-*lop*-uh-thee) *n. Medicine.* System of treating disease by inducing reactions opposite to those of the disease.—**al·lo·path** (*al*-uh-path), **al·lop·a·thist** (uh-*lop*-uh-thist) *n.* —**al·lo·path·ic** (al-uh-*path*-ik) *adj.*—**al·lo·path·i·cal·ly** *adv.*

al·lot (uh-*lot*) *v.* [al·lot·ted; al·lot·ting] To parcel out; grant; assign.—**al·lot·ment** *n.*

al·lot·ro·py (uh-*lot*-ruh-pee) *adj. Chemistry.* The occurrence of an element or compound in several different, but chemically related forms.—**al·lo·trope** (*al*-uh-trohp) *n.*—**al·lo·trop·ic** (al-uh-*trop*-ik) *adj.*

al·low (uh-*low*) *v.* 1. To permit; grant; give; yield. 2. To admit; acknowledge. 3. To set aside; take out of account.—**al·low·ed·ly** *adv.*—**al·low·er** *n.*

al·low·a·ble (uh-*low*-uh-b'l) *adj.* 1. Permissible; lawful. 2. Reasonable; admissible.—**al·low·a·bly** *adv.*

al·low·ance (uh-*low*-uns) *n.* 1. A set rate or quantity granted. 2. Charitable overlooking of faults. 3. Permission. 4. Admission. 5. Compensation, esp. a deduction for loss.

al·loy (*al*-oi) *n.* A mixture of two or more metals.—*v.* (uh-*loi*) 1. To mix metals to form an alloy. 2. To make less valuable by mixture; debase.

all right. Satisfactory; agreeable; permissible.

all-round *adj. Colloquial.* 1. General; talented. 2. All-around.—**all-round** *adv.*

all·spice *n.* An aromatic berry of the pimento tree used in powdered form for flavoring.

all-star *adj.* Composed of outstanding performers.—*n.* Player on an all-star team.

al·lude (uh-*lood*) *v.* [al·lud·ed; al·lud·ing] To refer to indirectly; hint at.

al·lure (uh-*loor*) *v.* [al·lured; al·lur·ing] To tempt; invite; entice.—**al·lure, al·lure·ment** *n.*—**al·lur·er** *n.*

al·lur·ing *adj.* Enticing; tempting; charming. —**al·lur·ing·ly** *adv.*—**al·lur·ing·ness** *n.*

al·lu·sion (a-*loo*-zh'n) *n.* An indirect reference; suggestion; hint.—**al·lu·sive** (uh-*loo*-siv) *adj.* —**al·lu·sive·ly** *adv.*—**al·lu·sive·ness** *n.*

A

al·lu·vi·al (uh-*loo*-vee-ul) *adj*. Deposited or washed up by running water.

al·lu·vi·um (uh-*loo*-vee-um) *n*. Water-deposited soil, etc.

al·ly (*al*-y, uh-*ly*) *n*. [*pl*. al·lies] 1. A person or nation united in friendship or by treaty to another. 2. Related form or being.—**al·ly** -(uh-*ly*) *v*. [al·lied; al·ly·ing].

alma mater (al-muh-*may*-ter, ahl-muh-*mah*-ter). One's university, college, or school.

al·ma·nac (*awl*-muh-nak) *n*. A book, usually issued annually, containing meteorological and other information for each day.

al·might·y (awl-*myt*-ee) *adj*. All-powerful; supreme.—*n*. [*cap*.] God.—**al·might·i·ly** *adv*. —**al·might·i·ness** *n*.

al·mond (*ah*-mund, *am*-und) *n*. A tasty, thin-shelled nut.

al·mond-eyed *adj*. With narrow, apparently slanting eyes.

al·mon·er (*al*-mun-er) *n*. One who offers charity on behalf of another.

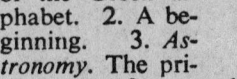
ALMOND

al·most (awl-*most*, *awl*-most) *adv*. Nearly; practically; coming just short.

alms (*ahmz*) *n*. A charitable gift; charity.

alms·house *n*. A poorhouse.

al·oe (*al*-oh) *n*. 1. [*pl*.] The spicy wood of a tree native to India. 2. A plant of the lily family, native to South Africa. 3. [*pl*.] A medicine distilled from the leaves of the aloe.

a·loft (uh-*loft*) *adv*. Above; on high; toward the top.

a·lone (uh-*lohn*) *adj*. 1. Single; solitary; by oneself. 2. Only; nothing else. 3. Unique; unequaled.—**a·lone** *adv*.

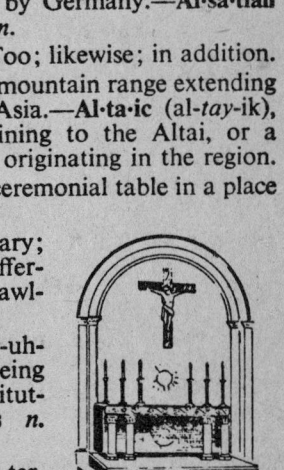
ALOE

a·long (uh-*long*) *prep*. By the side or the length of.—*adv*. 1. Lengthwise. 2. Onward. 3. In company; together.

a·long·side *prep*. Beside.—*adv*. By the side; beside one another.

a·loof (uh-*loof*) *adj*. Extremely reserved; distant; separated.—**a·loof, a·loof·ly** *adv*.—**a·loof·ness** *n*.

a·loud (uh-*lowd*) *adv*. In an audible tone; out loud.

A. L. P. *Abbreviation*. American Labor Party, a political party having its greatest influence in New York City.

al·pac·a (al-*pak*-uh) *n*. 1. A llamalike animal of the Andes. 2. Cloth made of the long staple wool of the alpaca. —**al·pac·a** *adj*.

ALPACA (1/45 life size)

al·pen·stock *n*. An iron-tipped staff used by mountain climbers.

al·pha (*al*-fuh) *n*. 1. The first letter of the Greek alphabet. 2. A beginning. 3. *Astronomy*. The primary star of a constellation.

al·pha·bet (*al*-fuh-bet) *n*. The letters of a language arranged in the usual order.—**al·pha·bet·ic** (al-fuh-*bet*-ik), **al·pha·bet·i·cal** *adj*.—**al·pha·bet·i·cal·ly** *adv*.

al·pha·bet·ize (*al*-fuh-buh-tyz) *v*. [al·pha·bet·ized; -iz·ing] 1. To arrange in alphabetical order. 2. To mark with the letters of the alphabet.—**al·pha·bet·i·za·tion** (al-fuh-buh-tuh-*zay*-sh'n) *n*.—**al·pha·bet·i·zer** *n*.

al·pine (*al*-pyn) *adj*. Denoting a lofty mountain. —**Al·pine** *adj*. Pertaining to the Alps.

Alps. A range of lofty mountains lying mainly in Switzerland.

al·read·y (awl-*red*-ee) *adv*. Prior to some specified time.

Al·sace (*al*-sas) *n*. A French province on the Rhine, twice seized by Germany.—**Al·sa·tian** (al-*say*-shun) *adj*. & *n*.

al·so (*awl*-soh) *adv*. Too; likewise; in addition.

Al·tai (al-*ty*). A vast mountain range extending easterly in central Asia.—**Al·ta·ic** (al-*tay*-ik), **Al·ta·ian** *adj*. Pertaining to the Altai, or a family of languages originating in the region.

al·tar (*awl*-ter) *n*. A ceremonial table in a place of worship.

al·ter *v*. To change; vary; make or become different.—**al·ter·a·tion** (awl-ter-*ay*-sh'n) *n*.

al·ter·a·ble (*awl*-ter-uh-b'l) *adj*. Capable of being changed or reconstituted.—**al·ter·a·ble·ness** *n*. —**al·ter·a·bly** *adv*.

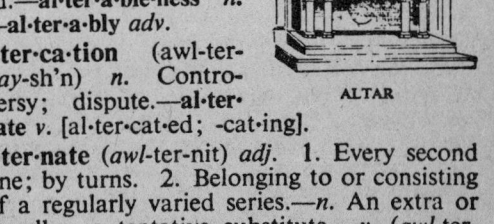
ALTAR

al·ter·ca·tion (awl-ter-*kay*-sh'n) *n*. Controversy; dispute.—**al·ter·cate** *v*. [al·ter·cat·ed; -cat·ing].

al·ter·nate (*awl*-ter-nit) *adj*. 1. Every second one; by turns. 2. Belonging to or consisting of a regularly varied series.—*n*. An extra or standby; a tentative substitute.—*v*. (*awl*-ter-nayt) [al·ter·nat·ed; -nat·ing] 1. To take turns; perform successively. 2. To change back and forth.—**al·ter·nate·ly** *adv*.—**al·ter·nate·ness** *n*.

alternating current. An electric current periodically undergoing a change in the direction of its motion. *Abbreviation:* A.C. or a.c.

al·ter·na·tion (awl-ter-*nay*-sh'n) *n.* Reciprocal succession; following and being followed successively.

al·ter·na·tive (awl-*ter*-nuh-tiv) *n.* 1. A choice between two possibilities. 2. One of two possibilities open to choice.—**al·ter·na·tive** *adj.* —**al·ter·na·tive·ly** *adv.*—**al·ter·na·tive·ness** *n.*

al·ter·nat·or (*awl*-ter-nayt-er) *n.* An alternating current generator or dynamo.

alt·horn *n.* A horn with the same range as the French horn used in brass bands.

al·though (awl-*thoh*) *conj.* Notwithstanding; even if.

al·tim·e·ter (al-*tim*-uh-ter; al-tuh-mee-ter) *n.* An instrument for measuring altitudes.—**al·tim·e·try** (al-*tim*-uh-tree) *n.* Altitude measurement, theory, or practice.

al·ti·tude (*al*-tih-tood) *n.* Height; distance above the ground or sea level.—**al·ti·tu·di·nal** (al-tih-*too*-dih-n'l) *adj.*

al·to (*al*-toh) *n.* [*pl.* al·tos, al·ti] *Music.* 1. A singer having the lowest range of female voices. 2. A composition sung by an alto. 3. The viola. —*adj.* Having a range similar to the alto voice. 'Alto clarinet.'

ALTHORN

al·to·geth·er (awl-tuh-*geth*-er) *adj.* Completely; wholly.

al·tru·ism (*al*-troo-izm) *n.* Consecration to the good of others; selflessness.—**al·tru·ist** *n.*—**al·tru·is·tic** *adj.*—**al·tru·is·ti·cal·ly** *adv.*

al·um (*al*-um) *n.* 1. A compound of aluminum sulphate and potassium sulphate. 2. One of a series of commercially important sulphate salts.

a·lu·mi·num (uh-*loo*-muh-num) *n.* A whitish, lightweight metallic element extracted from the ore bauxite. (*Symbol:* Al).—**a·lu·mi·num** *adj.*

a·lum·na (uh-*lum*-nuh) *n.* [*pl.* a·lum·nae (-nee)] A woman graduate of a school or college.

a·lum·nus (uh-*lum*-nus) *n.* [*pl.* a·lum·ni (-ny)] A graduate of a school or college.

al·ways *adv.* Perpetually; continually.

a·lys·sum (uh-*lis*-um) *n.* A family of yellow flowers of the mustard family.

a·mal·gam (uh-*mal*-gum) *n.* 1. A mixture of mercury and any other metal. 2. Any mixture or compound.

a·mal·gam·ate (uh-*mal*-guh-mayt) *v.* [a·mal·ga·mat·ed; -mat·ing] To mix together; merge; join; coalesce.—**a·mal·gam·a·ble** *adj.*—**a·mal·gam·a·tion** (uh-mal-guh-*may*-sh'n) *n.*—**a·mal·gam·a·tive** *adj.*

a·man·u·en·sis (uh-man-yoo-*en*-sis) *n.* [*pl.* -ses] A secretary; stenographer.

am·a·ranth (*am*-uh-ranth) *n.* 1. A family of coarse annual flowers native to warm regions.

2. An imaginary flower which never fades. —**am·a·ran·thine** *adj.*

am·a·ryl·lis (am-uh-*ril*-is) *n.* 1. A family of bulbous-rooted flowers native to South Africa. 2. [*cap.*] A heroine in pastoral romances.

a·mass (uh-*mas*) *n.* To collect; gather; accumulate.—**a·mass·a·ble** *adj.*—**a·mass·er** *n.*—**a·mass·ment** *n.*

am·a·teur (*am*-uh-choor; -tyoor) *n.* 1. One who pursues an art or study from interest rather than for a livelihood; a non-professional. 2. An inexperienced, unskillful person.—**am·a·teur** *adj.*—**am·a·teur·ism**, **am·a·teur·ship** *n.*

am·a·teur·ish (am-uh-*choor*-ish; -tyoor-) *adj.* Crude; lacking professional finish.—**am·a·teur·ish·ly** *adv.*—**am·a·teur·ish·ness** *n.*

am·a·tive (*am*-uh-tiv) *adj.* Having to do with physical passion or love.—**am·a·tive·ly** *adv.* —**am·a·tive·ness** *n.*

am·a·to·ry (*am*-uh-tor-ee) *adj.* Also **am·a·to·ri·al** (am-uh-*tor*-ee-ul). Pertaining to or expressing love; erotic.

a·maze (uh-*mayz*) *v.* [a·mazed; a·maz·ing] To overwhelm with surprise; astonish.—**a·maz·ed·ly** *adv.*—**a·maze·ment** *n.*

a·maz·ing *adj.* Startling; astounding; exciting wonder.—**a·maz·ing·ly** *adv.*

am·a·zon (*am*-uh-zon) *n.* 1. One of a fabled race of women warriors. 2. Any large and powerful woman. 3. [*cap.*] The great river of tropical South America.—**am·a·zon·ian** (am-uh-*zohn*-ee-un), **Am·a·zon·ian** *adj.*

am·bas·sa·dor (am-*bas*-uh-dor) *n.* 1. Highest-ranking minister representing his government in a foreign country. 2. Any envoy or representative.—**am·bas·sa·do·ri·al** (am-bas-uh-*dor*-ee-ul, -dohr-) *adj.*—**am·bas·sa·dor·ship** *n.*—**am·bas·sa·dress** *n.*

am·ber *n.* 1. Petrified or mineralized resin. 2. A translucent golden brown.—**am·ber** *adj.*

am·ber·gris (*am*-ber-grees) *n.* A solid, opaque, ash-colored, inflammable substance secreted by whales, valuable in the manufacture of perfumes.

am·bi·dex·trous (am-bih-*dek*-strus) *adj.* Able to use either hand with equal facility.—**am·bi·dex·trous·ly** *adv.*—**am·bi·dex·trous·ness**, **am·bi·dex·ter·i·ty** (am-bih-deks-*ter*-ih-tee) *n.*

am·bi·ent (*am*-bee-ent) *adj.* Surrounding; encompassing.

am·bi·gu·i·ty (am-bih-*gyoo*-ih-tee) *n.* [*pl.* -ties] 1. Lack of clarity in meaning. 2. A phrasing open to more than one interpretation.

am·big·u·ous (am-*big*-yoo-us) *adj.* Equivocal; doubtful or confusing in meaning.—**am·big·u·ous·ly** *adv.*—**am·big·u·ous·ness** *n.*

am·bi·tion (am-*bish*-un) *n.* 1. Aspiration; desire for pre-eminence or distinction. 2. Energy; drive; vigor. 3. End; goal; object of desire.

am·bi·tious (am-*bish*-us) *n.* 1. Desirous of self-advancement. 2. Energetic; hard-working.—**am·bi·tious·ly** *adv.*—**am·bi·tious·ness** *n.*

A

am·bi·vert (*am*-bih-vert) *n. Psychology.* One who is neither introvert nor extrovert.—**am·bi·ver·sion** (am-bih-*verzh*-un) *n.*

am·ble (*am*-b'l) *v.* [am·bled; am·bling] 1. To move along easily and gently, as a horse. 2. To walk in a loose-limbed, informal manner.—**am·ble** *n.*—**am·bler** *n.*

am·bro·si·a (am-*broh*-zhuh) *n.* 1. *Greek Mythology.* The food of the gods. 2. A delicacy; delicious or exotic food.—**am·bro·si·al, am·bro·si·an** *adj.*—**am·bro·si·al·ly** *adv.*

am·bu·lance (*am*-byoo-luns) *n.* A vehicle for transporting the sick or wounded.

am·bu·lant (*am*-byoo-l'nt) *adj.* Moving; walking.

am·bu·late (*am*-byoo-layt) *v.* [am·bu·lat·ed; -lat·ing] To walk; move about.—**am·bu·la·tion** (am-byoo-*lay*-shun) *n.*—**am·bu·la·tor** *n.*

am·bu·la·to·ry (*am*-byu-luh-tor-ee) *adj.* 1. Pertaining to walking or the ability to walk. 2. Not stationary; capable of movement or alteration.—*n.* 1. An aisle or walk. 2. Semicircular aisle behind the sanctuary in a church.

am·bus·cade (am-bus-*kayd*) *n.* 1. A preparation for surprise attack; ambush. 2. A group of ambushers.—*v.* [am·bus·cad·ed; -cad·ing]. —**am·bus·cad·er** *n.*

am·bush (*am*-bush) *v.* To attack unexpectedly from a hiding place.—*n.* 1. A trap. 2. Hidden place where surprise attackers lie concealed. 3. The troops posted for a surprise attack.—**am·bush·er** *n.*—**am·bush·ment** *n.*

a·me·ba. *Variant spelling of* **amoeba.**

a·meer. *Variant spelling of* **amir.**

a·mel·io·rate (uh-*meel*-yuh-rayt) *v.* [a·mel·io·rat·ed; -rat·ing] To make better; improve. —**a·mel·io·ra·tion** (uh-meel-yuh-*ray*-sh'n) *n.* —**a·mel·io·ra·tive** *adj.*—**a·mel·io·ra·tor** *n.*

a·men (ay-*men*, ah-*men*) *interjection.* So be it.

a·me·na·ble (uh-*mee*-nuh-b'l) *adj.* Agreeable; readily yielding or submitting.—**a·me·na·bil·i·ty** (uh-mee-nuh-*bil*-ih-tee), **a·me·na·ble·ness** *n.*

a·mend (uh-*mend*) *v.* To change; correct; reform.—**a·mends** *n. pl.* Compensation; satisfaction.—**a·mend·a·ble** *adj.*—**a·mend·er** *n.*

a·mend·ment *n.* 1. Correction; improvement; reform. 2. An alteration in or addition to a constitution or resolution.

a·men·i·ty (uh-*men*-ih-tee) *n.* [*pl.* a·men·i·ties] [*pl.*] Social courtesy; graceful convention.

A·mer·i·ca (uh-*meh*-rih-kuh) *n.* 1. Either continent of the Western Hemisphere; North, South, or Central America. 2. The United States.—**A·mer·i·can** *n. & adj.*

A·mer·i·ca·na (uh-mehr-ih-*kay*-nuh, -*kan*-uh, -*kah*-nuh) *n.* 1. All things American, collectively. 2. American folklore, literature, art, etc.

A·mer·i·can·ism (uh-*mehr*-ih-k'n-izm) *n.* 1. The patriotism Americans feel toward their country and its institutions. 2. A peculiarly American trait, idiom, etc.

A·mer·i·can·ize (uh-*mehr*-ih-k'n-yz) *v.* [A·mer·i·can·ized; -iz·ing] To assimilate into the American culture; make American.—**A·mer·i·can·i·za·tion** (uh-meh-rik-uh-niz-*ay*-sh'n) *n.*

American plan. An arrangement whereby hotels charge a flat rate including board and room for the period a guest stays.

American way. The collective social, political, and economic institutions of the U.S.

A·mer·i·ci·um (am-uh-*rish*-ee-um; uh-*mer*-ih-kum) *n.* An extremely rare, nonmetallic, radioactive element of the halogen family isolated during research on the atom bomb. (*Symbol:* Am).

am·e·thyst (*am*-uh-thist) *n.* A violet or purple semiprecious stone.—**am·e·thyst, am·e·thys·tine** *adj.* Made of or colored like amethyst.

A.M.G. *Abbreviation.* Allied Military Government.

a·mi·a·ble (*ay*-mee-uh-b'l) *adj.* Good-natured; agreeable; pleasant.—**a·mi·a·bil·i·ty** (ay-mee-uh-*bil*-ih-tee), **-a·ble·ness** *n.*—**a·mi·a·bly** *adv.*

am·i·ca·ble (*am*-ih-kuh-b'l) *adj.* Friendly; harmonious; agreeable.—**am·i·ca·bil·i·ty** (am-ih-kuh-*bil*-ih-tee), **-i·ca·ble·ness** *n.*—**-i·ca·bly** *adv.*

a·mid *prep.* Among; mingled with; in the center of.

a·mid·ships *adv.* Also **a·mid·ship.** In or toward the middle or keel of a ship.

a·midst *prep.* Among; amid.

amino acid. Any of several acids containing the group NH_2 and commonly found in proteins.

a·miss *adj.* Wrong; faulty; improper.—**a·miss** *adv.*

am·i·ty (*am*-ih-tee) *n.* [*pl.* am·i·ties] Friendship; harmony; peace.

am·me·ter (*am*-mee-ter) *n.* A device for measuring the intensity of electrical currents.

am·mo·ni·a (uh-*mohn*-yuh) *n.* 1. A suffocating gas composed of hydrogen and nitrogen. (*Symbol:* NH_3) 2. This gas dissolved in water.—**am·mo·ni·a·cal, am·mo·ni·ac** *adj.*

am·mo·ni·ac (uh-*moh*-nee-ak) *n.* Also **gum am·mo·ni·ac.** Rosin from an African and oriental tree, used medicinally as a stimulant.

am·mo·ni·um (uh-*moh*-nee-um) *n.* A hypothetical basic element represented by the radical NH_4.

am·mu·ni·tion (am-yoo-*nish*-un) *n.* All kinds of ordnance; explosives.

am·ne·si·a (am-*nee*-zhuh) *n. Psychology.* A functional loss of memory.—**am·ne·sic, -nes·tic** (-*nes*-tik) *adj.*

am·nes·ty (*am*-nes-tee) *n.* [*pl.* am·nes·ties] A general pardon for offenses against a state.

a·moe·ba (uh-*mee*-buh) *n.* [*pl.* a·moe·bae; a·moe·bas] Also **a·me·ba.** A microscopic one-celled animal of the protozoa family.—**a·moe·bic** (uh-*mee*-bik), **a·me·bic** *adj.*

AMOEBA (greatly magnified)

a·mok. *Variant spelling* of **amuck.**

a·mong (uh-*mung*) *prep.* 1. Mingled with; in. 2. Of; in the range of. 3. Between; in equal parts to each.

a·mon·til·la·do (uh-mon-tih-*lah*-doh) *n.* A kind of light, dry sherry wine.—**a·mon·til·la·do** *adj.*

a·mor·al (ay-*mor*-'l) *adj.* Without morals or morality.—**a·mor·al·ly** *adv.*—**a·mo·ral·i·ty** (ay-mor-*al*-ih-tee) *n.*

am·o·rous (*am*-er-us) *adj.* Loving; in love; passionate.—**am·o·rist** *n.* One addicted to romantic pursuits.—**am·o·rous·ly** *adv.*—**am·o·rous·ness** *n.*

a·mor·phous (uh-*mor*-fus, ay-) *adj.* 1. Shapeless; formless; irregular. 2. *Biology.* Undeveloped; without structure. 3. *Chemistry.* Having no crystallization. 4. *Geology.* Unstratified.—**a·mor·phism, a·mor·phous·ness** *n.* —**a·mor·phous·ly** *adv.*

a·mor·tize (*am*-or-tyz) *v.* [a·mor·tized; a·mor·tiz·ing] To liquidate a debt or equity.—**a·mor·tiz·a·ble** *adj.*—**a·mor·ti·za·tion** (uh-mor-tiz-*ay*-sh'n), **a·mor·tize·ment** *n.*

A·mos (*ay*-mus) *n.* 1. An Old Testament minor prophet. 2. The Book of Amos.

a·mount (uh-*mownt*) *n.* Sum; total; value; result.—*v.* To have worth or influence.

a·mour (uh-*moor*) *n.* A love affair, esp. illicit.

am·per·age (*am*-peer-ij) *n.* The intensity of electric current, expressed in amperes.

am·pere (*am*-peer) *n.* The unit of strength of electric current.

am·per·sand (*am*-per-sand) *n.* The character &.

am·phet·a·mine (am-*fet*-uh-meen) *n.* A drug used in inhalators and nasal sprays; benzedrine.

am·phib·i·a (am-*fib*-ee-uh) *n. pl. Zoology.* A class of animals able to live either on land or in water.

am·phib·i·an (am-*fib*-ee-un) *adj.* Able to live on land or in water.—*n.* 1. An animal of the class Amphibia. 2. A vehicle which can land or travel on either land or sea.

am·phib·i·ous (am-*fib*-ee-us) *adj.* Able to live or function on land or water.—**am·phib·i·ous·ly** *adv.*—**am·phib·i·ous·ness** *n.*

am·phi·ox·us (am-fee-*ok*-sus) *n.* A small marine animal, the lowest form of vertebrate life; lancelet.

am·phi·the·a·ter (*am*-fih-thee-uh-ter) *n.* Also **am·phi·the·a·tre.** A stadium or bowl having a central area surrounded by ascending rows of seats.—**am·phi·the·at·ric, am·phi·the·at·ri·cal** (am-fih-thee-*at*-rih-k'l) *adj.*—**am·phi·the·at·ri·cal·ly** *adv.*

AMPHITHEATER

am·ple (*am*-p'l) *adj.* 1. Sufficient; enough. 2. Large; spacious; extended.—**am·ple·ness** *n.*

am·pli·fi·ca·tion (am-plih-fih-*kay*-shun) *n.* 1. Enlargement; expansion; more exhaustive treatment. 2. Magnification of electric impulses.

am·pli·fi·er (*am*-plih-fy-er) *n. Electronics.* A vacuum tube or a device containing several such tubes for increasing the intensity of electrical waves.

am·pli·fy (*am*-plih-fy) *v.* [am·pli·fied; -fy·ing] 1. To make broader or more inclusive; enlarge upon. 2. To increase the strength of an electrical impulse.

am·pli·tude (*am*-plih-tood) *n.* 1. Ampleness; largeness; extent. 2. *Electricity.* Maximum of an alternating current. 3. *Physics.* Maximum variation of a regularly varying movement.

amplitude modulation. *Abbreviation*: A. M. or AM *Radio.* Process of varying the amplitude or strength of the carrier wave to conform to audio frequencies impressed on it; contrasted with **frequency modulation** (F.M. or FM) in which the frequency of the carrier wave is varied.

am·ply *adv.* Sufficiently; fully; abundantly.

am·pu·tate (*am*-pyoo-tayt) *v.* [am·pu·tat·ed; -tat·ing] To cut off; remove by surgical operation.—**am·pu·ta·tion** (am-pyoo-*tay*-sh'n) *n.* —**am·pu·ta·tor** *n.*

Amsterdam. A great port and chief city of the Netherlands.

a·muck, a·mok (uh-*muk*) *adv.* In a homicidal frenzy.—**a·muck, a·mok** *adj. & n.*

am·u·let (*am*-yoo-let) *n.* A charm or talisman worn to ward off evil.

a·muse (uh-*myooz*) *v.* [a·mused; a·mus·ing] To entertain; affect with mirth.—**a·mus·a·ble** *adj.* —**a·mus·ed·ly** *adv.*—**a·muse·ment** *n.*

a·mus·ing *adj.* Laughable; entertaining.—**a·mus·ing·ly** *adv.*—**a·mus·ing·ness** *n.*

an *Indefinite article.* One; a; used before words beginning with a vowel sound.

a·nab·o·lism (uh-*nab*-uh-lizm) *n.* The process by which food is assimilated and converted into living tissue.—**an·a·bol·ic** (an-uh-*bol*-ik) *adj.*

a·nach·ro·nism (uh-*nak*-ruh-nizm) *n.* A chronological error placing an event in a time in which it could not occur.—**a·nach·ro·nis·tic** (uh-nak-ruh-*nis*-tik) *adj.*

an·a·co·lu·thon (an-uh-kuh-*loo*-thon) *n. Rhetoric.* Sudden break in the grammatical sequence of a sentence.

an·a·con·da (an-uh-*kon*-duh) *n.* 1. A huge tropical snake which kills its victims by squeezing. 2. [*cap.*] A city of Montana noted for its copper smelter.

a·nae·mi·a, a·nae·mic. *Variant spelling* of **anemia, anemic.**

an·aes·the·si·a, an·aes·thet·ic. *Variant spelling* of **anesthesia, anesthetic.**

an·a·gram (*an*-uh-gram) *n.* Rearrangement of the letters in a word or phrase to make other words.—**an·a·gram·ma·tic** (an-uh-gruh-*mat*-ik), **an·a·gram·ma·ti·cal** *adj.*

a·nal (*ay*-n'l) *n.* Pertaining to or near the anus.

an·al·ge·si·a (an-al-*jeez*-ee-uh, -yuh) *n.* Lack of sensibility to pain.—**an·al·ge·sic** *n.* A pain-killing drug.—**an·al·ge·sic** *adj.*

a·nal·o·gous (uh-*nal*-uh-gus) *adj.* Comparable; resembling; similar, though having differences. —**a·nal·o·gous·ly** *adv.*—**a·nal·o·gous·ness** *n.*

a·nal·o·gy (uh-*nal*-uh-jee) *n.* [*pl.* a·nal·o·gies] A similarity between two basically different things.—**a·nal·o·gist** *n.*—**a·nal·o·gize** *v.* [a·nal·o·gized; -giz·ing].

an·a·lyse, ana·lys·er, etc. *Variant spelling of* analyze, etc.

a·nal·y·sis (un-*nal*-ih-sis) *n.* [*pl.* a·nal·y·ses] 1. Reduction to basic components and their relationship; a study. 2. *Chemistry.* Decomposition of a compound to determine its elements. 3. Freudian method of psychiatric treatment.—**an·a·lyst** *n.*

an·a·lyt·ic (an-uh-*lit*-ik) *adj.* Also **an·a·lyt·i·cal.** 1. Resolving into basic principles or elements. 2. Employing analysis. 3. *Philology.* Not employing inflection to modify meanings.—*n. pl.* The art or science of analysis.—**an·a·lyt·i·cal·ly** *adv.*

an·a·lyze, an·a·lyse *v.* [an·a·lyzed; -lyz·ing] To resolve into elements; separate into basic parts; scrutinize in detail; discuss meaning. —**an·a·lyz·a·ble, an·a·lys·a·ble** *adj.*—**an·a·lyz·er, an·a·lys·er** *n.*

an·a·pest (*an*-uh-pest) *n.* Also **an·a·paest.** *Prosody.* A metrical foot consisting of two unaccented and one accented beat.—**an·a·paes·tic** *adj.*

an·arch·ism (*an*-er-kizm) *n.* Belief in the abolition of all government.—**an·arch·ist** *n.*—**an·arch·ist, an·arch·is·tic** *adj.*

an·arch·y (*an*-er-kee) *n.* [*pl.* an·arch·ies] 1. A state having no law or government. 2. Chaos; terrorism.—**an·arch·ic** (an-*ark*-ik), **an·arch·i·cal** *adj.*—**an·arch·i·cal·ly** *adv.*

a·nath·e·ma (uh-*nath*-uh-muh) *n.* 1. A subject of repugnance and loathing. 2. A curse or denunciation. 3. Excommunication.

a·nath·e·ma·tize (uh-*nath*-uh-muh-tyz) *v.* [a·nath·e·ma·tized; -tiz·ing] To curse; denounce. —**a·nath·e·ma·ti·za·tion** (uh-nath-uh-muh-tuh-*zay*-sh'n) *n.*—**a·nath·e·ma·tiz·er** *n.*

an·a·tom·ic (an-uh-*tom*-ik) *adj.* Also **an·a·tom·i·cal.** Pertaining to bodily structure or dissection.—**an·a·tom·i·cal·ly** *adv.*

a·nat·o·mist (uh-*nat*-uh-mist) *n.* One skilled in the science of anatomy.

a·nat·o·mize (uh-*nat*-uh-myz) *v.* [a·nat·o·mized; -miz·ing] To dissect; examine part by part; expose and analyze minutely.—**a·nat·o·mi·za·tion** *n.*

a·nat·o·my (uh-*nat*-uh-mee) *n.* [*pl.* a·nat·o·mies] 1. The science of bodily structure. 2. The body; the physical structure of an organism.

an·ces·tor (*an*-ses-ter) *n.* A forefather; progenitor.—**an·ces·tress** *n.*—**an·ces·tral** (an-*ses*-trul) *adj.*—**an·ces·tral·ly** *adv.*

an·ces·try (*an*-ses-tree) *n.* [*pl.* an·ces·tries] Lineage; descent; forebears.

an·chor (*ank*-er) *n.* 1. A heavy hooked weight for holding a ship at rest in water. 2. Anything depended upon for stability or security.—**an·chor** *v.*

ANCHOR

an·chor·age (*ank*-uh-rij) *n.* 1. Dropping of an anchor. 2. An area of underwater floor where anchors hold firmly. 3. Immobility due to moorage by anchor.

an·cho·rite (*ang*-kuh-ryt) *n.* Also **an·cho·ret.** A hermit; one who retires to a solitary place to follow religious asceticism.—**an·cho·ress** *n.* —**an·cho·rit·ic** (ang-kuh-*rit*-ik), **-ret·ic** *adj.*

an·cho·vy (an-*choh*-vee, *an*-choh-vee) *n.* [*pl.* an·cho·vies] A small, warm-water fish having a rich, distinctive flavor.

ANCHOVY (1/3 life size)

an·cient (*ayn*-shunt) *adj.* 1. Very old; venerable. 2. Belonging to antiquity; pertaining to early civilization.—**an·cient·ly** *adv.*—**an·cient·ness** *n.*

and *conj.* Also; in addition to; plus.

An·da·lu·si·a (an-duh-*loo*-zhuh). The southern region of Spain, most influenced by Arab culture.—**An·da·lu·sian** *adj. & n.*

an·dan·te (ahn-*dahn*-teh) *adj. Music.* Slow, even, and graceful in progression.—*n.* A composition or movement in andante tempo.

An·des (*an*-deez). Lofty mountain chain which extends through western South America. —**An·de·an** (an-*dee*-un) *adj. & n.*

and·i·ron (*an*-dy-ern) *n. pl.* A standard for retaining logs in a fireplace.

an·dro·gen (*an*-droh-jen) *n.* A hormone which promotes masculinity. —**an·dro·gen·ic** (an-droh-*jen*-ik) *adj.*

an·ec·dote (*an*-ek-doht) *n.* A short, pointed, often humorous story, frequently biographical.—**an·ec·dot·age** (*an*-ek-doht-ij) *n.* Anecdotes collectively.—**an·ec·do·tal, an·ec·dot·ic, an·ec·dot·i·cal** *adj.*—**an·ec·dot·ist** *n.*

ANDIRON

a·ne·mi·a (uh-*nee*-mee-uh) *n.* Also **a·nae·mi·a.** *Medicine.* A deficiency of hemoglobin or red corpuscles in the blood.—**a·ne·mic, a·nae·mic** *adj.* 1. Deficient in red corpuscles. 2. Pallid; weak.

an·e·mom·e·ter (an-uh-*mom*-uh-ter) *n.* A wind-velocity measuring instrument.—**an·e·mom·e·try** *n.*—**an·e·mo·met·ric** *adj.*—**an·e·mo·met·ri·cal·ly** *adv.*

a·nem·o·ne (uh-*nem*-uh-nee) *n.* A large genus of flowers having small, bowl-shaped blossoms.

aneroid barometer (*an*-er-oid). An instrument

for measuring atmospheric pressure by mechanical means.

an·es·the·si·a (an-us-*theez*-ee-uh, -yuh) *n.* Also **an·aes·the·si·a.** A loss or impairment of the senses.

an·es·thet·ic (an-us-*thet*-ik) *adj.* Also **an·aes·thet·ic[** Causing loss of the senses. —*n.* A drug that produces insensibility. —**an·es·the·tist, an·aes·the·tist** (an-*es*-thuh-tist) *n.*—**an·es·the·tize, an·aes·the·tize** (an-*es*-thuh-tyz) *v.* [an·es·the·tized; -tiz·ing].

ANEMONE

a·new (uh-*nyoo*, -noo) *adv.* Again; once more.

an·gel (*ayn*-j'l) *n.* 1. A spiritual being having a human form. 2. A beautiful and good person.—**an·gel·ic, an·gel·i·cal** (an-*jel*-ik, -ik-'l) *adj.*—**an·gel·i·cal·ly** *adv.*

An·ge·lus (*an*-juh-lus) *n.* 1. A prayer said morning, noon, and night. 2. The bell rung to announce this prayer.

an·ger (*ang*-ger) *n.* An emotion of keen displeasure and hostility caused by a sense of injury; wrath; ire.—**an·ger** *v.*

an·gi·na (an-*jy*-nuh) *n. Medicine.* Any inflammatory disease of the throat.—**an·gi·nal** *adj.*

angina pectoris. *Medicine.* A constricting pain in the chest region caused by a heart disease.

an·gle *v.* [an·gled; an·gling] 1. To fish with hook and line. 2. To maneuver; elicit or entrap by wiles.—**an·gler** *n.*

an·gle *n.* 1. The meeting point of two straight lines, or the area between them; the arc of an angle. 2. A corner. *v.* [an·gled; an·gling] To form an angle.

angle iron. An L-shaped piece of iron, usually accurately squared for use in machining and inspection.

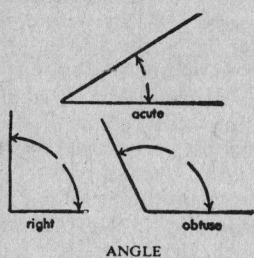
ANGLE

An·gles *n.* A Germanic tribe which occupied northern England from the 5th century.—**An·gli·an** *adj. & n.*

an·gle·worm *n.* An earthworm.

An·gli·can (*ang*-glih-k'n) *adj.* 1. Denoting the church of England. 2. English; pertaining to England.—*n.* A member of the Church of England.—**An·gli·can·ism** *n.*

an·gli·cize (*ang*-glih-syz) *v.* [an·gli·cized; -ciz·ing] To make English; to give an English pronunciation or form to foreign words.

an·gling *n.* Fishing with a line and rod.

Anglo-American *adj.* Denoting Americans of English descent; representing both English and American interests.—**Anglo-American** *n.*

An·glo·phile (*ang*-gloh-fyl) *n.* A lover of England and its traditions, etc.

An·glo·phobe (*ang*-gloh-fohb) *n.* One strongly adverse to England and its traditions.

An·glo-Sax·on *n.* 1. A descendant of the mixed race forming the British people. 2. The early Germanic language of England.—**Anglo-Saxon** *adj.*

An·go·ra (ang-*gor*-uh) *n.* 1. Cloth woven from the silken, long-staple wool of the Angora goat. 2. See Ankara.—**An·go·ra** *adj.*

angora cat. A large, long-furred domestic cat.

ANGORA CAT

an·gry (*ang*-gree) *adj.* [an·gri·er; an·gri·est] 1. Resentful; vexed; wrathful. 2. Reddened; stinging. —**an·gri·ly** *adv.* —**an·gri·ness** *n.*

an·guish (*ang*-gwish) *n.* Pain; grief; torment; agony.—**an·guish** *v.*

an·gu·lar (*ang*-gyoo-ler) *adj.* 1. Sharp-cornered; having tapering points or angles. 2. Bony; ungracefully thin.—**an·gu·lar·ly** *adv.* —**an·gu·lar·ness** *n.*

an·gu·lar·i·ty (ang-gyoo-*lair*-ih-tee) *n.* [pl. -ties] Sharpness; presence of corners or angles.

an·i·line (*an*-ih-lin) *n.* Also **an·i·lin.** A colorless, acrid fluid used in dyes.—**an·i·line, an·i·lin** *adj.*

an·i·mad·ver·sion (an-ih-mad-*ver*-zhun) *n.* Blame; criticism; reproving remarks.—**an·i·mad·vert** *v.*—**an·i·mad·vert·er** *n.*

an·i·mal (*an*-ih-m'l) *n.* 1. Any living organism distinguished from a plant, characteristically capable of sensation and voluntary motion. 2. Brute; beast.—**an·i·mal** *adj.*—**an·i·mal·ly** *adv.*

an·i·mal·cule (an-ih-*mal*-kyool) *n.* A minute or microscopic animal.—**an·i·mal·cu·lar** *adj.*

an·i·mal·ism *n.* Also **an·i·mal·i·ty.** Sensuality; resemblance to animals.—**an·i·mal·ist, an·i·mal·ist·ic** *adj.*

an·i·mate (*an*-ih-mayt) *v.* [an·i·mat·ed; an·i·mat·ing] 1. To give life to. 2. To inspire; heighten in power or effect; stimulate.—*adj.* (an-ih-mit) Living.—**an·i·mat·er** *n.*

an·i·mat·ed *adj.* 1. Lively; spirited; vivacious. 2. Endowed with life.—**an·i·mat·ed·ly** *adv.*

an·i·ma·tion (an-ih-*may*-shun) *n.* 1. Liveliness; vivacity. 2. Infusion of life; awakening to life.

an·i·ma·tism (*an*-ih-muh-tizm) *n.* Tendency of primitive civilizations to endow inanimate things with living qualities.

an·i·mism (*an*-ih-mizm) *n.* 1. Ascription of conscious life to all objects in nature. 2. A hypothesis that all matter is given form and

A

motion by a spiritual power.—**an·i·mist** *n.*
—**an·i·mis·tic** *adj.*

an·i·mos·i·ty (an-uh-*mos*-ih-tee) *n.* [*pl.* an·i·mos·i·ties] Enmity; hostility; opposition.

an·i·mus (*an*-ih-mus) *n.* 1. Intention; spirit; temper; purpose. 2. Enmity; ill-will.

an·ise (*an*-is) *n.* An annual aromatic herb of North Africa.

an·i·sette (an-ih-*zet*) *n.* An aromatic liqueur flavored with oil of anise seeds.

An·ka·ra (*ang*-kah-rah) *n.* Also **An·go·ra.** The capital city of Turkey.

an·kle (*ang*-kl) *n.* The joint between the leg and the foot.

an·klet (*angk*-let) *n.* 1. An ankle-length sock. 2. A bracelet worn around the ankle.

an·nal·ist (*an*'l-ist) *n.* A chronicler; historian. —**an·nal·is·tic** *adj.*

an·nals (*an*'lz) *n. pl.* 1. A chronological record of events. 2. A periodical history publication of a society.

An·nap·o·lis (uh-*nap*-uh-lis). 1. A port and city of Maryland, site of U. S. Naval Academy. 2. The U. S. Naval Academy.

an·neal (uh-*neel*) *v.* 1. *Metallurgy.* To soften stresses in metals by heat. 2. To heat; bake. 3. To crystallize; steel; harden.—**an·neal·er** *n.*

an·nex (uh-*neks*) *v.* To add to; connect to; be united to.—*n.* (*an*-eks) An addition, esp. a wing added to a larger structure.—**an·nex·a·ble** (uh-*neks*-uh-b'l).

an·nex·a·tion (an-ek-*zay*-shun) *n.* An addition, esp. a small nation taken over by a large one.

Annie Oakley. *Slang.* A free pass; complimentary ticket.

an·ni·hi·late (uh-*ny*-uh-layt) *v.* [an·ni·hi·lat·ed; -lat·ing] To wipe out; destroy; extirpate.—**-hi·la·tion** *n.*—**-hi·la·tive** *adv.*—**-hi·la·tor** *n.*

an·ni·ver·sa·ry (an-ih-*ver*-ser-ee) *n.* [*pl.* -ries] 1. A date commemorated yearly for its association with a previous event. 2. A celebration of an anniversary.—**an·ni·ver·sa·ry** *adj.*

An·no Dom·i·ni (*an*-oh *dom*-ih-nee). Year of our Lord. *Abbreviation:* **A.D.**

an·no·tate (*an*-oh-tayt) *v.* [an·no·tat·ed; -tat·ing] To add notes or commentaries.—**an·no·ta·tion** (an-oh-*tay*-shun) *n.*—**an·no·ta·tor** *n.*

an·nounce (uh-*nowns*) *v.* [an·nounced; an·nounc·ing] To give notice of; make known. —**an·nounc·er** *n.* 1. A person who introduces radio programs. 2. One who announces.

an·nounce·ment *n.* 1. Proclamation; publication. 2. A printed notice. 3. Act of making known.

an·noy (uh-*noy*) *v.* To displease; vex; disturb; molest.—**an·noy·ance** *n.*—**an·noy·er** *n.*

an·noy·ing *adj.* Troublesome; vexing; irritating.—**an·noy·ing·ly** *adv.*—**an·noy·ing·ness** *n.*

an·nu·al (*an*-yoo-ul) *adj.* Yearly.—*n.* 1. A publication appearing yearly. 2. A plant which lives one year only.—**an·nu·al·ly** *adv.*

an·nu·i·ty (uh-*nyoo*-ih-tee) *n.* [*pl.* an·nu·i·ties] A payment of money in a fixed sum per year.

an·nul (uh-*nul*) *v.* [an·nulled; an·nul·ling] To void; nullify; declare illegal.—**an·nul·la·ble** *adj.*—**an·nul·ment** *n.*

an·nu·lar (*an*-yoo-ler) *adj.* Pertaining to or resembling a ring.—**an·nu·lar·i·ty** (an-yoo-*lar*-ih-tee) *n.*—**an·nu·lar·ly** *adv.*

an·nun·ci·a·tion (uh-nun-see-*ay*-shun) *n.* 1. Announcement; proclamation. 2. [*cap.*] The appearance of Gabriel to the Virgin Mary, announcing the Incarnation.

an·ode (*an*-ohd) *n. Electricity.* The positive pole of a voltaic cell or electroplating device.—**an·od·ic** *adj.*

an·o·dize (*an*-oh-dyz) *v.* [an·o·dized; -diz·ing] To electroplate at the anode.

an·o·dyne (*an*-oh-dyn) *n.* A pain-deadening drug.—**an·o·dyne** *adj.*

a·noint (uh-*noynt*) *n.* 1. To rub with oil or grease. 2. To consecrate with oil.—**a·noint·er** *n.*—**a·noint·ment** *n.*

a·nom·a·ly (uh-*nom*-uh-lee) *n.* [*pl.* a·nom·a·lies] Also **a·nom·a·lism.** A freak; abnormality; irregularity.—**a·nom·a·lous** *adj.*— **-a·lous·ly** *adv.* — **-a·lous·ness** *n.*

a·non (uh-*non*) *adv.* 1. Again; another time. 2. Soon.

a·non·y·mous (uh-*non*-uh-mus) *adj.* Unacknowledged; unidentified; not named; of unknown authorship.—**an·o·nym·i·ty** (an-uh-*nim*-ih-tee), **a·non·y·mous·ness** *n.*—**-mous·ly** *adv.*

an·oth·er (uh-*nuth*-er) *adj.* 1. Not the same; different. 2. One more. 3. Anyone else; any other.—**an·oth·er** *pron.*

An·schluss (*ahn*-shlus) *n. German.* A joining; annexation, esp. the Nazi annexation of Austria in 1939.

an·swer (*an*-ser) *n.* 1. A reply. 2. The solution to a mathematical problem. 3. *Law.* A counterstatement; a confuting of testimony. —*v.* 1. To reply to. 2. To fit or serve a purpose. 3. To refute; reply to successfully. 4. To write a letter in reply. 5. To receive and accept a telephone call.

an·swer·a·ble (*an*-ser-uh-b'l) *adj.* 1. Admitting of a reply. 2. Liable; accountable; responsible.—**an·swer·a·ble·ness** *n.*—**-a·bly** *adv.*

ant *n.* A small gregarious insect living in burrows in the ground.

ant·ac·id (ant-*ass*-id) *n.* An alkali; solution for neutralizing stomach acidity.—**ant·ac·id** *adj.*

an·tag·o·nism (an-*tag*-uh-nizm) *n.* Hostility; opposition; ill will.

an·tag·o·nist (an-*tag*-uh-nist) *n.* A contender; opponent.—**an·tag·o·nis·tic** (an-tag-uh-*niss*-tik) *adj.*—**an·tag·o·nis·ti·cal·ly** *adv.*

ANT (larger than life size)

an·tag·o·nize (an-*tag*-uh-nyz) *v.* [an·tag·o·nized; -niz·ing] 1. To provoke opposition; cause contention. 2. To contend with; act in opposition.

ant·arc·tic (ant-*ark*-tik) *adj.* Pertaining to the South Pole and its regions.—**ant·arc·tic** *n.*

Antarctic Circle. The parallel of latitude

which divides the South Temperate and South Frigid zones.

an·te (*an*-tee) *n.* 1. *Card Playing.* A sum deposited as a stake before play starts. 2. *Slang.* Investment price; initial cost.—*v.* [an·teed; an·te·ing].

ant·eat·er (*ant*-eet-er) *n.* A large family of mammals feeding on ants.

an·te·ced·ent (an-tuh-*seed*-ent) *n.* 1. An ancestor. 2. Person or thing which precedes.

ANTEATER (1/60 life size)

3. *Grammar.* The substantive to which a pronoun refers. 4. [*pl.*] The earlier events and determinants of a man's life.—*adj.* Preceding; prior.—-**ced·ence, -ced·en·cy** *n.*—-**ced·ent·ly** *adv.*

an·te·cham·ber (*an*-teh-chaym-ber) *n.* A small room leading into a larger.

an·te·date (*an*-teh-dayt) *v.* [an·te·dat·ed; -dat·ing] 1. To give a date earlier than the true one. 2. To occur earlier.—**an·te·date** *n.*

an·te·di·lu·vi·an (an-teh-dih-*loo*-vee-un) *adj.* Before Noah's flood; ancient.

an·te·lope (*an*-teh-lohp) *n.* A group of hollow-horned ruminants related to sheep and goats.

an·te·me·rid·i·an (an-teh-mer-*id*-ee-un) *adj.* Before noon. *Abbreviation: a.m.* or *A.M.*

ANTELOPE (1/62 life size)

an·ten·na (an-*ten*-uh) *n.* [*pl.* an·ten·nae] The feelers of insects and other lower animals.—*n.* [*pl.* an·ten·nas] *Radio.* A conductor which radiates or receives radio waves.—**an·ten·na** *adj.*

an·te·ri·or (an *teer*-ee-er) *adj.* Before in time or place.—-**or·i·ty, -or·ness** *n.*—-**or·ly** *adv.*

an·te·room (*an*-teh-room) *n.* A room leading into another; antechamber.

an·them (*an*-them) *n.* A sacred or patriotic song.

an·ther (*an*-ther) *n.* The pollen-producing cell of a flower.—**an·ther·al** *adj.*

an·thol·o·gy (an-*thol*-uh-jee) *n.* [*pl.* -gies] A collection of poems or of prose passages.—**an·tho·log·i·cal** (an-thuh-*loj*-ih-k'l) *adj.*—**an·thol·o·gist** *n.*

an·thra·cite (*an*-thruh-syt) *n.* Hard or non-bituminous coal.—**an·thra·cit·ic** (an-thruh-*sit*-ik) *adj.*

ANTHER

an·thrax (*an*-thraks) *n.* 1. *Medicine.* A burning sore; carbuncle. 2. A bacterial disease usually infecting cattle.—**an·thra·coid** (*an*-thruh-koid) *adj.*

an·thro·poid (*an*-thruh-poyd) *adj.* Resembling man.—*n.* A member of the ape family closely resembling man.

an·thro·pol·o·gy (an-thruh-*pol*-uh-jee) *n.* The science of man and his physical and social history.—**an·thro·po·log·ic** (an-thruh-puh-*loj*-ik), **-i·cal** *adj.*—**-i·cal·ly** *adv.*—**-pol·o·gist** *n.*

an·thro·po·mor·phic (an-thruh-poh-*mor*-fik) *adj.* 1. Resembling man. 2. Assigning human form, character, etc., to non-human beings.—**an·thro·po·mor·phism** *n.*

an·ti- *Prefix.* Opposite; as:

anti-American   antifascist   anti-Polish
anti-Catnolic   anti-imperial   anti-Republican
anti-Communist   anti-New Deal   antislavery

an·ti *n.* [*pl.* an·tis] *Colloquial.* A person in opposition to a given law, philosophy, etc.

an·ti·air·craft (an-tee-*air*-kraft) *n.* Long-range, mobile, automatically aimed gun for firing on airplanes from the ground.—**an·ti·air·craft** *adj.*

an·ti·bod·y *n.* [*pl.* an·ti·bod·ies] *Medicine.* A serum in the body which combats germs or nullifies their effects.

an·tic *n.* An absurd gesture or action; caper; buffoonery.—**an·tic** *v.* & *n.*

an·ti·christ (*an*-tih-kryst) *n.* A person or power hostile to Christ.—**an·ti·chris·tian, an·ti·Chris·tian** *adj.*

an·tic·i·pate (an-*tis*-ih-payt) *v.* [an·ti·ci·pat·ed; -pat·ing] 1. To look forward to; 2. To foresee; deal with in advance; avert or fulfill ahead of time.—**an·tic·i·pant** *adj.*—-**pa·tion** (-*pay*-shun) *n.*—**an·tic·i·pa·tive** (an-*tis*-ih-pay-tive) *adj.*—-**pa·tive·ly** *adv.*—-**pa·tor** *n.*

an·tic·i·pa·to·ry (an-*tis*-ih-puh-tor-ee) *adj.* Expectant; awaiting; foreseeing.—-**to·ri·ly** *adv.*

an·ti·cli·max (an-tih-*kly*-maks) *n.* 1. A secondary situation or event following a high point or crisis of excitement and interest. 2. *Rhetoric.* A passage which weakens in concept and forcefulness toward the close.—**an·ti·cli·max** *v.*—**an·ti·cli·mac·tic** (an-tih-kly-*mak*-tik) *adj.*—**an·ti·cli·mac·ti·cal·ly** *adv.*

Anti-Comintern Pact. The treaty of alliance between Japan, Germany, and Italy against U.S.S.R. in 1936.

an·ti·dote (*an*-tih-doht) *n.* 1. A medicine which combats the effects of poison. 2. Any action which nullifies another.—**an·ti·dot·al** *adj.*—**an·ti·dot·al·ly** *adv.*

an·ti·freeze *n.* A substance added to water to lower the freezing point.—**an·ti·freeze, an·ti·freez·ing** *adj.* & *v.* [an·ti·froz·en; -freez·ing].

an·ti·gen (*an*-tih-jen) *n.* An agent which promotes the development of antibodies in the system—**an·ti·gen·ic** *adj.*

an·ti·im·pe·ri·al·ism *n.* A doctrine hostile to expansion of one country at the expense of another.—**an·ti·im·pe·ri·al·is·tic** *adj.*

an·ti·ma·cas·sar (an-tih-muh-*kas*-er) *n.* A tidy; cover for back and arms of a chair, sofa, etc.

A

an·ti·mo·ny (*an*-tih-moh-nee) *n.* A silver-white brittle metallic element similar to arsenic. —**an·ti·mo·ni·al** (*an*-tih-moh-nee-ul) *adj. & n.* (*Symbol:* Sb).

an·ti·pas·to (ahn-tee-*pahss*-toh) *n.* Italian hors d'oevres; varied appetizer, usually celery, anchovies, olives, etc.

an·tip·a·thy (an-*tip*-uh-thee) *n.* [*pl.* -thies] 1. Aversion; repugnance; distaste. 2. An object of dislike.—**an·ti·pa·thet·ic** (an-tip-uh-*thet*-ik), **an·ti·pa·thet·i·cal** *adj.*—**an·ti·pa·thet·i·cal·ly** *adv.*

an·tiph·o·ny (an-*tif*-uh-nee) *n.* [*pl.* -nies] Responsive or alternate singing; an answer of one choral group to another.—**an·tiph·o·nal** *adj.*

an·tip·o·des (an-*tip*-uh-deez) *n. pl.* The opposite; anything diametrically opposed; the opposite sides of the globe.—**an·tip·o·de·an** (an-tip-uh-*dee*-un) *adj.*

an·ti·py·ret·ic (an-tih-py-*ret*-ik) *n. Medicine.* A fever-relieving drug.—**an·ti·py·ret·ic** *adj.*

an·ti·py·rine (an-tih-*py*-reen) *n. Medicine.* A drug derived from coal tar, used to relieve fever, soothe pain, etc.

an·ti·quar·i·an (an-tih-*kwair*-ee-un) *n.* One devoted to studying ancient things.—**an·ti·quar·i·an** *adj.*

an·ti·quar·y (*an*-tih-kwair-ee) *n.* [*pl.* an·ti·quar·ies] An authority on the relics or lore of ancient times.

an·ti·quate (*an*-tih-kwayt) *v.* [an·ti·quat·ed; -quat·ing] To make obsolete; cause to fall into disuse.—**an·ti·qua·tion** (an-tih-*kway*-sh'n) *n.*

an·tique (an-*teek*) *n.* 1. Any relic of an earlier or ancient time; an old-fashioned object, esp. of house furnishings. 2. *Printing.* A type having each stroke of equal thickness.—*v.* [an·tiqued; an·tiqu·ing] To paint or finish an object to make it look antique.—**an·tique** *adj.*—**an·tique·ly** *adv.*—**an·tique·ness** *n.*

an·tiq·ui·ty (an-*tik*-wih-tee) *n.* [*pl.* an·tiq·ui·ties] 1. Ancient times. 2. Great age; oldness. 3. A relic of the past.

an·ti·scor·bu·tic (an-tih-skor-*byoo*-tik) *n. Medicine.* A preventive or cure for scurvy.—**an·ti·scor·bu·tic** *adj.*

an·ti·sep·sis (an-tih-*sep*-sis) *n.* Prevention of poisoning or putrefaction by destruction of micro-organisms.

an·ti·sep·tic (an-tih-*sep*-tik) *n. Medicine.* A chemical that destroys or hinders the action of bacteria and germs.—**an·ti·sep·tic, an·ti·sep·ti·cal** *adj.*—**an·ti·sep·ti·cal·ly** *adv.*

an·ti·slav·er·y (an-tih-*slay*-ver-ee) *adj.* Opposed to the enslavement of men.

an·ti·so·cial (an-tih-*soh*-shul) *adj.* Viciously hostile or harmful to society.

an·tith·e·sis (an-*tith*-uh-sis) *n.* [*pl.* an·tith·e·ses] Opposition; contrast; the opposite.—**an·ti·thet·ic, -i·cal** (-*thet*-ik) *adj.*—**-i·cal·ly** *adv.*

an·ti·tox·in (an-tih-*tok*-sin) *n. Medicine.* Also **an·ti·tox·ine.** A substance in blood serum that acts against a specific toxin or infection.

an·ti·trades *n. pl.* Tropical high-level winds blowing opposite to the trade winds.

ant·ler *n.* A horn of a deer or stag.—**ant·lered** *adj.*

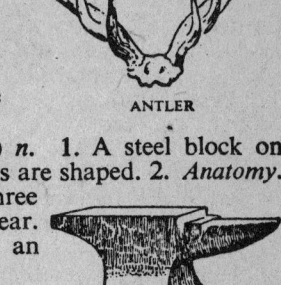

an·to·nym *n.* A word having the opposite, or nearly opposite, meaning to another.

a·nus (*ay*-nus) *n.* The opening at the posterior end of the digestive tract.

ANTLER

an·vil (*an*-v'l *an*-vil) *n.* 1. A steel block on which heated metals are shaped. 2. *Anatomy.* The middle of three bones of the inner ear. —*v.* To shape on an anvil.

anx·i·e·ty (ang-*zy*-uh-tee) *n.* [*pl.* anx·i·e·ties] 1. Worry; concern; disquietude; uneasiness. 2. Sincere desire.

anx·ious (*ank*-shus) *adj.* 1. Apprehensive; uneasy 2. Solicitous; desirous. 3. Causing worry.—**anx·ious·ly** *adv.*—**anx·ious·ness** *n.*

ANVIL

an·y (*en*-ee) *adj.* 1. Some; a quantity of. 2. One indiscriminately chosen from many. —*adv.* To an indefinite degree.—**any** *pron.*

an·y·bod·y *pron.* Some person; anyone.

an·y·how *adv.* In any case; at any rate; in any way.

any more. 1. Any indefinite amount more. 2. Now; at present; since an unspecified time.

an·y·one *pron.* Any person whatsoever.

an·y·thing *n.* Any object, fact, case, etc.

an·y·way *adv.* Nevertheless; anyhow.

an·y·where *adv.* At or to any place at all.

an·y·wise *adv.* In any way; anyhow.

An·zac (*an*-zak) *n. Colloquial.* A member of the Australian and New Zealand army corps. —**An·zac** *adj.*

A one. Also **A-1** or **A1.** *Colloquial.* First-rate; top-notch.

a·or·ta (ay-*or*-tuh) *n.* [*pl.* a·or·tas; a·or·tae] *Anatomy.* The main artery, leading from the heart's left ventricle.

a·pace (uh-*payss*) *adv.* Swiftly; fast.

A·pach·e (uh-*pach*-ee) *n.* [*pl.* Apaches, Apache] *n.* A tribe of fierce nomad Indians of SW U.S.

a·pache (uh-*pahsh*) *n.* 1. One of a gang of Parisian criminals. 2. A violent dance derived from the manners and customs of apaches.

ap·a·nage. *Variant spelling* of **appanage.**

a·part (uh-*part*) *adv.* 1. Separate from; independently. 2. Asunder; in pieces. 3. Aside; removed from.

a·part·ment (uh-*part*-m'nt) *n.* A division of a house separate from the rest; a suite of rooms.

—**apartment house.** A building containing a number of separate dwellings.

ap·a·thet·ic (ap-uh-*thet*-ik) *adj*. Also **ap·a·thet·i·cal.** Lacking feeling; indifferent.—**ap·a·thet·i·cal·ly** *adv*.

ap·a·thy (ap-uh-thee) *n*. [*pl*. ap·a·thies] Lack of interest or emotion; insensitivity.

ape *n*. 1. One of a family of large, tailless monkeys of Africa. 2. A mimic; servile imitator.—*v*. [aped; ap·ing] To mimic.

Ap·en·nines (ap-uh-nynz). A range of mountains of Central Italy.—**Ap·en·nine** *adj*.

a·pe·ri·ent *n. Medicine*. A mild laxative.—**a·pe·ri·ent** *adj*.

ap·er·ture (ap-er-choor) *n*. 1. An opening; hole. 2. *Optics*. The effective diameter of a lens.

a·pex (ay-peks) *n*. [*pl*. a·pex·es, a·pices (ap-i-seez)] 1. A summit; top. 2. Pointed tip; end.

a·pha·si·a (uh-*fay*-zhee-uh, -zhuh) *n*. Loss of the power of speech resulting from a brain disorder.

a·phid (ay-fid) *n*. A plant louse.—**a·phid·i·an** *n*. An insect which lives by sucking the juices of plants.—**a·phid·i·an** (uh-*fid*-ee-un) *adj*.

a·phis (ay-fis) *n*. [*pl*. aph·i·des (af-ih-dees)] A plant louse.

aph·o·rism (af-uh-rizm) *n*. A brief, pithy statement or precept.——**aph·o·rist** *n*.—**aph·o·ris·tic** (af-uh-*ris*-tik) *adj*.—**aph·o·ris·ti·cal·ly** *adv*.

aph·ro·dis·i·ac (af-ruh-*diz*-ee-ak) *n*. Any drug which arouses sexual impulse.—*adj*. Denoting sexual love.

Aph·ro·di·te (af-ruh-*dy*-tee) *n. Mythology*. The Greek goddess of love and beauty.

a·pi·ar·y (ay-pee-ehr-ee) *n*. [*pl*. a·pi·ar·ies] A building or area devoted to keeping bees.—**a·pi·a·rist** *n*. A bee keeper.

ap·i·ces (ap-ih-seez). Plural of **apex**.

a·piece *adv*. For each. 'Take only two apiece.'

ap·ish (ayp-ish) *adj*. Slavishly imitative; mimicking.—**ap·ish·ly** *adv*.—**ap·ish·ness** *n*.

a·plomb (uh-*plom*) *n*. Assurance; poise; self-possession.

a·poc·a·lypse (uh-*pok*-uh-lips) *n*. 1. Revelation; disclosure; discovery. 2. [*cap*.] *The Revelation of Saint John the Divine*, the last book of the New Testament.—**a·poc·a·lyp·tic** (uh-pok-uh-*lip*-tik), **a·poc·a·lyp·ti·cal** (uh-pok-uh-*lip*-tik; -ti-k'l) *adj*.—**a·poc·a·lyp·ti·cal·ly** *adv*.

a·poc·ry·pha (uh-*pok*-rih-fuh) *n. pl*. 1. Writings of unknown authorship. 2. [*cap*.]. The books of the Bible rejected by most Protestant churches.

a·poc·ry·phal (uh-*pok*-rih-f'l) *adj*. 1. Having no authority; false; spurious. 2. [*cap*.] Pertaining to the Apocrypha.—*n*. A writing of uncertain authority.

ap·o·gee (ap-uh-jee) *n*. 1. *Astronomy*. The point in the moon's orbit when it is farthest from earth. 2. A climax; high point.

A·pol·lo (uh-*pol*-oh) *n. Mythology*. The sun god; god of poetry, music, and prophecy, and patron of physicians.

a·pol·o·get·ic (uh-pol-uh-*jet*-ik) *adj*. Also **a·pol·o·get·i·cal.** 1. Begging forgiveness; asking pardon. 2. Defending; arguing in defense.—**a·pol·o·get·i·cal·ly** *adv*.

a·pol·o·gist (uh-*pol*-uh-jist) *n*. 1. A defender; one who presents an argument for a cause. 2. One who asks pardon.

a·pol·o·gize (uh-*pol*-uh-jyz) *v*. [a·pol·o·gized; -giz·ing] 1. To beg pardon or forgiveness. 2. To plead in defense of.—**a·pol·o·giz·er** *n*.—**a·pol·o·gy** *n*. [*pl*. -gies]

ap·o·plex·y (ap-uh-pleks-ee) *n. Medicine*. Sudden unconsciousness followed by paralysis, caused by rupture or stoppage of brain arteries.—**ap·o·plec·tic** *adj*. & *n*.—**ap·o·plec·ti·cal** (ap-uh-*plek*-tih-k'l) *adj*.—**ap·o·plec·ti·cal·ly** *adv*.

a·port *adv. Nautical*. On or toward the left.

a·pos·ta·sy (uh-*pos*-tuh-see) *n*. [*pl*. -ies] Desertion of one's belief.

a·pos·tate (uh-*pos*-tayt) *n*. One who abandons his principles.—**a·pos·tate** *adj*.

a·pos·tle (uh-*pos*'l) *n*. [*cap*.] 1. One of the twelve followers of Christ sent forth to preach the gospel. 2. One who pursues a mission.—**a·pos·tle·ship** *n*.

ap·os·tol·ic (ap-us-*tol*-ik) *adj*. Also **ap·os·tol·i·cal.** Pertaining to an apostle or his doctrines.—**ap·os·tol·i·cism, a·pos·to·lic·i·ty** (uh-pos-tuh-*lis*-ih-tee) *n*.—**ap·os·tol·i·cal·ly** *adv*.

a·pos·tro·phe (uh-*pos*-truh-fee) *n*. 1. A mark (') used in contractions, the possessive case, etc. 2. A transition in address from the reader or listener to another abstract subject.—**ap·os·troph·ic** (ap-us-*troh*-fik) *adj*.—**a·pos·tro·phize** (uh-*pos*-truh-fyz) *v*. [a·pos·tro·phized; -phiz·ing].

a·poth·e·car·y (uh-*poth*-uh-keh-ree) *n*. [*pl*. -ies] A pharmacist; druggist.

ap·o·thegm (ap-uh-them) *n*. A short, pithy statement; maxim.—**ap·o·theg·mat·ic** (ap-uh-theg-*mat*-ik), **ap·o·theg·mat·i·cal** *adj*.

a·poth·e·o·sis (uh-poth-ee-*oh*-sis, ap-uh-*thee*-uh-sis) *n*. [*pl*. a·poth·e·o·ses] Deification; elevation to godship.—**a·poth·e·o·size** *v*. (uh-*poth*-ee-uh-syz) [a·poth·e·o·sized; -siz·ing].

Ap·pa·lach·i·ans (ap-uh-*lay*-chee-uns, -*lach*-uns). The great system of mountain ranges of eastern U.S.—**Ap·pa·lach·i·an** *adj*.

ap·pall (uh-*pawl*) *v*. To dismay; confound with fright or horror.—**ap·pal·ling** *adj*.—**ap·pal·ling·ly** *adv*.

ap·pa·nage (ap-uh-nij) *n*. Also **ap·a·nage.** Rights and privileges accruing from birth or station.

ap·pa·ra·tus (ap-uh-*ray*-tus) *n*. [*pl*. ap·pa·ra·tus; ap·pa·ra·tus·es] 1. A machine; mechanical device or equipment for a specific operation. 2. *Physiology*. A group of organs performing a specific function.

ap·par·el (uh-*par*-'l) *n*. Clothing; dress; garments.—*v*. [ap·par·eled, ap·par·elled; ap·par·el·ing, ap·par·el·ling].

A

ap·par·ent (uh-*par*-'nt) *adj.* 1. Seeming; presenting the appearance of. 2. Obvious; evident; visible.—**ap·par·en·cy, ap·par·ent·ness** *n.* —**ap·par·ent·ly** *adv.*

ap·pa·ri·tion (ap-uh-*rish*-un) *n.* 1. A ghost; specter. 2. Appearance; sight; spectacle.—**ap·pa·ri·tion·al** *adj.*

ap·peal (uh-*peel*) *v.* 1. To call for; request; beg. 2. *Law.* To refer to a higher court. 3. To refer to an authority.—**ap·peal** *n.*—**ap·peal·a·bil·i·ty** (uh-peel-uh-*bil*-ih-tee) *n.*—**ap·peal·a·ble** *adj.*—**ap·peal·er** *n.*

ap·peal·ing *adj.* 1. Winning; touching; supplicating. 2. Attractive; interesting.—**ap·peal·ing·ly** *adv.*

ap·pear (uh-*peer*) *v.* 1. To become visible. 2. To seem; give the appearance of. 3. To be present.—**ap·pear·er** *n.*

ap·pear·ance (uh-*peer*-uns) *n.* 1. Coming; arrival. 2. Presence; attendance. 3. A thing seen; phenomenon. 4. [*often pl.*] External impression; effect. 5. Physical aspect; mien. 6. Presentation to the public. 7. *Law.* Being present; stating a defense.

ap·pease (uh-*peez*) *v.* [ap·peased; ap·peas·ing] 1. To conciliate; calm; reconcile. 2. To pacify by making concessions.—**ap·peas·a·ble** *adj.* —**ap·pease·ment** *n. & adj.*

ap·pel·lant (uh-*pel*-unt) *n.* One who appeals to a higher court or authority.—**ap·pel·lant** *adj.*

ap·pel·late (uh-*pel*-it) *adj.* Denoting or dealing with appeals.

ap·pel·la·tion (ap-eh-*lay*-shun) *n.* Name; title; designation.—**ap·pel·la·tive** *adj.* Pertaining to the naming of persons or things.

ap·pend (uh-*pend*) *v.* To add to; attach to a larger body.—**ap·pend·age** *n.*

ap·pen·dec·to·my *n.* Operation for removal of the appendix.

ap·pen·di·ces. *Plural* of **appendix.**

ap·pen·di·ci·tis (uh-pen-dih-*sy*-tis, -tus) *n.* *Medicine.* An inflammation of the vermiform appendix.

ap·pen·dix (uh-*pen*-diks) *n.* [*pl.* ap·pen·dixes; ap·pen·dices] 1. A wormlike outgrowth at the opening of the large intestine. 2. An addition, esp. a related but not essential addition to a book.

ap·per·tain (ap-er-*tayn*) *v.* To belong; relate.

ap·pe·tite (*ap*-uh-tyt) *n.* 1. Desire for nourishment; hunger. 2. Longing; desire; eagerness. —**ap·pe·ti·tive** *adj.*

APPENDIX

ap·pe·tiz·er (*ap*-eh-tyz-er) *n.* Small course served before the main dish of a meal; hors d'oevres.

ap·pe·tiz·ing *n.* Delectable; tempting; stimulating hunger.—**ap·pe·tiz·ing·ly** *adv.*

Appian Way. An ancient Roman road from Rome to Brindisi.

ap·plaud (uh-*plawd*) *v.* 1. To praise or approve by clapping. 2. To praise; command.—**ap·plaud·er** *n.*

ap·plause *n.* Handclapping; public demonstration of praise or approbation.—**ap·plau·sive** *adj.*

APPLE

ap·ple (*ap*-'l) *n.* 1. The most commonly cultivated and widely used of temperate climate fruits. 2. Any of certain fruits bearing some resemblance to an apple.

apple blossom	apple grower	applenut
apple cart	applejohn	apple-scented
apple-cheeked	applelike	apple-shaped
apple-faced	applemonger	appleworm

ap·ple·jack *n.* A brandy distilled from cider.

ap·ple·sauce *n.* Apples stewed, sweetened, and seasoned.

ap·pli·ance (uh-*ply*-uns) *n.* 1. A gadget; a device which permits or facilitates use of the unit of which it is a part. 2. Applying or using.

ap·pli·ca·ble (*ap*-lih-kuh-b'l) *adj.* Relevant; capable of being applied.—**ap·pli·ca·bil·i·ty** (ap-lih-kuh-*bil*-ih-tee), **ap·pli·ca·ble·ness** *n.*—**ap·pli·ca·bly** *adv.*

ap·pli·cant (*ap*-lih-k'nt) *n.* A candidate; petitioner; one who presents himself for a job or a concession.

ap·pli·ca·tion (ap-lih-*kay*-shun) *n.* 1. A written request for a job or concession. 2. Petitioning or requesting. 3. Putting or laying on. 4. A salve or other medicine used externally. 5. Close study; intense concentration. 6. Testing of a theory by putting it into practice.—**ap·pli·ca·tive** (*ap*-lik-uh-tiv), **ap·pli·ca·to·ry** *adj.*

ap·pli·qué (ap-lih-*kay*) *n.* Decorative detail superimposed on a solid ground.—*v.* [ap·pli·quéd; ap·pli·qué·ing].—**ap·pli·qué** *adj.*

ap·ply (uh-*ply*) *v.* [ap·plied; ap·ply·ing] 1. To put on; lay on. 2. To use in a particular case. 3. To concentrate; devote oneself. 4. To pertain; have bearing upon. 5. To request; solicit; petition. 6. To put into practice; test by use.—**ap·pli·er** *n.*

ap·point (uh-*point*) *v.* 1. To nominate; designate. 2. To settle; fix; name. 3. To adorn. 4. To determine.—**ap·point·ee** *n.* One nominated or designated.—**ap·point·er** *n.*—**ap·point·ive** *adj.*

ap·point·ment *n.* 1. A designation to office. 2. Office to which one is appointed. 3. A scheduled meeting; engagement.

ap·por·tion (uh-*por*-shun) *v.* To assign or allot equally.—**ap·por·tion·ment** *n.*

ap·po·site (*ap*-uh-zit) *adj.* Relevant; appropriate; applicable.—**ap·po·site·ly** *adv.*—**ap·po·site·ness** *n.*

ap·prais·al (uh-*prayz*-'l) *n.* 1. Valuation decided by an authority. 2. Estimation of value.

ap·praise (uh-*prayz*) *v.* [ap·praised; ap·prais·

A

ing] To set a value upon; evaluate; estimate worth.—**ap·prais·a·ble** *adj.*—**ap·prais·er** *n.*—**ap·praise·ment** *n.*—**ap·prais·ing·ly** *adv.*

ap·pre·ci·a·ble (uh-*pree*-shuh-b'l) *adj.* Noticeable; considerable; perceptible; enough to be considered.—**ap·pre·ci·a·bly** *adv.*

ap·pre·ci·ate (uh-*pree*-shee-ayt) *v.* [ap·pre·ci·at·ed; -at·ing] 1. To place a sufficiently high value on; be grateful for. 2. To recognize; grasp; understand. 3. To enjoy; have a sensitivity for. 4. To rise in value.—**ap·pre·ci·a·tion** *n.*—**ap·pre·ci·a·tor** *n.*

ap·pre·ci·a·tive (uh-*pree*-shee-ay-tiv; -uh-tiv) *adj.* Grateful; showing due appreciation.—**ap·pre·ci·a·tive·ly** *adv.*—**ap·pre·ci·a·tive·ness** *n.*

ap·pre·hend (ap-reh-*hend*) *v.* 1. To grasp; become cognizant of; notice. 2. To seize upon; arrest. 3. To dread; fear.—**ap·pre·hend·er** *n.* —**ap·pre·hen·si·ble** *adj.*—**ap·pre·hen·si·bil·i·ty** (ap-reh-hen-sih-*bil*-ih-tee) *n.*

ap·pre·hen·sion (ap-reh-*hen*-shun) *n.* 1. Dread; distrust or fear of future events. 2. Power of grasping new ideas; intellect. 3. An opinion; thought. 4. Arrest; capture by officers of the law.

ap·pre·hen·sive (ap-reh-*hen*-siv) *adj.* 1. Anticipating evil or misfortune; suspicious; fearful. 2. Pertaining to the intellect.—**ap·pre·hen·sive·ly** *adv.*—**ap·pre·hen·sive·ness** *n.*

ap·pren·tice (uh-*pren*-tiss) *n.* One who is learning a trade or subject.—*v.* [ap·pren·ticed; -tic·ing].

ap·pren·tice·ship (uh-*pren*-tiss-ship) *n.* 1. A period of training for a trade. 2. Learning a trade.

ap·prise (uh-*pryz*) *v.* [ap·prised; ap·pris·ing] To inform; give notice.

ap·proach (uh-*prohch*) *v.* 1. To come toward; draw close to. 2. To approximate; come near to.—**ap·proach** *n.*—**ap·proach·a·ble** *adj.*—**ap·proach·a·bil·i·ty** (uh-prohch-uh-*bil*-ih-tee) *adv.*

ap·pro·ba·tion (ap-ruh-*bay*-shun) *n.* Approval; praise; sanction.—**ap·pro·ba·tive** (*ap*-ruh-bay-tiv) *adj.*—**ap·pro·ba·tive·ness** *n.*—**ap·pro·ba·to·ry** (*ap*-ruh-buh-tor-ee) *adj.*

ap·pro·pri·ate (uh-*proh*-pree-it) *adj.* Suitable; fitting; proper.—**ap·pro·pri·ate·ly** *adv.*—**ap·pro·pri·ate·ness** *n.*

ap·pro·pri·ate (uh-*proh*-pree-ayt) *v.* [ap·pro·pri·at·ed; -at·ing] 1. To take or seize without compensation. 2. To claim or use exclusively. 3. To set apart for a specific use.—**ap·pro·pri·a·tive** (uh-*proh*-pree-uh-tiv) *adj.*—**ap·pro·pri·a·tive·ness** *n.*—**ap·pro·pri·a·tor** *n.*

ap·pro·pri·a·tion (uh-proh-pree-*ay*-shun) *n.* 1. Funds granted for a specific purpose; any reserve set apart for a specific use. 2. Taking for one's own use.

ap·prove (uh-*proov*) *v.* [ap·proved; ap·prov·ing] 1. To be pleased with; praise. 2. To sanction; ratify.—**ap·prov·a·ble** (uh-*proov*-uh-b'l) *adj.*—**ap·prov·al** *n.*—**ap·prov·er** *n.*—**ap·prov·ing·ly** *adv.*

ap·prox·i·mate (uh-*prok*-sih-mit) *adj.* Close but not exact; general.—**ap·prox·i·mate·ly** *adv.* About.

ap·prox·i·mate (uh-*prok*-suh-mayt) *v.* [ap·prox·i·mat·ed; -mat·ing] 1. To come close to; approach perfection or exactness. 2. To reach a reasonably accurate figure or estimate.—**ap·prox·i·mat·er** *n.*—**ap·prox·i·ma·tion** (uh-prok-suh-*may*-sh'n) *n.*

ap·pur·te·nance (uh-*per*-tuh-n'ns) *n.* Appendage; incidental detail; adjunct.—**ap·pur·te·nant** *adj.*

a·pri·cot (*ay*-prih-kot, *ap*-rih-kot) *n.* A small, round, pitted fruit closely related to the peach. —**a·pri·cot** *adj.* 1. Flavored with apricots. 2. Of the light orange color of the apricot.

A·pril (*ay*-pr'l) *n.* Fourth month of our calendar year.—**A·pril** *adj.*

a priori (ay pry-*oh*-rye). Denoting knowledge gained independently of experience.

a·pron (*ay*-prun) *n.* 1. A garment worn to protect the front of one's clothing. 2. A platform or flooring of a dock. 3. *Theater.* That part of a stage in front of the curtain. 4. The paved area in front of an airplane hangar.—**a·pron** *v.*

ap·ro·pos (ap-ruh-*poh*) *adj.* Opportune; to the point; seasonable.—*adv.* 1. Opportunely. 2. By the way; incidentally.

apse *n. Architecture.* A domed, many-sided, or semicircular recess of an edifice, esp. a church.

apt *adj.* 1. Ready; quick: adept. 2. Fit; suitable; pertinent. 3. Likely; having a tendency. —**apt·ly** *adv.*—**apt·ness** *n.*

ap·ti·tude (*ap*-tih-tood) *n.* Inherent ability or skill; bent; tendency; suitability.

aq·ua (*ak*-wuh) *n.* A pastel blue-green color; aquamarine.—**aq·ua** *adj.*

aq·ua·cade (*ak*-wuh-kayd) *n.* A water carnival or pageant.

aq·ua·ma·rine (ak-wuh-muh-*reen*) *n.* 1. A fine grade of beryl of a sea-green or bluish tint. 2. The color of an aquamarine.—**aq·ua·ma·rine** *adj.*

aq·ua·plane (*ak*-wuh-playn) *n.* A broad, short board towed behind a boat and ridden by a person standing on it.—*v.* [aq·ua·planed; -plan·ing] To ride an aquaplane.

AQUAPLANE

aqua regia (*ak*-wuh *ree*-juh). *Chemistry.* A mixture of nitric and hydrochloric acids capable of dissolving gold.

a·quar·i·um (uh-*kwair*-ee-um) *n.* [*pl.* a·quar·i·ums, a·quar·i·a] A case or enclosure usually of glass for displaying aquatic plants and animals.

a·quat·ic (uh-*kwat*-ik) *adj.* 1. Living in the water. 'Aquatic plants.' 2. Performed in or on the water. 'Aquatic sports.'—*n.* 1. A water-inhabiting plant. 2. [*pl.*] Water sports.

aq·ua·tint (*ak*-wuh-tint) *n.* 1. A process of

etching with nitric acid by which a water-color effect is obtained. 2. A print made by aquatint.—**aq·ua·tint** v.—**aq·ua·tint·er** n.

aq·ue·duct (*ak*-wuh-dukt) n. A conduit or channel for carrying water.

a·que·ous (*ay*-kwee-us, *ak*-wee-us) n. Watery; water-covered; made from water.—**a·que·ous·ness** n.

aq·ui·line (*ak*-wih-lyn, -lin) adj. 1. Prominent and curved like an eagle's beak. 'An aquiline nose.' 2. Pertaining to an eagle.

Ar·ab (*air*-ub) n. 1. A native of Arabia. 2. A horse of an Arabian breed. 3. [*Not cap.*] A street urchin.—**Ar·ab** adj.

ar·a·besque (air-uh-*besk*) n. 1. Fanciful ornamental pattern, either painted, inlaid, or carved. 2. *Ballet.* A graceful pose employed in adagio variations.—**ar·a·besque** adj.

Ar·a·bi·a (uh-*ray*-bee-uh). A peninsula at the southwest extremity of Asia. Approximate area: 1,000,000 sq. mi.—**A·ra·bi·an** n. & adj.

Ar·a·bic (*air*-uh-bik) n. The language of the Arabs.—adj. Pertaining to Arabs or Arabia.

Arabic numerals. The numbers in use in our arithmetic: 1, 2, 3, 4, 5, 6, 7, 8, 9, 0.

ar·a·ble (*air*-uh-b'l) adj. Fit for tilling or cultivation.—**ar·a·bil·i·ty** (air-uh-*bil*-uh-tee) adj.

a·rach·nid (uh-*rak*-nid) n. An invertebrate animal of the order which includes spiders and scorpions.—**a·rach·ni·dan** n. & adj.

Ar·a·gon (*air*-uh-gon). A former province of northern Spain.—**Ar·a·gon·ese** (ar-uh-guh-*neez*) n. & adj.

Ar·a·lac (*air*-uh-lak) n. Trade-mark for a synthetic fiber made from casein.—**ar·a·lac** adj.

Aral Sea (*air*-'l). A large inland sea of Siberia east of the Caspian.—**Ar·al** adj.

Ar·a·ma·ic (air-uh-*may*-ik) n. The northern group of the Semitic languages.—**Ar·a·ma·ic** adj.

ar·bi·ter (*ahr*-bih-ter) n. 1. A person who decides controversies. 2. A ruler or judge of unlimited power.—**ar·bi·tress** n.

ar·bit·ra·ment (ahr-*bit*-ruh-m'nt) n. 1. A final decision. 2. The right of judging.

ar·bi·trar·y (*ahr*-buh-trehr-ee) adj. 1. Decided without reference to logical necessity. 2. Tyrannical; absolute; despotic. 3. Established by will, choice, or decision.—**ar·bi·trar·i·ly** adv.—**ar·bi·trar·i·ness** n.

ar·bi·trate (*ahr*-buh-trayt) v. [ar·bi·trat·ed; -trat·ing] 1. To submit a dispute to an authorized person for decision. 2. To act as judge; decide.—**ar·bi·tra·tion** (ahr-buh-*tray*-shun) n. —**ar·bi·tra·tion·al, ar·bi·tra·tive** adj.—**ar·bi·tra·tor** n.

ar·bor (*ahr*-ber) n. 1. A tree. 2. *Machinery.* **a.** A shaft or spindle through rotating parts. **b.** A bar which holds cutting tools.

Arbor Day. A day officially designated in most states for planting trees.

ar·bor·e·al (ahr-*bor*-ee-ūl) adj. 1. Like or pertaining to a tree. 2. Living in trees. 'Arboreal animals.'

ar·bo·re·tum (ahr-ber-*ee*-tum) n. [*pl.* ar·bo·re·tums, ar·bo·re·ta] A botanical garden where trees and shrubs are grown for study.

ar·bor·vi·tae (ahr-ber-*vy*-tee) n. Also **arbor vi·tae.** Any of several hardy, compactly growing evergreens of the pine family.

ar·bu·tus (ahr-*byoo*-tus) n. A tiny, fragrant, trailing flower of the heath family.

ARBUTUS

arc n. 1. A section of the circumference of a circle. 2. *Electricity.* A bright glow produced between two electrodes. —v. [arced (*ahrkt*), arcked; arc·ing (*ahrk*-ing), arck·ing] To create an incandescent arc.

ar·cade (ahr-*kayd*) n. 1. A lane or passage in a building with shops on each side. 2 *Architecture.* A series of arches supported on pillars.

Ar·ca·di·a (ahr-*kay*-dee-uh). Also **Ar·ca·dy.** 1. Mountainous section of Greece celebrated in pastoral poetry. 2. Any idyllic, rural place. —**Ar·ca·di·an** adj. & n.

ARCADE

arch n. 1. *Architecture.* A structure composed of wedge-shaped pieces which form a curved or pointed span over an opening. 2. Any archlike curve or structure.—v. 1. To cover or span with an arch. 2. To curve or form like an arch.

ARCH

arch adj. Principal; chief; eminent.

arch adj. Sly; mischievous; roguish.

ar·chae·ol·o·gy. Variant spelling of **ar·che·ol·o·gy.**

ar·cha·ic (ahr-*kay*-ik) adj. Antiquated; no longer commonly used, but not completely obsolete.

ar·cha·ism (*ahr*-kay-izm) n. 1. An archaic word or idiom. 2. Antiquity of style.—**ar·cha·ist** n.—**ar·cha·is·tic** (ahr-kay-*ist*-ik) adj.

Arch·an·gel (*ahrk*-ayn-j'l), **Ar·khan·gelsk** (ahr-*kahn*-gelsk). An Arctic port of the U.S.S.R.

arch·an·gel (ark-*ayn*-j'l) n. An angel of the highest order.—**-an·gel·ic** (an-*jel*-ik), **-i·cal** adj.

arch·bish·op (arch-*bish*-up) *n*. Dignitary at the head of an ecclesiastical province in the Anglican and Roman Catholic Churches.—**arch·bish·op·ric** *n*. The authority or office of an archbishop.

arch·dea·con (arch-*deek*-'n) *n*. A church dignitary next below a bishop.—**arch·dea·con·ate, arch·dea·con·ry, arch·dea·con·ship** *n*. The office or authority of an archdeacon.

arch·duke (arch-*dyook*) *n*. A prince of the deposed royal families of Austria and Russia. —**arch·du·cal** *adj*.—**arch·duch·ess** (arch-*duch*-ess) *n*.—**arch·duch·y** *n*. [*pl*. arch·duch·ies].

arched *adj*. Curved; constituting an arch.

ar·che·ol·o·gy (ark-ee-*ol*-uh-jee) *n*. Also **archaeology**. The science that investigates human history as revealed by monuments and relics of ancient peoples.—**ar·che·ol·o·gist, ar·chae·ol·o·gist** *n*.—**ar·che·o·log·i·cal, ar·chae·o·log·i·cal** (ahr-kee-uh-*loj*-ih-k'l) *adj*.

arch·er *n*. One skilled in the use of bow and arrow.—**ar·cher·y** *n*.

ar·che·type (*ar*-kuh-type) *n*. Pattern; model; first form.—**ar·che·typ·al, ar·che·typ·i·cal** *adj*.

ar·chi·e·pis·co·pal (ar-kee-uh-*pisk*-uh-p'l) *adj*. Pertaining to an archbishop or archbishopric.

Ar·chi·me·des (ahr-kih-*mee*-deez) *n*. An ancient Greek physicist and inventor.—**Ar·chi·me·de·an** (ar-kih-*mee*-dee-un) *adj*.

ar·chi·pel·a·go (ar-kih-*pel*-uh-goh) *n*. [ar·chi·pel·a·goes, ar·chi·pel·a·gos] A chain of islands. —**ar·chi·pe·lag·ic** (ar-ki-pel-*aj*-ik) *adj*.

ar·chi·tect (*ar*-kih-tekt) *n*. One skilled in designing or constructing buildings.

ar·chi·tec·ture (*ar*-kih-tek-cher) *n*. Science of building or construction; workmanship.—**ar·chi·tec·tur·al** (ar-ki-*tek*-cher-ul) *adj*.—**ar·chi·tec·tur·al·ly** *adv*.

ar·chi·trave (*ar*-kih-trayv) *n*. The lintel or horizontal member immediately supported by a column.

ar·chive (*ar*-kyv) *n*. 1. [*pl*.] Historic records or documents; annals. 2. Vault or chamber where public records are kept.

arch·ly *adv*. Slyly; roguishly; wittily.—**arch·ness** *n*.

arch·way *n*. A passage under an arch.

arcked, arcking. See arc.

arc·tic (*ark*-tik) *n*. 1. The northern frigid region; the far north. 2. [*pl*.] Galoshes.—**arc·tic** *adj*. Pertaining to the North Pole or surrounding region.

Arctic Circle. The parallel of latitude which divides the North Temperate and North Frigid zones.

Arctic Ocean. The ocean covering most of the arctic regions.

Arc·tu·rus (ark-*tyoor*-us, -*toor*-) *n*. The major star in the constellation Boötes.

Ar·den *n*. A forest in Warwickshire, England. —**Ar·den** *adj*.

ar·dent (*ard*-'nt) *adj*. 1. Passionate; warm; zealous; intense; vehement. 2. Hot; burning. —**ar·dent·ly** *adv*.—**ar·dent·ness** *n*.

ar·dor (*ar*-der) *n*. 1. Warmth; eagerness; vehemence; passion. 2. Brilliancy; heat.

ar·du·ous (*ar*-dyoo-us) *adj*. 1. Difficult; trying. 2. Steep; hard to climb.—**ar·du·ous·ly** *adv*.—**ar·du·ous·ness** *n*.

a·re·a (*air*-ee-uh) *n*. [*pl*. a·re·as] 1. Region; any bounded plane surface. 2. *Geometry*. The surface measurement within any given dimensions.

a·re·na (uh-*ree*-nuh) *n*. 1. The enclosed space in the center of an amphitheater. 2. Any scene of action or contest.

ar·gent (*arj*-'nt) *adj*. Silver.

Ar·gen·ti·na (ar-jen-*tee*-nuh). A nation of southern South America. Area: 1,079,965 sq. mi. Capital: Buenos Aires.—**Ar·gen·tine, Ar·gen·tin·e·an** (ar-jen-*tin*-ee-un) *n*. & *adj*.

ar·gon (*ar*-gahn) *n*. An inert gas element found in the air in small quantities. (*Symbol*: A).

ar·go·naut (*ar*-guh-nawt) *n*. 1. A mollusk of the cuttlefish family. 2. [*cap*.] One who sailed with Jason on the "Argo." 3. One of the 'forty-niners.'—**ar·go·nau·tic, Ar·go·nau·tic** *adj*.

ar·go·sy (*ar*-guh-see) *n*. [*pl*. ar·go·sies] A large sail-propelled merchant ship, esp. one richly laden.

ar·gue (*ar*-gyoo) *v*. [ar·gued; ar·gu·ing] 1. To dispute; contend; debate. 2. To reason; offer reasons in support or contradiction of a proposition. 3. To evidence; indicate; bear testimony of.—**ar·gu·a·ble** *adj*.—**ar·gu·er** *n*.—**ar·gu·men·ta·tion** (ar-gyoo-men-*tay*-shun) *n*.

ar·gu·ment (*ar*-gyoo-m'nt) *n*. 1. Debate; controversy; discussion. 2. A statement presented for or against a proposition. 3. Theme; subject; summary or abstract of a book or play.

ar·gu·men·ta·tive (ar-gyoo-*men*-tuh-tiv) *adj*. 1. Addicted to argument; contrary. 2. Pertaining to argument or reasoning; open to debate.—**ar·gu·men·ta·tive·ly** *adv*.—**ar·gu·men·ta·tive·ness** *n*.

a·ri·a (*ah*-ree-uh) *n*. A song written for one voice.

ar·id (*ar*-id) *adj*. Dry; lifeless.—**a·rid·i·ty** (uh-*rid*-ih-tee) *n*.—**ar·id·ness** *n*.

Ar·i·el (*air*-ee-ul) *n*. The spirit enslaved by Prospero in Shakespeare's *Tempest*.

a·right (uh-*ryte*) *adv*. Rightly; without error.

a·rise (uh-*ryz*) *v*. [a·rose; a·ris·en] 1. To get up; get out of bed. 2. Ascend; go up. 3. To appear; become noticeable.

ar·is·toc·ra·cy (air-iss-*tok*-ruh-see) *n*. [*pl*. ar·is·toc·ra·cies] 1. The richest, or most influential, class of society; the nobility. 2. A government in which power is vested in a small wealthy class.

a·ris·to·crat (uh-*riss*-tuh-krat) *n*. 1. Possessor of inherited wealth and power; one having the traits of a member of the privileged class. 2. One who favors the continuance of an aristocracy.—**a·ris·to·crat·ic** (uh-riss-tuh-*krat*-ik) *adj*.—**a·ris·to·crat·i·cal·ly** *adv*.

Ar·is·to·te·li·an (air-iss-tuh-*tee*-lih-un) *n*. An

A

adherent of the doctrines of the Greek philosopher Aristotle, who taught that reason is dependable when it is exercised through formal logic.—Ar·is·to·te·li·an *adj.*—Ar·is·to·te·li·an·ism *n.*

a·rith·me·tic (uh-*rith*-muh-tik) *n.* The science of computing by positive real numbers.—ar·ith·met·i·cal (air-ith-*met*-ih-k'l) *adj.*—a·rith·me·ti·cian (uh-rith-muh-*tish*-un) *n.*

Ar·i·zo·na (air-ih-*zoh*-nuh). A state of southwestern U.S. between California and New Mexico. Area: 113,909 sq. mi. Capital: Phoenix.—Ar·i·zo·nan, Ar·i·zo·ni·an *n.* & *adj.*

ark *n.* 1. *Jewish History.* The repository of the stone tablets inscribed with the Ten Commandments. 2. *Bible.* The vessel which Noah built for the Deluge.

Ar·kan·sas (*ahr*-k'n-saw). A state between Missouri and Louisiana. Area: 53,102 sq. mi. Capital: Little Rock.—Ar·kan·san (ahr-*kan*-z'n) *n.* & *adj.*

Ar·kan·saw·yer *n.* A native of Arkansas.

arm *v.* 1. To equip with weapons or armor. 2. To push with the arms or elbows.

arm *n.* 1. The upper limb of the human body between the shoulder and the hand. 2. Something corresponding to or resembling the arm. 'An arm of the sea. The arm of a chair.' 3. Power; might; efficacy. 4. [*often pl.*] A weapon; implements of war.

ar·ma·da (ahr-*mah*-duh, ahr-*may*-duh) *n.* 1. A great fleet of naval ships. 2. [*cap.*] The fleet sent against England by Spain in 1588.

ar·ma·dil·lo (ahr-muh-*dil*-oh) *n.* A small, toothless mammal of South America covered with a bony armor.—ar·ma·dil·lo *adj.*

Ar·ma·ged·don (ahr-muh-*ged*-'n) *n. Bible.* The place of the final, great battle of the world predicted in The Revelation.

arm·a·ment (*ahrm*-uh-m'nt) *n.* 1. The total military strength of a nation, fort, ship, etc. 2. Process of equipping with weapons.—arm·a·ment *adj.*

ar·ma·ture (*ahr*-muh-cher) *n.* 1. The rotating part of a motor or generator consisting of a soft iron bar wound with wire, set in a magnetic field to produce current when rotated in a generator, or rotation when current is applied in a motor. 2. A covering, as of wire about a cable, for protection.

arm·chair *n.* A chair with supports for the elbows.

Armenian Soviet Socialist Republic. Country of SE Soviet Europe. Area: 11,661 sq. mi. Capital: Yerevan.

arm·ful *n.* [*pl.* arm·fuls] The quantity the arms can hold.

arm·hole *n.* 1. The armpit. 2. An opening in a garment for the arm.

ar·mi·stice (*arm*-iss-tiss) *n.* Truce; temporary cessation of hostilities.—Armistice Day. November 11, in celebration of the cessation of hostilities in World War I.

arm·let *n.* A bracelet for the upper arm.

ar·mor (*ar*-mer) *n.* 1. A suit of mail formerly worn in battle. 2. Metal plating for machines of war. 3. A protective covering; a defense; a shield.—ar·mor *v.*—ar·mor·er *n.* —ar·mor·ial (ar-*mor*-ee-ul) *adj.*

ar·mo·ry (*ar*-mer-ee) *n.* [*pl.* ar·mo·ries] 1. An arms factory; arsenal. 2. A storehouse for weapons.

ar·mour. *Variant spelling* of armor.

arm·pit *n.* The hollow under the arm at the shoulder.

ar·my *n.* [*pl.* ar·mies] 1. An organized body of soldiers. 2. A multitude; large number.

ARMOR

army worm. A voracious green striped caterpillar destructive to grain and forage.

ar·ni·ca (*arn*-ik-uh) *n.* 1. A family of perennial yellow-flowered, cluster-leaved herbs of the Temperate Zone. 2. *Medicine.* A liniment; heart stimulant.—ar·ni·ca *adj.*

a·ro·ma (uh-*roh*-muh) *n.* Fragrance; savor; odor.

ar·o·mat·ic (air-oh-*mat*-ik) *adj.* Also ar·o·mat·i·cal. Fragrant; agreeable in odor; spicy.—*n.* A fragrant, stimulating drug.—ar·o·mat·i·cal·ly *adv.*

a·rose. *Past tense* of arise.

a·round (uh-*rownd*) *prep.* 1. About; along the circumference of. 2. Encircling; enveloping. 3. *Colloquial.* From place to place. 'She gets around.' 4. Approximately.—a·round *adv.*

a·rouse (uh-*rowz*) *v.* [a·roused; a·rous·ing] To excite; stir up; animate; awaken.—a·rous·al *n.*

ar·peg·gio (ahr-*pej*-oh) *n. Music.* Rendering of the tones of a chord in rapid succession instead of simultaneously.

ar·que·bus. *Variant spelling* of harquebus.

ar·raign (uh-*rayn*) *v. Law.* To summon before a court; call for trial.—ar·raign·ment *n.*

ar·range (uh-*raynj*) *v.* [ar·ranged; ar·rang·ing] 1. To put in proper order; fix; place or dispose properly. 2. To agree upon; adjust; settle. 3. *Music.* To adapt music for voices or instruments other than as originally written by the composer.—ar·range·ment *n.*

ar·rant (air-'nt) *adj.* Notorious; confirmed; brazen.—ar·rant·ly *adv.*

ar·ras (air-us) *n.* Ornamental tapestry or hangings.

ar·ray (uh-*ray*) *n.* 1. Regular order or arrangement; an orderly display. 2. Apparel; dress. —ar·ray *v.*—ar·ray·al *n.*

ar·rears (uh-*reers*) *n. pl.* Unpaid amount; debt overdue.—ar·rear·age (uh-*reer*-ij) *n.*

ar·rest *v.* 1. To take into legal custody. 2. To stop; hinder; seize; retard. 3. To engage or attract the attention.—ar·rest·er, ar·rest·or *n.* —ar·rest·ment *n.*

ar·rest·ing *adj.* Striking; remarkable; vivid; spectacular.

ar·rive (uh-*ryv*) *v.* [ar·rived; ar·riv·ing] 1. To

A

reach; come; attain. 2. To achieve fame or success.—**ar·ri·val** n.

ar·ro·gance (*air*-uh-g'nss) n. Also **ar·ro·gan·cy.** Insolence; haughtiness; presumption.—**ar·ro·gant** adj.—**ar·ro·gant·ly** adv.

ar·ro·gate (*air*-uh-gayt) v. [ar·ro·gat·ed; -gat·ing] To claim or demand high-handedly without grounds.— **-ga·tion** (-*gay*-shun) n.

ar·row (*air*-oh) n. 1. A slender, barbed shaft with a feather at the end to be shot from a bow. 2. A symbol [——→] indicating direction.—**ar·row·y** adj.

arrowbeam	arrowplate	arrowsnake
arrowheaded	arrow-shaped	arrowstone
arrow-leaved	arrowshot	arrow-toothed
arrowlike	arrowsmith	arrow-worm
arrow maker	arrow-smitten	arrow-wounded

ar·row·head n. 1. The barb of an arrow. 2. A family of aquatic plants of the water-plantain group.

ar·row·root n. 1. A tropical herb, the roots of which yield tapioca and starch. 2. A starch made from arrowroot.

ar·roy·o (uh-*roy*-oh) n. [pl. ar·roy·os] 1. The dry bed of a stream. 2. A rivulet.

ar·se·nal (*ar*-suh-n'l) n. A factory or storehouse for arms and munitions.

ar·se·nate (*ar*-suh-nit) n. A salt formed of arsenic and a base.

ar·sen·ic (*ar*-suh-nik) n. A brittle, steel-blue, non-metallic element of the phosphorous group. (*Symbol:* As).—**ar·sen·ic** (ar-*sen*-ik) adj.

ar·sen·i·cal (ar-*sen*-ih-k'l) adj. Pertaining to or containing arsenic.—n. A drug containing arsenic.

ar·son n. Malicious or deliberate burning of a building.—**ar·son** adj.

art. Second person singular of **be**, used with **thou.**

art n. 1. Specialized skill or knowledge; facility; knack. 2. A medium of aesthetic expression unified by its own body of principles and historical development, as sculpture or music. 3. The representational arts; graphic or plastic art; painting, sculpture, and architecture. 4. A branch of academic learning. 5. Cunning; craftiness.

Ar·te·mis (*ar*-tuh-mis) n. Greek Mythology. The moon goddess.

ar·te·ri·al (ar-*teer*-ee-ul) adj. 1. Pertaining to the arteries of the human body. 2. Pertaining to a course or channel. 'Arterial highway.'

ar·te·ri·o·scle·ro·sis (ahr-teer-ee-oh-skler-*oh*-sis) n. Medicine. Hardening of the arteries.—**ar·te·ri·o·scle·rot·ic** (ahr-teer-ee-oh-skler-*ot*-ik)adj.

ar·ter·y (*art*-er-ee) n. [pl. ar·ter·ies] 1. Anatomy. One of a system of vessels which convey the blood from the heart to all parts of the body. 2. An avenue of communication.

artesian well. (ar-*tee*-zhun *wel*). A well bored deep into the ground through which water rises under pressure to the surface of the soil, in a constant flow.

art·ful adj. Wily; crafty; adroit.—**art·ful·ly** adv. —**art·ful·ness** n.

ar·thri·tis (ar-*thry*-tis) n. Medicine. Painful inflammation of the joints.—**ar·thrit·ic** (ar-*thrit*-ik), **ar·thrit·i·cal** adj.

ar·ti·choke (*art*-ih-chohk) n. An herb having a globular leafy head, considered a vegetable delicacy.

ar·ti·cle (*ar*-tih-k'l) n. 1. A thing; a particular commodity or substance. 2. An essay, report, or story appearing in a periodical. 3. A single clause, item, or point, as in a contract or treaty. 4. Grammar. A part of speech placed before nouns to limit their application: a, an, and the.—v. [ar·ti·cled; ar·tic·ling].

ar·tic·u·lar (ar-*tik*-yoo-ler) adj. Anatomy. Pertaining to the joints.

ar·tic·u·late (ar-*tik*-yoo-lit) adj. 1. Eloquent; communicative; expressive. 2. Lettered; distinctly spoken. 3. Integrated.—**ar·tic·u·late·ly** adv.—**ar·tic·u·late·ness** n.

ar·tic·u·late (ar-*tik*-yoo-layt) v. [ar·tic·u·lat·ed; ar·tic·u·lat·ing] To pronounce distinctly; enunciate.—**ar·tic·u·la·tive** (ar-*tik*-yoo-lay-tiv; -luh-tiv) adj.—**ar·tic·u·la·tor** n.

ar·tic·u·la·tion (ar-tik-yoo-*lay*-shun) n. 1. Integrity; organization. 2. Anatomy. Joint; suture. 3. Pronunciation.

ar·ti·fact (*ar*-tih-fakt) n. Also **ar·te·fact.** 1. Archaeology. An early example of human handicraft. 2. Biology. A postmortem formation or change in an animal tissue.

ar·ti·fice (*art*-ih-fis) n. Trick; maneuver.

ar·tif·i·cer (ar-*tif*-ih-ser) n. 1. Craftsman; artisan. 2. One who works on military explosives.

ar·ti·fi·cial (art-ih-*fish*-ul) adj. 1. Not natural; synthetic; imitation. 2. Affected.—**ar·ti·fi·ci·al·i·ty** (art-ih-fish-ee-*al*-ih-tee) n.— **-cial·ly** adv.

ar·til·ler·y (ar-*til*-er-ee) n. Cannon; ordnance; large guns.—**ar·til·ler·ist** n.—**ar·til·ler·y·man** n.

ar·ti·san (*art*-ih-zun) n. Worker; mechanic; craftsman.

ar·tist n. 1. One pre-eminent in a creative field. 2. One occupied in one of the fine arts. 3. A painter or sculptor.

ar·tiste (ar-*teest*) n. 1. A female entertainer. 2. Woman skilled in a creative occupation.

ar·tis·tic (ar-*tis*-tik) adj. 1. Pertaining to art. 2. Tasteful; aesthetically pleasing. 3. Having an inclination for art; creative.—**ar·tis·ti·cal** adj.—**ar·tis·ti·cal·ly** adv.

art·ist·ry (*art*-is-tree) n. Skillfulness of execution; workmanship.

art·less adj. Simple, unaffected; natural.—**art·less·ly** adv.—**art·less·ness** n.

art·y adj. Colloquial. Affectedly and superficially artistic.

Ar·y·an (*air*-ee-un, *ahr*-, -yun) adj. 1. Relating or belonging to the Caucasian peoples whose languages are derived from a common Indo-European source; Indo-European. 2. Belonging to a nonexistent "super race" invented by Nazi ideologists.—**Ar·y·an** n.

as (az) adv. 1. In the same degree; equally. 2. For example.—conj. 1. While; at the same time. 2. Thus; in like manner. 3. Since; because. 4. Though. 'Tired as I am, I will go.' —*pron.* That. 'Such art as there is.'—*prep.* In the status of. 'He worked as a writer.'

as·a·fet·i·da, as·a·foet·i·da (as-uh-*fet*-ih-duh) *n. Medicine.* A foul-smelling gum-resin used as an antispasmodic and stimulant.

as·bes·tos, as·bes·tus (as-*bes*-tus, az-) *n.* A group of fibrous minerals which can be manufactured into noncombustible fabrics for heat insulation and fire-resisting purposes.—**as·bes·tos, as·bes·tus** *adj.*

as·cend (uh-*send*) *v.* To rise; mount; go up. —**as·cend·a·ble, as·cend·i·ble** *adj.*

as·cend·ant (uh-*send*-'nt) *adj.* 1. Superior; predominant; surpassing. 2. Rising.—*n.* Predominance; superiority.

as·cend·an·cy, as·cend·en·cy (uh-*send*-'n-see) *n.* Supremacy; predominance.

as·cen·sion (uh-*sen*-shun) *n.* 1. A rising; act of ascending. 2. [*cap.*] The ascent of Jesus to Heaven forty days after His resurrection.—**as·cen·sion·al** *adj.*

as·cent (uh-*sent*) *n.* 1. A rise; mounting upward. 2. An upward slope.

as·cer·tain (ass-er-*tayn*) *v.* To discover; unearth; find out.—**as·cer·tain·a·ble** *adj.*—**as·cer·tain·a·bly** *adv.*—**as·cer·tain·ment** *n.*

as·cet·ic (uh-*set*-ik) *adj.* Severe; austere.—*n.* One who leads an austere existence to attain religious exaltation.—**as·cet·i·cal·ly** *adv.*

as·cet·i·cism (uh-*set*-uh-sizm) *n.* 1. The practice of ascetics. 2. The doctrine of self-denial as a method of attaining a high spiritual state.

ascorbic acid. Vitamin C, deficiency of which tends to produce scurvy.

as·cot (*as*-kot) *n.* A full, broad necktie; a scarf worn knotted over at the throat.—*adj.* [*cap.*] Pertaining to the Ascot Heath horse races in England.

as·cribe (uh-*skryb*) *v.* [as·cribed; as·crib·ing] To attribute; assign; impute.—**as·crib·a·ble** *adj.*—**as·crip·tion** (uh-*skrip*-shun) *n.*

as·dic *n.* A supersonic instrument for detection and location of underwater objects.

a·sep·sis (uh-*sep*-sis) *n.* Freedom from infection.

a·sep·tic (uh-*sep*-tik) *adj.* Free from bacteria; sterilized.—**a·sep·ti·cal·ly** *adv.*

a·sex·u·al (ay-*sek*-shoo-ul, uh-) *adj.* Without sex.—**a·sex·u·al·ly** *adv.*

ash *n.* [*pl.* ash·es] 1. Gray, powdery noncombustible residue of organic substances. 2. [*pl.*] The remains of a deceased person.

ash *n.* 1. A common, coarse-barked timber tree related to the olive. 2. The wood of the ash.

a·shamed (uh-*shaymd*) *adj.* Abashed; humiliated; having a sense of guilt; embarrassed; mortified.

ash·en *adj.* Pale; livid.—**ash·y** *adj.*

a·shore (uh-*shawr*) *adv.* On shore; on land.

Ash Wednesday. The first day of Lent.

A·sia (*ay*-zhuh). Largest of the six continents, containing Siberia, Asia Minor, India, etc. —**A·sian** *adj. & n.*

Asia Minor. The peninsula on the western margin of Asia, which includes most of Turkey.

A·si·at·ic (ay-zhee-*at*-ik) *adj.* Pertaining to Asia or its inhabitants.—**A·si·at·ic** *n.*

a·side *adv.* On or to one side; apart.—*n.* A parenthetical or confidential remark made among company not intended to hear.

as·i·nine (*ass*-ih-nyne) *adj.* Foolish; stupid.—**as·i·nine·ly** *adv.*—**as·i·nin·i·ty** (ass-ih-*nin*-ih-tee) *n.*

ask *v.* 1. To question; interrogate; query. 2. To solicit; request. 3. To invite. 4. To require; need; desire.—**ask·er** *n.*

a·skance (uh-*skanss*) *adv.* 1. Distrustfully; disdainfully. 2. Obliquely; in a sidelong manner.

a·skew (uh-*skyoo*) *adv.* Awry; obliquely.—**a·skew** *adj.*

a·slant (uh-*slant*) *adv.* At an angle; obliquely. —*prep.* Over in an oblique direction.—**a·slant** *adj.*

a·sleep (uh-*sleep*) *adv.* In or into a state of sleep. —*adj.* 1. Sleeping. 2. Inactive. 3. Dead.

a·slope (uh-*slohp*) *adj.* With leaning or inclination; deflected from the perpendicular.—**a·slope** *adv.*

asp *n.* A poisonous snake native to Africa.

as·par·a·gus (uh-*spair*-uh-gus) *n.* a perennial vegetable whose tender shoots are a popular food.

as·pect (*ass*-pekt) *n.* 1. Appearance; look; countenance. 2. Prospect; exposure. 3. Facet; phase.

ASP (1/5 life size)

as·pen *n.* A species of poplar, having leaves which move with any breeze.—**as·pen** *adj.*

as·per·i·ty (ass-*pehr*-ih-tee) *n.* [*pl.* as·per·i·ties] Severity; sharpness; harshness of temper.

as·perse (uh-*sperss*) *v.* [as·persed; as·pers·ing] To slander; vilify; defame.

as·per·sion (uh-*sper*-zhun) *n.* 1. Calumny; slander; a defamatory remark. 2. A sprinkling; spray.

as·phalt (*ass*-fawlt) *n.* A tough, gummy mineral product used for paving, etc.—*v.* To pave with asphalt.

as·pho·del (*ass*-fuh-del) *n.* A flowering plant of the lily family, bearing white or yellow clusters.

as·phyx·i·ate (ass-*fik*-see-ayt) *v.* [as·phyx·i·at·ed; as·phyx·i·at·ing] To suffocate; kill by excluding oxygen.— **-i·a·tion** (see-*ay*-sh'n) *n.*

as·pic (*ass*-pik) *n.* A gelatine product of meat, usually served in molds.

as·pi·dis·tra (ass-puh-*dis*-truh) *n.* A plant with large glossy leaves, used as a house plant.

as·pir·ant (uh-*spyr*-'nt) *n.* One who aspires; candidate; applicant.—**as·pir·ant** *adj.*

as·pi·rate (*ass*-per-ayt) *v.* [as·pi·rat·ed; as·pi·rat·ing] To pronounce with an audible emission of breath.—*n.* The sound of the letter H or a similar sound.—**as·pi·rate** (*ass*-puh-rit) *adj.*

as·pi·ra·tion (ass-per-*ay*-shun) *n.* 1. Ambition; strong desire for success. 2. Breathing.

as·pire (uh-*spyr*) *v.* [as·pired; as·pir·ing] 1. To aim; be ambitious; yearn. 2. To seat; to rise. —**as·pir·er** *n.*

as·pir·in (*ass*-per-in) *n.* A trade name for acetylsalicylic acid, used for relieving pain and reducing fever.

ass *n.* 1. A donkey; a small animal of the horse family having long ears and great endurance. 2. A dull, stupid person; a blockhead. 3. *Vulgar.* The buttocks.

ASS (1/40 life size)

as·sa·fet·i·da,as·sa·foet·i·da *Variant spellings of asafetida.*

as·sa·gai (*ass*-uh-gye) *n.* A javelin used by the Riffs of Africa.

as·sail (uh-*sayl*) *v.* To attack; assault.—**as·sail·a·ble** *adj.*—**as·sail·ant** *n.*—**as·sail·er** *n.*—**as·sail·ment** *n.*

as·sas·sin (uh-*sass*-in) *n.* A murderer, esp. a hired killer.

as·sas·si·nate (uh-*sass*-uh-nayt) *v.* [as·sas·si·nat·ed; as·sas·si·nat·ing] To murder; kill.—**as·sas·si·na·tion** (uh-sass-uh-*nay*-shun) *n.*—**as·sas·si·na·tor** *n.*

as·sault (uh-*sawlt*) *v.* To attack; storm; assail. —*n.* 1. Onslaught; attack. 2. *Law.* A direct attempt to strike a person. The actual striking is called **battery.**—**as·sault·er** *n.*

as·say (uh-*say*) *v.* 1. To attempt; endeavor. 2. To estimate; appraise.—*n.* (uh-*say*, *ass*-ay) Examination; analysis; measurement.—**as·say·a·ble** *adj.*—**as·say·er** *n.*

as·sem·blage (uh-*sem*-blij) *n.* Collection; gathering; congregation.

as·sem·ble (uh-*sem*-b'l) *v.* [as·sem·bled; as·sem·bling] To gather; collect.—**as·sem·bler** *n.*

as·sem·bly *n.* [*pl.* as·sem·blies] 1. Gathering; congregation; meeting. 2. In some states, the state legislature. 3. *Military.* Signal for troops to fall in. 4. Construction from individual pre-fabricated parts.

as·sem·bly·man *n.* [*pl.* as·sem·bly·men] A member of a legislative body, esp. a state legislature.

as·sent (uh-*sent*) *n.* Consent; acquiescence; approval; agreement.—**as·sent** *v.*—**as·sen·ta·tion** (ass-en-*tay*-sh'n) *n.*

as·sert (uh-*sert*) *v.* 1. To declare; aver; affirm. 2. To vindicate; defend.—**as·sert·er, -or** *n.*

as·ser·tion (uh-*ser*-shun) *n.* 1. Declaration; affirmation. 2. Vindication; defense.

as·ser·tive (uh-*ser*-tiv) *adj.* Aggressive; bold; positive.—**as·ser·tive·ly** *adv.*—**as·ser·tive·ness** *n.*

as·sess (uh-*sess*) *v.* 1. To value for taxation purposes. 2. To tax.—**as·sess·a·ble** *adj.*

as·sess·ment *n.* 1. Levy; tax. 2. A valuation of property for taxation.

as·ses·sor *n.* 1. An appraiser. 2. A judge's assistant. 3. A business associate.—**as·ses·so·ri·al** (ass-suh-*sor*-ee-ul) *adj.*

as·set (*ass*-et) *n.* 1. An advantage; a desirable possession or quality. 2. [*pl.*] Resources; means; total property.

as·sev·er·ate (uh-*sev*-uh-rayt) *v.* [as·sev·er·at·ed; as·sev·er·at·ing] To affirm; declare.—**as·sev·er·a·tion** (uh-sev-er-*ay*-shun) *n.*

as·si·du·i·ty (ass-sih-*dyoo*-ih-tee) *n.* [*pl.* as·si·du·i·ties] Diligence; attention; industriousness.

as·sid·u·ous (uh-*sid*-yoo-us) *adj.* Diligent; industrious.—**as·sid·u·ous·ly** *adv.*— **-ous·ness** *n.*

as·sign (uh-*syn*) *v.* 1. To fix; appoint; issue authoritatively. 2. To allot; apportion. 3. To attribute; ascribe. 4. To turn over to creditors.—**as·sign·a·ble** *adj.*—**as·sign·a·bil·i·ty** (uh-syn-uh-*bil*-ih-tee) *n.*—**as·sign·a·bly** *adv.* —**as·sign·er, as·sign·or** *n.*

as·sig·na·tion (ass-ig-*nay*-sh'n) *n.* 1. The act of allotting or assigning. 2. A rendezvous; tryst, esp. of lovers.

as·sign·ee (uh-syn-*ee*) *n.* Also **as·sign.** The recipient of an assignment.

as·sign·ment (uh-*syn*-m'nt) *n.* 1. The act of assigning, fixing, or specifying. 2. A task; job. 3. The transfer of property by legal instrument. 4. Property assigned.

as·sim·i·late (uh-*sim*-'l-ayt) *v.* [as·sim·i·lat·ed; as·sim·i·lat·ing] 1. To blend; merge; make or become similar. 2. *Physiology.* To absorb and incorporate food into the system.—**as·sim·i·la·ble** (uh-*sim*-'l-uh-b'l) *adj.*

as·sim·i·la·tion (uh-sim-uh-*lay*-shun) *n.* 1. Merging; blending. 2. *Physiology.* The process by which organisms convert and absorb nutriment into living tissue. 3. *Phonetics.* Modification of a speech sound by its proximity to a related sound.—**as·sim·i·la·tive** (uh-*sim*-ih-lay-tiv) *adj.*—**as·sim·i·la·tive·ness** *n.*

as·sist (uh-*sist*) *v.* To help; aid.—*n. Baseball.* A play in which one player throws the ball to another who puts the runner out.—**as·sis·tance** *n.*

as·sis·tant *adj.* Helping; auxiliary.—*n.* Aid: helper.

as·size (uh-*syz*) *n.* 1. A judicial inquiry before a jury; inquest. 2. A fixed or accepted standard, as of price, quantity, etc. 3. [*pl.*] Periodical sessions held by judges of the superior courts in each county of England.

as·so·ci·ate (uh-*soh*-shee-it, -et) *n.* Companion; colleague; partner.—*v.* (uh-*soh*-shee-ayt) [as·so·ci·at·ed; as·so·ci·at·ing] 1. To combine; unite. 2. To have social intercourse; consort; have dealings.—**as·so·ci·ate** (uh-*soh*-shee-it, -et) *adj.*—**as·so·ci·a·ble** (uh-*soh*-shuh-b'l) *adj.*

as·so·ci·a·tion (uh-soh-see-*ay*-shun) *n.* 1. Connection; relationship. 2. A society; an organization. 3. *Psychology.* An unconscious process by which a thought or image recalls a previous experience.—**as·so·ci·a·tion·al** (uh-soh-shee-*ay*-shun-ul) *adj.*—**as·so·ci·a·tive** (uh-*soh*-shee-ay-tiv) *adj.*—**as·so·ci·a·tive·ly** *adv.*

as·so·nance (*as*-uh-n'ns) *n.* The rhyming of words of like sound in the accented vowel, though with different consonants, as *move* and *illusion.*—**as·so·nant** *adj.* & *n.*

as·sort (uh-*sort*) *v.* 1. To classify; arrange. 2. To fit; belong.—**as·sort·ed** *adj.*

as·sort·ment *n.* 1. A mixed selection; variety; diversity. 2. Classification.

as·suage (uh-*swayj*) *v.* [as·suaged; as·suag·ing] To alleviate; pacify; mitigate.—**as·suage·ment** *n.*—**as·sua·sive** (uh-*sway*-siv) *adj.*

as·sume (uh-*syoom*, -*soom*) *v.* [as·sumed; as·sum·ing] 1. To take; arrogate; adopt. 2. To pretend; affect. 3. To postulate; suppose. —**as·sum·a·ble** *adj.*—**as·sum·ing** *adj.*

as·sump·tion (uh-*sump*-shun) *n.* 1. Presupposition; hypothesis. 2. Taking upon oneself; adoption. 3. [*cap.*] The ascension of the Virgin Mary.—**as·sump·tive** *adj.*

as·sur·ance (uh-*shoor*-uns) *n.* 1. Insurance. 2. Conviction; certainty. 3. Promise; pledge. 4. Arrogance; presumption.

as·sure (uh-*shoor*) *v.* [as·sured; as·sur·ing] 1. To convince; make confident. 2. To declare solemnly; assert earnestly. 3. To make certain; to insure.

as·sured *adj.* 1. Inevitable; certain to occur. 2. Confident; sanguine.—**as·sur·ed·ly** (uh-*shoor*-ed-lee) *adv.*—**as·sur·ed·ness** *n.*

As·syr·ia (uh-*seer*-ee-uh). An ancient empire located between the Tigris and Euphrates rivers in Mesopotamia.—**As·syr·i·an** *n.* & *adj.*

as·ter *n.* Hardy, autumnal garden plant related to the daisy family, bearing clustered flowers ranging in color from purple to white.

as·ter·isk (*as*-ter-isk) *n.* The sign [*] used in printing and writing usually as a reference mark.—*v.* To mark with an asterisk.

a·stern (uh-*stern*) *adv. Nautical.* 1. At or toward the back of a ship. 2. Behind a ship. 3. Backward; in reverse.

ASTER

as·ter·oid (*ass*-ter-oyd) *n.* One of the small planets between the orbits of Mars and Jupiter. —*adj.* Starlike.—**as·ter·oi·dal** (as-ter-*oy*-d'l) *adj.* —**as·ter·o·de·an** (as-ter-*oy*-dee-un) *adj.* & *n.*

asth·ma (*az*-muh) *n. Medicine.* A chronic respiratory disorder, characterized by difficulty of breathing, coughing, and expectoration.

—**asth·mat·ic** (az-*mat*-ik) *adj.* & *n.*—**asth·mat·i·cal** (az-*mat*-ih-k'l) *adj.*—**asth·mat·i·cal·ly** *adv.*

a·stig·ma·tism (uh-*stig*-muh-tizm) *n.* A malformation of a lens or of the eye causing a blurred image due to improper focusing. —**as·tig·mat·ic** (as-tig-*mat*-ik) *adj.*

a·stir (uh-*ster*) *adj.* & *adv.* Active; moving.

as·ton·ish (uh-*ston*-ish) *v.* To amaze; astound; inspire wonder or awe.—**as·ton·ish·er** *n.*

as·ton·ish·ing *adj.* Surprising; causing wonder. —**as·ton·ish·ing·ly** *adv.*

as·ton·ish·ment (uh-*ston*-ish-m'nt) *n.* 1. Amazement; stupefaction. 2. A cause of wonder.

as·tound (uh-*stownd*) *v.* To astonish, bewilder; amaze.—**as·tound·ing** *adj.*—**as·tound·ing·ly** *adv.*

a·strad·dle (uh-*strad*-'l) *adv.* Astride; with one leg on either side.

As·tra·khan (ass-truh-*kan*). A Soviet city on the Volga River, near the Caspian Sea.

as·tra·khan (*ass*-truh-kan) *n.* Also **as·tra·chan.** 1. The skins of young lambs with curly wool. 2. A head covering made of such skins.

as·tral (*as*-tr'l) *adj.* 1. Belonging to the stars; starry. 2. Composed of a supposedly spiritual substance beyond the perception of the senses.—**as·tral·ly** *adv.*

a·stray (uh-*stray*) *adv.* Amiss; wrong; away from the proper way.

a·stride (uh-*stryd*) *adv.* With one leg on each side.—**a·stride** *prep.*

as·trin·gent (uh-*strin*-j'nt) *adj.* 1. Binding; constricting; shrinking. 2. Severe; austere. —*n.* A medicine which contracts the tissues of the body.—**as·trin·gen·cy** *n.*

as·tro·labe (*ass*-truh-layb) *n.* An instrument formerly used for measuring the altitude of celestial bodies, now replaced by the sextant.

as·trol·o·gy (uh-*strol*-uh-jee) *n.* A pseudo science which claims to foretell future events by the heavenly bodies.—**as·trol·o·ger** *n.*—**as·tro·log·ic** (as-truh-*loj*-ik) **as·tro·log·i·cal** *adj.*—**as·tro·log·i·cal·ly** *adv.*

ASTROLABE

as·tron·o·my (uh-*stron*-uh-mee) *n.* The science which deals with the celestial bodies.—**as·tro·nom·ic** (ass-truh-*nom*-ik), **as·tro·nom·i·cal** *adj.*— **-i·cal·ly** *adv.*

as·tute (uh-*styoot*, -*stoot*) *adj.* Shrewd; crafty; sagacious.—**as·tute·ly** *adv.*—**as·tute·ness** *n.*

a·sun·der (uh-*sun*-der) *adv.* Apart; into pieces.

a·sy·lum (uh-*sy*-lum) *n.* 1. Retreat; sanctuary. 2. An institution for the housing and care of afflicted or homeless people.

a·sym·me·try (ay-*sim*-ih-tree, a-) *n.* The lack of symmetry or proportion.—**a·sym·met·ric** (ay-si-*met*-rik), **-met·ri·cal** *adj.*— **-met·ri·cal·ly** *adv.*

at *prep.* 1. Near; on; by; coincident in time or space. 'At the moment; at sea.' 2. To-

A

ward; in the direction of; with intention to-ward. 'Shoot at the enemy; guess at the solution.' 3. Occupied with; in a state of. 'At play; at rest.' 4. Due to; by reason of. 'Shudder at the thought.'

at·a·brine (*at*-uh-brin) *n.* A proprietary preparation for the treatment of malaria.

at·a·vism (*at*-uh-vizm) *n.* Reversion to features and characteristics of primitive ancestors. —**at·a·vist** *n.*—**at·a·vist·ic** (at-uh-*vis*-tik) *adj.*

a·tax·i·a (uh-*tak*-see-uh, -*taks*-yuh) *n.* Failure of muscular co-ordination.

at·el·ier (*at*-'l-ya'y) *n.* A workshop, esp. a sculptor's or painter's studio.

a·the·ism (*ay*-thee-izm) *n.* Disbelief in the existence of a Supreme Being.—**a·the·ist** *n.* — -**is·tic** (-*iss*-tik), -**ti·cal** *adj.*— -**is·ti·cal·ly** *adv.*

A·the·na, A·the·ne (uh-*thee*-nuh, -nee) *n. Greek Mythology.* The goddess of wisdom, arts, and sciences.

ath·e·nae·um, ath·e·ne·um (ath-uh-*nee*-um) *n.* 1. An institution or building devoted to study of literature, science, and art. 2. An ancient Roman school of literature and rhetoric.

Ath·ens (*ath*-enz). The capital and largest city of Greece.

a·thirst (uh-*therst*) *adj.* 1. Thirsty. 2. Avid; craving.

ath·lete (*ath*-leet) *n.* One trained and skilled in sports.

athlete's foot. Ringworm of the feet.

ath·let·ic (ath-*let*-ik) *adj.* 1. Pertaining to athletes or athletics. 2. Muscular; sinewy. —**ath·let·i·cal·ly** *adv.*—**ath·let·i·cism** *n.*

ath·let·ics (ath-*let*-iks) *n. sing. & pl.* Sports; contests of physical skill.

a·thwart (uh-*thwart*) *adv.* Obliquely; crosswise. —*prep.* Across; from side to side of.

At·lan·ta (at-*lan*-tuh). The capital and largest city of Georgia.

At·lan·tic (at-*lan*-tik) *n.* The sea dividing Europe and Africa from North and South America.—**At·lan·tic** *adj.*

Atlantic Charter. A document issued by Franklin D. Roosevelt and Winston Churchill on August 14, 1941, listing the post-war aims of the United States and Great Britain.

At·lan·tis (at-*lan*-tis). A legendary continent located in the Atlantic Ocean west of Portugal.

at·las (*at*-l's) *n.* [*pl.* at·las·es] A volume of maps or charts.

At·las (*at*-lus) *n. Mythology.* A giant in Greek legend who was portrayed as carrying the vault of heaven on his shoulders.

Atlas Mountains. A mountain range of North Africa.

at·mos·phere (*at*-mus-feer) *n.* 1. The gaseous mass, consisting mainly of nitrogen and oxygen, surrounding the earth. 2. Surrounding conditions; aura.

at·mos·pher·ic (at-mus-*fer*-ik) *adj.* Pertaining to the atmosphere.—*n.* [*pl.*] *Radio.* Prevailing weather conditions which determine quality

of reception; static.—**at·mos·pher·i·cal** *adj.* —**at·mos·pher·i·cal·ly** *adv.*

at·oll (*at*-ol) *n.* A small island or islands, made up of a coral reef encircling a lagoon.

at·om (*at*-um) *n.* The most minute particle of an element which retains the characteristics of matter.—**a·tom·ic** (uh-*tom*-ik) *adj.*— -**i·cal·ly** *adv.*

at·om bomb (*at*-um-bom), **atomic bomb.** A vastly destructive bomb whose explosive energy is liberated by disintegration of atoms.

atomic energy. Energy released by disintegration of atoms into their component charges of electrical energy.

atomic number. A serial number assigned an element based on the theoretical number of electrons outside its nucleus.

atomic theory. Theory developed around the hypothesis that matter is composed of chemically active atoms.

atomic weight. The weight of an atom of an element, expressed as a number derived comparatively from the value sixteen, assigned to oxygen.

at·om·ize *v.* 1. To pulverize; break into minute particles. 2. To devastate; disintegrate.

at·om·iz·er (*at*-uh-myz-er) *n.* A sprayer; vessel fitted with a syringe and perforated cap for spraying perfume, etc.

ATOMIZER

a·ton·al·ism (uh-*tohn*-uh-lizm) *n.* A theory of musical composition utilizing an even-tempered 12-tone scale with no tonic tones nor key relationships. —**a·ton·al·ist** *n.*

a·ton·al·i·ty (ay-toh-*nal*-ih-tee) *adj. Music.* Having no harmonic relation to a key tone or tonic.—**a·ton·al·ly** *adv.*—**a·ton·al·i·ty** *n.*

a·tone (uh-*tohn*) *v.* [a·toned; a·ton·ing] To expiate; make amends.—**a·ton·er** *n.*

a·tone·ment *n.* 1. Expiation; reparation. 2. The redemption of mankind by the death of Christ.

a·top *adv.* On or at the top.—**a·top** *prep.*

a·tri·um (*ay*-tree-um) *n.* [*pl.* a·tri·a] 1. *Architecture.* The entrance court of an ancient Roman dwelling. 2. An auricle of the heart.

a·tro·cious (uh-*troh*-shus) *adj.* Monstrous; terrible; outrageous.—**cious·ly** *adv.*—**cious·ness** *n.*

a·troc·i·ty (uh-*tros*-ih-tee) *n.* [*pl.* a·troc·i·ties] A brutal or outrageous act.

at·ro·phy (*at*-ruh-fee) *v.* [at·ro·phied; at·ro·phy·ing] To wither; suffer arrestment of development and function; become useless.—*n.* A wasting of the flesh due to lack of nutrition. —**at·ro·phied** *adj.*

at·ro·pine, at·ro·pin (*at*-ruh-peen) *n.* A crystalline alkaloid, used as a narcotic, sedative, and antispasmodic.

at·tach (uh-*tach*) *v.* 1. To tie; connect. 2. To ascribe. 3. *Law.* To take by legal authority. —**at·tach·a·ble** *adj.*

at·ta·ché (at-ash-*ay*) *n.* [*pl.* at·ta·chés] A member of the diplomatic staff of an embassy or legation, or of any other official body or group.

at·tach·ment *n.* 1. Affection; fidelity. 2. *Law.* Confiscation or taking into custody by a writ. 3. Connection; tie bond. 4. An adjunct; an appurtenance.

at·tack *v.* 1. To assault; assail; storm. 2. To criticize; censure; revile. 3. To begin to destroy; to seize. 4. To commence; set about; tackle.—**at·tack** *n.*

at·tain (uh-*tayn*) *v.* To achieve; reach.—**at·tain·a·ble** *adj.*—**at·tain·a·bil·i·ty** (uh-tayn-uh-*bil*-ih-tee) *n.*—**at·tain·a·ble·ness** *n.*

at·tain·der (uh-*tayn*-der) *n.* Cancellation of a person's civil rights and potentialities.

at·tain·ment *n.* Accomplishment; achievement.

at·taint (uh-*taynt*) *v.* To disgrace; shame; stain. —**at·taint** *n.*

at·tar (*at*-er) *n.* An oil made from rose petals, used as a perfume.

at·tempt (uh-*tempt*) *v.* To endeavor; try.—**at·tempt** *n.*—**at·tempt·a·ble** *adj.*

at·tend (uh-*tend*) *v.* 1. To take charge of; apply oneself; mind. 2. To be present. 3. To accompany; escort; wait on. 4. To be connected with.

at·tend·ance (uh-*tend*-uns) *n.* 1. Presence; appearance. 2. Service; attentions; waiting upon. 3. Number of persons present.

at·tend·ant *n.* 1. One who accompanies or performs service for another; servant; usher. 2. An accompaniment; concomitant.—*adj.* Accompanying; connected with.

at·ten·tion (uh-*ten*-shun) *n.* 1. Heedfulness; notice; consideration; devotion. 2. Concentration; application. 3. [*pl.*] Acts of courtesy.

at·ten·tive (uh-*ten*-tiv) *adj.* 1. Heedful; alert; concentrating. 2. Considerate; solicitous. —**at·ten·tive·ly** *adv.*—**at·ten·tive·ness** *n.*

at·ten·u·ate (uh-*ten*-yoo-ayt) *v.* [at·ten·u·at·ed; at·ten·u·at·ing] 1. To stretch out; make slender and elongated. 2. To separate or thin out; make less dense. 3. To diminish; weaken.—**at·ten·u·a·ble** *adj.*—**at·ten·u·a·tion** (uh-ten-yoo-*ay*-shun) *n.*

at·test (uh-*test*) *v.* 1. To certify; vouch for. 2. To indicate; prove.—**at·tes·tant** *n.*—**at·tes·ta·tion** (at-es-*tay*-shun) *n.*

at·tic (*at*-ik) *n.* A garret; room in the top of a house directly under the roof.

At·tic *adj.* 1. Pertaining to ancient Athens. 2. Classic; pure.—**At·tic** *n.*

at·tire (uh-*tyr*) *v.* [at·tired; at·tir·ing] To dress; array.—**at·tire** *n.*—**at·tire·ment** *n.*

at·ti·tude (*at*-uh-tyood) *n.* 1. Posture; bearing. 2. Position; viewpoint; outlook.

at·ti·tu·di·nize (at-uh-*tyoo*-dih-nyz) *v.* [at·ti·tu·di·nized; at·ti·tu·di·niz·ing] To posture; pose.

at·tor·ney (uh-*ter*-nee) *n.* [*pl.* at·tor·neys] A lawyer; one qualified to transact legal business for others.—**at·tor·ney·ship** *n.*

attorney general. [*pl.* attorneys general, attorney generals] The chief legal officer and member of the cabinet of the U.S. Government; the chief legal officer of a state.

at·tract (uh-*trakt*) *v.* 1. To draw; cause to move toward. 2. To allure; fascinate.—**at·tract·a·ble** *adj.*—**at·tract·a·ble·ness** *n.*—**at·trac·tor** *n.*

at·trac·tion (uh-*trak*-shun) *n.* 1. *Physics.* The tendency or force through which all particles of matter are drawn toward each other. 2. The power or act of alluring or enticing. 3. Fascination; charm; appeal.

at·trac·tive (uh-*trak*-tiv) *adj.* Charming; appealing; pleasant; handsome.—**at·trac·tive·ly** *adv.*—**at·trac·tive·ness** *n.*

at·tri·bute (*at*-rih-byoot) *n.* 1. Quality; property; unique characteristic. 2. *Art.* A symbol by which a figure is traditionally identified.

at·trib·ute (uh-*trib*-yoot) *v.* [at·trib·ut·ed; at·trib·ut·ing] To ascribe; assign.—**at·trib·ut·a·ble** *adj.*—**at·trib·u·ter, at·trib·u·tor** *n.*

at·tri·bu·tion (at-rih-*byoo*-shun) *n.* Ascription; designation.

at·trib·u·tive (uh-*trib*-yoo-tiv) *adj.* 1. Pertaining to or expressing an attribute. 2. *Grammar.* Pertaining to an adjective or other modifier placed before the noun it modifies.—**at·trib·u·tive** *n.*—**at·trib·u·tive·ly** *adv.*—**at·trib·u·tive·ness** *n.*

at·tri·tion (uh-*trish*-un) *n.* Abrasion; wearing down.

at·tune (uh-*tyoon*, -*toon*) *v.* [at·tuned; at·tun·ing] To harmonize; adapt.

au·burn (*aw*-bern) *n.* A reddish-brown color. —**au·burn** *adj.*

auc·tion (*awk*-shun) *n.* 1. A sale in which purchases are made by competitive bidding. 2. Also **auction bridge.** A card game based on competitive bidding.—**auc·tion** *v.*

auc·tion·eer (awk-shun-*eer*) *n.* Person who presides at an auction.—**auc·tion·eer** *v.*

au·da·cious (aw-*day*-shus) *adj.* 1. Bold; daring. 2. Brazen; insolent; contemptuous of law.—**au·da·cious·ly** *adv.*—**au·da·cious·ness** *n.*

au·dac·i·ty (aw-*das*-ih-tee) *n.* [*pl.* au·dac·i·ties] 1. Dash; daring. 2. Impudence; insolence.

au·di·ble (*awd*-uh-b'l) *adj.* Perceptible to the ear.—**au·di·bil·i·ty** (awd-uh-*bil*-ih-tee), **au·di·ble·ness** *n.*—**au·di·bly** *adv.*

au·di·ence (*aw*-dee-ens) *n.* 1. An assemblage of listeners or onlookers. 2. A hearing; opportunity to speak. 3. Act of hearing.

au·dit (*aw*-dit) *v.* To examine and check accounts or records.—**au·dit, au·dit·ing** *n.*

au·di·tion (aw-*dish*-un) *n.* A hearing; esp. an opportunity to demonstrate talent.

au·di·tor (*aw*-dit-er) *n.* 1. An examiner of accounting records. 2. A listener.

au·di·to·ri·um (aw-dih-*tor*-ee-um) *n.* [*pl.* au·di·to·ri·ums, au·di·to·ri·a] A building or room with large floor space for seating an audience.

au·di·to·ry (*aw*-dih-tor-ee) *adj.* Pertaining to sound detection; hearing.

au·ger (*aw*-ger) *n.* A tool for drilling holes in wood.

aught (awt) *n.* Anything; any part. —*adv.* In any way; at all.

aug·ment (awg-*ment*) *v.* To add to; increase; enlarge.—**aug·ment·a·ble** *adj.*—**aug·men·ta·tion** (awg-men-*tay*-shun) *n.*—**aug·ment·er** *n.*

au gratin (oh-*graht*-'n, oh-grah-*tan*). *French.* Cooked or prepared with bread crumbs and often cheese.

au·gur (*aw*-ger) *v.* 1. To presage; omen; forecast. 2. To predict; conjecture on a basis of omens. —*n.* A soothsayer.

AUGER

au·gu·ry (*awg*-yer-ee) *n.* [*pl.* aug·u·ries] 1. Any prediction deduced from omens or signs. 2. The practice of auguring.

au·gust (*aw*-gust) *adj.* Dignified and impressive; majestic; stately.—**au·gust·ly** *adv.*—**au·gust·ness** *n.*

Au·gust (*aw*-gust) *n.* The eighth month of our calendar year.

Au·gus·ta (uh-*gus*-tuh). The capital of Maine.

Au·gus·tan (uh-*gus*-tun) *adj.* Pertaining to the Roman emperor Augustus or his reign.—**Au·gus·tan** *n.*—**Augustan age.** The great period of Roman literature during the reign of Augustus; any brilliant literary era.

Au·gus·tine (*aw*-gus-teen) *n.* 1. Saint who preached Christianity in England in the sixth century. 2. A monk who follows monastic rules of St. Augustine.—**Au·gus·tin·ian** (aw-gus-*tin*-ee-un) *adj. & n.*

Au·gus·tus (uh-*gus*-tus) *n.* Emperor during the zenith of Rome's power and literary development.

auk (awk) *n.* One of a family of large, web-footed diving birds.

aunt (ant, ahnt) *n.* The sister of one's parent, or an uncle's wife.—**aunt·ie, aunt·y** *n.* Familiar term for aunt.

au·ra (*aw*-ruh) *n.* [*pl.* au·ras, au·rae] 1. An invisible atmosphere emanating from and encompassing a body. 2. A stream or current of air.

AUK (1/17 life size)

3. *Medicine.* A cool sensation rising from the body to the head just preceding hysteria or epilepsy.—**aur·al** *adj.*

au·ral (*aw*-rul) *adj.* Pertaining to the ear.

au·re·ate (*aw*-ree-it) *adj.* Gilded; ornate.

au·re·ole (*aw*-ree-ohl) *n.* Also **aureola.** 1. An encircling illumination; halo. 2. *Meteorology.* The misty radiance circling the sun.

au·ri·cle (*aw*-rih-k'l) *n.* 1. The outer ear. 2. One of the two heart chambers which receives circulated blood.—**au·ri·cled** *adj.*

au·ric·u·lar (aw-*rik*-yoo-ler) *adj.* 1. Pertaining to the ear or hearing. 2. Confided; secretly told. 3. Pertaining to the heart's auricles.

—au·ric·u·lar·ly *adv.*—**au·ric·u·late** (aw-*rik*-yoo-lit) *adj.*

au·rif·er·ous (aw-*rif*-er-us) *adj.* Containing or yielding gold.

au·ro·ra (uh-*ror*-uh) *n.* [*pl.* au·ro·ras] 1. Dawn; the morning light. 2. [*cap.*] The Roman goddess of dawn. 3. The aurora borealis.—**au·ro·ral, au·ro·re·an** *adj.*—**au·ro·ral·ly** *adv.*

aurora borealis (uh-*ror*-uh bor-ee-*al*-iss). Northern lights; electrical disturbances in the polar atmosphere with resulting spectacular display.

AURORA BOREALIS

aus·pice (*aws*-pis) *n.* 1. Omen; sign. 2. [*pl.*] Patronage; protection; sponsorship.—**aus·pi·cial** (aws-*pish*-ul) *adj.*

aus·pi·cious (aws-*pish*-us) *n.* Fortunate; favorable; auguring success.—**aus·pi·cious·ly** *adv.*—**aus·pi·cious·ness** *n.*

aus·tere (aws-*teer*) *adj.* 1. Stern; severe. 2. Harsh; sour to taste. 3. Rigorously plain; unadorned.—**aus·tere·ly** *adv.*—**aus·tere·ness** *n.* —**aus·ter·i·ty** (aws-*tehr*-ih-tee) *n.* [*pl.* -ities].

Aus·tin (*aws*-tin). Capital city of Texas.

Aus·tral·a·sia (aws-truh-*lay*-zhuh). All the island groups, including Australia, south of Asia.—**Aus·tral·a·sian** *adj. & n.*

Aus·tra·lia (aws-*trayl*-yuh). Continent in the southwest Pacific. Area: 2,974,581 sq. mi. Capital: Canberra.—**Aus·tral·ian** *adj. & n.*

Aus·tri·a (*aws*-tree-uh). Country in central Europe. Capital: Vienna.—**Aus·tri·an** *n. & adj.*

au·tar·chy (*aw*-tahr-kee) *n.* [*pl.* au·tar·chies] Absolute power; one-man rule.—**au·tar·chic** (aw-*tahr*-kik), **au·tar·chi·cal** *adj.*

au·then·tic (aw-*then*-tik) *adj.* 1. Genuine. 2. Authoritative; reliable.—**au·then·ti·cal·ly** *adv.*—**au·then·tic·i·ty** (aw-then-*tis*-i-tee) *n.*

au·then·ti·cate (aw-*then*-tih-kayt) *v.* [au·then·ti·cat·ed; -cat·ing] To prove by authoritative evidence.—**au·then·ti·ca·tion** (aw-then-tih-*kay*-sh'n) *n.*

au·thor (*aw*-ther) *n.* 1. Writer of a literary work. 2. One who creates; originator.—**au·thor·ess** *n.*—**au·tho·ri·al** *adj.*

au·thor·i·tar·i·an (aw-thor-ih-*tair*-ee-un) *adj.* Believing in obedience to authority rather than personal freedom.—**au·thor·i·tar·i·an** *n.*—**au·thor·i·tar·i·an·ism** *n.*

au·thor·i·ta·tive (aw-*thor*-ih-tay-tiv) *adj.* 1. Supported by authority. 2. Positive; dictatorial; imperative.—**au·thor·i·ta·tive·ly** *adv.* —**au·thor·i·ta·tive·ness** *n.*

au·thor·i·ty (aw-*thor*-ih-tee) *n.* [*pl.* -ties] 1. The ability or power to act or command. 2. Person or body with this power. 3. Source referred to for a final decision or expert opinion. 4. Influence created by superiority of mind or character.

A

au·thor·i·za·tion (aw-thor-ih-*zay*-shun) *n.* Act of authorizing; official sanction.

au·thor·ize (*aw*-ther-yz) *v.* [au·thor·ized; au·thor·iz·ing] 1. To charge with authority; empower. 2. To sanction; allow. 3. To warrant; justify.

au·thor·ship (*aw*-ther-ship) 1. Writing; profession of an author. 2. Origin or source.

au·to *n.* [*pl.* au·tos] *Colloquial.* An automobile.

au·to·bi·og·ra·phy (aw-toh-by-*og*-ruh-fee) *n.* [*pl.* -phies] Memoirs or history of a person written by himself.—**au·to·bi·og·ra·pher** *n.*—**au·to·bi·o·graph·ic** (aw-toh-by-uh-*graf*-ik), -graph·i·cal *adj.*— -graph·i·cal·ly *adv.*

au·toc·ra·cy (aw-*tok*-ruh-see) *n.* [*pl.* au·toc·ra·cies] 1. Unmitigated power; absolute control possessed by one individual. 2. A complete dictatorship.

au·to·crat (*aw*-tuh-krat) *n.* A ruler possessing unlimited authority.—**au·to·crat·ic** (aw-tuh-*krat*-ik) -crat·i·cal *adj.*—-crat·i·cal·ly *adv.*

au·to·da·fé (aw-toh-duh-*fay*) *n.* [*pl.* autos·da·fé] 1. A session or a judgment of the Inquisition. 2. Public ceremony during which the Inquisition court turned heretics over to the state executioner.

Au·to·gi·ro (aw-toh-*jy*-roh) *n.* Also **au·to·gy·ro.** Trade-mark name for a plane borne aloft by a large, horizontally rotating blade or blades.

au·to·graph (*aw*-tuh-graf) *n.* A person's written signature, esp. one given or preserved as a souvenir.—**au·to·graph·ic** (aw-tuh-*graf*-ik), **au·to·graph·i·cal** *adj.*—**au·to·graph·i·cal·ly** *adv.*

au·to·in·tox·i·ca·tion (aw-toh-in-tok-sih-*kay*-shun) *n. Medicine.* Poisoning of the body's tissues by absorption of toxins from bodily waste.

au·to·jec·tor (*aw*-toh-jek-ter) *n.* A resuscitating instrument able to revive animals which have been dead for several minutes.

au·to·mat (*aw*-tuh-mat) *n.* A cafeteria in which the customer serves himself by inserting coins in dispensing machines.

au·to·mat·ic (aw-tuh-*mat*-ik). Also **au·to·mat·i·cal.** 1. Mechanical reflex; performed without conscious thought. 2. Pertaining to self-acting machinery.—*n.* 1. A repeating pistol. 2. Any automatic device or instrument.—**au·to·mat·i·cal·ly** *adv.*

au·tom·a·ton (aw-*tom*-uh-ton) *n.* [*pl.* au·tom·a·ta, au·tom·a·tons] 1. One who follows a fixed pattern of existence with no original impulses. 2. An apparatus made to perform acts imitative of living beings.

au·to·mo·bile (aw-tuh-muh-beel) *n.* An engine-driven vehicle, esp. a passenger car.—*adj.* (aw-tuh-*moh*-bil) Self-propelling.—**au·to·mo·bil·ist** (aw-tuh-muh-*beel*-ist) *n.*

au·to·mo·tive (aw-tuh-*moh*-tiv) *adj.* 1. Self-propelling. 2. Relating to automobiles.

au·ton·o·mous (aw-*ton*-uh-mus) *adj.* Having self-government; independent. -mous·ly *adv.*

au·ton·o·my (aw-*ton*-uh-mee) *n.* [*pl.* au·ton·o·mies] 1. Self-government; independence.

2. A state or organization independent of outside control.

au·top·sy (*aw*-top-see) *Medicine.* Examination of a corpse to determine cause of death.

au·to·truck (*aw*-toh-truk) *n.* An automobile designed to carry freight.

au·to·type (*aw*-tuh-typ) *n.* 1. A duplicating process by which impressions are put on a metal plate for printing. 2. A print from an autotype plate.

au·tumn (*aw*-tum) *n.* The season of transition from summer to winter; fall.—**au·tum·nal** (au-*tum*-nul) *adj.*—**au·tum·nal·ly** *adv.*

aux·il·ia·ry (awg-*zil*-yu-ree) *adj.* 1. Helping; assisting. 2. Substitute; serving in place of. 3. *Grammar.* Denoting a verb used to form the tense, voice, or mood of another verb.—*n.* [*pl.* -ries] 1. A helper; assistant. 2. A subsidiary organization, esp. of a trade union, performing certain functions for a larger group. 3. *Grammar.* An auxiliary verb.

a·vail (uh-*vayl*) *v.* To work for the advantage of; profit; effect; benefit.—**a·vail** *n.*—**avail oneself of.** To put to use.

a·vail·a·ble (uh-*vayl*-uh-b'l) *adj.* Readily obtainable; accessible; usable.—**a·vail·a·bil·i·ty** (uh-vayl-uh-*bil*-ih-tee), **a·vail·a·ble·ness** *n.*—**a·vail·a·bly** *adv.*

av·a·lanche (*av*-uh-lanch) *n.* 1. A huge mass of ice, snow, or rocks sliding down a mountain. 2. Any overpowering weight or mass.—*v.* [av·a·lanched; av·a·lanch·ing].

av·a·rice (*av*-er-iss) *n.* Also **av·a·ri·cious·ness** (av-er-*ish*-us-niss). Greed; insatiable desire for wealth.—**av·a·ri·cious** *adj.*

a·vast (uh-*vast*) *interj. Nautical.* Stop!, Halt!, Cease!

av·a·tar (*av*-uh-*tahr*) *n.* 1. A descending from heaven; reincarnation. 2. An incarnate form; embodiment; personification.

a·vaunt (uh-*vawnt*) *interj.* Begone!

a·ve (*ay*-vee, *ah*-vay) *interj.* God bless you!, Be of good cheer!—*n.* An Ave Maria; prayer.

Ave Maria (ah-vuh-muh-*ree*-uh) *Roman Catholic Church.* Invocation to the Virgin Mary.

a·venge (uh-*venj*) *v.* [a·venged; a·veng·ing] To punish for a wrong done one; vindicate; deal vengeance.—**a·veng·er** *n.*

av·e·nue (*av*-uh-nyoo, -noo) *n.* 1. A wide passageway or street. 2. Way; opening; means. 'An avenue of attainment.'

a·ver (uh-*ver*) *v.* [a·ver·red; a·ver·ring] 1. To declare positively; assert. 2. *Law.* To vouch for or verify.

av·er·age (*av*-er-ij) *n.* 1. The sum of a group of quantities divided by the number of quantities. 2. A common or typical occurrence, person, or quality.—**av·er·age** *adj. & v.* [av·er·aged; -ag·ing] 1. To determine the arithmetical proportion. 2. To allot in proportional amounts.

a·verse (uh-*verss*) *adj.* 1. Feeling repugnance; opposed; reluctant. 2. Turned away from;

reversed. 3. Unfavorably disposed; malign. —a·verse·ly *adv.*—a·verse·ness *n.*

a·ver·sion (uh-*ver*-zhun) *n.* Strong dislike; repugnance; reluctance.

a·vert (uh-*vert*) *v.* To turn aside; avoid; prevent.

A·ver·tin (uh-*ver*-tin; *av*-er-tin) *n.* Trade-mark name for an anaesthetic given through the rectum.

a·vi·a·ry (ay-vee-ehr-ee) *n.* [*pl.* -ries] A cage or building for keeping birds.

a·vi·a·tion (ay-vee-*ay*-shun) *n.* The science, art, and industry dealing with airplanes and their flight.

a·vi·a·tor (ay-vee-ay-ter) *n.* The pilot or one connected with the navigation of an airplane.

av·id (*av*-id) *adj.* Eager; greedy; intensely desirous.—a·vid·i·ty *n.*—av·id·ly *adv.*

av·o·ca·do (av-uh-*kah*-doh) *n.* [*pl.* av·o·ca·dos] Alligator pear; the shiny green, pulpy fruit of a tropical evergreen.

av·o·ca·tion (av-uh-*kay*-shun) *n.* 1. A hobby; a pursuit chosen for enjoyment rather than profit. 2. A distraction; disturbing element.

av·o·cet, av·o·set (*av*-uh-set) *n.* A small, web-footed shore bird with a long, slender, upward-curving bill.

a·void (uh-*voyd*) *v.* 1. To shun; keep away from; evade. 2. To void; annul; disqualify. —a·void·a·ble *adj.*—a·void·ance *n.*

a·voir·du·pois (av-er-duh-*poyz*) *n.* 1. The common system of weights wherein sixteen ounces equals one pound. 2. *Colloquial.* Excess weight; stoutness.

a·vouch (uh-*vowch*) *v.* 1. To declare openly and positively. 2. To maintain; establish; substantiate.—a·vouch·ment *n.*

a·vow (uh-*vow*) *v.* To assert openly; acknowledge and justify.—a·vow·al *n.*—a·vow·ed *adj.* —a·vow·ed·ly *adv.*—a·vow·ed·ness *n.*

a·wait *v.* 1. To wait for; expect. 2. To be in store for.

a·wake *v.* [a·waked; a·wak·ing] To bestir oneself; wake up.—*adj.* Vigilant; active; not sleeping.

a·wak·en *v.* To be roused from sleep or inactivity.—a·wak·en·er *n.*—a·wak·en·ing *n.* & *adj.*

a·ward *v.* To bestow a prize; allot or assign a basis of judgment.—a·ward *n.*—a·ward·a·ble *adj.*—a·ward·er *n.*

a·ware *adj.* Informed; warned; acquainted. —a·ware·ness *n.*

a·wash *adj. Nautical.* Covered with water.—a·wash *adv.*

a·way *adv.* 1. At a distance; apart; absent. 2. Aside; to one side. 3. To another; out of one's possession. 4. Off; to the vanishing point; as, to fade away. 5. Intently; vigorously. 'Study away!' 6. *Colloquial.* Now; instantly. 'Right away.'

awe (*aw*) *v.* [awed; aw·ing] To strike with fear or reverence.—awe *n.*

a·weigh (uh-*way*) *adj. Nautical.* Hoisted clear; free on its cable, as an anchor.

awe·less. *Variant spelling* of awless.

awe·some (*aw*-sum) *adj.* Inspiring fear or reverence.—awe·some·ly *adv.*—awe·some·ness *n.*

awe·stricken, awe·struck *adj.* Filled with profound wonder or terror.

aw·ful *adj.* 1. Inspiring awe. 2. *Colloquial.* a. Great; excessive. b. Of grossly inferior quality.—aw·ful·ly *adv.*—aw·ful·ness *n.*

a·while *adv.* For some time, esp. a short time.

awk·ward (*awk*-werd) *adj.* 1. Wanting dexterity; clumsy. 2. Ungraceful; uncouth. 3. Unpleasant; embarrassing; compromising. —awk·ward·ly *adv.*—awk·ward·ness *n.*

awl *n.* A pointed tool for piercing holes.

aw·less, awe·less *adj.* Without reverence or dread.

AWL

awn·ing *n.* 1. A canvas roof for protection from sun or rain. 2. A projecting canvas window covering for screening out the sun.

a·woke. *Past tense* & *past participle* of awake.

A.W.O.L. (ay-duhb'l-yoo-oh-*el*, ay-wawl). *Military Abbreviation.* Absent without official leave.

a·wry (uh-*ry*) *adj.* 1. Twisted; turned; oblique. 2. Turned aside from truth or reason.—a·wry *adv.*

ax, axe *n.* [*pl.* ax·es] A cutting tool having a heavy wedged metal head on a handle.—ax *v.*

ax-adze	axhead	ax-shaped
ax grinder	ax maker	axstone
axhammer	axman	axtree

ax·i·al (*ak*-see-ul) *adj.* Pertaining to an axis. —ax·i·al·ly *adv.*

ax·i·om (*ak*-see-um) *n.* A self-evident, undeniable truth.—ax·i·o·mat·ic (ak-see-uh-*mat*-ik), ax·i·o·mat·i·cal *adj.*—ax·i·o·mat·i·cal·ly *adv.*

ax·is *n.* 1. A straight center line on which a body rotates or is assumed to rotate. 2. *Botany.* Stem or root of a plant. 3. [*cap.*] The coalition of Germany, Italy, and Japan (1936–1945).

ax·le (*ak*-s'l) *n.* The bar on which a wheel turns.

ax·le·tree *n.* An axle.

Ax·min·ster (aks-min-ster) *n.* A kind of carpet, formerly made by hand, now by machine.

AXIS

a·yah (ah-yuh) *n. India.* A personal maid.

aye, ay (ay) *adv.* Always; forever.

aye, ay (eye) *adv.* Yes; yea.—*n.* [*pl.* ayes] A vote, or voter, on the affirmative side.

Ayr·shire (ayr-shir) *n.* One of a breed of dairy cattle originating in Scotland.

a·za·lea (uh-*zayl*-yuh) *n.* A beautifully flowering group of plants of the heath family.

Azerbaidzhan Soviet Socialist Republic (ah-zur-by-*jahn*). Country SE Europe. Area: 33,345 sq. mi. Capital: Baku.

az·i·muth (az-ih-muth) n. *Astronomy*. The arc of the celestial horizon between the north or south point and an observed celestial body. —**az·i·muth·al** adj.— **-al·ly** adv.

Azores (uh-*zorz*). An archipelago of ten Portuguese islands in the Atlantic.

Az·tec (az-tek) n. 1. Tribe of Mexican Indians whose highly advanced civilization was disrupted by Cortes. 2. The Aztecs' language. —**Az·tec, Az·tec·an** adj.

az·ure (azh-er) n. 1. A sky-blue color or pigment. 2. The heavens; sky.—**az·ure** adj.

B

baa (bah) v. [baaed; baa·ing] To bleat, as a sheep.—**baa** n.

Baal (bay-'l) n. [pl. Ba·al·im, Ba·als] Deity of the ancient Canaanites and Phoenicians, usually the god of the sun or of fertility.—**Ba·al·ish** adj.—**Ba·al·ism** n.—**Ba·al·ist** n.

Bab·bitt (bab-it) n. A smug, conventional, middle-class American businessman, from Sinclair Lewis's novel *Babbitt*.—**Bab·bitt·ry** n.

babbitt metal. A soft alloy of copper, antimony, and tin.

bab·ble v. [bab·bled; bab·bling] 1. To talk foolishly or indistinctly; prattle. 2. To murmur, as a stream.—**bab·ble** n.—**bab·ble·ment** n.—**bab·bler** n.

babe n. 1. An infant; childlike person. 2. *Slang*. A girl; woman.

Ba·bel (bay-b'l) n. 1. *Bible*. Babylonian city whose inhabitants tried to build a tower to heaven, but failed when God divided their language. 2. [not cap.] Din; hubbub.

babies'-breath n. Tall herb with small, fragrant pink or white flowers.

ba·boo, ba·bu (bah-boo) n. 1. Hindu title for gentleman. 2. Native clerk who writes English. 3. A semiliterate native.

ba·boon (bab-oon) n. 1. Large Asiatic or African monkey with a doglike snout and short tail. 2. *Slang*. A stupid person. —**ba·boon·er·y** n.—**ba·boon·ish** adj.

ba·bush·ka (bah-boosh-kuh) n. Woman's triangular head scarf.

BABOON(1/30 life size)

ba·by (bay-bee) n. [pl. ba·bies] 1. An infant; young child. 2. Spoiled or childish person.—v. [ba·bied; ba·by·ing] To treat as a child.—adj. 1. Of, like, or for a baby. 2. Diminutive; small.—**ba·by·hood** n. —**ba·by·ish** adj.—**ba·by·like** adj.

baby farm. Establishment for paid nursing and care of babies.—**baby farmer, baby farming**.

Bab·y·lon (bab-uh-l'n) n. 1. Wicked, luxurious capital city of Babylonia. 2. Any city of wealth or sinful luxury.

Bab·y·lo·ni·a (-loh-nee-uh). Ancient, powerful empire in SW Asia.—**-lo·ni·an** n. & adj.

bac·ca·lau·re·ate (bak-uh-law-ree-ut) n. 1. University or college degree of bachelor. 2. Com-

mencement address delivered to a graduating class.

bac·ca·rat, bac·ca·ra (bak-uh-rah) n. Popular French card game, played for money.

bac·cha·nal (bak-uh-nal) adj. Pertaining to Bacchus.—n. 1. Reveler. 2. Drunken feast.

Bac·cha·na·li·a (bak-uh-nay-lee-uh) n. pl. 1. Festive rites in honor of Bacchus. 2. Drunken feast.—**Bac·cha·na·li·an** n. & adj.

Bac·chus (bak-us) n. *Mythology*. God of wine; Dionysus.—**Bac·chic, Bac·chi·cal** adj.

bach·e·lor (bach-uh-ler) n. 1. An unmarried man. 2. A person holding the lowest college or university degree.—**bach·e·lor·hood** n.—**bach·e·lor·ship** n.

bach·e·lor's-but·ton n. Any of several plants with flowers resembling buttons, esp. the cornflower.

ba·cil·lus (buh-sil-us) n. [pl. bacilli] Any of the microscopic, rod-shaped bacteria.—**bac·il·lary, ba·cil·lar** adj.

back n. 1. The rear; posterior part or section. 2. The posterior or upper part of the body, extending from the neck to the loins. 3. Part which covers or supports the back. 4. Backfield player in some team games.—adj. 1. Rear; posterior. 2. In or of the past; not up-to-date.—adv. 1. At or toward the back. 2. To a former place or condition. 3. In retort. 'He spoke back.' 4. In a state of restraint or concealment.—v. 1. To support; champion. 2. To retreat; move or cause to move backward. 3. To form or furnish a backing; reinforce.—**back down, back out**. To break a promise; withdraw; retreat.

backache	backlash	backwash
backboned	backspin	back way
back breaker	back-trail (v.)	back yard

back·bite v. [back·bit, back·bit·ten; back·bit·ing] To slander one absent; defame.—**back·bit·er** n.—**back·bit·ing** n.

back·bone n. 1. Spine; vertebral column. 2. Something resembling a backbone in appearance, position, or function. 3. Firmness; resolution.—**back·boned** adj.

back·drop n. 1. Any background. 2. *Theater*. A curtain providing the background of a scene.

back·er n. Supporter; advocate; guarantor.

back·field (bak-feeld) n. *Football*. Those players behind the line who handle the ball during offensive play.

back·fire v. [back·fired; back·fir·ing] **1.** To explode prematurely in a combustion chamber or its exhaust lines. **2.** To start and control a fire against a forest or prairie fire to stop the latter. **3.** To boomerang.—**back·fire** n.

back·gam·mon (bak-gam-'n) n. A game of chance played with dice. — **back·gam·mon** v.

back·ground (bak-grownd) n. **1.** That part of an action or scene farthest from the spectator. **2.** That part of an artistic creation upon which objects are projected. **3.** A position in which one tries to avoid notice. **4.** A person or thing's antecedents.

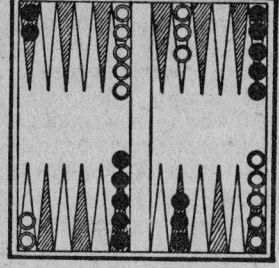

BACKGAMMON BOARD

back·hand n. **1.** Tennis. A stroke begun with the arm across the chest. **2.** A blow delivered with the back of the hand. **3.** Handwriting which slopes backward.

back·hand, back·hand·ed adj. **1.** With the hand turned backward. **2.** Indirect; not whole-hearted; sarcastic. **3.** Written with a back slope.— -hand·ed·ly adv.— -hand·ed·ness n.

back·ing n. **1.** Support; help. **2.** Reinforcement. **3.** Declaration of favor or approval.

back·log (bak-log) n. **1.** Log at the back of a fireplace. **2.** Any reserve or reservoir.

back·slide v. [back·slid; back·slid·ing] To return to improper conduct.—**back·slid·er** n.

back·stage adv. Behind the scenery of a theatrical performance.—n. The performers' dressing rooms.—**back·stage** adj.

back stairs. Stairs in the back of a house. —**back·stair, back·stairs** adj. **1.** Pertaining to such stairs. **2.** Underhand; indirect; intriguing.—**backstairs** gossip. Servants' rumors.

back·stay n. Nautical. A supporting cable running from the deck to the mast.

back·stroke n. Swimming. A style in which the swimmer lies on his back and brings his arms over his head to his sides; inverted crawl.—v. [back·stroked; back·strok·ing].

back·ward (bak-werd) adj. **1.** Rear; hind. **2.** Reversed. **3.** Dull; unprogressive; retarded. **4.** Bashful; not aggressive.—**back·ward·ly** adv.—**back·ward·ness** n.

back·ward, back·wards (bak-werdz) adv. **1.** Toward the rear; hind side foremost. **2.** In a reverse manner or direction. **3.** From a better to a worse condition.

back·wa·ter n. **1.** A body of water without a forward current or flow. **2.** Water pushed back or displaced by a disturbing force.—v. **1.** To reverse direction, esp. of a boat or swimmer. **2.** To retreat.

back·woods n. pl. Sparsely settled forest areas. —**back·wood, -woods** adj.— -woods·man n.

ba·con (bay-k'n) n. Smoked side-pork.

bac·te·ri·a (bak-tihr-ee-uh) n. pl. A large group of one-celled, vegetable micro-organisms. —**bac·te·ri·al** adj.—**bac·te·ri·al·ly** adv.

bac·te·ri·ol·o·gy (bak-tihr-ee-ol-uh-jee) n. The scientific study of bacteria.—**bac·te·ri·o·log·i·cal** adj.— -o·log·i·cal·ly adv.— -ol·o·gist n.

bad adj. [worse; worst] **1.** Evil; wicked; vicious; naughty. **2.** Incompetent; poor; valueless. **3.** Severe. **4.** Unwholesome; sick. **5.** Distressing; unfortunate.—**bad** n.—**bad·ly** adv.—**bad·ness** n.

bad blood. 1. Antagonism; hatred. **2.** Inherited criminal tendencies.

badge (baj) n. A mark; emblem; identification. —v. [badged; badg·ing].

badg·er (baj-er) n. A short-legged, burrowing, carnivorous mammal related to the bear family.—v. To tease; bait; harass.

BADGER

bad·i·nage (bad-'n-ij, bad-ih-nahzh) n. Banter; raillery; joshing.—v. [bad·i·naged; bad·i·nag·ing].

badlands n. pl. Rugged, desolate regions where erosion has shaped rocks into strange figures.

bad·min·ton (bad-min-t'n) n. A game similar to tennis played with rackets and shuttlecocks.

bad-tempered adj. Irritable; cross; sulky.

baf·fle v. [baf·fled; baf·fling] **1.** To puzzle; mystify. **2.** Frustrate; thwart; foil.—n. Mechanics. Any device which inhibits or redirects the flow of a gas or fluid.—**baf·fle·ment** n.—**baf·fler** n.—**baf·fling** adj.—**baf·fling·ly** adv.

baf·fle·board (baf-'l-bohrd) n. Also **baffle.** Radio. A piece of board used for mounting loudspeakers to improve sound reproduction.

bag n. **1.** A sack; container for carrying miscellaneous things. **2.** Animals taken in hunting. **3.** The quantity a bag contains. **4.** Anything that sags or bulges like a bag. **5.** Slang. A baggage; low or homely woman.—v. [bagged; bag·ging] **1.** To put into a bag. **2.** To capture; kill. **3.** To swell; bulge.

bag·a·telle (bag-uh-tel) n. **1.** A trifle; thing of no importance. **2.** A table game played with cue and balls. **3.** Music. Short composition in light style.

bag·gage (bag-ij) n. **1.** Clothing and other belongings carried by a traveler. **2.** Suitcases and trunks collectively. **3.** A minx; hussy.

bag·gy adj. [bag·gi·er; bag·gi·est] Loose; swelling; ill-fitting. —**bag·gi·ly** adv.—**bag·gi·ness** n.

bag·nio (ban-yoh) n. A brothel; house of prostitution.

BAGPIPE

bag·pipe n. A shrill wind instrument, now re-

garded as the national instrument of Scotland.
—**bag·pip·er** *n.*

ba·guette, ba·guet (bag-*get*) *n.* 1. A gem cut in an elongated diamond shape. 2. This shape itself.

bah *interjection.* An expression of disgust or contempt.

bail (*bayl*) *n.* 1. *Law.* Security given for the release of a prisoner from custody. 2. Release by posting this guarantee.—**bail** *v.* —**bail·ee** *n.*—**bail·ment** *n.*—**bail·or** *n.*

bail *n.* An arched half hoop used as handle, brace, etc.—**bail** *v.*

bail *v.* To empty of fluid by ladling or dipping. —**bail** *n.*—**bail·er** *n.*

bail·a·ble *adj.* 1. *Law.* Admitting of bail. 2. Capable of being emptied by ladling.

bail·iff (*bayl*-if) *n.* A sheriff's assistant.

bail·i·wick (*bayl*-uh-wik) *n.* 1. One's own provinc 2. Area of a bailiff's jurisdiction.

bail out. Also **bale out.** *Aviation.* To make a parachute jump from a plane in flight.

bait (*bayt*) *n.* Anything used to entice or lure. —*v.* 1. To put a bait on or in. 2. To harass; badger; annoy.—**bait·er** *n.*

baize (*bayz*) *n.* A coarse, solid-colored cloth with a nap on one side.

bake *v.* [baked; bak·ing] 1. To cook food in an oven. 2. To dry and harden by exposing to heat.—**bake** *n.*—**bak·er** *n.*

Ba·ke·lite (*bayk*-uh-lyte) *n.* Trade name of a synthetic plastic.—**Ba·ke·lite** *adj.*

baker's dozen. *Colloquial.* Thirteen.

bak·er·y (*bayk*-er-ee) *n.* [*pl.* bak·er·ies] An establishment where baked goods are made and sold.

bak·ing *n.* 1. Cooking by dry heat. 2. A single batch of baked goods.

baking powder. A leavening agent for quick baking.

baking soda. Bicarbonate of soda.

bak·sheesh, bak·shish (*bahk*-sheesh) *n.* A gift of money, esp. in the Near East; alms; tip.

Ba·laam (*bay*-l'm). A biblical prophet scolded by his donkey for slandering Israel.

ba·la·lai·ka (bal-uh-*ly*-kuh) *n.* A guitarlike stringed instrument.

bal·ance (*bal*-'ns) *n.* 1. A weighing instrument consisting essentially of a centered beam with a pan or scale on either arm; any test of value or quality. 2. Excess; surplus; remainder. 3. Poise; equilibrium; sanity. 4. Counterpoise; counterweight. 5. Equality between two sides of an account or ledger. 6. Regulatory wheel in a watch.—*v.* [bal·anced; bal·anc·ing] 1. To

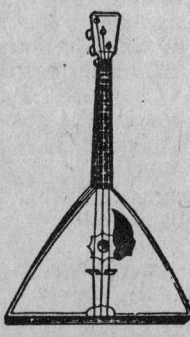

BALALAIKA

estimate; weigh. 2. To counteract; counterpoise. 3. To maintain or remain in equilibrium. 4. *Accounting.* To prove the equality of assets and liabilities. —**bal·anc·er** *n.*

SCALES IN BALANCE

balance of power. 1. Equality of military power between or among nations. 2. Ability of a small group to decide issues by siding with one or two larger factions, neither of which has a majority.

balance of trade. The difference between the values of commodities exported and imported.

balance sheet. *Accounting.* A periodic summary of the financial state of a business.

bal·bo·a (bal-*boh*-ah) *n.* A silver coin of Panama worth one U.S. dollar. 2. [*cap.*] The Pacific port of the Panama Canal.

bal·brig·gan (bal-*brig*-un) *n.* A knitted, ribbed, stretchable cotton fabric.

bal·co·ny (*bal*-kun-ee) *n.* [*pl.* bal·co·nies] 1. A platform projecting from the outside of a building and surrounded by a railing or parapet. 2. A ledge or gallery above a main floor.

bald (*bawld*) *adj.* 1. Destitute of covering or hair, esp. on the head. 2. Unadorned; plain. —**bald·ly** *adv.*—**bald·ness** *n.*

bald eagle. A North American eagle with contrasting white head and neck.

bal·der·dash (*bawl*-der-dash) *n.* Nonsense.

bal·dric (*bawl*-drik) *n.* A belt worn over the shoulder with certain uniforms.

Bald·win (*bawld*-win) *n.* A large, moderately tart apple.

bale *n.* A bulky, compressed bundle, usually wired or bound.—*v.* [baled; bal·ing] To press into a bale.—**bal·er** *n.*

ba·leen (buh-*leen*) *n.* A flexible bone taken from the jaw of certain whales.

bale·ful *adj.* Sinister; deadly; menacing.—**bale·ful·ly** *adv.*—**bale·ful·ness** *n.*

balk (*bawk*) *v.* 1. To frustrate; thwart. 2. To hesitate; demur.—*n. Baseball.* An incompleted motion, as if to pitch the ball.—**balk·er** *n.* —**balk·ing** *n.* & *adj.*—**balk·ing·ly** *adv.*

Bal·kan (*bawl*-k'n) *adj.* Pertaining to the people, countries, and institutions of the Balkan Peninsula: Yugoslavia, Greece, Bulgaria, etc.

balk·y (*bawk*-ee) *adj.* [balk·i·er; balk·i·est] Contrary; reluctant; stubborn.

ball (*bawl*) *n.* A large formal dancing party.

ball *n.* 1. A spherical body; globe. 2. One of the many round pellets or spheroids used in sports. 3. A sport in which a ball is used. 4. *Baseball.* A pitch not accurate enough to be judged a strike.—*v.* To make into a ball.

bal·lad (*bal*-ud) *n.* A short narrative poem often originating with the people and adapted to singing.—**bal·lad** *v.*— **-lad·eer** *n.*— **-lad·ry** *n.*

bal·last (*bal*-ust) *n.* Material carried in a ship or vehicle to stabilize it in the absence of cargo. 2. Anything that lends stability or firm foundation.—**bal·last** *v.*

ball bearing. A steel ball used, with others, to reduce friction in moving parts.

bal·le·ri·na (bal-uh-*ree*-nuh) *n.* A female ballet dancer, esp. one of great excellence.

bal·let (*bal*-ay, ba-*lay*) *n.* 1. Medium of artistic expression employing classical forms of pantomime, dancing, and music. 2. A performance of this style of dance.

bal·lis·tics (bal-*ist*-iks) *n.* Science of the firing of projectiles.—**bal·lis·tic** *adj.*

bal·loon (buh-*loon*) *n.* 1. A rubber sack which may be inflated. 2. A large bag filled with light gas and sent aloft.—*adj.* Inflated; puffed out.—**bal·loon** *v.*—**bal·loon·er, bal·loon·ist** *n.*

bal·lot (*bal*-ut) *n.* 1. Franchise; suffrage. 2. A list of electoral candidates on which a voter indicates his choices.—*v.* To vote.—**bal·lot·er** *n.*

ball·room (*bawl*-room) *n.* A large room for social dancing.

bal·ly·hoo (*bal*-ee-hoo) *n. Slang.* Sensational or extravagant publicity.—**bal·ly·hoo** *v.*

balm (bahm) *n.* 1. A soothing ointment; salve. 2. Anything soothing. 3. A resin from trees of the pine family.

Balm of Gilead. A resinous substance from the spring buds of a poplar of the same name.

balm·y (*bahm*-ee) *adj.* [balm·i·er; balm·i·est] 1. Aromatic; fragrant. 2. Gentle; refreshing. 3. *Slang.* Daft.—**balm·i·ly** *adv.*— **-i·ness** *n.*

bal·sa (*bawl*-suh) *n.* 1. A raft made of floats and a platform. 2. A strong, lightweight wood from a tropical American tree.

bal·sam (*bawl*-s'm) *n.* 1. An aromatic resin obtained from various trees and plants. 2. Any balm or healing agent. 3. A balsam-producing plant.—**bal·sam·ic** (-*sam*-) *adj.*

Bal·tic (*bawl*-tik) *adj.* Pertaining to the Baltic Sea and the countries bordering on it.

Baltimore oriole. A North American oriole with black and yellow-orange plumage.

bal·us·ter (*bal*-us-ter) *n.* A small column supporting a railing or balustrade.

bal·us·trade (bal-us-*strayd*) *n.* A railing; series of rails or columns joined by a heavy top rail.

bam·bi·no (bam-*bee*-noh) *n.* [*pl.* bam·bi·ni] *Italian.* 1. Any young child. 2. [*cap.*] A picture of the infant Jesus.

bam·boo (bam-*boo*) *n.* A tropical plant with a hollow, jointed stem.

bam·boo·zle (bam-*boo*-z'l) *v. Colloquial.* [bam·boo·zled; bam·boo·zling] To deceive; trick.— **-zle·ment** *n.*— **-zler** *n.*

BAMBOO

ban *v.* [banned; ban·ning] To prohibit; forbid.

—*n.* 1. A public announcement or proclamation. 2. A prohibition. 3. *Ecclesiastic.* Excommunication. 4. Public disapproval or ostracism. 5. [*pl.*] [Usually **banns**] Public announcement of an approaching marriage.

ba·nal (*bay*-n'l, buh-*nal*) *adj.* Hackneyed; commonplace; trite.—**ba·nal·i·ty** *n.*—**ba·nal·ly** *adv.*

ba·nan·a (buh-*nan*-uh) *n.* 1. A long, mealy, yellow fruit growing in clusters. 2. The tropical perennial plant it grows on.

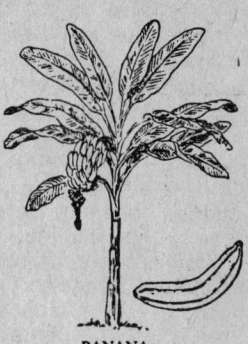
BANANA

banana oil. A synthetic organic compound used as solvent, etc.

band *n.* 1. Bond; tie. 2. Strip; ribbon. 3. A group of persons united by common interest. 4. An orchestra with a predominance of percussion and wind instruments. 5. *Physics.* A range of light or radio waves. 6. An encircling tie. 7. A border on a fabric. 8. A gradation of color or shade. —*v.* 1. To unite; associate. 2. To tie or border with a band.

band cutter	band pulley	bandstand
band man	band sawyer	bandstring
bandmaster	band-shaped	band-tailed

band·age (*band*-ij) *n.* A piece of gauze or other cloth used to dress wounds.—*v.* [band·aged; band·ag·ing].—**band·ag·er** *n.*

ban·dan·na, ban·dan·a (ban-*dan*-uh) *n.* A large kerchief, usually brightly figured.

band·box *n.* A box, usually pasteboard, used to contain hats or other attire.

ban·deau (ban-*doh*) *n.* [*pl.* ban·deaux] 1. A band worn as a tie in the hair. 2. A brassiere.

ban·dit (*ban*-dit) *n.* [*pl.* ban·dits; band·it·ti] A robber; highwayman; outlaw.—**ban·dit·ry** *n.*

band·saw *n.* Mechanical saw whose blade is a revolving saw-toothed hoop.

band·spread *n.* The width of a specific wave in the radio spectrum.

band·wagon *n.* 1. A high, large wagon or truck from which a band plays. 2. *Colloquial.* A metaphorical vehicle of popular support or enthusiasm for a winning side.

ban·dy (*ban*-dee) *v.* [ban·died; ban·dy·ing] To give and receive reciprocally; knock back and forth; interchange.—*adj.* Bent.

ban·dy-leg·ged *adj.* Having crooked or bowed legs.

bane *n.* 1. A destroyer of life, esp. poison. 2. Ruin; destruction.—*v.* [baned; ban·ing].— **bane·ful** *adj.*—**bane·ful·ly** *adv.*—**bane·ful·ness** *n.*

bang *v.* 1. To produce a loud, sudden noise. 2. To strike; hit.—**bang** *n.*

Bang·kok (*ban*-kok). The chief city and capital of Siam.

ban·gle *n.* An anklet or bracelet.

bangs *n. pl.* The front hair combed over the forehead and cut straight across.

ban·ian (*ban*-yun) *n.* 1. A Hindu tradesman. 2. A Bengal who handles money matters for Europeans. 3. A loose gown worn by Hindu men. 4. *Variant spelling* of banyan.

ban·ish *v.* 1. To exile; drive away. 2. Put from the mind. —**ban·ish·er** *n.*—**ban·ish·ment** *n.*

ban·is·ter (*ban*-is-ter) *n.* 1. A column or rail in a balustrade. 2. [*pl.*] A heavy hand-rail; balustrade.

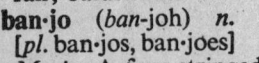

BANISTER

ban·jo (*ban*-joh) *n.* [*pl.* ban·jos, ban·joes] *Music.* A four-stringed instrument played by picking.—**ban·jo·ist** *n.*

bank *n.* 1. A slope; pile; embankment. 2. An area of shallow water in the sea. 3. Land bordering on a river. 4. The tilt of a plane when turning in. 5. *Billiards.* A shot made by bouncing the ball off the cushion.—**bank** *v.*

bank *n.* A row; tier; battery; series.—**bank** *v.*

bank *n.* 1. An establishment interested in various phases of finance. 2. A fund, esp. in gambling games.—*v.* 1. To place money in a bank. 2. To depend; count; rely.—**bank·er** *n.*

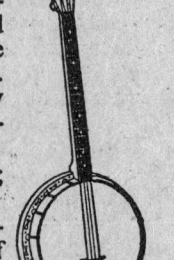

BANJO

bank·a·ble *n.* Acceptable by a bank.

bank·ing *n.* Profession or theory of money management.

bank note. A promissory note issued by a bank and payable in silver at the bearer's demand.

bank rate. Discount or interest rate set by a bank.

bank·rupt *n.* 1. A person legally declared insolvent, all his property being then forfeit to his creditors. 2. One devoid of hope or essential moral qualities.—**bank·rupt** *v. & adj.*

bank·rupt·cy (*bank*-rup-see) *n.* [*pl.* bank·rupt·cies] 1. Insolvency; failure in business. 2. Lack of hope, strength, morality, etc.

ban·ner *n.* A standard flag.—*adj.* Incomparable; superlative.

banner head. *Journalism.* A headline of large type, running the full width of the page.

ban·nis·ter. *Variant spelling* of banister.

banns *n. pl.* Also **bans.** Notices of forthcoming marriage posted in a church.

ban·quet (*bang*-kwit, *ban*-) *n.* A sumptuous or costly feast.—*v.* To feast.—**ban·quet·er** *n.*

Ban·quo (*bang*-kwoh, *ban*-) A character in Shakespeare's *Macbeth.*

ban·shee *n. Irish Folklore.* A noisy goblin or spirit.

ban·tam (*ban*-t'm) *n.* 1. A small and plucky or impudent person. 2. *Pugilism.* A boxer weighing in at no more than 118 pounds. 3. [*cap.*] A variety of dwarf chicken.—**ban·tam** *adj.*

ban·ter *v.* To ridicule good-humoredly; make fun of.—*n.* Humorous raillery; jesting.—**ban·ter·er** *n.*—**ban·ter·ing·ly** *adv.*

BANTAM (def. 3)

Ban·tu (*ban*-too) *n.* A family of languages in south and central Africa.—**Ban·tu** *adj.*

ban·yan, ban·ian (*ban*-y'n) *n.* A kind of fig tree noted for its vast, rooting branches.

ban·zai (*bahn*-zy) *interjection.* Japanese cry of salutation, congratulations, etc.

ba·o·bab (*bay*-oh-bab) *n.* Thick African tree which yields an edible fruit.

bap·tism (*bap*-tizm) *n.* 1. The application of water as a sacrament symbolizing spiritual cleansing or acceptance into the church. 2. Initial experience.—**bap·tis·mal** *adj.*—**bap·tis·mal·ly** *adv.*

Bap·tist (*bap*-tist) *n.* Member of a Christian denomination holding that baptism should be administered by immersion to believers only.

bap·tis·ter·y (*bap*-tist-ree) *n.* [*pl.* -teries]. Also **bap·tist·ry** [*pl.* -tries] A building or portion of a church set apart for baptisms.

bap·tize (bap-*tyze*) *v.* [bap·tized; bap·tiz·ing] 1. To administer the sacrament of baptism. 2. To name; christen.—**bap·tiz·er** *n.*

bar *n.* 1. A long, solid piece of wood, metal, etc. 2. A portion or quantity shaped like a bar. 3. An obstacle; barrier. 4. Shoal; bank. 5. A counter over which liquor is served; also a room or establishment serving liquor. 6. *Law.* **a.** Place in court where prisoners stand. **b.** The legal profession. 7. *Music.* The line drawn perpendicularly across the staff dividing it into measures.—*v.* [barred; bar·ring] To obstruct; exclude; impede.—*prep.* Excluding; excepting.

barb *n.* 1. The sharp point projecting backward on an arrow, fishhook, etc., to prevent its extraction. 2. Horizontal branch of a feather.—**barb** *v.* To fit with barbs.

barb *n.* 1. One of a breed of horses introduced into Spain by the Moors. 2. A black or dun pigeon with a short beak.

bar·bar·i·an (bahr-*bair*-ee-un) *n.* A savage; uncivilized person. 2. A rude, uncultured individual.—**bar·bar·i·an** *adj.*—**bar·bar·i·an·ism** *n.*

bar·bar·ic (bahr-*bair*-ik) *adj.* Uncivilized; crudely striking or splendid.

bar·ba·rism (*bahr*-buh-rizm) *n.* 1. Uncivilized condition. 2. A violation of correct style or usage.—**bar·ba·rize** *v.* [bar·ba·rized; bar·ba·riz·ing].—**bar·ba·ri·za·tion** *n.*

bar·bar·i·ty (bahr-*bair*-ih-tee) *n.* [*pl.* -ties] Cruelty; savagery.

bar·ba·rous (*bahr*-buh-rus) *adj.* 1. Uncivilized; rude. 2. Savage; cruel.—**bar·ba·rous·ly** *adv.*—**bar·ba·rous·ness** *n.*

bar·be·cue (*bahr*-bih-kyoo) *n.* 1. A festive open-air gathering at which animals are roasted whole and eaten. 2. A hog or other animal thus roasted.—*v.* [bar·be·cued; bar·be·cu·ing] To roast whole.

barbed *adj.* Having barbs or points.

barbed wire. A protective wire with barbs at regular intervals.

bar·ber *n.* One whose business is shaving and cutting the hair.—**bar·ber** *v.*

bar·ber·ry (*bahr*-behr-ee) *n.* [*pl.* bar·ber·ries] A spiny shrub having oblong red berries.

bar·bi·tal (*bahr*-bih-tawl) *n.* A white powder used as a hypnotic drug.

bar·ca·role, bar·ca·rolle (*bahr*-kuh-rohl) *n.* A Venetian gondolier's song or one resembling it.

Barcelona (bahr-s'l-*oh*-nuh). Port in NE Spain.

bard *n.* A poet; minstrel.—**bard·ic** *adj.*

bare (*behr*) *adj.* 1. Naked; uncovered; exposed. 2. Simple; unadorned. 3. Empty; unfurnished. 4. Just sufficient; mere.—*v.* [bared; bar·ing].—**bar·er** *n.*—**bare·ness** *n.*

bare-ankled	barehanded	bare-skinned
bare-armed	bare-kneed	bare-skulled
bare-branched	bare-legged	bare-throated
bare bone	bare-naked	bare-toed
bare-fingered	bare-necked	bare-worn

bare·back *adj. & adv.* On a saddleless horse.

bare·faced *adj.* Brazen; shameless.—**bare·fac·ed·ly** *adv.*—**bare·fac·ed·ness** *n.*

bare·foot *adj. & adv.* Also **bare·foot·ed.** With the feet bare.

bare·head·ed *adj. & adv.* Without a head covering.—**bare·head·ed·ness** *n.*

bare·ly *adv.* 1. Hardly; scarcely. 2. Nakedly; without covering.

bar·gain (*bahr*-gun) *n.* 1. A contract or mutual agreement. 2. Article bought or sold at a low price; advantageous transaction.—*v.* 1. To haggle over a purchase. 2. To trade; negotiate.—**bar·gain·er, bar·gain·or** *n.*

barge (*bahrj*) *n.* A flat-bottomed boat for transporting goods. —*v.* [barged; barging] To enter rudely, without invitation.—**barge·man** *n.* [*pl.* -men].

BARGE

bar·i·tone, bar·y·tone (*bair*-uh-tohn) *n. Music.* A male voice between tenor and bass; also a man with such a voice.—**bar·i·tone, bar·y·tone** *adj.*

bar·i·um (*behr*-ee-um) *n.* A silver-white metallic element in the alkaline-earth group. (*Symbol:* Ba).—**bar·ic** *adj.*

bark *n.* The rough outer covering of trees and other plants.—*v.* 1. To peel; scrape the surface of. 2. To cover with bark.—**bark·y** *adj.*

bark *n.* The loud, abrupt cry of a dog, or a similar sound.—**bark** *v.*

bark, barque *n. Nautical.* 1. A three-masted vessel, square-rigged except for the mizzenmast. 2. *Poetic.* A boat.

bar·keep·er, bar·keep *n.* One who dispenses liquor at a bar.

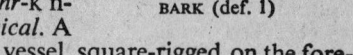

BARK (def. 1)

bark·en·tine, bar·quen·tine (*bahr*-k'n-teen) *n. Nautical.* A three-masted vessel, square-rigged on the foremast.

bark·er *n.* 1. An animal that barks. 2. *Slang.* A person stationed outside a show to announce the attraction within.

bar·ley (*bahr*-lee) *n.* A cereal used for food and malt beverages.

Barleycorn, John. A personification of whisky.

barm *n.* Yeast rising on fermented malt liquors.—**barm·y** *adj.*

barn *n.* A covered building for storing farm produce and stabling horses and cattle.

bar·na·cle (*bahr*-nuh-k'l) *n.* A small shellfish found clinging to rocks and ships' bottoms.

barn·storm *v.* To give performances throughout the country, esp. in rural areas.—**barn·storm·er** *n.*—**barn·storm·ing** *n. & adj.*

bar·o·graph (*bair*-uh-graf) *n.* A self-registering instrument for recording the variations in atmospheric pressure.—**bar·o·graph·ic** *adj.*

ba·rom·e·ter (buh-*rom*-uh-ter) *n.* An instrument for measuring the weight or pressure of the atmosphere.—**bar·o·met·ric, -ri·cal** *adj.* —**bar·o·met·ri·cal·ly** *adv.*—**ba·rom·e·try** *n.*

bar·on (*bair*-'n) *n.* Nobleman holding the lowest rank in the British peerage.—**bar·on·age** *n.* —**bar·on·ess** *n. fem.*

bar·on·et (*bair*-uh-net) *n.* Hereditary rank or title of honor below a baron, and not of the peerage.—**bar·on·et·age** *n.*— -et·cy *n.* [*pl.* -cies].

ba·ro·ni·al (buh-*roh*-nee-ul) *adj.* Pertaining to a baron or a barony.

bar·o·ny (*bair*-uh-nee) *n.* [*pl.* bar·o·nies] Rank and lands of a baron.

ba·roque (buh-*rohk*) *n.* Post-Renaissance school of art expressing the restless and fervent spirit of the Counter-Reformation.—*adj.* Ornate.

ba·rouche (buh-*roosh*) *n.* A four-wheeled carriage with a folding top.

BAROUCHE

bar·rack (*bair*-uk) *n.* [*usually pl.*] 1. A permanent building for lodging soldiers. 2. Temporary shelter for a group of workmen.— -rack *v.*— -rack·er *n.*

bar·ra·cu·da (bair-uh-*koo*-duh) *n.* A large, voracious fish, usually found in warm waters.

bar·rage (buh-*rahzh*) *n.* 1. *Military.* A curtain of concentrated artillery fire. 2. *Engineering.* Artificial obstruction placed in a stream to increase its depth.—*v.* [bar·raged; bar·rag·ing].

B

barrage balloon. Lighter-than-air balloons moored, in World War II, above merchant ships and cities as defense against air attack.

BARRAGE BALLOON

barred *adj.* 1. Blocked; obstructed. 2. Enclosed with bars. 3. Marked with bars. 'A barred hen.'

bar·rel (*bair*-'l) *n.* 1. A round wooden vessel, made of staves and bulging in the middle. 2. Quantity contained in a barrel. 3. A tube or cylinder.—*v.* [bar·reled, bar·relled; bar·rel·ing, bar·rel·ling].

bar·rel·house (*bair*-rul-howss) *n.* 1. *Jazz Music.* A style of jazz piano playing characterized by a heavily syncopated bass and a simple melodic line. 2. *Southern U.S.* A brothel.

BARREL

barrel organ. Small hand-operated musical instrument resembling an organ; a hurdy-gurdy.

bar·ren (*bair*-'n) *adj.* 1. Sterile; unfruitful; empty. 2. Unproductive; dull.—*n.* An unproductive tract of land.—**bar·ren·ly** *adv.*—**bar·ren·ness** *n.*

bar·rette (buh-*ret*) *n.* An ornamental hair clip.

bar·ri·cade (*bair*-uh-kayd) *n.* 1. A hastily erected fortification for obstructing the enemy's progress. 2. Any bar or obstruction. —*v.* (bair-uh-*kayd*) [bar·ri·cad·ed; -cad·ing].

bar·ri·er (*bair*-ee-er) *n.* Obstruction; boundary.

bar·ring *prep.* Excepting.

bar·ris·ter (*bair*-iss-ter) *n.* A lawyer who pleads in court; attorney.

bar·room (*bahr*-room) *n.* A room in which liquor is served over a bar.

bar·row (*bair*-oh) *n.* A box for conveying articles, set on a frame having one wheel and handles.

bar·row *n.* An ancient burial mound.

bar sinister. Popularly, the mark or social stigma of illegitimacy.

bar·tend·er (*bahr*-tend-er) *n.* Barkeeper; dispenser of liquor.

bar·ter (*bahr*-ter) *v.* To trade by exchanging one article for another.—**bar·ter** *n.*— -ter·er *n.*

Bart·lett (*bahrt*-lit) *n.* A fine variety of pear.

bas·al (*bays*-'l) *adj.* 1. Pertaining to the base. 2. Fundamental.—**bas·al·ly** *adv.*

basal metabolism. The heat production of the human body, measured when the body is fasting and at rest.

ba·salt (buh-*sawlt*) *n.* A dark, fine-grained rock of volcanic origin.—**ba·salt·ic** *adj.*

base *adj.* [bas·er; bas·est] 1. Low; mean; contemptible. 2. Of little value. 'The base metals.'—**base·ly** *adv.*—**base·ness** *n.*

base *n.* 1. Foundation; supporting part of an object. 2. *Chemistry.* A compound substance which unites with an acid to form a salt. 3. *Geometry.* The line forming the bottom part of a figure. 4. The main ingredient. 5. *Baseball.* One of the four points which a runner must touch to score. 6. *Military.* A protected place from which operations are directed.—*v.* [based; bas·ing].

base·ball *n.* 1. The national game of the U.S., played by two nine-man teams. 2. The ball used in this game.

base·board *n.* Mopboard; molding where the floor and wall meet.

base·less *adj.* Without foundation; invalid.

base·ment (*bays*-m'nt) *n.* Story or part of a building below the main floor.

bash *v.* *Slang.* To strike violently; crush out of shape.—**bash** *n.*

bash·ful (*bash*-f'l) *adj.* Shy; modest to excess. —**bash·ful·ly** *adv.*—**bash·ful·ness** *n.*

bas·ic (*bays*-ik) *adj.* 1. Essential; fundamental. 2. *Chemistry.* Alkaline.— -i·cal·ly *adv.*

Basic English. A copyrighted language of 850 English words with which, it is claimed, meaning can be adequately conveyed.

bas·il (*baz*-'l) *n.* A sweet flavoring herb of the mint family, used in cooking.

ba·sil·i·ca (buh-*sil*-ih-kuh) *n.* [*pl.* ba·sil·i·cas] 1. A building, esp. a church, whose central area is separated from the side aisles by rows of columns, with an apse at one end. 2. A code of laws of the Byzantine empire. —**ba·sil·i·can** *adj.*

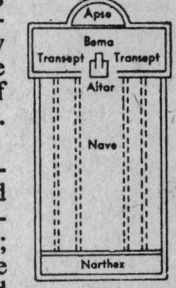
BASILICA

ba·sin (*bay*-s'n) *n.* 1. A circular, bowl-like utensil used to hold fluids. 2. A washbowl. 3. Any reservoir; pond; depression. 4. The whole tract of country drained by a river and its tributaries. 5. The amount held by a basin.—**ba·sined** *adj.*

ba·sis (*bay*-sis) *n.* [*pl.* ba·ses] Foundation; first principle; cause; major ingredient; essence.

bask *v.* 1. To relax in genial warmth. 2. To thrive; be exposed to a kindly influence.

bas·ket (*bas*-kit) *n.* 1. A receptacle of light, pliable materials interwoven or stapled. 2. The contents of a basket. 3. *Basketball.* a. A hoop strung with a knit web or netting. b. A goal or score.—**bas·ket·ry** *n.*

bas·ket·ball *n.* 1. A game played on an indoor court by two five-man teams, the object being to toss a ball through a basketlike hoop. 2. The large leather ball used in this sport.

Basque (*bask*) *n.* 1. The language spoken in the Basque provinces of NE Spain. 2. An inhabitant of the Basque provinces.—**Basque** *adj.*—**basque** *n.* A fitted bodice.

bas·re·lief (bah-rih-*leef*) *n.* A style of sculpturing figures so that they are only slightly raised above the background.

bass (*bass*) *n.* [*pl.* bass] A group of edible fishes of the perch family.

bass (*bayss*) *n.* [*pl.* basses] 1. *Music.* The lowest part in a musical score. 2. A voice adapted to the bass part. 3. The bass viol. 4. The singer or player of the bass notes.—**bass** *adj.*

bass drum. The largest drum, producing a deep, bass sound.

bas·set (*bass*-it) *n.* Also **basset hound.** A short-legged, stocky hunting dog.

bas·si·net (bass-uh-*net*) *n.* A padded wicker basket for holding an infant, often mounted on a mobile standard.

bas·soon (buh-*soon*) *n. Music.* An orchestral woodwind instrument producing deep notes.

bass viol (*bayss* vy-'l). *Music.* A large, violin-shaped orchestral string instrument of bass tone.

bass·wood (*bass*-wud) *n.* The American linden tree or wood cut from it.

bast *n.* Fibrous cordage material taken from linden trees, flax, etc.

bas·tard (*bass*-terd) *n.* 1. An illegitimate child. 2. *Colloquial.* A low, vicious person. 3. *Slang.* Chap; fellow.—*adj.* 1. Illegitimate. 2. Spurious; adulterated; not genuine. 3. Not standard; substandard.—**bas·tard·ize** *v.* [bas-tard-ized; bas·tard·iz·ing]—**bas·tard·i·za·tion** *n.* —**bas·tard·ly** *adj. & adv.*—**bas·tard·y** *n.*

bas·ti·na·do (bas-tuh-*nay*-doh) *n.* [*pl.* bas·ti·na·does] 1. A sound beating with a cudgel. 2. An oriental penalty consisting of beating the soles of the feet.—**bas·ti·na·do** *v.*

baste (*bayst*) *v.* [bast·ed; bast·ing] 1. To sew with long, usually temporary stitches. 2. *Cookery.* To pour drippings or other fat over meat while it roasts. 3. To beat; belabor; berate. —**bast·ing** *n.*

bas·tille, bas·tile (bass-*teel*) *n.* 1. A prison. 2. Fortification; tower. 3. [*cap.*] Political prison demolished by the French Revolutionaries, July 14, 1789.

bas·tion (*bass*-chun) *n. Fortification.* An outjutting from a rampart which allows protection of the rampart walls.

BASTION

bat *n.* A winged mammal of nocturnal habits.

bat *n.* 1. A heavy stick or club, esp. the tapered stick used in basball. 2. Lowgrade cotton batting.—*v.* [bat·ted; bat·ting] To hit with a club or bat.

BAT (1/7 life size)

BASSOON

batch *n.* Collection of similar things; group having a common origin. 'A batch of bread.'

bate *v.* [bat·ed; bat·ing] To lessen; reduce; soften in intensity. 'With bated breath.'

ba·teau (bat-*toh*) *n.* [*pl.* bateaux] A small, flat-bottomed river boat.

bath (*bath; bahth*) *n.* [*pl.* baths] 1. A tub for water in which to wash the body. 2. The act of bathing. 3. A liquid in which anything is immersed for chemical treatment. 4. Short for bathroom; lavatory.

bathe (*bayth*) *v.* [bathed; bath·ing] 1. To immerse in water or other fluid; surround with. 2. To apply a liquid with a sponge or cloth, for therapeutic purposes. 3. To swim. 4. To wash the body.—**bathe** *n.*—**bath·er** *n.*

ba·thos (*bay*-thos) *n.* An anticlimax; ludicrous descent from a noble plane to commonplaceness.—**ba·thet·ic** *adj.*

bath·room *n.* A lavatory; room for bathing.

bath·y·sphere (*bath*-iss-feer) *n.* A diving bell used for underwater exploration.

ba·tik, bat·tik (*bah*-tik) *n.* 1. A process of fabric color design in which areas to remain undyed are blotted out with wax. 2. A design or picture thus made. 3. The fabric containing it.—**ba·tik** *v.*

ba·tiste (buh-*teest*) *n.* A fine cotton cloth.

ba·ton (bat-*ahn*) *n.* 1. *Music.* A wand used by a conductor or teacher to indicate tempo. 2. A short, ornate staff or wand carried by a field marshal as a symbol of his rank.

ba·tra·chi·an (buh-*trayk*-ee-un) *adj.* Pertaining to such amphibious animals as frogs, toads, salamanders, etc.—**ba·tra·chi·an** *n.*

bats·man (*bats*-m'n) *n.* [*pl.* bats·men] *Baseball* and *Cricket.* The batter.

bat·tal·ion (buh-*tal*-yun) *n.* 1. *Military.* A unit commanded by a major or lieutenant colonel. 2. [*pl.*] Military forces collectively.

bat·ten (*bat*-'n) *v.* To grow fat in luxury.

bat·ten *n.* 1. A piece of wood used for flooring. 2. *Nautical.* A strip of steel used for fastening. 3. *Theater.* Strip of wood fastened to the bottom of a drop curtain to keep it taut.—*v.* To fasten with battens.

bat·ter *v.* 1. To beat; pound; belabor. 2. To dent; bruise; injure.—*n. Cookery.* A thin mixture of several ingredients beaten together.

bat·ter *n. Baseball* and *Cricket.* The player to whom the ball is being pitched.

bat·ter·ing-ram *n. Military.* In antiquity, a large beam with a head of iron, used to beat down the walls of besieged places.

bat·ter·y *n.* [*pl.* bat·ter·ies] 1. *Military.* A complement or series of heavy guns. 2. The personnel manning such a battery. 3. *Law.* Injury to an individual or his personal belongings through

BATTERING-RAM

beating. 4. *Baseball*. The pitcher and catcher of a team. 5. Any series, tier or set of related or identical things. 'A battery of floodlights.' 6. *Electricity*. A device for generating direct current by chemical means.

bat·ting *n*. Sheets or thin layers of fluffy cotton or wool.

bat·tle *n*. A great, long fight, esp. between two sizable forces.—*v*. [bat·tled; bat·tling].

bat·tle-ax, bat·tle-axe *n*. 1. An ax used in ancient warfare. 2. *Slang*. A shrewish woman.

battle fatigue. A psychoneurotic condition induced by the conflicts of modern warfare.

bat·tle·ment *n*. A notched or indented parapet. —**bat·tle·ment·ed** *adj*.

bat·tle·ship *n*. The most heavily armed and armored type of naval vessel.

bat·ty *adj*. [bat·ti·er; bat·ti·est] *Slang*. Silly; mentally deranged.

bau·ble (*baw*-b'l) *n*. A trifle; trinket; worthless finery.

baulk. *Variant spelling* of **balk.**

BATTLEMENT

baux·ite (*bawks*-yte) *n*. The ore which is the source of aluminum.

bawd *n*. A woman who procures prostitutes.

bawd·y *adj*. [bawd·i·er; bawd·i·est] Obscene; smutty; lewd.—**bawd·i·ly** *adv*.—**bawd·i·ness** *n*.

bawl *v*. 1. To cry out loud and long; bellow. 2. *Slang*. To cry; weep.—**bawl** *n*.—**bawl·er** *n*.

bawl out. To reprimand; reprove severely.

bay *adj*. Of a reddish-brown color.—*n*. An animal or pigment of this color.

bay *n*. 1. The deep-toned bark of a dog. 2. Impossibility of escape or avoiding a fight. 'A fox at bay.'—*v*. 1. To bark with a deep-chested note. 2. To corner.

bay *n*. 1. The water between two headlands or capes; inlet. 2. An isolated flatland between hills. 3. A subdivision of a building; bulkhead; stall. 4. A compartment in the fuselage of an airplane.

bay *n*. A family of glossy-leaved evergreen trees; laurel.

bay·ber·ry (*bay*-beh-ree) *n*. [*pl*. -ries] 1. A seacoast shrub with clusters of waxy gray berries used for making candles. 2. A tree found in Jamaica whose leaves furnish an oil used to perfume bay rum.

bay·o·net (*bay*-uh-net) *n*. A daggerlike knife attached to the muzzle-end of a rifle barrel.—**bay·o·net** *v*.

BAYONET

bay·ou (*by*-oo) *n*. [*pl*. bay·ous] A marshy outlet of a river or lake.

bay rum. An aromatic liquid with alcohol base, used as a skin and scalp lotion.

bay window. 1. *Architecture*. A window covering a recess or bay in a room. 2. *Slang*. A prominent abdomen.

ba·zaar, ba·zar (buh-*zahr*) *n*. 1. A market place; exchange. 2. A sale of miscellaneous items for charity.

ba·zoo·ka (buh-*zoo*-kuh) *n*. 1. A portable rocket gun used as an antitank weapon. 2. A hill-billy musical instrument remotely resembling a trombone.

BAY WINDOW

be *v*. [*present indicative*: am, is, are; *past*: was, were; *past participle*: been; *present participle*: being] 1. To exist. 'To think is to be.' 2. To have a certain condition. 'He was ill.' 3. To equal; represent. 'Six is a half dozen.' 4. To remain; stay; continue. 'The train is in motion.' 5. To happen; occur; befall. 'Woe be unto you.' 6. Auxiliary verb used to form tense or passive voice. 'I was elected; he is singing.'

be- *Prefix*. 1. Thoroughly; fully. 'Benight, bedew.' 2. Cover with; surround with. 'Besmear, bedabble.' 3. Over-ornately. 'Bejewel.' 4. Hence; in a direction away from. 'Betake.' 5. To cause; effect. 'Befoul.'

beach *n*. The shore of the sea or a lake.—*v*. To land on a beach.—**beach·y** *adj*.

beach·comb·er *n*. 1. In the tropics, a degraded white man who frequents the water front. 2. A long, sweeping wave.

beach·head *n*. *Military*. A position established on a beach in the face of enemy opposition.

beach wagon. A station wagon.

bea·con (*bee*-kun) *n*. 1. A signal to give warning or guidance. 2. A radio station that transmits signals to guide mariners and pilots. 3. Anything that guides or pilots.—**bea·con** *v*.

bead *n*. 1. A little, perforated ball or form strung on a thread and used as necklace, rosary, decoration, etc. 2. Any tiny, globular body; droplet; bubble. 3. A small projection on a gunbarrel for aiming. 4. An aim. 'He drew a bead on it.' 5. *Architecture*. A kind of molding, rounded and narrow. 6. [*pl*.] A string of beads.—**bead** *v*.—**bead·y** *adj*.

bead·ing *n*. 1. *Architecture*. A molding in imitation of a bead. 2. Embroidery or other work done in beads. 3. Beads collectively. 4. A decorative trimming.

bea·dle (*bee*-d'l) *n*. One who leads university or church processions; macebearer.

bea·gle (*bee*-g'l) *n*. A compactly built, short-haired hunting dog with drooping ears.

BEAGLE (1/18 life size)

beak *n*. 1. The bill of a bird or turtle. 2. *Slang*.

The nose. 3. Anything beak-like in form or function.—**beaked** *adj.*

beak·er *n.* A large glass cup, usually with a rudimentary spout.

beam (*beem*) *n.* 1. *Construction.* Long, rigid, strong piece of wood or metal to support or join. 2. A ray or stream of rays emitted from a radiant body. 3. The main axis of a deer's horns, bearing the antlers. 4. *Nautical.* The greatest width of a vessel. 5. The crossbar of a balance. 6. An arm or lever in an engine transferring force from the piston rod to the parts utilizing the power. 7. Roller on a loom which bears the warp or rolls off the finished textile. 8. *Radio.* Path of parallel radio waves transmitted by and received on directional antennas, as a guide to navigators.—*v.* 1. To emit rays. 2. To smile radiantly. —**beam·ing, beam·ish** *adj.*—**beam·ing·ly** *adv.*

bean (*been*) *n.* 1. A group of pod-producing plants of the pea family. 2. The green pod or ripened seed of this plant. 3. Any seed similar to a bean. 4. *Slang.* The head.—*v. Slang.* To hit someone on the head with a missile.

bear (*bair*) *n.* 1. A large, shaggy, five-toed mammal. 2. Any animal closely resembling a bear. 3. *Stock Market.* One who promotes or hopes for depreciation in the value of stocks and securities. 4. A grumpy, ill-mannered person. 5. [*cap.*] One of two constellations of the Northern Hemisphere; big or little dipper.—**bear** *v.* To attempt to drive down the price of stocks; sell short.—**bear** *adj.*

BEAR (1/80 life size)

bear *v.* [bore; borne, born; bear·ing] 1. To support; sustain. 2. To endure. 3. To carry; convey. 4. To give; render. 5. To harbor, as a grudge. 6. To possess, as an attribute or characteristic; contain; have. 7. To behave; comport. 8. To give birth to; yield. 9. To relate; pertain. 10. To spread. 'To bear tales.'

bear·a·ble (*bair*-uh-b'l) *adj.* Tolerable; endurable.—**bear·a·ble·ness** *n.*—**bear·a·bly** *adv.*

beard *n.* 1. The hair of the face. 2. Any beardlike growth, as corn tassels. 3. A barb or barb-shaped implement.—*v.* 1. To furnish with a beard. 2. To defy; confront boldly. —**beard·ed** *adj.*—**beard·less** *adj.*

bear·er (*bair*-er) *n.* 1. Carrier; one who holds a bill of exchange. 2. Pallbearer. 3. Tree or plant that produces a yield.

bear·ing *n.* 1. Deportment; mien; carriage. 2. Patient endurance. 3. Time, duration, or capability of producing. 4. Location of one object in reference to another or to the points of the compass. 5. *Radio.* A line of direction determined by a direction finder. 6. A yield or crop. 7. *Machinery.* A piece in which a shaft or other moving part revolves.

bear·ish *adj.* 1. Resembling a bear; grumpy.

2. Driving stock market prices down.—**bear·ish·ly** *adv.*—**bear·ish·ness** *n.*

bear out. To uphold; substantiate.

bear·skin *n.* 1. The hide of a bear. 2. A coat or other article of or like a bear's fur.

bear up. To have fortitude; maintain one's optimism or efficiency.

bear with. To endure patiently.

beast *n.* 1. Any large, four-footed mammal. 2. A brutal, animal-like person. 3. One's animal desires or nature. 'The beast in me.'

beast·ly *adj.* 1. Brutal; coarse; beastlike. 2. *Colloquial.* Deplorable; abominable. —**beast·li·ness** *n.*

beat *v.* [beat; beat·en; beat·ing] 1. To pound; strike repeatedly. 2. To hammer into shape. 3. To mix or agitate. 4. To step. 5. To drive game before one. 6. To defeat. 7. *Colloquial.* To baffle. 8. To pulsate. 9. To make progress against the wind by sailing zigzag. 10. To indicate tempo by regular strokes. 11. *Colloquial.* To cheat; swindle. 12. *Military.* To drum; sound an order.—*n.* 1. A pulsation; repeated blow. 2. A route frequently gone over. 'A policeman's beat.' 3. *Acoustics.* Pulsation resulting from the joint vibrations of two similar sounds. 4. *Music.* **a.** The motion of the hand or foot in indicating the tempo. **b.** A regularly recurring accent. 5. *Journalism.* **a.** An exclusive story; a scoop. **b.** A regular assignment.—**beat·er** *n.*

beat·en *adj.* 1. Worn smooth by use or treading. 2. Conquered. 3. Pounded; hammered. 4. Baffled. 5. Worn out. 6. Whipped or leavened by beating.

be·a·tif·ic (bee-uh-*tif*-ik) *adj.* Causing deep joy.

be·at·i·fy (bee-*at*-ih-fy) *v.* [be·at·i·fied; be·at·i·fy·ing] 1. To make blissfully happy. 2. *Roman Catholic Church.* To decree that a person is received into heaven and is to be reverenced as blessed.— **-fi·ca·tion** (-fih-*kay*-shun) *n.*

beat·ing *n.* 1. Flogging; punishment. 2. Pulsation; throbbing.

be·at·i·tude (bee-*at*-ih-tyood) *n.* 1. Blessedness; supreme bliss. 2. [*cap.*] In Christ's Sermon on the Mount, one of the nine statements that begin: "Blessed are . . ."

beau (*boh*) *n.* [*pl.* beaux, beaus] 1. A suitor; boy-friend. 2. A foppish dandy.

beau·te·ous (*byoo*-tee-us) *adj.* Sensuously lovely.— **-te·ous·ly** *adv.*— **-te·ous·ness** *n.*

beau·ti·ful (*byoo*-tih-ful) *adj.* Lovely; aesthetically pleasing.— **-ful·ly** *adv.*— **-ful·ness** *n.*

beau·ti·fy (*byoo*-tih-fy) *v.* [beau·ti·fied; beau·ti·fy·ing] To embellish; adorn; decorate.—**beau·ti·fi·ca·tion** (-*kay*-shun) *n.*—**beau·ti·fi·er** *n.*

beau·ty (*byoo*-tee) *n.* [*pl.* beau·ties] 1. Loveliness; elegance; those qualities giving pleasure to the mind or senses. 2. A particularly lovely or pleasing quality or thing.

beauty spot. A natural or simulated mole or patch on the face.

beaux-arts (boh-*zahr*) *n. pl.* The arts of design, poetry, music, the dance, and drama.

bea·ver *n.* 1. A fur-bearing rodent of the temperate regions, noted for its ability to dam up streams. 2. The fur of the beaver. 3. Cotton or woolen cloth in imitation of this fur.

BEAVER (1/23 life size)

be·calm (bih-*kahm*) *v.* 1. To make quiet; still. 2. *Nautical.* To stall for want of wind.

be·cause (bih-*kawz*) *conj.* For the reason that.

because of. Owing to; on account of.

beck *n.* 1. Bidding; command. 2. A sign or gesture of call.

beck·on (*bek*-un) *v.* 1. To signal; call by gesturing. 2. To entice; lure.—**beck·on** *n.* —**beck·on·er** *n.*—**beck·on·ing·ly** *adv.*

be·cloud (bih-*klowd*) *v.* To cloud over; veil as with a cloud.

be·come (bih-*kum*) *v.* [be·came; be·come; be·com·ing] 1. To pass from one condition to another. 2. To be suitable to; befit; grace. 3. To come to pass; occur.

become of. To happen to; be the fate of.

be·com·ing *adj.* 1. Suitable; appropriate; proper. 2. Attractive; pleasing.—**be·com·ing·ly** *adv.*—**be·com·ing·ness** *n.*

bed *n.* 1. Article of furniture for resting or sleeping. 2. Anything suggestive of a bed or a resting place. 3. The bottom of a body of water. 4. *Geology.* A stratum; layer. 5. A small, intensively tilled plot or area for plants. 6. A flat, bedlike heap.—*v.* [bed·ded; -ding].

bedchamber	bed lamp	bedspring
bedcover	bedpost	bedstead
bedfellow	bedquilt	bedtime

be·dab·ble (bih-*dab*-'l) *v.* [be·dab·bled; be·dab·bling] To splash; sprinkle.

be·daub (bih-*dawb*) *v.* To smear; rub over; soil.

Bedeaux system. Technique for increasing output per man in industrial plants; speed-up.

bed·bug *n.* A bloodsucking insect which infests household furnishings.

bed·clothes (*bed*-clohz) *n. pl.* Blankets and other bed coverings.

bed·ding *n.* 1. The placing in a bed. 2. Bedclothes or other bed-making materials. 3. *Geology.* Stratification. 4. Matrix; that in which something is embedded.—**bed·ding** *adj.*

be·deck (bih-*dek*) *v.* To adorn; decorate.

be·dev·il (bih-*dev*-'l) *v.* 1. To throw into confusion; befuddle. 2. To harass; torment. 3. To bewitch fiendishly.—**be·dev·il·ment** *n.*

be·dew (bih-*dyoo*, bee-, -*doo*) *v.* To moisten.

Bedford cord. A durable worsted fabric with a pronounced wale or rib.

bed·fel·low *n.* 1. A bed partner. 2. A partner or comrade, esp. in politics.

be·diz·en (bih-*diz*-'n; -*dye*-z'n) *v.* To adorn flashily.—**be·diz·en·ment** *n.*

bed·lam (*bed*-l'm) *n.* 1. Loud confusion; uproar. 2. A mental hospital. 3. A madman.

—bed·lam *adj.*—**bed·lam·ite** *n.*—**bed·lam·ize** *v.* [bed·lam·ized; bed·lam·iz·ing].

Bed·ou·in (*bed*-oo-in) *n.* One of a tribe of nomadic Arabs.—**Bed·ou·in** *adj.*—**Bed·ou·in·ism** *n.*

bed·pan *n.* 1. A shallow vessel for the excretions of bedridden persons. 2. A pan for preheating beds.

be·drag·gle (bih-*drag*-'l) *v.* [be·drag·gled; be·drag·gling] To make untidy by soiling or wetting.—**be·drag·gled** *adj.*

bed·rid·den *adj.* Also **bed·rid.** Kept in bed through illness or age.

bed·rock *n.* 1. *Geology.* The solid rock formation under the shale and other surface strata. 2. The basis; bottom; foundation.

bed·room *n.* A room used mainly for sleeping.

bed·side *n.* Location or station near the side of a bed.—**bed·side** *adj.*

bedside manner. A physician's cheerful, reassuring attitude toward bedridden patients.

bed·sore *n. Medicine.* A persistent sore appearing in patients long bedridden, caused by localized pressure.

bed·spread *n.* A decorative covering for a bed.

bed·stead *n.* A frame for supporting a bed.

bee *n.* 1. A hairy, thick-bodied winged insect, esp. a honey-producing one. 2. An industrious person. 3. A sociable meeting for communal work or spell-downs.

bee·bread *n.* Pollen of flowers collected by bees and prepared as food for their young.

beech *n.* [*pl.* beech·es] A hardwood tree with smooth gray bark, native of north temperate regions; also its wood or edible nuts.—**beech·en** *adj.*

beef *n.* [*pl.* beeves; beefs] 1. The flesh of cattle. 2. An adult bull or cow. 3. *Slang.* A grievance; complaint. 4. *Colloquial.* Brawn; physical strength or bulk.—*v. Slang.* To complain; state a grievance.

beef·y *adj.* [beef·i·er; beef·i·est] 1. Fleshy; brawny; stout. 2. Phlegmatic; stolid; dull. —**beef·i·ness** *n,*

beef·steak (*beef*-stayk) *n.* A cut of beef from the upper leg of a bull or cow.

bee·hive *n.* A compartmented box in which bees live and produce honeycomb. —**bee·hive** *adj.*

bee·line *n.* A direct route or course.

Be·el·ze·bub (bee-*el*-zih-bub) *n.* 1. A Philistine god. 2. Variously, the Devil himself or a demon immediately below him in rank.

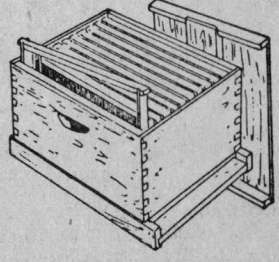

BEEHIVE

beer *n.* 1. An alcoholic liquor made from malted grain. 2. One of several fermented or carbonated beverages.

beer·y *adj.* [beer·i·er; beer·i·est] 1. Like or influenced by beer. 2. Maudlin.—**beer·i·ness** *n.*

bees·wax (*beez*-waks) *n.* The wax produced by bees in forming honeycomb.—**bees·wax** *v.*

beet *n.* A family of herbs grown for their edible roots or for greens.

bee·tle *n.* A flying insect, whose outer wings form a hard protective sheath.

bee·tle *n.* 1. A heavy wooden mallet or masher. 2. A fabric-finishing machine that rolls and hammers the cloth. —*v.* [bee·tled; bee·tling].—**bee·tler** *n.*

BEETLE (1/2 life size)

bee·tle *v.* [bee·tled; bee·tling] To protrude; hang or extend over.—**bee·tle, bee·tling** *adj.*

bee·tle-browed *adj.* 1. Having a jutting, overhanging forehead. 2. Lowering; scowling.

beeves. *Plural* of beef.

be·fall *v.* [be·fell; be·fall·en; be·fall·ing] To take place; come to pass.

be·fit *v.* [be·fit·ted; be·fit·ting] To be suitable to or worthy of; become.—**be·fit·ting** *adj.* —**be·fit·ting·ly** *adv.*

be·fog *v.* [be·fogged; be·fog·ging] To confuse; obscure.

be·fool *v.* To trick; dupe; make a fool of.

be·fore *prep.* 1. Preceding in time, space, order, value, etc.; ahead of. 2. In the presence of. 3. Being acted upon by.—*adv.* 1. In front; ahead. 2. Previously; priorly. 3. Ahead of time. 'Come for breakfast, not before.' —*conj.* 1. Rather than. 2. Prior to the time that.

be·fore·hand *adv.* In advance; in anticipation.

be·foul *v.* To soil; make foul.

be·friend (bee-*frend*) *v.* To assist; act as a friend to.

be·fud·dle *v.* [be·fud·dled; be·fud·dling] To confuse; bewilder.

beg *v.* [begged; beg·ging] 1. To ask for charity. 2. To entreat; implore. 3. To accept without evidence. 'To beg the question.'

be·gan. *Past tense* of begin.

be·get *v.* [be·got; be·got·ten, be·got; be·get·ting] To procreate; produce; cause. —**be·get·ter** *n.*

beg·gar (*beg*-er) *n.* 1. A humble supplicant or asker. 2. One who lives by charity; poverty-stricken person.—*v.* 1. To impoverish. 2. To exceed the possibilities of; exhaust.—**beg·gar·dom** *n.*—**beg·gar·er** *n.*—**beg·gar·hood** *n.*

beg·gar·ly *adj.* 1. Mean; wretched; despicable. 2. Penniless; indigent.—**beg·gar·li·ness** *n.*

beg·gar·y *n.* [*pl.* beg·gar·ies] 1. Extreme indigence. 2. Beggars generally.

be·gin *v.* [be·gan; be·gun; be·gin·ning] 1. To commence; start. 2. To become existent. 3. To invent; originate.—**be·gin·ner** *n.*

be·gin·ning *n.* 1. Commencement; inception; start. 2. Origin; cause.

be·gone (bee-*gawn*) *interj.* Depart; go away.

be·girt *adj.* Girded; bound about.

be·go·ni·a (beh-*gohn*-yuh) *n.* A family of tropical plants noted for their beautiful flowers and leaves.

be·grime *v.* [be·grimed; be·grim·ing] To soil deeply; make grimy.

be·grudge *v.* [be·grudged; be·grudg·ing] 1. To envy; covet. 2. Give grumblingly or unwillingly. —**be·grudg·ing·ly** *adv.*

be·guile (bee-*gyle*) *v.* [be·guiled; be·guil·ing] 1. To delude; deceive; cheat. 2. To entertain; amuse. 3. To while; make pass pleasingly.—**be·guile·ment** *n.*—**be·guil·er** *n.*

BEGONIA

be·guine (buh-*geen*) *n.* A Latin-American folk dance.

be·half (bee-*haf*) *n.* Advantage; benefit; interest; stead.

be·have *v.* [be·haved; be·hav·ing] 1. To act; comport. 2. To be good. 3. *Psychology.* To react to internal or environmental stimuli.

be·hav·ior (bee-*hayv*-yer) *n.* Also **be·hav·iour.** 1. Conduct; actions; deportment. 2. Any manifestation of physical or chemical properties. 3. *Psychology.* Total overt effect of an environment on a personality.

be·hav·ior·ism (bee-*hayv*-yer-izm) *n.* School of psychology which holds that all human behavior can be analyzed in terms of stimulus-response reactions, and denies the existence of consciousness, sensation, or will.—**be·hav·ior·ist** *n.* & *adj.*—**be·hav·ior·is·tic** *adj.*

be·head (bee-*hed*) *v.* To cut the head from the body.

be·he·moth (bee-*hee*-muth) *n.* A huge beast mentioned by Job in the Old Testament.

be·hest *n.* Bidding; command.

be·hind (bee-*hynde*) *adv.* 1. In the rear. 2. Backward. 3. Past in point of time. 4. Remaining after one's departure. 5. Slow; retardedly. 'The watch runs behind.'—*prep.* After in time, place, progress, rank, etc. 2. Remaining after. 3. Inferior to. 4. Giving support to; backing.—*n.* *Colloquial.* The buttocks; backside.—**be·hind** *adj.*

be·hind·hand *adv.* Tardily; overdue; in arrears. —**be·hind·hand** *adj.*

be·hold *v.* [be·held; be·held, be·hold·en; be·hold·ing] To see; gaze at; contemplate. —*interj.* Look!; observe!—**be·hold·er** *n.*

be·hold·en *adj.* Obligated; indebted.

be·hoove, be·hove *v.* [be·hooved; be·hoov·ing] To be necessary or appropriate.

beige (*bayzh*) *n.* An unbleached, undyed woolen fabric or its color.—*adj.* Of a light tan color.

be·ing. *Present participle* of be.—*n.* 1. Existence; living. 2. A creature; entity; organism.

be·jew·el (bih-*joo*-ul) *v.* To adorn with jewels, esp. too many of them.

B

be·la·bor (bih-*lay*-ber) *v.* 1. To beat long and hard; drub. 2. To give a tongue lashing to.

be·lat·ed (bih-*layt*-ed) *adj.* Overdue; tardy. —**be·lat·ed·ly** *adv.*—**be·lat·ed·ness** *n.*

be·lay (bih-*lay*) *v. Nautical.* To make fast by taking turns about a cleat or belaying pin.

belaying pin. *Nautical.* A small pin to which running ropes are fastened.

belch *v.* 1. To emit stomach gases through the mouth. 2. To eject violently.—**belch** *n.*

bel·dam (*bel*-dum), **bel·dame** (-daym) *n.* An old, ugly woman; hag.

be·lea·guer (bih-*lee*-ger) *v.* To besiege; blockade; surround.

bel·fry (*bel*-free) *n.* [*pl.* bel·fries] A bell tower, esp. of a church.—**bel·fried** *adj.*

Bel·gi·an (*bel*-jee-un, -jun) *n.* An inhabitant of Belgium.—**Bel·gi·an** *adj.*

Be·li·al (*bee*-lee-ul) *n.* 1. Satan. 2. An evil spirit or demon.

be·lie (bih-*lye*) *v.* [be·lied; be·ly·ing] 1. To contradict; give the lie to. 2. To represent falsely. 3. To show to be false. 4. To speak falsehoods of.

be·lief (bih-*leef*) *n.* 1. Conviction; confidence; trust. 2. Faith; creed; tenets. 3. Acceptance as truth.

be·lieve (bih-*leev*) *v.* [be·lieved; be·liev·ing] 1. To put credence in; have confidence in. 2. To suppose; have an opinion.—**be·liev·a·ble** *adj.*—**be·liev·er** *n.*—**be·liev·ing·ly** *adv.*

be·lit·tle (bih-*lit*-’l) *v.* [be·lit·tled; be·lit·tling] To disparage; minimize; make seem insignificant.

bell *n.* 1. A flare-mouth metal vessel or form that sounds a clear, ringing note when struck. 2. Any bell-shaped object. 3. *Nautical.* [*Usually pl.*] Division of time, based one bell per half hour for four hours.—**bell** *n.*

bel·la·don·na (bel-uh-*don*-uh) *n.* A poisonous plant whose juice dilates the pupils of the eyes.

bell·boy *n.* A service employee who responds to a bell or call, as in a hotel.

bell·buoy (*bel*-boy). *Nautical.* A buoy that, when agitated by waves, sounds a warning.

belle *n.* 1. A beautiful young woman. 2. The outstanding beauty of a particular group. —**belle·dom** *n.*

belles-lettres (bel-*let*-r’) *n. pl.* Pure literature as opposed to informative and practical writings.—**bel·le·tris·tic** (bel-leh-*tris*-tik) *adj.*

bell·hop *n. Slang.* A bellboy; porter.

bel·li·cose (*bel*-ih-kohs) *adj.* Pugnacious; quarrelsome.—**bel·li·cose·ly** *adv.*—**bel·li·cos·i·ty** *n.*

bel·li·ger·ent (buh-*lij*-er-unt) *adj.* Warlike; warring; likely to cause war.—*n.* A nation waging war; person engaged in fighting.—**bel·lig·er·ence, bel·lig·er·ency** *n.*—**bel·lig·er·ent·ly** *adv.*

bel·low (*bel*-oh) *v.* To roar; give a loud, deep noise; bawl.—**bel·low** *n.*—**bel·low·er** *n.*

bel·lows *n. sing. & pl.* 1. An instrument or machine for producing a forcible stream of air by compressing an air-filled bag. 2. The folding part of some cameras.

bell·weth·er (*bel*-weth-er) *n.* A belled sheep which leads the flock.

bel·ly *n.* [*pl.* bel·lies] 1. The abdomen. 2. The stomach or appetite. 3. Anything bellylike in form or location,—*v.* [bel·lied; bel·ly·ing] To fill; swell out.

belly·ache (*bel*-ee-ayk) *v.* [bel·ly·ached; -ach·ing] *Slang.* To complain.—**bel·ly·ach·ing** *n.*

belly-button *n. Colloquial.* The navel.

be·long (bih-*long*) *v.* 1. To be the property of. 2. To have a special relation to; be connected with. 3. To be a member of a group or community. 4. To be appropriately placed or classified; be suitable.

be·long·ing *n.* [*Usually pl.*] Property; possessions.

be·lov·ed (bih-*luh*-vid, -*luhvd*) *adj.* Dear to one; greatly loved.—**be·lov·ed** *n.*

be·low (bih-*loh*) *prep.* 1. Beneath; under. 2. Inferior or subordinate to. 3. Unworthy of; unbefitting.—*adv.* 1. Lower down; beneath. 2. At the bottom of a page; following. 3. Beneath heaven; in hell or on earth.

belt *n.* 1. A strap or tie encircling the waist. 2. A strip or area similar in color, climate, etc. 3. Any beltlike object or strip. 4. *Slang.* A blow. 5. *Machinery.* An endless strip of leather, fiber, etc., which conveys power or materials. 6. *Geography.* Narrow sound or strait.—*v.* 1. To encircle; surround. 2. *Slang.* To hit.—**belt·ed** *adj.*—**belt·ing** *n.*

be·moan (bih-*mohn*) *v.* To lament; bewail.

be·muse (bih-*myooz*) *v.* [be·mused; be·mus·ing] To make muddled or stupefied.—**be·mused** *adj.*

bench *n.* 1. A long seat. 2. A strong table on which mechanics prepare their work. 3. **a.** A seat reserved for judges in a courtroom. **b.** The court or judges collectively. 4. *Geography.* A narrow, raised flatland or terrace.—*v.* 1. To furnish with benches. 2. *Sports Slang.* To put a player among the reserves.—**bench·er** *n.*

benchboard	benchland	benchman
benchfellow	benchlike	bench mark
bench-hardened	bench-made	bench work

bend *v.* [bent; bend·ing] 1. To make crooked or curved. 2. To incline; turn. 3. To direct to a certain point. 4. To subdue; make submissive. 5. To tie a knot in; fasten. 6. To direct toward; focus upon. 7. To bow; humble oneself.—*n.* 1. A curve; turn. 2. A twisting or curving from a straight line. 3. [*pl.*] *Colloquial.* Serious disease caused by too rapid a change from a high to a low atmospheric pressure; caisson disease.—**bend·a·ble** *adj.*

Ben Day process. 1. A process of shading, tinting, or stippling engravings by a photographic-mechanical operation. 2. A print or background made by this process.

bend·er *n.* 1. *Slang.* A drinking spree. 2. Person or thing that bends.

be·neath *adv. & prep.* Below; under.

ben·e·dic·i·te (ben-uh-*dis*-uh-tee) *interj.* Bless you.—*n.* [*cap.*] A hymn or canticle.

ben·e·dict (*ben*-uh-dikt) *n.* A man recently married, esp. one who has long been a bachelor.

Ben·e·dic·tine (ben-uh-*dik*-tin) *n.* A member of a scholarly religious order founded by St. Benedict.—**Ben·e·dic·tine** *adj.*

ben·e·dic·tine (ben-uh-*dik*-teen) *n.* A sweet liqueur developed by Benedictine monks.

ben·e·dic·tion (ben-uh-*dik*-shun) *n.* 1. A blessing; grace; thanksgiving; well-wishing. 2. *Ecclesiastic.* Short prayer delivered at the end of a service.—**ben·e·dic·to·ry** *adj.*

ben·e·fac·tion (ben-uh-*fak*-shun) *n.* A charitable donation or gift.

ben·e·fac·tor (*ben*-uh-fak-ter) *n.* One who bestows a favor.—**ben·e·fac·tress** *n. fem.*

ben·e·fice (*ben*-uh-fis) *n. Ecclesiastical.* 1. An endowed church. 2. Revenue from church endowments.—*v.* [ben·e·ficed; ben·e·fic·ing].

be·nef·i·cence (buh-*nef*-ih-s'ns) *n.* 1. Generosity; goodness; kindness. 2. A kindly deed or donation.—**be·nef·i·cent** *adj.*— -i·cent·ly *adv.*

ben·e·fi·cial (ben-uh-*fish*-ul) *adj.* 1. Advantageous; wholesome; helpful. 2. *Law.* Getting income from property without owning it.

ben·e·fi·ci·ar·y (ben-uh-*fish*-uh-ree) *n.* [*pl.* ben·e·fi·ci·ar·ies] 1. The recipient of a gift, legacy, insurance policy, etc. 2. *Ecclesiastical.* Receiver of a benefice.—**ben·e·fi·ci·ar·y** *adj.*

ben·e·fit (*ben*-uh-fit) *n.* 1. Profit; advantage; anything beneficial. 2. A performance the proceeds of which go to some charitable cause. 3. A payment made on an insurance policy. —**ben·e·fit** *v.*

be·nev·o·lent (buh-*nev*-uh-l'nt) *adj.* Kindly; philanthropic; charitable.—**be·nev·o·lence** *n.* —**be·nev·o·lent·ly** *adv.*

ben·ga·line (*beng*-guh-leen) *n.* A finely ribbed dress fabric.

be·night·ed (bih-*nyte*-ed) *adj.* Ignorant; unenlightened.—**be·night·ed·ness** *n.*

be·nign (bih-*nyne*) *adj.* 1. Gracious; gentle; kindly. 2. *Medicine.* Mild; not malignant. —**be·nign·ly** *adv.*

be·nig·nant (bih-*nig*-n'nt) *adj.* 1. Kindly; benevolent; charitable. 2. *Medicine.* Not malignant; not dangerous.—**be·nig·nan·cy** *n.*—**be·nig·nant·ly** *adv.*

be·nig·ni·ty (bih-*nig*-nih-tee) *n.* [*pl.* be·nig·ni·ties] 1. Kindness; benevolence; generosity. 2. Kindly or altruistic deed.

benison (*ben*-ih-sun) *n.* Benediction; blessing.

bent. *Past tense & past participle* of **bend.**

bent *n.* Inclination; aptitude; disposition.—*adj.* Curved; crooked.

be·numb (bih-*num*) *v.* To deprive of sensation; anesthetize.

ben·ze·drine (*ben*-zuh-dreen) *n.* Trade name for amphetamine sulfate, used to stimulate the central nervous system and decrease fatigue.

ben·zene (*ben*-zeen) *n.* A colorless, pungent hydrocarbon liquid derived from coal tar.

ben·zine (*ben*-zeen) *n.* A petroleum product similar to gasoline, used for cleaning, fuel, etc.

ben·zo·in (*ben*-zoh-in) *n.* A thick, white, resinous juice, obtained from a Sumatran tree, used in cosmetics and medicinals.—**ben·zo·ic** *adj.*

ben·zol (*ben*-zohl) *n.* A coal-tar derivative used in dyes, as a solvent, etc.; benzene.

Be·o·wulf (*bay*-uh-wulf) *n.* Hero of an Anglo-Saxon epic poem of the same name.

be·queath (bih-*kweeth*) *v.* To leave as a legacy; will; hand down.—**be·queath·al** *n.*

be·quest (bih-*kwest*) *n.* A legacy; something willed.

be·rate (bih-*rayt*) *v.* [be·rat·ed; be·rat·ing] To scold harshly; reprimand.

Ber·ber (*ber*-ber) *n.* A group of North African tribes; also, their language.—**Ber·ber** *adj.*

be·reave (buh-*reev*) *v.* [be·reaved; be·reft; be·reav·ing] 1. To deprive; strip. 2. To desolate or sadden, as by a loved one's death.

be·ret (buh-*ray*) *n.* A soft, visorless cap with a billowing, round crown.

berg *n.* A large mass or mountain, usually of ice.

ber·ga·mot (*ber*-guh-mot) *n.* 1. A south European citrus fruit whose peel has a perfume-yielding oil. 2. A mint with a bergamot savor.

ber·i·ber·i (*behr*-ee-*behr*-ee) *n.* A vitamin-B deficiency disease marked by muscular atrophy and neuralgic pains.

ber·lin (ber-*lin*) *n.* 1. An automobile with a glass partition between front and back seats. 2. A worsted yarn spun of the highest quality, softest fibers.

berm, berme (*berm*) *n. Southern U.S.* The shoulder of a road.

Ber·mu·da (ber-*myoo*-duh). Chief of a group of British-owned islands about 600 mi. E of Georgia, U.S.A.—**Ber·mu·di·an** *n. & adj.*

Bermuda onion. A variety of large white onion, first developed in Bermuda.

Bern, Berne (*bern*, *behrn*). The capital of the Swiss Confederation.

ber·ry (*behr*-ee) *n.* [*pl.* ber·ries] 1. A small succulent or pulpy fruit containing many seeds. 2. Something similar to a berry.—*v.* [ber·ried; ber·ry·ing]. To gather berries.—**ber·ried** *adj.*

ber·serk (*ber*-serk) *adj.* Insanely violent; frenzied.

berth *n.* 1. *Nautical.* A station or place where a ship can dock or anchor. 2. A bunk or shelflike bed on a ship or train. 3. Job; situation; allotted place. 4. Ample room to avoid or maneuver in.—**berth** *v.*

ber·yl (*behr*-ul) *n.* A hard mineral gem crystallized in six-sided prisms, the emerald being a rich variety.—**ber·yl·line** *adj.*

be·ryl·li·um (ber-*il*-ee-um) *n.* A hard, silver-white metallic element related to and much lighter than aluminum. (*Symbol:* Be).

be·seech *v.* [be·sought; be·seech·ing] To entreat; beg; implore.—**be·seech·er** *n.*—**be·seech·ing·ly** *adv.*

be·seem *v.* To become; be fit or proper for.

be·set *v.* [be·set; be·set·ting] 1. To harass; plague. 2. To encircle.—**be·set·ting** *adj.*

be·shrew (bih-*shroo*) *v.* To curse mildly; wish bad luck to.

be·side *prep.* 1. At the side of. 2. Outside of;

aside from. 3. Besides.—**beside oneself.** In a state of great excitement.

be·sides *adv.* Moreover; furthermore.—*prep.* Other than; in addition to.

be·siege (bih-*seej*) *v.* [be·sieged; be·sieg·ing] To surround with armed forces; beleaguer; lay siege to.—**be·sieg·er** *n.*—**be·siege·ment** *n.*

be·smear (bih-*smihr*) *v.* To soil; daub; stain.

be·smirch (bih-*smerch*) *v.* To soil; discolor. —**be·smirch·er** *n.*—**be·smirch·ment** *n.*

be·som (*beh*-zum) *n.* A broom; brush made of twigs.

be·sot (bih-*sot*) *v.* [be·sot·ted; be·sot·ting] To stupefy, esp. with drink.—**be·sot·ted** *adj.*

be·span·gle (bih-*spang*-g'l) *v.* [be·span·gled; be·span·gling] To adorn with spangles.

be·spat·ter (bih-*spat*-er) *v.* To soil by spattering; splash.

be·speak (bih-*speek*) *v.* [be·spoke; be·spok·en; be·speak·ing] To attest; indicate; betoken.

Bessemer process (*bes*-uh-mer). A process for making steel by blowing compressed air through molten iron.

best *adj.* [*Superlative* of **good**] 1. Excellent in the highest degree. 2. Most useful, correct, worthy, etc. 3. Greatest; most; largest.—*adv.* [*Superlative* of **well**] In the highest degree; in the most excellent manner.—*n.* 1. That which is most excellent, useful, correct, etc. 2. The utmost. 'He did his best.'—*v.* To conquer.

bes·tial (*bes*-chul, *bess*-tee-ul) *adj.* Brutal; brutish; depraved.—**bes·tial·ly** *adv.*—**bes·ti·al·i·ty** (bes-tee-*al*-ih-tee) *n.* —*v.* [bes·tial·ized; -iz·ing].

be·stir (bih-*ster*) *v.* To arouse; cause to move.

best man. The bridegroom's attendant at a wedding.

be·stow (bih-*stoh*) *v.* 1. To confer; present. 2. To allot; apply.—**be·stow·al** *n.*

be·strew *v.* [be·strewed; be·strewed, be·strewn; be·strew·ing] To scatter over; sprinkle.

be·stride *v.* [be·strode; be·strid·den; be·strid·ing] 1. To stride over. 2. To stand or sit with the legs on either side of.

best-sel·ler (best-*sel*-er) *n.* A book which has or has had a very large sale.

bet *v.* [bet, bet·ted; bet·ting] To lay a wager; stake, as money, upon the outcome of a contest.—*n.* 1. That which is wagered. 2. A contestant to wager on; a means or agency chosen to place confidence in. 'When in doubt, your best bet is a dictionary.'

be·take (bih-*tayk*) *v.* [be·took; be·tak·en; be·tak·ing] To go; resort; repair.

be·ta ray (*bay*-tuh). A stream of electrons emitted at the speed of light by radio-active substances.

be·ta·tron (*bay*-tuh-tron) *n.* Electrical instrument for producing beta rays.

be·tel (*bee*-t'l) *n.* A climbing East Indian plant, whose leaves and nuts are chewed by natives.

Be·tel·geuse (*beet*-'l-jooz, *bet*-'l-jurz) *n.* A first-magnitude star in the constellation Orion.

beth·el (*beth*-'l) *n.* A place of worship, esp. a church for seamen.

be·think (bih-*think*) *v.* [be·thought; be·think·ing] To recall; recollect.

be·tide *v.* [be·tid·ed; be·tid·ing] To happen; befall.

be·times *adv.* 1. Early. 2. Quickly; in a brief time.

be·tok·en (bih-*toh*-kun) *v.* To presage; indicate. —**be·tok·en·er** *n.*

be·tray *v.* 1. To deceive; act treacherously; mislead. 2. To reveal; indicate unintentionally. 3. To disclose a secret.—**be·tray·al** *n.* —**be·tray·er** *n.*

be·troth (bih-*trawth*) *v.* To promise or pledge to marry.—**be·troth·al** *n.* Engagement to marry. —**be·tro·thed** *n.*

bet·ter *adj.* [*Comparative* of **good**] 1. Having good qualities in a greater degree than another. 2. Larger. 'The better part of a year.' —*adv.* [*Comparative* of **well**] 1. In a more excellent or superior manner. 2. In a higher or greater degree.—*v.* 1. To improve; ameliorate. 2. To exceed; surpass.—*n.* 1. [*usually pl.*] A superior person. 2. Advantage; superior position.

bet·ter, bet·tor *n.* One who makes wagers.

bet·ter·ment (*bet*-er-m'nt) *n.* Improvement, esp. an extensive improvement of real estate.

be·tween (bih-*tween*) *prep.* 1. In the space separating. 2. Passing from one to another. 3. In partnership among; in common to. 4. Mutually or in opposition. 'Strong feeling between the two.' 5. Out from two. 'Choose between us.'—**be·tween** *adv.*

be·twixt *prep. Chiefly Literary.* Between.—**be·twixt and between.** Indeterminate; occupying an equivocal position.

bev·el (*bev*-'l) *n.* 1. An oblique angle between two surfaces. 2. An instrument for measuring or forming a bevel.—*v.* [bev·eled; bev·elled; bev·el·ing; bev·el·ling] To make oblique; shape to an angle.—*adj.* Oblique.

BEVEL (def. 2)

bev·er·age (*bev*-er-ij) *n.* Any drink except water.

bev·y (*bev*-ee) *n.* [*pl.* bev·ies] 1. A group or company of women. 2. A flock of quail.

be·wail (bih-*wayl*) *v.* To bemoan; mourn.

be·ware (bih-*wehr*) *v.* To take care; to be cautious; to avoid.

be·wil·der (bih-*wil*-der) *v.* [be·wil·dered; be·wil·der·ing] To perplex; puzzle; mystify.—**be·wil·der·ed·ly** *adv.*— **-der·ing·ly** *adv.*— **-der·ment** *n.*

be·witch *v.* 1. To fascinate; charm. 2. To cast a magic spell, esp. an evil one, upon.

be·witch·ing *adj.* Fascinating; captivating; enchanting.—**be·witch·ing·ly** *adv.*

bey (*bay*) *n.* 1. A governor of a Turkish town or district. 2. The ruler of Tunis.

be·yond (bih-*yond*) *prep.* 1. On the farther side of. 2. Out of reach of; past. 3. Above;

exceeding; surpassing.—*adv*. At a distance; yonder.—*n*. Death; the after life.

bez·el (*bez*-'l) *n*. A facet, as of a gem; beveled surface, as of a tool.

be·zique (buh-*zeek*) *n*. A game of cards usually played by two persons.

bi·an·nu·al (by-*an*-yoo-'l) *adj*. Occurring twice a year.—**bi·an·nu·al·ly** *adv*.

bi·as (*by*-us) *n*. 1. Partiality; prejudice; bent. 2. A line or cut diagonal to the weave of cloth. —*adj*. Oblique; inclined.—*v*. [bi·ased, bi·assed; bi·as·ing; bi·ass·ing] To prejudice.—**bi·as** *adv*.

bib *n*. A cloth worn under the chin by children during meals to catch spilt food; the upper part of an apron, pinafore, or overalls.

Bi·ble (*by*-b'l) *n*. The book regarded by Christians as divinely inspired and having sacred authority.—**Bib·li·cal** (*bib*-lih-k'l) *adj*.— **-cal·ly** *adv*.

bib·li·og·ra·phy (bib-lee-*og*-ruh-fee) *n*. [*pl*. bib·li·og·ra·phies] A list of authors and titles, often with short descriptions, dealing with a given subject.—**bib·li·og·ra·pher** *n*.—**bib·li·o·graph·ic**, **bib·li·o·graph·i·cal** (bib-lee-uh-*graf*-ik, -ik'l) *adj*.

bib·li·o·phile (*bib*-lee-uh-fyl), **bib·li·o·phil** (*bib*-li-uh-fil) *n*. A booklover.

bib·li·o·phobe (*bib*-lee-uh-fohb) *n*. A book hater.— **-o·phob·i·a** (-*fohb*-ih-uh) *n*.

bib·u·lous (*bib*-yuh-lus) *adj*. 1. Addicted to intoxicating liquors. 2. Absorbent.— **-los·i·ty** (-*los*-uh-tee) *n*.— **-lous·ly** *adv*.— **-lous·ness** *n*.

bi·cam·er·al (by-*kam*-er-ul) *adj*. Consisting of two legislative chambers.

bi·car·bon·ate (by-*kahr*-bun-it) *n*. *Chemistry*. A compound of carbonic acid with a metallic element or radical.

bicarbonate of soda. Common household baking soda; sodium bicarbonate.

bi·cen·te·nar·y (by-*sen*-tuh-nehr-ee) *adj*. Pertaining to two hundred years.—*n*. Two-hundredth anniversary.

bi·cen·ten·ni·al (by-sen-*ten*-ee-ul) *n*. Two-hundredth anniversary.—*adj*. Occurring every two hundred years.

bi·ceps *n*. [*pl*. bi·ceps·es] *Anatomy*. A double-ended flexor muscle in the upper arm.

bi·chlor·ide (by-*klohr*-yde, -id) *n*. Also **bi·chlor·id**. A compound containing two atoms of chlorine with one atom of another element.

bick·er *v*. To quarrel; squabble.—**bick·er** *n*. —**bick·er·er** *n*.

bi·cus·pid (by-*kus*-pid) *adj*. Two-pointed; two-fanged.—*n*. A tooth having two points.

BICEPS

bi·cy·cle (*by*-sik-'l) *n*. A common two-wheeled vehicle, propelled by pedals which drive the rear wheel.—*v*. [bi·cy·cled; bi·cy·cling] To ride a bicycle.—**bi·cy·cler**, **bi·cy·clist** *n*.

bid *v*. [bade, bid; bid·den, bid; bid·ding] 1. To command; enjoin. 2. To make an offer. 3. To express. 'Bid farewell.'—*n*. 1. An offer. 2. *Colloquial*. An invitation.—**bid·der** *n*.

bid·ding *n*. Behest; order; invitation.

bide *v*. [bode, bid·ed; bid·ed; bid·ing] To await. —**bide one's time.** Await an opportunity.

bi·en·ni·al (by-*en*-ih-ul) *adj*. Occurring once in two years.—*n*. A plant which requires two seasons of growth to produce its flowers and fruit.—**bi·en·ni·al·ly** *adv*.

bier (bihr) *n*. 1. A frame on which a coffin is carried. 2. A coffin.

biff *v*. *Slang*. To strike; hit.—*n*. [*cap*.] A boy's nickname.

bi·fo·cal (by-*foh*-k'l) *adj*. Having two focuses. —**bi·fo·cals** *n*. *pl*. Spectacles having lenses in two sections for seeing at different distances.

bi·fur·cate (*by*-fer-kayt) *v*. [bi·fur·cat·ed; bi·fur·cat·ing] To divide into two branches.—**bi·fur·ca·tion** (by-fer-*kay*-shun) *n*.

big *adj*. [big·ger; big·gest] 1. Large; great; extensive. 2. Pregnant; ready to give birth. 3. Boastful. 4. Important.—**big·ness** *n*.

big·a·my (*big*-uh-mee) *n*. The state of being married to more than one person at one time. —**big·a·mist** *n*.—**big·a·mous** *adj*.—**big·a·mous·ly** *adv*.

big·horn *n*. [*pl*. big·horn; big·horns] Rocky Mountain sheep.

bight (byte) *n*. 1. A bend in a shore or coastline forming a bay. 2. The slack part of a rope between the ends; loop.

BIGHORN (1/40 life size)

Big Inch. An oil pipeline built in the U.S. during World War II, running from Texas to Philadelphia.

Big League. One of the two major baseball associations.—**big-league** *adj*. *Colloquial*. Top notch; A-1.

big·ot (*big*-ut) *n*. Fanatic; intolerant devotee of a single cause.

big·ot·ed (*big*-ut-id) *adj*. Intolerant; fanatical, —**big·ot·ed·ly** *adv*.—**big·ot·ry** *n*.

big shot. *Slang*. An important person.

big time. *Slang*. Upper ranks of an occupation; upper social strata.—**big-time** *adj*. *Slang*. Important; successful.

big tree. The giant sequoia; redwood.

bi·jou (*bee*-zhoo) *n*. [*pl*. bi·joux] A jewel; small and beautifully finished article.

bi·lat·er·al (by-*lat*-er-ul) *adj*. 1. Of or having two sides. 2. Between two parties.—**bi·lat·er·al·ly** *adv*.

bil·ber·ry (*bil*-behr-ee) *n*. [*pl*. bil·ber·ries] A small blue bush-grown berry of Europe.

bile *n*. 1. The yellowish, bitter liquid secreted by the liver. 2. Ill nature; bitter feeling.

bilge (bilj) *n*. 1. The bulging middle section of

a cask. 2. The section of a ship's bottom where it curves into the sides. 3. A drainage well running longitudinally along each side of a ship's hold. 4. Water collected there.

bi·lin·gual (by-*ling*-gwul) *adj*. Containing, using, or expressed in two languages.—**bi·lin·gual·ism** *n*.—**bi·lin·gual·ly** *adv*.

bil·ious (*bil*-yus) *adj*. Pertaining to or affected by bile.—**bil·ious·ly** *adv*.—**bil·ious·ness** *n*.

bilk *v*. 1. To frustrate; thwart; cheat; deceive. —**bilk** *n*.—**bilk·er** *n*.

bill *n*. The beak of a bird.—*v*. 1. To join beaks as doves. 2. To caress; handle tenderly, usually in 'bill and coo.'

bill *n*. An ancient military weapon consisting of a long staff with a hook-shaped blade.

bill *n*. 1. An account of goods sold or services rendered with prices attached; statement of debt. 2. Any written statement of particulars. 'Bill of fare.' 3. A draft of a law offered to a legislature, but not yet enacted. 4. *Law*. A written statement of a wrong suffered by the complainant, or of a case of lawbreaking. 5. An advertising poster; placard.—*v*. To make out a bill.—**bill·a·ble** *adj*.—**bill·er** *n*.

bill·board (*bil*-bohrd) *n*. A frame on which advertising material is displayed.

bil·let (*bil*-et) *n*. A small stick of wood.

bil·let (*bil*-et) *n*. A lodging for soldiers in a private house.—*v*. To quarter soldiers in a private house or houses.

bil·let-doux (*bil*-ay-*doo*) *n*. A love letter.

bill·fold *n*. A wallet.

bill·head *n*. A sheet of stationery used for making up a bill.

bill·hook *n*. A small variety of hatchet curved inward at the point of the cutting edge, used for pruning hedges, trees, etc.

bil·liards (*bil*-yerdz) *n. pl*. Any of several games played with balls and cues on a rectangular table.—**bil·liard** *adj*.

bil·lings·gate (*bil*-ingz-gayt) *n*. Vituperation; invective; abusive language.

bill of fare. A menu; list of dishes served by a restaurant.

bill of lading. A list of goods shipped, used as a receipt or acknowledgment of delivery.

bill of rights. A list of the liberties enjoyed by a people, esp. the first ten amendments to the Constitution of the U.S.

bill of sale. A formal instrument for the transfer of ownership of goods and chattels.

bil·lion (*bil*-yun) *n*. In the U.S., one thousand millions; the number one followed by nine zeros.—**bil·lion** *adj*.—**bil·lionth** *n*. & *adj*.

bil·lion·aire (*bil*-yun-*ehr*) *n*. One who has wealth in the billions; an extremely wealthy man.

bil·low (*bil*-oh) *n*. 1. A massive wave; breaker. 2. A rolling mass, as of smoke.—*v*. To swell; surge.

bil·low·y (*bil*-oh-ee) *adj*. Wavy; swelling or swelled into large waves.—**bil·low·i·ness** *n*.

bil·ly (*bil*-ee) *n*. [*pl*. bil·lies] A club; stick.

billy goat. A male goat.

bi·met·al·ism (by-*met*-'l-izm) *n*. A monetary system in which both gold and silver are established as standards.—**bi·met·al·lic** (by-muh-*tal*-ik) *adj*.—**bi·met·al·ist** (by-*met*-'l-ist) *n*.

bi·month·ly (by-*munth*-lee) *adj*. Occurring every two months.—*n*. A periodical published every two months.—**bi·month·ly** *adv*.

bin *n*. A box or enclosed place used for storage. —*v*. To put into a bin.

bi·na·ry (*by*-nuh-ree) *adj*. Twofold; dual.—*n*. A double star, whose members revolve around a common center of gravity.

bind (*bynde*) *v*. [bound; bind·ing] 1. To tie together; join. 2. To unite by bonds of affection or loyalty. 3. To constipate. 4. To sew together and cover. 'Bind a book.' 5. To hold together in a mass. 6. To place under legal obligation.—**bind over**. To oblige by bond to appear in court.

bind·er *n*. 1. One who binds. 2. The cover of a loose-leaf book. 3. A supporting abdominal bandage.

bind·er·y *n*. [*pl*. bind·er·ies] A plant where books are bound.

bind·ing *n*. 1. The act of fastening, as with a band. 2. The act of bringing under obligation or stipulations. 3. The cover and stitching of a book. 4. An ingredient which holds a mixture together. 5. A tape or strip edging a fabric.—*adj*. Serving to connect or fasten; obligatory.—**bind·ing·ly** *adv*. —**bind·ing·ness** *n*.

binge (*binj*) *n*. A drunken revel; a brannigan.—*v*. To carouse; debauch.

bin·go (*bing*-goh) *n*. A kind of lottery game, usually played for charity.

bin·na·cle (*bin*-uh-k'l) *n*. A case or box on a vessel's compass and lights for reading it at night.

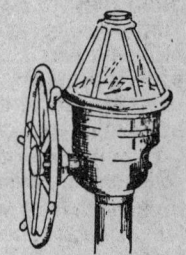

BINNACLE

bin·oc·u·lar (bin-*ok*-yoo-ler) *adj*. 1. Having two eyes. 2. Suited for the simultaneous use of both eyes.—*n*. [*pl*.] A pair of magnifying glasses connected by a frame; field glasses.—**bin·oc·u·lar·i·ty** (bin-ok-yoo-*lar*-ih-tee) *n*. —**bin·oc·u·lar·ly** *adv*.

BINOCULAR

bi·no·mi·al (by-*noh*-mee-ul) *n*. *Algebra*. An expression consisting of two terms connected by a plus or minus sign. —**bi·no·mi·al** *adj*.—**bi·no·mi·al·ly** *adv*.

bi·o·chem·is·try (by-oh-*kem*-iss-tree) *n*. The study of chemical processes in plants and animals.—**bi·o·chem·ic**, **bi·o·chem·i·cal** *adj*. —**bi·o·chem·i·cal·ly** *adv*.—**bi·o·chem·ist** *n*.

bi·og·ra·phy *n*. 1. The story of the life of a person. 2. Biographical writings in general. —**bi·o·graph·ic**, **bi·o·graph·i·cal** *adj*.—**bi·o·graph·i·cal·ly** *adv*.—**bi·og·raph·er** *n*.

bi·ol·o·gy *n.* The science which deals with living organisms.—**bi·o·log·ic, bi·o·log·i·cal** *adj.* Pertaining to biology.—**bi·o·log·i·cal** *n.* Drug; pharmaceutical.—**bi·o·log·i·cal·ly** *adv.*

bi·o·tin *n.* A basic factor in the vitamin-B complex, required by all forms of life.

bi·par·ti·san (by-*pahr*-tih-z'n) *adj.* Pertaining to a combination of two political parties.—**bi·par·ti·san·ship** *n.*

bi·part·ite (by-*pahr*-tyte) *adj.* In two parts, esp. two matching parts.—**bi·part·ite·ly** *adv.*—**bi·par·ti·tion** (by-pahr-*tish*-un) *n.*

bi·ped (*by*-ped) *n.* A two-legged animal.—**bi·ped, bi·ped·al** (*by*-ped'l) *adj.*

bi·plane (*by*-playn) *n.* An airplane with two pairs of wings, usually one above the other.

birch (berch) *n.* [*pl.* **birch·es**] 1. Any of a family of hardy trees with smooth outer bark which peels off in thin layers. 2. The hard-grained wood of the birch. 3. A birch branch or bundle of twigs used as a whip.—*v.* To whip with a birch.—**birch, birch·en** *adj.*

bird (berd) *n.* 1. A feathered, winged, warm-blooded animal. 2. *Slang.* A man, esp. an eccentric. 3. *Slang.* A jeer, usually in 'give the bird.'—*v.* To catch birds.—**bird·y** *adj.*

bird·lime *n.* A thick, sticky substance prepared from holly bark, used for entangling and snaring birds.—*v.* [bird·limed; bird·lim·ing].

bird of paradise. A brilliantly plumaged bird native to the Netherlands Indies.

bird of passage. 1. A migratory bird. 2. A migratory worker.

bird of prey. Any bird which feeds upon animals.

bird·man *n.* [*pl.* bird·men]. Also **bird man.** 1. A bird catcher; ornithologist. 2. *Slang.* An aviator.

bird's-eye *adj.* 1. Seen from above; general; embraced at a glance. 2. Having markings somewhat resembling bird eyes, as bird's-eye maple.—*n.* 1. A kind of diagonally woven cotton cloth, used esp. for diapers. 2. A yellow-eyed primrose.

bird's-foot violet. A common large-flowered violet, the state flower of Wisconsin.

bi·ret·ta (bih-*ret*-uh) *n.* Cap worn by members of the Roman Catholic clergy.

birth (berth) *n.* 1. Coming into the world; nativity. 2. Childbearing; parturition. 3. Lineage; descent. 4. Origin; beginning.

birth·day *n.* 1. The day when a person is born. 2. The anniversary of the day of birth.

BIRETTA

birth·mark *n.* A blemish of congenital origin on a person's body.

birth·place *n.* The location of birth or origin.

birth rate. The ratio of births to population in a given area.

birth·right *n.* A right or privilege held from the time of birth.

bis·cuit (*bis*-kit) *n.* 1. A kind of hard, flat wafer. 2. Light bread baked in small shapes.

bi·sect (by-*sekt*) *v.* To cut into two equal parts.—**bi·sec·tion** (by-*sek*-shun) *n.*—**bi·sec·tor** *n.*

bi·sex·u·al (by-*seks*-yoo-ul) *adj.* 1. Hermaphroditic; having the organs of both sexes in one individual. 2. Being attracted physically to both sexes. 3. *Botany.* Denoting flowers which contain both stamen and pistil.

bish·op (*bish*-up) *n.* 1. Clergyman having jurisdiction over a diocese. 2. A chess piece which moves diagonally.—**bish·op** *v.*

bish·op·ric (*bish*-up-rik) *n.* 1. The office of a bishop. 2. A diocese.

bis·muth (*biz*-muth) *n.* A brittle, white metal with a reddish tinge. (*Symbol:* Bi).—**bis·muth·al, bis·mu·thic, bis·muth·ous** *adj.*

bi·son (*by*-sun, -zun) *n. sing. & pl.* A bovine quadruped with short, rounded horns, a large hunch on the shoulders, and, in the male, a heavy mane.

bisque (bisk) *n.* Unglazed white porcelain after one baking.

BISON

bisque (bisk) *n.* 1. A thick soup containing fish, meat, or vegetable, usually creamed. 2. Ice cream made with crushed nuts or cookies.

bis·sex·tile (bih-*seks*-tul) *n.* The leap year.—*adj.* Denoting the extra day in leap year.

bis·ter, bis·tre (*bis*-ter) *n.* A brown pigment extracted from the soot of wood.

bis·tro (*bee*-stroh) *n.* A small café; pub.

bit *n.* 1. A particle; small piece; morsel. 2. *Colloquial.* Any small coin or quantity of money, esp. 12½ cents in the phrase *two bits* (25 cents). 3. *Colloquial.* A brief time.

bit *n.* 1. The metal part of a bridle which is inserted in the mouth of a horse. 2. A curb; restraining agent. 3. A boring tool inserted into a brace by which it is turned. 4. The part of a key which enters the lock and operates the tumblers.—*v.* [bit·ted; bit·ting] To put a bit in a horse's mouth.

bitch *n.* 1. The female of canine animals, as the dog and wolf. 2. *Vulgar Slang.* A vicious or immoral woman.—*v. Slang.* To complain irritably; whine; bellyache.

bite *v.* [bit; bit·ten, bit; bit·ing] 1. To penetrate or seize with the teeth. 2. To cause a smarting pain; sting. 3. To corrode or injure in various ways. 4. To grip, take fast hold of. 5. To fall victim of a lure.—*n.* 1. A seizing with the teeth. 2. Wound made by the teeth or a stinger. 3. A mouthful; bit. 4. Grasping power. 5. Action of acid in photoengraving or on an etcher's plate.—**bit·er** *n.*

bite the dust. To fall; be vanquished.

bit·ing (*byte*-ing) *adj.* Caustic; sarcastic; incisive.—**bit·ing·ly** *adv.*—**bit·ing·ness** *n.*

bitt *n.* A short post secured to the deck of a ship, usually in pairs, to make fast ropes or hawsers.

bit·ter *adj.* 1. Having an acrid, biting, disagreeable taste. 2. Severe; cruel; harsh. 3. Painful; biting. 4. Distressing; poignant. —**bit·ter·ish** *adj.*—**bit·ter·ly** *adv.*—**bit·ter·ness** *n.*

bit·tern (*bit*-ern) *n.* A wading bird with a long neck and long legs, which has a peculiar booming cry.

bit·tern (*bit*-ern) *n.* The brine remaining after a salt is crystallized from it.

bit·ters *n. pl.* A spirituous liquor in which bitter herbs or roots have been steeped.

bit·ter·sweet *n.* A trailing plant bearing decorative clustering berries.—*adj.* Having a combined bitter and sweet taste.

bi·tu·men (bih-*tyoo*-min) *n.* A resinous hydrocarbon substance appearing in a variety of forms, including petroleum, asphalt, peat, coal, etc.—**bi·tu·mi·nize** *v.* [bi·tu·mi·nized; bi·tu·mi·niz·ing]—**bi·tu·mi·nous** *adj.*

bituminous coal. Soft coal, with a lower carbon content and a higher proportion of volatile matter than anthracite.

bi·va·lent (by-*vay*-lent) *adj.* Pertaining to an element one of whose atoms can replace two of hydrogen.—**bi·va·lence, bi·va·len·cy** *n.*

bi·valve (*by*-valv) *n.* A mollusk with a shell consisting of two parts which open on an elastic hinge.—**bi·valve** *adj.*—**bi·val·vu·lar** (-*val*-) *adj.*

biv·ou·ac (*biv*-wak, *biv*-oo-ak) *n.* A temporary encampment of soldiers with little or no shelter.—*v.* [biv·ou·acked; biv·ou·ack·ing].

bi·week·ly (by-*week*-lee) *adj.* Occurring or appearing every two weeks; fortnightly.—*n.* A periodical published every two weeks.—**bi·week·ly** *adv.*

bi·zarre (bih-*zahr*) *adj.* Grotesque; outlandish; strange.—**bi·zarre·ly** *adv.*—**bi·zarre·ness** *n.*

blab *v.* [blabbed; blab·bing] To tattle; reveal secrets.—**blab** *n.*—**blab·ber** *n.*

black *adj.* 1. Of the darkest color; reflecting no light; opposite of white. 2. Dismal; gloomy. 3. Evil; wicked. 4. Dirty; filthy. —*n.* 1. The darkest color; the opposite of white. 2. Black dress; mourning clothes. 3. *Chess.* The side playing the dark-colored pieces.—**black** *v.*—**black·ish** *adj.*—**black·ness** *n.*

black·a·moor (*blak*-uh-moor) *n.* A Negro.

black art. Witchcraft; evil magic.

black·ball *v.* To exclude; debar.—**black·ball** *n.*—**black·ball·er** *n.*

black bass. An American fresh-water game fish.

black·ber·ry(*blak*-behr-ee)*n.* [*pl.* black·ber·ries] 1. A bush of the bramble family with berries which turn

BLACKBERRY

dark purple when ripe. 2. The berry of a blackberry bramble.

black·bird *n.* A bird with black plumage and an orange bill, related to the thrush.

black·board *n.* A board, usually of slate, written or drawn on with chalk.

black·cap *n.* 1. A small black-crowned warbling bird. 2. A black raspberry.

BLACKBIRD

black·en (*blak*-'n) *v.* 1. To darken; make or become black. 2. To defame; stain.

black eye. 1. A dark bruise surrounding the eye. 2. Disrepute; bad name.

black-eyed Susan. A yellow daisy with a dark brown, conical disk, the state flower of Maryland; coneflower.

black·guard (*blag*-erd) *n.* A scoundrel; knave; rogue.—*v.* To revile; abuse.—*adj.* Vicious; vile.—**black·guard·ly** *adv.* & *adj.*

black·head *n.* A skin opening clogged with dirt and skin oils.

black·ing *n.* A paste or liquid used for shining shoes, stoves, etc.

black·jack (*blak*-jak) *n.* 1. A small, flexible bludgeon. 2. A card game played with wagers. 3. A pirate's flag showing a skull and crossbones.—*v.* To strike with a blackjack.

black·leg (*blak*-leg) *n.* 1. *Slang.* A strikebreaker; scab. 2. A cheat; swindler.

BLACKJACK

blacklist *n.* A list of persons marked as dangerous, undesirable, or suspect.—**blacklist** *v.*

black·ly *adv.* Darkly; threateningly; sullenly.

black·mail *v.* To extort from a person by threatening to disclose secret facts which will bring disgrace upon the victim.—**black·mail** *v.* —**black·mail·er** *n.*

black maria (muh-*ry*-uh). *Colloquial.* A police wagon.

black market. 1. The exchange of commodities in violation of price, priority, or rationing laws. 2. A place for such exchange.—**black market** *adj.*

black·out (*blak*-owt) *n.* 1. The extinction of all lights in a city or other area so that enemy airplanes cannot distinguish their targets. 2. Temporary loss of consciousness, as from a maneuver in an airplane.—**black out** *v.* To cause or experience a blackout.—**black·out** *adj.*

Black Sea. A sea in SE Europe, bordered by the U.S.S.R., Turkey, Bulgaria, and Rumania.

Black Shirt. 1. A member of the Italian Fascisti. 2. A member of the German Schutzstaffel, the Nazi elite guard.

black·smith *n.* A craftsman who fashions and repairs iron articles.

black snake, black·snake *n.* 1. A large, agile, nonpoisonous North American snake. 2. A long rawhide whip.

black widow. A very poisonous spider, having a shiny black body.

blad·der *n.* A thin membranous bag in animals, which serves as the receptacle of some secreted fluid, esp. urine.

blade *n.* 1. The leaf of a grass. 2. The cutting part of an instrument. 3. The broad part of an oar or propeller. 4. A dashing young man. —**blad·ed** *adj.*

blam·a·ble (*blaym*-uh-b'l) *adj.* Culpable; blameworthy.— -**a·ble·ness** *n.*— -**a·bly** *adv.*

blame *v.* [blamed; blam·ing] To censure; hold at fault; reprehend.—*n.* 1. Culpability; guilt. 2. Censure.—**blame·ful** *adj.*—**blame·less** *adj.* —**blame·less·ly** *adv.*—**blame·less·ness** *n.*

blame·wor·thy (*blaym*-wer-thee) *adj.* Censurable; deserving blame.—**blame·wor·thi·ness** *n.*

blanch *v.* To whiten; make or become pale; bleach.—**blanch·er** *n.*

blanc·mange (bluh-*mahnzh*) *n.* A cornstarch pudding.

bland *adj.* 1. Suave; urbane. 2. Mild; gentle.—**bland·ly** *adv.*—**bland·ness** *n.*

blan·dish (*blan*-dish) *v.* To coax; flatter.—**blan·dish·er** *n.*—**blan·dish·ment** *n.*

blank *n.* 1. A void; vacancy. 2. A card or form prepared to be made out or filled in. 3. A lottery ticket which wins no prize. 4. A cartridge without a projectile. 5. A dash signifying an omitted word, as an oath.—*adj.* 1. Void; empty; vacant. 2. Expressionless. —*v.* 1. To erase. 2. *Baseball.* To prevent the opposition from scoring.—**blank·ness** *n.*

blank·et (*blank*-et) *n.* 1. A woven bed covering. 2. A thick, overspreading layer.—*v.* To cover completely.—*adj.* All-inclusive.

blank·ly *adv.* Vacantly; without expression.

blank verse. Lines written in unrhymed iambic pentameter.

blare *v.* [blared; blar·ing] To burst into loud, grating noise; sound harshly.—**blare** *n.*

blar·ney (*blar*-nee) *n.* Smooth, winning talk. —*v.* To flatter.

Blarney Stone. A stone in Castle Blarney near Cork, Ireland, traditionally endowing whoever kisses it with skill in flattery.

bla·sé (blah-*zay*) *adj.* World-weary; sated; bored with excessive pleasure; jaded.

blas·pheme (blas-*feem*) *v.* [blas·phemed; blas·phem·ing] 1. To curse; swear. 2. To abuse; denounce.—**blas·phem·er** *n.*

blas·phe·my (*blas*-fuh-mee) *n.* [*pl.* blas·phe·mies] Irreverent use of God's name.— -**phe·mous** *adj.*— -**mous·ly** *adv.*— -**mous·ness** *n.*

blast *n.* 1. A burst of wind. 2. The sound made by a wind instrument. 3. A destructive stroke; ruin. 4. Any continuous, forced ejection of air, as in a smelting furnace. 5. A violent explosion.—*v.* 1. To dynamite. 2. To demolish. 3. To shrivel.—**blast·ed** *adj.* 1. Shattered. 2. Damned; accursed.

blat *v.* [blat·ted; blat·ting] To bleat.

bla·tant (*blay*-t'nt) *adj.* 1. Crudely conspicuous or obvious; glaring. 2. Loud; vociferous; clamorous.— -**tan·cy** *n.*— -**tant·ly** *adv.*

blath·er (*blath*-er) *v.* To talk nonsense.—*n.* Gibberish; nonsense.—**blath·er·skite** (*blath*-er-skyt) *n.* 1. A talkative, silly person. 2. A reddish American duck.

blaze *n.* 1. Flame; light and heat radiating from a burning body. 2. Brilliance; effulgence. 3. Active or violent display; a bursting forth.—*v.* [blazed; blaz·ing].

blaze *v.* [blazed; blaz·ing] 1. To set a white mark on, as a tree, by paring off part of its bark. 2. To tell; publicize.—*n.* 1. A white spot on the forehead or face of a horse. 2. A white spot made on a tree by removing bark.

blaz·er (*blayz*-er) *n.* A sport jacket, often of variously colored striped material.

bla·zon (*blay*-z'n) *n.* 1. A coat of arms; symbol in heraldry. 2. Publication; celebration; pompous display.—*v.* To display; exhibit conspicuously; publish.—**bla·zon·ry** *n.*

bleach *v.* 1. To make white; remove color. 2. To dye blond.—**bleach** *n.*

bleach·er *n.* 1. One who bleaches. 2. [*pl.*] *Baseball.* The uncovered section of seats behind the outfield.

bleak *adj.* 1. Desolate; lonesome; forsaken. 2. Cold; raw. 3. Unpromising; dismal. —**bleak·ish** *adj.*—**bleak·ly** *adv.*—**bleak·ness** *n.*

blear *v.* To suffuse with tears; dim, as the vision.—*adj.* Inflamed and watery.—**blear** *n.* —**blear-eyed** *adj.*—**blear·i·ness** *n.*—**blear·y** *adj.*

bleat *v.* To cry as a sheep.—*n.* The cry of a sheep.—**bleat·er** *n.*—**bleat·ing·ly** *adv.*

bleed *v.* [bled; bleed·ing] 1. To lose blood. 2. To feel sorrow or sympathy. 3. To extract blood from. 4. To extort from.

bleed·er *n.* One afflicted with hemophilia.

blem·ish (*blem*-ish) *v.* To mar; impair; deface. —*n.* Defect; spot; flaw.—**blem·ish·er** *n.*

blench *v.* 1. To blanch; grow white. 2. To flinch; shrink; start back.

blend *v.* [blend·ed, blent; blend·ing] To fuse; merge; coalesce.—*n.* A mixture.

blend-word. A word made by combining parts of other words, as *brunch*, from *breakfast* and *lunch*.

bless *v.* [blessed, blest; bless·ing] 1. To confer a blessing or benediction upon. 2. To make happy and contented. 3. To consecrate; make holy. 4. To praise; extol.

bless·ed (*bles*-ed) *adj.* Also **blest.** 1. Highly favored; fortunate. 2. Sacred; hallowed; holy. 3. Enjoying spiritual blessings.—**bless·ed·ly** *adv.*—**bless·ed·ness** *n.*

bless·ing *n.* 1. A benediction; conferring of divine favor. 2. A gift; benefit.

blight (*blyte*) *n.* 1. A plant disease caused by condition of soil, atmospheric influences, insects, parasitic plants, etc. 2. A frustrating, dampening, or withering force or influence. —*v.* To blast; frustrate; wither.

blimp *n.* A small, nonrigid dirigible.

blind (*blynde*) *adj.* 1. Destitute of the sense of sight. 2. Performed without benefit of sight, as blind driving. 3. Without moral or intellectual understanding. 4. Unseen; hidden; concealed. 5. Indiscriminate; unconsidered; irrational; not directed by will or intellect. 6. Closed at one end.—*n.* 1. The sightless. 2. A window shade; sun screen. 3. A ruse; pretense.—*v.* 1. To deprive of sight. 2. To overwhelm with brilliancy; dazzle.—**blind·ing** *adj.*—**blind·ing·ly** *adv.*—**blind·ing·ness** *n.*

blind·er *n.* One of two leather flaps placed on either side of a horse's head, to prevent it from looking sideways.

BLINDERS

blind flying. *Aviation.* Navigation by instruments only.

blind·fold *v.* To bandage the eyes to cut off vision. —**blind·fold** *n. & adj.*

blindman's buff. A game in which a blindfolded player tries to tag one of the others.

blind spot. 1. A subject or situation regarding which one is ignorant or determinedly prejudiced. 2. The point of entrance of the optic nerve in the retina. 3. *Radio.* A region having bad reception.

blind tiger. *Slang.* A place where liquor is sold illegally.

blink *v.* 1. To wink; open and shut the eyes quickly. 2. To glimmer, as a lamp.—**blink** *n.*

blink·er *n.* 1. A blinder for horses. 2. A signal light.

bliss *n.* Utter happiness; joy; felicity.—**bliss·ful** *adj.*—**bliss·ful·ly** *adv.*—**bliss·ful·ness** *n.*

blis·ter *n.* 1. An elevated thin sac on the skin containing watery matter. 2. Any similar swelling; a surface bubble, as on a coat of paint.—*v.* To raise blisters.—**blist·er·y** *adj.*

blithe (*blythe*) *adj.* Merry; light-hearted; joyous.—**blithe·ly** *adv.*—**blithe·some** *adj.*

blitz, blitz·krieg (*blitz*-kreeg) *n.* 1. Lightning war; a plan developed by the Germans in World War II aiming at dispersal and disintegration of the enemy's defenses by sudden drastic attacks at strategic points. 2. In British usage, the Nazi air bombardments.

bliz·zard (*bliz*-erd) *n.* A snowstorm accompanied by powerful winds.

bloat (*bloht*) *v.* To inflate; cause to swell; puff up.—**bloat·ed** *adj.*

bloat·er (*bloht*-er) *n.* A salted and smoked herring.

blob *n.* A small drop or lump; blot.—*v.* [blob-bed; blob·bing].

bloc (*blok*) *n.* A combination of persons or groups for promoting a common cause.

block *n.* 1. A solid mass of matter, as wood, stone, etc. 2. Wooden support for the neck of a person being beheaded. 3. An obstacle; hindrance. 4. A grooved pulley mounted in a casing or shell furnished with an attaching hook or eye. 5. A connected group of buildings. 6. A city square or the length of one side. 7. A mold for shaping objects. 8. Platform on which articles are sold at auction.

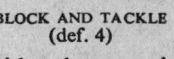
BLOCK AND TACKLE (def. 4)

9. A group or quantity considered as a unit. —*v.* 1. To obstruct; stop up. 2. To mold on a block. 3. To mark in general outline.

block·ade (blok-*ayd*) *n.* 1. The cutting off of a port or nation by preventing escape from it and hindering the entrance of supplies. 2. Blockading or obstructing force.—*v.* [block·ad·ed; block·ad·ing] To prevent exit or entrance; obstruct; shut up.—**block·ad·er** *n.*

blockade runner. A swift vessel for evading a blockade.

block buster. An enormous aerial bomb, capable of destroying an entire city block.

block·head (*blok*-hed) *n.* A stupid person; dolt.

block·house (*blok*-howss) *n. Military.* A fortified structure with openings for gunfire.

BLOCKHOUSE

block·y (*blok*-ee) *adj.* 1. Stocky; chunky. 2. Having color or shade in patches.

blond, blonde *adj.* 1. Having yellowish or light brown hair and fair skin. 2. Light-colored.—*n.* Person with light hair and skin.—**blond·ness, blonde·ness** *n.* Note: **blond,** *masculine;* **blonde,** *feminine.*

blood (*bluhd*) *n.* 1. The red fluid which circulates in the arteries and veins of animal bodies. 2. Lineage; descent; relationship. 3. Disposition; temper. 4. Bloodshed.—**in cold blood.** Without emotion; deliberately.

blood-bespattered	bloodletting	bloodstain
blood-colored	blood red	bloodstock
bloodcurdling	blood spot	bloodworm

blood bank. A store of human blood for giving emergency transfusions.

blood count. The number and ratio of white and red corpuscles in a sample of blood.

blooded *adj.* Also **blood.** Of pure blood or breed.

blood·hound (*bluhd*-hownd) *n.* A large dog noted for its acute sense of smell.

blood·less (*bluhd*-lis) *adj.* 1. Drained of blood; spiritless. 2. Without bloodshed. —**blood·less·ly** *adv.*—**blood·less·ness** *n.*

BLOODHOUND

B

blood money. Money earned by killing or betrayal.

blood poisoning. A condition caused by the presence of poisonous matter in the blood.

blood pressure. Pressure of the blood against the artery walls.

blood·root n. An American plant having a red root and red sap.

blood·shed n. Also **blood·shed·ding.** The spilling of blood; slaughter.

blood·shot adj. Congested with blood.

blood·stone n. A dark green variety of quartz, spotted with red.

blood·suck·er n. 1. Any bloodsucking animal, as a leech. 2. An extortioner; parasite.

blood·thirst·y adj. Murderous; cruel; ferocious. —**blood·thirst·i·ly** adv.—**blood·thirst·i·ness** n.

blood vessel. A tube of the body in which blood circulates, as a vein, artery, or capillary.

blood·y adj. [blood·i·er; blood·i·est] Pertaining to, covered with, or like blood; sanguinary; gory.—v. [blood·ied; blood·y·ing] To smear with blood.—**blood·i·ly** adv.—**blood·i·ness** n.

bloom n. 1. A blossom; flower of a plant. 2. State of flowering. 3. State of beauty and vigor; flourishing condition. 4. Rosy hue of the cheek. 5. A mass of iron from a puddling furnace.—v. 1. To produce blossoms. 2. To be in a state of vigor and beauty.

bloom·ers n. [pl.] 1. Loose-fitting trousers formerly worn by women for gymnastics and sports. 2. An undergarment similar in shape.

bloom·ing adj. 1. Flowering; blossoming. 2. Glowing; healthy.—**bloom·ing·ly** adv. —**bloom·y** adj.

blos·som (blos-'m) n. 1. The flower of a plant. 2. Blooming period or state.—v. 1. To flower. 2. To develop; prosper.—**blos·som·y** adj.

blot n. 1. A spot, as of ink; stain. 2. A blemish; disgrace.—v. [blot·ted; blot·ting] 1. To spot or stain. 2. To mar; tarnish; disgrace. 3. To obliterate; obscure. 4. To dry with blotting paper.

blotch n. 1. A red spot or eruption on the skin. 2. A large, irregular spot.—v. To mark with blotches.—**blotch·y** adj. [-i·er; -i·est].

blot·ter n. 1. A piece of blotting paper. 2. Book for recording events or transactions, usually in police stations.

blotting paper. A highly absorbent paper for soaking up excess ink.

blouse (blows, blowz) n. 1. A woman's upper garment; waist. 2. Undress jacket of the U.S. Army uniform. 3. Short, loose overgarment; smock.

blow (bloh) v. [blew; blown; blow·ing] To flower; blossom.—n. State of bloom.

blow (bloh) v. [blew; blown; blow·ing] 1. To make or form a current of air. 2. To expel forcefully. 3. To sound, as a wind instrument. 4. To impel; drive a current of air. 5. To shatter, as by explosion. 6. Slang. To brag; boast. 7. Slang. To spend freely; to

treat.—n. 1. Act of blowing. 2. A violent wind; gale.—**blow hot and cold.** To waver.

blow (bloh) n. 1. A heavy stroke with the hand or a weapon; assault. 2. A calamity; sudden misfortune.

blow·er n. One who or machine which blows.

blow·fish n. A kind of fish capable of inflating itself.

blow·gun n. A pipe or tube through which arrows or other missiles can be blown.

blow·hole n. 1. The nostril of a whale or other sea animal. 2. Hole for escaping gas or air. 3. Defect caused by an air or gas bubble.

blow·ing n. Noise made by the expulsion of gas or air.

blow·out (bloh-owt) n. 1. Compressed air rushing explosively out of a break in a tire. 2. The hole so made. 3. Slang. A big party.

blow·pipe (bloh-pyp) n. 1. An instrument for driving a current of air or gas through a flame to create an intense heat. 2. A blowgun.

blow·torch (bloh-torch) n. A mechanical torch that produces an intensely hot point of flame.

blow up. 1. To explode. 2. Slang. To lose one's temper. 3. To inflate; fill with air. 4. Photography. To enlarge.—**blow·up** n.

blowz·y (blowz-ee) adj. [blowz·i·er; blowz·i·est] Frowzy; slatternly; slovenly.—**blowzed** adj.

blub·ber (blub-er) n. 1. The fat of whales and other large sea animals. 2. Act of weeping noisily.—v. To weep violently and noisily. —**blub·ber·er** n.—**blub·ber·ing·ly** adv.

blub·ber·y (blub-er-ee) adj. 1. Weepy; lachrymose. 2. Containing or like blubber; fat.

bludg·eon (bluhj-un) n. A short club with a weighted end; cudgel.—v. To beat with a bludgeon; bully.—**bludg·eon·er** n.— **-eon·eer** n.

blue (bloo) n. 1. Color of the clear sky; spectrum color between violet and green. 2. The sea or sky. 3. A blue dye or pigment. 4. [pl.] Colloquial. Low spirits. 5. [pl.] A form of jazz music developed from Negro folksongs, characterized by a twelve-bar phrase in a minor key.—adj. 1. Of a blue color. 2. Livid, as from cold. 3. Colloquial. In low spirits; discouraged. 4. Puritanical. 'Blue laws.'—v. [blued; blu·ing, blue·ing] To color or become blue.—**blue·ly** adv.—**blue·ness** n.

Blue·beard (bloo-bihrd) n. 1. Folk tale villain who murdered six of his seven wives. 2. [not cap.] One who murders his wives.

blue·bell (bloo-bel) n. Any of several plants with bell-shaped blue flowers.

blue·ber·ry (bloo-behr-ee) n. [pl. blue·ber·ries] A small, edible blue berry or the shrub on which it grows.

blue·bird (bloo-berd) n. American songbird with a blue back and reddish breast.

blue blood. Aristocratic blood or descent.— —**blue-blooded** adj.

blue·book (bloo-book) n. 1. An English Parliamentary report. 2. Colloquial. Register of socially prominent persons.

blue·fish (*bloo*-fish) *n*. An edible salt-water fish.

blue flag. The blue-flowered iris, state flower of Tennessee.

blue·grass (*bloo*-gras) *n*. A pasture grass having bluish-green stems.

blue·jack·et (*bloo*-jak-it) *n*. A sailor.

blue jay. Chattering, crested bird with a blue back.

blue moon. An extremely long period of time.

BLUE JAY

blue-pen·cil *v*. To correct; edit; strike out.

blue·print *n*. A photograph of a plan of construction printed in white lines on blue paper.—**blue·print** *v*. —**blue·print** *adj*.

blue·stock·ing *n*. A highly intellectual or literary woman.—**blue·stock·ing·ism** *n*.

blue streak. Flash of tremendous speed.

blu·et (*bloo*-it) *n*. American plant with small blue flowers.

bluff (*bluhf*) *adj*. 1. Frank; roughly good humored; hearty. 2. Rising with a broad, flat front.—*n*. A high, often perpendicular, bank or cliff.—**bluff·ly** *adv*.—**bluff·ness** *n*.

bluff *v*. To deceive; mislead, esp. by a pretense of confidence or strength.—**bluff** *n*.—**bluff·er** *n*.

blu·ing, blue·ing (*bloo*-ing) *n*. A preparation used in laundering to retain whiteness or impart a slight bluish tinge.

blu·ish, blue·ish (*bloo*-ish) *adj*. Slightly blue. —**blu·ish·ness** *n*.

blun·der (*blun*-der) *v*. 1. To stumble; move clumsily. 2. To bungle; make a serious mistake.—*n*. A serious error.—**blun·der·er** *n*. —**blun·der·ing·ly** *adv*.

blun·der·buss (*blun*-der-buss) *n*. An ancient short gun with a large muzzle.

blunt *adj*. 1. Dull; having a thick edge. 2. Obtuse; slow in comprehending. 3. Curt; outspoken; brusque.—*v*. 1. To dull a point or edge. 2. To weaken; impair.—**blunt·ly** *adv*.—**blunt·ness** *n*.

BLUNDERBUSS

blur (*bler*) *v*. [blurred; blurr·ing] 1. To make indistinct; obscure. 2. To blot or soil.—*n*. 1. Dim, confused appearance. 2. A blot or stain.—**blur·ry** *adj*.

blurb (*blerb*) *n*. An enthusiastic description, as used in advertising.

blurt (*blert*) *v*. To utter suddenly or inadvertently.—**blurt** *n*.

blush *v*. 1. To redden, esp. in the cheeks. 2. To feel confusion or shame.—*n*. 1. A reddening of the cheeks. 2. A rosy or ruddy color.—*adj*. Rosy.—**blush·er** *n*.—**blush·ing** *adj*. —**blush·ing·ly** *adv*.

blus·ter (*bluhs*-ter) *v*. 1. To blow violently and noisily. 2. To swagger; talk loudly and violently.—*n*. 1. A noisy storm or commotion. 2. Loud, bragging talk; swaggering.—**blus·ter·er** *n*.—**blus·ter·ing·ly** *adv*.—**blus·ter·y** *adj*.

bo·a (*boh*-uh) *n*. 1. A woman's long scarf of fur or feathers. 2. A nonpoisonous tropical American snake.

boa constrictor. A large tropical snake which crushes its victims in its powerful coils.

boar (*bohr*) *n*. 1. A male swine. 2. A wild hog or pig.

board (*bohrd*) *n*.
1. A thin piece of timber of much greater length than width. 2. A flat piece of wood on which to do work, etc. 3. A table,

BOAR

esp. for food. 4. Food; meals. 5. A group of people who manage or direct a company, public institution, etc. 6. A thick, stiff paper. 7. [*pl*.] The stage of a theater. 8. The side or edge, esp. of a ship.—*v*. 1. To give or obtain meals or lodging for pay. 2. To cover with boards. 3. To step into or climb aboard, as a train or ship.

board·er (*bohrd*-er) *n*. 1. One who receives and pays for meals and sometimes lodging. 2. One who climbs aboard a ship.

board·ing (*bohrd*-ing) *n*. Boards, esp. when used as a covering.

boarding house. A house furnishing meals and sometimes lodging for pay.

boarding school. A school at which the pupils are lodged and fed.

board·walk (*bohrd*-wawk) *n*. An elevated walk, esp. along a beach.

boast (*bohst*) *v*. 1. To brag; extol one's accomplishments, property, etc. 2. To possess with pride.—*n*. 1. Act of bragging. 2. Cause of pride.—**boast·er** *n*.—**boast·ing·ly** *adv*.

boast·ful (*bohst*-f'l) *adj*. Bragging; immodest. —**boast·ful·ly** *adv*.—**boast·ful·ness** *n*.

boat (*boht*) *n*. 1. A small open craft for use on water. 2. A boat-shaped dish.—*v*. To travel or transport in a boat.—**boat·er** *n*.—**boat·ing** *n*.

boatbill	boatload	boatshop
boatbuilder	boatman	boatside
boatbuilding	boatmaster	boatwoman
boathouse	boat owner	boatwright

boat·hook *n*. An iron hook fixed to a long pole, for pulling or pushing a boat.

boat·swain (*boh*-s'n) *n*. Also **bosun, bos'n.** The foreman of the deck gang aboard ship.

bob *n*. 1. A round object hanging from the end of a cord, chain, etc. 2. A short feminine haircut. 3. A bobbing motion. 4. *Angling.* Bait used in fishing for eels.—*v*. [bobbed; bobb·ing] 1. To cut short. 2. To move in a short, jerking manner.—**bobbed** *adj*.—**bob·ber** *n*.—**bob up.** To appear suddenly.

bob·bin (*bob*-in) *n*. A contrivance for holding thread, as in a sewing machine; spool.

B

bob·by (*bob*-ee) *n.* [*pl.* bob·bies] *Colloquial British.* A policeman.

bobby pin. A slender, two-pronged metal pin for holding the hair in place.

bob·by·socks (*bob*-ee-soks) *n.* Ankle socks worn by young girls.

bob·cat (*bob*-kat) *n.* A North American variety of lynx; wildcat.

bob·o·link (*bob*-uh-link) *n.* Migratory bird named from its cry.

bob·sled *n.* Also **bobsleigh.** A long sled with a steering apparatus, capable of high speeds.—*v.* [bob·sled·ded; bob·sled·ding].

bob·tail (*bob*-tayl) *n.* A bobbed tail.—*v.* To cut short, as a tail.—*adj.* Cut short; bobbed.—**bob·tailed** *adj.*

bob·white (bob-*hwyt*) *n.* North American quail, named from its call.

bock *n.* Also **bock beer.** A kind of strong beer, usually made in the spring.

bode *v.* [bod·ed; bod·ing] To augur; presage.—**bode·ment** *n.*

bod·ice (*bod*-is) *n.* The close-fitting waist of a woman's dress.

bod·i·less (*bod*-ih-lis) *adj.* Having no material form.

bod·i·ly (*bod*-ih-lee) *adj.* Corporeal; physical.—*adv.* As one; entirely; completely.

bod·kin (*bod*-kin) *n.* 1. An instrument with a small blade and a sharp point for piercing holes. 2. A blunt needle with a large eye, for drawing thread through a loop. 3. *Printing.* A sharp-pointed instrument for picking out type in making corrections.

bod·y (*bod*-ee) *n.* [*pl.* bod·ies] 1. The physical or material structure of an animal. 2. The main part of an animal; trunk; the main part of any structure. 3. A person. 4. A corpse. 5. A group of associated individuals; unit. 6. Any separate or distinct portion of matter. 7. Consistency; solidity of texture.—*v.* [bod·ied; bod·y·ing] To provide with a body.

bod·y·guard (*bod*-ee-gahrd) *n.* A guard for protecting the life or person of an individual.

Bo·er (*bohr*) *n.* A South African of Dutch descent.—**Bo·er** *adj.*

bog *n.* A quagmire; section of wet, spongy ground.—*v.* [bogged; bog·ging] To sink or become stuck.—**bog·gish** *adj.*—**bog·gish·ness** *n.*

bo·gey (*boh*-gee) *n.* [*pl.* bo·geys] 1. *Golf.* The score against which players compete. 2. Bogy.

bog·gle (*bog*-'l) *v.* [bog·gled; bog·gling] 1. To hesitate; falter. 2. To bungle; botch.—**bog·gle** *n.*—**bog·gler** *n.*

bog·gy (*bog*-ee) *adj.* [bog·gi·er; bog·gi·est] Swampy; marshy.—**bog·gi·ness** *n.*

bog·trot·ter (*bog*-trot-er) *n.* A vagabond.

bo·gus (*boh*-gus) *adj.* Fraudulent; counterfeit.

bo·gy (*boh*-gee) *n.* [*pl.* bo·gies] Also **bo·gey, bo·gie.** Goblin; imaginary specter; bugbear.

bo·hea (boh-*hee*) *n.* Black tea.

Bo·he·mi·a (boh-*hee*-mee-uh) *n.* 1. A province in SW Czechoslovakia. 2. A colony of artists and writers.

Bo·he·mi·an (boh-*hee*-mee-un) *n.* 1. An inhabitant of Bohemia. 2. The language of Bohemia. 3. One who leads a free, unconventional life.—**Bo·he·mi·an** *adj.*—**-mi·an·ism** *n.*

boil *n.* An inflamed, pus-filled swelling on the skin.

boil *v.* 1. To bubble or be agitated by the action of heat. 2. To become violently agitated or excited. 3. To cook, sterilize, etc., in boiling water.—*n.* Act of boiling.

boil·er *n.* 1. One who boils. 2. A utensil for boiling. 3. A metallic container for generating steam.

bois·ter·ous (*bois*-ter-us) *adj.* Clamorous; cheerfully noisy.—**bois·ter·ous·ly** *adv.*—**-ous·ness** *n.*

bold (*bohld*) *adj.* 1. Courageous; intrepid. 2. Brazen; impudent. 3. Abrupt; precipitous. 4. Clearcut; sharp in outline.—**bold·ly** *adv.*—**bold·ness** *n.*

bold·face (*bohld*-fays) *n.* *Printing.* A type style characterized by heavy lines, usually used for emphasis. **This is boldface.**—**bold·face** *adj.*

bole *n.* A tree trunk.

bo·le·ro (boh-*lehr*-oh) *n.* 1. A Spanish dance in ¾ time. 2. A short jacket, usually worn open in front.

bol·i·var (*bol*-ih-ver) *n.* [*pl.* bol·i·vars, bol·i·va·res (boh-lih-*vah*-rayss)] Venezuelan monetary unit, valued at ⅓ the U.S. dollar.

bo·li·via·no (buh-lee-vee-*vyah*-noh) *n.* [*pl.* -nos] Bolivian monetary unit, valued at 60% of a U.S. dollar.

boll (*bohl*) *n.* The seed pod of a plant, esp. of cotton.—**boll weevil.** The destructive beetle that feeds on growing cotton bolls.

bo·lo (*boh*-loh) *n.* [*pl.* bo·los] A long single-edged knife common in the Philippines.

Bologna sausage (buh-*lohn*-uh). A large sausage of cold meat prepared of inferior cuts, ground, seasoned, and stuffed in a skin.

bo·lo·ney (buh-*lohn*-ee) *n.* 1. Bologna sausage. 2. *Slang.* Baseless talk; flattery.

Bol·she·vik (*bol*-shuh-vik) *n.* [*pl.* Bol·she·viki; Bol·she·viks] A member or supporter of the victorious left wing of the Russian Social Democratic party under the leadership of V. I. Lenin. This party is now the Communist party of the Soviet Union.—**Bol·she·vik** *adj.*

Bol·she·vism (*bol*-shuh-vizm) *n.* The theory and practice of the Bolsheviki.—**Bol·she·vist** *n.* & *adj.*—**Bol·she·vist·ic, bol-** (bol-shuh-*vist*-ik) *adj.*

bol·ster (*bohl*-ster) *n.* A long pillow or cushion on which to rest the head.—*v.* 1. To pad; stuff. 2. To support; hold up.—**bol·ster·er** *n.*

bolt (*bohlt*) *v.* 1. To sift; run through a sieve. 2. To examine closely.—**bolt·er** *n.*

bolt *n.* 1. A threaded pin or shaft for fastening. 2. A crash of thunder, or a flash of lightning. 3. A mechanism in a rifle which ejects an empty cartridge and inserts a new one. 4. A movable bar for locking doors, win-

BOLT

dows, etc. 5. A standard roll of cloth. 6. A sudden departure, esp. from a political party. 7. An arrow. 8. A gulp; sudden swallow. 9. A log from a young tree.—*adv.* 1. Suddenly; straight. 2. Upright; straight.—*v.* 1. To shoot forth suddenly. 2. To fasten with bolts. 3. To eat rapidly. 4. To flee, esp. to refuse to support the candidate of one's party.

bomb (*bom*) *n. Military.* An explosive charge, dropped from the air or hurled from a mortar. —**bomb** *v.*

bom·bard (bom-*bahrd*) *n.* To fire missiles upon; attack with bombs.—**bom·bard·ment** *n.*

bom·bard·ier (bom-ber-*dihr*) *n.* The member of a bomber crew who aims and releases bombs.

bom·bast (*bom*-bast) *n.* High-flown language; rant.

bom·bas·tic (bom-*bas*-tik) *adj.* Also **bom·bas·ti·cal.** Grandiloquent; flowery in language; pompous.—**bom·bas·ti·cal·ly** *adv.*

bom·ba·zine, bom·ba·sine (bom-buh-*zeen*) *n.* A light twill fabric having a silk or cotton warp and woolen weft.

bomb·er (*bom*-er) *n. Military.* Airplane designed to carry and drop bombs.

bomb·proof (*bom*-proof) *adj.* Protected from the explosion of bombs and shells.

bomb·shell (*bom*-shel) *n.* 1. A bomb. 2. Any sudden, violent surprise.

bomb·sight (*bomb*-syte) *n.* An aiming mechanism that permits precision aerial bombing.

bo·na fi·de (*boh*-nuh *fy*-dee). Genuine; authentic; without deception.

bo·nan·za (boh-*nan*-zuh) *n.* 1. A stroke of fortune; a lucky find. 2. A gold mine or rich vein of ore.

Bo·na·part·ist (*bohn*-uh-pahr-tist) *n. French History.* One favoring the policy or dynasty of Napoleon Bonaparte.

bon·bon (*bon*-bon) *n.* A kind of small candy.

bond *n.* 1. A sum of money posted as a guarantee or security. 2. A certificate bearing evidence of debt by a government or corporation. 3. Anything that binds or fastens; fetter. 4. A link; connection; tie. 5. A moral obligation. 6. The status of articles kept under government supervision until tax is paid on them.—*v.* 1. To place in bond. 2. To offer security for.—**bond·ed** *adj.*—**bond·er** *n.*

bond *adj.* Enslaved; in serfdom.

bond·age (*bond*-ij) *n.* 1. Slavery; involuntary servitude; captivity. 2. Obligation; duty.

bond·man (*bond*-m'n) *n.* [*pl.* bond·men] A male slave; indentured servant.—**bond·wo·man** *n.*

bonds·man (*bondz*-m'n) *n.* [*pl.* bonds·men] *Law.* One who pledges security for a bond.

bone *n.* 1. A part of a vertebrate animal's skeleton. 2. The calcium compound of which it is made. 3. [*pl.*] The skeleton. 4. [*pl.*] *Slang.* Dice. 5. [*pl.*] An end man in a minstrel show. 6. See **pick a bone.**—*v.* [boned; bon·ing] 1. To remove the bones from. 2. *Slang.* To study intensely; cram.—**bone·less** *adj.*

bon·er *n. Colloquial.* A ridiculous error.

bone·set (*bohn*-set) *n.* An herb of the aster family used as a tonic.

bon·fire *n.* A large open fire built outdoors, usually in celebration.

bo·ni·to (buh-*nee*-toh) *n.* [*pl.* bon·i·tos, bon·i·toes] A sea fish related to the mackerels.

bon·net (*bon*-it) *n.* 1. A woman's hat with an extended brim which fits about the face. 2. A woolen cap worn by Scotsmen.

bon·ny, bon·nie (*bon*-ee) *adj.* [bon·ni·er; bon·ni·est] Handsome; beautiful; pretty.

bo·nus (*boh*-nus) *n.* 1. A sum paid over and above a required amount. 2. An incentive or reward payment.

bon·y (*bohn*-ee) *adj.* [bon·i·er; bon·i·est] 1. Like or full of bones. 2. Having prominent or sparsely fleshed bones.—**bon·i·ness** *n.*

boo *interj.* 1. A call of disapproval or contempt, esp. at sports events. 2. An exclamation used to startle.—**boo** *v.*

boo·by (*boo*-bee) *n.* [*pl.* boo·bies] 1. Dunce; fool; oaf. 2. A sluggish fishing bird of the warm latitudes.—*adj.* [boo·bi·er; boo·bi·est].

booby trap. *Military.* A concealed bomb attached to a harmless-looking object so as to detonate when disturbed by an unwary person.

boo·dle *n. Slang.* 1. Bounty; prize; catch. 2. Large quantity; crowd. 3. Bribe money.

boo·gie woo·gie. Also **boo·gie.** *Jazz Music.* A style of jazz piano playing emphasizing a rolling bass in syncopated eighth notes, with rhythmic accents for the right hand, usually in twelve-bar blues form.

book *n.* 1. A number of pages bound together. 2. A main division of a literary work. 3. A record or list of bets accepted by a bookmaker. 4. A register; record. 5. [*pl.*] Accounting records. 6. *Bridge & Whist.* The first six tricks taken. 7. [*cap.*] The Bible. —*v.* 1. To make a reservation; schedule. 2. To enter in a book.

bookbinder	bookman	bookshop
bookcase	book rack	bookstack
book learning	bookroom	bookstall
book-lined	book rest	bookstand
booklore	book seller	bookstore
booklover	bookshelf	book work

book·end. One of a pair of supports to hold a row of books.

book·ish *adj.* 1. Pedantic; speaking in a literary vocabulary; formal. 2. Fond of books and study.— -ish·ly *adv.*— -ish·ness *n.*

book·keep·er (*book*-keep-er) *n.* One who keeps accounts.—**book·keep·ing** *n.* The art or theory of keeping business accounts.

book·let (*book*-lit) *n.* A small book.

book·mak·er *n.* 1. One who accepts and records bets, as on a horse race. 2. A compiler or publisher of books.

book·mark *n.* Any object used to indicate a place in a book.

book·plate *n.* A label for the inside front cover of a book, indicating ownership.

book·worm *n.* 1. A person deeply absorbed in

reading. 2. An insect which eats holes in bookbindings.

boom *n.* 1. A loud, explosive report or concussion. 2. A period of feverish prosperity or speculation.—**boom** *v.* & *adj.*

boom *n.* 1. *Nautical.* A long pole or spar, esp. one used in handling cargo. 2. An obstruction across a harbor mouth to block enemy ships. 3. *Logging.* **a.** A flow or run of floated logs. **b.** Timbers across a river to keep logs from floating away.

BOOM (def. 3 b)

boom·er·ang (*boom*-er-ang) *n.* 1. A curved blade which, when thrown, returns to the thrower. 2. Any scheme which plagues its originator by visiting its effects upon him.

BOOMERANG

boon *n.* A favor asked or given; benefit.

boon *adj.* Gay; merry. 'Boon companion.'

boon·dog·gle (*boon*-dog'l) *v.* [boon·dog·gled; dog·gling] To waste government money on useless projects.— -**dog·gling** *n.*— -**dog·gler** *n.*

boor *n.* 1. A crude person. 2. A rustic; peasant.—**boor·ish** *adj.*— -**ish·ly** *adv.*— -**ish·ness** *n.*

boost *v.* 1. To hoist; lift or push up. 2. *Slang.* To give favorable publicity to.—**boost·er** *n.*

boot *n.* 1. A covering, usually of leather, for the foot and leg. 2. *Baseball Slang.* An error. 3. *Naval slang.* A trainee.—**boot** *v.*

boot·black *n.* One who shines shoes.

boot·ee *n.* An infant's crocheted sock.

Bo·ö·tes (boh-*oh*-teez) *n.* A northern constellation to which the star Arcturus belongs.

booth *n.* 1. In a restaurant, an alcove or partitioned area for one party. 2. A stall; small, temporary stand or enclosure. 3. A closet for making calls on a public telephone.

boot·leg *v. Slang.* [boot·legged; boot·leg·ging] To sell illegally, esp. liquor.—**boot·leg** *adj.* —**boot·leg·ger** *n.*—**boot·leg·ging** *n.*

boot·less *adj.* Unavailing; unprofitable; useless. —**boot·less·ly** *adv.*—**boot·less·ness** *n.*

boo·ty *n.* [*pl.* boot·ies] Spoil; plunder.

booze *n. Slang.* Liquor, esp. of a strong, inferior quality.—*v.* [boozed; booz·ing] To guzzle; drink spirits to excess.—**booz·er** *n.*—**booz·y** *adj.* [booz·i·er; booz·i·est].

bo·rac·ic ac·id (bor-*ass*-ik). A soluble powder used as an antiseptic; boric acid.

bo·rax (*boh*-raks, *bor*-) *n.* A white boron salt used as water softener, flux, etc.

Bor·deaux (bor-*doh*) *n.* 1. A seaport and wine center of SW France. 2. Any of several wines from the Gironde district of France.

bor·der (*bor*-der) *n.* 1. Edge; margin; boundary. 2. Any decorative or reinforcing edging.

3. *Theater.* Overhead drop and side scenery. —**bor·der** *v.*—**bor·der·ed** *adj.*—**bor·der·er** *n.*

bor·der·land (*bor*-der-land) *n.* Frontier; land adjacent to another boundary.

bore *v.* [bored; bor·ing] To weary or annoy by dullness.—**bore** *n.*—**bore·dom** *n.*

bore *v.* 1. To drive a hole in; penetrate; squeeze through. 2. *Mechanics.* To enlarge and accurately finish a drilled hole.—*n.* 1. A drilled hole. 2. The size of a drilled hole; caliber.—**bor·er** *n.*

bore *n.* A very rapid rise in tide; tidal wave.

bo·re·al (*bor*-reh-ul) *adj.* Denoting the north or the north wind.

bor·ic (*boh*-rik, *bor*-) *adj.* Containing or pertaining to boron.— **boric acid.** Boracic acid.

born *adj.* 1. Given birth to; brought forth. 2. From time of birth. 'A born cheat.'

bo·ron (*boh*-rahn, *bor*-) *n.* A metallic element of the aluminum group, similar to carbon in its properties. (*Symbol:* B).

bor·ough (*ber*-oh) *n.* 1. Subdivision of a county. 2. One of the five governmental sections of New York City.

bor·row (*bor*-oh; *bahr*-) *v.* 1. To accept a loan. 2. To adopt; appropriate; take as one's own.—**bor·row·er** *n.*

borscht, borsch (borsht, borsh) *n.* A beef-stock soup or stew made of beets, usually served with sour cream.

bosk·y *adj.* Wooded; covered with groves or thickets.—**bosk·i·ness** *n.*

bos'n (*boh*-sun). *Variant spelling* of **boatswain.**

bos·om (*boo*-zum) *n.* 1. The breast. 2. The seat of thought, emotion, cogitation, etc. 3. Embrace; protection.—*adj.* Intimate; near; close.—*v.* 1. Enclose or harbor in the bosom; encompass. 2. To conceal; embrace; cherish intimately.

Bos·por·us (*bos*-per-us). Strait at the outlet of the Black Sea.

boss *n.* 1. A projecting mass; knob; stud. 2. *Mechanics.* An enlarged diameter on a shaft.—*v.* To ornament with bosses.—**bos·sy** *adj.*

boss *n.* 1. Foreman; superintendent; employer. 2. *Colloquial.* Master; one who has bested another. 3. *Colloquial.* A corrupt politician or political contriver.—**boss** *v.* —**boss·ism** *n.*—**bos·sy** *adj.* Dictatorial; authoritarian.

boss, boss·y *n. Colloquial.* A cow or calf.

Boston terrier. Small, smooth-haired, spotted breed of dog.

bo·tan·i·cal (buh-*tan*-ih-k'l) *adj.* Also **bo·tan·ic.** Pertaining to plants.—**bo·tan·i·cal·ly** *adv.*

bot·a·nist (*bot*-uh-nist) *n.* One skilled in the science of plants.

bot·a·nize (*bot*-uh-nyze) *v.* [bot·a·nized; -niz·ing] To make a scientific study of plants.

bot·a·ny (*bot*-uh-nee) *n.* [*pl.* bot·a·nies] The science of plants and vegetation.

botch *n.* 1. Bungled, unsatisfactory work. 2. A clumsy patch.—**botch** *v.*—**botch·er** *n.* —**botch·y** *adj.* [botch·i·er; botch·i·est].

B

both (*bohth*) *adj.* Two; the one and the other. —**both** *pron.*—*conj.* Not only this but also that; equally the former and the latter.

both·er (*both*-er) *v.* 1. To annoy; vex; tease. 2. To perplex. 3. To put oneself out; trouble oneself.—**both·er** *n.*—**both·er·some** *adj.*

both·er·a·tion (both-er-*ay*-shun) *interj.* Expression of annoyance or perplexity.—*n. Colloquial.* Vexation; trouble; perplexity.

bot·tle (*bot*-'l) *n.* A narrow-necked container for liquids, usually made of glass.—*v.* [bot·tled; bot·tling]—**bot·tler** *n.*

bot·tle·neck *n.* A focal point where the progress of a whole process or operation is retarded.—**bot·tle·necked** *adj.*

bot·tom (*bot*-um) *n.* 1. Lowest or deepest part; underside; base. 2. The land under a body of water. 3. The seat of a chair. 4. Low, sediment-deposited land along a river; valley. 5. A ship, esp. a cargo ship.—*adj.* 1. Undermost; lowest. 2. Denoting low alluvial lands.—**bot·tom** *v.*—**bot·tom·less** *adj.*

bot·u·lism (*bot*-yoo-lizm, *boch*-oo-) *n.* Poisoning caused by improperly canned foods.

bou·doir (*boo*-dwahr) *n.* A lady's bedroom.

bough (*bow*) *n.* Limb of a tree.

bouil·la·baisse (bool-yuh-*bayss*; bwee-yuh-*bess*) *n.* A fish soup.

bouil·lon (*bul*-yon; *bwee*-yon) *n.* Clear broth.

boul·der, bowl·der (*bohl*-der) *n.* A large, eroded stone.

bou·le·vard (*bul*-uh-vard, *bool*-) *n.* A broad avenue.

bounce (*bownss*) *v.* [bounced; bounc·ing] 1. To leap; spring. 2. To rebound. 3. *Slang.* To expel from a public place for disorderly conduct.—**bounce** *n.*—**bounc·er** *n.*

bounc·ing *adj.* Vigorous; sturdy; plump.

bound (*bownd*) *n.* 1. Limit; boundary; edge. 2. [*pl.*] An area forbidden to soldiers, students, etc. 3. Confine; restraint.—**bound** *v.*

bound *v.* 1. To leap; jump; progress in leaps. 2. To bounce back; rebound.—**bound** *n.*

bound *adj.* 1. Tied up; fettered; obliged. 2. Sure; destined. 'He is bound to win.'

bound·a·ry (*bown*-duh-ree) *n.* [*pl.* bound·a·ries] Limit; line of demarcation; border.

bound·er *n.* 1. *Colloquial.* A cad; contemptible, worthless fellow. 2. *Baseball.* A hit ball bouncing along the ground.

bound·less *adj.* Limitless; endless; unconfined. —**bound·less·ly** *adv.*—**bound·less·ness** *n.*

boun·te·ous (*bown*-tee-us) *adj.* Generous; liberal.—**boun·te·ous·ly** *adv.*—**boun·te·ous·ness** *n.*

boun·ti·ful (*bown*-tih-ful) *adj.* Bounteous; bestowing gifts.— -**ful·ly** *adv.*—**ful·ness** *n.*

boun·ty *n.* [*pl.* boun·ties] 1. Liberality in bestowing gifts and favors. 2. A gift generously given. 3. A premium or incentive reward.

bou·quet (boo-*kay*) *n.* 1. A bunch of cut flowers. 2. A flavor; pleasing odor; savor.

Bour·bon (*boor*-bun) *n.* 1. A European royal family which formerly ruled France and Spain. 2. Any extreme reactionary in politics.

3. [*not cap.*] (*ber*-b'n, *boor*-) An aged corn whisky, originated in Bourbon County, Ky.

bour·geois (boor-*zhwah*) *adj.* 1. Of the middle class. 2. Denoting capitalism or the capitalist class. 3. Of vulgar taste.—**bour·geois** *n.* —**bour·geoi·sie** *n.*

bour·geois (bur-*joiss*) *n. Printing.* A 9-point type.

bourn, bourne (*bohrn, born, bern*) *n.* 1. A stream; rivulet. 2. Destination.

bourse (*boors*) *n.* Also **boerse.** An exchange; esp. a European stock exchange.

bout (*bowt*) *n.* 1. Trial; contest; set-to. 2. A turn.

bo·vine (*boh*-vyne) *n.* The family of cud-chewing mammals to which cows belong.—**bo·vine** *adj.*

bow *v.* 1. To bend; curve. 2. To incline the head or body in greeting or reverence. 3. To depress; crush; subdue.—**bow** *n.*

bow *n.* The forward part of a ship.—**bow** *adj.*

bow (*boh*) *n.* 1. An elastic shaft with a string, designed to shoot arrows. 2. Anything bent like a bow. 3. *Music.* A shaft strung with horsehair and drawn over the strings of a violin, etc., to produce the tone. 4. An ornamental slipknot with two loops. 5. Something curved like a bow.—*v.* 1. To curve or bend. 2. *Music.* To produce a tone with a bow.

BOW AND ARROWS

bow arm	bow maker	bow-necked
bowback	bow making	bow-shaped
bowhead	bowman	bowwood

bowd·ler·ize (*bowd*-ler-yze) *v.* [bowd·ler·ized; -iz·ing] To expurgate; remove offensive or questionable words from.—**bowd·ler·ism** *n.*

bow·el (*bow*-ul) *n.* 1. [*usually pl.*] An intestine; gut. 2. [*pl.*] The interior or depths of anything. 'The bowels of the earth.'

bow·er (*bow*-er) *n.* A shelter of boughs or vines; arbor; shady recess.

Bow·er·y *n.* A street of New York City's lower East Side, once famous for its amusement establishments.

bowie knife (*boh*-ee, *boo*-ee). A long, broad-bladed hunting knife.

bow·knot (*boh*-not) *n.* A kind of slipknot with two loops.

bowl (*bohl*) *n.* 1. A round, concave, deep dish. 2. The contents of a bowl. 3. Any bowl-shaped depression or vessel.

bowl *v.* To roll balls at pins in the game of bowling.—**bowl·ing.** Also **bowls.** *n.* A game played with balls and pins on a level alley. —**bowl·er** *n.*

bow·leg·ged *adj.* Having crooked legs.—**bow·leg** *n.*

bow·line (*boh*-l'n) *n.* 1. A knot forming a non-slipping loop. 2. A line secured along the leach of a sail.

bow·shot *n.* The distance traveled by an arrow.

bow·sprit (*bow*-sprit) *n.* A large spar on the bow of a sailing vessel to which rigging, sails, etc., are secured.

BOWSPRIT

bow·string (*boh*-string) *n.* 1. The string of a bow. 2. Any cord used for strangling. —*v.* [bow·strung; bow·string·ing].

box *n.* 1. A case; receptacle; container; chest. 2. The quantity contained in a box. 3. A compartment or small enclosed seating area, esp. in a theater.—**box** *v.*

box *n.* A blow with the flat of the hand, esp. on the ear.—*v.* 1. To strike with the hand. 2. To fight with the fists according to pugilistic rules. —**box·er** *n.*

box, box·wood *n.* A family of evergreen shrubs or trees having leathery leaves and small flowers.

box·ing *n.* The theory or technique of fist fighting according to rules.

box office. 1. The ticket booth of an entertainment place. 2. *Slang.* Theatrically successful. '*Show Boat* is terrific box office.'

boy *n.* 1. A male child. 2. An immature young man. 3. A servant; waiter; porter.

boy·cott (*boy*-kot) *v.* To refuse to have dealings with; impose sanctions against.—**boy·cott** *n.*

boy·hood *n.* Period in the life of a male child from birth to puberty.

boy·ish *adj.* Like a boy; youthful; immature. —**boy·ish·ly** *adv.*—**boy·ish·ness** *n.*

Boy Scout. A member of the Boy Scouts an international boys' organization dedicated to character building.

brace *n.* 1. A support; a device which lends rigidity or strength. 2. A pair. 'A brace of ducks.' 3. *Printing & Music.* A connective symbol [}] 4. An angled stock or holder for bits, drills, reamers, and other cutting tools. 5. [*pl.*] Suspenders.—*v.* [braced; brac·ing] 1. To support. 2. To get set or ready.

brace·let (*brays*-let) *n.* A piece of jewelry worn around the wrist.

brac·er *n. Slang.* A drink of liquor or other stimulating agent.

brach·i·al (*bray*-kee-ul) *adj.* Pertaining to or resembling the arm.

brac·ing *adj.* Stimulating; invigorating.—*n.* A system of braces.

brack·et (*brak*-et) *n.* 1. A triangular brace projecting from a wall to support a shelf, beam, shaft, etc. 2. *Printing.* One of two symbols ([ ]) used to set off parenthetical matter.—**brack·et** *v.*

brack·ish *adj.* Salty in taste; unwholesome. —**brack·ish·ness** *n.*

bract *n. Botany.* A modified leaf growing on a flower stem to protect the bud.—**brac·te·al** *adj.* —**brac·te·ate** (*brak*-tee-it) *adj.*—**bract·ed** *adj.*

brag *v.* [brag·ged; brag·ging] To boast; vaunt; crow.—**brag** *n.*—**brag·ger** *n.*

brag·ga·do·ci·o (brag-uh-*doh*-shee-oh) *n.* 1. Empty boasting. 2. A boastful fellow.

brag·gart (*brag*-ert) *n.* A boastful, vaunting fellow.—**brag·gart** *adj.*

Brah·ma (*brah*-muh) *n. Hindu Religion.* 1. The creator of the universe. 2. The immaterial, self-existent force which produced the gods.

Brah·man *n.* [*pl.* Brah·mans]. Also **Brah·min.** 1. One of the highest or sacred caste of Hindus. 2. [always *Brahmin*]. An intellectual, esp. in 19th century New England—**Brah·man·ic** (brah-*man*-ik), **-man·i·cal** *adj.*— **-man·ism, -min·ism** *n.*— **-man·ist, -min·ist** *n.*

braid *v.* To plait; weave or twist three or more strands into a cord.—*n.* 1. A narrow band or tape. 2. A plait.—**braid·ing** *n.*

braille (*brayl*) *n.* [*often cap.*] An alphabet enabling the blind to read by sense of touch.

brain *n.* 1. The mass of nerve matter within the skull, the center of consciousness and all bodily functions. 2. Mentality; understanding; imagination.—*v.* To dash out the brain.

brain-born	brainfag	brainsick
brain-cracked	brain fever	brainstone
brain-crazed	brain-fevered	brain-tired

brain·less *adj.* Silly; flighty; stupid.—**brain·less·ly** *adv.*—**brain·less·ness** *n.*

brain·pan *n.* The cranium; bony case around the brain.

brain·storm *n. Slang.* An inspirational idea.

brain trust. A group of experts serving as advisers.—**brain-trust·er** *n.*

brain·y *adj.* [brain·i·er; brain·i·est] *Colloquial.* Intelligent; clever; brilliant.—**brain·i·ness** *n.*

braise (*brayz*) *v.* [braised; brais·ing] To sear and cook slowly in a covered dish with liquid.

brake *n.* A family of coarse ferns.—**brak·y** *adj.* [brak·i·er; brak·i·est].

brake *n.* A thicket; place rank with vegetation.

brake *n.* 1. An appliance to arrest the motion of a machine. 2. A machine for breaking flax or hemp.—*v.* [braked; brak·ing]—**brake·age** *n.*

brake drum. The rotating part of a braking mechanism.

brake lining. The abrasive surface which provides the friction to make a brake operative.

brake·man *n.* [*pl.* brake·men] A railway employee who applies the brakes.

brake shoe. The functional end of the lever which applies the braking pressure.

bram·ble (*bram*-b'l) *n.* 1. A large family of thorny berry-producing bushes. 2. Any prickly or thorny shrub.—**bram·bly** *adj.*

bran *n.* The outer coat of grains separated from the flour in grinding.

branch *n.* 1. The limb or bough of a plant. 2. Any offshoot from a main body; subdivision; section; tributary; ramification.

B

—**branch** v. & adj.—**branch·y** adj. [branch·i·er; branch·i·est].

brand n. 1. Trademark or identification; quality; kind. 2. A burning piece of wood. 3. A sword. 4. Lightning.—v. To mark; label.—**brand·er** n.

bran·dish (bran-dish) v. To flourish; vaunt; wave about defiantly or threateningly.—**bran·dish** n.—**bran·dish·er** n.

brand new. 1. Entirely unused. 2. Radically different or novel.

bran·dy (bran-dee) n. [pl. bran·dies] A potent alcoholic beverage obtained by distillation of wine.—v. [bran·died; bran·dy·ing] To flavor with brandy.

bran·ni·gan n. Slang. An extensive debauch; binge; bender.

brant n. A variety of small wild goose.

brash adj. Colloquial. Hasty; impetuous; indiscreet.—**brash·ness** n.—**brash·y** adj. [brash·i·er; brash·i·est].

brash n. Sludge ice.—**brash·i·ness** n.

brass n. 1. A metal alloy basically compounded of zinc and copper. 2. Colloquial. Impudence; brazenness. 3. Music. Wind instruments played by vibration of the lips rather than of a reed, as the trumpet, trombone, etc. —**brass** v. & adj.

brass hat. Slang. A military officer, esp. a pompous, inefficient, or high-ranking one.

bras·si·ca (bras-ih-kuh) n. The family of plants to which cabbage belongs.—**bras·si·ca·ceous** (bras-ih-kay-shus) adj.

brass·ie, brass·y n. Golf. A wooden-headed club used in distance shots; the number-two wood.

bras·si·ère (bruh-zeer; brah-see-air) n. A woman's undergarment fitted to support the breasts.

brass·y adj. [brass·i·er; brass·i·est] 1. Of or like brass. 2. Colloquial. Impudent; bold.—**brass·i·ly** adv.—**brass·i·ness** n.

brat n. A child; an ill-mannered, uncontrollable child.

braun·schwei·ger (brown-shwy-ger) n. A type of liverwurst.

bra·va·do (bruh-vah-doh) n. [pl. bra·va·does; bra·va·dos] Boastfulness; defiance; an effort at a brave gesture.—**bra·va·do** adj. & v.

BRASSIE

brave adj. 1. Daring; courageous; bold. 2. Cutting a fine figure.—n. A daring person, esp. a North American Indian warrior.—v. [braved; brav·ing]—**brave·ly** adv.—**brave·ness** n.—**brav·er·y** n.

bra·vo (brah-voh) n. [pl. bra·voes, bra·vos] A villain; hired assassin.—interj. Well done! Excellent! Also **brava** (feminine).—n. [pl. bra·vos] A shout of applause.

brawl v. To wrangle noisily; fight drunkenly or bestially.—n. Slang. A loud, rough party.—**brawl·er** n.

brawn n. Muscular strength; muscle.—**brawn·y** adj.—**brawn·i·ness** n.

bray v. To utter a loud, harsh sound. 'The donkey brays.'—**bray** n.—**bray·er** n.

braze v. [brazed; braz·ing] To adorn with brass.

braze v. To unite a copper alloy with some other metal in a soldering process.—**braz·er** n.

bra·zen (bray-z'n) adj. 1. Impudent; bold; callously forward. 2. Of or like brass.—**bra·zen** v.—**bra·zen·ness** n.

bra·zier (bray-zher) n. 1. A brass worker. 2. An open pan for holding burning coals.

Brazil nut. A large, semicircular, triangular nut with an oily center.—**Brazil-nut** adj.

breach (breech) n. 1. A break; gap; rupture. 2. Dissolution of relationship; estrangement. 3. Violation; commission of an offense; breaking of a law or code.—**breach** v.

bread (bred) n. 1. Kneaded dough baked in an oven. 2. Food; a living.—**bread** v. To dip in or cover with bread crumbs.

bread box	bread-faced	breadman
bread crumb	bread maker	breadmeal
breadearner	bread making	bread seller

bread and butter. Colloquial. A livelihood. —**bread-and-butter** adj.—**bread-and-butter letter.** A letter in appreciation of hospitality.

bread·bas·ket n. Slang. The stomach; abdomen.

bread·fruit n. A large, seedless, pulpy fruit grown in moist tropical areas.

bread line. A line of people waiting for a dole of food.—**bread·lin·er** n.

bread·stuff n. 1. Grain or flour. 2. Bakery goods; breads.

breadth (bredth) n. 1. Width; extent; scope. 2. Spaciousness; largeness; magnitude.

bread·win·ner n. One who earns the livelihood of the family; means of earning a living.

break (brayk) v. [broke; brok·en; break·ing] 1. To rend; tear apart; part. 2. To destroy; crush; impair; subdue. 3. To quell; tame. 4. To bankrupt. 5. Military. To demote or dismiss. 6. To violate, as a law. 7. To stop; interrupt; check. 8. To disclose cautiously. 'The attaché broke the news.' 9. To disrupt or interrupt a set or series.—n. 1. Slang. A lucky circumstance; opportunity to advance oneself. 2. An opening; rupture; interruption of continuity. 3. Communications. The signal BT indicating new paragraph or end of message. 4. A fracture; shattering. 5. Dancing. A temporary drawing apart of the partners. 6. Slang. A social error; an unfortunate slip. 7. Jazz Music. A hot phrase interpolated during a momentary suspension of the rhythmic accompaniment.—**break·a·ble** adj.

break·age (brayk-ij) n. 1. The quantity of goods broken, esp. in transit. 2. An allowance made for such loss.

break·down n. 1. A collapse; failure; inability to continue. 2. A reduction to small subdivisions or categories.

break·er n. A large wave.

break·fast (brek-fust) n. The first meal of the day.—**break·fast** v.

break·neck adj. Dangerous; hazarding life.

break·up n. A disintegration; separation.

break·wa·ter *n.* Wall built to break waves' force.

bream *n.* A family of fresh-water fishes having a flavorless meat; also the scup, a sea fish.

breast (*brest*) *n.* 1. Bosom; mammary gland; chest. 2. The figurative center of affections and emotions. 3. The front.—**breast** *v.*

breast band	**breast height**	**breastplate**
breastbeam	**breast high**	**breastrope**
breast-fed	**breastpin**	**breastwood**

breast·bone *n. Anatomy.* The sternum; the bone to which the ribs attach.

breast·work *n.* 1. A hastily raised defensive embankment. 2. A balustrade; parapet.

breath (*breth*) *n.* 1. The air inhaled and exhaled. 2. The ability to breathe; life. 3. A single respiration. 4. A slight breeze or scent.

breathe (*breeth*) *v.* [breathed; breath·ing] 1. To inhale and exhale. 2. To live. 3. To make a single exhalation. 4. To infuse; revive; inject. 5. To whisper; speak softly. 6. To give a respite from exercise. 'Breathe the horses.'—**breath·a·ble** *adj.*

breath·er (*breeth*-er) *n. Colloquial.* A period of relaxation after exertion.

breath·ing (*breeth*-ing) *n.* 1. Respiration. 2. A gentle breeze.—*adj.* Inhaling and exhaling breath; alive.

breath·less (*breth*-lis) *adj.* 1. Not breathing from wonder or other emotion; in suspense. 2. Respiring heavily; spent.—**breath·less·ly** *adv.*—**breath·less·ness** *n.*

breech *n.* 1. The hind or thick part of a cannon or gun. 2. The hinder part of anything.

breech·es (*brich*-iz) *n. pl.* Also **britches.** 1. Knee-length trousers, tight at the knees and full above. 2. *Colloquial.* Any trousers.

breeches buoy. *Nautical.* A life preserver with a trouserlike bottom secured to an endless line to convey survivors from a stranded ship.

breed *v.* [bred; breed·ing] 1. To beget; procreate. 2. To cause; originate; produce. 3. To rear; bring up.—*n.* 1. A class of animals related by heredity. 2. Kind; type. —**breed·er** *n.*

breed·ing *n.* 1. Refined social deportment; good manners. 2. Upbringing; rearing. 3. Generation; reproduction.

breeze *n.* A gentle wind; zephyr.—*v.* [breezed; breez·ing].

breez·y *adj.* [breez·i·er; breez·i·est] 1. Filled with soft winds; cool; refreshing. 2. Casual; sprightly.—**breez·i·ly** *adv.*—**breez·i·ness** *n.*

Bre·ton (*bret*-un) *n.* An inhabitant of the French province of **Brittany.**—**Bre·ton** *adj.*

breve (*breev*) *Printing.* Pronunciation symbol [˘] indicating a short vowel sound.

bre·vet (breh-*vet*) *n. Military.* A commission conferring a higher privilege or rank than that paid for.—**bre·vet** *adj.*—*v.* [bre·vet·ted; brev·et·ed; bre·vet·ting, brev·et·ing]—**bre·vet·cy** *n.*

bre·vi·ar·y (*bree*-vee-ehr-ee) *n.* [*pl.* -ries] A book of prayers, psalms, etc., for daily reading.

bre·vier (bruh-*vihr*) *n. Printing.* An 8-point type.

brev·i·ty (*brev*-uh-tee) *n.* [*pl.* brev·i·ties] Shortness; conciseness; succinctness.

B

brew (*broo*) *n.* Beverage produced by fermentation, boiling, etc.—*v.* 1. To make such a beverage. 2. To concoct; plot; prepare. 3. To be in preparation; be in the offing. —**brew·er** *n.*

brew·er·y (*broo*-er-ee) *n.* [*pl.* brew·er·ies] A building or factory for making malt liquors.

brew·ing (*broo*-ing) *n.* 1. Quantity of beverage brewed at one time. 2. Preparation of brewed beverages.

bri·ar, bri·er (*bry*-er) *n.* 1. A prickly or thorny shrub. 2. A European heath, whose roots are used for making smoking pipes. 3. A briar pipe.—**bri·ar·y, bri·er·y** *adj.*

bribe *v.* [bribed; brib·ing] To corrupt with a gift or favor.—**bribe** *n.*—**brib·a·ble** (*bribe*-uh-b'l) *adj.*—**brib·er** *n.*—**brib·er·y** *n.* [*pl.* -er·ies].

bric-a-brac (*brik*-uh-brak) *n.* A group of small decorative articles.

brick *n.* 1. A block of kneaded clay baked in an oven until hard. 2. Any bricklike mass or shape.—**brick** *adj.*—**brick·y** *adj.*

brick-built	**bricklayer**	**brick-paved**
brick-colored	**bricklaying**	**brick setter**
brickfield	**brick liner**	**brick-walled**
brick-fronted	**brickmaker**	**brickwork**
brickkiln	**brickmason**	**brickyard**

brick·bat *n.* 1 A broken piece of a brick. 2. An insult; vicious remark.

brid·al (*bryde*-'l) *adj.* Relating to a bride or a wedding.—*n.* A marriage ceremony.

bridal wreath. A flowering shrub of the spirea family.

bride *n.* A woman recently married, being married, or soon to be wed.

bride·groom (*bryde*-groom) *n.* A man recently married, being married, or soon to be wed.

brides·maid (*brydze*-mayd) *n.* A female attendant to a bride at her wedding.

bridge (*brij*) *n.* 1. A structure built for passage across a stream, ravine, etc. 2. The upper part of the nose. 3. *Music.* An arch on a stringed instrument over which the strings are stretched. 4. The runner or structure on which a mechanical crane operates. 5. A card game employing the entire deck, in which play is based on a system of bids. 6. *Dentistry.* An artificial tooth or teeth filling a gap between natural teeth. 7. *Nautical.* The deck from which a ship is piloted and navigated.—*v.* [bridged; bridg·ing]. To cross any intervening gap; overcome.—**bridge·a·ble** *adj.*

bridge builder	**bridge maker**	**bridgeward**
bridgekeeper	**bridgemaster**	**bridgeway**

bridge·head (*brij*-hed) *n. Military.* An area on the far bank of a river or other waterway secured from an enemy by invasion.

bridge·work (*brij*-werk) *n. Dentistry.* Bridges or artificial teeth collectively.

bridg·ing (*brij*-ing) *n.* A system of braces placed

between beams or other supports to prevent their drawing together.

bri·dle (*bry*-d'l) *n.* 1. The gear or harness fitted over a horse's head. 2. Any curb or restraint. —*v.* [bri·dled; bri·dling]. 1. To curb; control. 2. To assert one's dignity or express indignation at 'offense. 3. To put a bridle on.—**bri·dler** *n.*

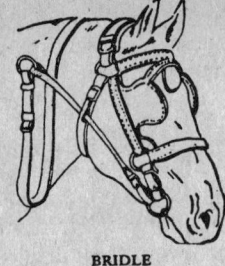

BRIDLE

bridle path. A trail passable to horses but not to vehicles.

brief (*breef*) *adj.* Short; concise; laconic.—*n.* 1. A summary; short statement. 2. *Law.* A concise statement of the facts of a case drawn up to guide a lawyer in court proceedings.—*v.* 1. To reduce to a summary. 2. To give concise instructions in preparation for a task.

brief case. A sheath or case, usually leather, for carrying documents, papers, and books.

brig *n.* 1. A type of square-rigged sailing ship. 2. A jail aboard ship.

bri·gade (brih-*gayd*) *n.* 1. A body of persons organized and acting under authority. 2. A body of troops consisting of two regiments.

BRIG

brig·a·dier (brig-uh-*dihr*) *n. Military.* An officer in charge of a brigade.

brigadier general. The lowest rank of general, between a colonel and major general.

brig·and (*brig*-und) *n.* A bandit; highwayman; robber.—**brig·and·age, brig·and·ism** *n.*

brig·an·tine (*brig*-un-teen) *n.* A kind of light, fast, two-masted sailing ship.

brig·gi·ty, brig·go·ty *adj. Colloquial.* Conceited; self-important; saucy.

bright (*bryte*) *adj.* 1. Shining; sparkling; luminous. 2. Glorious; illustrious. 3. Intelligent; brilliant. 4. Cheerful; vivacious. —**bright·ly** *adj.*—**bright·ness** *n.*

bright·en (*bryte*-'n) *v.* 1. To make luminous or lustrous. 2. To cheer; dispel gloom. 3. To make splendid or distinguished. 4. To make acute or witty. 5. To add brilliancy to a color.

Bright's disease. An inflammatory degeneration of the kidneys, usually fatal.

bril·liance (*bril*-yuns) *n.* Also **bril·lian·cy.** 1. Luster; great brightness. 2. High intelligence. 3. The evaluation of a color in terms of its lightness, or closeness to white.

bril·liant (*bril*-yunt) *adj.* 1. Brightly shining; flashing. 2. Highly intelligent or gifted. 3. Distinguished; splendid.—*n.* 1. A diamond cut to reflect maximum light. 2. *Printing.* A type with a 3½-point face.—**bril·liant·ly** *adv.*—**bril·liant·ness** *n.*

bril·lian·tine (*bril*-yun-teen) *n.* An oily preparation used to give a sheen to the hair.

brim *n.* 1. Edge; brink; margin. 2. A projecting rim or border. 3. The projecting edge of a hat.—*v.* [brimmed; brim·ming] To fill to the top.—**brim·ful** *adj.*—**brim·less** *n.*

brim·stone *n.* Sulphur.—**brim·ston·y** *adj.*

brin·dled (*brin*-d'ld) *adj.* Streaked; spotted; motley.—**brin·dle** *adj. & n.*

brine *n.* A salt-water solution; the sea.—*v.* [brined; brin·ing] To treat in brine.—**brin·ish** *adj.*

bring *v.* [brought; brought; bring·ing] 1. To carry; transport. 2. To guide; conduct; accompany. 3. To induce; persuade. 4. To procure; obtain.—**bring·er** *n.*

brink *n.* Edge; border; verge.

brin·y (*bry*-nee) *adj.* [brin·i·er; brin·i·est] Salty; pertaining to ocean water.—**brin·i·ness** *n.*

bri·oche (bree-*ohsh*) *n.* A rich breakfast roll.

bri·quette (brih-*ket*) *n.* Also **bri·quet.** Coal dust pressed into bricks.

brisk *adj.* 1. Quick; active; vigorous; lively; rapid. 2. Crisp; sharp.—**brisk** *v.*—**brisk·ly** *adv.*—**brisk·ness** *n.*

bris·ket (*bris*-ket) *n.* The breast of lamb, veal, or beef, when used as food.

bris·tle (*bris*-'l) *n.* A stiff, coarse hair.—*v.* [bris·tled; bris·tling] 1. To show anger or defiance. 2. To erect bristles. 3. To be thickly covered. 'The ship bristled with guns.'

Bristol board (*bris*-t'l-bohrd). A quality pasteboard with a smooth and glazed surface.

bri·tan·nia (brih-*tan*-yuh, -ee-uh) *n.* A whitish alloy of tin, antimony, zinc, and copper.

Bri·tan·nia. 1. Great Britain. 2. The female figure symbolizing Great Britain.

brit·ches (*brih*-chiz) *n.* [*pl.*] *Colloquial.* Pants; trousers; breeches.

Brit·ish *adj.* Denoting Great Britain, its dependencies and people.—**Brit·ish, Brit·ish·er** *n.*

British Empire. Great Britain and its dependencies and dominions.

Brit·on (*brit*-un) *n.* 1. One of the ancient inhabitants of England and Wales. 2. An Englishman.

Brit·ta·ny (*brit*-uh-nee). A province and former kingdom of western France.

brit·tle (*brit*-'l) *adj.* Crisp; easy to break or shatter.—**brit·tle·ness** *n.*

broach (*brohch*) *n.* 1. A highly precise machine tool used primarily to cut irregular holes. 2. The tapering notched cutting tool of this machine. 3. A narrow stone chisel. 4. A tapered, fluted reamer.—*v.* 1. To introduce; begin discussion of. 2. To tap; let out; shed. 3. To cut with a broach.—**broach·er** *n.*

broach to. *Nautical.* To incline suddenly to windward, endangering balance.

broad (*brawd*) *adj.* 1. Wide; extensive; vast. 2. Comprehensive; not limited. 3. Liberal; tolerant. 4. Off-color; vulgar. 5. Full; complete. 'Broad daylight.' 6. Bold; unre-

served.—*n. Slang.* Woman.—**broad·ish** *adj.*
—**broad·ly** *adv.*—**broad·ness** *n.*

broad-beamed	broadbrim	broadleaved
broadbill	broad-chested	broadsheet
broad-billed	broadleaf	broadtail

broad·ax, broad·axe *n.* 1. A large-bladed ax used for peeling logs. 2. A battleax.

broad·cast *n.* A performance or entertainment transmitted via radio waves.—*v.* [broad·cast; broad·cast·ing] 1. To put a show or performance on the air. 2. To disseminate; spread; propagate.—*adj.* Widely dispersed. —**broad·cast·er** *n.*—**broad·cast·ing** *n.*

broad·cloth *n.* 1. A firmly woven, select cotton or silk cloth. 2. A heavy, soft-napped, felted woolen fabric.

broad·en *v.* To make wider, more comprehensive, or more representative.

broad jump. A distance leap, esp. in athletic games.

broad·mind·ed *adj.* Tolerant; liberal; not bigoted; understanding.—**broad·mind·ed·ly** *adv.* —**broad·mind·ed·ness** *n.*

broad·side *n.* 1. A large advertising folder or poster printed on one side only. 2. A simultaneous firing of the guns of one side of a ship.

broad·sword *n.* A broad-bladed cutting sword.

Broad·way (*brawd*-way) *n.* 1. New York City's longest street. 2. The theatrical district of New York City.

Brob·ding·nag·i·an (brob-ding-*nag*-ee-an) *adj.* Denoting the race of giants in Swift's *Gulliver's Travels*; huge.—*n.* A giant.

bro·cade (broh-*kayd*) *n.* Rich cloth embroidered with raised ornamentation.—*v.* [bro·cad·ed; bro·cad·ing].

broc·co·li (*brok*-uh-lee) *n.* A loose green herb closely related to the cabbage.

bro·chure (broh-*shoor*) *n.* A pamphlet; extract.

bro·gan (broh-g'n) *n.* A stout, heavy shoe.

brogue (*brohg*) *n.* Speech with a strong dialectal accent, esp. Irish.

broil *v.* To roast under a flame.

broil *n.* A noisy quarrel; tumult; fight.

broil·er *n.* 1. A compartment of a stove for broiling food. 2. A young chicken dressed for broiling.

broke *adj. Slang.* Penniless.

bro·ken *adj.* 1. Parted; separated. 2. Shattered; fractured. 3. Out of order; not operating. 4. Interrupted; intermittent. 5. Crushed in spirit. 6. Infirm; weak. 7. Bankrupt. 8. Spoken with a foreign accent.—**bro·ken·ly** *adv.*—**bro·ken·ness** *n.*

broken-arched	broken-fortuned	broken-spirited
broken-backed	broken-nosed	broken-winded
broken down	broken-paced	broken-winged

bro·ken·heart·ed *adj.* Crushed with grief.

bro·ker *n.* 1. An agent or negotiator. 2. A stock-broker; dealer in stocks and bonds.

bro·ker·age (broh-ker-ij) *n.* 1. A broker's business. 2. The fee charged by brokers.

bro·mide, bro·mid (broh-*myde*) *n.* 1. *Chem*-istry. A salt, often used as a sedative, in which bromine is the electronegative element. 2. An oft-repeated commonplace remark or statement.—**bro·mid·ic** (broh-*mid*-ik) *adj.*

bro·mine (*broh*-meen) *n.* Also **bro·min.** A red-brown liquid element of the chlorine group. (*Symbol:* Br).

bron·chi (*bronk*-ee, -y) *n. pl. Anatomy.* [*sing.* bron·chus] The two main branches of the windpipe.

bron·chi·a (*bronk*-ee-uh) *n. pl. Anatomy.* A branching from the bronchi.

bron·chi·al (*bronk*-ee-ul) *adj.* Denoting the bronchi or bronchia. 'Bronchial pneumonia.'

bron·chi·tis (bron-*ky*-tis) *n.* An inflammation of the bronchial passages.—**bron·chit·ic** (bron-kit-ik) *adj.*

bron·co, bron·cho (*brong*-koh) *n.* [*pl.* bron·cos, bron·chos] A spirited saddle horse noted for its endurance, common in western U.S.

bron·co·bust·er *n.* Also **bron·cho·bust·er.** *Colloquial.* One who breaks or trains wild horses.

Bronx cheer. *Slang.* A derisive noise produced by vibrating the lips and tongue.

bronze *n.* 1. An alloy usually composed of copper and tin, with copper predominating. 2. A statue or other art work cast in bronze. 3. A bronze-colored pigment.—*v.* [bronzed; bronz·ing]—**bronz·y** *adj.*

brooch (*brohch, brooch*) *n.* An ornamental pin or clasp.

brood *n.* 1. A single hatching; family. 2. That which is produced or bred. 3. Offspring; progeny.—*v.* 1. To remain in anxious or dejected thought. 2. To hatch. 3. To cherish; nurture.—**brood** *adj.*—**brood·y** *adj.*

brood·er *n.* 1. An artificially heated compartment for rearing young fowl. 2. A brooding animal or person.

brook *v.* A small stream.—*v.* To endure; allow. —**brook·let** *n.* A small brook.

brook trout. A large, fighting gamefish of inland streams.

broom *n.* 1. A bundle of stiff stems or straws fixed to a handle, used for sweeping. 2. A woody shrub with yellow flowers.—**broom** *v.*

broom-leaved	broomshank	broomtail
broommaker	broomstaff	broom twine
broommaking	broomstraw	broomwood

broom·corn *n.* A tall, reedy grass from which brooms are made.

broom·stick *n.* The handle of a broom.

broth *n.* Clear meat soup; bouillon.

broth·el (*braw*-th'l) *n.* A house of prostitution.

broth·er *n.* 1. A male born to the same parents as oneself. 2. Anyone having close physical, intellectual, or professional relation. 3. One of a religious order.—**broth·er** *v.*

broth·er·hood *n.* 1. An association of men. 2. The state of being a brother.

broth·er-in-law *n.* [*pl.* broth·ers-in-law] The husband of one's sister, or the brother of one's spouse.

B

broth·er·ly *adj*. 1. Pertaining to brothers. 2. Kindly; affectionate; helpful.—**broth·er·ly** *adv*.—**broth·er·li·ness** *n*.

brougham (*broom*) *n*. 1. A car body similar to a coupé but accommodating more passengers. 2. A closed, horse-drawn carriage, with an outside driver's seat.

BROUGHAM (def. 2)

brow *n*. 1. The forehead. 2. The eyebrow. 3. The upper part of a slope; edge of a steep place.

brow·beat (*brow*-beet) *v*. [brow·beat; brow·beaten; brow·beat·ing] To bully; intimidate by harsh or overbearing action.

brown *n*. A dark, dull color composed of a mixture of yellow, red, and blue.—*adj*. 1. Of this color. 2. Dark-skinned; tanned.—*v*. To color brown; toast until brown.

brown betty. A baked pudding of fruit, breadcrumbs, etc.

brown bread. Any steamed or baked bread of graham or wheat flour.

brown·ie (*brown*-ee) *n*. 1. A rich chocolate cake, usually cut into cubes. 2. A helpful sprite or elf. 3. [*cap*.] A junior Girl Scout.

brown rice. Unpolished or natural rice.

Brown Shirt. 1. Member of an armed band of terrorists which supported Adolf Hitler in his rise to power. 2. [*pl*.] The Nazis.

brown·stone (*brown*-stohn) *n*. Brown sandstone used for building in late 19th century.

brown study. A deep reverie or absorption in thought.

browse (*browz*) *v*. [browsed; brows·ing] 1. To graze; feed; nibble. 2. To examine leisurely and at random.—*n*. Tender green shoots for feeding cattle.

bru·in (*broo*-in) *n*. A bear.

bruise (*brooz*) *n*. A contusion; injury which does not break the skin.—*v*. [bruised; bruis·ing] 1. To injure without breaking the skin. 2. To hurt or become hurt. 3. To crush.

bruis·er (*brooz*-er) *n*. 1. A boxer; prizefighter. 2. *Slang*. Big, tough person; bully.

bruit (*broot*) *v*. To noise about; rumor.

brunch *n*. A combined breakfast and lunch.

bru·net, bru·nette (broo-*net*) *n*. A person with dark eyes, hair, and skin.—**bru·net, bru·nette** *adj*. Note: **brunet**, *masculine*; -ette, *feminine*.

brunt *n*. The greatest concentration of force or violence, as of an attack.

brush *n*. 1. A cleaning or painting utensil of bristles or wires fixed in a back or handle. 2. Act of brushing; quick rub. 3. *Electricity*. A carbon or copper device for conducting current to or from a rotating part. 4. Bushy tail, as of a fox.—*v*. 1. To rub or paint with a brush. 2. To touch in passing. 3. To wipe; remove.—**brush·y** *adj*. [brush·i·er; brush·i·est].

brush *n*. A short, indecisive encounter.—*v*. To move quickly.

brush *n*. 1. Small trees and shrubs. 2. The cut branches of trees.—**brush·y** *adj*. [brush·i·er; brush·i·est].

brush-off *n*. *Slang*. A rebuff; repulse; snub.

brush·wood *n*. 1. Cut branches of trees. 2. Shrubs and small trees of a forest.

brusque (*brusk*) *adj*. Abrupt; blunt; curt. —**brusque·ly** *adv*.—**brusque·ness** *n*.

Brussels carpet. Carpet with a pattern formed by loops of colored worsted yarn.

Brussels sprouts. A variety of cabbage bearing small, edible heads on the plant stem.

bru·tal (*broo*-t'l) *adj*. Pertaining to or like a brute; cruel; bestial.—**bru·tal·i·ty** (broo-*tal*-uh-tee) *n*.—**bru·tal·ly** (*broo*-t'l-ee) *adv*.

bru·tal·ize (*broo*-t'l-yze) *v*. [bru·tal·ized; -iz·ing] To render brutal; degrade.—**bru·tal·i·za·tion** (broo-t'l-uh-*zay*-sh'n] *n*.

brute (*broot*) *n*. 1. An animal; beast. 2. A coarse or savage person.—*adj*. 1. Unreasoning; without feeling. 2. Savage; coarse.

brut·ish (*broot*-ish) *adj*. Like a brute; unreasoning; savage.—**brut·ish·ly** *adv*.— -**ish·ness** *n*.

bub·ble (*buhb*-'l) *n*. 1. A small blob of air or gas in a fluid or solid. 2. Thin liquid film filled with gas or air. 3. An unsafe speculative venture; a vain project.—*v*. [bub·bled; bub·bling]—**bub·bly** *adj*.

bubonic plague (byoo-*bon*-ik). A virulent infectious fever marked by chills and swelling of the lymph glands.

buc·ca·neer (buhk-uh-*nihr*) *n*. A pirate.

buck *n*. 1. The male of the rabbit, goat, deer, and certain other animals. 2. *Slang*. A man; male, esp. a dandy. 3. Act of bucking. 4. A sawhorse. 5. *Slang*. A dollar.—*v*. 1. To leap wildly with the hind legs raised high. 'A bucking horse.' 2. To fight or charge against.

buck·a·roo (buhk-uh-roo) *n*. *U.S.* A cowboy.

buck·board (*buhk*-bohrd) *n*. An open buggy with the seat fastened to a springy platform.

buck·et (*buhk*-it) *n*. A pail; container with an arched handle.—*v*. To carry or lift in a bucket. —**buck·et·ful** *n*.

buck·eye *n*. 1. Tree or shrub of the horse chestnut family. 2. [*cap*.] A native of Ohio.

buck·fev·er *n*. Extreme agitation upon sighting game, common among inexperienced hunters.

buck·le (*buhk*-'l) *n*. 1. A clasp or catch for fastening two ends, as of a belt. 2. An ornament of similar design. 3. A bulge or unnatural bend.—*v*. [buck·led; buck·ling]. 1. To fasten with a buckle. 2. To apply oneself energetically. 'Buckle down to the job.' 3. To bend; crumple.

buck·ler (*buhk*-ler) *n*. 1. Ancient shield used in fighting. 2. A defense or protection.

buck·pass·ing *n*. *Slang*. Avoiding responsibility or censure by referring a matter to somebody else.—**buck·pass·er** *n*.

buck·ram (*buhk*-rum) *n*. A coarse stiffened cloth.

buck·saw *n*. A saw set in a frame and used on light lumber.

B

buck·shot *n.* Large lead shot for hunting game.

buck·skin *n.* A soft, pliable leather formerly made from deerskin.—**buck·skin** *adj.*

buck·tooth *n.* [*pl.* -teeth] A protruding tooth.

buck·wheat *n.* A grain-producing grass closely related to wheat.

bu·col·ic (byoo-*kol*-ik) *adj.* Also **bu·col·i·cal.** Rural; rustic; pastoral.—*n.* A pastoral poem.—**bu·col·i·cal·ly** *adv.*

bud *n.* 1. An unopened flower or undeveloped shoot. 2. Any small, undeveloped protuberance. 3. Undeveloped person or thing.—*v.* [bud·ded; bud·ding] 1. To sprout buds; develop. 2. To graft by inserting a bud in the stem of another variety.—**bud·der** *n.*

Bud·dha (*boo*-duh) *n.* An Oriental philosopher and teacher, founder of Buddhism.

Bud·dhism *n.* Asiatic religion teaching that one can attain Nirvana, the escape from mortality, by right thinking and living.— -**dhist** *n.* & *adj.*

bud·dy (*buhd*-ee) *n.* [*pl.* bud·dies] *Colloquial.* A comrade; close friend.

budge (*buhj*) *v.* [budged; budg·ing] To move slightly; stir.—*n. Slang.* Pocket; pocketbook.

budg·et (*buhj*-it) *n.* 1. A carefully enumerated statement of income and necessary expenditures. 2. A stock; total amount.—**budg·et** *v.*—**budg·et·er** *n.*

buff *n.* 1. A strong soft leather made from the hide of the buffalo, elk, etc. 2. A dull tan or yellow color. 3. A leather-covered stick for polishing. 4. *Slang.* Bare skin.—*v.* To polish.—**buff** *adj.*

buf·fa·lo (*buhf*-uh-loh) *n.* [*pl.* buf·fa·loes, buf·fa·los, buf·fa·lo] 1. Any of several large animals related to the ox, as the water buffalo and cape buffalo. 2. *Colloquial.* The American bison.

WATER BUFFALO

buf·fer (*buhf*-er) *n.* 1. A shock-absorbing mechanism. 2. A polisher; buff. 3. A small state between two larger antagonistic nations. 4. *Radio.* An amplifying tube isolating the oscillator from following stages of radio-frequency amplification.

buf·fet (*buh*-fit) *n.* A blow of the fist; hence, any blow or violent force.—**buf·fet** *v.*—**buf·fet·er** *n.*

buf·fet (buh-*fay*) *n.* A sideboard; long low set of shelves for displaying china and bric-a-brac.

buffet luncheon. A meal at which the guests serve themselves.

bug *n.* 1. Any insect, esp. a crawling insect. 2. *Radio Slang.* A high-speed radio-telegraph key. 3. *Slang.* An obsessive idea. 4. *Slang.* A faulty technical detail in a new product or process.

bug·a·boo (*buhg*-uh-boo) *n.* An imaginary cause of terror; bogy.

bug·bear (*buhg*-bayr) *n.* A cause of needless fright; bugaboo.

bug·ger (*buh*-ger) *n.* 1. A sodomite. 2. *Slang.* A worthless fellow. —*v.* To commit sodomy.

bug·gy (*buhg*-ee) *n.* [*pl.* bug·gies] A light, one-horse carriage. —*adj.* [bug·gi·er; bug·gi·est] Having many bugs.

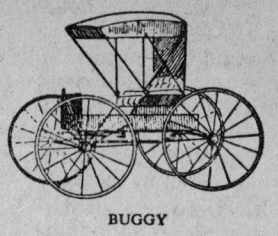
BUGGY

bu·gle (*byoo*-g'l) *n. Music.* A brass wind instrument similar to the trumpet.—*v.* [bu·gled; bu·gling] 1. To blow a bugle. 2. To summon by bugling. —**bu·gler** *n.*

BUGLE

bu·gle *n.* A long glass bead used for trimming or ornamentation.—**bu·gled** *adj.*

buhl (*bool*), **buhl·work** *n.* Elaborately patterned inlay work of metal, ivory, etc.

build (*bild*) *v.* [built; built; build·ing] 1. To construct; erect a structure. 2. To establish; create slowly and carefully. 'Build good will.' —*n.* Form; manner of construction; lines. —**build·er** *n.*

build·ing *n.* 1. An edifice; permanent structure. 2. Act or business of construction.

built. *Past tense* & *past participle* of **build.**

bulb *n.* 1. The rounded, underground bud of certain plants, as the onion. 2. Fleshy part of an underground stem. 3. The round glass enclosing an incandescent lamp. 4. Any bulblike projection or formation.—**bulb·ar** *adj.* —**bulb·ous** *adj.*

bul·bul *n.* Persian species of nightingale.

bulge (*buhlj*) *v.* [bulged; bulg·ing] To swell outward; protrude.—*n.* A protruding part.

bulk *n.* 1. Size; magnitude. 2. The largest portion; main part. 3. A mass or quantity before it has been subdivided and packaged. —*v.* 1. To have size or bulk. 2. To swell.

bulk·head *n.* 1. *Nautical.* A wall or partition. 2. A square wooden structure, above ground level, protecting a shaft or stairway down.

bulk·y (*buhlk*-ee) *adj.* [bulk·i·er; bulk·i·est] Large and hard to handle; having bulk.—**bulk·i·ly** *adv.*—**bulk·i·ness** *n.*

bull *n.* 1. Male of the bovine and certain other animals, as the whale. 2. *Stock Market.* One who buys in hope of a rise in stock values. 3. *Slang.* Exaggeration; boasting. 4. [*cap.*] Taurus, a sign of the Zodiac. 5. *Slang.* A policeman. 6. A ridiculous blunder in speech. —*adj.* 1. Male. 2. Of large size. 3. Attended by rising prices.—**bull** *v.*—**bull·ish** *adj.* —**bull·ish·ly** *adj.*—**bull·ish·ness** *n.*

bull baiting	bullfly	bullnose
bullberry	bullhide	bullnosed
bullcart	bull-like	bull-run
bull-faced	bull-necked	bull-voiced

bull *n.* A papal decree or order.

bull·dog *n.* A muscular, short-haired dog known for its courage.—*adj.* Like a bulldog; tenacious. —*v.* [bull·dogged; bull·dog·ging] To throw, as a steer, by grasping the horns and twisting the neck.

BULLDOG

bull·doze *v.* [bull·dozed; bull·doz·ing] 1. To level earth with a bulldozer. 2. *Colloquial.* To bully. —**bull·doz·er** *n.* 1. A high-powered tractor for leveling ground. 2. *Colloquial.* A bully.

bul·let (*bul*-it) *n.* A metal projectile to be fired from a gun.—**bul·let·proof** *adj.*

bul·le·tin (*bul*-uh-t'n) *n.* 1. An announcement of news just received. 2. An official report or release of information. 3. A publication appearing periodically —**bul·le·tin** *v.*

bull·fight *n.* A sport popular in Spanish-speaking countries, in which armed men enrage and fight a bull.—**bull·fight·er** *n.*—**bull·fight·ing** *n.*

bull·finch *n.* A songbird having bright plumage and a short, heavy bill.

bull·frog *n.* A large frog with a deep croak.

bull·head *n.* 1. A large-headed variety of fish, as the catfish. 2. *Slang.* An obstinate fellow.

bull·head·ed *adj. Slang.* Obstinate; stubborn.

bul·lion (*bul*-yun) *n.* Bars of gold or silver.

Bull Moose. Member of Theodore Roosevelt's Progressive party of 1912.

bull·ock (*bul*-uk) *n.* A castrated bull; steer.

bull pen. 1. An enclosure for bulls. 2. *Baseball.* Area where reserve pitchers warm up.

bull session. An informal discussion, esp. among men.

bull's-eye *n.* 1. Lens with a short focal length for concentrating light. 2. The center of a target; hence, a direct hit.

bull terrier. A white dog, crossbred of a terrier and a bulldog, known for its tenacity.

bul·ly, bul·ly beef *n.* Beef canned or pickled.

bul·ly *n.* [*pl.* bul·lies] One who intimidates or browbeats those weaker than himself.—*v.* [bul·lied; bul·ly·ing] To threaten with violence; intimidate.—*adj. Colloquial.* Good; fine.

bul·rush *n.* A large rush native to swampy land.

bul·wark (*bul*-werk) *n.* 1. Defensive wall; rampart. 2. Any defense against harm or annoyance. 3. Low wall-like structure rising from a ship's main deck.—**bul·wark** *v.*

bum (*buhm*) *n. Slang.* A tramp; beggar.—*v.* [bummed; bum·ming] *Slang.* To beg; obtain by sponging or begging.—*adj. Slang.* Inferior; poor in quality or tone.

bum·ble·bee (*buhm*-b'l-bee) *n.* A large honeybee which makes a loud, droning hum.

bum·boat (*buhm*-boht) *n.* A small boat for carrying stores to sell to ships.

bump *v.* To strike against; jar; thump.—*n.* 1. A heavy jar or blow. 2. A swelling.

bump·er *n.* A framework on a vehicle to protect from minor collisions.

bump·er *n.* A brimming cup or glass.—*adj.* Abundant; brimming over. 'Bumper crop.'

bump·kin (*bump*-kin) *n.* A rustic lout.

bump·tious (*bump*-shus) *adj.* Quarrelsome; domineering; loudly self-assertive.—**bump·tious·ly** *adv.*—**bump·tious·ness** *n.*

bump·y (*bump*-ee) *adj.* [bump·i·er; bump·i·est] Having pronounced surface irregularities. —**bump·i·ly** *adv.*—**bump·i·ness** *n.*

bun *n.* A roll or small loaf.

bunch *n.* 1. A cluster; group; collection. 2. *Slang.* Large quantity.—**bunch** *v.*—**bunch·y** *adj.* [bunch·i·er; bunch·i·est].

bun·combe, bun·kum (*buhnk*-um) *n.* Bombast; empty talk.

Bund *n.* Short for **German-American Bund.** A Nazi organization in the U.S., declared illegal in World War II.

bun·dle (*buhn*-d'l) *n.* 1. A package; parcel. 2. A number of articles bound together.—*v.* [-dled; -dling] 1. To tie together. 2. To dispose of unceremoniously.—**bun·dler** *n.*

bun·dling *n.* A Colonial custom of couples sharing a partitioned bed during courtship.

bung *n.* 1. A stopper for a cask. 2. A bunghole; mouth of a cask.—*v.* To stop; close up.

bun·ga·low (*buhng*-guh-loh) *n.* A small single-storied house.

bun·gle *v.* [bun·gled; bun·gling] To botch; deal with clumsily.—*n.* A botch; awkward work. —**bun·gler** *n.*—**bun·gling·ly** *adv.*

bun·ion (*buhn*-yun) *n.* A swelling on the joint of the large toe caused by inflammation.

bunk *n.* A sleeping berth, as on a ship.—*v.* To sleep in a bunk.—**bunk with.** *Colloquial.* To share quarters with.

bunk *n. Slang.* Deceptive talk; humbug.

bunk·er *n.* 1. A chest serving as a seat. 2. A large receptacle; bin. 3. *Golf.* A hazard; sand hole.—*v. Golf.* To shoot into an obstacle.

bun·ko *n.* [*pl.* bun·kos] Also **bun·co.** A conspiracy to swindle; confidence game.—**bun·ko** *v.*

bun·ny *n.* [*pl.* bun·nies] A pet name for a rabbit.

Bunsen burner. A laboratory burner having a short tube with perforations to immingle air with gas and produce hot blue flame.

bunt *v.* 1. *Baseball.* To hit the ball lightly. 2. To butt, as a goat.—*n.* 1. The middle part of a sail. 2. *Baseball.* A bunting movement with the bat. 3. A shove; butt. 4. A wheat blight.—**bunt·er** *n.*

bun·ting *n.* A thick-beaked European finch.

bun·ting *n.* Also **bun·tine.** 1. A thin woolen fabric used for flags. 2. Flags in general.

buoy (*boy*, *boo*-ee) *n.* A floating body moored in a position to indicate hazards, as shoals or rocks.

BUOY

—*v*. 1. To keep from sinking. 2. To sustain; keep cheerful.

buoy·an·cy (*boy*-un-see) *n*. 1. Ability to float; suspension on a liquid surface. 2. Light-heartedness; cheerfulness; elasticity of spirit. —**buoy·ance** *n*.

buoy·ant (*boy*-unt) *adj*. 1. Light; able to float. 2. Cheerful; hopeful.—**buoy·ant·ly** *adv*.

bur, burr (ber) *n*. A rough prickly seed case, as of the chestnut, etc.—*v*. To pick off burs.

bur·ble (*ber*-b'l) *v*. [bur·bled; bur·bling] 1. To gurgle, as water. 2. To babble.

bur·den (*ber*-d'n) *n*. A refrain; a chorus; the theme repeated in a song.

bur·den *n*. Also **bur·then**. 1. A load; weight. 2. An oppressive responsibility. 3. The freight capacity of a ship.—**bur·den** *v*.

burden of proof. Obligation to prove a point.

bur·den·some (*ber*-d'n-s'm) *adj*. Heavy; oppressive.— -**some·ly** *adv*.— -**some·ness** *n*.

bur·dock (*ber*-dok) *n*. A coarse, bur-bearing plant of temperate climates.

bu·reau (*byoor*-oh) *n*. [*pl*. bu·reaus, bu·reaux] 1. A chest of drawers for clothes. 2. A department for the transaction of public business. 3. A public or private service agency, as an employment bureau.

bu·reauc·ra·cy (byoor-*ok*-ruh-see) *n*. [*pl*. bu·reauc·ra·cies] 1. A system of government administration by departments, each under the control of a single chief. 2. Inflexibility and complexity of government. 3. A graded series of government officials.

bu·reau·crat (*byoor*-oh-krat) *n*. 1. An official of a government department. 2. An advocate of centralized administration by means of bureaus.—**bu·reau·crat·ic** (byoor-oh-*krat*-ik) -**i·cal** *adj*.—**bu·reau·crat·i·cal·ly** *adv*.

burg (berg) *n*. *Colloquial*. A town.

bur·gee (*ber*-jee) *n*. A double-pointed pennant used on yachts, merchant vessels, etc.

bur·geon (*ber*-jun) *n*. Also **bour·geon**. A budding leaf.—*v*. To sprout; expand.

bur·gess (*ber*-jes) *n*. 1. A resident; occupant; citizen. 2. *England*. The parliamentary delegate of a borough. 3. Before the American Revolution, a member of the lower house of the Virginia legislature. 4. *Local U.S*. Mayor of a village.

burgh (berg) *n*. A corporate town; borough.

burgh·er (*berg*-er) *n*. 1. A citizen of a corporate town, as in colonial New York. 2. Well-to-do citizen.

bur·glar (*berg*-ler) *n*. A thief; one who breaks into a building with intent to steal.

bur·gla·ry (*berg*-ler-ee) *n*. [*pl*. bur·gla·ries] Theft; illegal entry with the intent to steal. — -**glar·i·ous** (-*glayr*-ee-us) *adj*.— -**ous·ly** *adv*.

bur·go·mas·ter (*berg*-uh-mas-ter) *n*. A mayor, as in Holland, Flanders, or Germany.

Bur·gun·dy (*berg*-un-dee) *n*. A wine originated in the province of Burgundy, France.

bur·i·al (*behr*-ee-ul) *n*. The depositing of a body in a grave, tomb, or vault.—**bur·i·al** *adj*.

burl (berl) *n*. 1. A knot in thread or fabric. 2. A growth, usually flat and circular, on a tree trunk.—*v*. To finish cloth by picking knots, loose threads, etc.—**burled** *adj*. Knotted.—**burl·er** *n*.

bur·lap (*ber*-lap) *n*. Also **bur·laps**. A coarse, loosely woven cloth of hemp or jute, used for bagging, upholstery, etc.

bur·lesque (ber-*lesk*) *n*. 1. A type of spectacular musical theatrical entertainment depending upon broad humor. 2. A travesty; a caricature; a farcical representation.—**bur·lesque** *adj*. —*v*. [bur·lesqued; bur·les·quing] To make ludicrous; satirize; travesty.—**bur·les·quer** *n*. —**burlesque show**. A popular form of variety entertainment, featuring low humor and often the strip tease.

bur·ly *adj*. [bur·li·er; bur·li·est] Corpulent; husky.—*n*. *Slang*. Burlesque.—**bur·li·ness** *n*.

burn *v*. [burned, burnt; burn·ing] 1. To scorch; injure by heat. 2. To consume; reduce to ashes. 3. To be inflamed. 4. To process by fire, as clay, bricks, or lime. 5. *Chemistry*. To combine with oxygen. 6. *Surgery*. To cauterize. 7. To smolder. 8. To glow; gleam, as a light. 9. To experience the sensation of heat; feel hot.—*n*. 1. An injury caused by fire. 2. A sensation of heat.

burn·er *n*. The part of a stove from which the flame issues.

bur·nish (*bern*-ish) *v*. To polish; brighten; make lustrous.—*n*. Luster; gloss; brightness.— -**nish·er** *n*. Any device for polishing.— -**nish·ment** *n*.

bur·noose (ber-*noos*) *n*. A hooded cloak, esp. an Arabian mantle of wool.

burn·sides *n. pl*. Side whiskers; sideburns.

burp *n*. *Slang*. Expulsion, often involuntary, of stomach gas via the mouth; belch.—**burp** *v*.

burr *n*. Also **bur**. The guttural pronunciation of the rough *r*, esp. in the Scotch dialect.—*v*. [burred; burr·ing].

bur·ro *n*. [*pl*. bur·ros] A small donkey used as a pack animal in the Southwest.

bur·row *n*. A hole dug as a habitat by small animals.—**bur·row** *v*.

BURNOOSE

bur·ry *adj*. [bur·ri·er; bur·ri·est] Prickly; full of burrs.

bur·sa (*bers*-uh) *n*. [*pl*. bur·sae, bur·sas] *Anatomy*. A small sac between the movable parts of an organ or joint.—**bur·sal** *adj*.

bur·sar (*ber*-ser) *n*. A treasurer, as of a monastery or college.—**bur·sa·ry** *n*. A treasury.

bur·si·tis (ber-*sy*-tis) *n*. *Medicine*. Inflammation of a sac, cyst, or pouch.

burst (berst) *v*. [burst; burst·ing] 1. To disrupt; break asunder; fly open. 2. To explode, as a bomb. 3. To split, as a seam. 4. To be filled to overflowing.—*n*. 1. A disruption; an explosion. 2. An outburst; a spurt. —**burst·er** *n*.

bur·y (*beh*-ree) *v.* [bur·ied; bur·y·ing] 1. To inter; entomb; place in a final resting place. 2. To cover up; conceal. 3. To repress, as emotions or feelings.—**bury the hatchet.** Forget mutual grievances.

bus *n.* [*pl.* bus·ses, bus·es] Omnibus; motor vehicle for public conveyance.

bus boy. A restaurant attendant who clears tables.

bush *n.* 1. A shrub. 2. Woodland; a stretch of forest. 3. Uncultivated country. 4. *Machinery.* A perforated metal lining to guard against friction and corrosion. 5. A thick mass of hair or fur.—*v.* 1. To grow thick. 2. To set around with bushes.—**bush·i·ness** *n.*

bush·el (*bush*-'l) *n.* 1. A dry measure containing 4 pecks. 2. A receptacle holding 4 pecks.

bush·ing *n. Machinery.* A perforated metal lining to prevent corroding; a bush.

bush·y *adj.* [bush·i·er; bush·i·est] 1. Overgrown with shrubs. 2. Thick and unkempt.

bus·i·ly *adv.* Earnestly; steadfastly; with unceasing activity.

bus·i·ness (*biz*-nis) *n.* 1. Commerce; trade. 2. Occupation; employment; means of earning a livelihood. 3. Duty; task, concerns; province. 4. Customers; clientele; patronage.—*adj.* Pertaining to trade, finance, etc.

bus·i·ness·like *adj.* Practical; efficient.

bus·kin (*buhs*-kin) *n.* A laced halfboot worn by ancient tragedians.—**bus·kined** *adj.* 1. Wearing buskins. 2. Tragic.

buss *v.* To kiss; smack heartily.

bust *n.* 1. *Sculpture.* A representation of the head and shoulders. 2. The bosom; breasts.

bust *n. Slang.* 1. Bankruptcy; financial collapse; a crash. 2. A spree.—*v. Slang.* 1. To bankrupt. 2. To collapse. 'Tokyo or bust.' 3. To reduce in rank.

bus·tard (*bus*-terd) *n.* A large wading bird inhabiting southern and eastern Europe.

BUST (def. 1)

bust·er *n.* 1. *Slang.* A roisterer; a blade. 2. A spree. 3. An extravaganza; a spectacle.

bus·tle (*bus*-'l) *v.* [bus·tled; bus·tling] To hurry fussily about.—**bus·tle** *n.*—**bus·tling·ly** *adv.*

bus·tle *n.* A pad formerly worn to puff out the back of a skirt.

bus·y (*biz*-ee) *adj.* [bus·i·er; -i·est] Active; occupied; full of activity.—*v.* [bus·ied; -y·ing].

bus·y·bod·y *n.* [*pl.* bus·y·bod·ies] 1. A meddler; one concerned with the affairs of others. 2. Mirror affixed outside an upstairs window to afford a view of those who enter and leave the house.

bus·y·ness *n.* 1. Great activity. 2. Inquisitiveness; meddling.

but *prep.* Except; besides.—*conj.* 1. However; nevertheless. 2. Save that; excepting. 3. Yet; still; unless.—*adv.* Only; merely; simply.

bu·ta·di·ene (byoo-tuh-*dy*-een) *n.* A hydrocarbon gas used in the manufacture of synthetic rubber. (*Symbol:* C_4H_6).

butch·er (*buch*-er) *n.* 1. A dealer in meats. 2. A slaughterer.—*v.* 1. To slaughter for food. 2. To murder; massacre.—**butch·er·ly** *adj.* Cruel; savage; murderous.— -**er·li·ness** *n.*

butch·er·y *n.* [*pl.* butch·er·ies] 1. A slaughterhouse. 2. Slaughter; carnage; massacre.

but·ler (*buht*-ler) *n.* The chief servant of an establishment.—**but·ler·y** *n.* The art of being a butler.

butt *n.* A wine cask.

butt *n.* 1. The thick end, as of a gun, a fishing rod, etc. 2. The thickest part of tanned oxhide. 3. A rifle target. 4. A target of ridicule. 5. A thrust with the head. 6. *Slang.* A cigarette; its stub.—*v.* To thrust with the head.

butte (*byoot*) *n.* An isolated flat-topped hill.

but·ter (*but*-er) *n.* Fatty product obtained from churning milk or cream.—*v.* To spread with butter.

butter-and-eggs *n.* A flowering plant producing yellow flowers with a white center.

but·ter·cup *n.* A field plant having bright yellow cup-shaped flowers.

but·ter·fat *n.* The part of milk from which butter is obtained.

but·ter·fin·gered *adj.* Clumsy with the hands.

but·ter·fly *n.* [*pl.* but·ter·flies] An insect having four broad, bright-colored wings.

butterfly table. A drop-leaf table with wing-shaped leaves.

butterfly weed. An ornamental milkweed having bright orange flowers.

but·ter·milk *n.* Liquid left after butterfat has been separated from milk by churning.

BUTTERFLY

but·ter·nut *n.* The sweet edible nut of a large tree of the walnut family.

but·ter·scotch *n.* A candy made from brown sugar and butter.

but·ter·y (*but*-ter-ee) *adj.* Resembling or having the characteristics of butter.—*n.* A room where provisions are stored; a pantry.

but·tock (*but*-uk) *n.* The fleshy part of the human body back of the hip joints.

but·ton (*but*-'n) *n.* A plate-shaped or spherical fastener, often ornamental, sewed on clothing and secured through a corresponding hole. —*v.* To attach or fasten with buttons.

but·ton·hole *n.* The opening or loop through which a button is fastened.—*v.* To intercept or detain abruptly.

but·ton·wood *n.* The plane tree.

but·tress (*but*-riss) *n.* 1. A mass of masonry erected against an exterior wall to support or strengthen it. 2. Any mainstay or bolsterer.

bu·tyl (*byoo*-til) *n. Chemistry.* One of four univalent radicals. (*Symbol:* C_4H_9).

bu·tyl·ene (*byoo*-tih-leen) *n. Chemistry.* A hydrocarbon compound gas. (*Symbol:* C_4H_8).

bux·om (*buk*-sum) *adj.* Attractively plump; blooming and wholesome.—**bux·om·ly** *adv.* —**bux·om·ness** *n.*

buy (*by*) *v.* [bought; buy·ing] 1. To purchase; to acquire by paying a price. 2. To bribe. —**buy off.** To secure for a consideration.—**buy out.** To purchase one's share in a business.

buy·er *n.* A purchasing agent; one who buys.

buzz *n.* 1. A steady humming sound as of a bee. 2. Gossip.—**buzz** *v.* 1. To make a humming sound. 2. *Aviation.* To fly low over a field or populated area.

buzz bomb. Jet-propelled pilotless plane which makes a buzzing sound in flight.

buz·zard (*buz*-erd) *n.* Any hawklike bird of prey.

buzz·er (*buz*-er) *n.* A bell or other electric button which gives a buzzing signal.

buzz saw. A circular type of saw.

by *prep.* 1. At hand; close to. 2. Through or over. 'By way of.' 3. From. 'Death by drowning.' 4. Past. 'I drove by him.' 5. During. 'By night.' 6. Not after; no later than. 7. To the degree of. 'Taller by a foot.' 8. According to. 9. In regard to. 10. On; from. 'Hang by a thread.' 11. In the name of; with the witness of. 12. Through the agency of. 'Books written by Poe.'—*adv.* Near; aside; past. 'The car went by.'

by-and-by *n.* The near future.

bye *n.* 1. Not in the usual course of events. 2. *Cricket.* A passed ball. 3. *Golf.* The unplayed holes left after a game.

by·gone *adj.* Past.—**by·gone** *n.*

by·law *n.* [*usually pl.*] Law or rule established by an organization to regulate its affairs.

by·line *n.* Insertion of the name of the writer at the head of a newspaper article.

by·pass *n.* A highway to route traffic around an urban area.—*v.* To ignore; overlook.

by·path *n.* An indirect or secluded path.

by·play *n.* An aside; activity or interchange apart from the main situation.

by·prod·uct *n.* 1. A substance derived secondarily in the manufacture of another. 2. Any incidental development or outgrowth.

by·road *n.* A side road not much used.

by·stand·er *n.* A witness; one who looks on without participating.

by·way *n.* A side path.

by·word *n.* A catch phrase; a proverbial expression.

By·zan·tine (bih-*zan*-tin) *adj.* 1. Pertaining to Byzantium. 2. Denoting the richly ornamented, buoyant style of architecture developed in ancient Byzantium.—**By·zan·tine** *n.*

By·zan·ti·um (bih-*zan*-tee-um) Ancient Greek city founded in 658 B.C., now Istanbul, formerly Constantinople.

C

cab *n.* 1. Taxicab; automobile for passenger hire. 2. Enclosed driver's compartment of a truck or locomotive.

ca·bal (kuh-*bal*) *n.* 1. A small group secretly promoting its own interests. 2. Intrigue; secret scheming.—*v.* [ca·balled; ca·bal·ling].

cab·a·la (*kab*-uh-luh) *n.* 1. Secret religious code of Jewish theosophists for interpreting difficult Scripture passages. 2. Any occult science; mystery.—**ca·ba·lism** *n.*—**ca·ba·list** *n.* —**ca·ba·lis·tic** (kah-buh-*liss*-tik) *adj.*

ca·bal·le·ro (kah-bahl-*yay*-roh) *n.* [*pl.* -ros] Spanish gentleman or cavalier.

ca·bañ·a (kah-*bahn*-yah) *n.* Also **ca·ban·a.** A small house, usually at a resort; also, a small private bathhouse.

cab·a·ret (kab-uh-*ray*) *n.* 1. A night club featuring entertainment by singers and dancers. 2. Any tavern or café.

cab·bage (*kab*-ij) *n.* A vegetable having a round head of thick, edible leaves.—*v.* [cab·baged; cab·bag·ing] To form a head, as a cabbage.

cab·by *n.* [*pl.* -bies] *Colloquial.* A cabman.

cab·in *n.* 1. A small, crudely built house; hut. 2. An enclosed passenger compartment in a ship or airplane.—**cab·in** *v.*

cabin boy. A boy who attends a ship's officers and passengers.

cab·i·net (*kab*-uh-nit) *n.* 1. Chest, cupboard, or compartment for holding valued objects. 2. Private conference room. 3. Group of advisers selected by a chief executive.—**cab·i·net** *adj.*

cab·i·net·mak·er *n.* Furniture craftsman.

cab·i·net·work *n.* 1. Skillfully made furniture. 2. The art of making fine furniture.—**cab·i·net·work·er** *n.*

ca·ble (*kay*-b'l) *n.* 1. A strong rope or chain for sustaining heavy weights. 2. An insulated wire conductor for carrying undersea telegraphic messages. 3. A cablegram. 4. A cable's length.—*v.* [ca·bled; ca·bling] To send a message by cable.

ca·ble·gram (*kay*-b'l-gram) *n.* A message sent by undersea cable.

ca·bl·ese (kay-b'l-*eez*) *n.* A condensed, succinct style of writing, notable for its use of compounded words, used by newsmen to economize on cable charges for foreign dispatches.

cable's length. The length of a ship's cable, usually 720 feet.

cab·man *n.* [*pl.* -men] Taxicab driver.

ca·boo·dle (kuh-*boo*-d'l) *n. Slang.* Assorted group; lot. 'The whole caboodle.'

ca·boose (kuh-*boos*) *n.* Trainmen's rest car on a freight train, usually at the end.

cab·ri·o·let (kab-ree-uh-*lay*) *n*. A one-horse two-seated carriage.

ca·ca·o (kuh-*kay*-oh) *n*. A tropical American tree, yielding seeds from which cocoa and chocolate are prepared.

cach·a·lot (*kash*-uh-lot) *n*. The blunt-headed sperm whale.

cache (*kash*) *n*. 1. Hiding place for supplies or valuables. 2. Hidden store.—*v*. [cached; cach·ing] To hide, as in a cache.

ca·chet (kash-*ay*) *n*. 1. A seal. 2. Distinguishing quality.—**lettre de cachet** (letr'-duh-ka-*shay*) *French History*. Sealed order authorizing imprisonment or execution without trial.

cack·le *v*. [cack·led; cack·ling] 1. To utter a series of shrill, broken sounds, as a hen. 2. To laugh or chatter shrilly.—**cack·le** *n*.

ca·cog·ra·phy (kak-*og*-ruh-fee) *n*. Poor handwriting.—**ca·cog·ra·pher** *n*.—**cac·o·graph·ic, -i·cal** (kak-uh-*graf*-ik) *adj*.

ca·coph·o·ny (kak-*off*-uh-nee) *n*. [*pl*. -nies] Disagreeable sound; discord.—**ca·coph·a·nous** *adj*.

cac·tus *n*. [*pl*. cac·ti (*kak*-ty), cac·tus·es] Plant with spine-covered fleshy stems and no leaves.

cad *n*. Scoundrel; rascal.—**cad·dish** *adj*. —**cad·dish·ly** *adv*. —**cad·dish·ness** *n*.

ca·dav·er (kuh-*dav*-er) *n*. A corpse, esp. one for dissection.

ca·dav·er·ous *adj*. Resembling a corpse; ghastly; haggard. —**ous·ly** *adv*.—**ous·ness** *n*.

CACTUS

cad·die, cad·dy *n*. Person who carries a player's golf clubs and runs errands.—*v*. [cad·died; cad·dy·ing].

caddis fly (*kad*-is). Winged insect which lives under water at the larva stage.

caddis worm. Larva of the caddis fly.

cad·dy *n*. [*pl*. -dies] Small box or can, esp. for holding tea.

ca·dence (*kay*-d'ns) *n*. 1. Uniform measure or beat, as in poetry or marching; rhythm. 2. Modulation or fall of the voice. 3. *Music*. The closing of a phrase.—**ca·denced** *adj*.

ca·den·za (kuh-*den*-zuh) *n*. *Music*. Ornamental flourish usually ending a movement.

ca·det (kuh-*det*) *n*. 1. Student at a military, naval, or maritime academy; officer candidate. 2. Younger son or brother.—*adj*. 1. Younger. 2. Student. 'A cadet nurse.'—**ca·det·cy, ca·det·ship** *n*.

cadge (*kaj*) *v*. [cadged; cadg·ing] 1. To beg; sponge. 2. To peddle.—**cadg·er** *n*.

cad·mi·um (*kad*-mee-um) *n*. A pliant, whitish, metallic element. (*Symbol:* Cd.)

ca·dre (*kah*-der) *n*. Skeleton; framework.

ca·du·ce·us (kuh-*dyoo*-see-us, -doo-) *n*. [*pl*. -ce·i] 1. Mercury's wand. 2. Staff entwined with two serpents, symbol of the medical profession.—**ca·du·ce·an** *adj*.

cae·cum (*see*-k'm) *n*. [*pl*. -ca] Pouch joining the small and large intestine.—**cae·cal** *adj*.

Cae·sar (*see*-zer) *n*. *Roman History*. Title of Roman emperors, after Julius Caesar; dictator.—**Cae·sa·re·an, -ri·an** (sih-*zair*-ee-un) *adj*.

Caesarean section. *Surgery*. An operation removing a baby from the uterus after cutting through the abdominal wall.

Cae·sar·ism (*see*-zer-izm) *n*. Dictatorship; autocracy.—**Cae·sar·ist** *n*.

cae·su·ra (sih-*zyoo*-ruh) *n*. [*pl*. -ras, -rae] Metrical pause in a verse, usually for sense.—**cae·su·ral** *adj*.

ca·fé (kaf-*ay*) *n*. A restaurant.

caf·e·te·ri·a (kaf-uh-*tihr*-ee-uh) *n*. A self-service restaurant.

caf·feine, caf·fein (*kaf*-een) *n*. A stimulating organic substance found in coffee, tea, etc.

caf·tan (*kaf*-t'n) *n*. Wide-sleeved gown fastened by a sash, worn in the Middle East.

cage (*kayj*) *n*. 1. An openwork enclosure for keeping birds or animals. 2. Any framework resembling a cage, as an elevator car. 3. *Baseball*. Enclosed practice space.—*v*. [caged; cag·ing] To confine.—**caged** *adj*.

cage·ling (*kayj*-ling) *n*. Bird kept in a cage.

cage·y (*kay*-jee) *adj*. [cag·i·er; cag·i·est] *Slang*. Shrewd; wily.

ca·hoots (kuh-*hoots*) *n*. *Slang*. A combination; partnership.—**in cahoots.** In league.

Cain (*kayn*) *n*. First-born son of Adam and Eve, murderer of his brother, Abel.

ca·ique (kah-*eek*) *n*. A small Turkish skiff.

cairn (*kehrn*) *n*. Pile of stones marking a site.

cais·son (*kay*-s'n) *n*. 1. Wagon carrying artillery ammunition. 2. Watertight chamber for working under water. 3. Watertight structure for raising sunken vessels.

CAISSON

caisson disease. A disease caused by too rapid change in atmospheric pressure; the bends.

cai·tiff (*kay*-tif) *n*. Villian; wretch.—*adj*. Vile.

ca·jole (kuh-*johl*) *v*. [ca·joled; ca·jol·ing] To coax; wheedle; persuade by flattery.—**ca·jole·ment** *n*.—**ca·jol·er** *n*.

ca·jol·er·y (kuh-*johl*-er-ee) *n*. [*pl*. -er·ies] Coaxing; artful persuasion.

cake *n*. 1. Baked sweetened or flavored dough. 2. A small mass of solid matter. 'A cake of soap.' 3. Any small, flat mass of baked or fried food.—*v*. [caked; cak·ing] To solidify.

cake·walk *n*. Intricate dance step originated by American Negroes.— **-walk** *v*.— **-walk·er** *n*.

cal·a·bash (*kal*-uh-bash) *n*. 1. Shell-covered fruit of the tropical calabash tree. 2. A container made of a dried calabash shell.

cal·a·boose (*kal*-uh-boos) *n*. *Colloquial*. Prison.

ca·lam·i·tous (kuh-*lam*-ih-tus) *adj*. Disastrous; causing calamity.— **-tous·ly** *adv*.— **-tous·ness** *n*.

ca·lam·i·ty (kuh-*lam*-ih-tee) *n.* [*pl.* -ties] 1. Disaster; tremendous misfortune. 2. Misery.

ca·lash (kuh-*lash*) *n.* A light, horse-drawn carriage with a movable hood.

cal·car·e·ous (kal-*kehr*-ee-us) *adj.* Like or containing lime or calcium.

cal·cif·er·ous, cal·cif·ic (kal-*sif*-er-us) *adj.* Producing or containing calcite.

cal·ci·fy (*kal*-sih-fy) *v.* [cal·ci·fied; cal·ci·fy·ing] To harden by the deposit of lime salts.—**cal·ci·fi·ca·tion** *n.*

cal·ci·mine (*kal*-sih-myne) *n.* Also **kal·so·mine.** Whitewash for covering walls.—*v.* [cal·ci·mined; cal·ci·min·ing].

cal·cine (*kal*-syne) *v.* [cal·cined; cal·cin·ing] 1. To reduce a substance to powder by heat. 2. To oxidize.—**cal·ci·na·tion** *n.*—**cal·cin·a·to·ry** (kal-*sin*-uh-tor-ee) *adj.* & *n.*

cal·cite (*kal*-syte) *n.* A common form of calcium carbonate, as limestone or chalk.

cal·ci·um (*kal*-see-um) *n.* A soft, silvery-white, chemically active element. (*Symbol:* Ca).

calcium carbide. A compound of calcium and carbon, used to produce acetylene.

calcium carbonate. A mineral, composing limestone, marble, etc., from which lime and portland cement are refined.

calcium chloride. A white crystalline compound of calcium and chlorine.

cal·cu·la·ble (*kal*-kyuh-luh-b'l) *adj.* Ascertainable; computable.

cal·cu·late (*kal*-kyuh-layt) *v.* [cal·cu·lat·ed; cal·cu·lat·ing] 1. To reckon; estimate mathematically. 2. To decide by reasoning; estimate. 3. To rely; count. 4. To intend; design.—**cal·cu·lat·ing** *adj.* 1. Able to calculate. 2. Shrewd; scheming.

cal·cu·la·tion *n.* 1. Reckoning; estimate. 2. Deliberation.—**cal·cu·la·tive** *adj.*

cal·cu·la·tor *n.* Person or machine that computes.

cal·cu·lus (*kal*-kyuh-lus) *n.* [-li, -luses] 1. A stony mass formed in the body. 2. Branch of higher mathematics concerned with problems involving variable quantities, including differential calculus and integral calculus.

cal·dron, caul·dron (*kawl*-dr'n) *n.* A large kettle or boiler.

Cal·e·do·ni·a (kal-uh-*doh*-nee-uh) *n.* Ancient name for Scotland.—**Cal·e·do·ni·an** *n.* & *adj.*

cal·en·dar (*kal*-un-der) *n.* 1. System for fixing and recording the divisions of time. 2. Table of the days, weeks, and months in the year. 3. A schedule; list of events, as of cases standing for trial.—*v.* To register; list.

cal·en·der (*kal*-un-der) *n.* A machine for pressing and glazing cloth or paper.—*v.* To press in a calender.—**cal·en·der·er** *n.*

ca·lends, ka·lends (*kal*-undz) *n. pl.* The first day of the month, in the old Roman calendar.

ca·len·du·la (kuh-*lend*-dyuh-luh) *n.* [*pl.* -ae] Variety of marigold with yellow flowers.

calf (*kaf*) *n.* [*pl.* calves] 1. Young of the cow or other bovine. 2. Young of certain large animals, as the whale, elephant, etc. 3. *Colloquial.* Foolish young man; dolt. 4. Fine leather made from a calfskin.

calf (*kaf*) *n.* [*pl.* calves] The fleshy part of the leg, behind and below the knee.

calf·skin *n.* Hide of a calf; leather made from it.

Cal·i·ban (*kal*-uh-ban) *n.* The deformed slave in Shakespeare's *The Tempest.*

cal·i·ber, cal·i·bre (*kal*-uh-ber) *n.* 1. The inside diameter of a cylindrical body, as the barrel of a gun. 2. Mental capacity or quality.

cal·i·brate (*kal*-uh-brayt) *v.* [-bra·ted; -bra·ting] To find the caliber or adjust the graduations of any scale instrument.—**cal·i·bra·tion** *n.*

cal·i·co (*kal*-uh-koh) *n.* [*pl.* -coes, -cos] Cotton cloth, often printed.—**cal·i·co** *adj.*

California poppy. Golden poppy, the state flower of California.

cal·i·pers, cal·li·pers (*kal*-uh-perz) *n. pl.* Compass with curved legs for measuring diameter, thickness, etc.

ca·liph, ca·lif (*kay*-lif) *n.* Acknowledged successor of Mohammed; former title of Turkish sultans.—**ca·li·phate, ca·li·fate** *n.*

cal·is·then·ics (kal-iss-*then*-iks) *n. pl.* Also **cal·lis·then·ics.** Gymnastics; body-building exercises.—**cal·is·then·ic, -i·cal** *adj.*

CALIPERS

calk (*kawk*) *n.* Sharp-pointed projection on a shoe or a horseshoe to prevent slipping.—*v.* To furnish with calks.

calk, caulk (*kawk*) *v.* To stop up, as the seams of a ship, to prevent leakage.—**calk·er** *n.*

call (*kawl*) *v.* 1. To utter or address loudly; summon. 2. To assemble; call together. 3. To name; designate. 4. To pay a short visit. 5. To initiate a talk with a person by telephone. 6. To demand payment of. 7. *Poker.* To ask for a show of hands.—*n.* 1. A loud cry. 2. A summons; demand; request. 3. Characteristic cry, as of a bird. 4. A brief visit. 5. Divine assembly. 6. Demand for payment.—**call down.** 1. To reprimand. 2. Request to descend.—**call up.** 1. Bring to mind; recollect. 2. Telephone to.

cal·la (*kal*-uh) *n.* Also **calla lily.** Plant whose flower consists of a large white leaf around a yellow spike.

call·boy *n.* Person who calls actors on stage.

call·er *n.* One who calls; visitor.

cal·lig·ra·phy (kuh-*lig*-ruh-fee) *n.* Fine penmanship; handwriting.—**cal·lig·ra·pher** *n.*—**cal·li·graph·ic** (kal-uh-*graf*-ik) *adj.*—**cal·lig·ra·phist** (kuh-*lig*-ruh-fist) *n.*

call·ing *n.* 1. Act of calling. 2. Vocation; profession; occupation.—**calling card.** Small card imprinted with one's name for business or social use.

cal·li·o·pe (kuh-*ly*-uh-pee) *n.* 1. A musical instrument having steam whistles, and played like an organ. 2. [*cap.*] *Mythology.* The muse of heroic poetry.

CALLIOPE

cal·los·i·ty (kuh-*los*-uh-tee) *n.* [*pl.* -ties] 1. State of being hardened. 2. A callus.

cal·lous (*kal*-us) *adj.* 1. Having calluses; hardened. 2. Unfeeling; insensitive.—cal·lous·ly *adv.*—cal·lous·ness *n.*

cal·low (*kal*-oh) *adj.* 1. Inexperienced; immature. 2. Unfledged.

cal·lus *n.* [*pl.* calluses] 1. A thick, hardened spot on the skin. 2. New growth uniting ends of a broken bone.—*v.* To form a callus.

calm (*kahm*) *adj.* Placid; tranquil; still.—*n.* Freedom from motion or disturbance; tranquillity.—calm *v.*—calm·ly *adv.*—calm·ness *n.*

cal·o·mel (*kal*-uh-m'l) *n.* A white, tasteless powder used as a purgative.

ca·lor·ic (kuh-*lor*-ik) *n.* Heat.—*adj.* Pertaining to heat.—cal·o·ric·i·ty *n.*

cal·o·ry, cal·o·rie (*kal*-er-ee) *n.* Unit of heat energy,—often applied to the amount of energy produced in the body by various foods. —cal·o·ric (kal-*or*-ik) *adj.*

cal·o·rif·ic (kal-er-*if*-ik) *adj.* Producing heat.

cal·o·rim·e·ter (kal-er-*im*-uh-ter) *n.* *Physics.* Instrument for measuring quantities of heat. —cal·o·ri·met·ric, -i·cal *adj.*—cal·o·rim·e·try *n.*

ca·lotte, ca·lot (kuh-*lot*) *n.* A close-fitting cap.

cal·u·met (*kal*-yuh-met) *n.* Ceremonial peace pipe of North American Indians.

CALUMET

ca·lum·ni·ate (kuh-*lum*-nee-ayt) *n.* [ca·lum·ni·at·ed; ca·lum·ni·at·ing] To make false and injurious charges against; defame; slander.—ca·lum·ni·a·tion *n.* —ca·lum·ni·a·tor *n.*

ca·lum·ni·ous (kuh-*lum*-nee-us) *adj.* Slanderous; defamatory.—ca·lum·ni·ous·ly *adv.*

cal·um·ny (*kal*-um-nee) *n.* [*pl.* -nies] False and injurious accusation; defamation.

Cal·va·ry (*kal*-ver-ee) Site of the crucifixion of Christ; Golgotha.

calve (*kav*) *v.* [calved; calv·ing] To give birth to a calf.

Cal·vin·ism (*kal*-vin-izm) *n.* The austere religious doctrine, including predestination, of John Calvin, French leader of the Protestant Reformation.—Cal·vin·ist *n.* & *adj.*—Cal·vin·is·tic, -i·cal *adj.*

Ca·lyp·so (kuh-*lip*-soh) *n.* 1. A sea nymph in Homer's Odyssey. 2. A kind of extemporaneous singing with a distinctive syncopated rhythm, native to Trinidad. 3. A singer or composer of these songs.—ca·lyp·so *adj.*

ca·lyx (*kay*-liks) *n.* [*pl.* ca·lyx·es, ca·lyc·es] *Botany.* Supporting husk beneath the petals of a flower.

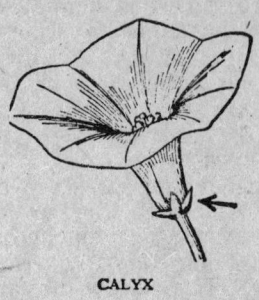
CALYX

cam *n.* A device, as on a wheel, for transforming the rotary motion of machinery into any required movement.

ca·ma·ra·de·rie (kah-muh-*rah*-der-ee) *n.* Good-fellowship; friendship.

cam·ber *n.* 1. Slight arch; curve, as of a bridge; a piece of timber so curved. 2. *Aeronautics.* Curve of the upper surface of a wing. —*v.* To arch; curve.

cam·bi·um (*kam*-bee-um) *n.* *Botany.* Layer of cellular tissue separating and forming new wood and bark.

Cam·bri·a (*kam*-bree-uh). Ancient name for Wales.—Cam·bri·an *n.* & *adj.*

Cam·bri·an (*kam*-bree-un) *adj.* *Geology.* Pertaining to the Cambrian period or system. —Cambrian period. The earliest division of the Paleozoic era.—Cambrian system. The oldest rocks containing fossils in any great number.

cam·bric (*kaym*-brik) *n.* A fine white linen or cotton fabric. —cambric tea. Weak tea with milk and sugar.

cam·el (*kam*-'l) *n.* Large pack animal having one fatty hump, as the Arabian camel or dromedary, or two humps, as the Bactrian camel. —cam·el·eer *n.* Camel driver.

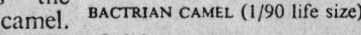

BACTRIAN CAMEL (1/90 life size)

ca·mel·li·a (kuh-*meel*-yuh) *n.* A shrub bearing red or white flowers similar to roses; the flower itself.

ca·mel·o·pard (kuh-*mel*-uh-pard) *n.* The giraffe.

Cam·e·lot (*kam*-uh-lot) *n.* Legendary home of King Arthur and the Knights of the Round Table.

CAMELLIA

camel's hair. 1. Hair of the camel. 2. Cloth made of or with it. 3. Squirrels' long hair used in brushes, etc.—cam·el's-hair *adj.*

Cam·em·bert, Cam·em·bert cheese (*kam*-em-behr). A soft, rich French cheese.

cam·e·o (*kam-ee-oh*) *n.* [*pl.* cam·e·os] Figure cut in relief on a precious or semi-precious stone.

cam·er·a (*kam-er-uh*) *n.* 1. A closed box with lens and sensitized plate for recording permanent images. 2. *Law.* A judge's private room.—**in camera.** *Law.* In a judge's chamber; privately.—**cam·er·al** *adj.*

cam·i·on (kahm-*yawn*) *n.* Truck for transporting military equipment.

cam·i·sole (*kam-ih-sohl*) *n.* 1. Woman's undershirt; chemise. 2. Short dressing gown.

cam·o·mile, cham·o·mile (*kam-uh-myle*) *n.* Plant of the aster family, having daisylike flowers which yield a bitter medicine.

Ca·mor·ra (kuh-*mor*-uh) *n.* A secret Italian terroristic society in the early 19th century. —**Ca·mor·rism** *n.*—**Ca·mor·rist** *n.*

cam·ou·flage (*kam*-uh-flahzh) *n.* 1. The art of disguising military objects. 2. A disguise or deceptive appearance.—*v.* [-flaged; flag·ing] To reduce the visibility of an object by disguise.—**cam·ou·flag·er** *n.*

camp *n.* 1. Collection of temporary shelters, esp. for an army; the ground on which they stand. 2. Outdoor summer resort having a regular schedule of activities. 3. Body of people actively supporting a person or doctrine.—*v.* To pitch or live in a camp; live a rugged, outdoor existence.—**camp·er** *n.*

cam·paign (kam-*payn*) *n.* 1. Series of related military operations directed toward a particular objective. 2. Series of related activities to accomplish a special purpose. 'An election campaign.'—**cam·paign** *v.*—**cam·paign·er** *n.*

cam·pa·ni·le (kam-puh-*nee*-lee) *n.* [*pl.* -ni·les; -ni·li] A bell tower.

cam·pan·u·la (kam-*pan*-yul-uh) *n.* Any of several plants having white or blue bell-shaped flowers, as the bluebell.—**cam·pan·u·late** (kam-*pan*-yuh-lit) *adj.* Bell-shaped.

camp·fire *n.* 1. Fire built for warmth or cooking needs. 2. Social gathering around a campfire.—**campfire girl.** Member of The Camp Fire Girls of America, an organization engaging in outdoor activities.

cam·phor (*kam*-fer) *n.* A translucent, aromatic substance derived mainly from the camphor tree and used in medicine, celluloid manufacturing, etc.—**cam·phor·ic** (kam-*for*-ik) *adj.*

cam·phor·ate (*kam*-fer-ayt) *v.* [-at·ed; -at·ing] To impregnate with camphor.—**-phor·at·ed** *adj.*

camphor ball. A small ball of camphor or naphthalene for protection against moths.

camphor ice. Ointment for external use made from camphor, white wax, etc.

cam·pus (*kam*-pus) *n.* College or school grounds.

can [could; *no past participle*] *v.* To be able; have the right to.

can *n.* A tin or metal container.—*v.* [canned; can·ning] 1. To preserve by sealing in cans or jars. 2. *Slang.* To discharge; fire.

Ca·naan (*kay*-nun). Region in Palestine west of Jordan River; the Israelites' Land of Promise; hence, paradise.—**Ca·naan·ite** *n.*

Canada balsam. A fluid resin obtained from the balsam fir.

Canada goose. Large, wild North American goose, with black head and neck.

ca·naille (kuh-*nayl*; -nye) *n.* Rabble; mob.

ca·nal (kuh-*nal*) *n.* 1. An artificial waterway. 2. *Anatomy.* Any tubular body cavity; duct. —*v.* [can-alled; ca·naled; ca·nal·ling, ca·nal·ing] To construct a canal.

canal boat. Narrow boat used on a canal.

ca·nal·ize (kuh-*nal*-yze, kan-ul-yze) *v.* [ca·nal·ized; ca·nal·iz·ing] 1. To cut a canal through; form like or into a canal. 2. To direct or supply an outlet for, as energy.

Canal Zone. The Panama Canal and a piece of land five miles wide on each side, leased permanently to U.S.A. Area: 549 sq. mi.

ca·na·pé (kan-uh-*pay*, kan-) *n.* Thin cracker or toasted bread spread with cheese, fish, meat, etc., and served as a relish.

ca·nard (kuh-*nard*) *n.* A fantastic story; lie.

ca·nar·y (kuh-*nayr*-ee) *n.* [*pl.* -ies] 1. Yellow songbird of the finch family. 2. *Slang.* Criminal who betrays his accomplices. 3. *Slang.* Female singer.—*adj.* Canary yellow.

canary yellow. A light, bright yellow.

can·can (*kan*-kan) *n.* A lively French dance characterized by high kicking.

can·cel (*kan*-s'l) *v.* [can·celed; can·celled; can·cel·ing, can·cel·ling] 1. To cross out; delete; obliterate. 2. *Mathematics.* To strike out a common factor, as from a numerator and denominator. 3. To void; neutralize.—**can·cel·er, can·cel·ler** *n.*

can·cel·la·tion (kan-s'l-*ay*-shun) *n.* Act or result of canceling; deletion.

can·cer (*kan*-ser) *n.* 1. *Medicine.* A malignant, spreading tissue growth. 2. Any spreading evil. 3. *Astronomy.* [*cap.*] A northern constellation; the fourth sign of the Zodiac.—**can·cer·ous** *adj.*

can·de·la·brum (kan-duh-*lay*-brum, -lah-, -lab-) *n.* [*pl.* -bra, -brums]. Also **can·de·la·bra** [*pl.* -bras]. An ornamental branched candlestick.

can·des·cent (kan-*des*-'nt), **can·dent** *adj.* Glowing with white heat; incandescent.

can·did (*kan*-did) *adj.* Honest; frank; unbiased. —**can·did·ly** *adv.*—**can·did·ness** *n.*

can·di·da·cy (*kan*-dih-duh-see) *n.* [*pl.* -cies]. Also **can·di·da·ture.** The state of being a candidate.

can·di·date (*kan*-dih-dayt) *n.* One who aspires to an office or honor; contestant in an election.

candid camera. Small camera, having a large lens and high-speed shutter, for taking unposed snapshots.

can·died (*kan*-deed, -did) *adj.* 1. Preserved in or turned into sugar. 2. Sweet; flattering.

can·dle (*kan*-d'l) *n.* 1. A cylindrical body of wax or tallow formed around a wick and burned to furnish light. 2. A unit of light intensity.—v. [can·dle; can·dling] To test, as eggs, by holding before a bright light.

can·dle·light n. Illumination by candles; the light of a candle.

can·dle·stick n. Utensil for holding a candle.

can·dor (kan-der) n. Frankness; sincerity.

can·dy (kan-dee) n. [pl. -dies] A confection prepared with sugar and flavoring, often with nuts, chocolate, fruits, etc.—v. [can·died; can·dy·ing] 1. To preserve with sugar. 2. To become candied; crystallize. 3. To make palatable; sweeten.

cane n. 1. Slender, jointed stem of certain grasses or other plants, as bamboo, rattan, etc. 2. Split rattan used in wickerwork. 3. A walking stick.—v. [caned; can·ing] 1. To beat with a cane. 2. To make or supply with rattan.

ca·nine (kay-nyne) adj. Pertaining to or like dogs or the dog family, including wolves, foxes, etc.—n. 1. A dog. 2. Anatomy. One of the four pointed teeth next to the incisors.

can·is·ter (kan-is-ter) n. A small box or can for holding coffee, tea, etc.

can·ker n. 1. An ulcerated sore, esp. in the mouth. 2. A cankerworm. 3. Any corroding or corrupting agent or influence.—v. To infect with canker; corrode.—**cank·er·ous** adj.

can·ker·worm n. An insect larva destructive to trees and plants.

can·na (kan-uh) n. A plant having large leaves and brightly colored flowers; the flower itself.

canned adj. 1. Preserved in cans. 2. Slang. Recorded or electrically transcribed, as music.

cannel coal, can·nel (kan-'l) n. A soft coal which burns with a bright flame.

can·ner n. One who cans food.

can·ner·y (kan-er-ee) n. [pl. can·ner·ies] A place where food is canned.

can·ni·bal (kan-uh-b'l) n. A person who eats human flesh; an animal that eats its own kind.—**can·ni·bal** adj.— **-bal·ism** n.— **-bal·is·tic** adj.

can·ni·kin (kan-ih-kin) n. A small can or cup.

can·ning n. Preserving foods in tins or jars.

can·non (kan-un) n. [pl. can·nons, can·non] A large gun, usually mounted, for long-distance firing.—**can·non** v.—**can·non·eer** n.

can·non·ade (kan-un-ayd) v. [can·non·ad·ed; -ad·ing] To bombard with artillery intensively or continuously.—**can·non·ade** n.

can·non·ry (kan-un-ree) n. [pl. -ries] 1. A cannonade. 2. Cannon collectively; artillery.

can·ny adj. [can·ni·er, can·ni·est] 1. Cautious; prudent; wary. 2. Skillful; expert; clever. —**can·ni·ly** adv.—**can·ni·ness** n.

ca·noe (kuh-noo) n. A light, narrow, round-bottomed boat, propelled by paddles. —v. [ca·noed; ca·noe·ing] To paddle or travel in a canoe. —**ca·noe·ing** n.—**ca·noe·ist** n.

CANOE

can·on (kan-un) n. 1. A law or rule, esp. of religious doctrine. 2. A standard; criterion. 3. Official list, esp. of the books of the Bible considered genuine. 4. A catalogue of saints. 5. Member of a group of clergymen forming a bishop's council. 6. Music. A form of composition of two or more voice parts, in which the voices imitate one another at irregular intervals.—**can·on·ess** n.

ca·non·i·cal (kuh-non-ih-k'l) adj. Relating to a canon or rule.—n. [pl.] The clothes worn by an officiating clergyman.—**ca·non·i·cal·ly** adv.

can·on·ize (kan-un-yze) v. [can·on·ized; -iz·ing] 1. To declare and glorify as a saint. 2. To sanction by canonical law.—**can·on·i·za·tion** (kan-un-ih-zay-shun) n.

canon law. Body of ecclesiastical law governing a church.

can·on·ry (kan-un-ree) n. [pl. -ries] Office and authority of a canon; also canons collectively.

can·o·py (kan-uh-pee) n. [pl. can·o·pies] A covering or shelter fixed over a bed or an entrance.—v. [can·o·pied; can·o·py·ing].

cant n. 1. The vernacular of a particular sect, profession, or group; jargon. 2. Insincere or hypocritical talk, esp. moral or religious phraseology.—**cant** adj.—**cant** v.

cant n. An angle; slope.—v. To turn; cut off at an angle.

can·ta·bi·le (kahn-tah-bee-lay) adj. Music. Graceful; flowing; melodious.

Can·ta·brig·i·an (kan-tuh-brij-ee-un) n. A resident of Cambridge; a student or graduate of Cambridge University.—**Can·ta·brig·i·an** adj.

can·ta·loupe, can·ta·loup (kan-tuh-lohp; -loop) n. A large round, sweet melon with a rough rind; muskmelon.

can·tan·ker·ous (kan-tank-er-us) adj. Quarrelsome; ill-tempered; perverse.—**can·tan·ker·ous·ly** adv.—**can·tan·ker·ous·ness** n.

can·ta·ta (kan-tah-tuh) n. Music. A short dramatic composition to be sung by a chorus.

can·teen (kan-teen) n. Military. 1. A shop where provisions are sold to servicemen; post exchange. 2. A bottle, usually of aluminum and encased in cloth, for carrying drinking water. 3. A recreation hall or organization providing entertainment for servicemen.

can·ter n. A moderate, easy gallop.—**can·ter** v.

Canterbury bell. Plant with blue or white bell-shaped flowers.

cant hook. A pole with an adjustable iron hook for handling logs.

CANT HOOK

can·ti·cle (kan-tih-k'l) n. 1. A short song or hymn for religious chanting. 2. [pl. cap.] Song of Solomon.

can·ti·le·ver (kan-tih-lev-er; -t'l-eev-er) n. Large, projecting beam fastened at one end.—**cantilever bridge.** Bridge formed of two meeting but not mutually supporting cantilevers.

can·tle (kan-t'l) n. 1. A section; corner. 2. The upturned rear part of a saddle.

can·to (*kan*-toh) *n.* [*pl.* can·tos] A main division of a long poem.

can·ton (*kan*-tun) *n.* Small political division of a country, esp. a state of the Swiss Confederation.—can·ton *v.*—can·ton·al *adj.*

can·ton·ment (kan-*ton*-m'nt) *n.* Temporary quarters for troops.

can·tor (*kan*-ter) *n.* 1. Soloist in a synagogue or temple. 2. Leader of a church choir.

can·vas (*kan*-vus) *n.* 1. A heavy coarse cloth used for tents, sails, etc. 2. *Nautical.* Sails. 3. Surface on which oil paintings are executed; an oil painting.—can·vas *adj.*

can·vas·back *n.* North American wild duck with grayish back feathers.

can·vass (*kan*-vus) *v.* 1. To go through, as a district, requesting votes, orders, or support. 2. To examine or scrutinize, often in discussion.—can·vass *n.*—can·vas·ser *n.* A door-to-door salesman.

can·yon, cañ·on (*kan*-yun) *n.* A deep narrow valley worn by a river.

caou·tchouc (*koo*-chook) *n.* Rubber, esp. natural rubber.

cap *n.* 1. Brimless head covering sometimes worn as a mark of rank, occupation, etc. 2. Object resembling a cap in use, shape, or position.—*v.* [capped; cap·ping] 1. To cover; crown. 2. To surpass. 'This caps the climax.'

ca·pa·bil·i·ty (kay-puh-*bil*-ih-tee) *n.* [*pl.* -ties] Ability; competence; power to perform.

ca·pa·ble (*kay*-puh-b'l) *adj.* 1. Able; competent; qualified or fitted. 2. Allowing for; open to.—ca·pa·ble·ness *n.*—ca·pa·bly *adv.*

ca·pa·cious (kuh-*pay*-shus) *adj.* Roomy; capable of holding much.—ca·pa·cious·ly *adv.*

ca·pac·i·ty (kuh-*pass*-ih-tee) *n.* [*pl.* -ties] 1. The power of receiving and holding; the power to contain; volume. 2. Ability; fitness. 3. Position; function. 'In her teaching capacity.'

cap-a-pie (*kap*-uh-pee) *adv.* Also **cap-à-pie.** From head to foot.

ca·par·i·son (kuh-*pair*-ih-sun) *n.* 1. Ornaments, or an ornamented covering, worn by a horse. 2. Elaborate attire.—ca·par·i·son *v.*

cape *n.* 1. A loose sleeveless outer garment, hung from the shoulders. 2. Land extending into water.

ca·per (*kay*-per) *n.* 1. A playful leap; skip. 2. A prank.—*v.* To frolic; prance.

ca·per (*kay*-per) *n.* A Mediterranean shrub whose buds are used as a condiment.

cap·il·lar·i·ty (kap-'l-*air*-ih-tee) *n.* 1. State of being capillary. 2. *Physics.* Force by which a liquid surface is raised when it comes in contact with a solid.

cap·il·la·ry (*kap*-'l-air-ee) *n.* [*pl.* -ies] 1. *Anatomy.* A hairlike blood vessel joining a vein and an artery. 2. Any tube with a small bore. —*adj.* 1. Slender; hairlike. 2. Pertaining to capillary tubes or vessels.

cap·i·tal (*kap*-uh-t'l) *n.* 1. Seat of government. 2. Large letter used to begin a sentence, proper name, etc. 3. *Economics.* Accumulated property of a person or business at a particular time; net worth; wealth used for future production. 4. Advantage; source of power. 'Make capital out of your reputation.' 5. Capitalists as a class.—*adj.* 1. Punishable by death. 'A capital crime.' 2. Major; principal; chief. 3. *Colloquial.* First-rate.

cap·i·tal (*kap*-uh-t'l) *n. Architecture.* Uppermost part or crown of a column, pillar, etc.

cap·i·tal·ism *n.* Economic system in which the means of production are privately owned, and goods are produced for profit, usually under competitive conditions.

cap·i·tal·ist *n.* Person who owns or controls capital, esp. large financial resources.—cap·i·tal·is·tic *adj.*—cap·i·tal·is·ti·cal·ly *adv.*

CAPITAL

cap·i·tal·i·za·tion *n.* 1. Act or result of capitalizing. 2. *Accounting.* The total face value of the capital stock of a corporation.

cap·i·tal·ize *v.* [cap·i·tal·ized; cap·i·tal·iz·ing] 1. To apply or convert into capital for business purposes; turn to profit or advantage. 2. To realize or compute periodically the value of a long-term payment. 'To capitalize rents.' 3. To write with a capital letter.

capital stock. Total capital of a corporation divided into shares; the total face value of these shares.

cap·i·ta·tion (kap-uh-*tay*-shun) *n.* Any direct tax or charge of the same amount for each person, as the poll tax.

cap·i·tol (*kap*-uh-t'l) *n.* 1. [*cap.*] The building in Washington, D. C., in which Congress meets. 2. Building in which a State legislature meets.

Cap·i·to·line (*kap*-uh-t'l-yne) *n.* Smallest of the seven hills of ancient Rome, site of ancient Capitol.—*adj.* Pertaining to the Capitol at Rome or the hill on which it once stood.

ca·pit·u·late (kuh-*pit*-choo-layt) *v.* [ca·pit·u·lat·ed; ca·pit·u·lat·ing] To surrender, as an army, under accepted terms or conditions.

ca·pit·u·la·tion (kuh-pit-choo-*lay*-shun) *n.* 1. A surrender on stipulated terms. 2. A treaty containing conditions of surrender or concessions. 3. Summary; statement of the main heading of a subject or discourse.

ca·pon (*kay*-pon) *n.* A cock castrated and raised for food.

ca·price (kuh-*preess*) *n.* 1. A whim; sudden fancy or notion. 2. Disposition to change suddenly. 3. *Music.* A lively composition in a free style.

ca·pri·cious (kuh-*prih*-shus, -*pree*-) *adj.* Fickle; changeable; guided by caprice.—ca·pri·cious·ly *adv.*—ca·pri·cious·ness *n.*

Cap·ri·corn (*kap*-rih-korn) *n.* 1. A southern constellation. 2. *Astrology.* The tenth sign of the Zodiac.

cap·si·cum (*kap*-sih-kum) *n.* Tropical plant

yielding a pungent, seedy pod, as the pepper or chili; the pod itself.

cap·size (*kap*-syze) *v.* [cap·sized; cap·siz·ing] To overturn; upset, as a boat.

cap·stan (*kap*-st'n) *n.* A grooved cylindrical apparatus fitted with rope for moving weights, weighing anchor, etc.—**capstan bar.** Lever for turning a capstan.

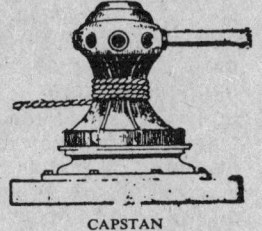

CAPSTAN

cap·sule (*kap*-s'l, *kap*--syool, -sool) *n.* 1. A small gelatin case enclosing a dose of medicine. 2. *Botany.* A seed pod. 3. *Anatomy.* The membranous sac enveloping an organ.—**cap·su·lar** *adj.*

cap·tain (*kap*-tin) *n.* 1. Chief; leader. 2. *Military.* Commissioned officer ranking above a first lieutenant and below a major. 3. *Naval.* Commissioned officer ranking above a commander and below a rear admiral. 4. Officer commanding a ship.—**cap·tain** *v.*—**cap·tain·cy** *n.*

cap·tion (*kap*-shun) *n.* 1. A heading; title of a chapter or section. 2. A newspaper headline. 3. *Journalism.* The text, usually brief, above a picture. 4. *Law.* The explanatory heading on a legal document.—**cap·tion** *v.*

cap·tious (*kap*-shus) *adj.* Critical; faultfinding. —**cap·tious·ly** *adv.*—**cap·tious·ness** *n.*

cap·ti·vate (*kap*-tih-vayt) *v.* [cap·ti·vat·ed; cap·ti·vat·ing] To charm; fascinate; enchant.—**cap·ti·vat·ing** *adj.*—**cap·ti·va·tion** *n.*—**cap·ti·va·tor** *n.*

cap·tive (*kap*-tiv) *n.* One confined against his will, as by an enemy; prisoner.—*adj.* 1. Held prisoner. 2. Captivated.—**cap·tiv·i·ty** *n.*

cap·tor (*kap*-ter) *n.* One who captures.

cap·ture (*kap*-cher) *v.* [cap·tured; cap·tur·ing] To seize by strategy.—*n.* 1. Seizure. 2. Person or thing captured.

cap·u·chin (*kap*-yoo-chin) *n.* 1. [*cap.*] A Franciscan monk. 2. A woman's hooded cloak. 3. A variety of South American monkey.

car *n.* 1. A wheeled vehicle, esp. an automobile. 2. A vehicle running on rails, as a streetcar. 3. An elevator cage.

car·a·ba·o (kahr-uh-*bah*-oh) *n.* [*pl.* **-os**] The water buffalo.

car·a·bi·neer, car·a·bi·nier (kair-uh-buh-*neer*) *n.* A cavalry soldier armed with a carbine.

car·a·cul (*kair*-uh-kul) *n.* Also **kar·a·kul.** Flat curly coat of newborn lambs, valued as fur.

ca·rafe (kuh-*raf*) *n.* A glass water bottle.

car·a·mel (*kair*-uh-m'l) *n.* 1. Burnt sugar used for coloring and flavoring. 2. A hard chewy candy.—**car·a·mel·ize** *v.* [-ized; -iz·ing]. To make into caramel.

car·a·pace (*kair*-uh-payss) *n.* Hard upper covering of certain animals, as the shell of a turtle.

ca·rat (*kair*-ut) *n.* 1. A unit of weight for precious stones. 2. A twenty-fourth part; unit expressing the amount of pure gold in an alloy.

car·a·van (*kair*-uh-van) *n.* 1. A group of travelers journeying together, esp. in desert regions. 2. A large covered wagon.

car·a·van·sa·ry (kair-uh-*van*-suh-rye; -ree) *n.* [*pl.* **-ries**]. Also **car·a·van·ser·ai.** 1. Large, unfurnished resting place for caravans. 2. Large inn; hotel.

car·a·vel (*kair*-uh-vel) *n.* Also **car·a·velle.** A light, fast sailing vessel.

car·a·way (*kair*-uh-way) *n.* A biennial plant yielding aromatic seeds used for flavoring.

CARAVEL

car·bide (*kahr*-byde) *n.* A compound of carbon, such as calcium carbide.

car·bine (*kahr*-byne) *n.* A short rifle used esp. by the cavalry.

car·bo·hy·drate (kahr-boh-*hy*-drayt) *n.* A compound of carbon, hydrogen, and oxygen, including sugars, starches, etc.

CARBINE

car·bol·ic (kahr-*bol*-ik) *adj.* Derived from carbon or coal tar.—**carbolic acid.** A corrosive, poisonous substance used in weakened form for disinfecting, etc.—**car·bo·lat·ed** (*kahr*-buh-lay-tid) *adj.* Containing carbolic acid.

car·bol·ize (*kahr*-buh-lyze) *v.* [-ized; -iz·ing] To blend or treat with carbolic acid.

car·bon (*kahr*-b'n) *n.* A non-metallic element found in all organic compounds. It occurs free as diamond and graphite, and in its impure state as coal. (*Symbol:* C).—*adj.* Of or resembling carbon.—**car·bo·na·ceous** *adj.*

car·bon·ate (*kahr*-buh-nit) *n.* A salt formed of carbonic acid.—*v.* (*kahr*-buh-nayt) [car·bon·a·ted; -at·ing]. —**-a·tion** (-*ay*-shun) *n.*

carbon dioxide. A heavy colorless gas caused by the oxidation of carbon.

car·bon·ic (kahr-*bon*-ik) *adj.* Derived from carbon.—**carbonic acid gas.** Carbon dioxide.

car·bon·if·er·ous (kahr-buh-*nif*-er-us) *adj.* 1. *Geology.* Pertaining to; **a.** A period of the Paleozoic Era. **b.** The strata of the earth containing coal beds. 2. Containing carbon.

car·bon·ize (*kahr*-buh-nyze) *v.* [car·bon·ized; car·bon·iz·ing] To convert into or cover with carbon.— **-i·za·tion** (-ih-*zay*-shun) *n.*

carbon monoxide. A colorless, tasteless, highly poisonous gas formed by the deoxidation of carbon dioxide.

carbon paper. A thin, chemically treated paper for copying imprints, esp. of a typewriter.

carbon tetrachloride. A colorless liquid used as a solvent and as a fire extinguisher.

Car·bo·run·dum (kahr-ber-*un*-dum) *n.* Trademark for a compound of carbon, used as an abrasive.

car·boy *n.* A large bottle encased in a box or basketwork, used for holding corrosive acids.

car·bun·cle (*kahr*-bunk-'l) *n.* 1. A large, painful boil under the skin. 2. A pimple. 3. The garnet.—**car·bun·cu·lar** *adj.*

car·bu·ret (*kahr*-buh-rayt) *n.* A carbide.—*v.* [-ret·ed; -ret·ted; ret·ing, ret·ting] To combine with carbon; charge with carbon compounds. —**car·bu·re·tion** *n.*—**car·bu·ret·ant** *n.*

car·bu·re·tor, car·bu·ret·tor (*kahr*-ber-ay-ter) *n.* An engine or apparatus for the conversion of gasoline into vapor mixed with air.

car·cass (*kahr*-kus) *n.* [*pl.* car·cas·ses]. Also **car·case.** *n.* 1. The dead body of an animal. 2. *Slang.* The human body. 3. Worthless framework; shell.

car·cin·o·gen (kahr-*sin*-uh-j'n) *n.* A substance producing cancer in living tissue.

car·ci·no·ma (kahr-suh-*no*-muh) *n.* [*pl.* -mata, -mas] A form of cancer.— -**nom·a·tous** *adj.*

card *n.* 1. Small flat rectangle of stiff paper or pasteboard, often imprinted with one's name, an invitation, or greetings. 2. One of a pack of cards printed with numbers and symbols for playing certain games. 3. [*pl.*] Any game played with cards. 4. *Slang.* An amusing fellow. 5. *Slang.* Entertainment bill or menu.

card *n.* An instrument for combing wool, flax, etc.—*v.* To comb, as wool.—**card·er** *n.*

card·a·mom (*kahrd*-uh-mum) *n.* Also **card·a·mum, card·a·mon.** 1. An aromatic Indian herb. 2. Its seeds, used in medicine and for seasoning.

card·board *n.* A stiff, thick pasteboard for making boxes, cards, etc.

car·di·ac (*kahr*-dee-ak) *adj.* Pertaining to the heart or to the upper stomach.—*n.* A stimulant medicine.

car·di·gan (*kahr*-dih-gun) *n.* A collarless jacket.

car·di·nal (*kahr*-d'n-ul) *adj.* 1. Chief; principal; fundamental. 2. Yellowish red.—*n.* 1. *Roman Catholic Church.* A member of the Pope's council, appointed by the Pope and second to him in the ecclesiastical hierarchy. 2. A light, bright-red color.—**car·di·nal·ly** *adv.* —**car·di·nal·ship** *n.*

car·di·nal·ate (*kahr*-d'n-ul-ayt) *n.* 1. The office or rank of cardinal. 2. Cardinals collectively.

cardinal bird. North American songbird with bright red plumage.

cardinal flower. The bright-red flower of a North American plant.

cardinal number. Number expressing quantity as one, two, etc., rather than degree, as first, second, etc.

cardinal points. The four main points of the compass: north, south, east, and west.

card·ing *n.* The process of combing wool, cotton, etc., for spinning.

car·di·o·gram (*kahr*-dee-uh-gram) *n.* The record made by a cardiograph.

car·di·o·graph (*kahr*-dee-uh-graph) *n.* An instrument for recording the movements of the heart.— -**o·graph·ic** *adj.*— -**og·ra·phy** *n.*

car·di·tis (kahr-*dy*-tis) *n.* Inflammation of the muscular tissue of the heart.

card·sharp *n.* Also **card·sharp·er.** One who cheats at cards, esp. professionally.

care (kehr) *n.* 1. Deep concern; anxiety; solicitude. 2. Oversight; charge. 'In a nurse's care.' 3. An object of concern or oversight. 4. Close attention; caution.—*v.* [cared; caring]. 1. To feel concern or exercise caution. 2. To wish; want; feel affection for; like. 3. To mind; object to.—**car·er** *n.*

ca·reen (kuh-*reen*) *v.* 1. To lean or tip to one side while at full speed, as a boat. 2. *Nautical.* To heave a ship to one side for repair.

ca·reer (kuh-*rihr*) *n.* 1. General course or progress, esp. in a particular field. 2. Vocation; profession, esp. when entered upon as a lifework.—*v.* To speed; dash.—**ca·reer·ist** *n.*

care·free *adj.* Without care; gay.

care·ful *adj.* 1. Done with care; painstaking. 2. Watchful; cautious; discreet.—**care·ful·ly** *adv.*—**care·ful·ness** *n.*

care·less *adj.* Without care; negligent; indifferent; inattentive.— -**less·ly** *adv.*— -**less·ness** *n.*

ca·ress (kuh-*ress*) *n.* A soft or affectionate touch or gesture; embrace.—**car·ess** *v.*—**ca·ress·er** *n.* —**ca·ress·ing·ly** *adv.*—**ca·res·sive** *adj.*

car·et (*kair*-ut) *n.* Proofreading symbol [∧] indicating an omission or material to be inserted.

care·tak·er *n.* Person who takes care of a residence or other property.

car·go *n.* [*pl.* -goes, -gos] Goods conveyed by a ship; freight; lading.

Car·ib (*kair*-ib) *n.* Member of an Indian tribe found in parts of Venezuela, Guiana, etc.

Car·ib·be·an (kair-ih-*bee*-un, kuh-*rib*-bee-un) *adj.* Relating to the Caribs or the Caribbean Sea.—**Caribbean Sea.** Sea bordered by the West Indies and Central and South America.

car·i·bou (*kair*-uh-boo) *n. sing. & pl.* The North American reindeer.

car·i·ca·ture (*kair*-ih-kuh-cher) *n.* 1. A portrait which exaggerates or ridicules by distortion. 2. A burlesque; grotesque exaggeration.—*v.* [car·i·ca·tured; car·i·ca·tur·ing].—**car·i·ca·tur·al** *adj.*—**car·i·ca·tur·ist** *n.*

CARIBOU

ca·ri·es (*kay*-rih-eez; commonly *kay*-reez) *n.* Bone or tooth decay.

car·il·lon (*kair*-uh-lon) *n.* 1. A set of fixed bells played by striking. 2. A melody played on these bells.—*v.* [car·il·lonned; car·il·lon·ning].—**car·il·lon·neur** (kair-ih-l'n-*er*) *n.*

car·i·ole, car·ri·ole (*kair*-ee-ohl) *n.* Small open carriage drawn by one horse.

car·i·ous (*kehr*-ee-us) *adj.* Affected with caries; decayed.—**car·i·os·i·ty** (kehr-ee-*os*-ih-tee) *n.*

car·load *n.* The capacity of a railroad car.

car·ma·gnole (kahr-m'n-*yohl*) *n.* 1. Popular

song of the French Revolution. 2. Costume worn by the Revolutionists.

car·min·a·tive (kahr-*min*-uh-tiv) *adj.* Expelling gas from the body. 'A carminative agent.'—*n.* A remedy for intestinal disorders.

car·mine (*kahr*-min) *n.* A red pigment derived from cochineal; a deep red color.

car·nage (*kahr*-nij) *n.* Slaughter; butchery.

car·nal (*kahr*-n'l) *adj.* Of the body; sensual; sexual.—**car·nal·i·ty** *n.*—**car·nal·ly** *adv.*

car·na·tion (kahr-*nay*-shun) *n.* Plant having fragrant flowers of various colors; the flower itself. 2. A bright pink.

car·ne·lian, cor·nel·ian (kahr-*neel*-yun) *n.* A translucent red stone used for jewelry.

car·ni·val (*kahr*-nuh-v'l) *n.* 1. A traveling circus or fair. 2. A noisy, unrestrained festival; revelry. 3. The season of rejoicing before Lent.

CARNATION

Car·niv·o·ra (kahr-*niv*-er-uh) *n. pl. Zoology.* The order of flesh-eating mammals.

car·niv·o·rous (kahr-*niv*-er-us) *adj.* Flesh-eating; feeding on animals.—**car·niv·o·rous·ly** *adv.*

car·ol (*kair*-ul) *n.* 1. A Christmas ballad. 2. A song of joy. 'The carol of birds.'—*v.* [car·oled, car·olled; car·ol·ing, car·ol·ling] To sing merrily.—**car·ol·er** *n.*

Ca·ro·lin·gi·an (kair-uh-*lin*-jee-un) *adj.* Relating to the second Frankish dynasty, rulers of France until 987.—**Ca·ro·lin·gi·an** *n.*

Car·o·lin·i·an (kair-uh-*lin*-ee-un) *n.* An inhabitant of North or South Carolina.— **-i·an** *adj.*

car·om (*kair*-um) *n.* 1. *Billiards.* A shot in which the cue ball strikes two other balls. 2. A striking and bouncing off.—*v.* [car·omed; car·om·ing] To strike and rebound.

ca·rot·id (kuh-*rot*-id) *n. Anatomy.* A large, double-branched artery in the neck.—**ca·rot·id, ca·rot·id·al** *adj.*

ca·rous·al (kuh-*rowz*-'l) *n.* A drunken feast; revel.

ca·rouse (kuh-*rowz*) *n.* Carousal; drinking party.—*v.* [ca·roused; ca·rous·ing] To revel; drink heavily.—**ca·rous·er** *n.*

car·ou·sel (kair-uh-*zel*) *n.* Also **car·rou·sel.** A merry-go-round; ring of seats, in the form of wooden animals, on a platform revolving to music.

carp *v.* To find fault; complain; quibble.

carp *n.* A large, edible fresh-water fish.

car·pal (*kahrp*-'l) *adj. Anatomy.* Pertaining to the wrist.—*n.* A wrist bone.

Carpathian Mountains (kahr-*pay*-thee-un). Mountain range in southern Poland, northern Czechoslovakia, and Rumania.

car·pel (*kahr*-p'l) *n. Botany.* A small seed vessel, resembling a leaf.—**car·pel·lar·y** *adj.*—**car·pel·late** *adj.*

car·pen·ter (*kahr*-p'n-ter) *n.* Man who works with wood or builds wooden structures.—*v.* To construct or repair with wood.—**car·pen·ter·ing** *n.* —**car·pen·try** *n.*

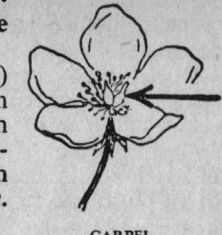

CARPEL

car·pet (*kahr*-pit) *n.* 1. A thick woven fabric for covering floors. 2. Any covering resembling a carpet.—*v.* [car·pet·ed; -pet·ing].—**on the carpet.** Facing a reprimand.

car·pet·bag *n. Now rare.* A fabric traveling bag.

car·pet·bag·ger *n.* A political adventurer; Northerner who went South after the Civil War to take advantage of the political disorganization.—**car·pet·bag·ging** *n.*

car·pet·ing *n.* The fabric for carpets; carpets.

carp·ing *adj.* Criticizing; captious; censorious.

car·pus (*kahr*-pus) *n.* [*pl.* -pi]. The wrist.

Carrara marble. A fine-grained Italian marble used esp. for sculpture.

car·riage (*kair*-ij) *n.* 1. A perambulator; wheeled cradle propelled by pushing. 2. A horse-drawn passenger vehicle. 3. A wheeled stand, as a gun carriage. 4. The part of a machine which moves another part, as a typewriter carriage. 5. *Business.* (*kair*-ee-ij) Transportation cost. 6. Bearing; conduct.

car·ri·er *n.* 1. A messenger; conveyor; bearer. 2. A transmitter of disease, as a typhoid carrier. 3. *Law.* A transport house or service.

carrier pigeon. Pigeon trained to carry messages.

car·ri·on (*kair*-ee-un) *n.* The decaying flesh of carcasses.—*adj.* Feeding on carrion.

carrion crow. The common European crow.

car·rot *n.* A garden plant with an edible, tapering, orange-colored root.—**car·rot·y** *adj.* Orange-colored, as hair.

car·ry *v.* [car·ried; car·ry·ing] 1. To convey; transport. 2. To bear; support. 3. To transmit. 'Water carries sound.' 4. *Arithmetic.* To transfer. 5. To win, as an election or a resolution. 6. To conduct. 'To carry oneself.' 7. To have on one's person. 'To carry matches.'—**carry away.** 1. To inspire. 2. To abduct.—**carry on.** To continue; maintain routine; misbehave.—**carry out.** Accomplish.

car·ry·all *n.* A four-wheeled carriage drawn by one horse.

car·ry·o·ver *n.* Remains; surplus.

cart *n.* An open, often two-wheeled, vehicle; wagon.—*v.* 1. To convey by cart. 2. *Colloquial.* To carry.—**cart·er** *n.*

cart·age *n.* The charge for conveying goods.

carte *n.* A bill of fare; menu.

carte blanche (*kahrt blahnsh*). [*pl.* cartes blanches] Unlimited authority granted.

car·tel (*kahr*-t'l, kahr-*tel*) *n.* 1. A monopoly;

pool. 2. A written international agreement. 3. A written personal challenge.

Car·te·sian (kahr-*tee*-zhun) *adj.* Pertaining to the philosophy of Descartes.— -**sian·ism** *n.*

Car·thage (*kahr*-thij). Ancient city on the N coast of Africa.—**Car·tha·gin·i·an** *adj.*

car·ti·lage (*kahr*-tih-lij) *n. Anatomy.* Gristle; elastic tissue connecting the joints.

car·ti·lag·i·nous(kahr-tih-*laj*-ih-nus)*adj.* 1.Pertaining to cartilage. 2. Having a skeleton chiefly constituted of cartilage.

car·tog·ra·phy (kahr-*tog*-ruh-fee) *n.* Map-drawing; chart-making.—**car·tog·ra·pher** *n.*—**car·to·graph·ic** (kahr-tuh-*graf*-ik) *adj.*

car·ton (*kahr*-tun) *n.* 1. A pasteboard container; box. 2. The white disk within the bull's eye of a target.

car·toon (kahr-*toon*) *n.* 1. A pictorial caricature; comic or satirical drawing. 2. *Painting.* The original drawing from which a fresco is traced.—*v.* [-toon·ed; -toon·ing]— -**toon·ist** *n.*

car·tridge (*kahr*-trij) *n.* 1. A case of metal or other material containing the charge of a firearm. 2. Protected film roll. —**blank cartridge.** A cartridge containing no bullet.

CARTRIDGE

cart wheel. 1. The wheel of a cart. 2. *Colloquial.* A silver dollar. 3. A handspring.

carve *v.* [carved; carv·ing] 1. To shape by cutting; to sculpture; hew. 2. To engrave on wood, stone, or other solid material. 3. To cut into portions, as meat.—**carv·er** *n.*

carv·ing *n.* 1. The art of cutting forms in stone, wood, etc. 2. A carved figure.

car·y·at·id (kair-ee-*at*-id) *n.* [*pl.* -ids, -ides] *Architecture.* A pillar scuptured in the form of a female figure.

ca·sa·ba (kuh-*sah*-buh) *n.* Also **casaba melon.** A muskmelon having a yellow rind.

cas·bah (*kas*-bah) *n.* Also **kas·bah.** Native quarter of a North African town.

cas·cade (kas-*kayd*) *n.* 1. A stream of water descending over a precipice; waterfall. 2. Any rippling descent.—*v.* To surge downward.

cas·car·a (kas-*kair*-uh) *n.* 1. The bark of the American bearwood. 2. The laxative **cascara sagrada** made from the bark.

case *n.* 1. Circumstances; situation; sum of conditions or facts. 2. Occurrence; instance. 3. A problem; plight. 4. A throng; prepared argument. 5. An attack or an instance of a disease. 6. A person considered as a subject of study. 7. A suit in court. 8. *Grammar.* A form in the declension of a noun, pronoun, or adjective. 'The genitive case.'

case *n.* 1. A receptacle designed to hold a specific article. 2. A box; container.—*v.* [cased; cas·ing].

case-hard·en *v.* 1. *Metallurgy.* To harden the outer surface of a metal, such as steel. 2. To become callous or hard.—**case-hard·en·ing** *n.* —**case-hard·ened** *adj.* Impudent; brazen.

ca·se·in (*kay*-see-in) *n.* A protein element of milk used in making cheese, plastics, etc.

case·mate *n. Military Engineering.* A bombproof chamber built on the parapet of a fortification for storing guns; magazine.—**case·mat·ed** *adj.* Furnished with a casemate.

case·ment *n.* A window frame secured by hinges and designed to turn outward.

ca·se·ous (*kay*-see-us) *adj.* Pertaining to or resembling cheese; cheesy.

cash *n.* Money on hand; ready money.—*v.* To convert into currency, as a check.

cash·book *n. Bookkeeping.* A ledger for recording money received and money paid out.

ca·shew (kuh-*shoo*) *n.* 1. A tropical nut tree from which is obtained an acid for varnish. 2. The rich nut of the cashew.

cash·ier (kash-*eer*) *n.* One in charge of money or cash accounts.—*v.* To dismiss dishonorably; throw away.

cash·mere (*kash*-meer) *n.* 1. Cloth of a soft, long-staple, high-quality goat fiber. 2. A shawl of mohair.—**cash·mere** *adj.*

Caspian Sea. A large inland sea east of the Caucasus and north of Iran.

cas·ing *n.* A case; covering; outer layer.

ca·si·no (kuh-*see*-noh) *n.* [*pl.* -noes, -ni] 1. A house or club for drinking, gambling, etc. 2. A card game.

cask *n.* A small barrel.

cas·ket *n.* 1. A coffin. 2. A small chest; jewel case.—**cas·ket** *v.*

Cas·san·dra (kuh-*san*-druh) *n.* A Greek princess whose dismal but accurate predictions were never believed.

cas·sa·tion (kuh-*say*-shun) *n.* An annulling or reversal of a judicial sentence.

cas·sa·va (kuh-*sah*-vuh) *n.* A tropical plant with large, starchy roots; the source of tapioca.

cas·se·role (*kas*-uh-rohl) *n.* 1. A covered baking dish. 2. A meat pie or other combination of foods served in the baking dish.

cas·si·a (*kash*-ee-uh) *n.* Large division of plants and trees of the pea family; a source of senna.

cas·si·mere (*kas*-ih-meer) *n.* A twill-woven woolen cloth in imitation of cashmere shawls.

Cas·si·o·pe·ia (kas-ee-oh-*pee*-ah) *n.* Also **Cas·si·e·pe·ia, Cas·si·a·pe·a.** A W-shaped constellation of the northern hemisphere.

cas·sock (*kas*-uk) *n.* Straight-cut garment worn by clergymen of certain churches.

cas·so·war·y (*kas*-uh-wair-ee) *n.* [*pl.* -ies] A large powerful, nonflying Australasian bird similar to an ostrich.

CASSOWARY

cast *v.* [cast; cast·ing] 1. To throw; hurl. 2. To assign a role in a play. 3. To direct. 'Cast your eyes upward.' 4. To shed; slough off. 5. To deposit. 'Cast a ballot.' 6. To mold; shape; form. 7. To throw away; reject. 8. To fish by throwing out a line on a reel. 9. To explore. 'He cast about for a subject.'—**cast·er** *n.*

cast *n.* 1. Act of casting. 2. A reproduction of a work of sculpture; mold form; impression. 3. The actors in a play. 4. Supporting surgical dressing of plaster. 5. Tinge; tint; slight coloring. 6. Distance traversed by an object thrown. 7. A throw of dice; gamble. 8. Mold; kind; type; character. 9. *Medicine.* Strabismus; in-co-ordination of the eyballs.

cas·ta·nets (kas-tuh-*nets*) *n.* Two small concave shells tied to the thumb and used by Spanish dancers to beat the tempo.

cast·a·way (*kast*-uh-way) *n.* One who is shipwrecked.—*adj.* Rejected; useless.

caste (*kast*) *n.* A division or stratification of society, esp. in India.

cas·tel·lat·ed (*kas*-tel-ayt-ed) *adj.* Built with turrets and battlements, like a castle.

cast·er, cast·or (*kast*-er) *n.* 1. A small, swiveling wheel on which furniture is mounted. 2. One who casts; instrument used in casting. 3. A cruet; container for table dressings.

cas·ti·gate (*kas*-tih-gayt) *v.* [cas·ti·gat·ed; -gat·ing] 1. To chastise; punish. 2. To criticize severely; correct.—**cas·ti·ga·tion** (kas-tih-*gay*-shun) *n.*—**cas·ti·ga·tor** *n.*

Cas·tile (kas-*teel*). Province of northern and central Spain, the speech of which became the literary language of Spain.—**Cas·til·i·an** (kas-*til*-yun) *n. & adj.*

castile soap. A mild soap made with olive oil and sodium hydroxide.

cast·ing *n.* 1. A metal or plastic object formed in a mold. 2. Act of casting.

cast iron. Iron melted, run into molds, and allowed to harden.—**cast-iron** *adj.*

cas·tle (*kass*-'l) *n.* 1. Fortified building or series of buildings; stately, imposing mansion; palace. 2. *Chess.* Rook; one of four pieces which occupy the corners of the board. 3. *Nautical.* A cabin or housing at either end of a ship.—*v.* [cas·tled; cas·tling] *Chess.* To move the king two squares and the rook to the square passed over by the king.

cast-off *adj.* Thrown away; rejected.

cas·tor (*kas*-ter) *n.* A large plant of the spurge family from whose bean castor oil is derived.

castor oil. A laxative, fixed oil extracted from the castor bean.

cas·trate (*kas*-trayt) *v.* [cas·trat·ed; cas·trat·ing] To remove the testicles; emasculate.—**cas·tra·tion** (kas-*tray*-shun) *n.*

cast steel. Steel melted, run into molds, and allowed to harden.

cas·u·al (*kaz*-yoo-l) *adj.* 1. Happening by chance; accidental. 2. Occasional; incidental. 3. Unconcerned; not serious.—*n. Military.* A soldier not officially attached to any unit where he is based.—**cas·u·al·ness** *n.*

cas·u·al·ty (*kaz*-yoo-ul-tee) *n.* [*pl.* -ties] 1. Accident; chance. 2. Mishap; serious misfor-

tune. 3. *Military.* a. A man unfit for duty because of wounds. b. One who has met death. 4. *pl. Military.* Losses in personnel due to enemy action. 5. Death from accident.

cas·u·ist·ry (*kaz*-yoo-iss-tree) *n.* [*pl.* -ries] 1. Misleading or rationalizing reasoning. 2. Branch of ethics dealing with cases of conscience.—**cas·u·ist** *n.*—**cas·u·is·tic, cas·u·is·ti·cal** (kaz-yoo-*iss*-tik, -tih-k'l) *adj.*

cat *n.* 1. A feline; one of a family of flesheating, claw-toed mammals. 2. A small type of feline kept as a pet. 3. A critical or gossiping woman. 4. A caterpillar tractor.

ca·tab·o·lism (kuh-*tab*-ul-izm) *n.* The process of deterioration of plant and animal tissues.—**cat·a·bol·ic** (kat-uh-*bol*-ik) *adj.*

cat·a·clysm (*kat*-uh-klizm) *n.* 1. A flood; deluge. 2. Violent change in the earth's crust. 3. Any violent upheaval.—**cat·a·clys·mal** (kat-uh-*kliz*-mul), **cat·a·clys·mic** *adj.*

cat·a·comb (*kat*-uh-kohm) *n.* [*usually pl.*] An underground recess or cave for burial.

cat·a·falque (*kat*-uh-falk) *n.* A framework used to hold a coffin during funeral services. ·

cat·a·lep·sy (*kat*-uh-lep-see) *n. Medicine.* A nervous condition marked by rigid immobility and unconsciousness.—**cat·a·lep·tic** (kat-uh-*lep*-tik) *n. & adj.*

cat·a·log (*kat*-uh-lawg, -log) *n.* Also **cat·a·logue.** A book which systematically lists and briefly describes persons or things.—*v.* [cat·a·loged; cat·a·log·ing] To arrange in a systematic list; list in a catalog.— **-log·er, -logu·er** *n.*

ca·tal·pa (kuh-*tal*-puh) *n.* A shade tree producing beautiful clusters of flowers and long pods.

ca·tal·y·sis (kuh-*tal*-uh-sis) *n.* [*pl.* -ses] Acceleration of a chemical or physical reaction by a substance which does not itself enter into the reaction.—**cat·a·lyst** (*kat*-uh-list) *n.* The accelerating substance.—**cat·a·lyt·ic** (kat-uh-*lit*-ik) *adj. & n.*

cat·a·lyze (*kat*-uh-lyze) *v.* [cat·a·lyzed; -lyz·ing] To speed a chemical or physical reaction by introduction of a catalyst.

cat·a·ma·ran (kat-uh-muh-*ran*) *n.* 1. A rude boat or raft of tied logs. 2. A vessel with two joined hulls.

cat·a·mount (*kat*-uh-mownt) *n.* Mountain lion.

cat·a·pult *n.* 1. An ancient military engine for hurling large missiles. 2. A slingshot. 3. A powerful machine to launch airplanes from a ship.—*v.* To hurl; to leap.

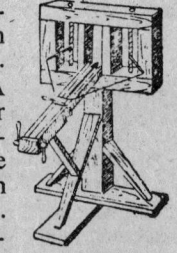

cat·a·ract (*kat*-uh-rakt) *n.* 1. A large waterfall; rushing or downpouring water. 2. *Medicine.* Opacity of the lens of the eye or its capsule, resulting in loss or impairment of vision.

ca·tarrh (kuh-*tahr*) *n. Medicine.* Inflammation of a mucous membrane.—**ca·tarrh·al** *adj.*

CATAPULT

ca·tas·tro·phe (kuh-*tas*-truh-fee) *n.* A disaster; calamity; culminating tragedy.—**cat·as·troph·ic** (kat-uh-*strof*-ik) *adj.*

Ca·taw·ba (kuh-*taw*-buh) *n.* 1. A red American grape. 2. Wine from catawba grapes.

cat·bird *n.* A dark gray thrush, one of whose calls resembles a kitten's wailing.

cat·boat *n.* A small one-masted, single-sailed pleasure boat.

cat·call *n.* A derisive hoot or scream showing disapproval. —**cat·call** *v.*

CATBOAT

catch *v.* [caught; catch·ing] 1. To seize; grasp. 2. To apprehend; arrest; trap. 3. To seize and hold an object passing through the air. 4. To observe; notice. 5. To be infected by. 6. To win the affection of; captivate. 7. To perform suddenly or quickly. 'Catch a nap.' 8. To become ensnarled or wedged in. 9. To take proper hold, as a lock. 10. To reach just in time. 'He caught the train.'

catch *n.* 1. A clasp, lock, or other holder. 2. *Colloquial.* A person highly desirable as a spouse. 3. A sudden break or stoppage. 4. A short scrap; snatch. 5. A game of tossing a ball between two or more persons.

catch·all *n.* A container for small articles.

catch·er *n.* *Baseball.* Player stationed behind the plate to receive the ball from the pitcher.

catch·ing *adj.* 1. Infectious; contagious. 2. Captivating; charming.

catch·pen·ny *n.* [*pl.* -nies] An attractive but worthless thing manufactured to sell quickly.

catch·word (*kach*-werd) *n.* 1. A slogan; glib phrase. 2. A word printed prominently to attract the attention.

catch·y (*kach*-ee) *adj.* [catch·i·er; catch·i·est] 1. Captivating; charming; attractive. 2. Deceptive; tricky, as a problem.

cat·e·chism (*kat*-uh-kizm) *n.* 1. Instruction by questions and answers, esp. in religion. 2. A book of the principles of a subject in the form of questions and answers.—**cat·e·chist** *n.*—**cat·e·chis·tic, cat·e·chis·ti·cal** *adj.*

cat·e·chize (*kat*-uh-kyze) *v.* [cat·e·chized; -chiz·ing] To instruct by question and answer.—**cat·e·chiz·er** *n.*

cat·e·gor·i·cal (kat-uh-*gor*-ih-k'l) *adj.* 1. Positive; absolute; unqualified. 2. Pertaining to a category.—**cat·e·gor·i·cal·ly** *adv.*

cat·e·go·ry (*kat*-uh-gor-ee) *n.* [*pl.* -ries] 1. A class; group or division in a system of classification. 2. *Logic.* One of the fundamental concepts or classes of thought.

cat·e·nate (*kat*-uh-nayt) *v.* [cat·e·nat·ed; cat·e·nat·ing] To link; connect in a series of ties. —**cat·e·na·tion** (kat-uh-*nay*-shun) *n.*

ca·ter (*kay*-ter) *v.* 1. To provide food and service, esp. for parties. 2. To supply whatever is desired.—**cat·er·er** *n.*—**cat·er·ess** *n. fem.*

cat·er-cor·nered (*kat*-er-kor-nerd) *adj.* Diagonal.—*adv.* Diagonally.

cat·er·pil·lar (*kat*-er-pil-er) *n.* 1. The larva of the moth or butterfly. 2. A caterpillar tractor or any similar machine.—**caterpillar tractor.** [*often cap.*] Trade-mark for a tractor able to cover rough ground on two endless belts.

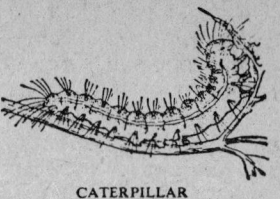

CATERPILLAR

cat·er·waul (*kat*-er-wawl) *v.* To cry or howl like a cat.—**cat·er·waul** *n.* Wail of a cat at mating time.

cat·fish *n.* Any of several scaleless fishes having feelers resembling a cat's whiskers.

cat·gut *n.* A strong, flexible cord made from the intestines of certain animals.

ca·thar·sis (kuh-*thar*-sis) *n.* 1. A purging or cleansing. 2. A purification of the emotions.

ca·thar·tic (kuh-*thar*-tik) *n.* A purgative medicine; strong laxative.—**ca·thar·tic, -i·cal** *adj.*

Ca·thay (kath-*ay*) *n.* Old or literary European name for China.

cat·head *n.* *Nautical.* Projecting beam near the bow of a ship.

ca·the·dra (kuh-*thee*-druh) *n.* 1. The bishop's seat in a cathedral. 2. Any chair of authority.

ca·the·dral (kuh-*thee*-dr'l) *n.* The principal church in a diocese; the bishop's official church.—**ca·the·dral** *adj.* Pertaining to the cathedra or bishop's authority.

cath·e·ter (*kath*-uh-ter) *n.* *Medicine.* A tube for draining an obstructed bladder.—*v.* [cath·e·ter·ized; cath·e·ter·iz·ing].

cath·ode (*kath*-ohd) *n.* Negative pole of an electric circuit.— **-thod·ic** (-*thod*-ik), **-thod·i·cal** *adj.*

cathode ray. A stream of electrons produced in a vacuum tube.

cath·o·lic (*kath*-uh-lik) *adj.* 1. Universal or general. 2. Understanding; liberal. 3. [*cap.*] Pertaining to the Roman Catholics.—*n.* [*cap.*] A member of the Roman Catholic Church.

ca·thol·i·cism (kuh-*thol*-uh-sizm) *n.* 1. Catholicity; universality. 2. [*cap.*] Faith, doctrines, and organization of the Roman Catholic Church.

cath·o·lic·i·ty (kath-uh-*lis*-uh-tee) *n.* State of being catholic; liberal-mindedness.

ca·thol·i·cize (kuh-*thol*-uh-syze) *v.* [-cized; -ciz·ing] 1. To make or become catholic; universalize. 2. [*cap.*] To convert to Catholicism.

cat·kin *n.* A spike of small, close-growing flowers, often shedding when mature.

cat·mint *n.* Catnip.

cat nap. A short nap.

cat·nip *n.* Flowering plant with a strong mint flavor, much liked by cats.

CATKIN

cat-o'-nine-tails *n.* A whip of knotted cords fastened to a handle.

C

cat rig. *Nautical.* Mast set far forward and carrying a single sail.

cat's cradle *n.* A child's game played with string looped between the fingers.

cat's-eye *n.* A hard gem exhibiting opalescence suggestive of a cat's eye.

cat's-paw *n.* 1. A dupe; tool of another. 2. *Nautical.* A light air rippling the water's surface during a calm.

cat·sup (*kat*-sup) *n.* Also **ketch·up.** A thick, highly seasoned tomato sauce.

cat·tail *n.* 1. A tall marsh plant tipped with spikes of brown flowers. 2. A catkin.

cat·ta·lo (*kat*-uh-loh) *n.* [*pl.* -loes, -los] A hybrid of the buffalo and domestic cattle.

cat·tish *n.* 1. Catlike. 2. Catty.—**cat·tish·ly** *adv.*—**cat·tish·ness** *n.*

cat·tle *n.* 1. Collectively, the large domestic animals, usually cows, bulls, and steers. 2. *Contemptuous.* Human beings.—**cat·tle·man** *n.* One who raises or tends cattle.

cat·ty *adj.* [cat·ti·er; cat·ti·est] 1. Pertaining to cats; catlike. 2. Malicious; spiteful.—**cat·ti·ly** *adv.*—**cat·ti·ness** *n.*

cat·walk *n.* Narrow path along a bridge, in an airship, etc.

cat whisker. *Radio.* A fine wire used to establish contact on a crystal detector.

Cau·ca·sia (kaw-*kay*-zhuh). Region on both sides of the Caucasus.

Cau·ca·sian (kaw-*kay*-zhun) *n.* 1. A division of mankind including the major races of Europe, SW Asia, North Africa, and the Western Hemisphere. 2. A native of the Caucasus.—**Cau·ca·sian** *adj.*

Cau·ca·sus (*kaw*-kuh-sus). Mountain range between the Black and Caspian seas in southern U.S.S.R.

cau·cus (*kaw*-kus) *n.* A meeting of leaders of a faction or political party to determine policy or select candidates.—**cau·cus** *v.*

cau·dal (*kawd*-'l) *adj.* Of or like a tail; near the tail or hind part.—**cau·dal·ly** *adv.*

cau·date (*kaw*-dayt) *adj.* Possessing a tail.

cau·dle (*kaw*-d'l) *n.* A warm drink for the sick, usually a gruel mixed with wine or ale.

caul (*kawl*) *n.* A membrane which occasionally covers the head at birth.

caul·dron. *Variant spelling* of **caldron.**

cau·li·flow·er (*kawl*-ih-flou-er) *n.* A variety of cabbage with a thickened, fleshy white head.

caus·al (*kaw*-z'l) *adj.* Expressing, implying, or relating to a cause or causes.—*n.* *Grammar.* A causative word.—**caus·al·ly** *adv.*

CAULIFLOWER

cau·sal·i·ty (kaw-*zal*-ih-tee) *n.* [*pl.* -ties] 1. Causal state or agent. 2. Relation of cause and effect.

cau·sa·tion (kaw-*zay*-shun) *n.* 1. Act of causing or producing. 2. Causality.

caus·a·tive (*kaw*-zuh-tiv) *adj.* 1. Operating as a cause or agent. 2. *Grammar.* Expressing causation.—**caus·a·tive** *n.*—**caus·a·tive·ly** *adv.*

cause (*kawz*) *n.* 1. That which produces an effect or result. 2. A reason or motive. 3. Any matter to be decided, esp. a suit or action in court. 4. The side of a question upheld or supported by a person or group.—*v.* [caused; caus·ing] To effect; bring about.

cause·less *adj.* Without reason or justification. —**cause·less·ly** *adv.*—**cause·less·ness** *n.*

cau·se·rie (*kaw*-zuh-ree) *n.* 1. An informal talk. 2. A short article.

cause·way (*kawz*-way) *n.* A raised road or path above wet ground.—**cause·way** *v.*

caus·tic (*kaws*-tik) *adj.* 1. Capable of corroding or destroying by chemical action. 2. Sharp; severe; cutting.—**caus·tic** *n.*—**caus·ti·cal** *adj.*—**caus·ti·cal·ly** *adv.*—**caus·tic·i·ty** *n.*

cau·ter·ize (*kaw*-ter-yze) *v.* [-ized; -iz·ing] To sear with a hot iron.—**cau·ter·i·za·tion** (kaw-ter-ih-*zay*-shun) *n.*

cau·ter·y (*kaw*-ter-ee) *n.* [*pl.* -ies] 1. A searing by a caustic or a hot iron. 2. The instrument used for cauterizing.

cau·tion (*kaw*-shun) *n.* 1. Prudence regarding danger; carefulness. 2. A warning or admonition. 3. *Slang.* A peculiar or extraordinary person or thing.—*v.* To warn of danger.—**cau·tion·ary** *adj.*

cau·tious (*kaw*-shus) *adj.* Prudent; wary; showing caution.— **-tious·ly** *adv.*— **-tious·ness** *n.*

cav·al·cade (kav-'l-*kayd*) *n.* 1. A horse-borne procession. 2. Historical procession of events.

cav·a·lier (kav-uh-*leer*) *n.* 1. An armed horseman; knight. 2. A chivalrous soldier; lady's escort. 3. [*cap.*] A follower of King Charles I of England.—*v.* To act the cavalier; be haughty.—*adj.* 1. Gay; careless. 2. Arrogant; haughty. 3. [*cap.*] Relating to followers of Charles I.—**cav·a·lier·ly** *adj. & adv.*

cav·al·ry (*kav*-'l-ree) *n.* [*pl.* -ries] *Military.* A body of mounted troops.—**cav·al·ry·man** *n.* [*pl.* -men] Member of a cavalry division.

cave. *n.* A cavern; den; natural or artificial hollow in the earth.—*v.* To fall in, as a mine. —**cave in.** To break down.—**cave-in** *n.*

cave man. 1. A cave dweller of a prehistoric race. 2. *Colloquial.* A man who acts primitively toward women.

cav·ern (*kav*-ern) *n.* 1. A large hollow. 2. A natural subterranean passage in rock.

cav·ern·ous (*kav*-ern-us) *adj.* Having hollows or caverns.—**cav·ern·ous·ly** *adv.*

cav·i·ar, cav·i·are (kav-ee-*ahr*) *n.* A delicacy prepared of fish roe, esp. sturgeon.

cav·il (*kav*-'l) *v.* [cav·iled; cav·illed; cav·il·ing; cav·il·ling] To quibble; split hairs.—*n.* An unreasonable objection.—**cav·il·er, cav·il·ler** *n.*

cav·i·ty (*kav*-ih-tee) *n.* [*pl.* -ties] A hole.

ca·vort (kuh-*vort*) *v.* To gambol; prance about.

ca·vy (*kay*-vee) *n.* [*pl.* -vies] A tropical rodent.

caw *v.* To cry like a crow.—*n.* A short harsh cry.

cay *n.* An islet, as of reef, rocks, etc., near the surface of the water.

cay·enne (ky-*en*; kay-). A pepper derived from the tropical capsicum.

cay·man *n.* [*pl.* -mans] An alligator.

Ca·yu·ga (kay-*yoo*-guh) *n.* [*pl.* -ga, -gas] 1. An Indian tribe formerly occupying central New York. 2. One of the Finger Lakes.

cay·use (ky-*yoos*) *n.* 1. [*cap.*] An Indian tribe settled in Oregon. 2. A breed of Indian pony.

C battery. *Electricity.* Battery which puts a negative charge on the grid of a vacuum tube.

cease (*seess*) *v.* [ceased; ceas·ing] 1. To discontinue; leave off. 2. To terminate; stop; come to an end.

cease·less *adj.* Continual; incessant; without end.—**cease·less·ly** *adv.*

cecropia moth (sih-*kroh*-pih-uh). A moth of the silkworm family.

ce·dar (*see*-der) *n.* A variety of evergreen furnishing light, durable wood.—*adj.* Relating to cedar; made of cedar.

cedar waxwing. Also **ce·dar·bird.** A small grayish brown bird with slate-colored wings.

cede (*seed*) *v.* [ced·ed; ced·ing] 1. To surrender; yield. 2. To grant.

ce·dil·la (seh-*dil*-uh) *n.* A mark placed under the letter *c* [ç] to indicate the sound of *s.*

ceil (*seel*) *v.* To place covering on a room.

ceil·ing (*seel*-ing) *n.* 1. The upper covering of a room. 2. The inner lining of a ship's frame. 3. *Aeronautics.* **a.** Top limit of flight visibility. 'Ceiling zero.' **b.** Maximum altitude possible under existing circumstances. 4. Top permissible limit. 'Ceiling price.'

cel·an·dine (*sel*-an-dyne) *n.* A cuplike yellow flower having heart-shaped leaves.

Cel·a·nese (*sel*-uh-nees) *n.* Trademarked name of a fabric made by processing cellulose fiber.

cel·e·brant (*sel*-uh-br'nt) *n.* 1. A participant in a ceremony or festivity. 2. *Roman Catholic Church.* The priest who conducts mass.

cel·e·brate (*sel*-uh-brayt) *v.* [cel·e·brat·ed; cel·e·brat·ing] 1. To commemorate, as a birthday, a holy day, etc. 2. To praise; honor. 3. To take part in a ceremony.—**cel·e·bra·tion** (sel-uh-*bray*-shun) *n.*

cel·e·brat·ed (*sel*-uh-brayt-ed) *adj.* Illustrious; famous; renowned.

ce·leb·ri·ty (suh-*leb*-ruh-tee) *n.* [*pl.* -ties] 1. Renown; fame. 2. A person of distinction.

ce·ler·i·ty (suh-*lehr*-uh-tee) *n.* Swiftness.

cel·er·y (*sel*-er-ee) *n.* A vegetable having edible stalks and yellowish green leaves.

ce·les·tial (suh-*les*-chul) *adj.* 1. Heavenly; ethereal; divine. 2. Relating to outer space. 'A star is a celestial body.' 3. Of the Chinese empire.—*n.* 1. An inhabitant of heaven. 2. [*cap.*] *Colloquial.* A native of China.—**ce·les·tial·ly** *adv.*

Celestial Empire. The former Chinese empire.

cel·i·ba·cy (*sel*-ih-buh-see) *n.* [*pl.* -cies] Bachelorhood; adherence to unmarried life.

cel·i·bate (*sel*-uh-bayt) *n.* A bachelor; an adherent of single life.—*adj.* Unmarried.

cell *n.* 1. A small chamber. 'A monk's cell'; 'a prison cell.' 2. The hollow chamber of a honeycomb. 3. A mass of protoplasm forming the smallest physiological unit of all organisms. 4. *Architecture.* The interspace in a vaulted roof. 5. A hermitage, a retreat. 6. *Electricity.* A unit containing electrodes in which current is induced by chemical action. 7. A unit of organization, esp. of a political group.

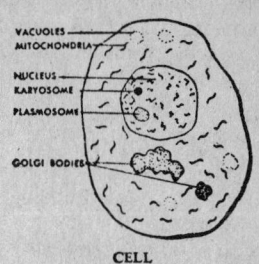

VACUOLES
MITOCHONDRIA
NUCLEUS
KARYOSOME
PLASMOSOME
GOLGI BODIES

CELL

cel·lar (*sel*-er) *n.* 1. A basement; the part of a house standing underground. 2. A storage chamber, under a building.—**cel·lar·age** (*sel*-er-ij) *n.* Cellar space.

cel·lar·et (sel-er-*et*) *n.* A liquor cabinet; a piece of furniture designed to hold bottles.

cel·lo, 'cel·lo (*chel*-oh) *n.* [*pl.* cel·los] A violoncello; a four-stringed instrument tuned one octave lower than the viola.—**cel·list, 'cel·list** *n.* One who plays the cello.

cel·lo·phane (*sel*-uh-fayn) *n.* [*cap.*] Trade name for a translucent wrapping paper.

cel·lu·lar (*sel*-yoo-ler) *adj.* Pertaining to cells, or consisting of cells, as cellular membrane, etc.

cel·lule (*sel*-yool) *n.* A small cell.

cel·lu·loid (*sel*-yuh-loyd) *n.* 1. [*cap.*] Trade name for xylonite; a composition of cotton and camphor used in combs, toilet articles, dental appliances, optical instruments, etc., as a substitute for bone. 2. Celluloid material.—*adj.* Made of celluloid.

cel·lu·lose (*sel*-yuh-lohs) *n.* A fibrous substance in plant tissue used for textiles, paper, synthetic silk, and similar products.

cellulose acetate. A compound used in the manufacture of synthetic silk.

cel·lu·lous (*sel*-yoo-lus) *adj.* Cellular.

Celt (*selt*) *n.* 1. An early inhabitant of northern or western Europe. 2. One of an ancient people represented by the modern Scotch, Welsh, Irish, and Bretons.—**Celt·ic** *adj.* Pertaining to the Celts.—*n.* The Celtic language.

ce·ment (suh-*ment*) *n.* 1. Mortar. 2. Any substance causing cohesion, as glue, putty, rubber cement, etc. 3. The outer layer of the teeth.—*v.* 1. To unite with cement. 2. To coat with cement as a floor. 3. To unify, as to *cement* relations.—**ce·ment·er** *n.*

cem·e·ter·y (*sem*-uh-ter-ee) *n.* [*pl.* -ies] A graveyard; a burial ground.

cen·o·bite (*sen*-uh-byte) *n.* A dweller in a religious community, as a convent or monastery.

cen·o·taph (*sen*-uh-taf) *n.* A commemorative

monument erected elsewhere than on the burial spot.

Ce·no·zo·ic (see-nuh-*zoh*-ik) *n. Geology.* Tertiary; the epoch when existing continents were formed.—*adj.* Manifesting recent life forms.

cen·ser (*sen*-ser) *n.* A vessel for burning incense.

cen·sor *n.* 1. A representative of an office which examines manuscripts, plays, motion pictures, etc., for morally objectionable content. 2. *Military.* An officer who prevents transmission of secret information by letter, radio, press, etc.—*v.* 1. To pass judgment; to criticize. 2. To ban; to prohibit, as publication, performance, etc.—**cen·so·ri·al** (sen-*sor*-ee-ul) *adj.* Severe.

cen·so·ri·ous (sen-*sor*-ee-us) *adj.* Critical; fault-finding; severe; apt to condemn.—**cen·so·ri·ous·ly** *adv.*—**cen·so·ri·ous·ness** *n.*

cen·sor·ship (*sen*-ser-ship) *n.* Supervision; restriction; subjection to examination.

cen·sure (*sen*-sher) *n.* Judgment; condemnation; reproof; criticism; disapproval.—*v.* [cen·sured; cen·sur·ing] To condemn; reprove; pass judgment.—**cen·sur·a·ble** *adj.* Reprehensible; deserving blame.—**cen·sur·a·bly** *adv.*

cen·sus (*sen*-sus) *n.* An official detailed enumeration of the population.

cent (sent) *n.* A penny; a coin valued at one hundredth part of a dollar.—**per cent.** In proportion to one hundred.

cen·taur (*sen*-tawr) *n.* 1. *Greek Mythology.* A creature with the head of a man and the body of a horse. 2. *Astronomy.* Centaurus; southern constellation.

CENTAUR

cen·ta·vo (sen-*tah*-voh) *n.* [*pl.* -vos] A South American coin; the hundredth part of a peso.

cen·te·nar·i·an (sen-teh-*nayr*-ee-un) *n.* A person one hundred years old.—*adj.* Denoting one hundred years.

cen·te·nar·y (*sen*-tuh-ner-ee) *n.* [*pl.* -ies] 1. The space of one hundred years. 2. A one-hundredth anniversary.—*adj.* 1. Occurring once every century. 2. Pertaining to a century.

cen·ten·ni·al (sen-*ten*-ee-ul) *adj.* 1. Happening every hundred years. 2. Consisting of a century, as an epoch.—*n.* The commemoration of a hundredth anniversary.— -**ni·al·ly** *adv.*

cen·ter, cen·tre (*sen*-ter) *n.* 1. The middle point, equally distant from all sides. 2. A point of concentration. 'A business center.' 3. The part of a target next to the bull's eye. 4. *Machinery.* A revolving pin on a lathe spindle. 5. *Football.* The player in the middle of the forward line.—*v.* [cen·tered; centr·ed; cen·ter·ing, centr·ing] 1. To place on a center. 2. To focus, as attention.

cen·ter·board *n.* A movable board passing through the keel of a boat.

center of gravity. The point about which a body will balance in any given position.

cen·ter·piece *n.* An ornament placed in the middle, as on a table, a mantel, shelf, etc.

cen·tes·i·mal (sen-*tes*-ih-m'l) *adj.* Hundredth. —*n.* A hundredth part.—**cen·tes·i·mal·ly** *adv.*

cen·ti- *Prefix.* Hundred; hundredth part.

cen·ti·grade (*sent*-ih-grayd) *adj.* 1. Consisting of a hundred degrees. 2. Graduated into a hundred degrees. 3. Pertaining to a centigrade thermometer.

centigrade thermometer. A thermometer having a scale graduated from zero to one hundred degrees, zero being the freezing point of water, and one hundred degrees the boiling point.

cen·ti·gram, cen·ti·gramme (*sen*-tih-gram) *n.* A metric unit of weight; a hundredth part of a gram.

cen·time (*sahn*-teem) *n.* A hundredth of a franc.

cen·ti·me·ter, cen·ti·me·tre (*sen*-tih-mee-ter) *n.* 0.39 inch; one hundredth of a meter.

cen·ti·pede (*sen*-tih-peed) *n.* A flat-bodied insect having numerous legs.

cen·tral (*sen*-tr'l) *adj.* 1. Situated in the center. 2. Relating to the center.—*n. Colloquial.* A telephone exchange. —**cen·tral·ly** *adv.*

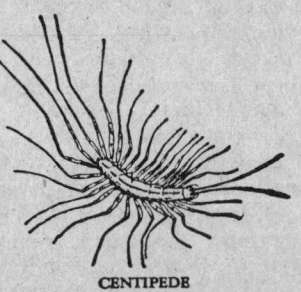

CENTIPEDE

cen·tral·ize (*sen*-tr'l-yze) *v.* [cen·tral·ized; cen·tral·iz·ing] 1. To concentrate at one point. 2. To bring under one control, as governmental agencies.—**cen·tral·i·za·tion** (sen-tr'l-ih-*zay*-shun) *n.*—**cen·tral·iz·er** *n.*

cen·tric, cen·tri·cal (*sen*-trik) *adj. Physics.* Moving toward or connected with a fixed center.—**cen·tric·i·ty** (sen-*tris*-uh-tee) *n.*

cen·trif·u·gal (sen-*trih*-fyuh-g'l) *adj. Physics.* 1. Moving away from the center. 2. Depending on centrifugal action. 'A centrifugal pump.' —*n.* Any cylindrical machine working by centrifugal action.—**cen·trif·u·gal·ly** *adv.*

centrifugal force. *Physics.* The force acting outward from a rotating center.

cen·tri·fuge (*sen*-trih-fyooj) *n.* A machine which produces centrifugal force for various operations, as separating fluids.

cen·trip·e·tal (sen-*trip*-uh-t'l) *adj. Physics.* Acting toward the center.—**cen·trip·e·tal·ly** *adv.*

centripetal force. The force drawing a body toward a rotating center.

cen·trist (*sen*-trist) *n.* A political moderate; a member of neither the left nor the right.

cen·tu·ple (*sen*-tyoo-p'l) *adj.* Hundredfold.—*v.* [cen·tu·pled; cen·tu·pling] To multiply a hundredfold.—**cen·tu·pli·cate** (sen-*tyoo*-plih-kayt) *v.* [cen·tu·pli·cat·ed; cen·tu·pli·cat·ing] To make

C

a hundredfold.—*adj.* 1. Containing a hundred copies. 2. Consisting of a hundred repetitions.—*n.* A hundredth copy.

cen·tu·ri·on (sen-*tyoor*-ee-un) *n.* A military commander in the armies of ancient Rome.

cen·tu·ry (*sen*-cher-ee) *n.* [*pl.* -ries] A hundred years. *Abbreviation*: cent.

century plant. The American aloe, erroneously supposed to bloom once every hundred years.

ce·phal·ic (seh-*fal*-ik) *adj.* Pertaining to the head.—*n.* A headache remedy.

ceph·a·lo·pod (*sef*-uh-loh-pahd) *n. Zoology.* A mollusk having tenacles attached to the head. —*adj.* Resembling a cephalopod.—**ceph·a·lop·o·dan** (sef-uh-*lop*-uh-dun) *adj. & n.*

ceph·a·lo·tho·rax (sef-uh-loh-*thor*-aks) *n.* A combined head and thorax, as in spiders, scorpions, and other arachnids.

ce·ram·ic (ser-*am*-ik) *adj.* 1. Pertaining to the plastic arts. 2. Pertaining to plastic materials, as pottery, earthenware, porcelain, etc.—**ce·ram·ics** *n.* 1. The manufacture of articles of porcelain, earthenware, etc. 2. Articles made of earthenware; pottery.

Cer·ber·us (*ser*-ber-us) *n. Greek Mythology.* The three-headed watchdog of Hades.—**Cer·be·re·an** (ser-*beer*-ee-un) *adj.* Resembling Cerberus.—**a sop to Cerberus.** An act designed to pacify.

cere (*seer*) *v.* [cered; cer·ing] To cover with waxed cloth, as an embalmed body.—*n. Ornithology.* The naked skin below the bill of some birds, as the parrot, hawk, etc.

ce·re·al (*seer*-ee-ul) *n.* 1. Edible grain, as wheat, barley, rye, oats, etc. 2. Any of various breakfast foods: corn flakes, oatmeal, etc. —*adj.* Pertaining to edible grain.

cer·e·bel·lum (ser-uh-*bel*-um) *n.* [*pl.* -lums, -la] The posterior lobe of the brain, believed to control equilibrium.— **-bel·lar** (-*bel*-er) *adj.*

cer·e·bral (*seh*-ruh-brul) *adj.* 1. Relating to the brain. 2. Of the brain. 'Cerebral hemorrhage.'

cer·e·brate (*seh*-ruh-brayt) *v.* [cer·e·brate; cer·e·brat·ing] To think.—**cer·e·bra·tion** (seh-ruh-*bray*-shun) *n.* Thought; mental activity.

cer·e·bro·spi·nal (seh-ruh-broh-*spy*-n'l) *adj.* Pertaining to the brain and spinal cord.

cerebrospinal meningitis. An infectious disease characterized by inflammation of the cerebral and spinal membranes.

cer·e·brum (*seh*-ruh-brum) *n.* [*pl.* -brums, -bra] The large lobe of the brain occupying the whole skull cavity.—**cer·e·bric** (*ser*-uh-brik) *adj.* Derived from the brain, as cerebric fluid.

cere·cloth (*seer*-kloth) *n.* A waxed cloth for wrapping embalmed bodies.

cere·ment (*seer*-m'nt) *n.* 1. A cerecloth. 2. [*pl.*] Grave clothes; a shroud.

cer·e·mo·ni·al (sehr-uh-*moh*-nee-ul) *adj.* Ritual; formal; elaborate; punctilious.—*n.* 1. The form prescribed for an observance or rite. 2. Ritual.—**cer·e·mo·ni·al·ism** *n.* 1. Ritualism. 2. Fondness for ceremony.

cer·e·mo·ni·ous (sehr-uh-*moh*-nee-us) *adj.* Formal; polite; punctilious; elaborate; conventional.— **-mon·i·ous·ly** *adv.*— **-mon·i·ous·ness** *n.*

cer·e·mo·ny (*sehr*-uh-moh-nee) *n.* [*pl.* -nies] 1. A traditional observance; a rite. 2. Formality; adherence to conventions.

Ce·res (*seer*-eez) *n.* [*cap.*] 1. A planet between Jupiter and Mars. 2. *Roman Mythology.* The goddess of agriculture.

ce·re·us (*seer*-ee-us) *n.* A large flowering cactus.

ce·rise (ser-*eez*, ser-*eess*) *n.* The color of a cherry.—*adj.* Cherry-colored.

ce·ri·um (*seer*-ee-um) *n.* A metallic element found in minerals. (*Symbol:* Ce).

cer·tain (*ser*-t'n) *adj.* 1. Sure; true. 2. Fixed; definite, as a certain rate. 3. Unfailing; infallible, as a certain remedy. 4. Inevitable, as certain death. 5. Undeniable; indisputable. 6. Particular, as a certain person.—**cer·tain·ly** *adv.* 1. Without doubt. 2. Without fail.

cer·tain·ty *n.* [*pl.* -ties] 1. State of being certain; lack of doubt. 2. An established truth or fact.

cer·tif·i·cate (ser-*tif*-ih-kit) *n.* 1. A written testimony or declaration of truth; legal voucher. 'A birth certificate.' 2. A diploma. —*v.* [cer·tif·i·cat·ed; -i·cat·ing] To attest in writing.— **-i·ca·to·ry** (-ih-kuh-tor-ee) *adj.*

cer·ti·fi·ca·tion (sert-ih-fih-*kay*-shun) *n.* Written attestation; authorized declaration.

cer·ti·fied (*sert*-ih-fyde) *adj.* Vouched for; endorsed; guaranteed.

cer·ti·fy (*sert*-ih-fy) *v.* [cer·ti·fied; cer·ti·fy·ing] 1. To attest in writing; verify. 2. To make certain; assure. 3. To endorse; guarantee. —**cer·ti·fi·able** *adj.*—**cer·ti·fi·er** *n.*

cer·ti·tude (*sert*-ih-tyood) *n.* Certainty.

ce·ru·le·an (ser-*ool*-yun) *adj.* Sky blue; azure.

ce·ru·men (ser-*oo*-m'n) *n.* The waxlike secretion of the ear.

cer·vi·cal (*serv*-ih-k'l) *adj.* Pertaining to the neck, as cervical vessels.

cer·vine (*ser*-vyne) *adj.* 1. Of the deer family. 2. Like a deer.

cer·vix (*serv*-iks) *n.* [*pl.* cer·vi·ces, -vix·es] 1. The neck. 2. The narrow part of an organ, esp. of the uterus.

ce·si·um (*see*-zee-um) *n.* A silvery alkali metal used in the photo-electric cell. (*Symbol:* Cs).

ces·sa·tion (seh-*say*-shun) *n.* A discontinuance; stopping.

ces·sion (*sesh*-un) *n.* A surrender; yielding, as of territory, rights, etc.

cess·pool *n.* 1. Underground cavity receiving the waste material of a drain. 2. Any receptacle or gathering place for filth.

ces·tode (*ses*-tohd) *n.* A tapeworm.

ce·ta·cean (seh-*tay*-shun) *adj.* Belonging to the order of marine mammals.—*n.* A marine mammal, as a whale, porpoise, dolphin, etc.

Cha·blis (shah-*blee*) *n.* A French white wine.

cha·bouk, cha·buk (*chah*-buk) *n.* A long oriental whip.

chafe (*chayf*) *v*. [chafed; chaf·ing] **1.** To rub; produce heat or wear away by friction. **2.** To vex; irritate; inflame.—*n*. **1.** Annoyance; irritation. **2.** Abrasion; friction.

chaf·er (*chayf-er*) *n*. One of several beetles which feed on plants.

chaff *n*. **1.** Grain husks separated from the seed. **2.** Worthless matter.—**chaf·fy** *adj*.

chaff *n*. Banter; good-natured jesting.—*v*. To banter; tease; make fun of good-naturedly.

chaf·fer *v*. To bargain; haggle.—*n*. Bargaining; haggling.—**chaf·fer·er** *n*.

chaf·finch (*chaf-inch*) *n*. A European song bird, often kept as a pet.

chafing dish. Metal dish with a heating device for cooking or warming food at the table.

cha·grin (shuh-*grin*) *n*. Mortification; vexation; acute disappointment.—**cha·grin** *v*.

chain *n*. **1.** A connected series of links, usually metal, for sustaining weight, transmitting power, ornamentation, etc. **2.** A connected series. 'A chain of events.' **3.** A bond; fetter; restraint. **4.** A measuring device resembling a chain.—*v*. **1.** To bind or unite with a chain. **2.** To restrain; enslave.

chain gang. A group of convicts chained together, often used as labor in certain sections of southern U.S.

chain letter. Letter intended to reach one person after another in a geometric progression.

chain·man *n*. *Surveying*. Man who carries the measuring chain.

chain stitch. An ornamental linked stitch forming a chain.

chain store. One of several retail stores selling similar merchandise and owned and managed by the same company.

chair *n*. **1.** A movable seat with a back and, often, arms, designed for one sitter. **2.** An office or dignity. **3.** A sedan chair. **4.** [with *the*] **a.** Chairman of a meeting. **b.** The electric chair.—*v*. To seat or install in office.

chair·man *n*. [*pl*. -men] **1.** One who presides over a meeting, heads a committee, etc. **2.** Man who carries or wheels a chair.—**chair·man·ship** *n*.—**chair·wom·an** *n*.

chaise (*shayz*) *n*. A light, often two-wheeled, carriage with a movable hood.

chaise longue (*shayz long*) [*pl*. chaise longues] An elongated, usually upholstered, chair for lounging.

CHAISE

chal·ce·do·ny (kal-*sed*-uh-nee) *n*. [*pl*. -nies] Lustrous kind of quartz often used in jewelry.

Chal·de·a (kal-*dee*-uh) *n*. Ancient empire in SW Asia.—**Chal·de·an** *adj*. & *n*.

cha·let (shal-*ay*) *n*. **1.** A Swiss mountain or cottage. **2.** A house built like a Swiss cottage.

chal·ice (*chal*-iss) *n*. **1.** An ornamental goblet holding wine for communion. **2.** A cup-shaped flower.—**cha·liced** *adj*. Having a cup shape, as a flower.

chalk (*chawk*) *n*. **1.** A soft, whitish variety of limestone. **2.** A drawing crayon of material resembling chalk.—*v*. **1.** To mark or draw with chalk; hence, to record; score. **2.** To whiten with chalk.—**chalk** *adj*.

chalk·y *adj*. [chalk·i·er; chalk·i·est] Containing or resembling chalk.

chal·lenge (*chal*-enj) *n*. **1.** A provocative invitation to a contest or duel; a dare. **2.** *Military*. A sentry's demand for identification. **3.** *Law*. A formal objection, as to a juror. **4.** Act of disputing or questioning. **5.** A claim or demand on.—*v*. [chal·lenged; chal·leng·ing].—**chal·lenge·a·ble** *adj*.—**chal·leng·er** *n*.

chal·lis (*shal*-ee) *n*. Also **chal·lie**. A fine, light woolen, cotton, or rayon fabric.

cham·ber (*chaym*-ber) *n*. **1.** A compartment; a hollow space. **2.** A room, esp. a bedroom. **3.** A room for conducting legal or government business. **4.** A legislature. **5.** A business advisory council.—**cham·ber** *v*.

cham·ber·lain (*chaym*-ber-lin) *n*. **1.** A steward; court official. **2.** The comptroller of a city or corporation.

cham·ber·maid (*chaym*-ber-mayd) *n*. A maid employed to clean bedrooms.

chamber music. Musical compositions requiring few instruments.

chamber of commerce. A local board for the promotion of trade.

cham·bray (*sham*-bray) *n*. A gingham cloth woven from white and colored threads.

cha·me·le·on (kuh-*meel*-yun) *n*. **1.** A lizard having the faculty of changing the color of its skin. **2.** A fickle person.—**cha·me·le·on·ic** (kuh-mee-lee-*on*-ik) *adj*.

CHAMELEON

cham·fer (*cham*-fer) *n*. The slanting surface formed by cutting off an angle or edge.—*v*. *Carpentry*. To groove; bevel.

cham·ois (*sham*-ee) *n*. *sing*. & *pl*. **1.** A kind of antelope habiting central and southern Europe. **2.** A soft velvety leather used for gloves, polishing clothes, etc.—*v*. To clean with chamois.

CHAMOIS

champ *v*. To bite or chew loudly, as a horse.—*n*. **1.** Act of champing. **2.** *Slang*. Champion.

cham·pagne (sham-*payn*) *n*. A sparkling white wine originated in Champagne, France.

cham·paign (sham-*payn*) *n.* A plain; flat, open country.—*adj.* Level; open.

cham·pi·on (*champ*-ee-un) *n.* 1. A defender; supporter, as of a cause. 2. The acknowledged victor over all competitors.—*adj.* Unrivaled; winning. 'The champion boxer.'—*v.* To defend; fight for.—**cham·pi·on·less** *adj.*

cham·pi·on·ship *n.* 1. Act of defending. 2. State of being champion; supremacy.

Champs Elysées (shahnz-ay-lee-*zay*) A beautiful boulevard in Paris.

chance *n.* 1. A happening; accident. 2. Fortune; fate; luck. 3. An opportunity. 4. A hazard; risk. 5. Possibility or probability. —*v.* [chanced; chanc·ing] 1. To happen. 2. To risk; hazard.—*adj.* Casual; accidental.

chan·cel (*chan*-s'l) *n.* The part of a church reserved for the altar and choir.

chan·cel·ler·y (*chan*-s'l-ree) *n.* [*pl.* -ies] 1. The office or position of a chancellor. 2. Office of a consulate, etc.

chan·cel·lor (*chan*-s'l-er) *n.* 1. Presiding judge in a court of equity. 2. The president of certain universities. 3. Official secretary of a king or prince. 4. High embassy official. —**chan·cel·lor·ship** *n.*

Chancellor of the Exchequer. The minister of finance in the British cabinet.

chan·cer·y (*chan*-ser-ee) *n.* [*pl.* -ies] 1. A court of equity. 2. A court or office containing public records. 3. Equity practice. 4. *Wrestling.* Head grip.—**in chancery.** 1. *Law.* Under equity proceedings. 2. Helpless; powerless.

chan·cre (*shank*-er) *n.* A venereal sore.

chanc·y (*chan*-see) *adj.* [chanc·i·er; chanc·i·est] *Colloquial.* Risky; perilous.

chan·de·lier (shan-duh-*leer*) *n.* A branched holder for candles or electric bulbs, usually suspended from the ceiling.

chan·dler (*chand*-ler) *n.* 1. A candle maker. 2. A grocery dealer.—**chan·dler·y** *n.* [*pl.* -ies].

change (*chaynj*) *v.* [changed; chang·ing] 1. To alter; make or become different; vary. 2. To substitute. 3. To exchange. 4. To give smaller pieces of currency in place of a larger. —*n.* 1. A changing; substitution or alteration. 2. Variety. 3. Money returned when the payment exceeds the price. 4. Small piece of currency exchanged for a larger; coins. —**change face.** To reverse oneself; face another way.—**change front.** To alter one's point of view.—**chang·er** *n.*

change·a·ble (*chayn*-juh-b'l) *adj.* Given to change; fickle; variable.—**change·a·bil·i·ty** *n.* —**change·a·ble·ness** *n.*—**change·a·bly** *adv.*

change·ling *n.* A child secretly left in place of another.

change of life. The menopause.

change ringing. The continuous ringing of bells in a certain order.

chan·nel (*chan*-'l) *n.* 1. A furrow; groove; passageway. 2. The bed of a stream. 3. The deepest part of a strait, river, etc. 4. A narrow sea between two pieces of land. 5. A medium of transmission. 'A channel of propaganda.'—*v.* [chan·neled, -nelled; chan·nel·ing, -nel·ling] 1. To furrow; form a channel. 2. To transmit through a channel.

chan·son (*shan*-sun) *n.* A song.

chant *v.* 1. To sing. 2. To celebrate in song, as to chant praises. 3. To repeat in a monotone.—*n.* A musical composition in which several syllables are sung in one tone.—**chant·er** *n.* 1. The chief singer of a chantry. 2. A singer.

chan·tey, chant·y (*chant*-ee, *shant*-) *n.* [*pl.* -eys, -ies] A sailor's air sung to the rhythm of his work.

chan·ti·cleer (*chan*-tih-kleer) *n.* A cock.

chan·try (*chan*-tree) *n.* [*pl.* -tries] An endowed chapel for saying daily mass for the donors.

cha·os (*kay*-ahss) *n.* 1. The confused state before the creation of the universe. 2. Utter confusion.—**cha·ot·ic** (kay-*ot*-ik), **-i·cal** *adj.*

chap *v.* [chapped; chap·ping] To crack; split, as the surface of the skin.—*n.* A cleft; chink.

chap *n.* 1. A fellow; young man. 2. Also **chop.** A jaw.

chap·ar·ral (chap-uh-*ral*) *n.* A thicket of shrubs and brambles.

chap·book *n.* A pamphlet of songs and stories popular in the eighteenth century.

cha·peau (shuh-*poh*) *n.* [*pl.* -peaux, -peaus] *French.* A hat.

chap·el (*chap*-'l) *n.* 1. A section of a church for private worship. 2. Small place of worship. 3. A chapel service.

chap·er·on, chap·er·one (*shap*-uh-rohn) *n.* One who escorts a young woman in public.—*v.* To protect; escort.—**chap·er·on·age** *n.*

chap·fall·en *adj.* Also **chop·fall·en.** Dejected; dispirited; weary.

chap·lain (*chap*-lin) *n.* A clergyman officiating in a public institution, army, navy, etc.

chap·let *n.* 1. A wreath for the head; garland. 2. A necklace. 3. A type of rosary.

chap·man *n.* [*pl.* -men] A peddler.

chap·ter *n.* 1. A principal division, as of a book, treatise, etc. 2. A branch of a society. 3. Meeting of a bishop's council.—*v.* To divide into chapters.

chapter house. A meeting house for a fraternity, religious council, etc.

char (*chahr*) *v.* [charred; char·ring] 1. To burn partially, esp. to reduce to charcoal. 2. To work as a cleaning woman, esp. by the day.

char·ac·ter (*kar*-ak-ter) *n.* 1. A written or printed letter or sign. 2. Moral traits. 3. Distinguishing quality. 4. Position; capacity. 5. Person in a work of fiction. 6. *Slang.* An odd person.—**char·ac·ter·less** *adj.*

char·ac·ter·is·tic (kar-ak-ter-*is*-tik) *adj.* Peculiar; distinctive.—*n.* A distinguishing trait or quality.— **-ti·cal** *adj.*— **-ti·cal·ly** *adv.*

char·ac·ter·ize (*kar*-ak-ter-yze) *v.* [char·ac·ter·

ized; char·ac·ter·iz·ing] 1. To stamp; distinguish. 2. To describe; portray.—**char·ac·ter·iz·a·tion** (kar-ak-ter-ih-*zay*-shun) n.

char·ac·ter·y (*kar*-ik-ter-ee) n. Expression of thought by symbols.

cha·rade (shuh-*rayd; -rahd*) n. A parlor game of guessing a word through the dramatic representation of each syllable.

char·coal (*chahr*-kohl) n. 1. A carbonic substance used for fuel, drawing pencils, etc. 2. A drawing made with charcoal.—v. To draw with charcoal.

chard n. 1. Prepared artichoke leaves. 2. Variety of beet, grown for its leaves; Swiss chard.

charge (chahrj) v. [charged; charg·ing] 1. To ask a price. 2. To record, as a debt. 3. To accuse. 4. To entrust, as with a task; commission. 5. To instruct, as a jury. 6. To attack; assault. 7. *Electricity*. To re-establish the normal voltage of, as a battery. 8. To load.—**charge** n.—**charge·able** adj.

charge·a·ble (*charj*-uh-b'l) adj. Subject to charge.

charg·er n. 1. A war horse. 2. *Electricity*. Contrivance for charging batteries.

char·i·ly (*chehr*-uh-lee) adv. 1. Warily; with caution. 2. Sparingly; frugally.— **-i·ness** n.

char·i·ot (*chair*-ee-ut) n. An ancient two-wheeled vehicle used in war, processions of state, racing, etc.

char·i·ot·eer n. A chariot driver.

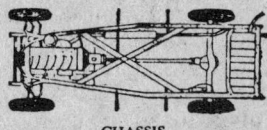
CHARIOT

char·i·ta·ble (*chair-ih*-tuh-b'l) adj. 1. Benevolent; of a kind disposition. 2. Liberal; generous. 3. Intended for charity. 'A charitable institution.'—**char·i·ta·ble·ness** n.—**char·i·ta·bly** adv.

char·i·ty (*chair*-ih-tee) n. [pl. -ties] 1. Benevolence; kindness. 2. Alms; anything offered for the relief of the poor. 3. A benevolent act. 4. An organization for aiding the poor.

cha·ri·va·ri (shuh-*riv*-uh-ree, *shiv*-uh-ree) n. A mock serenade of discordant music.

char·la·tan (*shahr*-luh-t'n) n. A pretender; fraud; quack.—**char·la·tan·ry** n. [pl. -ries].

charley horse. *Athletics*. A muscular strain caused by overexertion.

char·lotte russe (*shahr*-lut roos). A delicacy consisting of whipped cream within a folded layer of sponge cake.

charm n. 1. Allurement; the power to delight. 2. An enchantment; a spell; a supernatural implement. 3. A trinket worn on a chain. —v. 1. To allure; to delight; to please. 2. To bewitch; to cast a spell.—**charm·er** n.

charm·ing adj. Alluring; delightful; captivating.

char·nel (*chahr*-n'l) n. A repository for the dead. —**charnel house**. A vault for dead bodies.

Char·on (*kehr*-un) n. *Greek Mythology*. The ferryman who rowed dead souls across the river Styx.

chart n. 1. A sheet giving information in tabular or diagrammatic form. 2. A marine or air navigation map.—v. [chart·ed; chart·ing] To delineate; to map out.

char·ter n. 1. An official document bestowing rights, powers, or grants. 2. A permit to do business. 'A corporation charter.' 3. A private contract to lease a ship. 4. A statement of rights. 'The Atlantic Charter.'—v. 1. To establish by charter, as a bank. 2. To hire by contract, as a ship.—**char·ter·age** n.

char·treuse (shahr-*trerz*) n. 1. A cordial originated by the monks of Chartreuse, France. 2. A yellowish green color.—**char·treuse** adj.

char·wom·an n. [pl. -wom·en] 1. A cleaning woman, esp. one hired by the day.

char·y (*chayr*-ee) adj. [char·i·er; char·i·est] 1. Cautious; wary. 2. Frugal; sparing. 'Chary of compliments.'

chase v. [chased; chas·ing] 1. To pursue; to follow in pursuit. 2. To hunt game. 3. To drive off.—n. 1. A strenuous pursuit. 2. A hunt.—**chas·er** n. One who pursues.

chase n. 1. A groove; a furrow; a trench. 2. *Printing*. An iron frame for holding columns of type.—v. *Toolmaking*. To cut a groove into, as a screwthread.—**chas·er** n.

chase v. 1. To emboss metal; to decorate by engraving. 2. To place in a setting, as a gem. 3. To encrust with jewels.—**chas·er** n.

chas·er n. *Colloquial*. A mild drink taken after hard liquor.

chasm (*kazm*) n. 1. An abyss; a gorge; a deep crevice. 2. An opening in the earth.

chas·sé (shass-*ay*) n. *Dancing*. A glide.—v. [chas·séd; chas·sé·ing] To glide.

chas·seur (shas-*er*) n. 1. Soldier of a unit trained to move rapidly. 2. A uniformed attendant. 3. A hunter.

chas·sis (*shass*-ee) n. [pl. chas·sis (*shass*-eez)] 1. The framework of an automobile or airplane. 2. Framework on which a mounted gun moves.

CHASSIS

chaste adj. 1. Pure; virtuous; continent. 2. Simple in style or design.—**chaste·ly** adv. —**chaste·ness** n.

chast·en (*chays*-'n) v. 1. To chastise; punish. 2. To purify; reclaim from excess or evil.

chas·tise (*chass*-tyze) v. [chas·tised; chas·tis·ing] To discipline; correct by punishment, esp. by whipping.—**chas·tise·ment** n.—**chas·tis·er** n.

chas·ti·ty (*chass*-tuh-tee) n. 1. Abstinence; sexual purity; virginity. 2. Freedom from ornamentation; simplicity.

chas·u·ble (*chaz*-yuh-b'l) n. *Ecclesiastical*. Embroidered outer vestment worn by a priest saying mass.

chat v. [chat·ted; chat·ting] To converse in a pleasant, informal manner.—n. 1. Informal conversation. 2. A yellow-breasted American song bird.

châ·teau (shat-*toh*) n. [pl. -teaux] 1. A French castle. 2. An imposing country residence.

—*adj.* [*cap.*] Indicating certain French wines.

chat·e·laine (*shat*-uh-layn) *n.* 1. An ornamental chain and clasp holding a watch, keys, etc. 2. Mistress of a castle.

chat·tel (*chat*-'l) *n. Law.* Any property with the exception of real estate.

chat·ter (*chat*-er) *v.* 1. To jabber; utter rapid, indistinct sounds. 2. To talk rapidly or foolishly. 3. To make a clicking sound with the teeth.—*n.* Gibberish; idle talk.

chat·ter·box (*chat*-er-boks) *n.* A constant talker.

chat·ter·er (*chat*-er-er) *n.* 1. One who chatters. 2. A species of tropical bird.

chat·ty (*chat*-ee) *adj.* [chat·ti·er; chat·ti·est] 1. Talkative. 2. Informal. 'A chatty lecture.'

chauf·feur (*shoh*-fer) *n.* Driver of an automobile.—*v.* To work as a chauffeur; drive.

Chau·tau·qua, chau·tau·qua (shuh-*tawk*-wuh) *n.* A system of education based on home study with annual assemblies of students.

chau·vin·ism (*shoh*-v'n-izm) *n.* 1. Blind devotion to a cause, esp. fanatical patriotism. 2. Exaggerated loyalty to one's sex. 'Female chauvinism.'—**chau·vin·ist** *n.* & *adj.*—**chau·vin·is·tic** *adj.*—**chau·vin·is·ti·cal·ly** *adv.*

cheap (*cheep*) *adj.* 1. Inexpensive; low-priced. 2. Inferior; common; of small value.—**cheap·ly** *adv.*—**cheap·ness** *n.*

cheap·en (*cheep*-'n) *v.* 1. To lower the price. 2. To render common.—**cheap·en·er** *n.*

cheat (*cheet*) *n.* 1. A deception; fraud. 2. A swindler; one who defrauds; a deceiver.—*v.* 1. To deceive; act dishonestly. 2. To swindle; defraud. 3. To elude, as death.—**cheat·er** *n.*—**cheat·ing·ly** *adv.*

check *n.* 1. A sudden halt. 2. A restraint; a curb or control. 3. A comparison for verification; standard. 4. Also **cheque.** An order for money drawn on a bank. 5. A token issued for identification. 6. The mark (√) used in confirming or, in printing, to reduce spacing between words. 7. A pattern of squares or a single square. 8. *Chess.* Position of the king when in danger.—*v.* 1. To restrain; curb. 2. To bring to a halt. 3. To compare for accuracy. 4. *Chess.* To place an opponent's king in danger. 5. To confirm by a mark.—*adj.* Checkered.—**check·a·ble** *adj.*

checkbird	check-off	checkrope
checklist	checkrack	checkstrap
checkman	checkroll	check work

check·book *n.* A book holding blank checks on a bank.

check·er (*chek*-er) *n.* 1. One who checks. 2. A disk of light or dark color for playing checkers. 3. A square or pattern of squares. —*v.* 1. To pattern with squares. 2. To diversify; impart variety.

check·er·ber·ry (*chek*-er-behr-ee) *n.* [*pl.* -ries] 1. Wintergreen; a low shrub with scarlet berries. 2. The berry itself.

check·er·board (*chek*-er-bohrd) *n.* A square board for playing checkers.

check·ered *adj.* 1. Marked with squares. 2. Varied. 'A checkered career.'

check·ers *n.* A game played by two persons and based on the strategic placing of disks on a square board; draughts.

check·mate (*chek*-mayt) *n.* 1. *Chess.* The losing position of a king in check so that he cannot escape. 2. Complete defeat.—*b.* [check·mat·ed; check·mat·ing] 1. *Chess.* To put an opponent's king in checkmate. 2. To defeat.

check·rein *n.* A bearing rein; a short rein extending from bridle to saddle.

check·room *n.* A room in a public place for depositing parcels, outer clothing, etc.

Ched·dar (*ched*-er) *n.* A hard cheese originated in Cheddar, England; store cheese; rat cheese.

cheek *n.* 1. The side of the face below either eye. 2. *Mechanics.* Any piece having a corresponding side, as in a printing press, a turning lathe, a door, etc. 3. *Colloquial.* Impudence.—*v. Colloquial.* To assail with impudence.—**cheek by jowl.** Side by side.

cheek·bone *n.* The bone forming the prominence beneath the eye.

cheek·y *adj.* [cheek·i·er; -i·est] *Colloquial.* Impudent; brazen.—**cheek·i·ly** *adv.*— -i·ness *n.*

cheep *v.* To chirp; to pipe.—*n.* A tiny, shrill squeak.—**cheep·er** *n.*

cheer *n.* 1. Joy; animation. 2. Spirits; state of mind. 3. A shout of acclamation. 4. Refreshments; provisions; a feast.—*v.* 1. To gladden; to console. 2. To salute with shouts, applause, etc.—**cheer·er** *n.*

cheer·ful *adj.* Joyful; gladdening; blithe. —**cheer·ful·ly** *adv.*—**cheer·ful·ness** *n.*

cheer·less *adj.* Dismal; gloomy; mournful. —**cheer·less·ly** *adv.*—**cheer·less·ness** *n.*

cheer·y *adj.* [cheer·i·er; cheer·i·est] Good-humored; gay.—**cheer·i·ly** *adv.*—**cheer·i·ness** *n.*

cheese (*cheez*) *n.* 1. A product obtained from the curd of milk. 2. *Slang.* Anything of poor quality.—*v.* [chees·ed; chees·ing] *Slang.* To escape; get away. 'Cheese it, the cops!'

cheese·cake *n.* 1. Cake filled with a paste of sweetened soft curds. 2. *Slang.* A photograph which accents a woman's legs.

cheese·cloth *n.* A thin, loosely woven cloth; coarse gauze.

chees·y *adj.* [chees·i·er; chees·i·est] 1. Caseous; resembling cheese. 2. *Slang.* Of poor quality. — **chees·i·ness** *n.*

chee·tah (*chee*-tuh) *n.* The leopard of India, trained for hunting.

chef (*shef*) *n.* A cook, esp. the head cook of a hotel, restaurant, etc.

che·la (*kee*-luh) *n.* [*pl.* -lae] A claw adapted for holding, terminating the limbs of

CHEETAH (1/35 life size)

C

lobsters, crabs, and other crustaceans.—**che·late** (*kee*-layt) *adj.* Having a prehensile claw.

chem·i·cal (*kem*-ih-k'l) *adj.* 1. Pertaining to chemistry. 2. Pertaining to the laws of chemistry, as chemical affinity, chemical attraction, chemical combination, etc.—*n.* The product of a chemical action.—**chem·i·cal·ly** *adv.*

che·mise (sheh-*meez*) *n.* A woman's undergarment.

chem·ist (*kem*-ist) *n.* 1. An analyst. 2. A druggist; an apothecary.

chem·is·try (*kem*-is-tree) *n.* [*pl.* -tries] The science which investigates the properties of substances and the laws governing their change. See **physical chemistry.**

chem·o-, chem- *Prefix.* Relating to chemistry. 'Chemolysis; chemosmosis; chemotherapy.'

chem·ur·gy (*kem*-er-jee) *n.* Branch of organic chemistry concerned with industrial utilization of farm products.—**chem·ur·gic, -ur·gi·cal** *adj.*

che·nille (shuh-*neel*) *n.* 1. A thick, tufted cord used for fringes and other ornamental sewing. 2. A fabric trimmed with chenille.

Che·ops (*kee*-ops) *n.* Egyptian King of the Fourth Dynasty who built the Great Pyramids.

cher·ish (*cheh*-rish) *v.* 1. To care for tenderly; to guard and treasure. 2. To cling to; to harbor, as a principle.

Cher·o·kee (chehr-uh-*kee*) *n.* [*pl.* -kee, -kees] A North American Indian tribe formerly inhabiting southeastern states, now largely concentrated in Oklahoma.

Cherokee rose. The state flower of Georgia.

che·root (sheh-*root*) *n.* A tapering cigar having both ends cut square.

cher·ry (*chair*-ee) *n.* [*pl.* -ries] A small pulpy stone fruit found in all temperate climates. —*adj.* Of a cherry color; red.—**cher·ried** *adj.*

cher·ub (*cher*-ub) *n.* [*pl.* cher·ubs] 1. A winged representation of an angel, usually having the face of a child. 2. A beautiful child. 3. [*pl.* cher·u·bim] *Old Testament.* A class of angels next in order to the seraphim.

che·ru·bic (cheh-*roo*-bik) *adj.* Angelic.—**che·ru·bi·cal·ly** *adv.*

Cheshire cat. The grinning cat who gives noncommittal advice in *Alice's Adventures in Wonderland.*

chess *n.* A game based on the strategic placing of pieces on a squared board with the object of capturing an opponent's king.—**chess·board** *n.* —**chess·man** *n.* [*pl.* -men] A pawn; a piece used in playing chess.

chest *n.* 1. A box; trunk; case of wood, iron, etc., for holding foods. 2. The thorax; the bony part of the body from the neck to the abdomen. 3. An article of furniture fitted with drawers for clothing, utensils, etc.

ches·ter·field *n.* A kind of topcoat.

chest·nut (*ches*-nut) *n.* 1. A nut enclosed in a prickly pericarp and having two seeds. 2. *Slang.* A trite story.—*adj.* Reddish brown; the color of a chestnut.

chest·y *adj. Slang.* Conceited; arrogant.

chev·a·lier (shev-uh-*leer*) *n.* 1. A knight; a cavalier; a horseman. 2. A man known for his gallantry.

chev·i·ot (*chev*-ee-ut) *n.* 1. A rough, loosely woven wool or cotton fabric. 2. [*cap.*] A variety of large mountain sheep raised in the Cheviot Hills, Scotland.

chev·ron (*shev*-run) *n. Military.* A stripe; a sleeve badge worn by noncommissioned officers, denoting rank.—**chev·ron·ed** *adj.*

chev·y, chiv·y (*chev*-ee) *n.* [*pl.* -ies] A hunt; pursuit; chase. —*v.* [chev·ied; chev·y·ing, chiv·ied; chiv·y·ing] 1. To hunt; chase. 2. To goad; worry.

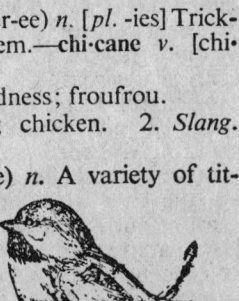

CHEVRONS

chew *v.* 1. To grind with the teeth; masticate, as food. 2. To ruminate; meditate.—*n.* 1. A mouthful. 2. A quid of tobacco.—**chewing gum.** Flavored gum mixed with chicle.

che·wink (cheh-*wink*) *n.* A North American finch.

Chey·enne (shy-*en*) *n.* [*pl.* -enne, -ennes] 1. A branch of the Algonquin Indian tribe living in Montana and Wyoming. 2. Capital city of Wyoming.

Chi·an·ti (kee-*an*-tee) *n.* A red Italian wine.

chi·a·ro·scu·ro (kih-ah-ruh-*skyoo*-roh) *n.* [*pl.* -ros] 1. The distribution of light and shadows in pictorial art. 2. A style of art using light and shade only.—**chi·a·ro·scu·rist** *n.*

chic (*sheek*) *n.* Artistic elegance; style, as in attire.—*adj.* [chic·quer; chic·quest] Elegant; stylish.

chi·can·er·y (chih-*kayn*-er-ee) *n.* [*pl.* -ies] Trickery; conniving stratagem.—**chi·cane** *v.* [chi·caned; chi·can·ing].

chi·chi *n. Slang.* Affectedness; froufrou.

chick *n.* 1. A young chicken. 2. *Slang.* Young woman.

chick·a·dee (*chik*-uh-dee) *n.* A variety of titmouse with gray and black feathers.

chick·a·ree (*chik*-uh-ree) *n.* American red squirrel.

chick·en (*chik*-'n) *n.* 1. A young domestic fowl. 2. A young or immature person. 3. *Slang.* A young woman.

CHICKADEE (1/4 life size)

chick·en·heart·ed *adj.* Cowardly; lacking courage.

chick·en·pox *n.* A contagious children's disease, marked by skin eruptions.

chick·weed (*chik*-weed) *n.* A flowering weed having leaves and seeds used as food for birds.

chi·cle (*chik*-'l) *n.* A milky product of the sapodilla tree used in making chewing gum.

chic·o·ry (*chik*-er-ee) *n.* [*pl.* -ries]. Also **chic·co·ry.** 1. A lettucelike plant whose root when roasted is used for mixing with coffee and whose leaves are used in salads.

chide *v.* [chid or chid·ed; chid, chid·den, or chid·ed; chid·ing] To scold; reprove; reproach. —**chid·er** *n.*—**chid·ing·ly** *adv.*

chief (*cheef*) *n.* 1. A leader; the person highest in authority of any group or organization. —*adj.* Principal; leading; most important. —**chief·ly** *adv.*

chief justice. The presiding judge, esp. of the U.S. Supreme Court, whose designation is Chief Justice of the United States.—**chief·jus·tice·ship** *n.*

chief·tain (*cheef*-tun) *n.* A chief, or commander, of a clan or tribe.— -**tain·cy** *n.*— -**tain·ship** *n.*

chif·fon (shif-*ahn*) *n.* A thin, gauzy fabric, esp. of silk.

chif·fo·nier (shif-uh-*nihr*) *n.* Also **chif·fon·nier.** Tall chest fitted with drawers and a mirror.

chig·ger (*chig*-er) *n.* 1. Chigoe. 2. A mite larva causing painful itching.

chig·non (*sheen*-yon) *n.* A roll of natural or artificial hair worn at the nape of the neck.

chig·oe (*chig*-oh) *n.* Also **chig·ger.** A South American flea which burrows beneath the skin, causing painful itching.

chil·blain (*chil*-blayn) *n.* Inflammatory skin condition caused by severe cold.

child (*chyld*) *n.* [*pl.* chil·dren] 1. A youth between the ages of infancy and adolescence. 2. Offspring; a son or daughter. 3. Descendant. 4. Outcome; product. 'The child of that bargain.'—**with child.** Pregnant.

child·bear·ing (*chyld*-behr-ing) *n.* Pregnancy; gestation.—**child·bear·ing** *adj.*

child·bed (*chyld*-bed) *n.* Labor; confinement; final stage of pregnancy.

child·birth (*chyld*-berth) *n.* Process of bringing forth a child.

child·hood (*chyld*-hood) *n.* Stage of development between infancy and puberty.

child·ish (*chyld*-ish) *adj.* Puerile; immature; foolish.—**child·ish·ly** *adv.*—**child·ish·ness** *n.*

child·less (*chyld*-lis) *adj.* Without children.

child·like (*chyld*-lyke) *adj.* Like a child; innocent; naïve.—**child·like·ness** *n.*

chil·i (*chil*-ee) *n.* [*pl.* chil·ies]. Also **chil·e, chil·li.** 1. A spicy red pepper, dried fruit of the chili plant. 2. Chili con carne.—**chili sauce.** Spicy sauce made from tomatoes and chilies.

chili con carne (*chil*-ee kon *kahr*-nee). Dish of diced meat, red peppers, and beans.

chill *n.* 1. A cold bodily sensation. 2. A sudden frost in the atmosphere. 3. Lack of friendliness.—*adj.* 1. Disagreeably cold. 2. Distant; discouraging; depressing.—*v.* 1. To make chilly or cold. 2. To depress; discourage.—**chill·er, chill·ness** *n.*

chill·y (*chil*-ee) *adj.* [chill·i·er; chill·i·est] Disagreeably cold; raw; damp.—**chill·i·ness** *n.*

chime *n.* 1. The sound produced by a set of bells. 2. [*pl.*] A set of bells tuned to musical scale.—*v.* [chim·ed; chim·ing] 1. To resound harmoniously. 2. To produce tones by striking. 3. To utter in sing-song.—**chime in.** To add to; agree with.—**chim·er** *n.*

chi·me·ra, chi·mae·ra (kuh-*mihr*-uh) *n.* [*pl.* -ras] 1. *Greek Mythology.* A fire-breathing monster with a lion's head and a goat's body. 2. Any monster of the imagination; a wild or foolish fancy.

chi·mer·i·cal (kuh-*mihr*-ih-k'l) *adj.* Also **chi·mer·ic.** 1. Imaginary; fanciful; unreal. 2. Given to wild fancies.—**chi·mer·i·cal·ly** *adv.*

chim·ney (*chim*-nee) *n.* [*pl.* -neys] 1. An erection on a building containing a passageway for the escape of smoke. 2. A glass tube enclosing a flame.

chimney piece. A mantel; structure ornamenting a fireplace.

chimney pot. A cylinder placed above a chimney for increasing the draft.

chimney sweep. A person hired to clean the soot from chimneys.

chim·pan·zee (chim-pan-*zee*) *n.* An anthropoid ape of West Africa.

CHIMPANZEE (1/32 life size)

chin *n.* The part of the face below the mouth. —*v.* [chinned; chinning] 1. To hang by the hands, raising oneself until the chin is at hand level. 2. *Slang.* To talk; chat.

china (*chy*-nuh) *n.* 1. A fine, glazed porcelain originated in China. 2. Dishes of china. —**chi·na** *adj.*

chi·na·ber·ry (*chy*-nuh-behr-ee) *n.* An ornamental tree bearing fruit resembling berries.

Chi·na·man (*chy*-nuh-m'n) *n.* A Chinese man.

Chi·na·town (*chy*-nuh-town) *n.* The section of a city inhabited by Chinese.

chi·na·ware (*chy*-nuh-wehr) *n.* Dishes, esp. when made of china.

chinch *n.* 1. The bedbug. 2. Chinch bug.

chinch bug. A small black bug destructive to grain.

chin·chil·la (chin-*chil*-uh) *n.* 1. A South American rodent. 2. The valuable, soft gray fur of the chinchilla. 3. A heavy, napped woolen cloth.

chine *n.* 1. The spine. 2. The backbone of an animal with surrounding meat for cooking. 3. A ridge. —*v.* [chin·ed; chin·ing] To cut through the backbone.

CHINCHILLA (1/5 life size)

Chi·nese (chy-*neez*, -nees) *n. sing. & pl.* 1. A native of China. 2. The language of China. —**Chi·nese** *adj.*

Chinese puzzle. An extremely involved puzzle; any intricate problem or device.

chink *n.* 1. A short sharp metallic sound. 2. A small fissure; crack.—**chink** *v.*

Chi·nook (chih-*nook; -nuhk*) *n.* 1. Member of an Indian tribe in NW United States. 2. The language of the Chinooks, mixed with French and English. 3. [*not cap.*] A warm ocean wind in NW U.S.—**Chin·ook·an** *adj.*

chin·qua·pin (*chink*-uh-pin) *n.* Also **chin·ca·pin, chin·ka·pin.** 1. The dwarf chestnut tree. 2. Its sweet edible nut.

chintz *n.* A glazed, multicolored cotton cloth.

chip *v.* [chipped; chip·ping] 1. To chop into small pieces. 2. To break off in small pieces, as earthenware.—*n.* 1. A fragmentary piece as of stone, wood, etc. 2. A cleft or mark left by chipping. 3. Flat disk for playing poker and other games. 4. A thin, dried piece of food.—**chip in.** To put in one's share.—**chip·per** *n.*

chip·munk (*chip*-munk) *n.* A small, striped American squirrel.

chipped beef. Thinly sliced dried or cured beef.

Chip·pen·dale (*chip*-un-dayl) *adj.* Denoting or resembling the furniture designed by Thomas Chippendale in the eighteenth century.

chip·per (*chip*-er) *adj. Colloquial.* Lively; cheerful; brisk.

CHIPMUNK (1/4 life size)

Chip·pe·wa, Chip·pe·way (*chip*-uh-wah; -way) *n.* A tribe of North American Indians also called Ojibway, or Ojibwa.

chipping sparrow. Also **chip·py.** The common North American sparrow.

chip·py (*chip*-ee) *n.* [*pl.* -pies] 1. The chipping sparrow. 2. *Slang.* A disreputable woman.

chi·rog·ra·phy (ky-*rog*-ruh-fee) *n.* Handwriting. —**chi·rog·ra·pher** *n.*—**chi·ro·graph·ic, -i·cal** *adj.*

chi·rop·o·dy (ky-*rop*-uh-dee) *n.* Treatment of minor foot ailments, as corns, bunions, etc. —**chi·rop·o·dist** *n.*

chi·ro·prac·tic (ky-ruh-*prak*-tik) *n.* A treatment for diseases based on hand manipulation of the spinal bones.—**chi·ro·prac·tor** (ky-ruh-*prak*-ter) *n.* A practitioner of chiropractic.

chirp (*cherp*) *v.* To utter a shrill sound, as a bird.—**chirp** *n.*—**chirp·er** *n.*

chirr (*cher*) *v.* To make a trilling sound, as a grasshopper.—**chirr** *n.*

chir·rup (*chir*-up) *v.* To utter a series of chirps. —**chir·rup** *n.*—**chir·rup·er** *n.*—**chir·rup·y** *adj.*

chi·rur·geon (ky-*rur*-jun) *n. Archaic.* A surgeon. —**chi·rur·ge·ry** *n.*—**chi·rur·gic, -i·cal** *adj.*

chis·el (*chih*-z'l) *n.* An edged tool for cutting wood, metal, or stone.—*v.* [chis·eled, chis·elled; chis·el·ing, chis·el·ling] 1. To engrave with a chisel. 2. *Slang.* To cheat; swindle. —**chis·el·er, chis·el·ler** *n.*

chit *n.* 1. A brief note; memorandum. 2. A signed bill for food or drink. 3. *Colloquial.* A pert child.

chit-chat (*chit*-chat) *n.* Small talk; gossip.

chi·tin (*ky*-tin) *n.* A hard substance present in the outer covering of insects, shellfish, etc. —**chit·in·ous** *adj.*

chi·ton (*ky*-t'n; -tahn) *n.* Loose garment worn next to the skin by ancient Greeks.

CHITON

chit·ter (*chih*-ter) *v.* To chirp; twitter.—**chit·ter-chat·ter** *n.* Lively small talk.

chit·ter·lings (*chih*-ter-lingz) *n. pl.* The small intestines, esp. of swine, fried for food.

chiv·al·ric (*shiv*-'l-rik; shiv-*al*-rik) *adj.* Chivalrous; pertaining to chivalry.

chiv·al·rous (*shiv*-'l-rus) *adj.* 1. Pertaining to chivalry. 2. Bold; gallant; courteous. —**chiv·al·rous·ly** *adv.*—**chiv·al·rous·ness** *n.*

chiv·al·ry (*shiv*-'l-ree) *n.* 1. Any quality associated with knighthood, as valor; gallantry; courtesy. 2. A medieval military and social system based on knighthood.

chive (*chyve*) *n.* A plant similar to the onion and used in soups, salads, etc.

chlo·ral (*klor*-'l) *n.* An oily fluid obtained by the mixture of chlorine and alcohol.—**chloral hydrate.** A chloral compound used as a narcotic.

chlo·rate (*klor*-ayt) *n.* A salt of chloric acid used in preparing oxygen.

chlo·ric (*klor*-ik) *adj.* Containing chlorine. —**chloric acid.** A colorless liquid having strong bleaching properties.

chlo·ride (*klor*-yde) *n.* A compound used in bleaching powders and disinfectants.

chlo·rine (*klor*-in) *n.* A greenish yellow gaseous element liquefied for varied purposes as medicinal solutions, disinfectants, bleaching preparations, etc. (*Symbol:* Cl).

chlo·rin·ate (*klor*-ih-nayt) *v.* [chlo·rin·at·ed; chlo·rin·at·ing] To treat with chlorine, for purification, etc.—**chlo·rin·a·tion** (klor-ih-*nay*-shun) *n.*—**chlo·rin·a·tor** *n.*

chlo·ro·form (*klor*-uh-form) *n.* A sweetish-tasting liquid compound used as an anaesthetic.—*v.* To administer chloroform.

chlo·ro·phyl (*klor*-uh-fil) *n.* Also **chlo·ro·phyll.** Green vegetable pigment of leaves which, under the action of sunlight, manufactures plant food from carbon dioxide and water.

chlo·ro·plast (*klor*-uh-plast) *n.* A granule of chlorophyl.

chock (*chok*) *n.* 1. A block of wood; wedge. 2. *Nautical.* Block with two curving arms through which a rope may be drawn.—*v.* To close or fasten with a chock.—*adv.* Tightly.

chock-a-block (*chok*-uh-blok) *adj.* Crowded.

chock full. Filled to capacity.

choc·o·late (*chawk*-lit, *chok*-uh-lit) *n.* 1. A flavoring or beverage prepared from ground cacao beans. 2. A chocolate candy. 3. The dark brown color of chocolate.—*adj.* Made or flavored with chocolate.

Choc·taw (*chok*-taw) *n.* [*pl.* -taw, -taws] Member of an Indian tribe now in Oklahoma, originally in Mississippi and Alabama.

choice (*choyss*) *n.* 1. Act or power of choosing; selection. 2. Variety from which to choose. 3. That which is chosen; preference.—*adj.* [choic·er, choic·est] Chosen with care; select; superior.—**choice·ly** *adv.*—**choice·ness** *n.*

choir (*kwyre*) *n.* 1. A chorus; group of singers, esp. in a church. 2. Portion of a church set aside for the singers.—*v.* To sing in chorus.

choke (*chohk*) *v.* [choked; chok·ing] 1. To strangle; throttle; suffocate. 2. To block up; obstruct. 3. To extinguish, as a fire. 4. To hinder growth or action. 5. To enrich the fuel mixture of a gasoline engine by shutting off the air supply.—*n.* 1. Sound or act of choking. 2. Valve in a gasoline engine for cutting off air supply.

choke·bore (*chohk*-bohr) *n.* Gun with a bore which tapers toward the muzzle.

choke·damp (*chohk*-damp) *n.* A heavy poisonous gas generated in coal mines.

chok·er (*choh*-ker) *n.* 1. One who chokes. 2. *Colloquial.* Object worn about the neck, as a high collar or necklace.

chok·ing (*choh*-king) *adj.* 1. Tending to choke. 2. Indistinct; strangled, as a voice.

chol·er (*kol*-er) *n.* Anger; irascibility.

chol·er·a (*kol*-uh-ruh) *n.* Acute infectious, usually epidemic, disease, characterized by diarrhea, cramps, and collapse.

chol·er·ic (*kol*-uh-rik) *adj.* Easily irritated or angered; irascible.

choose (*chooz*) *v.* [chose; chosen; choos·ing] 1. To select; make a choice. 2. To be inclined; think fit. 'He chose to stay.'

chop *v.* [chopped; chop·ping] 1. To mince; cut into pieces. 2. To sever by quick, sharp blows. 3. *Tennis, etc.* To hit a ball with a short downward stroke. 4. To veer; shift with the wind.—*n.* 1. Act of chopping; short stroke. 2. A cut of meat. 'A lamb chop.' 3. Short, irregular motion, as of waves. 4. [*pl.*] The jaws and mouth.—**chop·per** *n.*

chop·house (*chop*-howss) *n.* A restaurant specializing in meat dishes.

chop·py (*chop*-ee) *adj.* [chop·pi·er; chop·pi·est] Rough; moving irregularly; changeable.

chop·stick (*chop*-stik) *n.* One of two slender sticks used in China as eating implements.

chop suey (*soo*-ee). A dish of rice, noodles, onions, and meat served in Chinese restaurants.

cho·ral (*koh*-rul; *kaw*-rul) *adj.* 1. Pertaining to a choir or chorus. 2. Sung in concert.

cho·ral, chor·ale (kor-*ahl*) *n.* 1. A hymn sung in chorus. 2. A choir. 'Collegiate Chorale.'

chord (*kord*) *n. Music.* The simultaneous combination of different tones.—*v. Music.* To be in harmony.

chord (*kord*) *n.* 1. The string of a musical instrument. 2. *Geometry.* A straight line joining the ends of an arc. 3. *Anatomy.* A tendon or filament. 4. A particular feeling or emotion.—**chord·al** *adj.*

chore *n.* 1. A small or disagreeable task. 2. [*pl.*] The daily light work around a farm.

cho·re·a (kor-*ee*-uh) *n.* St. Vitus's dance; a nervous disease marked by twitchings of the limbs.

chor·e·og·ra·phy (kor-ee-*og*-ruh-fee) *n.* 1. The art of dance arrangement. 2. Dancing or ballet dancing.—**chor·e·o·graph·ic** *adj.*

chor·ic (*kor*-ik) *adj.* Pertaining to a chorus.

chor·is·ter (*kor*-iss-ter) *n.* 1. A choral singer. 2. A choir master.

chor·tle *v.* [chor·tled; chor·tling] To chuckle gleefully or triumphantly.—**chor·tle** *n.*—**-tler** *n.*

cho·rus (*kor*-us) *n.* 1. A group of singers or dancers in modern stage shows. 2. *Music.* a. A composition for several voices. b. A group singing in harmonious concert. c. Part of a song repeated after each stanza. 3. The simultaneous singing or utterance of several voices.—*v.* To sing or utter sounds in chorus.

chos·en (*chohz*-'n). *Past participle* of **choose**.—*adj.* Choice; select.

chow *n.* 1. A small, stocky, thickly coated dog originally bred in China. 2. *Slang.* Food.

chow·chow *n.* A preserve of mixed pickles.

chow·der (*chow*-der) *n.* A soup or stew of fresh fish or clams.

CHOW (1/28 life size)

chow mein (chow-*mayn*). A dish of stewed onions and celery, served with rice and fried noodles.

chrism (*krizm*) *n. Roman Catholic Church.* A consecrated oil used for baptism, confirmation, etc.—**chris·mal** *adj.*

Christ *n.* Jesus Christ, founder of the Christian religion.

chris·ten (*kris*-'n) *v.* 1. To baptize and name at baptism. 2. To name. 3. *Slang.* To use for the first time.—**chris·ten·ing** *n.*

Chris·ten·dom (*kris*-'n-dum) *n.* Christians and Christian countries collectively.

Chris·tian (*kris*-chun) *n.* 1. A believer in Christ's teachings. 2. A decent, kindly person.—*adj.* 1. Pertaining to or believing in Christ or Christianity. 2. Gentle; charitable.

Christian era. Period beginning with the birth of Christ.

Chris·tia·ni·a, Chris·tia·ni·a turn (krist-*yan*-ee-uh), *n.* Also **Chris·ty.** *Skiing.* A Norwegian swinging turn with the legs pressing inward.

Chris·ti·an·i·ty (kris-tee-*an*-uh-tee, -*chan*-) *n.*
1. The religion stemming from Christ's precepts. 2. Christians collectively. 3. State of being a Christian.

Chris·tian·ize (*kris*-chun-yze) *v.* [Chris·tian·ized; Chris·tian·iz·ing] To convert to Christianity.—**Chris·tian·i·za·tion** *n.*

Christian Science. A religion and healing method founded by Mary Baker Eddy, holding that apparent evils, such as disease, are errors of the mortal mind which can be eliminated by proper spiritual understanding.

Christ·like (*kryste*-lyke) *v.* Resembling Christ in holiness, goodness, etc.

Christ·ly (*kryste*-lee) *adj.* Pertaining to Christ; holy; saintly.—**Christ·li·ness** *n.*

Christ·mas (*kris*-m's) *n.* Annual celebration of the birth of Jesus Christ.—**Christmas Day.** December 25.

chro·mat·ic (kroh-*mat*-ik) *adj.* 1. Pertaining to color. 2. *Music.* Including notes not belonging to the diatonic scale, being either sharped or flatted.—**chro·mat·i·cal·ly** *adv.*

chro·mat·ics *n.* Branch of optics dealing with colors.—**chro·ma·tist** *n.*

chro·ma·tin (*kroh*-muh-tin) *n. Biology.* That part of a cell nucleus most easily stained by dyes for microscopic observation.

chrome (krohm) *n.* Chromium.

chrom·ic (*kroh*-mik) *adj.* Pertaining to or obtained from chromium.

chro·mi·um (*kroh*-mee-um) *n. Chemistry.* A brittle steel gray, rustproof metallic element. (*Symbol:* Cr).

chro·mo (*kroh*-moh) *n.* [*pl.* -mos] A chromolithograph.

chro·mo·lith·o·graph (kroh-moh-*lith*-uh-graf) *n.* A colored picture printed from specially prepared stones.—**chro·mo·li·thog·ra·pher** *n.*

chro·mo·some (*kroh*-muh-sohm) *n.* One of the microscopic bodies formed by the chromatin of a plant or animal cell during division.

chron·ic (*kron*-ik) *adj.* Continuing a long time; lasting; persistent.—**chron·i·cal·ly** *adv.*

chron·i·cle (*kron*-ih-k'l) *n.* A simple account of events, esp. historical, written in order of occurrence.—*v.* [chron·i·cled; chron·i·cling] To record events.—**chron·i·cler** *n.*

Chron·i·cles *n. pl.* Two books in the Old Testament.

chron·o·log·i·cal (kron-uh-*loj*-ih-k'l) *adj.* Also **chron·o·log·ic.** According to or arranged in the order of time or occurrence.— **-i·cal·ly** *adv.*

chro·nol·o·gy (kroh-*nol*-uh-jee) *n.* [*pl.* -gies] 1. The science of computing dates or arranging events in the order of time. 2. A list of events arranged thus.—**chro·nol·o·gist** *n.*

chro·nom·e·ter (kroh-*nom*-ih-ter) *n.* An accurate instrument for measuring time, esp. one not affected by temperature changes.—**chron·o·met·ric, -ri·cal** *adj.*—**chron·o·met·ri·cal·ly** *adv.*

chro·nom·e·try (kroh-*nom*-ih-tree) *n.* The science of measuring time.

chrys·a·lis (*krih*-s'l-is) *n.* [*pl.* chrys·a·lis·es; chry-

sal·i·des] Inactive form taken by certain insects between the larval and the winged state.

chrys·an·the·mum (kris-*an*-thuh-mum) *n.* Plant of the aster family having large, brightly colored flowers; also, the flower itself.

chrys·o·lite (kris-'l-yte) *n.* A green, usually transparent, gem.

chrys·o·prase (*kris*-uh-prayz) *n.* An apple-green variety of hard quartz, valued as a gem.

chub *n.* A fresh-water fish with a thick body and silvery sides.

CHRYSANTHEMUM

chub·by *adj.* [chub·bi·er; chub·bi·est] Plump; round; fat.—**chub·bi·ness** *n.*

chuck *v.* 1. To pat or tap in a playful manner. 2. To throw or toss a short distance.—**chuck** *n.*

chuck *n.* 1. A cut of beef including the neck, shoulder and first five ribs. 2. Device for holding a tool or work in a lathe. 3. A wedge.

chuckle (*chuk*-'l) *v.* [chuck·led; chuck·ling] To laugh quietly, in a suppressed manner.—**chuckle** *n.*—**chuck·ler** *n.*

chuck·le·head (*chuk*-'l-hed) *n. Colloquial.* A stupid person.—**chuck·le·head·ed** *adj.*

chug *n.* A short, harsh, explosive sound, as from an engine.—*v.* [chugged; chug·ging] To make, or move with, such sounds.

chuck·er, chuk·ker (*chuk*-er) *n.* One of the playing periods in polo.

chum *n. Colloquial.* A roommate or close friend. —*v.* [chummed; chum·ming].

chum·my *adj.* [chum·mi·er, chum·mi·est] *Colloquial.* Friendly; intimate.—**chum·mi·ly** *adv.*

chump *n.* 1. A small, thick block of wood. 2. *Colloquial.* A foolish person.—*v. Colloquial.* To chew noisily.

chunk *n.* 1. A short, thick piece. 2. *Colloquial.* A sizable piece or quantity.

chunk·y *adj.* [chunk·i·er, chunk·i·est] *Colloquial.* Short and thick; stocky.—**chunk·i·ly** *adv.*

church (*cherch*) *n.* 1. A building consecrated for divine worship, esp. Christian worship. 2. [*cap.*] The collective or a particular body of Christians. 3. The clerical profession or organization.—**church** *adj.*—**church·less** *adj.*

church·go·er (*cherch*-goh-er) *n.* One who attends church.—**church·go·ing** *n. & adj.*

church·ly *adj.* Ecclesiastical; of the church.

church·man (*cherch*-m'n) *n.* [*pl.* -men] 1. A member of the clergy. 2. [*cap.*] A member of a particular church.—**church·man·ly** *adj.*

Church of Christ, Scientist. Church, founded by Mary Baker Eddy, which maintains the doctrine of Christian Science.

Church of England. The Anglican communion; the established espiscopal church in England.

church·ward·en (*cherch*-ward-'n) *n.* 1. A lay guardian of the church and its property. 2. A long-stemmed clay pipe.

churl *n.* 1. A sullen, rude person. 2. A peasant or country fellow.

churl·ish (*cherl*-ish) *adj.* Surly; rude; unmanageable.—**churl·ish·ly** *adv.*—**churl·ish·ness** *n.*

churn *n.* Vessel or machine for agitating milk or cream to make butter.—*v.* 1. To make butter by agitating milk or cream. 2. To shake or stir violently.—**churn·er** *n.*—**churn·ing** *n.*

chute (*shoot*) *n.* 1. An inclined trough for sliding objects to a lower level. 2. A riverfall; rapids. 3. *Slang.* Parachute.

chut·ney (*chuht*-nee) *n.* A spicy Indian relish.

chyle (*kyle*) *n. Physiology.* A milky fluid, containing digested fat, which is assimilated into the blood.—**chy·lous** *adj.*

chyme (*kyme*) *n. Physiology.* Semiliquid mass of food digested by the stomach and passed into the small intestine.—**chy·mous** *adj.*

ci·bo·ri·um (sih-*bor*-ee-um) *n.* [*pl.* -ri·a] 1. *Roman Catholic Church.* Cup for holding the sacred wafers of the Eucharist. 2. A canopy over an altar.

ci·ca·da (sih-*kay*-duh) *n.* [*pl.* -das, -dae] A winged insect with a loud, shrill chirp.

cic·a·trix (*sik*-uh-triks) *n.* [*pl.* cic·a·tri·ces] 1. Also **cic·a·trice.** The scar of a healed wound. 2. *Botany.* Scar left by a detached part.—**ci·ca·tri·cial** (sik-uh-*trish*-ul) *adj.*

cic·a·trize (*sik*-uh-tryze) *v.* [cic·a·trized; cic·a·triz·ing] *Medicine.* To heal a wound by causing the formation of a scar.—**cic·a·tri·za·tion** *n.*

ci·ce·rone (sis-uh-*roh*-nee) *n.* [*pl.* roni, -rones] A guide who points out and explains the interesting sights of a building or locality.

Cic·e·ro·ni·an (sis-uh-*roh*-nee-un) *adj.* Pertaining to or resembling the style of Cicero, Roman orator noted for his eloquence.

ci·der (*sy*-der) *n.* The juice of apples.

ci·gar (sih-*gahr; see*-gahr) *n.* A cylindrical roll of tobacco leaf for smoking.

cig·a·rette (sig-uh-*ret,* sig-uh-ret) *n.* Also **cig·a·ret.** A small cylinder of cut tobacco rolled in paper for smoking.

cil·i·a (*sil*-ee-uh) *n. pl.* [*sing.* cil·i·um] 1. Eyelashes. 2. *Botany.* Hairs or bristles on the margin of a vegetable body. 3. *Biology.* Microscopic, vibrating, hairlike organs.—**cil·i·ary** *adj.* Pertaining to cilia.—**cil·i·ate** (*sil*-ee-it), **cil·i·at·ed** (*sil*-ee-ayt-ed) *adj.* Furnished with cilia.

Cim·me·ri·an (suh-*meer*-ee-un) *n.* Member of a mythical people described by Homer as living in perpetual darkness.—*adj.* Intensely dark.

cinch (*sinch*) *n.* 1. Sturdy girth for fastening a saddle. 2. *Colloquial.* A firm grip. 3. *Slang.* An easy or sure task.—*v.* To fasten securely; hence, to make certain or conclusive.

cin·cho·na (sin-*koh*-nuh) *n.* A South American tree whose bark yields quinine.—**cin·chon·ic** (sin-*kon*-ik) *adj.*

cinc·ture (*sink*-cher) *n.* 1. A belt or girdle worn around the waist. 2. An enclosure.

cin·der (*sin*-der) *n.* A small, partly burned particle, as of coal.—**cin·der** *v.*—**cin·der·y** *adj.*

Cin·der·el·la (sin-der-*el*-uh) *n.* Heroine of a fairy tale who was rescued from a life of drudgery by her fairy godmother and married to a prince.

cin·e·ma (*sin*-uh-muh) *n.* 1. A motion picture. 2. Motion-picture theater. 3. Motion pictures in general.—**cin·e·mat·ic** (sin-uh-*mat*-ik) *adj.*—**cin·e·mat·i·cal·ly** *adv.*—**cin·e·ma·tize** *v.*

cin·e·mat·o·graph (sin-uh-*mat*-uh-graf) *n.* Motion-picture camera.—**cin·e·ma·tog·ra·pher** (sin-uh-muh-*tog*-ruh-fer) *n.* Motion-picture cameraman.—**cin·e·mat·o·graph·ic** *adj.*—**cin·e·mat·o·graph·i·cal·ly** *adv.*—**cin·e·ma·tog·ra·phy** *n.*

cin·e·ra·ri·a (sin-uh-*rayr*-ee-uh) *n.* A flowering plant with heart-shaped leaves.

cin·e·ra·ri·um (sin-uh-*rayr*-ee-um) *n.* [*pl.* -ri·a] Place for holding the ashes of cremated bodies.

cin·er·a·tor (*sin*-uh-ray-ter) *n.* 1. A crematory. 2. A furnace or incinerator.

cin·na·bar (*sin*-uh-bahr) *n.* 1. A reddish mineral, the main source of mercury. 2. A red pigment for dyes, etc.; vermilion.

cin·na·mon (*sin*-uh-mun) *n.* 1. Tree yielding an aromatic bark used as a spice; also the spice itself. 2. A light, reddish-brown color.

cinque·foil (*sink*-foyl) *n.* 1. A plant with a compound leaf in five parts. 2. *Architecture.* Ornamental design with five curving points.

CIO. The Congress of Industrial Organizations, a group of American industrial unions.

ci·on (*sy*-un) *n.* Also **sci·on.** The shoot or bud of a plant used for grafting.

ci·pher (*sy*-fer) *n.* 1. The symbol 0. 2. A person or thing without any value. 3. A secret manner of writing; a code.—*v.* 1. To calculate by arithmetic. 2. To write in code.

cir·ca (*ser*-kuh) *prep.* About; approximately.

Cir·cas·si·a (ser-*kash*-uh) *n.* A part of Asia north of the Caucasus, once an independent nation, now integrated with the U.S.S.R.

Cir·ce (*ser*-see) *n.* A famous sorceress in Homer's *Odyssey.*—**Cir·ce·an** (ser-*see*-un) *adj.* Also **Cir·cae·an.** Fascinating but dangerous.

cir·cle (*ser*-k'l) *n.* 1. A plane figure bounded by a curved line every part of which is equidistant from the center. 2. Anything of similar shape; a ring. 3. A coterie; set. 'Circle of friends.' 4. A going around; a cycle; self-repeating series or succession. 5. *Logic.* An argument based on a hypothesis in which the conclusion is assumed. 6. A designated or special balcony in a large theater.—*v.* [circled; circling] 1. To surround; enclose. 2. To revolve about; move circularly.

CIRCLE

C

cir·clet (*serk*-let) *n*. A small circle; a ring-shaped ornament.

cir·cuit (*ser*-kit) *n*. 1. A revolving about; circular journey. 2 The distance around any space; circumference. 3. The unbroken path of an electric current. 4. *Radio.* A broadcasting system. 5. A route or course traveled to maintain a schedule.—*v*. To move in a circle; go around.

circuit breaker. *Electricity.* A magnetic device that interrupts a circuit when the current varies abnormally.

cir·cu·i·tous (ser-*kyoo*-ih-tus) *adj.* Like a circuit; roundabout.—**cir·cu·i·tous·ly** *adv.*—**cir·cu·i·tous·ness** *n*.—**cir·cu·i·ty** *n* [*pl.* -ties].

cir·cu·lar (*serk*-yoo-ler) *adj.* 1. In the shape of a circle; round. 2. Designed for circulation or distribution. 3. Circuitous; roundabout. 4. Describing or occurring in a circle. —*n*. A mechanically reproduced letter or advertisement which is widely distributed. —**cir·cu·lar·i·ty** *n*. [*pl.* -ties].—**cir·cu·lar·ly** *adv.*

cir·cu·lar·ize (*serk*-yuh-luh-ryze) *v*. [cir·cu·lar·ized; -iz·ing] 1. To make round. 2. To direct circulars to.—**cir·cu·lar·i·za·tion** (serk-yuh-luh-rih-*zay*-shun) *n*.—**cir·cu·lar·iz·er** *n*.

cir·cu·late (*serk*-yuh-layt) *v*. [cir·cu·lat·ed; -lat·ing] 1. To follow a circular course. 2. To change owners or location frequently. 'Money circulates.'—**cir·cu·la·tor** *n*.

circulating library. A library whose books may be borrowed by any responsible citizen.

cir·cu·la·tion (serk-yuh-*lay*-shun) *n*. 1. The number of subscribers to a newspaper or library. 2. *Medicine.* The circular flow of the blood. 3. A moving in an orbit or circuit. 4. Dissemination; diffuseness; a passing from hand to hand.—**cir·cu·la·tive** (*serk*-yoo-lay-tiv), **cir·cu·la·to·ry** (*serk*-yoo-luh-tor-ee) *adj.*

cir·cum *Prefix.* Around; about; circling; surrounding. 'Circumnavigation.'

cir·cum·am·bi·ent (ser-kum-*am*-bee-ent) *adj.* Encircling; encompassing; on all sides.—**cir·cum·am·bi·ence, cir·cum·am·bi·en·cy** *n*.

cir·cum·cise (*ser*-kum-syze) *v*. [cir·cum·cised; -cis·ing] 1. To cut off the foreskin of the penis. 2. To render spiritual or holy.—**cir·cum·cis·er** *n*.— -**ci·sion** (-*sizh*-un) *n*.

cir·cum·fer·ence (ser-*kum*-fuh-r'ns) *n*. The line that bounds a circle or sphere; distance of this line; periphery.—**cir·cum·fer·en·tial** *adj.*

cir·cum·flex (*ser*-kum-fleks) *n*. 1. *Phonetics.* An accent [∧] placed over vowels in various languages. 2. A rise and fall of the voice on the same syllable. 3. A bending or twisting about.—**cir·cum·flex** *v*. & *adj.*— -**flex·ion** *n*.

cir·cum·lo·cu·tion (ser-kum-loh-*kyoo*-shun) *n*. A wordy, roundabout way of speaking.—**cir·cum·loc·u·to·ry** (ser-kum-*lok*-yoo-tor-ee) *adj.*

cir·cum·nav·i·gate (ser-kum-*nav*-ih-gayt) *v*. [cir·cum·nav·i·gat·ed; -gat·ing] To pilot a ship or plane around. 'Circumnavigate the globe.' —**cir·cum·nav·i·ga·tion** (ser-kum-nav-ih-*gay*-shun) *n*.—**cir·cum·nav·i·ga·tor** *n*.

cir·cum·scribe (*serk*-um-skrybe) *v*. [cir·cum·scribed; -scrib·ing] 1. To mark out bounds or limits for; confine; restrain. 2. *Geometry.* To draw around. 'Circumscribe a circle.'

cir·cum·scrip·tion (ser-kum-*skrip*-shun) *n*. 1. A defining of the limits or form; restraint; enclosure. 2. The exterior line determining the form or size of something; periphery. 3. The area circumscribed. 4. An inscription on the periphery of anything.—**cir·cum·scrip·tive** *adj.*

cir·cum·spect (*serk*-um-spekt) *adj.* Watchful; wary; looking on all sides.—**cir·cum·spect·ly** *adv.*—**cir·cum·spec·tion** (ser-kum-*spek*-shun), **cir·cum·spect·ness** *n*.—**cir·cum·spec·tive** *adj.*

cir·cum·stance (*ser*-kum-stans) *n*. 1. Something relative to a fact or case; something that affects it. 2. An unessential detail. 3. A happening; occurrence. 4. [*pl.*] Condition; state; environment.—*v*. [cir·cum·stanced; -stanc·ing] To place in a particular situation.

cir·cum·stan·tial (ser-kum-*stan*-sh'l) *adj.* 1. Incidental; pertaining to but not fundamental. 2. Exhibiting all the circumstances; minute; particular. 3. Pertaining to or occasioned by circumstances.—**cir·cum·stan·tial·ly** *adv.*—**cir·cum·stan·ti·al·i·ty** (ser-kum-stan-shee-*al*-ih-tee).

circumstantial evidence. Evidence obtained from reasonably conclusive attendant facts as distinguished from eyewitness proof.

cir·cum·stan·ti·ate (ser-kum-*stan*-shee-ayt) *v*. [cir·cum·stan·ti·at·ed; -at·ing] To confirm by circumstances; describe in full detail.—**cir·cum·stan·ti·a·tion** (-*ay*-shun) *n*.

cir·cum·vent (ser-kum-*vent*) *v*. 1. To outwit; to get the better of by cunning. 2. To encircle; encompass. 3. To get or go around. —**cir·cum·vent·er, cir·cum·ven·ter** *n*.—**cir·cum·ven·tion** (ser-kum-*ven*-shun) *n*.— -**ven·tive** *adj.*

cir·cus (*ser*-kus) *n*. 1. An entertainment in which exotic animals, acrobatics, freaks, etc., are displayed. 2. The personnel or the exhibition of a circus. 3. In ancient Rome, an enclosed plot where horse races, athletic contests, and contests with wild beasts were held.

cirque (serk) *n*. *Geology.* A round, steep-walled valley among mountains.

cir·rho·sis (sih-*roh*-sis) *n*. *Medical.* A wasting away of an organ with consequent substitution of connective tissue.—**cir·rhot·ic** (sih-*rot*-ik) *adj.*

cir·ro·cu·mu·lus (sih-roh-*kyoom*-yuh-lus) *n*. *Meteorology.* A high-altitude cloud formation of roundish, fleecy, thickly grouped clouds.

cir·ro·stra·tus (sih-roh-*strayt*-us) *n*. *Meteorology.* A high cloud layer of haze or frozen particles arranged in groups or lines.

cir·rus (*sih*-rus) *n*. [*pl.* cir·ri] 1. *Meteorology.* A feather-shaped cloud of gauzelike appearance, usually white. 2. *Botany.* A tendril. 3. *Zoology.* A tiny appendage.

cis- (*siss*) *Prefix.* 1. On this side. 'Cispacific.' 2. Occurring after or since. 'Cis-Victorian.'

cis·al·pine (sis-*al*-pyne) *adj.* South of the Alps.

cis·co (sis-koh) *n*. [*pl.* cis·coes, cis·cos] A kind of herring or whitefish of the Great Lakes.

Cis·ter·cian (sis-*ter*-shun) *n*. A member of a

religious order founded in 1098 at Cîteaux, France.—**Cis·ter·cian** *adj.*

cis·tern (*sis*-tern) *n.* 1. A reservoir or tank for water or other liquids. 2. Any similar or analogous container.

cit·a·del (*sit*-uh-d'l) *n.* A fortress; castle; bastion.

ci·ta·tion (sy-*tay*-shun) *n.* 1. A call or notice to appear; summons. 2. A quoting of a passage from a work. 3. *Law.* Reference to a precedent decision. 4. Mention; enumeration. 'A citation for heroism.'—**ci·ta·to·ry** *adj.*

cite *v.* [cit·ed; cit·ing] To quote as authority.

cith·a·ra (*sith*-uh-ruh) *n. Music.* An ancient stringed instrument closely related to a lyre.

ci·ther (*sith*-er) *n. Music.* A cithara; a cittern.

cit·ied (*sit*-eed) *adj.* 1. Like a city. 2. Having many cities.

cit·i·fy (*sit*-ih-fy) *v.* [cit·i·fied; -fy·ing] To give metropolitan qualities or outlooks to.

cit·i·zen (*sit*-ih-zin) *n.* 1. A member of a state who has full political privileges and protection. 2. A legal resident; occupant. 3. A civilian as distinguished from the military or police.

cit·i·zen·ry (*sit*-ih-zin-ree) *n.* [*pl.* -ries] Citizens in mass.

cit·i·zen·ship (*sit*-ih-zin-ship) *n.* 1. The condition of having all civil rights and duties. 2. Nationality; official allegiance. 3. Behavior becoming a citizen.

cit·rate (*sit*-rit) *n. Chemistry.* A salt derived from citric acid.

cit·ric (*sit*-rik) *adj.* Denoting an organic acid extractable from lemons and other sour fruits.

citric acid. Colorless crystals extracted from citrous fruits or made synthetically.

cit·rine (*sit*-rin) *adj.* Resembling a lemon or citron; lemon-colored.—*n.* 1. Lemon color. 2. A yellow, pellucid quartz.

cit·ron (*sit*-run) *n.* 1. A large species of lemon; the tree on which it grows. 2. A small watermelon whose hard rind is preserved. 3. The candied or preserved rind of a citron.

cit·ron·el·la (sit-ruh-*nel*-uh) *n.* An Asiatic grass yielding a strong-scented oil used in repelling insects.

citron melon. A type of small watermelon, used as citron.

cit·rus *adj.* Also **cit·rous.** Pertaining to a family of trees and shrubs bearing pulpy, strong-scented fruit, as the orange or lemon.

cit·tern (*sit*-ern) *n.* Also **ci·thern.** A stringed instrument of the Middle Ages resembling a guitar.

cit·y (*sit*-ee) *n.* [*pl.* cit·ies] A large, important town; in the U.S., a municipality having fixed boundaries and deriving its powers from the state in which it is located.

city-state. A free, sovereign city having jurisdiction over outlying territories.

civ·et (*siv*-et) *n.* An offensive-smelling substance derived from the glands of civet cats, used in making perfumes.

civet cat. A catlike, meat-eating animal found in North Africa and Asia.

civ·ic (*siv*-ik) *adj.* Pertaining to a city or to public affairs.

civ·ics (*siv*-iks) *n.* The study of the relationship between the government and the people.

CIVET CAT (1/20 life size)

civ·il (*siv*-'l) *adj.* 1. Pertaining to the community and its government. 2. Courteous; obliging; well-bred.

civil disobedience. A policy initiated by the Indian leader, Mohandas K. Gandhi, which involves passive resistance to British rule.

civil engineer. An engineer engaged in construction of public utilities.

ci·vil·ian (sih-*vil*-yun) *n.* Anyone not in the armed forces.—**ci·vil·ian** *adj.*

ci·vil·i·ty (sih-*vil*-ih-tee) *n.* [*pl.* -ties] 1. Courtesy; good breeding. 2. An act of courtesy.

ci·vi·li·za·tion (siv-ih-lih-*zay*-shun) *n.* 1. Well-developed social and cultural life of a people. 2. A society possessing an organized learning.

civ·i·lize (*siv*-ih-lyze) *v.* [civ·i·lized; civ·i·liz·ing] To raise from barbarism; introduce order and civic organization among.—**civ·i·liz·a·ble** *adj.*

civil law. The legal system of a state, city, or country.—**civ·il-law** *adj.*

civil liberty. The political and personal privileges guaranteed individuals under a constitutional government.

civ·il·ly (*siv*-ih-lee) *adv.* 1. Politely; urbanely. 2. Not actually but in law. 'Civilly dead.'

civil marriage. A marriage performed by a civil, rather than an ecclesiastical, authority.

civil rights. The political and other privileges accorded a citizen.

civil service. Non-military government employment.

civil war. 1. A war between sections or population groups of the same state. 2. [*cap.*] The American Civil War, 1861–1865, fought between the northern and southern states.

civ·vies (*siv*-eez) *n. pl. Slang.* Civilian clothing; mufti.

clab·ber *n.* Milk turned sour and thick.—*v.* To curdle.

clack *v.* 1. To make a sudden sharp, flat noise. 2. To talk incessantly and sharply. —**clack** *n.*—**clack·er** *n.*

claim *v.* To assert a right.—*n.* 1. The assertion of a right. 2. A title to anything in another's possession. 3. Anything claimed. 4. A demand for workmen's compensation, or other insurance payment.—**claim·a·ble** *adj.*

claim·ant (*klaym*-unt) *n.* A person who places a claim.

clair·voy·ance (klayr-*voy*-uns) *n.* The power of seeing beyond accepted limits of vision in space and time.—**clair·voy·ant** *adj.*

clam *n.* A common shellfish of many varieties. —*v.* To dig clams.

clam·bake n. An outdoor meal of baked clams.

clam·ber (*klam*-ber) v. To climb with difficulty, on hands and feet.—n. The act of clambering.

clam·my adj. [clam·mi·er; clam·mi·est] Damp and sticky; chill.—**clam·mi·ly** adv.

clam·or (*klam*-er) n. Also **clam·our**. 1. A great outcry. 2. Any loud disturbance or noise. —**clam·or** v.—**clam·or·er, clam·our·er** n.

clam·or·ous (*klam*-uh-rus) adj. Vociferous; noisy.—**clam·or·ous·ly** adv.— **-ous·ness** n.

clamp n. A rigid device which fastens, binds, or compresses. —**clamp** v.—**clamp down**, To exert authority decisively.

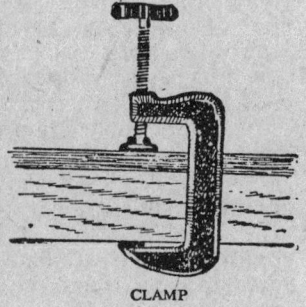

clamp·er n. A spiked iron frame to insure safe walking on ice; creeper.

clam·shell n. 1. A hinged dredging shovel. 2. Shell of a clam.

CLAMP

clan n. 1. A race; family; tribe. 2. A clique united by some common interest; coterie.

clan·des·tine (klan-*des*-t'n) adj. Secret; hidden; having evil designs.—**clan·des·tine·ly** adv.

clang v. To make a loud, metallic ring; to clank; resound.—**clang** n.

clan·gor (*klang*-ger, *klang*-er) n. Also **clan·gour**. A continued hard, metallic sound. —**clan·gor·ous** adj.—**clan·gor·ous·ly** adv.

clank n. A sharp, metallic sound less resounding than *clang* and deeper and stronger than *clink*.—**clank** v.

clan·nish adj. 1. Having the feelings and prejudices of a clique. 2. Reluctant to mix with a social group other than one's own.—**clan·nish·ly** adv.—**clan·nish·ness** n.

clans·man (*klanz*-m'n) n. [pl. -men] 1. One belonging to a clan. 2. Also **klans·man**. A member of the Ku Klux Klan.

clap v. [clapped; clap·ping] 1. To slap; tap. 2. To thrust; drive together; place by a sudden motion. 'Clap hands.' 'Clap on the shoulder.' 3. To applaud by beating the palms together. —n. 1. A bang; slap. 2. A peal of thunder or other sudden, loud noise. 3. Striking the hands together. 4. *Slang*. Gonorrhea.

clap·board (*klab*-erd) n. A board thin on one edge for covering houses; siding.—v. To cover with siding.

clap·per n. 1. One who applauds by clapping. 2. The hammer of a bell. 3. *Colloquial*. A tongue used too frequently. 4. A flat bone or stick used like a castanet.

clap·trap n. Any cheap trick or insincerity to secure applause.—**clap·trap** adj.

claque (*klak*) n. 1. A set of persons hired to applaud a theater performance or performer; hence, any group of fawning admirers.

clar·et (*klair*-et) n. A red Bordeaux table wine. —adj. Red-purple in color.

clar·i·fy (*klair*-uh-fy) v. [clar·i·fied; clar·i·fy·ing] 1. To make clear; illuminate; purify. 2. To establish a policy; enlighten.—**clar·i·fi·ca·tion** n.—**clar·i·fi·er** n.

clar·i·net (klair-ih-*net*, klair-ih-net) n. *Music*. A

CLARINET

reed musical wind instrument played by fingering vents and keys.—**clar·i·net·ist** n.

clar·i·on (*klair*-ee-un) n. 1. A shrill-noted trumpet. 2. A sound made on a clarion; trumpetlike blast.—adj. High-pitched and loud; rousing.—**clar·i·on** v.

clar·i·ty (*klair*-it-ee) n. Clearness.

clash v. 1. To come into violent collision. 2. To meet in opposition. 3. To make a loud, ringing noise.—**clash** n.

clasp v. 1. To fasten. 2. To catch and hold in embrace.—n. 1. A catch, as on a string of beads. 2. Grasp; embrace; hold.

class n. 1. An order or rank of persons. 2. Pupils of the same grade, standing, or study group. 3. *Natural History*. A large group of plants or animals formed by the association of several orders.—**class** v.—**class·a·ble** adj.

class·ic (*klas*-ik) adj. 1. Of the highest order, esp. literary; pure; correct; refined. 2. Pertaining to Greek or Roman antiquity.—n. A standard or literary work or its author.

clas·si·cal (*klas*-ih-k'l) adj. 1. Pertaining to ancient Greece or Rome or to the principles of formality, restraint, and clarity in their art; opposed to **romantic**. 2. Conforming to traditional or established structure and composition.—**clas·si·cal·ly** adv.

clas·si·cism (*klas*-ih-sizm) n. The principles of dignity, purity, and harmony in art originally developed by Greek and Roman culture.

clas·si·cist (*klas*-ih-sist) n. One versed in, or imitative of, the classics.

clas·si·cize (*klas*-ih-syze) v. [clas·si·cized; clas·si·ciz·ing] To imitate the manner of the classics.

clas·si·fi·ca·tion (klas-ih-fih-*kay*-shun) n. The technique of separating into sets, or ranks.

clas·si·fy (*klas*-ih-fy) v. [clas·si·fied; clas·si·fy·ing] To arrange in sets, sorts, or ranks.—**clas·si·fi·a·ble** adj.—**clas·si·fi·er** n.

class·mate n. A fellow pupil at school or college.

class·room n. A room in which school or college pupils meet for instruction.

clat·ter (*klat*-er) v. To make rattling sounds.— n. Rattling sounds; tumultuous and confused noise.—**clat·ter·er** n.

clause (*klawz*) n. 1. An article in a contract or other document. 2. *Grammar*. A part of a compound sentence containing a predicate and its subject.—**claus·al** adj.

claus·tral (*klawss*-tr'l) adj. Secluded.

claus·tro·pho·bi·a (klawss-truh-*foh*-bee-uh) n.

Medicine. A psychoneurosis characterized by terror of being enclosed or crowded.

clav·ate (*klay*-vayt) *adj.* Club-shaped.

clav·i·chord (*klav*-ih-kord) *n. Music.* Stringed instrument played by keys, the forerunner of the piano.

clav·i·cle (klav-ih-k'l) *n.* The collarbone.

clav·i·er (*klay*-vee-er) *n. Music.* The keyboard of a piano, organ, or concertina.

claw *n.* 1. The sharp hooked nail on the extremity of an animal or bird. 2. The pincers of a crustacean. 3. A scratch from a claw. —*v.* To tear; scratch; gash; gouge.

claw·ham·mer *n.* 1. A hammer with one end divided for drawing nails. 2. Dress coat with tails.

clay *n.* 1. A malleable variety of earth which hardens when dry, for making pottery, etc. 2. Earth; mud. 3. *Figurative.* The human body.—**clay·ey, clay·ish** *adj.*

clay·more *n.* The large two-edged sword of Scottish Highlanders.

clay pigeon. A target for shotgun practice.

clean (*kleen*) *adj.* 1. Free from dirt, imperfection, or moral impurity; clear; pure. 2. Trim; well-turned.—*adv.* 1. Wholly; perfectly. 2. Cleanly.—*v.* To purify; cleanse.—**clean out.** To empty; exhaust the resources of. —**clean up.** 1. Put in order; clean. 2. To finish. 3. *Slang.* To make a big profit.—**clean·a·ble** *adj.*

clean-bred   clean-hearted   clean-out (*n.*)
clean-faced   clean-limbed   clean-shaven
clean-handed   clean-minded   clean-up (*n.*)

clean-cut *adj.* 1. Sharply outlined; well-defined. 2. Having trim lines; well-shaped.

clean·er *n.* Person or device that cleans.

clean·ly (*klen*-lee) *adj.* [clean·li·er; clean·li·est] Habitually free from dirt; neat.—**clean·li·ly** *adv.*—**clean·li·ness** *n.*

clean·ly (*kleen*-lee) *adv.* In a clean manner.

clean·ness (*kleen*-ness) *n.* The condition or quality of being clean.

cleanse (*klenz*) *v.* [cleansed; cleans·ing] To make clean; purify.

clear *adj.* 1. Unclouded; light; bright. 2. Having no flaw; clean; innocent. 3. Easily comprehended; distinct; evident. 'A clear statement.' 4. Distinctly audible. 5. Unobstructed; open. 6. Net; free of charges. 'A clear profit.'—*adv.* 1. Clearly. 2. Wholly; entirely.—*v.* 1. To free from obscurity, ambiguity, imperfection, obstruction, debt, guilt, etc. 2. To leap over or pass without touching. 3. To remove in order to leave a clear space. 4. To pass, as a check, through a clearing-house; cash.—*n.* A clear surface.—**clear out.** *Slang.* Deport.—**clear up.** 1. To settle; explain. 2. Become clear, as weather.—**in the clear.** Innocent; free from guilt.—**clear·a·ble** *adj.*—**clear·er** *n.*

clear-eyed   clear-skinned   clear-up (*n.*)
clear-hearted   clear-tinted   clear-voiced
clear-minded   clear-toned   clear-witted

clear·ance (*kleer*-uns) *n.* 1. The act of clearing. 2. A certificate showing authoritative approval. 3. The distance or clear space between passing objects.

clear-cut *adj.* Formed with clear outlines.

clear-headed *adj.* Intelligent; understanding. —**clear-head·ed·ly** *adv.*—**clear-head·ed·ness** *n.*

clear·ing *n.* 1. The act of clearing. 2. A tract of land cleared of timber.

clear·ing·house *n.* An institution where banks exchange checks and settle their balances.

clear·ly *adv.* In a clear manner; plainly.

clear·ness *n.* The condition or quality of being clear.

clear-sighted *adj.* Having acute vision; discerning; perspicacious.—**clear-sight·ed·ly** *adv.*

clear·starch *v.* To stiffen with colorless starch.

cleat (*kleet*) *n.* 1. *Nautical.* A metal peg or shaft of different designs used on ships to retain ropes. 2. A strip of material worn on shoes, nailed on gangplanks, etc., to give traction. 3. *Carpentry.* A piece of wood used to secure or strengthen a joint.—*v.* To strengthen or provide with cleats.

cleav·age (*kleev*-ij) *n.* 1. A splitting or separating. 2. *Geology.* The way rocks and ores regularly or naturally split. 3. *Biology.* Division of a cell or cells into two similar cells or groups of cells.

cleave (*kleev*) *v.* [cleaved; cleav·ing] To cling; be fast together; be faithful.

cleave (*kleev*) *v.* [cleft, cleaved, clove; cleft cleaved, clo·ven; cleav·ing] 1. To split; pierce; crack open. 2. To part or open. 3. To chop or cut off.—**cleav·a·ble** *adj.*

cleav·er (*kleev*-er) *n.* A heavy butcher's ax or knife for cutting bones.

CLEAVER

cleek *n. Golf.* A driving iron.

clef *n. Music.* A character placed at the beginning of a staff to indicate the range of pitch according to its place on the staff.

TREBLE   TENOR   BASE
G CLEF   CLEF   F CLEF
CLEFS

cleft *n.* 1. A split; crevice. 2. A horses' disease causing a split hoof.

cleft *adj.* Split; having a line of separation.

clem·a·tis (*klem*-uh-tis) *n.* A group of woody climbing plants whose flowers are petalless.

clem·en·cy (*klem*-'n-see) *n.* [*pl.* -cies] 1. Mercy; leniency. 2. Moderateness of the weather. 3. A merciful deed.—**clem·ent** *adj.*

clench *v.* 1. To double up tightly; grip; hold together fiercely. 2. To clinch.—**clench** *n.*

Cle·o·pa·tra (klee-uh-*pay*-truh, -*pah*-, -*pa*-). An Egyptian queen noted for her beauty.

clep·sy·dra (*klep*-sih-druh) *n.* Device for keeping time by the regulated flow of a fluid.

clere·sto·ry, clear·sto·ry (*kleer*-stor-ee) *n.* [*pl.* -ries] The upper story of a structure perforated by a line of windows which light the interior.

cler·gy (*kler*-jee) *n.* [*pl.* -gies] The priesthood or ministry; ecclesiastics; clerics.

cler·gy·man *n.* [*pl.* -men] A churchman; priest.

cler·ic (*kler*-ik) *n.* A minister or priest; ecclesiastic.—**cler·ic** *adj.*

cler·i·cal (*kler*-ih-k'l) *adj.* 1. Pertaining to the clergy. 2. Denoting clerks or office workers.

cler·i·cal·ism (*kler*-ih-k'l-izm) *n.* Undue influence of the clergy.—**cler·i·cal·ist** *n.*

clerk *n.* 1. A general office worker; clerical employee. 2. A salesperson in a retail store. 3. Official of a court, society, corporation, etc., whose duty is to keep records and who has miscellaneous functions. 4. A preacher or lay assistant.—**clerk** *v.*—**clerk·ly** *adj. & adv.*

clev·er (*klev*-er) *adj.* Intelligent; ingenious; alert; smart.—**clev·er·ly** *adv.*—**clev·er·ness** *n.*

clev·is (*klev*-is) *n.* A U-shaped fastening or hitching device with a retaining pin through the punched ends of its arms.

clew *n.* 1. *Nautical.* One of the corners of a sail, or the metal hoop or ring on it. 2. *Variant spelling* of **clue.** 3. Yarn or small cordage wound in a ball.—**clew** *v.*

cli·ché (klee-*shay*) *n.* [*pl.* cli·chés] 1. Platitude; stereotyped expression; catchword. 2. *Printing.* A plate produced by electrotyping.

click *n.* A small sharp sound. 2. *Machinery.* A small ratchet or retaining stop.—*v.* 1. To make a small sharp sound. 2. *Slang.* To get along well together.—**click·er** *n.*

cli·ent (*kly*-unt) *n.* The customer or patron of a lawyer, shop, etc.—**cli·en·tal** (kly-*en*-t'l) *adj.*

cli·en·tele (kly-en-*tel*) *n.* Customers or clients collectively, esp. regular patrons.

cliff *n.* A precipice; lofty, perpendicular mountain.—**cliff·y** *adj.*

cliff dweller. 1. One of a prehistoric Indian tribe who built their homes in the cliffs of SW U.S. 2. *Slang.* A dweller in a penthouse or lofty building.—**cliff-dwelling** *adj.*

cliff swallow. A swallow which builds flasklike nests of mud on cliff walls.

cli·mac·ter·ic (kly-*mak*-ter-ik) *n.* 1. A period of major change in the human constitution, as the menopause or puberty. 2. Any critical change.—**cli·mac·ter·ic** *adj.*—**cli·mac·ter·i·cal** (kly-mak-*ter*-ih-k'l) *adj. & n.*

cli·mac·tic (kly-*mak*-tik) *adj.* Also **cli·mac·ti·cal.** Pertaining to, or rising to, a point of highest intensity.

cli·mate (*kly*-m't) *n.* 1. Prevailing temperature, humidity, and other life-determining factors. 2. The area where a certain grouping of these factors prevails. 'Warm climate.'—**cli·mat·ic** (kly-*mat*-ik) *adj.*

cli·ma·tol·o·gy (kly-muh-*tol*-uh-jee) *n.* The scientific study of climate.—**cli·ma·to·log·ic** (kly-muh-tuh-*loj*-ik), **cli·ma·to·log·i·cal** *adj.*

cli·max (*kly*-maks) *n.* 1. Culmination; point of greatest intensity. 2. *Rhetoric.* Ideas or arguments organized so that each succeeding one increases in force; the final of such a grouping.—**cli·max** *v.*

climb (*klyme*) *v.* 1. To mount; ascend. 2. To incline or slope upward. 3. To increase; advance.—**climb** *n.*—**climb·a·ble** *adj.*

climb·er (*klyme*-er) *n.* 1. One who ascends. 2. *Colloquial.* One avidly anxious to enhance his social prestige. 3. A vine that rises by attaching itself to some support.

climbing iron. A steel spike or framework strapped to the foot to assist in climbing wooden shafts.

clime *n.* Region or area of a given climate.

clinch *v.* 1. *Boxing.* To embrace an opponent so as to smother his blows. 2. *Slang.* To embrace. 3. To establish; settle, as an argument. 4. To bend the point of a driven nail.

clinch·er *n.* 1. *Slang.* A decisive retort; unanswerable argument. 2. A tool for fastening nails.

cling *v.* [clung; cling·ing] To cleave; hold fast; adhere; embrace.—**cling·er** *n.*—**cling·ing** *adj.*

cling·stone *n.* A variety of peach the pulp of which adheres closely to the pit.

clin·ic (*klin*-ik) *n.* 1. An institution offering medical treatment free or at a low cost. 2. Demonstrational treatment of patients before medical students.

clin·i·cal *adj.* Based on actual observation; not theoretical. 'Clinical research.'— -**cal·ly** *adv.*

clink *v.* To make a small, sharp sound.—**clink** *n.*—**clink·er** *n.*

clink *n.* *Slang.* Jail; prison.

clink·er *n. pl.* Ashes; cinders.—**clink·er** *v.*

cli·nom·e·ter (klih-*nom*-uh-ter) *n.* An instrument for measuring degrees of obliquity. —**cli·no·met·ric, cli·no·met·ri·cal** *adj.*

Cli·o (*kly*-oh). *Mythology.* The muse of history.

clip *v.* [clipped; clip·ping] 1. To shear; trim; shorten by cutting. 2. *Slang.* To hit with the fist. 3. *Slang.* To cheat.—*n.* 1. The quantity of wool shorn in a single season. 2. *Slang.* A punch. 3. A quick pace. 'At a fast clip.'

clip *n.* 1. A twisted metal wire for fastening papers together. 2. An ornamental clasp.

clip·per *n.* 1. One who clips. 2. A fast sailing ship, with a sharp, forward-raking bow and masts slanting backward. 3. [*pl.*] Scissors.

clip·ping *n.* 1. The act of cutting. 2. An article cut from a periodical.—**clip·ping** *adj.*

clipping bureau. A firm which clips and forwards articles on a special topic to a person or organization interested in it.

clique (*kleek*) *n.* A coterie; exclusive group. —*v.* [cliqued; cliq·uing]—**cli·quish** *adj.*—**cli·quish·ly** *adv.*—**cli·quish·ness** *n.*—**cli·quy** *adj.*

cli·to·ris (*klit*-uh-ris) *n.* A small, erectile female sex organ, homologous to the male penis.

clo·a·ca (kloh-*ay*-kuh) *n.* [*pl.* -cae] 1. An underground conduit for drainage; a sewer. 2. A water closet. 3. The termination of the intestinal canal in many lower animals. 4. An instrument or channel of degeneracy and corruption.—**clo·a·cal** *adj.*

cloak *n.* **1.** A loose, sleeveless outer garment; a long cape. **2.** A means of concealment; disguise; pretext.—*v.* **1.** To cover with a cloak. **2.** To hide; conceal.

cloche (*klohsh*) *n.* A type of woman's hat, close-fitting and deep-crowned.

clock *n.* A machine for measuring time, with hands revolving around a dial to indicate hours and minutes.—*v.* To measure the time of an action or event.—**clock·er** *n.*

clock *n.* An ornament woven or embroidered on the ankle of a stocking.—**clock** *v.*—**clock·er** *n.*

clock·wise *adv.* In the circular direction taken by the hands of a clock.—**clock·wise** *adj.*

clock·work *n.* The mechanical parts of a clock. —**like clockwork.** *Colloquial.* With precision.

clod *n.* **1.** A lump or mass, esp. of earth. **2.** A dull, gross, stupid person; a dolt.—**clod·dish** *adj.*—**clod·dish·ness** *n.*—**clod·dy** *adj.*

clod·hop·per *n.* A dolt; a boor.

clog *n.* **1.** An impediment or hindrance. **2.** A wooden shoe.—*v.* To impede; to choke up. —**clog·gy** *adj.* Adhesive; viscous.

clog dance. A tap dance done with wooden-soled shoes to emphasize the beat.—**clog dancer, clog dancing.**

cloi·son·né (kloy-zuh-*nay*) *n.* [*cap.*] A French enamel ware in which wire partitions outline the design.—**cloi·son·né** *adj.*

clois·ter (*kloys*-ter) *n.* **1.** A convent; a monastery. **2.** An arched way or covered walk running around the walls of monasteries or collegiate buildings.—*v.* **1.** To confine in a convent or monastery. **2.** To shut up in retirement from the world.—**clois·tral** *adj.*

clois·tered *adj.* **1.** Solitary; sheltered; withdrawn from the world. **2.** Inhabiting a convent.

close (*klohss*) *adj.* **1.** Strictly confined or watched, as a close prisoner. **2.** Secretive, reticent. **3.** Adjoining, with little intervening distance. **4.** Oppressive, as the air or weather. **5.** Almost evenly balanced, as a close election. **6.** Intimate. **7.** Undeviating, as a close translation. **8.** Stingy.—*adv.* **1.** Tightly, so as to leave no opening. **2.** In strict confinement. **3.** Very near in space or time.—**close·ly** *adv.*

close-annealed	close-coupled	close-hearted
close-banded	close-eared	close-herd
close-bodied	close-fertilize (*v.*)	close-mouthed
close-bred	close-fibered	close-packed
close-buttoned	close-fisted	close-reefed
close-clipped	close-grained	close-rounded
close-connected	close-handed	close-tongued

close (*klohz*) *v.* [closed; clos·ing] **1.** To come together; to unite. **2.** To end. **3.** To engage in close encounter.—**close with.** To come to an agreement with.—*n.* Conclusion.

close (*klohs*) *n.* An enclosed place; any place surrounded by wall, fence, or hedge.

closed shop. An industrial or commercial establishment in which only union members in good standing are permitted to work.

close-fist·ed *adj.* Miserly; niggardly.

close-hauled *adj.* Sailing into the wind.

clos·et (*kloz*-et) *n.* **1.** A small room or recess for storing clothing, utensils, etc. **2.** Any small room.—*v.* To place in a closet for concealment or consultation.—*adj.* Secluded.

close-up *n.* A photograph, esp. a motion-picture scene, taken very near the subject.

clo·sure (*kloh*-zher) *n.* **1.** The act of shutting; a closing. **2.** A parliamentary device for ending debate. **3.** Enclosure. **4.** Conclusion.

clot *n.* A coagulated mass of soft or fluid matter, as blood.—*v.* To form into clots; to coagulate.

cloth (*kloth*) *n.* [*pl.* cloths] **1.** A woven fabric of wool, cotton, or other material. **2.** Fabric put to a particular use, as table cloth.—*adj.* Of or pertaining to cloth.—**the cloth.** The clergy.

clothe (*klohth*) *v.* [clothed; cloth·ing] **1.** To dress. **2.** To cover.

clothes (*klohz*) *n. pl.* **1.** Garments for the human body. **2.** Bed covers.

clothes bag	clothesline	clothes-moth
clothes basket	clothesman	clothes-press
clothes brush	clothesmonger	clothes-rack

clothes·horse *n.* **1.** A frame to hang clothes on. **2.** *Slang.* One who makes a fetish of fine wearing apparel.

clothes·pin *n.* A forked piece of wood by which clothes are attached to a line for drying.

clothes tree. A stand on which to hang clothes.

cloth·ier (*klohth*-ee-er) *n.* A seller or manufacturer of clothes.

cloth·ing (*klohth*-ing) *n.* Garments in general.

clot·ty *adj.* Full of clots or small hard masses.

clo·ture (*kloh*-cher) *n.* A parliamentary device for ending debate; a closure.

cloud (*klowd*) *n.* **1.** A visible collection of watery particles suspended above the earth. **2.** Any nebulous mass, as smoke, dust, etc. **3.** A threat; a foreboding, concealing, overshadowing element.—*v.* **1.** To spread over with clouds. **2.** To obscure; to darken.—**in the clouds.** Inspired.—**under a cloud.** In disrepute.

cloud·ber·ry *n.* A small herbaceous plant with large white flowers found in Great Britain.

cloud·burst *n.* A violent rainfall.

cloud·less *adj.* Clear; bright.—**cloud·less·ly** *adv.*

cloud·let *n.* A small cloud.

cloud·y *adj.* [cloud·i·er, cloud·i·est] **1.** Obscured with clouds; overcast. **2.** Dimmed; marked with dark areas; opaque. **3.** Not easily understood; unclear.—**cloud·i·ly** *adv.*

clough (*kluf*) *n.* **1.** A ravine or cleft in a hillside. **2.** A sluice for irrigating farm lands.

clout (*klowt*) *n.* **1.** A cloth or leather patch. **2.** A blow with the hand.—*v.* **1.** To patch; to mend. **2.** To strike a blow.

clove *n.* A pungent aromatic spice, native to the Molucca Islands.

clove *n. Botany.* A small bulb found in the axils of the scales of a mother bulb, as in garlic.

clo·ven (*kloh*-vun) *adj.* Split; divided.

C

cloven foot, or **hoof.** A symbol of Satan.—**clo·ven-foot·ed, clo·ven-hoofed** adj. 1. Evil; devilish. 2. Having the foot or hoof cleft.

clo·ver n. Common, low-growing herb having three-lobed leaves and white to purplish close-headed flowers.—**in clover.** Well-off; luxuriously situated.

clown n. 1. A circus jester. 2. A person of rude manners. 3. A rustic.—v. To act like a clown.—**clown·er·y** n. [pl. -ies]

clown·ish (klown-ish) adj. Joking; rude; awkward. —**clown·ish·ly** adv.—**clown·ish·ness** n.

CLOVER

cloy (kloy) v. To gratify to excess so as to cause loathing; satiate; surfeit.

club n. 1. A thick heavy stick of wood; a cudgel. 2. A golf stick. 3. A playing card suit. 4. An organization of men or women devoted to a common purpose. 5. A clubhouse.—v. 1. To beat with a club. 2. To join together for some common purpose.

club-armed	clubhouse	clubroom
club-fisted	clubman	clubwoman

club·foot n. A short deformed foot.—**club·footed** adj.

club grass. A grass with club-shaped leaves.

club steak. A small cut of beef for broiling.

cluck v. To make, or imitate, the sound of a hen.—**cluck** n.

clue (kloo) n. An aid to unraveling a mystery.

clump n. 1. A shapeless mass. 2. A cluster of trees or shrubs.—v. To form into clumps.

clum·sy adj. [clum·si·er; clum·si·est] Awkward; ungainly.—**clum·si·ly** adv.—**clum·si·ness** n.

Cluny lace. A net lace originating in the French city of Cluny.

clus·ter n. 1. A number of things, such as fruit or berries, growing naturally together. 2. A group of persons or things gathered closely together.—v. To grow or collect in clusters. —**clus·ter·y** adj. Growing in clusters.

clutch v. To seize or grip with the hand.—n. 1. A grasp; seizure. 2. Mechanics. A device for smoothly engaging and disengaging moving parts of a machine.

clut·ter n. Litter; confusion.—v. To crowd together in disorder.

coach n. 1. A horse-drawn passenger conveyance; railroad car; autobus. 2. A private tutor.—v. To tutor.—**coach and four.** A large four-wheeled carriage drawn by four horses. —**coach·er.**

coach dog. A Dalmatian.

coach·man n. [pl. -men] The driver of a coach. —**coach·man·ship** n. Skill in driving a coach.

co·ad·ju·tor (koh-aj-oo-ter, -aj-oo-) n. An associate; an assistant; a helper.—**co·ad·ju·tant** adj.

co·ag·u·late (koh-ag-yoo-layt) v. [co·ag·u·lat·ed; co·ag·u·lat·ing] To congeal; clot; crystal-lize.—**co·ag·u·la·ble** adj.—**co·ag·u·la·bil·i·ty** n.

co·ag·u·la·tion (koh-ag-yoo-lay-sh'n) n. The act of changing from fluid to a thickened or solid state.—**co·ag·u·la·tive** adj.—**co·ag·u·la·tor** n. That which causes coagulation.

coal (kohl) n. 1. A solid, black, inflammable mineral used for fuel. 2. A burning or charred substance.—v. 1. To supply with coal, as a ship. 2. To burn to coal.—**coal·er** n.

coal bag	coal dealer	coalmouse
coal bagger	coal-faced	coalpit
coal bin	coal-fired	coal rake
coal black	coalhole	coal shed
coal box	coal-laden	coal-whipper
coal dark	coalmonger	coalyard

co·a·lesce (koh-uh-less) v. [co·a·lesced; co·a·lesc·ing] To grow together; unite; combine. —**co·a·les·cence** n.—**co·a·les·cent** adj.

coal gas. 1. Illuminating gas made from coal. 2. The gas given off by burning coal.

coaling station. A place where ships stop for refueling.

co·a·li·tion (koh-uh-lih-sh'n) n. 1. The union of separate entities in a combined mass. 2. Voluntary alliance of persons, political parties, etc., for united action.— -**tion·ist** n.

coal measures. Geology. Strata of the earth containing coal beds.

coal oil. 1. Petroleum. 2. Kerosene.

coal·sack n. Astronomy. Large dark space in the Milky Way.

coal tar. A thick, black, sticky fluid produced by the distillation of coal.

coam·ing (kohm-ing) n. A raised edge around a hatch, well, etc., to prevent flooding.

coarse (kohrs) adj. 1. Rough in texture; comprised of large particles or grains. 2. Gross; indelicate; vulgar. 3. Poor; inferior.—**coarse·ly** adv.—**coars·en** v.—**coarse·ness** n.

coarse-featured	coarse-handed	coarse-spun
coarse-fibered	coarse-lipped	coarse-tongued
coarse-grained	coarse-minded	coarse-toothed
coarse-haired	coarse-skinned	coarse-wrought

coast (kohst) n. 1. The shore; land bordering the sea. 2. A slide or ride down an incline. —v. 1. To sail along the shore. 2. To slide or roll down an incline. 3. To move forward under momentum.—**coast·al** adj.

coast·er n. 1. A ship which sails coastwise. 2. A sled or other coasting vehicle. 3. A pad set under glasses to protect furniture.

coaster brake. A bicycle brake which works like a clutch, disengaging pedals for coasting.

Coast Guard. United States. Armed naval force under the authority of the Treasury department, responsible for the suppression of smuggling, guarding the coastline, etc.

coast·ward adj. Toward the shore.—**coast·ward, coast·wards** adv.

coast·wise adj. & adv. By or along the coast.

coat (koht) n. 1. A sleeved outer garment. 2. External covering of an animal. 3. A layer of one substance covering another; coating. —v. To cover with a coat.—**coat·less** adj.

coat·ee n. A short, close-fitting coat.

C

co·a·ti (koh-*ah*-tee) *n.* [*pl.* -tis] An animal similar to the raccoon, with a long body and snout and a long, striped tail.

coat·ing (*koht*-ing) *n.* 1. A covering; layer over a surface. 2. Material for coats.

coat of arms. The armorial insignia of a noble family; shield.

coat of mail. [*pl.* coats of mail] A flexible metal outer garment worn as armor.

coax (*kohks*) *v.* To cajole; wheedle; persuade by flattery. —**coax·er** *n.* —**coax·ing·ly** *adv.*

co·ax·i·al (koh-*aks*-yul) *adj.* Also **co·ax·al.** Having a common axis. —**coaxial cable.** A complex transmission cable used in telegraph, telephone, and television.

COAT OF ARMS

cob (kob) *n.* 1. Spiked shoot on which corn kernels grow. 2. A sturdy horse with short legs. 3. A male swan.

co·balt (*koh*-bawlt) *n.* A strong silver-white metallic element. (*Symbol:* Co).—**co·bal·tic, co·bal·tous** *adj.*

cobalt blue. A beautiful dark blue pigment derived from cobalt.

cob·ble (*kob*-b'l) *n.* A round stone for paving; cobblestone.—*v.* [cob·bled; cob·bling].

cob·ble *v.* [cob·bled; cob·bling] To patch; repair, as shoes.

cob·bler (*kob*-bler) *n.* 1. A shoe repairer. 2. An iced beverage of wine, sugar, lemon, etc. 3. A deep dish fruit pie.

cob·ble·stone (*kob*-b'l-stohn) *n.* A round stone for paving roads.

co·bra (*koh*-bruh) *n.* An extremely poisonous snake which, when irritated, dilates its neck into a hoodlike form.

COBRA (1/20 life size)

cob·web (*kob*-web) *n.* 1. The delicate web spun by a spider. 2. That which is delicate or entangling.—*v.* [cob·webbed; cob·web·bing].—**cob·web·ber·y** *n.*—**cob·web·by** *adj.*

co·ca (*koh*-kuh) *n.* South American plant whose dried leaves are the source of cocaine.

co·caine, co·cain (koh-*kayn*) *n.* A narcotic used as a stimulant and local anaesthetic.

coc·cus (*kok*-us) *n.* [*pl.* coc·ci] 1. A carpel. 2. A sphere-shaped bacterium.—**coc·coid** *adj.*

coc·cyx (*kok*-siks) *n.* [*pl.* coc·cy·ges (kok-*sy*-jees)] *Anatomy.* Small bone at the lower extremity of the spinal column.—**coc·cyg·e·al** (kok-*sij*-ee-ul) *adj.*

Co·chin (*koh*-chin) *n.* A variety of large domestic fowl, originally from Cochin-China.

coch·i·neal (koch-ih-*neel*) *n.* A dye derived from dried bodies of a tropical American insect.

coch·le·a (*kok*-lee-uh) *n.* [*pl.* -leae] *Anatomy.* A cavity in the inner ear resembling a snail shell in shape.—**coch·le·ar** *adj.*

cock *n.* 1. A male domestic fowl; rooster. 2. A weathercock. 3. A valve; faucet. 4. A gun hammer. 5. Act of turning up or cocking.—*v.* 1. To turn or tip up. 2. To pull back the hammer of a gun for firing.

cock *n.* A conical stack of hay, etc.—**cock** *v.*

cock·ade (kok-*ayd*) *n.* A knot of ribbon or rosette worn on a hat.—**cock·ad·ed** *adj.*

Cock·aigne (kok-*ayn*) *n.* A mythical country of idleness and enjoyment.

cock·a·lo·rum (kok-uh-*lor*-um) *n.* A bantam cock; hence, a diminutive pompous man.

cock-and-bull story. A fantastic tale.

cock·a·too (*kok*-uh-too) *n.* A beautifully-crested bird of the parrot family, native to Australia and the south Pacific islands.

cock·a·trice (*kok*-uh-tris) *n.* A mythical monster supposed to have been hatched by a serpent from a cock's egg.

cock·boat *n.* Also **cock·le·boat.** A small boat.

cock·cha·fer (*kok*-chayf-er) *n.* A common European beetle, injurious to trees.

cock·crow *n.* Early morning.

cocked hat. Hat worn in the eighteenth century having the brim turned up in peaks.

cock·er·el (*kok*-uh-r'l) *n.* A young cock.

cock·eye *n.* A crossed eye.—**cock·eyed** *adj.* 1. Crosseyed. 2. *Slang.* Crazy. 3. Drunk.

cock·horse *n.* A child's rocking horse.

cock·le (*kok*-'l) *n.* An edible, common mollusk.

cock·le·boat. *Variant spelling* of **cock·boat.**

cock·le·bur *n.* A prickly weed of the ragweed family.

cock·le·shell *n.* The ribbed, curved shell of a cockle.

cock·ney (*kok*-nee) *n.* [*pl.* -neys] 1. A native of the East End of London. 2. Cockney speech.—**cock·ney** *adj.*—**cock·ney·dom** *n.*—**cock·ney·ish** *adj.*—**cock·ney·ism** *n.*—**cock·ney·ese** *n.*

cock·pit *n.* 1. Enclosed space in an airplane in which the pilot sits. 2. An enclosed area in which cock fights took place.

cock·roach *n.* A common insect pest prevalent in warm places.

cocks·comb *n.* 1. A coarse-textured, tall, vivid garden flower, usually deep red or yellow. 2. A fop; a dandy.—**cocks·combed** *adj.*

cock·sure *adj.* Aggressively positive; certain.

cock·tail *n.* 1. A short mixed drink, usually served before dinner. 2. An appetizer, usually of seafood or fruit. 3. A cross-bred horse.

cock·y *adj.* [cock·i·er; cock·i·est] Jaunty; defiantly self-confident.

co·co (*koh*-koh) *n.* [*pl.* co·cos] Also **co·coa.** A tall palm which produces coconuts; coconut palm or tree.—*adj.* Made from the inner fiber of the coconut.

co·coa (*koh*-koh) *n.* 1. The pulverized seeds of the cacao tree, after removal of fat. 2. The drink made by cooking this powder with milk and sugar. 3. A reddish-brown color.

co·co·nut (*koh*-kuh-nut) *n.* Also **co·coa·nut.** The hard-shelled fruit of the coco palm; also its white meaty lining, used as food.

co·coon (kuh-*koon*) *n.* The silky envelope which the larvae of many insects spin as a covering for themselves during the chrysalis state.

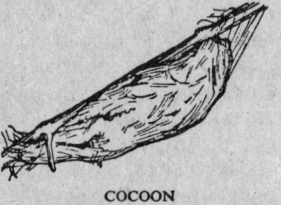

COCOON

co·cotte (kuh-*kot*) *n.* A loose woman.

cod *n.* A voracious, edible fish with a large club-shaped head, abounding off the shores of New England and Newfoundland.

cod·dle *v.* [cod·dled; cod·dling] 1. To pamper; baby. 2. To simmer slowly in water, as an egg.—**cod·dler** *n.*

code (kohd) *n.* 1. An organized collection or body of laws, principles, etc. 2. A system in which symbols are substituted for letters or words to preserve secrecy, or save wordage. 3. Morse code.—*v.* [cod·ed; cod·ing].

co·de·ine, co·de·in (*koh*-dee-in, *koh*-deen) *n.* A sedative drug derived from opium.

co·dex (*koh*-dex) *n.* [*pl.* co·di·ces] 1. A systematic body of laws. 2. A manuscript volume of a classic, esp. of the Scriptures.

cod·fish *n.* [*pl.* -fish, -fishes] The cod or its meat prepared for eating.

codg·er (*koj*-er) *n. Colloquial.* An eccentric old man.

cod·i·cil (*kod*-uh-sil) *n.* 1. A limiting supplement or postscript to a will. 2. Any added supplement or appendix.—**cod·i·cil·la·ry** (kod-uh-*sil*-uh-ree) *adj.*

cod·i·fy (*kod*-uh-fy, *kohd*-uh-fy) *v.* [cod·i·fied; -fy·ing] To reduce to a code or system.—**cod·i·fi·ca·tion** *n.*—**cod·i·fi·er** *n.*

cod·ling *n.* An immature cod; also a hake.

cod·ling, cod·lin *n.* 1. A green apple. 2. A variety of long, tapering apple.

cod·ling moth. Also **cod·lin moth.** A small dark gray moth whose larvae bore into fruit.

cod-liver oil. A vitamin-rich oil extracted from the liver of the cod for therapeutic purposes.

co·ed, co-ed (*koh*-ed) *n.* A female student in a college enrolling both sexes.

co·ed·u·ca·tion (koh-ed-yoo-*kay*-sh'n) *n.* An educational system in which men and women attend classes together.—**co·ed·u·ca·tion·al** *adj.*

co·ef·fi·cient (koh-uh-*fish*-'nt) *n.* 1. That which unites with something else to produce an effect. 2. *Algebra.* A known quantity placed before variable or unknown quantities to express multiplication. 3. A constant ratio

expressed as a whole or decimal number.—**co·ef·fi·cient** *adj.*

co·e·qual (koh-*ee*-kw'l) *adj.* Equivalent in size, rank, power, etc.—**co·e·qual** *n.*

co·erce (koh-*erss*) *v.* [co·erced; co·erc·ing] 1. To compel obedience or acquiescence highhandedly. 2. To repress; restrain forcibly. 3. To enforce.—**co·er·ci·ble** *adj.*

co·er·cion (koh-*er*-sh'n) *n.* 1. Compulsion; force. 2. Restraint; curb; check.—**co·er·cion·ary** *adj.*—**co·er·cion·ist** *n.*

co·er·cive (koh-*er*-siv) *adj.* 1. Compelling; forcing. 2. Restraining; inhibiting.—**co·er·cive·ly** *adv.*—**co·er·cive·ness** *n.*

co·e·ter·nal (koh-ee-*ter*-n'l) *adj.* Coexisting forever or perpetually.—**co·e·ter·nal·ly** *adv.*

co·e·val (koh-*ee*-v'l) *adj.* Of equal age; having existed the same number of years.— -**val·ly** *adv.*

co·ex·ist (koh-egz-*ist*) *v.* To live or have existence at the same time as another.—**co·ex·is·tence** *n.*—**co·ex·is·tent** *n.*

co·ex·tend (koh-eks-*tend*) *v.* To occupy the same space or time as another; extend equally.—**co·ex·ten·sion** *n.*—**co·ex·ten·sive** *adj.*

cof·fee (*kaw*-fee) *n.* 1. A stimulating beverage made from the berry of a small tropical tree. 2. The color or flavor of coffee.—**cof·fee** *adj.*

coffee cake	coffee grower	coffeepot
coffee-colored	coffee growing	coffee room
coffeecup	coffee house	coffee shop
coffee-faced	coffee making	coffeetime

cof·fer (*kaw*-fer) *n.* 1. A chest; trunk; casket. 2. An ornate sunken panel or compartment. 3. A cofferdam. 4. [*pl.*] Treasury; hoard.

cof·fer·dam *n.* A watertight compartment or structure in which men can work below the water line.

cof·fin (*kaw*-fin) *n.* The chest or case in which a corpse is buried.—**cof·fin** *v.*

cog *n.* 1. The tooth of a gear wheel. 2. A projecting tooth on a timber fitting a corresponding notch in an adjoining member. 3. A primitive type of ship.—*v.* [cog·ged; cog·ging].

co·gent (*koh*-j'nt) *adj.* Forceful; compelling; convincing.—**co·gen·cy** *n.*—**co·gent·ly** *adv.*

cog·i·tate (*koj*-uh-tayt) *v.* [cog·i·tat·ed; -tat·ing] To meditate; ponder; plan.—**cog·i·ta·tor** *n.*

cog·i·ta·tion (koj-uh-*tay*-sh'n) *n.* Deep thought; meditation.—**cog·i·ta·tive** (*koj*-uh-tay-tiv) *adj.*

co·gnac (*kohn*-yak) *n.* A fine French brandy; liquor distilled from wine.

cog·nate (*kog*-nayt) *adj.* Allied; related; having an affinity or a common origin.—**cog·nate** *n.*—**cog·na·tion** (kog-*nay*-sh'n) *n.*

cog·ni·tion (kog-*nish*-un) *n.* Knowledge; mental awareness; power to know; perception.—**cog·ni·tion·al, cog·ni·tive** (*kog*-nuh-tiv) *adj.*

cog·ni·za·ble (*kog*-niz-uh-b'l) *adj.* Capable of being known or perceived.—**cog·ni·za·bly** *adv.*

cog·ni·zance (*kog*-nih-z'ns) *n.* 1. Knowledge; heed; awareness. 2. A symbol; a distinguishing device. 3. Legal jurisdiction.—**cog·ni·zant** *adj.* Acquainted; having knowledge of.

cog·no·men (kog-*noh*-m'n) *n.* [*pl.* -no·mens,

nom·i·na] A surname.—**cog·nom·i·nal** (kog-nom-ih-n'l) *adj.*

cog·wheel *n.* A wheel with teeth.

co·hab·it (koh-*hab*-it) *v.* To live together as man and wife.—**co·hab·i·tant, co·hab·i·ter** *n.*—**co·hab·i·ta·tion** (koh-hab-ih-*tay*-shun) *n.*

COGWHEEL

co·here (koh-*heer*) *v.* [co·hered; co·her·ing] 1. To hold together; stick; fasten. 2. To be logically connected.—**co·her·er** *n.*

co·her·ence (koh-*heer*-enss) *n.* Also **co·her·en·cy.** 1. Consistency; clarity of structure or continuity. 2. A sticking or cleaving together.

co·her·ent (koh-*heer*-ent) *adj.* 1. Connected; lucidly developed; logical. 2. Sticking together.—**co·her·ent·ly** *adv.*

co·he·sion (koh-*hee*-zhun) *n.* Unity; relation; holding together.

co·he·sive (koh-*heez*-iv) *adj.* Sticking together.

co·hort (*koh*-hort) *n.* 1. A body of warriors. 2. A supporter; a group in league.

coif (*koyf*) *n.* A close-fitting cap or headdress.

coif·fure (kwah-*fyoor*) *n.* Style of hair arrangement.

coil (*koyl*) *v.* To twist or wind spirally.—*n.* 1. A series of spirals into which any other pliant material is wound. 2. *Radio.* A length of wire wound around some core to provide inductance.—**coil·er** *n.*

coin *n.* 1. A small disk of metal used as money; metallic currency. 2. A corner or wedge.—*v.* 1. To stamp and convert into money; mint. 2. To invent, as a word.—**coin·a·ble** *adj.*—**coin·er** *n.*

coin·age (*koyn*-ij) *n.* 1. The art or practice of stamping money. 2. Metallic currency. 3. Invention; fabrication.

co·in·cide (koh-in-*syde*) *v.* [co·in·cid·ed; co·in·cid·ing] 1. To happen at the same time; be contemporaneous. 2. To agree; correspond.

co·in·cid·ence (koh-*in*-sih-d'ns) *n.* 1. Accidental and striking parallel or affinity. 2. Agreement; correspondence.—**co·in·ci·dent, co·in·ci·den·tal** *adj.*—**co·in·ci·dent·ly, -den·tal·ly** *adv.*

co·in·sur·ance (koh-in-*shoor*-uns) *n.* Insurance carried jointly with others.

Coin·treau (*kwan*-troh) *n.* Trade-mark name for an orange-flavored liqueur originally made only in Angers, France.

coir (*koyr*) *n.* A type of yarn manufactured from the husk of coconuts, and formed into cordage, sailcloth, etc.

co·i·tion (koh-*ish*-un) *n.* Copulation; sexual intercourse.

co·i·tus (*koh*-ih-tus) *n.* Sexual intercourse.

coke *n.* Coal deprived of its bitumen and other volatile matter by a heating process.—*v.* [coked; cok·ing] To convert into coke.

col·an·der (*kol*-en-der) *n.* A large perforated pot for straining.

cold *adj.* 1. Chilly; at low temperatures; frigid; icy. 2. Emotionless; not easily affected; reserved; unyielding. 3. Objective; detached. 4. *Painting.* Having a blue cast. 5. *Colloquial.* Far afield in perception; off the track. —*n.* 1. Absence of heat; chilliness. 2. *Medicine.* A common malady of the respiratory tract.—**cold·ly** *adv.*—**cold·ness** *n.*

cold-blooded *adj.* 1. Without sensitivity or feeling. 2. *Zoology.* Denoting animals, such as fish and reptiles, whose blood maintains approximately the same temperature as their habitat.—**cold-blood·ed·ly** *adv.*— **-ed·ness** *n.*

cold chisel. A chisel having a cutting edge formed of tempered steel for cutting cold metal.

cold pack. *Medicine.* Enveloping of a patient in sheets dipped in cold water.

cold sore. Eruption on the lip following fever or cold.

cole *n.* Any of a family of edible greens, including the cabbage.

cole·slaw *n.* Finely chopped, seasoned cabbage used as a salad.

cole·wort (*kohl*-wort) *n.* A loosely heading cabbage.

col·ic (*kol*-ik) *n.* A painful intestinal condition accompanied by fever.—**col·ick·y** *adj.*

col·i·se·um (kol-uh-*see*-um) *n.* A large building for theatrical performances or sports.

co·li·tis (koh-*ly*-tis) *n. Medicine.* Inflammation of the large intestine.

col·lab·o·rate (kuh-*lab*-uh-rayt) *v.* [-rat·ed; -rat·ing] 1. To work with someone in a joint enterprise. 2. To aid the enemies of one's country in wartime.—**col·lab·o·ra·tion** (kuh-lab-uh-*ray*-shun) *n.*—**col·lab·o·ra·tive** *adj.*—**col·lab·o·ra·tor** *n.*

col·lab·o·ra·tion·ist (kuh-lab-uh-*ray*-shun-ist) *n.* A citizen of one of the occupied countries in World War II who worked with the fascist invaders; a quisling.

col·lage (koh-*lahzh*) *n.* An abstract composition made by utilizing the textures of various commonplace substances, such as newspapers, sand, etc., glued on a flat ground.

col·lapse (kuh-*laps*) *v.* [col·lapsed; col·laps·ing] 1. To fall in; break down. 2. To faint; to suffer sudden failure of strength or health. —**col·lapse** *n.*—**col·laps·i·ble** *adj.*

col·lar (*kol*-er) *n.* 1. An item of apparel worn around the neck. 'Shirt collar, coat collar.' 2. *Machinery.* A metal ring or flange encircling another part, as a collar nut on a bolt.—*v.* 1. To place a collar on. 2. To grasp by the neck.

col·lar·bone *n.* A bone extending from the shoulder to the breastbone; the clavicle.

col·lard (*kol*-erd) *n.* A variety of leafy greens, of the cabbage family.

col·lar·et (kol-er-*et*) *n.* Also **col·lar·ette.** A small collar of linen, fur, etc., worn by women.

col·late (kol-*layt*) *v.* [col·lat·ed; col·lat·ing] 1. To bring together and compare; examine critically. 2. To gather and place in order.

C

col·lat·er·al (kuh-*lat*-er-ul) *adj.* 1. Auxiliary; subordinate. 2. Parallel; coincidental. 3. *Genealogy*. Stemming from the same ancestors but by different lines of descent. 4. Guaranteed or assured by supplementary security. 'A collateral loan.'—*n. Commerce*. Additional security.—**col·lat·er·al·ly** *adv.*

col·la·tion (kuh-*lay*-sh'n) *n.* 1. A meal, esp. a light lunch. 2. A text which is collated.

col·league (*kol*-eeg) *n.* An associate; partner. —*v.* To ally; conspire.—**col·league·ship** *n.*

col·lect (*kol*-lekt) *n.* 1. A brief, ritualistic prayer asking some specific blessing. 2. An opening prayer in some church rituals.

col·lect (kuh-*lekt*) *v.* 1. To bring together; accumulate. 2. To assemble; convene. 3. To get money upon demand or request. 4. To accumulate a group of objects: stamps, paintings, etc. 5. To re-establish control over oneself.—*adj. & adv.* Chargeable to the addressee. —**col·lect·i·ble, col·lect·a·ble** *adj.*—**col·lec·tion** *n.*

col·lect·ed *adj.* 1. Cool; self-possessed; composed. 2. Brought or grouped together.—**col·lect·ed·ly** *adv.*—**col·lect·ed·ness** *n.*

col·lec·tive (kuh-*lek*-tiv) *adj.* 1. Pertaining to or produced by a group. 2. Expressing a number or multitude united. 3. Able to bring together.—*n.* 1. A Soviet farm, whose members own and work the land in common. 2. A group of entities conceived as a unit. 3. *Grammar*. Collective noun.

collective bargaining. Negotiations on a basis of equality between an employer and a union representing his employees.

col·lec·tiv·ism (kuh-*lek*-t'v-ism) *n.* 1. A form of nonrevolutionary Socialism. 2. Loosely, any form of government ownership or control. —**col·lec·tiv·ist** *n.*—**col·lec·tiv·is·tic** *adj.*

col·lec·tor *n.* 1. One who gathers things together, esp. one who systematically accumulates. 2. A government official who receives taxes, customs, etc.—**col·lec·tor·ship** *n.*

col·leen (*kol*-een) *n.* A young Irish woman.

col·lege (*kol*-ij) *n.* 1. An institution of higher learning or specialized instruction. 2. A group having common interests professionally, scholastically, etc. 3. The building or buildings that house a college. 4. One of the schools of a university.—**col·le·gi·an** *n.*

col·le·gi·ate (kol-*eej*-ee-uht) *adj.* 1. Pertaining to colleges or college students. 2. Sportive.

col·lide (kuh-*lyde*) *v.* [col·lid·ed; col·lid·ing] 1. To strike or dash against; meet violently. 2. To have conflicting interests; clash.

col·lie *n.* A large, sharp-nosed, shaggy sheep dog.

col·lier (*kol*-yer) *n.* 1. A coal miner or merchant. 2. A coal-carrying ship.—**col·lier·y**

COLLIE (1/32 life size)

n. [*pl.* -ies] A coal mine with its auxiliary machinery and structures.

col·li·mate (*kol*-uh-mayt) *v.* [col·li·mat·ed; -mat·ing] *Optics.* 1. To redirect a line of sight. 2. To cause to be parallel, as light beams.—**col·li·ma·tion** (kol-uh-*may*-sh'n) *n.*

col·li·sion (kuh-*lih*-zh'n) *n.* 1. A striking together of two bodies. 2. Opposition; antagonism. 3. *Physics*. An exertion of force between two near or striking particles of matter so that energy is dissipated.

col·lo·ca·tion (kol-oh-*kay*-sh'n) *n.* Arrangement; organization; a placing side by side. —**col·lo·cate** (*kol*-oh-kayt) *v.*

col·lo·di·on (kuh-*loh*-dee-uhn) *n.* A syrupy, fast-drying liquid solution of a nitrate in ether, used for covering minor wounds, etc.

col·loid (*kol*-oyd) *n.* A form of matter in which submicroscopic particles disperse through, without dissolving in, a medium and show continuous random movement.—**col·loid·al** (kol-*oy*-d'l) *adj.*—**col·loid·al·i·ty** (kol-oyd-*al*-uh-tee) *n.*

col·lop (*kol*-uhp) *n.* A slice or small portion of food, esp. meat.

col·lo·qui·al (kuh-*loh*-kwee-ul) *adj.* Used in everyday speech but not in formal writing; familiar; informal.— **-al·ly** *adv.*— **-al·ness** *n.*

col·lo·qui·al·ism *n.* 1. A word or phrase peculiar to everyday speech. 2. A familiar style of speech or writing.

col·lo·quy (*kol*-oh-kwee) *n.* [*pl.* -quies] Dialogue; mutual conversation, esp. of a formal nature.—**col·lo·quist** *n.*

col·lude (kol-*lood*) *v.* [col·lud·ed; col·lud·ing] To connive; conspire in a fraud.—**col·lud·er** *n.*

col·lu·sion (kol-*oo*-zhun) *n.* Secret cooperation for a fraudulent purpose.—**col·lu·sive** *adj.*—**col·lu·sive·ly** *adv.*—**col·lu·sive·ness** *n.*

col·lyr·i·um (kuh-*leer*-ee-um) *n.* [*pl.* -i·a, -i·ums] A medicated eyewash.

co·logne (kuh-*lohn*) *n.* A toilet water of essences dissolved in alcohol.

co·lon (*koh*-l'n) *n. Punctuation.* A character [:] used (1) to indicate that a series or quotation is to follow; (2) after the salutation in a business letter; (3) in time records, to indicate hours, minutes, and seconds.

co·lon *n.* [*pl.* co·lons, cola] *Anatomy.* The large intestine.—**co·lon·ic** (kuh-*lohn*-ik) *adj.*

colo·nel (*ker*-n'l) *n. Army.* Head of a regiment; rank between lieutenant colonel and brigadier general.—**colo·nel·cy, colo·nel·ship** *n.*

co·lo·ni·al (kuh-*lohn*-ee-ul) *adj.* 1. Pertaining to a colony. 2. Denoting the American states when they were British colonies.—*n.* A resident in a colony.

col·o·nist (*kol*-uh-nist) *n.* A member of a colonizing group; settler.

col·o·nize (*kol*-uh-nyze) *v.* [col·o·nized; col·o·niz·ing] 1. To establish a colony or migrate and settle in new territories.—**col·o·ni·za·tion** (kol-uh-nuh-*zay*-sh'n) *n.*—**col·o·ni·za·tion·ist** *n.* —**col·o·niz·er** (*kol*-uh-nyze-'r) *n.*

col·on·nade (kol-uh-*nayd*) *n. Architecture.* Any series of columns or pillars placed at regular intervals.—**col·on·nad·ed** *adj.*

COLONNADE

col·o·ny (*kol*-uh-nee) *n.* [*pl.* -nies] 1. Group of settlers in a new land remaining subject to their mother country. 2. District settled by these people; any territory ruled by a distant state. 3. A number of animals or plants living or growing together.

col·o·phon (*kol*-uh-fon) *n.* An inscription or publisher's emblem placed at the end of a book, or frequently on the title page.

col·or (*kul*-er) *n.* 1. Sensation produced by the stimulating effect on the eye of certain visible wave lengths. 2. The visible distribution of the light given off or reflected by a surface, or any degree or variety of this; hue. 3. Complexion, esp. **a.** Ruddy color. **b.** The complexion of people not considered white. 4. Coloring matter; paint; pigment. 5. Pretext; guise. 6. A vivid or graphic quality. 7. [*pl.*] National or regimental flag.—*v.* 1. To give color to; paint; dye. 2. To flush; become red. 3. To misrepresent.—**col·or·er** *n.*

color bearer	color line	colorman
colorfast	color maker	colortype (*n.*)
color-free	color making	color-washed

col·or·a·ble (*kul*-er-uh-b'l) *adj.* Plausible; capable of taking color; specious; deceptive. —**col·or·a·bil·i·ty, -a·ble·ness** *n.*— **-a·bly** *adv.*

col·or·a·tion (kul-er-*ay*-sh'n) *n.* Pigmentation; coloring.

col·o·ra·tu·ra (kul-er-uh-*tyoo*-ruh; kol-er-) *n. Music.* 1. Ornamental flourishes to vocal music. 2. A coloratura soprano.

coloratura soprano. 1. Clear soprano voice suited to singing coloratura music. 2. Singer with this type of voice.

co·lor-blind·ness *n.* Whole or partial inability to distinguish colors.—**col·or-blind** *adj.*

col·ored (*kul*-erd) *adj.* 1. Having color. 2. Of or pertaining to any race other than white. 3. Misrepresented; biased.

col·or·ful (*kul*-er-ful) *adj.* Vivid; full of color; picturesque.—**col·or·ful·ly** *adv.*— **-ful·ness** *n.*

col·or·ing *n.* 1. The act or art of applying colors. 2. Appearance in relation to color; pigmentation. 3. Coloring matter; dye.

col·or·ist *n.* Artist skilled in use of color.

col·or·less *adj.* 1. Without color. 2. Dull; uninteresting.

color transparency. A color photograph on film, usually framed for projection on a screen.

co·los·sal (kuh-*los*-'l) *adj.* Immense; huge.

Col·os·se·um (kol-uh-*see*-um) *n.* 1. Famous Roman amphitheater, built about A.D. 80.

2. [*not cap.*] Also **col·i·se·um.** A large theater or arena.

Co·los·si·ans (kuh-*losh*-uns) *n. Bible.* An Epistle in the New Testament.

co·los·sus (kuh-*los*-us) *n.* [*pl.* -si, -sus·es] 1. A gigantic statue. 2. Any huge person or object.—**Colossus of Rhodes.** A great statue of Apollo destroyed about 224 B.C.

colt (*kohlt*) *n.* 1. A young male horse. 2. A youth.—**colt·ish** *adj.* Frisky.

col·ter (*kol*-ter) *n.* Also **coul·ter.** An iron blade on a plow for cutting the ground.

col·um·bar·y (*kol*-um-buh-ree) *n.* [*pl.* -ies] A dovecot.

Co·lum·bi·a (kuh-*lum*-bee-uh). United States.

Co·lum·bi·an *adj.* Pertaining to the United States or to Christopher Columbus.

col·um·bine (*kol*-um-byne) *n.* 1. Any of several plants of the buttercup family, esp. one bearing showy blue flowers; state flower of Colorado. 2. [*cap.*] A character in old Italian comedy.

co·lum·bi·um (kol-*um*-bee-um) *n.* Also **ni·o·bi·um** (*Symbol:* Nb). A steel-gray metallic element, related to tantalum. (*Symbol:* Cb).

Columbus Day. October 12, the day, in 1492, when Columbus discovered the New World.

col·umn (*kol*-um) *n.* 1. *Architecture.* A solid, upright shaft serving as support. 2. *Military.* A long, narrow formation of troops, ships, etc. 3. *Printing.* A perpendicular series of lines ruled off or spaced from a parallel series. 4. A newspaper or magazine feature appearing regularly under a fixed title. —**col·um·nar** *adj.*—**col·umned** *adj.*

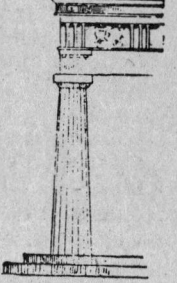

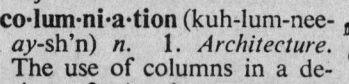

COLUMN (def. 1)

co·lum·ni·a·tion (kuh-lum-nee-*ay*-sh'n) *n.* 1. *Architecture.* The use of columns in a design. 2. A columnar arrangement.

col·um·nist (*kol*-um-nist) *n.* A journalist who writes regularly for a by-lined column.

col·za (*kol*-zuh) *n.* A variety of cabbage whose seeds provide an illuminating oil.

co·ma (*koh*-muh) *n. Medicine.* Deep, prolonged unconsciousness.

co·ma (*koh*-muh) *n.* [*pl.* -co·mae] *Astronomy.* The nebulous envelope about the nucleus of a comet, helping to form the head.—**co·mal** *adj.*

Co·man·che (kuh-*man*-chee) *n.* [*pl.* -ches] One of a tribe of Indians native to northern Texas.

com·a·tose (*kom*-uh-tohs) *adj.* Listless; drowsy; pertaining to a coma.—**com·a·tose·ly** *adv.*

comb (*kohm*) *n.* 1. A small, toothed hair-grooming implement. 2. The red fleshy tuft growing on a fowl's head. 3. The crest of a wave. 4. A honeycomb. 5. Any toothed tool for disentangling fibers.—**comb** *v.*

com·bat (kum-*bat*) *v.* [com·bat·ed, com·bat·ted; com·bat·ing, com·bat·ting] To oppose; fight; battle.—*n.* (*kom*-bat) Fight; struggle; battle. —**com·bat·a·ble** (kum-*bat*-uh-b'l) *adj.*

C

com·ba·tant (*kom*-bat-'nt) *n.* An opponent; one involved in a struggle.—**com·ba·tant** *adj.*

com·ba·tive (kum-*bat*-iv) *adj.* Pugnacious; resisting; belligerent.—**com·ba·tive·ly** *adv.*—**com·ba·tive·ness** (kum-*bat*-iv-nes) *n.*

comb·er (*kohm*-er) *n.* 1. A long, sweeping wave. 2. One who combs or operates a combing machine.

com·bi·na·tion (kom-buh-*nay*-sh'n) *n.* 1. Union; aggregate; merger; a grouping together. 2. *Mathematics.* One of the possible ways in which a series may be grouped without regard to order. 3. The formula for opening certain keyless locks.—**com·bi·na·tion·al** *adj.*

com·bine (kum-*byne*) *v.* [com·bined; com·bin·ing] To unite; merge; coalesce.—**com·bin·a·ble** (kum-*byne*-uh-b'l) *adj.*—**com·bin·er** *n.*

com·bine (*kom*-byne) *n.* 1. A trust; association of similar interests, often with dishonest intent. 2. A machine which harvests and threshes grain in a single operation.

combined operations. A co-ordinated assault, usually amphibious, of land, sea, and air units.

comb·ings (*kohm*-ings) *n. pl.* Fibers, etc., removed by a comb.

com·bus·ti·ble (kom-*bus*-tuh-b'l) *adj.* 1. Capable of burning. 2. Easily aroused to violence; fiery.—*n.* Any inflammable substance.—**com·bus·ti·bil·i·ty** (kum-bus-tuh-*bil*-uh-tee) *n.*

com·bus·tion (kum-*bus*-chun) *n.* 1. Oxidation; burning; any chemical union attended with heat. 2. Great furor or tumult.

come (*kum*) *v.* [came; come; com·ing] 1. To advance nearer; move toward. 2. To arrive at; reach a certain stage. 3. To happen; befall. 4. To result from; appear.

come-at-a·ble (kum-*at*-uh-b'l) *adj. Colloquial.* Capable of being reached or obtained.

come·back *n.* 1. *Colloquial.* Retort; reply. 2. Return to success.

co·me·di·an (kuh-*mee*-dee-un) *n.* A jokester; one who entertains with quips and jests.

co·me·di·enne (kuh-mee-dee-*en*) *n.* [*pl.* -ennes] A comic actress.

come·down *n. Slang.* A drop in prestige or rank.

com·e·dy (*kom*-uh-dee) *n.* [*pl.* -dies] 1. A humorous dramatic production; an amusing play. 2. Wit; humor.

come-hith·er *adj. Colloquial.* Alluring.

come·ly (*kum*-lee) *adj.* [come·li·er; come·li·est] Fair; lovely; handsome.—**come·li·ness** *n.*

com·er (*kum*-'r) *n. Slang.* A newcomer rapidly progressing in the field of creative arts, business, or politics. 'That young actor is a comer.'

co·mes·ti·ble (kuh-*mes*-tuh-b'l) *adj.* Edible; eatable. —*n.* (*pl.*) Food.

com·et (*kom*-et) *n.* A rapidly moving celestial body accompanied by a train of light, appearing at regular intervals.—**com·e·tary** *adj.*

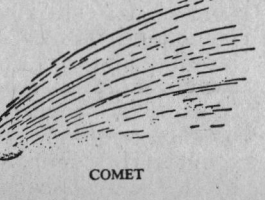

COMET

com·fit (*kum*-fit) *n.* A bonbon; a sweet.

com·fort (*kum*-fert) *v.* To cheer; console; gladden.—*n.* 1. Satisfaction; content; well-being. 2. That which gives satisfaction.

com·fort·a·ble (kum-*fert*-uh-b'l) *adj.* 1. Restful; cozy; contented. 2. Sufficient. 'A comfortable income.'—*n. Colloquial.* A padded quilt.—**com·fort·a·ble·ness** *n.*— **-a·bly** *adv.*

com·fort·er (*kum*-fert-er) *n.* 1. One who consoles. 2. A muffler; scarf. 3. A quilted bedcover.

com·fort·ing (*kum*-fert-ing) *adj.* Consoling; heartening.—**com·fort·ing·ly** *adv.*

com·fort·less *adj.* Without contentment or well-being; desolate; forlorn.

com·ic *adj.* Amusing; funny.—*n.* A comedian.

com·i·cal (*kom*-ih-kul) *adj.* Droll; funny; amusing.—**com·i·cal·i·ty** (kom-ih-*kal*-uh-tee) *n.* —**com·i·cal·ly** *adv.*—**com·i·cal·ness** *n.*

com·ing (*kum*-ing) *adj.* Approaching; advancing; attaining importance.—**com·ing** *n.*

Com·in·tern (kom-in-*turn*) *n.* The Third or Communist International, an organization founded in Moscow in 1919 to promote the world-wide spread of Socialism. It was dissolved in 1943.

com·i·ty (*kom*-uh-tee) *n.* [*pl.* -ties] Courtesy.

com·ma (*kom*-uh) *n. Punctuation.* A mark [,], denoting the shortest pause in reading, and separating a sentence into minor divisions, as in a series of phrases, or in setting off parenthetical elements.

comma bacillus. A curved microscopic organism, believed to be the cause of cholera.

com·mand (kuh-*mand*) *v.* 1. To order; bid; direct. 2. To govern; rule; dominate. 3. To be capable of obtaining. 'This auto commands a high price.'—*n.* 1. Order; injunction. 2. Supreme power; control; mastery. 3. A body of men serving under an officer.

com·man·dant (kom-un-*dant*) *n.* Commander of a post or station.

com·man·deer (kom-un-*deer*) *v.* 1. To take for military purposes. 2. To take by force.

com·man·der (kuh-*man*-der) *n.* 1. A leader; chief; head of a military unit. 2. *Naval.* A rank above that of lieutenant commander and below that of captain.—**com·mand·er·ship** *n.*

commander in chief [*pl.* commanders in chief] 1. The President of the United States. 2. The head of all military or naval forces of a nation. 3. Chief of all military or naval forces in a specific theater of operations.

com·mand·ing *adj.* 1. Governing; exercising supreme authority. 2. Impressive; imposing. 'A commanding appearance.'— **-ing·ly** *adv.*

com·mand·ment *n.* An injunction; a precept, esp. one of the ten precepts [the Decalogue] given by God to Moses.

com·man·do *n.* [*pl.* -dos, -does] A soldier rigorously trained in hand-to-hand combat.

com·mem·o·rate *v.* [-rat·ed; -rat·ing] To celebrate; keep; observe.

com·mem·o·ra·tion (kuh-mem-uh-*ray*-sh'n) *n.*

The act of celebrating by solemn rites.—**com·mem·o·ra·tion·al** *adj.*

com·mem·o·ra·tive (kuh-*mem*-ruh-tiv) *adj.* Memorial.—**com·mem·o·ra·tive·ly** *adv.*

com·mence (kuh-*menss*) *v.* [com·menced; com·menc·ing] To begin; start; originate.—**com·menc·er** *n.*

com·mence·ment (kuh-*menss*-m'nt) *n.* 1. Beginning; start; origin. 2. Graduation day in educational institutions.

com·mend (kuh-*mend*) *v.* 1. To recommend; represent as worthy of confidence. 2. To extol; praise; laud.—**com·mend·a·ble** *adj.*

com·men·da·tion (kom-'n-*day*-sh'n) *n.* Praise; declaration of esteem.

com·mend·a·to·ry (kuh-*mend*-uh-toh-ree) *adj.* Eulogizing; laudatory; praising.

com·men·su·ra·ble (kuh-*men*-shoor-uh-b'l) *adj.* Reducible to a common measure; able to be measured in the same units.—**com·men·su·ra·bil·i·ty** *n.*—**com·men·su·ra·bly** *adv.*

com·men·su·rate (kuh-*men*-shoor-ayt) *v.* [-rat·ed, -rat·ing] To reduce to the same measure. —*adj.* (kuh-*men*-shoor-it) 1. Reducible to the same unit of measurement. 2. Adequate; sufficient. 'A salary commensurate with his needs.'—**com·men·su·rate·ly** *adv.*—**com·men·su·ra·tion** *n.*

com·ment (*kom*-ent) *n.* A remark; observation; note.—*v.* To remark; criticize.

com·men·tar·y (*kom*-'n-tair-ee) *n.* [*pl.* -ies] 1. A series of annotations, footnotes, or comments explaining a writing or a difficult passage. 2. An historical narrative. 3. *Motion Pictures.* A spoken narrative accompanying a film.

com·men·ta·tor (*kom*-'n-*tay*-ter) *n.* 1. *Radio.* A speaker who regularly discusses topical questions. 2. Any writer or speaker who comments on affairs of the day.

com·merce *n.* 1. Trade; interchange of merchandise. 2. Sexual intercourse.

com·mer·cial (kuh-*mer*-sh'l) *adj.* Pertaining to trade.—*n. Radio.* An advertisement for the program sponsor's product.— -**cial·ly** *adv.*

com·mer·cial·ism *n.* The methods and practices of modern business—often used in derogation, as indicating a debasement of business ethics.

com·mer·cial·ize *v.* [com·mer·cial·ized; com·mer·cial·iz·ing] 1. To distribute or promote a commodity solely for financial gain. 2. To lower or cheapen artistic standards for greater profits.—**com·mer·cial·i·za·tion** *n.*

com·mi·na·tion (kom-ih-*nay*-sh'n) *n.* Threat; denunciation.—**com·min·a·to·ry** (kuh-*min*-uh-tor-ee) *adj.*

com·min·gle (kuh-*ming*-'l) *v.* [com·min·gled; com·min·gling] To mix together; blend.

com·mi·nute (*kom*-ih-nyoot) *v.* [com·mi·nut·ed; com·mi·nut·ing] To pulverize; reduce to tiny particles.—**com·mi·nu·tion** *n.*

com·mis·er·ate (kuh-*miz*-uh-rayt) *v.* [com·mis·er·at·ed; com·mis·er·at·ing] To sympathize with; pity; feel for.—**com·mis·er·a·ble** *adj.*

com·mis·er·a·tion *n.* Condolence; sympathy; compassion.—**com·mis·er·a·tive** *adj.*

com·mis·sar (*kom*-ih-sar) *n.* 1. Formerly in Soviet Union: **a.** A political officer attached to a military unit. **b.** A government official in charge of one sector of the nation's activities; a minister. 2. Any commissioner, esp. in Germany and Russia.—**com·mis·sar·i·al** *adj.*

com·mis·sar·i·at (kom-ih-*sair*-ee-ut) *n.* 1. Ministry; government department headed by a commissar. 2. An army's supply department.

com·mis·sar·y (*kom*-ih-sair-ee) *n.* [*pl.* -ies] 1. A deputy; subordinate official. 2. A store selling food and supplies, esp. in an army camp. 3. *Military.* An army supply officer.

com·mis·sion (kuh-*mish*-'n) *n.* 1. Act of committing; perpetration. 2. Warrant; authorization. 3. A group of persons authorized to carry out a certain function. 4. Payment based on a percentage of the business transacted. 5. *Military & Naval.* Written order conferring rank.—*v.* 1. To empower; appoint; authorize. 2. Place in service, as a ship.

com·mis·sion·aire (kuh-mih-sh'n-*air*) *n.* An attendant entrusted with petty commissions.

com·mis·sion·er *n.* 1. Member of a commission; a person authorized to perform some task. 2. An official in charge of a government department.—**com·mis·sion·er·ship** *n.*

com·mit (kuh-*mit*) *v.* [com·mit·ted; com·mit·ting] 1. To entrust; consign. 2. To obligate; pledge. 3. To imprison; confine. 4. To do; esp. something wrong; perpetrate.

com·mit·ment (kuh-*mit*-m'nt) *n.* 1. Act of committing or condition of being committed; imprisonment. 2. A written order for imprisonment or confinement. 3. Obligation; pledge.—**com·mit·tal** *n.*

com·mit·tee (kuh-*mit*-ee) *n.* A group of persons elected or appointed to act upon certain measures or business.

com·mit·tee·man, com·mit·tee·wom·an *n.* Member of a committee.

com·mode (kuh-*mohd*) *n.* A chest of drawers, often with a cupboard below.

com·mo·di·ous (kuh-*mohd*-ee-us) *adj.* 1. Spacious; roomy. 2. Convenient; comfortable. —**com·mo·di·ous·ly** *adv.*—**com·mo·di·ous·ness** *n.*

com·mod·i·ty (kuh-*mod*-ih-tee) *n.* [*pl.* -ties] 1. An article of merchandise. 2. Article holding economic usefulness.

com·mo·dore (*kom*-uh-dohr) *n.* 1. *Naval.* A commissioned officer ranking between captain and rear admiral. 2. The president of a yachting club.

com·mon (*kom*-'n) *adj.* 1. Belonging or pertaining equally to all; universal; general; public. 2. Ordinary; usual; familiar. 3. Vulgar; coarse; inferior,—*n.* Land belonging to the community.—**in common.** Shared.—**com·mon·ly** *adv.*—**com·mon·ness** *n.*

com·mon·al·ty (*kom*-mon-ul-tee) *n.* [*pl.* -ties] 1. The common people. 2. Membership of a corporation.

com·mon·er (*kom*-mon-er) *n.* A person not of the nobility.

common law. Law whose binding force is based on long usage and universal acceptance; unwritten law.—**com·mon-law** *adj.*

common-law marriage. *Law.* A marital relation entered into without formal civil or ecclesiastical sanction.

com·mon·place (*kom*-m'n-playss) *n.* 1. A common occurrence or object. 2. A platitude; trite saying.—*adj.* Trite; common; usual.

com·mons (*kom*-'ns) *n. pl.* 1. The common people. 2. [*cap.*] The House of Commons, lower house of the British Parliament. 3. Large common dining hall, esp. in a school. 4. Food; rations.

common school. A public grade school.

common sense. Sound judgment; good sense. —**com·mon-sense** *adj.*

com·mon·weal (*kom*-'n-weel) *n.* The public welfare.

com·mon·wealth (*kom*-'n-welth) *n.* 1. The public; body of people constituting a state; hence, the state itself. 2. [*cap.*] The English government under the Cromwells, 1649–1660.

com·mo·tion (kuh-*moh*-sh'n) *n.* Agitation; violent disturbance; tumult.

com·mu·nal (*kom*-yoo-n'l) *adj.* Pertaining to a community; public.—**com·mu·nal·ly** *adv.*

com·mu·nal·ism (*kom*-yoo-nul-ism) *n.* Theory or system of government by communes.—**com·mu·nal·ist** *n.*—**com·mu·nal·ist·ic** *adj.*

com·mune (kum-*yoon*) *v.* [com·muned; com·mun·ing] 1. To converse privately; confer. 2. To receive the sacrament of Communion.

com·mune (*kom*-yoon) *n.* 1. The smallest French administrative unit. 2. Any local, self-governing community.

com·mu·ni·ca·ble (kuh-*myoo*-nih-kuh-b'l) *adj.* Capable of being communicated.—**com·mu·ni·ca·bil·i·ty** *n.*—**com·mu·ni·ca·ble·ness** *n.*

com·mu·ni·cant (kuh-*myoo*-nih-k'nt) *n.* 1. One who communicates. 2. Participant in Holy Communion.—**com·mu·ni·cant** *adj.*

com·mu·ni·cate (kuh-*myoo*-nih-kayt) *v.* [-cated; -cat·ing] 1. To impart; disclose; reveal. 2. To engage in communication.— -ca·tor *n.*

com·mu·ni·ca·tion (kuh-myoo-nih-*kay*-sh'n) *n.* 1. The act of communicating. 2. Exchange of thoughts, information, etc., by conversation or writing. 3. A message; news. 4. A means of communication; connection. 5. [*pl.*] System, as by telephone, for communicating.

com·mu·ni·ca·tive (kuh-*myoo*-nuh-kay-tiv) *adj.* Talkative; articulate; not reserved.—**com·mu·ni·ca·tive·ly** *adv.*—**com·mu·ni·ca·tive·ness** *n.*

com·mun·i·on (kuh-*myoon*-yun) *n.* 1. Intercourse; intimate conversation. 2. Act of sharing or holding in common. 3. [*cap.*] The sacrament of the Eucharist, celebration of the Lord's Supper.

com·mu·ni·qué (kuh-myoo-nih-*kay*) *n.* [*pl.* -qués] Official report; news bulletin.

com·mu·nism (*kom*-yoo-nism) *n.* 1. A classless system of society in which the community or government owns the means of production and aims at an equitable distribution of wealth. 2. Loosely, the system of government practiced in U.S.S.R. today.

com·mu·nist (*kom*-yoo-nist) *n.* 1. A believer in communism. 2. [*cap.*] A member of the Communist party.—**com·mu·nist** *adj.*—**com·mu·nist·ic, -nist·i·cal** *adj.*— -i·cal·ly *adv.*

Communist party. 1. A working-class party whose program is based on Marxist principles and whose ultimate aim is the establishment of communism. 2. The political party controlling the government in the U.S.S.R.

com·mu·ni·ty (kuh-*myoo*-nih-tee) *n.* [*pl.* -ties] 1. Common possession. 2. A body of people living in a certain area and having common rights, responsibilities, and interests. 3. A group of plants or animals living together. 4. The public; people in general.

com·mu·ta·tion (*kom*-yoo-tay-sh'n) *n.* 1. Substitution; change; esp. the reduction or softening of an obligation or punishment. 2. Act of traveling back and forth on a commutation ticket.—**commutation ticket.** Transportation ticket sold at a reduced rate for a certain number of trips.

com·mu·ta·tor (*kom*-yoo-tay-ter) *n.* 1. *Electricity.* A device on an armature to reverse the direction of a current.—**com·mu·tate** *v.*

com·mute (kuh-*myoot*) *v.* [com·mut·ed; com·mut·ing] 1. To lessen the severity of, as a punishment. 2. To travel, esp. to and from a city, using a commutation ticket.— -mut·er *n.*

com·pact (kum-*pakt*) *adj.* 1. Close; dense; firmly consolidated. 2. Concise; brief.—*v.* To consolidate; unite firmly.—**com·pact·ly** *adv.*

com·pact (*kom*-pakt) *n.* 1. Agreement; contract; treaty. 2. A small case carried in a woman's handbag for face powder.

com·pan·ion (kum-*pan*-yun) *n.* 1. A friend; comrade; escort. 2. One of a pair; mate.—*v.* To accompany.—**com·pan·ion·less** *adj.*

com·pan·ion·a·ble *adj.* Friendly; sociable; amiable.—**com·pan·ion·a·bil·i·ty, com·pan·ion·a·ble·ness** *n.*—**com·pan·ion·a·bly** *adv.*

com·pan·ion·ate *adj.* Pertaining to or like companions.

com·pan·ion·ship *n.* Fellowship; friendship; association.

com·pan·ion·way *n. Nautical.* The staircase from the deck to a cabin below.

com·pa·ny (*kum*-puh-nee) *n.* [*pl.* -nies] 1. Fellowship, society; companionship. 2. A group of people joined in a common purpose, as for carrying on a business. 3. *Colloquial.* Guests; visitors. 4. *Military.* An infantry unit normally commanded by a captain.

company union. An employees' union which is under the control of the company's management and not affiliated with a trade union.

com·pa·ra·ble (*kom*-p'r-uh-b'l) *adj.* Analogous; capable of being compared.—**com·pa·ra·ble·ness** *n.*—**com·pa·ra·bly** *adv.*

com·par·a·tive (kum-*pair*-uh-tiv) *adj.* 1. Pertaining to or measured by comparison; not absolute. 2. *Grammar.* Expressing an increased degree.—*n.* The comparative form of an adjective.—**com·par·a·tive·ly** *adv.*

com·pare (kum-*pair*) *v.* [com·pared; com·par·ing] 1. To bring together and study, as two objects, in order to ascertain their similarities or differences. 2. To liken; consider as similar.—**com·pare** *n.*

com·par·i·son (kum-*pair*-ih-s'n) *n.* 1. The act of comparing. 2. *Grammar.* The change or modification of an adjective to show degree.

com·part·ment (kum-*pahrt*-m'nt) *n.* Division of an enclosed space or structure.

com·pass (*kum*-pus) *n.* 1. An instrument which indicates direction, usually by a magnetic needle pointing north. 2. A mechanical drawing instrument for describing circles, measuring, etc. 3. Limits; boundary; reach. —*v.* 1. To extend around; embrace; surround. 2. To plot or scheme.

COMPASS CARD

compass card. The dial on which the points of a compass are indicated.

com·pas·sion (kum-*pash*-'n) *n.* Pity; sympathy commiseration.—**com·pas·sion·ate** *adj.*—**com·pas·sion·ate·ly** *adv.*—**com·pas·sion·ate·ness** *n.*

com·pat·i·ble (kum-*pat*-uh-b'l) *adj.* Agreeable; congruous; existing together harmoniously. —**com·pat·i·bil·i·ty** (kum-pat-uh-*bil*-uh-tee).

com·pa·tri·ot (kum-*payt*-ree-ut) *n.* One of the same country.—**com·pa·tri·ot** *adj.*

com·peer (kum-*peer*) *n.* Companion; equal.

com·pel (kum-*pel*) *v.* [com·pelled; com·pel·ling] 1. To oblige; force; constrain. 2. To exact by force.—**com·pel·la·ble** (kum-*pel*-uh-b'l) *adj.* —**com·pel·ler** *n.*

com·pel·la·tion (kom-puh-*lay*-sh'n) *n.* Act of addressing or calling by a name; designation.

com·pen·di·ous (kum-*pen*-dee-us) *adj.* Abridged; condensed.—**com·pen·di·ous·ly** *adv.*

com·pen·di·um (kum-*pen*-dee-um) *n.* [*pl.* -di·ums, -di·a] A summary; abridgment.

com·pen·sate (*kom*-p'n-sayt) *v.* [com·pen·sat·ed; -sat·ing] 1. To recompense; give equal value to. 2. To make up for; counterbalance. —**com·pen·sa·ble** (kum-*pen*-suh-b'l) *adj.*—**com·pen·sa·tive, com·pen·sa·to·ry** *adj.*

com·pen·sa·tion *n.* 1. Act or instance of compensating. 2. Recompense; pay; equal return. 3. *Physiology.* Over-functioning, as of an organ, to make up for deficiency in another organ or another part of the same organ.

com·pete (kum-*peet*) *v.* [com·pet·ed; com·pet·ing] To vie; contend; rival.

com·pe·tence (*kom*-pih-t'ns) *n.* Also **com·pe·ten·cy.** 1. Ability; proficiency. 2. Means; sufficiency. 3. *Law.* Legal capacity, qualification, or authority.—**com·pe·tent** *adj.*

com·pe·ti·tion (kom-pih-*tish*-un) *n.* 1. Mutual striving for the same object; rivalry. 2. A contest; trial. 3. *Economics.* Condition existing when two or more enterprises actively contend for the same market.—**com·pet·i·to·ry** (kum-*pet*-ih-tor-ee) *adj.*

com·pet·i·tive (kum-*pet*-ih-tiv) *adj.* Relating to, caused by, or based on competition.—**com·pet·i·tive·ly** *adv.*—**com·pet·i·tive·ness** *n.*

com·pet·i·tor (kum-*pet*-ih-ter) *n.* 1. A rival; opponent. 2. One of two or more business men buying or selling the same goods or service in an open market.

com·pile (kum-*pyle*) *v.* [com·piled; com·pil·ing] 1. To collect; amass. 2. To organize materials from many sources into one presentation. —**com·pi·la·tion** (kom-pih-*lay*-shun) *n.*—**com·pil·er** *n.*

com·pla·cence (kum-*play*-s'ns) *n.* Also **com·pla·cen·cy.** 1. Self-satisfaction; smugness. 2. Gratification; satisfaction.—**com·pla·cent** *adj.*—**com·pla·cent·ly** *adv.*

com·plain (kum-*playn*) *v.* 1. To find fault; whine; murmur. 2. To lodge a charge or accusation. 3. To report. 'Patient complains of a headache.'— **-plain·er** *n.*— **-ing·ly** *adv.*

com·plain·ant (kum-*play*-n'nt) *n.* 1. A complainer. 2. *Law.* A plaintiff; one who institutes a lawsuit.

com·plaint (kum-*playnt*) *n.* 1. Expression of hurt, sickness, resentment, etc. 2. Ailment; minor illness. 3. *Law.* The plaintiff's statement of charges. 4. A grievance; objection.

com·plai·sant (kom-*play*-s'nt) *adj.* Amiable; obliging; genial.—**com·plai·sance** *n.*—**com·plai·sant·ly** *adv.*

com·ple·ment (*kom*-plih-m'nt) *n.* 1. Full quantity, set, crew, etc. 2. What is necessary to complete or supplement. 3. *Geometry.* An angle which added to another equals ninety degrees. 4. An antitoxin substance in the blood which combats bacteria. 5. An interval which added to a given interval completes an octave.—**com·ple·ment** *v.*—**com·ple·ment·al** (kom-plih-*ment*-'l) *adj.*—**com·ple·men·ta·ry** *adj.*

C

complete (kum-*pleet*) *adj.* 1. Thorough; painstaking. 2. Full; total; entire; perfect. 3. Brought to fruition or conclusion.—*v.* [com·plet·ed; com·plet·ing]—**com·plete·ly** *adv.*

com·ple·tion (kum-*plee*-shun) *n.* Fruition; fulfillment; termination; perfection.—**com·ple·tive** (kum-*plee*-tiv) *adj.*

com·plex (kom-*pleks*) *adj.* 1. Complicated; intricate; not simple. 2. Composed of many elements.—**com·plex·i·ty** *n.* [*pl.* -ties] Intricacy.—**com·plex·ly** *adv.*—**com·plex·ness** *n.*

com·plex (*kom*-pleks) *n.* 1. *Psychology.* An emotionally colored idea or idea pattern that has been repressed. 2. A complicated system of integral parts.

complex fraction. A fraction having a fractional quantity in its numerator, denominator, or both.

com·plex·ion (kum-*plek*-shun) *n.* 1. The color or hue of the face. 2. General appearance; aspect. 3. Temperament; disposition.

complex sentence. *Grammar.* A sentence containing one independent clause and one or more subordinate clauses.

com·pli·a·ble (k'm-*ply*-uh-b'l) *adj.* 1. Pliant; flexible; capable of being bent. 2. Acquiescent; yielding; willing to agree.—**com·pli·a·ble·ness** *n.*—**com·pli·a·bly** *adv.*

com·pli·ance (k'm-*ply*-'ns) *n.* Also **com·pli·an·cy.** 1. Concession; acquiescence; readiness to agree or oblige. 2. Submission; willingness to obey.—**com·pli·ant** *adj.*—**com·pli·ant·ly** *adv.*

com·pli·cate (*kom*-plih-kayt) *v.* [com·pli·cat·ed; -cat·ing] To involve; entangle; make intricate or formidable.

com·pli·cat·ed *adj.* 1. Complex; involved; intricate. 2. Confusing; difficult to understand.—**com·pli·cat·ed·ly** *adv.*—**-ed·ness** *n.*

com·pli·ca·tion (kom-pluh-*kay*-sh'n) *n.* 1. Entanglement; complexity. 2. Impediment; obstacle; hindrance. 3. *Pathology.* A condition or disease further aggravating an illness.

com·plic·i·ty (k'm-*plis*-ih-tee) *n.* [*pl.* -ties] Participation, esp. in crime; abetment.

com·pli·ment (*kom*-plih-m'nt) *n.* 1. A commending; praising; flattering. 2. [*pl.*] Best wishes; friendly greeting.—*v.* To praise.

com·pli·men·ta·ry (kom-plih-*men*-ter-ee) *adj.* 1. Praising; laudatory; expressing esteem. 2. Bestowed for advertising purposes. 'A complimentary ticket.'—**com·pli·men·ta·ri·ly** *adv.*

com·plot (*kom*-plot) *n.* A conspiracy; scheme; plot.—*v.* (kom-*plot*) [com·plot·ted; com·plot·ting]—**com·plot·ter** *n.*

com·ply *v.* [com·plied; com·ply·ing] To yield; acquiesce; do as directed.—**com·pli·er** *n.*

com·po·nent (k'm-*poh*-n'nt) *adj.* Composing; constituting; integral.—*n.* 1. A factor; a constituent. 2. One of the elements into which any force, emotion, quality, etc., may be analyzed or resolved.

com·port (k'm-*port*) *v.* 1. To behave; conduct. 2. To suit; accord; fit.—**com·port·ment** *n.*

com·pose (k'm-*pohz*) *v.* [com·posed; com·pos-

ing] 1. To make; fashion; put together. 2. To write; create; be the author of. 3. To make up; constitute; comprise. 4. *Printing.* To prepare type for printing. 5. To calm; allay agitation. 6. *Music.* To write music.

com·posed *adj.* 1. Calm; tranquil; unagitated. 2. Poised; self-possessed; cool.—**com·pos·ed·ly** *adv.*—**com·pos·ed·ness** *n.*

com·pos·er (k'm-*poh*-zer) *n.* An author of music or literature, esp. the former.

composing stick. *Printing.* A small adjustable tray for setting lines of type.

com·pos·ite (k'm-*poz*-it) *adj.* 1. Compounded; formed of distinct units. 2. Denoting a flower compounded of densely packed smaller flowers. 3. *Architecture.* Describing a pillar having Corinthian, Ionic, and often other elements.—**com·pos·ite** *n.*—**com·pos·ite·ly** *adv.*

com·po·si·tion (kom-poh-*zih*-sh'n) *n.* 1. Arrangement; structure; disposition. 2. A mixture; material containing separate ingredients. 3. A musical, literary, or artistic creation. 4. *Pedagogy.* An assigned exercise in the art of writing. 5. *Printing.* Typesetting. 6. Synthesis; bringing together of parts. 7. Settlement of a dispute. 8. Make-up of a substance or structure.—*adj.* 1. Synthetic, as composition leather, etc. 2. Made with an alloy. 'Composition metal.'

com·pos·i·tor (kum-*poz*-ih-ter) *n. Printing.* A typesetter; one who directs composition of matter to be printed.

compos mentis. *Law.* Sound of mind; competent; responsible.

com·post (*kom*-pohst) *n.* A fertilizer of manure and various other soil enrichers.

com·pos·ure (k'm-*poh*-zher) *n.* Freedom from agitation; poise; equanimity; serenity.

com·pote (*kom*-poht) *n.* Fruit stewed in syrup.

com·pound (*kom*-pownd) *adj.* 1. Composed of two or more parts. 2. *Electricity.* Denoting a field excited by a series winding as well as shunt or parallel winding.—*n.* 1. A combination; mixture; substance formed by chemical reactants in definite proportions. 2. A word formed of two or more words.—*v.* (kom-*pownd*) 1. To mix; combine. 2. To resolve, as a dispute; compromise. 3. *Banking.* To add an accruing interest to a principal, which in turn draws interest. 4. *Law.* To fail to prosecute an offense for a consideration, as to compound a felony.—**com·pound·er** *n.*

compound fracture. The breaking of a bone so that it pierces the skin.

compound interest. Interest accruing from interest plus principal, rather than from principal alone.

compound number. A quantity containing both whole and fractional numbers.

compound sentence. A sentence composed of two or more independent clauses.

com·pre·hend (kom-pree-*hend*) *v.* 1. To understand; grasp; perceive. 2. To embrace; comprise; contain.—**com·pre·hend·i·ble** *adj.*

com·pre·hen·si·ble *adj.* Admitting of comprehension; understandable.—**com·pre·hen·si·bil·i·ty** (kom-pree-hen-suh-*bil*-uh-tee) *n.*—**com·pre·hen·si·bly** (kom-pree-*hen*-suh-blee) *adv.*

com·pre·hen·sion (kom-pree-*hen*-sh'n) *n.* 1. Understanding; perception; mental capacity. 2. *Logic.* All the attributes essential to the perception of an object or a concept. 3. Inclusiveness; an encompassing.

com·pre·hen·sive *adj.* 1. All-embracing; wide in scope; inclusive. 2. Understanding much; having broad intellectual grasp.—**com·pre·hen·sive·ly** *adv.*—**com·pre·hen·sive·ness** *n.*

com·press (*kom*-press) *n.* A cloth or pad used as a bandage or for bringing pressure, heat, cold, etc., to a part of the body.

com·press (k'm-*press*) *v.* 1. To condense; force into a smaller area. 2. To summarize; make brief. 3. To thrust or squeeze together; distort. 'Lips compressed in anger.'—**com·press·i·ble** *adj.*—**com·press·i·bil·i·ty** *n.*

com·press·ion (k'm-*presh*-un) *n.* 1. Condensation; reduction of volume of a substance by pressure. 2. *Mechanics.* Condensation of a gas by a piston prior to combustion or expansion.—**com·pres·sion** *adj.*

com·pres·sor *n.* 1. *Anatomy.* A muscle that contracts so as to compress an organ. 2. An instrument for compressing a blood vessel. 3. A machine for compressing gases.

com·prise (k'm-*pryze*) *v.* [com·prised; com·pris·ing]. Also **com·prize.** To embrace; embody; include; be composed of.—**com·pris·al, com·priz·al** *n.* An embodiment; summary.

com·pro·mise (*kom*-proh-myze) *n.* 1. Adjustment of a controversy by reciprocal concession. 2. An agreement to refer a controversy to an arbitrator. 3. A partial sacrifice, as of principles, desires, etc.—*v.* [com·pro·mised; com·pro·mis·ing] 1. To resolve a conflict by reciprocal concessions. 2. To jeopardize; put to risk, as one's reputation.— -mis·er *n.*

comp·tom·e·ter *n.* Trade name of a rapid-calculation machine.

comp·trol·ler (k'n-*trohl*-er) *n.* An account overseer; an official who checks on expenditures. —**comp·trol·ler·ship** *n.*

com·pul·sion (k'm-*pul*-sh'n) *n.* 1. Coercion; application of force. 2. A necessity; urge; strong or irrational desire.—**com·pul·sive** *adj.*

com·pul·so·ry *adj.* 1. Compelling; overcoming resistance. 2. Obligatory; prescribed; forced upon.—**com·pul·so·ri·ly** *adv.*

com·punc·tion (k'm-*punk*-sh'n) *n.* Contrition; remorse; uneasiness of conscience.

com·pu·ta·tion (kom-pyoo-*tay*-sh'n) *n.* 1. Reckoning; calculation; estimation. 2. A sum; an ascertained amount.

com·pute (k'm-*pyoot*) *v.* [com·put·ed; com·put·ing] To calculate; estimate; determine, as a sum.—**com·put·a·ble** *adj.*—**com·put·a·bil·i·ty** *n.*—**com·put·er, com·put·ist** *n.*

com·rade (*kom*-rad) *n.* 1. A close companion; friend. 2. An associate. 3. A Communist's designation of a fellow member of his party;

hence, a Communist.—**comrade·ship, com·rade·ry** *n.* Fellowship; intimacy.

Com·ti·an (*kom*-tee-un) *adj.* Denoting Auguste Comte (1789–1857) or his philosophy of Positivism.—**Comt·ism** *n.*—**Comt·ist** *n.* & *adj.*

Co·mus (*koh*-mus) *n.* [*cap.*] 1. *Classical Mythology.* God of festivity and mirth. 2 One given to revelry. 3. A masque or poetic drama by Milton.

con *v.* [conned; con·ning] To memorize; study.

con *adv.* Opposed to; against; negatively.—*n.* The negative side, voter, argument, etc.

con *adj. Slang.* Relating to a confidence game; swindling. 'A con man.'

co·na·tion (koh-*nay*-sh'n) *n. Psychology.* The will or power to act or expend effort.—**con·a·tive** (*kon*-uh-tiv) *adj.*

con·cat·e·na·tion (k'n-kat-uh-*nay*-sh'n) *n.* 1. A related series; chain; configuration. 2. Interdependence; interrelationship.—**con·cat·e·nate** (k'n-*kat*-uh-nayt) *adj.*—*v.* [-nat·ed; -nat·ing].

con·cave (kon-*kayv*) *adj.* Hollowed out; arched or curved inward.—*v.* [con·caved; con·cav·ing]—*n.* (*kon*-kayv) A hollow; cavity.—**con·cave·ly** (kon-*kayv*-lee) *adv.*—**con·cave·ness** *n.*

con·cav·i·ty (k'n-*kav*-uh-tee) *n.* [*pl.* -ties] Hollowness; internal surface of a hollow, spherical body

con·ca·vo·con·vex (kon-*kay*-voh-kon-*veks*) *adj.* Presenting an incurve on one side and a convexity CONCAVE on the other.

con·ceal (k'n-*seel*) *v.* 1. To hide; secrete; keep from knowledge. 2. To disguise; cover; cloak.—**con·ceal·a·ble** *adj.*—**con·ceal·ment** *n.*

con·cede (k'n-*seed*) *v.* [con·ced·ed; con·ced·ing] 1. To surrender; yield. 2. To permit; allow; give. 3. To admit; let pass undisputed; acknowledge defeat in.—**con·ced·er** *n.*

con·ceit (k'n-*seet*) *n.* 1. Vanity; egotism. 2. A trifling or inane thought pompously expressed. 3. A clever phrasing or expression; quip. 4. A fantastic or eccentric notion.

con·ceit·ed *adj.* 1. Egotistical; vain; self-important. 2. Expressed in flowery language. —**con·ceit·ed·ly** *adv.*—**con·ceit·ed·ness** *n.*

con·ceiv·a·ble (k'n-*seev*-uh-b'l) *adj.* 1. Imaginable; possible; plausible. 2. Understandable; intelligible.—**con·ceiv·a·bil·i·ty** (k'n-seev-uh-*bil*-uh-tee), -a·ble·ness *n.*— -a·bly *adv.*

con·ceive *v.* [con·ceived; con·ceiv·ing] 1. To think; imagine; suppose possible. 2. To comprehend; understand. 3. To devise; form in the mind, as a plan. 4. To become pregnant. 5. To hold an opinion.—**con·ceiv·er** *n.*

con·cen·trate (*kon*-sen-trayt) *v.* [con·cen·trat·ed; -trat·ing] 1. To bring to a small area; compress. 2. To intensify; increase the strength of, as chemical solutions. 3. To focus on one point; think or study intensively. 4. To specialize in a subject or field of endeavor.—*n.* A substance purified or intensified. —**con·cen·tra·tion** (kon-sen-*tray*-sh'n) *n.*

concentration camp. A prison camp, esp. one for political prisoners.

con·cen·tric (k'n-*sent*-rik) *adj.* Also **con·cen·tri·cal.** 1. Sharing a common center. 'Concentric circles.' 2. Having the center line exactly at right angles to a machined surface; having the center precisely located with respect to a circumference. —**con·cen·tri·cal·ly** *adv.* In a common center.—**con·cen·tri·ci·ty** (kon-s'n-*tris*-uh-tee) *n.*

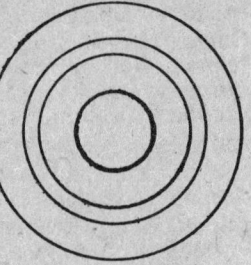

CONCENTRIC CIRCLES

con·cept (*kon*-sept) *n.* 1. A notion; belief; thought. 2. An idea or group of perceptions. 3. An abstract thought or phenomenon grasped by the mind.

con·cep·tion (kun-*sep*-sh'n) *n.* 1. Act or power of conceiving. 2. The state of being conceived; beginning of pregnancy. 3. Idea; mental impression.—**con·cep·tion·al** *adj.*

con·cep·tu·al (kun-*sep*-choo-ul) *adj.* 1. Relating to the process of conception. 2. Conceived by the mind.—**con·cep·tu·al·ly** *adv.*

con·cern (kun-*sern*) *v.* 1. To affect; be of importance to. 2. To disturb; interest.—*n.* 1. Business; affair; interest. 'Peace is the concern of all mankind.' 2. Solicitude; care; anxiety. 'This concern for the poor.' 3. A commercial establishment.—**con·cerned** *adj.*

con·cern·ing *prep.* Regarding; relating to.

con·cern·ment *n.* 1. Importance; moment. 2. Solicitude; worry. 3. Reference; relation.

con·cert (*kon*-sert) *n.* 1. Accord; harmony; mutual agreement. 2. A musical program presented by several instruments, voices, or both.—**con·cert** *adj.*—*v.* To plan by conferring.

con·cert·ed (kun-*ser*-tid) *adj.* Mutually devised or executed; combined.—**con·cert·ed·ly** *adv.*

con·cer·ti·na (kon-ser-*tee*-nuh) *n.* A small musical instrument played like the accordion.

con·cert·mas·ter *n.* Assistant to the conductor of an orchestra, usually the first violinist.

CONCERTINA

con·cer·to (kun-*chehr*-toh) *n.* [*pl.* -tos] A musical composition for one or more principal instruments with a full orchestra.

con·ces·sion (kun-*sesh*-un) *n.* 1. A government or commercial grant, as of land, privileges, rights, etc. 2. Act of granting or yielding. 3. That which is conceded; admission; acknowledgment.—**con·ces·sion·a·ry** *adj.* Pertaining to a concession.—*n.* [*pl.* -aries] A concessionaire.

con·ces·sion·aire (kun-sesh-uh-*nehr*) *n.* A grantee; receiver of a concession.

conch (*konk, konch*) *n.* [*pl.* conchs (*konks*), conches (*kon*-chuz)] The large spiral shell of certain marine mollusks.

con·chol·o·gy (kon-*kol*-uh-jee) *n.* The study of shells or mollusks. —**con·chol·o·gist** *n.*

CONCH (1/8 life size)

con·ci·erge (kon-see-*erzh*) *n.* A janitor; doorkeeper.

con·cil·i·ate (kun-*sil*-ee-ayt) *v.* [-at·ed; -at·ing] 1. To reconcile; bring together, as disputants. 2. To appease by friendly acts; pacify; win over.—**con·cil·i·a·ble** *adj.*—**con·cil·i·a·tive** *adj.*

con·cil·i·a·tion (kun-sil-ee-*ay*-sh'n) *n.* 1. Act or process of conciliating. 2. Settlement of labor disputes by mutual agreement through the mediation of a court-appointed conciliator.—**con·cil·i·a·tor** *n.*

con·cil·i·a·to·ry (kun-*sil*-ee-uh-toh-ree, -taw-ree) *adj.* Calculated to conciliate or win over. —**con·cil·i·a·to·ri·ly** *adv.*— -to·ri·ness *n.*

con·cise (kun-*syse*) *adj.* Brief; succinct; employing as few words as possible.—**con·cise·ly** *adv.*—**con·cise·ness** *n.*

con·clave (*kon*-klayv) *n.* 1. A private meeting; secret assembly. 2. *Roman Catholic Church.* The meeting of cardinals for the election of a pope. 3. The special apartment reserved for this assembly.

con·clude (kun-*klood*) *v.* [con·clud·ed; con·clud·ing] 1. To infer; deduce by reasoning; decide. 2. To terminate; finish; bring to an end. 3. To settle; effect. 'To conclude a peace.'

con·clu·sion *n.* 1. The end; close; termination. 2. A decision; inference; deduction. 3. Outcome; final result. 4. Settlement.

con·clu·sive *adj.* Final; convincing; satisfactory.—**con·clu·sive·ly** *adv.* Decisively.

con·coct (kon-*kokt*, kun-*kokt*), *v.* To devise; prepare; invent, as a story, dish, etc.

con·coc·tion (kon-*kok*-sh'n) *n.* 1. A preparation containing various ingredients. 2. A plan; scheme. 3. Act of concocting.

con·com·i·tant (kon-*kom*-uh-t'nt) *adj.* Accompanying; concurrent; attending.—*n.* An accompanying factor or circumstance.—**con·com·i·tance, -tan·cy** *n.*—**con·com·i·tant·ly** *adv.*

con·cord (*kon*-kawrd) *n.* 1. Harmony; accord; agreement. 2. *Music.* Harmonious combination of sounds. 3. An agreement; treaty.

con·cord (*kon*-kerd) *n.* A large, sweet blue grape.

con·cord·ance (kon-*kawrd*-n's) *n.* 1. Agreement; accord. 2. A glossary; index.

con·cor·dant (kon-*kawrd*-n't) *adj.* Agreeing; harmonious.—**con·cor·dant·ly** *adv.*

con·cor·dat (kon-*kawr*-dat) *n.* 1. An agreement; compact. 2. An agreement between the papacy and a government determining ecclesiastical powers.

con·course (*kon*-kawrs) *n.* 1. A confluence; meeting; coming together. 2. An assemblage; throng; crowd. 3. A junction; place where several roads meet; boulevard.

con·crete (kon-*kreet*) *adj.* 1. Solid; forming a mass. 2. Tangible; real; existing in nature. 3. Particular; specific. 4. (*kon*-kreet) Made of concrete.—**con·crete·ly** *adv.*

con·crete (*kon*-kreet) *n.* 1. A mixture of gravel, sand, cement, and water for paving roads, etc. 2. A solid mass; a term; tangible object.—*v.* [con·cret·ed; con·cret·ing] 1. (kon-*kreet*) 1. To solidify; combine into a mass. 2. (*kon*-kreet) To cover with concrete.

con·cre·tion (kon-*kree*-sh'n) *n.* 1. Act or state of concreting; solidifying. 2. Solidified formation or mass.—**con·cre·tion·ar·y** *adj.*—**con·cre·tive** *adj.*—**con·cre·tive·ly** *adv.*

con·cu·bin·age (kon-*kyoo*-bin-ij) *n.* 1. Common-law marriage. 2. The state of being a concubine.

con·cu·bi·nar·y *adj.* Living in concubinage.—*n.* [*pl.* -nar·ies] One who engages in concubinage.

con·cu·bine (*kon*-kyoo-byne) *n.* A mistress; woman who lives with a man without being legally married to him.

con·cu·pis·cence (kon-*kyoo*-pih-s'ns) *n.* Lust; sexual desire.—**con·cu·pis·cent** *adj.*

con·cur *v.* (kun-*ker*) [con·curred; con·cur·ring] 1. To agree; assent. 2. To act; happen together; combine; coincide.

con·cur·rence *n.* Also **con·cur·ren·cy.** 1. Agreement; assent. 2. Combination; union. 3. A sharing of equal powers.

con·cur·rent *adj.* 1. Concomitant; coincident; existing together. 2. Acting jointly; co-operating. 3. Equal; join, as concurrent powers.

con·cus·sion (kun-*kuh*-sh'n) *n.* 1. An agitation; tremor, caused by collision. 2. *Medicine.* Injured condition caused by blows, shock, etc.—**con·cus·sion·al, con·cus·sive** *adj.*

con·demn (kun-*dem*) *v.* 1. To disapprove of; censure; declare guilty. 2. To doom; sentence. 3. To pronounce unfit or not suitable for use. 4. *Law.* To appropriate for public use.—**con·dem·na·ble** *adj.* —**con·dem·ner** *n.*

con·dem·na·tion (kon-dem-*nay*-sh'n) *n.* 1. Censure; act of condemning. 2. Reason or cause for condemning.—**con·dem·na·to·ry** *adj.*

con·den·sa·tion (kon-d'n-*say*-sh'n) *n.* 1. Consolidation, the process of bringing into closer union. 2. Reduction of words; an abridgment, as of a book. 3. *Chemistry & Physics.* The process of reducing a gas to a denser form.

con·dense (k'n-*denss*) *v.* [con·densed; con·dens·ing] 1. To compress; contract; make compact. 2. *Chemistry & Physics.* To change to a denser form, as from a vapor to a liquid. 3. To reduce to fewer words.—**con·den·sa·ble** *adj.*—**con·den·sa·bil·i·ty** (-*bil*-uh-tee) *n.*

con·den·ser (k'n-*denss*-er) *n.* 1. A machine for compressing gases. 2. An apparatus or chamber for changing a gas to a liquid or solid. 3. A mirror lens for concentrating light. 4. An apparatus for storing electricity.

con·de·scend (kon-dih-*send*) *v.* To deign; submit haughtily.—**con·de·scend·ing** *adj.*

con·de·scen·sion (kon-dih-*sen*-sh'n) *n.* Act of condescending; patronizing civility.

con·dign (kun-*dyne*) *adj.* Deserved; merited; suitable.—**con·dign·ly** *adv.*

con·di·ment (*kon*-duh-m'nt) *n.* A seasoning; substance for giving flavor or relish to food.

con·di·tion (kun-*dih*-sh'n) *n.* 1. State of being, esp. good condition. 2. Rank; position. 3. A modification; limitation. 4. A stipulation; provision. 5. A prerequisite.—*v.* 1. To make fit; to make healthy. 2. To contract; stipulate. 3. To limit; modify. 4. *Psychology.* To form a reflex action by repetition.

con·di·tion·al *adj.* Depending upon or expressing a condition; limited.—**con·di·tion·al·ly** *adv.*

con·di·tioned *adj.* 1. Conditional. 2. In a state or condition. 3. *Psychology.* Learned by repetition, as a conditioned reflex.

con·dole (kun-*dohl*) *v.* [con·doled; con·dol·ing] Commiserate; extend sympathy, as to a mourner.—**con·dole·ment** *n.*—**con·dol·er** *n.*

con·do·lence (kun-*doh*-luns; *kon*-duh-) *n.* Sympathy; commiseration.

con·do·na·tion (kon-doh-*nay*-sh'n) *n.* Implied forgiveness, as of a crime, by ingoring it.

con·done (kun-*dohn*) *v.* [con·doned; con·don·ing] To pardon; forgive; overlook.

con·dor (*kon*-der) *n.* A large South American vulture.

con·duce (kun-*dyoos*) *v.* [con·duced; con·duc·ing] To contribute; lead.—**con·duc·i·ble** *adj.* —**con·duc·i·ble·ness** *n.* —**con·duc·i·bly** *adv.*

con·duc·ive *adj.* Favorable; helpful. 'Actions conducive to happiness.'— **-duc·ive·ness** *n.*

CONDOR (1/25 life size)

con·duct (*kon*-dukt) *n.* 1. Behavior; deportment. 2. Management; administration.

con·duct (kun-*dukt*) *v.* 1. To guide; lead. 2. To direct; manage. 3. To direct or lead, as an orchestra. 4. To behave. 5. To transmit; convey.— **-duct·i·bil·i·ty** *n.*— **-i·ble** *adj.*

con·duct·ance (kun-*duk*-tunss) *n. Electricity.* Conduction capacity.

con·duc·tion (kun-*duk*-sh'n) *n.* 1. Act of transmitting or conveying. 2. *Physics.* Transmission by means of a conductor.

con·duc·tiv·i·ty (kon-duk-*tiv*-uh-tee) *n.* [*pl.* -ties] *Physics.* The power of conducting, as electricity, etc.—**con·duc·tive** *adj.*

con·duc·tor (kun-*duk*-ter) *n.* 1. A guide; one who leads. 2. The director of a chorus or orchestra. 3. Attendant who collects fares on a public vehicle. 4. *Physics.* A body which transmits, as heat, electricity, etc.—**con·duc·tor·ship** *n.*

con·du·it (*kon*-dit; -doo-it) *n.* **1.** A channel for conveying liquids; pipe. **2.** A protective tube.

cone (*kohn*) *n.* **1.** A solid figure rising from a circular base and tapering to a point. **2.** *Geometry.* A surface generated by a straight line passing through a fixed point and moving around a circumference. **3.** Any cone-shaped object or formation, as an ice cream cone. **4.** A small, scaly, seed-bearing cluster on trees of the pine family.

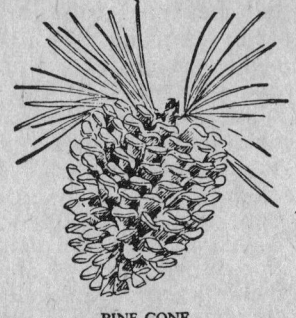

PINE CONE

cone·flow·er *n.* The black-eyed Susan.

Coney Island. **1.** A popular seaside resort in the borough of Brooklyn, New York. **2.** A frankfurter and roll sandwich, with chili.

con·fab (*kon*-fab) *v.* [con·fabbed; con·fab·bing] *Colloquial.* To confabulate.—**con·fab** *n.*

con·fab·u·late (kun-*fab*-yoo-layt) *v.* [con·fab·u·la·ted; -lat·ing] **1.** To chat; talk informally. **2.** To confer.— **-la·tion** (-*lay*-sh'n) *n.*

con·fect (k'n-*fekt*) *v.* **1.** To prepare; construct; build. **2.** To make candy, preserves, and other sweets.—**con·fec·tion** *n.*—**con·fec·tion·er** *n.*

con·fec·tion·er·y (k'n-*fek*-sh'n-er-ee) *n.* [*pl.* -ies] Candy and sweets of all sorts.

con·fed·er·a·cy (k'n-*fed*-er-uh-see) *n.* [*pl.* -cies] **1.** A loose league or union of states. **2.** A combination of persons. **3.** [*cap.*] The league of southern states which seceded from the Union in 1861.

con·fed·er·ate (k'n-*fed*-er-ayt) *v.* [con·fed·er·at·ed; -at·ing] To band together into a loose union; unite; work together.—*n.* (kun-*fed*-er-it) **1.** One who bands with one or more others, usually for a dishonest purpose; assistant; abettor. **2.** [*cap.*] A member of or sympathizer with the Army of The Confederacy [1861–65].—**con·fed·er·ate, con·fed·er·a·tive** *adj.*

con·fed·er·a·tion (k'n-fed-er-*ay*-sh'n) *n.* **1.** A league of states previously independent; union; alliance. **2.** [*cap.*] The U.S. government prior to the adoption of the Federal Constitution in 1789.

con·fer (k'n-*fer*) *v.* [con·ferred; con·fer·ring] **1.** To consult together; converse. **2.** To bestow; give.—**con·fer·ment** *n.*—**con·fer·ra·ble** *adj.*—**con·fer·ee** (kon-fer-*ee*)—**con·fer·rer** *n.*

con·fer·ence (*kon*-fer-ens) *n.* **1.** Consultation; formal conversation, usually leading to a decision. **2.** A convention; meeting to which delegates are sent.—**con·fer·en·tial** *adj.*

con·fess (k'n-*fess*) *v.* [con·fessed; con·fess·ing] **1.** To admit formally; avow; own. **2.** To unburden one's sins to a priest or other authorized auditor. **3.** To admit to a crime or misdeed.—**con·fess·er** *n.*—**con·fess·ed·ly** *adv.*

con·fes·sion (k'n-*fesh*-'n) *n.* **1.** A formal admission either written or oral, usually of a misdeed; avowal. **2.** A disclosing of sins to a priest for absolution.—**con·fes·sion·al** *adj.*

con·fes·sion·al (kun-*fesh*-uh-n'l) *n.* **1.** Enclosure in which a priest hears confessions. **2.** Act of confessing to a priest.

con·fes·sor (k'n-*fess*-er) *n.* **1.** One who confesses. **2.** A priest who hears confessions.

con·fet·ti (k'n-*fet*-ee) *n. pl.* Bits of colored paper thrown in the air at carnivals.

con·fi·dant (*kon*-fih-dent) *n.* Person entrusted with one's secrets.—**con·fi·dante** *n. fem.*

con·fide (kun-*fyde*) *v.* [con·fid·ed; con·fid·ing] **1.** To trust; entrust. **2.** To tell, as secrets in confidence.—**con·fid·er** *n.*

con·fi·dence (*kon*-fih-d'ns) *n.* **1.** Trust; faith. **2.** Belief in one's own competence; assurance. **3.** A secret confidential communication.

confidence game. A swindle.—**confidence man.** A swindler; one who takes dishonest advantage of the trust placed in him.

con·fi·dent (*kon*-fih-d'nt) *adj.* **1.** Assured; having confidence in oneself. **2.** Sure; believing firmly.—*n.* A close friend.—**con·fi·dent·ly** *adv.*

con·fi·den·tial (kon-fih-*den*-sh'l) *adj.* **1.** Secret; told in confidence. **2.** Entrusted with secrets.

con·fid·ing (kun-*fyde*-ing) *adj.* Trusting; having faith.—**con·fid·ing·ly** *adv.*

con·fig·u·ra·tion (kun-fig-yuh-*ray*-shun) *n.* Form; shape; arrangement of parts.—**con·fig·u·ra·tion·al** *adj.*—**con·fig·u·ra·tion·al·ly** *adv.*

con·fine (kun-*fyne*) *n.* [*Usually pl.*] Border; boundary.—*v.* [con·fined; con·fin·ing] **1.** To enclose; imprison; shut up. **2.** To limit; restrain.—**con·fin·a·ble, con·fine·a·ble** *adj.*

con·fined *adj.* **1.** Limited; narrow. **2.** In childbed.

con·fine·ment *n.* The state of being confined, esp. when giving birth.

con·firm (kun-*ferm*) *v.* **1.** To settle; establish; make certain. **2.** To sanction; ratify; corroborate. **3.** To make firmer; strengthen. **4.** *Ecclesiastical.* To administer the rite of confirmation to.—**con·firm·a·ble** *adj.*—**con·firm·a·tive, con·firm·a·to·ry** *adj.*—**con·firm·er** *n.*

con·fir·ma·tion (kon-fer-*may*-shun) *n.* **1.** The act of confirming; validation. **2.** *Ecclesiastical.* The ceremony in which members of some churches take on their full duties and privileges. **3.** That which confirms; proof.

con·firmed (kun-*fermd*) *adj.* **1.** Established; settled; habitual. **2.** *Ecclesiastical.* Admitted to the full privileges of the church.

con·fis·cate (*kon*-fis-kayt) *v.* [-cat·ed; -cat·ing] To appropriate, with legal authority, as forfeited.—**con·fis·cate** *adj.*—**con·fis·ca·tor** *n.*

con·fis·ca·tion (kon-fuh-*skay*-shun) *n.* The act of appropriating legally.

con·fla·gra·tion (kon-fluh-*gray*-shun) *n.* A blazing fire.—**con·fla·grant** (kon-*flay*-grunt) *adj.*

con·flict (kon-*flikt*) *v.* To be in opposition; contend; clash.—*n.* (*kon*-flikt) **1.** A struggle for mastery; battle. **2.** An opposition or clash, as of beliefs, interests, etc.—**con·flic·tive** *adj.*

con·flu·ence (*kon*-floo-uns) *n.* 1. The junction of two streams. 2. A crowd; throng.

con·flu·ent (*kon*-floo-ent) *adj.* Flowing together; meeting.—*n.* A tributary stream.

con·flux (*kon*-fluks) *n.* A confluence.

con·form (kun-*form*) *v.* 1. To make or be similar; adapt; correspond. 2. To act in compliance or agreement, as with laws or customs. —**con·form·ance** *n.*—**con·form·er** *n.*

con·form·a·ble (kun-*form*-uh-b'l) *adj.* 1. Compliant; submissive. 2. Consistent; adaptive; agreeing.—**con·form·a·bil·i·ty** (kun-form-uh-bil-ih-tee), **-a·ble·ness** *n.*—**con·form·a·bly** *adv.*

con·for·ma·tion (kon-for-*may*-shun) *n.* 1. The manner in which anything is formed; structure. 2. The act of conforming.

con·form·ist (kun-*form*-ist) *n.* One who conforms or complies, esp. in religious matters.

con·form·i·ty (kun-*form*-ih-tee) *n.* [*pl.* -ties] 1. Correspondence; agreement; congruity. 2. Submission, esp. in religious matters.

con·found (kun-*fownd*) *v.* 1. To throw into consternation or disorder; confuse; dismay. 2. To damn; curse mildly.—**con·found·er** *n.*

con·found·ed *adj.* 1. Odious; damned. 2. Confused.—**con·found·ed·ly** *adv.*

con·fra·ter·ni·ty (kon-fruh-*tern*-ih-tee) *n.* [*pl.* -ties] A brotherhood; group of men united for a purpose.

con·frere (*kon*-frayr) *n.* A colleague; fellow member; associate.

con·front (kun-*frunt*) *v.* 1. To face; meet in hostility. 2. Set face to face; place before. —**con·front·a·tion** (kon-frun-*tay*-shun) *n.*

Con·fu·cian·ism *n.* The Chinese system of morality taught by Confucius.—**Con·fu·cian·ist** *n.*

Con·fu·cius (kun-*fyoo*-shus). Great Chinese philosopher primarily concerned with the development of harmony through man's realization of his social duties.

con·fuse (kun-*fyooz*) *v.* [con·fused; con·fus·ing] 1. To mix up; disorder; jumble; mistake one for another. 2. To perplex; disconcert; confound.—**con·fus·ed·ly** *adv.*—**con·fus·ed·ness** *n.*

con·fu·sion (kun-*fyoo*-zhun) *n.* 1. An indiscriminate mingling; disorder. 2. Perturbation of mind; embarrassment; shame. 3. Overthrow; defeat; ruin.—**con·fu·sion·al** *adj.*

con·fu·ta·tion (kon-fyoo-*tay*-shun) *n.* The act of disproving.— **-ta·tive** (kun-*fyoo*-tuh-tiv) *adj.*

con·fute (kun-*fyoot*) *v.* [con·fut·ed; con·fut·ing] To disprove.—**con·fut·er** *n.*

con·geal (kun-*jeel*) *v.* To freeze; stiffen; coagulate.—**con·geal·a·ble** *adj.*—**con·geal·er**, **con·geal·ment** *n.*

con·gen·i·al (kun-*jeen*-y'l) *adj.* 1. Partaking of the same characteristics; sympathetic. 2. Naturally suited or adapted. 'Congenial work.' —**con·ge·ni·al·i·ty** (kun-jeen-ee-*al*-ih-tee) *n.* —**con·gen·ial·ly** *adv.*

con·gen·i·tal (kun-*jen*-ih-t'l) *adj.* 1. Belonging to an individual from birth. 2. Not hereditary but dating from the prenatal, fetal stage of de-velopment.—*n.* A person born with an affliction.—**con·gen·i·tal·ly** *adv.*

con·ger (*kong*-ger) *n.* Also **con·ger eel.** A large edible sea eel sometimes eight feet long.

con·ge·ri·es (kon-*jeer*-eez) *n. sing. & pl.* An aggregate; combination.

con·gest (kon-*jest*) *v.* 1. To gather into a mass; heap together; become jammed. 2. *Medicine.* To cause an unnatural accumulation of blood in an organ.—**con·ges·tive** *adj.*

con·ges·tion (kun-*jes*-chun) *n.* 1. A crowded or choked condition. 2. *Medicine.* An excessive accumulation of blood in an organ.

con·glom·er·ate (kun-*glom*-uh-rayt) *v.* [-ated; -at·ing] To gather into a round body.—(kun-*glom*-uh-rit) *adj.* Gathered into a ball; crowded together; clustered.—*n. Geology & Mineralogy.* Rounded fragments of various rocks found cemented together.

con·glom·er·a·tion (kun-glom-uh-*ray*-shun) *n.* A mixed mass; collection; accumulation.

congo snake. A short-legged amphibian eel found in southern U.S.

con·grat·u·late (kun-*grat*-yoo-layt) *v.* [-lated; -lat·ing] To express pleasure to another at his good fortune.—**con·grat·u·la·tor** *n.*—**con·grat u·la·to·ry** (kun-*grat*-yoo-luh-tor-ee) *adj.*

con·grat·u·la·tion (kun-grat-yoo-*lay*-shun) *n.* [*Also pl.*] Expression of pleasure at some one's good fortune; felicitations.

con·gre·gate (*kong*-gruh-gayt) *v.* [-gat·ed; -gat·ing] To assemble; gather in a group.—**con·gre·gate** (*kong*-gruh-git) *adj.* Collected; compact; close.—**con·gre·ga·tor** *n.*

con·gre·ga·tion (kong-gruh-*gay*-shun) *n.* 1. The act of assembling; an assembly of persons or things. 2. **a.** Persons attending a religious service. **b.** Membership of a church.

con·gre·ga·tion·al *adj.* Pertaining to a congregation, or, [*cap.*] to the Congregationalists.

Con·gre·ga·tion·al·ism (kong-gruh-*gay*-shun-ul-izm) *n.* A denomination of the Protestant Church in which each parish regulates all its affairs.—**Con·gre·ga·tion·al·ist** *n. & adj.*

con·gress (*kong*-gress) *n.* 1. A meeting; assembly; convention. 2. [*cap.*] The Federal legislative body of the United States.

con·gres·sion·al (kun-*gresh*-uh-n'l) *adj.* Pertaining to the United States Congress, or any congress.—**con·gres·sion·al·ist** *n.*

con·gress·man *n.* [*pl.* -men] A member of the United States Congress, esp. a Representative. —**con·gress·wom·an** *n.*

con·gru·ent (*kong*-groo-unt) *adj.* Agreeing; corresponding; suitable.—**con·gru·ence**, **con·gru·en·cy** *n.*—**con·gru·ent·ly** *adv.*

con·gru·i·ty (kon-*groo*-ih-tee) *n.* [*pl.* -ties] 1. Agreement; consistency; fitness. 2. *Geometry.* Coincidence; ability to match exactly.

con·gru·ous (*kong*-groo-us) *adj.* Well-adapted; harmonious; appropriate.—**con·gru·ous·ly** *adv.*

con·ic (*kon*-ik) *adj.* Having the shape of a cone; round and tapering to a point.—*n. Geometry.*

A conic section; a figure formed by cutting a cone with a plane.—**con·i·cal** *adj.*— **-cal·ly** *adv.*

con·ics (*kon*-iks) *n. Geometry.* A branch of higher geometry dealing with cones and curved lines rising from sections of it.

conic section. A geometric figure formed by cutting a cone with a plane.

conic sections. *Geometry.* The study of the ellipse, parabola, and hyperbola.

co·ni·fer (*koh*-nih-fer) *n.* A tree or shrub bearing cones.—**co·nif·er·ous** *adj.* Bearing cones.

con·jec·tur·al (kun-*jek*-tyoor-ul) *adj.* Depending upon guesswork.—**con·jec·tur·al·ly** *adv.*

con·jec·ture *n.* Formation of opinion without proof; a guess; surmise.—*v.* **con·jec·tur·a·ble** *adj.*—**con·jec·tur·a·bly** *adv.*—**con·jec·tur·er** *n.*

con·join (kun-*joyn*) *v.* To unite; connect.

con·joint (kun-*joynt*) *adj.* 1. United; combined. 2. Formed by two or more; joint.

con·ju·gal (*kon*-joo-g'l) *adj.* Pertaining to marriage; marital; matrimonial.—**con·ju·gal·i·ty** *n.*

con·ju·gate (*kon*-joo-gayt) *v.* [-gat·ed; -gat·ing] 1. *Grammar.* To inflect (a verb) through its voices, moods, tenses, etc. 2. To unite; fuse. —*adj.* 1. United in pairs; coupled. 2. *Grammar.* Of the same root or derivation.—*n.* A word having the same derivation as another and hence a similar meaning.—**con·ju·ga·tor** *n.*

con·ju·ga·tion (kon-joo-*gay*-sh'n) *n.* 1. *Grammar.* Systematic arrangement of a verb's inflected forms. 2. Act of conjugating.—**con·ju·ga·tion·al** *adj.*—**con·ju·ga·tion·al·ly** *adv.* **con·ju·ga·tive** (*kon*-joo-gay-tiv) *adj.*

con·junc·tion (kon-*junk*-sh'n) *n.* 1. Union; association; act or instance of conjoining. 2. *Astronomy.* A meeting of stars or planets in the same degree of the Zodiac. 3. *Grammar.* A word connecting sentences, clauses, phrases, or words as *and, but, or,* etc.— **-tion·al** *adj.*

con·junc·ti·va (kon-junk-*ty*-vah) *n.* [*pl.* -vas, -vae] The mucous membrane lining the eyelids' inner surface.

con·junc·tive (kun-*junk*-tiv) *adj.* 1. Serving to unite or connect. 2. Combined; united.

con·junc·ti·vi·tis (kun-junk-tih-*vy*-tis) *n. Medicine.* Pinkeye; an inflammation of the conjunctiva.

con·junc·ture (kun-*junk*-choor) *n.* Combination of events; crisis.

con·jur·a·tion (kon-joor-*ay*-sh'n) *n.* The act of conjuring; incantation; magic spell.

con·jure (*kon*-jer) *v.* [con·jured; con·jur·ing] 1. To summon, as a spirit, by incantation. 2. To bring about, as if by magic. 3. To practice magic. 4. (*kon*-joor) To entreat.

con·jur·er, con·jur·or (*kon*-jer-er) *n.* A sorcerer; magician; juggler.

conk out. *Aviation.* To stop suddenly during flight.

con·nect (kuh-*nekt*) *v.* 1. To fasten together; join; unite. 2. To associate mentally. 3. To join by association.—**con·nec·ter, con·nec·tor** *n.*

connecting rod. *Mechanics.* A rod which connects a piston with an engine crankshaft.

con·nec·tion (kuh-*nek*-shun) *n.* 1. Junction; association; union; relationship. 2. An acquaintance; associate. 3. [*pl.*] Transfer or continuation in travel. 'He made good connections.' 4. [*pl.*] *Colloquial.* Influential acquaintance; means of access.

con·nec·tive (kuh-*nek*-tiv) *adj.* Connecting; joining.—*n.* 1. *Grammar.* A conjunction, preposition, or relative pronoun. 2. A link; a joining factor.—**con·nec·tive·ly** *adv.*—**con·nec·tiv·i·ty** (kuh-nek-*tiv*-ih-tee) *n.*

connective tissue. *Anatomy.* Fibrous white tissue which supports and joins the other tissues of the body.

conning tower. The bulletproof pilothouse of a warship.

con·nip·tion *n.* Also **conniption fit.** *Colloquial.* A spell of hysteria or fury.

con·niv·ance (kuh-*ny*-v'ns) *n.* Voluntary blindness to an act; tacit consent to wrongdoing.

con·nive (kuh-*nyve*) *v.* [con·nived; con·niv·ing] 1. To close the eyes on a fault; pretend ignorance of guilt. 2. To co-operate under cover.

con·nois·seur (kon-ih-*sur*) *n.* A competent critic; a well-equipped judge of a specific subject.

con·no·ta·tion (kon-uh-*tay*-shun) *n.* The attributes of a word or term; associations called up; implications.

con·note (kuh-*noht*) *v.* [con·not·ed; con·not·ing] To include in its meaning; imply.

con·nu·bi·al (kuh-*noo*-bee-ul) *adj.* Pertaining to marriage; nuptial.—**con·nu·bi·al·i·ty** *adv.*

co·noid (*koh*-noyd) *adj.* Shaped like a cone. —*n.* A solid produced by the revolution of a conic section about its axis.—**co·noi·dal** *adj.*

con·quer (*kong*-ker) *v.* To vanquish; overcome; subdue; win; triumph.—**con·quer·a·ble, con·quer·ing** *adj.*—**con·quer·ing·ly** *adv.*

con·quer·or (*kong*-ker-er) *n.* One who conquers.

con·quest (*kong*-kwest) *n.* 1. The act of conquering; victory. 2. The act of gaining as a result of conflict; also the gains established.

con·quis·ta·dor (kon-*kwis*-tuh-dor) *n.* [*pl.* -dors, -dores] A conqueror, esp. one of the invaders of Spanish America.

con·san·guin·e·ous (kon-sang-*gwin*-ee-us) *adj.* Of the same blood; related by birth.

con·san·guin·i·ty (kon-sang-*gwin*-ih-tee) *n.* Relation by blood.

con·science (*kon*-sh'ns) *n.* An individual's sense of right and wrong; the faculty of judging one's actions morally.

con·science·less *adj.* Without a moral sense.

conscience money. Money paid in compensation for a wrong done.

con·sci·en·tious (kon-shee-*en*-shus) *adj.* Scrupulous; faithful; upright.—**con·sci·en·tious·ly** *adv.*—**con·sci·en·tious·ness** *n.*

con·scion·a·ble (*kon*-shun-uh-b'l) *adj.* Governed by conscience; reasonable; just.— **-a·bly** *adv.*

con·scious (*kon*-shus) *adj.* 1. Aware of; knowing; understanding. 'Conscious of her loud voice.' 2. In full possession of one's senses.

'He became conscious in the fresh air.' 3. Deliberate; intentional. 'His was a conscious lie.' —**con·scious·ness** *n.* State of being awake and aware. 'Regain consciousness after ether.'

con·script (*kon*-skript) *adj.* Forced into service, usually military.—*n.* A person drafted into service.—*v.* (kon-*skript*) To draft or compel into service.

con·scrip·tion (kun-*scrip*-sh'n) *n.* A draft or enforced enrollment of military personnel.

con·se·crate (*kon*-suh-krayt) *v.* [con·se·crat·ed; con·se·crat·ing] 1. To make or declare sacred; dedicate to God. 2. To hallow; dedicate; devote.—*adj.* Sacred; dedicated. —**con·se·cra·tor** *n.*—**con·se·cra·to·ry** *adj.*

con·se·cra·tion (kon-suh-*kray*-shun) *n.* The act or ceremony of dedicating to sacred uses.

con·sec·u·tive (kun-*sek*-yoo-tiv) *adj.* 1. Following in uninterrupted order; successive. 2. Made up of logically successive stages.

con·sen·sus *n.* Unanimity; agreement; concord.

con·sent (kun-*sent*) *v.* To assent; grant permission or approval.—*n.* Approval.— -**sent·er** *n.*

con·se·quence (*kon*-suh-kwens) *n.* 1. An effect produced by some act or cause; result. 2. *Logic.* A deduction; inference. 3. Significance; importance, often of position.

con·se·quent (*kon*-suh-kwent) *adj.* 1. Following as the natural effect. 2. Having logical sequence.—*n.* 1. *Mathematics.* A conclusion or inference. 2. A result; consequence.

con·se·quen·tial (kon-suh-*kwen*-sh'l) *adj.* 1. Following as a logical effect or result. 2. Self-important; pompous.—**con·se·quen·ti·al·i·ty** (kon-suh-kwen-shee-*al*-ih-tee) *n.*

con·se·quent·ly *adv.* As a logical result.

con·ser·va·tion (kon-ser-*vay*-shun) *n.* 1. Preservation; act of guarding against loss, decay, or injury. 2. Official protection of natural resources. 3. A forest, etc., under such care. —**con·ser·va·tion·al** *adj.*— -**va·tion·ist** *n.*

conservation of energy. The physical law stating that energy cannot be lost, but merely changed in form.

con·serv·a·tism (kun-*serv*-uh-tism) *n.* 1. The practice of preserving what is established; tendency to oppose change. 2. [cap.] Principles of the British Conservative party.

con·serv·a·tive (kun-*serv*-uh-tiv) *adj.* 1. Preservative. 2. Opposed to innovations or change; desirous of maintaining established conditions and institutions. 3. Moderate; prudent. 4. [cap.] Belonging or pertaining to a British political party opposed to change. —*n.* 1. A preservative. 2. A conservative person. 3. Conservative party member.—**con·ser·va·tive·ly** *adv.*—**con·ser·va·tive·ness** *n.*

con·ser·va·tor (*kon*-ser-vay-ter) *n.* A guardian.

con·serv·a·to·ry (kun-*serv*-uh-tor-ee) *n.* [pl. -ries] 1. A greenhouse. 2. A music school. —*adj.* Having a preservative quality.

con·serve (kun-*serv*) *v.* [con·served; con·serv·ing] 1. To keep safe; protect from loss or decay. 2. To preserve in sugar, as fruit.—*n.*

(*kon*-serv, kon-*serv*) Fruit preserved by boiling in sugar.—**con·ser·ver** *n.*

con·sid·er (kun-*sid*-er) *v.* 1. To ponder; contemplate; study, esp. in order to make a decision. 2. To judge; believe to be. 3. To regard; be thoughtful of, as people's feelings.

con·sid·er·a·ble (kun-*sid*-uh-ruh-b'l) *adj.* Deserving attention, esp. because of size or amount; moderately large.— -**er·a·bly** *adv.*

con·sid·er·ate (kun-*sid*-uh-rit) *adj.* Thoughtful of other people; reflective; discreet.—**con·sid·er·ate·ly** *adv.*—**con·sid·er·ate·ness** *n.*

con·sid·er·a·tion (kun-sid-uh-*ray*-shun) *n.* 1. Deliberation. 2. Respect for others; thoughtful regard. 3. A motive for action; reason. 4. Remuneration; payment.

con·sid·ered (kun-*sid*-erd) *adj.* 1. Thoughtfully decided upon; deliberate. 2. Respected.

con·sid·er·ing *prep.* Taking into account.

con·sign (kun-*syne*) *v.* 1. To deliver; commit; entrust. 2. To assign. 3. To transmit; send, esp. to an agent.—**con·sign·a·ble** *adj.*

con·sign·ee (kon-sy-*nee*) *n.* A person to whom goods are delivered for sale.

con·sign·ment (kun-*syne*-m'nt) *n.* 1. The act of consigning or depositing with. 2. Quantity of goods consigned.

con·sign·or (kon-*syne*-er) *n.* Also **con·sign·er.** A person who delivers goods for resale.

con·sist (kun-*sist*) *v.* To be composed or formed.

con·sis·ten·cy *n.* [pl. -cies] 1. State of cohering; firmness. 2. Degree of density or firmness. 3. Uniformity; harmony; agreement.

con·sis·tent *adj.* 1. Solid; firm. 2. Keeping to the same pattern; uniform. 3. In accord; compatible.—**con·sis·tent·ly** *adv.*

con·sis·to·ry (kon-*sis*-tuh-ree) *n.* [pl. -ries] 1. An ecclesiastical court or assembly. 2. Any solemn council.—**con·sis·to·ri·al** (kon-sis-*tor*-ee-ul) *adj.*

con·so·la·tion (kon-suh-*lay*-shun) *n.* Comfort; alleviation of mental distress.

con·sol·a·to·ry (kun-*sol*-uh-tor-ee) *adj.* Tending to relieve grief; consoling.

con·sole (kun-*sohl*) *v.* [con·soled; con·sol·ing] To alleviate grief; soothe.—**con·sol·a·ble** *adj.*

con·sole (*kon*-sole) *n.* 1. *Architecture.* An ornamental bracket supporting a cornice or other decoration. 2. A console table. 3. Desk-like structure containing the keyboard, pedals, etc., of an organ. 4. Radio cabinet.

console table. Narrow table, set against a wall.

con·sol·i·date (kun-*sol*-ih-dayt) *v.* [-dat·ed; -dat·ing] 1. To unite; combine; compress into a single mass or body. 2. To secure and strengthen, as a position.—**con·sol·i·da·tor** *n.*

con·sols (*kon*-solz) *n. pl.* British government bonds.

con·som·mé (kon-suh-*may*) *n.* A thin, clear soup made from meat.

con·so·nance (*kon*-suh-n'ns) *n.* 1. Harmony of sounds. 2. Agreement; accord; consistency.—**con·so·nan·cy** *n.*

C

con·so·nant (*kon*-suh-n'nt) *adj.* 1. Agreeing; consistent. 2. Having similar sounds; harmonious. 3. Consonantal.—*n.* 1. Speech sound enunciated with a partial or entire closing of the breath channel. 2. Letter representing such a sound, as *r, g, t, s,* etc.

con·sort (*kon*-sort) *n.* 1. Companion; intimate associate, esp. a wife or husband. 2. *Nautical.* A vessel accompanying another.—*v.* (kon-*sort*) 1. To accompany; associate. 2. To accord; agree.

con·sor·ti·um (kon-*sor*-shee-um) *n.* 1. *Law.* Partnership; union. 2. International financial agreement esp. to aid another nation.

con·spec·tus (kun-*spek*-tus) *n.* A synopsis.

con·spic·u·ous (kun-*spik*-yoo-us) *adj.* 1. Easily seen; obvious; prominent. 2. Distinguished; remarkable.—**con·spic·u·ous·ness** *n.*

con·spir·a·cy (kun-*speer*-uh-see) *n.* [*pl.* -cies] Secret combination of persons; plot.

con·spir·a·tor (kun-*speer*-uh-ter) *n.* One who conspires or plots criminal action.—**con·spir·a·to·ri·al** (kun-speer-uh-*tor*-ee-ul) *adj.*

con·spire (kun-*spyre*) *v.* [con·spired; con·spiring] 1. To plan a crime in concert with others; plot. 2. To concur; act in concert.

con·sta·ble (*kon*-stuh-b'l) *n.* 1. A policeman; peace officer. 2. An official of high rank in several medieval monarchies.— **-sta·ble·ship** *n.*

con·stab·u·lar·y (kun-*stab*-yoo-leh-ree) *n.* [*pl.* -ries] The police force of a city, district, or country.—*adj.*—**con·stab·u·lar** *adj.*

con·stan·cy (*kon*-stan-see) *n.* Immutability; a permanent state; resolution; steadfastness.

con·stant (*kon*-st'nt) *adj.* Unchanging; permanent; firm; steadfast.—**con·stant** *n.* That which cannot change.—**con·stant·ly** *adv.*

Con·stan·ti·no·ple (kon-stan-tih-*noh*-p'l) *n.* Formerly capital of Turkey, now called Istanbul.

con·stel·la·tion (kon-stuh-*lay*-shun) *n.* Any group of fixed stars named for its resemblance to an actual form.—**con·stel·la·to·ry** (kon-*stel*-uh-tor-ee) *adj.*

con·ster·na·tion (kon-ster-*nay*-shun) *n.* Horror; dismay; perturbation.

con·sti·pa·tion (kon-stih-*pay*-shun) *n.* *Medicine.* Infrequency or difficulty of evacuating the bowels.—**con·sti·pate** *v.*—**con·sti·pat·ed** *adj.*

con·stit·u·en·cy (kun-*stit*-yoo-un-see) *n.* [*pl.* -cies] An electorate; body of voters.

con·stit·u·ent (kun-*stit*-yoo-unt) *adj.* 1. Forming an essential part. 2. Having the power of appointing. 3. Empowered to devise a constitution.—*n.* 1. An essential part. 2. An elector; voter.

con·sti·tute (*kon*-stih-toot) *v.* [con·sti·tut·ed; con·sti·tut·ing] 1. To form; make up; give existence to. 2. To establish; enact. 3. To appoint; depute; elect.

con·sti·tu·tion (kon-stih-*too*-shun) *n.* 1. The structure and characteristics of a body or system. 2. A system of principles and laws for governing a state or nation.

con·sti·tu·tion·al *adj.* 1. Inherent in the mind

or body; inborn; innate. 2. Consistent with the constitution. 3. Pertaining to a constitution.—*n.* A walk taken for health.

con·sti·tu·tion·al·i·ty (kon-stih-too-shun-*al*-ih-tee) *n.* [*pl.* -ties] The quality of being consistent with the constitution.

con·sti·tu·tion·al·ly *adv.* 1. Legally; in accordance with the constitution. 2. Naturally. 'He is constitutionally humane.'

con·sti·tu·tive (*kon*-stih-too-tiv) *adv.* 1. Elemental; essential. 2. Having power to enact or establish; instituting.—**con·sti·tu·tive·ly** *adv.*

con·strain (kun-*strayn*) *v.* 1. To compel; force. 2. To bind; restrain.—**con·strain·a·ble** *adj.*—**con·strain·er** *n.*

con·strained *adj.* Repressed; bound; forced; produced unnaturally, as a constrained voice.

con·straint *n.* 1. Compulsion; urgency. 2. Restraint; inhibition; awkwardness.

con·strict (kun-*strikt*) *v.* To cramp; contract.

con·stric·tion (kun-*strik*-shun) *n.* Contraction; a cramping.—**con·stric·tive** *adj.*

con·stric·tor (kun-*strik*-ter) *n.* 1. Anything that contracts; a muscle which closes a body orifice. 2. Any snake which crushes its prey, as the boa constrictor.

con·stru·a·ble (kun-*stroo*-uh-b'l) *adj.* Understandable; explainable; translatable.

con·struct (kun-*strukt*) *v.* 1. To build; put together in proper form. 2. To devise and arrange mentally.—**con·struct·er, -struct·or** *n.*

con·struc·tion (kun-*struk*-shun) *n.* 1. The act of building. 2. A building; structure. 3. *Grammar.* Syntactical arrangement. 4. Interpretation.—**con·struc·tion·al** *adj.*

con·struc·tion·ist (kun-*struk*-shun-ist) *n.* One who interprets, or places a particular construction on, the law, a paper, or public document.

con·struc·tive (kun-*struk*-tiv) *adj.* 1. With creative or helpful intent. 'Constructive measures.' 2. By construction; created or deduced by construction.—**con·struc·tive·ly** *adv.*

con·strue (kun-*stroo*) *v.* [con·strued; con·struing] To interpret; discover the meaning of; explain; analyze.—**con·stru·er** *n.*

con·sub·stan·tial (kon-sub-*stan*-shul) *adj.* Having the same substance or essence.

con·sue·tude (*kon*-swuh-tyood) *n.* Custom; usage.—**con·sue·tu·di·nar·y** *adj.*

con·sul (*kon*-s'l) *n.* 1. An agent stationed in a foreign country to protect the commercial and other rights of his government's nationals. 2. The chief magistrates of ancient Rome.—**con·su·lar** *adj.*—**con·sul·ship** *n.*

con·su·late (*kon*-suh-lit) *n.* 1. The office of a consul. 2. The extent of a consul's authority. 3. The dwelling of a consul. 4. [*cap.*] The government of France 1799–1804.

con·sult (kun-*sult*) *v.* To ask another's opinion; deliberate in common.—**con·sult·a·ble** *adj.*

con·sul·tant (kun-*sul*-t'nt) *n.* 1. One who advises professionally. 2. One who seeks advice.

con·sul·ta·tion (kon-sul-*tay*-shun) *n.* A meeting to form a decision; deliberation of experts, working together.—**con·sult·a·tive** (kun-*sul*-tuh-tiv), **con·sult·a·to·ry** *adj.*

con·sume (kun-*soom*) *v.* [con·sumed; con·sum·ing] 1. To destroy; burn up. 2. To dissipate; use up. 3. To eat; devour. 4. To permeate; obsess; engross.—**con·sum·a·ble** *adj.*

con·sum·ed·ly *adv.* Greatly; hugely.

con·sum·er (kun-*soom*-er) *n.* One who spends, wastes, or destroys: an economic term applied to purchasers for use, to distinguish them from labor, management, and capital.

con·sum·mate (kun-*sum*-it) *adj.* Complete; perfect.—**con·sum·mate·ly** *adv.*

con·sum·mate (*kon*-suh-mayt) *v.* [-mat·ed; -mat·ing] 1. To complete; perfect; bring to fulfillment. 2. To realize a marriage by coitus. —**con·sum·ma·tive** (*kon*-suh-may-tiv) *adj.*

con·sum·ma·tion (kon-suh-*may*-shun) *n.* Completion; perfection; climax.

con·sump·tion (kun-*sump*-shun) *n.* 1. Destruction by burning, use, decay, etc. 2. *Economics.* The using up of industrial products. 3. *Medicine.* Tuberculosis.

con·sump·tive (kun-*sump*-tiv) *adj.* 1. Destructive; wasting; exhausting. 2. Tuberculous.—*n.* A tuberculous person.—**con·sump·tive·ly** *adv.*—**con·sump·tive·ness** *n.*

con·tact (*kon*-takt) *n.* 1. A touching; meeting. 2. *Electricity.* The uniting of two conductors. 3. *Colloquial.* An influential acquaintance.—*v.* 1. To touch physically. 2. *Slang.* To reach; get in touch with.

con·ta·gion (kun-*tay*-jun) *n.* 1. *Medicine.* Communication of disease by contact. 2. Infectiousness; transmission from one to another.

con·ta·gious (kun-*tay*-jus) *adj.* Catching; propagatable.— -**gious·ly** *adv.*— -**gious·ness** *n.*

con·tain (kun-*tayn*) *v.* To hold; enclose; include.—**con·tain·a·ble** *adj.*

con·tain·er *n.* Anything that holds or encloses, as a carton, box, etc.

con·tam·i·nate (kun-*tam*-ih-nayt) *v.* [-nat·ed; -nat·ing] To pollute; defile; taint.—**con·tam·i·na·tion** *n.*—**con·tam·i·na·tor** *n.*

con·temn (kun-*tem*) *v.* [con·temned; con·temn·ing] To despise; scorn; slight; reject with disdain.—**con·temn·er, con·temn·or** *n.*

con·tem·plate (*kon*-tem-playt) *v.* 1. To consider; ponder. 2. To plan; intend.—**con·tem·pla·ble** *adj.*—**con·tem·pla·tor** *n.*

con·tem·pla·tion (-*play*-shun) *n.* Meditation.

con·tem·pla·tive (kon-*tem*-pluh-tiv) *adj.* Meditative; thoughtful.—**con·tem·pla·tive·ly** *adv.*

con·tem·po·ra·ne·ous (kun-tem-puh-*ray*-nee-us) *adj.* Existing at the same time.—**con·tem·po·ra·ne·ous·ly** *adv.*— -**ne·ous·ness** *n.*

con·tem·po·ra·ry (kun-*tem*-puh-rer-ee) *adj.* Existing at the same time.—*n.* [*pl.* -ies] One who lives at the same time as another.

con·tempt (kun-*tempt*) *n.* 1. Scorn; disdain. 2. *Law.* Disobedience to the orders of a court or legislative assembly.

con·tempt·i·ble (kun-*tempt*-ih-b'l) *adj.* Despica-

ble; vile; base.—**con·tempt·i·bil·i·ty, con·tempt·i·ble·ness** *n.*—**con·tempt·i·bly** *adv.*

con·temp·tu·ous (kun-*tempt*-yoo-us) *adj.* Scornful; haughty; insulting.— -**u·ous·ly** *adv.*

con·tend (kun-*tend*) *v.* To struggle; oppose; vie with; contest; dispute; debate.—**con·tend·er** *n.*

con·tent (*kon*-tent) *n.* 1. [*usually pl.*] Whatever is held or contained. 'The contents of a ship.' 2. Capacity. 3. Meaning; substance.

con·tent (kon-*tent*) *adj.* Placid; satisfied.—*v.* To please; gratify; satisfy.—*n.* Quietness of mind; satisfaction.

con·tent·ed *adj.* Quiet; mentally at ease; satisfied.—**con·tent·ed·ly** *adv.*—**con·tent·ed·ness** *n.*

con·ten·tion (kun-*ten*-shun) *n.* Struggle; controversy; quarrel; discord.

con·ten·tious (kun-*ten*-shus) *adj.* Quarrelsome; litigious; perverse; pugnacious.—**con·ten·tious·ly** *adv.*—**con·ten·tious·ness** *n.*

con·tent·ment (kun-*tent*-m'nt) *n.* Placidity; ease; satisfaction.

con·test (kun-*test*) *v.* To dispute; contend; oppose; argue.—(*kon*-test) *n.* 1. Conflict; combat; dispute; debate; controversy. 2. A competition.—**con·test·a·ble** *adj.*—**con·test·er** *n.*

con·test·ant (kun-*tes*-t'nt) *n.* A disputant.

con·text (*kon*-tekst) *n.* The parts of a writing or statement preceding and following a quoted passage.—**con·tex·tu·al** *adj.*— -**tu·al·ly** *adv.*

con·ti·gu·i·ty (kon-tih-*gyoo*-ih-tee) *n.* Contact; nearness; continuousness.

con·tig·u·ous (kon-*tig*-yoo-us) *adj.* Touching; bordering; adjoining.—**con·tig·u·ous·ly** *adv.*

con·ti·nence (*kon*-tih-n'ns) *n.* Also **con·ti·nen·cy.** Self-command; sexual self-denial.

con·ti·nent (*kon*-tih-n'nt) *adj.* Restrained; temperate; moderate; refraining from sexual indulgence.—**con·ti·nent·ly** *adv.*

con·ti·nent *n.* A great mass of land; one of the six largest geographic divisions, as Asia, Africa, etc.—**the continent.** Europe.

con·ti·nen·tal (kon-tih-*nen*-t'l) *adj.* 1. Pertaining to a continent. 2. European; polished; cosmopolitan. 3. *American History.* Pertaining to the American colonies during the Revolution. 'Continental money.'—*n.* 1. A European. 2. *American History.* An American soldier in the War of Independence.

con·tin·gen·cy (kun-*tin*-jun-see) *n.* [*pl.* -cies] Possibility; chance; accident.

con·tin·gent (kun-*tin*-j'nt) *adj.* Possibly occurring; undeterminable; accidental; incidental. —*n.* 1. A doubtful future situation; a fortuitous event. 2. A quota. 'Contingent of troops.'—**con·tin·gent·ly** *adv.*

con·tin·u·al (kun-*tin*-yoo-ul) *adj.* Unceasing; often repeated.—**con·tin·u·al·ly** *adv.*

con·tin·u·ance (kun-*tin*-yoo-uns) *n.* 1. Permanence; a lasting state; prolongation of existence. 2. *Law.* Deferring of a trial.

con·tin·u·a·tion (kun-tin-yoo-*ay*-shun) *n.* Extension; carrying on to a further point; prolongation; protraction.

con·tin·ue (kun-*tin*-yoo) *v.* [con·tin·ued; con-

C

tin·u·ing] **1.** To keep on; last; be permanent; persevere. **2.** To protract; extend.

con·ti·nu·i·ty (kon-tih-*nyoo*-ih-tee) *n.* [*pl.* -ties] **1.** Close union of parts; uninterrupted connection; cohesion. **2.** A movie or radio script.

con·tin·u·ous (kun-*tin*-yoo-us) *adj.* Uninterrupted.—**con·tin·u·ous·ly** *adv.*— -ous·ness *n.*

con·tin·u·um (kon-*tin*-yoo-um) *n.* [*pl.* -u·a] Any factor which is continuous and unchanging.

con·tort (kun-*tort*) *v.* To twist; writhe.—**con·tor·tion** *n.*—**con·tor·tive** *adj.*

con·tor·tion·ist (kun-*tor*-shun-ist) *n.* A performer who entertains with unusual twistings of the body.

con·tour (*kon*-toor) *n.* The outline of a figure or body; periphery.—*v.* To make an outline.

contour line. A line on a map connecting points having the same height above sea level.

contour map. A map with contour lines to indicate height above sea level of various areas.

con·tra- *Prefix.* Against; in opposition.

con·tra·band (*kon*-truh-band) *n.* Articles illegally imported or exported.—**con·tra·band** *adj.*—**con·tra·band·ist** *n.* A smuggler.

con·tra·bass (kon-truh-*bayss*) *n. Music.* The largest and deepest-toned instrument of the viol family.—**con·tra·bass** *adj.*— -bass·ist *n.*

con·tra·cep·tion (kon-truh-*sep*-sh'n) *n.* Prevention of conception, usually by mechanical or chemical means.—**con·tra·cep·tive** *adj.*—*n.* A means of or device for contraception.

con·tract (*kon*-trakt) *n.* **1.** A compact; agreement; bargain; obligation. **2.** The written terms of such an agreement. **3.** *Cards.* **a.** A form of bridge wherein the winning team receives credit only for points they have bid in their contract. **b.** The contract so bid.

con·tract (kun-*trakt*) *v.* **1.** To compress; diminish; draw together; shrink. **2.** To bring on; incur. 'Contract a disease.' **3.** To make an agreement.—**con·tract·i·bil·i·ty, con·tract·i·ble·ness** *n.*—**con·tract·i·ble** *adj.*

con·tract·ed (kun-*trak*-ted) *adj.* **1.** Drawn together; shrunk. **2.** Incurred; bargained for.

con·trac·tile (kun-*trak*-t'l) *adj.* Tending to contract; having the power to contract.—**con·trac·til·i·ty** (kon-trak-*til*-ih-tee) *n.*

con·trac·tion (kun-*trak*-sh'n) *n.* **1.** The act of shrinking; state of being shrunk. **2.** The act of abridging; shortening. **3.** Abbreviation.—**con·trac·tive** *adj.*— -tive·ly *adv.*

con·trac·tor (kun-*trak*-ter) *n.* **1.** One of the parties to a bargain. **2.** A builder or supplier who contracts to provide his goods or services at a stipulated price.

con·trac·tu·al (kun-*trak*-tyoo-ul) *adj.* Having the force or characteristics of a contract.

con·tra·dict (kon-truh-*dikt*) *v.* To deny; correct; assert the contrary.—**con·tra·dict·a·ble** *adj.*—**con·tra·dict·er, con·tra·dict·or** *n.*

con·tra·dic·tion (kon-truh-*dik*-shun) *n.* **1.** A denial; contrary declaration. **2.** Inconsistency.

con·tra·dic·to·ry (kon-truh-*dik*-tuh-ree) *adj.* **1.** Affirming the contrary; implying a denial.

2. Inconsistent.—**con·tra·dic·tive** *adj.*—**con·tra·dic·tive·ly** *adv.*—**con·tra·dic·tive·ness** *n.*

con·tra·dis·tinc·tion (kon-truh-dis-*tink*-shun) *n.* Differentiation by opposing qualities.—**con·tra·dis·tinc·tive** *adj.*— -tive·ly *adv.*

con·tral·to (kun-*tral*-toh) *n.* [*pl.* -tos, -ti] **1.** The lowest female singing voice. **2.** A singer having a contralto voice.

con·trap·tion (kun-*trap*-shun) *n. Colloquial.* A device; piece of machinery; gadget.

con·tra·pun·tal (kon-truh-*pun*-t'l) *adj.* Pertaining to counterpoint.—**con·tra·pun·tal·ly** *adv.*— -pun·tist *n.* One skilled in counterpoint.

con·tra·ri·e·ty (kon-truh-*ry*-uh-tee) *n.* [*pl.* -ties] Inconsistency; discrepancy; disagreement.

con·tra·ri·wise (*kon*-trer-ee-wyze) *adv.* On the contrary; oppositely.

con·tra·ry (*kon*-trer-ee) *adj.* **1.** Adverse; moving in the opposite direction. **2.** Contradictory; inconsistent; repugnant. **3.** Perverse; self-willed.—*n.* [*pl.* -ries] A thing or proposition contrary to another.—**con·tra·ri·ly** *adv.*— -ri·ness *n.*—**by contraries.** By opposites.

con·trast (kun-*trast*) *v.* To show differences between.—(*kon*-trast) *n.* **1.** Comparison by dissimilarities; a dissimilarity. **2.** *Art.* Degree of difference between light and dark areas in a painting or photograph.—**con·trast·a·ble** *adj.*

con·tra·vene (kon-truh-*veen*) *v.* [con·tra·vened; con·tra·ven·ing] **1.** To obstruct; nullify; defeat. **2.** To violate.—**con·tra·ven·er** *n.*

con·tra·ven·tion (kon-truh-*ven*-shun) *n.* The act of contravening; opposition; violation.

con·tre·temps (*kon*-truh-tahm) *n.* [*pl.* -temps] An unexpected and embarrassing coincidence.

con·tri·bute (kun-*trib*-yoot) *v.* [con·trib·ut·ed; con·trib·ut·ing] **1.** To give along with others; pay a share; aid in a common effort or cause. **2.** To submit for publication.—**con·trib·u·ta·ble** *adj.*—**con·trib·u·tor** *n.*

con·tri·bu·tion (kon-trih-*byoo*-shun) *n.* **1.** The act of contributing. **2.** A sum or article contributed; donation. **3.** A literary work offered to a periodical.—**con·trib·u·tive** (kon-*trib*-yoo-tiv) *adj.*— -tive·ly *adv.*— -tive·ness *n.*

con·trib·u·to·ry (kun-*trib*-yoo-tor-ee) *adj.* Promoting the same end.

con·trite (*kon*-tryte) *adj.* Affected with remorse; penitent; humble.—**con·trite·ly** *adv.*

con·tri·tion (kun-*trish*-un) *n.* Sorrow; penitence; remorse; compunction.

con·triv·ance (kun-*tryve*-uns) *n.* **1.** The act of devising, inventing, or planning. **2.** Device; invention; design; scheme; plan.

con·trive (kun-*tryve*) *v.* [con·trived; con·triv·ing] To invent; devise; plan; scheme; manage.—**con·triv·a·ble** *adj.*—**con·triv·er** *n.*

con·trol (kun-*trohl*) *v.* [con·trolled; con·trolling] To restrain; direct; rule.—*n.* **1.** Power; authority; command. **2.** Steering or driving apparatus of a machine or vehicle. **3.** Self-command; self-restraint.—**con·trol·la·ble** *adj.*

con·trol·ler (kun-*trohl*-er) *n.* **1.** One who governs or restrains. **2.** An official who oversees the accounts of others; as the controller of the mint.—**con·trol·ler·ship** *n.*

control stick. An airplane instrument by means of which banking and elevation are changed.

con·tro·ver·sial (kon-truh-*versh*-ul) *adj.* Pertaining to or leading to disputation; unsettled; open to argument.—**con·tro·ver·sial·ist** *n.* A disputant.—**con·tro·ver·sial·ly** *adv.*

con·tro·ver·sy (*kon*-truh-vers-ee) *n.* [*pl.* -sies] A dispute; debate; quarrel; contest.

con·tro·vert (*kon*-truh-vert) *v.* To dispute; contend against in words; deny and attempt to disprove.—**con·tro·vert·er** *n.*—**con·tro·vert·i·ble** (kon-truh-*vert*-uh-b'l) *adj.*

con·tu·ma·cious (kon-tyoo-*may*-shus) *adj.* Obstinate; proud; headstrong; perverse.—**con·tu·ma·cious·ly** *adv.*—**con·tu·ma·cious·ness** *n.*

con·tu·ma·cy (*kon*-tyoo-muh-see) *n.* [*pl.* -cies] Contempt of lawful authority; stubbornness; perverseness; haughtiness.

con·tu·me·ly (*kon*-tyoo-mee-lee) *n.* [*pl.* -lies] Rudeness; insolence; contemptuous language. —**con·tu·me·li·ous** (kon-tyoo-*meel*-ee-us) *adj.* —**con·tu·me·li·ous·ly** *adv.*—**-li·ous·ness** *n.*

con·tu·sion (kun-*tyoo*-zhun) *n.* 1. A bruise. 2. The act of beating or bruising; the state of being bruised.—**con·tuse** *v.*

co·nun·drum (kuh-*nun*-drum) *n.* A riddle.

con·va·lesce (kon-vuh-*les*) *v.* [con·va·lesced; -lesc·ing] To become better after sickness.

con·va·les·cence (kon-vuh-*les*-ens) *n.* Gradual recovery of health and strength after a sickness.—**con·va·les·cent** *adj.* & *n.*

con·vec·tion (kun-*vek*-shun) *n.* 1. The act of carrying or conveying. 2. Transfer of heat or electrical energy by surging particles of matter. —**con·vec·tion·al, con·vec·tive** *adj.*

con·vene (kun-*veen*) *v.* [con·vened; con·ven·ing] To come together; meet; assemble; call together.—**con·ven·er** *n.*

con·ven·ience (kun-*veen*-y'ns) *n.* Also **con·ven·ien·cy.** 1. Opportune conjunction of affairs. 'Do it at your convenience.' 2. Suitableness; freedom from discomfort or trouble; ease. 3. Any feature providing ease or comfort.

con·ven·ient (kun-*veen*-y'nt) *adj.* Accommodating; opportune.—**con·ven·ient·ly** *adv.*

con·vent (*kon*-vent) *n.* A nunnery; abbey.

con·ven·ti·cle (kon-*ven*-tih-k'l) *n.* A meeting of dissenters from an established church; a secret meeting; any assembly.— **-ven·ti·cler** *n.*

con·ven·tion (kun-*ven*-shun) *n.* 1. A meeting; assembly. 2. An agreement or contract. 3. Custom; the accepted ways.

con·ven·tion·al (kun-*ven*-sh'n-ul) *adj.* 1. Stipulated; formed by agreement. 2. Formal; traditional; sanctioned by custom and general agreement. 3. Trite.—**con·ven·tion·al·ism, con·ven·tion·al·ist** *n.*—**con·ven·tion·al·ly** *adv.*

con·ven·tion·al·i·ty (kun-ven-sh'n-*al*-ih-tee) *n.* [*pl.* -ties] Living, acting, or speaking according to accepted arbitrary rules, rather than impulse.

con·ven·tion·al·ize (kun-*ven*-sh'n-uh-lyze) *v.*

[-ized; -iz·ing] To make conform to a traditional pattern.—**con·ven·tion·al·i·za·tion** *n.*

con·ven·tu·al (kun-*ven*-choo-ul) *adj.* Belonging to a convent; monastic.—*n.* A monk or nun.

con·verge (kun-*verj*) *v.* [con·verged; con·verg·ing] To move toward one point; draw together.

con·ver·gence (kun-*verj*-'ns) *n.* Also **con·ver·gen·cy.** Tendency to draw together at one point.—**con·ver·gent** *adj.*

con·vers·a·ble (kun-*vers*-uh-b'l) *adj.* Inclined to talk; sociable.— **-a·ble·ness** *n.*— **-a·bly** *adv.*

con·ver·sant (kun-*ver*-s'nt) *adj.* 1. Intimately associated with; acquainted; well-versed. 2. Acquainted by use or study.—**con·ver·sance, con·ver·san·cy** *n.*—**con·ver·sant·ly** *adv.*

con·ver·sa·tion (kon-ver-*say*-sh'n) *n.* 1. Talk; dialogue; discourse. 2. Sexual intercourse. —**con·ver·sa·tion·al** *adj.*— **-al·ly** *adv.*

con·ver·sa·tion·al·ist (kon-ver-*say*-sh'n-uh-list) *n.* Also **con·ver·sa·tion·ist.** A person who talks well or at length.

con·verse (kon-*verss*) *v.* [con·versed; con·vers·ing] To talk familiarly.—*n.* (*kon*-verse) Conversation.

con·verse (*kon*-verss) *adj.* Turned around; opposite; reciprocal.—*n.* A complement; counterpart; opposite; reverse.— **-verse·ly** *adv.*

con·ver·sion (kun-*ver*-zhun) *n.* 1. Change from one condition to another; as conversion of water into ice. 2. Change from one religion to another; from one side or political party to another. 3. *Mathematics.* Alteration in the form of an expression. 'Conversion of a fraction to a decimal.'— **-sion·al, -sion·ar·y** *adj.*

con·vert (kun-*vert*) *v.* To change from one form or condition to another; from one religion or party to another; from one use to another.—*n.* (*kon*-vert) A person who is converted to a new religion or party.

con·vert·er (kun-*ver*-ter) *n.* Also **con·vert·or.** 1. A person or thing that converts. 2. Apparatus used in the Bessemer process for making steel from pig iron. 3. A device for changing alternating to direct current or (**inverted converter**) from direct to alternating.

con·vert·i·ble (kun-*vert*-uh-b'l) *adj.* Capable of change; transformable; interchangeable.—*n.* An automobile with a top which may be lowered or raised.—**con·vert·i·bil·i·ty, con·vert·i·ble·ness** *n.*—**con·vert·i·bly** *adv.*

con·vex (*kon*-veks; *kun*-veks) *adj.* Rising or swelling into spherical or rounded form.—*n.* A convex body.— **-vex·ly** *adv.*

con·vex·i·ty (kun-*veks*-ih-tee) *n.* [*pl.* -ties] Roundness; globular form.

con·vey (kun-*vay*) *v.* 1. To carry; transport. 2. To transmit or transfer. 3. *Law.* To transfer; pass title. 'Convey an estate from father to son.' 4. To impart; communicate. —**con·vey·a·ble** *adj.*—**con·vey·or, con·vey·er** *n.*

con·vey·ance (kun-*vay*-uns) *n.* 1. Transmission; transference. 2. *Law.* The

CONVEX

act of transferring title to property; the document or instrument by which it is transferred. 3. Anything that carries or transports.

con·vey·anc·ing (kun-*vay*-uns-ing) *n.* The practice of drawing deeds and leases, investigating title, etc., for transferring legal title.

con·vict (kun-*vikt*) *v.* To find or prove guilty. —*n.* (*kon*-vikt) A person found guilty of crime.

con·vic·tion (kun-*vik*-sh'n) *n.* 1. The act of finding a person guilty of crime. 2. The act of convincing. 3. A settled persuasion; the state of being convinced.—**con·vic·tion·al** *adj.*

con·vince (k'n-*vinss*) *v.* [con·vinced; con·vinc·ing] To induce or compel belief; satisfy by evidence.—**con·vince·ment** *n.*—**con·vinc·er** *n.*

con·vinc·ing (k'n-*vin*-sing) *adj.* Compelling belief or assent; undeniable.—**con·vinc·ing·ly** *adv.*

con·viv·i·al (k'n-*viv*-ee-ul) *adj.* Jovial; festive; marked by, or fond of, eating and drinking in company.—**con·viv·i·al·ist** *n.*—**con·viv·i·al·i·ty** (k'n-viv-ee-*al*-uh-tee) *n.*—**con·viv·i·al·ly** *adv.*

con·vo·ca·tion (kon-voh-*kay*-sh'n) *n.* 1. An assembly; a calling together. 2. An ecclesiastical convention or conference.—**con·vo·ca·tion·al** *adj.*—**con·vo·ca·tor** (*kon*-voh-kay-ter) *n.*

con·voke (k'n-*vohk*) *v.* [con·voked; con·vok·ing] To convene; assemble; call or bring together.

con·vo·lute (*kon*-vuh-loot) *v.* [con·vo·luted; -lut·ing] To roll together overlappingly; wind; twist.—**con·vo·lute** *adj.*—**con·vo·lute·ly** *adv.*

con·vo·lu·tion (kon-vuh-*loo*-sh'n) *n.* 1. A rolling or folding together so as to overlap. 2. An irregular elevation on the brain surface.

con·vol·vu·lus (k'n-*volv*-yoo-lus) *n.* [*pl.* -lus·es, -li] A family of climbing plants including the morning glory.

con·voy (*kon*-voy) *n.* 1. A formation of ships under protective escort. 2. Any formation or file of vehicles.—*v.* To escort.

con·vulse *v.* [con·vulsed; con·vuls·ing] 1. To cause violent laughter. 2. To shake; agitate.

con·vul·sion *n.* 1. Spasm; a violent, involuntary muscular contraction. 2. Any violent, irregular movement. 3. An uncontrollable fit of laughter.—**con·vul·sion·ar·y** *adj.*

con·vul·sive (k'n-*vul*-siv) *adj.* Producing or marked by convulsions.—**con·vul·sive·ly** *adv.*

co·ny, co·ney (*koh*-nee) *n.* [*pl.* -nies, -neys] 1. A rabbit. 2. Fur of the rabbit.

coo *v.* [cooed; coo·ing] 1. To utter the call of a dove. 2. To converse affectionately.—**coo** *n.*—**coo·er** *n.*—**coo·ing·ly** *adv.*

cook *v.* 1. To prepare, as food, by the action of heat. 2. To undergo cooking. 3. *Slang.* To ruin; destroy.—*n.* One who prepares food.

cook·book *n.* A book containing directions and recipes for cooking.

cook·er·y *n.* [*pl.* -ies] The practice of cooking.

cook·ie, cook·y *n.* [*pl.* -ies] A small, sweet cake.

cook up. To fabricate; concoct; make up.

cool *adj.* 1. Somewhat cold. 2. Producing coolness. 'Cool clothing.' 3. Poised; self-possessed: deliberate. 4. Showing dislike or apathy; indifferent. 5. Without qualification. 'A cool billion.'—*v.* To make or become cool. —**cool·ly** *adv.*—**cool·ness** *n.*

cool·er *n.* 1. *Slang.* A jail. 2. A refrigerator. 3. That which produces coolness.

cool-head·ed *adj.* Not easily excited; calm.

coo·lie, coo·ly *n.* [*pl.* -lies] An oriental porter or unskilled laborer.

cool·ish *adj.* Slightly cool.

coon (*koon*) *n. Colloquial.* Raccoon.

coop (*koop*) *n.* A pen; enclosure.—*v.* To confine in a narrow space.

co-op (*koh*-op) *n.* A co-operative.

coop·er *n.* One who makes or repairs barrels and casks.—**coop·er** *v.*

coop·er·age (*koop*-er-ij) *n.* 1. A place where barrels and casks are made. 2. The business of a cooper. 3. Work performed by a cooper or the pay received for it.

co-op·er·ate (koh-*op*-uh-rayt) *v.* [co-op·er·at·ed; -at·ing] Also **co·op·er·ate, co·öp·er·ate.** To act or work with others to achieve a common objective.—**co-op·er·a·tor** *n.*

co-op·er·a·tion (koh-op-uh-*ray*-sh'n) *n.* Also **co·op·er·a·tion, co·öp·er·a·tion.** Joint effort or labor toward a common end, esp. to promote profit or general prosperity.

co-op·er·a·tive (koh-*op*-er-uh-tiv) *adj.* Also **co·op·er·a·tive, co·öp·er·a·tive.** 1. Helpful. 2. Operating jointly to the same end.—*n.* An enterprise owned by its members, each of whom shares in the profits of the organization in proportion to the amount of business he does with it.— -tive·ly *adv.*— -tive·ness *n.*

co-or·di·nate (koh-*or*-dih-nut) *adj.* Also **co·or·di·nate, co·ör·di·nate.** 1. Being of the same rank or degree. 2. Denoting mathematical co-ordinates.—*v.* [-at·ed; -at·ing] To organize different groups or parts into a functioning whole.—*n.* 1. A person or thing that is co-ordinate. 2. [*pl.*] *Mathematics.* Numerical quantities by means of which points, lines, etc., are plotted or determined.—**co-or·di·nate·ly** *adv.*— -nate·ness *n.*— -na·tor *n.*

co-or·di·na·tion (koh-or-d'n-*ay*-sh'n) *n.* Also **co·or·di·na·tion, co·ör·di·na·tion.** 1. An organizing of different parts or groups into a functioning whole. 2. Ability to function harmoniously.

co-or·di·na·tive (koh-*or*-din-uh-tiv) *adj.* Also **co·or·di·na·tive, co·ör·di·na·tive.** 1. Of equal importance, power, etc. 2. Co-ordinating.

coot *n.* An aquatic bird with a bald forehead and a black body.

coot·ie (*koot*-ee) *n. Slang.* The body louse.

cop *n. Slang.* A policeman.—*v. Slang.* [copped; cop·ping] To snatch; grab; steal.

COOT (1/16 life size)

co·pa·cet·ic (koh-puh-*set*-ik) *adj. Slang.* Excellent; okay; fine.

co·pal (*koh*-p'l) *n*. A hard, shining resin used for varnish, lacquer, etc.

co·part·ner (koh-*part*-ner) *n*. Partner; associate; colleague.—**co·part·ner·ship** *n*.

cope (kohp) *v*. [coped; cop·ing] To contend with; deal with; meet on equal terms.

cope *n*. 1. A heavily draped, sleeveless ecclesiastic cloak. 2. An arched covering or canopy. 3. The vault of the sky. 4. A wall's top surface; coping.—*v*. [coped; cop·ing].

Co·per·ni·can (kuh-*per*-nih-k'n) *adj*. Pertaining to the astronomer Copernicus or to his theory that the earth revolves around the sun.

cope·stone (*kohp*-stohn) *n*. Head or top stone.

cop·i·er (*kop*-ee-er) *n*. Imitator; transcriber.

cop·ing (*kohp*-ing) *n*. The top or cover of a wall, often sloping to carry off water.

co·pi·ous (*koh*-pee-us) *adj*. Abundant; plentiful; ample; containing much.—**co·pi·ous·ly** *adv*. —**co·pi·ous·ness** *n*.

cop·per (*kop*-er) *n*. 1. A soft, widely distributed, reddish metal that conducts electricity well. (*Symbol*: Cu). 2. A copper coin; small change. 3. *Slang*. A policeman.—*v*. To plate or cover with copper.—**cop·per** *adj*.

copper-alloyed	copper-faced	coppersidesman
copper-bottomed	copper-headed	copperware
copper-coated	copper-nosed	copper works
copper-colored	copperplated	copperworm

cop·per·as *n*. Iron sulphate, a green dyestuff and pigment.

cop·per·head *n*. 1. A poisonous moccasin snake with a thick body. 2. [*cap*.] A Northerner during the American Civil War who sympathized with the South.

cop·per·plate (*kop*-er-playt) *n*. 1. A burnished copper plate on which engravings are made. 2. A print or impression from such an engraving. 3. A layer of copper deposited by electroplating.—*v*. [cop·per·plated; -plat·ing].

cop·per·smith *n*. One who makes copper articles.

cop·per·y *adj*. Made of or containing copper.

cop·pice (*kop*-iss) *n*. An area overgrown with small trees or brushwood.

cop·ra (*kop*-ruh) *n*. Also **cop·rah, cop·pra, cop·per·ah**. The dried meat of the coconut from which coconut oil is extracted.

Copt *n*. 1. A member of a sect of Egyptian Christians. 2. One of ancient Egyptian ancestry.—**Cop·tic** *n*.—The language of ancient Egypt.—**Cop·tic** *adj*.

cop·u·late (*kop*-yoo-layt) *v*. [cop·u·lat·ed; cop·u·lat·ing] To join, esp. in sexual intercourse; cohabit.— **-la·tion** (kop-yoo-*lay*-sh'n) *n*.

cop·u·la·tive (*kop*-yoo-luh-tiv) *adj*. 1. Uniting; coupling; connecting. 2. *Grammar*. Denoting a word that connects phrases, words, etc. 'Man *and* wife.' 3. Pertaining to sexual union. —**cop·u·la·tive** *n*.—**cop·u·la·tive·ly** *adv*.

cop·y (*kop*-ee) *n*. [*pl*. -ies] 1. An imitation; reproduction; duplicate. 2. The written matter of advertisements, catalogues, etc. 3. Manuscript matter awaiting typesetting. 4. A single item of an edition of books or periodicals. 5. An original or model to be copied. —*v*. [cop·ied; cop·y·ing] To imitate; duplicate.

cop·y·book *n*. A book having models or examples to be copied.

copy boy. *Journalism*. A messenger who carries copy, galleys, etc., between the editorial department and composing room.

cop·y·cat (*kop*-ee-kat) *n*. *Slang*. An uncritical imitator.

copy desk. *Journalism*. The semicircle or group of desks where rewrite men and copy editors work.

copy editor. *Journalism*. An editor in charge of making up the newspaper.

cop·y·hold·er (*kop*-ee-hohl-der) *n*. One who reads a manuscript aloud to the proofreader.

cop·y·ist (*kop*-ee-ist) *n*. 1. One who imitates, duplicates, or transcribes. 2. *Music*. One who writes the instrumental parts of an orchestral composition.

cop·y·right (*kop*-ee-ryte) *n*. A right granted an author or publisher to be sole exploiter of a literary or artistic work for 28 years, with option of renewal for a similar period.—*v*. To obtain this right.—**cop·y·right** *adj*.—**cop·y·right·a·ble** *adj*.—**copy·right·er** *n*.

co·quet *v*. [co·quet·ted; co·quet·ting] Also **co·quette**. To flirt; trifle with a person's affections.

co·quet·ry *n*. [*pl*. -ries] Flirtation calculated to win amorous attention.

co·quette *n*. A woman who flirts for the purpose of getting attention.—**co·quet·tish** *adj*. —**co·quet·tish·ly** *adv*.—**co·quet·tish·ness** *n*.

co·qui·na (kuh-*keen*-uh) *n*. A fragile, white limestone composed of shells, coral, etc.

cor·a·cle (*kor*-uh-k'l) *n*. A small boat of canvas, leather, etc., stretched over a framework.

cor·al (*kor*-ul) *n*. 1. A porous, limy stone secreted as the external skeleton of various low marine animals. 2. Any of these animals. 3. A pink-orange color.—**cor·al** *adj*.

cor·bel (*kor*-b'l) *n*. *Architecture*. A piece projecting from the vertical face of a wall to support weight.—*v*. [cor·belled; cor·bel·ling].

cord *n*. 1. String or a small rope composed of several strands twisted together. 2. A pile of wood eight feet long, four feet high and usually four feet broad. 3. The welt or rib in a fabric. 4. A fabric having such ribs, as Bedford Cord. 5. *Electricity*. An insulated wire with plugs at each end, used to carry current from an outlet to an appliance. 6. *Anatomy*. Any round, stringy, flexible organ.—*v*. 1. To tie with a cord. 2. To pile wood in cords.—**cord·er** *n*.

cord·age (*kord*-ij) *n*. 1. Ropes and string. 2. A quantity of wood expressed in cords.

cor·date (*kor*-dut) *adj*. In the form of a heart.

cord·ed *adj*. 1. Fastened with cords. 2. Composed of or furnished with welts or cords. 3. Stacked or piled in cords, as wood.

cor·dial (*kor*-j'l) *adj*. Genial; warm; friendly; cheering.—*n*. 1. A sweet, aromatized liqueur. 2. Any tonic or stimulating preparation.

C

cor·dial·i·ty (kor-*jal*-ih-tee) *n.* [*pl.* -ties] Warmth; friendliness; sincere affection.

cor·dil·le·ra (kor-*dil*-er-uh, kor-dih-*yehr*-uh) *n.* A major range or system of mountains.

cord·ite (*kor*-dyte) *n.* A smokeless explosive made from nitroglycerine, guncotton, etc.

Cor·do·ba (*kor*-doh-buh). A city and province in southern Spain, once a center of Moorish culture.—**cor·do·ba** *n.* Nicaraguan unit of money worth one dollar.

cor·don (*kor*-d'n) *n.* 1. *Military.* A line of military posts or sentinels enclosing a place to prevent entrance or exit. 2. A buffer of hostile states ringing a country to isolate it economically. 3. A ribbon decoration.

Cor·do·van (*kor*-doh-v'n) *adj.* Pertaining to Cordoba, Spain.—**cor·do·van** *n.* A superior grade of fine, soft, dyed leather.

cor·du·roy (*kor*-duh-roy) *n.* 1. A thick cotton material heavily corded or ribbed. 2. A roadbed of logs laid over swampy land. 3. [*pl.*] Trousers made of corduroy cloth.

cord·wain·er (*kord*-wayn-er) *n.* A worker in leather, often a shoemaker.

cord·wood *n.* Wood cut for sale by the cord.

core *n.* 1. The seed-bearing center of certain fruits. 2. Any heart or center. 3. *Foundry.* A form which assures a hole or indentation in a casting. 4. *Electricity.* An iron bar used to increase the magnetism of a coil. 5. The fabric center of some steel cables. 6. The substance, essence, or central point of a truth, book, etc.—*v.* [cored; cor·ing] To remove the core.—**cor·er** *n.*—**core·less** *adj.*

co·re·li·gion·ist (koh-ree-*lij*'n-ist) *n.* Also **co·re·li·gion·ar·y.** One of the same religion.

co·re·op·sis (kor-ee-*op*-sis) *n.* A genus of bright red or yellow flowers of the aster family.

co·re·spond·ent (koh-rih-*spond*-'nt) *n. Law.* A joint defendant, esp. in a divorce case involving adultery.—**co·re·spond·en·cy** *n.*

co·ri·an·der (kor-ee-*an*-der) *n.* 1. A small group of plants of the parsley family. 2. The strongly flavored seed of such a plant.

Cor·inth (*kor*-inth). A Greek city on the Peloponnesian peninsula.

Co·rin·thi·an (kor-*in*-thee-un) *n.* An inhabitant of Corinth.—**Co·rin·thi·an** *adj.* 1. The most ornate and intricate of the three basic Greek styles of architecture. 2. Denoting Corinth.

Co·rin·thi·ans (kor-*in*-thee-uns) *n. pl.* One of two New Testament epistles by St. Paul.

cork *n.* 1. The light, resilient bark of a kind of oak tree. 2. The inner, growing tissue or bark of trees and higher plants. 3. A stopper for a bottle.—*v.* 1. To smudge with burned cork. 2. To stopper with a cork.—**cork·ed** *adj.*

cork·er *n. Slang.* 1. Any remarkable or wonderful thing. 2. A clever person.

cork·ing *adv. Slang.* Exceedingly; notably; superlatively.—*adj.* Excellent.

cork·screw (*kork*-skroo) *n.* A screw-bladed tool for extracting corks from bottles.—*v.* To direct in or follow a twisting way.—**cork·screw** *adj.*

cork·y (*kor*-kee) *adj.* [cork·i·er, cork·i·est] Consisting of or resembling cork.—**cork·i·ness** *n.*

corm *n. Botany.* The solid bulblike lower stem of such plants as the gladiolus.

cor·mo·rant (*kor*-muh-r'nt) *n.* A large webfooted, extremely voracious bird of the pelican family.—*adj.* Greedy; rapacious.

corn *n.* A thickening or callus of the skin caused by friction.

corn *n.* 1. A single grain or kernel, esp. of a cereal plant. 2. Maize; the plants which produce maize. 3. *Slang.* Inferior or rural humor.—*v.* To preserve and season with salt, as corned beef.

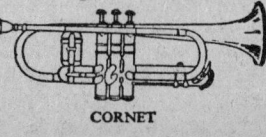
CORMORANT (1/20 life size)

corn bin	corn eater	cornland
cornbird	corn-fed	corn meal
corn cake	cornfield	cornpipe
corn-colored	cornfly	corn pit
corncrib	corn grower	cornstalk
corn crusher	corn husk	cornworm

Corn Belt. The predominantly farm area from Ohio to Nebraska.

corn borer. A moth which in its larva is very destructive to green corn.

corn bread. Johnnycake; slightly leavened bread made from corn meal.

corn·cob *n.* 1. The shaft or stem on which maize kernels grow. 2. A tobacco pipe made from a corncob.

corn cockle. A flowering weed which grows among grain fields and spoils the flour.

cor·ne·a (*kor*-nee-uh) *n.* [*pl.* -ne·as] A hard transparent membrane in the fore part of the eye protecting the pupil.—**cor·ne·al** *adj.*

cor·nel (*kor*-n'l) *n.* A family of decorative shrubs and small trees, esp. the dogwood.

cor·ner *n.* 1. The point where two lines or surfaces meet; angle. 2. A condition in which a commodity or service is under monopolistic control. 3. Any part, area, or region. 4. A position in which no retreat is possible. 5. A nook; retreat; secluded place. 6. A place where two or more streets intersect. 7. A remotely distant place or quarter.—*v.* 1. To force into a place from which there is no escape; surround. 2. To shape into a corner.

cor·ner·stone *n.* 1. The stone at the corner of a building's foundation, esp. one that is laid with ceremony. 2. Any basic matter.

cor·ner·wise (*kor*-ner-wyze) *adv.* Also **cor·ner·ways.** Having the corner in front; diagonally.

cor·net (*kor*-net; -net) *n.* 1. A brass wind instrument very similar to a trumpet. 2. A cone-shaped receptacle.— **-net·ist, -net·tist** *n.*

CORNET

corn·flow·er *n.* Bachelor's button; an annual plant, of the aster family, with blue flowers.

cor·nice (*kor*-niss) *n.* 1. *Architecture.* Any decorated projection which crowns or finishes the part to which it is affixed. 2. A decorative molding on a wall near the ceiling.—*v.* [cor·niced; cor·nic·ing]

Cor·nish *adj.* Pertaining to Cornwall in England.—*n.* The ancient Celtic dialect formerly spoken in Cornwall.—**Cor·nish·man** *n.*

corn pone. A flat bread whose basic ingredient is corn meal.

corn·starch *n.* A concentrated, commercial starch used esp. in cooking.

corn sugar. A dextrose extracted from corn, about half as sweet as cane sugar.

cor·nu·co·pi·a (korn-uh-*koh*-pee-uh) *n.* [*pl.* -pi·as] *Classical Antiquity.* 1. A horn, filled to overflowing with fruit and flowers, a symbol of plenty. 2. A cone-shaped container. — -co·pi·an *adj.*

CORNUCOPIA

corn·y (*kor*-nee) *adj.* [corn·i·er; corn·i·est] 1. *Slang.* Crude; unsophisticated. 2. Pertaining to or producing corn.

co·rol·la (kor-*ol*-luh) *n.* *Botany.* The delicate leaves or petals of a flower.—**cor·ol·late, cor·ol·lat·ed** *adj.*

cor·ol·lar·y (*kor*-uh-lair-ee) *n.* [*pl.* -ies] 1. A deduction; inference; result. 2. *Mathematics.* A truth or proposition which logically follows from a preceding proof.

CdROLLA

co·ro·na *n.* [*pl.* -nas, -nae] 1. A halo or luminous circle around one of the heavenly bodies. 2. A crown; crest; garland. 3. Any crownlike part or location. 4. An electric arc or discharge.

Corona Australis. The Southern Crown, a twelve-starred constellation of the Southern Hemisphere.

Corona Borealis. The Northern Crown, a constellation of the Northern Hemisphere.

cor·o·nal (*kor*-uh-n'l) *n.* A crown; garland. —*adj.* (kuh-*roh*-n'l) 1. Belonging to the top of the head. 2. Crownlike.

cor·o·nar·y (*kor*-uh-nair-ee) *adj.* 1. Like a crown or circlet; circling. 2. *Anatomy.* Denoting one of two arteries which nourish the heart's muscles.

cor·o·ner (*kor*-uh-ner) *n.* An official who investigates cases of accidental or unexplained death.—**cor·o·ner·ship** *n.*

cor·o·na·tion (kor-uh-*nay*-sh'n) *n.* Act or rites of crowning a king or queen.

cor·o·net (*kor*-uh-net) *n.* 1. An inferior crown worn by princes and noblemen. 2. A band or other ornamental headdress. 3. The part of a horse's foot where the hoof joins the flesh.

cor·po·ral (*kor*-puh-r'l) *adj.* Bodily; denoting the body as distinct from the mind.—**cor·po·ral·ly** *adv.*

cor·po·ral *n.* *Military.* The lowest non-commissioned officer of the army.— -ral·ship *n.*

corporal punishment. Physical chastisement, including flogging, death, imprisonment, etc.

cor·po·rate (*kor*-puh-rut) *adj.* Joined into a single body; joint; united. Pertaining to a city or business enterprise with a charter of incorporation.—**cor·po·rate·ly** *adv.*

cor·po·ra·tion (kor-per-*ay*-sh'n) *n.* 1. A business or government legally authorized to act as an individual; limited liability firm. 2. *Colloquial.* An enlarged abdomen.—**cor·po·ra·tive** (*kor*-puh-ruh-tiv) *adj.*—**cor·po·ra·tor** *n.*

cor·po·re·al *adj.* Material; physical; bodily; not mental or immortal.—**cor·po·re·al·ly** *adv.*

corps (*kor*) *n.* [*pl.* corps.] 1. An organized body of persons, esp. troops. 2. A part of an army having at least two divisions.

corpse *n.* Cadaver; dead body, esp. of a human.

cor·pu·lence (*kor*-pyoo-lenss) *n.* Also **cor·pu·len·cy.** Fleshiness; excessive fatness.—**cor·pu·lent** *adj.*—**cor·pu·lent·ly** *adv.*

cor·pus *n.* [*pl.* cor·po·ra] 1. A body, esp. a dead one. 2. Any main body or principal part.

cor·pus·cle (*kor*-pus-'l) *n.* 1. *Physiology.* A minute protoplasm cell floating in animal body fluids. 2. A minute particle, often electrically charged.—**cor·pus·cu·lar** (kor-*pus*-kyoo-lar) *adj.*

corpus delicti. *Law.* The basic facts of a crime.

cor·ral (kuh-*ral*) *n.* A pen or enclosure for livestock.—*v.* [cor·ralled; cor·ral·ling] 1. To drive animals into an enclosed area; pen up. 2. *Slang.* To get possession of; seize; catch.

cor·rect (kuh-*rekt*) *v.* 1. To rectify; improve; remedy; make conform to a standard. 2. To punish; chastise.—*adj.* Right; precise; meeting all requirements of truth, accuracy, etiquette, etc.—**cor·rect·ly** *adv.*—**cor·rect·ness** *n.*

cor·rec·tion (kuh-*rek*-shun) *n.* 1. Removal of faults or errors. 2. The right material or condition substituted in place of what is objectionable. 3. Punishment; chastisement.

cor·rec·tive *adj.* Tending to rectify, or re-establish normality.—**cor·rec·tive** *n.*— -tive·ly *adv.*

cor·re·late (*kor*-uh-layt) *v.* [cor·re·lated; -lating] 1. To establish a systematic connection; interdependence, or reciprocal relationship. —**cor·re·late** (*kor*-uh-lut) *adj.*—**cor·re·la·tion** (kor-uh-*lay*-sh'n) *n.*

cor·rel·a·tive (kuh-*rel*-uh-tiv) *adj.* 1. Interrelated; correspondent; reciprocal. 2. *Grammar.* Denoting conjunctions always used together, as neither . . . nor.—**cor·rel·a·tive** *n.*

cor·res·pond (kor-us-*pond*) *v.* 1. To fit; agree; conform. 2. To communicate by writing.

cor·res·pond·ence *n.* 1. Relation; conformity; agreement; similarity. 2. Intercourse between persons through writing. 3. The letters passing between correspondents.

cor·res·pond·ent (kor-us-*pon*-d'nt) *n.* 1. A letter writer. 2. *Journalism.* An out-of-town reporter.—*adj.* 1. Fitting; suitable; answering. 2. Similar; comparable.— **-ent·ly** *adv.*

cor·res·pond·ing *adj.* 1. Answering; suiting. 2. Similar; analogous. 3. Letter writing.

cor·ri·dor (*kor*-uh-dor) *n.* 1. Passage; hallway. 2. A belt of territory allowing an inland country access to a port. 'Polish Corridor.'

cor·ri·gi·ble (*kor*-ij-uh-b'l) *adj.* Correctable; amendable; not beyond reform.—**cor·ri·gi·bil·i·ty** *n.*—**cor·ri·gi·bly** *adv.*

cor·ri·val (kuh-*ry*-v'l) *n.* A competitor; rival.

cor·rob·o·rate *v.* [cor·rob·o·rat·ed; -rat·ing] To verify; confirm; prove.—**cor·rob·o·ra·tion** *n.* —**cor·rob·o·ra·tive** *adj.*— **-ra·tive·ly** *adv.*

cor·rode (kuh-*rohd*) *v.* [cor·rod·ed; cor·rod·ing] To wear away; rust; deteriorate by chemical action.—**cor·rod·i·ble** *adj.*

cor·ro·sion *n.* 1. A gradual wearing away. 2. Rust or other evidence of corroding.

cor·ro·sive *adj.* Deteriorating; wearing away. —*n.* A substance that causes corrosion.—**cor·ro·sive·ly** *adv.*—**cor·ro·sive·ness** *n.*

cor·ru·gate (*kor*-uh-gayt) *v.* [cor·ru·gat·ed; -gat·ing] 1. To wrinkle; crinkle; crimp. 2. To shape materials into frequent folds in order to increase strength or rigidity.—**cor·ru·gat·ed** *adj.*—**cor·ru·ga·tion** (kor-uh-*gay*-sh'n) *n.*

cor·rupt *adj.* 1. Debased; depraved; dishonest; accepting bribes. 2. Having many errors. 3. Rotten; spoiled.—*v.* 1. To impair; debase; pervert. 2. To bribe.—**cor·rupt·er** *n.*—**cor·rupt·ing** *adj.*—**cor·rupt·ing·ly** *adv.*—**cor·rupt·ly** *adv.*—**cor·rupt·ness** *n.*

cor·rupt·i·ble (kuh-*rupt*-uh-b'l) *adj.* Susceptible to depravation, contamination, or dishonesty. —**cor·rupt·i·bil·i·ty** (kuh-rupt-uh-*bil*-ih-tee).

cor·rup·tion (kuh-*rup*-sh'n) *n.* 1. Debasement; pollution; decay. 2. Bribery; venality. 3. An erroneous alteration.—**cor·rup·tive** *adj.*

cor·sage (kor-*sahzh*) *n.* An arrangement of flowers to be worn on the bodice or waist.

cor·sair (*kor*-sehr) *n.* 1. Pirate; freebooter; privateer. 2. A pirate ship.

corse·let, cors·let (*kors*-let) *n.* A suit of armor worn in medieval times.

cor·set (*kor*-s't) *n.* A close-fitting garment often reinforced, worn by women to give shape to the body.—**cor·set** *v.*

cor·tege (kor-*tezh*) *n.* Also **cor·tège.** A procession, funeral train; retinue.

cor·tex *n.* [*pl.* cor·ti·ces] Outer wall of a tree or root. 2. Rind of a fruit. 3. *Anatomy.* The outer covering or envelope of an organ, esp. the gray top layer of the brain.

cor·ti·cal (*kor*-tih-k'l) *adj.* Pertaining to the outer layer of a body; external.— **-cal·ly** *adv.*

cor·ti·cate, cor·ti·cat·ed (*kor*-tih-kayt) *adj.* Resembling or having bark, or any cortex.

co·run·dum (kuh-*run*-dum) *n.* Aluminum oxide, a mineral used as an abrasive and as a gem.

cor·us·cate (*kor*-us-kayt) *v.* [cor·us·cat·ed; -cat·ing] To flash; sparkle; be intellectually brilliant.—**cor·us·ca·tion** (kor-us-*kay*-sh'n) *n.*

cor·vette, cor·vet (kor-*vet*) *n.* A small war craft, used esp. in submarine patrol.

cor·vine *adj.* Like or characteristic of the crow.

Cor·y·bant (*kor*-ih-b'nt) *n.* [*pl.* -ban·tes, -bants] A priest of Cybele, an Asiatic goddess who was worshiped with orgiastic dances.—**cor·y·bant** *n.* A wild reveler.—**Cor·y·ban·tic** (kor-ih-*ban*-tik), **Cor·y·ban·tine, Cor·y·ban·ti·an** *adj.*

co·ry·phee (kor-uh-*fay*) *n.* A ballet dancer.

co·ry·za (kuh-*ryze*-uh) *n. Medicine.* Inflammation and oversecretion of the nasal mucous membranes; the common cold.

co·se·cant (koh-*see*-kant) *n. Trigonometry.* Ratio of the hypotenuse of a right triangle divided by its side; reciprocal of a sine.

co·sig·na·to·ry (koh-*sig*-nuh-tor-ee) *n.* [*pl.* -ries] Joint signer of a document.— **-na·to·ry** *adj.*

co·sign·er (*koh*-syne-er) *n.* One who signs a document, especially a guarantee for a loan, jointly with another.

co·sine (*koh*-syne) *n. Trigonometry.* The ratio of the base of a right triangle divided by its hypotenuse.

cos·met·ic (koz-*met*-ik) *adj.* Promoting or enhancing beauty.—*n.* An externally applied preparation that enhances beauty, esp. of the complexion.

cos·mic (*koz*-mik) *adj.* Also **cos·mi·cal.** Pertaining to the universe or its laws; hence, **a.** Vast. **b.** Well ordered or organized.—**-cal·ly** *adv.*

cosmic ray. A complex, penetrating radiation that bombards the earth from outer space.

cos·mism (*koz*-mizm) *n.* A theory or philosophy of the evolutionary development of the universe.—**cos·mist** *n.*

cos·mog·o·ny (koz-*mog*-uh-nee) *n.* [*pl.* -nies] A theory of the origin of the world or universe. —**cos·mog·o·nist** *n.*

cos·mog·ra·phy (koz-*mog*-ruh-fee) *n.* [*pl.* -phies] 1. The science which treats of the disposition and relation of the various parts of the universe. 2. A treatise on this subject.—**cos·mog·ra·pher** *n.*—**cos·mo·graph·ic** (koz-moh-*graf*-ik), **cos·mo·graph·i·cal** *adj.*

cos·mol·o·gy (koz-*mol*-uh-gee) *n.* The theory or metaphysics of the universe as an ordered integration or whole.—**cos·mol·o·gist** *n.*

cos·mo·pol·i·tan (koz-muh-*pol*-ih-t'n) *adj.* 1. Worldly; not provincial or local; feeling at home in any country. 2. Having people of many nationalities, as a city. 3. *Biology.* Dispersed over much of the earth, as a plant.—**cos·mo·pol·i·tan** *n.*—**cos·mo·pol·i·tan·ism** *n.*

cos·mos (*koz*-mus) *n.* 1. The universe, conceived as a well-organized system; hence, any such system. 2. A family of tall, annual, composite flowers.—**cos·mic** *adj.*

Cos·sack (*kos*-suk, *kos*-sak) *n.* One of a hardy people of the Russian and Siberian steppes.

cos·set (*kos*-et, *kos*-it) *v.* To caress; pamper. —*n.* A pet, esp. a pet lamb.

cost (*kawst*) *n.* **1.** Amount expended to procure a result or commodity; price; value. **2.** Outlay or loss of any kind; pain; suffering. **3.** [*pl.*] *Law.* The cost of the legal process, borne by the loser of a suit or one found guilty on criminal charges.—*v.* [cost; cost·ing].

cos·tal (*kos*-t'l) *adj.* Also **cos·tate.** Pertaining to the ribs, region of the ribs, or a riblike object.

cos·ter·mong·er (*kos*-ter-mung-ger) *n.* A push-cart peddler.

cos·tive (*kos*-tiv) *adj.* Causing or having constipation.—**cos·tive·ly** *adv.*—**cos·tive·ness** *n.*

cost·ly (*kawst*-lee) *adj.* [cost·li·er; cost·li·est] Expensive; costing much.—**cost·li·ness** *n.*

cos·tume (*kos*-tyoom) *n.* **1.** An established mode of dress in any age. **2.** A masquerade outfit.—*v.* (kos-*tyoom*) [-tumed; -tum·ing].

cos·tum·er *n.* **1.** One who provides costumes for theaters, balls, etc. **2.** An upright on which to hang clothes; a clothes rack.

cot *n.* A light, narrow bed, often collapsible.

cot *n.* Small house; hut; cottage.

co·tan·gent (*koh*-tan-jent) *n.* *Trigonometry.* Ratio of the base of a right triangle divided by its side; a tangent's reciprocal.—**co·tan·gen·tial** (koh-tan-*jen*-ch'l) *adj.*

cote (*koht*) *n.* A cage or shelter for domestic animals or doves.

co·ten·ant (koh-*ten*-ant) *n.* One of two or more joint tenants.—**co·ten·an·cy** *n.*

co·ter·ie (*koh*-tuh-ree) *n.* A circle; exclusive set.

co·til·lion (koh-*til*-yun) *n.* Also **co·til·lon.** **1.** A lively dance in which at least eight persons participate. **2.** The music for this dance.

Cots·wold (*kots*-wold) *n.* A breed of large sheep noted for long, fleecy wool.

cot·tage (*kot*-ij) *n.* Small rural house.

cottage cheese. A soft cheese made of sour milk curds.

cottage pudding. Plain cake with a sauce.

cot·tag·er *n.* One who lives in a cottage.

cot·ter, cot·tar (*kot*-er) *n.* A Scottish tenant farmer; peasant.

cot·ter *n.* A wedge of wood or iron for fastening or tightening parts of machinery.—**cotter pin.** Split pin used as a cotter.

cot·ton (*kot*-'n) *n.* **1.** The soft white fibers growing around the seeds of certain plants. **2.** The plant producing this substance. **3.** Cloth or thread made of cotton.—*v. Colloquial.* To take a liking; agree; get along.

cot·ton·mouth *n.* The water moccasin, a large poisonous snake.

cot·ton·seed *n.* The seed of the cotton.

cottonseed oil. Oil obtained from cottonseed.

cot·ton·tail *n.* The common American rabbit.

cot·ton·wood *n.* **1.** A variety of poplar with cottony tufts covering its seeds. **2.** Its wood.

cot·ton·y *adj.* Downy; soft; like cotton.

cot·y·le·don (kot'l-*ee*-d'n) *n.* First leaf or one of the first leaves growing from seed plants.—**cot·y·le·don·al** *adj.*—**cot·y·le·don·ar·y** *adj.*

couch (*kowch*) *n.* A long, low piece of furniture for sitting, resting, or sleeping.—*v.* **1.** To lie down; rest. **2.** To lie hidden; lurk. **3.** To express; phrase.—**couch·er** *n.*

couch·ant (*kow*-ch'nt) *adj.* Lying down.

cou·gar (*koo*-ger) *n.* A large American wildcat.

cough (*kawf*) *v.* To expel air from the lungs with a violent effort and explosive noise.—*n.* **1.** Act of coughing. **2.** Diseased condition causing constant fits of coughing.—**cough·er** *n.* —**cough up. 1.** To expel by coughing. **2.** *Slang.* To pay out; hand over.

cou·lee (*koo*-lee) *n.* **1.** *Geology.* A stream of lava. **2.** Ravine.

cou·lisse (koo-*leess*) *n.* **1.** Piece of grooved lumber. **2.** Side scene of a theater stage.

cou·lomb (koo-*lom*) *n.* *Physics.* Amount of electricity transferred by a current of one ampere in one second.

coun·cil (*kown*-s'l) *n.* **1.** Assembly; group of people gathered for consultation, etc. **2.** Legislative body.—**coun·cil·man** *n.* [*pl.* -men].

coun·ci·lor (*kown*-s'l-er) *n.* A member of a council.—**coun·cil·or·ship** *n.*

coun·sel (*kown*-s'l) *n.* **1.** Advice; opinion. **2.** Consultation; interchange of opinions. **3.** Legal adviser; lawyer or lawyers conducting a case.—*v.* [coun·seled; -selled; -sel·ing, -sel·ling] **1.** To advise; instruct. **2.** To consult; take counsel.

coun·se·lor (*kown*-s'l-er) *n.* Also **coun·sel·lor.** An adviser, esp. a legal adviser; lawyer.

count (*kownt*) *v.* **1.** To number; add up; compute. **2.** To consider; esteem; reckon. **3.** To name the numerals in correct order. **4.** To be accounted; be of value.—*n.* **1.** Reckoning; act or result of counting. **2.** *Law.* A particular charge in an indictment.—**count·a·ble** *adj.* —**count on or upon.** To depend or reckon on.

count *n.* A European nobleman about equal in rank to an English earl.

coun·te·nance (*kown*-tuh-nunss) *n.* **1.** Face; visage. **2.** Expression of the face or features. **3.** Favor; approval.—*v.* [coun·te·nanced; nanc·ing] To favor; endorse.— **-nanc·er** *n.*

coun·ter (*kown*-ter) *n.* **1.** A table over which goods are sold in a store, restaurant, etc. **2.** A token or disk used to keep an account or score, as in games.

coun·ter *adv.* Contrary; in opposition.—*adj.* Adverse; opposed; antagonistic.—*v.* To oppose; act counter to; parry.—*n.* **1.** The act of parrying or returning a blow. **2.** Part of a ship from the water line to the end of the stern swell. **3.** Stiff support for the back of a shoe.

coun·ter- *Prefix.* Denoting opposition or contrary action. 'Counterblast.'

coun·ter·act *v.* To neutralize; offset.—**coun·ter·ac·tion** *n.*—**coun·ter·ac·tive** *adj.*

coun·ter·bal·ance *v.* [coun·ter·bal·anced; coun·ter·bal·anc·ing] To act against with equal power or effect.—*n.* Equal weight or power opposing another.

coun·ter·claim *n.* A claim made in opposition to another.—**coun·ter·claim** *v.*— **-claim·ant** *n.*

coun·ter·clock·wise *adj. & adv.* Moving in a direction opposite to that taken by the hands of a clock.

coun·ter·feit (*kown*-ter-fit) *v.* 1. To sham. 2. To copy or imitate without authority; forge.—*adj.* Forced; spurious.—*n.* A copy or imitation passed as genuine with intent to defraud.—**coun·ter·feit·er** *n.*

coun·ter·foil *n.* Part, as of a receipt or check, kept as a record.

coun·ter·ir·ri·tant *n. Medicine.* A substance producing a secondary irritation in order to relieve a primary one.

counter jumper. *Colloquial.* An aggressive clerk.

coun·ter·mand *v.* To reverse or revoke, as an order.—**coun·ter·mand** *n.*

coun·ter·march *v.* To march back; reverse direction.—**coun·ter·march** *n.*

coun·ter·mine (*kown*-ter-myne) *n.* 1. *Military.* A mine to detonate enemy mines. 2. A tactic or plan to counteract an opponent's strategy. —(kown-ter-*myne*) *v.* [-mined; -min·ing].

coun·ter·pane (*kown*-ter-payn) *n.* A bedspread.

coun·ter·part *n.* 1. A person resembling or corresponding to another; match. 2. A part which fits into or works as complement of another part. 3. Corresponding part; duplicate.

coun·ter·plot (kown-ter-*plot*) *v.* [coun·ter·plot·ted; -plot·ting] To conspire against a plot. —**coun·ter·plot** (*kown*-ter-plot) *n.*

coun·ter·point (*kown*-ter-poynt) *n. Music.* 1. A combination of melodies so as to produce harmony. 2. Accompanying music or the art of writing it.

coun·ter·poise (*kown*-ter-poyz) *n.* 1. A weight equal to and acting in opposition to another weight. 2. A power or force acting to oppose an equal; equilibrium.—*v.* [-poised; -pois·ing].

coun·ter·rev·o·lu·tion (kown-ter-rev-uh-*loo*-sh'n) *n.* A revolt by the Right; reactionary revolution.—**coun·ter·rev·o·lu·tion·ar·y** *adj. & n.* —**coun·ter·rev·o·lu·tion·ist** *n.*

coun·ter·shaft (*kown*-ter-shaft) *n.* A shaft which transfers power from a driveshaft to moving parts.

coun·ter·sign (*kown*-ter-syne) *v.* To sign with someone else to attest to a document's authenticity.—**coun·ter·sig·na·ture** (kown-ter-*sig*-nuh-choor) *n.* 1. An authenticating signature. 2. A secret password; watchword; sign, esp. one used by the military as a signal to a sentry.

coun·ter·sink (*kown*-ter-sink) *v.* [coun·ter·sunk; -sink·ing] *Machinery.* To make a shallow depression concentric with and larger than a bored hole.—**coun·ter·sink** *n.*

coun·ter·vail (kown-ter-*vayl*) *v.* To balance; compensate; offset.

coun·ter·weight (*kown*-ter-wayt) *n.* An opposing or balancing weight or force.—**coun·ter·weigh** (kown-ter-*way*) *v.*

coun·tess (*kown*-tess) *n.* The wife or widow of a count or earl.

coun·ting·house (*kown*-ting-hows) *n.* Office, house, or room where tradesmen keep accounts and transact business.

count·less (*kownt*-les) *adj.* Innumerable; many.

coun·tri·fied (*kun*-trih-fyde) *adj.* Also **coun·try·fied.** Bucolic; with rural manners or looks.

coun·try (*kun*-tree) *n.* [*pl.* -tries] 1. A nation; state; region. 2. Rural parts of a nation. 3. The public; people. 4. The land of which one is a citizen; fatherland.—**coun·try** *adj.*

country dance. A dance in which the partners are arranged in lines opposite each other.

coun·try·man (*kun*-tree-man) *n.* [*pl.* -men] 1. A native of the same country as another; compatriot. 2. A farmer; rustic.—**coun·try·wom·an** *n.* [*pl.* -wo·men].

country seat. A rural mansion; villa.

coun·try·side (*kun*-tree-syde) *n.* 1. A rural area. 2. Inhabitants of these regions.

coun·ty (*kown*-tee) *n.* [*pl.* -ties] A governmental unit between a township and a state.

county seat. The capital or governmental center of a county.

coup (koo) *n.* [*pl.* coups (kooz)] 1. A sudden maneuver. 2. Overthrow of a government.

coup d'état (koo-day-tah). A sudden, revolutionary seizure of government power.

cou·pé (koo-*pay*; koop) *n.* 1. A two-doored automobile usually having only one wide seat. 2. A two-seater, cabin-type airplane.

cou·ple (*kup*-'l) *n.* 1. Two connected, similar things. 2. A husband and wife; man and a woman. 3. *Electricity.* Two connected dissimilar elements which may be induced to generate a current. 4. A bond; connection; link. 5. *Mechanics.* Two equal, parallel forces acting in opposite directions to produce turning.—*v.* [cou·pled; cou·pling] 1. To link one with another. 2. *Colloquial.* To wed.

cou·pler (*kup*-ler) *n.* That which links or connects; coupling.

cou·plet (*kup*-let) *n.* Two consecutive rhymed lines of poetry.

cou·pling (*kup*-ling) *n.* 1. A joining or connecting mechanism, esp. a connective shackle between railway cars. 2. *Electricity.* A passing of electricity between two circuits without an actual connection, as by a transformer.

cou·pon (*koo*-pon, *kyoo*-pon) *n.* 1. A certificate entitling one to purchase at decreased cost, redeem at face value, obtain premiums, etc. 2. A detachable certificate on a bond designating the date of interest due. 3. A ticket stub.

cour·age (*ker*-ij; *kuhr*-) *n.* Bravery; mettle; fearlessness.—**cou·ra·geous** (kuh-*ray*-j's) *adj.*

cour·i·er (*koor*-ee-er) *n.* 1. A messenger. 2. One who arranges the details of a journey.

course (korss) *n.* 1. Movement; continuous or gradual progression or advance. 2. Direction; path; flow. 3. Ground, distance, or path traversed. 4. A direction of progress indicated by a compass. 5. *Architecture.* An uninterrupted layer or line of masonry. 6. Established sequence of events. 7. A separate dish or section of a meal. 8. Conduct; comportment; behavior. 9. A systematized series of classes or lectures in a given subject or field. —*v.* [coursed; cours·ing] 1. To run; move rapidly. 2. To hunt; chase. 3. To lope over.

court (*kort*) *n.* 1. An uncovered space bounded by buildings or walls. 2. Open space marked off for a particular game, as a tennis court. 3. Residence or retinue of a sovereign. 4. The chamber where legal justice is administered. 5. The judges and attendants assembled for this purpose. 6. Homage; flattery; act of courting.—*v.* 1. To attempt to gain the favor of by praise and attention. 2. To woo; make love to. 3. To seek; solicit.

cour·te·ous (*ker*-tee-us) *adj.* Polite; civil; considerate.—**cour·te·ous·ly** *adv.*— **-ous·ness** *n.*

cour·te·san, **cour·te·zan** (*kor*-tuh-zan) *n.* A prostitute; harlot.

cour·te·sy (*ker*-tuh-see) *n.* [*pl.* -sies] 1. Politeness; civility. 2. A favor; kindness.

court·house (*kort*-howss) *n.* Building in which courts of justice are held.

cour·ti·er (*kor*-tee-er) *n.* One who attends or frequents the court of a sovereign.

court·ly (*kort*-lee) *adj.* [-li·er, -li·est] Elegant; dignified; polite.—**court·li·ness** *n.*

court martial. [*pl.* courts martial] A tribunal of officers for trying offenses against military or naval law.—**court-martial** *v.* [-tialed, -tialled; -tial·ing, -tial·ling] To try before such a court.

court·plas·ter *n.* Thin adhesive tape for covering slight scratches, etc.

court·room *n.* Chamber in which a court of law is held.

court·ship *n.* The act of wooing.

court·yard *n.* A court adjacent to or surrounded by a house.

cous·in (*kuz*-'n) *n.* 1. Also **first cousin.** The child of one's uncle or aunt. 2. A relative descended from a common ancestor.—**cous·in·hood** *n.*—**cous·in·ly** *adv.*—**cous·in·ship** *n.*

cous·in-ger·man (kuz-'n-*jer*-m'n) *n.* [*pl.* cous·ins-ger·man] A first cousin.

cou·tu·rier (koo-tyoor-*yay*) *n.* A dress designer. —**cou·tu·rière** (-*yair*) *n. fem.*

cove (*kohv*) *n.* 1. A small inlet; sheltered recess. 2. *British Slang.* An odd chap.

cov·e·nant (*kuv*-uh-nunt) *n.* 1. Solemn agreement; compact. 2. *Theology.* The promises of God as recorded in the Bible. 3. [*cap.*] Either of two agreements made by Scottish Presbyterians to uphold their faith. 4. *Law.* A valid promise or contract.—*v.* To contract.

cov·e·nan·ter (*kuv*-uh-nun-ter) *n.* 1. One who makes a covenant. 2. [*cap.*] Supporter of either of the Scottish Covenants.

Cov·en·try (*kuv*-'n-tree). A town in central England.—**send to Coventry.** Exclude from society; ostracize.

cov·er (*kuv*-er) *v.* 1. To spread over; place a lid or cover over. 2. To conceal; shelter; protect. 3. To clothe; invest; envelop. 4. To be equivalent to; compensate for. 5. To

travel over. 6. To have within range; aim at. 7. To include; comprehend. 8. *Journalism.* To report on, as a sports event.—*n.* 1. Object or substance spread over another object; wrapping; lid. 2. Protective concealment. 3. A disguise; screen. 4. Table utensils and cloth for one person.—**cov·er·er** *n.*

cov·er·age (*kuv*-er-ij) *n.* 1. Sum of risks provided for, as in an insurance contract. 2. *Finance.* Amount on hand to cover liabilities. 3. *Journalism.* Act or manner of covering, as a news event.

cov·er·ing (*kuv*-er-ing) *n.* 1. Any object or substance which covers or conceals. 2. Clothing; garments.

cov·er·let (*kuv*-er-let) *n.* Also **co·ver·lid.** A blanket or bedspread.

cov·ert (*kuh*-vert) *adj.* Protected; concealed; disguised; surreptitious.—*n.* 1. A shelter; protective covering. 2. A thicket providing shelter for game. 3. Also **covert cloth.** A fine, twilled woolen fabric.—**cov·ert·ly** *adv.*

cov·er·ture (*kuv*-er-choor) *n.* 1. Covering; shelter; disguise. 2. *Law.* Status of a woman during marriage.

cov·et (*kuv*-et) *v.* To long for; crave, esp. that which belongs to another.—**cov·et·a·ble** *adj.*

cov·et·ous (*kuv*-uh-tus) *adj.* Greedy; avaricious.—**cov·et·ous·ly** *adv.*—**cov·et·ous·ness** *n.*

cov·ey (*kuv*-ee) *n.* [*pl.* -eys] A small flock; group, as of quail.

cow (*kow*) *n.* [*pl.* cows] The mature female of the bovine and certain other animals, esp. that domestic dairy animal which provides milk.

cow (1/75 life size)

cowbell	cowhand	cowpath
cow-eyed	cow horse	cow pony
cow gate	cowleech	cowshed
cowgirl	cow-nosed	cowyard

cow (*kow*) *v.* To intimidate; daunt; frighten.

cow·ard (*kow*-erd) *n.* One lacking courage; craven.—**cow·ard** *adj.*

cow·ard·ice (*kow*-er-dis) *n.* Lack of courage.

cow·ard·ly (*kow*-erd-lee) *adj.* Lacking courage; fearful; craven.—**cow·ard·ly** *adv.*— **-li·ness** *n.*

cow·bird (*kow*-berd) *n.* A small, black North American migratory bird.

cow·boy *n.* Man who herds cattle, esp. on the western plains of the U.S.

cow·catch·er *n.* 1. A wedge-shaped frame in front of a locomotive for clearing the track ahead. 2. *Advertising.* Slogan or commercial appearing at the beginning of a radio program.

cow·er (*kow*-er) *v.* To quail; shrink.

cow·herd *n.* Person employed to tend cows.

cow·hide *n.* 1. The hide of a cow made into leather. 2. A heavy whip of cowhide.—*v.* [hid·ed; -hid·ing] To whip with a cowhide.

cowl (*kowl*) *n.* 1. A monk's hood. 2. A hood-shaped chimney covering for increasing drafts.

C

3. Cowling. 4. Upper front portion of an automobile body; hood.—**cowl** v.—**cowled** adj.

cow·lick n. A tuft of hair turned about, or sticking up, on the forehead.

cowl·ing n. A metal covering over an airplane engine.

cow·man n. A rancher; one who raises cattle.

co-work·er (koh-werk-er) n. A collaborator.

cow·pea (kow-pee) n. A plant having long pods and a seed used for food.

cow·pox n. An eruptive disease of cows which immunizes humans against smallpox.

cow·punch·er n. Colloquial. A cowboy.

cow·rie, cow·ry (kow-ree) n. [pl. -ries] A marine mollusk whose shell is used for money and ornamentation by various primitive tribes.

cow·slip n. A yellow wildflower.

cox (koks) n. [pl. coxes] Colloquial. Coxswain. —v. To act as a coxswain for.

cox·comb n. 1. A fop; vain fellow; dandy. 2. A cockscomb.—**cox·comb·ic, -com·bi·cal** adj.

cox·swain (kok-s'n) n. Man who steers a boat, esp. a racing shell.

coy (koy) adj. Shy; coquettishly bashful or demure.—**coy·ly** adv.—**coy·ness** n.

coy·o·te (ky-oht; ky-oh-tee) n. The American prairie wolf.

coy·pu (koy-poo) n. A South American water rodent bearing a valuable brown fur called nutria.

COYOTE (1/75 life size)

coz (kuz) n. Colloquial. Cousin.

coz·en (kuz-'n) v. To cheat; deceive, esp. in a petty way.—**coz·en·age** n.—**coz·en·er** n.

co·zy, co·sy (koh-zee) adj. [co·zi·er, co·si·er; co·zi·est, cos·i·est] Snug; comfortable; warm. —**coz·i·ly** adv.—**coz·i·ness** n.

co·zy (koh-zee) n. [pl. co·zies] A knitted covering for a teapot. Also **co·sy, co·sey.**

crab n. 1. An edible, ten-footed, short-tailed c r u s t a c e a n. 2. [cap.] Cancer, a sign in the Zodiac. 3. A mechanism fitted with hooks, used for hoisting. —v. [crabbed; crab·bing] To fish for crabs.—**crab·ber** n.—**catch a crab.** To miss a stroke when rowing a boat.

CRAB (1/15 life size)

crab n. A louse infesting the pubic region.

crab n. 1. A small, wild, sour apple. 2. A morose sour-tempered person.—adj. Sour.

crab v. [crabbed; crab·bing] Slang. To be irritable; criticize.

crab apple. Also **crab.** A small, wild apple.

crab·bed adj. 1. Morose; peevish; bitter. 2. Cramped.—**crab·bed·ly** adv.— **-bed·ness** n.

crack (krak) v. 1. To break without an entire separation of the parts; fracture. 2. Slang. To utter quips or jokes. 3. To snap; cause to

make a sharp, sudden noise. 4. To make crazy. 5. To open. 'Crack a new bottle of whisky.'—n. 1. A fissure; chink; narrow breach. 2. A sharp, sudden sound. 3. Slang. Witticism, quip.—adj. Excellent, first-rate.

crack·a·jack (krak-uh-jak) n. Also **crack·er·jack.** 1. A caramel, popcorn, and nut confection. 2. Slang. An expert; virtuoso.—adj. Slang. Skillful; expert; topnotch.

crack-brained adj. Crazy; eccentric; mad.

cracked adj. 1. Split; rent. 2. Crazy; insane.

crack·er n. 1. A small hard biscuit. 2. A firework which explodes with a noise. 3. Southern U.S. A poor white person.

crack·ing n. 1. Breaking. 2. Process of heating petroleum under pressure to obtain a larger yield of gasoline.

crack·le (krak-'l) v. [crack·led; crack·ling] 1. To make small abrupt noises rapidly. 2. To make or become marked by a network of fine lines.—**crack·le** n.

crack·ling n. 1. Small abrupt noises frequently repeated. 2. Crisp, brittle skin of roasted pork. 3. [pl.] Small bits of deep-fried pork.

crack·ly (krak-lee) adj. Making a series of short, popping noises.

crack·nel n. A hard brittle biscuit.

cracks·man n. A burglar; safe-cracker.

crack·up n. 1. A collision between two vehicles. 2. Smash-up of an airplane. 3. A nervous breakdown.

cra·dle (kray-d'l) n. 1. A movable crib for rocking infants. 2. Birthplace. 3. Infancy. 4. Agriculture. A frame of wood with long bending teeth, fastened to a scythe, for laying oats and other cereal grasses in a swath as they are cut. 5. A low platform equipped with casters, on which mechanics work under automobiles.—v. [cra·dled; cra·dling].

cradle song. A lullaby.

craft (kraft) n. 1. Guile; cunning; artifice. 2. Trade; manual art. 3. A vessel; ship; airplane. 4. Ships or planes viewed collectively.

crafts·man (krafts-m'n) n. [pl. -men] A skilled artisan.—**crafts·man·ship** n.

craft·y (kraf-tee) adj. [craf·ti·er; craf·ti·est] Cunning; sly; tricky.—**craft·i·ly** adv.— **-i·ness** n.

crag (krag) n. A steep rough-surfaced rock or cliff.—**crag·ged** adj. Rough; rugged.—**crag·gi·ness** n.—**crag·gy** adj.

crake (krayk) n. A migratory wading bird.

cram (kram) v. [crammed; cram·ming] 1. To stuff; crowd; fill to superfluity. 2. To prepare for an examination by last-minute study.

cram n. 1. Colloquial. A state of being crammed; crush. 2. Colloquial. The act of studying in haste for an examination.—**cram·mer** n.

cramp n. 1. Medical. A painful muscular contraction. 2. Restraint; confinement.—v. 1. To affect with spasms. 2. To confine; restrain. 3. To turn the front wheels of a vehicle far to one side.—**cramp** adj.

cram·pon (kram-p'n) n. Also **cram·poon.** One

of a pair of large hooks used to raise heavy objects.

cran·ber·ry (*kran*-bair-ree) *n.* A dark red, globular berry used to make sauce, tarts, etc.

crane (*krayn*) *n.* 1. A migratory, wading bird, with long neck and legs. 2. A machine for raising great weights and depositing them at some distance from their original place.—*v.* [craned; cran·ing] To stretch out one's neck.

crane's-bill, cranes·bill *n.* The geranium family, esp. the wild geranium.

cra·ni·al (*kray*-nee-ul) *adj.* Pertaining to the skull.—**cra·ni·al·ly** *adv.*

cra·ni·ol·o·gy (kray-nee-*ol*-uh-jee) *n.* Science dealing with the size and shape of the skull. —**cra·ni·o·log·i·cal·ly** *adv.*—**cra·ni·ol·o·gist** *n.*

cra·ni·om·e·try (kray-nee-*om*-uh-tree) *n.* The study of the measurements of the human head. — **-o·met·ric** (-uh-*meh*-trik), **-ri·cal** *adj.*— **-ri·cal·ly** *adv.*— **-om·e·trist** (-*om*-uh-trist) *n.*

cra·ni·um (*kray*-nee-um) *n.* [*pl.* -ni·ums; -ni·a] The skull.

crank (*krank*) *n.* 1. *Mechanics.* **a.** A tool used to turn over or start an engine. **b.** Any bent arm rotating on a straight shaft to convert circular motion to up-and-down motion. 2. A crotchety person; eccentric.—**crank** *v.*

crank·case *n. Mechanics.* The housing or covering about a crankshaft.

crank·shaft *n. Mechanics.* A shaft which turns or is driven by a crank.

crank·y *adj.* [crank·i·er; crank·i·est] Irritable; cross; peevish.—**crank·i·ly** *adv.*— **-i·ness** *n.*

cran·ny (*kran*-ee) *n.* [*pl.* -nies] A small narrow opening or crevice.—**cran·nied** *adj.*

crape (*krayp*) *n.* A gauzy, crinkled fabric, often black and associated with mourning.—**crape·hang·er** *n. Slang.* A gloomy, morose person.

crap·pie (*krap*-ee) *n.* A fresh-water fish of North America, related to the sunfish.

craps (*kraps*) *n., sing.* Also **crap shooting.** A gambling game played with a pair of dice. —**crap·shoot·er** *n.*

crash (*krash*) *v.* 1. To break with a loud noise; collide violently. 2. *Slang.* To enter uninvited. 3. *Aeronautics.* To make a bad or emergency landing, damaging the plane.

crash *n.* A coarse linen cloth.

crass (*kras*) *adj.* 1. Dense; stupid. 2. Coarse; crude; gross.—**crass·ly** *adv.*—**crass·ness** *n.*

crate (*krayt*) *n.* 1. A box with wooden slats. 2. A worn-out airplane.—*v.* [crat·ed; crat·ing] To put into a crate or box.—**crat·er** *n.*

cra·ter (*krayt*-er) *n.* 1. The mouth of a volcano. 2. *Military.* A shell-hole; cavity made by an exploding mine or bomb.

cra·vat (kruh-*vat*) *n.* A necktie.

crave (*krayv*) *v.* [craved; crav·ing] 1. To hunger for; desire; need. 2. To beg for earnestly.—**crav·er** *n.*

cra·ven (*kray*-v'n) *adj.* Cowardly; base.—*n.* A coward; weak-hearted person.—*v.* To make cowardly.—**cra·ven·ly** *adv.*—**cra·ven·ness** *n.*

Cra·ven·ette (krav-uh-*net*) *n.* 1. A trade-mark for a waterproofed fabric or leather. 2. A raincoat made of such material.

crav·ing (*kray*-ving) *n.* Strong desire; hunger.

craw (*kraw*) *n.* 1. Stomach of an animal. 2. Crop of a bird or insect.

craw·fish *n.* Also **cray·fish.** An edible, lobster-like crustacean.—*v.* To back out.

crawl *n.* An enclosure for fish, turtles, etc.

crawl (*krawl*) *v.* 1. To creep; move slowly on the hands and knees. 2. To abase oneself. 3. To have, or have the sensation of, insects, creeping over the body. 4. To move slowly. —*n.* 1. The act of crawling. 2. *Swimming.* An overhand stroke made while resting flat on the stomach.—**crawl·er** *n.* 1. A reptile. 2. An angleworm.—**crawl·ing·ly** *adv.*

craw·ly *adj. Colloquial.* Feeling as if insects were creeping over one.

cray·fish (*kray*-fish) *n.* Crawfish.

cray·on (*kray*-un) *n.* 1. A cylinder of colored clay, chalk, or charcoal used in drawing. 2. A crayon drawing.—**cray·on** *v.*

craze (*krayz*) *v.* [crazed; craz·ing] To render insane; drive mad.—*n.* Fad; rage.

cra·zy (*kray*-zee) *adj.* [cra·zi·er; cra·zi·est] 1. Insane; mad. 2. Cracked; flawed; unsound.—**cra·zi·ly** *adv.*—**cra·zi·ness** *n.*

crazy bone. A point on the elbow where a nerve comes near the surface; funny bone.

crazy quilt. A patchwork quilt.

creak (*kreek*) *v.* To make a squeaking or grating sound.—**creak** *n.*

creak·y *adj.* [creak·i·er, creak·i·est] Grating; broken down.—**creak·i·ly** *adv.*—**creak·i·ness** *n.*

cream (*kreem*) *n.* 1. The richer part of milk, which rises to the top. 2. The choice part; best portion.

cream cheese. A cheese made from new milk to which cream has been added.

cream·er *n.* 1. A cream pitcher. 2. A machine for separating cream from milk.

cream·er·y *n.* [*pl.* -ies] An establishment where cream is turned into butter and cheese; a shop where dairy products are sold.

cream of tartar. Purified tartar used in cooking and medicine.

cream·y *adj.* [cream·i·er; cream·i·est] Thick; full of or resembling cream; rich.—**cream·i·ly** *adv.*—**cream·i·ness** *n.*

crease (*krees*) *n.* A line or mark made by folding or doubling a material.—*v.* [creased; creas·ing]—**creas·er** *n.*

create (kree-*ayt*) *v.* [cre·at·ed; cre·at·ing] To produce; cause to exist; bring about.

cre·a·tion (kree-*ay*-sh'n) *n.* 1. The act of bringing into existence. 2. That which is produced.—**cre·a·tion·al** *adj.*

cre·a·tive *adj.* Productive; original.—**cre·a·tive·ly** *adv.*—**cre·a·tive·ness** *n.*

cre·a·tor *n.* 1. One who creates or produces. 2. [*cap.*] God.

crea·ture (*kree*-cher) *n.* 1. Any living being. 2. One subject to the will of another; a tool.

C

—**crea·tur·al** *adj.*—**crea·ture·ly** *adv.*—**creature comfort.** Anything, like food or drink, that contributes to physical enjoyment.

crèche (*kresh*) *n.* 1. A nursery; day nursery. 2. A home for foundlings. 3. A representation of the Nativity displayed in churches and homes at Christmas time.

cre·dence (*kree*-d'ns) *n.* Belief; trust.

cre·den·tial (kruh-*den*-sh'l) *adj.* Accrediting; certifying a claim.—*n.* An identifying document; accreditation.

cre·den·za (kreh-*den*-zuh) *v.* An ornamental bookcase, usually with rounded ends.

cred·i·ble (*kred*-uh-b'l) *adj.* Believable; worthy of confidence.—**cred·i·bil·i·ty, cred·i·ble·ness** *n.*

cred·it (*kreh*-dit) *n.* 1. Belief; trust; confidence. 2. Source of pride. 'A credit to the community.' 3. *Business.* Confidence in future payments for goods delivered. 4. *Business.* The reputation of solvency and honesty which entitles a man to be trusted. 5. *Bookkeeping.* The side of an account in which a payment received is entered. 6. A sum of money due a person. 7. *Education.* Official acceptance that a course of study has been completed; unit of academic work accepted.—**cred·it** *v.*

cred·it·a·ble *adj.* 1. Worthy of belief; credible. 2. Estimable; reputable.—**cred·it·a·bil·i·ty** *n.*—**cred·it·a·bly** *adv.*

credit line. A line of type on or below a reproduction of a photograph, map, etc., giving the name of its creator.

cred·i·tor (*kred*-ih-ter) *n.* 1. A person to whom money is owed. 2. *Bookkeeping.* An amount shown on the credit side of the ledger.

cre·do (*kree*-doh) *n.* [*pl.* cre·dos] 1. A creed; system of beliefs. 2. [*cap.*] The Nicene Creed sung during the mass.

cre·du·li·ty (kruh-*dyoo*-luh-tee) *n.* [*pl.* -ties] Gullibility; overreadiness to believe.

cred·u·lous (*kreh*-joo-lus) *adj.* Overready to believe; gullible.— **-lous·ly** *adv.*— **-lous·ness** *n.*

Cree (*kree*) *n.* [*pl.* Cree, Crees] An American Indian of the Algonquin tribes.

creed (*kreed*) *n.* 1. A set of beliefs. 2. Religion; faith.

creek (*kreek*; *krik*) *n.* A rivulet; small river.

Creek *n.* A member of a southern U.S. Indian tribe.

creel (*kreel*) *n.* A wicker fishing basket.

creep (*kreep*) *v.* [crept; creep·ing] 1. To move with the body close to the ground; crawl. 2. To move slowly or feebly. 3. To move secretly; enter unobserved. 4. To feel as though insects were moving on one's skin.—*n. Mining.* A sinking down of the strata overlying a working.—**the creeps.** A terrified feeling.

creep·er *n.* 1. One who creeps. 2. *Botany.* A plant which spreads along the surface of the earth, or attaches itself to some other body. 3. A small bird with a curved bill, resembling the woodpecker. 4. A grapnel. 5. A device for moving material slowly to or from a machine. 6. An infant's rompers.

creep·y *adj.* [creep·i·er; creep·i·est] 1. Frightened; crawly. 2. Marked by creeping.

cre·mate (*kree*-mayt) *v.* [cre·mat·ed; cre·mat·ing] To incinerate a corpse.—**cre·ma·tion** *n.*

cre·ma·tor *n.* One who incinerates corpses.

cre·ma·to·ry (*kree*-muh-taw-ree) *n.* [*pl.* -ries] A place where corpses are incinerated.

crème de menthe. A mint-flavored liqueur.

Cre·mo·na (kree-*moh*-nuh) *n.* A type of violin made at Cremona, Italy, in the seventeenth and eighteenth centuries.

cre·nate (*kree*-nayt) *adj.* Notched; indented; scalloped.—**cre·nat·ed** *adj.*—**cre·nate·ly** *adv.*

cren·el·ate, cren·el·late (*kreh*-n'l-ayt) *v.* [cren·el·ated, cren·el·lat·ed; cren·el·at·ing, cren·el·lat·ing] To provide with battlements or loopholes.—**cren·el·at·ed, cren·el·lat·ed** *adj.*

Cre·ole (*kree*-ohl) *n.* 1. A Frenchman or Spaniard born and raised in the American colonies. 2. A white descendant of the French settlers of Louisiana. 3. The French dialect spoken in Louisiana. 4. [*not cap.*] A person of mixed Creole and Negro parentage.—*adj.*

cre·o·sole (*kree*-uh-sohl) *n.* A colorless, oily antiseptic.

cre·o·sote (*kree*-uh-soht) *n.* An oily, heavy preservative distilled from coal tar and wood tar.—*v.* [cre·o·sot·ed; cre·o·sot·ing].

crepe, crêpe (*krayp*) *n.* A light, crinkly, closely woven fabric of various materials; crape.

crêpe de Chine (krayp-duh-*sheen*) A sheer silk crepe.

crêpe paper. A thin, crinkly paper.

crep·i·tate (*krep*-uh-tayt) *v.* [-tat·ed; tat·ing] To crackle; snap.—**crep·i·tant** *adj.*— **-ta·tion** *n.*

cre·pus·cu·lar (kruh-*pus*-kyoo-ler) *adj.* Pertaining to twilight.

cre·scen·do (kruh-*shen*-doh) *n.* [*pl.* -dos] Swelling volume of noise or music.—**cre·scen·do** *adj. & adv.*

cres·cent (*kres*-ent) *n.* 1. The new moon. 2. The Turkish flag; Mohammedanism. 3. Anything shaped like the new moon.—**cres·cent** *adj.*

cre·sol (*kree*-sohl) *n.* Any of three oily, colorless solids or liquids obtained from coal tar and used as disinfectants.

CRESCENT

cress *n.* A plant the leaves of which are used for making salads.

cres·set (*kres*-et) *n.* A fixed candlestick in a great hall; firepan carried in a procession.

crest *n.* 1. A tuft on the top of an animal's head. 2. Plume or tuft of feathers on an ancient helmet. 3. The foamy top of a wave. 4. The summit of a hill or mountain range. 5. *Heraldry.* Part of a coat of arms used as an ornament.—**crest** *v.*—**crest·ed** *adj.*

crest·fall·en *adj.* Dejected; abashed; dispirited. —**crest·fall·en·ly** *adv.*—**crest·fall·en·ness** *n.*

cre·ta·ceous (kreh-*tay*-shus) *adj.* 1. Chalky. 2. [*cap.*] *Geology.* Relating to the period between the Jurassic and Tertiary.—*n.* [*cap.*] *Geology*. The Cretaceous period.

cre·tin (*kree*-tin) *n.* One affected with cretinism.

cre·tin·ism *n.* A state of arrested development of mind and body due to lack of thyroid secretion.

cre·tonne (kree-*ton*, *kree*-ton) *n.* A printed cotton cloth.

cre·vasse (kruh-*vass*) *n.* 1. A broad crack in a glacier. 2. A break in a levee.

crev·ice (*krev*-iss) *n.* A fissure; crack.

crew *n.* 1. A band; gang. 2. The personnel of a ship or airplane. 3. *Sports*. The members of a rowing team.

crew·el (*kroo*-ul) *n.* A worsted thread of silk or wool, used in embroidery and fancy work.

crew·man *n.* A member of a plane's operating personnel.

crib *n.* 1. A manger; rack for feeding cattle. 2. A stall in a stable. 3. A bin for grain; small room; nut. 4. A small, fenced bed for children. 5. A key or translation used by students to avoid work or to cheat. 6. The bank of discards in cribbage. 7. *Thieves' Slang*. A place to be robbed. 8. A brothel. —*v.* [cribbed; crib·bing] *Slang*. To plagiarize.

crib·bage (*krib*-ij) *n.* A card game in which the purpose is to obtain counting combinations.

crick (*krik*) *n.* A spasm of muscular pain in some part of the body.—**crick** *v.*

crick·et (*krick*-et) *n.* A black, leaping insect related to the grasshopper, which produces a distinctive chirping sound by rubbing its wings together.

crick·et *n.* An English game, similar to baseball, played by eleven-man teams.—*v.* To play cricket.—**crick·et·er** *n.*

crick·et *n.* A small footstool.

cri·er (*kry*-er) *n.* 1. Formerly, one who made public proclamations. 2. An official who proclaims orders at a court.

crim. con. *Law*. Criminal conversation.

crime *n.* 1. A violation of law or morality, esp. a serious one. 2. Acts of wrongdoing and organized lawbreaking collectively.

Cri·me·a (kryme-*ee*-uh) *n.* A Russian peninsula on the north coast of the Black Sea.—**Cri·me·an** *adj. & n.*

crim·i·nal (*krim*-uh-n'l) *n.* One who breaks the law seriously or habitually.—**crim·i·nal** *adj.* —**crim·i·nal·i·ty** (krim-uh-*nal*-uh-tee) *n.*

criminal conversation. Illegal sexual intercourse, esp. with a married woman; adultery.

crim·i·nate (*krim*-uh-nayt) *v.* [-nat·ed; -nat·ing] 1. To charge with a crime. 2. To involve in a crime.—**crim·i·na·tion** *n.*—**crim·i·na·tive**, **crim·i·na·to·ry** *adj.*

crim·i·nol·o·gy (krim-uh-*nol*-uh-jee) *n.* The organized study of crime and criminals.—**crim·i·no·log·ic**, **-log·ic·al** *adj.*—**crim·i·nol·o·gist** *n.*

crimp (*krimp*) *v.* 1. To curl; flute. 2. To bend the edge of, as metal, so as to hold fast. 3. To gash fish or other meat in preparation for cooking.—**crimp** *n.*—**crimp·er** *n.*

crimp *n.* One who, by underhand means, gets a seaman to sign on a ship.—**crimp** *v.*

crimp·y *adj.* [crimp·i·er; crimp·i·est] Curly; kinky.

crim·son (*krim*-z'n) *n.* A deep red color.—*v.* To blush.—**crim·son** *adj.*

cringe (*krinj*) *v.* [cringed; cring·ing] To cower; shrink; quail; fawn.—**cringe** *n.*—**cring·er** *n.*

crin·gle (*kring*-g'l) *n.* *Nautical*. A ring, loop, or eyelet at the edge of a sail.

crin·kle (*kring*-k'l) *v.* [crink·led; crin·kling] 1. To wrinkle; bend. 2. To rustle.—*n.* A wrinkle.—**crin·kly** *adj.*

cri·noid (*kry*-noyd) *adj.* 1. Shaped like a lily. 2. Pertaining to a flowerlike class of marine animals.—**cri·noid** *n.*

crin·o·line (*krin*-uh-lin) *n.* 1. Stiff material used to reinforce dress fabrics. 2. A hoop skirt.

crip·ple (*krip*-'l) *n.* One who has lost the use of a limb or limbs; a lame person.—*v.* [crip·pled; -pling] 1. To lame; disable by injuring the limbs. 2. To disable; weaken.—**crip·pler** *n.*

cri·sis (*kry*-sis) *n.* [*pl.* cri·ses] 1. A turning point; emergency. 2. *Medicine*. A critical moment or stage of development in a disease.

crisp (*krisp*) *adj.* 1. Fresh; firm; brittle. 2. Neat, sharp. 'Crisp outlines.' 3. Incisive, trenchant; terse. 4. Brisk; lively. 'Crisp dialogue.' 5. Bracing. 'Crisp air.'—*n.* Anything crisp.—*v.* 1. To cook to a brittle state. 2. To curl; ripple.—**crisp·ly** *adv.*—**crisp·ness** *n.*

crisp·y (*krisp*-ee) *adj.* [crisp·i·er; crisp·i·est] 1. Brittle. 2. Closely curled.

criss·cross (*kriss*-kross) *n.* A pattern of lines crossing each other.—*adj.* Intersecting.—*adv.* So as to cross something.—*v.* To make a crisscross pattern.

cri·te·ri·on (kry-*tihr*-ee-un) *n.* [*pl.* -ri·a] A standard for judging; yardstick.

crit·ic (*krit*-ik) *n.* 1. One who criticizes or finds fault. 2. One who judges works of literature, music, and art.

crit·i·cal (*krit*-ih-k'l) *adj.* 1. Relating to criticism. 2. Faultfinding; carping; fastidious. 3. Crucial; decisive. 4. Dangerous; hazardous.—**crit·i·cal·ly** *adv.*—**crit·i·cal·ness** *n.*

critical angle. 1. *Optics*. The smallest angle of incidence at which total reflection occurs. 2. *Aeronautics*. The angle of flight at which airflow changes suddenly around the ailerons, rudder, etc., with consequent changes in lift and drag.

crit·i·cism (*krit*-uh-sizm) *n.* 1. Censure; rebuke. 2. Evaluation of musical, literary, or artistic works.

crit·i·cize (*krit*-uh-syze) *v.* [crit·i·cized; crit·i·ciz·ing] Also **crit·i·cise**. To judge critically; censure; find fault.—**crit·i·ciz·a·ble** *adj.*

cri·tique (krih-*teek*) *n.* 1. A critical examination of any subject. 2. The art of criticism.

croak (*krohk*) *v.* 1. To make a low, hoarse noise in the throat, as a frog, raven, or crow. 2. *Slang*. To die; murder. 3. To foretell disaster; grumble.—**croak** *n.*—**croak·er** *n.*

C

croak·er (*krohk*-er) *n.* One of several fishes which make grunting sounds.

Cro·at (*kroh*-at) *n.* An inhabitant of Croatia.

Cro·a·tia (kroh-*ay*-shuh) A part of Yugoslavia.

cro·chet (kroh-*shay*) *n.* A kind of knitting done with a small hook.—*v.* [-cheted; -chet·ing].

crock (*krok*) *n.* 1. An earthen vessel; pitcher. 2. *Slang.* A worn-out horse or person.

crock·er·y (*krok*-er-ee) *n.* Earthenware.—**crock·er·y·ware** *n.*

croc·o·dile (*krok*-uh-dyle) *n.* A large, long-tailed, tough-skinned, carnivorous aquatic reptile, found in the tropics.—**croc·o·dil·i·an** *adj.* & *n.*

CROCODILE (1/90 life size)

crocodile tears. Superfluous, insincere lamentation.

cro·cus (*kroh*-kus) *n.* [*pl.* -cus·es, -ci] 1. A bulbous herb of the iris family, with a singular tubular flower. 2. A saffron coloring matter.

Croe·sus (*kree*-sus). A fabulously rich king of Lydia in Asia Minor.

croft (*kroft*) *n.* A small field or farm.—**croft·er** *n.*

Croix de Feu (krwah-duh-*fer*). A French fascist organization.

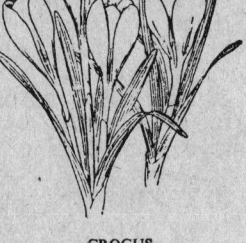
CROCUS

Cro-Mag·non (kroh-*man*-yon) *adj.* Referring to a prehistoric race of men that had stone and bone but not metal implements.—**Cro-Mag·non** *n.*

crom·lech (*krom*-lek) *n. Archaeology.* A large flat stone laid across others as a sepulchral monument; dolmen.

crone (*krohn*) *n.* An old woman; hag.

cro·ny (*kroh*-nee) *n.* [*pl.* -nies] An intimate; comrade; chum.

crook *n.* 1. A sharp bend; curve; turn. 2. A shepherd's or bishop's staff. 3. Anything hooked or bent. 4. *Colloquial.* Cheat; thief; swindler.—*v.* To bend; curve.—**crooked** *adj.* Having a sharp bend.

crook·ed (*krook*-id) *adj.* 1. Bent; curved; winding. 2. *Slang.* Dishonest; nefarious; deceitful.—**crook·ed·ly** *adv.*—**crook·ed·ness** *n.*

crook·neck *n.* A variety of squash with a curved neck.

croon *v.* 1. To hum; sing softly. 2. *Slang.* To sing songs in an intimate style.—**croon·er** *n.*

crop *n.* 1. An organ in the gullet of a fowl where food is stored and digestion of it begun; craw. 2. The produce of the earth; harvest· 3. Hair cut close; short haircut. 4. A stout riding whip.—*v.* [cropped; crop·ping] 1. To cut close; mow; reap. 2. To trim a photograph, esp. in order to improve its composition.—**crop up.** To appear; become manifest.

crop·per *n.* One who cultivates another's land for a share of the crop.

crop·per *n.* A fall; collapse; failure.

cro·quet (kroh-*kay*) *n.* An outdoor game played with mallets and balls by two teams, the object being to drive the balls through hoops or wickets in a certain order.—*v.* [croqueted (-*kayd*); cro·quet·ing (-*kay*-ing)].

cro·quette (kroh-*ket*) *n.* Any chopped food combined with thick sauce, rolled in egg and crumbs, and fried.

cro·sier, cro·zier (*kroh*-zher) *n.* A bishop's or abbot's staff bearing a cross at the top.

cross (*krawss*) *n.* 1. An ancient instrument of execution made of two crossed pieces of timber, esp. the one [*cap.*] on which Christ was crucified. 2. The symbol of the Christian religion. 3. A figure made by two straight lines intersecting, esp. when used as a signature. 4. Act of crossing; state of being crossed. 5. Burden; trial. 6. A hybrid.—*v.* 1. To draw a line or lay an object across another. 2. To make the sign of the cross over something or someone as a devotional act. 3. To move across; traverse; pass. 4. To thwart, obstruct. 5. To interbreed.—*adj.* 1. Transverse; oblique; lying athwart. 2. Peevish; ill-humored; fretful. 3. Cross-breed. 4. Contrary; opposed.—**cross·ly** *adv.*—**cross·ness** *n.*

cross-armed	cross-handed
cross-banded	cross haul
cross beam	cross-headed
cross belt	cross-index
cross-bias	cross-interrogate
cross bolt	cross-laced
cross channel	cross-over
cross-check	crosspiece
cross-cultivation	cross-plow
cross-drain	cross rail
cross-file	cross rule
cross-fire	cross-shaped
cross-fissured	cross tie
cross flow	cross-town
cross-folded	cross-voting
cross-gartered	cross walk

cross bar. A transverse bar or line.—*v.* [cross-barred; cross-bar·ring] To furnish with cross bars.—**cross-barred** *adj.*

cross·bill *n.* A bird of the finch family with a curved and crossed bill.

cross·bones *n. pl.* Two crossed bones, usually beneath a skull, symbolizing death.

cross·bow *n.* An old weapon for hurling missiles, formed by placing a bow across a stock.—**cross·bow·man** *n.*

cross·breed *n.* A hybrid; breed produced from a male and female of different kinds.—**cross·breed** *v.* [-bred; -breed·ing]—**cross·bred** *adj.*

CROSSBOW

cross·cut *n.* A short cut; direct line or route

oblique to the main one.—*v.* [cross·cut; cross·cut·ting] To cut across.—**cross·cut** *adj.*

crosse (*krawss*) *n.* A stick ending in a basketlike net used in the game of lacrosse.

cross-ex·am·ine *v.* [cross-ex·am·ined; cross-ex·am·in·ing] To question an opposition witness thoroughly, esp. in a court of law.—**cross-ex·am·i·na·tion** *n.*—**cross-ex·am·in·er** *n.*

cross eye. A squint in which one or both eyes are turned toward the nose.—**cross-eyed** *adj.*

cross-fer·ti·li·za·tion *n. Botany.* The fertilization of one plant by the pollen of another.—**cross-fer·ti·lize** *v.* [-ized; -iz·ing].

cross-grained *adj.* 1. Having an irregular grain. 2. Contrary; perverse.

cross-hatch *v.* To mark or shade with many parallel lines crossing each other.

cross·ing *n.* 1. Act of crossing. 2. Intersection; place of crossing.

cross·patch *n. Slang.* An ill-natured person.

cross-pol·li·na·tion *n.* Cross-fertilization.—**cross-pol·li·nate** *v.* [-nat·ed; -nat·ing].

cross-ques·tion *v.* To cross-examine.

cross-reference *n.* A reference to an item in another part of a book or catalogue.

cross road. A road which crosses or connects with a main road.—**cross·roads** *n. pl.* Place where roads intersect.

cross section. 1. A piece cut directly across. 2. A representative selection or sample.

cross-stitch. A stitch crossed diagonally over another.—**cross·stitch** *v.*

cross·trees *n. pl. Nautical.* Two short pieces of timber supporting a mast.

cross·wise *adv.* Also **cross·ways.** 1. Across; in the form of a cross. 2. Contrarily.

crossword puzzle. A word puzzle with sets of squares to be filled in with letters forming words, both vertically and horizontally.

crotch (*kroch*) *n.* Angle at the parting of two legs or branches.—**crotched** *adj.*

crotch·et (*kroch*-it) *n.* 1. A whim; odd fancy. 2. A small hook or hooklike device.

crotch·et·y *adj.* Full of crotchets; queer; eccentric.—**crotch·et·i·ness** *n.*

cro·ton (*kroh*-t'n) *n.* A tropical shrub yielding croton oil.—**croton oil.** A brownish, bitter-tasting liquid used as a cathartic.

Croton bug. A small winged cockroach.

crouch (*krowch*) *v.* To stoop; bend low, esp. as in fear or hiding; cower.—**crouch** *n.*

croup (*kroop*) *n.* An inflammatory condition of the larynx and trachea marked by a constant hoarse cough.—**croup·y** *adj.*

croup *n.* The rump of a horse.

crou·pi·er (*kroop*-ee-er) *n.* One who superintends and collects the stakes at a gaming table.

crou·ton (kroo-*ton*) *n.* A small cube of toast used esp. in soups.

crow (*kroh*) *n.* 1. A large black bird which feeds on grain. 2. A crowbar.—**as the crow flies.** In a straight line.

crow (*kroh*) *v.* [crew, crowed; crowed; crow·ing] 1. To make the shrill noise of a cock. 2. To boast; exult.—*n.* The cry of a cock.

Crow *n.* Member of a tribe of Indians from the western plains of the U.S.—**Crow** *adj.*

crow·bar (*kroh*-bahr) *n.* An iron bar with a bent end, used as a lever.

crowd *v.* 1. To press close or forward; shove. 2. To fill to excess; pack; cram.—*n.* 1. A throng; multitude; large, unorganized group of persons. 2. *Colloquial.* A clique.—**crowd sail.** *Nautical.* To carry a large amount of sail in order to increase speed.

crow·foot (*kroh*-foot) *n.* [*pl.* -feet] 1. A number of small cords of varying lengths for suspending an object. 2. A zinc electrode in certain batteries. 3. [*pl.* -foots] The buttercup or any plant with similarly shaped leaves.

crown *n.* 1. An ornamental head covering worn as a symbol of royalty or sovereignty. 2. Regal power; royalty. 3. Garland; wreath for the head. 4. The topmost part; highest state. 5. The portion of a tooth above the gum. 6. A British coin worth five shillings.—*v.* 1. To invest with a crown; install as a sovereign. 2. To honor; reward. 3. To top; surmount. 4. To complete; consummate.

crown colony. A British possession having little autonomy.

crown glass. A fine window glass, blown in circular sheets.

crown prince. The heir apparent to the throne.—**crown princess.**

crow's-foot *n.* [*pl* -feet] 1. A fine wrinkle at the outer corner of the eye. 2. A crowfoot.

crow's-nest *n. Nautical.* The position near the top of a mast where the lookout man is stationed.

Croydon. A city in SE England, site of one of the world's largest airports.

cru·cial (*kroo*-shul) *adj.* 1. Critical; decisive. 2. Trying; severe.—**cru·cial·ly** *adv.*

cru·ci·ble (*kroo*-suh-b'l) *n.* 1. A heat-resistant vessel for melting ores, etc.

cru·ci·fix (*kroos*-uh-fiks) *n.* A representation of Christ crucified upon the cross.

cru·ci·fix·ion (kroos-uh-*fik*-shun) *n.* 1. The act of crucifying; state of being crucified. 2. [*cap.*] The crucifying of Christ.

cru·ci·form (*kroo*-sih-form) *adj.* Cross-shaped.

cru·ci·fy (*kroo*-sih-fye) *v.* [cru·ci·fied; cru·ci·fy·ing] 1. To put to death by nailing the hands and feet to a cross. 2. To subject to extreme torture.

crude (*krood*) *adj.* 1. Unfinished; immature; raw. 2. Rude; vulgar; gross.—**crude·ly** *adv.*—**crude·ness** *n.*

cru·di·ty (*kroo*-dih-tee) *n.* [*pl.* -ties] 1. That which is crude. 2. Crassness; rudeness.

cru·el (*kroo*-ul) *adj.* [cru·el·er; cru·el·est] Pitiless; merciless; causing pain or misery.—**cru·el·ly** *adv.*—**cru·el·ness** *n.*

cru·el·ty (*kroo*-ul-tee) *n.* [*pl.* -ties] Ferocity; brutality; inhumanity.

C

cru·et (*kroo*-it) *n.* A small glass vial for holding vinegar, oil, etc.

cruise (*krooz*) *v.* [cruised; cruis·ing] 1. To make a sea voyage, esp. for pleasure, without a fixed destination. 2. To prowl a city's streets in an auto. 'Police cars and taxis cruise.'—*n.* A pleasure trip.

cruis·er (*krooz*-er) *n.* 1. A heavily armed, fast warship. 2. A power-driven pleasure boat with living accommodations. 3. A police patrol car with radio. 4. A forester who marks trees for cutting.

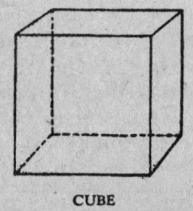

CRUET

crul·ler (*krul*-er) *n.* A fried cake made of egg batter; doughnut.

crumb (*krum*) *n.* 1. A small fragment or piece, esp. of bread or cake. 2. *Slang.* An oaf.—*v.* 1. To cover with bread crumbs. 2. To break into crumbs.—**crumb·er** *n.*—**crum·by** *adj.*

crum·ble (*krum*-b'l) *v.* [crum·bled; crum·bling] To break into pieces; fall apart.—**crum·ble** *n.*

crum·bly (*krum*-blee) *adj.* [crum·bli·er; crum·bli·est] Brittle; apt to crumble.—**crum·bli·ness** *n.*

crum·pet (*krum*-pit) *n.* A light, flat cake.

crum·ple (*krum*-p'l) *v.* [crum·pled; crum·pling] 1. To press into wrinkles or folds; crush. 2. To faint and fall to the ground.—*n.* An irregular fold.—**crum·pled** *adj.*

crunch *v.* 1. To press or grind with a crushing sound. 2. To chew a brittle substance noisily.

crup·per (*krup*-er) *n.* 1. The rump of a horse. 2. A harness strap fitting under a horse's tail.

cru·sade (kroo-*sayd*) *n.* 1. [*cap.*] One of a series of military expeditions undertaken by Christians in the Middle Ages for the recovery of the Holy Land from the Mohammedans. 2. Any zealous undertaking against evil.—*v.* [cru·sad·ed; cru·sad·ing]—**Cru·sad·er, cru·sad·er** *n.*

cruse (*krooz*) *n.* A small cup.

crush *v.* 1. To press out of shape. 2. To break to pieces by pressure. 3. To subdue; conquer.—*n.* 1. Strong pressure. 'The crush of a crowd.' 2. A fruit drink.—**crush·er** *n.*

crust (*krust*) *n.* 1. A hard surface layer or external covering, esp. of bread or pie. 2. Any dry hard piece of bread. 3. *Geology.* The observable exterior portion of the earth.

Crus·ta·cea (krus-*tay*-shuh) *n. pl.* A class of aquatic, segmented animals which breathe through gills and have a bony outer covering.—**crus·ta·cean** *n. & adj.*—**crus·ta·ceous** *adj.*

crust·ed (*krus*-tid) *adj.* Having a hard covering.

crust·y *adj.* [crust·i·er; crust·i·est] 1. Like or pertaining to crust; hard. 2. Gruff; brusque; surly.—**crust·i·ly** *adv.*—**crust·i·ness** *n.*

crutch (*kruch*) *n.* 1. A staff with a curving cross piece at the top, to be placed under the arm for supporting the lame while walking. 2. That which resembles a crutch in use or appearance.—**crutch** *v.*

crux (*kruks*) *n.* [*pl.* crux·es, cru·ces] 1. A difficult problem. 2. The essence; substance.

cry *n.* [*pl.* cries] 1. A loud, forceful call or utterance. 2. The characteristic sound of an animal; call. 3. Slogan; watchword.—*v.* [cried; cry·ing] 1. To utter a loud sound, as in anger, pain, etc. 2. To shout; proclaim. 3. To lament; weep.—**a far cry.** A long way. —**cry·down.** To depreciate; undervalue.

cry·ing *adj.* Demanding notice; extreme.

cry·o·lite (*kry*-oh-lyte) *n.* A hard, brittle, glassy crystal from which aluminum is extracted.

crypt (*kript*) *n.* 1. An underground cell or cave. 2. Part of a church below ground level.

cryp·tic (*krip*-tik) *adj.* Also **cryp·ti·cal.** Hidden; secret; occult.—**cryp·ti·cal·ly** *adv.*

cryp·to·gam (*krip*-tuh-gam) *n.* A large class of plants which seed from spores and do not bear true flowers.—**cryp·to·gam·ic, cryp·tog·a·mous** (krip-tuh-*gam*-ik; krip-*tog*-uh-mus) *adj.*

cryp·to·gram (*krip*-tuh-gram) *n.* 1. A code writing. 2. A secret cipher.

cryp·to·graph (*krip*-tuh-graf) *n.* 1. A secret code or cipher. 2. A writing in code.

cryp·tog·ra·phy (krip-*tog*-ruh-fee) *n.* [*pl.* -phies] 1. Art or science of writing in secret code. 2. Secret characters or code.—**cryp·tog·ra·pher, cryp·tog·ra·phist** (krip-*tog*-ruh-fer, -fist] *n.*—**cryp·to·graph·ic, cryp·to·graph·i·cal** (krip-tuh-*graf*-ik, -ih-k'l) *adj.*—**-i·cal·ly** *adv.*

crys·tal (*kris*-t'l) *n.* 1. A natural form of a substance having plane faces arranged in a symmetrical fashion. 2. The glass face of a watch. 3. A kind of high-grade, sparkling glass. 4. Any crystalline substance.—**crys·tal, crys·tal·line** (*kris*-t'l-een) *adj.*

crystal detector. *Radio.* A quartz crystal which rectifies a signal voltage.

crys·tal·ize (*kris*-t'l-yze) *v.* [crys·tal·ized; -liz·ing] 1. To form into crystals. 2. To become definite or lucid.—**crys·tal·liz·a·ble** *adj.*—**crys·tal·li·za·tion** (kris-t'l-ih-*zay*-shun) *n.*

crys·tal·log·ra·phy (kris-tuh-*log*-ruh-fee) *n.* The science dealing with crystals; theory of crystal structure.—**crys·tal·log·ra·pher** *n.*

crys·tal·loid (*kris*-tuh-loyd) *n. Chemistry.* A crystallizable substance which passes through a semipermeable animal membrane in solution.—**crys·tal·loid** *adj.*

crystal set. A radio receiver employing a galena crystal detector.

cub *n.* 1. The young of the bear, lion, and various other animals. 2. *Journalism.* An inexperienced reporter.—**cub·bish** *adj.*

cub·by·hole (*kuhb*-ee-hohl) *n.* A small snug compartment.

cube (*kyoob*) *n.* 1. A right-angled solid having six equal sides. 2. *Mathematics.* The product of a number multiplied by its square; third power of a number. —*v.* [cubed; cub·ing] 1. To multiply a number by its square. 2. To form into cubes.

CUBE

cu·beb (*kyoo*-beb) *n.* The dried, unripe fruit of a plant of the pepper family, used medicinally.

cube root. *Mathematics.* One of three equal factors of a number.

cu·bic (*kyoo*-bik) *adj.* Also **cu·bi·cal.** 1. Shaped like a cube. 2. Denoting the third power or cube root.—**cu·bi·cal·ly** *adv.*—**cu·bi·cal·ness** *n.*

cu·bi·cle (*kyoo*-bih-k'l) *n.* A tiny room or compartment, esp. a small sleeping alcove.

cub·ism (*kyoob*-izm) *n.* School of modern painting developed by Picasso and Bracque, aiming at the reduction of natural forms to their essential geometrical elements and emphasizing abstract pattern in monochrome.—**cub·ist** *n.*

cu·bit (*kyoo*-bit) *n.* A unit of measurement based on the distance from a man's elbow to the end of the middle finger; eighteen inches.

cu·boid (*kyoo*-boyd) *adj.* 1. Resembling a cube in shape. 2. Denoting a square-shaped bone of the foot.—*n.* 1. A right-angled solid whose opposite sides are equal. 2. The cuboid bone.

cuck·old (*kuhk*-'ld) *n.* The husband of an adultress.—*v.* To be unfaithful to a husband.—**cuck·old·ly** *adv.*—**cuck·old·ry** *n.*

cuck·oo (*kook*-oo) *n.* 1. A large song bird that lays its eggs in other birds' nests. 2. The note or call of this bird.—*v.* To repeat monotonously.—*adj.* (*koo*-koo) *Slang.* Daft; crazy.

cu·cul·late (*kyoo*-kuh-layt) *adj.* Also **cu·cu·lat·ed.** Covered with a hood or similar covering.

cu·cum·ber (*kyoo*-kum-ber) *n.* A deep-green, seeded vegetable grown on a trailing vine.

cud *n.* Food brought up from the first stomach of ruminant animals and rechewed at leisure.

cud·dle (*kuhd*-'l) *v.* [cud·dled; cud·dling] To lie or hold close; embrace; fondle.—**cud·dle** *n.*—**cud·dle·some** *adj.*—**cud·dly** *adv.*

cud·dy *n.* [*pl.* cud·dies] 1. A small after cabin where ship's officers and passengers eat. 2. A cook shanty on a barge.

cudg·el (*kuhj*-ul) *n.* A club; thick stick, esp. used for beating.—*v.* [cudg·eled, cudg·elled; -el·ing, -el·ling] To beat.—**cudg·e·ler, -el·ler** *n.*

cue *n.* 1. Line of dialogue serving as a signal to another actor. 2. A hint; prompter; signal. 3. A long single-file line; queue. 4. A straight tapered shaft used in pool.—*v.* [cued; cu·ing].

cuff *n.* A band or fold at the end of a sleeve or trouser leg.

cuff *v.* To rap or slap smartly.—**cuff** *n.*

cui·rass (kwih-*rass*) *n.* Armor to protect the chest region.—**cui·rass** *v.*

cui·sine (kwih-*zeen*) *n.* Cooking; the kitchen.

cuisse (*kwiss*) *n.* Defensive armor for the thighs.

cul-de-sac (*kul*-duh-*sak*) *n.* [*pl.* cul-de-sacs, culs-de-sac] A one-way street; blind alley.

cu·lex (*kyoo*-leks) *n.* One of a genus of mosquitoes including the household mosquito of America.

cu·li·nar·y (*kyoo*-lih-ner-ee; popularly *kuh*-) *adj.* Pertaining to cooking.

cull *n.* Waste remnants; discarded part.—**cull** *v.*

culm (*kulm*) *n.* An impure, shaly kind of coal.

culm *n. Botany.* A jointed stem or trunk.

cul·mi·nate (*kul*-mih-nayt) *v.* [cul·mi·nat·ed; -nat·ing] 1. To reach a climax; to arrive at the maximum point. 2. *Astronomy.* To be at the zenith or meridian.—**cul·mi·na·tion** (kuhl-mih-*nay*-shun) *n.*

cu·lottes (kuh-*lots*) *n. pl.* Loose, skirtlike slacks of dress length.

cul·pa·ble (*kuhl*-puh-b'l) *adj.* Guilty; blameworthy; faulty.—**cul·pa·bil·i·ty** (kuhl-puh-*bil*-ih-tee), **cul·pa·ble·ness** *n.*—**cul·pa·bly** *adv.*

cul·prit (*kuhl*-prit) *n.* One arraigned in court for a crime; guilty person.

cult *n.* 1. A system of religious belief; sect. 2. An intellectual obsession; fad.—**cult·ist** *n.*

cul·ti·vate (*kul*-tih-vayt) *v.* [cul·ti·vat·ed; -vat·ing] 1. To till; prepare for planting; raise or produce by tilling. 2. To improve socially by study or labor; refine. 3. To give special attention to; foster. 4. To loosen soil with a cultivator.—**cul·ti·va·ble, cul·ti·vat·a·ble** (kul-tih-*vayt*-uh-b'l) *adj.*—**cul·ti·va·tion** *n.*

cul·ti·vat·ed *adj.* Cultured; refined.

cul·ti·va·tor *n.* An agricultural implement with teeth or blades for loosening the earth.

cul·tu·ral (*kul*-cher-'l) *n.* 1. Educational; artistic; refining. 2. Pertaining to culture. 3. Bred; produced by breeding.

cul·ture *n.* 1. The total intellectual and institutional heritage of a civilization. 2. A preparation in which bacteria thrive. 3. Intellectual refinement. 4. Tilling the earth; cultivation.—*v.* [cul·tured; cul·tur·ing].

cul·tured *adj.* Well educated; refined; cultivated; possessing highly aesthetic tastes.

cul·vert (*kul*-vert) *n.* An arched drain or waterway under a bridge, road, etc.

cum·ber (*kum*-ber) *v.* To load down; overburden.—**cum·ber** *n.*—**cum·ber·er** *n.*

cum·ber·some (*kum*-ber-sum) *adj.* Burdensome; bulky; unwieldy; troublesome.—**cum·ber·some·ly** *adv.*—**cum·ber·some·ness** *n.*

cum·in (*kum*-in) *n.* Also **cum·min.** A small herb producing aromatic seeds.

cu·mu·late (*kyoo*-myoo-layt) *v.* [cu·mu·lat·ed; -lat·ing] To gather to one place; accumulate.—**cu·mu·la·tion** (kyoo-myoo-*lay*-shun) *n.*

cu·mu·la·tive (*kyoo*-myoo-luh-tiv) *adj.* 1. Increasing by successive additions. 2. Aggregated; heaped; amassed.—**cu·mu·la·tive·ly** *adv.*

cu·mu·lus (*kyoom*-yoo-lus) *n.* [*pl.* -li] A white cloud appearing in large, rounded masses.

cu·ne·ate (*kyoo*-nee-it) *adj.* Also **cu·ne·at·ed.** Wedge-shaped.—**cu·ne·ate·ly** *adv.*

cu·ne·i·form (kyoo-*nee*-ih-form) *n.* The wedge-shaped characters of an alphabet developed by ancient civilizations.—**cu·ne·i·form** *adj.*

cun·ning *adj.* 1. Shrewd; crafty; sly; designing. 2. Skillful; adroit; experienced. 3. *Colloquial.* Charming; attractive.—*n.* Shrewdness; craft.—**cun·ning·ly** *adv.*

cup *n.* 1. A small round vessel with a handle. 2. Any cup-shaped object. 3. The contents of a cup. 4. One's lot; portion.—**in one's cups.** Intoxicated; drunk.—*v.* [cupped; cup·ping]. 1. To form in the shape of a cup. 'He

C

cupped his hands.' 2. *Medicine*. To draw blood to the surface of the body by producing a vacuum with a glass cup.

cup·bear·er *n*. 1. An attendant who serves liquors. 2. Anciently, an officer who sampled wine before his master drank of it.

cup·board (*kub*-erd) *n*. A closet or locker in which food or eating utensils are kept.

cup·cake *n*. A small cake baked in a cup-shaped pan.

cup·ful *n*. [*pl*. cup·fuls] 1. The quantity contained in a full cup. 2. *Cooking*. A unit of fluid measure equal to ½ pint.

Cu·pid (*kyoo*-pid) *n. Roman Mythology*. 1. The god of love, son of Venus. 2. [*not cap.*] A personification of love as a naked, winged boy who shoots arrows into the heart.

cu·pid·i·ty (kyoo-*pid*-uh-tee) *n*. An inordinate desire for wealth; avarice; covetousness.

cu·po·la (*kyoo*-puh-luh) *n*. A rounded vault on a building; dome.

cup·ping (*kup*-ing) *n*. 1. Formation of a depression or hollow. 2. *Medicine*. Application of a vacuum cup to the flesh to draw blood to the surface.—**cup·per** *n*.

CUPOLA

cu·pre·ous (*kyoo*-pree-us) *adj*. Like or composed of copper.

cu·pric (*kyoo*-prik) *adj*. Containing copper in a valence of 2.

cu·prous (*kyoo*-prus) *adj*. Containing copper in a valence of 1.

cur (ker) *n*. 1. A mongrel; mediocre or mixed-breed dog. 2. A despicable man.

cur·a·ble (*kyoor*-uh-b'l) *adj*. Able to be healed or remedied.—**cur·a·bil·i·ty** (kyoor-uh-*bil*-uh-tee) *n*.—**cur·a·bly** *adv*.

cu·ra·çao (kyoo-ruh-*soh*) *n*. [*pl*. -çaos] Also **cu·ra·çao**. A liqueur flavored with orange peel, cinnamon, and mace.

cu·ra·cy (*kyoo*-ruh-see) *n*. [*pl*. -cies] The office of a curate.

cu·ra·re, cu·ra·ri (kyoo-*rah*-ree) *n*. Also **cu·ra·ra**. A brown-black resin used by South American Indians to poison arrows.

cu·rate (*kyoo*-rit) *n*. A clergyman who acts as assistant to a rector or a vicar.

cur·a·tive (*kyoor*-uh-tiv) *adj*. Healing; remedial; used in curing.—**cur·a·tive** *n*.

cu·ra·tor (kyoo-*ray*-ter) *n*. One who superintends a museum, library, exhibition, etc.—**cu·ra·to·ri·al** (kyoo-ruh-*tor*-ih-ul) *adj*.

curb (kerb) *n*. 1. The raised side of a gutter; border of a pavement. 2. A check; restraint; inhibition. 3. Part of a bridle which restrains by pulling the lower jaw.—*v*. To restrain; guide; check.

curb bit. A stiff bit with an attached strap fastening under the horse's jaw.

curb·ing *n*. Material for making a curb.

curb·stone *n*. A raised border of stone.

curd (kerd) *n*. The coagulated part of milk.—*v*. To curdle.—**curd·y** *adj*.

cur·dle (*ker*-d'l) *v*. [cur·dled; cur·dling] 1. To coagulate; thicken. 2. To run slow because of terror; freeze. 'His blood curdled.'

cure (kyoor) *v*. [cured; cur·ing] 1. To restore to health; heal. 2. To prepare for preservation by drying, salting, etc.—*n*. 1. Act or method of healing; remedy. 2. Spiritual charge or care.—**cur·er** *n*.—**cure·less** *adj*.

cu·ré (kyoo-*ray*) *n*. A curate; parish priest.

cure-all *n*. A panacea.

cur·few (*ker*-fyoo) *n*. 1. Regulation requiring all outdoor activity to cease at a certain hour. 2. Signal announcing this hour.

Cu·ri·a (*kyoo*-ree-uh) *n*. Organization and officials assisting the Pope in governing the Roman Catholic Church; papal court.

cu·rie (*kyoo*-ree) *n. Chemistry*. A unit of radio activity.

cu·ri·o (*kyoo*-ree-oh) *n*. [*pl*. -ri·os] A curiosity; unusual artistic object.

cu·ri·os·i·ty (kyoor-ee-*oss*-ih-tee) *n*. [*pl*. -ties] 1. Inquisitiveness; strong desire to know, or inquire into, affairs. 2. A rare thing.

cu·ri·ous (*kyoor*-ee-us) *adj*. 1. Inquisitive; eager to know. 2. Strange; queer; unusual.—**cu·ri·ous·ly** *adv*.—**cu·ri·ous·ness** *n*.

cu·ri·um (*kyoor*-ee-um) *n*. An inert, radioactive element, isolated during research on the atom bomb. (*Symbol:* Cm).

curl (kerl) *v*. 1. To shape into curls. 2. To move or rise in spirals or curves.—*n*. 1. A ringlet; twisted lock of hair. 2. A curved or spiral form.—**curl·er** *n*.

cur·lew (*ker*-loo) *n*. A bird of the snipe family having long legs and slender, curved bill.

cur·li·cue (*ker*-lih-kyoo) *n*. Also **curl·y·cue**. An ornamental twist; flourish, in handwriting.

curl·ing (*ker*-ling) *n*. An ice game in which contending parties slide flattened, circular stones from one target to another.—**curling stone**.

curling iron. An instrument for curling the hair by application of heat.

curl·y *adj*. [curl·i·er; curl·i·est] Having or resembling curls.—**curl·i·ly** *adv*.—**curl·i·ness** *n*.

cur·mudg·eon (ker-*muj*-un) *n*. A mean, grasping person; miser.—**cur·mudg·eon·ly** *adj*.

cur·rant (*kur*-'nt) *n*. 1. A small, sour berry used for jelly, etc. 2. Shrub bearing currants. 3. A small seedless raisin.

cur·ren·cy (*kur*-un-see) *n*. [*pl*. -cies] 1. Money; legal tender. 2. Circulation; general use.

cur·rent (*kur*-'nt) *adj*. 1. Prevailing; generally accepted; customary. 2. Of the present time; occurring now. 3. In circulation.—*n*. 1. Stream; flow. 2. Drift; trend; course. 3. A movement or flow of electricity.—**cur·rent·ly** *adv*.—**cur·rent·ness** *n*.

cur·ri·cle (*kur*-ih-k'l) *n*. A two-wheeled carriage drawn by two horses.

cur·ric·u·lum (kuh-*rik*-yuh-lum) *n*. [*pl*. -lums,

-la] 1. A specified course of study. 2. The collective courses offered by an educational institution.—**cur·ric·u·lar** adj.

cur·ri·er (kur-ee-er) n. 1. One who dresses tanned leather. 2. Person who curries horses.

cur·rish (kur-ish) adj. Nasty; ill-bred; quarrelsome.—**cur·rish·ly** adv.

cur·ry (kur-ee) v. [cur·ried; cur·ry·ing] 1. To dress and color (leather) after tanning. 2. To rub and clean the coat of, as a horse.—**curry favor.** To seek favor by flattery.

cur·ry n. [pl. cur·ries] Also **cur·rie.** 1. A sauce or powder much used in India, containing strong spices. 2. A stew cooked with curry. —v. [cur·ried; cur·ry·ing] To flavor with curry.

cur·ry·comb n. An iron comb with short teeth for currying horses.—**cur·ry·comb** v.

curse (kers) n. 1. Malediction; oath; prayer for harm or evil to visit. 2. Torment; evil; great vexation. 3. Person or object cursed. —v. [cursed, curst; curs·ing.] 1. To execrate; pray for evil to fall upon. 2. To afflict; to bring evil upon. 3. To use profane language.

curs·ed (ker-sid) adj. 1. Under a curse; damned; afflicted. 2. Hateful; detestable. —**curs·ed·ly** adv.—**curs·ed·ness** n.

cur·sive (ker-siv) adj. Running together; flowing.—**cur·sive·ly** adv.—**cur·sive** n.

cur·so·ry (ker-suh-ree) adj. Superficial; desultory; hastily performed.—**cur·so·ri·ly** adv.

curt (kert) adj. 1. Short; brief. 2. Brusque; peremptory.—**curt·ly** adv.—**curt·ness** n.

cur·tail (ker-tayl) v. To cut short; abridge; reduce.—**cur·tail·er** n.—**cur·tail·ment** n.

cur·tain (ker-t'n) n. 1. A hanging of cloth, lace, etc., over a window. 2. Any hanging cloth or screen. 3. The movable screen in a theater serving to conceal the stage from the spectators.—**cur·tain** v.

curtain call. A performer's return to the stage to acknowledge the applause of the audience.

curtain raiser. An overture; short introductory piece.

cur·te·sy (ker-tuh-see) n. [pl. -sies] Law. Right of a husband to the property left by his wife upon her death.

curt·sy, curt·sey (kert-see) n. [pl. -sies, -seys] A woman's bow made by sinking the body slightly and bending the knees.—v. [curt·sied; curt·seyed; curt·sy·ing, curt·sey·ing].

cu·rule (kyoo-rool) adj. Pertaining to the special seat of the high magistrates in ancient Rome.

cur·va·ture (kerv-uh-cher) n. A bending.

curve (kerv) n. 1. A bending with no straight part; flexure. 2. Geometry. A line in which no three consecutive points lie in the same direction. 3. Baseball. A pitched ball which breaks to the left or the right as it approaches the plate.—v. [curved; curv·ing] To swerve from a course; bend.—**curve** adj.—**curv·ed·ness** n.

cur·vet (ker-vit) v. [cur·vet·ted, cur·vet·ed; cur·vet·ting, cur·vet·ing] To leap; bound; cause to spring upward.—n. A leap of a horse in which all four legs are off the ground at once.

cur·vi·lin·e·ar, cur·vi·lin·e·al (ker-vuh-lin-ee-er, -ul) adj. Consisting of curved lines.

cush·ion (koosh-un) n. 1. A pillow or soft pad for a seat. 2. Any stuffed or padded surface. —v. 1. To furnish with cushions. 2. To soften; mitigate.—**cush·ioned** adj.

cusk n. A fish of the cod family.

cusp n. 1. Any pointed end, esp. on a tooth. 2. Astronomy. The point or horn of a crescent. 3. Architecture. The point of a small arc or foliation.—**cusp·al** adj.

cus·pid (kus-pid) n. A tooth with one cusp or point; canine tooth.—**cus·pi·dal** adj.

cus·pi·date, cus·pi·dat·ed (kus-pih-dayt, -ed) adj. Having a sharp end or point.

cus·pi·dor (kus-pih-dor) n. A spittoon.

cuss n. Slang. 1. A curse. 2. An irritating or good-for-nothing person.—v. To curse.

cuss·ed (kuss-ed) adj. 1. Obstinate; unmanageable. 2. Cursed.—**cuss·ed·ly** adv.—**cuss·ed·ness** n.

cus·tard n. A light, sweetened, baked pudding of milk and eggs.

cus·to·di·al (kus-toh-dee-ul) adj. Pertaining to guardianship.—n. A vessel for holy objects.

cus·to·di·an (kus-toh-dee-un) n. Caretaker or keeper, as of a public building.— **-an·ship** n.

cus·to·dy (kus-tuh-dee) n. [pl. -dies] 1. Guard; safe keeping. 2. Confinement; imprisonment.

cus·tom (kus-tum) n. 1. Frequent or common use; habitual practice. 2. Patronage; practice of frequenting, as a shop. 3. Accepted usage; established mode of conduct in a community. 4. Tax on imports or exports.—**cus·tom** adj.

cus·tom·ar·y (kus-tuh-meh-ree) adj. Usual; accustomed; habitual.—n. [pl. -ies] Book containing an account of the customs and rights of a city, province, etc.—**cus·tom·ar·i·ly** adv.

cus·tom·er (kus-tuh-mer) n. 1. One who deals regularly with a business place; patron; buyer. 2. Colloquial. Chap. 'A tough customer.'

cus·tom·house n. Building where customs are paid.

cus·tom-made adj. Made to one's order.

cut v. [cut; cut·ting] 1. To slice, part, or stab with a sharp instrument. 2. To reduce. 'Prices were cut.' 3. To wound the sensibilities of; affect deeply. 4. To intersect; cross. 5. To divide a pack of cards and change their order. 6. To function as a severing instrument. 7. To admit of cutting. 'This bread cuts easily.' 8. To dilute. 9. To pierce the gum. 'Baby is cutting his teeth.' 10. Sports. To strike a ball so as to cause it to spin. 11. Motion Pictures. To stop the camera and action of a scene. 12. To refuse to acknowledge a greeting from an acquaintance.—n. 1. A minor wound. 2. A reduction. 3. A wound to one's feelings. 4. A sharp, quick stroke or blow. 5. A segment or portion severed from the rest. 6. A shorter way of arriving at a point; shortcut. 7. The plate on which an illustration is engraved for printing; print from an engraved plate. 8. Division and regrouping of a pack of cards. 9. The manner in which a thing is cut. 'The cut of his clothes.'—**cut** *adj.*—**cut back.** 1. To reduce or decrease. 2. To return to a previous event in a sequence.—**cut off.** 1. To disinherit. 2. To interrupt; halt before completed.—**cut out.** 1. To design; fit. 2. *Colloquial.* To cease.

cut and dried. Settled beforehand.

cu·ta·ne·ous (kyoo-*tay*-nee-us) *n.* Of or denoting the skin.

cut·a·way *n.* A coat tapering back from the waist to tails in the back.

cut-back *n.* A reduction: decrease, esp. in the output of a manufacturing plant.

cute (*kyoot*) *adj.* 1. *Colloquial.* Pretty; charming; attractive. 2. Clever; shrewd; acute. —**cute·ly** *adv.*—**cute·ness** *n.*

cut glass. 1. Ornamental glass having a design cut into it. 2. Glass ground and polished, as distinguished from molded glass.

cu·ti·cle (kyoo-tih-k'l) *n.* 1. The skin of the body, esp. the skin about the fingernails. 2. Any thin, external coat or covering.

cut·lass (*kut*-lus) *n.* Also **cut·las.** A short, heavy, curved sword.

cut·ler *n.* One who makes, sells, or repairs cutlery.

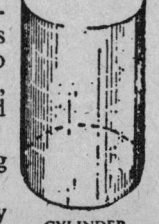

CUTLASS

cut·ler·y *n.* [*pl.* -ies] Sharp-bladed implements collectively.

cut·let (*kut*-lit) *n.* A small cut of meat, esp. veal, taken from near the rib.

cut line. *Journalism.* Brief descriptive statement below an illustration.

cut·off *n.* 1. A nearer passage or route. 2. That which cuts off or is cut off. 3. *Steam Engines.* A device that prevents the flow of steam to the compression chamber when the piston has made part of its stroke.

cut-out *n.* 1. A valve in the exhaust pipe of a gasoline engine which allows the gas to escape directly into the air. 2. *Electricity.* A circuit breaker; any device which interrupts a circuit.

cut·purse *n.* A thief; pickpocket; robber.

cut·ter *n.* 1. A cutting agent. 2. One who cuts cloth that is to be made into garments. 3. A cutting tool. 4. A small fast, trim ship. 5. A small, light sleigh.

cutter-built	cutterman	cutter rig
cutter-down	cutter-off	cutter-rigged
cutter head	cutter-out	cutter-up

cut·throat *n.* A murderous villain; assassin; ruffian.—*adj.* Barbarous; cruel; unethical. 'Cutthroat competition.'

cut·ting *adj.* 1. Penetrating; severing; dividing. 2. Hurting the feelings; sarcastic; severe. —*n.* 1. The amount cut at one time. 2. A slip; piece of a plant from which a new plant can be grown.—**cut·ting·ly** *adv.*

cut·tle·bone (*kut*-'l-bohn) *n.* The outer skeleton of cuttlefish, used as a polishing agent, etc.

cut·tle·fish (*kut*-'l-fish) *n.* Also **cut·tle.** A ten-tentacled mollusk which gives off an inky fluid when alarmed.

cut-up *n. Slang.* A lively, mischievous person.

cut·wa·ter *n.* Any sharp forward end of the prow of a ship.

cut·worm *n.* One of several moth larvae destructive to young plants.

cy·a·nate (*sy*-uh-nayt) *n.* A salt of cyanic acid.

cy·an·ic (*sy-an*-ik) *adj.* Denoting or containing cyanogen.

cyanic acid *n.* A poisonous, colorless liquid composed of cyanogen, oxygen, and hydrogen.

cy·a·nide (*sy*-uh-nyde) *n.* Also **cy·a·nid.** A poisonous substance compounded of cyanogen and a metallic base; potassium cyanide.

cy·an·o·gen (sy-*an*-uh-jin) *n.* 1. A colorless, highly poisonous gas with the odor of bitter almonds. 2. A radical of carbon and nitrogen having a valence of 1.

cy·a·no·sis (sy-uh-*noh*-sis) *n.* A blueness of the skin, usually caused by lack of oxygen in the bloodstream.—**cy·a·not·ic** (sy-uh-*not*-ik) *adj.*

cy·cad (*sy*-kad) *n.* A family of palmlike trees whose stiff, evergreen leaves grow in a cluster at the top of a trunk.

cyc·la·men (*sy*-kluh-m'n) *n.* A beautifully flowering plant with heart-shaped leaves.

cy·cle *n.* 1. A regularly recurring sequence in time or space. 'The life cycle.' 2. A group of literary works on a single theme.—*v.* [cy·cled; cy·cling] 1. To occur in cycles. 2. To ride a bicycle or similar vehicle.—**cy·cler** *n.*

cy·clic *adj.* Also **cy·cli·cal.** Occurring in cycles.

cy·clist *n.* One who rides a bicycle.

cy·cloid (*sy*-kloyd) *adj.* A curved line drawn by a point on the circumference of a circle that is rolled along a straight line.—*adj.* Having a circular form.—**cy·cloi·dal** *adj.*

cy·clom·e·ter (sy-*klom*-eh-ter) *n.* An instrument to record the revolutions of a wheel.

cy·clone (*sy*-klohn) *n.* A spiraling, violent destructive storm; tornado.—**cy·clon·ic** (sy-*klon*-ik), **cy·clon·i·cal** *adj.*—**cy·clon·i·cal·ly** *adv.*

cy·clo·pe·di·a, cy·clo·pae·di·a (sy-kluh-*pee*-dee-uh) *n.* A comprehensive reference book or series of books.—**cy·clo·pe·dic, cy·clo·pae·dic** *adj.*—**cy·clo·pe·di·cal·ly** *adv.*—**cy·clo·pe·dist** *n.*

Cy·clops (*sy*-klops) *n. Greek Mythology.* A race of one-eyed giants who helped Vulcan forge thunderbolts for Jupiter.

cy·clo·ra·ma (sy-kloh-*rah*-muh) *n.* 1. A series of pictures extended circularly so as to appear in natural perspective to the spectator. 2. Curved wall, or curtains so hung, at the back of a stage.—**cy·clo·ram·ic** (sy-kloh-*ram*-ik) *adj.*

cy·clo·tron (*sy*-kloh-tron) *n. Physics.* A machine which imparts terrifically high velocities to electrified particles of matter, these particles then being used to bombard atoms.

cyg·net (*sig*-net) *n.* A young swan.

cyl·in·der (*sil*-in-der) *n.* 1. Any body having length, a constant diameter, and ends parallel to each other. 2. *Mechanics.* A chamber in an engine or

CYLINDER

motor where gases expand or explode to drive the piston. 3. *Printing*. A roller by which an impression is made. 4. The barrel or body of a pump.—**cy·lin·dri·cal** (sih-*lin*-drih-k'l) Also **cy·lin·dric** *adj*.—**cy·lin·dri·cal·ly** *adv*.

cym·bal (*sim*-b'l) *n*. A dish-like brass musical instrument struck against another to produce a sharp ringing sound.—**cym·bal·er, cym·bal·eer** (sim-buh-*leer*), **cym·bal·ist** *n*.

Cym·ric, Kym·ric (*sim*-rik; *kim*-) *adj*. Relating to the Cymry or Welsh.—**cym·ric, kym·ric** *n*.

Cym·ry, Kym·ry (*sim*-ree; *kim*-) *n*. The Welsh people.

cyn·ic (*sin*-ik) *n*. 1. A misanthrope; habitually sneering person; disbeliever. 2. [*cap*.] A member of an ancient Greek philosophical school which despised riches, arts, sciences, and amusements.—**cyn·ic** *adj*.

cyn·i·cal (*sin*-ih-k'l) *adj*. Sneering; disbelieving; mistrustful of human motives.—**cyn·i·cal·ly** *adv*.—**cyn·i·cal·ness** *n*.

cyn·i·cism (*sin*-ih-sizm) *n*. Misanthropy; disillusionment; distrust of accepted values.

cy·no·sure (*sy*-noh-shoor) *n*. 1. A center of attention; a focus. 2. [*cap*.] An old name for the constellation Ursa Minor, or Little Bear, which includes the pole-star.

Cyn·thi·a (*sin*-thee-uh) *n*. 1. Artemis, goddess of the moon. 2. The moon.

cy·press (*sy*-prus) *n*. Family of long-lived, picturesque evergreens, varying widely in shape.

Cyp·ri·an (*sip*-ree-un) *n*. 1. A native of the island Cyprus. 2. A lewd woman; courtesan; strumpet.—**Cyp·ri·an** *adj*.

cyst (*sist*) *n*. A sac, often abnormally developed, in a human or animal body, containing fluid matter.—**cyst·ic** *adj*.

Cyth·er·e·a (sith-uh-*ree*-uh) *n*. Venus or Aphrodite, goddess of love.—**Cyth·er·e·an** *adj*.

cy·tol·o·gy (sy-*tol*-uh-jee) *n*. The branch of biology specializing in the study of cell structure and the functions of cell parts.—**cy·to·log·i·cal** (sy-tuh-*loj*-ih-k'l) *adj*.—**cy·tol·o·gist** *n*.

cy·to·plasm (*sy*-toh-plazm) *n*. *Biology*. The protoplasm or living substance of a cell, aside from its nucleus.—**cy·to·plas·mic** *adj*.

czar, tsar (*zahr*) *n*. 1. The emperor or king of Russia before the revolution of 1917. 2. *Colloquial*. A dictator; chief; autocratic leader.

cza·ri·na, tsa·ri·na (zah-*ree*-nuh) *n*. The empress or queen of Russia before the revolution of 1917.

czar·ism, tsar·ism (*zahr*-izm) *n*. Autocratic rule.

Czech (*chek*) *n*. 1. A Bohemian; native of Bohemia, Moravia, or Silesia in western Czechoslovakia. 2. The Czechoslovak language; Bohemian.—**Czech·ic, Czech·ish** *adj*.

Czech·o·slo·vak, Czecho-Slo·vak (chek-oh-*sloh*-vak) *n*. 1. A native or inhabitant of Czechoslovakia. 2. The language of Czechoslovakia.—**Czech·o·slo·vak** *adj*.

D

D

dab [dabbed; dab·bing] 1. To pat; strike gently. 2. To apply a liquid by gentle pats. —*n*. 1. A soft blow. 2. *Colloquial*. A small quantity.

dab *n*. Any of several flatfish, esp. the flounder.

dab·ble (*dab*-'l) *v*. [dab·bled; dab·bling] 1. To sputter; dip. 2. To tinker; play at superficially.—**dab·bler** *n*. An amateur; dilettante.

dab·ster *n*. *Colloquial*. An expert; master.

dace (*dayss*) *n*. [*pl*. dace; dac·es] A small freshwater fish of the carp family.

dachs·hund (*dahks*-hund) *n*. A German breed of dog having a very long body, short legs, and a sleek black or brown coat.

DACHSHUND (1/17 life size)

dac·tyl, dac·tyle (*dak*-t'l) *n*. *Prosody*. A foot consisting of one long and two short syllables. —**dac·tyl·ic** (dak-*til*-ik) *adj*. & *n*.

da·da·ism (*dah*-dah-izm) *n*. Cult developed in Paris following World War I, proposing a deliberate irrationality in art and society.—**da·da·ist** *n*.

dad·dy *n*. *Familiar*. Father.

daddy longlegs. A species of globular-bodied longlegged crane fly related to the spider family.

da·do (*day*-doh) *n*. [*pl*. da·does] 1. The part of a pedestal directly above the base. 2. The baseboard of a room.

Daed·a·lus (*ded*-uh-lus) *n*. 1. *Greek Mythology*. Cretan inventor whose son Icarus perished on wax wings, after venturing too near the sun.

dae·mon (*dee*-mun) *n*. [*pl*. daemons, dae·mones] 1. *Variant spelling* of demon. 2. *Greek mythology*. An instructing spirit; mentor.

daf·fo·dil (*daf*-uh-dil) *n*. A bright-yellow flower of the narcissus variety.

daf·fo·dil·ly *n*. [*pl*. -lies] Also **daf·fy·down·dil·ly, daf·fa·dil·ly, daf·fa·down·dil·ly.** *Variants of* daf·fo·dil.

daf·fy (*daf*-ee) *adj*. [daf·fi·er; daf·fi·est] *Slang*. Crazy; foolish; giddy.

DAFFODIL

daft *adj*. Insane; foolish; giddy.—**daft·ly** *adv*.—**daft·ness** *n*.

dag·ger (*dag*-er) *n.* 1. A short pointed weapon, usually having a flat triangular blade and a rounded grip. 2. An editorial reference mark [†].—*v.* To stab; pierce with a dagger.

da·guerre·o·type (duh-*gehr*-uh-type) *n.* A picture produced on a silver plate by an early photography process.—*v.* To produce a daguerreotype.—**da·guerre·o·typ·er, da·guerre·o·typ·ist** *n.*

da·ha·be·ah (dah-huh-*bee*-uh) *n.* Also **da·ha·bee·ah, da·ha·bi·ah, da·ha·bi·yeh.** A narrow, masted passenger boat used on the Nile.

DAGGERS

dahl·ia (*dal*-yuh; *dahl*-; *dayl*-) *n.* A large, bright-colored flower of the aster family.

Dail Eireann (doyl ayr-in; dyle). The Chamber of Deputies of the Irish legislature in Dublin.

dai·ly (*day*-lee) *adj.* Occurring or appearing every day.—*n.* [*pl.* -lies] A newspaper issued every day.—**dai·ly** *adv.*

dain·ty (*dayn*-tee) *adj.* [-ti·er; -ti·est] 1. Delicate; petite; feminine. 2. Elegant; fastidious; squeamish. 3. Choice; palate-pleasing.—*n.* [*pl.* -ties] Delicacies.—**dain·ti·ly** *adv.*

dai·qui·ri (*dy*-kuh-ree) *n.* A cocktail containing rum, lime or lemon juice, and sugar.

dair·y (*dayr*-ee) *n.* [*pl.* -ies] 1. A farm house or room for storing and processing milk. 2. A shop specializing in milk and milk products. —*adj.* Relating to milk and milk products. —**dair·y·ing** *n.* The business of producing milk and milk products.—**dair·y·maid** *n.* A woman working in a dairy.—**dair·y·man** *n.*

da·is (*day*-iss) *n.* [*pl.* da·is·es] A raised platform.

dai·sy (*day*-zee) *n.* [*pl.* -sies] A common wild flower having a yellow center and white–or yellow petals.—**dai·sied** *adj.*

Da·ko·ta (duh-*koh*-tuh). *n.* An Indian group of the Sioux tribe.—**Da·ko·ta** *adj.*

Dalai Lama (dah-*ly lah*-muh). Head of the Lamaist monks of Tibet.

dale *n.* A valley; dell; pocket between hills.

dal·li·ance (*dal*-ee-uns) *n.* Idle amusement; trifling.

dal·ly (*dal*-ee) *v.* [dal·lied; dal·ly·ing] To linger; delay; waste time.—**dal·li·er** *n.*

Dal·ma·tia (dal-*may*-shuh). A province of Austria.—**Dal·ma·tian** *n.* 1. An inhabitant of Dalmatia. 2. A white spotted breed of dog related to the pointer.–**Dal·ma·tian** *adj.*

Dal·ton·ism (*dawl*-t'n-izm) *n.* Color-blindness. —**Dal·to·ni·an** (dawl-*toh*-nee-un), **Dal·ton·ist** *n.*

dam *n.* 1. A barrier built to confine or divert a current of water. 2. An artificial basin for supplying water.—*v.* [dammed; dam·ming].

dam *n.* A female parent, esp. of animals.

dam·age (*dam*-ij) *n.* 1. Injury; harm; detriment; loss. 2. *Law.* Money recovered for a loss or injury.—*v.* [dam·aged; dam·ag·ing] —**dam·age·a·ble** *adj.*—**dam·ag·ing·ly** *adv.*

dam·a·scene (*dam*-uh-seen) *n.* 1. The process of inlaying one metal with another. 2. [*cap*]. A native of Damascus.—**dam·a·scene** *adj.*

Da·mas·cus (duh-*mas*-kus). Capital of Syria.

dam·ask (*dam*-usk) *n.* 1. Fabric, usually table linen, ornamented with raised woven figures. 2. Damask steel. 3. A shade of red.—**dam·ask** *adj.*—**dam·ask** *v.*

damask steel. Also **Damascus steel.** A type of sword blade having a variegated surface.

dame (daym) *n.* 1. A lady; wife of a nobleman. 2. *Slang.* A woman.

damn (dam) *v.* [damned; damn·ing] 1. To condemn; denounce; judge unfavorably. 2. *Theology.* To curse; sentence to hell.—*n.* A malediction; curse.

dam·na·ble (*dam*-nuh-b'l) *adj.* Detestable; meriting condemnation.—**dam·na·bly** *adv.*

dam·na·tion (dam-*nay*-shun) *n.* 1. Condemnation; censure. 2. *Theology.* Eternal punishment.—**dam·na·to·ry** (*dam*-nuh-tor-ee) *adj.*

damned *adj.* 1. *Theology.* Lost; consigned to eternal punishment. 2. Condemned. 3. *Profane.* Hateful; detestable.—**the damned.** Those consigned to hell.

Dam·o·cles (*dam*-uh-kleez) *n.* A citizen of ancient Syracuse who was placed by the king under a sword suspended by a single hair. —**Dam·o·cle·an** (dam-uh-*klee*-un) *adj.* Imminent; threatening; dangerous.—**under the sword of Damocles.** In a precarious position.

Da·mon (*day*-m'n) *n.* 1. A Sicilian philosopher who offered himself for punishment in place of his friend Pythias. 2. A loyal friend.

damp *n.* 1. Moisture; humidity; fog. 2. A dangerous gas found in coal mines.—*adj.* 1. Moist; humid. 2. Dejected; depressed.—*v.* Also **dampen.** 1. To moisten. 2. To depress; deject. 3. To restrain; check. 4. To reduce the vibration of. 'Damp a harp string.' —**damp·ly** *adv.*—**damp·ness** *n.*

damp·en (*damp*-'n) *v.* To damp.—**damp·en·er** *n.*

damp·er (*damp*-er) *n.* 1. A restraint; check. 2. A valve regulating the draft in a furnace. 3. A device for deadening the vibrations of a musical instrument. 4. *Slang.* A pistol.

dam·son (*dam*-z'n) *n.* A small purple plum.

dance *v.* [danced; danc·ing] 1. To move in a series of measured steps governed by the rhythm of music. 2. To leap; frisk; move nimbly.—*n.* 1. A measured series of body movements governed by the rhythm of music. 2. A tune intended to accompany a dance. 3. A ball.—**danc·er** *n.*—**danc·ing** *n.*

dan·de·li·on (*dan*-duh-ly-un) *n.* A common weed, bearing toothed leaves and yellow flowers.

dan·der *n.* *Colloquial.* Anger; rage.

dan·di·fy (*dan*-duh-fy) *v.* [dan·di·fied; dan·di·fy·ing] To make foppish.—**dan·di·fi·ca·tion** *n.*

dan·dle (*dan*-d'l) *v.* [dan·dled; dan·dling] 1. To fondle; pet. 2. To handle playfully, as a child.

dan·druff (*dan*-druf) *n.* A scale which forms on the scalp.—**dan·druf·fy** *adj.*

dan·dy n. [pl. -dies] 1. A fop; coxcomb; elegant dresser. 2. *Slang*. An excellent article. —adj. *Colloquial*. High grade; excellent.—**dan·dy·ish** adj. Like a fop.—**dan·dy·ism** n.

Dane n. A native of Denmark.

dan·ger (*dayn*-jer) n. Peril; jeopardy; hazard.

dan·ger·ous (*dayn*-jer-us) adj. Perilous; hazardous; unsafe.— -**ger·ous·ly** adv.— -**ous·ness** n.

dan·gle (*dang*-g'l) v. [dan·gled; dan·gling] 1. To hang loosely. 2. To oscillate; swing back and forth while hanging. 3. To leave or be left unconnected.—**dan·gler** n. A trifler.

Dan·ish (*day*-nish) n. The language of Denmark.—adj. Relating to Denmark.

dank adj. Damp; humid—**dank·ly** adv.

dan·seuse (dahn-*serz*) n. [pl. -seuses] A woman ballet dancer.—**premiere** (prem-*yehr*) **dan·seuse**. The leading ballerina of a company.

Dan·ube (*dan*-yoob). Famous central European river running from Black Forest (Germany) to the Black Sea.

dap·per (*dap*-er) adj. 1. Brisk; lively. 2. Small; active; neat.

dap·ple (*dap*-'l) n. 1. A spot on an animal. 2. A spotted animal.—v. [dap·pled; dap·pling] To spot; mark with spots.—adj. Spotted; marked with patches of different color.—**dap·pled** adj.

Dardenelles, The. Strait connecting the Black and Aegean Seas.

dare v. [dared, durst; dared; dar·ing] 1. To venture; be bold; brave a danger. 2. To challenge.—n. A challenge.—**dar·er** n.

dare-dev·il n. An adventure-seeker; reckless person.—**dare-dev·il** adj.—**dare-dev·il·try,** n.

dar·ing n. Courage; boldness; fearlessness. —adj. Bold; courageous; intrepid.—**dar·ing·ly** adv. Boldly; courageously.—**dar·ing·ness** n.

dark (dahrk) adj. 1. Obscure; destitute of light. 2. Disheartening; depressing; ominous. 3. Concealed; mysterious; ambiguous. 4. Sinister; wicked. 5. Black; deep-hued. 6. Dark-complexioned; not fair.—n. Darkness.—**dark·ly** adv.—**dark·ness** n.

Dark Ages. Medieval period characterized by a lack of knowledge and learning.

dark·en v. 1. To grow dim; be deprived of light. 2. To discourage; make cheerless. 3. To make less white. 4. To obscure; cloud.

dark horse. 1. An unpublicized candidate nominated unexpectedly. 2. *Horse Racing*. A horse that wins, contrary to expectation.

dark·ish adj. Dusky; dim.—**dark·ish·ness** n.

dark lantern. A lamp for signaling at night.

dark·room n. *Photography*. A light-tight room for developing plates or films.

dark·some adj. Dark; gloomy; obscure.

dar·ling n. A favorite; one beloved or cherished.—**dar·ling** adj.

darn v. To mend with crossing stitches; patch; sew up a rent.—n. A mended place.—**darn·er** n.

darn v. *Slang*. To damn mildly.—**darn** adj. & n.

darning needle. 1. A large-eyed needle for darning. 2. The dragonfly.

dart n. 1. A short arrow. 2. A lance; missile; any pointed weapon thrown by hand. 3. *Sewing*. A short seam for drawing a garment in.—v. 1. To hurl; send; emit. 2. To spring and run; flit.

dart·er n. 1. The snakebird; web-footed tropical pelican. 2. A type of fresh-water fish.

Dar·win·ism (*dahr*-win-izm) n. The theory of natural selection, as developed by Charles Darwin; evolution.—**Dar·win·i·an** (dahr-*win*-ee-un) adj.—**Dar·win·ist** n. & adj.

dash v. 1. To throw violently. 2. To shatter; break. 3. To daub hastily. 4. To rush; run. —n. 1. Collision; striking together of bodies. 2. A sprinkling; small admixture. 3. A sudden rush. 4. Vigor; flourish; bluster. 5. *Printing*. A mark [—] to indicate a pause or break. —**dash off.** 1. To sketch or write hastily. 2. To depart fast.

dash·board n. 1. A mudguard on a vehicle. 2. The instrument board of a motorcar.

dash·er n. 1. A dashboard; mudguard. 2. *Slang*. An impetuous person.

dash·ing adj. Impetuous; spirited; blustering.

dash·y adj. [dash·i·er; dash·i·est] Ostentatious.

das·tard n. A sneaky coward.—**das·tard** adj. —**das·tard·ly** adv. & adj.—**das·tard·ness** n.

da·ta (*day*-tuh) n. *Plural*. Pertinent facts or premises, as in a mathematical problem, a treatise, an argument, etc.

date n. 1. A notation of the day, month, and year. 2. The time, esp. the year of an historical event. 3. A specific division in time consisting of the day, the month, and the year. 4. *Slang and Colloquial*. An appointment.—v. [dat·ed; dat·ing] 1. To affix a date to. 2. To begin; originate. 3. *Slang and Colloquial*. To have an appointment with.—**dat·er** n.

date n. An edible Asiatic palm fruit, often dried.

date·less adj. 1. Bearing no date. 2. Ageless; eternal.

date line. 1. The line on which a document, letter, newspaper article, etc., is dated. 2. The 180th meridian, established as the origin of the calendar day, so that when it is Monday noon at this line it is Monday in the Western Hemisphere and Sunday in the Eastern Hemisphere. Ships crossing the date line change the date one day.

da·tive (*day*-tiv) adj. *Grammar*. Denoting the indirect object of a verb.—n. The case of an indirect object.—**da·ti·val** (duh-*ty*-v'l) adj.

daub (dawb) v. 1. To smear, as with plaster, paint, mud, etc. 2. To paint amateurishly. 3. To besmear; soil.—**daub** n.—**daub·y** adj.

daugh·ter (*daw*-ter) n. A female offspring. —**daugh·ter·ly** adj. Dutiful; filial.

daugh·ter-in-law n. [pl. daughters-in-law] A son's wife.

daunt (dawnt) v. To intimidate; dishearten.

daunt·less adj. Bold; fearless; daring.—**daunt·less·ly** adv.—**daunt·less·ness** n.

dau·phin (*daw*-fin) n. Formerly the eldest son of the King of France.—**dau·phin·ess, dau·phine** (*daw*-feen) n. The wife of the dauphin.

D

dav·en·port (*dav*-en-port) *n.* A high-backed couch convertible for sleeping.

dav·it (*dav*-it) *n. Nautical.* One of the projections on the side of a vessel for hoisting a boat.

Davy Jones. *Nautical.* A sea devil; spirit of the sea. —**Davy Jones's Locker.** Bottom of the sea.

Davy lamp. Also **Davy's lamp, safety lamp.** A miner's kerosene lamp enclosed in wire.

DAVIT

daw *n.* A jackdaw; bird of the crow family.

daw·dle (*daw*-d'l) *v.* [daw·dled; daw·dling] To idle; waste time.—**daw·dler** *n.*

dawn *v.* 1. To break; grow light as the day. 2. To become visible; begin to appear or be understood.—*n.* 1. Daybreak; the first morning light. 2. The beginning; first appearance.

day *n.* 1. The period between sunrise and sunset or between one night and the next. 2. The space of 24 hours from one midnight to the next. 3. A specific day; appointed time. 4. Period of life or of history; age. 5. A working day; hours normally spent in work.

day·book *n.* 1. An accounting book listing the transactions of the day. 2. Diary.

day·break *n.* The dawn; time when the first morning light appears.

day·dream *n.* A pleasant reverie; vain hope or fancy.—**day·dream·er** *n.*

day laborer. A laborer hired by the day.

day·light *n.* 1. The light of the sun; daytime. 2. Clear understanding.—**daylight saving.** Practice of setting the clock ahead at certain seasons to obtain greater use of daylight.

day room. Recreation room or hall.

days of grace. *Law.* The customary period allowable for payment of a note after the date it is due.

day·time *n.* Interval between sunrise and -set.

daze (*dayz*) *v.* [dazed; daz·ing] To stun; stupefy; bewilder.—*n.* Stupefaction; condition of being dazed.—**daz·ed·ly** *adv.*

daz·zle (*daz*-'l) *v.* [daz·zled; daz·zling] 1. To blind momentarily; overpower with light. 2. To overcome with splendor.—**daz·zling** *adj.*

D Day (*dee*-day). 1. Day on which any large-scale military assault commences, esp. the day (June 6, 1944) on which the Allied invasion of the continent of Europe began. 2. Day of beginning or commencement.

DDT. A hydrocarbon compound developed in World War II, highly effective as an insecticide.

de- *Prefix.* 1. Down. 'Depose; descend.' 2. Away; off. 'Decamp; debark.' 3. The opposite of; reverse. 'Demobilize; decode.' 4. Completely; utterly. 'Debase; denude.'

dea·con (*dee*-k'n) *n.* An assistant to a minister. —**dea·con·ry, dea·con·ship** *n.*

dea·con·ess (*dee*-k'n-iss) *n.* A feminine assistant to a minister; woman church worker.

dead (*ded*) *adj.* 1. Deceased; not living; lifeless. 2. Resembling death; without sensation or vitality. 3. Not in use. 4. Not transmitting current. 'A dead wire.' 5. Forgotten; extinct. 'A dead issue.' 6. Lacking resiliency. 7. *Colloquial.* Extremely tired. 8. Complete; certain; absolute. 'It's a dead loss.'—*n.* The time of greatest intensity. 'The dead of night.' —*adv.* 1. Totally; entirely. 'Dead right.' 2. Directly. 'Stop dead.'—**dead·ness** *n.*

dead afraid	dead drunk	dead house
dead-born	dead-drunkenness	deadlatch
dead cold	dead end	deadlight
dead color	dead-eyed	dead set
dead-colored	dead-hearted	dead weight

dead beat. *Slang.* A loafer; sponger; one who does not pay his debts.

dead center. *Machinery.* Position of an engine when the crank and connecting rod are in the same straight line.—**dead-center** *adj.*

dead·en (*ded*-'n) *v.* To deprive of force, vigor, sensibility, etc.; dull.—**dead·en·er** *n.*

dead·eye *n. Nautical.* A large wooden disk for setting up the shrouds.

dead·fall *n.* A trap made so that a weight falls on, and either kills or imprisons, the animal.

dead·head *n.* One who rides on public vehicles, attends amusements, etc., without paying. —**dead·head** *v.* To travel without payment.

dead heat. A contest which ends in a tie.

dead letter. 1. An unclaimed letter. 2. An unenforced law, rule, etc.

dead·line *n.* A specified time set for the completion of an activity, piece of work, etc.

dead·lock *n.* An impasse; situation in which no progress or decision can be made.—*v.* To reach an impasse.

dead·ly (*ded*-lee) *adj.* [dead·li·er; dead·li·est] 1. Mortal; fatal; causing or capable of causing death. 2. Resembling death. 3. Intense; very great.—*adv.* Deathly; extremely; intensely.—**dead·li·ness** *n.*

deadly nightshade. A poisonous plant whose leaves are used as a narcotic; belladonna.

dead·pan *adv. Slang.* Without facial expression.

dead reckoning. *Nautical.* The calculation of a ship's position at sea without the use of celestial observations.

Dead Sea. Salt sea bounding eastern Palestine.

dead·wood *n.* 1. Dead branches. 2. Unsalable merchandise; useless articles; inefficient personnel.

deaf (*def*) *adj.* 1. Incapable of hearing. 2. Refusing to listen.—**deaf·ly** *adv.*—**deaf·ness** *n.*

deaf·en (*def*-'n) *v.* 1. To make deaf; impair the hearing of. 2. To overpower with noise; drown out.—**deaf·en·ing·ly** *adv.*

deaf-mute *n.* A person incapable of speaking and hearing.—**deaf-mute** *adj.*

deal (*deel*) *v.* [dealt; deal·ing] 1. To distribute; give out in shares. 'Deal the cards.' 2. To have to do; carry on relations. 3. To trade;

traffic in. 4. To negotiate; contend; take action. 'Deal with the offenders.' 5. To behave; act.—*n.* 1. Act of dealing; distribution. 2. *Card Playing.* A hand. 3. A business arrangement or negotiation. 4. Treatment.—**a good deal, a great deal.** Much; a large, indefinite quantity.

deal *n.* The wood of the fir tree cut into planks.

deal·er (*deel*-er) *n.* 1. A trader; shopkeeper. 2. One who distributes cards to the players.

deal·ing (*deel*-ing) *n.* 1. Conduct of affairs; behavior.—2. [*pl.*] Relations; traffic.

dean (*deen*) *n.* 1. The presiding officer of a church or other ecclesiastical institution. 2. The president; administrative officer of a school or group of students. 3. The senior member of a group.—**dean·ship** *n.*

dean·er·y (*deen*-er-ee) *n.* [*pl.* -ies] The office or residence of a dean.

dear (*deer*) *adj.* 1. Loved; cherished; valued. 2. Expensive; high-priced. 3. Earnest.—*adv.* At high or expensive rate.—*n.* Darling; beloved person.—*Interjection.* An exclamation of surprise, distress, etc.—**dear·ly** *adv.*

dear·ie (*deer*-ee) *n. Colloquial.* Dear.

dearth (*derth*) *n.* Scarcity; lack; want.

death (*deth*) *n.* 1. Lifelessness; departure of life; dying; perishing. 2. Way or cause of dying. 3. Total loss; extinction; cessation. 4. Execution; murder. 5. [*cap.*] The spirit of death, personified as a skeleton.

death·bed *n.* 1. A person's last sickness. 2. The bed on which a person dies.

death·blow *n.* 1. Anything which extinguishes or finishes decisively. 2. The blow or wound which causes death.

death cup. A poisonous mushroom having a sac at its base.

death·less *n.* Immortal; not subject to extinction or oblivion.—**death·less·ly** *adv.*

death·ly *adj.* 1. Fatal; mortal; deadly. 2. Resembling death.—**death·ly** *adv.*

death rate. The proportion of deaths per year in relation to the population.

death's-head *n.* A human skull, symbol of death and mortality.

death watch. 1. The group which guards a criminal on the night before his execution. 2. A type of small beetle making a clicking sound, superstitiously believed a harbinger of death.

de·ba·cle (deh-*bah*-k'l) *n.* 1. A confused rout; stampede. 2. A sudden, great surge of water.

de·bar (dee-*bahr*) *v.* [de·barred; de·bar·ring] To prevent; exclude; render impossible or unattainable.—**de·bar·ment** *n.*

de·bark (dee-*bark*) *v.* To land from a ship or boat; disembark.—**de·bar·ka·tion** (dee-bar-*kay*-shun) *n.*

de·base (dee-*bayss*) *v.* [de·based; de·bas·ing] To reduce in rank, quality, etc.; degrade. —**de·base·ment** *n.*—**de·bas·er** *n.*

de·bat·a·ble (dee-*bayt*-uh-b'l) *adj.* Open to question; controvertible; disputable.

de·bate (dee-*bayt*) *v.* [de·bat·ed; de·bat·ing] To argue; reason; present a point of view in a contest of opinion.—**de·bate** *n.*—**de·bat·er** *n.*

de·bauch (dee-*bawch*) *v.* 1. To indulge freely in vice; be intemperate; revel. 2. To corrupt; vitiate.—**de·bauch** *n.*—**de·bauch·ee** (deb-aw-*shee*) *n.*—**de·bauch·er** *n.*—**de·bauch·ment** *n.*

de·bauch·ed *adj.* Corrupted through vice; given over to sensual pleasure; lewd.

de·bauch·er·y *n.* 1. Intemperate indulgence in sensual pleasures. 2. Seduction; immorality.

de·ben·ture (dee-*ben*-cher) *n.* A document acknowledging a debt, mortgage, or rebate due.

de·bil·i·tate (dee-*bil*-ih-tayt) *v.* [de·bil·i·tat·ed; -tat·ing] To weaken; make feeble; enervate. —**de·bil·i·ta·tion** *n.*

de·bil·i·ty (dee-*bil*-ih-tee) *n.* [*pl.* -ties] Weakness; faintness; languor.

deb·it (*deb*-it) *v.* 1. To charge with as a debt. 2. To enter on the debtor side of an account book.—**deb·it** *n.*

deb·o·nair (deb-uh-*nayr*) *adj.* Also **deb·on·naire.** Charming; courteous; well-bred; spirited.—**deb·o·nair·ly** *adv.*—**deb·o·nair·ness** *n.*

de·bris, dé·bris (deh-*bree*) *n.* Rubble; wreckage; remains.

debt (*det*) *n.* Amount owed; obligation; due.

debt·or (*det*-er) *n.* One who owes or is obligated to another.

de·bunk (dee-*bunk*) *v. Slang.* To belittle; puncture; divest of pretensions.

de·but (*day*-byoo) *n.* 1. First appearance before the public. 2. First attempt; beginning. 3. Formal introduction of a girl to society.

deb·u·tante (*deb*-yoo-tahnt, -tant) *n.* A girl being presented, or recently presented, to society.

dec·ade (*dek*-ayd) *n.* A ten-year period.

de·ca·dence (dee-*kay*-d'ns; *dek*-uh-d'ns) *n.* Also **de·ca·den·cy.** 1. Deterioration; decay; disintegration. 2. Lapse of a culture to a lethargic, artificial, and overrefined state; loss of vigor and inventiveness.—**de·ca·dent** *adj.*

dec·a·gon (*dek*-uh-gon) *n.* A plane figure having ten sides and ten angles. —**de·cag·o·nal** (dek-*ag*-uh-n'l) *adj.*

dec·a·he·dron (dek-uh-*hee*-drun) *n.* [*pl.* -drons, -dra] A figure or body bounded by ten sides. —**dec·a·he·dral** *adj.*

de·cal (dee-*kal*) Also **de·cal·co·ma·ni·a** (dee-kal-koh-*may*-nee-uh) *n.* 1. Transfer of patterns, words, or pictures from specially treated paper to chinaware, glass, etc. 2. The resulting print.

DECAGON

Dec·a·log (*dek*-uh-log) *n.* Also **Dec·a·logue.** The Ten Commandments.

de·camp (deh-*kamp*) *v.* 1. To depart; leave suddenly. 2. To break camp; march off.

de·cant (deh-*kant*) *v.* To pour off gently.—**de·can·ta·tion** (dee-kan-*tay*-shun) *n.*

de·cant·er (deh-*kant*-er) *n*. A glass bottle from which wine is served.

de·cap·i·tate (deh-*kap*-ih-tayt) *v*. [de·cap·i·tat·ed; -tat·ing] To behead; remove the head from. —**de·cap·i·ta·tion** (deh-kap-ih-*tay*-shun) *n*.—**de·cap·i·ta·tor** *n*.

dec·a·pod (*dek*-uh-pod) *n*. *Zoology*. 1. A ten-legged order of crustaceans. 2. A cuttlefish having ten grasping arms.—*adj*. Ten-footed.

de·cath·lon (deh-*kath*-lun) *n*. *Athletics*. A single competition of ten different events.

DECANTER

de·cay (deh-*kay*) *v*. To deteriorate; decompose; rot; weaken.—**de·cay** *n*.

de·cease (deh-*sees*) *v*. [de·ceased; de·ceas·ing] To die.—**de·cease** *n*.

de·ceased *n*. A dead person.—*adj*. Dead.

de·ce·dent (deh-*see*-d'nt) *n*. A dead person.

de·ceit (deh-*seet*) *n*. Fraud; fallacy; deception.

de·ceit·ful *adj*. Fraudulent; deceptive; insincere.—**de·ceit·ful·ly** *adv*.—**de·ceit·ful·ness** *n*.

de·ceive (deh-*seev*) *v*. [de·ceived; de·ceiv·ing] To violate a confidence; delude; cheat; beguile.—**de·ceiv·er** *n*.—**de·ceiv·ing·ly** *adv*.

de·cel·er·ate (dee-*sel*-er-ayt) *v*. [de·cel·er·at·ed; -at·ing] To slow down; retard.—**de·cel·er·a·tion** (dee-sel-er-*ay*-shun) *n*.—**de·cel·er·a·tor** *n*.

De·cem·ber (deh-*sem*-ber) *n*. The final month of our calendar year; the twelfth month.

de·cen·cy (*dees*-en-see) *n*. [*pl*. -cies] 1. Propriety of conduct; becoming comportment. 2. *Colloquial*. Goodness; generosity.

de·cen·ni·al (deh-*sen*-ee-ul) *adj*. 1. Occurring every ten years. 2. Continuing for ten years. —*n*. A tenth anniversary.—**de·cen·ni·al·ly** *adv*.

de·cent (*deess*-ent) *adj*. 1. Respectable; seemly; modest; decorous. 2. Moderate; tolerable; passable. 3. *Colloquial*. Generous; kind. —**de·cent·ly** *adv*.—**de·cent·ness** *n*.

de·cen·tral·ize (dee-*sen*-truh-lyze) *v*. [de·cen·tral·ized; -iz·ing] 1. To distribute powers of administration among a number of agencies or governmental bodies rather than vest them in one center. 2. To distribute; spread out from a focal point.—**de·cen·tral·i·za·tion** (dee-sen-truh-liz-*ay*-shun) *n*.

de·cep·tion (deh-*sep*-shun) *n*. 1. Act of misleading or deceiving. 2. An unscrupulous scheme; fraud; imposition; deceit.

de·cep·tive (deh-*sep*-tiv) *adj*. Able to mislead or give false impressions; illusory; deceitful.—**de·cep·tive·ly** *adv*.—**de·cep·tive·ness** *n*.

de·cide (deh-*syde*) *v*. [de·cid·ed; de·cid·ing] To determine a course of action; settle; conclude.

de·cid·ed *adj*. Definite; well marked; unmistakable; pronounced.—**de·cid·ed·ly** *adv*.

de·cid·u·ous (deh-*sij*-oo-us) *adj*. Applied to plants whose leaves fall in autumn or to animals who periodically shed hair, horns, etc.

de·cil·lion (dee-*sil*-yun) *n*. The numeral one followed by 33 zeros.—**de·cil·lion·th** *adj*. & *n*.

dec·i·mal (*dess*-ih-m'l) *n*. 1. Any number expressed in terms of ten as the basic number. 2. A decimal fraction. 3. The point [.] used to indicate a decimal fraction.—**dec·i·mal** *adj*.

decimal fraction. A fraction whose denominator is a power of ten, expressed in numbers preceded by a decimal point. '.017 is a decimal fraction representing 17/1000.'

dec·i·mate (*dess*-ih-mayt) *v*. [dec·i·mat·ed; dec·i·mat·ing] 1. To take or destroy a tenth part of. 2. To destroy a great portion of.—**de·ci·ma·tion** (dess-ih-*may*-shun) *n*.—**dec·i·ma·tor** *n*.

de·ci·pher (deh-*sy*-fer) *v*. To figure out a paper written in secret code or in badly formed or partly obliterated letters.—**de·ci·pher·a·ble** *adj*.

de·ci·sion (deh-*sizh*-un) *n*. 1. A judgment arrived at after deliberation; resolution of doubt or uncertainty. 2. Unwavering firmness; prompt and definite determination.

de·ci·sive (deh-*sy*-siv) *adj*. 1. Having the power of settling a question. 2. Conclusive; definite; showing decision.—**de·ci·sive·ly** *adv*.

deck *n*. 1. One of the horizontal surfaces of a ship, corresponding to a floor. 2. A pack of cards. 3. *Journalism*. One of the lines into which a headline is divided.—*v*. 1. To dress in one's best; adorn. 2. To furnish with a deck.

deck hand. A seaman; unlicensed member of the deck department of a ship.

deck house. A cabin or structure on the main deck of a ship.

deck·le *n*. Also **deck·el**. A thin wooden frame on a wood pulp mold which regulates rough or raw edge of paper.—**deck·le-edged** *adj*.

de·claim (deh-*klaym*) *v*. To deliver a formal oration or rhetorical speech.—**de·claim·er** *n*.

dec·la·ma·tion (dek-luh-*may*-shun) *n*. 1. A rhetorical exercise or harangue; oration; formal or set speech. 2. The use of pretentious, inflated language; bombast.—**de·clam·a·to·ry** (deh-*klam*-uh-tor-ee) *adj*.

dec·la·ra·tion (dek-ler-*ay*-shun) *n*. 1. Publication, announcement; proclamation. 2. *Law*. a. The plaintiff's opening statement of his complaint. b. A solemn affirmation made in place of the oath.

de·clar·a·tive, de·clar·a·to·ry (deh-*klair*-uh-tiv; -tor-ee) *adj*. Making an assertion.

de·clare (deh-*klayr*) *v*. [de·clared; de·clar·ing] 1. To assert; affirm. 2. To publish; announce. 3. To make a statement of taxable articles in one's possession.—**de·clar·er** *n*.

de·clen·sion (deh-*klen*-shun) *n*. 1. Decline; deterioration; decay. 2. Slope; slant. 3. *Grammar*. The inflection of nouns, adjectives, and pronouns.—**de·clen·sion·al** *adj*.

dec·li·na·tion (dek-lin-*ay*-shun) *n*. 1. Withdrawal; refusal. 2. Decline; deterioration. 3. A slanting or bending down. 4. *Astronomy*. The angular distance of a body north or south of the celestial equator, corresponding

D

to latitude on the earth. 5. The angle between true north and the direction indicated by a magnetic needle; compass error.—**de·clin·a·to·ry** (deh-*klin*-uh-tor-ee) *adj.*

de·cline (deh-*klyne*) *v.* [de·clined; de·clin·ing] 1. To refuse; reject; avoid. 2. To fail; sink in character or value; become diminished or impaired. 3. To deviate. 4. To bend or slant down.—**de·cline** *n.*—**de·clin·a·ble** *adj.*

dec·li·nom·e·ter (dek-lin-*om*-uh-ter) *n.* An instrument for measuring the declination of the magnetic needle from the true north.

de·cliv·i·ty (deh-*kliv*-ih-tee) *n.* [*pl.* -ties] A slope.

de·coct (deh-*kokt*) *v.* To prepare by boiling.

de·coc·tion *n.* 1. Liquid in which a substance has been boiled. 2. Process of boiling.

de·code (deh-*kohd*) *v.* [de·cod·ed; de·cod·ing] To translate from code into ordinary language.

de·col·late (deh-*kol*-ayt) *v.* [de·col·lat·ed; -lat·ing] To behead.—**de·col·la·tion** (dee-kuh-*lay*-shun) *n.*—**de·col·la·tor** (dee-kuh-lay-ter) *n.*

dé·col·le·té (day-kol-*tay*) *adj.* Not covering the neck and shoulders. 'A décolleté gown.'

de·com·pose (dee-kum-*pohz*) *v.* [de·com·posed; de·com·pos·ing] To decay; disintegrate; separate.—**de·com·pos·a·ble** *adj.*—**de·com·po·si·tion** (dee-kom-puh-*zish*-un) *n.*

de·com·press (dee-kum-*pres*) *v.* To lessen or remove pressure.—**de·com·pres·sion** *n.*

de·con·tam·i·na·tion (dee-kun-tam-ih-*nay*-shun) *n.* The removal or destruction of contaminating substances; cleansing.—**de·con·tam·i·nate** *v.* [-i·nat·ed; -i·nat·ing].

dé·cor (*day*-kor; day-*kor*) *n.* Decorative background.

dec·o·rate (*dek*-er-ayt) *v.* [dec·o·rat·ed; dec·o·rat·ing] 1. To adorn; embellish; beautify. 2. To award a medal to.

dec·o·ra·tion (dek-er-*ay*-shun) *n.* 1. The act of adorning. 2. An ornament; embellishment. 3. A medal awarded as an honor.

Decoration Day. May 30th, a day dedicated to the memory of the dead U.S. servicemen.

dec·o·ra·tive (*dek*-er-ay-tiv) *adj.* Ornamental; embellishing; pretty.—**dec·o·ra·tive·ly** *adv.*

dec·o·ra·tor (*dek*-er-ay-ter) *n.* One who plans the decorative ensemble of a building interior.

dec·o·rous (*dek*-er-us) *adj.* Proper; fitting; seemly.—**dec·o·rous·ly** *adv.*—**dec·o·rous·ness** *n.*

de·cor·ti·cate (dee-*kor*-tih-kayt) *v.* [-cat·ed; -cat·ing] To strip off the bark; peel; husk.—**de·cor·ti·ca·tion** (dee-kor-tih-*kay*-shun) *n.*

de·co·rum (deh-*kor*-um) *n.* [*pl.* -rums, -ra] 1. Propriety; dignity; observance of conventions. 2. The moral and social code.

de·coy (dee-*koy*, *dee*-koy) *n.* 1. Lure; bait. 2. A person or thing who lures another into a dangerous situation.—*v.* (dee-*koy*) To lure; entice.—**de·coy·er** *n.*

de·crease (dee-*krees*) *v.* [de·creased; de·creas·ing] To lessen; diminish; dwindle.—**de·crease** (*dee*-krees, dee-*krees*) *n.*—**de·creas·ing·ly** *adv.*

de·cree (deh-*kree*) *n.* An order; edict; law.—*v.* [-creed; -cree·ing] To order; command.

dec·re·ment (*dek*-ruh-m'nt) *n.* 1. Decrease; diminution. 2. The quantity lost by waste.

de·crep·it (deh-*krep*-it) *adj.* Infirm; aged; worn out.—**de·crep·it·ly** *adv.*—**de·crep·i·tude** *n.*

de·cre·scen·do (dee-kruh-*shen*-doh, day-) *n.* [*pl.* -dos] *Music.* A gradual decrease in volume of sound.—**de·cre·scen·do** *adj. & adv.*

de·cry (deh-*kry*) *v.* [de·cried; de·cry·ing] To depreciate; condemn; censure; criticize.—**de·cri·al** *n.*—**de·cri·er** *n.*

de·cum·bent (deh-*kum*-b'nt) *adj.* 1. Lying down; reclining. 2. *Botany.* Growing along the ground with tips upright.

de·cur·rent (deh-*kur*-unt) *adj.* Extending downward, esp. of leaves growing down a stem.

ded·i·cate (*ded*-ih-kayt) *v.* [ded·i·cat·ed; ded·i·cat·ing] 1. To consecrate; hallow; set apart. 2. To give wholly or earnestly up to. 3. To inscribe or address a work to a patron, friend, etc., as a compliment.—**ded·i·cate** *adj.*

ded·i·ca·tion (ded-ih-*kay*-shun) *n.* 1. Consecration; hallowing. 2. A setting aside for a purpose. 3. An address prefixed to a book or composition honoring a friend, patron, etc.—**ded·i·ca·tive** *adj.*—**ded·i·ca·tor** *n.*—**ded·i·ca·to·ry** (*ded*-ih-kuh-tor-ee) *adj.*— -to·ri·ly *adv.*

de·duce (dih-*dyoos*) *v.* [de·duced; de·duc·ing] To derive by reasoning.—**de·duc·i·ble** *adj.*

de·duct (deh-*dukt*) *v.* To subtract; take away. **de·duct·i·ble** *adj.*

de·duc·tion (deh-*duk*-shun) *n.* 1. An amount subtracted. 2. Inference; conclusion. 3. Reasoning which proceeds from a universal premise to a particular conclusion.—**de·duc·tive** *adj.*

deed *n.* 1. Act; exploit, achievement. 2. *Law.* A document conveying real estate to a purchaser, or donee.—*v.* To transfer by deed.

deem *v.* To consider; think; suppose.

deep *adj.* 1. Extending or lying far below the surface. 2. Extending or lying a great way back from the front or outside. 3. Absorbed; engrossed. 4. Difficult to comprehend; abstruse. 5. Sagacious; profound. 6. Artful; crafty. 7. Low in sound or pitch. 8. Intense; dark or vivid, as in color.—*n.* 1. A deep place or part. 2. The sea; ocean. 3. The most profound or intense part.—**deep**, **deep·ly** *adv.* —**deep·ness** *n.*—**go off the deep end.** *Colloquial.* Become overenthusiastic or overzealous.

deep asleep	deep-eyed	deep-skirted
deep-bellied	deep-felt	deep-stapled
deep-bosomed	deep-grown	deep-sunk
deep-browed	deep-mouthed	deep-tangled
deep-buried	deep-piled	deep-throated
deep-chested	deep-pitched	deep-toned
deep-colored	deep-set	deep-vaulted
deep-cut	deep-settled	deep-voiced
deep-dyed	deep-sided	deep water
deep-engraven	deep-sighted	deep-worn

deep·en (*deep*-'n) *v.* To make or become deeper.

deep laid *adj.* Formed with great skill; planned carefully.

deep-root·ed *adj.* Strong; deeply embedded; inveterate.

deep-seat·ed *adj.* Buried deep; fixed.

deer *n. sing. & pl.* A large, swift animal bearing

horns or antlers which are shed and grow anew each year.

deer·hound n. A large, shaggy hound formerly used for hunting deer.

deer mouse. A small North American mouse.

deer·skin n. The skin of a deer or the leather made from it.

de·face (deh-*fayss*) v. [de·faced; de·fac·ing] To mar; disfigure; injure the appearance of. —**de·face·a·ble** adj.—**de·face·ment** n.—**de·fac·er** n.

de·fal·cate (deh-*fal*-kayt) v. [-cat·ed; -cat·ing] To steal money; embezzle.—**de·fal·ca·tor** n.

de·fal·ca·tion (dee-fal-*kay*-sh'n) n. Embezzlement; theft or misuse of money.

def·a·ma·tion (def-uh-*may*-shun) n. Slander; calumny.

de·fam·a·to·ry (deh-*fam*-uh-toh-ree) adj. Slanderous.

de·fame (deh-*faym*) v. [-famed; -fam·ing] To slander; vilify; harm the reputation of.—**de·fam·er** n.

de·fault (deh-*fawlt*) n. 1. A failing; neglect to do what law or duty requires. 2. Failure to pay a debt. 3. Failure to appear, as in court, or to engage in a contest.—v. 1. To fail in meeting an obligation or payment. 2. To fail to do or appear. 3. *Sports.* To forfeit a contest by not appearing for or finishing it. —**de·fault·er** n.

de·feat (deh-*feet*) v. 1. To vanquish; subdue; beat. 2. To frustrate; nullify.—**de·feat** n.

de·feat·ism n. Pessimism; expectation or admission of defeat.—**de·feat·ist** n. & adj.

def·e·cate (*def*-uh-kayt) v. [def·e·cat·ed; def·e·cat·ing] 1. To make or become pure. 2. To discharge excrement from the bowels.—**def·e·ca·tion** (def-uh-*kay*-shun) n.—**def·e·ca·tor** n.

de·fect (deh-*fekt*, dee-fekt) n. 1. A fault; flaw; imperfection. 2. A deficiency; lack.

de·fec·tion (deh-*fek*-shun) n. Desertion; a falling away; failure.

de·fec·tive adj. 1. Imperfect; faulty; incomplete; subnormal. 2. *Grammar.* Lacking one or more of the usual inflected forms.—**de·fec·tive·ly** adv.—**de·fec·tive·ness** n.

de·fend (deh-*fend*) v. 1. To protect; guard against attack or injury. 2. *Law.* To oppose; contest.—**de·fend·er** n.

de·fend·ant n. *Law.* Party required to answer a complaint, or charge.—**de·fend·ant** adj.

de·fen·es·tra·tion (dee-fen-uh-*stray*-shun) n. Act of throwing out through a window.

de·fense, de·fence (deh-*fenss*) n. 1. Justification; vindication. 2. Protection from or resistance against assault; security; guard. 3. *Law.* A defendant's plea or answer. 4. *Sports.* The protection or guarding of a goal.

de·fense·less adj. Unprotected; helpless; unarmed.— -**less·ly** adv.— -**less·ness** n.

defense mechanism. *Psychology.* Any reaction by which a person conceals or protects sensitive convictions or emotions.

de·fen·si·ble (deh-*fen*-suh-b'l) adj. 1. Capable of being defended. 2. Justifiable.—**de·fen·si·bil·i·ty** (deh-fen-suh-*bil*-uh-tee), **de·fen·si·ble·ness** n.—**de·fen·si·bly** adv.

de·fen·sive (deh-*fen*-siv) adj. 1. Suitable for or devoted to defense. 2. In an attitude of defense. 3. Apologetic; self-justifying.—n. Position or weapon of defense.—**de·fen·sive·ly** adv.—**de·fen·sive·ness** n.

de·fer (deh-*fer*) v. [de·ferred; de·fer·ring] 1. To delay; postpone. 2. To yield; submit.

def·er·ence (*def*-er-uns) n. Respect; regard.

def·er·en·tial (def-er-*en*-shul) adj. Respectful; expressing deference.—**def·er·en·tial·ly** adv.

de·fer·ment (deh-*fer*-munt) n. Postponement; delay.—**de·ferred** adj.—**de·fer·rer** n.

de·fi·ance (deh-*fy*-uns) n. 1. A challenge. 2. Contempt of opposition or danger.

de·fi·ant adj. Challenging; bold; belligerent.

de·fi·cien·cy (deh-*fish*-un-see) n. [pl. -cies] A lack; imperfection; shortage.

de·fi·cient adj. Wanting; not sufficient; lacking; incomplete.—**de·fi·cient** n.—**de·fi·cient·ly** adv.

def·i·cit (*def*-uh-sit) n. Shortage; deficiency.

de·fi·er n. A challenger; one who defies.

de·file (deh-*fyle*) v. [de·filed; de·fil·ing] 1. To sully; befoul; make filthy. 2. To pollute; contaminate; corrupt.—**de·file·ment** n.

de·file v. To march off in a line; file off.—n. A long, narrow pass between hills.

de·fine (deh-*fyne*) v. [de·fined; de·fin·ing] 1. To prescribe; limit; establish the boundaries or character of. 2. To explain; determine and express the meaning of; describe.—**de·fin·a·ble** adj.—**de·fin·er** n.

def·i·nite (*def*-in-it) adj. 1. Explicit; precise; clear. 2. Having certain limits; restricted. 3. Limiting; designating.—**def·i·nite·ly** adv.—**def·i·nite·ness** n.—**definite article.** *Grammar.* The designating article *the*.

def·i·ni·tion (def-in-*ish*-un) n. 1. An explanation of the meaning of a word or term. 2. Act of defining or making clear.

de·fin·i·tive (deh-*fin*-it-iv) adj. Conclusive; final; decisive; defining exactly.—n. *Grammar.* A word, as *some, all, this*, used to define or limit the meaning of a noun.—**de·fin·i·tive·ly** adv.

def·la·grate (*def*-luh-grayt) v. [-grat·ed; -grat·ing] To burn suddenly.—**def·la·gra·tion** (def-luh-*gray*-shun) n.

de·flate (deh-*flayt*) v. [-flat·ed; -flat·ing] To collapse; contract; reduce in size.— -**fla·tor** n.

de·fla·tion n. A contraction, esp. in the amount of purchasing power in circulation.—**de·fla·tion·ar·y** adj.—**de·fla·tion·ist** n.

de·flect (deh-*flekt*) v. To turn aside; divert.

de·flec·tion n. Deviation; swerving; turning aside.—**de·flec·tive** adj.—**de·flec·tor** n.

def·lo·ra·tion (def-lor-*ay*-shun) n. Rape; deflowering.

de·flow·er (deh-*flow*-er) v. 1. To violate; ravish; rape. 2. To strip of flowers.

de·fo·li·ate (deh-*foh*-lee-ayt) v. [-at·ed; -at·ing] To deprive of leaves.—**de·fo·li·a·tion** n.

D

de·for·est (deh-*for*-ist) *v.* To clear of trees.—**de·for·est·a·tion** *n.*—**de·for·est·er** *n.*

de·form (deh-*form*) *v.* To disfigure; distort; spoil the shape or form of.

de·for·ma·tion (deh-for-*may*-sh'n) *n.* Distortion; mutilation; disfiguration.

de·formed *adj.* Distorted; warped; crippled.

de·form·i·ty *n.* [*pl.* -ties] 1. Distortion; disfigurement. 2. A deformed person or part.

de·fraud (deh-*frawd*) *v.* To swindle; cheat; deprive of, as money, by deceit.—**de·frau·da·tion** (deh-fraw-*day*-shun) *n.*—**de·fraud·er** *n.*

de·fray (deh-*fray*) *v.* To pay; bear, as expense. —**de·fray·a·ble** *adj.*—**de·fray·al** *n.*— -**fray·er** *n.*

de·frost (dee-*frawst*) *v.* To remove ice from by raising the temperature.—**de·frost·er** *n.*

deft *adj.* Dexterous; skillful; adroit.—**deft·ly** *adv.*—**deft·ness** *n.*

de·funct (deh-*funkt*) *adj.* Deceased; dead.

de·fy (deh-*fy*) *v.* [de·fied; de·fy·ing] 1. To challenge; dare. 2. To withstand; brave.—*n.* [*pl.* de·fies] *Colloquial.* A challenge.

de·gauss (deh-*gows*) *v.* To eliminate the magnetic attraction of ships, for protection against magnetic mines.

de·gen·er·ate (deh-*jen*-er-ayt) *v.* [de·gen·er·at·ed; de·gen·er·at·ing] 1. To decline; become corrupt; deteriorate. 2. *Biology.* To become a lower type; deteriorate gradually.—*adj.* (deh-*jen*-er-it) Degraded; perverted; having declined far below normal.—*n.* A debased person, esp. a sexual pervert.—**de·gen·er·a·cy** *n.*—**de·gen·er·ate·ly** *adv.*—**de·gen·er·ate·ness** *n.*

de·gen·er·a·tion (deh-jen-er-*ay*-sh'n) *n.* 1. Deterioration; degradation. 2. *Medicine.* Deterioration in tissues or organs.—**de·gen·er·a·tive** (deh-*jen*-ruh-tiv) *adj.*

de·gra·da·tion (deg-ruh-*day*-shun) *n.* 1. Act of degrading. 2. Debasement; degeneration.

de·grade (deh-*grayd*) *v.* [de·grad·ed; de·grad·ing] 1. To reduce in rank or dignity; humiliate. 2. To debase; corrupt; lower in quality. 3. *Geology.* To wear down or away by erosion.—**de·grad·ing** *n.* & *adj.*—**de·grad·ing·ly** *adv.*—**de·grad·ing·ness** *n.*

de·grad·ed *adj.* Debased; corrupted; perverted. —**de·grad·ed·ly** *adv.*—**de·grad·ed·ness** *n.*

de·gree (deh-*gree*) *n.* 1. A step in a series. 2. Grade; rank; station. 3. Measure; relative extent or quantity. 4. The 360th part of the circumference of any circle. 5. A unit of measure or interval marked on a mathematical, meteorological, or other instrument, as a thermometer. 6. A rank attained by scholastic achievement, in a college or university. 7. *Music.* Line on the staff marking the position of the notes; interval between notes. —**by degrees.** Gradually.—**to a degree.** Exceedingly; rather.

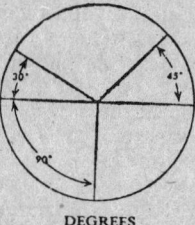

DEGREES

de·horn (dee-*horn*) *v.* To strip of horns.

de·hu·man·ize (dee-*hyoo*-mun-yze) *v.* [-ized; -iz·ing] To deprive of human characteristics.—**de·hu·man·i·za·tion** (dee-hyoo-mun-iz-*ay*-shun) *n.*

de·hu·mid·i·fy (dee-hyoo-*mid*-uh-fy) *v.* [-fied; fy·ing] To remove moisture from, as the air.

de·hy·drate (dee-*hy*-drayt) *v.* [-drat·ed; -drat·ing] To remove water from; dry up.—**de·hy·dra·tion** (dee-hy-*dray*-shun) *n.*

de·i·cer (dee-*eye*-ser) *n.* Device for removing ice from the wings of an airplane.

de·i·fi·ca·tion (dee-uh-fih-*kay*-sh'n) *n.* The act of exalting; deifying.

de·i·fy (*dee*-uh-fy) *v.* [de·i·fied; de·i·fy·ing] 1. To make a god of. 2. To exalt; worship.

deign (*dayn*) *v.* To condescend; believe fit for or worthy of one.

de·ism (*dee*-izm) *n.* The religious belief that God exists but exerts no influence on man or his world.—**de·ist** *n.*—**de·is·tic** (dee-*is*-tik) *adj.*

de·i·ty (*dee*-ih-tee) *n.* [*pl.* -ties] A god.

de·ject·ed (deh-*jek*-ted) *adj.* Downcast; dispirited; discouraged; depressed.—**de·ject·ed·ly** *adv.*—**de·ject·ed·ness** *n.*

de·jec·tion *n.* Sadness; melancholy; depression.

Del·a·ware (*del*-uh-wair) *n.* 1. State situated on Delaware Bay. Area: 2,057 sq. mi. Capital: Dover. 2. A river which rises in New York and empties into Delaware Bay south of New Jersey.—**Del·a·war·e·an** (del-uh-*wair*-ee-un) *adj.*

de·lay (deh-*lay*) *v.* 1. To retard; slow up; detain. 2. To postpone; put off.—**de·lay** *n.*

de·le (*dee*-lee) *v. Printing.* Take out; delete.

de·lec·ta·ble (deh-*lek*-tuh-b'l) *adj.* Delicious; tasty; pleasing.—**de·lec·ta·ble·ness** *n.*—**de·lec·ta·bly** *adv.*

de·lec·ta·tion (dee-lek-*tay*-shun) *n.* Delight; great pleasure.

del·e·gate (*del*-uh-gayt) *v.* [-gat·ed; -gat·ing] 1. To entrust; commit to another's care. 2. To appoint as a representative.—*n.* A representative; deputy; one sent to a convention.

del·e·ga·tion (del-uh-*gay*-shun) *n.* 1. A body of representatives or deputies; commission. 2. Appointment of a delegate; relinquishing of authority to an agent or representative.

de·lete (deh-*leet*) *v.* [-let·ing; -let·ed] 1. To blot or cross out; erase. 2. *Printing.* To take out, indicated by symbol [ϑ].—**de·le·tion** *n.*

del·e·te·ri·ous (del-uh-*tihr*-ee-us) *adj.* Injurious; pernicious; depriving of health or life. —**del·e·te·ri·ous·ly** *adv.*—**del·e·te·ri·ous·ness** *n.*

delft·ware *n.* Also **delft, delf.** A richly designed, glazed earthenware or pottery.

de·lib·er·ate (deh-*lib*-er-it) *adj.* 1. Not sudden or rash; well considered. 2. Carefully weighing facts or considering the consequences of an act.—*v.* [de·lib·er·at·ed; -at·ing] To weigh facts carefully; consider thoroughly.—**de·lib·er·ate·ly** *adv.*—**de·lib·er·ate·ness** *n.*

de·lib·er·a·tion (deh-lib-er-*ay*-shun) *n.* 1. A thoughtful weighing of evidence or consequences. 2. Caution; prudence.— -**er·a·tor** *n.*

de·lib·er·a·tive (deh-*lib*-er-ay-tiv) *adj.* Pertaining to deliberation; having the right or function of deliberating.—**de·lib·er·a·tive·ness** *n.*

del·i·ca·cy (*del*-ih-kuh-see) *n.* 1. A luxury; delight to the senses. 2. Lack of robustness or good health. 3. Acuteness of aesthetic perception. 4. Nicety in observing the laws of propriety. 5. Exquisiteness or delightfulness of tint, texture, flavor, etc. 6. Fineness; slenderness; smallness.

del·i·cate (*del*-ih-kut) *adj.* 1. Pleasing; dainty; agreeable. 2. Fine in texture. 3. Softly tinted. 4. Tiny; slender; fine. 5. Sensitive to beauty. 6. Refined in social intercourse. 7. Tender; easily injured; fragile. 8. Requiring careful, tactful handling.—**del·i·cate·ly** *adv.*—**del·i·cate·ness** *n.*

del·i·ca·tes·sen (del-ih-kuh-*tes*-'n) *n. sing. & pl.* 1. A store where food, esp. prepared meat, is sold. 2. Table delicacies.

de·li·cious (deh-*lish*-us) *adj.* 1. Tasty; delightful to the senses. 2. Gratifying to the mind.—**de·li·cious·ly** *adv.*—**de·li·cious·ness** *n.*

de·light (deh-*lyte*) *n.* 1. Exquisite pleasure; joy. 2. That which affords keen pleasure.—*v.* To please highly; enrapture.—**de·light·er** *n.*

de·light·ed *adj.* Thrilled with pleasure; greatly pleased.—**de·light·ed·ly** *adv.*—**de·light·ed·ness** *n.*

de·light·ful *adj.* Causing pleasure; fascinating; rapturous; gratifying.—**de·light·ful·ly** *adv.*

De·li·lah (duh-*ly*-luh) *n.* 1. In the Old Testament, the treacherous mistress of Samson.

de·lim·it (deh-*lim*-it) *v.* To bound; put a limit to; demark.—**de·lim·i·ta·tion** *n.*

de·lin·e·ate (deh-*lin*-ee-ayt) *v.* [-at·ed; -at·ing] 1. To describe fully; portray to the mind. 2. To paint or make a likeness of. 3. To mark out with lines; sketch; design.—**de·lin·e·a·tion** *n.*—**de·lin·e·a·tive** *adj.*—**de·lin·e·a·tor** *n.*

de·lin·quen·cy (deh-*lin*-kwun-see) *n.* [*pl.* -cies] An omission of duty; law violation; misdeed.

de·lin·quent (deh-*lin*-kw'nt) *adj.* Failing or remiss in duty; violating the law; criminal.—**de·lin·quent** *n.*—**de·lin·quent·ly** *adv.*

del·i·quesce (del-ih-*kwes*) *v.* [-quesced; -quesc·ing] To change from solid to liquid by absorbing moisture from the air; melt.—**del·i·ques·cence** *n.*—**del·i·ques·cent** *adj.*

de·lir·i·ous (deh-*leer*-ee-us) *adj.* Disordered in mind; having wild, incoherent ideas, esp. in fever.—**de·lir·i·ous·ly** *adv.*—**de·lir·i·ous·ness** *n.*

de·lir·i·um *n.* [*pl.* -i·ums, -i·a] 1. A temporary mental derangement caused by fever, injury, etc. 2. Violent excitement; mirth.

delirium tremens (*tree*-munz). A disease, commonest among alcoholics, marked by mental derangement and physical trembling.

de·liv·er (deh-*liv*-er) *v.* 1. To free; release; rescue. 2. To give or transfer; put into another's possession. 3. To give birth to a child. 4. To yield; render. 5. To utter; speak. 6. To direct; send forth.

de·liv·er·ance *n.* 1. Release; rescue; liberation. 2. Bringing forth of children. 3. A transferring, giving, or rendering. 4. Utter-

ance; pronouncement; affirmation. 5. Acquittal of a person being tried.

de·liv·er·y *n.* [*pl.* -ies] *n.* 1. A distribution. transfer; transportation. 2. Childbirth. 3. Surrender; giving up. 4. Liberation; release. 5. Speaking or manner of utterance.

dell *n.* A ravine; small valley between hills.

de·louse (dee-*lowss*) *v.* [de·loused; de·lous·ing] To exterminate vermin; free of lice.

Del·phi (*del*-fy) *n.* A famous oracle of ancient Greece.—**Del·phi·an** (*del*-fee-un), **Del·phic** *adj.*

del·phin·i·um (del-*fin*-ee-um) *n.* A family of hardy flowering plants; larkspur.

del·ta (*del*-tuh) *n.* 1. The branching of a river at its mouth caused by alluvial islands or deposits. 2. The fourth letter [∆, δ] of the Greek alphabet.—**del·ta·ic** (del-*tay*-ik) *adj.*

del·toid (*del*-toyd) *adj.* Triangular; trowel-shaped.—*n.* The triangular-shaped shoulder muscle which raises the arm.

de·lude (deh-*lood*, -*lyood*) *v.* [de·lud·ed, de·lud·ing] To deceive; mislead; cheat; beguile.—**de·lud·er** *n.*—**de·lud·ing·ly** *adv.*

del·uge (*del*-yooj) *n.* A great overflow of water; flood.—*v.* [del·uged; del·ug·ing] To overwhelm; cover.

de·lu·sion (deh-*loo*-zhun, deh-*lyoo*-zhun) *n.* 1. Deception; a misleading. 2. False impression or belief. 3. An insanely fixed notion of something false.—**de·lu·sion·al** *adj.*

de·lu·sive (deh-*loo*-siv, deh-*lyoo*-siv) *adj.* Deceptive; misleading; illusory.—**de·lu·sive·ly** *adv.*

de luxe (deh-*looks*, deh-*luhks*). Of prime quality; having special features.

delve (*delv*) *v.* [delved; delv·ing] 1. *Dial.* To dig; spade. 2. To fathom; study deeply; penetrate.—**delv·er** *n.*

de·mag·net·ize (dee-*mag*-nuh-tyze) *v.* [de·mag·net·ized; -iz·ing] To deprive of magnetic polarity.—**de·mag·net·i·za·tion** (dee-mag-nih-tih-*zay*-shun) *n.*—**de·mag·net·i·zer** *n.*

dem·a·gog·ic (dem-uh-*goj*-ik). Also **dem·a·gog·i·cal** *adj.* Like a demagogue; unprincipled; quarrelsome; corrupt.—**dem·a·gog·i·cal·ly** *adv.*

dem·a·gogue, **dem·a·gog** (*dem*-uh-gog) *n.* One who grasps power by playing on the prejudices and ignorance of the masses; an unprincipled, persuasive orator.—**dem·a·gog·ism** (-gog-ism), **dem·a·gog·uer·y** (-gog-er-ee) **-gog·y** (goh-jee) *n.*

de·mand (deh-*mand*) *n.* 1. An imperative request made with or without reason; claim; order. 2. The amount of a commodity which will be sold if offered at a specific price. 3. Earnest inquiry; question. 4. Desire to possess. 5. *Law.* Asking what is due or claimed.—*v.* 1. To call for a claim with authority. 2. To inquire peremptorily. 3. To require. 'Language demands study.'

de·mar·cate (deh-*mahr*-kayt) *v.* [de·mar·cat·ed; -cat·ing] To define the limits of; mark off; separate.—**de·mar·ca·tion, de·mar·ka·tion** *n.*

dé·marche (day-*marsh*) *n.* A plan of action, esp. one involving alteration in diplomatic policy.

de·mean (deh-*meen*) *v.* 1. To debase; lower;

corrupt. 2. To behave; conduct. 'Demean ourselves with humility.'

de·mean·or, de·mean·our (deh-*meen*-er) *n*. Behavior; deportment; manner.

de·ment (deh-*ment*) *v*. To make insane.

de·ment·ed *adj*. Insane; crazy; out of one's mind.—**de·ment·ed·ly** *adv*.—**de·ment·ed·ness** *n*.

de·men·ti·a (deh-*men*-shuh) *n*. 1. A form of insanity in which the powers of attention and reflection are lost, and perception eventually becomes indistinct. It sometimes accompanies old age. 2. Absence of intellect; mental deterioration.

dementia praecox (*pree*-koks). A psychosis most common to adolescence and shortly after but also appearing in maturity. It is marked by disorientation, loss of contact with reality, delusions, and general mental deterioration.

de·mer·it (dee-*mehr*-it) *n*. 1. Something punishable or blamable. 2. A black mark; unit of discredit in a person's record.

de·mesne (deh-*mayn*) *n*. 1. A manor house and nearby land used by a lord and his family. 2. Any landed estate. 3. *Law*. The right of possession of land. 4. A region; sphere.

dem·i·god (*dem*-ih-god) *n*. A half-god; inferior deity; fabulous hero.—**dem·i·god·dess** *n*.

dem·i·john (*dem*-ih-jon) *n*. A large bottle or jug with a small neck, enclosed in basket work.

de·mil·i·tar·ize (dee-*mil*-ih-ter-yze) *v*. [ized; -iz·ing] To disarm; reduce military and naval strength to ineffectiveness.—**de·mil·i·ta·ri·za·tion** (dee-mil-ih-ter-ih-*zay*-shun) *n*.

dem·i·monde (*dem*-ih-mond) *n*. Disreputable female society; courtesans as a class.—**dem·i·mon·daine** (dem-ih-mon-*dayn*) *n*. A harlot.

de·mise (deh-*myze*) *n*. 1. Death, esp. of a distinguished person. 2. *Law*. Transfer of property for life or a term of years.—*v*. *Law*. To lease; bequeath.—**de·mis·er** *n*.

dem·i·tasse (*dem*-ih-tas) *n*. A small cup of coffee.

de·mo·bi·lize (dee-*moh*-bih-lyze) *v*. [-lized; -liz·ing] To disband; relieve from military service. —**de·mo·bi·li·za·tion** *n*.

de·moc·ra·cy (duh-*mok*-ruh-see) *n*. [*pl.* -cies] 1. A form of government vesting sovereignty in the people, who exercise it either directly or through elected representatives. 2. [*cap*.] The principles of the Democratic party of the U.S.

dem·o·crat (*dem*-uh-krat) *n*. 1. One who adheres to democracy. 2. [*cap*.] A member of the U.S. Democratic party.

dem·o·crat·ic (dem-uh-*krat*-ik) *adj*. 1. Pertaining to or characteristic of democracy. 2. Socially equal; not snobbish. 3. [*cap*.] Denoting the Democratic party.—**dem·o·crat·i·cal** *adj*.—**dem·o·crat·i·cal·ly** *adv*.

de·moc·ra·tize (duh-*mok*-ruh-tyze) *v*. [-tized; -tiz·ing] To place under popular administration; organize according to principles of equality and freedom.—**de·moc·ra·ti·za·tion** (duh-mok-ruh-tih-*zay*-shun) *n*.

dem·oi·selle (dem-wah-*zel*) *n*. 1. A young

French lady; maiden. 2. A small crane found in warm climates of the Eastern Hemisphere. 3. A common dragonfly having a long, narrow body.

de·mol·ish (duh-*mol*-ish) *v*. To destroy; ruin; tear down.—**de·mol·ish·er** *n*.— -ish·ment *n*.

dem·o·li·tion (dem-uh-*lish*-un) *n*. Destruction; wrecking; pulling down, as of condemned buildings.—**dem·o·li·tion·ist** *n*.

de·mon (*dee*-mun) *n*. 1. An evil spirit. 2. A fiendish person. 3. *Slang*. One having a particular obsession. 'A demon for work.'—**de·mon·ic** (duh-*mon*-ik) *adj*.

de·mon·e·tize (dee-*mon*-uh-tyze) *v*. [-tized; -tiz·ing] To withdraw from circulation; cease to use as money.—**de·mon·e·ti·za·tion** (dee-mon-uh-tih-*zay*-shun) *n*.

de·mo·ni·ac (duh-*moh*-nee-ak) *adj*. Also **de·mo·ni·a·cal** (dee-muh-*ny*-uh-k'l). 1. Possessed by evil spirits. 2. Fiendish.— -a·cal·ly *adv*.

de·mon·ism (*dee*-mun-izm) *n*. Belief in demons. —**de·mon·ist** *n*.

de·mon·ol·a·try (dee-mun-*ol*-uh-tree) *n*. [*pl.* -tries] Worship of evil spirits.—**de·mon·ol·a·ter** *n*.

de·mon·ol·o·gy (dee-mun-*ol*-uh-jee) *n*. [*pl.* -gies] Study of demon worship.— -ol·o·gist *n*.

de·mon·stra·ble (duh-*mon*-struh-b'l) *adj*. Capable of proof or demonstration.—**de·mon·stra·bil·i·ty** (duh-mon-struh-*bil*-ih-tee), **de·mon·stra·ble·ness** *n*.—**de·mon·stra·bly** *adv*.

dem·on·strate (*dem*-un-strayt) *v*. [dem·on·strat·ed; -strat·ing] 1. To prove; show to be true. 2. To point out; indicate; show. 3. To try out publicly; exhibit in action.

dem·on·stra·tion (dem-un-*stray*-shun) *n*. 1. Manifestation; display. 2. Public exhibition of a commercial product. 3. Conclusive proof. 4. Public rally.—**dem·on·stra·tion·al** *adj*.—**dem·on·stra·tion·ist** *n*.

de·mon·stra·tive (duh-*mon*-struh-tiv) *adj*. 1. Conclusive; beyond doubt. 2. *Grammar*. Used to indicate the thing referred to. 'A demonstrative pronoun.' 3. Effusive; openly expressing affection.—*n*. *Grammar*. A specifying word; pronoun.—**de·mon·stra·tive·ly** *adv*.

dem·on·stra·tor (*dem*-un-stray-ter) *n*. 1. One who publicly shows the use of a product. 2. A product used for commercial exhibition.

de·mor·al·ize (duh-*mor*-'l-yze) *v*. [-ized; -iz·ing] 1. To undermine courage and optimism; cause to lose spirit. 2. To corrupt morally; undermine principles. 3. To disorganize; play havoc with.—**de·mor·al·i·za·tion** (duh-mor-'l-ih-*zay*-shun) *n*.—**de·mor·al·i·zer** *n*.

De·mos·the·nes (duh-*mos*-thuh-neez) *n*. Famous Greek orator.

de·mote (dee-*moht*) *v*. [-mot·ed; -mot·ing] To reduce in rank or grade.—**de·mo·tion** (dee-*moh*-shun) *n*.

de·mot·ic (dee-*mot*-ik) *adj*. Denoting the common people; popular; in the vernacular.

de·mur (deh-*mer*) *v*. [de·murred; de·mur·ring] To offer objections; hesitate; withhold compliance.—**de·mur, de·mur·ral** *n*.

D

de·mure (deh-*myoor*) *adj.* Prim; coquettishly proper and retiring.—**de·mure·ly** *adv.*

de·mur·rage (deh-*mer*-ij) *n. Law.* Holding up of a freight or cargo carrier by the loader. 2. The recompense paid for such delay.

de·mur·rer (deh-*mer*-er) *n. Law.* A plea for dismissal of a case on grounds of insufficient cause; an objection.

den *n.* 1. A wild animal's lair or cave; recess for concealment or security. 2. Any squalid, low place. 'An opium den.' 3. A comfortable, informal sitting room in a home.

de·nar·i·us (deh-*nayr*-ee-us) *n.* [*pl.* -i·i] A Roman silver coin worth nearly two dollars.

de·na·tion·al·ize (dee-*nash*-un-uh-lyz) *v.* [-ized; -iz·ing] To remove national character or rights. —**de·na·tion·al·i·za·tion** *n.*

de·nat·u·ral·ize (dee-*nach*-er-uh-lyze) *v.* [-ized; -iz·ing] 1. To deprive of naturalization or citizenship acquired in a foreign country. 2. To render unnatural or unlike nature.—**de·nat·u·ral·i·za·tion** *n.*

de·na·ture (dee-*nay*-cher) *v.* [de·na·tured; -tur·ing] To change in nature or composition, esp. to render unfit for human consumption.—**de·na·tur·a·tion** (dee-nay-cher-*ay*-shun) *n.*

de·na·zi·fy (dee-*naht*-sih-fy) *n.* [-fied; -fy·ing] To purge a people or culture of Nazi philosophy and institutions.—**de·na·zi·fi·ca·tion** *n.*

den·drite (*den*-dryte) *n.* 1. A minute nerve ending. 2. A stone or ore in which there are branching, treelike lines.—**den·drit·ic, den·drit·i·cal** *adj.*—**den·trit·i·cal·ly** *adv.*

den·gue (*deng*-ee, *deng*-ay) *n.* An infectious, eruptive fever caused by a filterable virus.

de·ni·al (duh-*ny*-ul) *n.* 1. An assertion that a statement made is untrue; negation. 2. Refusal to grant a request. 3. A rejection; refusal to accept as true or valid.—**de·ni·er** *n.*

den·i·grate *v.* To disparage, defame, blacken.

den·im (*den*-um) *n.* A coarse, twill-woven cotton cloth used for overalls.—**den·im** *adj.*

den·i·zen (*den*-uh-zun) *n.* An inhabitant; dweller; citizen.—**den·i·zen** *v.*

de·nom·i·nate (duh-*nom*-ih-nayt) *v.* [-nat·ed; -nat·ing] To name; call; designate; indicate. —*adj.* (duh-*nom*-uh-nit) Having a specified denomination, quantity, etc.

de·nom·i·na·tion (duh-nom-uh-*nay*-shun) *n.* 1. A sect; religious group. 2. Appellation; category.—**de·nom·i·na·tion·al** *adj.*

de·nom·i·na·tive (duh-*nom*-uh-nay-tiv) *adj.* Conferring or receiving a name; calling.—*n.* 1. A denomination or name. 2. *Grammar.* A verb formed from a noun.— **-na·tive·ly** *adv.*

de·nom·i·na·tor (duh-*nom*-uh-nay-ter) *n.* 1. *Mathematics.* The number appearing under the line in a fraction. 2. One who names or serves as namesake.

de·no·ta·tion (dee-noh-*tay*-shun) *n.* 1. Indication; distinguishing mark. 2. Meaning; signification.—**de·not·a·tive** (duh-*noht*-uh-tiv) *adj.*

de·note (duh-*noht*) *v.* [-not·ed; -not·ing] 1. To mark; indicate; point out. 2. To mean; signify; betoken.—**de·not·a·ble** *adj.*— **-note·ment** *n.*

dé·noue·ment (day-*noo*-mahn) *n.* The unraveling or outcome of a situation; solution; revelation.

de·nounce (duh-*nownss*) *v.* [de·nounced; de·nounc·ing] 1. To censure or berate solemnly; declare bad or vicious. 2. To threaten by open expression. 3. To accuse; point out as guilty.—**de·nounce·ment** *n.*—**de·nounc·er** *n.*

dense *adj.* 1. Compact; thick; crowded together; teeming. 2. *Colloquial.* Slow-witted; stupid.—**dense·ly** *adv.*—**dense·ness** *n.*

den·si·ty (*den*-suh-tee) *n.* [*pl.* -ties] 1. The mass or quantity of matter per unit of volume. 2. Compactness; frequency of occurrence in a restricted area. 3. *Colloquial.* Stupidity.

dent *n.* A small hollow or depression caused by an impact.—**dent** *v.*

den·tal (*dent*-'l) *n.* 1. Denoting the teeth; pertaining to dentistry. 2. *Phonetics.* Pronounced with the tip of the tongue against the teeth, as the consonant *th.*

den·tate (*den*-tayt) *adj.* Toothed; having sharp toothlike projections.—**den·tate·ly** *adv.*—**den·ta·tion** (den-*tay*-shun) *n.*

den·ti·frice (*den*-tuh-friss) *n.* Any tooth-cleansing substance.

den·tine, den·tin (*den*-teen, *den*-tin), *n.* The hard tissue, under the enamel, which makes up the main body of a tooth.

den·tist (*den*-tist) *n.* A licensed medical practitioner who treats the teeth and gums.

den·tist·ry *n.* Branch of medicine specializing in treatment of teeth.

den·ti·tion (den-*tish*-'n) *n.* The growing or cutting of teeth; time at which this occurs.

den·ture (*den*-cher) *n.* A complete set of teeth, either natural or artificial.

de·nude *v.* [-nud·ed; -nud·ing] To strip naked; bare; uncover.—**den·u·da·tion** *n.*—**de·nud·er** *n.*

de·nun·ci·a·tion (duh-nun-see-*ay*-shun) *n.* 1. Condemnation; severe criticism; censure. 2. Solemn declaration accompanied by a threat.—**de·nun·ci·a·tive** *adj.*—**de·nun·ci·a·tor** *n.*

de·nun·ci·a·to·ry (duh-*nun*-see-uh-tor-ee, -shuh-) *adj.* 1. Condemning; stigmatizing. 2. Menacing; containing a public threat.

de·ny (duh-*ny*) *v.* [de·nied; de·ny·ing] 1. To declare false; contradict. 2. To refuse to give; withhold. 3. To refuse to acknowledge or confess; disown.

de·o·dor·ant (dee-*oh*-der-unt) *n.* A substance used to counteract offensive odors.—**de·o·dor·ant** *adj.*

de·o·dor·ize (dee-*oh*-der-yze) *v.* [-dor·ized; -iz·ing] To free of odor; destroy an odor.—**de·o·dor·i·za·tion** (dee-oh-der-uh-*zay*-shun) *n.*—**de·o·dor·iz·er** *n.*

de·ox·i·dize (dee-*ok*-suh-dyze) *v.* [-dized; -diz·ing] To deprive of oxygen; reduce an oxide compound to a simple substance.—**de·ox·i·di·za·tion** *n.*—**de·ox·i·diz·er** *n.*

de·part (deh-*pahrt*) *v.* 1. To leave; go away. 2. To die. 3. To deviate; vary.

de·part·ed *adj.* 1. Gone from; left. 2. Dead. —*n. sing. & pl.* The dead; deceased.

de·part·ment *n.* 1. A separate branch or sphere of operations; distinct province or field. 2. A governmental division of France. —**de·part·men·tal** (dee-pahrt-*men*-t'l) *adj.*

department store. A store where an extensive range of consumer goods is sold.

de·par·ture *n.* 1. A leaving or going forth. 2. Death. 3. Time of leaving. 4. Abandonment; deviation.

de·pend (duh-*pend*) *v.* 1. To rely on; trust in; have full confidence in. 2. To be contingent upon; be caused by. 3. To be undetermined; be pending or in suspense. 4. To hang down.

de·pend·a·ble (duh-*pen*-duh-b'l) *adj.* Trustworthy; responsible.—**de·pend·a·bil·i·ty** (duh-pen-duh-*bil*-uh-tee), **de·pend·a·ble·ness** *n.*

de·pend·ence (duh-*pen*-denss) *n.* 1. Necessity of accepting support from another; inability to exist or flourish alone. 2. Mutual connection; interrelation. 3. Reliance; trust. 4. Lack of sovereignty; subordination.

de·pend·en·cy (duh-*pen*-den-see) *n.* [*pl.* -cies] A territory controlled by another state.

de·pend·ent (duh-*pen*-dent) *n.* One who relies on another for support.—**de·pend·ent** *adj.*

de·pict (deh-*pikt*) *v.* 1. To paint; portray. 2. To describe in words.—**de·pic·tion** *n.*

dep·i·late (*dep*-ih-layt) *v.* [-lat·ed; -lat·ing] To remove the hair from.—**dep·i·la·tion** (dep-ih-*lay*-shun) *n.*—**dep·i·la·tor** *n.*

de·pil·a·to·ry (duh-*pil*-uh-tor-ee) *n.* A preparation for removing hair.—**de·pil·a·to·ry** *adj.*

de·plete (duh-*pleet*) *v.* [-plet·ed; -plet·ing] 1. To empty; exhaust; drain. 2. *Medicine.* To let blood; purge.—**de·ple·tion** *n.*

de·plor·a·ble (deh-*plor*-uh-b'l) *adj.* Lamentable; pitiable; wretched; miserable.—**de·plor·a·ble·ness** *n.*—**de·plor·a·bly** *adv.*

de·plore (deh-*plor*) *v.* [de·plored; de·plor·ing] To lament; mourn; bewail.

de·ploy (deh-*ploy*) *v.* 1. To extend front ranks, in a formation of troops. 2. To arrange for battle.—**de·ploy·ment** *n.*

de·pone (deh-*pohn*) *v.* [de·poned; de·pon·ing] To swear to; bear witness under oath.

de·po·nent *adj. Grammar.* In passive form but having active meaning, as a group of Greek and Latin verbs.—*n.* 1. A witness. 2. A deponent verb.

de·pop·u·late (dee-*pop*-yoo-layt) *v.* [-lat·ed; -lat·ing] To strip of inhabitants.—**de·pop·u·la·tion** (dee-pop-yoo-*lay*-shun) *n.*—**de·pop·u·la·tor** *n.*

de·port (deh-*port*) *v.* 1. To banish from a country. 2. To conduct oneself.

de·por·ta·tion (dee-por-*tay*-shun) *n.* Legal banishment of an alien; exile.

de·port·ment *n.* Behavior; conduct; demeanor.

de·pose (deh-*pohz*) *v.* [de·posed; de·pos·ing] 1. To dethrone; put out of office. 2. *Law.* To give testimony.—**de·pos·a·ble** *adj.*

de·pos·it (deh-*poz*-it) *v.* 1. To place; put. 2. To commit to safekeeping, as of a bank;

entrust.—*n.* 1. Entrusting of property to safekeeping. 2. Money placed in a bank. 3. A natural mineral formation.

de·pos·i·ta·ry *n.* [*pl.* -ries] 1. One to whom property is committed. 2. A place for storing property; depository.

dep·o·si·tion (dep-uh-*zish*-'n) *n.* 1. Depriving of position or high station; dethronement. 2. *Law.* Attested written testimony of a witness; an affidavit. 3. A deposit.

de·pos·i·tor (deh-*poz*-ih-ter) *n.* One who places money in a bank account.

de·pos·i·to·ry *n.* A place where goods are lodged for safekeeping; warehouse.

de·pot (*dee*-poh) *n.* 1. A railway station. 2. A warehouse; storehouse. 3. *Military.* A magazine where ammunition and stores are kept.

de·prave (deh-*prayv*) *v.* [de·praved; de·prav·ing] To corrupt.—**dep·ra·va·tion** (dep-ruh-*vay*-shun) *n.*—**de·prav·er** *n.*

de·praved *adj.* Corrupt; perverted; evil-minded.

de·prav·i·ty (deh-*prav*-uh-tee) *n.* [*pl.* -ties] Vice; perversion; moral corruption.

dep·re·cate (*dep*-ruh-kayt) *v.* [-cat·ed; -cat·ing] 1. To criticize; belittle. 2. To try to avoid; evade.—**dep·re·cat·ing** *adj.*—**dep·re·ca·tion** *n.*

dep·re·ca·to·ry (*dep*-ruh-kuh-tor-ee) *adj.* Self-effacing; apologetic; excusing.

de·pre·ci·ate (deh-*pree*-shee-ayt) *v.* [-at·ed; -at·ing] 1. To fall in value. 2. To disparage; represent as of little value.—**de·pre·ci·a·ble** *adj.*

de·pre·ci·a·tion *n.* 1. Decline in value; reduction of worth. 2. Disparagement.—**de·pre·ci·a·tive** (duh-*pree*-shee-ay-tive) *adj.* Undervaluing.—**de·pre·ci·a·tive·ly** *adv.*

dep·re·date (*dep*-ruh-dayt) *v.* [-dat·ed; -da·ting] To plunder; rob; lay waste.—**dep·re·da·tor** *n.*—**dep·re·da·tion** (dep-ruh-*day*-sh'n) *n.*

de·press (deh-*press*) *v.* 1. To sadden; dispirit. 2. To degrade; lower in value. 3. To push down. 'Depress the tongue.'— -press·ing *adj.*

de·pressed *adj.* 1. Sad; dispirited; melancholy. 2. Flat; sinking.

de·pres·sion (deh-*presh*-un) *n.* 1. Dejection; melancholy; low spirits. 2. Reduction; deceleration; lowering of rate. 3. A period of economic poverty. 4. *Medicine.* A drop in physical resistance and energy. 5. A sub-horizon angle of measurement. 6. A hollow. —**de·pres·sive** *adj.*—**de·pres·sive·ly** *adv.*

de·pres·sor (deh-*pres*-er) *n.* 1. A depressing factor. 2. A muscle which operates to pull down. 3. *Physiology.* A nerve which decelerates an organ's function. 4. *Medicine.* An instrument for keeping aside a bodily part during examination. 'Tongue depressor.'

dep·ri·va·tion (dep-rih-*vay*-sh'n) *n.* 1. The act of taking away. 2. Loss; want; need.

de·prive (deh-*pryve*) *v.* [de·prived; de·priv·ing] To take away from; bereave; dispossess.—**de·priv·a·ble** *adj.*—**de·priv·al** *n.*

depth *n.* 1. Lowness; penetration below normal level. 2. A deep place; abyss. 3. a. Measurement of distance downward. b. Distance

D

from front to back. 4. Midst; center. 5. Profundity; significance. 6. Lowness of pitch, tone, etc. 7. [*pl.*] The sea; ocean.

depth bomb. Also **depth charge.** An anti-submarine charge set to explode at a predetermined depth.

dep·u·ta·tion (dep-yoo-*tay*-sh'n) *n.* 1. Authority commissioned to transact business for another. 2. Appointment of a representative.

de·pute (deh-*pyoot*) *v.* [-put·ed; -put·ing] 1. To assign. 2. To appoint as a substitute.

dep·u·tize (*dep*-yoo-tyze) *v.* To empower to act for another. 'A deputy sheriff.'

dep·u·ty (*dep*-yoo-tee) *n.* [*pl.* -ties] Substitute; representative; agent.—**dep·u·ty** *adj.*

de·range (deh-*raynj*) *v.* [-ranged; -rang·ing] 1. To disturb action or function. 2. To disorder; confuse. 3. To make insane.—**deranged** *adj.* Insane.

de·range·ment (deh-*raynj*-m'nt) *n.* Disorder, esp. of the reason; disturbance; confusion.

der·by (*der*-bee) *n.* 1. A stiff, domecrowned hat. 2. A horse race with a rich prize.

Der·by·shire (*dahr*-bee-shir) A county of central England.

der·e·lict (*dehr*-uh-likt) *n.* 1. An abandoned, drifting ship. 2. One who has sunk to the lowest level of society. 3. Any abandoned thing.—*adj.* 1. Failing to perform a duty; in arrears. 2. Forsaken; cast off.— -lic·tion *n.*

de·ride (dch-*ryde*) *v.* [de-rid·ed; de-rid·ing] To laugh at; ridicule; jeer; insult.—**de·rid·er** *n.* A scoffer.—**de·rid·ing·ly** *adv.*

de·ri·sion (deh-*rizh*-un) *n.* Scorn; mockery.

de·ri·sive (deh-*ry*-siv) *adj.* Mocking; ridiculing. —**de·ri·sive·ly** *adv.*—**de·ri·sive·ness** *n.*

de·ri·va·tion (dehr-uh-*vay*-sh'n) *n.* 1. Tracing a word to its root. 2. An origin; source; beginning. 3. A drawing or receiving from a source.

de·riv·a·tive (deh-*riv*-uh-tiv) *n.* 1. That which is deduced, obtained, or extracted from something else. 2. A word which stems from a similar, older form. 3. *Chemistry.* A substance which is obtained from a similar substance.—*adj.* Secondary; having an origin.

de·rive (deh-*ryve*) *v.* [de-rived; de-riv·ing] 1. To draw from; deduce. 2. To stem from; branch from. 3. To trace to an origin or root. 4. To extract or obtain a substance from a related, more complex substance.

der·ma (*der*-muh) *n.* The under layer of skin containing blood vessels and nerves.—**der·mal, der·mic** *adj.*

der·ma·tol·o·gy (der-muh-*tol*-uh-jee) *n.* Branch of medicine specializing in skin diseases. —**der·ma·to·log·i·cal** (der-muh-tuh-*loj*-ih-k'l) *adj.*—**der·ma·tol·o·gist** *n.*

der·mis *n.* The skin, esp. that below the epidermis.—**der·mic** *adj.*

der·o·gate (*dehr*-uh-gayt) *v.* [-gated; -gat·ing] To decrease in value, rank, etc.; detract from; deteriorate.—**der·o·ga·tion** (der-uh-*gay*-shun) *n.*—**de·rog·a·tive** (deh-*rog*-uh-tiv) *adj.*

de·rog·a·to·ry (deh-*rog*-uh-tor-ee) *adj.* Belittling; disparaging; disdaining.—**de·rog·a·to·ri·ly** *adv.*—**de·rog·a·to·ri·ness** *n.*

der·rick (*dehr*-ik) *n.* 1. An arrangement of booms, tackle, etc., for hoisting ponderous weights. 2. An upward-tapering steel framework supporting drilling tools over oil and mineral wells.

DERRICK

der·ring-do *n.* A bold exploit or deed.

der·rin·ger (*dehr*-in-jer) *n.* A short, large-calibered revolver for firing at short range.

der·vish (*der*-vish) *n.* One of an order of Mohammedan monks noted for ecstatic religious dances.

des·cant (*des*-kant) *n.* 1. A song or melody. 2. Art of composing music for several voices or parts. 3. A discussion or discourse on a single subject.—*v.* (des-*kant*) 1. To sing; play. 2. To discourse in lengthy detail.

de·scend (deh-*send*) *v.* 1. To move, come, or go downward; fall; flow down. 2. To invade or assault suddenly. 3. To stem from; be derived. 4. To lower oneself socially.

de·scend·ant (duh-*send*-unt) *n.* Offspring in a direct family line.—**de·scend·ant** *adj.*

de·scend·ent *adj.* 1. Proceeding from an origin or ancestor. 2. Advancing from a higher to a lower level.

de·scend·i·ble *adj.* Also **de·scend·a·ble.** 1. *Law.* Able to be handed down from generation to generation. 2. Admitting of being brought to a lower state or level.

de·scent (deh-*sent*) *n.* 1. Ancestry; lineage; family line. 2. A lowering or descending. 3. A hill, stairway, or any sloping formation. 4. The passing on of a heritage.

de·scribe (dih-*skrybe*) *v.* [-scribed; -scrib·ing] 1. To represent something orally or by writing; relate; explain; depict. 2. To outline; trace a figure.—**de·scrib·a·ble** *adj.*— -scrib·er *n.*

de·scrip·tion (dih-*skrip*-sh'n) *n.* 1. Account; statement. 2. Sketch; depiction; representation. 3. Kind; sort; variety. 4. A list of physical characteristics, as of a criminal. 5. An outlining; marking; delimitation.

de·scrip·tive *adj.* 1. Representing or depicting by words, signs, figures, etc.—**de·scrip·tive·ly** *adv.*—**de·scrip·tive·ness** *n.*

de·scry (dih-*skry*) *v.* [de-scried; de-scry·ing] 1. To detect; behold from a distance; espy. 2. To learn or determine by examination.

des·e·crate (*des*-uh-krayt) *v.* [-crat·ed; -crat·ing] To perform a profane sacrilegious act. —**des·e·crat·er, -crat·or** *n.*—**des·e·cra·tion** *n.*

de·sen·si·tize (dee-*sen*-sih-tyze) *v.* [-tized; -tiz·ing] 1. To anaesthetize; numb. 2. To render unsusceptible to; dispel an allergy.—**de·sen·si·ti·za·tion** (dee-sen-sih-tih-*zay*-shun) *n.*— -tiz·er *n.*

de·sert (duh-*zert*) *n.* A due reward or penalty; that which is deserved; worth.

des·ert (*deh*-zert) *n.* A vast, dry, often sandy expanse devoid of vegetation; desolate waste. —*adj.* Uninhabited; uncultivated; waste.

de·sert (duh-*zert*) *v.* 1. *Military.* To leave or quit unlawfully. 2. To forsake; relinquish. 3. To be lacking when most needed.—**de·sert·er** *n.*

de·ser·tion (duh-*zer*-shun) *n.* 1. Any dereliction of duty. 2. An illegal withdrawing from, or fleeing the authority of, an armed force. 3. *Law.* Abandonment of one's dependents.

de·serve (duh-*zerv*) *v.* [-served; -serv·ing] To merit; be entitled to.—**de·serv·ed** *adj.*—**de·serv·ed·ly** *adv.* Justly.— **-ed·ness** *n.*—**de·serv·er** *n.*

de·serv·ing *adj.* Having merit; worthy of recognition.—**de·serv·ing·ly** *adv.*—**de·serv·ing·ness** *n.*

des·ha·bille. *Variant spelling of* **dishabille.**

des·ic·cant, des·ic·ca·tive (*des*-uh-kay-tiv) *n.* A medical application for drying up secretions.

des·ic·cate (*des*-uh-kayt) *v.* [-cat·ed; -cat·ing] 1. To dry out; deprive of moisture. 2. To preserve food by dehydration.— **-ca·tion** *n.*

de·sid·er·a·tum (deh-sid-er-*ay*-tum) *n.* [*pl.* -a·ta] Anything agreed to be needed.

de·sign (deh-*zyne*) *v.* 1. To outline; invent; draw up; devise. 2. To project; purpose; plan; intend. 3. To inscribe or work in a decorative pattern.—*n.* 1. A representation of a thing by an outline; sketch; plan. 2. A scheme or plan; intention; aim. 3. Decorative figuring upon fabric and other materials. 4. A secret or ulterior plan.

des·ig·nate (*dez*-ig-nayt) *v.* [-nat·ed; -nat·ing] 1. To mark out or show; point out; name; characterize. 2. To appoint or assign.—*adj.* Appointed. 'Cardinal designate.'

des·ig·na·tion (dez-ig-*nay*-sh'n) *n.* 1. Appointment; assignment. 2. A title or sign which distinguishes. 3. A pointing out; indication. —**des·ig·na·tive** *adj.*—**des·ig·na·tor** *n.*

de·signed (deh-*zynde*) *adj.* Planned; intentional; purposeful.—**de·sign·ed·ly** *adv.*

de·sign·ing *n.* 1. A sketching, outlining, or planning; patterning. 2. A conspiring; scheming.—*adj.* 1. Purposive; rational. 2. Full of intrigue; scheming; crafty.—**de·sign·ing·ly** *adv.*

de·sir·a·ble (deh-*zyre*-uh-b'l) *adj.* 1. Eagerly wished or longed for. 2. Pleasant; agreeable; gratifying. 3. Having merit; advantageous. —**de·sir·a·bil·i·ty, -ble·ness** *n*—**de·sir·a·bly** *adv.*

de·sire (deh-*zyre*) *n.* 1. Wish; craving; longing; aspiration. 2. Passion; erotic drive; ardor. 3. The object of one's wishing.—*v.* [de·sired; de·sir·ing] To wish or long for; covet. 2. To request; ask.—**de·sir·er** *n.*

de·sir·ous *adj.* 1. Wishing for; wanting. 2. Avid; eager to obtain.—**de·sir·ous·ly** *adv.*

de·sist (deh-*zist*) *v.* To stop; leave off; discontinue; cease.—**de·sist·ance** *n.*

desk *n.* A table used by writers and readers, usually with drawers or storage space.

desk space. Space rented in another's office.

des·o·late (*des*-uh-lit) *adj.* 1. Uninhabited; lonely; forsaken. 2. Wasted; destroyed. 3. Depressed; forlorn; sad.—*v.* [des·o·lat·ed; -lat·ing] 1. To lay waste; strip of inhabitants; ruin. 2. To depress; make gloomy or miserable. 3. To forsake; abandon.—**des·o·late·ly** *adv.*—**des·o·late·ness** *n.*

des·o·la·tion (des-uh-*lay*-shun) *n.* 1. Destruction; devastation. 2. Sadness; gloominess; misery. 3. A lonely, barren region.

de·spair (dis-*payr*) *n.* 1. Hopelessness; despondency. 2. That which promotes a feeling of futility.—*v.* To give up all hope or expectation; lose confidence.—**de·spair·er** *n.*

de·spair·ing *adj.* Despondent; devoid of hope or confidence.—**de·spair·ing·ly** *adv.*

des·per·a·do (des-per-*ay*-doh, -*ah*-) *n.* [*pl.* -does, -dos] A reckless lawbreaker.

des·per·ate (*des*-per-it) *adj.* Reckless in despair; rash; frantic. 2. Beyond hope; past cure. —**des·per·ate·ly** *adv.*—**des·per·ate·ness** *n.*

des·per·a·tion (des-per-*ay*-shun) *n.* Disregard of danger; fury; boldness bred of despair.

des·pi·ca·ble (*des*-pik-uh-b'l) *adj.* Contemptible; vile; low; worthless; degraded.—**des·pi·ca·ble·ness** *n.*—**des·pi·ca·bly** *adv.*

de·spise (dis-*pyze*) *v.* [-spised; -spis·ing] To have a low opinion of; scorn; detest.—**de·spis·er** *n.*

de·spite (dis-*pyte*) *n.* Spite; hate; aversion.

des·pite *prep.* Notwithstanding; in spite of.

de·spoil (dis-*poil*) *v.* To deprive of belongings; rob; plunder; strip.—**de·spoil·er** *n.*—**de·spo·li·a·tion, de·spoil·ment** *n.*

de·spond (dis-*pond*) *v.* To be depressed or dejected; lose heart.—**de·spond·ing** *adj.*

de·spond·en·cy *n.* [*pl.* -cies]. Also **des·pon·dence.** A sinking or dejection of spirit through hopelessness; loss of heart.

de·spond·ent *adj.* Profoundly discouraged; depressed; melancholy.—**de·spond·ent·ly** *adv.*

des·pot (*des*-put) *n.* 1. One who rules or domineers with no regard to the rights of others; tyrant. 2. A ruler with unlimited authority.

des·pot·ic (dih-*spot*-ik) *adj.* Also **des·pot·i·cal.** Unlimited in power; arbitrary; tyrannical.

des·pot·ism (*des*-puh-tizm) *n.* 1. An arbitrary government; absolutism; autocracy. 2. Absolute power or control ruthlessly exercised.

des·qua·mate (*des*-kwuh-mayt) *v.* [des·qua·mat·ed; -mat·ing] *Medicine.* To peel; cast off epidermis.—**des·qua·ma·tion** *n.*

des·sert (deh-*zert*) *n.* The last course of a meal, usually a sweet dish.—**des·sert** *adj.*

des·sert·spoon *n.* A spoon approximately midway between a teaspoon and a tablespoon in capacity.—**des·sert·spoon·ful** *n.*

des·ti·na·tion (des-tin-*ay*-sh'n) *n.* 1. The place to which something is sent; end of a journey. 2. Purpose; end; ultimate design.

des·tine (*des*-tin) *v.* [-tined; -tin·ing] To appoint or ordain to a use, purpose, or state; decree.

des·ti·ny *n.* [*pl.* -nies] 1. A predetermined state or condition; ultimate fate; inescapable circumstances. 2. Fate; doom; luck.

D

des·ti·tute (*des*-tih-toot) *adj.* 1. Lacking the basic necessities of life; needy. 2. Devoid; wanting; without.—*n. sing. & pl.* The needy. —**des·ti·tu·tion** (des-tih-*too*-shun) *n.*

de·stroy (dih-*stroy*) *v.* 1. To ruin; smash; demolish; kill; annihilate. 2. To put an end to; wipe out; extirpate.—**de·stroy·a·ble** *adj.*

de·stroy·er *n.* 1. One who or that which demolishes or kills. 2. *Naval.* A fast, lightly armored ship smaller than a light cruiser.

de·struct·i·ble (dih-*struk*-tih-b'l) *adj.* Capable of being annihilated or ruined.—**de·struc·ti·bil·i·ty** (dih-struk-tih-*bil*-ih-tee) *n.*

de·struc·tion (dih-*struk*-sh'n) *n.* 1. Ruination; demolition; murder; extermination. 2. The cause or agency of downfall.

de·struc·tive (dih-*struk*-tiv) *adj.* 1. Causing ruin; pernicious; vicious. 2. Negative; carping; tearing down. 'Destructive criticism.'

destructive distillation. *Chemistry.* Process of breaking a substance down, usually by heat, and collecting and concentrating the vapors.

des·ue·tude (*des*-wih-tood) *n.* Obsoleteness; a passing out of date, use, or fashion.

des·ul·to·ry (*des*-ul-tor-ee) *adj.* 1. Unconnected; erratic; aimless. 2. Inconstant; unstable.—**des·ul·to·ri·ly** *adv.*—**des·ul·to·ri·ness** *n.*

de·tach (deh-*tach*) *v.* 1. To part from; separate; disunite; disengage. 2. To appoint to a mission or assignment.—**de·tach·a·bil·i·ty** (deh-tach-uh-*bil*-ih-tee) *n.*—**de·tach·a·ble** *adj.*

de·tached *adj.* 1. Objective; unemotional; impersonal. 2. Separated from; disunited.

de·tach·ment *n.* 1. Objectivity or aloofness based on lack of personal considerations. 2. A small body of troops dispatched on a special mission. 3. A separation.

de·tail (dih-*tayl*) *v.* 1. To give an exhaustive account of; particularize. 2. To assign to a special task.—*n.* (*dee*-tayl) 1. A minute account. 2. *Military.* A detachment. 3. A minor part of a picture, routine, or building. 4. An enlargement of a section of a drawing.

de·tain (deh-*tayn*) *v.* 1. To delay; hinder departure; stop. 2. To withhold; retain; hold in custody.—**de·tain·er** *n.*—**de·tain·ment** *n.*

de·tect (deh-*tekt*) *v.* 1. To discover; find out. 2. To perceive; note; apprehend. 3. *Radio.* To convert an alternating current wave into a direct current wave.—**de·tect·a·ble, de·tect·i·ble** *adj.*—**de·tec·tion** *n.*—**de·tec·tor** *n.*

de·tec·tive (deh-*tek*-tiv) *n.* A solver of crimes, esp. those of a baffling nature.—*adj.* Denoting a detective or a story about a detective.

de·ten·tion (deh-*ten*-sh'n) *n.* 1. State of being forcibly restrained; confinement. 2. A withholding of something from its owner.

de·ter (deh-*ter*) *v.* [-terred; -ter·ring] To discourage; restrain; prevent.—**de·ter·ment** *n.*

de·terge (deh-*terj*) *v.* [de·terged; de·terg·ing] To clean; render free of dirt or offensive matter.

de·ter·gent (deh-*ter*-junt) *n.* A cleansing, purifying medicine or substance.—**de·ter·gent** *adj.*

de·te·ri·o·rate (deh-*tihr*-ee-uh-rayt) *v.* [-rat·ed; -rat·ing] To grow worse; degenerate; lower in quality.—**de·te·ri·o·ra·tion** *n.*—**-ra·tive** *adj.*

de·ter·mi·nant (deh-*ter*-min-'nt) *n.* 1. That which exerts a deciding influence. 2. *Mathematics.* A system of symbols arranged in a square, their use being to study and solve linear equations.

de·ter·mi·nate (deh-*ter*-min-it) *adj.* 1. Definitely fixed; marked out. 2. Deciding; decisive; most influential. 3. Positive; resolute in purpose.—**de·ter·mi·nate·ly** *adv.*—**-nate·ness** *n.*

de·ter·mi·na·tion (deh-ter-min-*ay*-shun) *n.* 1. Inflexibility of purpose or intent; firmness; resolution. 2. Definite establishment of value, extent, or character; measurement. 3. A concluding or deciding.—**de·ter·min·a·tive** (deh-*ter*-min-ay-tiv) *adj.* Decisive; resolving.—**de·ter·min·a·tive·ly** *adv.*—**-tive·ness** *n.*

de·ter·mine (deh-*ter*-min) *v.* [-mined; -min·ing] 1. To settle ultimately; establish. 2. To confine; limit. 3. To decide; conclude; resolve on. 4. To cause to decide.—**de·ter·min·a·ble** *adj.*—**de·ter·min·er** *n.*

de·ter·mined (deh-*ter*-mind) *adj.* Having a firm purpose; resolute.—**de·ter·mined·ly** *adv.*—**de·ter·mined·ness** *n.*

de·ter·min·ism *n.* Theory that man's behavior is a result of circumstances beyond his control.—**de·ter·min·ist** *n. & adj.*—**-min·is·tic** *adj.*

de·ter·rent (deh-*ter*-unt) *adj.* Retarding action; inhibiting; causing inaction through fear of consequences.—**de·ter·rent** *n.*

de·test (deh-*test*) *v.* To despise; loathe; abhor. —**de·test·a·ble** *adj.*—**de·test·a·bil·i·ty, de·test·a·ble·ness** *n.*—**de·test·a·bly** *adv.*—**de·test·er** *n.*

de·tes·ta·tion (deh-tes-*tay*-shun) *n.* 1. Loathing; abhorrence; contemptuous hatred. 2. A despised thing or act; abomination.

de·throne (dee-*throhn*) *v.* [-throned; -thron·ing] To force from a throne; divest of supreme power.—**de·throne·ment** *n.*—**de·thron·er** *n.*

det·o·nate (*det*-uh-nayt) *v.* [-nat·ed; -nat·ing] To explode; set off.— **-na·tion** *n.*— **-na·tor** *n.*

de·tour (*dee*-toor; deh-*toor*) *n.* 1. Deviation from the shortest or most direct way. 2. Temporary route around an obstruction or a repair.—**de·tour** *v.*

de·tract (deh-*trakt*) *v.* 1. To take away; lessen, esp. a merit or reputation. 2. To defame; underrate.—**de·trac·tion** *n.*—**de·tract·or** *n.*

de·trac·tive *adj.* Tending to diminish, take away, or underrate.—**de·trac·tive·ly** *adv.*—**de·trac·to·ry** *adj.*

det·ri·ment (*det*-ruh-m'nt) *n.* 1. Loss; disadvantage; damage; harm; injury. 2. Cause of injury.—**det·ri·men·tal** *adj.*— **-tal·ly** *adv.*

de·tri·tus (deh-*try*-tus) *n.* Rock rubble; débris broken from a large formation.—**de·tri·tal** *adj.*

de trop (duh-*troh*) *French.* Superfluous.

de·trun·cate (dee-*trunk*-ayt) *v.* [-cat·ed; -cat·ing] To cut off; prune.—**de·trun·ca·tion** (duh-trunk-*ay*-shun) *n.*

deuce (*doos*) *n.* 1. A playing card with two pips; two spot. 2. A die having two spots or a throw in which two aces turn up. 3. *Tennis.* A tied score at forty-all. 4. Bad luck.

deu·ced *adj.* Unfortunate; like a plague; cursed. —*adv.* Very; exceedingly.—**deu·ced·ly** *adv.*

deu·te·ri·um (dyoo-*teer*-ee-um) *n.* An isotope of hydrogen twice the atomic weight of ordinary hydrogen.

Deu·ter·on·o·my (dyoo-ter-*on*-uh-mee). The fifth book of the Old Testament.

de·val·u·ate (dee-*val*-yoo-ayt) *v.* [-at·ed; -at·ing] To reduce in value; debase.—**de·val·u·a·tion** (dee-val-yoo-*ay*-shun) *n.*

dev·as·tate (*dev*-uh-stayt) *v.* [-tat·ed; -tat·ing] To ravage; plunder; desolate; wreck completely.—**dev·as·tat·ing·ly** *adv.*—**dev·as·ta·tor** *n.*

dev·as·ta·tion (dev-uh-*stay*-sh'n) *n.* 1. Destruction; ruin; pillage. 2. Laying waste.

de·vel·op (deh-*vel*-up) *v.* 1. To grow; evolve; advance; expand. 2. *Photography.* To render an image visible. 3. To show step by step; disclose gradually or in detail.— -op·a·ble *adj.*

de·vel·op·er *n. Photography.* A chemical which reacts with the exposed area of a film to bring out the image.

de·vel·op·ment *n.* 1. A gradual growth through progressive changes; an unfolding; evolution. 2. Preparation of land for use, esp. residential use; the land prepared. 3. Occurrence. 'Late developments.' 4. *Mathematics.* The transformation of any function into the form of a series; also the process by which a mathematical expression is changed into another equivalent value or meaning of more expanded form. 5. *Photography.* Process through which the image is made visible.—**de·vel·op·men·tal** *adj.*

de·vest (deh-*vest*) *v.* 1. *Law.* To alienate; take away from. 2. To divest; undress.

de·vi·ate (*dee*-vee-ayt) *v.* [-at·ed; -at·ing] 1. To digress from the usual or right course; turn aside from; wander; differ; err. 2. To change the course or position of.—**de·vi·a·tor** *n.*

de·vi·a·tion (dee-vee-*ay*-sh'n) *n.* Digression from the normal course; turning aside.

de·vice (deh-*vysse*) *n.* 1. A contrivance; invention; instrument. 2. A scheme; project. 3. An emblem or crest of metaphorical meaning; motto.

dev·il (*dev*-'l) *n.* 1. A wicked or sadistic person. 2. A wretched person. 'Poor devil.' 3. A printer's errand boy. 4. A machine which prepares clothing fibers for carding. 5. [*cap.*] The evil spirit. Satan.—*v.* [dev·iled, dev·illed; dev·il·ing, dev·il·ling] 1. *Cookery.* To chop up and season highly. 2. To tease or annoy; be cruel to. 3. To subject cloth fibers to the devil machine.

dev·il·fish *n.* A large fish of unusual shape; the giant octopus; gigantic ray.

dev·il·ish *adj.* 1. Evil; wicked. 2. Mischievous; impish. 3. Exceeding; great; enormous. —*adv. Colloquial.* Very; excessively. 'Devilish awkward.'—**dev·il·ish·ly** *adv.*—**dev·il·ish·ness** *n.*

dev·il·try *n.* [*pl.* -tries] 1. Roguishness; malicious trickery. 2. A prank; mischievous sport.—**dev·il·ment** *n.*—**dev·il·ry** *n.* [*pl.* -ries].

de·vi·ous (*dee*-vee-us) *adj.* 1. Not in the usual course or way; roundabout; rambling. 2. Disingenuous; not frank or straightforward.—**de·vi·ous·ly** *adv.*—**de·vi·ous·ness** *n.*

de·vis·a·ble (deh-*vyze*-uh-b'l) *adj.* 1. Able to be invented or contrived. 2. Capable of being bequeathed or willed.

de·vise *v.* [-vised; -vis·ing] 1. To invent; contrive; plan; compose; concoct. 2. *Law.* To give by will; bequeath.—*n.* A will or testament; also a gift of property by will.—**de·vi·see** *n.* Receiver of a bequest.—**de·vis·er, de·vis·or** *n.*

de·vi·tal·ize (dee-*vyte*-uh-lyze) *v.* [-tal·ized; -tal·iz·ing] To deprive of life or vitality.—**de·vi·tal·i·za·tion** (dee-vy-tuh-luh-*zay*-shun) *n.*

de·void (deh-*voyd*) *adj.* Destitute of; not possessing; lacking completely.

de·volve (deh-*volv*) *v.* [-volved; -volv·ing] To pass from one person to another; transfer; hand over.—**de·vo·lu·tion** (dev-uh-*loo*-shun) *n.*

Dev·on (*dev*-un). 1. A county of southwestern England. 2. A small tough breed of cattle originated in Devon.—**De·von·i·an** (deh-*voh*-nee-un) *adj.* 1. Relating to Devonshire. 2. *Geology.* Relating to a period of the Paleozoic era between the Silurian and Mississippian.—**De·von·i·an** *n.*

de·vote (deh-*voht*) *v.* [-vot·ed; -vot·ing] To dedicate; consecrate; direct wholly.—**de·vot·ed** *adj.* 1. Dedicated; strongly attached. 2. Ardent; faithful.—**de·vot·ed·ly** *adv.*

dev·o·tee (dev-oh-*tee*) *n.* One passionately fond of or devoted to a pursuit, religion, sport, etc.

de·vo·tion (deh-*voh*-shun) *n.* 1. Affection manifested by constant attention; love. 2. Consecration; dedication. 3. Religious zeal or devoutness. 4. [*pl.*] Prayer; performance of religious duties.—**de·vo·tion·al** *adj.*— -al·ly *adv.*

de·vour (deh-*vowr*).*v.* 1. To eat ravenously. 2. To destroy or consume with violence. 3. To enjoy avidly.—**de·vour·ing·ly** *adv.*

de·vout (deh-*vowt*) *adj.* 1. Pious; religious. 2. Sincere; earnest.—**de·vout·ness** *n.*

dew (*dyoo*; *doo*) *n.* 1. Droplets of moisture which precipitate on bodies colder than the surrounding atmosphere. 2. Anything with the appearance of dew.—**dew** *v.*

dew-bent	dew-dipped	dewflower
dew bright	dew-drenched	dew-gemmed
dew-clad	dewdrop	dew-laden
dew damp	dew-fed	dew-sprinkled

dew·ber·ry *n.* Trailing blackberry vine; its fruit.

dew·claw *n.* 1. Rudimentary claw on the foot of a dog. 2. False hoof on a deer or other animal.

dew·lap *n.* 1. Fold of skin hanging from an animal's neck, esp. a dog's or cow's. 2. The skin of the human throat sagging with age.

dew point. The temperature at which water vapor precipitates as dew or rain.

dew·y *adj.* [-i·er; -i·est] Moist with, having the appearance of, or pertaining to, dew.—**dew·i·ness** *n.*

D

dex·ter·i·ty (deks-*tehr*-ih-tee) *n.* 1. Physical or manual adroitness; skill; ability. 2. Readiness of mind; cleverness.—**dex·ter·ous** *adj.*

dex·tral (dek-str'l) *adj.* Right, as opposed to left; on the right hand or side.—**dex·tral·i·ty** (dek-*stral*-ih-tee) *n.*—**dex·tral·ly** *adv.*

dex·trin (dek-strin) *n.* Also **dex·trine.** Carbohydrate obtain from transforming starch into sugar, used as mucilage, etc.

dex·trose (dek-strohs). *n.* Glucose; grape sugar.

dhow (dow) *n.* A small Arabian sailing vessel with projecting bow and high poop.

di- (dy) *prefix.* Twofold; double; two times.

di·a·be·tes (dy-uh-*bee*-tiss; -teez) *n.* Derangement of metabolism marked by over-secretion of urine and great thirst, treated by insulin.

DHOW

di·a·bol·ic (dy-uh-*bol*-ik) *adj.* Devilish; infernal; fiendishly wicked.—**di·a·bol·i·cal·ly** *adv.*

di·ac·o·nate (dy-*ak*-uh-nit) *n.* 1. A deaconship; authority of a deacon. 2. Deacons collectively or in a group.—**di·ac·o·nal** *adj.*

di·a·crit·ic (dy-uh-*krit*-ik) *n.* Also **diacritical mark.** A sign used to indicate pronunciation of letters in some dictionaries.

di·a·crit·i·cal *adj.* Indicating pronunciation; distinguishing.—**di·a·crit·i·cal·ly** *adv.*

di·a·dem (*dy*-uh-dem) *n.* A rich band worn on the head; crown.—*v.* To crown.

di·aer·e·sis *n.* Variant of **di·er·e·sis.**

di·ag·nose (dy-ug-*nohs*) *v.* [-nosed; -nos·ing] To analyze; assign cause to; identify.

di·ag·no·sis (dy-ug-*noh*-sis) *n.* The establishing of a cause from symptoms or effects.—**di·ag·nos·tics** (dy-ug-*noss*-tiks) *n. sing.* Science of ascertaining diseases on the basis of symptoms.—**di·ag·nos·ti·cian** *n.*—**di·ag·nos·tic** *adj.*—**di·ag·nos·ti·cal·ly** *adv.*

di·ag·o·nal (dy-*ag*-uh-n'l) *n.* 1. Straight line drawn between two angles of a rectangle or other polygonal figure. 2. Slanting or oblique line, formation, pattern, direction, etc.—**di·ag·o·nal** *adj.*— -nal·ly *adv.*

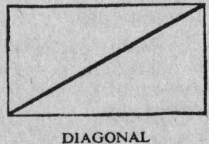
DIAGONAL

di·a·gram (*dy*-uh-gram) *n.* 1. Illustrative figure, sketch, or drawing making understanding easier. 2. *Geometry.* Figure or representation.—*v.* [-gramed, -grammed; di·a·gram·ing, di·a·gram·ming]—**di·a·gram·mat·ic, -mat·i·cal** *adj.*

di·al (*dy*-ul) *n.* 1. A circle graduated in units, as on the face of a watch. 2. Any instrument or gauge in which a pointer or indicator revolves. 3. A numbered circular device on a telephone for making calls automatically. 4. A compass used by miners, surveyors, etc.—*v.* [-aled, -alled; -al·ing, -al·ling].

di·a·lect (*dy*-uh-lekt) *n.* 1. Vernacular; idiom or form of a language peculiar to a region or population segment. 2. Terminology or cant of a particular profession or trade.—**di·a·lect, di·a·lec·tal** *adj.*—**di·a·lec·tal·ly** *adv.*

di·a·lec·tic (dy-uh-*lek*-tik) *n.* 1. A logical method of developing thought; logic; reasoning. 2. Also **di·a·lec·tics.** Art of logical discussion.—**di·a·lec·tic, di·a·lec·ti·cal** *adj.* Pertaining to discussion or logical development.—**di·a·lec·ti·cal·ly** *adv.*—**di·a·lec·ti·cian** (dy-uh-lek-*tish*-un) *n.*

dialectical materialism. The science of logic developed by Karl Marx on a solely materialistic basis.

di·al·ing, di·al·ling (*dy*-ul-ing) *n.* 1. Constructing or working a dial. 2. Measurement of time on a dial. 3. *Mining.* Compass surveying. 4. Getting a telephone number by dial system; locating a radio station's frequency on a dial.

di·a·log (*dy*-uh-log) *n.* Also **di·a·logue.** 1. Conversation in literary work. 2. Discourse; colloquy.—**di·a·log·er** *n.*—**di·a·lo·gist** *n.*

di·al·y·sis (dy-*al*-ih-sis) *n.* [*pl.* -ses] *Chemistry.* Process of separating the crystalloid elements of a body from the colloid.—**di·a·lyt·ic** (dy-uh-*lit*-ik) *adj.*—**di·a·lyt·i·cal·ly** *adv.*—**di·a·lyze** *v.*

di·am·e·ter (dy-*am*-uh-ter) *n.* 1. A straight line passing through the center of a circular figure, dividing it into two equal parts. 2. The length of a straight line passing through the center of any object from one side to the other; width; thickness.—**di·am·e·tral** (dy-*am*-uh-tr'l) *adj.*

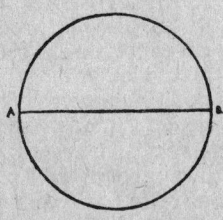
DIAMETER

di·a·met·ric·al (dy-uh-*met*-rik-ul) *adj.* 1. Completely opposite; at the other extreme. 2. Pertaining to a diameter.—**di·a·met·ri·cal·ly** *adv.*

di·a·mond (*dy*-mund) *n.* 1. Hardest known mineral, formed of crystalline carbon, transparent and colorless, valued as a precious stone. 2. A plane figure formed of two isosceles triangles joined base to base; lozenge. 3. A glasscutting tool. 4. *Baseball.* Infield. 5. Playing card marked with red diamonds. 6. *Printing.* A small type (4½ points).—*v.* To ornament with diamonds.

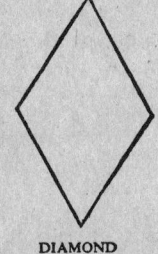
DIAMOND

diamondback   diamond-paved   diamond-shaped
diamond-headed   diamond-pointed   diamond-tipped

diamond anniversary. 1. A 60th anniversary. 2. A 75th anniversary.

diamondback terrapin. A turtle valued as table delicacy found along the Atlantic coast.

Di·an·a (dy-*an*-uh) *n.* Latin name of the virgin goddess of the hunt and moon.

di·a·pa·son (dy-uh-*pay*-z'n) *n. Music.* 1. The

perfect consonance of tones an octave apart. 2. Organ stop which produces tones in unison or octaves with notes being played. 3. Standard of pitch, as a tuning fork. 4. An octave.

di·a·per (*dy*-uh-per) *n*. A soft fabric covering for an infant's buttocks.—**di·a·per** *v*.

di·aph·a·nous (dy-*af*-uh-nus) *adj*. Filmy; sheer. —**di·aph·a·nous·ly** *adv*.—**di·aph·a·nous·ness** *n*.

di·a·pho·re·sis (dy-uh-fuh-*ree*-sis) *n*. *Medicine*. Abnormal degree of perspiration, artificially stimulated.—**di·a·pho·ret·ic** (dy-uh-for-*et*-ik) *n*. A stimulus for perspiration.— -**ret·ic** *adj*.

di·a·phragm (*dy*-uh-fram) *n*. 1. A muscle separating the chest from the abdomen. 2. A membrane partition or film. 3. *Optics*. A ring used in optical instruments to cut off parts of a beam of light as at the focus of a telescope. 4. *Medicine*. A woman's contraceptive; circular rubber device covering mouth of uterus. —**di·a·phrag·mat·ic** (dy-uh-frag-*mat*-ik) *adj*.

di·a·rist (*dy*-er-ist) *n*. One who keeps a diary.

di·ar·rhe·a (dy-er-*ee*-uh) *n*. Also **di·ar·rhoe·a**. *Medicine*. Abnormally frequent discharge of feces.—**di·ar·rhe·al**, **di·ar·rhoe·al**, **di·ar·rhe·ic**, **di·ar·rhoe·ic** *adj*.

di·a·ry (*dy*-er-ee) *n*. [*pl*. -ries] 1. A written account of daily events and observations. 2. A blank book dated for the recording of daily occurrences.

di·a·stase (*dy*-uh-stayss) *n*. A solid, white substance able to convert starch to maltose.—**di·a·stas·ic**, **di·a·stat·ic** (dy-uh-*stat*-ik) *adj*.

di·as·to·le (dy-*ass*-tuh-lee) *n*. *Medicine*. Regular dilation of the heart.—**di·as·tol·ic** (dy-uh-*stol*-ik) *adj*.

di·as·tro·phism (dy-*ass*-truh-fizm) *n*. Deformation of the earth's crust.—**di·a·stroph·ic** (dy-uh-*strohf*-ik) *adj*.

di·a·ther·my (*dy*-uh-ther-mee) *n*. Treatment by high-frequency radio waves.

di·a·tom·ic (dy-uh-*tom*-ik) *adj*. *Chemistry*. Consisting of two atoms.

di·a·ton·ic (dy-uh-*ton*-ik) *adj*. Designating or derived from the seven-tone major and minor scales forming the basis of Western music.

di·a·tribe (*dy*-uh-trybe) *n*. Abuse; invective.

dib·ble (*dib*-'l) *n*. A pointed instrument used to make holes for planting seeds, bulbs, etc.—*v*. [dib·bled; dib·bling].

dice *n*. [*pl*. of die] 1. A game played by casting small numbered cubes. 2. The cubes used.—*v*. [diced; dic·ing]. 1. To cut into cubes. 2. To gamble away; lose at dice. 3. To pattern with cubes.—**dic·er** *n*.

DICE

di·chot·o·my (dy-*kot*-uh-mee) *n*. [*pl*. -mies] 1. A division; split. 2. *Botany*. Repeated equal forking of a branch.—**di·chot·o·mous**, **di·cho·tom·ic** (dy-kuh-*tom*-ik) *adj*.

di·chro·ma·tism (dy-*kroh*-muh-tizm) *n*. 1. Consistence of two colors. 2. *Medicine*. Seeing only two colors.—**di·chro·mat·ic** *adj*.

dick *n*. *Slang*. A detective.

dick·ens *n*. & *interj*. Bother; the deuce.

dick·er *v*. To bargain; haggle; barter.—*n*. 1. A number or quantity of ten, esp. ten hides or skins. 2. A small bargain.

dick·ey, **dick·y** *n*. [*pl*. -eys, -ies] 1. A yoke or sleeveless shirt front worn in place of a shirt, esp. with dress suit. 2. A donkey. 3. A small bird. 4. A seat at the rear of a carriage.

dic·ta. *Plural* of **dictum**.

Dic·ta·phone (*dik*-tuh-fohn) *n*. Trade-mark name for a dictation instrument which both records and reproduces for stenographic transcription.

dic·tate (*dik*-tayt) *v*. -[tat·ed; -tat·ing] 1. To order; prescribe; impose. 2. To give commands; rule authoritatively. 3. To utter what is to be written down by another.—*n*. A command; order.

dic·ta·tion (dik-*tay*-shun) *n*. Material uttered aloud to be transcribed.

dic·ta·tor (*dik*-tay-ter) *n*. A person invested with absolute authority and unlimited power over a country or state.—**dic·ta·tress** *n*.

dic·ta·to·ri·al (dik-tuh-*toh*-ree-ul) *adj*. Pertaining to a dictator; absolute; unlimited.—**dic·ta·to·ri·al·ly** *adv*.—**dic·ta·to·ri·al·ness** *n*.

dic·ta·tor·ship *n*. Office, term, or government of one given absolute authority.

dic·tion (*dik*-shun) *n*. Choice or selection of words; manner of expressing ideas in words; style of speaking; enunciation.

dic·tion·ar·y (*dik*-sh'n-eh-ree) *n*. [*pl*. -ies] A book containing the words of a language, or a special subject, in alphabetical order, giving definitions and pronunciations; wordbook.

Dic·to·graph (*dik*-tuh-graf) *n*. Trade-mark name of a telephone instrument used to record sounds or conversation without detection.

dic·tum (*dik*-tum) *n*. [*pl*. dic·ta] 1. An authoritative or current saying; dogmatic statement. 2. *Law*. Judicial opinion.

di·dac·tic (dy-*dak*-tik) *adj*. Also **di·dac·ti·cal**. Intended to instruct; adapted or inclined to teach.—*n*. [*pl*.] The art or science of teaching. —**di·dac·ti·cal·ly** *adv*.—**di·dac·ti·cism** *n*.

did·dle (*did*-'l) *v*. [-dled; -dling] 1. *Colloquial*. To cheat; fleece. 2. To fritter; waste time.

Di·do (*dy*-doh) *n*. Legendary queen of Carthage, who, in Vergil's *Aeneid*, entertains and falls in love with Aeneas, and later kills herself.

di·do *n*. [*pl*. di·dos, di·does] *Colloquial*. A trick.

die (*dy*) *v*. [died; dy·ing] 1. To perish; cease to live. 2. To lose strength; fade; become extinct. 3. To desire intensely; long for.

die *n*. 1. [*pl*. dice] A small cube used for gambling. 2. [*pl*. dies] Any of several tools for cutting, shaping, or stamping.—*v*. [died; die·ing] To stamp or shape with a die.—**the die is cast**. The decision is made.

die-cast	die maker	die sinking
die-cut	die making	die square

die-hard *n*. A fanatic; one who resists doggedly to, and often beyond, the end.—**die-hard** *adj*.

D

di·e·lec·tric (dy-uh-*lek*-trik) *n.* Any nonconducting medium or substance.—**di·e·lec·tric, di·e·lec·tri·cal** *adj.*—**di·e·lec·tri·cal·ly** *adv.*

di·er·e·sis (dy-*ehr*-uh-sis) *n.* [*pl.* -ses]. Also **di·aer·e·sis.** A mark ['] placed over the second of two succeeding vowels to indicate that it is pronounced in a separate syllable, as in coöperation.—**di·e·ret·ic, di·ae·ret·ic** *adj.*

Die·sel (*deez*-'l) *n.* 1. A principle utilized in heavy motors or engines whereby combustion is caused by heat evolved from compression of air on the piston's offstroke. 2. A motor or engine using this principle.—**Die·sel** *adj.*

die sinker. An engraver of dies for stamping or embossing.—**die-sunk** *adj.*

di·et *n.* A legislative or ecclesiastical assembly.

di·et (*dy*-it) *n.* 1. Course of food prescribed by a physician or regulated by physical requirements. 2. Normally consumed food and drink; usual fare.—*v.* To eat according to prescribed rules, esp. to attempt to lose weight by abstaining from certain foods.—**di·et·er** *n.*—**di·e·tet·ic, di·e·tet·i·cal** *adj.*—**di·e·tet·i·cal·ly** *adv.*

di·e·tar·y (*dy*-uh-tehr-ee) *n.* [*pl.* -ies] System or course of food allowance.—**di·e·tar·y** *adj.*

di·e·tet·ics (dy-uh-*tet*-iks) *n.* Science of nutrition and regulation of diet.

di·e·ti·cian, di·e·ti·tian (dy-uh-*tih*-sh'n) *n.* One who practices or teaches dietetics.

dif·fer (*dif*-er) *v.* 1. To disagree; dispute. 2. To be unlike or different; be distinct.

dif·fer·ence (*dif*-runss) *n.* 1. State or instance of being different; unlikeness; distinction. 2. Controversy; dispute; disagreement. 3. *Arithmetic.* The amount by which one quantity differs from another; quantity remaining after subtraction of a lesser sum.

dif·fer·ent (*dif*-runt) *adj.* 1. Distinct; not the same; dissimilar. 2. Unusual.— **-ent·ly** *adv.*

dif·fer·en·tial (dif-uh-*ren*-shul) *adj.* 1. Relating to or showing difference. 2. Having or causing different effects. 3. Pertaining to or involving differentials.—*n.* 1. *Mathematics.* A delicate difference between the changes of a variable. 2. A differential gear. 3. The difference involved in transportation rates between the same points over variant routes.

differential calculus. Branch of higher mathematics analyzing the rate of change of a variable.

differential gear. An arrangement of gears connecting two shafts and allowing one to revolve at a greater rate of speed than the other.

dif·fer·en·ti·ate (dif-er-*en*-shee-ayt) *v.* [-at·ed; -at·ing] 1. To distinguish by unlike quality; to produce or develop difference in. 2. To note difference in or between. 3. To acquire a separate character.—**dif·fer·en·ti·a·tion** *n.*

dif·fi·cult (*dif*-uh-kult) *adj.* 1. Hard to do; laborious; arduous. 2. Hard to understand; not accommodating.—**dif·fi·cult·ly** *adv.*

dif·fi·cul·ty (*dif*-uh-kul-tee) *n.* [*pl.* -ties] 1. Condition or quality of being difficult. 2. What is difficult to do or overcome; obstacle; objection. 3. Laborious effort; trouble.

dif·fi·dence (*dif*-uh-dunss) *n.* Shyness.—**dif·fi·dent** (*dif*-uh-d'nt) *adj.* Retiring; timid; lacking self-confidence.—**dif·fi·dent·ly** *adv.*

dif·frac·tion (dif-*frak*-shun) *n. Physics.* Deflection; the peculiar modifications undergone by light when it passes by the edge of an opaque body.—**dif·fract** *v.*—**dif·frac·tive** *adj.*

dif·fuse (dif-*yoos*) *adj.* 1. Dispersed; widely spread. 2. Wordy; verbose.—**dif·fuse·ly** *adv.*

dif·fuse (dif-*yooz*) *v.* [-fused; -fus·ing] 1. To spread widely; circulate. 2. *Physics.* To undergo, or cause to undergo, diffusion.—**dif·fus·er, dif·fu·sor** *n.*—**dif·fus·i·bil·i·ty** *n.*

dif·fu·sion (dif-*yoo*-zh'n) *n.* 1. Dispersion; spread; expansion. 2. *Physics.* The breaking up of light rays on a rough surface. 3. *Physics & Chemistry.* Process by which variant physical conditions in a medium are equalized spontaneously.

dig *v.* [dug, digged; dig·ging] 1. To turn up or work with a spade. 2. To excavate; unearth. 3. To obtain or form by removing earth. 4. To poke; stab.—*n. Colloquial.* A poke or stab, esp. verbal.—**dig in.** To entrench; prepare for a siege.

dig·a·my (*dig*-uh-mee) *n.* A legal second marriage.—**dig·a·mous** *adj.*

di·gest (duh-*jest*; dy-*jest*) *v.* 1. To arrange in suitable classes; summarize. 2. To prepare in the mind; absorb mentally. 3. To change (food) into a form which can be absorbed in the body. 4. To undergo digestion. 5. *Chemistry.* To dissolve.—*n.* (*dy*-jest) A compilation, as of laws, or information, brought under proper heads; abridgment.—**di·gest·er** *n.*

di·gest·i·ble (duh-*jes*-tuh-b'l) *adj.* Able to be digested.—**di·ges·ti·bil·i·ty** *n.*—**di·ges·ti·bly** *adv.*

di·ges·tion (duh-*jes*-chun) *n.* The process of decomposing food in the body and preparing it for circulation and absorption.

di·ges·tive (duh-*jes*-tiv) *adj.* Pertaining to or promoting digestion.—**di·ges·tive** *n.*

dig·ger (*dig*-er) *n.* 1. One who digs. 2. An implement for digging. 3. [*cap.*] A member of an American Indian tribe of low culture.

dig·ging (*dig*-ing) *n.* 1. Act of a digger. 2. [*pl.*] Site of digging. 3. [*pl.*] Material dug or unearthed. 4. [*pl.*] *Colloquial.* Residence.

dig·it (*dij*-it) *n.* 1. A finger or toe. 2. *Arithmetic.* Any figure under 10.—**dig·it·al** *adj.* & *n.*

dig·i·tal·is (dij-uh-*tayl*-iss, dij-uh-*tal*-iss) *n.* The dried leaf of the foxglove plant, used as a narcotic and heart stimulant.

dig·ni·fied (*dig*-nuh-fyde) *adj.* Stately in manner; having dignity; lofty.—**dig·ni·fied·ly** *adv.*

dig·ni·fy (*dig*-nuh-fy) *v.* [dig·ni·fied; dig·ni·fy·ing] To make dignified; honor; ennoble.

dig·ni·tar·y (*dig*-nuh-tehr-ee) *n.* [*pl.* -ies] One who holds an exalted rank or office. 'A dignitary of the church.'—**dig·ni·tar·y** *adj.*

dig·ni·ty (*dig*-nuh-tee) *n.* [*pl.* -ties] 1. Nobility of the mind and character; worth. 2. Stateliness of manner or carriage. 3. Degree of importance. 4. Office or position bestowing honor; high rank.

di·gress (duh-*gres*, dy-*gres*) v. To depart from the main subject of a discourse; turn aside. —**di·gres·sive** adj.—**di·gres·sive·ly** adv.

di·gres·sion (duh-*gresh*-un) n. Departure from a main course or subject.—**di·gres·sion·al** adj.

di·he·dral (dy-*hee*-drul) adj. 1. Having two sides, as a figure. 2. Having or formed by two plane faces, as a crystal.—**di·he·dral** n.

dike (*dyke*) n. Also **dyke**. 1. A mound of earth or stone defending lowlands from flooding by sea or river. 2. A channel for water. 3. *Geology*. A vein of igneous rock driven into fissures.—v. [diked; dik·ing] To secure or surround by a dike.—**dik·er** n.

di·lap·i·date (duh-*lap*-uh-dayt) v. [-dat·ed; -dat·ing] 1. To fall into partial ruin. 2. To bring into decay; allow to fall into disrepair.—**di·lap·i·da·tion** n.

di·lap·i·dat·ed adj. Partly ruined; neglected.

di·late (dy-*layt*) v. [-lat·ed; -lat·ing] To expand; distend; enlarge.—**di·lat·a·bil·i·ty** n.—**di·lat·a·ble** adj.—**di·lat·er, di·lat·or** n.

di·la·tion (dy-*lay*-shun) n. Also **dil·a·ta·tion**. Act of dilating; expansion; distention.

dil·a·to·ry (*dil*-uh-toh-ree) adj. Causing or tending to delay; slow; procrastinating.—**dil·a·to·ri·ly** adv.—**dil·a·to·ri·ness** n.

di·lem·ma (duh-*lem*-uh) n. A difficult choice; argument or situation requiring choice between two equally distasteful alternatives.

dil·et·tan·te (dil-uh-*tan*-tee) n. [pl. -tan·ti, -tan·tes] One who engages in artistic, political, or scientific pursuits in a casua' manner.—**dil·et·tan·te** adj.—**dil·et·tant·ism, di·let·tan·te·ism** n.

dil·i·gence (*dil*-uh-juns) n. Constant, steady effort to accomplish a task; application.

dil·i·gent (*dil*-uh-junt) adj. Industrious; careful; steadily attentive.—**dil·i·gent·ly** adv.

dill n. A spicy herb used in cooking.

dil·ly-dal·ly v. [-lied; -ly·ing] To delay; loiter.

di·lute (dih-*loot*, dy-) v. [-lut·ed; -lut·ing] 1. To thin; make more liquid by mixture. 2. To weaken; reduce the strength of.—adj. Weakened; thinned.—**di·lute·ness** n.—**di·lu·tion** n.

di·lu·vi·al, di·lu·vi·an adj. Pertaining to a flood, esp. the Deluge in Noah's time.

dim adj. [dim·mer; dim·mest] 1. Not clearly seen; obscured; faint; vague. 2. Dull; not bright. 3. Of weak vision or understanding.—v. [dimmed; dim·ming] 1. To render less distinct or visible; cloud; obscure. 2. To dull; weaken, as vision.—**dim·ly** adv.—**dim·ness** n.

dime n. A U.S. silver coin worth ten cents or the tenth part of a dollar.—**dime novel**. A cheap, sensational novel of low literary value.

di·men·sion (dih-*men*-shun) n. 1. Extension in a single line or direction as *length, height, breadth*. 2. [pl.] Measurements; size. 3. Consequence; extent; importance.— -sion·al adj.

dime store. Store selling inexpensive articles.

di·min·ish (dih-*min*-ish) v. 1. To lessen; reduce in size. 2. To degrade; impair; reduce in importance or quality. 3. To shrink.—**di·min·ish·a·ble** adj.—**di·min·ish·ing·ly** adv.

dim·in·u·en·do (dih-min-yoo-*en*-doh) adj. & adv. *Music*. Gradually decreasing in volume.—n. [pl. -dos] Gradual reduction in volume.

dim·i·nu·tion (dim-ih-*nyoo*-shun) n. Act of lessening or diminishing; reduction.

di·min·u·tive (dih-*min*-yoo-tiv) adj. Very small; tiny.—n. *Grammar*. A derivative word designating a small thing of its kind.—**dim·in·u·tive·ly** adv.—**di·min·u·tive·ness** n.

dim·i·ty (*dim*-uh-tee) n. [pl. -ties] A thin cotton fabric woven with raised stripes or figures.

dim·mer n. Device for dimming a light.

dim-out n. A moderate or incomplete blackout.

dim·ple n. A slight indentation or depression in a surface, esp. in flesh of the cheek or chin.—v. [dim·pled; dim·pling].—**dim·ply** adj.

dim·wit n. *Slang*. A fool; stupid person.

din n. An uproar; loud, continued noise.—v. [dinned; din·ning] 1. To stun with noise. 2. To repeat constantly. 'Din the lesson into him.'

dine v. [dined; din·ing] 1. To eat a meal, esp. dinner. 2. To furnish with a dinner.

din·er (*dy*-ner) n. 1. One who is eating dinner. 2. A railroad coach in which meals are served; restaurant resembling a railroad diner.

di·nette (dy-*net*) n. A small room or alcove where meals are eaten.

ding v. 1. *Colloquial*. To chatter noisily and at length. 2. To emit a sharp, bell-like sound.

ding·dong n. 1. Sound of bells or other similar strokes. 2. Tiresome repetition.—adj. *Colloquial*. Hotly contested; vigorously competed for.

din·gey, dingh·y, ding·y (*ding*-ee) n. [pl. ding·eys, dingh·ies, ding·ies] Small rowboat.

din·gle n. A narrow, secluded dale or valley.

din·go (*ding*-goh) n. A wolflike Australian dog.

ding·y (*din*-jee) adj. [-gi·er; -gi·est] Soiled; dull-colored; grimy.—**din·gi·ly** adv.—**din·gi·ness** n.

dink·ey (*dink*-ee) n. A locomotive below standard size.—adj. *Slang*. Small; tiny.

din·ner (*din*-er) n. The principal meal of the day; banquet; feast.

di·no·saur (*dy*-nuh-sawr) n. A class of gigantic, prehistoric reptiles.—**di·no·sau·ri·an** adj.

dint n. 1. Means; force. 'By dint of hard work.' 2. Mark made by a blow; dent.—**dint** v.

DINOSAUR

di·o·cese (*dy*-uh-sees) n. A bishop's district; bishopric.—**di·oc·e·san** (dy-*os*-eh-s'n) n. & adj.

di·oe·cious (dy-*ee*-shus) adj. *Botany*. Bearing flowers in which male and female reproductive organs never occur together in the same flower.

Di·og·e·nes (dy-*oj*-un-eez). Greek philosopher.

Di·o·ny·sus (dy-uh-*ny*-sus) n. *Greek Mythology*. The god of wine and revelry; Bacchus.—**Di·o·nys·i·ac, Di·o·ny·si·a·cal** adj.— -a·cal·ly adv.

D

di·o·ra·ma (dy-uh-*ram*-uh) *n.* A painting in which lighting and projection produce spectacular effects.—**di·o·ram·ic** *adj.*

di·ox·ide (dy-*ok*-syde) *n.* Also **di·ox·id.** An oxide having two oxygen atoms in its molecule.

dip *v.* [dipped; dip·ping] 1. To immerse for a short time in a fluid; plunge and withdraw. 2. To scoop or take out. 3. To settle or sink suddenly. 4. To lower and bring up again quickly. 5. To investigate in an unsystematic way; look cursorily. 6. To incline downward; slant; slope.—*n.* 1. Immersion in fluid; plunge; bath. 2. A sloping incline. 3. A candle. 4. *Slang.* A pickpocket. 5. A bath into which objects are plunged.

diph·the·ri·a (dif-*thihr*-ee-uh, dip-) *n.* Infectious inflammatory disease of the throat characterized by formation of a false membrane over the air passages.—**diph·the·ri·al, -the·rit·ic** *adj.*

diph·thong (*dif*-thawng; dip-) *n.* A union of two vowels pronounced as one sound.—**diph·thon·gal** *adj.*—**diph·thon·gal·ly** *adv.*

di·plo·ma (dih-*ploh*-muh) *n.* 1. A document or letter, usually sealed or signed by an authority, conferring a privilege, power, or honor. 2. A certificate granted by a school to its graduates.

di·plo·ma·cy (dih-*ploh*-muh-see) *n.* [*pl.* -cies] 1. Tact; skill in managing negotiations or affairs without friction. 2. Practice of international relations. 3. Skillful management to gain an advantage; tact.

dip·lo·mat (*dip*-luh-mat) *n.* 1. Person authorized to represent his government, esp. in international affairs. 2. A tactful person.

dip·lo·mat·ic, dip·lo·mat·i·cal·ly *adj.* 1. Relating to international diplomacy. 2. Tactful; skillful in the manner of a diplomat.—**dip·lo·mat·i·cal·ly** *adv.*—**di·plo·ma·tist** *n.*

dip·per *n.* 1. A long handled cup; ladle. 2. [*cap.*] The seven brightest stars (Big Dipper) of the constellation Ursa Major; also several stars (Little Dipper) in Ursa Minor.

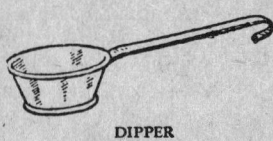

DIPPER

3. Any of several types of diving water birds.

dip·so·ma·ni·a (dip-suh-*may*-nee-uh) *n.* Uncontrollable craving for alcoholic drink.—**dip·so·ma·ni·ac** *n.*—**dip·so·ma·ni·a·cal** (dip-suh-muh-*ny*-ih-k'l) *adj.*

Dip·ter·a (*dip*-ter-uh) *n. Zoology.* An order of insects having only two wings, including the housefly and mosquito —**dip·ter·ous** *adj.*

dip·tych (*dip*-tik) *n.* 1. Picture painted on a hinged tablet. 2. Ancient writing tablet.

dire *adj.* [dir·er; dir·est] 1. Dreadful; disastrous; horrible. 2. Ill-omened. 3. Extreme.

di·rect (duh-*rekt*, dy-*rekt*) *adj.* 1. Straight; following the shortest or simplest course. 2. Straightforward; blunt; artless. 3. In lineal descent. 4. *Electricity.* Designating current flowing in one direction.—*v.* 1. To point out the proper direction. 2. To aim;

point. 3. To govern; control. 4. To order; command.—**di·rect** *adv.*

di·rec·tion (duh-*rek*-shun) *n.* 1. Management; control; guidance. 2. Path along which anything is aimed or pointed. 3. Instruction; command; order. 4. Course; line of motion. 'In a westerly direction.'—**di·rec·tion·al** *adj.*

direction finder. Radio equipped with directional loop antenna to obtain bearings for navigation.

di·rec·tive (duh-*rek*-tiv) *n.* An order; edict; command.—**di·rec·tive** *adj.*

di·rect·ly (duh-*rekt*-lee) *adv.* 1. In a straight unbroken manner. 2. Immediately; at once.

di·rec·tor (duh-*rek*-ter) *n.* 1. One who governs, manages, or guides. 2. An officer of a corporation.—**di·rec·tor·ship** *n.*

di·rec·to·rate (duh-*rek*-ter-it) *n.* 1. A body of directors. 2. The position of a director.

di·rec·to·ry (duh-*rek*-ter-ee) *n.* [*pl.* -ries] 1. A guide, esp. a book containing an alphabetical list of inhabitants of an area, members of a profession, etc. 2. A board of directors.

dire·ful (*dyre*-ful) *adj.* Calamitous; terrible; dreadful.—**dire·ful·ly** *adv.*—**dire·ful·ness** *n.*

dirge (derj) *n.* 1. Song or chant expressing sorrow or mourning. 2. Rites for the dead.

dir·i·gi·ble (dihr-*ij*-ih-b'l) *n.* A rigid, lighter-than-air craft.—*adj.* Able to be steered.

dirk *n.* A small dagger.—*v.* To stab.

dirn·dl (*dern*-d'l) *n.* A dress with tight-fitting waist and full skirt.—**dirn·dl** *adj.*

DIRIGIBLE

dirt *n.* 1. Earth; soil. 2. Any unclean or filthy substance, as mud, excrement, etc. 3. Sordidness; vile language. 4. *Music Slang.* Jazz played with a rough attack and often a growling tone; the blues.

dirt·y *adj.* [dirt·i·er; dirt·i·est] 1. Unclean; soiled. 2. Low; mean; despicable. 3. Off-color; obscene. 4. Squally; stormy. 5. Dull and muddy; not clear in tone,—*v.* [dirt·ied; dirt·y·ing].—**dirt·i·ly** *adv.*—**dirt·i·ness** *n.*

dirty-colored   dirty-handed   dirty-shirted
dirty-faced   dirty-minded   dirty-souled

dis·a·bil·i·ty (dis-uh-*bil*-uh-tee) *n.* [*pl.* -ties] 1. A lack of a bodily or mental power or faculty; incapacity. 2. Want of legal qualification or capacity.

dis·a·ble (dis-*ay*-b'l) *v.* [dis·a·bled; dis·a·bling] 1. To deprive of natural strength or faculties; incapacitate. 2. To disqualify legally.—**dis·a·bled** *adj.*—**dis·a·ble·ment** *n.*

dis·a·buse (dis-uh-*byooz*) *v.* [dis·a·bused; dis·a·bus·ing] To undeceive; inform of the truth.

dis·ad·van·tage (dis-ad-*van*-tij) *n.* 1. An unfavorable circumstance; drawback; handicap. 2. A loss; detriment.

dis·ad·van·ta·geous (dis-ad-van-*tay*-jus) *adj.* Unfavorable; inconvenient.— **-ta·geous·ly** *adv.*

dis·af·fect (dis-uh-*fekt*) v. To alienate; estrange.—**dis·af·fect·ed** *adj.*

dis·af·fec·tion (dis-uh-*fek*-shun) n. Alienation; dislike; unfriendliness; hostility.

dis·a·gree (dis-uh-*gree*) v. [-agreed; -a·gree·ing] 1. To hold a contrary opinion; dissent. 2. To be unsuitable or disturbing. 'Late meals disagree with him.'

dis·a·gree·a·ble (dis-uh-*gree*-uh-b'l) *adj.* Unpleasant; repugnant.—**dis·a·gree·a·bil·i·ty** (-*bil*-uh-tee), **dis·a·gree·a·ble·ness** n.—**a·bly** *adv.*

dis·a·gree·ment (dis-uh-*gree*-m'nt) n. 1. Discrepancy; difference; variance. 2. Dispute.

dis·al·low (dis-uh-*low*) v. To refuse permission; disapprove.—**dis·al·low·ance** n.

dis·ap·pear (dis-uh-*peer*) v. 1. To vanish; go from sight. 2. To exist no longer. 'Hoopskirts have disappeared.'—**dis·ap·pear·ance** n.

dis·ap·point (dis-uh-*poynt*) v. To defeat in an expectation; frustrate; thwart.

dis·ap·point·ment n. Failure of an expectation; miscarriage of a plan or design.

dis·ap·pro·ba·tion (dis-ap-ruh-*bay*-shun) n. Disapproval; censure.

dis·ap·prov·al (dis-uh-*proov*-'l) n. Condemnation; dislike; unfavorable judgment.

dis·ap·prove v. [-proved; -prov·ing] 1. To censure; judge unfavorably. 2. To reject; decline to pass upon.—**dis·ap·prov·ing** *adj.*

dis·arm (dis-*ahrm*) v. To deprive of weapons; reduce defenses to peacetime status.

dis·ar·ma·ment (dis-*ahrm*-uh-m'nt) n. Reduction of military forces to peacetime status.

dis·ar·range (dis-uh-*raynj*) v. [-ranged; -rang·ing] To unsettle; disorder.—**-range·ment** n.

dis·ar·ray (dis-uh-*ray*) n. 1. Disorder; confusion. 2. Undress.—v. 1. To disrobe. 2. To throw into confusion.

dis·as·sem·ble (dis-uh-*sem*-b'l) v. [-sembled; -semb·ling] To separate into component parts.

dis·as·so·ci·ate (dis-uh-*soh*-shee-ayt) v. To remove from connection with.

dis·as·ter (diz-*as*-ter) n. A sudden misfortune; calamity; adversity; catastrophe.

dis·as·trous *adj.* 1. Calamitous; causing serious misfortune. 2. Ill-omened.—**-trous·ly** *adv.*

dis·a·vow (dis-uh-*vow*) v. To renounce; disown.

dis·band v. 1. To break up; demobilize, as a regiment. 2. To disperse; scatter.

dis·bar v. [-barred; -bar·ring] To deprive an attorney of the right to practice law.—**dis·bar·ment** n.

dis·be·lief (dis-buh-*leef*) n. Refusal to credit or accept as truthful; lack of credence.

dis·be·lieve (dis-buh-*leev*) v. [-lieved; -liev·ing] To hold to be untrue or nonexistent; deny.

dis·bur·den (dis-*ber*-d'n) v. 1. To rid of oppressive weight; relieve of anything oppressive.

dis·burse (dis-*berss*) v. [-bursed; -burs·ing] To pay out; spend; lay out.—**dis·burs·a·ble** *adj.*

dis·burse·ment n. 1. A paying out, esp. of money. 2. What is paid out; expenditure.

disc. *Variant spelling* of **disk.**

dis·card (dis-*kahrd*) v. 1. *Card Playing.* To throw out of the hand; reject; thrust away. 2. To dismiss from service or employment; cast off.—(*dis*-kahrd) n. 1. That which is cast off as useless. 2. A throwing of unnecessary cards out of the hand; the cards so removed. 3. Rejection; repudiation.

dis·cern (dih-*zern*, dih-*sern*) v. 1. To distinguish; make out; detect. 2. To discover; perceive by intellect. 3. To show a distinction or differentiation.—**dis·cern·er** n.—**-cern·i·ble** *adj.*

dis·cern·ing *adj.* Capable of discriminating or judging; acute.—**dis·cern·ing·ly** *adv.*

dis·cern·ment n. Acuteness of judgment; clearsightedness; penetration.

dis·charge (dis-*chahrj*) v. [-charg·ed; -charg·ing] 1. To unload; relieve of a charge or burden. 2. To shoot; fire, as a gun. 3. To release; remit; let go; dismiss. 4. To pay; satisfy, as a debt or obligation. 5. To acquit; absolve. 6. To perform; execute. 7. To emit. 'Discharge pus.'—**dis·charge** n.—**dis·charge·a·ble** *adj.*—**dis·charg·er** n.

dis·ci·ple (dih-*sy*-p'l) n. A pupil; follower; adherent.—**dis·ci·ple·ship** n.—**the disciples.** The twelve companions of Christ; the apostles.

dis·ci·pli·na·ri·an (dis-ih-plin-*air*-ee-un) *adj.* Pertaining to discipline.—n. One who enforces discipline; martinet.

dis·ci·pli·nar·y (*dis*-ih-plin-air-ee) *adj.* Pertaining to or promoting proper conduct.

dis·ci·pline (*dis*-ih-plin) n. 1. Corrective training. 2. Correction; punishment. 3. Rules for regulating conduct. 4. Control or order maintained by enforcing obedience.—v. [-ci·plined; -plin·ing] To train; control; punish.—**dis·ci·plin·a·ble** *adj.*—**dis·ci·plin·er** n.

dis·claim (dis-*klaym*) v. To disavow; repudiate.

dis·claim·er n. Renunciation or denial.

dis·close (dis-*klohz*) v. [-closed; -clos·ing] To open to view; reveal; divulge.—**dis·clos·er** n.

dis·clo·sure (dis-*kloh*-zher) n. 1. The act of divulging. 2. Something revealed.

dis·coid (*dis*-koyd) *adj.* Having the form of a disk.—n. Any disk-shaped object.

dis·col·or (dis-*kuh*-ler) v. To alter the color of; stain; blemish.—**dis·col·or·a·tion** n.

dis·com·fit (dis-*kum*-fit) v. 1. To defeat; rout; frustrate. 2. To disconcert; upset; embarrass.—**dis·com·fi·ture** n. Embarrassment.

dis·com·fort (dis-*kum*-fert) n. Suffering; uneasiness.—v. To distress; make uncomfortable.

dis·com·mode (dis-kuh-*mohd*) v. [-mod·ed; -mod·ing] To trouble; inconvenience; disturb.

dis·com·pose (dis-kum-*pohz*) v. [-posed; -pos·ing] 1. To disturb; agitate; fluster. 2. To disarrange; unsettle.—**dis·com·po·sure** n.

dis·con·cert (dis-kun-*sert*) v. To embarrass; confuse; fluster.—**dis·con·cert·ing·ly** *adv.*—**dis·con·cer·tion** n.—**dis·con·cert·ed** *adj.*—Confused; discomfited; disturbed.—**dis·con·cert·ed·ly** *adv.*

dis·con·nect (dis-kuh-*nekt*) v. To separate; unfasten; disunite.—**dis·con·nec·tion** n.

dis·con·nect·ed *adj.* 1. Detached; separate.

D

2. Lacking in logic; disjointed.—**dis·con·nect·ed·ly** *adv.*—**dis·con·nect·ed·ness** *n.*

dis·con·so·late (dis-*kon*-sul-it) *adj.* Dejected; sorrowful; desolate; hopeless.—**dis·con·so·late·ly** *adv.*— **-late·ness** *n.*— **-la·tion** *n.*

dis·con·tent (dis-kun-*tent*) *n.* Dissatisfaction; unrest.—*v.* To dissatisfy.— **-tent·ment** *n.*

dis·con·tent·ed *adj.* Dissatisfied; displeased and uneasy; rebellious.—**dis·con·tent·ed·ly** *adv.* —**dis·con·tent·ed·ness** *n.*

dis·con·tin·u·ance (dis-kun-*tin*-yoo-'ns) *n.* 1. A cessation; interruption. 2. *Law.* Termination of an action.—**dis·con·tin·u·a·tion** *n.*

dis·con·tin·ue (dis-kun-*tin*-yoo) *v.* [-tin·ued; -tin·u·ing] To stop; interrupt.— **-con·tin·u·er** *n.*

dis·con·ti·nu·i·ty (dis-kon-tih-*noo*-ih-tee) *n.* Lack of connection or cohesion.

dis·con·tin·u·ous (dis-kun-*tin*-yoo-us) *adj.* Interrupted; broken off.—**dis·con·tin·u·ous·ly** *adv.*—**dis·con·tin·u·ous·ness** *n.*

dis·cord (*dis*-kawrd) *n.* 1. Disagreement; contention; strife. 2. *Music.* Lack of harmony; dissonance. 3. Any harsh sound.—*v.* (dis-*kawrd*) To disagree; clash.—**dis·cord·ance, dis·cord·an·cy** *n.*

dis·cord·ant (dis-*kawrd*-'nt) *adj.* 1. Incompatible; disagreeing; contradictory. 2. Dissonant; jarring.—**dis·cord·ant·ly** *adv.*

dis·count (*dis*-kownt) *v.* 1. To deduct (a percentage or sum) from an amount, price, etc. 2. To lend money, deducting the interest from the principal in advance. 3. To disregard; leave out of account. 4. To allow for exaggeration, inaccuracy, etc., in. 'Discount his stories.' 5. To reduce the value of by anticipating.—**dis·count** *n.*—**dis·count·a·ble** *adj.*

dis·coun·te·nance (dis-*kown*-tuh-n'ns) *v.* [-nanced; -nanc·ing] 1. To embarrass; abash. 2. To discourage; refuse to approve; oppose.

dis·cour·age (dis-*kur*-ij) *v.* [-aged; -ag·ing] 1. To dishearten; deprive of confidence. 2. To dissuade; attempt to prevent.—**dis·cour·ag·er** *n.*—**dis·cour·ag·ing** *adj.*— **-ag·ing·ly** *adv.*

dis·cour·age·ment (dis-*kur*-ij-m'nt) *n.* 1. The act or means of disheartening or deterring. 2. Depression; pessimism.

dis·course (*dis*-kors) *n.* 1. Talk; conversation. 2. A lecture; formal treatment of a subject. —*v.* (dis-*kors*) [-coursed; -cours·ing].

dis·cour·te·ous (dis-*ker*-tee-us) *adj.* Rude; impolite.—**dis·cour·te·ous·ly** *adv.*—**dis·cour·te·ous·ness** *n.*—**dis·cour·te·sy** *n.* [*pl.* -sies].

dis·cov·er (dis-*kuhv*-er) *v.* To ascertain; learn of for the first time; unearth.—**dis·cov·er·a·ble** *adj.* —**dis·cov·er·er** *n.*—**dis·cov·er·y** *n.* [*pl.* -ies].

dis·cred·it (dis-*kred*-it) *v.* 1. To disbelieve. 2. To destroy trust in; disgrace; bring into disfavor.—**dis·cred·it** *n.*

dis·cred·it·a·ble (dis-*kred*-it-uh-b'l) *adj.* Disreputable; disgraceful.—**dis·cred·it·a·bly** *adv.*

dis·creet (dis-*kreet*) *adj.* Prudent; showing good judgment; circumspect.—**dis·creet·ly** *adv.*

dis·crep·an·cy (dis-*krep*-'n-see) *n.* [*pl.* -cies] Disagreement; difference.

dis·crep·ant (dis-*krep*-'nt) *adj.* Inconsistent; disagreeing; differing.

dis·cre·tion (dis-*kreh*-shun) *n.* 1. Prudence; caution; good judgment. 2. Power of acting freely; uncontrolled choice or decision.—**dis·cre·tion·al** *adj.*—**dis·cre·tion·al·ly** *adv.*

dis·cre·tion·ar·y (dis-*kresh*-'n-ehr-ee) *adj.* Unrestrained except by will or discretion.

dis·crim·i·nate (dis-*krim*-uh-nayt) *v.* [-nat·ed; -nat·ing] 1. To distinguish; make or observe difference between. 2. To favor one person or group over another.—*adj.* (dis-*krim*-uh-nit) Having a difference marked.—**dis·crim·i·nate·ly** *adv.*—**dis·crim·i·nat·ing** *adj.*— **-nat·ing·ly** *adv.*

dis·crim·i·na·tion (dis-krim-uh-*nay*-shun) *n.* 1. Insight; acumen; judgment. 2. Act of discriminating. 3. Favoring of one group or individual over another.—**dis·crim·i·na·tive** *adj.* — **-na·tive·ly** *adv.*—**dis·crim·i·na·to·ry** *adj.*

dis·cur·sive (dis-*ker*-siv) *adj.* Rambling; digressing.—**dis·cur·sive·ly** *adv.*— **-sive·ness** *n.*

discus (*dis*-kus) *n.* [*pl.* -cus·es, dis·ci] A heavy disk thrown in tests of skill and strength.

dis·cuss (dis-*kuss*) *v.* To debate; argue; talk from all angles.

dis·cus·sion (dis-*kuh*-shun) *n.* Talk; debate; conversational consideration of a question.

dis·dain (dis-*dayn*) *v.* To scorn; look upon with contempt; spurn.—**dis·dain** *n.*

dis·dain·ful (dis-*dayn*-ful) *adj.* Contemptuous; scornful; overbearing.—**dis·dain·ful·ly** *adv.*

dis·ease (diz-*eez*) *n.* Sickness; malady; pathological condition of the body or one of its parts.—*v.* [dis·eased; -eas·ing]—**dis·eased** *adj.*

dis·em·bark (dis-im-*bahrk*) *v.* To leave or remove from ship.—**dis·em·bar·ka·tion** *n.*

dis·em·bar·rass (dis-im-*bair*-us) *v.* To free from embarrassment or perplexity; extricate.

dis·em·bod·y (dis-im-*bod*-ee) *v.* [-bod·ied; -bod·y·ing] To divest of bodily form.— **-bod·i·ment** *n.*

dis·em·bow·el (dis-im-*bow*-ul) *v.* [-eled, -elled; -el·ing, -el·ling] To take out the intestines of.

dis·en·chant (dis-in-*chant*) *v.* To free from fascination or illusion.—**dis·en·chant·ment** *n.*

dis·en·cum·ber (dis-in-*kum*-ber) *v.* To free from a burden.

dis·en·fran·chise. *Variant of* disfranchise.

dis·en·gage (dis-in-*gayj*) *v.* [-gaged; -gag·ing] 1. To loose; detach. 2. To disentangle; extricate.—**dis·en·gage·ment** *n.*

dis·en·tan·gle (dis-in-*tang*-'l) *v.* [-tan·gled; -tan·gling] To untwist; free from entanglement; extricate.—**dis·en·tan·gle·ment** *n.*

dis·es·tab·lish (dis-uh-*stab*-lish) *v.* To deprive of its established state; to withdraw, as a church, from connection with the state.–**dis·es·tab·lish·ment** *n.*— **-lish·men·tar·i·an·ism** *n.*

dis·es·teem (dis-uh-*steem*) *v.* To dislike; slight. —*n.* Dislike; want of esteem.

dis·fa·vor (dis-*fay*-ver) *n.* 1. Dislike; unfavorable regard; disapproval. 2. State of being out of favor. 3. An unkindness.—**dis·fa·vor** *v.*

dis·fig·ure (dis-*fig*-yer) *v.* [-ured; -ur·ing] To mar in appearance; deface.—**dis·fig·ure·ment** *n.*

dis·fran·chise (dis-*fran*-chyze) *v.* [-chised; -chis·ing] To deprive of the rights of citizenship; strip of a privilege.—**dis·fran·chise·ment** *n.*—**dis·fran·chis·er** *n.*

dis·gorge (dis-*gorj*) *v.* [-gorged; -gorg·ing] To eject; vomit; discharge, esp. with reluctance.

dis·grace (dis-*grayss*) *n.* 1. A cause for shame; disfavor. 2. Shame; dishonor; loss of respect or favor.—*v.* [-graced; -grac·ing]— -**grac·er** *n.*

dis·grace·ful (dis-*grayss*-ful) *adj.* Shameful; dishonorable; infamous.—**dis·grace·ful·ly** *adv.*

dis·grun·tle (dis-*grun*-t'l) *v.* [-tled; -tling] To dissatisfy; make discontented.— -**grun·tled** *adj.*

dis·guise (dis-*gyze*) *v.* [-guised; -guis·ing] 1. To change or conceal one's appearance by unusual dress or a mask. 2. To conceal; dissemble; change the appearance of.—**dis·guise** *n.*—**dis·guis·ed·ly** *adv.*—**dis·guis·er** *n.*

dis·gust (dis-*gust*) *n.* Aversion; loathing; repugnance.—**dis·gust** *v.* To arouse aversion or strong dislike in; revolt; nauseate.

dis·gust·ed (dis-*gus*-tid) *adj.* 1. Revolted; sickened. 2. Annoyed; bored.—**dis·gust·ed·ly** *adv.*—**dis·gust·ed·ness** *n.*—**dis·gust·ing** *adj.*—**dis·gust·ing·ly** *adv.*

dish *n.* 1. An open vessel for serving food. 2. The food served in a dish. 3. Any dishlike object or form.—*v.* To serve.

dishboard	dish-headed	dishwasher
dishcloth	dish maker	dishwashing
dish-crowned	dishmonger	dishwater
dish-faced	dishpan	dishwiper

dis·ha·bille (dis-uh-*beel*) *n.* State of partial undress; informal or careless dress.

dis·har·mo·ny (dis-*hahr*-muh-nee) *n.* [*pl.* -nies] Discord; want of harmony; conflict.

dis·heart·en (dis-*hahr*-t'n) *v.* To discourage; dispirit; depress.—**dis·heart·en·ing·ly** *adv.*—**dis·heart·en·ment** *n.*

di·shev·el (dih-*shev*-'l) *v.* [-eled, -elled; -el·ing, -el·ling] To disorder; rumple, as the hair.—**di·shev·el·ment** *n.*

dis·hon·est (dis-*on*-ist) *adj.* 1. Devoid of honesty; fraudulent. 2. Perfidious; deceitful. —**dis·hon·est·ly** *adv.*

dis·hon·es·ty (dis-*on*-iss-tee) *n.* Deceitfulness; lack of probity and integrity.

dis·hon·or (dis-*on*-er) *n.* 1. Disgrace; loss of honor; shame. 2. Nonpayment of a check. —*v.* 1. To disgrace; degrade. 2. To refuse to pay.—**dis·hon·or·er** *n.*

dis·hon·or·a·ble (dis-*on*-er-uh-b'l) *adj.* Shameful; disgraceful; base.—**dis·hon·or·a·ble·ness** *n.* —**dis·hon·or·a·bly** *adv.*

dis·il·lu·sion (dis-ih-*loo*-zh'n) *v.* To free from illusions.—**dis·il·lu·sion** *n.*—**dis·il·lu·sion·ment** *n.*—**dis·il·lu·sive** *adj.*

dis·in·cli·na·tion (dis-in-kluh-*nay*-sh'n) *n.* Unwillingness; distaste.—**dis·in·cline** (dis-in-*klyne*) *v.* [-clined; -clin·ing] To be or make unwilling.

dis·in·fect (dis-in-*fekt*) *v.* To free from germs or contagion.—**dis·in·fec·tion** *n.*— -**fec·tor** *n.*

dis·in·fec·tant (dis-in-*fekt*-'nt) *n.* An agent or solution for destroying germs.

dis·in·fest (dis-in-*fest*) *v.* To rid of lice, fleas, rats, etc.—**dis·in·fes·ta·tion** *n.*

dis·in·gen·u·ous (dis-in-*jen*-yoo-us) *adj.* Insincere; crafty; cunning.—**dis·in·gen·u·ous·ly** *adv.*

dis·in·her·it (dis-in-*hehr*-it) *v.* To deprive of an inheritance.—**dis·in·her·it·ance** *n.*

dis·in·te·grate (dis-*in*-tuh-grayt) *v.* [-grat·ed; -grat·ing] To decompose; crumble; break into small bits.—**dis·in·te·gra·tion** (dis-in-tuh-*gray*-sh'n) *n.*—**dis·in·te·gra·tor** *n.*

dis·in·ter (dis-in-*ter*) *v.* 1. To exhume; take out of a grave. 2. To bring to light; disclose.

dis·in·ter·est·ed (dis-*in*-ter-es-tid) *adj.* 1. Indifferent; unconcerned. 2. Unselfish; not influenced by personal motives.—**dis·in·ter·est·ed·ly** *adv.*—**dis·in·ter·est·ed·ness** *n.*

dis·join (dis-*joyn*) *v.* To separate; put apart.

dis·joint (dis-*joynt*) *v.* 1. To take apart at the joints; dislocate. 2. To break up into parts.

dis·joint·ed *adj.* Disconnected; incoherent. —**dis·joint·ed·ly** *adv.*—**dis·joint·ed·ness** *n.*

dis·junc·tive (dis-*junk*-tiv) *adj.* 1. Tending to separate; disjoining. 2. *Grammar.* A conjunction which denotes separation, as *or*, *nor*.

disk *n.* Also **disc.** 1. Any flat circular object or body. 2. *Botany.* The flat central part of a flower head. 3. A phonograph record.

disk harrow. A farm implement with a series of revolving disks for cutting soil.

disk jockey. *Radio Slang.* An announcer on programs of recordings and transcriptions.

dis·like (dis-*lyke*) *v.* [-liked; -lik·ing] To disfavor; disapprove of; object to.—*n.* Aversion; a feeling of antipathy.—**dis·lik·a·ble** *adj.*

dis·lo·cate (dis-loh-*kayt*) *v.* [-cat·ed; -cat·ing] To put out of joint; displace; upset.—**dis·lo·ca·tion** (dis-loh-*kay*-sh'n) *n.*

dis·lodge (dis-*loj*) *v.* [-lodged; -lodg·ing] To displace; drive or remove from a position.

dis·loy·al (dis-*loy*-ul) *adj.* False; perfidious; unfaithful.—**dis·loy·al·ly** *adv.*

dis·loy·al·ty (dis-*loy*-ul-tee) *n.* [*pl.* -ties] 1. Faithlessness; breach of allegiance. 2. A disloyal act.

dis·mal (*diz*-m'l) *adj.* Dreary; gloomy; sad; woeful.—**dis·mal** *n.*—**dis·mal·ly** *adv.*—**dis·mal·ness** *n.*

dis·man·tle (dis-*man*-t'l) *v.* [-tled; -tling] To strip; divest; take to pieces.— -**man·tle·ment** *n.*

dis·may (dis-*may*) *v.* To discourage or disable through fear; daunt; frighten.—**dis·may** *n.*

dis·mem·ber (dis-*mem*-ber) *v.* To tear limb from limb; mutilate; rend.—**dis·mem·ber·ment** *n.*

dis·miss (dis-*miss*) *v.* 1. To discharge; remove from office or employment. 2. To eject; oust; send or put away. 3. *Law.* To refuse to consider; reject. 4. To end a session of a class.—**dis·miss·al** *n.*

dis·mount (dis-*mownt*) *v.* 1. To alight from a horse or vehicle. 2. To remove from a mount, support, or setting.—**dis·mount** *n.*

dis·o·be·di·ence (dis-uh-*beed*-ee-enss) *n.* Failure or refusal to obey.—**dis·o·be·di·ent** *adj.*

D

dis·o·bey (dis-uh-*bay*) *v.* To fail to obey; refuse to submit.—**dis·o·bey·er** *n.*

dis·o·blige (dis-uh-*blyje*) *v.* [-bliged; -blig·ing] 1. To offend by unkindness or incivility; inconvenience. 2. To refuse accommodation.—**dis·o·blig·ing** *adj.*—**dis·o·blig·ing·ly** *adv.*

dis·or·der (dis-*or*-der) *n.* 1. Confusion; lack of order; disturbance. 2. Indisposition; sickness.—*v.* To confuse; upset; derange.

dis·or·der·ed (dis-*or*-derd) *adj.* Disarranged; out of order; deranged.

dis·or·der·ly (dis-*or*-der-lee) *adj.* 1. Out of order; upset. 2. Tumultuous; unruly; lawless. 3. *Law.* Contrary to decency and good morals.—**dis·or·der·ly** *adv.*—**dis·or·der·li·ness** *n.*

dis·or·gan·ize (dis-*or*-guh-nyze) *v.* [-ized; -iz·ing] To disturb organization of; throw into confusion or disorder.—**dis·or·gan·i·za·tion** (dis-or-guh-nih-*zay*-sh'n) *n.*— **-gan·iz·er** *n.*

dis·own (dis-*ohn*) *v.* To repudiate; refuse to claim or acknowledge.

dis·par·age (dis-*pair*-ij) *v.* [-aged; -ag·ing] To depreciate; belittle; attempt to lessen the importance of.—**dis·par·age·ment** *n.*—**dis·par·ag·ing** *adj.*—**dis·par·ag·ing·ly** *adv.*

dis·pa·rate (*dis*-puh-rit) *adj.* Dissimilar; unlike.—**dis·par·ate·ly** *adv.*—**dis·par·ate·ness** *n.*

dis·par·i·ty (dis-*pair*-ih-tee) *n.* [*pl.* -ties] Inequality; unlikeness; disproportion.

dis·pas·sion·ate (dis-*pash*-'n-it) *adj.* Calm; without emotion; objective.—**dis·pas·sion·ate·ly** *adv.*—**dis·pas·sion·ate·ness** *n.*

dis·patch (dis-*patch*) *v.* 1. To send off. 2. To put to death; kill. 3. To perform promptly; execute speedily.—*n.* 1. Speed; celerity. 2. Act of dispatching. 3. A message; letter.—**dis·patch·er** *n.*

dis·pel (dis-*pel*) *v.* [-pelled; -pel·ling] To scatter; disperse; drive away.

dis·pen·sa·ble (dis-*pen*-suh-b'l) *adj.* 1. Not vital; able to be dispensed with. 2. Able to be distributed.—**dis·pen·sa·bil·i·ty, dis·pen·sa·ble·ness** *n.*

dis·pen·sa·ry (dis-*pen*-suh-ree) *n.* [*pl.* -ries] 1. Hospital department for dispensing medicines. 2. A clinic; place where medical treatment is dispensed free or at a low cost.

dis·pen·sa·tion (dis-p'n-*say*-sh'n) *n.* 1. The act of distributing. 2. *Theological.* License to do what is forbidden by vows or canons. 3. Provision; management.— **-sa·tion·al** *adj.*

dis·pen·sa·to·ry (dis-*pen*-suh-toh-ree) *n.* 1. A dispensary. 2. A book of medicines and their uses.—**dis·pen·sa·tor** (dis-p'n-*say*-tor) *n.*

dis·pense (dis-*penss*) *v.* [-pensed; -pens·ing] 1. To distribute; dole out. 2. To administer; distribute. 'Judges dispense justice.' 3. To excuse; free from obligation.—**dis·pens·er** *n.* —**dispense with.** To do without; relinquish.

dis·perse (dis-*perss*) *v.* [-persed; -pers·ing] To scatter; dissipate; spread from a central point.—**dis·per·sal** *n.*—**dis·pers·ed·ly** *adv.*—**dis·pers·er** *n.*—**dis·pers·i·ble** *adj.*—**dis·per·sive** *adj.*

dis·per·sion (dis-*per*-zh'n) *n.* 1. Scattering. 2. *Physics.* The division of a beam of light into its colored rays.

dis·pir·it (dis-*pir*-it) *v.* To deprive of spirit; dishearten; depress.—**dis·pir·it·ed** *adj.*—**dis·pir·it·ed·ly** *adv.*—**dis·pir·it·ed·ness** *n.*

dis·place (dis-*playss*) *v.* [-placed; -plac·ing] 1. To take out of the normal or proper place. 2. To take the place of; replace. 3. To oust.

displaced person. A national of a Nazi-occupied country forcibly removed from his home or country.

dis·place·ment (dis-*playss*-m'nt) *n.* 1. Act of removing from its proper place. 2. Quantity of water displaced by a floating object.

dis·play (dis-*play*) *v.* 1. To show; open to view; exhibit. 2. To spread out.—*n.* 1. Act of showing. 2. Ostentation; excessive show. 3. Arrangement of merchandise in a shop window.

dis·please (dis-*pleez*) *v.* [-pleased; -pleas·ing] To offend; dissatisfy; incur the dislike of.

dis·pleas·ure (dis-*pleh*-zher) *n.* Dissatisfaction; distaste; annoyance.

dis·port (dis-*port*) *v.* To sport; frolic; amuse.

dis·pos·al (dis-*poh*-z'l) *n.* 1. Disposition; arrangement; management. 2. A giving away.

dis·pose (dis-*pohz*) *v.* [-posed; -pos·ing] 1. To arrange; place; adjust. 2. To give; bestow; get rid of. 3. To incline.—**dis·pos·a·ble** *adj.*

dis·po·si·tion (dis-puh-*zih*-sh'n) *n.* 1. The act of disposing; management; distribution; arrangement. 2. Natural inclination or tendency. 3. Temper; psychological outlook.

dis·pos·sess (dis-puh-*zess*) *v.* To deprive of possession, esp. of living quarters; oust.—**dis·pos·ses·sion** *n.*—**dis·pos·ses·sor** *n.*

dis·praise (dis-*prayz*) *v.* [-praised; -prais·ing] To blame; censure; disapprove of.—**dis·prais·ing·ly** *adv.*

dis·proof *n.* Disproving; refutation.

dis·pro·por·tion (dis-pruh-*por*-sh'n) *n.* Lack of proportions or symmetry; inequality.—**dis·pro·por·tion** *v.*—**dis·pro·por·tion·al** *adj.*

dis·pro·por·tion·ate (dis-pruh-*por*-sh'n-it) *adj.* Unsymmetrical; out of proper proportion.—**dis·pro·por·tion·ate·ly** *adv.*—**dis·pro·por·tion·ate·ness** *n.*

dis·prove (dis-*proov*) *v.* [-proved; -prov·ing] To refute; prove false.—**dis·prov·a·ble** *adj.*

dis·pu·ta·ble (dis-*pyoo*-tuh-b'l; *dis*-pyoot-) *adj.* Debatable; of doubtful certainty.—**dis·pu·ta·bil·i·ty** (dis-pyoot-uh-*bil*-ih-tee) *n.*—**dis·pu·ta·bly** *adv.*

dis·pu·tant (*dis*-pyoo-t'nt) *n.* One who argues or debates.—**dis·pu·tant** *adj.*

dis·pu·ta·tion (dis-pyoo-*tay*-sh'n) *n.* Verbal controversy; argument; act of disputing.—**dis·pu·ta·tious, dis·pu·ta·tive** *adj.*—**dis·pu·ta·tious·ly** *adv.*—**dis·pu·ta·tious·ness** *n.*

dis·pute (dis-*pyoot*) *v.* [-put·ed; -put·ing] 1. To contest; question; argue; debate. 2. To argue noisily or angrily. 3. To question the validity of. 'Dispute an election.'—*n.* An argument, quarrel, or controversy.

dis·qual·i·fy (dis-*kwol*-ih-fy) v. [-fied; -fy·ing] To render unsuitable; bar from participation; deprive of capacity, power, or right.—**dis·qual·i·fi·ca·tion** (dis-kwol-ih-fih-*kay*-shun) n.

dis·qui·et (dis-*kwy*-ut) v. To disturb; fret; vex; worry.—n. Uneasiness; disturbance; anxiety.—**dis·qui·et·ing** adj.—**dis·qui·et·ing·ly** adv.

dis·qui·e·tude (dis-*kwy*-uh-tood) n. Disquiet; agitation; anxiety.

dis·qui·si·tion (dis-kwih-*zish*-un) n. A formal treatise on a subject; dissertation.

dis·re·gard (dis-ree-*garhd*) v. To fail to observe; ignore; neglect; snub.—**dis·re·gard·ful** adj.

dis·re·mem·ber (dis-ree-*mem*-b'r) v. Colloquial. To forget; fail to recall.

dis·re·pair (dis-reh-*pair*) n. Poor condition.

dis·rep·u·ta·ble (dis-*rep*-yoo-tuh-b'l) adj. Dishonorable; discreditable; low; mean.—**dis·rep·u·ta·bil·i·ty** (dis-rep-yoo-tuh-*bil*-uh-tee), **dis·rep·u·ta·ble·ness** n.—**dis·rep·u·ta·bly** adv.

dis·re·pute (dis-ree-*pyoot*) n. Loss of reputation; discredit; dishonor; lack of integrity.

dis·re·spect (dis-ree-*spekt*) n. Irreverence; incivility; rudeness.—**dis·re·spect** v.

dis·re·spect·a·ble (dis-ree-*spekt*-uh-b'l) adj. Undeserving of esteem or respect.—**dis·re·spec·ta·bil·i·ty** (dis-ree-spekt-uh-*bil*-uh-tee) n.

dis·re·spect·ful (dis-ree-*spekt*-ful) n. Uncivil; discourteous; rude.—**dis·re·spect·ful·ly** adv.

dis·robe v. [-robed; -rob·ing] To remove clothing; strip.

dis·rupt v. To break up; tear apart; interrupt the smooth functioning of.—**dis·rupt·er, dis·rupt·or** n.—**dis·rup·tion** (dis-*rup*-sh'n) n.

dis·rup·tive (dis-*rup*-tiv) adj. Causing disruption; interrupting an orderly functioning.

dis·sat·is·fac·tion (dih-sat-iss-*fak*-sh'n) n. Discontent; disappointment; lack of approval.

dis·sat·is·fy (dih-*sat*-iss-fy) v. [-fied; -fy·ing] To displease; cause discontent; leave unsatisfied.

dis·sect (dih-*sekt*) v. 1. To divide or cut into pieces so as to study carefully. 2. To analyze; describe in minute detail.—**dis·sec·tion** (dih-*sek*-shun) n.—**dis·sec·tor** n.

dis·sem·ble (dih-*sem*-b'l) v. [-bled; -bling] 1. To conceal; disguise; cover up. 2. To pretend; feign; simulate. 3. To feign not to notice; pass over.—**dis·sem·blance** n.— -**bler** n.

dis·sem·i·nate (dih-*sem*-uh-nayt) v. [-nat·ed; -nat·ing] To spread; diffuse; promulgate; circulate; scatter.—**dis·sem·i·na·tion** (dih-sem-uh-*nay*-shun) n.—**dis·sem·i·na·tive** adj.

dis·sen·sion (dih-*sen*-sh'n) n. Disagreement; contention; discord; strife.

dis·sent (dih-*sent*) v. 1. To disagree; differ. 2. To hold unconventional beliefs.—n. 1. A statement of differing opinion. 2. Disagreement. 3. Nonconformity.—**dis·sent·er** n.

dis·sen·tient (dih-*sen*-sh'nt) adj. Disagreeing; dissenting.—**dis·sen·tient** n.—**dis·sen·tience** n.

dis·ser·ta·tion (dih-ser-*tay*-sh'n) n. A formal discourse; thesis embodying the research of a doctoral candidate.—**dis·ser·tate** (*dis*-er-tayt) v. [-tat·ed; -tat·ing]—**dis·ser·ta·tor** n.

dis·serv·ice (dis-*ser*-vis) n. Harm.

dis·sev·er (dis-*sev*-er) v. To separate; disunite; cut apart.—**dis·sev·er·ance, dis·sev·er·ment** n.

dis·si·dent (*dis*-uh-d'nt) adj. Varying; disagreeing; unorthodox.—**dis·si·dent** n.— -**si·dence** n.

dis·sim·i·lar (dih-*sim*-ih-ler) adj. Unlike; varying.—**dis·sim·i·lar·ly** adv.—**dis·sim·i·lar·i·ty** n.

dis·si·mil·i·tude (dis-sih-*mil*-uh-tyood) n. Lack of resemblance; difference.

dis·sim·u·late (dih-*sim*-yoo-layt) v. [-lated; -lat·ing] To try to deceive; hide true motives; make pretense.—**dis·sim·u·la·tion** (dih-sim-yoo-*lay*-sh'n) n.—**dis·sim·u·la·tive** adj.— -**u·la·tor** n.

dis·si·pate (*dis*-uh-payt) v. [-pat·ed; -pat·ing] 1. To spend too much money or time in drunken or riotous living; squander; waste. 2. Physics. To convert energy into heat or another form of energy. 3. To waste or vanish away. 4. To scatter; disperse; dispel.—**dis·si·pat·er, dis·si·pa·tor** n.

dis·si·pat·ed (*dis*-uh-payt-ed) adj. 1. Loose; extravagant; devoted to pleasure and vice. 2. Showing physical effects of a dissolute life.—**dis·si·pat·ed·ly** adv.—**dis·si·pat·ed·ness** n.

dis·si·pa·tion (dis-uh-*pay*-sh'n) n. 1. A scattering; dispersal; being dispersed. 2. Excessive pursuit of pleasure; wasteful living. 3. Expenditure of energy.—**dis·si·pat·ive** adj.

dis·so·ci·a·tion (dih-soh-see-*ay*-sh'n) n. 1. To separate; divide; break up into parts. 2. Psychology. Thrusting a body of ideas from normal consciousness so that they integrate, operate as a unit, and form the basis for a split personality. 3. Chemistry. A breakdown of a molecule into ions or less complex molecules.—**dis·so·ci·ate** v. [-at·ed; -at·ing].—**dis·so·ci·a·tive** (dih-*soh*-see-ay-tiv) adj.—**dis·so·ci·a·ble** (dih-*soh*-see-uh-b'l) adj.

dis·sol·u·ble (dih-*sol*-yoo-b'l) adj. 1. Capable of going into solution. 2. Decomposable; separable.—**dis·sol·u·bil·i·ty** (dih-sol-yoo-*bil*-uh-tee), -**sol·u·ble·ness** (dih-*sol*-yoo-b'l-niss) n.

dis·so·lute (*dis*-uh-loot) adj. Inclined to vice and dissipation; wanton; lewd; debauched.—**dis·so·lute·ly** adv.—**dis·so·lute·ness** n.

dis·so·lu·tion (dis-uh-*loo*-sh'n) n. 1. A dissolving or liquefying. 2. Decomposition; disintegration. 3. Death; separation of body and soul. 4. Breaking up. 'Dissolution of a government.' 5. Complete liquidation of a business enterprise.

dis·solve (dih-*zolv*) v. [-solved; -solv·ing] 1. To mix a substance with another so that they become relatively inseparable; blend. 2. To melt; liquefy. 3. To separate; break up; decompose. 4. To remove; annul; rescind. 5. To vanish gradually; lose intensity. 6. To arrive at a solution; settle.—**dis·solv·a·ble** adj.

dis·so·nance (*dis*-uh-n'ns) n. Also **dis·so·nan·cy.** 1. Discord; mixture of inharmonious sounds. 2. Disagreement; inconsistency; incongruity.—**dis·so·nant** adj.—**dis·so·nant·ly** adv.

dis·suade (dih-*swayd*) v. [-suad·ed; -suad·ing] To advise against; render averse to; persuade against.—**dis·suad·er** n.—**dis·sua·sion** n.

D

dis·sua·sive (dih-*sway*-siv) *adj*. Persuading not to follow a proposed course.—**dis·sua·sive·ly** *adv*.—**dis·sua·sive·ness** *n*.

dis·syl·la·ble (dih-*sil*-uh-b'l) *n*. A word of two syllables.—**dis·syl·lab·ic** (dih-sih-*lab*-ik) *adj*.

dis·taff (*dis*-taf) *n*. 1. The female sex; women. 2. The staff which holds fibers in spinning.

dis·tance (*dis*-t'ns) *n*. 1. Interval or space between two points or times; remoteness. 2. Faraway region or point. 3. Aloofness or formality of manner. 4. *Music*. Tonal difference between two notes.—*v*. [-tanced; -tanc·ing] 1. To leave behind; outrun; outdo. 2. To make seem remotely distant.

dis·tant (*dis*-t'nt) *adj*. 1. Remote; far away; obscure; separated. 2. Slight; faint, as a sound. 3. Aloof; not cordial; reserved. 4. Divided by a wide space.—**dis·tant·ly** *adv*.

dis·taste (dis-*tayst*) *n*. Dislike; disrelish; repugnance.—*v*. [-tast·ed; -tast·ing] 1. To feel dislike or aversion for. 2. To offend; vex.

dis·taste·ful (dis-*tayst*-f'l) *adj*. Offensive to the taste; unpleasant; causing dislike; repulsive. —**dis·taste·ful·ly** *adv*.—**dis·taste·ful·ness** *n*.

dis·tem·per *n*. 1. Ill humor; inability to control one's temper. 2. A sickness, esp. a catarrhal virus disease of puppies. 3. Political strife; disorder.—*v*. 1. To disorder; ruffle; put out of sorts. 2. To derange the health of.

dis·tem·per *n*. 1. A paint compounded of pigment and sizing or egg. 2. A mural or painting using this paint; the art of such painting. —*v*. To mix distemper paint.

dis·tend (dis-*tend*) *v*. To expand; swell; increase in bulk or area.—**dis·ten·si·ble** *adj*.

dis·ten·tion (dis-*ten*-shun) *n*. Also **dis·ten·sion**. A distending; spreading; breadth.

dis·tich (*dis*-tik) *n*. A couplet; two lines of verse.

dis·till (dih-*stil*) *v*. [dis·tilled; dis·till·ing] Also **dis·til**. 1. To condense; purify. 2. To subject to or obtain by distillation. 3. To trickle; drip.—**dis·till·a·ble** *adj*.—**dis·till·er** *n*.

dis·til·la·tion (dis-tih-*lay*-sh'n) *n*. 1. Extracting an essence by evaporation and condensation; separation of substances by a controlled heat process. 2. The essence extracted by distillation.—**dis·til·late** (*dis*-tuh-lut) *n*. A concentrated or distilled product.

dis·til·ler·y (dih-*stil*-er-ee) *n*. [*pl*. -ies] A factory where distilling, esp. of alcohol, is done.

dis·tinct (dis-*tinkt*) *adj*. 1. Clearly distinguished or defined; markedly different. 2. Easily heard, seen, or understood.—**dis·tinct·ly** *adv*.

dis·tinc·tion (dis-*tink*-sh'n) *n*. 1. Eminence; superiority. 2. A mark of difference. 3. The power to distinguish. 4. Act of distinguishing or noting differences. 5. Recognition of merit or eminence; honor. 6. Variation.

dis·tinc·tive (dis-*tink*-tiv) *adj*. 1. Having eminence or distinction. 2. Marking a clear difference.—**dis·tinc·tive·ly** *adv*.— -tive·ness *n*.

dis·tin·gué (dis-tang-*gay*). *French*. Distinguished; elegant in bearing or appearance.

dis·tin·guish (dis-*ting*-gwish) *v*. 1. To find or indicate a difference; draw a distinction. 2. To perceive; be able to see or apprehend. 3. To confer an honor upon; make outstanding.—**dis·tin·guish·a·ble** *adj*.— -guish·a·bly *adv*.

dis·tin·guished (dis-*ting*-gwishd) *adj*. 1. Eminent; noted; conspicuous.

dis·tort (dis-*tort*) *v*. 1. To twist from a natural shape. 2. To give a biased interpretation; pervert a meaning.—**dis·tort·er** *n*.

dis·tort·ed *adj*. Misrepresented; ill-proportioned; twisted; perverted.—**dis·tort·ed·ly** *adv*.

dis·tor·tion (dis-*tor*-sh'n) *n*. 1. Wrenching out of normal shape. 2. Perversion or twisting of meaning or context.—**dis·tor·tion·al** *adj*.

dis·tract (dis-*trakt*) *v*. 1. To divert; cause to consider a different factor. 2. To drive insane; craze.—**dis·tract·ed·ly** *adv*.

dis·trac·tion (dis-*trak*-sh'n) *n*. 1. A drawing away; diversion. 2. Puzzlement; confusion; wild disorder. 3. Insanity.—**dis·trac·tive** *adj*.

dis·train (dis-*trayn*) *v*. *Law*. To make legal seizure of goods for debt or as security.—**dis·traint**, **dis·train·ment** *n*. Legal seizure of goods.

dis·trait (dis-*tray*) *adj*. 1. Forgetful; inattentive. 2. Distracted; crazy. 3. Distraught.

dis·traught (dis-*trawt*) *adj*. Perplexed; torn by mental anxiety; distracted.

dis·tress *n*. 1. Suffering; anguish. 2. Affliction; adversity. 3. A hazardous situation. 'Ship in distress.' 4. *Law*. Seizure of goods to insure payment; goods so seized.—*v*. 1. To pain; afflict; grieve; annoy. 2. *Law*. To seize for debt.—**dis·tress·ful** *adj*.—**dis·tress·ful·ly** *adv*.

dis·trib·ute (dis-*trib*-yoot) *v*. [-ut·ed; -ut·ing] 1. To dispense; apportion; allot. 2. To scatter over or cover a wide area. 3. To classify; group.—**dis·trib·u·ta·ble** *adj*.— -ut·er *n*.

dis·tri·bu·tion (dis-trib-*yoo*-sh'n) *n*. 1. A dividing among a number; dispensation. 2. Classification; systematic arrangement. 3. Apportionment; allotment. 4. A range or dispersal. 'A distribution of test scores.' 5. Making the products of industry available to consumers.

dis·trib·u·tive (dis-*trib*-yoo-tiv) *adj*. Expressing separation or division; alloting portions.—**dis·trib·u·tive·ly** *adv*.—**dis·trib·u·tive·ness** *n*.

dis·trib·u·tor (dis-*trib*-yoo-ter) *n*. 1. An outlet or agent for marketing merchandise. 2. *Mechanics*. A rotating switch that conducts electricity from one source to several circuits.

dis·trict (*dis*-trikt) *n*. A portion of a country, city, etc.; region; precinct; locality.—*v*. To make into districts.

district attorney. The prosecuting official of a local government or district.

dis·trust (dis-*trust*) *v*. To doubt integrity of; disbelieve.—*n*. Suspicion; lack of confidence.

dis·trust·ful *adj*. Feeling or showing suspicion; apprehensive.— -trust·fully *adv*.— -ful·ness *n*.

dis·turb (dis-*terb*) *v*. 1. To stir; move; arouse. 2. To cause deviation; make irregular; interfere with; disrupt. 3. To agitate; trouble;

perplex. 4. To put out; inconvenience.—**dis·turb·er** n.

dis·tur·bance (dis-*terb*-'ns) n. 1. A stirring; disquiet; excitement. 2. Interruption of a settled state of things; violent change. 3. Agitation of mind; perturbation.

dis·u·nite (dis-yoo-*nyte*) v. [-nit·ed; -nit·ing] 1. To separate; divide; fall apart. 2. Set at variance; interrupt harmony of.— **-un·ion** n.

dis·use (dis-*yooss*) n. Obsolescence; neglect; lack of use.—v. (dis-*yooz*) [-used; -us·ing].

ditch n. A shallow trench dug in earth, esp. to conduct water.—v. 1. To make a ditch; drain by or surround with a ditch. 2. *Slang*. To get rid of; cast aside. 3. *Aviation*. To make a forced landing, esp. in water.—**ditch·er** n.

ditchbank	ditch digger	ditch spade
ditchbur	ditch hand	ditch water

dith·er n. *Colloquial*. Agitation; nervous tremor; irritation.—v. To bother; irritate; agitate.

dith·y·ramb (*dith*-uh-ram) n. 1. Ancient Greek hymn or lyric poem. 2. Poem written with wild enthusiasm.—**dith·y·ram·bic** (dith-uh-*ram*-bik) adj.

dit·to (*dit*-oh) n. [pl. dit·tos] 1. The same thing. 2. A symbol (") indicating repetition.

dit·ty (*dit*-ee) n. [pl. dit·ties] A simple song.

ditty bag. Also (rarely) **ditty box.** *Nautical*. A sack for small personal possessions.

di·u·ret·ic (dy-uh-*ret*-ik) adj. Also **di·u·ret·i·cal.** Producing or tending to produce urination.—n. A medicine that increases urination.

di·ur·nal (dy-*er*-n'l) adj. 1. Occurring daily. 2. Pertaining to the daytime; enduring for a day. 3. Active or thriving during daylight hours. 'A diurnal plant.'—**di·ur·nal·ly** adv.

di·va (*dee*-vuh) n. [pl. di·vas, di·ve] Female lead in an opera; prima donna.

div·a·gate (*dy*-vuh-gayt) v. [-gat·ed; -ga·tion] To wander; stray; digress.—**div·a·ga·tion** n.

di·van (*dy*-van; duh-*van*) n. 1. A low sofa or couchlike seat. 2. An oriental council chamber or reception room. 3. A salon for smoking or taking coffee.

di·var·i·cate (duh-*vair*-uh-kayt) v. [-cat·ed; -cat·ing] To divide into two branches; fork; diverge.—adj. (duh-*vair*-uh-kut) Spreading; ramifying.—**di·var·i·ca·tion** n.

dive v. [dived, dove; div·ing] 1. To plunge hurriedly or deeply into a substance, subject, activity, etc. 2. To descend at high speed, as an airplane.—n. 1. Act of diving. 2. Cheap or low resort, esp. for drinking or gambling.

dive bomber. A warplane designed to release bombs during a steep dive at its objective.

div·er (*dy*-ver) n. 1. One who dives. 2. Professional underwater worker who descends in a diving suit. 3. Any of several diving birds.

di·verge (duh-*verj*) v. [-verg·ed; -verg·ing] 1. To deviate as from a given course; branch out. 2. To differ from the normal; vary.

di·ver·gence (duh-*verj*-enss) n. Act of diverging; deviation; variance.—**di·ver·gen·cy** n. [pl. -cies]—**di·ver·gent** adj. Differing

di·vers (*dy*-verz) adj. Various; several

di·verse (duh-*vers*) adj. Unlike; differing; varied.—**di·verse·ly** adv.—**di·verse·ness** n.

di·ver·si·fied (duh-*vers*-uh-fyde) adj. Varied.

di·ver·si·fy (duh-*vers*-uh-fy) v. [-fied; -fy·ing] To vary; give variety to.—**di·ver·si·fi·ca·tion** (duh-vers-ih-fih-*kay*-shun) n.—**di·ver·si·fi·er** n.

di·ver·sion (duh-*ver*-zh'n) n. 1. The act of turning aside as from a course or pursuit. 2. Diverting activity; sport; pastime. 3. *Military*. Minor attack to draw attention from the main action.

di·ver·si·ty (duh-*ver*-suh-tee) n. [pl. -ties] Variety; difference.

di·vert (duh-*vert*) v. 1. To turn aside; draw off. 2. To entertain; amuse.—**di·vert·er** n.

di·vert·ing adj. Entertaining; distracting.

di·ver·tisse·ment (dee-vehr-tees-*mahn*) n. 1. Diversion; entertainment. 2. Short entertainment, as a ballet, between acts of a play.

di·vest (duh-*vest*) v. To undress; strip; deprive.—**di·vest·i·ture** (duh-*vest*-uh-choor), **di·ves·ture** n. 1. The act of stripping or depriving. 2. *Law*. The act of surrendering possession.

di·vide (duh-*vyde*) v. [-vid·ed; -vid·ing] 1. To separate into parts or pieces; sever. 2. To keep apart; separate. 3. To disunite; make discordant. 4. To share; separate into equal parts. 5. To separate into classes.—n. A watershed; ridge between two drainage areas.—**di·vid·a·ble** adj.—**di·vid·ed** adj.—**di·vid·er** n.

div·i·dend (*div*-uh-dend) n. 1. The share of profits distributed among stockholders. 2. *Arithmetic*. The number to be divided.

di·vi·ders (duh-*vyde*-ers) n. pl. Pair of adjustable pointed arms to describe circles and divide lines; compass.

div·i·na·tion (div-uh-*nay*-sh'n) n. Foretelling the future; prediction.—**di·vin·a·to·ry** (duh-*vin*-uh-tor-ee) adj.

di·vine (duh-*vyne*) adj. Devoted to, coming from, or like God; sacred; religious.—n. A clergyman; theologian.—v. 1. To foretell; predict. 2. To make out by observation; guess; conjecture.—**di·vine·ly** adv.—**di·vine·ness** n.—**di·vin·er** n.

diving bell. A metal chamber in which men can descend deep under water.

diving suit. A heavy waterproof suit and helmet for working under water.

divining rod. A rod formerly thought useful in discovering water or minerals underground.

di·vin·i·ty (duh-*vin*-uh-tee) n. [pl. -ties] 1. The state of being divine. 2. A deity. 3. Supernatural power or quality. 4. Theology.

di·vis·i·ble (duh-*viz*-uh-b'l) adj. Capable of division; separable.—**di·vis·i·bil·i·ty** (duh-viz-uh-*bil*-uh-tee), **di·vis·i·ble·ness** n.— **-i·bly** adv.

di·vi·sion (duh-*vizh*-un) n. 1. The act of dividing; state of being divided. 2. Object which separates; partition. 3. The part separated; segment; section. 4. *Military*. An army unit consisting of two or three infantry brigades, with artillery and supply forces, normally

D

commanded by a major general. **5.** Section of a fleet. **6.** Disunion; discord. **7.** *Arithmetic.* Process of discovering how many times one number is contained in another.—**di·vi·sion·al** *adj.*

di·vi·sor (duh-*vy*-zer) *n. Arithmetic.* The number by which another is divided.

di·vorce (duh-*vohrs, -vawrs*) *n.* **1.** A legal dissolution of a marriage. **2.** Separation.—*v.* [-vor·ced; -vorc·ing] **1.** To separate from by divorce. **2.** To separate; sever.—**di·vor·cé** (dih-vawr-*say*) *n.* A divorced man.—**di·vor·cée** *n.* A divorced woman.—**di·vorc·er** *n.*

di·vorce·ment *n.* Divorce.

div·ot (*div*-ut) *n. Golf.* A piece of sod chipped out in making a shot.

di·vulge (duh-*vulj*) *v.* [di·vulged; di·vulg·ing] To reveal; disclose; make known.—**di·vulge·ment** *n.*—**di·vulg·er** *n.*

di·vul·gence (duh-*vul*-j'ns) *n.* The act of disclosing; revelation.

Dix·ie (*dik*-see) *n.* Also **Dixie Land.** The southern section of the United States.

Dix·ie·land *n. Jazz.* A New Orleans style of playing, with a strongly syncopated rhythm.

diz·en (*diz*-'n, *dy*-z'n) *v.* To dress gaudily.

diz·zy (*diz*-ee) *adj.* [diz·zi·er; diz·zi·est] **1.** Giddy; confused. **2.** Causing giddiness. **3.** *Colloquial.* Thoughtless; unstable; silly.—**diz·zi·ly** *adv.*—**diz·zi·ness** *n.*

do (*doo*) *v.* [did; done; do·ing] **1.** To perform; exert; produce; transact. **2.** To prepare; treat. 'To do the meat thoroughly.' **3.** To work at. **4.** To hoax; cheat. **5.** *Colloquial.* To inspect the sights of. 'Do the town.' **6.** To behave; conduct oneself. **7.** To fare. 'She's doing well.' **8.** To succeed; serve a purpose. 'Will this plan do?'—**do away with.** To destroy. —**do for. 1.** To serve; wait on. **2.** To ruin; kill.—**do in. 1.** To wear out. **2.** To kill. —**do up.** To arrange; tidy; prepare; launder.

do (*doh*) *n. Music.* First note of diatonic scale.

do·a·ble (*doo*-uh-b'l) *adj.* Able to be done.

do·all *n.* One who attends to everything; general factotum.

dob·bin (*dob*-in) *n.* A gentle farm or work horse.

Doberman pinscher. A large terrier.

doc·ile (*doss*-'l) *adj.* Tractable; teachable; easily managed.—**doc·ile·ly** *adv.*—**doc·ile·ness** *n.*

do·cil·i·ty (dos-*sil*-ih-tee) *n.* Gentleness; manageability.

dock *n.* **1.** A pier; quay; space in a harbor for the reception of ships. **2.** An artificial basin of water confined by walls for ship's repairing.—*v.* To bring a ship into a dock.

dock *n.* A prisoner's chair in court.

dock *n.* The stump of an animal's tail.—*v.* **1.** To cut short; clip, as the tail of an animal. **2.** To deduct from; curtail, as wages.

dock·age (*dok*-ij) *n.* **1.** The charge for using a dock. **2.** Docking facilities. **3.** Deduction.

dock·et (*dok*-it) *n.* **1.** *Law.* A summary; register of judgments; calendar of court cases. **2.** A list of matters to be considered. **3.** A

ticket tied to a package; label.—*v.* **1.** To record. **2.** To label.

dock·yard *n.* **1.** A storage place for naval equipment. **2.** Place where ships are built.

doc·tor (*dok*-ter) *n.* **1.** A licensed physician. **2.** A high academic degree; a holder of this degree.—*v.* **1.** *Colloquial.* To treat for illness; mend. **2.** To practice medicine. **3.** To falsify; tamper with. 'Doctor an account.'—**doc·tor·al** *adj.*—**doc·tor·ship** *n.*

doc·tor·ate (*dok*-ter-it) *n.* The degree or title of doctor, esp. Doctor of Philosophy (Ph.D.).

doc·tri·naire (dok-trih-*nair*) *n.* A theorizer; impractical thinker.—**doc·tri·nair·ism** *n.*

doc·trine (*dok*-trin) *n.* A principle or position in any science; tenet; article of faith.—**doc·tri·nal** *adj.*—**doc·tri·nal·ly** *adv.*

doc·u·ment (*dok*-yoo-ment) *n.* An official or authoritative paper.—*v.* To furnish with papers proving the facts.—**doc·u·men·tal, doc·u·men·ta·ry** *adj.*—**doc·u·men·ta·tion** *n.*

dod·der *v.* To shake with age.—**dod·der·ing** *adj.*

do·dec·a·he·dron (doh-dek-uh-*hee*-dron) *n.* A solid with twelve plane surfaces.

dodge *v.* [dodged; dodg·ing] To shift suddenly aside; evade.—*n.* A trick; artifice; evasion.

dodg·er *n.* **1.** One who evades; a trickster. **2.** [*cap.*] Member of the Brooklyn National League baseball team.

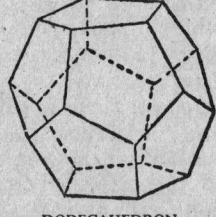

DODECAHEDRON

do·do (*doh*-doh) *n.* [*pl.* -does, -dos] A large, extinct bird.

doe (*doh*) *n.* A female deer.

do·er (*doo*-er) *n.* One who performs what is required. 'Talkers are no great doers.'

doe·skin *n.* **1.** The skin of a female deer. **2.** A compact twilled woolen cloth.—**doe·skin** *adj.*

doff *v.* To take off; strip; divest.

dog *n.* **1.** A four-legged domestic animal of various breeds. **2.** A contemptible, worthless fellow or thing. **3.** A gay young man. **4.** A mechanical screw fastening for ships' ports. —*v.* To follow closely; hunt; urge; worry with importunities.

DOG (1/30 life size)

dog bite	dogfall	dog mad
dog-bitten	dog-fashion	dog poor
dogboat	dogfoot	dogshore
dogbush	dog-footed	dog sick
dog catcher	dog-headed	dogskin
dog-draw	dog hole	dog sleep
dog-driven	dog hungry	dog stone
dog-eyed	dog lame	dog trick
dog-faced	dog-legged	dogtrot

dog·ber·ry *n.* The berry of the dogwood.

dog·cart *n.* A light cart with seats back to back.

dog days. The hot, muggy period from early July to early September.

dog down. *Nautical*. To fasten with dogs. 'Dog down the port.'

doge (*dohj*) *n*. The chief magistrate of the Venetian and Genoan republics.—**doge·dom** *n*.

dog-ear (*dog*-eer) *h*. Also **dog's-ear**. Turned-down corner of a page.—**dog-eared, dog's-eared** *adj*.

dog fight. 1. A fight between two dogs. 2. Any savage contest characterized by disregard of the rules. 3. A battle of warplanes.

dog·fish *n*. A kind of shark.

dog·ged *adj*. Obstinate; determined; sullen. —**dog·ged·ly** *adv*.—**dog·ged·ness** *n*.

dog·ger·el (*dog*-uh-r'l) *adj*. 1. Illiterate; lacking sense or rhythm. 2. Pertaining to an informal comical style of verse.—**dog·ger·el** *n*.

dog·gish *adj*. Churlish; snappish; growling; brutal.—**dog·gish·ly** *adv*.—**dog·gish·ness** *n*.

dog·gy, dog·gie *n*. [*pl*. -gies] Diminutive for dog.

dog·gy *adj*. [-gi·er] -gi·est] Stylish; natty.

dog house. *Slang*. Disfavor; bad graces.

do·gie (*doh*-gee) *n*. A motherless calf.

dog in the manger. One who will neither use something himself nor let anyone else use it.

dog·ma (*dog*-muh) *n*. [*pl*. -mas, ma·ta] 1. Settled opinion; principle; belief. 2. Indisputable doctrine.

dog·mat·ic (*dog*-mat-ik) *adj*. Also **dog·mat·i·cal**. Opinionated; dictatorial; arrogantly assertive.—**dog·mat·i·cal·ly** *adv*.— **-cal·ness** *n*.

dog·ma·tism (*dog*-muh-tizm) *n*. Positiveness in assertion; assurance of infallibility; arrogance. —**dog·ma·tist** *n*.

dog·ma·tize (*dog*-muh-tyze) *v*. [-tized; -tiz·ing] Treat a subject one-sidedly and overconfidently; propound without proof.—**dog·ma·ti·za·tion** *n*.—**dog·ma·tiz·er** *n*.

dog star. Sirius, the brightest star in the sky.

dog tag. *Slang*. An identification tag.

dog tired. *Slang*. Exhausted; bone weary.

dog·tooth *n*. Eye tooth; one of four fanglike teeth between the incisors and premolars.

dogtooth violet. Also **dog's-tooth violet.** 1. A lilylike spring flower native to southern Europe. 2. A related American flower.

dog·trot *n*. An easy, untiring running pace.

dog·watch *n*. *Nautical*. A two-hour watch from four to six or six to eight p.m.

dog·wood *n*. A family of hardy trees or shrubs bearing lovely white or pink flowers.

doi·ly *n*. [*pl*. -lies] A small, sometimes intricately patterned mat under dishes at table.

do·ings (*doo*-ingz) *n. pl.* 1. Actions; behavior; conduct. 2. Stir; bustle.

dol·drums (*dol*-dr'mz) *n*. 1. Low spirit; listlessness. 2. Parts of the ocean near the equator abounding in calms and erratic squalls.

dole (*dohl*) *n*. 1. A gratuity; charitable gift. 2. A system of relief for the needy unemployed.—*v*. [doled; dol·ing] To give out; allot.

dole·ful *adj*. Sorrowful; suffering or causing grief.—**dole·ful·ly** *adv*.—**dole·ful·ness** *n*.

doll *n*. 1. A figure or puppet used as plaything by children, 2. Girl or woman more pretty than intelligent. 3. Tiny, pretty woman.—*v*. *Slang*. To dress in one's best clothes. 'She dolled up.'—**dol·lish** *adj*.—**dol·lish·ly** *adv*.

dol·lar (*dol*-er) *n*. 1. The standard monetary unit of the United States; one hundred cents. 2. A one-dollar bill or coin. 3. A symbol ($).

dollar diplomacy. Carrying on a nation's foreign policy as an adjunct of its business interests.

dol·ly (*dol*-ee) *n*. [*pl*. -lies] 1. A low cart or platform with wheels or rollers for moving objects. 2. *Mining*. A perforated board used in washing ore. 3. A bar for holding a rivet while it is being installed; bucking bar. 4. Child's diminutive of doll.

dol·man (*dol*-m'n) *n*. 1. Long robe worn by Turks over other garments. 2. A woman's jacket with capelike sleeves.

dol·men *n*. *Archeology*. A large ancient, monumental stone, unhewn and raised on smaller stones.

do·lor (*doh*-ler) *n*. Also **do·lour.** Suffering; distress; grief; sorrow.

dol·or·ous (*dohl*-er-us) *adj*. 1. Sad; griefstricken. 2. Giving or expressing pain.—**do·lor·ous·ly** *adv*.—**do·lor·ous·ness** *n*.

dol·phin (*dol*-fin) *n*. A frisky marine mammal six to ten feet long. 2. A piling or buoy.

dolphin striker. *Nautical*. A small spar perpendicular to the bowsprit.

DOLPHIN (1/60 life size)

dolt (*dohlt*) *n*. Blockhead; dull, stupid person.—**dolt·ish** *adj*.—**dolt·ish·ly** *adv*.

-dom. *Suffix*. 1. State; condition; quality. 'Freedom.' 2. Rank; station; dominion. 'Kingdom.' 3. A body or collective group. 'Christendom.'

do·main (doh-*mayn*) *n*. 1. *Law*. Ownership of property. 2. Province; sphere; field; forte. 3. Estate having much land. 4. Territory which a sovereign rules.

dome *n*. 1. *Architecture*. A roof or cupola shaped like a steep-walled inverted bowl. 2. Any dome-shaped figure. 3. *Slang*. The head.—*v*. [domed; dom·ing] To cover a building or part of one with a dome.

Domesday Book (*doomz*-). The register of the first land survey of England in 1085–86.

do·mes·tic (duh-*mes*-tik) *adj*. 1. Pertaining to the home or family. 2. Preferring home life. 3. Tame; useful to man. 'Domestic animals.' 4. Relating to one's own country; not foreign. —*n*. A servant; household worker.—**do·mes·ti·cal·ly** *adv*.

do·mes·ti·cate (duh-*mes*-tih-kayt) *v*. [-cat·ed; -cat·ing] To make or become tame.—**do·mes·ti·ca·tion** *n*.

D

do·mes·tic·i·ty (doh-mes-*tis*-uh-tee) *n.* The state of being domestic; preference for home life.

dom·i·cile (*dom*-uh-s'l) *n.* Also **dom·i·cil.** Place of residence; home.—*v.* [-ciled; cil·ing] To reside; dwell.—**dom·i·cil·i·ar·y** *adj.*

dom·i·nance (*dom*-uh-nuns) *n.* Also **dom·i·nan·cy.** Ascendancy; rule; authority.

dom·i·nant (*dom*-uh-nunt) *adj.* 1. Ruling; predominant; commanding; governing. 2. *Music.* Based on, or relating to, the fifth note of the scale.—*n. Music.* The fifth note of the diatonic scale.

dom·i·nate (*dom*-uh-nayt) *v.* [-nat·ed; -nat·ing] To exercise control over; command; rule.

dom·i·na·tion (dom-uh-*nay*-sh'n) *n.* The act of dominating; controlling authority.

dom·i·neer (dom-uh-*neer*) *v.* To tyrannize.

dom·i·neer·ing (dom-uh-*neer*-ing) *adj.* Overbearing; tyrannical.—**dom·i·neer·ing·ly** *adv.* —**dom·i·neer·ing·ness** *n.*

Do·min·i·can (duh-*min*-ih-k'n) *adj.* Relating to St. Dominic or the religious orders named for him.—*n.* A member of the Dominican order.

dom·i·nie (*dom*-uh-nee) *n.* 1. *Colloquial.* A schoolmaster. 2. A minister; clergyman.

do·min·ion (duh-*min*-yun) *n.* 1. Power to govern or control; government. 2. Territory under a government. 3. [*cap.*] Self-governing unit of the British Commonwealth of Nations, as Canada, etc.

Dom·i·nique (dom-uh-*neek*) *n.* Also **Dom·i·nick.** An American breed of hens having striped plumage.

dom·i·no (*dom*-ih-noh) *n.* [*pl.* -noes, -nos] 1. A wide-sleeved robe and hood worn as a masquerade costume. 2. A half mask. 3. [*pl.*] Game played with flat, oblong pieces dotted variously on one side. 4. A piece of wood used in dominoes.

don *n.* 1. [*cap.*] Spanish courtesy title meaning *Sir* or *Mr.* 2. A college official or dignitary.

don *v.* [donned; don·ning] To put on, as clothes.

Doñ·a (*dohn*-yuh) *n.* A Spanish title signifying *Lady* or *Madam.*

do·nate (*doh*-nayt) *v.* [-nat·ed; -nat·ing] To give; contribute, as to a charity.—**do·na·tor** *n.*

do·na·tion (doh-*nay*-sh'n) *n.* 1. The act of giving. 2. A contribution or gift.

don·a·tive (*don*-uh-tiv) *n.* A gift; dole.

done (*dun*). Past participle of **do.**—*adj.* 1. Finished; through. 2. *Colloquial.* Cheated.

do·nee (doh-*nee*) *n.* Person who receives a gift.

don·jon (*dun*-j'n) *n.* The main tower of a castle.

Don Juan (don *wahn*; don *joo*-un). 1. Legendary dissolute Spanish nobleman. 2. A seducer; man attractive to women.

don·key (*don*-kee) *n.* [*pl.* -keys] 1. An ass; small animal resembling a horse. 2. A stupid, obstinate fellow.—**donkey engine.** A small engine used for subsidiary operations.

don·na (*don*-uh) *n.* [*pl.* don·ne] A lady; as prima donna, the leading woman singer in an opera.

do·nor (*doh*-ner) *n.* 1. One who gives. 2. One who gives his blood for a transfusion.

Don Quixote (don-kee-*hoh*-tee; -k*wik*-sut). Hero of Cervantes' famous satire of chivalry.

doo·dle *v.* [doo·dled; doo·dling] *Slang.* To draw idly or unconsciously while concentrating on other things.—**doo·dling** *n.*

doo·dle·bug (*doo*-d'l-bug) *n.* Any of several devices supposed to locate mineral deposits.

doom *n.* 1. Judgment; passing of sentence; final judgment. 2. Fate; state to which one is doomed or destined. 3. Ruin; destruction. —*v.* To sentence; condemn; destine.

dooms·day (*doomz*-day) *n.* Day of judgment.

door (*dohr*) *n.* 1. An opening into a house, room, or closet through which persons pass; entrance. 2. A hinged panel of metal or wood blocking a doorway. 3. Means of approach or access.

door·man (*dohr*-m'n) *n.* [*pl.* -men] One who attends the entrance of a building.

door·nail *n.* Nail against which the knocker strikes.—**dead as a doornail.** Wholly dead.

door·plate *n.* A metal plate on a door bearing the resident's name and sometimes his business.

door·step *n.* A step leading to an outer door.

door·way *n.* An entrance into a room or house.

door·yard *n.* A yard near a house's front door.

dope *n.* 1. *Colloquial.* Drug; narcotic. 2. *Slang.* A stupid person. 3. *Southern U.S.* A soft drink. 4. Water-proofing and tightening liquid used on airplane fabric.—*v.* To drug; administer narcotics to.—**dop·er** *n.*—**dope fiend.** A drug addict.

Dor·ic (*dor*-ik) *adj.* 1. Relating to the Dorians, who lived near Parnassus in ancient Greece. 2. *Architecture.* In the oldest and simplest Greek style.—**Dor·ic** *n.* The Dorian dialect.

dor·mant (*dor*-m'nt) *adj.* 1. Sleeping; at rest; inactive. 2. *Heraldry.* In a sleeping position. 3. Neglected; disused. 'Dormant privileges.'

dor·mer (*dor*-mer) *n.* Also **dormer window.** A window standing vertically on a sloping roof.

DORMER

dor·mi·to·ry (*dor*-muh-tor-ee) *n.* [*pl.* -ries] Room or building for sleeping, esp. in a school.

dor·mouse (*dor*-mowss) *n.* [*pl.* -mice] A small hibernating rodent found in Europe and Asia.

dor·my, dor·mie (*dor*-mee) *n. Golf.* A situation in which one player leads another by as many holes as there are left to play.

DORMOUSE (2/5 life size)

dor·sal (*dor*-s'l) *adj.* Relating to the back. 'Dorsal fin.'— **-sal·ly** *adv.*

do·ry (*doh*-ree) *n.* [*pl.* **do·ries**] A small boat with a flat bottom and a broad flare.

dos·age (*dohs*-ij) *n.* Prescribed amount of medicine.

DORY

dose (*dohs*) *n.* 1. The quantity of medicine prescribed to be taken at one time. 2. Anything offensive that must be taken. 3. A quantity in general.—*v.* 1. To give medicine to. 2. To give anything unpleasant to.—**dos·er** *n.*

dos·si·er (*doss*-ee-ay; -er) *n.* A file of confidential data about a person or organization.

dot *n.* 1. A speck or small spot, usually circular. 2. Dowry.—*v.* To mark with dots.

dot·age (*doh*-tij) *n.* Senility; childishness or feeble-mindedness in old age.

do·tard (*doh*-terd) *n.* A person in second childhood; one whose mind is impaired by age.

dote *v.* [**dot·ed**; **dot·ing**] 1. To love excessively. 'He dotes on her.' 2. To be silly; have a mind impaired by age.—**dot·er** *n.*

dot·ing (*doht*-ing) *adj.* Foolish; extravagantly fond.—**dot·ing** *n.*—**dot·ing·ly** *adv.*— **-ing·ness** *n.*

dot·ty (*dot*-ee) *adj.* 1. *Colloquial.* Insane; eccentric; feeble-minded. 2. Covered with dots.

Dou·ay Bible (doo-*ay*). Also **Douay Version.** An English translation of the Bible sanctioned by the Roman Catholic Church.

dou·ble (*dub*-'l) *adj.* 1. Coupled; in pairs; twofold. 2. Twice as much. 3. Deceitful; two-faced. 4. Bent or folded over; having two thicknesses.—*n.* 1. Twice as much or many. 2. A turn in flight to escape pursuers; any trick or artifice. 3. A counterpart; duplicate. 4. A bid in the game of bridge, making gains or penalties twofold. 5. A fold or plait. 6. A small roofing slate. 7. *Printing.* Several words, lines, or sentences set twice. 8. An understudy, esp. for an actor. 9. *Baseball.* A two-base hit. 10. [*pl.*] A game, esp. tennis, played between two sets of partners. 11. *Theater.* An actor who plays two or more parts in a play.—*adv.* 1. Folded over. 2. By twos or pairs; doubly.—**dou·ble** *v.* [-**bled**; **bling**].

double-armed	double-dye (*v.*)	double-loaded
double-barred	double-edged	double-manned
double barrel	double-engined	double-pointed
double-bedded	double-eyed	double-rivet (*v.*)
double-bitted	double-fronted	double-sided
double-bladed	double geared	double-sighted
double-bottomed	double-handed	double-stitched
double-buttoned	double-hearted	double threaded
double-charged	double-jointed	double tongue
double concave	double-keeled	double-tongued
double convex	double leaf	double track
double-distilled	double line	double trouble
double-doored	double-lined	double-windowed

dou·ble-banked *adj.* 1. Equipped with two tiers of oars. 2. Having two rowers on the same bench.

dou·ble-bar·reled *adj.* 1. Having two barrels, as a shotgun. 2. Dual in purpose or result.

double bass (*bayss*). *Music.* The largest violin.

dou·ble-breast·ed *adj.* With one side overlapping the other on the breast. 'A double-breasted coat.'

double cross. *Slang.* An act of treachery; breach of trust.—**dou·ble-cross** *v.*—**dou·ble-cross·er** *n.*

double dagger. *Printing.* The mark [‡].

dou·ble-deal·ing *n.* Duplicity; artifice; deceit. —*adj.* Treacherous; two-faced.— **-deal·er** *n.*

dou·ble-deck·er *adj.* Having one level above another. 'Double-decker bus.'

double entry. *Bookkeeping.* A form of bookkeeping in which entries are made on both the credit and debit sides of the ledger for each transaction.

dou·ble-faced *adj.* 1. Deceitful; hypocritical. 2. With both sides finished or intended for use, as a fabric.—**doub·le-fac·ed·ness** *n.*

dou·ble-head·er *n. Baseball.* Two games played on the same day for a single admission price.

dou·ble-mind·ed *adj.* Undecided; irresolute.

dou·ble-quick *adj. Military.* Very quick or rapid; at the rate of 180 paces a minute.—*n.* A march in double time.—**dou·ble-quick** *v.*

dou·bler (*duh*-bler) *n. Radio.* A stage of amplification in which a signal's frequency is doubled.

dou·blet (*duh*-blit) *n.* 1. A close-fitting jacket. 2. One of a couple; a pair. 3. *Printing.* Repetition of a word or phrase not intended.

double talk. Meaningless or intentionally confusing patter.

double time. *Military.* Double-quick time.

double up. To make a facility serve twice what it was designed to accommodate; share.

dou·bloon (*duh*-bloon) *n.* An old Spanish gold coin once worth sixteen dollars.

dou·bly (*duh*-blee) *adv.* 1. In twice the quantity or degree. 2. Insincerely; deceitfully.

doubt (*dowt*) *v.* 1. To question or hold questionable; suspect; distrust; be uncertain. 2. To be apprehensive of; fear.—**doubt** *n.* —**doubt·a·ble** *adj.*—**doubt·er** *n.*

doubt·ful (*dowt*-ful) *adj.* 1. Dubious; hesitating; undetermined. 2. Ambiguous; not clear. 3. Questionable; hazardous; equivocal. 4. Untrustworthy; suspicious.— **-ful·ly** *adv.*

doubting Thomas. A doubter; a pessimist; one difficult to convince.

doubt·less (*dowt*-l's) *adv.* Assuredly; without doubt.—**doubt·less** *adj.*—**doubt·less·ly** *adv.* Unquestionably; indubitably.—**doubt·less·ness** *n.*

douche (*doosh*) *n.* 1. A fluid for flushing a body passage. 2. A syringe; device for flushing a body orifice. 'Vaginal douche.'—*v.* [**douch·ed**; **douch·ing**].

dough (*doh*) *n.* 1. A kneaded batter of flour and other ingredients for baking. 2. *Slang.* Money.

dough·boy *n. World War I.* An infantryman.

dough·nut *n.* A customarily ring-shaped cake fried in deep fat.

D

dough·ty (*dow-tee*) *adj*. [-ti·er; -ti·est] Brave; valiant; illustrious.—**dough·ti·ly** *adv*. Valiantly.

dough·y *adj*. [dough·i·er; -i·est] Moist and spongy.

Douglas fir. Also **red fir, Oregon pine.** A giant timber pine of western U.S.

dour (dewr; dowr) *adj*. Gloomy; sullen; morose.

douse (*dowss*) *v*. [doused; dous·ing] 1. To drench; to immerse; to plunge into water. 2. To extinguish; to put out. 'Douse the lights.' 3. *Nautical*. To slacken hastily. 'Douse the topsail.'—**dous·er** *n*.

dove (duv) *n*. 1. The pigeon. 2. A term of endearment. 3. [*cap*.] The symbol of the Holy Ghost.

dove·cot *n*. Also **dove·cote.** A pigeon house; a small elevated structure for breeding pigeons.

dove·tail *n*. *Carpentry*. Joint made of interlocking wedges.—*v*. 1. To join by interlocking. 2. To adapt; to fit; to work together.

dow·a·ger (*dow-uh-jer*) *n*. 1. An elderly woman, esp. in society. 2. *Law*. Widow endowed with an estate.

dow·dy *adj*. [-di·er; -di·est] Drab; unfashionable; ungroomed.—*n*. [*pl*. -dies] 1. Shabby woman. 2. A fruit cobbler. 'Apple pan dowdy'—**dow·di·ly** *adv*.—**dow·di·ness** *n*.

dow·el *n*. Also **dowel pin.** A pin inserted into a grooved edge, as of a board, a stone slab, etc., for fastening.—*v*. [-eled, -elled; -el·ing, -el·ling] To fasten by inserting dowels.

dow·er *n*. 1. A gift. 2. The part of an estate awarded to a widow by law. 3. A dowry.

down *n*. 1. Soft feathers on the breasts of birds. 2. The soft hair of the face. 3. A tract of hilly pasture land.

down *adv*. 1. In a descending direction. 2. On the ground; at the bottom. 'He is down.' 3. To a smaller bulk. 'Boil it down.' 4. Condescendingly. 'To look down upon.'—*prep*. 1. Along a descent. 'Down a hill.' 2. Along a current. 'Down a stream.'—*v*. 1. To descend. 2. To overthrow; to subdue; to put down.—*n*. 1. A downward fluctuation; depression. 2. A low state. 'Ups and downs.' 3. *Football*. The length of a play; a play itself. —**down and out.** Poor; without funds.—**down at the heel.** Seedy; unprosperous looking. **down at the mouth.** Dejected; dispirited. —**down with.** Overthrow; put down.—**to be down on.** To have a grudge against.

down·cast *adj*. Dejected; dispirited.

down·fall *n*. 1. Ruin; destruction; loss. 2. A heavy descent.—**down·fall·en** *adj*.

down·heart·ed *adj*. Dejected; discouraged. —**down·heart·ed·ly** *adv*.—**down·heart·ed·ness** *n*.

down·hill *adv*. With a descending tendency; toward the bottom.—*adj*. Descending; sloping downward.

down·pour *n*. A heavy rain.

down·right *adj*. 1. Blunt; unceremonious. 2. Complete; thorough.—**down·right·ly** *adv*.

down·stairs *adv*. Below; to a lower floor.—*adj*. Pertaining to or located on the lower floor.—*n*.

down·stream *adv*. & *adj*. In the current's direction.

down·town *adv*. Toward the business section of a town, city, etc.—**down·town** *adj*. & *n*.

down·trod·den *adj*. Oppressed; tyrannized over.

down·ward, down·wards *adv*. 1. To a lower place. 2. From the source; from the origin.

down·ward *adj*. 1. Descending; moving toward a lower place, position, etc. 2. Descending from a source.—**down·ward·ly** *adv*. In a descending course.—**down·ward·ness** *n*.

down·wind *adv*. & *adj*. In the wind's direction.

down·y *adj*. [down·i·er; down·i·est] 1. Soft; calm; soothing. 2. Made of soft feathers. 3. Covered with fine hairs, as a plant.—**down·i·ness** *n*.

dow·ry (*dow-ree*) *n*. [*pl*. -ries] Property brought by a woman in marriage.

dox·ol·o·gy (dok-*sol*-uh-jee) *n*. [*pl*. -gies] A hymn in praise of God.—**dox·o·log·i·cal** (dok-suh-*loj*-uh-k'l) *adj*. Giving praise to God.

dox·y (*dok*-see) *n*. [*pl*. -ies] A wench; strumpet.

doze *v*. [dozed; doz·ing] To drowse; to sleep lightly.—*n*. A nap.—**doz·er** *n*.

doz·en (*duz*-'n) *n*. [*pl*. doz·ens, doz·en (preceding a noun)] Twelve of anything regarded as a unit.—**doz·enth** *adj*. Twelfth.

doz·y *adj*. [doz·i·er; doz·i·est] Drowsy; sluggish; inclined to sleep.—**doz·i·ly** *adv*.

drab *n*. A strumpet; prostitute; disreputable woman.—*v*. [drabbed; drab·bing] To associate with such women.

drab *adj*. [drab·ber; drab·best] 1. Dull; uninteresting; dreary; monotonous. 2. Of a dull color. 3. Brownish-yellow.—*n*. 1. A brownish-yellow color. 2. A coarse brown woolen cloth; khaki.—**drab·ly** *adv*.—**drab·ness** *n*.

drach·ma (*drak*-muh) *n*. [*pl*. -mas, -mae, -mai] A Greek coin worth less than a U.S. cent.

Dra·co·ni·an (druh-*koh*-nee-un) *adj*. 1. Pertaining to certain severe Athenian laws. 2. Concerning Draco, Athenian lawmaker. 3. *Astronomy*. Pertaining to the northern constellation, Draco.—**Dra·con·ic, -i·cal** *adj*.—**Dra·con·i·cal·ly** *adv*.

draft *n*. Also **draught.** 1. A call to military service. 2. An order upon a bank or individual directing payment. 3. An outline; a rough sketch. 4. A drawing; a plan. 5. A current of air. 6. A drink; a single inhalation of smoke.—*v*. 1. To call to military service. 2. To compose an outline.—*adj*. 1. For drawing. 'Draft horse; draft beer.' 2. Pertaining to compulsory military service. 'Draft notice.'—**draft·er** *n*. One who originates a plan.

draft·ee *n*. One ordered to military service.

drafts·man *n*. [*pl*. -men] A planner or designer, esp. of blueprints.—**drafts·man·ship** *n*.

draft·y *adj*. [draft·i·er; -i·est] Exposed to air currents; chilly.—**draft·i·ly** *adv*.—**draft·i·ness** *n*.

drag *v*. [dragged; drag·ging] 1. To pull; haul; draw along the ground. 2. To harrow; break land. 3. To search a body of water. 4. To proceed slowly.—*n.* 1. A net. 2. A kind of harrow for breaking ground. 3. Any weight retarding progress. 4. A skid; a device for stopping a wheel. 5. A heavy sled for hauling stones. 6. A laborious movement.

drag·gle *v.* [drag·gled; drag·gling] 1. To draw through mud. 2. To trail behind.

drag·gle·tail *n.* An unkempt woman.—**drag·gle·tail·ed** *adj.* Untidy; slatternly.

drag·net *n.* 1. Net drawn along a river bottom. 2. Any device for rounding up varied items.

drag·o·man (*drag*-oh-man) *n.* [*pl.* -mans, -men]. An interpreter; a guide, esp. in Egypt.

drag·on (*drag*-'n) *n.* 1. A mythical fire-breathing serpent having a crested head and enormous claws. 2. A small species of winged reptile of Asia and Africa. 3. Draco; a northern constellation. 4. A tyrannous and severe woman.

drag·on·fly *n.* An insect having a long, slender body, large eyes, and transparent gauzelike wings.

dra·goon (druh-*goon*) *n.* A British cavalry soldier. —*v.* To harass; to persecute; to coerce.

DRAGONFLY (life size)

drain *v.* 1. To filter; dry; empty of water or other liquid. 2. To exhaust; sap. —*n.* 1. A sewer; channel for carrying off excess water. 2. The process of emptying. —**drain·er** *n.* A stand or basket where articles are placed to drain.

drain·age (*drayn*-ij) *n.* 1. The means by which water is drawn off. 2. Water conveyed by a channel. 3. A flowing of liquid, as from a wound. 4. Area drained by a river system.

drake *n.* A male duck.

dram *n.* Also **drachm.** 1. A unit of weight for drugs; ⅛ ounce. 2. A small quantity of liquor. —*v.* [drammed; dram·ming] To drink spirits.

dra·ma (*drah*-muh; *dram*-) *n.* 1. A play; composition to be acted on the stage. 2. Arts connected with theatrical representation, as playwriting, acting, etc. 3. Excitement; emotional intensity; suspense.

dra·mat·ic (druh-*mat*-ik) *adj.* Also **dra·mat·i·cal.** 1. Theatrical; colorful; filled with suspenseful interest. 2. Vivid; striking. 3. Pertaining to the drama.—**dra·mat·i·cal·ly** *adv.*

dra·mat·ics *n. sing.* & *pl.* 1. Histrionics; acting. 2. Pretenses; guiles; behavior for effect.

dramatis personae (*dram*-uh-tis per-*soh*-nee). The cast of characters in a play.

dram·a·tist (*dram*-uh-tist) *n.* A playwright.

dram·a·tize (*dram*-uh-tyze) *v.* [-tized; -tiz·ing] 1. To compose in the form of a play. 2. To adapt for stage, radio, etc. 3. To make vivid. —**dram·a·ti·za·tion** (dram-uh-tih-*zay*-shun) *n.* —**dram·a·ti·zer** *n.*

dram·a·tur·gy (*dram*-uh-ter-jee) *n.* The technique of theatrical presentation, esp. the rules of staging.—**dram·a·tur·gic, -i·cal** *adj.* 1. Pertaining to theatrical presentation. 2. Theatrical; unreal.— **-tur·gi·cal·ly** *adv.*— **-tur·gist** *n.*

drape *v.* [draped; drap·ing] 1. To arrange cloth over. 2. To arrange in folds.—*n.* 1. A cloth covering. 2. A window hanging. 3. Part of a garment arranged in folds.

drap·er *n.* A dealer in fabrics.

dra·per·y *n.* [*pl.* -ies] Fabric used for hangings, esp. window hangings.—**dra·per·ied** *adj.*

dras·tic (*dras*-tik) *adj.* Extreme; harsh; severe. 'A drastic measure.'—**dras·ti·cal·ly** *adv.*

draughts (*drafts*) *n. British.* Checkers.

Dra·vid·i·an (druh-*vid*-ee-un) *n.* 1. A race of southern India. 2. A group of related languages of southern India.—**Dra·vid·ian** *adj.*

draw *v.* [drew; drawn; draw·ing] 1. To pull; haul; drag; bring; cause to move. 2. To extract. 'Draw water.' 3. To attract; compel; induce. 4. To inhale. 5. To pull together; pull apart. 'Draw a curtain.' 6. To delineate; represent by lines; form a picture. 7. To deduce; derive. 'Draw conclusions.' 8. To receive money. 'Draw a salary.' 9. To compose; draft. 10. To extend; sketch. 11. To disembowel. 'Draw and quarter.' 12. To take by chance. 'Draw a number.'—*n.* A game ending in equal scores.—**drawn** *adj.* 1. Gaunt; haggard. 2. Disemboweled.

draw·back *n.* An impediment; a hindrance.

draw·bridge *n.* A bridge built of movable platforms for the passage of vessels or to prevent passage of foot traffic.

DRAWBRIDGE

draw·er *n.* 1. A sliding compartment in a piece of furniture. 'Desk drawer.' 2. One who orders the payment of money, as on a draft. 3. [*pl.*] Shorts; trunks; underwear worn about the hips and legs.

draw·ing *n.* 1. A pictorial sketch. 2. The act of sketching. 3. Selection of winning chances in a lottery.—**draw·ing** *adj.*

drawing card. *Theater.* A feature, esp. a leading actor, effective in attracting audiences.

drawing room. A salon; living room; parlor for the reception of company.—**drawing-room** *adj.* Polite; formal. 'Drawing-room chat.'

draw·knife *n.* Also **drawing knife.** *Carpentry.* A knife used to cut the guide lines for a saw.

drawl *v.* To speak in a slow, dragging tone. —**drawl** *n.*—**drawl·er** *n.*—**drawl·ing·ly** *adv.*

drawn work. An ornamental pattern of thread running through a material, esp. linen.

draw·shave *n.* A drawknife; a knife used to cut the guide lines for a saw.

dray *n.* A low cart for heavy loads.—*v.* To cart.

dray·man *n.* One who loads or drives a dray.

D

dread (*dred*) *v.* To fear; to anticipate with alarm.—*n.* Awe; alarm; terror.—**dread** *adj.*

dread·ful *adj.* Frightening; inspiring terror; shocking.—**dread·ful·ly** *adv.*—**dread·ful·ness** *n.*

dread·naught, dread·nought (*dred*-nawt) *n.* 1. An obsolete type of battleship. 2. A fearless, redoubtable person.

dream *n.* 1. An illusion, esp. in sleep; a fancy. 2. A hope; a strong desire.—*v.* [dreamed, dreamt; dream·ing] 1. To have a hallucination in sleep. 2. To envision; imagine. 'Don't dream of such a thing!' 3. To muse; indulge in reverie.—**dream·ing·ly** *adv.*

dream·er *n.* A visionary; one given to inactive, often impractical musing.

dream·land *n.* Fairyland; any fanciful place.

dream·less *adj.* Without dreams.

dream·y *adj.* [dream·i·er; dream·i·est] 1. Indistinct; far away, as in a dream. 2. Visionary; musing; imbued with or inspiring dreams. —**dream·i·ly** *adv.* Abstractedly; in a preoccupied way.—**dream·i·ness** *n.*

drear *adj.* Dismal; mournful; dreary.

drear·y *adj.* [drear·i·er; drear·i·est] Dismal; gloomy; monotonous; tiresome; uninteresting.—**drear·i·ly** *adv.*—**drear·i·ness** *n.*

dredge *n.* A scoop; a dragnet; an apparatus for scooping under water.—*v.* [dredged; dredging] To scoop under water. 2. To dip in or sprinkle with flour.—**dredg·er** *n.* A machine for cleaning the beds of canals, rivers, harbors.

dregs *n. pl.* 1. Sediment; grounds; waste matter. 2 Something worthless.—**dreg·gy** *adj.*

drench *v.* 1. To saturate; wet completely; soak. 2. To purge forcibly, esp. an animal. —*n.* 1. A drink; a dose of liquid. 2. A solution for soaking.—**drench·er** *n.*

dress *n.* 1. Apparel; clothing; attire. 2. A gown; feminine outer garment. 3. Outer appearance; guise.—*v.* [dressed, drest; dress·ing] 1. To attire; clothe; put on clothes, esp. formal attire. 2. To prepare; ready for use; arrange. 3. To adorn; embellish; trim. 4. *Medicine.* To apply bandages or medication to. 'Dress a wound.' 5. *Military.* To form in a straight line.—*adj.* Formal; requiring evening clothes. 'A dress affair.'—**dress down.** 1. To understate; employ restraint. 2. To scold; rebuke.—**dress up.** To dress formally or showily; deck out.

dress·er *n.* 1. One who dresses; decorator. 2. A low chest of drawers, usually with a mirror. 3. A sideboard; cupboard.

dress·ing *n.* 1. A bandage; application for a wound. 2. Fertilizer; manure for crops. 3. A trimming for a dish, as sauce, stuffing, etc. 4. Act of clothing or preparing.

dressing gown. A robe for informal wear at home.

dressing room. A room for costume changes.

dress·mak·ing *n.* Craft or process of making dresses.—**dress·mak·ing** *adj.*— **-mak·er** *n.*

dress parade. A military review in dress uniform.

dress rehearsal. A practice performance in costume.

dress suit. A man's suit for formal occasions.

dress·y (*dres*-ee) *adj.* [dress·i·er; -i·est] Elaborate; for wear on gala occasions; showy. —**dress·i·ly** *adv.*—**dress·i·ness** *n.*

drib·ble (*drib*-'l) *v.* [-bled; -bling] 1. To trickle; fall in steady drops. 2. To drool; slobber. 3. *Sports.* To move a ball or puck by light kicks or taps.—*n.* 1. Act of dribbling a ball. 2. A trickling, as of water.—**drib·bler** *n.*

drib·let (*drib*-lit) *n.* A bit; small piece or amount; drop.

dri·er, dry·er *n.* A drying apparatus or agent.

drift *n.* 1. Act or direction of drifting; course; tendency. 2. That which drives; compelling force. 3. That which is driven, esp. by the wind. 'Drift of snow.' 4. *Geology.* Deposit formed by a river, glacier, etc. 5. *Mining.* A passage connecting shafts. 6. A tool for driving, esp. through metal. 7. Driftage.—*v.* 1. To be driven or carried along as by water or wind current. 2. To be driven into heaps by the wind.—**drift·er** *n.*—**drift·y** *adj.*—[drift·i·er; drift·i·est].

drift·age (*drift*-ij) *n.* 1. *Nautical.* Leeway; the amount of a ship's deviation from its course. 2. Act or result of drifting.

drift·wood *n.* Pieces of wood cast up on a shore or floating on water.

drill *n.* Also **drilling.** A coarse cotton cloth with a diagonal rib.

drill *n.* 1. A tool for perforating metal or other hard substances. 2. An implement for planting seeds in furrows. 3. A furrow; row of seeds in a furrow.—*v.* 1. To bore; perforate or pierce as with a drill. 2. To plant in furrows.—**drill·er** *n.*

drill *n.* 1. Repeated practice, exercise, or training. 2. Military exercise or training, esp. in the manual of arms.—*v.* 1. To teach by repeated exercise or practice. 2. To exercise military trainees.—**drill·er** *n.*

drill·mas·ter *n.* 1. A military trainer. 2. Instructor of gymnastic exercises.

dri·ly (*dry*-lee). *Variant spelling* of **dryly.**

drink *v.* [drank; drunk, drunk·en; drink·ing] 1. To imbibe; take liquid through the mouth. 2. To take alcoholic liquors, esp. habitually. 3. To absorb; take in through the senses. —*n.* 1. A swallow of liquid. 2. A beverage. 3. Alcoholic liquor.

drink·a·ble *adj.* Safe or suitable for drinking.

drink·er *n.* One who drinks; drunkard.

drip *v.* [dripped, dript; drip·ping] To leak; fall in slow drops.—*n.* 1. A slow fall of drops. 2. *Architecture.* A protecting cornice or strip to allow water to run off. 3. *Slang.* A dolt.

dripping pan. A utensil for receiving drippings.

drip·pings *n. pl.* Melted fat from roasted meat.

drive *v.* [drove; driv·en; driv·ing] 1. To impel; move before one by force. 2. To press; urge; constrain. 3. To propel; guide; keep in motion while directing the course of. 'Drive an automobile.' **4.** To force through, as by hammering. **5.** To hit hard, as a ball.—*n.* **1.** A short ride. **2.** A road; driveway. **3.** An onslaught; attack. **4.** Pressure; compulsion. 'The drive of business.' **5.** Energy; forcefulness. **6.** An impulse; compulsion. **7.** A special, sustained effort. 'A charity drive.' —**drive at.** To aim at; insinuate.—**drive off.** To chase; scatter.

drive-in *n.* Roadside cafe where waitresses bring trays of food out to customers in automobiles.

drive-in theater. An open-air motion picture theater located near a highway, so automobiles may drive in and park while the occupants view the film.

driv·el (*driv*-'l) *v.* [-eled, -elled; -el·ing, -el·ling] **1.** To drool at the mouth. **2.** To babble; talk senselessly.—*n.* **1.** Nonsense; meaningless talk. **2.** Saliva running from the mouth. —**driv·el·er, driv·el·ler** *n.*

driv·er (*dryve*-er) *n.* **1.** A chauffeur; coachman; engineer; one who propels a vehicle. **2.** *Mechanics.* A shaft, wheel, etc., for imparting force to machinery. **3.** A wooden-headed golf club for hitting the ball from the tee. **4.** A hammer or mallet. **5.** *Nautical.* A spanker; square sail.

drive·way (*dryve*-way) *n.* **1.** An alley; passage leading into a garage. **2.** A drive; highway.

driv·ing *n.* Process of propelling a vehicle or imparting energy.—*adj.* **1.** Tempestuous; violent; having great force. 'A driving wind.' **2.** Propelling a vehicle. 'A driving wheel.'

driz·zle (*driz*-'l) *v.* [driz·zled; driz·zling] To fall in tiny beads of moisture, as rain.—*n.* A rain of fine droplets.—**drizz·ly** *adj.*

droll (*drohl*) *adj.* Comic; queer; inspiring laughter.—*n.* **1.** A buffoon; clown; jester. **2.** A farce; laughter-inspiring exhibition.—*v.* To jest; play the clown.

droll·er·y (*drohl*-er-ee) *n.* [*pl.* -ies] **1.** Buffoonery; jesting; humor. **2.** A show, story, exhibition, etc., designed to cause mirth.

-drome *Suffix.* Runway, driveway, course, speedway. 'An airdrome.'

drom·e·dar·y (*drom*-uh-der-ee) *n.* [*pl.* -ies] A speedy, high-bred camel, having one hump.

drone *v.* [droned; dron·ing] **1.** To utter a low, humming sound, as a bee. **2.** To speak in dull, monotonous tones.—*n.* **1.** One who talks expressionlessly and tiresomely. **2.** A male bee. **3.** An idler.

DROMEDARY (1/70 life size)

drool *v.* **1.** To drivel; slobber; dribble at the mouth. **2.** To talk nonsensically.—*n.* Drivel.

droop *v.* **1.** To stoop; bend downward, as the head, the shoulders, etc. **2.** To hang limply. **3.** To languish; decline. 'His spirits drooped.' —*n.* **1.** A sag or decline. **2.** *Slang.* An uninteresting person.—**droop·ing·ly** *adv.*—**droop·y** *adj.* [-i·er; -i·est].

drop *v.* [dropped; drop·ping] **1.** To let fall. **2.** To dismiss; let go. **3.** To utter casually. 'Drop a hint.' **4.** To lower; fall; descend abruptly. **5.** To come down in small globules. **6.** To knock or bring down. **7.** *Cookery.* To poach, as eggs. **8.** To write informally. 'Drop me a note.'—*n.* **1.** A small liquid globule. **2.** A contrivance for lowering weights. **3.** *Theater.* A stage hanging representing scenery. **4.** An abrupt fall or decline. **5.** An object resembling a drop. 'Lemon drop.' **6.** The distance of a fall. **7.** An advantage gained by speedy action. 'Get the drop on them.' **8.** An aperture through which letters are let fall. **9.** [*pl.*] A medicinal dosage administered in drops.

drop-forge *v.* [-forged; -forg·ing] To shape metal by hammering with dies while it is hot. —**drop-forg·ing** *n.* **1.** Forging of metal by hammering with dies. **2.** A metal article so shaped.—**drop-forg·er** *n.*

drop hammer *n.* Also **drop press.** A machine for stamping or forging metal.

drop in. To pay an informal call.

drop kick. *Football.* A kick made after first bouncing the ball on the ground.—**drop-kick** *v.*—**drop-kick·er** *n.*

drop·let (*drop*-lit) *n.* A tiny drop.

drop·per (*drop*-er) *n.* **1.** A glass tube, often with rubber bulb, for medicated drops. **2.** *Mining.* A vein branching off from the main lode.

drop·pings *n. pl.* Manure; dung.

drop·sy (*drop*-see) *n.* Disease characterized by infiltration of fluid in body cavities or tissues. —**drop·si·cal, drop·sied** *adj.*—**drop·si·cal·ly** *adv.*

drosh·ky, dros·ky (*drosh*-kee) *n.* [*pl.* -kies] A light, four-wheeled Russian carriage, esp. one in which the passengers ride by straddling a bench.

DROSHKY

Dro·soph·i·la (druh-*sof*-ih-luh) *n.* [*pl.* -lae] A family of insects to which the fruitfly belongs.

dross *n.* **1.** Slag; waste derived from processing metal. **2.** Refuse; scum; waste matter.

drought (*drowt*) *n.* Also **drouth.** Aridity; dry weather; lack of rain.—**drought·y** *adj.*

drove (*drohv*) *n.* **1.** A flock; herd; collection of animals. **2.** A crowd advancing together. **3.** A stonecutter's chisel.—*v.* [droved; drov·ing] **1.** To herd; drive animals. **2.** To finish the surface of stone.

dro·ver *n.* **1.** A driver of cattle to market. **2.** A cattle dealer.

drown *v.* **1.** To suffocate in fluid, esp. water. **2.** To overpower; negate; overwhelm. **3.** To submerge; put out of mind. 'Drown your sorrows.'

drowse (*drowz*) v. [drowsed; drows·ing] To doze; nap intermittently.—**drowse** n.

drow·sy (*drow*-zee) adj. [drow·si·er; drow·si·est] 1. Sleepy; half awake. 2. Lethargic; sluggish; dull.—**drow·si·ly** adv.—**drow·si·ness** n.

drub v. [drubbed; drub·bing] 1. To thump; rap or beat with a stick; thrash. 2. To defeat or vanquish. 3. To stamp the feet.—**drub** n.

drub·bing n. A cudgeling; thrashing; sound beating; defeat.

drudge (*druj*) v. [drudged; drudg·ing] 1. To toil; work hard, esp. at menial tasks. 2. To do monotonous, fatiguing work at small pay. —n. A worker at menial or monotonous tasks.

drudg·er·y (*druj*-er-ee) n. [pl. -ies] 1. Menial, tiresome labor. 2. Monotonous toil.

drug n. 1. A medical preparation. 2. A narcotic; habit-forming preparation. 3. An item for which there is little or no sale. 'A drug on the market.'—v. [drugged; drug·ging] 1. To dose with narcotics. 2. To anesthetize.

drug·gist (*drug*-ist) n. 1. A pharmacist; apothecary; mixer of drugs. 2. A drug store owner.

drug store n. A pharmacy; shop that sells drugs and miscellaneous small articles.

dru·id (*droo*-id) n. Member of an ancient Celtic religion.—**dru·id·ic** (droo-*id*-k), **-i·cal** adj.

drum n. 1. A percussion instrument composed of a hollow cylinder covered with hide. 2. The hollow part of the inner ear; ear drum. 3. A large, round, metal container or barrel. 4. The revolving cylinder in a machine. 5. A sound of or like a drum. —v. [drummed; drum·ming] 1. To beat a drum. 2. To tap with the fingers. 3. To din; resound. 4. To instruct by tireless repetition. 5. To rap or beat in a rhythmic pattern.—**drum up**. To recruit; solicit; garner, esp. business or sales.

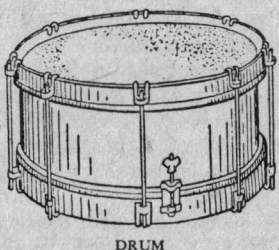

DRUM

drum·fire n. A rapid staccato discharge of guns.

drum·head (*drum*-hed) n. 1. The top of a drum. 2. The end of a capstan that holds levers for turning. 3. The tympanum or eardrum.

drum major. 1. The chief drummer of a regiment. 2. The leader of a military band.

drum·mer n. 1. A performer on a drum. 2. A traveling salesman.

drum·stick n. 1. A stick used to beat a drum. 2. The lower joint of a fowl's leg.

drunk adj. 1. Intoxicated; inebriated; overcome by alcohol. 2. Frenzied; stupefied.—n. 1. *Slang*. An intoxicated person. 2. A fit of drunkenness.

drunk·ard (*drunk*-erd) n. An inebriate; an alcoholic; a person addicted to liquor.

drunk·en adj. 1. Habitually intoxicated. 2. Done in a state of intoxication.—**drunk·en·ly** adv.—**drunk·en·ness** n.

drupe n. *Botany*. A fruit whose single seed is inside a hard pit surrounded by pulpy flesh, as the peach.—**dru·pa·ceous** (droo-*pay*-shus) adj.

drupe·let (*droop*-let) n. *Botany*. A fruit with many small drupes, as a blackberry.

dry adj. [dri·er; dri·est] 1. Arid; not moist. 2. Thirsty; craving drink. 3. Boring; uninteresting. 4. Without tears. 5. Not yielding milk. 6. Unsweetened, as dry wine. 7. Laconic; characterized by understatement. 'Dry humor.'—v. [dried; dry·ing] 1. To desiccate; free of moisture. 2. To deprive of sap, juice, etc. 'Dry hay.'—**dry·ness** n.—**dry up**. To wither; shrivel.—n. [pl. drys] A prohibitionist.

dry·ad (*dry*-ad) n. [pl. -ads, -ades] *Greek Mythology*. A wood nymph.—**dry·ad·ic** adj.

dry cell. A battery whose electrolyte is absorbed and sealed to prevent its escape.

dry-clean v. To clean garments, draperies, etc., by chemical treatment.—**dry cleaner**. A person or establishment cleaning with chemicals. —**dry cleaning**. Process of cleaning fabric by chemical treatment.

dry dock. A dock, from which water may be pumped, for repairing ships.—**dry-dock** v. To bring a ship in for repairs.

dry farming. The raising of drought-resistant crops.—**dry-farm** v. 1. To conserve the natural moisture of farmland. 2. To raise crops needing little moisture.—**dry farm, dry farmer**.

dry goods. Textile fabrics; cloth, ribbon, etc.

Dry Ice. Trade-mark for a refrigerant made of solidified carbon dioxide.

dry law. *Colloquial*. A law enforcing prohibition.

dry·ly adv. Also **drily**. 1. With quiet humor; sarcastically. 2. Without embellishment.

dry measure. A system for measuring the volume of solid articles, in pecks, bushels, etc.

dry point. 1. Process of engraving without acid. 2. An etching engraved without acid.

dry rot. A decay of timber caused by fungi.

dry run. *Aviation Slang*. Practice flight, esp. one without ammunition.

d.t.'s *Slang*. Delirium tremens; mental incapacity caused by alcoholic poisoning.

du·al (*doo*-ul) adj. 1. Double; twofold. 'A dual personality.' 2. Expressing the number 2.—**du·al·i·ty** (doo-*al*-ih-tee) n. 1. A division; separation into two parts. 2. State of being twofold.

du·al·ism (*doo*-ul-izm) n. 1. A twofold division. 2. A philosophical theory based on two divergent principles, the materialistic and the spiritual elements in human nature. 3. A theological doctrine based on two divergent assertions, as the coexistence of good and evil. —**du·al·ist** n.—**du·al·is·tic** (doo-uh-*lis*-tik) adj.

dub v. [dubbed; dub·bing] 1. To name; refer to as. 2. To knight. 3. To dress or rub till smoothly finished. 4. *Slang*. To execute clumsily. 5. *Motion Pictures*. To incorporate sound upon a film. 'To dub in.'

dub *n. Slang*. A clumsy player.

du·bi·e·ty (doo-*by*-uh-tee) *n.* [*pl.* -ties] Doubtfulness; uncertainty.

du·bi·ous (doo-bee-us) *adj.* 1. Doubtful; uncertain. 2. Open to unpleasant interpretation.—**du·bi·ous·ly** *adv.*—**du·bi·ous·ness** *n.*

du·cal (doo-k'l) *adj.* Pertaining to a duke.

duc·at (duk-it) *n.* 1. [*pl.*] *Slang*. Money. 2. The gold monetary unit of several European countries.

du·ce (doo-cheh) *n. Colloquial*. A dictator.—**Il Duce**. The title of Benito Mussolini, former Italian fascist leader.

duch·ess (duch-is) *n.* The consort of a duke.

duch·y (duch-ee) *n.* [*pl.* -ies] A dukedom; the dominion of a duke.

duck *n.* 1. A domestic web-footed water fowl. 2. A swimming wild fowl. 3. *Military*. An amphibious weapon and personnel carrier.

duck *n.* 1. A coarse cloth resembling canvas, for sails, bed ticking, etc. 2. [*pl.*] *Colloquial*. Trousers made of duck.

DUCK (1/15 life size)

duck *v.* 1. To stoop into water. 2. To plunge the head into water. 3. To make a dodging movement with the head. 4. *Slang*. To dodge; stoop in hiding. —*n.* 1. A nod; dodging movement of the head, as in boxing. 2. *Slang*. A chap.

duck·bill *n.* Also **duck mole**. The platypus; an egg-laying, aquatic Australian mammal having webbed feet and the bill of a duck.

ducking stool. A chair fixed at the end of a beam, on which evildoers were ducked as punishment.

duck·ling (duk-ling) *n.* A young duck.

duck·pin. A small tenpin; target in bowling.

duck·weed *n.* A fresh-water plant eaten by ducks.

duck·y (duk-ee) *adj. Slang*. Pleasing; satisfying.

duct *n.* 1. A canal; tube; passage for water or other fluid. 2. An enclosed passage for wires, cables, etc.

duc·tile (duk-t'l) *adj.* 1. Capable of being drawn out in threads. 'A ductile metal.' 2. Tractable; pliant; yielding.—**duc·til·i·ty** (duk-til-uh-tee) *n.* 1. Flexibility; compliance. 2. The property enabling metals to be drawn out in threads.

ductless gland. A gland discharging its secretion directly into the blood stream.

dud *n.* 1. An unexploded shell. 2. *Slang*. Any failure. 3. [*pl.*] *Slang*. Attire; clothes.

dude (dooc?) *n.* An overdressed, affected man; dandy; fop.—**dud·ish** *adj.*

dude ranch. A resort styled after a western ranch.

dudg·eon (duj-un) *n.* Bad temper; ill humor.

due (dyoo; doo) *adj.* 1. Owing. 'Respect due to age.' 2. Appropriate; suitable; required by circumstances. 'With due solemnity.' 3. Expected; stipulated to arrive. 'Mail is due.'—*n.* 1. Right; just title. 'Obedience is his due.' 2. [*pl.*] A fee; monetary obligation, esp. to an organization.—*adv.* Directly. 'Due east.'

du·el (dyoo-ul; doo-) *n.* 1. A formal combat between two persons with deadly weapons. 2. Any contest between two persons.—*v.* [-eled, -elled; -el·ing, -el·ling] To engage in a duel.—**du·el·er, du·el·ler, du·el·ist, du·el·list** *n.*

du·el·lo (doo-el-oh) *n.* [*pl.* -los] The code of rules regulating dueling.

du·en·na (doo-en-uh) *n.* [*pl.* -nas] A governess; companion to a young woman, esp. in Spain.

du·et (doo-et) *n. Music*. A composition intended for two voices or instruments.

duff *n.* A pudding made by boiling flour and other ingredients in a bag.

duf·fel (duf-'l) *n.* 1. A cloth having a thick nap. 2. *Colloquial*. Camping supplies.—**duffel bag**. *Military*. A heavy cloth bag for personal gear.

duf·fer (duf-er) *n.* 1. *Slang*. A fogey; person of old-fashioned habits. 2. An ineffectual person. 3. A peddler. 4. *Golf*. A dub.

dug *n.* A pap; teat; udder; breast.

dug·out *n.* 1. A canoe hewn out of a log. 2. An excavation, as on the side of a hill, for the protection of soldiers. 3. *Baseball*. The sideline shelter where players await their turn at bat, the manager watches play, etc.

duke (dyook; dook) *n.* Hereditary nobleman next under prince.—**duke·dom** (dyook-d'm) *n.* The jurisdiction or title of a duke.

dul·cet (dul-sit) *adj.* Harmonious; sweet-sounding.

dul·ci·mer (dul-sih-mer) *n.* A musical instrument with wire strings struck by padded hammers.

dul·cin·e·a (dul-sin-ee-uh) *n.* 1. [*cap.*] Beloved of Don Quixote. 2. Object of one's love.

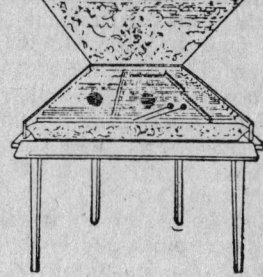

DULCIMER

dull *adj.* 1. Stupid; slow of understanding. 2. Heavy; sluggish; without spirit. 'To feel dull.' 3. Sleepy; drowsy. 4. Cheerless; not exhilarating. 'A dull party.' 5. Dim; not bright. 'A dull glow.' 6. Cloudy; overcast. 'Dull weather.' 7. Blunt; not sharp. 'A dull blade.'—*v.* 1. To stupefy; make insensible. 'To dull the mind.' 2. To tarnish; cloud. 'To dull a mirror.' 3. To blunt; make less sharp.—**dull·ish** *adj.*—**dul·ly** *adv.*—**dull·ness, dul·ness** *n.*

D

dull·ard (*dul*-erd) *n.* A dunce; dolt; stupid person.

dulse (*dulss*) *n.* An edible seaweed.

du·ly (*doo*-lee) *adv.* 1. Properly; in a suitable manner. 2. At the proper time.

Du·ma (*doo*-muh) *n.* The lower house of the Russian parliament from 1905 to 1917.

dumb (*dum*) *adj.* 1. Mute; incapable of speech. 2. *Colloquial.* Stupid; ignorant.—**dumb·ly** *adv.*—**dumb·ness** *n.*—**to strike dumb.** To confound; astonish; render speechless.

Dumbarton Oaks (dum-*bahr*-t'n). The place in Washington, D. C., where preliminary plans were drawn in 1944 for the United Nations.

dumb·bell (*dum*-bell) *n.* 1. An exercising weight with large round ends. 2. *Slang.* A dolt; stupid person.

dumb show. A pantomime.

dumb·wait·er *n.* An elevator moving on pulleys to convey food or refuse between floors.

dum·dum *n.* A soft-nosed bullet which expands on striking and makes a large wound.

dum·my (*dum*-ee) *n.* [*pl.* -mies] 1. A counter test article for display. 'A dummy carton.' 2. A manikin; figure for practicing football tackles, etc. 3. *Bridge.* The player holding an exposed hand. 4. *Printing.* A plan of make-up for a publication. 5. *Slang.* A dumb or silent person; stupid person. 6. One who acts for another while pretending to act for himself.—**dum·my** *adj.*

dump *v.* 1. To toss in a heap. 2. To unload dirt, rubbish, etc. 3. To sell at a low price. —*n.* 1. A depositing ground for rubbish; outdoor storage place. 2. *Slang.* A hovel; mean residence.—**dump·er** *n.*—**dump cart.** Cart with a movable body for unloading.

dump·ling (*dump*-ling) *n.* A round piece of baked or steamed dough served with meat, fruit, etc.

dumps *n. pl.* Low spirits.

dump·y (*dump*-ee) *adj.* [-i·er; -i·est] 1. Squat; short and thick. 2. Sullen; sulky; gloomy.

dun *n.* [dunned; dun·ning] To make emphatic demands for payment.—*n.* 1. An urgent demand for payment. 2. A person who duns.

dun *n.* Grayish brown.—*adj.* 1. Of a grayish brown color. 2. Dull; of a drab color.

dunce (*dunss*) *n.* An ignoramus; dullard; dolt. —**dunce·cap, dunce's cap.** A pointed cap formerly worn by schoolboys as a penalty for learning slowly.

dun·der·head (*dun*-der-hed) *n.* A dunce; blunderer; blockhead.—**dun·der·head·ed** *adj.*

dune (*doon*) *n.* A low hill or ridge of sand.

dung *n.* Manure; animal excrement.—*v.* To spread with dung.—**dung·y** *adj.* 1. Resembling dung. 2. Covered with dung.

dun·ga·ree (dung-guh-*ree*) *n.* 1. A coarse cotton fabric. 2. [*pl.*] Coarse work clothes.

dun·geon (*dun*-jun) *n.* 1. A medieval prison. 2. A dark underground cell.

dung·hill *n.* 1. A manure pile; dung heap. 2. Anything low or vile.

dunk *v. Slang.* To dip in liquid before eating.

Dun·kirk (*dun*-kerk). The French coastal town from which British army remnants fled the continent in May, 1940.

dun·nage (*dun*-ij) *n.* 1. Baggage. 2. *Nautical.* Boards, paper, etc., placed around cargo.

du·o (*doo*-oh) *n.* [*pl.* du·os, du·i] A duet; harmony by two singers or musical instruments.

du·o·dec·i·mal (doo-oh-*des*-ih-m'l) *adj.* 1. Consisting of twelve. 2. Computed by twelves. —*n.* 1. Computation by twelves. 2. A twelfth. 3. [*pl.*] System of numbers computed by twelves rather than tens.

du·o·dec·i·mo (doo-oh-*des*-ih-moh) *n.* [*pl.* -mos] 1. Sheet folded into twelve leaves. 2. Book made up of such leaves. *Abbreviation:* 12mo or 12°.—*adj.* Having twelve leaves to a sheet. 'Duodecimo form.'

du·o·de·num (doo-oh-*dee*-num) *n.* [*pl.* -na] The first part of the small intestine, near the stomach.—**du·o·den·al** *adj.*

dupe (*doop*) *n.* Person who is easily deceived; one who has been tricked.—*v.* [duped; duping] To trick; deceive.—**dup·a·ble** *adj.*—**dup·er** *n.*—**dup·er·y** *n.* [*pl.* -ies].

du·ple (*dyoo*-p'l, *doo*-p'l) *adj.* Double.

du·plex (*doo*-pleks) *adj.* Double; twofold.—**du·plex·i·ty** (doo-*plek*-suh-tee) *n.*

duplex apartment. An apartment with rooms on two floors.—**duplex house.** Two-family house.

du·pli·cate (*doo*-plih-kayt) *adj.* 1. Double; twofold. 2. Resembling or corresponding to another.—*n.* 1. An exact copy; carbon; facsimile. 2. A form of whist or bridge.—*v.* [-cat·ed; -cat·ing] To make an exact copy of.

du·pli·ca·tion (doo-plih-*kay*-shun) *n.* 1. The act of duplicating. 2. A duplicate.—**du·pli·ca·tive** (*doop*-luh-kay-tiv) *adj.*

du·pli·ca·tor *n.* A duplicating machine.

du·plic·i·ty (doo-*plis*-uh-tee) *n.* [*pl.* -ties] Deceit; treachery; double-dealing.

du·ra·ble (*dyoor*-uh-b'l) *adj.* Lasting; strong; enduring.—**du·ra·bil·i·ty** (dyoor-uh-*bil*-uh-tee), **du·ra·ble·ness** *n.*—**du·ra·bly** *adv.*

Du·ral·u·min (dyoo-*ral*-yuh-min, doo-) *n.* Trade-mark name of a strong, lightweight aluminum alloy.

dur·ance (*dyoor*-'ns, door-) *n.* Imprisonment.

du·ra·tion (dyoo-*ray*-sh'n, doo-*ray*-sh'n) *n.* Continuance in time; length of existence.

dur·bar (*der*-bahr) *n.* An official reception or levee in India.

du·ress (dyoo-*ress*; -ress) *n.* Coercion; force.

Dur·ham (*der*-um) *n.* A variety of beef cattle, first bred in Durham, England.

dur·ing (*doo*-ring, dyoo-) *prep.* In the time, or throughout the course of.

Du·roc-Jer·sey (dyoo-*rok-jer*-zee, doo-) *n.* An American variety of red hog.

du·rum (*dyoo*-rum, doo-) *n.* Also **durum wheat.** Wheat used in making flour for macaroni, etc.

dusk *n.* 1. Late twilight. 2. Shade; gloom darkness.—*adj.* Swarthy.—*v.* To darken.

dusk·y (*dus*-kee) *adj.* [-i·er; -i·est] **1.** Obscure; gloomy. **2.** Swarthy; dark-colored.—**dusk·i·ly** *adv.*—**dusk·i·ness** *n.*

dust *n.* **1.** Fine dry particles of earth; any fine powder. **2.** Remains of a dead body; decayed matter. **3.** Humble or worthless object or condition. **4.** *Slang.* Money; cash.—*v.* **1.** To wipe or sweep away dust. **2.** To strew with dust or powder; sprinkle.—**dust·less** *adj.*

dust-begrimed	dust counter	dustpan
dust box	dust-covered	dust plate
dust brush	dust dry	dust-polluted
dust cloth	dust gray	dustproof
dust-colored	dust-laden	dust-soiled

dust bowl. A western plains area of the U.S. where drought has destroyed vegetation, enabling dust storms to carry away the topsoil.

dust·er (*dus*-ter) *n.* **1.** Person or implement that dusts. **2.** A light overcoat.

dust·pan *n.* A pan with a short handle for holding dust brushed from the floor.

dust storm. Strong hot wind carrying dust.

dust·y (*dus*-tee) *adj.* [-i·er; -i·est] Like or covered with dust.—**dust·i·ly** *adv.*—**dust·i·ness** *n.*

Dutch *adj.* **1.** Pertaining to the Netherlands or its inhabitants. **2.** *Slang.* German.—*n.* **1.** The inhabitants of the Netherlands. **2.** The language of the Dutch.—**beat the Dutch.** To be amazing; outdo everything.—**go Dutch.** To pay for one's own share.—**in Dutch.** In trouble.

Dutch door. A door divided so that the top and bottom halves may be opened separately.

Dutch·man *n.* **1.** A native or inhabitant of the Netherlands. **2.** *Slang.* A German.

Dutch·man's-breeches *n. sing. & pl.* A wild spring plant bearing white flowers.

Dutch oven. **1.** A heavy pan with a close-fitting cover for baking or braising over a flame. **2.** An oven, usually next to a fireplace, in which baking or roasting is done by accumulated heat.

Dutch treat. *Colloquial.* A treat at which each person pays for himself.

Dutch uncle. *Colloquial.* One who criticizes severely, but fairly.

du·te·ous (*dyoo*-tee-us, *doo-*) *adj.* Obedient; dutiful.—**du·te·ous·ly** *adv.*—**du·te·ous·ness** *n.*

du·ti·a·ble (*dyoo*-tee-uh-b'l, *doo-*) *adj.* Subject to a duty or customs tax.

du·ti·ful (*dyoo*-tif-'l; *doo-*) *adj.* Obedient; respectful; proceeding from a sense of duty.—**du·ti·ful·ly** *adv.*—**du·ti·ful·ness** *n.*

du·ty (*dyoo*-tee; *doo-*) *n.* [*pl.* du·ties] **1.** Obligation; responsibility; required conduct or service. **2.** Task; job; assignment. **3.** A tax; payment made to the government on manufactured, imported, or exported articles.

du·ve·tyn (*doo*-vuh-teen) *n.* Also **du·ve·tine, du·ve·tyne.** A soft, velvety woolen fabric.

dwarf *n.* Any person, animal, or plant much below the ordinary size of its kind.—*v.* **1.** To stunt; make or keep small. **2.** To cause to look small by comparison.—**dwarf** *adj.*

dwarf·ish *adj.* Extremely small; like a dwarf. —**dwarf·ish·ly** *adv.*—**dwarf·ish·ness** *n.*

dwell *v.* [dwelt, dwelled; dwell·ing] **1.** To live; reside; lodge. **2.** To remain.—**dwell·er** *n.*

dwell·ing (*dwel*-ing) *n.* House; residence.

dwin·dle (*dwin*-d'l) *v.* [-dled; -dling] To decrease; shrink.

DX. *Radio.* Distance.

Dy·ak (*dy*-ak) *n.* Member of a primitive tribe in Borneo.

dye *v.* [dyed; dye·ing] To stain; give a new and permanent color to.—*n.* **1.** Liquid coloring matter. **2.** Color imparted by dyeing.—**dy·er** *n.*—**dye·ing** *n.*—**dyed·in·the·wool.** Complete.

dye·stuff *n.* Substance used in dyeing.

dy·ing. *Present participle* of **die.**—*adj.* **1.** Pertaining to death. **2.** Perishing; about to die; drawing to a close.—*n.* Death; loss of life.

dy·nam·ic (dy-*nam*-ik) *adj.* Also **dy·nam·i·cal.** **1.** Intense; forceful; potent. **2.** *Physics.* Pertaining to force or energy.— **-i·cal·ly** *adv.*

dy·nam·ics (dy-*nam*-iks) *n.* **1.** Branch of physics dealing with the action of force in the motion of bodies. **2.** Forces of any kind or their study. **3.** *Music.* Variations in volume.

dy·na·mism (*dy*-nuh-mizm) *n.* **1.** *Philosophy.* Any doctrine that regards force as the basis of the universe. **2.** *Anthropology.* A primitive religious attitude, which worships the forces of nature in themselves, not as gods.

dy·na·mite (*dy*-nuh-myte) *n.* Highly explosive substance mainly composed of nitroglycerine. —*v.* To destroy with dynamite.—**dy·na·mit·er** *n.*

dy·na·mo (*dy*-nuh-moh) *n.* [*pl.* -mos] A machine which converts mechanical into electrical energy.

dy·na·mo·e·lec·tric *adj.* Also **dy·na·mo·e·lec·tri·cal.** Used in converting mechanical energy into electrical energy or vice versa.

dy·na·mom·e·ter (dy-nuh-*mom*-uh-ter) *n.* An instrument for measuring power.

dy·na·mo·tor (*dy*-nuh-moh-ter) *n.* A dynamo usable either as a generator or as a motor.

dy·nast *n.* A ruler; governor; prince.

dy·nas·ty (*dy*-nus-tee) *n.* [*pl.* -ties] A succession of rulers of the same family line.

dy·na·tron (*dy*-nuh-tron) *n.* A three-electrode vacuum tube in which the current is decreased as the voltage increases.

dyne *n.* *Physics.* A unit of force sufficient to accelerate a one-gram mass one centimeter per second, during a period of one second.

dys·en·ter·y (*dis*-un-tehr-ee) *n.* Inflammation of the large intestine, accompanied by pain in the abdomen and rectal discharge of blood.—**dys·en·ter·ic** (dis-un-*tehr*-ik) *adj.*

dys·gen·ics (dis-*jen*-iks) *n.* The science which deals with inherited defects.

dys·pep·si·a (dis-*pep*-shuh) *n.* Indigestion.

dys·pep·tic (dis-*pep*-tik) *n.* A person suffering from indigestion.—**dys·pep·tic, dys·pep·ti·cal** *adj.*—**dys·pep·ti·cal·ly** *adv.*

dys·pro·si·um (dis-*proh*-zee-um) *n.* A rare earth element, highly magnetic. (*Symbol:* Dy).

D

E

each (*eech*) *adj.* Every.—*pronoun.* Everyone.
—*adv.* Apiece; separately; for each.

ea·ger (*ee*-ger) *adj.* Earnest; enthusiastic; ardent; impetuous.—**ea·ger·ly** *adv.*— -ger·ness *n.*

ea·gle (*ee*-g'l) *n.* 1. A large, powerful, keen-eyed predatory bird of the falcon family. 2. A ten-dollar gold piece. 3. The U.S. national emblem.

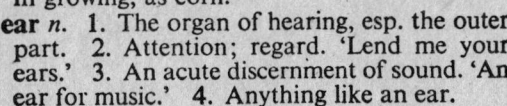

eagle-billed   eagle-sighted
eagle eye   eaglestone
eagle-eyed   eagle-winged

ea·glet (*ee*-glit) *n.* An immature eagle.

ear (*eer, ihr*) *n.* The seed-bearing part of a grain plant.—*v.* To form an ear in growing, as corn.

EAGLE (1/35 life size)

ear *n.* 1. The organ of hearing, esp. the outer part. 2. Attention; regard. 'Lend me your ears.' 3. An acute discernment of sound. 'An ear for music.' 4. Anything like an ear.

earache   ear-minded   eartab
earhole   earpiece   earwitness
earlap   earplug   earworm

ear·drop *n.* 1. A pendant type of earring. 2. Medicated fluid dropped into the ear.

ear·drum *n.* Membrane of the ear, whose vibrations cause sounds to be heard; tympanum.

earl (*erl*) *n.* A British nobleman ranking just below a marquis.—**earl·ship** *n.*—**earl·dom** *n.* The title, privileges, and property of an earl.

ear·ly (*er*-lee) *adj.* [-li·er; -li·est] 1. Ahead in time; advanced; premature. 2. Denoting ancient times. 3. In the near future; occurring soon.—*adv.* Soon; in good season.

ear·mark *n.* A distinctive characteristic or mark.—*v.* 1. To brand; identify with a mark. 2. To single out.

earn (*ern*) *v.* 1. To receive compensation for service rendered. 2. To deserve or merit recognition.—**earn·er** *n.*

ear·nest (*er*-nest) *n.* Pledge to bind a bargain. —*adj.* 1. Ardent; eager; zealous. 2. Sincere; serious.—**ear·nest·ly** *adv.*— -nest·ness *n.*

earn·ings (*ern*-ingz) *n. pl.* Wages; income.

ear·phone *n.* A set of telephonic receivers which clamp over the ears.

ear·ring *n.* An ear ornament.—**ear·ringed** *adj.*

ear·shot *n.* Distance over which sounds may be heard.

earth (*erth*) *n.* 1. Planet inhabited by the human race. 2. Dry land as opposed to sea. 3. Dirt and other materials which form the surface of the globe. 4. Inhabitants of the globe

EARPHONE

collectively. 5. Any noncrystalline, easily pulverized mineral.

earthbank   earthlight   earth sounds
earth-bred   earth maker   earth-stained
earthfast   earth making   earth-strewn
earth-fed   earthnut   earth wall
earth god   earthshock   earth-wide

earth-born *adj.* 1. Mortal; human; not godly. 2. Stemming from worldly desires; ignoble.

earth-bound *adj.* Literal-minded; unimaginative.

earth·en (*er*-thun) *adj.* Made of clay or soil.

earth·en·ware *n.* Pottery and other articles made of fire-hardened clay.

earth·ling (*erth*-ling) *n.* A mortal; creature of human frailties; worldly person.

earth·ly (*erth*-lee) *adj.* 1. Belonging to this world or this life; worldly; not spiritual. 2. *Colloquial.* Possible. 'What earthly use is it?'—**earth·li·ness** *n.*

earth·quake (*erth*-kwayk) *n.* A tremor of the earth produced by subterranean volcanic forces.

earth·ward (*erth*-werd), **earth·wards** *adv.* Toward the earth.—**earth·ward** *adj.*

earth·work *n.* 1. Removal of, or banking up of, earth. 2. Embankment; earthen fortification.

earth·worm *n.* One of several worms which live in rich, moist soil.

earth·y (*erth*-ee) *adj.* [-i·er; -i·est] 1. Relating to the earth. 2. Gross; coarse; indelicate. 3. Wholesome; elemental; strong and uncomplex.—**earth·i·ness** *n.*

ear·wax *n.* The secretion of the outer ear.

ear·wig *n.* 1. A beetlelike plant pest. 2. Any of several types of centipede.

ease (*eez*) *n.* Rest; tranquillity; freedom from pain, difficulty, or formality.—**at ease.** 1. Free from anxiety. 2. *Military.* Relaxing while holding ranks.—**ill at ease.** In a disturbed state. —*v.* [eased; eas·ing] 1. To relieve; free from pain or anxiety. 2. To release from pressure. —*Nautical.* **ease off** or **ease away.** To slacken a ship's line gradually.—**ease the helm** or **ease her.** To return a ship's wheel to center.

ea·sel (*ee*-z'l) *n.* A tripod for supporting a painter's canvas.

ease·ment (*eez*-m'nt) *n.* 1. A comfort; accommodation; convenience. 2. *Law.* Some right one may have over another's land, such as a right of way.

eas·i·ly (*eez*-uh-lee) *adv.* Without difficulty; readily; smoothly; gently.

eas·i·ness (*eez*-ee-nes) *n.* 1. Ease; freedom from difficulty. 2. Affability; flexibility; compliability. 3. Freedom from constraint.

east *n.* 1. One of the four cardinal points of the compass, directly opposite west. 2. Territory lying toward the east. 3. [*cap.*] **a.** The countries of Asia; the Orient. **b.** *U.S.* Area lying east of the Mississippi River.—*adj.* At, from, in, or of the east.—*adv.* To or in the east.

east by north, east by south. See compass.

East·er (*ees*-ter). Feast day of the Christian Church to celebrate the Resurrection of Christ; first Sunday after the full moon on, or next following, March 21.

Easter egg. A colored or ornamented egg used as an Easter gift or decoration.

east·er·ly (*eest*-er-lee) *n.* [*pl.* -lies] A wind blowing from the east.—*adj. & adv.* To, toward, from, or of the east.—**east·er·li·ness** *n.*

east·ern (*eest*-ern) *adj.* 1. Of, to, in, toward, or from the east. 2. [*cap.*] Pertaining to the East; Oriental.—**east·ern·most** *adj.*

east·ern·er *n.* 1. A dweller in the east. 2. [*cap.*] Native of eastern U.S.

Eastern Hemisphere. The half of the earth which includes Europe, Asia, and Africa.

East·er·tide (*ees*-ter-tyde) *n.* A period variously calculated from Easter to Ascension Day, Whitsunday, or Trinity Sunday.

East Indies. 1. A term first used to distinguish India and the Malay Archipelago from the West Indies. 2. Indonesia; the Dutch East Indies.—**East Indian** *adj. & n.*

east-northeast, east-southeast. See compass.

east·ward (*eest*-werd) *adj. & adv.* Toward the east.—**east·ward·ly** *adj. & adv.*—**east·wards** *adv.*

eas·y (*eez*-ee) *adj.* [-i·er; -i·est] 1. Not difficult; simple. 2. Free from pain or anxiety. 3. Not stiff or formal.

easy chair. A cushioned armchair.

eas·y·go·ing *adj.* Good-natured; mild-tempered; unexcitable.—**eas·y·go·ing·ness** *n.*

eat *v.* [ate; eat·en; eat·ing] 1. To consume; take food. 2. To corrode; gnaw at; wear away.—**eat crow.** To accept the inevitable. —**eat humble pie.** To suffer humiliation.—**eat one's words.** To retract an assertion.

eat·a·ble *adj.* Edible; fit to eat.—*n.* Food.

Eau de Cologne (oh-duh-kuh-*lohn*). Toilet water.

eaves (eevz) *n. pl.* The projecting edge of a roof.

eaves·drop *v.* [-dropped; -drop·ping] To listen to others' private conversation.—**eaves·drop·per** *n.*—**eaves·drop·ping** *n. & adj.*

ebb *n.* 1. The flowing back of the tide. 2. A decline; decay; decrease.—*v.* 1. To recede; flow back. 2. To sink; decline; decrease.

ebb tide. The tide flowing out.

eb·on (*eb*-un) *adj.* Made of ebony; black.

eb·on·ite (*eb*-uh-nyte) *n.* A variety of vulcanite used for ornaments, combs, handles, etc.

eb·on·y (*eb*-uh-nee) *n.* [*pl.* -ies] Hard, heavy, durable wood, usually black.

e·bul·li·ence (eh-*bul*-y'ns) *n.* A boiling over; effervescence; enthusiasm.—**e·bul·li·en·cy** *n.*

e·bul·li·ent *adj.* Overenthusiastic.

e·bul·li·tion (eb-uh-*lish*-un) *n.* 1. An outburst; pouring forth; sudden display of feeling. 2. *Physics.* Effervescence; process of boiling.

é·car·té (ay-kahr-*tay*) *v.* A card game played by two persons with 32 cards.

ec·cen·tric (ek-*sen*-trik) *adj.* 1. Extraordinary; unusual; odd. 2. *Geometry.* Not having the same center. 3. *Mechanics.* Having an off-center action.—*n.* 1. An irregular person or thing. 2. *Mechanics.* A disk with an off-center axis for changing circular motion into back-and-forth motion.—**ec·cen·tri·cal** *adj.*

ec·cen·tric·i·ty (ek-sen-*tris*-ih-tee) *n.* [*pl.* -ties] Irregularity; oddity; departure from normal.

Ec·cle·si·as·tes (uh-klee-zee-*ass*-teez) *n.* A canonical book of the Old Testament.

ec·cle·si·as·tic *adj.* Relating to the church.—*n.* A clergyman; member of a holy order.—**ec·cle·si·as·ti·cal** *adj.* Relating to the church.—**ec·cle·si·as·ti·cal·ly** *adv.*

Ec·cle·si·as·ti·cus (uh-klee-zee-*as*-tih-kus) *n.* One of the four canonical books of the Apocrypha.

ec·dem·ic (ek-*dem*-ik) *adj.* Of foreign origin.

ech·e·lon (*esh*-uh-lon) *n.* 1. *Aviation.* A wedge or V-shaped formation of planes in flight. 2. *Military.* A stage in the chain of command. 3. *Nautical.* A flanking formation of warships designed to furnish each the maximum protection when attacking.—*v.* To arrange in echelon formation, in a series of steps.

ech·o (*ek*-oh) *n.* 1. The repercussion of a sound. 2. [*cap.*] *Mythology.* A nymph who vanished leaving only her voice.—*v.* [ech·oed; -o·ing] 1. To reflect a sound. 2. To reverberate; sound out loud. 'Trumpets echo loudly.' 3. To repeat the words of others. —**ech·o·er** *n.*—**ech·o·ic** *adj.*

é·clair (ay-*klair*) *n.* An elongated cream-filled pastry covered with chocolate or sugar.

é·clat (ay-*klah*) *n.* 1. Acclamation; approbation. 2. Brilliancy; luster. 3. Renown.

ec·lec·tic (ek-*lek*-tik) *adj.* Selecting the best from different systems, doctrines, sources, etc. —*n.* A follower of the eclectic method in philosophy, religion, etc.—**ec·lec·ti·cal·ly** *adv.*

ec·lec·ti·cism (ek-*lek*-tih-sizm) *n.* System based on the combination of various principles.

e·clipse (uh-*klips*) *n.* 1. Blotting out of the light of sun, moon, etc., by another body coming between it and earth. 2. Darkness; obscurity.—*v.* To darken or hide; degrade.

e·clip·tic (uh-*klip*-tik) *n.* The apparent path of the sun during the year.—*adj.* Relating to the ecliptic.—**e·clip·ti·cal** *adj.*

ec·logue (*ek*-log) *n.* A bucolic poem.

e·co·nom·ic (eek-uh-*nom*-ik; ek-) *adj.* Relating to the study of monetary and other resources of mankind and their permutations.

e·co·nom·i·cal (eek-uh-*nom*-uh-k'l; ek-), *adj.* Frugal; thrifty; prudent.— **-nom·i·cal·ly** *adv.*

e·co·nom·ics *n.* 1. Study of the application of wealth and resources to mankind's needs. 2. Also **home economics.** Science of domestic management.

E

e·con·o·mist (uh-*kon*-uh-mist) *n.* Economics expert.

e·con·o·mize (uh-*kon*-uh-myze) *v.* [-mized; -miz·ing] To spend money with care; reduce expenses.

e·con·o·my (uh-*kon*-uh-mee) *n.* [*pl.* -mies] 1. Organization of resources. 2. Careful expenditure of money or effort.

ec·ru (*ek*-roo) *adj.* Beige.

ec·sta·sy (*ek*-stuh-see) *n.* [*pl.* -sies] 1. Excessive joy; rapture; extreme delight. 2. A trance.—*v.* [-sied; -sy·ing] To imbue with rapture.

ec·stat·ic (ek-*stat*-ik) *adj.* 1. Thrilling; extremely delightful. 2. Exhilarated; joyful. —**ec·stat·i·cal** *adj.*—**ec·stat·i·cal·ly** *adv.*

ec·to·derm (*ek*-tuh-derm) *n.* The outer layer of an animal's skin.—**ec·to·der·mal** (ek-tuh-*der*-m'l), **ec·to·der·mic** *adj.*

ec·to·plasm (*ek*-tuh-plazm) *n.* 1. *Biology.* A cell wall. 2. *Spiritualism.* A luminous substance supposed to come from a medium's body.—**ec·to·plas·mic** (ek-tuh-*plaz*-mik) *adj.*

ec·u·men·i·cal (ek-yoo-*men*-ik-ul) *adj.* Also **ec·u·men·ic.** *Ecclesiastic.* Universal; general; representing all denominations of the Church.

ec·ze·ma (*ek*-suh-muh) *n.* Eruptive skin disease.

Edam cheese (*ee*-dam). A mild cheese, usually coated red, originated in Edam, Holland.

Ed·da (*ed*-uh) *n.* One of two collections of Icelandic myths.—**Ed·da·ic, Ed·dic** *adj.*

ed·dy (*ed*-ee) *n.* [*pl.* -dies] A current of air or water running against the main stream; minor whirlpool.—*v.* [ed·died; ed·dy·ing]. To whirl.

e·del·weiss (ayd-'l-vysse) *n.* A perennial Alpine plant.

e·de·ma (ee-*dee*-muh) *n.* [*pl.* -ma·ta]. Also **oe·de·ma.** A swelling; dropsy.—**e·dem·a·tous** (ee-*dem*-uh-tus), **e·dem·a·tose** *adj.*

E·den (*ee*-d'n) *n.* 1. The garden where God placed Adam and Eve. 2. Any delightful place.

e·den·tate (ee-*den*-tayt) *adj.* Having no teeth.

edge (ej) *n.* 1. Thin cutting side of an instrument. 2. The margin of anything; brink; border. 3. Keenness; sharpness.—*v.* [edged; edg·ing] 1. To move slowly. 2. To fringe or border. 3. To sharpen.—**on edge.** Anxious.

edg·ing (*ej*-ing) *n.* Fringe; border; trimming.

edge·ways, edge·wise *adv.* 1. With the edge turned forward; in the direction of the edge. 2. Sideways; with the side foremost.

ed·i·ble (*ed*-uh-b'l) *adj.* Eatable; fit to eat.—*n.* —**ed·i·ble·ness, ed·i·bil·i·ty** (-*bil*-ih-tee) *n.*

e·dict (*ee*-dikt) *n.* Proclamation; ruling; law; command.—**e·dic·tal** (ee-*dik*-t'l) *adj.*

ed·i·fi·ca·tion (ed-ih-fih-*kay*-shun) *n.* Instruction; improvement of the mind.

ed·i·fice (*ed*-uh-fis) *n.* A building; structure.

ed·i·fy (*ed*-uh-fy) *v.* [ed·i·fied; ed·i·fy·ing] To instruct; make morally better.

ed·it (*ed*-it) *v.* To prepare for publication; direct publication of a newspaper, periodical, or book.

e·di·tion (uh-*dish*-un) *n.* 1. The whole number of copies of a work published at one time. 2. A work bearing a special stamp or form. 'A first edition.'

ed·i·tor (*ed*-it-er) *n.* Person who superintends, revises, and prepares material for publication. —**ed·i·to·ri·al** *adj.*—**ed·i·tor·ship** *n.*

ed·i·to·ri·al (ed-ih-*tor*-ee-ul) *n.* An article written by an editor, usually given featured position.—**ed·i·to·ri·al** *adj.*—**ed·i·to·ri·al·ly** *adv.*

ed·u·cate (*ej*-oo-kayt) *v.* [-cat·ed; -cat·ing] To instruct; inform and enlighten; indoctrinate.

ed·u·ca·tion (ej-oo-*kay*-shun) *n.* 1. The techniques and practices of teaching; instruction. 2. All agencies and people involved in public instruction.—**ed·u·ca·tion·al** *adj.*—**ed·u·ca·tion·al·ist, -tion·ist** *n.*—**ed·u·ca·tive** *adj.*

ed·u·ca·tor (*ej*-oo-kay-ter) *n.* An instructor; one eminent in the teaching field.

e·duce (eh-*doos*) *v.* [-duced; -duc·ing] To bring out; draw out; extract.—**e·duc·i·ble** *adj.*—**e·duc·tion** (eh-*duk*-sh'n) *n.*

eel *n.* A snakelike fish, usually 1 to 2 feet long, found in both fresh and salt water.—**eel·y** *adj.*

eel·grass *n.* A long-leafed underwater plant common along the eastern coast of North America.

EEL (1/12 life size)

e'en (een) *adv. Poetic.* Contraction of **even.**

e'er (air) *adv. Poetic.* Contraction of **ev·er.**

ee·rie, ee·ry (*eer*-ee) *adj.* [-ri·er; -ri·est] Weird; fearsome; unnatural.—**ee·ri·ly** *adv.*—**-ri·ness** *n.*

ef·face (eh-*fayss*) *v.* [-faced; -fac·ing] To wipe out; obliterate; expunge; erase.—**ef·face·a·ble** *adj.*—**ef·face·ment, ef·fac·er** *n.*

ef·fect (eh-*fekt*) *n.* 1. Result; consequence. 2. Purport; general intent. 3. Impression produced on the observer. 4. Validity; importance. 5. [*pl.*] Household goods. 6. Actuality; fact; truth. 7. Operation; force. 'The law goes into effect.'

ef·fect *v.* To produce; cause; accomplish; bring to pass.—**ef·fect·er** *n.*—**ef·fect·i·ble** *adj.*

ef·fec·tive (eh-*fek*-tiv) *adj.* Efficient; active; able to produce a result.—*n.* [*pl.*] *Military.* Soldiers fit for combat.—**ef·fec·tive·ly** *adv.*

ef·fec·tu·al (ef-*fek*-choo-ul) *adj.* Producing a result desired; having power to gain an end. —**ef·fec·tu·al·ly** *adv.*

ef·fec·tu·ate (eh-*fek*-choo-ayt) *v.* [-at·ed; -at·ing] To achieve; accomplish; fulfill.—**ef·fec·tu·a·tion** (eh-fek-choo-*ay*-sh'n) *n.*

ef·fem·i·nate (ef-*fem*-ih-nit) *adj.* Womanish; weak; delicate; unmanly.—**ef·fem·i·na·cy** *n.*

ef·fen·di (eh-*fen*-dee) *n.* Turkish term of respect; sir.

ef·fer·vesce (ef-er-*ves*) *v.* [-vesced; -vesc·ing] 1. To bubble and hiss; boil. 2. To show excitement; exhibit high spirits.

ef·fer·ves·cence (ef-er-*ves*-ens) *n.* 1. Gaseous bubbling disturbance in a fluid. 2. Excitement; high spirits.—**ef·fer·ves·cent** *adj.*

ef·fete (eh-*feet*) *adj.* Exhausted; barren; without vigor; no longer productive.— **-fete·ness** *n.*

ef·fi·ca·cious (ef-ih-*kay*-shus) *adj.* Powerful; producing the result desired.— **-ca·cious·ly** *adv.*

ef·fi·ca·cy (*ef*-ih-kuh-see) *n.* [*pl.* -cies] Power to produce effects; force; efficiency.

ef·fi·cien·cy (uh-*fish*-en-see) *n.* [*pl.* -cies] Competency; ability to achieve results desired with minimum waste. 'Efficiency is required.'

ef·fi·cient (eh-*fish*-ent) *adj.* Competent; capable; effective —**ef·fi·cient·ly** *adv.*

ef·fi·gy (*ef*-ih-jee) *n.* [*pl.* -gies] The image or likeness of a person or thing.

ef·flo·resce (ef-ler-*es*) *v.* [-resced; -resc·ing] 1. To burst into bloom; break out in full flower. 2. *Chemistry.* To change gradually to powder on exposure to the air.

ef·flo·res·cence *n.* Also **ef·flo·res·cen·cy.** 1. Full flowering; outburst; climax of development. 2. *Medicine.* A rash; skin eruption. 3. *Chemistry.* A powder or crust on the surface of certain bodies.—**ef·flo·res·cent** *adj.*

ef·flu·ence (*ef*-loo-ens) *n.* A flowing out; emanation.—**ef·flu·ent** *adj. & n.*

ef·flu·vi·um (eh-*floo*-vee-um) *n.* [*pl.* -vi·a, -vi·ums] An invisible outflowing; emanation; exhalation, esp. a noxious one.—**ef·flu·vi·al** *adj.*

ef·fort (*ef*-ert) *n.* Exertion; struggle; attempt.—**ef·fort·less** *adj.* Easy; without strain.

ef·fron·ter·y (eh-*frun*-ter-ee) *n.* [*pl.* -ter·ies] Impudence; boldness; audacity.

ef·ful·gence (eh-*fuhl*-juns) *n.* A flood of light; splendor.—**ef·ful·gent** *adj.* Shining brightly.

ef·fuse (eh-*fyooz*) *v.* [ef·fused; ef·fus·ing] To pour out; spill; shed; emanate.

ef·fu·sion (eh-*fyoo*-zhun) *n.* An outpouring; fulsome or gushing speech.

ef·fu·sive (eh-*fyoo*-siv) *adj.* Gushing; voluble. —**ef·fu·sive·ly** *adv.*—**ef·fu·sive·ness** *n.*

eft *n.* A newt; small, amphibious salamander.

e·gad (eh-*gad*) *interj.* By God.

egg *n.* A body developed in the females of many animals and birds in which, after impregnation by sperm from the male, the primary development of the young animal occurs. It is usually roundish and often enclosed in a shell.

egg *v.* To urge; incite; produce.

egg·nog *n.* A drink made of eggs, milk, sugar, nutmeg, and often brandy.

egg·plant *n.* A plant bearing large egg-shaped, purple fruit, eaten as a vegetable.

egg·shell *n.* The outside, usually brittle, covering of an egg.

EGGPLANT

eg·lan·tine (*eg*-lan-tyne) *n.* Sweetbrier; a plant similar to honeysuckle.

e·go (*ee*-goh) *n.* [*pl.* egos] 1. The conscious self. 2. Excessive love of self; conceit.

e·go·cen·tric (ee-goh-*sen*-trik) *adj.* Self-centered; wrapped up in one's own concerns. —*n.* A self-centered person.—**ego·cen·tric·i·ty, ego·cen·trism** *n.*

e·go·ism (*ee*-goh-izm) *n. Philosophy.* 1. Belief that all action is based on selfish, personal motives. 2. Love of self; egocentricity.

e·go·ist *n.* A selfish person; believer in egoism. —**e·go·is·tic, e·go·is·ti·cal** *adj.*— **-ti·cal·ly** *adv.*

e·go·ma·ni·a (ee-goh-*mayn*-yuh; -*may*-nee-uh) *n.* Extreme or morbid self-esteem, often to the point of insanity.—**e·go·ma·ni·ac** *n.*—**e·go·man·ic** (ee-goh-*man*-ik) *adj.*

e·go·tism (*ee*-goh-tizm) *n.* Excessive outward display of self-esteem; conceit.

e·go·tist *n.* One who is blatant and outspoken in self-esteem.—**e·go·tis·tic, -ti·cal** *adj.*

e·gre·gious (eh-*gree*-jus) *adj.* Very bad; flagrant.—**e·gre·gious·ly** *adv.*—**e·gre·gious·ness** *n.*

e·gress (*ee*-gres) *n.* 1. Way out; exit. 2. Act of leaving.—*v.* To go out; depart.—**e·gres·sion** (ee-*gresh*-'n) *n.*

e·gret (*ee*-grit; -gret) *n.* 1. Bird of the heron family notable for its beautiful plumage. 2. One of its long plumes; aigrette.

E·gyp·tol·o·gy (ec-jip-*tol*-uh-jee) *n.* Study of the relics of ancient Egyptian civilization. —**-to·log·i·cal** *adj.* —**-tol·o·gist** *n.*

eh (*ay*, *eh*) *interj.* Expressing doubt or surprise.

EGRET (1/30 life size)

ei·der (*eye*-der) *n.* A species of northern sea duck.

eider down. The down or soft breast feathers of the eider, valued for lightness and warmth.

Eiffel Tower (*eye*-f'l). Famous steel structure erected for the exposition of 1889 in Paris.

eight (*ayt*) *n.* 1. One of the cardinal numbers, represented by the symbol 8. 2. A crew in intercollegiate boat racing.—**eight** *adj.*—**eight·fold** *adj.* Eight times the quantity.—**eight·fold** *adv.*

eight·een (ay-*teen*) *n.* The number represented by the symbol 18.—**eight·een** *adj.*

eight·eenth (ay-*teenth*) *n.* 1. One of eighteen equal parts. 2. *Music.* An interval covering two octaves and a fourth.—**eight·eenth** *adj.*

eighth (*aytth*) *n.* 1. One of eight equal parts. 2. *Music.* An interval covering the full diatonic scale; octave.—**eighth** *adj.*

eight·i·eth (*ay*-tee-uth) *n.* One of 80 equal parts. —**eight·i·eth** *adj.*

eight·y (*ay*-tee) *n.* [*pl.* -ies] The number represented by the symbol 80.—**eight·y** *adj.*—**eight·y·fold** *adj.* Eighty times.—**eight·y·fold** *adv.*

ei·ther (*ee*-ther; *eye*-) *adj.* 1. One or the other.

E

'Either team.' 2. Both. 'On either side of the river.'—*pronoun*. One or the other.—*conj.* Used as correlative to and preceding *or*. 'Either one or the other.'—*adv*. Any more than the other.

e·jac·u·late (ee-*jak*-yuh-layt) *v*. [-lat·ed; -lat·ing] 1. To eject; emit suddenly. 2. To exclaim; blurt.— -u·la·tive *adj*.— -u·la·tor *n*.

e·jac·u·la·tion (ee-jak-yuh-*lay*-shun) *n*. 1. The act of emitting or ejecting suddenly. 2. An exclamation; sudden brief remark.

e·jac·u·la·to·ry (ee-*jak*-yuh-luh-toh-ree) *adj*. Suddenly ejected or uttered.

e·ject (ee-*jekt*) *v*. To throw out; expel.—**e·jec·tion** *n*.—**e·jec·tive** *adj*.—**e·jec·tor** *n*.

e·ject (*ee*-jekt) *n*. A mental condition or idea considered from without the mind.

eke (*eek*) *v*. [eked; ek·ing] *Archaic*. To enlarge; lengthen.—**eke out**. 1. To have barely enough, as a living. 2. To add to; supplement.

el *n*. *Colloquial*. Elevated railroad.

e·lab·o·rate (uh-*lab*-er-it) *adj*. Worked out with care; executed with great detail and exactness. —*v*. (uh-*lab*-er-ayt) [-rat·ed; -rat·ing] 1. To make with great labor or care. 2. To improve or develop; add particulars to.—**e·lab·o·rate·ly** *adv*.—**e·lab·o·rate·ness** *n*.—**e·lab·o·ra·tive** *adj*.

e·lab·o·ra·tion (uh-lab-uh-*ray*-shun) *n*. Extension; development; improvement.

e·land (*ee*-lund) *n*. A large African antelope.

e·lapse (uh-*laps*) *v*. [e·lapsed; e·laps·ing] To pass or slip away. 'Time elapsed.'

e·las·tic (uh-*las*-tik) *adj*. 1. Capable of springing back to its original shape after being stretched, squeezed, or expanded. 2. Buoyant; resilient, as a temperament.—*n*. A band of or containing rubber.—**e·las·ti·cal·ly** *adv*.

e·las·tic·i·ty (uh-las-*tiss*-uh-tee) *n*. Resiliency.

e·late (uh-*layt*, ee-*layt*) *v*. [-lat·ed; -lat·ing] To raise in spirit; make proud or happy.—**e·lat·ed** *adj*.—**e·lat·ed·ly** *adv*.—**e·lat·er** *n*.

e·la·tion (uh-*lay*-shun) *n*. A feeling of exultation; great joy or pride.

El·ba (*el*-buh). Island off the coast of Italy, to which Napoleon I was exiled in 1814.

El·be (*el*-buh). River in central Germany.

el·bow (*el*-boh) *n*. 1. The joint uniting the upper arm with the forearm, esp. its outer angle when bent. 2. Any turn or bend resembling the elbow.—*v*. To push; jostle. 'Elbow through the crowd.'

el·bow·room *n*. Space for movement or action.

eld·er (*el*-der) *adj*. Older; senior; earlier.—*n*. 1. An older or aged person. 2. An ancestor. 3. A person who exerts influence because of his age; church or community officer.

el·der *n*. A tree or shrub akin to the honeysuckle.—**el·der·ber·ry** *n*. The fruit of the elder.

eld·er·ly (*el*-der-lee) *adj*. Bordering on old age.

eld·est (*el*-dist) *adj*. Oldest.

El Dorado [*pl.* -dos]. Also **El·do·ra·do**. A legendary country overflowing with gold and other precious resources.

e·lect (eh-*lekt*) *adj*. 1. Chosen; taken by preference. 2. *Theology*. Chosen for eternal life. 3. Chosen but not inaugurated. 'Governor-elect.'—**the elect**. Those especially favored. —**elect** *v*. To choose; select for office by vote.

e·lec·tion (eh-*lek*-shun) *n*. 1. Act of choosing. 2. Selection for office. 3. Power of choice; free will.

e·lec·tion·eer (uh-lek-shun-*ihr*) *v*. To work for a candidate's election.—**e·lec·tion·eer·er** *n*.

e·lec·tive *adj*. 1. Chosen or bestowed by election. 2. Exerting the power of choice.—*n*. *Education*. A course of study freely chosen by the pupil.—**e·lec·tive·ly** *adv*.—**e·lec·tive·ness** *n*.

e·lec·tor (eh-*lek*-ter) *n*. One who has the right to elect; voter.—**e·lec·tor·al** *adj*.—**electoral college**. Body of men selected by popular vote to name the U.S. President and Vice-President.

e·lec·tor·ate (eh-*lek*-ter-it) *n*. 1. The whole body of voters. 2. The territory once ruled by an elector in the Holy Roman Empire.

E·lec·tra (eh-*lek*-truh). A daughter of Agamemnon, who commanded the Greek army at Troy.

Electra complex. *Psychoanalysis*. Abnormal love of a daughter for her father. See **Oedipus complex**.

e·lec·tric, e·lec·tri·cal (eh-*lek*-trik) *adj*. 1. Relating to electricity. 2. Spirited; vigorous. 'Electric personality.'—**e·lec·tri·cal·ly** *adv*.

electrical transcription. *Radio*. A large phonograph record, often containing a complete program.

electric chair. A device for executing condemned criminals by electricity.

electric eel. A large eel-like fish capable of producing electric shocks.

electric eye. The photoelectric cell; a vacuum tube that produces changes in electric current corresponding to changes in light striking it.

e·lec·tri·cian (eh-lek-*trish*-un) *n*. One skilled in repairing or installing electrical devices.

e·lec·tric·i·ty (eh-lek-*tris*-ih-tee) *n*. 1. A form of energy manifested by the action of electrons and protons, minute particles bearing electrical attraction. Electricity can be generated by friction, by chemical action, as in a battery, or by motion of a conductor in a magnetic field, as in a dynamo. It is employed in heating, lighting, and innumerable mechanical processes. 2. The science of electricity.

e·lec·tri·fy (eh-*lek*-truh-fy) *v*. [-fied; -fy·ing] 1. To charge with electricity. 2. To excite; shock; thrill. 3. To wire for electricity. —**e·lec·tri·fi·ca·tion** *n*.—**e·lec·tri·fi·er** *n*.

e·lec·tro- *prefix*. Electric; produced electrically.

e·lec·tro·chem·is·try (eh-lek-troh-*kem*-iss-tree) *n*. The science concerned with the interaction of electricity and chemical changes.—**e·lec·tro·chem·i·cal** *adj*.—**e·lec·tro·chem·ist** *n*.

e·lec·tro·cute (eh-*lek*-truh-kyoot) *v*. [-cut·ed; -cut·ing] To kill or execute by electric shock. —**e·lec·tro·cu·tion** (eh-lek-truh-*kyoo*-shun) *n*.

e·lec·trode (eh-*lek*-trohd) *n*. A terminal of an electric circuit, esp. of an electrolytic cell.

e·lec·tro·dy·nam·ics (eh-lek-troh-dy-*nam*-iks) *n.* Science dealing with electricity in current. —**e·lec·tro·dy·nam·ic, e·lec·tro·dy·nam·i·cal** *adj.*

e·lec·tro·lier (eh-lek-truh-*lihr*) *n.* A wall bracket or hanging fixture for electric lights.

e·lec·trol·y·sis (eh-lek-*trol*-uh-sis) *n.* 1. The breaking down, by electric current, of chemical compounds into their several elements. 2. Passage of an electric current through an ionized solution, causing molecules of the substance dissolved to form at the electrodes.

e·lec·tro·lyte (eh-*lek*-truh-lyte) *n.* 1. A compound which ionizes in solution. 2. A solution containing ions of such a compound. — **-ly·tic** (-*lit*-ik), **-i·cal** *adj.*— **-i·cal·ly** *adv.*

e·lec·tro·lyze (eh-*lek*-truh-lyze) *v.* [-lyzed; -lyzing] To pass electric current through an electrolyte.—**e·lec·tro·ly·za·tion, e·lec·tro·lyz·er** *n.*

e·lec·tro·mag·net (eh-lek-troh-*mag*-nit) *n.* A soft iron core wound with wire, through which an electric current passes, creating a magnetic field.— **-net·ic, -i·cal** *adj.*— **-net·i·cal·ly** *adv.*

e·lec·tro·mag·net·ism *n.* 1. The magnetic force exerted by an electromagnet. 2. The science of the relationship between magnetism and electricity.

e·lec·trom·e·ter (eh-lek-*trom*-it-er) *n.* Instrument measuring difference of electric potential.

e·lec·tro·mo·tive (eh-lek-troh-*moh*-tiv) *adj.* 1. Producing current. 2. Run by electricity.

electromotive force. The force that maintains a flow of electricity; it is measured in volts. *Abbreviation*: **e.m.f.**

e·lec·tro·mo·tor (eh-lek-troh-*moh*-ter) *n.* 1. An engine using electricity to produce mechanical effect. 2. An electric generator.

e·lec·tron (eh-*lek*-tron) *n.* Basic unit of negative electricity which associates with a positively charged nucleus to form the atom. Chemical and physical properties of matter are determined by the action and grouping of electrons.

e·lec·tro·neg·a·tive (eh-lek-troh-*neg*-uh-tiv) *adj.* 1. Having a negative electrical charge. 2. Acidic.—*n. Chemistry.* An acid.

e·lec·tron·ics (eh-lek-*tron*-iks) *n.* The physical science dealing with the actions of electrons, esp. in instruments, such as radio and radar, employing cathode-ray tubes.

e·lec·troph·o·rus (eh-lek-*trof*-er-us) *n.* A device for storing an electric charge by induction.

e·lec·tro·plate (eh-*lek*-truh-playt) *v.* To coat with metal by electrolysis.—*n.* An article so coated.—**e·lec·tro·plat·er** *n.*— **-plat·ing** *n.*

e·lec·tro·pos·i·tive (eh-lek-troh-*poz*-uh-tiv) *adj.* 1. Having a positive electric charge. 2. Basic; collecting at the cathode in electrolysis.—*n. Chemistry.* A base.

e·lec·tro·scope (eh-*lek*-truh-skohp) *n.* An instrument for detecting electric charges and determining their polarity.— **-scop·ic** *adj.*

e·lec·tro·stat·ics (eh-lek-truh-*stat*-iks) *n.* Science of static electricity.— **-stat·ic** *adj.*

e·lec·tro·type (eh-*lek*-truh-type) *n.* A printing plate made by electrolytically coating a mold or mat of the type page to be reproduced. — **-typ·er** *n.*— **-typ·y** *n.*— **-typ·ist** *n.*

e·lec·trum (eh-*lek*-trum) *n.* 1. A silver-bearing gold ore. 2. A gold-and-silver alloy.

el·ee·mos·y·nar·y (el-uh-*mos*-uh-nehr-ee) *adj.* Relating to charity, esp. organized charity.

el·e·gance (*el*-uh-gunss) *n.* Refinement; beauty resulting from perfect propriety.—**el·e·gan·cy** *n.*

el·e·gant (*el*-uh-gunt) *adj.* 1. Refined; polished; graceful; well-mannered. 2. *Colloquial.* Excellent.—**el·e·gant·ly** *adv.*

el·e·gi·ac (eh-*lee*-jee-ak, el-uh-*jy*-ik) *adj.* Expressing sorrow; lamenting.—*n.* A style of verse used in writing elegies.

el·e·gy (*el*-uh-jee) *n.* [*pl.* -ies] A mournful poem; dirge; lamentation.—**el·e·gist** *n.*—**el·e·gize** *v.*

el·e·ment (*el*-uh-munt) *n.* 1. A fundamental, irreducible part. 2. Proper environment. 'John is in his element.' 3. A fact; value. 'These are elements to consider.' 4. *Chemistry.* One of the 98 substances which join in compounds to make up all matter. Elements cannot be broken down into other substances by ordinary chemical means. 5. Fire, Earth, Air, or Water—the four elements once thought to comprise the universe.—**the elements.** Manifestations of bad weather.

el·e·men·tal (el-uh-*men*-t'l) *adj.* 1. Fundamental; relating to first principles. 2. Pertaining to fire, air, earth, or water. 3. Constituting a part. 4. Primitive; savage.—**el·e·men·tal·ly** *adv.*

el·e·men·ta·ry (el-uh-*men*-ter-ee) *adj.* 1. Primary; simple; rudimentary. 2. *Chemistry.* Composed of or relating to a single element.

elementary school. A school for beginners.

el·e·phant (*el*-uh-funt) *n.* A large mammal of Asia and Africa having valuable ivory tusks and a long sensitive trunk.

ELEPHANT (1/140 life size)

el·e·phan·ti·a·sis (el-uh-fun-*ty*-uh-sis) *n. Medicine.* A disease of humans characterized by great enlargement of limbs and hardening of skin.

el·e·phan·tine (el-uh-*fan*-teen) *adj.* Resembling or pertaining to an elephant; huge; clumsy.

el·e·vate (*el*-uh-vayt) *v.* [-vat·ed; -vat·ing] 1. To lift. 2. To exalt; raise to a higher station. 3. To improve. 'Elevate the mind.' 4. To cheer; animate; elate.

el·e·vat·ed *adj.* Raised; exalted; elated; excited; stimulated.—*n. Colloquial.* A streetcar or railroad running on tracks raised some distance above the ground.

el·e·va·tion (el-uh-*vay*-shun) *n.* 1. The act of raising or lifting; state of being elevated. 2. A high place. 3. Altitude. 4. *Military.* The angle with the horizontal at which a gun is

E

fired. 5. *Ballet*. The skill of a dancer in appearing to leap high with apparent ease.

el·e·va·tor (*el*-uh-vay-ter) *n.* 1. A muscle that raises any part of the body. 2. An apparatus in large buildings for raising and lowering passengers and freight; lift. 3. A building for storing grain. 4. A movable surface in the tail assembly of an airplane causing it to rise or descend.

el·ev·en (eh-*lev*-un) *n.* 1. One of the cardinal numbers, represented by the symbol 11. 2. An American football team.—**e·lev·en** *adj.*

el·ev·enth (eh-*lev*-unth) *n.* One of 11 equal parts.—*adj.* Occurring in order after 10.

elf *n.* [*pl.* elves] 1. An imaginary being; fairy; goblin. 2. A mischievous or wicked person. 3. A diminutive person; dwarf.

elf·in (*elf*-in) *adj.* Relating to or suggesting an elf.—*n.* A little elf; urchin.

elf·ish (*elf*-ish) *adj.* Resembling an elf; mischievous.—**elf·ish·ly** *adv.*—**elf·ish·ness** *n.*

e·lic·it (eh-*lis*-it) *v.* To draw out; bring to light; educe.—**e·lic·i·ta·tion** *n.*—**e·lic·i·tor** *n.*

e·lide (eh-*lyde*) *v.* [e·lid·ed; e·lid·ing] To cut off or suppress in pronunciation, as a syllable.

el·i·gi·ble (*el*-ij-uh-b'l) *adj.* Worthy; capable; qualified to be chosen.—**el·i·gi·bil·i·ty** (el-ih-juh-*bil*-uh-tee) *n.*—**el·i·gi·bly** *adv.*

e·lim·i·nate (eh-*lim*-uh-nayt) *v.* [-nat·ed; -nat·ing] 1. To expel; discharge. 2. To leave out or set aside as unimportant.—**e·lim·i·na·tion** *n.*

e·li·sion (eh-*lizh*-un) *n.* Suppression or omission of a vowel or syllable in speech.

e·lite (eh-*leet*, ay-*leet*) *n.* 1. A choice or select body. 'The elite of society.' 2. A typewriter type which allows 12 characters to the inch.

e·lix·ir (eh-*lik*-ser) *n.* 1. *Pharmacy*. A compound tincture held in solution by alcohol. 2. *Alchemy*. **a.** A mixture for transforming other metals into gold. **b.** A potion intended to extend life.

E·liz·a·be·than (eh-liz-uh-*bee*-thun, -*beth*-'n) *adj.* Pertaining to Queen Elizabeth or her times.—*n.* One who lived in England at the time of Elizabeth.

elk *n. sing. & pl.* The largest species of deer.

ell *n.* A standard of measure for cloth.

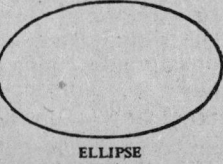

ELK (1/90 life size)

ell *n. Architecture*. A wing extending at right angles to a building.

el·lipse (uh-*lips*) *n.* An oval-shaped geometrical figure produced by cutting a cone with a plane.

el·lip·sis (uh-*lip*-sis) *n.* [*pl.* -lip·ses] *Grammar*. Omission of words not necessary to the sense of a passage. 'You will go your way, I mine.'

ELLIPSE

el·lip·tic (uh-*lip*-tik), **el·lip·ti·cal** *adj.* 1. Hav-

ing a part left out; defective. 2. Having the form of an ellipse.—**el·lip·ti·cal·ly** *adv.*

Ellis Island. An island in New York Bay, used as a place of entry for immigrants.

elm *n.* 1. A large, graceful shade tree. 2. The tough hard wood of this tree.

el·o·cu·tion (el-uh-*kyoo*-shun) *n.* The art of public speaking; oratory.

e·lon·gate (eh-*long*-gayt) *v.* [-gat·ed; -gat·ing] To lengthen; extend— **-gate** *adj.*— **-ga·tion** *n.*

e·lope (uh-*lohp*) *v.* [-loped; -lop·ing] To run away with a lover.—**e·lope·ment** *n.*—**e·lop·er** *n.*

el·o·quence (*el*-uh-kwunss) *n.* Vivid fluency.

el·o·quent *adj.* Expressive; vivid and fluent in speech.—**el·o·quent·ly** *adv.*

else *adj.* Other; one or something besides. —*adv.* Elsewhere; otherwise.—*conj.* Otherwise; if the facts were different.

else·where (*elss*-whair) *adv.* In another place.

e·lu·ci·date (uh-*loo*-sih-dayt) *v.* [-dat·ed; -dat·ing] To explain; clarify.—**e·lu·ci·da·tion** *n.* —**e·lu·ci·da·tive** *adj.*—**e·lu·ci·da·tor** *n.*

e·lude (el-*ood*) *v.* [-lud·ed; -lud·ing] To evade; escape; avoid deftly.—**e·lu·sion** (el-*oo*-zhun) *n.*

e·lu·sive (el-*oo*-siv) *adj.* Slippery; fugitive; intangible; difficult to grasp.—**e·lu·sive·ly** *adv.* —**e·lu·sive·ness** *n.*—**e·lu·so·ry** *adj.*

elv·ish (*elv*-ish) *adj.* Mischievous; playful.

E·ly·sian (uh-*lizh*-un) *adj.* Pertaining to paradise.—**Elysian Fields.** Heaven.

E·ly·si·um (uh-*lizh*-ee-um). Paradise.

em *n. Printing*. 1. A unit of measurement theoretically equal to the width of the upper case M of any font. 2. A pica.—**em** *adj.*

em- *prefix*. A variant of **en-** used before the letters *b*, *m*, and *p*.

e·ma·ci·ate (uh-*may*-shee-ayt) *v.* [-at·ed; -at·ing] To become thin; waste away.—**e·ma·ci·a·tion** (uh-may-shee-*ay*-shun; -see-) *n.*

em·a·nate (*em*-uh-nayt) *v.* [-nat·ed; -nat·ing] To flow out; issue; originate; proceed.—**em·a·na·tion** (em-uh-*nay*-shun) *n.*—**em·a·na·tive** *adj.*

e·man·ci·pate (eh-*man*-sih-payt) *v.* [-pat·ed; -pat·ing] To free; liberate.—**e·man·ci·pa·tor** *n.*

e·man·ci·pa·tion (eh-man-sih-*pay*-shun) *n.* Liberation; deliverance.

e·mas·cu·late (eh-*mas*-kyoo-layt) *v.* [-lat·ed; -lat·ing] 1. To castrate; take away virility. 2. To soften; vitiate.—**e·mas·cu·la·tion** *n.* —**e·mas·cu·la·tor** *n.*—**e·mas·cu·la·to·ry** *adj.*

em·balm (em-*bahm*) *v.* To delay putrefaction of a dead body by infusion of preservatives.—**em·balm·er** *n.*—**em·balm·ment** *n.*

em·bank (em-*bank*) *v.* To enclose with an earthen bank.

em·bank·ment *n.* A mound or bank of earth, stones, etc., raised for any purpose.

em·bar·go (em-*bahr*-goh) *n.* [*pl.* -goes] A government ban on the movement of ships; government stoppage of trade.—**em·bar·go** *v.*

em·bark (em-*bahrk*) *v.* 1. To place or go on board a ship. 2. To start an enterprise.

em·bar·ka·tion (em-bahr-*kay*-shun) *n.* The act of going aboard ship.

em·bar·rass (im-*bair*-us) *v.* 1. To disconcert; cause to feel uneasy or constrained; confuse. 2. To impede; involve in difficulties. 3. To complicate.— -**rass·ing** *adj.*— -**rass·ing·ly** *adv.*

em·bar·rass·ment *n.* 1. Condition of being embarrassed. 2. That which embarrasses.

em·bas·sy (*em*-buh-see) *n.* [*pl.* -sies] The office, entourage, or residence of an ambassador.

em·bat·tle (em-*bat*-'l) *v.* [-tled; -tling] 1. To form or prepare for battle; fortify. 2. To provide with battlements.

em·bay (em-*bay*) *v.* To shut off from the sea.

em·bed (im-*bed*) *v.* [-bed·ded; -bed·ding] To set or lay in surrounding matter.

em·bel·lish (im-*bel*-ish) *v.* 1. To adorn; decorate; beautify. 2. To enhance by adding imaginary details.

em·bel·lish·ment (im-*bel*-ish-m'nt) *n.* 1. Decoration; ornament. 2. Act of embellishing.

em·ber (*em*-ber) *n.* 1. A small coal, piece of wood, etc., still glowing in ashes. 2. [*pl.*] Smoldering ashes of a fire.

Em·ber *adj. Church.* Relating to certain days or weeks of fasting and prayer in each season.

em·bez·zle (im-*bez*-'l) *v.* [em·bez·zled; em·bez·zling] To steal what has been entrusted to one's care.—**em·bez·zle·ment** *n.*—**em·bez·zler** *n.*

em·bit·ter (im-*bit*-er) *v.* To make bitter; to anger.—**em·bit·ter·ment** *n.*

em·bla·zon (em-*blayz*-un) *v.* 1. To ornament with heraldic figures. 2. To decorate brightly; display; extol.—**em·bla·zon·ment** *n.*

em·bla·zon·ry *n.* [*pl.* -ries] The act or art of emblazoning; heraldic decoration.

em·blem (*em*-bl'm) *n.* Symbol; visible representation of a quality or idea; flag.—**em·blem** *v.*

em·blem·at·ic, em·blem·at·i·cal (em-bl'm-*at*-ik, -ik-'l) *adj.* Symbolic.—**em·blem·at·i·cal·ly** *adv.*—**em·blem·at·i·cal·ness** *n.*

em·bod·i·ment (im-*bod*-ee-m'nt) *n.* 1. Act of embodying. 2. Bodily representation.

em·bod·y (im-*bod*-eė) *v.* [-bod·ied; -bod·y·ing] 1. To invest with material form; express visibly. 2. To include in; incorporate.

em·bold·en (im-*bohl*-d'n) *v.* To encourage; make bold.

em·bo·lism (*em*-buh-liz-'m) *n. Medicine.* The obstruction of a vessel by a foreign particle.

em·bo·lus (*em*-buh-lus) *n.* [*pl.* -li] An obstructing particle, as a clot, moving in the blood stream.—**em·bol·ic** (em-*bol*-ik) *adj.*

em·bos·om (em-*booz*-'m) *v.* To cherish; hold dear; shelter or enclose.

em·boss (im-*bawss*) 1. To fashion raised work. 2. To cause to stand out.—**em·boss·ment** *n.*

em·bou·chure (ahm-boo-*shoor*; ahm-) *n.* 1. A mouth, as of a river or valley. 2. The position of the lips for playing a wind instrument.

em·bow (em-*boh*) *v.* To curve; arch.—**em·bowed** *adj.*—**em·bow·ment** *n.*

em·bow·er (em-*bow*-er) *v.* To shelter with trees or branches.

em·brace (im-*brayss*) *v.* [em·braced; em·bracing] 1. To clasp in the arms; press to the bosom; encircle. 2. To adopt; accept eagerly. 3. To comprehend; include.—**em·brace** *n.*

em·bra·sure (em-*bray*-zher) *n.* 1. An opening in a wall through which guns are fired. 2. The enlargement on the inside of a door or window.

em·bro·cate (*em*-broh-kayt) *v.* [-cat·ed; -cat·ing] *Medicine.* To bathe and rub with a soothing liquid.—**em·bro·ca·tion** *n.*

em·broi·der (em-*broy*-der) *v.* 1. To fashion or adorn with needlework. 2. To add fictitious details to; embellish.—**em·broid·er·er** *n.*—**em·broi·der·y** *n.* [*pl.* -ies].

em·broil (em-*broyl*) *v.* 1. To involve or entangle, esp. in a dispute or difficulty. 2. To throw into disorder; confuse.—**em·broil·ment** *n.*

em·brown (em-*brown*) *v.* To tan; darken.

em·bry·o (*em*-bree-oh) *n.* [*pl.* -os] 1. *Physiology.* An animal in the first stages of development in the womb. 2. *Botany.* The rudimentary plant contained in the seed. 3. Any rudimentary or early state.—**em·bry·o** *adj.*

em·bry·ol·o·gy (em-bree-*ol*-uh-jee) *n.* The scientific study of the formation and development of the embryo.—**em·bry·o·log·ic, em·bry·o·log·i·cal** *adj.*—**em·bry·ol·o·gist** *n.*

em·bry·on·ic (em-bree-*on*-ik) *adj.* Rudimentary.

e·mend (eh-*mend*) *v.* To amend by correction of the text; free from errors.—**e·mend·a·ble** *adj.*

e·men·da·tion (ee-men-*day*-sh'n; em-en-) *n.* Alteration; correction.—**e·man·da·tor** *n.*

em·er·ald (*em*-er-'ld) *n.* 1. A hard, deep-green, precious stone. 2. The color of an emerald. —*adj.* Of an emerald color.

Emerald Isle. Ireland.

e·merge (eh-*merj*) *v.* [e·merged; e·merg·ing] To rise out of a fluid; appear; come into view. —**e·mer·gence** *n.*—**e·mer·gent** *adj.*

e·mer·gen·cy (ih-*mer*-j'n-see) *n.* [*pl.* -cies] Exigency; unexpected situation requiring immediate action.

e·mer·i·tus (eh-*mehr*-uh-tus) *adj.* Honorably relieved of the duty, but not the rank or title, of a position. 'A professor emeritus.'

e·mersed (ee-*merst*) *adj.* Rising from a surface, esp. from a fluid.—**e·mer·sion** *n.* Emergence.

em·er·y (*em*-er-ee) *n.* An impure variety of corundum used for grinding and polishing.

e·met·ic (eh-*met*-ik) *n. Medicine.* A medicine which produces vomiting.—**e·met·ic** *adj.*

em·i·grate (*em*-uh-grayt) *v.* [-grat·ed; -grat·ing] To leave a country or area in order to settle in another.—**em·i·grant** *n.* & *adj.*

em·i·gra·tion (em-uh-*gray*-sh'n) *n.* 1. Act of emigrating. 2. A group of emigrants.

em·i·nence (*em*-uh-nunss) *n.* 1. Rising ground; hill. 2 High position or rank; fame. 3. [*cap.*] *Roman Catholic Church.* A title of honor given to cardinals.—**em·i·nen·cy** *n.* [*pl.* -cies].

em·i·nent (*em*-uh-n'nt) *adj.* 1. High; elevated. 2. Famous; distinguished; exalted. 3. Outstanding; evident; conspicuous.— -**nent·ly** *adv.*

E

eminent domain. *Law.* The right of a government to commandeer private property for public use upon reasonable payment.

e·mir, e·meer (uh-*meer*) *n.* A Mohammedan title for an official or chief.

em·is·sar·y (*em*-uh-sehr-ee) *n.* [*pl.* -ies] Person sent on a secret or delicate mission; private agent.—**em·is·sar·y** *adj.*

e·mis·sion (eh-*mish*-'n) *n.* 1. The act of issuing or emitting. 2. That which is sent out or emitted.—**e·mis·sive** *adj.*—**e·mis·siv·i·ty** *n.*

e·mit (eh-*mit*) *v.* [e·mit·ted; e·mit·ting] To send forth; issue; give off.—**e·mit·ter** *n.*

e·mol·lient (im-*ol*-y'nt) *adj.* Softening; soothing.—*n.* A balm; salve.

e·mol·u·ment (im-*ol*-yuh-m'nt) *n.* Salary; compensation; profit from an office or position.

e·mo·tion (eh-*moh*-sh'n) *n.* Any strong feeling.

e·mo·tion·al *adj.* 1. Pertaining to, or exciting emotion. 2. Tending to, or affected by, emotion.—**e·mo·tion·al·ly** *adv.*

e·mo·tion·al·ism *n.* Emotional character or condition; tendency toward strong feelings.

e·mo·tion·al·ize *v.* [-ized; -iz·ing] To regard, or treat with, emotion.

e·mo·tive (eh-*moh*-tiv) *adj.* Marked by or showing emotion.—**e·mo·tive·ly** *adv.*—**-tive·ness** *n.*

em·pan·el (im-*pan*-'l) *v.* [-eled, -elled; el·ing, -el·ling] To impanel; select a jury.

em·per·or (*em*-per-er) *n.* The supreme ruler of an empire.—**em·per·or·ship** *n.*

em·pha·sis (*em*-fuh-sis) *n.* [*pl.* -ses] 1. Stress; special importance. 2. A particular weight given to certain words or syllables in speaking.

em·pha·size (*em*-fuh-syze) *v.* [-sized; -siz·ing] 1. To stress; give emphasis to; make important. 2. To dwell upon; call attention to.

em·phat·ic (em-*fat*-ik) *adj.* 1. Marked by emphasis; energetic; forceful. 2. Striking; especially noticeable.—**em·phat·i·cal·ly** *adv.*

em·pire (*em*-pyre) *n.* 1. Imperial power; supreme dominion. 2. Territory, state, or group of states under the dominion of an emperor or any single powerful government or sovereign. 3. [*cap.*] Any specific empire. 'The British Empire.'—*adj.* 1. Pertaining to a specific empire. 2. [*cap.*] Denoting a style of dress and furniture developed under the first French Empire (1804–1815).

em·pir·ic (em-*pir*-ik) *n.* 1. One who relies on experience and observation rather than scientific training. 2. A quack; pretender to medical skill.—**em·pir·i·cal** (em-*pir*-ih-k'l) *adj.* Also **em·pir·ic.** Based solely on experience and observation.—**em·pir·i·cal·ly** *adv.*

em·pir·i·cism (em-*pir*-uh-sizm) *n.* 1. The philosophy which maintains that all knowledge is based on experience. 2. Empirical methods or use, esp. the unscientific practice of medicine; quackery.—**em·pir·i·cist** *n.* & *adj.*

em·place·ment (em-*playss*-m'nt) *n.* 1. A foundation or space for a heavy gun. 2. Assignment to, or placing in, a specific location.

em·ploy (em-*ploy*) *v.* 1. To use. 2. To occupy; engage the time or attention of. 3. To engage in one's service; hire.—**em·ploy** *n.*

em·ploy·ee (em-*ploy*-ee) *n.* [*pl.* -ees] Also **em·ploy·é, em·ploy·e.** One who works for salary or wages.

em·ploy·er (em-*ploy*-er) *n.* One who hires the service of a person or persons.

em·ploy·ment (em-*ploy*-m'nt) *n.* 1. Utilization; use; act of hiring. 2. Work, occupation; business.

em·po·ri·um (em-*poh*-ree-um) *n.* [*pl.* -ri·ums, -ri·a] 1. A trade center. 2. A store which carries many commodities; department store.

em·pow·er (em-*pow*-er) *v.* To authorize; commission; permit.

em·press (*em*-pris) *n.* The wife of an emperor; feminine ruler of an empire.

emp·ty (*emp*-tee) *adj.* [-ti·er; -ti·est] 1. Containing nothing; void of contents or occupants; vacant. 2. Lacking in reality, sense, or sincerity; meaningless; vain. 3. *Colloquial.* Hungry.—*v.* [-tied; -ty·ing] To remove the contents from; become empty; discharge.—**emp·ti·ly** *adv.*—**emp·ti·ness** *n.*

empty-armed	empty-headed	empty-minded
empty-barreled	empty-hearted	empty-mouthed
empty-handed	empty looking	empty-skulled

em·pur·ple (em-*per*-p'l) *n.* [-pled; -pl·ing] To make purple.—**em·pur·pled** *adj.*

em·py·e·ma (em-pih-*ee*-muh; em-py-) *n.* [*pl.* -ma·ta] *Medicine.* A collection of pus in a body cavity, esp. the chest.—**em·py·e·mic** *adj.*

em·pyr·e·al (em-*pir*-ee-ul) *adj.* Pure; celestial.

em·py·re·an (em-puh-*ree*-un) *n.* 1. The highest and purest region of heaven. 2. The firmament; sky.—**em·py·re·an** *adj.*

e·mu (*ee*-myoo) *n.* A large Australian nonflying bird, related to the ostrich.

em·u·late (*em*-yuh-layt) *v.* [-lat·ed; -lat·ing] To vie with; try to equal or surpass.

em·u·la·tion (em-yuh-*lay*-sh'n) *n.* Rivalry; ambition to equal. —**em·u·la·tive** *adj.* — **-tive·ly** *adv.*

EMU (1/40 life size)

em·u·lous (*em*-yuh-lus *adj.* Desirous of equaling or excelling another. —**em·u·lous·ly** *adv.*—**em·u·lous·ness** *n.*

e·mul·si·fy (eh-*mul*-suh-fye) *v.* [-fied; -fy·ing] To make into or subject to an emulsion.—**e·mul·si·fi·ca·tion** *n.*—**e·mul·si·fi·er** *n.*

e·mul·sion (eh-*mul*-sh'n) *n.* 1. One liquid suspended in another. 2. *Photography.* A light-sensitive silver compound mixed with gelatin. 3. Any milky fluid.—**e·mul·sive** *adj.*

en *n. Printing.* Half the width of an em.

en- *prefix.* 1. Into; put in or on. 2. Make; cause to be like. 3. Intensity.

-en *suffix.* 1. Made of. 2. To make; cause to be or have. 3. To become; gain. 4. Past participle ending of certain verbs.

en·a·ble (en-*ay*-b'l) *v.* [-bled; -bling] To make able; furnish with power, ability, etc.

en·act (en-*akt*) *v.* 1. To decree; make into a legislative act. 2. To play the part of; act out.

en·act·ment (en-*akt*-m'nt) *n.* 1. The act of making into law or playing as a role. 2. A law; act.

en·am·el (eh-*nam*-'l) *n.* 1. A glasslike substance for coating pottery, metal, etc. 2. A paint or coating which forms a smooth, hard, glossy surface. 3. *Anatomy.* The hard outer layer of a tooth.—*v.* [-el·ed; -elled; -el·ing; -el·ling] To cover with enamel.—**en·am·el·er, en·am·el·ler** *n.*—**en·am·el·ist, en·am·el·list** *n.*

en·am·or (eh-*nam*-er) *v.* To arouse love; captivate.—**en·am·ored** *adj.*

en bloc. All together; as a whole.

en·camp (en-*kamp*) *v.* To pitch tents; make a camp.—**en·camp·ment** *n.*

en·case (en-*kayss*) *v.* [en·cased; en·cas·ing] To enclose; cover entirely.

en·caus·tic (en-*kaw*-stik) *n.* The art of painting or decorating by burning in the colors or fixing them by means of heat.—**en·caus·tic** *adj.*

-ence (-*enss*) *suffix.* State; quality; act or degree.

en·ceinte (ahn-*sant*) *adj.* Pregnant; with child.

en·ce·phal·ic (en-suh-*fal*-ik) *adj.* Pertaining to or situated in the brain or cranial cavity.

en·ceph·a·li·tis (en-sef-uh-*lye*-tis) *n.* Inflammation of the brain.— **-a·lit·ic** (-uh-*lit*-ik) *adj.*

en·chain (en-*chayn*) *v.* To bind or hold in chains; fetter.—**en·chain·ment** *n.*

en·chant (en-*chant*) *v.* 1. To charm; fascinate. 2. To work a spell upon.—**en·chant·er** *n.*—**en·chant·ress** *n.*

en·chant·ing *adj.* Charming; delightful; fascinating.—**en·chant·ing·ly** *adv.*— **-chant·ment** *n.*

en·chase (en-*chayss*) *v.* [en·chased; en·chas·ing] 1. To surround with an ornamental setting. 2. To adorn with embossed work.

en·cir·cle (en-*serk*-'l) *v.* [-cir·cled; -cir·cling] To encompass; surround.—**en·cir·cle·ment** *n.*

en·clit·ic (en-*klit*-ik) *adj. Grammar.* Suffixed; subjoined.—**en·clit·ic** *n.*

en·close (en-*klohz*) *v.* [-closed; -clos·ing]. Also **inclose.** To surround; shut in; encompass.

en·clo·sure (en-*kloh*-zher) *n.* 1. A fenced-in or shut-off area. 2. The surrounding of an area with a wall or fence. 3. A surrounding wall.

en·co·mi·ast (en-*koh*-mee-ast) *n.* One who praises another; panegyrist.—**en·co·mi·as·tic** (en-koh-mee-*as*-tik), **en·co·mi·as·ti·cal** *adj.*

en·co·mi·um (en-*koh*-mee-um) *n.* [*pl.* -mi·ums, -mi·a] Praise; eulogy; panegyric.

en·com·pass (en-*kuhm*-p's) *v.* To encircle; enclose; surround.—**en·com·pass·ment** *n.*

en·core (*on*-kor; *on*-kor) *interj.* Again; once more.—*v.* [en·cored; en·cor·ing] To call for a repeated or additional performance.—*n.* Repeated or additional number performed at the request of the audience.

en·coun·ter (en-*kown*-ter) *v.* 1. To meet; come upon. 2. To meet in conflict.—**en·coun·ter** *n.*

en·cour·age (en-*kur*-ij) *v.* [-aged; -ag·ing] 1. To inspirit; cheer. 2. To foster; promote.

en·cour·age·ment (en-*kur*-ij-m'nt) *n.* Aid; support; cheer; hope; favorable conditions.

en·cour·ag·ing *adj.* Hopeful; favorable; cheering; inspiriting.—**en·cour·ag·ing·ly** *adv.*

en·croach (en-*krohch*) *v.* To trespass; infringe. —**en·croach·er** *n.*—**en·croach·ment** *n.*

en·crust (en-*krust*) *v.* Also **in·crust.** To cover with a crust or hard outer layer.

en·cum·ber (en-*kum*-ber) *v.* To load; burden.

en·cum·brance (en-*kum*-br'nss) *n.* 1. A hindrance; hampering burden; impediment. 2. *Law.* Liability resting in an estate.

en·cy·cli·cal (en-*sy*-klih-k'l) *adj.* Sent out to many persons or places.—*n. Roman Catholic Church.* A letter issued by the Pope for widespread circulation.

en·cy·clo·pe·di·a, en·cy·clo·pae·di·a (en-sy-kluh-*pee*-dee-uh) *n.* A work separately treating all branches of human knowledge.

en·cy·clo·pe·dic, en·cy·clo·pae·dic (en-sy-kluh-*pee*-dik) *adj.* Also **en·cy·clo·pe·di·cal, -pae·di·cal.** Universal in knowledge and information.

en·cy·clo·pe·dist, en·cy·clo·pae·dist (en-sy-kluh-*pee*-dist) *n.* The compiler of an encyclopedia.

en·cyst (en-*sist*) *v.* To enclose in a cyst or vesicle.—**en·cyst·ment** *n.*

end *n.* 1. The extreme point or edge; tip. 2. Termination; conclusion. 3. Death; decease. 4. Consequence; result. 5. Purpose; aim.—*v.* To terminate; conclude.—**end·er** *n.*

end-all	end grain	end-rack
endboard	end-match	endways
endgate	endpiece	endwise

en·dan·ger (en-*dayn*-jer) *v.* To imperil; expose to injury.

en·dear (en-*deer*) *v.* To bind by ties of affection and love; attach.—**en·dear·ing·ly** *adv.*

en·dear·ment *n.* 1. Caress; tender expression. 2. Attachment; bond of affection.

en·deav·or (en-*dev*-er) *v.* To try; attempt; aim. —**en·deav·or** *n.*—**en·deav·or·er** *n.*

en·dem·ic (en-*dem*-ik) *adj.* Also **en·dem·i·cal.** Peculiar to a particular people, nation, or region.—*n.* A disease attacking a particular district or people.—**en·dem·i·cal·ly** *adv.*

end·ing *n.* 1. Termination; conclusion. 2. *Grammar.* A word's final inflective syllable or letter.

en·dive (*en*-dyve; *on*-deev) *n.* A curly-leafed salad herb.

end·less *adj.* Interminable; unceasing; boundless; deathless.— **-less·ly** *adv.*— **-less·ness** *n.*

end·most *adj.* Farthest; most remote.

en·do- *prefix.* Within.

en·do·crine (*en*-duh-kryne) *adj.* Producing an internal secretion, as certain glands.—**en·do·crine, en·do·crin** *n.* 1. An internal secretion. 2. An internally secreting gland.

en·dog·a·my (en-*dog*-uh-mee) *n.* Prohibition of

marriage outside one's tribe or group.—**en·do·gam·ic** (en-duh-*gam*-ik), **en·dog·a·mous** *adj.*

en·dog·e·nous (en-*doj*-uh-nus) *adj.* Internal; originating from within.—**en·dog·e·nous·ly** *adv.*

en·do·plasm (*en*-duh-plazm) *n.* Inner mass of cell material.—**en·do·plas·mic** (-*plaz*-mik) *adj.*

en·dorse (en-*dorss*) *v.* [-dorsed; -dors·ing]. Also **in·dorse.** 1. To approve; sanction. 2. To transfer by writing one's name on the back. 'Endorse a check.'—**en·dors·a·ble** *adj.*—**en·dors·er** *n.*

en·dorse·ment *n.* Also **in·dorse·ment.** 1. Approval; sanction. 2. Signature on the back of a check.

en·do·skel·e·ton (en-doh-*skel*-uh-tun) *n. Anatomy.* The bony structure of man and other animals.

en·do·sperm (*en*-doh-sperm) *n. Botany.* The tissue surrounding the embryo in seeds.

en·dow (en-*dow*) *v.* 1. To provide for a permanent fund. 2. To bestow.

en·dow·ment *n.* 1. Property, fund, or revenue permanently established for a particular object. 2. Natural capacity or gifts.

en·due (en-*dyoo*) *v.* [-dued; en·du·ing] To invest; clothe.

en·dur·a·ble (en-*dyoor*-uh-b'l) *adj.* Bearable.

en·dur·ance (en-*dyoor*-'nss) *n.* Fortitude; strength; ability to bear pain, hardship, etc.

en·dure *v.* [-dured; -dur·ing] 1. To bear; put up with; tolerate. 2. To last; continue.

en·dur·ing *adj.* 1. Lasting long. 2. Long-suffering.—**en·dur·ing·ly** *adv.*—**-ing·ness** *n.*

end·wise *adv.* Also **end·ways.** On the end; in an upright position.

en·e·ma (*en*-uh-muh) *n.* Injection of a liquid into the rectum for medicinal purposes.

en·e·my (*en*-uh-mee) *n.* [*pl.* -mies] Foe; antagonist.—**en·e·my** *adj.*

en·er·get·ic (en-er-*jet*-ik) *adj.* Forceful; vigorous; dynamic.—**en·er·get·i·cal·ly** *adv.*

en·er·gize (*en*-er-jyze) *v.* [-gized; -giz·ing] To vitalize; stimulate.—**en·er·giz·er** *n.*

en·er·gy (*en*-er-jee) *n.* [*pl.* -gies] 1. Force; vigor; power. 2. Ability to perform work.

en·er·vate (*en*-er-vayt) *v.* [-vat·ed; -vat·ing] To weaken; debilitate.— **-va·tion** *n.*— **-va·tor** *n.*

en·fee·ble (en-*fee*-b'l) *v.* [-bled; -bling]. To weaken; deprive of strength.—**en·fee·ble·ment** *n.*

en·fi·lade (en-fil-*ayd*) *n. Military.* An objective which may be raked by fire through its whole length.—*v.* [-lad·ed; -lad·ing].

en·fold *v.* Also **in·fold.** To embrace.

en·force (en-*forss*) *v.* [-forced; -forc·ing] 1. To put into execution; make effective. 2. To strengthen; invigorate. 3. To use force; effect by force.—**en·force·a·ble** *adj.*—**en·forc·er** *n.*

en·force·ment *n.* A carrying out.

en·fran·chise (en-*fran*-chyze) *v.* [-chised; -chis·ing] 1. To give the right to vote. 2. To make free and independent.—**en·fran·chise·ment** *n.*

en·gage (en-*gayj*) *v.* [-gaged; -gag·ing] 1. To bind, as by pledge, contract, or promise; obligate. 2. To employ; hire. 3. To win and attach; draw to. 4. To occupy; take up. 'Engage in business.' 5. To betroth. 6. To enter into contest with. 7. To mesh.

en·gaged *adj.* 1. Affianced; betrothed. 2. Hired. 3. Occupied. 4. Enmeshed.

en·gage·ment *n.* 1. Betrothal. 2. Appointment. 3. Battle; conflict.

en·gag·ing *adj.* Attractive; pleasing.— **-ing·ly** *adv.*

en·gen·der (en-*jen*-der) *v.* To produce; create.

en·gine (*en*-jun) *n. Mechanics.* A machine for applying any mechanical or physical power to effect a particular purpose.

en·gi·neer (en-jin-*eer*) *n.* 1. One skilled in the principles and practice of building, construction, sanitation, electricity, etc. 2. A locomotive driver; one who attends to the machinery on board a steam vessel.

en·gi·neer (en-jin-*eer*) *v.* To guide; manage; direct.—**en·gi·neer·ing** *n.* 1. The art of construction or the use of engines or machines. 2. Management; maneuvering.

Eng·lish *adj.* Pertaining to England or its inhabitants.—*n.* 1. The people of England. 2. The chief language spoken in England, the United States, etc. 3. *Billiards.* Spin put on a ball to make it deviate from its normal direction.

English-born English-hearted English-minded
English-bred English-made English-rigged
English-built English-manned English speaking

English horn. A double-reed wind instrument; the alto oboe.

Eng·lish·man *n.* A native of England.—**Eng·lish·wo·man** *n.*

English setter. A large breed of setter having a white coat spotted with black and tan.

en·gorge (en-*gorj*) *v.* [en·gorged; en·gorg·ing] 1. To devour; swallow large quantities. 2. *Medicine.* To fill; congest.

en·graft (en-*graft*) *v.* To insert; introduce.

en·grave (en-*grayv*) *v.* [-graved; -grav·ing] 1. To cut figures, letters, or devices on stone, metal, etc. 2. To print from a prepared plate. 3. To impress deeply.—**en·grav·er** *n.*

en·grav·ing (en-*grayv*-ing) *n.* 1. The art of putting designs on metal plates or wooden blocks for reproduction by printing. 2. A reproduction from an engraved plate; print.

en·gross (en-*grohss*) *v.* 1. To absorb; monopolize the attention of. 2. To copy in large handwriting.—**en·gross·er** *n.*—**en·gross·ment** *n.*

en·grossed *adj.* Absorbed; intent.—**en·gross·ing** *adj.* Absorbing; fascinating.— **-ing·ly** *adv.*

en·gulf (en-*guhlf*) *v.* To swallow up; overcome.

en·hance (en-*hanss*) *v.* [en·hanced; en·hanc·ing] To heighten; increase.—**en·hance·ment** *n.*

e·nig·ma (eh-*nig*-muh) *n.* [*pl.* -mas] A riddle; mystery.—**e·nig·mat·ic** (en-ig-*mat*-ik) *adj.* Obscure; ambiguous; puzzling.— **-i·cal·ly** *adv.*

en·join (en-*joyn*) *v.* 1. To order; command. 2. *Law.* To prohibit; forbid.—**en·join·er** *n.*

en·joy (en-*joy*) *v.* 1. To receive satisfaction

from; relish. 2. To possess; have and use. —en·joy·a·ble *adj.* —en·joy·a·bly *adv.*

en·joy·ment *n.* Pleasure; delight; satisfaction.

en·kin·dle (en-*kin*-d'l) *v.* [en·kin·dled; en·kin·dling] To excite; inflame; kindle.

en·lace (en-*layss*) *v.* [en·laced; en·lac·ing] To encircle; surround; enfold. —en·lace·ment *n.*

en·large (en-*lahrj*) *v.* [en·larged; en·larg·ing] 1. To expand; increase; augment. 2. To amplify; elaborate. —en·larg·er *n.*

en·large·ment *n.* 1. An increase in size or quantity; augmentation. 2. *Photography.* A positive print made by projecting a magnified image of the negative on sensitized paper.

en·light·en (en-*lyte*-'n) *v.* To inform; instruct; illuminate. —en·light·en·er *n.* —en·light·en·ment *n.* 1. Act of informing. 2. State of being informed.

en·list (en-*list*) *v.* 1. To volunteer for military service. 2. To engage; enroll; secure. 'Enlist his sympathy.' —en·list·ment *n.*

en·liv·en (en-*ly*-v'n) *v.* To animate; vivify; invigorate. —en·liv·en·er *n.*

en masse (en-*mass*). In a mass or whole body.

en·mesh (en-*mesh*) *v.* To entangle; ensnare; net.

en·mi·ty (*en*-muh-tee) *n.* [*pl.* -ties] Hostility; hatred; ill will; malignant disposition.

en·no·ble (en-*oh*-b'l) *v.* [en·no·bled; en·no·bling] 1. To dignify; elevate; promote; make noble. 2. To bestow a title upon. —en·no·ble·ment *n.*

en·nui (*on*-wee) *n.* [*pl.* en·nuis] Boredom; listlessness from want of interest. —en·nuied *adj.*

e·nor·mi·ty (eh-*nor*-muh-tee) *n.* [*pl.* -ties] 1. Hugeness; vastness. 2. Atrocity; outrage.

e·nor·mous (eh-*nor*-mus) *adj.* 1. Huge; vast. 2. Wicked; atrocious. —e·nor·mous·ly *adv.* — -mous·ness *n.*

e·nough (eh-*nuf*) *adj.* Satisfying; adequate. —*adv.* 1. Sufficiently; adequately. 2. Quite. —*n.* Sufficiency. —*interj.* Stop!, No more!

en·plane (en-*playn*) *v.* [en·planed; en·plan·ing] To board or climb into an airplane.

en·rage (en-*rayj*) *v.* [en·raged; en·rag·ing] To rouse to great anger; exasperate.

enrapt (en-*rapt*) *adj.* Transported with joy or enthusiasm; ecstatic.

en·rap·ture (en-*rap*-cher) *v.* [-tured; -tur·ing] To render ecstatic; transport with delight.

en·rich (en-*rich*) *v.* 1. To make wealthy; supply with riches. 2. To fertilize; render more productive. 3. To fill with abundance. 4. To adorn; ornament. — -rich·er *n.* — -rich·ment *n.*

en·roll, en·rol (en-*rohl*) *v.* [-rolled; -roll·ing] 1. To become a member; enlist. 2. To enter a name in a register. —en·roll·ment, en·rol·ment *n.*

en route (on-*root*). On the way.

en·san·guine (en-*sang*-gwin) *v.* [en·san·guined; -guin·ing] To cover or smear with blood.

en·sconce (en-*skonss*) *v.* [-sconced; -sconc·ing] 1. To settle; install. 2. To protect; hide.

en·sem·ble (on-*som*-b'l) *n.* 1. The general effect of a whole. 2. *Music.* a. The union of several performers in a concerted composition. b. A group of musicians who perform together.

en·shrine (en-*shryne*) *v.* [-shrined; -shrin·ing] 1. To cherish; preserve with care. 2. To enclose in a shrine. —en·shrine·ment *n.*

en·shroud (en-*shrowd*) *n.* To cover; conceal.

en·sign *n.* 1. (*en*-s'n, *en*-syne) A flag; banner, esp. a national flag. 2. (*en*-s'n) The lowest-ranking commissioned officer in the U.S. navy. 3. (*en*-syne) A badge or symbol of office. —en·sign·cy, en·sign·ship *n.*

en·si·lage (*en*-suh-lij) *n.* Cattle fodder stored in a silo. —en·sile *v.* To lay up fodder.

en·slave (en-*slayv*) *v.* [-slaved; -slav·ing] To reduce to slavery; deprive of liberty; make a slave or pawn of. — -slave·ment *n.* — -slav·er *n.*

en·snare (en-*snair*) *v.* [-snared; -snar·ing] To trap; lure to destruction; catch.

en·sue (en-*syoo*, en-*soo*) *v.* [-sued; -su·ing] To follow; succeed; happen after. — -su·ing·ly *adv.*

en·sure (en-*shoor*) *v.* [-sured; -sur·ing]. Also insure. To make secure or certain; guarantee.

en·tab·la·ture (en-*tab*-luh-cher) *n. Architecture.* Vertical part of a structure resting on columns.

en·tail (en-*tayl*) *v.* 1. To include; have as consequence. 2. *Law.* To limit the inheritance of property to a particular heir or line in perpetuity. —*n. Law.* 1. Rule of descent established for a property. 2. Property so bequeathed.

en·tan·gle (en-*tang*-g'l) *v.* [-gled; -gling] 1. To make or become snarled, fouled, or confused. 2. To involve in anything complicated or difficult of extrication. 3. To perplex; confuse. —en·tan·gler *n.* —en·tan·gle·ment *n.*

en·tente (ahn-*tahnt*) *n.* An alliance between nations.

en·ter (*en*-ter) *v.* 1. To come or go in; pass into. 2. To embark upon; be initiated into.

en·ter·ic (en-*tehr*-ik) *adj.* Of the intestines. —en·teric fever. Typhoid fever.

en·ter·prise (*en*-ter-pryze) *n.* 1. A business undertaking. 2. A project, esp. of a daring nature. 3. Adventurous spirit; initiative.

en·ter·pris·ing (*en*-ter-pryze-ing) *adj.* Bold; venturesome; competitive. —en·ter·pris·ing·ly *adv.*

en·ter·tain (en-ter-*tayn*) *v.* 1. To receive as guest; offer hospitality. 2. To amuse; divert; please. 3. To consider; weigh or hold in the mind. —en·ter·tain·er *n.*

en·ter·tain·ing *adj.* Diverting; amusing; interesting. — -tain·ing·ly *adv.* — -tain·ing·ness *n.*

en·ter·tain·ment *n.* 1. A performance which serves to amuse or divert. 2. Amusement; pleasure derived from diversion. 3. Hospitable provision for guests; hospitable reception.

en·thrall, en·thral (en-*thrawl*) *v.* [-thralled; -thrall·ing] 1. To captivate; charm. 2. To hold in bondage; enslave. —en·thrall·er *n.* —en·thrall·ing·ly *adv.* —en·thrall·ment, en·thral·ment *n.*

en·throne (en-*throhn*) *v.* [-throned; -thron·ing] 1. To exalt; dignify; raise to a high position. 2. To crown —en·throne·ment *n.*

E

en·thuse (en-*thooz*) *v.* [-thused; -thus·ing] *Colloquial*. To be or make enthusiastic.

en·thu·si·ast *n.* A zealot; devotee.

en·thu·si·as·tic *adj.* Eager; ardent; fervent. —**en·thu·si·asm** *n.*—**en·thu·si·as·ti·cal·ly** *adv.*

en·tice (en-*tysse*) *v.* [-ticed; -tic·ing] To allure; attract; tempt.—**en·tic·er** *n.*—**en·tice·ment** *n.* —**en·tic·ing·ly** *adv.*

en·tire (en-*tyre*) *adj.* Whole; unbroken; complete; full.—**en·tire·ly** *adv.*

en·tire·ty (en-*tyre*-uh-tee) *n.* [*pl.* -ties] Wholeness; a complete whole; total.

en·ti·tle (en-*ty*-t'l) *v.* [-tled; -tling] 1. To name; call; designate. 2. To offer a right or claim to; furnish with grounds for a claim.

en·ti·ty (*en*-tih-tee) *n.* [*pl.* -ties] 1. A being; thing. 2. Existence; essence; being.

en·tomb (en-*toom*) *v.* To bury; inter; place in a tomb.—**en·tomb·ment** *n.*

en·to·mol·o·gy (en-tuh-*mol*-uh-jee) *n.* [*pl.* -gies] Branch of zoology concerned with insects.—**en·to·mo·log·ic** (en-tuh-muh-*loj*-ik), **-i·cal** *adj.* — **-i·cal·ly** *adv.*— **-mol·o·gist** (-*mol*-uh-jist) *n.*

en·tou·rage (ahn-toor-*ahzh*) *n.* Retinue; group of attendants or followers.

en·tr'acte (ahn-*trakt*) *n.* 1. An intermission; interval between the acts of a drama. 2. A short musical piece performed in this interval.

en·trails (*en*-traylz) *n. pl.* 1. Viscera of animals; guts. 2. Internal parts.

en·train (en-*trayn*) *v.* To board a train.

en·trance (*en*-trunss) *n.* 1. A passage into; opposite of *exit*. 2. A coming or entering into. 3. Power or right to enter; admission. 4. An anticipated or ostentatious entry. 'she made a sweeping entrance.' 5. Beginning; debut; initiation.

en·trance (en-*transs*) *v.* [-tranced; -tranc·ing] To fascinate; hold spellbound; enrapture. —**en·trance·ment** *n.*—**en·tranc·ing·ly** *adv.*

en·trance·way (*en*-trunss-way) *n.* Means of entry; passageway or door leading in.

en·trap (en-*trap*) *v.* [-trapped; -trap·ping] To ensnare; entangle; involve in difficulties.

en·treat (en-*treet*) *v.* To beg; plead; beseech. —**en·treat·y** (en-*treet*-ee) *n.* [*pl.* -ies] An earnest request; plea; prayer.—**en·treat·ing·ly** *adv.*

en·tree (*ahn*-tray) *n.* 1. A dish served before the meat course. 2. The main course of a meal. 3. Freedom of access.

en·trench (en-*trench*) *v.* Also **in·trench.** 1. To install or establish securely. 'Well entrenched in the job.' 2. To make a trench about. 3. To trespass.—**en·trench·ment** *n.*

en·tre·pôt (*ahn*-truh-poh) *n.* A depot for goods, esp. warehouse for dutiable goods.

en·tre·pre·neur (ahn-truh-pruh-*ner*) *n.* The owner and manager of a business or artistic enterprise.

en·trust (en-*trust*) *v.* Also **in·trust.** To commit to another's care.

en·try (*en*-tree) *n.* [*pl.* en·tries] 1. An item recorded in an accounting record book. 2. En-tranceway; passage in. 3. An entering into; ingress. 4. Right to enter upon or into. 5. Legal procedure followed to import dutiable goods.

en·twine (en-*twyne*) *v.* [en·twined; en·twin·ing] To twist or twine about.

e·nu·mer·ate (eh-*noo*-mer-ayt) *v.* [-at·ed; -at·ing] To list; mention in detail; recount; recapitulate.— **-a·tion** *n.*— **-a·tive** *adj.*— **-a·tor** *n.*

e·nun·ci·ate (eh-*nun*-see-ayt) *v.* [-at·ed; -at·ing] 1. To give utterance; announce; proclaim. 2. To speak; pronounce; articulate.—**e·nun·ci·a·tion** *n.* Pronunciation; articulation.—**e·nun·ci·a·tive** *adj.*— **-a·tive·ly** *adv.*— **-a·to·ry** *adj.*

en·vel·op (en-*vel*-up) *v.* 1. To cover; enwrap; surround. 2. To conceal by covering or surrounding.—**en·vel·op·er** *n.*—**en·vel·op·ment** *n.*

en·ve·lope (*en*-vuh-lohp) *n.* 1. A wrapper or enclosing cover. 2. Any sheath or covering.

en·ven·om (en-*ven*-um) *v.* To poison; taint; render deadly. 'An envenomed tongue.'

en·vi·a·ble (*en*-vee-uh-b'l) *adj.* Highly desirable; exciting covetousness.—**en·vi·a·bly** *adv.*

en·vi·ous (*en*-vee-us) *adj.* Jealous; covetous. —**en·vi·ous·ly** *adv.*—**en·vious·ness** *n.*

en·vi·ron (en-*vy*-run) *v.* To surround; encircle.

en·vi·ron·ment *n.* The sum of external influences affecting an individual's development; surroundings.—**en·vi·ron·men·tal** (en-vy-run-*men*-t'l) *adj.*—**en·vi·ron·men·tal·ly** *adv.*

en·vi·rons (en-*vy*-runz) *n. pl.* Neighborhood.

en·vis·age (en-*viz*-ij) *v.* [-aged; -ag·ing] To visualize; picture; apprehend.

en·vi·sion (en-*vizh*-un) *v.* To imagine; picture; see in the mind's eye.

en·voy (*en*-voy) *n.* 1. A representative; delegate; one dispatched on a special mission. 2. Also **envoi.** A brief stanza at the end of a ballade.

en·vy (*en*-vee) *n.* [*pl.* en·vies] 1. Jealousy; discontent at another's good fortune. 2. The object of jealousy; that which is coveted.—*v.* [-vied; -vy·ing] To be jealous or covetous of. —**en·vi·er** *n.*—**en·vy·ing·ly** *adv.*

en·wrap (en-*rap*) *v.* [en·wrapped; en·wrap·ping] To envelop; swathe; cover about.

en·zyme (*en*-zyme) *n.* An organic secretion which hastens the transmutation of food and other substances.—**en·zy·mat·ic** (en-zy-*mat*-ik) *adj.*

E·o·cene (*ee*-uh-seen) *adj. Geology.* Of the epoch in which living things were first coming into being.—*n.* The Eocene epoch.

e·o·lith·ic (ee-uh-*lith*-ik) *adj. Archaeology.* Denoting the period in which primitive man developed the use of crude stone tools.

e·on, aeon (*ee*-on) *n.* An age; long period of time; epoch.

E·os (*ee*-os). *Greek Mythology.* The dawn goddess, corresponding to the Roman Aurora.

e·o·sin (*ee*-uh-sin) *n.* Also **e·o·sine.** A rose-colored dye or stain compounded of bromine and other elements. (*Symbol:* $C_{20}H_8Br_4O_5$). —**e·o·sin·ic** (ee-uh-*sin*-ik) *adj.*

ep·au·let, ep·au·lette (*ep*-uh-let) *n.* A distinguishing shoulder piece for military uniforms.

e·pergne (eh-*pern*) *n.* An ornamental stand with a large dish and branchings, used as centerpiece.

e·phed·rine (uh-*fed*-rin) *n.* Also **e·phe·drin.** An organic medicinal alkaloid which dilates the upper passages of the nose, affects circulation, etc.

EPAULET

e·phem·er·al (uh-*fem*-er-'l) *adj.* Temporary; transient; existing only a day or for a short time.—**e·phem·er·al** *n.*—**e·phem·er·al·ly** *adv.*

e·phem·er·id (uh-*fem*-er-id) *n. Zoology.* A family of insects which live in their adult stage only about a day.

E·phe·sians (eh-*feezh*-unz) *n.* Epistle written by St. Paul to the Christians of Ephesus.

ep·ic (*ep*-ik) *adj.* Also **ep·i·cal.** In a lofty, narrative style; heroic.—*n.* A narrative poem in an exalted style, having a great hero as its subject.—**ep·i·cal·ly** *adv.*

ep·i·cene (*ep*-ih-seen) *n.* 1. *Grammar.* A noun having one form to indicate both genders. 2. A person with characteristics of both sexes. —**ep·i·cene** *adj.*

ep·i·cen·ter (*ep*-ih-sen-ter) *n.* 1. The point on the earth's surface above the center of an earthquake. 2. The crux; focus.

ep·i·cure (*ep*-ih-kyoor) *n.* 1. One with a taste for fine foods. 2. One devoted to sensual enjoyments.

ep·i·cu·re·an (ep-ih-kyoor-*ee*-un) *adj.* 1. Loving luxury, esp. table delicacies; luxurious. 2. [*cap.*] Pertaining to the Greek philosopher Epicurus.—**ep·i·cur·ean** *n.*—**Ep·i·cu·re·an·ism** *n.*

ep·i·dem·ic (ep-ih-*dem*-ik) *n.* A widespread contagion, as a disease; an uncontrollably generalized condition.—*adj.* Prevalent; affecting many over a large area.—**ep·i·dem·i·cal·ly** *adv.*

ep·i·der·mis (ep-ih-*der*-mis) *n.* The outermost layer of skin of animals and plants.—**ep·i·der·mal, ep·i·der·mic** *adj.*

ep·i·glot·tis (ep-ih-*glot*-is) *n.* A cartilage behind the tongue covering the glottis in swallowing.

ep·i·gram (ep-ih-gram) *n.* A thought presented pointedly and pungently in few words.—**ep·i·gram·mat·ic** (-*mat*-ik), **-i·cal** *adj.*— **-i·cal·ly** *adv.*

ep·i·graph (*ep*-ih-graf) *n.* 1. A quotation or motto at the beginning of a literary work. 2. An inscription on a monument, edifice, etc.

e·pig·ra·phy (eh-*pig*-ruh-fee) *n.* The science or study of inscriptions; the inscriptions themselves.—**e·pig·ra·pher, e·pig·ra·phist** *n.*

ep·i·lep·sy (*ep*-ih-lep-see) *n.* A chronic, functional nervous disease manifested by fits and convulsions.—**ep·i·lep·tic** (ep-uh-*lep*-tik) *adj.* —*n.* A victim of epilepsy.—**ep·i·lep·ti·cal·ly** *adv.*

ep·i·logue (*ep*-ih-log) *n.* Also **ep·i·log.** 1. An appended section, as of a literary work, rounding out the structure, and often bringing the narrative back to the present time. 2. A speech delivered to the audience by one of the actors or a narrator at the end of a play.

E·piph·a·ny (eh-*pif*-uh-nee) *n.* [*pl.* -nies] A Christian festival celebrated on January 6 to commemorate the manifestation of Christ to the Gentiles in the visit of the Magi.

e·pis·co·pa·cy (eh-*pis*-kuh-puh-see) *n.* Administration of the church by bishops.

e·pis·co·pal *adj.* 1. Pertaining to or under the authority of a bishop. 2. [*cap.*] Denoting the churches of the Anglican communion.—**e·pis·co·pal·ly, E·pis·co·pal·ly** *adv.*

e·pis·co·pa·li·an (eh-pis-kuh-*payl*-yun) *n.* 1. [*cap.*] A member of the Episcopal Church. 2. A believer in the administration of the church by bishops, rather than a Pope.—**e·pis·co·pal·ian, E·pis·co·pal·ian** *adj.*—**E·pis·co·pa·li·an·ism** *n.*

e·pis·co·pate (eh-*pis*-kuh-pit) *n.* 1. A bishopric; bishop's office and authority. 2. Bishops collectively.—*v.* [-pat·ed; -pat·ing]. To act as a bishop.

ep·i·sode (*ep*-uh-sohd) *n.* 1. An incident; occurrence. 2. *Music.* A variation. 3. An incidental narrative, as in a play or novel.—**ep·i·sod·ic, -i·cal** (ep-uh-*sod*-ik) *adj.*— **-i·cal·ly** *adv.*

e·pis·te·mol·o·gy (eh-pis-tuh-*mol*-uh-jee) *n. Philosophy.* The science investigating the nature and validity of knowledge.—**e·pis·te·mo·log·i·cal** (-muh-*loj*-ih-k'l) *adj.*— **-i·cal·ly** *adv.*

e·pis·tle (eh-*pis*-'l) *n.* 1. A letter. 2. [*cap.*] A section of the New Testament containing a letter of an Apostle.

e·pis·to·lar·y (eh-*pis*-tuh-lehr-ee) *adj.* In the form of a letter.

ep·i·taph (*ep*-ih-taf) *n.* 1. An inscription on a tombstone. 2. A brief eulogy.— **-taph·ic** *adj.*

ep·i·tha·la·mi·um (ep-ih-thuh-*lay*-mee-um) *n.* [*pl.* -mi·ums, -mi·a] A song or poem honoring a couple at their wedding.

ep·i·the·li·um (ep-ih-*thee*-lih-um) *n.* [*pl.* -li·ums, -li·a] The tissue lining body cavities.—**ep·i·the·li·al** *adj.*

ep·i·thet (*ep*-ih-thet) *n.* An appellation; descriptive name. 'Honest Abe.'

e·pit·o·me (eh-*pit*-uh-mee) *n.* 1. A digest; summary. 2. A complete representation.

e·pit·o·mize (eh-*pit*-uh-myze) *v.* [-mized; -miz·ing] 1. To condense; summarize. 2. To contain all the qualities of.—**e·pit·o·mist** *n.*

ep·i·zo·ot·ic (ep-ih-zoh-*ot*-ik) *adj.* Infecting animals. *n.* Also **ep·i·zo·o·ty.** An epidemic among animals other than humans.

ep·och (*ep*-uk) *n.* An era; age; period in history. —**ep·och·al** *adj.*—**ep·och·al·ly** *adv.*

ep·ode (*ep*-ohd) *n.* 1. A lyric poem with alternate long and short verses. 2. Last part of an ode.

Epsom salts (*ep*-sum). Sulphate of magnesium used as a cathartic.

eq·ua·ble (*ek*-wuh-b'l) *adj.* 1. Even; steady;

not varying. 2. Proportionate; uniform; tranquil.—**e·qua·bil·i·ty, e·qua·ble·ness** n.

e·qual (ee-kw'l) adj. 1. Exactly the same in number, extent, degree, etc. 2. Equivalent; parallel; commensurate. 3. Adequate; qualified for. 'Equal to the task.'—n. A person of equivalent station.—v. [-qualed, -qualled; -qual·ing, -qual·ling].

e·qual·i·ty (eh-kwol-uh-tee) n. [pl. -ties] Equivalence; likeness in station; value; quality, etc.

e·qual·ize (eek-wuh-lyze) v. [e·qual·ized; -iz·ing] To adjust; balance; make equal or uniform. —**e·qual·i·za·tion** (eek-wul-iz-ay-sh'n) n.—**e·qual·iz·er** n. Slang. A pistol.

e·qual·ly (eek-wuh-lee) adv. 1. Alike; in the same manner. 2. Uniformly; in equal parts. 3. Equitably; impartially.

e·qua·nim·i·ty (eek-wuh-nim-ih-tee) n. Calmness; serenity of temper; lack of agitation.

e·quate (eh-quayt) v. [-quat·ed; -quat·ing] 1. To adjust equally; reduce to a common denominator. 2. Mathematics. To express by an equation.

e·qua·tion (eh-quay-zhun) n. Mathematics. 1. One quantity being expressed as the equal of another. 2. Chemistry. A collection of symbols representing a chemical reaction.

e·qua·tor (eh-quay-ter) n. 1. The imaginary line dividing the earth into two equal parts. 2. Astronomy. The equinoctial extension of the earth's equator so that it bisects the vault or sphere of the heavens.

EQUATOR

e·qua·to·ri·al (eek-wuh-tor-ee-ul) adj. Pertaining to the equator; having climate and other conditions like the equator's.—n. A telescopic device for keeping a star in view independently of the earth's rotation.

eq·uer·ry (ek-wer-ee) n. [pl. -ries] An officer in charge of the horses of nobles or royalty.

e·ques·tri·an (eh-ques-tree-un) adj. 1. Relating to horses or to horsemanship. 2. Mounted on horseback.—n. A horseman; highly skilled rider.—**e·ques·tri·enne** n.

e·qui- prefix. Equal. 'Equipoise; equilateral.'

e·qui·dis·tant (eek-wih-dis-t'nt) adj. Equally distant from a point.—**e·qui·dis·tant·ly** adv.

e·qui·lat·er·al (eek-wih-lat-er-ul) adj. Having all sides of equal length.—n. Geometry. A figure with equal sides.—**e·qui·lat·er·al·ly** adv.

e·quil·i·brant (eh-kwil-ih-br'nt) n. Physics. Any force which can balance or bring to equilibrium an opposing force or forces.

e·qui·li·brate (ee-kwih-ly-brayt) v. [-brat·ed; -brating] To balance; maintain equilibrium; steady with equal weights.—**e·qui·li·bra·tion** (ee-kwih-lih-bray-sh'n) n.—**-li·bra·tor** n.

e·qui·lib·ri·um (eek-wih-lib-ree-um) n. [pl. -ri·ums, -ri·a] 1. Equipoise; balance; equality of

weight, force, power, etc. 2. The state of a chemical reaction which has been completed.

e·quine (ee-kwyne) adj. 1. Relating to horses. 2. Of the horse species.—n. A horse.

e·qui·noc·tial (ee-kwih-nok-shul) adj. 1. Pertaining to the equinox or the equator. 2. Designating days and nights of equal length.—n. Also **equinoctial line**. The sky's equator, which is in the same plane as the earth's equator.

e·qui·nox (eek-wih-noks) n. Time at which the sun is over the earth's equator, giving 12 hours of daylight and darkness everywhere.

e·quip (eh-kwip) v. [-quipped; -quip·ping] 1. To furnish; fit out; provide apparatus. 2. To prepare; qualify for. 3. To dress.

eq·ui·page (ek-wih-pij) n. 1. Provisions for an expedition or excursion. 2. A retinue; body of traveling attendants. 3. A carriage.

e·quip·ment (eh-kwip-m'nt) n. sing. & pl. 1. Apparatus; facilities; necessary articles for an undertaking. 2. Qualifications as to mental capacity, physical powers, etc.

e·qui·poise (ee-kwih-poyz) n. Equilibrium; even balance; equality of weights or forces.

eq·ui·se·tum (ek-wih-see-tum) n. [pl. -tums, -ta] The horsetail; a genus of flowerless marsh plants which reproduce from spores.

eq·ui·ta·ble (ek-wih-tuh-b'l) adj. Just; fair; equal as to deserts.—**eq·ui·ta·ble·ness** n.—**eq·ui·ta·bly** adv.

eq·ui·ty (ek-wih-tee) n. [pl. -ties] 1. Colloquial. The value of an asset over and above debts outstanding against it. 2. Justice; impartiality. 3. Interpretation according to the spirit, not merely the letter, of the law. 4. A debt held against or outstanding against. 5. A legal system which has jurisdiction in such cases as cannot be adequately settled by common law. 6. [cap.] Actors Equity Association, a union of theatrical performers.

e·quiv·a·lence (eh-kwiv-uh-l'ns) n. Also̍ **e·quiv·a·len·cy**. Interchangeableness; equality of value, quantity, significance, etc.

e·quiv·a·lent (eh-kwiv-uh-l'nt) adj. 1. Interchangeable; equal; having the same value. 2. Synonymous; having the same meaning. 3. Geometry. Equal in area or volume but dissimilar in shape.—n. 1. Anything of equal value, power, effect, etc. 2. A synonym.

e·quiv·o·cal (eh-kwiv-uh-k'l) adj. 1. Ambiguous; having a double meaning; uncertain. 2. Dubious; open to suspicion.

e·quiv·o·cate (eh-kwiv-uh-kayt) v. [-cat·ed; -cat·ing] To prevaricate; be ambiguous; mislead by vague words.—**e·quiv·o·ca·tion** n.

-er suffix. 1. One who; that which. 'Polisher.' 2. Inhabitant of. 'New Zealander.' 3. Doer of. 'Worker.' 4. Occupied or employed to. 'Miller.' 5. More. 'Prettier; stupider.'

e·ra (eer-uh) n. An epoch; age; period; succession of years starting from a fixed point.

e·rad·i·ca·ble (uh-rad-ih-kuh-b'l) adj. 1. Effaceable; capable of being erased. 2. Capable of being destroyed.

e·rad·i·cate (uh-*rad*-ih-kayt) *v.* [-cat·ed; -cat·ing] 1. To exterminate; destroy utterly. 2. To obliterate; erase; blot out.—**e·rad·i·ca·tion** *n.*—**e·rad·i·ca·tive** *adj.*—**e·rad·i·ca·tor** *n.*

e·rase (uh-*rayss*) *v.* [-rased; -ras·ing] To efface; obliterate; remove traces of.—**e·ras·a·ble** *adj.*

e·ras·er *n.* 1. A piece of rubber for removing pencil marks. 2. Any device for effacing.

e·ra·sure (uh-*ray*-zher, -sher) *n.* 1. Obliteration; the rubbing out of a mark, word, etc. 2. Evidence that erasing was done.

er·bi·um (*er*-bee-um) *n.* A rare metallic element found in gladolinite. (*Symbol:* Er).

ere (*air*) *prep.* & *conj.* Before.

Er·e·bus (*er*-uh-bus). *Greek Mythology.* The dark, gloomy place through which damned souls passed en route to Hades.

e·rect (eh-*rekt*) *adj.* Upright; in a perpendicular position; pointed upward.—*v.* 1. To build; construct; raise up. 2. To set upright.—**e·rect·ly** *adv.*—**e·rect·ness** *n.*—**e·rect·or** *n.*

e·rect·ile (eh-*rek*-til) *adj.* Capable of elevating or rising up.

e·rec·tion (eh-*rek*-sh'n) *n.* 1. Construction; building. 2. Establishment; formation. 3. A structure; building. 4. *Physiology.* Rigidity or distention of erectile tissues, esp. of the penis, during stimulation or excitement.

ere·long (air-*long*) *adv.* Soon; before long.

ere·while (air-*hwyl*) *adv.* Some time ago.

erg (*erg*) *n.* *Physics.* A unit of energy equal to one dyne of work operative through one centimeter of distance.

er·go (*er*-goh) *conj.* Therefore; consequently.

er·gos·ter·ol (er-*gos*-ter-ohl) *n.* A preparation which, irradiated, supplies Vitamin D.

er·got (*er*-got) *n.* A fungus growth on rye and other grasses, the source of many medicines.

E·rie (*eer*-ee). 1. One of the Great Lakes, located north and northeast of Ohio. 2. A tribe of Indians related to the Iroquois.

Er·in (*air*-in). Sentimental name for Ireland.

E·ris (*eer*-is). *Greek Mythology.* The goddess of strife.

Er·i·tre·a (ehr-uh-*tree*-uh). An Italian colony north of Ethiopia. Area: 89,274. Capital: Mogadiscio.—**Er·i·tre·an** *n.* & *adj.*

erl·king (*erl*-king). *Scandinavian Mythology.* The king of the elves, who harms children.

er·mine (*er*-min) *n.* 1. A weasel which has a white coat in winter. 2. The highly prized fur of the ermine.

erne, ern *n.* The white-tailed sea eagle.

e·rode (uh-*rohd*) *v.* [e·rod·ed; e·rod·ing] 1. To wear away, esp. by running water. 2. To corrode; eat away; disintegrate.

ERMINE (1/9 life size)

E·ros (*eer*-os). *Mythology.* Cupid; the god of love.

e·rose (uh-*rohs*) *adj.* Irregularly shaped as if partially eroded; notched along the margin.

e·ro·sion (uh-*roh*-zhun) *n.* 1. Disintegration or wearing away. 2. Corrosion; the process of eating away.—**e·ro·sive** *adj.*

e·rot·ic (uh-*rot*-ik) *adj.* Also **e·rot·i·cal.** 1. Amorous; relating to love. 2. Exciting sexual desire.—**e·rot·i·cal·ly** *adv.*

e·rot·i·cism (uh-*rot*-iss-izm) *n.* Arousing of sexual desire; sexual love.

err *v.* 1. To make a mistake. 2. To fall into error; be led astray.—**er·ran·cy** *n.*

er·rand (*eh*-r'nd) *n.* 1. A mission; task to be performed at a distance. 2. A task for a messenger.

er·rant (*eh*-r'nt) *adj.* 1. Roving; wandering, esp. in search of adventure. 2. Deviating; astray; in error.—**er·rant·ly** *adv.*

er·rant·ry (*eh*-r'nt-ree) *n.* [*pl.* -ries] A wandering; roaming in search of adventure.

er·rat·ic (er-*at*-ik) *adj.* 1. Irregular; changeable; having no fixed course. 2. Eccentric; having peculiar habits.—**er·rat·i·cal·ly** *adv.*

er·ra·tum (er-*ay*-tum; -*ah*-) *n.* [*pl.* -ta] A mistake in writing or printing.

err·ing *adj.* 1. Transgressing; misbehaving. 2. Acting with poor judgment.—**err·ing·ly** *adv.*

er·ro·ne·ous (er-*oh*-nee-us) *adj.* Incorrect; fallacious; misleading; untrue.—**er·ro·ne·ous·ly** *adv.*

er·ror (*ehr*-er) *n.* 1. A mistake; fallacy; deviation from the truth. 2. A transgression; mistake in conduct. 3. A false belief. 4. *Baseball.* A misplay by a player in the field.

er·satz (ehr-*zahts*) *n.* *German.* An inferior substitute or synthetic.—*adj.* Made of inferior ingredients; substitute.

Erse (*erss*) *n.* 1. The Gaelic or Celtic speech of Scotland. 2. Any Celtic tongue.—**Erse** *adj.*

erst·while (*erst*-hwyle) *adj.* Former.

e·ruct (uh-*rukt*) *v.* Also **e·ruc·tate.** 1. To erupt; break forth. 2. To belch; eject stomach gas.—**e·ruc·ta·tion** (ee-ruk-*tay*-sh'n) *n.* A belch; burp.—**e·ruc·tive** *adj.*

er·u·dite (*ehr*-uh-dyte) *adj.* Scholarly; profoundly learned.— **-dite·ly** *adv.*— **-dite·ness** *n.*

er·u·di·tion (ehr-uh-*dish*-'n) *n.* Learning; scholarship; book knowledge.—**er·u·di·tion·al** *adj.*

e·rupt (uh-*rupt*) *v.* 1. To burst forth; eject violently. 2. To break out; form a skin rash.

e·rup·tion (uh-*rup*-sh'n) *n.* 1. An emission; ejection of matter. 2. A skin rash or blemish. 3. Any violent outbreak.—**e·rup·tive** *adj.*

er·y·sip·e·las (er-ih-*sip*-uh-l'ss) *n.* An acute, inflammatory skin disease attended by high fever.

E·sau (*ee*-saw) *n.* *Bible.* The brother of Jacob, who sold his birthright for a mess of pottage.

es·ca·drille (es-kuh-*dril*) *n.* A squadron of military ships or planes.

es·ca·lade (es-kuh-*layd*) *v.* [-lad·ed; -lad·ing] To storm a fortified place by scaling ladders.—**es·ca·lade** *n.*

Es·ca·la·tor (*es*-kuh-lay-ter) *n.* Trade-mark name for a moving stairway.

es·ca·pade (*es*-kuh-payd) *n.* 1. A prank; rash or scandalous adventure. 2. An escape.

es·cape (es-*kayp*) *v.* [-caped; -cap·ing] 1. To elude; evade; avoid. 2. To flee from; be set free. 3. To flow or be pressed out of. 4. To elude the notice, perception, or memory of.—*n.* 1. Flight; deliverance; freedom from danger. 2. That through which a person or thing escapes. 3. Leakage; emanation. 4. *Psychology.* A flight from reality and the conflicts of one's environment.—es·cap·er *n.*

es·cape·ment (es-*kayp*-m'nt) *n.* 1. Mechanism for regulating watches, meters, etc. 2. *Mechanics.* Device to keep a machine from operating until it can safely do so.

es·cap·ism (es-*kayp*-izm) *n.* A tendency to flee from or ignore reality.—es·cap·ist *adj.* & *n.*

es·carp·ment (es-*karp*-m'nt) *n.* A cliff; precipice, esp. one made for military use.

es·cheat (es-*cheet*) *n.* Reverting of land to the state when no legal heirs exist.—es·cheat *v.*

es·chew (es-*choo*) *v.* To shun.

es·cort (*es*-kort) *n.* 1. A convoy; armed guard. 2. A person's companion in public.—es·cort (es-*kort*) *v.* 1. To convoy; guard. 2. To accompany for protection or out of courtesy.

es·cri·toire (es-krih-*twahr*) *n.* A desk; writing table; secretary.

es·crow (*es*-kroh, es-*kroh*) *n. Law.* A deed held by a third party until certain obligations are fulfilled between the two interested parties.

es·cu·do (es-*koo*-doh) *n.* [*pl.* -dos] A Portuguese monetary unit and coin, worth about U.S. $1.

es·cu·lent (*es*-kyuh-l'nt) *n.* Edible; good as food.

es·cutch·eon (es-*kuch*-'n) *n.* 1. A shield bearing a coat of arms. 2. A name plate.

-ese *suffix.* Origin in; native of; language of. 'Chinese, Portuguese.'

Es·ki·mo (*es*-kim-oh). [*pl.* -mos, -mo] A race inhabiting the North Frigid Zone.

Eskimo dog. A husky, wolflike Arctic dog used as a beast of burden and draft.

e·soph·a·gus (uh-*sof*-uh-gus) *n.* [*pl.* -gi] The gullet; tube between the mouth and stomach.

es·o·ter·ic (es-uh-*tehr*-ik) *adj.* Also **es·o·ter·i·cal.** 1. Intelligible to a few; abstruse; taught only to a select few. 2. Private; confidential. —es·o·ter·i·cal·ly *adv.*

E S P (ee-es-*pee*). Extrasensory perception.

es·pe·cial (es-*pesh*-'l) *adj.* Particular; special; not ordinary or common.—es·pe·cial·ly *adv.*

Es·pe·ran·to (es-per-*on*-toh, -*an*-) *n.* A language constructed from Latin roots for an international language.

es·pi·al (es-*py*-ul) *n.* 1. Surveillance by a spy. 2. Observation; discovery.

es·pi·o·nage (es-pee-uh-*nij*) *n.* 1. A spying; gaining of information by close, secret watching. 2. Utilization of spies.

es·pla·nade (es-pluh-*nayd*) *n.* 1. A boardwalk; promenade beside a body of water. 2. Any open, level area.

es·pous·al (es-*powz*-'l) *n.* 1. A betrothal; marriage. 2. Decision to support a cause.

es·pouse (es-*powz*) *v.* [-poused; -pous·ing] 1. To marry; wed. 2. To adopt; embrace; take to oneself, as a cause, doctrine, etc.

es·prit (es-*pree*) *n.* Wit; cleverness.

esprit de corps (es-*pree* duh *kor*). A spirit or drive animating an entire group; morale.

es·py (es-*pye*) *v.* [-pied; -py·ing] To discern; discover; see unexpectedly.

-esque *suffix.* Like; having the features or qualities of. 'Picturesque; Romanesque.'

es·quire (es-*kwyre*) *n.* [*cap.*] Mister. 'John Smith, Esquire. *Abbreviation*: Esq.

-ess *suffix.* Feminine; female. 'Actress; princess.'

es·say (es-*ay*) *v.* To endeavor; attempt; try; test; analyze.—es·say·er *n.*

es·say (*es*-ay) *n.* 1. An endeavor; test; try. 2. A treatise; short, expository composition on a particular subject.

es·say·ist (*es*-ay-ist) *n.* An author of essays.

es·sence (*es*-'ns) *n.* 1. An extract; concentrated preparation. 2. Scent; perfume. 3. The basic characteristic or element of anything.

es·sen·tial (eh-*sen*-sh'l) *adj.* 1. Necessary; indispensable; basic. 2. Volatile; diffusible. 'Essential oils.'—*n.* A necessity; requirement. —es·sen·ti·al·i·ty *n.*—es·sen·tial·ly *adv.*

es·tab·lish (es-*tab*-lish) *v.* 1. To set; fix; make firm or stable. 2. To found; institute; settle. 3. To place in a secure position. 4. To prove; confirm; make valid or legal.—es·tab·lish·er *n.*

es·tab·lish·ment *n.* 1. A residence, place of business, or institution. 2. A fixed estate; settlement; confirmation. 3. Proof; validation. 4. Act of establishing.

es·tate *n.* 1. A plantation; large place of residential property. 2. Property willed or inherited. 3. Condition; circumstances; state. 4. An order or class of citizens.—*v.* [-tat·ed; -tat·ing] To endow with an estate.

es·teem (eh-*steem*) *n.* Respect; favorable opinion; regard.—es·teem *v.*

es·ter *n.* Compound formed from an organic acid and an alcohol by eliminating water.

Es·ther (*es*-ter) *n.* 17th book of the Old Testament.

es·ti·ma·ble (*es*-tim-uh-b'l) *adj.* 1. Worthy of respect or high regard. 2. Capable of estimation.—es·ti·ma·ble·ness *n.*—es·ti·ma·bly *adv.*

es·ti·mate (*es*-tih-mayt) *v.* [-mat·ed; -mat·ing] 1. To calculate cost; reckon; appraise. 2. To form a judgment of; rate.—es·ti·mate *n.*—es·ti·ma·tive** (*es*-tih-may-tiv) *adj.*—es·ti·ma·tor *n.*

es·ti·ma·tion (es-tih-*may*-sh'n) *n.* 1. Appraisal; calculation; judgment. 2. Esteem; regard.

es·ti·val (es-tiv-'l) *adj.* Also **aes·ti·val.** Denoting or continuing throughout the summer.

es·ti·vate (*es*-tih-vayt) *v.* [es·ti·vat·ed; -vat·ing] Also **aes·ti·vate.** To pass the summer.

es·top (es-*top*) *v.* [-topped; -top·ping] *Law.* To impede or bar an action by one's prior deed or oath.—es·top·page (es-*top*-ij), es·top·pel *n.*

es·trange (es-*traynj*) *v.* [-tranged; -trang·ing]

1. To alienate; suspend cordial or affectionate relations with. 2. To divert; alter; change. —es·trange·ment *n.*—es·trang·er *n.*

es·trone (*es*-trohn) *n.* A female hormone extracted from urine of pregnant animals. (*Symbol:* $C_{18}H_{22}O_2$).

es·tu·ar·y (*es*-choo-ehr-ee) *n.* [*pl.* -ies] The wide mouth of a river in which the tide ebbs and flows.—es·tu·ar·i·al (es-choo-*ehr*-ee-ul) *adj.*

et cetera (et-*set*-er-uh). And so forth.

etch *v.* To mark or make designs by subjecting to the action of a corrosive agent.—etch·er *n.* —etch·ing *n.* A print from an etched plate.

e·ter·nal (ee-*ter*-n'l) *adj.* Everlasting; without beginning or end; immortal; ceaseless; unchangeable.—*n.* 1. That which is everlasting. 2. [*cap.*] God.— -nal·ly *adv.*— -nal·ness *n.*

e·ter·ni·ty (ee-*tern*-ih-tee) *n.* [*pl.* -ties] 1. Endlessness of past and future. 2. The after life.

e·ter·nize (ee-*tern*-yze) *v.* [-nized; -niz·ing] To render immortal; prolong indefinitely; perpetuate.—e·ter·ni·za·tion (ee-tern-ih-*zay*-sh'n) *n.*

eth·ane (*eth*-ayn) *n.* A gaseous hydrocarbon found in natural gas. (*Symbol:* CH_3CH_3).

e·ther (*ee*-ther) *n.* 1. An anaesthetic obtained by the action of sulphuric acid on alcohol. 2. A hypothetical, all-pervading fluid which serves to transmit heat and light waves.

e·the·re·al (eh-*theer*-ee-ul) *adj.* Celestial; spiritual; of another world; unearthly.—e·the·re·al·ly *adv.*—e·the·re·al·ness *n.*

e·the·re·al·ize (eh-*theer*-ee-ul-yze) *v.* [-ized; -iz·ing] To purify and refine; spiritualize.

e·ther·ize (ee-ther-yze) *v.* [-ized; -iz·ing] To anaesthetize with ether.—e·ther·i·za·tion (ee-ther-iz-*ay*-sh'n) *n.*—e·ther·iz·er *n.*

eth·ic (*eth*-ik) *adj.* Pertaining to morality or manner; moral.—*n.* Ethics.

eth·i·cal (*eth*-ih-k'l) *adj.* 1. Conforming to a moral standard; honorable. 2. Pertaining to morality.—eth·i·cal·ly *adv.*—eth·i·cal·ness *n.*

eth·ics *n.* 1. The science of morality and ideal conduct. 2. A set of moral principles.

E·thi·op (*ee*-thee-op) *n. & adj.* Ethiopian.

E·thi·op·ic (ee-thee-*op*-ik) *n.* The language of Ethiopia.—*adj.* Relating to Ethiopia.

eth·nic (*eth*-nik) *adj.* Also eth·ni·cal. 1. Pertaining to race; racial; ethnological. 2. Neither Jewish nor Christian.—eth·ni·cal·ly *adv.*

eth·nog·ra·phy (eth-*nog*-ruh-fee) *n.* Branch of learning describing and classifying the races of mankind.—eth·nog·ra·pher *n.*—eth·no·graph·ic (eth-nuh-*graf*-ik), eth·no·graph·i·cal *adj.*

eth·nol·o·gy (eth-*nol*-uh-jee) *n.* The science of races and racial divisions.—eth·no·log·ic (eth-nuh-*loj*-ik), eth·no·log·i·cal *adj.*—eth·no·log·i·cal·ly *adv.*—eth·nol·o·gist *n.*

e·thos (*ee*-thos) *n.* 1. The characteristic genius of a people, institution, or system. 2. The objective moral element in an artistic work.

eth·yl (*eth*-'l) *n. Chemistry.* 1. A radical composed of two molecules of carbon and five of hydrogen, derived from ethane. (*Symbol:*

C_2H_5 or CH_3CH_2). 2. [*cap.*] Trade-mark name for a motor fuel.—e·thyl·ic (eh-*thil*-ik) *adj.*

ethyl alcohol. The type of alcohol found in whisky, wine, etc.

eth·y·lene (*eth*-ih-leen) *n.* A colorless, poisonous gas used as an anesthetic, fuel, etc. (*Symbol:* C_2H_4 or $CH_2{:}CH_2$).

e·ti·ol·o·gy (ee-tee-*ol*-uh-jee) *n.* Also ae·ti·ol·o·gy. The science of discovery of causes, esp. of diseases.— -log·i·cal (loj-ih-k'l) *adj.*— -log·i·cal·ly *adv.*— -ol·o·gist *n.*

et·i·quette (*et*-uh-ket) *n.* Polite manners; rules for social conduct; decorous conventions.

Et·na (*et*-nuh) *n.* Also Aet·na. A Sicilian volcano.

E·to·ni·an (ee-*toh*-nee-un) *n.* A schoolboy or graduate of Eton.—E·to·ni·an *adj.*

E·tru·ri·a (eh-*troor*-ee-uh). An ancient district in central Italy.—E·tru·ri·an *adj. & n.* Etruscan.

E·trus·can (eh-*trus*-k'n) *adj.* Relating to Etruria.—E·trus·can *n.*

é·tude (ay-*tyood*) *n. Music.* A composition designed as an exercise; study.

et·y·mol·o·gy (et-uh-*mol*-uh-jee) *n.* [*pl.* -gies] The study of the derivation of words.—et·y·mo·log·i·cal (et-uh-muh-*loj*-ih-k'l) *adj.*—et·y·mo·log·i·cal·ly *adv.*—et·y·mol·o·gist *n.*

eu·ca·lyp·tus (yoo-kuh-*lip*-tus) *n.* [*pl.* -ti, -tus·es] An Australian tree having thick, leathery leaves, from which medicinal oil is obtained.

Eu·cha·rist (*yoo*-kuh-rist) *n.* 1. The sacrament of the Lord's Supper. 2. The consecrated elements, bread and wine.—Eu·cha·ris·tic (yoo-kuh-*ris*-tik), Eu·cha·ris·ti·cal *adj.*

eu·chre (*yoo*-ker) *n.* A game of cards which may be played by two, three, or four players with the 32 highest cards of the pack.—*v.* [euchred; eu·chring] To trick; manipulate.

Eu·clid (*yoo*-klid). A great Greek geometrician. —Eu·clid·e·an (yoo-*klid*-ee-un) *adj.*

eu·gen·ic, eu·gen·i·cal (yoo-*jen*-ik) *adj.* Relating to development of healthy, happy children. —eu·gen·i·cal·ly *adv.*

eu·gen·ics (yoo-*jen*-iks) *n.* The study of hereditary influences affecting human beings.—eu·gen·ist *n.*

eu·lo·gist (*yoo*-luh-jist) *n.* One who praises; panegyrist.—eu·lo·gis·tic (yoo-luh-*jis*-tik), eu·lo·gis·ti·cal *adj.* Laudatory; commendatory.

eu·lo·gize (*yoo*-luh-jyze) *v.* [-gized; -giz·ing] To praise; extol.—eu·lo·giz·er *n.*

eu·lo·gy (*yoo*-luh-jee) *n.* [*pl.* -gies] Tribute; encomium, esp. a burial address.

Eu·men·i·des (yoo-*men*-ih-deez) *n. pl. Mythology.* The Furies.

eu·nuch (*yoo*-nuk) *n.* A castrated human male.

eu·pep·sia (yoo-*pep*-shuh) *n.* Good digestion. —eu·pep·tic *adj.*

eu·phe·mism (*yoo*-fuh-mizm) *n.* A mild term used to convey a disagreeable or repugnant idea.—eu·phe·mist *n.*—eu·phe·mist·ic (yoo-fuh-*mis*-tik), -i·cal *adj.*— -i·cal·ly *adv.*

E

eu·phon·ic, eu·phon·i·cal (yoo-*fon*-ik, -ih-k'l) *adj.* Pleasing to the ear; agreeable in sound. —**eu·phon·i·cal·ly** *adv.*—**eu·phon·i·cal·ness** *n.*

eu·pho·ni·ous (yoo-*foh*-nee-us) *adj.* Agreeable in sound; harmonious.—**eu·pho·ni·ous·ly** *adv.* —**eu·pho·ni·ous·ness** *n.*

eu·pho·ni·um *n. Music.* A brass bass instrument with three or four valves.

eu·pho·ny (*yoo*-fuh-nee) *n.* [*pl.* -nies] Agreeable sound.

eu·phor·bi·a (yoo-*for*-bee-uh) *n.* A widely distributed family of flower-bearing herbs.

eu·pho·ri·a (yoo-*for*-ee-uh) *n.* A feeling of comfort and well-being.—**eu·pho·ric** *adj.*

Eu·phra·tes (yoo-*fray*-teez). A large Mesopotamian river which flows into the Persian Gulf.

Eu·phros·y·ne (yoo-*fros*-ih-nee). 1. A small planet or asteroid between Mars and Jupiter. 2. *Greek Mythology.* One of the three Graces.

eu·phu·ism (*yoo*-fyoo-izm) *n.* Excessive elegance of language; high-flown diction.—**eu·phu·ist** *n.* —**eu·phu·is·tic, -ti·cal** *adj.*— -**ti·cal·ly** *adv.*

Eu·ra·sia (yoor-*ayzh*-uh). Europe and Asia as a whole.—**Eu·ra·sian** *n.* & *adj.*

eu·re·ka (yoo-*ree*-kuh) *interjection.* An expression of triumph at a discovery.

Eu·ro·pa (yoo-*roh*-puh). 1. *Greek Mythology.* A princess abducted by Zeus. 2. A small planet between the orbits of Mars and Jupiter.

Eur·ope (*yoor*-up). The continent which lies between the Atlantic Ocean and Asia, and between the Mediterranean Sea and the Arctic Ocean.—**Eu·ro·pe·an** (yoor-uh-*pee*-un) *n.* An inhabitant of Europe.—**Eu·ro·pe·an** *adj.*

Eu·ro·pe·an·ize (yoor-uh-*pee*-un-yze) *v.* [-yzed; -iz·ing] To cause to become European in characteristics or manners.

European plan. Hotel accommodations without board.

eu·ro·pi·um (yoo-*roh*-pee-um) *n.* A rare earth metal. (*Symbol:* Eu).

eustachian tube (yoo-*stay*-kee-un; -*stay*-shun). The tube which communicates between the internal ear and the back of the mouth cavity.

eu·tha·na·si·a (yoo-thuh-*nay*-zhuh) *n.* Inducement of painless death; death induced as a relief from suffering.

eu·then·ics (yoo-*then*-iks) *n.* The science dealing with the environmental factors affecting human beings and their improvement.

Euxine Sea. The Black Sea.

e·vac·u·ate (eh-*vak*-yoo-ayt) *v.* [-at·ed; -at·ing] 1. To discharge; eject. 2. To withdraw from.

e·vac·u·a·tion (eh-vak-yoo-*ay*-shun) *n.* 1. The act of emptying or clearing of the contents; act of withdrawing from, as an army or garrison. 2. A bowel movement.

e·vade (ee-*vayd*) *v.* [e·vad·ed; e·vad·ing] To elude; avoid; escape.—**e·vad·a·ble, e·vad·i·ble** *adj.*—**e·vad·er** *n.*

e·val·u·ate (eh-*val*-yoo-ayt) *v.* [-at·ed; at·ing] To assess; appraise; estimate.—**e·val·u·a·tion** (eh-val-yoo-*ay*-shun) *n.*

ev·a·nesce (ev-uh-*nes*) *v.* [ev·a·nesced; ev·a·nesc·ing] To vanish; disappear.— -**nes·cence** *n.*

ev·a·nes·cent (ev-uh-*nes*-ent) *adj.* Fleeting; ephemeral.—**ev·a·nes·cent·ly** *adv.*

e·van·gel (eh-*van*-j'l) *n.* 1. Good tidings. 2. The Gospel.

e·van·gel·i·cal (ee-van-*jel*-ih-k'l) *adj.* Also **e·van·gel·ic.** 1. According to or pertaining to the Gospel. 2. Denoting those Protestant Churches which profess to base their principles on Scripture alone.—**e·van·gel·i·cal** *n.*—**e·van·gel·i·cal·ism** *n.*—**e·van·gel·i·cal·ly** *adv.*

e·van·gel·ism (eh-*van*-juh-lizm) *n.* The promulgation of the Gospel; revivalism.

e·van·ge·list (eh-*van*-juh-list) *n.* 1. [*cap.*] One of the authors of the first books of the New Testament: Matthew, Mark, Luke, and John. 2. A traveling preacher; revivalist.—**e·van·ge·lis·tic** (eh-van-juh-*lis*-tik) *adj.*— -**ti·cal·ly** *adv.*

e·van·ge·lize (eh-*van*-juh-lyze) *v.* [-lized, -liz·ing] To convert to a belief in the Gospel.— -**li·za·tion** (eh-van-juh-liz-*ay*-shun) *n.*— -**liz·er** *n.*

e·vap·o·rate (eh-*vap*-uh-rayt) *v.* [-rat·ed; -rat·ing] To pass off in vapor; dry up; become concentrated by loss of liquid.—**e·vap·o·ra·ble** *adj.* — -**o·ra·bil·i·ty** (eh-vap-uh-ruh-*bil*-ih-tee) *n.*

e·vap·o·ra·tion (eh-vap-uh-*ray*-shun) *n.* The conversion of a solid or liquid by heat into vapor or a concentrate.—**e·vap·o·ra·tive** (eh-*vap*-uh-ray-tiv) *adj.*—**e·vap·o·ra·tor** *n.*

e·va·sion (eh-*vay*-zhun) *n.* Subterfuge; equivocation; excuse; avoidance.

e·va·sive (eh-*vay*-siv) *adj.* Elusive; not frank. —**e·va·sive·ly** *adv.*—**e·va·sive·ness** *n.*

eve *n.* 1. Evening. 2. Night or evening before a holiday. 3. Any immediately preceding period.

Eve. *Bible.* The mate of Adam.

e·ven *adj.* 1. Level; smooth; flat. 2. Calm; not easily disturbed. 3. Balanced; fair; equitable. 4. Having accounts balanced; square. 5. Capable of being divided by two without a remainder.—*adv.* 1. Just as; exactly in consonance with. 2. Exactly; precisely. 3. So much as. 4. Yet; still. 'It grew even colder.' 5. The very. 'Even the stones seemed to shout.'—*v.* 1. To level; make smooth. 2. To balance accounts with. —**e·ven·er** *n.*—**e·ven·ly** *adv.*—**e·ven·ness** *n.*

e·ven *n. Poetic.* Evening.

e·ven·fall *n.* Twilight; early evening.

e·ven-hand·ed *adj.* Impartial; just; equitable.

even if. Although.

eve·ning (*eev*-ning) *n.* The latter part of the day; the beginning of the night.—**eve·ning** *adj.*

evening primrose. A plant bearing yellow flowers which open in the evening.

evening star. A western planet visible in early evening; Venus.

e·ven·song *n.* The Anglican vesper service.

e·vent (eh-*vent*) *n.* 1. Incident; happening; occurrence; case. 2. Result; upshot; consequence. 3. An important occurrence. 4. A single contest in an athletic series.

e·vent·ful *n.* Full of incident; important.—**e·vent·ful·ly** *adv.*

e·ven·tide *n.* Evening.

e·ven·tu·al (eh-*ven*-choo-ul) *adj.* Ultimate; final.— **-tu·al·ly** *adv.*— **-al·i·ty** (eh-ven-choo-al-ih-tee) *n.* [*pl.* -ties] Event; contingency.

e·ven·tu·ate (eh-*ven*-choo-ayt) *v.* [-at·ed; -at·ing] To result; happen ultimately.

ev·er *adv.* 1. At any time. 2. Always; forever. 3. In any degree; in any case.

ever abiding	ever durable	everliving
ever active	ever during	ever loving
ever admiring	ever echoing	evermore
everbearing	ever-esteemed	ever new
ever-beloved	ever faithful	ever present
ever-blessed	ever fast	ever ready
everblooming	ever friendly	ever smiling
ever-celebrated	ever going	ever strong
ever changing	ever growing	ever victorious
ever constant	ever-honored	ever wearing

Ev·er·est (*ev*-er-est). A mountain in the Himalayas, the highest in the world.

ev·er·glade *n.* A low marshy tract of inundated land.—**the Everglades.** Marshy region covering a large part of southern Florida.

ev·er·green *adj.* Verdant through the year; always green.—*n.* A plant which retains its verdure throughout the year, as the fir.

ev·er·last·ing *adj.* 1. Eternal; immortal. 2. Endless; continual.—*n.* A plant whose flowers retain their form and color for many months after being gathered.— **-last·ing·ly** *adv.* **-last·ing·ness** *n.*—**The Everlasting.** God.

ev·er·more *adv.* Always; forever.

e·vert (eh-*vert*) *v.* To turn inside out.—**e·ver·si·ble** *adj.*—**e·ver·sion** (eh-*versh*-un) *n.*

ev·er·y (*ev*-er-ee) *adj.* 1. Each individual or part. 2. All; complete; full.

ev·er·y·bod·y *pronoun.* Every person.

ev·er·y·day *adj.* Common; usual; weekday.

ev·er·y·one *pronoun.* Every person.

ev·er·y·thing *pronoun.* Each thing; all things.

ev·er·y·where *adv.* In every place; in all places.

e·vict (eh-*vikt*) *v.* To dispossess; expel from home or property.—**e·vic·tion** (eh-*vik*-shun) *n.*

ev·i·dence (*ev*-ih-d'ns) *n.* 1. Proof; facts; confirmation. 2. *Law.* Material submitted by parties at a trial to substantiate their claim.—*v.* [-denced; -denc·ing] To indicate; evince.

ev·i·dent (*ev*-ih-d'nt) *adj.* Clear; apparent; manifest.—**ev·i·dent·ly** *adv.*

ev·i·den·tial (ev-ih-*den*-sh'l) *adj.* Indicative; clearly proving.

e·vil (*ee*-v'l) *adj.* 1. Bad; wicked. 2. Calamitous; unfortunate.—*n.* 1. Calamity; misfortune; injury. 2. Malignity; depravity.—*adv.* Unfortunately; not happily.—**e·vil·ly** *adv.*

evil boding	evil-hued	evil sounding
evil-disposed	evil looking	evilspeaker
evildoer	evil-mannered	evilspeaking
evildoing	evil-minded	evil-starred
evil-faced	evil-savored	evil-taught
evil-favored	evilsayer	evil-tongued
evil-featured	evil-shaped	evil-willed
evil-hearted	evil smelling	evil wishing

e·vil·do·er *n.* A wrongdoer; sinner; criminal. —**e·vil·do·ing** *n.*

evil eye. The power superstitiously ascribed to certain persons, to do harm to others by casting a hostile look upon them.

e·vil·mind·ed *adj.* Depraved; lascivious.

e·vince (eh-*vinss*) *v.* [e·vinced; e·vinc·ing] To manifest; indicate.—**e·vin·ci·ble** *adj.*

e·vis·cer·ate (eh-*vis*-er-ayt) *v.* [-at·ed; -at·ing] To disembowel; take out the intestines.—**e·vis·cer·a·tion** (eh-vis-er-*ay*-shun) *n.*

ev·o·ca·ble (*ev*-uh-kuh-b'l) *adj.* Capable of being called or summoned.

e·vo·ca·tion (ev-uh-*kay*-shun) *n.* A calling forth; a summoning.

e·voc·a·tive (eh-*vok*-uh-tiv) *adj.* Calling forth; drawing out.

e·voke (eh-*vohk*) *v.* [e·voked; e·vok·ing] To elicit; summon forth; draw out.

ev·o·lu·tion (ev-uh-*loo*-shun, ev-uh-*lyoo*-shun) *n.* 1. Development; growth; gradual change. 2. One of a series of movements. 3. Something developed from a simpler form. 4. *Biology.* Development of complex forms from simpler forms; the theory that all existing species developed from simpler forms by changes adapting them to their environment. —**ev·o·lu·tion·al, ev·o·lu·tion·ar·y** *adj.*—**evo·lu·tion·al·ly** *adv.*—**ev·o·lu·tion·ist** *n.*

e·volve (eh-*volv*) *v.* [e·volved; e·volv·ing] To unfold; develop.—**e·volve·ment** *n.*

ewe (*yoo*) *n.* A female sheep.

ew·er (*yoo*-er) *n.* A water pitcher.

ex *prep.* 1. Out of. 2. Off; from; out. 3. Beyond.

ex- *prefix.* 1. Out. 2. Former. 3. Beyond. 4. Completely.

ex·ac·er·bate (eg-*zass*-er-bayt) *v.* [-bat·ed; -bat·ing] 1. To irritate; exasperate. 2. Aggravate; intensify.—**ex·ac·er·ba·tion** *n.*

ex·act (eg-*zakt*) *adj.* 1. Precise; conforming to a standard or pattern. 2. Methodical; strict; careful. 3. Accurate.

ex·act (eg-*zakt*) *v.* 1. To demand; extort. 2. To require; necessitate.—**ex·act·a·ble** *adj.* —**ex·act·or, ex·act·er** *n.*

ex·act·ing (eg-*zakt*-ing) *adj.* Severe; strict; demanding.—**ex·act·ing·ly** *adv.*—**ex·act·ing·ness** *n.*

ex·ac·tion (eg-*zak*-shun) *n.* 1. Extortion; coercive demands. 2. Tribute; that which is extorted.

ex·act·i·tude (eg-*zak*-tuh-tyood) *n.* Exactness; accuracy; precision.

ex·act·ly (eg-*zakt*-lee) *adv.* Precisely; with accuracy.

ex·act·ness *n.* Precision; accuracy.

ex·ag·ger·ate (eg-*zaj*-er-ayt) *v.* [-at·ed; -at·ing] To enlarge beyond the truth; amplify.— **-at·ed·ly** *adv.*— **-a·tive** *adj.*— **-a·tor** *n.*—**ex·ag·ger·a·tory** *adj.*

ex·ag·ger·a·tion (eg-zaj-er-*ay*-shun) *n.* Magnification; overstatement.

ex·alt (eg-*zawlt*) *v.* 1. To elevate; elate. 2. To magnify; praise; extol.—**ex·alt·er** *n.*

E

ex·al·ta·tion (eg-zawl-*tay*-shun) *n.* Mental elevation; spiritual delight.

ex·alt·ed (eg-*zawlt*-id) *adj.* Sublime; elevated; lofty.—**ex·alt·ed·ly** *adv.*—**ex·alt·ed·ness** *n.*

ex·am (eg-*zam*) *n. Colloquial.* Examination.

ex·am·i·na·tion (eg-zam-uh-*nay*-shun) *n.* 1. Inspection; scrutiny. 2. Interrogation; questioning. 3. A test prescribed for investigating qualifications or knowledge.

ex·am·ine (eg-*zam*-in) *v.* [-ined; -in·ing] 1. To inspect; scrutinize. 2. To interrogate; query. 3. To inquire into qualifications or knowledge.—**ex·am·in·a·ble** *adj.*—**ex·am·in·er** *n.*

ex·am·in·ee *n.* One who is examined.

ex·am·ple (eg-*zam*-p'l) *n.* 1. Specimen; sample. 2. Model; pattern; ideal. 3. Punishment to be a warning to others. 'Make an example of the thief.' 4. A problem designed to illustrate a rule.

ex·arch (eg-*zark*) *n. Greek Orthodox Church.* An inspector of the clergy in a given area, commissioned by the patriarch.—**ex·arch·ate** *n.*

ex·as·per·ate (eg-*zass*-per-ayt) *v.* [-at·ed; -at·ing] To irritate; provoke.— **-at·ing·ly** *adv.*

ex·as·per·a·tion (eg-zass-per-*ay*-shun) *n.* Irritation; annoyance; anger.

Ex·cal·i·bur (eks-*kal*-uh-ber) *n.* The mythological sword of King Arthur given him by the Lady of the Lake.

ex cathedra (eks kuh-*thee*-druh). Authoritatively; with proper power and authority.

ex·ca·vate (*eks*-kuh-vayt) *v.* [-vat·ed; -vat·ing] 1. To hollow out. 2. To dig up and remove. 3. To disinter; expose by uncovering.

ex·ca·va·tion (eks-kuh-*vay*-shun) *n.* 1. Digging out. 2. A hole where earth has been excavated.

ex·ca·va·tor (*eks*-kuh-vay-ter) *n.* Digging machine.

ex·ceed (ek-*seed*) *v.* To surpass; transcend; outdo; pass the proper bounds.

ex·ceed·ing *adj.* Great in extent or quantity; unusually large.—**ex·ceed·ing·ly** *adv.*

ex·cel (ek-*sel*) *v.* [-celled; -cell·ing] 1. To surpass; outdo. 2. To perform well; be expert.

ex·cel·lence (*ek*-suh-lunss) *n.* Virtue; goodness; perfection; merit.

ex·cel·len·cy (*ek*-suh-lun-see) *n.* [*pl.* -cies] 1. Valuable quality. 2. [*cap.*] A title of honor given to certain distinguished personages.

ex·cel·lent (*ek*-suh-lunt) *adj.* Good; choice; valuable; virtuous.—**ex·cel·lent·ly** *adv.*

ex·cel·si·or (ek-*sel*-see-er) *adj.* Always upward. —*n.* A packing material of fine shavings.

ex·cept (ek-*sept*) *v.* 1. To leave out; exclude. 2. To object; take exception.—*prep.* Excluding; with the exception of.

ex·cept·ing (ek-*sept*-ing) *prep.* Excluding.

ex·cep·tion (ek-*sep*-shun) *n.* 1. Exclusion. 2. That which is excluded or separated from others in a general description. 3. Offense; slight anger or resentment. 4. *Law.* The denial of what is alleged by the other party.

ex·cep·tion·a·ble (ek-*sep*-shun-uh-b'l) *adj.* Objectionable; undesirable.— **-tion·a·bly** *adv.*

ex·cep·tion·al (ek-*sep*-shun-ul) *adj.* Extraordinary; unusual.—**ex·cep·tion·al·ly** *adv.*

ex·cerpt (ek-*serpt*) *v.* To make an extract from; pick out; select.—**ex·cerp·tion** *n.*

ex·cerpt (*ek*-serpt) *n.* An extract; selection; passage copied from a written source.

ex·cess (ek-*sess*) *n.* 1. Superfluity; superabundance; more than necessary or usual. 2. Intemperance.—**ex·cess** *adj.*

ex·ces·sive (ek-*sess*-iv) *adj.* Immoderate; extreme; unreasonable.—**ex·ces·sive·ly** *adv.*

ex·change (eks-*chaynj*) *n.* 1. Giving one thing or commodity for another; barter. 2. A place where stocks, etc. are bought and sold. —*v.* [-changed; -chang·ing]—**ex·change·a·bil·i·ty** *n.*—**ex·change·a·ble** *adj.*

ex·cheq·uer (eks-*chek*-er) *n.* A state treasury.

ex·cise (ek-*syze*) *n.* A tax.—**ex·cis·a·ble** *adj.*

ex·cise (ek-*syze*) *v.* [ex·cised; ex·cis·ing] 1. To levy a duty on. 2. To cut out, as a tumor. —**ex·cis·a·ble** *adj.*—**ex·ci·sion** (ek-*sizh*-un) *n.*

ex·cise·man *n.* [*pl.* -men]. A customs officer.

ex·cit·a·ble (ek-*syte*-uh-b'l) *adj.* High-strung; temperamental.— **-a·bil·i·ty** *n.*— **-a·ble·ness** *n.*

ex·ci·ta·tion (ek-sy-*tay*-shun) *n.* The act of arousing or stimulating.—**ex·cit·a·tive** (ek-*syte*-uh-tiv) *adj.*—**ex·cit·a·to·ry** *adj.*

ex·cite (ek-*syte*) *v.* [ex·cit·ed; ex·cit·ing] To stimulate; rouse; agitate.—**ex·cit·ed** *adj.* Aroused; wrought up; agitated.—**ex·cit·ed·ly** *adv.*

ex·cite·ment (ek-*syte*-m'nt) *n.* 1. Stimulation. 2. Commotion; turbulence; agitation.

ex·cit·ing *adj.* Stimulating; stirring; interesting.

ex·claim (eks-*klaym*) *v.* To cry out; utter vehemently.—**ex·claim·er** *n.*

ex·cla·ma·tion (eks-kluh-*may*-shun) *n.* 1. An outcry; ejaculation. 2. *Grammar.* A word expressing outcry; an interjection.—**exclamation point.** *Printing.* A punctuation mark [!] put after an emphatic remark.

ex·clam·a·to·ry (eks-*klam*-uh-tor-ee) *adj.* Containing or expressing exclamation.

ex·clude (eks-*klood*) *v.* [-clud·ed; -clud·ing] To keep out; eliminate.—**ex·clud·a·ble** *adj.*

ex·clu·sion (eks-*kloozh*-un) *n.* A shutting out; debarring.

ex·clu·sive (eks-*kloo*-siv) *adj.* 1. Possessed; enjoyed or controlled singly or privately. 2. Not including or comprehending. 3. Snobbish; socially restricted; illiberal.—**ex·clu·sive·ly** *adv.*—**ex·clu·sive·ness** *n.*

ex·com·mu·ni·cate (eks-kuh-*myoon*-ih-kayt) *v.* [-cat·ed; -cat·ing] 1. *Ecclesiastical.* To eject from the communion of a church by an ecclesiastical sentence. 2. To debar; exclude.—**ex·com·mu·ni·cate** *n. & adj.*—**ex·com·mu·ni·ca·ble** *adj.*—**ex·com·mu·ni·ca·tor** *n.*—**ex·com·mu·ni·ca·tion** (eks-kuh-myoo-nih-*kay*-shun) *n.* Expulsion; debarment.— **-ni·ca·tive** (eks-kuh-*myoo*-nih-kuh-tiv) *adj.*

ex·co·ri·ate (eks-*kor*-ee-ayt) *v.* [-at·ed; -at·ing]

To flay; strip off the skin.—**ex·co·ri·a·tion** (eks-kor-ee-*ay*-sh'n) *n.*

ex·cre·ment (*eks*-krih-m'nt) *n.* The waste products of digestion ejected from the body; feces.—**ex·cre·men·tal** *adj.*

ex·cres·cence (iks-*kreh*-s'ns) *n.* 1. A superfluous or objectionable growth, as a wart. 2. Any normal outgrowth, as fingernails.

ex·cres·cen·cy (iks-*kreh*-s'n-see) *n.* [*pl.* -cies] An excrescent condition, esp. superfluous growth.

ex·cres·cent (iks-*kreh*-s'nt) *adi.* Growing abnormally out of something else; superfluous.

ex·cre·ta (eks-*kree*-tuh) *n. pl.* Excreted or waste matter: feces, sweat, urine, etc.

ex·crete (iks-*kreet*) *v.* [ex·cret·ed; ex·cret·ing] To isolate and discharge (waste matter) from the tissues or blood.

ex·cre·tion (iks-*kree*-sh'n) *n.* 1. Elimination; process of separating and discharging bodily waste products. 2. Excreted material.

ex·cre·to·ry (*eks*-krih-toh-ree) *adj.* Pertaining to excretion; able to excrete.—*n.* A small duct or vessel which excretes waste fluids.

ex·cru·ci·ate (iks-*kroo*-shee-ayt) *v.* [ex·cru·ci·at·ed; -at·ing] To agonize; torture; pain exceedingly.—**ex·cru·ci·a·tion** *n.*

ex·cru·ci·at·ing (iks-*kroo*-shee-ay-ting) *adj.* Tormenting; severe; causing great agony.

ex·cul·pate (*eks*-k'l-payt) *v.* [ex·cul·pat·ed; -pat·ing] To clear of a charge of guilt; relieve of blame.—**ex·cul·pa·ble** *adj.*—**ex·cul·pa·tion** *n.*

ex·cur·sion (iks-*ker*-zh'n) *n.* 1. A short journey, esp. for pleasure or health. 2. Digression; progression beyond usual limits.

ex·cur·sive (iks-*kur*-siv) *adj.* Rambling; wandering; digressive.—**ex·cur·sive·ly** *adv.*

ex·cuse (iks-*kyooz*) *v.* [ex·cused; ex·cus·ing] 1. To absolve of guilt or blame; exculpate. 2. To pardon; forgive. 3. To apologize for; try to justify. 4. To release, as from a duty or obligation.—**ex·cus·a·ble** *adj.*— **-a·bly** *adv.*

ex·cuse (iks-*kyooss*) *n.* 1. An apology; plea for forgiveness. 2. That which justifies a fault or omission; adequate reason. 3. Act of excusing.

ex·e·cra·ble (*eks*-ih-kruh-b'l) *n.* Worthy of abomination; extremely bad; detestable.

ex·e·crate (*eks*-ih-krayt) *v.* [ex·e·crat·ed; ex·e·crat·ing] To curse; denounce; abominate. —**ex·e·cra·tive** *adj.*—**ex·e·cra·tor** *n.*

ex·e·cra·tion (eks-ih-*kray*-sh'n) *n.* 1. A curse; expression of utter abomination. 2. That which is abominated.—**ex·e·cra·to·ry** *adj.*

ex·e·cute (*eks*-ih-kyoot) *v.* [ex·e·cut·ed; -cut·ing] 1. To do; effect; carry out; complete. 2. To enforce; put into effect. 3. To put to death legally. 4. To make valid or legal. 5. To make or perform according to a pattern or design, as a work of art.—**ex·e·cut·a·ble** *adj.* —**ex·e·cut·er** (*eks*-ih-kyoo-ter) *n.*

ex·e·cu·tion (eks-ih-*kyoo*-sh'n) *n.* 1. Performance; accomplishment. 2. *Law.* Power to effect a sentence or judgment. 3. Capital punishment; legal infliction of death. 4. Style; manner of performance.

ex·e·cu·tion·er (exs-ih-*kyoo*-sh'n-er) *n.* Person who carries out a death sentence.

ex·ec·u·tive (ig-*zek*-yuh-tiv) *n.* 1. An official who administers or carries out accepted or legal policy. 2. Administrative branch or power of a government.—*adj.* 1. Pertaining to execution or management of affairs. 2. Having the power to execute, as laws.

ex·ec·u·tor (ig-*zek*-yuh-ter) *n.* 1. Person appointed to carry a will into effect. 2. (*eks*-ih-kyoo-ter) One who performs or effects.—**ex·ec·u·to·ri·al** *adj.*—**ex·ec·u·trix** *n. fem.*

ex·e·ge·sis (eks-uh-*jee*-sis) *n.* [*pl.* -ses] An exposition or interpretation of a literary work, esp. the Bible.—**ex·e·get·ic, -i·cal** *adj.*— **-i·cal·ly** *adv.*

ex·em·plar (ig-*zem*-pler) *n.* An example; pattern; model to be followed.

ex·em·pla·ry (ig-*zem*-pluh-ree) *adj.* 1. Worthy of being followed or imitated; model. 2. Serving as an example or warning.—**ex·em·pla·ri·ly** *adv.*—**ex·em·pla·ri·ness** *n.*

ex·em·pli·fy (ig-*zem*-pluh-fye) *v.* [ex·em·pli·fied; -fy·ing] 1. To show by example; be a model for. 2. To copy; transcribe.—**ex·em·pli·fi·ca·tion** *n.*

ex·empt (ig-*zempt*) *v.* To grant immunity, or release from a responsibility or restraint to which others are subject.—*n.* One who is exempt.—*adj.* Not liable or subject to.—**ex·empt·i·ble** *adj.*

ex·emp·tion (ig-*zemp*-sh'n) *n.* 1. Freedom from tax or other obligations. 2. An amount of income free from taxation.

ex·er·cise (*eks*-er-syze) *n.* 1. Exertion of the muscles to maintain bodily health. 2. A practice lesson or example. 3. Use; putting into action; employment. 4. [*pl.*] A program or ceremony.—*v.* [ex·er·cised; -cis·ing] 1. To exert; use actively or repeatedly. 2. To train; discipline, as the organs. 3. To trouble; harass.—**ex·er·cis·a·ble** *adj.*—**ex·er·cis·er** *n.*

ex·ert (ig-*zert*) *v.* To activate; put into operation; execute.—**ex·er·tion** *n.*—**ex·er·tive** *adj.*

ex·e·unt (*eks*-ee-'nt) *v.* Stage direction for several actors to quit the scene.

ex·fo·li·ate (eks-*foh*-lee-ayt) *v.* [ex·fo·li·at·ed; -at·ing] To flake off; come off in scales or splinters.—**ex·fo·li·a·tion** *n.*

ex·hale (eks-*hayl*) *v.* [ex·haled; ex·hal·ing] 1. To breathe or send out; emit. 2. To evaporate; cause emission in vapor.— **-ha·la·tion** *n.*

ex·haust (ig-*zawst*) *v.* 1. To use up; consume; expend all of. 2. To wear out; tire exceedingly. 3. To empty completely. 4. To study or develop thoroughly; leave nothing unsaid or undone. 5. To drain, as of strength.—*n.* 1. Vapors which escape from the cylinder of an engine after their energy has been dissipated. 2. The vent or pipe through which they are passed.—**ex·haust·er** *n.*—**ex·haust·i·bil·i·ty** *n.*—**ex·haust·i·ble** *adj.*

E

ex·haus·tion (ig-*zaws*-chun) *n*. 1. Act of exhausting. 2. State of being emptied or used up; utter weariness.

ex·haus·tive (ig-*zaws*-tiv) *adj*. Thorough; treating or covering all angles.—**ex·haus·tive·ly** *adv*.

ex·haust·less (ig-*zawst*-lis) *adj*. Incapable of being exhausted.—**ex·haust·less·ly** *adv*.

ex·hib·it (ig-*zib*-it) *v*. 1. To show; present to view, esp. public view; display. 2. *Law*. To submit as evidence in court.—*n*. 1. Act of showing publicly. 2. An article or group of articles exhibited; part of an exhibition. 3. *Law*. An object submitted as evidence in court.—**ex·hib·i·tor, ex·hib·i·ter** *n*.

ex·hi·bi·tion (eks-uh-*bih*-shun) *n*. 1. A public showing or display. 2. Act of exhibiting. 3. Articles displayed publicly.

ex·hi·bi·tion·ism (eks-uh-*bih*-sh'n-izm) *n*. 1. An inordinate desire to attract notice. 2. *Psychology*. Display of one's body, esp. the genitals, to attract sexual interest.—**ex·hi·bi·tion·ist** *n*.

ex·hil·a·rate (ig-*zil*-uh-rayt) *v*. [ex·hil·a·rat·ed; -rat·ing] To invigorate; animate; cheer.—**ex·hil·a·rat·ing** *adj*.—**ex·hil·a·ra·tion** *n*.

ex·hil·a·ra·tive (ig-*zil*-er-ay-tiv) *adj*. Also **ex·hil·a·ra·to·ry**. Animating; causing joy or cheer; enlivening.

ex·hort (ig-*zawrt*) *v*. To incite or urge by words; warn or admonish urgently.—**ex·hort·er** *n*.

ex·hor·ta·tion (eg-zer-*tay*-sh'n) *n*. 1. Persuasive or inciting speech or language. 2. Act of warning or urging.— **-ta·tive, -ta·to·ry** *adj*.

ex·hume (ig-*zyoom*) *v*. [ex·humed; ex·hum·ing] To dig up (what is buried); disinter.—**ex·hu·ma·tion** *n*.

ex·i·gen·cy (*eks*-uh-jun-see) *n*. [*pl*. -cies]. Also **ex·i·gence**. 1. An urgent need; that which requires immediate action. 2. Specific needs; requirements.—**ex·i·gent** *adj*.

ex·ig·u·ous (ig-*zig*-yoo-us) *adj*. Slender; scanty; minute.—**ex·i·gu·i·ty, ex·ig·u·ous·ness** *n*.

ex·ile (*eg*-zyle, *eks*-yle) *n*. 1. Banishment from one's home or native country; forced or voluntarily prolonged absence from one's home. 2. A person so banished or absent.—*v*. [ex·iled; ex·il·ing] To banish from one's home.

ex·ist (ig-*zist*) *v*. 1. To be; live; have actual existence. 2. To continue to be; live. 3. To occur; be present or manifest.—**ex·is·tent** *adj*.

ex·ist·ence (ig-*zis*-t'ns) *n*. 1. An entity; a being. 2. Act or condition of existing; life. 3. Occurrence; continued presence or manifestation.—**ex·is·ten·tial** *adj*.

ex·it (*eg*-zit) *n*. 1. A passage or way out. 2. Departure from the stage. 3. Act of going out; departure.

ex·it. A stage direction denoting departure from the stage.

ex·o·don·tia (eks-uh-*don*-chuh) *n*. The science or art of tooth extraction.—**ex·o·don·tist** *n*. Dentist specializing in tooth extraction.

ex·o·dus (*eks*-uh-dus) *n*. 1. A migration; departure of a large number. 2. [*cap*.] Departure of the Israelites from Egypt. 3. [*cap*.] The second book of the Old Testament.

ex officio. By virtue of office; without special authorization.

ex·o·gen (*eks*-uh-j'n) *n*. A plant whose stem is formed by successive additions to the outside of the wood.—**ex·og·e·nous** *adj*.—**ex·og·e·nous·ly** *adv*.

ex·on·er·ate (ig-*zon*-uh-rayt) *v*. [ex·on·er·at·ed; -at·ing] To clear, as of blame or guilt; vindicate; absolve.—**ex·on·er·a·tion** *n*.—**ex·on·er·a·tive** *adj*.

ex·or·bi·tance (ig-*zawr*-buh-t'ns) *n*. Also **ex·or·bi·tan·cy**. Quality or state of being exorbitant.

ex·or·bi·tant (ig-*zawr*-buh-t'nt) *adj*. Exceeding customary limits; extravagant.—**ex·or·bi·tant·ly** *adv*.

ex·or·cise (*eks*-awr-syze) *v*. [ex·or·cised; -cis·ing]. Also **ex·or·cize**. 1. To drive out, as evil spirits, by holy rituals. 2. To free of the influence of demons.—**ex·or·cis·er, ex·or·ciz·er** *n*.

ex·or·cism (eks-*awr*-sizm) *n*. Act or ceremony of exorcising.—**ex·or·cist** *n*.

ex·or·di·um (ig-*zawr*-dee-um) *n*. [*pl*. -di·ums, di·a] Introductory part, as of a speech or composition.—**ex·or·di·al** *adj*.

ex·o·skel·e·ton (eks-oh-*skel*-uh-t'n) *n*. *Zoology*. A hard external shell or covering grown by crustaceans, turtles, etc.

ex·o·ter·ic (eks-uh-*tehr*-ik) *adj*. Evident; not secret or private; easily understood; opposite of *esoteric*.

ex·ot·ic (ig-*zot*-ik) *adj*. Foreign; strange.—*n*. An exotic person or thing.

ex·pand (ek-*spand*) *v*. 1. To grow larger; spread out; swell. 2. To increase in scope or importance; grow. 3. To unfold; develop. —**ex·pand·er** *n*.—**ex·pan·si·ble** *adj*.

ex·panse (ek-*spanss*) *n*. A large extent of space; wide area.

ex·pan·sion (ek-*span*-shun) *n*. 1. A becoming larger or more spread out. 2. That which is increased, enlarged, or extended. 3. Amount of space or area; immensity. 4. *Physics*. Increase in the amount of space occupied without an increase in substance.

ex·pan·sive (ek-*span*-siv) *adj*. 1. Capable of becoming larger; increasing. 2. Warm; friendly; sympathetic. 3. Operating by expansion.—**ex·pan·sive·ly** *adv*.— **-sive·ness** *n*.

ex parte (eks *pahr*-tay). From one part only; one-sided.

ex·pa·ti·ate (eks-*pay*-shee-ayt) *v*. [ex·pa·ti·at·ed; -at·ing] To enlarge upon in a discourse or in writing; expand.—**ex·pa·ti·a·tion** *n*.

ex·pa·tri·ate (eks-*pay*-tree-ayt) *v*. [ex·pa·tri·at·ed; -at·ing] 1. To leave or be driven from one's native land. 2. To lose citizenship in one country by naturalization in another. —*adj*. (eks-*pay*-tree-ut) Exiled; emigrant; expatriated.—*n*. An exile; emigrant.—**ex·pa·tri·a·tion** (eks-pay-tree-*ay*-shun) *n*.

ex·pect (ek-*spekt*) *v*. 1. To look for; await. 2. To anticipate; look forward to as likely or due.   3. To require; obligate; consider due.

ex·pec·tan·cy (ek-*spek*-tun-see) *n*. [*pl*. -cies]. Also **ex·pec·tance**. 1. Anticipation; expectation. 2. That which seems due or likely.

ex·pec·tant (ek-*spek*-tunt) *adj*. 1. Awaiting; looking for; anticipating. 2. Pregnant.—**ex·pec·tant** *n*.—**ex·pec·tant·ly** *adv*.

ex·pec·ta·tion (ek-spek-*tay*-shun) *n*. 1. An anticipating; awaiting.   2. That which is deemed due or probable; prospect; likelihood of success or benefit.

expectation of life. Also **life expectancy.** Average anticipated life span of a person.

ex·pec·to·rant (ek-*spek*-ter-unt) *adj*. Inducing mucus discharge from the lungs or windpipe; causing coughing up or spitting out.—*n*. A medicine which induces discharge of mucus.

ex·pec·to·rate (ek-*spek*-ter-ayt) *v*. [ex·pec·to·rat·ed; -rat·ing] Cough up; spit out.—**ex·pec·to·ra·tion** (ek-spek-ter-*ay*-shun) *n*.

ex·pe·di·en·cy (ek-*spee*-dee-un-see) *n*. [*pl*. -cies]. Also **ex·pe·di·ence**. 1. Fitness; advisability. 2. That which serves one's immediate, practical ends.   3. Furtherance of one's aims with little regard to ethics or ultimate consequence.

ex·pe·di·ent (ek-*spee*-dee-unt) *adj*. Convenient; suitable for an immediate purpose; profitable; advantageous.—*n*. That which is advisable or politic.—**ex·pe·di·ent·ly** *adv*.

ex·pe·dite (*ek*-spuh-dyte) *v*. [ex·pe·dit·ed; -dit·ing] To facilitate; speed up; remove impediments.—*adj*. Quick; easy; convenient.

ex·pe·di·tion (ek-spuh-*dish*-un) *n*. 1. Voyage; journey made by several people for a definite purpose. 2. A body of persons so journeying, plus their gear.   3. Speed; dispatch.

ex·pe·di·tion·ar·y (ek-spuh-*dish*-un-ehr-ee) *adj*. Making up or similar to an expedition.

ex·pe·di·tious (ek-spuh-*dish*-us) *adj*. Quick; fast; prompt.— -tious·ly *adv*.— -tious·ness *n*.

ex·pel (ek-*spel*) *v*. [ex·pelled; ex·pel·ling] 1. To force out; eject. 2. To dismiss; exclude.—**ex·pel·la·ble** *adj*.

ex·pel·lant (ek-*spel*-unt) *adj*. Also **ex·pel·lent**. Ejecting; purgative; forcing out.—*n*. A purging medicine.

ex·pend (ek-*spend*) *v*. To use up; consume; dissipate; disburse.—**ex·pend·a·ble** *adj*. 1. Able to be dispensed with. 2. Capable of use or consumption.

ex·pend·i·ture (ek-*spend*-uh-cher) *n*. 1. Amount disbursed or spent. 2. A paying out, as of money. 3. A using up; dissipation.

ex·pense (ek-*spenss*) *n*. 1. A laying out or spending. 2. Cost; amount spent.   3. A financial burden; drain on one's resources.

ex·pen·sive (ek-*spen*-siv) *adj*. Costly; high-priced; occasioning great expense.—**ex·pen·sive·ly** *adv*.—**ex·pen·sive·ness** *n*.

ex·pe·ri·ence (ek-*spihr*-ee-unss) *n*. 1. An encounter; ordeal; event. 2. Knowledge or skill gained from doing a particular thing. 3. Amount of knowledge gained from practice.   4. The sum total of the events of one's life. 5. Knowledge gained from personal observation.—*v*. [ex·per·i·enced; -enc·ing] To have; know; encounter; undergo.

ex·pe·ri·enced *adj*. Practiced; tried; wise.

ex·per·i·ment (ek-*spehr*-uh-munt) *n*. 1. A trial; test; attempt to gain new knowledge. 2. That which is doubtful as opposed to what is tried or certain.—**ex·per·i·ment** *v*.

ex·per·i·men·tal (ek-spehr-uh-*men*-t'l) *adj*. Pertaining to a test or trial; derived from practice rather than theory.—**ex·per·i·men·tal·ly** *adv*.

ex·per·i·men·ta·tion (ek-spehr-uh-m'n-*tay*-shun) *n*. Conducting of a test or trial; carefully or scientifically controlled testing.

ex·pert (ek-*spert*, ek-spert) *adj*. Skilled; proficient.—**ex·pert·ly** *adv*.—**ex·pert·ness** *n*.

ex·pert (*ek*-spert) *n*. A person highly trained or learned in a particular field; authority.

ex·pi·ate (*ek*-spee-ayt) *v*. [ex·pi·at·ed; ex·pi·at·ing] To redeem; atone for; give satisfaction for.—**ex·pi·a·ble** *adj*.— -a·tion *n*.— -a·tor *n*.

ex·pi·a·to·ry (*eks*-pee-uh-tor-ee) *adj*. Atoning; making amends in restitution or suffering.

ex·pi·ra·tion (ek-spuh-*ray*-shun) *n*. 1. A breathing out or forcing air from the lungs. 2. An end; conclusion.—**ex·pir·a·to·ry** *adj*.

ex·pire (ek-*spyre*) *v*. [ex·pired; ex·pir·ing] 1. To breathe out. 2. To die; pass away. 3. To come to an end; draw to a close.

ex·plain (ek-*splayn*) *v*. To make clear; elucidate; give a reason for.—**ex·plain·a·ble** *adj*.

ex·pla·na·tion (ek-spluh-*nay*-shun) *n*. 1. Elucidation; interpretation; exposition; excuse. 2. That which simplifies the comprehension of or gives reason for.

ex·plan·a·to·ry (ek-*splan*-uh-tor-ee) *adj*. Also **ex·plan·a·tive**. Interpretative; containing an explanation; showing why or how.— -to·ri·ly *adv*.

ex·ple·tive (*eks*-pluh-tiv) *adj*. Also **ex·ple·to·ry**. Filling up space; extra; redundant.—*n*. 1. A word or thing inserted to fill a vacancy. 2. An interjection; profanity.

ex·pli·ca·ble (*eks*-plih-kuh-b'l) *adj*. Able to be explained or solved.

ex·pli·cate (*eks*-plih-kayt) *v*. [ex·pli·cat·ed; -cat·ing] To explain; unfold; expand; interpret. —**ex·pli·ca·tive** *adj*.—**ex·pli·ca·tion** *n*.

ex·plic·it (eks-*pliss*-it) *adj*. 1. Clear; plain; definite. 2. Unmistakably and openly stated. —**ex·plic·it·ly** *adv*.—**ex·plic·it·ness** *n*.

ex·plode (eks-*plohd*) *v*. [ex·plod·ed; ex·plod·ing] 1. To burst or break with a loud noise. 2. To use violent, angry language. 3. To disprove; show as false.—**ex·plod·er** *n*.

ex·ploit (*eks*-ployt) *n*. A daring deed; heroic or noteworthy act.

ex·ploit (eks-*ployt*) *v*. 1. To utilize; get use or value from. 2. To use unfairly or unscrupulously to further one's own profit or interests.

ex·ploi·ta·tion (eks-ploy-*tay*-shun) *n*. 1. Utilization. 2. Base or selfish use of a person. —**ex·ploit·a·tive** *adj*.

ex·plo·ra·tion (eks-plor-*ay*-shun) *n*. 1. Search;

E

probe; careful examination. 2. A journey of discovery through new regions.—**ex·plor·a·to·ry** (eks-*plor*-uh-tor-ee), **-a·tive** *adj.*

ex·plore (eks-*plor*) *v.* [ex·plored; ex·plor·ing] 1. To search through; examine carefully; scrutinize. 2. To range over new or uncharted areas to discover new facts.—**ex·plor·er** *n.*

ex·plo·sion (ek-*sploh*-zhun) *n.* 1. A bursting with a loud report; detonation. 2. A sudden, violent outburst of feeling or language.

ex·plo·sive (eks-*ploh*-siv) *adj.* 1. Bursting with sudden violence. 2. Causing or caused by explosion. 3. Easily detonated.—*n.* 1. A munition or other violent substance. 2. *Phonetics.* A consonant pronounced with a sudden breath after having the air passages shut off. —**ex·plo·sive·ly** *adv.*—**ex·plo·sive·ness** *n.*

ex·po·nent (*eks*-poh-n'nt) *n.* 1. One who supports or upholds a principle or theory. 2. *Mathematics.* The small figure placed slightly above a root to denote how many times the root is multiplied by itself, as 2^2. 3. A person or thing that exemplifies or serves as prototype.—**ex·po·nen·tial** *adj.*

ex·port (eks-*port*) *v.* To ship or transport to another country.—**ex·port·a·ble** *adj.*—**ex·por·ta·tion** *n.*—**ex·port·er** *n.*

ex·port (*eks*-port) *n.* 1. Merchandise shipped out of a country. 2. The act or business of exportation.

ex·pose (eks-*pohz*) *v.* [ex·posed; ex·pos·ing] 1. To disclose; unearth; uncover. 2. To put forward; exhibit. 3. To submit to danger or to any power or influence. 4. *Photography.* To subject a sensitized surface to light rays. —**ex·pos·er** *n.*—**ex·pos·al** *n.*

ex·po·sé (eks-poh-*zay*) *n.* A disclosure of something discrediting or embarrassing.

ex·posed (eks-*pohzd*) *adj.* Unprotected; unsheltered; open.

ex·po·si·tion (eks-puh-*zish*-un) *n.* 1. A great public exhibition or fair. 2. Explanation; exposure. 3. A kind of prose which describes or presents information; example of this literary art.—**ex·pos·i·tor** (eks-*poz*-uh-ter) *n.* One who explains or writes expositions.

ex·pos·i·to·ry (eks-*poz*-uh-tor-ee) *adj.* Also **ex·pos·i·tive.** Serving to explain or illustrate; denoting an exposition.

ex post facto (eks pohst *fak*-toh). Retrospective; retroactive; denoting an event occurring after another but retroactive to the first.

ex·pos·tu·late (eks-*poss*-chuh-layt) *v.* [ex·pos·tu·lat·ed; -lat·ing] To reason with someone to turn him from an unwise course.—**ex·pos·tu·lat·or** *n.*

ex·pos·tu·la·tion (eks-poss-chuh-*lay*-shun) *n.* Remonstrance; dissuasion; reasoning against. —**ex·pos·tu·la·tive** (eks-*poss*-chuh-lay-tiv) *adj.* —**ex·pos·tu·la·to·ry** (-luh-tor-ee) *adj.*

ex·po·sure (eks-*poh*-zher) *n.* 1. Disclosure; exposition; exposé. 2. Side or direction a dwelling faces. 'A room with a southern exposure.' 3. A weakened condition of the body from inadequate protection from cold. 4. *Photography.* Subjection of a sensitized emulsion to light.

ex·pound (eks-*pownd*) *v.* 1. To explain; interpret. 2. Set forth or state in detail.

ex·press (eks-*pres*) *adj.* 1. Precise; definite; clearly stated. 2. Specialized; particularized. 3. Traveling with a limited schedule of stops, as an elevator.—*n.* 1. Any passenger conveyance stopping only at important points and traveling with speed. 2. A method of rapid transport of goods or money. 3. A special, fast message or messenger.—*adv.* By express; with infrequent stops.—*v.* 1. To state; tell; present. 2. To speak in a particular manner. 'He expresses himself well.' 3. To send or ship on rapid transit. 4. To mean; be the equivalent; represent. 5. To extract by squeezing.—**ex·press·er** *n.*—**ex·press·i·ble** *adj.*

ex·press·age (eks-*pres*-ij) *n.* 1. The conveying of goods by express. 2. The fee charged for such transit.

ex·pres·sion (eks-*presh*-'n) *n.* 1. Utterance; representation, esp. by words. 2. A look, gesture, or other outward aspect of an emotion or feeling tone. 3. A phrase; idiom; term. 4. Expressiveness; intensity or accuracy of presentation. 5. *Mathematics.* A group of numbers or symbols having a value. 6. That which is squeezed out; a squeezing.

ex·pres·sion·ism (eks-*presh*-un-izm) *n.* Theory or practice of showing or expressing one's innermost thoughts or feelings by the arts or other outward means.—**ex·pres·sion·ist** *n.* & *adj.*—**ex·pres·sion·is·tic** *adj.*

ex·pres·sive (eks-*pres*-iv) *adj.* 1. Outwardly displayed; demonstrative. 2. Eloquent; forceful. 3. Full of meaning or significance.—**ex·pres·sive·ly** *adv.*—**ex·pres·sive·ness** *n.*

ex·press·ly *adv.* 1. Explicitly; in direct terms; plainly. 2. Particularly; especially.

ex·press·man *n.* An agent or employee of an express company.

ex·pro·pri·ate (eks-*proh*-pree-ayt) *v.* [ex·pro·pri·at·ed; -at·ing] 1. To deprive of belongings or property rights. 2. To transfer possession to another or to the public.—**ex·pro·pri·a·tion** (eks-proh-pree-*ay*-shun) *n.*—**ex·pro·pri·a·tor** *n.*

ex·pul·sion (eks-*pul*-sh'n) *n.* A driving out; ejection.—**ex·pul·sive** *adj.*

ex·punge (eks-*punj*) *v.* [ex·punged; ex·pung·ing] To strike or blot out; obliterate; erase.—**ex·punc·tion** *n.*—**ex·pung·er** *n.*

ex·pur·gate (*eks*-per-gayt) *v.* [-gat·ed; -gat·ing] To cleanse; purge; purify of anything offensive, esp. a book.—**ex·pur·ga·tion** *n.*— **-ga·tor** *n.*— **-ga·tor·i·al** (-guh-*tor*-ee-ul), **-ga·to·ry** *adj.*

ex·qui·site (*eks*-kwiz-it) *adj.* 1. Fine; lovely; delicately made. 2. Nicely discriminating; highly appreciative of fine things. 3. Keen; exciting intense emotion.—*n.* One who is affected in dress or manner; dandy.—**ex·qui·site·ly** *adv.*—**ex·qui·site·ness** *n.*

ex·tant (ek-*stant*, eks-*tunt*) *adj.* Existing; living.

ex·tem·po·ral (eks-*tem*-per-ul) *adj.* Unstudied; not premeditated.—**ex·tem·po·ral·ly** *adv.*

ex·tem·po·ra·ne·ous (eks-tem-per-*ay*-nee-us) *adj.* 1. Offhand; spontaneous; unpremeditated. 2. Gifted in making speeches without preparation.— -**ne·ous·ly** *adv.*— -**ne·ous·ness** *n.*

ex·tem·po·ra·ry , (eks-*tem*-per-ehr-ee) *adj.* 1. Done on the spur of the moment; impromptu; improvised. 2. Growing out of the occasion; unexpected.— -**ri·ly** *adv.*

ex·tem·po·re (eks-*tem*-puh-ree) *adj.* Impromptu; done without preparation.—**ex·tem·po·re** *adv.*

ex·tem·po·rize (eks-*tem*-puh-ryze) *v.* [ex·tem·po·rized; -riz·ing] To speak or do without forethought; improvise.— -**ri·za·tion** *n.*— -**riz·er** *n.*

ex·tend (ek-*stend*) *v.* 1. To reach; continue; stretch. 2. To prolong; drag out in time. 3. To offer; bestow. 4. To increase the scope of one's power or influence. 5. To reach out; outstretch. 6. To increase a time limit previously set.—**ex·tend·i·ble** *adj.*

ex·tend·ed *adj.* 1. Occupying space; stretched out. 2. *Printing.* Wider than is usual in a given type face.—**ex·tend·ed·ly** *adv.*

ex·ten·si·ble (ek-*sten*-sih-b'l) *adj.* Able to be extended or stretched.—**ex·ten·si·bil·i·ty, ex·ten·si·ble·ness** *n.*

ex·ten·sion (ek-*sten*-shun) *n.* 1. Lengthening; stretching out. 2. An additional portion or section that adds length; continuation. 3. An allowance of more time. 4. *Physics.* The property of a substance that causes it to occupy space.

ex·ten·sive (ek-*sten*-siv) *adj.* 1. Wide; far reaching; long in time or space. 2. *Farming.* Opposite of intensive; basing one's expectations upon quantity of land rather than care in cultivation.—**ex·ten·sive·ly** *adv.*— -**sive·ness** *n.*

ex·ten·sor (ek-*sten*-ser) *n. Physiology.* A muscle which straightens or extends a member.

ex·tent (ek-*stent*) *n.* 1. The amount of space a thing occupies; area; volume. 2. Compass; range; reach; degree. 'The extent of his influence.' 3. *Law.* A writ permitting temporary seizure of a debtor's lands.

ex·ten·u·ate (eks-*ten*-yoo-ayt) *v.* [ex·ten·u·at·ed; -at·ing] 1. To underestimate; minimize; lessen. 2. To paint an ill deed as less serious than it seems; mitigate.—**ex·ten·u·a·tor** *n.*

ex·ten·u·a·tion (eks-ten-yoo-*ay*-shun) *n.* Treating of a fault or crime as if it were of little importance; excuse.—**ex·ten·u·a·tive, -a·to·ry** *adj.*

ex·te·ri·or (eks-*tihr*-ee-er) *adj.* 1. Outer; external; outside; surface. 2. Outlying; foreign. —*n.* 1. Outside; external surface. 2. Aspect; mien; outward deportment.— -**or·ly** *adv.*

ex·ter·mi·nate (eks-*ter*-muh-nayt) *v.* [-nat·ed; -nat·ing] 1. To destroy; abolish; wipe out. 2. To rid a place of vermin.—**ex·ter·mi·na·tor** *n.*

ex·ter·mi·na·tion (eks-ter-muh-*nay*-shun) *n.* Utter destruction.— -**na·tive, -na·to·ry** *adj.*

ex·ter·nal (ek-*ster*-n'l) *adj.* 1. Outward; outer; on the outside. 2. Visible from the outside; physical. 3. On the surface; super-

ficial. 4. Foreign; international.—*n.* An outward part or form.—**ex·ter·nal·ly** *adv.*

ex·tinct (ek-*stinkt*) *adj.* 1. Extinguished; inactive. 2. No longer existing; having died out.

ex·tinc·tion (ek-*stink*-sh'n) *n.* 1. Act of extinguishing; extinct state. 2. Destruction; suppression.—**ex·tinc·tive** *adj.*

ex·tin·guish (ek-*sting*-gwish) *v.* 1. To put out, as a flame; quench; destroy. 2. Eclipse; obscure.—**ex·tin·guished** *adj.*— -**guish·er** *n.*

ex·tir·pate (*ek*-ster-payt) *v.* [ex·tir·pat·ed; ex·tir·pat·ing] To pull up by the roots; destroy completely.—**ex·tir·pa·tion** *n.*—**ex·tir·pa·tive** *adj.*—**ex·tir·pa·tor** *n.*

ex·tol, ex·toll (ek-*stol*, ek-*stohl*) *v.* [ex·tolled; ex·tol·ling] To praise highly; celebrate; glorify. —**ex·tol·ler** *n.*—**ex·tol·ment, ex·toll·ment** *n.*

ex·tort (ek-*stawrt*) *v.* To obtain by force.—**ex·tort·er** *n.*—**ex·tor·tive** *adj.*

ex·tor·tion (ik-*stawr*-sh'n) *n.* 1. Act of extorting. 2. That which is obtained by force or fraud.

ex·tor·tion·ate (ek-*stawr*-sh'n-it) *adj.* Unreasonable; oppressive; marked by extortion. Also **ex·tor·tion·ar·y.**—**ex·tor·tion·ate·ly** *adv.*

ex·tor·tion·er (ek-*stawr*-sh'n-er) *n.* Also **ex·tor·tion·ist.** One who uses extortion.

ex·tra (*ek*-struh) *adj.* Additional; beyond; more or better than what is normal or necessary.—*n.* 1. That which is added; accessory. 2. A special edition of a newspaper. 3. An added worker, esp. one hired by the day to play minor parts in motion pictures.—*adv.* Beyond the usual standard or size.

extra allowance	extra dry	extra long
extra binding	extra fine	extra mild
extra bound	extra good	extra session
extra condensed	extra hazardous	extra special
extra current	extra large	extra strong

ex·tra- *prefix.* Beyond; outside of; aside from.

extra-acinous	extra-Britannic
extra-alimentary	extra-European
extra-American	extrajudicial
extra-analogical	extramarginal
extra-anthropic	extrapolar
extra-articular	extraterrestrial
extra-atmospheric	extravascular

ex·tract (ek-*strakt*) *v.* 1. To draw out; remove; obtain, esp. with effort. 2. To derive; deduce. 3. To select; take out for quotation, as a passage.—**ex·tract·a·ble, ex·tract·i·ble** *adj.* —**ex·tract·or** *n.*

ex·tract (*ek*-strakt) *n.* 1. Matter, object, or substance extracted; essence. 2. Excerpt or quotation, as from a speech or writing.

ex·trac·tion (ek-*strak*-sh'n) *n.* 1. Act of extracting. 2. Lineage; descent. 3. That which is extracted; extract.

ex·trac·tive (ek-*strak*-tiv) *adj.* Capable of being extracted; extracting.—*n.* Extract.

ex·tra·cur·ri·cu·lar, ex·tra·cur·ri·cu·lum (ek-struh-kuh-*rik*-yuh-ler, -l'm) *adj.* Not included in the prescribed schedule or course of study.

ex·tra·dite (*ek*-struh-dyte) *v.* [ex·tra·dit·ed; ex-

E

tra·dit·ing] To deliver or surrender to an outside legal authority.—**ex·tra·dit·a·ble** *adj.*

ex·tra·di·tion (ek-struh-*dih*-sh'n) *n.* Surrender of a prisoner or fugitive from justice to another government or authority.

ex·tra·ne·ous (ek-*stray*-nee-us) *adj.* Foreign; unessential.—**ex·tra·ne·ous·ly** *adv.*—**ex·tra·ne·ous·ness** *n.*

ex·traor·di·nar·i·ly (ek-*strawr*-d'n-ehr-uh-lee) *adv.* Remarkably; not in the ordinary manner.

ex·traor·di·nar·y (ek-*strawr*-d'n-ehr-ee) *adj.* 1. Unusual; remarkable. 2. Exceeding or unlike that which is ordinary or usual; special; singular.

extrasensory perception. Also **ESP.** *Psychology.* Clairvoyant and telepathic phenomena purportedly observed under laboratory test conditions by certain scientists.

ex·tra·ter·ri·to·ri·al (ek-struh-tehr-uh-*toh*-ree-ul) *adj.* Beyond the boundaries or jurisdiction of a state or territory.—**ex·tra·ter·ri·to·ri·al·ly** *adv.*

ex·tra·ter·ri·to·ri·al·i·ty *n.* The exemption from local jurisdiction granted to foreign representatives, diplomats, etc.

ex·trav·a·gance (ek-*strav*-uh-g'ns) *n.* 1. Excess; lack of restraint; lavish expenditure or display. 2. An extravagant act or article. Also **ex·trav·a·gan·cy** [*pl.* -cies].

ex·trav·a·gant (ek-*strav*-uh-g'nt) *adj.* 1. Excessive; profuse. 2. Spending lavishly; wasteful.—**ex·trav·a·gant·ly** *adv.*

ex·trav·a·gan·za (ek-strav-uh-*gan*-zuh) *n.* A spectacular or extravagantly elaborate show.

ex·treme (ek-*streem*) *adj.* 1. Utmost; farthest possible. 2. Last; at the very end. 3. In or to the greatest degree; violent; intense.—*n.* 1. An extreme degree or condition. 2. That which is extreme. 3. The first or last term in a mathematical series or proportion.—**ex·treme·ly** *adv.*—**ex·treme·ness** *n.*

ex·trem·ism (ek-*streem*-izm) *n.* State of being extreme or favoring extreme measures.

ex·trem·i·ty (ek-*strem*-uh-tee) *n.* [*pl.* -ties] 1. The farthest point; point or border of termination. 'The extremities of a country.' 2. [*pl.*] Limbs; hands or feet.

ex·tri·cate (*eks*-trih-kayt) *v.* [ex·tri·cat·ed; ex·tri·cat·ing] To free; disentangle.—**ex·tric·a·ble** (*eks*-trih-kuh-b'l) *adj.*—**ex·tri·ca·tion** (eks-trih-*kay*-shun) *n.*

ex·trin·sic (eks-*trin*-sik) *adj.* Outward; external; unessential.—**ex·trin·si·cal·ly** *adv.*

ex·tro·ver·sion (eks-truh-ver-shun) *n.* Also **ex·tra·ver·sion.** *Psychology.* Habitual tendency to take greater interest in events and other people than in one's own thought and imagination; opposite of *introversion.*

ex·tro·vert (*eks*-truh-vert) *n.* Also **ex·tra·vert.** *Psychology.* One who habitually directs his interest outward.

ex·trude (eks-*trood*) *v.* [ex·trud·ed; ex·trud·ing] To expel; thrust out; protude.—**ex·tru·sion** (eks-*troo*-zhun) *n.*—**ex·tru·sive** *adj.*

ex·u·ber·ance (eg-*zyoo*-ber-unss, -*zoo*-) *u.* 1. An abundance; excess; overflowing quantity. 2. Effusiveness; lavishness.

ex·u·ber·ant (eg-*zyoo*-ber-unt, -*zoo*-) *adj.* 1. Abundant; plenteous. 2. Effusive; overflowing with spirit.—**ex·u·ber·ant·ly** *adv.*

ex·ude (eks-*yood*, eg-*zyood*) *v.* [ex·ud·ed; ex·ud·ing] To discharge through the pores; give forth.—**ex·u·da·tion** (eks-yoo-*day*-shun) *n.*

ex·ult (eg-*zult*) *v.* To rejoice; triumph; glory, as in victory.—**ex·ult·ing·ly** *adv.*

ex·ul·tant (eg-*zul*-tunt) *adj.* Rejoicing; jubilant. —**ex·ult·ant·ly** *adv.*

ex·ul·ta·tion (eg-zul-*tay*-shun) *n.* Rejoicing; gladness; great delight. 'The exultation of the victor knew no bounds.'

eye *n.* 1. The organ of sight. 2. That which resembles an eye. 'The eye of a needle.' 3. The ability to see. 'The artist has an eye for beauty.'—*v.* To observe attentively; stare.

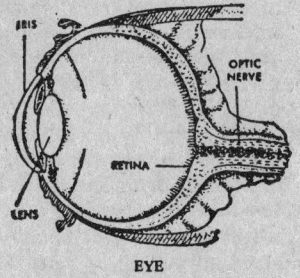

EYE

eye·ball *n.* The orb or spherical part of the eye.

eye·brow *n.* The arched line of hair on the forehead over the eye.

eye·glass *n.* 1. A lens to aid the sight. 2. Lens contained in the eyepiece of an optical instrument. 3. [*pl.*] Spectacles; a pair of lenses to correct defects of vision.

eye·hole *n.* 1. A peephole; hole to look through. 2. A round opening to receive a rope, pin, etc. 3. The socket for the eyeball.

eye·lash *n.* 1. A thin protective line of hair growing on the edge of the eyelid. 2. One hair of this line.

eye·less *adj.* Without eyes; sightless; blind.

eye·let *n.* 1. A small hole through which a cord or small rope can be threaded. 2. A small decorative hole in cloth.

eye·lid *n.* The covering of skin over the eye by which it opens and closes.

eye opener. *Colloquial.* 1. A startling sight; dazzling spectacle. 2. A remarkable or unexpectedly informing fact. 3. *Slang.* A short alcoholic drink, esp. one taken upon arising.

eye·piece *n.* The part of an optical instrument which is placed to the eye.

eye·sight *n.* The sense of sight; observation.

eye·sore *n.* An ugly or sordid structure or view.

eye·strain *n.* A morbid condition caused by excessive use of the eyes.

eye·tooth *n.* A pointed tooth in the upper jaw; the upper canine tooth.

eye·wash *n.* A solution to bathe the eyes.

eye·wink·er *n.* A hair of the eyelashes.

eye·wit·ness *n.* One who sees an event occur.

ey·rie, ey·ry. *Variant spellings* of **aerie.**

F

fa (*fah*) *n. Music.* The fourth note of the diatonic scale.

Fa·bi·an (*fay*-bee-'n) *adj.* 1. Using a harassing strategy; delaying; cautious. 2. Denoting an English society working for the adoption of socialism through education and gradual reform.—*n.* Member of this society.—**Fa·bi·an·ism** *n.*—**Fa·bi·an·ist** *n.* & *adj.*

fa·ble (*fay*-b'l) *n.* 1. A legend; story pointing a moral, often through the medium of animal characters that talk and act like people. 2. A falsehood; fictitious story.—*v.* [fa·bled; fa·bling] To fabricate; feign; speak falsely.

fab·ric (*fab*-rik) *n.* 1. Cloth; textile; woven goods. 2. Structure; framework; craftsmanship. 3. Texture.

fab·ri·cate (*fab*-rih-kayt) *v.* [-cat·ed; -cat·ing] 1. To build; manufacture; construct; fit together. 2. To invent; make up; devise.—**fab·ri·ca·tion** *n.*—**fab·ri·ca·tor** *n.*

Fab·ri·koid (*fab*-rih-koid) *n.* Trade-mark for an imitation-leather fabric.

fab·u·list (*fab*-yuh-list) *n.* A liar; fabler.

fab·u·lous (*fab*-yuh-lus) *adj.* 1. Incredible; legendary; amazing. 2. Imaginary; fictitious.

fa·çade (fuh-*sahd*) *n.* 1. The front of a building. 2. The face of any object.

face (*fayss*) *n.* 1. The front part of the head. 2. The countenance; expression. 3. Façade; front; principal or outer surface. 4. A grimace; distorted expression. 5. Boldness. 6. Dignity; self-respect; prestige. 7. Proper value or amount. 8. *Printing.* Style or variety of type.—*v.* [faced; fac·ing] 1. To confront; turn or have the face toward. 2. To resist; oppose. 3. To line or cover with a different material.—**face·a·ble** *adj.*—**in the face of.** In the presence of; in spite of.

face-about	face-harden	faceplate
face-centered	face maker	facewise
facecloth	facemark	face work

face card. A playing card bearing a picture; that is, a king, queen, or jack.

face lifting. *Colloquial.* Plastic-surgery operation lifting the contours of the face.

fac·er (*fayss*-er) *n. Colloquial.* A staggering blow; unexpected check or difficulty.

fac·et (*fass*-it) *n.* 1. An aspect; angle; side. 2. Any of the plane surfaces of a cut gem.—*v.* To cut plane surfaces on, as a diamond.

fa·ce·tious (fuh-*see*-shus) *adj.* Humorous; witty; marked by levity.—**fa·ce·tious·ly** *adv.* **fa·ce·tious·ness** *n.*

face value. Surface or nominal value; worth estimated from the outward appearance or amount stated in the face.

fa·cial (*fay*-sh'l) *adj.* Relating to the face.—*n.* A face massage or freshening treatment.

fa·cile (*fass*-'l) *adj.* 1. Easy; not difficult.

2. Skillful; dexterous; fluent. 3. Agreeable; compliant.—**fa·cile·ly** *adv.*—**fa·cile·ness** *n.*

fa·cil·i·tate (fuh-*sil*-ih-tayt) *v.* [-tat·ed; -tat·ing] To aid; make easy.—**fa·cil·i·ta·tion** *n.*

fa·cil·i·ty (fuh-*sil*-ih-tee) *n.* [*pl.* -ties] 1. Ease; freedom from difficulty. 2. Dexterity; skill. 3. [*pl.*] Equipment; that which aids or eases any action or course. 4. Compliancy.

fac·ing (*fayss*-ing) *n.* An ornamental lining or covering.

fac·sim·i·le (fak-*sim*-ih-lee) *n.* An exact reproduction or copy, as of a picture.

facsimile transmission. Also **facsimile broadcasting.** A communication system transmitting by radio text or pictures which are reproduced in facsimile at the receiving end.

fact (*fakt*) *n.* 1. That which is known to exist or to have existed or occurred; event; act. 2. That which is known to be true; reality.

fac·tion (*fak*-sh'n) *n.* 1. A clique; coterie; partisan group. 2. Discord; dissension.—**fac·tion·al** *adj.*—**fac·tion·al·ism** *n.*

fac·tious (*fak*-shus) *adj.* Opposing; clashing; marked by or given to dissent.

fac·ti·tious (fak-*tih*-shus) *adj.* Artificial; unnatural.— **-tious·ly** *adv.*— **-tious·ness** *n.*

fac·tor (*fak*-ter) *n.* 1. A contributing element; constituent. 2. *Mathematics.* One of two numbers which, multiplied, give a product. 3. One who does business for another; agent. —*v. Mathematics.* To resolve into factors.

fac·tor·age (*fak*-ter-ij) *n.* Business of, or commission paid to, a factor.

fac·to·ry (*fak*-ter-ee) *n.* [*pl.* -ries] Building in which goods are manufactured.

fac·to·tum (fak-*toh*-tum) *n.* One who does all sorts of jobs.

fac·tu·al (*fak*-choo-ul) *adj.* Pertaining to, or consisting of, facts.—**fac·tu·al·ly** *adv.*

fac·ul·ty (*fak*-'l-tee) *n.* [*pl.* -ties] 1. Capacity; mental or physical power; ability. 2. A natural gift; knack. 3. Teaching staff of a school or college. 4. Department or branch of learning in a college. 5. The collective members of any profession.

fad *n.* A passing fashion or custom; craze.—**fad·dish, fad·dy** *adj.*—**fad·dist** *n.*

fade (*fayd*) *v.* [fad·ed; fad·ing] 1. To become dim; lose color or brilliance. 2. To languish; wither; lose strength. 3. To die away; disappear gradually; vanish.—**fade·less** *adj.*

fade-in *n. Motion Pictures.* A change in negative density from minimum to normal.

fade-out *n.* 1. *Motion Pictures.* A change in negative density from normal to minimum. 2. *Slang.* A disappearance.

faer·y *adj.* Also **faer·ie.** Fairy.

fag *v.* [fagged; fag·ging] 1. To tire; exhaust. 2. To drudge; work until exhausted.—*n.* 1. A drudge; one who does menial labor. 2. *Slang.* A cigarette.

fag end. The dregs; leavings.

fag·ot, fag·got (*fag*-ut) *n.* 1. A bundle of twigs or branches. 2. A bundle or pile of scrap iron.—*v.* To bind together, as in a fagot.

fag·ot·ing, fag·got·ing (*fag*-uh-ting) *n.* Decorative stitch made by drawing the horizontal threads from a fabric and tying bunches of the remaining cross threads in the center.

Fahr·en·heit (*far*-un-hyte) *adj.* According to or denoting the Fahrenheit scale.—*n.* A thermometer scale ranging from a 32° freezing point to a 212° boiling point of water.

fa·ïence (*fy*-ahns) *n.* A kind of glazed pottery.

fail (*fayl*) *v.* 1. To be unsuccessful; neglect; be found wanting or of no use. 2. To fall short; be wanting or lacking. 3. To waste away; decline. 4. To become bankrupt; be unable to pay debts.—*n.* Uncertainty; failure. 'Without fail.'

fail·ing (*fayl*-ing) *adj.* Ailing; weakening; unsuccessful.—*n.* A shortcoming; fault; deficiency in.—*prep.* Lacking.—**fail·ing·ly** *adv.*

faille (*fyle*) *n.* A twilled silk or rayon fabric.

fail·ure (*fayl*-yer) *n.* 1. A failing; deficiency; defeat. 2. An omission; neglect. 3. Lack of success. 4. Bankruptcy. 5. One who has failed.

fain (*fayn*) *adj.* Eager; content; willing.—*adv.* Gladly; with pleasure. 'I would fain dance.'

faint (*faynt*) *adj.* 1. Feeble; weak; inclined to lose consciousness. 2. Indistinct; barely perceptible; dim. 3. Spiritless; timorous; not vigorous. 4. Done weakly.—*n.* A sudden loss of consciousness; act of fainting.—*v.* To lose consciousness; swoon.—**faint·er** *n.*—**faint·ish** *adj.*—**faint·ly** *adv.*—**faint·ness** *n.*

faint·heart·ed *adj.* Timid; lacking courage. — **-heart·ed·ly** *adv.*— **-heart·ed·ness** *n.*

fair (*fayr*) *adj.* 1. Impartial; equitable; just; according to the rules. 2. Beautiful; attractive; pleasing to view. 3. Light-colored, as hair or skin. 4. Passable; moderately good. 5. Clear; not stormy. 6. Clean; spotless. 7. Favorable; promising.—*adv.* In a fair manner.—**fair·ness** *n.*—**fair and square.** Honest; straightforward.

fair-breasted fair-faced fair head
fair-browed fair-featured fair-hued
fair-cheeked fair-fronted fair-natured
fair-colored fairground fair-sized
fair-complexioned fair-haired fair-skinned

fair *n.* 1. A bazaar; display and sale of goods, often accompanied by entertainment. 2. A manufacturer's or industry exposition. 'A book fair.'

fair ball. *Baseball.* A ball batted between the foul lines.

fair catch. *Football.* Catch of a punt or kick-off made, without interference, by a player who signals that he will not run with or forward the ball.

fair-haired boy. *Colloquial.* A man specially

favored, protected, and esteemed by his political or business group.

fair·ing (*fayr*-ing) *n. Engineering.* A structure or part which provides a smooth line.

fair·ish (*fayr*-ish) *adj.* Moderately fair.

fair·ly (*fayr*-lee) *adv.* 1. In a fair manner; impartially; moderately. 2. Distinctly.

fair-mind·ed *adj.* Just; impartial; without prejudices.—**fair-mind·ed·ness** *n.*

fair-spok·en *adj.* Speaking smoothly or plausibly.

fair·way *n.* 1. An open passageway, as of a river. 2. *Golf.* The unobstructed part of a course between the tees and putting greens.

fair·y (*fayr*-ee, *fehr*-ee) *n.* [*pl.* -ries]. Also **faer·y, faer·ie.** 1. A sprite; small, delicate, supernatural being supposedly able to influence human beings. 2. *Slang.* A homosexual. —*adj.* Pertaining to or like fairies.

fair·y·land *n.* 1. Place inhabited by fairies. 2. A place of great charm or beauty.

fairy tale. 1. A fanciful children's story. 2. An incredible tale; falsehood.

faith (*fayth*) *n.* 1. Belief; trust, esp. in God or religion. 2. Fidelity, loyalty. 3. A creed; esp. a religious doctrine.—*interj.* In truth.

faith·ful (*fayth*-f'l) *adj.* 1. Loyal; trustworthy. 2. True; honest; accurate. 3. Trusting; having faith.— **-ful·ly** *adv.*— **-ful·ness** *n.*

faith·less (*fayth*-less) *adj.* 1. Disloyal; unfaithful. 2. Unbelieving; without a faith. 3. Deceptive.— **-less·ly** *adv.*— **-less·ness** *n.*

fake (*fayk*) *v.* [faked; fak·ing] 1. To falsify. 2. To sham; pretend; feign.—*n.* A fraud; deception.—*adj.* Sham; imitation; fraudulent.

fak·er (*fayk*-er) *n.* A fraud; swindler; deceiver.

fa·kir (fuh-*keer*, *fayk*-er) *n.* Also **fa·keer.** 1. A Mohammedan mendicant priest; dervish. 2. A Hindu ascetic; yogi.

Fa·lange (fuh-*lanj*) *n.* Spanish fascist organization aiming at the re-establishment of a Spanish Empire. It has branches in Latin America, esp. Argentina.—**Fa·lan·gist** *n.*

fal·cate (*fal*-kayt) *adj.* Scythe-shaped; curved.

fal·chion (*fawl*-ch'n) *n.* A short curved sword with a broad blade.

fal·con (*fawl*-k'n) *n.* A variety of hawk having a hooked beak and long wings, used in hunting.

fal·con·er *n.* 1. A sportsman using a falcon for hunting. 2. A trainer of falcons.

fal·con·ry *n.* 1. The sport of hunting wild birds with a trained hawk. 2. The training of hawks for hunting.

fal·de·ral, fal·de·rol, fol·de·rol (*fahl*-duh-rahl) *n.* Nonsense; idle fancy; meaningless trifle.

FALCON
(1/15 life size)

fall (*fawl*) *v.* [fall; fall·en; fall·ing] 1. To descend; drop down. 2. To drop to the ground; sink from an erect posture. 3. To fell a tree.

F

4. To die in war. 5. To deteriorate; decline; come to ruin. 6. To decrease; diminish. 7. To happen; come by chance; take place. 8. To become; pass into a new state. 'To fall asleep.' 9. To occur; assume proper position.—*n.* 1. A sudden descent. 2. Downfall; degradation; ruin. 3. A decrease. 4. A cascade; cataract; descent of water. 5. A tumble; spill. 6. Autumn.—**fall flat.** To fail. —**fall in.** 1. To collapse. 2. *Military.* To assemble in formation.—**fall through.** To fail to materialize.

fall-away	fallfish	falltime
fall-back	fall-plow (*v.*)	fall-trap
fall-board	fall-sow (*v.*)	fallway

fal·la·cious (fuh-*lay*-shus) *adj.* False; misleading; deceptive.— -**cious·ly** *adv.*— -**cious·ness** *n.*

fal·la·cy (*fal*-uh-see) *n.* [*pl.* -cies] 1. An error; untruth. 2. A deception; misleading appearance.

fall·en (*fawl*-'n) *adj.* 1. Degraded; ruined. 2. Dropped; descended.

fall guy. *Slang.* The victim of a hoax.

fal·li·ble (*fal*-ih-b'l) *adj.* Liable to err or fail. — -**li·bil·i·ty** (fal-uh-*bil*-ih-tee) *n.*— -**li·bly** *adv.*

falling sickness. *Colloquial.* Epilepsy.

falling star. A shooting star; meteor.

Fallopian tube (fuh-*loh*-pee-un). A duct from the ovary to the uterus.

fal·low (*fal*-oh) *n.* Untilled land.—*adj.* Uncultivated; unproductive.—*v.* To leave unseeded.

fallow deer. A small spotted European deer.

false (*fawlss*) *adj.* [fals·er; fals·est] 1. Untrue; unfounded. 2. Imitation; sham; counterfeit. 3. Dishonest; disloyal; perfidious. 4. *Music.* Not in tune. 5. *Architecture.* Inorganic; superficial.—**false·ly** *adv.*—**false·ness** *n.*

false·hood *n.* A lie.

false keel. *Nautical.* A protective piece of timber under the main keel.

false ribs. *Anatomy.* The pair of ribs unconnected to the sternum.

fal·set·to (fawl-*set*-oh) *n.* [*pl.* -tos] A high artificial voice tone.—**fal·set·to** *adj.*

fal·si·fy (*fawl*-sih-fy) *v.* [fal·si·fied; fal·si·fy·ing] 1. To counterfeit; forge; represent falsely. 2. To lie.— -**si·fi·ca·tion** *n.*— -**si·fi·er** *n.*

fal·si·ty (*fawl*-sih-tee) *n.* [*pl.* -ties] Untruth; deception.

Fal·staff (*fawl*-staf) *n.* 1. A witty, rotund, convivial Shakespearean character. 2. A braggart.—**Fal·staff·i·an** (fawl-*staf*-ee-un) *adj.*

falt·boat (*fawlt*-boht) *n.* A light collapsible boat; kayak.

fal·ter (*fawl*-ter) *v.* 1. To hesitate; waver. 2. To stammer; stutter. 3. To totter; tremble; be unsteady.—*n.* Hesitation; wavering; vacillation.—**fal·ter·er** *n.*—**fal·ter·ing** *adj.*

fame *n.* 1. Renown; celebrity. 2. Public report; reputation.—**famed** *adj.*

fa·mil·iar (fuh-*mil*-yer) *adj.* 1. Intimate; well acquainted. 2. Affable; easy; not formal. 3. Well known; common. 4. Offensively intimate.—*n.* An intimate; close companion.

fa·mil·i·ar·i·ty (fuh-mil-ee-*ar*-ih-tee) *n.* [*pl.* -ties] 1. Intimacy; close acquaintance. 2. Informality. 3. Unwarranted intimacy.

fa·mil·iar·ize (fuh-*mil*-yer-yze) *v.* [-ized; -iz·ing] 1. To make accustomed to. 2. To make acquainted with.—**fa·mil·iar·i·za·tion** *n.*

fam·i·ly (*fam*-ih-lee) *n.* [*pl.* -lies] 1. A social group consisting of a husband, a wife, and a child or children. 2. A household; relatives living in one home. 3. Lineage; the descendants of a common ancestor. 4. Kindred; group related by birth or marriage. 5. A scientific classification below an *order*.

fam·ine (*fam*-in) *n.* 1. Scarcity of food; starvation. 2. A lack; dearth; want.

fam·ish (*fam*-ish) *v.* To starve; suffer extreme hunger.—**fam·ish·ment** *n.*—Starvation.

fa·mous (*faym*-us) *adj.* 1. Noted; illustrious; renowned; celebrated. 2. Well known; talked of.—**fa·mous·ly** *adv.*—**fa·mous·ness** *n.*

fan *n.* 1. An apparatus for circulating the air, as an electric fan, a palm leaf fan, etc. 2. An ornamented wing-shaped device of paper, silk, etc., waved by hand to stir a breeze. 3. *Aviation Slang.* A propeller.—*v.* [fanned; fan·ning] 1. To cool; produce ventilation; agitate the air. 2. To winnow; separate chaff from grain. 3. To increase; stir up; stimulate. —**fan·ner** *n.*

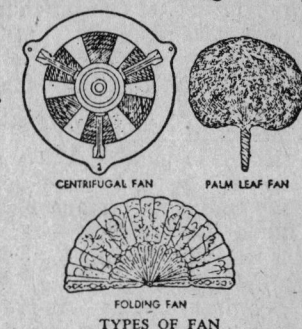

CENTRIFUGAL FAN   PALM LEAF FAN

FOLDING FAN
TYPES OF FAN

fan *n.* *Slang.* An enthusiast; devotee; admirer.

fa·nat·ic (fuh-*nat*-ik) *adj.* Zealous; blindly attached; obsessed by a particular subject, esp. religion.—**fa·nat·ic** *n.*—**fa·nat·i·cal** *adj.*

fa·nat·i·cism (fuh-*nat*-ih-sizm) *n.* Religious frenzy; bigotry; excessive enthusiasm.

fan·ci·er (*fan*-see-er) *n.* 1. A breeder of birds, dogs, or other pets. 2. A collector; enthusiast; one indulging a hobby.

fan·ci·ful (*fan*-sih-ful) *adj.* 1. Imaginary; chimerical; unreal. 2. Imaginative; whimsical.—**fan·ci·ful·ly** *adv.*—**fan·ci·ful·ness** *n.*

fan·cy (*fan*-see) *n.* [*pl.* -cies] 1. The imagination; faculties. 2. A notion; whim; caprice. 3. Inclination; liking; fondness.—*v.* [fan·cied; fan·cy·ing] 1. To imagine; suppose. 2. To like; have a fondness for.

fan·cy *adj.* [fan·ci·er; fan·ci·est] 1. Elegant; fine. 2. Ornamented; embellished. 3. *Slang.* Exorbitant. 'Fancy prices.' 4. Specially bred or cultivated; of a superior kind.

fancy dress. A masquerade costume.—**fancy-dress** *adj.*

fancy-free *adj.* Not in love.

fan·cy·work *n.* Needlework, as crocheting, embroidery, etc.

fan·dan·go (fan-*dang*-goh) n. [pl. -gos] Spanish dance in triple time derived from the bolero.

fane n. A church; temple.

fan·fare (*fan*-fayr) n. 1. A flourish of trumpets. 2. Noisy acclaim; boisterous reception.

fang n. 1. A tusk; long pointed tooth. 2. The poison tooth of a snake.—**fanged** adj.

fan·light n. Architecture. A semicircular window over a door.

fan·tail n. 1. The Australian flycatcher. 2. A variety of pigeon. 3. The projecting stern of a ship.

fan·tan n. A Chinese gambling game.

fan·ta·si·a (fan-*tayzh*-uh) n. 1. A musical composition not restricted by the usual forms. 2. A melody of popular tunes.

fan·tas·tic (fan-*tass*-tik) adj. Grotesque; incongruous; having no basis in reality.—**fan·tas·ti·cal** adj.—**fan·tas·ti·cal·ly** adv.

fan·ta·sy (*fant*-uh-see) n. [pl. -sies] 1. A highly imaginative composition, as a story or play, portraying unrealistic characters and events; fairy tale. 2. Vagary; fancy; unreality.

far adj. [far·ther; far·thest] 1. Distant; separated by time. 2. More distant. 'The far side.' —adv. 1. At a distance. 2. Remotely. 'Searched far in the past.' 3. For the most part. 'Far gone.' 4. To a great extent. 'Far better.' 5. To a certain point. 'You have gone far enough.'—**far and away.** Much; unquestionably; decidedly.—**far and wide.** Everywhere; all over.

far·ad (*fair*-ad, -ud) n. Electricity. A unit of electrical capacity.—**fa·rad·ic** (fuh-*rad*-ik) adj. Relating to induced electric currents.

far·a·way adj. 1. Distant. 2. Abstracted; dreamy.

farce n. 1. A dramatic piece characterized by grotesquerie and exaggeration; broad comedy. 2. Show; empty display.—**far·ci·cal** adj.—**far·ci·cal·i·ty** (fahrss-ih-*kal*-ih-tee) n.— -**cal·ly** adv.

far cry. A great difference or distance.

fare v. [fared; far·ing] 1. To progress; proceed along. 2. To do. 'To fare badly.' 3. To happen; come to pass. 4. To eat; be dined. —n. 1. A passage charge; the sum paid for riding on a public conveyance. 2. A passenger in a public vehicle. 3. Food; provisions.

Far East. Eastern Asia.

fare·well interj. Goodbye.—n. Departure.—adj. Last; final; parting.

far·fetched adj. Forced; strained.

far·flung adj. Extending to a great distance.

fa·ri·na (fuh-*reen*-uh) n. 1. A meal from various grains used for breakfast cereals and puddings. 2. A white flour obtained from potatoes.—**far·i·na·ceous** (far-ih-*nay*-shus) adj. 1. Made of meal or flour. 2. Mealy.

farm n. A tract of land for agricultural, stock-raising, or dairy purposes.—v. To be employed in agriculture; cultivate the soil.—**farm out.** To turn over an enterprise to another operator in return for a percentage guarantee.

farm·er n. 1. An agriculturist; breeder; cultivator of land. 2. Anyone deriving income from the cultivation of the earth.

farm·house n. A dwelling house on a farm.

farm·ing n. The occupation of cultivating land.

farm·stead n. Farm property.

farm·yard n. A barnyard; enclosure near a barn.

far·o (*fayr*-oh) n. A game played by betting on the order of cards drawn from a box.

far·off adj. 1. Faraway; distant; remote. 2. Abstracted.

far·ra·go (fer-*ay*-go, -*ah*-) n. [pl. -goes] A hodgepodge; confused mixture.

far·reach·ing adj. Extensive; reverberating; having effect in remote times or places.

far·ri·er (*fair*-ee-er) n. A shoer of horses.—**far·ri·er·y** n. The art of shoeing horses.

far·row (*fair*-oh) n. A litter of pigs.—v. Of pigs, to give birth.

far·see·ing adj. Farsighted; having forethought.

far·sight·ed adj. 1. Wise; farseeing; having good judgment. 2. Unable to see clearly objects near at hand; hypermetropic.— -**ed·ly** adv.— -**ed·ness** n.

far·ther adj. More remote; more distant than. —adv. Beyond; more remotely; at a greater distance. 'Without looking farther.'

far·ther·most adj. Most distant.

far·thest adj. Most distant; most remote.—adv. At the greatest distance.

far·thing n. An English coin worth about ¼c.

far·thin·gale (*fahr*-thing-gayl) n. A hoopskirt common in the 17th century.

fas·ces (*fass*-eez) n. pl. 1. A bundle of rods containing an axe, carried by ancient Roman guards. 2. Any symbol of tyranny. 3. The symbol of the Italian Fascists.—**fas·ci·al** (*fash*-'l) adj. Resembling the fasces.

fas·ci·a (*fash*-uh) n. [pl. -ci·ae] 1. A fillet; belt; bandage. 2. Anatomy. Layer of tissue connecting or supporting an organ.— -**ci·al** adj.

fas·ci·cle (*fass*-ih-k'l) n. 1. A cluster; collection; bundle. 2. A section of a work printed in parts.—**fas·ci·cled** adj.—**fas·cic·u·lar** (fas-*ik*-yoo-ler) adj.

fas·ci·nate (*fass*-ih-nayt) v. [-nat·ed; -nat·ing] To enchant; captivate; exert an irresistible influence.—**fas·ci·nat·ed·ly** adv.

fas·ci·nat·ing adj. 1. Captivating; enchanting. 2. Having an irresistible attraction.—**fas·ci·nat·ing·ly** adv.

fas·ci·na·tion (fass-ih-*nay*-sh'n) n. Enchantment; allure; irresistible appeal.

fas·ci·na·tor (*fass*-ih-nay-ter) n. 1. An enchanter; captivator. 2. A crocheted head-scarf.

fas·cism (*fash*-izm) n. 1. [cap.] The nationalistic and anti-democratic principles and practices of the Italian Fascisti. 2. A political philosophy and movement of extreme nationalism, militaristic imperialism, suppression of civil rights, and opposition to democratic social progress, expressed through the efforts of a fanatic minority to seize complete political power.

fas·cist (*fash*-ist) *n.* 1. [*cap.*] A member of the Italian Fascisti or other political party based on fascism. 2. One who supports the principles of fascism.—*adj.* Also **fas·cist·ic.** 1. [*cap.*] Relating to the Fascisti. 2. Characteristic of fascism.

Fas·cis·ti (fah-*sheess*-tee) *n. pl.* An Italian fascist political party organized by Benito Mussolini in 1919.

fash·ion (*fash*-un) *n.* 1. Style; custom; prevailing mode. 2. Manner; way; kind of behavior. 'In his sour fashion.' 3. Society.—*adj.* Relating to clothes.—*v.* To form; shape; make by molding.—**fash·ion·er** *n.*

fash·ion·a·ble (*fash*-un-uh-b'l) *adj.* 1. Stylish; modish. 2. According to the prevailing mode. —*n.* A stylish person.—**fash·ion·a·ble·ness** *n.* —**fash·ion·a·bly** *adv.*

fashion plate. 1. A style illustration. 2. A fop; person overly concerned with dress.

fast *v.* To abstain from eating.—*n.* 1. Abstinence from food. 2. *Nautical.* A mooring rope or chain.

fast *adj.* [fast·er; fast·est] 1. Swift; speedy; quick. 2. Firm; steadfast; secure. 3. Durable; not fading, as a color. 4. *Colloquial.* Dissipated; wild.

fast-bound	fast going	fast moving
fast-dyed	fast-grounded	fast-rooted
fast fading	fast growing	fast running
fast-fettered	fasthold	fast-settled
fast fleeting	fast knit	fast stepping

fas·ten (*fass*-'n) *v.* 1. To secure; fix; make firm. 2. To lock; close firmly. 3. To attach; tie; join together. 4. To place upon; set; fix. 'Fasten your attention.'—**fast·en·er** *n.* A snap, hook and eye, etc., esp. for fastening clothing.

fas·ten·ing *n.* A lock; bolt; clasp.

fas·tid·i·ous (fass-*tid*-ee-us) *adj.* 1. Squeamish; delicate; overnice. 2. Hard to please. 3. Meticulous; neat.— *-ous·ly adv.— -ous·ness n.*

fast·ness *n.* 1. A fortification; stronghold. 2. Strength; security.

fat *adj.* [fat·ter; fat·test] 1. Obese; corpulent; fleshy; stout. 2. Adipose; containing fat. 3. Lucrative; profitable. 'Fat fees.'—*n.* 1. A yellowish greasy substance making up part of animal tissue. 2. The richest part of anything. 3. Shortening.—*v.* [fat·ted; -ting] To fatten; make fleshy.—**fat·ly** *adv.*—**fat·ness** *n.*

fat-bellied	fat-free	fat-rumped
fat-bodied	fathead	fat-soluble
fat-cheeked	fat-hipped	fat-tailed
fat-fed	fat-legged	fat-witted

fa·tal (*fay*-t'l) *adj.* 1. Deadly; mortal. 2. Calamitous; of great moment.—**fa·tal·ly** *adv.*

fa·tal·ism (*fay*-t'l-izm) *n.* The doctrine that all things happen by inevitable necessity.—**fa·tal·ist** *n.*—**fa·tal·is·tic** *adj.*—**fa·tal·is·ti·cal·ly** *adv.*

fa·tal·i·ty (fay-*tal*-ih-tee; fuh-), *n.* [*pl.* -ties] 1. Destiny; inevitability. 2. A calamity; disastrous occurrence. 3. A death.

Fata Morgana. A mirage seen at the Strait of Messina, between Sicily and Italy.

fate *n.* 1. Destiny; the force believed to determine events; inevitable necessity. 2. One's lot; that which befalls. 3. Death; destruction; doom.—**the Fates.** The three goddesses, Clotho, Lachesis, and Atropos, ruling the destiny of men.

fat·ed *adj.* Destined; decreed by fate.

fate·ful *adj.* Momentous; filled with significance or foreboding; predestined.—**fate·ful·ly** *adv.*—**fate·ful·ness** *n.*

fa·ther (*fah*-ther) *n.* 1. A male parent; male producing offspring. 2. A founder; inventor; originator. 3. A guardian. 4. A priest. 5. [*cap.*] God. 6. [*pl.*] The early ecclesiastical writers.—*v.* 1. To beget; procreate. 2. To originate; be author of.

fa·ther·hood *n.* Paternity.

fa·ther-in-law *n.* [*pl.* fa·thers-in-law] The father of one's wife or husband.

fa·ther·land *n.* Homeland; native country.

fa·ther·less *adj.* Orphaned; without a father.

fa·ther·ly *adj.* Paternal; protective.— *-li·ness n.*

fath·om (*fath*-um) *n. Nautical.* A depth of six feet.—*v.* To penetrate; comprehend.—**fath·om·a·ble** *adj.*—**fath·om·less** *adj.*

fa·tigue (fuh-*teeg*) *n.* 1. Weariness; exhaustion. 2. [*pl.*] *Military.* Work clothes.—*v.* [fatigued; fa·tig·uing]—**fat·i·ga·ble** *adj.*

fatigue duty. *Military.* Work connected with the upkeep of a post.

Fa·ti·ma (*fat*-ih-muh) *n.* 1. The daughter of Mohammed. 2. A wife of Bluebeard.

fat·ling *n.* A young animal fattened for slaughter.

fat·ten *v.* 1. To make fat; feed for slaughter. 2. To grow plump. 3. To enrich.— *-ten·er n.*

fat·ty [-ti·er; -ti·est] 1. Containing fat; having deposits of fat. 2. Greasy; oily.—**fat·ti·ly** *adv.* —**fat·ti·ness** *n.*

fatty degeneration. A disease characterized by the conversion of body protein into fat.

fa·tu·i·ty (fuh-*tyoo*-ih-tee) *n.* [*pl.* -ties] Weakmindedness; foolishness; folly.— *-i·tous adj.*

fat·u·ous (*fat*-choo-us) *adj.* 1. Asinine; silly. 2. Empty; unreal.—*-ous·ly adv.*—*-ous·ness n.*

fau·ces (*faw*-seez) *n. pl. Anatomy.* The part of the throat from the mouth to the gullet.—**faucal, fau·ci·al** *adj.*

fau·cet (*faw*-set) *n.* A spigot; spout; tap; pipe with valves for drawing liquid.

faugh *interj.* An exclamation of derision.

fault *n.* 1. A weakness; shortcoming; failing. 2. A mistake; error. 3. A defect; flaw. 4. A misdemeanor; misdeed.—*v.* To cause a defect in.

FAUCET

fault·find·ing *n.* A tendency to be overly critical.—**fault·find·ing** *adj.*—**fault·find·er** *n.*

fault·less adj. Flawless; perfect; without defect.—**fault·less·ly** adv.—**fault·less·ness** n.

faul·ty adj. [fault·i·er; -i·est] 1. Defective; imperfect; containing flaws. 2. Blamable; worthy of censure.—**fault·i·ly** adv.—**fault·i·ness** n.

faun n. Mythology. A deity having the ears and tail of a goat, torso and face of a man.

fau·na (fawn-uh) n. The animal life of a region or period.—**fau·nal** adj.—**fau·nal·ly** adv.

Faust (fowst) n. In Goethe's play, the hero who sold his soul to the devil.

faux pas (foh-pah). A breach of etiquette.

fa·vor (fay-ver) n. 1. A kindness; benevolent act. 2. Good will; benevolence. 3. Patronage, partiality. 4. A token; souvenir, as of a party.—v. 1. To prefer; be partial to. 2. To facilitate; make easier. 3. To resemble.

fa·vor·a·ble (fay-ver-uh-b'l) adj. 1. Propitious; advantageous. 2. Friendly; kind.—**fa·vor·a·ble·ness** n.—**fa·vor·a·bly** adv.

fa·vored adj. 1. Preferred; favorable. 2. Aided. 3. Featured; looking. 'A well-favored man.'

fa·vor·ite (fay-ver-it) n. 1. An object of affection or esteem. 2. The competitor picked to win.—adj. Best-liked; preferred.

fa·vor·it·ism (fay-ver-it-izm) n. Partiality; one-sidedness.

fawn n. A young deer.—adj. Yellowish brown.

fawn v. To wheedle; flatter servilely; court favor.—**fawn·er** n.—**fawn·ing·ly** adv.

fay n. A fairy; elf.

fay v. To fit; to join, as wood.

faze v. [fazed; faz·ing] To disconcert; take aback.

F.B.I. U.S. Federal Bureau of Investigation.

F.C.C. U. S. Federal Communications Commission.

fe·al·ty (fee-ul-tee) n. Loyalty; fidelity.

fear n. 1. Dread; apprehension; alarm. 2. Anxiety; solicitude; worry. 'Fear for his safety.' 3. Awe; respect; reverence.—v. To be alarmed about or in awe of.—**fear·er** n.

fear-broken	fear-frozen	fear-shaken
fear-crested	fearnaught	fear-struck
fear-free	fear-pursued	fear-taught

fear·ful adj. 1. Apprehensive; afraid. 2. Timid; lacking courage. 3. Terrible; horrible; shocking.—**fear·ful·ly** adv.—**fear·ful·ness** n.

fear·less adj. Brave; daring; courageous.—**fear·less·ly** adv.—**fear·less·ness** n.

fear·some adj. Fearful; frightful; dreadful. —**fear·some·ly** adv.—**fear·some·ness** n.

feas·i·ble (feez-uh-b'l) adj. Practicable; advisable; desirable.—**feas·i·bil·i·ty** n.—**feas·i·ble·ness** n.—**feas·i·bly** adv.

feast n. 1. A banquet; sumptuous repast, esp. in commemoration of an event. 2. A church festival. 3. A delicious meal.—v. 1. To eat sumptuously. 2. To entertain with rich food. 3. To gratify. 'Feast the eyes.'—**feast·er** n.

feat n. Accomplishment; exploit; show of skill.

feath·er (feth-er) n. 1. A plume; one of the shaftlike appendages forming the plumage of a bird. 2. Kind; species. —v. 1. To cover with feathers. 2. To keep in light motion, as oars, an airplane propeller, etc. —**feather in one's cap.** An achievement; victory. —**feather one's nest.** To collect wealth.

FEATHERS

feath·er·brain n. A scatterbrain; giddy person. —**feath·er·brained** adj.

feath·er·less adj. Having no feathers.

feath·er·y adj. 1. Covered with feathers. 2. Light, as a cake.—**feath·er·i·ness** n.

feat·ly adv. Neatly; correctly.—**feat·li·ness** n.

fea·ture (fee-cher) n. 1. A part of the face. 2. A prominent part. 'The features of a treaty.' 3. [pl.] The physiognomy; facial characteristics. 4. Material, as a magazine article, played up as a special selling attraction. 5. The main film on a motion-picture bill.—v. [fea·tured; fea·tur·ing] 1. To give an important place to. 2. To offer as an attraction.

fea·tured adj. 1. Having a particular facial cast. 2. Displayed prominently; advertised for sales appeal.

fea·ture·less adj. Having nondescript features.

feb·ri·fuge (feb-rih-fyooj) n. A medicine dispelling fever.—**feb·ri·fuge** adj.—**fe·bri·fu·gal** (feh-brif-yoo-g'l) adj.

fe·brile (fee-bril; feb-ril) adj. Feverish.

Feb·ru·ar·y (feb-roo-er-ee) n. [pl. -aries] The second month of the year.

fe·ces, fae·ces (fee-seez) n. pl. Excrement. —**fe·cal, fae·cal** (fee-k'l) adj.

feck·less adj. Shiftless; morally weak.—**feck·less·ly** adv.—**feck·less·ness** n.

fe·cund (fee-kund, fek-und) adj. Fruitful; prolific; fertile.—**fe·cun·di·ty** (fek-un-dih-tee) n. 1. Fruitfulness; fertility. 2. Creativeness; richness of imagination.

fed·er·a·cy (fed-er-uh-see) n. [pl. -cies] A confederation; union of self-governing states having a central control.

fed·er·al (fed-er-ul) adj. 1. United; founded on alliance by mutual agreement. 2. [cap.] Relating to the U.S. Government. 3. [cap.] Supporting the Union in the Civil War.—n. [cap.] A supporter of the Union cause.—**fed·er·al·ly** adv.

fed·er·al·ism (fed-er-ul-izm) n. 1. The doctrine of centralized government. 2. [cap.] The principle of those advocating federal union of the colonies after the Revolution.

fed·er·al·ize (fed-er-ul-yze) v. [-ized; -iz·ing] To bring together under a central government. —**fed·er·al·i·za·tion** (fed-er-ul-ih-zay-sh'n) n.

Federal party. The party which favored adoption of the Constitution, and strong central government.

federal union. A union local not affiliated to an international union but directly to either AFL or CIO, and responsible only to the national body.

fed·er·ate (*fed*-er-ayt) *v.* [-at·ed; -at·ing] To unite; bring as sovereign states under a central government.—*adj.* (*fed*-er-it).

fed·er·a·tion (fed-er-*ay*-sh'n) *n.* 1. The union of several states retaining their sovereignty. 2. A union; league.—**fed·er·a·tive** (*fed*-er-uh-tiv) *adj.*—**fed·er·a·tive·ly** *adv.*

fe·do·ra (feh-*dor*-uh) *n.* A type of man's felt hat.

fee *n.* 1. Compensation; recompense; charge for services. 2. A tax; duty; dues. 3. An inherited estate.—*v.* To pay for services.—**fee simple.** Property unconditionally granted to heirs.—**fee tail.** Property granted to designated heirs.

fee·ble (*fee*-b'l) *adj.* [fee·bler; fee·blest] 1. Weak; infirm; without strength. 2. Dim; faint; inefficient; ineffectual.—**fee·ble·ness** *n.* **fee·bly** *adv.*

feeble-bodied	**feeble-eyed**	**feeble-lunged**
feeble-brained	**feeble-hearted**	**feeble-voiced**

fee·ble-mind·ed *adj.* Mentally weak; lacking intellectual powers.—**fee·ble·mind·ed·ly** *adv.*

feed *v.* [fed; feed·ing] 1. To nourish; give food to. 2. To eat; subsist on. 3. To supply; provide with material. 'Feed a machine.'—*n.* 1. Fodder; food for animals. 2. A supply of material for a machine. 3. *Slang.* A meal. —**fed up.** *Colloquial.* Satiated with; disgusted.

feed bin	**feed box**	**feedstuff**
feedboard	**feedhead**	**feedway**

feed·er *n.* 1. A branch, as of a canal, railway, etc. 2. *Mining.* A cross vein passing into a lode. 3. One who fattens cattle for slaughter.

feeder line. *Aviation.* Auxiliary airline which transports cargo and passengers from rural areas to main-line airports.

feel *v.* [felt; feel·ing] 1. To perceive by the touch. 2. To experience; be conscious of, as pain, love, etc. 3. To understand; sympathize; be emotionally moved. 4. To know oneself to be. 'Feel certain; feel willing.' 5. To appear to the touch. 'Velvet feels smooth.'—*n.* 1. Sensation; feeling. 2. Tactile impression. —**feel out.** To test; investigate by a stratagem.

feel·er *n.* 1. An antenna; tactile organ of the lower animals. 2. A stratagem for ascertaining the opinions of others.

feel·ing *n.* 1. Sense of touch; physical sensation. 2. Emotion; sentiment. 3. Intuition; conviction; belief. 4. [*pl.*] Sensitivity. 'I hurt his feelings.'—**feel·ing·ly** *adv.*

feet. *Plural* of **foot.**

feign (fayn) *v.* 1. To pretend; present falsely. 2. To vent; imagine.—**feigned** *adj.*—**feign·er** *n.*

feint (faynt) *n.* 1. A pretended attack to mislead a defender. 2. A trick; pretense.—**feint** *v.*

feld·spar (*feld*-spahr) *n.* A quartzlike mineral consisting principally of aluminum silicates.

fe·lic·i·tate (fuh-*liss*-uh-tayt) *v.* [-tat·ed; -ta·

ting] 1. To congratulate; express pleasure. 2. Make very happy.

fe·lic·i·ta·tion (feh-liss-ih-*tay*-sh'n) *n.* Congratulation.

fe·lic·i·tous (feh-*liss*-ih-tus) *adj.* Appropriate; apt; fortunate.— **-tous·ly** *adv.*— **-tous·ness** *n.*

fe·lic·i·ty (feh-*liss*-ih-tee) *n.* [*pl.* -ties] 1. Happiness; bliss. 2. Source of happiness; blessing. 3. Skillfulness; facility.

fe·line (*fee*-lyne) *adj.* Pertaining to the cat family; like a cat.—**fe·line** *n.*—**fe·line·ly** *adv.*—**fe·lin·i·ty** (feh-*lin*-ih-tee) *n.*

fell *v.* 1. To cause to fall by striking, cutting, etc. 2. To sew a seam level with the cloth.

fell *adj.* Cruel; fierce.—**fel·ly** *adv.*

fell *n.* 1. A skin or hide of an animal. 2. Seam sewed down level with the cloth. 3. A barren hill; high land not fit for pasture.

fel·lah (*fel*-uh) *n.* [*pl.* fel·la·hin, fel·lahs] Egyptian or Syrian peasant.

fell·er *n.* 1. One who fells or knocks down. 2. Attachment on a machine for sewing seams. 3. *Humorous & Dialect.* Fellow (sense 1).

fel·low (*fel*-oh) *n.* 1. *Colloquial.* A person; individual. 2. A companion; associate. 3. An equal in rank; peer. 4. One of a pair, or of two articles used together. 5. A student who receives a stipend from a university for teaching and research.—*adj.* Having community or equality in nature, position, employment, etc.

fellow feeling. Sympathy; kindred feeling.

fel·low·ship *n.* 1. Companionship. 2. Fitness and liking for festivities. 3. Partnership; joint interest. 4. Association of persons on a basis of similar tastes, occupations, etc. 5. A grant of a stipend from a university for teaching and research.

fellow traveler. *Political Slang.* One who sympathizes with the ideals of a political organization without being affiliated with it.

fel·on (*fel*-un) *n.* 1. *Law.* A person who has committed a felony. 2. A criminal; convict; culprit.—*adj.* Malignant; fierce; malicious. —**fel·on·ry** *n.* A body of criminals.

fel·on *n.* *Medical.* A pus-filled infection or abscess at the edge of the fingernail or toenail.

fe·lo·ni·ous (feh-*loh*-nee-us) *adj.* Malignant; villainous.— **-ous·ly** *adv.*— **-ous·ness** *n.*

fel·o·ny (*fel*-uh-nee) *n.* [*pl.* -ies] 1. *Law.* A crime next in gravity to a misdemeanor. 2. A crime for which punishment is meted out in accordance with the degree of guilt.

fel·spar. *Variant spelling* of **feldspar.**

felt *n.* 1. Cloth of wool, or wool with hair or fur, made by rolling, beating, and pressure. 2. A hat made of felted wool.—**felt** *adj.*—*v.* 1. To make felt cloth. 2. To cover with felt.

felt-jacketed	**felt maker**	**feltmonger**
felt-lined	**felt making**	**feltwork**

fe·luc·ca (feh-*luhk*-uh) *n.* *Nautical.* A long, swift sailing vessel, which may also be rowed.

fe·male (*fee*-mayl) *n.* 1. Among animals, one of the sex which conceives and brings forth

F

young. 2. Among plants, that which produces fruit.—*adj.* 1. Belonging to the female sex. 2. Pertaining to or characteristic of females. 3. Feminine; soft; delicate. 4. *Botany*. Pistil-bearing.

fem·i·na·cy (*fem*-in-uh-see) *n.* [*pl.* -cies] Female nature.

fem·i·nine (*fem*-in-in) *adj.* 1. Pertaining to the female sex; womanly; delicate; dainty. 2. Effeminate; lacking manly qualities. 3. *Grammar*. Denoting the gender of words which signify females, or which employ the grammatical terminations of such words.—*n.* A female; woman; feminine sex.—**fem·i·nine·ly** *adv.* —**fem·i·nine·ness** *n.*

feminine rhyme. Rhyming of words of more than one syllable having an unaccented final syllable, as *garden* and *pardon*.

fem·i·nin·i·ty (fem-ih-*nin*-ih-tee) *n.* [*pl.* -ties] Womanliness; delicacy; daintiness.

fem·i·nism (*fem*-ih-nizm) *n.* 1. Belief in according women equal status with men, politically, socially, and economically. 2. The characteristics of women.—**fem·i·nist** *n.*—**fem·i·nis·tic** *adj.*

fe·mur (*fee*-mer) *n.* [*pl.* fe·murs, fem·o·ra] 1. In vertebrate animals, the first bone of the leg or pelvic extremity. 2. *Entomology*. The third joint of the leg, long and usually compressed. 3. *Architecture*. The interstitial space between the channels in the triglyph of the Doric order.—**fem·o·ral** *adj.* Belonging to the thigh.

fen *n.* Boggy land; moor; marsh.

fence *n.* 1. A wall, hedge, or line of posts, boards, or pickets, etc., to confine or to keep out. 2. Art of self-defense either by weapons or skill in debate. 3. A purchaser or receiver of stolen goods.—*v.* [fenced; fenc·ing] 1. To enclose with a hedge, wall, etc. 2. To guard; fortify. 3. To ward off or parry by argument or reasoning. 4. To practice the art of fencing.—**on the fence.** Straddling, as of political issues; undecided; neutral.

fenc·er *n.* 1. One skilled in the art of fencing with sword or foil. 2. A horse good at leaping fences. 3. One who repairs fences.

fenc·ing *n.* 1. The art of using a sword or foil skillfully. 2. Material used in making fencing. 3. That which fences; enclosure.

fend *v.* To ward off; parry; resist.—**fend for oneself.** To be resourceful; shift for oneself.

fend·er *n.* 1. A shell-like covering over the wheels of an automobile, preventing the body from being splashed. 2. A frame on the front of a train or car to reduce impact in case of collision.

fen·es·tra·tion (fen-ess-*tray*-sh'n) *n.* *Architecture*. The series or arrangement of windows in a building.—**fe·nes·trate** (*fen*-es-trit) *adj.* Pertaining to a window.—**fe·nes·trat·ed** *adj.* Having windows.

Fe·ni·an (*fee*-nee-un, *feen*-yun) *n.* A member of an association of Irish refugees whose aim was the independence of Ireland.—**Fe·ni·an** *adj.*

fen·nel (*fen*-'l) *n.* A fragrant, flowering plant often used in medicine.

fe·ral (*fehr*-ul) *adj.* Wild, esp. of animals.

fer-de-lance (fehr-duh-*lahnss*) *n.* A lance-headed, poisonous member of the rattlesnake family, found in Brazil and the West Indies.

fer·ment (fer-*ment*) *v.* 1. To undergo or cause fermentation. 2. To be agitated or excited. 3. To cause agitation or excitement.—*n.* (*fer*-ment) 1. Any substance which produces fermentation; an enzyme. 2. Commotion; tumult; agitation.—**fer·ment·a·ble** *adj.*

fer·men·ta·tion (fer-men-*tay*-shun) *n.* 1. Conversion of an organic substance into new compounds in the presence of an enzyme. 2. State of agitation or excitement.

fern *n.* A seedless, nonflowering plant with long divided leaves.

fern·er·y (*fern*-er-ee) *n.* [*pl.* -ies] A place where ferns are cultivated.

fe·ro·cious (fer-*oh*-shus) *adj.* Fierce; savage; wild; rapacious.—**·cious·ly** *adv.*—**·cious·ness** *n.*

FERN

fe·roc·i·ty (fer-*oss*-uh-tee) *n.* [*pl.* -ties] Fierceness; savageness.

fer·ret (*fehr*-it) *n.* A weasellike animal found in Africa and Europe, used for hunting rabbits.—*v.* 1. To search out by cunning and perseverance. 2. To drive out of a lurking place.—**fer·ret·ter** *n.*—**fer·ret·y** *adj.*

FERRET (1/15 life size)

fer·ric (*fehr*-ik) *adj.* Pertaining to or extracted from iron, esp. in its greater valence of three.

fer·ris wheel (*fehr*-iss). An amusement apparatus consisting of a vertical revolving wheel with seats hung about its rim.

fer·ro·con·crete (fehr-oh-*kon*-kreet) *n.* Steel-reinforced concrete.

fer·rous (*fehr*-us) *adj.* Pertaining to or containing iron, esp. in its smaller valence of two.

fer·ru·gi·nous (fer-*roo*-jin-us) *adj.* 1. Partaking of iron; containing iron. 2. Rust-colored.

fer·rule (*fehr*-ul, *fehr*-ool) *n.* A metal ring used to provide additional strength or to prevent splitting of a stick, etc.

fer·ry (*fehr*-ee) *n.* [*pl.* -ries] 1. A ferryboat. 2. The place where ferryboats dock.—*v.* [ferried; fer·ry·ing] 1. To transport. 2. To pass or carry over water in a boat.

fer·ry·boat *n.* A boat for transporting passengers, vehicles, and freight over short distances.

fer·ry·man *n.* [*pl.* -men] One who owns, looks after, or operates a ferry.

fer·tile (*fer*-t'l) *adj.* 1. Fruitful; rich. 2. Prolific; inventive; able to produce abundantly.

fer·til·i·ty (fer-*til*-uh-tee) *n.* [*pl.* -ties] 1. Fruitfulness; productiveness. 2. Richness; abundancy of resources; inventiveness.

fer·til·i·za·tion (fer-t'l-ih-*zay*-shun) n. 1. Rendering fertile, fruitful, or productive. 2. Impregnation; union of the male and female reproductive cell.

fer·ti·lize (*fer*-tuh-lyze) v. [fer·ti·lized; fer·ti·liz-ing] 1. To make fertile, fruitful, or productive. 2. To enrich, as soil.—**fer·ti·liz·a·ble** adj.

fer·ti·liz·er (*fer*-tuh-lyze-er) n. A substance that enriches the soil.

fer·ule (*fehr*-ool) n. A flat piece of wood or cane used to punish school children.—v. [fer·uled; fer·ul·ing] To punish with a ferule.

fer·vent (*fer*-vunt) adj. 1. Ardent; earnest; zealous. 2. Vehement. 3. Hot; glowing. —**fer·ven·cy** n.—**fer·vent·ly** adv.

fer·vid (*fer*-vid) adj. 1. Vehement; eager; warmly zealous. 2. Hot; burning; boiling. —**fer·vid·ly** adv.—**fer·vid·ness** n.

fer·vor (*fer*-ver) n. 1. Intensity of feeling; ardor; earnestness. 2. Heat; warmth.

fess n. Also **fesse heraldry.** A horizontal band forming the center third part of an escutcheon.

fes·tal (*fess*-t'l) adj. 1. Joyous; gay; mirthful. 2. Pertaining to a feast.—**fes·tal·ly** adv.

fes·ter (*fess*-ter) v. 1. To generate or discharge pus. 2. To grow virulent; to rankle. 3. To cause to fester or rankle.—n. 1. A small inflammatory sore. 2. Act of festering or rankling.

fes·ti·val (*fess*-tih-v'l) adj. 1. Joyous; mirthful. 2. Pertaining to a feast.—n. A festive celebration; day of joy; time of feasting.

fes·tive (*fess*-tiv) adj. 1. Joyous; gay; mirthful. 2. Pertaining to a feast.—**fes·tive·ly** adv.

fes·tiv·i·ty (fess-*tiv*-uh-tee) n. [pl. -ties] 1. Gaiety; joyfulness. 2. A festival.

fes·toon (fess-*toon*) n. A chain of flowers or other materials suspended between two points. —**fes·toon** v.—**fes·toon·er·y** n.

fe·tal, foe·tal (*fee*-t'l) adj. Pertaining to a fetus; postembryonic stage of the unborn young.

fetch v. 1. To go and bring; bring. 2. To derive; draw from a source. 3. To bring back; recall. 4. To obtain as a price. 5. To move or turn about.—n. A stratagem; trick; artifice.—**fetch·er** n.—**fetch up.** 1. To bring up. 2. To stop suddenly. 3. To overtake.

fetch·ing adj. Colloquial. Attractive; fascinating.

fete, fête (fayt) n. 1. A holiday; festival day. 2. Feast.—v. To honor with a feast or entertainment.

fet·id (*fet*-id) adj. Having an offensive smell; stinking.—**fet·id·ly** adv.—**fet·id·ness** n.

fe·tish, fe·tich (*fet*-ish) n. 1. An object awfully regarded as having mysterious powers or as representing a deity. 2. Psychoanalysis. An object which arouses erotic feelings, though of no sexual significance in itself. 3. An object arousing unreasonable devotion.—**fe·tish·ism**, **fe·tich·ism** n.—**fe·tish·is·tic, fe·tich·is·tic** adj.

fet·lock (*fet*-lok) n. 1. A tuft of hair growing behind the pastern joint of a horse's leg. 2. The projection on which the tuft grows.

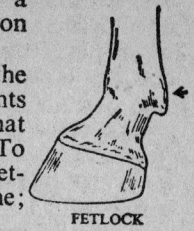

FETLOCK

fet·ter n. 1. A shackle for the feet or hands which prevents free motion. 2. Anything that confines; a restraint.—v. 1. To shackle with a chain; put fetters on. 2. To bind; confine; restrain.

fet·tle n. Preparation; condition; order.

fe·tus, foe·tus (*fee*-tus) n. [pl. -tus·es] The young of viviparous animals in the womb, and of oviparous animals in the egg, after it is perfectly formed.

F

feud (fyood) n. 1. A quarrel; hostility; enmity. 2. War waged by one family or small group on another to avenge the death or injury of one of its members. 3. Land held from a lord on condition of performance of military and other services.

feu·dal (*fyoo*-d'l) adj. Pertaining to or consisting of feuds, fiefs, or fees; pertaining to the system of feudalism.—**feu·dal·ly** adv.

feu·dal·ism (*fyood*-'l-izm) n. The system of society, economics, and politics of the Middle Ages, based on the holding of land by serfs under a land-owning lord.—**feu·dal·ist** n. 1. A supporter of the feudal system. 2. One versed in feudal law.—**feu·dal·is·tic** adj.

feu·da·to·ry (*fyoo*-duh-tor-ee) n. [pl. -ries] A tenant who holds his land from a superior on condition of military service; tenant of a feud or fee.—adj. Holding on conditional tenure.

fe·ver (*fee*-ver) n. 1. A diseased state of the body characterized by an increase of heat, accelerated pulse, deranged functions, diminished strength, and often excessive thirst. 2. Heat; agitation; passionate excitement.—v. To put in a fever.—**fe·vered** adj.

fe·ver·ish (*fee*-ver-ish) adj. 1. Having fever, esp. a slight fever. 2. Indicating or pertaining to fever. 3. Hot; sultry; burning. 4. Frantic; excited.—**fe·ver·ish·ly** adv.— -**ish·ness** n.

fe·ver·ous adj. 1. Affected with fever. 2. Having the nature of fever. 3. Having a tendency to produce fever.—**fe·ver·ous·ly** adv.

fever sore. An ulcer in the mouth: a cold sore.

few (fyoo) adj. Not many; small in number. —pronoun. A small number.

fez n. [pl. fez·zes] A close-fitting red cap with a tassel hanging from the crown, worn esp. in Turkey and the Near East.

fi·an·cé (fee-ahn-*say*, fee-*ahn*-say) n. A man who is betrothed.—**fi·an·cée** n. A woman who is betrothed.

FEZ

fi·as·co (fee-*ass*-koh) n. [pl. -coes, -cos] An ignominious failure.

fi·at (*fy*-at) *n.* 1. An effective command; order; decree. 2. *Law.* A short order or warrant by a judge.

fiat money. Paper money legally issued but bearing no promise of redemption.

fib *n.* A trivial lie; falsehood.—*v.* [fibbed; fibbing].—**fib·ber** *n.*

fi·ber (*fy*-ber) *n.* Also **fi·bre.** 1. A thread; filament. 2. Material composed of threadlike parts. 'Muscle fiber.' 3. The small slender root of a plant. 4. Character. 'A man of strong fiber.'

fi·bril (*fy*-bril) *n.* A small fiber; branch of a fiber; very slender thread.

fi·brin (*fy*-brin) *n.* A whitish, insoluble protein which forms the basic portion of a blood clot.

fi·broid (*fy*-broyd) *adj.* Resembling fibrous tissue.

fi·brous (*fy*-brus) *adj.* Containing or consisting of fibers.

fib·ster (*fib*-ster) *n.* One who tells lies; fibber.

fib·u·la (*fib*-yoo-luh) *n.* [*pl.* -lae, -las] The outer and smaller bone of the leg below the knee. —**fib·u·lar** *adj.*

fich·u (*fish*-oo) *n.* A lady's decorative neckerchief or cape whose ends cross in front.

fick·le (*fik*-'l) *adj.* Inconstant; capricious.

fic·tion (*fik*-shun) *n.* 1. Imaginative prose literature, esp. novels. 2. Anything imagined, invented, or feigned.—**fic·tion·al** *adj.*

fic·ti·tious (fik-*tish*-us) *adj.* Imaginary; not real; false.—**fic·ti·tious·ly** *adv.*—**fic·ti·tious·ness.**

fid *n. Nautical.* A tapered pin used to open strands of rope in splicing.

fid·dle (*fid*-'l) *n.* 1. *Colloquial.* A violin. 2. *Nautical.* A rack or frame for holding dishes, etc., on a table in rough weather.—*v.* [fid·dled; fid·dling] 1. To play a fiddle. 2. To trifle; waste time; potter.—**fid·dler** *n.*

fid·dle-fad·dle *n.* Trifle; chatter; fussing.—*v.* [fid·dle-fad·dled; -fad·dling].

fid·dle·stick (*fid*-'l-stik) *n.* 1. The bow with which a violin is played. 2. [*pl.*] *interj.* Nonsense!

fi·del·i·ty (fih-*del*-uh-tee, fy-) *n.* [*pl.* -ties] 1. Faithfulness; trust; loyalty. 2. Strict adherence to the marriage vow. 3. The accuracy with which a sound is reproduced, a copy is made, etc.

fid·get (*fij*-it) *v.* To move uneasily or nervously. —*n.* 1. Restlessness. 2. [*pl.*] Abrupt movements manifesting nervousness.

fidg·e·ty (*fij*-it-ee) *adj.* Restless; impatient; uneasy.—**fidg·et·i·ness** *n.*

Fido *n.* Fog Investigation Dispersal Operation; device for burning fog off airport runways.

fi·du·cial (fih-*dyoo*-shee-ul) *adj.* 1. Of or like a trust; fiduciary. 2. Confident; undoubting.

fi·du·ci·ar·y (fih-*dyoo*-shee-ehr-ee) *adj.* 1. Held in trust. 2. In strict confidence; private. 3. Believed in; trusted.—*n.* [*pl.* -ies] One who holds in trust; trustee.

fie *interj.* For shame!

fief (*feef*) *n.* A feudal estate held in exchange for military or other service.

field (*feeld*) *n.* 1. A piece of land; part of a farm. 2. Ground where battle is fought; battle or warring. 3. Space; compass. 'Field of opportunity.' 4. *Sport.* Those taking part in a competition. 5. A locality rich in subsoil resources. 'An oil field.' 6. [*pl.*] The out-of-doors; open country. 7. An area where a sport is played. 8. The practical situation; area covered by field workers. 9. An area or scope of operations. 10. A background of a painting, projection, etc. 11. A sphere of specialization. 12. *Physics.* A space permeated by magnetic lines of force.—*v.* 1. To take to or put in the field. 2. *Baseball.* To recover a hit ball.

field artillery. *Military.* Mobile guns of heavy caliber used to open the way for infantry; branch of the army that operates them.

field·er (*feeld*-er) *n. Baseball.* A player who catches or stops hit balls.

fielder's choice. *Baseball.* A ball so taken by a fielder that he has choice of whom to put out.

field glass. A small telescope, usually binocular, for better vision of distant objects.

field goal. *Football.* A drop-kick or place-kick made during a regular series of downs.

field marshal. [*pl.* field marshals] *Military.* The highest rank of field general.

field·piece *n.* A field artillery cannon.

field·work (*feeld*-werk) *n. Military.* A temporary earthwork or other protection thrown up by troops in the field.

field work. Scientific research away from headquarters.—**field·work·er** *n.*

fiend (*feend*) *n.* 1. A devil; excessively wicked, cruel, or malicious person. 2. *Colloquial.* An addict; one excessively devoted to a practice.

fiend·ish (*feend*-ish) *adj.* Diabolic; excessively wicked, cruel or malicious.—**fiend·ish·ly** *adv.* —**fiend·ish·ness** *n.*

fierce (*feerss*) *adj.* [fierc·er; fierc·est] Savage; ferocious.—**fierce·ly** *adv.*—**fierce·ness** *n.*

fi·er·y (*fyre*-ee) *adj.* [fi·er·i·er; fi·er·i·est] 1. Burning; flaming; hot. 2. Passionate; fierce; easily provoked.—**fi·er·i·ly** *adv.*—**fi·er·i·ness** *n.*

fies·ta (*fyess*-tah) *n. Spanish.* Feast; party; holiday; social gathering.

fife *n.* A small flutelike musical instrument.—*v.* [fifed; fif·ing]
To play a fife.
—**fif·er** *n.*

FIFE

fif·teen (fif-*teen*) *n.* The cardinal number represented by the symbol 15.—**fif·teen** *adj.*—**fif·teenth** *n.* One of fifteen equal parts.—*adj.* Next in order after the fourteenth.

fifth *n.* 1. One of five equal parts. 2. *Music.* The interval comprising five degrees of the scale.—*adj.* Next after fourth.—**fifth·ly** *adv.* In the fifth place.

fifth column. An organization of spies, saboteurs, agents provocateurs, etc., working to overthrow a country from within.

fifth wheel. *Colloquial.* Something useless and in the way.

fif·ty (*fif*-tee) *n.* A cardinal number represented by the symbol 50.—**fif·ty** *adj.*—**fif·ti·eth** *n.* One of fifty equal parts.—*adj.* Next after 49th.

fif·ty-fif·ty *adv. & adj. Colloquial.* Evenly; in equal shares. 'He split fifty-fifty with me.'

fig *n.* 1. The edible fruit of the fig tree, native to the Mediterranean area, but transplanted elsewhere. 2. An expression of contempt. 'I don't care a fig for him.'

fig *v.* [figged; fig·ging] 1. *Colloquial.* To dress. 'All figged out.' 2. To make a contemptuous gesture with the fingers. 3. To treat a horse with some irritant so as to make him appear lively.—*n. Colloquial.* Dress.

fight (*fyte*) *n.* 1. A battle; combat; struggle. 2. Power or inclination for fighting. 'Full of fight.'—*v.* [fought; fight·ing] 1. To wage battle; engage in a struggle or combat. 2. To contend against. 3. To cause to fight. 'He fights cocks.'—**fight·a·ble** *adj.*—**fight·er** *n.* —**fight shy of.** To avoid because of mistrust, dislike, etc.

fig·ment (*fig*-m'nt) *n.* Something imagined; an invention; fiction.

fig·u·ra·tion (fig-yuh-*ray*-shun) *n.* 1. The act of giving determinate form. 2. *Music.* A mixture of discords and concords.

fig·ur·a·tive (*fig*-yer-uh-tiv) *adj.* 1. Metaphorical; not literal. 2. Abounding with figures of speech; ornate; flowery.—**fig·ur·a·tive·ly** *adv.*—**fig·ur·a·tive·ness** *n.*

fig·ure (*fig*-yur) *n.* 1. Shape; form. 2. Representation of any form, as a drawing, embroidery, etc. 3. An eminent person. 4. Appearance. 'A sorry figure.' 5. *Arithmetic.* A character [1, 2, 3, etc.] standing for a number. 6. Price; value. 'He set a high figure.' 7. The pattern of steps in dancing or skating. 8. *Geometry.* A group of lines or curves enclosing a space or surface. 9. A figure of speech.—*v.* [fig·ured; fig·ur·ing] 1. To adorn or mark with figures. 2. To imagine. 3. To indicate by numerals; calculate. 4. To make a figure; be distinguished. 'He figured in the rebellion.' 5. *Colloquial.* To reckon; calculate.

fig·ured *adj.* 1. Adorned with figures. 2. *Music.* Marked with numbers to represent the chords. 'Figured bass.'

fig·ure·head (*fig*-yur-hed) *n.* 1. An ornamental statue or bust on the prow of a ship. 2. A person of prominent position who does nothing really important.

figure of speech. A symbolic manner of expression in which words are given other than their ordinary meanings for the sake of vividness.

fig·u·rine (fig-yur-*een*) *n.* A small statue.

fil·a·ment (*fil*-uh-m'nt) *n.* A thread; fiber; fine wire.—**fil·a·men·ta·ry, fil·a·men·tous** *adj.*

fil·bert (*fil*-bert) *n.* An egg-shaped hazel nut.

filch *v.* To steal; pilfer.—**filch·er** *n.*

file *n.* 1. A folder containing papers; any orderly collection of papers. 2. A line of troops one behind the other.—*v.* [filed; fil·ing] 1. To put away in order for preservation or reference. 2. *Law.* To present in court for trial. 3. To march one behind the other.

file *n.* A tool with abrasive surfaces for cutting or smoothing wood, metal, etc.—*v.* To cut or smooth.—**fil·er** *n.*

file·fish *n.* A fish with rough, filelike skin.

fi·let (fih-*lay*) *n.* A fleshy cut of meat or fish, usually without bones; fillet.

fil·i·al (*fil*-ee-ul) *adj.* Relating to a son or daughter; proper for a child in relation to his parents.—**fil·i·al·ly** *adv.*

fil·i·bus·ter (*fil*-uh-bus-ter) *n.* 1. A buccaneer; pirate; adventurer. 2. A parliamentary device common in the U.S. Congress through which a minority blocks passage of legislation by holding the floor for extended periods.—**fil·i·bus·ter** *v.*—**fil·i·bus·ter·er** *n.*

fil·i·gree (*fil*-uh-gree) *n.* Ornamental openwork of fine gold or silver wire; sculptured work resembling this.—*v.* To ornament with filigree.

fil·ing (*fyle*-ing) *n.* A particle, as of metal, rubbed off with a file.

Fil·i·pi·no (fil-uh-*pee*-noh) *n.* [*pl.* -nos] A native of the Philippine Islands, usually one of Maylayan blood.—**Fil·i·pi·no** *adj.*

fill *v.* 1. To make or grow full; occupy the whole space of. 2. To supply with an incumbent. 'Fill an office.' 3. *Nautical.* To belly out; dilate. 'Wind fills the sails.' 4. To satisfy, esp. with food. 5. To plug up. 6. To fulfill the instructions of. 'A pharmacist fills prescriptions.'—*n.* 1. A full supply; enough to satisfy. 2. A place where earth has been poured in to fill a cavity.—**fill in.** 1. To insert. 2. To take another's place.—**fill out.** 1. To write desired information, as on a form. 2. To grow stouter.

fill·er *n.* 1. One that fills. 2. A priming composition to fill the pores of a surface to be painted. 3. Pad of paper to fit a looseleaf notebook. 4. The roll of tobacco forming the inside of a cigar.

fil·let (*fil*-it) *n.* 1. A small band for the hair. 2. *Architecture.* A small molding. 3. Any of several things resembling a band, as, in carpentry, a strip nailed to a wall to support a shelf. 4. A filet of meat or fish.—*v.* To bind, furnish, or adorn with a small band.

fill·ing (*fil*-ing) *n.* 1. Material used to fill up a space, cavity, etc. 2. *Weaving.* The weft; horizontal threads.

filling station. A retail establishment where automobiles are supplied with gasoline, oil, water, etc.

fil·lip (*fil*-ip) *v.* 1. To flick with the fingers. 2. To goad; stimulate.—*n.* 1. A flick of the fingers; any sharp blow or stroke. 2. A stimulus; goad.

fil·ly *n.* [*pl.* -lies] 1. A young mare. 2. *Slang.* A young woman.

F

film *n.* 1. A thin skin; membrane; thin layer. 2. A chemical-coated cellulose material on which photographic impressions are registered. 3. A moving picture.—*v.* 1. To cover with thin skin or membrane. 2. To take moving pictures of. 'He filmed the rebellion.'

film-coated filmgoing filmlike
filmgoer filmland film-struck

film·y *adj.* [film·i·er; film·i·est] Composed of thin membranes or fine threads; having such an appearance.—**film·i·ly** *adv.*—**film·i·ness** *n.*

fil·ter (*fil*-ter) *n.* A strainer; porous material for purifying a liquid.—*v.* To strain; purify.—**fil·ter·a·ble, fil·tra·ble** *adj.* Capable of passing through a filter.—**fil·ter·er** *n.*

filth *n.* 1. Dirt; foul matter. 2. Nastiness; indecency.

filth·y *adj.* [filth·i·er; filth·i·est] 1. Dirty; foul. 2. Morally impure; obscene.—**filth·i·ly** *adv.* —**filth·i·ness** *n.*

fil·trate (*fil*-trayt) *n.* Liquid that has passed through a filter.

fil·tra·tion (fil-*tray*-shun) *n.* The act or process of filtering.

fin *n.* 1. A projecting winglike organ used by a fish to balance or move in the water. 2. Anything resembling a fish's fin. 'A submarine fin.' 3. *Slang.* $5.

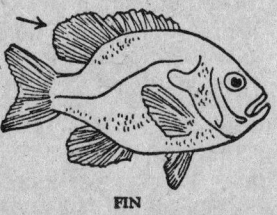

FIN

fi·na·gle (fih-*nay*-g'l, -nig-) *v. Slang.* To wangle; secure by trickery or underhanded method.—**fi·na·gler** *n.*

fi·nal (*fy*-n'l) *adj.* 1. Last; ultimate. 2. Conclusive; decisive. 3. Relating to the purpose or end in view. 'Final as opposed to immediate causes.'—*n.* 1. *Colloquial.* An examination at the end of a course. 2. The last edition of a newspaper in a day.—**fi·nal·ly** *adv.*

fi·na·le (fih-*nah*-lay, fuh-*nal*-ee) *n.* The closing part of a theatrical presentation.

fi·nal·ist (*fy*-n'l-ist) *n. Sports.* A player who reaches the last stage in an elimination tournament.

fi·nal·i·ty (fy-*nal*-uh-tee) *n.* [*pl.* -ties] 1. The state or quality of being concluded, settled, or arranged; completeness. 2. A final event.

fi·nance (fin-*anss*, *fy*-nanss) *n.* 1. The science of managing money, on either a public or private scale. 2. [*pl.*] Public or private monetary resources.—*v.* (fin-*anss*) [fi·nanced; fi·nanc·ing] 1. To support a business operation by providing capital. 2. To manage the monetary problems of.

fi·nan·cial (fih-*nan*-shul) *adj.* Concerning money or money matters.—**fi·nan·cial·ly** *adv.*

fi·nan·cier (fin-un-*seer*, fy-nan-*seer*) *n.* 1. An expert in money matters. 2. A large-scale invester or banker.

fin·back (*fin*-bak) *n.* Also **finback whale.** A whale with a dorsal hump or fin.

finch *n.* Any of several types of small singing bird, including sparrows and grosbeaks.

FINCH (1/6 life size)

find (*fynde*) *v.* [found; find·ing] 1. To discover; come upon. 2. To learn; discover by experiment, as to find bottom. 3. To gain; acquire. 'Find leisure for study.' 4. To catch; detect. 'Find in a lie.' 5. *Law.* To determine and declare, or award, by verdict. 'Found guilty.'—*n.* A discovery of something valuable.—**find fault.** To criticize; blame; censure.—**find out.** To detect; discover; solve.

find·er (*fynde*-er) *n.* 1. One who discovers something either by accident or by searching. 2. A small telescope used to find objects for observation by a large telescope. 3. A device on a camera showing the view being photographed.

find·ing *n.* 1. A discovery; something found. 2. *Law.* A verdict.

fine *n.* A payment of money as penalty for a legal offense.—*v.* [fined; fin·ing] To inflict a money penalty.—**in fine.** In conclusion.

fine *adj.* [fin·er; fin·est] 1. Not coarse; small; thin; delicate. 2. Keen; sharp. 'A fine edge.' 3. Clear; pure. 'Fine gold.' 4. Refined; perceptive. 'Fine sense of rhythm.' 5. Handsome; beautiful; accomplished. 6. Sunshiny; free from rain. 7. Noble; excellent. 8. Showy; splendid. 9. Affected; stilted; overornate.—**fine·ly** *adv.*

fine arts. The arts that appeal aesthetically, as painting, sculpture, architecture, etc.

fine grain developer. *Photography.* A developing agent designed to permit great enlargement without coarse grain.

fine-grained (*fyne*-graynd) *adj.* With the graining close together. 'Fine-grained walnut.'

fine·ness *n.* 1. Quality of being fine, as sharpness, tenuity, subtlety. 2. The proportion of pure silver or gold in coins. 3. *Marine Architecture.* The ratio of the volume of the underwater section of a hull to the volume of a rectangular block of the same dimensions.

fin·er·y (*fyne*-er-ee) *n.* [*pl.* -ies] Ornament; clothing, esp. showy raiment.

fine·spun *adj.* Drawn to a fine thread; overrefined; overelaborated.

fi·nesse (fin-*ess*) *n.* 1. Artifice; sublety. 2. *Bridge.* Playing through a strong hand so as to take a trick with a lower card than one has in the suit.—*v.* [fi·nessed; fi·ness·ing].

fin·ger (*fing*-ger) *n.* 1. One of a hand's five extremities; digit. 2. Anything resembling a finger.—*v.* 1. To touch with the fingers; handle. 2. *Music.* To use the fingers in playing an instrument.—**fin·ger·er** *n.*

finger bowl. A dish or bowl of water for cleansing the fingers at the table after a meal.

fin·ger·ing (*fing*-ger-ing) *n.* 1. The act of touching lightly in handling. 2. *Music.* Management of the fingers in playing an instrument; also marking notes on a score to aid in playing. 3. A thick loose woolen yarn.

fin·ger·nail (*fing*-ger-nayl) *n.* The hard brittle formation at the end of each finger.

finger post. Guide sign with a pointing finger.

fin·ger·print (*fing*-ger-print) *n.* An impression of the skin pattern on the human fingertip taken for identification.—**fin·ger·print** *v.* To take such an impression with ink, etc.

finger wave. A method of curling the hair.

fin·i·al (*fin*-ee-ul) *n. Architecture.* An ornamental apex for a pinnacle, gable, or the like.

fin·i·cal (*fin*-ih-k'l) *adj.* Fastidious, overparticular of details.—**fin·i·cal·i·ty** (fin-ih-*kal*-uh-tee) *n.*—**fin·i·cal·ly** *adv.*—**fin·i·cal·ness** *n.*

fin·ick·ing, fin·ick·y (*fin*-ik-ing, -ik-ee) *adj.* Also **fin·i·kin.** Precise about trifles; finical.

fi·nis (*fy*-niss) *n.* [*pl.* **fi·nis·es**] End; conclusion.

fin·ish (*fin*-ish) *v.* 1. To bring or come to an end; complete. 2. To perfect; elaborate carefully.—*n.* 1. Polish; careful elaboration. 2. The last smooth coat of plaster on a wall. 3. *Colloquial.* An end; ruin; death. 4. See *photo finish.*—**fin·ish·er** *n.*

fin·ished *adj.* 1. Complete. 2. Ended. 3. Polished; perfected.

finishing school. A girls' private school.

fi·nite (*fy*-nyte) *adj.* Having a limit; bounded; —**fi·nite** *n.* Concrete; definable.—**fi·nite·ly** *adv.*

finite verb. Any mood of a verb limited by number or person.

fink *n. Labor Slang.* A person paid by the employer to disrupt union activities.

Finn *n.* A native of Finland.—**Fin·nic** *adj.*

finnan haddie (*fin*-'n *had*-ee). Smoked haddock.

Fin·nish *adj.* Relating to Finland or the Finns. —*n.* The language of Finland.

fiord (*fyord*) *n.* Also **fjord.** An inlet of the sea between steep cliffs.

fir *n.* A kind of pine tree; tall straight evergreen tree of many varieties.

fire *n.* 1. Combustion. 2. A destructive burning, as of a house. 3. The discharge of firearms. 4. The ardor of any passion; animation; force of sentiment.—*v.* [fired; fir·ing] 1. To shoot. 2. To discharge from employment. —**fire away.** To begin; go on.—**fire up.** To become angry.—**hang fire.** Fail to come off or happen.—**on fire.** Burning; passionate.—**under fire.** In combat.

fireback	firefanged	fire-resistant
firebird	fire-free	fire-retardant
fireboat	fireguard	fire-robed
firebolt	fire-hardened	fireroom
fire-born	fire hot	firesafe
fireboy	fire house	fire-scarred
firebreak	firelight	firespout
fire-burnt	firelighted	fire swift
fire clay	fire-lit	firetight
firecoat	firemaster	firetrap
fire-crowned	fireplow	fire warden
fire-cure (*v.*)	fire-polish	fire-warmed

fire·arm *n.* A weapon discharged by the combustion of gunpowder or a similar explosive.

fire·ball *n.* A meteor appearing as a globular mass of light.

fire·box *n.* The insulated metal box in which a locomotive's fuel is burned to provide steam for power.

fire·brand *n.* 1. A burning piece of wood. 2. An inflammatory person; one who arouses contention.

fire·brick *n.* A heat-resistant brick.

fire·bug *n. Colloquial.* An incendiary.

fire·crack·er *n.* A small paper cylinder filled with gunpowder, discharged for amusement.

fire·damp *n.* A light hydrogen gas or marsh gas, highly inflammable, appearing in mines from decomposition of partially carbonized coal.

fire·dog *n.* An andiron.

fire-eat·er *n.* 1. An entertainer who pretends to swallow flames. 2. *Colloquial.* A belligerent person; fighter.

fire engine. A mobile engine which pumps water to extinguish a fire.

fire escape. An arrangement of metal ladders for escaping from a burning building.

fire extinguisher. A portable mechanism using chemicals for putting out small fires.

fire·fly *n.* A luminous winged insect of several varieties.

fire·less *adj.* Without flame.

fire·lock *n.* An old musket in which flint and steel set off the discharge.

fire·man *n.* [*pl.* -men] 1. A professional fire fighter. 2. A fire-tender; stoker.

fire·place *n.* A hearth; structure for an open fire in a room.

FIREPLACE

fire·plug *n.* A street hydrant for drawing water from the mains.

fire·proof *adj.* Incombustible; made of heat-resistant materials.

fire·side *n.* Vicinity of the fireplace; home.

fire·stone *n.* A heat-resistant sandstone.

fire·wat·er *n. Slang.* Liquor; spirits.

fire·weed *n.* An erect coarse annual with whitish flowers, which appears on burnt-over land.

fire·wood *n.* Wood for fuel.

fire·works *n.* 1. Pyrotechnics; an exhibition of Roman candles, sky rockets, pinwheels, etc., usually on some public holiday. 2. Any exciting display; explosion; violence.

fir·ing *n.* 1. The act of discharging firearms. 2. The application of fire.

firing line. *Military.* The line from which troops fire.

fir·kin (*fer*-kin) *n.* A small wooden cask for butter, tallow, etc.

firm *adj.* 1. Compact; hard; solid. 2. Fixed;

F

stable; not easily moved.—*v.* To render firm or solid; solidify.—**firm·ly** *adv.*—**firm·ness** *n.*

firm *n.* A business house; partnership; association; corporation.

firm·a·ment (*ferm*-uh-m'nt) *n.* The sky; heavens.—**fir·ma·men·tal** *adj.*

fir·man (*fer*-m'n) *n.* [*pl.* -mans] An oriental decree, order, grant, passport, permit, etc., issued by a sovereign.

first *adj.* Preceding all others in order, time, excellence, etc.; the ordinal of one; primary.
—*adv.*—*n.* 1. The leading one. 2. The first day of the month. 3. *Music.* The upper part of a duet, trio, etc.

first aid. Emergency treatment of a sick or injured person.—**first-aid** *adj.*—**first-aid·er** *n.*

first-born *n.* Eldest offspring.—**first-born** *adj.*

first-class *adj. Colloquial.* Of the highest excellence or quality.—*adv.* In the best manner.

first fruits. 1. The first produce harvested in a season. 2. The first profits of any enterprise. 3. The earliest effect or result.

first-hand *adj.* Obtained directly from the source.—**first-hand** *adv.*

first lieutenant. *Military.* A commissioned officer in the U.S. Army or Marine Corps between second lieutenant and captain.

first·ling *n.* First offspring, produce, etc.

first·ly *adv.* In the first place.

first-rate *adj.* Of the highest excellence.—*adv.*

first water. The highest quality; purest luster.

firth *n.* A large inlet from the sea; fiord; bayou.

fis·cal (*fiss*-k'l) *adj.* Relating to the public treasury or revenue.—*n.* A treasurer.

fish *n.* [*pl.* fish, fish·es] 1. Any vertebrate animal living in water. 2. The flesh of fish used for food. 3. *Colloquial.* A person. 'A queer fish.' 4. *Carpentry.* A strengthening joint.—*v.* 1. To attempt to catch fish. 2. To search; seek to obtain. 'Fish for information.' 3. To take hold and draw out, esp. from water. 4. *Carpentry.* To strengthen with a piece of wood above or below a joint, sometimes both.

fish-backed	fish-fed	fishpool
fishbed	fish god	fishpot
fish-bellied	fish goddess	fishpound
fish-blooded	fishhook	fish-shaped
fishbolt	fish house	fishskin
fishbone	fish-joint	fishway
fish-culturist	fishman	fishwoman
fisheye	fish meal	fishwood
fisheyed	fishmouth	fish works
fishfall	fishpond	fishworm

fish ball, fish cake. A patty made of flaked fish, usually cod, bound with mashed potato, and fried.

fish·er *n.* 1. A kind of weasel. 2. A fisherman.

fish·er·man *n.* [*pl.* -men] 1. One whose occupation or avocation is catching fish. 2. A fishing vessel.

FISHER (1/27 life size)

fish·er·y *n.* [*pl.* -ies] 1. The business of catch-

ing fish. 2. A place where fish are commonly caught.

fish hawk. The osprey, bald buzzard, or fishing eagle; a bird of prey which lives on fish.

fish·hook *n.* A barbed hook for catching fish.

fish·ing *n.* The art or practice of catching fish.

fish·mon·ger *n.* A seller of fish.

fish·plate *n.* A metal plate which secures the juncture of two railroad rails.

fish story. *Colloquial.* A fabricated or exaggerated tale.

fish·tail *v. Aviation Slang.* To swing an airplane from side to side in reducing speed.

fish·wife *n.* [*pl.* -wives] 1. A shrew. 2. A woman who sells fish.

fish·y *adj.* [fish·i·er; fish·i·est] 1. Consisting of fish; inhabited by fish. 2. *Slang.* Equivocal; doubtful; unreliable. 3. Cold. 'A fishy eye.'
—**fish·i·ly** *adv.*—**fish·i·ness** *n.*

fis·sile (*fiss*-il) *adj.* Capable of being split with the grain, as wood.—**fis·sil·i·ty** (fih-*sil*-ih-tee) *n.*

fis·sion (*fish*-un) *n.* 1. A splitting up into parts. 2. Multiplication of cells by self-division.

fis·sure *n.* A cleft; crack; narrow slit.—*v.* To cleave; divide; crack apart.

fist *n.* The hand clenched, with fingers doubled into the palm.—*v.* To strike with the fist.

fist·ic (*fist*-ik) *adj.* Pugilistic; relating to boxing.

fist·i·cuff (*fist*-ih-kuf) *n.* A blow with the fist.
—**fist·i·cuff** *v.*—**fist·i·cuff·er** *n.*

fis·tu·la (*fiss*-tyoo-luh) *n.* [*pl.* -las, -lae] 1. A reed; pipe; wind instrument. 2. *Medicine.* An ulcerous passage between some internal part and the skin.—**fis·tu·lar, fis·tu·lous** *adj.*

fit *adj.* [fit·ter; fit·test] 1. Meet; appropriate. 2. Adapted; qualified; suitable. 3. Ready; competent.—*v.* [fit·ted; fit·ting] 1. To adapt; make suitable. 2. To prepare; provide with proper accessories. 3. To make ready or qualified. 4. To suit; be the correct size.—**fit** *n.* Proper adjustment.—**fit·ly** *adv.*—**fit·ness** *n.*

fit *n.* 1. An attack of a disease. 2. A sudden, violent disorder. 3. A violent temporary emotion. 4. A brief irregular period of any activity.—**by fits and starts.** Irregularly; spasmodically.

fitch, fitch·ew (*fich*-oo) *n.* Also **fitchet.** A polecat; its skin.

fit·ful *adj.* Spasmodic; checkered.—**fit·ful·ly** *adv.*—**fit·ful·ness** *n.*

fit·ter *n.* A workman who puts the parts of equipment together; one who adapts.

fit·ting *n.* 1. A fixture. 2. An appointment with a tailor at which clothes are adapted to the person.—*adj.* Appropriate; suitable; proper.—**fit·ting·ly** *adv.*—**fit·ting·ness** *n.*

five *n.* The cardinal number represented by the symbol 5.—*adj.* **five·fold.** Five times repeated.

five-bar	five-master	fivescore
five-cornered	fivepence	five-shooter
five-fingered	fivepenny	five-spotted
five-gaited	five-ply	fivestones
five-leaved	five-pointed	five-story
five-lobed	five-reeler	five-toed

five-and-ten *n. Colloquial.* A ten-cent store.

five hundred. A card game similar to euchre.

Five Nations. A league of American Indian tribes, the Iroquois confederation.

fiv·er (*fy*-ver) *n. Slang.* A five-dollar bill.

fives *n.* The game of handball.

fix *v.* 1. To make firm or fast; establish. 2. To attach firmly. 3. To direct steadily, as the attention. 4. To repair; put in order; arrange. 5. *Photography.* To make a film image permanent by removing residual silver deposit in a hypo bath.—**fix** *n.* A predicament; difficulty.—**fix·a·ble** *adj.*

fix·a·tion (fiks-*ay*-sh'n) *n.* 1. *Psychiatry.* An obsessive attachment, esp. one formed in childhood, arresting the development of adult sexual desires. 2. *Chemistry.* Solidification of gas on uniting with a solid body.

fix·a·tive (*fiks*-uh-tiv) *n.* 1. A varnish applied with a blower for the preservation of charcoal sketches, etc. 2. Any adhesive medium.—**fix·a·tive** *adj.*

fixed *adj.* 1. Settled; established; firm; stable. 2. Repaired. 3. Arranged. 4. *Chemistry.* Nonvolatile; compounded.—**fix·ed·ness** *n.*

fixed charge. An unvarying expense, as rent.

fixed star. *Astronomy.* A star which always has the same apparent position.

fix·ing *n.* 1. Consolidation; establishment. 2. [*pl.*] *Colloquial.* Trimmings.

fix·i·ty (*fiks*-ih-tee) *n.* Stability; firmness.

fix·ture (*fiks*-cher) *n.* 1. An object or person situated in a firm or well-established position. 'Light fixture.' 2. A stable state; firmness.

fizz, fiz *v.* [fizzed; fizz·ing] To make a hissing, gurgling sound.—**fizz** *n.*—**fizz·er** *n.*

fiz·zle (*fiz*-'l) *v.* [fiz·zled; fiz·zling] To fail in an undertaking.—**fiz·zle** *n.*—**fizzle out.** To die away gradually.

fiz·zy *adj.* [fiz·zi·er; fiz·zi·est] Bubbling; gaseous.

flab·ber·gast (*flab*-er-gast) *v. Colloquial.* To astonish; confound.

flab·by *adj.* [flab·bi·er; flab·bi·est] Soft; flaccid; yielding to the touch.—**flab·bi·ly** *adv.*—**flab·bi·ness** *n.*

flac·cid (*flak*-sid) *adj.* Soft; weak; lax; drooping; flabby.—**flac·cid·i·ty** (flak-*sid*-ih-tee) *n.*

flag *n.* An ensign; banner; standard; colors.—*v.* [flagged; flag·ging] 1. To signal to, as with a flag. 2. To deck with flags.

flag bearer	flagfall	flag-signal (*v.*)
flag-bedizened	flag maker	flagworm

flag *n.* A plant with sword-shaped leaves; iris.

flag *n.* A flat paving stone.—*v.* To lay with flat stones.—**flag·ger** *n.*

flag *v.* [flagged; flag·ging] To droop; sink; languish; fail.

Flag Day. June 14, commemorating the adoption by Congress in 1777 of the design of the American flag.

flag·el·lant (*flaj*-uh-l'nt) *n.* One who whips himself in religious frenzy.—*adj.* **flag·el·lant** *adj.*

flag·el·late (*flaj*-uh-layt) *v.* [-lat·ed; -lat·ing] To whip; scourge.—*adj.* Also **flag·el·lat·ed.** *Natural History.* Furnished with lashlike appendages.—**flag·el·la·tion** *n.*—**flag·el·la·tor** *n.*

fla·gel·lum (fluh-*jel*-um) *n.* [*pl.* -lums, -la] 1. *Botany.* A runner; weak branch creeping out from the stem, with leaves and roots at its end. 2. *Zoology.* A lashlike appendage.

flag·eo·let (flaj-uh-*let*) *n. Music.* A small wind instrument with a piccololike tone.

flag·ging *n.* 1. The act of laying with flagstones. 2. A pavement of flagstones.

flag·ging *adj.* Weary; drooping; spiritless.

flag·gy *adj.* 1. Weak; limber. 2. Pertaining to flagstone. 3. Abounding with or resembling the plants called flags.

fla·gi·tious (fluh-*jish*-us) *adj.* Villainous; heinous; corrupt; profligate; atrocious.—**fla·gi·tious·ly** *adv.*

flag·man *n.* A signaler.

flag officer. An admiral or other naval officer commanding a squadron.

flag of truce. A white flag under which troops wishing to parley advance toward enemy lines.

flag·on (*flag*-un) *n.* A narrow-mouthed vessel for holding liquors.

fla·grant (*flay*-gr'nt) *adj.* Glaring; flaming into notice; enormous.—**fla·gran·cy, fla·grance** *n.*—**fla·grant·ly** *adv.*

flag·ship *n.* The ship bearing the squadron or fleet commander, and flying his flag.

flag·staff *n.* [*pl.* -staffs, -staves] A pole from which a flag flies.

flag·stone *n.* 1. A flat stone used for paving. 2. Any fissile sandstone that splits up into flags.

flail *n.* A manual instrument for threshing grain.—*v.* To thresh with a flail.

flair *n.* A special aptitude or ability.

flak *n. Slang.* 1. Anti-aircraft artillery fire. 2. A press agent.

flake *n.* A loose, thin, scalelike fragment; small flat particle. —*v.* [flaked; flak·ing] To peel or scale off; form into flakes.

flak·y *adj.* [flak·i·er; flak·i·est] Flakelike; light; tender. 'Flaky pastry.'—**flak·i·ly** *adv.*—**flak·i·ness** *n.*

flam·beau (*flam*-boh) *n.* [*pl.* -beaux, -beaus] A torch.

flam·boy·ant (flam-*boy*-unt) *adj.* 1. Fiery; bright; conspicuous; colorful; garish. 2. *Architecture.* A term applied to a French Gothic style of architecture distinguished by flamelike tracery in the windows.—**flam·boy·ance, flam·boy·an·cy** *n.*—**flam·boy·ant·ly** *adv.*

flame *n.* 1. An open light; illumination from combustion; fire. 2. Heat of any emotion.

F

FLAGEOLET

FLAIL

'Flame of love, anger.' 3. *Colloquial.* Sweetheart.—*v.* [flamed; flam·ing]—**flam·er** *n.*

flame-colored flame-feathered flame-shaped
flame-cut   flame-haired   flametight
flame-eyed   flame-robed   flame-tipped

fla·men (*flay*-men) *n.* Any ancient Roman priest serving a single deity.

flam·ing (*flaym*-ing) *adj.* 1. Bright in color; red. 2. Exciting; violent.—**flam·ing·ly** *adv.*

fla·min·go (fluh-*ming*-goh) *n.* [*pl.* -gos, -goes] A tall, wading bird having pinkish plumage and scarlet wings.

flam·y *adj.* Like a flame.

flâ·neur (flah-*ner*) *n.* A trifler; idler.

flange (*flanj*) *n.* A projecting shoulder, edge, or rim.—*v.* [flanged; flang·ing] To furnish with a flange.—**flang·er** *n.*

flank *n.* 1. The meaty part of an animal between the ribs and the hip. 2. The side of an army or a formation. 3. The side of any structure or object.—*v.* To be next to.—**flank·er** *n.*

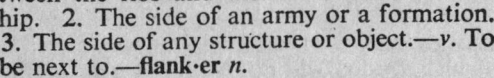
FLAMINGO
(1 / 25 life size)

flan·nel (*flan*-'l) *n.* A soft, nappy woolen cloth.—*v.* [flan·neled, flan·nelled; flan·nel·ing, flan·nel·ling] To wrap in flannel.—**flan·nel·ly** *adv.*

flan·nel·et, flan·nel·ette (flan-el-*et*) *n.* A coarse cotton cloth with a fleecy nap.

flap *n.* 1. A loose-hanging patch or fold. 2. A slapping or waving movement, as of a flag in the wind.—*v.* [flapped; flap·ping].

flap·doo·dle *n. Colloquial.* Nonsense.

flap·jack *n.* A pancake; griddlecake.

flap·per *n.* 1. *Colloquial.* A young girl of the 1920's regarded as frivolous and wild. 2. Anything which flaps.

flare *v.* [flared; flar·ing] 1. To shine dazzlingly, suddenly, and unsteadily. 2. To break into sudden anger. 3. To spread outward.—*n.* 1. A sudden bright light; a signal fire. 2. An explosion; outburst, as of anger. 3. A billowing or spreading out, as of a skirt.

flare·back *n.* An outburst taking a reverse or unusual direction.

flare·up *n.* 1. A sudden, angry quarrel or argument. 2. Recurrence or attack of disease.

flash *n.* 1. A sudden burst of light. 2. Any sudden, brilliant burst, as of wit. 3. An instant, fraction of a second. 4. *Slang.* A late news bulletin.—*v.* 1. To burst forth; appear suddenly. 2. To shine brilliantly and momentarily. 3. To move or do with lightning speed. 4. *Building.* To cover with waterproof sheathing.—**flash·er** *n.*—**flash·ing·ly** *adv.*

flash·back *n.* A break in the continuity of a literary or dramatic work to introduce action which has occurred previously.

flash bulb. *Photography.* A light bulb which burns suddenly and brilliantly, so as to illuminate the subject being photographed.

flash·ing *n. Engineering.* 1. Creation of a flood in a river by releasing pent-up waters. 2. Pieces of noncorrosive metal for protecting and waterproofing roof angles.

flash in the pan. A brilliant but transient success.

flash·light *n.* 1. A flashing or revolving light. 2. A hand torch operated by dry-cell batteries. 3. A flash bulb.—**flash·light** *adj.*

flash·y *adj.* [flash·i·er; flash·i·est] 1. Momentarily brilliant or dazzling. 2. Showy; sensational.—**flash·i·ly** *adv.*—**flash·i·ness** *n.*

flask *n.* 1. A bottle, esp. a chemical retort. 2. A flat bottle designed to be carried in one's pocket.

flat *n.* A story of a building; apartment or group of rooms on one floor.

flat *adj.* [flat·ter; flat·test] 1. Having an even surface; level; unbroken. 2. Prostrate; fallen; spread out. 3. *Fine Arts.* Wanting relief, gloss, or color contrast. 4. Tasteless; stale; without flavor. 5. Dull; lacking spirit or interest; monotonous. 6. Having little depth or thickness. 7. Exact; unchangeable; positive. 'A flat rate.' 'A flat rejection.' 8. *Music.* Slightly below the natural or true pitch. 9. Not sharp or clear in sounding. 10. Without sufficient air; deflated.—*n.* 1. A level tract or surface. 2. The broad surface or portion. 3. A deflated tire. 4. *Music.* The symbol (♭) indicating a note dropped one half step.—*adv.* 1. *Music.* Below the true pitch. 2. Flatly.—*v.* [flat·ted; flat·ting] To become or cause to become flat.—**flat·ly** *adv.*—**flat·ness** *n.*—**flat·tish** *adj.*

FLASK (def. 1)

flat-armed   flat-faced   flat-ribbed
flat-backed flat-fold (v.) flat-roofed
flat-billed flat-handled flat-sided
flat-bosomed flatheaded   flat-topped
flat-bottomed flat-knit   flat-waisted
flat-compound flat-nosed   flatway
flat-decked flat-packed   flatworm

flat·boat *n.* A broad flat-bottomed boat for use in shallow water.

flat·car *n.* A railroad freight car with neither sides nor top; gondola.

flat·fish *n.* [*pl.* -fish; -fish·es]. Any fish having a flattened body and both eyes on the upper side.

flat·foot *n.* 1. Deformed foot condition in which the arch of the foot is flattened. 2. *Slang.* A policeman.

flat·foot·ed *adj.* 1. Having flattened arches. 2. *Colloquial.* Firm; resolute; uncompromising.—**flat·foot·ed·ly** *adv.*—**flat·foot·ed·ness** *n.*

flat·head *n.* 1. *Slang.* An ignoramus. 2. [*cap.*] A Chinook Indian.

flat·i·ron *n.* A flat-surfaced, top-handled device for pressing cloth.

flat·ten (*flat*-'n) *v.* To level; depress; make or become flat.—**flat·ten·er** *n.*

flat·ter (*flat*-er) v. 1. To gratify someone's vanity by unwarranted praise or attention; praise insincerely or extravagantly. 2. To inspire with vain hope.—**flat·ter·ing·ly** adv.

flat·ter·y (*flat*-er-ee) n. [pl. -ies] Insincere or unwarranted praise; act of flattering.

flat-top n. Slang. An aircraft carrier.

flat·u·lent (*flat*-shuh-l'nt) adj. 1. Windy; abounding in or generating stomach and intestinal gas. 2. Pretentious; empty; pompous.—**flat·u·lence, -len·cy** n.— **-u·lent·ly** adv.

flat·ware n. Flat tableware, as platters, plates, silverware, etc.

flat·wise adv. Also **flat·ways.** With the flat or broad side down or touching, not edgewise.

flat·work n. Laundry, such as sheets and towels, ironed by machine.

flaunt (*flawnt*) v. To make an ostentatious, impudent, or boastful show of; display proudly. —n. An impudent or boastful display. **flaunter** n.—**flaunt·ing·ly** adv.

flau·tist (*flawt*-ist) n. A flute player; flutist.

fla·vor (*flay*-ver) n. 1. Taste; quality affecting the gustatory sense; savor. 2. Odor; aroma. 3. The dominant or characteristic quality. 4. Flavoring.—v. To imbue with a flavor. —**flav·or·er** n.—**flav·or·ous** adj.

flav·or·ing (*flay*-ver-ing) n. A substance or extract which imparts a certain flavor.

flaw n. 1. A defect; mar; blemish. 2. A defective part; crack.—v. To crack; make or become faulty.—**flaw·less** adj.—**flaw·less·ly** adv.

flax n. 1. A small slender plant with blue flowers. 2. The fibers of this plant, which are made into linen.—**flax·y** adj. [flax·i·er; flax·i·est] Resembling flax.

flax·en adj. Of or like flax; blond; fair.

flay v. 1. To skin; strip the hide from. 2. To scold mercilessly.—**flay·er** n.

flea (*flee*) n. A small, wingless parasitic insect able to leap relatively great distances.

flea·bane n. A plant related to the aster, supposed to drive away fleas.

flea-bit·ten adj. 1. Bitten by fleas. 2. Flecked with reddish spots on a lighter background, as a horse. 3. Slang. Rundown; motheaten.

fleck (*flek*) n. 1. A small spot; dapple; speck. 2. A small flake.—**fleck** v. To speckle; spot. —**fleck·y** adj. [fleck·i·er; fleck·i·est].

flec·tion, flex·ion (*flek*-sh'n) n. 1. Act of bending or flexing. 2. A bend.—**flec·tion·al, flex·ion·al** adj.

fledge (*flej*) v. [fledged; fledg·ing] 1. To grow the feathers required for flying. 2. To provide with feathers; feather. 3. To prepare for flight, or independent existence.

fledg·ling, fledge·ling (*flej*-ling) n. 1. A young bird ready for flight. 2. Any young, immature person.

flee v. [fled; flee·ing] 1. To run away; escape; take shelter from. 2. To vanish; move away rapidly.—**flee·er** n.

fleece (*fleess*) n. 1. The sheep's coat of wool, esp. that shorn at one time. 2. That which resembles fleece in quality or looks. 3. A soft heavy, napped woolen fabric.—v. [fleeced; fleec·ing] 1. To shear, as sheep. 2. To rob or cheat; swindle ruthlessly.—**fleece·a·ble** adj.

fleec·y (*fleess*-ee) adj. [fleec·i·er; fleec·i·est] Of, like, or covered with fleece.—**fleec·i·ly** adv. —**fleec·i·ness** n.

fleer v. To grin in contempt; leer scornfully; mock.—n. Expression of derision or mockery.

fleet n. 1. A squadron of warships. 2. The naval strength of a nation. 3. A group, as of vehicles, moving or operating together.

fleet adj. Swift; light and quick in motion; rapidly passing.—v. To move swiftly; flit.—**fleet·ly** adj.—**fleet·ness** n.

fleet·ing (*fleet*-ing) adj. Passing rapidly; transient; ephemeral.—**fleet·ing·ly** adv.

Flem·ing (*flem*-ing) n. A native of Flanders; Belgian who speaks Flemish.

Flem·ish (*flem*-ish) adj. Pertaining to Flanders. —n. The language or people of Flanders.

flesh n. 1. The soft or edible part of an animal body, consisting mainly of muscle, fat, etc. 2. The body, in contrast to the soul. 3. Mankind; humanity; human nature. 4. Kindred; close relatives. 5. The pulpy, edible part of fruits and vegetables. 6. The pinkish yellow color normally associated with a white person's skin.—v. 1. To glut; satiate. 2. To incite by an initial taste or experience.

flesh·ings (*flesh*-ingz) n. pl. Clinging flesh-colored tights worn esp. by circus performers.

flesh·ly (*flesh*-lee) adj. 1. Of the body; corporeal. 2. Carnal; worldly.—**flesh·li·ness** n.

flesh·pot n. 1. A kettle for cooking meat. 2. [pl.] Luxury; good living.

flesh·y (*flesh*-ee) adj. [flesh·i·er; flesh·i·est] 1. Fat; plump. 2. Of or like flesh. 3. Pulpy. —**flesh·i·ness** n.

fleur-de-lis (fler-duh-*lee*) n. [pl. fleurs-de-lis] 1. Iris; tall plant with multicolored flowers. 2. Flower design used in heraldry; device of the French Bourbons.

flex (*fleks*) v. To bend. 'He flexed his arm.'

flex·i·ble (*fleks*-uh-b'l) adj. 1. Easily bent; pliable. 2. Capable of persuasion; docile; easily managed or influenced. 3. Plastic; malleable; easily changed or molded. 4. Adaptable; not restricted in use, purpose, etc.—**flex·i·bil·i·ty** n.

flex·ile (*fleks*-'l) adj. Flexible.

flex·or (*fleks*-er) n. A muscle which bends a joint.

FLEUR-DE-LIS
(def. 1)

flex·u·ous (*flek*-shoo-us) adj. Also **flex·u·ose.** Winding; turning; bending frequently.

flex·ure (*flek*-sher) n. 1. A bend; curve; fold. 2. A bending or flexing.

flib·ber·ti·gib·bet (*flib*-er-tih-jib-it) n. A silly chattering person, esp. a woman.

flick *n.* A sharp, sudden stroke; flip.—**flick** *v.*

flick·er *v.* 1. To fluctuate or waver, as a flame. 2. To flutter; move the wings rapidly without flying.—**flick·er** *n.*—**flick·er·ing·ly** *adv.*

flick·er *n.* A colorful bird of the woodpecker family, which is especially destructive to ants.

FLICKER (1/9 life size)

flied (*flyde*). *Past tense & past participle* of **fly**, meaning to hit a fly baseball. 'He flied out to center field.'

fli·er, fly·er *n.* 1. One that flies. 2. An aviator. 3. A fast vehicle. 4. *Slang.* A risky project.

flight (*flyte*) *n.* A running away; hasty departure, as from danger.

flight *n.* 1. The power or act of moving through the air. 2. A number of birds or planes flying in company. 3. Distance flown or time spent in flight. 4. A soaring of the intellect. 'A flight of fancy.' 5. The stairway between two landings.

flight·y (*flyte-ee*) *adj.* [flight·i·er, flight·i·est] 1. Giddy; fickle; capricious; emotionally unstable. 2. Fleeting; transient; swift.—**flight·i·ly** *adv.*—**flight·i·ness** *n.*

flim·flam *n.* A trick; humbug.—*v.* [flim·flammed; flim·flam·ming] To trick; cheat; fool.—**flim·flam·mer** *n.*—**flim·flam·mer·y** *adj. & n.*

flim·sy (*flim-zee*) [flim·si·er; flim·si·est] 1. Feeble; insubstantial. 2. Without good reason or plausibility; vain; superficial.—*n.* Thin paper; onionskin.—**flim·si·ly** *adv.*—**flim·si·ness** *n.*

flinch *v.* To shrink; wince; cringe.—**flinch·er** *n.*

flin·der (*flin-der*) *n.* A splinter; fragment.

fling *v.* [flung; fling·ing] 1. To throw; hurl. 2. To throw down; prostrate; defeat. 3. To move suddenly and violently. 'Fling the arms about.'—*n.* 1. *Slang.* A spree; romp; round of pleasures. 2. A vigorous Scottish dance. 3. A throw; cast.—**fling·er** *n.*

flint *n.* Hard, brittle kind of quartz.—*v.* To provide with flint.

flint·y *adj.* [flint·i·er; flint·i·est] Hard; obdurate; severe.—**flint·i·ness** *n.*

flip *v.* [flipped; flip·ping] To turn quickly, as the pages of a book; hit with a light quick blow. —**flip** *n.*

flip *n.* A drink of sherry, brandy, etc., usually beaten with an egg and sweetening.

flip *adj. Slang.* Impertinent; saucy.

flip·pan·cy (*flip-un-see*) *n.* [*pl.* -cies] A saucy manner; undue levity; frivolous attitude.

flip·pant (*flip-unt*) *adj.* Saucy; frivolous. —**flip·pant·ly** *adv.*—**flip·pant·ness** *n.*

flip·per (*flip-er*) *n.* 1. The broad propelling fin of a marine mammal, limb of a sea turtle, etc. 2. *Slang.* The human hand or arm.

flirt (*flert*) *v.* 1. To coquet; entice romantically. 2. To flip; move spasmodically. 3. To

play, as with an idea.—*n.* 1. One who flirts. 2. A quick toss.—**flirt·er** *n.*—**flirt·y** *adj.*

flir·ta·tion (fler-*tay*-shun) *n.* Coquetry; casual courtship.—**flir·ta·tious** *adj.*

flit *v.* [flit·ted; flit·ting] To fly short distances rapidly; move quickly about.—**flit** *n.*—**flit·ter** *n.*

flitch *n.* 1. A cured strip from the side of a hog. 'Flitch of bacon.' 2. A board combined with others to make a strong beam or girder.—*v.* To slice off in strips.

flit·ter·mouse (*flit*-er-mowss) *n.* A bat.

fliv·ver (*fliv*-er) *n. Colloquial.* A small, cheap old car or airplane, often in poor repair.

float (*floht*) *v.* 1. To stay on the surface of a fluid; be buoyed up. 2. To move easily and gently, as through the air. 3. To sell, as a bond issue. 'Float a loan.'—*n.* 1. Anything that stays on the surface of a liquid, esp. a raft for swimmers, cork on a fishing line, hollow sphere in a tank to indicate or regulate the level of fluid, etc. 2. A flat tool to smooth plaster. 3. A platformed vehicle to carry a display in a procession.—**float·a·ble** *adj.*

float·er (*floh*-ter) *n. Slang.* One who votes illegally several times in an election by casting ballots at different polling places.

float·ing (*floht*-ing) *adj.* 1. Lying flat on the surface of the water. 2. Circulating; free to be used as occasion requires. 3. Free; disconnected.—**float·ing·ly** *adv.*

floating island. 1. An island in a lake or other quiet water, consisting of a little earth floating on vegetation. 2. A dessert of custard, whipped cream, and beaten white of egg.

floating ribs. *Anatomy.* In man the lowest two pairs of ribs; any ribs not articulated with the sternum.

floc·cu·lent (*flok*-yoo-l'nt) *adj.* Pertaining to or resembling wool or flocks of wool.—**floc·cu·lence** *n.*—**floc·cu·lent·ly** *adv.*

flock *n.* 1. A collection of living creatures, esp. applied to birds and sheep. 2. A church congregation.—*v.* To gather in crowds.

flock *n.* A lock or tuft of wool or hair.—**flock** *v.*

floe (*floh*) *n.* A large mass of ice floating in ocean or lake; flat iceberg.

flog *v.* [flogged; flog·ging] To whip; chastise. —**flog·ger** *n.*—**flog·ging** *n.*

flood (*fluhd*) *n.* 1. A great flow of water inundating the land; torrent. 2. The flowing in of the tide. 3. A great quantity; an inundation; abundance.—*v.* To overflow; inundate.—**the flood.** The deluge in Noah's time.

floodboard	floodhatch	floodtime
floodcock	floodmark	floodwater

flood·gate *n.* 1. A gate or sluice to permit, stop, or control the flow of water. 2. An obstruction; restraint.

flood·light *n.* An artificial light with a wide, intense beam; the lamp producing such a light.

flood·tide *n.* The rising tide.

floor (*flor*) *n.* 1. The bottom or lower part of a room. 2. A story in a building. 3. In legislative assemblies, the part of the house assigned to the members.—**the floor.** The parliamentary right to speak from one's place. —*v.* 1. To cover with a floor. 2. To beat down; silence by decisive retort or argument.

floorcloth	floor load	floorway
floorhead	floorman	floor work

floor·ing *n.* Materials for floors.

floor leader. The leader of a group on the floor of a legislature or convention.

floor show. An entertainment in a night club or cabaret.

floor·walk·er *n.* A section or floor supervisor in a department store.

flooz·y *n. Slang.* A cheap, vulgar woman.

flop *v.* [flopped; flop·ping] *Colloquial.* 1. To strike or fall clumsily. 2. To fail humiliatingly.—*n. Slang.* A play that fails.—**flop·per** *n.*

flop·house *n. Colloquial.* A cheap rooming house.

flop·py *adj.* [flop·pi·er; flop·pi·est] Soft and flexible; flapping.

flo·ra (*flor*-uh) *n.* [*pl.* flo·ras, flo·rae] The plants of any district, country, region, or period. —**Flora.** Roman goddess of flowers.

flo·ral (*flor*-ul) *adj.* Pertaining to flowers.

floral emblem. The symbolic flower or plant of any state, region, or country.

flo·res·cence (flor-*ess*-unss) *n. Botany.* A bursting into flower.—**flo·res·cent** *adj.*

flo·ret (flor-*et*) *n.* A tiny flower; one of the tiny flowers in the head of a composite flower.

flo·ri·cul·ture (*flor*-ih-kul-cher) *n.* The cultivation of flowering plants.—**flo·ri·cul·tur·al** *adj.*

flor·id (*flor*-id) *adj.* 1. Flushed; red. 2. Ornate; flowery.—**flo·rid·i·ty** *n.*—**flo·rid·ly** *adv.*

flor·in (*flor*-in) *n.* 1. A Florentine gold coin of the late Middle Ages. 2. A present-day English coin worth two shillings.

flo·rist (*flor*-ist) *n.* One who sells flowers.

floss (*flawss*) *n.* Unusable silk fibers; soft silky matter in the husks of various plants.

floss·y *adj.* [floss·i·er; floss·i·est] 1. Silky. 2. *Slang.* Fancy; overdressed.

flo·ta·tion (floh-*tay*-shun) *n.* 1. The act or state of floating. 2. The act of marketing securities to finance a business venture. 3. *Mining.* The process of separating particles of crushed ore according to their relative abilities to float in a prepared liquid.

flo·til·la (floh-*til*-uh) *n.* A small fleet of ships; fleet of small craft.

flot·sam (*flot*-s'm) *n.* The portion of wrecked ship and its cargo which continues to float on the surface; driftage of any kind.—**flotsam and jetsam.** Things or persons drifting as a result of accident and jettison.

flounce (*flounss*) *v.* [flounced; flounc·ing] To make rapid angry movements with the body. —**flounce** *n.*

flounce *n.* A strip of cloth sewed horizontally with the lower border loose and spreading.—*v.* [flounced; flounc·ing]—**flounc·ing** *n.*

floun·der (*floun*-der) *n.* A small, edible flat fish.

floun·der (*floun*-der) *v.* 1. To thrash about, as a mired animal. 2. To muddle.—**floun·der** *n.*—**floun·der·ing·ly** *adv.*

FLOUNDER (1 / 14 life size)

flour (*flour*) *n.* The finely ground meal of wheat or of any other grain.—*v.* 1. To convert into flour. 2. To sprinkle with flour.—**flour·y** *adj.*

flour·ish (*flur*-ish) *v.* 1. To thrive; grow vigorously. 2. To prosper; increase in wealth or happiness. 3. To brandish; wave.—*n.* 1. Ostentatious embellishment; show. 2. A brandishing; waving of something held in the hand. 3. *Music.* The decorative notes which a singer or instrumental performer adds to a passage.—**flour·ish·er** *n.*—**flour·ish·ing** *adj.*

flout (*flout*) *v.* To scoff; scorn; insult.—**flout·er** *n.*—**flout·ing·ly** *adv.*

flow (*floh*) *v.* 1. To run or spread, as a liquid. 2. To proceed; issue. 3. To be full; copious. 4. To hang free and waving.—*n.* 1. A stream of fluid; current. 2. Abundance; copiousness. 3. Outpouring; stream. 4. Fluency. —**flow·ing·ly** *adv.*—**flow·ing·ness** *n.*

flow·er (*flour*) 1. *Botany.* The reproductive part of a plant. 2. A blossom. 3. Any ornamental plant developed for its blossoms. 4. The prime; youthful vigor. 5. The most valuable part.—*v.* To blossom; bloom; flourish.—**flow·er** *adj.*

FLOWER

flower bud	
flower-crowned	
flower cup	flowerpiece
flowerdecked	flower-scented
flower-embroidered	flower stalk

flow·er·et (*flour*-et) *n.* A small flower; floret.

flow·er·ing (*flour*-ing) *adj.* Blossoming.

flow·er·pot (*flour*-pot) *n.* A pot in which flowering plants or shrubs are grown.

flow·er·y (*flour*-ee) *adj.* [flow·er·i·er; flow·er·i·est] 1. Full of flowers. 2. Florid; grandiloquent.—**flow·er·i·ly** *adv.*—**flow·er·i·ness** *n.*

flu (*floo*) *n. Colloquial.* Influenza.

fluc·tu·ate (*fluk*-choo-ayt) *v.* [fluc·tu·at·ed; fluc·tu·at·ing] To rise and fall; be in an unsettled state; oscillate.— **-tu·ant** *adj.*— **-tu·a·tion** *n.*

flue (*floo*) *n.* 1. A passage for smoke in a chimney. 2. A pipe or tube for conveying heat to water in certain kinds of steam boilers.

flu·en·cy (*floo*-un-see) *n.* 1. Volubility; ease of expression. 2. The quality of fluidity as applied to a person's motion, etc.

flu·ent (*floo*-unt) *adj.* 1. Articulate; voluble. 2. Freely flowing.—**flu·ent·ly** *adv.*

fluff *n.* 1. Light down or nap. 2. *Slang.* A miscue or error in performance.—**fluff** *v.*

fluff·y *adj.* [fluff·i·er; fluff·i·est] Light and soft.—**fluff·i·ly** *adv.*—**fluff·i·ness** *n.*

flu·id (*floo*-id) *n.* A body whose particles on the slightest pressure move and change their relative position without separation; a liquid or gas.—**flu·id** *adj.*—**flu·id·ic** *adj.*—**flu·id·ly** *adv.*

fluid dram. One eighth of a fluid ounce; approximately a teaspoonful.

flu·id·i·ty (floo-*id*-uh-tee) *n.* The quality of being able to flow.

fluid ounce. A liquid measure equivalent to $\frac{1}{16}$ pint.

fluke (*flook*) *n.* 1. The crook of an anchor that catches in the ground. 2. One of the two triangular divisions of a whale's tail. 3. A harpoon head or one of its barbs.

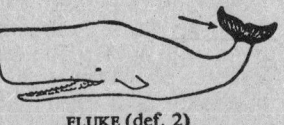

FLUKE (def. 2)

fluke *n.* A flounder or flatfish.

fluke *n. Slang.* An unusually lucky happening against expectation.—**fluk·y, fluk·ey** *adj.*

flume (*floom*) *n.* An artificial passage or channel carrying water for power or some other specific purpose.

flum·mer·y (*flum*-er-ee) *n.* [*pl.* -ies] Nonsense.

flum·mox (*flum*-uks) *v. Slang.* To embarrass; bewilder.

flung. *Past tense & past participle* of **fling.**

flunk *v. Slang.* To fail, as in an examination.—**flunk** *n.*

flunk·y, flunk·ey *n.* [*pl.* -ies; -eys] 1. A male servant in livery. 2. A servile person; cringing flatterer.

flu·o·resce (floo-er-*ess*) *v.* [flu·o·resced; flu·o·resc·ing] To become luminous when excited by radiation from another source.

flu·o·res·cence (floo-er-*ess*-unss) *n. Physics.* The property owned by certain substances of absorbing light rays of one wavelength and emitting rays of another, usually greater, wavelength.—**flu·o·res·cent** *adj.*

flu·o·ride (*floo*-er-yde) *n.* Also **flu·o·rid** (*floo*-er-id). Any substance compounded of fluorine and some other element.

flu·o·rine (*floo*-er-een; -in) *n.* Also **flu·o·rin.** A poisonous, highly reactive gaseous element similar to chlorine. (*Symbol:* F).—**flu·or·ic** *adj.*

flu·o·rite (*floo*-er-yte) *n.* A compound of calcium and chlorine much used as a flux.

flu·o·ro·scope (*floo*-er-uh-skohp) *n.* An apparatus containing a fluorescent screen, for examining deep structures by means of X-rays.

flu·or·spar (*floo*-er-spahr) *n.* Fluorite.

flur·ry *n.* [*pl.* -ries] 1. A sudden, short-lived shower or strong wind. 2. Agitation; bustle; commotion.—*v.* [flur·ried; flur·ry·ing] To excite; disturb.

flush *v.* 1. To become suddenly red; glow; blush. 2. To elate; animate with joy. 3. To wash out with a strong flow of water. 4. *Hunting.* To cause to start up or fly off.—*n.* 1. Redness of face caused by a sudden rush of blood; glow, warm coloring. 2. A strong, rapid flow, as of water for cleansing. 3. Sudden impulse or excitement. 4. *Card Playing.* A run of cards of the same suit.—**flush·er** *n.*

flush *adj.* 1. Having the surface even or level with the neighboring or contiguous surface. 2. Plentiful; very abundant. 3. Prosperous; well supplied, as with money.—*adv.* Evenly.

flush paragraph. *Printing.* A paragraph having no indentation.

flus·ter (*fluss*-ter) *v.* To agitate; disturb; confuse.—*n.* Agitation; disordered condition.

flute (*floot*) *n.* 1. *Music.* A long, slender, tube-like instrument with a series of holes stopped by keys or the player's fingers. 2. A rounded groove in a column or pillar. 3. Any similar groove in material.—*v.* [flut·ed; flut·ing] 1. To play on a flute. 2. To play or sing with flutelike tones. 3. To make grooves in, as material or a pillar.—**flut·ed** *adj.*

flut·ing (*floot*-ing) *n.* Decorative grooves or flutes.

flut·ist (*floot*-ist) *n.* One who plays a flute.

flut·ter (*flut*-er) *v.* 1. To flap or beat the wings without flying. 2. To move rapidly and irregularly back and forth. 3. To tremble; quiver; move agitatedly. 4. To confuse; upset.—**flut·ter** *n.*—**flut·ter·er** *n.*—**flut·ter·ing·ly** *adv.*—**flut·ter·y** *adj.*

FLUTE

flu·vi·al (*floo*-vee-ul) *adj.* Relating to, or produced in, rivers.

flux *n.* 1. A state of continuous change or movement. 2. Any flow or discharge of liquid matter. 3. *Metallurgy.* Any substance aiding the fusion of metals or minerals. 4. *Physics.* Rate of flow of energy or a fluid across a particular surface.—**flux** *v.*

flux·ion (*fluhk*-shun) *n.* Act of flowing; continuous flow.—**flux·ion·al** *adj.*—**flux·ion·al·ly** *adv.*

fly *v.* [flew; flown; fly·ing] 1. To rise into or move through or in the air. 2. To cause to move in the air, esp. to guide an aircraft. 3. To move, pass, or be spent rapidly. 4. To run away; flee; avoid. 5. To travel over or carry by flying.—*n.* [*pl.* flies] 1. A fold or cloth for concealing buttons or a slide fastener. 2. The flyleaf of a book. 3. The flywheel or regulating wheel of a machine. 4. The extent of a flag from the mast to the outer edge. 5. *Baseball.* A ball hit high into the air.

fly *n.* [*pl.* flies] 1. Any of a large family of insects with two transparent wings, including the housefly. 2. A fishhook covered with feathers and made to resemble an insect.

fly-back	fly-fisher	flyproof
flyblow	fly-fishing	flytail
flyboat	flyflap	fly trap
fly-fish (*v.*)	flypaper	flywinch

fly·a·way (*fly*-uh-way) *adj.* Flighty; frivolous.

fly·blown (*fly*-blohn) *adj.* 1. Containing fly eggs or larvae. 2. Spoiled; contaminated; tainted.

fly-by-night *adj.* Unreliable; irresponsible.

fly·catch·er (*fly*-kach-er) *n.* Any of a family of broad-billed birds which feed on flying insects.

fly cop. *Slang.* A plainclothesman; policeman in civilian clothes; detective.

fly·ing *n.* Act of a flier.—*adj.* 1. Moving through or in the air. 2. Swift; hasty.

flying boat. A large aircraft equipped with pontoons and a hull.

flying buttress. *Architecture.* A buttress or support arching out from a solid mass of masonry.

Flying Dutchman. A legendary Dutch sea captain, or his derelict ship, supposedly doomed to wander over the sea till Judgment Day.

fly·ing·fish. Any of a family of fish with enlarged pectoral fins for sailing short distances through the air.

Flying Fortress. A large, heavily armored bomber developed in World War II; B 17.

flying machine. An airplane or airship.

flying squirrel. A small squirrel able to leap considerable distances by means of weblike folds of skin between the front and hind legs.

flying wing. An airplane with all lifting surfaces, engines, and controls incorporated into one wing.

fly·leaf *n.* [*pl.* -leaves] A blank page at the beginning or end of a book.

fly·speck *n.* The excremental stain of a fly.—**fly·speck** *v.*

fly·weight *n.* A boxer weighing no more than 112 pounds.

fly·wheel *n.* A heavy wheel whose momentum regulates and stabilizes the speed of a machine.

FM. *Radio.* Frequency modulation.

f: number. *Photography.* Ratio of the effective diameter of the lens to its focal length. 'f:3.5'.

foal (*fohl*) *n.* A colt or filly; young horse.—*v.* To bear (a foal).

foam (*fohm*) *n.* Spume; the bubbly mass accumulated on liquids or in the mouth from fermentation or extreme agitation.—**foam.** *v.*

foam-born	foam-flanked	foam-lit
foambow	foam-flecked	foam-painted
foam-crested	foam-girt	foam white

foam·y (*fohm*-ee) *adj.* [foam·i·er; foam·i·est] Covered with, or resembling, foam.—**foam·i·ly** *adv.*—**foam·i·ness** *n.*

fob *n.* 1. A watch pocket. 2. A short chain or ribbon, as for a watch, or an ornament suspended from it.

fob *v.* [fobbed; fob·bing] To cheat; trick.—**fob off.** To put aside, or get rid of, by trickery.

fo·cal (*foh*-k'l) *adj.* Relating to a focus.

focal length. Also **focal distance.** *Optics.* Distance from the center of lens surface to the focal point, as in a camera.

fo·cal·ize (*foh*-k'l-yze) *v.* [fo·cal·ized; fo·cal·iz·**

ing] To converge; bring into or to focus.—**fo·cal·i·za·tion** *n.*

fo·cus (*foh*-kus) *n.* [*pl.* -cus·es, -ci] 1. *Optics.* A point where any number of rays, as of light, meet and form an image after being reflected or refracted by a mirror or lens. 2. Focal length. 3. Proper adjustment (of the eye or a lens) in order to see clearly. 4. A point of centralization—*v.* [fo·cused, fo·cussed; fo·cus·ing, fo·cus·sing] 1. To bring or come to a focus. 2. To adjust the eye or a lens in order to see clearly. 3. To concentrate.

fod·der (*fod*-er) *n.* Food, such as hay, for cattle, horses, and ·heep.—**fod·der** *v.*

foe *n.* An enemy; antagonist; opponent.

·foe·man (*foh*-m'n) *n.* An enemy, esp. in war.

fog (*fog*, *fawg*) *n.* 1. A dense watery vapor hanging low over the ground. 2. Bewilderment. 3. *Photography.* Blurred portion or condition of a negative or print.—*v.* [fogged; fog·ging] To cover with fog; blur; confuse.

fogbow	fogeater	fog gage
fogdog	fogfruit	fogman

fog·gy *adj.* [fog·gi·er; fog·gi·est] 1. Cloudy; covered with fog; misty. 2. Confused; bewildered.—**fog·gi·ly** *adv.*—**fog·gi·ness** *n.*

fog·horn *n.* 1. A horn sounded to warn ships in foggy weather. 2. A deep, harsh sound.

fog·y (*foh*-gee) *n.* [*pl.* -gies] Also **fo·gey.** A stuffy, old-fashioned person.—**fo·gy·ish** *adj.*

foi·ble (*foy*-b'l) *n.* A weak point; failing.

foil *n.* A long, light blunt sword with a covered point used in fencing.—*v.* To outwit; thwart.

foil *n.* 1. An extremely thin sheet of metal. 2. Person or thing which, by comparison or contrast, shows the superiority of another person or object. 3. *Architecture.* A small arc in Gothic design; an ornamental leaflike design.—*v.* 1. To cover with foil. 2. To show the superiority of, by contrast.

foist *v.* To palm off by trickery; insert secretly.

fold (*fohld*) *v.* 1. To double; lay one part over another. 2. To bring close to the body. 3. To enclose; embrace.—*n.* 1. A folded layer; folding. 2. *Geology.* A bend or curve in a rock layer produced after its formation.

fold *n.* 1. A sheep pen. 2. A flock; church or congregation.—**fold** *v.*

fold·er *n.* 1. A paper cover or binder for documents, etc. 2. One who folds.

fol·de·rol *n.* Nonsense; trivia.

fo·li·a·ceous (foh-lee-*ay*-shus) *adj.* Leaflike.

fo·li·age (*foh*-lee-ij) *n.* Leafage; the leaves of growing plants.—**fo·li·aged** *adj.*

fo·li·ate (*foh*-lee-it) *adj.* *Botany.* Bearing leaves. —*v.* [fo·li·at·ed; fo·li·at·ing] To decorate with foils, leaves, etc.

fo·li·a·tion (foh-lee-*ay*-sh'n) *n.* 1. *Botany.* The leafing of plants. 2. The beating of a metal into a thin plate. 3. *Architecture.* Ornamentation of windows with foils and tracery. 4. The operation of spreading foil over the back of a mirror.

F

fo·li·o (*foh*-lee-oh) *n.* [*pl.* -os] 1. A sheet of paper folded once; leaf of a book. 2. A book of the largest size, formed of sheets once doubled.—**fo·li·o** *adj.*—*v.* [fo·li·oed; fo·li·o·ing] To page; paginate.

folk *n.* [*pl.* folk, folks] 1. People. 2. The majority of a people, who form and preserve a national tradition and culture. 3. [*pl.*] *Colloquial.* 1. People. 2. The family.—*adj.* Popularly developed, as art and culture.

folk·lore *n.* The tales or traditions of a people.

folk·sy (*fohk*-see) *adj.* Plain; simple.

folk·way *n.* A custom; a social tradition.

fol·li·cle (*fol*-ih-k'l) *n.* 1. *Botany.* A dry seed pod opening on one side. 2. *Anatomy.* A minute cavity; the pore containing a hair root. —**fol·lic·u·lar** (fuh-*lik*-yoo-ler) *adj.*

fol·low (*fol*-oh) *v.* 1. To proceed after; move behind. 2. To pursue; chase. 3. To be led or guided by; accept and adhere to the teachings or leadership of. 4. To copy; take as an example. 5. To result from. 6. To pursue with the eye. 7. To watch the progress of; keep informed upon. 8. To understand; comprehend. 'Do you follow me?'—**fol·low** *n.*

fol·low·er *n.* An adherent; disciple.

fol·low·ing *n.* Adherents; body of disciples; public.—*adj.* Being next after; succeeding.

fol·low-through *n.* A completing action.

fol·low-up *n.* A second or repeated action or attempt; a tracer.—**fol·low-up** *adj.*

fol·ly *n.* [*pl.* -lies] Stupidity; thoughtless action; silliness.

fo·ment (fuh-*ment*) *v.* To incite; instigate; provoke.—**fo·ment·er** *n.*

fo·men·ta·tion (foh-men-*tay*-sh'n) *n.* Instigation; provocation.

fond *adj.* 1. Liking; enjoying; having a preference for. 2. Affectionate; caring for.—**fond·ly** *adv.*—**fond·ness** *n.*

fon·dant (*fon*-d'nt) *n.* A cream used as a filling for chocolates, bonbons, or other candies.

fon·dle (*fon*-d'l) *v.* [fon·dled; fon·dling] To caress; pat.—**fon·dler** *n.*

fon·du (fon-*dyoo*) *adj.* Dissolving one into another, as colors.

fon·due (fon-*doo*) *n.* A soufflé with crumbs.

font *n.* *Printing.* A complete assortment of all the different characters of a particular size and style of type.

font *n.* A baptismal basin.

food *n.* Nutriment; victuals; nourishment taken in by organic bodies.

food·stuff *n.* A food.

fool *n.* 1. A simpleton; a silly person. 2. A jester; clown; buffoon. 3. A dupe; one upon whom a deception is practiced.—*v.* To deceive; trick.

fool-born	**fool-frequented**	**fool-headed**
foolfish	**fool happy**	**fool-heady**

fool·er·y *n.* [*pl.* -ies] Habitual foolishness; folly.

fool·har·dy *adj.* [-har·di·er; -har·di·est] Rash; imprudently daring; incautious.—**fool·hard·i·ly** *adv.*—**fool·har·di·ness** *n.*

fool·ish *adj.* 1. Brainless; silly; imprudent. 2. Preposterous.— -ish·ly *adv.*— -ish·ness *n.*

fool·proof *adj.* Absolutely secure and reliable; flawlessly planned or constituted; perfect.

fools·cap *n.* 1. Paper cut in sheets of about 12 by 16 inches. 2. A jester's hood.

fool's gold. Iron pyrites.

fool's paradise. Deceptive happiness; blissful ignorance.

foot *n.* [*pl.* feet] 1. The lower extremity of the leg on which an animal stands. 2. The lower end of anything that supports a body. 3. The lowest part or foundation; bottom; last of a row or series. 4. *Military.* Infantry. 5. A unit of measure consisting of 12 inches. 6. *Poetry.* A certain number of syllables, usually 2 or 3, constituting a metrical unit of a verse.—*v.* 1. To dance or walk. 2. To add up a column of figures. 3. *Colloquial.* To be liable for; pay.

footband	footlining	footslog
foot binding	foot-loose	footstalk
footboy	foot mark	footstall
footcloth	footpace	footstone
footfight	footplate	foot-ton
foot-free	foot race	footwalk
footgear	footrail	footwall
foot-grain	footrest	foot-weary
foothalt	footroom	footworm
foothook	footrope	foot-worn

foot·age *n.* 1. Length measured in feet. 2. *Motion Pictures.* Amount of film used in any particular picture.

foot-and-mouth disease. A highly contagious disease of cattle.

foot·ball *n.* 1. An oval-shaped inflated pigskin ball. 2. One of three games, American football, Rugby, or association football (soccer), played with a football between two teams.

foot·board *n.* 1. A support for the foot as on an automobile, boat, etc. 2. The foot end of a bed.

foot·bridge *n.* A narrow bridge for pedestrians.

foot-can·dle *n.* A unit of measurement of light equal to the illumination of a standard candle one foot away.

foot·fall *n.* A footstep; tread of the foot.

foot·hill *n.* A hill lying at the base of mountains.

foot·hold *n.* A firm footing; a stable entering wedge.

foot·ing *n.* Ground for the foot; firm foundation to stand on.

foot·lights *n. pl.* 1. *Theater.* A row of lights at the front of the stage. 2. The theater.

foot·man *n.* [*pl.* -men] A male servant with various duties; attendant.

foot·note *n.* A note of reference or further exposition at the bottom of a page.

foot·pad *n.* A robber.

foot·path *n.* A narrow path for pedestrians.

foot·pound *n.* A unit of energy required to raise one pound a distance of one foot.

foot·print n. The impression left by a foot.

foot·sore adj. Having painful feet.

foot·step n. Tread; footfall; sound of the step.

foot·stool n. A stool to support the feet.

foot·way n. A path for pedestrians.

foot·wear n. Shoes, slippers, boots, etc.

foot·work n. Sports. Movements of the feet.

foo·zle v. [foo·zled; foo·zling] 1. To fumble; juggle. 2. Bowling. To roll the ball off the alley into the side gutter.—**foo·zle** n.

fop n. A dandy; man vain about his appearance.—**fop·per·y** n.—**fop·pish** adj.—**fop·pish·ly** adv.—**fop·pish·ness** n.

for prep. 1. In place of. 'Substitute for butter.' 2. Corresponding to; accompanying. 3. In the character of. 'I took him for a cad.' 4. Toward; to. 'Train for Boston.' 5. For the sake of. 'Fight for freedom.' 6. Conducive to; beneficial to. 'Good for you.' 7. Leading or inducing to. 'For better or for worse.' 8. Suitable for; proper to. 'Dress for the occasion.' 9. Notwithstanding. 'For all your persuasion, I refuse.' 10. Because; on account of. 'For these beliefs I stand.' 11. In consideration of. 'Penny for your thoughts.' 12. Through a certain space; during a certain time. 'Employed for ten years.' 13. Notwithstanding. 'Old for his years.' 14. In honor of. 'Dinner for the Duchess.' 15. Liable to the amount of. 'I owe this for meal.'—conj. Because; by reason that.

for·age (for-ij) n. 1. Food for horses and cattle such as grass, pasture, hay. 2. Act of searching for provisions.—v. [-aged; -ag·ing] 1. To wander about in search of food. 2. To ravage; raid.—**for·ag·er** n.

forasmuch as. Since; seeing that.

for·ay v. To ravage; pillage.—n. A predatory excursion.—**for·ay·er** n.

for·bade, for·bad. Past tense of for·bid.

for·bear (for-behr) v. [-bore; -borne; -bear·ing] 1. To refrain from proceeding; pause; delay. 2. To abstain; refrain.—**for·bear·ance** n.

for·bid (for-bid) v. [-bade, -bad; -bid·den; -bid·ding] To prohibit; interdict; refuse to allow. —**for·bid·ding** adj. Threatening; menacing. —**for·bid·ding·ly** adv.

force (forss) n. 1. Manifestation of energy. 2. Strength; power; vigor. 3. Physics. That which causes or tends to cause changes in the motion of bodies. 4. Violence; coercion. 5. Validity; binding power. 6. Troops; an army or navy; a body of policemen.—v. [forced; forc·ing] 1. To compel; coerce. 2. To drive; impel. 3. To assault; storm. 4. To assume; compel oneself to give expression to.—**force·a·ble** adj.—**forc·er** n.

forced (forst) adj. 1. Coercive; obligatory. 2. Affected; unnatural.

force·ful (forss-f'l) adj. Powerful; telling; convincing; effective.— -**ful·ly** adv.— -**ness** n.

force·meat n. Cookery. Chopped and seasoned meat, often used for stuffing.

for·ceps (for-seps) n. [pl. -ceps] A two-bladed instrument on the principle of pincers or tongs, used for seizing, holding, or extracting objects.

for·ci·ble (for-suh-b'l) adj. 1. Violent; accomplished by force. 2. Powerful; strong.—**for·ci·bly** adv.

ford n. A shallow place in a river where one may cross on foot.—**ford** v.—**ford·a·ble** adj.

FORCEPS

fore adj. 1. Anterior; preceding. 2. Being in front or toward the face. 3. Nautical. Pertaining to parts of a ship at or near the bow.—adv. Nautical. Toward the front of a ship.

fore! interj. Golf. Watch out, ball coming!

fore and aft. Nautical. From bow to stern; at the bow and stern.—**fore-and-aft** adj. Longitudinal; running lengthwise.

fore·arm n. Anatomy. That part of the arm between the elbow and wrist.

fore·arm v. To prepare for attack or resistance.

fore·bear, for·bear (for-behr) n. An ancestor.

fore·bode (for-bohd) v. [-bod·ed; -bod·ing] To portend; augur; to be ominous.—**fore·bod·er** n. —**fore·bod·ing** n. A premonition.

fore·cast (for-kast) v. [-cast, -cast·ed; -cast·ing] Predict; prophesy.—**fore·cast·er** n.

fore·cast (for-kast) n. A prediction; calculation of future conditions, as of the weather.

fore·cas·tle (fohk-s'l) n. Nautical. 1. Raised section of a ship's bow, formerly containing crew's quarters. 2. Crew's quarters wherever located.

fore·close v. [-closed; -clos·ing] To deprive of the right of redemption, as of a mortgage.—**fore·clo·sure** n.

fore·doom v. To doom beforehand.

fore·fath·er n. An ancestor; progenitor.

fore·fin·ger n. The finger beside the thumb.

fore·foot n. [pl. -feet] One of the front feet of a four-footed animal.

fore·front n. The most advanced position.

fore·go v. [-went; -gone; -go·ing] 1. To go ahead of; precede. 2. To renounce; give up.—**fore·go·er** n.

fore·go·ing adj. Preceding; antecedent.

fore·gone adj. Predetermined; settled beforehand.—**fore·gone·ness** n.

fore·ground n. The part of a picture or scene between the observer and the principal subject.

fore·hand n. The parts of a horse in front of the rider.—adj. Done in advance.

fore·hand·ed adj. Timely; early.—**fore·hand·ed·ness** n.

fore·head n. The brow; the part of the face between the eyes and hairline.

for·eign (for-in) adj. 1. Belonging or relating to another nation. 2. Alien; unfamiliar.

for·eign·er *n.* Citizen of another country; alien.

fore·know *v.* [-knew; -know·ing; -known] To know ahead; anticipate.—**fore·know·a·ble** *adj.*

fore·knowl·edge *n.* Previous knowledge of an event.

fore·land *n.* A promontory; cape; headland.

fore·leg *n.* One of the front legs of an animal.

fore·man *n.* 1. One who superintends the work of a group of employees. 2. The chief member of a jury, who acts as their speaker.

fore·mast *n.* The mast closest to the bow.

fore·most *adj.* Chief; leading; principal.—**fore·most** *adv.*

fore·name *n.* The given name.

fore·noon *n.* The part of the day from morning to noon; first part of the day.—**fore·noon** *adj.*

fo·ren·sic (fuh-*ren*-sik) *adj.* Argumentative; open to discussion.—**fo·ren·si·cal·ly** *adv.*

fore·or·dain *v.* To predetermine; ordain beforehand.—**fore·or·dain·ment** *n.*

fore part. Also **fore·part.** The front part.

fore·run *v.* [-ran; -run; -run·ning] To precede.—**fore·run·ner** *n.* A predecessor; precursor.

fore·sail *n.* The lowest sail on the foremast.

fore·see *v.* [-saw, -seen; -see·ing] To anticipate.

fore·shad·ow *v.* To portend, presage; point to.—**fore·shad·ow·er** *n.*

fore·shore *n.* The sloping part of a shore between the high and low watermarks.

fore·short·en *v. Painting.* To depict in proper perspective to produce a realistic effect.

fore·show *v.* [-showed; -shown; -show·ing] To indicate; betoken.

fore·sight *n.* Prudence; perspicacity; forethought.—**fore·sight·ed** *adj.*— -**sight·ed·ness** *n.*

fore·skin *n.* Fold of skin over the glans penis.

for·est (*for*-est) *n.* Woodlands; large area densely covered with trees.—*v.* To fill with trees.—**for·est** *adj.*

fore·stall (for-*stawl*) *v.* 1. To avert; stop; prevent. 2. To buy and hold large quantities of goods for rising prices.—**fore·stall·er** *n.*

for·est·a·tion (for-ess-*tay*-sh'n) *n.* The preservation and development of wooded areas.

fore·stay *n.* A longitudinal brace running from the crosstrees of a mast to the forward deck.

for·est·er (*for*-ess-ter) *n.* 1. A forest warden; a ranger. 2. A kind of moth. 3. A giant antelope.

for·est·ry *n.* The science of preserving and developing woodlands.

fore·taste *n.* An advance sample.—*v.* [fore·tast·ed; fore·tast·ing].

fore·tell *v.* [fore·told; fore·tell·ing] To predict; prognosticate; forecast.—**fore·tell·er** *n.*

fore·thought (*for*-thawt) *n.* Prudence; wisdom.

fore·to·ken (*for*-toh-k'n) *n.* An omen; sign of the future.—*v.* (for-*toh*-k'n) To foretell.

fore·top *n.* 1. Hair on the front of the head. 2. *Nautical.* A platform at the foremost head.

for·ev·er (for-*ev*-er) *adv.* For all time; always.

for·ev·er·more *adv.* For eternity.

fore·warn *v.* To caution; admonish beforehand.

fore·word *n.* A preface; explanatory note at the beginning of a book.

for·feit (*for*-fit) *n.* A penalty; fine.—*adj.* Lost or alienated for an offense.—**for·feit** *v.*

for·fei·ture (*for*-fih-choor) *n.* 1. Loss of right or property by breach of conditions. 2. A fine.

for·gath·er *v.* Also **fore·gath·er.** To convene.

forge (forj) *v.* [forged; forg·ing] To move on slowly and laboriously.

forge *n.* 1. Furnace in which metal is heated to be shaped. 2. Workshop in which iron or other metal is wrought.—*v.* 1. To form by heating and hammering. 2. To counterfeit a signature or signed document.—**forg·er** *n.*

for·ger·y (*for*-jer-ee) *n.* [*pl.* -ies] 1. Crime of fraudulently counterfeiting any record, signature, etc. 2. Something counterfeited.

for·get (for-*get*) *v.* [for·got; for·got·ten or for·got; for·get·ting] To lose memory of; cease to have in mind.—**for·get·ta·ble** *adj.*

for·get·ful (for-*get*-f'l) *adj.* 1. Apt to forget; easily losing remembrance. 2. Careless; neglectful.—**for·get·ful·ly** *adv.*—**for·get·ful·ness** *n.*

for·get-me-not *n.* A plant of the genus myosotis, whose flowers are usually bright blue.

for·give (for-*giv*) *v.* [-gave; -giv·en; -giv·ing] To pardon; absolve; cease to feel resentment against.—**for·giv·a·ble** *adj.*—**for·giv·er** *n.*

for·give·ness *n.* Pardon; absolution.

for·giv·ing *adj.* Inclined to overlook offenses; compassionate.—**for·giv·ing·ly** *adv.*—**for·giv·ing·ness** *n.*

for·go (for-*goh*) *v.* Also **fore·go** [for·went; for·gone; for·go·ing] To give up; renounce.

fork *n.* 1. An instrument consisting of a handle terminating in two or more prongs, used for piercing or lifting something. 2. The point where something, as a road, river, etc., divides into branches.—*v.* To divide into extensions.

fork out or **over.** *Slang.* To hand or pay over.

forked (*forkt*) *adj.* Opening into two or more parts; pronged.

for·lorn (for-*lorn*) *adj.* Downcast; abject; hopeless.—**for·lorn·ly** *adv.*—**for·lorn·ness** *n.*

form *n.* 1. The shape or external appearance of a body. 2. Regularity; method; order. 3. *British.* A grade or class in school. 4. The stated method; established practice; ceremony. 5. A shape; phantom. 6. Likeness; image. 7. System; manner of arrangement. 8. *Printing.* A page of type and material arranged for printing and locked in a chase. 9. Excellent condition or fitness for an undertaking. 10. State; condition.—*v.* 1. To shape; mold. 2. To devise; invent; create. 3. To be an element or constituent of; go to make up.

for·mal (*for*-m'l) *adj.* 1. Ceremonious; precise; punctilious. 2. According to regular method; not incidental or sudden. 3. Having form without substance.—**for·mal·ly** *adv.*

for·mal·de·hyde (for-*mal*-duh-hyde) *n.* A colorless gas, used in solution as a preservative.

for·mal·ism (*for*-m'l-izm) *n.* Strict compliance with established forms and procedure.

for·mal·i·ty (for-*mal*-uh-tee) *n.* [*pl.* -ties] 1. Conventionality; conformity to customary procedures. 2. Established order, method.

for·mal·ize (*for*-m'l-yze) *v.* [for·mal·ized; for·mal·iz·ing] To reduce to a certain form.—**for·mal·i·za·tion** (for-m'l-uh-*zay*-shun) *n.*

for·mat (*for*-mat) *n.* General layout, style, and size of a publication.

for·ma·tion (for-*may*-shun) *n.* 1. Creation; generation; production. 2. The manner in which a thing is formed. 3. *Geology.* Any series of rocks referred to a common origin or period. 4. *Military.* An arrangement of troops, airplanes, or ships.

form·a·tive (*for*-muh-tiv) *adj.* 1. Plastic; malleable. 2. Molding; creating form.

form·er (*for*-mer) *adj.* 1. First mentioned; earlier of two things mentioned together. 2. Prior; previous.—**for·mer·ly** (*for*-mer-lee) *adv.* Previously; in time past.

formic acid. A colorless acid compound, occurring in plants and insects.

for·mi·da·ble (*for*-mid-uh-b'l) *adj.* Menacing; threatening; awe-inspiring; dreadful.—**for·mi·da·bil·i·ty** *n.*— -da·ble·ness *n.*— -da·bly *adv.*

form·less (*form*-liss) *adj.* Shapeless; irregularly formed.—**form·less·ly** *adv.*—**form·less·ness** *n.*

for·mu·la (*for*-myuh-luh) *n.* [*pl.* -las, -lae] 1. A prescribed form; a fixed method in which anything is to be done, arranged, or said. 2. A recipe; prescription. 3. *Mathematics.* A rule or principle expressed in algebraic symbols. 4. *Chemistry.* An expression by means of symbols and letters of the constituents of a compound.

for·mu·lar·ize (*for*-myuh-luh-ryze) *v.* [-ized; iz·ing] To reduce to a formula; express tersely in systematic form.

for·mu·late (*for*-myuh-layt) *v.* [-lat·ed; -lat·ing] To put into a precise and logical form.—**for·mu·la·tion** *n.*—**for·mu·la·tor** *n.*

for·ni·cate *v.* [-cat·ed; -cat·ing] To have illicit sexual intercourse, esp. while unmarried.—**for·ni·ca·tion** *n.*—**for·ni·ca·tor** *n.*

for·sake (fer-*sayk*) *v.* [-sook; -sak·en; -sak·ing] 1. To desert; abandon. 2. To give up.

for·sooth (fer-*sooth*) *adv.* In truth, in fact.

for·swear (for-*swehr*) *v.* [-swore; -sworn; -swear·ing] 1. To renounce; reject solemnly. 2. Deny on oath, esp. falsely.—**for·swear·er** *n.*

for·sworn (for-*sworn*) *adj.* False to a promise or oath; perjured.

for·syth·i·a (fer-*sith*-ee-uh) *n.* Shrub bearing yellow flowers in early spring.

fort *n.* An enclosed, strongly fortified place.

forte (fort) *n.* A peculiar talent; strong point.

for·te (*for*-teh, -tay) *adj. Music.* Loud.—*adv.* Loudly.—*n.* Passage to be played loudly.

forth *adv.* 1. On; forward. 2. Out; into sight.

forth·com·ing *adj.* Approaching; coming into view.—**forth·com·ing** *n.*

forth·right (forth-*ryte*) *adv.* Straight or directly forward; immediately.—*adj.* (*forth*-ryte) Honest; direct; frank.

forth·with *adv.* At once; without delay.

for·ti·eth (*for*-tee-ith) *n.* One of forty equal parts; last of a series of forty.—**for·ti·eth** *adj.*

for·ti·fi·ca·tion (fort-uf-uh-*kay*-sh'n) *n.* 1. The act of strengthening or fortifying. 2. A fortified place; defensive structure.

for·ti·fy (*fort*-ih-fye) *v.* [-fied; -fy·ing] 1. To strengthen; support. 2. To render defensible against an attack; secure.—**for·ti·fi·er** *n.*

for·tis·si·mo (for-*teess*-uh-moh) *adj. & adv. Music.* With the greatest strength or loudness.

for·ti·tude (*for*-tih-tood) *n.* Enduring courage; resolution; hardihood.—**for·ti·tud·i·nous** *adj.*

fort·night (*fort*-nyte) *n.* Two weeks.—**fort·night·ly** *adj.* Happening once in two weeks. —**fort·night·ly** *adv.*

for·tress (*for*-tress) *n.* Stronghold.—**for·tress** *v.*

for·tu·i·tous (for-*tyoo*-ih-tus) *adj.* Accidental; occurring by chance.—**for·tu·i·tous·ly** *adv.* —**for·tu·i·tous·ness** *n.*—**for·tu·i·ty** (for-*tyoo*-ih-tee) *n.* [*pl.* -ties] Accident; chance.

for·tu·nate (*for*-chun-it) *adj.* Lucky; having or bringing good fortune; successful.—**for·tu·nate·ly** *adv.*—**for·tu·nate·ness** *n.*

for·tune (*for*-chun) *n.* 1. Luck; fate; chance; whatever befalls a person. 2. What the future may bring; destiny. 3. Great wealth; prosperity; a large sum of money.—*v.* [for·tuned; for·tun·ing] To happen; befall.

fortune hunter. One who marries for money.

for·tune·tel·ler *n.* One who pretends to know and reveal forthcoming events.—**for·tune·tell·ing** *n.*

for·ty (*for*-tee) *n.* [*pl.* -ties] The number represented by the symbol 40.—**for·ty** *adj.*—**for·ty·fold** *adj. & adv.*

for·ty-nin·er *n. Colloquial.* One of the adventurers in the California gold rush of 1849.

fo·rum (*foh*-rum) *n.* [*pl.* -rums, -ra] 1. A tribunal; judicial assembly. 2. A formal discussion of a subject from various points of view.

for·ward (*for*-werd) *adj.* 1. Near or at the front; anterior. 2. Bold; aggressive; pushing. 3. Precocious; advanced. 4. Onward. —*adv.* Onward; toward a place before or in front.—*v.* 1. To promote; advance. 2. To transmit.—*n. Sports.* A player who plays toward the opponents' goal.—**for·ward·er** *n.* An agent who forwards transported goods.

for·ward·ly (*for*-werd-lee) *adv.* 1. Boldly; belligerently. 2. At the front; eagerly.

for·ward·ness (*for*-werd-ness) *n.* 1. Overbearance; brashness. 2. Precocity. 3. Zealousness.

forward pass. *Football.* Throwing the ball past the line of scrimmage toward opponent's goal.

for·wards (*for*-werdz) *adv.* Forth; forward.

fos·sil *n.* 1. Prehistoric plant or animal pre-

F

served in the earth. 2. *Colloquial*. A fogey; old-fashioned person.—fos·sil *adj.*—fos·sil·if·er·ous *adj.*

fos·sil·ize (*foss*-'l-yze) *v.* [-ized; -iz·ing] 1. To convert into a fossil. 2. To become antiquated, rigid, or fixed.—fos·sil·i·za·tion *n.*

fos·ter (*foss*-ter) *v.* 1. To nourish; feed. 2. To promote the growth of; further; champion; support.—*adj.* Caring for or receiving care, though not of kin. 'Foster father.'—fos·ter·er *n.*

foul (*fowl*) *adj.* 1. Filthy; dirty. 2. Obscene; abusive. 3. Loathsome; defiling. 4. Wicked; shameful. 5. *Nautical*. Entangled.—*v.* 1. To make filthy; dirty; defile. 2. *Nautical*. To become entangled or clogged. 3. *Sports*. To commit a foul.—*n.* 1. *Baseball*. A ball hit outside of the first or third base line. 2. *Boxing*. An illegal blow.—foul·ly *adv.*—foul·ness *n.*

fou·lard (foo-*lahrd*) *n.* A kind of silk material.

foul play. An underhand attack.

found *v.* To base; establish; set up.—found·er *n.*

found *v.* To cast; form by melting a metal and pouring it into a mold.—found·er *n.*

foun·da·tion (fown-*day*-shun) *n.* 1. The act of establishing or beginning to build. 2. That part of a building which is under the surface of the ground. 3. The basis or groundwork for anything. 4. An endowed institution.

foun·der (*fown*-der) *v.* 1. To fall; stumble; fail. 2. To fill with water; sink.

found·ling *n.* An infant abandoned by its parents.

found·ry *n.* [*pl.* -ries] 1. A factory or works where metal is cast. 2. The casting of metals.

foundry proof. *Printing*. The last impression or proof before electrotyping.

fount *n.* A fountain; source; wellspring.

foun·tain (*fown*-t'n) *n.* 1. A spring; natural source of water. 2. A jet or spout which supplies drinking water.

foun·tain·head *n.* A source; origin.

fountain pen. A pen which contains ink.

four (*for*) *n.* 1. The number 4. 2. Any group composed of four persons or things.—four *adj.*—four·fold *adj. & adv.*

four-ball	four-headed	fourpence
four-colored	four-leaved	fourpenny
four-cornered	four-legged	four-ply
four-cylindered	four-lettered	four-sided
four-eyed	four-lobed	four-storied
four-eyes	four-masted	four-striped
four-footed	four-master	four-striper
four-handed	four-oared	four-wheeled

four-bag·ger *n. Baseball*. A home run.

four-flush·er *n. Slang*. One who bluffs his way. —four-flush *v.*—four-flush·ing *adj.*

Four Hundred, the. The traditionally wealthy and exclusive group of a community.

Fou·ri·er·ism (*foor*-ee-er-izm) *n.* A form of socialism proposed by F. M. C. Fourier in the early 19th century, based on division of society into small co-operative communities.

four-in-hand *n.* A slipknot necktie.—four-in-hand *adj.*

four-poster *n.* A bed with a post at each corner.

four-score *adj.* Eighty.

four-some *n. Golf*. Two sets of partners.

four-square *adj.* 1. Having four equal sides and four equal angles. 2. With firmness; without equivocation.—*n.* A square.—four-square, four-square·ly *adv.*—four-square·ness *n.*

four-teen (for-*teen*) *n.* The number 14.—*adj.* Having fourteen units.—four-teenth *adj.* Being one equal part of fourteen units; last of a series of fourteen.—four-teenth *n.*

fourth (*forth*) *n.* A quarter.—*adj.* The last of four.—fourth·ly *adv.* In the fourth place.

fourth dimension. The factor of time, as involved in velocity, introduced by Einstein's theory of relativity as a necessary consideration in physical measurement. This time element is not regarded separately, but as a relative dimension in the concept of space-time. See relativity.

fourth estate. The press; journalism.

fowl *n.* A bird, esp. one raised for food.—*v.* To hunt birds.—fow·ler *n.*

fowling piece. A small-calibered gun for bird-hunting.

fox *n.* 1. An animal of the dog family, smaller than the wolf, noted for his cunning. 2. A sly, designing fellow. 3. The fur of the fox.—*v.* To outsmart.

FOX (1/30 life size)

fox-colored		
fox-faced		
foxfish		
fox hunting		
foxlike	foxskin	fox-visaged
fox-nosed	foxskinned	fox wolf
foxship	foxtailed	foxwood

fox·glove *n.* A widely dispersed flowering plant yielding digitalis.

fox hole. A hole hastily dug in the earth, esp. as protection from gunfire.

fox·hound *n.* A large, swift, keen-scented hound.

fox terrier. A small, quick terrier with a white mottled coat.

fox·trot *n.* A ballroom dance step in four-four tempo.—*v.* [fox·trot·ted; fox·trot·ting].

fox·y *adj.* [fox·i·er; fox·i·est] Sly; clever.—fox·i·ly *adv.*—fox·i·ness *n.*

FOXGLOVE

foy·er (*foy*-er) *n.* A hallway; lobby.

fra (*frah*) *n.* A monk's title; brother.

fra·cas (*fray*-kuss) *n.* [-cas·es] Disturbance; noisy quarrel.

frac·tion (*frak*-shun) *n.* 1. A part; fragment. 2. A quotient of unity.—frac·tion *v.*—frac·tion·al *adj.*—frac·tion·al·ly *adv.*

frac·tious (*frak*-shuss) *adj.* Quarrelsome; peevish.—frac·tious·ly *adv.*—frac·tious·ness *n.*

frac·ture (*frak*-cher) *n.* A break, esp. of a bone. —*v.* [-tured; -tur·ing]—**frac·tur·al** *adj.*

frag·ile (*fraj*-il) *adj.* Easily broken; delicate. —**frag·ile·ly** *adv.*—**frag·ile·ness, fra·gil·i·ty** *n.*

frag·ment (*frag*-m'nt) *n.* A detached part; small piece.—**frag·men·tal** *adj.*

frag·men·tar·y (*frag*-m'n-tehr-ee) *adj.* Incomplete; broken up; disconnected.

fra·grance (*fray*-grunss) *n.* Also **fra·gran·cy.** A pleasing, sweet, or aromatic odor; scent. —**fra·grant** *adj.*—**fra·grant·ly** *adv.*

frail (*frayl*) *adj.* 1. Weak; fragile; slight. 2. Morally weak.—*n. Slang.* A woman or girl. —**frail·ly** *adv.*—**frail·ness** *n.*

frail·ty (*frayl*-tee) *n.* [*pl.* -ties] Weakness.

frame *v.* [framed; fram·ing] 1. To silhouette; outline. 2. To construct; fit together. 3. To make; originate. 4. To fit to a specific aim; conform. 5. *Colloquial.* To make an innocent person seem guilty.—*n.* 1. The framework of a structure; inner construction. 2. Body build; physique. 3. Any supporting structure. 4. Form; structure. 5. Disposition; state, as of mind. 6. A border surrounding a picture. 7. *Photography.* Any individual negative on a strip of motion picture film. —*adj.* Built about a unifying idea. 'A frame story.'—**fram·er** *n.*

framed (*fraymd*) *adj. Colloquial.* Trapped by prearranged design; hoaxed; rigged.

frame-up *n.* A plot to make an innocent person seem guilty; rigging of evidence; hoax.

frame·work (*fraym*-werk) *n.* An inner structure; strengthening frame.

franc (*frank, frahnk*) *n.* The chief monetary unit of France and Switzerland.

fran·chise (*fran*-chyze) *n.* 1. The right to vote. 2. A special grant or privilege, esp. an operating privilege granted public-utility corporations.

Fran·cis·can (fran-*siss*-k'n) *n.* A member of an order of friars sworn to absolute poverty. **Fran·cis·can** *adj.*

Fran·co·phile, Fran·co·phil (*frank*-oh-fyle) *n.* A lover of the culture, institutions, etc., of France.—**Fran·co·phile** *adj.*

Fran·co·phobe (*frank*-oh-fohb) *n.* A hater of France and things French.—**Fran·co·phobe** *adj.*—**Fran·co·pho·bia** *n.*

fran·gi·ble (*fran*-jih-b'l) *adj.* Fragile; brittle; easily broken.—**fran·gi·bil·i·ty, -ble·ness** *n.*

frank *adj.* Open; candid; not hypocritical.

frank *n.* 1. The privilege of sending mail free of postage. 2. That mark or signature which secures free postage.—**frank** *v.*

Frank·en·stein (*frank*-'n-styne) *n.* A character in Mary Shelley's novel of the same name who is destroyed by the monster he created. Often wrongly used as the monster's name.

frank·furt·er (*frank*-fer-ter) *n.* Also **frank·furt.** A wiener; ground meat in membrane casing.

frank·in·cense (*frank*-in-senss) *n.* Incense; a yellow resin that burns with a fragrant odor.

frank·lin (*frank*-lin) *n.* A medieval landowner of large holdings, free-born but not a noble.

fran·tic (*fran*-tik) *adj.* Also **fran·ti·cal.** 1. Desperate; greatly worried. 2. Frenzied; distracted.—**fran·ti·cal·ly** *adv.*—**fran·tic·ness** *n.*

frap·pé (frap-*pay*) *adj.* Chilled with chopped ice; frozen.—*n.* A dessert or drink filled with chopped ice or frozen to a mushy consistency.

fra·ter·nal (fruh-*ter*-n'l) *adj.* Brotherly; comradely.—**fra·ter·nal·ism** *n.*—**fra·ter·nal·ly** *adv.*

fra·ter·ni·ty (fruh-*ter*-nih-tee) *n.* [*pl.* -ties] 1. Condition of being brothers. 2. A social or honorary association of men of similar interests or pursuits. 3. The whole body of men in some profession, class, etc. 'The advertising fraternity.'

frat·er·nize (*frat*-er-nyze) *v.* [-nized; -niz·ing] 1. To associate in a friendly or brotherly spirit. 2. To be overintimate with enemy nationals.—**fra·ter·ni·za·tion** *n.*—**fra·ter·niz·er** *n.*

frat·ri·cide (*frat*-ruh-syde) *n.* Murder of one's brother.—**frat·ri·cid·al** *adj.*

Frau (*frow*) *n.* [*pl.* Frau·en] *German.* A married woman; equivalent to *Mrs.*

fraud (*frawd*) *n.* A cheat; swindle; trick.

frau·du·lent (*fraw*-juh-lunt) *adj.* 1. Deceitful; cheating. 2. Not genuine; false.—**fraud·u·lence, fraud·u·len·cy** *n.*—**fraud·u·lent·ly** *adv.*

fraught (*frawt*) *adj.* Laden; charged; abounding.

Fräu·lein (*froy*-lyne) *n.* [*sing. & pl.*] *German.* An unmarried girl; equivalent to *Miss.*

fray *n.* A battle; fight.

fray *v.* To wear into shreds; rub to tatters.—*n.* A wearing or shredding.

freak (*freek*) *n.* 1. A sudden causeless change; whim. 2. A monstrosity; deviation from the normal.—**freak·ish** *adj.*—**freak·ish·ness** *n.*

freck·le (*frek*-'l) *n.* A brownish spot in the skin caused by a local excess of skin pigment.—*v.* [freck·led; freck·ling]—**freck·ly** *adj.*

free *adj.* [fre·er; fre·est] 1. Not subject to necessity or restraint; at liberty. 2. Not under arbitrary or despotic rule; subject only to democratic laws. 3. Instituted by a free people. 4. Without cost or charge; gratuitous. 5. Unrestricted; available. 6. Not obstructed; clear. 7. Open; candid; frank. 8. Without care; unconcerned. 9. Liberal; profuse; unrestrained. 10. Clear of offense; guiltless; innocent. 11. Unrestrained; immoderate. 12. *Chemistry.* Not chemically combined with any other element. 13. Devoid of tariffs and other impediments to trade. 14. Not strict in observance of law or convention.—*v.* [freed; free·ing] 1. To remove any encumbrance or obstruction; disengage; clear. 2. Rescue; release from slavery or confinement. 3. To exempt. 4. To clear from guilt or a charge.—**free, free·ly** *adv.*

free acting	free-footed	free-mouthed
free-armed	free-grown	free-quarter
free-blown	free-hearted	free-spirited
freeboat	freemartin	free swimming
free-bred	free-minded	free-tongued

F

free·board (*free*-bord) *n.* A ship's side between the gunwale and the water line.

free·boot·er (*free*-boo-ter) *n.* Robber; pirate.

free·born *adj.* Not born in slavery or serfdom.

free·dom (*free*-d'm) *n.* 1. Exemption from power or control by another; liberty; independence. 2. Frankness; openness. 3. Liberality. 4. Special privilege; immunity. 5. Exemption from necessity. 6. Facility; ease. 7. License; violation of rules of decorum. 8. A free, unconditional grant.

free-for-all *n.* A general brawl; mass fight.

free·hand *adj.* Drawing or sketching without special instruments or aids.

free·hand·ed *adj.* Liberal; free in giving.

free·hold *n.* Land which may be held for life or be given in inheritance.—**free·hold·er** *n.*

free lance. 1. *Colloquial.* A literary or artistic worker who sells his labor or his product on a piece-work basis. 2. One who speaks or acts solely on his own authority.—**free-lance** *adj.*

free loader. *Slang.* A moocher; sponge; one who presumes on another's generosity.

free love. Doctrine or practice of sexual relationship sanctioned only by the will of the lovers.

free·man *n.* [*pl.* free·men] One who has liberty or all the privileges of citizenship.

Free·mason *n.* Member of a fraternal order with secret ritual based on principles of tolerance, brotherly love, and intellectual freedom.

free·ma·son·ry (*free*-may-s'n-ree) *n.* 1. A natural sentiment of brotherhood or common interest. 2. [*cap.*] The rules, secret ceremonies, etc., of the fraternal order of Freemasons.

free on board; f.o.b. Having the cost of delivery to means of transport included in the price.

free silver. The free, unrestricted coinage of silver at a ratio to gold established by law.

Free-Soil party. A party in the United States which opposed the extension of slavery.

free-spok·en *adj.* Frank; unreserved in speech.

free·stone *adj.* With the stone adhering loosely to the flesh. 'A freestone peach.'

free·think·er *n.* One who avoids the conventional and thinks for himself on religious matters; a deist, an agnostic, or an atheist. —**free·think·ing** *n.* & *adj.*

free trade. Trade or commerce free from tariffs which would hinder the importation of raw materials or products from other countries. —**free trad·er.** An advocate of free trade.

free verse. Poetry with no regular meter or rhyme-scheme.

free will. The power of directing one's own actions by spontaneous, uncontrolled decision.—**free-will** *adj.*

freeze *v.* [froze; froz·en; freez·ing] 1. To change from a liquid to a solid state by coldness; congeal; harden into ice. 2. To become chilled; suffer greatly from the cold. 3. To chill.—*n.* The act of freezing; frost.—**freez·er** *n.*

freezing point. The temperature at which a liquid becomes solid, esp. of water at 32° F.

freight (*frayt*) *n.* 1. The cargo of a ship, railroad, or vehicle; goods carried commercially. 2. Charge for the transportation of goods. 3. Transportation of freight.—*v.* 1. To load with goods; burden. 2. To send or carry as freight.

freight·age (*frayt*-ij) *n.* Freight; freight charges.

freight·er *n.* 1 A cargo ship. 2. One who sends, loads, or forwards freight.

French *adj.* Pertaining to France or its inhabitants.—*n.* 1. The language of France. 2. The French people collectively.

French-born	French-grown
French-bred	French looking
French chop	French-made
French-fashioned	French-minded

French chalk. Soft, white talc for marking cloth.

French horn. A curved brass wind instrument.

FRENCH HORN

French·i·fy (*french*-uh-fye) *v.* Also **french·i·fy.** [-fied; -fy·ing] To become or make French or like the French.

French leave. Departure without permission.

French·man *n.* [*pl.* -men] A native or citizen of France.—**French·wom·an** *n.* [*pl.* -wom·en].

French pancake. A thin, rolled pancake, generally used for dessert.

French toast. Bread dipped in beaten egg and milk, fried, and served with sirup.

French window. Long casement window, hinged at the sides and opening in the middle.

fre·net·ic, fre·net·i·cal. *Variant spellings* of phrenetic, phrenetical.

fren·zied (*fren*-zeed) *adj.* Frantic; maddened.

fren·zy (*fren*-zee) *n.* [*pl.* -zies] Violent fury or excitement; madness; distraction.—*v.* [-zied; -zy·ing] To incite to madness; make frenzied.

Fre·on (*free*-on) *n.* Trade-mark for a nonpoisonous, odorless gas used in refrigerating.

fre·quen·cy (*free*-kw'n-see) *n.* [*pl.* -cies] 1. Frequent repetition; repeated occurrence. 2. Rate of occurrence. 3. *Physics.* Rate of vibration or oscillation of any periodic motion.

frequency modulation. *Abbreviation:* FM. *Radio.* Process of varying the frequency of a carrier wave to conform to audio frequencies impressed upon it. *See* **amplitude modulation.**

fre·quent (*free*-kw'nt) *adj.* 1. Occurring often. 2. Accustomed; habitual.—**fre·quent·ly** *adv.*

fre·quent (free-*kwent*) *v.* To visit often or habitually.—**fre·quen·ta·tion** *n.*—**fre·quent·er** *n.*

fres·co (*fress*-koh) *n.* [*pl.* -coes, -cos] 1. A method of painting on wet, fresh plaster. 2. A fresco painting.—*v.* [fres·coed; fres·co·ing] To paint in fresco.—**fres·co·er** *n.*

fresh *adj.* 1. Undecayed; in good condition; not stale. 2. Not exhausted or wearied; vigorous or renewed in strength. 3. Refreshing; pure. 4. Vivid; bright; not faded. 5. New; recently grown, made, or obtained; not canned or preserved. 6. Not salt. 7. *Slang.* Impolite; impudent. 8. Brisk; strong, as a wind.—*n.* 1. A spring or small stream of fresh water. 2. An overflowing.—**fresh, fresh·ly** *adv.*

fresh-baked	fresh-cut	fresh-leaved
fresh-caught	fresh-faced	fresh looking
fresh-cleaned	fresh-fallen	fresh-made
fresh-colored	fresh-killed	fresh-picked
fresh-cooked	fresh-laid	fresh-watered

fresh·en *v.* 1. To make or become fresh. 2. *Nautical.* To relieve (a rope) by altering the position of a part exposed to friction.

fresh·et *n.* An overflowing of a river or stream.

fresh·man *n.* A first-year student in a school.

fresh-water *adj.* 1. Pertaining to, or living in, water that is fresh, not salt. 2. Having sailed in fresh waters only; raw; unskilled.

fret *v.* [fret·ted; fret·ting] 1. To be irritated; become vexed or peevish. 2. To rub or eat away; chafe; impair. 3. To agitate; disturb; irritate; vex.—*n.* 1. Act or state of agitating or wearing away. 2. A rubbed or frayed spot.

fret *n.* 1. Ornamental carved or perforated work. 2. An ornamental design formed of a series of small straight lines arranged in continuing rectangular forms.—**fret** *v.*

fret *n. Music.* One of the cross bars on the finger boards of some stringed instruments.

fret·ful *adj.* Peevish; ill-humored.—**fret·ful·ly** *adv.*—**fret·ful·ness** *n.*—**fret·some** *adj.*

fret saw. Saw with a fine-toothed blade.

fret·ty *adj.* [fret·ti·er; fret·ti·est] 1. Fretful. 2. Ornamented with fretwork.

fret·work *n.* Ornamental design of frets, esp. when carved or in relief.

Freud·i·an (*froy*-dee-'n) Pertaining to, or derived from, the theories of Sigmund Freud, esp. regarding the causes and treatment of psychopathic disorders and the explanation of dreams, through knowledge of the subconscious. See **psychoanalysis.**—**Freud·i·an** *n.*—**Freud·i·an·ism** *n.*

fri·a·ble (*fry*-uh-b'l) *adj.* Easily crumbled or pulverized.—**fri·a·bil·i·ty** *n.*—**fri·a·ble·ness** *n.*

fri·ar (*fry*-er) *n. Roman Catholic Church.* Male member of a religious order.

fri·ar·y (*fry*-er-ee) *n.* [*pl.* -ries] 1. Home of friars; monastery. 2. Brotherhood of friars. —*adj.* Belonging to a friary.

frib·ble (*frib*-'l) *adj.* Trifling; silly.—*n.* A frivolous person or act.— **frib·ble** *v.*—**frib·bler** *n.*

fric·as·see (frik-uh-*see*) *n.* A dish of meat cut up and cooked in its gravy.—**fric·as·see** *v.*

fric·tion (*frik*-sh'n) *n.* 1. State or act of one body rubbing against another. 2. Relative resistance to motion of touching surfaces. 3. Clash in opinion or scope of activity; disagreement.—**fric·tion·al** *adj.*—**fric·tion·al·ly** *adv.*

Fri·day (*fry*-dee) *n.* The sixth day of the week.

friend (*frend*) *n.* 1. An intimate; close acquaintance. 2. A supporter; adherent. 3. An ally; nation not hostile. 4. [*cap.*] A member of a religious sect who stress meditation in worship; Quaker.—**friend·less** *adj.*

friend·ly (*frend*-lee) *adj.* [friend·li·er; friend·li·est] 1. Affable; congenial; sympathetic. 2. Having peaceful intentions; not hostile, as a nation. 3. Propitious; favorable. 'A friendly breeze.'—**friend·ly** *adv.*—**friend·li·ly** *adv.*—**friend·li·ness** *n.*

friend·ship (*frend*-ship) *n.* 1. Intimacy; fellowship; close attachment. 2. Alliance; good will; amity.

frieze (*freez*) *n. Architecture.* 1. The flat surface or tablet above a column, ornamented by sculpture. 2. A horizontal, ornamenting strip on a wall.

FRIEZE (def. 1)

frig·ate (*frig*-ut) *n.* A square-rigged warship smaller than a capital ship.

frigate bird. An ocean bird having a hooked upper bill and long tail and wings.

fright (*fryte*) *n.* 1. Alarm; terror; sudden fear. 2. *Colloquial.* Anything unpleasing to the eye.

fright·en (*fryte*-un) *v.* To scare; terrify; strike with sudden fear.—**fright·ened** *adj.*—**fright·en·er** *n.*—**fright·en·ing·ly** *adv.*

FRIGATE BIRD (1 / 28 life size)

fright·ful (*fryte*-ful) *adj.* 1. Terrible; shocking; causing alarm. 2. Grotesque; disagreeable.—**fright·ful·ly** *adv.*—**fright·ful·ness** *n.*

frig·id (*frij*-id) *adj.* 1. Icy; extremely cold. 2. Haughty; distant; unfeeling. 3. Sexually unexcitable.—**fri·gid·i·ty** *n.*—**frig·id·ly** *adv.*—**frig·id·ness** *n.*

Frigid Zone. The frozen parts of the earth between the parallels 66°33′ and the poles.

fri·jol, fri·jole (free-*hohl*, free-*hoh*-lay) *n.* [*pl.* -joles] A dark or black Mexican bean.

frill *n.* 1. A ruffle; crimped edging of material; wrinkle. 2. [*pl.*] Ornamentation; nonessential decorations, esp. in dress. 3. Any non-essential or luxurious practice or commodity. 4. *Slang.* A girl.—*v.* 1. To ruffle the feathers, as a bird. 2. To ornament; decorate with frills.—**frill·er** *n.*

fringe (*frinj*) *n.* 1. A tassel; ornamental edging consisting of loose threads. 2. A border; edging. 3. Borderline; outer circle; approach; verge.—*v.* [fringed; fring·ing]—**fring·y** *adj.*

F

frip·per·y (*frip*-er-ee) *n.* [*pl.* -ies] Showy or tawdry finery; cheap bauble.

frisk *v.* 1. To frolic; gambol; caper. 2. *Slang.* To search (a person) for concealed objects.—*n.* A frolic; fit of gaiety.—*adj.* Frisky.

frisk·y *adj.* [frisk·i·er; -i·est] Lively; sprightly; animated.—**frisk·i·ly** *adv.*—**frisk·i·ness** *n.*

frith *n.* Also **firth**. A strait; inlet; estuary.

frit·il·lar·y (*frit*-uh-lehr-ee) *n.* [*pl.* -ies] 1. Family of bulb-bearing plants with single, mottled flowers. 2. Species of spotted butterfly.

frit·ter *n.* 1. A piece of batter or batter-covered food fried in deep fat. 2. A fragment; bit.—*v.* To waste by small degrees.—**frit·ter·er** *n.*

fri·vol·i·ty (frih-*vol*-uh-tee) *n.* [*pl.* -ties] 1. Levity; lightness; silliness. 2. Triviality.

friv·o·lous (*friv*-uh-lus) *adj.* 1. Trivial; unimportant. 2. Silly; gay; giddy.

friz, frizz *v.* [frizzed; friz·zing] To make small, tight curls or tufts.—*n.* Any tightly curled material.—**friz·er, friz·zer** *n.*

friz·zle *v.* [-zled; -zling] To crimp; make small, tight curls.—**friz·zly** *adj.* Kinky; tightly curled.

friz·zle *v.* [friz·zled; -zling] To sizzle; fry.

fro (*froh*) *adv.* From; away. 'Walk to and fro.'

frock *n.* 1. A dress; gown. 2. A monk's outer robe.—*v.* 1. To put on a dress. 2. To invest with the office of monk.

frock coat. A man's double-breasted dress coat.

frog *n.* 1. A tailless, web-footed amphibian. 2. The horny growth on the sole of a horse's hoof. 3. A crossplate; device in a railway track which permits switching. 4. A braided loop on a garment.—*v.* [frogged; frog·ging] To hunt frogs.—**frog·gy** *adj.* [-gi·er; -gi·est].

frol·ic (*frol*-ik) *adj.* 1. Gay; jubilant. 2. Mischievous; playing pranks.—*n.* Play; sport; fun-making; prank.—*v.* [frol·icked; frol·ick·ing]—**frol·ick·er** *n.*—**frol·ick·ly** *adj.*

frol·ic·some (*frol*-ik-sum) *adj.* 1. Gay; sportive. 2. Mischievous; given to pranks.

from *prep.* 1. Away; toward a more distant place. 2. Out of; off. 3. Originating with; starting at. 4. Since 'From 1776 on.'

frond *n. Botany.* 1. A fern leaf. 2. The leafy shoot of a lichen, etc.—**frond·ed** *adj.*

front (*frunt*) *n.* 1. The forepart; face; forward surface. 2. Countenance; outward behavior or appearance. 3. *Colloquial.* Pretense of wealth or position. 4. Battleground; scene of military action. 5. Land facing a street, water, etc.—*adj.* Relating to or at the front. —*v.* To face, stand opposite, confront.

front·age (*frunt*-ij) *n.* 1. The front surface or exposure of a building. 2. Front part of a lot; land between a building and the street.

fron·tal (*frunt*-'l) *n.* 1. A forehead bone. 2. A head or face band.—*adj.* Relating to the front or forehead.—**fron·tal·ly** *adv.*

fron·tier (frun-*teer*) *n.* 1. The boundary or border of a country. 2. The farthest region of civilization or human settlement. 3. An un-

explored or undeveloped region; outpost, as of science.—*adj.* Bordering; outlying.

fron·tiers·man (frun-*teerz*-m'n) *n.* [*pl.* -men] A frontier dweller.

fron·tis·piece (*frun*-tiss-peess) *n.* Picture or design facing the title page of a book.

frost (*frawst*) *n.* 1. Freezing temperature or condition. 2. Also **hoarfrost.** Frozen particles of moisture or vapor. 3. Coldness of spirit or manner.—*v.* 1. To cover with frost or frosting. 2. To harm by frost.

frost-beaded	**frost-fettered**	**frostproof**
frostbird	**frost-free**	**frost pure**
frost-bound	**frost-hardy**	**frost-rent**
frostbow	**frost-killed**	**frost-riven**
frost-burnt	**frost-nipped**	**frostwork**

frost·bite *v.* [-bit; -bit·ten; -bit·ing] To injure or blight by frost.—*n.* Injury caused by exposure to severe cold.—**frost·bit·ten** *adj.*

frost·ing *n.* 1. Icing; a sugared preparation for covering cakes. 2. A mat finish on glass.

frost·y *adj.* [-i·er; -i·est] 1. Icy; wintry. 2. Cold; distant. 3. Hoar; resembling frost. —**frost·i·ly** *adv.*—**frost·i·ness** *n.*

froth *n.* 1. Foam; surface bubbles on a liquid. 2. A foam of saliva running from the mouth. 3. Anything airy, unsubstantial, or trivial.—*v.* 1. To foam or cause to foam. 2. To emit a foam of saliva.—**froth·er** *n.*

froth·y *adj.* [-i·er; -i·est] Foamy; unsubstantial. —**froth·i·ly** *adv.*—**froth·i·ness** *n.*

frou·frou (*froo*-froo) *n.* Fussy femininity.

fro·ward (*froh*-erd) *adj.* Perverse; ungovernable; willful.—**fro·ward·ly** *adv.*— **-ward·ness** *n.*

frown *v.* 1. To scowl; wrinkle the brow, as in thought or anger. 2. To show disapproval; act or look displeased.—*n.* 1. A scowl; stern or displeased look. 2. Expression of disapproval.—**frown·er** *n.*—**frown·ing·ly** *adv.*

frowz·y (*frow*-zee) *adj.* [-i·er; -i·est] Also **frows·y.** Slovenly; slatternly; unkempt. —**frowz·i·ly** *adv.*—**frowz·i·ness** *n.*

fro·zen (*froh*-z'n) *adj.* 1. Icy; characterized by severe cold. 2. Congealed or benumbed by cold; turned into ice. 3. Not easily sold or converted into cash. 'Frozen assets.'

fruc·ti·fy (*fruk*-tuh-fye) *v.* [-ti·fied; -fy·ing] To bear fruit; make fruitful or productive.—**fruc·tif·er·ous** *adj.*—**fruc·ti·fi·ca·tion** *n.*

fruc·tose (*fruk*-tohss) *n. Chemistry.* Fruit sugar.

fru·gal (*froo*-g'l) *adj.* 1. Thrifty; economical; avoiding waste. 2. Meager; scanty. 'A frugal meal.'—**fru·gal·ly** *adv.*—**fru·gal·ness** *n.*

fru·gal·i·ty (froo-*gal*-uh-tee) *n.* [*pl.* -ties] Thrift.

fruit (*froot*) *n.* 1. The edible product of a plant, tree, etc. 2. The ripened part of a plant containing the seeds. 3. The result; consequence; product. 4. [*pl.*] All useful plant products.—*v.* To produce or develop fruit.

fruit grower	**fruitman**	**fruitwoman**
fruit growing	**fruitstalk**	**fruitworm**

fruit cake. A heavy spiced cake filled with raisins, currants, and chopped candied fruit.

fruit·er·er *n.* A dealer in fruits.

fruit fly. The Drosophila; a small fly, used in the study of eugenics, whose larvae feed on decaying or fermenting fruit.

fruit·ful *adj.* 1. Productive; fertile. 2. Profitable; rewarding; bringing results.—**fruit·ful·ly** *adv.*—**fruit·ful·ness** *n.*

fru·i·tion (froo-*ih*-sh'n) *n.* 1. Realization; consummation; fulfillment. 2. Enjoyment; pleasure of use.

fruit·less *adj.* 1. Barren; unproductive. 2. Vain; futile; useless.—**fruit·less·ly** *adv.*

fruit'sugar. Fructose; levulose.

fruit·y *adj.* [fruit·i·er; fruit·i·est] Resembling fruit, esp. in taste.—**fruit·i·ness** *n.*

fru·men·ty (*froo*-m'n-tee) *n.* A hulled wheat and milk pudding.

frump *n.* A dowdy or old-fashioned woman. —**frump·ish** *adj.*—**frump·y** *adj.*

frus·trate (*fruss*-trayt) *v.* [-trat·ed; -trat·ing] 1. To thwart; balk; prevent from succeeding. 2. To defeat; render null.—*adj.* Frustrated. —**frus·trat·er** *n.*—**frus·tra·tive** *adj.*

frus·tra·tion (fruss-*tray*-sh'n) *n.* 1. Defeat; disappointment. 2. Embitterment caused by failure.

frus·tum (*fruss*-t'm) *n.* [*pl.* -tums, -ta] *Geometry.* 1. Portion of a conical solid left after the top is cut off parallel to the base. 2. The part of a solid between any two of its parallel planes.

FRUSTUM

fry *n.* [*pl.* fry] 1. Young fish or small adult fish living in schools. 2. Group or brood of young; offspring. 3. Group of unimportant persons or things. 'Small fry.'

fry *v.* [fried; fry·ing] 1. To cook in fat over a flame. 2. *Slang.* To die in the electric chair.—*n.* [*pl.* fries] A dish, esp. of animal entrails, prepared by frying.

fry·er, fri·er *n.* 1. A pan for frying. 2. One who fries. 3. A young fowl.

fuch·sia (*fyoo*-shuh) *n.* 1. A garden plant with drooping red and purple flowers. 2. A deep bluish red color.— **fuch·sia** *adj.*

fud·dle (*fud*-'l) *v.* [fud·dled; fud·dling] To stupefy with drink.

fudge (*fuhj*) *n.* 1. A confection of butter, sugar and often chocolate. 2. A fictitious story; nonsense.—*inter.* Nonsense!—*v.* [fudged; fudg·ing] To bungle; patch; contrive imperfectly.

FUCHSIA

fu·el (*fyoo*-'l) *n.* 1. Combustible material producing fire or power. 2. That which inflames or excites.—*v.* [fu·eled, fu·elled; fu·el·ing, fu·el·ling] To supply with or obtain fuel.—**fu·el·er, fu·el·ler** *n.*

fu·gi·tive (*fyoo*-juh-tiv) *adj.* 1. Fleeing; escaping; straying. 2. Impermanent; passing; evanescent. 'Fugitive delights.' 3. Dealing with temporary interests.—*n.* A runaway; refugee.—**fu·gi·tive·ly** *adv.*—**fu·gi·tive·ness** *n.*

fugue (*fyoog*) *n. Music.* A composition of several themes arranged in counterpoint.

Füh·rer (*feer*-er, *fyoor*-er) *n. German.* Leader, esp. the title assumed by Adolf Hitler.

Fu·ji·ya·ma (fyoo-jee-*yah*-muh). Also **Fu·ji.** Mountain on the island of Honshu, in Japan.

-ful *suffix.* Denoting: 1. Full of; marked by; having. 'Delightful.' 2. Amount to fill. 'Spoonful.'

ful·crum (*ful*-kr'm) *n.* [*pl.* crums, -cra] A prop, support, esp. for a lever.

ful·fill, ful·fil (ful-*fil*) *v.* [-filled; -fill·ing] To execute; carry out; complete by performance.—**ful·fill·er** *n.* —**ful·fill·ment, ful·fil·ment** *n.*

ful·gent (*ful*-j'nt) *adj.* Radiant; dazzling. —**ful·gent·ly** *adv.*

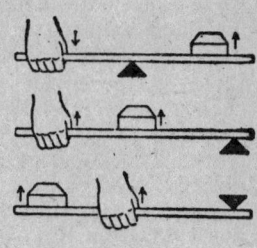
FULCRUM

full *adj.* 1. Replete; filled; having no empty space. 2. Abundant; well-supplied; sated. 3. Complete; entire; at its greatest size, development, etc. 'A full moon.' 4. Sonorous; loud; distinct. 5. Plump; filled out. 6. Wide; made with gathers.—*n.* Maximum or utmost in measure, extent, etc.—*adv.* Fully; completely. —*v.* To make full.— **full·ness, ful·ness** *n.*—**fully** *adv.*

full-attended	full-drawn	full-powered
full-banked	full face	full-rigged
full-bearded	full-faced	full ripe
full bearing	full-grown	full-ripened
full-bellied	full hand	full scale
full-bloomed	full-handed	full-size
full-bodied	full-laden	full-sized
full-bosomed	full load	full speed
full charge	full mouth	full strength
full-charged	full-mouthed	full-toned
full depth	full-paid	full-weighted

full·back *n. Football.* A backfield player.

full-blooded *adj.* Thoroughbred; of unmixed breed.

full dress. Formal clothes for evening wear.

full·er (*ful*-er) *n.* One who thickens cloth.

fuller's earth. A substance resembling powdered clay, for cleaning cloth.

full-fledged *adj.* Completed; fully developed; having met all necessary requirements.

full house. *Poker.* Three of a kind and a pair.

ful·mi·nate (*ful*-muh-nayt) *v.* [-nat·ed; -nat·ing] 1. To explode; detonate. 2. To utter with violence or threats; thunder. 3. To strike violently, as a disease.—*n.* An explosive crystalline salt.—**ful·mi·na·tion** *n.*—**ful·mi·na·tor** *n.*—**ful·mi·na·to·ry** *adj.*

F

ful·some (*ful*-s'm) *adj.* Sickeningly excessive; disgusting; offensive. 'His fulsome praise.'

fu·ma·to·ry (*fyoo*-muh-toh-ree) *n.* [*pl.* -ries] An airtight place for disinfecting plants.—*adj.* Pertaining to smoking.

fum·ble (*fum*-b'l) *v.* [-bled; -bling] 1. To grope; search about awkwardly. 2. To handle clumsily. 3. *Sports.* To fail to catch or hold (the ball).—*n.* A fumbling motion or action.—**fum·bler** *n.*

fume (*fyoom*) *n.* 1. A vapor; smoke; any stifling or fragrant gas. 2. A fit of temper.—*v.* [fumed; fum·ing] 1. To emit smoke or vapor. 2. To rage; rant angrily.—**fum·ing·ly** *adv.*

fu·mi·gate (*fyoom*-uh-gayt) *v.* [-gat·ed; -gat·ing] 1. To disinfect with a germicidal gas. 2. To render the air fragrant with incense. —**fu·mi·ga·tion** *n.*—**fu·mi·ga·tor** *n.*

fum·y (*fyoom*-ee) *adj.* [-i·er; -i·est] Producing or filled with vapors.—**fum·i·ly** *adv.*—**fum·i·ness** *n.*

fun *n.* Amusement; enjoyment; sport.—*v.* [funned; fun·ning] To joke; make sport of.

func·tion (*funk*-shun) *n.* 1. Office; purpose; duty. 2. A faculty; operation; anything performed by an organ. 3. An important public ceremony. 4. *Mathematics.* A quantity varying in relation to another quantity. 5. Anything which varies according to another variable.—*v.* To perform; act; work.

func·tion·al (*funk*-shun-ul) *adj.* 1. *Physiology.* Relating to the operation of an organ. 2. Having a function; designed for use; practical. 3. *Medical.* Affecting the use of a bodily part without affecting the part itself.

func·tion·al·ism (*funk*-shun-ul-izm) *n.* Any theory or doctrine that stresses practicality and function over other considerations.

func·tion·ar·y (*funk*-shun-ehr-ee) *n.* [*pl.* -ies] An official; officeholder.

fund *n.* 1. Money set aside for a specific purpose. 2. A permanent debt owed by a government. 3. Stock; capital for conducting a business. 4. An ample stock; abundant supply. 5. [*pl.*] Money.—*v.* 1. To put a debt in the form of long-range stocks or bonds. 2. To provide money.

fun·da·ment·al (fun-duh-*men*-t'l) *adj.* 1. Elementary; primary; basic. 2. Essential; of principal importance.—*n.* 1. A requisite; essential. 2. A basic principle. 3. *Physics.* In a complex light or sound wave, that wave having the lowest frequency of vibration.

fun·da·men·tal·ism (fun-duh-*men*-t'l-izm) *n.* 1. [*cap.*] *Theology.* Adherence to a literal interpretation of the Scriptures. 2. Rigid observance of an original creed.— -**tal·ist** *n.* & *adj.*

fund·ing *n.* Conversion of a short-range debt or equity into interest-bearing securities to be paid off over a long period.—**fund·ed** *adj.*

fu·ner·al (*fyoo*-ner-ul) *adj.* Relating to burial of corpses.—*n.* A burial; interment.

fu·ne·re·al (fyoo-*nihr*-ee-ul) *adj.* Mournful; gloomy; solemn.—**fu·ne·re·al·ly** *adv.*

fun·gi·cide (*fun*-jih-syde) *n.* Disinfectant for mold, bacteria, and other fungi.— -**cid·al** *adj.*

fun·goid (*fun*-goyd) *adj.* Like a fungus in growth or other characteristics.—*n.* A fungus plant.

fun·gous (*fung*-gus) *adj.* 1. Like or caused by fungi. 2. Springing up; growing swiftly.

fun·gus (*fung*-gus) *n.* [*pl.* -gi, -gus·es] 1. A colorless parisitic spore plant, as mold, mushrooms, etc. 2. A spongy growth attacking animal bodies.—*adj.* Having the properties of a fungus.

fu·nic·u·lar (fyoo-*nik*-yuh-ler) *adj.* Towed or held taut by a cord or cable.

funk *n. Colloquial.* 1. Panic; fear. 2. One stricken with fear.—*v. Colloquial.* 1. To shrink fearfully. 2. To frighten.

fun·nel (*fun*-'l) *n.* 1. A hollow cone used to prevent spilling in pouring liquids. 2. The smokestack of a steamship. 3. A flue or pipe for vapors and gases.—*v.* [-neled, -nelled; -nel·ing, -nel·ling] To convey or pour through a funnel.

fun·ny (*fun*-ee) *adj.* [-ni·er; -ni·est] 1. Humorous; comical. 2. *Colloquial.* Strange; surprising; peculiar.—**fun·ni·ly** *adv.* —**fun·ni·ness** *n.*

FUNNEL (def. 1)

funny bone. A projection on the elbow which tingles when bumped.

fur *n.* 1. The thick, hairy covering of certain mammals. 2. A pelt; animal skin. 3. A garment of fur. 4. Fuzz; matter collected on the tongue.—*v.* [furred; fur·ring] To cover or line with fur or a fuzzy material.—**fur** *adj.*

fur·be·low (*fer*-buh-loh) *n.* 1. A pleat, crimp or frill, esp. on women's clothes. 2. [*pl.*] Frilly ornamentation.—**fur·be·low** *v.*

fur·bish (*fer*-bish) *v.* 1. To polish; burnish. 2. To renovate; restore.—**fur·bish·er** *n.*

fu·ri·ous (*fyoor*-ee-us) *adj.* 1. Raging; moved by anger. 2. Frenzied; vehement. 3. Turbulent; violent.— -**ous·ly** *adv.*— -**ous·ness** *n.*

furl *v.* To gather or roll up; wind.—*n.* A roll; bundle.—**furl·er** *n.*

fur·long (*fer*-lawng) *n.* An eighth of a mile.

fur·lough (*fer*-loh) *n. Military.* An official leave of absence.—*v.* To grant a leave.

fur·nace (*fer*-nuss) *n.* A chamber where heat is produced by burning fuel.

fur·nish (*fer*-nish) *v.* 1. To equip; supply with. 2. To install furniture and other housekeeping necessities.—**fur·nish·er** *n.*

fur·nish·ing (*fer*-nish-ing) *n.* 1. [*pl.*] Fixtures; furniture. 2. Any basic requirement.

fur·ni·ture (*fer*-nih-cher) *n.* 1. Any necessary furnishings or equipment, esp. for the household. 2. Pieces of wood or metal used to fill out blank spaces in a form.

fu·ror, fu·rore (*fyoor*-or) *n.* 1. Commotion; an outburst of excitement. 2. A current enthusiasm; fad. 3. Rage; wild enthusiasm.

furred (*furd*) *adj.* Ornamental or coated with fur.

fur·ri·er (*fur*-ee-er) *n.* 1. A dealer in furs. 2. A dresser of fur.

fur·ring (*fur*-ing) *n.* Material used to level the surface of a wall or floor. 2. Fur trimmings.

fur·row (*fur*-oh) *n.* 1. A trench; rut; wrinkle. 2. A groove made by a plow.—*v.* 1. To plow. 2. To wrinkle, as the brow.— -**row·er** *n.*

fur·ry (*fur*-ee) *adj.* [fur·ri·er; fur·ri·est] 1. Covered with or resembling fur. 2. Coated with fuzz, as the tongue.—**fur·ri·ness** *n.*

fur·ther (*fer*-ther) *adj.* 1. More remote in time or degree. 2. Additional; more.—*adv.* 1. To a greater extent. 2. Moreover; in addition. —*v.* To promote; advance; help.

fur·ther·ance (*fer*-ther-unss) *n.* Promotion; aid.

fur·ther·more (*fer*-ther-mor) *adv.* Moreover; in addition; besides.

fur·ther·most (*fer*-ther-mohst) *adj.* Most remote.

fur·thest (*fer*-thist) *adj. & adv.* Most remote in time or extent; to the greatest degree.

fur·tive (*fur*-tiv) *adj.* Stealthy; sly; secret.

fu·ry (*fyoor*-ee) *n.* [*pl.* -ries] 1. Rage; anger. 2. Turbulence; impetuous motion; frenzy. 3. [*cap.*] *Mythology.* An avenging goddess or spirit.

furze (*ferz*) *n.* Gorse; a spiny, evergreen shrub of the pea family.—**fur·zy** *adj.*

fuse, fuze (*fyooz*) *n.* 1. A small tube of explosive material for detonating a main explosive charge. 2. A protective device containing a thin strip of metal which melts under an overload of electricity, breaking the circuit.

fuse *v.* [fused; fus·ing] 1. To melt; be reduced to fluid by heat. 2. To unite; intermingle.

fu·see, fu·zee (fyoo-*zee*) *n.* 1. A friction match not easily extinguished by the wind. 2. A railroad warning flare. 3. *Slang.* A firecracker which does not explode.

fu·se·lage (*fyoo*-z'l-ij; -ahj) *n. Aviation.* The main, central chamber of an airplane.

fusel oil (*fyoo*-z'l). An oily, poisonous, colorless alcohol found in poorly distilled liquor.

fu·si·ble (*fyoo*-zuh-b'l) *adj.* Capable of being liquefied or melted.—**fu·si·bil·i·ty, fu·si·ble·ness** *n.*—**fu·si·bly** *adv.*

fu·sil·lade (fyoo-z'l-*ayd*) *n.* A volley; firing of guns in rapid succession.—*v.* [-lad·ed; -lad·ing] To shoot by a fusillade.

fu·sion (*fyoo*-zhun) *n.* 1. Liquefaction by heat. 2. A blending, mingling; union.

fu·sion·ism (-izm) *n.* Advocation of the union or coalition of two or more political parties.

fuss *n.* 1. Bustle; unnecessary activity. 2. Tumult; confusion.—*v.* To bustle; indulge in trifling activity; fidget.—**fuss·er** *n.*

fuss·y *adj.* [fuss·i·er; fuss·i·est] Concerned with trifles; meticulous about small details.—**fuss·i·ly** *adv.*—**fuss·i·ness** *n.*

fus·tian (*fuss*-chun) *n.* 1. A coarse, twill-woven cotton. 2. Bombastic speech or writing; pompousness.—**fus·tian** *adj.*

fust·y (*fuss*-tee) *adj.* [fust·i·er; fust·i·est] 1. Rancid; moldy. 2. Antiquated; old-fogyish.—**fust·i·ly** *adv.*—**fust·i·ness** *n.*

fu·tile (*fyoo*-t'l) *adj.* Vain; useless; trifling.—**fu·tile·ly** *adv.*— -**tile·ness** *n.*— -**til·i·ty** *n.* [-ties].

fu·ture (*fyoo*-cher) *adj.* Forthcoming; in time to come.—*n.* 1. Any time after the present. 2. Prospect; outlook. 3. [*pl.*] Commodities bought or sold for delivery at a later date.

fu·tur·ism (*fyoo*-cher-izm) *n.* A school translating the idea of motion and energy into painting and the plastic arts.—**fu·tur·ist** *n. & adj.*

fu·tur·i·ty (fyoo-*tyoor*-ih-tee) *n.* [*pl.* -ties] 1. Contingency; coming event. 2. The future.

fuzz *n.* 1. Minute fibers; fluff. 2. Down; fine hairs.—*v.* To remove or cover with fuzz.

fuzz·y *adj.* [fuzz·i·er; fuzz·i·est] Like or covered with down.—**fuzz·i·ly** *adv.*—**fuzz·i·ness** *n.*

G

gab *n. Colloquial.* Chatter; idle talk.—*v.* [gabbed; gab·bing].—**gab·by** *adj.* [gab·bi·er; gab·bi·est].

gab·ar·dine (gab-er-*deen*) *n.* 1. A finely ribbed woolen, rayon, or cotton fabric. 2. Gaberdine.

gab·ble (*gab*-'l) *v.* [gab·bled; gab·bling] To talk or utter sounds rapidly and inarticulately; jabber.—**gab·ble** *n.*—**gab·bler** *n.*

gab·er·dine (gab-er-*deen*) *n.* Also **gab·ar·dine.** Long, loose coat worn, esp. by Jews, in the Middle Ages.

ga·ble (*gay*-b'l) *n.* 1. *Architecture.* The triangular end of a building from the eaves to the top. 2. A triangular ornament on a building.—*v.* [ga·bled; ga·bling]—**ga·bled** *adj.*

Ga·bri·el (*gay*-bree-ul) *n. Bible.* Archangel heralding the coming of the Messiah; bringer of good news and comfort.

gad *v.* [gad·ded; gad·ding] To move about idly or restlessly, esp. seeking pleasure.—**gad·der** *n.*

gad *n.* A small rod; goad.

gad. Interjection expressing surprise, annoyance, etc.

gad·a·bout (*gad*-uh-bowt) *n. Colloquial.* One who wanders about purposelessly.—**gad·a·bout** *adj.*

gad·fly (*gad*-fly) *n.* 1. A fly which stings cattle, horses, etc. 2. An annoying person.

gadg·et (*gaj*-it) *n.* 1. Device; small contrivance, esp. mechanical, for performing a function. 2. *Colloquial.* An ingenious ornament.

gad·o·lin·i·um (gad-uh-*lin*-ee-um) *n.* A rare metallic element. (*Symbol:* Gd).

Gael (*gayl*) *n.* A Scottish Highlander or Celt. —**Gael·ic** *n.* Celtic language.—**Gael·ic** *adj.*

gaff *n.* 1. Strong iron hook or spear for pulling in large fish. 2. *Nautical.* Spar on the upper edge of a fore-and-aft sail. 3. *Slang.* Strain; difficulties.—**gaff** *v.*

gaffe (*gaf*) *n.* A mistake; error; faux pas.

gaf·fer (*gaf*-er) *n.* An old man.

gag *v.* [gagged; gag·ging] 1. To prevent from speaking by covering or obstructing the mouth. 2. To silence. 3. To choke with nausea; retch. 4. *Slang.* To joke.—*n.* 1. Object thrust into the mouth to prevent speech; forcible hindrance of free speech. 2. *Slang.* An amusing remark; clever joke or trick.

gage (*gayj*) *n.* A pledge; pawn; security.

gage, gag·er. *Variant spelling* of **gauge, gauger.**

gai·e·ty (*gay*-uh-tee) *n.* [*pl.* -ties] 1. Light-heartedness; merriment. 2. Brilliance; finery.

gai·ly (*gay*-lee) *adv.* Also **gay·iy.** In a gay manner; merrily; brightly.

gain (*gayn*) *n.* 1. A profit; increase, advantage. 2. Acquisition.—*v.* 1. To acquire; earn; obtain. 2. To win. 3. To reach; arrive at.

gain·ful *adj.* Profitable; advantageous.—**gain·ful·ly** *adv.*—**gain·ful·ness** *n.*

gain·less *adj.* Profitless.—**gain·less·ness** *n.*

gain·ly *adj.* Shapely; well-formed.— **-li·ness** *n.*

gain·say *v.* [gain·said; gain·say·ing] To contradict; deny; dispute.—**gain·say·er** *n.*

'gainst, gainst (*genst*) *prep. & conj.* Against.

gait (*gayt*) *n.* 1. Manner of walking. 2. Movement of the feet in stepping along, esp. of horses.—**gait·ed** *adj.*

gai·ter (*gay*-ter) *n.* 1. A cloth or leather covering for the lower leg or ankle. 2. An overshoe with a cloth upper.

ga·la (*gay*-luh) *n.* Festive occasion; holiday.

ga·lac·tic (guh-*lak*-tik) *adj. Astronomy.* Pertaining to the Galaxy.

Gal·a·had (*gal*-uh-had) *n.* King Arthur's purest knight, finder of the Holy Grail.

gal·an·tine (*gal*-'n-teen) *n.* A dish of boned and stuffed meat or fish, served cold in aspic.

Ga·la·tia (guh-*lay*-shuh). Ancient Roman province in Asia Minor.—**Ga·la·ti·an** *adj. & n.*

Gal·a·ti·ans *n.* Paul's Epistle to the Galatians, book of the New Testament.

gal·ax·y (*gal*-uks-ee) *n.* [*pl.* -ies] 1. [*cap.*] *Astronomy.* Luminous band of stars; the Milky Way. 2. Brilliant company of beauty or talent.

gale *n.* 1. *Nautical.* A wind of 25- to 75-miles-per-hour velocity. 2. A strong wind. 3. An outburst. 'A gale of laughter.'

Ga·len (*gay*-len) *n.* Second-century Greek physician.

ga·le·na (guh-*lee*-nuh) *n.* Sulphide of lead. (*Symbol:* PbS).

Gal·i·le·an (gal-ih-*lee*-un) *n.* 1. A native of Galilee, in Judea. 2. Member of a Jewish sect which opposed the payment of tribute to the Romans.—*adj.* 1. *Geography.* Pertaining to Galilee. 2. Pertaining to Galileo.

Gal·i·le·o (gal-ih-*lay*-oh). Italian physicist and astronomer of the Renaissance.

gal·i·ot, gal·li·ot (*gal*-ee-ut) *n.* A Dutch or Flemish sailing vessel for cargoes.

gall (*gawl*) *n.* 1. *Physiology.* Bile; a bitter yellowish-green secretion of the liver. 2. Bitter feeling; rancor. 3. Painfully wounding experience. 4. *Colloquial.* Impudence.

gall *n.* 1. Sore produced by chafing of the skin. 2. A cause of vexation or chagrin. —*v.* To vex; irritate.

gall *n.* On plants, a growth produced by insects and used in dyes, ink, and medicine.

gal·lant (*gal*-'nt) *adj.* 1. Brave; chivalrous; noble. 2. (guh-*lant*) Attentive to women. —(*gal*-'nt) *n.* A gay, dashing young man, esp. one who pays court to women.—**gal·lant** (guh-*lant*) *v.*—**gal·lant·ly** *adv.*

gal·lant·ry (*gal*-un-tree) *n.* [*pl.* -ries] 1. Bravery; heroism. 2. Great attention to women.

gall bladder. *Anatomy.* A small pear-shaped sac which receives the gall from the liver.

gal·le·on (*gal*-ee-un) *n.* A large sailing ship, used esp. by Spain during colonial expansion.

GALLEON

gal·ler·y (*gal*-er-ee) *n.* [*pl.* -ies] 1. Seating space above the main floor of churches, theaters, etc. 2. An exhibition hall. 'An art gallery.' 3. A corridor; hall. 4. *Nautical.* A balcony-like projection from a ship. 5. Porch.

gal·ley (*gal*-ee) *n.* [*pl.* -leys] 1. *Printing.* A tray used for holding composed types. 2. A sea-going vessel navigated by oars and sails, once common in the Mediterranean. 3. A ship's kitchen.

GALLEY (def. 2)

galley proof. *Printing.* Trial impressions taken for corrections, before making up pages.

galley slave. A convict condemned to work at the oars of a galley.

gall·fly *n.* An insect which produces gall, a vegetable excrescence, by depositing its eggs in a plant.

gal·liard (*gal*-yerd) *n.* 1. A gay, dashing person. 2. A sprightly 16th-century dance.

Gal·lic (*gal*-ik) *adj.* Pertaining to Gaul or France.

gallic acid *n.* A crystalline product of the decomposition of tannic acid, used in dyes and inks. (*Symbol:* $C_7H_6O_5$).

Gal·li·cism, gal·li·cism (*gal*-ih-sizm) *n.* A French idiom.

Gal·li·cize (*gal*-ih-syze) *v.* [gal·li·cized; gal·li·ciz·ing] To make an expression conform to the French idiom.

gal·li·gas·kins (gal-ih-*gass*-kins) *n. pl.* 1. Large loose breeches. 2. Leather guards worn on the legs by sportsmen.

gal·li·mau·fry (gal-ih-*maw*-free) *n.* [*pl.* -fries] 1. A meat stew. 2. A jumbled mixture.

Gal·li·na·ce·ae (gal-ih-*nay*-see-ee) *n.* Group of birds including domestic fowls.— -ceous *adj.*

gall·ing (*gawl*-ing) *adj.* Vexing; aggravating.

gal·li·pot (*gal*-ih-pot) *n.* 1. A small pot used by druggists for medicines. 2. A kind of resin.

gal·li·um (*gal*-ee-um) *n. Chemistry.* A rare, malleable metal, liquid above 26° F. (*Symbol:* Ga).

gal·li·vant (gal-ih-*vant*) *v.* To gad; go out frequently for pleasure.

gall·nut *n.* A vegetable excrescence in plants.

gal·lon (*gal*-un) *n.* A liquid and dry unit of measure containing four quarts.

gal·loon (guh-*loon*) *n.* A kind of lace or binding used as trimming.—**gal·looned** *adj.*

gal·lop (*gal*-up) *n.* A leaping gait, esp. of a horse.—**gal·lop·er** *n.*—**gal·lop** *v.*

Gal·lo·way (*gal*-uh-way) *n.* A small horse originally bred in Galloway, Scotland.

gal·lows (*gal*-ohz) *n.* [*pl.* -lows·es] A framework on which criminals are hanged.

gallows bird. One who deserves to be hanged.

gall·stone (*gawl*-stohn) *n.* A solid substance formed abnormally in the gall bladder.

gal·op (*gal*-up) *n.* 1. A lively dance. 2. The music for the dance in 2/4 time.

GALLOWS

ga·losh (guh-*losh*) *n.* [*pl.* ga·losh·es]An overshoe.

ga·lore (guh-*lor*) *adv. Colloquial.* Abundantly.

gal·va·nism (*gal*-vuh-nizm) *n.* 1. Current electricity produced by chemical action, esp. from the decomposition of metals. 2. Branch of physics dealing with electric current.

gal·va·nize *v.* [gal·va·nized; gal·va·niz·ing] 1. To treat with a continuous electric current. 2. To plate with zinc by electrolysis. 3. To excite.—**gal·va·ni·za·tion** *n.*—**gal·va·niz·er** *n.*

galvanized iron. Zinc-coated, rust-resisting iron.

gal·va·nom·e·ter (gal-vuh-*nom*-it-er) *n.* An instrument for determining the strength of weak electric current.—**gal·va·no·met·ric** (gal-van-uh-*met*-rik) *adj.*—**gal·va·nom·e·try** *n.*

gal·van·o·scope (gal-*van*-uh-skohp) *n.* An instrument for detecting the existence and direc-tion of an electric current.—**gal·van·o·scop·ic** (gal-van-uh-*skop*-ik) *adj.*—**gal·va·nos·co·py** *n.*

gam *n. Slang.* The leg, esp. a woman's.

gam·bit (*gam*-bit) *n. Chess.* Sacrifice of a pawn at the opening of a game to gain an advantage.

gam·ble (*gam*-b'l) *v.* [gam·bled; gam·bling] 1. To play for money or other stake. 2. To participate in a game of chance. 3. To take a risk.—*n.* A risky project.—**gam·bling** *n.*

gam·boge (gam-*bohj*) *n.* A yellow gum-resin obtained from certain trees and used as a purgative.

gam·bol (*gam*-b'l) *v.* [gam·boled, gam·bolled; gam·bol·ing, gam·bol·ling] To frolic; dance and skip about in sport or joy.—**gam·bol** *n.*

gam·brel (*gam*-brul) *n.* The hock, esp. of a horse.

gambrel roof. A roof having a double slope on each side.

game *n.* 1. Sport of any kind. 2. Play; pastime; amusement. 3. A contest between two or more players. 4. Wild animals or birds which are hunted; any object of pursuit.—*v.* [gamed; gam·ing] 1. To play for a stake or prize; gamble. 2. To play at a sport or diversion.—*adj.* 1. Plucky; courageous; resolute. 2. Ready; prepared to do something.—**game·ly** *adv.*—**game·ness** *n.*

game *adj.* Crippled; lame. 'A game leg.'

game·cock *n.* A cock bred for fighting.

game·keep·er *n.* One who is employed to look after and protect animals kept for sport.

game·some (*gaym*-sum) *adj.* Playful; gay.

game·ster (*gaym*-ster) *n.* A gambler.

gam·ete (*gam*-eet) *n.* A fully developed reproductive cell, capable of uniting with a cell from the opposite sex to form a new individual.

gam·in (*gam*-in) *n.* A child of the streets.

gam·ing (*gaym*-ing) *n.* Gambling.

gamma ray. One of the three types of radiation emitted by radium and other radioactive elements, used in treatment of cancer.

gam·mon (*gam*-un) *n. Colloquial.* Humbug; hoax; imposition.—*v.* To delude.

gam·ut *n.* 1. *Music.* The entire scale. 2. A complete series; entire range.

gam·y (*gaym*-ee) *adj.* [gam·i·er; -i·est] Pungent; ripe; high.—**gam·i·ly** *adv.*—**gam·i·ness** *n.*

gan·der (*gan*-der) *n.* A male goose.

gang *n.* 1. A number of persons associated together for a particular purpose, esp. for a criminal or questionable purpose. 2. A number of workmen under the supervision of one person. 3. *Colloquial.* Group of friends; companions.

Ganges (*gan*-jeez). Sacred river in India.

gan·gling (*gang*-gling) *adj.* Tall and loose-jointed; clumsy.

gan·gli·on (*gang*-lee-un) *n.* [*pl.* -gli·a, -gli·ons] 1. An enlargement in a nerve; nerve center. 2. A small tumor on a tendon.—**gan·gli·on·ic** *adj.*

gan·gly (*gang*-glee) *adj.* Lanky and awkward; gangling.

G

gang·plank *n.* A plank or narrow platform for boarding or leaving a vessel.

gan·grene (*gang*-green, gang-*green*) *n.* Early stage of mortification of the flesh; decay or death of a tissue.—*v.* [gan·grened; gan·gren·ing] To mortify; produce gangrene in.—**gan·gre·nous** *adj.*

gang·ster *n.* Member of a criminal gang.

gang·way *n.* A temporary passageway.—*Interjection.* Clear the road!

gan·net (*gan*-it) *n.* A pelicanlike sea bird.

gan·oid (*gan*-oyd) *adj.* Pertaining to the Ganoidei, an order of scaled fishes including the bony pike and sturgeon.—*n.* A ganoid fish.

gant·let (*gant*-lit, *gawnt*-lit) *n.* 1. An old punishment requiring the offender to run between two rows of men who struck him as he passed. 2. A series of unpleasant events.

gan·try, gaun·try (*gan*-tree) *n.* [*pl.* -tries] A wooden frame for holding casks horizontally.

Gan·y·mede (*gan*-uh-meed) *n. Mythology.* A beautiful youth whom Jupiter carried off to be his cupbearer.

gaol. *British spelling* of **jail.**

gap *n.* 1. A break or opening; breach; chasm. 2. An interval; vacant space.—*v.* [gapped; gap·ping].

gape (*gayp*) *v.* [gaped; gap·ing] 1. To yawn; open the mouth wide, as in sleepiness or wonder. 2. To show a wide opening or chasm. 3. To stare in wonder.—**gape** *n.* 1. The act of gaping. 2. *Zoology.* The width of the open mouth, as in birds.—**gap·er** *n.*—**gap·ing** *adj.* —**gap·ing·ly** *adv.*—**the gapes** *n.* A disease of young poultry, marked by gaping.

G.A.R. *Abbr.* Grand Army of the Republic.

gar (*gahr*) *n.* Garfish.—*v.* To force; compel.

ga·rage (guh-*rahzh*) *n.* A building or shop where motor cars are kept and repaired.—*v.* [ga·raged; ga·rag·ing].

Garand rifle. A semiautomatic rifle used by the American infantry in World War II.

garb (*gahrb*) *n.* Clothing; attire.—*v.* To attire.

gar·bage (*gahr*-bij) *n.* 1. Animal or household refuse. 2. Any worthless or offensive matter.

gar·ble (*gahr*-b'l) *v.* [gar·bled; gar·bling] To pervert; mutilate; repeat misleadingly.—**gar·ble** *n.*—**gar·bler** *n.*

gar·den (*gahr*-d'n) *n.* 1. A plot of ground, usually enclosed, where fruits, vegetables, or flowers are cultivated. 2. Any rich, cultivated ground.—*v.* To cultivate a garden; grow plants.—**garden** *adj.*—**gar·den·ing** *n.*

gar·den·er (*gahrd*-ner) *n.* One who makes and tends a garden.

gar·de·ni·a (gahr-*deen*-yuh) *n.* A variety of shrub bearing fragrant white flowers.

gar·fish (*gahr*-fish) *n.* Any of several fishes with a very long, slender body and snout.

Gar·gan·tu·a (gahr-*gan*-choo-uh) *n.* A gluttonous giant, hero of Rabelais's satire *Gargantua.*—**gar·gan·tu·an** *adj.* Enormous; prodigious.

gar·gle (*gahr*-g'l) *v.* [gar·gled; gar·gling] To rinse the mouth or throat.—*n.* A liquid so used.

gar·goyle (*gahr*-goyl) *n. Architecture.* A grotesquely carved spout for draining water from the gutters of a building.—**gar·goyled** *adj.*

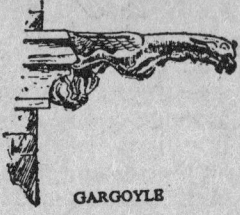
GARGOYLE

gar·ish (*gehr*-ish, *gar*-ish) *adj.* Gaudy; showy; glaringly bright.—**gar·ish·ly** *adv.*—**gar·ish·ness** *n.*

gar·land (*gahr*-l'nd) *n.* 1. A wreath, as of flowers, leaves, etc. 2. A collection of printed pieces; anthology.—*v.* To adorn with a garland.

gar·lic (*gahr*-lik) *n.* A hardy bulb plant with a strong odor and pungent taste.—**gar·lick·y** *adj.*

gar·ment (*gahr*-m'nt) *n.* An article of clothing.

gar·ner (*gahr*-ner) *n.* A granary; place where grain is stored.—*v.* To gather and store.

gar·net (*gahr*-nit) *n.* 1. A family of hard, translucent minerals, generally red. 2. The dark red of the precious garnet.—**gar·net** *adj.*

gar·nish (*gahr*-nish) *v.* 1. *Cookery.* To give a dish added flavor or ornamentation. 2. To adorn; decorate. 3. *Law.* To warn.—**gar·nish** *n.*—**gar·nish·er** *n.*

gar·nish·ee (*gahr*-nish-ee) *n. Law.* A person warned not to pay money or deliver effects to a defendant.—*v.* [gar·nish·eed; gar·nish·ee·ing] 1. *Law.* To secure or warn by garnishment. 2. *Law.* To attach the property of a debtor, esp. the wages of a workman.

gar·nish·ment *n.* 1. Ornament; decoration. 2. *Law.* Warning not to pay money, etc., to a defendant, but to appear and answer a creditor's suit.

gar·ni·ture (*gahr*-nih-cher) *n.* Ornamental appendages; decoration.

gar·ret (*gair*-it) *n.* Attic; story or room immediately under the roof.

gar·ri·son (*gair*-uh-s'n) *n.* 1. Troops stationed in a fort or town. 2. A fort or town occupied by troops.—*v.* To supply or man with troops.

gar·rote, gar·otte (guh-*roht*, guh-*raht*) *n.* 1. An instrument for strangling, used in Spain for capital punishment. 2. Strangulation.—*v.* [gar·rot·ed, -rot·ted; -rot·ing, -rot·ting] To strangle with a garrote.—**gar·rot·er, gar·rot·ter** *n.*

gar·ru·li·ty (guh-*rool*-uh-tee) *n.* Talkativeness.

gar·ru·lous (*gair*-uh-lus) *adj.* Talkative; loquacious; wordy.—**gar·ru·lous·ly** *adv.*—**lous·ness** *n.*

gar·ter (*gahr*-ter) *n.* 1. A band or support, usually elastic, for holding up a stocking. 2. The badge of the highest order of knighthood in Great Britain. 3. [*cap.*] The Order of the Garter.—**gar·ter** *v.*

garter snake. A harmless American snake.

gas *n.* 1. Matter in its most rarefied state; a fluid with no fixed volume or shape. 2. A gaseous mixture used for lighting and fuel.

3. *Colloquial.* Gasoline. 4. *Slang.* Empty or bragging talk.—*v.* [gassed; gas·sing] 1. To expose to the action of gas. 2. *Slang.* To boast; talk idly. 3. To poison by gas.

gas bag	gas-heated	gasman
gas-charged	gas house	gas-operated
gas-driven	gas-laden	gastight
gas-filled	gaslock	gas worker
gas-fired	gas maker	gas works

Gas·con (*gass*-k'n) *n.* 1. A native of Gascony, France. 2. [*not cap*] A boaster; braggart.

gas·con·ade (gass-kuh-*nayd*) *n.* Boasting; bragging; bravado.—*v.* [gas·con·ad·ed; gas·con·ad·ing] To boast; brag.—**gas·con·ad·er** *n.*

Gas·co·ny (*gass*-kuh-nee). A former province in SW France.

gas engine. An internal-combustion engine utilizing gasoline as its motive power.

gas·e·ous (*gass*-ee-us, *gass*-yus) *adj.* Having the nature or form of gas.

gas fitter. A workman who lays pipes and installs burners and gas fixtures.

gas fixture. A bracket or fixture for utilizing gas supplied for lighting or fuel.

gas furnace. A furnace using gas as a fuel.

gas gauge. An instrument for determining the pressure of gas.

gash *v.* To make a gash in.—*n.* A deep, long cut, as in flesh.

gas·i·fy (*gass*-uh-fye) *v.* [gas·i·fied; gas·i·fy·ing] To convert into or become gas.—**gas·i·fi·a·ble** *adj.*—**gas·i·fi·ca·tion** *n.*—**gas·i·fi·er** *n.*

gas jet. 1. A burner on a gas fixture. 2. A spout of flame issuing from such a burner.

gas·ket (*gass*-kit) *n.* 1. A piece of material used between two surfaces as an airtight seal. 2. *Nautical.* A cord used to furl or tie a sail to the yard.

gas·light (*gass*-lyte) *n.* Light from burning gas.

gas main. The main pipe supplying or conveying gas.

gas mask. A covering for face and head, protecting against the fumes of gas.

gas meter. Apparatus for measuring gas.

gas·o·line (*gass*-uh-leen) *n.* Also **gas·o·lene.** An inflammable liquid obtained by distilling petroleum and used for heating and power.

gas·om·e·ter (gass-*om*-uh-ter) *n.* 1. *Chemistry.* An instrument for measuring or mixing gases. 2. A gas reservoir.

gasp *v.* 1. To breathe laboriously or convulsively. 2. To pant violently, esp. in desire.—**gasp** *n.*—**gasp·ing** *adj.*—**gasp·ing·ly** *adv.*

gas·sing (*gass*-ing) *n.* 1. Act of subjecting to gas, esp. poisoning by gas. 2. *Slang.* Idle talk.

gas·sy (*gass*-ee) *adj.* [gas·si·er; gas·si·est] 1. Related to or containing gas; gaseous. 2. *Slang.* Given to pretentious or idle talk.

gas·tric (*gass*-trik) *adj.* Pertaining to the stomach.

gastric juice. The principal agent in digestion, secreted by the membrane of the stomach.

gas·tri·tis (gass-*try*-tiss) *n. Medicine.* Inflammation of the mucous membrane of the stomach.

gas·tro- (*gass*-troh). *Combining form* denoting stomach or belly.

gas·tro·nome (*gass*-truh-nohm) *n.* One who likes good living; epicure.

gas·tron·o·my (gass-*tron*-uh-mee) *n.* The art of good living and eating; epicurism.—**gas·tro·nom·ic, -i·cal** *adj.*— **-i·cal·ly** *adv.*

gas·tro·pod (*gass*-truh-pod) *n.* Also **gas·ter·o·pod.** A univalve mollusk, such as the snail, having a broad, muscular foot attached to its belly.—**gas·tro·pod, gas·trop·o·dous** *adj.*

gat *n. Slang.* Gun; pistol.

gate (*gayt*) *n.* 1. Movable frame of wood, iron, etc., closing an entrance to a passage or an opening in a wall or fence. 2. Means of entrance or exit. 3. A valve regulating the flow of water. 4. The amount of admission money received from spectators at a sports event.

gatehouse	gatepost	gatewise
gatekeeper	gate tender	gatewoman
gateman	gateward	gate works
gate money	gatewayman	gatewright

gate-leg table. Also **gate-legged table.** A drop-leaf table with legs that can fold in when the leaves are dropped.

gate·way *n.* 1. A means of entrance or exit. 2. Opening in which a gate is hung.

gath·er (*gath*-er) *v.* 1. To bring or come together; assemble; congregate. 2. To harvest; pick; pluck. 3. To accumulate; amass. 4. To fold or pull together with stitches. 5. To infer; deduce by inference; conclude. 6. To come to a head, as a sore, and form pus. —*n.* A fold, esp. in fabric.—**gath·er·er** *n.*

gath·er·ing (*gath*-er-ing) *n.* 1. Act or result of collecting; assembling. 2. An assembly; crowd. 3. An informal parley. 4. A gather.

Gatling gun. Early form of machine gun having a revolving cluster of barrels.

gauche (*gohsh*) *adj.* Awkward; clumsy.—**gauche·ly** *adv.*—**gauche·ness** *n.*

gau·cher·ie (*gohsh*-er-ee) *n.* 1. An awkward action. 2. Awkwardness; bungling.

gau·cho (*gow*-choh) *n.* [*pl.* gau·chos] South American cowboy.

gaud (*gawd*) *n.* A cheap ornament; trinket.

gaud·y *adj.* [gaud·i·er; gaud·i·est] Showy; vulgarly bright.—**gaud·i·ly** *adv.*—**gaud·i·ness** *n.*

gauge, gage (*gayj*) *v.* [gauged; gaged; gaug·ing; gag·ing] 1. To ascertain the contents or capacity of; measure. 2. To appraise; estimate. —*n.* 1. A standard measure; scale; measure. 2. A measuring instrument. 3. The distance between railroad rails or the wheels of a vehicle. 4. *Nautical.* Position of one ship in relation to another or to the wind. 5. Extent; measurements; size.—**gaug·er, gag·er** *n.*

Gaul (*gawl*) *n.* 1. An ancient European country including France, Belgium, and Holland. 2. An inhabitant of Gaul. 3. A Frenchman. —**Gaul·ish** *adj. & n.*

gaunt *adj.* 1. Lean with hunger or suffering; haggard. 2. Desolate; grim.—**gaunt·ly** *adv.* —**gaunt·ness** *n.*

G

gaunt·let (*gawnt*-lit) *n.* 1. Large iron or heavy leather glove formerly worn with armor. 2. A challenge. 3. Glove with a wide, flaring cuff. — **gaunt·let·ed** *adj.*

GAUNTLET

gauss (*gowss*) *n. Electricity.* Unit of magnetic attraction.

gauze (*gawz*) *n.* An extremely thin, transparent fabric.—**gauze** *adj.*

gauz·y *adj.* [gauz·i·er; gauz·i·est] Like gauze; transparent.—**gauz·i·ly** *adv.*—**gauz·i·ness** *n.*

gav·el (*gav*-'l) *n.* Small mallet used by a presiding officer or judge.

ga·votte, ga·vot (guh-*vot*) *n.* 1. A lively French dance. 2. The music to which the dance is performed.

gawk *n.* An awkward fool; simpleton.—*v.* To gape; stare.

gawk·y *adj.* [gawk·i·er; gawk·i·est] Awkward; ungainly.—**gawk·i·ly** *adv.*—**gawk·i·ness** *n.*

gay *adj.* [gay·er; gay·est] 1. Merry; light-hearted; frolicsome. 2. Showy; bright-colored. 3. Dissolute; loose.—**gay·ness** *n.*

GAVEL

gay-colored gay-humored gay-spent
gay-flowered gay looking gay-spotted
gay-hued gay-painted gay-throned

ga·za·bo, ga·ze·bo (guh-*zay*-bo) *n. Slang.* Guy; gink; fellow; chap.

gaze *v.* [gazed; gaz·ing] To look long and intently.—*n.* A fixed look.—**gaz·er** *n.*

ga·ze·bo (gaz-*ee*-boh) *n.* [*pl.* -bos, -boes] A summer house having an extended balcony.

ga·zelle (guh-*zel*) *n.* Small, graceful, soft-eyed antelope.

ga·zette (guh-*zet*) *n.* 1. A newspaper. 2. Official journal.—*v.* [ga·zet·ted; ga·zet·ting] To publish in a gazette.

gaz·et·teer (gaz-uh-*teer*) *n.* 1. A news writer; officer who publishes news. 2. A geographical dictionary.

GAZELLE
(1/40 life size)

gear (*geer*) *n.* 1. A toothed wheel fitted into and working on another. 2. Proper adjustment or working order. 3. A mechanism for some particular purpose, as steering gears. 4. Equipment, esp. tackle, harness, household goods, etc. 5. Clothes.—*v.* To connect by, or provide with, gears.—**geared** *adj.*

gear·ing *n.* A system of toothed wheels for transmitting motion.

gear·shift *n.* Mechanism for meshing any of various sets of gears connected with an engine.

gear wheel. Toothed wheel which fits into another.

geck·o (*gek*-oh) *n.* [*pl.* -os, -oes] A small, insect-eating variety of lizard.

gee (*jee*) *n. & interj.* Command directing horses, etc., to turn to the right.—*v.* Turn to the right.

geese. *Plural* of **goose.**

gee·zer (*gee*-zer) *n. Slang.* Funny old man.

Ge·hen·na (guh-*hen*-uh) *n. Bible.* Place for burning refuse; hell.

gei·sha (*gay*-shuh) *n.* [*pl.* -sha, -shas] A specially trained singing and dancing girl of Japan.

gel (*jel*) *n.* A jellylike substance formed from a colloidal solution.—*v.* [gelled; gel·ling].

gel·a·tin, gel·a·tine (*jel*-uh-t'n) *n.* 1. Nutritious animal substance which dissolves in hot water and forms a jelly when cooled. 2. Any substance similar to or made from this, as gelatin desserts, glue, etc.

ge·lat·i·nize (juh-*lat*-in-yze) *v.* [-nized; -niz·ing] To treat with, or make into, gelatin.

ge·lat·i·nous (juh-*lat*-in-us) *adj.* Pertaining to, consisting of, or resembling gelatin.

geld (*geld*) *v.* [geld·ed, gelt; geld·ing] To castrate; emasculate.

geld·ing *n.* Castrated horse or other animal.

gel·id (*jel*-id) *adj.* Frozen; ice-cold; frosty.—**ge·lid·i·ty** *n.*—**gel·id·ly** *adv.*

gelt *n. Slang.* Money.

gem (*jem*) *n.* 1. A jewel; cut and polished precious stone. 2. That which is remarkable for beauty, rarity, or perfection.—*v.* [gemmed; gem·ming] To ornament with gems.

gem·i·nate (*jem*-uh-nayt) *v.* [-nat·ed; -nat·ing] To double; make or become paired.—*adj.* Coupled; combined in pairs.—**gem·i·na·tion** *n.*

Gem·i·ni (*jem*-uh-nye) *n. pl.* 1. *Astronomy.* Northern constellation having two bright stars. 2. The third sign of the Zodiac.

gem·ma (*jem*-uh) *n.* [*pl.* -mae] *Biology.* A bud or growth resembling a bud.—**gem·mate** *adj.*

gem·mule (*jem*-yool) *n. Biology.* A small bud.

gems·bok (*gemz*-bok) *n.* Large, straight-horned African antelope.

gen·darme (*zhahn*-dahrm) *n.* [*pl.* -darmes] A policeman, esp. in France.—**gen·darm·er·y, gen·dar·me·rie** *n.* Force of gendarmes.

gen·der (*jen*-der) *n.* 1. Male or female sex. 2. *Grammar.* Category into which words are divided often according to the sex (masculine, feminine, or neuter) of the beings or things they denote.

gene (*jeen*) *n. Biology.* The element in a germ cell which transmits or determines a hereditary trait.

ge·ne·al·o·gist (jee-nee-*al*-uh-jist, jen-) *n.* One engaged in tracing descent or genealogies.

ge·ne·al·o·gy *n.* [*pl.* -gies] 1. A record of the ancestry or descent of a person or family. 2. Lineage; descent; pedigree. 3. The making or study of family descent records.— **-log·i·cal** (-*loj*-ih-k'l) *adj.*— **-log·i·cal·ly** *adv.*

gen·er·a (*jen*-er-uh). *Plural* of **genus.**

gen·er·a·ble (*jen*-er-uh-b'l) *adj.* Able to be generated.

gen·er·al (*jen*-er-'l) *adj.* 1. Prevalent; widespread; common. 2. Relating to a whole class or order. 'A general law for animals.' 3. Relating to the whole community; public. 'The general welfare.' 4. Not specific; vague; indefinite. 5. Not specialized. 'A general practitioner.'—*n.* 1. The people as a whole; public. 2. *Military.* A chief military officer; commander of an army, division, or brigade. 3. Leader of a religious order.—**in general.** Usually; generally.

gen·er·al·cy *n.* Rank of a general.

gen·er·al·is·si·mo *n.* [*pl.* -mos] Chief commander of both military and naval forces; commander of several field armies.

gen·er·al·i·ty *n.* [*pl.* -ties] 1. The condition of being general. 2. A general statement of principle. 3. The mass; main body.

gen·er·al·i·za·tion *n.* A general inference or proposition.

gen·er·al·ize (*jen*-er-ul-yze) *v.* 1. To reduce or relate to general laws or facts; apply generally. 2. To infer, as a general principle, from specific facts. 3. To speak vaguely or generally.

gen·er·al·ly (*jen*-er-ul-ee) *adv.* 1. Usually; ordinarily. 2. On the whole; for the most part. 3. In a general way or sense.

gen·er·al·ship *n.* 1. The office, command, or skill of a general. 2. Skillful management.

general staff. The directing staff of an army.

gen·er·ate (*jen*-er-ayt) *v.* [gen·er·at·ed; gen·er·at·ing] 1. To produce, as children; propagate. 2. To bring into being; form; make.

gen·er·a·tion (jen-er-*ay*-shun) *n.* 1. Act of begetting children; propagation. 2. Production by natural or artificial means; formation. 3. A single step in descent; usual length of time between the birth of father and child. 4. Persons, animals, etc., born within this time.—**gen·er·a·tive** *adj.* Able to produce.

gen·er·a·tor (*jen*-er-ay-ter) *n.* One that generates, esp. an apparatus for converting kinetic energy into electrical.

gen·er·ic (juh-*nehr*-ik) *adj.* Also **ge·ner·i·cal.** 1. Pertaining to or characteristic of a genus. 2. Comprehensive; general; not specific.

gen·er·os·i·ty (jen-er-*oss*-uh-tee) *n.* [*pl.* -ties] 1. Magnanimity; liberality; openhandedness. 2. A generous act.

gen·er·ous (*jen*-er-us) *adj.* 1. Magnanimous; noble; unselfish. 2. To give or share. 3. Abundant; copious; rich.—**gen·er·ous·ly** *adv.*—**gen·er·ous·ness** *n.*

gen·e·sis (*jen*-uh-siss) *n.* [*pl.* -ses] 1. [*cap.*] First book of the Old Testament, describing the creation. 2. Origin; generation; formation.

ge·net·ic (juh-*net*-ik) *adj.* Also **ge·net·i·cal.** 1. Pertaining to generation or origin. 2. Relating to genetics or genes.—**ge·net·i·cal·ly** *adv.*—**ge·net·i·cist** *n.*

ge·net·ics *n. pl.* The science dealing with inherited characteristics of the individual.

Ge·ne·va (juh-*nee*-vuh) *n.* 1. City in SW Switzerland, headquarters of the League of Nations. 2. A gin made in Holland.—**Ge·ne·van** *adj.* 1. Relating to Geneva. 2. Calvinistic.—**Ge·ne·van** *n.*

Gen·e·vese (jen-uh-*veez*) *n.* [*sing.* & *pl.*] A native of Geneva.—*adj.* Pertaining to Geneva.

gen·ial (*jeen*-yul) *adj.* 1. Cheerful and social; cordial; kindly. 2. Promoting growth; comforting.—**gen·ial·ly** *adv.*—**gen·ial·ness** *n.*

ge·ni·al·i·ty (jeen-ee-*al*-uh-tee) *n.* Warmth; kindliness; cordiality.

ge·nie (*jeen*-ee) *n.* [*pl.* ge·ni·i] Jinni; spirit or goblin in Mohammedan folk tales.

ge·ni·i (*jeen*-ee-eye). *Plural* of genius, genie.

gen·i·tal (*jen*-uh-t'l) *adj.* Pertaining to reproduction or the organs of sex.

gen·i·tals *n. pl.* The external organs of sex.

gen·i·tive (*jen*-uh-tiv) *adj. Grammar.* Indicating source, origin, possession, etc.—*n.* A genitive or possessive word or case.—**gen·i·ti·val** *adj.*

gen·ius (*jeen*-yus) *n.* [*pl.* gen·ius·es] 1. Outstanding intellectual prowess; extraordinary imaginative, creative, or inventive ability. 2. Person gifted with any of these qualities. 3. Distinguishing character or quality, as of a nation, person, religion, historical period, etc. 4. [*pl.* ge·ni·i] A good or evil spirit presiding over a person or place. 5. Person who exerts great influence over another.

gen·o·cide (*jen*-uh-syde) *n.* The deliberate extermination or destruction of large racial, religious, or national groups.

Gen·o·ese (jen-uh-*weez*) *n. sing.* & *pl.* Inhabitant or native of Genoa.—**Gen·o·ese** *adj.*

gen·re (*zhahn*-ruh) *n.* 1. Kind; category; style. 2. *Painting.* Realistic portrayal of scenes from ordinary life.

gent *n. Slang.* Gentleman.

gen·teel (jen-*teel*) *adj.* Well-bred; refined; polite.—**gen·teel·ly** *adv.*—**gen·teel·ness** *n.*

gen·tian (*jen*-sh'n) *n.* Plant bearing flowers, usually bright blue.

gen·tile (*jen*-tyle) *n.* 1. One who is not a Jew, esp. a Christian. 2. Among Mormons, one who is not a Mormon.—**gen·tile** *adj.*

gen·til·i·ty (jen-*til*-uh-tee) *n.* 1. High or gentle birth. 2. Politeness; refinement.

GENTIAN

gen·tle (*jen*-t'l) *adj.* [gent·ler; gent·lest] 1. Mild; meek; tractable. 2. Soft; peaceful. 3. Wellborn; polite; refined. 4. Moderate.—*v.* [gen·tled; gen·tling] To make gentle or tractable.

gentle-born	gentle-handed	gentle-minded
gentle-bred	gentle-hearted	gentle-mouthed
gentle-browed	gentle looking	gentle-natured
gentle-eyed	gentle-mannered	gentle-spoken

G

gen·tle·folk *n. pl.* Also **gen·tle·folks.** Persons of good breeding, family, or position.

gen·tle·man *n.* [*pl.* -men] 1. Well-bred, considerate, polite man. 2. Courteous term for any man. 3. A man of good family or social position.

gen·tle·man·like *adj.* Like, or suitable for, a gentleman.—**gen·tle·man·like·ness** *n.*

gen·tle·man·ly *adj.* Gentlemanlike; having the qualities of a gentleman.—**gen·tle·man·li·ness** *n.*

gentleman of fortune. An adventurer; one seeking to profit by danger or chance.

gentleman's agreement. An unwritten or informal agreement, esp. one not legally binding.

gentleman's gentleman. A valet.

gen·tle·ness *n.* Mildness; docility; kindness.

gen·tle·wom·an *n.* Woman of good breeding or social position; lady.

gent·ly *adv.* Softly; mildly; in a gentle manner.

gen·try (*jen*-tree) *n.* 1. People of wealth, good breeding, or social position. 2. People of any special class.

gen·u·flect (*jen*-yoo-flekt) *v.* To bend the knee, esp. in worship.

gen·u·flec·tion, gen·u·flex·ion (jen-yoo-*flek*-shun) *n.* Act of genuflecting.

gen·u·ine (*jen*-yoo-in) *adj* 1. Real; true; authentic. 2. Unadulterated; pure; natural. 3. Honest; sincere.— -ine·ly *adv.*— -ine·ness *n.*

ge·nus (*jee*-nus) *n.* [*pl.* gen·er·a] 1. *Logic.* A class which includes subordinate species. 2. *Science.* Group of animals or plants having certain common characteristics, usually including several species. 3. Kind; class.

ge·o·cen·tric, ge·o·cen·tri·cal (jee-oh-*sen*-trik, -trih-k'l) *adj.* Having the earth as a center.

ge·od·e·sy (jee-*od*-uh-see) *n. Mathematics.* The science of computing the shape and size of great portions of the earth.—**ge·o·det·ic** (jee-uh-*det*-ik), **ge·o·det·i·cal** *adj.*—**ge·o·det·i·cal·ly** *adv.*—**ge·od·e·sist** (jee-*od*-uh-sist) *n.*

ge·og·ra·pher (jee-*og*-ruh-fer) *n.* One learned in geography.

ge·og·ra·phy (jee-*og*-ruh-fee) *n.* [*pl.* -phies] 1. Science describing the earth's surface and physical features, political and natural divisions, climates, populations, resources, etc. 2. A book on geography.—**ge·o·graph·i·cal, -graph·ic** (-*graf*-ik) *adj.*— -i·cal·ly *adv.*

ge·ol·o·gy (jee-*ol*-uh-jee) *n.* [*pl.* -gies] Science dealing with the earth's crust, its structure, composition, strata, etc.—**ge·o·log·ic** (jee-uh-*loj*-ik), **ge·o·log·i·cal** *adj.*—**ge·ol·o·gist** *n.*

ge·o·man·cy (*jee*-uh-man-see) *n.* Interpretation of lines and symbols.—**ge·o·man·cer** *n.*—**ge·o·man·tic** (jee-uh-*man*-tik) *adj.*

ge·o·met·ric, ge·o·met·ri·cal *adj.* Pertaining to or determined by geometry.—**ge·o·met·ri·cal·ly** *adv.*—**ge·o·me·tri·cian** (jee-uh-meh-*trish*-un) *n.*

ge·om·e·trid (jee-*om*-uh-trid) *n.* A common, large-winged moth, the larvae of which move in a humping fashion.

ge·om·e·try (jee-*om*-uh-tree) *n.* [*pl.* -tries]

Branch of mathematics dealing with properties and relations of magnitudes in space.

ge·o·phys·ics (jee-uh-*fiz*-iks) *n. Geology.* The study of the forces and factors which bring about changes in the earth's surface.—**ge·o·phys·i·cal** *adj.*—**ge·o·phys·i·cist** *n.*

ge·o·pol·i·tics (jee-oh-*pol*-ih-tiks) *n.* The study of the relationship between a nation's political life and its geography.—**ge·o·po·lit·i·cal** *adj.*

Georgette crepe (jor-*jet*). Also **Geor·gette.** Trade-mark name for a thin silk dress material.

Geor·gi·an (*jor*-j'n) *n.* 1. An inhabitant of Georgia in the U.S.A. 2. An inhabitant of Georgian Soviet Socialist Republic.—*adj.* Pertaining to the four Georges, kings of England.

ge·o·stat·ics (jee-oh-*stat*-iks) *n. Physics.* The study of rigid bodies in equilibrium.

ge·ot·ro·pism (jee-*ot*-ruh-pizm) *n. Biology.* The determination by the force of gravity of the direction followed by an organism.—**ge·o·trop·ic** (jee-uh-*trop*-ik) *adj.*— -trop·i·cal·ly *adv.*

ge·ra·ni·um (jer-*ay*-nee-um) *n.* A hardy family of plants bearing pink or purple pungent flowers, found in temperate regions.

ger·i·at·rics (jeh-ree-*at*-riks) *n. Medicine.* The study of the medical problems of old age.—**ger·i·a·tri·cian** (jeh-ree-uh-*trish*-un) *n.*

germ (*jerm*) *n.* 1. A microbe, esp. one which causes disease. 2. The rudimentary form of any organism; embryo; seed.—**germ** *adj.*

ger·man (*jer*-m'n) *adj.* 1. Having the same parents. 2. Being the cousin of.

ger·man (*jer*-m'n) *n.* A set of ballroom dances.

Ger·man (*jer*-m'n) *n.* 1. A native of Germany. 2. The language of Germany.—*adj.* Pertaining to Germany, its inhabitants, or its language.

ger·mane (jer-*mayn*) *adj.* Closely akin; allied; relevant; pertinent.—**ger·mane·ly** *adv.*

Ger·man·ic (jer-*man*-ik) *adj.* 1. Pertaining to Germany. 2. Teutonic.

Ger·man·ism (*jer*-m'n-izm) *n.* 1. A German phrase or expression. 2. A theory or approach regarded as characteristically German. 3. Affectation of German characteristics.

ger·ma·ni·um (jer-*may*-nee-um) *n. Chemistry.* A grayish metallic element. (*Symbol:* Ge).

German measles. A mild, contagious disease, having some of the symptoms of measles.

German shepherd dog. A breed of dog often trained for police work.

German silver. A white alloy of nickel, zinc, and copper.

German text. A black-letter type similar to old English and modern German.

ger·mi·cide (*jer*-mih-syde) *n.* An agent for killing germs, esp. disease germs.—**ger·mi·cid·al** (jer-mih-*sy*-d'l) *adj.*

ger·mi·nal (*jer*-min-ul) *adj.* 1. Pertaining to a germ. 2. In the earliest stage of development.

ger·mi·nate (*jer*-min-ayt) *v.* [ger·mi·nat·ed; ger·mi·nat·ing] To become fertile; sprout; bud. —**ger·mi·nant** *adj.*

ger·mi·na·tion (jer-mih-*nay*-shun) *n.* The first

act of growth of an embryo plant.—**ger·mi·na·tive** (*jer*-mih-nay-tiv) *adj.*

germ plasm. *Biology.* Material in the germ cells transmitting the hereditary characters.

ger·ry·man·der (*gehr*-ee-man-der, *jehr*-) *v.* To arrange the political divisions of a region so as to gain advantage in an election.

ger·und (*jehr*-und) *n. Grammar.* A verbal noun.

ge·run·dive (jer-*un*-div) *adj.* Pertaining to a verbal noun.—*v.* The adjective form of the gerund.

gest, geste (*jest*) *n. Archaic.* Gesture; action.

Gestalt psychology (geh-*shtahlt*) *n.* A school of psychology which regards a perception as a unified whole whose totality is qualitatively greater than the mere sum of its parts.

Ge·sta·po (geh-*stah*-poh) *n.* The political police of Nazi Germany.

ges·ta·tion (jess-*tay*-shun) *n.* Pregnancy.—**ges·tate** (*jess*-tayt) *v.*

ges·tic·u·late (jess-*tik*-yoo-layt) *v.* [-lat·ed; -lat·ing] To make motions, usually while speaking. —**ges·tic·u·la·tive** *adj.*—**ges·tic·u·la·tor** *n.*

ges·tic·u·la·tion (jess-tik-yuh-*lay*-shun). *n.* A gesture made in order to illustrate speech. —**ges·tic·u·la·to·ry** (jess-*tik*-yuh-luh-tor-ee) *adj.*

ges·ture (*jess*-cher) *n.* 1. An expressive motion. 2. An action performed out of courtesy.—*v.* [ges-tured; ges·tur·ing]—**ges·tur·er** *n.*

get *v.* [got; got or got·ten; get·ting] 1. To procure; obtain. 2. To gain; win. 'He got the upper hand.' 3. To receive. 4. To contract, as an ailment. 5. To induce; persuade. 'I got him to come.' 6. To reach; come; arrive. 'We'll get there tonight.' 7. To cause to be; make. 'Get ready.' 8. To take; take oneself. 'Get away.' 9. To beget. 10. *Slang.* To strike; kill. 'It gets them in the end.' 11. *Slang.* To receive punishment. 'He is going to get it.' 12. *Slang.* To baffle. 'This gets me.'

get·a·way (*get*-uh-way) *n.* Escape.

Geth·sem·a·ne (geth-*sem*-uh-nee) 1. *Biblical.* The garden outside Jerusalem in which Jesus prayed before his arrest. 2. Any spiritual ordeal.

get·ta·ble (*get*-uh-b'l) *adj.* Able to be obtained.

get-to·geth·er *n. Colloquial.* Meeting.

get-up *n. Colloquial.* Style of dress or costume.

gew·gaw (*gyoo*-gaw) *n.* A trifle; toy; bauble; gaudy plaything.—**gew·gaw** *adj.*

gey·ser (*gy*-zer) *n.* A spring throwing up at intervals a column of steaming water.

ghast·ly (*gast*-lee) *adj.* [-li·er; -li·est] Horrible; shocking; dreadful; deathlike.—**ghast·li·ness** *n.*

ghat, ghaut (*gawt*) *n.* 1. *India.* A ravine. 2. [*pl.*] The ranges bordering the peninsula of India. 3. A porch and staircase to a river bank for bathing, Hindu cremations, etc.

gher·kin (*ger*-kin) *n.* Small variety of cucumber, used for pickling.

ghet·to (*get*-oh) *n.* [*pl.* -tos, -ti] Section of a city to which Jews were confined.

ghost (*gohst*) *n.* 1. Apparition; specter; phan-tom. 2. Shadow; trace. 'Not a ghost of a chance.' 3. The spirit; soul.—**ghost·like** *adj.* —**ghost·ly** *adj.*—**ghost·li·ness** *n.*

ghost writer. One employed to do writing in another's name.

ghoul (*gool*) *n.* In eastern tales, a spirit which preys upon human bodies.—**ghoul·ish** *adj.* —**ghoul·ish·ly** *adv.*—**ghoul·ish·ness** *n.*

G.I. (*jee eye*) *Abbreviation.* Government Issue, stamped on U.S. military equipment.—*n. Slang.* An enlisted soldier in the U.S. Army. —**G. I.** *adj.*

gi·ant (*jy*-unt) *n.* 1. *Mythology.* One of a race of men of superhuman size and strength. 2. An abnormally tall person. 3. A person of extraordinary ability, courage, strength, etc. —*adj.* Of enormous size.

gi·ant·ess (*jy*-unt-ess) *n.* Female giant.

giant panda. A rare bearlike mammal found in NW China and Tibet.

giaour (*jowr*) *n.* Turkish name for a non-Moham-medan, esp. a Christian.

gib·ber (*jib*-er) *v.* To speak rapidly and inarticulately; chatter.—**gib·ber** *n.*

gib·ber·ish *n.* Babbling, inarticulate talk.

GIANT PANDA
(1/50 life size)

gib·bet (*jib*-et) *n.* A gallows. —*v.* 1. To hang and expose on gallows. 2. To expose to ridicule, scorn, or infamy.

gib·bon (*gib*-un) *n.* A species of long-armed ape, esp. those of the Indian archipelago.

gib·bos·i·ty (gih-*boss*-ih-tee) *n.* [*pl.* -ties] Protuberance; convexity.

gib·bous, gib·bose (*gib*-us) *adj.* 1. Swollen; protuberant; convex. 2. Hunched; humpbacked.—**gib·bous·ness** *n.*

gibe, jibe (*jybe*) *v.* [gibed; gib·ing] To sneer; jeer; taunt; flout.—**gibe** *n.* An expression of sarcastic scorn.—**gib·er, jib·er** *n.*

GIBBON
(1/20 life size)

gib·lets (*jib*-lits) *n. pl.* Edible entrails of a fowl: the heart, liver, gizzard, etc.

Gi·bral·tar (jib-*rawl*-ter) *n.* 1. British fortress on the Rock of Gibraltar on the Spanish peninsula. 2. An invulnerable, unshakable stronghold.

gid·dy (*gid*-ee) *adj.* [gid·di·er; gid·di·est] 1. Dizzy. 2. Inconstant; unstable; heedless; excitable; frivolous. 3. Causing dizziness. —**gid·di·ly** *adv.*—**gid·di·ness** *n.*

gift *n.* 1. A present; donation; property voluntarily transferred without compensation. 2. A natural talent or faculty.—**gift** *v.*

gift·ed *adj.* Endowed with a natural power or faculty; talented.

gig (*gig*) *n.* 1. A top; whirligig. 2. Light, two-wheeled carriage, drawn by one horse.

G

3. *Nautical.* Long, light, narrow rowboat, adapted for racing; also a ship's boat.

gig *n. Military Slang.* Minor punishment.—*v.* [gigged; gig·ging] To penalize for a minor infraction.

gi·gan·tic (jy-*gan*-tik) *adj.* Huge; enormous.

gig·gle (*gig*-'l) *n.* A titter; small trill of laughter. —*v.* [gig·gled; gig·gling]—**gig·gly** *adj.*

gig·o·lo (*jig*-uh-loh) *n.* 1. A man who lives by accepting money from women. 2. A hired male escort.

gig·ot (*jig*-ut) *n.* Also **gigot sleeve.** A leg-of-mutton sleeve.

Gila monster (*hee*-luh). A large, poisonous, orange-spotted black lizard found in western U.S.

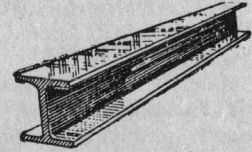
GILA MONSTER (1/10 life size)

gild *v.* [gilded, gilt; gild·ing] 1. To paint over with a thin layer of gold. 2. To make shining; touch with light; illuminate; brighten. 3. To impart a superficially attractive appearance to. —**gild·a·ble** *adj.*—**gild·er.**

gild·ing *n.* 1. The art of applying gold to surfaces. 2. Gold coating. 3. Adornment.

gill (jil) *n.* A liquid measure of ¼ of a pint.

gill (gil) *n.* 1. Respiratory organ in fishes and other water-breathing animals. 2. Wattle or dewlap of fowls; flesh under or about the chin. 3. One of the vertical radiating plates on the under side of a mushroom.

gil·lie, gil·ly (*gil*-ee) *n.* [*pl.* -lies] *Scotland.* A manservant.

gil·ly·flow·er (*jil*-ee-flour) *n.* Also **gil·li·flow·er.** 1. The clove-scented pink. 2. The common stock. 3. The wallflower.

gilt. *Past tense & past participle* of **gild.**

gilt *n.* Gilding; gold applied to a surface; any brilliant, superficial veneer.—*adj.* Gilded.

gilt-edged *adj.* 1. Having a coat of gold applied to the edges. 2. Of the first quality.

gim·bals (*jim*-b'lz) *n. pl.* A device for maintaining the proper position of an object, as a compass, level, or lamp, regardless of the shifting of its mounting.

gim·crack (*jim*-krak) *n.* Cheap article; knick-knack; useless ornament.—**gim·crack** *adj.*

gim·let (*gim*-let) *n.* A tool, somewhat similar to a corkscrew, for boring holes. —*v.* [gim·let·ed; gim·let·ing] To bore with a gimlet; move like a gimlet.

gim·let-eyed *adj.* Keen-eyed.

gim·mick (*gim*-ik) *n.* 1. *Slang.* A concealed device for setting a gambling wheel. 2. Any deceptive trick. 3. A gadget; gizmo.

gimp (*gimp*) *n.* 1. A kind of silk twist or edging. 2. Spirit; vigor. 'The loss took the gimp out of him.'

GIMLET

gin (jin) *n.* A strong spirit distilled from grain and aromatically flavored.

gin *n.* 1. A hoisting apparatus used instead of a crane; kind of windlass. 2. A machine for separating the seeds from cotton. 3. A trap; snare.—*v.* [ginned; gin·ning] 1. To separate the seeds from cotton by means of cotton gin. 2. To catch in a trap.

gin·ger (*jin*-jer) *n.* 1. A plant with a hot, spicy root used in cooking and medicine. 2. Mettle; spirit; pluck.—**gin·ger** *v.*

ginger ale. A carbonated, ginger-flavored beverage.

gin·ger·bread *n.* 1. Cake made with molasses and flavored with ginger. 2. Superfluous and petty ornamentation, esp. on a house.

gin·ger·ly *adv.* Cautiously; fastidiously.

gin·ger·snap *n.* Thin, crisp cooky flavored with ginger.

gin·ger·y *adj.* Hot-tasting; spicily sweet.

ging·ham (*ging*-um) *n.* Striped or checked cotton cloth.

gink *n. Slang.* Guy; chap; fellow.

gink·go (*gink*-goh) *n.* [*pl.* -goes]. Also **ging·ko.** A tree with fan-shaped leaves, native to northern China and often grown in America.

gin rummy *n.* A card game.

gin·seng (*jin*-seng) *n.* 1. A Chinese plant bearing scarlet berries. 2. A similar North American plant.

gip, gipsy. *Variant spellings* of **gyp, gypsy.**

gi·raffe (jih-*raf*) *n.* Long-necked, cud-chewing spotted quadruped found in remote sections of Africa.

gird *v.* [girt or gird·ed; gird·ing] 1. To bind or encircle, esp. the waist, as with a belt. 2. To clothe; dress. 3. To surround; enclose; encompass. 4. To prepare for action.

GIRAFFE (1/200 life size)

gird·er *n.* Main beam supporting a floor, the upper wall of a house, the roadway of a bridge, etc.

gir·dle (*gerd*-'l) *n.* 1. A band or belt worn around the waist. 2. An elastic corset. 3. That part of a cut gem embraced by the setting.—*v.* [gir·dled; gir·dling] 1. To bind with a belt; gird. 2. To enclose; shut in. 3. To make an incision around the trunk of a tree in order to kill it. —**gir·dler** *n.* One who girdles.

GIRDER

gird·ler *n.* 1. A type of beetle which girdles twigs, laying its eggs upon them. 2. One who makes girdles.

girl *n.* 1. A female child or adolescent; young woman. 2. A woman servant. 3. *Colloquial.* Sweetheart.

girl·hood *n.* Period of adolescence and early womanhood.

girl·ish *adj.* Like or pertaining to a girl.—**girl·ish·ly** *adv.*—**girl·ish·ness** *n.*

Girl Scout. A member of the Girl Scouts, American girls' organization formed in 1912.

girth *n.* 1. The distance around a cylindrical body; waist measurement; circumference. 2. The band by which a saddle is made fast on a horse.—*v.* To bind, encircle.

gist (*jist*) *n.* Main point; substance; pith.

git·tern (*git*-ern) *n.* A stringed instrument of the Middle Ages.

give (*giv*) *v.* [gave; given; giv·ing] 1. To bestow gratuitously; bequeath. 2. To deliver; hand over. 3. To devote; dedicate. 4. To provide, as a party. 5. To present; offer; show. 'Give me a reason.' 6. To perform. 7. To impart; be the source of. 8. To allot; assign; grant. 9. To yield as a product or result. 10. To collapse; yield to pressure; shrink. 11. To open out on; overlook. 12. *Slang.* To tell; talk.—**give in.** To surrender.—**give up.** To abandon; yield.—**give way.** To yield.

give-and-take *n.* Fair exchange; well-matched interchange, as in a dispute.

give·a·way *n.* A revealing or betraying circumstance.

giv·en *adj.* 1. Bestowed; granted; imparted. 2. Addicted; disposed. 3. Fixed; specified. 4. *Mathematics.* Assuming; granted.

given name. The first name; Christian name.

giv·er *n.* Bestower; donor.

giz·mo *n. Slang.* A gadget; doodad; what-you-may-call-it.

giz·zard (*giz*-erd) *n.* 1. The thick-walled second stomach in birds. 2. *Colloquial.* The stomach.

gla·brous (*glay*-brus) *adj.* Smooth; hairless.

gla·cé (glass-*ay*) *adj.* 1. Smooth; polished, as cloth, leather, etc. 2. Iced; sugared. 3. Frozen.—*v.* [gla·céed; gla·cé·ing].

gla·cial (*glay*-sh'l) *adj.* 1. Icy; frozen. 2. *Chemistry.* Crystallized. 3. *Geology.* Pertaining to the glacial period, when most of the Northern Hemisphere was ice-covered.—**gla·cial·ly** *adv.*

gla·ci·ate (*glay*-shee-ayt) *v.* [-at·ed; -at·ing] 1. To convert into ice; freeze. 2. To mark as a result of ice formations.—**gla·ci·a·tion** *n.*

gla·cier (*glay*-sher) *n.* Slow-moving mass of ice formed by the accumulation of snow on high ground.

gla·cis (*glay*-siss) *n.* Sloping bank in front of a fort; easy slope.

glad *adj.* [glad·der; glad·dest] 1. Pleased; gratified; delighted. 2. Cheerful; joyous; joyful. —**glad·ly** *adv.*—**glad·ness** *n.*

glad·den *v.* To make glad; please; cheer; comfort; delight.—**glad·den·er** *n.*

glade *n.* Open place in a wood or forest.

glad·i·a·tor (*glad*-ee-ay-ter) *n.* 1. An athlete trained to fight with a sword or other weapons in ancient Roman entertainments. 2. A fighter; champion of a cause.— -**a·to·ri·al** *adj.*

glad·i·o·la (glad-ee-*ohl*-uh; gluh-*dy*-uh-luh) *n.* A gladiolus.

glad·i·o·lus (glad-ee-*oh*-lus; gluh-*dy*-uh-lus) *n.* [*pl.* glad·i·o·li (glad-ee-*oh*-lye), -lus·es] Tall bulbous-rooted plant with sword-shaped leaves and bright flowers.

glad rags. *Slang.* Best clothes.

glad·some *adj. Poetry.* 1. Pleased; joyful; cheerful. 2. Pleasing.—**glad·some·ly** *adv.* —**glad·some·ness** *n.*

glair *n.* 1. Egg-white, or a glaze made from it. 2. Any viscous, translucent substance. —**glair·e·ous, glair·y** *adj.*

GLADIOLI

glam·or·ous (*glam*-er-us) *adj.* Enchanting; having a dazzling beauty.

glam·our (*glam*-er) *n.* 1. Magical or brilliant beauty. 2. Witchery; fascination.

glance *v.* [glanced; glanc·ing] 1. To look at briefly. 2. To flash; dart; gleam. 3. To fly off in an oblique direction; dart aside, as a weapon. 4. To pass quickly over, as in conversation.—*n.* A hasty look.

gland *n. Physiology.* An organ consisting of cells which form secretions from certain constituents of the blood.

glan·ders (*glan*-derz) *n.* Dangerous, highly contagious disease of horses, affecting the nostrils and lower jaw, and communicable to man. —**glan·dered, glan·der·ous** *adj.*

glan·du·lar (*glan*-dyoo-ler) *adj.* Pertaining to glands; containing or supporting glands.

glans (*glanz*) *n.* The head or end of the penis or clitoris.

glare *n.* 1. A bright, dazzling light; strong, disagreeable light. 2. A fierce, fixed stare. 3. Gaudiness; glitter.—*v.* [glared; glar·ing] —**glar·ing** *adj.*—**glar·ing·ly** *adv.*— -ing·ness *n.*

glass *n.* 1. Hard, brittle, transparent substance, made by fusing sand with potash and other ingredients. 2. A drinking vessel. 3. A mirror; looking-glass. 4. [*pl.*] Spectacles.—**glass** *adj.* Made of glass.

glass-bottomed	glass hard	glass rope
glass-built	glass-lined	glass-topped
glass-coated	glassmaker	glassweed
glass-colored	glassmaking	glass wool
glass-covered	glassman	glasswork
glass eater	glass-paneled	glassworker
glass-eyed	glass paper	glass works
glass-fronted	glass-paper (*v.*)	glassworm

glass blowing. Method of manufacturing glassware by means of a blowpipe.—**glass blower.**

glass·ful *n.* [*pl.* glass·fuls] The quantity a glass holds.

glass·house *n.* A greenhouse; conservatory.

glass·ware *n.* Articles or utensils made of glass.

glass·y *adj.* [glas·si·er; glas·si·est] 1. Like glass; smooth; brittle; transparent. 2. Beady; fixed; blank.—**glass·i·ly** *adv.*—**glass·i·ness** *n.*

glau·co·ma (glaw-*koh*-muh) *n. Medicine.* A disease of the eye, involving gradual loss of sight.— -**co·ma·tous** (-*koh*-muh-tus) *adj.*

G

glau·cous (*glaw*-kus) *adj.* 1. Sea-green. 2. *Botany.* Covered with a fine bluish powder.

glaze *v.* [glazed; glaz·ing] 1. To fit with glass, as a window, picture, etc. 2. To cover with a shining, vitreous substance, as pottery, etc. 3. *Painting.* To apply a thin layer of medium which enriches the undertone. 4. To become glassy and staring, as the eye.—**glaze** *n.*—**glaz·er** *n.*—**glaz·i·ness** *n.*

gla·zier (*glay*-zher) *n.* One who sets window glass.

glaz·ing *n.* 1. The fitting of glass panes, or the glass itself. 2. A vitreous finish applied to a surface; the glaze itself.

gleam (*gleem*) *n.* Beam; ray; small stream of light.—*v.* To shine.—**gleam·y** *adj.*

glean *v.* 1. To gather grain left by reapers. 2. To collect in small or fragmentary portions; scrape together.—**glean·er** *n.*—**glean·ing** *n.*

glee *n.* 1. Joy; mirth; gaiety. 2. *Music.* Composition for three or more voices.

glee club. A singing society.

glee·ful *adj.* Merry; gay; joyous.

glen *n.* Narrow secluded valley; dale.

glib *adj.* [glib·ber; glib·best] Fluent; ready; voluble; smooth-spoken.

glide *v.* [glid·ed; glid·ing] 1. To move silently and smoothly. 2. To pass gently, imperceptibly, or gradually. 3. *Aviation.* To descend at lower engine power than must be maintained in flight. 4. *Phonetics.* To join two separate sounds with an intermediary sound.—**glide** *n.* —**glid·ing** *adj.*—**glid·ing·ly** *adv.*

glid·er *n.* 1. A planelike aircraft having no engine. 2. Anything having an easy, smooth movement.

glim·mer *v.* To shine faintly; flicker.—**glim·mer** *n.*—**glim·mer·ing** *n.* 1. Faint, unsteady light; glimmer. 2. Faint view or notion; inkling.

glimpse *v.* [glimpsed; glimps·ing] To see faintly, imperfectly, or momentarily.—**glimpse** *n.*

glint *v.* To gleam; flash; glitter.—**glint** *n.*

glis·sade (glih-*sahd*) *v.* [glis·saded; glis·sad·ing] 1. To slide down a steep slope, esp. of ice and snow. 2. *Ballet.* A sliding step to one side.

glis·ten (*gliss*-'n) *v.* To glitter; sparkle; shine fitfully.—**glis·ten** *n.*

glit·ter (*glit*-er) *v.* 1. To shine with a brilliant broken light; sparkle. 2. To create a showy display.—**glit·ter** *n.*—**glit·ter·y** *adj.*

gloam·ing (*gloh*-ming) *n.* Twilight.

gloat *v.* To regard with baleful complacency.

glob·al (*glohb*-'l) *adj.* 1. World-wide. 'Global war.' 2. Spherical. —**glob·al·ly** *adv.*

globe *n.* 1. Spherical body; ball. 2. The earth. 3. Spherical model of the earth or any celestial body. —*v.* To shape or become like a sphere.

GLOBE

globe·fish *n.* A fish which inflates itself into a globular shape by swallowing air.

globe·trot·ter *n.* *Colloquial.* An habitual tourist.—**globe·trot·ting** *n.* & *adj.*

glob·u·lar (*glob*-yoo-ler) *adj.* Also **glo·bose** (*gloh*-bahss). 1. Spherical; ball-like. 2. Composed of globules.

glob·ule (*glob*-yool) *n.* Small globe; spherical particle.—**glob·u·lous** *adj.*

glock·en·spiel (*glok*-'n-speel) *n.* *Music.* An instrument, usually portable, of tuned metal bars, played with hammers.

glom·er·ate (*glom*-er-it) *adj.* Clustered; collected into a rounded mass.—**glom·er·a·tion** (glom-er-*ay*-shun) *n.*

gloom *n.* 1. Obscurity; partial darkness; shade. 2. Dejection; depression; melancholy.—**gloom** *v.*

gloom·y *adj.* [gloom·i·er; gloom·i·est] 1. Obscure; dark; dim; cloudy. 2. Melancholy; dejected; dismal.—**gloom·i·ly** *adv.* —**gloom·i·ness** *n.*

GLOCKENSPIEL

Glo·ri·a *n.* 1. *Ecclesiastical.* One of several hymns of praise. 2. [*not cap.*] A halo. 3. [*not cap.*] A lustrous part-silk fabric.

glo·ri·fy (*glo*-rih-fy) *v.* [glo·ri·fied; glo·ri·fy·ing] To exalt; invest with splendor; irradiate; honor.—**glo·ri·fi·ca·tion** (glor-if-ih-*kay*-shun) *n.* —**glo·ri·fi·er** *n.*

glo·ri·ous (*glor*-ee-us) *adj.* 1. Illustrious; noble; excellent; renowned; celebrated. 2. Splendid; magnificent.—**glo·ri·ous·ly** *adv.*,— **-ous·ness** *n.*

glo·ry (*glor*-ee) *n.* [*pl.* -ries] 1. Public praise, honor, and admiration; greatness; renown. 2. Brightness; luster; splendor. 3. The bliss of heaven.—*v.* [glo·ried; glo·ry·ing] 1. To exult with joy; rejoice. 2. To take pride in.

gloss *n.* 1. Brightness; polish; luster; sheen. 2. Deceptive appearance.—*v.* To shine.

gloss *n.* Interpretation; explanation; marginal comment.—**gloss** *v.* 1. To explain; illustrate. 2. To make plausible; palliate.

glos·sa·ry *n.* [*pl.* -ries] 1. Lexicon of selected words in a work, esp. those which are obsolete, foreign, technical, etc. 2. A limited and partial dictionary.—**glos·sar·i·al** (gloss-*air*-ee-ul) *adj.*—**glos·sar·i·al·ly** *adv.*—**glos·sa·rist** *n.*

gloss·y *adj.* [gloss·i·er; gloss·i·est] 1. Smooth and shining; highly polished. 2. Outwardly plausible.—**gloss·i·ly** *adv.*—**gloss·i·ness** *n.*

glot·tis (*glot*-iss) *n.* The mouth of the windpipe.

glove (*gluhv*) *n.* A cover for the hand, or hand and arm, with a separate sheath for each finger.—*v.* [gloved; glov·ing] To put on a glove.—**glov·er** *n.* One who makes gloves, or deals in them.

glow (*gloh*) *v.* 1. To give forth light and heat, or either, esp. without flame. 2. To feel heat; become red. 3. To be ardent or animated. —**glow** *n.*—**glow·ing** *adj.*—**glow·ing·ly** *adv.*

glow·er (*glou*-er) *v.* To frown; scowl.—**glow·er·ing** *adj.* Scowling.—**glow·er·ing·ly** *adv.*

glow·worm *n.* Female wingless insect, resembling a caterpillar, which emits a greenish light.

gloze *v.* [glozed; gloz·ing] 1. To explain; expound; gloss; comment. 2. To gloss over; extenuate.—**gloze** *n.*

glu·ci·num (gloo-*sy*-num) *n.* Also **glu·cin·i·um** (gloo-*sin*-ee-um). *Chemistry.* A white metal, also known as beryllium. (*Symbol:* Gl).

glu·cose (*gloo*-kohss) *n.* A sugar, less sweet than cane sugar, produced from dried grapes, cane sugar, dextrin, starch, etc. (*Symbol:* $C_6H_{12}O_6$).

glue (*gloo*) *n.* Common or impure gelatin, obtained by boiling the skins, hoofs, etc., of animals, and used for sticking objects together. —*v.* [glued; glu·ing] 1. To join with glue or any adhesive substance. 2. To unite; hold together; fix.—**glue·y** *adj.* Sticky; viscous.

glum *adj.* [glum·mer; glum·mest] Sullen; morose.—**glum·ly** *adv.*—**glum·ness** *n.*

glut *v.* [glut·ted; glut·ting] 1. To gorge; supply to excess. 2. To cloy; sate; satiate.—**glut** *n.* Superabundance; excessive supply.

glu·ten (*gloo*-t'n) *n.* Grayish, tough, elastic substance found in wheat flour and other grains. —**glu·te·nous** *adj.*

glu·te·us (gloo-*tee*-us) *n.* [*pl.* -te·i] *Anatomy.* A buttock muscle.—**glu·te·al** *adj.*

glu·ti·nous (*gloo*-tin-us) *adj.* Viscous; tenacious; resembling glue.—**glu·ti·nous·ly** *adv.* —**glu·ti·nous·ness** *n.*

glut·ton (*gluht*-'n) *n.* 1. One who eats to excess. 2. One who indulges to excess in anything.—**glut·ton·ous** *adj.*—**glut·ton·ous·ly** *adv.* —**glut·ton·ous·ness** *n.*—**glut·ton·y** *n.*

glyc·er·in, glyc·er·ine (*gliss*-er-in) *n.* A thick, oily, colorless, sweet liquid, formed in the decomposition of fats and used in soaps, etc.

gly·co·gen (*gly*-kuh-j'n) *n.* A white, amorphous compound found in the liver.—**gly·co·gen·ic** (gly-kuh-*jen*-ik) *adj.*

G-man *n. Slang.* Abbreviation for *government man:* a member of the U.S. Federal Bureau of Investigation.

gnarl (*narl*) *n.* A knot; protuberance on the outside of a tree.—**gnarl** *v.*—**gnarled, gnarl·y** *adj.*

gnash (*nash*) *v.* To grind or clamp together, as the teeth.

gnat (*nat*) *n.* A small insect, the female of which has a blood-sucking sting.

gnaw (*naw*) *v.* [gnawed; gnawed or gnawn; gnaw·ing] 1. To wear away by biting; nibble at. 2. To waste; corrode.—**gnaw·er** *n.*

gneiss (*nysse*) *n. Geology.* Species of rock, composed of quartz, feldspar, and mica, arranged in layers.—**gneiss·ic** *adj.*

gnome (*nohm*) *n.* Fabled elflike being, supposed to be a guardian of mines, quarries, etc.

gno·mon (*noh*-mon) *n.* Any object, as the marker on a sundial, whose shadow acts as an indicator.

GNOMON

Gnos·tic (*noss*-tik) *n.* Member of a cult of early Christian philosophers who believed that only they had a true knowledge of Christianity.—*adj.* Pertaining to the Gnostics or their doctrines. —**gnos·ti·cism** *n.*

gnu (*noo, nyoo*) *n.* An oxlike antelope inhabiting South Africa.

go (*goh*) *v.* [went; gone; going] 1. To move; proceed; progress. 2. To walk. 3. To depart; start. 4. To judge or act upon. 'A good rule to go by.' 5. To have recourse to. 'He went to law.' 6. To release. 'Let go.' 7. To extend; reach; lead. 'This road goes to New York.' 8. To be habitually in a specified state. 'To go hungry.' 9. To become. 'She has gone mad.' 10. To be current. 'The story goes thus.'—*n.* 1. *Colloquial.* An attempt. 2. *Colloquial.* A situation; set of circumstances. 3. *Colloquial.* Spirit; spunk.—**go under.** To fail; succumb; become bankrupt. —**no go.** *Colloquial.* Unsuccessful; hopeless. —**on the go.** Busy; restless.

GNU
(1/40 life size)

goad (*gohd*) *n.* 1. A pointed stick used to urge animals. 2. A stimulus; prod; spur.—*v.* 1. To prick; drive with a goad; incite; stimulate; irritate.

goal (*gohl*) *n.* 1. The point marking the end of a race. 2. The final purpose. 3. Destination. 4. Area, mark, structure or the like serving as the objective in certain games. 5. A score in certain games.

goal·keep·er *n.* Also **goal tender.** *Sports.* A player stationed to protect the goal.

goat *n.* 1. Four-legged, cud-chewing, horned animal, the male of which is generally bearded. 2. *Slang.* Scapegoat.—**goat·ish** *adj.*—**goat·ish·ly** *adv.* —**goat·ish·ness** *n.*—**goat·like** *adj.*

GOAT
(1/30 life size)

goat-bearded	goat-footed	goat-kneed
goat drunk	goat-headed	goatland
goat-eyed	goat-hoofed	goatstone
goatfish	goat-horned	goat-toothed

goat·ee (goh-*tee*) *n.* A pointed beard.

goat·herd *n.* One who tends goats.

G

goat·skin *n.* Garment or bottle made of a goat's skin.

goat·suck·er *n.* Nocturnal bird, known as the whippoorwill in the U.S.

gob *n. Slang.* A sailor.

gob *n.* Also **gob·bet.** A small mass or lump.

gob·ble (*gob-*'l) *v.* [gob·bled; gob·bling] 1. To eat hastily and noisily. 2. To make a noise in the throat, like a turkey.—**gob·ble** *n.* A noise made in the throat, as that of a turkey-cock.

gob·bler *n* 1. A greedy, rapid, and noisy eater. 2. A turkey-cock.

Gob·e·lin (*gob-*eh-lin; goh-*blan*) *adj.* Pertaining to a type of tapestry made in Paris, France.

go-be·tween (*goh-*beh-tween) *n.* An intermediary.

gob·let *n.* A stemmed drinking glass.

gob·lin (*gob-*lin) *n.* An evil or mischievous spirit; gnome; elf.

go·cart *n.* A small cart, usually four-wheeled, for young children.

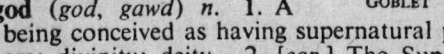

GOBLET

god (god, gawd) *n.* 1. A being conceived as having supernatural powers; divinity; deity. 2. [*cap.*] The Supreme Being; the Creator; the infinite spirit of the universe. 3. A person who is highly honored or deified.

god·child *n.* [*pl.* -chil·dren] A child sponsored by one at baptism.

god·daugh·ter *n.* A girl godchild.

god·dess (*god-*iss) *n.* 1. A female deity. 2. A woman who is adored.

god·fath·er *n.* A man who sponsors a godchild.

god·head *n.* 1. Divine nature or essence. 2. [*cap.*] God; Supreme Being.

god·less (*god-*liss) *adj.* Acknowledging no god; impious; atheistic; irreligious.—**god·less·ness** *n.*

god·like (*god-*lyke) *adj.* Resembling a god or goddess; divine.

god·ly (*god-*lee) *adj.* [god·li·er; -li·est] Pious; religious; devout.—**god·li·ness** *n.*

god·moth·er *n.* A woman who sponsors a child in baptism.

god·send *n.* An unexpected piece of good fortune.

god·son *n.* A boy godchild.

god·speed *n.* Success; prosperous journey.

go-get·ter *n.* An enterprising, ambitious, aggressive person.

gog·gle (*gog-*'l) *v.* [gog·gled; gog·gling] To strain or roll the eyes about.—*adj.* Protuberant. —*n.* A strained or affected rolling of the eyes.

gog·gles (*gog-*'lz) *n. pl.* A kind of spectacles, often with colored glasses, for protecting the eyes against glare, dust, etc.

GOGGLES

go·ing (*goh-*ing) *adj.* Operating successfully.

—*n.* 1. Departure. 2. Ease or difficulty of progressing. 'The going is rough ahead.'

goi·ter, goi·tre *n.* Enlargement of the thyroid gland, often showing as a large swelling in the neck.—**goi·trous** *adj.*

gold *n.* 1. Precious, yellow metallic element, both ductile and malleable. (*Symbol:* Au). 2. Money; riches; wealth. 3. Bright yellow color.—*adj.* Made of, or resembling, gold.

gold-banded	gold-enwoven	gold-plated
gold beater	gold-framed	gold-ribbed
gold-bound	gold-fringed	gold-rimmed
gold-braided	gold-haired	gold-robed
gold-breasted	goldhammer	goldstone
gold bright	goldhead	gold-striped
gold-broidered	gold-headed	gold-strung
goldbug	gold-hilted	gold-studded
gold-crested	gold-inlaid	goldtail
gold-daubed	gold-laced	goldwater
gold-decked	gold-laden	gold-winged
gold-edged	gold-lit	goldwork
gold-embossed	gold-mounted	goldworker
gold-embroidered	gold-plate (*v.*)	gold-wrought

gold-brick *v. Army Slang.* To idle; loaf; evade work and duties.—**gold brick.** *Slang.* Imitation of a brick of gold in a swindling sale; any form of cheating by means of false representation. —**gold-brick·er** *n.*—**gold-brick·ing** *n.*

gold·en *adj.* 1. Made of, or containing, gold. 2. Like gold; bright yellow; shining; splendid. 3. Excellent; valuable; precious. 4. Happy; favorable; auspicious.—**gold·en·ly** *adv.*—**gold·en·ness** *n.*

Golden Gate. Entrance to San Francisco harbor.

golden mean. Moderate course; careful avoidance of extremes.

gold·en·rod *n.* Long-stemmed plant with spikes of small, bright-yellow flowers.

golden rule. The rule that we should treat others as we ourselves wish to be treated.

golden wedding. The fiftieth anniversary of a wedding ceremony.

gold-filled *adj.* Having a surface layer of hard gold, as jewelry.

gold·finch *n.* 1. Bright-colored European songbird with a patch of yellow on its wings. 2. A small American songbird, the male being bright yellow, with black wings and tail.

gold·fish *n.* A small reddish-yellow fish, often kept as a household pet or ornament.

gold leaf. An extremely thin sheet of gold for gilding.—**gold-leaf** *adj.*

gold·smith *n.* One who fashions articles of gold.

golf *n.* A game played with a small, hard ball and long clubs with variously shaped heads, on a course provided with nine or eighteen small holes, and scattered obstacles.—*v.* To play golf.—**golf-club** *n.*

gol·go·tha (*gol-*guh-thuh) *n.* 1. [*cap.*] Site of the crucifixion of Christ. 2. A place where dead bodies are piled.

Go·li·ath (guh-*ly*-uth) *n.* Biblical giant slain by David.

Go·mor·rah, Go·mor·rha (guh-*mor*-uh) *n. Biblical.* A city of great wickedness.

gon·ad (*gon*-ad) *n. Anatomy.* A sexual gland. —**gon·ad·al** (*gon*-uh-d'l), **go·na·di·al** (guh-*nay*-dee-ul)—**go·nad·ic** (guh-*nad*-ik) *adj.*

gon·do·la (*gon*-duh-luh) *n.* 1. A long, narrow, flat-bottomed boat, with a high point at each end, and a cabin in the center, used on the canals of Venice, Italy. 2. A railroad freight car with no top and very low sides.

GONDOLA

gon·do·lier (gon-duh-*leer*) *n.* One who propels a gondola.

gone (*gawn*) *past participle* of go.—*adj.* 1. Lost; hopeless. 2. Past; bygone.

gon·er *n. Colloquial.* A doomed person.

gon·fa·lon (*gon*-fuh-lon) *n.* Banner or standard, often with streamers, hung from a pole.

gong *n.* A saucer-shaped bell; percussion instrument having a clanging tone.

go·ni·om·e·ter (goh-nee-*om*-uh-ter) *n.* Instrument for measuring angles.—**go·ni·o·met·ric** (goh-nee-uh-*met*-rik), **go·ni·o·met·ri·cal** *adj.* —**go·ni·om·e·try** (goh-nee-*om*-uh-tree) *n.*

gon·or·rhe·a, gon·or·rhoe·a (gon-er-*ee*-uh) *n.* Contagious inflammation of the urethra or vagina attended by a discharge of mucus. —**gon·or·rhe·al, -rhoe·al** *adj.*

goo·ber (*goo*-ber) *n. Southern U.S.* Peanut.

good *adj.* [bet·ter; best] 1. Serviceable; advantageous; beneficial; wholesome; suitable; right. 2. Virtuous; worthy; righteous; dutiful; moral. 3. Kind; benevolent; humane. 4. Clever; skillful. 5. Adequate; valid. 6. Full; complete. 'A good measure.' 7. Unsullied; immaculate; honorable. 'A good name.'—**good** *n.* 1. Benefit; advantage. 2. Welfare; prosperity.—*interj.* Fine!

good fellow
good-fellowhood
good-fellowship
good-for-nothingness
good-looker
good looking

good-by, good-bye *n. & interj.* Farewell.

good-for-noth·ing *n.* An idle, worthless person.—**good-for-noth·ing** *adj.*

good-heart·ed *adj.* Kind; humane.—**good·heart·ed·ly** *adv.*—**good·heart·ed·ness** *n.*

good-hu·mored *adj.* Cheerful; amiable.—**good·hu·mored·ly** *adv.*

good·ly *adj.* [good·li·er; good·li·est] 1. Graceful; well favored; handsome. 2. Pleasant; agreeable. 3. Large; considerable. 'A goodly number.'—**good·li·ness** *n.*

good-na·tured *adj.*—Kindly; obliging.—**good·na·tured·ly** *adv.*—**good·na·tured·ness** *n.*

good·ness *n.* 1. Virtue. 2. Excellence. 3. Benevolence; generosity.—*interj.* My!

goods *n. pl.* 1. Wares; merchandise; commodities. 2. Movable property.

good-tem·pered *adj.* Free from irritability. **good-tem·pered·ly** *adv.*

good will. 1. Benevolence; kindly feeling. 2. Heartiness; zeal. 3. Privilege granted a purchaser of a business to trade as the recognized successor of the seller.

good·y *n.* [*pl.* -ies] *Colloquial.* A delicacy; particularly tasty morsel of food, esp. a candy. —*adj.* Unnaturally or excessively good.

good·y-good·y *adj. Colloquial.* Excessively or unnaturally good; sissyish.

goof *n. Slang.* A silly or stupid person; fool. —**goof·y** *adj.*—**goof·i·ly** *adv.*—**goof·i·ness** *n.*

goof off. *Slang.* To err; act stupidly.

goon *n. Slang.* 1. A fool; simpleton; goof. 2. A hired thug; tough.

goon squad. *Union Slang.* A group of strong-arm strike breakers.

goose *n.* [*pl.* geese] 1. A web-footed, long-necked bird between a duck and a swan in size. 2. A silly person; fool. 3. [*pl.* goos·es] Tailor's pressing iron.

GOOSE

goosebeak
goose cackle
goosecap
goose-eyed
goose-footed
goose-headed
gooseherd
goose house
goose-pimply
goose-shaped
goosewing
goose-winged

goose·ber·ry *n.* [*pl.* -ries] 1. Shrub bearing a small sour berry used in tarts, preserving, etc. 2. The berry itself.

goose-flesh *n.* Also **goose flesh.** Bristling of the skin, produced by cold or fright. Also **goose pimples, goose skin.**

goose·neck *n.* Object curved like a goose's neck.

goose step. Stiff, straight-legged military drill or parade step, esp. as used by the German army.—**goose-step** *v.*

go·pher (*goh*-fer) *n.* A ratlike burrowing animal.

Gordian knot. A difficult problem or task, from Gordius, King of Phrygia, who tied an intricate knot cut later by Alexander the Great.

gore (*gor*) *n.* Blood shed from the body; clotted blood.

gore *n.* Gusset; triangular piece inserted, as in a skirt, often to increase width.—*v.* [gored; gor·ing]. To fit with gores.

GOPHER
(1/10 life size)

gore *v.* [gored; gor·ing] To stab; pierce.

gorge (*gorj*) *n.* 1. The throat; gullet. 2. That which is swallowed; food caused to rise in the throat by nausea or disgust. 3. Deep, narrow passage between hills.—*v.* [gorged; gorg·ing] 1. To swallow greedily and in large quantities. 2. To satiate; glut; surfeit.

gor·geous (*gor*-jus) *adj.* Splendid; richly colored; magnificent.—**gor·geous·ly** *adv.*

Gor·gon (*gor*-g'n) *n.* 1. *Greek Mythology.* One of three female monsters whose hideous looks and snaky hair turned beholders to stone. 2. [*not cap.*] Horrible woman.

Gor·gon·zo·la (gor-gon-*zoh*-luh) *n.* A rich Italian cheese.

G

go·ril·la (guh-*ril*-uh) *n.* Large, powerful, ferocious, tree-dwelling ape.

gor·man·ize (*gor*-mund-yze) *v.* [gor·mand·ized; gor·mand·iz·ing] To eat voraciously. —**gor·mand·iz·er** *n.*

gorse *n.* Prickly, yellow-flowered shrub; furze. —**gors·y** *adj.*

gor·y (*gor*-ee) *adj.* [gor·i·er; gor·i·est] 1. Covered with congealed or clotted blood. 2. Bloody; murderous. —**gor·i·ness** *n.*

GORILLA (1/45 life size)

gos·hawk (*goss*-hawk) *n.* A large, powerful hawk.

Go·shen (*goh*-sh'n) *n.* 1. *Biblical.* The rich land given the Israelites in Egypt. 2. A place of plenty.

gos·ling (*goz*-ling) *n.* A young goose.

gos·pel (*goss*-p'l) *n.* 1. [cap.] The history of the life and doctrines of Jesus Christ; one of the first four books of the New Testament. 2. System or principle which determines one's conduct and beliefs.—**gos·pel** *adj.*

gos·sa·mer (*goss*-uh-mer) *n.* A fine, filmy substance, esp. cobwebs, floating in calm, clear air or spread over grass.—**gos·sa·mer, gos·sa·mer·y** *adj.* Flimsy; filmy; unsubstantial.

gos·sip (*goss*-ip) *n.* 1. Idle talk; groundless rumor. 2. Idle talker; tattler. 3. Easy, familiar personal conversation.—**gos·sip** *v.* [gos·siped; gos·sip·ing] 1. To tell idle tales; tattle. 2. To write in gossipy style.—**gos·sip·er** *n.*—**gos·sip·ing·ly** *adv.*—**gos·sip·y** *adj.*

Goth *n.* 1. One of an ancient German tribe which invaded the Roman Empire. 2. Rude or uncivilized person; barbarian.

goth·ic (*goth*-ik) *adj.* 1. *Architecture.* Denoting the pointed-arch style of architecture prevalent in western Europe from the 12th to 16th century. 2. Pertaining to the Goths. 3. Rude; barbarous. 4. Pertaining to medieval art.—*n.* 1. Gothic architecture. 2. The language of the Goths. 3. *Printing.* A kind of boldfaced type.

GOTHIC (def. 1)

gouache (*gwahsh*) *n.* 1. Opaque watercolor. 2. A painting in this medium.

gouge (*gowj*) *n.* A rounded, hollow chisel for cutting holes or grooves.—*v.* [gouged; gouging] 1. To cut with a gouge. 2. To force out, esp. a person's eye, with the thumb.

gou·lash (*goo*-lash) *n.* A beef or veal stew.

gourd (*gord*) *n.* 1. Trailing or climbing plant or its large, fleshy fruit, such as the pumpkin, squash, watermelon. 2. The dried rind of the fruit, used as a bottle, etc.

gour·mand (*goor*-mand) *n.* An epicure; connoisseur of good eating.—**gour·mand·ism** *n.*

gour·met (*goor*-may) *n.* A connoisseur of food and wines.

gout (*gowt*) *n.* 1. Painful disease with inflammation of the joints, esp. of the big toe. 2. A drop; spot; clot.—**gout·y** *adj.*—**gout·i·ly** *adv.* —**gout·i·ness** *n.*

gov·ern (*guv*-ern) *v.* 1. To direct or control, as the actions of men or the affairs of the state, either despotically or constitutionally. 2. To regulate; influence; rule. 3. To curb; restrain. 4. *Grammar.* To require a particular case. 'A transitive verb governs the accusative case.' —**gov·ern·a·ble** *adj.*

gov·ern·ess *n.* A woman teacher, esp. of children in a private household.

gov·ern·ment (*guv*-ern-m'nt) *n.* 1. System of ruling; principles by which a state is administered. 2. Exercise of authority; direction and control over the actions of persons in a community. 3. The administration; executive power. 4. Direction; regulation; guidance. 5. A province, etc., ruled by a governor. —**gov·ern·men·tal** *adj.*—**gov·ern·men·tal·ly** *adv.*

gov·er·nor (*guv*-er-ner) *n.* 1. The executive head of each of the United States. 2. Official appointed to govern a province, territory, etc. 3. One of a governing body of an institution. 4. An automatic regulator of the supply of gas, steam, water, etc., to a machine, insuring an even speed.

governor general. [pl. governors general] A governor with subordinate governors under him; viceroy.

gov·er·nor·ship *n.* The office of governor.

gown *n.* 1. A dress; evening dress. 2. A night dress. 3. Official dress worn by judges, clerics, academies, etc.—*v.* To put on a gown.

goy *n.* *Yiddish.* Any non-Jewish person, esp. a Christian.

grab *v.* [grabbed; grab·bing] 1. To seize; grip suddenly. 2. To snatch or appropriate greedily or unscrupulously.—**grab** *n.*—**grab·ber** *n.*

grace *n.* 1. Good will; kindness; mercy. 2. Ease and harmony of contour or movement. 3. [pl.] Favor. 'In his good graces.' 4. A winning attribute; charm. 5. Respite; reprieve. 6. Blessing; prayer said before a meal. 7. [cap.] Divine mercy or salvation. 8. Title accorded a duke or archbishop. 9. [pl. cap.] *Greek Mythology.* Three beautiful sister goddesses. 10. *Music.* Small accessory notes embellishing the melody.—*v.* [graced; grac·ing] To adorn.

grace·ful *adj.* Beautiful in form or motion; having a natural ease.—**grace·ful·ly** *adv.*—**grace·ful·ness** *n.*

grace·less *adj.* 1. Unregenerate; irrepressible; hapless. 2. Awkward.—**grace·less·ly** *adv.* —**grace·less·ness** *n.*

gra·cious (*gray*-shus) *adj.* Cordial; affable; pleasant; courteous; warm in manner.—**gra·cious·ly** *adv.*—**gra·cious·ness** *n.*

grack·le (*grak-'l*) *n.* A blackbird; any of several American birds of dark, glossy plumage.

gra·da·tion (*gray-day*-shun) *n.* 1. Arranging in order according to size, quality, rank, etc.; being arranged in series or ranks; regular advance from one degree to another.

GRACKLE (1/8 life size)

2. A degree or relative position in any order or series. 3. *Fine Arts.* Blending; subordination of parts for best effect. 4. *Music.* An ascending or descending succession of chords.—**gra·da·tion·al** *adj.*

grade *n.* 1. A degree or rank in any series; relative position or standing. 2. Rate of ascent or descent of a slope; gradient. 3. *Breeding.* A hybrid. 4. *Education.* A class or division of the course in elementary schools.—*v.* [grad·ed; grad·ing] 1. To arrange in order according to size, quality, rank, etc. 2. To reduce to an even inclination.—**grad·er** *n.*

gra·di·ent (*gray*-dee-unt) *adj.* 1. Moving by steps. 2. Rising or descending by regular degrees of inclination.—*n.* 1. Rate of ascent or descent, increase or decrease, etc. 2. A sloping portion of a road.

grad·u·al (*grad*-joo-ul) *adj.* Proceeding by steps or degrees; regular and slow; progressive.—*n. Ecclesiastical.* 1. An ancient book of hymns and prayers. 2. Part of the mass sung between the Epistle and Gospel.—**grad·u·al·ly** *adv.*—**grad·u·al·ness** *n.*

grad·u·ate (*grad*-joo-it) *adj. & n.* 1. A recipient of a diploma or degree from an educational institution. 2. A measuring container. —(*grad*-joo-ayt) *v.* [grad·u·at·ed; -at·ing] 1. To receive a diploma or degree. 2. To grade; arrange or scale progressively.—**grad·u·a·tion** (grad-joo-*ay*-sh'n) *n.*

graft *n.* 1. A tree shoot or cutting inserted into another plant. 2. Political corruption; bribes; dishonest gains through use of official position. 3. Transferred skin or other living tissue.—**graft** *v.*—**graft·age** *n.*—**graft·er** *n.*

graham flour (*gray*-um). A kind of wholewheat flour.—**gra·ham** *adj.*

Grail *n.* Also **Holy Grail.** The chalice used by Christ at the Last Supper.

grain *n.* 1. Cereal; seed of one of the cereal grasses. 2. A small particle. 3. In troy weight, $\frac{1}{24}$ of a pennyweight. 4. Quality of a surface with regard to the direction of its texture; vein or fiber pattern, as of wood. —**grain** *v.*—**grain·y** *adj.* [grain·i·er; grain·i·est].

grain alcohol. Ethyl alcohol. (*Symbol:* C_2H_5OH).

gram, gramme *n.* In the metric system, a weight equal to one cubic centimeter of water at maximum density.

gram·mar (*gram*-er) *n.* 1. Body of principles which govern language usage. 2. Language or construction with reference to these principles. 3. A textbook of grammar.—**gram·mar·i·an** (gruh-*mair*-ee-un) *n.*

grammar school. Elementary school.

gram·mat·i·cal *adj.* Pertaining or conforming to grammar.—**gram·mat·i·cal·ly** *adv.*

gram molecule. Also **gram-molecular weight.** *Chemistry.* The number of grams of a substance numerically equal to its molecular weight.

Gram·o·phone (*gram*-uh-fohn) *n.* Trade-mark name for a phonograph.

gram·pus (*gram*-pus) *n.* A ferocious, carnivorous member of the porpoise family.

gran·a·ry (*gran*-er-ee) *n.* [*pl.* -ries] A storehouse for grain.

grand *adj.* 1. Great; noble; illustrious. 2. Sublime; splendid; fine.—*n. Slang U.S.* A thousand dollars.—**grand·ly** *adv.*—**grand·ness** *n.*

gran·dam (*gran*-dam) *n.* Also **gran·dame.** An elderly woman, esp. a grandmother.

grand·aunt *n.* The sister of one's grandfather or grandmother; aunt of one's parents.

Grand Canyon. Famous canyon in the valley of the Colorado River.

grand·child *n.* The son or daughter of one's offspring.

grand·dad, grand·dad·dy *n. Colloquial.* Grandfather.

grand·daugh·ter *n.* The daughter of one's child.

grand duke. 1. In certain monarchies, the male heir to the throne. 2. A male member of the old imperial family of Russia.

gran·dee (gran-*dee*) *n.* A nobleman.

gran·deur (*gran*-jer) *n.* Sublimity; splendor.

grand·fa·ther *n.* The father of one's parent. —**grand·fa·ther·ly** *adv. & adj.*

gran·dil·o·quence (gran-*dil*-uh-kwenss) *n.* Also **grandiloquentness.** Bombast; inflated or lofty manner of expression.—**gran·dil·o·quent** *adj.*—**gran·dil·o·quent·ly** *adv.*

gran·di·ose (*gran*-dee-ohss) *adj.* 1. Impressive; magnificent. 2. Spectacularly magnificent; ostentations.—**gran·di·ose·ly** *adv.*—**-ose·ness** *n.*

grand jury. A jury, composed of up to 24 members, which studies cases and arrives at a decision in the form of an indictment.

grand·ma, grand·ma·ma *n.* A grandmother.

grand·moth·er *n.* The mother of one's parent. —**grand·moth·er·ly** *adj. & adv.*

grand·neph·ew *n.* The son of one's nephew or niece.

grand·niece *n.* The daughter of one's nephew or niece.

grand opera. *Music.* Drama in which the entire dialogue is sung.

grand·pa, grand·pop, grand·pap, grand·pap·py *n. Colloquial.* A grandfather.

grand·par·ent *n.* A parent of one's parents.

grand·sire *n. Archaic.* A grandfather; old man.

grand·stand *n.* A seating construction arranged

G

in tiers about a race course or other spectacle.

grand·un·cle *n.* The brother of one's grandparent; uncle of one's parent.

grange *n.* 1. A society or combination of farmers. 2. A farm.—**gran·ger** *n.*

gran·ite (*gran*-it) *n.* A hard, unstratified stone used in building.— -**it·ic** (gruh-*nit*-ik) *adj.*

gran·ny, gran·nie *n.* [*pl.* -nies] 1. A grandmother; old woman. 2. *Colloquial.* A fussy, officious person.

granny knot. A landlubber's imitation of a square knot.

grant *v.* 1. To give; bestow; confer. 2. To concede; admit as true what has not been proved.—*n.* 1. Conferment or concession. 2. A gift; donation; subsidy.—**grant·ee** *n.* —**grant·a·ble** *adj.*—**grant·er, grant·or** *n.*

gran·u·lar (*gran*-yoo-ler) *adj.* Grainy; rough-textured; showing a crystallike formation. —**gran·u·lar·i·ty** (gran-yoo-*lair*-ih-tee) *n.*

gran·u·late (*gran*-yoo-layt) *v.* [gran·u·lat·ed; -lat·ing] 1. To form into grains. 2. To roughen the surface by small, pebbly protuberances.—**gran·u·lat·ed** *adj.*—**gran·u·lat·er gran·u·lat·or** *n.*—**gran·u·la·tion** *n.*

gran·ule (*gran*-yool) *n.* A grain; small, hard particle.

grape *n.* A vine-growing, clustering berry from which wine is made.

grape-hued	graperoot	grapeskin
grape juice	grape-shaped	grapestalk
grape-leaved	grape-sized	grapestone

grape·fruit *n.* A large, yellow citrus fruit related to the orange and lemon.

grape·shot *n.* A small missile formerly used in cannons in dispersed firing.

grape sugar. Dextrose.

grape·vine *n.* 1. Also **grapevine telegraph.** Rumor; gossip. 2. The vine on which grapes grow.

graph (*graf*) *n.* A chart; diagrammatic representation of quantities by points joined to show their relative values.—**graph** *v.*

graph·ic (*graf*-ik) *adj.* Also **graphical.** 1. Vivid; easily seen or grasped. 2. Pertaining to the representational art based on linear expression. 3. Pertaining to writing, graphs, or diagrams.—**graph·i·cal·ly** *adv.*

graph·ite (*graf*-yte) *n.* A soft form of carbon used in pencils, etc.— -**phit·ic** (gruh-*fit*-ik) *adj.*

grap·nel (*grap*-n'l) *n.* An anchor with four or five flukes for holding small boats.

grap·ple (*grap*-'l) *v.* [grap·pled; grap·pling] 1. To fight, wrestle, or struggle. 2. To seize; lay hold of.—*n.* 1. Close struggle. 2. Grappling iron.—**grap·pler** *n.*

grappling iron. An instrument equipped with claws for seizing and holding.

grap·y *adj.* Of or resembling grapes.

grasp *v.* 1. To seize hold of; clasp. 2. To understand; comprehend.—*n.* 1. A handclasp; grip. 2. Possession; reach; control. 3. Mentality; comprehension.—**grasp·er** *n.*

grasp·ing *adj.* Selfish; greedy; miserly.—**grasp·ing·ly** *adv.*—**grasp·ing·ness** *n.*

grass *n.* 1. Herbage; pasture; green growth covering fields, lawns, etc. 2. Any of a family of narrow-leaved plants including the canes, cereals, and decorative lawn grasses. 3. Land covered with grass.—**grass** *v.*

grassbird	grass-fed	grassnut
grass blade	grass green	grassplot
grass-clad	grass-grown	grass-roofed
grass-covered	grassland	grasswork
grass cutter	grass-leaved	grassworker

grass·hop·per *n.* Any of a family of winged, leaping insects.

grass widow. A woman separated or divorced from her husband.

grass·y *adj.* [grass·i·er; grass·i·est] Abounding in, or like, grass; green.—**grass·i·ness** *n.*

grate (*grayt*) *v.* [grat·ed; grat·ing] 1. To rub so as to produce a harsh sound; grind. 2. To wear away in small particles. 3. To vex; irritate; affect unpleasantly.—**grat·ing·ly** *adv.*

grate *n.* A barred, usually metal framework, as before a fire or window.—**grate** *v.*

grate·ful *adj.* 1. Feeling or showing appreciation for favors received; thankful. 2. Agreeable; gratifying.— -**ful·ly** *adv.*— -**ful·ness** *n.*

grat·i·fi·ca·tion (grat-ih-fih-*kay*-sh'n) *n.* 1. Enjoyment; satisfaction; indulgence. 2. A reward; payment; remuneration.

grat·i·fy *v.* [grat·i·fied; -fy·ing] To satisfy; give pleasure to; indulge.—**grat·i·fi·er** *n.*—**grat·i·fy·ing·ly** *adv.*

grat·ing *n.* A framework of crossed bars.

gra·tis (*grayt*-iss; *grat*-iss) *adj.* Free of charge; done or given for nothing.—**gra·tis** *adv.*

grat·i·tude (*grat*-ih-tood) *n.* Appreciation; feeling of good will, as toward a benefactor.

gra·tu·i·tous (gruh-*too*-ih-tus) *adj.* 1. Freely given; voluntary; granted without payment. 2. Without reasonable cause; not warranted.

gra·tu·i·ty (gruh-*too*-ih-tee) *n.* [*pl.* -ties] A tip; donation; gift.

grave (*grayv*) *adj.* 1. Solemn; sober; not bright or gay. 2. Important; vital; serious. 3. *Music.* Low, as a sound; not shrill. 4. Having a grave accent.—*n.* Also **grave accent.** A mark [`] denoting inflection, quality of sound, or pronunciation of a syllable.—**grave·ly** *adv.*

grave *v.* [graved; grav·en, graved; grav·ing] 1. To carve; shape or cut, as with a chisel. 2. Imprint deeply.—**grav·er** *n.*

grave *n.* A hole in the earth for burying a corpse; tomb.

grave-born	gravedigger	graveship
grave-bound	grave maker	graveside
graveclod	grave making	graveward

grave·clothes *n. pl.* The garments in which a corpse is buried.

grav·el (*grav*-'l) *n.* 1. Pebbles; small stone fragments. 2. Gallstones; small, hard deposits in the bladder or kidneys.—*v.* [graveled, grav·elled; grav·el·ing, grav·el·ling] To sprinkle or lay with gravel.—**grav·el·ly** *adv.*

grav·en (*gray*-v'n) *adj*. Engraved; carved.—**graven image**. A statue; idol.

grave·stone *n*. A monument or marker for a grave.

grave·yard *n*. A cemetery; burying place.

grav·i·tate (*grav*-uh-tayt) *v*. [grav·i·tat·ed; -tat·ing] To move by, or as by, gravitation.

grav·i·ta·tion (grav-uh-*tay*-sh'n) *n*. 1. *Physics*. Attraction toward a center; force of attraction between bodies. 2. A natural attraction or tendency toward any point.—**grav·i·ta·tion·al** *adj*.—**grav·i·ta·tion·al·ly** *adv*.

grav·i·ty (*grav*-uh-tee) *n*. [*pl*. -ties] 1. Force that draws toward a center of attraction, esp. the natural tendencies of bodies toward the earth's center. 2. Gravitation. 3. Solemnity; serious character or quality; importance.—*adj*. Functioning by gravity.

grav·ure (*grayv*-yer) *n*. 1. Process of printing from an engraved block or plate. 2. Such a plate, or the print produced by it.

gra·vy (*gray*-vee) *n*. [*pl*. -vies] 1. A sauce or dressing, usually from its own juices, for meat or other foods. 2. *Slang*. Net profit, esp. when unearned; easy money.

gray, grey *n*. 1. A shade intermediate between, and formed by mixing, black and white. 2. A gray person, animal, object.—*adj*. 1. Gray in color. 2. Old; gray-haired. 3. Wearing gray; dull; somber.—*v*. To turn gray.—**gray·ly, grey·ly** *adv*.—**gray·ness, grey·ness** *n*.

grayback	gray-eyed	gray-leaved
gray-bearded	grayfish	graypate
gray-clad	grayfly	gray-toned
graycoat	gray-haired	gray-winged

gray·beard, grey·beard *n*. An old man.

gray·ish, grey·ish *adj*. Slightly gray.

gray·ling *n*. A tasty freshwater fish resembling the trout.

gray matter. 1. Grayish tissue in the brain and spinal column, containing the nerve endings. 2. *Colloquial*. Intelligence.

graze (*grayz*) *v*. [grazed; graz·ing] 1. To feed on growing plants; furnish with pasture. 2. To tend while pasturing, as cattle, sheep.

graze *v*. To skin or brush against in passing; scrape.—*n*. A rubbed surface; scrape.—**graz·er** *n*.—**graz·ing·ly** *adv*.

gra·zier (*gray*-zher) *n*. A cattleman; rancher.

graz·ing *n*. Grass for feeding; pasture.

grease (*greess*) *n*. A heavy lubricant; animal fat; petroleum product.—*v*. (*greess*; *greez*) [greased; greas·ing] 1. To apply lubricant to; smear with grease. 2. *Slang*. To bribe.

grease·bush *n*. Also **grease·wood**. A bush or small tree common in the arid regions of western U.S.

grease monkey. *Slang*. A mechanic.

greas·y (*greess*-ee, *greez*-ee) *adj*. [greas·i·er; greas·i·est] Oily; soiled with grease; unctuous. —**greas·i·ly** *adv*.—**greas·i·ness** *n*.

great (*grayt*) *adj*. 1. Large; weighty. 2. Important; eminent; accomplished. 3. Swollen; pregnant. 4. Denoting a degree of relationship once removed in lineal descent, as great-grandfather.—**the great**. Important persons. —**great·ly** *adv*.—**great·ness** *n*.

great-aunt *n*. A grandaunt.

Great Bear. A familiar, easily visible constellation; Big Dipper; Ursa Major.

great·coat *n*. An overcoat, esp. a heavy one.

Great Dane. A breed of large short-haired dog, noted for its strength and gentleness.

Great Divide. The Rocky Mountain watershed.

great-heart·ed *adj*. Noble; generous; courageous.

Great Lakes. The group of five large lakes including Erie, Huron, Michigan, Ontario and Superior, in the northern U. S. and Canada.

great seal. The official seal or stamp of a nation.

Great White Way. The legendary theatrical district of Broadway in New York City.

greave (*greev*) *n*. Armor for the leg below the knee.

grebe *n*. A tailless diving bird.

GREBE (1/12 life size)

Gre·cian (*gree*-shun) *adj*. Relating to Greece.—*n*. A native of Greece.

Greece (*greess*). A small country in the NE Mediterranean region. Area: 50,269 sq. mi. Capital: Athens.

greed *n*. Rapacity; covetousness; avidity; gluttony.

greed·y *adj*. [greed·i·er; greed·i·est] Avaricious; rapacious; gluttonous.—**greed·i·ly** *adv*.—**greed·i·ness** *n*.

Greek *n*. 1. A native of Greece. 2. The language of Greece. 3. Something incomprehensible. 'It's all Greek to me.'—**Greek** *adj*.

Greek Church, Greek Orthodox Church. The Orthodox Catholic Church of Greece, recognizing the headship of the patriarch of Constantinople.

green *adj*. 1. Of the color green. 2. Unripe; immature; inexperienced.—*n*. The color made by combining blue and yellow. 2. A grass-covered area. 3. [*pl*.] Green vegetables.—*v*. To make or become green.—**green·ness** *n*.

green·back *n*. *Colloquial*. A bill of U.S. paper money.

green·bri·er (*green*-bry-er) *n*. A thorny climbing shrub with yellowish-green stem, thick leaves, and small bunches of flowers.

green·er·y (*green*-er-ee) *n*. [*pl*. -ies] 1. A mass of green plants or foliage. 2. A place where green plants are raised.

green-eyed *adj*. 1. Having green eyes. 2. *Slang*. Jealous; envious.

greengage (*green*-gayj) *n*. A variety of large greenish plum.

G

green·groc·er (*green*-groh-ser) *n.* A seller of vegetables.

green·horn (*green*-horn) *n. Colloquial.* A novice; inexperienced person.

green·house (*green*-howss) *n.* A heated, glass-enclosed structure for cultivating plants.

green·ing *n.* An apple that is green when ripe.

green·ish (*green*-ish) *adj.* Somewhat green.

green·room *n.* A room in a theater for actors not occupied on the stage.

Green·wich (*gren*-ij, *grin*-ij) A town in SE England, site of a famous observatory from which longitude is measured around the earth.

green·wood *n.* 1. A forest in full foliage. 2. Any wood that acquires a green color from a type of fungus.

greet *v.* To welcome; salute; hail.—**greet·er** *n.*

greet·ing *n.* A salutation; expression of welcome.

gre·gar·i·ous (gruh-*gehr*-ee-us) *adj.* Inclined to gather in a flock or herd; liking company; not solitary.— **-i·ous·ly** *adv.*— **-ous·ness** *n.*

Gre·go·ri·an (grih-*gor*-ee-un) *adj.* Relating to Gregory, esp. Pope Gregory XIII.

Gregorian Calendar. The calendar, now in common use, reformed under Pope Gregory XIII in 1582, taking leap-years into account so as to harmonize the civil year with the solar: —adopted in America and Great Britain, 1752.

grem·lin (*grem*-lin) *n. Slang.* The name facetiously given by military fliers to an imaginary imp that causes mechanical failures in their planes; 20th-century leprechaun.

gre·nade (gruh-*nayd*) *n. Military.* An anti-personnel fragmentation missile, set off by a fuse and usually thrown by hand.

gren·a·di·er (gren-uh-*deer*) *n.* 1. *Military.* Originally a soldier designated to throw grenades, later a member of an elite company or regiment. 2. A small red-and-black bird inhabiting the Cape Colony.

gren·a·dine (gren-uh-*deen*) *n.* 1. A red, sweet flavoring syrup. 2. A thin gauzy fabric for women's dresses, shawls, etc.

Gretna Green (*gret*-nuh). 1. A town in Scotland noted for elopement marriages. 2. Any town of like character.

grey. *Variant spelling of* gray.

grey·hound (*gray*-hownd) *n.* A tall, slender, exceptionally fleet dog used for hunting and racing.

grid *n. Electricity.* 1. One of the elements of a vacuum tube. 2. A lead plate in a storage battery. 3. A grating.

GREYHOUND (1/35 life size)

grid·dle (*grid*-'l) *n.* An iron plate for cooking hotcakes, etc.—*v.* [grid·dled; grid·dling].

grid·dle·cake (*grid*-'l-kayk) *n.* A hotcake; pancake; thin cake fried on a griddle.

grid·i·ron (*grid*-eye-ern) *n.* 1. A grate for broiling food over coals. 2. A football field.

grief (*greef*) *n.* 1. Sorrow; sadness. 2. Calamity; disaster.

griev·ance *n.* A cause of grief; ground for complaint; insult; injustice.

grievance committee. Elected committee of workers which meets with management to adjust complaints about working conditions, etc.

grieve (*greev*) *v.* [grieved; griev·ing] 1. To afflict; give mental pain to. 2. To mourn; sorrow over.—**griev·er** *n.*—**griev·ing·ly** *adv.*

griev·ous (*greev*-us) *adj.* 1. Painful; harmful; severe. 2. Serious;heinous;atrocious. 3. Expressing grief or pain.—**griev·ous·ly** *adv.*

grif·fin (*grif*-in) *n.* Also **grif·fon.** 1. *Mythology.* An imaginary animal, part eagle and part lion. 2. A vulture found in Europe, North Africa, and Turkey.

GRIFFIN

grift *v. Colloquial.* To operate a concession, esp. dishonestly, at a carnival, etc.—**grift·er** *n.*

grig *n.* 1. A cricket; grasshopper. 2. A sand eel.

grill *n.* 1. A gridiron; grate for broiling food over coals. 2. Grillroom.—*v.* 1. To broil over a grate. 2. *Colloquial.* To torment; examine or question unmercifully.—**grill·er** *n.*

grille *n.* A latticework or grating, usually ornamental.—**grilled** *adj.*

grill·room *n.* Also **grill.** An informal restaurant.

grilse (*grilss*) *n.* [*pl.* grilse] A young salmon when first returning to fresh water from the sea.

grim *adj.* [grim·mer; grim·mest] Of forbidding aspect; stern; surly; fierce; frightful; ghastly. —**grim·ly** *adv.*—**grim·ness** *n.*

gri·mace (gruh-*mayss*) *n.* A distortion of the face expressing strong emotion, humor, etc. —*v.* [gri·maced; gri·mac·ing]—**gri·mac·er** *n.*

gri·mal·kin (gruh-*mal*-kin) *n.* An old cat, esp. a female.

grime *n.* Dirt; ingrained dirt; foul matter.—*v.* [grimed; grim·ing] To soil deeply.

grim·y (*gryme*-ee) *adj.* [grim·i·er; grim·i·est] Dirty; foul.—**grim·i·ly** *adv.*—**grim·i·ness** *n.*

grin *v.* [grinned; grin·ning] To smile broadly. —**grin·ning·ly** *adv.*

grind (*grynde*) *v.* [ground; grind·ing] 1. To wear down, smooth, or sharpen by friction. 2. To suppress. 3. *Slang.* To study laboriously.—*n. Colloquial.* 1. Hard work. 2. A plodding, hard-working person. 3. *Slang.* A cheap motion-picture theater.

grind·er (*grynde*-er) *n.* 1. One that grinds. 2. A double tooth; molar.

grind·stone (*grynde*-stohn) *n.* A stone used for sharpening tools.

grip *n.* 1. The act of grasping by the hand; any special manner of grasp, as that of a fraternity; strength of grasp. 2. A hilt or handle. 3. Power; domination. 4. *Colloquial.* A small traveling bag. 5. *Theater.* A stage hand. 6. *Motion Pictures.* An electrician.—*v.* [gripped; gripping]—**grip·per** *n.*—**grip·ping·ly** *adv.*

GRINDSTONE

gripe (*grype*) *v.* [griped; grip·ing] 1. To clutch; embrace closely; clench. 2. To give pain to the bowels; pinch; straiten; distress. 3. *Slang.* To complain·bitterly.—**grip·en** *n.*—**grip·er** *n.*

grippe (*grip*) *n.* A form of influenza.

grip·sack *n. Colloquial.* A traveling bag.

gri·sette (grih-*zet*) *n.* A French working girl.

gris·ly (*griz*-lee) *adj.* [gris·li·er; gris·li·est] Frightful; grim; gruesome.—**gris·li·ness** *n.*

grist *n.* Something ground, esp. grain.

gris·tle (*griss*-'l) *n. Anatomy.* A tough elastic substance found in the body; cartilage.—**gris·tly** *adj.*—**grist·li·ness** *n.*

grist·mill (*grist*-mil) *n.* A place where grain is ground.

grit *n.* 1. Sand or gravel; rough hard particles. 2. The coarse part of meal. 3. *Colloquial.* Courage; determination.—*v.* [grit·ted; grit·ting] To grate; grind; make a grating sound.

grits *n. pl.* Coarsely ground grain, esp. hominy.

grit·ty *adj.* [grit·ti·er; grit·ti·est] 1. Containing sand or grit; full of hard particles. 2. *Colloquial.* Courageous.—**grit·ti·ly** *adv.*— **-ti·ness** *n.*

griz·zled (*griz*-'ld) *adj.* Gray; streaked with white and black.

griz·zly (*griz*-lee) *adj.* [griz·zli·er; griz·zli·est] Grayish.—*n.* [*pl.* -zlies] A grizzly bear.

grizzly bear. A large ferocious bear of western North America.

groan (*grohn*) *v.* To utter a moaning sound, as in pain or sorrow.—*n.* A low moaning sound, as in pain, sorrow, or disapprobation.—**groan·er** *n.*—**groan·ing·ly** *adv.*

groat (*groht*) *n.* 1. An old English coin worth fourpence. 2. Any small sum.

gro·cer (*groh*-ser) *n.* A retailer of foodstuffs.

gro·cer·y (*groh*-ser-ee) *n.* [*pl.* -ies] 1. A grocer's shop. 2. [*pl.*] Foodstuffs sold by a grocer.

grog *n.* A mixture of rum and water; strong drink in general.

grog·ger·y (*grog*-er-ee) *n.* [*pl.* -ies] Saloon.

grog·gy (*grog*-ee) *adj.* [grog·gi·er; grog·gi·est] Stupefied; stumbling; tipsy.—**grog·gi·ness** *n.*

grog·ram (*grog*-rum) *n.* A coarse material of silk and mohair or strong coarse silk.

grog·shop *n.* Place where liquors are sold; saloon.

groin *n.* 1. The forepart of the human body where the thighs join the trunk. 2. *Architecture.* The angular curve made by simple vaults crossing each other.

GROIN

grom·met (*grom*-it) *n.* An eyelet in a sail, tarpaulin, flag, etc., to receive a rope.

groom *n.* 1. A stable man or boy. 2. A man newly married or about to be married; bridegroom.—*v.* To tend or care for; train.—**groom·er** *n.*

grooms·man *n.* An attendant on a bridegroom.

groove *n.* A furrow; rut; channel; long hollow. —*v.* [grooved; groov·ing] To cut a groove or channel.—**in the groove.** *Swing Music Slang.* Well-played; performed in the jazz idiom.

grope *v.* [groped; grop·ing] To feel with the hands; search in the dark by feeling; attempt anything blindly.—**grop·er** *n.*—**grop·ing·ly** *adv.*

gros·beak (*grohss*-beek) *n.* A thick-billed bird resembling a finch.

gros·grain (*groh*-grayn) *n.* A ribbed fabric of silk or rayon used in ribbons.

gross (*grohss*) *adj.* 1. Thick; fat; large. 2. Coarse; rough; vulgar. 3. Heinous; enormous; shameful. 4. Stupid; dull. 5. Whole; entire; total. 'Gross profit.'—*n.* 1. Bulk; mass; main body. 2. Twelve dozen. —**gross·ly** *adv.*—**gross·ness** *n.*

GROSBEAK (1/7 life size)

gro·tesque (groh-*tesk*) *adj.* Of extravagant, irregular form; antic; whimsical.—**gro·tesque** *n.* —**gro·tesque·ly** *adv.*—**gro·tesque·ness** *n.*

grot·to (*grot*-oh) *n.* [*pl.* -toes, -tos] A cave; natural cavity in the earth.

grouch (*growch*) *v. Colloquial.* To be surly; complain overmuch.—*n.* 1. A surly, ill-tempered person. 2. A fit of ill temper.

grouch·y (*growch*-ee) *adj.* [grouch·i·er; grouch·i·est] Ill-tempered; complaining; surly.—**grouch·i·ly** *adv.*—**grouch·i·ness** *n.*

ground (*grownd*) *n.* 1. The surface of the earth; land. 2. A foundation; basis. 3. A background. 4. *Electricity.* The connection of a circuit with the earth. 5. [*pl.*] Sediment; lees; dregs.—*v.* 1. To set on the ground; connect with the ground. 2. To fix; settle firmly; base. 3. *Nautical.* To run ashore. 4. To deny permission for an aviator or plane to fly, as for some offense.—**ground** *adj.*

ground·er *n. Baseball.* A ball hit low and bounding.

ground hog. A woodchuck.

ground·less *adj.* False; without foundation or reason.—**ground·less·ly** *adv.*— **-less·ness** *n.*

G

ground·ling n. 1. A fish that stays near the bottom of a stream, etc. 2. Anyone who stays on the ground.

ground·nut n. 1. A peanut. 2. A related vine bearing tubers on its roots.

ground-pea n. *Southern U.S.* The peanut.

ground pine. A fernlike moss with evergreen leaves.

ground squirrel. 1. A squirrellike rodent, having a striped back. 2. The chipmunk.

ground swell. A swell in the sea occurring at a distance from the gale or earthquake which produced it.

ground·work (*grownd*-werk) n. Basis; foundation; the fundamental part.

group (*groop*) n. 1. An assemblage; collection of objects. 2. A crowd; assembly. 3. Organisms having similar characteristics. 4. A geological division.—*adj.* Performed by a group. —*v.* To arrange together.

grouse (*growss*) n. The partridge; red-and-black game bird inhabiting marshes, heaths, etc.

grouse v. [groused; grous·ing] 1. To hunt grouse. 2. *Slang.* To complain; grumble.

grove n. 1. A small wood. 2. A collection of fruit trees.

grov·el (*gruv*-'l) v. [grov·eled, grov·elled; grov·el·ing, grov·el·ling] 1. To move with the body prostrate. 2. To debase oneself.

grow (*groh*) v. [grew; grown; grow·ing] 1. To develop by a natural process. 2. To increase; accrue. 3. To become taller. 4. To become. 'To grow pale.' 5. To produce; cultivate; raise.—**grow·er** n.—**grow out of.** To result from.—**grow up.** To become adult.

growl v. To snarl; utter an angry rumbling sound, as a dog.—*n.* A snarl; surly murmur.

growl·er n. 1. A small iceberg. 2. A beer can.

grown-up adj. Mature; adult.—*n.* An adult.

growth (*grohth*) n. 1. The process of development. 2. Advancement; improvement; progress. 'Growth of an idea.' 3. Increase. 'Growth of population.' 4. A beard. 5. An excrescence; tumor. 6. A yield, as of grain.

grub v. [grubbed; grub·bing] To dig up; root out of the ground.—*n.* 1. The larva of an insect; a caterpillar, maggot, etc. 2. *Slang.* Food; victuals.—**grub·ber** n.

grub·by adj. [grub·bi·er; -bi·est] Dirty; soiled; unclean.—**grub·bi·ly** adv.—**grub·bi·ness** n.

grub·stake n. Equipment lent to a gold prospector for a share of his finds.—*v.*

grub street. 1. Hack literary works or their authors. 2. [*cap.*] A former street in London. —**grub·street** adj. Of no literary value.

grudge (*gruj*) v. [grudged; grudg·ing] 1. To envy. 2. To begrudge; grant with reluctance. —*n.* 1. Ill will; malice; enmity. 2. Aversion; dislike.—**grudg·ing** adj.— **-ing·ly** adv.

gruel (*groo*-ul) n. Broth; thin mixture of water and oats, meal, etc.

gru·el·ing, gru·el·ling adj. *Colloquial.* Incessantly tortuous; exhausting.

grue·some, grew·some (*groo*-sum) adj. Hideous; repulsive; inspiring horror.—**grue·some·ly** adv.—**grue·some·ness** n.

gruff adj. 1. Rough; coarse in manner. 2. Surly; severe. 3. Hoarse.—**gruff·ly** adv.

grum·ble (*grum*-b'l) v. [grum·bled; grum·bling] 1. To complain; express discontent. 2. To growl; snarl.—**grum·bler** n.—**grum·bling** adv.

grump·y (*grum*-pee) adj. [grump·i·er; grump·i·est] Surly; angry; gruff.—**grump·i·ly** adv.

grunt v. To snort; groan; utter a short guttural sound, as a pig.—*n.* A short guttural sound. —**grunt·er** n.—**grunt·ing·ly** adv.

Gruy·ère (*groo-yehr*) n. A creamy pressed Swiss cheese.

gua·no (*gwah*-noh) n. The dung of sea birds found on the west coast of South America and used as fertilizer.

guar·an·tee (gair-un-*tee*) v. [guar·an·teed; guar·an·tee·ing] 1. To warrant; answer for. 2. To insure; be responsible for. 3. To undertake to uphold, as rights, claims, etc.—*n.* An undertaking to secure the fulfillment of an agreement.

guar·an·ty (*gair*-un-tee) n. [*pl.* -ties] A guarantee; security; undertaking rendering one person responsible for the obligation of another. —*v.* [-tied; -ty·ing] To assume responsibility for the obligations of another.—**guar·an·tor** n.

guard (*gahrd*) v. To protect; watch; shield; defend; take care.—*n.* 1. Caution; watch; heed. 'Take on guard.' 2. A watchman; sentinel. 3. A body of men equipped for defense, as the Home Guard, etc. 4. Any safety device.

guard·ed adj. 1. Protected; defended. 2. Circumspect; cautious.— **-ed·ly** adv.— **-ed·ness** n.

guard·house n. *Military.* A temporary prison.

guard·i·an (*gahrd*-ee-un) n. 1. Anyone caring for the person or property of another. 2. The legal custodian of a child or an incompetent. —*adj.* Protecting.—**guard·i·an·ship** n.

guard·room n. 1. The room of a military guard. 2. A temporary place of confinement for military prisoners.

guards·man n. [*pl.* -men] 1. A watchman; guard. 2. A soldier of the guard.

gua·va (*gwah*-vuh) n. A pear-shaped South American fruit used in making jelly, etc.

gua·yu·le (gwah-*yoo*-lay) n. Also **huayule.** A rubber plant of Central Mexico.—**guayule rubber.** An India-rubber substitute.

gu·ber·na·to·ri·al (goo-ber-nuh-*tor*-ee-ul) adj. Relating to a governor.

gudg·eon (*guhj*-un) n. 1. A small-scaled freshwater fish used for bait. 2. A dupe; person easily cheated.

guer·don (*ger*-dun) n. A reward; recompense.

Guern·sey (*gern*-zee) n. [*pl.* -seys] One of a breed of dairy cattle originally from Guernsey.

guer·ril·la (ger-*il*-uh) n. Also **gue·ril·la.** A member of an irregular band carrying on raids against a military enemy.

guess (*gess*) v. 1. To conjecture; form a random opinion. 2. To surmise; suspect; think; believe.—**guess** n.—**guess·er** n.

guess·work n. Guessing; conjecture; construed conclusions.

guest (gest) n. 1. A visitor; anyone staying at the home of another. 2. A lodger; resident at a hotel. 3. Anyone receiving the hospitality of another.

guf·faw (guh-faw) n. A sudden shout of laughter.—**guf·faw** v.

guid·ance n. Advice; counsel; direction.

guide (gyde) v. [guid·ed; guid·ing] 1. To lead; direct; point a way. 2. To motivate; inflame. 3. To advise; counsel.—n. 1. A director; anyone leading or directing another. 2. An influence; a motivator.—**guid·a·ble** adj.

guide·board n. A signboard giving direction to travelers.

guide·book n. A book of information for tourists, travelers, etc.

guide·post n. A signpost giving directions.

gui·don (gy-dun) n. A notched flag for troops.

guild, gild (gild) n. A trade union; society for mutual protection for men in the same occupation. 2. An association.—**guilds·man** n.

guil·der (gil-der) n. A Dutch coin; gulden.

guild·hall n. The meeting hall of a guild.

guile (gyle) n. 1. Craft; cunning. 2. Artifice; deceit.—**guile·ful** adj.—**guile·less** adj.

guil·le·mot (gil-uh-mot) n. A species of auk found in northern seas.

guil·lo·tine (gil-uh-teen) n. 1. An apparatus for beheading a criminal, used in France. 2. A machine for cutting paper.—v. (gil-uh-teen) [-tined; -tin·ing] To behead.

guilt (gilt) n. 1. Criminality; liability to punishment for a breach of law. 2. Sin. 3. Responsibility for a breach of conduct.

guilt·less adj. Innocent; without guilt.—**guilt·less·ly** adv.— **·less·ness** n.

guilt·y adj. [guilt·i·er; guilt·i·est] 1. Delinquent; criminal; not innocent. 2. Conscience-stricken; aware of guilt.— **guilt·i·ly** adv.—**guilt·i·ness** n.

guimpe (gamp; gimp) n. A sleeveless low-necked garment worn over a blouse.

guin·ea (gin-ee) n. British coin worth 21 shillings.

guinea fowl. Also **guinea hen.** A gray-spotted species of pheasant native to Africa, now domesticated.

GUINEA FOWL
(1/14 life size)

guinea pig. A prolific South American rodent extensively used for experimental purposes.

Guin·e·vere (gwin-uh-veer) n. Also **Guin·ever.** The wife of King Arthur, and paramour of Lancelot.

GUINEA PIG (1/7 life size)

guise (gyze) n. 1. Mask; assumed appearance or shape. 2. Mien; habitual conduct.

gui·tar (git-ahr) n. A flat-backed stringed instrument related to the lute.

gulch n. A narrow rocky valley.

gul·den (gul-d'n) n. A Dutch silver coin.

gules (gyoolz) n. Heraldry. An emblem composed of close-set perpendicular lines and denoting red.

gulf n. 1. An arm of the sea extending into the land. 2. An abyss; chasm; deep place in the earth. 3. A wide separation. 4. A whirlpool; eddy.—v. To swallow; engulf.—**gulf·y** adj.

GUITAR

G

Gulf Stream. A warm ocean current flowing from the Gulf of Mexico to and across the Atlantic.

gull n. [pl. gulls] A web-footed, hook-billed sea bird having long wings.

gull v. To cheat; defraud; trick.—n. One who is easily cheated.

Gul·lah (gul-uh) n. 1. One of a Negro group inhabiting the coastal and island sections of Georgia and South Carolina. 2. The dialect of the Gullahs, based on English.

GULL (1/15 life size)

gul·let (gul-it) n. The esophagus; passage from the pharynx to the stomach.

gul·li·ble (gul-uh-b'l) adj. Easily deceived.—**gul·li·bil·i·ty** (gul-uh-bil-ih-tee) n.—**gul·li·bly** adv.

gul·ly (gul-ee) n. [pl. -lies] A ravine; channel worn in the earth by a current of water.—v. [gul·lied; gul·ly·ing] To wear into a gully.

gulp v. 1. To swallow in large drafts. 2. To swallow convulsively, as in embarrassment or shock.—**gulp** n.—**gulp·er** n.—**gulp·ing·ly** adv.

gum n. [pl.] The fleshy part of the jaws surrounding the teeth.

gum n. 1. A sticky substance derived from plants and used as an adhesive, thickener, etc. 2. Chewing gum; flavored preparation made from chicle.—v. [gummed; gum·ming] To smear with gum.

gum arabic. A gum derived from the acacia and used as an adhesive.

gum·bo (gum-boh) n. 1. The green pod of the okra plant. 2. A dish containing okra pods. 3. A Creole dialect.—**gum·bo** adj.

gum·boil n. An abscess near the jacket of a tooth.

gum·drop n. A kind of candy made with gelatin.

gum·my adj. [gum·mi·er; gum·mi·est] Sticky; viscous; resembling gum.—**gum·mi·ness** n.

gump·tion (gump-sh'n) n. Colloquial. Courage.

gum resin. Sap extracted from various plants, as myrrh or aloes.

gum·shoe *n*. 1. A rubber overshoe; sneaker. 2. *Slang*. A detective.—*v*. [-shoed; -shoe·ing] *Slang*. To proceed stealthily.—*adj*. *Slang*. Surreptitious; secretive.

gum·wood *n*. Wood of any of the gum trees.

gun *n*. A firearm; any implement for discharging shot.—*v*. [gunned; gun·ning] 1. *Slang*. To seek out with the intention to punish. 2. To go hunting. 3. To accelerate. 'Gun the motor.'

gun bearer	gunpaper	gun-rivet (*v*.)
gun bright	gunplay	gun shop
gunfire	gunpowder	gunshot
gunflint	gunpower	gun-shy
gun house	gun rack	gunsight
gun maker	gunreach	gunwall

gun·boat *n*. A small vessel armed with guns.

gun·cot·ton *n*. An explosive formed by the action of nitric acid on cotton.

gung ho. Work together—a Chinese slogan used as a battle cry by Gen. Evans Carlson's U.S. Marine raiders in World War II.

gun·lock *n*. The firing mechanism of a gun.

gun·man *n*. [*pl*. -men] An armed robber or killer.

gun metal. An alloy of copper and tin.—**gun·metal** *adj*. Of neutral-gray color.

gun·ner *n*. A person operating a gun, esp. a huntsman.

gun·ner·y (*gun*-er-ee) *n*. The science and practice of shooting guns.

gun·ning *n*. The shooting of game.

gun·ny (*gun*-ee) *n*. [*pl*. -nies] 1. A coarse sackcloth of hemp and jute. 2. A burlap bag.

gun·pow·der *n*. An explosive compound used to charge bullets.

gun running. Smuggling of firearms.—**gun runner.** An arms smuggler.

gun·shot *n*. 1. The distance which a shot bullet travels. 2. A gun's effective range.

gun·smith *n*. A maker or repairer of small arms.

gun·stock *n*. The frame which mounts the barrel and lock.

gun·wale (*gun*-'l) *n*. Also **gun·nel**. Upper edge of a ship's or boat's side.

gup·py (*gup*-ee) *n*. [*pl*. -pies] A brilliant-hued, minnowlike fish which breeds rapidly.

gur·gle (*ger*-g'l) *v*. [gur·gled; gur·gling] To flow with a broken, bubbling sound.—**gur·gle** *n*.

gush *v*. 1. To flow violently and suddenly. 2. To show effusive sentiment; wax enthusiastic over trifles.—*n*. An outburst of liquid or of affected sentiment.—**gush·i·ness** *n*.—**gush·ing** *adj*.—**gush·ing·ly** *adv*.

gush·er *n*. 1. An oil well which flows violently without pumping. 2. A person given to extravagant sentimentality.

gus·set (*guss*-it) *n*. 1. A triangular piece of cloth inserted in a garment. 2. A steel bracket for strengthening an angle of a structure.—**gus·set** *v*.

gust *n*. A sweeping rush of wind.

gus·ta·to·ry (*guss*-tuh-tor-ee) *adj*. Relating to taste for food.

gus·to *n*. Relish; zest; enjoyment.

gust·y (*guss*-tee) *adj*. [gust·i·er; gust·i·est] Stormy; subject to sudden blasts of wind. —**gust·i·ly** *adv*.—**gust·i·ness** *n*.

gut *n*. 1. The intestinal tract. 2. Catgut. 3. *Slang*. The abdomen; paunch. 4. [*pl*.] Viscera; entrails. 5. [*pl*.] *Slang*. Daring; pluck.—*v*. [gut·ted; gut·ting] 1. To eviscerate; remove the entrails. 2. To plunder; take or burn out completely.—**gut·ter** *n*.

gut·buck·et *n*. *Music Slang*. Slow, dirty blues.

gut·ta·per·cha (*gut*-uh-*per*-chuh) *n*. A substance extracted from a Malayan evergreen, used for insulation in cements, etc.

gut·ter *n*. 1. A channel or depression beside a curb for carrying away water. 2. Lowly source or origin.—*v*. To flow in a defined path or channel.—**gut·ter·y** *adj*.

gut·ter·snipe (*gut*-er-snype) *n*. *Slang*. A street urchin; child allowed to run the streets.

gut·tur·al (*gut*-er-ul) *adj*. Formed in the throat; throaty.—*n*. A sound seemingly pronounced in the throat; as *g* or *k*.—**gut·tur·al·ly** *adv*.—**gut·tur·al·ness** *n*.

guy (*gye*) *n*. *Slang*. A fellow; man.—*v*. [guyed; guy·ing] To tease; ridicule.—**guy·er** *n*.

guy *n*. A rope or cable for steadying a heavy body.—*v*. To guide or steady with a guy.

guz·zle *v*. [guz·zled; guz·zling] To gulp; drink liquor intemperately or frequently.—**guz·zler** *n*.

gym (*jim*) *n*. Short for **gymnasium.**

gym·na·si·um (jim-*nay*-zee-um) *n*. [*pl*. -si·ums, -si·a] A building for athletic games or calisthenics.

gym·nast (*jim*-nast) *n*. An athlete; expert in gymnastics.

gym·nas·tic (jim-*nass*-tik) *adj*. Also **gym·nas·ti·cal**. Relating to body-building exercises.

gym·nas·tics *n*. *pl*. 1. Athletic or calisthenic exercises. 2. Science of muscle building through exercise.

gym·no·sperm (*jim*-nuh-sperm) *n*. A plant having seeds not enveloped by an ovary.—**gym·no·sper·mous** *adj*.

gyn·e·col·o·gy, gyn·ae·col·o·gy (gyne-uh-*kol*-uh-jee; jyne-) *n*. Branch of medicine treating of female diseases.—**gyn·e·co·log·ic, gyn·ae·co·log·ic** *adj*.—**gyn·e·col·o·gist** *n*.

gyn·i·a·trics (jin-ee-*at*-riks) *n*. Treatment of woman's diseases.

gyp (*jip*) *n*. *Slang*. 1. A swindle. 2. A cheat; swindler.—*v*. [gyped; gyp·ping] To swindle; cheat; defraud.

gyp·sum (*jip*-sum) *n*. Plaster of Paris; selenite.

gyp·sy, gip·sy (*jip*-see) *n*. [*pl*. -sies] 1. One of a wandering, dark-skinned race of Indo-European origin. 2. The language of the gypsies. 3. A girl who flouts convention.—*adj*. Resembling or relating to a gypsy or a gypsy dialect.—**gyp·sy·dom, gip·sy·dom** *n*.—**gyp·sy·hood, gip·sy·hood** *n*.

gypsy moth. A moth whose larva is destructive of trees.

gy·rate (*jy*-rayt) *v.* [gy·rat·ed; gy·rat·ing] To rotate; revolve around a center.—*adj.* Winding; circular.—**gy·ra·tion** (jy-*ray*-sh'n) *n.*—**gy·ra·tor** (*jy*-ray-t'r) *n.*—**gy·ra·to·ry** (*jy*-ruh-tor-ee) *adj.*

gyre *v.* [gyred; gyr·ing] To revolve; gyrate; move spirally.—**gyre** *n.*

gy·ro (*jy*-roh) *n.* [*pl.* -ros] *Colloquial.* 1. A gyroscope. 2. A gyro compass.

gyrocar	gyro mechanism	gyroplane
gyrochrome	gyrometer	gyrostabilizer
gyrograph	gyro pelorus	gyrowheel

gy·ro·com·pass (*jy*-roh-kum-pus) *n.* A compass operated by a gyroscope so that it is not disturbed by nearby magnetic metal.

gy·ro·scope (*jy*-roh-skohp) *n.* Also **gy·ro·stat.** A device employing a heavy revolving disk which stabilizes by resisting any change in its axis of rotation.—**gy·ro·scop·ic** (jy-ruh-*skop*-ik) *adj.*—**gy·ro·scop·i·cal·ly** *adv.*

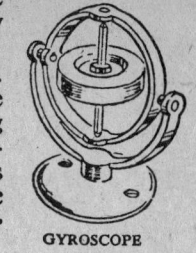
GYROSCOPE

gyve (*jyve*) *n.* A fetter; shackle.—*v.* [gyved; gyv·ing] To bind in fetters.

H

ha *interj.* An exclamation denoting astonishment, pleasure, distaste, suspicion, etc.

Ha·bak·kuk (huh-*bak*-kuk) *n.* 1. A Hebrew prophet. 2. The book of the Old Testament that gives his prophecies.

habeas corpus (*hay*-bee-us *kor*-pus). *Law.* A writ to secure a hearing for a person held in jail.

hab·er·dash·er·y (*hab*-er-dash-er-ee) *n.* [*pl.* -ies] 1. A store where small items of men's apparel, such as neckties and shirts, are sold. 2. The goods sold there.—**hab·er·dash·er** *n.*

ha·bil·i·ment (huh-*bil*-uh-munt) *n.* [*usually pl.*] Clothing; articles of dress.

ha·bil·i·tate (huh-*bil*-uh-tayt) *v.* [-tat·ed; -tat·ing] 1. To qualify; entitle. 2. To equip. 3. To attire; clothe. — **ha·bil·i·ta·tion** (-*tay*-shun) *n.*

hab·it (*hab*-it) *n.* 1. An ingrained behavior pattern; tendency resulting from repetition. 2. A characteristic act or way of acting. 3. Dress; garb, esp. for a certain purpose or occupation. 'A riding habit.'—*v.* To dress.

hab·it·a·ble (*hab*-it-uh-b'l) *adj.* Capable of being lived in or of sustaining life.—**hab·it·a·bil·i·ty, -a·ble·ness** *n.*—**hab·it·a·bly** *adv.*

hab·i·tant (*hab*-it-unt) *n.* Resident; inhabitant.

hab·i·tat (*hab*-ih-tat) *n.* 1. The natural element or abode of a plant or animal. 2. The place where a person or thing habitually is.

hab·i·ta·tion (hab-ih-*tay*-shun) *n.* 1. Home; dwelling place. 2. Occupancy; an inhabiting.

ha·bit·u·al (huh-*bich*-oo-ul) *adj.* Customary; acquired by habit; regular.—**hab·it·u·al·ly** *adv.*

ha·bit·u·ate (huh-*bich*-oo-ayt) *v.* [-at·ed; -at·ing] To accustom; cause to become used to.

hab·i·tude (*hab*-ih-tyood) *n.* Custom; habit.

ha·bit·u·é (huh-*bich*-oo-ay) *n.* A frequenter; one who is habitually present in a place.

ha·ci·en·da (hah-see-*en*-duh) *n.* An estate; ranch; ranch house.—**ha·cen·da·do** (ah-then-*dah*-do) *n.* *Spanish.* The owner of a hacienda.

hack *v.* 1. To mangle by cutting or chopping; notch. 2. To cough.—**hack** *n.*—**hack·er** *n.*

hack *n.* 1. A horse or buggy let out for hire; a taxicab. 2. A worn-out horse. 3. A drudge; person who does routine writing or editorial work.—*adj.* Hired; hackneyed. 2. Worn out; overworked.—*v.* 1. To let out for hire. 2. To operate a taxicab.

hack·a·more (*hak*-uh-mor) *n.* *Chiefly Western U.S.* A rope or rawhide halter used in breaking horses.

hack·le *n.* 1. A comb for dressing flax. 2. An unspun, flimsy fiber. 3. A neck feather of a fowl. 4. *Fishing.* An artificial fly made from a rooster's neck feather.—*v.* [hack·led; hack·ling] 1. To comb out, as hemp. 2. To provide with an artificial fly.—**hack·ler** *n.*

hack·le *v.* To hack; tear in cutting.

hack·ney (*hak*-nee) *n.* [*pl.* -neys] A horse or carriage for hire; hack.—*v.* To use too often; make trite.—*adj.* 1. Trite, commonplace. 2. Let for hire. 3. Prostituted; mercenary.

hack·neyed *adj.* Trite; used too often.

hack saw. Also **hack·saw.** A metal-cutting saw with a narrow blade and fine teeth.

had·dock (*had*-uk) *n.* A long-bodied, brown-backed fish related to the cod.

HACKSAW

Ha·des (*hay*-deez) *n.* *Mythology.* Abode of the dead.

haf·ni·um (*haf*-nee-um) *n.* A metallic element similar to zirconium. (*Symbol:* Hf).

haft *n.* A handle, esp. of an ax or sword.—*v.* To provide with a haft.

hag *n.* An ugly old woman; witch.—*v.* To annoy; torment.

hag·ga·da, hag·ga·dah (huh-*gah*-dah) *n.* [*pl.* -doth] A rabbinical explanation of an Old Testament passage by parable, narrative, or other imaginative, lively method.

hag·gard (*hag*-erd) *adj.* Gaunt; wasted; wan; wild-eyed.—*n.* *Falconry.* A hawk caught in maturity.—**hag·gard·ly** *adv.*—**hag·gard·ness** *n.*

hag·gle (*hag*-'l) *v.* [hag·gled; hag·gling] To bargain pettily; higgle.—*n.* The act of haggling.

hag·i·ol·o·gy (hag-ee-*ol*-uh-jee) *n.* [*pl.* -gies] The study of the lives and writings of the saints. —**hag·i·o·log·ic** (hag-ee-oh-*loj*-ik), **hag·i·o·log·i·cal** *adj.*—**hag·i·ol·o·gist** *n.*

hag·rid·den *adj.* Affected with nightmares; harassed by witches.

hail (*hayl*) *n.* Ice particles falling from the sky. —*v.* To pour down with violence.

hail *interj.* Good health! Good cheer! Salute! —*n.* A call; greeting; salute.—**hail** *v.*—**hail·er** *n.*

hail fellow. A phrase used as a noun, adjective, or adverb denoting friendliness or familiarity.

hail from. To come from; be a native of.

hail·stone *n.* Pellet or particle of frozen rain.

hail·storm *n.* A shower of hailstones.

hair *n.* 1. A small filament growing from the skin of mammals. 2. A coat or collection of hairs; fur. 3. A small distance or quantity.

hair band	haircap	hairlock
hairbrain	hair-check	hairstone
hairbrained	haircut	hairstreak
hair brush	hair-fibered	hairwork

hair·breadth *n.* Also **hairs·breadth.** The diameter of a hair; minute distance.—*adj.* Very narrow.

hair·cloth *n.* A coarse, prickly cloth woven of or containing horse's or camel's hair.

hair-do *n.* Manner or style of hairdress, coiffure.

hair·dress·er *n.* A barber; beautician; coiffeur. —**hair·dress·ing** *n.* 1. An oil or other application for the hair. 2. Beautifying the hair.

hair·line *n.* 1. A slender written, printed, or drawn stroke. 2. A line marking the limit of hair growth on the head.

hair·pin *n.* A U-shaped wire used to keep hair in place.—*adj.* Denoting an abrupt turn.

hair·split·ter *n.* One who makes over-fine or trifling distinctions.—**hair·split·ting** *n.* & *adj.*

hair trigger. A trigger which discharges a gun at the slightest touch.

hair·y *adj.* [hair·i·er; hair·i·est] Covered with, like, or made of hair.—**hair·i·ness** *n.*

Hai·ti (*hay*-tee). An island republic between Cuba and Puerto Rico. Area: 10,206 sq. mi. Capital: Port-au-Prince.—**Hai·ti·an** *n.* & *adj.*

hake (*hayk*) *n.* A broad-headed sea fish of the cod family.

ha·keem, ha·kim (hah-*keem*) *n.* In Moslem regions, a physician, judge, or ruler.

Ha·ken·kreuz (*hah*-ken-kroyts) *n.* German. Swastika.

hal·berd, hal·bert (*hal*-berd) *n.* A long-handled medieval weapon designed for stabbing and chopping. —**hal·berd·ier** *n.*

hale *v.* [haled; hal·ing] To pull or draw. 'To hale to court.'

hale *adj.* Healthy; robust.

half (*haf, hahf*) *n.* [*pl.* halves] 1. One of two equal portions; 50%. 2. *Golf.* A hole or round not won by either competitor or side. 3. *Football.* One of the two equal periods of a game, divided by a rest interval.—**half** *adj.* & *adv.*

HALBERD

—**half** *v.* To split; to divide into two equal parts.

half a crown	half-dressed	half-rigger
half-admitted	half-feed	half ripe
half afraid	half-grown	half-sailed
half alive	halfhold	half-share (v.)
half angry	half-leaded	half-size
halfbeak	half-marked	half-sized
half-bred	half-miler	half speed
half-buried	half-monthly	half-speeded
half-cleaned	half-necked	half strength
half clear	half-paced	half-timer
half day	half-paid	half title
half-decked	half-rater	half true
half-decker	half-rigged	half-truth

half-and-half *n.* A mixture of two ingredients in equal proportions.—**half-and-half** *adj.* & *adv.*

half·back *n.* *Football.* One of two backfield men who carry the ball most in offensive play.

half-baked *adj.* *Colloquial.* Hastily planned; not thought out; lacking in judgment; silly.

half-blood *n.* 1. A person whose parents differ racially.; half-breed. 2. One related to another by one parent only.—**half·blood·ed** *adj.*

half-breed *adj.* Being part white and part American Indian; half-blooded.—**half-breed** *n.*

half brother. A man who has only one parent in common with his sisters or brothers.

half-caste *n.* Person with one Hindu or Moslem and one European parent; half-blood. —**half-caste** *adj.*

half cock. The halfway stage of retracting a gun's hammer, where the trigger cannot discharge the gun.—**half·cock** *v.*—**half-cocked** *adj.* *Colloquial.* Insufficiently prepared.

half crown. British coin worth $2\frac{1}{2}$ shillings.

half dollar. A fifty-cent piece; 50c.

half-hearted *adj.* Indifferent; lukewarm; unenthusiastic.—**-heart·ed·ly** *adv.*—**-heart·ed·ness** *n.*

half hitch. A simple knot made by placing a rope end over a line and through the eye thus formed.

half-mast *n.* A position below the top of a flagpole where a flag is flown to indicate mourning or distress.—**half-mast** *n.*

half nelson. *Wrestling.* A one-armed hold, usually from behind, under the opponent's arm and around his neck.

half·pen·ny (*hay*-p'n-ee, *hayp*-nee) *n.* [*pl.* -pence, -pen·nies] British coin worth 1c.

half sister. A woman or girl who has one parent in common with her brothers or sisters.

half sole. The sole of a shoe from the toe to the middle of the arch.—*v.* [half-soied; half-sol·ing].

half step. 1. *Military.* A marching step half as long as a standard step; in the U.S. Army a 15-inch pace. 2. *Music.* A semitone; smallest interval of the scale.

half-timbered *adj.* *Architecture.* Partly of wood and partly of masonry or plaster. 'A half-timbered wall.'

half tone. *Music.* The smallest interval of the modern scale; semitone. 2. Also **half-tone** *n.* *Fine Arts.* A neutral color tone in painting, engraving, etc., neither light nor dark.

half·tone n. Photoengraving. A reproduction of a picture by use of small screened dots on the negative and plate to represent degrees of light and shadow.—**half-tone** adj.

half·way adj. In the middle; equidistant from beginning and end; partly.—**half·way** adv.

half·wit n. A fool; mental defective.—**half-wit·ted** adj.—**half·wit·ted·ly** adv.—**-wit·ted·ness** n.

hal·i·but (hal-uh-but) n. An edible flat fish, sometimes reaching a length of ten feet

hal·i·to·sis (hal-uh-toh-siss) n. Offensive breath.

hall (hawl) n. 1. A building or large room devoted to public gatherings. 2. A vestibule; entrance lobby. 3. A connecting passage between rooms. 4. A British landowner's house.

HALIBUT

hal·le·lu·jah, hal·le·lu·iah (hal-uh-loo-yuh) n. & interj. Praise to God!

hall·mark n. 1. Symbol or stamp indicating quality. 2. The official mark of purity on gold and silver articles, stamped at Goldsmiths' Hall, London.

hal·loo (huh-loo) n. A cry; shout.—interj. A call to invite attention.—v. [hal·looed; -loo·ing].

hal·low (hal-oh) v. To make holy; consecrate.

Hal·low·een n. Eve of All Saints' Day (Oct. 31), celebrated by children's pranks.

hal·lu·ci·na·tion (huh-loo-sin-ay-sh'n) n. A delusion; mirage; morbid mental condition causing imaginary objects to seem real.—**hal·lu·ci·na·to·ry** adj.

hall·way n. A corridor; passage between rooms.

ha·lo (hay-loh) n. [pl. -los, -loes] 1. A luminous ring appearing around the sun or moon. 2. Art. A circle of light around the head of a holy person.—v. [ha·loed; ha·lo·ing].

hal·o·gen (hal-oh-jen) n. Chemistry. A group of elements including chlorine, fluorine, iodine.

halt (hawlt) n. A stop.—v. 1. To stop; cease to advance. 2. To stammer in speaking.

halt adj. Lame; limping.—n. pl. Lame people. 'The halt and the blind.'

hal·ter n. 1. A noose for leading or confining a horse. 2. A kind of woman's blouse supported by a cord about the neck.—**hal·ter** v.

halt·ing adj. Slow; awkward; stammering.—**halt·ing·ly** adv.

halve (hav, hahv) v. [halved; halv·ing] To divide into two equal parts.

hal·yard (hal-yerd) n. Nautical. Line for hoisting sails.

ham n. 1. Anatomy. The inner or hind part of the knee joint. 2. The thigh of a hog, often salted and cured. 3. Theater. A performer who overacts.—**ham** v. & adj. 'A ham actor.'

ham n. Colloquial. An amateur radio operator.

ham·a·dry·ad (ham-uh-dry-ad) n. Mythology. A wood nymph.

Ham·ble·to·ni·an (ham-b'l-toh-nee-un) n. 1. A type of American trotting horse. 2. A famous trotting sweepstakes.

Ham·burg. Second largest city in Germany.

ham·burg·er (ham-ber-ger) n. Also **hamburg, hamburg steak.** Chopped beef, often fried in a patty and served in a roll.

Hamitic languages (ham-it-ik). A language family which includes Egyptian and some modern languages.

ham·let n. A small village.

Ham·let. Title character in Shakespeare's Hamlet.

ham·mer (ham-er) n. 1. Instrument consisting usually of an iron head fixed at right angles to a handle, used to drive nails, beat metals, etc. 2. That part of a gunlock which detonates the charge.—v. 1. To beat with a hammer. 2. To produce by much effort. 'He hammered away at the job.'—**ham·mer·er** n.

Hammer and Sickle. Emblem first used as a symbol of unity between agricultural and industrial workers, and since 1923 as part of the national flag of the U.S.S.R.

ham·mer·head n. 1. A rapacious shark whose head resembles in shape that of a double-headed hammer. 2. Slang. A dolt; oaf.

HAMMER AND SICKLE

ham·mock (ham-uk) n. A cloth bed suspended by cords and hooks.

ham·per n. A large covered basket.

ham·per v. To impede; hinder; frustrate.

ham·string n. One of the tendons behind the knee.—v. [ham·strung; ham·string·ing] 1. To lame by cutting the tendons behind the knee. 2. To cripple.

Han·chow. Important seaport in central China.

hand n. 1. The extremity of the arm, consisting of the palm and fingers, joined to the arm at the wrist. 2. Side; direction, either right or left. 3. A burst of applause. 4. Possession; power. 'In my rival's hands.' 5. Card Playing. a. The cards held by a single player. b. A single round in a game. 6. Something acting as a finger in pointing. 'The hands of a clock.' 7. An employee. 'Hired hand.' 8. Style of penmanship. 9. In measuring an animal's height, four inches.—**hand** adj.—**at hand.** Near; here.—**on hand.** In present possession. —**out of hand.** Out of control.

hand-bank	hand-embroidered	hand-pick
hand-beaten	hand-fed	handpost
hand-blocked	handgrip	handprint
handbow	hand gun	handrail
hand-built	hand-hewn	handsale
handcar	hand high	handshake
hand-carve	handhold	handstaff
handclasp	hand lock	hand-tailored
hand-colored	hand-off	hand-tied
hand-cut	hand-operated	hand tool

H

hand *v.* To give; transmit by hand.—**hand down.** To transmit in succession.—**hand on.** To pass along.

hand·bag *n.* A woman's purse.

hand·ball *n.* A game the object of which is to hit a ball against a wall so that the next player cannot return it.

hand·bar·row *n.* A litter with handles at each end, carried between two persons.

hand·bill *n.* Circular; sheet, usually printed, carrying an advertisement.

hand·book *n.* 1. A manual; guidebook; compendium. 2. Book for recording bets on horses, carried in the hand to evade the law.

hand·cuff *n.* A manacle consisting of two metal rings worn around the wrists, and usually connected by a short chain. —**hand·cuff** *v.*

HANDCUFF

hand·ed *adj.* Having a hand possessed of any special property. 'Left-handed; heavy-handed.'

hand·ful *n.* [*pl.* -fuls] A small amount; as much as may be grasped or held in one hand.

hand·i·cap (*han*-dih-kap) *n.* 1. A disadvantage; encumbrance. 2. *Sports.* An advantage allowed to inferior competitors to make a more even match. 3. A race in which handicaps are allowed.—*v.* [hand·i·capped; -cap·ping] 1. To give an advantage to an inferior competitor in a contest. 2. To hamper; encumber; hinder.—**hand·i·cap·per** *n.*

hand·i·craft (*han*-dih-kraft) *n.* Work performed by hand, as basket-weaving; manual dexterity. —**hand·i·crafts·man** *n.*— **-man·ship** *r.*

hand·i·work *n.* Work performed by the hands.

hand·ker·chief *n.* A piece of cloth for wiping the nose or face, for ornamentation, etc.

han·dle (*han*-d'l) *v.* [han·dled; han·dling] 1. To touch; feel with the hand. 2. To wield; ply; manage. 3. To behave. 'This car handles well.'—*n.* 1. The part of an object intended to be grasped by the hand when using it. 2. *Slang.* A person's name.

han·dler *n.* A trainer, esp. of prizefighters.

hand·made *adj.* Manufactured by hand.

hand·maid *n.* Also **handmaiden.** A female attendant.

hand-me-down *adj. Colloquial.* 1. Used; second hand. 2. Ready-made.—**hand-me-down** *n.* [*pl.* hand-me-downs].

hand organ. A portable or barrel organ.

hand·out *n. Slang.* Food, clothing, etc., given to a beggar.

hand·saw *n.* A saw used with the hand.

hand·some (*han*-sum) *adj.* 1. Good looking; beautiful; exquisite; noble. 2. Generous; lavish. 'A handsome donation.'— -some·ly *adv.*

hand·spike *n.* A short bar used as a lever.

hand-to-hand *adj.* At close quarters.

hand-to-mouth *adj.* Poverty-stricken; indigent.

hand·writ·ing (*hand*-ryte-ing) *n.* The form of penmanship peculiar to a person.

hand·y *adj.* [hand·i·er; hand·i·est] 1. Dexterous; skillful. 2. Convenient; near.—**hand·i·ly** *adv.*—**hand·i·ness** *n.*

handy man. A man of all work.

hang *v.* [hung or hanged; hang·ing] 1. To suspend. 2. To suspend by the neck till dead. 3. To furnish or decorate with suspended material or objects. 4. To droop; lean forward. 5. To fasten in proper position. 'Hang a door.' 6. To depend; be contingent. 7. To cling; loiter; linger.—*n.* 1. Style in which an object hangs. 2. Meaning; draft; knack. 3. A bit; small amount. 'I don't give a hang.'

hang-back	hang-fair	hang net
hangbird	hang-head	hangworm
hang-choice	hangnest	hangworthy

hang·ar (*hang*-er) *n.* A building in which aircraft are housed.

hang·dog *n.* Base, degraded person.—*adj.* Ashamed; degraded.

hang·er-on *n.* [*pl.* hang·ers-on] A useless follower; dependent; parasite.

hang fire. To be undecided; hesitate.

hang·ing *n.* 1. Death by suspension. 2. [*pl.*] Drapery or other suspended objects.—*adj.* 1. Leaning forward or down; inclined. 2. Deserving of, or causing, death by suspension.

hang·man *n.* [*pl.* -men] One who executes by hanging.

hang·nail *n.* A bit of torn skin at the side of a fingernail.

hang·out *n. Slang.* 1. A place regularly frequented. 2. A low resort; a dive.

hang-over *n.* 1. *Slang.* A temporary feeling of illness caused by overindulgence in liquor. 2. That which remains from a previous time.

hank *n.* A looped piece; one or more skeins of yarn or thread tied together.

han·ker *v.* To desire keenly.—**han·ker·er** *n.*

han·ky-pan·ky (*hank*-ee-*pank*-ee) *n. Colloquial.* Trickery; juggling; chicanery.

Han·o·ver (*han*-uh-ver). 1. A province of western Germany. 2. Family name, until 1917, of the royal house of Great Britain.—**Han·o·ver·i·an** (han-uh-*veer*-ee-un) *adj.*

Hanseatic League. A trading confederacy embracing most of the commercial Germanic cities during the Renaissance.

han·som (*han*-sum) *n.* Also **hansom cab.** A two-wheeled carriage for two passengers, having an elevated driver's seat in the rear.

hap *n.* Accident; contingency; chance.—*v.* [happed; hap·ping] To chance; happen.

hap·haz·ard (hap-*haz*-erd) *adj.* Happening by chance; casual; random.—*n.* Chance.—**hap·haz·ard, hap·haz·ard·ly** *adv.*— -ard·ness *n.*

hap·less *adj.* Unfortunate; unlucky.—**hap·less·ly** *adv.*—**hap·less·ness** *n.*

hap·ly *adv.* Perhaps; by chance.

hap·pen (*hap*-'n) *v.* 1. To occur; take place. 2. To chance; occur accidentally.—**happen on.** To find or come upon by chance.—**hap·pen·ing** *n.* Occurrence; event.

hap·py (*hap*-ee) *adj.* [hap·pi·er; hap·pi·est] 1. Contented; satisfied; pleased; delighted. 2. Prosperous; enjoying good fortune. 3. Apt; fitting; well suited to a particular situation.—**hap·pi·ly** *adv.*—**hap·pi·ness** *n.*

hap·py-go-luck·y *adj.* Irresponsible; carefree.

Haps·burg (*haps*-berg) *n.* Member of the former royal house of Austria.

ha·ra-ki·ri (hair-uh-*keer*-ee) *n.* The elaborate Japanese rite of suicide by cutting open the abdomen, done to atone for failure or disgrace.

ha·rangue (huh-*rang*) *v.* [-rangued; -rangu·ing] To orate; speechify.—*n.* A public address; declamation; noisy, pompous speech.—**ha·rangu·er** *n.*

har·ass (*hair*-us, huh-*rass*) *v.* 1. To molest or raid repeatedly; harry. 2. To weary; pursue with annoyance; vex.—**har·ass·er** *n.*—**har·ass·ment** *n.*

har·bin·ger (*hahr*-bin-jer) *n.* A forerunner; one that announces or hints of coming events. —**har·bin·ger** *v.*

har·bor (*hahr*-ber) *n.* 1. A port; part of a body of water enclosed as a shelter for ships. 2. A refuge; shelter; haven.—*v.* 1. To shelter. 2. To entertain; cherish, as a notion.

har·bor·age *n.* Shelter; haven; refuge.

harbor master. One who has charge of ship moorings and enforcement of harbor rules.

hard (hahrd) *adj.* 1. Resisting pressure; solid. 2. Difficult; not easily done, managed, or understood. 3. Oppressive; severe; painful. 4. Unfeeling; harsh; unpleasant; rigid. 5. Earnest; energetic. 'A hard worker.' 6. Nasty; violent, as weather. 7. Alcoholic. 8. Containing mineral impurities. 'Hard water.' 9. *Phonetics.* Denoting unvoiced sounds, as *p*, *t*, *k*.—*adv.* 1. Close; near. 2. Vigorously; severely; firmly. 3. With effort or difficulty. 4. Fully; utterly.

hard-acquired	hard-fated	hard-natured
hardback	hard-favored	hard-plucked
hard-baked	hard-featured	hard-ridden
hardbeam	hard-fed	hard-set
hard-billed	hard-finished	hard-skinned
hard-boned	hard-fired	hard-spun
hard-bought	hard-fleshed	hard-surfaced
hard-contested	hard-got	hardtail
hard-cooked	hard-grained	hard-used
hard-cured	hard-hit	hard-visaged
hard-dried	hard-learned	hardway
hard-driven	hard looking	hard-won
hard-earned	hardmouth	hard-worked
hard-faced	hard-mouthed	hard-wrung

hard-bit·ten *adj.* Dogged; unyielding; tough.

hard-boiled *adj.* 1. Made firm or solid by heat, as an egg. 2. *Slang.* Tough; callous; unfeeling.

hard·en *v.* 1. To render or become firm or hard. 2. To fix; confirm. 3. To render insensitive; inure.—**hard·en·er** *n.*

hard·fist·ed *adj.* Miserly; close.— -fist·ed·ness *n.*

hard-head·ed *adj.* 1. Shrewd; hard to deceive. 2. Willful; headstrong.—**hard-head·ed·ness** *n.*

hard-heart·ed *adj.* Cruel; unfeeling; pitiless.

har·di·hood (*hahr*-dee-hood) *n.* Courage; boldness; endurance.

hard·ly *adv.* 1. Scarcely; barely; without probability. 2. Not easily or readily; grudgingly. 3. Harshly; with severity.

hard·pan *n.* A stratum of rock beneath the soil; any hard, solid foundation.

hard sauce. A stiff mixture of sugar, butter, and flavoring used on puddings, gingerbread, etc.

hard-shell *adj.* Also **hard-shelled.** 1. Covered with a hard shell. 2. *Colloquial.* Uncompromising; stubborn.

hard·ship *n.* Privation; bodily oppression; that which is difficult to endure.

hard·tack *n.* Sea biscuit; coarse, hard bread.

hard up. *Colloquial.* In difficult straits; in need.

hard·ware *n.* Metal goods, household equipment, etc.—**hard·ware·man** *n.*

hard·wood *n.* Any wood of a close, solid texture, as oak.—**hard·wood, hard·wood·ed** *adj.*

har·dy *adj.* [har·di·er; har·di·est] 1. Strong; robust; having good powers of endurance. 2. Bold; brave—**har·di·ly** *adv.*—**har·di·ness** *n.*

hare *n.* A rabbit.

harebell	hare-footed	harelip
harebrain	hare-hearted	hare-mad
hare-eyed	hare hound	harewood

hare and hounds. A game similar to hide and seek, played by a large group.

hare·brained *adj.* Giddy; irresponsible.

hare·lip *n.* A fissure or breach in the lip existing from birth.

ha·rem (*hair*-'m) *n.* 1. The living quarters of a Mohammedan's wives or concubines. 2. The women in such quarters.

har·i·cot (*hair*-ih-coh) *n.* 1. A well-seasoned lamb stew. 2. Shelled string beans.

hark *v.* To listen; harken.—**hark back.** To go back; revert; revive; recall. 'The styles hark back to the last century.'

hark·en *v.* Also **hearken.** To listen attentively.

Har·lem (*hahr*-lum). Uptown section of New York City, populated mainly by Negroes and people of Spanish or Portuguese extraction.

Har·le·quin (*hahr*-luh-kwin) *n.* 1. A traditional character in pantomime and comedy, costumed as a clown. 2. [*not cap.*] A buffoon.

har·le·quins *n. pl.* Eyeglasses designed with the frame of each lens tilted upward at the outer corner.—**har·le·quin** *adj.*

har·lot (*hahr*-lut) *n.* A whore; prostitute.—**har·lot·ry** *n.* [*pl.* -ries]. Prostitution.

harm *n.* 1. Hurt; injury. 2. Moral wrong; evil.—*v.* To hurt; wrong. —**harm·ful** *adj.* Causing damage. —**harm·ful·ly** *adv.*—**harm·ful·ness** *n.*

HARLEQUIN

harm·less *adj.* Inoffensive; not harmful.

har·mon·ic (hahr-*mon*-ik) *n.* 1. *Music.* A tone produced on a stringed instrument which is stopped by lightly touching a nodal point of a string. 2. *Physics.* A sound, light, or radio wave whose frequency of vibration is a multiple of a given wave; an overtone.—*adj.* Agreeable; harmonious.—**har·mon·i·cal·ly** *adv.*

har·mon·i·ca (hahr-*mon*-ik-uh) *n.* A mouth organ.

har·mon·ics *n.* Science of musical sounds; art of musical composition.—**har·mo·nist** *n.*

har·mo·ni·ous (hahr-*moh*-nee-us) *adj.* 1. Symmetrical; well-proportioned. 2. Musical; agreeable in sound. 3. Living in peace and friendship.— -**ni·ous·ly** *adv.*— -**ni·ous·ness** *n.*

har·mo·ni·um *n.* A small reed organ.

har·mon·ize (*hahr*-mun-yze) *v.* To blend musically; be in harmony and concord.—**har·mo·ni·za·tion** (hahr-mun-iz-*ay*-shun) *n.*— -**niz·er** *n.*

har·mo·ny (*hahr*-muh-nee) *n.* [*pl.* -nies] 1. Agreement; amity; concord. 2. Symmetry; proportion. 3. *Music.* **a.** Agreeable proportion of sound. **b.** A succession of chords. **c.** Harmonics.

har·ness *n.* The working gear or tackle of a draft horse.—**har·ness** *v.* To restrain; bridle.

HARNESS

harp *n.* A large, triangular stringed instrument played by plucking.—*v.* 1. To play a harp. 2. To repeat or dwell on tiresomely or vexatiously. —**harp·ist** *n.* Harp player.

har·poon *n.* A large barbed spear for catching whales.—**har·poon** *v.*—**har·poon·er** *n.*

harp·si·chord *n.* An early keyboard instrument, precursor of the piano.

HARPSICHORD

har·py *n.* [*pl.* -pies] 1. A rapacious or vicious person. 2. [*cap.*] *Mythology.* A ravenous, filthy, winged monster with the head of a woman.

har·que·bus (*hahrk*-wih-bus) *n.* Also **har·que·buss.** A portable firearm, forerunner of the musket.—**har·que·bus·ier, -bus·sier** *n.*

har·ri·dan (*hair*-ih-d'n) *n.* Hag; harlot; jade.

har·ri·er *n.* 1. A dog trained for rabbit hunting. 2. A long-distance runner. 3. A species of hawk.

har·row *n.* A drag; agricultural instrument dragged over plowed or seeded ground,—**har·row** *v.* 1. To plow. 2. To vex; trouble.

HARROW

har·ry *v.* [har·ried; har·ry·ing] 1. To harass; annoy; tease. 2. To plunder.

harsh (hahrsh) *adj.* 1. Grating. 2. Rough;

severe; abusive.—**harsh·ly** *adv.*—**harsh·ness** *n.*

hart *n.* A male deer.

har·te·beest *n.* A South African antelope.

har·um-scar·um (*hair*-um-*skair*-um) *adj.* Harebrained; rash.—*n.* A giddy, irresponsible person.

ha·rus·pex (huh-*rus*-peks) *n.* [*pl.* -pi·ces (huh-*rus*-pih-seez)] *Roman Religion.* A prophet.

Har·vard (*hahr*-verd, *hah*-vud) *n.* An old, highly endowed world-famous university at Cambridge, Massachusetts.—**Harvard beets.** Beets cooked and served in a sauce containing butter, cornstarch, sugar, and vinegar.

har·vest (*hahr*-vest) *n.* 1. A crop; reaping. 2. The season for gathering in crops. 3. Any product of labor.—**har·vest** *v.*—**har·vest·er** *n.*

har·vest·man *n.* [*pl.* -men] 1. A long-legged spider commonly found in gardens; daddy longlegs. 2. A crop gatherer.

has-been (*haz*-bin) *n. Slang.* One who has lost popularity, prosperity, or fame.

ha·sen·pfef·fer (*hah*-zen-fef-er) *n.* Hare, highly seasoned, and stewed in own juice and wine; jugged hare.

hash *n.* 1. A dish of vegetables and meat chopped together and seasoned. 2. A mass; a slovenly job.—*v.* To chop into bits; mince and mix.—**hash over.** To discuss; mull over.

hash·ish (*hash*-eesh) *n.* Also' **hash·eesh.** A narcotic prepared from Indian hemp; marijuana.

has·let (*hass*-let) *n.* Edible internal organs of an animal, esp. hog.

hasp *n.* A clasp or punctured hinge which passes over a staple to be fastened by a padlock.—**hasp** *v.*

has·sock (*hass*-uk) *n.* 1. A stuffed leather or cloth-covered footstool. 2. A clump; tussock.

haste *n.* 1. Hurry; speed. 2. Urgency.—*v.* [hast·ed; has·ting].

has·ten (*hayss*-'n) *v.* 1. To quicken; speed up; accelerate. 2. To speed; hurry.—**has·ten·er** *n.*

hast·y (*hayss*-tee) *adj.* [hast·i·er; hast·i·est] 1. Quick; speedy; hurried. 2. Rash; unconsidered; indiscreet. 3. Easily angered.—**hast·i·ly** *adv.*—**hast·i·ness** *n.*

hasty pudding. *New England.* Cornmeal mush.

hat *n.* A head covering.—*v.* [hat·ted; hat·ting] —**hat·ter** *n.*

hat band	hat making	hat rail
hat box	hatpin	hat-shaped
hat brim	hat rack	hat stand

hatch *v.* 1. To incubate; produce young from eggs. 2. To create; contrive.—*n.* A brood.

hatch *n.* An opening in the deck of a ship.

hatch *v. Fine Arts.* To shade with fine lines.

hatch·er·y *n.* [*pl.* -ies] A place where eggs are incubated.

hatch·et *n.* A small, short-handled ax.

hatch·way *n.* An opening in a deck for stairs.

hate *v.* [hat·ed; hat·ing] To feel enmity or bitter aversion for; dislike intensely.—**hate, ha·tred** *n.*—**hate·a·ble** *adj.*—**hat·er** *n.*

hate·ful *adj.* Detestable; obnoxious; spiteful.

hau·berk (*haw*-berk) *n.* A coat of mail.

haugh·ty *adj.* [haugh·ti·er; haugh·ti·est] Arrogantly proud; disdainful; supercilious.—**haugh·ti·ly** *adv.*—**haugh·ti·ness** *n.*

haul (*hawl*) *v.* 1. To transport; drag along; tow. 2. *Nautical.* To alter course closer to the wind.—*n.* 1. Transport; transit. 2. Quantity taken or procured at one time; booty.—**haul·age** *n.* 1. Transportation. 2. Fee paid for hauling.—**haul·er** *n.*

haunch (*hawnch*) *n.* Hip; part of the body between the ribs and the thigh.

haunt (*hawnt*) *v.* 1. To visit habitually. 2. To pervade; revisit constantly, as a spirit, ghost, memory, etc.—*n.* A favorite retreat; place one frequents.—**haunt·ing·ly** *adv.*

haut·boy (*hoh*-boy; *oh*-boy) *n.* An oboe.

hau·teur (haw-*ter*) *n.* Insolent pride; superciliousness.

Ha·van·a (huh-*van*-uh) *n.* 1. Capital, largest city, and cultural center of Cuba. 2. A Cuban cigar.

have (*hav*) *v.* [had; hav·ing] 1. To possess; hold in possession or power. 2. To accept. 3. To regard; hold. 4. To procure; gain. 5. To be obliged. 'He has to go.' 6. To contain; include. 7. To cause; make to be. 8. To give birth to. 9. To experience; participate in. 10. To claim; affirm. 11. To endure; allow; allow to be. 12. To entrap; place at a loss. 'Now we have him.'

ha·ven (*hay*-v'n) *n.* A refuge; place of safety.

have-not *n.* A poor person or nation.—**have-not** *adj.*

hav·er·sack (*hav*-er-sak) *n.* A bag for carrying provisions.

hav·oc (*hav*-uk) *n.* Wide destruction; devastation.—*v.* [hav·ocked; hav·ock·ing].

haw *n.* 1. The hawthorn or its fruit. 2. A pause in one's speech; hesitation.—**haw** *v.*

haw *v.* Of a horse-team, to turn to the left.

hawk *n.* A family of rapacious birds having hooked beaks, cloven tongue, and head thickly set with feathers.—*v.* To hunt with trained hawks.—**hawk·ing** *n.* The sport of hunting with hawks.

HAWK

hawk-beaked   hawk-headed
hawk bill   hawk moth
hawk-billed   hawk-nosed
hawk-faced   hawkweed

hawk *v.* To clear the throat of phlegm.—**hawk** *n.*

hawk *v.* To peddle; vend.—*n.* A huckster.

hawk-eyed *adj.* Keen-sighted; discerning.

hawks·bill *n.* Also **hawksbill turtle.** A sea turtle with a snout shaped like a hawk's beak.

hawse hole. A hole in the bow of a ship through which a hawser or cable passes.

haw·ser (*haw*-zer) *n.* A stout rope for towing or securing a vessel.

haw·thorn *n.* Shrub having long thorns and clusters of fragrant flowers.

hay *n.* Grass, clover, etc., cut and dried for fodder.—*v.* To cut for hay.

hay band   hayfield   hayrack
haybird   hay fork   hay rake
hay cap   hay grower   hay scented
hay cart   hayloft   haystack
hay-colored   hay market   haytime

hay·cock (*hay*-kok) *n.* A small pile of hay.

hay fever. An allergic respiratory reaction akin to asthma, often caused by plant pollen.

hay·mak·er *n.* 1. Blow of a fist delivered in a wide arc. 2. One who cuts and dries hay.

hay·mow (*hay*-mow) *n.* Place for storing hay.

hay·rick *n.* A haystack.

hay·seed *n.* 1. *Slang.* Rustic; hick. 2. The seed or chaff from hay.

hay·stack *n.* A pile of hay left in a field to cure.

hay·wire *adj. Slang.* Wrong; not according to plan; crazy.—*n.* Wire for securing bales of hay.

haz·ard (*haz*-erd) *n.* 1. A risk; chance; danger. 2. *Golf.* An obstruction on the course.—*v.* To risk; chance.—**haz·ard·ous** *adj.*—**-ous·ly** *adv.*

haze *n.* 1. Mist; slight vapor or dimness in the air. 2. Mental confusion; fog.

haze *v.* [hazed; haz·ing] 1. To harass with work so as to break a person's spirit. 2. *School.* To plague with rough or humiliating tricks.—**haz·er** *n.*—**haz·ing** *n.*

ha·zel (*hayz*-'l) *n.* 1. A small, nut-bearing tree related to the birch. 2. The color of the hazelnut; light brown.—*adj.* Light-brown.—**ha·zel·ly** *adj.*—**ha·zel·nut** *n.* The fruit of the hazel.

ha·zy (*hay*-zee) *adj.* [ha·zi·er; ha·zi·est] 1. Misty; obscured by haze. 2. Vague; not clear or defined.—**ha·zi·ly** *adv.*—**ha·zi·ness** *n.*

he (*hee*) *pronoun.* 1. The male person mentioned previously. 2. Any man; anyone.

head (*hed*) *n.* 1. Part of the human or animal body above, or forward of, the neck. 2. The intelligence; mental powers or balance. 3. A chief; leader; commander. 4. Top; foremost or upper part; any headlike piece. 5. The source (of a stream). 6. An individual or individuals. 'Six head of sheep.' 7. Pressure of a liquid. 'A head of steam.' 8. Crisis; point of decision. 9. A major division; heading. 10. The foam on carbonated or fermented beverages.—*v.* 1. To direct or set a course. 2. To form, or furnish with, a head. 3. To lead; direct.—*adj.* 1. Principal; chief. 2. At or coming from the head or front.

head band   head mold   headsail
head-bander   headmost   head set
headboard   headplate   head shake
head cap   headpost   head sill
head chair   head race   headspring
headchute   headrail   headstall
headcloth   head rent   headstream
head drop   headrest   head-turned
head-ender   head ring   head waiter
head frame   headroom   headward
headlock   headrope   headwork

H

head·ache n. A pain in the head.— **-ach·y** adj.

head·cheese n. Boiled pressed meat, usually from a hog's head.

head·dress n. Any head covering or adornment.

head·ed adj. Having a head.

head·er n. 1. Colloquial. A headlong tumble; dive. 2. Person or tool that heads pins, nails, etc. 3. Thing having a specified number of units. 'We played a double-header.'

head·first, head·fore·most adv. With the head preceding the rest of the body.

head·gear n. Covering for the head; hat.

head hunter. A primitive tribesman who beheads his captives and shrinks the heads. —**head hunting.**

head·ing n. Title; indication of matter to follow; that which acts as a head.

head·land n. A cape; small peninsula.

head·light n. An electric lamp with reflector, on the front of a vehicle.

head·line n. A title in large print above a newspaper article, etc.

head·long adv. 1. Headfirst. 2. Rashly; too hurriedly; thoughtlessly.—adj. 1. Hurried; rash. 2. Pitching headfirst.

head·man n. [pl. -men] A chief; leader.

head·mas·ter n. The principal of a school or seminary.—**head·mas·ter·ship** n.

head·on adj. & adv. Contacting directly; with the front first.

head·phone n. A telephone receiver worn directly over the ear.

head·piece n. 1. A hat; helmet; head armor or covering. 2. Flexible metal band linking a pair of headphones.

head·quar·ters n. pl. 1. Any central military or administrative command. 2. Place from which a business or organization is conducted or directed.

head·ship n. Chief position.

heads·man n. [pl. -men] An executioner; beheader.

head·stock n. The frame which supports the centers of a lathe.

head·stone n. 1. Stone marking the head of a grave. 2. Cornerstone.

head·strong adj. Willful; stubborn; unruly.

head·waters n. pl. Also **head·water.** Source or upper part of a stream.

head·way n. 1. Progress; motion forward. 2. Clear space overhead, as under a bridge.

head·y adj. [head·i·er; head·i·est] 1. Intoxicating. 2. Rash; not deliberate or careful; impetuous.—**head·i·ly** adv.—**head·i·ness** n.

heal (heel) v. To cure of a disease; mend, as a wound; restore to a sound or healthy condition.—**heal·er** n.—**heal·ing·ly** adv.

health (helth) n. 1. Bodily or mental state in which all organs function normally; soundness; freedom from illness. 2. Toast; wish for health, pledged with a drink.

health·ful adj. Wholesome; salubrious; aiding health.—**health·ful·ly** adv.—**health·ful·ness** n.

health·y adj. [health·i·er; health·i·est] 1. Hale; sound; vigorous. 2. Showing good health.

heap (heep) n. 1. A pile; an accumulation. 2. Colloquial. A large amount or quantity.—v. 1. To pile up; accumulate. 2. To give liberally; fill more than full.

hear (heer) v. [heard; hear·ing] 1. To perceive by the auditory sense. 2. To listen to; be told; receive as news. 3. To try in a court of justice.—**hear·er** n.

hear·ing n. 1. Perception of sound; auditory sense. 2. A chance to be heard; audience; trial. 3. Extent to which sound carries.

heark·en (hahr-k'n). Variant spelling of **harken.**

hear·say n. Rumor; gossip.—**hear·say** adj.

hearse (herss) n. A carriage or automobile for carrying the dead to the grave.

heart (hahrt) n. 1. Anatomy. Muscular organ which pumps or circulates the blood throughout the body. 2. Anything shaped like a heart or like the conventional figure of a heart. 3. The center; middle; most vital part; core. 4. Courage; spirit; soul; emotion. 5. One of a suit of playing cards marked with a red heart.—**at heart.** Really; substantially.—**by heart.** Committed to memory.—**with all one's heart.** Completely; without reservatipn.

heartbeat	heart-hardened	heartsore
heartbird	heart-heaviness	heart-stricken
heart blood	heartheavy	heart-swollen
heartbroken	heartnut	heartthrob
heart-burdened	heartquake	heartwater
heart complaint	heartroot	heart-weariness
heartgrief	heart-shaped	heart-wounded

heart·ache (hahrt-ayk) n. Anguish; grief.

heart·break (hahrt-brayk) n. Overwhelming sorrow or grief.—**heart·break·er** n. A person or thing that causes sorrow.— **-break·ing** adj.

heart·burn n. A burning sensation in the lower esophagus.

heart·en v. To encourage; inspire.

heart·felt adj. Profoundly felt; genuine.

hearth (hahrth) n. 1. The part of a fireplace, furnace, or stove on which the fire burns. 2. The fireside; household.

hearth·stone n. The stone with which the hearth is paved.

heart·less adj. Cruel; unfeeling.—**heart·less·ly** adv.—**heart·less·ness** n.

heart·rend·ing adj. Pathetic; piteous.

heart·sick adj. Despondent; melancholy; distressed.

heart·strings n. pl. Feelings; tender sentiments or emotions.

heart-to-heart adj. Frank; open; intimate.

heart·wood n. The hard, central wood of a tree.

heart·y (hahr-tee) adj. [heart·i·er; heart·i·est] 1. Warm; sincere; unfeigned. 2. Large; abundant. 3. Healthy; vigorous.—n. [pl. -ies] Intimate friend; good shipmate.—**heart·i·ly** adv.—**heart·i·ness** n.

heat (heet) n. 1. A form of energy which raises temperature. 2. High temperature; concentration of extreme warmth. 3. *Sports.* A trial or semifinal race. 4. Agitation; vehemence; excitement. 5. A period of sexual excitement in animals. 6. *Metallurgy.* Amount of metal from the loading of one furnace.—*v.* 1. To make hot; communicate heat to. 2. To excite; make feverish.—**heat·ed·ly** *adv.*

heat-cracked	heat-laden	heatproof
heat drops	heat maker	heat-resistant
heat-killed	heat making	heat-softened

heat·er *n.* 1. A stove or other appliance for raising temperature. 2. *Slang.* A gun.

heath *n.* 1. A desolate tract of land. 2. A family of plants including the blueberry, heather, rhododendron, etc.—**heath·y** *adj.*

hea·then *n.* [*pl.* -thens, -then] One who worships idols; pagan.—**hea·then** *adj.*—**hea·then·ish** *adj.* —**hea·then·ism** *n.*

heath·er (*heth*-er) *n.* An evergreen heath plant with white to red-purple flowers.— -**er·y** *adj.*

heat lightning. Reflection of lightning far distant from the observer.

heat·stroke *n.* Prostration caused by prolonged exposure to heat.

heat treatment. Heating of a metal to near its critical temperature to relieve internal stresses.

heave (*heev*) *v.* [heaved; hove; heav·ing] 1. To pick up; lift. 2. To give vent to, as a sigh. 3. To rise and fall; swell. 4. To apply power to; pull; force in any direction. 5. To vomit; retch.—*n.* 1. An upward motion; swell, as of the waves of the sea. 2. A throw. 3. [*pl.*] A disease of horses, characterized by heavy breathing and coughing.—**heave to.** To bring a ship's head into the wind and stop her.

heav·en (*hev*-'n) *n.* 1. [*pl.*] The space surrounding the earth; skies. 2. *Religion.* The final abode of the blessed. 3. A place or condition of supreme happiness.

heav·en·ly (*hev*-'n-lee) *adj.* 1. Denoting heaven or the skies. 2. Beautiful; pure. 3. Delightful; extremely pleasant.—**heav·en·li·ness** *n.*

heav·en·ward, heav·en·wards *adv. & adj.* Toward heaven; skyward.

heaviside layer. An ionized layer in the outer atmosphere which deflects radio waves and greatly increases the range of high-frequency transmission.

heav·y (*hev*-ee) *adj.* [heav·i·er; heav·i·est] 1. Weighty; ponderous. 2. Burdensome; oppressive. 3. Afflicted with grief or cares. 4. Sluggish; lifeless. 5. Great in strength, intensity, size. 6. Gloomy; lowering. 7. Not spongy or leavened. 8. Having much body or strength, as wines. 9. Pregnant.—*n.* [*pl.* -ies] *Theater.* The villain or his role.—**heav·i·ly** *adv.*—**heav·i·ness** *n.*

heavy-armed	heavy-handed	heavy-laden
heavy-boned	heavy-hearted	heavy looking
heavy-gaited	heavy-jawed	heavy-set

heavy hydrogen. An isotope of hydrogen twice the atomic weight of ordinary hydrogen.

heavy water. An oxide of heavy hydrogen; deuterium oxide.

heav·y·weight (*hev*-ee-wayt) *n.* A boxer weighing over 175 pounds.

He·bra·ic (hee-*bray*-ik) *adj.* Pertaining to the Hebrews or their language.

He·bra·ism *n.* An expression or manner of speaking peculiar to the Hebrew language. —**He·bra·ist** *n.*—**He·bra·is·tic, -is·ti·cal** *adj.*

He·brew (*hee*-broo) *n.* 1. One of a group of northern Semites; Israelite. 2. An adherent of the Jewish faith. 3. The Semitic language of the Hebrews.—**He·brew** *adj.*

He·brews *n. sing.* New Testament epistle written by St. Paul.

Heb·ri·des, The. A group of more than 500 islands off the west coast of Scotland.

Hec·a·te, Hek·a·te (*hek*-uh-tee) *n. Mythology.* The goddess of witchcraft and sorcery.

hec·a·tomb (*hek*-uh-toom) *n.* A great slaughter of persons or animals.

heck·le (*hek*-'l) *v.* [heck·led; heck·ling] To bait; jeer; interrupt noisily.—**heck·ler** *n.*

hec·tare *n.* An area of approximately $2\frac{1}{2}$ acres.

hec·tic (*hek*-tik) *adj.* 1. Chronic; habitual. 2. *Colloquial.* Agitated; feverish; restless. 3. Consumptive; wasted by disease.—*n.* A consumptive fever, flush, or victim.—**hec·ti·cal·ly** *adv.*

hec·to·graph (*hek*-tuh-graf) *n.* A duplicating apparatus which produces printed copies from a moist gelatin or clay mat.— -**graph·ic** *adj.*

Hec·tor (*hek*-ter) *n.* The warrior son of Priam, king of Troy.

hec·tor *v.* To badger; bully; annoy.—*n.* A bully.

hedge (*hej*) *n.* A fence of closely growing bushes or small trees.—*v.* [hedged; hedg·ing] 1. To attempt to retreat from a previous stand or position; be purposely equivocal or vague. 2. To encircle; surround for defense. 3. To bet upon both sides; to guard against. 4. *Stock Exchange.* To buy produce futures in such a way as to cut down losses from price fluctuation. 5. To enclose with a hedge.—*adj.* Poor in quality; low.—**hedg·er** *n.*

hedgeberry	hedge breaker	hedgepig
hedge-born	hedge maker	hedgestraw
hedge-bound	hedge making	hedgewood

hedge·hog *n.* A European animal very similar to the porcupine.

hedge·hop *v.* [hedge·hop·ped; hedge·hop·ping] *Aviation.* To fly at a low level.—**hedge·hop·ping** *n.*—**hedge·hop·per** *n.*

hedge·row (*hej*-roh) *n.* A row of growing shrubs or trees.

HEDGEHOG

he·don·ism (*hee*-dun-izm) *n.* The doctrine that life's greatest good lies in the pursuit of pleasure.—**he·don·ist** *n. & adj.*— -**is·ti·cal·ly** *adv.*

hee·bie-jee·bies *n. Slang.* Frightened, nervous feelings; jitters.

heed v. To regard; pay attention.—n. Care; attention; regard.—**heed·er** n.

heed·ful adj. Attentive; careful; cautious.

heed·less adj. Thoughtless; negligent; inattentive.

heel n. Slang. An unprincipled person.

heel v. To tilt from the vertical.—**heel** n.

heel n. 1. The hind part of a foot or of footwear. 2. A part left over; remainder.—v. 1. Slang. To furnish with money. 2. To follow close at the heels of. 3. To canvass votes or support. 4. To put heels on, as on shoes.

heelball	heel maker	heelplate
heel band	heel making	heelprint
heelcap	heelpiece	heelstrap

heel·tap n. A thickness of metal, rubber, etc., for a shoe heel; lift.

heft v. Colloquial. To lift so as to try the weight of.—n. Colloquial. Weight; influence.

heft·y adj. [heft·i·er; -i·est] Heavy; ponderous.

he·gem·o·ny (heh-jem-uh-nee; hee-) n. Predominance; leadership; authority.—**heg·e·mon·ic** (hej-eh-mon-ik) adj.

he·gi·ra (heh-jy-ruh) n. Also **he·ji·ra**. 1. [cap.] The flight of Mohammed from Mecca, 622 A.D., from which date Mohammedans reckon their time. 2. Any flight or exodus.

heif·er (hef-'r) n. A young cow.

height (hyte) n. 1. Elevation; eminence. 2. The distance which something rises above its foundation or the earth; altitude. 3. A summit; mountain. 4. Extent; degree.

height·en v. To increase; intensify.— -**en·er** n.

hei·nous (hay-nus) adj. Monstrous; atrocious; hateful.—**hein·ous·ly** adv.—**hein·ous·ness** n.

heir (air) n. One who inherits property from another on the latter's death.—**heir** v.—**heir·dom** n.—**heir·ess** n.—**heir·ship** n.

heir apparent. [pl. heirs apparent] One whose right of inheritance is unchallengeable.

heir·loom n. Any piece of personal property which has belonged to a family for a long time.

heir presumptive. One whose right of inheritance may be defeated by the birth of a closer relative.

Helen of Troy. The beautiful wife of Menelaus, King of Sparta.

hel·i·cal (hel-ih-k'l) adj. Having a spiral form.

hel·i·cop·ter (hel-ih-kop-ter) n. An airplane whose propeller or propellors are on top, and which rises almost straight up.

HELICOPTER

he·li·o·cen·tric (hee-lee-oh-sen-trik) adj. Also **heliocentrical.** Astronomy. Relating to the sun as a center.

he·li·o·graph (hee-lee-oh-graf) n. An instrument for signaling by reflecting the sun's rays.—**he·li·o·graph** v.

he·li·o·ther·a·py n. Treatment of disease by sunlight.

he·li·o·trope (hee-lee-uh-trohp) n. 1. A fragrant flower with small purple or white blossoms. 2. A shade of purple.

HELIOTROPE

he·li·um (hee-lee-um) n. A colorless, noninflammable, very light gas. (Symbol: He).

he·lix (hee-liks) n. [pl. hel·i·ces (hel-ih-seez), he·lix·es] 1. Any spiral. 2. Thread of a screw.

hell n. 1. Religion. The place of punishment for evildoers after death. 2. Hate or misery. 3. Printing. Box for broken or pied type.

Hel·las n. Greece.

hell·bend·er n. 1. A large North American salamander. 2. A riotous spree; debauch; drinking bout.

hell box. Receptacle into which a printer throws discarded type.

hell·cat n. 1. A witch; hag. 2. A vicious person. 3. [cap.] A fast Navy pursuit plane in World War II.

Hel·len·ic (hel-en-ik) adj. Pertaining to the Greeks; Grecian.—**Hel·len·ic** n.

Hel·len·ist (hel-en-ist) n. One who studies or adopts the language and customs of the Greeks.—**Hel·len·ism** n.

Hel·len·is·tic adj. Also **Hellenistical.** Relating to Greek culture after Alexander the Great.

Hel·les·pont. The Dardanelles.

Hell Gate. Strait in the East River, New York.

Hel·lene (hel-een) n. [pl. -lenes] A Greek.

hel·lion (hel-yun) n. A roisterer; rowdy; mischievous person.

hell·ish adj. Diabolical; infernal.

hel·lo [pl. -los] interj. A greeting used to attract attention, esp. on the telephone.

helm n. 1. The steering apparatus of a ship; wheel. 2. The post of direction or management.—**helm** v.

hel·met n. A protective covering for the head.—**hel·met·ed** adj.

helms·man n. [pl. -men] Nautical. Steersman of a ship.

Hel·ot (hel-ut) n. A serf or slave, esp. in ancient Sparta.—**hel·ot·ism, hel·ot·ry** n.

help v. 1. To aid; assist; succor. 2. To prevent; remedy. 3. To avoid.—n. 1. Assistance; aid. 2. Relief. 3. [pl.] Servants. 'The help have eaten.'—**help·er** n.

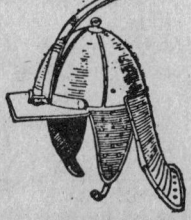
HELMET

help·ful adj. Useful; obliging.—**help·ful·ly** adv.—**help·ful·ness** n.

help·ing *n.* A serving of food; portion.

help·less *adj.* Feeble; powerless; impotent.

help·mate, help·meet *n.* A wife; companion.

hel·ter-skel·ter *adv.* Hurriedly and confusedly. —*adj.* Confused; disorderly.—**hel·ter·skel·ter** *n.*

helve *n.* A hatchet or axe handle.—*v.* [helved; helv·ing]—**helv·er** *n.*

Hel·ve·tia (hel-*vee*-shuh). Switzerland.—**Hel·ve·tian** *adj. & n.*

hem *n.* The border of a garment, doubled and sewed to strengthen it and prevent raveling. —*v.* [hemmed; hem·ming]—**hem in.** To surround; confine.

hem and haw. To stammer; act ill at ease.

hem·a·tite (*hem*-uh-tyte) *n.* A reddish-brown iron ore.

he·ma·to·ma (hem-uh-*toh*-muh) *n.* [*pl.* -ma·ta, -mas] A blood-filled tumor.

hem·i- *prefix.* Half.

he·mip·ter·ous (hem-*ip*-ter-us) *adj.* Denoting an order of insects, including all bugs.

hem·i·sphere (*hem*-ih-sfeer) *n.* A half sphere, esp. half of the terrestrial globe, or earth's surface.—**hem·i·spher·i·cal, hem·i·spher·ic** *adj.*

hem·lock *n.* 1. A tall, poisonous plant bearing white flowers. 2. An evergreen tree related to the pine.

hem mer *n.* Person, or sewing-machine attachment, that hems.

he·mo·glo·bin, hae·mo·glo·bin (hee-moh-gloh-bin) *n.* Pigment which colors the red-blood corpuscles and carries oxygen to the tissues.

he·mo·phil·i·a, hae·mo·phil·i·a (hee-moh-*fil*-ee-uh) *n.* A hereditary tendency to bleed excessively, due to improper clotting of the blood.—**he·mo·phil·i·ac** *n.*—**he·mo·phil·ic** *adj.*

hem·or·rhage, hae·mor·rhage (*hem*-er-ij) *n.* A copious discharge of blood from blood vessels.

hem·or·rhoid, haem·or·rhoid (*hem*-er-oyd) *n.* A painful swelling of the veins at the anus; [*pl.*] piles.

hemp *n.* 1. An annual Asiatic plant whose strong fibers are made into rope and coarse fabrics. 2. Narcotic obtained from hemp; hashish; marijuana.—**hemp·en** *adj.*

hem·stitch *n.* A stitch made by drawing a few parallel threads from a fabric and, with a needle, tying the remaining cross threads in small bunches.—**hem·stitch** *v.*—**hem·stitch·er** *n.*

hen *n.* 1. A female domestic fowl. 2. The female of certain other birds.

HEN

hen·bane *n.* Malodorous plant bearing yellowish-brown flowers, and poisonous to fowls.

hence (henss) *adv.* 1. From this source, place, or time; in the future. 2. In consequence of this; therefore.

hence·forth, hence·for·ward *adv.* From now on.

hench·man (hench-m'n) *n.* [*pl.* -men] Adherent; follower.

hen·e·quen (*hen*-uh-kin) *n.* Also **henequin.** Plant yielding a strong yellow fiber for rope.

hen·na (*hen*-uh) *n.* 1. A tropical shrub whose leaves yield a reddish dye, esp. for tinting hair. 2. A reddish-brown color.—**hen·na** *v.*

hen·ner·y (*hen*-er-ee) *n.* [*pl.* -ies] An enclosed place for hens.

hen·peck *v.* To nag; dominate. 'She henpecked her husband.'—**hen·pecked** *adj.*

hen·ry (*hen*-ree) *n.* [*pl.* -rys, -ries] *Electricity.* A unit of inductance.

hep *adj. Slang.* Discerning; in the know.

he·pat·ic (hih-*pat*-ik) *adj.* Pertaining to, or like, the liver.—*n.* A medicine acting on the liver.

he·pat·i·ca (hih-*pat*-ik-uh) *n.* Plant bearing early blooming white, pink, or blue flowers.

Hep·ple·white (*hep*-'l-hwyte) *adj.* Denoting a light, graceful style of furniture developed by George Hepplewhite in 18th-century England.

hep·ta·gon (*hep*-tuh-gon) *n. Geometry.* A plane figure consisting of seven sides and seven angles. —**hep·tag·o·nal** *adj.*

hep·tam·e·ter (hep-*tam*-uh-ter) *n.* A line of verse having seven metrical feet.

HEPTAGON

her *pron.* 1. *Objective case* of **she.** 2. *Possessive case* of **she.**—*adj.* Of or belonging to a particular female.

He·ra (*heer*-uh), **He·re** (*heer*-ee). *Greek Mythology.* The supreme goddess of Heaven.

Her·a·kles, Her·a·cles (*hehr*-uh-kleez). *Greek Mythology.* Hercules.

her·ald (*hehr*-'ld) *n.* 1. Formerly, an officer who announced war, carried messages, challenged to battle, etc. 2. A messenger; forerunner; harbinger. 3. Officer in charge of coats of arms and genealogies.—*v.* To indicate; usher in.

he·ral·dic (hehr-*al*-dik) *adj.* Concerning heraldry.

her·ald·ry (*hehr*-'ld-ree) *n.* [*pl.* -ries] The art or practice of tracing and recording genealogies and armorial bearings.

herb (erb, herb) *n.* Any plant with a succulent stem which dies to the root every year, esp. those used for medicine or flavoring.

her·ba·ceous (her-*bay*-shus) *adj.* Pertaining to or resembling herbs.

herb·age (*er*-bij; *her*-) *n.* Grass; green plants.

herb·al (*her*-b'l; *er*-) *adj.* Of herbs.—*n.* Book containing names and descriptions of plants.

herb·al·ist *n.* A collector of herbs; dealer in medicinal plants.

her·bar·i·um (her-*behr*-ee-um) *n.* [*pl.* -i·ums, -i·a] A systematic collection of dried plants.

H

Her·cu·le·an (her-*kyoo*-lee-un) *adj*. Having or requiring great strength or prowess.

Her·cu·les (her-kyoo-leez) *n. Greek Mythology*. A hero who performed twelve superhuman feats.

herd (*herd*) *n*. 1. A group of animals. 2. A crowd; rabble.—*v*. 1. To drive animals. 2. To associate; flock; group.—**herder** *n*.

herds·man (*herdz*-mun) *n*. [*pl*. -men] A shepherd; tender of a flock.

here (*heer*) *adv*. 1. In or at this place or state. 2. In this direction; to this place.—**here and there**. In a dispersed manner.

hereamong	hereinafter	hereunder
hereat	hereinto	hereunto
herebefore	hereof	hereupon
herefrom	hereon	herewith
hereinabove	hereto	herewithal

here·a·bout (*heer*-uh-bowt), **here·a·bouts** *adv*. Near this place.

here·aft·er *adv*. At a future time; still to come. —*n*. The after life.

here·by *adv*. By this means.

he·red·i·ta·ble (hehr-*ed*-it-uh-b'l) *adj*. Capable of inheriting or being inherited.—**he·red·i·ta·bil·i·ty** *n*.—**he·red·i·ta·bly** *adv*.

he·red·i·ta·ry (hehr-*ed*-ih-tehr-ee) *adj*. 1. Received or passed on from an ancestor; ancestral. 2. Inheritable.—**he·red·i·tar·i·ly** *adv*.

he·red·i·ty (hehr-*ed*-ih-tee) *n*. [*pl*. -ties] Inheritance of characteristics from one's ancestors.

Her·e·ford (*hehr*-uh-ferd) *n*. A kind of cattle noted for the amount and quality of its beef.

here·in *adv*. Here; in this.

her·e·sy (*hehr*-uh-see) *n*. [*pl*. -sies] An opinion opposed to the orthodox belief, esp. a disruptive opinion.—**her·e·tic** *n*. Exponent of an unorthodox opinion.—**he·ret·i·cal** *adj*.—**he·ret·i·cal·ly** *adv*.

here·to·fore *adv*. Before this; in the past.

her·it·a·ble (*hehr*-it-uh-b'l) *adj*. Able to inherit or be inherited.—**her·it·a·bil·i·ty** *n*.

her·i·tage (*hehr*-uh-tij) *n*. Inheritance; that which is passed on from ancestors.

her·maph·ro·dite (her-*maf*-roh-dyte) *n*. An animal or plant which has, or seems to have, both male and female sex organs.—**her·maph·ro·dite, -dit·ic, -dit·i·cal** *adj*.— **-dit·i·cal·ly** *adv*.

Her·mes (*her*-meez) *n. Greek Mythology*. The messenger of the gods; Mercury.

her·met·ic, her·met·i·cal (her-*met*-ik) *adj*. Tight; close; airtight.—**her·met·i·cal·ly** *adv*.

her·mit *n*. 1. One who retires from society and lives alone. 2. A molasses cookie, usually with raisins.—**her·mit·age** *n*. A hermit's home.

hermit crab. A crustacean which lives in cast-off mollusk shells.

her·nia (*her*-nee-uh) *n*. [*pl*. -ni·as] Rupture; protrusion of an internal organ or other tissue beyond the cavity normally containing it.

he·ro (*heer*-oh) *n*. [*pl*. -roes] 1. A doer of great or brave deeds. 2. The central male character in a literary work or a celebration.

he·ro·ic (hee-*roh*-ik) *adj*. Also **heroical**. 1. Denoting or like a hero or his accomplishments. 2. Epic. 'Heroic poetry.' 3. Larger than life size. 'A heroic statue.'—**he·ro·i·cal·ly** *adv*.

heroic verse. Rhyming iambic-pentameter couplets.

Her·o·in (*hehr*-oh-in) *n*. Trade-mark name for a powerful narcotic derived from opium.

her·o·ine *n*. 1. A female hero. 2. The leading female character of a literary work.

her·o·ism *n*. Courage; gallantry; fortitude.

her·on (*hehr*-un) *n*. A long-legged wading bird related to the stork. —**her·on·ry** [*pl*. -ries] Breeding place for herons.

her·pes (*her*-peez) *n. Medical*. A skin disease marked by spreading blisters.

her·pe·tol·o·gy (her-peh-*tol*-uh-jee) *n*.

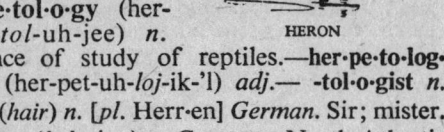

HERON

Science of study of reptiles.—**her·pe·to·log·i·cal** (her-pet-uh-*loj*-ik-'l) *adj*.— **-tol·o·gist** *n*.

Herr (*hair*) *n*. [*pl*. Herr·en] *German*. Sir; mister.

her·ring (*hehr*-ing) *n*. Common North Atlantic food fish.

her·ring·bone *n*. A pattern in which rows of wedge-shaped designs parallel each other.—**her·ring·bone** *adj*.

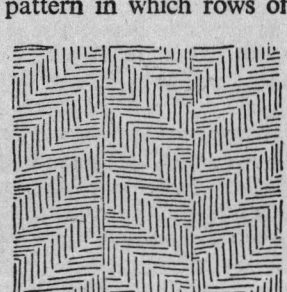

HERRINGBONE

hers (*herz*) *Possessive pron*. Belonging to her.

her·self *pron*. Intensive or reflexive form of **her**.

Hertz·i·an (*hertz*-ee-un) *adj*. Denoting electromagnetic or radio-wave radiation.

hes·i·tan·cy (*hez*-ih-tun-see) *n*. [*pl*. -cies]. Also **hesitance**. Indecisiveness; vacillation; delay. —**hes·i·tant** *adj*.—**hes·i·tant·ly** *adv*.

hes·i·tate (*hez*-ih-tayt) *v*. [hes·i·tat·ed; hes·i·tat·ing] 1. To pause indecisively; be in doubt. 2. To stammer.— **-tat·ing·ly** *adv*.— **-i·ta·tion** *n*.

Hes·pe·ri·an (hess-*peer*-ee-un) *adj*. Western.

Hes·per·us (*hess*-per-us) *n*. The evening star.

Hes·sian (*hesh*-un) *n*. An inhabitant of Hesse, Germany, esp. the mercenary soldiers from Hesse that fought in the American Revolution.—**Hes·si·an** *adj*.

Hessian fly. A small, blackish, two-winged fly whose larvae destroy young wheat.

he·tae·ra, he·tai·ra (hee-*teer*-uh) *n*. [*pl*. -rae, -rai] In ancient Greece, an attractive accomplished woman, usually a slave, who entertained men; not necessarily a courtesan.

het·er·o-, he·ter- (*het*-er-oh) *prefix*. Mixed different.

het·er·o·dox *adj.* Contrary to standardized opinion; not orthodox.—**het·er·o·dox·y** [*pl.* -ies] *n.* Heresy.

het·er·o·dyne *adj. Radio.* Beating a low frequency against a high one so as to produce a wave of intermediate frequency.

het·er·o·ge·ne·ous (het-er-oh-*jee*-nee-us) *adj.* Dissimilar; differing.—**het·er·o·ge·ne·i·ty** *n.*

het·er·o·nym (*het*-er-oh-nim) *n.* A word with the same spelling as another word, but wholly different in meaning and pronunciation.

het·er·o·sex·u·al (-*sek*-shoo-ul) *adj.* Sexually attracted to a member of the opposite sex.—**het·er·o·sex·u·al** *n.*—**het·er·o·sex·u·al·i·ty** *n.*

hew (*hyoo*) *v.* [hewed, hewn; hew·ing] 1. To cut; fell. 2. To carve; shape. 3. To hack; chop.—**hew·er** *n.*

hex *n.* A witch's spell or curse.—**hex** *v.*

hex·a-, hex- *prefix.* Six; six times.

hex·a·gon *n.* A six-sided plane figure.—**hex·ag·o·nal** *adj.*—**hex·ag·o·nal·ly** *adv.*

hex·am·e·ter (heks-*am*-uh-ter) *n.* Verse of six metrical feet, common in Greek and Latin poetry.

hex·a·ped, hex·a·pod *adj.* Six-footed.—*n.* A six-footed animal; insect.

HEXAGON

hey (*hay*) *interj.* An expression of surprise; call to secure attention.

hey·day *n.* Prime of life; season of vigor.

hi·a·tus (hy-*ay*-tus) *n.* [*pl.* -tus·es, -tus] A gap; space or gulf; interruption.

Hi·a·wa·tha (hy-uh-*woth*-uh) *n.* The American Indian hero of Longfellow's *Hiawatha*.

hi·ber·nate (*hy*-ber-nayt) *v.* [hi·ber·nat·ed; -nat·ing] To winter; spend the winter in sleep or inactivity.—**hi·ber·nal** (hy-*bern*-ul) *adj.* Wintry; denoting winter.—**hi·ber·na·tion** *n.*

Hi·ber·ni·a (hy-*ber*-nee-uh). Ancient name of Ireland.—**Hi·ber·ni·an** *n. & adj.*

hi·bis·cus (hy-*biss*-kus, hih-*biss*-kus) *n.* Plant or small tree bearing large bell-shaped flowers.

hic·cup (*hik*-up) *n.* Also **hiccough.** A spasm in the diaphragm causing a quick, voiced intake of air.—**hic·cup** *v.*

hick (*hik*) *n. Slang.* A farmer.—*adj.* Countrified.

hick·o·ry (*hik*-er-ee) *n.* [*pl.* -ries] A tree valuable for its nuts and hard, strong wood.

hi·dal·go (hih-*dal*-goh) *n.* [*pl.* -gos] A lower-class Spanish nobleman.

hid·den (*hid*-'n) *Past participle* of **hide.**—*adj.* Concealed; not readily apparent; secret.

hide *n.* The skin of an animal.—*v.* [hid·ed; hid·ing] 1. To flay; strip of skin. 2. *Colloquial.* To whip; lash.

hide *v.* [hid; hid·den or hid; hid·ing] 1. To conceal; withhold from sight or knowledge. 2. To cover; bar from view. 3. To keep oneself concealed.—**hid·er** *n.*

hide·bound *adj.* Narrow-minded; conservative.

hid·e·ous (*hid*-ee-us) *adj.* Shockingly ugly; revolting to the mind or senses.—**hid·e·ous·ly** *adv.*—**hid·e·ous·ness** *n.*

hide·out *n.* A hiding place, esp. for criminals.

hid·ing (*hy*-ding) *n.* 1. *Colloquial.* A severe beating; flaying. 2. Concealment; hiding place.

hie (*hy*) [hied; hy·ing, hie·ing] To hasten; go.

hi·er·arch (*hy*-er-ahrk) *n.* Leader of a religious order.

hi·er·arch·y *n.* [*pl.* -ies] 1. Body of persons, esp. ecclesiastics, in whom authority is vested and who are organized in successive ranks. 2. Any group arranged in ranks.—**hi·er·arch·ic, hi·er·arch·i·cal** *adj.*—**hi·er·arch·i·cal·ly** *adv.*

hi·er·at·ic (hy-er-*at*-ik) *adj.* Also **hieratical.** Sacred; priestly; holy.—**hi·er·at·i·cal·ly** *adv.*

hi·er·o·glyph·ic (hy-er-uh-*glif*-ik) *n.* Also **hieroglyphical.** 1. A picture or symbol representing a letter, word, or idea in primitive picture alphabets. 2. Secret or unintelligible symbol or letter.— **-og·ly·phist** (-*og*-lih-fist) *n.*

hig·gle (*hig*-'l) *v.* [hig·gled; hig·gling] To bargain pettily; haggle.—**hig·gler** *n.*

hig·gle·dy-pig·gle·dy (*hig*-'l-dee-*pig*-'l-dee) *adj. & adv.* In confusion; mixed up.—*n.* A confused tangle; jumble.

high (*hy*) *adj.* 1. Elevated; lofty; raised. 2. Tall; of a particular height. 3. Great in rank, importance, degree, intensity, etc. 4. Of great moral or intellectual qualities; noble. 5. Arrogant; proud. 6. *Slang.* Tipsy; affected by a narcotic. 7. Expensive. 8. Sharp; shrill, as sound. 9. Having a strong odor; gamy.—**high** *n.* 1. An elevated place. 2. A peak in a cycle.—**high, high·ly** *adv.*

high-arched	high-mettled
high back	high-motived
high-backed	high-mounted
high-blooded	high-necked
high-boned	high pass
high-breasted	high-peaked
high-built	highpitched
high caliber	high-placed
high caste	high-pooped
high-ceilinged	high potential
high class	high-powered
high climber	high-priced
high-collared	high-principled
high-colored	high-prized
high-complexioned	high-raised
high-crested	high reaching
high-crowned	high-reared
high-cut	high-roofed
high-flavored	high-seasoned
high-flushed	high-seated
high grade	high-sided
high-headed	high-souled
high-heaped	high speed
high-hung	high-stepper
high intensity	high-tempered
high-keyed	high-waisted

high·ball *n.* A tall drink made with distilled liquor, ice, and a carbonated beverage.

high·born *adj.* Born into a noble family.

H

high·boy *n.* High chest of drawers mounted on legs.

high-bred *adj.* Refined in manner; of aristocratic breeding.

high·brow *n. Slang.* An intellectual snob.—**high·brow, high-browed** *adj.*

High Church. Group within the Church of England laying stress on symbolism and ceremony.—**High-Church** *adj.*—**High-Churchman** *n.*

HIGHBOY

high comedy. Comedy depending on wit and character, not situation.

high·fa·lu·tin, high·fa·lu·ting (hy-fuh-*loo*-t'n) *adj. Colloquial.* Pompous; affected; bombastic.—*n.* Affected superiority; bombast.

high-flown *adj.* 1. Lofty; proud. 2. Extravagant; bombastic.

high-fly·er, high-fli·er *n.* One extravagant in pretensions or manner.—**high-fly·ing** *adj.*

high-hand·ed *adj.* Arbitrary; domineering.—**high-hand·ed·ly** *adv.*—**high-hand·ed·ness** *n.*

high-hat *v.* [high-hat·ted; high-hat·ting] *Slang.* To snub; treat as inferior or inconsequential.—*adj. Slang.* Pretentious; snobbish.

high·jack·er, hi·jack·er *n.* A thug or robber who waylays trucks, esp. those with illegal cargoes.—**high·jack** *v.*—**high·jack·ing** *n.*

High·lands, The. The scenic mountain regions of northern Scotland.—**High·land·er** *n.*

highland fling. Spirited dance originating in the Scottish Highlands.

high light. 1. Part of a painting, etc., marked by the brightest light. 2. Most interesting or effective portion of a book, speech, etc.

High Mass. *Roman Catholic Church.* The complete Mass sung with assistance of a choir.

high-mind·ed *adj.* Of lofty principles; proud.—**high-mind·ed·ness** *n.*

high-muckety-muck, high-muck-a-muck *n. Colloquial.* An important person, or one who fancies himself important.

high·ness *n.* 1. [*cap.*] Title given to royalty. 2. Elevation; state or quality of being high.

high-pres·sure *adj.* 1. *Slang.* Glib-tongued; fast-talking; aggressive. 2. Exceeding normal or atmospheric pressure.—*v.* [high-pres·sured; -sur·ing] *Slang.* To be repugnantly aggressive.

high proof. Of high alcoholic content.

high·road *n.* 1. Highway. 2. Expedient way.

high school. A secondary school; grades following elementary school.

high seas. Open sea, outside the territorial limits of any nation.

high-sound·ing *adj.* Pompous; pretentious.

high-spir·it·ed *adj.* Mettlesome; proud.

high-strung *adj.* Tense; sensitive; nervous.

high tension. Large voltage; great electrical potential.—**high-tension** *adj.*

high-test *adj.* 1. Containing a high degree of power per unit. 2. Meeting difficult requirements.

high time. 1. Just in time; with no time to spare. 2. *Slang.* An extremely gay party.

high-toned *adj.* 1. *Colloquial.* Fashionable; sophisticated. 2. High in pitch; shrill.

high·way *n.* A public or main road.

high·way·man *n.* Robber who attacks travelers on a public road.

hi·jack·er, *Variant spelling* of highjacker.

hike *v.* [hiked; hik·ing] To march or tramp a long distance, esp. through the countryside.—*n.* A long walk or march.—**hi·ker** *n.*

hi·lar·i·ous *adj.* (hil-*air*-ee-us) Excessively or noisily gay; extremely merry.—**hi·lar·i·ous·ly** *adv.*—**hi·lar·i·ous·ness** *n.*

hi·lar·i·ty *n.* Noisy mirth; jollity.

hill *n.* 1. A sizeable elevation in the earth. 2. A heap; mound. 'An anthill.' 3. A cluster of plants. 'A hill of beans.'—**hill** *v.*

hill·bil·ly (*hil*-bil-ee) *n.* [*pl.* -lies] *Colloquial.* A rustic mountaineer.—**hill·bil·ly** *adj.*

hill·ock (*hil*-uk) *n.* A small hill or mound.—**hill·ock·y** *adj.*

hill·y (*hil*-ee) *adj.* [hill·i·er; hill·i·est] Marked by frequent hills; unevenly surfaced.—**hill·i·ness** *n.*

hilt *n.* A guard between the blade and handle of a knife or sword.

Hi·ma·la·yas (hih-*mahl*-uh-yuz). A central Asian mountain range, the highest in the world.—**Hi·ma·la·yan** *adj.*

him·self *pron.* Emphatic or reflexive form of *he.*

hind (hynde) *n.* The female of the red deer.

hind *adj.* [hind·er; hind·most, hind·er·most] Rear; back; posterior.

hin·der (*hin*-der) *v.* To impede; obstruct; retard; prevent; interrupt.—**hin·der·er** *n.*

hind·quar·ter (hynde-kwawr-ter) *n.* The posterior part of a half of a meat carcass.

hin·drance (*hin*-drunss) *n.* Obstruction; impediment; obstacle.

hind·sight (hynde-syte) *n.* Opposite of foresight; understanding of an event after it has happened.

Hin·du, Hin·doo (*hin*-doo) *n.* 1. A member of a native race of India. 2. A follower of Hinduism.—**Hin·du, Hin·doo** *adj.*

Hin·du·ism (*hin*-doo-izm) *n.* A religious and social doctrine followed by most of the people of India.

Hin·du·stan, Hin·do·stan (hin-doo-*stahn*). India, esp. the central section, where the language of the Hindus originated.

Hin·du·sta·ni, Hin·doo·sta·ni (hin-doo-*stah*-nee) *n.* The language spoken over almost all of India.—*adj.* Relating to Hindustan.

hinge (hinj) *n.* 1. A swinging or pivoted joint on which doors and the like turn. 2. That on which anything depends or turns.—*v.* [hinged; hing·ing]—**hing·er** *n.*

hint *n.* Intimation; insinuation; suggestion.—*v.* To suggest; allude to vaguely.—**hint·er** *n.*—**hint·ing·ly** *adv.*

hin·ter·land (*hin*-ter-land) *n.* The back country.

hip *n.* The protrusion of the pelvic bone or the region about the pelvis.

hip *n.* The ripe fruit of the rose plant.

Hip·po·crat·ic oath (hip-uh-*krat*-ik). A code of medical ethics sworn to by physicians upon receiving the M.D. degree.

hip·po·drome (*hip*-uh-drohm) *n.* A racing course; arena, esp. for horseshows.

hip·po·pot·a·mus (hip-uh-*pot*-uh-mus) *n.* [*pl.* -mus·es, -mi] A huge, thick-skinned African river animal related to the pig.

hir·cine (*her*-seen) *adj.* Resembling a goat.

hire *v.* [hired; hir·ing] 1. To employ; rent; let. 2. To bribe.—*n.* Rent; payment; wages.—**hire·a·ble** *adj.*—**hir·er** *n.*

HIPPOPOTAMUS (1/125 life size)

hire·ling (*hyre*-ling) *n.* One who works merely for pay, not for principle.—**hire·ling** *adj.*

hiring hall. Labor union hall where men gather to await announcement of jobs available.

Hir·o·shi·ma (hihr-oh-*shee*-muh). Large Japanese city almost wholly destroyed by an atom bomb on August 6, 1945.

hir·sute (her-*soot*) *adj.* Hairy; shaggy; full of bristles.—**hir·sute·ness** *n.*

his (hiz) *pron.* Of or belonging to him. Possessive case of **he.**—*adj.* Of him.

His·pan·io·la (hiss-pan-*yoh*-luh). Island in the Caribbean Sea including Dominican Republic and Republic of Haiti.

his·pid (*hiss*-pid) *adj.* Covered with stiff bristles.—**his·pid·ly** *adv.*—**his·pid·i·ty** (hiss-*pid*-uh-tee) *n.*

hiss *n.* The voiceless sound of *s*, used to express disapprobation, derision, etc.—**hiss** *v.*

hist *interj.* Silence! Hush!

his·to·ri·an (hiss-*tor*-ee-un) *n.* A writer of or specialist in history.

his·tor·ic (hiss-*tor*-ik) *adj.* Momentous; great.

his·tor·i·cal *adj.* Pertaining to history.—**his·tor·i·cal·ly** *adv.*—**his·tor·i·cal·ness** *n.*

his·to·ri·og·ra·pher (hiss-toh-ree-*og*-ruh-fer) *n.* Historian; historical writer.—**-og·ra·phy** *n.*

his·to·ry (*hiss*-ter-ee) *n.* [*pl.* -ries] 1. Branch of knowledge dealing with past experience of mankind. 2. A narrative or chronicle.

his·tri·on·ic (hiss-tree-*on*-ik) *adj.* Also **his·tri·on·i·cal.** Pertaining to acting or the stage; theatrical.—**his·tri·on·ic** *n.* 1. A stage player. 2. [*pl.*] Dramatics.—**his·tri·on·i·cal·ly** *adv.*

hit *v.* [hit; hit·ting] 1. To strike; deal a blow; knock; come into forceful contact with. 2. To attain; produce successfully. 3. To fit; suit.—*n.* 1. A great success; any venture scoring great popularity. 2. A blow; collision. 3. *Baseball.* Batting of the ball so as to get safely on base. 4. A cutting, deftly calculated remark.—**hit·ter** *n.*

hit-and-miss *adj.* Haphazard; random.

hitch *n.* 1. An impediment; snag; breakdown;

stoppage. 2. A device for coupling. 3. A kind of easily loosened knot. 4. A tug; yank.—*v.* 1. To couple; make fast. 2. To hobble; move jerkily; fidget. 3. To raise by jerks.—**hitch·er** *n.*

hitch·hike *v.* [hitch·hiked; hitch·hik·ing] To travel by begging rides in passing automobiles.—**hitch·hike** *n.*—**hitch·hik·er** *n.*

hith·er (*hith*-er) *adv.* In this direction; to this place.—*adj.* Close; near.

hith·er·most *adj.* Nearest; closest.

hith·er·to *adv.* Previously; before this time.

hith·er·ward, hith·er·wards *adv.* Toward this place.

Hit·ler·ism *n.* The fascist doctrine and practice of the Nazi party in Germany under Adolf Hitler.—**Hit·ler·ite** *n.* A follower of Nazism.

hit or miss. At random.—**hit-or-miss** *adj.*

Hit·tite *n.* One of an ancient Indo-European people of Asia Minor.—**Hit·tite** *adj.*

hive *n.* 1. A habitation for bees; colony or swarm of bees. 2. A place buzzing with activity.—*v.* [hived; hiv·ing] To put in a hive.

hives *n.* An eruptive skin disorder.

hoar (hor) *adj.* 1. White. 2. Gray or whitish through age.—*n.* Antiquity; hoariness.

hoard (hord) *n.* Hidden stock; treasure.—*v.* To collect in secret.—**hoard·er** *n.*

hoard·ing *n.* 1. Laying up a store. 2. A board wall around a building under construction.

hoar·frost *n.* White particles of frozen dew.

hoarse (horss) *adj.* Harsh; grating.—**hoarse·ly** *adv.*—**hoarse·ness** *n.*

hoar·y *adj.* [hoar·i·er; hoar·i·est] White; gray; hoar.—**hoar·i·ness** *n.*

hoax (hohks) *n.* [*pl.* hoax·es] A trick played for deception; practical joke.—*v.* To deceive; play a trick without malice.—**hoax·er** *n.*

hob *n.* 1. The part of a grate on which things are placed to be kept warm. 2. A sprite; elf. 3. Mischief. 'The storm played hob with our plans.'

hob·ble *v.* [-bled; -bling] 1. To limp; walk awkwardly. 2. To move irregularly; wriggle. 3. To tie the legs together to prevent free motion; clog.

hob·ble·de·hoy (hob-'l-dee-hoy) *n.* A raw, gawky youth.

hob·by *n.* [*pl.* -bies] 1. Any favorite pursuit followed persistently. 2. A hobbyhorse.

hob·by·horse *n.* A child's wooden horse.

hob·gob·lin *n.* A kind of fairy or elf.

hob·nail *n.* A thick-headed nail used for shoeing horses and for the soles of heavy boots.—**hob·nailed** *adj.*

hob·nob *v.* [-nobbed; -nobbing] To drink familiarly (with); be very familiar with.—*adv.* At random.

HOBBYHORSE

ho·bo (*hoh*-boh) *n.* [*pl.* -bos, -boes] A vagrant.

H

Hob·son's choice. A choice which one has no option but to accept.

hock *n.* 1. In horses, etc., the joint between the knee and fetlock. 2. In man, the posterior part of the knee joint; ham.—*v.* To disable by cutting the tendons of the ham.

hock *n.* A white Rhine wine.

hock *v. Slang.* To pawn.—**hock·shop** *n.* Pawnbroker's shop.

hock·ey (*hok*-ee) *n.* A game played on either ice or grass by teams which use a ball or puck, and curved clubs. —**hockey stick.** The curved club used in hockey.

hocus-pocus (*hoh*-kus-*poh*-kus) *n.* 1. A juggler's trick; conjurer's wiles. 2. Trickery; deception.—*v.* To cheat.

hod *n.* 1. A long-handled trough for carrying mortar or bricks on the shoulder. 2. A coal scuttle.

hodge·podge (*hoj*-poj) *adj.* A mixed mass; medley.

HOD

hoe (*hoh*) *n.* A long-handled garden instrument for cutting weeds, loosening earth, etc.—*v.* [hoed; hoe·ing] To use a hoe.—**ho·er** *n.*

hoe·cake *n.* A bread made of corn meal.

hog *n.* 1. Swine; pig; boar. 2. A mean, filthy, or greedy person.—*v.* [hogged; -ging] 1. *Slang.* To act selfishly or greedily. 2. To scrape a ship's bottom under water. —**go whole hog.** Pursue a course to the end.

HOE

hog·gish *adj.* Filthy, greedy, or selfish.—**hog·gish·ly** *adv.*—**hog·gish·ness** *n.*

hognose snake. A non-venomous snake which flattens its head when about to strike.

hogs·head (*hogz*-hed) *n.* 1. A measure of capacity containing 63 gallons. 2. A large cask.

hog·wash *n.* 1. Swill; kitchen refuse given to swine. 2. *Slang.* Flapdoodle; baloney.

Hoh·en·zol·lern (*hoh*-en-tsol-ern) *n.* A member of a dynasty ruling Prussia from 1701, and Germany from 1871 until 1918.

hoicks *interj.* A hunting cry.—**hoicks** *v.*

hoi polloi (*hoy* puh-*loy*). Derogatively, the masses of the people.

hoist *v.* [hoist·ed; hoist·ing] To lift, heave, esp. raise by means of block and tackle.—*n.* 1. A lift; act of hoisting. 2. Any machine for lifting; elevator. 3. *Nautical.* **a.** The perpendicular height of a flag in position to fly from a staff. **b.** The extent to which a sail may be hoisted.

hoi·ty-toi·ty (*hoy*-tee-*toy*-tee) *adj.* Huffy; snobbish.—**hoi·ty·toi·ty** *n.*

ho·key-po·key (*hoh*-kee-*poh*-kee) *n.* Hocuspocus.

ho·kum (*hoh*-kum) *n. Colloquial.* Use of devices to create a poignant effect; contrived sentimentality.

hold *v.* [held; hold·ing] 1. To have or grasp; support; sustain. 2. To bear, manage, or maintain in a certain way. 3. To regard; think; judge. 4. To contain; have capacity. 5. To retain within itself; keep from flowing out. 6. To maintain; retain; uphold, defend. 7. To occupy; possess; have power over. 8. To have; keep. 9. To stop; restrain; limit; withhold. 10. To bind or oblige. 11. To guard or keep under restraint. 12. To continue; prosecute or carry on; pursue. 13. To preside over; celebrate; solemnize. 14. To engage the attention of; occupy. 15. To continue firm; stand fast; not give way. 16. To be true or valid. 17. To refrain.—*n.* 1. A clutch; grip; mental grasp. 2. Anything which can be seized for support. 3. Power of keeping. 4. Authority to seize or keep; claim. 5. Prison. 6. Fort; stronghold. 7. *Music.* The character which indicates a pause.—**hold forth.** To declaim.—**hold off.** 1. To delay action. 2. To keep away. —**hold out.** To last; endure.—**hold over.** To continue.—**hold up.** 1. To accost and rob. 2. To delay.—**hold with.** To side with.

hold *n.* The interior of a ship.

hold·back *n.* 1. Check; hindrance; restraint. 2. A contrivance which enables an animal to hold back a vehicle when going down hill.

hold·er *n.* 1. A container, stand, etc. 2. One who holds. 3. Payee of a bill of exchange or promissory note.

hold·fast *n.* 1. Support; hold. 2. A catch; hook; long nail with short flat head.

hold·ing *n.* 1. Land or other property held from a superior. 2. Property in one's possession, esp. securities.

holding company. *Finance.* A company which controls the stock of subordinate companies.

hold·up *n. Colloquial.* An armed robbery.

hole *n.* 1. A hollow place or cavity. 2. A torn space; tear. 3. A poverty-stricken living place. 4. An animal's burrow. 5. A circumstance not covered; defect. 'A hole in his story.' 6. *Colloquial.* A difficult position; spot.—*v.* [holed; hol·ing] 1. To make a hole in. 2. To drive into a hole.—**hole·y** *adj.*

hol·i·day (*hol*-ih-day) *n.* 1. A day set apart for commemoration. 2. A gay, festive occasion. 3. A day of exemption from labor. 4. [*often pl.*] A vacation.—**hol·i·day** *adj.*

ho·li·ly (*hoh*-lih-lee) *adv.* Piously; sacredly.

ho·li·ness *n.* 1. Sacredness; consecration to God. 2. Piousness; sanctity; freedom from sin. 3. [*cap.*] A title of the pope.

hol·la *interj.* Stop! Hey! Ho, there!

hol·land (*hol*-und) *n.* Coarse linen fabric used for window blinds, carpets, etc.

hollandaise sauce (*hol*-un-dayz). A tart dressing of butter and egg yolks seasoned with lemon or vinegar, used on vegetables.

Holland gin. A gin imported from Holland.

hol·ler (*hol*-er) *v.* To shout.—**hol·ler** *n.*

hol·low (*hol*-oh) *adj.* 1. Having an empty space or cavity within. 2. Concave; sunken. 3. Deep; low; reverberating. 4. False; deceitful; not sound.—*n.* A cavity; den; hole; channel.—*v.* To make hollow; excavate.—*adv. Colloquial.* Utterly; completely.

HOLLY

hol·ly (*hol*-ee) *n.* [*pl.* -lies] An evergreen plant with shiny leaves and red berries.

hol·ly·hock (*hol*-ee-hok) *n.* A tall garden flower.

Hol·ly·wood (*hol*-ee-wood). A section of Los Angeles, the center of the motion-picture industry.

hol·mi·um (*hohl*-mee-um) *n.* A rare-earth metallic element. (*Symbol:* Ho).

holm oak. A European evergreen oak.

HOLLYHOCK

hol·o·caust (*hol*-uh-kost) *n.* 1. A great slaughter or sacrifice of life, esp. by fire. 2. A burnt sacrifice to be entirely consumed by fire.—**hol·o·caus·tal** (hol-uh-*koss*-t'l) *adj.*—**hol·o·caus·tic** *adj.*

hol·o·graph (*hol*-uh-graf) *n.* A document written entirely by the person signing or sending it.—**hol·o·graph, hol·o·graph·ic** (hol-uh-*graf*-ik), **hol·o·graph·i·cal** *adj.*

Hol·stein-Frie·sian (*hohl*-steen-*free*-zhun). Also **Holstein.** One of a breed of largest-sized beef and dairy cattle.

hol·ster (*hohl*-ster) *n.* A sheath for a pistol.

ho·ly (*hoh*-lee) *adj.* [ho·li·er; ho·li·est] 1. Hallowed; consecrated; sacred. 2. Godly; pious; pure.—*n.* [*pl.* -lies].

Holy Communion. The Eucharist; the Christian sacrament of the Lord's Supper.

holy day. Also **holyday.** A day of religious commemoration.

Holy Ghost. The third person in the Trinity.

Holy Grail. The cup used by Christ at the Last Supper. The search for it formed a medieval-legend theme.

Holy Land. Palestine.

holy of holies. *Bible.* The innermost recess of the Jewish temple, where the Ark was kept.

holy orders. The positions of the Christian clergy: bishop, priest, deacon, etc.

Holy Roman Empire. The loosely organized Germanic federation of central Europe from the 9th to the 19th century.

Holy Spirit. The Holy Ghost; third person in the Trinity.

ho·ly·stone (*hoh*-lih-) *n.* A soft sandstone used to clean the decks of ships.—*v.* To scrub a deck.

Holy Week. The week before Easter; last week of Lent.

Holy Writ. The Scriptures.

hom·age (*hom*-ij) *n.* 1. Deference; obeisance; reverential tribute. 2. Symbolical acknowledgment made by a feudal tenant to his lord.

home *n.* 1. One's own dwelling; abode of one's family; the family unit. 2. One's own country; birthplace. 3. Place of origin; source. 4. An institution, usually charitable, for the sick, homeless, etc. 5. The after-life; heaven. 6. The pith; heart.—*adj.* 1. Connected with one's home or residence. 2. Domestic, esp. as opposed to foreign. 3. Pointed; close. —*adv.* 1. To one's home or residence. 2. To one's country. 3. To the point; effectively; thoroughly; closely.—*v.* [homed; hom·ing].

home-baked	homefarer	homelikeness
homebody	home-fed	homemaking
home-born	home-felt	home owner
home-bound	home goer	homeplace
home-brewed	home-grown	home-raised
home-built	homekeeper	home-reared
homecomer	homekeeping	home seeker
homecoming	homeland	home site
homecraft	homelander	homewort
home-driven	homelike	home-woven

home-bred *adj.* 1. Uncultivated; plain; unpolished. 2. Domestic; not foreign.

home brew. Liquor, esp. beer, made at home.

home economics. The study of the needs of a family, esp. diet, budget, child care, etc.

home·less *adj.* Without a home.

home·like *adj.* Pleasant; cozy; cheery.

home·ly *adj.* [home·li·er; home·li·est] 1. Plain-featured; not handsome. 2. Coarse; plain; for common use.—**home·li·ness** *n.*

home·made *adj.* Made at home or on the premises.

home·mak·er *n.* A housewife; one who manages a home.—**home·mak·ing** *n.*

ho·me·op·a·thy (hoh-mee-*op*-uh-thee) *n.* The treatment of diseases by administering small doses of medicines which produce in healthy persons symptoms similar to those of the disease being treated.—**ho·me·o·path** (*hoh*-mee-uh-path) *n.*— **-o·path·ic** *adj.*— **-op·a·thist** *n.*

home plate. *Baseball.* The fourth or home base.

Ho·mer (*hoh*-mer). The great epic poet of ancient Greece, to whom the *Iliad* and the *Odyssey* are traditionally ascribed.

ho·mer (*hoh*-mer) *n. Baseball.* A home run.

Ho·mer·ic (hoh-*mehr*-ik) *adj.* Also **Homerical.** Pertaining to Homer; resembling Homer's verse or style.—**Ho·mer·i·cal·ly** *adv.*

home rule. The vesting of local and internal legislative power of a part of an empire in a native parliament, esp. as in the programs of the Irish Separatist party and Indian Nationalist Movement.

home run. *Baseball.* A hit allowing the batter to complete the circuit of the bases.

home·sick *adj.* Unhappy at being away from home; pining.—**home·sick·ness** *n.*

home·spun *adj.* 1. Plain; unpolished; homely.

2. Spun or made at home.—*n.* Cloth made at home.

home·stead (*hohm*-sted) *n.* The home and grounds; place of residence.

home·stead·er *n.* One who has developed his home under protection from creditors assured by the homestead laws.

home·stretch *n.* 1. *Racing.* The last curve of the track. 2. The final stint.

home·ward (*hohm*-werd) *adj.* In the direction of home; toward one's habitation or native land. —**home·ward, home·wards** *adv.*

home work. 1. *Education.* Assignments to be done outside of school. 2. Piece-work given out by a manufacturer to be done in the employee's home.

home·y *adj.* [hom·i·er; hom·i·est] Cozy; warmly informal; hospitable.

hom·i·cide (*hom*-ih-syde) *n.* The killing of one human being by another.—**hom·i·cid·al** *adj.*

hom·i·let·ic (hom-ih-*let*-ik) *adj.* Also **homiletical.** Pertaining to preaching; like a sermon.

hom·i·let·ics *n.* The art of writing or preaching sermons.

hom·i·ly (*hom*-ih-lee) *n.* [*pl.* -lies] Sermon; long talk on morality.—**hom·i·list** *n.*

homing pigeon. A pigeon that finds its way home from distant places, used to carry messages.

hom·i·ny (*hom*-ih-nee) *n.* Ground corn, usually served boiled.

ho·mo- (*hoh*-moh) *prefix.* Same; similar; resembling.

ho·mo *n.* [*pl.* hom·i·nes] 1. Man. 2. [*cap.*] *Zoology.* Mankind as a genus.

ho·mo·ge·ne·i·ty (hoh-moh-jen-*ee*-uh-tee) *n.* [*pl.* -ties] Uniformity; similarity; identity.

ho·mo·ge·ne·ous (hoh-muh-*jee*-nee-us) *adj.* Uniform; of like nature; consisting of like parts. —**ho·mo·ge·ne·ous·ly** *adv.*— **-ge·ne·ous·ness** *n.*

ho·mo·gen·ize (hoh-*moj*-uh-nyze) *v.* [-ized; -iz·ing] To disperse the globules of cream uniformly throughout milk.—**ho·mo·ge·ni·za·tion** (hoh-moj-eh-nih-*zay*-sh'n) *n.*— **-gen·iz·er** *n.*

ho·mo·graph (*hoh*-moh-graf) *n. Philology.* A word which has exactly the same form as another, though of a different origin and meaning.

ho·mol·o·gous (hoh-*mol*-uh-gus) *adj.* Similar in structure, proportion, position, or value; corresponding.—**hom·o·logue** *n.* That which is homologous to something else.

ho·mol·o·gy *n.* Correspondence of structure, proportion, position, or value; relation.

hom·o·nym (*hom*-uh-nim) *n.* A word which agrees with another in sound, and sometimes in spelling, but differs from it in meaning.

ho·mop·ter·ous (hoh-*mop*-ter-us) *adj. Zoology.* Relating to an order of insects including cicadas, scale insects, etc.— **-ter·an** *adj. & n.*

Homo sapiens (*say*-pee-unz) Mankind; the human race.

ho·mo·sex·u·al·i·ty (hoh-moh-sek-shoo-*al*-uh-

tee) *n.* Erotic relationship between persons of the same sex.—**ho·mo·sex·u·al** *adj. & n.*

ho·mun·cu·lus (hoh-*mun*-kyoo-lus) *n.* [*pl.* -li] A dwarf; little man.

hone (hohn) *n.* A stone used for sharpening instruments which require a fine edge.—*v.* [honed; hon·ing].

hon·est (*on*-est) *adj.* 1. Upright; just; equitable. 2. Sincere; candid; unreserved. 3. Unadulterated; genuine.—**hon·est·ly** *adv.*

hon·es·ty (*on*-ess-tee) *n.* Integrity; probity; veracity; straightforwardness.

hon·ey (*hun*-ee) *n.* [*pl.* -eys] 1. A sweet, sticky substance made by the honeybee from the liquid it collects from flowers. 2. Darling; sweet one. 3. Sweetness; syrupy quality.—*v.* [hon·eyed or hon·ied; hon·ey·ing] To sugar; sweeten.—**hon·ey** *adj.*

honeyballs	honey-hearted	honey-steeped
honey-colored	honey-laden	honey sweet
honeydrop	honey-mouthed	honey-tongued
honeyflower	honeypot	honey-voiced

hon·ey·bee *n.* A bee which produces honey.

hon·ey·comb *n.* 1. A waxy, many-celled structure formed by honeybees for storing their honey. 2. Any similar structure. —*v.* To break up into many small cells or compartments.—**hon·ey·comb, hon·ey·combed** *adj.*

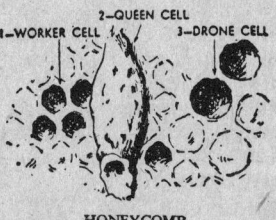

2—QUEEN CELL 1—WORKER CELL 3—DRONE CELL

HONEYCOMB

hon·ey·dew *n.* A sweet substance found in small drops on plant leaves.

honeydew melon. A sweet white muskmelon.

hon·eyed (*hun*-eed) *adj.* Sweet; cloying.

honey locust. A tall tree of the senna family bearing crescent-shaped seed pods.

hon·ey·moon *n.* The vacation period spent by a newly married couple.—**hon·ey·moon** *v.*

hon·ey·suck·le (*hun*-ee-suk-'l) *n.* Any of several climbing shrubs with white, red, or yellow flowers.

Hong Kong (*hong kong*). A British crown colony including Hong Kong island off the SE coast of China.

honk *n.* 1. The cry of a goose. 2. A similar sound. 'The honk of an automobile horn.' —**honk** *v.*

honky-tonk (*honk*-ee-tonk) *n.* A disreputable nightclub or roadhouse.

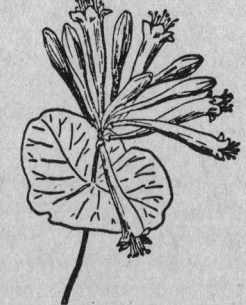

HONEYSUCKLE

Ho·no·lu·lu (hon-uh-*loo*-loo). Capital of the territory of Hawaii on SE Oahu Island.

hon·or (*on*-er) *n.* 1. High estimation; reverence. 2. A token of esteem; mark of respect.

3. Dignity; distinction; exalted rank. **4.** Reputation; good name. **5.** Loyalty and uprightness. **6.** *Bridge.* The ace, king, queen, jack, or ten of trumps, or the four aces in no-trump. **7.** [*pl.*] Civilities paid. **8.** [*pl.*] Academic distinction. **9.** [*cap.*] Title of respect or distinction.—*v.* **1.** To revere; respect. **2.** To elevate in rank; exalt. **3.** *Business.* To accept as valid, as a note or check.

hon·or·a·ble (*on-er-uh-b'l*) *adj.* **1.** Upright; just; honest. **2.** Receiving the marks of honor. **3.** [*cap.*] A title of respect or distinction.—hon·or·a·ble·ness *n.*—hon·or·a·bly *adv.*

hon·o·rar·i·um (*on-er-ehr-ee-um*) *n.* [*pl.* -i·a] A fee paid for services which have no fixed price.

hon·or·ar·y (*on-or-ehr-ee*) *adj.* Denoting a title which entails no services or compensation.

Hon·shu (*hon-shoo*). The main island of Japan. Area: 878,028 sq. mi.

hooch *n. Slang.* Whisky.

hood *n.* **1.** A soft covering for the head and neck; cowl. **2.** The metal cover of an automobile engine. **3.** Any covering like a cowl.

hood *n. Underworld Slang.* A gangster; gunman.

hood·lum (*hood-lum*) *n.* A ruffian; tough.

hoo·doo *n. Colloquial.* A person or object supposed to bring bad luck.—hoo·doo *v.*

hood·wink *v.* To deceive; dupe; trick.—hood·wink·er *n.*

hoo·ey *interj. & n. Slang.* Nonsense; absurdity.

hoof *n.* [*pl.* hoofs, hooves] The horny covering of the feet of horses, oxen, sheep, deer, etc.—*v.* To walk.—hoofed *adj.*

HORSE'S HOOFS
(side and bottom view)

hoofbeat	hoofmark	hoofprint
hoof-cut	hoof-plowed	hoof-shaped

hoof·er *n. Slang.* A dancer.

hook *n.* **1.** A bent implement for catching or holding objects. **2.** A trap; that which ensnares. **3.** A cape of land. **4.** *Golf.* The curve of a ball toward the left side of the player. **5.** *Boxing.* A short blow with bent elbow.—*v.* **1.** To catch or seize with a hook. **2.** To entrap; ensnare.—by hook or (by) crook. By fair means or foul.

hook·ah, hook·a *n.* A pipe with a long flexible tube, in which smoke passes through a bowl of water to be cooled.

hook·ed *adj.* Curved; bent.

hook·er *n. Nautical.* A small two-masted vessel, esp. one in poor repair.

hook-up *n. Radio.* An arrangement of wiring for transmission or reception.

hook·worm *n.* A parasitic worm which causes serious disorders when present in the small intestine.

hoo·li·gan (*hoo-lih-gun*) *n.* A ruffian; tough; hoodlum.—hoo·li·gan *adj.*—hoo·li·gan·ism *n.*

hoop *n.* **1.** A circular band, as on a barrel.

2. A circle of whalebone or other material, used to expand the skirts of ladies' dresses.

hoop·skirt. A formerly fashionable style of skirt extended by a framework of hoops.

hoo·ray *interj.* A cheer; shout of joy.

hoose·gow (*hooss-gow*) *n. Slang.* Jail.

Hoo·sier (*hoo-zher*) *n.* A native of Indiana.

hoot *v.* **1.** To cry out or shout in contempt. **2.** To cry as an owl.—hoot *n.*

hop *v.* [hopped; hop·ping] **1.** To move by sudden starts; skip; spring. **2.** *Colloquial.* To dance. **3.** *Colloquial.* To get aboard. 'Hop a bus.'—*n.* **1.** A leap on one leg. **2.** *Slang.* A brief flight in an airplane. **3.** *Slang.* A dance.

hop *n.* A vine with long twining stems whose dried flowers are used in malt liquors.

hope *n.* **1.** Yearning with expectation; anticipation. **2.** One in whom trust or confidence is placed. **3.** That which is desired and expected.—*v.* [hoped; hop·ing].

hope·ful *adj.* **1.** Optimistic; displaying hope. **2.** Inspiring expectation of success. 'The situation is hopeful.'— -ful·ly *adv.*— -ful·ness *n.*

hope·less *adj.* **1.** Despondent; despairing. **2.** Incurable; irreparable.—hope·less·ly *adv.*

hop·per *n.* A receptacle designed to pass its contents to another compartment, machine, etc., as grain into the hold of a ship.

hop·scotch (*hop-skoch*) *n.* A children's game in which the participants hop from one square to another in a figure drawn upon the ground.

HOPPER

horde *n.* Multitude; mob; crowd.

hore·hound (*hohr-hownd*) *n.* **1.** A mint plant which produces a bitter aromatic oil. **2.** Its oil used to flavor candy, etc.

ho·ri·zon (*huh-ry-z'n*) *n.* The apparent junction of the earth and sky; circle bounding that part of the earth's surface visible to a spectator from a given point.

hor·i·zon·tal (*hor-ih-zon-t'l*) *adj.* Level; flat. —hor·i·zon·tal *n.*—hor·i·zon·tal·ly *adv.*

hor·mone (*hor-mohn*) *n.* A secretion of a ductless gland carried by the bloodstream to the organs upon which it acts.—hor·mo·nal (*hor-mohn-'l*), hor·mon·ic (*hor-mon-ik*) *adj.*

horn *n.* **1.** A hard projection, usually bent or curving, growing on the heads of certain hoofed animals. **2.** *Music.* A metal wind instrument. —horn *v.*—hornless *adj.*

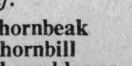

HORN (def. 2)

hornbeak	hornfish	horn-shaped
hornbill	horn-footed	horntail
horn blower	hornplant	horn work

H

horn·beam (*horn*-beem) *n*. Any of a family of nut-bearing, smooth-barked trees.

horn·blende (*horn*-blend) *n*. A common black aluminous mineral; amphibole.

horn·book *n*. 1. Formerly, a printed sheet covered with transparent horn, from which children learned the alphabet. 2. A primer.

horned *adj*. Having horns.

horned pout. A species of bullhead, a large-headed fish native to the eastern U.S.

horned toad. A short-legged North American lizard having long, hornlike spines on its head.

hor·net (*hor*-nit) *n*. An insect larger and fiercer than the wasp.

horn of plenty. The cornucopia.

horn·pipe *n*. A lively sailor's dance, or the music for it.

horn·swog·gle (*horn*-swog-'l) *v*. [horn·swog·gled; -swog·gling] *Slang*. To trick; deceive.

horn·y *adj*. [horn·i·er; horn·i·est] Calloused; hard.

hor·o·loge (*hor*-uh-lohj) *n*. A timepiece; clock.

hor·ol·o·gy (hor-*ol*-uh-jee) *n*. The principles and art of constructing devices for measuring time. —**hor·o·log·ic** (hor-uh-*loj*-ik), **hor·o·log·i·cal** *adj*.—**hor·ol·o·gist** *n*.

hor·o·scope (*hor*-uh-skohp) *n*. A chart of the zodiac, showing the relative positions of its signs, by which astrologers calculate their predictions.

hor·ren·dous (hor-*en*-dus) *adj*. Fearful; frightening.—**hor·ren·dous·ly** *adv*.

hor·ri·ble (*hor*-ih-b'l) *adj*. Dreadful; shocking; terrible.—**hor·ri·ble·ness** *n*.—**hor·ri·bly** *adv*.

hor·rid (*hor*-id) *adj*. Dreadful; hideous; shocking.—**hor·rid·ly** *adv*.—**hor·rid·ness** *n*.

hor·ri·fy (*hor*-ih-fy) *v*. [hor·ri·fied; hor·ri·fy·ing] To appall; dismay.—**hor·ri·fi·ca·tion** *n*.

hor·ror (*hor*-er) *n*. Fear; dread; terror.

hors d'oeuvre (*or derv*). [*pl*. d'oeuvres] An appetizer; canape.

horse *n*. 1. Large, hoofed, plant-eating animal used by man as a beast of burden and mount. 2. A wooden frame or support. 3. *Slang*. A tall, heavy-bodied woman.—*v*. [horsed; hors·ing] 1. *Slang*. To manhandle; jest roughly. 2. To mount or provide with a horse.—**horse around**. *Slang*. To be skittish or playful, esp. in a rough way.

horse-bitten	horsehaired	horseload
horse-drawn	horsehide	horsepipe
horse eye	horse hoof	horsepond
horse-eyed	horse-hour	horsepox
horse-faced	horse jockey	horsewhip

horse car. A streetcar drawn by horses.

horse chestnut. A large, leaf-shedding, shapely shade tree which bears large flowers and burry nuts.

horse·flesh *n*. 1. Horses in general. 2. Horse meat.

horse·fly *n*. A large, blood-sucking fly.

horse·hair *n*. The mane and tail hairs of horses. —**horse·hair** *adj*.

horse latitudes. An area of calm between the trade-wind belt and the prevailing westerly winds.

horse·laugh *n*. A loud, coarse, boisterous laugh.—**horse·laugh·er** *n*.—**horse·laugh·ter** *n*.

horse·man *n*. [*pl*. -men] A professional rider; mounted man.—**horse·man·ship** *n*. Riding skill.

horse·play *n*. Rough, coarse, or rude play.

horse·pow·er *n*. Unit of work equal to 550 foot-pounds per second.

horse·rad·ish *n*. A plant whose white pungent roots are used as a condiment.

horse sense. Common sense; intuition.

horse·shoe *n*. A U-shaped steel shoe for horses, often considered a good-luck symbol; any similarly shaped object.—*v*. [horse·shoed; horse·shod; horse·shoe·ing]. —**horse·shoe·er** *n*.

horse·tail *n*. A family of rush-like, spore-bearing plants.

horse wrangler. *Western U.S.* One who herds horses.

HORSESHOE

hors·y *adj*. [hors·i·er; hors·i·est] Like a horse; fond of horses.—**hors·i·ness** *n*.

hor·ta·tive (*hor*-tuh-tiv) *adj*. Advisory; exhorting.—**hor·ta·tive·ly** *adv*.

hor·ta·to·ry (*hor*-tuh-tor-ee) *adj*. Encouraging.

hor·ti·cul·ture (*hor*-tih-kul-choor) *n*. The study of fruit and vegetable gardening.—**hor·ti·cul·tur·al** *adj*.—**hor·ti·cul·tur·ist** *n*.

ho·san·na (hoh-*zan*-uh) *interj*. Praise God!

hose (hohz) *n*. [*pl*. -hose] 1. A flexible fibrous or rubber tubing. 2. Stockings; socks.—*v*. [hosed; hos·ing]. To water. 'Hose the lawn.'

ho·sier·y (*hoh*-zher-ee) *n*. [*pl*. -ies] 1. Stockings. 2. A stocking factory or shop.—**ho·sier** *n*.

hos·pice (*hoss*-piss) *n*. A lodging house, esp. one maintained by a religious order.

hos·pi·ta·ble (*hoss*-pit-uh-b'l) *adj*. Generous and gracious to guests; cordial.—**hos·pi·ta·bly** *adv*.

hos·pi·tal (*hoss*-pit-'l) *n*. A medical institution for the care of the sick.

hos·pi·tal·i·ty (hoss-pih-*tal*-it-ee) *n*. [*pl*. -ties] Considerate and generous entertainment of guests; cordiality; warmth.

hos·pi·tal·ize (*hoss*-pit-'l-yze) *v*. [hos·pi·tal·ized; -iz·ing] To remove to a hospital for care.—**hos·pi·tal·i·za·tion** (hoss-pit-'l-iz-*ay*-shun) *n*.

host *n*. 1. One, esp. a man, who entertains guests. 2. *Biology*. The organism upon which a parasite lives. 3. [*cap*.] *Ecclesiastical*. The consecrated communion wafer. 4. A crowd.

hos·tage (*hoss*-tij) *n*. A captive held to secure fulfillment of conditions.

hos·tel (*hoss*-t'l) *n*. An inn where hikers or bicycle travelers put up over night.

hos·tess (*hohss*-tiss) *n*. 1. A woman who entertains guests. 2. A woman employed to take charge of guests or passengers, as in a restaurant, an airplane, etc.

hos·tile (*hoss*-t'l) *n*. Unfriendly; showing enmity.

hos·til·i·ty (hoss-*til*-ih-tee) *n.* [*pl.* -ties] 1. Enmity; ill will; unfriendliness. 2. [*pl.*] War.

hos·tler (*hoss*-ler) *n.* A groom; stableboy.

hot *adj.* [hot·ter; hot·test] 1. High in temperature; extremely warm. 2. *Slang.* Passionate; sexually excited. 3. Sharp-flavored; highly seasoned. 4. Ardent; easily excited or angered. 5. *Slang.* Functioning with unusual efficiency. 6. *Jazz Music.* Played with uninhibited improvisation, esp. in rapid tempo. 7. *Labor Slang.* Manufactured or distributed by a firm whose employees are on strike. 'Union truckmen refuse hot freight.'—hot, hot·ly *adv.*—hot·ness *n.*

hot·bed *n.* 1. A place promoting rapid growth or development. 2. A glass-covered box where plants are protected from cold by decomposition of manure.

hot·blood·ed *adj.* Spirited; easily excited; passionate.—hot·blood *n.*

hot·box *n.* On a railway car, an overheated journal box.

hot·cake. A pancake; wheatcake; flapjack.

hotch-potch *n.* A hodgepodge; mixture.

hot dog. *Slang.* A wiener; frankfurter, esp. one heated, spread with mustard sauce, and served in a long split roll.

ho·tel (hoh-*tel*) *n.* An establishment where guests purchase accommodations.

hot·foot *n. Slang.* Lighting a match between the sole and upper of a person's shoe as a prank. —*v.* To rush; run.—*adv.* Swiftly.

hot·head·ed *adj.* Easily angered; vehement. —hot·head *n.* A violent-tempered person. —hot·head·ed·ly *adv.*—hot·head·ed·ness *n.*

hot·house *n.* A glass house where plants are grown, often out of season; greenhouse.

hot·shot *n. Slang.* An expert,—a term of mock praise.

hot·spur *n.* A man of violent, impetuous temperament.

Hot·ten·tot (*hot*-en-tot) *n.* A South African tribe or their language.—Hot·ten·tot *adj.*

hound (hownd) *n.* A family of long-eared, keen-scented hunting dogs.—*v.* To harry; chase.

hour (owr) *n.* 1. Unit of time equal to 60 minutes. 2. A particular or appointed time.

hour·glass *n.* An instrument which measures time by the dropping of sand from the upper to the lower of two glass bulbs joined neck to neck.

hou·ri (*hoo*-ree) *n.* [*pl.* -ris] One of the beautiful nymphs of the Mohammedan Garden of Allah.

hour·ly (*owr*-lee) *adj.* Occurring every hour; continual.—*adv.* Every hour.

house (howss) *n.* 1. A building or structure serving as a dwelling; abode. 2. A tribe; family. 3. A parliament; representative or consulta-

HOURGLASS

tive body. 4. Audience; attendance. 5. Those inhabiting a house; household. 6. A firm; commercial establishment.—*v.* (*howz*) [housed; hous·ing] To provide with a residence.

housebug	housemaiding	house owner
house builder	houseman	houseroom
house cap	housemaster	housetop
house father	housemate	housewear
housekept	houseminder	housewright

house·boat *n.* A water craft used primarily as a dwelling.

house·break·ing *n.* Forceful entry into a house to commit a felony, esp. robbery.—house·break·er *n.*

house·brok·en, house·broke *adj.* Trained in proper toilet and behavior habits necessary to indoor life.

house·fly *n.* [*pl.* -flies] The common black, two-winged, household pest fly.

house·hold *n.* A family; those living in quarters as a unit.—*adj.* Domestic; pertaining to the house or family.—house·holder *n.*

house·keep·er *n.* A woman who cares for a house or household.—house·keep·ing *n.*

house·maid *n.* A female domestic.

housemaid's knee. A swelling of the knee joint caused by frequent pressure from kneeling.

house mother. A woman who superintends and chaperons a students' residence hall.

House of Commons. The elected branch of the British and Canadian Parliaments.

house of correction. A reformatory; penal institution for minor offenders.

House of Lords. The less powerful, upper branch of the British Parliament.

House of Representatives. The lower branch of the U.S. Congress.

house organ. *Colloquial.* A publication for the employees and customers of a business firm.

house party. 1. A social gathering at which the guests stay over one or more nights. 2. These guests collectively.

house·warm·ing *n.* A party to celebrate occupancy of a new home.

house·wife *n.* [*pl.* -wives] A woman who manages a household.—*v.* [house·wifed; -wif·ing] To manage with economy and skill.—house·wif·er·y *n.*

house·wife·ly *adj.* Thrifty; neat; domestic. —house·wife·ly *adv.*—house·wife·li·ness *n.*

house·work *n.* The details of caring for a house.

hous·ing (*howz*-ing) *n.* 1. Houses collectively. 2. A covering; receptacle for a mechanism. 3. A provision of shelter.

hov·el (*huv*-'l) *n.* A shack; small, mean house. —*v.* [hov·eled; hov·elled; hov·el·ing, hov·el·ling] To shelter in a shanty.

hov·er (*huv*-er) *v.* 1. To fly or be suspended over a restricted area. 2. To move to and fro threateningly, commiseratingly, or observantly.—hov·er·er *n.*—hov·er·ing·ly *adv.*

how *adv.* In what manner, degree, or quantity; by what means.—*n. Colloquial.* The manner or method of accomplishment.

H

how·dah n. A seat, usually covered, for persons riding an elephant.

how·ev·er adv. 1. In whatever manner; to whatever degree. 2. In any case.

how·itz·er (how-it-zer) n. Military. A short-barreled artillery piece.

howl v. 1. To wail; utter a loud, mournful sound. 2. To shriek or roar.—n. 1. A wailing cry. 2. A derisive shout.—**howl·er** n. Slang. A silly or ludicrous blunder.

how·so·ev·er adv. In any manner or degree.

hoy·den, hoi·den (hoy-d'n) n. A tomboy; boisterous girl.—**hoy·den, hoi·den** adj.

hub n. 1. The center of a wheel where the spokes converge. 2. Any similar center. —**The Hub.** A nickname for Boston, Mass.

hub·bub n. Uproar; tumult.

huck·a·back (huk-uh-bak) n. A napped linen-and-cotton cloth much used as toweling.

huck·le·ber·ry (huk-'l-behr-ee) n. [pl. -ries] A fruit-bearing marsh plant of the heath family; whortleberry.

huck·ster (huk-ster) n. A vendor of small articles; peddler.

hud·dle (hud-'l) v. [hud·dled; hud·dling] 1. To crowd together in disorder. 2. To draw oneself together compactly.—n. 1. A compact jumble. 2. A strategy-mapping conference.

Hudson Bay. A great inland sea of Canada.

Hudson River. A much-traveled river which empties into the sea at New York City.

Hudson Seal. Muskrat fur treated to resemble sealskin.

hue (hyoo) n. A color; shade of color; tint. —**hued** adj.

hue n. A shouting.—**hue and cry.** Law. The clamor raised by a victim of or witness to a robbery to bring aid.

huff v. 1. To swell; puff up. 2. To become angry or sulky.—n. A sudden anger; fit of peevishness.—**huff·ish** adj.—**huff·ish·ly** adv.

huff·y (huf-ee) adj. [-i·er; -i·est] Petulant; sulky; touchy.—**huff·i·ly** adv.—**huff·i·ness** n.

hug v. [hugged; hug·ging] 1. To embrace; clasp. 2. To cherish in the mind. 3. To keep close to.—n. A warm embrace.

huge (hyooj) adj. Very great; enormous; expansive.—**huge·ly** adv.—**huge·ness** n.

hug·ger-mug·ger n. Confusion; secrecy.—adj. 1. In disorder; muddled. 2. Secret; clandestine.—v. To proceed in haste or secrecy; hush up.

Hu·gue·not (hyoo-guh-not) n. A French Protestant of the 16th- and 17th-century religious wars.

hu·la-hu·la (hool-uh-hool-uh) n. A sinuous, sensual Hawaiian ceremonial dance.

hulk n. 1. An old ship unfit for service. 2. A clumsy, unmanageable ship. 3. Anything bulky and unwieldy.

hulk·ing, hulk·y adj. Bulky; unwieldy; loutish.

hull n. 1. An outer covering; husk. 2. The body or main structure of a ship or plane.—v. 1. To strip the husk from. 2. To pierce a ship's hull.—**hull·er** n.—**hull down.** Being so distant that only its masts may be seen over the horizon—said of a ship.

hul·la·ba·loo (hul-uh-buh-loo) n. Uproar; noisy confusion.

hul·lo interj. Hello.

hum, hmm interj. An expression of doubt, hesitation, etc.; ahem.

hum v. [hummed; hum·ming] 1. To make a dull prolonged sound; drone; buzz. 2. To sing without forming words. 3. To be brisk or spirited.—n. A droning sound.

hu·man (hyoo-mun) adj. Relating to or having the qualities of a man or mankind.

hu·mane (hyoo-mayn) adj. 1. Sympathetic; kind. 2. Tending to ennoble or refine.—**hu·mane·ly** adv.—**hu·mane·ness** n.

hu·man·ism (hyoo-mun-izm) n. 1. Liberal or cultural education, esp. training in the classics. 2. A philosophy or attitude based on human needs rather than religion. 3. Mankind; human nature.—**hu·man·ist** n. & adj.—**hu·man·is·tic** adj.

hu·man·i·tar·i·an (hyoo-man-ih-tehr-ee-un) n. One who loves humanity; philanthropist. —adj. Loving mankind.—**hu·man·i·tar·i·an·ism** n. Philanthropy; love of humanity.

hu·man·i·ty (hyoo-man-ih-tee) n. [pl. -ties] 1. The quality of being human. 2. Mankind collectively. 3. Kindness; benevolence.—**the humanities.** Classical literature. 'He studies the humanities.'

hu·man·ize v. [-ized; -iz·ing] To render human or humane; civilize.—**hu·man·i·za·tion** n.

hu·man·kind n. The race of man; human species.

hu·man·ly adv. In the manner of mankind.

hum·ble (hum-b'l) adj. 1. Unpretentious; mean. 'A humble cottage.' 2. Modest; meek; unassuming.—v. [hum·bled; hum·bling] To bring down; lower; abase.—**hum·ble·ness** n.—**hum·bler** n.—**hum·bly** adv.

hum·ble·bee (hum-b'l-bee) n. A bumblebee.

humble pie. A pie made of a deer's heart, liver, kidneys, and entrails.—**eat humble pie.** To submit to humiliation; abase one's self.

hum·bug (hum-buhg) n. 1. A hoax. 2. Spirit of deception or falseness. 3. An impostor; teller of tall tales.—v. [hum·bugged; -bug·ging] To deceive; hoax.—**hum·bug·ger·y** n.

hum·drum adj. Dull; monotonous; commonplace.—n. 1. A bore. 2. Monotony. 3. A droning tone of voice.

hu·mer·us (hyoo-mer-us) n. [pl. -mer·i] The arm bone from the elbow to the shoulder.—**hu·mer·al** adj.

hu·mid (hyoo-mid) adj. Moist; damp.—**hu·mid·ly** adv.—**hu·mid·ness** n.

hu·mid·i·fy (hyoo-mid-uh-fye) v. [-fied; -fy·ing] To make humid; add moisture to.—**hu·mid·i·fi·ca·tion** n.—**hu·mid·i·fi·er** n.

hu·mid·i·ty (hyoo-*mid*-uh-tee) *n.* 1. Moisture; dampness, esp. in the air. 2. *Meteorology.* Relative humidity; the amount of water vapor in the air, at a given temperature, in ratio to the greatest possible saturation regarded as 100%.

hu·mi·dor (*hyoo*-muh-dor) *n.* A decorative box to keep cigars from drying out.

hu·mil·i·ate (hyoo-*mil*-ee-ayt) *v.* [-at·ed; -at·ing] To humble; lower in esteem.—**hu·mil·i·at·ing·ly** *adv.*—**hu·mil·i·a·tion** *n.*

hu·mil·i·ty (hyoo-*mil*-uh-tee) *n.* [*pl.* -ties] Freedom from pride or arrogance; humbleness.

hum·ming·bird *n.* A tiny bird whose wings move with great rapidity in flight, producing a humming sound.

HUMMINGBIRD

hum·mock (*hum*-uk) *n.* 1. A hillock; slight rise of ground, or of ice in an ice field. 2. *Florida.* Fertile, timbered lands.

hu·mor (*hyoo*-mer, *yoo*-mer) *n.* 1. Turn of mind; temper; mood. 2. The mental quality that produces ludicrous mirthful ideas. 3 Caprice; whim. 4. An animal fluid: blood, lymph, etc. 5. Whimsicality; comicality.—*v.* To indulge; soothe by compliance; adapt oneself to.—**out of humor.** Displeased; in temper.

hu·mor·esque (hyoo-mer-*esk*, yoo-) *n.* A light, playful musical composition.

hu·mor·ist *n.* An amusing, witty person; humorous writer.

hu·mor·ous *adj.* Witty; merry; jocular; exciting laughter.—**hu·mor·ous·ly** *adv.*— **-ous·ness** *n.*

hump *n.* 1. A protuberance; swelling; hunch, esp. on the back. 2. A hummock; rise of the ground.—*v.* 1. To bend over so as to crook the back. 2. *Slang.* To apply; work; exert. 'Hump yourself to the job.'—**hump·y** *adv.*

hump·back *n.* A person with a crooked back. —**hump·backed** *adj.*

Humpty Dumpty (*hump*-tee *dump*-tee). A nursery-rhyme character who fell from a wall.

hu·mus (*hyoo*-mus) *n.* Vegetable mold; decayed vegetation.

Hun *n.* 1. A member of a savage Asiatic tribe that overran Europe in the 5th century. 2. [*not cap.*] A wantonly destructive person.

hunch *v.* 1. To push with the elbow; push or thrust with a sudden jerk. 2. To crook, as the back.—*n.* 1. A hump; protuberance. 2. A push or jerk with fist or elbow. 3. *Colloquial.* A premonition.

hunch·back *n.* A humpback.— **-backed** *adj.*

hun·dred (*hun*-dred) *n.* 1. A cardinal number represented by the symbol 100. 2. *England.* A part of a county.—**hun·dred** *adj.*

hun·dred·fold *adv.* & *adj.* Multiplied by 100.

hun·dred·per·cent·er *n.* A person completely in favor of a cause.

hun·dredth *n.* One of 100 equal parts.—*adj.* Next after 99.

hun·dred·weight *n.* A measure of weight equivalent to 100 pounds.

Hun·gar·i·an (hung-*gehr*-ee-un) *adj.* Relating to Hungary.—*n.* 1. A national of Hungary. 2. The language of Hungary.

hun·ger (*hung*-ger) *n.* 1. A craving for food. 2. Any strong desire.—**hun·ger** *v.*

hunger strike. A protest expressed by refusal to eat.

hun·gry (*hung*-gree) *adj.* [hun·gri·er; hun·gri·est] Craving food; desirous.—**hun·gri·ly** *adv.*

hunk *n. Slang.* A chunk. 'A hunk of cheese.'

hunk·y-do·ry (hunk-ee-*dor*-ee) *adj. Colloquial.* Fine; excellent; in good condition.

Hun·nish (*hun*-ish) *adj.* Beastly; wanton; vicious.—**Hun·nish·ly** *adv.*

hunt *v.* 1. To pursue or seek out, as wild animals. 2. To course with hounds. 3. To search carefully. 4. To persecute; drive.—*n.* 1. A chase; pursuit of animals. 2. A search. 3. A group of hunters.

hunt·er *n.* 1. One who pursues and kills wild game. 2. A horse or dog used in the chase.

hunting case. A sturdy covering for a watch.

hunt·ress (*hunt*-riss) *n.* A female hunter.

hunts·man (*hunts*-mun) *n.* [*pl.* -men] A hunter.

hur·dle (*her*-d'l) *n.* 1. A movable wooden frame used to support boards, as an obstacle in races, etc. 2. A portable enclosure for animals. 3. An obstacle.—*v.* [hur·dled; hur·dling] 1. To jump over. 2. To enclose in a hurdle. 3. To overcome obstacles.—**hur·dler** *n.*

hur·dy-gur·dy (*her*-dee-ger-dee) *n.* [*pl.* -dies] A portable musical organ operated by a crank.

hurl *v.* To throw with violence.—*n.* A throw; fling.—**hur·ler** *n.* 1. One who hurls. 2. *Baseball.* A pitcher.

hur·ly-bur·ly (*her*-lee-ber-lee) *n.* [*pl.* -lies] Tumult; bustle; confusion.

Hu·ron (*hyoo*-ron) *n.* 1. A member of an American Indian tribe. 2. One of the Great Lakes. 3. [*not cap.*] A perchlike food fish.

hur·rah (her-*aw*, hoo-*raw*, -*rah*) *interj.* An exclamation of joy, acclamation, encouragement.

hur·ray (her-*ay*). *Variant form of* **hurrah.**

hur·ri·cane (*hur*-ih-kayn, *hur*-ih-k'n) *n.* A violent cyclonic storm, with wind generally between 75 and 100 miles per hour.

hurricane deck. The upper deck of an inland steamship.

hur·ried (*hur*-eed) *adj.* Done in a hurry; hasty. —**hur·ried·ly** *adv.*—**hur·ried·ness** *n.*

hur·ry (*hur*-ee) *v.* [hur·ried; hur·ry·ing] 1. To urge or impel to greater speed. 2. To cause to be performed too fast for effectiveness. 3. To perform with haste.—*n.* Haste; rush.

hur·ry-scur·ry, hur·ry-skur·ry (hur-ee-*skur*-ee) *n.* The confusion of haste; bustle.

hurt *v.* [hurt; hurt·ing] 1. To injure; inflict or cause pain. 2. To damage; impair; cause

H

harm. 3. To offend; wound the feelings.—*n.* 1. A wound; injury. 2. Harm; damage; detriment.—**hurt·er** *n.*

hurt·ful *adj.* Harmful; injurious; causing damage.—**hurt·ful·ly** *adv.*—**hurt·ful·ness** *n.*

hur·tle (*hert*-'l) *v.* [hur·tled; hur·tling] To hurl; fling; rush violently.

hus·band (*huz*-b'nd) *n.* A spouse; married man.—*v.* 1. To manage economically. 2. To marry; become husband to.

hus·band·man *n.* [*pl.* -men] A farmer; tiller of the soil.

hus·band·ry *n.* 1. Agriculture. 2. Thrift.

hush *v.* To still; silence; repress noise.—*n.* Quiet; stillness; silence.—*interj.* Be still! Be silent!—**hush up.** To withhold from publicity.

hush money. A bribe given to insure silence.

husk *n.* 1. Hull; shuck; the outer covering, esp. of an ear of corn. 2. Rough, worthless exterior.—*v.* To remove the outer covering of. —**husk·er** *n.*

husk·ing *n.* Also **husking bee.** A social gathering to assist in husking corn.

husk·y (*hus*-kee) *adj.* [husk·i·er; husk·i·est] Hoarse; harsh in tone; throaty.—**husk·i·ly** *adv.*

husk·y *adj.* [husk·i·er; husk·i·est] Burly; robust; strapping.—*n.* [*pl.* -kies] A strong, burly person.—**hus·ki·ly** *adv.*—**hus·ki·ness** *n.*

hus·ky *n.* A rough-coated Eskimo dog.

hus·sar (huh-*zahr*) *n.* A light-cavalry soldier.

Hus·site (*hus*-ite) *n.* A follower of the Bohemian reformer, John Huss.—**Hus·site** *adj.*

hus·sy (*huz*-ee) *n.* [*pl.* -sies] 1. A saucy, sprightly girl. 2. A jade; harlot.

hus·tings *n. pl.* A place for making political speeches.

hus·tle (*hus*-'l) *v.* [hus·tled; hus·tling] 1. To hurry. 2. To jostle; push roughly, as in a crowd.—**hus·tle** *n.*—**hus·tler** *n.*—**hustle and bustle.** Feverish activity.

hut *n.* A small, rough cabin, usually having one room.—*v.* [hut·ted; hut·ting] To take lodging in a hut.

hutch *n.* 1. A coop; pen for rabbits. 2. A box; bin; receptacle for storing grain, food, etc.—*v.* To store up; hoard.

huz·za (huh-*zah*) *interj.* Hurrah!—*n.* A cheer; hurrah; shout of acclaim.—*v.* To cheer; shout.

hy·a·cinth (*hy*-uh-sinth) *n.* A bulbous plant having broad leaves and bell-shaped flowers.

hy·a·line (*hy*-uh-lin) *adj.* Glossy; crystalline; transparent.—*n.* 1. A glossy surface. 2. Hyaloplasm, the fluid portion of protoplasm.

hy·brid (*hy*-brid) *n.* 1. *Biology.* The offspring produced by crossing two different species. 2. Anything of mixed origin.—*adj.* Mongrel; produced by the union of different species.—**hy·brid·ism** *n.*

hy·brid·ize (*hy*-brid-yze) *v.* [-ized; -iz·ing] To cross breed; produce from the

HYACINTH

union of two different species.— **-i·za·tion** *n.*

Hy·dra (*hy*-druh) *n.* 1. *Greek Mythology.* A monster having nine heads, each of which grew back double when cut off. 2. Any evil not easily overcome. 3. *Astronomy.* A southern constellation at the south of Cancer.

hy·dra *n.* [*pl.* -dras, -drae] A cylindrical polyp attaching itself to weeds in fresh-water ponds.

hy·dran·ge·a (hy-*dran*-jee-uh) *n.* A large round flower of the saxifrage family.

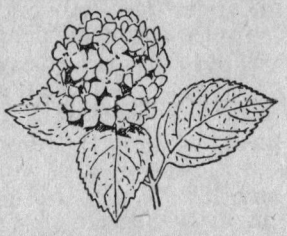

HYDRANGEA

hy·drant (*hy*-drunt) *n.* A pipe having a valve and outlets to supply water from a main pipe, esp. one on a public road or street.

hy·drate (*hy*-drayt) *n.* A chemical compound containing hydrogen and oxygen in the same proportion as water.—*v.* [hy·drat·ed; hy·drat·ing] To combine with water chemically.—**hy·dra·tion** (hy-*dray*-shun) *n.*

hy·drau·lic (hy-*draw*-lik) *adj.* Relating to the actions of fluids in motion; operated by fluid pressure.—**hy·drau·li·cal·ly** *adv.*

HYDRANT

hy·drau·lics *n.* The branch of engineering which deals with the application of the motion of liquids to machinery.

hy·dric (*hy*-drik) *adj.* Relating to hydrogen; containing hydrogen.

hy·dride (*hy*-dryde, *hy*-drid) *n.* Also **hydrid.** *Chemistry.* Hydrogen combined with another element or radical.

hy·dro·car·bon (hy-druh-*kahr*-bun) *n. Chemistry.* A fat, bitumen, or other compound composed of hydrogen and carbon.

hy·dro·chlor·ic (hy-druh-*klor*-ik) *adj.* Compounded of chlorine and hydrogen.—**hydrochloric acid.** A colorless, pungent acid gas, often dissolved in water.

hy·dro·cy·an·ic (hy-droh-sy-*an*-ik) *adj.* Derived from the combination of hydrogen and cyanogen.—**hydrocyanic acid.** A poisonous, colorless compound having the odor of almonds, used as an insecticide; prussic acid.

hy·dro·dy·nam·ics (hy-droh-dy-*nam*-iks) *n.* The branch of physics teaching of the application of forces producing motion in fluids.—**hy·dro·dy·nam·ic, -i·cal** *adj.*

hy·dro·e·lec·tric (hy-droh-el-*ek*-trik) *adj.* Relating to the production of electricity by water power.—**hy·dro·e·lec·tric·i·ty** *n.*

hy·dro·flu·or·ic (hy-droh-floo-*or*-ik) *adj.* Composed of fluorine and hydrogen.—**hydrofluoric acid.** A volatile acid used in etching glass.

hy·dro·gen (*hy*-druh-jun) *n.* A light, colorless gaseous element combining with oxygen to produce water. (*Symbol:* H).

hy·dro·gen·ate (*hy*-druh-juh-nayt) *v.* [-at·ed; -at·ing] To combine with hydrogen.—**hy·dro·gen·a·tion** (hy-druh-juh-*nay*-shun) *n.*—**hy·drog·e·nous** (hy-*droj*-uh-nus) *adj.*

hydrogen peroxide. A liquid chemical (H_2O_2) used as a disinfectant when diluted.

hy·drog·ra·phy (hy-*drog*-ruh-fee) *n.* The geography of the waters of the earth.—**hy·dro·graph·ic, -i·cal** (hy-druh-*graf*-ik, -ih-k'l) *adj.*

hy·drol·y·sis (hy-*drol*-uh-siss) *n.* [*pl.* -ses] *Chemistry.* The decomposition of a chemical compound by the addition of water.—**hy·dro·lyt·ic** (hy-druh-*lit*-ik) *adj.* Causing decomposition by means of water.—**hy·dro·lyze** (*hy*-druh-lyze) *v.*

hy·drom·e·ter (hy-*drom*-uh-ter) *n. Physics.* An instrument measuring the density of fluids. —**hy·dro·met·ric, -i·cal** (hy-druh-*met*-rik, -ih-k'l) *adj.*—**hy·drom·e·try** (hy-*drom*-uh-tree) *n.*

hy·drop·a·thy (hy-*drop*-uh-thee) *n.* The method of treating diseases by internal and external use of water.—**hy·dro·path·ic, -i·cal** (hy-druh-*path*-ik, -ih-k'l) *adj.*

hy·dro·pho·bi·a (hy-druh-*foh*-bee-uh) *n.* 1. *Medicine.* Rabies, a disease communicated by the bite of an infected animal. 2. Morbid fear of water.—**hy·dro·pho·bic** *adj.*

hy·dro·phone (*hy*-druh-fohn) *n.* An instrument for transmitting sounds through water.

hy·dro·plane (*hy*-druh-playn) *n.* 1. An airplane equipped to take off from the water. 2. A small fast motorboat which skims the surface of the water at high speeds.—*v.* To take flight from the water.

hy·dro·sphere (*hy*-drus-feer) *n.* 1. The water enveloping the earth—oceans, rivers, etc. 2. The water vapor of the atmosphere.

hy·dro·stat·ics (hy-druh-*stat*-iks) *n.* The branch of physics treating of the equilibrium of fluids. —**hy·dro·stat·ic, -i·cal** *adj.*

hy·dro·ther·a·py (hy-druh-*thehr*-uh-pee) *n.* Treatment of disorders by various kinds of water baths.

hy·drous (*hy*-drus) *adj.* Watery; containing water in chemical composition.

hy·drox·ide (hy-*drok*-syde) *n.* Also **hydroxid.** *Chemistry.* A chemical compound containing the hydroxyl radical, composed of one atom each of oxygen and hydrogen.

hy·drox·yl (hy-*drok*-sil) *n. Chemistry.* A unit composed of one atom of hydrogen and one of oxygen, found in bases and many organic compounds. (*Symbol:* OH).

hy·dro·zo·an (hy-druh-*zoh*-un) *n. Zoology.* A member of a class of marine animals, including the polyp and jellyfish.

hy·ena, hy·ae·na (hy--*ee*-nuh) *n.* A wolf-like quadruped native to Africa and Asia.

Hy·ge·ia (hy-*jee*-uh) *n. Greek Mythology.*

HYENA
The goddess of health.

hy·gi·ene (*hy*-jeen) *n.* The preservation of health.—**hy·gi·en·ist** (*hy*-jee-en-ist) *n.*

hy·gi·en·ic (hy-jee-*en*-ik) *adj.* 1. Relating to health. 2. Healthy. 3. Sanitary; free of germs.—**hy·gi·en·i·cal·ly** *adv.*

hy·grom·e·ter (hy-*grom*-uh-ter) *n. Physics.* An instrument measuring the degree of atmospheric moisture.—**hy·gro·met·ric** (hy-gruh-*met*-rik) *adj.*—**-grom·e·try** (hy-*grom*-uh-tree) *n.*

hy·gro·scope *n. Physics.* An instrument indicating the presence and variations of moisture in the atmosphere.—**hy·gro·scop·ic, -i·cal** (hy-gruh-*skop*-ik, -ih-k'l) *adj.*—**-scop·i·cal·ly** *adv.*

hy·la (*hy*-luh) *n.* A tree toad.

Hy·men (*hy*-men) *n.* 1. *Greek Mythology.* The god of marriage. 2. [*not cap.*] Marriage.

hy·men *n. Anatomy.* The membrane partly closing the vaginal entrance; maidenhead.

hy·me·ne·al (hy-muh-*nee*-ul) *adj.* Nuptial; relating to marriage.—*n.* A wedding song.

hy·men·op·ter·ous (hy-men-*op*-ter-us) *adj.* Relating to a class of four-winged insects.—**hy·men·op·ter·an** *adj. & n.*

hymn (*him*) *n.* A sacred song; song of adoration.—*v.* To sing in praise or adoration.

hym·nal (*him*-nul) *adj.* Relating to hymns.—*n.* A collection of hymns used in public worship.

hym·no·dy (*him*-nuh-dee) *n.* 1. Anthology of hymns. 2. Hymnology; study of hymns.

hym·nol·o·gy (him-*nol*-uh-jee) *n.* 1. Study of hymns. 2. Group or types of hymns.

hy·per·bo·la (hy-*per*-buh-luh) *n.* [*pl.* -lae] *Geometry.* A curve formed by cutting a cone in a direction parallel to its axis.

hy·per·bole (hy-*per*-buh-lee) *n.* Overstatement; exaggeration for emphasis.—**hy·per·bo·lism** *n.* The use of exaggeration.—**hy·per·bo·lize** *v.* [hy·per·bo·lized; hy·per·bo·liz·ing].

hy·per·bol·ic (hy-per-*bol*-ik) *adj.* 1. Relating to the hyperbola. 2. Exaggerating; exceeding the truth.

Hy·per·bo·re·an (hy-per-*bor*-ee-un) *n. Greek Mythology.* A race inhabiting a northern paradise.—*adj.* Northern; frigid.

hy·per·crit·i·cal (hy-per-*krit*-ih-k'l) *adj.* Over-critical; captious; faultfinding.

hy·per·o·pi·a (hy-per-*oh*-pee-uh) *n. Medicine.* Farsightedness.—**-op·ic** (hy-per-*op*-ik) *adj.*

hy·per·pla·si·a (hy-per-*play*-zhee-uh) *n. Medicine.* Overgrowth of an organ.—**hy·per·plas·ic** (hy-per-playz-ik), **-plas·tic** (-*plass*-tik) *adj.*

hy·per·sen·si·tive (hy-per-*sen*-sit-iv) *adj.* Over-sensitive; easily injured.—**hy·per·sen·si·tive·ness** *n.*—**hy·per·sen·si·tiv·i·ty** *n.*

hy·per·thy·roid·ism (hy-per-*thy*-royd-izm) *n. Medicine.* Oversecretion of the thyroid gland. —**hy·per·thy·roid** *n. & adj.*

hy·phen (*hy*-fun) *n.* A mark [-] joining two words or syllables.—**hy·phen** *v.*

hy·phen·ate (*hy*-fun-ayt) [-at·ed; -at·ing] To join by a hyphen.— **-a·tion** (-*ay*-shun) *n.*

hyp·no·sis (hip-*noh*-siss) *n.* [*pl.* -ses] Sleep induced by suggestion.

hyp·not·ic (hip-*not*-ik) *adj.* Inducing sleep.—*n.* An opiate; sleep-inducing drug.—**hyp·not·i·cal·ly** *adv.*

hyp·no·tism (*hip*-nuh-tizm) *n.* The study of inducement of sleeplike state by suggestion.—**hyp·no·tist** *n.*

hyp·no·tize (*hip*-nuh-tyze) *v.* [-tized; -tiz·ing] To induce a sleeplike trance by suggestion.—**hyp·no·tiz·a·ble** *adv.*—**hyp·no·ti·za·tion** (hip-nuh-tiz-*ay*-shun) *n.*—**hyp·no·tiz·er** *n.*

hy·po (*hy*-poh) *n. Colloquial.* 1. A hypodermic. 2. *Photography.* An abbreviation of *sodium hyposulphite.* 3. A hypochondriac.

hy·po·chlo·rous (hy-puh-*klor*-us) *adj.* Having bleaching properties.—**hypochlorous acid.** An acid for bleaching obtained by passing chlorine gas through water.

hy·po·chon·dri·a (hy-poh-*kon*-dree-uh) *n.* Morbid and fanciful anxiety over one's health.

hy·po·chon·dri·ac *n.* One who has hypochondria.—**hy·po·chon·dri·ac** *adj.*—**hy·po·chon·dri·a·cal** (hy-poh-kun-*dry*-uh-k'l) *adj.*

hy·poc·ri·sy (hip-*ok*-ruh-see) *n.* [*pl.* -sies] Dissimulation; false pretense, as of piety or virtue.

hyp·o·crite (*hip*-uh-krit) *n.* A dissembler; one given to false pretenses.—**hyp·o·crit·i·cal** *adj.*

hy·po·der·mic (hy-puh-*der*-mik) *adj.* 1. Relating to parts under the skin. 2. Introduced under the skin.—*n.* 1. Medication introduced under the skin. 2. A hypodermic syringe.

hypodermic syringe. A vial and needle for injecting medication under the skin.

hy·po·gas·tric (hy-puh-*gass*-trik) *adj. Anatomy.* Relating to the lower abdomen.

hy·po·phos·pho·rous (hy-puh-*foss*-fer-us) *adj. Chemistry.* Denoting an acid containing less oxygen than phosphorous acid.

hy·poph·y·sis (hy-*pof*-ih-siss) *n. Anatomy.* The pituitary gland at the base of the brain.

hy·po·pla·si·a (hy-puh-*play*-zhee-uh) *n. Medicine.* Incomplete development of a part.—**hy·po·plas·tic** (hy-puh-*plas*-tik) *adj.*

hy·po·sul·phite (hy-puh-*sul*-fyt) *n. Photography.* An acid salt (thiosulphate) for fixing.

hy·pot·e·nuse, hy·poth·e·nuse (hy-*pot*-uh-nyooss) *n. Geometry.* The longest side of a right triangle.

hy·poth·e·cate (hy-*poth*-uh-kayt) *v.* [-cat·ed; -cat·ing] To mortgage; pledge property without giving up possession.—**hy·poth·e·ca·tion** (hy-poth-uh-*kay*-shun) *n.*—**hy·poth·e·ca·tor** *n.*

hy·poth·e·sis (hy-*poth*-uh-siss) *n.* [*pl.* -ses] A supposition; conditions assumed for the sake of argument.

hy·poth·e·size (hy-*poth*-uh-syze) *v.* [-sized; -siz·ing] To theorize; form assumptions.

hy·po·thet·i·cal (hy-puh-*thet*-ih-k'l) *adj.* Also **hypothetic.** Conjectural; conditional; assumed without proof.—**hy·po·thet·i·cal·ly** *adv*

hy·po·thy·roid·ism (hy-puh-*thy*-royd-izm) *n. Medicine.* Undersecretion of the thyroid gland.—**hy·po·thy·roid** *n. & adj.*

hy·son (*hy*-sun) *n.* A green Chinese tea.

hys·sop (*hiss*-up) *n.* A pungent herb of the mint family, having blue flowers.

hys·ter·ec·to·my (hiss-ter-*ek*-toh-mee) *n.* Removal of the uterus by surgery.

hys·te·ri·a (hiss-*teer*-ee-uh) *n.* 1. A nervous fit characterized by alternate paroxysms of crying and laughter. 2. Extreme nervousness; panic; violent emotional excitement.

hys·ter·i·cal (hiss-*tehr*-ih-k'l) *adj.* 1. Irrational; violently emotional. 2. Caused by hysteria. 3. *Colloquial.* Hilarious.— -**cal·ly** *adv.*

hys·ter·ics (hiss-*tehr*-iks) *n. pl.* 1. Hysteria; nervous fit. 2. *Colloquial.* Uncontrollable laughter.

hys·ter·oid (*hiss*-ter-oyd) *adj.* Also **hysteroidal.** *Medicine.* Resembling hysteria; characterized by nervous paroxysms.

hys·ter·ot·o·my (hiss-ter-*ot*-uh-mee) *n. Medicine.* Caesarean operation; incision of the uterus for removing a fetus.

HYPOTENUSE

I

I *pron.* The first person singular, nominative case; oneself.—*n.* The self or ego.

I·a·go (ee-*ah*-goh) *n.* The perfidious villain of Shakespeare's *Othello.*

i·amb (*eye*-am) *n.* A metrical foot consisting of an unaccented syllable followed by an accented one.—**i·am·bic** *adj.*—**iambic** *n.* An iambic foot or line.

-i·at·rics (ee-*at*-riks) *Suffix. Medicine.* Treatment (of the specified disease).

-i·a·try *Suffix.* Curing; treatment.

I·be·ri·a (eye-*beer*-ee-uh). Ancient name for Spain and Portugal.—**I·be·ri·an** *adj. & n.*

i·bex (*eye*-beks) *n.* [*pl.* ib·ex·es, ib·i·ces] A mountain goat with huge curving horns.

i·bis (*eye*-biss) *n.* A long-legged wading bird related to the stork. —**sacred ibis.** A variety of ibis held sacred by ancient Egyptians.

-ic *Suffix.* 1. Of, pertaining or belonging to, or like. 'Angelic,' 'artistic,' 'dramatic.' 2. Made of or by. 'Alcoholic,' 'telephonic.'

IBIS (1/30 life size)

-i·cal *Suffix.* 1. Same as -ic. 2. Forming the adjectives for nouns ending in -ic. 'Magical,' 'tragicomical,' 'historical,' hysterical.'

Ic·a·rus (*ik*-uh-rus) *n. Mythology.* Youth who flew too near the sun, which melted his artificial wax wings, causing his death.—**I·car·i·an** (eye-*kair*-ee-un) *adj.* Flying too high.

ice *n.* 1. Water solidified by cold. 2. Sherbet; frozen dessert. 3. Icing. 4. *Slang.* Diamonds; jewels.—*v.* [iced; ic·ing] 1. To make into ice; chill. 2. To spread with icing.—**ice** *adj.*

icebird	ice cold	iceland
ice-blind	ice-cooled	ice-locked
ice-blindness	ice-covered	ice maker
icebone	icecraft	ice making
ice breaking	icefall	iceman
ice-built	icefield	icemaster
icecap	ice-free	icequake
ice-capped	ice hook	ice water
ice-clad	ice house	icework

ice·berg *n.* A floating mountain of ice.

ice·boat *n.* 1. A light sailboat on runners for traveling on ice. 2. Also **ice breaker.** A high-powered ship for cutting a passage through ice.

ice·bound *adj.* Rendered inaccessible or impassable by ice; imprisoned by ice.

ice box *n.* A compartment cooled by ice, for storing perishable food; refrigerator.

ICEBOAT

ice cream. A frozen dessert made of cream or butter, sugar, and flavoring.

Ice·land moss. An edible arctic lichen.

ich·neu·mon (ik-*nyoo*-m'n) *n.* A brownish weasel-like animal of Egypt.—**ichneumon fly.** Insect whose larvae live on or in other larvae.

ich·thy·ol·o·gy (ik-thee-*ol*-uh-jee) *n.* Branch of zoology treating of fishes.—**ich·thy·o·log·ic, ich·thy·o·log·i·cal** *adj.*—**ich·thy·ol·o·gist** *n.*

ich·thy·o·saur, ich·thy·o·saur·us (ik-thee-uh-*sawr*, -*sawr*-us) *n.* An extinct fishlike lizard.

i·ci·cle (*eye*-sik-'l) *n.* A hanging cone of ice formed by dripping water.—**i·ci·cled** *adj.*

i·ci·ly *adv.* Frigidly; coldly.

i·ci·ness *n.* Coldness; frigidity.

ic·ing *n.* Frosting; sugary covering for cakes.

i·con (*eye*-kon) *n.* Also **i·kon.** *n.* [*pl.* i·cons, i·co·nes; i·kons, i·kon·es] 1. An image; representation. 2. A sacred image. —**i·con·ic, i·con·i·cal** *adj.*

i·con·o·clast (eye-*kon*-uh-klast) *n.* 1. One hostile to the use of images in worship. 2. One who attacks or exposes established beliefs as hypocrisies or shams. —**i·con·o·clas·tic** *adj.*

ICICLE

-ics *Suffix.* 1. Science; principles. 'Mathematics,' 'physics.' 2. Activities. 'Athletics.'

i·cy *adj.* [i·ci·er; i·ci·est] 1. Frigid; frosty; ice-like. 2. Extremely indifferent; cold in manner.

id *n. Psychoanalysis.* Totality of impulses or instincts comprising the true unconscious mind.

i·de·a (eye-*dee*-uh) *n.* [*pl.* i·deas] 1. A mental concept, image, or plan. 2. A fancy; notion. 3. An opinion; thought.

i·de·al (eye-*dee*-ul) *adj.* 1. Existing in the mind or imagination; visionary. 2. Pertaining to an ideal; perfect.—*n.* A model of perfection; superiority.—**i·de·al·ly** *adv.*

i·de·al·ism *n.* 1. *Philosophy.* Doctrine that reality is spiritual or mental rather than material in essence. 2. Inclination to form or follow ideals.

i·de·al·ist *n.* 1. A visionary. 2. A believer in the doctrine of idealism.—**i·de·al·is·tic, i·de·al·is·ti·cal** *adj.*—**i·de·al·is·ti·cal·ly** *adv.*

i·de·al·ize *v.* [i·de·al·ized; -iz·ing] To set up or think of as an ideal; embody in a perfect form. **i·de·al·i·za·tion** *n.*—**i·de·al·iz·er** *n.*

i·den·ti·cal (eye-*den*-tik-'l) *adj.* 1. The same. 2. Equal; corresponding; equivalent.—**i·den·ti·cal·ly** *adv.*—**i·den·ti·cal·ness** *n.*

i·den·ti·fi·ca·tion (eye-den-tuh-fih-*kay*-sh'n) *n.* 1. A proof or proving of identity. 2. Establishment of an exactly corresponding relationship.

i·den·ti·fy (eye-*den*-tuh-fye) *v.* [i·den·ti·fied; -fy·ing] 1. To establish the ownership or identity of. 2. To associate with; treat or represent as being the same.—**i·den·ti·fi·er** *n.*

i·den·ti·ty (eye-*den*-tuh-tee) *n.* [*pl.* -ties] 1. Individuality; who or what one is. 2. Sameness; correspondence.

id·e·o·gram (*id*-ee-uh-gram) *n.* Ideograph.

id·e·o·graph (*id*-ee-uh-graf) *n.* A symbol or picture suggesting an object or idea without actually expressing its name; picture writing. —**id·e·o·graph·ic, -i·cal** *adj.*— -i·cal·ly *adv.*

id·e·ol·o·gy (eye-dee-*ol*-uh-jee) *n.* [*pl.* -gies] 1. A political or social philosophy, esp. of a certain class. 'Proletarian ideology.' 2. The science of ideas. 3. Theorizing; impractical thinking.—**id·e·o·log·i·cal** (eye-dee-uh-*loj*-ik-'l) *adj.*—**id·e·o·lo·gist** *n.*

ides (eydz) *n. pl.* A day in each ancient Roman month: 15th March, May, July, October; 13th of other months.

id·i·o·cy (*id*-ee-uh-see) *n.* [*pl.* -cies] The mentality or condition of an idiot; stupidity.

id·i·om (*id*-ee-um) *n.* 1. A phrase with a meaning other than that logically derived from each word in it. 2. The language or construction peculiar to a country, district, or group. 3. Individual style of expression.—**id·i·o·mat·ic, id·i·o·mat·i·cal** *adj.*—**id·i·o·mat·i·cal·ly** *adv.* —**id·i·o·mat·i·cal·ness** *n.*

id·i·o·syn·cra·sy (id-ee-uh-*sin*-kruh-see) *n.* [*pl.* -sies] A trait or habit peculiar to an individual. —**id·i·o·syn·crat·ic** *adj.*— -crat·i·cal·ly *adv.*

I

id·i·ot (*id*-ee-ut) *n.* 1. A person with a mental age of two or three years. 2. A fool; stupid person.—**id·i·ot·ic, id·i·ot·i·cal** *adj.* Grossly stupid.—**id·i·ot·i·cal·ly** *adv.*

i·dle (eye-d'l) *adj.* [i·dler; i·dlest] 1. Unoccupied; inactive; unemployed. 2. Lazy; indolent. 3. Useless; ineffectual; without foundation.—*v.* [i·dled; i·dling] 1. To waste time in action; dissipate, as time. 2. To operate without applying available power, as a motor.—**i·dle·ness** *n.*—**id·ler** *n.*—**i·dly** *adv.*

idle-brained   idle-headed   idle-minded
idle-handed   idle looking   idle-witted

i·dol (eye-d'l) *n.* 1. Worshiped image of a divinity. 2. An object of great love or admiration.—**i·dol·a·ter** *n.* An idol worshiper.

i·dol·a·try (eye-*dol*-uh-tree) *n.* [*pl.* -tries] 1. Worship of idols. 2. Extreme attachment or veneration.—**i·dol·a·trous** *adj.*—**i·dol·a·trous·ly** *adv.*—**i·dol·a·trous·ness** *n.*

i·dol·ize (eye-d'l-yze) *v.* [i·dol·ized; -iz·ing] To worship or love as an idol; adore; revere to excess.—**i·dol·i·za·tion** *n.*—**i·dol·iz·er** *n.*

i·dyl, i·dyll (eye-d'l) *n.* 1. A short portrayal of the delights of pastoral life. 2. A life or scene suitable for an idyl.—**i·dyl·ist, i·dyll·ist** *n.*

i·dyl·lic (eye-*dil*-ik) *adj.* Delightfully simple or rural; pertaining to an idyl.—**i·dyl·li·cal·ly** *adv.*—**i·dyl·li·cism** *n.*

if *conj.* 1. Provided or supposing that; in case that. 2. Whether.—*n.* A possibility; uncertainty.

if·fy *adj.* *Colloquial.* Tentative; uncertain.

ig·loo, ig·lu *n.* Eskimo dome-shaped snow hut.

ig·ne·ous (*ig*-nee-us) *adj.* Of or like fire; produced by fire or heat. 'Igneous rocks.'

ig·nite *v.* [ig·nit·ed; ig·nit·ing] To set afire; kindle; make intensely hot.—**ig·ni·ter, ig·ni·tor** *n.*—**ig·nit·i·ble, ig·nit·a·ble** *adj.*

ig·ni·tion (ig-*nish*-'n) *n.* 1. Act or means for setting aflame. 2. Electrical system for producing the spark to start combustion in a motor.

ig·no·ble (ig-*noh*-b'l) *adj.* 1. Base; despicable; dishonorable. 2. Of humble birth.—**ig·no·ble·ness** *n.*—**ig·no·bly** *adv.*

ig·no·min·i·ous (ig-nuh-*min*-ee-us) *adj.* Shameful; infamous; marked by or deserving ignominy.—**ig·no·min·i·ous·ly** *adv.*

ig·no·min·y (*ig*-nuh-min-ee) *n.* [*pl.* -ies] 1. Public disgrace; dishonor. 2. Vile, shameful action.

ig·no·ra·mus (ig-nuh-*ray*-mus) *n.* Ignorant or stupid person.

ig·no·rance (*ig*-ner-unss) *n.* Lack of knowledge.

ig·no·rant *adj.* 1. Lacking knowledge; untaught; illiterate. 2. Uninformed; not aware.—**ig·no·rant·ly** *adv.*

ig·nore (ig-*nohr*) *v.* [ig·nored; ig·nor·ing] To disregard; pass without notice.—**ig·nor·er** *n.*

I·go·rot (ig-uh-rot) *n.* [*pl.* -rot, -rots] Also **I·gor·ro·te.** Member of a northern Luzon tribe in the Philippine Islands.

i·gua·na (ig-*wah*-nuh) *n.* A large, tree-dwelling tropical lizard.

i·kon *n.* Variant spelling of **icon.**

il- *prefix.* Not. 'Illegible, illegal, illiterate.'

Il Duce (eel *doo*-chay). Benito Mussolini, former dictator of Italy.

IGUANA (1/20 life size)

Il·i·ad (*il*-ee-ud) *n.* A Greek epic poem of the Trojan wars, supposedly written by Homer.

ilk *n.* Kind; sort; class.

ill *adj.* [worse; worst] 1. Sick; unhealthy; indisposed. 2. Causing misfortune; bad; unlucky; unfavorable. 3. Improper; harmful; unkind.—*n.* 1. Evil; calamity; trouble. 2. Disease; illness.—**ill** *adv.*

ill-accoutered   ill-born   ill-timed
ill-accustomed   ill breeding   ill-willer
ill afford   ill-featured   ill-wisher

ill-advised *adj.* Unwise; resulting badly.

ill-bred *adj.* Rude; impolite; poorly reared.

il·le·gal (il-*ee*-g'l) *adj.* Contrary to law; illicit.—**il·le·gal·i·ty** *n.* [*pl.* -ties] Unlawfulness; action violating law.—**il·le·gal·ly** *adv.*

il·leg·i·ble (il-*ej*-uh-b'l) *adj.* Hard to read or decipher.—**il·leg·i·bil·i·ty, il·leg·i·ble·ness** *n.*—**il·leg·i·bly** *adv.*

il·le·git·i·mate (il-lij-*it*-ih-mit) *adj.* 1. Born out of wedlock. 2. Unlawful; not authorized; irregular.—**il·le·git·i·ma·cy** *n.* [*pl.* -cies].—**il·le·git·i·mate·ly** *adv.*—**il·le·git·i·mate·ness** *n.*

ill-fa·vored *adj.* Lacking beauty; ugly.—**ill-fav·ored·ly** *adv.*—**ill-fav·ored·ness** *n.*

ill-hu·mored *adj.* Bad-tempered; fretful; cross.—**ill-hu·mored·ly** *adv.*—**ill-hu·mored·ness** *n.*

il·lib·er·al (il-*ib*-er-ul) *adj.* 1. Stingy; niggardly; not generous. 2. Narrow in view or opinions; lacking culture or broadmindedness.—**il·lib·er·al·i·ty** *n.*— **-al·ly** *adv.*— **-al·ness** *n.*

il·lic·it (il-*iss*-it) *adj.* Prohibited; unlawful; improper.—**il·lic·it·ly** *adv.*—**il·lic·it·ness** *n.*

il·lim·it·a·ble (il-*im*-it-uh-b'l) *adj.* Boundless; too vast to measure.—**il·lim·it·a·bil·i·ty, il·lim·it·a·ble·ness** *n.*—**il·lim·it·a·bly** *adv.*

il·lit·er·a·cy (il-*it*-er-uh-see) *n.* [*pl.* -cies] 1. Inability to read or write; ignorance. 2. Error cause by illiteracy.

il·lit·er·ate (il-*it*-er-it) *adj.* Unable to read or write; ignorant; uneducated.—*n.* One who is illiterate.—**il·lit·er·ate·ly** *adv.*— **-er·ate·ness** *n.*

ill-man·nered *adj.* Rude; uncivil.—**ill-man·nered·ly** *adv.*—**ill-man·nered·ness** *n.*

ill-na·tured *adj.* Disagreeable; surly; cross.—**ill-na·tured·ly** *adv.*—**ill-na·tured·ness** *n.*

ill·ness *n.* Sickness; physical or mental disorder.

il·log·i·cal (il-*oj*-ik-'l) *adj.* Contrary to reason or logic.—**il·log·i·cal·ly** *adv.*—**il·log·i·cal·ness** *n.*

ill-o·mened *adj.* Marked for misfortune; unlucky.

ill-starred *adj.* Unfortunate; unlucky.

ill-tem·pered *adj.* Cross; peevish; crabbed.

ill-treat *v.* To be cruel to; abuse.—**ill-treat·ed** *adj.*

il·lu·mi·nate (il-*oo*-min-ayt) *v.* [il·lu·mi·nat·ed; -nat·ing] 1. To light up; flood with light. 2. To enlighten; make clear or understandable. 3. To adorn with illustrations or ornamented letters.—**il·lum·in·a·tive** *adj.*—**-na·tor** *n.*

il·lu·mi·na·tion *n.* 1. Act of lighting up. 2. Light; brightness; splendor.

il·lu·mine (il-*oom*-in) *v.* [il·lu·mined; -min·ing] To light up; illuminate.—**il·lu·min·a·ble** *adj.*

ill-use *v.* [ill·used; ill·us·ing] To treat badly; misuse.—**ill-use, ill-us·age** *n.*

il·lu·sion (il-*oo*-zhun) *n.* 1. That which deceives the senses; deceptive appearance; hallucination. 2. Deception; false conception or impression. 3. A thin gauzy net for veils, etc. —**il·lu·sion·ist** *n.* One who sees or produces illusions.

il·lu·sive (il-*oo*-siv) *adj.* deceiving; misleading; unreal.—**il·lu·sive·ly** *adv.*—**il·lu·sive·ness** *n.*

il·lu·so·ry (il-*oo*-zer-ee) *adj.* Tricking the senses; false; illusive.

il·lus·trate (*il*-uh-strayt) *v.* [-trat·ed; -trat·ing] 1. To explain or ornament by pictures or other graphic means. 2. To give an example of; explain by comparison or example.—**il·lus·tra·tor** *n.*

ILLUSION

(Two simple optical illusions: the perpendicular lines are parallel; the horizontal lines are of equal length.)

il·lus·tra·tion (il-us-*tray*-shun) *n.* 1. A picture or other decorative or explanatory representation. 2. An explanatory example; sample case. 3. Explanation; act of illustrating.

il·lus·tra·tive *adj.* Explanatory; used to illustrate.—**il·lus·tra·tive·ly** *adv.*

il·lus·tri·ous (il-*us*-tree-us) *adj.* Famous; great; eminent.—**il·lus·tri·ous·ly** *adv.*— **-tri·ous·ness** *n.*

ill-will *n.* Malice; enmity.

im- *prefix.* Not; opposite or lack of. 'Imperfect.'

im·age (*im*-ij) *n.* 1. A representation or likeness, esp. one perceptible visually. 2. An idol; icon. 3. A copy; embodiment; symbol. 4. A mental picture; idea. 5. *Optics.* The duplication of an object in rays of light.—*v.* [im·aged; im·ag·ing] 1. To mirror; form or be an image of; typify. 2. To form a mental likeness of; imagine. 3. To describe in images.

im·age·ry (*im*-ij-ree) *n.* [*pl.* -ries] 1. Mental pictures; imagination. 2. Representation by images; descriptive language.

im·ag·i·na·ble (im-*aj*-in-uh-b'l) *adj.* Conceivable; within the realm of the imagination.—**im·ag·i·na·bly** *adv.*

im·ag·i·nar·y (im-*aj*-in-ehr-ee) *adj.* Unreal; existing in the imagination.

im·ag·i·na·tion *n.* 1. Ability to form mental images; power of the mind to combine separate experiences into new ideas or patterns. 2. A mental creation; idea; fancy.

im·ag·i·na·tive (im-*aj*-in-uh-tiv) *adj.* 1. Invented or conceived by the imagination; fanciful. 2. Having an active imagination.—**im·ag·i·na·tive·ly** *adv.*—**im·ag·i·na·tive·ness** *n.*

im·ag·ine (im-*aj*-in) *v.* [-ined; -in·ing] 1. To form a picture or notion of in the mind; invent by imagination. 2. To think; suppose.

im·a·gist (*im*-uh-jist) *n.* A poet who expresses his feelings and thoughts in graphic images. —**im·a·gism** *n.*—**im·a·gist, im·a·gis·tic** *adj.*

im·be·cile (*im*-buh-sul) *n.* 1. A feeble-minded person, esp. one with a mental age of three to seven years. 2. A fool; idiot.—*adj.* Feebleminded; foolish.—**im·be·cil·i·ty** *n.* [*pl.* -ties].

im·bed *v.* To set firmly into a substance.

im·bibe (im-*bybe*) *v.* [im·bibed; im·bib·ing] To drink; absorb; take in.—**im·bib·er** *n.*

im·bro·glio (im-*brohl*-yoh) *n.* [*pl.* -glios] Quarrel; fracas; dispute.

im·brue (im-*broo*) *v.* [im·brued; im·bru·ing] To soak; drench.

im·bue (im-*byoo*) *v.* [im·bued; im·bu·ing] To ingrain; infuse; impregnate.

im·i·tate (*im*-uh-tayt) *v.* [im·i·tat·ed; im·i·tat·ing] To copy; counterfeit; mimic.—**im·i·ta·ble** (*im*-it-uh-b'l) *adj.*

im·i·ta·tion (im-ih-*tay*-shun) *n.* 1. The act of copying or mimicking. 2. Copy; counterfeit; simulation.—**im·i·ta·tion** *adj.*

im·i·ta·tive (*im*-ih-tay-tiv) *adj.* 1. Formed after a model; copied after. 2. Mimicking.

im·i·ta·tor *n.* 1. A copyist. 2. Impersonator.

im·mac·u·late (im-*ak*-yoo-lit) *adj.* Spotless; pure; unstained.—**im·mac·u·late·ly** *adv.*—**im·mac·u·late·ness** *n.*

Immaculate Conception. *Ecclesiastical.* The conception and birth of the Virgin Mary without stain of original sin.

im·ma·nence, im·ma·nen·cy (*im*-uh-nunss; -see) *n.* Dwelling within; inherence.

im·ma·nent *adj.* Remaining within; internal; subjective.—**im·ma·nent·ly** *adv.*

Im·man·u·el *n. Biblical.* Christ.

im·ma·te·ri·al (im-uh-*teer*-ee-ul) *adj.* 1. Spiritual; incorporeal. 2. Unimportant; without weight.—**im·ma·te·ri·al·ly** *adv.*— **-al·ness** *n.*

im·ma·ture (im-uh-*tyoor*) *adj.* Unripe; not fully developed; youthful.—**im·ma·ture·ly** *adv.*—**im·ma·ture·ness** *n.*—**im·ma·tu·ri·ty** *n.*

im·meas·ur·a·ble (im-*ezh*-er-uh-b'l) *adj.* Immense; indefinitely extensive.— **-a·bly** *adv.*

im·me·di·a·cy (im-*ee*-dee-uh-see) *n.* Nearness; proximity.

im·me·di·ate (im-*ee*-dee-it) *adj.* 1. Placed in the closest relation; proximate. 2. Present; instant.—**im·me·di·ate·ness** *n.*

im·me·di·ate·ly *adv.* Directly; instantly.

im·med·i·ca·ble (im-*ed*-ih-kuh-b'l) *adj.* Incurable.

im·me·mo·ri·al (im-em-*or*-ee-ul) *adj.* Beyond

memory; of unrecorded ancientness.—im·me·mo·ri·al·ly *adv.*

im·mense (im-*enss*) *adj.* Vast; tremendous; enormous.—im·mense·ly *adv.*— -mense·ness *n.*

im·men·si·ty (im-*en*-sih-tee) *n.* [*pl.* -ties] Vastness; greatness.

im·merse (im-*erss*) *v.* [im·mersed; im·mers·ing] 1. To dip; submerge; soak. 2. To engross; engage profoundly.—im·mersed *adj.*

im·mer·sion (im-*er*-zhun) *n.* Soaking; dipping.

im·mi·grant (*im*-ih-grunt) *n.* One who enters a country to establish a permanent home.

im·mi·grate (*im*-ih-grayt) *v.* [-grat·ed; -grat·ing] To move to and settle in another country.

im·mi·gra·tion (im-ih-*gray*-shun) *n.* Entrance of permanent settlers into a country or region.

im·mi·nent (*im*-ih-nunt) *adj.* Impending; near at hand; threatening.—im·mi·nence, im·mi·nen·cy *n.*—im·mi·nent·ly *adv.*

im·mis·ci·ble (im-*iss*-ih-b'l) *adj.* Incapable of being mixed.

im·mo·bile (im-*oh*-bil) *adj.* Unmoving; unchanging; fixed.— -bil·i·ty (-*bil*-it-ee) *n.*

im·mo·bil·ize (im-*oh*-bil-yze) *v.* [i-zed; -iz·ing] To paralyze; prevent from moving.—im·mo·bi·li·za·tion (im-oh-b'l-iz-*ay*-shun) *n.*

im·mod·er·ate (im-*od*-er-it) *adj.* Excessive; unreasonable; inordinate.—im·mod·er·a·cy *n.*—im·mod·er·ate·ly *adv.*— -a·tion (-*ay*-shun) *n.*

im·mod·est (im-*od*-est) *adj.* 1. Indecent; shameful; obscene. 2. Arrogant; boastful.—im·mod·est·ly *adv.*—im·mod·es·ty *n.*

im·mo·late (*im*-uh-layt) *v.* [-lat·ed; -lat·ing] To kill, as a victim offered in sacrifice.—im·mo·la·tion (im-uh-*lay*-shun) *n.*—im·mo·la·tor *n.*

im·mor·al (im-*or*-'l) *adj.* 1. Licentious; lascivious; lewd. 2. Wicked; sinful.— -al·ly *adv.*

im·mo·ral·i·ty (im-or-*al*-it-ee) *n.* [*pl.* -ties] Vice; wickedness; lewdness; licentiousness.

im·mor·tal (im-*or*-t'l) *adj.* Eternal; deathless; imperishable.—*n.* One exempt from death.

im·mor·tal·i·ty (im-or-*tal*-it-ee) *n.* Unending existence; exemption from death.

im·mor·tal·ize *v.* [-ized; -iz·ing] To perpetuate; cause to live forever; make eternally great.

im·mov·a·ble (im-*oov*-uh-b'l) *adj.* 1. Firmly fixed; fast. 2. Unalterable; unchangeable; steadfast. 3. Unfeeling; unyielding; unimpressible.—*n.* [*pl.*] *Law.* Land and the buildings and trees on it.—im·mov·a·bil·i·ty (im-oov-uh-*bil*-it-ee), im·mov·a·ble·ness *n.*

im·mune (im-*yoon*) *adj.* 1. Free from; exempt from. 2. Not subject to a disease.

im·mu·ni·ty *n.* [*pl.* -ties] 1. Exemption; nonliability. 2. Power of resistance to a disease.

im·mu·nize (*im*-yoo-nyze) *v.* [-nized; -niz·ing] To make the body resistant to a disease.—im·mu·ni·za·tion (im-yoo-niz-*ay*-shun) *n.*

im·mure (im-*yoor*) *v.* [im·mured; im·mur·ing] To imprison; jail; confine.—im·mure·ment *n.*

im·mu·ta·ble (im-*yoot*-uh-b'l) *adj.* Unchangeable; invariable; unalterable.—im·mu·ta·bil·i-

ty (-uh-*bil*-it-ee), -ble·ness *n.*— -ta·bly *adv.*

imp *n.* A mischievous child.

im·pact (im-*pakt*) *v.* To drive close; press firmly together.—(*im*-pakt) *n.* 1. Collision; forcible meeting or continued contact of two bodies. 2. Impression; effect.—im·pact·ed *adj.*—im·pac·tion (im-*pak*-shun) *n.*

im·pair (im-*payr*) *v.* To damage; injure; weaken.—im·pair·er *n.*—im·pair·ment *n.*

im·pale (im-*payl*) *v.* [im·paled; im·pal·ing] To fix on an upright sharp stake; pierce.—im·pale·ment *n.*—im·pal·er *n.*

im·pal·pa·ble (im-*pal*-puh-b'l) *adj.* Intangible; not concrete; indefinable.—im·pal·pa·bil·i·ty (im-pal-puh-*bil*-it-ee) *n.*—im·pal·pa·bly *adv.*

im·pan·el (im-*pan*-'l) *v.* [im·pan·eled; -elled] -el·ing, -el·ling] To enroll or list, esp. jurors.

im·part (im-*pahrt*) *v.* To communicate; share; dispense; divulge.—im·part·a·ble *adj.*—im·par·ta·tion (im-pahr-*tay*-shun) *n.*—im·part·er *n.*

im·par·tial (im-*pahr*-shul) *adj.* Unbiased; equitable; objective.—im·par·tial·ly *adv.*

im·par·ti·al·i·ty *n.* Objectivity; freedom from prejudice.

im·pass·a·ble (im-*pass*-uh-b'l) *adj.* Incapable of being passed.—im·pass·a·bil·i·ty (im-pass-uh-*bil*-ih-tee), im·pass·a·ble·ness *n.*— -a·bly *adv.*

im·passe (im-*pass*, *im*-pass) *n.* [*pl.* -pass·es] A dead end; bottleneck; deadlock.

im·pass·si·ble (im-*pass*-ib-'l) *adj.* Insensitive; without feeling.—im·pas·si·bil·i·ty (im-pass-ih-*bil*-it-ee), im·pas·si·ble·ness *n.*— -si·bly *adv.*

im·pas·sioned (im-*pash*-und) *adj.* Fervent; ardent; excited.

im·pas·sive (im-*pass*-iv) *adj.* Phlegmatic; unresponsive; betraying no emotion.—im·pas·sive·ly *adv.*—im·pas·sive·ness, im·pas·siv·i·ty *n.*

im·pa·tience (im-*pay*-shunss) *n.* 1. Excessive eagerness; restless anticipation. 2. Irritability; want of forbearance.

im·pa·tient *adj.* 1. Overly eager or anxious; restive. 2. Testy; sharp; irritable.

im·peach (im-*peech*) *v.* 1. To bring charges against an official before a tribunal. 2. To discredit; challenge; question. — im·peach·a·bil·i·ty (im-peech-uh-*bil*-it-ee) *n.*—im·peach·a·ble *adj.*—im·peach·er *n.*—im·peach·ment *n.*

im·pearl (im-*perl*) *v.* To decorate with pearls.

im·pec·ca·ble (im-*pek*-uh-b'l) *adj.* Faultless; flawless; errorless.—im·pec·ca·bil·i·ty (im-pek-uh-*bil*-it-ee) *n.*—im·pec·ca·bly *adv.*

im·pe·cu·ni·ous (im-peh-*kyoo*-nee-us) *adj.* Poor; indigent; poverty-stricken.—im·pe·cu·ni·os·i·ty (im-peh-kyoo-nee-*oss*-it-ee) *n.*—im·pe·cu·ni·ous·ly *adv.*—im·pe·cu·ni·ous·ness *n.*

im·ped·ance (im-*peed*-unss) *n. Electricity.* The combined resistance in a conductor resulting from simple resistance and inductance.

im·pede (im-*peed*) *v.* [im·ped·ed; im·ped·ing] To hinder; obstruct; make difficult.— -ped·er *n.*

im·ped·i·ment (im-*ped*-im-'nt) *n.* Hindrance; obstruction; obstacle.—im·ped·i·men·tal (im-ped-im-*en*-t'l), im·ped·i·men·ta·ry *adj.*

im·ped·i·men·ta (im-ped-im-*en*-tuh) *n. pl.* Luggage, esp. military supplies.

im·pel (im-*pel*) *v.* [im·pelled; im·pel·ling] To drive; excite to action; urge.—**im·pel·ler** *n.*

im·pend (im-*pend*) *v.* To hang over; await.

im·pend·ing *adj.* Imminent; approaching.

im·pen·e·tra·ble (im-*pen*-eh-truh-b'l) *adj.* 1. Impregnable; affording no means of access. 2. Closed; inflexible; adamant. 3. Defying understanding; mysterious.—**im·pen·e·tra·bil·i·ty** (im-pen-eh-truh-*bil*-it-ee), **im·pen·e·tra·ble·ness** *n.*—**im·pen·e·tra·bly** *adv.*

im·pen·i·tent (im-*pen*-it-'nt) *adj.* Unrepentent; hard-hearted; obdurate.—**im·pen·i·tence, im·pen·i·ten·cy** *n.*— **-tent·ly** *adv.*— **-tent·ness** *n.*

im·per·a·tive (im-*pehr*-uh-tiv) *adj.* 1. Obligatory; essential; compulsory. 2. Authoritative; peremptory; commanding. 3. *Grammar.* Pertaining to the mood or form of a verb which expresses command or exhortation. —**im·per·a·tive** *n.*—**im·per·a·tive·ly** *adv.*

im·pe·ra·tor (im-per-*ay*-ter) *n.* King; emperor. —**im·per·a·to·ri·al** (im-per-uh-*tor*-ee-ul) *adj.*

im·per·cep·ti·ble (im-per-*sep*-tib-'l) *adj.* Indiscernible; so minute as to be unnoticed.—**im·per·cep·ti·bil·i·ty** (im-per-sep-tih-*bil*-it-ee), **im·per·cep·ti·ble·ness** *n.*—**im·per·cep·ti·bly** *adv.*

im·per·fect (im-*per*-fekt) *adj.* Defective; wanting; faulty.—*n. Grammar.* A tense expressing an uncompleted action or state, esp. in time past.—**im·per·fect·ly** *adv.*—**im·per·fect·ness** *n.*

im·per·fec·tion (im-per-*fek*-shun) *n.* Flaw; defect; blemish.

im·per·fo·rate (im-*per*-fer-it) *adj.* Also **imperforated.** 1. Having no openings or perforations. 2. *Philately.* Having no perforations between the stamps.

im·pe·ri·al (im-*peer*-ee-ul) *adj.* 1. Pertaining to an emperor or empire. 2. Regal; majestic; noble; grand.—**im·pe·ri·al·ly** *adv.*

im·pe·ri·al·ism (im-*peer*-ee-ul-izm) *n.* A national foreign policy of extending areas of political or economic control, often by force. —**im·pe·ri·al·ist** *n. & adj.*—**im·pe·ri·al·is·tic** (im-peer-ee-uh-*liss*-tik) *adj.*— **-ti·cal·ly** *adv.*

im·per·il (im-*pehr*-ul) *v.* [im·per·iled, -illed; im·per·il·ing, -il·ling] To endanger.

im·pe·ri·ous (im-*peer*-ee-us) *adj.* Domineering; dictatorial.— **-ous·ly** *adv.*— **-ous·ness** *n.*

im·per·ish·a·ble (im-*pehr*-ish-ub-'l) *adj.* Not subject to decay; enduring permanently.—**im·per·ish·a·bil·i·ty** (im-pehr-ish-uh-*bil*-it-ee), **im·per·ish·a·ble·ness** *n.*—**im·per·ish·a·bly** *adv.*

im·per·ma·nent (im-*per*-muh-nunt) *adj.* Not enduring; perishable.

im·per·me·a·ble (im-*per*-mee-uh-b'l) *adj.* Impenetrable; impervious.—**im·per·me·a·bil·i·ty** (im-per-mee-uh-*bil*-it-ee), **im·per·me·a·ble·ness** *n.*—**im·per·me·a·bly** *adv.*

im·per·son·al (im-*per*-sun-'l) *adj.* Objective; unemotional.—**im·per·son·al·i·ty** (im-per-sun-al-it-ee) *n.*—**im·per·son·al·ize** (im-*per*-sun-ul-yze) *v.* [-ized; -iz·ing]—**im·per·son·al·ly** *adv.*

im·per·son·ate (im-*per*-sun-ayt) *v.* [-at·ed; -at·ing] To imitate; mimic; adopt the appearance and mannerisms of another person.—**im·per·son·a·tion** (-sun-*ay*-shun) *n.*— **-son·a·tor** *n.*

im·per·ti·nence (im-*per*-tin-unss) *n.* [*pl.* -nen·cies]. Also **impertinency.** Impudence; presumptousness; brazenness.

im·per·ti·nent (im-*per*-tin-unt) *adj.* 1. Impudent; insolent. 2. Irrelevant.— **-ti·nent·ly** *adv.*

im·per·turb·a·ble (im-per-*terb*-uh-b'l) *adj.* Calm; cool; unmoved.—**im·per·turb·a·bil·i·ty** (im-per-terb-uh-*bil*-it-ee), **im·per·turb·a·ble·ness** *n.*

im·per·vi·ous (im-*per*-vee-us) *adj.* 1. Impenetrable; incapable of being pierced. 2. Unyielding; immovable; inflexible.—**im·per·vi·ous·ly** *adv.*—**im·per·vi·ous·ness** *n.*

im·pe·ti·go (im-peh-*ty*-goh) *n. Medicine.* A skin eruption with itching pustules.—**im·pe·tig·i·nous** (im-peh-*tij*-in-us) *adj.*

im·pet·u·os·i·ty (im-pet-choo-*oss*-it-ee) *n.* [*pl.* -ties] Impulsiveness; rashness; precipitateness.

im·pet·u·ous (im-*pet*-choo-us) *adj.* Impulsive; abrupt.—**im·pet·u·ous·ly** *adv.*— **-ous·ness** *n.*

im·pe·tus (im-peh-tus) *n.* [*pl.* -tus·es] 1. Force of motion; momentum. 2. Stimulus; impulse.

im·pi·e·ty (im-*py*-eh-tee) *n.* [*pl.* -ties] Irreverence; ungodliness.

im·pinge (im-*pinj*) *v.* [im·pinged; im·ping·ing] To come into contact with; strike; collide. —**im·pinge·ment** *n.*—**im·ping·er** *n.*

im·pi·ous (im-pee-us) *adj.* Blasphemous; sacrilegious; profane.—**im·pi·ous·ly** *adv.*

imp·ish (*imp*-ish) *adj.* Mischievous; roguish; playful.—**imp·ish·ly** *adv.*—**imp·ish·ness** *n.*

im·pla·ca·ble (im-*plak*-uh-b'l; -*playk*-) *adj.* Relentless; unforgiving.—**im·plac·a·bil·i·ty, im·plac·a·ble·ness** *n.*—**im·plac·a·bly** *adv.*

im·plant (im-*plant*) *v.* To inculcate; instil; insert.—**im·plan·ta·tion** (im-plan-*tay*-shun) *n.*

im·ple·ment (*im*-pleh-m'nt) *n.* An instrument; tool; utensil.—*v.* To fulfill; carry into execution.—**im·ple·men·tal** (im-pleh-*men*-t'l) *adj.* —**im·ple·men·ta·tion** (im-pleh-men-*tay*-shun) *n.*

im·pli·cate (*im*-plih-kayt) *v.* [-cat·ed; -cat·ing] 1. To involve; bring into association with. 2. To imply. 3. To intertwine.

im·pli·ca·tion (im-plih-*kay*-shun) *n.* Hint; suggestion; intimation.—**im·pli·ca·tion·al, im·pli·ca·tive** (*im*-plih-kuh-tiv) *adj.*— **-tive·ly** *adv.*

im·plic·it (im-*pliss*-it) *adj.* 1. Implied; suggested; tacitly recognized; actual. 2. Undoubting; complete; full and unquestioning.

im·plied *adj.* Intimated; conveyed; suggested.

im·plore (im-*plohr*) *v.* [im·plored; im·plor·ing] To entreat; beseech.—**im·plor·er** *n.*—**im·plor·ing·ly** *adv.*—**im·plor·ing·ness** *n.*

im·ply (im-*ply*) *v.* [-plied; -ply·ing] 1. To involve; include; mean. 2. To suggest; insinuate. 'I imply by my tone that I consider you wrong.'

im·po·lite (im-puh-*lyte*) *adj.* Rude; discourteous; uncivil.—**im·po·lite·ly** *adv.*—**im·po·lite·ness** *n.*

im·pol·i·tic (im-*pol*-it-ik) *adj.* Imprudent; indiscreet; injudicious.— -tic·ly *adv.*— -tic·ness *n.*

im·pon·der·a·ble (im-*pon*-der-uh-b'l) *adj.* Intangible; without appreciable weight.—im·pon·der·a·ble *n.*—im·pon·der·a·bil·i·ty (im-pon-der-uh-*bil*-it-ee), -a·ble·ness *n.*— -a·bly *adv.*

im·port (im-*port*) *v.* 1. To bring into a country from abroad; introduce from without. 2. To mean; signify.—(*im*-port) *n.* 1. A commodity brought into a country from abroad. 2. Meaning; purport. 3. Weight; importance.—im·port·a·bil·i·ty (im-port-uh-*bil*-ih-tee) *n.*—im·port·a·ble *adj.*—im·port·er *n.*

im·por·tance (im-*port*-'nss) *n.* Consequence; weight; significance.

im·por·tant (im-*por*-t'nt) *adj.* Weighty; consequential; influential.—im·por·tant·ly *adv.*

im·por·ta·tion (im-por-*tay*-shun) *n.* Bringing in foreign products; the commodities themselves.

im·por·tu·nate (im-*por*-choo-nit) *adj.* Incessantly soliciting; unreasonably demanding.— -por·tu·na·cy *n.*— -nate·ly *adv.*— -nate·ness *n.*

im·por·tune (im-por-*tyoon*) *adj.* Unreasonable; vexatious.—*v.* [-tuned; -tun·ing] To beg; implore; harry.—im·por·tune·ly *adv.*— -tun·er *n.*

im·por·tu·ni·ty (im-por-*tyoo*-nih-tee) *n.* [*pl.* -ties] Pressing request; troublesome demand.

im·pose (im-*pohz*) *v.* [-posed; -pos·ing] 1. To levy; inflict. 2. To take advantage of.

im·pos·ing *adj.* Stately; majestic; magnificent; impressive.—im·pos·ing·ly *adv.*

im·po·si·tion (im-puh-*zish*-un) *n.* 1. An advantage taken; inconsiderate use made of a situation. 2. Levy; taxation. 3. Laying on of hands, as in the sacrament of Confirmation.

im·pos·si·bil·i·ty (im-poss-ih-*bil*-it-ee) *n.* [*pl.* -ties] 1. Incapability of occurrence or performance. 2. An impossible task.

im·pos·si·ble (im-*poss*-ib-'l) *adj.* 1. Incapable of being done or endured; unachievable; impracticable. 2. *Colloquial.* Not to be dealt with; not worth bothering with.— -si·ble·ness *n.*— -si·bly *adv.*

im·post (*im*-pohst) *n.* Tax; levy; duty.

im·pos·tor (im-*poss*-ter) *n.* One who pretends to be someone else; a fraud.

im·pos·ture (im-*poss*-cher) *n.* Fraud; cheat.

im·po·tence (*im*-puh-tunss) *n.* Also **impotency.** 1. Weakness; feebleness. 2. Lack of sexual power, esp. in the male.

im·po·tent (*im*-puh-tunt) *adj.* 1. Weak; feeble; powerless. 2. Unable to copulate.—im·po·tent·ly *adv.*—im·po·tent·ness *n.*

im·pound *v.* 1. To take into custody. 2. To store up water for irrigating, etc.

im·pov·er·ish (im-*pov*-er-ish) *v.* To make poor; bankrupt; deplete.—im·pov·er·ish·er *n.*—im·pov·er·ish·ment *n.*

im·prac·ti·ca·ble (im-*prak*-tik-uh-b'l) *adj.* Unfeasible; not useful.—im·prac·ti·ca·bil·i·ty (im-prak-tik-uh-*bil*-it-ee), im·prac·ti·ca·ble·ness *n.*

im·prac·ti·cal (im-*prak*-tik-'l) *adj.* 1. Not

workable; inefficient; ineffective. 2. Visionary; dreaming.— -cal·ly *adv.*— -cal·ness *n.*

im·pre·cate (*im*-preh-kayt) *v.* [-cat·ed; -cat·ing] To invoke a curse upon.—im·pre·ca·tor *n.*—im·pre·ca·to·ry (*im*-preh-kuh-tor-ee) *adj.*

im·pre·ca·tion (im-preh-*kay*-shun) *n.* Curse.

im·preg·na·ble (im-*preg*-nuh-b'l) *adj.* Unassailable; invulnerable; unconquerable.—im·preg·na·bil·i·ty (im-preg-nuh-*bil*-ih-tee), im·preg·na·ble·ness *n.*—im·preg·na·bly *adv.*

im·preg·nate (im-*preg*-nayt) *v.* [-nat·ed; -nat·ing] 1. To make pregnant; cause to conceive. 2. To infuse; imbue.—im·preg·nate *adj.*—im·preg·na·tion (im-preg-*nay*-shun) *n.*

im·pre·sa·ri·o (im-preh-*sah*-ree-oh) *n.* [*pl.* -ri·os, -sa·ri] A manager of theatrical presentations.

im·press (im-*press*) *v.* 1. To mark by pressure; stamp. 2. To affect; touch; move.—*n.* (*im*-press) Mark; influence.—im·press·er *n.*

im·press (im-*press*) *v.* To compel to enter into public service.—im·press *n.*

im·pres·sion (im-*presh*-'n) *n.* 1. A mark made by pressure; stamp; imprint. 2. A copy taken by pressure from type, from an engraved plate, etc. 3. Profound, vivid, or spectacular effect; emotional reaction produced. 4. Notion; thought; idea.—im·pres·sion·al *adj.*

im·pres·sion·a·ble (im-*presh*-un-uh-b'l) *adj.* Susceptible; easily affected; sensitive.—im·pres·sion·a·bil·i·ty (im-presh-un-uh-*bil*-it-ee), im·pres·sion·a·ble·ness *n.*

im·pres·sion·ism *n.* 1. *Painting.* A movement to achieve momentary visual realism by close study of light effects, and use of a high, pure, sparkling palette. 2. *Music.* A style of descriptive, evocative composition.—im·pres·sion·ist *n.*—im·pres·sion·is·tic *adj.*

im·pres·sive (im-*press*-iv) *adj.* Moving; imposing; majestic; remarkable.—im·pres·sive·ly *adv.*—im·pres·sive·ness *n.*

im·press·ment (im-*press*-m'nt) *n.* Enforcement into public service.

im·pri·ma·tur (im-prim-*ay*-ter) *n.* A mark of approval.

im·print (im-*print*) *v.* To stamp; fix deeply; impress.—(*im*-print) *n.* The name of publisher, date and place of publication, usually on the title page of a book.

im·pris·on (im-*priz*-un) *v.* To jail; confine.—im·pris·on·ment *n.*

im·prob·a·bil·i·ty (im-prob-uh-*bil*-it-ee) *n.* [*pl.* -ties] Unlikelihood.

im·prob·a·ble (im-*prob*-uh-b'l) *adj.* Unlikely; not expected.— -a·ble·ness *n.*— -a·bly *adv.*

im·promp·tu (im-*promp*-too) *adv. & adj.* Offhand; unplanned; extemporaneous.

im·prop·er (im-*prop*-er) *adj.* 1. Inappropriate; unfitting; inapt. 2. Indecent; indelicate; unseemly.—im·prop·er·ly *adv.*

im·pro·pri·e·ty (im-pruh-*pry*-uh-tee) *n.* [*pl.* -ties] Indecency; incorrectness; poor taste.

im·prove (im-*proov*) *v.* [-proved; -prov·ing] 1. To better; ameliorate; correct. 2. To modernize; remodel.—**im·prov·a·bil·i·ty** (im-proov-uh-*bil*-ih-tee) *n.*—**im·prov·a·ble** *adj.*— -**a·ble·ness** *n.*— -**a·bly** *adv.*— -**im·prov·er** *n.*

im·prove·ment (im-*proov*-munt) *n.* 1. The act of bettering or reforming. 2. A desirable addition or change; modernization.

im·prov·i·dent (im-*prov*-id-'nt) *adj.* Thriftless; extravagant.—**im·prov·i·dence** *n.*— -**dent·ly** *adv.*

im·pro·vi·sa·tion (im-pruh-vih-*zay*-shun) *n.* Extemporizing.—**im·pro·vi·sa·tion·al** *adj.*

im·pro·vise (*im*-pruh-vyze) *v.* [im·pro·vised; im·pro·vis·ing] 1. To perform or elaborate on the spur of the moment; extemporize. 2. To create or devise resourcefully.—**im·pro·vis·er** *n.*

im·pru·dence (im-*proo*-d'nss) *n.* Indiscretion; rashness; lack of caution.

im·pru·dent (im-*proo*-d'nt) *adj.* Indiscreet; reckless; heedless.—**im·pru·dent·ly** *adv.*

im·pu·dence (*im*-pyoo-d'nss) *n.* Also **impu·dency.** Impertinence; effrontery; audacity.

im·pu·dent (*im*-pyoo-d'nt) *adj.* Impertinent; brazen.—**im·pu·dent·ly** *adv.*—**im·pu·dent·ness** *n.*

im·pugn (im-*pyoon*) *v.* To gainsay; challenge; controvert.—**im·pugn·a·ble** *adj.*—**im·pug·na·tion** (im-pug-*nay*-shun) *n.*

im·pulse (*im*-pulss) *n.* 1. Thrust; push. 2. Sudden idea or inclination; spontaneous desire. 3. Instinct; feeling; motive.

im·pul·sion (im-*pul*-shun) *n.* 1. Impetus; driving influence. 2. Impulse.

im·pul·sive (im-*pul*-siv) *adj.* Spontaneous; impetuous; unreflecting.— -**sive·ly** *adv.*— -**sive·ness** *n.*

im·pu·ni·ty (im-*pyoo*-nih-tee) *n.* Exemption from punishment, injury, etc.

im·pure (im-*pyoor*) *adj.* 1. Adulterated; tainted; foul. 2. Obscene; lewd; unclean. —**im·pure·ly** *adv.*—**im·pure·ness** *n.*

im·pu·ri·ty (im-*pyoor*-it-ee) *n.* [*pl.* -ties] 1. Pollution; lewdness. 2. Adulterating matter.

im·pu·ta·tion (im-pyoo-*tay*-shun) *n.* Attribution; ascription.—**im·put·a·tive** (im-*pyoot*-uh-tiv) *adj.*—**im·put·a·tive·ly** *adv.*— -**tive·ness** *n.*

im·pute (im-*pyoot*) *v.* [im·put·ed; im·put·ing] To attribute; ascribe.—**im·put·er** *n.*

in *prep.* Within; surrounded by; during.—*adv.* Inward; within; inside.—*n.* An officeholder; one of the party in power.—**in** *adj.*

in- *Prefix.* 1. Not; opposite to. 'Inactive; inefficient.' 2. Lack of; devoid of. 'Incivility; incompatibility.'

Note: Many words formed with this prefix and representing a simple negation of the meaning of the root word do not require definition. Such words are listed to indicate spelling, beginning at the foot of this page.

in·ac·ti·vate (in-*ak*-tiv-ayt) *v.* [in·ac·ti·vated; -vat·ing] To make functionless.

in·ad·ver·tence (in-ad-*ver*-t'nss) *n.* Also **in·ad·ver·ten·cy.** Negligence; oversight; inattention; error.— -**ver·tent** *adj.* Negligent.— -**tent·ly** *adv.*

in·am·o·ra·ta (in-am-er-*ah*-tuh) *n.* A sweetheart; mistress.—**in·am·o·ra·to** *n.* A lover.

in·ane (in-*ayn*) *adj.* Silly; pointless.

in·a·ni·tion (in-uh-*nish*-un) *n.* 1. Emptiness; lack of sense. 2. Exhaustion from lack of nutrition.

in·an·i·ty (in-*an*-it-ee) *n.* [*pl.* -ties] Emptiness; vacuity; senselessness.

inasmuch as. Also **in as much as.** In that; since; considering that.

in·au·gu·ral (in-*aw*-gyoo-r'l) *adj.* Pertaining to installation in a public office.—*n.* The speech made at an inauguration.

in·au·gu·rate (in-*aw*-gyoo-rayt) *v.* [-rat·ed; -rat·ing] 1. To install formally in office. 2. To initiate officially; set in action.—**in·au·gu·ra·tion** (in-aw-gyoo-*ray*-shun) *n.*— -**ra·tor** *n.*

in·board *adv. Nautical.* Toward the center or keel of a ship.—**in·board** *adj.*

in·born *adj.* Inherent; implanted by heredity.

in·bred (*in*-bred) *adj.* 1. Innate; natural. 2. (in-*bred*) Pertaining to inbreeding.

in·breed (in-*breed*) *v.* [in·bred; in·breed·ing] To mate members of the same or a closely related family.—**in·breed·ing** *n.*

In·ca (*ing*-kuh) *n.* A tribe of Peruvian Indians whose highly developed civilization was destroyed by Pizarro.—**In·can** *n. & adj.*

in·can·des·cence (in-kan-*dess*-'nss) *n.* Light cast by a heated body; luminosity.—**in·candesce** *v.* [in·candesced; -des·cing] To glow.—**in·can·des·cent** *adj.*—**in·can·des·cent·ly** *adv.*

in·can·ta·tion (in-kan-*tay*-shun) *n.* Magic words or evocations; spell-binding language; enchantment.

I

in·ca·pac·i·tate (in-kuh-*pass*-it-ayt) v. [in·ca·pac·i·tat·ed; -tat·ing] To render unfit or incapable; disqualify.—**in·ca·pac·i·ta·tion** (in-kuh-pass-ih-*tay*-shun), **in·ca·pac·i·ty** n.

in·car·cer·ate (in-*kahr*-ser-ayt) v. [in·car·cer·at·ed; -at·ing] To imprison; jail; confine; enclose.—**in·car·cer·a·tion** (in-kahr-ser-*ay*-shun) n.—**in·car·cer·a·tor** n.

in·car·na·dine (in-*kahr*-nuh-din) n. Flesh color; red.—v. [in·car·na·dined; -din·ing]—**in·car·na·dine** adj. & adv.

in·car·nate (in-*kahr*-nit) adj. 1. Embodied in flesh; in human form; personified. 2. Flesh-colored.—v. [in·car·nat·ed; -nat·ing].

in·car·na·tion (in-kahr-*nay*-shun) n. 1. Assumption of a human form and nature. 2. [cap.] *Theology.* The union of God and man in Christ. 3. One who exemplifies strikingly a quality or type.

in·case (in-*kayss*) v. [in·cased; in·cas·ing] To enclose; cover or surround with a case or shell.—**in·case·ment** n.

in·cen·di·ar·y (in-*sen*-dee-er-ee) adj. 1. Pertaining to the malicious setting of fires. 2. Agitating; exciting quarrels. 3. Pertaining to explosives which ignite upon bursting. —n. [pl. -ies] 1. An arsonist; one who sets fire to property. 2. A bomb which ignites on exploding. 3. An agitator; trouble-maker.

in·cense (in-*senss*) v. [in·censed; in·cens·ing] To anger; arouse indignation.—**in·cense·ment** n.

in·cense (*in*-senss) n. 1. A preparation which gives off perfumed vapors when burned. 2. Fragrance.—v. [in·censed; in·cen·sing].

in·cen·tive (in-*sen*-tiv) n. A motivation; spur; goad; stimulus.—**in·cen·tive** adj.

in·cep·tion (in-*sep*-shun) n. Beginning; commencement.—**in·cep·tive** adj.

in·ces·sant (in-*sess*-'nt) adj. Continual; constant; ceaseless.—**in·ces·san·cy** n.—**-sant·ly** adv.

in·cest (*in*-sest) n. Sexual intercourse between persons too closely related to be legally married.—**in·cest·u·ous** adj.—**in·cest·u·ous·ly** adv.

inch n. 1. $\frac{1}{12}$ of a foot. 2. Any small measure or degree.—v. To advance slowly.

inch·meal adv. Little by little; slowly.

in·cho·ate (in-*koh*-it) adj. Just commenced; incipient.—**in·cho·ate·ly** adv.—**in·cho·ate·ness, in·cho·a·tion** (in-koh-*ay*-shun) n.

inch·worm n. The larva of a large-winged moth; looper; measuring worm.

in·ci·dence (*in*-sih-d'nss) n. 1. The angle or direction in which a ray or a body strikes a surface. 2. Occurrence; accident.

in·ci·dent (*in*-sih-d'nt) n. An event; happening; minor or accidental occurrence.—adj. 1. Caused by; connected with. 2. Likely to occur. 3. Striking at an angle.

in·ci·den·tal (in-sih-*den*-t'l) adj. 1. Occurring haphazardly; accidental. 2. Not essential; subordinate. 3. Following from; apt to proceed from.—n. A subordinate matter.—**in·ci·den·tal·ly** adv. 1. Without intent or design. 2. By the way.

in·cin·er·ate (in-*sin*-er-ayt) v. [in·cin·er·at·ed; -at·ing] To burn; reduce to ashes.—**in·cin·er·a·tion** (in-sin-er-*ay*-shun) n.—**in·cin·er·a·tor** n.

in·cip·i·ence (in-*sip*-ee-unss) n. Also **incipiency.** A beginning; commencing to be evident. —**in·cip·i·ent** adj.—**in·cip·i·ent·ly** adv.

in·ci·sion (in-*sizh*-un) n. 1. A gash; cut; esp. a surgical wound. 2. Sharpness; trenchancy. —**in·cise** v. [in·cised; in·cis·ing] To cut.

in·ci·sive (in-*sy*-siv) adj. Cutting; sharp; penetrating; clearly expressive.—**in·ci·sive·ly** adv. —**in·ci·sive·ness** n.

in·ci·sor (in-*sy*-zer) n. *Zoology.* A front tooth, adapted for biting.—**in·ci·so·ry** adj.

in·cite (in-*syte*) v. [in·cit·ed; in·cit·ing] To stir up; stimulate to action.—**in·ci·ta·tion** (in-sy-*tay*-shun), **in·cite·ment** n.—**in·cit·er** n.

in·cli·na·tion (in-klih-*nay*-shun) n. 1. Disposition; tendency; proneness. 2. Aptitude; bent. 3. Slope; leaning; slant.

in·cline (in-*klyne*) v. [in·clined; in·clin·ing] 1. To deviate from the normal direction; slant; bend. 2. To tend; be disposed.—**in·cline** n. A slope.—**in·clin·er** n.

inclined plane. *Physics.* A plane or surface which makes an acute angle with the horizon.

in·cli·nom·e·ter (in-klin-*om*-uh-ter) n. 1. An instrument for measuring magnetic dip. 2. An instrument for indicating the angle of an aircraft with the horizontal.

in·close (in-*klohz*) v. [in·closed; in·clos·ing] To enclose; shut in; confine.

in·clo·sure (in-*kloh*-zher) n. An enclosure.

in·clude (in-*klood*) v. [in·clud·ed; in·clud·ing] 1. To contain; comprise. 2. To enclose; surround.—**in·clud·a·ble, in·clud·i·ble** adj.

in·clu·sion (in-*kloo*-zhun) n. 1. That which is contained or added. 2. A comprising.

incoherent	incommunicability	inconceivability	inconsiderateness
incoherently	incommunicable	inconceivable	inconsideration
incombustibility	incommunicableness	inconceivableness	inconsistence
incombustible	incommunicably	inconceivably	inconsistencies
incombustibleness	incompetence	inconclusive	inconsistency
incombustibly	incompetency	inconclusively	inconsistent
incommensurability	incomplete	inconclusiveness	inconsistently
incommensurable	incompletely	inconsequence	inconsolability
incommensurableness	incompleteness	inconsequent	inconsolable
incommensurably	incompletion	inconsequential	inconsolableness
incommensurate	incomprehensibility	inconsequentially	inconsolably
incommensurately	incomprehensible	inconsequently	inconsonance
incommensurateness	incomprehensibleness	inconsiderable	inconsonant
incommodious	incomprehensibly	inconsiderably	inconsonantly
incommodiously	incompressibility	inconsiderate	inconspicuous
incommodiousness	incompressible	inconsiderately	inconspicuously

in·clu·sive (in-*kloo*-siv) *adj.* 1. Comprehended in a sum; contained within limits. 2. Tending to comprise.— -sive·ly *adv.*— -sive·ness *n.*

in·cog·ni·to (in-*kog*-nit-oh) *adj. & adv.* In disguise; in an assumed identity.—*n.* [*pl.* -tos] 1. Disguise; feigned character. 2. One in disguise.

in·come (*in*-kum) *n.* Revenue; money received from labor or property.

in·com·mode (in-kuh-*mohd*) *v.* [-mod·ed; -mod·ing] To inconvenience; cause difficulty for.

in·com·mu·ni·ca·do (in-kuh-myoon-ih-*kah*-doh) *adj.* Debarred from communication. 'The offender was held incommunicado.'

in·com·pa·ra·ble (in-*kom*-per-uh-b'l) *adj.* Unequaled; not comparable with others.—in·com·pa·ra·bil·i·ty, -ble·ness *n.*— -ra·bly *adv.*

in·com·pat·i·ble (in-kum-*pat*-uh-b'l) *adj.* Incapable of harmonizing or being in accord with others; not compatible.—in·com·pat·i·bil·i·ty, in·com·pat·i·ble·ness *n.*— -pat·i·bly *adv.*

in·com·pe·tent (in-*kom*-puh-tunt) *adj.* 1. Lacking competence; without ability. 2. *Law.* Lacking the qualifications required by law.—*n.* An incompetent person.— -pe·tent·ly *adv.*

in·con·gru·i·ty (in-kong-*groo*-it-ee) *n.* [*pl.* -ties] Unsuitableness of one thing to another; absurdity; one of two or more things that do not go together.

in·con·gru·ous (in-*kon*-groo-us) *adj.* Unsuitable; not fitting; inappropriate.—in·con·gru·ous·ly *adv.*—in·con·gru·ous·ness *n.*

in·con·ven·ience (in-kun-*veen*-yunss) *n.* Also **inconveniency.** 1. A disadvantage; troublesome or embarrassing factor; hindrance. 2. Want of convenience.—*v.* [in·con·ven·ienced; -ienc·ing]

in·con·ven·ient (in-kun-*veen*-yunt) *adj.* Hindering; difficult to use; causing trouble or annoyance.—in·con·ven·ient·ly *adv.*

in·cor·po·rate (in-*kor*-per-it) *adj.* United in one body; joined; associated.—*v.* (-*rayt*) [in·cor·po·rat·ed; -rat·ing] 1. To form a commercial or political corporation; unite into a body. 2. To mix together.

in·cor·po·ra·tion (in-kor-per-*ay*-shun) *n.* 1. Formation of a limited liability company or a political entity; corporation. 2. A mixing or joining together.—in·cor·po·ra·tive *adj.* —in·cor·po·ra·tor *n.*

in·cor·ri·gi·ble (in-*kawr*-ij-ih-b'l) *adj.* Beyond correction or reform.—*n.* One who cannot be reformed.—in·cor·ri·gi·bil·i·ty, in·cor·ri·gi·ble·ness *n.*—in·cor·ri·gi·bly *adv.*

in·crease (in-*kreess*) *v.* [in·creased; in·creas·ing] 1. To make larger, more intense, more frequent, higher, or better; augment. 2. To reproduce; be fruitful.—*n.* (*in*-kreess).—in·creas·a·ble (in-*kreess*-uh-b'l) *adj.*—in·creas·er *n.*—in·creas·ing·ly *adv.*

in·cred·i·ble (in-*kred*-uh-b'l) *adj.* Unbelievable; too extraordinary or improbable to accept. —in·cred·i·bil·i·ty, -ble·ness *n.*— -cred·i·bly *adv.*

in·cre·du·li·ty (in-kreh-*dyoo*-luh-tee) *n.* Skepticism; unbelief.

in·cred·u·lous (in-*kred*-yoo-lus) *adj.* 1. Sceptical; withholding belief. 2. Caused by unbelief.—in·cred·u·lous·ly *adv.*— -lous·ness *n.*

in·cre·ment (*in*-kruh-munt) *n.* An increase; addition to; augmentation.— -men·tal *adj.*

in·crim·i·nate (in-*krim*-uh-nayt) *v.* [in·crim·i·nat·ed; -nat·ing] To fix guilt upon; make suspect; accuse of a crime.—in·crim·i·na·tion (in-krim-uh-*nay*-shun) *n.*—in·crim·i·na·tor *n.*—in·crim·i·na·to·ry *adj.*

in·crust (in-*krust*) *v.* To cover with a crust or film; coat.— -crus·ta·tion (in-krus-*tay*-shun) *n.*

in·cu·bate (*in*-kyoo-bayt) *v.* [in·cu·bat·ed; -bat·ing] To provide an environment suitable to hatching of eggs, growth of bacteria, etc.—in·cu·ba·tive *adj.*—in·cu·ba·tion *n.*—in·cu·ba·tor *n.*

in·cu·bus (*in*-kyoo-bus) *n.* [*pl.* -bi, -bus·es] 1. A nightmare. 2. Oppressive worry; mental burden.

in·cul·cate (in-*kul*-kayt) *v.* [-cat·ed; -cat·ing] To teach or impress upon thoroughly.—in·cul·ca·tion (in-kul-*kay*-shun) *n.*—in·cul·ca·tor *n.*

in·cul·pate (in-*kul*-payt) *v.* [in·cul·pat·ed; -pat·ing] To blame; accuse; incriminate.—in·cul·pa·tion (in-kul-*pay*-shun) *n.*—in·cul·pa·to·ry *adj.*

in·cum·ben·cy (in-*kum*-ben-see) *n.* [*pl.* -cies] 1. Burden; obligation. 2. Tenure of office.

in·cum·bent (in-*kum*-bent) *adj.* 1. Imposed; obligatory; devolving upon. 2. Resting upon; bearing upon.—*n.* An officeholder.—in·cum·bent·ly *adv.*—in·cum·bent·ness *n.*

in·cum·ber. *Variant spelling of* encumber.

in·cum·brance. *Variant of* encumbrance.

in·cu·nab·u·la (in-kyoo-*nab*-yoo-luh) *n. pl.* [*sing.* -lum] 1. Period of inception; earliest phase of development. 2. Printed works in circulation prior to 1500 A.D.— -nab·u·lar *adj.*

in·cur (in-*ker*) *v.* [in·curred; in·cur·ring] To contract; bring upon oneself; expose self to.

in·cur·sion (in-*kerzh*-un) *n.* An invasion not followed by occupation; inroad; raid.—**in·cur·sive** (in-*kerss*-iv) *adj.*

in·curve (*in*-kerv) *n.* Also **in-curve, in curve.** *Baseball.* A pitched ball that breaks inward.

in·debt·ed (in-*det*-ed) *adj.* Being under obligation to; owing; obliged.—**in·debt·ed·ness** *n.*

in·de·cen·cy (in-*deess*-en-see) *n.* [*pl.* -cies] Unbecomingness; obscenity; offensiveness; immodesty.—**in·de·cent** *adj.*—**in·de·cent·ly** *adv.*

in·de·ci·sion (in-deh-*sizh*-un) *n.* Irresolution; wavering of the mind.

in·de·ci·sive (in-deh-*sy*-siv) *adj.* 1. Not conclusive; not determining; not settled upon. 2. Prone to vacillate or hesitate.—**in·de·ci·sive·ly** *adv.*—**in·de·ci·sive·ness** *n.*

in·deed (in-*deed*) *adv.* In reality; in fact.—*interjection.* Is that so! Do tell!

in·de·fat·i·ga·ble (in-deh-*fat*-ig-uh-b'l) *adj.* Tireless; unwearying; unflagging.—**in·de·fat·i·ga·bil·i·ty** (in-deh-fat-ig-uh-*bil*-it-ee) **in·de·fat·i·ga·ble·ness** *n.*—**in·de·fat·i·ga·bly** *adv.*

in·de·fea·si·ble (in-deh-*feez*-ih-b'l) *adj.* Not to be defeated or invalidated.—**in·de·fea·si·bil·i·ty** (in-deh-feez-ih-*bil*-it-ee) *n.*— **-si·bly** *adv.*

in·def·i·nite (in-*def*-in-it) *adj.* Not well-defined; unclear; uncertain; indeterminate.—**in·def·i·nite·ly** *adv.*—**in·def·i·nite·ness** *n.*

indefinite article. *Grammar.* The word *a* or *an.*

in·del·i·ble (in-*del*-uh-b'l) *adj.* Incapable of erasure or obliteration.—**in·del·i·bil·i·ty** (in-del-uh-*bil*-it-ee), **-ble·ness** *n.*—**in·del·i·bly** *adv.*

in·del·i·cate (in-*del*-ih-kit) *adj.* Indecent; indecorous; lewd.—**in·del·i·ca·cy** *n.*—**in·del·i·cate·ly** *adv.*—**in·del·i·cate·ness** *n.*

in·dem·ni·fi·ca·tion (in-dem-nih-fih-*kay*-shun) *n.* Security against loss, damage, or penalty.

in·dem·ni·fy (in-*dem*-nih-fy) *v.* [in·dem·ni·fied; -fy·ing] 1. To secure against loss or damage. 2. To reimburse; compensate.— **-dem·ni·fi·er** *n.*

in·dem·ni·ty (in-*dem*-nit-ee) *n.* [*pl.* -ties] 1. Compensation for loss or injury suffered; reimbursement. 2. Exemption from loss.

in·dent (in-*dent*) *v.* 1. *Printing.* To begin a line farther in from the margin than the rest of the paragraph. 2. To notch; make jagged.—*n.* (*in*-dent) An indentation; notch.—**in·dent·or** *n.*

in·den·ta·tion (in-den-*tay*-shun) *n.* 1. *Printing.* An indention. 2. A cut or notch.

in·den·tion (in-*den*-shun) *n.* *Printing.* A space before a line in addition to the margin.

in·den·ture (in-*den*-cher) *n.* 1. Bond or contract of apprenticeship. 2. Indentation.—*v.* [-tured; -tur·ing] To bind to service.

in·de·pend·ence (in-dih-*pen*-dunss) *n.* Also **in·de·pend·en·cy.** 1. Freedom; lack of restraint or dependence. 2. Income sufficient to free one from reliance on others.

Independence Day. The Fourth of July, celebrated in the U.S. in honor of the signing of the Declaration of Independence.

in·de·pend·ent (in-dih-*pen*-dunt) *adj.* 1. Free to direct oneself; not under the power of others. 2. Not subject to bias or influence; objective. 3. Bold; unconstrained.—*n.* One who is not partisan; one who has not taken sides or made commitments.— **-pen·dent·ly** *adv.*

in·dex (*in*-dekss) *n.* [*pl.* in·dex·es, in·di·ces] 1. That which points out or indicates; pointer. 2. A printer's sign [☜]. 3. The first or pointing finger. 4. An alphabetical list of the contents of a book. 5. A statistical table or summary.—*v.* To provide with or arrange in an index.—**in·dex·er** *n.*

India ink. Black, opaque, indelible pigment.

In·di·a·man *n.* [*pl.* -men] *Nautical.* A ship employed in trade with India, esp. the large sailing vessels operated by the East India Company.

In·di·an (*in*-dee-un) *n.* 1. A native of India. 2. An American aboriginal. 3. An American Indian language.—**In·di·an** *adj.*

Indian club. An object shaped like a bowling pin, used in calisthenics.

Indian corn. American corn; maize.

Indian file. Single row or file.

Indian giver. One who takes back a gift after bestowing it.

Indian Ocean. The section of the earth's water area lying south of Asia between Africa and Australia.

Indian pipe. A leafless herb bearing hanging white blossoms.

Indian pudding. A dish made from cornmeal, molasses, and spices.

Indian summer. A brief period of balmy weather occurring in the fall.

India paper. A thin, strong paper.

in·di·a·rub·ber, India rubber. Common commercial rubber.

In·dic (*in*-dik) *adj.* Pertaining to the class of Indo-European languages spoken in India.

in·di·cate (*in*-duh-kayt) *v.* [in·di·cat·ed; in·di·cat·ing] To show; point out; signify; evidence.

in·di·ca·tion (in-duh-*kay*-shun) *n.* Mark; sign; suggestion; symptom.

in·dic·a·tive (in-*dik*-uh-tiv) *adj.* 1. Pointing out; bringing to notice; showing. 2. *Grammar.* Denoting the mood of a verb that affirms, denies, or asks a direct fact.— **-a·tive·ly** *adv.*

in·di·ca·tor *n.* 1. A gauge which visibly registers some quantitative fact. 2. *Chemistry*. A substance which indicates the nature of a solution by changing color.

in·di·ces (*in*-duh-seez). *Plural* of **index**.

in·dict (in-*dyte*) *v.* 1. To incriminate; charge; accuse. 2. *Law*. To charge with a crime or misdemeanor by the finding of a grand jury. **in·dict·a·ble** *adj*.—**in·dict·er, in·dict·or** *n.*

in·dict·ment (in-*dyte*-m'nt) *n.* 1. Accusation; charge. 2. *Law*. A written accusation of a crime or a misdemeanor presented upon oath by a grand jury.

In·dies. The East Indies.

in·dif·fer·ence (in-*dif*-er-unss) *n.* Detachment; lack of interest; unconcern.

in·dif·fer·ent (in-*dif*-er-ent) *adj.* 1. Disinterested; unconcerned: aloof. 2. So-so; mediocre; neither good nor bad.— **-fer·ent·ly** *adv.*

in·di·gence (*in*-dih-junss) *n.* Poverty; destitution; want.

in·dig·e·nous (in-*dij*-in-us) *adj.* Native; endemic; innate.— **-nous·ly** *adv.*— **-nous·ness** *n.*

in·di·gent (*in*-dih-junt) *adj.* Poor; needy; destitute.

in·di·ges·tion (in-dih-*jess*-chun) *n.* Dyspepsia; difficulty in digesting food.—**in·di·ges·tive** *adj.*

in·dig·nant (in-*dig*-nunt) *adj.* Angry from injustice; righteously wrathful.—**in·dig·nant·ly** *adv.*

in·dig·na·tion (in-dig-*nay*-shun) *n.* Righteous anger; dignified wrath.

in·dig·ni·ty (in-*dig*-nih-tee) *n.* [*pl.* -ties] Affront; injury; wrong.

in·di·go (*in*-dig-oh) *n.* [*pl.* -gos; -goes] 1. A valuable blue dye obtained from an Asiatic shrub, or produced synthetically. 2. A rich blue color.—**in·di·go** *adj.*

indigo bunting. Also indigo bird. An American bird belonging to the finch family.

indirect tax. A tax which eventually falls upon persons other than those directly taxed, by being passed on in the form of increased prices.

in·dis·cre·tion (in-diss-*kresh*-un) *n.* Imprudence; rash or unconventional act.— **-tion·ar·y** *adj.*

in·dis·crim·i·nate (in-diss-*krim*-in-it) *adj.* Unselecting; undistinguishing; sweeping; miscellaneous.—**in·dis·crim·i·nate·ly** *adv.*—**in·dis·crim·i·nate·ness** *n.*—**in·dis·crim·i·na·tion** *n.*

in·dis·pose (in-diss-*pohz*) *v.* [in·dis·posed; in·dis·pos·ing] 1. To disincline; make averse. 2. To affect with illness.—**in·dis·posed** *adj.* 1. Averse; disinclined. 2. Slightly ill.—**in·dis·po·si·tion** (in-diss-puh-*zish*-un) *n.*

in·dite (in-*dyte*) *v.* [in·dit·ed; -dit·ing] To compose; write.—**in·dit·er** *n.*

in·di·um (*in*-dee-um) *n.* A rare, soft, silver-white metallic element. (*Symbol:* In).

in·di·vi·du·al (in-dih-*vij*-yoo-ul) *adj.* 1. Single; one. 2. Peculiar to; characteristic of. 3. Personal; having character; unusual.—*n.* A person; human being.—**in·di·vid·u·al·ly** *adv.*

in·di·vid·u·al·ism *n.* 1. The theory that the common interest will be best served by allowing each individual the maximum freedom; laissez-faire. 2. Self-interest; selfishness. 3. Personal identity.—**in·di·vid·u·al·ist** *n.* & *adj.*—**in·di·vid·u·al·is·tic** *adj.*

in·di·vid·u·al·i·ty (in-dih-vij-yoo-*al*-it-ee) *n.* [*pl.* -ties] 1. Qualities distinguishing one person or object from another. 2. Separate identity and existence.

in·di·vid·u·al·ize (in-dih-*vij*-yoo-ul-yze) *v.* [-ized; -iz·ing] 1. To endow with personality and identity. 2. To specify; treat separately.—**in·di·vid·u·al·iz·a·tion** (in-dih-vij-yoo-ul-ih-*zay*-shun) *n.*—**in·di·vid·u·al·iz·er** *n.*

in·di·vis·i·ble (in-div-*iz*-ib-'l) *adj.* Incapable of being separated into parts.—*n. Geometry*. An infinitely small element or principle into which a figure may be resolved.—**in·di·vis·i·bil·i·ty** (in-div-iz-ib-*il*-it-ee), **in·di·vis·i·ble·ness** *n.*

In·do-Chi·nese *adj.* 1. Pertaining to the people or culture of Indo-China. 2. Pertaining to a language group of India.

in·doc·tri·nate (in-*dok*-trin-ayt) *v.* [-nat·ed; -nat·ing] To inculcate; instruct.—**in·doc·tri·na·tion** (in-dok-trin-*ay*-shun) *n.*— **-na·tor** *n.*

In·do-Eu·ro·pe·an (*in*-doh-yoor-uh-*pee*-un) *adj.* Pertaining to a family of languages generally classified into six branches: Indic, Iranian, Celtic, Graeco-Latin, Teutonic, and Slavonic.

In·do-Ger·man·ic (*in*-doh-jer-*man*-ik) *adj.* Indo-European.

in·do·lence (*in*-duh-lunss) *n.* Laziness; lethargy.

in·do·lent *adj.* Lazy; lethargic; listless.—**in·do·lent·ly** *adv.*

in·dom·i·ta·ble (in-*dom*-it-uh-b'l) *adj.* Invincible; unconquerable; intrepid.— **-ta·bly** *adv.*

In·do·ne·sia (in-do-*nee*-shuh; -zhuh). The area including the East Indies, East Indian archipelago, and the Philippines.—**In·do·ne·sian** *adj. & n.*

in·door (in-*dor*) *adj.* 1. Pertaining to an interior. 2. Taking place or belonging indoors.

in·doors *adv.* Inside a building.

in·dorse, etc. *Variants* of **endorse**, etc.

In·dra (*in*-druh) *n.* A Hindu deity originally symbolizing the sky or heavens.

in·draft (*in*-draft) *n.* Also **indraught.** 1. The inward sea current. 2. Any inward pull.

in·du·bi·ta·ble (in-*dyoo*-bih-tuh-b'l) *adj.* Unquestionable; undeniable; incontrovertible. —**in·du·bi·ta·ble·ness** *n.*—**in·du·bi·ta·bly** *adv.*

in·duce (in-*dyooss*) *v.* [in·duced; in·duc·ing] To persuade; prevail upon; incite.—**in·duce·ment** *n.*—**in·duc·er** *n.*—**in·duc·i·ble** *adj.*

in·duct (in-*dukt*) *v.* 1. To install; put in formal possession of office. 2. To introduce.

in·duc·tance *n. Electricity.* The property of a conductor which produces a current in a neighboring conductor when receiving a varying current itself.

in·duc·tile (in-*duk*-til) *adj.* Not malleable or pliant.—**in·duc·til·i·ty** (in-duk-*til*-it-ee) *n.*

in·duc·tion (in-*duk*-shun) *n.* 1. Installation in an office or position. 2. Prologue; prelude. 3. A process of demonstration in which a general truth is gathered from an examination of particular cases. 4. *Physics.* The property by which one body with electrical or magnetic polarity induces or causes it in another without contact.

induction coil. A coil that causes an electric current to vary from that of its external source.

in·duc·tive (in-*duk*-tiv) *adj.* 1. Using induction as a method of reasoning. 2. Relating to electrical induction.—**in·duc·tive·ly** *adv.*

in·duc·tor (in-*duk*-ter) *n.* An electrical device which operates by induction.

in·due (in-*dyoo*) *v.* [in·dued; in·du·ing] To furnish; supply; endow; clothe.

in·dulge (in-*dulj*) *v.* [in·dulged; in·dulg·ing] 1. To pamper; spoil; humor. 2. To give free course to; give way to.—**in·dulg·er** *n.*

in·dul·gence (in-*dul*-junss) *n.* 1. Forbearance; tolerance; leniency. 2. *Roman Catholic Church.* Remission of punishment.

in·dul·gent (in-*dul*-junt) *adj.* Lenient; tolerant; kindly.—**in·dul·gent·ly** *adv.*

in·du·rate (*in*-dyoo-rit) *adj.* Hardened; unfeeling; insensitive.—*v.* [-rat·ed; -rat·ing] To harden.—**in·du·ra·tion** *n.*—**in·du·ra·tive** *adj.*

In·dus (*in*-dus) *n.* A great river of northern India which empties into the Arabian Sea.

in·dus·tri·al (in-*duss*-tree-ul) *adj.* Relating to industries or workers in industries.—**in·dus·tri·al·ly** *adv.*

in·dus·tri·al·ism *n.* An economic system based on the organization of work into large industries.

in·dus·tri·al·ist *n.* An owner or executive of an industry.

in·dus·tri·al·ize *v.* [-ized; -iz·ing] To bring an area or country to industrialism.—**in·dus·tri·al·i·za·tion** *n.*

in·dus·tri·ous *adj.* Diligent; hard-working; assiduous.—**in·dus·tri·ous·ly** *adv.*— **-ous·ness** *n.*

in·dus·try (*in*-duss-tree) *n.* [*pl.* -ties] 1. Diligence; assiduity. 2. Any branch of economically productive activity, esp. a large-scale activity. 'The publishing industry.'

in·e·bri·ate (in-*ee*-bree-ayt) *v.* [-at·ed; -at·ing] To intoxicate; make drunk.—*n.* A drunkard. —**in·e·bri·ate, in·e·bri·at·ed** *adj.*— **-a·tion** *n.*

in·e·bri·e·ty (in-eh-*bry*-uh-tee) *n.* Drunkenness.

in·ef·fa·ble (in-*ef*-uh-b'l) *adj.* Unutterable; unspeakable.—**in·ef·fa·bil·i·ty, in·ef·fa·ble·ness** *n.* —**in·ef·fa·bly** *adv.*

in·ef·fec·tu·al (in-eh-*fek*-choo-ul) *adj.* Weak; powerless; vain.—**in·ef·fec·tu·al·i·ty** (in-eh-fek-choo-*al*-uh-tee) *n.*—**in·ef·fec·tu·al·ly** *adv.*

in·ept (in-*ept*) *adj.* 1. Awkward; clumsy. 2. Inappropriate; unsuitable.—**in·ep·ti·tude** (in-*ep*-tih-tyood), **in·ept·ness** *n.*—**in·ept·ly** *adv.*

in·ert (in-*ert*) *adj.* Inactive; lifeless; inanimate. —**in·ert·ly** *adv.*—**in·ert·ness** *n.*

in·er·tia (in-*er*-shuh) *n.* 1. Passiveness; inactivity. 2. *Physics.* The property of matter by which it remains immobile or in unvaried motion until exertion of an external force.

in·es·ti·ma·ble (in-*ess*-tim-uh-b'l) *adj.* Priceless; too valuable to be fully appreciated.—**in·es·ti·ma·bly** *adv.*

in·ev·i·ta·ble (in-*ev*-it-uh-b'l) *adj.* Unavoidable; inescapable.—**in·ev·i·ta·bil·i·ty, in·ev·i·ta·ble·ness** *n.*—**in·ev·i·ta·bly** *adv.*

in·ex·o·ra·ble (in-*eks*-er-uh-b'l) *adj.* Inflexible; relentless; implacable; merciless.—**in·ex·o·ra·bil·i·ty** (in-eks-er-uh-*bil*-it-ee), **in·ex·o·ra·ble·ness** *n.*—**in·ex·o·ra·bly** *adv.*

in·ex·pen·sive (in-eks-*pen*-siv) *adj.* Cheap; reasonable.— **-sive·ly** *adv.*— **-sive·ness** *n.*

in·ex·pli·ca·ble (in-*eks*-plik-uh-b'l) *adj.* Unexplainable; incomprehensible.—**in·ex·pli·ca·bil·i·ty, in·ex·pli·ca·ble·ness** *n.*—**in·ex·pli·ca·bly** *adv.*

in·fal·li·ble (in-*fal*-ib-'l) *adj.* Unerring; never failing; incapable of making mistakes.—**in·fal·li·bil·i·ty** *n.*—**in·fal·li·bly** *adv.*

in·fa·mous (*in*-fuh-mus) *adj.* Nefarious; iniquitous; shameful.—**in·fa·mous·ly** *adv.*

in·fa·my (*in*-fuh-mee) *n.* [*pl.* -mies] Ignominy; shame; odium; public disgrace.

in·fan·cy (*in*-fun-see) *n.* [*pl.* -cies] 1. Early childhood; first stage of life. 2. *Law.* The period from birth to 21 years.

in·fant (*in*-funt) *n.* 1. A baby. 2. *Law.* A person under 21.—*adj.* Young; tender.

in·fan·ti·cide (in-*fan*-tih-syde) *n.* Murder of a young child.

in·fan·tile (*in*-fun-tyle) *adj.* Pertaining to infants; childish.

infantile paralysis. An acute infectious disease which causes muscle atrophy and often permanent deformity; poliomyelitis.

in·fan·til·ism (in-*fan*-tul-izm) *n. Medicine.* Arrested development of mind or body.

in·fan·try (*in*-fun-tree) *n.* [*pl.* -tries] Foot soldiers.—**in·fan·try·man** *n.* [*pl.* -men].

in·fat·u·ate (in-*fach*-oo-ayt) *v.* [in·fat·u·at·ed; -at·ing] 1. To cause an ardent, temporary love. 2. To deprive of sound judgment; cap-

inexpedient	inexpiable	inexpressibleness	inextinguishable
inexpediently	inexpiableness	inexpressibly	inextinguishably
inexperience	inexpiably	inexpressive	inextricability
inexperienced	inexpressibility	inexpressively	inextricable
inexpert	inexpressible	inexpressiveness	inextricableness

tivate.—*adj.* Stricken with a passion or obstinate desire.—**in·fat·u·a·tion** *n.*

in·fect *v.* To taint with disease or germs; contaminate.—**in·fec·tor** *n.*

in·fec·tion *n.* 1. A sore or other evidence of diseased tissue. 2. Contamination by disease.

in·fec·tious (in-*fek*-shus) *adj.* 1. Communicated by a parasite, as a disease. 2. Corrupting; tainting. 3. Easily spread from person to person. 'Infectious laughter.'—**in·fec·tious·ly** *adv.*—**in·fec·tious·ness** *n.*

in·fer (in-*fer*) *v.* [in·ferred; in·fer·ring] To deduce; conclude. 'I infer from your statement that you imply that I am wrong.'—**in·fer·a·ble** *adj.*—**in·fer·er** *n.*

in·fer·ence (*in*-fer-unss) *n.* A deduction; conclusion.—**in·fer·en·tial** *adj.*— **-tial·ly** *adv.*

in·fe·ri·or (in-*feer*-ee-er) *adj.* 1. Lower in position, age, value, importance, quality, etc.; subordinate. 2. *Printing.* At the base of a line. 'Inferior figures, as in H_2SO_4.'—*n.* One lower in social or intellectual rank.—**in·fer·ior·i·ty** (in-feer-ee-*or*-uh-tee) *n.* [*pl.* -ties]—**in·fer·ior·ly** *adv.*

inferiority complex. An irrational feeling of inferiority which operates in the unconscious to produce timidity or overaggressiveness.

in·fer·nal *adj.* 1. Of, in, or appropriate to hell; diabolical; evil; detestable. 2. *Colloquial.* Extreme; great. 'His infernal nerve.' —**in·fer·nal·ly** *adv.*

infernal machine. A bomb; explosive for assassination.

in·fer·no *n.* [*pl.* -nos] Hell; any hellish place.

in·fest (in-*fest*) *v.* To overrun; occupy in order to commit depredations; harass.—**in·fest·er** *n.*

in·fi·del (*in*-fuh-dul) *n.* A disbeliever of a particular religious belief; one skeptical of the divine origin of a religion.—*adj.* Disbelieving.

in·fi·del·i·ty (in-fid-*el*-it-ee) *n.* [*pl.* -ties] 1. Adultery; unfaithfulness. 2. Religious disbelief or skepticism. 3. A breach of trust.

in·field (*in*-feeld) *n.* 1. The area of a baseball diamond that is inside or near the baseline. 2. The players who are stationed there.—**in·field·er** *n.* An infield player.

in·fil·trate (in-*fil*-trayt) *v.* [in·fil·trat·ed; -trat·ing] 1. To enter or pass through small breaches or openings. 2. To diffuse through the pores of a substance.—**in·fil·tra·tion** *n.*

in·fi·nite (*in*-fih-nit) *adj.* Without limit; endless; boundless.—*n.* 1. An infinity. 2. [*cap.*] God. —**in·fin·ite·ly** *adv.*—**in·fin·ite·ness** *n.*

in·fin·i·tes·i·mal (in-fin-uh-*tess*-um-ul) *adj.* Microscopically or infinitely small; minute.—*n.* A minute or infinitely small quantity.—**in·fin·i·tes·i·mal·ly** *adv.*

in·fin·i·tive (in-*fin*-it-iv) *n.* A verb form usually preceded by *to*, used as a noun with verbal

force.—*adj.* Not limiting or restricting.—**in·fin·i·ti·val** (in-fin-uh-*ty*-v'l) *adj.*

in·fin·i·tude (in-*fin*-ih-tyood) *n.* Boundlessness; infinity; endless quantity.

in·fin·i·ty (in-*fin*-uh-tee) *n.* [*pl.* -ties] Limitless extent of time, space, power, number, etc.

in·firm (in-*ferm*) *adj.* 1. Sickly; feeble; diseased. 2. Not solid; unstable. 3. Irresolute; unsteadfast.—**in·firm·i·ty** *n.* Sickness; weakness.—**in·firm·ly** *adv.*—**in·firm·ness** *n.*

in·fir·ma·ry (in-*ferm*-er-ee) *n.* [*pl.* -ries] A hospital.

in·flame (in-*flaym*) *v.* [in·flamed; in·flam·ing] 1. To set on fire; kindle. 2. To excite; stimulate passion or other violent emotions. 3. To become red and painful from infection.—**in·flam·er** *n.*—**in·flam·ing·ly** *adv.*

in·flam·ma·ble (in-*flam*-uh-b'l) *adj.* 1. Capable of being set afire; readily kindled. 2. Violent; excitable; explosive.—*n.* Combustible material.—**in·flam·ma·bil·i·ty** (in-flam-uh-*bil*-it-ee) **in·flam·ma·ble·ness** *n.*— **-ma·bly** *adv.*

in·flam·ma·tion (in-fluh-*may*-shun) *n.* A redness or swelling in the body caused by infection.

in·flam·ma·to·ry (in-*flam*-uh-tor-ee) *adj.* 1. Tending to inflame or cause fire. 2. Inciting violent emotional reaction.

in·flate (in-*flayt*) *v.* [in·flat·ed; in·flat·ing] 1. To puff up; swell; distend. 2. To raise above real value; increase the volume of money without increasing its total value.—**in·flat·a·ble** *adj.*—**in·flat·er, in·flat·or** *n.*

in·fla·tion (in-*flay*-shun) *n.* 1. Increase in price above real value; expansion of credit or money. 2. Pompousness; conceit.—**in·fla·tion·ar·y** *adj.*

in·fla·tion·ism (in-*flay*-shun-izm) *n.* An economic policy of cheap money.—**in·fla·tion·ist** *n.*—**in·fla·tion·is·tic** (in-flay-shun-*iss*-tik) *adj.*

in·flect (in-*flekt*) *v.* 1. *Grammar.* To vary the ending of a word to change its tense, gender, number, etc. 2. To modulate, as the voice. 3. To bend.—**in·flec·tive** *adj.*—**in·flec·tor** *n.*

in·flec·tion (in-*flek*-shun) *n.* 1. Change in voice pitch or tone. 2. *Grammar.* Variation in word forms by word endings. 3. A bending or diffraction.—**in·flec·tion·al** *adj.*—**in·flec·tion·al·ly** *adv.*

in·flex·i·ble (in-*fleks*-ib-'l) *adj.* Rigid; unbending; firm; obstinate; unrelenting.—**in·flex·i·bil·i·ty** (in-fleks-ih-*bil*-it-ee), **in·flex·i·ble·ness** *n.* —**in·flex·i·bly** *adv.*

in·flict (in-*flikt*) *v.* To apply; impose; cause to experience or suffer.—**in·flic·tion** *n.* The act of administering punishment; imposition.—**in·flict·er, in·flict·or** *n.*—**in·flic·tive** *adj.*

in·flo·res·cence (in-flor-*ess*-enss) *n.* Flowering; arrangement of flowers on their stems.—**in·flo·res·cent** *adj.*

I

in·flu·ence (*in*-floo-enss) *n.* 1. Power; ability to produce an effect. 2. Authority; means of getting other persons to further one's interests. 3. A contributing factor.—*v.* [in·flu·enced; -enc·ing].—**in·flu·enc·er** *n.*

in·flu·en·tial (in-floo-*en*-shul) *adj.* Important; largely contributive.—**in·flu·en·tial·ly** *adv.*

in·flu·en·za (in-floo-*en*-zuh) *n.* Flu; a highly contagious respiratory disease caused by a filterable virus.

in·flux (*in*-fluhks) *n.* 1. Infusion; a flowing into. 2. The mouth of a stream.

in·fold (in-*fohld*) *v.* To clasp; embrace; wrap.

in·form (in-*form*) *v.* To tell; impart information.—**in·form·er** *n.* One whose information implicates or incriminates another.

in·for·mal (in-*form*-'l) *adj.* Unceremonious; not adhering to convention; casual.—**in·for·mal·i·ty** (in-for-*mal*-it-ee) *n.*—**in·for·mal·ly** *adv.*

in·form·ant (in-*form*-ent) *n.* A giver or divulger of information; informer.

in·for·ma·tion (in-fer-*may*-shun) *n.* 1. News; intelligence; knowledge. 2. Informing or communicating.—**in·for·ma·tion·al** *adj.*

in·form·a·tive (in-*form*-uh-tiv) *adj.* Communicating knowledge or information.

in·fra- (*in*-fruh) *prefix.* Beneath; lower than.

in·frac·tion (in-*frak*-shun) *n.* Violation; infringement; nonobservance.—**in·fract** *v.* To break, as a law.—**in·frac·tor** *n.*

in·fran·gi·ble (in-*fran*-jib-'l) *adj.* 1. Unbreakable; inseparable. 2. Not to be violated or infringed.—**in·fran·gi·bil·i·ty** (in-fran-jih-*bil*-ih-tee), **-ble·ness** *n.*—**in·fran·gi·bly** *adv.*

in·fra·red (*in*-fruh-red) *adj.* Denoting radiation the wave lengths of whose rays are greater than those of visible light rays.

in·fringe (in-*frinj*) *v.* [in·fringed; in·fring·ing] 1. To violate; transgress. 2. To hinder; hurt.—**in·fringe·ment** *n.*—**in·fring·er** *n.*

in·fu·ri·ate (in-*fyoor*-ee-ayt) *v.* [in·fu·ri·at·ed; -at·ing] To anger; enrage.—**in·fu·ri·ate·ly** *adv.*—**in·fu·ri·a·tion** (in-fyoor-ee-*ay*-shun) *n.*

in·fuse (in-*fyooz*) *v.* [in·fused; in·fus·ing] 1. To instill; put into; pour; introduce.—**in·fus·er** *n.*—**in·fu·sion** (in-*fyoo*-zhun) *n.*

in·fu·si·ble (in-*fyooz*-ib-'l) *adj.* Incapable of being fused, melted, or dissolved.—**in·fu·si·bil·i·ty** (in-fyooz-ih-*bil*-ih-tee) *n.*

in·gen·ious (in-*jeen*-yus) *adj.* 1. Skillful; inventive; resourceful; clever at devising. 2. Produced by unusual talent or cleverness.—**in·gen·ious·ly** *adv.*—**in·gen·ious·ness** *n.*

in·gé·nue (*an*-juh-noo) *n.* [*pl.* -nues] The role of a naïve young girl; an actress playing this part.

in·ge·nu·i·ty (in-jun-*oo*-it-ee) *n.* Cleverness; facility in invention; resourcefulness.

in·gen·u·ous (in-*jen*-yoo-us) *adj.* 1. Frank; candid; not dissimulating. 2. Honorable;

noble; generous.—**in·gen·u·ous·ly** *adv.*—**in·gen·u·ous·ness** *n.*

in·gest (in-*jest*) *v.* To take in, as food; swallow.—**in·ges·tion** (in-*jess*-chun) *n.*—**in·ges·tive** *adj.*

in·glo·ri·ous (in-*gloh*-ree-us) *adj.* Shameful; disgraceful; ignominious.—**in·glo·ri·ous·ly** *adv.*

in·got *n.* A bar or mass of unwrought metal.

in·graft. *Variant spelling* of **engraft.**

in·grain (in-*grayn*) *v.* To imbue or work in deeply; dye or impregnate thoroughly.—**in·grained** *adj.* Dyed-in-the-wool.

in·grate (*in*-grayt) *n.* An ungrateful person.

in·gra·ti·ate (in-*gray*-shee-ayt) *v.* [-at·ed; -at·ing] To insinuate oneself; commend oneself to another's attention.—**in·gra·ti·at·ing·ly** *adv.*—**in·gra·ti·a·tion** (in-gray-shee-*ay*-shun) *n.*

in·grat·i·tude (in-*grat*-ih-tood) *n.* Unthankfulness; ungratefulness.

in·gre·di·ent (in-*gree*-dee-ent) *n.* A component part of any compound; element.

in·gress (*in*-gress) *n.* Entrance.

in·grown (*in*-grohn) *adj.* Grown inward, esp. into the flesh.

in·gui·nal (*ing*-gwin-'l) *adj.* Of or near the groin.

in·gulf. *Variant spelling* of **engulf.**

in·hab·it (in-*hab*-it) *v.* To live or dwell in; make one's home in.—**in·hab·it·a·bil·i·ty** (in-hab-it-uh-*bil*-it-ee) *n.*—**in·hab·it·a·ble** *adj.*—**in·hab·i·ta·tion** (in-hab-ih-*tay*-shun) *n.*—**in·hab·it·er** *n.*

in·hab·i·tant *n.* One who lives in a place permanently.

in·hal·ant (in-*hayl*-ent) *adj.* Drawing or breathing in.—*n.* A medicine effective when breathed.

in·hale *v.* [in·haled; in·hal·ing] To draw, breathe, or suck into the lungs.—**in·hal·er** *n.* 1. A device aiding inhalation of medicinal vapors. 2. Gas mask; respirator. 3. Type of brandy glass.—**in·hal·a·tion** (in-huh-*lay*-shun) *n.*

in·here *v.* [in·hered; in·her·ing] To reside in as an inseparable quality; belong in.

in·her·ent (in-*heer*-'nt) *adj.* Innate; inseparable; inborn.—**in·her·ence** *n.*—**in·her·ent·ly** *adv.*

in·her·it (in-*hehr*-it) *v.* To receive by descent from an ancestor.—**in·her·it·a·bil·i·ty, in·her·it·a·ble·ness** *n.*—**in·her·it·a·ble** *adj.*—**in·her·i·tor** *n.*

in·her·i·tance (in-*hehr*-it-unss) *n.* 1. A characteristic or a property derived from one's ancestors; heritage. 2. The right of an heir to an estate.

in·hib·it (in-*hib*-it) *v.* 1. To hinder; repress; check. 2. To forbid; prohibit.—**in·hib·it·a·ble** *adj.*—**in·hib·i·ter, in·hib·i·tor** *n.*—**in·hib·i·tive, in·hib·i·to·ry** *adj.*

in·hi·bi·tion (in-hih-*bish*-'n) *n.* Repression; restraint; arresting of an activity.

in·hu·man (in-*hyoo*-m'n) *adj.* Cruel; unfeeling; savage.—**in·hu·man·ly** *adv.*—**in·hu·man·ness** *n.*

in·hu·man·i·ty *n.* Extreme cruelty.

---

in·hume (in-*hyoom*) *v.* [in·humed; in·hum·ing] To bury; inter.—**in·hu·ma·tion** *n.*

in·im·i·cal (in-*im*-ik-'l) *adj.* Hostile; unfriendly; harmful.—**in·im·i·cal·ly** *adv.*

in·im·i·ta·ble (in-*im*-ih-tuh-b'l) *adj.* Not to be copied or imitated; without peer.—**in·im·i·ta·bil·i·ty, -ble·ness** *n.*—**in·im·i·ta·bly** *adv.*

in·iq·ui·tous (in-*ik*-wit-us) *adj.* Wicked; unrighteous; unjust.— **-tous·ly** *adv.* **-tous·ness** *n.*

in·iq·ui·ty *n.* [*pl.* -ties] 1. A sin; grievous offense. 2. Foul dealing; injustice.

in·i·tial (in-*ish*-'l) *adj.* First; beginning.—*n.* The first letter of a name or word.—*v.* [-tialed, tialled; -tial·ing, -tial·ling] To sign or mark by initials.—**in·i·tial·ly** *adv.*

in·i·ti·ate (in-*ish*-ee-ayt) *v.* [-at·ed; -at·ing] 1. To introduce; begin. 2. To admit ceremoniously into a society. 3. To guide or direct by teaching of elementary principles. —**in·i·ti·a·tor** *n.*

in·i·ti·a·tion *n.* 1. Admission into an organization; rites and ceremonies of entrance. 2. Introduction; commencement.

in·i·ti·a·tive (in-*ish*-yuh-tiv) *n.* 1. Ability to take the lead or originate; aggressiveness, energy. 2. The first step; introductory act.—*adj.* Initiatory.—**in·i·ti·a·tive·ly** *adv.*

in·i·ti·a·to·ry (in-*ish*-yuh-tor-ee) *adj.* 1. Of, like, or appropriate to a beginning. 2. Introducing; initiating.—**in·i·ti·a·to·ri·ly** *adv.*

in·ject *v.* To put or squirt in; force in by mechanical means.—**in·jec·tion** *n.*—**in·jec·tor** *n.*

in·ju·di·cious (in-joo-*dish*-us) *adj.* Unwise; impolitic.—**in·ju·di·cious·ly** *adv.*

in·junc·tion (in-*junk*-sh'n) *n.* 1. *Law.* A writ or process by which a court commands the doing of, or refraining from, certain acts. 2. Command; direction; order.

in·jure (in-jer) *v.* [in·jured; in·jur·ing] To hurt; harm; impair; damage; grieve.—**in·jur·er** *n.*

in·ju·ri·ous (in-*joor*-ee-us) *adj.* Hurtful; harmful; unwholesome.— **-ous·ly** *adv.*— **-ous·ness** *n.*

in·ju·ry *n.* [*pl.* -ries] 1. A wound; physical hurt. 2. Damage; harm; detriment; loss.

ink *n.* A colored liquid used in writing and the graphic arts.—*v.* To mark or daub with ink. —**ink·er** *n.*

ink-blurred	inkpot	inkstain
ink-colored	inkslinger	inkstone
inkfish	ink-spotted	ink-written

ink·ling *n.* Hint; suspicion; intimation.

ink·stand *n.* Container for ink and pens.

ink·well *n.* A small receptacle for ink.

ink·y *adj.* [ink·i·er; ink·i·est] Of, like, or smeared with ink; black.—**ink·i·ness** *n.*

in·laid *adj.* Ornamented with decorative materials set in.

in·land (*in*-land; -lund) *n.* The interior of a country.—*adj.* (*in*-lund) 1. Interior; far from the sea. 2. Domestic; carried on within a country.—**in·land** *adv.*—**in·land·er** *n.*

in·law (*in*-law) *n.* A relative of one's mate.

in·lay *v.* [in·laid; in·lay·ing] To place or insert in; ornament by imbedding decorative materials.—*n.* 1. A metal or other substance used to insert or fill. 2. A semi-permanent tooth filling.—**in·lay·er** *n.*

in·let *n.* 1. A channel; small bay in a shore. 2. A narrow opening; entrance.

in·ly (*in*-lee) *adv.* Internally; inwardly.

in·mate *n.* 1. A person in a prison, asylum, or similar institution. 2. A dweller; occupant.

in memoriam (in mem-*or*-ee-um). In memory of.

in·most *adj.* Farthest in; remotest from the surface or external part.

inn *n.* Small hotel; lodging house for travelers.

in·nards (*in*-erdz) *n. pl. Colloquial.* The insides; internal organs of the body.

in·nate *adj.* Inborn; natural; inseparable.—**in·nate·ly** *adv.*—**in·nate·ness** *n.*

in·ner *adj.* 1. Internal; farther inward. 2. Not obvious; obscure.—*n.* The inside.

in·ner·most (*in*-er-mohst) *adj.* Farthest in.

in·ning *n.* 1. *Baseball.* A team's time at bat. 2. A period of prosperity or luck.

inn·keep·er *n.* Operator of an inn.

in·no·cence (*in*-uh-senss) *n.* Also **in·no·cen·cy.** 1. Freedom from guilt. 2. Naïveté; lack of worldly experience.

in·no·cent *adj.* 1. Not guilty; blameless. 2. Harmless; not injurious. 3. Pure; sinless; not worldly.—*n.* A pure, guiltless, naïve, or inoffensive person.—**in·no·cent·ly** *adv.*

in·noc·u·ous (in-*ok*-yoo-us) *adj.* Harmless.—**in·noc·u·ous·ly** *adv.*—**in·noc·u·ous·ness** *n.*

in·no·vate (*in*-noh-vayt) *v.* [-vat·ed; -vat·ing] To change by introducing a new factor; start something new.—**in·no·va·tive** *adj.*— **-va·tor** *n.*

in·no·va·tion *n.* A new fashion; novelty. 2. Initiation of something new.— **-tion·al** *adj.*

in·nu·en·do (in-yoo-*en*-doh) *n.* [*pl.* -does] A sly remark or hint; depreciatory insinuation.

in·nu·mer·a·ble (in-*yoo*-mer-uh-b'l) *adj.* Countless; myriad.— **-a·ble·ness** *n.*— **-a·bly** *adv.*

in·oc·u·la·ble *adj.* Capable of being transmitted by inoculation.

in·oc·u·late (in-*ok*-yoo-layt) *v.* [-lat·ed; -lat·ing] 1. To introduce a virus or microbe toxin into the body in small quantities for preventive, curative, or experimental reasons. 2. To infect; contaminate.—**in·oc·u·la·tion** *n.*—**in·oc·u·la·tive** *adj.*—**in·oc·u·la·tor** *n.*

in·of·fen·sive (in-uh-*fen*-siv) *adj.* Harmless; innocuous; mild.— **-sive·ly** *adv.*— **-sive·ness** *n.*

in·op·er·a·ble *adj.* 1. Not capable of operation. 2. *Surgical.* Not fit for operation.

in·op·er·a·tive (in-*op*-er-uh-tiv) *adj.* Not functioning; yielding no effect.— **-tive·ness** *n.*

I

in·op·por·tune (in-op-per-*toon*) *adj.* Inconvenient; unseasonable.— -tune·ly *adv.*

in·or·di·nate (in-*ord*-in-it) *adj.* Excessive; outlandish; irregular.—in·or·di·nate·ly *adv.*

in·or·gan·ic (in-or-*gan*-ik) *adj.* 1. Not living; not of or like an organism. 2. Relating to the branch of chemistry that deals with substances other than organic.

in·put *n.* 1. *Mechanics.* Amount of energy put into a machine. 2. Anything that is put in.

in·quest (*in*-kwest) *n. Law.* An inquiry conducted by a judge or coroner.

in·quire (in-*kwyre*) *v.* [in·quired; in·quir·ing] To ask; seek for information; investigate; examine.—in·quir·er *n.*—in·quir·ing·ly *adv.*

in·quir·y (in-*kwyre*-ee; in-kwir-ee) *n.* [*pl.* -ies] 1. A question; query. 2. Search for information; research; examination.

in·qui·si·tion (in-kwiz-*ish*-'n) *n.* 1. [*cap.*] *Roman Catholic Church.* A court for punishing heretics. 2. Any severe grilling or harsh method of questioning. 3. Inquiry; inquest; investigation.—in·qui·si·tion·al *adj.*—in·qui·si·tor, in·qui·si·tion·ist *n.*

in·quis·i·tive (in-*kwiz*-uh-tiv) *adj.* 1. Asking questions; addicted to inquiry. 2. Overly curious; prying.—in·quis·i·tive·ly *adv.*—in·quis·i·tive·ness *n.*

in·quis·i·to·ri·al (in-kwiz-uh-*tor*-ee-ul) *adj.* 1. Pertaining to or like an inquisitor; earnestly or cruelly questioning. 2. Relating to judicial proceedings in which the judge acts as prosecutor.— -al·ly *adv.*— -al·ness *n.*

in·road (*in*-rohd) *n.* Incursion; encroachment.

in·sal·i·vate (in-*sal*-iv-ayt) *v.* [-vat·ed; -vat·ing] To mix saliva with.—in·sal·i·va·tion *n.*

in·sane (in-*sayn*) *adj.* 1. Mentally deranged; crazy. 2. Pertaining to or used by deranged persons. 3. Foolish; impractical. 'An insane project.'—*n.* Crazy people collectively.—in·sane·ly *adv.*—in·sane·ness *n.*

in·san·i·ty (in-*san*-it-ee) *n.* 1. Mental disorder; madness. 2. Complete folly.

in·sa·ti·a·ble (in-*say*-shuh-b'l) *adj.* Incapable of being satisfied; infinitely greedy.—in·sa·ti·a·bil·i·ty, -a·ble·ness *n.*—in·sa·ti·a·bly *adv.*

in·sa·ti·ate (in-*say*-shee-it) *adj.* Incapable of satisfaction; always greedy.

in·scribe (in-*skrybe*) *v.* [in·scribed; in·scrib·ing] 1. To write on; engrave; mark with letters or other characters. 2. To commend, address, or assign. 3. To impress or print deeply. 4. *Geometry.* To draw one figure within another with all possible points in contact.—in·scrib·er *n.*

in·scrip·tion (in-*skrip*-shun) *n.* 1. The act of writing on or engraving. 2. The wording inscribed, as a dedication in a book.—in·scrip·tion·al *adj.*

in·scru·ta·ble (in-*scroo*-tuh-b'l) *adj.* Incapable of being understood; beyond comprehension; mysterious.—in·scru·ta·bil·i·ty, in·scru·ta·ble·ness *n.*—in·scru·ta·bly *adv.*

in·sect *n.* One of a class of small invertebrate animals having segmented bodies and jointed legs.

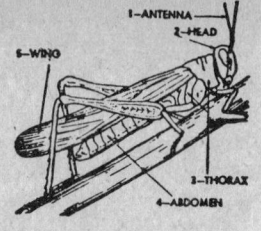

TYPICAL INSECT (Grasshopper)

in·sec·ti·cide (in-*sek*-tuh-syde) *n.* A poison designed to kill insects.

in·sec·tiv·o·rous (in-sek-*tiv*-er-us) *adj.* Feeding on insects.—in·sec·ti·vore (in-*sek*-tih-vohr) *n.* An animal that eats insects.

in·sen·sate (in-*sen*-sit) *adj.* 1. Unfeeling; inanimate. 2. Bestial; stupid.— -sate·ly *adv.*

in·sep·a·ra·ble (in-*sep*-ruh-b'l) *adj.* Permanently joined or united; indissoluble.—*n.* [*pl.*] Persons or things always found together.—in·sep·a·ra·bil·i·ty, -ble·ness *n.*—in·sep·a·ra·bly *adv.*

in·sert (in-*sert*) *v.* To set in or among; put or thrust in.—(*in*-sert) *n.* That which is added between or thrust into.—in·sert·er *n.*

in·ser·tion (in-*ser*-shun) *n.* 1. The thing set in, as lace among the plain materials of a dress. 2. A placing into or among other things. 3. *Advertising.* Each publication of an advertisement.

in·set (in-*set*) *v.* [in·set; in·set·ting] To set in; make an insertion.—*n.* (*in*-set) 1. Something inserted. 2. An inflow.

in·shore *adj. & adv.* Shoreward; near or toward the coast or beach.

in·side *prep.* Within; in.—*n.* 1. The interior. 2. [*pl.*] *Colloquial.* The inwards; internal organs or mechanisms.—*adj.* 1. Interior; internal. 2. *Colloquial.* Supposedly secret and authentic. 'Inside story.'—in·side *adv.*

in·sid·er *n.* One of a limited group; an intimate of a clique or circle, with confidential knowledge of its activities.

in·sid·i·ous (in-*sid*-ee-us) *adj.* Sly; pernicious; treacherous; entrapping.—in·sid·i·ous·ly *adv.*

in·sight (*in*-syte) *n.* Discernment; understanding.

in·sig·ni·a (in-*sig*-nee-uh) *n. pl.* [*sing.* in·sig·ne (in-*sig*-nee)] Badges; distinguishing marks.

in·sig·nif·i·cant (in-sig-*nif*-ik-unt) *adj.* 1. Unimportant; trivial. 2. Pitiful; puny; contemptible.—in·sig·nif·i·cance *n.*— -cant·ly *adv.*

in·sin·cere (in-sin-*seer*) *adj.* Deceitful; false; dissembling.—in·sin·cere·ly *adv.*— in·sin·cer·i·ty *n.*

MEDICAL CORPS

ORDNANCE

CHEMICAL WARFARE

SIGNAL CORPS AIR CORPS

INSIGNIA

in·sin·u·ate (in-*sin*-yoo-ayt) *v.* [-at·ed; -at·ing] 1. To introduce slyly or gradually. 'He insinuated himself into their confidence.' 2. To hint; suggest; intimate.—**in·sin·u·at·ing·ly** *adv.*—**in·sin·u·a·tion** *n.*—**in·sin·u·a·tive** *adj.*

in·sip·id (in-*sip*-id) *adj.* 1. Vapid; tasteless. 2. Lifeless; unanimated; characterless.—**in·si·pid·i·ty, in·sip·id·ness** *n.*—**in·sip·id·ly** *adv.*

in·sist (in-*sist*) *v.* To be persistent; be pressing; demand.

in·sis·tent (in-*siss*-tunt) *adj.* Persistent; unyielding; demanding.—**in·sis·tence, in·sis·ten·cy** *n.* —**in·sis·tent·ly** *adv.*

in·snare. *Variant spelling* of ensnare.

in·so·bri·e·ty (in-soh-*bry*-uh-tee) *n.* Drunkenness; intemperance.

in·sole (*in*-sohl) *n.* The inner sole of a shoe.

in·so·lent (*in*-suh-lunt) *adj.* Arrogant; overbearing; insulting; rude.—**in·so·lence** *n.*—**in·so·lent·ly** *adv.*

in·sol·vent (in-*sol*-vunt) *adj.* Bankrupt; unable to pay debts.—*n.* A bankrupt.—**in·sol·ven·cy** *n.*

in·som·ni·a (in-*som*-nee-uh) *n.* Inability to sleep; sleeplessness.—**in·som·ni·ous** *adj.*

in·so·much (in-soh-*much*) *adv.* So; to such a degree.

in·sou·ci·ance (in-*soo*-see-unss) *n.* Unconcern; indifference.—**in·sou·ci·ant** *adj.*— **-ant·ly** *adv.*

in·spect (in-*spekt*) *v.* 1. To examine; scrutinize; scan. 2. To examine with an official ceremony. 'Inspect troops.'—**in·spec·tion** *n.* —**in·spec·tion·al** *adj.*—**in·spec·tive** *adj.*

in·spec·tor (in-*spek*-ter) *n.* 1. One who examines or oversees. 2. A police officer.

in·spi·ra·tion (in-sper-*ay*-shun) *n.* 1. Any external influence which quickens and fires the mind or emotions. 2. *Theology.* A divine visitation or revelation. 3. Inhaling. 4. A highly awakened, creative state of mind.—**in·spi·ra·tion·al** *adj.*—**in·spi·ra·tion·al·ly** *adv.*

in·spire (in-*spyre*) *v.* [in·spired; in·spir·ing] 1. To animate; quicken; fill with inspiration. 2. To excite; cause in the mind. 'Inspire fear.' 3. To inhale.—**in·spir·er** *n.*—**in·spir·ing·ly** *adv.*

in·spir·it (in-*spihr*-it) *v.* To encourage; animate; infuse with life.—**in·spir·it·ing·ly** *adv.*

in·stall (in-*stawl*) *v.* 1. To induct into an office. 2. To put in and connect a fixture or piece of equipment.—**in·stal·la·tion** (in-stul-*ay*-shun) *n.*—**in·stall·er** *n.*

in·stall·ment, in·stal·ment *n.* 1. One of a number of successive parts. 2. One of the sections of a serial story or article. 3. One of a series of payments made over a period of time. 4. The ceremony of putting in office.

in·stance (*in*-stunss) *n.* 1. A time; occasion. 2. Example; case; sample. 3. Suggestion; initiative.—*v.* [in·stanced; in·stanc·ing] To cite; offer as illustration.

in·stant (*in*-stunt) *adj.* Immediate; without intervening time.—*n.* Moment; second.—**in·stant·ly** *adv.*

in·stan·ta·ne·ous (in-stan-*tay*-nee-us) *adj.* Immediate; done in an instant.—**in·stan·ta·ne·ous·ly** *adv.*—**in·stan·ta·ne·ous·ness** *n.*

in·stan·ter (in-*stan*-ter) *adv.* *Law.* Immediately; without delay.

in·stant·ly (*in*-stant-lee) *adv.* Immediately; directly; forthwith.

in·stead (in-*sted*) *adv.* In place of; rather than.

in·step (*in*-step) *n.* The upper, arching side of the human foot.

in·sti·gate (*in*-stih-gayt) *v.* [-gat·ed; -gat·ing] To incite; provoke; set on.—**in·sti·ga·tion** (in-stih-*gay*-shun) *n.*— **-ga·tive** *adj.*— **-ga·tor** *n.*

in·still, in·stil (in-*stil*) *v.* [in·stilled; in·still·ing] To inculcate; implant; infuse.—**in·stil·la·tion** (in-stil-*ay*-shun) *n.*—**in·still·er** *n.*

in·stinct (*in*-stinkt) *n.* A natural and inborn urge or motivation.—**in·stinct** *adj.*

in·stinc·tive (in-*stink*-tiv) *adj.* Spontaneous; automatic; habitual.—**in·stinc·tive·ly** *adv.*

in·sti·tute (*in*-stih-toot) *v.* [-tut·ed; -tut·ing] To establish; found; set up.—*n.* 1. An organization; institution; public establishment; society. 2. [*pl.*] A book dealing with the basic principles of a subject.—**in·sti·tu·ter, -tu·tor** *n.*

in·sti·tu·tion (in-stih-*too*-shun) *n.* 1. Establishment; public foundation; society. 2. Established method or custom. 3. Founding; setting up.—**in·sti·tu·tion·al** *adj.*—**in·sti·tu·tion·al·ize** *v.* [-al·ized; -al·iz·ing]— **-al·ly** *adv.*

in·struct (in-*strukt*) *v.* [in·struct·ed; in·struct·ing] 1. To teach; educate. 2. To direct; order.—**in·struc·tion** *n.*—**in·struc·tion·al** *adj.*

in·struc·tive *adj.* Enlightening; informative. —**-tive·ly** *adv.*— **-tive·ness** *n.*

in·struc·tor *n.* A teacher, esp. a college teacher below the rank of assistant professor.

in·stru·ment (*in*-struh-m'nt) *n.* 1. A tool; implement. 2. Means; agency; vehicle. 3. Any musical apparatus. 4. *Law.* A document, contract, writ, etc.

in·stru·men·tal (in-struh-*men*-t'l) *adj.* 1. Useful; prominently contributive; serving as a means. 2. Pertaining to a musical instrument. 3. Pertaining to a tool. 4. *Grammar.* Pertaining to a mood expressing means or way. — **-tal·i·ty** (-men-*tal*-ih-tee) *n.*— **-tal·ly** *adv.*

in·stru·men·ta·tion *n.* *Music.* Arrangement of music for a group of instruments.

in·sub·or·di·nate (in-sub-*or*-din-it) *adj.* Recalcitrant; unruly; ungovernable.— **-nate·ly** *adv.* —**in·sub·or·di·na·tion** (in-sub-or-din-*ay*-shun) *n.*

in·suf·fer·a·ble (in-*suf*-er-uh-b'l) *adj.* 1. Intolerable; unendurable. 2. *Colloquial.* Detestable.— **-a·ble·ness** *n.*— **-a·bly** *adv.*

in·su·lar (*in*-suh-ler) *adj.* 1. Pertaining to an island. 2. Narrow; provincial; intolerant. —**in·su·lar·i·ty** (in-suh-*lair*-it-ee) *n.*

in·su·late (*in*-suh-layt) *v.* [in·su·lat·ed; in·su·lat·ing] 1. To isolate; segregate; keep apart. 2. To seal against conductance of temperature, electricity, sound, etc., by the interposing of non-conducting material.—**in·su·la·tion** (in-suh-*lay*-shun) *n.* 1. Sealing against transferral of atmosphere, electricity, etc. 2. Non-conducting material used for insulating.

in·su·la·tor *n.* A device, usually of glass or porcelain, used to prevent passage of electric current.

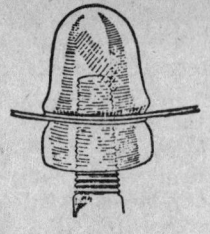

INSULATOR

in·su·lin (*in*-suh-lin) *n.* 1. [*cap.*] A trade-mark for a pancreatic extract used in the treatment of diabetes. 2. The secretion of the islands of Langerhans in the pancreas promoting the oxidation of sugar.

in·sult (in-*sult*) *v.* To affront; outrage; offend. —in·sult (*in*-sult) *n.*—in·sult·er *n.*—in·sult·ing *adj.*—in·sult·ing·ly *adv.*

in·su·per·a·ble (in-*soo*-per-uh-b'l) *adj.* Insurmountable; unconquerable.—in·su·per·a·bil·i·ty (in-soo-per-uh-*bil*-it-ee) *n.*— -a·bly *adv.*

in·sur·a·ble (in-*shoor*-uh-b'l) *adj.* Capable of being insured against loss, injury, death, etc. —in·sur·a·bil·i·ty (in-shoor-uh-*bil*-it-ee) *n.*

in·sur·ance (in-*shoor*-unss) *n.* 1. A contract by which a company, in consideration of a sum of money or percentage, agrees to indemnify the insured against loss by certain risks. 2. The business of an insurance firm. 3. The premium which one's insurance costs. 4. The amount for which one is insured.

in·sure (in-*shoor*) *v.* [in·sured; in·sur·ing]. Also **ensure.** To safeguard; secure against possible loss or damage.—in·sured *n.*—in·sur·er *n.*

in·sur·gent (in-*ser*-junt) *adj.* Rebellious; insubordinate.—in·sur·gent *n.*— -gence, -gen·cy *n.*

in·sur·rec·tion (in-ser-*ek*-shun) *n.* Rebellion; uprising.—in·sur·rec·tion·ar·y *adj.* & *n.*—in·sur·rec·tion·ist *n.*

in·tact (in-*takt*) *adj.* Whole; entire; complete.

in·tagl·io (in-*tal*-yoh) *n.* [*pl.* -ios, -i] Sunken relief from which a raised relief may be impressed, as in sealing-wax.

in·take (*in*-tayk) *n.* 1. Consumption; amount absorbed. 2. Point of reception of a fluid. 3. Suction. 4. Contraction; shrinking.

in·tan·gi·ble (in-*tan*-jib-'l) *adj.* Impalpable; imperceptible; incapable of being touched. —in·tan·gi·ble *n.*—in·tan·gi·bil·i·ty (in-tan-jih-*bil*-it-ee), -ble·ness *n.*—in·tan·gi·bly *adv.*

in·te·ger (*in*-teh-jer) *n. Arithmetic.* A whole number.

in·te·gral (*in*-teh-grul) *adj.* 1. Composite; entire; complete. 2. Constituent; essential. 3. *Mathematics.* Relating to whole numbers. —*n.* A whole.—in·te·gral·ly *adv.*

in·te·grate (*in*-teh-grayt) *v.* [-grat·ed; -grat·ing] To fuse; combine; unite into a whole.—in·te·gra·tive *adj.*—in·te·gra·tion *n.*—in·te·gra·tor *n.*

in·teg·ri·ty (in-*teg*-rit-ee) *n.* 1. Wholeness; entireness. 2. Honesty; uprightness.

in·teg·u·ment (in-*teg*-yuh-m'nt) *n.* A skin; covering.—in·teg·u·men·ta·ry *adj.*

in·tel·lect (*in*-t'l-ekt) *n.* 1. Power to know or comprehend; understanding. 2. Person of great mental powers.—in·tel·lec·tive *adj.*—in·tel·lec·tive·ly *adv.*

in·tel·lec·tu·al (in-t'l-*ek*-choo-ul) *adj.* 1. Mental; performed by or pertaining to the mind. 2. Having or requiring great mental powers. —*n.* Person having or presuming to have a high degree of intelligence.—in·tel·lec·tu·al·i·ty *n.*—in·tel·lec·tu·al·ly *adv.*

in·tel·lec·tu·al·ism *n.* 1. Intellectual nature. 2. The doctrine that all knowledge derives from reason.— -al·ist *n.*— -al·is·tic *adj.*

in·tel·li·gence (in-*tel*-uh-junss) *n.* 1. The mind, esp. its capacity to deal with new situations or problems. 2. News; information.

intelligence department. The government department whose task is obtaining information necessary to the successful operation of its army and navy.

intelligence quotient. Also **IQ.** *Psychology.* Number indicating a person's mental capacity.

in·tel·li·gent (in-*tel*-uh-junt) *adj.* Having intelligence; clever; mentally alert or aware. —in·tel·li·gent·ly *adv.*

in·tel·li·gent·si·a (in-tel-uh-*jent*-see-uh) *n.* Intellectuals as a group.

in·tel·li·gi·ble (in-*tel*-ij-uh-b'l) *adj.* Understandable; clear; comprehensible.—in·tel·li·gi·bil·i·ty *n.*—in·tel·li·gi·bly *adv.*

in·tem·per·ate (in-*tem*-per-it) *adj.* 1. Addicted to excessive use of alcoholic liquor. 2. Excessive; immoderate; violent.—in·tem·per·ate·ly *adv.*—in·tem·per·ance, in·tem·per·ate·ness *n.*

in·tend (in-*tend*) *v.* To mean; be determined; plan.

in·tend·ant (in-*ten*-d'nt) *n.* A superintendent; manager.—in·ten·dan·cy *n.*

in·tend·ed *adj.* Meant; proposed; prospective. —*n. Colloquial.* A betrothed.

in·tense (in-*tenss*) *adj.* 1. Concentrated; in an extreme degree; strained. 2. Violent; ardent; earnest.—in·tense·ly *adv.*—in·tense·ness *n.*

in·ten·si·fy (in-*ten*-suh-fye) *v.* [-fied; -fy·ing] To heighten; make intense; enhance.— -fi·ca·tion (in-ten-suh-fih-*kay*-sh'n) *n.*— -fi·er *n.*

in·ten·si·ty (in-*ten*-suh-tee) *n.* [*pl.* -ties] 1. Extreme strength or severity; high degree. 2. Violence; earnestness. 3. *Physics.* The amount or degree of force of electricity, radiation, or other manifestations of energy.

in·ten·sive (in-*ten*-siv) *adj.* 1. Assiduous; thorough; marked by intensity; unremitting. 2. *Grammar.* Giving emphasis. —*n.* An intensive word, as *very.*—in·ten·sive·ly *adv.*—in·ten·sive·ness *n.*

in·tent (in-*tent*) *adj.* Engrossed; absorbed; fixed attentively.—*n.* Purpose; object; significance. —in·tent·ly *adv.*—in·tent·ness *n.*

in·ten·tion (in-*ten*-sh'n) *n.* 1. Aim; purpose; determination. 2. [*pl.*] *Colloquial.* Marital aim or object. 'His intentions are honorable.'

in·ten·tion·al *adj.* Deliberate; intended; willful. —in·ten·tion·al·ly *adv.*

in·ter (in-*tur*) *v.* [in·terred; in·ter·ring] To bury.

in·ter- *Prefix.* Among; between; together; intermediate; mutual; reciprocal.

interagree	interknit
interallied	interknot
inter-Allied	interlaminate
inter-American	interlay
inter-Andean	interleave
interatomic	interlink
interblend	intermesh
interbonding	intermigration
intercellular	intermingle
interchapter	intermolecular
interchurch	intermunicipal
intercollege	internode
intercollegiate	interoceanic
intercolonial	interosculate
intercolumnar	interplanetary
intercommunicate	interplay
interconnection	interpolar
intercontinental	interracial
intercross	interscholastic
intercurrent	intersexual
interdenominational	interstellar
interdental	interstratify
interdepartmental	interterritorial
interflow	intertribal
interfold	intertwine
intergrow	intertwist
intergrowth	interwreathe
interjoin	inter-war

in·ter·act *v.* To influence one another.—**in·ter·ac·tion** *n.*—Mutual effect.

in·ter·breed *v.* To breed by crossing one variety of animals or plant with another.

in·ter·cede (in-ter-*seed*) *v.* [-ced·ed; -ced·ing] 1: To mediate; intervene. 2. To plead or beg in another's behalf.—**in·ter·ced·er** *n.*—**in·ter·ces·sion** *n.*—**in·ter·ces·sor** *n.*—**-ces·so·ry** *adj.*

in·ter·cept (in-ter-*sept*) *v.* To stop on its passage; seize while en route.—**in·ter·cep·tion** *n.*—**in·ter·cep·tive** *adj.*

in·ter·change *v.* [-changed; -chang·ing] 1. To exchange; reciprocate; give and take. 2. To vary; intermingle.—*n.* Exchange; interspersing.—**in·ter·chang·er** *n.*

in·ter·change·a·ble *adj.* Readily changed or substituted for another.—**in·ter·change·a·bil·i·ty, -ble·ness** *n.*—**in·ter·change·a·bly** *adv.*

in·ter·cos·tal (in-ter-*koss*-tul) *adj. Anatomy.* Located between the ribs.—**in·ter·cos·tal·ly** *adv.*

in·ter·course (*in*-ter-korss) *n.* 1. Communication; commerce; dealings. 2. Sexual union.

in·ter·de·pend·ence *n.* Mutual dependence.—**in·ter·de·pend·ent** *adj.*— **-de·pend·ent·ly** *adv.*

in·ter·dict *n.* A prohibition; decree forbidding an act.—*v.* To prohibit; forbid.—**in·ter·dic·tion** *n.*—**in·ter·dic·tive** *adj.*—**in·ter·dic·tor** *n.* **in·ter·dic·to·ry** *adj.*

in·ter·est *n.* 1. Premium paid for the use of money. 2. Advantage; benefit. 3. Share; part use of money. 4. Concern; regard; sympathy. 5. Lack of boredom; attention. 6. Persons or corporations in a specific phase of industry.—**in·ter·est** *v.*

in·ter·est·ed *adj.* 1. Affected; moved. 2. Concerned in a cause; liable to be biased by personal considerations.—**in·ter·est·ed·ly** *adv.*

in·ter·est·ing *adj.* Holding the attention; exciting the imagination.—**in·ter·est·ing·ly** *adv.*

in·ter·fere (in-ter-*feer*) *v.* [-fered, -fer·ing] 1. To meddle; intervene; intrude. 2. To conflict with. 3. *Sports.* To jostle or hinder another player.— **-fer·er** *n.*— **-fer·ing·ly** *adv.*

in·ter·fer·ence (in-ter-*feer*-'nss) *n.* 1. Meddling; intrusion. 2. *Physics.* The mutual action of waves of any sort upon each other. 3. *Sports.* A deliberate jostling or colliding with another player.

in·ter·fuse (in-ter-*fyooz*) *v.* [-fused; -fus·ing] 1. Intermix; cause to flow together or blend. 2. To permeate; diffuse through.—**in·ter·fu·sion** *n.*

in·ter·im *n.* The meanwhile; time between.—**in·ter·im** *adj.*

in·te·ri·or (in-*teer*-ee-er) *adj.* 1. Internal; inside. 2. Inland; remote from the frontier or coast.—*n.* The inside; inland; internal affairs of a nation.—**in·te·ri·or·i·ty** *n.*— **-or·ly** *adv.*

in·ter·ject *v.* To insert; introduce; throw in. —**in·ter·jec·tor** *n.*— **-to·ri·ly** *adv.*— **-to·ry** *adj.*

in·ter·jec·tion (in-ter-*jek*-sh'n) *n.* An exclamation; a word suddenly expressing some emotion.—**in·ter·jec·tion·al** *adj.*— **-tion·al·ly** *adv.*

in·ter·lace (in-ter-*layss*) *v.* [-laced; -lac·ing] To unite; intertwine.—**in·ter·lace·ment** *n.*

in·ter·lard (in-ter-*lahrd*) *v.* To mix in irrelevant or unrelated material; vary by interspersing.

in·ter·line (in-ter-*lyne*) *v.* [-lined; -lin·ing] To provide an additional lining between the lining and the outside of a garment.—**in·ter·lin·ing** *n.*

in·ter·line *v.* [in·ter·lined; in·ter·lin·ing] To write between written or printed lines.—**in·ter·lin·e·ar** *adj.*—**in·ter·lin·e·a·tion** *n.*

in·ter·lock (in-ter-*lok*) *v.* To connect by linking together; overlap.—**in·ter·lock·ing** *adj.*

in·ter·loc·u·tor (in-ter-*lok*-yuh-ter) *n.* 1. One who speaks questions in a dialogue. 2. In a minstrel show, the person whose questions elicit the end men's humor.— **-loc·u·to·ry** *adj.*

in·ter·lop·er (*in*-ter-loh-per) *n.* An intruder; interferer.

in·ter·lude (*in*-ter-lood) *n.* 1. An intervening time between two events. 2. A short entertainment between the acts of a play or other parts of a performance.

in·ter·mar·riage (in-ter-*mair*-ij) *n.* Marriage between members of different races, tribes, or creeds.—**in·ter·mar·ry** *v.* [-mar·ried; -mar·ry·ing].

in·ter·med·dle (in-ter-*med*-'l) *v.* [·med·dled; -med·dling] To interfere; intrude in others' affairs.—**in·ter·med·dler** *n.*

in·ter·me·di·ar·y (in-ter-*mee*-dee-ehr-ee) *n.* [*pl.* -ies] An agent; mediator; contact man.—*adj.* Serving as a go-between.

in·ter·me·di·ate (in-ter-*mee*-dee-it) *adj.* In the middle place or degree; coming between.—*n.* An intermediary.—**in·ter·me·di·ate·ly** *adv.*—**in·ter·me·di·ate·ness** *n.*

in·ter·ment (in-*ter*-m'nt) *n.* Burial of the dead.

in·ter·mez·zo (in-ter-*met*-soh) *n.* [*pl.* -zi, -zos] A short, sparkling ballet or composition performed between the acts of a major work.

in·ter·mi·na·ble (in-*ter*-min-uh-b'l) *adj.* Endless; unlimited; boundless.— **-na·bly** *adv.*

in·ter·mis·sion (in-ter-*mish*-'n) *n.* Cessation for a time; pause, esp. between two parts of a dramatic or literary work.

in·ter·mit·tent (in-ter-*mit*-'nt) *adj.* Ceasing at intervals; periodic.—**in·ter·mit·tence, in·ter·mit·ten·cy** *n.*—**in·ter·mit·tent·ly** *adv.*

in·ter·mix (in-ter-*miks*) *v.* To combine by mixing together.—**in·ter·mix·ture** *n.*

in·tern (in-*tern*) *v.* To confine, as within an area or country; detain on suspicion, esp. during wartime.—**in·tern·ment** *n.*

in·tern (*in*-tern) *n.* Also **interne.** A medical graduate who resides and serves in a hospital prior to obtaining his doctor's license.—**in·tern** *v.*—**in·tern·ship** *n.*

in·ter·nal (in-*ter*-n'l) *adj.* 1. Inner; interior; inward. 2. Domestic; national. 3. To be taken inwardly, as medicine.—*n.* [*pl.*] The organs inside the body.—**in·ter·nal·i·ty** *n.*

internal-combustion engine. An engine in which timed explosions of fuel vapors in a cylinder furnish motive power.

in·ter·na·tion·al (in-ter-*nash*-uh-n'l) *adj.* Pertaining to or affecting more than one nation. —*n.* [*cap.*] Any one of several international workers' organizations.—**in·ter·na·tion·al·ize** *v.* [-al·ized; -al·iz·ing]—**in·ter·na·tion·al·ly** *adv.*

Internationale, The. A revolutionary workingmen's song, formerly the national anthem of the USSR.

in·ter·na·tion·al·ism *n.* Belief in co-operation among nations.—**in·ter·na·tion·al·ist** *n.*

in·terne. *Variant spelling* of **intern.**

in·ter·ne·cine (in-ter-*nee*-sin) *adj.* Mutually destructive; deadly.

in·ter·pel·late (in-ter-*pel*-ayt) *v.* [-lat·ed; -lat·ing] To question in formal procedure, as an official action.— **-la·tion** *n.*— **-la·tor** *n.*

in·ter·pen·e·trate (in-ter-*pen*-uh-trayt) *v.* [-trat·ed; -trat·ing] To penetrate deeply or mutually. —**in·ter·pen·e·tra·tion** *n.*

in·ter·play *n.* Reciprocal action or influence.

in·ter·po·late (in-*ter*-poh-layt) *v.* [-lat·ed; -lat·ing] 1. To insert, as a word, passage, etc. 2. To change by inserting new material. 3. *Mathematics.* To introduce intermediate terms in, as to complete a series.—**in·ter·po·la·ter, in·ter·po·la·tor** *n.*—**in·ter·po·la·tion** *n.*

in·ter·pose (in-ter-*pohz*) *v.* [-posed; -pos·ing] 1. To introduce or thrust between. 2. To intervene; intercede. 3. To interrupt.—**in·ter·pos·er** *n.*—**in·ter·pos·ing·ly** *adv.*—**in·ter·po·si·tion** (in-ter-puh-*zish*-'n) *n.*

in·ter·pret (in-*ter*-pret) *v.* 1. To elucidate; explain; translate. 2. To understand; construe. —**in·ter·pret·a·bil·i·ty** *n.*—**in·ter·pret·a·ble** *adj.* —**in·ter·pret·ive** *adj.*—**in·ter·pre·tive·ly** *adv.*

in·ter·pre·ta·tion (in-ter-pruh-*tay*-sh'n) *n.*

1. Explanation; translation. 2. One's characteristic conception or treatment of a theme or artistic work.—**in·ter·pre·ta·tion·al** *adj.*—**in·ter·pre·ta·tive** *adj.*—**in·ter·pre·ta·tive·ly** *adv.*

in·ter·pret·er *n.* A translator; one who explains or expounds.

in·ter·reg·num (-*reg*-num) *n.* [*pl.* -na] 1. The period between the reigns of two successive rulers; time during which a country lacks a government. 2. Pause; break.

in·ter·re·lat·ed *adj.* Mutually connected.—**in·ter·re·la·tion·ship** *n.*

in·ter·ro·gate (in-*tair*-uh-gayt) *v.* [-gat·ed; -gat·ing] To question; examine; query.—**in·ter·ro·gat·ing·ly** *adv.*—**in·ter·ro·ga·tion** *n.*—**in·ter·ro·ga·tion·al** *adj.*—**in·ter·ro·ga·tor** *n.*

in·ter·ro·ga·tion point, mark (in-tair-uh-*gay*-sh'n) *n.* The sign [?] indicating that the sentence it follows is a question.

in·ter·rog·a·tive (in-ter-*rog*-uh-tiv) *adj.* Asking or expressing a question.—*n.* Word which asks a question, as *who?*, *which?*, *why?*.—**in·ter·rog·a·tive·ly** *adv.*

in·ter·rog·a·to·ry *adj.* Asking a question; questioning.—*n.* A question or questioning.—**in·ter·rog·a·to·ri·ly** *adv.*

in·ter·rupt *v.* 1. To break the uniformity or motion of. 2. To break in upon; check, as a conversation.—**in·ter·rup·ter** *n.*—**in·ter·rup·tion** *n.*—**in·ter·rup·tive** *adj.*

in·ter·sect *v.* To cut across; cross mutually.

in·ter·sec·tion (in-ter-*sek*-sh'n) *n.* 1. Place where lines, roads, etc., cross. 2. Act of cutting across.—**in·ter·sec·tion·al** *adj.*

in·ter·sperse *v.* [-spersed; -spers·ing] To scatter or place among others; vary at random.—**in·ter·spers·ed·ly** *adv.*—**in·ter·sper·sion** *n.*

in·ter·state *adj.* Relating to, or between, different states. 'Interstate commerce.'

in·ter·stice (in-*ter*-stiss) *n.* [*pl.* -sti·ces] A narrow space between parts; crevice.—**in·ter·sti·tial** (in-ter-*stish*-'l) *adj.*—**in·ter·sti·tial·ly** *adv.*

in·ter·ur·ban (in-ter-*er*-b'n) *adj.* Between cities.

in·ter·val (*in*-ter-v'l) *n.* 1. A space or distance between conditions or objects. 2. Space of time between two definite dates or events. 3. *Music.* The relation of the pitch of two given tones.

in·ter·vene (in-ter-*veen*) *v.* [-vened; -ven·ing] 1. To come or fall between; lie between. 2. To intercede; come into for the purpose of settling, as a dispute.—**in·ter·ven·er, in·ter·ven·or** *n.*—**in·ter·ven·tion** (-in-ter-*ven*-sh'n) *n.*—**in·ter·ven·tion·al** *adj.*—**in·ter·ven·tion·ist** *n.*

in·ter·view (*in*-ter-vyoo) *v.* To question a person as to his views, background, or qualifications for purposes of publication or employment.—*n.* 1. A meeting for the purpose of interviewing someone. 2. A written report of such a meeting.—**in·ter·view·er** *n.*

in·ter·weave (in-ter-*weev*) *v.* [-wove; -wov·en or -wove; -weav·ing] To unite or connect intimately; intermix.

in·tes·tate (in-*tess*-tit) *adj.* Having made no valid will.—*n.* One who dies without making a will.—**in·tes·ta·cy** *n.*

in·tes·tine (in-*tess*-tin) *adj.* Internal.—*n.* The tube which extends from the stomach to the anus and plays a vital part in the digestive process.—**in·tes·tin·al** *adj.*

in·ti·ma·cy (*in*-tuh-muh-see) *n.* [*pl.* -cies] 1. Intimate friendship or association; comradeship. 2. [*pl.*] Sexual relations.

in·ti·mate (*in*-tuh-mit) *adj.* 1. Familiar; close; closely united or associated. 2. Personal; private. 3. Having sexual relations.—*n.* A confidant; comrade.—**in·ti·mate·ly** *adv.*—**in·ti·mate·ness** *n.*

in·ti·mate (*in*-tuh-mayt) *v.* [-mat·ed; -mat·ing] To hint; suggest.—**in·ti·mat·er** *n.*—**in·ti·ma·tion** *n.*

in·tim·i·date (in-*tim*-uh-dayt) *v.* [-dat·ed; -dat·ing] To deter through fear; terrorize; frighten; browbeat.—**in·tim·i·da·tion, in·tim·i·da·tor** *n.*

in·to (*in*-too) *prep.* 1. To the interior or inside of. 2. To the state or form of. 'Changed into glass.'

in·tol·er·a·ble (in-*tol*-er-uh-b'l) *adj.* Unbearable; insufferable; not endurable.—**in·tol·er·a·bil·i·ty, -ble·ness** *n.*—**in·tol·er·a·bly** *adv.*

in·tol·er·ance (in-*tol*-er-'nss) *n.* Dogmatism; bigotry; inability to tolerate or endure, as beliefs or opinions of others.

in·tol·er·ant (in-*tol*-er-'nt) *adj.* Dogmatic; narrow-minded; showing or marked by intolerance.—**in·tol·er·ant·ly** *adv.*

in·to·na·tion (in-toh-*nay*-sh'n) *n.* 1. The style or manner of sounding tones or words; rise and fall of the voice. 2. Act of intoning.

in·tone (in-*tohn*) *v.* [in·toned; in·ton·ing] To utter, or modulate the voice, in a singsong or monotonous way.—**in·ton·er** *n.*

in·tox·i·cant (in-*tok*-sih-k'nt) *adj.* Producing drunkenness.—*n.* An intoxicating liquor.

in·tox·i·cate (in-*tok*-sih-kayt) *v.* [-cat·ed; -cat·ing] 1. To make drunk. 2. To excite or elate beyond control.—*adj.* Drunk.—**in·tox·i·ca·tive** *adj.*—**in·tox·i·ca·tor** *n.*

in·tox·i·ca·tion (in-tok-sih-*kay*-sh'n) *n.* Drunkenness; frenzy; wild exhilaration.

in·tra- (*in*-truh) *prefix.* Within; inside.

    intracellular   intramolecular   intratelluric
    intramarginal intramuscular   intravenous

in·trac·ta·ble (in-*trak*-tuh-b'l) *adj.* Ungovernable; stubborn; unruly.—**in·trac·ta·bil·i·ty, in·trac·ta·ble·ness** *n.*—**in·trac·ta·bly** *adv.*

in·tra·mu·ral (in-truh-*myoo*-r'l) *adj.* 1. Played between teams from the same institution. 2. Limited to or within boundaries or walls.

in·tran·si·gent (in-*tran*-suh-junt) *adj.* Uncompromising; politically radical or irreconcilable.—*n.* A radical.—**in·tran·si·gence, in·tran·si·gen·cy** *n.*—**in·tran·si·gent·ly** *adv.*

in·tran·si·tive (in-*tran*-suh-tiv) *adj.* *Grammar.* Denoting a class of verbs which do not take a direct object.—**in·tran·si·tive·ly** *adv.*

in·tra·state (in-truh-*stayt*) *adj.* Within the borders of a state.

in·trench (in-*trench*) *v.* 1. To dig or fortify with trenches; furrow. 2. To encroach; trespass.—**in·trench·er** *n.*—**in·trench·ment** *n.*

in·trep·id (in-*trep*-id) *adj.* Brave; valiant; dauntless.—**in·tre·pid·i·ty** *n.*—**in·trep·id·ly** *adv.*

in·tri·ca·cy (*in*-truh-kuh-see) *n.* [*pl.* -cies] Complication; entanglement; perplexity.

in·tri·cate (*in*-truh-kit) *adj.* Highly involved; complicated; hard to understand.— **-cate·ly** *adv.*

in·trigue (in-*treeg*) *v.* [in·trigued; in·tri·guing] 1. To plot; scheme; contrive underhandedly. 2. To captivate; excite the interest or curiosity of.—*n.* 1. Plotting or scheming by complicated and underhand means; secret plot. 2. A secret or illicit love affair.—**in·tri·guer** *n.*—**in·tri·guing·ly** *adv.*

in·trin·sic (in-*trin*-sik) *adj.* Also **in·trin·si·cal**. 1. Inherent; belonging by nature; essential. 2. Internal.—**in·trin·si·cal·ly** *adv.*

in·tro- (*in*-troh) *prefix.* Within; into.

in·tro·duce (in-truh-*dyoos*) *v.* [in·tro·duced; -duc·ing] 1. To make known or acquainted; present, esp. formally. 2. To bring into fashion or use; bring or usher in. 3. To lead up to or begin, as a topic. 4. To insert.—**in·tro·duc·er** *n.*—**in·tro·duc·tive** *adj.*

in·tro·duc·tion (in-truh-*duk*-sh'n) *n.* 1. A making known; ushering in; bringing into use or practice. 2. A preface; preliminary discourse, as of a book.—**in·tro·duc·to·ry** *adj.*—**in·tro·duc·tor·i·ly** *adv.*

in·tro·spect (in-truh-*spekt*) *v.* To examine one's own thoughts and feelings; look within oneself.—**in·tro·spec·tion** *n.*—**in·tro·spec·tive** *adj.*—**in·tro·spec·tive·ly** *adv.*

in·tro·ver·sion (in-truh-*ver*-zhun) *n.* A condition in which all interests or desires are directed inward; inclination to live within oneself.—**in·tro·ver·sive** *adj.*

in·tro·vert (*in*-truh-vert) *n.* One completely absorbed in his own thoughts and dreams to the exclusion of the outer world.—*v.* (in-truh-*vert*) To turn inward; be unduly concerned with one's own thoughts.—**in·tro·vert** *adj.*

in·trude (in-*trood*) *v.* [in·trud·ed; in·trud·ing] To force, esp. oneself, upon; enter when unwelcome or uninvited.—**in·trud·er** *n.*

in·tru·sion (in-*troo*-zhun) *n.* Entry without welcome or invitation.—**in·tru·sive** *adj.*—**in·tru·sive·ly** *adv.*—**in·tru·sive·ness** *n.*

in·trust. *Variant spelling* of **entrust.**

in·tu·i·tion *n.* The supposed power of the mind to grasp a truth without recourse to reason; knowledge by quick apprehension.—**in·tu·i·tion·al** *adj.*

in·tu·i·tive *adj.* 1. Able to discover truth without reasoning. 2. Perceived or marked by intuition.—**in·tu·i·tive·ly** *adv.*— **-tive·ness** *n.*

in·un·date *v.* [in·un·dat·ed; -dat·ing] To flood; submerge; overflow.— **-da·tion** *n.*— **-da·tor** *n.*

in·ure v. [in·ured; in·ur·ing] To make or become used or hardened to; accustom.—**in·ure·ment** n.

in·vade v. [in·vad·ed; in·vad·ing] 1. To enter with a view to conquer or rob. 2. To encroach on; violate.—**in·vad·er** n.

in·va·lid (*in*-vuh-lid) adj. Unhealthy; weak; of, or suitable for, one who is ill.—n. A chronically sick or bedridden person.—v. To make an invalid of; retire or dismiss because of sickness.—**in·va·lid·ism** n.

in·val·id (in-*val*-id) adj. Not legal or effective; null and void; having no force.—**in·va·lid·i·ty** n.

in·val·i·date (in-*val*-ih-dayt) v. [in·val·i·dat·ed; -dat·ing] To nullify; render ineffective or void. —**in·val·i·da·tion** n.—**in·val·i·da·tor** n.

in·val·u·a·ble (in-*val*-yoo-uh-b'l) adj. Precious beyond measure; priceless.—**in·val·u·a·bly** adv.

in·var·i·a·ble adj. Unalterable; unchangeable; immutable.—**in·var·i·a·bil·i·ty** (in-vair-ee-uh-*bil*-it-ee), -ble·ness n.—**in·var·i·a·bly** adv.

in·va·sion (in-*vay*-zhun) n. 1. Hostile entry; attack for conquest or plunder. 2. An infringement of rights; violation.—**in·va·sive** adj.

in·vec·tive (in-*vek*-tiv) n. Violent reproach or slander; reviling or abusive words.—adj. Violently insulting; reviling.—**in·vec·tive·ly** adv. —**in·vec·tive·ness** n.

in·veigh (in-*vay*) v. To rail; revile; use bitter language.—**in·veigh·er** n.

in·vei·gle (in-*vee*-g'l; -*vay*-g'l) v. [in·vei·gled; in·vei·gling] To persuade by flattery or other deception; entice.— -gle·ment n.— -vei·gler n.

in·vent (in-*vent*) v. 1. To originate or contrive something new. 2. To devise in the mind; concoct.—**in·ven·tor, -ter** n.—**in·vent·i·ble** adj.

in·ven·tion (in-*ven*-shun) n. 1. An original contrivance. 2. A fabrication; lie. 3. Power or act of producing something new; creative imagination.

in·ven·tive (in-*ven*-tiv) adj. Original; creative; good at invention.—**in·ven·tive·ness** n.

in·ven·to·ry (in-v'n-*tor*-ee) n. [pl. -ries] 1. A survey or listing of current resources or assets· 2. Amount of stock or resources on hand.—v. [-to·ried; -ry·ing] To take stock of; catalogue. — -to·ri·al adj.— -to·ri·al·ly adv.

In·ver·ness (in-ver-*ness*) n. Also **Inverness cape**. A long, full cape.

in·verse (in-*verss*) adj. Opposite; inverted; reversed.—n. That which is reversed or a direct opposite.—**in·verse·ly** adv.

in·ver·sion (in-*ver*-zhun) n. 1. Reversal in order or succession. 2. *Music*. Change of position of the parts of a phrase, interval, or chord.—**in·ver·sive** adj.

in·vert (in-*vert*) v. 1. To turn upside down or around; reverse in order or position. 2. *Music*. To change by inversion.—**in·vert·er** n.—**in·vert·i·ble** adj.

in·vert (*in*-vert) n. Person or thing which is inverted, esp. a homosexual.—**in·vert** adj.

in·ver·te·brate (in-*ver*-tuh-brit) adj. Having no backbone or spinal column; relating to inver-

tebrates.—n. An animal with no backbone.

in·vest (in-*vest*) v. 1. To spend money or capital in expectation of a profitable return. 2. To install in office; clothe with authority. 3. To surround; cover. 4. To surround with military forces; besiege.—**in·ves·tor** n.

in·ves·ti·gate (in-*vest*-tih-gayt) v. [-gat·ed; -gat·ing] To search or inquire into; scrutinize; examine.—**in·ves·ti·ga·ble** adj.—**in·ves·ti·ga·tive** adj.—**in·ves·ti·ga·tor** n.— -ga·to·ry adj.

in·ves·ti·ga·tion n. Examination; painstaking research; scrutiny.

in·ves·ti·ture (in-*vess*-tuh-cher) n. 1. Installation; bestowing of an office. 2. Vestments.

in·vest·ment (in-*vest*-m'nt) n. 1. Spending of money or capital for a profitable return. 2. Money or capital invested or property thus acquired.

in·vet·er·ate (in-*vet*-er-it) adj. Habitual; firmly established; confirmed.—**in·vet·er·a·cy** n.—**in·vet·er·ate·ly** adv.—**in·vet·er·ate·ness** n.

in·vid·i·ous (in-*vid*-ee-us) adj. Tending to provoke ill will or envy; offensive; hateful.—**in·vid·i·ous·ly** adv.—**in·vid·i·ous·ness** n.

in·vig·or·ate (in-*vig*-er-ayt) v. [-at·ed; -at·ing] To exhilarate; add vigor or energy to; refresh. —**in·vig·or·at·ing·ly** adv.—**in·vig·or·a·tive** adj.

in·vig·o·ra·tion (in-vig-er-*ay*-sh'n) n. Animation; energy.

in·vin·ci·ble (in-*vin*-suh-b'l) adj. Unconquerable; insuperable.—**in·vin·ci·bil·i·ty, in·vin·ci·ble·ness** n.—**in·vin·ci·bly** adv.

in·vi·o·la·ble (in-*vy*-uh-luh-b'l) adj. 1. Sacred; hallowed; not to be violated. 2. Not to be injured or harmed.—**in·vi·o·la·bil·i·ty, in·vi·o·la·ble·ness** n.—**in·vi·o·la·bly** adv.

in·vi·o·late (in-*vy*-uh-lit) adj. Not broken or profaned.— -late·ly adv.— -late·ness n.

in·vis·i·ble (in-*viz*-uh-b'l) adj. Not perceptible or capable of being seen; indistinct.—n. 1. Invisible being. 2. [*cap.*] God.—**in·vis·i·bil·i·ty, in·vis·i·ble·ness,** n.—**in·vis·i·bly** adv.

in·vi·ta·tion (in-vuh-*tay*-sh'n) n. Solicitation; request to attend; enticement.— -tion·al adj.

in·vite (in-*vyte*) v. [in·vit·ed; in·vit·ing] 1. To ask courteously to attend; request the presence of. 2. To tempt; solicit; entice.—**in·vit·er** n.

in·vit·ing adj. Tempting; attractive.—**in·vit·ing·ly** adv.—**in·vit·ing·ness** n.

in·vo·ca·tion (in-voh-*kay*-shun) n. 1. A prayer; entreaty. 2. Incantation; summoning of aid, inspiration, etc.

in·voice (*in*-voyss) n. Itemized statement of quantities, values, and charges of merchandise.—v. [in·voiced; in·voic·ing] To enter the record of a shipment.

in·voke (in-*vohk*) v. [in·voked; in·vok·ing] 1. To address in prayer. 2. To call up solemnly; appeal.—**in·vok·er** n.

in·vol·un·tar·y (in-*vol*-un-tehr-ee) adj. Forced; not done by choice; not willed.—**in·vol·un·tar·i·ly** adv.—**in·vol·un·tar·i·ness** n.

in·volve (in-*volv*) v. [in·volved; in·volv·ing]

1. To implicate; entangle; affect. 2. To envelop; entwine; roll up.—**in·volve·ment** *n.* Entanglement.—**in·volv·er** *n.*

in·vul·ner·a·ble (in-*vul*-ner-uh-b'l) *adj.* Impregnable; invincible; unassailable.—**in·vul·ner·a·bil·i·ty** (in-vul-ner-uh-*bil*-ih-tee), **in·vul·ner·a·ble·ness** *n.*—**in·vul·ner·a·bly** *adv.*

in·ward, in·wards (*in*-werd, -werdz) *adv.* 1. Toward the inside. 2. Within onself.

in·ward *adj.* 1. Interior; placed within; inland. 2. Private; hidden; unspoken.—*Colloquial.* *n. pl.* (*in*-erdz) The bowels; internal organs.

in·ward·ly *adv.* 1. Internally. 2. Privately; secretly. 3. Toward the center.

in·ward·ness *n.* 1. Internal state; inner meaning. 2. Spiritual quality.

in·wrap. *Variant spelling of* **enwrap.**

in·wrought (in-*rawt*) *adj.* Worked into a pattern; woven together.

i·o·dide (*eye*-uh-dyde) *n.* Also **i·o·did.** A compound of iodine.

i·o·dine (*eye*-uh-dyne, -din) *n.* Also **i·o·din.** A nonmetallic element, grayish-black in luster, with a chlorine odor when vaporized. (*Symbol:* I).

i·o·do·form (eye-*oh*-duh-form) *n. Chemistry.* A crystalline compound of iodine used as an antiseptic in dressing wounds or cuts.

i·on (*eye*-un) *n.* A particle of matter bearing an electric charge.—**i·on·ic** (eye-*on*-ik) *adj.*

I·o·ni·a (eye-*oh*-nee-uh) *n.* Ancient Greek colony on the west coast of Asia Minor.—**I·o·ni·an** *n. & adj.*

I·on·ic (eye-*on*-ik) *adj.* 1. Pertaining to the order of Greek architecture distinguished esp. by spiral scrolls of the capital. 2. *Prosody.* Of the Ionic form of verse, foot, or meter.—*n. Prosody.* 1. A foot of four syllables, two long and two short, or two short and two long. 2. A meter or verse in Ionic feet.

IONIC (def. 1)

i·o·ni·um (eye-*oh*-nee-um) *n.* A radioactive element. (*Symbol:* Io).

i·on·ize (*eye*-uh-nyze) *v.* [i·on·ized; i·on·iz·ing] To change into ions.—**i·on·i·za·tion** (eye-un-iz-*ay*-shun) *n.* Formation of ions.—**i·on·iz·er** *n.*

i·o·ta (eye-*oh*-tuh) *n.* 1. A minute quantity; bit. 2. The Greek letter I.

IOU (eye oh *yoo*). A paper bearing the letters *IOU*, the sum owed, and a signature, as an acknowledgment of debt.

ip·e·cac (*ip*-eh-kak), **ip·e·cac·u·an·ha** (ip-eh-kak-yoo-*an*-uh) *n.* An emetic made from the dried roots of a South American plant.

i·ras·ci·ble (ih-*rass*-ib-'l) *adj.* Easily provoked; irritable.—**i·ras·ci·bil·i·ty** (ih-rass-ih-*bil*-it-ee), **i·ras·ci·ble·ness** *n.*—**i·ras·ci·bly** *adv.*

i·rate (*eye*-rayt, eye-*rayt*) *adj.* Enraged; incensed.—**i·rate·ly** *adv.*

ire *n.* Wrath; strong resentment.—**ire·ful** *adj.* —**ire·ful·ly** *adv.*

Ire·land *n.* Island west of Great Britain, comprising the Irish Free State, or Eire, and northern Ireland, a part of the British Empire.

ir·i·des·cence (ir-ih-*dess*-enss) *n.* A shimmering play of colors, as in a rainbow.—**ir·i·des·cent** *adj.*—**i·ri·des·cent·ly** *adv.*

i·rid·i·um (ih-*rid*-ee-um) *n.* A hard, brittle, rare metallic element resembling platinum. (*Symbol:* Ir).—**i·rid·ic** *adj.*

i·ris (*eye*-riss) *n.* [*pl.* i·ris·es] 1. A family of plants with sword-shaped leaves and iridescent flowers having three upright and three drooping petals. 2. [*cap.*] Greek goddess of the rainbow. 3. The colored part of the eye surrounding the pupil. 4. A rainbow.

I·rish (*eye*-rish) *adj.* Pertaining to Ireland, its people, or its Celtic language.—*n.* 1. [*pl.*] Natives of Ireland. 'The Irish.' 2. The Hibernian-Celtic language.

IRIS

Irish Free State. Former name of Eire, an independent state of the British Empire, in central and southern Ireland.

I·rish·man *n.* [*pl.* -men] A person of Irish birth or ancestry.—**I·rish·wom·an** *n.* [*pl.* -wom·en].

Irish potato. The common white potato.

Irish setter. A hunting dog with a long, reddish, silky coat.

Irish stew. A thick stew made of meat, potatoes, and onions.

Irish terrier. A small but sturdy breed of dog with a wiry brown coat.

Irish wolfhound. A large hunting dog of ancient breed.

irk (erk) *v.* To annoy; vex; bore.

irk·some (*erk*-sum) *adj.* Tedious; dull; tiresome.—**irk·some·ly** *adv.*—**irk·some·ness** *n.*

i·ron (*eye*-ern) *n.* 1. Most common and useful metallic element, silver-white in color, found widely over the earth in combined forms. (*Symbol:* Fe). 2. Tool, utensil, or weapon made of iron. 3. Firmness; strength; rigidity. 4. [*pl.*] Shackles; fetters. 5. *Golf.* An iron-headed club.—*adj.* 1. Made of iron. 2. Like iron; strong; inflexible; harsh.—*v.* 1. To smooth, esp. clothes, with a flatiron. 2. To handcuff; fetter. 3. To make or furnish with iron.—**i·ron·er** *n.*

iron-banded	iron-forged	iron mold
ironbark	iron-handed	iron-ribbed
iron-barred	iron hard	iron-sided
iron-branded	iron-hearted	ironsmith
iron-cased	iron-jawed	ironstone
iron casing	ironlike	iron-tipped
iron-faced	iron-lined	iron-winged
iron-fastened	iron maker	ironwood
iron-fisted	ironman	iron works

i·ron·clad *adj.* 1. Covered with iron plates.

2. Unchangeable; binding.—*n.* An armored warship.

Iron Guard. Rumanian fascist party.

i·ron·i·cal (eye-*ron*-ih-k'l) *adj.* Also **i·ron·ic.** Saying one thing and meaning the opposite; sarcastic; marked by, or using, irony.—**i·ron·i·cal·ly** *adv.*—**i·ron·i·cal·ness** *n.*

i·ron·mas·ter *n.* One who manufactures iron.

iron pyrites. A mineral resembling gold in appearance; fool's gold.

i·ron·side *n.* 1. [*pl.*] An armor-clad warship. 2. A strong, brave man. 3. [*cap.*] Also **Ironsides.** Oliver Cromwell or a member of his troops.

i·ron·ware *n.* Hardware; light tools, utensils, etc., of iron.

i·ron·work *n.* 1. Parts or objects of iron. 2. [*pl.*] Mill where iron is smelted or cast. —**i·ron·work·er** *n.*

i·ro·ny (*eye*-ruh-nee, *eye*-er-nee) *n.* [*pl.* -nies] 1. A manner of speech or ridicule expressing a sense contrary to its literal meaning. 2. An event or result just the reverse of normal. 'The irony of his condition.'

Ir·o·quois (*ihr*-uh-kwoy) *n.* A member of a group of five powerful Indian tribes, originally living in New York State.—**Ir·o·quoi·an** *adj.*

ir·ra·di·ate (ih-*ray*-dee-ayt) *v.* [-at·ed; -at·ing] 1. To illuminate; cast rays, or shine, upon. 2. To shine; emit rays. 3. To treat by radiation, as of radium.—*adj.* Illuminated.—**ir·ra·di·ance, ir·ra·di·an·cy** *n.* Luster; radiance.—**ir·ra·di·ant** *adj.* Illuminating.—**ir·ra·di·a·tive** *adj.*

ir·ra·di·a·tion (ih-ray-dee-*ay*-sh'n) *n.* 1. The process of emitting beams of light. 2. Exposure to, or treatment with, certain rays, as radium, ultra-violet, or X-rays.

ir·ra·tion·al (ih-*rash*-'n-'l) *adj.* 1. Lacking in reason; witless. 2. Contrary to reason; absurd; senseless.—**ir·ra·tion·al·i·ty, ir·ra·tion·al·ness** *n.*—**ir·ra·tion·al·ly** *adv.*

ir·re·claim·a·ble (ih-rih-*klaym*-uh-b'l) *adj.* Incapable of being restored or reformed.—**ir·re·claim·a·bil·i·ty, ir·re·claim·a·ble·ness** *n.*—**ir·re·claim·a·bly** *adv.*

ir·rec·on·cil·a·ble (ih-rek-'n-*syle*-uh-b'l) *adj.* 1. Implacable; unappeasable. 2. Incongruous; incompatible.—**ir·rec·on·cil·a·bil·i·ty, -a·ble·ness** *n.*—**ir·rec·on·cil·a·bly** *adv.*

ir·re·cov·er·a·ble (ih-rih-*kuhv*-er-uh-b'l) *adj.* Incapable of being regained, restored, or remedied.—**ir·re·cov·er·a·bly** *adv.*

ir·re·deem·a·ble (ih-rih-*deem*-uh-b'l) *adj.* 1. Not available at its original value; not exchangeable for coin. 2. Beyond change or help. —**ir·re·deem·a·bly** *adv.*

Ir·re·den·tist (ih-rih-*den*-tist) *n.* Member of an Italian political party agitating for Italian control over neighboring regions with large Italian populations but belonging to other countries. —**Ir·re·den·tism** *n.*

ir·re·duc·i·ble (ih-rih-*dyoo*-suh-b'l) *adj.* Not capable of being reduced.

ir·ref·ra·ga·ble (ih-*ref*-ruh-guh-b'l) *adj.* Incontestable; undeniable; indisputable.—**ir·ref·ra·ga·bil·i·ty** *n.*—**ir·ref·ra·ga·bly** *adv.*

ir·ref·u·ta·ble (ih-*ref*-yoo-tuh-b'l) *adj.* Not capable of being disproved.—**ir·ref·u·ta·bil·i·ty** *n.*—**ir·ref·u·ta·bly** *adv.*

ir·reg·u·lar (ih-*reg*-yuh-ler) *adj.* 1. Not according to rules or customs; contrary to nature; anomalous. 2. Not straight or uniform; lackin symmetry. 3. *Grammar.* Deviating from common forms of inflection. 4. Not belonging to a regular organization, esp. military.—*n.* A soldier not in the regular army.—**ir·reg·u·lar·ly** *adv.*

ir·reg·u·lar·i·ty (ih-reg-yuh-*lair*-uh-tee) *n.* [*pl.* -ties] Deviation from established methods, rules, or orders; divergence from normal.

ir·rel·e·vant (ih-*rel*-uh-v'nt) *adj.* Not pertinent; inapplicable; not serving to support.—**ir·rel·e·vance, -van·cy** *n.* [*pl.* -cies]— **-vant·ly** *adv.*

ir·re·li·gion (ih-rih-*lij*-'n) *n.* Lack of religion; impiety.

ir·re·li·gious *adj.* 1. Not religious; impious. 2. Contrary to religion; profane; wicked. —**ir·re·li·gious·ly** *adv.*

ir·re·me·di·a·ble (ih-rih-*mee*-dee-uh-b'l) *adj.* Incurable; without a remedy.—**ir·re·me·di·a·ble·ness** *n.*—**ir·re·me·di·a·bly** *adv.*

ir·re·miss·i·ble (ih-rih-*miss*-uh-b'l) *adj.* Unpardonable.

ir·rep·a·ra·ble (ih-*rep*-er-uh-b'l) *adj.* Incapable of being repaired or recovered.—**ir·rep·a·bil·i·ty, -ble·ness** *n.*—**ir·rep·a·ra·bly** *adv.*

ir·re·pres·si·ble (ih-rih-*press*-uh-b'l) *adj.* Not restrainable or controllable.—**ir·re·press·i·bil·i·ty, -ble·ness** *n.*—**ir·re·press·i·bly** *adv.*

ir·re·proach·a·ble (ih-rih-*prohch*-uh-b'l) *adj.* Faultless; beyond reproach.—**ir·re·proach·a·ble·ness** *n.*— **-a·bly** *adv.*

ir·re·sist·i·ble (ih-rih-*ziss*-tuh-b'l) *adj.* Incapable of being resisted; overpowering.—**ir·re·sist·i·bil·i·ty, -i·ble·ness** *n.*

ir·res·o·lute (ih-*rez*-uh-loot) *adj.* Undecided; wavering; hesitant.—**ir·res·o·lute·ly** *adv.*—**ir·res·o·lu·tion, ir·res·o·lute·ness** *n.*

ir·re·spec·tive (ih-rih-*spek*-tiv) *adj.* Regardless; independent.—**ir·re·spec·tive·ly** *adv.*

ir·re·spon·si·ble (ih-rih-*spon*-suh-b'l) *adj.* Not liable or able to answer for consequences; having no responsibility.—**ir·re·spon·si·bil·i·ty** *n.*—**ir·re·spon·si·bly** *adv.*

ir·re·triev·a·ble (ih-rih-*treev*-uh-b'l) *adj.* Beyond recall, recovery, or repair.—**ir·re·triev·a·bil·i·ty** *n.*—**ir·re·triev·a·bly** *adv.*

ir·rev·er·ence (ih-*rev*-er-'nss) *n.* 1. Want of veneration or due regard; disrespect. 2. A disrespectful or profane act.—**ir·rev·er·ent** *adj.* —**ir·rev·er·ent·ly** *adv.*

ir·re·vers·i·ble (ih-rih-*ver*-suh-b'l) *adj.* Incapable of inversion or reversal.—**ir·re·vers·i·bil·i·ty** *n.*—**ir·re·vers·i·bly** *adv.*

ir·rev·o·ca·ble (ih-*rev*-uh-kuh-b'l) *adj.* Not capable of being revoked or set aside.—**ir·rev·o·ca·bil·i·ty, -ca·ble·ness** *n.*—**ir·rev·o·ca·bly** *adv.*

ir·ri·gate (*ihr*-uh-gayt) *v.* [-gat·ed; -gat·ing] To

water land by running a stream over or through it. To direct a stream of fluid upon.—**ir·ri·ga·ble** *adj.*—**ir·ri·ga·tor** *n.*

ir·ri·ga·tion (ih-ruh-*gay*-sh'n) *n.* 1. A watering of land by a system of canals or flooding. 2. Direction of a stream of fluid upon, as for cleansing.—**ir·ri·ga·tion·al** *adj.*

ir·ri·ta·ble (*ihr*-uh-tuh-b'l) *adj.* 1. Easily irritated, excited, or vexed; sensitive. 2. *Medicine.* Responding to stimuli.—**ir·ri·ta·bil·i·ty, ir·ri·ta·ble·ness** *n.*—**ir·ri·ta·bly** *adv.*

ir·ri·tant (*ihr*-uh-t'nt) *n.* A poison or other substance which irritates.—*adj.* Causing irritation; soreness, etc.—**ir·ri·tan·cy** *n.*

ir·ri·tate (*ihr*-uh-tayt) *v.* [-tat·ed; -tat·ing] 1. To exasperate; vex; annoy. 2. To render sensitive or sore; inflame; stimulate.—**ir·ri·tat·ing** *adj.*—**ir·ri·tat·ing·ly** *adv.*—**ir·ri·ta·tion** *n.*—**ir·ri·ta·tive** *adj.*

ir·rup·tion (ih-*rup*-sh'n) *n.* A sudden rushing or bursting in; invasion; raid.—**ir·rup·tive** *adj.*

Is·car·i·ot (iss-*kair*-ee-ut) *n.* 1. Judas Iscariot, betrayer of Christ, 2. Any betrayer; traitor.

-ish *Suffix.* 1. Having the unfavorable traits of; resembling. 2. Somewhat; to a degree.

Ish·ma·el (*ish*-mee-ul) *n.* 1. *Old Testament.* Son of Abraham, who was driven into the desert. 2. An outcast.—**Ish·ma·el·ite** *adj. & n.*

i·sin·glass (*eye*-zing-glass) *n.* 1. A gelatinous plastic made from the air bladders of certain fish. 2. Mica, in thin translucent layers.

I·sis (*eye*-siss) *n.* Egyptian goddess of fertility.

Is·lam (*iss*-lum) *n.* Mohammedanism; Mohammedans collectively.—**Is·lam·ic** (is-*lam*-ik) *adj.*

is·land (*eye*-l'nd) *n.* 1. A tract of water-surrounded land. 2. Any isolated, completely surrounded area.—**is·land·er** *n.*

isle (*yle*), **is·let** *n.* A small island.

ism (*iz'm*) *n.* An ideology; theory; doctrine.

i·so·bar (*eye*-suh-bahr) *n.* 1. A line drawn on a weather map connecting places with equal barometric pressure. 2. *Chemistry.* An atom having the same atomic weight as another, though a different atomic number.—**i·so·bar·ic** (eye-suh-*bair*-ik) *adj.*

i·so·gon·ic (eye-suh-*gon*-ik) *adj.* Having equal angles.

i·so·late (*eye*-suh-layt) *v.* [-lat·ed; -lat·ing] 1. To put by itself; place apart; segregate. 2. *Chemistry.* To obtain a substance free from all its combinations. 3. *Medicine.* To quarter for treatment away from non-infected persons.—**i·so·la·tion** (eye-suh-*lay*-shun) *n.*

i·so·la·tion·ism *n.* A nationalistic philosophy opposed to political co-operation with other nations.—**i·so·la·tion·ist** *n.*

i·som·er·ism (eye-*som*-er-izm) *adj. Chemistry.* Difference in chemical or physical properties between two elements of the same proportionate weight.—**i·so·mer·ic** (eye-suh-*mehr*-ik).

i·so·met·ric (eye-suh-*met*-rik) *adj.* Also **i·so·met·ri·cal.** Denoting or marked by equality of measure.—**i·so·met·ri·cal·ly** *adv.*

i·sos·ce·les (eye-*soss*-uh-leez) *adj. Geometry.* Having or bounded by two equal sides.

i·so·therm (*eye*-suh-therm) *n.* A line on a map marking areas of equal temperature.—**i·so·ther·mal** (eye-suh-*ther*-m'l) *adj.*

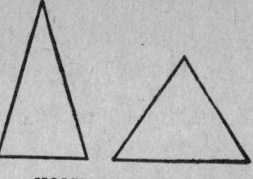

ISOSCELES TRIANGLES

i·so·tope (*eye*-suh-tohp) *n.* A substance or element having the same place in the atomic table as another but an abnormal atomic weight.—**i·so·top·ic** (eye-suh-*top*-ik) *adj.*

i·so·trop·ic (eye-suh-*trop*-ik) *adj.* Having identical physical properties in every direction.

Is·ra·el (*iz*-ree-ul). The nation founded by Jacob; the Jewish people.—**Is·ra·el·ite** *n. & adj.*

Is·sei (*ee*-say) *n.* A Japanese-born inhabitant of the U.S.

is·sue (*ish*-oo) *v.* [is·sued; is·su·ing] 1. To flow or run out; emerge. 2. To discharge. 3. To result; proceed; be derived or produced. 4. To deliver for use; put into official or public circulation; publish.—*n.* 1. A controversial point. 2. Offspring; child; children. 3. Emanation; delivery; a flowing or sending out. 4. The copy or quantity sent out at a single time. 5. Event; result. 6. Outlet; exit.—**is·su·ance** *n.* An issuing.— **-a·ble** *adj.*—**is·su·er** *n.*

isth·mi·an (*iss*-mee-un) *adj.* Pertaining to, or on, an isthmus.—*n.* Inhabitant of an isthmus.

isth·mus (*iss*-muss) *n.* [*pl.* -mus·es, -mi] A narrow neck of land connecting two land masses.

it *pronoun.* A neuter, third-person singular pronoun used in place of a neuter or indefinite noun, or an indefinite term. 'How is it done?'

I·tal·i·an (ih-*tal*-yun) *n.* 1. A citizen or native of Italy. 2. The language of Italy.—*adj.* Of Italy, its language, or people.

i·tal·ic (ih-*tal*-ik) *adj.* Denoting a right-sloping type used to emphasize or distinguish. *This is italic type.*—*n.* An italic type or letter.

i·tal·i·cize (ih-*tal*-uh-syze) *v.* [-cized; -ciz·ing] To write or print in italic characters.

itch (*ich*) *n.* 1. Contagious skin disease, marked by an irritation inclining the patient to rub or scratch the affected area. 2. A prickling skin sensation causing one to scratch. 3. A constant, teasing desire.—**itch** *v.*—**itch·y** *adj.*

i·tem (*eye*-t'm) *n.* 1. A detail; particular; separate article. 2. *Journalism.* A paragraph; scrap of news.

i·tem·ize (*eye*-t'm-yze) *v.* [i·tem·ized; i·tem·iz·ing] To list or note by items.

it·er·ate (*it*-er-ayt) *v.* [-at·ed; -at·ing] To repeat; say or do again.— **-a·tion** *n.*— **-a·tive** *adj.*

i·tin·er·a·cy (eye-*tin*-er-uh-see) *n.* Also **i·tin·er·an·cy.** 1. A wandering from place to place. 2. Work or duty requiring frequent travel.

i·tin·er·ant (eye-*tin*-er-'nt) *adj.* Wandering; roving; traveling here and there.—*n.* A wanderer, esp. a roving preacher.— **-ant·ly** *adv.*

I

i·tin·er·ar·y (eye-*tin*-er-ehr-ee) *n*. [*pl*. -ies] 1. List of stops on a traveler's route; outline or record of a journey. 2. A guidebook. —*adj*. Relating to traveling or routes.

-i·tis (eye-tiss) *Suffix*. Inflammatory condition, or disease, of.

its *adj*. Belonging or pertaining to it.

it·self (it-*self*) *pron*. Emphatic or reflexive form of it.

i·vied (eye-veed) *adj*. Covered with trailing ivy.

i·vo·ry (eye-ver-ee) *n*. [*pl*. -ries] 1. The hard whitish substance composing the tusks of elephants. 2. [*pl*.] *Slang*. Certain objects made of or resembling, ivory, as teeth, piano keys, etc. 3. The yellow-white color of ivory. —**i·vo·ry** *adj*.

Ivory Coast. A French colony on the west coast of Africa.

ivory tower. Seclusion; withdrawal from the everyday world.

i·vy (eye-vee) *n*. [*pl*. i-vies] A climbing plant with smooth shiny green leaves.

-ize *Suffix*. 1. To make or become. 2. Treat with or subject to. 3. To practice; use.

iz·zard *n*. *Colloquial*. The letter *z*. 'From A to izzard.'

IVY

J

jab *v*. [jab·bed; jab·bing] To poke; hit with a sharp object.—*n*. A poke; thrust; light blow.

jab·ber (*jab*-er) *v*. To talk rapidly or foolishly; chatter.—*n*. Rapid, indistinct chatter.

jab·ber·wock·y (*jab*-er-wok-ee) *n*. 1. [*cap*.] Title of a nonsense poem in Lewis Carroll's *Through the Looking-Glass*. 2. Any meaningless language or talk; doubletalk.

ja·bot (zhah-*boh*) *n*. A frill at the neck or down the front of a blouse or dress.

jack *n*. 1. A mechanical device for raising heavy weights a short distance. 2. The male of certain animals, as the rabbit or ass. 3. A fellow, esp. one who does odd jobs. 4. *Nautical*. A flag or ensign for signaling. 5. *Cards*. A knave. 6. [*pl*.] A children's game played with a set of metal pieces and a small ball. 7. One of the pieces in this game.—**jack up.** 1. To lift up by means of a jack; raise, as prices. 2. *Colloquial*. To reprimand.

jack·al (*jak*-'l) *n*. 1. A doglike wild animal not as large or ferocious as a wolf. 2. Person who does another's dirty work. 3. A traitor.

jack·a·napes (*jak*-uh-naypz) *n*. An impertinent person; upstart.

jack·ass (*jak*-ass) *n*. A donkey; male ass. 2. A foolish or stupid person.

JACKAL (1/25 life size)

jack boot. Also **jack·boot** *n*. A long, heavy boot.

jack·daw (*jak*-daw) *n*. A small black, bird, related to the crow.

jack·et (*jak*-it) *n*. 1. A short, usually hip-length coat. 2. An outer covering or wrapper.—*v*. To cover with a jacket.

jack-in-the-box *n*. [*pl*. -box·es] A toy consisting of a figure which pops out of a box when the lid is opened.

jack-in-the-pulpit *n*. A small yellow flower covered by a leaflike canopy.

Jack Ketch *n*. *England*. A public executioner.

jack·knife (*jak*-nyfe) *n*. [*pl*. -knives] A large, strong clasp-knife for the pocket.

jack-of-all-trades *n*. A person who can do many different kinds of work.

jack-o'-lantern (*jak*-uh-lan-tern) *n*. 1. A glow that appears at night in low, marshy lands. 2. A lantern made of a hollowed pumpkin, carved into a grotesque face.

jack pot. *Poker*. A pool of money which remains closed until a player has a pair of jacks or better.

jack rabbit. One of several species of large, long-eared American hares.

jack·straw *n*. 1. One of a set of straws or thin strips of wood, etc., used in a child's game. 2. [*pl*.] The game played with jackstraws.

Ja·co·be·an (jak-uh-*bee*-un) *adj*. Pertaining to the time of James I of England.

Jac·o·bin (*jak*-uh-bin) *n*. 1. A member of a revolutionary club during the first French Revolution. 2. An ardent revolutionary. —**Jac·o·bin·ic** (jak-uh-*bin*-ik) *adj*.

Ja·co·bite (*jak*-uh-byte) *n*. Adherent of James II of England after he abdicated in 1688.—**Ja·co·bite** *adj*. Pertaining to the Jacobites.—**Jac·o·bit·ic** (jak-uh-*bit*-ik) *adj*.—**Jac·o·bit·ism** *n*.

Jacob's ladder (*jay*-kubz). 1. A common garden plant with blue flowers. 2. *Nautical*. A rope ladder with wooden steps.

jade *n*. 1. Green mineral, very hard and tough, used for making ornaments. 2. The color jade green.

JACK-IN-THE-PULPIT

jade *n.* **1.** A tired, worthless horse. **2.** A hussy; loose woman.—*v.* [jad·ed; jad·ing] To tire or become weary.

jad·ed *adj.* Worn out through excessive indulgence. 'A jaded appetite.'

jag *n.* Sharp projection; notch; indentation.—*v.* [jagged; jag·ging] To notch; cut or tear in an uneven manner.

jag *n. Slang.* A drunken spree.

jag·ged (*jag*-id) *adj.* Rough-edged; uneven; angular.—**jag·ged·ly** *adv.*—**jag·ged·ness** *n.*

jag·uar (*jag*-wahr) *n.* Large, four-legged, carnivorous animal of the cat family, found in America.

Jah·ve, Jah·veh (*yah*-veh). *Variant forms of* **Jehovah.**

jail (*jayl*) *n.* A prison. —*v.* To put in prison; imprison.

JAGUAR (1/50 life size)

jail·bird *n. Slang.* A prisoner or ex-prisoner.

jail·er *n.* Also **jail·or.** The keeper of a jail.

ja·lop·y (juh-*lop*-ee) *n.* [*pl.* -ies] *Slang.* An old, worn-out automobile.

jam *v.* [jammed; jam·ming] **1.** To crowd; wedge in; squeeze tight. **2.** To disrupt mechanically. **3.** *Radio.* To interfere with the reception of radio broadcasts. **4.** To block, fill up a passage, etc., by crowding into it.—*n.* A crush; squeeze; crowded mass.

jam *n.* A fruit preserve.

jam *v. Jazz Music.* **1.** To improvise informally, esp. for the performer's own pleasure. **2.** To improvise in ensemble. 'Jam out the last chorus.'—**jam session.** A gathering of jazz musicians improvising together for pleasure.

jamb *n.* Also **jambe.** *Architecture.* The vertical side piece of a door, window, chimney, etc.

jam·bo·ree (*jam*-ber-ee) *n. Slang.* Celebration; merry-making.

jan·gle (*jang*-g'l) *v.* [jan·gled; jan·gling] **1.** To make a harsh, discordant noise. **2.** To speak discordantly or noisily.—*n.* Discordant sound; harsh noise.

jan·i·tor (*jan*-uh-ter) *n.* **1.** One who looks after the maintenance of a building. **2.** Door-keeper.

Jan·i·zar·y (*jan*-uh-zehr-ee) *n.* [*pl.* -ies]. Also **Jan·is·sar·y. 1.** A Turkish infantry soldier. **2.** An instrument of tyranny.

Jan·u·ar·y (*jan*-yoo-air-ee) *n.* The first month of the year.

Ja·nus (*jayn*-us) *n.* The Roman god of gates represented with two faces looking in opposite directions.—**Ja·nus-faced** *adj.* Two-faced; double dealing; deceitful.

ja·pan (juh-*pan*) *n.* **1.** Work lacquered and figured in Japanese style. **2.** The lacquer used in japanning articles.—*v.* [ja·panned; ja·pan·ning] To lacquer with a thick glossy coat.

Jap·a·nese (jap-uh-*neez*) *n.* A native of Japan; the language of Japan.—**Japanese** *adj.*

Japanese beetle. An extremely destructive widespread, plant-eating insect originally native to Japan.

jape (*jayp*) *v.* [japed; jap·ing] To jest.—*n.* A jest; trick.—**jap·er** *n.*—**jap·er·y** *n.*

ja·pon·i·ca (juh-*pon*-ih-kuh) *n.* A camellia-flowered, ornamental, evergreen shrub.

jar (*jahr*) *n.* A wide-mouthed vessel made of earthenware, glass, etc.

jar *v.* [jarred; jar·ring] **1.** To make a harsh, discordant sound. **2.** To vibrate or resound harshly. **3.** To send a shock through the nerves. **4.** To clash; quarrel.—*n.* **1.** A rattling vibration; harsh sound. **2.** A shock to the nerves or feelings. **3.** Disagreement; quarrel.—**jar·ring·ly** *adv.*

jar·di·niere (jahr-duh-*neer*) *n.* An ornamental stand for plants and flowers.

jar·gon (*jahr*-gun) *n.* **1.** Confused, unintelligible talk; gibberish. **2.** Phraseology peculiar to an art, profession, etc. 'Medical jargon.' —**jar·gon,** **jar·gon·ize** *v.* To talk jargon.

jas·mine (*jaz*-min, *jass*-min) *n.* Also **jas·min.** Erect or climbing shrub with fragrant white or yellow flowers.

jas·per (*jass*-per) *n.* Opaque, colored quartz.

jaun·dice (*jawn*-diss) *n.* **1.** A disease characterized by yellowness of the eyes, skin, and body fluids. **2.** Emotion, such as jealousy or envy, which distorts the judgment.—*v.* [jaun·diced; jaun·dic·ing] **1.** To affect with jaundice. **2.** To affect with envy, prejudice, etc.

jaunt (*jawnt*) *v.* To take an excursion, esp. for pleasure; ramble.—*n.* An excursion; ramble.

jaun·ty *adj.* [jaun·ti·er; jaun·ti·est] Airy; sprightly; gay and easy.—**jaunt·i·ly** *adv.*

ja·va (*jah*-vuh, *jav*-uh) *n. Slang.* Coffee.

Jav·a·nese (jah-vuh-*neez*) *n.* A native of Java; the language of Java.—**Jav·a·nese** *adj.*

jave·lin (*jav*-lin) *n.* A light spear.

jaw *n.* **1.** The bones of the mouth in which the teeth are fixed; maxillary bones. **2.** *pl.* The mouth. **3.** *Slang.* Loquacity. **4.** Anything resembling a jaw in form or use. 'The jaws of a vise.'—**jaw** *v. Slang.* To talk tediously.

jaw·bone *n.* The bone of the lower jaw.

jaw·break·er *n. Colloquial.* A word hard to pronounce; a long word.

jay *n.* A chattering bird of the crow family.

jay·walk *v. Colloquial.* To cross a street in disregard of traffic regulations.—**jay·walk·er** *n.* —**jay·walk·ing** *n.*

jazz *n.* A form of American dance music derived from Negro folk songs and the music of marching bands. It is characterized by syncopated rhythms and freely improvised instrumental variations.—*v. Slang.* To liven up. —**jazz** *adj.*—**jazz·y** *adj.*

jeal·ous (*jel*-us) *adj.* **1.** Pained by preference being given to another. **2.** Solicitous to defend the honor, rights, etc., of. **3.** Envious. **4.** Suspiciously vigilant; anxiously fearful. —**jeal·ous·ly** *adv.*—**jeal·ous·y, jeal·ous·ness** *n.*

J

jean *n.* 1. Twilled cotton cloth. 2. [*pl.*] Pants or trousers made of jean, usually blue.

jeep *n. Military.* A small, rugged automobile.

jeer *v.* To scoff; deride; taunt.—**jeer** *n.*—**jeer·er** *n.*—**jeer·ing·ly** *adv.*

Jef·fer·so·ni·an *adj.* Pertaining to Thomas Jefferson, third president of the U.S.A., his beliefs and philosophy. 'Jeffersonian democracy.'

Je·ho·vah (jeh-*hoh*-vuh) *n.* Principal name for God in the Old Testament.

Je·hu (*jee*-hyoo) *n.* 1. *Bible.* The son of Nimshi [2 Kings ix.20]. 2. [*not cap.*] One fond of driving; a fast driver.

je·june (jeh-*joon*) *adj.* Meagre; scanty; barren; uninteresting.—**je·june·ly** *adv.*—**je·june·ness** *n.*

jell *v. Colloquial.* 1. To set in the form of a jelly. 2. To hold together; be plausible, as a story; succeed.

jel·lied (*jel*-eed) *adj.* Having the consistency of jelly.

jell·i·fy (*jel*-uh-fye) *v.* [-fied; -fy·ing] To cause to set as jelly; congeal.—**jell·i·fi·ca·tion** *n.*

jel·ly (*jel*-ee) *n.* [*pl.* -lies] 1. Soft pliable, semitransparent substance, consisting usually of gelatin in solution. 2. Fruit juice congealed with sugar.—*v.* [jel·lied; jelly·ing].

jel·ly·fish *n.* 1. The medusa or sea-nettle, a soft umbrella-shaped marine animal with long tentacles. 2. *Colloquial.* A person with no will of his own; a spineless person.

JELLYFISH

jen·net (*jen*-it) *n.* A small Spanish horse.

jeop·ard·ize (*jep*-er-dyze) *v.* [jeop·ard·ized; jeop·ard·iz·ing]. Also **jeop·ard.** To endanger; risk loss or injury.

jeop·ard·y (*jep*-er-dee) *n.* 1. Danger; hazard; risk. 2. *Law.* The position of a person being tried for a criminal offense.

jer·e·mi·ad (jehr-uh-*my*-ad) *n.* Lamentation; tale of grief or complaint.

Jer·e·mi·ah (jehr-uh-*my*-uh) *n. Bible.* A Hebrew prophet, author of Jeremiah and Lamentations in the Old Testament.

jerk *v.* 1. To pull, thrust, twist, etc., suddenly. 2. To throw with a quick, sudden motion. 3. To move with a start. —*n.* 1. A short, sudden thrust, push, twist, etc. 2. Involuntary muscle contraction.

jerk *v.* To cure meat by cutting in long, thin slices and drying in the sun.

jerk *n. Slang.* A boorish, stupid person; lout.

JERKIN

jer·kin (*jer*-kin) *n.* Close-fitting jacket or waistcoat.

jerk·wa·ter *adj. Slang.* Countrified; rural.

jerk·y (*jerk*-ee) *adj.* [jerk·i·er, jerk·i·est] Sudden and uneven; spasmodic.—**jerk·i·ly** *adv.*

jerry·build *v.* [-built; -build·ing] To build flimsily with cheap materials.— -**build·er** *n.*

jer·sey (*jer*-zee) *n.* [*pl.* -seys] 1. A kind of elastic close-fitting fabric. 2. A tight-fitting jacket of jersey. 3. [*cap.*] A breed of cow notable for high butter-fat content of its milk.

Je·ru·sa·lem (jer-*ooss*-uh-lum). The capital city of Palestine; holy city of Christians and Jews.

Jerusalem artichoke. A tall sunflower whose tubers are eaten as a vegetable.

jest *n.* 1. A joke; banter. 2. Humor; fun. —**jest** *v.*—**jest·ing·ly** *adv.*

jest·er *n.* 1. A clown; buffoon kept to amuse royalty. 2. Anyone who habitually jokes.

Jes·u·it (*jez*-yoo-it) *n.* A member of the Society of Jesus.—**Jes·u·it·ic, Jes·u·it·i·cal** *adj.*

Jes·u·it·ry (*jez*-yoo-it-ree) *n.* 1. Pertaining to the Society of Jesus. 2. [*not cap.*] Manipulation of logic for predetermined ends; casuistry.

Je·sus (*jee*-zus) *n.* Founder of Christianity.

jet *n.* 1. A variety of black lignite. 2. A deep black.—**jet** *adj.*

jet *n.* A spray; a sudden spouting.—*v.* [jet·ted; jet·ting]. To spout.

jet propulsion. A method of powering aircraft by the reaction of heated, compressed gases blown out against the air.

jet·sam (*jet*-sum) *n.* Goods thrown overboard to lighten a vessel.

jet·ti·son (*jet*-ih-sun) *v.* To throw cargo overboard to lighten a ship.—**jet·ti·son** *n.*

jet·ty (*jet*-ee) *n.* [*pl.* -ties] 1. A breakwater extending out into water. 2. A pier.

Jew (*joo*) *n.* A Hebrew; Israelite; a believer in Judaism.—**Jew·ess** *n.*

jew·el (*joo*-ul) *n.* 1. A gem; precious stone. 2. An ornament of precious stones. 3. A cherished object or person. 4. A bearing for a watch.—*v.* [jew·el·ed, jew·elled; jew·el·ing, jew·el·ling] To ornament with jewels; stud.

jew·el·er *n.* A dealer in gems.

jew·el·ry *n.* Jewels.

jew·fish *n.* A giant sea bass weighing up to six pounds.

Jew·ish *adj.* Relating to the Jews.

Jew·ry *n.* [*pl.* -ries] Jews collectively.

jew's-harp, jews'-harp *n.* A lyre-shaped instrument placed between the teeth when played.

Jez·e·bel (*jez*-uh-bel) *n.* 1. The Israelite queen who persecuted Elijah. 2. A shameless or wicked woman.

JIB

jib *n.* A triangular sail extending beyond the bowsprit of a ship.—*v.* [jibbed; jib·bing] To jibe; to shift a sail from one side to the other.

jib *v.* To balk; rear; move sideways.—*n.* A balky horse.—**jib·ber** *n.*

jib·boom *n. Nautical.* An extension of the bowsprit holding the jib sails.

jibe (*jybe*) *v.* [jibed; jib·ing] *Nautical.* To jib; shift a sail from one side to the other.

jibe *v. Colloquial.* To coincide; agree.

jif·fy *n.* [*pl.* -fies]. Also **jiff.** *Colloquial.* An instant; moment. 'It cooks in a jiffy.'

jig *v.* [jigged; jig·ging] 1. To move with light, jolting motion. 2. To dance a jig.—*n.* A lively Irish country dance.—**The jig is up.** The day of reckoning has come.

jig·ger *n.* Also **chig·ger.** A small tropical flea which penetrates the skin of humans.

jig·ger *n.* 1. A dram of liquor. 2. A small glass for liquor. 3. A gadget; small appliance or device. 4. *Nautical.* a. A small yawlike vessel. b. A small mast mounted on the rear of a sailing boat.

jig·gle (*jig-'l*) *v.* [jig·gled; jig·gling] To move with quick small jerks.—*n.* A rapid, jerky motion.

jig·saw (*jig*-saw) *n.* A small saw; a fine-toothed saw for cutting ornamental patterns.—**jig·saw** *v.*

jigsaw puzzle. A puzzle consisting of parts to be pieced together, usually to form a picture.

jilt *n.* A coquette; flirt. —*v.* To reject a lover. —**jilt·er** *n.*

jim crow. Also **Jim Crow.** The practice of discriminating against Negroes, esp. by segregation in housing and transportation, and by denial of the voting franchise.—**jim-crow** *v.* To discriminate against Negroes, esp. by segregation.—**jim-crow** *adj.*

jim·jams (*jim*-jamz) *n. Slang.* Delirium tremens.

jim·my (*jim*-ee) *n.* [*pl.* -mies] A crowbar; burglar's tool for opening doors and windows.—*v.* [jim·mied; jim·my·ing] To pry open.

Jimmy Higgins. *Labor Slang.* A conscientious, hard-working person who performs many routine tasks within a union.

Jimson weed. The poisonous thorn apple.

jin·gle (*jing*-g'l) *v.* [jin·gled; jin·gling] To make a rattling metallic sound.—*n.* 1. A tinkling. 2. A light, rhymed chant.—**jin·gly** *adj.*

jin·go (*jing*-goh) *n.* [*pl.* -goes] A chauvinist; a believer in an aggressive foreign policy.—**jin·go** *adj.*—**jin·go·ism** *n.*—**jin·go·ist** *n.*—**is·tic** *adj.*

jin·ni, jin·nee (jih-*nee*) *n.* [*pl.* jinn]. Also **genie.** *Mohammedan Mythology.* A spirit capable of doing good or evil.

jin·rik·i·sha (jin-*rik*-shaw) *n.* Also **jin·rick·sha, rick·shaw.** An Oriental two-wheeled carriage drawn by one or more men.

jinx (*jinks*) *n. Slang.* Anything bringing bad luck.—*v.* To bring misfortune upon.—**jinx up.** To confuse; disorder.

JINRIKISHA

jit·ney (*jit*-nee) *n. Slang.* 1. A nickel. 2. A bus.

jit·ter (*jit*-ter) *v. Slang.* To tremble; shake.

jit·ter·bug *n. Slang.* A devotee of jazz.—*v.* To dance in frenzied and acrobatic fashion.

jit·ters *n. pl. Slang.* Nervousness; fear.—**jit·ter·y** *adj.* High strung.

jiu·jit·su, jui·jit·su. *Variant spelling of* **jujitsu.**

jive *n. Slang.* Jazz.

job *n.* 1. A piece of work. 2. An employment; occupation. 3. Duty; task; obligation. 4. *Slang.* A robbery. 5. *Colloquial.* Situation; set-up. 6. *Colloquial.* A difficult task. —*adj.* Of a miscellaneous nature. 'Job lots.' —*v.* [jobbed; job·bing] 1. To buy in quantity and sell in smaller lots. 2. To let out for hire.

Job (*johb*) *n.* 1. An Old Testament hero epitomizing patience. 2. A book of the Old Testament.

job·ber (*job*-er) *n.* 1. A middleman; a person buying from a producer and selling to a wholesaler. 2. One who takes work by the job.

job·ber·y (*job*-er-ee) *n.* Political intrigue for private gain.

job lot. A miscellaneous assortment of articles bought for resale.

jock·ey (*jok*-ee) *n.* A rider of a race horse.—*v.* 1. To cheat; swindle. 2. To take advantage of in business.

jo·cose (joh-*kohss*) *adj.* Funny; droll; given to jesting.—**jo·cose·ly** *adv.*—**jo·cose·ness** *n.*

joc·u·lar (*jok*-yoo-ler) *adj.* Droll; facetious, amusing; not serious.—**joc·u·lar·i·ty** (jok-yoo-*lair*-uh-tee) *n.*—**joc·u·lar·ly** *adv.*

joc·und (*jok*-und) *adj.* Cheerful; mirthful; light-hearted.—**joc·und·ly** *adv.*

jodh·purs (*jod*-perz) *n. pl.* Riding breeches worn with short boots.

joe-pye weed. A plant of the aster family, having purple flowers.

jog *v.* [jogged; jog·ging] 1. To stimulate; to give a start to. 2. To move at a trot.—*n.* 1. A push; a slight shake. 2. A trotting pace. 3. A jut; a sharp angle.

jog·gle *v.* [jog·gled; jog·gling] 1. To jog; to trot; to amble. 2. To jolt back and forth. 3. *Carpentry.* To join by notches.—*n.* A notch in a joint to prevent slipping.

jog trot. A slow monotonous pace.

John (*jon*) *n.* 1. John the Baptist. 2. One of the Apostles, author of a Gospel.

John Bull. *Colloquial.* The English people; a typical Englishman.

john·ny·cake *n.* A cake made of cornmeal and milk or water.

john·ny-jump-up *n.* 1. A type of pansy. 2. A violet.

join *v.* 1. To unite; bring together. 2. To combine; couple. 3. To annex; attach. 4. To become a member of; become connected with.

join·er *n.* 1. A mechanic who finishes the woodwork on houses, ships, etc. 2. *Colloquial.* One who belongs to many clubs.

J

joint *n.* 1. *Anatomy.* An articulation; joining of two or more bones. 2. A fork; juncture; meeting of the rails, roads, lines, etc. 3. *Carpentry.* The connection between two pieces of wood. 4. A hinge. 5. A large cut of meat. 6. *Slang.* A disreputable saloon or night club. —*adj.* 1. United; combined; acting in concert. 2. Shared by two or more as property. —*v.* 1. To unite to; join. 2. To fit together; as pieces of timber.—**joint·ly** *adv.*

joint stock. Capital of firm owned jointly.

join·ture (*joyn*-cher) *n.* A settlement left to a widow.

joist *n.* A beam; horizontal timber to which floor boards or a ceiling is attached.

joke *n.* 1. A jest; raillery. 2. An act or saying exciting mirth.—*v.* [joked; jok·ing] To jest; banter; excite mirth.—**jok·ing·ly** *adv.*

jok·er *n.* 1. A jester. 2. An extra card in a deck of playing cards. 3. A deceptive clause or condition, as in a law.

jol·li·ty (*jol*-uh-tee) *n.* [*pl.* -ties] Mirth; gaiety.

jol·li·fi·ca·tion (jol-uh-fih-*kay*-shun) *n.* Festivity; merrymaking.

jol·ly (*jol*-ee) *adj.* [-li·er; -li·est] Gay; lively; full of mirth.—**jol·li·ly** *adv.*—**jol·li·ness** *n.*

jol·ly *v.* [jol·lied; jol·ly·ing] *Colloquial.* 1. To tease; to poke fun at. 2. To humor along.

jolly boat. A ship's small boat.

jolt (*johlt*) *v.* 1. To shake abruptly. 2. To jerk suddenly.—*n.* 1. A shock; a start. 2. A sudden blow.—**jolt·er** *n.*

Jo·nah (*joh*-nuh) *n.* A Hebrew prophet of the book of Jonah in the Old Testament.

Jon·a·than (*jon*-uh-thun) *n.* A kind of red apple ripening late in autumn.

jon·gleur (*jong*-gler) *n.* A juggler; a wandering entertainer of medieval times.

jon·quil (*jon*-kwil) *n.* A species of yellow narcissus; the daffodil.

Jo·seph. 1. *Old Testament.* The eleventh son of Jacob who became chief minister to the Pharoh. 2. *New Testament.* the husband of Mary.

josh *n. Slang.* To tease.—*n.* A hoax; joke.

Josh·u·a (*josh*-yoo-uh) *n.* 1. *Bible.* The successor to Moses as leader of the Israelites. 2. A book of the Old Testament.

joss *n.* A Chinese god.

joss house. A Chinese Temple. —**joss stick.** Stick of Chinese incense.

jos·tle (*joss*-'l) *v.* [jos·tled; jos·tling] To hustle; to shove, as in a crowd.—*n.* A crowding.—**jost·ler** *n.*

JONQUIL

jot *n.* A tittle; an iota; a small particle.—*v.* [jot·ted; jot·ting] To set down; make a memorandum.—**jot·ting** *n.* A memorandum; a note.

joule (*jool*) *n. Physics.* The unit of energy generated by one watt in one second.

jounce (*jownss*) *v.* [jounced; jounc·ing] To jolt; shake roughly.

jour·nal (*jer*-n'l) *n.* 1. A diary. 2. *Bookkeeping.* A record of daily transactions. 3. A log; ship's record. 4. A newspaper. 5. The section of an axle which turns in a bearing.

jour·nal·ese (jer-n'l-*eez*, -*eess*) *n. Slang.* The style or language of a newspaper.

jour·nal·ism (*jer*-n'l-izm) *n.* The occupation of writing for newspapers, magazines, etc.

jour·nal·ist (*jer*-n'l-ist) *n.* 1. A correspondent; reporter; newspaperman. 2. A writer or editor of a newspaper or periodical.—**jour·nal·ist·ic** *adj.*—**jour·nal·ist·i·cal·ly** *adv.*

jour·ney (*jer*-nee) *n.* A trip; passage from one place to another.–*v.* To travel; make a trip.

jour·ney·man (*jer*-nee-m'n) *n.* [*pl.* -men] A craftsman who has finished his apprenticeship.

joust (*just, jowst*) *v.* Also **just.** To tilt; engage in mock combat on horseback.—*n.* A mock combat; tournament.—**joust·er, just·er** *n.*

Jove (*johv*) *n.* Jupiter; the chief Roman god.

jo·vi·al (*joh*-vee-ul) *adj.* Gay; joyous; mirthful; —**jo·vi·al·ly** *adv.*—**jo·vi·al·ness** *n.*—**jo·vi·al·i·ty** *n.*

Jo·vi·an *adj.* Relating to Jove.

jowl *n.* 1. The cheek; jaw. 2. Sagging chin.

joy *n.* 1. Pleasure; delight; happiness. 2. Ecstasy; bliss.—*v.* To rejoice; exult.

joy·ful *adj.* Exultant; blissful; happy.—**joy·ful·ly** *adv.*—**joy·ful·ness** *n.*

joy·less *adj.* Grim; without joy.—**joy·less·ly** *adv.*—**joy·less·ness** *n.*

joy·ous (*joy*-us) *adj.* Gay; joyful; happy.—**joy·ous·ly** *adv.*—**joy·ous·ness** *n.*

joy ride. *Slang.* A reckless automobile ride.

ju·bi·lant (*joo*-buh-lunt) *adj.* Exultant; joyful. —**ju·bi·lance** *n.*—**jub·i·lant·ly** *adv.*

ju·bi·la·tion (joo-bih-*lay*-shun) *n.* Exultation; rejoicing.

ju·bi·lee (*joo*-bih-lee) *n.* 1. A public festivity. 2. An anniversary (usually 50th) of an event. 3. A Jewish festival celebrated every 50th year.

Ju·da·ic (joo-*day*-ik) *adj.* Also **Ju·da·i·cal.** Relating to the Jews.

Ju·da·ism (*joo*-duh-izm) *n.* The religious doctrines of the Jews.—**Ju·da·ist** *n.*—**Ju·da·ist, Ju·da·is·tic** *adj.*

Ju·das (*joo*-dus) *n.* 1. Iscariot; the betrayer of Christ. 2. A betrayer; informer.

Judas tree. Traditionally, the tree on which Judas Iscariot hanged himself; a shrub with rosy-purple flowers, also called *redbud.*

Jude *n. Biblical.* The writer of the Epistle of Jude; traditionally, a brother of Jesus.

Ju·de·a (joo-*dee*-uh) *n.* Also **Ju·dae·a.** The home of the Jews; Palestine under the Romans.

judge (*judj*) *n.* 1. The presiding official in a court having power to arbitrate cases. 2. A critic; connoisseur. 3. A person appointed to choose the winner of a contest.—*v.* [judged; judg·ing] 1. To decide; arbitrate. 2. To determine; hear and pass sentence. 3. To esteem; think.—**judge·ship** *n*. The office of a judge.

judge advocate. [*pl.* judge advocates] *Military*. An officer acting as legal adviser in a court martial.

Judg·es *n*. The seventh book of the Old Testament.

judg·ment, judge·ment *n*. 1. Discernment; understanding; intelligence. 2. A verdict of a court; sentence. 3. Opinion; estimation. 'In my judgment.'

ju·di·ca·ture (*joo*-dih-kuh-cher) *n*. 1. Judges. 2. The power of administering justice. 3. A court of justice.

ju·di·cial (joo-*dish*-ul) *adj*. 1. Relating to a judge or a court of justice. 2. Proceeding from a court. 3. Impartial; critical.—**ju·di·cial·ly** *adv*.

ju·di·ci·ar·y (joo-*dish*-ee-ehr-ee) *adj*. 1. Passing judgment. 2. Relating to courts of justice. —*n*. 1. Judges. 2. The system of courts of a government.

ju·di·cious (joo-*dish*-uss) *adj*. 1. Prudent; according to sound judgment. 2. Wise; sagacious.—**ju·di·cious·ly** *adv*.—**ju·di·cious·ness** *n*.

Ju·dith (*joo*-dith) *n*. A book of the Old Testament Apocrypha.

jug *n*. 1. A pitcher; vessel for liquids having a short, narrow neck and a handle. 2. *Slang*. Jail.—*v*. [jugged; jug·ging] 1. To stew in a jug. 2. *Slang*. To imprison.

jug·ger·naut (*jug*-er-nawt) *n*. 1. An object of unreasoning devotion or sacrifice. 2. [*cap*.] A Hindu idol, borne on a large car, under which victims formerly threw themselves.—*v*. To crush; ride over.

jug·gle (*jug*-'l) *v*. [jug·gled; jug·gling] 1. To do tricks with, esp. keep several objects in the air at once. 2. To deceive or change by trickery. —*n*. A deception; trick; act of juggling.—**jug·gler** *n*.—**jug·gler·y** *n*. [*pl.* -ies] -**gling** *n. & adj*.

jug·u·lar (*jug*-yuh-ler) *adj*. Relating to the throat, the neck, or a jugular vein.—*n*. Also **jugular vein**. One of the large veins in the neck.

juice (*jooss*) *n*. 1. Sap; the fluid in fruits, vegetables, etc. 2. The liquid content of animal bodies. 3. *Slang*. Electrical power.—**juice·less** *adj*.

juic·y *adj*. [juic·i·er; juic·i·est] 1. Full of juice; not dry. 2. Full of interest; lively; racy. —**juic·i·ly** *adv*.—**juic·i·ness** *n*.

ju·jit·su (joo-*jit*-soo) *n*. Also **jui·jut·su, jiu·jit·su**. A Japanese method of wrestling, which uses an opponent's weight against him.

ju·jube (*joo*-joob) *n*. 1. East Indian tree bearing fruit resembling the plum. 2. The fruit itself. 3. A confection flavored with jujubes.

juke box. *Slang*. Automatic, coin-operated phonograph.—**juke** *adj*.

ju·lep (*joo*-lip) *n*. Also **mint ju·lep**. A tall drink made of brandy or whisky, sugar, fresh mint, and ice.

Ju·li·an (*jool*-yun) *adj*. Of Julius Caesar.

Julian Calendar. The calendar adjusted by Julius Caesar, 46 B.C., and replaced by the Gregorian Calendar.

ju·li·enne (joo-lee-*en*) *adj*. Cut in thin strips. 'Julienne potatoes.'—*n*. A clear soup containing shredded vegetables.

Ju·ly (joo-*lye*) *n*. The seventh month of the year.

jum·ble (*jum*-b'l) *v*. [jum·bled; jum·bling] To mix without order; confuse; disorder.—*n*. Confusion; a disordered mixture.

jum·bo (*jum*-boh) *n*. [*pl.* -bos] Any large, clumsy person or thing.—*adj*. Huge; large.

jump *v*. 1. To leap; spring up from the ground, by or as by, leaping. 2. To jolt; move with a sudden start or jerk. 3. To steal possession of, as a claim. 4. To leave or evade, as by leaping. 5. *Checkers*. To move over and capture an opponent's piece.—*n*. 1. A leap; spring; bound. 2. Distance leaped.

jump *adj*. *Jazz Music*. 1. Denoting rapid syncopated tempo. 'Tempo di jump.' 2. Denoting a piece in rapid tempo with simple melodic figures repeated many times.—*n*. A composition or dance in rapid tempo.

jump·er *n*. 1. A sleeveless bodice and skirt worn over a blouse. 2. A loose blouse or jacket; smock.

jump·er *n*. 1. A person or device that jumps. 2. Chisel for boring holes in rock.

jumping bean. The seed of a Mexican plant, containing the larva of a moth.

jumping jack. A toy figure with movable joints.

jump·y *adj*. [jump·i·er; jump·i·est] 1. Nervous; jittery. 2. Tending to jump; jerky.

jun·co (*jung*-koh) *n*. [*pl.* -cos] A small North American finch.

junc·tion (*junk*-sh'n) *n*. 1. A union; coalition; joining. 2. A point where railroad lines meet.

junc·ture (*junk*-cher) *n*. 1. A junction; meeting of two lines, etc. 2. A decisive point in time; crisis.

June (*joon*) *n*. The sixth month of the year.

June bug, June beetle. 1. A large brown beetle appearing in early June. 2. A green beetle which feeds on peaches, figs.

jun·gle (*jung*-g'l) *n*. 1. Thick, tangled forest; dense tropical thicket. 2. Any thick, tangled mass.

jungle fowl. An Asiatic wild fowl.

jun·ior (*joon*-yer) *adj*. 1. Younger. 2. Of lower standing or position. 3. Of or relating to juniors.—*n*. 1. Younger person. 2. Person of lower standing, esp. a third-year student in schools and universities.—**jun·ior·i·ty** *n*.

junior college. A school which gives the first two years of a college course.

junior high school. A school combining the 7th and 8th grades of grammar school with the first year of high school.

ju·ni·per (*joon*-uh-per) *n*. An evergreen shrub having small blue berries used in preparing gin, medicines, etc.

J

junk *n.* A Chinese sailing boat with high stern and shallow draft.

junk *n.* 1. Discarded material; trash. 2. Scraps of metal, paper, glass, etc.—*v.* To discard; scrap.

JUNK

Junk·er (*yoonk*-er) *n.* A Prussian aristocrat.—**junk·er** *adj.*

junk·et (*jung*-kit) *n.* 1. A picnic; excursion, esp. one at public expense. 2. A dessert made of curds and cream or sweetened milk.—*v.* To picnic.

Ju·no (*joon*-oh) *n.* [*pl.* -nos] *Mythology.* The chief Roman goddess, wife of Jupiter.

jun·ta (*hoon*-tuh) *n.* A Spanish or Latin American legislative council.

jun·to (*jun*-toh) *n.* A cabal; intriguing faction.

Ju·pi·ter (*joop*-uh-ter) *n. Mythology.* 1. The chief Roman god. 2. The largest planet of the solar system.

ju·rid·i·cal (joo-*rid*-ih-k'l) *adj.* Also **ju·rid·ic.** Relating to law or justice; legal.— **-cal·ly** *adv.*

ju·ris·dic·tion (joor-iss-*dik*-shun) *n.* 1. Legal authority or control. 2. The extent of control or scope of legal authority.—**ju·ris·dic·tion·al** *adj.*—**ju·ris·dic·tion·al·ly** *adv.*

ju·ris·pru·dence (joor-iss-*proo*-d'nss) *n.* 1. The science or study of law. 2. A country's system of laws.—**ju·ris·pru·dent** *n.* A jurist.—**ju·ris·pru·dent, ju·ris·pru·den·tial** *adj.*

ju·rist (*joor*-ist) *n.* A legal expert; one skilled in, or practicing, law.

ju·rist·ic *adj.* Legal; relating to law.—**ju·ris·ti·cal** *adj.*—**ju·ris·ti·cal·ly** *adv.*

ju·ror (*joor*-er) *n.* A person serving on a jury.

ju·ry (*joor*-ee) *n.* [*pl.* -ries] 1. A body of men sworn to judge evidence in court. 2. A committee chosen to award prizes in a competition.

ju·ry·man *n.* [*pl.* -men] A juror; jury member.

ju·ry-rigged *adj. Nautical.* Temporary.

just *adj.* 1. Impartial; fair; equitable. 2. According to human or spiritual law; righteous; proper. 3. Based on truth or reason.—*adv.* 1. Closely; nearby. 2. Exactly; precisely. 'Just at that moment.' 3. Narrowly; barely; only. 'He just escaped.' 4. *Colloquial.* Quite; completely. 'Just exhausted.'—**just·ly** *adv.*

jus·tice (*juss*-tiss) *n.* 1. The fair rendering of what is just or due. 2. The principle of fair dealing; integrity. 3. Rightfulness. 'The justice of his claims.' 4. A magistrate; judge. —**jus·tice·ship** *n.*

justice of the peace. A local magistrate with minor powers.

jus·ti·fi·a·ble (juss-tih-*fye*-uh-b'l) *adj.* Defensible; capable of being proven just; excusable. —**jus·ti·fi·a·bil·i·ty, jus·ti·fi·a·ble·ness** *n.*

jus·ti·fi·ca·tion (juss-tih-fih-*kay*-sh'n) *n.* Defense; vindication; act of justifying.—**jus·ti·fi·ca·tive** *adj.*

jus·ti·fy (*juss*-tih-fye) *v.* [jus·ti·fied; jus·ti·fy·ing] 1. To show just reason for; vindicate; prove to be right. 2. To pardon; absolve; exonerate.—**jus·ti·fi·er** *n.*

jut *v.* [jut·ted; jut·ting] To project; incline forward or outward.—*n.* A projection.

jute (*joot*) *n.* 1. An East Indian plant whose fiber is used for ropes, sacking, etc. 2. The fiber itself.—*adj.* Made of jute.

ju·ve·nes·cent (joo-veh-*ness*-'nt) *adj.* Becoming young.—**ju·ve·nes·cence** *n.*

ju·ve·nile (*joo*-veh-n'l) *adj.* 1. Young; immature. 2. Characteristic of or belonging to the young.—*n.* 1. A youth; young person. 2. An actor portraying youthful roles. 3. A child's book.—**ju·ve·nil·i·ty** (joo-veh-*nil*-ih-tee) *n.* [*pl.* -ties].

jux·ta·po·si·tion (juks-tuh-puh-*zish*-'n) *n.* Contiguity; placing side by side.

K

Kaa·ba (*kah*-buh) *n.* Also **Caa·ba.** A building in the great mosque at Mecca where the Black Stone, sacred to Mohammedans, is contained.

Kaf·fir, Ka·fir (*kaf*-er) *n.* A member of a native race in South Africa.

kai·ser (*ky*-zer) *n.* 1. King; ruler. 2. [*cap.*] The ruler of Germany under the monarchy. 3. [*cap.*] The ruler of the Holy Roman Empire.

kale *n.* 1. A variety of curly-leaved cabbage. 2. *Slang.* Money.

ka·lei·do·scope (kuh-*ly*-duh-skohp) *n.* 1. An optical instrument through which is viewed a great variety of colors and designs. 2. A changing pattern of scenes.—**ka·lei·do·scop·ic, ka·lei·do·scop·i·cal** *adj.*—**ka·lei·do·scop·i·cal·ly** *adv.*

kal·so·mine. *Variant spelling* of **calcimine.**

Ka·mi·ka·ze (kam-uh-*kaz*-ee) *n.* Japanese airplane for suicide attacks.—**ka·mi·ka·ze** *adj.*

Kan·a·ka (*kan*-uh-kuh; kuh-*nak*-uh) *n.* A native of the Hawaiian or South Sea Islands.

kan·ga·roo (kang-ger-*oo*) *n.* An Australian mammal with short forelegs and powerful hind legs for leaping. The female has a pouch in front for carrying her young.

KANGAROO (1/50 life size)

kangaroo rat. Small pouched rodent of SW U.S.

ka·o·lin (*kay*-uh-lin) *n.* Also **ka·o·line.** A fine, white clay used in chinaware and porcelain.

ka·pok (*kay*-pok) *n.* Silky fiber of a West Indian tree used for stuffing pillows, life jackets, etc.

ka·put (kah-*put*) *adj. Slang.* Finished; done.

kar·a·kul, kar·a·kule. *Variants of* **caracul.**

kar·at *n.* 1. Unit of weight of gems. 2. One twenty-fourth part; index of fineness of gold.

ka·ty·did (*kay*-tee-did) *n.* A large, green variety of grasshopper emitting a shrill cry.

kay·ak *n.* A light, completely covered Eskimo fishing boat.

ke·a (*kay*-uh) *n.* A large New Zealand parrot which feeds on animal flesh.

KAYAK

kedge (*kej*) *v.* [kedged; kedg·ing] *Nautical.* To warp; move a ship by means of an anchor.—*n.* Also **kedge anchor.** A small anchor for hauling a ship around a harbor.

keel *n.* 1. The main longitudinal structural member of a ship. 2. Part of an aircraft corresponding to a ship's keel. 3. A coal barge. —*v.* To turn over.—**keel over.** To capsize; turn upside down; fall over suddenly.

keel·haul (*keel*-hawl) *v.* To punish by dragging under the bottom of a ship.

keel·son, kel·son *n.* Beam or plates fastened along the top of a keel to stiffen and support it.

keen *adj.* 1. Sharp; thin-edged. 2. Acute; shrewd. 3. Intense; penetrating; vehement. —**keen·ly** *adv.*—**keen·ness** *n.*

keen-eared	keen-eyed	keen-sighted
keen-edged	keen-scented	keen-witted

keen *n.* A lament for the dead; mourning wail. —*v.* To wail; cry for the dead.—**keen·er** *n.*

keep *v.* [kept; kept; keep·ing] 1. To hold; retain. 2. To detain; hold at a place. 3. To tend; take care of. 4. To remain; continue; stay. 5. To last; stay fresh, as food. 6. To maintain; have available. 7. To provide support for. 8. To withhold; prevent knowing. 9. To perform; manage; look after.—*n.* 1. Dungeon; jail. 2. Subsistence; provision. 3. [*pl.*] The right to own what is won.—**keeping company.** *Colloquial.* Courtship.

keep one's distance. 1. To stay away; refrain from coming near. 2. To refrain from becoming intimate; remain aloof.

keep·er *n.* 1. A caretaker; custodian; superintendent. 2. A guard, as a jail keeper. 3. One who tends animals.

keep·ing *n.* 1. Custody; care; charge. 2. Harmony; conformity.

keep·sake *n.* A souvenir; token of remembrance.

keg *n.* A cask; barrel of less than 10 gallons.

kelp *n.* 1. Coarse brown seaweed. 2. The ashes of seaweed for making iodine.

kel·pie, kel·py *n.* [*pl.* -pies] *Gaelic Folklore.* A water sprite.

ken *v.* [kenned; ken·ning] To know; be acquainted with; understand.—*n.* Knowledge; understanding.

ken·nel *n.* 1. A dog house; place for raising dogs. 2. A pack of dogs.—*v.* [ken-neled, -nelled; -nel·ing, -nel·ling] To lodge or put in a kennel.

ke·no (*kee*-noh) *n.* A game played with numbered balls and cards; bingo.

kep·i (*kep*-ee) *n.* A round military cap with a visor.

ker·chief (*ker*-chif) *n.* 1. A cloth covering the head or neck. 2. A handkerchief.—**ker·chiefed** *adj.*

kerf *n.* A notch; slit; the cut made by an ax.

kern *n. Printing.* The overhanging or projecting part of a type face.

ker·nel *n.* 1. A grain; seed; anything enclosed in a shell. 2. The core; nucleus; essence.

ker·o·sene (*kehr*-uh-seen) *n.* A thin fuel oil refined from petroleum.

ketch *n.* A small two-masted sailboat.

ketch·up *n.* Also **cat·sup.** A condiment sauce prepared from tomatoes and spices.

KETCH

ke·tone (*kee*-tohn) *n. Chemistry.* One of a large group of hydrocarbons with a carbon-and-oxygen radical.

ket·tle *n.* 1. A metal vessel or pot. 2. A teakettle.

ket·tle·drum *n.* A bowl-shaped tunable copper drum.

key (*kee*) *n.* A small, low reef or islet.

key *n.* 1. An instrument for operating a lock. 2. Any device for fastening or wedging in. 3. A lever on a musical instrument, typewriter, or similar device. 4. Pitch; tone; flavor; style. 5. A clue; factor in solving anything.—*v.* 1. To lock; close firmly. 2. To fasten with a key.—*adj.* Principal; strategically placed; major.—**key up.** To become excited; cause tension.

KETTLE

key holder	key ring	keysmith
keynotes	keyseat	key-stringed

key·board *n.* The row or rows of keys on a piano, typewriter, or other instrument.

key·hole *n.* An opening in a lock for receiving the key.

key·man. A person entrusted with the most important details of an organization or project.

KEYBOARD (piano)

key·note *n.* 1. *Music.* The first or basic tone of

K

any key. 2. The guiding principle; essential or central idea.—*v.* [-not·ed; -not·ing] *Colloquial*. To make the principal address at a meeting.

key·stone *n.* The center stone of an arch.

KEYSTONE

Keystone State. Pennsylvania.

kha·ki (*kak*-ee; *kah*-kee) *adj.* Olive-drab; brownish.—*n.* A cloth of this color, used esp. for uniforms.

khan (*kahn*) *n.* An Asiatic prince.

khan *n.* A caravansary; an Eastern inn.

khe·dive (keh-*deev*) *n.* A governor or viceroy of Egypt.

khor·a·san (koh-ruh-*sahn*) *n.* A type of Persian carpet or rug.

kibe *n.* A split or crack in the flesh caused by chapping.

kib·itz (*kib*-its) *v.* [kib·itzed; kib·itz·ing] *Colloquial*. To heckle; give unsolicited advice, usually by a spectator to a player.—**kib·it·zer** *n.*

ki·bosh (*ky*-bosh) *n.* 1. Dry cement spread over sculpture. 2. *Slang*. Humbug; nonsense.—**put the kibosh on**. Thwart; quash.

kick *v.* 1. To strike with the foot. 2. *Slang*. To complain. 3. To recoil; as a gun.—*n.* 1. A blow with the foot. 2. The recoil of a firearm. 3. *Slang*. **a.** A complaint. **b.** A thrill; pleasure.—**kick·er** *n. Slang*. A complainer.

kick·back *v. Slang*. To pay an unauthorized commission.—*n.* 1. A rebate. 2. A commission.

kick·off *n. Football*. A kick from the center of the field, after a touchdown or at the start of a half.

kick·shaw (*kik*-shaw), **kick·shaws** *n.* 1. A delicacy. 2. A fantastic trifle.

kid *n.* 1. A young goat. 2. Goat hide. 3. *Colloquial*. A child; young person.—*v.* [kid·ded; kid·ding] 1. To bear a goat. 2. *Slang*. To tease; joke.

kid·nap (*kid*-nap) *v.* [kid·naped, -napped; -nap·ing, -nap·ping] To abduct; carry off unlawfully, esp. a child.—**kid·nap·er, kid·nap·per** *n.*

kid·ney (*kid*-nee) *n.* 1. One of two oblong flattened organs secreting urine. 2. Temperament; type.

kidney bean. A reddish kidney-shaped bean.

kill *v.* 1. To slay; destroy; deprive of life. 2. To deaden; quell, as pain. 3. To delete; discard, as a news story. 4. *Slang*. To strike one as hilarious.—*n.* 1. Prey; slain animal. 2. A stream; creek.

kill·deer (*kil*-deer) *n.* Also **kill·dee**. A small brown aquatic bird of North America.

kill·er *n.* 1. A slayer; murderer. 2. *Slang*. A hilarious story. 3. Also **killer whale**. A large predatory dolphin.

kill·ing *n.* A murder; slaying.—*adj.* 1. Dangerous; cruelly exhausting. 2. *Colloquial*.

Overpowering. 3. *Colloquial*. Hilariously funny.

kiln (*kil*; *kiln*) *n.* An oven; stove for drying, heating, baking, etc.—*v.* To dry in a kiln, as grain, meal, etc.

ki·lo (*kee*-loh) *n.* [*pl.* -los] Shortened form of **kilogram**, **kilometer**.

ki·lo·cy·cle (*kil*-uh-sy-k'l) *n.* A measurement of radio frequency denoting 1,000 electrical impulses per second.

kil·o·gram, kil·o·gramme (*kil*-uh-gram) *n.* 1,000 grams; 2.2046 lbs.

kil·o·lit·er, kil·o·lit·re (*kil*-uh-leet-er) *n.* 1,000 liters; about 264 gallons.

kil·o·me·ter, kil·o·me·tre (*kil*-uh-mee-ter) *n.* A unit of linear measurement; 3,280.8 feet; about 3/5 of a mile.—**kil·o·met·ric** (kil-uh-*met*-rik), **kil·o·met·ri·cal** *adj.*

kil·o·watt (*kil*-o-wot) *n.* A unit of electrical activity; 1,000 watts.

KILT

kil·o·watt-hour *n.* The amount of energy spent by a kilowatt during one hour.

kilt *n.* A pleated knee-length skirt worn by Scotch Highlanders.—*v.* To pleat like a kilt.

kil·ter *n. Colloquial*. Arrangement; proper condition, focus, etc.—**out of kilter**. Disarranged.

ki·mo·no (kuh-*moh*-nuh) *n.* [*pl.* -nos] 1. A loose Japanese outer robe. 2. A woman's dressing gown.

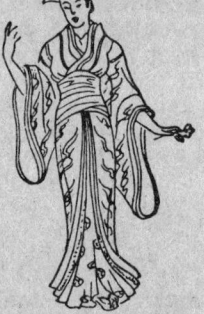

KIMONO

kin *n.* Relative; kindred; family.—*adj.* Kindred; of the same nature.

kind (*kynde*) *adj.* Benevolent; doing good to others.

kind *n.* Sort; variety; nature; character; style.

kin·der·gar·ten (*kin*-der-gahr-t'n) *n.* A play school for children of pre-school age, aimed at developing initiative and proper social attitudes.

kind·heart·ed *adj.* Benevolent; sympathetic; well-disposed toward others.—**kind·heart·ed·ly** *adv.*—**kind·heart·ed·ness** *n.*

kin·dle (*kin*-d'l) *v.* [kin·dled; kin·dling] 1. To light; inflame; set on fire. 2. To provoke; rouse; excite to action.

kin·dling (*kin*-dling) *n.* Small piece of firewood; material for starting a fire.

kind·ly *adj.* [kind·li·er; kind·li·est] Sympathetic; genial; inclined to do good.—**kind·ly** *adv.*

kind·ness *n.* 1. Benevolence; generosity; compassion. 2. A favor; act of good will.

kin·dred (*kin*-drid) *n.* 1. Relations; relatives; kin. 2. Relationship; connection; kin.—*adj.* 1. Related; allied. 2. Congenital.

kin·e·mat·ics (kin-eh-*mat*-iks) *n.* The science of pure motion.—**kin·e·mat·ic, -i·cal** *adj.*

kin·e·tics (kih-*net*-iks) *n.* The study of the forces causing motion.—**kin·e·tic** *adj.* Active; indicating motion.

king *n.* 1. A monarch, ruler, male sovereign. 2. One who holds a controlling position. 3. A representation of a king, as a card or chess piece.—*adj.* Chief; most powerful.

king·bird *n.* A North American flycatcher having a white-edged tail and erectile crest.

king·bolt *n.* A vertical bolt connecting the running gear with the front axle of a railway car.

king·dom (*king*-dum) *n.* 1. The dominion of a king. 2. A domain; realm; sphere.

king·fish *n.* A carnivorous fish of the Atlantic coast.

king·fish·er *n.* A fish-eating bird with blue and green plumage.

King Lear. The aged hero of the Shakespearean tragedy of the same name.

king·let *n.* A weak king; little king.

king·ly *adj.* [king·li·er; king·li·est] Majestic; imperial; becoming a king. —**king·li·ness** *n.*

KINGFISHER (1/10 life size)

king·pin *n.* 1. The bowling pin at the front apex. 2. *Colloquial.* The leader of an enterprise.

Kings *n. pl.* The eleventh and twelfth books of the Old Testament.

king·ship *n.* The office of a king.

king size. *Colloquial.* Large; giant size.

kink *n.* 1. A loop; twist, as in rope. 2. A muscular tightness or crick.—*v.* To twist into knots.

kin·ka·jou (*kink*-uh-joo) *n.* A catlike South American animal, easily tamed.

kink·y *adj.* [kink·i·er; kink·i·est] Twisted; knotted; having small, tight curls.—**kink·i·ly** *adv.*

kin·ship *n.* Relationship.

kins·man *n.* [*pl.* -men] A relative.—**kins·wom·an** *n.*

ki·osk (kee-*osk*) *n.* A boxlike structure, usually round, used as a newstand, etc.

kip *n. Tanning.* The hide of a young animal.

kip·per *n.* 1. A male salmon. 2. A salmon split, salted, and dried or smoked.—*v.* To cure and preserve by use of salt, pepper, and a smoking process.

kirk *n.* 1. A church. 2. [cap.] The established church of Scotland.

kirsch, kirsch·was·ser (*kersh*-vahss-er) *n.* A liquor distilled from the fermented juice of the small black cherry.

kir·tle (*ker*-t'l) *n.* A woman's gown; petticoat.

kis·met (*kiz*-met) *n.* Fate; destiny.

kiss *v.* 1. To touch with the lips in salutation or affection; join lips in love; caress. 2. To touch gently; come into light contact with.—*n.* 1. A salute or caress given with the lips. 2. A baked confection made of egg whites, powdered sugar, etc.—**kiss·er** *n. Slang.* Face.

kit *n.* A case designed to hold a set of equipment; outfit.

kitch·en (*kich*-en) *n.* 1. A room which is used for cooking. 2. Cuisine; cookery.—*adj.* Belonging to or used in a kitchen.

kitch·en·ette (kich-en-*et*) *n.* A small, compactly laid-out kitchen.

kitchen police. *Military.* The tasks connected with the cooking and serving of meals; a man or men assigned to kitchen detail.

kitch·en·ware *n.* Domestic utensils for use in the kitchen.

kite *n.* 1. A carnivorous bird of the falcon family. 2. A light frame of wood and paper which is flown in the air for amusement. 3. *Business.* Fictitious or nominal commercial paper used to mislead others as to one's real monetary resources. 4. A rascal; rogue. —*v.* 1. To fly kites. 2. To raise money by use of fictitious paper.

kith *n. Archaic.* Acquaintances or friends collectively.—**kith and kin.** Friends and relatives.

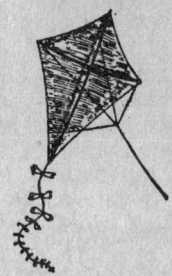
KITE (def. 1)

KITE (def. 2)

kit·ten *n.* A young cat; the young of a cat.—*v.* Of cats, to give birth.—**kit·ten·ish** *adj.* Playful; frivolous.

kit·ty *n.* [*pl.* -ties] 1. A kitten. 2. *Card Playing.* The pooled stakes.

ki·wi (*kee*-wee) *n.* 1. An almost extinct, non-flying, large New Zealand bird. 2. *Slang.* An aviation cadet.

Klan *n.* The Ku Klux Klan.—**klans·man** *n.*

klep·to·ma·ni·a (klep-toh-*may*-nee-uh) *n.* An irresistible desire to steal.—**klep·to·ma·ni·ac** *n.*

klieg light. An actinic arc light, used in motion picture photography.

knack (*nak*) *n.* 1. Readiness; dexterity; adroitness. 2. A knickknack; ingenious trifle, toy.

knap·sack (*nap*-sak) *n.* A bag of leather or canvas for carrying personal articles on the back.

knave (*nayv*) *n.* 1. A false, deceitful fellow. 2. *Card Games.* The jack; card next above a 10.

knav·er·y *n.* [*pl.* -ies] Dishonesty; petty villainy.

knav·ish (*nayv*-ish) *adj.* Dishonest; fraudulent; rascally.—**knav·ish·ly** *adv.*—**knav·ish·ness** *n.*

knead (*need*) *v.* 1. To work, usually by hand, pressing dough, etc., into a well-mixed mass. 2. To pummel; massage.—**knead·er** *n.*

knee (*nee*) *n.* 1. The joint connecting the thigh and lower leg. 2. Anything resembling the

K

knee in shape. 3. Portion of a garment covering the knee.—*v.* To thrust with the knee.

knee-bent	knee halter	kneepiece
knee-bowed	knee-haltered	knee-shaped
knee-braced	knee high	knee-sprung
knee-breeched	kneehole	kneestone
kneebrush	knee-jointed	knee-tied
knee deep	knee pad	knee-worn

knee·cap *n.* The flat, movable bone forming the front of the knee; patella.

kneel (*neel*) *v.* [knelt or kneeled; kneeling] To bend the knee; fall or remain on one or both knees.—**kneel·er** *n.*

knee·pan *n.* The kneecap; patella.

knell (*nel*) *v.* 1. To indicate or summon by a knell. 2. To toll; sound as an omen or warning.—*n.* The sound of a bell striking slowly, esp. for a funeral; mourning sound.

Knick·er·bock·er (*nik-er-bok-er*). A descendant of the early New York settlers.

knick·er·bock·ers *n. pl.* Loose trousers gathered just below the knee.

knick·ers (*nik-erz*) *n. pl.* Knickerbockers.

knick·knack (*nik-nak*) *n.* Trifle; small toy or ornament.

knife (*nyfe*) *n.* [*pl.* -knives] 1. A cutting instrument with a sharp-edged blade and a handle. 2. A cutting blade in certain machines.—*v.* [knifed; knif·ing] 1. To stab or cut with a knife. 2. *Slang.* To betray; fight unfairly.

knife-backed	knife-jawed	knife-shaped
knife-bladed	knifelike	knifesmith
knife-edged	knifeman	knife-stripped

knife-edge *n.* A sharp, accurately ground edge serving as the axis of a balance.

knight (*nyte*) *n.* In medieval times, a man of military rank, pledged to chivalry. 2. A man on whom a nonhereditary distinction, carrying the title of *Sir*, has been conferred. 3. A chess piece bearing a horse's head.—*v.* To confer knighthood on.

knight-errant *n.* [*pl.* knights-errant] A knight wandering in search of adventure.—**knight·er·rant·ry** *n.* [*pl.* -ries].

knight·hood *n.* 1. The rank or distinction of a knight. 2. Knights collectively.

knight·ly *adj.* Pertaining to or suitable for a knight.—**knight·ly** *adv.*—**knight·li·ness** *n.*

Knight Templar. 1. [*pl.* Knights Templars] Member of a medieval armed religious order formed to protect the Holy Sepulcher. 2. [*pl.* Knights Templar] Member of an order of Freemasons.

knit (*nit*) *v.* [knit, knit·ted; knit·ting] 1. To make a garment or fabric by looping and knotting yarn with needles. 2. Draw together; consolidate; contract.—**knit·ter, knit·ting** *n.*

knives (*nyvz*). *Plural of* knife.

knob (*nob*) *n.* 1. A round or ball-shaped handle. 2. A rising; rounded lump or swelling. 3. A rounded hill.—**knobbed** *adj.*—**knobby** *adj.* [knob·bi·er; knob·bi·est].

knock (*nok*) *v.* 1. To strike; hit, esp. with a noise. 2. To drive against; crash. 3. To rattle, as loose machinery. 4. *Slang.* To criticize destructively.—*n.* 1. A blow; forceful contact; rap. 2. *Slang.* A destructive criticism.—**knock·er** *n.*—**knock off.** 1. To cease an activity. 2. *Slang.* To kill.

knock about. To go around with no purpose; wander.—**knock·a·bout** *n.* A small sailboat for open water.—*adj.* 1. Suitable for rough or traveling use. 2. Rough; noisy.

knock down. 1. To take apart. 2. To sell to the highest bidder. 3. To reduce in price.—**knock·down** *n.* 1. A price reduction. 2. Object capable of being taken apart.—*adj.* 1. Spirited; aggressive; forceful. 2. Capable of being taken apart.

knock-kneed *adj.* With the legs curving inward at the knee so they knock together in walking.—**knock·knee** *n.*

knock out. To render unconscious or ineffectual.—**knock-out** *n.* 1. *Slang.* A beautiful or striking person or thing. 2. A rendering unconscious.—**knock·out** *adj.*

knoll *n.* A mound; small, round hill.

knot (*not*) *n.* 1. A fastening or tie in a rope or other flexible material. 2. A bond; close association or union. 3. A cluster; group. 4. Something hard to solve; problem, perplexity. 5. A mark or plug in timber, growing against its grain. 6. A swelling; lump; protuberance. 7. A unit of speed equal to one nautical mile (6,082.2 feet) per hour.—*v.* [knot·ted; knot·ting] 1. To tie a knot; entangle; complicate. 2. To unite.

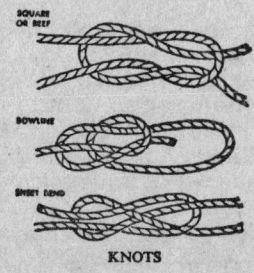
KNOTS

knot·hole *n.* A hole in wood left when a knot is removed.

knot·ty (*not-ee*) *adj.* [knot·ti·er; knot·ti·est] 1. Marked with or like a knot. 2. Intricately tangled; complicated.—**knot·ti·ness** *n.*

knout (*nowt*) *n.* A whip; lash.—*v.* To flog; whip.

know (*noh*) *v.* [know; known; know·ing] 1. To understand clearly. 2. To be acquainted or familiar with. 3. To be informed or convinced of. 4. To distinguish between. 5. *Bible.* To cohabit with.—**in the know.** *Slang.* Having special knowledge of a situation.—**know·a·ble** *adj.*—**know·er** *n.*

know-how *n. Colloquial.* Specialized skill or knowledge.

know·ing (*noh-ing*) *adj.* 1. Expressive of knowledge or cunning. 'A knowing look.' 2. Conscious; intelligent. 3. Well informed; skillful.—**know·ing·ly** *adv.*—**know·ing·ness** *n.*

knowl·edge (*nol-ij*) *n.* [*pl.* -edg·es] 1. Learning; erudition. 2. Skill; experience. 3. Acquaintance. 4. What is known or knowable. 5. Clear perception. 6. Information. 7. *Archaic.* Sexual intercourse.— -**edge·a·ble** *adj.*

know-noth·ing *n.* A fool.

knuck·le (*nuk*-'l) *n*. A finger joint.—*v*. [knuckled; knuck·ling] 1. To yield; submit. 2. To thrust with the knuckles.

knurl (*nerl*) *n*. 1. A series of shallow beads on a surface to make it easier to grasp. 2. A knot; protuberance.—**knurl·y** *adj*.

ko·a·la (koh-*ah*-luh) *n*. A pouched, almost tailless, tree-dwelling animal of Australia.

Ko·be (*koh*-beh). Japanese city on the southern end of Honshu.

Ko·dak *n*. A trade-mark name for a camera.—*v*. To take pictures with a Kodak.

KOALA (1/20 life size)

Koh·i·noor (*koh*-in-oor) *n*. A famous diamond acquired by the British crown in 1849.

kohl·ra·bi (*kohl*-rah-bee) *n*. [*pl*. -bies] A variety of cabbage having a large edible stem.

ko·lin·sky (koh-*lin*-skee) *n*. A fine mink fur from northeastern U.S.S.R.

Kom·in·tern. *Variant spelling* of **Comintern.**

ko·pek (*koh*-pek) *n*. Also **ko·peck.** A small coin of the U.S.S.R.

Ko·ran (koh-*ran*, koh-ran) *n*. The Mohammedan book of faith, containing God's revelations to Mohammed.

ko·sher (*koh*-sher) *adj*. 1. Designated as clean and proper by Jewish dietary law. 2. *Colloquial*. Proper; correct; orthodox.

kow·tow (*kow*-tow) *v*. 1. To fawn obsequiously. 2. To salute by prostrating the body.

kraal (*krahl*) *n*. In South Africa, a group of huts; native village.

Krem·lin (*krem*-lin) *n*. 1. The old fortress of Moscow, now containing government offices. 2. [*not cap.*] Any Russian citadel.

Krish·na (*krish*-nuh) *n*. A widely worshiped Hindu deity; one of the forms of Vishnu.

kro·na (*kroh*-nuh) *n*. [*pl*. kro·nor] A silver coin of Sweden.

kro·ne (*kroh*-neh) *n*. [*pl*. kro·ner] A coin of Norway and Denmark.

kro·ne (*kroh*-nuh) *n*. [*pl*. kro·nen] 1. A former German coin worth ten marks. 2. A former coin of Austria-Hungary.

kryp·ton (*krip*-ton) *n*. A chemically inert gaseous element found in minute quantities in the air. (*Symbol*: Kr).

KRISHNA

ku·dos (*kyoo*-doss, *koo*-) *n*. Glory; fame.

ku·du (*koo*-doo) *n*. The striped antelope.

Ku-Klux (*koo*-kluks, often, erroneously, *kloo*-kluks) *n*. Also **Ku Klux Klan.** 1. A secret organization formed in the South following the Civil War to maintain political control by the whites, often through terrorism. 2. (Knights of the Ku-Klux Klan). An organization incorporated in Georgia in 1915, advocating the supremacy of American-born white Protestants.—**Ku-Klux·er, Klux·er** *n*.

ku·lak (koo-*lahk*) *n*. In Czarist Russia, a wealthy peasant.

ku·miss (*koo*-miss) *n*. A liquor made by the Tartars from mare's milk distilled or fermented.

küm·mel (*kim*-ul) *n*. A caraway-flavored liqueur, originated in Germany.

kum·quat (*kum*-kwot) *n*. 1. A variety of Chinese tree bearing small orangelike fruit. 2. The fruit of this tree.

Kuo·min·tang (*kwoh*-min-*tahng*) *n*. The nationalist party in the Chinese Republic.

Kurd *n*. An inhabitant of Kurdistan.—**Kurd·ish** *adj*.

L

la (*lah*) *n*. *Music*. The sixth note of the diatonic scale.

la·bel (*lay*-b'l) *n*. 1. Slip affixed to an object indicating contents, ownership, etc. 2. A name indicating classification.—*v*. [la·beled, la·belled; la·bel·ing, la·bel·ling] To affix a label to.—**la·bel·er, la·bel·ler** *n*.

la·bi·al (*lay*-bee-ul) *adj*. Pertaining to, or formed by, the lips.—*n*. A consonant formed chiefly by the lips, as *b, p, m*.

la·bor (*lay*-ber) *n*. 1. Exertion involved in doing work; toil. 2. Workers collectively. 3. A task. 4. Pangs of childbirth.—*v*. 1. To exert muscular strength; work. 2. To endeavor; strive. 3. To undergo childbirth. 4. To pitch or roll, as a ship.

lab·o·ra·to·ry (*lab*-ruh-tor-ee) *n*. [*pl*. -ries]

Building or workshop designed for scientific research or production.—**lab·o·ra·to·ry** *adj*.

la·bored (*lay*-berd) *adj*. Done with labor; showing constraint or effort.

la·bor·er (*lay*-ber-er) *n*. One who does work, esp. physical or unskilled work.

la·bo·ri·ous (luh-*bor*-ee-us) *adj*. 1. Involved; entailing heavy work. 2. Industrious.

la·bor move·ment. The sum of all workers organized into trade and industrial unions.

labor union. An organization of workers formed for mutual welfare and collective bargaining with employers.

Labour Party. British political party representing, and supported by, workers.

La·bour·ite (*lay*-ber-yte) *n*. Member of the British Labour Party.

la·bur·num (luh-*bern*-um) *n.* Shrub or small tree bearing yellow flowers.

lab·y·rinth (*lab*-er-inth) *n.* 1. A structure of winding passages, difficult to get out of; maze. 2. Any intricate business. 3. Part of the inner ear.—**lab·y·rin·thi·an, -rin·thic, -rin·thi·cal** *adj.*

lab·y·rin·thine (lab-er-*in*-thin) *adj.* Having numerous winding passages; intricate.

lac *n.* A resinous substance, used to make shellac.

lace (*layss*) *n.* 1. A string or cord for fastening shoes, corsets, etc. 2. Delicate network of silk or cotton thread, elaborately patterned. —*v.* [laced; lac·ing] 1. To fasten with cord, etc. 2. To add spirits to tea, soda, etc. 3. To beat; lash.

lace-bordered	lace-fronted	lace-trimmed
lace-curtained	lace maker	lacewoman
lace-edged	lacepiece	lacework

lac·er·ate (*lass*-er-ayt) *v.* [lac·er·at·ed; lac·er·at·ing] 1. To tear; mangle. 2. To wound; harrow.—**lac·er·ate, -at·ed** *adj.*—**lac·er·a·tion** *n.*

lach·ry·mal (*lak*-rih-m'l) *adj.* Also **lac·ri·mal.** Pertaining to, or secreting tears.—*n.* [*pl.*] The tear-producing organs.

lach·ry·mose (*lak*-rih-mohss) *adj.* Shedding tears; mournful.—**lach·ry·mose·ly** *adv.*

lac·ing (*layss*-ing) *n.* 1. Binding or fastening through eyelet holes. 2. A cord. 3. A beating.

lack *v.* 1. To want; require. 2. To be without; be short.—*n.* 1. Failure; being without. 2. A want; thing needed.

lack·a·dai·si·cal (lak-uh-*day*-zik-'l) *adj.* Slow-moving; languid; indolent.—**lack·a·dai·si·cal·ly** *adv.*—**lack·a·dai·si·cal·ness** *n.*

lack·ey *n.* [*pl.* -eys, -ies] 1. A servant; footman. 2. A submissive follower.

lack·lus·ter, lack·lus·tre *n.* Want of brightness or luster.—**lack·lus·ter, lack·lus·tre** *adj.*

lac·on·ic (luh-*kon*-ik) *adj.* Concise; short; terse. —**la·con·i·cal·ly** *adv.*

lac·quer (*lak*-er) *n.* Varnish made from shellac. —*v.* To cover with lacquer.—**lac·quer·er** *n.*

la·crosse (luh-*kross*) *n.* A game of ball played with long-handled, loose-netted rackets.

lac·ta·tion (lak-*tay*-shun) *n.* 1. The act of suckling. 2. The secreting or yielding of milk.

lac·te·al (*lak*-tee-ul) *adj.* 1. Of or like milk; milky. 2. Holding or carrying chyle.—*n.* One of numerous small tubes which carry the chyle to the thoracic duct.

lac·tic (*lak*-tik) *adj.* Of milk; from sour milk.

lac·to·fla·vin (*lak*-toh-flay-vin) *n.* A yellow fluorescent pigment found in milk and containing Vitamin B_2.

lac·tose (*lak*-tohss) *n.* The sugar of milk.

la·cu·na (luh-*kyoo*-nuh) *n.* [*pl.* -nae, -nas] 1. Small blank or empty space; gap; hiatus. 2. Minute cavity in bone or tissue.

lac·y (*lay*-see) *adj.* [lac·i·er; lac·i·est] Made of, or like, lace.

lad *n.* Young man or boy; fellow.

lad·der (*lad*-er) *n.* 1. Two sidepieces of wood, metal, or rope, joined by rungs at intervals to form steps for climbing. 2. A wide run in a stocking or sweater.

lad·die *n.* A boy or young man.

lade (*layd*) *v.* [lad·ed; lad·ed or lad·en; lad·ing] 1. To load; put a cargo in. 2. To lift or scoop, as with a ladle.

lad·ing *n.* 1. Cargo; freight; burden. 2. Act of loading.

la·dle (*lay*-d'l) *n.* A long-handled, cup-shaped utensil for dipping out liquids from a vessel. —*v.* [la·dled; la·dling] To scoop up and carry in a ladle.—**la·dler** *n.*

la·dy (*lay*-dee) *n.* [*pl.* -dies] 1. Term applied by courtesy to any woman, esp. one of social position or refinement. 2. [*cap.*] The title of certain women of the British nobility; courtesy title given to wives and daughters of some members of the British peerage. 3. Woman one loves; sweetheart; wife.—**la·dy** *adj.*

la·dy·bug *n.* Also **lady·bird.** A small spotted insect of the beetle family.

la·dy·fin·ger *n.* A small narrow spongecake, shaped like a finger.

la·dy·kill·er *n.* A man irresistible to women.

la·dy·like *adj.* Refined; well-bred; like, or suitable for, a lady.

LADYBUG

la·dy·love *n.* A sweetheart; beloved.

la·dy·ship *n.* 1. The rank or character of a lady. 2. Address or designation for a woman with the title of *Lady.* 'Her ladyship returned.'

la·dy's-slip·per *n.* Also **la·dy-slip·per.** An orchid whose blossom slightly resembles a slipper.

lag *v.* [lagged; lag·ging] To slacken speed or move slowly; loiter or hang back.—*n.* 1. The retardation of a movement. 2. Delay between related actions.

lager beer (*lah*-ger). A light beer which is stored for some months before use.

lag·gard (*lag*-erd) *adj.* Slow; backward.—*n.* One who loiters or moves slowly.

la·gniappe, la·gnappe (lan-*yap*) *n. Southern U.S.* A small present traditionally given by trades-people to their customers.

la·goon (luh-*goon*) *n.* 1. Shallow lake connected with a sea or river. 2. Body of water surrounded by a coral atoll.

lair *n.* Retreat; hiding or resting place, esp. the den of a wild beast.

laird *n.* Landowner in Scotland.

lais·sez-faire (leh-say-*fair*) *adj.* A policy of government allowing undirected and unrestrained business competition.

la·i·ty (*lay*-it-ee) *n.* [*pl.* -ties] Those outside a particular profession, esp. outside the clergy.

lake *n.* A large body of water surrounded by land.

lam *v. Slang.* [lammed; lam·ming] 1. To punch; strike. 2. To flee, esp. from the police.

la·ma (*lah*-muh) *n.* A priest of Lamaism.

La·ma·ism (*lah*-muh-iz'm) *n.* A form of Buddhism followed chiefly in Tibet and Mongolia.

lamb (*lam*) *n.* 1. A young sheep. 2. A gentle, beloved person.

lam·baste (lam-*bayst*) *v.* [lam·bast·ed; lam·bast·ing] To chastise vigorously; beat; scold.

lam·bent (*lam*-b'nt) *adj.* 1. Touching lightly; gliding over; licking. 2. Gleaming; twinkling; flickering.—**lam·ben·cy** *n.*—**-bent·ly** *adv.*

lamb·kin (*lam*-kin) *n.* 1. A small lamb. 2. A term of endearment.

la·mé (lam-*ay*) *n.* A brilliant metallic fabric.

lame *adj.* 1. Crippled; disabled in the leg or foot; limping. 2. Imperfect; weak; unsatisfactory.—*v.* [lamed; lam·ing] To cripple or disable.—**lame·ly** *adv.*—**lame·ness** *n.*

lame duck. 1. An ineffectual or incapacitated person. 2. A speculator who cannot meet his contracts. 3. A man in public office who is completing his term after he has been defeated for re-election.

la·ment (luh-*ment*) *v.* To express sorrow; weep.—*n.* A mournful song or chant of grief.—**la·ment·ed** *adj.*—**la·ment·er** *n.*

la·men·ta·ble (*lam*-en-tuh-b'l) *adj.* Piteous; grievous; miserable; deplorable.— **-ta·bly** *adv.*

la·men·ta·tion (lam-en-*tay*-shun) *n.* Expression of sorrow; cries of grief; bewailing.

La·men·ta·tions *n.* A book of the Scriptures ascribed to Jeremiah.

lam·i·na (*lam*-in-uh) *n.* [*pl.* -nae, -nas] A thin plate or scale; layer.

lam·i·nate (*lam*-in-it) *adj.* Plated; consisting of scales or layers.—*v.* (*lam*-in-ayt) [-nat·ed; -nat·ing] To separate into or cover with thin plates or layers.—**lam·i·na·tion** (lam-in-*ay*-shun) *n.*

lamp *n.* A device, usually movable, for producing light by electricity or flame.

lamp·black (*lamp*-blak) *n.* Finely powdered carbon, used in pigments.

lam·poon (lam-*poon*) *n.* An abusive attack on a person in prose or verse; written personal satire.—**lam·poon** *v.*—**lam·poon·er** *n.*—**lam·poon·er·y** *n.*—**lam·poon·ist** *n.*

lam·prey (*lam*-pree) *n.* Name of several species of eel-like, scaleless, sucker-mouthed fishes found in both salt and fresh water.

lance (*lanss*) *n.* 1. A long spear tipped with metal. 2. A weapon or instrument resembling a lance.—*v.* [lanced; lanc·ing] To pierce or cut.

Lan·ce·lot (*lan*-sch-lot; *lahn*-). The bravest and most famous of the legendary knights of the Round Table.

lan·ce·o·late (*lan*-see-oh-layt) *adj. Botany & Zoology.* Shaped like a lance head.

lanc·er *n.* Cavalry soldier armed with a lance.

LANCET

lan·cet (*lanss*-et) *n.* A small, sharp, surgical instrument for opening abscesses, etc.

lance·wood *n.* A kind of wood with a high degree of toughness and elasticity.

land *n.* 1. Any portion of the earth's surface not covered by water. 2. A region; country. 3. Soil; earth. 4. [*pl.*] Real estate; property.—*v.* 1. To go ashore, or put anything ashore, from a vessel. 2. To pilot an airplane to earth. 3. *Colloquial.* To catch; secure. 4. To arrive.

land-born	landlock	land-sheltered
land-cast	landlook	landsick
landfall	landman	landslip
landfast	land-obsessed	landstorm
landfolk	landplane	land-surrounded
land-girt	land-poor	land-taxer
land grabber	landraker	landways
land grabbing	land sale	land wire

lan·dau (*land*-aw) *n.* 1. A four-wheeled carriage. 2. An automobile with a folding top.

land·ed *adj.* Owning, or consisting of, real estate.

land·hold·er *n.* An owner or occupant of land. —**land·hold·ing** *n. & adj.*

land·ing *n.* 1. A place where passengers or goods are discharged from vessels. 2. A platform at the end of a flight of stairs. 3. A putting ashore; descent from the air.

landing gear. Equipment necessary to land.

land·la·dy *n.* [*pl.* -dies] 1. The mistress of a lodging house. 2. A female owner of real estate for rent or lease.

land·less *adj.* Owning no land.

land·locked *adj.* Surrounded by land; cut off from open water.

land·lord *n.* 1. The holder of real estate to be leased or rented. 2. The host or master of an inn or lodging.

land·lub·ber *n.* 1. One who spends his life on land. 2. Any poor, clumsy sailor.

land·mark *n.* 1. A prominent physical feature by which a locality or boundary is known. 2. An event which marks a new phase in development.

land·scape *n.* 1. A portion of territory which can be comprehended in a single view. 2. A picture showing a country view.—*v.* [-scaped; -scap·ing] To beautify land by grading, gardening, etc.

landscape architect. One who beautifies land by rearranging its physical features.

land·slide *n.* 1. Sliding of a quantity of earth from a higher to a lower level; land mass which slides. 2. A huge majority of votes.

lands·man *n.* [*pl.* -men] A landlubber; seaman on his first voyage.

land·ward *adj. & adv.* Toward land from the sea.—**land·wards** *adj.*

lane (*layn*) *n.* 1. A narrow passage between hedges or buildings; narrow street; alley. 2. Any opening resembling such a passage, as between lines of people. 3. A route regularly traveled by ships. 4. A highway strip designated for one-way traffic.

lan·guage (*lang*-gwij) *n.* 1. The sum total of words used by a tribe, race, or nation for in-

L

tercommunication. 2. The expression of thoughts by spoken sounds or other symbols. 3. Style of speaking; ability to use words.

lan·guid (*lang*-gwid) *adj.* Indisposed to exertion; drooping; slow; tired.—**lan·guid·ly** *adv.*

lan·guish (*lang*-gwish) *v.* 1. To lose vigor or animation; become dull or inactive. 2. To droop; wither; fade. 3. To look appealingly or sentimentally.—**lan·guish·er** *n.*

lan·guish·ing *adj.* 1. Pining; losing strength; fading. 2. Having a soft, sentimental look. 3. Long continuing, as a sickness.—**-ing·ly** *adv.*

lan·guor (*lang*-er) *n.* 1. Weariness of body or mind. 2. A lazy, dreamy state. 3. Dullness; sluggishness; listlessness.—**lan·guor·ous** *adj.*

lank *adj.* 1. Thin; emaciated; meager. 2. Loose; drooping; not curly.—**lank·ly** *adv.*

lank·y *adj.* [lank·i·er; lank·i·est] Lean and tall of body; loose-jointed; clumsy.—**lank·i·ly** *adv.*

lan·o·lin (*lan*-uh-lin) *n.* A fat obtained from washing newly sheared wool.

lan·tern (*lan*-tern) *n.* 1. A lamp with a glass shield to protect the flame from wind. 2. The upper part of a lighthouse. 3. *Architecture.* A structure in the roof of a building that admits light to the interior.

lan·tern-jawed *adj.* Having a long, thin face and jutting jaw.

lan·tha·num (*lan*-thuh-num) *n.* A gray-white, scarce element of the cerium subgroup of metals. (*Symbol:* La).

LANTERN

lan·yard (*lan*-yerd) *n. Nautical.* A short piece of cordage used for fastening and tying down.

lap *v.* 1. To take up fluid or food with the tongue; feed or drink by licking. 2. To splash or wash against.—*n.* The sound made by splashing or licking liquid.

lap *n.* 1. The part of clothing that lies on the knees and upper part of the legs when sitting. 2. The knees and upper legs in this position.

lap *v.* [lapped; lap·ping] 1. To fold; bend and lay over. 2. To lay one thing partly covering another. 3. To infold; involve. 4. To polish or cut with a lap.—*n.* 1. The part of one object which partly covers another. 2. A revolving machine used for precision grinding, cutting, or polishing. 3. A part of a race course; once around a race track.

la·pel (luh-*pel*) *n.* The folded part of a coat which drops from the collar.

lap·i·dar·y (*lap*-uh-dair-ee) *n.* [*pl.* -ies] An artisan who cuts and mounts precious stones.

la·pin (*lap*-in; luh-*pan*) *n.* Rabbit fur.

lapis lazuli (*lap*-iss *laz*-yuh-lee). Stone of a rich blue color.

Lap·land. A barren area in northern Europe extending from Norway through northern Soviet Union.—**Lap·land·er** *n.*

Lapp *n.* A Laplander.

lapse *n.* 1. Gradual decline; an unnoticed passing, as of time. 2. Error; a failing in duty or morality.—*v.* [lapsed; laps·ing] 1. To pass slowly or silently. 2. To make an error; deviate from moral conduct. 3. To become legally void through failure to retain option.

lap·wing *n.* A crested plover whose plumage is green above and white below, with a black crest.

lar·board (*lahr*-bohrd; -b'd) *n. Nautical.* The lefthand side of a ship facing the bow; port.—**lar·board** *adj. & adv.*

lar·ce·ny (*lahr*-sun-ee) *n.* [*pl.* -nies] Theft of property. In U.S. law, **grand larceny** is classed as a felony, while **petty larceny** is a misdemeanor.—**lar·cen·er** *n.*—**lar·ce·nous** *adj.*—**-ous·ly** *adv.*

LAPWING

larch *n.* A cone-bearing tree of the pine family that sheds its needlelike leaves.

lard *n.* Pork fat melted down.—**lard** *v.* 1. To add lard to. 2. To insert strips of bacon or salt pork into a roast.—**lar·da·ceous, lard·y** *adj.*

lard·er *n.* Room or cabinet where food is kept.

la·res and penates (*lair*-eez and puh-*nayt*-eez). 1. Roman household gods. 2. Domestic possessions.

large (*lahrj*) *adj.* [larg·er; larg·est] 1. Of great size or quantity; big; extensive. 2. Unrestrained; lavish.—**large·ly** *adv.* 1. Chiefly. 2. In a large manner.—**large·ness** *n.*

lar·gess, lar·gesse (*lahr*-jess; *-jess*) *n.* A liberal gift or donation.

lar·go (*lahr*-goh) *adj. & adv. Music.* Slow.—*n.* A slow movement.

lar·i·at (*lair*-ee-ut) *n.* A long rope fitted with a noose for catching livestock.

lark *n.* 1. A small crested bird noted for its lovely song. 2. A sportive prank or frolic.—*v. Colloquial.* To frolic; sport; skylark.—**lark·er** *n.*

lark·spur *n.* A plant of the crowfoot family noted for its red, pink, or white flowers.

lar·rup (*lair*-up) *v. Colloquial.* To flog; whip.—**lar·rup** *n.*

LARKSPUR

lar·va (*lahr*-vuh) *n.* [*pl.* -vae] The early form of animal or insect life which during primary development is unlike the adult form of its parent.—**lar·val** *adj.*

la·ryn·ge·al (luh-*rin*-jee-ul) *adj.* Pertaining to the larynx.

lar·yn·gi·tis (lair-in-*jy*-tus) *n.* Inflammation of the larynx.—**lar·yn·gi·tic** (lair-in-*jit*-ik) *adj.*

LARVA

lar·ynx (*lair*-inks) *n.* [*pl.* la·rin·ges; lar·ynx·es]

Upper part of the windpipe containing membranes which produce vocal sounds.

las·car (*lass*-ker) *n*. East Indian sailor.

las·civ·i·ous (luh-*siv*-ee-us) *adj*. Lewd; lustful; exciting voluptuous emotions.—**las·civ·i·ous·ly** *adv*.—**las·civ·i·ous·ness** *n*.

lash *n*. 1. Whip; cord or thong used for striking. 2. A sharp, stinging blow.—**lash** *v*. 1. To strike with a whip; flog. 2. To strike out quickly and sharply. 3. To bind or secure with rope.—**lash** *n*.

lash·ing *n*. A piece of rope for binding or making fast one thing to another.

lass, las·sie *n*. Young woman; girl.

las·si·tude (*lass*-ih-tood) *n*. Weakness or weariness of body.

las·so (*lass*-oh) *n*. [*pl*. -sos, -soes] A rope with a noose used to catch wild horses and cattle. —**las·so** *v*.—**las·so·er** *n*.

last *n*. A foot-shaped form on which shoes are molded.—**last** *v*.—**last·er** *n*.

last *adj*. 1. Final; concluding; ultimate. 2. Most recent. 'Last night.' 3. Most unlikely. 'The last man I'd consult.'—*adv*. 1. Just before the present. 2. Finally; conclusively.—*n*. The end; conclusion; final unit of a group.—**at last**. Finally.

last *v*. To endure; continue; survive.

Las·tex (*lass*-teks) *n*. Trade name for an elastic fabric woven from strands of rubber wound with textile filaments.

last·ing *adj*. Durable; long continuing; permanent.—**last·ing·ly** *adv*.—**last·ing·ness** *n*.

last·ly *adv*. Finally; in conclusion.

Last Supper. The supper eaten by Christ and his disciples just prior to his betrayal.

latch (*lach*) *n*. A device for fastening a door or other movable structure.—*v*. To fasten; secure.

latch·key *n*. A door key.

late (*layt*) *adj*. [lat·er, lat·ter; lat·est, last] 1. Done or arrived after the usual or appointed time; advanced in time. 2. Past; recent; former; deceased.—**late** *adv*.—**late·ness** *n*.—**of late**. Recently; lately.

late-begun latecoming late-lost
late-born late-embarked late-practiced
late-built late-found late-taken
latecomer late-lamented late-won

lateen sail. *Nautical*. A triangular sail set obliquely and raking forward on a low mast.

late·ly *adv*. Recently; not long since.

la·tent (*layt*-'nt) *adj*. Not visible or apparent; concealed; potential.—**-ten·cy** *n*. —**-tent·ly** *adv*.

lat·er·al (*lat*-er-'l) *adj*. pertaining to the side; directed forward or proceeding from the side.—**lat·er·al·ly** *adv*.

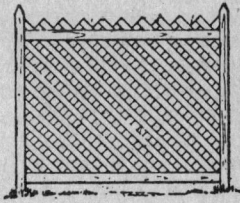
LATEEN SAIL

Lat·er·an (*lat*-er-un) *n*. The episcopal church of the Pope a principal church of Rome.

la·tex (*lay*-teks) *n*. [*pl*. lat·i·ces; la·tex·es] A milky sap, found in many plants, from which rubber may be made.

lath *n*. A thin wooden strip, wire netting, etc., nailed to the framework of a building to retain plaster.—*v*. To furnish with laths.—**lath·er** *n*.

lathe (*layth*) *n*. Machine for rapidly turning stock against a cutting tool.

lath·er (*lath*-er) *n*. Thick foam or froth often made by soap and water.—*v*. 1. To spread soap foam over a surface. 2. To become flecked with sweaty foam.—**lath·er·er** *n*.

lath·ing (*lath*-ing) *n*. A covering of laths.

Lat·in (*lat*-'n) *n*. 1. The language of the ancient Romans.—*adj*. Pertaining to peoples and countries whose language derives from Latin.

Latin America. The nations of the Western Hemisphere south of the U.S.

Latin Quarter. A Parisian district inhabited largely by students.

lat·i·tude (*lat*-ih-tood) *n*. 1. Distance in degrees north or south from the equator. 2. Freedom from restriction; scope; range. —**lat·i·tu·di·nal** *adj*. —**lat·i·tu·di·nal·ly** *adv*.

lat·i·tu·di·nar·i·an (-in-*air*-ee-un) *n*. A freethinker; liberal.—*adj*. Tolerant; unorthodox. —**-nar·i·an·ism** *n*.

DEGREES OF LATITUDE

L

la·trine (luh-*treen*) *n*. *Chiefly Military*. A toilet or privy, often furnished with a washroom.

lat·ter (*lat*-er) *adj*. Following something else; more recent.—**lat·ter·ly** *adv*. Recently.

Latter-day Saint. A Mormon.

lat·tice (*lat*-iss) *n*. Network made by fastening laths or sticks at right angles to each other.—*v*. [-ticed; -tic·ing] To furnish with such a network.

lat·tice·work *n*. A grill or network of small bars.

LATTICE

laud (*lawd*) *v*. To praise; acclaim.

laud·a·ble *adj*. Commendable; praiseworthy. —**laud·a·bil·i·ty, laud·a·ble·ness** *n*.— **-a·bly** *adv*.

lau·da·num (*lawd*-uh-num) *n*. Tincture of opium.

lau·da·to·ry (*lawd*-uh-tor-ee) *adj*. Referring to or expressing praise.

laugh (*laf, lahf*) *n*. 1. Expression of amusement or pleasure by deep, convulsive vocal sounds and a wide smile. 2. The sound so made.—*v*. 1. To show pleasure or other feelings with a laugh. 2. To influence by laughter. 3. To deride; ridicule.—**laugh·er** *n*.

laugh·a·ble *adj.* Ridiculous; funny; silly. —**laugh·a·ble·ness** *n.*—**laugh·a·bly** *adv.*

laugh·ing *adj.* Merry; gay; having no serious consequences.—**laugh·ing·ly** *adv.*

laughing gas. Nitrous oxide, which when first inhaled produces exhilaration.

laugh·ing·stock *n.* A butt of jokes; ridiculous person.

laugh·ter *n.* An expression of mirth produced by partially involuntary movements of chest and throat muscles creating a series of hilarious sounds.

launch *n.* A fast high-powered motor boat.

LAUNCH

launch (*lawnch*) *v.* 1. To throw or set into motion, as a spear or rocket. 2. To move a ship from land into water. 3. To enter or plunge into a new field of activity.

laun·der (*lawn*-der) *v.* 1. To wash and iron clothes. 2. To be washable.—**laun·dress** *n.*

laun·dry (*lawn*-dree) *n.* [*pl.* -dries] 1. Place or room where washing is done. 2. Articles to be washed and ironed.—**laun·dry·man** *n.*

lau·re·ate (*law*-ree-it) *adj.* Decked or crowned with laurel; worthy of highest honor.—*n.* The recipient of a great honor for excellence of accomplishment. 'A poet laureate.'

lau·rel (*lawr*-el) *n.* 1. An evergreen tree of southern Europe bearing tough, aromatic leaves; bay tree. 2. [*pl.*] Honor; fame; distinction. 3. Various trees and shrubs similar to the true laurel.

la·va (*lav*-uh, *lah*-vuh) *n.* Molten rock matter from a volcano, or its solidified form.

LAUREL

lav·a·liere, lav·a·lier (lav-uh-leer) *n.* An ornament worn about the neck on a chain.

lav·a·to·ry (*lav*-uh-tor-ee) *n.* [*pl.* -ries] 1. A bathroom; toilet. 2. A bowl or basin for washing the hands and face.

lave (*layv*) *v.* [laved; lav·ing] To bathe; wash.

lav·en·der (*lav*-'n-der) *n.* 1. A warm-climate plant with spikes of small red-purple flowers. 2. A delicate reddish-purple tint. 3. The oil obtained from the lavender's flowers.

lav·ish (*lav*-ish) *adj.* 1. Expending in profusion; wasteful. 2. Unrestrained; abundant; sumptuous.—*v.* To give generously; waste; squander.—**lav·ish·ly** *adv.*—**lav·ish·ness** *n.*

law *n.* 1. A rule or principle laid down by authority or recognized among men by consent. 2. A collection or code of such rules. 3. A statement of a predictable, unvarying order of events. 4. The legal profession. 5. The legal process. 6. The science of law; jurisprudence. 7. *Slang.* One or more enforcement officers.

law abiding	law-fettered	law writer
lawbook	law-ridden	law-worthy

law·break·er *n.* One who violates a legal code. —**law·break·ing** *n.* & *adj.*

law·ful *adj.* Legal; legitimate; rightful.—**lawful·ly** *adv.*—**law·ful·ness** *n.*

law·giv·er *n.* A legislator; codifier of laws. —**law·giv·ing** *adj.* & *n.*

law·less *adj.* 1. Unrestrained by rule or custom; unruly. 2. Unauthorized by law; illegal. —**law·less·ness** *n.*—**law·less·ly** *adv.*

law·mak·er *n.* A legislator; formulator or enacter of laws.—**law·mak·ing** *n.* & *adj.*

lawn *n.* A kind of fine linen or cotton cloth.

lawn *n.* A level expanse of closely cut grass.

lawn mower. A machine for cutting grass.

lawn tennis. Tennis played on a grass court.

law·suit *n.* A legal process instituted to compel conviction or settlement of a claim.

law·yer (*law*-yer) *n.* One licensed to practice law; one versed in jurisprudence.

lax (*laks*) *adj.* 1. Loose; slack; flabby. 2. Not strict or rigorous; careless; inaccurate.—**lax·ly** *adv.*—**lax·ness** *n.*

lax·a·tive (*laks*-uh-tiv) *n.* Physic; medicine that relieves constipation.—*adj.* Cathartic.

lax·i·ty (*laks*-uh-tee) *n.* Looseness; slackness.

lay *adj.* Pertaining to people outside of a specific profession, esp. those not of the clergy.

lay *n.* A ballad or poem designed to be sung.

lay *v.* [laid; laid; lay·ing] 1. To put or place. 2. To place in a lying position; knock down. 3. To bring to any condition or state. 'To lay bare.' 4. To settle; still; allay. 5. To scheme; plan. 'To lay a plot.' 6. To produce eggs. 7. To bet; wager; risk. 8. To cover; spread; press out. 9. To impose; make; enact; exercise. 10. To prepare; make ready. 11. To charge with; assess blame.

lay *n.* The related elements or configuration of a situation or locality. 'Lay of the land.'

lay·er (*lay*-'r, *lair*) *n.* 1. One thickness of a substance; stratum; coating. 2. (*lay*-er) A hen regularly producing eggs.

lay·ette (lay-*et*) *n.* Clothes, bedding, and all the other outfitting for a new-born baby.

lay·man (*lay*-m'n) *n.* [*pl.* -men] One not belonging to a certain profession, esp. the clergy.

lay-off (*lay*-off) *n.* 1. Temporary dismissal of workers. 2. The period of their nonproductivity.

lay·out (*lay*-owt) *n.* 1. An orderly arrangement, esp. of type and illustrations on the printed page. 2. The art of marking out or indicating how a job is to be done. 3. That which is furnished; supply.—**lay·out·man** n.

la·zar (*lay*-zer) n. A leper; person affected with a pestilential disease.

laz·a·ret·to (laz-er-*et*-oh) n. Also **laz·a·ret, laz·a·rette.** 1. A hospital for persons with infectious diseases. 2. A building or vessel used to quarantine persons or goods. 3. A place on a ship where provisions are stored.

Laz·a·rus (*laz*-er-us). *New Testament.* A friend of Jesus whom He raised from the dead.

la·zy (*lay*-zee) adj. [la·zi·er; la·zi·est] 1. Averse to work and other exertion; indolent; unambitious. 2. Sluggish; slow-moving.—**la·zi·ly** adv.—**la·zi·ness** n.

lea (lee) n. A meadow; grassy plain; pasture.

leach v. To run or percolate a liquid through a substance so as to dissolve part of it.—n. The solution so obtained.—**leach·er** n.

lead (leed) v. [led; led; lead·ing] 1. To guide or conduct; show the way. 2. To direct and govern. 3. To go first; precede. 4. To pass; spend. 'Lead a gay life.' 5. To have preeminence or prominence. 6. To influence to take a course; allure. 7. To rule; be in command. 8. To go to a specified destination. —n. 1. Precedence; going before. 2. An idea or contact which promises further activity. 3. *Electricity.* A conductor connected to an appliance. 4. The principal actor or actress of a play; his or her role or part. 5. The introductory part of a newspaper story. 6. Guidance; leadership.

lead (led) n. 1. A soft, heavy, gray metal which resists the passage of X-rays and similar radiation. (*Symbol:* Pb). 2. Small stick of graphite in a pencil. 3. *Printing.* Thin plate of metal used to give space between lines. 4. *Nautical.* A plummet.—adj. Composed of lead.—v. 1. To space between lines of type. 2. To line with or apply lead.

lead·en (led-'n) adj. 1. Like lead in being soft, heavy, dull, gray, etc. 2. Composed of lead. —**lead·en·ly** adv.—**lead·en·ness** n.

lead·er (*leed*-er) n. 1. Guide; one who shows or conducts the way. 2. A chief; commander. 3. One who conducts a band or orchestra. 4. A person or product of pre-eminence. 5. A quality product sold at a low price to attract trade. 6. The main editorial of a newspaper. 7. A catgut line on the end of a fish-line. 8. [*pl.*] *Printing.* A series of dots [......] to direct the reader to a specific point.—**lead·er·ship** n.

lead·ing (*leed*-ing) n. 1. Act of guiding or conducting. 2. Guidance; example; leadership. —adj. Most important; chief; principal.

lead·ing (led-ing) n. *Printing.* Spacing between type with thin strips.

leads·man (ledz-m'n) n. [*pl.* -men] *Nautical.* The man who heaves the lead for sounding.

leaf (leef) n. [*pl.* leaves] 1. An extension or expansion of a plant's stem or branches, through which the plant obtains nourishment from air

and sunlight. 2. A page of a book. 3. The hinged section of a table or door. 4. Metal beaten into thin sheets.—adj. Of or like a leaf; thin; flat.—v. 1. To sprout or make leaves. 2. To flip through, as a book.—**leaf·age** n. Foliage.—**leaf·less** adj.

leaf-clad	leafmold	leaf-shaped
leaf forming	leaf red	leaf-sheltered
leaf-fringed	leaf-shaded	leaf-strewn

leaf·let (*leef*-lit) n. 1. A small sheet of printed paper, usually folded; folder. 2. A small leaf.

leaf·y adj. [leaf·i·er; leaf·i·est] 1. Full of leaves. 2. Of or like a leaf.

league (leeg) n. 1. A union of two or more persons, nations, or groups promoting their mutual interest; alliance. 2. A measure of length of about three miles. 3. A group of sporting teams that maintain a season schedule of games among themselves.—v. [leagued; lea·guing] To form an alliance; confederate.

League of Nations. An organization of many nations, formed in January, 1920, for the promotion of international peace and co-operation; dissolved in April, 1946.

leak n. 1. An unintentional hole or crack in a vessel permitting liquid to escape or enter. 2. The oozing or dripping of liquid. 3. The undesirable escape of information, etc.—v. 1. To pass, as water, through a crack or hole in a vessel. 2. To become known, or escape unintentionally. 'The story leaked out.'

leak·age (*leek*-ij) n. 1. The passing, as of fluid in or out through a leak. 2. The quantity which enters or issues by leaking.

leak·y adj. [leak·i·er; leak·i·est] Allowing liquid to pass in or out.—**leak·i·ness** n.

leal adj. *Poetic.* Loyal.

lean v. [leaned or leant; lean·ing] 1. To slope or slant from a straight or perpendicular position. 2. To tend or turn in feeling or opinion. 3. To rest for support; depend; rely.

lean adj. 1. Slender; not fat or fleshy. 2. Poor; barren.—n. Flesh consisting of muscle without fat.—**lean·ly** adv.—**lean·ness** n.

lean-cheeked	lean-headed	lean looking
lean-faced	lean-jawed	lean-necked
lean-fleshed	lean-limbed	lean-ribbed

lean-to n. A structure whose roof slopes to rest against another building or wall.—adj. Having a simple slope, as a roof.

leap (leep) v. [leaped or leapt; leap·ing] 1. To spring or rise from the ground by the feet; bound; jump. 2. To pass over by jumping. —n. 1. The act of springing or jumping. 2. The space covered in a jump.

leap·frog n. Game in which one player crouches and another jumps over him.

leap year. A year exactly divisible by four, or even hundred years if divisible by 400, containing 366 days; the extra day is added to February, giving it 29 days.

learn (lern) v. [learned, learnt; learn·ing] 1. To acquire adequate knowledge of or skill in. 2. To find out about; hear.—**learn·er** n.

L

learn·ed (*lern*-id) *adj.* Possessing great knowledge acquired through study.—**learn·ed·ly** *adv.*

learn·ing *n.* Knowledge acquired through study; erudition.

lease (*leess*) *n.* An agreement providing for rental or tenancy of property for a specified period at a certain rent.—*v.* [leased; leas·ing] To grant or hold temporary possession of, as property, under terms of an agreement with the owner.

lease-lend. See **lend-lease.**

leash (*leesh*) *n.* A line or strap for leading or checking a dog or other animal.—*v.* To hold in by a line or strap; check.

least (*leest*) *adj.* Slightest; smallest; most insignificant.—*n.* The smallest degree or amount. —*adv.* In or to the smallest degree.—**at least.** At the very lowest or smallest; in any case.

least·wise *adv.* Also **least·ways.** *Colloquial.* At least.

leath·er (*leth*-er) *n.* The skin of an animal prepared for use.—*v.* 1. To make or cover with leather. 2. To thrash with a strap.—**leath·er, leath·ern** *adj.*

leather-backed	leathercraft	leather making
leatherbark	leatherhead	leatherware
leather-bound	leather-lined	leatherwork
leather-covered	leather maker	leatherworker

leath·er·neck *n. Slang.* A marine.

leath·er·y *adj.* Like leather; tough.— -i·ness *n.*

leave (*leev*) *v.* [left; leav·ing] 1. To withdraw or depart from. 2. To allow to remain; not to disturb or remove. 3. To let remain at death; bequeath. 4. To refer; commit or entrust to; relinquish. 5. To set out.—*n.* 1. The act of parting. 2. Permission; liberty granted, esp. to be absent.—**leave off.** To quit; desist from.—**leave out.** To omit.

leave, *v.* [leaved; leav·ing] To grow leaves. —**leaved** *adj.*

leav·en (*lev*-'n) *v.* 1. To rise or lighten, as by fermentation of yeast. 2. To permeate and change; imbue.—*n.* 1. That which changes by mixture, or lightens. 2. A doughy substance producing fermentation, as in bread dough; yeast.—**leav·en·ing** *n.*

leav·ings (*leev*-ingz) *n. pl.* Remnants; refuse.

Le·bens·raum (*lay*-b'nz-rowm). *German.* Room to grow or expand.

lech·er (*lech*-er) *n.* A lewd, lustful man.—**lech·er·ous** *adj.*—**lech·er·ous·ly** *adv.*—**lech·er·ous·ness, lech·er·y** *n.*

lec·tern (*lek*-tern). High desk or stand in a church, from which scriptures are read.

lec·ture (*lek*-cher) *n.* 1. A formal discourse or speech meant for instruction. 2. A formal scolding or reprimand.—*v.* [lec·tured; lec·tur·ing] 1. To deliver a discourse for instruction. 2. To scold; reprimand.—**lec·tur·er** *n.*

ledge (*lej*) *n.* A surface projecting horizontally; shelf; ridge.

ledg·er (*lej*-er) *n.* 1. An account book containing financial data and records of business transactions. 2. A timber supporting the horizontal part of a scaffolding.

lee *n.* A place or side sheltered, or away, from the wind.—*adj.* Relating to the direction or side toward which the wind is blowing.

leech *n.* 1. A small blood-sucking worm formerly much used by doctors for letting blood. 2. A grasping, parasitic person.

leek *n.* A bulbous vegetable similar to, but milder than, the onion.

leer *v.* To look sidelong; to cast a sly glance expressing lewdness, contempt, etc.—*n.* A sly, lewd look.

lees (*leez*) *n. pl.* Sediment; dregs.

lee·ward (*lee*-werd, *loo*-erd) *adj.* Relating to the lee direction or side.—*adv.* Toward the lee direction.—*n.* Lee side.

lee·way *n.* 1. *Nautical.* Movement of a vessel to the lee side of its course. 2. Extra space for movement; margin.

left *adj.* 1. On the west side of one facing north. 2. Relating to political opinions or groups supporting social changes.—*n.* The side opposite the right; port side. 2. Political radicals and radicalism collectively.—**left·ish** *adj.* Somewhat left.

left-hand·ed *adj.* 1. More proficient in using the left hand than the right. 2. Accomplished with the left hand. 3. Insincere; insulting. 4. Awkward; clumsy.—**left-hand·ed·ly** *adv.*

left·ist *n.* An advocate of radical social and political changes.—*adj.* Politically radical.

left wing. Radical political sympathizers and organizations.—**left-wing** *adj.* Radical politically.—**left-wing·er** *n.*—**left-wing·ism** *n.*

leg *n.* 1. An appendage or limb used in walking. 2. One of the supports or standards of an article of furniture. 3. The part of a garment worn on the leg. 4. One fork or section of a divided instrument. 5. A section of a journey. 6. A side of a triangle other than the base.

leg·a·cy (*leg*-uh-see) *n.* [*pl.* -cies] A bequest; something willed or handed down from one generation to the next.

le·gal·i·ty (lee-*gal*-ih-tee) *n.* [*pl.* -ties] Observance of or conformity to law; lawfulness.

le·gal (*lee*-g'l) *adj.* 1. According to law; lawful. 2. Related to law or jurisprudence.—**le·gal·ly** *adv.*

le·gal·ize (*lee*-g'l-yze) *v.* [-ized; -iz·ing] To render lawful; authorize.—**le·gal·i·za·tion** *n.*

legal tender. Money which a creditor is legally obliged to accept in payment of a debt.

leg·ate (*leg*-it) *n.* An ambassador; authorized respresentative, esp. of the pope.

leg·a·tee (leg-uh-*tee*) *n.* The recipient of a legacy or willed property.

le·ga·tion (leh-*gay*-sh'n) *n.* 1. A group sent out as envoys to another government; embassy. 2. The headquarters or residence of envoys.

leg·end (*lej*-end) *n.* 1. A traditional story

passed on from one generation to the next. 2. An inscription; caption explaining an illustration.—**leg·end·ar·y** (*lej*-en-der-ee) *adj.* 1. Inspiring legends. 2. Fabulous; not real.

leg·er·de·main (lej-er-duh-*mayn*) *n.* Sleight of hand; trick based on manual quickness.

leg·gings *n. pl.* Outer coverings for the legs.

leg·horn (*leg*-ern) *n.* 1. A hat of plaited straw. 2. [*cap.*] A small breed of chicken noted for its egglaying.

leg·i·ble (*lej*-ib-'l) *adj.* Capable of being read; plain; decipherable.—**leg·i·bil·i·ty** (lej-ih-*bil*-ih tee), **-ble·ness** *n.*—**-i·bly** *adv.*

le·gion (*lee*-jun) *n.* 1. A great number; multitude. 2. An armed force; army.

le·gion·a·ry (*lee*-jun-ehr-ee) *adj.* Innumerable; many.—*n.* [*pl.* **-ies**] A soldier of a legion.

leg·is·late (*lej*-iss-layt) *v.* [**-lat·ed**; **-lat·ing**] To make or pass laws; limit or foster by laws. —**leg·is·la·tive** *adj.* Engaged in or related to lawmaking.—**leg·is·la·tive·ly** *adv.*—**-la·tor** *n.*

leg·is·la·tion (lej-iss-*lay*-shun) *n.* 1. Laws passed by a lawmaking body; proposals being considered by such a body. 2. Lawmaking; enactment of legislators.

leg·is·la·ture (*lej*-iss-lay-cher) *n.* A law-enacting body; a congress or parliament.

le·git (luh-*jit*) *Slang. adj.* Legitimate; aboveboard.—*n.* The legitimate stage; theater.

le·git·i·ma·cy (luh-*jit*-ih-muh-see) *n.* 1. Birth in lawful wedlock. 2. Legality; justice.

le·git·i·mate (luh-*jit*-ih-mit) *adj.* 1. Genuine; real; true. 2. Born or conceived in wedlock. 3. Abiding by recognized standards. 4. Legal; lawful.—*v.* (luh-jit-ih-*mayt*) [**-mat·ed**; **-mat·ing**] To validate; legalize; justify.—**le·git·i·mate·ly** *adv.*—**legitimate stage.** Drama as enacted on the stage, as contrasted with vaudeville or motion pictures.

leg·man *n.* [*pl.* **-men**] A newspaper man who reports news to be written up by others.

le·gume (*leg*-yoom) *n.* 1. A family of plants including the pea which converts atmospheric nitrogen into a form usable by plants. 2. A pod from such a plant.—**le·gu·mi·nous** *adj.*

le·i (*lay*-ih) *n.* [*pl.* **le·is**] A Hawaiian necklace or wreath of flowers.

lei·sure (*leezh*-er, *lezh*-er) *n.* Freedom from occupation or work; ease; convenience. —**lei·sure·ly** *adv. & adj.*

lem·ming *n.* A small, short-tailed Arctic rodent.

lem·on (*lem*-un) *n.* A citrus fruit, growing in warm climates, having a sour juice used for beverages and flavoring.—**lem·on·ade** *n.* A beverage made from lemon juice, water, and sugar.

LEMUR (1/13 life size)

le·mur (*lee*-mer) *n.* A monkeylike animal having soft fur and a pointed muzzle.

lend *v.* [**lent**; **lend·ing**] 1. To grant to another for temporary use. 2. To grant or furnish in general. 'Lend assistance.' 3. To let for hire or compensation. 4. To accommodate. 'The dress lent itself to her figure.' 5. To devote. 'He lent himself to the scheme.'—**lend·er** *n.* **lend a hand.** To assist.

lend-lease, lease-lend *n.* System in effect during World War II by which the U.S. supplied war material to enemies of the Axis.

length *n.* 1. The longest dimension of any object as distinct from depth, thickness, breadth, or width. 2. A certain extent measured longwise.—**at length.** 1. To the full extent. 2. At last; finally.

length·en (*leng*-thun) *v.* 1. To make or grow long or longer. 2. To expand or prolong.

length·wise (*length*-wyze) *adv. & adj.* In the direction of the length.—**length·ways** *adv.*

length·y (*leng*-thee) *adj.* [**length·i·er**; **length·i·est**] Long; protracted—applied chiefly to speeches or arguments.— **-i·ly** *adv.*— **-i·ness** *n.*

le·ni·en·cy (*lee*-nee-un-see) *n.* Also **len·i·ence.** Mildness; mercy; clemency.

le·ni·ent (*lee*-nee-unt, -yunt) *adj.* Mild; gentle; merciful.—**le·ni·ent·ly** *adv.*

Len·in·ism (*len*-in-izm) *n.* Communism as developed from the doctrines of Karl Marx by V. I. Lenin, Bolshevist leader.—**Len·in·ist** *n.*

len·i·ty (*len*-ih-tee) *n.* [*pl.* **-ties**] 1. Clemency; mercy. 2. A lenient act.

lens (*lenz*) *n.* A transparent substance, usually glass, designed to refract light rays passing through it so as to form an image.

LENS

Lent *n.* A fast of forty days, beginning at Ash Wednesday and continuing until Easter.

lent. *Past tense & past participle of* **lend.**

Len·ten (*len*-tun) *adj.* Pertaining to or suitable for Lent.

len·til (*lent*-'l) *n.* A type of pea vine bearing two small edible peas to a pod; its seed.

le·o·nine (*lee*-oh-nyne) *adj.* Lionlike; resembling a lion.

leo·pard (*lep*-erd) *n.* A meat-eating animal of the cat family inhabiting Central Africa, Persia, etc.

lep·er (*lep*-er) *n.* A victim of leprosy.

le·pre·chaun (*lep*-ruh-kawn) *n.* A mischievous dwarf of Irish folklore.

LEOPARD (1/50 life size)

lep·ro·sy (*lep*-ruh-see) *n.* A disease characterized by thickening of the skin, sores, loss of hair, and deformity.—**lep·rous** *adj.*

les·bi·an (*lez*-bee-un) *n.* A woman who engages in homosexual practices.

lese majesty (leez-*maj*-ess-tee, mah-zhess-*tay*).

L

An offense against sovereign power, esp. a crime against a monarch.

le·sion (*lee*-zhun) *n.* Any pathological condition of the body structure caused by disease or injury, as cuts or sores.

less *adj.* Smaller; fewer.—*adv.* In lower degree. —*n.* 1. The lower, smaller, etc., of two. 2. A smaller amount.—*prep.* Minus. 'Ten less four equals six.'

·less. *Suffix.* 1. Without; not having. 'Shameless; thankless.' 2. Not to be; incapable of being.

les·see (less-*ee*) *n.* One who holds by a lease; tenant of leased property.

les·sen (*less*-'n) *v.* To diminish; reduce.

les·ser (*less*-er) *adj.* Smaller; not so great.

les·son (*less*-'n) *n.* 1. Anything studied or taught. 2. A study assignment made by a teacher to a pupil. 3. Anything learned from experience. 4. A portion of Scripture read in a church service. 5. A severe lecture; rebuke.

les·sor (*less*-er) *n.* One who grants property rights under a lease.

lest *conj.* For fear that; so that. 'He hurried lest he fail to accomplish the mission.'

let *n.* 1. *Law.* An obstacle; hindering force. 'Without let.' 2. *Lawn Tennis.* A ball which strikes the net, but lands in the proper court.

let *v.* [let; let·ting] 1. To permit; allow. 2. To lease; grant possession and use for compensation. 3. To leave. 'Let him alone.'—**let blood.** To open a vein and allow the blood to flow out.—**let down.** 1. To relax. 2. *Colloquial.* To betray or disappoint.

let·down *n.* Release; relaxation; disappointment.

le·thal (*lee*-th'l) *adj.* Fatal; causing or relating to death.

le·thar·gic (leh-*thahr*-jik) *adj.* Also **le·thar·gi·cal.** Drowsy; dull; indifferent.

leth·ar·gy (*leth*-er-jee) *n.* [*pl.* -gies] 1. Dullness; inaction. 2. Unnatural sleepiness.

Le·the (*lee*-thee) *n.* 1. *Greek Mythology.* A river of Hades whose waters destroyed memory. 2. Forgetfulness; oblivion.—**Le·the·an** (luh-*thee*-un) *adj.*

let·ter (*let*-er) *n.* 1. A character of the alphabet; symbol representing a speech sound. 2. A written message or communication. 3. Exact meaning; literal expression. 'The letter of the law.' 4. [*pl.*] Learning; erudition. 'A man of letters.'—*v.* To impress or form letters on.

let·tered *adj.* 1. Learned; educated. 2. Marked with letters.

let·ter·head *n.* An identifying heading printed or engraved on letter paper.

let·ter·ing *n.* 1. The act of marking with letters. 2. The letters marked or drawn.

let·tuce (*let*-iss) *n.* Any of several varieties of crisp, leafy plant used in salads, etc.

let·up *n. Colloquial.* Cessation; respite.

leu·co·cyte (*loo*-kuh-syte) *n.* A white corpuscle of the blood.

Le·vant (leh-*vant*) *n.* The lands forming the east coast of the Mediterranean.—**Lev·an·tine** (luh-van-tin; *lev*-un-tyne) *adj.* & *n.*

lev·ee (*lev*-ee) *n.* An embankment built on the margin of a river to confine it within its channel.

lev·ee (*lev*-ee, leh-*vee*) *n.* 1. A reception held in the morning. 2. A gathering of distinguished guests.

lev·el (*lev*-'l) *adj.* 1. Having an even surface. 2. Horizontal. 3. Equal in quality, condition, etc. 4. Uniform; smooth. 5. Calm; cool. 'Keep a level head.'—*v.* 1. To make or become smooth or even. 2. To destroy; lay waste. 3. To aim; point.—*n.* 1. An instrument for determining a horizontal plane. 2. A horizontal plane. 3. A rank; social position.—**lev·el·er, lev·el·ler** *n.*

lev·er (*lev*-er, *lee*-ver) *n.* 1. *Mechanics.* A rigid bar turning on a point (the fulcrum) so that force results at one point on it in the opposite direction to a force applied at another point. 2. A crowbar, handle, pry, etc.

LEVER

lev·er·age (*lev*-er-ij, *leev*-) *n.* 1. The mechanical advantage derived from application of a lever. 2. The motion of a lever.

le·vi·a·than (leh-*vy*-uh-thun) *n.* 1. A sea monster, of uncertain description, mentioned in the Bible. 2. Any monstrous, formidable thing.

lev·i·ta·tion (lev-uh-*tay*-shun) *n.* The illusion of being without weight; a rising up without support.

lev·i·ta·tor (*lev*-uh-tay-ter) *n.* A fabulous vehicle which moves with equal facility in every direction, including straight up.

Le·vite (*lee*-vyte) *n. Jewish History.* One of the tribe of Levi, esp. one assigned certain duties in the temple.

Le·vit·i·cal (luh-*vit*-ik-'l) *adj.* 1. Relating to the Levites. 2. Relating to the Book of Leviticus.

Le·vit·i·cus (luh-*vit*-ih-kuss) *n.* A book of the Old Testament.

lev·i·ty (*lev*-uh-tee) *n.* [*pl.* -ties] Lightness of conduct; lack of seriousness; frivolity.

lev·y (*lev*-ee) *v.* [lev·ied; lev·y·ing] 1. To collect or conscript by legal authority. 'Levy taxes; levy troops.' 2. To impose. 'Levy a fine as punishment for a crime.'

lewd (*lood*) *adj.* Lascivious; sensual; coarse. —**lewd·ly** *adv.*—**lewd·ness** *n.*

lew·is·ite (*loo*-iss-yte) *n.* A military poison gas which causes blistering.

lex·i·cog·ra·pher (leks-ih-*kog*-ruh-fer) *n.* An author or editor of, or writer for, a dictionary. —**lex·i·cog·ra·phy** *n.*—**lex·i·co·graph·ic** (leks-ih-koh-*graf*-ik), **-i·cal** *adj.*— **-ic·al·ly** *adv.*

lex·i·con (*lek*-sih-k'n) *n.* A dictionary.—**lex·i·cal** *adj.*

Leyden jar (*lye*-d'n). A primitive form of electrical condenser, consisting of a glass jar coated with tinfoil inside and out.

li·a·bil·i·ty (ly-uh-*bil*-uh-tee) *n.* [*pl.* -ties] 1. An obligation; debt. 2. State of responsibility.

li·a·ble (*ly*-uh-b'l) *adj.* 1. Obliged in law or equity; responsible; answerable for consequences. 2. Apt to incur something undesirable. 'Liable to be injured.'

LEYDEN JAR

li·ai·son (lee-*ay*-zun) *n.* 1. A bond; co-ordination of activities; intercommunication. 2. An illicit intimacy between a man and a woman. 3. *Military.* Communication between two branches of a service, between two armies, etc.

li·ar (*ly*-er) *n.* One who knowingly utters a falsehood; prevaricator.

li·ba·tion (ly-*bay*-shun) *n.* 1. A sacrificial ceremony in which wine is poured on the ground or on the sacrifice. 2. *Colloquial.* An intoxicating drink.

li·bel (*ly*-b'l) *n.* 1. *Law.* The defamation of a person by publication of written or pictorial matter tending to injure his reputation. 2. A defamatory statement, writing, or picture.—*v.* [-beled; -belled; -bel·ing, -bel·ling]. To defame.

li·bel·ous, li·bel·lous *adj.* 1. Defamatory; slanderous. 2. Constituting a libel.

lib·er·al (*lib*-er-ul) *adj.* 1. Munificent; generous. 2. Favorable to reform or progress; not bound by orthodox or established tenets in politics or religion; not conservative. 3. Free; open; candid. 'A liberal communication of thoughts.' 4. Not too literal or strict.—*n.* 1. A person who believes in progressive reform, esp. in the direction of conferring more power on the people. 2. [*cap.*] A member of the Liberal Party in England.—**lib·er·al** *adv.*

lib·er·al·ism *n.* Attitude favoring reforms in the economic, social, and political fields.—**lib·er·al·ist·ic** *adj.*

lib·er·al·i·ty (lib-er-*al*-uh-tee) *n.* [*pl.* -ties] 1. Disposition to give largely; generosity. 2. Broadness of mind; impartiality. 3. A particular act of generosity; donation.

lib·er·ate (*lib*-er-ayt) *v.* [lib·er·at·ed; lib·er·at·ing] To set at liberty; free; deliver.—**lib·er·a·tion** *n.*—**lib·er·a·tor** *n.*

lib·er·tine (*lib*-er-teen) *n.* One who leads a dissolute, licentious life.—*adj.* Licentious; morally loose.—**lib·er·tin·ism** (*lib*-er-tin-izm) *n.*

lib·er·ty (*lib*-er-tee) *n.* [*pl.* -ties] 1. Freedom; exemption from restraint. 2. Permission granted. 3. The total rights and privileges of a free people. 4. Freedom from occupation or engagements. 5. Action or speech exceeding the bounds of propriety. 6. *Naval.* Permission granted to sailors to go ashore for any time less than 72 hours.

Liberty Ship. A cargo ship of approximately 10,000 gross tons, equipped with a reciprocating steam engine, hastily turned out in large numbers during World War II.

li·bid·i·nous (lih-*bid*-in-us) *n.* Lustful; lecherous.— -nous·ly *adv.*— -nous·ness *n.*

li·bi·do (lih-*by*-doh) *n.* 1. Sexual energy. 2. *Psychoanalysis.* A desire or drive associated with the sexual instinct or the instinct to live.

li·brar·i·an (ly-*brair*-ee-un) *n.* One who cares for a collection of books or manuscripts.

li·brar·y (*ly*-brair-ee) *n.* [*pl.* -ies] 1. A collection of books belonging to an individual, public institution, organization, school, etc. 2. The building or room in which such a collection of books is kept.

li·bret·to (lih-*bret*-oh) *n.* [*pl.* -tos, -ti] The text of an opera, choral composition, etc.—**li·bret·tist** *n.*

li·cense (*ly*-sunss) *n.* Also **li·cence.** 1. Authority or liberty given for a specified act; permit. 2. Excessive liberty; undue freedom. 3. Conscious deviation from the rules of an art for the sake of effectiveness.—*v.* [li·censed; li·cens·ing] To permit by grant of authority.—**li·cens·er, li·cenc·er** *n.*

li·cen·tiate (ly-*sen*-shee-it) *n.* A holder of a degree entitling him to practice a profession.

li·cen·tious (ly-*sen*-shus) *adj.* Wanton; loose; lascivious.—**li·cen·tious·ly** *adv.*—**-tious·ness** *n.*

li·chen (*ly*-ken) *n.* A type of growth on rocks, trees, etc., some varieties of which are used for dyeing.—**li·chen·ose, li·chen·ous** *adj.*

lic·it (*liss*-it) *adj.* Legal; lawful.—**-it·ly** *adv.*

lick *v.* 1. To draw the tongue over. 2. To lap, take in by the tongue. 3. *Colloquial.* Flog; beat.—*n.* 1. A rub with the tongue. 2. *Colloquial.* A hasty or superficial stroke, performance, etc. 'Not a lick of work.' 3. A salt deposit which animals come to lick up.

lic·o·rice (*lik*-er-iss, -ish) *n.* A flowering European plant from the root of which a flavoring extract is derived.

lid *n.* 1. Cover of a pan, box, chest, etc. 2. An eyelid.—**lid·ded** *adj.*

lie *v.* [lied; ly·ing] To utter a falsehood; deceive.—*n.* A falsehood.

lie *v.* [lay; lain; ly·ing] 1. To be in a recumbent or prostrate position; recline. 2. To be situated in a specific place or condition. 3. To lodge; stop off at.—**lie to.** *Nautical.* To head a ship into the sea, keeping bare steerageway.

Lie·der·kranz (*lee*-der-kranss) *n.* Trademark for an American cheese similar to Camembert but notable for its strong odor.

lief (*leef*) *adv.* Gladly; willingly.

liege (*leej*) *adj.* Relating to the feudal bond between vassal and chief.—*n.* 1. A vassal. 2. A lord or superior.

li·en (*lee*-en) *n.* A legal claim; right of one party to attach the property of another until his claim is satisfied.

lieu (*loo*) *n.* Stead; place.—**in lieu of.** Instead of.

lieu·ten·ant (loo-*ten*-'nt) *n.* 1. a. A commissioned officer in the Army next in rank below a captain. b. A commissioned officer in the

L

Navy, ranking next below a lieutenant commander. 2. An officer who supplies the place of a superior in his absence.—**lieu·ten·an·cy** *n.*

lieutenant colonel. A commissioned Army officer ranking above a major and below a colonel.

lieutenant commander. A commissioned officer in the Navy next in rank below a commander.

lieutenant general. Commissioned Army officer ranking below general and above major general.

lieutenant governor. *U.S.* An official in a state government ranking below the governor.

life *n.* [*pl.* lives] 1. That property of a plant or animal involving the functions of growth, nutrition, respiration, reproduction, etc., distinguishing organic from inorganic bodies. 2. Existence; period of existence. 3. Mode or manner of existence; sum of individual experience. 4. Animation; spirit. 5. A person; people. 'Great loss of life.' 6. Biographical study. 7. Social state, as high or low life. 8. That which is as dear to one as one's existence; beloved. 9. The living reality; original. 'Painted from life.'

lifeblood   lifelike   lifesize
lifegiving   lifelong   lifetime

life belt. A cork or rubber ring for supporting the body in the water; life preserver.

life·boat *n.* A fully provisioned boat carried aboard a ship to be launched in case of disaster.

life buoy. A floating ring for supporting persons in the water in emergency.

life·guard *n.* An experienced swimmer stationed at bathing places for the protection of bathers.

life insurance. A contract maintained by regular premiums providing for payment to a designated beneficiary in the event of the insured's death.

life·less *adj.* 1. Dead. 2. Destitute of force, spirit, or vigor; dull; inactive.—**life·less·ly** *adv.* —**life·less·ness** *n.*

life preserver. Also **life jacket.** A buoyant apparatus designed to maintain a person afloat in the water.

lift *v.* 1. To raise; pick up; elevate. 2. To rise. 'The fog lifts.' 3. To plagiarize; steal.—*n.* 1. A rise; boost; elevation. 2. Help; assistance. 3. A free ride given by one on the same route. 4. An inspiriting or invigorating influence.

LIFE PRESERVER

lig·a·ment (*lig*-uh-m'nt) *n. Anatomy.* A white, inelastic, sinewy tissue connecting bones.

lig·a·ture (*lig*-uh-cher) *n.* 1. A link; bond; tie; joining. 2. *Printing.* A pair of joined letters (œ). 3. *Music.* A slur, or the combination of

notes it connects. 4. *Surgery.* A thread used to tie off blood vessels, etc.

light (*lyte*) *n.* 1. A wave motion of radiant energy which renders the environment visible. 2. A radiation of this energy from a body, as the sun. 3. A body which radiates light. 4. The day, as contrasted with night. 5. Understanding; that which aids perception. 'Throw light on the problem.' 6. Public knowledge. 7. Appearance. 8. A flame to light a cigarette, etc.—*adj.* 1. Abounding in light. 2. Pale; of a color containing white.—*v.* 1. To ignite; cause to burn or give off light. 2. To provide light for; illuminate. 3. To brighten; become illuminated or animated. 'His face lighted up.' 4. To burst into flame.

light *adj.* 1. Having little weight. 2. Not burdensome; not oppressive. 3. Not heavily armed. 'Light troops.' 4. Active; nimble. 5. Trifling; unimportant. 6. Dizzy. 'Her head felt light.' 7. Delicate; fine. 8. Not serious; frivolous.—*v.* [light·ed; lit; light·ing] 1. To land; come to rest. 2. To dismount. 3. To strike. 4. To come down.

lightarmed   light-fingered   light-robed
lightbearded   light-footed   light-rooted
light-bodied   light-headed   light-skinned
light-brained   light-hearted   light-spirited
light-colored   light-limbed   light-winged
light-complexioned   light proof   light-year

light·en *v.* To illuminate; make less dark.

light·en *v.* 1. To relieve of a certain amount of weight. 2. To make less burdensome or oppressive; alleviate.

light·er *n.* 1. A large open flat-bottomed barge, often used in lightening or loading and unloading ships. 2. A device for kindling.

light-head·ed *adj.* 1. Delirious from fever; giddy; dizzy. 2. Silly; witless; scatterbrained. —**light-head·ed·ly** *adv.*—**light-head·ed·ness** *n.*

light-heart·ed *adj.* Gay; blithe; happy; unworried.—**light-heart·ed·ly** *adv.*—**light-heart·ed·ness** *n.*

light·house *n.* A tower or other structure equipped with a light to aid navigation.

light·ing *n.* 1. Illumination. 2. Arrangement of light and dark tones in a painting.

light·ly *adv.* 1. Without heaviness; easily; nimbly. 2. For reasons of little weight. 3. Cheerfully.

light-mind·ed *adj.* Silly; frivolous; fickle. —**light-mind·ed·ly** *adv.*—**light-mind·ed·ness** *n.*

LIGHTHOUSE

light·ness *n.* 1. Lack of weight. 2. Frivolity.

light·ness *n.* 1. Amount of illumination; quality of light. 2. Paleness of color.

light·ning (*lyte*-ning) *n.* A flash of light resulting from a discharge of static electricity from one cloud to another, or from a cloud to the earth.

lightning bug. A firefly.

light·ship n. An anchored vessel equipped with a powerful light to aid navigation.

light·some adj. 1. Nimble; agile; lithe. 2. Gay; blithe.

light·weight (-wayt) n. 1. Boxing. A fighter who weighs between 127 and 135 pounds. 2. Colloquial. A person considered of little worth or influence.—**light·weight** adj.

light-year n. Astronomy. The distance light can travel during one solar year, approximately six trillion miles.

lig·nite (lig-nyte) n. A combustible substance resembling coal and peat partially mineralized, but retaining its woody texture.

lik·a·ble, like·a·ble (lyke-uh-b'l) adj. Of a nature to attract approval and affection.

like v. [liked; lik·ing] To have a preference or fondness for; choose.—**likes** n. pl. Preferences.

like adj. & prep. Resembling; indicative or characteristic of.—adv. In a similar manner or degree.

like·a·ble. Variant spelling of likable.

-like Suffix. Characteristic of. Note: Compounds of -like are usually spelled as solid words (bearlike) except those formed with words ending in double l, which are hyphenated (bell-like, hall-like).

like·li·hood (lyke-lee-hood) n. Probability.

like·ly adj. [like·li·er; like·li·est] 1. Credible; probable. 2. Suitable; promising. 'A likely account.'—**like·ly** adv.

lik·en v. To compare.

like·ness n. 1. Similarity; resemblance. 2. A portrait; picture.

like·wise adv. Also; too; thus.

lik·ing n. Pleasure; satisfaction; fondness.

li·lac (ly-lak) n. 1. A tall fragrant shrub whose flower, a cluster of small blossoms, ranges from white to purple. 2. Pale violet color.—**li·lac** adj.

Lil·li·pu·tian (lil-ih-pyoo-shun) adj. Tiny; very small—from Lilliput, a mythical kingdom of pygmies in Swift's Gulliver's Travels.—**Lil·li·pu·tian** n.

LILAC

lilt n. 1. Lift; spring. 2. Bright, rhythmic tune.—**lilt** v.—**lilt·ing** adj.—**lilt·ing·ly** adv.

li·ly n. [pl. -ies] A plant with large handsome flowers, often white.

li·ly-liv·ered adj. Weak; craven; cowardly.

lily of the valley. Small perennial herb with tiny, fragrant bell-shaped flowers.

Lima bean (lyme-uh). A flat green-white bean.

limb (lim) n. 1. One of the extremities of the human or animal body. 2. Branch of a tree.

3. An agent. 'Limb of the law.'—**limbed** adj. Having legs. 'Sleek-limbed girl.'

lim·ber (lim-ber) v. To make pliant.—adj. Supple; pliant.—n. Front detachable part of a gun carriage.

lim·bo (lim-boh) n. 1. A region beyond this world where souls are detained till the final judgment. 2. A place of exile or neglect.

lim·burg·er n. A mild, crusted, semi-soft, natural cheese of pronounced odor.

lime n. 1. Caustic earth, obtained by exposing chalk and other kinds of limestones to heat. 2. A tropical evergreen tree bearing a small, strongly acid fruit. 3. The linden tree.

lime·kiln n. Furnace where limestone is reduced to lime.

lime·light n. 1. A very strong light. 2. Theater. Position securing prominence and publicity.

lim·er·ick n. A rhymed humorous verse of five lines, often bawdy.

lime·stone n. A kind of stone containing varieties of calcium carbonate.

lime·wat·er n. 1. Water to which calcium carbonate has been added. 2. Natural water containing a high concentration of calcium carbonate.

li·mey (lye-mee) n. Slang. An Englishman, esp. a British sailor.

lim·i·nal (lim-in-'l; ly-min-'l) adj. Verging on; at the threshold of.

lim·it n. Boundary; border; anything that terminates, restrains, or encloses.—v. To restrict.

lim·i·ta·tion (lim-ih-tay-sh'n) n. Restriction; restraining condition; qualification.

lim·it·ed (lim-it-ed) adj. 1. Narrow; confined; circumscribed. 2. Bigoted; provincial; prejudiced. 3. Undeveloped; scanty. 'Limited resources.' 4. Railroads. Designating a fast train making few stops.—n. A limited train. '20th Century Limited.'

lim·it·less adj. Unbounded; unending.

limn (lim) v. [limned; lim·ning] To paint; delineate.

lim·ou·sine (lim-uh-zeen) n. A luxurious, closed automobile, with a separate compartment for the driver.

limp v. To walk haltingly.—n. A halting step. —adj. Pliant; flaccid.—-ly adv.—-ness n.

lim·pet n. A small shellfish which clings to rocks, timbers, etc.

lim·pid adj. Clear; transparent.—**lim·pid·ly** adv. —**lim·pid·ness, lim·pid·i·ty** n.

lim·y (lye-mee) adj. [lim·i·er; lim·i·est] Containing or covered with lime.

lin·age, line·age (lyne-ij) n. Amount of printed matter, esp. advertising, measured by the number of lines it occupies.

lin·den (lin-d'n) n. A tall shade tree with heart-shaped leaves and fragrant yellowish flowers.

line n. 1. A rope, string, or cord. 2. A pipe conveying oil, natural gas, etc. 3. Theater. [often pl.] An actor's speeches. 4. Colloquial.

L

Exaggerated boastful chatter. 5. *Printing.* A row of words, figures, etc., usually column-width. 6. A boundary; limit. 7. A wrinkle on the hand or face. 8. Sphere of business activity. 'His line is books.' 9. *Railroads.* Course; route. 'Main-line trains.' 10. *Art.* Stroke in delineation of contour, distinguished from coloring, perspective, etc.—*v.* [lined; lin·ing] 1. To place or put in symmetrical alignment. 'Line up those troops!' 2. To mark or crease. 3. To place a lining in. 'Line my coat with satin.'

lin·e·age (*lin*-ee-ij) *n.* 1. Descendants in line from a common ancestor; family. 2. Linage.

lin·e·al (*lin*-ee-ul) *adj.* 1. In direct line from an ancestor; hereditary. 2. Composed of lines.

lin·e·a·ment (*lin*-ee-uh-ment) *n.* The outline or exterior of a body, particularly of the face.

lin·e·ar (*lin*-ee-er) *adj.* Pertaining to a line; consisting of lines.—**linear measure.** Measurement by length.

line charge. *Radio.* Telegraph or telephone fee for carrying messages or programs by wire between transmitting points.

line·man *n.* [*pl.* -men] 1. One who strings or repairs telephone or telegraph wires. 2. One who carries a surveyor's line. 3. A football forward.

lin·en (*lin*-'n) *n.* 1. Cloth finely woven of flax or, sometimes, hemp fibers. 2. Tablecloths, sheets, shirts, etc., made of linen. 3. High-quality correspondence paper.—**lin·en** *adj.*

lin·er (*lye*-ner) *n.* 1. A ship or airplane traveling between regular destinations. 2. Something which fills, supports, or reinforces. 'A vacuum-bottle liner.' 3. *Baseball.* A low-flying hard drive with an almost flat trajectory.

lines·man *n.* [*pl.* -men] *Sports.* An official who decides if a play or player is out of bounds.

line-up, lineup *n.* 1. Persons, esp. criminals, drawn up for close inspection. 2. Arrangement of players at the start of a game or individual play. 3. Any organization or list of individuals. 'Metro has a line-up of stars.'

ling *n.* A slender, flat-headed fish.

lin·ger (*ling*-ger) *v.* 1. To delay; loiter. 2. To remain long in any condition.—**lin·ger·ing** *adj.* Protracted.—**lin·ger·er** *n.*

lin·ge·rie (*lan*-jeh-ree; *lahn*-jeh-ray) *n.* Women's underclothing.

lin·go (*ling*-goh) *n.* [*pl.* -goes] Jargon; informal, often localized speech.

lin·guist (*ling*-gwist) *n.* Person who speaks one or more foreign languages fluently.

lin·guis·tics (ling-*gwiss*-tiks) *n.* The science of languages and all aspects of human speech. —**lin·guis·tic, -tic·al** *adj.*—**lin·guis·tic·al·ly** *adv.*

lin·i·ment (*lin*-uh-m'nt) *n.* A medicated liquid rubbed into the skin to ease aching muscles.

lin·ing *n.* The covering of the inner surface of anything. 'Jacket lining.'

link *n.* 1. A single round of chain. 2. *Surveying.* A distance of 7.92 inches. 3. Any con-

necting or binding device or person. 'Law is the link between labor and capital.'—*v.* To join together.—**link·age** (*link*-ij) *n.* Any system or device by which things are joined together.

links *n.* Golf course.

lin·net (*lin*-et) *n.* A small singing bird; finch.

li·no·le·um (lin-*oh*-lee-um) *n.* A hard, stiff, washable floor covering.

Lin·o·type (*lyne*-oh-type) *n.* *Printing.* Trade-mark name for a mechanical type-setter which casts type in line-length slugs.—**lin·o·type** *v.*

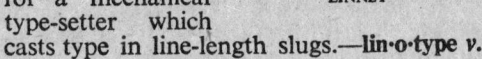

LINNET

lin·seed (*lin*-seed) *n.* The seed of flax.—**linseed oil.** A yellow oil pressed from flaxseed.

lin·sey-wool·sey *n.* Coarse burlaplike cloth.

lint *n.* 1. Scraped linen fibers. 2. Ravelings of thread.

lin·tel *n.* *Architecture.* A horizontal piece of timber or stone over a door, window, or other opening.

lint·er *n.* 1. Machine or device for removing lint. 2. Short fibers used in cotton batting.

LINTEL

li·on *n.* 1. Large, meat-eating animal of the cat family found in Africa and southern Asia. 2. Cynosure of all eyes. 'The lion of the occasion.'—**lionhearted.** Having great courage. —**lion's share.** The largest portion.

LION

li·on·ize *v.* [-ized; -iz·ing] To regard with awe; treat with fatuous deference.—**li·on·i·za·tion** *n.*

lip *n.* 1. Either of the two fleshy borders of the mouth. 2. The edge of a container. 'Lip of a pitcher.' 3. *Slang.* Impertinent rejoinder. 'Don't give me any lip!' 4. *Music.* Embouchure, esp. of brass players.—*v.* [lipped; lipping] To put lips to.

lip·stick *n.* Cosmetic stick used to color the lips.

liq·ue·fac·tion (lik-wih-*fak*-sh'n) *n.* Conversion of a solid to a liquid.

liq·ue·fy (*lik*-wih-fy) *v.* [liq·ue·fied; liq·ue·fy·ing] To make liquid.—**liq·ue·fi·a·ble** *adj.*

liq·ueur (lee-*ker*) *n.* A cordial; sweet liquor.

liq·uid (*lik*-wid) *n.* A substance, neither gas nor solid, which flows freely.—*adj.* 1. Easily flowing. 2. Translucent. 3. Not frozen;

easily convertible. 'Liquid assets.'—**li·quid·i·ty** (lik-*wid*-ih-tee), **liq·uid·ness** n.—**liq·uid·ly** adv.

liq·ui·date (*lik*-wih-dayt) v. [-dat·ed; -dat·ing] 1. To pay off. 'Liquidate a debt.' 2. To wind up financial affairs. 3. To kill off or render harmless.—**liq·ui·da·tion** n.—**liq·ui·da·tor** n.

liquid measure. Method of measuring liquids, by pints, quarts, gallons, etc.

liq·uor (*lik*-er) n. 1. Any fluid. 2. A potent alcoholic beverage, as whiskey, rum, gin.—v. *Slang*. To drink; ply another with liquor.

li·ra (*lee*-ruh) n. [*pl*. -re, -ras] An Italian metal coin; theoretically worth 5c.

lisle (*lyle*) n. A closely woven cotton fabric, esp. used in stockings.—**lisle** adj.

lisp v. To speak the sibilant sounds *s* and *z* poorly, giving them the value of *th* or *dh*.—n. The act of lisping.—**lisp·er** n.—**lisp·ing·ly** adv.

lis·some (*liss*-um) adj. Also **lis·som**. Supple; slender and graceful. 'That lissome blonde.' —**lis·some·ly** adv.—**lis·some·ness** n.

list n. 1. An index; catalog, esp. of names or items. 2. *Nautical*. Sidewise inclination of a ship. 'Port list.' 3. [*pl*.] Field or area of contest. 'He entered the lists against vice.'—v. 1. To enter on a list. 2. To tilt or veer.

lis·ten (*liss*-'n) v. To hear; pay close attention to.—**lis·ten·er** n.

listening post. 1. An advanced outpost where observers can eavesdrop on the enemy. 2. Radio station designed to monitor broadcasts, esp. from foreign sources.

list·less (*list*-liss) adj. Languid; indifferent; without animation.— **-less·ly** adv.— **-less·ness** n.

lit v. *Past tense & past participle* of **light.**—adj. *Slang*. Drunk.

lit·a·ny (*lit*-uh-nee) n. [*pl*. -nies] A solemn form of supplication used in public worship.

litchi nut (*lee*-chee). Edible dried fruit of a Chinese evergreen tree.

li·ter, li·tre (*lee*-ter) n. A unit of metric measurement equal to 1.0567 U.S. liquid quarts or 0.9081 dry quart.

lit·er·a·cy (*lit*-er-uh-see) n. Ability to read and write.

lit·er·al (*lit*-er-ul) adj. Accurate; true; undeviating; precise; original.—**lit·er·al·ly** adv.—**lit·er·al·ness** n.

lit·er·ar·y (*lit*-er-air-ee) adj. 1. Given to reading or the study of books. 2. Pertaining to literature.

lit·er·ate (*lit*-er-it) adj. Able to read and speak intelligently.—n. One versed in literature.

lit·er·a·ture (*lit*-er-uh-cher) n. 1. The mass of the world's books, letters, etc.; the writings of a particular race or nation. 2. Artistic writing, as distinguished from hack work. 3. Body of writings on any one subject. 'Literature of the trade-union movement.' 4. *Colloquial*. Any printed matter.

lithe adj. Supple; flexible; lissome.—**lithe·ly** adv.—**lithe·ness** n.—**lithe·some** adj.

lith·i·um (*lith*-ee-um) n. Very light, silver-white, malleable metallic element. (*Symbol*: Li).

lith·o·graph (*lith*-uh-graf) n. A print produced from a design cut in stone, aluminum, etc.—v. To print by lithography.—**li·thog·ra·pher** (lith-*og*-ruh-fer) n.—**li·thog·ra·phy** n.— **-o·graph·ic** (lith-uh-*graf*-ik), **-i·cal** adj.— **-i·cal·ly** adv.

lith·o·sphere (*lith*-uh-sfeer) n. Solid crust of the earth.

lit·i·gant (*lit*-ih-gunt) n. Person involved in a lawsuit.—**lit·i·gant** adj.

lit·i·gate (*lit*-ih-gayt) v. [-gat·ed; -gat·ing] To bring legal action.—**lit·i·ga·tor** n.

lit·i·ga·tion n. Legal proceedings; dispute.

li·ti·gious (lih-*tij*-us) adj. Disposed to sue; contentious; quarrelsome.—**li·ti·gious·ly** adv.—**li·ti·gious·ness** n.

litmus paper. Paper containing a purple dye which turns red when exposed to acid, blue when exposed to alkali.

lit·ter n. 1. A portable bed, usually of canvas. 2. Objects scattered topsy-turvy. 3. Animal offspring produced at one birth. 'A litter of kittens.'—v. 1. To scatter things about in a slovenly manner. 2. To bear a litter.

lit·tle (*lit*-'l) adj. [less, less·er; least] *Colloquial*. 1. Small; tiny; short. 2. Trivial; petty. 3. Niggardly.—n. A small amount.—adv. 1. Slightly. 2. Not at all. 'He little thinks we know all.'—**lit·tle·ness** n.

lit·to·ral (*lit*-er-ul) n. The coast; shore.—**lit·to·ral** adj.

li·tur·gi·cal, li·tur·gic (lih-*terj*-ih-k'l) adj. Concerning public religious ceremonies.—**li·tur·gi·cal·ly** adv.

lit·ur·gy (*lit*-er-jee) n. [*pl*. -gies] Formal rites of public religious ceremonies.

liv·a·ble (*liv*-uh-b'l) adj. Pleasant; fit or agreeable to live in.

live v. (*liv*) [lived; liv·ing] 1. To exist; be alive. 2. To be permanent; remain in memory. 'Lincoln lives on.' 3. To spend a period of time in a particular manner. 'He lived soberly.' 4. To abide; dwell. 5. To feed; subsist. 'Horses live on grass.'—**live down.** To obliterate the memory of.

live (*lyve*) adj. 1. Having life; alive. 2. Ignited; not extinct. 'A live coal.' 3. Under pressure and imparting power. 'Live steam.' 4. *Colloquial*. Timely; immediate. 'Democracy is a live issue.'

live·li·hood (*lyve*-lih-hood) n. Means of earning a living.

live·long (*liv*-long) adj. Entire; slowly passing.

live·ly (*lyve*-lee) adj. [live·li·er; live·li·est] Animated; spirited; vivacious; quick.—**live·li·ly** adv.—**live·li·ness** n.

liv·en (*ly*-vun) v. *Colloquial*. To rouse; enliven.

liv·er (*liv*-er) n. A dweller; resident.

liv·er n. The gland which secretes bile, essential to digestion.—**liv·er·ish** adj. Sickly; crabbed.

liv·er·ied (*liv*-er-eed) adj. Wearing a characteristic outfit or uniform.

L

liv·er·wort (*liv*-er-wert) *n.* A family of flower-less plants resembling the mosses.

liv·er·wurst *n.* A sausage of ground and sea-soned liver; braunschweiger.

liv·er·y *n.* [*pl.* -ies] 1. A characteristic dress or uniform. 2. A stable where horses are kept or vehicles rented. 3. *Law.* Relinquishment of property.—**liv·er·y·man** *n.* [*pl.* -men].

live·stock (*lyve*-stok) *n.* Farm animals, as horses, goats, cows.

liv·id (*liv*-id) *adj.* Black and blue; of a leaden hue; discolored.—**li·vid·i·ty** (liv-*id*-uh-tee); **liv·id·ness** *n.*—**liv·id·ly** *adv.*

liv·ing *n.* 1. Power of continuing life. 2. Means of subsistence; livelihood. 3. The benefice or charge of a clergyman. 4. Manner or mode of life. 5. Those who are alive.

liv·ing *adj.* 1. Alive; animate. 2. Active; in motion or operation. 3. Producing action or vigor; quickening.

living wage. A wage sufficient to maintain an employee in a minimum standard of decency.

liz·ard (*liz*-erd) *n.* A small, four-legged reptile with a scaly body and movable eyelids.

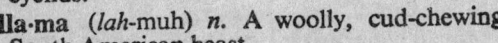

LIZARD (1/5 life size)

lla·ma (*lah*-muh) *n.* A woolly, cud-chewing South American beast of burden related to the camel.

lla·no (*lah*-no) *n.* [*pl.* -nos] A vast grassy plain of South America.

lo *interjection.* Behold! Observe!

load (*lohd*) *n.* 1. A burden; weight; encumbrance. 2. The

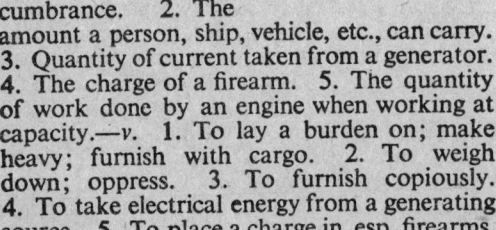

LLAMA (1/50 life size)

amount a person, ship, vehicle, etc., can carry. 3. Quantity of current taken from a generator. 4. The charge of a firearm. 5. The quantity of work done by an engine when working at capacity.—*v.* 1. To lay a burden on; make heavy; furnish with cargo. 2. To weigh down; oppress. 3. To furnish copiously. 4. To take electrical energy from a generating source. 5. To place a charge in, esp. firearms. —**load·er** *n.*

load·stone, lode·stone (*lohd*-stohn) *n.* 1. Magnetic iron ore. 2. Anything strongly attracting.

loaf (*lohf*) *n.* [*pl.* loaves] A molded mass, esp. of bread.

loaf *v. Colloquial.* To pass time in idleness; loiter or lounge.—**loaf·er** *n.*

loam (*lohm*) *n.* A good farming soil of clay mixed with various earths and organic matter. —*v.* To put loam on.—**loam·y** *adj.*

loan (*lohn*) *n.* Anything furnished for tempo-rary use on the condition that it or its equivalent be returned; sum of money lent, usually at interest.—*v.* To lend; let at interest.

loath, loth *adj.* Unwilling; reluctant; filled with disgust or aversion.

loathe *v.* [loathed; loath·ing] To dislike greatly, detest; feel disgust for.—**loath·ing** *n.*

loath·some (*lohth*-sum) *adj.* Disgusting; detest-able.—**loath·some·ly** *adv.*—**loath·some·ness** *n.*

lob *v.* [lobbed; lob·bing] To throw with gentle force; hit a ball in an easy, looping arc.—*n.* A ball tossed or hit easily or in a high arc.—**lob·ber** *n.*

lob·by (*lob*-ee) *n.* [*pl.* -bies] 1. A small hall; waiting room; foyer. 2. Persons or interests who seek to influence legislation.—*v.* [lob-bied; lob·by·ing] To solicit legislators to vote for or against proposed measures.—**lob·by·ist** *n.*

lobe (*lohb*) *n.* A rounded projection or division, esp. of the ear.—**lobed** *adj.*

lo·be·li·a (loh-*beel*-yuh) *n.* A family of leafy stemmed herbs with irregular flowers in spike-like clusters.

lob·lol·ly *n.* [*pl.* -lies] A coarse-grained pine tree of southern U.S.

lo·bo (*loh*-boh) *n.* A large, gray timber wolf.

lob·ster *n.* A large stalk-eyed crustacean with powerful fore claws and flat, plated tail; the ed-ible flesh of this animal.

LOBSTER (1/14 life size)

lo·cal (*loh*-kul) *adj.* 1. Limited to a small area; confined to a definite district. 2. Pertaining to a particular place. 3. Of conveyances, making all stops. 4. Of interest to one locality only.—*n.* 1. An item of news which has reference in a particu-lar locality. 2. A conveyance making all stops. 3. A chapter or unit, as of a labor union.—**lo·cal·ly** *adv.*

local color. Characteristics of a particular lo-cality, esp. as used in fiction.

lo·cale (loh-*kal*) *n.* A scene, esp. of an event.

lo·cal·ism (*loh*-kul-ism) *n.* Local idiom or custom.

lo·cal·i·ty (loh-*kal*-uh-tee) *n.* [*pl.* -ties] 1. A community; neighborhood; vicinity. 2. Lim-itation to a small or local area.

lo·cal·ize (*loh*-kuh-lyze) *v.* [-ized; -iz·ing] To restrict to a limited area; fix in a particular place.—**lo·cal·i·za·tion** *n.*

local option. The right of small governmental units to adopt Prohibition.

lo·cate (*loh*-kayt) *v.* [lo·cat·ed; lo·cat·ing] 1. To determine the place of; select; designate by limits. 2. To set in a particular spot; place. 3. To find; discover. 4. *Colloquial.* To settle in; adopt a fixed residence.—**lo·ca·tor** *n.*

lo·ca·tion (loh-*kay*-shun) *n.* 1. A placing or setting; marking out of boundaries, etc. 2. Situation with respect to place. 3. A tract of land designated or marked out. 4. Locale outside a studio where motion pictures are taken.

loch (*lok*) *n. Scottish.* 1. A lake; pond. 2. A narrow or landlocked bay.

lock *n.* 1. A tuft, wisp, or bunch of fibers or hair. 2. [*pl.*] Tresses; the hair.

lock *n.* 1. A device for securing doors, chests, drawers, machines, etc., opened only by key or combination. 2. A fastening together; fixity; immovability. 3. *Wrestling.* A restraining hold or grapple. 4. An enclosure in a canal, with gates at each end, used to raise or lower water levels. 5. The mechanism by which a gun is fired.—*v.* 1. To secure with a lock. 2. To fasten so as to impede motion. 3. To shut up or confine; close fast; seal. 4. To join firmly, as by intertwining or enfolding. 5. To come to grips; grapple. 6. To furnish with locks; float a ship through a lock.

lockbox	lock maker	lockpole
lock-down	lock making	lock pouch
lockfast	lockpin	lockspit

lock·er *n.* A small cupboard or compartment, esp. one that may be closed with a lock.

lock·et *n.* Little case worn as a pendant.

lock·jaw *n.* A disease in which there is spasmodic rigidity of voluntary muscles, esp. those of the lower jaw; tetanus.

lock out. To refuse employment to a staff of workers in order to force them to accept their employer's terms.—**lock-out** *n.*

lock·smith *n.* A craftsman who makes locks.

lock·up *n. Colloquial* A jail.

lo·co (*loh*-koh) *adj. Slang.* Crazy; frenzied.—*n.* 1. Also **loco weed.** A plant of the pea family which poisons cattle. 2. Also **loco disease.** The debilitated condition of cattle which have eaten loco.—*v.* [lo·coed; lo·co·ing] *Colloquial.* To drive mad.

lo·co·mo·tion (loh-kuh-*moh*-shun) *n.* The power or act of movement; travel.—**lo·co·mo·tor** *adj.*

lo·co·mo·tive (loh-kuh-*moh*-tiv) *n.* An engine which powers or moves railroad cars. —*adj.* 1. Moving from place to place. 2. Having power to propel or produce a motion. 3. Pertaining to a locomotive.

DIESEL LOCOMOTIVE

locomotor ataxia. A disease caused by degeneration of part of the spinal nerve, attended by loss of muscular co-ordination.

lo·cust (*loh*-kust) *n.* 1. An insect closely related to the grasshopper which swarms in large numbers, destructive of vegetation. 2. A pod-bearing shrub or tree of the pea family.

lo·cu·tion (loh-*kyoo*-shun) *n.* 1. Discourse; mode of speech. 2. A peculiar turn of phrase.

lode *n. Mining.* A vein of ore imbedded in a rock fissure.

lode·star, load·star (*lohd*-stahr) *n.* 1. A star

which guides navigators, esp. the North Star. 2. Anything strongly attractive.

lode·stone. *Variant spelling* of **loadstone.**

lodge *n.* 1. A small house in a park or forest; temporary habitation. 2. A fraternal society, or its place of meeting. 3. A den; cave; lair. 4. A wigwam; tepee.—*v.* [lodged; lodg·ing]. 1. To set; vest; deposit; place. 2. To furnish with or have a temporary habitation; accommodate. 3. To take up fixed residence; settle. 4. To become imbedded in.—**lodg·er** *n.*

lodg·ing *n.* 1. Temporary habitation; accommodation. 2. [*pl.*] Rented place of residence. —**lodging house.** A rooming house.

lodg·ment, lodge·ment *n.* 1. Accommodation; rented room. 2. A depositing at rest.

loft *n.* 1. An attic; top or upper story. 2. Upper floor in a barn; hayloft. 3. Large upper-story room in a warehouse or office building. —*v.* To place in, or furnish with, a loft.

loft·y *adj.* [loft·i·er; loft·i·est] 1. Elevated; rising high. 2. Dignified; stately; exalted. 3. Haughty; proud.—**loft·i·ly** *adv.*— **-i·ness** *n.*

log *n.* 1. A long, bulky piece of timber. 2. Any of several devices for measuring the rate of a ship's speed. 3. The complete record of a ship's or an aircraft's progress; logbook. —*v.* [logged; log·ging] 1. To cut down trees for logs. 2. To record in a log book.

lo·gan·ber·ry (*loh*-g'n-behr-ee) *n.* [*pl.* -ries] 1. A bramble related to the blackberry. 2. Its red fruit.

log·a·rithm (*log*-er-ith-'m) *n.* The exponent of a chosen base number, usually ten, which produces a given number. Logarithms arranged in tables are used to simplify multiplication and division.—**log·a·rith·mic, log·a·rith·mi·cal** *adj.*—**log·a·rith·mi·cal·ly** *adv.*

log·book *n.* A book containing the complete daily record of a ship's voyage.

loge (*lohzh*) *n.* Box or box section in a theater.

log·ger *n.* A person or machine employed to cut or haul logs.

log·ger·head (*log*-er-hed) *n.* 1. A blockhead; dunce. 2. An iron sphere attached to a long handle for heating tar, etc. 3. A large turtle found in the South Atlantic.—**at loggerheads.** Engaged in a dispute or fight.

log·gi·a (*loj*-ee-uh) *n.* [*pl.* -gi·as, -gie] *Architecture.* A gallery open to the air on one side.

log·ging *n.* The business of cutting logs and hauling them to market.

log·ic (*loj*-ik) *n.* 1. The science dealing with the basic principles or methods of valid reasoning. 2. Basic principles or structure of any art or science. 3. Sensible or convincing reasoning or argument. 4. An exposition or book of logic.

log·i·cal (*loj*-ih-k'l) *adj.* 1. Pertaining to or using logic. 2. Reasonable; natural; expected.—**log·i·cal·i·ty** *n.*—**log·i·cal·ly** *adv.*

lo·gi·cian (loh-*jish*-'n) *n.* Skilled user or teacher of logic.

L

lo·gis·tics (loh-*jiss*-tiks) *n. Military.* Business of transporting or quartering troops and supplies. —**lo·gis·tic, lo·gis·ti·cal** *adj.*

log·roll·ing *n.* 1. The collecting and communal handling of logs. 2. The giving of mutual assistance in carrying political or legislative measures.—**log·roll** *v.*—**log·roll·er** *n.*

lo·gy (*loh*-gee) *adj.* [lo·gi·er; lo·gi·est] Sluggish; heavy.

loin *n.* 1. Portion of the human or animal body between the ribs and the hip bone. 2. Cut of meat from this part, as of mutton.

loin·cloth *n.* Garment covering the loins, worn by primitive peoples.

loi·ter (*loy*-ter) *v.* To move slowly; lag; delay.

loll (*lol*) *v.* 1. To lounge; lean; relax lazily. 2. To hang loosely; dangle.—**loll** *n.*—**loll·er** *n.*

lol·li·pop (*lol*-ee-pop) *n.* A hard, often round, candy on the end of a small stick.

Lom·bard (*lom*-berd) *n.* 1. Member of a Teutonic tribe which conquered and settled Lombardy, in northern Italy. 2. A native of Lombardy.—**Lom·bard·ic** *adj.*

lone (*lohn*) *adj.* 1. Solitary; retired; unfrequented. 2. Without companion or fellow.

lone·ly *adj.* [-li·er; -li·est] 1. Unfrequented by man; solitary; sequestered. 2. Not having others near; apart from companions; lacking company. 3. Sad from want of companionship; lonesome.—**lone·li·ly** *adv.*—**lone·li·ness** *n.*

lone·some (*lohn*-sum) *adj.* 1. Sad or dreary from want of company and sympathy. 2. Solitary; secluded; desolate.— -**some·ly** *adv.*

long *adj.* [long·er; long·est] 1. Drawn out in the direction of length; drawn out or extended in time; greater in length than in any other dimension. 2. Extended to any specified measure. 3. Extending far in prospect or time. 4. Lingering; tedious. 5. Having a characteristic or ingredient to a high degree. 'He is long on courage.' 6. *Phonetics.* Of extended duration, as a vowel.—*adv.* 1. For a long time or at a distant point in time. 2. Throughout.

long-awaited	long-expected	long-necked
longbeard	long-fingered	long-parted
long-bearded	long-forgotten	long-planned
long-borne	long-haired	long-settled
long-clawed	long-handled	long-sleeved
long-delayed	long-hid	long-sought
long-desired	long-jawed	long-tailed
long distance	long-legged	long-tongued
long-drawn-out	longlegs	long-waisted

long *v.* [longed; long·ing] To crave; yearn; feel a great desire for.

long·boat *n.* General-purpose boat carried on certain large vessels.

long·bow *n.* A large wooden hand-drawn bow.

lon·gev·i·ty (lon-*jev*-uh-tee) *n.* Long span of life.

long·hand *n.* Ordinary writing or script as distinguished from shorthand or typewriting.

long·horn *n.* A species of cattle with long horns, formerly raised in southwestern U.S.

long·ing (*lawng*-ing) *n.* A desire; yearning. —**long·ing** *adj.*—**long·ing·ly** *adv.*

lon·gi·tude (*lon*-jih-tood) *n.* Angular distance east or west of the prime meridian running through Greenwich, England, to the meridian of any place.

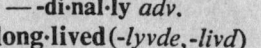
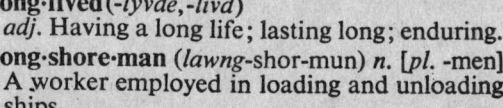

lon·gi·tu·di·nal (lon-jih-*too*-dih-n'l) *adj.* Pertaining to length; running lengthwise. — -**di·nal·ly** *adv.*

DEGREES OF LONGITUDE

long·lived (-*lyvde*, -*livd*) *adj.* Having a long life; lasting long; enduring.

long·shore·man (*lawng*-shor-mun) *n.* [*pl.* -men] A worker employed in loading and unloading ships.

long·sight·ed *adj.* 1. Able to see at a great distance; having foresight. 2. Far-sighted; able to see objects distinctly at a distance, but not close at hand.— -**ed·ness** *n.*

long·suf·fer·ing *adj.* Patient; not easily provoked; having much endurance.

long·wind·ed *adj.* Tedious in speaking; wearisome.— -**ed·ly** *adv.*— -**ed·ness** *n.*

look *v.* 1. To gaze. 2. To consider; examine. 3. To seem; appear. 'The sky looks cloudy.' —*n.* 1. A glance, gaze, etc. 2. Appearance; aspect.

look·er *n.* 1. One who looks. 2. *Slang.* A pretty girl.

look·er-on *n.* [*pl.* look·ers-on] An observer.

looking glass. A mirror.

look·out *n.* 1. A careful watch for an object or event. 2. A place where such observation is made. 3. A person engaged in watching.

loom *v.* 1. To come into sight. 2. To appear indistinctly and larger than life. 'The ship looms large.'—*n.* 1. A vague distorted appearance. 2. *Nautical.* The reflection of a light against the sky before it crosses the horizon.

loom *n.* 1. A machine for weaving thread or yarn into fabric. 2. *Nautical.* The cylindrical shaft of an oar.

loon *n.* 1. Any of several water birds, as the diver or ember-goose. 2. *Colloquial.* A crazy person.

loon·y (*loon*-ee) *adj.* [loon·i·er; loon·i·est] *Slang.* Mad; mentally deranged.—**loon·y** [*pl.* -ies] *n.* A lunatic.

LOON (1/25 life size)

loop *n.* A noose; a turn in the bight of a line. —*v.* 1. To form into a loop or loops; fasten or enclose with a loop. 2. A maneuver in which an airplane describes a vertical circle keeping its transverse axis horizontal.

loop·hole *n.* 1. *Military.* In the wall of a fortification or ship, a slit to shoot through. 2. An outlet; means of escape or evasion.

loose (*looss*) *adj.* 1. Unfastened; free; not confined. 2. Not tight or close. 3. Not dense or compact. 4. Vague; not precise. 5. Morally lax; dissolute.—*v.* [loosed; loos·ing] 1. To set free; liberate. 2. To relax; loosen. 3. To free from obligation, etc. 4. To unfasten; undo.—**loose·ly** *adv.*—**loose·ness** *n.*—**cut loose.** To break away from restraint.—**on the loose.** *Slang.* Free; unrestrained.

loose-joint·ed *adj.* Free in movement; ungracefully free of bodily restraint.

loos·en (*looss-'n*) *v.* 1. To free from tightness or tension. 2. To free from restraint. 3. To make less dense or compact.

loot *n.* Booty; plunder; spoils.—*v.* To plunder.

lop *v.* [lopped; lop·ping] To cut off; shorten; trim. 'Lop off the branches of a tree.'

lop *v.* [lopped; lop·ping] To hang limply.—*adj.* Hanging down; limp; pendulous.—**lop·py** *adj.*

lope *v.* [loped; lop·ing] To run with a long, bounding stride, as a dog.—**lope** *n.*—**lop·er** *n.*

lop-eared *adj.* Having ears which hang down.

lop·sid·ed *adj.* Heavier at one side than at the other; unevenly balanced.

lo·qua·cious (*loh-kway-shus*) *adj.* Talkative; garrulous; voluble.—**lo·qua·cious·ly** *adv.*—**lo·quac·i·ty** (*loh-kwass-uh-tee*) *n.*

lo·ran (*loh-ran*) *n.* Long-range radar navigational equipment.

lord *n.* 1. Master; ruler; governor. 2. [*cap.*] The supreme being; God. 3. [*cap.*] Jesus Christ. 4. A nobleman, a title of honor in Great Britain.—*v.* 1. To invest with the title of lord. 2. To rule as a lord. 3. To rule despotically.

lord·ly (*lord-lee*) *adj.* [lord·li·er; lord·li·est] 1. Fit for a lord; pertaining to a lord. 2. Haughty; imperious.—**lord·li·ness** *n.*

lord·ship (*lord-ship*) *n.* 1. The state or jurisdiction of a lord. 2. [*cap.*] Title of address given to noblemen and judges in Great Britain. 3. Sovereignty; authority.

Lord's Prayer. In the New Testament, the prayer which Christ gave his disciples.

Lord's Supper. Sacrament of the Eucharist instituted by Christ at his last meal with his disciples.

lore *n.* 1. Learning; erudition; knowledge. 2. The space between the bill and eye of a bird.

Lor·e·lei (*lor-uh-lye*) *n.* A siren of the Rhine who lured sailors to shipwreck.

lor·gnette (*lorn-yet*) *n.* 1. A pair of eyeglasses on a long handle. 2. Long-handled opera glasses.

lorn *adj.* Lonely; bereft; forsaken; lost.

lor·ry (*lor-ee*) *n.* [*pl.* -ries] 1. A motor truck for transporting heavy loads. 2. A four-wheeled platform wagon for carrying goods.

lo·ry (*loh-ree*) *n.* A bird of the parrot family with brilliant plumage, common in New Guinea.

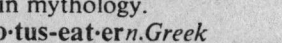

LORGNETTE

lose (*looz*) *v.* [lost; los·ing] 1. To part with by accident; mislay. 2. To forfeit; fail to gain or win. 'Lose a prize.' 3. To be deprived or bereaved of. 4. To squander; waste. 5. To miss. 'Lose an opportunity.'—**los·er** *n.*

los·ing (*looz-ing*) *n.* Loss.—*adj.* Causing or incurring loss.

loss (*lawss*) *n.* 1. Privation; deprivation; forfeiture. 2. Failure to win, gain, or keep. 3. That which is lost. 4. Damage; injury.

lost (*lawst*) *v.* Past tense & past participle of **lose**. —*adj.* 1. Missing; not to be found; parted with. 2. Forfeited. 3. Misspent; squandered; wasted. 4. Bewildered; perplexed. 5. Ruined, physically or morally. 6. Ignorant of one's whereabouts.

lot *n.* 1. Destiny; chance; fate. 2. Anything, as dice or straws, used to determine something by chance. 3. A separate or distinct collection or parcel of things. 'A lot of goods.' 4. A division of land. 5. A large number or amount. 'A lot of people.'—*v.* [lot·ted; lot·ting] 1. To divide by lot. 2. Allot; apportion.

Lo·tha·ri·o (*loh-thehr-ee-oh*) *n.* A libertine; rakehell; wastrel.

lo·tion (*loh-shun*) *n.* A liquid preparation applied to the skin.

lot·ter·y (*lot-er-ee*) *n.* [*pl.* -ies] A procedure for distributing prizes determined by chance.

lo·tus (*loh-tuss*) *n.* 1. Any of the several species of plant of the water-lily family. 2. A genus of plants consisting of creeping herbs and undershrubs, with yellow, red, or white flowers. 3. A name given to many different plants famous in mythology.

LOTUS

lo·tus-eat·er *n.* *Greek Mythology.* One of the Lotophagi, people who, in legend, lived in happy indolence as a result of eating the fruit of the lotus-tree.

loud *adj.* 1. Noisy; of great aural intensity. 2. Making a great noise. 'A loud instrument.' 3. Clamorous; vociferous. 4. Flashy; vulgarly showy.—**loud·ly** *adv.*—**loud·ness** *n.*

loud-mouthed *adj.* 1. Having a loud, clamorous voice. 2. Incautiously talkative.

loud-speak·er *n.* An electromagnetic device which amplifies sound.

lounge (*lownj*) *v.* [lounged; loung·ing] To loaf; loll; dawdle.—*n.* 1. The act of reclining at ease; lolling. 2. A lounging place. 3. A couch; sofa.—**loung·er** *n.* An idler; a lazy person.—**loung·ing** *adj.*

louse (*lowss*) *n.* [*pl.* lice] Small parasitic insect which sucks the blood of man and other animals.

lous·y (*lowz-ee*) *adj.* [lous·i·er; lous·i·est] 1. Infested with lice. 2. *Slang.* Mean; low; contemptible.—**lous·i·ly** *adv.*—**lous·i·ness** *n.*

L

lout (*lowt*) *n.* An awkward, boorish person; clown.—**lout·ish** *adj.* Clumsy; awkward; boorish.—**lout·ish·ly** *adv.*—**lout·ish·ness** *n.*

lou·ver (*loo*-ver) *n. Architecture.* A window, as in a church tower, partially closed by sloping slats, called **louver boards.**

Louvre (*loov*-r') *n.* An ancient palace of French kings in Paris, now used as an art museum.

lov·a·ble (*luv*-uh-b'l) *adj.* Worthy of love; amiable; endearing.—**lov·a·bil·i·ty** *n.*—**lov·a·ble·ness** *n.*—**lov·a·bly** *adv.*

love (*luv*) *v.* [loved; lov·ing] 1. To feel devotedly attached to or affectionate toward. 2. To feel strong tenderness and passion for. 3. To like; take pleasure in. 4. To caress.—*n.* 1. A strong feeling of affection, devotion, attachment. 2. Great tenderness and passion for another person. 3. Liking; inclination; fondness. 4. One who is beloved; sweetheart. 5. A personification of love, as Cupid, Eros, Venus. 6. *Tennis.* No score.

lovebird	lovelock	lovesick
love-bitten	lovelorn	love-smitten
love-crossed	love-mad	love-starved
love-entangled	lovemaking	love-stricken

love apple. The tomato.

love·bird *n.* A member of a group of small, beautiful parrots, remarkable for their attachment to their mates.

love·less *adj.* Devoid of love; unloved.—**love·less·ly** *adv.*—**love·less·ness** *n.*

love·lorn *adj.* 1. Forsaken by a lover. 2. Pining for a lover.

love·ly *adj.* [love·li·er; love·li·est] Attractive; beautiful; charming; delightful; enchanting.—**love·li·ly** *adv.*—**love·li·ness** *n.*

lov·er *n.* 1. Person in love. 2. One who has a strong liking for a particular thing. 'A lover of books.'—**lov·er·ly** *adj. & adv.*

love·sick *adj.* Sick with love or amorous desire.—**love·sick·ness** *n.*

lov·ing (*luv*-ing) *adj.* Fond; affectionate; tender.—**lov·ing·ly** *adv.*—**lov·ing·ness** *n.*

loving cup. A large two-handled cup, usually of silver or gold, given as a prize.

low (*loh*) *v.* To moo, as an ox or cow.—**low** *n.*

low *adj.* 1. Having comparatively little elevation. 2. Below the usual level; depressed. 3. Having less than average height. 4. Below the usual rate or amount. 5. Soft; not loud. 6. Dejected. 'Low in mind.' 7. Humble in rank. 8. Mean; abject; vulgar; base. 9. Feeble; weak.—*adv.* 1. Not high; near the ground. 2. At a low price. 3. In a humble condition. 4. Softly; on a low key.—**low, low·ness** *n.*

low-born	low-geared	low-spoken
low-bowed	low-heeled	low-tongued
low-bred	low-minded	low-voiced
lowbrowed	low-pitched	low-waisted
low caste	low-principled	low wattage
low-ceilinged	low-purposed	low-wheeled
low-flung	low-set	low-witted

low·boy *n.* A kind of buffet table.

low·brow *n. Slang.* One not interested in culture or intellect.—**low·brow** *adj.*

Low Countries. The Netherlands.

low-down *n. Slang.* Inside story.

low·er, lour (*lou*-er) *v.* 1. To appear dark or gloomy; be clouded; threaten a storm. 2. To frown; look sullen.

low·er (*loh*-er) *v.* 1. To let or take down. 2. To degrade or humble. 3. To diminish.—*n. Colloquial.* A lower berth in a train or ship.

lower case. Small letters of printing type.—**low·er-case** *v.* To set in small letters.—**low·er-case** *adj.*

Lower House. Lower branch of a legislature.

low·er·ing, lour·ing *adj.* 1. Cloudy; overcast. 2. Sullen.—**low·er·ing·ly, lour·ing·ly** *adv.*

low·er·most *adj.* Lowest.

low·land *n.* A level, flat country.

low·ly *adj.* [low·li·er; low·li·est] Humble; meek; unpretentious.—**low·ly** *adv.*—**low·li·ness** *n.*

Low Mass. *Roman Catholic Church.* A shortened version of the Mass, without music or choral responses.

low-mind·ed *adj.* Vulgar; mean; base.—**low-mind·ed·ly** *adv.*—**low-mind·ed·ness** *n.*

low-pitched *adj.* Low in key or tone.

low-spir·it·ed *adj.* Dejected; discouraged.—**low-spir·it·ed·ly** *adv.*—**low-spir·it·ed·ness** *n.*

lox (*loks*) *n.* Smoked salmon.

loy·al (*loy*-ul) *adj.* True or faithful to duty, love, or obligation; faithful in allegiance to government, country, etc.—**loy·al·ly** *adv.*

loy·al·ist *n.* 1. A person who supports the existing authority in a period of rebellion. 2. [*cap.*] Supporter of the Spanish government against the fascist rebels during the Spanish Civil War (1936–9).

loy·al·ty *n.* [*pl.* -ties] Faithfulness; constancy.

loz·enge (*loz*-enj) *n.* 1. *Geometry.* A figure with four equal sides, and two acute and two obtuse angles; a diamond. 2. A small medicine or candy tablet, originally lozenge-shaped.

lub·ber *n.* 1. A heavy, clumsy fellow; lout. 2. An inexpert sailor.—**lub·ber·ly** *adj. & adv.*

lu·bri·cant (*loo*-brik-unt) *n.* An oily or greasy substance applied to make a surface smooth or slippery.—**lu·bri·cant** *adj.*

lu·bri·cate *v.* [-cat·ed; -cat·ing] To make smooth or slippery.—**lu·bri·ca·tive** (*loo*-brih-kuh-tiv) *adj.*—**-ca·tion** (-*kay*-shun) *n.*

lu·bric·i·ty (*loo-briss*-it-ee) *n.* [*pl.* -ties] 1. Smoothness; slipperiness; oiliness. 2. Lewdness; lechery; lasciviousness.—**lu·bri·cous** (*loo*-brih-kus) *adj.*

lu·cent (*loo*-s'nt) *adj.* Shining; bright; luminous.

lu·cern (*loo-sern*) *n.* Also **lu·cerne.** Alfalfa, a cloverlike plant used for fodder.

lu·cid (*loo*-sid) *adj.* 1. Clear; intelligible. 2. Sane; rational. 3. Shining; pure.—**lu·cid·i·ty** (*loo-sid*-ih-tee) *n.*

Lu·ci·fer (*loo*-sif-er) *n.* 1. Satan; the prince of darkness; the devil. 2. The planet Venus when it appears before sunrise; the morning star.   3. A type of friction match.

Lu·cite (*loo*-syte) *n*. Trade-mark name for a crystalline translucent synthetic resin.

luck *n*.   1. Fortune; chance; accident.   2. Good fortune; success due to chance.

luck·less *adj*. Unfortunate; unpropitious; unsuccessful.—**luck·less·ly** *adv*.—**luck·less·ness** *n*.

luck·y *adj*. [luck·i·er; luck·i·est]   1. Fortunate; attended by good luck.   2. Favorable; auspicious.—**luck·i·ly** *adv*.—**luck·i·ness** *n*.

lu·cra·tive (*loo*-kruh-tiv) *adj*. Profitable; yielding gain.—**lu·cra·tive·ly** *adv*.—**lu·cra·tive·ness** *n*.

lu·cre (*loo*-ker) *n*. Money; pecuniary profit.

lu·cu·brate (*loo*-kyuh-brayt) *v*. [lu·cu·brat·ed; lu·cu·brat·ing] To study laboriously; burn the midnight oil.

lu·cu·bra·tion *n*.   1. Nocturnal study.   2. A literary work, esp. a pedantic or elaborate one.

Lu·cul·lan, Lu·cul·li·an (loo-*kul*-an, loo-*kul*-ee-un) *adj*. Pertaining to the Roman Lucullus, noted for his sumptuous feasts.

lu·di·crous (*loo*-dih-krus) *adj*. Absurd; droll; ridiculous.— -**crous·ly** *adv*.— -**crous·ness** *n*.

luff *n. Nautical*.   1. The weather part of a fore-and-aft sail, next to the mast or stay.   2. The broadest part of a ship's bow.—**luff** *v*. To steer closer to the wind.

Luft·waf·fe (*luft*-vahf-uh) *n*. The air force of Nazi Germany.

lug *v*. [lugged; lug·ging] To haul; drag; carry.

lug *n*.   1. An earlike projection on a piece of machinery by which it may be fixed in place.   2. *Scottish*. The ear.

lug·gage (*lug*-ij) *n*. A traveler's baggage.

lug·ger (*lug*-er) *n*. A small ship carrying two or three masts with a running bowsprit and lugsails.

lug·sail, lug *n. Nautical*. A four-sided sail hung upon a yard that hangs obliquely to the mast at one third of its length.

lu·gu·bri·ous (luh-*goo*-bree-us) *adj*. Mournful; doleful; sad.— -**ous·ly** *adv*.— -**ous·ness** *n*.

Luke *n. Biblical*. The author of the third of the four Gospels, traditionally a physician.

luke·warm *adj*.   1. Moderately warm; tepid.   2. Indifferent; unenthusiastic.—**luke·warm·ly** *adv*.—**luke·warm·ness** *n*.

lull *v*.   1. To quiet; soothe to sleep; compose.   2. To subside; cease; become calm.—**lull** *n*. An interval of quiet after a storm.

lull·a·by (*lul*-uh-by) *n*. [*pl*. -bies] A song to soothe babies to sleep.

lum·ba·go (lum-*bay*-goh) *n. Medicine*. Rheumatism in the lumbar region or loins.

lum·bar (*lum*-ber) *adj*. Pertaining to the loins.

lum·ber (*lum*-ber) *n*. Timber sawed and split for use as beams, joists, boards, planks, etc.—*v*. To cut and prepare forest lumber.—**lum·ber·er** *n*. One who cuts timber.

lum·ber *v*.   1. To move in a heavy, blundering way.   2. To heap together haphazardly.

3. To fill with useless, cumbersome material.—*n*. Any useless, bulky rubbish.

lum·ber·ing *n*. The felling of timber.

lum·ber·ing *adj*. Clumsy, blundering, noisy.—**lum·ber·ing·ly** *adv*.—**lum·ber·ing·ness** *n*.

lum·ber·jack *n*. One who cuts and prepares timber.

lu·mi·nar·y (*loo*-min-ehr-ee) *n*. [*pl*. -ies]   1. Any body which gives natural light, esp. a celestial body.   2. Any outstanding leader.

lu·mi·nes·cence (loo-min-*ess*-enss) *n*. A power of emitting light possessed by certain bodies which have been exposed to light or radiant energy.—**lu·mi·nes·cent** *adj*.

lu·mi·nous (*loo*-min-us) *adj*.   1. Shining; emitting light; bright.   2. Clear; lucid; perspicuous.—**lu·mi·nous·ly** *adv*.—**lu·mi·nous·ness** *n*.—**lu·mi·nos·i·ty** (loo-min-*os*-ih-tee) *n*.

lum·mox (*lum*-uks) *n*. A fat, ungainly person.

lump *n*.   1. A compact mass of matter of no definite shape.   2. Protuberance; swelling; bruise.   3. Aggregate; gross.   4. A heavy, dull person.—*v*. To mass together without regard to differences; speak of or regard collectively. 'A lump sum.'

lump *v. Colloquial*. To put up with ungraciously. 'If you don't like it, lump it.'

lump·ish *adj*.   1. Heavy; bulky.   2. Dull; lethargic.—**lump·ish·ly** *adv*.—**lump·ish·ness** *n*.

lump·y *adj*. [lump·i·er; lump·i·est] Full of or covered with lumps.—**lump·i·ly** *adv*.— -**i·ness** *n*.

Lu·na (*loo*-nuh) *n*. The moon.

lu·na·cy (*loo*-nuh-see) *n*. [*pl*. -cies] Insanity.

lu·nar (*loo*-ner) *adj*.   1. Pertaining to the moon.   2. Measured by the revolutions of the moon. 'Lunar months.'   3. Resembling the moon; crescent-shaped.

lu·na·tic (*loo*-nuh-tik) *n*. A madman; insane person.—**lu·na·tic** *adj*. Also **lu·nat·i·cal** (loo-*nat*-ih-k'l).   1. Mad; insane.   2. Foolish; frantic; eccentric.—**lu·na·tic a·sy·lum**. Hospital for the insane.

lunch *n*. A light meal, usually eaten at midday.—**lunch** *v*.—**lunch·er** *n*.

lunch·eon (*lunch*-un) *n*. A lunch, esp. one regarded as a special occasion.

lunch·eon·ette (lunch-un-*et*) *n*. A small restaurant, usually with seats at a counter, where light meals can be bought.

lung *n*. Either of the pair of respiratory organs in man and other air-breathing vertebrates.

lunge (*lunj*) *v*. [lunged; lung·ing]   1. To move forward suddenly; plunge; rush.   2. To make a thrust, as with a sword or rapier.   3. To deliver a blow from the shoulder in boxing.   4. To kick out, as a horse.—**lunge** *n*.—**lung·er** *n*.

lung·er *n. Colloquial*. A person suffering from tuberculosis.

lu·pine (*loo*-pyne) *adj*. Pertaining to a wolf.

lu·pine (*loo*-pin) *n*. Family of garden and fodder plants, with flowers of various colors.

lurch (*lerch*) *n*. A sudden stagger or roll to one side, as of a drunken person.—**lurch** *v*.

L

lurch *n.* A difficult or embarrassing situation—used only in 'left in the lurch.'

lure (*loor*) *n.* 1. *Falconry.* An object resembling a bird used to recall a hawk. 2. Any enticement. 3. A decoy for catching fish.—*v.* [lured; lur·ing] 1. To catch or call by means of a lure. 2. To entice; attract.—**lur·er** *n.*

lu·rid (*loor*-id) *adj.* 1. Ghastly pale; glaring; terrible in color or light. 2. *Botany.* Of a dingy, clouded brown color.—**lu·rid·ly** *adv.*—**lu·rid·ness** *n.*

lurk *v.* 1. To lie hidden; lie in wait. 2. To escape notice; be latent.—**lurk·er** *n.*—**lurk·ing** *adj.*—**lurk·ing·ly** *adv.*

lus·cious (*lush*-us) *adj.* 1. Richly sweet in taste or smell; delicious. 2. Excessively sweet; cloying; fulsome.— **-cious·ly** *adv.*— **cious·ness** *n.*

lush *adj.* Luxuriant; succulent. 'Lush grass.' —**lush·ness** *n.*

lush *n. Slang.* 1. A drunkard. 2. Alcoholic liquor.—*v. Slang.* To become or make drunk.

lust *n.* 1. Eager desire. 2. Animal passion for sexual indulgence.—**lust** *v.*

lus·ter, lus·tre (*luss*-ter) *n.* 1. Brilliance; gloss. 2. Splendor; renown; distinction. 3. A branched chandelier with drops of cut glass. 4. Thin, lustrous-surfaced dress material. 5. The quality and intensity of light reflected from the surface of minerals.—*v.* To put luster on cloth, pottery, etc.— **-ter·less** *adj.*

lus·ter·ware, lus·tre·ware *n.* Brilliantly glazed earthenware.

lust·ful *adj.* 1. Eagerly desirous. 2. Having a strong passion for sexual gratification; libidinous.—**lust·ful·ly** *adv.*—**lust·ful·ness** *n.*

lus·trous (*luss*-trus) *adj.* Brilliant; shining; radiant.—**lus·trous·ly** *adv.*—**lus·trous·ness** *n.*

lus·trum *n.* [*pl.* -trums; tra] 1. A purification ceremony, esp. of the ancient Roman people every five years. 2. A five-year period.

lust·y *adj.* [lust·i·er; lust·i·est] Vigorous; robust; healthy; strong.—**lust·i·ness** *n.*

lute (*loot*) *n.* A stringed musical instrument of the guitar family.

lute, lu·ting *n.* A composition of clay, used to make joints or seams airtight.—*v.* To close or coat with lute.

lu·te·ci·um (loo-*tee*-shee-um) *n.* A rare metallic element. (*Symbol:* Lu).

Lu·ther·an (*loo*-ther-un) *adj.* Pertaining to Martin Luther, German reformer, or his church and its doctrines.—*n.* A member of the Lutheran Church; follower of Luther.—**Lu·ther·an·ism** *n.*

lux·u·ri·ance (luk-*shoor*-ee-unss) *n.* 1. Abundance; excess. 2. Floridness; rich ornament.

lux·u·ri·ant *adj.* 1. Prolific; abundant; rank.

LUTE

'Luxuriant growth of grass.' 2. Florid; ornamented.—**lux·u·ri·ant·ly** *adv.*

lux·u·ri·ate *v.* [-at·ed; -at·ing] 1. To grow unrestrainedly. 2. To live sybaritically. 3. To indulge without restraint.—**lux·u·ri·a·tion** *n.*

lux·u·ri·ous (luk-*shoor*-ee-us) *adj.* Given to luxury; voluptuous.—**lux·u·ri·ous·ly** *adv.*—**lux·u·ri·ous·ness** *n.*

lux·u·ry (*luk*-sher-ee) *n.* [*pl.* -ries] 1. Indulgence in expensive food, drink, clothes, furniture, etc. 2. A rare delicacy. 3. A thing that is desirable, but not necessary for life.

ly·can·thrope (*ly*-kun-throhp) *n.* Person suffering a delusion that he is a wolf.—**ly·can·thro·py** (ly-*kan*-throp-ee) *n.* 1. Belief that man can change into a wolf. 2. Belief in existence of werewolves.—**ly·can·throp·ic** *adj.*

ly·ce·um (ly-*see*-um) *n.* 1. An academy; lecture hall. 2. A literary association.

lydd·ite (*lid*-yte) *n.* A powerful explosive with a picric-acid base.

lye *n.* Strong alkaline solution used as a cleansing agent and in soap-making.

ly·ing (*ly*-ing) *Present participle* of **lie.** 1. Being prostrate. 2. Telling a falsehood.—**ly·ing** *adj.* False; deceitful.—**ly·ing·ly** *adv.*

ly·ing-in *n.* Childbirth.—**ly·ing-in** *adj.*

lymph (*limf*) *n. Physiology.* In animal bodies, a colorless, alkaline fluid, like blood, but without red corpuscles.

lym·phat·ic (lim-*fat*-ik) *adj.* 1. Of lymph or the lymphatics. 2. Flabby; sluggish.—**lym·phat·ics** *n. pl.* Small, transparent, lymph-bearing vessels.

lynch (*linch*) *v.* To inflict illegal and summary punishment, often death by hanging, upon someone, as by a mob or unauthorized persons.—**lynch·er** *n.*

lynx (*links*) *n.* A spotted, catlike animal with proverbially keen vision; bobcat.

lynx-eyed *adj.* keen-eyed; sharp-sighted.

ly·on·naise (ly-uh-*nayz*) *adj.* Fried with slices of onion. 'Lyonnaise potatoes.'

LYNX (1/25 life size)

lyre *n. Music.* Ancient stringed instrument of the harp family.

lyre·bird *n.* Australian bird, the male of which has lyre-shaped tail feathers.

lyr·ic (*lih*-rik) *adj.* Suited to or designed for singing. 'Lyric poetry.' —*n.* A verse with singable qualities.—**lyr·i·cal** *adj.*—**lyr·i·cal·ly** *adv.*

lyr·i·cist, lyr·ist *n.* A lyric writer.

lyric writer. *Theater.* Person who writes the words for popular tunes; lyricist.

LYRE

M

ma'am (*mam*) *n. Colloquial.* Madam.

ma·ca·bre (muh-*kah*-bruh, muh-*kah*-ber) *adj.* Also **ma·ca·ber.** Weird; gruesome; suggesting death or horror.

mac·ad·am (muh-*kad*-um) *n.* 1. A type of drained roadway paved with finely broken stone. 2. The stone used for this road.—**mac·ad·am·ize** *v.* [-ized; -iz·ing].

mac·a·ro·ni (mak-er-*oh*-nee) *n.* [*pl.* -nis] 1. An Italian preparation of hardened flour paste in tubular form. 2. A fop; dude.

mac·a·roon (mak-er-*oon*) *n.* A small almond-flavored cookie.

ma·caw (muh-*kaw*) *n.* A large, South American parrot of brilliant plumage.

Mac·beth (mak-*beth*). The general who murdered the king of Scotland in Shakespeare's *Macbeth.*

mace *n.* 1. An ornamental staff borne before dignitaries during ceremonial processions. 2. One who bears this staff.

mace *n.* A spice ground from the dried outermost shell of the nutmeg.

Mac·e·do·ni·a (mas-uh-*doh*-nee-uh) *n.* A country north of ancient Greece. —**Mac·e·do·ni·an** *adj. & n.*

mac·er·ate (*mass*-er-ayt) *v.* [-at·ed; -at·ing] 1. To soften into pulp; waste or wear away; extract by steeping. 2. To harass; annoy. —**mac·er·a·tion** (mass-er-*ay*-shun) *n.*

MACE

mach (*mock*) *n.* Ratio between speed of airflow and speed of sound, used instead of conventional miles-per-hour ratio in calculating speed of trans- and super-sonic aircraft.

ma·che·te (mah-*tshay*-tay) *n.* A long, heavy knife.

Mach·i·a·vel·li·an (mak-ee-uh-*vel*-ee-un) *adj.* Also **Mach·i·a·vel·i·an.** Cunning; grossly unscrupulous; double-dealing, esp. in politics.—**Mach·i·a·vel·li·an·ism** *n.* 1. Political chicanery. 2. Belief that any means used to maintain a strong central government are justifiable.

MACHETE

mach·i·na·tion (mak-ih-*nay*-shun) *n.* 1. Plotting; intrigue. 2. A plot; evil scheme.—**mach·i·nate** [-nat·ed; -nat·ing] *v.* To plot; contrive; scheme.—**mach·i·na·tor** *n.*

ma·chine (muh-*sheen*) *n.* 1. A complicated tool; mechanical device for converting energy into useful work. 2. A vehicle, as an automobile. 3. A political group that controls, usually unethically, a party or organization. 4. A person or organization that acts with precision or unfeelingness like a machine.—*adj.* Pertaining to machinery or a machine.—*v.* [ma·chined;

ma·chin·ing] 1. To shape or work. 2. To contrive; engineer; bring about.

machine-cut   machine-finished   machine-made
machine-drilled   machine-forged   machineman
machine-driven   machine-hour   machine work

machine gun. A self-cooled gun designed for rapid, continuous shooting.

ma·chin·er·y (muh-*sheen*-er-ee) *n.* 1. A mechanism; component parts of a machine. 2. A collection of machines. 3. A working system; combination of operating factors.

machine tool. A machine, such as a lathe or drill press, used in manufacturing.

ma·chin·ist (muh-*sheen*-ist) *n.* 1. One who designs, makes, or repairs machines. 2. *U.S. Navy.* An engine room assistant.

mack·er·el (*mak*-er-ul) *n.* An edible blue-barred fish of the north Atlantic.

mackerel sky. A sky with many small clouds.

mack·i·naw (*mak*-in-aw) *n.* A short heavy doubled-breasted jacket, often plaid.

mack·in·tosh (*mak*-in-tosh) *n.* A raincoat made of rubberized fabric of the same name.

mac·ro·cosm (*mak*-ruh-kozm) *n.* The universe; world exclusive of man.—**mac·ro·cos·mic** *adj.*

mad *adj.* [mad·der; mad·dest] 1. Deranged; frantic; crazy. 2. Angry; furious. 3. Infatuated; blindly devoted. 4. Irrepressibly gay. 5. Afflicted with rabies.—**mad·ness** *n.*

mad·am (*mad*-'m) *n.* 1. [*pl.* mes·dames] A form of courteous address to a woman. 2. [*pl.* mad·ams] Mistress of a brothel.

mad·ame (muh-*dam*) *n.* [*pl.* mes-dames] A French form of address to a married woman. *Abbreviation:* Mme.

mad·cap (*mad*-kap) *n.* A person given to wild antics or escapades.—*adj.* Rash; reckless.

mad·den *v.* To enrage; infuriate; exasperate. —**mad·den·ing** *adj.*—**mad·den·ing·ly** *adv.*

mad·der *n.* A large family of mainly tropical plants including the coffee tree.

made *adj.* Constructed; contrived; artificially or synthetically created.

Ma·dei·ra (muh-*deer*-uh) *n.* A sweet wine made in Madeira.

ma·de·moi·selle (mad-'m-wuh-*zel*) *n.* [*pl.* mes-de·moi·selles] Miss; French title used in addressing an unmarried woman. *Abbr.:* Mlle.

made-up *adj.* 1. Artificial; unreal; covered with cosmetics. 2. Faked; imagined.

mad·house *n.* 1. A hospital for the insane. 2. A house or scene of noisy confusion.

mad·man *n.* [*pl.* -men] A lunatic; frenzied or berserk person.

mad-mon·ey *n.* A small sum carried by a woman against an emergency.

M

Ma·don·na (muh-*don*-uh) *n.* The Virgin Mary; a picture or sculpture of her.

ma·dras (muh-*drass*) *n.* A fine cotton printed material for sport shirts, kerchiefs, etc.

Ma·dras (muh-*drass*). Third largest city of India and the best port on its east coast.

mad·ri·gal (*mad*-rih-g'l) *n.* 1. A short lyric or love poem adapted to singing. 2. A vocal composition in two or more parts.

mael·strom (*mayl*-strum) *n.* 1. A destructive influence; catastrophe. 2. [*cap.*] A whirlpool on the coast of Norway.

mae·stro (*my*-stroh) *n.* [*pl.* mae·stros; mae·stri] A virtuoso; outstanding performer in an art, esp. music.

Mae West. *Slang.* A pneumatic life preserver.

mag·a·zine (*mag*-uh-zeen) *n.* 1. A periodical; publication containing miscellaneous articles and stories issued at regular intervals. 2. A storage room for ammunition. 3. In a gun, the chamber retaining the ammunition.

Mag·da·len, Mag·da·lene (*mag*-duh-lin) *n.* 1. Mary of Magdala, an associate of Jesus and the disciples. 2. [*not cap.*] A reformed harlot.

Ma·gel·lan, Strait of (muh-*jel*-un). A 360-mile strait at the southern tip of South America, very treacherous and hazardous to navigate.

ma·gen·ta (muh-*jen*-tuh) *n.* A red-purple, coal-tar dye or its color.

mag·got (*mag*-ut) *n.* A grub; worm; the larva of a fly.—**mag·got·y** *adj.*

Ma·gi (*may*-jy) *n. pl.* The three wise men who brought gifts to the infant Christ.

MAGGOT

mag·ic (*maj*-ik) *n.* 1. Sorcery; the art of producing supernatural results. 2. Any manifestation of seemingly supernatural powers. —*adj.* Also **mag·i·cal.** Using or showing extraordinary powers.—**mag·i·cal·ly** *adv.*

ma·gi·cian (muh-*jish*-un) *n.* 1. A sleight-of-hand artist; conjurer. 2. One skilled in sorcery or witchcraft.

magic lantern. Apparatus for showing still-picture slides magnified on a screen.

Maginot line (*mah*-zhin-oh). Line of forts erected by France as a barrier to German aggression prior to World War II.

mag·is·te·ri·al (maj-iss-*teer*-ee-ul) *adj.* 1. Authoritative; lofty; domineering. 2. Of or like a magistrate.—**mag·is·te·ri·al·ly** *adv.*

mag·is·tra·cy (*maj*-iss-truh-see) *n.* [*pl.* -cies] 1. The office or jurisdiction of a magistrate. 2. The body of magistrates.

mag·is·trate (*maj*-iss-trayt) *n.* 1. A judge; justice of the peace. 2. A high governmental official.

Magna Carta (*mag*-nuh *kahr*-tuh). Also **Magna Charta.** 1. The document of King John, 1215, granting civil liberties to the English people. 2. A bill of rights.

mag·na·nim·i·ty (mag-nuh-*nim*-it-ee) *n.* [*pl.* -ties] 1. Nobility; high-mindedness; generosity. 2. A chivalrous or lofty deed.

mag·nan·i·mous (mag-*nan*-ih-mus) *adj.* Of high principles; honorable; benevolent.—**mag·nan·i·mous·ly** *adv.*—**mag·nan·i·mous·ness** *n.*

mag·nate (*mag*-nayt) *n.* A person of high rank or wide influence, esp. an industrial or financial czar.

mag·ne·sia (mag-*nee*-shuh) *n.* White oxide of magnesium used as a laxative.—**mag·ne·si·an, mag·ne·sic** *adj.*

mag·ne·si·um (mag-*nee*-shee-um) *n.* A light, tough, silver-white metal element which burns with a brilliant flash. (Symbol: Mg).

mag·net (*mag*-nit) *n.* 1. Any device or loadstone that attracts iron and steel. 2. Anything that attracts.

mag·net·ic (mag-*net*-ik) *adj.* Also **mag·net·i·cal.** 1. Pertaining to magnetism; attracting; drawn by magnetism. 2. Having personal effect; attractive.—**mag·net·i·cal·ly** *adv.*

magnetic field. The area permeated by lines of force about a magnet.

magnetic needle. The needle of a compass magnetized to point north.

magnetic north. The direction of the north magnetic pole.

magnetic pole. A point at which magnetic lines of force converge, esp. those of the earth.

mag·net·ism (*mag*-nuh-tizm) *n.* 1. A force of attraction or repulsion between two bodies caused by a polarized alignment of their molecules. 2. The science treating of magnetic attraction. 3. Personal appeal or attraction.

mag·ne·tite (*mag*-nuh-tyte) *n.* Loadstone; iron ore which is sometimes found polarized in its native form.

mag·net·ize (*mag*-nuh-tyze) *v.* [-ized; -iz·ing] 1. To impart magnetism to. 2. To attract; charm.—**mag·net·iz·a·ble** *adv.*—**mag·net·iz·a·bil·i·ty** (mag-nuh-tyze-uh-*bil*-ih-tee) *n.*—**mag·net·i·za·tion** (mag-nuh-tih-*zay*-shun) *n.*—**mag·net·iz·er** *n.*

mag·ne·to (mag-*nee*-toh) *n.* [*pl.* -tos] A small generator with permanent magnets for producing ignition current in some internal-combustion engines.

mag·ni·fi·ca·tion (mag-nih-fih-*kay*-shun) *n.* Increase of the apparent size or importance of an object or concept.

mag·nif·i·cence (mag-*nif*-ih-s'nss) *n.* Grandeur; splendor; sumptuousness.

mag·nif·i·cent *adj.* 1. Grand; glorious; lavish. 2. Sublime; exalted.—**mag·nif·i·cent·ly** *adv.*

mag·ni·fy (*mag*-nih-fy) *v.* [-fied; -fy·ing] 1. To enlarge; increase in size. 2. To make to appear larger or more significant; exaggerate. —**mag·ni·fi·er** *n.*

mag·nil·o·quent (mag-*nil*-uh-kwunt) *adj.* Bombastic; pompous in speech.—**mag·nil·o·quence** *n.*—**mag·nil·o·quent·ly** *adv.*

mag·ni·tude (*mag*-nih-tood) *n*. 1. Dimension; size; extent; quantity. 2. *Astronomy*. Relative amount of light intensity.

mag·no·li·a (*mag-nohl*-yuh) *n*. A family of trees and shrubs with spectacularly beautiful, large flowers.

mag·num (*mag*-num) *n*. A liquor bottle of two-quart capacity.

magnum opus. A masterpiece; chief work of an artist.

MAGNOLIA

mag·pie *n*. 1. An incessantly noisy bird of the crow family. 2. A chatter-box; loquacious person.

mag·uey (*mag*-way) *n*. The Mexican century plant.

Mag·yar (*mag*-yahr) *n*. 1. Member of the predominating race of Hungary. 2. The Hungarian language.—**Mag·yar** *adj*.

MAGPIE

ma·ha·ra·ja, ma·ha·ra·jah (mah-huh-*rah*-juh) *n*. A ruling Hindu prince, esp. the head of one of the principal Indian states.—**ma·ha·ra·ni, -nee** *n. fem.*

ma·hat·ma (muh-*hat*-muh) *n*. A Hindu sage; person of great powers.—**ma·hat·ma·ism** *n*.

Mah·di (*mah*-dee) *n*. The Messiah of the Mohammedans.—**Mah·dism** *n*. Doctrine of the coming of the Mahdi.—**Mah·dist** *n*.

mah-jongg, mah-jong (mah-*jong*) *n*. Game of Chinese origin using tiles resembling dominoes.

ma·hog·a·ny (muh-*hog*-uh-nee) *n*. [*pl*. -nies] 1. A tropical tree yielding a valuable reddish-brown wood. 2. The wood of this tree, used for furniture. 3. The color of mahogany. —*adj*. Of or like mahogany.

maid (*mayd*) *n*. 1. A woman servant. 2. A maiden; unmarried woman; virgin.

maid·en (*may*-d'n) *n*. A maid.—*adj*. 1. Virgin; unsullied; untried. 2. Relating to a young woman or virgin. 3. First; initial.

maid·en·hair *n*. Also **maidenhair fern.** A delicate variety of fern.

maid·en·head *n*. 1. The hymen; vaginal membrane. 2. Maidenhood.

maid·en·hood *n*. An unmarried state; virginity.

maid·en·ly *adj*. Modest; proper; of or like a maiden.—**maid·en·li·ness** *n*.

maid of honor. A bride's principal unmarried attendant.

maid·serv·ant *n*. A maid; woman servant.

mail (*mayl*) *n*. 1. Armor; a defensive covering. 2. A flexible metal armor formerly worn in battle.—*v*. To envelop or arm with mail.

mail *n*. 1. Anything conveyed by government post, as letters, packages, etc. 2. The postal system or service.—*v*. To send, as letters, by post.—**mail** *adj*.—**mail·a·ble** *adj*.—**mail·er** *n*.

mail bag   mail-checked   mail plane
mail box   mail guard   mail pouch

mail·man *n*. [*pl*. -men] A postman; government employee who delivers mail.

maim (*maym*) *v*. To mutilate; injure; cripple.

main (*mayn*) *adj*. 1. Principal; most important; chief. 2. Utter; extreme.—*n*. 1. A large pipe for conducting gas, water, etc. 2. The open sea; ocean.

main brace   mainsheet   main-topmast
mainpin   maintopman   main-topsail

main·land *n*. The continent; largest area of land adjacent to water.—**main·land·er** *n*.

main·ly *adv*. Chiefly; primarily; mostly.

main·mast (*mayn*-mast, *mayn*-m'st) *n. Nautical*. The tallest or principal mast of a vessel.

main·sail (*mayn*-sayl, *mayn*-s'l) *n*. The largest or principal sail of a vessel.

main·spring *n*. 1. The principal spring, as in a watch. 2. The main motivating force.

main·stay *n*. 1. The chief support. 2. *Nautical*. The brace supporting the mainmast.

main·tain *v*. 1. To hold; sustain; carry on. 2. To support; keep up. 3. To allege; declare to be true; defend.—**main·tain·a·ble** *adv*.

main·te·nance (*mayn*-tuh-nunss) *n*. 1. Upkeep; support; sustenance. 2. Protection; defense. 3. Act of keeping or carrying on.

maintenance of membership. Clause in a contract between union and management providing that workers belonging to union when contract is signed must retain membership for the life of the contract.

maître d'hôtel (meh-truh-doh-*tel*) 1. A head waiter. 2. A steward; manager of a home or hotel. 3. A sauce of parsley, lemon juice, etc., in melted butter.

maize (*mayz*) *n*. 1. Indian corn. 2. Light yellow color.

ma·jes·tic (muh-*jess*-tik) *adj*. Also **ma·jes·ti·cal**. Regal; grand; having or showing great dignity.—**ma·jes·ti·cal·ly** *adv*.

maj·es·ty (*maj*-iss-tee) *n*. [*pl*. -ties] 1. Stateliness; dignity; grandeur. 2. [*cap*.] The dignity, person, or title of a sovereign.

ma·jol·i·ca (muh-*jol*-ih-kuh) *n*. A kind of richly enameled pottery.

ma·jor (*may*-jer) *adj*. 1. Greater; the larger part. 2. More important. 3. Chief; principal; main. 4. *Music*. Standard; normal, as a major interval.—*n*. 1. *Military*. An officer ranking above a captain. 2. *Law*. An adult; contrasted with **minor**.—*v*. To specialize; emphasize a particular subject of study.

major-domo (*may*-jer-*doh*-moh) *n*. [*pl*. -do·mos] The steward of a household.

major general. *Military*. An officer ranking just below a lieutenant general and commanding a division.—**ma·jor-gen·er·al·cy** *n*.—**ma·jor-gen·er·al·ship** *n*.

M

ma·jor·i·ty (muh-*jor*-ih-tee) *n.* [*pl.* -ties] 1. The greater number. 2. Adulthood.

Major Leagues. The National and American baseball leagues.

major scale. *Music.* The seven-tone diatonic scale, arranged in five whole-tone and two half-tone intervals within the octave.

make *v.* [made; mak·ing] 1. To produce; create; fashion. 2. To compel; occasion; cause. 'He should be made to go.' 3. To prepare, as a fire, a meal, etc. 4. To cause to become. 'Make public.' 5. To serve as. 'He will make a good soldier.' 6. To reach; arrive at. 'To make port; make Chicago.' 7. To gain; acquire. 'He makes money.' 8. To attain. 'He made the team.'—**to make as if.** To act as though.—**to make believe.** To pretend.—**to make good.** To succeed.—**to make out.** 1. To fare; do. 2. To decipher.—**to make up.** 1. To compensate. 2. To use cosmetics. 3. To settle differences with another.

make *n.* Construction; design.—**on the make.** *Slang.* On the alert for a flirtation.

make and break. *Electricity.* A device for making and breaking a circuit at regular intervals.

make-believe *n.* 1. Pretending; pretext. 2. Unreality.—*adj.* Unreal; pretended; feigned.

mak·er *n.* 1. A manufacturer; producer. 2. [*cap.*] God; the Creator.

make·shift *n.* A temporary substitute.—*adj.* Constructed of odds and ends; serving in an emergency; for temporary use.

make-up *n.* 1. Arrangement; composition. 2. *Printing.* The arrangement of type lines and illustrations into page forms. 3. Cosmetics. 4. *Colloquial.* Character; personality traits.

mak·ing *n.* 1. Workmanship. 2. Basic elements; potential qualities. 3. Creation; development. 'In the making.'

Malacca cane (muh-*lak*-uh). A walking stick made of palm stem.

Mal·a·chi (*mal*-uh-ky) *n.* 1. A Hebrew prophet. 2. A book of the Old Testament.

mal·a·chite (*mal*-uh-kyte) *n.* A greenish carbonate of copper.

mal·ad·just·ed (mal-uh-*jus*-ted) *adj.* Neurotic; unstable; erratic; out of kilter.

mal·ad·just·ment *n.* *Psychology.* Emotional instability.

mal·ad·min·is·ter (mal-ad-*min*-iss-ter) *v.* To manage badly, esp. public affairs.—**mal·ad·min·is·tra·tion** (mal-ad-min-is-*tray*-shun) *n.*

mal·a·droit (mal-uh-*droyt*) *adj.* Clumsy; awkward; unhandy.—**mal·a·droit·ly** *adv.*

mal·a·dy (*mal*-uh-dee) *n.* [*pl.* -dies] An ailment; disorder; illness.

Mal·a·ga (*mal*-uh-guh) *n.* 1. A variety of grape. 2. A white wine from Malaga grapes.

ma·laise (muh-*layz*) *n.* A vague feeling of physical uneasiness.

Malaprop, Mrs. (*mal*-uh-prop). A character in Sheridan's *The Rivals.*—**mal·a·prop·ism** *n.* The grotesque misuse of elegant words.

mal·ap·ro·pos (mal-ap-ruh-*poh*) *adj.* Inopportune; unsuitable.—*adv.* Unseasonably.

ma·lar·i·a (muh-*lair*-ee-uh) *n.* An infectious disease transmitted by the bite of anopheles mosquitoes.—**ma·lar·i·al, ma·lar·i·ous** *adj.*

mal·con·tent (*mal*-kun-tent) *adj.* Discontented. —*n.* 1. A crank; chronically discontented person. 2. A political agitator.

mal de mer (mahl duh *mair*). *French.* Seasickness.

male *adj.* 1. Masculine; relating to men. 2. *Botany.* Having stamens but no pistils.—*n.* A member of the masculine sex.

mal·e·dic·tion (mal-eh-*dik*-shun) *n.* An imprecation; curse.—**mal·e·dic·to·ry** *adj.*

mal·e·fac·tor (*mal*-uh-fak-ter) *n.* A culprit; evildoer; criminal.—**mal·e·fac·tion** (mal-uh-*fak*-shun) *n.* A crime.—**ma·le·fac·tress** *n.*

ma·lef·ic, mal·ef·i·cent (muh-*lef*-ik, muh-*lef*-ih-s'nt) *adj.* Doing mischief.—**mal·ef·i·cence** *n.*

ma·lev·o·lent (muh-*lev*-uh-l'nt) *adj.* Malicious; hostile; evilly disposed.—**ma·lev·o·lence** *n.* **ma·lev·o·lent·ly** *adv.*

mal·fea·sance (mal-*fee*-z'nss) *n.* A wrong; misdeed; misdemeanor; act unbecoming to one's position.—**mal·fea·sant** *n.* A wrongdoer.

mal·for·ma·tion (mal-for-*may*-shun) *n.* A faulty structure of an organism.

mal·ice (*mal*-iss) *n.* Ill-will; malevolence; rancor.—**with malice aforethought.** With evil intent.

ma·li·cious (muh-*lish*-us) *adj.* Ill-disposed; hostile; evil.—**ma·li·cious·ly** *adv.*—**-cious·ness** *n.*

ma·lign (muh-*lyne*) *v.* To defame; to vilify; to injure.—*adj.* 1. Malicious; hostile; tending to injure. 2. Pernicious; hurtful.—**ma·lign·er** *n.*—**ma·lign·ly** *adv.*

ma·lig·nant (muh-*lig*-nunt) *adj.* 1. Virulent; pernicious. 2. Malicious; bitter; spiteful. —**ma·lig·nance, -nan·cy** *n.*—**ma·lig·nant·ly** *adv.* —**ma·lig·ni·ty** [*pl.* -ties] *n.*

ma·lin·ger (muh-*ling*-ger) *v.* To pretend illness in order to shirk a task.—**ma·lin·ger·er** *n.*

mall (*moll*) *n.* A shaded walk; greensward.

mal·lard (*mal*-erd) *n.* The common wild duck.

mal·le·a·ble (*mal*-ee-uh-b'l) *adj.* Capable of being stretched out or shaped by pressure, as metal.—**mal·le·a·bil·i·ty** (mal-ee-uh-bil-ih-tee), **mal·le·a·ble·ness** *n.*

mal·let (*mal*-it) *n.* A broad-headed hammer, usually of wood.

mal·low (*mal*-oh) *n.* A pink-flowered herbaceous plant.

malm·sey (*mahm*-zee) *n.* 1. A variety of grape. 2. A sweet white wine made in Madeira.

MALLET

mal·nu·tri·tion (mal-noo-*trish*-un) *n.* Ill health caused by lack of food or improper diet.

mal·o·dor·ous (mal-*oh*-der-us) *adj.* Having offensive smell.—**mal·o·dor·ous·ly** *adv.*

mal·prac·tice (mal-*prak*-tiss) *n.* Professional misconduct; illegal practice.

malt (*mawlt*) *n.* Fermented grain for brewing. —*adj.* Made with malt.—*v.* To make into malt.

Mal·tese (mawl-*teez*) *n.* 1. A native of Malta. 2. The language of Malta.—**Mal·tese** *adj.*

Maltese cat. A cat having long bluish-gray fur.

Mal·thu·si·an (mal-*thoo*-zhun) *adj.* Relating to the doctrine of Malthus.—**Malthusian theory.** The theory, promulgated by Malthus, that economic ills are caused by overpopulation.

malt·ose (*mawl*-tohss) *n.* Sugar obtained from starch.

mal·treat (mal-*treet*) *v.* To abuse; mistreat. —**mal·treat·ment** *n.* Ill usage; abuse.

mam·ma (*mum*-uh) *n.* Also **ma·ma.** A child's word for *mother.*

mam·ma (*mam*-uh) *n.* [*pl.* -mae] A breast; an organ for the secretion of milk.

mam·mal (*mam*-'l) *n.* The highest order of vertebrates, having hair and suckling their young.— **-ma·li·an** (-*mayl*-ee-un) *n.* & *adj.*

mam·ma·ry (*mam*-er-ee) *adj.* Relating to the breasts. 'Mammary glands.'

mam·mon (*mam*-un) *n.* Riches; worldly gain.

mam·moth (*mam*-uth) *n.* An extinct species of elephant.—*adj.* Gigantic; huge.

man *n.* [*pl.* men] 1. An adult male human being. 2. An individual; person; one. 3. Mankind; human beings collectively. 4. A male servant or employee. 5. A manly person. 6. A chess piece.—*v.* [manned; man·ning] 1. To furnish with men. 2. To strengthen; brace. 3. To tend; operate, as a machine.—*adj.* Masculine.

MAMMOTH (1/130 life size)

man-bodied	man-hater	man-slayer
man-born	man high	man-slaying
man-brute	man keen	man-stealer
man-changed	man-killer	man-stealing
man child	man-made	man-stopper
man-created	man-minded	man-stopping
man-devised	man-minute	man-taught
maneater	manpower	man trap
man-enslaved	man-ridden	manward
man-fashion	man rope	manway
man-god	man-shaped	man-wise
man-grown	man-size	man-woman

Man, Isle of. Small island in the North Sea, between England and Ireland.

man·a·cles (*man*-uh-k'lz) *n.* Handcuffs; shackles; a set of iron rings for confining the hands. —*v.* [man·a·cled; man·a·cling] 1. To fasten handcuffs on. 2. To confine; restrain.

man·age (*man*-ij) *v.* [man·aged; man·ag·ing] 1. To administer; conduct; direct; handle. 2. To govern; control. 3. To contrive; succeed in doing.

man·age·a·ble (*man*-ij-uh-b'l) *adj.* Tractable; docile; controllable.—**man·age·a·bil·i·ty, man·age·a·ble·ness** *n.*—**man·age·a·bly** *adv.*

man·age·ment *n.* 1. Conduct; administration; handling. 2. A body of directors. 3. Managing ability or skill.

man·ag·er *n.* A director; one who manages a business or affair, esp. with skill.— **-er·ship** *n.*

man·a·ge·ri·al (man-uh-*jeer*-ee-ul) *adj.* Relating to management or a manager.— **-ri·al·ly** *adv.*

man-at-arms *n.* [*pl.* men-at-arms] A mounted, heavily armed soldier.

man·a·tee (*man*-uh-tee) *n.* The sea cow; an aquatic mammal with a broad, flat tail.

Man·chu (*man*-choo) *adj.* Relating to Manchuria.—*n.* 1. A native of Manchuria. 2. The Manchu language.

MANATEE (1/90 life size)

man·da·mus (man-*day*-muss) *n. Law.* A writ issued by a superior court ordering the performance of a specific act.

man·da·rin (*man*-der-in) *n.* 1. A Chinese magistrate or high-ranking public official. 2. [*cap.*] The main and official dialect of Chinese. 3. A tangerine.

man·da·tar·y (*man*-duh-tair-ee) *n.* [*pl.* -tar·ies] A person receiving a mandate.

man·date (*man*-dayt) *n.* 1. An order; command. 2. *Law.* An order delivered from a higher court or authority to an inferior one. 3. Directions given to their representatives by a group of voters. 4. Commission assigned by the League of Nations to one of its members to administer a colony, territory, etc. 5. Territory thus assigned.—*v.* [man·dat·ed; man·dat·ing] To order or govern under a mandate.—**man·da·tor** *n.*

man·da·to·ry (*man*-duh-toh-ree) *adj.* 1. Obligatory; containing a command. 2. Relating to a League of Nations mandate.—*n.* [*pl.* -ries] Receiver of a mandate.

man·di·ble (*man*-duh-b'l) *n.* 1. The lower jaw of a vertebrate. 2. Either jaw of a bird. 3. Either of the anterior jaws of an insect.

man·do·lin (*man*-duh-lin) *n.* A musical instrument with four pairs of strings.—**man·do·lin·ist** *n.*

MANDOLIN

man·drake (*man*-drik, *man*-drayk) *n.* 1. The May apple. 2. A plant root of the nightshade family, used as a narcotic.

man·drel, man·dril (*man*-drul) *n.* 1. The revolving spindle of a lathe. 2. Core about which metal is shaped or cast.

man·drill (*man*-dril) *n.* Large, ferocious West African ape.

mane (*mayn*) *n.* The long, coarse neck hair of certain animals, as the horse and lion.—**maned** *adj.*

M

ma·nège (man-*ezh*) *n.* Also **ma·nege.** 1. Horsemanship. 2. The gaits of trained horses. 3. A riding school.

ma·nes (*may*-neez) *n. pl. Roman Mythology.* The souls of the dead inhabiting Hades.

ma·neu·ver, ma·noeu·vre (muh-*noo*-ver) *n.* 1. A stratagem; skillful move. 2. A military operation. 3. [*pl.*] *Military.* Extensive practice operations.—*v.* 1. To manage adroitly; manipulate. 2. To effect by manipulation or stratagem. 3. *Military.* To move or change positions in order to secure an advantage.—**ma·neu·ver·a·bil·i·ty** *n.*—**ma·neu·ver·a·ble** *adj.*

man·ful (*man*-ful) *adj.* Courageous; resolute; manly.—**man·ful·ly** *adv.*—**man·ful·ness** *n.*

man·ga·nese (*man*-guh-neess, -neez) *n.* A brittle, grayish metal used for bleaching, making glass, etc. (*Symbol:* Mn).

mange (*maynj*) *n.* A parasite-caused skin disease common to domestic animals.

man·gel-wur·zel (*mang*-g'l-*wer*-z'l) *n.* A coarse beet fed to cattle.

man·ger (*mayn*-jer) *n.* A feeding trough for cattle or horses.

man·gle (*mang*-g'l) *v.* [man·gled; man·gling] 1. To lacerate; mutilate by cutting. 2. To spoil in doing; make a mess of.—**man·gler** *n.*

man·gle *n.* An ironing machine with rollers for pressing flat cloth.—*v.* [man·gled; man·gling] To press with a mangle.—**man·gler** *n.*

man·go (*mang*-goh) *n.* [*pl.* -goes, -gos] A tart, juicy tropical fruit with a thick reddish rind.

man·grove (*man*-grohv) *n.* A tropical tree whose roots dropping from branches grow new trees.

man·gy (*mayn*-jee) *adj.* [man·gi·er; man·gi·est] 1. Scabby; infected with mange. 2. Unkempt; soiled and shabby; mean.—**man·gi·ly** *adv.*—**man·gi·ness** *n.*

man·han·dle (*man*-han-d'l) *v.* [man·han·dled; man·han·dling] 1. To abuse; handle roughly. 2. To move solely by human strength.

Man·hat·tan *n.* A cocktail made of rye or bourbon whisky, either dry or sweet vermouth, and often a dash of bitters.

man·hole (*man*-hohl) *n.* A man-sized opening in a sewer, pipe, etc.

man·hood *n.* 1. Adulthood; maturity; state of an adult male. 2. Resolution; courage; manliness. 3. Men in general.

man-hour *n.* Amount of work accomplished by one man in one hour.

ma·ni·a (*may*-nee-uh) *n.* 1. Violent insanity; madness. 2. An uncontrolled desire or enthusiasm; craze.

ma·ni·ac (*may*-nee-ak) *n.* A lunatic; madman. —**ma·ni·ac** *adj.*—**ma·ni·a·cal** (mun-*eye*-uh-k'l), *adj.*—**ma·ni·a·cal·ly** *adv.*

man·ic (*mayn*-ik; *man*-ik) *adj. Medicine.* Of, suffering from, or resembling, mania.

man·ic-de·pres·sive (*mayn*-; *man*-ik-duh-*press*-iv) *adj.* Characterized by alternate depression and violent insanity.

man·i·cure (*man*-ih-kyoor) *n.* Care or grooming of the fingernails.—*v.* [man·i·cured; man·i·curing] To groom the fingernails.—**man·i·cur·ist** *n.*

man·i·fest (*man*-ih-fest) *adj.* Visible; apparent; obvious; evident.—*v.* 1. To reveal; display; show. 2. To prove; evidence.—*n.* An invoice of a vessel's cargo to be examined by a customs officer.—**man·i·fest·ly** *adv.*

man·i·fes·ta·tion (man-ih-fess-*tay*-shun) *n.* 1. A display; evidence; demonstration, as of power. 2. A materialization, as of a spirit.

man·i·fes·to (man-ih-*fess*-toh) *n.* [*pl.* -toes] A public declaration of political principles.

man·i·fold (*man*-ih-fohld) *adj.* 1. Numerous; many in number and kind. 2. Having many sides, parts, or features. 3. Doing or operating many things at once.—*n.* 1. One of several machine-made copies. 2. A pipe with openings for connecting with other pipes.—*v.* To make several copies of, as a letter.—**man·i·fold·ly** *adv.*—**man·i·fold·ness** *n.*

man·i·kin (*man*-ih-kin) *n.* 1. A midget; dwarf. 2. A mannequin.

Manila hemp. A tough fiber, used for cordage, obtained from a Philippine banana plant.

Manila paper. A strong yellow or brown paper once made from Manila hemp.

ma·nip·u·late (muh-*nip*-yuh-layt) *v.* [-lat·ed; -lat·ing] 1. To handle; wield; operate, esp. skillfully. 2. To manage or control with skill, often fraudulently.—**ma·nip·u·lat·a·ble** *adj.* —**man·ip·u·la·tion** *n.*—**ma·nip·u·la·tive, ma·nip·u·la·to·ry** *adj.*—**ma·nip·u·la·tor** *n.*

man·i·to, man·i·tou, man·i·tu (*man*-uh-toh, *man*-ih-too) *n.* A nature spirit worshiped by certain North American Indians.

man·kind *n.* The human race; men.

man·like *adj.* Manly; masculine.

man·ly *adj.* [man·li·er; man·li·est] Like a man; virile; resolute; dignified; honorable.—**man·ly** *adv.*—**man·li·ness** *n.*

man·na (*man*-uh) *n.* Divinely or unexpectedly supplied food; spiritual sustenance.

man·ne·quin (*man*-uh-kin) *n.* 1. A model; woman who models clothes. 2. A tailor's figure for fitting clothes.

man·ner (*man*-er) *n.* 1. Method; style; mode of action. 2. Customary or normal behavior; way of living. 3. [*pl.*] Deportment; civil or social behavior. 4. Distinctive style or deportment.

man·nered (*man*-erd) *adj.* Artificial; affected.

man·ner·ism (*man*-er-izm) *n.* Peculiarity of style or manner; affectation.—**man·ner·ist** *n.*

man·ner·less *adj.* Lacking proper manners.

man·ner·ly *adj.* Civil; having good manners; courteous.—**man·ner·ly** *adv.*—**man·ner·li·ness** *n.*

man·nish *adj.* Like or suitable to a man; masculine; unwomanly.—**man·nish·ly** *adv.*

man-of-war *n.* [*pl.* men-of-war] An armed naval ship.

ma·nom·e·ter (mun-*om*-un-ter) *n.* An instrument for gauging the pressure of gases.—**man·o·met·ric, man·o·met·ri·cal** adj.

man·or (man-er) n. The estate and home of a feudal noble.—**ma·no·ri·al** adj.

manor house. The large house of a manor.

mansard roof. A roof formed with an upper and lower slope on each side.

manse (manss) n. A minister's residence.

man·serv·ant (man-ser-v'nt) n. [pl. **men·serv·ants**] A male servant.

man·sion (man-shun) n. A large house.

man·slaugh·ter (man-slaw-ter) n. Law. The unlawful, but unpremeditated killing of a person.—**man·slay·er** n.

man·tel (man-t'l) n. The ledge above a fireplace.

man·tel·et (man-t'l-et) n. 1. A short cloak or cape. 2. Large, protective screen formerly used by attacking soldiers.

MANTEL

man·tel·piece n. Also **man·tel·shelf.** An ornamental mantel.

man·til·la (man-til-uh) n. A veil or headscarf covering the shoulders, worn by Spanish women.

man·tis (man-tiss) n. [pl. -tes, -tis·es] A voracious insect which holds its front legs bent as if praying.

man·tle (man-t'l) n. 1. Cloak; loose outer garment without sleeves. 2. A covering; that which envelops or conceals. 3. Lacy hood which gives light by glowing when placed over a flame.—v. [man·tled; man·tling]

MANTILLA

1. To cloak; disguise; obscure. 2. To become coated or covered, as with scum. 3. To blush.

man·tu·a (man-choo-uh) n. A loose robe or cloak formerly worn by women.

man·u·al (man-yoo-ul) adj. Pertaining to or performed by the hand.—n. 1. A small book of directions or rules. 2. Military. Designated drill for handling a weapon.—**man·u·al·ly** adv.

manual training. Training in crafts, esp. woodworking, or other manual work.

man·u·fac·ture (man-yuh-fak-cher) v. [-tured; -tur·ing] 1. To produce; fabricate goods by hand or machinery. 2. To make into a useful form. 3. To invent; concoct.—n. 1. A producing or making, esp. by hand or machinery. 2. That which is so made; the finished article.—**man·u·fac·tur·ing** n.

man·u·fac·tur·er n. An industrialist; factory owner.

man·u·mit (man-yuh-mit) v. [man·u·mit·ted; man·u·mit·ting] To free from slavery; emancipate.—**man·u·mis·sion** n.

ma·nure (muh-noor) n. Substance, often animal excrement, used to fertilize the soil; dung.—v. [ma·nured; ma·nur·ing] To enrich soil with fertilizer.—**ma·nur·er** n.

man·u·script (man-yuh-skript) n. A book or paper written by hand or typewriter, as opposed to printed material.—**man·u·script** adj.

Manx (manks) adj. Of or belonging to the Isle of Man.—n. 1. Manxman. 2. The native Celtic tongue of the Manxmen.—**Manx·man** n. A native of the Isle of Man.

manx cat. Domestic cat with almost no tail.

man·y (men-ee) adj. [more; most] Numerous; composed of a large number.—n. A great number.—pron. Many people.

many-acred	many-fold	many-leaved
many-angled	many-forked	many-legged
many-blossomed	many-handed	many-lived
many-branched	many-headed	many-loved
many-celled	many-hued	many-mouthed
many-colored	many-jointed	many-pointed
many-eyed	many-knotted	many-sided
many-faced	many-languaged	many-spotted
many-faceted	many-layered	many-tailed

Ma·o·ri (mow-ree, mah-uh-ree) n. [pl. -ris] 1. One of the Polynesian inhabitants of New Zealand. 2. Their language.—**Ma·o·ri** adj.

map n. 1. A delineation of the earth's surface or any part of it. 2. Slang. The face.—v. [mapped; map·ping] 1. To draw or show, as on a map. 2. To plan, esp. in detail; survey.

ma·ple (may-p'l) n. 1. Shade tree valuable for its sap and its hard, light-colored wood. 2. Wood of this tree, used for furniture.—**ma·ple** adj.—**maple syrup.** A sweet syrup from the sap of the sugar maple.

Ma·quis (mah-kee) n. World War II. A French guerilla organization, formed to resist the Germans and sabotage their conquest.

mar (mahr) v. [marred; mar·ring] To injure; deface; impair.

mar·a·bou, mar·a·bout (mair-uh-boo) n. 1. A large African stork. 2. Its long, curly wing- or tail-feathers, used as a trimming.

mar·a·schi·no (mair-uh-skee-noh) n. A cordial distilled from a small wild cherry.

maraschino cherries. Cherries preserved in a maraschino-flavored syrup.

Mar·a·thon (mair-uh-thun) n. The plain near Athens where the Greeks defeated the Persians in 490 B.C.

mar·a·thon n. 1. Also **marathon race.** Foot race covering 26 miles and 385 yards. 2. Any long-distance race or lengthy contest.

ma·raud (muh-rawd) v. To pillage; ravage; raid for plunder.—n. Pillaging.—**ma·raud·er** n.

mar·bel·ize (mahr-b'l-yze) v. [-ized; -iz·ing] To stain or otherwise mark in imitation of marble.

mar·ble (mahr-b'l) n. 1. Any limestone of a compact texture which takes a fine polish. 2. A slab or work of marble. 3. A small

M

glass or stone ball used by children in play.—*v.* [mar·bled; mar·bling] To vein or color like marble.—**mar·ble** *adj.*

marble cake. Any cake made from a two-colored batter, giving the appearance of marble.

mar·ble·ize *v.* To marbelize.

mar·cel (mahr-*sel*) *v.* [mar·celled; mar·cel·ling] To set hair in deep waves.—**mar·cel** *n.*

March (*mahrch*) *n.* The third month of the year.

march *n.* A frontier; border.—*v.* To border.

march *v.* 1. To walk with a steady, regular tread, esp. in formation; move in a military manner. 2. To advance steadily; progress. —*n.* 1. The measured and uniform progress of a body of men. 2. Steady advance; progress. 3. Distance covered in a march. 4. *Music.* A rhythmic composition designed to accompany marching.—**march·er** *n.*

mar·chion·ess (*mahr*-shun-iss) *n.* The wife of a marquis.

march·pane (*mahrch*-payn) *n.* Marzipan.

mar·co·ni·gram (mahr-*koh*-nih-gram) *n.* A radio message.

Mardi Gras (*mahr*-duh grah). An annual pre-lenten festival; carnival.

mare *n.* A female horse.

mare's-nest *n.* A deceptively dramatic discovery; a hoax.

mare's-tail *n.* 1. A long streaky cloud, supposed to indicate rain. 2. A common aquatic plant.

mar·ga·rine (*mahr*-jer-een, -in) *n.* Oleomargarine; a butter substitute made of vegetable or animal fats, water, salt, and milk solids.

mar·gin (*mahr*-jin) *n.* 1. A border; edge, esp. the blank border of a printed or written page. 2. Percentage of profit. 3. *Stock Exchange.* Cash deposited with a broker to insure him against loss.—**mar·gin** *v.*—**mar·gi·nal** *adj.* Barely covering costs of tilling or production. 'Marginal land.'

mar·gue·rite (mahr-ger-*eet*) *n.* 1. A single-flowered chrysanthemum. 2. The daisy.

mar·i·gold (*mair*-ih-gold) *n.* A popular garden plant with orange-colored or yellow blossoms.

ma·ri·jua·na (mair-uh-*wah*-nuh). Also **ma·ri·hua·na.** A type of hemp which produces a temporary feeling of exhilaration when smoked in a cigarette.

ma·rim·ba (muh-*rim*-buh) *n.* A type of xylophone.

mar·i·nate (*mair*-ih-nayt) *v.* [-nat·ed; -nat·ing] To soak in a tart dressing or to pickle before serving.—**mar·in·ate** *n.*

MARIGOLD

ma·rine (muh-*reen*) *adj.* Pertaining to the sea. —*n.* A member of the U.S. Marine Corps, a branch of the Navy, used in land operations.

mar·i·ner (*mair*-in-er) *n.* A seaman; sailor.

mar·i·o·nette (mair-ee-uh-*net*) *n.* A puppet animated by strings.

mar·i·tal (*mair*-ih-t'l) *adj.* Pertaining to marriage.—**mar·i·tal·ly** *adv.*

mar·i·time (*mair*-ih-tyme) *adj.* Pertaining to the sea, esp. to the merchant marine.

mar·jo·ram (*mahr*-jer-'m) *n.* An aromatic herb, some varieties of which are used in cooking.

Mark *n.* The author of the second Gospel in the New Testament.

mark *n.* 1. A sign; indication; symptom; symbol. 2. Importance; distinction. 3. Goal; target. 4. Grade attained by a student. 5. A character, usually x-shaped, made in place of a signature by a person unable to write.—*v.* 1. To make a mark upon. 2. To single out; characterize. 3. To notice; regard; observe. 4. To grade; assign marks to. 5. To tag with a price.—**mark·er** *n.*

mark *n.* The German monetary unit, formerly equal to about 24 cents.

marked *adj.* Definite; outstanding.— -**ed·ly** *adv.*

mark·er *n.* A counter used in card playing.

mar·ket (*mahr*-ket) *n.* 1. A public place where goods are displayed for sale. 2. A nation or region receptive to a particular import. 3. Buying and selling.—*v.* To buy or sell.

mar·ket·a·ble (*mahr*-kut-uh-b'l) *adj.* Saleable; fit for the market.—**mar·ket·a·bil·i·ty** *n.*

market price. Current price of securities.

marks·man *n.* [*pl.* -men] A sharpshooter; one skilled with a gun.—**marks·man·ship** *n.*

marl *n.* An earthy substance used as a fertilizer. —*v.* To manure with marl.—**mar·ly** *adj.*

mar·lin (*mahr*-lin) *n.* A large deep-sea fish, prized by sportsmen.

mar·line (*mahr*-lin) *n.* Also **mar·ling.** *Nautical.* Small, two-strand, left-laid line used for light lashings.

mar·lin·spike (*mahr*-lun-spyke) *n.* Also **mar·line·spike.** *Nautical.* A pointed metal tool used chiefly in splicing wire or rope.

mar·ma·lade (*mahr*-muh-layd) *n.* A preserve made from various citrus fruits.

mar·mo·set (*mahr*-muh-zet) *n.* A small, tropical American monkey with a long tail.

MARLINSPIKE

mar·mot (*mahr*-mut) *n.* A squirrel-like rodent with a bulky body, living in burrows and hibernating in winter; woodchuck.

ma·roon (muh-*roon*) *n.* A deep brownish-crimson color.—**ma·roon** *adj.*

ma·roon *v.* To abandon; desert; forsake.

MARMOT (1/15 life size)

marque (*mahrk*) *n.* A license to make reprisals on the belongings of a public enemy.

mar·quee (mahr-*kee*) *n.* An awninglike projection over the entrance to a building.

mar·que·try (*mahr*-kuh-tree) *n.* Also **mar·que·te·rie.** Varicolored inlaid work in furniture, etc.

mar·quis (*mahr*-kwiss) *n.* 1. A title of nobility in Britain next in rank to that of duke. 2. (mahr-*kee*) Formerly a similar title in France.

mar·quise (mahr-*keez*) *n.* The wife of a marquis.

mar·qui·sette (mahr-kih-*zet*) *n.* A sheer fabric used in dresses.

mar·riage (*mair*-ij) *n.* 1. The legal union of a man and woman; wedlock. 2. Intimate union.

mar·riage·a·ble (*mair*-ij-uh-b'l) *adj.* Of an age suitable for marriage.—**mar·riage·a·bil·i·ty, mar·riage·a·ble·ness** *n.*

mar·ried *adj.* 1. Connubial; conjugal. 2. United in wedlock.

mar·row (*mair*-oh) *n.* 1. The tissue contained in bones. 2. The essence; best part. 3. A kind of edible gourd or squash.

mar·ry (*mair*-ee) *v.* [mar·ried; mar·ry·ing] 1. To unite or be united in marriage. 2. To take for a mate.—**mar·ri·er** *n.*

Mars (*mahrz*) *n.* 1. A bright, reddish planet, the fourth in order of distance from the sun. 2. Roman god of war.

Mar·seil·laise (mahr-suh-*layz*, mahr-seh-*yez*) *n.* The national anthem of France, composed during the French Revolution.

marsh *n.* A tract of swampy land; bog.

mar·shal (*mahr*-shul) *n.* 1. The highest military officer in some countries. 2. In the U.S. a civil officer appointed by the Federal Government in each judicial district.—*v.* [mar·shaled, mar·shalled; mar·shal·ing, mar·shal·ling] To arrange; order; organize. — **-shal·cy** *n.*

marsh·mal·low (*marsh*-mal-loh) *n.* A soft, white confection composed of sugar, syrup, starch, and gelatin.

marsh marigold. A plant of the crowfoot family, with bright yellow flowers, found in marshy places; sometimes called *cowslip.*

marsh·y *adj.* [marsh·i·er; marsh·i·est] Swampy; boggy.—**marsh·i·ness** *n.*

mar·su·pi·al (mahr-*soop*-ee-ul) *adj.* Pertaining to or having a pouch.—*n.* An animal having a pouch covering the mammary glands where the young are kept until sufficiently developed.

mart *n.* A place where goods are sold; market.

mar·ten *n.* A carnivorous quadruped, inhabiting woody and rocky localities, valued for its fur.

mar·tial (*mahr*-shul) *adj.* Pertaining to warfare; military.—**mar·tial·ly** *adv.*

martial law. An arbitrary system of law imposed by military authority suspending all civil law.

MARTEN (1/20 life size)

Mar·ti·an (*mahr*-shun) *adj.* Pertaining to the planet Mars.—*n.* An inhabitant of Mars.

mar·tin *n.* A bird of the swallow family.

mar·ti·net (mahr-tuh-*net*) *n.* A strict taskmaster.

mar·tin·gale, mar·tin·gal (*mahr*-tin-gayl, -gal) *n.* 1. A strap running from a horse's girth to the bit to hold its head down. 2. *Nautical.* A stay beneath the jib boom.

mar·tyr (*mahr*-ter) *n.* One who suffers death or persecution in defense of a cause.—*v.* To make a martyr of.—**mar·tyr·dom** *n.*

mar·vel (*mahr*-v'l) *n.* A wonder; miracle.—*v.* [mar·veled, mar·velled; mar·vel·ing, mar·vel·ling] To wonder; be astonished.

mar·vel·ous, mar·vel·lous (*mahr*-vuh-luss) *adj.* Wonderful; miraculous; splendid.—**mar·vel·ous·ly, mar·vel·lous·ly** *adv.*—**mar·vel·ous·ness, mar·vel·lous·ness** *n.*

Marx·i·an (*mahrk*-see-un) *adj.* Pertaining to the doctrines of Karl Marx.—**Marx·i·an** *n.*

Marx·ism (*mahrk*-sizm) *n.* The philosophical, political, and economic doctrines of Karl Marx.—**Marx·ist** *n.*

Ma·ry (*mehr*-ee) *n.* The mother of Jesus Christ.

mar·zi·pan (*marts*-ih-pan) *n.* Also **march·pane.** A confection made of sugar, ground almonds, and egg-whites.

mas·car·a (mass-*kair*-uh) *n.* A cosmetic for darkening the eyelashes.

mas·cot (*mass*-kot) *n.* A person or animal supposed to bring good luck.

mas·cu·line (*mass*-kyuh-lin) *adj.* 1. Of the male sex. 2. Manly; virile; robust. 3. *Grammar.* Pertaining to the gender of words regarded grammatically as male.—**mas·cu·line** *n.*—**mas·cu·line·ly** *adv.*—**mas·cu·lin·i·ty** (mass-kyuh-*lin*-uh-tee) *n.*

mash *n.* 1. A mixture of ingredients crushed together. 2. *Brewing.* A mixture of ground malt and warm water.—**mash** *v.*

mash·er *n. Slang.* A man who forces his attentions on a strange woman.

mash·ie, mash·y (*mash*-ee) *n.* [pl. -ies] *Golf.* An iron club with a broad, wide-angled blade.

mask *n.* 1. A disguise covering the face. 2. That which hides or conceals. 3. Also **masque.** A masquerade. 4. A sculptured mold of the face. 5. The face of an animal, as a dog. 6. A protective face covering. 7. *Theater.* a. In ancient Greece, a covering for the face serving to identify the actors. b. Also **masque.** An early form of drama wherein the actors are masked.—*v.* To conceal; disguise; cover.

MASKS (def. 7a.)

mas·o·chism (*mass*-uh-kizm) *n. Psychiatry.* A sexual perversion in which pleasure is obtained by being maltreated and injured by others.—**mas·o·chist** *n.*

M

ma·son (*may*-s'n) *n.* **1.** A builder in stone or brick. **2.** [*cap.*] A Freemason.—**ma·son** *v.*

Mason-Dixon Line. The border between Pennsylvania and Maryland regarded as the dividing line between the North and the South, esp. before 1860.

Ma·son·ic (muh-*son*-ik) *adj.* Pertaining to the Freemasons and their ritual.

ma·son·ry (*may*-s'n-ree) *n.* [*pl.* -ries] **1.** The art of building in bricks or stones. **2.** The work produced by a mason. **3.** [*cap.*] The principles and practices of Freemasons.

masque *n.* Also **mask.** **1.** A masquerade. **2.** A drama in which the actors wear masks.

mas·quer·ade (mass-ker-*ayd*) *n.* **1.** A ball where the participants wear masks. **2.** Disguise.—*v.* [-ad·ed; -ad·ing] To go in disguise.

Mass *n.* A service in the Roman Catholic, Greek Orthodox, and Anglican churches in which the consecration of the sacramental bread and wine takes place.

mass *n.* **1.** A quantity of matter forming a body. **2.** A heap; pile. **3.** Bulk; volume. **4.** The main body; the bulk. **5.** *Physics.* The quantity of matter in any body, determined by its inertia.—*v.* To gather; assemble.—**mass** *adj.* —**the masses.** The common people.

mas·sa·cre (*mass*-uh-ker) *n.* Slaughter; wanton butchery.—*v.* [mas·sa·cred; mas·sa·cring].

mas·sage (muh-*sahzh*) *n.* A method of treatment by rubbing or kneading the body.—*v.* [mas·saged; mas·sag·ing]—**mas·sag·er** *n.*

mas·sé (mass-*say*) *n.* Also **mas·sé shot.** *Billiards.* A shot making the cue ball follow a curved path by striking it on the side almost vertically.

mas·seur (mass-*ser*) *n.* One whose occupation is massaging.—**mas·seuse** *n. fem.*

mas·sive (*mass*-iv) *adj.* Immense; monumental; heavy; huge.—**mas·sive·ly** *adv.*— **-sive·ness** *n.*

mass production. The fabrication by machine of a great quantity of exactly similar articles. —**mass-produced** *adj.*

mass·y (*mass*-ee) *adj.* Bulky; substantial; big.

mast *n.* A long spar set vertically on a ship to support the sails and rigging.

mast *n.* Nuts; acorns.

mas·ter (*mass*-ter) *n.* **1.** The owner of slaves; employer of servants. **2.** The captain of a merchant ship. **3.** The head of or a teacher in a school. **4.** Respectful title of address to a boy. **5.** One extremely proficient in an occupation or art; an adept. **6.** A degree next above bachelor in colleges and universities. 'Master of Arts.'—*v.* **1.** To subdue; conquer. **2.** To understand so as to be able to apply. 'To master a science.'—**mas·ter** *adj.*

mas·ter·ful (*mass*-ter-ful) *adj.* **1.** Domineering; imperious; dictatorial. **2.** Able; powerful.—**mas·ter·ful·ly** *adv.*—**mas·ter·ful·ness** *n.*

mas·ter-at-arms *n.* A sailor assigned to keep order. *Abbr.:* M.A.A.

mas·ter·ly (*mass*-ter-lee) *adj.* Excellent; skillfully done.—**mas·ter·li·ness** *n.*

master of ceremonies. One who introduces speakers or performers at a show, club, etc.

mas·ter·piece (*mass*-ter-peess) *n.* An extraordinarily fine performance or piece of work.

mas·ter·y (*mass*-ter-ee) *n.* [*pl.* -ies] **1.** Control; power. **2.** Pre-eminence; superiority. **3.** Thorough acquaintance with or skill in an art.

mast·head (*mast*-hed) *n.* **1.** A legend or summary of title, proprietor, rates, etc., appearing in each issue of a periodical or newspaper. **2.** The top of a ship's mast.

mas·tic (*mass*-tik) *n.* A resin gathered from the bark of a southern European evergreen shrub, used in making varnish.

mas·ti·cate (*mass*-tih-kayt) *v.* [-cat·ed; -cat·ing] To chew; prepare food for the stomach by chewing.—**mas·ti·ca·tion** *n.*—**mas·ti·ca·tor** *n.*

mas·tiff (*mass*-tif) *n.* A large, stoutly built, powerful-jawed watchdog.

mas·to·don (*mass*-tuh-don) *n.* An extinct species of mammal resembling the elephant, but larger.

MASTIFF (1/35 life size)

mas·toid (*mass*-toid) *n.* A prominence or bone in the temple at the opening for the ear. —*adj.* **1.** Shaped like a breast or nipple. **2.** Pertaining to the mastoid.

mas·tur·ba·tion (mass-ter-*bay*-shun) *n.* Sexual stimulation or release by artificial friction of the genitals.—**mas·tur·bate** *v.* [-bat·ed; -bat·ing]—**mas·tur·ba·tor** *n.*

ma·su·ri·um (mas-*soor*-ee-um) *n.* A chemical element discovered by spectroscope in platinum. (*Symbol:* Ma).

mat *n.* **1.** A covering or rug made of coarse interwoven fibers. **2.** Anything appearing closely interwoven. 'A mat of hair.'—*v.* [mat·ted; mat·ting] **1.** To cover with a mat. **2.** To interweave; entangle; grow thickly.

mat *adj.* Not glossy; dull and even on the surface; uniform in color throughout.—*n.* **1.** A border on a picture. **2.** A lusterless, flat surface. **3.** *Printing.* A matrix.—*v.* To produce a mat surface.

mat·a·dor (*mat*-uh-dor) *n.* In bullfighting, the man who slays the bull.

match *n.* A splint of wood or cardboard with a tip lighted by friction.

matchboard	match lining	match safe
match box	matchlock	matchstick
match-lined	match mark	matchwood

match *n.* **1.** An equal; mate; companion; complement. **2.** A competition; contest. **3.** Union by marriage.—*v.* **1.** To make or be equal. **2.** To be suitable; harmonize. **3.** To be an equal of; meet on equal terms. **4.** To combine; marry. **5.** To complement; go well with; fit. **6.** To flip a coin, betting it will fall the same side up as another coin. —**match·a·ble** *adj.*—**match·er** *n.*

match·less *adj.* Unequaled; unrivaled; best. —**match·less·ly** *adv.*—**match·less·ness** *n.*

match·mak·er *n.* 1. One who instigates or schemes to arrange marriages of others. 2. A manufacturer of matches.—**match·mak·ing** *n.*

mate *n.* 1. Companion; associate. 2. Husband or wife; one of an animal pair. 3. A complement; one of a set. 4. One of a merchant ship's deck officers. 5. *U.S. Navy.* A petty officer; rated man. 'Pharmacist's mate.' —*v.* [mated; mat·ing] 1. To breed; unite sexually; marry. 2. To match; complement.

mate *v. Chess.* To checkmate.—*n.* A checkmate.

ma·té; ma·te (*mah*-tay) *n.* A bitter South American tea prepared from the leaves of a kind of holly.

ma·ter (*may*-ter, *mah*-ter) *n.* Mother.

ma·ter fa·mil·i·as (fuh-*mil*-ee-us). Mother of a family.

ma·te·ri·al (muh-*teer*-ee-ul) *n.* 1. Matter; substance; that of which anything is made. 2. Cloth from which garments are made; fabric.—*adj.* 1. Important; essential. 2. Denoting matter; physical rather than spiritual. —**ma·te·ri·al·ly** *adv.*

ma·te·ri·al·ism *n.* 1. Preoccupation with the present, physical world. 2. *Philosophy.* Doctrine that all world processes, including thought, consist of or are entirely dependent on matter and energy.—**ma·te·ri·al·ist** *n.* & *adj.*—**ma·te·ri·al·ist·ic** *adj.*—**ist·i·cal·ly** *adv.*

ma·te·ri·al·ize (muh-*ter*-ee-uh-lyze) *v.* [-ized; -iz·ing] 1. To come into being. 2. To regard as matter; clothe with material characteristics. —**ma·te·ri·al·i·za·tion** (-iz-*ay*-sh'n) *n.*

ma·te·ri·a med·i·ca (muh-*tee*-ree-uh *med*-ih-kuh). Branch of medical science dealing with medicines and their uses; medicines collectively.

ma·té·ri·el (muh-teer-ee-*el*) *n.* Apparatus; equipment, esp. military supplies.

ma·ter·nal (muh-*ter*-n'l) *adj.* 1. Motherly. 2. Of or from the mother's side of a family.

ma·ter·ni·ty *n.* [*pl.* -ties] Motherhood; process of becoming a mother.—**ma·ter·ni·ty** *adj.*

math·e·mat·i·cal (math-eh-*mat*-ik-ul) *adj.* Pertaining to or like mathematics; precise; exact. —**math·e·mat·i·cal·ly** *adv.*

math·e·mat·ics *n.* The science of the properties and relations of quantities, and methods of finding unknown from known quantities; arithmetic.—**math·e·ma·ti·cian** (math-em-uh-*tish*-'n) *n.*

mat·in *n.* 1. The morning. 2. [*pl.*] Morning devotions.—**mat·in, mat·in·al** *adj.*

mat·i·nee (mat-ih-*nay*) *n.* An afternoon theatrical or motion-picture show.—**mat·i·nee** *adj.*

ma·tri·arch (*may*-tree-ahrk) *n.* A female ruler of a house or tribe.—**ma·tri·arch·al** (-*ahr*-k'l) *adj.*

ma·tri·arch·y *n.* A society in which woman is dominant and descent is traced through the mother rather than the father.—**ma·tri·ar·chic** *adj.*

ma·tri·cide (*may*-trih-syde; *mat*-) *n.* 1. Murder of one's mother. 2. One who murders his mother.—**ma·tri·cid·al** *adj.*

ma·tric·u·late *v.* [-lat·ed; -lat·ing] To enroll in a college or university for credit toward a degree; register.—**ma·tric·u·la·tion** *n.*

mat·ri·mo·ny (*mat*-rih-moh-nee) *n.* [*pl.* -nies] Marriage; nuptials.—**mat·ri·mo·ni·al** *adj.*

ma·trix (*may*-triks) *n.* [*pl.* mat·ri·ces; ma·trix·es] 1. Anything that encloses or gives origin to. 2. A mold, often papier-maché, for making a stereotype; mat. 3. A womb; uterus. 4. A copper mold for casting type.

ma·tron (*may*-tron) *n.* 1. A wife; mother. 2. Female supervisor of an institution.—**ma·tron·age** *n.* 1. Married women collectively. 2. The status of a matron.—**ma·tron·ly** *adv.* —**ma·tron·li·ness** *n.*

mat·ter (*mat*-er) *n.* 1. The elementary substance of the universe. 2. Event; affair; business. 3. Importance; consequence. 4. The content or subject of speech or writing. 5. An indefinite quantity. 6. Pus; fluid discharge from an abscess. 7. *Printing.* Copy.—*v.* To be of import; make a difference.

mat·ter-of-fact *adj.* Commonplace; factual.

Mat·thew (*math*-yoo). One of Christ's apostles; author of the first book of the New Testament.

mat·ting *n.* Materials for mats; matwork.

mat·tock (*mat*-uk) *n.* A pickax with one or both of its ends broad instead of pointed.

mat·tress (*mat*-ress)*n.* A pad or tick stuffed with resilient material for comfort in sleeping.

mat·u·rate (*mat*-cher-ayt) *v.* [-rat·ed; -rat·ing] To ripen; come to or develop toward maturity.—**mat·u·ra·tion** *n.* —**ma·tur·a·tive** *adj.*

MATTOCK

ma·ture (muh-*tyoor*) *adj.* 1. Ripe; full grown; developed. 2. Payable; arrived at the date set for payment.—*v.* [ma·tured; ma·tur·ing] 1. To arrive at or advance toward fruition or perfection. 2. To reach the date set for payment. —**ma·ture·ly** *adv.*

ma·tu·ri·ty *n.* 1. Full development; fruition 2. The date a bill or note comes due.

matz·oth (*mat*-sohth) *n. pl.* Unleavened bread eaten by Jews, esp. on certain holidays.

maud·lin (*mawd*-lin) *adj.* 1. Overly sentimental. 2. Tearfully intoxicated.

maul *n.* A large mallet or hammer.—*v.* To beat or bruise; disfigure by rough usage; manhandle.—**maul·ing** *n.* & *adj.* Beating; cudgeling.—**maul·er** *n.*

maun·der (*mawn*-der) *v.* 1. To talk incoherently or idly; drivel. 2. To speak whiningly or grumblingly.

MAUL

Mau·ser (*mow*-zer) *n.* Trade-mark of a kind of German automatic firearm.

mau·so·le·um (maw-soh-*lee*-um) *n.* [*pl.* -le·ums, -lea] A stately tomb; large, pretentious building where the dead are buried.

mauve (*mohv*) *n.* A purple or lilac color.

mav·er·ick (*mav*-er-ik) *n.* 1. An unbranded calf, esp. a stray. 2. *U.S. Politics.* One who plays a lone hand, following no party line.

maw *n.* 1. A bird's crop. 2. The stomach.

mawk·ish (*mawk*-ish) *adj.* Nauseating; sickeningly sentimental.—**mawk·ish·ly** *adv.*—**mawk·ish·ness** *n.*

max·il·la (mak-*sil*-uh) *n.* [*pl.* -lae] The jawbone, esp. the upper.— **-il·lar·y** (*mak*-sih-lehr-ee) *adv.*

max·im (*mak*-sim) *n.* A short statement of an important truth; established principle; adage.

max·i·mum (*mak*-sim-um) *n.* [*pl.* -ma, -mums] The greatest quantity or degree; highest point. —**max·i·mum, max·i·mal** *adj.*

max·well *n.* Unit of magnetic flux.

may *v.* [*past tense:* might] To be able, permitted, or likely.

May *n.* The fifth month of the year.

Ma·ya *n.* A tribe of ancient, highly civilized Yucatan Indians.—**Ma·yan** *n.* & *adj.*

May apple. A plant with a single cuplike flower blossoming in May, followed by small, yellow, sweetish fruit.

may·be *adv.* Perhaps; possibly.

May Day. The first day of May, celebrated both as a festival of spring and as an international symbol of working-class solidarity.

may day. Radiotelephone distress call, equivalent to radiotelegraphy SOS. From French: *m'aider.*

may·flow·er *n.* 1. One of several flowers that bloom in May, esp. the arbutus. 2. [*cap.*] The ship that brought the Pilgrims to Plymouth.

may·hem *n. Law.* Maiming a person by mutilation or by destroying the use of a part of the body essential for self-defense.

may·on·naise (may-uh-*nayz*) *n.* A salad dressing of egg yolks, salad oil, and seasonings.

may·or (*may*-er) *n.* The chief administrative officer of a municipality.

may·or·al·ty (*may*-er-ul-tee) *n.* [*pl.* -ties] The office or tenure of a mayor.

May·pole *n.* A pole decked with flowers and ornaments set up to be danced around on May Day.

Maz·da (*maz*-duh) *n.* Trade-mark for a type of electric-light bulb.

maze (*mayz*) *n.* An intricate and baffling network of paths; labyrinth.

ma·zur·ka (muh-*zer*-kuh) *n.* Also **ma·zour·ka.** A lively polkalike Slavic dance; music for this dance.

ma·zy (*may*-zee) *adj.* [ma·zi·er; ma·zi·est] Intricate; full of turns and windings.—**ma·zi·ly** *adv.*

M.C. (*em-see*). Master of ceremonies.

McCoy, The. Also **The real McCoy.** *Slang.*
The original or genuine article or person; something indubitably authentic.

mead (*meed*) *n.* 1. A fermented liquor made from honey, spices, and water. 2. *Poetic.* A meadow.

mea·dow (*med*-oh) *n.* A flat, grassy plot of land.

meadow lark. A brown-colored hedge bird with a beautiful song.

mea·ger, mea·gre (*mee*-ger) *adj.* Scant; scarce; slight; barren; emaciated.—**mea·ger·ly, mea·gre·ly** *adv.*—**mea·ger·ness, mea·gre·ness** *n.*

meal (*meel*) *n.* Edible ground grain.

meal *n.* A repast; partaking of food.

meal·y (*meel*-ee) *adj.* [meal·i·er; meal·i·est] Like or of meal; of the color or texture of meal.

meal·y·mouthed *adj.* Unwilling to speak the plain truth; using soft words.

mean (*meen*) *v.* [mean; mean·ing] 1. To signify; denote; indicate. 2. To intend; have in mind.

mean *adj.* 1. *Colloquial.* Cruel; disagreeable. 2. Stingy; miserly. 3. Insignificant; humble; inferior.—**mean·ly** *adv.*—**mean·ness** *n.*

mean *adj.* 1. Intermediate; middle. 2. *Mathematics.* Average; lying exactly intermediate between two or more quantities.—*n.* 1. An average. 2. [*pl.*] a. Method; instrumentality; agency. b. Resources; income; substance.

me·an·der (mee-*an*-der) *v.* To pursue a wandering course; wind and turn.—*n.* 1. A winding; haphazard course. 2. A maze.

mean·ing (*meen*-ing) *adj.* Significant; denoting much.—*n.* 1. That which is meant to be expressed; import. 2. Intention; purpose; object. 3. Significance; sense.—**mean·ing·ful** *adj.*—**mean·ing·ful·ly** *adv.*

mean·ing·less *adj.* Devoid of sense or import. —**mean·ing·less·ly** *adv.*—**mean·ing·less·ness** *n.*

mean·time *n.* Also **mean·while.** The time between two events.—*adv.* During an interval between two events.

mea·sles (*mee*-z'lz) *n. pl. used as sing.* A contagious fever accompanied by dark-red skin eruptions.

meas·ly (*meez*-lee) *adj.* 1. *Colloquial.* Worthless; mean. 2. Ill with measles.

meas·ur·a·ble (*mezh*-er-uh-b'l) *adj.* Capable of being ascertained as to size or amount.—**mea·sur·a·bil·i·ty** (mezh-er-uh-*bil*-uh-tee) *n.*

meas·ure (*mezh*-er) *n.* 1. The extent of a thing in size. 2. A unit of capacity or extent. 3. The complement of sizes necessary to make a garment. 4. Moderation. 5. Means to an end. 6. *Music.* A section of music between two bars on the staff. 7. *Prosody.* Meter; rhythm. 8. A graceful dance. 9. *Printing.* Width of type line.—*v.* [meas·ured; meas·ur·ing] 1. To compute; reckon; ascertain the amount of. 2. To estimate; judge. 3. To allot or distribute by measure.—**meas·ur·er** *n.*

meas·ured (*mezh*-erd) *adj.* 1. Computed; adjusted; proportioned. 2. Deliberate; slow and steady.—**meas·ured·ly** *adv.*

meas·ure·less *adj*. Too great to be computed; boundless.

meas·ure·ment *n*. 1. The act of computing. 2. Size; bulk; area or content.

meat (*meet*) *n*. 1. The flesh of animals used as food. 2. The core; gist. 'Get to the meat of the subject.'—**meat·less** *adj*.—**meat·man** *n*.

meat·y *adj*. [meat·i·er; meat·i·est] Pithy; containing many facts; substantial.

Mec·ca (*mek*-uh) *n*. 1. A town in Saudi Arabia, Holy City of the Moslems. 2. Goal; sought-after result.

me·chan·ic (meh-*kan*-ik) *n*. A skilled workingman, esp. one who makes or repairs machinery.—**me·chan·ic** *adj*.—**mech·a·ni·cian** *n*.

me·chan·i·cal (meh-*kan*-ik-'l) *adj*. 1. Pertaining to machinery. 2. Automatic. 3. Hackneyed; stereotyped.—**me·chan·i·cal·ly** *adv*.

me·chan·ics *n*. 1. The science which deals with motion and force. 2. Routine details. 'Mechanics of dictionary making.'

mech·a·nism (*mek*-uh-nism) *n*. The arrangement of the parts of a machine, engine, or instrument.

mech·a·nize (*mek*-uh-nyze) *v*. [-nized; -niz·ing] To provide with machinery; replace workers by machines.—**mech·a·ni·za·tion** *n*.

med·al (*med*-'l) *n*. A small piece of inscribed metal, given as a reward for some meritorious service.—**med·al·ist, med·al·list** *n*. One who designs or receives a medal.—**me·dal·lic** *adj*.

me·dal·lion (meh-*dal*-yun) *n*. A large medal or tablet, esp. one bearing a reproduction of a scene or portrait in bas relief.

med·dle (*med*-'l) *v*. [med·dled; med·dling] To interfere; deal with affairs which are not one's concern.—**med·dler** *n*.

med·dle·some *adj*. Interfering; officious; impertinent; prying.—**med·dle·some·ness** *n*.

Mede (*meed*) *n*. An inhabitant of Media.

me·di·a (*mee*-dee-uh). Plural of *medium*, now esp. used to denote such advertising media as newspapers, magazines, and radio.

Me·di·a. An ancient Asiatic kingdom in NW Iran.—**Me·di·an** *adj. & n*.

me·di·al (*mee*-dee-ul) *adj*. Mean; pertaining to an average; in the middle.—**me·di·al·ly** *adv*.

me·di·an (*mee*-dee-un) *adj*. Situated in or pertaining to the middle.—*n*. Middle number of a series.

me·di·ate (*meed*-ee-ayt) *v*. [-at·ed; -at·ing] To intercede; conciliate; attempt to reconcile two contending parties.—**me·di·ate·ly** *adv*.

me·di·a·tion *n*. Intercession; intervention; attempt at reconciliation.—**me·di·a·tive** *adj*.—**me·di·a·tor** *n*.

med·ic *n*. 1. *Slang*. Doctor. 2. *Army*. Medical aid man.

med·i·ca·ble (*med*-ih-kuh-b'l) *adj*. Curable; remediable.

med·i·cal (*med*-ih-k'l) *adj*. Relating to medicine.—**med·i·cal·ly** *adv*.

me·dic·a·ment (meh-*dik*-uh-m'nt) *n*. A medicine; curative agent.

med·i·cate (*med*-ih-kayt) *v*. [-cat·ed; -cat·ing] 1. To treat medically. 2. To impregnate with drugs. 'Medicated ointment.'—**med·i·ca·tion** *n*.

me·dic·i·nal (meh-*diss*-in-'l) *adj*. Having curative or healing properties.—**me·dic·i·nal·ly** *adv*.

med·i·cine (*med*-ih-sin) *n*. 1. A remedy for disease; drug. 2. The science of the cure, mitigation, and prevention of disease.

medicine ball. A large, heavy ball, tossed back and forth for exercise.

medicine man. One who was supposed by the American Indians to possess supernatural powers.

me·di·e·val, me·di·ae·val (med-ih-*ee*-vul; mee-dee-*ee*-vul) *adj*. Pertaining to the Middle Ages.—**me·di·e·val·ly, me·di·ae·val·ly** *adv*.

me·di·e·val·ism, me·di·ae·val·ism *n*. Study of or belief in the characteristics and institutions of the Middle Ages.—**me·di·e·val·ist, me·di·ae·val·ist** *n*.

Me·di·na (may-*dee*-nah). A Holy Mohammedan city in Arabia where Mohammed is buried.

me·di·ocre (mee-dee-*oh*-ker) *adj*. Average; indifferent; second-rate; poor.

me·di·oc·ri·ty (mee-dee-*ok*-rih-tee) *n*. [pl. -ties] 1. A person of no great ability or intelligence. 2. Modest ability; second-rate talent.

med·i·tate (*med*-ih-tayt) *v*. [-tat·ed; -tat·ing] To cogitate; ruminate; think deeply.

med·i·ta·tion *n*. Cogitation, continued mental reflection.—**med·i·ta·tive** *adj*.—**-tive·ly** *adv*.

Med·i·ter·ra·ne·an Sea (med-ih-ter-*ay*-nec-un). A large body of water between Europe and Africa, from Straits of Gibraltar to Asia.

me·di·um (*mee*-dee-um) *n*. [pl. -ums, -a] 1. Agency; instrumentality. 2. One supposed to be capable of communicating with the spirits of the deceased. 3. The liquid vehicle with which dry colors are ground and prepared for painting. 4. Environment; surroundings. 5. Means; channel.—*adj*. Middle.

med·ley (*med*-lee) *n*. 1. A mixture; jumble. 2. A musical piece composed of parts of a number of tunes.

me·dul·la (meh-*duhl*-uh) *n*. [pl. -lae] Marrow.

medulla oblongata (ob-long-*gay*-tuh) [pl. medullae oblongatae] The upper enlarged portion of the spinal cord, connecting with the base of the brain.

Me·du·sa (meh-*doo*-suh) *n*. 1. *Mythology*. One of the three Gorgons, originally a beautiful maiden, whose hair was turned into serpents. 2. [*not cap*.] A jellyfish.—**Me·du·san, Me·du·soid** *adj*.

meek *adj*. Mild; submissive; compliant.—**meek·ly** *adv*.—**meek·ness** *n*.

meer·schaum (*meer*-shum) *n*. A soft white clay, found chiefly in Asia Minor, used for pipes and cigarette holders.

meet *v*. [met; meet·ing] 1. To encounter. 2. To come together; assemble. 3. To find.

M

4. To satisfy; answer. 'That meets my objection.'—*n.* A sports contest. 'A track meet.'

meet *adj.* Fit; proper.—**meet·ly** *adv.*

meet·ing *n.* **1.** An assemblage; gathering. **2.** Conjunction. 'Meeting of the rivers.'

meet·ing·house *n.* A place of worship.

meg·a-, meg-, meg·a·lo-. *Prefix.* **1.** Great; large. 'Megalith.' **2.** A million; a million times. 'Megacycle; megamho.'

meg·a·cy·cle (*meg*-uh-sy-k'l) *n.* *Electricity.* A million cycles.

meg·a·lo·ceph·a·ly (meg-uh-loh-*sef*-uh-lee) *n.* Condition of having a head larger than normal.—**meg·a·lo·ceph·al·ic** *adj.*

meg·a·lo·ma·ni·a (meg-uh-loh-*may*-nee-uh) *n.* *Psychiatry.* An exaggerated belief in one's own intelligence or greatness.—**meg·a·lo·ma·ni·ac** *n.*

meg·a·phone (*meg*-uh-fohn) *n.* A cone-shaped instrument used to magnify the voice.—*v.* [-phoned; -phon·ing].

me·grim (*mee*-grim) *n.* A periodical, extremely painful headache; migraine.

mel·an·cho·li·a (mel-un-*koh*-lee-uh) *n.* A psychosis marked by severe depression and inactivity.—**mel·an·cho·li·ac** *adj.* & *n.*

MEGAPHONE

mel·an·chol·ic (mel-un-*kol*-ik) *adj.* Gloomy; depressed; despondent.—**i·cal·ly** *adv.*

mel·an·chol·y *n.* [*pl.* -ies] Sadness; dejection; depression.—*adj.* Doleful; forlorn; sad.

Mel·a·ne·si·a (mel-uh-*nee*-zhuh). A group of islands in the central and western Pacific including New Caledonia, Fiji, New Hebrides.—**Mel·a·ne·sian** *adj.* & *n.*

mé·lange (may-*lahnzh*) *n.* A mixture.

melba toast. A dry, very thin toast.

me·lee (mel-*ay*, may-lay) *n.* A fracas; row.

mel·io·rate (*meel*-yer-ayt) *v.* To improve; better.—**mel·io·ra·tion** *n.*—**mel·io·ra·tor** *n.*

mel·lif·lu·ent (mel-*if*-loo-ent) *adj.* Sweet flowing.—**mel·lif·lu·ence** *n.*—**mel·lif·lu·ent·ly** *adv.*

mel·lif·lu·ous (-loo-us) *adj.* Fluent; flowing; smooth.—**mel·lif·lu·ous·ly** *adv.*

mel·low (*mel*-oh) *adj.* **1.** Matured; ripe. **2.** Genial; warm. **3.** *Slang.* Partially intoxicated. **4.** *Jazz Music.* Powerful and dynamic, yet restrained.—**mellow** *v.*—**mel·low·ly** *adv.*

me·lo·de·on (meh-*loh*-dee-un) *n.* A small old-fashioned reed organ.

me·lod·ic (meh-*lod*-ik) *adj.* Pertaining to melody.—**me·lod·i·cal·ly** *adv.*

me·lo·di·ous (meh-*loh*-dee-us) *adj.* Musical; dulcet; pleasant to the ear.—**me·lo·di·ous·ly** *adv.*—**me·lo·di·ous·ness** *n.*

mel·o·dra·ma (*mel*-uh-dram-uh) *n.* A play in which dramatic effect is sought by startling incidents, exaggerated sentiment, and a thrilling dénouement.

mel·o·dra·mat·ic (mel-uh-druh-*mat*-ik) *adj.*

Exaggerated; sensational; histrionic.—**mel·o·dra·mat·i·cal·ly** *adv.*—**mel·o·dra·mat·ics** *n.*

mel·o·dy (*mel*-oh-dee) *n.* [*pl.* -dies] **1.** Sweetness of sound; music. **2.** The chief theme of a musical composition. **3.** A tune; song.

mel·on (*mel*-'n) *n.* **1.** A climbing or trailing plant with rich, fleshy fruit. **2.** *Slang.* Surplus profits divided among shareholders.

melt *v.* [melt·ed; melt·ing] **1.** To liquefy; dissolve; fuse. **2.** To soften; mollify. **3.** To blend. 'The buildings melted into the fog.' **4.** To disappear; dwindle.—**melt·a·ble** *adj.*

mel·ton (*melt*-'n) *n.* A short-napped woolen cloth used for topcoats.

mem·ber *n.* **1.** A link; vital organ. **2.** An individual belonging to an organization. **3.** A single part.

mem·ber·ship *n.* **1.** The state of belonging to a group. **2.** All of the members of an association. 'The membership voted to strike.'

mem·brane *n.* A thin layer of tissue covering an organ.—**mem·bra·nous** (mem-*bray*-nus) *adj.*

me·men·to (mem-*en*-toh) *n.* [*pl.* -tos, -toes] A souvenir.

mem·o (*mem*-oh) *n.* [*pl.* -os] *Colloquial.* Memorandum.

mem·oir (*mem*-wahr) *n.* **1.** An informal history. **2.** A biography or autobiography.

mem·or·a·ble (*mem*-er-uh-b'l) *adj.* Noteworthy; remarkable; celebrated.—**mem·o·ra·bil·i·ty** *n.*

mem·o·ran·dum (mem-er-*an*-dum) *n.* [*pl.* -dums; -da] **1.** A note to aid the memory; an informal report. **2.** A summary of the pros and cons of a question.

me·mo·ri·al (mem-*or*-ee-ul) *n.* **1.** Anything, esp. a monument or statue, that serves to keep in memory. **2.** A written statement of facts addressed to a legislative body as ground for a petition.—**me·mo·ri·al** *adj.*

Memorial Day. Decoration Day, May 30th.

me·mo·ri·al·ize (mem-*mor*-ee-uh-lyze) *v.* [-ized; -iz·ing] To petition by memorial. **2.** To commemorate.—**me·mo·ri·al·i·za·tion** *n.*

mem·o·rize (*mem*-er-yze) *v.* [-rized; -riz·ing] To commit to memory; learn by rote.—**mem·o·ri·za·tion** *n.*—**mem·o·riz·er** *n.*

mem·o·ry (*mem*-er-ee) *n.* [*pl.* -ries] **1.** The power of the mind to retain knowledge of past events or ideas. **2.** A recollection; remembrance. **3.** The time within which one can recall past events. 'The Revolution was within my memory.'

mem·sa·hib (*mem*-sah-ib) *n.* Respectful title of address used by Indian servants to European women; lady.

men·ace (*men*-iss) *v.* [men·aced; men·ac·ing] To threaten; terrify; presage evil.—*n.* **1.** A threat. **2.** *Motion Pictures.* The villain.—**men·ac·ing** *adj.*—**men·ac·ing·ly** *adv.*

mé·nage, me·nage (may-*nahzh*) *n.* A household.

me·nag·er·ie (men-*aj*-er-ee) *n.* A collection of animals on exhibition; zoo.

mend *v.* 1. To repair; patch up. 2. To correct; rectify.—**mend·er** *n.*—**on the mend.** Improving, esp. in health.

men·da·cious (men-*day*-shus) *adj.* Dishonest; untruthful.—**men·da·cious·ly** *adv.*—**men·dac·i·ty** (men-*dass*-ih-tee) *n.* [*pl.* -ties].

Mendel's Law. Law, discovered by G. J. Mendel, that characteristics of plants and animals are transmitted from generation to generation according to definitely determinable combinations.—**Men·de·li·an·ism, Men·del·ism** *n.*

men·di·cant (*men*-dik-unt) *adj.* Poor to the point of beggary.—*n.* A begger.—**-can·cy** *n.*

Men·e·la·us (men-eh-*lay*-us) *n.* A Spartan King, husband of Helen of Troy.

me·ni·al (*meen*-yul) *adj.* Servile; low; mean. —*n.* A domestic servant.—**me·ni·al·ly** *adv.*

men·in·gi·tis (men-in-*jy*-tiss) *n.* Inflammation of the membranes of the brain or spinal cord.

me·nis·cus (meh-*niss*-kus) *n.* [*pl.* -cus·es; -ci] 1. A lens, convex on one side, concave on the other. 2. Concave or convex surface of liquid in a narrow container, caused by capillary action.

Men·non·ite (*men*-un-yte) *n.* One of a sect which does not believe in original sin, taking oaths, making war, or marriage outside the group.

men·o·pause (*men*-uh-pawz) *n.* Change of life; time when final cessation of menstrual flow occurs.

MENISCUS LENS

men·ses (*men*-seez) *n. pl.* A monthly discharge of bloody fluid from the uterus.

Men·she·vik (*men*-shuh-vik) *n.* [*pl.* -vi·ki; -viks] A member of the minority or reformist wing of the Russian Social Democrats.

men·stru·al (*men*-stroo-ul) *adj.* 1. Monthly. 2. Relating to the menses.

men·stru·ate (*men*-stroo-ayt) *v.* [-at·ed; -at·ing] To discharge the menses.—**men·stru·a·tion** *n.*

men·sur·a·ble (*men*-sher-uh-b'l) *adj.* Measurable; with fixed limits.—**men·sur·a·bil·i·ty** *n.*

men·su·ra·tion (men-sher-*ay*-sh'n) *n.* 1. The act of measuring. 2. Branch of geometry dealing with methods of ascertaining length, volume, or area.

men·tal (*men*-t'l) *adj.* Intellectual; pertaining to the mind.—**men·tal·ly** *adv.*

men·tal·i·ty (men-*tal*-ih-tee) *n.* Intelligence; intellect.

men·thol (*men*-thol) *n.* Peppermint camphor, used medicinally for colds and headaches. —**men·tho·lat·ed** *adj.*

men·tion (*men*-shun) *n.* A brief remark or notice; hint.—**men·tion** *v.*—**men·tion·a·ble** *adj.* —**men·tion·er** *n.*

men·tor (*men*-ter) *n.* A teacher; counselor.

men·u (*men*-yoo, *mayn*-yoo) *n.* [*pl.* -us] A bill of fare; food list.

Meph·i·stoph·e·les (mef-iss-*tof*-uh-leez) *n.* The devil in the Faust legend who wins the soul of Dr. Faustus.

Me·phis·to·phe·li·an, -le·an (meh-fiss-toh-*fee*-lee-an) *adj.* Diabolical; devilish; sardonic.

me·phi·tic (meh-*fit*-ik) *adj.* Noxious; foul.—**me·phi·tis** (meh-*fy*-tis) *n.* A foul odor.

mer·can·tile (*mer*-k'n-til) *adj.* Pertaining to trade; commercial.

mer·can·til·ism (*mer*-k'n-til-izm) *n.* An economic doctrine holding that a nation's wealth is enhanced when it has a favorable balance of trade with other nations.

Mercator's projection. A method of representing the surface of the earth on a chart, in which the lines are projected as if the chart were rolled into a cylinder about the earth.

mer·ce·nar·y (*mer*-s'n-ehr-ee) *adj.* Acting or done solely for money or gain; selfish; venal. —*n.* [*pl.* -ies] A soldier who serves in a foreign army for pay.

mer·cer·ize (*mer*-ser-yze) *v.* [-ized; -iz·ing] To treat cotton with an alkali to strengthen it and give it a silky gloss.

mer·chan·dise (*mer*-chun-dyze) *n.* Commodities; goods bought and sold.—*v.* [-ised; -is·ing] 1. To trade; buy and sell. 2. To package and advertise; promote.

mer·chant (*mer*-chunt) *n.* 1. A trader, esp. on an international scale. 2. A storekeeper; retailer.—**mer·chant** *adj.*

mer·chant·a·ble *adj.* Saleable; fit for market.

mer·chant·man *n.* [*pl.* -men] A commercial vessel.

merchant marine. The commercial or trade ships of a country and their crews.

mer·ci·ful (*mer*-sih-ful) *adj.* Showing mercy; compassionate; lenient.—**mer·ci·ful·ly** *adv.*

mer·ci·less (*mer*-sih-liss) *adj.* Pitiless; without mercy; relentless.—**mer·ci·less·ly** *adv.*

mer·cu·ri·al (mer-*kyoo*-ree-'l) *adj.* 1. Changeable; unstable; quick; capricious. 2. Caused by or containing mercury.—**mer·cu·ri·al·ly** *adv.* —**mer·cu·ri·al·ness** *n.*

mer·cu·ric (mer-*kyoo*-rik) *adj.* Containing mercury, esp. in compound.

Mer·cu·ro·chrome (mer-*kyoor*-uh-krohm) *n.* Trade name of a deep-red dye used in solution as an antiseptic.

mer·cu·rous (mer-*kyoo*-rus) *adj. Chemistry.* Pertaining to compounds which have a larger quantity of mercury than mercuric compounds.

Mer·cu·ry (*mer*-kyer-ee) *n.* 1. *Mythology.* The god of commerce, trickery, and eloquence, messenger of Jupiter. 2. *Astronomy.* The smallest planet, and that nearest the sun.

mer·cu·ry *n.* 1. A heavy, gray-white liquid metal; quicksilver. (*Symbol:* Hg). 2. The mercury column in a thermometer.

mer·cy (*mer*-see) *n.* [*pl.* -cies] 1. Forbearance; compassion; willingness to forgive or be kind; leniency. 2. Kind treatment. 3. A blessing.

mere *adj.* [*superl.* mer·est] Simple; bare.

mere·ly *adv.* Only; simply; and nothing else.

mer·e·tri·cious (mer-uh-*trish*-us) *adj.* Gaudy; tawdry; deceptively attractive.—**mer·e·tri·cious·ly** *adv.*—**mer·e·tri·cious·ness** *n.*

M

mer·gan·ser (mer-*gan*-ser) *n.* A large fish-eating duck with a long, slender bill.

merge (*merj*) *v.* [merged; merg· ing] 1. To blend; cause to combine or be absorbed. 2. Become ab- sorbed or swal- lowed up; mingle.

MERGANSER (1/14 life size)

merg·er *n.* A com- bination; amalgamation of corporations.

me·rid·i·an (mer-*id*-ee-un) *n.* 1. An imaginary circle on the surface of the earth passing through both poles. 2. The projection of a meridian on the celestial sphere. 3. The highest point reached by a heavenly body in its daily passage; noon. 4. Culmination; high point.—**me·rid·i·an** *adj.*

me·ringue (mer-*ang*) *n.* A light confection of beaten egg white and sugar, for covering cakes and pies or as a shell for ice cream.

me·ri·no (mer-*een*-oh) *n.* [*pl.* -nos] 1. A va- riety of sheep valued for its long fine wool. 2. The wool of this sheep or yarn made from it.—**me·ri·no** *adj.*

mer·it (*mehr*-it) *n.* 1. Due reward; desert. 2. Worth; value. 3. Intrinsic quality. 4. Mark of praise.—*v.* To deserve; earn.

mer·i·to·ri·ous (mehr-ih-*toh*-ree-us) *adj.* Com- mendable; deserving reward; praiseworthy. —**mer·i·to·ri·ous·ly** *adv.*—**mer·i·to·ri·ous·ness** *n.*

mer·lin (*mer*-lin) *n.* A small hawk or falcon.

Mer·lin *n.* The magician and sorcerer in the Arthurian legends.

mer·maid (*mer*-mayd) *n.* A mythical marine creature with a woman's body ending in a fish's tail.—**mer·man** *n.*

mer·ri·ment (*mehr*-ih-m'nt) *n.* Hilarity; mirth.

mer·ry (*mehr*-ee) *adj.* [mer·ri·er; mer·ri·est] 1. Gay; joyful; jolly. 2. Amusing; laugh- able.—**mer·ri·ly** *adv.*—**mer·ri·ness** *n.*

mer·ry-go-round *n.* A revolving circular plat- form, fitted with wooden horses or seats, on which children ride; carousel.

mer·ry·mak·ing *adj.* Producing mirth; gay.—*n.* Entertainment; festivity.—**mer·ry·mak·er** *n.*

me·sa (*may*- suh) *n.* A small elevat- ed plateau.

mes·cal (mess-*kal*) *n.* Small cactus whose but- ton-shaped

MESA

stem tops are used medicinally. 2. A liquor distilled from mescal juice.

mesh *n.* 1. Space between the threads or knots of a netting, as a screen. 2. A net; network. —*v.* 1. To catch in a net; become entangled. 2. To engage the teeth of gears.—**mesh** *adj.*

mes·mer·ism (*mess*-mer-iz'm; *mez*-) *n.* Hypno- tism; art of putting a person into a comatose state in which his actions and thoughts are controlled by another.—**mes·mer·ic** *adj.*—**mes· mer·i·cal·ly** *adv.*—**mes·mer·ist** *n.*

mes·mer·ize (*mess*-mer-yze; *mez*-) *v.* [mes· mer·ized; mes·mer·iz·ing] To put into a hyp- notic state.

Mes·o·po·ta·mi·a (mess-uh-puh-*tay*-mee-uh). Ancient country between the Tigris and Eu- phrates Rivers in Western Asia, now called Iraq.—**Mes·o·po·ta·mi·an** *adj. & n.*

mes·o·tron (*mess*-uh-tron) *n.* A heavy electron.

Mes·o·zo·ic (mess-uh-*zoh*-ik) *adj.* Pertaining to the secondary era of geological development, the period of great reptiles.—*n.* The Mesozoic period.

mes·quite (*mess*-keet) *n.* A tree or shrub bearing sweet pods used as cattle fodder.

mess *n.* 1. *Col- loquial.* A con- fused or sloppy mixture; disor- der; muddle. 2. Food pre- pared or served for one meal. 3. Those who habitually eat together.—*v.* 1. To eat at the same table. 2. To confuse; disorder; muddle.

MESQUITE

mes·sage (*mess*-ij) *n.* 1. A communication from one person to another. 2. An official address not delivered in person. 3. A spirit- ual communication.

mes·sa·line (*mess*-uh-leen) *n.* A lightweight material with a satiny surface.

mes·sen·ger (*mess*-'n-jer) *n.* 1. One who car- ries a message; person who does errands. 2. A forerunner; harbinger.

Mes·si·ah (muh-*sy*-uh) *n.* 1. The awaited de- liverer of the Jews; Savior. 2. Christ.—**mes· si·ah·ship** *n.*—**Mes·si·an·ic** *adj.*

mes·sieurs (*mess*-erz). 1. *Plural* of monsieur. 2. *Plural* of Mister. Abbreviation: Messrs.

mess·mate *n.* One of a group which eats to- gether.

mess·y *adj.* [mess·i·er; mess·i·est] Disordered; dirty; confused; distasteful.—**mess·i·ness** *n.*

mes·ti·zo (mess-*tee*-zoh) *n.* [*pl.* -zos, -zoes] One of mixed blood, esp. Spanish and American Indian.—**mes·ti·za** *n. fem.*

met·a-, met- *Prefix.* 1. Beyond; after; with. 2. Change; transformation.

me·tab·o·lism (muh-*tab*-uh-liz'm) *n.* The total of the processes which keep the body alive, nourished, and functioning.—**met·a·bol·ic** *adj.*

met·al (*met*-'l) *n.* 1. Any element, having mal- leability and luster, which conducts heat and electricity, and replaces the hydrogen of an acid. 2. Substance; spirit.—**me·tal·lic** *adj.* —**me·tal·li·cal·ly** *adv.*

met·al·lur·gy (*met*-'l-er-jee) *n*. The science of extracting and refining metals.—**met·al·lur·gic, met·al·lur·gi·cal** *adj*.—**met·al·lur·gist** *n*.

me·tal·work·ing *n*. The art of converting metals into useful commodities.—**met·al·work** *n*. & *v*.

met·a·mor·phism (met-uh-*mor*-fizm) *n*. *Geology*. A change in chemical or mineral composition, structure, or texture of sedimentary or igneous rocks.

met·a·mor·phose(met-uh-*mor*-fohz)*v*.[-phosed; -phos·ing] To change in shape of form.

met·a·mor·pho·sis (met-uh-*mor*-fuh-siss, -*foh*-siss) *n*. [*pl*. -ses] 1. A change in shape, form, or structure. 2. A marked change in the shape and function of a living body, as in the development from tadpole to frog.

met·a·phor (*met*-uh-for, -fer) *n*. A figure of speech in which similarity of one object to another is implied. 'He plowed through the crowd.'—**met·a·phor·i·cal** (met-uh-*for*-ih-k'l), -**phor·ic** *adj*. Not literal.— -**phor·i·cal·ly** *adv*.

met·a·phys·i·cal (met-uh-*fiz*-ih-k'l) *adj*. 1. Existing only in thought; abstract. 2. Pertaining to the principles of metaphysics.

met·a·phys·ics (met-uh-*fiz*-iks) *n*. Abstract philosophy dealing with problems of being, of absolute nature, and of ultimate causes.—**met·a·phy·si·cian** (met-uh-fih-*zish*-un) *n*.

mete (*meet*) *v*. [met·ed; met·ing] 1. To measure exactly; define. 2. To allot; apportion by measure.—*n. pl*. Limits; boundaries.

me·temp·sy·cho·sis (meh-temp-sy-*koh*-siss) *n*. [*pl*. -ses] Transmigration of the soul, after death, to another body.

me·te·or (*mee*-tee-er) *n*. A cosmic body visible in its fall through the earth's atmosphere; shooting star.

me·te·or·ic (mee-tee-*or*-ik) *adj*. 1. Consisting of or like a meteor. 2. Flashing but transitory; sudden.

me·te·or·ite (*mee*-tee-er-yte) *n*. A mass of stony matter which falls from outer space to the earth's surface.

me·te·or·ol·o·gy (mee-tee-er-*ol*-uh-jee) *n*. The science of the atmosphere, esp. as related to weather, climate, and atmospheric electricity. —**me·te·or·o·log·ic, -i·cal** *adj*.— -**ol·o·gist** *n*.

me·ter, me·tre (*mee*-ter) *n*. 1. Rhythmical arrangement of syllables in poetry; measure; rhythm. 2. The French standard measure of length equal to 39.37 inches, based on the measurement of one ten-millionth of an arc of the earth's meridian from pole to equator. 3. *Music*. Rhythm; the arrangement of notes and rests according to their time value.

me·ter *n*. An instrument, usually automatic, for measuring quantities by means of indicating and recording devices.

meth·ane (*meth*-ayn) *n*. A colorless, odorless gas, formed in coal mines and swamps, which burns when ignited in air; marsh gas.

meth·a·nol (*meth*-uh-nol) *n*. Methyl alcohol; wood alcohol, chiefly used as a solvent in the preparation of lacquers and varnishes.

meth·od (*meth*-ud) *n*. 1. Manner of procedure; mode; course. 2. System; regularity; order.

me·thod·i·cal (meh-*thod*-ih-k'l) *adj*. Also **me·thod·ic**. Systematic; orderly; carefully regulated.—**me·thod·i·cal·ly** *adv*.— -**i·cal·ness** *n*.

Meth·od·ist (*meth*-ud-ist) *n*. 1. Member of a Christian denomination founded by John Wesley, following a strict personal observance of religious duties. 2. [*not cap*.] One who adheres to order and method.—*adj*. Pertaining to the Methodists.— -**od·ism** *n*.— -**od·is·tic** *adj*.

meth·od·ize *v*. [-ized; -iz·ing] To arrange in orderly manner; follow a system.

Me·thu·se·lah (muh-*thoo*-zuh-luh) *n*. A Biblical figure said to have lived 969 years.

meth·yl (*meth*-'l) *n*. *Chemistry*. A radical or chemically combining form composed of three molecules of hydrogen and one of carbon.

me·tic·u·lous (meh-*tik*-yuh-luss) *adj*. Particular; careful about details.—**me·tic·u·lous·ly** *adv*.

me·tier (may-*tyay*) *n*. Specialty; profession.

me·ton·y·my (meh-*ton*-uh-mee) *n*. The substitution of one word for another closely related, as the *heart* for *affection*.

Met·ra·zol (*met*-ruh-zol) *n*. Trade-mark for a respiratory stimulant.

me·tre. *Variant spelling* of **meter**.

met·ric (*met*-rik) *adj*. Designating a system of measurement based on decimal subdivisions and multiples of the meter and gram.

met·ri·cal (*met*-rih-k'l) *adj*. 1. Relating to measurement. 2. Pertaining to rhythm; compose in rhythmic verse form.— -**ri·cal·ly** *adv*.

metric system. The decimal subdivisions and multiples of the meter and gram, named by the following Latin and Greek prefixes:

deci- = one-tenth.
centi- = one-hundredth.
milli- = one-thousandth.
deka- = ten.
hecto- = one hundred.
kilo- = one thousand.

met·ro·nome (*met*-ruh-nohm) *n*. An instrument for indicating the exact time of music.

me·trop·o·lis (meh-*trop*-uh-liss) *n*. [*pl*. -lis·es] 1. A very large or important city. 2. The capital of a country. 3. The see of a metropolitan bishop.

METRONOME

met·ro·pol·i·tan (met-ruh-*pol*-ih-tun) *adj*. 1. Belonging to a large city. 2. Having the authority of a metropolitan. —*n*. 1. Resident of a large city. 2. The title of a bishop having the authority over other bishops of a province or see; archbishop.

met·tle (*met*-'l) *n*. Courage; spirit; temper.—**on one's mettle**. Ready to do the utmost.

met·tle·some (*met*-'l-sum) *adj*. Brisk; fiery; high-spirited.

mew (*myoo*) *n*. A European seagull.

M

mew v. Also **me·ow, mi·aou.** To cry as a cat. —n. The cry of a cat.

mew n. 1. A cage for moulting hawks. 2. A place of confinement. 3. [pl. used as sing.] A row of stables or garages.—v. To enclose.

mewl (myool) v. To whimper; cry as a child.

mez·za·nine (mez-uh-neen) n. 1. Architecture. A half story, usually placed between the ground floor and second story. 2. Theater. The first several rows of the balcony.

mez·zo (met-zoh) adj. Music. Moderate. Mezzo piano means moderately soft.

mez·zo-so·pra·no n. [pl. -nos, -ni] 1. A singer whose voice range is lower than soprano and higher than contralto. 2. The range of a mezzo-soprano.—adj. Medium in range.

mez·zo·tint (met-zoh-tint) n. A process of engraving a copper or steel plate with minute punctures to hold ink, then smoothing the surface to produce variations of light and shade. —v. To engrave in mezzotint.

mho (moh) n. Electricity. Unit of conductance; opposite of ohm, unit of resistance.

mi·as·ma (my-az-muh) n. [pl. -ma·ta, -mas] A poisonous mist or vapor.—mi·as·mat·ic, mi·as·mat·i·cal, mi·as·mic, mi·as·mal adj. Having an evil or injurious effect; poisonous.

mi·ca (my-kuh) n. A lustrous mineral used as an insulator of high-frequency current.—mi·ca, mi·ca·ce·ous adj.

Mi·cah (my-kuh) n. A Hebrew prophet of the Old Testament book bearing his name.

mice. Plural of mouse.

Mi·chael (my-k'l) n. New Testament. One of the seven archangels.

Mi·chael·mas (mih-k'l-mus) n. Also **Michaelmas Day.** The feast of the archangel Michael, September 29.

mick·ey n. Slang. 1. Radar operator. 2. Radar equipment.

Mickey Finn. Slang. A doped drink causing diarrhea and eventual unconsciousness.

mi·cro- Prefix. 1. Small, minute; microscopically and infinitesimally small, as in

microbar	microgeology	micromineralogy
microbarograph	micromechanics	micropathology
microbattery	micrometallurgy	micropin
microbiology	micro-movie	microphysics
microburner	micro-needle	microzoology

2. One millionth of, as in

microammeter	microfarad	microjoule
microampere	microgram	microliter
microcoulomb	microhenry	microsecond
microerg	microhm	microvolt

mi·crobe (my-krohb) n. A germ; minute organism, esp. of the plant kingdom.—mi·cro·bic (my-kroh-bik) mi·cro·bi·al adj.

mi·cro·cop·y (my-kruh-kop-ee) n. [pl. -ies] A tiny photographic duplicate or copy.

mi·cro·cosm (my-kruh-kozm) n. 1. An organic whole which contains within itself all the elements of a universe; a little world.

2. Philosophy. Man seen as epitomizing a world.— -cos·mic (my-kruh-koz-mik),-i·cal adj.

mi·cro-film (my-kruh-film) n. A recording of a manuscript or book on small film; film designed for this use.

mi·crol·o·gy (my-krol-uh-jee) n. Undue attention to small matters.

mi·crom·e·ter (my-krom-uh-ter) n. 1. Also **mi·crom·e·ter cal·i·per.** A precision gauge employing a fine screw and a vernier. 2. An instrument which measures small distances with high precision,

MICROMETER

often attached to microscopes.—mi·crom·e·try n. The measurement of small dimensions or distances with a micrometer.

mi·cron (my-kron) n. [pl. -crons, -cra] One millionth of a meter.

Mi·cro·ne·si·a (my-kruh-nee-zhuh). The section of the Pacific embracing the Mariana, Marshall, and Gilbert Islands.—Mi·cro·ne·sian adj. & n.

mi·cro·or·gan·ism (my-kroh-or-gun-izm) n. A life form seen only by microscope; microbe.

mi·cro·phone (my-kruh-fohn) n. An instrument which transforms sound waves into audiofrequency electrical impulses for transmission. —mi·cro·phon·ic (my-kruh-fon-ik) adj. Intensifying sound.

mi·cro·scope (my-kruh-skohp) n. An optical instrument whose magnifying lenses render minute forms visible.

mi·cro·scop·ic (my-kruh-skop-ik) adj. Also **mi·cro·scop·i·cal.** 1. Tiny, minute. 2. Seen only with the aid of a microscope.—mi·cro·scop·i·cal·ly adv.

mi·cro·wave (my-kroh-wayv) n. A radiation with an extremely high frequency of vibration.

mid- Prefix. Middle.—mid adj. Occupying or pertaining to a middle position.

Mi·das (my-dus) n. Greek Mythology. A king who turned everything that he touched to gold.

mid·day (mid-day) n. Noon; the hours about noon.—adj. Occurring at or near noon.

mid·dle (mid-'l) adj. 1. Center; equally distant from the ends or a circumference; mean; medium. 2. Intermediate; between a first and a final.—n. 1. The center; mean; equidistant point. 2. The waist; midsection of the body.

mid·dle-aged adj. Past the age of youth, but not old.

Middle Ages. The period between the fall of the Roman Empire and the Renaissance.

middle class. The portion of society between the rich and the working class; bourgeoisie —mid·dle-class adj. Bourgeois; conventional; culturally like those of the middle class.

mid·dle·man n. [pl. -men] A wholesaler; dealer between the producer and the consumer.

mid·dle·most adj. Midmost; most centrally located.

mid·dle·weight *n.* A boxer weighing 147–160 pounds.

Middle West. Also **Mid·west.** The central portion of the U.S., roughly north of 39° North Latitude.—**Middle Western** *adj.*—**Middle Westerner** *n.*

mid·dling *adj.* Ordinary; average; moderate. —*adv.* Passably; moderately.—*n.* [*pl.*] Coarse flour or fine bran.

mid·dy *n.* [*pl.* -dies] 1. A naval cadet, esp. a student at Annapolis. 2. Also **middy blouse.** A loose-fitting girls' blouse with a sailor collar.

midg·et (*mij*-it) *n.* A dwarf; person of stunted growth.—*adj.* Abnormally small.

mid·i·ron (*mid*-eye-ern) *n. Golf.* A club with the head so pitched as to lift the ball moderately.

mid·land (*mid*-l'nd) *adj.* Inland; located in the interior.—*n.* 1. The central region; interior. 2. [*pl.*] The central counties of England.

mid·most *adj.* Nearest the middle; most central.

mid·night *n.* Twelve o'clock at night, or time near that hour.—*adj.* 1. Dark as midnight. 2. Occurring at midnight.

mid·riff (*mid*-rif) *n.* The diaphragm; muscle separating the chest and the stomach.—*adj.* Exposing the middle. 'A midriff bathing suit.'

mid·ship (*mid*-ship) *adj.* Relating to the middle of a ship. 'A midship beam.'

mid·ship·man (*mid*-ship-m'n) *n.* [*pl.* -men] A U.S. Maritime Service or Navy cadet.

midst *n.* The middle; central or inner part. —*prep.* In the middle of; among.

mid·sum·mer *n.* The middle of the summer, when the heat is greatest.—*adj.* Occurring in midsummer.

mid·way *n.* A lane or avenue where the amusements of a fair or exposition are concentrated. —*adj. & adv.* Halfway.

Mid·west *n.* The Middle West.—**Mid·west,** **Mid·west·ern** *adj.*—**Mid·west·ern·er** *n.*

mid·wife *n.* [*pl.* -wives] A woman assisting at childbirth.—**mid·wife·ry** *n.*

mid·win·ter *n.* The middle of the winter.

mid·year *adj.* Occurring in the middle of the year.—*n. Colloquial.* An examination in the middle of the college year.

mien (*meen*) *n.* Demeanor; air; external appearance; aspect; bearing.

miff *n.* A minor or trivial quarrel.—*v.* To take offense; vex.—**miff·y** *adj.* Touchy; easily offended.

might (*myte*) *n.* Power; strength; great force.

might·y *adj.* [might·i·er; might·i·est] 1. Powerful; strong. 2. Influential. 3. Vast; momentous; great.—*adv. Colloquial.* Very; greatly. —**might·i·ly** *adv.*—**might·i·ness** *n.*

mi·gnon·ette (min-yun-*et*) *n.* A coarse, thick-stemmed flower.

mi·graine (*my*-grayn) *n.* A nervous disorder marked by violent, periodic headaches.

mi·grant (*my*-gr'nt) *adj.* Migratory; of no fixed abode.—*n.* A wanderer; migrating animal.

mi·grate (*my*-grayt) *v.* [mi·grat·ed; mi·grat·ing] 1. To move from one place to another. 2. To move periodically so as to follow the seasons

mi·gra·tion (my-*gray*-shun) *n.* 1. Change of residence from one country or climate to another. 2. A group or flock making this change.—**mi·gra·tion·al** *adj.*

mi·gra·to·ry (*my*-gruh-tor-ee) *adj.* 1. Wandering; nomadic; given to changing residence. 2. Participating in a migration.

mi·ka·do (mih-*kah*-doh) *n.* Japanese emperor.

mike *n. Slang.* A microphone.

mil *n.* A unit in measuring diameter of wire: .001 inch.

mi·la·dy (mih-*lay*-dee) *n.* 1. A very fashionable woman. 2. An English gentlewoman.

mil·age. *Variant spelling* of mileage.

milch *adj.* Producing milk. 'A milch goat.'

mild *adj.* 1. Moderate; temperate. 2. Gentle; placid; not violent. 3. Malleable and easily worked, as steel.—**mild·ly** *adv.*—**mild·ness** *n.*

mild-aired	mild-faced	mild-scented
mild-aspected	mild-flavored	mild-spirited
mild-brewed	mild-hearted	mild-spoken
mild-cured	mild-mannered	mild-tempered
mild-eyed	mild-savored	mild-tongued

mil·dew (*mil*-doo) *n.* 1. Mold; fungi which thrive in dampness and decay. 2. Stain caused by these fungi.—*v.* To become moldy.

mile *n.* A unit of distance: 5,280 feet.

mile·age (*myle*-ij) *n.* 1. Distance in miles. 2. An allowance paid for traveling. 3. Charge based on miles transported.

mile·post *n.* A signpost indicating the distance to a given point.

mile·stone *n.* 1. A stone showing mileage. 2. An outstanding event.

mi·lieu (meel-*yer*) *n.* Setting; environment.

mil·i·tant (*mil*-ih-t'nt) *adj.* Fighting; warlike; aggressive.—*n.* An aggressive person; fighter. —**mil·i·tan·cy** *n.*—**mil·i·tant·ly** *adv.*

mil·i·ta·rism (*mil*-ih-ter-izm) *n.* 1. The institutions and ideals of a society dominated by warmongers. 2. Exaltation of the military. 3. Avid willingness to fight.—**mil·i·ta·rist** *n.* —**mil·i·ta·ris·tic** (mil-ih-ter-*iss*-tik) *adj.*—**mil·i·ta·ris·ti·cal·ly** *adv.*

mil·i·ta·rize (*mil*-ih-ter-yze) *v.* [-rized; -riz·ing] To equip with armies; prepare for war psychologically and militarily.—**mil·i·ta·ri·za·tion** *n.*

mil·i·tar·y (*mil*-ih-ter-ee) *adj.* Martial; adapted to war; in an armed organization.—*n.* The armed forces; soldiery.—**mil·i·tar·i·ly** *adv.*

military police. Also **M. P.** A police force which keeps order among soldiers.

mil·i·tate (*mil*-ih-tayt) *v.* [-tat·ed; -tat·ing] 1. To war; contend against. 2. To oppose.

mi·li·tia (muh-*lish*-uh) *n.* Civilians trained for emergency military duty; national guard. —**mi·li·tia·man** *n.* [*pl.* -men].

milk *n.* 1. A nourishing white fluid secreted by the mammary glands of the female. 2. Any milk-like fluid.—*v.* 1. To draw milk from.

M

2. *Slang*. To exhaust of funds; drain; exploit.

milk-blended	milkfish	milkshed
milk-borne	milkhead	milksick
milk-faced	milk-hued	milkstone
milk-fed	milk-livered	milk white

milk·er *n*. 1. A person or machine for milking cows. 2. A cow giving milk.

milk·maid *n*. A female employee of a dairy.

milk·man *n*. [*pl*. -men] A dairy's deliveryman.

milk of magnesia. A white hydroxide of magnesia used as a laxative, antacid, etc.

milk·sop *n*. An effeminate man.

milk tooth. A temporary tooth of a young mammal; baby tooth.

milk·weed *n*. A plant yielding a milky juice and bearing pods of downy seeds.

milk·y *adj*. [milk·i·er; milk·i·est] Of or re-sembling milk; white. —**milk·i·ness** *n*.

milky way. A dimly luminous band across the night skies, composed of many distant stars.

MILKWEED

mill *n*. One tenth of a cent.

mill *n*. 1. A machine for grinding grain and other hard foods. 2. A machine for extracting juices. 3. A plant; factory. 4. A milling machine. 5. *Slang*. A typewriter. 6. *Slang*. Wide range of chastening experiences. 'She's been through the mill.'—*v*. 1. To grind, as grain. 2. To press; crush in a mill. 3. To flute the edges of a coin. 4. To machine metal surfaces on a mill. 5. To move about in a confused mass or in a vague circle.

mill course	millman	mill site
mill dam	mill owner	mill stock
millfeed	mill post	millstream
mill hand	mill ring	milltail
mill-headed	mill run	millwork
mill house	mill-run (*v*.)	millworker

mill·board *n*. A stiff pasteboard used for book covers.

mil·len·ni·um (mih-*len*-ee-um) *n*. [*pl*. -ni·ums, -ni·a] 1. A thousand years. 2. *New Testament*. The time when Christ will reign on earth.

miller *n*. 1. A maker of flour. 2. A moth having its body covered with a pollenlike dust.

mil·let (*mil*-et) *n*. A cereal grass grown for hay and grain.

mil·li- *Prefix*. 1. Thousand; thousand times. 2. One-thousandth.

mil·li·gram, mil·li·gramme (*mil*-ih-gram) *n*. One thousandth of a gram.

mil·li·me·ter, mil·li·me·tre (*mil*-ih-mee-ter) *n*. One thousandth of a meter; .039 of an inch.

mil·li·ner·y (*mil*-ih-nehr-ee) *n*. [*pl*. -ies] 1. The occupation of hat making or hat selling. 2. Women's hats.—**mil·li·ner** *n*.

mill·ing *n*. Processing or manufacturing in a mill.

milling machine. A machine tool that cuts straight, helical, or irregular grooves.

mil·lion (*mil*-yun) *n*. & *adj*. Ten hundred thousand.—**mil·lionth** *n*. & *adj*.

mil·lion·aire (mil-yun-*air*) *n*. A person having a million or more dollars.

mill·pond *n*. A reservoir of water for turning a mill wheel.

mill·race *n*. 1. The current of water driving a mill. 2. Canal from millpond to mill wheel.

mill·stone *n*. 1. A stone for grinding grain. 2. An oppressive weight; heavy burden.

mill wheel. A wheel which imparts waterpower to mill machinery.

mill·wright (*mil*-ryte) *n*. A mechanic who in-stalls or maintains mills and other machinery.

milque·toast (*milk*-tohst) *n*. *Colloquial*. A weak-willed person.

mil·reis (*mil*-rayss) *n*. *sing*. & *pl*. 1. A Portu-guese coin, now obsolete. 2. A Brazilian coin.

milt *n*. 1. The spleen. 2. Sperm-filled repro-ductive organs of male fishes; the sperm itself. —**milt·er** *n*. Male fish in breeding season.

mime (*myme*) *n*. 1. An actor; esp. a comedian. 2. Ancient Greek comedy.—*v*. [mimed; mim-ing] To act, esp. in pantomime; perform comedy.—**mim·er** *n*.

Mim·e·o·graph (*mim*-ee-oh-graf) *n*. Trade-mark name of a stenciling machine for dupli-cating letters, etc.—*v*. [*not cap*.] To reproduce by stencil.

mim·ic (*mim*-ik) *n*. A person imitating another. —*v*. [mim·icked; mim·ick·ing] To imitate; mock; ape.—**mim·ick·er** *n*.

mim·i·cry *n*. Imitation, esp. for ridicule.

mi·mo·sa (mih-*moh*-suh) *n*. A plant of the bean family having prickly leaves and pink or white flowers.

min·a·ret (min-er-*et*) *n*. A tall slender tower on a mosque, whence the muezzin calls faithful Moslems to prayer.

mince (*minss*) *v*. [minced; minc·ing] 1. To chop into tiny pieces. 2. To make excuses; cover over. 'Mince matters.' 3. To walk with short, prim steps. 4. To talk with affected elegance.—*n*. Mincemeat.

mince·meat *n*. Meat finely chopped, with raisins, lemon peel, etc.—**mince pie.** Pie filled with mincemeat.

minc·ing *adj*. Prim; affectedly elegant; simper-ing.—**minc·ing·ly** *adv*.

mind (*mynde*) *n*. 1. The intellect; understand-ing; reasoning faculty. 2. Opinion; belief. 3. Inclination; disposition.—*v*. 1. To heed; obey; pay attention to. 2. To watch over; take care of. 3. To object. 'Do you mind if I join you?' 4. To remember.—**mind·er** *n*.—**of sound mind.** Sane.—**to have, or be, half a mind.** To be inclined.

mind·ful *adj*. Heedful; attentive; bearing in mind.—**mind·ful·ly** *adv*.—**mind·ful·ness** *n*.

mind·less *adj.* 1. Heedless; forgetful. 2. Stupid; unthinking.—**mind·less·ly** *adv.*

mind reading. Reading the thoughts of others. —**mind·reader** *n.*

mine *pron.* Belonging to me.—*adj. Archaic.* My. 'Mine eyes have seen the glory.'

mine *n.* 1. A pit; a digging from which a substance is extracted. 'A coal mine.' 2. A rich supply. 3. a. Explosive in or under water. b. Anti-personnel or anti-tank explosive in land warfare.—*v.* [mined; min·ing] 1. To dig for minerals or other substances. 2. To set explosives.—**min·er** *n.*

min·er·al (*min*-er-ul) *n.* An inorganic chemical compound found in the earth.—*adj.* 1. Consisting of minerals. 2. Containing minerals.

min·er·al·ize *v.* [-ized; -iz·ing] 1. To convert into a mineral. 2. To impregnate with minerals.—**min·er·al·i·za·tion** *n.*—**min·er·al·iz·er** *n.*

min·er·al·o·gy (min-er-*al*-uh-jee; -*ahl*-) *n.* [*pl.* -gies] Study of the properties of minerals. —**min·er·al·og·i·cal** *adj.*—**min·er·al·og·i·cal·ly** *adv.*—**min·er·al·o·gist** *n.*

mineral oil. Any liquid hydrocarbon mixture found in the earth, as petroleum, naphtha, etc.

mineral water. Water impregnated with minerals and having curative properties.

Mi·ner·va (mih-*ner*-vuh) *n. Roman Mythology.* The goddess of wisdom.

mi·ne·stro·ne (min-ess-*troh*-ne) *n.* A thick Italian vegetable soup.

Ming *n.* A Chinese dynasty ruling from the 14th to the 17th century.

min·gle (*ming*-g'l) *v.* [min·gled; min·gling] 1. To join in; intermix; combine; blend. 2. To associate with.—**min·gler** *n.*

min·i·a·ture (*min*-ee-uh-cher) *n.* 1. A very small portrait on vellum, ivory, etc. 2. A delineation on a smaller scale.—*adj.* Tiny; dimunitive; done on a smaller scale.

min·im (*min*-im) *n.* 1. An iota; particle; drop. 2. $\frac{1}{60}$ of a fluid dram; $\frac{1}{480}$ of a fluid ounce. 3. *Music.* A half note.—*adj.* Minute; very small.—**min·i·mal** *adj.* Smallest possible. 'A minimal fraction.'

min·i·mize (*min*-im-yz) *v.* [-mized; -miz·ing] To reduce to the smallest degree.—**min·i·mi·za·tion** (min-im-iz-*ay*-shun) *n.*—**min·i·miz·er** *n.*

min·i·mum (*min*-im-um) *n.* [*pl.* -ma, -mums] 1. The smallest amount. 2. The lowest degree.—*adj.* Smallest possible.

minimum wage. 1. The lowest wage possible for a reasonable living standard. 2. The lowest wage fixed by law or by contract which an employer may pay a worker.

min·ing *n.* The process of obtaining minerals from the earth.

min·ion (*min*-yun) *n.* 1. A henchman; crony. 2. A sycophant; servile flatterer. 3. *Printing.* Seven-point type.—*adj.* Delicate; fine.

min·is·ter (*min*-iss-ter) *n.* 1. A clergyman, as a priest, parson, preacher, etc. 2. A director of a department of state. 3. An ambassador;

delegate to a foreign country.—*v.* To attend; care for.

min·is·te·ri·al (min-iss-*teer*-ee-ul) *adj.* 1. Attending; performing service. 2. Administrative; not judicial. 'Ministerial office.' 3. Sacerdotal; relating to the clergy.—**min·is·te·ri·al·ly** *adv.*

minister plenipotentiary. [*pl.* ministers plenipotentiary] An ambassador empowered to negotiate with a foreign country.

min·is·trant (*min*-iss-trunt) *adj.* Administering; performing service.—*n.* A servant; attendant.

min·is·tra·tion (min-iss-*tray*-shun) *n.* Administration; service; stewardship, esp. in a church. —**min·is·tra·tive** (*min*-iss-tray-tiv) *adj.* Ministering; serving.

min·is·try (*min*-iss-tree) *n.* [*pl.* -tries] 1. The function of a clergyman; the clergy in general. 2. The office of a director of state. 3. The body of government ministers.

min·i·ver (*min*-iv-er) *n.* The Siberian squirrel.

mink *n.* A semiaquatic mammal of the weasel family yielding valuable dark-brown fur.

min·ne·sing·er (*min*-eh-sing-er) *n.* A German poet minstrel of the 14th century.

min·now (*min*-oh) *n.* A small fresh-water fish.

Mi·no·an (mih-*noh*-un) *adj.* Relating to ancient Crete.

MINK (1/16 life size)

mi·nor (*my*-ner) *adj.* 1. Less; smaller; not major. 2. Unimportant; petty; inconsiderable. 3. *Music.* Less than major by a half step. —*n.* 1. A juvenile; child; person under legal age. 2. Secondary field of concentration in a course of studies.

mi·nor·i·ty (min-*or*-ih-tee) *n.* [*pl.* -ties] 1. The smaller portion. 2. *Law.* The period between birth and legal age. 3. A racial, political, or religious group totalling under 50 per cent of the population.—*adj.* Belonging to the smaller group.

Mi·nos (*my*-nus) *n. Greek Mythology.* One of the judges of the dead.

Min·o·taur (*min*-uh-tawr) *n. Greek Mythology.* A monster, half man and half bull, who devoured seven maidens and seven youths annually.

min·ster (*min*-ster) *n.* The church of a monastery; any large church.

min·strel (*min*-str'l) *n.* 1. An entertainer giving performances of Negro songs, dances, etc. 2. A medieval troubadour.—**minstrel show.** A variety show performed by a troupe of minstrels.

min·strel·sy *n.* Musical entertainment, esp. the performance of folk music.

mint *n.* 1. An aromatic pungent herb for flavoring. 2. A mint-flavored candy.

mint *n.* A government coining plant.—*adj.* Relating to the mint.—*v.* 1. To coin; manufacture money. 2. Invent; fabricate.—**mint·er** *n.*

min·tage (*min*-tij) *n.* 1. Coin produced in a mint. 2. Duty paid the mint for coining gold or silver.

mint julep. A long drink of bourbon whiskey, mint, sugar, and finely crushed ice.

min·u·end (*min*-yoo-end) *n. Arithmetic.* The number from which a smaller number, the subtrahend, is subtracted.

min·u·et (min-yoo-*et*) *n.* 1. A slow 18th-century dance. 2. A musical piece in $\frac{3}{4}$ time for accompanying the minuet.

mi·nus *adj.* Less; to be subtracted.—*prep. Colloquial.* Without. 'He returned minus his hat.'—*n.* The sign [—] of subtraction.

min·us·cule (mih-*nuss*-kyool) *adj.* Tiny, very small.

min·ute (*min*-it) *n.* 1. $\frac{1}{60}$ of an hour; 60 seconds. 2. A brief space of time. 3. *Geometry & Geography.* $\frac{1}{60}$ of a degree. 4. [*pl.*] A record of the proceedings of a meeting.

mi·nute (my-*nyoot*) *adj.* 1. Small; infinitesimal. 2. Trivial; insignificant. 3. Detailed; noting all particulars.—**min·ute·ly** *adv.* Exactly; precisely; with full details.—**min·ute·ness** *n.*

minute hand. The large hand, marking the minutes on a timepiece.

min·ute·man *n.* [*pl.* -men] A militiaman of the American Revolution, pledged to serve on instant notice in an emergency.

minute steak (*min*-it). A small steak, thinly sliced for quick cooking.

mi·nu·ti·ae (mih-*nyoo*-shee-ee) *n. pl.* Trivia; details.

minx *n.* A saucy girl.

Mi·o·cene (*my*-uh-seen) *adj. Geology.* Relating to an epoch of the Tertiary period.—*n. Geology.* The epoch of the Tertiary period between the Eocene and the Pliocene.

mir·a·cle (*mihr*-uh-k'l) *n.* A wonder; marvel; supernatural event.

miracle play. An ancient dramatization of a Christian legend, esp. the life of a saint.

mi·rac·u·lous (mih-*rak*-yoo-lus) *adj.* 1. Extraordinary; incredible; astonishing. 2. Involving supernatural powers.—**mi·rac·u·lous·ly** *adv.*—**mi·rac·u·lous·ness** *n.*

mi·rage (mer-*ahzh*) *n.* An optical illusion caused by the reflection of light through different densities of air.

mire *n.* Mud.—*v.* [mired; mir·ing] 1. To sink in mud. 2. To soil; sully.

mir·ror (*mihr*-er) *n.* 1. A looking-glass; glass or other surface reflecting images. 2. An example; representation. 'Mirror of grace.'—*v.* To reflect.

mirth (*merth*) *n.* Merriment; hilarity; glee.—**mirth·less** *adj.*—**mirth·less·ly** *adv.*

mirth·ful *adj.* 1. Joyous; gleeful. 2. Festive.—**mirth·ful·ly** *adv.*—**mirth·ful·ness** *n.*

mir·y (*myre*-ee) *adj.* [mir·i·er; mir·i·est] 1. Muddy. 2. Sullied; soiled.—**mir·i·ness** *n.*

mis- *prefix.* Wrong; badly.

misadvise	misformation	misrecite
misarrange	misgauge	misreckon
misbecome	misinfer	misregulate
misbecoming	misinstruct	misremember
misbestow	misintend	misreport
misbrand	mislabel	missend
mis-citation	mislocate	mistaught
mis-cite	mismake	misteach
misclassify	mismarriage	mistell
miscounsel	mismatch	misterm
miscreate	mismove (*n.*)	misthink
misdate	misnumber	misthrow
misdeem	mispage	mistime
misdemean	misplant	mistranscribe
misderive	mispronounce	mistranslate
misemploy	mispronunciation	mistranslation
misesteem	misproportion	mistreat
misestimate	mispunctuate	misvalue
misestimation	mispunctuation	misword
misform	misqualify	miswrite

mis·ad·ven·ture (miss-ad-*ven*-cher) *n.* 1. Misfortune; bad luck. 2. An unfortunate accident.

mis·al·li·ance (miss-uh-*ly*-unss) *n.* An undesirable marriage; bad match.

mis·an·thrope (*miss*-en-throhp) *n.* One who hates people.—**mis·an·throp·ic** (miss-en-*throp*-ik), -**i·cal** *adj.*—**mis·an·throp·i·cal·ly** *adv.*

mis·an·thro·py (mis-*san*-thruh-pee) *n.* Hatred of mankind.—**mis·an·thro·pist** *n.*

mis·ap·ply (miss-uh-*ply*) *v.* [mis·ap·plied; mis·ap·ply·ing] To use for the wrong purpose.—**mis·ap·pli·ca·tion** (miss-ap-lih-*kay*-shun) *n.*

mis·ap·pre·hend (miss-ap-reh-*hend*) *v.* To misunderstand; misconceive.—**mis·ap·pre·hen·sion** (miss-ap-reh-*hen*-shun) *n.*

mis·ap·pro·pri·ate (miss-uh-*proh*-pree-ayt) *v.* [-at·ed; -at·ing] To apply to a wrong use, esp. public funds.—**mis·ap·pro·pri·a·tion** *n.*

mis·be·got·ten (miss-bih-*got*-'n) *adj.* 1. Wretched; doomed to live miserably. 2. Illegitimate; born out of wedlock.

mis·be·have (miss-bih-*hayv*) *v.* [mis·be·haved; mis·be·hav·ing] To misconduct oneself; behave improperly.—**mis·be·hav·ior** *n.*

mis·be·lieve (miss-buh-*leev*) *v.* [-lieved; -lieving] To have an erroneous belief, esp. in a religion.—**mis·be·lief** *n.*—**mis·be·liev·er** *n.*

mis·cal·cu·late (miss-*kal*-kyoo-layt) *v.* [-lat·ed; -lat·ing] To make a wrong estimate; make an error in judgment.—**mis·cal·cu·la·tion** *n.*

mis·call (miss-*kawl*) *v.* To name erroneously.

mis·car·riage (miss-*kair*-ij) *n.* 1. Failure to operate effectively. 2. Abortion; premature expulsion of a fetus.

mis·car·ry (miss-*kair*-ee) *v.* [-car·ried; -car·ry·ing] 1. To fail; suffer defeat. 2. To fail to reach a destination. 3. To expel a fetus prematurely.

mis·ce·gen·a·tion (miss-seh-jeh-*nay*-shun) *n.* Interbreeding between members of different races.

mis·cel·la·ne·ous (miss-uh-*lay*-nee-us) *adj.* Varied; diversified; mixed; of different kinds.—**mis·cel·la·ne·ous·ly** *adv.*— -**ous·ness** *n.*

mis·cel·la·ny (*miss*-uh-lay-nee) *n.* [*pl.* -nies] A mixture; assortment of different things.

mis·chance (miss-*chanss*) *n.* A mishap; unfortunate accident.

mis·chief (*miss*-chif) *n.* 1. Wrong-doing; acts causing annoyance. 2. Harm; damage. 3. A mischievous child.

mis·chie·vous (*miss*-chiv-us) *adj.* Prankish; given to vexing others.—**mis·chie·vous·ly** *adv.*

mis·ci·ble (*miss*-ih-b'l) *adj.* Capable of being mixed.—**mis·ci·bil·i·ty** (miss-ih-*bil*-ih-tee) *n.*

mis·con·ceive (miss-kun-*seev*) *v.* [-ceived; -ceiv·ing] To misunderstand; misapprehend; understand erroneously.— **-con·cep·tion** *n.*

mis·con·duct (miss-*kon*-dukt) *n.* Wrong conduct; improper behavior.—*v.* (miss-kun-*dukt*) To manage wrongly.

mis·con·strue (miss-kun-*stroo*) *v.* [-strued; -stru·ing] To misinterpret; take in a wrong sense.—**mis·con·struc·tion** (miss-kun-*struhk*-shun) *n.*

mis·count (miss-*kownt*) *v.* To add wrongly; miscalculate.

mis·cre·ant (*miss*-kree-ent) *adj.* Unscrupulous; conscienceless.—**mis·cre·ant** *n.*

mis·cue (miss-*kyoo*) *n.* 1. *Billiards.* An ineffectual stroke. 2. An error.—*v.* [mis·cued; mis·cu·ing] 1. To miss the ball with a billiard cue. 2. *Theater.* To fail to answer the cue.

mis·deal (mis-*deel*) *v.* [mis·dealt; mis·deal·ing] To distribute the wrong playing cards to each player.—**mis·deal** *n.*—**mis·deal·er** *n.*

mis·de·mean·or (mis-duh-*meen*-er) *n.* 1. A misdeed; transgression; trespass. 2. *Law.* A petty offense, as disorderly conduct, an ordinance violation, etc.

mis·di·rect (mis-dih-*rekt*) *v.* To give wrong instructions to.—**mis·di·rec·tion** *n.*

mis·do (mis-*doo*) *v.* [mis·did, mis·done; mis·do·ing] To do amiss; do wrong.—**mis·do·er** *n.*

mis·doubt (mis-*dowt*) *v.* To suspect; lack faith in.—**mis·doubt** *n.*

mi·ser (*my*-zer) *n.* A niggard; skinflint; hoarder of wealth.

mis·er·a·ble (*miz*-er-uh-b'l) *adj.* 1. Abject; forlorn; unhappy. 2. Mean; worthless; wretched.—**mis·er·a·bly** *adv.*

mi·ser·ly (*my*-zer-lee) *adj.* Parsimonious; stingy; given to hoarding.—**mi·ser·li·ness** *n.*

mis·er·y (*miz*-er-ee) *n.* [*pl.* -ies] Wretchedness; torment; agony.

mis·fea·sance (mis-*fee*-zunss) *n.* 1. A legal offense. 2. The misuse of power in office.

mis·fire (mis-*fyre*) *v.* [mis·fired; mis·fir·ing] To fail to discharge at the proper time.

mis·fit (mis-*fit*) *n.* 1. A badly fitting garment. 2. A maladjusted person; one unable to adapt to his environment.—*v.* [mis·fit·ted; mis·fit·ting] To match, as garments, badly.

mis·for·tune (mis-*for*-chun) *n.* 1. A mishap; misadventure. 2. Harm; calamity. 3. Bad luck.

mis·give (mis-*giv*) *v.* [mis·gave, mis·giv·en; mis·giv·ing] To be suspicious; be in doubt of.

mis·gov·ern (mis-*guhv*-ern) *v.* To mismanage; administer badly.—**mis·gov·ern·ment** *n.*

mis·guide (mis-*gyde*) *v.* [mis·guid·ed; mis·guid·ing] To exert a bad influence upon; lead astray. —**mis·guid·ance** *n.*—**mis·guid·er** *n.*

mis·han·dle (mis-*han*-d'l) *v.* [mis·han·dled; mis·han·dling] 1. To mismanage, as funds. 2. To abuse; treat badly.

mis·hap (*mis*-hap) *n.* An accident; stroke of bad luck.

mis·in·form (mis-in-*form*) *v.* To advise incorrectly; furnish with untrue data.—**mis·in·form·ant** *n.*—**mis·in·for·ma·tion** (mis-in-fer-*may*-shun) *n.*—**mis·in·form·er** *n.*

mis·in·ter·pret (mis-in-*ter*-pret) *v.* To misconstrue; put a wrong meaning on.—**mis·in·ter·pre·ta·tion** (mis-in-ter-pruh-*tay*-shun) *n.*

mis·judge (mis-*juj*) *v.* [mis·judged; mis·judg·ing] To form a wrong opinion; miscalculate; reckon wrongly.—**mis·judg·ment, mis·judge·ment** *n.*

mis·lay (mis-*lay*) *v.* [mis·laid; mis·lay·ing] To misplace; lose.—**mis·lay·er** *n.*

mis·lead (mis-*leed*) *v.* [mis·led; mis·lead·ing] To deceive; delude; lead astray.—**mis·lead·ing** *adj.*

mis·like (mis-*lyke*) *v.* [-liked; -lik·ing] To dislike; disapprove; have an aversion to.—**mis·like** *n.*—**mis·lik·er** *n.*

mis·man·age (mis-*man*-ij) *v.* [mis·man·aged; mis·man·ag·ing] To handle or conduct inefficiently.—**mis·man·age·ment** *n.*

mis·name (mis-*naym*) *v.* [mis·named; mis·nam·ing] To miscall; call wrongly.

mis·no·mer (mis-*noh*-mer) *n.* A misappellation; name wrongly applied.

mi·sog·a·my (mih-*sog*-uh-mee) *n.* Hatred of marriage.—**mi·sog·a·mist** *n.*

mi·sog·y·ny (mih-*soj*-in-ee) *n.* Hatred of women. —**mi·sog·y·nist** *n.*—**mi·sog·y·nous** *adj.*

mis·place (miss-*playss*) *v.* [mis·placed; mis·plac·ing] 1. To mislay; lose temporarily. 2. To put in the wrong place. 'Misplaced her affections.'—**mis·place·ment** *n.*

mis·play (mis-*play*) *n.* An ill-advised move.

mis·print (mis-*print*) *v.* To make an error in printing.—*n.* (*mis*-print) A typographical error.

mis·quote (mis-*kwoht*) *v.* [mis·quot·ed; mis·quot·ing] To cite incorrectly.

mis·read (mis-*reed*) *v.* [-read (mis-*red*); -read·ing] To misconstrue; misinterpret written matter.

mis·rep·re·sent (mis-rep-ree-*zent*) *v.* To give a false impression of; represent incorrectly. —**mis·rep·re·sen·ta·tion** (-*tay*-shun) *n.*

mis·rule (mis-*rool*) *v.* [mis·ruled; mis·rul·ing] To govern oppressively or inefficiently.—*n.* Confusion; tyranny.

miss *v.* 1. To fail to hit, attain, or meet; miscarry. 2. To be lonely for; feel the want of. 3. To omit; go without.—*n.* A failure to hit.

miss *n.* [*pl.* miss·es] 1. [*cap.*] Title of an unmarried woman. 2. A girl; young woman.

M

mis·sal (*miss-'l*) *n. Ecclesiastical.* The book of the Mass.

mis·shape *v.* [mis·shaped; mis·shap·ing] To deform; shape badly.—**mis·shap·en** *adj.*

mis·sile (*miss-'l*) *n.* A weapon which is hurled; projectile.—*adj.* Designed to be thrown.

miss·ing *adj.* Lost; lacking; not present.

missing link. The hypothetical biped between man and the apes in the scale of evolution.

mis·sion (*mish-un*) *n.* 1. Duty or business of a messenger or agent. 2. Persons sent by authority on some special business. 3. Task in life; calling. 4. Missionary work. 5. A religious charitable organization.—*v.* To send on a mission.—**mis·sion·al** *adj.*—**mis·sion·er** *n.*

mis·sion·ar·y (*mish-un-ehr-ee*) *n.* [*pl.* -ies] One sent to propagate religion.—**mis·sion·ar·y** *adj.*

mis·sis (*miss-iz*) *n. Colloquial.* Mrs.; wife.

Mis·sis·sip·pi (mis-ih-*sip*-ee) *n.* The greatest river of North America, flowing south through central U.S.—**Mis·sis·sip·pi·an** *n. & adj.*

mis·sive (*mis-iv*) *n.* A letter; message.—*adj.* Proceeding from some special source.

Mis·sou·ri (mih-*zoor*-ee) *n.* A large tributary of the Mississippi that joins it near St. Louis. —**Mis·sou·ri·an** *n. & adj.*

mis·spell (miss-*spel*) *v.* [mis·spelled, mis·spelt; mis·spell·ing] To spell incorrectly.—**mis·spel·ling** *n.*

mis·spend (miss-*spend*) *v.* [mis·spent; mis·spend·ing] To waste; consume to no purpose.

mis·state (miss-*stayt*) *v.* [mis·stat·ed; mis·stat·ing] To put incorrectly; misrepresent.—**mis·state·ment** *n.*

mis·step (miss-*step*) *n.* A wrong step or move.

mist *n.* 1. Water vapor suspended in the air; fog. 2. Any obscuring cloud.—**mist** *v.*

mis·tak·a·ble (miss-*tayk*-uh-b'l) *adj.* Ambiguous; capable of being misunderstood.—**mis·tak·a·bly** *adj.*

mis·take (miss-*tayk*) *v.* [mis·took, mis·tak·en; mis·tak·ing] 1. To misunderstand; misjudge; misconceive. 2. To take erroneously for another; select wrongly. 3. To commit an error.—*n.* An error; blunder; slip; misconception.

mis·tak·en (miss-*tayk*-en) *adj.* Erroneous; false; wrong.

Mis·ter (*miss*-ter) *n.* 1. A title prefixed to the name of a man, written in the abbreviated form *Mr.* 2. *Colloquial.* Sir; chap.

mis·tle·toe *n.* A green, parasitic, berry-bearing plant, used in Christmas decorations.

MISTLETOE

mis·tral (*miss*-tr'l) *n.* A cold, violent wind of the northern Mediterranean.

mis·treat (miss-*treet*) *v.* To abuse; deal cruelly or unjustly with.— -treat·ment *n.*

mis·tress (*miss*-triss) *n.* 1. [*cap.*] *Archaic & Southern U.S.* Miss or Mrs. 2. A female paramour; an illicit sweetheart. 3. A woman supervisor in some establishment or sphere.

mis·tri·al (*miss*-try-ul) *n. Law.* A trial invalidated by some error in procedure.

mis·trust (miss-*trust*) *v.* To suspect; doubt; regard with jealousy.—*n.* Suspicion.—**mis·trust·er** *n.*—**mis·trust·ing·ly** *adv.*

mis·trust·ful *adj.* Suspicious; lacking confidence.— -trust·ful·ly *adv.*— -trust·ful·ness *n.*

mist·y *adj.* [mist·i·er; mist·i·est] 1. Foggy; hazy; filled with vapor. 2. Dim; obscured; uncertainly defined.— -i·ly *adv.*— -i·ness *n.*

mis·un·der·stand (miss-un-der-*stand*) *v.* [-stood; -stand·ing] To misinterpret a meaning; mistake; misconceive.—**mis·un·der·stand·ing** *n.*

mis·un·der·stood *adj.* Unappreciated; not apprehended.

mis·us·age (miss-*yooss*-ij) *n.* 1. Incorrect application, as of a word. 2. Abuse; maltreatment.

mis·use (miss-*yooss*) *n.* Incorrect or abusive use; ill treatment.—*v.* (miss-*yooz*) [mis·used; mis·us·ing].—**mis·us·er** *n.*

mite *n.* 1. One of a large group of small insects with chewing, rather than sucking, mouth parts. 2. *Colloquial.* A tiny person or thing.

mi·ter, mi·tre (*myte*-er) *n.* 1. An ecclesiastical cap or head ornament, pointed and cleft at the top. 2. Also **miter·joint.** A juncture, usually right-angled, formed by two pieces, each of which has a 45° bevel.—*v.* 1. To adorn with a miter; raise to episcopal rank. 2. To join with a miter joint.

miter box. A small, square trough with guides in the vertical sides to allow cutting a 45° angle.

mit·i·gate (*mit*-uh-gayt) *v.* [-gat·ed; -gat·ing] To make less painful or harsh; lessen; alleviate.—**mit·i·ga·ble** *adj.*—**mit·i·ga·tion** *n.*—**mit·i·ga·tive** *adj.*—**mit·i·ga·tor** *n.*

mitt *n.* 1. A hand covering having a thumb but no individual finger sheathes. 2. *Baseball.* A protective covering for the hand having a large round pad over the palm and fingers.

mit·ten (*mit*-'n) *n.* A mitt to protect the hand from cold.

mix *v.* [mixed, mixt; mix·ing] 1. To blend; unite by mingling. 2. To associate; hold intercourse with.—*n.* A blended or scrambled preparation.—**mix·er** *n.* 1. A sociable, friendly person. 2. A machine that mixes or scrambles. 3. A beverage used in mixed alcoholic drinks.

mixed (*mikst*) *adj.* 1. Consisting of both sexes or of various kinds. 2. Blended; mingled.

mixed number. A number containing both whole and fractional quantities.

mix·ture (*miks*-cher) *n.* 1. An assortment;

mass of miscellaneous ingredients.   2. A scrambling or throwing together.

mix-up *n.* A mistake arising out of confusion; misunderstanding.

miz·zen *n.* Fore-and-aft sail on the mizzenmast. —*adj.* Relating to the mizzenmast.

miz·zen·mast *n.* The third mast aft in a vessel having more than two masts; the after mast of a yawl or ketch.

mo·a (*moh*-uh) *n.* A large, wingless bird of New Zealand, now extinct.

moan (*mohn*) *n.* A low, dull sound caused by grief or pain; lamentation.—*v.* To utter a distressed sound; grieve.—**moan·ing·ly** *adv.*

moat (*moht*) *n.* A defensive trench surrounding a castle and often filled with water.

mob *n.* A disorderly crowd; multitude of people.—*v.* [mobbed; mob·bing] To attack in a crowd; assail.—**mob·ber** *n.*—**mob·bish** *adj.*

mob·cap (*mob*-kap) *n.* A women's knit cap, completely covering the hair.

mo·bile (*moh*-b'l, -beel) *adj.* 1. Easily movable. 2. Changeable.—**mo·bil·i·ty** (moh-*bil*-uh-tee) *n.* 1. Adaptibility to motion. 2. Readiness to move or change.

mo·bile (moh-*beel*) *n.* An ornamental structure of finely balanced parts which move in a slight breeze.

mo·bi·lize (*moh*-buh-lyze) *v.* [mo·bi·lized; mo·bi·liz·ing] 1. *Military.* To assemble and prepare for active service, as an army. 2. To make movable.—**mo·bil·i·za·tion** *n.*

moc·ca·sin (*mok*-uh-sin) *n.* 1. A soft-soled shoe made of deerskin or other soft leather, originated by North American Indians. 2. A venomous, dark brown water snake of the southern U.S. Also called *water moccasin* and *cotton-mouth.*

MOCCASIN

moccasin flower. The common name of any flower of the orchid family; ladyslipper, the state flower of Minnesota.

Mo·cha (*moh*-kuh) *n.* 1. A coffee grown in Arabia. 2. A soft leather.

mo·cha (*moh*-kuh) *n.* 1. A flavor of coffee and chocolate combined. 2. A beverage of chocolate and coffee.

mock *v.* 1. To mimic; ape. 2. To ridicule; deride; laugh at.—*n.* A sneer; gibe; contempt; derision.—*adj.* Counterfeit; false; assumed. —**mock·er** *n.*—**mock·er·y** *n.*—**mock·ing·ly** *adv.*

mock-he·ro·ic *adj.* Parodying the heroic.

mock·ing·bird *n.* A bird of the thrasher family, of ash-brown color above and lighter below, with a fine song of its own and a faculty for imitating other birds' songs.

mock orange. A family of shrubs with creamy white, fragrant flowers.

mock-up *n.* Full-scale replica, usually in plaster-board or papier-mâché, of an airplane for test or instruction purposes.—**mock-up** *v.*

mod·al *adj.* 1. Relating to a manner or form. 2. Pertaining to mode, not essence.—**mo·dal·i·ty** *n.*

mode *n.* 1. Manner; way. 2. Fashion; style; custom. 3. *Music.* The arrangement of intervals within a scale establishing the tonality of music based upon it.

mod·el (*mod*-'l) *n.* 1. A form in miniature; pattern. 2. A copy; imitation. 3. A worthy example; pattern; standard. 4. A person who poses for an artist. 5. A woman who wears clothing to display it for sale.—*v.* [mod·eled, mod·elled; mod·el·ing, mod·el·ling] 1. To shape; form; imitate. 2. To work in plastic material. 3. To act as a subject in painting, sculpture, etc.—**mod·el·er, mod·el·ler** *n.*

mod·er·ate (*mod*-er-it) *adj.* Temperate; not extreme; not violent.—*n.* One who holds views neither reactionary nor radical; a believer in a middle course.—*v.* (*mod*-er-ayt) [mod·er·at·ed; -at·ing] 1. To mitigate; restrain; lessen; quiet. 2. To act as a moderator.—**mod·er·ate·ly** *adv.* —**mod·er·ate·ness** *n.*

mod·er·a·tion (mod-er-*ay*-shun) *n.* Restraint; freedom from excess; forbearance.

mod·er·a·tor (*mod*-er-ay-ter) *n.* 1. A presiding officer, as of a debate. 2. *Presbyterian Church.* One who presides at any meeting of church officers.

mod·ern (*mod*-ern) *adj.* Pertaining to the present; recent; new; up-to-date.—*n.* 1. A person having up-to-date attitudes. 2. An artist of the modern school. 3. *Printing.* A style of regularly formed heavy type, contrasted with *old style.*—**mod·ern·ly** *adv.*—**mod·ern·ness** *n.*

mod·ern·ism (*mod*-ern-izm) *n.* 1. A current custom or usage. 2. [*cap.*] A movement in the churches seeking to reconcile modern scientific discovery and method with traditional dogma.—**mod·ern·ist** *n.* & *adj.*

mod·ern·is·tic (mod-ern-*iss*-tik) *adj.* Pertaining to an exaggerated form of modern design.

mo·der·ni·ty (muh-*der*-nih-tee) *n.* [*pl.* -ties] Contemporaneousness; newness.

mod·ern·ize (*mod*-ern-yze) *v.* [mod·ern·ized; mod·ern·iz·ing] To adapt to present mode or design; give an up-to-date appearance.—**mod·ern·i·za·tion** (mod-ern-ih-*zay*-shun) *n.*

mod·est *adj.* 1. Unobtrusive; retiring; unassuming. 2. Decorous; chaste. 3. Moderate; not excessive.—**mod·est·ly** *adv.*

mod·es·ty (*mod*-ess-tee) *n.* 1. Propriety; decency. 2. Humility; diffidence in displaying one's accomplishments.

mod·i·cum (*mod*-ih-kum) *n.* [*pl.* -cums] A small quantity; a little.

mod·i·fi·ca·tion (mod-ih-fih-*kay*-shun) *n.* Change; alteration; reduction.

mod·i·fy (*mod*-ih-fy) *v.* [mod·i·fied; mod·i·fy·ing] 1. To alter; change; vary. 2. To reduce; limit; make more conservative.—**mod·i·fi·a·ble** *adj.*—**mod·i·fi·er** *n.*

M

mod·ish (*mohd*-ish) *adj.* Fashionable; stylish. —**mod·ish·ly** *adv.*—**mod·ish·ness** *n.*

mo·diste (moh-*deest*) *n.* A milliner or dressmaker.

mod·u·lar (*mod*-yoo-ler) *adj.* Pertaining to a standard unit of measurement of some condition, activity, effect, etc.

mod·u·late (*mod*-yoo-layt) *v.* [mod·u·lat·ed; mod·u·lat·ing] 1. To vary or inflect in tone; adjust pleasingly; tone down. 2. *Music.* To change from one key to another. 3. *Electricity.* To vary wave frequency by imposition of lower frequency waves.—**mod·u·la·tor** *n.* —**mod·u·la·to·ry** (*mod*-yoo-luh-tor-ee) *adj.*

mod·u·la·tion (mod-yoo-*lay*-shun) *n.* 1. Softening of tone; variation of inflection. 2. *Music.* Transition from one key to another. 3. *Radio.* Variation of a high-frequency carrier wave by a signal wave. *See:* **amplitude modulation** and **frequency modulation.**

mod·ule (*mod*-yool) *n. Architecture.* A dimension selected to measure the relative proportions of various parts of a building.

mod·u·lus (*mod*-yoo-lus) *n.* [*pl.* -li] A constant quantity expressing a unit measurement of a function or property which varies proportionately with another property.

Mo·gul (*moh*-g'l) *n.* 1. A Mongolian; one of the founders of the Mongol Empire in India. 2. [*not cap.*] A person wielding great power or influence.

mo·hair (*moh*-hair) *n.* Hair of the Angora goat of Asia Minor, or the cloth woven from it.

Mo·ham·med (moh-*ham*-ed) *n.* Also **Mo·ham·mad, Ma·hom·et.** The prophet and founder of the religious system of Islam as recorded in the Koran.

Mo·ham·me·dan (moh-*ham*-uh-d'n) *adj.* Pertaining to Mohammed or to his religious system.—*n.* A believer in Islam.—**Mo·ham·me·dan·ism** *n.*

Mo·hawk (*moh*-hawk) *n.* One of a small but aggressive tribe of Iroquois Indians once living along the Mohawk Valley of New York State.

Mo·hi·can (moh-*hee*-k'n) *n.* Also **Mo·he·gan.** One of an Indian tribe found in Connecticut and along the Hudson Valley.

moi·e·ty (*moy*-uh-tee) *n.* [*pl.* -ties] Portion; share; half.

moil *v.* To labor; toil.—**moil·er** *n.*

moire (mwahr) *n.* Watered silk.

moi·ré (mwahr-*ay*) *adj.* Having a watered effect. —*n.* A watered effect in textiles.

moist *adj.* Damp; moderately wet.—**moist·ness** *n.*

mois·ten (*moy*-s'n) *v.* To dampen; wet slightly; become moist.—**mois·ten·er** *n.*

mois·ture (*moyss*-cher) *n.* A slight wetness.

mo·lar (*moh*-ler) *n.* Grinding tooth, one of three back teeth on each side of each jaw. —*adj.* Grinding.

mo·las·ses (muh-*lass*-ez) *n.* [*pl.* mo·las·ses] A syrup derived from sugar during refining.

mold, mould (mohld) *n.* Soft, rich earth; humus.

mold, mould *n.* One of a number of minute parasitic fungi; the woolly patches caused by fungi, esp. on vegetable matter.—*v.* To undergo fungous decay.

mold, mould *n.* 1. Matrix of clay or metal into which a liquid metal or plastic is cast to receive its form; pattern. 2. Shape; form; character.—*v.* To shape; model; fashion. —**mold·a·ble, mould·a·ble** *adj.* Capable of being formed.—**mold·er, mould·er** *n.*

mold·board *n.* Curved section of a plow which turns over the furrow.

mold·er, mould·er *v.* To crumble; turn into dust; waste away gradually.

mold·ing, mould·ing *n. Architecture.* Variation of the flat surface of a projection or cavity by ornamentation with a continuous, decorative, profiled surface.

MOLDING

mold·y *adj.* [mold·i·er, mold·i·est]. Also **mould·y.** Covered with mold; musty; decaying.—**mold·i·ness, mould·i·ness** *n.*

mole *n.* A small, brownish, raised spot on human skin.

mole *n.* Small animal with tiny concealed eyes and very soft, shining fur, which burrows just under the ground surface.

mole *n.* A massive stone pier used as a breakwater.

mo·lec·u·lar (mol-*ek*-yoo-ler) *adj.* Pertaining to, or consisting of, molecules.

molecular film. A layer of a substance one molecule in thickness; thinnest possible film.

mol·e·cule (*mol*-uh-kyool) *n.* The smallest unit of a chemical substance in which its chemical properties are retained.

mole·hill *n.* 1. Small hill of earth thrown up by moles burrowing underground. 2. Something insignificant.

mole·skin *n.* A strong cotton fabric with a soft texture, used for work clothing.

mo·lest (muh-*lest*) *v.* To trouble; disturb; harass; vex.—**mo·lest·er** *n.*

mo·les·ta·tion (moh-less-*tay*-shun) *n.* Disturbance; harassment; annoyance.

moll *n. Slang.* A female tough, esp. a companion of gangsters.

mol·li·fy (*mol*-ih-fy) *v.* [mol·li·fied; mol·li·fy·ing] 1. To soften; assuage. 2. To calm; appease.—**mol·li·fi·ca·tion** (mol-ih-fih-*kay*-shun) *n.*—**mol·li·fi·er** *n.*—**mol·li·fy·ing·ly** *adv.*

mol·lusk (*mol*-usk) *n.* One of a large group of invertebrate animals, the mollusca, including scallops, oysters, mussels, snails, slugs, cuttlefish, squids, etc.—**mol·lus·can** *n. & adj.*

mol·ly·cod·dle (*mol*-ee-kod-'l) *n.* An effeminate or pampered person.—*v.* [-dled; -dling] To pamper.—**mol·ly·cod·dler** *n.*

Mo·loch (*moh*-lok) *n.* Also **Mo·lech.** God of the Phoenicians worshiped by offering human sacrifices; any deadly influence demanding sacrifice.

molt, moult (*mohlt*) *v.* To shed, as feathers, hair, horns, etc.—*n.* Shedding or changing, as feathers in birds.—**molt·er, moult·er** *n.*

mol·ten (*mohl*-t'n) *adj.* Melted; made of melted metal.

Molotov cocktail. A grenade consisting of a bottle of gasoline, used by the Red Army against tanks, early in World War II.

mo·lyb·de·num (muh-*lib*-deh-num) *n.* Silvery white metallic element, used on steel alloys. (*Symbol:* Mo).—**-lyb·de·nous, -lyb·dic** *adj.*

mo·ment (*moh*-m'nt) *n.* 1. Brief space of time; instant. 2. Importance; value; consequence.

mo·men·ta·ry (*moh*-m'n-tehr-ee) *adj.* Lasting only a moment; of brief duration.—**mo·men·tar·i·ly** *adv.*—Briefly.—**mo·men·tar·i·ness** *n.*

mo·ment·ly *adv.* From minute to minute; at any instant.

mo·men·tous (moh-*men*-tus) *adj.* Very important; weighty.—**mo·men·tous·ly** *adv.*

mo·men·tum (moh-*men*-tum) *n.* [*pl.* -ta, -tums] Force in motion; the product of mass and velocity; impetus.

mon·ad (*moh*-nad) *n.* 1. Ultimate unit; the primary constituent of matter. 2. *Zoology.* Single-celled organism. 3. *Chemistry.* Univalent element.—**mo·nad·ic** (moh-*nad*-ik), **mo·nad·i·cal** *adj.*

mon·arch (*mon*-erk) *n.* 1. A sovereign; supreme ruler; potentate. 2. One like a supreme ruler; one superior to all others of his kind.—**mo·nar·chal** (muh-*nahr*-k'l), **mo·nar·chi·al** *adj.* Pertaining to a ruler; sovereign.

mo·nar·chic (muh-*nahr*-kik) *adj.* Also **mo·nar·chi·cal.** 1. Vested in a single ruler. 2. Pertaining to monarchy.—**mo·nar·chi·cal·ly** *adv.*

mon·arch·ist (*mon*-er-kist) *n.* A believer in, or advocater of, the ruling power of a single individual.—**mon·arch·ism** *n.*—**mon·arch·is·tic** (mon-er-*kiss*-tik) *adj.*

mon·arch·y (*mon*-er-kee) *n.* [*pl.* -ies] 1. A state ruled, absolutely or nominally, by a hereditary sovereign. 2. Kingdom; empire.

mon·as·ter·y (*mon*-ess-tehr-ee) *n.* [*pl.* -ies] Religious house of retirement from worldly concerns; usually, a house for monks.—**mon·as·te·ri·al** (mon-ess-*teer*-ee-ul) *adj.*

mo·nas·tic (muh-*nass*-tik) *adj.* Pertaining to a monastery, or to the vows of poverty, chastity, and obedience; secluded; retired.—*n.* Member of a monastery; monk.—**mo·nas·ti·cal** *adj.*—**mo·nas·ti·cal·ly** *adv.*

Mon·day (*mun*-dee) *n.* The second day of the week.

Mo·nel (moh-*nel*) *n.* Also **Monel metal.** Trademark name of a copper-nickel alloy.

mon·e·tar·y (*mon*-uh-tehr-ee) *adj.* Pertaining to, or consisting of, money or currency.—**mon·e·tar·i·ly** *adv.*

mon·e·tize (*mon*-uh-tyze) *v.* [mon·e·tized; mon·e·tiz·ing] To accept officially as a medium of exchange; to designate as money.—**mon·e·ti·za·tion** (mon-eh-tih-*zay*-shun) *n.*

mon·ey (*mun*-ee) *n.* [*pl.* mon·eys] 1. Stamped metal or paper used as a medium of exchange. 2. A standard of value and an equivalent for commodities; a circulating medium, as banknotes, letters of credit. 3. Wealth; riches.

money bag	money grubber	money making
money-bloated	money grubbing	moneymonger
money-bound	money tender	money mongering
money box	money-mad	money saver
money changer	money maker	money saving

mon·eyed (*mun*-eed) *adj.* Rich; wealthy.

money order. A post-office form for the transfer, at small charge, of money by mail.

mon·ger (*mung*-ger) *n.* Trader; dealer, esp. an unscrupulous one.

Mon·gol (*mong*-g'l) *n.* Native of Mongolia. —*adj.* Pertaining to its people or language.

Mon·go·li·an *adj.* 1. Pertaining to Mongolia. 2. Denoting a people inhabiting most of Asia.

Mon·gol·ism (*mong*-g'l-izm) *n.* Also **Mon·go·li·an** or **Mongoloid idiocy.** *Medicine.* Mental deficiency marked by a flattened skull, slanted eye-slits, small fingers, and happy disposition.

mon·goose (*mong*-gooss) *n.* [*pl.* -goos·es] A weasel-like animal of India, a dexterous serpent-killer.

mon·grel (*mong*-gr'l) *n.* Any creature of a mixed breed.—*adj.* Of different kinds.

M

mon·i·ker, mon·ick·er (*mon*-ik-er) *n. Slang.* A name or nickname.

MONGOOSE (1/15 life size)

mon·ism (*mon*-izm) *n. Philosophy.* A doctrine holding that there is but one ultimate substance from which all things and events are developed.—**mon·ist** *n.* A believer in monism. —**mo·nis·tic** (muh-*niss*-tik), **mo·nis·ti·cal** *adj.*

mo·ni·tion (muh-*nish*-un) *n.* Warning; admonition; intimation.

mon·i·tor (*mon*-ih-ter) *n.* 1. One who gives advice or caution. 2. A pupil appointed to supervise his classmates. 3. *Radio.* A listening post for policing the air lanes.—*v. Radio.* To check carefully the content and quality of a broadcast.—**mon·i·to·ri·al** (mon-ih-*tor*-ee-ul) *adj.* Pertaining to supervision by a student.

mon·i·to·ry (*mon*-ih-tor-ee) *adj.* Cautioning.

monk (*munk*) *n.* A man who retires from worldly things to devote himself to religion; member of a monastic order.

mon·key (*munk*-ee) *n.* [*pl.* -keys] 1. Any of the Primates having long tails, and nails on all toes and fingers, as opposed to apes, lemurs, or baboons. 2. A mischief maker.—*v.* To finger; meddle with.—**mon·key·ish** *adj.*

MONKEY

mon·key·shine *n. Colloquial.* Prank; antic.

monkey wrench. A grasping tool with a jaw adjustable to the size of the nut to be turned.

monk·ish *adj.* Like a monk; monastic; usually applied opprobriously.—**monk·ish·ly** *adv.*— **-ish·ness** *n.*

MONKEY WRENCH

monks·hood *n.* A plant with helmet-shaped flowers. Its poisonous roots yield the drug aconite.

mon·o·chord (*mon*-uh-kord) *n. Music.* An ancient Greek instrument with a single string and a movable bridge, used to measure the scale.

mon·o·chrome (*mon*-uh-krohm) *n.* A painting in one color, with variations only in light and shade.—**mon·o·chro·mic, -mi·cal** *adj.*—**mon·o·chro·mist** *n.*

mon·o·cle (*mon*-uh-k'l) *n.* Eyeglass with a single lens, held by muscular contraction in one eye.—**mon·o·cled** *adj.*

mon·o·cot·y·le·don (mon-uh-kot-uh-*lee*-dun) *n. Botany.* Plant having a single seed leaf and flower parts in multiples of three, as lilies, orchids, cereal grains.

mon·o·dy (*mon*-uh-dee) *n.* [*pl.* -dies] 1. A mournful song. 2. Song for a single voice.—**mo·nod·ic, mo·nod·i·cal** *adj.*

mo·nog·a·my (muh-*nog*-uh-mee) *n.* Marriage to one person at a time.—**mo·nog·a·mist** *n.*—**mo·nog·a·mous** *adj.*

mon·o·gram (*mon*-uh-gram) *n.* A figure containing two or more interwoven letters.—**mon·o·gram·mat·ic** (mon-uh-gruh-*mat*-ik) *adj.*

mon·o·graph (*mon*-uh-graf) *n.* A detailed description dealing with a single subject.—*v.* To write a monograph.—**mo·nog·ra·pher** (muh-*nog*-ruh-fer) *n.*—**mon·o·graph·ic** *adj.*

mon·o·lith (*mon*-uh-lith) *n.* Pillar or column made of a single stone.—**mon·o·lith·ic** (mon-uh-*lith*-ik) *adj.*

mon·o·log, mon·o·logue (*mon*-uh-lawg) *n.* 1. Soliloquy; a long dissertation; monopoly of conversation. 2. *Theater.* A play, or part of one, in which the actor speaks alone.—**mon·o·log·ic** (mon-uh-*loj*-ik), **-i·cal** *adj.*—**mon·ol·o·gist** (*mon*-uh-lawg-ist; mon-*ol*-uh-jist) *n.*

mon·o·ma·ni·a (mon-uh-*may*-nee-uh) *n.* Abnormal concentration on a single subject.—**mon·o·ma·ni·ac** *n.*—**mon·o·ma·ni·a·cal** (mon-uh-muh-*ny*-ik-ul), *adj.*

mon·o·met·al·lism (mon-uh-*met*-'l-izm) *n.* System of currency based on a single metallic standard.—**mon·o·me·tal·lic** (mon-uh-muh-*tal*-ik) *adj.*

mon·o·plane (*mon*-uh-playn) *n.* Airplane with one wing.

mo·nop·o·lize (muh-*nop*-uh-lyze) *v.* [-lized; -lizing] To control exclusively; engross.—**mo·nop·o·li·za·tion** (muh-nop-uh-liz-*ay*-shun) *n.*—**mo·nop·o·liz·er** *n.*

mo·nop·o·ly (mon-*op*-uh-lee) *n.* [*pl.* -lies] 1. An exclusive privilege or power. 2. Possession to

the exclusion of others. 3. A corporation or cartel which effectively controls the production and selling price of any commodity. 4. [*cap.*] Trade-mark name of a game of chance.—**mo·nop·o·lism** *n.* Lack of free competition.—**mo·nop·o·list** *n. & adj.*—**mo·nop·o·lis·tic** *adj.*

mon·o·rail (*mon*-oh-rayl) *adj.* Having a single rail. 'Monorail train.'

mon·o·syl·la·ble (*mon*-uh-sil-uh-b'l) *n.* A word having only one syllable. '*An* and *be* are monosyllables.'—**mon·o·syl·lab·ic** (mon-uh-sil-*ab*-ik) *adj.*—**mon·o·syl·lab·i·cal·ly** *adv.*

mon·o·the·ism (*mon*-uh-thee-ism) *n.* Worship of a single god.—**mon·o·the·ist** *n. & adj.*—**mon·o·the·is·tic, -ti·cal** *adj.*— **-ti·cal·ly** *adv.*

mon·o·tone (*mon*-uh-tohn) *n.* Monotony of sound; speech or sound of unvaried pitch.

mo·not·o·nous (muh-*not*-uh-nuss) *adj.* Tiresome; boring through lack of variety in tone or pitch.— **-nous·ly** *adv.*— **-nous·ness** *n.*

mo·not·o·ny (muh-*not*-uh-nee) *n.* 1. Sameness; fatiguing lack of variation. 2. Continued uniformity of pitch or sound.

Mon·o·type (*mon*-uh-type) *n. Printing.* Trade name for a keyboard-operated typesetting machine which perforates a ribbon; also, the machine which casts type from the perforated tape.

mon·ox·ide (mon-*oks*-yde) *n.* A compound of one oxygen atom combined with a positive ion.

Monroe Doctrine (mun-*roh*). A declaration by President Monroe in 1823 that the U.S. would permit no interference in Western Hemisphere affairs by a foreign power.

mon·sieur (meh-*syer*) *n.* [*pl.* messieurs] French title corresponding to *Mr.* or *sir.*

mon·si·gnor (mon-*seen*-yer) *n.* [*pl.* -gnor·i] A title of honor conferred on prelates of the Roman Catholic Church. *Abbr. Mgr., Msgr.*

mon·soon (mon-*soon*) *n.* A periodic wind, esp. a trade wind in the Indian Ocean which blows in one direction for several months, then reverses.

mon·ster (*mon*-ster) *n.* Any departure from the normal type; abnormal being, esp. a horrible creature.—*adj.* Horrible; monstrous.

mon·stros·i·ty (mon-*stross*-uh-tee) *n.* [*pl.* -ties] A freak; abnormal being or condition.

mon·strous (*mon*-struss) *adj.* 1. Abnormal; unnatural; freakish; extraordinary. 2. Horrible; loathsome; ridiculous. 3. Enormous; huge.—**mon·strous·ly** *adv.*—**mon·strous·ness** *n.*

mon·tage (mon-*tahzh*) *n. Photography.* Several pictures, or elements thereof, imposed upon a single background to create a unified effect.

mon·te (*mon*-tay) *n.* A Spanish card game.

Monte Carlo (mon-teh *kahr*-loh). A famous gambling center on the Riviera, located in Monaco.

month (*munth*) *n.* One of the twelve divisions of the year.

month·ly (*munth*-lee) *adj.* 1. Occurring once a month or every month. 2. Lasting for a month.—*adv.* Once a month; every month. —*n.* [*pl.* -lies] 1. A periodical issued each month. 2. Menstrual period.

mon·u·ment (*mon*-yoo-m'nt) *n.* 1. A stone pillar or other memorial perpetuating the memory of a person or event. 2. Any enduring evidence or example.—mon·u·men·tal *adj.* Worthy of long remembering; great; transcendingly important. '*King Lear* is a monumental tragedy.'—mon·u·ment·al·ly *adv.*

moo *n.* The vocal sound made by a cow.—moo *v.*

mooch *v. Slang.* To sponge; borrow with no intent of repayment.—mooch·er *n.*

mood *n. Grammar.* An indication by verb form of the manner of concept of an action or fact. English has three moods: indicative ('I am'), subjunctive ('If I were'), and imperative ('Go home').

mood *n.* 1. State of mind; disposition. 2. A morbid, sulky, or distracted state of mind.

mood·y (*mood*-ee) *adj.* [mood·i·er; mood·i·est] 1. Depressed; peevish; melancholy. 2. Alternately withdrawn and sociable; changing mood frequently.—mood·i·ly *adv.*—mood·i·ness *n.*

moo·la (*moo*-luh) *n. Slang.* Money.

moon *n.* 1. A satellite of a planet. 2. The large, luminous heavenly body, a satelite of the earth, which shines at night by light reflected from the sun. 3. A lunar month.—*v.* To act as if dazed; pine; be moody.

moon-blanched	moonfaced	moonray
moon-blind	moonfall	moonrise
moon-born	moonfish	moonsail
moon bright	moon gazing	moonset
moon-charmed	moon glade	moonshade
moon-crowned	moonglow	moonshining
moondown	moonlight	moonsick
moondrop	moonmad	moontide
mooneyed	moonpath	moon-touched

moon·beam (*moon*-beem) *n.* A ray of light from the moon.

moon calf. A fool; dolt; moody lad.

moon·lit *adj.* Illuminated by moonbeams.

moon·mad·ness *n.* A form of temporary introspective dementia induced by overmuch exposure to and study of the moon.—moon·mad *adj.*—moon·mad·ly *adv.*

moon·shine *n.* 1. *Slang.* Illegal, home-distilled whisky. 2. Light from the moon.

moon·shin·er *n.* A clandestine distiller of, or dealer in, whisky.

moon·stone *n.* A gem of translucent feldspar.

moon·struck, -strick·en *n.* Crazy; lunatic.

moon·y *adj.* [moon·i·er; moon·i·est] *Colloquial.* Bewildered; in a daze.

moor *n.* A heath; barren tract of land; peat bog. —moor·ish *adj.*—moor·land *n.*

moor *v.* To tie a ship securely; anchor; tie up. —moor·age *n.* A place for mooring.

Moor *n.* An Arab; native of North Africa. —Moor·ish *adj.*

moor·ing *n.* 1. Securing a ship by anchors or lines. 2. Place where ships are moored.

moose (*mooss*) *n.* The largest member of the deer family, common in Canada.

moot *adj.* Debatable; arguable. 'The closed shop is a moot point.'—*n.* A debate; presentation of arguments. —moot *v.*— -er *n.*

mop *n.* 1. A cleaning device consisting of cloth or fibers fixed to a long handle. 2. A head of stringy, unkempt hair.—*v.* [mopped; mop·ping] To clean or wipe up.

MOOSE

mope (*mohp*) *v.* [moped; mop·ing] To move sluggishly; be listless or dispirited.—*n.* A drone; dull or listless person.—mop·ish *adj.* —mop·ish·ly *adv.*—mop·ish·ness *n.*

mop·pet (*mop*-et) *n.* A rag doll; small child.

mo·raine (moh-*rayn*) *n.* Sand, rock, and other debris deposited by glaciers.—mo·rain·ic *adj.*

mor·al (*mor*-ul) *adj.* 1. Ethical; good; not transgressing. 2. Pertaining to morality or character. 3. Sufficient for all practical purposes, but not demonstrable. 'A moral certainty that he is wrong.'—*n.* 1. Essence; truth. 'The moral is: don't hurry.' 2. [*pl.*] Behavior in respect to accepted standards of conduct. 3. [*pl.*] Ethics. 4. Truth inculcated by a fable or other story.—mor·al·ly *adv.*

mo·rale (mor-*al*) *n.* 1. Mental and moral fiber. 2. Spirit; enthusiasm. 3. Unified feeling among a group. 'The morale of the men is good.'

mor·al·ist (*mor*-uh-list) *n.* One who preaches conformity to accepted standards of behavior and conduct.—mor·al·is·tic *adj.*

mo·ral·i·ty (mor-*al*-ih-tee) *n.* [*pl.* -ties] 1. The science of ethics. 2. Virtue; exemplary behavior. 3. Conformity to accepted patterns of behavior.

mor·al·ize(mor-uh-lyze) *v.* [-ized; -iz·ing] 1. To draw a moral from; make a lesson of. 2. To induce morality; make moral.—mor·al·i·za·tion (mor-uh-liz-*ay*-shun) *n.*—mor·al·iz·er *n.*

mo·rass (muh-*rass*) *n.* A bog; swamp; fen.

mor·a·to·ri·um (mor-uh-*tor*-ee-um) *n.* [*pl.* -ri·a] *Law.* A period of respite granted in fulfilling obligations, esp. in certain emergencies.

Mo·ra·vi·an (muh-*ray*-vee-un) *n.* 1. Inhabitant of the Czechoslovakian province of Moravia. 2. One of a religious sect more commonly called United Brethren.—Mo·ra·vi·an *adj.*

mor·bid (*mor*-bid) *adj.* 1. Despondent; abnormally melancholic. 2. Diseased.—mor·bid·i·ty (mor-*bid*-ih-tee) *n.*—mor·bid·ly *adv.* —mor·bid·ness *n.*

mor·dant (*mor*-d'nt) *adj.* 1. Biting; sarcastic; caustic; severe. 2. A fixing color or dye.—*n.* A substance which fixes a dye.

more *adj.* [*compar.* of *many, much*; *superl.* most] Greater; additional; opposed to *less.*—*adv.*

M

1. In a greater extent or quantity. 2. Further; besides; in addition.—*n.* 1. A greater amount or degree. 2. Anything in addition.

more·o·ver (mor-*oh*-ver) *adv.* Besides; in addition; likewise.

mo·res (*mor*-eez) *n. pl.* Customs; moral principles developed out of usage; folkways.

nor·ga·nat·ic (mor-guh-*nat*-ik) *adj.* Denoting a marriage between royalty and one of low rank, in which the husband or wife and the children do not share the rank or succeed to the entailed estate.—**mor·ga·nat·i·cal·ly** *adv.*

morgue *n.* 1. A public building where corpses are kept while awaiting identification, autopsy, etc. 2. The reference files of a newspaper.

mor·i·bund (*mor*-ih-bund) *adj.* Dying; near death.—**mor·i·bun·di·ty** (mor-ih-*bun*-dih-tee) *n.* —**mor·i·bund·ly** *adv.*

Mor·mon (*mor*-mun) *n.* A member of a religious sect founded by Joseph Smith; Latter-Day Saint.—**Mor·mon** *adj.*—**Mor·mon·ism** *n.*

morn·ing, morn *n.* 1. The part of the day from midnight to noon. 2. The initial or early part; beginning.—**morn·ing** *adj.*

morn·ing-glo·ry *n.* [*pl.* -ries] A climbing plant bearing funnel-shaped flowers.

morning star. The planet Venus seen in the early morning.

Mo·ro (*moh*-roh) *n.* [*pl.* -ros] A member of any of several tribes of Mohammedan Filipinos. —**Mo·ro** *adj.*

mo·roc·co *n.* [*pl.* -cos]. Also **morocco leather.** A fine goat leather, characteristically wrinkled, used for purses, bookbinding, etc.

mo·ron (*moh*-ron) *n.* A person with a mental age of eight to twelve years; any feeble-minded person.—**mo·ron·ic** (muh-*ron*-ik) *adj.*—**mo·ron·ism, mo·ron·i·ty** *n.*

mo·rose (muh-*rohss*) *adj.* Sullen; gloomy; crabbed; sour.— -**rose·ly** *adv.*— -**rose·ness** *n.*

Mor·phe·us (*mor*-fee-us) *n. Greek Mythology.* The god of sleep and dreams.

mor·phine (*mor*-feen) *n.* A crystalline alkaloid of opium used to induce sleep.—**mor·phin·ism** (*mor*-fin-ism) *n.* Habitual use of morphine; illness resulting therefrom.

mor·phol·o·gy (mor-*fol*-uh-jee) *n.* 1. The science dealing with the structure of plants and animals. 2. *Linguistics.* Study of the evolution of word forms and inflections.—**mor·pho·log·ic, -i·cal** (mor-fuh-*loj*-ik; -ik-al) *adj.*—**mor·pho·log·i·cal·ly** *adv.*—**mor·phol·o·gist** *n.*

mor·ris (*maw*-riss) *n.* Also **morris dance.** Spectacular old-English folk dance.

Morris chair. A type of easy chair with adjustable back, designed by William Morris, English poet and social reformer.

mor·row (*maw*-roh) *n.* The day after today or after any given day; tomorrow.

Morse (*morss*) *n.* Morse code; now, loosely, any of several telegraphic codes.

Morse code. An alphabet of dits and dahs, visually represented as dots and dashes, invented by S. F. B. Morse for use in telegraphy.

mor·sel (*morss*-'l) *n.* Small piece; bit.

mor·tal (*mor*-t'l) *adj.* 1. Liable to die; human. 2. Bringing death; final. 3. Deadly; fatal. —*n.* A human; any being subject to death. —**mor·tal·ly** *adv.*

mor·tal·i·ty (mor-*tal*-ih-tee) *n.* [*pl.* -ties] 1. Death or casualty rate. 'Mortality is high among radio programs.' 2. State of being subject to death.

mor·tar (*mor*-ter) *n.* 1. A short, thick artillery piece. 2. A mixing bowl in which solids are broken up and ground with a pestle. 3. Building material, similar to plaster, but heavier.

mor·tar·board *n.* 1. A square board used by plasterers to hold mortar. 2. A square-crowned cap worn at graduation ceremonies.

MORTAR AND PESTLE

mort·gage (*mor*-gij) *n.* 1. Pledging of property as security for money borrowed. 2. The deed which records this transaction.—**mort·ga·gee** *n.* Holder of a mortgage.—*v.* [mort·gaged; mort·gag·ing].

mort·ga·gor, mort·ga·ger *n.* One whose property is mortgaged.

mor·ti·cian (mor-*tish*-'n) *n.* Undertaker.

mor·tif·i·ca·tion (mor-tif-ih-*kay*-shun) *n.* 1. Humiliation; chagrin. 2. Subduing of passions and normal desires by harsh repression. 3. *Medical.* Gangrene; decay.

mor·ti·fy (*mor*-tih-fy) *v.* [-fied; -fy·ing] 1. To humiliate; embarrass deeply. 2. To restrain basic urges by rigorous self-denial. 3. To affect with gangrene.—**mor·ti·fi·er** *n.*

mor·tise (*mor*-tiss) *n.* Also **mor·tice.** A deep slot in which a corresponding projection fits to form a joint. —*v.* [mor·tised; mor·tis·ing].

MORTISE

mor·tu·ar·y (*mor*-choo-air-ee) *n.* [*pl.* -ies] 1. A place for the temporary reception of the dead. 2. A burial place.—**mor·tu·ar·y** *adj.*

mo·sa·ic (moh-*zay*-ik) *n.* An inlaid surface design worked out by the arrangement of particles of varicolored stone, marble, etc.—**mo·sa·ic** *adj.*—**mo·sa·i·cist** *n.*

Mo·sa·ic *adj.* Designating Moses or his code of law.

Mo·selle (moh-*zel*) *n.* A variety of French white wine.

Mo·ses (*moh*-zez) *n.* The great Hebrew lawgiver who led the Israelites out of Egypt to Canaan.

mo·sey (*moh*-zee) *v. Colloquial.* To move; go; get under way.

Mos·lem (*moz*-lem) *n.* [*pl.* -lems, -lem] A Mohammedan.—**Mos·lem** *adj.*—**Mos·lem·ism** *n.*

mosque (*mosk*) *n.* A Mohammedan temple.

mos·qui·to (mus-*kee*-toh) *n.* [*pl.* -toes] A gnatlike insect which sucks blood.—**mos·qui·tal** *adj.*

mosquito boat. A small naval attack craft; PT-boat.

MOSQUE

moss *n.* A small green plant with leafy stems and rudimentary roots which grows as part of a cushionlike cluster.

mossbacked	moss-clad	moss-grown
moss-bordered	moss-covered	mosshead
moss-bound	moss green	moss-lined

moss·back *n. Slang.* A reactionary person.

moss·y (*moss*-ee) *adj.* [moss·i·er; moss·i·est] Like or abounding in moss.—**moss·i·ness** *n.*

most (*mohst*) *adj.* [*superlative* of **much, many**] Highest or greatest in extent, number, quantity, quality, etc.—*n.* Greatest number; greatest value, degree, effect, etc.—**most** *adv.*

most·ly *adv.* For the most part; chiefly; mainly.

mot (*moh*) *n.* A witty or pithy saying.

mote *n.* A spot; small particle.

moth *n.* A family of winged insects distinguished from butterflies by pointed, instead of knob-ended, feelers.—**moth·y** *adj.*

moth ball. A ball of white, aromatic crystals, used to repel clothes moths.

MOTH

moth-eat·en *adj.* Eaten by moths; full of holes; threadbare; shabby.

moth·er (*muth*-er) *n.* 1. A female parent. 2. Source; origin; parent. 3. An abbess; a woman holding an important position in a religious institution.—*v.* 1. To adopt. 2. To behave tenderly and parentally.—**moth·er** *adj.*

moth·er *n.* A tnick slimy substance which forms in liquors, esp. in vinegar.

moth·er·hood *n.* The state of being a mother.

Mother Hubbard. 1. Character in a favorite nursery rhyme. 2. A loose-fitting dressing gown.

moth·er-in-law *n.* [*pl.* moth·ers-in-law] The mother of one's husband or wife.

moth·er·land *n.* The land of one's origin.

moth·er·less *adj.* Without a mother.

moth·er·ly *adj.* 1. Pertaining to a mother. 2. Parental; tender.—**moth·er·li·ness** *n.*

moth·er-of-pearl *n.* The hard, silvery, brilliant internal layer of many shells, esp. of oysters from the Indian seas.—**moth·er-of-pearl** *adj.*

mother tongue. 1. The language of one's motherland. 2. A language to which other languages owe their origin.

mo·tif (moh-*tiff*) *n.* Theme; dominant symbol, figure, idea, etc., in a work of art.

mo·tile (*moh*-t'l) *adj.* Having an inherent spontaneous power or motion.—**mo·til·i·ty** *n.*

mo·tion (*moh*-shun) *n.* 1. The process or act of changing place or position. 2. The power of moving. 3. A single movement. 4. Tendency of the desires or passions; internal impulse. 5. Proposal made; formal proposition made in a deliberative assembly.—*v.* To make a significant movement or gesture.

mo·tion·less *adj.* Without motion; at rest.—**mo·tion·less·ly** *n.*—**mo·tion·less·ness** *n.*

motion picture. A photoplay; a series of photographs so rapidly presented as to merge in effect into a continuous moving image; a movie; a film.

mo·ti·vate (*moh*-tih-vayt) *v.* [mo·ti·vat·ed; mo·ti·vat·ing] To furnish a reason for; prompt; incite.—**mo·ti·va·tion** (moh-tih-*vay*-shun) *n.*

mo·tive (*moh*-tiv) *n.* 1. The cause; reason; inducement. 2. The prevailing design; theme. —**mo·tive** *adj.* Causing motion; having power or tendency to move.—**motive power.** The whole power acting on any quantity of matter to move it.

mot·ley (*mot*-lee) *adj.* 1. Varied in color. 2. Composed of discordant elements; heterogeneous; diversified.—*n.* An outfit variously colored, used by a clown.

mo·tor (*moh*-ter) *n.* A mechanical source of power; prime mover; engine.—*adj.* Imparting motion; moving; driving.—*v.* To drive, or travel by, a motor-powered vehicle.

M

motorcab	motordrome	motorship
motor camper	motorman	motortruck
motor-driven	motor-minded	motorway

mo·tor·boat *n.* A small boat driven by motor.

mo·tor·bus *n.* A bus for conveying passengers.

mo·tor·cade (*moh*-ter-kayd) *n.* A column or convoy of vehicles.

mo·tor·car *n.* An automotive vehicle.

mo·tor·cy·cle (*moh*-ter-sy-k'l) *n.* A motor-driven vehicle similar to, but of heavier construction than, a bicycle.—*v.* [-cy·cled; -cy·cling].—**mo·tor·cy·clist** *n.*

motor generator. A machine composed of a motor which operates a generator to produce current.

mo·tor·ist *n.* An automobile driver or passenger.

mo·tor·ize (*moh*-ter-yze) *v.* [mo·tor·ized; mo·tor·iz·ing] To provide with a motor; provide with automotive vehicles.—'Motorized cavalry.' —**mo·tor·i·za·tion** (moh-ter-iz-*ay*-shun) *n.*

mo·tor·man (*moh*-ter-mun) *n.* [*pl.* -men] The driver of a public conveyance, esp. a street-car.

mot·tle (*mot*-'l) *v.* [mot·tled; mot·tl·ing] To mark with blotches; variegate.—*n.* An irregularly spotted surface.

mot·to (*mot*-oh) *n.* [*pl.* -toes] A brief phrase expressing the guiding principle of a person or organization.

mou·jik. *Variant spelling* of **muzhik.**

mound (*mownd*) *n.* A hillock; small elevation; knoll.—*v.* To heap; make a mound of.

mount (*mownt*) *n.* A mountain.

mount *v.* 1. To ascend; climb up or upon. 2. To grow in intensity. 3. To place in a setting, as a jewel. 4. To fix onto a frame, backing, etc., as a picture. 5. To set in position for use. 'Mount a cannon.'—*n.* A setting, holder, frame, etc. 'Gun mount.'

moun·tain (*mown*-t'n) *n.* 1. A high elevation of land. 2. A great heap; pile.

mountain ash. A tree bearing white clustered flowers and leaves similar to the ash.

moun·tain·eer (mown-t'n-*eer*) *n.* 1. A dweller in a mountainous region. 2. A mountain climber.—*v.* To climb mountains for sport.

mountain goat. A hairy-coated, white, climbing goat common in the Rocky Mountains.

mountain laurel. A glossy-leafed evergreen shrub bearing clusters of white or pink flowers.

mountain lion. A cougar; a wildcat common to the mountains of western U.S.

moun·tain·ous (*mown*-t'n-us) *adj.* 1. Covered with mountains. 2. Huge.

moun·te·bank (*mown*-tuh-bank) *n.* A quack doctor; charlatan.

mount·ed *adj.* 1. On horseback. 2. Set in a mount; supported.

mourn (*morn*) *v.* To grieve; feel deep sorrow. —**mourn·er** *n.*

mourn·ful *adj.* Doleful; sorrowful; sad. —**mourn·ful·ly** *adv.*—**mourn·ful·ness** *n.*

mourn·ing *n.* 1. An expression of grief. 2. The black clothing worn by a mourner. —**mourn·ing** *adj.*

mouse (*mowss*) *n.* [*pl.* mice] 1. A small rodent infesting populous areas. 2. *Slang.* A black eye.

mous·er (*mowz*-er) *n.* A cat or dog which catches mice.

mousse (*mooss*) *n.* A fluffy ice cream made from whipped cream.

mous·y *adj.* Small; timid; meek; mouselike.

mouth (*mowth*) *n.* [*pl.* mouths] 1. The orifice in the face leading into the digestive tract. 2. Any opening like a mouth.—*v.* 1. To speak in an affected manner. 2. To mumble.

mouth·ful *n.* [*pl.* -fuls] 1. The amount taken into the mouth at one time. 2. *Slang.* Plenty.

mouth organ. A harmonica.

mouth·piece *n.* 1. Something serving as a mouthlike opening. 2. The part of a musical wind instrument which is placed to the lips. 3. *Slang.* A spokesman; attorney. 'The mob's mouthpiece.'

mouth·y *adj.* [mouth·i·er; mouth·i·est] Bombastic; garrulous.

mov·a·ble, move·a·ble *adj.* 1. Not fixed; able to be moved. 2. Varying; changeable. —*n.* An object, as a piece of furniture, which may be readily moved about.—**mov·a·bly, move·a·bly** *adv.*—**mov·a·bil·i·ty** (moov-uh-*bil*-ih-tee), **move·a·bil·i·ty** *n.*

move (*moov*) *v.* [moved; mov·ing] 1. To change position in space. 2. To cause to change position; stir. 3. To arouse emotion. 4. To present as a motion in parliamentary proceedings. 5. To set in action. 6. *Colloquial.* To leave; depart. 7. To change one's domicile. —*n.* Movement.

move·ment (*moov*-m'nt) *n.* 1. Change; regulated motion; passage. 2. *Music.* **a.** Portion of a symphony, concerto, etc. **b.** Rhythm. 3. Activity; performance. 4. Action of the bowels. 5. A trend; the activities of a group tending toward a large-scale change. 'The labor movement.' 6. The mechanism of a watch.

mov·ie (*moov*-ee) *n. Slang.* A motion picture.

mov·ing (*moov*-ing) *adj.* 1. Impelling; stirring. 2. Touching; arousing emotion. 3. In motion.—**mov·ing·ly** *adv.*

moving picture. A motion picture; movie.

mow *n.* 1. A heap of hay or grain. 2. The place in a barn where hay is put.

mow (*moh*) *v.* [mowed; mowed, mown; mowing] 1. To cut with a sickle, scythe or machine. 'Mowed grain.' 2. To cause to fall. 'The machine gun mowed down the close ranks.'—**mow·er** *n.* 1. A mowing machine. 2. One who cuts grass.

mowing machine. A machine with revolving blades designed to cut down grain, hay, etc.

MP, M.P. (*em pee*). 1. Military Police; a member of the Military Police. 2. Member of Parliament.

much *adj.* [more; most] Great in quantity; abundant.—*n.* A great deal.—*adv.* 1. Greatly; in a great degree. 2. Nearly.

mu·ci·lage (*myoo*-suh-lij) *n.* A liquid adhesive made from certain seeds or roots.

mu·ci·lag·i·nous (myoo-suh-*laj*-uh-nuss) *adj.* Slimy; ropy; gluey; sticky.

muck *n.* 1. Moist dung or vegetable mold. 2. Anything filthy, nasty, or vile.—*v.* 1. To fertilize with muck. 2. *Colloquial.* To soil; foul; mess up.—**muck·y** *adj.*

muck·er *n. Slang.* An ill-mannered person.

muck·rake (*muk*-rayk) *v.* [muck·raked; muck·rak·ing] To bring corrupt activities to public attention.—**muck·rak·er** *n.*

mu·cous (*myoo*-kuss) *adj.* 1. Pertaining to or like mucus. 2. Secreting mucus.

mucous membrane. Membrane lining all bodily passages and cavities, such as the mouth, nose, lungs, etc., and secreting mucus.

mu·cus (*myoo*-kuss) *n.* A transparent, slimy fluid secreted by the mucous membrane, forming a protective layer.

mud *n.* Moist, sticky earth; mire.—*v.* [mudded; mud·ding] To cover with mud; bedaub.

mud·dle (*mud*-'l) *v.* [mud·dled; mud·dling] 1. To make muddy or filthy; foul. 2. To

WOODWIND

HORN

CORNET

OBOE
MOUTHPIECES

stupefy; partially intoxicate. 3. To misuse; waste; cause confusion.—*n.* Confusion; disorder; bewilderment.—**mud·dler** *n.*

mud·dy *adj.* [mud·di·er; mud·di·est] 1. Miry; turbid; foul with mud. 2. Mentally confused; stupid. 3. Of the color of mud. 4. Obscure. —*v.* [mud·died; mud·dy·ing] 1. To soil; dirty. 2. To cloud; make dull; confuse. —**mud·di·ly** *adv.*—**mud·di·ness** *n.*

mud·guard *n.* A fender for protection from splashing mud.

mud puppy. A large salamander.

mu·ez·zin (myoo-*ez*-in) *n.* Mohammedan crier who, five times a day, gives a summons to prayer.

muff *n.* 1. Cylindrical cover, usually fur, into which the hands are thrust for warmth. 2. A useless, poor-spirited person. 3. A bungling attempt. —*v.* To muddle; spoil; do badly.

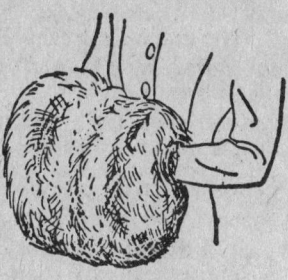

MUFF

muffin (*muf*-in) *n.* 1. A cup-shaped biscuit of egg batter or yeast dough. 2. A butter cake; biscuit baked on a griddle. 'English muffin.'

muf·fler (*muf*-ler) *n.* 1. Heavy scarf used for warmth. 2. Device designed to reduce exhaust noises in a gasoline engine.

muf·fle (*muf*-'l) *v.* [muf·fled; muf·fling] 1. To wrap up; cover closely; conceal; protect. 2. To deaden sound. 3. To wrap a fabric around the neck or face.—*n.* 1. A muffler. 2. The end of the muzzle of certain animals.

muf·ti (*muf*-tee) *n.* 1. In Islam, a lawyer consulted on points of the sacred law. 2. *Colloquial.* Civilian clothes, in contrast to uniforms.

mug *n.* 1. Cup-shaped drinking vessel, usually with a handle. 2. *Slang.* Face; mouth.—*v. Slang.* [mugged; mug·ging] 1. To make a face; grimace. 2. To cram for an examination. 3. To garrote; strangle.

mug·gy (*mug*-ee) *adj.* [mug·gi·er; mug·gi·est] Warm and humid; damp; close. —**mug·gi·ness** *n.*

MUG

mug·wump *n.* An independent voter, esp. one who bolts an established party.

mu·jik. *Variant spelling of* **muzhik.**

mu·lat·to (muh-*lat*-oh) *n.* [*pl.* -toes] A person with one white and one Negro parent; anyone of mixed descent.—*adj.* **mu·lat·to.**

mul·ber·ry (*mul*-ber-ee) *n.* Any of a number of trees, as the black mulberry, whose fruit is edible, and the white mulberry, whose leaves are used to feed silkworms.

mulch *n.* A mixture of manure with leaves or straw used to protect newly planted roots from dryness, heat, or cold by checking evaporation.—*v.* 1. To cover with a mulch. 2. To cultivate surface soil.

mulct *n.* Penalty; fine.—*v.* 1. To punish by fine. 2. To deprive by fraud; embezzle.

mule *n.* Hybrid offspring, usually sterile, of an ass and a mare.

mule *n.* A slipper covering the toes only.

MULE (1/65 life size)

mu·le·teer (myoo-luh-*teer*) *n.* A mule driver.

mul·ish *adj.* Stubborn; obstinate; dogged.—**mul·ish·ly** *adv.*—**mul·ish·ness** *n.*

mull *v.* To heat and flavor with spices. 'To mull wine.'—*n.* A thin soft muslin material.

mull *v. Colloquial.* To ponder. 'Mull over.'

mul·lein (*mul*-in) *n.* Also **mul·len.** A tall, downy-leaved weed of the figwort family.

mul·let (*mul*-it) *n.* A moderate-sized tasty foodfish found in the Atlantic.

mul·li·gan (*mul*-ih-g'n) *n. Slang.* A stew made from meat and miscellaneous vegetables.

mul·li·ga·taw·ny (mul-ih-guh-*taw*-nee) *n.* A highly seasoned meat soup.

mul·lion (*mul*-yun) *n. Architecture.* Vertical divisions between adjacent window lights.—*v.* To shape into divisions by mullions.

mul·ti- *Prefix.* Many; much.

multiangular	multimotored	multispeed
multicellular	multipartile	multispiral
multicylinder	multiphase	multistoried
multifold	multipolar	multitoned
multilineal	multiradial	multitubular
multilinear	multirooted	multivalved
multimolecular	multisegmented	multivoiced

mul·ti·far·i·ous (mul-tih-*fair*-ee-us) *adj.* Having great variety; diverse; manifold.—**mul·ti·far·i·ous·ly** *adv.*—**mul·ti·far·i·ous·ness** *n.*

mul·ti·form (*mul*-tih-form) *adj.* Having many shapes or appearances.—**mul·ti·for·mi·ty** (mul-tih-*for*-mih-tee) *n.* [*pl.* -ties] Diversity of forms.

Mul·ti·graph (*mul*-tih-graf) *n.* A trademark name for a small printing press with rollers slotted to receive detachable type.

mul·ti·lat·er·al (mul-tih-*lat*-er-ul) *adj.* 1. Many-sided. 2. Affecting more than two nations. —**mul·ti·lat·er·al·ly** *adv.*

mul·ti·mil·lion·aire (-mil-yun-*air*) *n.* One who possesses two or more millions of dollars.

mul·tip·a·rous (mul-*tip*-er-us) *adj.* Producing more than one offspring at a single delivery.

mul·ti·ple (*mul*-tih-p'l) *adj.* Manifold; having many parts or repetitions.—*n.* A number which may be divided by certain others an exact number of times.

M

mul·ti·pli·cand (mul-tih-plih-*kand*) *n.* The number which multiplied by another gives the product.

mul·ti·pli·ca·tion (mul-tih-plih-*kay*-shun) *n.* 1. Increase; augmentation; reproduction. 2. *Arithmetic.* An operation by which a given number is added to itself a given number of times.

mul·ti·plic·i·ty (mul-tih-*pliss*-ih-tee) *n.* [*pl.* -ties] 1. A large number. 2. Variety; manifoldness.

mul·ti·pli·er (*mul*-tih-ply-er) *n.* 1. The number which shows how many times another is to be multiplied. 2. *Physics.* A device that increases intensity, wave frequency, and other factors.

mul·ti·ply *v.* [-plied; -ply·ing] 1. To increase; augment; reproduce. 2. *Arithmetic.* To add a given number to itself as many times as the multiplier indicates.

mul·ti·tude (*mul*-tih-tood) *n.* Crowd; throng; host.—**mul·ti·tu·di·nous** (mul-tih-*too*-din·ous) *adj.* — **mul·ti·tu·di·nous·ly** *adv.* — **mul·ti·tu·di·nous·ness** *n.*

mum *adj.* Speechless; silent; not speaking.

mum·ble (*mum*-b'l) *v.* [mum·bled; mum·bling] To mutter; speak inarticulately.—*n.* Indistinct speech or locution.—**mum·bler** *n.*—**mum·bling·ly** *adv.*

mumbo jumbo. Rigamarole; hocus-pocus.

mum·mer *n.* A masked person who entertains in holiday festivities.

mum·mer·y *n.* [*pl.* -ies] 1. Performance by masked entertainers; masquerade. 2. Farcical show; hypocritical display.

mum·mi·fy (*mum*-ih-fy) *v.* [-fied; -fy·ing] To embalm and dry a corpse; desiccate.—**mum·mi·fi·ca·tion** (mum-ih-fih-*kay*-shun) *n.*

mum·my *n.* [*pl.* -mies] 1. A corpse dried and embalmed. 2. A rich brown pigment or color.

mumps *n.* An inflammation of the salivary glands accompanied by painful swelling along the side of the throat.

munch *v.* To chew audibly; crunch.—**munch·er** *n.*

mun·dane (mun-*dayn*) *adj.* Worldly; earthly; secular.—**mun·dane·ly** *adv.*

mun·go *n.* Reprocessed wool of fair quality.

Mun·ich (*myoo*-nik). A large city of southern Germany, capital of Bavaria.

mu·nic·i·pal (myoo-*nih*-sih-p'l) *adj.* Pertaining to a city or its government.

mu·ni·ci·pal·i·ty (myoo-nih-sih-*pal*-uh-tee) *n.* A city; incorporated town.

mu·nif·i·cence (myoo-*nih*-fih-senss) *n.* Generosity; liberality; bounty.—**mu·nif·i·cent** *adj.*

mu·ni·tion (myoo-*nish*-un) *n.* 1. Ammunition. 2. [*pl.*] Military material and stores.—**mu·ni·tion** *v.*

mu·ral (*myoor*-ul) *n.* A wall painting.—*adj.* Like, on, or pertaining to a wall.

mur·der (*mer*-der) *n.* Killing of a human being, either maliciously or while committing a crime. —**mur·der** *v.*—**mur·der·er** *n.*—**mur·der·ess** *n.*

mur·der·ous *adj.* 1. Savage; cruel; bloodthirsty. 2. Pertaining to murder or a murderer.—**mur·der·ous·ly** *adv.*

murk, mirk *n.* Darkness; obscurity.—**murk** *adj.*

murk·y *adj.* [murk·i·er; murk·i·est]. Also **mirk·y.** Obscure; dark; muddy; casting gloom.—**murk·i·ly** *adv.*—**murk·i·ness** *n.*

mur·mur *n.* 1. A soft, confused, unclear sound. 2. Grumbling; half-suppressed complaint. 3. *Medicine.* A gentle sound, often abnormal, heard when listening to the heart or lungs.—**mur·mur** *v.*—**mur·mur·er** *n.*—**mur·mur·ing** *adj.*—**mur·mur·ing·ly** *adv.*

mur·rain (*mer*-in) *n.* Any fatal disease of cattle.

mus·ca·dine (*mus*-kuh-din) *n.* A musk-flavored grape of southern U.S.

mus·cat (*mus*-kat) *n.* 1. Muscatel wine. 2. The grape from which it is made.

mus·ca·tel (mus-kuh-*tel*) *n.* A sweet; amber-colored wine.

mus·cle (*muss*-'l) *n.* 1. An animal tissue which effects movement of the bodily parts. 2. The extent of muscular development.—*v.* [mus·cled; mus·cling].—**muscle in.** *Slang.* Intrude; encroach on another's rights or possessions.

Muscle Shoals. A portion of the Tennessee River in northern Alabama, site of a great federal hydroelectric power project.

Mus·co·vite (*mus*-koh-vyte) *n.* An inhabitant of Moscow.—**Mus·co·vite** *adj.*

mus·cu·lar (*mus*-kyoo-ler) *adj.* 1. Pertaining to or performed by the muscles. 2. Sinewy; brawny; strong.—**mus·cu·lar·i·ty** (muhs-kyoo-*lair*-uh-tee) *n.*—**mus·cu·lar·ly** *adv.*

muse (*myooz*) *v.* [mused; mus·ing] To ponder; be lost in thought; meditate.—*n.* Deep or pensive thought.—**mus·er** *n.*

muse *n.* 1. A writer's inspiration or creative urge. 2. [*cap.*] *Mythology.* One of nine goddesses who are guardians of literature, arts, and sciences.

mu·se·um (myoo-*zee*-um) *n.* A building housing a collection of scientific or artistic specimens.

mush *n.* 1. Cornmeal gruel. 2. Any slushy mixture. 3. Maudlin sentimentality.—*v.* To make mushy.

mush *v.* To travel with a dog team.—*n.* A journey over snow with a dog team.—**mush·er** *n.*

mush·room *n.* 1. A large, fleshy fungus rich in protein. 2. Anything which springs or grows up rapidly like mushrooms.—*v.* To spring up; develop quickly. —*adj.* Phenomenally quick in growth.

MUSHROOMS

mush·y *adj.* [mush·i·er; mush·i·est] 1. Soft; sludgy; yielding. 2. Overly sentimental; silly.—**mush·i·ness** *n.*

mu·sic (*myoo*-zik) *n.* 1. Any combination of sounds that pleases the ear; melody. 2. The science and art of harmonic sounds. 3. Composition of harmony and melody. 4. The score of a musical composition.

mu·si·cal (*myooz*-ih-k'l) *adj.* 1. Pleasing to the ear. 2. Of or pertaining to music. 3. Musically talented.—*n.* A musical comedy.—**mu·si·cal·ly** *adv.*—**mu·si·cal·ness** *n.*

musical comedy. A theatrical entertainment in which plot is subordinated to singing parts.

mu·si·cale (myoo-zih-*kal*) *n.* A party where music is offered as the main entertainment.

music box. 1. A box enclosing a clockwork mechanism which plays music. 2. An automatic coin-operated phonograph.

mu·si·cian (myoo-*zish*-un) *n.* A musical composer or performer.—**mu·si·cian·ly** *adj. & adv.*

mus·ing (*myooz*-ing) *adj.* Preoccupied; absent-minded.—*n.* Meditation; daydreaming.—**mus·ing·ly** *adv.*

musk *n.* 1. A potently and diffusively odorous substance obtained from the musk deer. 2. An aroma; perfume.

musk deer. A small Asiatic deer with a musk-producing gland.

mus·kel·lunge (*musk*-uh-lunj) *n.* A large, fighting gamefish of the pike family.

musk·et (*musk*-it) *n.* A rifle, esp. a muzzle-loader.—**mus·ket·eer** *n.* An infantryman; musket-bearing soldier.

mus·ket·ry (*musk*-it-ree) *n.* [*pl.* -ries] 1. The fire of rifles. 2. The art of firing small arms. 3. Muskets collectively.

musk·mel·on (*musk*-mel-un) *n.* An oblong, fragrant, ribbed melon with sweet edible flesh.

musk·rat *n.* An American rodent akin to the beaver, and valued for its fur.

musk·y *adj.* Strongly fragrant; having the odor of musk.

mus·lin (*muz*-lin) *n.* A thin, fine cotton fabric.—**mus·lin** *adj.*

muss *n. Colloquial.* A scramble; mess; disorder.—*v.* To rumple; tousle.

MUSKRAT (1/15 life size)

mus·sel (*muss*-'l) *n.* An edible mollusk which attaches itself to rocks, etc.

Mus·sul·man (*muss*-'l-m'n) *n.* [*pl.* -mans, -men] A Moslem; follower of Mohammed.

muss·y *adj. Colloquial.* [muss·i·er; muss·i·est] In a state of disorder; rumpled.

must *v.* To be obliged or required; be bound.

must *n.* Unfermented, or new, wine.

mus·tache, mous·tache (muss-*tash*, mus-tash) *n.* Unshaven hair on the upper lip.

mus·ta·chi·o (mus-*tah*-shoh) *n.* [*pl.* -chios] Mustache, esp. when large or impressive. —**mus·ta·chi·oed** *adj.*

mus·tang (*muss*-tang) *n.* A small, often wild horse of western U.S.

mus·tard (*muss*-terd) *n.* A plant whose seeds, when ground, form a pungent condiment.

MUSTARD

mustard gas. A poisonous military gas which blisters the skin.

mus·ter (*muss*-ter) *v.* 1. To collect or assemble, esp. troops. 2. To gather; summon up, as courage.—*n.* 1. A collection or assembling, esp. of troops for review. 2. A roll call; register.

mus·ty (*muss*-tee) *adj.* [mus·ti·er; mus·ti·est] 1. Moldy; damp and foul. 2. Stale; vapid; dull and spiritless. —**mus·ti·ly** *adv.*— -ti·ness *n.*

mu·ta·ble (*myoo*-tuh-b'l) *adj.* 1. Capable of being altered; changeable. 2. Inconstant; unstable; unsettled.—**mu·ta·bil·i·ty, mu·ta·ble·ness** *n.*—**mu·ta·bly** *adv.*

mu·ta·tion (myoo-*tay*-shun) *n.* Change; alteration.—**mu·ta·tion·al** *adj.*—**mu·ta·tive** *adj.*

mute (*myoot*) *adj.* 1. Silent; still. 2. Incapable of utterance; dumb. 3. *Phonetics.* Silent; unpronounced.—*n.* 1. A silent or speechless person. 2. One incapable of speech or utterance. 3. *Phonetics.* A silent letter. 4. A device designed to soften or muffle the tone of a musical instrument.—*v.* [mut·ed; mut·ing] To silence; tone down.—**mute·ly** *adv.*— -ness *n.*

mu·ti·late (*myoo*-tuh-layt) *v.* [mu·ti·lat·ed; mu·ti·lat·ing] To maim; deprive of any part; render imperfect.—**mu·ti·la·tion** (myoo-tuh-*lay*-shun) *n.*—**mut·i·la·tive** *adj.*—**mu·ti·la·tor** *n.*

mu·ti·neer (myoo-tuh-*neer*) *n.* One who engages in a mutiny.

mu·ti·nous (*myoo*-tuh-nuss) *adj.* Engaged in mutiny; disposed to resist or rebel against authority.—**mu·ti·nous·ly** *adv.*— -ti·nous·ness *n.*

mu·ti·ny (*myoo*-tuh-nee) *n.* [*pl.* -nies] A revolt against authority, esp. open resistance of soldiers or sailors to their commanding officers. —*v.* [mu·ti·nied; mu·ti·ny·ing] To rise against or disobey lawful authority.

mutt *n. Slang.* 1. A dog of indeterminate breed. 2. A dull-witted person.

mut·ter (*mut*-ter) *v.* 1. To utter indistinctly; grumble; complain in a low voice. 2. To sound with a deep, rumbling noise.—**mut·ter** *n.* —**mut·ter·er** *n.*—**mut·ter·ing·ly** *adv.*

mut·ton (*mut*-'n) *n.* The meat of sheep.

mutton chop. A single cut of mutton from the loin, rib, or shoulder.

mu·tu·al (*myoo*-choo-ul) *adj.* 1. Reciprocal; pertaining to both sides; interchangable. 2. Common to two or more.—**tu·al·i·ty** (-choo-al-uh-tee) *n.*— -tu·al·ly *adv.*— -tu·al·ness *n.*

mu·zhik, mu·zjik (moo-*zhik*) *n.* A peasant in Czarist Russia.

muz·zle (*muz*-'l) *n.* 1. The projecting nose and

M

mouth of an animal. 2. The mouth or end, as of a tube. 3. A binding or cage for the mouth of a dog.—*v.* [muz·zled; -zling] 1. To stop the mouth of. 2. To prevent from speaking freely.—**muz·zler** *n.*

muz·zle-load·er *n.* An obsolete type of gun loaded through its muzzle.

my *pron.* Of or belonging to me.

My·ce·nae (my-*see*-nee). A city of Argolis which was the seat of the culture preceding the Greek.—**My·ce·nae·an** (-suh-*nee*-un) *adj.* & *n.*

Myn·heer (myne-*hehr*) *n.* 1. The title of address among Dutchmen; sir; Mr. 2. [*not cap.*] A Dutchman.

my·o·pi·a (my-*oh*-pee-uh) *n. Medicine.* Near-sightedness; inability to see clearly at a distance.—**my·op·ic** (my-*op*-ik) *adj.*

myr·i·ad (*mihr*-ee-ud) *n.* 1. Ten thousand. 2. An immense number.—*adj.* Innumerable.

Myr·mi·don (*mer*-muh-don,-d'n) *n.* [*pl.* -dons, -dones] 1. Member of an ancient Greek race ruled by Achilles. 2. [*not cap.*] One who executes ruthless orders; henchman.

myrrh (*mer*) *n.* 1. A gummy resinous substance used in cosmetics and perfume. 2. The tree exuding this substance.

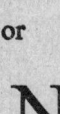

MYRTLE

myr·tle (*mer*-t'l) *n.* A plant bearing small white or yellow flowers.

my·self (my-*self*) *pro.* [*pl.* our·selves] I, or me, personally. Reflexive and emphatic form of *I.*

mys·ter·i·ous (miss-*teer*-ee-us) *adj.* Containing mystery; obscure; secret; unintelligible.—**mys·ter·i·ous·ly** *adv.*—**mys·ter·i·ous·ness** *n.*

mys·ter·y (*miss*-ter-ee) *n.* [*pl.* -ies] 1. Something incomprehensible and awe-inspiring. 2. A secret; anything kept hidden from knowledge or difficult to understand; enigma. 3. A story or play whose outcome is concealed.

mys·tic (*miss*-tik) *adj.* 1. Obscure; hidden from human knowledge. 2. Having a secret meaning; allegorical. 3. Of mystics or mysticism.—*n.* One professing to have direct contact with God, or direct insight into truth.

mys·ti·cal (*miss*-tih-k'l) *adj.* Mystic; understandable only through mysticism.—**mys·ti·cal·ly** *adv.*—**mys·ti·cal·ness** *n.*

mys·ti·cism (*miss*-tuh-sizm) *n.* 1. Supposed insight into truth or contact with God through an exaltation of the mind or soul. 2. Visionary dreaming.

mys·ti·fy (*miss*-tuh-fye) *v.* [mys·ti·fied; mys·ti·fy·ing] To perplex, bewilder.—**mys·ti·fi·ca·tion** (miss-tih-fih-*kay*-shun) *n.*— **-ti·fi·cat·ing·ly** *adv.*

myth (*mith*) *n.* 1. Fable; legend, esp. one with a religious background. 2. Falsehood.

myth·i·cal *adj.* Fabled; imaginary; existing only in myths.—**myth·i·cal·ly** *adv.*

my·thol·o·gy *n.* 1. A collection or system of myths belonging to a particular culture. 2. The science or study of myths.—**myth·o·log·i·cal** *adj.*— **-cal·ly** *adv.*—**my·thol·o·gist** *n.*

N

nab *v.* [nabbed; nab·bing] *Slang.* To grab; seize unexpectedly, esp. in arrest.

na·bob (*nay*-bob) *n.* 1. Wealthy man; millionaire. 2. Native ruler in India.—**na·bob·ish** *adj.* —**na·bob·ism** *n.*

na·celle (nuh-*sel*) *n.* Enclosed portion of an airplane, for the engines or passengers.

na·cre (*nay*-ker) *n.* Mother-of-pearl.—**na·cre·ous** *adj.* Iridescent.

na·dir (*nay*-der) *n.* 1. The point of the celestial sphere directly opposite to the zenith and beneath where one is standing. 2. The lowest or worst point.

nag *n.* A small or jaded horse.

nag *v.* [nagged; nag·ging] To find fault with constantly; pester; harry.—**nag·ger** *n.*—**nag·ging·ly** *adv.*

Na·ga·sa·ki (nah-guh-*sah*-kee). An important shipbuilding center on the SW coast of Japan, partially destroyed by an atomic bomb, Aug. 9, 1945.

nai·ad (*nye*-ad) *n.* [*pl.* -ads, -a·des] *Mythology.* A water nymph.

nail (*nayl*) *n.* 1. The thin horny scale growing at the upper ends of fingers and toes. 2. A slim, pointed piece of metal, with a head, driven into wood to hold separate pieces together.—*v.* 1. To fasten with nails; secure. 2. To trap; seize.

nail bin	nail-pierced	nailsick
nail brush	nail-print	nailsmith
nail hole	nail-shaped	nail-studded
nail maker	nail shop	nail-tailed

nail·head *n.* Small metal disk used to trim shoes, belts, dresses, etc.

nain·sook (*nayn*-suk) *n.* A thin, fine cotton fabric.

na·ïve (nah-*eev*) *adj.* Also **na·ive.** Simple; unsophisticated; artless.—**na·ïve·ly** *adv.*—**na·ïve·ness** *n.*—**na·ïve·te, na·ive·te** (nah-eev-*tay*) *n.*

na·ked (*nay*-kid) *adj.* 1. Bare; nude; uncovered; stripped. 2. Plain; evident; undisguised. 3. Unprotected.—**na·ked·ly** *adv.*—**na·ked·ness** *n.*

nam·by-pam·by (*nam*-bee-*pam*-bee) *adj.* Weak; insipid; effeminate.—**nam·by-pam·by** *n.*

name (*naym*) *n.* 1. Word or words by which a person or thing is designated. 2. Descriptive title; epithet. 3. Reputation; fame; eminence. 4. Semblance; appearance only. 'A friend in name.'—*v.* [named; nam·ing] 1. To entitle; designate. 2. To choose; **nominate.**

3. To mention by name; identify; fix.—**nam·a·ble, name·a·ble** *adj.*—**nam·er** *n.*

name·less *adj.* 1. Anonymous; not named. 2. Obscure; undistinguished. 3. Illegitimate. —**name·less·ly** *adv.*—**name·less·ness** *n.*

name·ly *adv.* To wit; that is to say.

name·sake *n.* One named after another.

nan·keen (nan-*keen*) *n.* Also **nan·kin.** A durable cotton cloth, usually yellow.

nan·ny·goat (*nan*-ee-goht) *n.* Female goat.

nap *v.* [napped; nap·ping] 1. To doze; take a short sleep. 2. To be unwary.—**nap** *n.*

nap *n.* The soft woolly surface of certain fabrics, as velvet or wool.—*v.* [napped; nap·ping] To raise the nap of.—**nap·per** *n.* Machine for raising a nap.

nape (nayp) *n.* The back of the neck.

nap·er·y (*nayp*-er-ee) *n.* Linens for the table.

naph·tha (*nap*-thuh, *naf*-thuh) *n.* A mixture of low-boiling oils distilled from petroleum and used in dry cleaning, etc.

naph·tha·lene (*naf*-thuh-leen; *nap*-) *n.* A colorless, aromatic hydrocarbon fluid used in dyes, moth preventives, etc.

naph·thol (*naf*-thol, *nap*-thol) *n.* An antiseptic, crystalline compound derived from naphthalene.

nap·kin (*nap*-kin) *n.* 1. A small cloth for wiping the fingers and lips after eating. 2. A diaper.

na·po·le·on (nuh-*pohl*-yun; -*pohl*-ee-un) *n.* 1. Formerly, a French gold coin. 2. A light, rich pastry with a cream filling.

Na·po·le·on·ic (nuh-pohl-ee-*on*-ik) *adj.* Pertaining to, or like, Napoleon Bonaparte.

nar·cis·sism (nahr-*siss*-izm) *n.* Sexual feeling excited by one's own body.—**nar·cis·sist** *n.*

nar·cis·sus (nahr-*siss*-uss) *n.* 1. Any of several flowering spring plants, including the daffodil. 2. [*cap.*] *Mythology.* A beautiful youth who pined away after falling in love with his own reflection and was changed into a narcissus.

nar·co·sis (nahr-*koh*-siss) *n.* A comatose state produced by a narcotic.

nar·cot·ic (nahr-*kot*-ik) *n.* A drug; substance which relieves pain by dulling sensibility and inducing sleep. 2. A constant user of narcotics.—**nar·cot·ic** *adj.*

nard (nahrd) *n.* Fragrant ointment obtained from the spikenard.

NARCISSUS

na·res (*nay*-reez) *n. pl.* [*sing.* -ris] The nostrils.

nar·ghi·le, nar·gi·le (*nahr*-guh-lee, -lay) *n.* An oriental tobacco pipe in which the smoke is passed through water.

nar·rate (nair-*ayt*) *v.* [nar·rat·ed; nar·rat·ing] To recount; tell; recite.—**nar·ra·tion** *n.*—**nar·ra·tor, nar·ra·ter** *n.*

nar·ra·tive (*nair*-uh-tiv) *n.* A tale; story; recital. —**nar·ra·tive** *adj.*—**nar·ra·tive·ly** *adv.*

nar·row (*nair*-oh) *adj.* 1. Of little breadth or extent; not wide; limited. 2. Close; careful. 3. Bare; with little margin. 4. Bigoted; provincial; not liberal.—*v.* To make or become smaller in breadth; limit.—*n.* [*pl.*] A strait; contracted part, as of a waterway.—**nar·row·ly** *adv.*—**nar·row·ness** *n.*

narrow-backed
narrow-bladed
narrow-brained
narrow-breasted
narrow-celled
narrow-chested
narrow-ended
narrow-eyed
narrow-faced
narrow-gauged
narrow-headed

narrow-hearted
narrow-mouthed
narrow-necked
narrow-nosed
narrow-petaled
narrow-shouldered
narrow-souled
narrow-streeted
narrow-trimmed
narrow-visioned
narrow-waisted

nar·row-mind·ed *adj.* Intolerant; bigoted; provincial.—**nar·row-mind·ed·ly** *adv.* —**nar·row-mind·ed·ness** *n.*

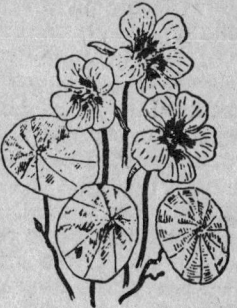

NARWHAL (1/150 life size)

nar·whal (*nahr*-hw'l, -w'l) *n.* Also **nar·wal, nar·whale.** An Arctic whale less than 20 feet long, the male of which has a long protective tusk.

na·sal (*nay*-z'l) *adj.* Pertaining to, as nasal catarrh, or uttered through the nose, as *m, n, ng.* —**na·sal·i·ty** (nuh-*zal*-ih-tee) *n.*—**na·sal·ly** *adv.*

nas·cent (*nass*-n't; *nayss*-) *adj.* Coming into being; beginning.—**nas·cen·cy, nas·cence** *n.*

nas·tur·tium (nuhss-*ter*-shum) *n.* A hardy, decorative plant whose yellow and red flowers, as well as seeds, are sometimes used in salads.

nas·ty (*nass*-tee) *adj.* [nas·ti·er; nas·ti·est] 1. Foul; dirty. 2. Vile; obscene. 3. Nauseous; disgusting; 4. Disagreeable; unpleasant; vicious. —**nas·ti·ly** *adv.*—**nas·ti·ness** *n.*

NASTURTIUM

na·tal (*nay*-t'l) *adj.* 1. Relating to one's birth. 2. Native.

na·tant (*nay*-t'nt) *adj.* Floating; swimming. —**na·ta·tion** *n.*—**na·ta·tion·al** *adj.*

na·ta·to·ri·um (nay-tuh-*toh*-ree-um) *n.* [*pl.* -ri·ums, -ri·a] An artificial swimming pool.

na·tion (*nay*-shun) *n.* 1. A people living within established political boundaries, united under a central government. 2. A group having a linguistic and cultural homogeneity.

na·tion·al (*nash*-uh-n'l) *adj.* Pertaining to a nation; federal.—*n.* A citizen; compatriot.

National Formulary. A book issued by the American Pharmaceutical Association containing approved formulas for many standard medical preparations. *Abbr.* **N.F., & n.f.**

N

na·tion·al·ism (*nash*-un-'l-izm) *n*. An ambitious and intensely loyal feeling for the nation-state, esp. for its political interests.

na·tion·al·ist (*nash*-un-'l-ist) *n*. 1. One motivated by a strong sense of his country's importance. 2. A chauvinist; isolationist; jingoist.—**na·tion·al·ist** *adj*.—**na·tion·al·ist·ic** (nash-un-'l-*iss*-tik) *adj*.—**na·tion·al·is·ti·cal·ly** *adv*.

na·tion·al·i·ty (nash-un-*al*-ih-tee) *n*. [*pl*. -ties] The people constituting a nation as determined by common language and character.

na·tion·al·iz·a·tion (nash-un-'l-ih-*zay*-shun) *n*. The taking over of a company or industry by a government to be administered as a public enterprise.—**na·tion·al·ize** *v*. [-ized; -iz·ing].

na·tive (*nay*-tiv) *adj*. 1. Pertaining to one's birth or birthplace; indigenous. 2. Not artificial or acquired; natural.—*n*. One born in a specific place or country.—**na·tive·ly** *adv*.

na·tiv·i·ty (nuh-*tiv*-ih-tee) *n*. [*pl*. -ties] 1. Birth. 2. [*cap*.] The birth of Christ.

nat·ty (*nat*-ee) *adj*. [nat·ti·er; nat·ti·est] Neat; spruce; dapper.—**nat·ti·ly** *adv*.—**nat·ti·ness** *n*.

nat·u·ral (*nat*-cher-'l) *adj*. 1. Pertaining to or caused by nature. 2. In conformity with the laws of nature. 3. Typical; usual; customary. 4. Unaffected; artless; simple.—*n*. 1. A fool; idiot. 2. An illegitimate child. 3. *Slang*. Anything showing great promise of success. —**nat·u·ral·ly** *adv*.—**nat·u·ral·ness** *n*.

natural history. Informal or primary study of botany and zoology.

nat·u·ral·ism (*nat*-cher-'l-izm) *n*. 1. State of nature. 2. The theory that the universe functions according to fixed, natural laws, without the aid of supernatural power. 3. The school of painting and literature holding that art should express reality or scientific observation.

nat·u·ral·ist (*nat*-cher-'l-ist) *n*. 1. Person skilled in natural history. 2. A believer in naturalism; atheist.—**nat·u·ral·is·tic** *adj*.

nat·u·ral·ize (*nat*-cher-'l-yze) *v*. [-ized; -iz·ing] 1. To make natural or habitual. 2. To bestow the rights and responsibilities of citizenship upon. 3. To adopt or accept as if native. —**nat·u·ral·i·za·tion** (nat-cher-'l-ih-*zay*-shun) *n*.

natural science. History or study of nature in its widest sense.

natural selection. The process of the weeding out of weaker forms of life, emphasized by Darwin as the basic factor in evolution, and resulting in the survival of the fittest.

na·ture (*nay*-cher) *n*. 1. The universe, as distinguished from the creator; whatever exists naturally. 2. The creator of all things; power carrying on the process of creation. 3. Essential qualities or attributes. 4. Disposition; temper; character.

naught (nawt) *n*. Zero.—*adv*. Not at all.

naught. *Variant spelling* of nought.

naugh·ty (*naw*-tee) *adj*. [naugh·ti·er; naugh·ti·est] Mischievous; bad; impish; risqué.—**naugh·ti·ly** *adv*.—**naugh·ti·ness** *n*.

nau·se·a (*naw*-shuh) *n*. 1. Sickness or squeamishness of the stomach, marked by a desire to vomit. 2. Loathing.

nau·se·ate (*naw*-shee-ayt) *v*. [nau·se·at·ed; nau·se·at·ing] 1. To feel nausea; create nausea in. 2. To loathe.—**nau·se·a·tion** *n*.

nau·seous (*naw*-shus) *adj*. Exciting nausea; loathsome; disgusting.—**nau·seous·ly** *adv*.

nautch (nawch) *n*. An East Indian entertainment consisting mainly of dancing by professionals called *nautch girls*.

nau·ti·cal (*naw*-tih-k'l) *adj*. Pertaining to seamen or navigation.—**nau·ti·cal·ly** *adv*.

nau·ti·lus (*naw*-til-us) *n*. [*pl*. -lus·es; -li] A mollusk having a smooth, spiral, chambered shell.

Nav·a·ho, Nav·a·jo (*nah*-vuh-hoh) *n*. [*pl*. -hos, -hoes, -jos, -joes] One of a tribe of Indians located in the SW U.S.

na·val (*nay*-v'l) *adj*. Pertaining to a navy or to ships.

nave *n*. The long middle section of a church.

na·vel (*nay*-v'l) *n*. 1. A scar in the center of the abdomen, left by severing the umbilical cord. 2. The middle or central part.

navel orange. A variety of seedless orange with a small navellike growth at one end.

nav·i·cert (*nav*-ih-sert) *n*. Certificate of assurance from a warring power that a neutral ship may pass a blockade unmolested.

nav·i·ga·ble (*nav*-ih-guh-b'l) *adj*. 1. Capable of being steered. 2. Open to the passage of vessels.—**nav·i·ga·bil·i·ty, nav·i·ga·ble·ness** *n*. —**nav·i·ga·bly** *adv*.

nav·i·gate (*nav*-ih-gayt) *v*. [nav·i·gat·ed; nav·i·gat·ing] 1. To steer; direct a ship or airplane. 2. To sail on, as the ocean.

nav·i·ga·tion (nav-ih-*gay*-shun) *n*. 1. The science of directing the course of a ship or aircraft. 2. Sailing; passage through water. —**nav·i·ga·tion·al** *adj*.

nav·i·ga·tor (*nav*-ih-gay-ter) *n*. A person skilled in directing a ship or aircraft.

nav·vy (*nav*-ee) *n*. [*pl*. -vies] *Colloquial*. A laborer, as on docks, in shipyards, etc.

na·vy (*nay*-vee) *n*. [*pl*. -vies] 1. An armed force operating on water, including the fleet, personnel, etc. 2. [*cap*.] The government department directing naval affairs.—**navy blue.** A dark shade of blue.

nay *adv*. 1. No, esp. when used in a voice vote. 2. A prohibition; refusal.—*n*. A person voting against a measure.

Naz·a·rene (*naz*-er-een) *n*. 1. An inhabitant of Nazareth. 2. Jesus Christ. 3. A Christian.

Naz·a·reth (*naz*-er-ith). The town in Palestine where Christ grew to maturity.

Na·zi (*naht*-see, *nat*-see) *n*. [*pl*. -zis] 1. A member of the National Socialist Party of Germany. 2. A fascist, following the principles of this party.—*adj*. Characteristic of or pertaining to German fascism.

Na·zism (*naht*-sizm, *nat*-sizm) *n*. Also **Na·zi·ism.** German fascism; the doctrine of the

National Socialist Party, advocating racial and religious intolerance, military aggression, etc.

Ne·an·der·thal (nee-*an*-der-tahl) *adj. Geology.* Relating to the paleolithic era.—**Neanderthal man.** A man of the early stone age, whose remains were found in the Rhine valley.

neap tide (*neep*). The lowest tide during the lunar month.

Ne·a·pol·i·tan (nee-uh-*pol*-uh-tun) *adj.* Relating to Naples, Italy.—*n.* An inhabitant of Naples.

near (*nihr*) *adv.* 1. At a short distance. 2. Within close degree.—*adj.* [near·er; nearest] 1. Adjacent; not far distant. 2. Close; intimate. 3. Not deviating.—*prep.* Close to. —*v.* To approach; come close to.—**near·ly** *adv.* —**near·ness** *n.*

near·by *adv.* At a short distance.—*adj.* Adjacent; close.

Near East. Area about the eastern Mediterranean; the Balkan States and SW Asia.

near·sight·ed *adj.* Myopic; short-sighted; not able to see clearly at a distance.—**near·sight·ed·ly** *adv.*—**near·sight·ed·ness** *n.*

neat (*neet*) *adj.* 1. Tidy; orderly. 2. Spruce; trim. 3. Unadulterated; unmixed. 'Neat brandy.' 4. Nice; exact; skillfully executed. —**neat·ly** *adv.*—**neat·ness** *n.*

neat *n. sing. & pl.* An ox or oxen. 'Neat's foot oil.'

Neb·u·chad·nez·zar, Neb·u·chad·rez·zar (neb-yuh-kud-*nez*-er; -*rez*-er) *n.* A Babylonian King who captured Jerusalem.

neb·u·la (*neb*-yoo-luh) *n.* [*pl.* -lae, -las] A luminous gaseous substance in outer space.—**neb·u·lar** *adj.* Relating to nebulae.

neb·u·lous (*neb*-yoo-luss) *adj.* 1. Cloudy; misty. 2. Hazy; confused; vague.—**neb·u·lous·ly** *adv.*—**neb·u·lous·ness** *n.*

nec·es·sar·y (*ness*-uh-sehr-ee) *adj.* 1. Essential; indispensable; requisite. 2. Inevitable; certain to occur.—*n.* [*pl.* -ies] An essential; a necessity.—**nec·es·sar·i·ly** *adv.*

ne·ces·si·tate (nuh-*sess*-uh-tayt) *v.* [-tat·ed; -tat·ing] To oblige; compel; make necessary. —**ne·ces·si·ta·tion** *n.*—**ne·ces·si·ta·tive** *adj.*

ne·ces·si·tous (nuh-*sess*-uh-tuss) *adj.* Destitute; poor; needy.—**ne·ces·si·tous·ly** *adv.*

ne·ces·si·ty (nih-*sess*-uh-tee) *n.* [*pl.* -ties] 1. An essential; a necessary; anything indispensable. 2. Compulsion; constraint. 3. Poverty.

neck *n.* 1. The part of the body between the head and trunk. 2. The narrow part of a bottle, jug, etc. 3. The finger board of a stringed instrument.—*v. Slang.* To fondle; caress; make love.—*adj.* 1. Worn around the neck. 2. Relating to the neck.

neck band. A band supporting the collar of a garment.

neck·cloth *n.* A kerchief or the like worn about the neck.

neck·er·chief (*nek*-er-chif) *n.* A triangular piece of material worn around the neck.

neck·tie *n.* An ornamental band worn around the neck and knotted in front; cravat.

neck·lace (*nek*-luss) *n.* An ornamental strand of beads, stones, etc., worn around the throat.

ne·crol·o·gy (neh-*krol*-uh-jee) *n.* [*pl.* -gies] An obituary; a list of deaths.—**nec·ro·log·i·cal** (nek-ruh-*loj*-ih-k'l) *adj.*—**ne·crol·o·gist** *n.*—**nec·ro·log·i·cal·ly** *adj.*

nec·ro·man·cy (*nek*-ruh-man-see) *n.* 1. Conjuration; the exercise of magic. 2. The art of supposed communication with the dead.—**nec·ro·man·cer** *n.* A conjurer; sorcerer; wizard.

ne·crop·o·lis (neh-*krop*-uh-liss) *n.* [*pl.* -lis·es] A cemetery.

nec·tar (*nek*-ter) *n.* 1. The wine of the gods. 2. A delicious beverage.

nec·tar·ine (*nek*-ter-een) *n.* A type of peach having a smooth skin.

nee (*nay*) *adj.* Born; used to indicate a married woman's maiden name. 'Mrs. Robert Jones, nee Jane Smith.'

need *n.* 1. Necessity; want. 2. Destitution; poverty. 3. A condition of emergency, requiring help.—*v.* 1. To require; have want of. 2. To have to; to be necessary.—**need·er** *n.*

need·ful *adj.* 1. Needy; distressful. 2. Necessary; requisite.—**need·ful·ly** *adv.*— **-ful·ness** *n.*

nee·dle *n.* 1. A small pointed instrument for sewing. 2. A pointed steel device balanced on a pivot. 'A phonograph needle; a dipping needle.' 3. An implement of wood, ivory, or metal for knitting, crocheting, etc. 4. A slender, hollow rod for inserting fluids. 'A hypodermic needle.'—*v.* [nee·dled; nee·dling] 1. To pierce. 2. *Slang.* To vex; irritate; goad into action.

nee·dle·ful *n.* [*pl.* -fuls] As much thread as is put into a needle.

need·less *adj.* Unnecessary; not required. —**need·less·ly** *adv.*—**need·less·ness** *n.*

nee·dle·wom·an *n.* [*pl.* -wom·en] A seamstress.

nee·dle·work *n.* Handiwork done with needle and thread, as sewing, embroidery.

needs *adv.* Necessarily (with *must*). 'He must needs be weary.'

need·y *adj.* [need·i·er; need·i·est] Poor; in need. —*n. pl.* The poor.—**need·i·ness** *n.*

ne'er (*nehr*). *Poetic contraction* of **never.**

ne'er-do-well *n.* 1. An idler; an incompetent. 2. An unreliable person.—*adj.* Good-for-nothing.

ne·far·i·ous (neh-*fehr*-ee-uss) *adj.* Villainous; infamous; characterized by evil.—**ne·far·i·ous·ly** *adv.*—**ne·far·i·ous·ness** *n.*

ne·ga·tion (nih-*gay*-shun) *n.* 1. Denial; contradiction; repudiation. 2. An assertion of denial.

neg·a·tive (*neg*-uh-tiv) *adj.* 1. Asserting denial. 2. Refusing. 'A negative answer.' 3. Vetoing; refusing to concur. 4. Defeatist. —*n.* 1. An assertion of denial. 2. The side not assenting, as in a debate. 3. *Photography.* The original film, having lights and shadows

N

in opposite relation to the final print. 4. *Electricity.* The pole of a circuit toward which the current flows.—*v.* [neg·a·tived; neg·a·tiv·ing] To disprove; deny.—**neg·a·tiv·i·ty, -tive·ness** *n.*

neg·a·tiv·ism (*neg*-uh-tiv-izm) *n.* Agnosticism; skepticism; the doctrine denying man's knowledge of God.—**neg·a·tiv·ist** *n.* & *adj.*—**neg·a·tiv·ist·ic** *adj.*

neg·lect (nug-*lekt*) *v.* 1. To slight; pay little attention to. 2. To overlook; leave undone.—*n.* 1. Disregard; indifference; heedlessness. 2. Carelessness; negligence.—**neg·lect·er** *n.*—**neg·lect·ful** *adj.*—**neg·lect·ful·ly** *adv.*—**neg·lect·ful·ness** *n.*

neg·li·gee, né·gli·gé (neg-luh-*zhay*, *neg*-) *n.* A woman's light dressing gown.

neg·li·gence (*neg*-lih-junss) *n.* 1. Neglectfulness; carelessness. 2. Oversight; indifference to duty.

neg·li·gent *adj.* Careless; neglectful.—**neg·li·gent·ly** *adv.*

neg·li·gi·ble (*neg*-lih-juh-b'l) *adj.* Unimportant; trifling; of little value.—**neg·li·gi·bil·i·ty** *n.*—**neg·li·gi·ble·ness** *n.*—**neg·li·gi·bly** *adv.*

ne·go·ti·a·ble (neh-*goh*-shee-uh-b'l) *adj.* 1. Capable of being effected. 2. Transferable. 'Negotiable notes.'—**ne·go·ti·a·bil·i·ty** *n.*

ne·go·ti·ate (neh-*goh*-shee-ayt) *v.* [-at·ed; -at·ing] 1. To conduct a transaction. 2. To bargain by discussion. 3. To transfer or sell. 4. *Colloquial.* To accomplish successfully.—**ne·go·ti·a·tion** *n.*—**ne·go·ti·a·tor** *n.*

Ne·gress (*nee*-gress) *n.* A woman of the black-skinned race.

Ne·gri·to (neh-*gree*-toh) *n.* [*pl.* -tos, -toes] A diminutive Negroid race of the Malay Archipelago.

Ne·gro (*nee*-groh) *n.* [*pl.* -groes] 1. A member of the black-skinned race, esp. the aborigines of Africa. 2. A person having Negro blood.

Ne·groid (*nee*-groyd) *adj.* Resembling Negroes.—*n.* Member of a race with characteristics similar to those of the Negroes.

neigh (*nay*) *n.* A whinny; the cry of a horse.—*v.* To whinny or nicker, as a horse.

neigh·bor (*nay*-ber) *n.* 1. A person dwelling near another. 2. A country adjacent to another.—*adj.* 1. Adjoining; adjacent; next. 2. Being in the same vicinity.—*v.* To adjoin.

neigh·bor·hood (*nay*-ber-hood) *n.* 1. A vicinity; a district; an area in a community. 2. The inhabitants of a district.

neigh·bor·ing (*nay*-ber-ing) *adj.* Bordering; adjacent; adjoining.

neigh·bor·ly *adj.* Friendly; mutually helpful.

nei·ther (*nee*-ther; *ny*-ther) *pron.* & *adj.* & *conj.* Not one of the two.

nem·e·sis (*nem*-uh-siss) *n.* [*pl.* -ses] 1. Justifiable vengeance; retribution. 2. [*cap.*] A Greek goddess who visited retribution on men.

ne·o- (*nee*-oh) *Prefix:* New.

neoclassic	neo-Darwinism	Neo-Latin
neocosmic	neo-Hellenism	neopaganism

ne·o·dym·i·um (nee-oh-*dim*-ee-um) *n.* A metallic element of the rare-earth group. (*Symbol:* Nd).

ne·o·lith·ic (nee-oh-*lith*-ik) *adj.* Characteristic of or denoting the age of human culture characterized by polished stone implements.

ne·ol·o·gism (nee-*ol*-og-jizm) *n.* A new word or expression.

ne·ol·o·gist *n.* A coiner of words.—**ne·ol·o·gy** *n.*

ne·on (*nee*-on) *n.* A colorless gaseous element used in one type of electric lamp. (*Symbol:* Ne).

neon lamp. An electric lamp consisting of a tube filled with an incandescent gas, such as neon, widely used for display lighting.

ne·o·phyte (*nee*-oh-fyte) *n.* A novice; beginner.

ne·o·prene (*nee*-oh-preen) *n.* A flexible waterproof and oilproof plastic.

neph·ew (*nef*-yoo) *n.* The son of a brother or a sister.

ne·phri·tis (neh-*fry*-tiss) *n.* Inflammation of the kidney.—**ne·phrit·ic** (neh-*frit*-ik) *adj.*

nep·o·tism (*nep*-uh-tizm) *n.* Favoritism; patronage, esp. to relatives.—**nep·o·tist** *n.*

Nep·tune (*nep*-tyoon) *n.* 1. *Roman Mythology.* The god of the sea. 2. The most distant planet of the solar system.—**Nep·tu·ni·an** *adj.*

nep·tu·ni·um (nep-*tyoo*-nee-um) *n.* A radioactive element processed from uranium ore and used in the atomic bomb. (*Symbol:* Np)

Ne·re·id (*neer*-ee-id) *n.* A sea nymph.

nerve *n.* 1. *Anatomy.* One of the fibers conveying sensation to the brain. 2. Courage; daring; self-command. 3. *Slang.* Audacity; presumptuousness.—*v.* [nerved; nerv·ing] To strengthen; steel; brace.

nerve center. A group of nerve cells performing a function as a unit.

nerve·less *adj.* 1. Weak; powerless to move. 2. Having no nerves.—**nerve·less·ly** *adv.*—**nerve·less·ness** *n.*

nerv·ous (*nerv*-us) *adj.* 1. Easily overwrought; excitable; unstable. 2. Apprehensive; worried. 3. Vigorous; flexible; forceful. 4. Consisting of nerves.—**nerv·ous·ly** *adv.*—**nerv·ous·ness** *n.*

nervous system. The collective nerve cells of an organism.

nerv·y *adj.* [nerv·i·er; nerv·i·est] *Slang.* 1. Daring. 2. Audacious.

nest *n.* 1. A dwelling of twigs, clay, etc., prepared by a bird; a bed prepared for laying and hatching eggs. 2. A number of creatures dwelling together. 3. A cozy retreat.—*v.* To live in or build a nest.

NEST

nest egg. 1. An egg for enticing a hen into a nest. 2. A savings fund.

nes·tle (*ness*-'l) *v.* [nes·tled; nes·tling] To snuggle; settle cozily.—**nest·ler** *n.*

nest·ling *n.* A newly hatched bird.

net *n.* 1. A snare of cord, twine, or other fiber for catching birds, fishes, etc. 2. Any article made of meshed fiber, as a hairnet, mosquito net, etc.—*v.* [net·ted; net·ting] 1. To snare; capture. 2. To take in a net.

net *adj.* 1. Clear, after deducting. 'Net profit.' 2. Exclusive of container, wrapping, etc. 'Net weight.'—*v.* To take as profit.

neth·er (*neth*-er) *adj.* 1. Lower; lying beneath. 2. Belonging to the underworld.

neth·er·most (*neth*-er-mohst) *adj.* Lowest; farthest down.

net·ting *n.* Fabric of meshed material for nets.

net·tle (*net*-'l) *n.* An herb having leaves with stinging hairlike follicles.—*v.* [net·tled; net·tling] To irritate; provoke.

net·work *n.* 1. A system of intercrossing threads, channels, routes, etc.; mesh. 2. A radio chain.

neu·ral (*noo*-r'l) *adj.* Relating to the nerves.

neu·ral·gia (nuh-*ral*-juh) *n.* Pain in a nerve. —**neu·ral·gic** *adj.* Characterized by neuralgia.

neu·ras·the·ni·a (noo-rus-*thee*-nee-uh) *n.* Nervous prostration; exhaustion of nervous energy.—**neu·ras·then·ic** (noo-rus-*then*-ik) *adj.*

neu·ri·tis (noo-*ry*-tiss) *n.* Inflammation of a nerve.—**neu·rit·ic** (noor-*it*-ik) *adj.* Characterized by neuritis.

neu·rol·o·gy (noor-*ol*-uh-jee) *n.* The science of the nervous system.—**neu·rol·o·gist** *n.*—**neu·ro·log·i·cal** *adj.*

neu·ro·sis (noor-*oh*-siss) *n.* [*pl.* -ses] A nervous disorder affecting the action but not the structure of the nervous system, esp. one caused by mental influences and not directly traceable to a physical injury.

neu·rot·ic (noo-*rot*-ik) *n.* A person suffering from abnormal personal conflicts; one afflicted with a neurosis.—*adj.* 1. Having a neurosis. 2. Pertaining to the nerves.

neu·ter (*noo*-ter) *adj.* 1. *Grammar.* Of neither masculine nor feminine gender. 2. Sexless; of neither sex. 3. Castrated.—**neu·ter** *n.*

neu·tral (*noo*-tr'l) *adj.* 1. Impartial; indifferent; taking no sides. 2. *Chemistry.* Neither acid nor alkaline. 3. Of colors, pure; containing no other pigment.—*n.* 1. A person taking no sides. 2. A noncombatant nation during a war.—**neu·tral·i·ty** (noo-*tral*-ih-tee) *n.*

neu·tral·ize (*noo*-truh-lyze) *v.* [neu·tral·ized; neu·tral·iz·ing] 1. *Chemistry.* To reduce to an inactive state. 2. To cancel out; nullify by counterbalancing.—**neu·tral·i·za·tion** (noo-truh-lih-*zay*-shun) *n.*—**neu·tral·i·zer** *n.*

neu·tron (*noo*-tron) *n.* *Chemistry.* A mass produced by the union of a proton and an electron.

nev·er (*nev*-er) *adv.* 1. Not ever; at no time. 2. Not at all.

nev·er·more *adv.* Never again.

nev·er·the·less *adv.* Yet; however; notwithstanding.

new *adj.* 1. Modern; of recent origin; not old. 2. novel; unfamiliar. 3. Unaccustomed; inexperienced. 4. Fresh; unused. 5. Commencing again. 'A new week.' 6. Recently discovered; not formerly known.—*adv.* Newly; lately.—**new·ness** *n.*

new·born *adj.* Recently born; just come into the world.

new·com·er (*noo*-kum-er) *n.* A person recently arrived; stranger.

new·el (*noo*-ul) *n.* The post at the bottom of a stairway.

New England. Northeastern U.S., comprising Maine, New Hampshire, Vermont, Massachusetts, Rhode Island, and Connecticut. —**New Englander** *n.*

new·fan·gled *adj.* Novel; newly invented.

NEWEL

Newfoundland dog (noo-*found*-land). A large shaggy dog originating in Newfoundland.

new·ly *adv.* 1. Lately; recently. 2. Freshly; anew.

news (*nooz*) *n.* 1. Tidings; recent information. 2. The report of public events.

news·boy *n.* A boy delivering or selling newspapers.

news·cast *n.* The report of a radio news commentator.—**news·cast·er** *n.*—**news·cast·ing** *n.*

news·pa·per *n.* A regularly published journal consisting mainly of news reports.

news·reel *n.* A motion picture of news events.

news·y *adj.* [news·i·er; news·i·est] *Colloquial.* Full of news.

newt *n.* A salamander; amphibian of the lizard family.

New Testament. The portion of the Bible dealing with the life and teachings of Jesus Christ and his apostles.

New World. America.

New Year's Day, New Year's. The first day of the calendar year; January 1.

NEWT (1/4 life size)

next *adj.* 1. Nearest. 2. Adjacent; adjoining. 3. Following; immediately succeeding.—*adv.* At the following time.

nex·us (*nek*-suss) *n.* Connection; tie; interdependence.

N.F., n.f. *Abbreviations for* **National Formulary.**

ni·a·cin (*ny*-uh-sin) *n.* The factor in the vitamin B complex which prevents pellagra; nicotinic acid.

Ni·ag·a·ra Falls (ny-*ag*-ruh). A famous waterfall in the Niagara River, 160 feet high, 1,400 feet wide.

nib *n.* 1. A bill or beak. 2. A point, esp. of a pen.—*v.* [nibbed; nib·bing] 1. To supply with a point. 2. To repair the nib of, as a pen.

N

nib·ble (*nib*-'l) *v.* [nib·bled; nib·bling] To bite at gently; eat in small bits.—*n.* A little bite; seizing with the mouth.—**nib·bler** *n.*

Ni·be·lung·en·lied (*nee*-buh-lung-un-leed) *n.* A cycle of medieval German epic poems of which Siegfried is the hero.

nib·lick (*nib*-lik) *n.* A golf club with metal head deep-tilted for maximum lift.

nice (*nysse*) *adj.* [nic·er; nic·est] 1. Pleasant; agreeable. 2. Accurate; precise. 3. Discerning; apprehending slight differences; subtle. 4. Overscrupulous; fastidious; squeamish. —**nice·ly** *adv.*—**nice·ness** *n.*

ni·ce·ty (*nysse*-uh-tee) *n.* [*pl.* -ties] 1. A minute distinction. 2. Delicate management; exactness in treatment. 3. Delicacy of perception; subtlety. 4. Minuteness of observation; precision. 5. Fastidiousness; delicacy.

niche (*nich*) *n.* 1. A recess in a wall for a bust or monument. 2. A special place or position allotted to a person or thing.

nick *n.* 1. A notch; chip. 2. The exact time required; critical time.—*v.* 1. To mar by chipping. 2. To try for at the most favorable moment. 3. *Slang.* To obtain by cheating.

Nick, Old Nick *n.* The devil.

NICHE

nick·el (*nik*-'l) *n.* 1. A five-cent piece. 2. A hard, ductile, whitish, noncorrosive metal. (*Symbol:* Ni).—*v.* To plate with nickel.

nick·el·o·de·on (nik-uh-*loh*-dee-un) *n.* An early moving picture theater where admission was a nickel.

nick·el-plate *v.* [-plat·ed; -plat·ing] To cover the surface of a metal with nickel by electroplating.

nickel silver. A durable alloy of two parts copper, one zinc, and one nickel.

nick·nack. *Variant spelling* of **knickknack.**

nick·name (*nik*-naym) *n.* A shortened or familiar name given a person in place of his real one.—**nick·name** *v.* [-named; -nam·ing].

nic·o·tine (*nik*-uh-teen) *n.* Also **nic·o·tin.** A poisonous, volatile alkaloid found in tobacco.

nicotinic acid (nik-uh-*tin*-ik). Niacin.

niece (*neess*) *n.* The daughter of one's sister or brother.

nif·ty (*nif*-tee) *adj.* [nif·ti·er; nif·ti·est] *Slang.* Smart; neat; very good.

nig·gard (*nig*-erd) *n.* A mean, stingy person; miser.—**nig·gard, nig·gard·ly** *adj.* Stingy.—**nig·gard·li·ness** *n.*—**nig·gard·ly** *adv.*

Ni·ger (*ny*-jer). A river of central west Africa.

nigh (*nye*) *adv.* 1. Close in place, time, or relationship; near. 2. Almost; nearly.—*adj.* Near, close.—**nigh·ness** *n.*

night (*nyte*) *n.* 1. The hours during which the earth is not illuminated by the sun. 2. A state

or time of darkness, misfortune, obscurity, ignorance, etc.—**night** *adj.*

night black	nightfly	night-struck
night blindness	nightfowl	night swift
nightcapped	night-haired	nighttime
night-cloaked	night-haunted	night-veiled
night-cradled	night-hid	nightwake
night dark	nightman	nightwalking
nightdress	night-mantled	nightward
night-enshrouded	night-overtaken	nightwear
night-filled	night-scented	night work
nightfish	nightshirt	night worker

night·cap *n.* 1. A cap worn while sleeping. 2. A drink or toddy taken before going to bed.

night·fall *n.* The close of day; twilight.

night·gown *n.* A loose gown worn in bed.

night·hawk *n.* 1. A bird of the whippoorwill family which preys on large insects. 3. One who habitually keeps late hours.

night·in·gale (*nyte*-'n-gayl) *n.* A small, migratory bird known for its sweet song.

night letter. A long telegram sent without priority at low rates during the night.

night·ly *adj.* Done or appearing at night or every night.—*adv.* Every night.

night·mare *n.* A fearful dream induced by upset nerves or stomach.

NIGHTINGALE (1/5 life size)

night·shade *n.* Any of a family of plants which includes potatoes, eggplant, and others. —**deadly nightshade.** Belladonna.

night·walk·er *n.* 1. A large earthworm which appears at night. 2. One who roams around at night.

ni·hil·ism (*ny*-ul-izm) *n.* 1. Nothingness. 2. The denial of all existence and the possibility of valid knowledge. 3. [*cap.*] The belief that there can be no social or economic progress until all existing institutions have been destroyed.—**ni·hil·ist** *n.*—**ni·hil·ist, ni·hil·is·tic** *adj.*

Nile. Great African river flowing mainly through Egypt.

nil *n.* Nothing; none at all.

nim·ble (*nim*-b'l) *adj.* 1. Agile; lively; speedy. 2. Quick-witted; bright.—**nim·ble·ness** *n.*—**nim·bly** *adv.*

nimble-brained	nimble-headed	nimble-spirited
nimble-fingered	nimble-jointed	nimble-tongued
nimble-footed	nimble-mouthed	nimble-witted

nim·bus (*nim*-bus) *n.* [*pl.* -bi, -bus·es] 1. A halo or circle of rays, used esp. in art to show divinity. 2. A rain cloud.

nim·rod (*nim*-rod) *n.* A devotee of hunting.

nin·com·poop (*nin*-kum-poop) *n.* A dunce; fool.

nine *adj.* Having or composed of one less than ten units.—*n.* 1. The number 9. 2. Any group of nine units or members.—**the nine.** The Muses.—**ninth** *adj.*

nine·pins (*nyne*-pinz) *n.* A game in which a ball is bowled at nine upright wooden pins.

nine·teen (nyne-*teen*) *n.* The number composed of ten and nine, or one less than twenty.—**nine·teen, nine·teenth** *adj.*—**nine·teenth** *n.*

nine·ty (*nyne*-tee) *n.* The product of nine times ten; ten less than a hundred.—**nine·ty, nine·ti·eth** *adj.*—**nine·ti·eth** *n.*

nin·ny (*nin*-ee) *n.* [*pl.* -nies] A fool; nincompoop.

ni·o·bi·um (ny-*oh*-bee-um) *n.* Columbium, a rare metallic element. (*Symbol:* Nb).

nip *v.* [nipped; nip·ping] 1. To pinch; bite lightly. 2. To cut off the end; pinch off. 3. To destroy, as by frost; halt the development of. 4. To chill; frost.—**nip** *n.*—**nip and tuck.** See-saw; with the advantage shifting.

nip *n.* A sip or small draft of liquor.—*v.* To sip, as liqueur.

nip·per *n.* 1. [*pl.*] A pair of sharp-nosed pliers for cutting wire. 2. That which nips.

nip·ple (*nip*-'l) *n.* 1. The protuberance by which milk is drawn from the breast of a female; teat. 2. An artificial pap or teat. 3. Anything that projects like a nipple.

Nip·pon (nih-*pon*) Japan.—**Nip·pon·ese** (nip-'n-eez) *n. & adj.* Japanese.

nip·py (*nip*-ee) *adj.* [nip·pi·er; nip·pi·est] Biting; pungent in taste; chilling or frosting.

Nir·va·na (ner-*van*-uh) *n. Buddhism & Hinduism.* Total conquest by the mind of the drive to live and the absorption of the soul by God.

Ni·sei (*nee*-say) *n.* One born to Japanese parents in the U.S.; a Japanese-American.

nit *n.* The egg or the young of a louse or similar parasite.—**nit·ty** *adj.*

ni·ter, ni·tre (*nyte*-er) *n.* A nitrate salt, esp. potassium nitrate.

ni·ton (*ny*-ton) *n.* An inert gaseous element emanating from radium; radon. (*Symbol:* Nt).

ni·trate (*ny*-trayt) *n.* A nitric-acid salt.—*v.* [ni·trat·ed; ni·trat·ing] To convert to a nitric salt; react with nitric acid.

ni·tric (*ny*-trik) *adj.* Pertaining to nitrogen compounds having more nitrogen than nitrous compounds have.

nitric acid. *n.* A powerful acid containing hydrogen, nitrogen, and oxygen.

ni·tride (*ny*-tryde) *n.* Also **ni·trid.** A compound of nitrogen with a positively charged element or radical.

ni·tri·fy (*ny*-truh-fy) *v.* [-fied; -fy·ing] 1. To convert into a nitrate. 2. To cover or sprinkle with nitrates.—**ni·tri·fi·ca·tion** *n.*

ni·tro·gen (*ny*-truh-jin) *n.* A heavy, odorless, gaseous element which constitutes about four-fifths of the air and exists in all living matter. (*Symbol:* N).—**ni·trog·e·nous** *adj.*

ni·tro·glyc·er·in, ni·tro·glyc·er·ine (ny-troh-*gliss*-er-in) *n.* An oily, highly explosive compound made from glycerin combined with a concentrated solution of nitric and sulphuric acids.

ni·trous (*ny*-truss) *adj. Chemistry.* Denoting nitrogen compounds in which the nitrogen's valence is three.

nitrous oxide *n.* A gas composed of two molecules of nitrogen to one of oxygen; laughing gas.

nit·wit (*nit*-wit) *n.* A foolish or giddy person.

nix, nix·ie *n.* [*pl.* nix·es] A water sprite.

nix *adv. Slang.* No; nothing doing; I refuse.

NLRB. National Labor Relations Board; a Department of Labor agency established under the Wagner Act to deal with labor disputes and to establish collective-bargaining machinery.

no *n.* [*pl.* noes] 1. A denial or refusal. 2. A negative vote. 3. [*pl.*] Those who cast a negative vote.—*adv.* 1. Not; in no degree. 2. The opposite of yes.—*adj.* Not any; none.

No·ah (*noh*-uh) *n. Old Testament.* The builder of the ark which saved all animal species during the flood.

nob *n. Slang.* The head.

nob·by *adj. Slang.* Stylish; swell.

Nobel prizes (noh-*bel*). Annual cash awards given to persons judged to have made outstanding contributions to the welfare of humanity in science, literature, and the preservation of peace.

no·bil·i·ty (noh-*bil*-uh-tee) *n.* [*pl.* -ties] 1. Greatness; dignity of mind. 2. Peerage; persons of titled rank collectively.

no·ble (*noh*-b'l) *adj.* 1. High in excellence or worth; great; honorable. 2. Lofty; superior intellectually and morally. 3. Magnificent; stately; grand. 4. *Chemistry.* Inactive; slow to react. 5. Pertaining to the aristocracy.—*n.* A nobleman; person of rank.—**no·ble·ness** *n.* —**no·bly** *adv.*

noble-born	noble looking	noble-spirited
noble-featured	noble-minded	noble-tempered
noble-hearted	noble-natured	noblewoman

no·ble·man (*noh*-b'l-m'n) *n.* [*pl.* -men] A peer; titled person.

no·bod·y (*noh*-bod-ee) *pron.* No one.—*n.* [*pl.* -ies] An unimportant person.

noc·tur·nal (nok-*tern*-ul) *adj.* 1. Pertaining to the night; done at night. 2. Habitually active at night.—**noc·tur·nal·ly** *adv.*

noc·turne (*nok*-tern) *n.* 1. *Music.* A piece pertaining to impressions of the night; an emotional, dreamy composition. 2. *Painting.* A work depicting night.

nod *v.* [nod·ded; nod·ding] 1. To bend the head either forward or sideways with a quick motion, as while falling asleep. 2. To commit an oversight through carelessness. 3. To incline the head by way of assent, greeting, or summons. 4. To bend or incline the top with a quick motion, as trees.—**nod** *n.*—**nod·der** *n.*

nod·al (*noh*-d'l) *adj.* Pertaining to a node or nodes; knotty.

nod·dle (*nod*-'l) *n. Colloquial.* The head.

node *n.* 1. A knot; knob; protuberance. 2. *Medical.* A swelling. 3. A center point

N

where parts join. 4. *Physics*. In a vibrating body, a point which does not vibrate.

nod·ule (*nod*-yool) *n.* A little knot or lump. —**nod·u·lar** (*nod*-yuh-ler) *adj.*

no·el (noh-*el*) *n.* 1. A Christmas carol. 2. [*cap.*] Christmas; Christmas joy.

nog·gin (*nog*-in) *n.* 1. A small mug or its contents. 2. A gill; unit of fluid measure.

noise (*noyz*) *n.* 1. A sound. 2. An outcry; clamor; loud talk. 3. Frequent talk; much public conversation.—*v.* [noised; nois·ing] 1. To spread by rumor. 2. To disturb with noise. 3. To sound loud.—**noise·less** *adj.* — -**less·ly** *adv.*— -**less·ness** *n.*

noi·some (*noy*-sum) *adj.* 1. Noxious; unwholesome; destructive. 2. Offensive to the smell or other senses; disgusting.—**noi·some·ly** *adv.*—**noi·some·ness** *n.*

noi·sy (*noy*-zee) *adj.* [nois·i·er; nois·i·est] 1. Making a loud sound; clamorous. 2. Full of noise.—**nois·i·ly** *adv.*—**nois·i·ness** *n.*

nol-pros (nol-*pross*) *v.* [nol-prossed; nol-prossing]. Also **nol·le pros·e·qui.** *Law.* To discontinue any further action by the plaintiff.

no·mad (*noh*-mad) *n.* One of a race or tribe which has no fixed abode, but wanders from place to place.—**no·mad** *adj.*

no·mad·ic (noh-*mad*-ik) *adj.* Wandering; pastoral; nomad.—**no·mad·i·cal·ly** *adv.*

nom de plume (nom-duh-*ploom*). An assumed name taken by an author; pen name.

no·men·cla·ture (*noh*-m'n-klay-cher) *n.* The system of terms used in any one branch of knowledge; vocabulary; terminology.

nom·i·nal (*nom*-in-'l) *adj.* Existing in name only; not real; so-called.

nom·i·nate (*nom*-in-ayt) *v.* [nom·i·nat·ed; nom·i·nat·ing] 1. To propose as a candidate for an election or appointment. 2. To appoint. 3. To name; mention by name.— -**na·tor** *n.*

nom·i·na·tion (nom-in-*ay*-shun) *n.* 1. The act of proposing a name for an office or election. 2. The state of being nominated. 3. The power of appointing or suggesting for office.

nom·i·na·tive (*nom*-in-uh-tiv) *adj.* *Grammar.* Denoting the case of a noun or pronoun used as the subject of a sentence, an appositive of the subject, or a predicate complement.—*n.* The nominative case.

nom·i·nee (nom-ih-*nee*) *n.* A person appointed or proposed for a position or office.

non- *prefix.* Not.

Note: This prefix indicates a simple negative with no implication of opposite force. The compounds formed with *non-* the meanings of which are obvious are listed to indicate spelling, beginning at the foot of this page.

non·age (*non*-ij) *n.* 1. Minority; period before a person comes of legal age. 2. Immaturity.

non·a·ge·nar·i·an (non-uh-jen-*ehr*-ee-un) *adj.* Between 90 and 100 years old.—*n.* A person of that age.

nonce (*nonss*) *n.* Present occasion or purpose; used esp. in the phrase, *for the nonce.*

non·cha·lance (*non*-shuh-lunss, non-shuh-*lonss*) *n.* Carelessness; coolness; indifference; want of earnestness.—**non·cha·lant** *adj.*

non·com (non-*kom*) *n.* *Slang.* A non-commis-

nonabsorbent	nonchargeable	noncontemporary	nondetachable
nonacceptance	non-Christian	noncontiguous	nondevotional
nonadhesive	noncivilized	noncontinuous	nondictatorial
nonadjacent	nonclerical	noncontraband	nondiffusing
nonadvantageous	noncoalescing	noncontradictory	nondirectional
non-African	noncoercive	noncontributing	nondirigible
nonaggression	noncollapsible	noncontroversial	nondisciplinary
nonaggressive	noncollectable	nonconventional	nondiscovery
nonalcoholic	noncollegiate	nonconvergent	nondiscriminatory
non-American	noncombat	nonconversant	nondisparaging
non-Anglican	noncombining	nonconvertible	nondisposal
nonantagonistic	noncombustible	nonconvivial	nondistribution
nonapostolic	noncommercial	non-co-operative	nondiversification
nonappearance	noncommunicable	noncorresponding	nondivisible
non-Arabic	noncommunicant	noncorrodible	nondoctrinal
non-Aryan	non-Communist	noncorrosive	nondutiable
non-Asiatic	non-Communistic	noncreative	nonedible
nonassessable	noncompensating	noncriminal	noneducational
nonassimilable	noncompeting	noncritical	non-Egyptian
nonattendance	noncompetitive	noncrystallized	nonelectrical
nonauthoritative	noncompletion	noncrystallizing	nonelimination
nonbeliever	noncompliance	nonculpable	nonenforcement
nonbelieving	noncompressible	noncumulative	non-English
nonbelligerent	noncompulsion	nondamageable	nonepiscopal
non-Biblical	nonconcealment	non-Darwinian	nonequivalent
nonblooming	nonconcordant	nondeceptive	nonerotic
non-Bolshevik	nonconcurrent	nondeciduous	nonessential
non-Bolshevist	noncondensable	nondefensive	nonethical
non-Brahmanical	nonconditioned	nondefilement	non-Euclidean
nonbreakable	nonconducive	nondefinitive	non-European
non-British	nonconducive	nondeliquescent	noneviction
nonbureaucratic	nonconflicting	nondelivery	nonexclusive
noncategorical	nonconformance	nondemocratic	nonexecution
non-Catholic	nonconforming	nondepartmental	nonexempt
non-Caucasian	non-Congressional	nondeportation	nonexistent
noncellular	nonconsecutive	nondepreciating	nonexisting
non-Celtic	nonconsent	nonderivable	nonexplosive
noncerebral	nonconstructive	nonderogatory	nonexportable
noncertified	noncontagious	nondestructive	nonextortion

sioned officer in the Army or Marine Corps.

non·com·bat·ant (non-*kom*-buh-tunt) *n.* Anyone connected with a military force who is not supposed to fight; a civilian in a place occupied by troops.

non·com·mis·sioned (non-kuh-*mish*-und) *adj.* Not holding rank by commission, as a noncommissioned officer, an appointed officer below the rank of warrant officer.

non·com·mit·tal (non-kuh-*mit*-ul) *adj.* Not decisive; not committed or pledged.—**non·com·mit·tal·ly** *adv.*

non·con·duc·tor (non-k'n-*duk*-ter) *n.* A substance that does not transmit heat or electrical energy.

non·con·form·ist (non-k'n-*form*-ist) *n.* 1. A dissenter; unconventional person. 2. [*cap.*] One of several Protestant groups who broke away from the Church of England.—**non·con·form·i·ty** *n.*

non·de·script (non-deh-*skript*) *adj.* 1. Not easily classified; indescribable; odd. 2. Of no special character; vague.—*n.* A person or thing not easily classified.

none (nun) *pron.* Not any; no part; no one. —*adv.* No; in no degree or extent.

non·en·ti·ty (non-*en*-tuh-tee) *n.* [*pl.* -ties] 1. Nonexistence; nothingness. 2. An insignificant person.

none·such (*nun*-such) *n.* A person or thing that has no peer.

none·the·less (nun-thuh-*less*) *adv.* Nevertheless; all the same.

no·nil·lion (noh-*nil*-yun) *n.* A number represented by the figure 1 followed by 30 zeroes.

non·in·ter·ven·tion (non-in-ter-*ven*-shun) *n.* A policy of not interfering in the internal affairs of another nation or in a dispute between other nations.

non·met·al (non-*met*-'l) *n. Chemistry.* Any element that is not a metal; one which forms acidic rather than basic compounds.—**non·me·tal·lic** (non-muh-*tal*-ik) *adj.*

non·objective *adj.* Denoting a school of painting seeking to express the mind or spirit in forms other than those of the objective world.

non·pa·reil (non-per-*el*) *adj.* Without parallel; supreme.—*n.* 1. A nonesuch. 2. *Printing.* A size of type measuring six points.

non·par·ti·san (non-*pahr*-tih-zun) *adj.* Not taking sides; neutral.

non·plus (non-*pluss*) *v.* [non·plused, non·plussed; non·plus·ing, non·plus·sing] To puzzle; stop; confound.—*n.* Quandary.

non·pro·duc·tive (non-pruh-*duk*-tiv) *adj.* 1. Not producing. 2. Denoting labor which does not directly produce goods or values.

non·pros *v.* [non·prossed; non·pross·ing]. Also **non prosequitur.** *Law.* To discontinue prosecution.

non·rep·re·sen·ta·tion·al (non-rep-reh-zen-*tay*-shun-ul) *adj. Art.* Denoting graphic art which does not represent forms of the objective world.

non·res·i·dent (non-*rez*-uh-dunt) *n.* One who does not live permanently in a given place. —*adj.* Transient; not residing at a specified place.—**non·res·i·dence, non·res·i·den·cy** *n.*

non·sense (*non*-senss) *n.* 1. Silly talk or ac-

N

nonfactual	nonimpairment	nonloving	nonpagan
nonfascist	nonimperative	nonmagnetic	nonpalatal
nonfastidious	nonimperial	nonmagnetizable	nonparallel
nonfermentable	nonimpregnated	non-Malay	nonparental
nonfermentation	nonindictable	non-Malayan	nonparishioner
nonfertility	non-Indo-European	nonmalleable	nonparochial
nonfestive	noninfectious	nonmarital	nonpaying
nonfeudal	noninflammatory	nonmarrying	nonpayment
nonfiction	noninheritable	nonmartial	nonpensionable
nonfictional	noninjurious	nonmaterial	nonperforated
nonfinancial	noninstrumental	nonmaterialistic	nonperformance
nonfiscal	nonintelligent	nonmaternal	nonperformer
nonflowing	nonintercourse	nonmechanistic	nonpermanent
nonfluctuating	noninterfering	nonmedicinal	nonpermeability
nonforfeitable	noninternational	nonmember	nonpermeable
nonfortuitous	nonintoxicant	nonmilitant	nonpermissible
non-French	nonintoxicating	nonministerial	nonpersistent
nonfulfillment	nonintuitive	nonmobile	nonphilanthropic
nonfunctional	noninvidious	non-Mohammedan	nonpoisonous
nongaseous	non-Irish	non-Mongolian	non-Polish
nongelatinous	nonirrigable	nonmoral	nonporous
nongenerative	nonirrigated	non-Moslem	non-Portuguese
nongentile	nonirrigation	nonmunicipal	nonpredatory
non-German	nonirritant	nonnational	nonprejudicial
non-Government	nonirritating	nonnaval	non-Presbyterian
nongovernmental	non-Islamic	nonnavigable	nonproducer
non-Greek	non-Israelite	nonnegotation	nonproducing
nonhabitable	non-Italian	non-Negro	nonprofessional
nonhazardous	non-Japanese	non-neutral	nonprofessorial
non-Hellenic	non-Jew	nonnutritious	nonprofit
nonhereditary	non-Jewish	nonobedience	nonprofiteering
nonheritable	nonjudicial	nonobservance	nonprohibitive
non-Homeric	nonjuristic	nonobstructive	nonpromiscuous
nonhostile	nonlegal	nonoccupational	nonproportional
nonhumorous	nonlimiting	nonodorous	nonproprietary
nonidentity	nonliquefying	nonoperating	nonprotective
nonimaginary	nonliquidation	nonoperative	non-Protestant
nonimmune	nonliterary	nonoriental	nonpunishable
nonimmunized	nonliturgical	nonorthodox	nonputrescent

tions; absurdity. 2. Trifles; worthless things.
—**non·sen·si·cal** *adj.*—**non·sen·si·cal·ly** *adv.*

non sequitur (non *sek*-wih-ter). *Logic.* An inference or conclusion that does not follow from the premises.

non·stop (*non*-stop) *adj.* & *adv.* Traveling continuously, without pausing, until destination is reached.—**non·stop** *n.*

non·suit (*non*-soot) *n.* Stoppage of a lawsuit by a judge when the plaintiff fails to make out a legal case or bring sufficient evidence.

non·sup·port (non-suh-*port*) *n.* Failure to maintain dependents.

non·un·ion (non-*yoon*-yun) *adj.* Not unionized; not covered by a labor-union contract.

non·un·ion·ism *n.* Nonexistence of labor unions in plants or factories.—**non·un·ion·ist** *n.* One who is not a member of a labor union or does not favor labor unionism.—**non·un·ion·ist** *adj.*

noo·dle (*noo*-d'l) *n. Colloquial.* 1. A simpleton; fool. 2. The head.

noo·dles (*noo*-d'lz) *n. pl.* Strips or strands of rolled dough, used in soup, etc.

nook *n.* A corner; recess; secluded retreat.

noon *n.* Midday; twelve hours after midnight; the time of day when the sun reaches its highest point.—**noon** *adj.*

noon·day *n.* Midday; twelve o'clock.

noon·tide *n.* & *adj.* The time of noon; midday.

noose *n.* A running knot which binds closer as it is drawn, as in a snare, lasso, hangman's noose, etc.—*v.* [noosed; noos·ing] To tie in a noose; ensnare; entrap.

nor *conj.* And not; and no more; neither; and not either. 'He had neither courage nor strength.'

Nor·dic (*nor*-dik) *adj.* Northwestern European; Scandinavian.—**Nor·dic** *n.*

Norfolk jacket (*nor*-fuk) *n.* A man's loose, belted jacket.

norm *n.* A pattern; type; authoritative standard.

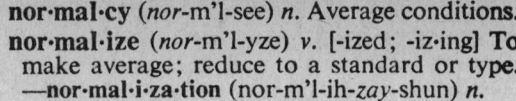

NOOSE

nor·mal (*nor*-mul) *adj.* 1. Conforming to a standard; usual typical. 2. *Geometry.* Perpendicular; standing at right angles. 3. *Psychology.* Of average mental development.—*n.* 1. A usual state, condition, etc. 2. *Geometry.* A perpendicular. 3. *Physics.* The average of observed quantities. 4. The normal temperature (98.6°) of the human body.—**nor·mal·i·ty** (nor-*mal*-ih-tee) *n.* —**nor·mal·ly** *adv.*—**nor·mal·ness** *n.*

nor·mal·cy (*nor*-m'l-see) *n.* Average conditions.

nor·mal·ize (*nor*-m'l-yze) *v.* [-ized; -iz·ing] To make average; reduce to a standard or type. —**nor·mal·i·za·tion** (nor-m'l-ih-*zay*-shun) *n.*

normal school. A school for training teachers.

Nor·man (*nor*-mun) *n.* Inhabitant or native of Normandy, a former province of France. —**Nor·man** *adj.* Pertaining to Normandy, the Normans, or a style of architecture introduced into England by them, characterized by the rounded arch and massive square towers.

Norse *n.* The language of Norway.—*adj.* Norwegian; pertaining to Norway.

Norse·man *n.* [*pl.* -men] A native or inhabitant of Norway.

north *n.* 1. One of the four cardinal points of the compass, directly opposite south. 2. Territory lying toward the north. 3. [*cap.*] Area of the U.S. lying north of the Mason and Dixon line.—*adj.* At, toward, from, in, or of the north.—*adv.* To or in the north.

north·east (north-*eest*) *n.* A compass point halfway between north and east.—*adj.* At, toward, from, in, or of the northeast.—*adv.* Toward the northeast.—**north·east·ern** *adj.*

north·east·er (north-*eest*-er) *n.* A wind blowing from the northeast.

north·east·er·ly *adj.* Toward or from the northeast.

north·er (*nor*-ther) *n.* Strong gale from the north which prevails in the Gulf of Mexico from September to March.

north·er·ly (*nor*-ther-lee) *adj.* & *adv.* To, toward, from, or of the north.—**north·er·li·ness** *n.*

north·ern (*nor*-thern) *adj.* 1. Of, to, in, toward, or from the north. 2. [*cap.*] Pertaining to the North of the U.S.—**north·ern·most** *adj.* Situated at the point farthest north.

north·ern·er (*nor*-thern-er) *n.* 1. A resident of the northern part of any country. 2. [*cap.*] A native of one of the Northern states of the U.S.

northern lights. *n.* Aurora borealis.

north·ing *n.* Northward progress or deviation in sailing or traveling.

north·land *n.* Northern lands; northern part of a country.—**north·land·er** *n.*

North·man *n.* [*pl.* -men] A Norseman; one of the early Scandinavians.

North Pole. The northern extremity of the earth's axis.—**North Pol·ar** *adj.*

North Star *n.* The polestar or North Polar star, used by navigators to determine true north.

north·ward (*north*-werd) *adj.* & *adv.* Toward the north.—*n.* The northern part; the north end.

—**north·ward·ly** adj. & adv.—**north·wards** adv.

north·west (north-west) n. A compass point halfway between north and west.—adj. At, toward, from, in, or of the northwest.—adv. Toward, from, or in the northwest.—**north·west·ern** adj.

north·west·er n. A wind blowing from the northwest.

north·west·er·ly adj. & adv. Toward or from the northwest.

Northwest Passage. A passage from the Atlantic to the Pacific along the northern coasts of America, for which explorers long searched.

Nor·we·gian (nor-wee-jun) n. 1. A native of Norway. 2. The language of Norway.

nose (nohz) n. 1. The projection of the face between the mouth and the eyes; the olfactory organ. 2. Sense of smell. 'A nose for trouble.' 3. A protuberance resembling a nose, as the nozzle of a bellows, pipe, tube, etc. 4. Projecting part.—v. [nosed; nos·ing] 1. To smell out; discover by smelling; detect. 2. To touch the nose. 3. To pry into the affairs of others.

nose band	nose bone	nose-led
nose-belled	nose high	nose piece
nosebleed	nose-leafed	nose-pulled

nose-bag n. A horse's fodder bag.

nose dive. 1. An airplane's downward plunge. 2. Colloquial. An abrupt drop.—**nose-dive** v.

nose·gay (nohz-gay) n. Bunch of flowers; bouquet.

nos·tal·gi·a (noss-tal-juh) n. Homesickness. —**nos·tal·gic** adj. Homesick.

Nos·tra·da·mus (noss-truh-day-mus) n. 1. A 16th-century French physician and prophet. 2. [not cap.] One who makes predictions; a professed seer.

nos·tril (noss-tr'l) n. Either opening in the nose, admitting air.

nos·trum (noss-trum) n. 1. A quack medicine. 2. Any pet scheme or special device.

nos·y (noh-zee) adj. [nos·i·er; nos·i·est] Colloquial. Inquisitive.

not adv. A word expressing negation, denial, refusal, prohibition, etc. 'He will not go.'

no·ta·bil·i·ty (noht-uh-bil-ih-tee) n. [pl. -ies] 1. Worthiness of notice. 2. A prominent person.

no·ta·ble (noht-uh-b'l) adj. 1. Worthy of notice; memorable; distinguished; eminent. 2. Easily seen; evident.—**no·ta·ble** n. A distinguished person.—**no·ta·ble·ness** n.— -bly adv.

no·ta·ry (noht-er-ee) n. [pl. -ries] A person publicly authorized to attest contracts and deeds,

administer oaths, etc.—**no·tar·i·al** (noh-tair-ee-ul) adj.—**no·tar·i·al·ly** adv.

no·ta·tion (noh-tay-shun) n. 1. A note; comment; jotting. 2. A system of signs, symbols, figures, or abbreviations used in any art or science, as arithmetic, algebra, music, chemistry, etc.—**no·ta·tion·al** adj.

notch n. 1. A nick; indentation. 2. A narrow passage through a mountain or hill; pass; defile. 3. Colloquial. A degree; peg.—**notch** v. 1. Make notches in; nick; indent. 2. To place in a notch. 3. To mark or score by notches.—**notched** adj.—**notch·er** n.

note (noht) n. Music. 1. A written symbol representing the pitch and duration of a musical sound. 2. Single tone of definite pitch made by a musical instrument, voice, etc. 3. A musical sound, as a bird's call.

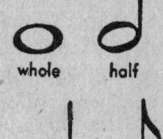

whole   half

note n. 1. A jotting; annotation; comment; memorandum. 2. A short, informal letter. 3. A written promise to pay a sum of money at a specified time. 4. A formal diplomatic communication. 5. Notice; attention. 'Worthy of note.' 6. Reputation; eminence. 'A critic of note.'

quarter   eighth
NOTES

note v. [not·ed; not·ing] 1. To observe carefully; heed. 2. To set down in writing; make a memorandum of. 3. To set down in musical characters. 4. To furnish with notes; annotate.

note·book n. A blank book in which notes or memoranda are written.

not·ed adj. Eminent; prominent; celebrated. —**not·ed·ly** adv.—**not·ed·ness** n.

note paper. Paper used for private correspondence.

note·worth·y adj. Outstanding; striking; worth attention.—**note·worth·i·ly** adv.

noth·ing (nuth-ing) n. 1. Not anything; nought; nonexistence. 2. A trifle; inconsequential thing. 3. Arithmetic. A cipher representing no amount or nought; zero.

noth·ing·ness n. 1. Nonexistence. 2. Insignificance; worthlessness.

no·tice (noh-tiss) n. 1. The act of noting or observing. 2. Intimation; warning, esp. of dismissal from employment. 3. Information; directions; instructions. 'Till further notice.' 4. Heed; attention; cognizance. 'He took no notice.' 5. A publicly displayed sign; published information.—v. [no·ticed; no·tic·ing]

N

1. To take cognizance of; observe. 2. Remark upon; speak of. 3. To treat politely or condescendingly. 4. To give notice to

no·tice·a·ble (*noh*-tiss-uh-b'l) *adj.* Apparent; obvious.—**no·tice·a·bly** *adv.*

no·ti·fi·ca·tion (noh-tih-fih-*kay*-shun) *n.* 1. The issuing of a piece of information. 2. An announcement; notice.

no·ti·fy (*noh*-tih-fy) *v.* [no·ti·fied; no·ti·fy·ing] To make known; inform; announce; declare.

no·tion (*noh*-shun) *n.* 1. A conception; idea. 2. A belief; opinion; view. 3. Inclination; intention; whim. 4. [*pl.*] *Colloquial.* Small miscellaneous personal or household articles.

no·tion·al *adj.* 1. Pertaining to a notion or conception; speculative. 2. Imaginary; visionary; fanciful.— -**al·ist** *n.*— -**al·ly** *adv.*

no·to·ri·e·ty (noh-ter-*eye*-eh-tee) *n.* [*pl.* -ties] 1. Exposure to public knowledge; publicity. 2. Spectacular, often unfavorable, reputation.

no·to·ri·ous (noh-*tor*-ee-us) *adj.* Widely known, usually unfavorably.—**no·to·ri·ous·ly** *adv.*—**no·to·ri·ous·ness** *n.*

not·with·stand·ing *prep.* In spite of; not the less for. 'He is rich notwithstanding his loss.' —*adv.* Nevertheless; yet; however.—*conj.* Although.

nou·gat (*noo*-g't) *n.* A confection of nuts and sugar paste.

nought (*nawt*) *n.* 1. Nothing. 2. Zero; cipher.

noun (*nown*) *n. Grammar.* A substantive; the name of any person, place or thing.—**noun·al** *adj.* Having the qualities of a noun.— -**al·ly** *adv.*

nour·ish (*nur*-ish) *v.* 1. To feed; keep alive with food. 2. To nurture; cause to thrive. — -**ish·er** *n.*— -**ish·ing** *adj.*— -**ish·ing·ly** *adv.*

nour·ish·ment (*nur*-ish-m'nt) *n.* Food; nutriment.

nov·el (*nov*-'l) *adj.* 1. Strange; unusual. 2. Of recent origin.—*n.* A long prose narrative having a complex plot.—**nov·el·is·tic** (nov-uh-*lis*-tik) *adj.*—**nov·el·is·ti·cal·ly** *adv.*

nov·el·ist (*nov*-uh-list) *n.* An author of novels.

nov·el·ty (*nov*-'l-tee) *n.* [*pl.* -ties] 1. A rarity; an infrequent happening. 2. A new and unfamiliar occurrence. 3. [*pl.*] Small, inexpensive, manufactured articles, esp. jewelry.

No·vem·ber (noh-*vem*-ber) *n.* The eleventh month of the year.

nov·ice (*nov*-iss) *n.* 1. A beginner; neophyte. 2. A probationary member of a religious order.

no·vi·ti·ate, no·vi·ci·ate (noh-*vish*-ee-it) *n.* A probationary period for a nun, apprentice, etc.

No·vo·cain (*noh*-vuh-kayn) *n.* A trade-mark for procaine hydrochloride used in a local anesthetic.

now *adv.* 1. At the present. 2. By this time. 'It was now too late.'—*conj.* Since; it being so that.—*n.* The present.—*interj.* I entreat you!

now·a·days *adv.* At present; in these days.

no·way, no·ways *adv.* Not at all.

no·where *adv.* Not in any place.

no·wise *adv.* In no way.

nox·ious (*nok*-shus) *adj.* Poisonous; pernicious; injurious.—**nox·ious·ly** *adv.*—**nox·ious·ness** *n.*

noz·zle (*noz*-'l) *n.* A spout; an attachment on a pipe, hose, etc., for regulating the flow of a liquid.

nth (*enth*) *adj.* Final; last. —**nth degree.** The top limit; highest degree or number possible.

nu·ance (*noo*-ahnss) *n.* A slight difference; a shade.

NOZZLE

nub *n.* A knob; protuberance; gist of a story.

nub·bin *n.* A small or imperfect ear of corn.

Nu·bi·a (*noo*-bee-uh). A section of the Anglo-Egyptian Sudan and Egypt.—**Nu·bi·an** *adj.* & *n.*

nu·bile (*noo*-b'l) *adj.* Of marriageable age. —**nu·bil·i·ty** (noo-*bil*-ih-tee) *n.*

nu·cle·us (*noo*-klee-us) *n.* [*pl.* -cle·us·es, -cle·i] 1. The kernel; core; center. 2. *Biology.* The protoplasmic body in a cell. 3. *Astronomy.* The head of a comet.—**nu·cle·ar** *adj.*

nude *adj.* 1. Naked; bare; unclothed. 2. *Law.* Bearing no weight. 'A nude contract.'—*n.* A naked figure in painting, sculpture, etc.—**nude·ly** *adv.*—**nude·ness** *n.*

nudge *v.* [nudged; nudg·ing] To push gently.

nud·ism (*nood*-izm) *n.* The practice of going unclothed.—**nud·ist** *n.* & *adj.*

nu·di·ty (*noo*-dih-tee) *n.* [*pl.* -ties] Nakedness.

nu·ga·to·ry (*noo*-guh-tor-ee) *adj.* Worthless; without significance; inoperative; ineffectual.

nug·get (*nug*-it) *n.* A lump, esp. of gold.

nui·sance (*noo*-sunss) *n.* 1. An annoyance. 2. A pest; anyone or anything causing vexation. 3. *Law.* Anything causing public inconvenience.

null *adj.* 1. Ineffectual; inoperative. 2. Negative; not any.—**null and void.** Invalid; having no legal force.

nul·li·fy (*nul*-ih-fy) *v.* [nul·li·fied; nul·li·fy·ing] 1. To annul; void; make invalid. 2. To deprive of legal force.—**nul·li·fi·ca·tion** (nul-ih-fih-*kay*-shun) *n.*—**nul·li·fi·er** *n.*

nul·li·ty (*nul*-ih-tee) *n.* [*pl.* -ties] Ineffectuality; lack of force.

numb (*num*) *adj.* Insensible; deprived of sensation.—*v.* To stupefy; deaden; deprive of sensation.—**numb·ly** *adv.*—**numb·ness** *n.*

num·ber (*num*-ber) *n.* 1. A numeral; a mathematical symbol representing a unit. 2. An aggregate; collection of objects, people, etc. 3. A multitude; many. 'A number of things to do.' 4. An issue of a periodical. 5. [*pl.*] Verses. 6. A single act, song, etc., on an entertainment program.—*v.* 1. To reckon as; to count as. 2. To amount to. 3. To mark with numbers.—**num·ber·er** *n.*

num·ber·less *adj.* Innumerable; countless.

Num·bers *n.* The fourth book of the Pentateuch.

numbers pool. A lottery.

nu·mer·a·ble (*noo*-mer-uh-b'l) *adj.* Capable of being counted.

nu·mer·al (*noo*-mer-'l) *n*. A symbol representing a number.—*adj*. 1. Relating to number. 2. Expressing number. 'Numeral letters.'

nu·mer·ate (*noo*-mer-ayt) *v*. [nu·mer·at·ed; nu·mer·at·ing] To count; reckon.

nu·mer·a·tion (noo-mer-*ay*-shun) *n*. Numbering; the process of recording numerical quantities by symbols.

nu·mer·a·tor (*noo*-mer-ay-ter) *n*. *Arithmetic*. In a fraction, the figure above the line, showing the number of units taken.

nu·mer·i·cal (noo-*mehr*-ih-k'l) *adj*. 1. Relating to numbers. 2. Represented by numbers. —**nu·mer·i·cal·ly** *adv*.

nu·mer·ous (*noo*-mer-us) *adj*. Many.—**nu·mer·ous·ly** *adv*.—**nu·mer·ous·ness** *n*.

nu·mis·mat·ic (noo-miz-*mat*-ik) *adj*. Also **nu·mis·mat·i·cal**. Relating to coins.

nu·mis·mat·ics (noo-miz-*mat*-iks) *n*. The study of coins.—**nu·mis·ma·tist** (noo-*miz*-muh-tist) *n*. A collector of coins.

num·skull (*num*-skuhl) *n*. A dunce; blockhead; fool.

nun *n*. A woman living under religious vows in a convent.

nun·ci·o (*nun*-shee-oh) *n*. [*pl*. -os] 1. A papal ambassador. 2. A messenger.

nun·ner·y (*nun*-er-ee) *n*. [*pl*. -ies] A convent.

nup·tial (*nup*-shul) *adj*. Relating to marriage —*n*. [*pl*.] A wedding; marriage ceremony.

nurse (nerss) *n*. 1. A person having the care of the sick, esp. a woman trained as a doctor's assistant. 2. A nursemaid; woman tending a child.—*v*. [nursed; nurs·ing] 1. To suckle; feed at the breast. 2. To nurture; rear. 3. To tend; care for. 4. To consume with economy. —**nurs·er** *n*.

nurse·maid *n*. A nurse; woman having the care of a child.—**nur·ser·y maid**.

nurs·er·y (*nerss*-er-ee) *n*. [*pl*. -ies] 1. Quarters set aside for children. 2. An establishment caring for children of pre-school age. 3. A greenhouse; a place for rearing plants, etc.

nur·ser·y·man *n*. [*pl*. -men] A gardener, esp. in a greenhouse.

nursery school. School for pre-primary school children.

nurs·ling *n*. Also **nurse·ling**. An infant.

nur·ture (*ner*-cher) *n*. Food; nutriment; diet. *v*.— [nur·tured; nur·tur·ing] 1. To feed; nourish. 2. To cause to thrive.—**nur·tur·er** *n*.

nut *n*. 1. A fruit having the seed enclosed in a hard shell. 2. A small metal cylinder for holding a screw in place. 3. *Slang*. An eccentric person.—*v*. [nut·ted; nut·ting] To gather nuts.

nut·crack·er *n*. 1. An implement for cracking nuts. 2. A bird of the crow family.

nut·gall *n*. A growth found on the bark of oaks.

nut·hatch *n*. A shorttailed climbing bird feeding on nuts.

NUTCRACKER

nut·meg *n*. A spice seed derived from tropical ever-greens.

nu·tri·a (*noo*-tree-uh) *n*. The fur of the South American coypu, resembling beaver.

NUTHATCH

nu·tri·ent (*noo*-tree-ent) *adj*. Nourishing; nutritious.—*n*. Any substance taken for nourishment.

nu·tri·ment (*noo*-trih-m'nt) *n*. Nourishment; sustenance; food.

nu·tri·tion (noo-*trish*-un) *n*. The process of absorbing food for the growth of body tissue. —**nu·tri·tion·al** *adj*.—**nu·tri·tion·al·ly** *adv*.

nu·tri·tious (noo-*trish*-us) *adj*. Nourishing; promoting health.—**nu·tri·tious·ly** *adv*.—**nu·tri·tious·ness** *n*.

nu·tri·tive (*noo*-trih-tiv) *adj*. Nourishing; nutritious.—**nu·tri·tive·ly** *adv*.—**nu·tri·tive·ness** *n*.

nut·shell *n*. The hard shell of a nut.—**in a nut-shell**. In short.

nut·ting *n*. Nut-gathering.

nut·ty *adj*. [nut·ti·er; nut·ti·est] 1. Nut-flavored. 2. *Slang*. Crazy; insane.—**nut·ti·ness** *n*.

nux vomica (nuks *vom*-ih-kuh). An East-Indian fruit yielding strychnine.

nuz·zle (*nuz*-'l) *v*. [nuz·zled; nuz·zling] 1. To nestle. 2. To touch with the nose.

Ny·lon (*ny*-lon) *n*. Trade-mark of synthetic silk-like fabric of great durability and elasticity, made from coal, air, and water.

nymph (nimf) *n*. 1. *Mythology*. Any goddess of nature inhabiting forests, streams, etc. 2. A graceful young woman.—**nymph·al** *adj*.

nym·pho·ma·ni·a (nim-foh-*may*-nee-uh) *n*. Abnormally strong sexual desire in the female. —**nym·pho·ma·ni·ac** *adj*. & *n*.

N

O

oaf (*ohf*) *n.* A stupid, clumsy fellow—**oaf·ish** *adj.* —**oaf·ish·ly** *adv.*—**oaf·ish·ness** *n.*

oak *n.* 1. Massive tree of North Temperate Zone. 2. The blondish hard wood of the oak. 3. Plant similarly leafed, as poison oak.—**oak·en** *adj.*

oak-beamed   oak-crested   oak-timbered
oak-boarded   oak-crowned   oak-wainscoted
oak-clad   oak-leaved   oakwood

oa·kum (*oh*-kum) *n.* Fiber rope strands usually tarred for filling seams in boats.

oar (*ohr*) *n.* A flat-bladed pole for rowing small boats.—**oar** *v.*

oared *adj.*—

OAR

oar·lock *n.* Fork swivel in which an oar rests.—**oars·man** *n.*—**oars·man·ship** *n.*

o·a·sis (oh-*ay*-siss) *n.* [*pl.* o·a·ses] Fertile watering spot in a desert.

oat (*oht*) *n.* 1. Grass cultivated for its edible grain. 2. [*pl.*] Cereal or kernels of oat.

oat bin   oat-fed   oatland
oatcake   oatfield   oat seed
oat ear   oatfowl   oat-shaped

oath (*ohth*) *n.* 1. Solemn promise or affirmation. 2. A curse; profanity; blasphemy.

oat·meal *n.* Cereal of rolled oats.

ob·bli·ga·to (ob-lih-*gah*-toh) *n. Music.* Variation for a single instrument scored as accompaniment to a main theme.

ob·dur·ate (ob-*dyoor*-rit) *adj.* 1. Hard-hearted; callous; insensitive. 2. Rugged; unyielding.—**ob·du·ra·cy** *n.* (**ob·du·rately** *adv.*

o·be·di·ent (oh-*bee*-dee-'nt) *adj.* Compliant; submissive to authority; docile.—**o·be·di·ence** *n.*—**o·be·di·ent·ly** *adv.*

o·bei·sance (oh-*bay*-sunss) *n.* 1. A deep bow. 2. Homage; honor; respect.—**o·bei·sant** *adj.*

ob·e·lisk *n.* 1. Tapering rectangular stone column, usually ancient Egyptian. 2. *Printing.* A reference sign now usually called *dagger* (†).— *v.* To mark with an obelisk.

o·bese (oh-*beess*) *adj.* Fat; abnormally stout.—**o·bes·i·ty**, **o·bese·ness** *n.*—**o·bese·ly** *adv.*

o·bey (oh-*bay*) *v.* To comply; submit; do as directed.

o·bit·u·ar·y (oh-*bit*-yoo-er-ee) *n.* 1. Death notice. 2. Church memorial register of the deceased.—**o·bit·u·ar·y** *adj.*

OBELISK

ob·ject (*ob*-jikt) *n.* 1. Any material thing; concrete reality. 2. Goal; aim. 3. A spectacle; a sight arousing emotion. 4. *Grammar.* The noun which takes the action of the verb.—**ob·ject·less** *adj.* Purposeless.—**object lesson.** Example.—**ob·jec·ti·fy** *v.* [ob·jec·ti·fied; ob·jec·ti·fy·ing] To view externally.

ob·ject (ob-*jekt*) *v.* To oppose; dissent; disapprove.—**ob·jec·tion** *n.*—**ob·jec·tion·a·ble** *adj.* —**ob·jec·tion·a·bly** *adv.*—**ob·jec·tor** *n.*

ob·jec·tive (ob-*jek*-tiv) *n.* 1. Goal; aim; target. 2. *Grammar.* Word or phrase which takes the action of a verb.—*adj.* 1. Detached; impartial; impersonal. 2. Extrinsic; complete in itself. 3. *Grammar.* Pertaining to accusative case.—**ob·jec·tive·ly** *adv.*—**ob·jec·tive·ness**, **ob·jec·tiv·i·ty** *n.*

ob·jur·gate (*ob*-jer-gayt) *v.* To scold; reprove; censure.—**ob·jur·ga·tion** *n.*—**ob·jur·ga·tor** *n.*—**ob·jur·ga·to·ry** *adj.*—**ob·jur·ga·tor·i·ly** *adv.*

ob·late (ob-*layt*) *adj. Geometry.* Flattened at the poles.—**ob·late·ly** *adv.*—**ob·late·ness** *n.*

ob·li·gate (*ob*-lih-gayt) *v.* [ob·li·gat·ed; ob·li·gat·ing] To bind; make indebted.—**ob·li·ga·tion** *n.* A debt; duty; claim.—**ob·lig·a·to·ry** (ob-*lig*-uh-taw-ree) *adj.* Binding.—**ob·lig·a·to·ri·ly** *adv.*

o·blige (oh-*blyge*) *v.* [o·bliged; o·blig·ing] 1. To accommodate; do a favor. 2. To compel; force.—**o·blig·ing** *adj.* Agreeable; accommodating.—**o·blig·er** *n.*—**o·blig·ing·ly** *adv.*—**o·blig·ing·ness** *n.*

ob·lique (ob-*leek*) *adj.* 1. Slanting; at an angle. 2. Devious; cagy.—**left oblique** (ob-*lyke*), **right oblique.** *Military.* Marching order calling for an oblique progression. —**ob·lique·ly** *adv.* —**ob·lique·ness** *n.*

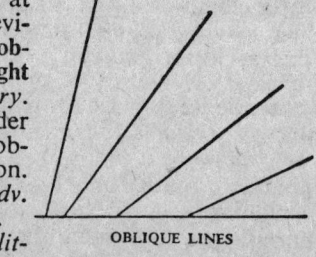

OBLIQUE LINES

ob·lit·er·ate (ob-*lit*-er-ate) *v.* [ob·lit·er·ated; on·lit·er·at·ing] To erase; efface; wipe out.—**ob·lit·er·a·tion** *n.*—**ob·lit·er·a·tive** *adj*—**ob·lit·er·a·tor** *n.*

ob·liv·i·on (ob-*liv*-ee-un) *n.* Complete forgetfulness.—**ob·liv·i·ous** *adj.*—**ob·liv·i·ous·ly** *adv.*

ob·long (*ob*-long) *n.* A rectangle.

ob·lo·quy (*ob*-loh-kwee) *n.* 1. Censure; abuse. 2. Disgrace; shame.

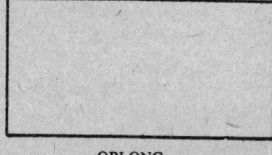

OBLONG

ob·nox·ious (ob-*nok*-shus) *adj.* Annoying; offensive; odious; irritating; hateful.—**ob·nox·ious·ly** *adv.*

o·boe (*oh*-boh) *n.* Musical wind instrument. —o·bo·ist *n.* Oboe-player.

ob·scene (ob-*seen*) *adj.* Indecent; lewd. —ob·scene·ly *adv.*—ob·scene·ness, ob·scen·i·ty (ob-*sen*-uh-tee) *n.* [*pl.* -i·ties].

ob·scure (ob-*skyoor*) *adj.* 1. Dark; dim. 2. Unclear; ambiguous. 3. Humble; unknown.—*v.* [ob·scured; ob·scur·ing] 1. To darken. 2. To hide; cover.—ob·scur·ant *n.* & *adj.*—ob·scure·ly *adv.*—ob·scur·i·ty *n.* [*pl.* ob·scur·i·ties].

ob·se·quies (*ob*-seh-kweez) *n. pl.* Funeral rites.

ob·se·qui·ous (ob-*see*-kwee-us) *adj.* Servile; too deferential.—ob·se·qui·ous·ly *adv.*—ob·se·qui·ous·ness *n.*

ob·serv·a·ble *adj.* Perceivable.—ob·serv·a·ble·ness *n.*—ob·serv·a·bly *adv.*

ob·serv·ance (ob-*zer*-v'nss) *n.* 1. Performance; celebration; keeping. 2. Rite; ceremony. 3. Observation.—ob·serv·ant *adj.* Attentive; wide-awake; aware.—ob·serv·ant·ly *adv.*

ob·ser·va·tion (ob-zer-*vay*-sh'n) *n.* 1. Notice; attention; perception. 2. Discovery; gathered data. 3. A remark; comment.

ob·serv·a·to·ry (ob-*zer*-vuh-taw-ree) *n.* Building for astronomical study.

ob·serve (ob-*zerv*) *v.* [ob·served; ob·serv·ing] 1. To watch; regard; appraise; notice. 2. To study scientifically. 3. To remark; mention. 4. To celebrate; keep. 5. To obey; comply with.—ob·serv·er *n.*—ob·serv·ing *adj.*—ob·serv·ing·ly *adv.*

ob·sess (ob-*sess*) *v.* To haunt; possess; beset. —ob·ses·sive *adj.*—ob·ses·sor *n.*

ob·ses·sion (ob-*seh*-shun) *n.* 1. Possession by evil spirits. 2. Undue preoccupation with an idea.

ob·so·les·cent (ob-suh-*less*-unt) *adj.* Disappearing; falling into disuse.—ob·so·les·cence *n.* —ob·so·les·cent·ly *adv.*

ob·so·lete (*ob*-suh-leet) *adj.* 1. Outdated; antiquated. 2. *Biology.* Rudimentary; imperfectly developed.—ob·so·lete·ly *adv.*—ob·so·lete·ness *n.*

ob·sta·cle (*ob*-stuh-k'l) *n.* Hindrance; impediment.

ob·stet·rics (ob-*stet*-riks) *n.* The science of childbirth.—ob·stet·ric, ob·stet·ri·cal *adj.*—ob·ste·tri·cian *n.* Obstetric physician.

ob·sti·nate (*ob*-stuh-nit) *adj.* Stubborn; dogged. —ob·sti·nate·ly *adv.*—ob·sti·nate·ness, ob·sti·na·cy *n.*

ob·strep·er·ous (ob-*strep*-er-us) *adj.* Boisterous; uncontrollable.—ob·strep·er·ous·ly *adv.*—ob·strep·er·ous·ness *n.*

ob·struct (ob-*strukt*) *v.* To hinder; block.—ob·struc·ter, ob·struc·tor *n.*—ob·struc·tive *adj.* —ob·struc·tive·ly *adv.*

ob·struc·tion *n.* 1. Obstacle; impediment. 2. Blocking; hindering.—ob·struc·tion·ist *n.* A hamperer of legislation, esp. progressive legislation.—ob·struc·tion·ism *n.*

ob·tain (ob-*tayn*) *v.* 1. To acquire; get; procure. 2. To continue in use.—ob·tain·er *n.*

ob·trude (ob-*trood*) *v.* [ob·truded; ob·trud·ing] To force upon; interlope; thrust forward. —ob·trud·er *n.*—ob·tru·sion *n.*

ob·tru·sive *adj.* Unduly conspicuous; pushing. —ob·tru·sive·ly *adv.*—ob·tru·sive·ness *n.*

ob·tuse *adj.* 1. *Mathematics.* Having an angle of more than ninety degrees; blunt. 2. Dull; slow; imperceptive.—ob·tuse·ly *adv.*—ob·tuse·ness, ob·tus·i·ty *n.*

ob·verse (*ob*-verss) *n.* 1. Side of a coin bearing the head; the foremost part. 2. A corresponding part. 3. *Logic.* Negative statement of the opposite of a proposition.—ob·vert *v.* To turn toward.—ob·verse *adj.*—ob·verse·ly *adv.*—ob·ver·sion *n.*

ob·vi·ate (*ob*-vee-ayt) *v.* [ob·vi·at·ed; ob·vi·at·ing] To preclude; avert.—ob·vi·a·tion *n.*—ob·vi·a·tor *n.*

ob·vi·ous (*ob*-vee-us) *adj.* 1. Plain; evident; apparent. 2. Unoriginal; superficial.—ob·vi·ous·ly *adv.*—ob·vi·ous·ness *n.*

oc·a·ri·na (ok-uh-*ree*-nuh) *n.* Small wind instrument with finger vents; sweet potato.

OCARINA

oc·ca·sion (uh-*kay*-zh'n) *n.* 1. Time of an event. 2. Opportunity; chance. 3. Cause; reason. 4. Social function; affair.—*v.* To cause; produce.—oc·ca·sion·al *adj.*—oc·ca·sion·al·ly *adv.*—oc·ca·sion·er *n.*

Oc·ci·dent (*ok*-sih-d'nt) *n.* Western Hemisphere, as distinguished from the Orient.—Oc·ci·den·tal *adj.*—Oc·ci·den·tal·ly *adv.*—Oc·ci·den·tal·ism. Western culture.—Oc·ci·den·tal·ist *n.* —Oc·ci·den·tal·ize *v.*—Oc·ci·den·tal·i·za·tion *n.*

oc·ci·put (*ok*-sih-put) *n.* Back part of the head. —oc·cip·i·tal (ok-*sip*-ih-tal) *adj.*— -tal·ly *adv.*

oc·clu·sion (ok-*kloo*-zh'n) *n.* 1. Closure; obstruction. 2. *Medicine.* Contact of the teeth when the jaws are closed. 3. *Chemistry.* Molecular adhesion without an actual chemical union.—oc·clude *v.* [oc·clud·ed; oc·clud·ing] —oc·clud·ent, oc·clu·sive *adj.*

oc·cult (ok-*kult*) *adj.* Magical; supernatural; mysterious.—oc·cul·ta·tion *n.* Eclipse of one heavenly body by another.—oc·cult·ism *n.* —oc·cult·ist *n.*—oc·cult·ly *adv.*

oc·cu·pan·cy (*ok*-yoo-pun-see) *n.* 1. Possession. 2. *Law.* Acquisition of unowned property.—oc·cu·pant, oc·cu·pi·er *n.* One in possession.

oc·cu·pa·tion *n.* 1. Vocation; employment; profession. 2. Possession. 3. Military administration of a conquered land.—oc·cu·pa·tion·al *adj.*—oc·cu·pa·tion·al·ly *adv.*

oc·cu·py (*ok*-yoo-pye) *v.* [oc·cu·pied; oc·cu·py·ing] 1. To seize; take possession. 2. To fill; cover. 3. To hold; inhabit. 4. To employ; keep busy.

oc·cur (uk-*ker*) *v.* [oc·curred; oc·cur·ring]

O

1. To happen; take place. 2. To come to mind.—**oc·cur·rence** *n.*

o·cean (*oh*-sh'n) *n.* 1. The sea; the water covering over three-fifths of the globe. 2. Vast quantity.—**o·cean, o·ce·an·ic** (oh-shee-*an*-ik) *adj.*

ocean-born	ocean-girdled	oceanside
ocean-borne	oceangoing	ocean-skirted
ocean-bound	ocean-guarded	ocean-sundered
ocean-compassed	ocean-rocked	ocean wide
ocean-flooded	ocean-severed	ocean-wise

o·ce·a·nog·ra·phy (oh-shee-uh-*nog*-ruh-fee) *n.* Science of the sea.—**o·ce·a·nog·ra·pher** *n.* —**o·ce·a·no·graph·ic** (oh-shee-h-noh-*graf*-ik), **o·ce·a·no·graph·i·cal** *adj.*— **-i·cal·ly** *adv.*

o·ce·lot (*oh*-suh-lot) *n.* Large, spotted catlike animal of southwest U.S. and South America.

OCELOT

o·cher, o·chre, (*oh*-ker) *n.* 1. A clay colored with an iron oxide, used as pigment. 2. A tan color.—**o·cher, o·cher·ous, o·cher·y, o·chre** *adj.*

o'clock (uh-*klok*) *Contraction* for **of the clock.**

oct·a·gon (*ok*-tuh-gon) *n.* Eight-angled figure. —**oc·tag·o·nal** (ok-*tag*-un-ul) *adj.*—**oc·tag·o·nal·ly** *adv.*

OCTAGON

oc·ta·he·dron (ok-tuh-*hee*-drun) *n.* *Geometry.* A solid with eight equal and equilateral triangles.—**oc·ta·he·dral** *adj.*

oc·tane (*ok*-tayn) *n.* 1. One of a group of hydrocarbons of the methane series. 2. A number indicating the anti-knock quality of motor fuel.

oc·tant (*ok*-tunt) *n.* *Geometry.* 1. The eighth part of a circle. 2. An angle-measuring instrument. 3. *Mathematics.* One of eight divisions of an area made by three co-ordinate planes.

oc·tave (*ok*-tayv) *n.* *Music.* The eight-tone interval between two notes which comprises a full scale.—*adj.* Eighth.—**oc·ta·val** *adj.*

oc·ta·vo (ok-*tay*-voh) *n.* 1. The size of one of eight leaves into which a sheet of paper is folded. 2. A book of eight-leaf sheets.

oc·ten·ni·al (ok-*ten*-ee-ul) *adj.* Occurring every eighth year.—**oc·ten·ni·al·ly** *adv.*

oc·tet, oc·tette (ok-*tet*) *n.* 1. *Music.* A composition for eight voices or instruments. 2. The first eight lines of a sonnet.

oc·til·lion (ok-*til*-yun) *n.* The product of one million raised to the eighth power.—**oc·til·lionth** *adj. & n.*

Oc·to·ber (ok-*toh*-ber) *n.* Tenth month of our calendar year.

oc·to·ge·nar·i·an (ok-tuh-jeh-*nair*-ee-un) *n.* A person in his eighties.—**oc·to·ge·nar·i·an, oc·tog·e·nar·y** (ok-*toj*-uh-nair-ee) *adj.*

oc·to·pus (*ok*-tuh-pus) *n.* An eight-tentacled animal of the cuttlefish family; a giant squid.

oc·u·lar (*ok*-yoo-ler) *adj.* Pertaining to the eye or vision.—*n.* *Optics.* Eyepiece of an optical instrument.—**oc·u·list** *n.* An eye specialist.—**oc·u·lar·ly** *adv.*

OCTOPUS

o·da·lisque, o·da·lisk (*oh*-duh-lisk) *n.* A female slave or concubine in a harem.

odd *adj.* 1. Not even; not divisible by two. 2. Belonging to a broken pair or set; left over. 3. Peculiar; strange; queer.—**od·di·ty** *n.* —**odd·ly** *adv.*—**odd·ness** *n.*

odd-fangled	odd-jobman	odd-numbered
odd-humored	odd looking	odd-shaped
odd-jobber	odd-mannered	odd-toed

odds *n. pl.* 1. Discrepancy in relative advantages. 2. Equalization of advantage. 3. Probability; likelihood; advantage.—**at odds.** In dispute.—**odds and ends.** Miscellany.

ode *n.* A stately lyric poem.

O·din (*oh*-din) *n.* The chief god of Norse mythology.

o·di·ous (*oh*-dee-us) *adj.* Hateful; repugnant; disgusting.—**o·di·ous·ly** *adv.*—**o·di·um, o·di·ous·ness** *n.*

o·dom·e·ter (oh-*dom*-uh-ter) *n.* Instrument for measuring distance.—**o·do·met·ri·cal** (oh-duh-*met*-rik-'l) *adj.*— **-e·try** (oh-*dom*-uh-tree) *n.*

o·dor (*oh*-d'r) *n.* 1. Scent; smell; fragrance. 2. A perfume.—**o·dor·ous** *adj.*—**o·dor·ous·ly** *adv.*—**o·dor·ous·ness** *n.*—**o·dor·less** *adj.*

O·dys·seus (oh-*diss*-yooss) Legendary Greek hero; Ulysses.

od·ys·sey (*od*-ih-see) *n.* 1. [*cap.*] Epic poem attributed to Homer, celebrating the journey of Odysseus. 2. A tale of wandering.—**od·ys·se·an** *adj.*

Oed·i·pus (*ed*-ih-pus) Prince of ancient Thebes who killed his father and married his mother.

Oedipus complex. Unnatural love of a child for the parent of the opposite sex.

o'er (ohr) *Contraction,* usually poetic, for **over.**

of *prep.* 1. From. 'Ill of a cold.' 2. Belonging to. 'Wage of a worker.' 3. Attribute; quality; condition. 'Man of the people.' 4. Made with. 'Crown of thorns.' 5. Belonging to a whole. 'Some of my friends.' 6. About. 'Think of the day.' 7. Identical with. 'City of Moscow.' 8. On. 'Often going there of an evening.'

off *adv.* Away from; out from; apart from. —*adj.* 1. Removed; absent; discontinued. 2. Inaccurate; mistaken. 3. Inferior; below standard.—*prep.* 1. Removed from. 2. Absent from. 3. Diverging or leading from.

off-cutting	offprint	offtype
off-flavor	offscape	offward
offgrade	offshoot	offwheel
off-lying	offshore	offwhite

of·fal (*awf*-ul) *n.* 1. Waste meat; rejected parts of a butchered animal. 2. Rubbish; refuse.

off and on. Intermittently.

off·beat *n. Music.* Point between two beats of tempo.

off-color *adj.* Risqué; obscene. 'An off-color joke.'

of·fend (uh-*fend*) *v.* 1. To affront; insult; annoy. 2. To sin; violate law.—**of·fend·er** *n.*

of·fense (uh-*fenss*) *n.* 1. Resentment; umbrage. 2. An affront; injustice. 3. A misdemeanor. 4. Attack; aggression.—**of·fense·less** *adj.*

of·fen·sive (uh-*fen*-siv) *adj.* 1. Disagreeable; repulsive; disgusting. 2. Aggressive; used for attack.—*n.* Assault; attack.—**of·fen·sive·ly** *adv.*

of·fer (*awf*-er, *ahf*-er) *v.* 1. To proffer; present. 2. To sacrifice. 3. To attempt; do. 'To offer violence.' 4. To bid; name a price.—*n.* 1. A proposal. 2. A bid.—**of·fer·able** *adj.*—**of·fer·er** *n.*—**of·fer·ing** *n.* A sacrifice; gift to a deity.

off·hand (awf-*hand*) *adv.* & *adj.* Casual; unpremeditated.

of·fice (*awf*-fiss, *ahf*-fiss) *n.* 1. Post; position; function. 2. Room or building where administrative and clerical work is performed. 3. Act of kindness; service.

of·fi·cer (*awf*-ih-ser, *ahf*-ih-ser) *n.* 1. Holder of commission in the armed forces. 2. Person authorized to perform a public duty. 3. A policeman. 4. An executive of an organization.—*v.* To direct as an executive.

of·fi·cial (uh-*fish*-'l) *adj.* 1. Pertaining to a public trust or charge. 2. Authorized; legal. —*n.* One holding a civil appointment.—**of·fi·cial·dom** *n.* Public-office holders.—**-cial·ly** *adv.*

of·fi·ci·ate (uh-*fish*-ee-ate) *v.* [of·fi·ci·at·ed; of·fi·ci·at·ing] To preside; conduct.—**of·fi·ci·a·tion** *n.*—**of·fi·ci·a·tor** *n.*

of·fi·cious (uh-*fish*-us) *adj.* Meddlesome; intrusive; bossy.—**of·fi·cious·ly** *adv.*—**of·fi·cious·ness** *n.*

off·ing *n.* The near distance; near future.

off·ish *adj.* Shy; aloof; distant.—**off·ish·ly** *adv.*

off·scour·ing (awf-scowr-ing) *n.* Refuse material.

off·set (awf-*set*) *v.* [off·set; off·set·ting] To negate; counterbalance.—*n.* 1. *Lithography.* Method of reproducing inked impressions via a rubber-covered roller to paper. 2. *Printing.* Smudges on the back of a sheet from the underlying sheet.

off·shoot *n.* 1. Tributary; branch from a main body. 2. A sprout; child.

off·side *n. Football.* Violation of the rules by crossing the line of play before the ball is put in motion.—**off·side** *adj.* & *adv.*

off·spring *n.* [*pl.* off·spring] Child; descendant.

of·ten (*awf*-'n) *adv.* Frequently; repeatedly.

of·ten·times, oft·times *adv.* Often.

o·gle (*oh*-g'l) *v.* [o·gled; o·gling] To leer; stare. —**o·gle** *n.*—**o·gler** *n.*

o·gre (*oh*-ger) *n.* A fabled, hideous monster who lived on human flesh.—**o·gre·ish** *adj.*—**o·gre·ism, o·grism** *n.*—**o·gress** *n.*

oh *interj.* Exclamation of surprise, pain, pleasure, comprehension, etc.

ohm (*ohm*) *n. Electricity.* Unit of resistance. —**ohm·me·ter** *n.* Instrument for measuring resistance.—**ohm·ic** *adj.*—**ohm·age** *n.*

Ohm's law. *Electricity.* Equation showing that the intensity of a current is directly proportional to voltage and inversely proportional to resistance. (*Formula:* $I = E/R$).

oil *n.* Inflammable fatty liquid obtained from various plant, animal, and mineral products. —*v.* To lubricate or saturate with oil.—**oil·er** *n.*

oilcan	oil-hardened	oilseed
oilcoat	oilhole	oilsoaked
oil-driven	oil-insulated	oilstock
oil-fed	oil-laden	oilstone
oil-filled	oil-lit	oilstoned
oil-finished	oilman	oilstoning
oil-fitted	oilmonger	oilstove
oilfish	oilpaper	oil-tempered
oil forming	oilproof	oiltight
oil-fueled	oilproofing	oilway

oil·cloth *n.* Painted or oiled cloth or canvas.

oil·skin *n.* 1. Waterproofed cloth. 2. [*pl.*] Waterproof outfit.

oil·y *adj.* [oil·i·er; oil·i·est] 1. Of or like oil. 2. Fat; greasy. 3. Suave; unctous; bland. —**oil·i·ly** *adv.*—**oil·i·ness** *n.*

oint·ment *n.* An unctuous, greasy medicament.

O·jib·way (oh-*jib*-way) *n.* Also **O·jib·wa.** A mid-continental tribe of American Indians.

o.k., OK, o·kay *adj.* & *adv.* All right; agreed; correct.—*v.* To approve.—*n.* Approval; agreement.

o·kra (*oh*-kruh) *n.* Tall, pod-bearing tropical herb.

old *adj.* 1. Advanced in years. 2. Not freshly or recently made. 3. Ancient; formerly existent. 4. Of any duration. 'One day old.' 5. Experienced; practiced. 6. Term of cordiality. 'Dear old boy.'—**old·ster** *n.* Aged person.—**old·en** *adj.* & *v.* —**old·ish** *adj.*—**old·ness** *n.*

OKRA

old-aged	old-new
old-established	old-sighted
old-faced	old standing
old-gentlemanly	old time
old-hearted	old-womanish
old looking	old-womanly

old-fash·ioned *adj.* Antiquated; obsolete; loving the past.—*n.* Cocktail made of whisky, bitters, sugar, and fruit.

old-fo·gy·ish *adj.* Fussy; fastidious; officious. —**old-fo·gy·ism** *n.*

old maid. 1. Spinster. 2. A fussy woman. 3. A card game.—**old-maid·ish** *adj.*

old style. Outmoded.—*n. Printing.* An early type face with oblique serifs.

Old Testament. The section of the Bible dealing with Hebrew canonical law.

old·timer *n.* An aged person; veteran.—**old·time** *adv.* & *adj.*

O

old world. Eastern Hemisphere.—**old-world** *adj.*

o·le·ag·i·nous (oh-lee-*aj*-ih-nus) *adj.* Greasy; oily; suave; smooth.—**o·le·ag·i·nous·ly** *adv.*

o·le·an·der (oh-lee-*an*-der) *n.* Family of poisonous evergreen shrubs used as decoration.

o·le·as·ter (oh-lee-*ass*-ter) *n.* Hardy shrub having fragrant, ornamental foliage.

o·le·o·graph (*oh*-lee-oh-graph) *n.* A colored lithograph similar to an oil painting.—**o·le·o·graph·ic** *adj.*—**o·le·og·ra·phy** (oh-lee-*og*-ruh-fee) *n.*

o·le·o·mar·ga·rine, o·le·o·mar·ga·rin (oh-lee-oh-*mar*-juh-rin) *n.* Butter substitute made of vegetable fats, water, salt, and milk solids.

o·le·om·e·ter (oh-lee-*om*-eh-ter) *n.* Instrument for measuring the weight and purity of oils.

ol·fac·to·ry (ol-*fak*-tuh-ree) *adj.* Pertaining to the sense of smell.—*n.* An organ of smelling; sense of smell.—**ol·fac·tion** *n.*

ol·i·gar·chy (*ol*-ih-gahr-kee) *n.* 1. Government by a small group. 2. A ruling minority.—**ol·i·garch** *n.* Member of an oligarchy.—**ol·i·gar·chic, ol·i·gar·chi·cal** *adj.*— **-chi·cal·ly** *adv.*

o·li·o (*oh*-lee-oh) *n.* 1. A miscellany; medley. 2. A stew.

ol·ive (*ol*-iv) *n.* 1. Family of evergreen shrubs and trees. 2. Small, edible, pitted fruit of the olive tree.—**ol·i·va·ceous** (ol-ih-*vay*-shus) *adj.* —**ol·i·va·ry** *adj.*—**o·live** *adj.*—**olive branch.** The emblem of peace.—**olive oil.** A food oil obtained from ripe olives.

olive-bordered   olive-complexioned   olive-sided
olive-cheeked   olive-shaded   olive-skinned
olive-colored   olive-shadowed   olive wood

O·lym·pic *adj.* Pertaining to Olympus, the mountain home of the Greek gods.—**Olympic games.** Modern international sports competition.

o·me·ga (oh-*mee*-guh) *n.* 1. Last letter of the Greek alphabet. 2. The end; the last.

om·e·let, om·e·lette (*om*-uh-let) *n.* Fried beaten eggs, with water or milk added.

o·men *n.* Augury; sign of a future event.

om·i·nous (*om*-ih-nus) *adj.* Sinister; threatening; forboding.—**om·i·nous·ly** *adv.*— **-nous·ness** *n.*

o·mit (oh-*mit*) *v.* [o·mit·ted; o·mit·ting] To leave out; pass over.—**o·mis·si·ble** *adj.* Unessential. —**o·mis·sion** *n.*—**o·mis·sive** *adj.*— **-sive·ly** *adv.*

om·ni·bus (*om*-nih-bus) *n.* A bus; public conveyance.—*adj.* All inclusive.—**omnibus bill.** Legislative measure covering many different items.

om·nip·o·tent (om-*nip*-uh-t'nt) *adj.* All powerful; supreme.—**om·nip·o·tence, om·nip·o·ten·cy** *n.*—**om·nip·o·tent·ly** *adv.*

om·ni·pres·ent (-nih-*prez*-'nt) *adj.* Ubiquitous; being everywhere at once.—**om·ni·pres·ence** *n.*

om·nis·cient (om-*nish*-'nt) *adj.* All knowing; having infinite knowledge.—**om·nis·cience** *n.*—**om·nis·cien·cy** *n.*—**om·nis·cient·ly** *adv.*

om·niv·o·rous (om-*niv*-uh-rus) *adj.* Eating both meat and vegetable food.—**om·niv·o·rous·ly** *adv.*—**om·niv·o·rous·ness** *n.*

on *adv.* 1. Forward; in continuance. 2. Upon. 3. *Theater.* Before the audience.—*prep.* 1. Resting upon; touching the surface of. 2. At or near. 3. In addition to. 4. At the time of. 5. Toward. 6. In consequence of.

oncoming   onhanger   onrush
onflowing   onlay   onrushing
on-going   onlooker   onshore

o·nan·ism (*oh*-nun-izm) *n.* 1. Incomplete sexual intercourse. 2. Masturbation.

once (wunss) *adv.* 1. Occurring a single time. 2. Formerly.—*conj.* When; if. 'Once done, it is done.'—**once** *n.*—**at once.** Immediately.

one *adj.* 1. Consisting of a single unit. 2. Same. 3. Undivided; closely united.—*n.* First cardinal number represented by 1.—*pron.* Any person.—**one-horse** *adj. Slang.* Backward; small-townish.—**one·ness** *n.*

one-acter   one-colored   one-footed
one-armed   one-cusped   one-grained
one-blade   one-decker   one-handed
one-bladed   one-eared   one-handedness
one-buttoned   one-eyed   one-legged
one-celled   one-eyedness   one-leggedness
one-chambered   one-finned   one-striper
one-classer   one-flowered   one-two-three

on·er·ous (*oh*-ner-us) *adj.* Burdensome; oppressive; troublesome.—**on·er·ous·ly** *adv.*—**on·er·ous·ness** *n.*

one·self *pron.* Also **one's self.** Emphatic and reflexive form of **one.**

one-sid·ed *adj.* Partial; prejudiced; unevenly matched.—**one-sid·ed·ly** *adv.*—**one-sid·ed·ness** *n.*

one-step *n.* Popular ballroom dance step.

on·ion (*un*-yun) *n.* Herb producing a sharp-flavored bulb.

on·ion·skin *n.* A tissuelike writing paper.

on·ly (*ohn*-lee) *adj.* Single; one alone; solitary.—*adv.* 1. Simply; merely; barely. 2. Solely. 3. Singly.—*conj.* But; excepting that.—**on·li·ness** *n.*

on·o·mat·o·poe·ia (on-uh-mat-uh-*pee*-yuh) *n.* 1. Development of words in imitation of sounds. 2. Suggestion of a sound by choice and arrangement of words.—**o·nom·a·tope** (uh-*nom*-uh-tohp) *n.* A word formed to represent a sound. —**on·o·mat·o·po·et·i·cal** *adj.*— **-i·cal·ly** *adv.*

ONION

on·set (*on*-set) *n.* 1. Rushing upon; assault. 2. A beginning.—*v.* [on·set·ted; on·set·ting].

on·slaught (*on*-slawt) *n.* Attack; assault.

on·to *prep.* On; upon. Also **on to.**

on·tol·o·gy (on-*tol*-uh-jee) *n.* The doctrine of being; branch of metaphysics which investigates existence.—**on·to·log·i·cal** *adj.*—**on·to·log·i·cal·ly** *adv.*—**on·tol·o·gist** *n.*

o·nus (*oh*-nus) *n.* Burden; blame.

on·ward (*on*-werd), **on·wards** *adv.* Forward; on.—**on·ward** *adj.*

on·yx (*on*-iks) *n.* Translucent gem veined with various colors.—**on·yx** *adj.*

o·öl·o·gy (oh-*ol*-uh-jee) *n*. Science of birds' nesting habits.—**o·ö·log·i·cal** *adj*.—**o·öl·o·gist** *n*.

ooze *v*. [oozed; ooz·ing] To leak out; flow gradually.—*n*. Soft mud; slime—**ooz·i·ness** *n*.

o·pac·i·ty (oh-*pass*-ih-tee) [*pl*. -ties] Denseness; imperviousness to light.

o·pal (*oh*-p'l) *n*. An iridescent, white gem. —**o·pal·esce** *v*. [o·pal·esced; o·pal·es·cing] To shimmer in rainbowlike colors.—**o·pal·es·cence** *n*.—**o·pal·es·cent, o·pal·ine** *adj*.

o·paque (oh-*payk*) *adj*. 1. Impervious to light; not transparent. 2. Dark; obscure.—**o·paque·ly** *adv*.—**o·paque·ness** *n*.

o·pen *v*. 1. To unclose; expose; make accessible. 2. To begin; start. 3. To broaden; expand. 4. To reveal; disclose.—*adj*. 1. Unclosed. 2. Available; unrestricted. 3. Candid; frank. 4. Unobstructed; clear. 5. Spread out. 6. Undetermined; free. 7. Responsive; generous; outgoing.—*n*. A clear space. —**o·pen·er** *n*.—**o·pen·ly** *adv*.—**o·pen·ness** *n*.

open-airishness	open-pitted
open-airness	open-roofed
open back	open-rounded
open-backed	open-shelved
openbeak	open-shopper
openbill	open-sleeved
open-cast	open-spaced
open-chested	open-spacedly
open-countenanced	open-spacedness
open-cut	open-spoken
open-eyed	open-spokenly
open-faced	open-throated
open-flowered	open-visaged
open-fronted	open-webbed
open-minded	open-webbedness
open-mindedness	open-windowed
open-mouthed	openwork

open city. A city declared defenseless by its occupants in wartime.

open door. Policy extending trade indiscriminately to all nations.—**o·pen-door** *adj*.

o·pen-hand·ed *adj*. Generous; liberal.—**o·pen-hand·ed·ly** *adv*.—**o·pen-hand·ed·ness** *n*.

o·pen-heart·ed *adj*. Frank; sincere.—**o·pen-heart·ed·ly** *adv*.—**o·pen-heart·ed·ness** *n*.

o·pen·ing *n*. 1. Unclosing. 2. Hole; aperture. 3. Beginning; first showing. 4. Opportunity; vacancy; unfilled job.

open shop. A firm having both union and nonunion employees.

op·er·a *n*. [*pl*. op·er·as] 1. Musical drama. 2. Score or presentation of a musical drama. —**op·er·at·ic** *adj*.—**op·er·at·i·cal·ly** *adv*.

op·er·a glass or **glasses.** Small binoculars.

op·er·ate *v*. [op·er·at·ed; op·er·at·ing] 1. To act; function; have effect. 2. To treat by surgery. 3. *Military*. To carry out campaign plans. —**op·er·a·tion** *n*. —**op·er·a·tive** *n*. & *adj*. —**op·er·a·tive·ly** *adv*.

OPERA GLASSES

op·er·a·tor *n*. 1. One who runs an apparatus, especially a switchboard. 2. Manager of a mine, ships, etc.

o·per·cu·lum (oh-*per*-kyoo-lum) *n*. *Biology*. Protective covering.

op·er·et·ta (op-er-*et*-uh) *n*. Short light musical drama.

oph·i·ol·o·gy (of-ee-*ol*-uh-jee) *n*. Branch of biology dealing with snakes.—**oph·i·o·log·i·cal** *adj*. —**oph·i·ol·o·gist** *n*.

oph·thal·mi·a (of-*thal*-mee-uh) *n*. Inflammation of the eye.—**oph·thal·mic** *adj*.

oph·thal·mol·o·gy (of-thal-*mol*-uh-jee) *n*. Science dealing with the eye or its diseases.—**oph·thal·mo·log·i·cal** *adj*.—**oph·thal·mol·o·gist** *n*.

o·pi·ate (*oh*-pee-ayt) *n*. 1. Medicine containing opium. 2. Balm.—*adj*. Sleep-inducing.

o·pine (oh-*pyne*) *v*. [o·pined; o·pin·ing] To think; suppose. *Chiefly humorous*.

o·pin·ion (oh-*pin*-yun) *n*. View; belief; conviction.—**o·pin·ion·at·ed** *adj*. Bigoted; prejudiced.—**o·pin·ion·at·ed·ness** *n*.—**o·pin·ion·a·tive** *adj*.—**o·pin·ion·a·tive·ly** *adv*.—**-tive·ness** *n*.

o·pi·um (*oh*-pee-um) *n*. Narcotic extracted from the white poppy.—**o·pi·um·ism** *n*. Addiction to opium.

o·pos·sum *n*. American tree-dwelling mammal which carries its young in a pouch.— **play possum.** To feign death; deceive.

OPOSSUM (1/13 Life-size)

O

op·po·nent (uh-*poh*-nunt) *n*. Antagonist; adversary.—**op·po·nen·cy** *n*.—**op·po·nent** *adj*.

op·por·tune (op-er-*toon*) *adj*. Timely; convenient.—**op·por·tune·ly** *adv*.—**-tune·ness** *n*.

op·por·tun·ism *n*. Seizure of every opportunity without regard for principle.—**op·por·tun·ist** *n*. & *adj*.—**op·por·tun·is·tic** *adj*.

op·por·tu·ni·ty *n*. Favorable chance; fit time.

op·pose (uh-*pohz*) *v*. [op·posed; op·pos·ing] 1. To resist; contradict; set against. 2. To place in a balancing position.—**op·pos·a·ble** *adj*.—**op·pos·a·bil·i·ty** *n*.—**op·pos·er** *n*.

op·po·site (*op*-uh-zit) *adj*. 1. Facing; across from; directly before. 2. Contrasting; antagonistic.—*n*. Contrary; antithesis.—**op·po·site·ly** *adv*.—**op·po·site·ness** *n*.

op·po·si·tion (op-uh-*zish*-'n) *n*. 1. Resistance; disagreement; obstruction. 2. Organized group in disagreement; minority party.—**op·po·si·tion** *adj*.

op·press (uh-*press*) *v*. 1. To persecute; overburden. 2. To depress; weigh down.—**op·pres·sion** *n*.

op·pres·sive *adj*. Tyrannical; burdensome; heavy.—**op·pres·sive·ly** *adv*.—**op·pres·sive·ness** *n*.—**op·pres·sor** *n*.

op·pro·bri·ous (uh-*proh*-bree-us) *adj*. Abusive; contemptuous; insulting.—**op·pro·bri·ous·ly** *adv*.—**op·pro·bri·ous·ness** *n*.—**op·pro·bri·um** *n*.

op·tic (*op*-tik) *adj.* Pertaining to the eye.—*n.*
1. An eye. 2. [*pl.*] Science dealing with light
phenomena.—**op·ti·cal** *adj.*—**op·ti·cal·ly** *adv.*
—**op·ti·cian** *n.* Dealer in or maker of lenses.

op·ti·mism *n.* Hopefulness; faith in favorable
outcome.—**op·ti·mist** *n.*—**op·ti·mis·tic, op·ti·**
mis·ti·cal *adj.*—**op·ti·mis·ti·cal·ly** *adv.*

op·ti·mum (*op*-tih-mum) *n.* [*pl.* -ma; -mums]
Maximum; best.—**op·ti·mum** *adj.*

op·tion (*op*-sh'n) *n.* 1. Choice; right of decision. 2. Time clause in a contract.—**op·**
tion·al *adj.*—**op·tion·al·ly** *adv.*

op·tom·e·try (op-*tom*-uh-tree) *n.* Prescription
of lenses for correcting vision.—**op·tom·e·ter** *n.*
Instrument measuring the eye's focal length.
—**op·tom·e·trist** *n.* Doctor who prescribes lenses.

op·u·lence, op·u·len·cy (*op*-yoo-lenss, -see) *n.*
Wealth; luxury.—**op·u·lent** *adj.*— **-lent·ly** *adv.*

o·pus (*oh*-pus) *n.* [*pl.* op·er·a] A work, esp. a
musical composition.

or *conj.* Alternatively; on the other hand; else.
'Sink or swim.'

or·a·cle (*or*-uh-k'l) *n.* A prophet; seer; medium
of supernatural revelation.—**o·rac·u·lar** *adj.*
—**o·rac·u·lar·i·ty** *n.*—**o·rac·u·lar·ly** *adv.*

or·al *adj.* Spoken; verbal.—**o·ral·ly** *adv.*

or·ange (*or*-inj) *n.* Citrous fruit of an evergreen
tree.—*adj.* Colored or flavored like an orange.

orangebird   orange-hued   orange-striped
orange-colored   orangeman   orange-tailed
orange-crowned   orange peel   orange-tipped
orange-flowered   orange-shaped   orangewood

or·ange·ade (or-enj-*ayd*) *n.* An orange-flavored
beverage.

orange blossom. 1. Fragrant flower of the
orange, traditionally worn by brides.
2. [*cap.*] Cocktail of gin and orange juice.

orange pekoe. Kind of black tea.

or·ange·stick *n.* Wooden manicure stick.

o·rang·u·tan, o·rang·ou·tang (oh-*rang*-uh-tan,
-tang) *n.* Large red-
dish brown ape,
closest to man in
development.

o·rate (oh-*rayt*) *v.*
[o·rat·ed; o·rat·ing]
To speak pomp-
ously; declaim.—
o·ra·tion *n.* Speech;
address.—**or·a·tor**
n.—**or·a·tor·i·cal**
adj.— **-cal·ly** *adv.*

or·a·to·ry *n.* 1. Public speaking. 2. A
private chapel.

ORANGUTAN (1/65 Life-size)

or·a·to·ri·o (or-uh-*tawr*-ee-oh) *n.* Sacred musical composition.

orb *n.* A ball; spherical body.—**or·bic·u·lar** *adj.*
Formed like an orb or sphere; roundish.
—**or·bic·u·lar·i·ty** *n.*—**or·bic·u·lar·ly** *adv.*—**or·**
bic·u·late, or·bic·u·lat·ed *adj.*—**orb·y** *adj.*

or·bit *n. Astronomy.* Path of a celestial body,
usually elliptical.—**or·bit·al** *adj.*

or·chard (*or*-cherd) *n.* Plot of cultivated fruit
trees.—**or·chard·ist** *n.*

or·ches·tra (*or*-kess-truh) *n.* 1. A full instrumental ensemble. 2. Section of an auditorium occupied by the musicians. 3. Ground
floor of a theater.—**or·ches·tral** (or-*kes*-trul)
adj.—**or·ches·tral·ly** *adv.*

or·ches·tra·tion *n.* Instrumental arrangement
of a musical composition.—**or·ches·trate** *v.*
[or·ches·trat·ed; or·ches·trat·ing].

or·chid (*or*-kid) *n.* 1. Family of plants bearing
a large three-pet-
aled, highly prized
flower. 2. A laven-
der color.—**or·chi·**
da·ceous (or-kih-
day-shus) *adj.*—**or·**
chid·ol·o·gy *n.* Or-
chid horticulture.

or·dain (or-*dayn*) *v.*
1. To decree; com-
mand. 2. To con-
secrate as a Chris-
tian clergyman.
—**or·dain·er** *n.*
—**or·dain·ment** *n.*

ORCHID

or·de·al (or-*dee*-ul)
n. 1. A trying ex-
perience; a severe test. 2. Medieval trial by
torture on theory of divine intervention for the
innocent.

or·der *n.* 1. Neat arrangement; proper condition. 2. Established usage. 'The motion is not
in order.' 3. Tranquillity; peace. 4. Mandate; command. 5. Written commission to
buy or supply. 6. A money draft. 7. A
rank; class. 8. An association; fraternity.
9. A biological subclassification. 10. [*pl.*]
Final instructions given a ship upon sailing.
—**or·der** *v.*—**or·der·er** *n.*—**order of the day.**
1. *Parliamentary Law.* Business regularly
recorded for consideration in the minutes.
2. *Military.* Specific directions or information
issued by an officer to his troops.—**take or-**
ders. 1. To obey. 2. To be ordained to the
priesthood.—**to order.** In specific fulfillment.
—**in order to.** So that.

or·der·ly *adj.* 1. Well regulated; methodical;
neat. 2. *Military.* Pertaining to duty.—*n.*
1. Soldier who delivers messages for an officer.
2. Male attendant in a hospital.—**or·der·li·**
ness *n.*—**or·der·ly** *adv.*

or·di·nal *adj.* Denoting order or succession.—*n.*
1. Number denoting ordered succession, as
first, second, third. 2. A Roman Catholic
prayerbook.—**or·di·nal·ism** *n.*

or·di·nance *n.* Law; decree; rule.

or·di·nar·y *adj.* 1. Common; usual; habitual.
2. Mediocre; undistinguished.—**or·di·nar·y** *n.*
[*pl.* or·di·nar·ies] Bishop; archbishop.—**or·**
di·nar·i·ly *adv.*—**or·di·nar·i·ness** *n.*—**ordinary**
seaman. *Nautical.* The least skilled of the deck
department workers.

or·di·nate (*or*-dih-nit) *n. Mathematics.* A line of

reference which determines the position of a point.

or·di·na·tion *n.* Conferment of religious orders.

ord·nance *n.* Artillery; armament.

or·dure *n.* Manure; excrement.—**or·dur·ous** *adj.*

ore *n.* Material mined for metallic content.

o·re·ad (*or*-ee-ad) *n. Greek Mythology.* A mountain nymph.

or·gan *n. Music.* Large, powerful wind instrument consisting of sets of pipes and bellows and played on one or several keyboards.—**or·gan·ist** *n.*

or·gan *n.* 1. Part of a living body performing a vital function. 2. Means; instrument; device. 3. Medium of communication, esp. a newspaper. — **organic disease.** Ailment causing structural deterioration of the organ it attacks. —**or·gan·ic** *adj.*—**or·gan·i·cal·ly** *adv.*

or·gan·dy, or·gan·die (*or*-g'n-dee) *n.* A stiff sheer muslin.

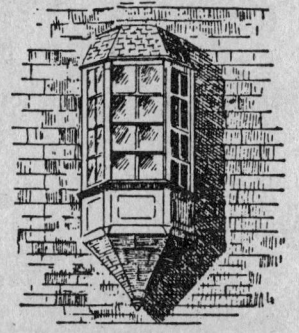

ORGAN

organic chemistry. Branch of chemistry dealing with carbon compounds.

or·gan·ism *n.* A body consisting of mutually dependent parts; living structure.

or·gan·ize (*or*-gan-yze) *v.* [or·gan·ized; or·gan·iz·ing] 1. To systematize; arrange. 2. To establish; found. 3. To recruit for a labor union.—**or·gan·i·za·tion** *n.*—**or·gan·iz·a·ble** *adj.*

or·ga·non (*or*-guh-non) *n. Philosophy.* Body of rules governing inductive or logical reasoning.

or·gasm *n.* Climax of sexual excitement.

or·gy *n.* [*pl.* or·gies] 1. Wild revelry. 2. A great excess.—**or·gi·as·tic** *adj.*

o·ri·el (or-ee-el) *n. Architecture.* Bay window.

o·ri·ent *n.* 1. [*cap.*] The East; eastern Asia. 2. The east; point on the horizon on which the sun appears.—*v.* 1. To become adjusted or acclimated. 2. *Surveying.* To define a position relative to the east of a compass point.—**o·ri·en·tal** *n.* Inhabitant of the eastern world. — **o·ri·en·tal** *adj.*—**O·ri·en·tal·ism** *n.*—**O·ri·en·tal·ist** *n.*

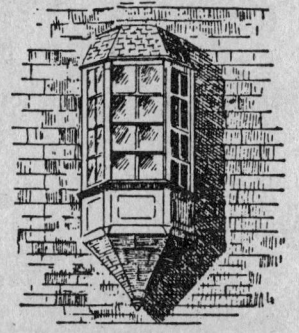

ORIEL

o·ri·en·ta·tion (oh-ree-en-*tay*-shun) *n.* 1. Process of getting one's bearings; adjustment. 2. Understanding of one's situation.

or·i·fice (*oh*-rih-fiss) *n.* Aperture; hole; opening.

or·i·gin (*oh*-rih-jin, *or*-ih-jin) *n.* Beginning; source.

o·rig·i·nal (oh-*rij*-ih-n'l) *adj.* 1. First; early; pristine. 2. Creative; fresh; firsthand.—*n.* 1. Archetype; a new work. 2. Work from which copies are made.—**o·rig·i·nal·i·ty** *n.*

o·rig·i·nate *v.* [o·rig·i·nat·ed; o·rig·i·nat·ing] To create.—**o·rig·i·na·tion** *n.*—**o·rig·i·na·tor** *n.*—**o·rig·i·na·tive** *adj.*— **-tive·ly** *adv.*

o·ri·ole *n.* Any of a family of migratory wild birds, usually with yellow and black plumage.

O·ri·on (oh-*ry*-un) *n. Astronomy.* A constellation in the Southern Hemisphere.

or·i·son *n.* A prayer.

or·mo·lu (*or*-muh-loo) *n.* Kind of brass used in cheap jewelry.

ORIOLE (1/5 Life-size)

or·na·ment (*or*-nuh-ment) *n.* Decoration; embellishment.—**or·na·ment** *v.*—**or·na·men·tal** *adj.*—**or·na·men·tal·ly** *adv.* —**or·na·men·ta·tion** *n.*

or·nate *adj.* Florid; overembellished.—**or·nate·ly** *adv.*—**or·nate·ness** *n.*

or·ner·y *n. Colloquial.* Disagreeable; mean-tempered; vicious.—**or·ner·i·ness** *n.*

or·ni·thol·o·gy (or-nih-*thol*-uh-jee) *n.* The science of birds.—**or·ni·tho·log·i·cal** (or-nih-thuh-*loj*-ih-kul) *adj.*—**or·ni·thol·o·gist** *n.*

o·ro·tund (oh-roh-tund) *n.* Mellow; rich; musical.—**o·ro·tund·i·ty** *n.*

or·phan (*or*-fun) *n.* Child whose parents are dead.—**or·phan·age** *n.* Home for orphans. —**or·phan** *v.*—**or·phan·hood** *n.*

Or·pheus (*or*-fee-us) *n.* A legendary poet and musician of ancient Greece.—**Or·phic** *adj.*

or·ris, or·rice *n.* Plant whose root is a common base for cosmetics.

or·tho·don·ti·a (or-thuh-*don*-shuh) *n.* Practice of straightening teeth.—**or·tho·don·tist** *n.*

or·tho·dox (*or*-thuh-doks) *adj.* Conforming to commonly accepted opinion or faith.—**or·tho·dox·ly** *adv.*—**or·tho·dox·y** *n.* [*pl.* -ies].

or·thog·ra·phy (or-*thog*-ruh-fee) *n.* Art of correct spelling; spelling.—**or·thog·ra·pher** *n.* —**or·tho·graph·i·cal** *adj.*—**or·tho·graph·i·cal·ly** *adv.*—**orthographic projection.** A drawing in which all points lie perpendicular to the plane of projection.

or·tho·pe·dics (or-thuh-*pee*-diks) *n.* Science of correcting bodily deformities.—**or·tho·pe·dic** *adj.*—**or·tho·pe·dist** *n.*

or·to·lan (*or*-toh-lun) *n.* Small bird much prized for its flesh.

os·cil·late (*oss*-ih-layt) *v.* [-lat·ed; -lat·ing] To swing; fluctuate; vibrate.—**os·cil·la·tion** *n.*

os·cil·la·tor (*os*-sil-lay-ter) *n. Electricity.* Device for converting direct current to alternating current.

O

os·cil·lo·graph (os-*sil*-oh-graph) *n.* Instrument for recording electrical vibrations.

os·cu·late (*oss*-kyoo-layt) *v.* [os·cu·lat·ed; os·cu·lat·ing] To kiss; to greet with a kiss.—**os·cu·la·tion** *n.*—**os·cu·la·tor** *n.*—**os·cu·la·to·ry** *adj.*

o·sier (*oh*-zher) *n.* A group of shrubs and trees of the willow family.

os·mo·sis (oz-*moh*-sis) *n.* Impulse of fluids to pass through a porous membrane.—**os·mot·ic** (oz-*mot*-ik) *adj.*—**os·mot·i·cal·ly** *adv.*

os·mi·um (*oz*-mee-um) *n.* Hard, bluish-white metallic element; the heaviest element. (*Symbol:* Os).—**os·mic, os·mi·ous** *adj.*

os·prey (*oss*-pree) *n.* Large fishing hawk.

os·se·ous (*os*-see-us) *adj.* Bony; resembling bone.—**os·se·ous·ly** *adv.*

os·si·fy (*oss*-ih-fy) *v.* [os·si·fied; os·si·fy·ing] To form bone; to harden.—**os·si·fi·ca·tion** *n.*

os·ten·si·ble (oss-*ten*-sih-b'l) *adj.* Apparent seeming; manifest.—**os·ten·si·bil·i·ty** *n.*—**os·ten·si·bly** *adv.*

os·ten·sive (oss-*ten*-siv) *adj.* Showing; appearing; exhibiting.—**os·ten·sive·ly** *adv.*

OSPREY (1/10 Life-size)

os·ten·ta·tion (oss-ten-*tay*-shun) *n.* Vain or pretentious display; flamboyant show.—**os·ten·ta·tious** *adj.*—**-tious·ly** *adv.*—**-tious·ness** *n.*

os·te·ol·o·gy (oss-tee-*ol*-uh-jee) *n.* The science dealing with bone tissue.—**os·te·o·log·i·cal** *adj.*—**os·te·ol·o·gist** *n.*

os·te·op·a·thy (oss-tee-*op*-uh-thee) *n.* Therapeutic system based upon manipulation of affected parts of the body.—**os·te·o·path** (*oss*-tee-oh-path) *n.*—**os·te·o·path·ic** *adj.*

os·tra·cism (*oss*-truh-sizm) *n.* Expulsion; banishment; exclusion from social intercourse.—**os·tra·cize** *v.* [os·tra·cized; os·tra·ciz·ing].

os·trich (*oss*-trich, *awss*-trich) *n.* A large, nonflying desert bird.

oth·er (*uth*-er) *adj.* 1. Second of two; additional; remaining. 2. Opposite. 'The other side of the street.'—*pron.* 1. Anything else. 'No one could do other than stare.' 2. [*pl.*] Those not specified.

oth·er·wise *adv.* Differently; not so; in other respects.—*conj.* Else; but for this.

oth·er·world·ly *adj.* 1. Concerned with a prospective after-life. 2. Transcendental; beyond earthly affairs.—**oth·er·world·li·ness** *n.*

o·ti·ose (*oh*-shee-ohss) *adj.* Vain; idle; empty.

OSTRICH (1/75 Life-size)

Ot·ta·wa (*ot*-tuh-wuh). 1. Tribe of North American Indians. 2. Capital of Canada.

ot·ter *n.* Amphibious, fur-bearing animal of the weasel family.

ot·to·man (*ot*-oh-m'n) *n.* 1. Kind of couch or sofa. 2. [*cap.*] A tribe of Turks. 3. [*cap.*] The first great Turkish emperor.—**Ot·to·man** *adj.* Turkish.

OTTER (1/35 Life-size)

ought (*awt*) *n.* Anything; aught.

ought (*awt*) *auxiliary. v.* To be bound or obliged—with an infinitive.

Oui·ja (*wee*-juh) *n.* A board used in fortune telling. The name is trade-marked.

ounce (*ounss*) *n.* 1. One-sixteenth of a pound (avoirdupois); one-twelfth of a pound (troy weight). 2. Fluid ounce; one-sixteenth of a pint.—*Abbreviation:* oz. (*sing.* and *pl.*).

our *adj.* Belonging to us.—**ours** *pron.* That which belongs to us.

our·selves *pron.* Reflexive form of we.

oust (*owst*) *v.* To put out; expel.—**oust·er** *n.* Dispossession.

out *adv.* 1. Forth; away; beyond. 2. Not at home. 3. Lacking; without. 'Out of funds.' 4. Extinguished. 5. To the end. 'Hear me out.'—*adj.* 1. *Slang.* Unconscious. 2. *Baseball.* Unsuccessful in attaining a base.—*n.* 1. *Printing.* An omission. 2. *Politics.* One out of office (usually used in plural).—**out-and-out** *adj.* Thorough; complete.

out- *prefix.* 1. Exceeding; surpassing. 2. Beyond; apart.

out-and-outer	outbuilding	out-group
outbox	outburst	outhouse
outbrag	outdo	out-kneed
outbreak	outgeneral	outperform
outbribe	outgo	outswim

out·board *adj. Nautical.* Away from the center or keel; outside a ship.—*n.* Small racing craft powered by an **outboard motor.**—**out·board** *adv.*

out·cast *n.* Exile; an unaccepted person.

out·come *n.* Result; issue; consequence.

out·door *adj.* Open-air; unclosed.—**out·doors** *n.*

out·er *adj.* External; outside.—**out·er·most** *adj.* Farthest from the center.

OUTBOARD MOTOR

out·field *n. Baseball.* Area beyond the diamond.—**out·field·er** *n.*

out·fit *n.* 1. Paraphernalia; equipment. 2. A suit; ensemble. 3. Aggregation; team; group.—*v.* [out·fit·ted; out·fit·ting].—**out·fit·ter** *n.*

out·flank *v.* To outmaneuver; surround the wing of an opposing army.

out·grow *v.* [out·grew; out·grown; out·growing] To discard; go beyond; become too large for.—**out·growth** n. 1. Growth; excrescence. 2. Result; consequence.

out·ing n. Picnic; excursion.

outing flannel. A soft-napped cotton cloth.

out·land·ish adj. Strange; bizarre; fantastic. —**out·land·ish·ly** adv.—**out·land·ish·ness** n.

out·last v. To survive; outlive.

out·law n. Criminal; desperado.—v. To declare illegal.—**out·law·ry** n.

out·lay n. Expenditure; disbursement.

out·let n. Vent; escape; exit.

out·line v. [out·lined; out·lin·ing] 1. To draw in contour. 2. To sketch; describe briefly. 3. To organize under headings.—**out·line** n.

out·live v. [out·lived; out·liv·ing] To live after; survive.—**out·liv·er** n.

out·look n. View; perspective; vision.

out·mod·ed adj. Obsolete; unfashionable.

out·pa·tient (out-pay-shent) n. A person who is treated at a hospital, though not an inmate. —**out·pa·tient** adj.

out·post n. Military. 1. Post or station in an outlying area. 2. An outpost garrison.

out·put n. Production; work turned out.

out·rage n. Abuse; atrocity.—v. [out·raged; out·rag·ing]—**out·ra·geous** adj.—**out·ra·geous·ly** adv.—**out·ra·geous·ness** n.

out·rank v. To surpass in rank.

out·rig·ger n. Narrow sailing boat or canoe, with a buoyant extension to prevent capsizing.

out·right adj. Complete; unmitigated.

out·set n. Beginning; start.

out·side n. 1. Surface; exposed part.

OUTRIGGER

2. Exterior; the far side of an enclosure. 3. Utmost; extreme limit.—**out·side** adj.

out·skirt, out·skirts n. Portion far from the middle; suburb.

out·spok·en n. Frank; candid; bold.—**out·spok·en·ly** adv.—**out·spok·en·ness** n.

out·stand·ing adj. 1. Notable; prominent; salient. 2. Unpaid, as a debt or bill.

out·strip v. [out·stripped; out·strip·ping] To exceed; outrun.

out·ward adj. External; superficial; outer. —**out·ward·ly** adv.—**out·ward·ness** n.

out·weigh v. To exceed in importance; carry greater weight.

out·wit v. [out·wit·ted; out·wit·ting] To frustrate; defeat; outmatch in ingenuity.

o·va plural of **ovum.**

o·val (oh-v'l) adj. Elliptical; egg-shaped.—**o·val** n.—**o·val·ly** adv.—**o·val·ness** n.

o·var·y n. [pl. o·var·ies] Female reproductive organ.—**o·vate** adj. Egg-shaped.—**o·var·i·an** adj.

OVAL

o·va·tion n. Demonstration in honor of a public figure; enthusiastic reception.

ov·en (uv-en) n. Chamber in a stove for baking or roasting.

o·ver (oh-ver) prep. 1. Above; in a higher position. 2. In greater degree than. 3. Across. 4. Upon the surface of; about; along. 5. During; throughout.—adv. 1. Above. 2. Across. 3. Away from an erect position. 'To fall over.' 4. In excess; beyond. 5. Again. —adj. 1. Upper; excessive; surplus. 2. Completed; ended.

o·ver- prefix 1. Above; too much; greater than; more than. 2. Covering; outer. See list of compounds given for spelling purposes below.

o·ver·all adj. Total; inclusive. 'An over-all estimate.'

o·ver·alls n. pl. Loose-fitting work trousers, with attached bib and shoulder straps.

o·ver·arm adj. Sports. Thrown or struck with the arm above the shoulder.

o·ver·bal·ance v. [o·ver·bal·anced; o·ver·bal·anc·ing] 1. To outweigh. 2. To knock off balance.

o·ver·bear v. [o·ver·borne; o·ver·bear·ing] To domineer; treat haughtily.—**o·ver·bear·ing** adj. Arrogant; insolent.—**o·ver·bear·ing·ly** adv.

o·ver·board adv. Over a ship's side.

o·ver·cast v. [o·ver·cast; o·ver·cast·ing] 1. To become cloudy; darken. 2. Sewing. To bind rough edges of a fabric.—n. A low-hanging layer of clouds.—**o·ver·cast** adj.

o·ver·cloud v. To become cloudy.

o·ver·coat n. Heavy coat worn over the other clothes; heavy topcoat.

o·ver·come v. [o·ver·came; o·ver·com·ing] To subdue; conquer.—**o·ver·com·er** n.

o·ver·de·vel·op v. Photography. To leave a film too long in developing solution.

O

overabound	overbashful	overcapitalize	overcomplex
overabundance	overbid	overcaptious	overcompliant
overabundant	overblow	overcaptiousness	overconfidence
overaccentuate	overboastful	overcareful	overconfident
overact	overbold	overcareless	overconscientious
overactive	overbounteous	overcaution	overconscious
overage	overbrilliant	overcautious	overconsciousness
overambitious	overbrutal	overcharge	overconservative
overanxious	overbuild	overcharitable	overconsiderate
overapprehensive	overburden	overcheap	overcontribute
overarch	overburdensome	overchildish	overcook
overassertive	overburn	overcivil	overcool
overassessment	overbusy	overcivilized	overcorrupt
overattentive	overbuy	overclean	overcourteous
overawe	overcapacity	overclever	overcovetous

o·ver·draft *n. Banking.* Sum drawn in excess of the depositor's credit.

o·ver·draw *v. Banking.* [o·ver·drew; o·ver·draw·ing] To draw in excess of one's credit.

o·ver·drive *v.* [o·ver·drove; o·ver·driv·en; o·ver·driv·ing] 1. To drive animals to exhaustion. 2. *Golf.* To hit the ball too fast.—*n.* A high-ratio gear which meshes automatically at high speed.

o·ver·due *adj.* Late; past the time of payment, delivery, arrival, etc.

o·ver·dye *v.* [o·ver·dyed; o·ver·dye·ing] To apply one color over another.

o·ver·ex·pose *v. Photography.* To expose a sensitized surface to light for too great a time.

o·ver·flow *v.* 1. To spill over the brim of a container. 2. To inundate; cover with liquid. *n.* 1. Surplus liquid. 2. Extra amount.

o·ver·grow *v.* To make or become covered with hair, weeds, herbage, etc.

o·ver·hand *adj. Sports.* With the hand describing an arc above the shoulder.— **-hand** *adv.*

o·ver·haul *v.* 1. To examine and repair thoroughly. 2. To overtake; catch.

o·ver·head *adv.* Aloft; above.—*n.* 1. Indirect charges incurred in operating a business. 2. *Naval.* Ceiling.—**o·ver·head** *adj.*

o·ver·hear *v.* [o·ver·heard; o·ver·hear·ing] To hear remarks addressed to others.

o·ver·lap *v.* [o·ver·lapped; o·ver·lap·ping] To extend beyond; cover partially.

o·ver·lay *v.* [o·ver·laid; o·ver·lay·ing] To cover; superimpose.—*n.* 1. Ornamental veneer. 2. *Printing.* Paper pasted to the tympan to make the impression stronger.

o·ver·leap *v.* 1. To skip; omit. 2. To go beyond one's goal.

o·ver·look *v.* 1. To view from a higher place. 2. To forget; omit. 3. To excuse; pass over.

o·ver·lord *n.* One who rules others.

o·ver·match *v.* To prove more than a match for.

o·ver·night *adj.* 1. During the night. 2. Of one night's duration.

o·ver·pass *n.* Bridge over a railway or road.

o·ver·play *v. Golf.* To drive the ball too far.

o·ver·pow·er *v.* To overwhelm; subdue. —**o·ver·pow·er·ing** *adj.* —**-ing·ly** *adv.*

OVERPASS

o·ver·reach *v.* 1. To extend beyond. 2. To deceive by cunning; outwit. 3. To overextend; attempt too much.—**o·ver·reach·er** *n.*

o·ver·ride *v.* [o·ver·rid·den; o·ver·rid·ing] To supersede; annul; overrule.

o·ver·rule *v.* [o·ver·ruled; o·ver·rul·ing] To rule against; reject.—**o·ver·rul·er** *n.*—**o·ver·rul·ing** *adj.*—**o·ver·rul·ing·ly** *adv.*

o·ver·run *v.* [o·ver·ran; o·ver·run·ning] 1. To run too far. 2. To conquer; take possession. 3. To flow over a brim. 4. To invest; beset. 5. *Printing.* To rearrange copy by shifting words or lines.

o·ver·sea, o·ver·seas *adj.* Foreign; beyond the ocean.

o·ver·see *v.* [o·ver·saw; o·ver·seen; o·ver·see·ing] To superintend; look after.—**o·ver·seer** *n.* —**o·ver·seer·ship** *n.*

overcredulous	overexercise	overgreedy	overlarge
overcritical	overexert	overhang	overlaudatory
overcrowd	overexertion	overhappy	overlavish
overcultivate	overexpand	overharden	overlax
overcunning	overexpansion	overhardy	overlearned
overcurious	overexpose	overharsh	overleaven
overdainty	overexposure	overhasty	overliberal
overdear	overexuberant	overhaughty	overlively
overdecorate	overfacile	overheat	overload
overdeliberate	overfamiliar	overheavy	overlogical
overdelicate	overfanciful	overhigh	overlong
overdemand	overfastidious	overidealistic	overlusty
overdesirous	overfar	overillustrate	overluxuriant
overdignified	overfat	overimaginative	overmany
overdiligence	overfatigue	overimpress	overmasterful
overdiligent	overfearful	overinclined	overmature
overdo	overfeed	overindividualistic	overmeanness
overdose	overfluent	overindulge	overmeasure
overdress	overfond	overindulgence	overmeek
overdrive	overfoolish	overindustrialize	overmellow
overdry	overfrail	overinflate	overmerciful
overeager	overfrank	overinflation	overmerry
overearly	overfree	overinfluence	overmild
overearnest	overfreely	overinsistent	overmodest
overeasy	overfrequency	overinsure	overmodesty
overeat	overfrequent	overinventoried	overmoist
overeducate	overfull	overinvest	overmortgage
overelaborate	overfullness	overirrigate	overmournful
overelegant	overgenerous	overirrigation	overmuch
overembellish	overgenial	overissue	overmultiply
overemotional	overgentle	overjealous	overnear
overemphasize	overgloomy	overjoy	overneat
overemphatic	overgracious	overjoyful	overnegligence
overenthusiastic	overgrasping	overjudicious	overnegligent
overestimate	overgrateful	overkeen	overnervous
overestimation	overgratify	overkind	overnice
overexcitable	overgraze	overlabor	overnourish
overexcite	overgreasy	overlade	overnumerous

o·ver·set *v.* [o·ver·set; o·ver·set·ting] To turn over; tip; overthrow.—*n. Journalism.* Excess news matter beyond the need of the edition.

o·ver·shad·ow *v.* 1. To throw a shadow upon. 2. To dominate; eclipse by superior importance.—**o·ver·shad·ow·er** *n.*

o·ver·shoes *n. pl.* Waterproof shoes worn over regular ones.

o·ver·shoot *v.* [o·ver·shot; o·ver·shoot·ing] 1. To exceed; miss by passing beyond the mark. 2. To excel another in shooting. 3. To tax oneself in shooting.—**o·ver·shot** *adj.* —1. Drunk. 2. Jutting; projecting. 3. Actuated from above, as a mill wheel.—**o·ver·shot** *n.*

o·ver·sight *n.* 1. Accidental omission. 2. Supervision; direction.

o·ver·soul *n. Philosophy.* Absolute being; containing all reality.

o·ver·spread *v.* To cover; envelop; spread out.

o·ver·state *v.* [o·ver·stat·ed; o·ver·stat·ing] To exaggerate.—**o·ver·state·ment** *n.* 1. Exaggeration. 2. Overcharged account.

o·ver·stay *v.* [o·ver·stayed; o·ver·stay·ing] To stay too long.

o·ver·step *v.* [o·ver·stepped; o·ver·step·ping] To exceed; transgress.

o·ver·strung *adj.* Tense; sensitive.

o·ver·stuff *v.* [o·ver·stuffed; o·ver·stuff·ing] 1. To cram to excess. 2. To upholster heavily. —**o·ver·stuffed** *adj.*

o·vert (oh-*vert*) *adj.* Open; manifest; outward. —**o·vert·ly** *adv.*—**o·vert·ness** *n.*

o·ver·take *v.* [o·ver·took; o·ver·tak·en; o·ver·tak·ing] To pass; reach.

o·ver-the-counter *adj.* [Pertaining to cash-and-carry sales.

o·ver·throw *v.* [o·ver·threw; o·ver·thrown; o·ver·throw·ing] To overturn; defeat.

o·ver·time *n.* 1. Work done after hours. 2. Pay for such work.—**o·ver·time** *adj. & adv.*

o·ver·tone. 1. *Music.* Harmonic; a secondary tone produced by independent vibration of a part of the vibrating body. 2. Implication; hidden significance.

o·ver·ture *n.* 1. Proposal; advance. 2. *Music.* A composition introductory to a long work.

o·ver·turn *v.* To upset; capsize; overthrow. —**o·ver·turn** *n.*

o·ver·ween·ing *adj.* Arrogant; overbearing. —**o·ver·ween** *v.*—**o·ver·ween·ing·ly** *adv.*

o·ver·weight *adj.* Heavier than normal.—**o·ver·weight** *n.*—**o·ver·weigh** *v.*

o·ver·whelm *v.* [o·ver·whelmed; o·ver·whelm·ing] To conquer; best.—**o·ver·whelm·ing** *adj.*

o·ver·wrought *adj.* 1. Distracted; upset. 2. Overworked. 3. Exaggerated.

o·vi·form *adj.* Egg shaped.

o·vine *adj.* Pertaining to sheep.

o·vip·a·rous (oh-*vip*-uh-rus) *adj. Biology.* Egg-laying.—**o·vi·par·i·ty** *n.*

o·void *adj.* Egg-shaped.

o·vule *n.* Seed or egg in early stage.—**o·vu·lar, o·vu·lar·y** *adj.*—**o·vu·late** *v.* [o·vu·lat·ed; o·vu·lat·ing]—**o·vu·la·tion** *n.*

o·vum *n.* [*pl.* o·va] Egg; vesicle in the ovary, forming the basis of the embryo.

owe (oh) *v.* [owed; ow·ing] To be indebted to; be obliged.—**ow·ing to.** Because of.

O

overobedient	overpunish	oversilent	oversystematic
overobese	overpunishment	oversimple	oversystematize
overobsequious	overquick	oversimplicity	overtalkative
overoffensive	overquiet	oversimplify	overtame
overofficious	overrash	oversize	overtask
overpartial	overrate	overskeptical	overtax
overpassionate	overrationalize	oversleep	overtaxation
overpatriotic	overready	overslight	overtechnical
overpay	overrealistic	overslow	overtedious
overpayment	overrefined	oversolemn	overteem
overpeople	overrefinement	oversolicitous	overtenacious
overpessimistic	overreligious	oversoon	overtender
overplausible	overremiss	oversophisticated	overthrifty
overplentiful	overresolute	overspecialize	overthrust
overplump	overrestrain	overspeculate	overtimid
overply	overrich	overspeculation	overtimorous
overpolite	overrighteous	overspend	overtire
overpopular	overripe	oversqueamish	overtrain
overpopulate	overripen	overstiff	overtrim
overpopulous	overroast	overstimulate	overtrustful
overpositive	overrude	overstimulation	overunionized
overpotent	oversad	overstock	overuse
overpowerful	oversalt	overstrain	overvaluation
overpraise	oversanguine	overstress	overvalve
overprecise	oversaturate	overstrict	overvehement
overpress	oversaucy	overstrident	overventuresome
overpresumptuous	overscented	overstrong	overventurous
overprize	overscrupulous	overstudious	overviolent
overproduce	overseason	overstudy	overvote
overproduction	oversell	oversubscribe	overwarm
overproficient	oversensitive	oversubscription	overwary
overprolific	oversentimental	oversubtle	overweaken
overprominent	overserious	oversubtlety	overwealthy
overprompt	overservile	oversufficient	overwear
overprosperous	oversevere	oversupply	overwet
overproud	overseverity	oversure	overwise
overprovide	oversharp	oversusceptible	overwork
overprovism	overshort	oversuspicious	overworry
overprovoke	overshorten	oversweet	overzealous

OWI *Abbreviation.* Office of War Information; the U.S. propaganda agency during World War II.

owl *n.* Night-flying, carnivorous bird.—**owl·et** *n.* Owl; young owl.—**owl·ish** *adj.*

own (*ohn*) *v.* **1.** To possess; hold. **2.** To admit; confess; acknowledge. —*adj.* Belonging to one. —**own·er** *n.*—**own·er·less** *adj.*—**own·er·ship** *n.*

ox *n.* [*pl.* ox·en] **1.** A bovine animal. **2.** A steer. **3.** A doltish or clumsy person.

OWL
(1/11 life-size)

oxbird	oxfly	oxhorn
oxblood	oxgall	ox house
ox bow	oxgang	oxlike
oxboy	oxgate	oxman
oxbrake	oxgoad	oxshoe
oxcart	oxhide	oxskin
ox-eyed	oxhoft	oxtail

ox·al·ic (oks-*al*-ik) *n.* A poisonous fatty acid.

ox·ford *n.* **1.** A low shoe. **2.** [*cap*]. A famous English university, specializing in humanistic studies.—**oxford gray.** Dark gray.

ox·i·da·tion *n.* Conversion to an oxide.—**ox·i·date** *v.* [-dat·ed; -dat·ing]—**ox·i·da·tive** *adj.*

ox·ide *n.* A compound of oxygen and an element.—**ox·i·dize** *v.* [ox·i·dized; ox·i·diz·ing] To convert into an oxide.—**ox·i·diz·a·ble** *adj.* —**ox·i·diz·er** *n.*

Ox·o·ni·an (oks-*oh*-nee-un) *adj.* Pertaining to Oxford.

ox·y·gen (*oks*-ih-jen) *n.* A common element, gaseous at earth temperatures and necessary for respiration. (*Symbol:* O).

oys·ter *n.* **1.** A common edible bivalve mollusk. **2.** *Slang.* A silent or uncommunicative person.

o·zone (*oh*-zohn) *n.* An allotropic form of oxygen, produced by chemical union of three oxygen atoms.—**o·zon·ic** (oh-*zon*-ik) *adj.*—**o·zo·nize** (*oh*-zuh-nyze) *v.* [o·zo·nized; o·zo·niz·ing]—**o·zo·nous** *adj.*

P

pab·u·lum (*pab*-yoo-lum) *n.* Food; nourishment; intellectual stimulation.

pace (*payss*) *v.* [paced; pac·ing] **1.** To step; walk. **2.** To measure by walking over. **3.** To set the speed.—*n.* **1.** A step. **2.** The length of one step. **3.** Manner of walking; gait. **4.** Rate of speed.—**pac·er** *n.*—**pace·mak·er, pace·set·ter** *n.* One who establishes a rate of speed.

pach·y·derm (*pak*-ih-derm) *n.* Any of certain large thick-skinned animals, as the elephant.

pa·cif·ic (puh-*sif*-ik). Also **pa·cif·i·cal.** *adj.* **1.** Tranquil; peaceable; conciliatory. **2.** [*cap*.] Relating to the Pacific Ocean.

pac·i·fism (*pass*-ih-fizm) *n.* Doctrine of opposition to war for any purpose.—**pac·i·fist** *n.*

pa·cif·i·cate (puh-*sif*-ih-kayt) *v.* [pa·cif·i·cat·ed; pa·cif·i·cat·ing] To placate; pacify.—**pac·i·fi·ca·tion** *n.*—**pa·cif·i·ca·to·ry** *adj.*

pac·i·fy (*pass*-ih-fy) *v.* [pac·i·fied; pac·i·fy·ing] To calm; mollify.—**pac·i·fi·a·ble** *adj.*—**pac·i·fi·er** *n.*

pack *n.* **1.** A tied bundle; knapsack; package. **2.** A collection; aggregate. **3.** Set of playing cards. **4.** Group of animals or people banded together, usually for evil purposes. **5.** Large area of floating ice.—*v.* **1.** To place in containers for transportation. **2.** To stow; stuff; tampon. **3.** To fill an audience with one's supporters. 'To pack the galleries.' **4.** To can; preserve. **5.** *Medicine.* To envelop in sheets or compresses. **6.** To be adapted to neat stowage. **7.** *Slang.* To carry, as a gun. —**pack·er** *n.*—**pack** *adj.*

pack·age *n.* A compact bundle.—*v.* [pack·aged; pack·ag·ing].

pack·et *n.* **1.** A small package; parcel.

2. Small ship making scheduled trips with mail, passengers, and cargo.

pack·ing *n.* Stuffing; filling.

pact *n.* Agreement; compact.

pad *n.* **1.** Cushion; soft, stuffed material. **2.** Tablet of writing paper.—*v.* [pad·ded; pad·ding] **1.** To stuff with soft material. **2.** To walk softly.—**pad·ding** *n.* Stuffing.

pad·dle *n.* Short broad oar used to propel certain small boats.—*v.* [pad·dled; pad·dling] **1.** To propel with a paddle. **2.** To row lightly. **3.** To swim effortlessly or playfully. —**pad·dler** *n.*

paddle-beam	paddlecock
paddle-board	paddlefish
paddle-box	paddlewood

paddle wheel. *Nautical.* Wheel with extending surfaces for propulsion of light vessels.

pad·dock *n.* Small field or enclosure used for pasturing horses.

pad·dy *n.* **1.** Rice in the husk, growing or cut. **2.** A rice field.

paddy wagon. *Slang.* A police van.

pad·lock *n.* Portable lock with a shackle for fastening through a staple. —**pad·lock** *v.*

pa·dre (*pah*-dray) *n.* **1.** *Spanish & Italian.* Priest; monk. **2.** *Colloquial.* Chaplain.

pae·an, pe·an *n.* A joyous, triumphant song.

pa·gan (*pay*-g'n) *n.* A heathen; idolator; person who adheres to none of the accepted reli-

PADDLE

PADLOCK

gions.—**pa·gan** *adj.*—**pa·gan·ish** *adj.*—**pa·gan·ism** *n.*—**pa·gan·ize** *v.* [-gan·ized; -gan·iz·ing].

page (*payj*) *n.* 1. Young attendant of a royal court. 2. Attendant; one employed to carry messages, etc.—*v.* [paged; pag·ing] To summon, as by a page.

page *n.* One side of a leaf of a book or other printed matter.—*v.* [paged; pag·ing] To number the pages of.

pag·eant (*paj*-'nt) *n.* Spectacle; display for public entertainment.—**pag·eant·ry** *n.* Splendid show or spectacle.

pag·i·nal (*paj*-ih-n'l) *adj.* Consisting of pages.

pag·i·nate (*paj*-ih-nayt) *v.* To number pages. —**pag·i·na·tion** *n.*

pa·go·da (puh-*goh*-duh) *n.* Many-tiered oriental tower, usually a shrine.

pail (*payl*) *n.* Bucket; cylindrical vessel with an arched handle. —**pail·ful** *n.*

pain 1. Physical suffering. 2. Distress; sorrow. 3. [*pl.*] Careful labor; trouble.—*v.* 1. To hurt; ache. 2. To distress; grieve. —**pain·ful** *adj.*—**pain ful·ly** *adv.*—**pain·ful·ness** *n.*—**pain·less** *adj.* —**pain·less·ness** *n.*

PAGODA

pains·tak·ing *adj.* Meticulous; industrious

paint *v.* 1. To apply color. 2. To depict; execute a picture.—*n.* Pigment; coloring preparation.—**paint·er** *n.*—**paint·ing** *n.*—1. A picture. 2. The art of composing in colors. —**painter's colic.** Lead poisoning.

paint-bespattered	paint filler	paint-spotted
paintbox	paint pot	paint-stained
paint brush	paint-splashed	paintwork

pair *n.* 1. A couple; two corresponding parts. 2. Two legislative members of opposite parties who agree not to vote on an issue; the compact itself.—**pair** *v.*

pais·ley (*payz*-lee) *n.* Figured in a small, plume-like pattern.—**paisley shawl.** Woolen shawl originally made in Scotland.

pa·ja·ma, py·ja·ma (puh-*jah*-muh, -*jam*-uh) *n.* 1. In *pl.*, Loose trousers and jacket worn for sleeping or lounging. 2. Costume of India.

pal *n. Slang.* Chum; comrade.—*v.* To associate with.

pal·ace (*pal*-iss) *n.* 1. Imperial or ecclesiastical residence. 2. A mansion; public building.

pal·a·din (*pal*-uh-din) *n.* 1. A knight-errant; hero. 2. [*cap.*] One of the twelve knights of Charlemagne.

pal·an·quin, pal·an·keen (pal-un-*keen*) *n.* Covered conveyance supported by poles on the shoulders of four bearers.

pal·at·a·ble (*pal*-it-uh-b'l) *adj.* 1. Tasty. 2. Acceptable; agreeable.—**pal·at·a·bil·i·ty** *n.* —**pal·at·a·ble·ness** *n.*—**pal·at·a·bly** *adv.*

pal·ate (*pal*-it) *n.* Roof of the mouth.—**pal·a·tal**

n. Phonetics. Sound formed with the tongue touching the palate; *ch, j, sh,* and *zh;* short *i* and long *e.*—**pal·a·tal** *adj.*—**pal·a·tal·i·za·tion** *n.*

pa·la·tial (puh-*lay*-sh'l) *adj.* Like a palace; magnificent.—**pa·la·tial·ly** *adv.*

pa·lav·er (puh-*lav*-er) *n.* Flattery; idle chatter. —**pa·lav·er** *v.*—**pa·lav·er·er** *n.*

pale *adj.* 1. Faint in color. 2. Pallid; colorless; wan.—*v.* [paled; pal·ing] To lose color; blanch.—**pale** *n.*—**pale·ly** *adv.*—**pale·ness** *n.* —**pal·ish** *adj.*

palebelly	pale dried	pale looking
pale-blooded	pale-eared	pale-reddish
pale blue	pale-eyed	pale-refined
palebreast	paleface(n.)	pale-souled
palebright	pale-faced	pale-spirited
pale buck	pale-hearted	pale-spotted
pale-cheeked	pale-hued	pale-striped
pale-colored	pale-leaved	pale-tinted

pale *n.* 1. Narrow pointed stake in a fence. 2. Enclosure; precincts; jurisdiction or protection. 'Beyond the pale.'—*v.* To enclose.

pa·le·o·lith·ic (pay-lee-oh-*lith*-ik) *adj.* Pertaining to the early Stone Age.—**paleolithic man.** Prehistoric man of the early stone period.

pa·le·on·tol·o·gy, pa·lae·on·tol·o·gy (payl-ee-on-*tol*-uh-jee) *n.* Study of extinct forms of life by interpretation of fossil remains.—**pa·le·on·to·log·ic, -i·cal** *adj.*—**pa·le·on·tol·o·gist** *n.*

Pal·es·ti·ni·an (pal-ess-*tin*-ee-an) *adj.* Pertaining to Palestine.—**Pal·es·tin·i·an** *n.*

pal·ette (*pal*-et) *n.* 1. Tablet for laying out and mixing artists' pigments. 2. Range or quality of colors used. —**pal·ette-knife** *n.* Flexible steel spatula for scraping a palette, or mixing and applying colors.

PALETTE

pal·frey *n.* Mount; horse trained to carry ladies.

pal·imp·sest (*pal*-imp-sest) *n.* A parchment which has been written upon after the erasure of previous writing.—**pal·imp·sest** *adj.*—**pal·imp·sest** *v.*

pal·ing *n.* 1. Construction of a fence. 2. A fence.

pal·in·gen·e·sis (pal-in-*jen*-eh-siss) *n.* 1. Regeneration; rebirth; baptism. 2. Reincarnation. 3. *Biology.* Identical inheritance of ancestral characteristics. — **pal·in·ge·ne·si·an** *adj.*—**pal·in·gen·et·ic** *adj.*

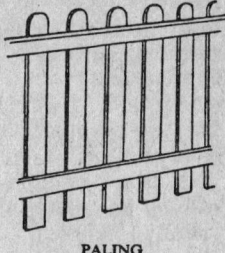

PALING

pal·i·sade (pal-uh-*sayd*) *n.* 1. Fence of tall closely planted stakes; stockade. 2. A single stake in a stockade. 3. A long, natural rock embankment.—*v.* [pal·i·sad·ed; pal·i·sad·ing] To fortify with palisades.

pall (*pawl*) *n.* 1. A dismal obscuring mass. 2. Black cloth on a coffin.—*v.* To shroud.

pall *v.* To cloy; satiate.

P

pal·la·di·um (puh-*lay*-dee-um) *n.* Rare metallic element of the platinum group used in dentistry, jewelry, etc. (*Symbol:* Pd).—**pal·la·di·um·ize** *v.*—**pal·lad·ic, pal·la·dous** *adj.*

Pal·las (*pal*-us) *n.* 1. *Mythology*. Appellation of Athena, Greek goddess of wisdom. 2. *Astronomy*. Asteroid between Mars and Jupiter.

pall·bear·er *n.* One who carries or escorts the coffin at a funeral.

pal·let *n.* 1. An oval wooden instrument used in pottery making. 2. A part of a clock connected with the pendulum. 3. A sleeping mat.

pal·li·ate (*pal*-ee-ayt) *v.* [pal·li·at·ed; pal·li·at·ing] 1. To soothe; ease superficially; mitigate. 2. To gloss over; extenuate.—**pal·li·a·tor** *n.* —**pal·li·a·tion** *n.*— -**a·tive** *adj.*— -**a·tive·ly** *adv.*

pal·lid (*pal*-id) *adj.* Pale; wan.—**pal·lid·ly** *adv.* —**pal·lid·ness, pal·lor** *n.*

pall-mall (*pel*-mel) *n.* A 17th-century ball game, played with a mallet.—**Pall Mall.** London street on the location of an old pall-mall alley.

palm (*pahm*) *n.* Common tropical tree.—**palm branch.** Emblem of victory.

palm *n.* 1. The inner part of the hand. 2. Lineal measure equal to length or breadth of a hand. 3. Broad part of an anchor. 4. *Nautical*. Instrument for sewing canvas. 5. Blade of an oar. 6. Broad part at the top of the buck's horn.—*v.* [palmed; palming] 1. To handle; stroke. 2. To hide in the hand.—**palm off on.** To delude into taking.

PALM

pal·met·to (pal-*met*-oh) *n.* Palm tree with fanshaped leaves common in southern U. S.

palm·is·try (*pahm*-iss-tree) *n.* Fortune telling by reading palms.—**palm·ist** *n.*

Palm Sunday. Sunday before Easter, commemorating Christ's triumphant ride into Jerusalem.

palm·y *adj.* 1. Rich in palms. 2. Flourishing; prosperous.

pal·my·ra (pal-*my*-ruh) *n.* Common African palm bearing edible fruit.

pa·lo·mi·no (pal-oh-*mee*-noh) *adj.* Blond or creamy tan horse.

pal·pa·ble *adj.* 1. Plain; obvious. 2. Perceptible to touch; tangible.—**pal·pa·bil·i·ty** *n.*—**pal·pa·bly** *adv.*—**pal·pa·ble·ness** *n.*

pal·pi·tate (*pal*-pih-tayt) *v.* [pal·pi·tat·ed; pal·pi·tat·ing] 1. To beat rapidly; pulsate violently. 2. To quiver.—**pal·pi·tant** *n.*— -**ta·tion** *n.*

pal·sy (*pawl*-zee) *n.* Paralysis.—*v.* [pal·sied; pal·sy·ing] To paralyze.—**pal·sied** *adj.*

pal·ter (*pawl*-ter) *v.* To prevaricate; quibble; hedge.—**pal·ter·er** *n.*

pal·try (*pawl*-tree) *adj.* Worthless; insignificant.—**pal·tri·ly** *adv.*—**pal·tri·ness** *n.*

pam·pas (*pam*-puz) *n. pl.* Large treeless grassy plains of Argentina.—**pampas grass.** Long-leaved grass.—**pam·pe·an** (pam-*pee*-an) *adj.*

pam·per *v.* To spoil; indulge.—**pam·pered** *adj.* —**pam·pered·ness** *n.*—**pam·per·er** *n.*

pam·phlet (*pam*-flet) *n.* A small, paper covered booklet.—**pam·phlet·eer** *n.*—**pam·phlet·eer** *v.* To publish pamphlets to influence public opinion.

pan *n.* 1. Shallow, metal vessel. 2. Part of a flintlock holding the priming.—*v.* 1. To wash over, or sift, in a pan. 2. *Slang*. To criticize severely.

pan-broil (*v.*)	pan fish	paniron
pancake	panhandle	panman
pan drop	panhead	panside
pandrop	panheaded	pansmith

pan- *Prefix*. All; entire.

Pan-American	Pan-Europe	Panhellenist
Pan-Anglican	Panhellenism	Panhellenium
Pan-Cosmic	Panhellenic	Pan-Slavic

Pan *n.* *Greek Mythology*. God of pasture and forest life.—**pan's pipes** or **Pandean pipes.** A shepherd's flute.

pan·a·ce·a (pan-uh-*see*-uh) *n.* A cure-all; universal remedy.

Pan·a·ma (*pan*-uh-mah). Latin-American republic between Costa Rica and Colombia. Area: 34,169 sq. mi.—**Panama Canal.** Waterway connecting the Atlantic and Pacific Oceans through the Isthmus of Panama.—**Panama hat.** Hat made of young leaves of a stemless screw pine.—**Pan·a·man·i·an** (pan-uh-*mayn*-ee-un) *adj.*

pan·chro·mat·ic *adj.* *Photography*. Sensitive to all colors.—**pan·chro·ma·tism** *n.*

pan·cre·as (*pan*-kree-us) *n.* Large gland whose secretion aids digestion; sweetbread.

pan·da *n.* See **Giant Panda.**

pan·dect *n.* Compendium; digest.

pan·dem·ic (pan-*dem*-ik) *adj.* Epidemic.

pan·de·mo·ni·um (pan-duh-*moh*-nee-um) *n.* Uproar; din.

pan·der *n.* A pimp; procurer.—**pan·der** *v.* To serve slavishly.—**pan·der·er** *n.*

pan·dow·dy *n.* Pudding of bread and apples.

pane *n.* Plate of glass in the frame of a window or door.

pan·e·gyr·ic (pan-eh-*jihr*-ik) *n.* Eulogy; tribute.—**pan·e·gyr·i·cal** *adj.*—**pan·e·gyr·i·cal·ly** *adv.*—**pan·e·gyr·ist** *n.*—**pan·e·gy·rize** *v.* [pan·e·gy·rized; pan·e·gy·riz·ing] To praise fulsomely.

PANEL

pan·el *n.* 1. *Architecture*. Inset section of a wall. 2. *Art*. A canvas or tempera board. 3. Vertical inset in a dress. 4. *Law*. A jury list.   5. A discussion group within a larger assemblage.—*v.* [pan·el·ed, pan·el·led; pan·el·ing, pan·el·ling] To fit with panels.

pang *n.* Pain; acute twinge; throe.

pan·han·dle *v. Slang.* To beg.—**pan·han·dler** *n.*

pan·ic (*pan*-ik) *n.*   1. Terror; alarm; distraction.   2. Wave of fear precipitating economic collapse.—**pan·ick·y** *adj.*

> panic-driven panic-stricken panic-stulted
> panicmonger panic-struck panic-stunned

pan·nier (*pan*-ee-er) *n.*   1. A wicker-basket.   2. Skirt-hoop.   3. Overskirt gathered up in a bustle effect on each side.

PANNIER

pa·no·cha, pa·nu·che (pah-*noh*-kah, p'*noo*-chee) *n.* Candy made of nuts and brown sugar.

pan·o·ply (*pan*-uh-plee) *n.* Full armor.—**pan·o·plied** *adj.*—**pan·o·plist** *n.*

pan·o·ra·ma (pan-uh-*ram*-uh, -*rahm*-) *n.* Wide-stretching view; vista.—**pan·o·ram·ic** *adj.*—**pan·oramic sight.** Wide periscopic view.

pan·pipe *n.* A simple wind instrument.

pan·sy *n.*   1. Velvety-textured garden flower of the violet family.   2. *Slang.* A homosexual.

pant *v.*   1. To gasp; breathe rapidly and laboriously.   2. To desire ardently.—*n.* A gasp.—**pant·ing** *adj.*—**pant·ing·ly** *adv.*

PANSY

pan·ta·lets, pan·ta·lettes (pan-tuh-*lets*) *n. pl.* Loose drawers worn by women and children in the middle of the 19h century.

pan·ta·loon (pan-tuh-*loon*)   1. [*pl.*] Trousers.   2. [*cap.*] Clown in old comedy.

pan·the·ism (*pan*-thee-izm) *n.*   1. Belief in the identity of the forces of nature with the Deity.   2. Worship of all gods.—**pan·the·ist** *n.*—**pan·the·is·tic, pan·the·is·ti·cal** *adj.*—**pan·the·is·ti·cal·ly** *adv.*

pan·the·on *n.*   1. [*cap.*] Ancient temple at Rome, dedicated to all the gods.   2. Burial place for national heroes.   3. All deities worshiped by a people.

PANTALETS

pan·ther *n.* Ferocious, catlike animal with tawny, black-spotted skin, native to Africa and Asia.—**pan·ther·ess** *n.*

pan·to·graph *n.* Instrument for mechanical copying maps, etc. according to desired scale.

pan·to·mime (*pan*-tuh-myme) *n.* Mute theatrical show, played only by gesture, mimicry, and movements.—**pan·to·mim·ic** *adj.*—**pan·to·mim·i·cal·ly** *adv.*— -mim·i·cry *n.*— -mim·ist *n.*

pan·try *n.* Kitchen closet or anteroom for storing food and utensils.—**pan·try·man** *n.*

pants *n. pl.* Trousers.

pan·zer (*pahnt*-ser) *adj.* Armored.—**Panzer Division.** A German division of armored vehicles.

pap *n.*   1. Semisolid infant food.   2. Nipple.

pa·pa (*pah*-puh; puh-*pah*) *n.* Father (a child's nickname).

pa·pa·cy (*pay*-puh-see) *n.*   1. [*cap.*] Central administration of the Roman Catholic Church.   2. Succession of popes.   3. Period of a pope's reign.—**pa·pal** *adj.*

pa·paw, paw·paw *n.* Tall tropical tree bearing edible fruit.

pa·pa·ya (puh-*py*-uh) *n.*   1. Tropical American tree.   2. Fruit or fruit juice of the papaya.

pa·per *n.*   1. Thin sheets of pressed fibrous material.   2. A journal; newspaper.   3. Essay.   4. [*pl.*] Documents.   5. Wall covering made of paper.—*adj.* Made of paper; thin; frail.—*v.* To cover with paper.—**pa·per·er** *n.*—**pa·per·y** *adj.*

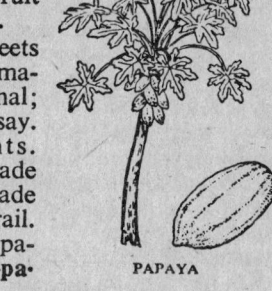

PAPAYA

> paperback (*n.*) paper cutter papermill
> paper-backed paper faced paper money
> paper bark paper file paper-shelled
> paper board paper folder paper-shuttered
> paper-bound paperhanger paper thick
> paper-capped paper hanging paper thin
> paper clip paper knife paper weight
> paper coal paper maker paper whiteness
> paper currency paper making paper-windowed

pa·pier·mâ·ché (pay-per-muh-*shay*) *n.* Hard drying pulp of paper and a binding agent.

pa·pil·la (puh-*pil*-uh) *n.*   1. A nipple; protuberance of vessels and nerves.   2. *Botany.* Hairlike projection.—**pap·il·lar·y** *adj.*—**pap·il·lo·ma** *n.* A wart.—**pap·il·lose** *adj.*—**pap·il·los·i·ty** *n.*

pa·pist (*pay*-pist) *n.* Devoted adherent of the Pope—disparagingly used.—**pa·pis·tic, pa·pis·ti·cal** *adj.*—**pa·pis·ti·cal·ly** *adv.*

pa·poose (puh-*pooss*) *n.* North American Indian child.

pap·py *adj.* Soft; mushy.—*n. Dialectal.* Dad.

pap·ri·ka, pap·ri·ca (puh-*pree*-kuh) *n.* Red spice derived from the fruit of pepper plant.

Pap·u·an (pap-*yoo*-an) *n.* Inhabitant of Papua or New Guinea.—**Pap·u·an** *adj.*

pa·py·rus (puh-*py*-rus) *n.* [*pl.* pa·py·ri] 1. Plant found in the Nile valley.   2. Ancient writing scrolls made of papyrus pulp.

P

par (*pahr*) *n.* State of equality. 2. Average; norm of the original price of shares of a corporation.—**par of exchange.** The standard value of the money unit of one country expressed in the coin of another.—**par** *adj.*

par·a- *prefix.* Beside; beyond; against; apart from.

para-analgesia   paracentral   para-equilibrium
para-anesthesia   paradysentery   parapsychology

par·a·ble (*pair-uh-b'l*) *n.* 1. A fable; allegory presenting a moral.—*v.* [-a·bled; -a·bling].

pa·rab·o·la *n.* 1. A curve formed by cutting a cone with a plane parallel to one of its sides.

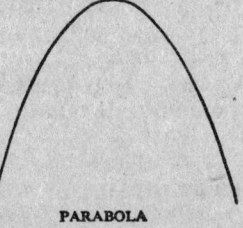

PARABOLA

par·a·bol·ic (pair-uh-*bol*-ik) *adj.* Also **par·a·bol·i·cal.** 1. Resembling or pertaining to a parabola. 2. Pertaining to a parable.—**par·a·bol·i·cal·ly** *adv.*—**pa·rab·o·lize** (puh-*rab*-uh-lyze) *v.* To tell by parables.

pa·rab·o·loid (puh-*rab*-uh-loyd) *n.* The solid generated by the revolution of a parabola about its axis.—**pa·rab·o·loid·al** *adj.*

par·a·chute (*pair*-uh-shoot) *n. Aeronautics.* An umbrella-shaped device used for jumps from airplanes.—**par·a·chute** *v.*

par·a·clete (*pair*-uh-kleet) *n.* 1. Helper. 2. [*cap.*] The Holy Ghost.

pa·rade (puh-*rayd*) *n.* 1. A procession, esp. a military march. 2. Ostentatious display.—*v.* [pa·rad·ed; pa·rad·ing] 1. To march in a procession. 2. To display; flaunt.—**pa·rad·er** *n.*

par·a·digm (*pair*-uh-dim, -dyme) *n.* 1. Example; model; illustration. 2. *Grammar.* Example of a word in its inflections.—**par·a·dig·mat·ic** (pair-uh-dig-*mat*-ik) *adj.*

par·a·dise (*pair*-uh-dysse) *n.* 1. Garden of Eden. 2. Supreme happiness. 3. Heaven.—**par·a·di·si·a·cal** *adj.*—**par·a·di·si·a·cal·ly** *adv.*

par·a·dox (*pair*-uh-doks) *n.* A self-contradictory statement.—**par·a·dox·i·cal** *adj.*—**par·a·dox·i·cal·ly** *adv.*—**par·a·dox·i·cal·ness** *n.*

par·af·fin, par·af·fine (*pair*-uh-fin, -feen) *n.* Fatty, odorless substance obtained from oil and used for making candles, drugs, etc.—*v.* To coat with paraffin.

par·a·gon (*pair*-uh-gon) *n.* Pattern or model of perfection.

par·a·graph (*pair*-uh-graf) *n.* 1. Subdivision of a chapter or piece of writing. 2. Short passage. 3. Marginal notation [¶] to indicate change of subject.—*v.* To write in sections.—**par·a·graph·er, par·a·graph·ist** *n.*—**par·a·graph·ic, par·a·graph·i·cal** *adj.*—**-cal·ly** *adv.*

Par·a·guay (*pair*-uh-gway). Republic of South America. Capital: Asuncion. Area: 154,165 sq. mi.—**Par·a·guay·an** *n. & adj.*

par·a·keet (*pair*-uh-keet) *n.* Also **paroquet, parrakeet.** Small bird of the parrot family.

par·al·lax (*pair*-uh-laks) *n.* The apparent alteration of an object when viewed from different positions.—**par·al·lac·tic** *adj.*

par·al·lel *n.* 1. Line equally distant from another line at all points. 2. *Geography.* Line on the globe or map marking latitude. 3. Similarity; resemblance; counterpart. 4. *Printing.* Reference mark [‖] to direct attention to footnotes.—*v.* [par·al·leled; par·al·lel·ing].—**par·al·lel·ism** *n.*—**par·al·lel, par·al·lel·is·tic** *adj.*—**par·al·lel·ize** *v.*

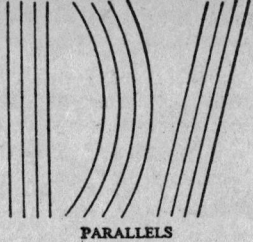

PARALLELS

par·al·lel·o·gram (pair-uh-*lel*-uh-gram) *n. Geometry.* A four-sided figure having parallel and equal opposite sides. —**par·al·lel·o·gram·mic, par·al·lel·o·gram·mi·cal** *adj.*

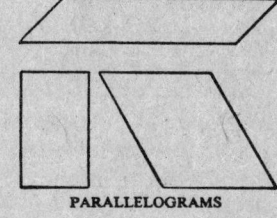

PARALLELOGRAMS

pa·ral·y·sis (puh-*ral*-ih-sis) *n.* Loss of power of action or sensation in a part of the body; palsy.—**par·a·lyt·ic** *n.*—**par·a·lyze** *v.*

par·a·me·ci·um (pair-uh-*mee*-see-um) *n.* [*pl.* -cia] One-celled, microscopic aquatic animal, oval-shaped and moving by means of hairlike protuberances.

par·a·mount (*pair*-uh-mount) *adj.* Supreme; dominant; pre-eminent.—**par·a·mount·cy** *n.*

par·a·mour (*pair*-uh-moor) *n.* Lover, esp. an illicit one.

pa·rang (pah-*rahng*) *n.* A short Malayan knife or sword.

par·a·noi·a (pair-uh-*noy*-uh) *n. Psychiatry.* Chronic mental disorder marked by delusions of persecution and grandeur.—**par·a·noid** *adj.*

par·a·pet *n.* (*pair*-uh-pet) 1. *Military.* Wall covering soldiers from frontal attacks; breastwork. 2. *Architecture.* Ramparts on balconies, roofs, bridges, etc., to prevent people from falling over.—**par·a·pet·ed** *adj.*

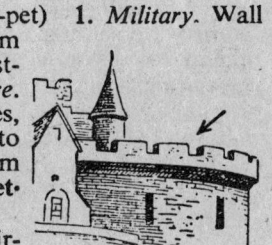

PARAPET

par·a·pher·na·li·a (pair-uh-fer-*nayl*-yuh) *n.* Equipment; gear; appendages.

par·a·phrase (*pair*-uh-frayz) *n.* Condensed rendering; restatement. —*v.* [par·a·phrased; par·a·phras·ing] To interpret; translate clearly.—**par·a·phras·er, par·a·phrast** *n.*—**-phras·tic, par·a·phras·ti·cal** *adj.*

par·a·site (*pair*-uh-syte) *n.* 1. A sycophant; hanger-on; one who lives at the expense of others. 2. Animal or plant deriving its nourishment from another living organism.—**par·a·sit·ic, par·a·sit·i·cal** *adj.*—**par·a·sit·i·cal·ly** *adv.*

par·a·sol (*pair*-uh-sawl) *n.* Small umbrella used for protection from the sun.

par·a·troops *n. pl.* Air-borne infantry. —**par·a·troop·er** *n.*

par·boil (*pahr*-boyl) *v.* To cook in water till partly tender.

Par·cae (*pahr*-see) *n. pl.* Latin name of the Fates.

par·cel (*pahr*-s'l) *n.* 1. Bundle; package. 2. Part; piece.—*v.* [par·celled; par·cel·ling] 1. To divide; apportion. 2. *Nautical.* To bind a rope with canvas. —**par·cel·ing, par·cel·ling** *n.*—**parcel post.** A system for mailing packages.

PARASOL

parch *v.* To dry; bake; scorch.—**parched** *adj.* —**parch·ed·ness** *n.*—**parch·ing·ly** *adv.*

par·chee·si (pahr-*chee*-zee) *n.* Also **pa·chi·si, par·che·si, par·chi·si.** A children's game, similar to backgammon played with dice, colored disks, and a ruled board.

parch·ment (*pahrch*-m'nt) *n.* Heavy writing paper originally made of animal skins.

par·don (*pahr*-d'n) *v.* To forgive; absolve; remit.—*n.* Remission of penalty; forgiveness; amnesty.—**par·don·a·bly** *adv.*—**par·don·er** *n.* —**pardon me.** Excuse me.

pare *v.* 1. To skin; cut or shave off. 2. To diminish.—**par·ing** *n.* A clipped-off piece; rind.—**par·ing** *adj.*

par·e·gor·ic (pair-uh-*gor*-ik) *n.* Camphorated tincture of opium, a sedative.—**par·e·gor·ic, par·e·gor·i·cal** *adj.* Relieving pain.

par·ent (*pair*-'nt) *n.* 1. A father or mother. 2. Source; original.—**par·ent·age** *n.*—**par·en·tal** (puh-*rent*-al) *adj.*—**-al·ly** *adv.*—**-ent·hood** *n.*

pa·ren·the·sis (puh-*ren*-thuh-siss) *n.* 1. Explanatory insertion in a complete sentence. 2. *Printing.* The parenthetical sign ( ).—**pa·ren·the·size** *v.*—**par·en·thet·ic, -i·cal** *adj.*

pa·re·sis (puh-*ree*-sis) *n. Pathology.* Slight paralysis affecting movement but not sensation. —**pa·ret·ic** *adj.*

par·fait (pahr-*fay*) *n.* A frozen dessert; sundae.

pa·ri·ah (puh-*ry*-uh) *n.* An outcast; member of the lowest caste in India.

pa·ri·e·tal (puh-*ry*-eh-tal) *adj.* Pertaining to a wall or enclosure.

pa·ri·mu·tu·el (*pair*-ee-*myoo*-tyoo-el) *n.* A form of registered horse-race betting by machine.

paris green. Artists' pigment and insect poison containing arsenic.

par·ish (*pair*-ish) *n.* A church; division of a diocese under one rector.—**pa·rish·ion·er** *n.*

par·i·ty (*pair*-ih-tee) *n.* 1. equality. 2. *Medicine.* Condition of having borne children.

park *n.* 1. Area preserved in its natural state as a decorative or recreational feature. 2. A train of artillery; artillery encampment.—*v.* To stop and leave an automobile standing.—**park·way** *n.* Highway; avenue.

par·lance (*pahr*-l'nss) *n.* 1. Conversation; discourse; talk. 2. Way of speaking.

par·lay *v.* To bet the winnings from one horse-race on subsequent races.—**par·lay** *n.*

par·ley *v.* 1. To confer, esp. with envoys of the enemy.—*n.* Conference; meeting.

par·lia·ment (*pahr*-lih-m'nt) *n.* 1. Council; legislative body. 2. Supreme legislative assembly of Great Britain consisting of the House of Lords and the House of Commons. —**par·lia·men·tar·i·an** *n.* Person versed in parliamentary law and procedure.—**par·li·a·men·ta·ry** *adj.*

par·lor, par·lour (*pahr*-ler) *n.* Living room; sitting room.—**parlor car.** Lounge car on a train.—**parlor maid.**

Par·me·san (*pahr*-muh-zan) *adj.* Of Parma, in Italy.—**parmesan cheese.** A pungent Italian cheese, sometimes grated for seasoning.

Par·nas·sus *n. Greek Mythology.* Mountain sacred to Apollo and the Muses.—**Par·nas·si·an** *adj.* 1. Pertaining to Parnassus. 2. Pertaining to a school of poetry in 19th-century France.—**Par·nas·si·an** *n.*

pa·ro·chi·al (puh-*roh*-kee-al) *adj.* 1. Pertaining to a parish or to the church. 2. Narrow; limited; provincial.—**pa·ro·chi·al·ly** *adv.*

par·o·dy (*pair*-uh-dee) *n.* Comic literary imitation; caricature.—*v.* [par·o·died; par·o·dy·ing] —**par·o·dist** *n.*

pa·role (puh-*rohl*) *n.* A conditional pardon and release from prison.—**pa·role** *adj.*—**pa·role** *v.*

pa·rot·id (puh-*rot*-id) *n. Anatomy.* Salivary gland in front of the ear connected by a duct with the mouth.—**par·o·tid** *adj.*—**par·o·tit·ic** *adj.*—**par·o·ti·tis** *n.* Mumps.

par·ox·ysm (*pair*-ok-sizm) *n. Medicine.* Fit; attack; spasm. —**par·ox·ys·mal** *adj.*

par·quet (pahr-*kay*) *n.* 1 Wooden inlay used for floors. 2. Section of a theater between the orchestra rail and the parquet circle.—**par·quet circle.** Section of the orchestra under the balcony.

par·ri·cide (*pair*-ih-syde) *n.* 1. Murder of a parent by his child. 2. Murderer of one's own parent.—**par·ri·cid·al** *adj.*

par·rot (*pair*-ut) *n.* Tropical bird with colorful plumage and hooked bill, able to imitate human speech.—*v.* To repeat by rote; imitate.

PARROT (1/10 life size)

par·ry *v.* [par·ried; par·ry·ing] To ward off; counter.

parse *v. Grammar.* To analyze grammatically. —**pars·er** *n.*

Par·see, Par·si (*pahr*-see) *n.* Zoroastrian adherent in India.—**par·see·ism, par·si·ism** *n.*

P

par·si·mo·ni·ous (pahr-sih-*moh*-nee-us) *adj.* Stingy; niggardly.—**par·si·mo·ni·ous·ness** *n.* —**par·si·mo·ny** *n.* Miserliness.

pars·ley *n.* Garden vegetable used as flavoring and garnish.

pars·nip *n.* Herb with edible, turniplike root.

par·son *n.* 1. Rector of a parish. 2. *Colloquial.* A clergyman.

par·son·age (*pahr*-s'n-ij) *n.* House and land provided for a parson.

part *n.* 1. Piece; portion; fraction. 2. Share. 3. Region; area. 4. Dividing line in the hair. 5. *Music.* A single voice or instrument in ensemble music. 6. *Theater.* A role in a drama. —*v.* 1. To separate; divide. 2. To break; fall into pieces. 3. To go away; depart.

part-created   part-heard   part time
part-earned   part-opened   part-time (adj.)

par·take *v.* [par·took; par·tak·en; par·tak·ing] To participate; share.—**par·tak·er** *n.*

par·terre (pahr-*tair*) *n.* 1. Arrangement of flower beds between spaces of gravel or turf. 2. Back orchestra seats in a theater.

par·the·no·gen·e·sis (pahr-then-oh-*gen*-eh-sis) *n.* Reproduction by means of unfertilized eggs. —**par·the·no·ge·net·ic** *adj.*

Par·the·non (*pahr*-theh-non, -nun) *n.* Famous Greek doric temple of Athena Parthenos in Athens on the Acropolis.

PARTHENON

Par·thi·a (*pahr*-thee-uh). Ancient country SE of Caspian Sea, today a province of Iran, called **Khurasan.—Par·thi·an** *adj.*

par·tial (*pahr*-shul) *adj.* 1. Incomplete; not total. 2. Biased; prejudiced. 3. Devoted; attached.—**par·ti·al·i·ty** *n.*—**par·tial·ly** *adv.*

par·tic·i·pate (pahr-*tiss*-ih-payt) *v.* [par·tic·i·pated; par·tic·i·pat·ing] To partake; share. —**par·tic·i·pa·tion** *n.*—**par·tic·i·pa·tor** *n.*—**par·tic·i·pance** *n.*—**par·tic·i·pan·cy** *n.*— **-pant** *n.*

par·ti·ci·ple (*pahr*-tih-sip-'l) *n.* Present or past verb form (as, *writing, written*) used as verb, adjective or noun.—**par·ti·cip·i·al** *adj.*

par·ti·cle (*pahr*-tik-'l) *n.* Small section; fraction.

par·ti-col·ored *adj.* Of various colors.

par·tic·u·lar (per-*tik*-yoo-ler) *adj.* 1. Single; lone. 2. Special; specific. 3. Fastidious; meticulous.—*n.* Item; detail.—**par·tic·u·lar·i·ty** *n.*—**par·tic·u·lar·ize** *v.* [par·tic·u·lar·ized; -iz·ing]— **-i·za·tion** *n.*—**par·tic·u·lar·ly** *adv.*

part·ing *n.* 1. Division; separation; leaving. 2. A farewell.—**parting** *adj.*

par·ti·san, par·ti·zan *n.* 1. An ardent adherent. 2. *Military.* Member of an armed band of civilians operating against the enemy. —**par·ti·san** *adj.*—**par·ti·san·ship** *n.*

par·ti·tion (pahr-*tish*-'n) *n.* 1. Separation; breaking up. 2. A dividing wall.—**par·ti·tion** *v.*—**par·ti·tion·er** *n.*—**par·ti·tion·ment** *n.*

par·ti·tive *n. Grammar.* Word expressing partition.—*adj. Grammar.* Expressing relation of a part to a whole.—**par·ti·tive·ly** *adv.*

part·ly *adv.* Not wholly; to some degree.

part·ner *n.* 1. Associate; mate; comrade; sharer. 2. Joint owner of a business. 3. Dancing companion. 4. Spouse.—**partner·ship** *n.* 1. Joint interest; participation with another. 2. Association of persons in business.

par·tridge (*pahr*-tridj) *n.* Gamebird of the grouse family.

par·tu·ri·tion (pahr-tyoo-*rish*-'n) *n.* Reproduction; childbirth; delivery. —**par·tu·ri·ent** (pahr-*tyoo*-ree-'nt) *adj.*—**par·tu·ri·en·cy** *n.*

PARTRIDGE (1/10 life-size)

par·ty *n.* [*pl.* par·ties] 1. A political faction or organization. 2. A group; number of persons. 3. Festive entertainment. 4. *Law.* Person involved in a suit. 5. *Slang.* A person.—**party line.** 1. The doctrine of a political group. 2. One telephone circuit accommodating several numbers. 3. Property boundary.

par·ve·nu (*pahr*-veh-nyoo) *n.* An upstart; one recently made wealthy.

pas·chal (*pass*-kal) *adj.* Pertaining to Easter.

pa·sha, pa·cha *n.* High honorary Turkish title. —**pa·sha·lik, pa·sha·lic, pa·cha·lic** *n.* A pasha's sphere of authority.

pass *v.* 1. To go; go by or beyond; 2. To vanish; die. 3. To elapse. 4. To enact; ratify. 5. To be acceptable. 6. To occur. 7. To give judgment. 8. To succeed in. 'To pass a test.' 9. To spend; live through. 10. To give; make proceed. 11. To utter; pronounce. 12. To excrete; void. 13. *Cardplaying.* To refrain from bidding. 14. *Football.* To throw the ball. 15. *Baseball.* To give a base on balls.—*n.* 1. A free ticket. 2. *Cardplaying.* Failing to bid. 3. *Football.* Act of throwing the ball. 4. *Baseball.* A base on balls. 5. A movement of the hand. 6. A state or condition. 7. A narrow road between two mountains.—**pass·er** *n.*—**pass·er-by** *n.*

passback   passman   passover
passkey   pass-out (n.)   password

pass·a·ble *adj.* 1. Capable of being traversed. 2. Acceptable; allowable. 3. Fair; mediocre. —**pass·a·bly** *adv.*

pass·age (*pass*-ij) 1. Transit; movement. 2. Access. 3. A corridor; way. 4. A selection from a literary work. 5. Enactment by a legislature.—**pas·sage·way** *n.* Corridor; hall.

pass·book *n.* A bankbook.

pas·sé (pah-*say*) *adj.* Out of date; antiquated.

pas·sen·ger *n.* A traveler on a conveyance.

pas·si·ble *adj.* Able to feel or suffer.

pas·sim *adv.* Skimmingly; here and there.

passing *adv.* Very; exceedingly.—*adj.* 1. Transient. 2. Casual.—*n.* 1. Going past. 2. Death.

pas·sion *n.* 1. Strong emotion; rage; frenzy. 2. Ardent love; sexual desire. 3. [*cap.*] The last sufferings of Christ.—**pas·sion·al** *adj.* —**pas·sion·ate** *adj.*—**pas·sion·ate·ly** *adv.*—**pas·sion·ate·ness** *n.*—**pas·sion·less** *adj.*

pas·sion·flow·er *n.* A family of flowering tendrilled vines.

pas·sive *adj.* 1. Unresisting; inert; inactive. 2. *Grammar.* Indicating that the subject (rather than the object) is acted upon.—**pas·sive·ly** *adj.*—**pas·sive·ness** *n.*—**pas·siv·i·ty** *n.*—**pas·siv·ism** *n.*

PASSIONFLOWER

Pass·o·ver *n.* Jewish spring feast commemorating the exodus of the Hebrews from Egypt.

pass·port *n.* An official identification permit, esp. for travelers abroad.

pass·word *n.* A word or countersign for identification.

past *adj.* Gone by; previous.—*n.* A former time.—*prep.* Beyond.—*adv.* By; beyond. —**past participle,** *Grammar.* The past form of the verb used with auxiliaries, as *given, written.* —**past perfect,** *Grammar.* A tense composed of an auxiliary and a past participle, as *have gone.*

paste *n.* 1. Thick homogeneous food preparation. 2. A viscous substance for cementing surfaces together. 3. A kind of glass used for imitation gems.—*v.* [past·ed; past·ing] 1. To glue; cement. 2. *Slang.* To hit.—**past·er** *n.*

paste·board (*payst*-bohrd) *n.* 1. Stiff paper board. 2. *Slang.* A ticket.—**paste·board** *adj.*

pas·tel (pass-*tel*) *adj.* Pale or unsaturated in color.—*n.* 1. A kind of colored crayon. 2. A drawing made with this crayon.—**pas·tel·ist, pas·tel·list** *n.*

pas·tern *n.* Part of the foot of a horse.

pas·teur·ize (*pass*-ter-yze) *v.* [pas·teur·ized; pas·teur·iz·ing] 1. To destroy certain bacteria by heating liquid to a critical temperature. —**pas·teur·i·za·tion** *n.*

pas·tille, pas·til *n.* 1. An incense or fumigating stick. 2. A lozenge.

pas·time *n.* Diversion; sport; recreation.

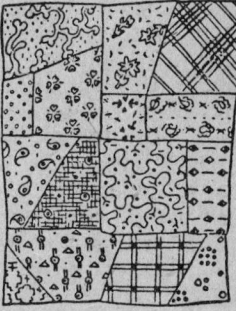

PASTERN

pas·tor (*pass*-ter) *n.* The minister of a congregation.—**pas·tor·ate** *n.* Also **pas·tor·age, pas·tor·ship.** Office and charge of a minister.

pas·to·ral (*pass*-ter-'l) *n.* 1. Pertaining to shepherds; rural. 2. Ministerial.—**-ral·ly** *adv.*

pas·tra·mi (puh-*strah*-mee) *n.* A kind of spiced smoked beef.

pas·try (*payss*-tree) *n.* [*pl.* pas·tries] Food made of dough, as pies, tarts, etc.

pas·ture (*pass*-cher) *n.* 1. Grazing ground. 2. Grass on which cattle feed.—**pas·ture** *v.* [pas·tured; pas·tur·ing]—**pas·tur·a·ble** *adj.* —**pas·tur·age** *n.*—**pas·tur·er** *n.*

past·y *adj.* (*payss*-tee) Resembling paste.

pat *v.* [pat·ted; pat·ting] To tap gently with the fingers or hand.—*n.* 1. A gentle rap. 2. Small, regular lump of butter.

pat *adj.* 1. Fitting; glib; neat. 2. Firm. 'Stand pat.'—**pat·ly** *adv.*—**pat·ness** *n.*

Pat·a·go·ni·a (pat-uh-*goh*-nee-uh). The part of South America below 40° south latitude. —**Pat·a·go·ni·an** *n.* & *adj.*

patch *n.* 1. Material used to repair. 2. Scrap; small piece. 3. Small plot different from its surroundings.—**patch** *v.*—**patch·er** *n.*—**patch·y** *adj.* [patch·i·er; patch·i·est].

patch·work *n.* 1. Quilting covered with sewed patches. 2. Anything composed of ill-assorted parts. —**patch·work** *adj.*

pate *n.* The head, esp. the top of the head.

pa·tel·la (puh-*tel*-luh) *n. Anatomy.* The kneecap.—**pa·tel·lar, pa·tel·late** *adj.*

pat·en (*pat*-'n) *n.* 1. *Church.* Plate for the sacrificial bread. 2. Any thin plate, esp. of metal.

PATCHWORK

pat·ent *n.* Legal right to be the sole exploiter of an invention for a period up to 14 years.—*adj.* 1. Open; obvious. 2. Secured by patent. —**pat·ent** *v.*—**pat·ent·a·ble** *adj.*—**pat·en·tor** *n.*

patent leather. Leather having a permanent glossy polish and hard surface.

pa·ter·nal *n.* 1. Fatherly. 2. Hereditary. —**pa·ter·nal·ly** *adv.*—**pa·ter·ni·ty** *n.*

pa·ter·nal·ism (puh-*ter*-n'l-izm) *n.* Practice of treating subordinates or subjects with fatherly discipline.—**pa·ter·nal·is·tic** *adj.*—**-ti·cal·ly** *adv.*

pa·ter·nos·ter (*pay*-ter-*noss*-ter) *n.* The Lord's Prayer.

path *n.* 1. Footway; trail; narrow road. 2. Course; route.—**path·less** *adj.*—**path·less·ness** *n.*—**path·way** *n.*

pa·thet·ic (puh-*thet*-ik) *adj.* Arousing sorrowful emotions; sad; pitiable.—**pa·thet·i·cal·ly** *adv.*

pa·thol·o·gy (puh-*thol*-uh-jee) *n.* 1. Science of disease. 2. Diseased condition.—**path·o·log·ic** (path-uh-*loj*-ik), **-i·cal** *adj.*—**pa·thol·o·gist** *n.*

pa·thos (*pay*-thoss) *n.* Quality which arouses deep feelings of tender sorrow.

pa·tient (*pay*-shent) *adj.* Long suffering; enduring; not hasty.—*n.* Person under medical care. —**pa·tience** *n.*—**pa·tient·ly** *adv.*

pat·i·na (*pat*-in-uh) *n.* A corroded film on a surface; discoloration from age.

P

pa·ti·o (*pah*-tee-oh) *n.* A court or open space within a house.

pat·ois (*pat*-wah) *n.* [*pl.* pat·ois] Dialect of provincial or uneducated people.

pa·tri·arch (*pay*-tree-ark) *n.* 1. A venerable old man. 2. High-ranking dignitary of several churches. 3. The ruler of a tribal government.—**pa·tri·arch·al** *adj.*—**pa·tri·arch·ate** *n.* —**pat·ri·arch·y** *n.* [*pl.* pat·ri·arch·ies].

pa·tri·cian (puh-*trish*-un) *adj.* Upper class; of noble birth.—**pa·tri·cian** *n.*

pat·ri·cide (*pat*-rih-syde) *n.* 1. Murder of one's father. 2. A murderer of his father.—**pat·ri·cid·al** *adj.*

pat·ri·mo·ny (*pat*-rih-moh-nee) *n.* [*pl.* pat·ri·mo·nies] 1. Inheritance; legacy. 2. Property of a religious organization.—**pa·tri·mo·ni·al** *adj.*

pa·tri·ot (*pay*-tree-ot) *n.* One who loves or zealously supports his country.—**pa·tri·ot·ic** *adj.* —**pa·tri·ot·i·cal·ly** *adv.*—**pa·tri·ot·ism** *n.*

pa·tris·tic (puh-*triss*-tik) *adj.* Also **pa·tris·ti·cal** Pertaining to the ancient fathers of the Christian church.—**pa·tris·ti·cal·ly** *adv.*

pa·trol (puh-*trohl*) *n.* 1. A roving guard or security detachment. 2. *Military.* Small reconnoitering force. 3. Roving guard duty. —*v.* [pa·trolled; pa·trol·ling]—**pa·trol** *adj.* —**pa·trol·ler** *n.*

pa·trol·man *n.* Policeman on a regular beat.

pa·tron (*pay*-tr'n) *n.* 1. A customer or client. 2. A subsidizer of artistic production. 3. Also **patron saint**. *Church*. A saint who is entrusted with the care of a person or institution.—**pa·tron·ess** *n.*

pa·tron·age (*pay*-tr'n-ij) *n.* 1. Status of a patron. 2. Support given by a patron. 3. Clientele; customers. 4. Condescension. 5. Favors bestowed by an elected official for political gain.

pa·tron·ize (*pay*-tr'n-yze) *v.* [pa·tron·ized; pa·tron·iz·ing] 1. To act as patron. 2. To assume a condescending attitude toward.—**pa·tron·iz·er** *n.*—**pa·tron·iz·ing·ly** *adv.*

pa·troon (puh-*troon*) *n.* A holder of a feudal land-grant under the Dutch governments of New York and New Jersey.

pat·ter *v.* 1. To strike or move with a succession of small sounds. 2. To talk glibly or rapidly.—**pat·ter** *n.*—**pat·ter·er** *n.*

pat·tern *n.* 1. A model; mold or design to be copied. 2. An ornamental design or figure. 3. A configuration; interrelated whole. 'A behavior pattern.'—**pat·tern** *v.*

pat·ty *n.* [*pl.* pat·ties]. A small pie.

pau·ci·ty (*paw*-sih-tee) *n.* Scarcity; dearth.

paunch (*pawnch*) *n.* The belly, esp. a bulging one.—**paunch·y,** *adj.* [paunch·i·er; -i·est].

pau·per (*paw*-per) *n.* A poor person, esp. one who is a public charge.—**pau·per·ism** *n.*—**pau·per·ize** *v.* [pau·per·ized; pau·per·iz·ing].

pause (*pawz*) *v.* [paused; paus·ing] To stop temporarily; hesitate.—**pause** *n.*—**paus·er** *n.*

pave *v.* [paved; pav·ing] To cover with a hard surface.—**pav·er** *n.*—**pav·ing** *n.*—**pave·ment** *n.*

pa·vil·ion (puh-*vil*-yun) *n.* 1. Large tent. 2. *Architecture.* **a.** Turret with a tent-shaped roof. **b.** Projecting wing or unit of a building. 3. A light open shelter.

paw *n.* The claw-bearing foot of certain animals. —*v.* 1. To caress awkwardly. 2. To scrape with the forefoot.—**paw·er** *n.*

pawl *n.* Pivoted tongue that fits into a notched wheel to prevent back motion.

pawn *n.* *Chess.* 1. The piece of lowest rank. 2. Person in a powerless position.

PAWL

PAWN

pawn *n.* An article posted as security for borrowed money.—*v.* To pledge as security.—**pawn·a·ble** *adj.*—**pawn·age** *n.*—**pawn·er** *n.*

pawn·bro·ker (*pawn*-broh-ker) *n.* One who lends money on goods given as security.—**pawn·brok·ing** *n.*

pawn·shop *n.* Pawnbroker's place of business.

pay *v.* [paid; pay·ing] 1. To remunerate; compensate; discharge a debt. 2. To give or offer. 'To pay a compliment.'—*n.* 1. Salary; wages; remuneration. 2. Retribution; retaliation.—**pay·a·ble** *adj.*—**pay·er** *n.*

pay·ee *n.* Receiver of pay.

pay·mas·ter *n.* Cashier in charge of paying wages.—**pay·mis·tress** *n.*

pay·ment *n.* What is given in return for work, service, or goods; remuneration.

pay·roll 1. List of employees entitled to pay. 2. Money for paying them.

pea (*pee*) *n.* 1. Low-growing, viny vegetable grown for its edible seed. 2. A small particle.

peabird	peafield	pea-sized
peachick	peajacket	peastick
pea cod	pea shooter	peasticking

peace *n.* 1. Tranquillity; calm; harmony. 2. Freedom from war. 3. Law and order. 4. Armistice; cessation of hostilities.—**peace·a·ble** *adj.*—**peace·a·ble·ness** *n.*—**peace·a·bly** *adv.* —**peace·ful·ly** *adv.*—**peace·ful·ness** *n.*

peace-blessed	peace-enamored	peacemonger
peacebreaker	peacemaker	peacetime
peacebreaking	peaceman	peace-trained

peach *n.* 1. Tree bearing a pitted fruit with juicy, yellowish flesh. 2. *Slang.* A lovely girl; fine person. —*adj.* Yellowish pink.—**peach·y** *adj.* [peach·i·er; peach·i·est].

PEACH

pea·coat *n.* Thick, woolen jacket worn by seamen.

pea·cock *n.* Large, beautifully plumaged, male

PEACOCK (1/20 life-size)

bird of the turkey family.—**pea·cock·ish** *adj.* Vain; proud.—**pea·cock·ish·ly** *adv.*—**pea·fowl** *n.* A peacock of either sex.—**pea·hen** *n.* Female of the peacock.

peak *n.* 1. Topmost point; summit. 2. Climax.—**peaked** *adj.* 1. Pointed. 2. (*peek*-ed) Tired; worn-out.

peal *n.* 1. Resounding sound. 2. *Music.* A series of bells.—*v.* To sound; ring.

pea·nut *n.* Seed produced by the roots of a trailing herb; goober; pinder; ground-pea.—**pea· nut butter.** Spread made of crushed peanuts.

pear (*pair*) *n.* Bulb-shaped, pulpy fruit grown on a tree of the apple family.

pearl (*perl*) *n.* 1. Hard. lustrous, white substance secreted by the pearl oyster. 2. *Printing.* A kind of small type. 3. A valuable object; treasure.—*v.* 1. To deck with pearls. 2. To form into grains. 3. To make pearl-like. 4. To fish for pearl oysters.—**pearl** *adj.* —**pearl·er** *n.*—**pearl·y** *adj.*

pearl-div·er *n.* 1. One who dives for pearl oysters. 2. *Slang.* A dishwasher.

pearl·ite *n.* Form of iron alloyed with 85% or more of carbon.—**pearl·it·ic** *adj.*

peas·ant (*pez*-ent) *n.* European small farmer. —**peas·ant** *adj.*—**peas·ant·ry** *n.* [*pl.* -ries].

peat (*peet*) *n.* A kind of turf used for fuel.

pea·vey (*pee*-vee) *n.* Log-turning tool consisting of handle and pike.

peb·ble *n.* 1. Small stone. 2. A quartz used for lenses.—*v.* [peb·bled; peb·bling] 1. To pave with pebbles. 2. To press a grainy crinkle into.—**peb·bly** *adj.*

pe·can (pee-*kan*, *pee*-kan) *n.* Large tree of the hickory family producing edible nuts.

pec·ca·ble (*pek*-uh-b'l) *adj.* Subject to or capable of sinning.—**pec·ca·bil·i·ty** *n.*

pec·ca·dil·lo (pek-uh-*dil*-oh) *n.* [*pl.* pec·ca·dil·loes, pec·ca·dil·los] A petty offense or fault.

pec·cant (*pek*-ant) *adj.* Sinning; criminal; bad. —**pec·can·cy** *n.*—**pec·cant·ly** *adv.*

pec·ca·ry (*pek*-uh-ree) *n.* [*pl.* pec·ca·ries] A wild hog of South America.

peck *n.* A dry measure, usually ¼ bushel.

peck *v.* 1. To strike with the beak. 2. *Colloquial.* To kiss lightly and quickly. —*n.* 1. Blow of a fowl's beak. 2. Quick light kiss.

PECCARY (1/30 life-size)

pec·tin *n.* A fruit acid used as a thickening agent.—**pec·tic** *adj.*

pec·to·ral *adj.* Pertaining to the chest.

pec·u·late *v.* [pec·u·lat·ed; pec·u·lat·ing] To embezzle; abscond with public funds.—**pec·u· la·tion** *n.*—**pec·u·la·tor** *n.*

pe·cul·iar (peh-*kyool*-yer) *adj.* 1. Singular; striking; strange. 2. Characteristic; individual; owned by one alone.—**pe·cu·li·ar·i·ty** *n.*

pe·cu·ni·ar·y (peh-*kyoo*-nee-er-ee) *adj.* Monetary; financial.

ped·a·gog *n.* Also **ped·a·gogue.** Teacher; instructor.—**ped·a·gog·ic,** **ped·a·gog·i·cal** *adj.* —**-cal·ly** *adv.*—**ped·a·go·gy** *n.* [*pl.* -gies].

ped·al *n.* 1. Treadle; foot-operated lever. 2. Pertaining to the feet.—**ped·al** *adj.*—**ped·al** *v.*

ped·ant *n.* An ostentatiously erudite person. —**pe·dan·tic** *adj.*—**pe·dan·ti·cal·ly** *adv.*—**ped·an·try** *n.* [*pl.* ped·an·tries].

ped·dle *v.* [ped·dled; ped·dling] To hawk; travel about selling small wares.—**ped·dler,** **ped·lar** *n.*—**ped·dler·y, ped·lar·y** *n.*—**ped·dling** *n.*

ped·es·tal (*ped*-ess-t'l) *n.* 1. Base or stand. 2. An idealized plan or conception.—*v.* 1. To exalt in one's estimation. 2. To place on a pedestal.

pe·des·tri·an (peh-*dess*-tree-an) *n.* A walker; one traveling on foot.—**pe·des·tri·an** *adj.* Mediocre; plodding.—**pe·des·tri·an·ism** *n.*

pe·di·at·rics (pee-dee-*at*-riks) *n.* Branch of medicine dealing with children's disease.—**pe· di·at·ric** *adj.*—**pe·di·a·tri·cian, pe·di·a·trist** *n.*

pe·dic·u·lar (peh-*dik*-yoo-ler) *adj.* Pertaining to, or infected with, lice.—**pe·dic·u·lo·sis** *n.* —**pe·dic·u·lous** *adj.* Lousy.

ped·i·cure (*ped*-ih-kyoor) *n.* 1. Chiropody; chiropodist. 2. A foot manicure.

ped·i·gree *n.* Line of descent; recorded ancestry.—*v.* To breed animals selectively.

ped·i·ment *n.* *Architecture.* A triangular gable. —**ped·i·men· tal** *adj.*

pe·dom·e·ter (peh-*dom*-eh-ter) *n.* Instrument by which miles walked are numbered.—**pe·do·met·ric** *adj.*

PEDIMENT

pe·dun·cle (peh-*dunk*-'l) *n.* *Botany.* Fruit stem. —**pe·dun·cled, pe·dun·cu·lar, pe·dun·cu·late** *adj.*

peek *v.* To look slyly or surreptitiously.—*n.* Glance; peep.

peel *v.* To skin; pare; slough off.—**peel** *n.* Rind; skin.—**peel·er** *n.*

peen *n.* Ball or nose of a hammer.—*v.* To pound with a peen.

peep *v.* 1. To peek; peer through a crevice. 2. To chirp, as chickens. 3. To emerge gradually.—**peep** *n.*—**peep·er** *n.* 1. A chirper. 2. A spying person. 3. *Slang.* [*pl.*] The eyes.

pee-pee (*pee*-pee) *n.* A small chicken.

peep·show. Any exhibition viewed through an aperture.

P

peeping Tom. A prying or indecently curious person.

peer *n.* 1. An equal; one of the same station. 2. A nobleman.—*v.* To look narrowly; stare. —**peer·age** *n.*—**peer·ess** *n.*—**peer·less** *adj.*

peeve *v.* [peeved; peev·ing] *Colloquial.* To irritate; exasperate.—**peev·ish** *adj.* Bad-tempered; fretful; complaining.—**peev·ish·ly** *adv.*

pee·wee *n. Slang.* A tiny person.—**pee·wee** *adj.*

peg *n.* 1. Wooden nail or pin. 2. A degree; notch. 3. A wooden leg.—*v.* [pegged; peg·ging] 1. To fix or stabilize, as prices. 2. To affix with a peg. 3. To throw. 4. To work diligently. 5. *Cribbage.* To score points on a board.—**take down a peg.** To humble.

Peg·a·sus (*peg*-uh-sus) *n.* 1. Mythological winged horse. 2. A constellation of the Northern Hemisphere.

peign·oir (payn-*wahr*) *n.* A negligee.

Pe·king·ese, Pe·kin·ese (pee-k'n-*eez*) *adj.* Pertaining to Peking, old capital of China.—*n.* A small pug-nosed dog with a silky coat.

PEKINGESE (1/14 life-size)

pe·koe (*pee*-koh) *n.* A grade of black tea.

pe·lag·ic (peh-*laj*-ik) *adj.* Marine; oceanic.

pelf *n. sing.* Money; riches.—**pelf·ish** *adj.*

pel·i·can (*pel*-ih-kan) *n.* Large, scoop-billed fishing bird.

pe·lisse (puh-*leess*) *n.* Fur-trimmed cloak formerly worn by women.

pel·la·gra (peh-*lay*-gruh) *n.* Skin disease found in southern U.S., caused by deficiencies in diet. —**pel·la·grous** *adj.*

pel·let *n.* A little ball; bullet.

PELICAN (1/25 life-size)

pell-mell, pell·mell *adv.* Confusedly; precipitously; disorderly.—**pell-mell, pell·mell** *adj.*

pel·lu·cid (pel-*oo*-sid, pel-*yoo*-sid) *adj.* 1. Limpid; transparent. 2. Clear; understandable. —**pel·lu·cid·i·ty, pel·lu·cid·ness** *n.*— **-cid·ly** *adv.*

Pel·o·pon·ne·sus (pel-uh-pon-*nee*-sus) *n.* Part of Greece south of the Isthmus of Corinth. —**Pel·o·pon·ne·sian** *n. & adj.*

pelt *n.* An untanned hide.

pelt *v.* To strike with a series of blows or missiles.—**pelt·er** *n.*

pel·vis *n.* Cavity formed by the hip and pubic bones.—**pel·vic** *adj.*

pem·mi·can (*pem*-ik-'n) *n.* Also **pem·i·can.** A dried preparation, used for emergency ration.

pen *n.* 1. Instrument for writing with fluid ink. 2. Small enclosure or cage.—*v.* [penned; pen·ning]—**pen name.** Name assumed by an author.

pe·nal (*pee*-n'l) *adj.* Relating to punishment.

pe·nal·ize (*peen*-uh-lyze; *pen*-uh-lyze) *v.* [pe·nal·ized; pe·nal·iz·ing] To punish; impose penalty upon.

pen·al·ty (*pen*-al-tee) *n.* [*pl.* pen·al·ties] Punishment; fine; loss from violation of rules.

pen·ance (*pen*-anss) *n.* Expiation; atonement.

pence *n.* British plural of *penny.*

pen·chant (*pen*-chant) *n.* Inclination; liking.

pen·cil (*pen*-s'l) *n.* 1. Slender stick of wood encasing graphite or chalk for writing or drawing. 2. Artist's brush. 3. *Optics.* System of converging or diverging light rays.—*v.* [penciled; pen·cilled; pen·cil·ing, pen·cil·ling] To mark or write with a pencil.—**pen·cil·er, pen·cil·ler** *n.*

pend *v.* To await; be in a process of settlement.

pend·ant *n.* 1. A suspended ornament. 2. A matching piece. 3. *Architecture.* Gothic hanging decoration. 4. *Electricity.* A ceiling light.

pen·dent *adj.* 1. Hanging; suspended. 2. Overhanging; outjutting. 3. Undecided upon. —**pen·den·cy** *n.* [*pl.* pen·den·cies]—**pen·dent·ly** *adv.*—**pend·ing** *adj.*

pen·den·tive (pen-*den*-tiv) *n.* Concave triangular corner supporting a dome over a square floor plan.

pend·ing *adj.* Unfinished; undecided.—*prep.* Until.

pen·du·lous *adj.* Hanging; swinging; vacillating.—**pen·du·lous·ly** *adv.*—**pen·du·lous·ness** *n.*

pen·du·lum *n.* A body swinging freely from a fixed point.

pen·e·tra·ble (*pen*-eh-truh-b'l) *n.* Capable of being pierced.—**pen·e·tra·bil·i·ty** *n.*—**pen·e·tra·bly** *adv.*

pen·e·trate *v.* [pen·e·trated; pen·e·trat·ing] 1. To pierce; enter; permeate. 2. To understand; discern.

pen·e·trat·ing *adj.* Shrewd; acute. —**pen·e·trat·ing·ly** *adv.*

pen·e·tra·tion *n.* Acuteness; insight; discrimination.

pen·guin (*pen*-gwin) *n.* A large, non-flying antarctic waterbird.

PENDULUM

pen·i·cil·lin (pen-ih-*sil*-in) *n.* An effective anti-infection drug extracted from a fungus of the mold family.

pen·in·su·la (pen-*in*-suh-luh) *n.* Land extending into water.—**pen·in·su·lar** *adj.*

pe·nis (*pee*-niss) *n.* The male organ of generation.

pen·i·tent (*pen*-ih-tent) *adj.* Repentant; remorseful; contrite.—**pen·i·tent** *n.*—**pen·i·tence** *n.*—**pen·i·tent·ly** *adv.* —**pen·i·ten·tial** *adj.*—**pen·i·ten·tial·ly** *adv.*

pen·i·ten·tia·ry (-*ten*-shuh-ree *n.* [*pl.* -ries]. Prison; house of correction.

PENGUIN (1/15 life-size)

pen·knife *n.* Small pocket knife.

pen·man *n.* 1. One using a pen; one having a good handwriting. 2. A writer.—**pen·man·ship** *n.*

pen·nant *n.* 1. Small flag; banner. 2. *Nautical.* A tackle for hoisting goods.

pen·nate (*pen*-ayt) *adj.* Winged or feathered.

pen·ni·less *adj.* Poverty-stricken; destitute.

pen·non *n.* Small pointed flag or streamer.

pen·ny *n.* [*pl.* pen·nies; *Brit. pl.* pence] 1. A coin having, in the U. S., $\frac{1}{100}$ the value of a dollar; in England, $\frac{1}{12}$ of a shilling; a cent. 2. Unit of measurement of the length of nails.

pen·ny-a-lin·er *n.* A hack writer.—**pen·ny-a-line** *adj.*

pen·ny-pinch·ing *adj. Slang.* Stingy; miserly.

pen·ny-wise *adj.* Saving small sums at the hazard of larger.

pe·nol·o·gy (peh-*nol*-uh-jee) *n.* The scientific study of criminal prisons.—**pe·nol·o·gist** *n.*

pen·sile *adj.* 1. Hanging; suspended; pendulous. 2. *Ornithology.* Building hanging nests.

pen·sion (*pen*-sh'n) *n.* 1. Periodical payment to a retired person. 2. *French.* (*pahn*-see-ahn) Continental boarding house or school.—**pen·sion** *v.*—**pen·sion·a·ble** *adj.*—**pen·sion·ar·y** *n.* [*pl.* pen·sion·ar·ies]—**pen·sion·er** *n.*

pen·sive (*pen*-siv) *adj.* Thoughtful; meditative;—**pen·sive·ly** *adv.*—**pen·sive·ness** *n.*

pen·ta·gon (*pen*-tuh-gon) *n.* A five-sided figure.—**pen·tag·o·nal** (pen-*tag*-uh-nal) *adj.*

pen·tam·e·ter (pen-*tam*-eh-ter) *n. Prosody.* A line having five feet.—**pen·tam·e·ter** *adj.*

Pen·ta·teuch (*pen*-tuh-took) *n.* The first five books of the Old Testament.—**pen·ta·teuch·al** *adj.*

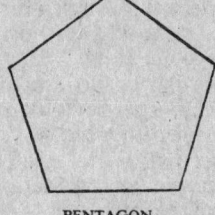

PENTAGON

Pen·te·cost *n.* 1. Jewish feast celebrated on the 50th and 51st days after Passover. 2. Whitsunday.—**pen·te·cos·tal** *adj.*

pent·house *n.* Private dwelling built on the roof of a building.

pe·nult (*pee*-nult) *n.* The next to last syllable of a word.—**pe·nul·ti·mate** *adj.*

pe·num·bra *n.* 1. Partial shadow; shaded area. 2. *Painting.* Boundary of light and shade.—**pe·num·bral**, **pe·num·brous** *adj.*

pen·u·ry (*pen*-yoor-ee) *n.* 1. Poverty; destitution. 2. Miserliness; stinginess.—**pe·nu·ri·ous** *adj.*—**pe·nu·ri·ous·ly** *adv.*—**-ous·ness** *n.*

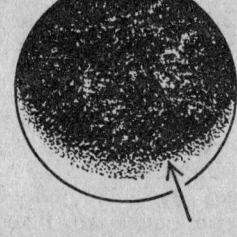

PENUMBRA

pe·on (*pee*-un; *pay*-on) *n.* Involuntary agricultural worker in Spanish-speaking countries; laborer; peasant.—**pe·on·age** *n.*—**pe·on·ism** *n.*

pe·o·ny *n.* [*pl.* pe·o·nies] Perennial, flowering cultivated plant.

peo·ple *n.* 1. A race; nation. 2. Populace; persons. 3. Relatives; ancestors.—*v.* [peo·pled; peo·pling]—**peo·pler** *n.*

pep *n. Colloquial.* Enthusiasm; energy; verve.—**pep·pi·ness** *n.*—**pep·py** *adj.* [pep·pi·er; pep·pi·est].

pep·per *n.* 1. Large family of plants producing pungent fruit used in seasoning. 2. The ground berries of a pepper plant—**pep·per** *v.*—**pep·per·y** *adj.*—**pep·per·i·ness** *n.*

PEONY

pep·per·corn *n.* Dried berry of the black pepper.

pep·per·mint *n.* The most aromatic plant of the mint family, from which a flavoring oil is obtained.

pepper pot. A highly seasoned West Indian or Philadelphian stew.

pep·sin, pep·sine *n.* A protein-digesting enzyme in gastric juice.—**pep·sin·ate** *v.*—**pep·tic** *adj.*

pep·tone *n.* A protein derivative formed during digestion.—**pep·ton·ic** *adj.*—**pep·to·nize** *v.* [pep·to·nized; pep·to·niz·ing]—**pep·to·ni·za·tion** *n.*

Pe·quot (*peek*-waht) *n.* A tribe of American Indians.

per- *prefix.* For; through; by; by means of; over the whole extent.

per *prep.* 1. Through; by way of. 2. Each. 'A dollar per day.'

per·ad·ven·ture *adv.* Perhaps; it may be.

per·am·bu·late (per-*am*-byoo-layt) *v.* [per·am·bu·lat·ed; per·am·bu·lat·ing] To walk across or through.—**per·am·bu·la·tor** *n.* 1. One who perambulates. 2. A baby carriage.—**per·am·bu·la·tion** *n.*—**per·am·bu·la·tor·y** *adj.*

per annum. Yearly; by the year.

per·cale *n.* A closely woven cotton fabric.

per capita. For each person.

per·ceive (per-*seev*) *v.* [per·ceived; per·ceiv·ing] 1. To observe; notice; discern. 2. To understand.—**per·ceiv·a·ble** *adj.*—**per·ceiv·a·bly** *adv.*

per cent. Part or unit in proportion to 100.—**per·cent·age** *n.* Rate or commission on a hundred.—**per·cen·tile** *adj.* Expressing percentage.—*n.* One of the 100 equal parts into which a group or distribution is divided.

per·cept *n.* An image; sensation.—**per·cep·ti·ble** *adj.*—**per·cep·ti·bly** *adv.*

per·cep·tion *n.* 1. Consciousness; sight; knowledge. 2. Insight; discernment.—**per·cep·tion·al** *adj.*—**per·cep·tive·ness, -tiv·i·ty** *n.*

perch *n.* 1. A family of tasty fresh-water fish found in the temperate regions. 2. A roost; elevated seat.—**perch** *v.*—**perch·er** *n.*

per·chance *adv.* Perhaps; maybe.

per·cip·i·ent (per-*sip*-ee-ent) *adj.* Able to know or understand.—**per·cip·i·ence, per·cip·i·en·cy** *n.*

per·co·late (*per*-kuh-layt) *v.* [per·co·lat·ed; per-

P

co·lat·ing] To flow through; filter.—**per·co·la·tion** n.—**per·co·la·tor** n. A filter coffeepot.

per·cus·sion (per-*kush*-'n) n. Impact; collision; concussion.—adj. Music. Producing its tone when struck, as a piano or drum.—**per·cuss** v.—**per·cus·sive** adj.—**per·cus·sive·ly** adv.

per diem (per *dy*-em; *dee*-em) Law. Per day.

per·di·tion (per-*dish*-'n) n. Utter ruin; complete loss; damnation.

per·e·gri·nate (*pehr*-eh-grih-nayt) v. [per·e·gri·nat·ed; per·e·grin·at·ing] To wander; roam.—**per·e·gri·na·tor** n.—**per·e·gri·na·tion** n.

per·emp·to·ry (per-*emp*-tor-ee) adj. Arbitrary; dogmatic; decisive.—**per·emp·to·ri·ly** adv.

per·en·ni·al adj. 1. Botany. Blossoming annually. 2. Continuous; undying.—**-al·ly** adv.

per·fect adj. 1. Flawless; ideal; complete. 2. Grammar. Pertaining to a verb form designating a completed action.—**per·fect** (per-*fect*) v.—**per·fect·er** n.—**per·fect·i·ble** adj.—**-i·bil·i·ty** n.—**per·fect·ly** adv.—**per·fec·tion, -fect·ness** n.

per·fec·tion·ism (per-*fek*-shun-izm) n. Belief that man's moral perfection is possible.—**per·fec·tion·ist** n.—**per·fec·tion·is·tic** adj.

per·fec·tive adj. Tending to make perfect.—**per·fec·tive·ly** adv.—**per·fec·tive·ness** n.

per·fec·to (per-*fek*-toh) n. A type of cigar which tapers from the middle toward both ends.

per·fid·y (*per*-fih-dee) n. [pl. per·fid·ies] Treachery; faithlessness; disloyalty.—**per·fid·i·ous** adj.—**per·fid·i·ous·ly** adv.—**per·fid·i·ous·ness** n.

per·fo·rate (*per*-fer-ayt) v. [per·fo·rat·ed; per·fo·rat·ing] To puncture; put holes in.—**per·fo·rate** adj.—**per·fo·ra·tion** n.—**per·fo·ra·tive** adj.—**per·fo·ra·tor** n.

per·force (per-*forss*) adv. Of necessity.

per·form (per-*form*) v. 1. To do; bring to completion; fulfill. 2. To act a part; show off.—**per·form·a·ble** adj.—**per·form·ance** n.—**per·form·er** n.

per·fume (*per*-fyoom) n. 1. Fragrance; sweet odor. 2. A commercially prepared scenting fluid.—**per·fume** (per-*fyoom*) v. [per·fumed; per·fum·ing]—**per·fum·er** n.—**per·fum·er·y** n.

per·func·to·ry (per-*funk*-tor-ee) adj. Routine; mechanical; indifferent.—**per·func·to·ri·ly** adv.

per·fuse (per-*fyooz*) v. [per·fused; per·fus·ing] To sprinkle; suffuse; fill.—**per·fu·sion** n.

per·go·la (*per*-guh-luh) n. A trellised balcony; arbor.

per·haps adv. Possibly; maybe

per·i·car·di·um (pehr-ih-*kahr*-dee-um) n. [pl. per·i·car·dia] Membranous sac enclosing the heart.—**pe·ri·car·di·ac, pe·ri·car·di·al** adj.—**pe·ri·car·di·tis** n.

PERGOLA

Per·i·cle·an (pehr-ih-*klee*-an) adj. Pertaining to Pericles, ruler of Athens during its Golden Age.

per·i·gee (*pehr*-ih-jee) n. Point on the moon's orbit nearest the earth.—**per·i·ge·al, per·i·ge·an** adj.

pe·ri·he·li·on (pehr-ih-*heel*-y'n) n. Point on a planet's orbit nearest the sun.

per·il (*pehr*-il) n. Danger; risk; jeopardy.—**per·il·ous** adj.—**per·il·ous·ly** adv.

per·im·e·ter (per-*im*-eh-ter) n. The distance or boundary around a body.—**per·i·met·ric, per·i·met·ri·cal** adj.—**per·i·met·ri·cal·ly** adv.

per·i·od n. 1. An interval; duration of time; era. 2. The dot [.] that indicates the end of a sentence.—**per·i·od·ic, per·i·od·i·cal** adj. Recurrent; intermittent.—**per·i·od·i·cal·ly** adv.

per·i·od·i·cal (peer-ee-*od*-ih-k'l) n. Magazine.

periodic table. Chemistry. A chart of the elements listed in order of atomic number.

per·i·os·te·um (per-ee-*os*-tee-um) n. [pl. per·i·os·te·a] Thick, vascular membrane covering a bone.—**per·i·os·ti·tis** n. Inflammation of the periosteum.—**per·i·os·te·al** adj.—**per·i·os·ti·tic** adj.

per·i·pa·tet·ic (pehr-ih-puh-*tet*-ik) adj. 1. Itinerant. 2. Pertaining to a follower of Aristotle.

pe·riph·er·y (peh-*rif*-er-ee) n. [pl. pe·riph·er·ies] Circumference; perimeter; edge.—**pe·riph·er·al** adj.—**pe·riph·er·al·ly** adv.

pe·riph·ra·sis (peh-*rif*-ruh-sis) n. [pl. pe·riph·ra·ses] Redundancy; circumlocution.—**per·i·phras·tic** adj.—**per·i·phras·ti·cal·ly** adv.

per·i·scope n. A system of mirrors or prisms by which images are reflected through a tube.—**per·i·scop·ic, per·i·scop·i·cal** adj.

per·ish v. To die; decay.—**per·ish·a·ble** adj.—**per·ish·a·ble·ness** n.

per·i·stal·sis n. The muscular contractions of the intestines.—**per·i·stal·tic** adj.

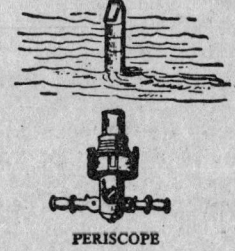
PERISCOPE

per·i·style n. Architecture. Colonnade; lines of columns surrounding an area.—**per·i·sty·lar** adj.

per·i·to·ne·um, per·i·to·nae·um (pehr-ih-tuh-*nee*-um) n. [pl. -nea] Membranous sac covering most of the viscera of the abdominal cavity.—**per·i·to·ni·tis** n. Inflammation of the peritoneum.—**per·i·to·ne·al** adj.

per·i·wig n. A wig, esp. an old-fashioned peruke.

per·i·win·kle n. 1. A family of edible mollusks. 2. Popular name for the vinca, a trailing perennial with lilac-blue flowers.

per·jure v. [per·jured; per·jur·ing] To lie while under oath; give false testimony.—**per·jur·er** n.—**per·jury** n. [pl. per·jur·ies].

perk v. 1. To cock; lift. 2. To spruce; make trim; revive. 3. Short for percolate.—**perk·y** adj. [perk·i·er; perk·i·est]. Cocky.

per·ma·nent adj. Fixed; durable; lasting; unchanging.—**per·ma·nence, per·ma·nen·cy** n.

per·me·a·bil·i·ty (per-mee-uh-*bil*-ih-tee) n. Perviousness; availability to penetration.—**per·me·a·ble** adj.

per·me·ate (*per*-mee-ayt) v. [per·me·at·ed; per·me·at·ing] To penetrate; pervade; saturate. —**per·me·a·tion** n.—**per·me·a·tive** adj.

per·mis·sion n. Consent; authorization; leave. —**per·mis·si·ble** adj.—**per·mis·si·bil·i·ty** n.—**per·mis·si·bly** adv.—**per·mis·sive** adj.— **-sive·ly** adv.

per·mit (per-*mit*) v. [per·mit·ted; per·mit·ting] To allow; consent to; tolerate.—n. (*per*-mit) A written permission or license.—**per·mit·ter** n.

per·mu·ta·tion (per-myoo-*tay*-sh'n) n. 1. Transformation; change. 2. *Mathematics*. Any regrouping of a series.—**per·mut·a·ble** adj.—**per·mute** v. [per·muted; per·mut·ing].

per·ni·cious (per-*nish*-us) adj. Injurious; deadly; evil.—**per·ni·cious·ly** adv.— **-cious·ness** n.

per·nick·et·y (per-*nik*-et-ee) adj. Fussy; fastidious.

per·o·rate (*pehr*-or-ayt) v. [per·o·rated; per·o·rat·ing] 1. To declaim. 2. To sum up impressively.—**per·o·ra·tion** n. Conclusion of a speech.

per·ox·ide (per-*ok*-syde) n. An oxide containing the greatest possible number of oxygen atoms.

per·pen·dic·u·lar (per-pen-*dik*-yoo-ler) adj. Vertical; at right angles. —n. A perpendicular line.—**per·pen·dic·u·lar·i·ty** n.—**per·pen·dic·u·lar·ly** adv.

per·pe·trate (*per*-peh-trayt) v. [per·pe·trat·ed; per·pe·trat·ing] To commit; perform. —**per·pe·tra·tor** n.

PERPENDICULAR

per·pet·u·al (per-*pet*-choo-al) adj. Everlasting; continual; eternal. —**per·pet·u·al·ly** adv.—**per·pet·u·ate** v. [-u·at·ed; -u·at·ing]—**per·pet·u·a·tion** n. **-u·a·tor** n.

per·pe·tu·i·ty (per-peh-*tyoo*-ih-tee) n. Eternity; endless duration.

per·plex (per-*pleks*) v. To puzzle; bewilder; confound.—**per·plex·ed·ly** adv.—**per·plex·i·ty** n.

per·qui·site (*per*-kwih-zit) n. 1. Pay; income. 2. Bonus; gain; tip.

per se. By itself.

per·se·cute (*per*-seh-kyoot) v. [per·se·cut·ed; per·se·cut·ing] To harass; oppress; afflict unjustly.—**per·se·cu·tion** n.—**per·se·cu·tive** adj. —**per·se·cu·tive·ness** n.—**per·se·cu·tor** n.

Per·seph·o·ne (per-*sef*-uh-nee) n. *Greek Mythology*. Wife of Pluto; goddess of vegetation.

Per·seus (*per*-syooss; *per*-see-us) n. *Greek Mythology*. 1. A son of Zeus who slew the Medusa. 2. A constellation.

per·se·ver·ance (per-seh-*veer*-enss) n. Persistence; steadfastness; singleness of purpose. —**per·se·vere** v. [per·se·vered; per·se·ver·ing]. —**per·se·ver·ing·ly** adv.

Per·sia (*per*-zhuh) Former name of Iran.—**Per·sian** adj. Persian lamb, The valuable skin of a species of Asiatic sheep.—**Persian rug.** An oriental rug with a thick nap.

per·si·flage (*per*-sih-flahzh) n. Idle banter; chaff.

per·sim·mon n. 1. A tree of the ebony group. 2. The juicy, seeded fruit of the persimmon.

per·sist (per-*sist*) v. 1. To persevere; remain unyielding. 2. To continue; last.—**per·sis·tence, per·sis·ten·cy** n.—**per·sis·tent** adj.

per·snick·et·y adj. Fussy; snippy.

per·son n. 1. Any individual. 2. One's body; one's physical self. 3. *Grammar*. Differentiation in nouns and pronouns to indicate relation of people.—**per·son·a·ble** adj. Attractive; well-appearing.—**per·son·age** n. An individual, esp. a distinguished one.

per·son·al adj. 1. Peculiar; individual. 2. By oneself; in person. 3. *Grammar*. Having the modification of one of the three persons. 'Personal pronoun.'—**per·son·al·ly** adv.—**per·son·al·ize** v. [-ized; -iz·ing]. To make personal.

per·son·al·i·ty (per-son-*al*-ih-tee) n. [*pl.* per·son·al·i·ties] 1. Individuality; character. 2. External manner. 3. Pleasing or ingratiating manner. 4. A vivid public figure. 4. [*pl.*] Reference to individuals. 'To indulge in personalities.'

per·son·ate v. [per·son·at·ed; per·son·at·ing] 1. To masquerade; act a part. 2. To make personal.—**per·son·a·tion** n.—**per·son·a·tive** adj.

per·son·i·fi·ca·tion (per-son-ih-fih-*kay*-shun) n. 1. Representation of qualities or objects as living things. 2. Embodiment.—**per·son·i·fy** v. [-fied; -fy·ing].—**per·son·i·fi·er** n.

per·son·nel n. Employees; staff.—**per·son·nel** adj.

per·spec·tive (per-*spek*-tiv) n. 1. Science of representing depth on a flat surface. 2. Impersonal and removed vision; co-ordinated outlook; total comprehension.—**per·spec·tive** adj.—**per·spec·tive·ly** adv.

per·spi·ca·cious (per-spih-*kay*-shus) adj. Astute; shrewd.— **-cious·ly** adv.—**per·spi·cac·i·ty** n.

per·spi·cu·i·ty (per-spih-*kyoo*-ih-tee) n. Clearness; limpidity; lucidity.—**per·spic·u·ous** adj. —**per·spic·u·ous·ly** adv.—**per·spic·u·ous·ness** n.

per·spire (per-*spyre*) v. [per·spired; per·spir·ing] To sweat; excrete fluid waste through the pores of the skin.—**per·spir·a·tion** n.— **-a·to·ry** adj.

per·suade (per-*swayd*) v. [per·suad·ed; per·suad·ing] 1. To will; coax. 2. To induce; convince. —**per·suad·a·ble** adj.—**per·suad·er** n.

per·sua·sion n. 1. Convincing. 2. Conviction; belief; religion.—**per·sua·sive** adj.—**per·sua·sive·ly** adv.—**per·sua·sive·ness** n.

pert adj. Saucy; lively; brisk.—**pert·ly** adv. —**pert·ness** n.

per·tain v. To relate; apply.

per·ti·na·cious (per-tih-*nay*-shus) adj. 1. Stubborn; obstinate; resolute.—**per·ti·na·cious·ly** adv.—**per·ti·na·cious·ness, per·ti·nac·i·ty** n.

per·ti·nence, per·ti·nen·cy n. Relevance; appropriateness.—**per·ti·nent** adj.— **-nent·ly** adv.

per·turb (per-*terb*) v. To disturb; agitate.—**per·turb·a·ble** adj.—**per·tur·ba·tion** n.

per·tus·sis (per-*tuss*-iss) n. *Medicine*. Whooping cough.—**per·tus·sal** adj.

pe·ruke (peh-*rook*) n. A wig.

P

pe·ruse (peh-*rooz*) *v.* [pe·rused; pe·rus·ing] 1. To read; examine carefully.—**pe·rus·a·ble** *adj.*—**pe·rus·al** *n.*—**pe·rus·er** *n.*

Peruvian bark. Bark of cinchona tree from which quinine is made.

per·vade *v.* [per·vad·ed; per·vad·ing] To permeate; infuse. **per·va·sion** *n.*—**per·va·sive·ly** *adv.*—**per·va·sive·ness** *n.*

per·verse (per-*verss*) *adj.* Stubborn; contrary. —**per·verse·ly** *adv.*—**per·verse·ness, -ver·si·ty** *n.*

per·ver·sion (per-*ver*-zhun) *n.* 1. Distortion; falsification. 2. *Psychology.* Sexual maladjustment inducing unnatural practices.—**per·ver·sive** *adj.*

per·vert *v.* 1. To corrupt; distort. 2. To miscomprehend; misapply.—*n.* 1. Renegade. 2. One given to unnatural sexual acts.—**per·vert·ed·ly** *adv.*—**per·vert·er** *n.*— **-vert·i·ble** *adj.*

per·vi·ous (*per*-vee-us) *adj.* Penetrable.—**per·vi·ous·ness** *n.*

pe·se·ta (peh-*say*-tah) *n.* The Spanish monetary unit.

pes·ky *adj.* Annoying; troublesome.—**pes·ki·ly** *adv.*

pe·so (*pay*-soh) *n.* A South American monetary denomination.

pes·sa·ry (*pess*-uh-ree) *n.* [*pl.* pes·sa·ries] *Medicine.* 1. A uterine support. 2. A diaphragm.

pes·si·mism (*pess*-ih-mizm) *n.* 1. Hopelessness; gloominess. 2. *Philosophy.* Doctrine teaching the irrationality and, therefore, the unhappiness of the world.—**pes·si·mist** *n.*—**pes·si·mis·tic, pes·si·mis·ti·cal** *adj.*— **-ti·cal·ly** *adv.*

pest *n.* 1. Epidemic; plague. 2. A tease; annoying person. 3. Vermin; destructive animal.—**pest·er** *v.*—**pest·er·er** *n.*

pest·house *n.* *Colloquial.* An isolation ward for contagious diseases.

pes·tif·er·ous (pess-*tif*-er-us) *adj.* 1. Noxious; infectious. 2. *Colloquial.* Annoying; bothersome.—**pes·tif·er·ous·ly** *adv.*— **-ous·ness** *n.*

pes·ti·lence (*pess*-tih-lenss) *n.* An epidemic disease.—**pes·ti·lent** *adj.*—**pes·ti·lent·ly** *adv.*—**pes·ti·len·tial** *adj.*

pes·tle (*pess*-'l) *n.* A tool for pounding and crushing, used with a mortar.

pet *n.* 1. A domesticated animal. 2. A favorite.—**pet** *adj.*—**pet** *v.* [pet·ted; pet·ting] To fondle.

pet·al *n.* A lobe or segment of a flower.—**pet·aled, pet·alled,** *adj.* —**pet·al·ine, pet·al·ous** *adj.*

pe·tard (peh-*tahrd*) *Military.* A small explosive formerly used against fortifications. —**hoist by one's own petard.** Destroyed by one's own trickery.

pet cock, pet·cock *n.* Valve; tap; lever.

pe·ter (*pee*-ter) *Colloquial.* To become exhausted; die out.

PETAL

pe·ter·sham *n.* 1. A heavy, napped cloth. 2. Overcoat made of it.

pet·i·ole (*pet*-ee-ohl) *n.* A leaf-supporting stalk. —**pet·i·o·lar** *adj.*—**pet·i·o·late, pet·i·o·lated** *adj.*

pe·tit (*pet*-ee) *adj. Law.* Trivial; minor.—**petit jury.** Twelve-man panel which decides court cases;—distinguished from **grand jury.**

pe·tite (peh-*teet*) *adj.* Tiny; small.

pe·ti·tion (peh-*tish*-un) *n.* 1. Earnest entreaty; prayer. 2. A written request or demand.—**pe·ti·tion** *v.*—**pe·ti·tion·er** *n.*

petits fours (peh-tee *foor*). Rich, decorated cookies.

pet·rel (*pet*-rel) *n.* An ocean bird closely related to the albatross.—**stormy petrel,** Small black petrel believed a bad omen.

pet·ri·fy (*pet*-rih-fy) *v.* [pet·ri·fied; pet·ri·fy·ing] 1. To change to stone; harden. 2. To paralyze with emotion.—**pet·ri·fac·tion** *n.*

pe·tro·le·um (peh-*troh*-lee-um) *n.* Crude oil; the bituminous hydrocarbon mixture as it comes from the earth.—**pe·trol·e·um** *adj.*

pe·trol·o·gy (peh-*trol*-uh-jee) *n.* Branch of geology dealing with composition and history of rocks.—**pet·ro·log·ic, pet·ro·log·i·cal** *adj.*—**pet·ro·log·i·cal·ly** *adv.*—**pe·trol·o·gist** *n.*

pet·ti·coat *n.* A woman's underskirt; half-slip.

pet·ti·fog *v.* [pet·ti·fogged; pet·ti·fog·ging] To practice law in a petty or dishonest fashion. —**pet·ti·fog·ger** *n.*—**pet·ti·fog·ger·y** *n.*

pet·tish *adj.* Irritable; peevish.—**pet·tish·ly** *adv.* —**pet·tish·ness** *n.*

pet·ty (*pet*-ee) *adj.* Small; unimportant; mean. —**pet·ti·ness** *n.*

petty cash. Money kept for paying small expenses.

petty officer. *Navy.* Noncommissioned officer below the rank of warrant officer.

pet·u·lant (*pet*-yoo-l'nt) *adj.* Cross; fretful. —**pet·u·lance, pet·u·lan·cy** *n.*—**pet·u·lant·ly** *adv.*

pe·tu·ni·a (peh-*tyoon*-yuh, peh-*toon*-yuh) *n.* A flowering herb of the nightshade family.

pew (*pyoo*) *n.* A seat or bench in a church, often partially enclosed.

pe·wee (*pee*-wee) *n.* A small North American songbird.

pe·wit (*pee*-wit) *n.* 1. The lapwing plover. 2. The black-headed gull.

pew·ter (*pyoo*-ter) *n.* 1. A tin alloy. 2. Utensils of pewter.—**pew·ter** *adj.*—**pew·ter·er** *n.*

pfen·nig (*fen*-ig) *n.* German coin; $\frac{1}{100}$ of a mark.

phae·ton (*fay*-uh-t'n) *n.* 1. An open carriage. 2. A two-seated open automobile.

pha·lanx (*fay*-langks) *n.* [*pl.* pha·lanx·es] 1. Close massed group; unified organization. 2. [*pl.* pha·lan·ges (fay-*lan*-jeez)] *Anatomy.* Bones of the fingers or toes.

PHAETON

phal·li·cism (*fal*-ih-sizm) *n.* Worship of the principle of reproduction.—**phal·li·cist** *n.*

phal·lus (*fal*-us) *n.* 1. The penis. 2. An ancient Greek symbol of reproductive power. —**phal·lic, phal·li·cal** *adj.*

phan·tasm (*fan*-tazm) *n.* 1. An apparition; ghost. 2. A vision; illusion.—**phan·tas·mal, phan·tas·mic** *adj.*

phan·tas·ma·go·ri·a, phan·tas·ma·go·ry (fan-taz-muh-*goh*-ree-uh, -*goh*-ree) *n.* A series of illusions or hallucinations.—**phan·tas·ma·go·ri·al, -go·ric** *adj.*

phan·ta·sy. *Variant spelling* of fantasy.

phan·tom (*fan*-tum) *n.* A specter; apparition. —**phan·tom** *adj.*

phar·a·oh (*fayr*-oh) *n.* A king of ancient Egypt. —**phar·a·on·ic, phar·a·on·i·cal** *adj.*

phar·i·sa·ic, phar·i·sa·i·cal *adj.* Sanctimonious; hypocritical.—**phar·i·sa·i·cal·ly** *adv.* —**phar·i·sa·i·cal·ness** *n.*—**phar·i·sa·ism** *n.*

Phar·i·see (*fair*-ih-see) *n.* Member of an ancient Jewish sect, noted for strict adherence to traditional rituals.—**phar·i·see·ism** *n.*

phar·ma·ceu·tic, phar·ma·ceu·ti·cal (fahr-muh-*soo*-tik, -ih-cal) *adj.* Pertaining to drugs or druggists.—**phar·ma·ceu·tics** *n.* Pharmacy. —**phar·ma·ceu·tist** *n.* A druggist.

phar·ma·cist *n.* Druggist; specialist in preparation and dispensing of drugs.—**pharmacist's mate.** Naval petty officer who administers medical treatment.

phar·ma·col·o·gy (fahr-muh-*kol*-uh-jee) *n.* The science of drugs in all their relationships. —**phar·ma·co·log·i·cal** *adj.* **-col·o·gist** *n.*

phar·ma·co·poe·ia (fahr-muh-koh-*pee*-uh) *n.* Authorized book on medicines. **-poe·ial** *adj.*

phar·ma·cy (*fahr*-muh-see) *n.* [*pl.* phar·ma·cies] 1. Science or practice of drug preparation. 2. A drugstore.

phar·ynx (*fair*-ingks) *n.* [*pl.* phar·yn·ges (fuh-*rin*-jees), phar·ynx·es (*fair*-ingk-sez)] Passage between the esophagus and the cavities of the nose and mouth.—**pha·ryn·gi·tis** *n.* Inflammation of the pharynx.—**pha·ryn·ge·al** *adj.*

phase (*fayz*) *n.* 1. An aspect; stage. 2. *Physics.* The status, at a given instant, of a constantly changing phenomenon.

pheas·ant (*fez*-ant) *n.* A family of large game birds with beautifully colored plumage.

phe·nix. *Variant spelling* of phoenix.

phe·no·bar·bi·tal. *n.* Sleep-inducing drug.

phe·nol (*fee*-nohl) *n.* Carbolic acid; coaltar acid.—**phe·nol·ic** *adj.*

phe·nom·e·non (feh-*nom*-eh-non) *n.*1.[*pl.* phe·nom·e·na] A natural event of scientific importance, esp. a deviation from the normal. 2. [*pl.* phe·nom·e·nons] An extraordinary happening or circumstance.—**phe·nom·e·nal** *adj.*— -**nal·ly** *adv.*

PHEASANT (1/15 life-size)

phew (*fyoo*) *interj.* An ejaculation of relief or exhaustion.

phi·al (*fy*-ul) *n.* A small glass bottle; vial.

phi·lan·der (fih-*lan*-der) *v.* To make love promiscuously.—**phi·lan·der·er** *n.*

phi·lan·thro·py (fih-*lan*-throh-pee) [*pl.* -thro·pies] *n.* Charity; benevolence.—**phil·an·throp·ic, phil·an·throp·i·cal** *adj.*—**phil·an·throp·i·cal·ly** *adv.*—**phi·lan·thro·pist** *n.*—**phi·lan·thro·pize** *v.* [phi·lan·thro·pized; -piz·ing].

phi·lat·e·ly (fih-*lat*-eh-lee) *n.* The systematic collection and study of postage stamps.—**phil·a·tel·ic, -i·cal** *adj.*— -**cal·ly** *adv.*—**phi·lat·e·list** *n.*

phil·har·mon·ic (fil-hahr-*mon*-ik) *adj.* Pertaining to music lovers.—*n.* A musical society.

Phi·lip·pi·ans (fih-*lip*-ee-anz)*n. Bible.* The Epistle of Paul to the Philippians.

phi·lip·pic (fih-*lip*-ik) *n.* A venomous public speech.

Phi·lis·tine (fih-*liss*-teen) *n.* One having no taste or culture.—**phi·lis·tine** *adj.*—**phi·lis·tin·ism** *n.*

phi·log·y·ny (fil-*oj*-uh-nee) *n.* Fondness for women.—**phi·log·y·nist** *n.*—**phi·log·y·nous** *adj.*

phi·lol·o·gy (fil-*ol*-uh-jee) *n.* Science of the evolution of languages.—**phi·lol·o·ger** *n.*—**phi·lo·log·ic, -i·cal***adj.*—-**i·cal·ly***adv.*—**phi·lol·o·gist** *n.*

phil·o·mel (*fil*-uh-mel) *n.* The nightingale.

phi·los·o·pher (fil-*oss*-uh-fer) *n.* 1. One who seeks to unify and interpret existence and experience through systematic methods of thought. 2. One who meets difficulties with rational calmness.

phil·o·soph·ic, phil·o·soph·i·cal (fil-oh-*sof*-ik, -k'l) *adj.* 1. Relating to philosophy. 2. Calm; rational; temperate.—**phil·o·soph·i·cal·ly** *adv.*

phi·los·o·phize (fil-*oss*-uh-fyze) *v.* [phi·los·o·phized; -phiz·ing] To reason systematically; theorize.—**phi·los·o·phiz·er** *n.*

phi·los·o·phy (fil-*oss*-uh-fee) *n.* Science which seeks to systematize and interpret knowledge through basic concepts of reality, validity, and value.

phil·o·pro·gen·i·tive (fil-uh-proh-*jen*-ih-tiv) *adj.* Pertaining to love of one's children.—**phil·o·pro·gen·i·tive·ness** *n.*

phil·ter, phil·tre (*fil*-ter) *n.* A love potion.

phle·bot·o·my (fleh-*bot*-uh-mee) *n. Medicine.* Practice of bleeding.—**phle·bot·o·mize** *v.* [-mized; -miz·ing] —**phle·bot·o·mist** *n.*

phlegm (*flem*) *n.* Mucus secreted in respiratory and digestive passages.—**phlegm·y** *adj.* [phlegm·i·er; phlegm·i·est].

phlegm (*flem*) *n.* Stolidity; impassiveness. —**phleg·mat·ic** *adj.*— **phleg·mat·i·cal·ly** *adv.*

PHLOX

phlox (*floks*) *n.* A family of decorative plants with red, purple, or white flowers.

pho·bi·a (*foh*-bee-uh) *n.* An unreasonable, uncontrollable fear.—**phobe** *n.*—**pho·bic** *adj.*

phoe·be (*fee*-bee) *n.* A small crested bird native to eastern U.S.

Phoe·bus. Apollo; the sun.

Phoe·ni·ci·a (feh-*niss*-ee-uh, fuh-*nish*-uh). Ancient commercial nation of Asia Minor. —**Phoe·ni·ci·an** *adj.*

phoe·nix, phe·nix (*fee*-niks) *n.* **1.** Mythological bird which revives from its own ashes every 500 years. **2.** Emblem of immortality.

phone (*fohn*) *n.* **1.** A telephone. **2.** An earphone.—*v.* [phoned; phon·ing]. To telephone.

pho·net·ic, pho·net·i·cal (foh-*net*-ik) *adj.* Pertaining to voice sounds or to alphabetic characters representing articulated sounds.—**pho·net·i·cal·ly** *adv.*

pho·net·ics *n.* Scientific study of vocal sounds of languages.—**pho·ne·ti·cian, pho·net·ist** *n.*

phon·ics (*fon*-iks) *n.* Study of sounds or pronunciation.—**phon·ic** *adj.*

pho·no·graph (*foh*-nuh-graf) *n.* Machine for playing records or recording sounds.—**pho·no·graph·ic, -i·cal** *adj.*—**pho·no·graph·i·cal·ly** *adv.*

phonograph pickup. Microphone that takes up sound from a recording, converts it to electrical energy, and transmits it to an amplifying device.

pho·nol·o·gy (foh-*nol*-uh-jee) *n.* The study of speech sounds.—**pho·no·log·ic, pho·no·log·i·cal** *adj.*—**pho·no·log·i·cal·ly** *adv.*

pho·ny (*foh*-nee) *adj.* [pho·ni·er; pho·ni·est]. *Slang.* Counterfeit; fake.—*n.* [*pl.* pho·nies].

phos·gene, phos·gen (*foss*-jeen) *n.* A poisonous gas made from chlorine and carbon dioxide.

phos·phate (*foss*-fayt) *n.* Any salt of phosphoric acid.—**phos·phat·ic** *adj.*—**phos·pha·tize** *v.*

phosphor bronze. A durable alloy of copper, tin, and phosphorus.

phos·pho·res·cent (foss-fuh-*ress*-ent) *adj.* Radiating light without heat; shining in the dark. —**phos·pho·res·cence** *n.*

phos·pho·rus (*foss*-for-us) *n.* [*pl.* phos·pho·ri] A solid nonmetallic element. (*Symbol:* P).—**phos·phor·ic** *adj.*

pho·to- *prefix.* **1.** Light. **2.** Photography.

photoactive
photochemical
photoelectrotype
photographometer
photoheliograph
photolithography
photomicography
photo-oxidation
photophobia
photorelief
photosculpture
phototelegraph

pho·to *n.* Short for **photograph.**—**photo finish.** A race won by a margin discernible only in a photograph.

pho·to·e·lec·tric (foh-toh-ih-*lek*-trik) *adj.* Relating to electrical changes caused by light, as in the **photoelectric cell,** a device used in various automatic controls.

pho·to·en·grav·ing *n.* Process of preparing printing plates in relief by mechanical etching from photographs.—**pho·to·en·grave** *v.* [-graved; -grav·ing].—**pho·to·en·grav·er** *n.*

pho·to·flash *n.* **1.** An electric bulb producing an intense flash of light for taking photographs. **2.** Photograph taken by photoflash.

pho·to·flood *n.* An extremely bright electric floodlamp used in photography.

pho·to·gen·ic (foh-tuh-*jen*-ik) *adj.* **1.** *Biology.* Phosphorescent. **2.** Attractive as a subject for photography.

pho·to·graph (*foh*-tuh-graph) *n.* A picture recorded on the sensitive film in a camera.—**pho·to·graph·ic, -i·cal** *adj.*—**-i·cal·ly** *adv.*

pho·tog·ra·phy (fuh-*tog*-ruh-fee) *n.* Art and science of reproducing images upon a sensitized surface by the action of light through a lens.

pho·to·gra·vure (foh-tuh-gruh-*vyoor*) *n.* Process of making printing plates by chemical-and-light action on a prepared metal surface.

pho·tom·e·try (foh-*tom*-eh-tree) *n.* Measurement of light intensity.—**pho·tom·e·ter** *n.*—**pho·to·met·ric, -i·cal** *adj.*—**pho·tom·e·trist** *n.*

pho·to·mon·tage *n.* A mounting of several photographs, combined to make one display.

pho·to·mur·al (foh-toh-*myoo*-r'l) *n.* Large photograph used to decorate a wall space.

pho·to·stat *n.* **1.** Trade-marked process of photographically reproducing documents. **2.** A photographed document.—*v.* [pho·to·stat·ted; pho·to·stat·ting].

phrase *n.* **1.** *Grammar.* A construction of words having fragmentary meaning. **2.** An expression; idiom. **3.** Two or more bars of music.—*v.* [phrased; phras·ing].—**phras·al** *adj.*

phra·se·ol·o·gy (fray-zee-*ol*-uh-jee) *n.* [*pl.* -o·gies] Manner or style of expression; diction. —**phra·se·o·log·i·cal** *adj.*—**phra·se·ol·o·gist** *n.*

phras·ing *n.* Construction; styling.

phre·net·ic (freh-*net*-ik) *adj.* Also **phre·net·i·cal.** Deranged; frenzied.—**phre·net·ic** *n.*—**phre·net·i·cal·ly** *adv.*

phre·nol·o·gy (freh-*nol*-uh-jee) *n.* Pseudoscience dealing with brain structure as a personality index.—**phren·o·log·ic, -i·cal,** *adj.*—**phre·nol·o·gist** *n.*

phthi·sis (*thy*-siss) *n.* Pulmonary tuberculosis. —**phthis·ic, phthis·ick·y** *adj.*

phy·lac·ter·y (fih-*lak*-ter-ee) *n.* [*pl.* -ter·ies] Charm containing biblical passages and worn as a preservative from harm.

phy·lum (*fy*-lum) *n.* A basic or principal biological classification.

phys·ic (*fiz*-ik) *n.* A medicine, esp. a laxative. —*v.* [phys·icked; phys·ick·ing].

phys·i·cal (*fiz*-ih-k'l) *adj.* **1.** Corporeal; material. **2.** Pertaining to physics. **3.** Somatic; bodily.—**phys·i·cal·ly** *adv.*—**physical chemistry.** Branch of chemistry dealing with divisions of matter and their fundamental laws.—**physical education.** Theory and practice of training the body.—**physical geography.** Science of the external features and changes of the earth. —**physical science.** Physics.

phy·si·cian (fih-*zish*-an) *n.* A doctor of medicine.

phys·ics *n.* Science dealing with the laws and properties of matter.—**phys·i·cist** *n.*

phys·i·og·no·my (fiz-ee-*og*-nuh-mee) *n.* [*pl.* -no·mies] 1. Fortune-telling from facial features. 2. Face; countenance.—**phys·i·og·nom·ic, phys·i·og·nom·i·cal** *adj.*—**phys·i·og·nom·i·cal·ly** *adv.*—**phys·i·og·no·mist** *n.*

phys·i·og·ra·phy (fiz-ee-*og*-ruh-fee) *n.* Physical geography; study of the earth's physical features.—**phys·i·og·ra·pher** *n.*—**phys·i·o·graph·ic, -i·cal** *adj.*—**phys·i·o·graph·i·cal·ly** *adv.*

phy·si·ol·o·gy (fiz-ee-*ol*-uh-jee) *n.* Science which treats of the functions of organisms.—**phys·i·o·log·ic, -i·cal** *adj.*—**phys·i·o·log·i·cal·ly** *adv.* —**phys·i·ol·o·gist** *n.*

phy·si·o·ther·a·py (fiz-ee-oh-*thehr*-uh-pee) *n.* Branch of medicine dealing with nonmedical remedies, such as heat or massage.

phy·sique (fih-*zeek*) *n.* Physical structure of an individual.

pi (*pye*) *n.* 1. The sixteenth character of the Greek alphabet [π]. 2. *Mathematics.* The letter π representing the ratio of a circle's circumference to its diameter, about 3.1416.

pi *v.* [pi·ed; py·ing] *Printing.* To scramble or unsort type.

pi·a·nis·si·mo (pee-uh-*niss*-ih-moh) *adj. Music.* Very soft.

pi·a·no, pi·a·no·for·te (pee-*ah*-noh, -*for*-tee) *n. Music.* A stringed instrument played from a keyboard. –*adj. & adv. Music.* Soft.—**pi·an·ist** (pee-*an*-ist, *pee*-uh-nist) *n.* Piano player.

PIANO

pi·as·ter, pi·as·tre (pee-*ass*-ter) *n.* A coin of Egypt, Turkey, and Syria.

pi·az·za (pee-*az*-uh) *n.* A porch; veranda.

pi·broch (*pee*-brok) *n.* Funeral or martial bagpipe music.

pi·ca (*py*-kuh) *n.* 1. *Printing.* A size of type and a unit of measurement ⅙ of an inch. 2. A size of typewriter type which allows ten characters to the inch.

pic·a·dor (*pik*-uh-dor) *n.* 1. Bullfight rider who agitates the bull with a pointed shaft. 2. A deft speaker.

pic·a·resque (pik-uh-*resk*) *n. Literature.* Pertaining to the theme (originally Spanish) of a wandering, scoundrelly hero.

pic·a·yune (pik-ih-*yoon*) *n.* 1. A copper coin. 2. An insignificant matter.—**pic·a·yune, pic·a·yun·ish** *adj.* Petty; trivial.

pic·ca·lil·li *n.* A sharp, spicy relish of pickles.

PICCOLO

pic·co·lo (*pik*-uh-loh) *n.* Small flute ranging an octave higher than a regular flute.— -**lo·ist** *n.*

pick *v.* 1. To apply a pointed instrument to. 2. To pluck; harvest; reap. 3. To select. 4. To pull apart. 5. To open without the proper key.—*n.* 1. A heavy pointed tool for breaking stone or hard soil. 2. Choice; selection. 3. *Printing.* Extraneous matter on type. —**pick·er** *n.*—**pick·ing** *n.* Opportunity for gain or profit. 'Easy pickings.'—**pick a bone** or (*southern U.S.*) **pick a crow.** To quarrel; dispute.—**pick a fight.** To precipitate a fight. —**pick-me-up.** A stimulant or refresher.

pick·a·back. See **piggyback.**

pick·ax, pick·axe *n.* A pick; tool for breaking earth and cutting roots.

pick·er·el (*pik*-er-el) *n.* A freshwater game fish of the pike family.

pick·et *n.* 1. A labor union striker stationed at the place struck. 2. A sharpened stake.—**pick·et** *v.*—**pick·et·er** *n.*

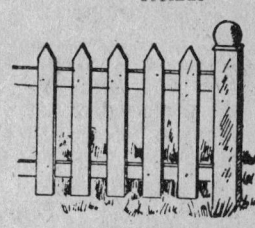
PICKAX

picket fence. Fence of wooden palings.

pick·le *v.* [pick·led; pick·ling] 1. To preserve by sealing in salt brine or vinegar. 2. *Metallurgy.* To place in an acid bath to remove surface impurities. [—**pick·le** *n.* 1. A preserved cucumber or other vegetable. 2. A preservative. 3. *Slang.* Difficulty; trouble.

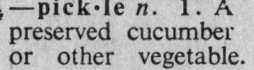
PICKET FENCE

pick·pock·et *n.* One who steals from purses or pockets.

pick·up *n.* 1. *Slang.* Invigoration; renewal of activity. 2. *Slang.* Promiscuous sexual companion. 3. Speed of acceleration, as of an automobile. 4. *Radio.* System for relaying a broadcast to the transmitting station. 5. A phonograph pickup.

pic·nic (*pik*-nik) *n.* An outdoor meal, esp. one eaten in the open country.—*v.* [pic·nicked; pic·nick·ing]—**pic·nic** *adj.*—**pic·nick·er** *n.*

picric acid. An acid used in explosives.

Pict *n.* An ancient Scotch people.—**Pict·ish** *adj.*

pic·to·ri·al *adj.* 1. Of or like pictures. 2. Graphic; vivid.—**pic·to·ri·al·ly** *adv.*

pic·ture (*pik*-cher) *n.* A representation; likeness. —*v.* [pic·tured; pic·tur·ing] 1. To represent pictorially. 2. To bring before the mind's eye.

pic·tur·esque *adj.* Vivid; colorful; attractive. —**pic·tur·esque·ly** *adv.*—**pic·tur·esque·ness** *n.*

pid·dle *v.* [pid·dled; pid·dling] To deal in trifles; dawdle.—**pid·dling** *adj.*

pidgin English. Chinese-English dialect.

pie *n.* 1. A filled pastry crust. 2. *Printing.* Also **pi.** Jumbled or unsorted type.

pie-eyed	piepan	pie-stuffed
pieman	pieprint	pie tin
pie market	pie shop	piewoman

P

pie·bald *adj.* Dappled; splotched; spotted.—*n.* A dappled animal.

pie card. *Slang.* A union official who fails to perform his job. Also **pie card artist.**

piece (*peess*) *n.* 1. Part; fragment. 2. Item 3. An artistic composition. 4. A coin. 5. A firearm.—*v.* [pieced; piec·ing]—**piec·er** *n.*—**piece goods** *n. pl.* Cloth sold by the piece.

piece·meal *adj.* Made of pieces or parts.—*n.* A fragment.—*adv.* Little by little.

piece·work *n.* Work paid by measure of output instead of time.—**piece·work·er** *n.*

pied (*pyde*) *adj.* Spotted; parti-colored.

pied-billed   pied-colored   pied-marked
pied-coated   pied-faced   pied-winged

pie·plant *n. U.S.* Rhubarb.

pier (*peer*) *n.* 1. A dock; breakwater. 2. A pillar; vertical support.

pierce (*peers*) *v.* [pierced; pierc·ing] To penetrate; perforate.—**pierc·er** *n.*—**pierc·ing·ly** *adv.*

pierhead jump. *Nautical Slang.* A job procured on a ship just before she sails.

PIER

pi·e·tis·tic (py-eh-*tiss*-tik) *adj.* 1. Hypocritical; affectedly devout. 2. [*cap.*] Pertaining to the sect of Pietists in 17th-century Germany.—**pi·e·tism** *n.*—**pi·e·tist** *n.*

pi·e·ty (*py*-eh-tee) *n.* Devoutness; reverence.

pie wagon. *Slang.* A police van or wagon.

pi·e·zo·e·lec·tric·i·ty (py-ee-zoh-ih-lek-*triss*-ih-tee) *n.* A current generated by certain crystals when compressed.—**pi·e·zo·e·lec·tric** *adj.*—**pi·e·zo·e·lec·tri·cal·ly** *adv.*

pif·fle *interj.* Nonsense.—**pif·fle** *n.*

pig *n.* 1. A young swine; pork-producing mammal. 2. Oblong mass of unforged metal.—*v.* [pigged; pig·ging]—**pig·ger·y** *n.* [*pl.* pig·ger·ies]—**pig·gy** *adj.* [pig·gi·er; pig·gi·est]—**pig·gie** *adj.*—**pig in a poke.** A blind bargain; unknown quantity.

PIG (1/40 life-size)

pig·boat *n. Nautical Slang.* A submarine.

pi·geon (*pih*-jun) *n.* A dove; a common family of birds eaten as a delicacy.

pigeonberry   pigeon-hearted   pigeontail
pigeon-breasted pigeon-livered   pigeon wing
pigeon express   pigeonman   pigeonwood

pi·geon·hole *n.* A desk compartment for papers.—*v.* [pi·geon·holed; pi·geon·hol·ing].

pi·geon-toed *adj.* Having the toes turned in.

pig·gish *adj.* Slovenly; greedy.—**pig·gish·ly** *adv.*—**pig·gish·ness** *n.*

pig·gy·back *adv.* Also, now less common, **pick·a·back.** On the back or shoulders of another.

pig·head·ed *adj.* Stubborn; obstinate.—**pig·head·ed·ly** *adv.*—**pig·head·ed·ness** *n.*

pig·ment *n.* Coloring matter; paint.—**pig·men·ta·ry** *adj.*—**pig·men·ta·tion** *n.*

pig·my *n.* Also **pyg·my.** 1. [*cap.*] A small-statured people of central Africa. 2. A dwarf.

pig·skin *n.* 1. Leather from the hide of a swine. 2. *Slang.* A football.—**pig·skin** *adj.*

pig·tail *n.* 1. A swine's tail. 2. *Colloquial.* A short tight braid of hair.—**pig·tailed** *adj.*

pike *n.* 1. A sharp-pointed instrument. 2. A road; highway. 3. A ferocious long-headed fresh-water game-fish.

pike-eyed   pikemonger   pikestaff
pikeman   pike-snouted   piketail

pik·er (*pyke*-er) *n. Slang.* 1. A gambler who plays for small stakes. 2. A stingy person.

pi·laf, pi·laff (pih-*lahf*) *Variant spellings* of **pilau.**

pi·las·ter (pih-*lass*-ter) *n.* Pillar adjoining a wall.

pi·lau, pi·law *n.* An oriental dish of spiced rice and meat.

pile *n.* 1. A heap; stack; large quantity. 2. A pointed timber driven into the ground. 3. Nap; woolly fabric surface. 4. *Medical.* A hemorrhoid.—*v.* [piled; pil·ing] 1. To heap. 2. To crowd.—**pil·er** *n.*

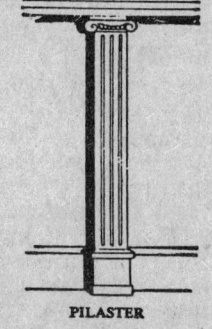
PILASTER

pil·fer *v.* To steal; purloin.—**pil·fer·age** *n.*

pil·grim *n.* A traveler; one who journeys to a holy or venerated place.—**pil·grim·age** *n.*

pill *n.* 1. A medicine tablet. 2. *Slang.* An annoying person.

pil·lage (*pil*-ij) *v.* [pil·laged; pil·lag·ing] To plunder; sack.—**pil·lage** *n.*—**pil·lag·er** *n.*

pil·lar *n.* 1. A column; pier. 2. A stanch supporter.—**pil·lared** *adj.*

pill·box *n.* A small concrete-and-steel fortification. 2. A small brimless hat.

pil·lo·ry (*pil*-er-ee) *n.* [*pl.* pil·lo·ries] A wooden frame formerly used for punishment of minor crimes.—*v.* [pil·lo·ried; pil·lo·ry·ing] 1. To punish. 2. To ridicule; abuse.

pil·low *n.* A cushion; case filled with down to support the head during sleep.—**pil·low** *v.*—**pillow case, pillow slip.** A changeable sack or covering for a pillow.

PILLORY

pi·lot (*py*-lut) *n.* 1. A navigator authorized to bring vessels through a harbor or dangerous waters. 2. A flier of an

airplane.—**pil·ot** v.—**pi·lot·age** n.—**pilot light.**
1. A permanent kindling flame. 2. Small light to indicate operation of a mechanism.

pi·men·to (pih-*men*-toh) n. [pl. pi·men·tos]
1. The Spanish paprika; pimiento. 2. Allspice, a dried unripe fruit used for flavoring.

pi·mi·en·to (pih-*myen*-toh) n. [pl. pi·mi·en·tos] Ripe red fruit of the pepper family, used as a garnish or stuffing of olives.

pimp n. A procurer; pander.—**pimp** v.

pim·per·nel (*pim*-per-nel) n. Family of small red-flowered annual herbs.

pim·ple (*pim*-p'l) n. A small elevated skin blemish or infection.—**pim·pled, pim·ply** adj.

pin n. 1. A pointed metal wire used for fastening. 2. A peg; bolt; retaining key. 3. *Colloquial*. A leg. 4. Badge or piece of jewelry fastened to the clothing.—v. [pinned; pin·ning].—**pin·cush·ion** n. Small stuffed pad for holding pins.—**pin·head** n. A small-headed person. —**pin money.** Spending money.

pin case	pin fold	pinprick
pin-eyed	pin folding	pinrail
pinfeathering	pinhold	pintail
pin fire	pinhole	pin-tailed
pinfish	pin maker	pinwheel
pin flat	pin making	pinworm

PINS

pin·a·fore n. An apron designed like a dress.

pinball machine. A coin-operated gaming device with a spring-driven pin for shooting balls at targets.

pince-nez (*panss*-nay) n. Spectacles worn clipped to the nose.

pin·cers, pinch·ers n. pl. 1. A scissorlike tool for gripping objects. 2. The claws of some of the lower animals.

pinch v. 1. To squeeze hard; nip. 2. To distress; afflict. 3. *Slang*. To arrest. 4. To be sparing or frugal.—**pinch** n.—**pinch·er** n.

pinch bar	pinchcock	pinchgut
pinchbeck	pinchfist	pinchpenny

PINAFORE

pinch-hit v. To substitute for, esp. in an emergency.—**pinch hitter** n.

pin·der n. *Southern U.S.* Peanut.

pin·dling adj. *Colloquial*. Sickly; slight.

pine n. 1. A family of conebearing evergreen trees. 2. The wood of this tree.

pine bearing	pine-covered	pineland
pine-bordered	pine-crested	pinesap
pine-built	pine-crowned	pine-shaded
pine-capped	pine-dotted	pinewood
pine-clad	pine-fringed	pine woods

pine v. [pined; pin·ing] To languish; yearn.

pineal gland. Body of unknown function at the base of the brain.

pine·ap·ple (*pyne*-ap-p'l) n. 1. Large, juicy, semitropical fruit. 2. *Slang*. A bomb.

piney woods. *Southern U.S.* A pine forest.

pin·feath·er (*pin*-feth-er) n. A small feather.—**pin-feath·ered** adj.

Ping-pong n. Trade name for table tennis.

pin·ion (*pin*-yun) n. 1. The smaller of two meshing gears. 2. A wing.—v. To bind; fetter; tie arms.

PINEAPPLE

pink n. 1. A family of flowers related to the carnation. 2. A pale red color. 3. Perfection. 'The pink of condition.' 4. *Colloquial*. A person of leftish political tendencies.—**pink** adj.—**pink·ish** adj.

pink v. 1. To scallop a border with an ornamental pattern. 2. To wound; pierce.

pink·eye n. A contagious inflammation of the membranes of the eye.

pin·na·cle (*pin*-uh-k'l) n. 1. A spine; peak. 2. Zenith; culmiration.

pin·nate (*pin*-ayt) n. Formed like a feather. —**pin·nate·ly** adv.—**pin·na·tion** n.

pi·noch·le, pi·noc·le (*pee*-nuk-'l) n. A card game played with a special 48-card deck.

pi·ñon (*peen*-yohn, *pin*-yun) n. Small pine of western U.S. bearing edible seeds.

pint (*pynte*) n. Unit of measure of 34.66 cubic inches; ½ quart.

pin·tle n. *Nautical*. The pin to which a rudder is hinged.

pin·to adj. Dappled; pied; varicolored.—n. An animal, esp. a horse, of motley coat.

pin-up n. *Slang*. A picture of a woman, pinned or hung up for admiration.—adj. Attractive. 'A pin-up girl.'

pin·y (*pyne*-ee) adj. [pin·ier; pin·i·est] 1. Resembling pine wood or trees. 2. Thickly grown with pines.

pi·o·neer (py-uh-*neer*) n. Trail blazer; one who leads the way. 2. Settler; colonist. 3. *Military*. Member of an advanced engineering unit.

pi·ous (*py*-us) adj. Reverent; devout; religious. —**pi·ous·ly** adv.—**pi·ous·ness** n.

pip n. 1. A small seed. 2. *Colloquial*. A mild illness.

pipe n. 1. A tubular musical wind instrument. 2. A tube for conveying fluids. 3. A tube with a bowl for smoking tobacco. 4. A shrill call or sound. 5. *Nautical*. A boatswain's whistle. 6. A large container for wine.—v. [piped; pip·ing] 1. To play a pipe. 2. To sing or whistle shrilly. 3. To convey through

P

pipes.   4. To order with a boatswain's pipe. 5. To apply piping.—**pip·er** *n.*

> pipe clay   pipe lining   pipe-shaped
> pipeline (*n.*)   pipe-necked   pipestem

pip·ing (*pype*-ing) *n.*   1. A shrill sound. 2. A system of ducts or tubes. 3. *Sewing.* A rolled or folded trimming applied to seams.—*adj.* Shrill; highpitched.—*adv.* Sizzling; boiling.

pip·kin *n.* An earthen pot glazed on the inside.

pip·pin *n.* A variety of apple.

pip·squeak (*pip*-skweek) *n. Colloquial.* An insignificant person.—**pip·squeak** *adj.*

pip·y (*pype*-ee) *adj.*   1. Tubular; hollow-stemmed. 2. Shrill.

pi·quant (*pee*-kunt) *adj.*   1. Tart; sharp; pungent. 2. Provocative; arch.—**pi·quan·cy** *n.*

pique (*peek*) *n.* Slight anger; hurt pride; resentment.—*v.* [piqued; piqu·ing]

pi·qué (pee-*kay*) *n.* A ribbed cotton cloth.

pi·ra·cy (*py*-ruh-see) *n.* [*pl.* -cies] 1. Robbery on the high seas. 2. Any infringement on a copyright or patent.

pi·rate (*py*-rit) *n.*   1. A sea-robber or his ship. 2. Violator of a copyright.—*v.* [pi·rat·ed; pi·rat·ing].—**pi·rat·ic, -i·cal** *adj.*— **-cal·ly** *adv.*

pi·rogue (pih-*rohg*) *n.* A dugout; canoe made of a single timber.

pir·ou·ette (pih-roo-*et*) *n. Dancing.* Rapid whirl on the toes.—*v.* [pir·ou·et·ted; pir·ou·et·ting].

pis·ca·to·ry (*piss*-kuh-tor-ee) *adj.* Also **pis·ca·to·ri·al.** Pertaining to fishing.— **-al·ly** *adv.*

pis·mire (*piss*-myre) *n.* An ant.

pis·ta·chi·o (piss-*tah*-shee-oh, -*tash*-oh) *n.* Also **pis·tache.** A small tree growing in Asia Minor and southern Europe and producing a green-kerneled, pleasant-tasting nut.—*adj.* Flavored with pistachio nuts.

PISTIL

pis·til (*piss*-til, -t'l) *n.* The seed-bearing organ of a flower.—**pis·til·late** *adj.*

pis·tol (*piss*-t'l) *n.* Small fire-arm designed to be shot with one hand; revolver.

pis·tole (piss-*tohl*) *n.* An old European coin worth about $4.

PISTOL

pis·ton (*piss*-tun) *n. Mechanics.* Sliding disk in a cylinder driven by or against pressure in the chamber.

piston ring. A band insuring the snug fit of a piston in a cylinder.

piston rod. The shaft to which the piston delivers its force.

pit *n.*   1. A hollow in the earth. 2. A depression in the flesh. 3. Seating area in a theater behind the orchestra, on the main floor. 4. The stone of a fruit.—*v.* [pit·ted; pit·ting] 1. To make indentations. 2. To

PISTON

set in competition or combat.   3. To remove the stone from a fruit.

pitch *n.* Black, gummy substance derived from the distillation of tar.

pitch *v.*   1. To throw; hurl. 2. To set up or raise. 'To pitch a tent.' 3. *Music.* To set the tone. 4. To fall; plunge. 5. *Nautical.* To rise and fall longitudinally.—**pitch·er** *n.* —**pitch** *n.*—**pitch in.** To help.

pitch·blende *n.* A valuable ore containing uranium, rare earths, and radioactive substances.

pitch·er *n.* A vessel with a handle and spout for fluids.—**pitcher plant.** A family of plants with flask-shaped leaves which trap insects.

pitch·er *n. Baseball.* The player who hurls the ball to the batter.

pitch·fork *n.* Farming implement used for moving hay.—**pitch·fork** *v.*

pitch·man *n.* A hawker, esp. a side-walk salesman.

pitch·y *adj.*   1. Resembling pitch. 2. Black; dismal.—**pitch·i·ness** *n.*

pit·e·ous (*pit*-ee-us) *adj.* Pitiful; pathetic.—**pit·e·ous·ly** *adv.*—**pit·e·ous·ness** *n.*

pit·fall (*pit*-fawl) *n.*   1. An excavation concealed to trap animals. 2. A snare; menace.

pith *n.*   1. The paperlike center of certain plant stalks. 2. Care; quintessence. 3. Energy; force. —**pith·y** *adj.* [pith·i·er; pith·i·est] —**pith·i·ly** *adv.*—**pith·i·ness** *n.*

pith·e·can·thro·pus (pith-eh-kan-*throh*-pus) *n.* Java man; an extinct form of man similar to the anthropoid ape.

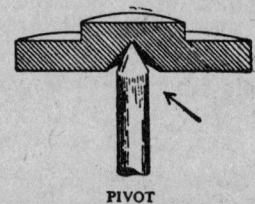

PITCHFORK

pit·i·a·ble (*pit*-ee-uh-b'l) *adj.*   1. Piteous; pathetic. 2. Sorry; despicable.—**pit·i·a·ble·ness** *n.*—**pit·i·a·bly** *adv.*

pit·i·less *adj.* Hard-hearted; cruel; unrelenting. —**pit·i·less·ly** *adv.*—**pit·i·less·ness** *n.*

pit·tance *n.* A small portion; meager allotment.

pit·ter-pat·ter *n.* Successive quick light beats.

pit·ty-pat *adv.* Fluttering; beating quickly.

pi·tu·i·ta·ry (pih-*tyoo*-ih-ter-ee) *n.* [*pl.* -ries] A gland near the brain, influencing growth.

pit·y (*pit*-ee) *n.* [*pl.* pit·ies] 1. Compassion; commiseration. 2. An unfortunate happening.—*v.* [pit·ied; pit·y·ing].—**pit·y·ing·ly** *adv.*

piv·ot (*piv*-ut) *n.*   1. Axis; swivel. 2. Swift turn.—**piv·ot** *v.* —**piv·ot·al** *adj.*—**piv·ot·al·ly** *adv.*

pix·y, pix·ie *n.* [*pl.* pix·ies] An elf; fairy.

piz·zi·ca·to (pit-seh-*kah*-toh) *adj. Music.* Direction to pluck the strings instead of to play by bow.—**piz·zi·ca·to** *n.* [*pl.* -ti].

PIVOT

pla·ca·ble (*play*-kuh-b'l) *adj.* Appeasable; willing to forgive.—**pla·ca·bil·i·ty** n.—**pla·ca·ble·ness** n.—**pla·ca·bly** adv.

plac·ard (*plak*-'rd) n. A handbill or poster.—**pla·card** v.—**pla·card·er** n.

pla·cate (*play*-kayt) v. [pla·cat·ed; pla·cat·ing] To appease; pacify; conciliate.—**pla·cat·er** n.—**pla·ca·tion** n.—**pla·ca·tive, pla·ca·to·ry** adj.

place (*playss*) v. [placed; plac·ing] 1. To put; establish. 2. To file; register. 3. To recollect; identify. 4. To secure a job for. 5. *Horse racing*. To come in second.—n. 1. Spot; location; area. 2. An allotted position. 3. Station in life; office. 4. Building having a special function. 5. A one-block street.—**place·ment** n.—**place kick**. *Football*. Kicking a carefully held ball from a point near the goal posts.

pla·ce·bo (pluh-*see*-boh) 1. First antiphon of the Roman Catholic vespers for the dead. 2. *Medicine*. A neutral medicine administered for its moral effect. 3. A placating action.

pla·cen·ta (pluh-*sen*-tuh) n. In most mammals, communicating organ between the fetus and the mother, providing respiration and nutrition.—**pla·cen·tal, pla·cen·tar·y** adj.

plac·er n. Gravelly land containing valuable mineral deposits.—**plac·er** adj.

plac·id (*plass*-id) n. Serene; undisturbed; quiet.—**plac·id·ly** adv.—**plac·id·ness** n.—**pla·cid·i·ty** n.

pla·gi·a·rize (*play*-juh-ryze) v. [pla·gi·a·rized; pla·gi·a·riz·ing] To steal from the writings of another.—**pla·gi·a·riz·er** n.—**plag·i·a·rism** n.—**plag·i·a·rist** n.—**plag·i·a·rist·ic** adj.

plague (*playg*) v. [plagued; plagu·ing] 1. To vex; trouble. 2. To afflict; visit with calamity.—**plague** n. 1. Disaster; vexation. 2. Epidemic. 3. Pest; nuisance. **plagu·er** n.—**pla·guy** n.—**pla·gui·ly** adv.

plaid (*plad*) n. Woolen cloth, cross-barred in different colors.—**plaid, plaid·ed** adj.

plain adj. 1. Simple; unadorned. 2. Clear; obvious. 3. Without beauty; homely. 4. Frank; sincere.—**plain, plain·ly** adv.—**plain·ness** n.

PLAID

plainback	plain-featured	plain-pranked
plain-bodied	plain-garbed	plain-soled
plain-bred	plain-headed	plain speaking
plain-clothed	plain-hearted	plain-spoken
plain-edged	plain looking	plain-spokenness
plain-faced	plain-mannered	plaintail

plain (*playn*) n. A flat stretch of land.

plain-clothes·man n. A detective.

plaint n. 1. A sad song; lamentation. 2. A complaint.

plain·tiff (*playn*-tif) n. One who takes a dispute to court; initiator of a lawsuit.

plain·tive (*playn*-tiv) adj. Mournful; sad.—**plain·tive·ly** adv.—**plain·tive·ness** n.

plait (*playt*) n. 1. A braid. 2. A pleat; pressed fold.—**plait** v.

plan n. 1. A scheme; project. 2. Diagram, blueprint.—v. [planned; -ning]—**plan·ner** n.

plane adj. Level; flat.—n. 1. A two-dimensional surface. 2. Level; scale. 3. Tool used to smooth a surface.—v. [planed; plan·ing]—**plan·er** n. 1. One who planes. 2. A large cutting machine for smoothing or squaring metals.

PLANE

plane n. Short for **air·plane.**—**plane** adj.

plane n. Also **plane tree**. Ornamental shade tree having large leaves and mottled bark.

plan·et (*plan*-et) n. A celestial body which revolves around a star; one of the nine celestial bodies of our solar system.—**plan·e·tar·y** adj.

plan·e·tar·i·um (plan-eh-*tayr*-ee-um) n. [pl. -i·ums, -i·a] 1. Mobile model of the heavens. 2. Building in which celestial movements are represented.

plan·gent (*plan*-jent) adj. Making a deep, echoing noise.—**plan·gent·ly** adv.

plan·ish v. 1. To toughen and dent metal ornamentally by blows of a hammer. 2. To polish.—**plan·ish·er** n.

plank n. 1. A broad piece of sawed timber; slab. 2. A principle in a political platform.

plant n. 1. A living organism without power of movement or sensation. 2. A young tree or bush. 3. A factory. 4. *Slang*. Prearranged deceptive evidence.—v. 1. To set in the earth. 2. To set down firmly; fix; establish. 3. To place deceptive or incriminating evidence.—**plant·er** n.

plan·tain (*plan*-tin) n. 1. Family of weeds with large leaves and inconspicuous flowers. 2. Tropical tree of the banana family.

plan·ta·tion (plan-*tay*-shun) n. A large tropical or semitropical agricultural estate.

plaque (*plak*) n. A commemorative tablet; ornamental plate.

plas·ma (*plaz*-muh) n. The fluid component of the blood.—**plas·mat·ic, plas·mic** adj.

plas·ter n. 1. A lime-and-sand mortar used for finishing walls. 2. A medicated adhesive pad to be applied to the skin.—**plas·ter** v.—**plas·tered** adj. 1. Smeared; bedaubed. 2. *Slang*. Intoxicated.—**plas·ter·er** n.

plaster cast. 1. Reproduction made of plaster of Paris. 2. A rigid surgical bandage.

plaster of Paris. A gypsum composition which hardens when mixed with water.

plas·tic adj. 1. Pliable; malleable. 2. Sculptural; three-dimensional.—**plas·tic** n.—**plas·ti·cal·ly** adv.—**plas·tic·i·ty** n.

plas·tic n. Any of various synthetic materials chemically created from organic substances.

plastic surgery. Science of restoring or altering human tissue by grafting.

P

plate 442 **pliable**

plate *n.* 1. Round shallow vessel for food. 2. Sheet of material uniform in thickness. 3. Original etching block; print; illustration. 4. Gold or silver utensils; flatware. 5. *Baseball.* Home base. 6. *Printing.* A page of electrotype or stereotype.—*v.* [plat·ed; plat·ing] To electroplate; overlay with a thin coating. —**plat·ing** *n.* 1. Art of electroplating. 2. The metallic overlay deposited.—**plat·er** *n.*—**plate·ful** *n.* [*pl.* plate·fuls].—**plate glass.** A thick pane of glass, used for mirrors, windows, etc.

plate carrier	plate layer	plate-rolled
plate-glazed	platemaking	plateway
plate holder	plateman	plate work
plate-encased	plate-roll	plate worker

pla·teau (plat-*toh*) *n.* A tableland; elevated plain.

plat·en (*plat*-'n) *n. Printing.* The part of a press which takes the impression from the form.

plat·form *n.* 1. A flat, raised structure; stage. 2. A body of principles adopted by a group, esp. a political party.

plat·i·num (*plat*-ih-num) *n.* A white, soft precious metal. (*Symbol:* Pl).—**plat·i·num, pla·tin·ic** *adj.*—**plat·i·nize** *v.* [-nized; -niz·ing].

plat·i·tude (*plat*-ih-tyood) *n.* A trite observation; truism.—**plat·i·tud·di·nous** *adj.*—**plat·i·tu·di·nize** *v.* [plat·i·tu·di·nized; plat·i·tu·di·niz·ing].

Pla·ton·ic (pluh-*ton*-ik) *adj.* Also **Pla·ton·i·cal.** 1. Relating to the philosophy of Plato, ancient Athenian idealist. 2. Not sensual or sexual; based upon ideals. 'Platonic love.'

pla·toon (pluh-*toon*) *n.* A detachment of troops, forming part of a company.

plat·ter *n.* 1. A large serving plate. 2. *Slang.* A phonograph record.

plat·y·pus (*plat*-ih-pus) *n.* An egg-laying Australian mammal which suckles its young.

plau·dit (*plaw*-dit) *n.* [*usually pl.*] Applause; praise.

plau·si·ble (*plaw*-zih-b'l) *adj.* Believable.—**plau·si·bil·i·ty** *n.*—**plau·si·ble·ness** *n.*— -**si·bly** *adv.*

play *v.* 1. To amuse oneself; sport. 2. To trifle; toy. 3. To perform upon a musical instrument. 4. To act in a stage production; be staged. 5. To take part in a game. 6. To focus upon; aim at.—**play** *n.*—**play·a·ble** *adj.* —**play off.** To decide a contest.—**play on words.** Pun.—**play out.** To exhaust; become tired out.

play-act (*v.*)	playfellow	play-off
play actor	playfolk	play reader
play-back (*n.*)	playgoer	playroom
play bill	playgoing	play script
play box	playground	plaything
play broker	play maker	playtime
playcraftsman	playmate	play writer

play·boy *n.* Man devoted to expensive dissipation in public.

play·er *n.* 1. A gamester; sportsman. 2. Performer on a musical instrument. 3. Actor.

player piano. Automatic piano which produces music from a perforated paper roll.

play·ful *adj.* Frolicsome; sportive.—**play·ful·ly** *adv.*—**play·ful·ness** *n.*

play·house *n.* 1. A theater. 2. A house for children to play in.

playing card. One of a deck of pasteboard cards used in games of skill or chance.

play·wright *n.* A dramatist; composer of plays. —**play·wright·ing, play·writ·ing** *n.*

pla·za (*plah*-zuh) *n.* An open square in a city.

plea (*plee*) *n.* 1. An urgent entreaty or request. 2. *Law.* a. The defendant's answer to the plaintiff. b. A suit or action.

plead (*pleed*) *v.* 1. To beseech; beg. 2. *Law.* a. To argue in court. b. To allege.—**plead·a·ble** *adj.*—**plead·er** *n.*—**plead·ing** *n.*— -**ing·ly** *adv.*

pleas·ant (*plez*-ant) *n.* 1. Agreeable; gratifying. 2. Cheerful; jocular.—**pleas·ant·ly** *adv.*

pleas·ant·ry (*plez*-ant-ree) *n.* [*pl.* pleas·ant·ries] A jest; lively talk.

please (*pleez*) *v.* [pleased; pleas·ing] To gratify; delight; satisfy.—**pleas·ing·ly** *adv.*

pleas·ur·a·ble (*plezh*-er-uh-b'l) *adj.* Agreeable; gratifying.— -**ble·ness** *n.*— -**ur·a·bly** *adv.*

pleas·ure (*plezh*-er) *n.* 1. Gratification; enjoyment. 2. Will; choice; desire.—*v. Southern U.S.* To give pleasure to; indulge in pleasure.

pleasure-bent	pleasureman	pleasure-tired
pleasure-bound	pleasuremonger	pleasure-wasted
pleasure-greedy	pleasure-tempted	pleasure-weary

pleat *n.* A tuck; sewed-in fold.—**pleat** *v.*

ple·be·ian (pleh-*bee*-un) *adj.* Common; popular; vulgar.—**ple·be·ian** *n.*—**ple·be·ian·ism** *n.*

pleb·i·scite (*pleb*-ih-syte) *n.* A universal vote on a specific question.

plec·trum (*plek*-trum) *n.* A pick for plucking stringed instruments.

pledge *v.* [pledged; pledg·ing] 1. To guarantee; promise. 2. To deposit as security. 3. To drink a toast.—**pledge** *n.*—**pledg·er** *n.*

ple·ia·des (*plee*-yuh-deez) *n. pl.* Also **ple·iad.** A seven-star cluster in the constellation Taurus.

ple·na·ry (*plee*-nuh-ree, *plen*-) *adj.* 1. Full; complete. 2. Fully attended.— -**na·ri·ly** *adv.*

plen·i·po·ten·ti·ar·y (plen-ih-poh-*ten*-shee-er-ee) *n.* A representative invested with full powers, esp. an ambassador to a foreign nation. —**plen·i·po·ten·ti·ar·y** *adj.*

plen·i·tude (*plen*-ih-tyood, -tood) *n.* Plenty; abundance; fullness.

plen·te·ous (*plen*-tee-us) *adj.* Abundant; ample; full.—**plen·te·ous·ly** *adv.*—**plen·te·ous·ness** *n.*

plen·ti·ful (*plen*-tih-ful) *adj.* Copious; abundant.—**plen·ti·ful·ly** *adv.*—**plen·ti·ful·ness** *n.*

plen·ty *n.* Abundance; copiousness.—*adv. Colloquial.* Very. 'It's plenty good.'—**plen·ty** *adj.*

pleth·o·ra (*pleth*-uh-ruh) *n.* 1. An overabundance. 2. *Medicine.* Congestion or oversupply of blood in the body.—**ple·thor·ic** *adj.*

pleu·ra (*ploor*-uh) *n.* [*pl.* -ae] Thin membrane covering the inside of the chest.—**pleu·ral** *adj.*

pleu·ri·sy (*ploor*-ih-see) *n.* Inflammation of the pleura.—**pleu·rit·ic** *adj.*

plex·us (*plek*-sus) *n.* [*pl.* plex·us·es, plex·us] *Anatomy.* Network of nerves, vessels, or fibers.

pli·a·ble (*ply*-uh-b'l) *adj.* 1. Plastic; flexible.

2. Compliant; easily persuaded.—**pli·a·bil·i·ty** *n.*—**pli·a·ble·ness** *n.*—**pli·a·bly** *adv.*

pli·ant (*ply*-ant) *adj.* 1. Flexible; limber. 2. Yielding; docile. 3. Adaptable.—**pli·an·cy** *n.*—**pli·ant·ly** *adv.*—**pli·ant·ness** *n.*

pli·ers (*ply*-erz) *n. pl.* Small long-jawed pinchers.

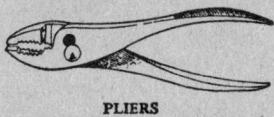

PLIERS

plight (*plyte*) *n.* Predicament; quandary.

plight *v.* To pledge; promise.

Plim·soll, Plimsoll mark. *Nautical.* Mark on a ship's side indicating maximum legal draft.

plinth *n. Architecture.* Square base of a column.

plod *v.* [plod·ded; plod·ding] 1. To trudge. 2. To walk laboriously.—**plod·der** *n.*—**plod·ding·ly** *adv.*

plot *v.* [plot·ted; plot·ting] 1. To diagram; represent graphically. 2. To conspire; intrigue.—*n.* 1. A defined tract of land. 2. A scheme; conspiracy. 3. The story or narrative thread of a play, novel, or the like.—**plot·tage** *n.*—**plot·ter** *n.*

plough *v.* Plow.

plov·er (*pluh*-ver) *n.* A short-billed meadow and marsh bird related to the sandpiper.

PLOVER (1/9 life-size)

plow, plough *v.* 1. To turn the earth for tilling. 2. To make furrows in. 3. To advance laboriously.—*n.* Bladed implement for turning the soil.—**plow·er, plough·er** *n.*

PLOW

plow·share, plough·share *n.* The metal point or cutting edge of a plow.

pluck *v.* 1. To pull; tug. 2. To pick, as fruit. 3. To jerk; twang, as a string. 4. *Slang.* To rob; fleece.—**pluck·er** *n.*

pluck *n.* Courage; spirit; resolution.—**pluck·y** *adj.* [pluck·i·er; pluck·i·est] Brave; determined.—**pluck·i·ly** *adv.*—**pluck·i·ness** *n.*

plug *n.* 1. A stopper for a hole. 2. A cake of tobacco. 3. *Slang.* **a.** A statement of praise. **b.** A decrepit horse.—*v.* [plugged; plug·ging] 1. To stop up. 2. *Slang.* To advertise repetitiously. 3. *Slang.* To kill or wound with a gun. 4. To plod; drudge.

plug·ger *n.* 1. Plodder. 2. *Radio Slang.* Announcer who reads commercials.

plug hat. *Slang.* Hat with a tall, round crown; top hat.

plug-ugly *n. Slang.* A tough; criminal; thug.

plum *n.* 1. The fleshy fruit of a small tree of the peach family. 2. A choice article.

plum·age (*ploom*-ij) *n.* Feathers of a bird.

plumb (*plum*) *n.* A weight hung on a line to determine vertical direction, or depth.—*adj.* 1. Vertical. 2. *Colloquial.* Downright; complete.—**plumb** *adv.*—*v.* 1. To fathom; determine depth. 2. To make perpendicular.

plumb·er (*plum*-er) *n.* One who installs and repairs piping systems.

plumb·ing (*plum*-ing) *n.* System of gas and water fixtures in a building.—**plumb·ing** *adj.*

plume (*ploom*) *n.* A feather or tuft of feathers.—*v.* [plumed; plum·ing] To preen; pride.

PLUME

plume-crowned	plume-fronted	plume making
plume-decked	plumelike	plume-plucked
plume-embroidered	plume maker	plume-stripped

plum·met (*plum*-et) *n.* A plumb; leaded line for measuring.—*v.* To fall or plunge swiftly.

plum·my *adj.* 1. Rich in plums. 2. *Slang.* Profitable; desirable.

plump *adj.* Fleshy; buxom; chubby.—*v.* To fall heavily and suddenly.—**plump·ly** *adv.*—**plump·ness** *n.*

plum·y (*ploom*-ee) *adj.* Feathery; covered with plumes.

plun·der *v.* To rob; loot.

plunge (*plunj*) *v.* [plunged; plung·ing] 1. To dive; thrust; immerse. 2. To rush into a dangerous situation. 3. *Colloquial.* To gamble in stocks or speculative ventures.—**plunge** *n.*

plu·per·fect (ploo-*per*-fekt) *n. Grammar.* Tense of the verb formed by *had* and a past participle to express completed action.—**plu·per·fect** *adj.*

plu·ral (*ploor*-al) *adj. Grammar.* Denoting more than one.—**plu·ral** *n.*—**plu·ral·ize** *v.* [-ized; -iz·ing].—**plu·ral·ly** *adv.*

plu·ral·i·ty (ploo-*ral*-ih-tee) *n.* [*pl.* -ities] 1. Numerousness. 2. The majority. 3. Number by which a candidate's votes exceed those of the runner-up.

plus *n.* The sign (+) indicating addition.—*adj.* More; increased; positive.—*prep.* And; in addition to.

plush *n.* Heavy fabric with a deep velvet nap.—**plush·y**—*adj.* [plush·i·er; plush·i·est] Rich.

Plu·to (*ploo*-toh) *n.* 1. *Greek Mythology.* God of the underworld. 2. The farthest planet of the solar system.—**Plu·to·ni·an** *adj.*

plu·toc·ra·cy (ploo-*tok*-ruh-see) *n.* [*pl.* -ra·cies] Government by a wealthy minority.

plu·to·crat (*ploo*-tuh-krat) *n.* Possessor of great wealth.—**Plu·to·crat·ic, plu·to·crat·i·cal** *adj.*

plu·to·ni·um (ploo-*toh*-nee-um) *n.* A heavy, radioactive element formed from uranium and employed in the release of atomic energy. (*Symbol:* Pu).

plu·vi·al (*ploo*-vee-al) *adj.* Also **plu·vi·ous.** Pertaining to rain; rainy.

P

ply v. [plied; ply·ing] 1. To work basely at; wield. 2. To supply continually; shower. 3. To go regularly back and forth upon.—n. [pl. plies] 1. A twist; cord; bias; thickness. 'Three-ply carpet.'—ply·er n.

Plymouth Rock. A variety of fowl.

ply·wood n. A sturdy sheet wood made of several thin layers pressed together.

pneu·mat·ic (nyoo-mat-ik, noo-) adj. Pertaining to air or air pressure.—pneu·mat·i·cal·ly adv.

pneu·mo·ba·cil·lus (nyoo-moh-buh-sil-us) n. A bacterium present in respiratory inflammations.

pneu·mo·ni·a (nyoo-moh-nee-uh, noo-mohn-yuh) n. Acute inflammation of the lungs. —pneu·mon·ic adj.

poach v. 1. To cook (an egg) by dropping contents of the shell into hot water. 2. To rob of game.—poach·er n.

pock n. A skin pustule caused by an eruptive disease.—pock·y adj. [pock·i·er; pock·i·est].

pock·et n. 1. A pouch sewed into a garment. 2. Pool. Small net to receive the balls. 3. Small rock cavity containing a deposit of ore.—pock·et v.

pocket battleship. Small heavily armed warship developed by Germany for World War II.

poc·ket·book n. A purse; wallet.

pock·et·knife n. [pl. pock·et·knives] A jackknife; penknife.

pocket veto. Power of the President of the U.S. to prevent passage of a bill by failure to sign it within the ten days before the end of a session of Congress.—pocket-veto v.

pock·mark n. A skin blemish from smallpox.

pod n. A seed-bearing vessel of certain plants. —v. [pod·ded; pod·ding] 1. To produce pods; become distended. 2. To hull.

podg·y adj. Dumpy; pudgy.—podg·i·ness n.

po·di·a·try (puh-dy-uh-tree) n. Branch of medicine dealing with foot ailments.— -a·trist n.

po·di·um n. [pl. po·di·a] Small platform on which an orchestra conductor stands.

po·em n. A composition in verse.

po·et n. A composer of poetry.—po·et·ess n.

poet laureate. Official poet of England.

po·et·as·ter n. A rhymester; versifier.

po·et·ic adj. Also po·et·i·cal. 1. Pertaining to poetry. 2. Lyrical; idyllic.—po·et·i·cal·ly adv. —po·et·ics n. sing. The theory of poetry.—po·et·ize v. [po·et·ized; -iz·ing].—po·et·iz·er n.

po·et·ry n. [pl. po·et·ries] Rhythmic language stimulating to the imagination.

po·go stick. A single jumping stilt with a spring base and two foot-brackets.

po·grom (pog-rum) n. Organized slaughter of a racial or religious minority group.

po·gy (poh-gee) n. [pl. po·gies] A flounderlike fish.

poign·ant (poyn-yunt) adj. 1. Affecting; moving; pathetic. 2. Pungent; keen.—poign·an·cy n.—poign·ant·ly adv.

poi·lu (pwah-loo) n. A French army private.

poin·set·ti·a (poyn-set-ee-uh) n. Tall tropical plant having red, flower-like leaves, commonly used as a Christmas pot plant.

POINSETTIA

point n. 1. Sharp top; tapering end. 2. Stem; section. 3. A stage; step. 4. A period or decimal point [.]. 5. Navigation. A division of the compass card. 6. A spot occupying position without area. 7. A thought; observation. 8. A characteristic; trait. 9. Purpose; climax; meaning. 10. Moment; juncture. 11. Printing. Measurement of type size: $\frac{1}{72}$ of an inch. 12. A unit in a score; tally. 13. Needleworked lace. 14. Education. A credit.—v. 1. To sharpen an end. 2. To indicate; aim. 3. To make more forceful or meaningful. 4. To replace old mortar between bricks.

point-blank adj. Direct; frank; outright.

point·ed adj. 1. Sharp. 2. Expressly aimed. 'A pointed remark.'—point·ed·ly adv.—point·ed·ness n.

point·er n. 1. Rod used to indicate or point out. 2. A dog closely related to the foxhound, used in game hunting. 3. Advice; tip.

POINTER (1/40 life-size)

point·less adj. Without meaning; futile; silly. —point·less·ly adv.—point·less·ness n.

poise (poyz) n. 1. Composure; self-confidence. 2. Balance; equilibrium. 3. Posture; carriage.—v. [poised; pois·ing] To balance.

poi·son n. An agent harmful to living organisms.—poi·son v. —poi·son·er n.— poi·son·ous adj.— poi·son·ous·ly adv. —poi·son·ous·ness n.

poison ivy. A plant with shiny green leaves which causes a skin rash upon contact with the human body.

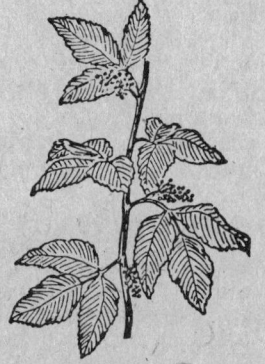
POISON IVY

poke v. [poked; pok·ing] 1. To prod; give a push. 2. To investigate; pry. 3. To dawdle.—n. A thrust.—poke fun. To make sport of; ridicule.

pok·er (poh-ker) n. A rod, usually metal, for stirring up fires.

pok·er *n.* A popular card game usually played for stakes.

poke bonnet. Woman's bonnet having a wide projecting brim.

poke·weed *n.* Common Western Hemisphere plant bearing poisonous berries and purplish flowers.

pok·y, poke·y *adj.* [pok·i·er; pok·i·est] 1. Small; poor. 2. Uninteresting; wearisome.

POKE BONNET

po·lar (*poh*-ler) *adj.* 1. Pertaining to the regions of the North and South Pole. 2. Pertaining to the centers of magnetism, or poles, of a magnetized body. 3. Cold; frigid.

po·lar bear. Ferocious white bear inhabiting the Arctic regions.

po·lar·im·e·ter (poh-ler-*im*-eh-ter) *n.* Instrument demonstrating or measuring light polarization.

Po·la·ris (pohlay-riss) *n. Astronomy.* The North Star.

POLAR BEAR (1/90 life-size)

po·lar·i·ty (poh-*lair*-ih-tee) *n.* The opposing forces or charges at opposite ends of electromagnetic substances.

po·lar·i·za·tion (poh-ler-ih-*zay*-shun) *n.* 1. *Optics.* Alteration of light rays so that their vibrations form a definite pattern. 2. *Electricity.* Formation of gas bubbles on the plates of a storage battery, reducing efficiency. 3. *Electromagnetism.* Realignment of molecules in a substance creating magnetic polarity.—**po·lar·ize** *v.* [po·lar·ized; -iz·ing]—**po·lar·iz·a·ble** *adj.* —**po·lar·iz·er** *n.*

Po·lar·oid (*poh*-ler-oyd) *n.* Trade name for a glass which reduces glare by polarizing light.

pole *n.* Long slender wooden rod or shaft. —*v.* [poled; pol·ing] 1. To push with a pole. 2. To support with poles. 3. [*cap.*] A native of Poland.—**pol·er** *n.*

pole *n.* 1. One of the extremities of the earth's axis. 2. One of the points on a body where its electromagnetic force is concentrated.

pole·cat *n.* A long-bodied, short-legged animal, similar to the weasel.

po·lem·ics (puh-*lem*-iks) *n. sing.* Art or practice of controversy, esp. theological.—**po·lem·ic, po·lem·i·cist, po·lem·ist** *n.* A disputer.—**polem·ic** *adj.*—**po·lem·i·cal·ly** *adv.*

pole·star *n.* 1. Polaris; the North Star. 2. A guide.

pole-vault *v. Sports.* To leap over a high bar with the aid of a pole.—**pole-vault** *n.*

po·lice (puh-*leess*) *n.* Government department in charge of maintaining order, enforcing laws, and prosecuting crime.—*v.* [po·liced; po·lic·ing].—**po·lice** *adj.*—**po·lice·man** *n.*

police dog. 1. A dog trained to assist the police. 2. A large dog of the wolfhound family, esp. the German shepherd.

pol·i·clin·ic (pol-ih-*klin*-ik) *n.* Dispensary of a hospital treating outpatients.

pol·i·cy (*pol*-ih-see) *n.* [*pl.* pol·i·cies] 1. Course; principles determining action. 2. Practical procedure; wise management.

pol·i·cy *n.* [*pl.* pol·i·cies] An insurance contract. —**pol·i·cy·hold·er** *n.*

policy racket. *Slang.* Illegal gambling based on a numbers pool.

pol·i·o·my·e·li·tis (pol-ee-oh-my-eh-*ly*-tiss) *n. Medicine.* Infantile paralysis.

pol·ish *v.* 1. To make glossy by rubbing. 2. To refine; groom.—*n.* 1. Luster; sheen. 2. Commercial product for shining a surface. 3. Refinement of manners.—**pol·ished** *adj.*

Pol·ish (*pohl*-ish) *adj.* Pertaining to Poland or its people.—*n.* The language of Poland.

po·lite (puh-*lyte*) *adj.* Courteous; well mannered; civil.— **po·lite·ly** *adv.*—**po·lite·ness** *n.*

pol·i·tic (*pol*-ih-tik) *adj.* 1. Pertaining to government. 2. Expedient; practical. 3. Diplomatic; discreet.

po·lit·i·cal (puh-*lit*-ih-k'l) *adj.* Pertaining to theory or management of government.—**po·lit·i·cal·ly** *adv.*

pol·i·ti·cian (pol-ih-*tish*-'n) *n.* 1. One skilled in the science of government. 2. One active in political parties; office seeker; one adept in gaining favor.

pol·i·tics *n.* 1. The theory and practice of government. 2. Social conniving for personal gain.

pol·i·ty (*pol*-ih-tee) *n.* [*pl.* pol·i·ties] 1. The constitution or fundamental laws of a government. 2. A state; nation.

pol·ka (*pohl*-kuh) *n.* 1. A vigorous round dance performed by couples to music in $\frac{2}{4}$ time. 2. The music for a polka.—**pol·ka** *v.*

polka dot. A pattern with small dots uniformly spaced.

poll (*pohl*) *n.* 1. Election vote. 2. A canvassing of public opinion. 3. [*pl.*] Voting place. 4. The head. 5. A register of persons. 6. Blunt end of an implement.—**poll** *v.*

pol·lack, pol·lock (*pol*-ak) *n.* An edible ocean fish of the cod family.

pol·len *n.* A yellow dust produced by the anthers of flowers, containing reproductive cells.

pol·li·nate (*pol*-ih-nayt) *v.* [pol·li·nat·ed; -nat·ing] *Botany.* To fertilize by transfer of pollen from anther to stigma.—**pol·li·na·tion** *n.*

pol·li·wog *n.* A tadpole.

poll tax. 1. Any per-capita tax, esp. one assessed for the right to vote. 2. *U.S.* Such a tax now levied in a few Southern states.

pol·lute (puh-*loot*) *v.* [pol·lut·ed; pol·lut·ing] To defile; taint; make impure.—**pol·lu·tion** *n.*

P

po·lo (*poh*-loh) *n.* A game played on horseback, with mallets and a wooden ball.—**po·lo·ist** *n.*

po·lo·naise (poh-luh-*nayz*) *n.* 1. A stately Polish dance. 2. Music in ¾ time for the polonaise.

po·lo·ni·um (puh-*loh*-nee-um) *n.* A radioactive element derived from pitchblende. (*Symbol:* Po).

pol·ter·geist (*pol*-ter-gyste) *n.* An uncouth ghost, esp. a malicious or mischievous spirit.

pol·troon (pol-*troon*) *n.* An abject coward. —**pol·troon** *adj.*—**pol·troon·er·y** *n.*

pol·y·an·drous (pol-ee-*an*-drus) *adj.* 1. Having more than one husband. 2. *Botany.* Having more than 20 stamens.—**pol·y·an·dry** *n.*

pol·y·an·thus (pol-ee-*an*-thus) *n.* 1. An American primrose. 2. A variety of narcissus.

pol·y·chro·mat·ic (pol-ee-kroh-*mat*-ik) *adj.* Also **pol·y·chrome, pol·y·chro·mic.** Many-colored.

pol·y·clin·ic (pol-ee-*klin*-ik) *n.* Clinic or hospital treating all diseases.

po·lyg·a·my (puh-*lig*-uh-mee) *n.* Marriage to more than one person at the same time.—**po·lyg·a·mist** *n.*—**po·lyg·a·mous** *adj.*

pol·y·glot (*pol*-ee-glot) *adj.* Speaking or containing many languages.—**pol·y·glot** *n.*

pol·y·gon (*pol*-ee-gon) *n. Geometry.* A closed plane figure comprised of straight line segments.—**po·lyg·o·nal** (puh-*lig*-gon-'l) *adj.* —**po·lyg·o·nal·ly** *adv.*

po·lyg·y·ny (puh-*lij*-ih-nee) *n.* Practice of having more than one wife. —**po·lyg·y·nous** *adj.*

pol·y·he·dron (pol-ee-*hee*-drun) *n. Geometry.* A solid bounded by many faces or planes.—**pol·y·he·dral** *adj.*

POLYGONS

pol·y·morph (*pol*-ee-morf) *n.* Matter capable of assuming different forms or shapes.—**pol·y·mor·phous, -mor·phic** *adj.*—**poly·mor·phism** *n.*

Pol·y·ne·sian (pol-ih-*nee*-shan, -zhan) *adj.* Pertaining to a region of many islands in the South Pacific.—*n.* Inhabitant or language of the Polynesian islands.

pol·y·no·mi·al (pol-ih-*noh*-mee-al) *n. Algebra.* A proportion of more than two terms.—**pol·y·no·mi·al** *adj.*

pol·yp (*pol*-ip) *n.* 1. A tiny, tropical, tube-shaped marine animal. 2. *Medicine.* Distention of the mucous membrane.—**pol·y·pous** *adj.*

po·lyph·o·ny (puh-*lif*-uh-nee) *n.* [*pl.* po·lyph·o·nies] 1. Combination of sounds. 2. *Music.* A composition harmonizing several melodies; counterpoint.—**pol·y·phon·ic** (pol-ih-*fon*-ik), **po·lyph·o·nous** (puh-*lif*-uh-nus) *adj.*

POLYP

pol·y·syl·lab·ic (pol-ee-sih-*lab*-ik) *n.* Consisting of over three syllables.—**pol·y·syl·la·ble** *n.*

pol·y·tech·nic (pol-ee-*tek*-nik) *adj.* Also **pol·y·tech·ni·cal.** Pertaining to a teaching of the mechanical arts.—*n.* A school specializing in technical training.

pol·y·the·ism (pol-ee-*thee*-izm) *n.* Belief in many gods rather than in one.—**pol·y·the·ist** *n.* —**pol·y·the·is·tic, pol·y·the·is·ti·cal** *adj.*

pom·ace (*pum*-iss) *n.* A ground pulp, esp. of apples.

po·made (puh-*mayd*) *n.* A scented salve for the hair.

po·man·der (puh-*man*-der) *n.* A ball of mixed scents, formerly worn as a safeguard against infection.

pome·gran·ate (*pom*-gran-it) *n.* An acidic seedy fruit with a red pulp and a hard rind.

Pom·er·a·ni·an (pom-er-*ay*-nee-an) *n.* A small, soft-coated dog with pointed ears and a plumelike tail.

pom·mel (*pum*-'l) *n.* A saddlehorn.—*v.* [pommelled; pom·mel·ling] To beat; pummel.

po·mol·o·gy (poh-*mol*-uh-jee) *n.* The study of fruit growing.—**po·mo·log·i·cal** *adj.*— -**o·gist** *n.*

pomp *n.* Splendor; magnificence.

pomp·a·dour (*pomp*-uh-dohr) *n.* A style of rolling the hair upward from the forehead.

pom·pa·no (*pom*-puh-noh) *n.* Edible fish found in the coastal waters of North America.

Pom·pe·ii (pom-*pay*-ee). City in Italy buried in 79 A.D. by an eruption of Mt. Vesuvius. —**Pom·pe·ian** *adj.*

pom·pom, pom·pon (*pom*-pom; -pon) *n.* 1. A ball-shaped tassel. 2. A compact, buttonlike variety of chrysanthemum.

pomp·ous (*pomp*-us) *adj.* 1. Self-important; pretentious. 2. Splendid; regal.—**pom·pos·i·ty** *n.* —**pom·pous·ly** *adv.*—**pom·pous·ness** *n.*

pon·cho (*pon*-choh) *n.* Blanketlike cloak worn in South America.

pond *n.* Small body of still water.

pon·der *v.* To reflect; meditate; consider carefully. —**pon·der·er** *n.*

POMPOM (def. 1)

pon·der·a·ble *adj.* Appreciable; tangible.—**pon·der·a·ble** *n.*—**pon·der·a·bil·i·ty** *n.*

pon·der·ous *adj.* Heavy; unwieldy.—**pon·der·os·i·ty** *n.*—**pon·der·ous·ly** *adv.*—**pon·der·ous·ness** *n.*

pone *n. Southern U.S.* Bread made of corn meal; corn pone; loaf; lump.

pon·gee (pon-*jee*) *n.* Cloth of unbleached silk.

pon·iard (*pon*-yerd) *n.* A long dagger with a faceted blade.

pon·tiff (*pon*-tif) *n.* 1. The Pope. 2. A high priest. 3. A bishop.—**pon·tif·i·cate** *n.* The office of a Pope or high priest.—**pon·tif·i·cate** *v.*

To offer opinions pompously.—**pon·tif·i·cal** *adj.*—**pon·tif·i·cal·ly** *adv.*

pon·ton (*pon*-tun) *n. U.S. Army.* A pontoon.

pon·toon (pon-*toon*) *n.* Also **pon·ton.** A watertight buoyant structure used to float heavy bodies. 'A pontoon bridge.'

po·ny *n.* [*pl.* po·nies] 1. A small or immature horse. 2. *Slang.* Hidden information used for cheating in examinations.—**pony up.** To pay.

poo·dle *n.* A breed of small, intelligent dog with curly, coarse hair.

pooh-pooh (*poo-poo*) *v.* To sneer at; ridicule.

pool *n.* 1. Small body of water. 2. A swimming tank. 3. An aggregate fund. 4. A trust; monopoly. 5. A type of billiards played on a six-pocketed table.—*v.* To combine; amalgamate.

poop *n.* The highest, aftermost deck of certain ships.

poor *adj.* 1. Poverty-stricken; needy. 2. Inferior; wretched. 3. Pitiable.—*n. pl.* Indigent people.—**poor·ly** *adv.* —**poor·ness** *n.*

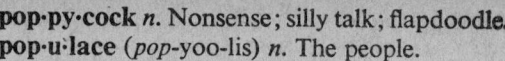

POOP

poor·house *n.* An institution for persons incapable of self-support.

pop *v.* [popped; pop·ping] 1. To split or break. 2. To bulge; protrude. 3. To move suddenly. 4. To explode; go off; burst with a short report. 5. *Slang.* To shoot.—*n.* 1. *Colloquial.* Soft drink. 2. A small, sharp report.

pop·corn *n.* Type of corn which explodes under heat into a white fluffy foodstuff.

pop·gun *n.* A toy gun which shoots a cork by compressed air.

Pope *n.* The head of the Roman Catholic Church.

pop·in·jay (*pop*-in-jay) *n.* A gay, trifling young man; fop.

pop·lar (*pop*-ler) *n.* A kind of tall, slender tree. —**pop·lar** *adj.*

pop·lin *n.* A ribbed, tightly woven cotton or worsted cloth.

Po·po·ca·te·petl (poh-poh-*kat*-uh-pet-'l, poh-poh-kuh-*tep*-uh-t'l). The second highest mountain peak in Mexico.

pop·o·ver *n.* A hollow, muffin-shaped quick bread, leavened by steam.

pop·per *n.* A pan or mesh basket in which corn is roasted or popped.

pop·py *n.* [*pl.* pop·pies] A family of large, decorative flowers, commonly red, a type of which is the source of opium.—**poppied** *adj.*

POPPY

pop·py·cock *n.* Nonsense; silly talk; flapdoodle.

pop·u·lace (*pop*-yoo-lis) *n.* The people.

pop·u·lar (*pop*-yoo-ler) *adj.* 1. Well liked. 2. Prevailing; widespread; common. 3. Pertaining to the people. 4. Available to the public; inexpensive. 5. Understandable to the layman.—**pop·u·lar·ly** *adv.*—**-lar·i·ty** *n.*

popular front. Combination of the democratic parties against fascism.

pop·u·lar·ize (*pop*-yoo-ler-yze) *v.* [pop·u·lar·ized; -iz·ing] To adapt for public appreciation. —**pop·u·lar·i·za·tion** *n.*—**pop·u·lar·iz·er** *n.*

pop·u·la·tion (pop-yoo-*lay*-shun) *n.* 1. The number of inhabitants of a region. 2. The act of peopling.—**pop·u·la·tion** *adj.*—**pop·u·late** *v.* [pop·u·lat·ed; -lat·ing].

Pop·u·list *n.* Member of the People's party in the agrarian revolt against big business during the 1890's.

pop·u·lous (*pop*-yoo-lus) *adj.* Thickly inhabited. —**pop·u·lous·ly** *adv.*—**pop·u·lous·ness** *n.*

por·ce·lain (*por*-seh-lin) *n.* A high-quality, glazed white earthenware.—**por·ce·lain, por·ce·la·ne·ous, por·cel·la·ne·ous** *adj.*

porch *n.* A roofed, elevated structure adjoining a building; veranda.

por·cine (*por*-syne) *adj.* Pertaining to swine.

por·cu·pine (*por*-kyoo-pyne) *n.* A rodent covered with defensive quills.

pore *n.* A tiny surface opening, esp. in the skin of living organisms.

pore *v.* [pored; por·ing] To read with deep concentration.

por·gy (*por*-jee) *n.* [*pl.* por·gies] A family of small, edible sea fish.

PORCUPINE (1/23 life-size)

P

pork *n.* The meat of the pig.—**pork·er** *n. Colloquial.* A pig.—**pork·y** *adj.*

pork barrel. *Colloquial.* The favors and jobs to be secured from the Federal Government through political patronage.

por·no·graph·ic (por-nuh-*graf*-ik) *adj.* Lewd; obscene.—**por·nog·ra·phy** [*pl.* -ra·phies] *n.*

por·ous (*por*-us) *adj.* Having small perforations or openings.—**po·ros·i·ty** *n.*—**por·ous·ness** *n.*

por·phy·ry (*por*-fih-ree) *n. Geology.* A silicate rock embedded with feldspar or other mineral crystals.—**por·phy·rit·ic** *adj.*

por·poise (*por*-pus) *n.* Black-backed, white-bellied marine mammal; dolphin.

por·ridge *n.* Cooked cereal.

por·rin·ger (*por*-in-jer) *n.* A small bowl.

port *n.* 1. A harbor. 2. A mercantile city or town. 3. The left side of a ship. 4. A porthole.—*adj.* Left.—*v.* To turn left.

port *n.* A sweet red wine.

port·a·ble *adj.* Easily carried.—*n.* A portable typewriter.—**port·a·ble·ness, port·a·bil·i·ty** *n.*

por·tage (*por*-tij) *n.* 1. The carrying of boats over a stretch of land lying between water communications. 2. The distance that boats are so carried.—**por·tage** *v.*

por·tal *n.* An entrance.

port·cul·lis *n.* A sliding iron or timber grating in the gate of a castle or fort.

porte-co·chère (*port*-koh-shair) *n.* 1. The extension of a roof over a driveway. 2. A wide gate.

por·tend *v.* To augur; presage.

por·tent *n.* A foreshadowing; omen.—**por·ten·tous** *adj.*—**por·ten·tous·ly** *adv.*—**por·ten·tous·ness** *n.*

PORTCULLIS

por·ter *n.* 1. One employed to carry luggage; attendant on a train. 2. A dark malt liquor.

por·ter·house *n.* A choice beefsteak cut.

port·fo·li·o *n.* 1. A carrying case for papers, drawings, etc. 2. A cabinet or ministerial post.

port·hole *n.* An opening in the side of a ship, esp. one used as a window.

por·ti·co *n.* [*pl.* por-ti-coes, por-ti-cos] A roofed porch surrounded by columns.

por·ti·ere (por-tee-air) *n.* A door curtain.

por·tion *n.* 1. A part; allotment. 2. Destiny; fate.—**por·tion** *v.*—**por·tion·er** *n.*—**por·tion·less** *adj.*

PORTICO

Portland cement. Lime mixed with clay or alum, used in concrete.

port·ly *adj.* [port-li-er, port-li-est] Bulky; stout.—**port·li·ness** *n.*

port·man·teau (port-*man*-toh) *n.* A case; valise.

portmanteau word. A word made by blending two or more words, as *brunch*, from *breakfast* and *lunch*.

port of embarkation. Any port from which ships clear to go to a foreign destination.

por·trait (*por*-trit) *n.* A pictorial likeness or photograph, esp. of a face.—**por·trait·ist** *n.*—**por·trai·ture** *n.*

por·tray (por-*tray*) *v.* 1. To produce a likeness. 2. To depict; describe. 3. *Drama.* To play a role.—**por·tray·a·ble** *adj.*—**por·tray·al** *n.*

por·tu·lac·a (por-choo-*lak*-uh) *n.* A hardy succulent flowering herb of the purslane group.

pose *v.* [posed; pos-ing] 1. To assume a studied attitude. 2. To set; assert; propose. 3. To masquerade; be affected and unnatural. 4. To arrange.—**pose** *n.*

Po·sei·don (poh-*sy*-dun). *Greek Mythology.* The god of the sea.

pos·er (*pohz*-er) *n.* 1. A difficult question or problem. 2. One who assumes attitudes.

pos·eur (poh-*zer*) *n.* One who poses (in sense 2).

pos·it (*poz*-it) *v. Logic.* To state as fact; accept as immediately real.

po·si·tion (poh-*zish*-un) *n.* 1. Location; standing; condition. 2. Attitude; viewpoint; thesis.—**po·si·tion** *v.*—**po·si·tion·al** *adv.*

pos·i·tive (*poz*-ih-tiv) *adj.* 1. Affirmative; sure. 2. Certain; real; existing in fact. 3. *Photography.* Like the original in regard to light and dark. 4. *Electricity.* Having a deficiency of electrons. 5. *Mathematics.* Greater than zero.—**pos·i·tive** *n.*—**-tive·ly** *adv.*—**tive·ness** *n.*

pos·i·tiv·ism *n.* The system of Comte limiting the scope of philosophy to the examination of knowable phenomena.—**pos·i·tiv·ist** *n.*—**pos·i·tiv·is·tic** *adj.*

pos·se (*poss*-ee) *n.* A group of men informally deputized to hunt down a criminal.

pos·sess (puh-*zess*) *v.* 1. To own; hold. 2. To take; seize.—**pos·sess·or** *n.*

pos·ses·sion (puh-*zesh*-un) *n.* 1. Ownership; having in one's power. 2. Belongings. 3. A colony; country subject to the rule of another.

pos·ses·sive *adj.* 1. Desirous of owning exclusively. 2. *Grammar.* Indicating ownership; genitive, as possessive case of a noun or pronoun.—**pos·ses·sive** *n.*—**pos·ses·sive·ly** *adv.*

pos·set *n.* A drink made of hot milk, liquor, and spices.

pos·si·ble *adj.* Capable of being or happening.—**pos·si·bil·i·ty** *n.* [*pl.* -i-ties].—**pos·si·bly** *adv.*

pos·sum *n.* An opossum.

post- *prefix.* After; behind; since; subsequent.

post-audit (*v.*)	postfact	postnuptial
post bellum	postfix	postprandial
postclassic	postnote	postsentence

post (*pohst*) *n.* A large stake or pole.

post *n.* 1. A station; position. 2. Job; appointment. 3. The postal system.—*v.* 1. To mail. 2. To hang up or display in a public place. 3. To make an entry in a ledger.

post·age (*pohst*-ij) *n.* Charge for sending mail.

postage stamp. Seal put on mail in token of payment.

post·al *adj.* Pertaining to the mail system.

postal card. Also **post card.** *U.S.* 1. Government card bearing a printed stamp. 2. A card admitted to the mails when stamped.

post·boy *n.* A mail carrier.

post·date *v.* [post-dated; post-dat-ing] To set down a date in advance of the actual date.

post·en·try *n. Bookkeeping.* An additional or subsequent entry in a ledger.

post·er *n.* An advertising bill or placard.

pos·te·ri·or (poss-*teer*-ee-er) *adj.* Rear; hind; later; subsequent.—**pos·te·ri·or** *n.* The hind part of an animal.—**-or·ly** *adv.*—**-or·i·ty** *n.*

pos·ter·i·ty (poss-*tehr*-ih-tee) *n.* Descendants; succeeding generations.

pos·tern (*pohss*-tern) *n*. A small or private gate. —**pos·tern** *adj*.

post exchange. An army canteen selling small stores. *Abbreviation*: PX.

post·grad·u·ate (pohst-*grad*-yoo-it) *n*. A student who continues study after graduation; graduate student.—**post·grad·u·ate** *adj*.

post·haste *adv*. Quickly; immediately.

post·hu·mous (*poss*-choo-mus) *adj*. 1. Born after the father's death. 2. Published after the author's death. 3. Taking place after one's death.

pos·til·ion, pos·til·lion (poh-*stil*-yun) *n*. Rider of the left horse of a team hitched to a coach.

post·im·pres·sion·ism *n*. *Painting*. A movement, dominated by Cézanne, which sought to restore form and self-expression while retaining the brilliant palette of the impressionists. —**post·im·pres·sion·ist** *n*.—**post·im·pres·sion·ist·ic** *adj*.— **·ic·al·ly** *adv*.

post·lude (*pohst*-lyood) *n*. *Music*. An afterpiece, esp. a piece following the recessional.

post·man *n*. A mailman; mail carrier.

post·mark *n*. The mark of a post office on a piece of mail.—**post·mark** *v*.

post·mas·ter *n*. The official in charge of a post office.

postmaster general [*pl.* postmasters general]. Official in charge of all the post offices in the country.

post·me·rid·i·an (pohst-mer-*id*-ee-an) *adj*. After noon.—*n*. The afternoon. *Abbreviation*: P.M.

post·mor·tem *adj*. After death.—*n*. An autopsy.

post office. 1. Agency charged with handling the mails. 2. Building where mail is handled. —**post-office** *adj*.

post·paid *adj*. Having postage prepaid.

post·pone (pohst-*pohn*) *v*. [post·poned; post·pon·ing] To put off; defer.—**post·pon·a·ble** *adj*. —**post·pon·er** *n*.—**post·pone·ment** *n*.

post·script (*pohst*-skript) *n*. An addition to a letter following the closing. *Abbreviations*: P.S., p.s.

pos·tu·late (*poss*-choo-late) *v*. [pos·tu·lat·ed; -lat·ing] To assume; posit.—**pos·tu·late, pos·tu·la·tion** *n*.—**pos·tu·la·tor** *n*.

pos·ture (*poss*-cher) *n*. Position or carriage of the body.—**pos·ture** *v*. [pos·tured; pos·tur·ing] To pose; assume an attitude.—**pos·tur·ize** *v*. [pos·tur·ized; -iz·ing] To pose.—**pos·tur·er, pos·tur·ist** *n*. 1. A poser. 2. An acrobat.

post·war *adj*. After the war.

po·sy *n*. [*pl*. po·sies] A flower; bouquet.

pot *n*. 1. A deep cooking vessel. 2. A mug; large cup. 3. An earthen jar for plants. 4. *Foundry*. A crucible. 5. *Colloquial*. A gambling stake or prize.—*v*. [pot·ted; pot·ting]. 1. To put into a pot. 2. To shoot. —**pot·ted** *adj*. *Slang*. Drunk.

po·ta·ble (*poh*-tuh-b'l) *adj*. Suitable for drinking.—[*n. pl*.] Drinks.

po·tage (puh-*tahzh*) *n*. A thick soup.

pot·ash (*pot*-ash) *n*. An impure potassium compound obtained from wood ashes.

po·tas·si·um (puh-*tas*-ee-um) *n*. A light metallic element which oxidizes violently. (*Symbol*: K).

po·ta·tion (poh-*tay*-shun) *n*. 1. Act of drinking. 2. A drink.

po·ta·to (puh-*tay*-toh) *n*. [*pl*. po·ta·toes] 1. A tuber-producing perennial herb of tropical and temperate zones. 2. The starchy tuber vegetable of the potato.

pot·bel·ly *n*. A prominent belly.—**pot·bel·lied** *adj*.

POTATO

pot·boil·er *n*. A literary or artistic work produced merely to make money.

po·tent (*poh*-tent) *adj*. 1. Strong; powerful. 2. Virile.—**po·tence, po·ten·cy** *n*.—**po·tent·ly** *adv*.—**po·tent·ness** *n*.

po·ten·tate (*poh*-ten-tayt) *n*. King; ruler; sovereign.

po·ten·tial (po-*ten*-sh'l) *adj*. Ultimately possible; latent; existent, but unrealized.—*n*. 1. A possibility. 2. *Electricity*. Voltage; electromotive force.—**po·ten·tial·ly** *adv*.—**po·ten·ti·al·i·ty** *n*. [*pl*. -i·ties].

poth·er *n*. Bustle; confusion; tumult.—**poth·er** *v*.

pot·herb *n*. 1. A plant bearing leaves used for boiled greens. 2. An herb used for seasoning.

pot·hook *n*. 1. A hook on which kettles are hung. 2. A written letter used as a model for penmanship.

po·tion (*poh*-shun) *n*. A drink or dose, esp. one producing a strange or aphrodisiac effect.

pot·luck *n*. A casual, unplanned meal.—**pot·luck** *adj*.

Po·to·mac (puh-*toh*-mak). A navigable river having its source in the Alleghenies, emptying into Chesapeake Bay.

pot·pie *n*. 1. A meat pie. 2. A fricassee with dumplings.

pot·pour·ri (poh-*poo*-ree) *n*. 1. A miscellaneous collection; medley. 2. A meat and vegetable stew.

pot·roast *n*. Meat cooked slowly in a pot with very little water.—**pot-roast** *v*.

pot·shot *n*. A shot fired without careful aim. —**pot·shoot** *v*. [pot·shot; pot·shoot·ing].

pot·tage (*pot*-ij) *n*. Boiled meat with vegetables; creamed soup.

pot·ter *n*. A maker of crockery.

pot·ter *v*. To dawdle; waste time on trifles. —**pot·ter·er** *n*.—**pot·ter·ing·ly** *adv*.

potter's field. A cemetery or part of one where paupers are buried.

potter's wheel. The revolving disk on which a potter shapes clay.

pot·ter·y *n*. [*pl*. pot·ter·ies] 1. Earthenware; baked-clay vessels. 2. The business or factory of a potter.

pouch (*powch*) *n*. 1. A bag; small sack. 2. *Zoology*. A sac or cyst in an animal.—*v*. To form a pouch.—**pouched** *adj*.—**pouch·y** *adj*.

P

poul·tice (*pohl*-tiss) *n.* A soft dressing applied to an inflamed area of the body.

pounce (*pownss*) *v.* [pounced; pounc·ing] To dive upon; seize.—**pounce** *n.*—**pounc·er** *n.*

poul·try (*pohl*-tree) *n.* Domesticated fowls. —**poul·ter·er**, **poul·try·man** *n.*

pound (*pownd*) *n.* 1. Standard unit of weight consisting of 16 ounces avoirdupois or 12 ounces troy weight. 2. English monetary unit [symbol £] worth approximately $4.—**pound·age** *n.* Weight in terms of pounds.—**pound·er** *n.* That which weighs a pound.

pound (*pownd*) *v.* To beat upon; strike; break into pieces.—**pound** *n.*—**pound·er** *n.*

pound (*pownd*) *n.* A public enclosure for stray animals; place of confinement.

pound·al *n.* A unit of force able to accelerate one pound mass one foot per second.

pound cake. A plain, rich cake, originally made from one pound of each ingredient.

pound-fool·ish *adj.* Neglectful of large matters by preoccupation with small ones.

pour (*pohr*) *v.* 1. To cause to flow or stream forth. 2. To give vent to. 3. To flow; rush. —**pour·er** *n.*—**pour·ing·ly** *adv.*

pout (*powt*) *v.* To thrust out or purse the lips; look sullen.—**pout** *n.*—**pout·er** *n.*

pov·er·ty (*pov*-er-tee) *n.* 1. Want; indigence. 2. A lack; deficiency.—**pov·er·ty-strick·en** *adj.*

pow·der *n.* 1. A dry, fine-grained substance. 2. A grainy nitrate explosive; gunpowder. —**pow·der** *v.* 1. To spread with powder. 2. To grind to particles; pulverize.—**pow·der·er** *n.*—**pow·der·y** *adj.*

pow·er *n.* 1. Ability to act. 2. Strength; force. 3. Sway; authority. 4. Legal authority. 5. A nation. 6. *Mechanics.* Capacity for doing work. 7. *Mathematics.* The number of times a number is to be multiplied by itself. 8. *Optics.* Amount of multiplication. —**power of attorney.** Authority given to one person to act for another.

pow·er·ful *adj.* Strong; forceful; influential.

pow·er·less *adj.* Impotent; incapable of action. —**pow·er·less·ly** *adv.*—**pow·er·less·ness** *n.*

pow·wow *n.* 1. A ceremony among North American Indians. 2. A conference; meeting.

pox *n.* A disease manifested by skin pustules.

prac·ti·ca·ble (*prak*-tih-kuh-b'l) *adj.* Feasible; possible.—**prac·ti·ca·bil·i·ty**, **prac·ti·ca·ble·ness** *n.*—**prac·ti·ca·bly** *adv.*

prac·ti·cal (*prak*-tih-k'l) *adj.* 1. Functional; workable. 2. Matter-of-fact; realistic.—**prac·ti·cal·i·ty** *n.*—**prac·ti·cal·ness** *n.*

practical joke. An annoying or injurious trick played upon another.

prac·ti·cal·ly (*prak*-tik-'l-ee) *adv.* 1. In a practical manner. 2. Almost; in effect.

prac·tice, **prac·tise** (*prak*-tiss) *v.* To drill. —**prac·tice** *n.* 1. Custom. 2. Mode. 3. Actual performance, as distinguished from theory. 4. A profession. 5. Drill, exercise.—**prac·**

ticed, **prac·tised** *adj.* Expert; accomplished. —**prac·tic·er**, **prac·tis·er** *n.*—**prac·ti·tion·er** *n.*

prae·tor, **pre·tor** (*pree*-ter) *n.* A Roman magistrate; sometimes governor of a province. —**prae·to·ri·an**, **pre·to·ri·an** *adj.*

prag·mat·ic (prag-*mat*-ik) *adj.* 1. Practical. 2. Pertaining to pragmatism.

prag·mat·i·cal *adj.* 1. Practical. 2. Meddlesome; officious.—**prag·mat·ical·ly** *adv.*

prag·ma·tism (*prag*-muh-tizm) *n.* A philosophic conception based on the practical utility of any given function or conception.—**prag·ma·tist** *n.*

prai·rie *n.* An extensive plain in central U.S.

prairie chicken. A large grouse of the Mississippi Valley.

prairie dog. A rodent resembling a woodchuck, found on the plains west of the Mississippi.

prairie schooner. A long canvas-covered wagon used to carry the early settlers to the West.

PRAIRIE DOG
(1/12 life-size)

prairie wolf. The coyote.

praise *v.* [praised; prais·ing] To commend; extol.—**praise** *n.*—**prais·er** *n.*

praise·wor·thy *adj.* Commendable; meritorious.—**praise·wor·thi·ly** *adv.*— **-thi·ness** *n.*

pra·line (*prah*-leen, *praw*-leen) *n.* A New Orleans confection made of brown sugar, butter, water, and pecans.

prank *n.* Mischievous trick; antic.—*v.* To deck; dress out.—**prank·ish** *adj.*

pra·se·o·dym·i·um (pray-zee-uh-*dim*-ee-um) *n.* A metallic element of the rare-earth group. (*Symbol:* Pr).

prate (*prayt*) *v.* [prat·ed; prat·ing] To chatter; talk loquaciously.—**prat·er** *n.*—**prat·ing·ly** *adv.*

prat·tle *v.* [prat·tled; prat·tling] To babble; chatter.—**prat·tle** *n.*—**prat·tler** *n.*—**-tling·ly** *adv.*

prawn *n.* A reddish, edible shellfish common around the British Isles; shrimp.—**prawn** *v.*

pray *v.* 1. To worship; offer up prayers. 2. To entreat; plead.

pray·er *n.* 1. Worship; offering of supplication or thanksgiving to the Deity. 2. Words so addressed; a set form used in worship. 3. A religious service. 4. A plea; appeal; hope.—**pray·er·ful** *adj.*—**pray·er·ful·ly** *adv.*

pre- *prefix.* Before in space, time, rank, etc.

preacceptance	precondemn	premarital
preacknowledge	preconvention	premodern
preadmission	precook	prenotify
pre-American	precool	prenuptial
prearrangement	pre-election	preobserve
pre-Aryan	pre-engage	prerelease
prebaptismal	preheat	preremit
precampaign	prehuman	presurvey
precast	preindebted	pre-Victorian
preclassic	preinstruct	prewar

preach *v.* 1. To deliver a sermon; discourse on a religious subject. 2. To lecture; sermonize.—**preach·er** *n.* 1. A clergyman. 2. A moralizer.—**preach·ing** *n.* —**preach·ing·ly** *adv.*

preach·i·fy *v.* [preach·i·fied; preach·i·fy·ing] To speak bombastically and loquaciously. —**preach·ment** *n.* A tedious sermon.

pre·am·ble (*pree*-am-b'l) *n.* 1. The introductory part of a statute or constitution. 2. Preface.

pre·car·i·ous (preh-*kayr*-ee-us) *adj.* Uncertain; doubtful; insecure.—**pre·car·i·ous·ly** *adv.*—**pre·car·i·ous·ness** *n.*

pre·cau·tion (preh-*kaw*-shun) *n.* A protective measure; care taken beforehand.—**pre·cau·tion·al** *adj.*—**pre·cau·tion·ar·y** *adj.*—**pre·cau·tious** *adj.*

pre·cede (pree-*seed*) *v.* [pre·ced·ed; pre·ced·ing] To go before; be ahead of.—**pre·ced·ence** (pre-*seed*-ens) *n.* 1. Priority. 2. Superiority. —**pre·ced·en·cy** (preh-*seed*-en-see) *n.*—**pre·ced·ent** (preh-*seed*-ent) *adj.*

prec·e·dent (*press*-ih-dent) *n.* An example serving as a future rule.—**prec·e·dent·ed** *adj.*—**prec·e·den·tial** *adj.*

pre·ced·ing *adj.* Occurring just before.

pre·cept (*pree*-sept) *n.* A rule of action; guide to moral conduct.—**pre·cep·tive** *adj.* Admonitive.—**pre·cep·tive·ly** *adv.*

pre·cep·tor (pree-*sep*-ter) *n.* A teacher; tutor. —**pre·cep·to·ral, pre·cep·to·ri·al** *adj.*

pre·ces·sion (pree-*sesh*-un) *n.* The act of going before; precedence.

pre·cinct (*pree*-sinkt) *n.* 1. An area within certain boundaries. 2. One of various city divisions made for policing, voting, etc.

pre·ci·os·i·ty (presh-ee-*oss*-ih-tee) *n.* [*pl.* pre·ci·os·i·ties] Meticulousness; finicalness, esp. in writing; overrefinement.

pre·cious (*presh*-us) *adj.* 1. Valuable; rare; of great worth. 2. Dear; cherished. 3. Out-and-out; arrant. 4. Fastidious; overnice. —**pre·cious·ly** *adv.*—**pre·cious·ness** *n.*

prec·i·pice (*press*-ih-pis) *n.* A very steep or overhanging cliff.

pre·cip·i·tant (preh-*sip*-ih-t'nt) *adj.* 1. Falling headlong; rushing. 2. Rash; hasty.—*n. Chemistry.* A substance which, when added to a solution, separates its constituents and causes one or more to settle in solid form. —**pre·cip·i·tance, pre·cip·i·tan·cy** *n.*

pre·cip·i·tate (preh-*sip*-ih-tayt) *v.* [pre·cip·i·tat·ed; pre·cip·i·tat·ing] 1. To fall or throw headlong. 2. To hasten; urge on too quickly. 3. To condense vapor into liquid form, as rain. 4. *Chemistry.* To dissolve and re-form a solution.—*n.* The solid substance resulting from chemical changes in a solution.—*adj.* (preh-*sip*-ih-tit) 1. Rash; hasty. 2. Falling.—**pre·cip·i·tate·ness** *n.*—**pre·cip·i·ta·tive** *adj.*—**pre·cip·i·ta·tor** *n.*

pre·cip·i·ta·tion (preh-sip-ih-*tay*-shun) *n.* 1. Rapid movement; tumultuous haste. 2. A falling downward. 3. *Chemistry.* The separation of a solution into its various visible ingredients. 4. The falling of condensed vapor, as rain, hail, snow, etc.

pre·cip·i·tous (preh-*sip*-ih-tus) *adj.* 1. Steep. 2. Headlong; abrupt.—**pre·cip·i·tous·ly** *adv.* —**pre·cip·i·tous·ness** *n.*

pre·cise (preh-*syse*) *adj.* Exact; definite; accurate.—**pre·cise·ly** *adv.*—**pre·cise·ness** *n.*

pre·ci·sion (preh-*sizh*-un) *n.* Accuracy; definiteness.—**pre·ci·sion·ist** *n.*

pre·clude (preh-*klood*) *v.* [pre·clud·ed; pre·clud·ing] To prevent; obviate.—**pre·clu·sion** *n.* —**pre·clu·sive** *adj.*—**pre·clu·sive·ly** *adv.*

pre·co·cious (preh-*koh*-shus) *adj.* Mentally matured at an early age.—**pre·co·cious·ly** *adv.* —**pre·co·cious·ness** *n.*—**pre·coc·i·ty** *n.*

pre·con·ceive (pree-kun-*seev*) *v.* [pre·con·ceived; pre·con·ceiv·ing] To form an opinion beforehand.—**pre·con·cep·tion** *n.*

pre·con·cert (pree-kun-*sert*) *v.* To settle by previous agreement.—**pre·con·cert·ed·ly** *adv.*

pre·cur·sor (preh-*ker*-ser) *n.* A forerunner; harbinger.—**pre·cur·sive** *adj.*—**pre·cur·so·ry** *adj.*

pred·a·to·ry (*pred*-uh-tor-ee) *adj.* Devouring; pillaging; preying.—**pred·a·to·ri·ly** *adv.*

pred·e·ces·sor (pred-eh-*ses*-er) *n.* One who has previously occupied another's place.

pre·des·ti·nate (preh-*des*-tih-nit) *v.* [pre·des·ti·nated; pre·des·ti·nat·ing] To predetermine; ordain beforehand.—**pre·des·ti·nar·i·an** *n.*

pre·des·ti·na·tion (pree-des-tih-*nay*-shun) *n.* 1. Fate; the act of foreordaining events. 2. *Theology.* The belief that God has decreed all events unchangeably from eternity.

pre·des·tine (pree-*des*-tin) *v.* [pre·des·tined; pre·des·tin·ing] To foreordain; settle beforehand.

pre·de·ter·mine (pre-de-*ter*-min) *v.* [pre·de·ter·mined; pre·de·ter·min·ing] To decide beforehand; to settle in advance.—**pre·de·ter·mi·nate** *adj.*—**pre·de·ter·mi·na·tion** *n.*

pred·i·ca·ble (*pred*-ih-kuh-b'l) *adj.* Affirmable. —*n.* A property; attribute.—**pred·i·ca·bil·i·ty** *n.*—**pred·i·ca·ble·ness** *n.*—**pred·i·ca·bly** *adv.*

pre·dic·a·ment (preh-*dik*-uh-m'nt) *n.* A plight; trying situation.

pred·i·cate (*pred*-ih-kayt) *v.* [pred·i·cat·ed; pred·i·cat·ing] 1. To affirm. 2. To base; found. —*n. Grammar.* The word or words which express what is affirmed or denied of the subject.—*adj. Grammar.* Belonging in the predicate; not attributive.—**pred·i·ca·tion** *n.*—**pred·i·ca·tive** *adj.*—**pred·i·ca·tive·ly** *adv.*

pre·dict (preh-*dikt*) *v.* To prophesy; foretell. —**pre·dict·a·ble** *adj.*—**pre·dic·tion** *n.*

pre·di·gest (pree-dih-*jest*) *v.* To create artificial digestion of proteins and starches before they are eaten.—**pre·di·ges·tion** *n.*

pre·di·lec·tion (pree-dih-*lek*-shun) *n.* A preference; partiality.

pre·dis·pose (pree-dis-*pohz*) *v.* [pre·dis·posed; pre·dis·pos·ing] 1. To incline beforehand; 2. To make susceptible.—**pre·dis·po·si·tion** *n.* A previous tendency; bias.

P

pre·dom·i·nant (preh-*dom*-ih-n'nt) *adj.* Prevailing; controlling; superior.—**pre·dom·i·nance** *n.* Supremacy; preponderance.— **-nant·ly** *adv.*

pre·dom·i·nate (preh-*dom*-ih-nayt) *v.* [pre·dom·i·nat·ed; pre·dom·i·nat·ing] To be superior; to prevail over.—**pre·dom·i·na·tion** *n.*

pre-em·i·nence, pre·ëm·i·nence (pree-*em*-ih-nence) *n.* Superiority; distinction.—**pre-em·i·nent** *adj.*—**pre-em·i·nent·ly** *adv.*

pre-empt, pre·empt (pree-*empt*) *v.* 1. To establish a first claim to purchase. 2. To take possession in advance of others; appropriate. —**pre-emp·tion** *n.*—**pre-emp·tive** *adj.*—**pre-emp·tor** *n.*—**pre-emp·to·ry** *adj.*

preen *v.* 1 To clean and trim with the beak, as a bird. 2. To groom oneself.—**preen·er** *n.*

pre-ex·ist, pre·ex·ist (pree-eg-*zist*) *v.* To exist before the present life.—**pre-ex·ist·ence** *n.* —**pre-ex·ist·ent** *adj.*

pre·fab·ri·cate (pree-*fab*-rih-kayt) *v.* [pre·fab·ri·cat·ed; pre·fab·ri·cat·ing] To manufacture standardized sections of a structure for rapid assembly.—**pre·fab·ri·ca·tion** *n.*

pre·face (*pref*-iss) *n.* 1. An introduction, as to a book. 2. A series of preliminary remarks. —*v.* [pre·faced; pre·fac·ing] To introduce; begin with an introduction.—**pref·a·to·ry** *adj.*

pre·fect (*pree*-fekt) *n.* 1. A chief magistrate or governor of a district in ancient Rome. 2. In France, a departmental official.—**pre·fec·ture** *n.* The office of a district governor; residence of a prefect.—**pre·fec·tur·al** *adj.*

pre·fer (preh-*fer*) *v.* 1. To hold in greater favor; choose. 2. To offer or present, as a claim. —**pre·fer·rer** *n.*—**pre·ferred stock,** Stock entitled to receive the first payment of dividends.

pref·er·a·ble (*pref*-er-uh-b'l) *adj.* More desirable; better.—**pref·er·a·bil·i·ty** *n.*—**pref·er·a·ble·ness** *n.*—**pref·er·a·bly** *adv.*

pref·er·ence (*pref*-er-enss) *n.* 1. Choice of one over another. 2. A chosen object.

pref·er·en·tial (pref-uh-*ren*-sh'l) *adj.* 1. In a position of choice or favor.—**pref·er·en·tial·ism** *n.*—**pref·er·en·tial·ist** *n.*— **-en·tial·ly** *adv.*

pre·fer·ment (preh-*fer*-m'nt) *n.* 1. Promotion; advancement to a higher office, rank, etc. 2. A superior office, esp. in the church.

pre·fig·ure (pree-*fig*-yer) *v.* [pre·fig·ured; pre·fig·ur·ing] 1. To foreshadow; symbolize a future event. 2. To foresee.—**pre·fig·u·ra·tion** *n.* —**pre·fig·u·ra·tive** *adj.*—**pre·fig·ure·ment** *n.*

pre·fix (*pree*-fiks) *v.* To put before; act at the beginning.—*n.* A letter, syllable, or word placed at the beginning of a word to vary its meaning.

preg·na·ble (*preg*-nuh-b'l) *adj.* Capable of being won by force; vulnerable.—**preg·na·bil·i·ty** *n.*

preg·nant (*preg*-n'nt) *adj.* 1. Great with child; carrying the unborn. 2. Significant; meaningful; fertile.—**preg·nan·cy** *n.*—**preg·nant·ly** *adv.*

pre·hen·sile (pree-*hen*-sil) *adj.* Naturally adapted for clinging, as the tails of certain tree-dwelling animals.

pre·his·tor·ic (pree-hiss-*tor*-ik) *adj.* Also **pre·his·tor·i·cal.** Pertaining to the period preceding written history.

pre·judge (pree-*juj*) *v.* [pre·judged; pre·judg·ing] To decide before hearing; condemn in advance.—**pre·judg·er** *n.*—**pre·judg·ment, pre·judge·ment** *n.*

prej·u·dice (*prej*-uh-diss) *n.* A partiality; bias; —*v.* [pre·ju·diced; prej·u·dic·ing] To bias the mind by unfair opinions.—**prej·u·di·cial** *adj.*

prel·a·cy (*prel*-uh-see) *n.* [*pl.* prel·a·cies] 1. The office of a prelate. 2. The system of church government by clergy of the higher order. —**pre·late** *n.* An ecclesiastic of high rank.

pre·lim·i·nar·y (preh-*lim*-ih-nair-ee) *adj.* Introductory; prefatory.—*n.* [*pl.* pre·lim·i·nar·ies] A preparatory act.—**pre·lim·i·nar·i·ly** *adv.*

prel·ude (*prel*-yood) *n.* 1. A preface; introduction. 2. *Music.* A short introductory strain or movement preceding the main theme. —*v.* [prel·ud·ed; prel·ud·ing] To precede; introduce.—**pre·lud·er** *n.*—**pre·lu·sion** *n.*—**pre·lu·sive, pre·lu·so·ry** *adj.*—**pre·lu·sive·ly** *adv.*

pre·ma·ture (pree-muh-*tyoor*) *adj.* Untimely; occurring before the proper time.—**pre·ma·ture·ly** *adv.*—**pre·ma·ture·ness, pre·ma·tu·ri·ty** *n.*

pre·med·i·tate (pree-*med*-ih-tayt) *v.* [pre·med·i·tat·ed; pre·med·i·tat·ing] To deliberate; contrive beforehand.—**pre·med·i·ta·tion** *n.*—**pre·med·i·ta·tive** *adj.*—**pre·med·i·ta·tor** *n.*

pre·mi·er (*pree*-mee-er) *adj.* Principal; chief. —*n.* The chief minister of state; prime minister.—**pre·mi·er·ship** *n.*

prem·ise (*prem*-iss) *n.* 1. An assumption; supposition. 2. *Logic.* One of the first two propositions of a syllogism. 3. *Law.* That part of a deed stating the subject matter. 4. [*pl.*] A building and its land.—*v.* [prem·ised; prem·is·ing] To postulate; assume.

pre·mi·um (*pree*-mee-um) *n.* 1. A reward; prize; bonus. 2. An added sum above stated value. 3. A sum paid periodically for insurance.—**at a premium.** Above normal value.

pre·mo·ni·tion (pree-muh-*nish*-un) *n.* A foreboding; advance warning.— **-mon·i·to·ry** *adj.*

pre·na·tal (pree-*nay*-t'l) *adj.* Before birth.

pre·oc·cu·pied (pree-*ok*-yoo-pyde) *adj.* 1. Abstracted; deep in thought. 2. Already occupied.

pre·oc·cu·py (pree-*ok*-yoo-py) *v.* [pre·oc·cu·pied; pre·oc·cu·py·ing] 1. To take possession before another. 2. To engross.—**pre·oc·cu·pan·cy** *n.* [*pl.* pre·oc·cu·pan·cies].—**pre·oc·cu·pa·tion** *n.*

pre·or·dain (pree-or-*dayn*) *v.* To decree beforehand; determine ahead.— **-or·di·na·tion** *n.*

prep·a·ra·tion (prep-uh-*ray*-shun) *n.* 1. The process of making ready. 2. A mixture compounded for a particular purpose.

pre·par·a·to·ry (preh-*pair*-uh-tor-ee) *adj.* Serving to make ready; introductory.

pre·pare (preh-*pair*) *v.* [pre·pared; pre·par·ing] 1. To make ready; adapt to a definite purpose. 2. To warn; give notice. 3. To compound; make.—**pre·par·er** n.

pre·par·ed·ness (preh-*pair*-ed-nes) n. The state of being in readiness.

pre·pay (pree-*pay*) v. [pre·paid; pre·paying] To pay in advance.—**pre·pay·ment** n.

pre·pon·der·ance (pree-*pon*-der-unss) n. A predominance; a superiority of weight.—**pre·pon·der·ant** adj.—**pre·pon·der·ant·ly** adv.

pre·pon·der·ate (pree-*pon*-der-ayt) v. [pre·pon·der·at·ed; pre·pon·der·at·ing] To overpower; exceed in influence.—**pre·pon·der·at·ing·ly** adv.

prep·o·si·tion (prep-uh-*zish*-un) n. Grammar. A part of speech showing the objective relation of a noun or pronoun to another word in a sentence. 'He works *for* money.'—**prep·o·si·tion·al** adj.—**prep·o·si·tion·al·ly** adv.

pre·pos·sess (pree-poh-*zess*) v. 1. To occupy in advance; take previous possession. 2. To prejudice usually favorably; influence.

pre·pos·sess·ing adj. Attractive; inviting favor.

pre·pos·ses·sion (pree-poh-*zesh*-un) n. A bias; partiality; prejudice.

pre·pos·ter·ous (pree-*poss*-ter-us) adj. Absurd; ridiculous; irrational.—**pre·pos·ter·ous·ly** adv.

pre·req·ui·site (pree-*rek*-wih-zit) adj. Necessary. —n. Something necessary to a proposed end.

pre·rog·a·tive (preh-*rog*-uh-tiv) n. An exclusive privilege based on position; hereditary right.

pres·age (*pres*-ij) n. A sign; omen; foreboding. —v. (preh-*sayj*) [pre·saged; pre·sag·ing] To predict; prophesy; portend.—**pre·sag·er** n.

pres·by·ter (*prez*-bih-ter) n. 1. An elder of the early Christian church. 2. A priest. 3. A minister or elder of a Presbyterian church.

Pres·by·te·ri·an (prez-bih-*teer*-ee-an) adj. 1. Pertaining to a church or churches governed by presbyters. 2. [*not cap.*] Pertaining to a presbyter.—n. A member of the Presbyterian Church; believer in Presbyterianism.

Pres·by·te·ri·an·ism (prez-bih-*teer*-ee-an-izm) n. A system of church policy vesting the powers of government in the body of believers to be exercised by their chosen representatives, the presbyters.

pres·by·ter·y (*prez*-bit-er-ee) n. [*pl.* pres·by·ter·ies] In the Presbyterian Church, the body of ministers and representative elders acting as judicational and spiritual overseers.

pre·sci·ence (*pree*-shee-enss) n. Foreknowledge; foresight.—**pre·sci·ent** adj.—**pre·sci·ent·ly** adv.

pre·scribe (preh-*skrybe*) v. [pre·scribed; pre·scrib·ing] 1. To order authoritatively; dictate. 2. To give medical directions.

pre·scrip·tion (preh-*skrip*-shun) n. 1. Direction; precept. 2. *Medical.* A written direction for a remedy and its use by a patient.—**pre·scrip·tive** adj.—**pre·scrip·tive·ly** adv.

pres·ence (*prez*-enss) n. 1. Existence in a certain place. 2. Nearness; immediate vicinity. 3. Appearance; mien.

pres·ent (*prez*-ent) adj. 1. Being in a certain place. 2. Being in company. 3. Real; actual. 4. Now existing; not past or future.

5. *Grammar.* The tense of a verb expressing action now.—n. 1. Time now. 2. A gift. 3. [*pl.*] *Legal.* A term specifying a deed or document.—**at present.** Right now.—**for the present.** Temporarily.

pre·sent (pree-*zent*) v. 1. To introduce. 2. To display; exhibit. 3. To give; bestow a gift upon. 4. To act; personate. 5. To proffer; submit. 6. To nominate.—**pre·sent·er** n.

pre·sent·a·ble (preh-*zent*-uh-b'l) adj. Adequate in appearance; pleasing.—**pre·sent·a·bil·i·ty** n.—**pre·sent·a·ble·ness** n.

pres·en·ta·tion (prez-en-*tay*-shun) n. 1. An offering. 2. An exhibition; display. 3. A formal introduction—**pre·sen·ta·tion·al** adj.

pre·sen·ti·ment (preh-*zen*-tih-ment) n. A misgiving; foreboding.

pre·sent·ly (*prez*-ent-lee) adv. In a short time.

pre·sent·ment (preh-*zent*-m'nt) n. 1. The act of presenting. 2. Appearance; representation.

pres·er·va·tion (prez-er-*vay*-shun) n. 1. Remaining safe from injury or delay. 2. Escape from danger.

pre·serv·a·tive (preh-*zerv*-uh-tiv) n. An agent for preventing injury or decay.—adj. Tending to preserve.

pre·serve (preh-*zerv*) v. [pre·served; pre·serv·ing] 1. To keep safe from injury or destruction; to secure. 2. To guard; uphold. 3. To conserve food by canning, pickling, cooking with sugar, etc. 4. To protect fish or game from hunting.—n. [*pl.*] 1. Fruit cooked with sugar. 2. Area set aside for the protection of game or fish.—**pre·serv·a·ble** adj.— -**serv·er** n.

pre·side (preh-*zyde*) v. [pre·sid·ed; pre·sid·ing] To direct; supervise; hold the leading position.—**pre·sid·er** n.

pres·i·den·cy (*prez*-ih-den-see) n. [*pl.* pres·i·den·cies] 1. Superintendence. 2. The office or term of a president.

pres·i·dent (*prez*-ih-dent) n. 1. An officer selected or appointed to preside over a company, society, college, etc. 2. The chief executive officer of a republic.—**pres·i·den·tial** adj.

pre·sid·i·um (preh-*sid*-ee-um) n. *U.S.S.R.* A government committee having administrative powers.

press n. 1. The act of pressure; urgency. 2. A crowd; throng. 3. A machine for squeezing or crushing into more compact form. 4. A printing press. 5. Printed literature collectively, esp. newspapers or periodicals. 6. An upright case or cupboard. 7. A wine vat.

PRESS (def. 4)

P

press agent	press-made	press-pack (v.)
pressfeeder	pressman	pressroom
press-forge (v.)	pressmaster	presswork
press gang	press-noticed	pressworker

press *v.* 1. To bear heavily; compress. 2. To extract by squeezing. 3. To iron. 4. To embrace; hug. 5. To urge on. 6. To strive eagerly. 7. To crowd; throng. 8. To entreat; importune. 9. To hasten; speed.

press *v.* To force into service, esp. armed service.

press·ing *adj.* Urgent; demanding.—**press·ing·ly** *adv.*

pres·sure (*presh*-er) *n.* 1. A squeezing. 2. *Mechanics.* The force of one body acting on another by weight or applied power. 3. Influence; compelling force. 4. Stress; turmoil. —**pressure gauge.** An apparatus registering the pressure of steam.

pres·ti·dig·i·ta·tion (press-tih-dij-ih-*tay*-shun) *n.* Sleight of hand.—**pres·ti·dig·i·ta·tor** *n.*

pres·tige (*press*-teezh) *n.* Influential reputation.

pres·to (*press*-toh) *adv.* 1. Quickly; immediately. 2. *Music.* Rapidly.—*adj.* Rapidly performed.

pre·sume (preh-*zoom*) *v.* [pre·sumed; pre·sum·ing] 1. To take for granted; presuppose. 2. To venture; dare. 3. To act arrogantly; take undue liberties.—**pre·sum·a·ble** *adj.* Probable.—**pre·sum·a·bly** *adv.*—**pre·sum·ed·ly** *adv.*

pre·sump·tion (preh-*zump*-shun) *n.* 1. Arrogance; assurance. 2. A supposition; strong probability. 3. *Law.* A conclusion derived from an ascertained fact.—**pre·sump·tive** *adj.* Based on probable evidence.— **-tive·ly** *adv.*

pre·sump·tu·ous (preh-*zump*-choo-us) *adj.* Bold; self-confident; temerarious.—**pre·sump·tu·ous·ly** *adv.*—**pre·sump·tu·ous·ness** *n.*

pre·sup·pose (pree-sup-*pohz*) *v.* [pre·sup·posed; pre·sup·pos·ing] 1. To take for granted. 2. To postulate; imply as antecedent.—**pre·sup·po·si·tion** *n.* 1. A surmise. 2. A premise.

pre·tend (preh-*tend*) *v.* To make believe; feign; sham.—**pre·tend·ed** *adj.*—**pre·tend·er** *n.*

pre·tense, pre·tence (preh-*tenss*) *n.* 1. A false appearance; show. 2. A pretext. 3. A claim.

pre·ten·sion (preh-*ten*-shun) *n.* 1. Ostentation; show. 2. An unwarranted assumption; claim. 3. A deception; pretext.

pre·ten·tious (preh-*ten*-shus) *adj.* 1. Showy; ostentatious. 2. Ambitious; attempting to impress.—**pre·ten·tious·ly** *adv.*— **-tious·ness** *n.*

pret·er·it, pret·er·ite (*pret*-er-it) *adj. Grammar.* Past; expressing finished action or state.—*n. Grammar.* The past tense.

pre·ter·nat·u·ral (pree-ter-*nach*-er-al) *adj.* Extraordinary; not in the natural course of things; inexplicable.—**pre·ter·nat·u·ral·ism** *n.* —**pre·ter·nat·u·ral·ly** *adv.*

pre·text (*pree*-tekst) *n.* A guise; deception; pretended motive.

pret·ti·fy (*prit*-ih-fye) *v.* [pret·ti·fied; pret·ti·fy·ing] To overembellish; make more detailed.

pret·ty (*prit*-ee) *adj.* [pret·ti·er; pret·ti·est] 1. Pleasing; attractive. 2. Nice; fine—used ironically. 3. Affected; foppish.—*adv.* Moderately; in some degree.—**pret·ties** *n. pl.* Dainty or pretty things.—**pret·ti·ly** *adv.*—**pret·ty·ish** *adj.*—**pret·ti·ness** *n.*

pret·zel (*pret*-sel) *n.* A hard twisted biscuit, glazed and salted.

pre·vail (preh-*vayl*) *v.* 1. To overcome; gain victory; succeed. 2. To influence; persuade; induce. 3. To be prevalent; become general. —**pre·vail·ing** *adj.* 1. Predominant. 2. Common; general.—**pre·vail·ing·ly** *adv.*

prev·a·lence (*prev*-uh-lenss) *n.* General existence; frequent occurrence.—**prev·a·lent** *adj.* Current; rife.—**prev·a·lent·ly** *adv.*

pre·var·i·cate (preh-*vair*-ih-kayt) *v.* [pre·var·i·cat·ed; pre·var·i·cat·ing] To evade the truth; lie; patter.—**pre·var·i·ca·tion** *n.*— **-ca·tor** *n.*

pre·vent (preh-*vent*) *v.* 1. To hinder or stop from happening. 2. To thwart; obstruct. —**pre·vent·a·ble, pre·vent·i·ble** *adj.*—**pre·vent·er** *n.*—**pre·ven·tion** *n.*

pre·ven·tive (preh-*ven*-tiv) *adj.* Precautionary. —*n.* A means of hindering, esp. of averting disease.—**pre·ven·tive·ly** *adv.*— **-tive·ness** *n.*

pre·view (*pree*-vyoo) *n.* Also **pre·vue.** 1. A private showing of an exhibition before its public opening. 2. *Motion Pictures.* An advance showing of excerpts of a movie as advertisement; trailer.

pre·vi·ous (*pree*-vee-us) *adj.* 1. Prior; earlier. 2. *Colloquial.* Premature.—**pre·vi·ous·ly** *adv.* Formerly; beforehand.—**pre·vi·ous·ness** *n.*

pre·vi·sion (preh-*vizh*-un) *n.* Foresight.

prey (*pray*) *n.* 1. An animal seized by another for food. 2. A victim; quarry.—*v.* 1. To plunder; pillage. 2. To seize and devour. 3. To rest heavily upon; wear away gradually.—**prey·er** *n.*

Pri·am (*pry*-am). *Greek Mythology.* The last king of Troy, father of Hector and Paris.

Pri·a·pus (*pry*-uh-pus, pry-*ay*-pus). *Mythology.* 1. The god of fruitfulness and virility. 2. [*not cap.*] The penis.—**Pri·a·pe·an** *adj.*

price *n.* 1. Exchange value; worth. 2. Amount for which an article is sold; cost. 3. Reward; recompense.—*v.* [priced; pric·ing] 1. To value; set a price on. 2. *Colloquial.* To ask the price of.

price·less *adj.* 1. Invaluable; inestimable. 2. *Slang.* Amusingly absurd.

prick *n.* 1. A puncture made by a pointed instrument; dot. 2. A small sharp-pointed implement; thorn. 3. A stinging sensation or thought; remorse.—*v.* 1. To puncture; pierce. 2. To affect with sharp pain; sting with remorse. 3. To spur on; incite. 4. To mark; trace by puncturing.—**prick·er** *n.*—**prick·ing·ly** *adv.*—**prick up one's ears.** To listen eagerly.

prick·le (*prik*-'l) *n.* 1. A small sharp point, esp. a projection on the bark of a plant. 2. A slight piercing sensation.—*v.* [prick·led; prick·ling] To pierce slightly; tingle.

prick·ly *adj.* [prick·li·er; prick·li·est] 1. Full of sharp points. 2. Stinging; tingling.

prickly heat. An acute inflammation of the

sweat glands causing an eruption of red pimples.

prickly pear. An American cactus with fleshy stems and pear-shaped edible fruit covered with thorns.

pride *n.* 1. Arrogance; loftiness; conceit. 2. Self-respect; dignity. 3. Complacency; smugness.—*v.* [prid·ed; prid·ing] To value oneself; take credit; glory.

pri·er, pry·er *n.* An inquisitive person.

priest (*preest*) *n.* 1. One who officiates in sacred religious rites. 2. A member of the clergy.—**priest·ess** *n.*

priest·craft *n.* A temporal material attitude toward priestly policy.

priest·hood *n.* 1. The office of a priest. 2. Priests collectively.

priest·ly *adj.* [priest·li·er; priest·li·est] 1. Sacerdotal; pertaining to a priest. 2. Befitting a priest.—**priest·li·ness** *n.*

prig *n.* A smug, self-satisfied person.

prig·gish *adj.* Prudish; narrowly virtuous. —**prig·gish·ly** *adv.*—**prig·gish·ness** *n.*

prim *adj.* [prim·mer; prim·mest] Demure; decorous.—*v.* [primmed; prim·ming] To prink; deck with affected nicety.—**prim·ly** *adv.*

pri·ma·cy (*pry*-muh-see) *n.* [*pl.* pri·ma·cies] 1. Priority; precedence. 2. The office or dignity of a primate, esp. the supreme power of the Pope.

prima donna (pree-muh-*don*-uh) [*pl.* prima donnas]. The leading female singer in an opera or concert.

pri·mal (*pry*-m'l) *adj.* 1. Initial; fundamental. 2. Most important; chief.

pri·ma·ry *adj.* 1. First in time; original. 2. First in importance; principal. 3. Elementary; preparatory, as primary schools. 4. Fundamental; basic, as primary colors.—*n.* [*pl.* pri·ma·ries] 1. One highest in rank, importance, place, etc. 2. A meeting of party members to name candidates for a coming election. 3. *Zoology.* One of the large feathers or the joint of a bird's wing. 4. *Astronomy.* A planet as opposed to its satellites. —**pri·ma·ri·ly** *adv.*

pri·mate (*pry*-mit) *n.* 1. Highest ranking archbishop of a nation. 2. *Zoology.* Animal of the order of Primates.—**pri·ma·tal** *adj.*—**pri·mate·ship** *n.*—**pri·ma·ti·al** *adj.*

Pri·ma·tes (pry-*may*-teez) *n. Zoology.* The highest order of mammals, including man, the apes, monkeys, marmosets, and lemurs.

prime *adj.* 1. First; original. 2. Highest; chief. 3. *Mathematics.* Divisible by no number except itself and 1.—*n.* 1. The earliest stage; dawn; the morning. 2. Most active period of life; youth. 3. The best in quality. 4. *Mathematics.* A prime number.—*v.* [primed; prim·ing] 1. To prepare an apparatus for operating. 2. To cover with the first coat of paint. 3. To make ready; to instruct beforehand. 'To prime a witness.'—**prime·ly** *adv.*

prim·er (*pryme*-er) *n.* Powder cap to ignite an explosive.

prim·er (*prim*-er) *n.* 1. An elementary book for teaching children to read and spell. 2. *Printing.* One of two sizes of type; **great primer** (18 point), or **long primer** (10 point).

pri·me·val (pry-*mee*-v'l) *adj.* Primitive; original; belonging to the earliest age.— **-val·ly** *adv.*

prim·ing (*pryme*-ing) *n.* 1. The powder or other material used to ignite an explosive charge. 2. The first coat of paint or sizing laid on a surface to be painted.

prim·i·tive (*prim*-ih-tiv) *adj.* 1. Belonging to earlier ages; original; first. 2. Crude; simple; in the style of early times.—*n.* 1. Member of an early uncivilized society. 2. *Art.* **a.** A medieval painter. **b.** An untrained modern painter, usually primarily interested in flat pattern and finely observed detail, executed in a brilliant palette.

pri·mo·gen·i·tor (pry-moh-*jen*-ih-ter) *n.* A forefather; ancestor.

pri·mo·gen·i·ture (pry-moh-*jen*-ih-choor) *n.* 1. Being born first among children in one family. 2. The right of inheritance of the first-born son of a family.

pri·mor·di·al (pry-*mor*-dee-al) *adj.* First in order; original; primitive.—**pri·mor·di·al·ly** *adv.*

primp *v.* To bedeck; doll up; preen.

prim·rose *n.* An early-blooming perennial herb bearing pale reddish-yellow flowers. —*adj.* Resembling a primrose in color.

PRIMROSE

P

prim·u·la (*prim*-yoo-luh) *n.* The family name of the primrose.

prince *n.* 1. A sovereign; holder of the highest rank. 2. The son of a sovereign. 3. A member of a royal family or of the higher nobility. 4. A distinguished leader of a class, profession, etc.—**prince·dom** *n.*

Prince Albert. A man's long frock coat for formal morning wear.

Prince of Darkness. Satan.

prince·ly *adj.* [prince·li·er; prince·li·est] 1. Pertaining to a prince; royal; regal. 2. Like a prince; stately; dignified. 3. Magnificent; bountiful.—**prince·li·ness** *n.*

prin·cess (*prin*-sess) *n.* 1. The daughter or granddaughter of a sovereign. 2. The wife of a prince.—**Princess royal,** The eldest daughter of a sovereign.

prin·cesse (prin-*sess*) *adj.* Also **princess.** Denoting a closely fitting one-piece slip or dress.

prin·ci·pal (*prin*-sih-pal) *adj.* Chief; main; highest.—*n.* 1. A head; leader. 2. The head of a school. 3. A capital sum drawing interest. 4. *Law.* **a.** The perpetrator of a crime or an abettor. **b.** A person employing another to act for him as agent. **c.** A person for whom another becomes surety. 5. *Architecture.* One of the main rafters of a building. 6. *Music.* A row of metallic stops in an organ tuned an octave higher than the diapason.—**prin·ci·pal·ly** *adv.*—**prin·ci·pal·ship** *n.*

prin·ci·pal·i·ty (prin-sih-*pal*-ih-tee) *n.* The territory ruled by a prince.

prin·ci·ple (*prin*-sih-p'l) *n.* 1. A source or origin. 2. A basic truth or law. 3. A guide to action; tenet; doctrine; ideal. 4. A primary component.

prink *v.* To dress for show; preen.—**prink·er** *n.*

print *n.* 1. An impression; mark or imprint. 2. A mold or die for making an impression; result of an impression. 3. Type; printed characters. 4. Any product of impression, as engraving, typesetting, etc. 5. A printed publication, esp. a newspaper. 6. A cloth figured with colored stampings. 7. *Photography.* A positive picture.—**print** *v.*—**print·a·ble** *adj.* —**print·er** *n.*—**print·er·y** *n.* [*pl.* print·er·ies]. —**in print.** Published; in a printed form.—**out of print.** No longer being published.

print·ing *n.* The art and practice of putting reading matter into type.

printing press. A machine for making impressions on paper, cloth, etc., by the pressure of the inked surface of type, plates, etc.

pri·or (*pry*-er) *adj.* Preceding; earlier; previous.

pri·or (*pry*-er) *n.* 1. The head of a religious house. 2. The head of a priory or monastery ranking just below an abbot.—**pri·or·ate** *n.*

pri·or·i·ty (pry-*or*-ih-tee) *n.* [*pl.* pri·or·i·ties] 1. The state of being earlier in time, or first in rank or place. 2. A U.S. government control over the production, use, distribution, and price of every material or product vitally necessary to the winning of World War II.

pri·or·y (*pry*-er-ee) *n.* [*pl.* pri·or·ies] An establishment for a religious order, ranking just below an abbey.

prism (*prizm*) *n.* 1. *Geometry.* A solid whose ends are in parallel planes identical in size and shape, and whose sides are parallelograms. 2. A transparent solid, usually triangular in shape, used to refract light and break it into its component colors.

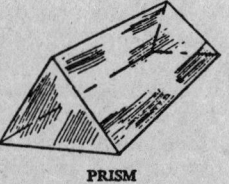

PRISM

pris·mat·ic (priz-*mat*-ik) *adj.* Also **pris·mat·i·cal.** 1. Resembling a prism. 2. Formed by a prism. 3. Colorful.—**pris·mat·i·cal·ly** *adv.*

prismatic colors. The three primary colors (red, yellow, blue) and their secondary tints (orange, green, violet) formed by the passage of light through a prism.

pris·on (*priz*-un) *n.* A jail; place of confinement or custody for criminals.

pris·on·er (*priz*-un-er) *n.* Captive; person under arrest or confined in prison.

pris·tine (*priss*-teen) *adj.* 1. Original; primitive. 2. Pure; uncorrupted; unspoiled.

prith·ee *interj. Archaic.* Please; I pray thee.

pri·va·cy (*pry*-vuh-see) *n.* [*pl.* pri·va·cies] Solitude; retirement; retreat; seclusion; secrecy.

pri·vate (*pry*-vit) *adj.* 1. Personal; not social. 2. Secret; not in public knowledge. 3. Not public; not governmental or political. 4. Solitary; sequestered.—*n.* The lowest-ranking enlisted soldier.—**pri·vate·ly** *adv.*—**pri·vate·ness** *n.*

pri·va·teer (pry-vuh-*teer*) 1. Privately owned ship licensed by government to act against enemy shipping. 2. A commander or seaman of a privateer.—*v.* To cruise as a privateer.

pri·va·tion (pry-*vay*-shun) *n.* 1. Want; destitution; lack of the necessary comforts of life. 2. Absence; negation.

priv·a·tive (*priv*-uh-tiv) *adj.* 1. Causing privation. 2. Negative; indicating absence.—*n.* 1. A negation. 2. *Grammar.* A prefix (*a-, in-, un-, non-*) or suffix (*-less*) giving a word its opposite meaning.—**priv·a·tive·ly** *adv.*

priv·et (*priv*-et) *n.* An evergreen shrub with dense clusters of small white flowers, widely used for hedges.

priv·i·lege (*priv*-ih-lij) *n.* A prerogative; special right; favor.—*v.* [priv·i·leged; priv·i·leg·ing] To grant a right or exemption.

priv·i·ty (*priv*-ih-tee) *n.* [*pl.* -ties] Secrecy; shared private knowledge.

priv·y (*priv*-ee) *adj.* 1. Private; for private uses. 2. Privately informed; secretly aware.—*n.* [*pl.* -ies] 1. *Law.* A person having an interest in an action or an estate. 2. A water closet; toilet.—**priv·i·ly** *adv.*

PRIVET

privy purse. The sum set apart in the civil list for the private use of the sovereign of England.

privy seal. In Great Britain, the seal placed on grants which are to pass the great seal, and on documents of minor importance.

prize, prise *v.* [prized; priz·ing] To force up; raise by means of a lever; pry.—*n.* A lever; leverage.

prize *n.* 1. A reward given the winner of a contest. 2. A gain; privilege; thing of value. 3. Goods taken from an enemy in war, esp. a captured ship.—*v.* [prized; priz·ing] 1. To value highly; esteem. 2. To rate; set the value.—*adj.* 1. Worthy of a prize. 2. Awarded as a prize.

prize court. A court passing judgment on captures made at sea.

prize fight. A boxing match for a wager or prize.—**prize fighter** *n.*—**prize fighting** *n.*

prize money. The money made from the sale of a captured ship divided in certain proportions among the officers and crew.

pro *adv.* For.—*n. Slang.* 1. Professional. 2. Prophylaxis; prophylactic.

pro and con. For and against.

prob·a·bil·i·ty *n.* [*pl.* prob·a·bil·i·ties] 1. Likelihood; favorable chance. 2. An event to be reasonably expected.

prob·a·ble (*prob*-uh-'b'l) *adj.* Likely; appearing.—**prob·a·bly** *adv.*

prc·bate (*proh*-bayt) *n. Law.* Proof of establishment of a will.—**pro·bate** *adj.*—*v.* [pro·bat·ed; pro·bat·ing] To prove a document genuine.

pro·ba·tion (proh-*bay*-shun) *n.* 1. A trial period; testing procedure. 2. *Law.* Conditional release of a prisoner. 3. *Education.* Conditional retention of a student.—**pro·ba·tion·al, pro·ba·tion·ar·y** *adj.*—**pro·ba·tion·er** *n.*

probe *v.* [probed; prob·ing] To search deeply; examine; explore.—*n.* 1. A surgical instrument for examining cavities or wounds. 2. An investigation; inquiry.—**prob·er** *n.*

prob·i·ty (*prob*-ih-tee, *prohb*-) *n.* Integrity; high character.

prob·lem *n.* A difficult question or situation.

prob·lem·at·i·cal (prob-lem-*at*-ih-k'l) *adj.* Also **prob·lem·at·ic.** Questionable; disputable.

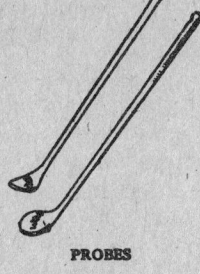

PROBES

pro·bos·cis (proh-*boss*-iss) *n.* [*pl.* pro·bos·ci·ses, pro·bos·cid·es] 1. A snoutlike projection; trunk. 2. *Colloquial.* The nose.

pro·ce·dure (proh-*see*-jer) *n.* 1. An established course of action. 2. Moving forward; progress.—**pro·ce·dur·al** *adj.*

pro·ceed (proh-*seed*) *v.* 1. To go forward. 2. To carry on methodical action. 3. To issue forth; come from.—**pro·ceed·er** *n.*

pro·ceeds (*proh*-seedz) *n. pl.* Sum received from a transaction or commercial deal.

pro·ceed·ing (proh-*seed*-ing) *n.* 1. Advancement; course of action. 2. Transaction; step taken in the course of business. 3. *pl.* Transactions of an organization or record thereof.

proc·ess (*pross*-ess) *n.* 1. Progress; course of action. 2. Related series of changes producing a definite result. 3. *Biology.* A projecting outgrowth of tissue. 4. *Law.* A written court order, as a summons.—*v.* 1. To subject to a methodical procedure. 2. *Law.* To serve court order upon.—*adj.* Produced by a special process.

pro·ces·sion (proh-*seh*-shun) 1. A formal march or parade. 2. Continuous progression.

pro·ces·sion·al (proh-*seh*-shun-'l) *n. Church.* A hymn for religious processions.—*adj.* Pertaining to a procession.

pro·claim (proh-*claym*) *v.* 1. To announce; publish. 2. To govern by proclamation.

proc·la·ma·tion (prok-luh-*may*-shun) *n.* 1. A public announcement. 2. A decree set forth by a sovereign.

pro·cliv·i·ty (proh-*kliv*-ih-tee) *n.* [*pl.* -ties] Tendency; inclination; readiness.

pro·cras·ti·nate (proh-*krass*-tih-nayt) *v.* [pro·cras·ti·nat·ed; -nat·ing] To put off; delay.—**pro·cras·ti·na·tion** *n.*—**pro·cras·ti·na·tor** *n.*

pro·cre·ate *v.* [pro·cre·at·ed; -ating] To produce offspring.—**pro·cre·ant** *adj.*—**pro·cre·a·tion** *n.*—**pro·cre·a·tive** *adj.*—**pro·cre·a·tor** *n.*

proc·tor (*prok*-ter) *n.* A university official charged with maintaining order.—**proc·tor** *v.*—**proc·to·ri·al** *adj.*—**proc·tor·ship** *n.*

pro·cum·bent (proh-*kum*-bent) *n.* Prone; lying face downward.

proc·u·ra·tion (prohk-yoo-*ray*-shun) *n.* 1. Managing the affairs of another. 2. Document empowering one to act for another.—**proc·u·ra·tor** *n.*—**proc·u·ra·to·ri·al, -to·ry** *adj.*

pro·cure (proh-*kyoor*) *v.* [pro·cured; pro·cur·ing] 1. To obtain; get. 2. To recruit women for prostitution.—**pro·cur·a·ble** *adj.*—**pro·cure·ment** *n.*—**pro·cur·er** *n.*—**pro·cur·ess** *n.*

prod *v.* [prod·ded; prod·ding] To goad; urge to greater effort.—*n.* A pointed instrument used to induce greater activity.—**prod·der** *n.*

prod·i·gal (*prod*-ih-g'l) *adj.* Wasteful; given to lavish expenditure.—*n.* A spendthrift.—**prod·i·gal·i·ty** (-*gal*-ih-tee) *n.* [*pl.* -ties] Wasteful expenditure; lavishness.—**prod·i·gal·ly** *adv.*

pro·di·gious (proh-*dih*-jus) *adj.* 1. Extraordinary. 2. Great in size, degree, intensity, etc.—**pro·di·gious·ly** *adv.*—**pro·di·gious·ness** *n.*

prod·i·gy (*prod*-ih-jee) *n.* [*pl.* prod·i·gies] 1. A wonder; extraordinary thing. 2. A gifted child.

pro·duce (proh-*dyoos*, -*dooss*) *v.* [pro·duced; pro·duc·ing] 1. To make. 2. To bring forth, as an offspring. 3. To cause. 4. To manufacture. 5. *Economics.* To impart social values to.—**pro·duc·er** *n.*

prod·uce (*prod*-dooss) *n.* The yield of farm land; vegetables, etc.

prod·uct (*prod*-ukt) *n.* 1. A result of a deliberate or natural process. 2. Quantity produced. 3. *Mathematics.* The quantity obtained by multiplication.

pro·duc·tion (proh-*duk*-sh'n) *n.* 1. That which is made or created. 2. Process of creating. 3. Output; total or quota of manufactured goods.—**pro·duc·tion** *adj.*

pro·duc·tive (proh-*duk*-tiv) *adj.* 1. Having the power to create or make. 2. Fertile; yielding results.—**pro·duc·tive·ly** *adv.*—**pro·duc·tive·ness** *n.*—**pro·duc·tiv·i·ty** (proh-duk-*tiv*-ih-tee) *n.*

pro·fa·na·tion (proh-fuh-*nay*-shun) *n.* Violation or irrevelant treatment of sacred things.

pro·fane *adj.* 1. Not sacred; worldly. 2. Irreligious; irreverent.—*v.* [pro·faned; pro·fan·ing] To desecrate; treat with irreverence.—**pro·fane·ly** *adv.*—**pro·fane·ness** *n.*—**pro·fan·er** *n.*

pro·fan·i·ty (proh-*fan*-ih-tee) *n.* [*pl.* pro·fan·i·ties] Blasphemy; cursing.

pro·fess (proh-*fess*) *v.* 1. To acknowledge or declare solemnly, often hypocritically. 2. To

P

follow a profession. 3. To subscribe to a religious faith.—**pro·fess·ed·ly** adv.

pro·fes·sion n. 1. Occupation; employment. 2. The body of persons following a specified calling. 3. That which is asserted.

pro·fes·sion·al adj. 1. Pertaining to a profession. 2. Following a calling as means of livelihood; not amateur. 3. Consistently following a formula of conduct.—**pro·fes·sion·al** n.—**pro·fes·sion·al·ism** n. Acceptance of money for services.—**pro·fes·sion·al·ly** adv.

pro·fes·sor (proh-fess-er) n. 1. A college teacher or lecturer, esp. one holding an appointment of professorial rank. 2. One who declares his beliefs.—**pro·fes·so·ri·al** adj.—**pro·fes·so·ri·al·ly** adv.—**pro·fes·sor·ship** n.

prof·fer v. To offer; tender.—**prof·fer** n.

pro·fi·cient (proh-fish-ent) adj. Well versed; expert.—**pro·fi·cient** n.—**pro·fi·cien·cy** n.—**pro·fi·cient·ly** adv.—**pro·fi·cient·ness** n.

pro·file (proh-fyle) n. 1. Contour, esp. of human features seen from the side; side view. 2. A biographical sketch. 3. Engineering. A vertical cross section.—v. [pro·filed; pro·fil·ing].

Pro·fil·o·me·ter. Mechanical Engineering. Trade-mark name for precision inspection instrument used for measuring irregularities of machine surfaces.

prof·it n. 1. Gain; advantage. 2. Excess of income over one's investment.—**prof·it** v.—**prof·it·less** adj. —**prof·it·less·ly** adv.

PROFILE

prof·it·a·ble adj. 1. Yielding gain; lucrative. 2. Advantageous.—**prof·it·a·ble·ness** n.—**prof·it·a·bly** adv.

prof·it·eer (prof-ih-teer) n. One who makes large profits at the expense of the general public.—**prof·it·eer** v.—**prof·it·eer·ing** n.

prof·li·gate (prof-lih-git) adj. 1. Debauched; dissolute. 2. Extravagant; prodigal.—**prof·li·ga·cy** n.—**prof·li·gate·ly** adv.— -**gate·ness** n.

pro·found (proh-found) adj. 1. Deep; searching; penetrating. 2. Deep-seated; strong; sincere.—**pro·found·ly** adv.—**pro·fun·di·ty, pro·found·ness** n.

pro·fuse (proh-fyoos) adj. Abundant; lavish; extravagent.—**pro·fuse·ly** adv.—**pro·fuse·ness** n. —**pro·fu·sion** n.

pro·gen·i·tor (proh-jen-ih-ter) n. A parent; ancestor.—**pro·gen·i·tor·ship** n.

prog·e·ny (proj-eh-nee) n. Offspring; children.

prog·no·sis n. Medicine. Estimate of the probable outcome of a disease.—**prog·nos·tic** adj.

prog·nos·ti·cate (prog-nos-tih-kayt) v. [prog·nos·ti·cat·ed; -cat·ing] To predict; foretell.—**prog·nos·ti·ca·tion** n.—**prog·nos·ti·ca·tor** n.

pro·gram, pro·gramme (proh-gram) n. 1. An announcement or outline of a public entertainment. 2. A plan; schedule.

prog·ress (prog-res) n. Advancement; movement forward; development; improvement.—

(proh-gres) v. To advance.—**pro·gres·sion** (proh-gresh-un) n. 1. Advancement. 2. Mathematics. A regular succession of numbers. —**pro·gres·sion·al** adj.

pro·gres·sive (proh-gres-iv) adj. Advancing; improving.—n. A believer in progress.—n. [cap.] 1. A liberal political party formerly having strength in Wisconsin. 2. A member of this party.—**pro·gres·sive·ly** adv.— -**sive·ness** n.

pro·hib·it (proh-hib-it) v. To forbid; prevent.

pro·hi·bi·tion (proh-hih-bish-un) n. 1. Act of forbidding. 2. An injunction forbidding a specified practice. 3. The outlawing of alcoholic liquors.—**pro·hi·bi·tion·ist** n.

pro·hib·i·tive (proh-hib-ih-tiv) adj. Also **pro·hib·i·to·ry**. Forbidding; precluding.—**pro·hib·i·tive·ly, pro·hib·i·to·ri·ly** adv.

pro·ject (proh-jekt) v. 1. To cast or shoot forward; throw; transfer; objectify. 2. To stick out; jut. 3. To plan; contrive. 4. To chart; represent; depict.—n. (proj-ekt) Scheme; plan.—**pro·jec·tor** n.

pro·jec·tile (proh-jek-t'l) n. A body forcibly propelled by an external force, esp. a missile from a firearm.—adj. Forcibly impelled.

pro·jec·tion (proh-jek-shun) n. 1. A representation of a three-dimensional object on a flat surface. 2. Act of shooting out. 3. A jutting section or object. 4. Act of planning. 5. Psychology. Objectifying of a subjective element.—**pro·jec·tive** adj.

pro·late (proh-layt) adj. Elongated at the poles.

pro·le·tar·i·an (proh-leh-tair-ee-an) n. A member of the working class.—**pro·le·tar·i·an** adj.—**pro·le·tar·i·at** n. The working class.—**pro·le·tar·i·an·ism** n.

pro·lif·ic (proh-lif-ik) adj. Fruitful; highly productive.—**pro·lif·i·cal·ly** adv.—**pro·lif·ic·ness** n.

pro·lix (proh-liks, proh-liks) adj. Wordy; profuse; tedious.—**pro·lix·i·ty** n.—**pro·lix·ly** adv. —**pro·lix·ness** n.

pro·loc·u·tor (proh-lok-yoo-ter) n. 1. A spokesman. 2. In Great Britain, the chancellor of the House of Lords.

pro·logue, pro·log (proh-log) n. Introduction to a literary work, as a drama.

pro·long (proh-long) v. To extend in duration. —**pro·long·er** n.—**pro·long·ment** n.

pro·lon·gate (proh-long-gayt) v. [pro·lon·gat·ed; -gat·ing] To lengthen; prolong.— -**ga·tion** n.

prom·e·nade (prom-uh-nahd, -nayd) n. 1. A leisurely stroll. 2. A public path or walk.—v. [prom·e·nad·ed; -nad·ing].

Pro·me·theus (proh-mee-thyus) n. Greek Mythology. A titan who gave the secret of fire to mankind.—**Pro·me·the·an** adj. 1. Like Prometheus. 2. Life giving.

prom·i·nent (prom-ih-n'nt) adj. 1. Conspicuous; obvious; noticeable. 2. Distinguished; well known. 3. Jutting; protruding.—**prom·i·nence** n.—**prom·i·nent·ly** adv.

pro·mis·cu·ous (proh-miss-kyoo-us) adj. 1. Heterogeneous; assorted. 2. Undiscriminating;

generalized; loose. 3. Sexually indiscrimi-
nate.—**prom·is·cu·i·ty** *n.*—**pro·mis·cu·ous·ly** *adj.*

prom·ise (*prom*-iss) *v.* [prom·ised; prom·is·ing]
1. To pledge; give one's word. 2. To give
hope; portend. 3. To assure; vouch.—**prom·
ise** *n.*—**prom·is·er** *n.*

prom·is·ing *adj.* Auguring well; hopeful; probable.—**prom·is·ing·ly** *adv.*

prom·is·so·ry (*prom*-ih-sor-ee) *adj.* Containing
a binding declaration.

promissory note. A pledge to pay a specified
sum on a date named.

prom·on·to·ry (*prom*-un-tor-ee) *n.* [*pl.* -to·ries]
A small, elevated peninsula.

pro·mote (proh-*moht*) *v.* [pro·mot·ed; pro·mot·
ing] 1. To raise to a higher rank or grade.
2. To contribute to; assist; spread. 3. To
organize a financial undertaking.—**pro·mot·er**
n.—**pro·mo·tion** *n.*

prompt *adj.* Quick; ready.—*v.* 1. To move to
action; suggest. 2. To give a reminder; supply a cue, as to an actor.—*n.* A hint; vocal cue.
—**prompt·er** *n.*—**prompt·ly** *adv.*—**prompt·ness,
promp·ti·tude** *n.*

pro·mul·gate(proh-*mul*-gayt)*v.*[pro·mul·gat·ed;
-gat·ing] To make public formally as the articles of a law or belief.—**pro·mul·ga·tion** *n.*
—**pro·mul·ga·tor** *n.*

prone *adj.* 1. Tending; inclined. 2. Lying
face downward; prostrate.—**prone·ly** *adv.*

prong *n.* 1. A pointed projection. 2. A tine
of a fork.—**prong** *v.*

prong·horn *n.* A hollow-horned antelope of
western North Amer-
ica.

pro·nom·i·nal *adj.*
Grammar. Referring
to a pronoun.—**pro·
nom·i·nal·ly** *adv.*

pro·noun (*proh*-nown)
n. Grammar. A word
used in the place of a
noun.

pro·nounce (proh-
nownss) *v.* [pro·
nounced; pro·nounc·
ing] 1. To utter dis-
tinctly and carefully.

PRONGHORN
(1/40 life-size)

2. To declare; affirm. 3. To speak formally
or officially.—**pro·nounce·a·ble** *adj.*—**pro·
nounc·er** *n.*

pro·nounced *adj.* Strongly marked or defined.
—**pro·nounc·ed·ly** *adv.*

pro·nounce·ment *n.* A formal announcement.

pron·to *adv. Slang.* Quickly; soon.

pro·nun·ci·a·men·to (proh-nun-shee-uh-*men*-
toh) *n. Spanish.* A manifesto or proclamation.

pro·nun·ci·a·tion (proh-nun-see-*ay*-shun) *n.* Articulation; manner of utterance.

proof *n.* 1. An ascertaining or evidence of
truth. 2. *Printing & Engraving.* A sample impression taken for correction. 3. *Photography.* Semipermanent test print. 4. *Mathe-*

matics. The series of logical steps in solving a
problem. 5. The concentration of alcohol in
a liquor. 'Ninety proof bourbon.'

proof·read (*proof*-reed) *v.* [proof·read; proof·
read·ing] To read and mark the mistakes in a
printer's proof.—**proof·read·er** *n.*— **-read·ing** *n.*

prop *v.* [propped; prop·ping] 1. To support
with a brace; shore. 2. To encourage; aid.
—*n.* A brace; support.

prop *n.* 1. *Aviation.* Short for **propeller.**
2. *Theater.* Short for **property.**

prop·a·gan·da (prop-uh-*gan*-duh) *n.* 1. Any
means of influencing opinion in favor of a
cause. 2. Group or plan devoted to propaganda. 3. [*cap.*] College of the Roman Catholic Church for training missionaries.—**prop·a·
gan·dism** *n.*—**prop·a·gan·dist** *n.*

prop·a·gan·dize (prop-uh-*gan*-dyze) *v.* [prop·a·
gan·dized; -diz·ing] To spread a doctrine, by
speeches, writing, etc.

próp·a·gate (*prop*-uh-gayt) *v.* [prop·a·gat·ed;
-gat·ing] 1. To produce offspring; originate.
2. To spread; transmit; diffuse.—**prop·a·ga·
tion** *n.*—**prop·a·ga·tive** *adj.*—**prop·a·ga·tor** *n.*

pro·pel (pro-*pel*) *v.* [pro·pelled; pro·pel·ling]
To drive forward; cause to advance.—**pro·pel·
lent** *adj.*

pro·pel·ler (proh-*pel*-ler) *n.* Revolving hub
fitted with blades, for driving ships, airplanes,
etc.

pro·pen·si·ty (proh-*pen*-sih-tee) *n.* [*pl.* -si·ties]
Bent of mind; aptitude.

prop·er *adj.* 1. Fit; suitable; correct. 2. Respectable; well comported. 3. Peculiar; distinctive. 4. Relating to a well-defined part
or section. 5. *Grammar.* Particularized.
6. *Mathematics.* Denoting a fraction with
numerator less than the denominator.

prop·er·ty (*prop*-er-tee) *n.* [*pl.* prop·er·ties]
1. Material wealth; goods, esp. real estate.
2. A quality or characteristic. 3. [*usually pl.*]
Theater. Furnishings and articles on a stage
other than the scenery.—**prop·er·tied** *adj.* Owning property, esp. real estate.

proph·e·cy (*prof*-eh-see) *n.* [*pl.* proph·e·cies] A
foretelling; prediction.

proph·e·sy (*prof*-eh-sy) *v.* [proph·e·sied; -sy·ing]
To forecast; predict.—**proph·e·si·er** *n.*

proph·et *n.* 1. Person disclosing divine revelation. 2. A spokesman; advocate. 3. One
who foretells the future.—**proph·et·ess** *n.*

pro·phet·ic (proh-*fet*-ik) *adj.* Also **pro·phet·i·
cal.** Pertaining to prediction; foretelling **or**
foretold.—**pro·phet·i·cal·ly** *adv.*

pro·phy·lac·tic *adj.* Preventive; protecting from
disease, esp. venereal.—**pro·phy·lac·tic** *n.*

pro·phy·lax·is *n.* A preventive treatment.

pro·pin·qui·ty (proh-*pin*-kwi-tee, *-ping-*) *n.*
Nearness; closeness.

pro·pi·ti·ate (proh-*pish*-ee-ayt) *v.* [pro·pi·ti·at·
ed; -at·ing] To appease; pacify; make atonement to.—**pro·pi·ti·a·tion** *n.*—**pro·pi·ti·a·tive**
adj.—**pro·pi·ti·a·tor** *n.*—**pro·pi·ti·a·to·ry** *adj.*

P

pro·pi·tious (proh-*pish*-us) *adj.* Favorable; helpful; fortunate.—**pro·pi·tious·ly** *adv.*—**pro·pi·tious·ness** *n.*

pro·po·nent (proh-*poh*-nent) *n.* One who makes a proposal; advocate.—**pro·po·nent** *adj.*

pro·por·tion *n.* 1. The comparative relation of one quantity to another. 2. The relative size and arrangement of parts; symmetry. 3. *Mathematics.* Equal ratios.—*v.* To arrange symmetrically.—**pro·por·tion·ment** *n.*

pro·por·tion·al (proh-*por*-shun-'l) *adj.* Arranged according to comparative quantity. —**pro·por·tion·al·i·ty** *n.*—**pro·por·tion·al·ly** *adv.*

pro·por·tion·ate (proh-*por*-shun-it) *adj.* According to a comparative relationship; proportional.—**pro·por·tion·ate·ly** *adv.*

pro·pose (proh-*pohz*) *v.* [pro·posed; pro·pos·ing] 1. To suggest; broach; offer. 2. To offer marriage. 3. To plan; intend.—**pro·pos·al** *n.*—**pro·pos·er** *n.*

prop·o·si·tion (prop-uh-*zish*-un) *n.* 1. Proposal; offer; suggestion. 2. An assertion either set forth to be demonstrated as in geometry or assumed true as in the premises of a syllogism. 3. *Colloquial.* An undertaking; project, esp. a business venture. 4. *Colloquial.* Person, situation, plan, etc., under consideration.—*v. Slang.* To make an offer.—**prop·o·si·tion·al** *adj.*

pro·pound (proh-*pound*) *v.* To offer for consideration; set forth.—**pro·pound·er** *n.*

pro·pri·e·ta·ry (proh-*pry*-eh-ter-ee) *adj.* Pertaining to ownership or an owner.—*n.* [*pl.* pro·pri·e·ta·ries] 1. An owner or group of owners. 2. *Pharmacy.* An unpatented medicine produced from a private formula.

pro·pri·e·tor (proh-*pry*-eh-ter) *n.* 1. Owner; holder of the legal title to property. 2. Manager.—**pro·pri·e·tor·ship** *n.*—**pro·pri·e·tress** *n.*

pro·pri·e·ty (proh-*pry*-eh-tee) *n.* [*pl.* -ties] 1. Fitness; correctness. 2. Decorum; social custom.

pro·pul·sion (proh-*pul*-shun) *n.* A driving forward.—**pro·pul·sive** *adj.*

pro·rate (proh-*rayt*) *v.* [pro·rat·ed; pro·rat·ing] To assess or distribute on a proportional basis. —**pro·rat·a·ble** *adj.*

pro·sa·ic (proh-*zay*-ik) *adj.* 1. Like prose; unpoetic. 2. Monotonous; commonplace.—**pro·sa·i·cal·ly** *adv.*

pro·sce·ni·um (proh-*see*-nee-um) *n. Theater.* The part of a stage between the curtain and the orchestra.

pro·scribe (proh-*skrybe*) *v.* [pro·scribed; pro·scrib·ing] To outlaw; banish; prohibit; damn. —**pro·scrib·er** *n.*

pro·scrip·tion (proh-*skrip*-shun) *n.* Denunciation; prohibition.—**pro·scrip·tive** *adj.*—**pro·scrip·tive·ly** *adv.*

prose *n.* 1. Language in ordinary usage, as opposed to verse. 2. Flat, unstimulating language.—**prose** *adj.*

pros·e·cute (*pros*-eh-kyoot) *v.* [pros·e·cut·ed; -cut·ing] 1. To follow through; pursue; continue in. 2. *Law.* a. To bring to trial. b. To sue by legal process.—**pros·e·cu·tion** *n.*—**pros·e·cu·tor** *n.*

pros·e·lyte (*pros*-eh-lyte) *v.* [pros·e·lyt·ed; -lyt·ing] To convert to an opinion or belief.— *n.* A new convert.—**pros·e·lyt·ism** *n.*—**pros·e·lyt·ize** *v.* [pros·e·lyt·ized; -iz·ing] To recruit followers.

Pro·ser·pi·na (proh-*ser*-pih-nuh) *n.* Also **Pro·ser·pi·ne** (-pih-nee, *pross*-ser-pyne), **Per·seph·o·ne.** *Classical Mythology.* Goddess of spring and vegetation.

pros·o·dy (*pros*-uh-dee) *n.* The study of the technique of versification.—**pros·o·dist** *n.*

pros·pect (*pros*-pekt) *n.* 1. A view; vista; scene. 2. Expectation; anticipation. 3. Future; probable outcome. 4. An anticipated client, customer, etc. 5. A newly located deposit.—*v. Mining.* To search for mineral deposits.—**pros·pec·tor** *n.*

pro·spec·tive (proh-*spek*-tiv) *adj.* Future; expected; anticipated.—**pro·spec·tive·ly** *adv.*

pro·spec·tus (proh-*spek*-tus) *n.* A brief outline of a publication or enterprise to arouse public interest.

pros·per *v.* To thrive; be successful.

pros·per·i·ty *n.* Success; economic well-being.

Pros·per·o (*pros*-per-oh) *n.* The hero of Shakespeare's *Tempest.*

pros·per·ous (*pros*-per-us) *adj.* 1. Thriving; successful. 2. Conducive; propitious.—**pros·per·ous·ly** *adv.*—**pros·per·ous·ness** *n.*

pros·tate (*pros*-tayt) *n.* A gland situated at the outlet of the bladder in males.

pros·ti·tute (*pros*-tih-tyoot, -toot) *n.* A woman who sells her body; whore.—*v.* [pros·ti·tut·ed; -tut·ing]. 1. To whore. 2. To use for material gain.—**pros·ti·tute** *adj.*

pros·trate (*pros*-trayt) *v.* [pros·trat·ed; pros·trat·ing] 1. To throw down; fall prone. 2. To exhaust; bring low; crush.—**pros·trate** *adj.* —**pros·tra·tion** *n.*

pros·y (*prohz*-ee) *adj.* [pros·i·er; pros·i·est] 1. Resembling prose; plodding. 2. Prosaic; humdrum.—**pros·i·ly** *adv.*—**pros·i·ness** *n.*

pro·tag·o·nist (proh-*tag*-uh-nist) *n.* Leading figure; hero.

pro·te·an (*proh*-tee-an) *adj.* Changeable in shape; variable.

pro·tect (proh-*tekt*) *v.* To shelter; shield; safeguard; defend.—**pro·tect·ing** *adj.*—**pro·tect·ing·ly** *adv.*—**pro·tect·ing·ness** *n.*

pro·tec·tion (proh-*tek*-shun) *n.* 1. Care; defense; guardianship. 2. An advantage given to national home industries by a tariff on imports.—**pro·tec·tion·ism** *n.* The doctrine opposed to free trade.—**pro·tec·tion·ist** *n.*

pro·tec·tive (proh-*tek*-tiv) *adj.* Sheltering; affording security.—**pro·tec·tive·ly** *adv.*

protective tariff. A duty imposed on imports to foster home industry.

pro·tec·tor (proh-*tek*-ter) *n.* 1. Guardian; defender. 2. A regent.—**pro·tec·tor·ship** *n.*

pro·tec·tor·ate (proh-*tek*-ter-it) *n.* 1. A state under the jurisdiction of a more powerful nation; the administrator of one nation by another. 2. Government by a protector or regent. 3. [*cap.*] The Cromwell interregnum in England.

pro·té·gé (*proh*-teh-zhay) *n.* One under the care or patronage of another.—**pro·té·gée** *n. fem.*

pro·te·in (*proh*-tee-in) *n.* A major food element found in animal products; an amino acid or its derivatives.—**pro·te·in** *adj.*

pro tem. Temporary; for the time being.

pro·test (*proh*-test) *n.* 1. A complaint; objection; dissent; opposition. 2. *Law.* A formal objection filed against an act or condition, or against a party liable for loss, damages, etc. —*v.* (proh-*test*).—**pro·test·er** *n.*—**pro·test·ing·ly** *adv.*

Prot·es·tant *adj.* Pertaining to non-Catholic Christians stemming from the Reformation. —**Prot·es·tant** *n.*

prot·es·ta·tion (prot-ess-*tay*-shun) *n.* A declaration; avowal.

Pro·teus (*proh*-tyooss, *proh*-tee-us). *Classical Mytholohy.* 1. A marine deity who assumed various shapes. 2. A turncoat.

pro·to·ac·tin·i·um (proh-toh-ak-*tin*-ee-um) *n.* A radioactive element occurring with radium in pitchblende. (*Symbol:* Pa).

pro·to·col (*proh*-tuh-kol) *n.* 1. The first draft of a diplomatic document. 2. Etiquette of diplomacy.—**pro·to·col** *v.*

pro·ton (*proh*-ton) *n.* The positively charged unit of mass in the nucleus of the atom.

pro·to·plasm (*proh*-toh-plazm) *n.* A colloidal substance forming the essential matter of all living organisms.—**pro·to·plas·mic** *adj.*

pro·to·type (*proh*-toh-type) *n.* An original; model; first instance.—**pro·to·typ·al, -typ·ic** *adj.*

Pro·to·zo·a (proh-toh-*zoh*-uh) *n.* Family of one-celled, usually microscopic, aquatic animals. —**pro·to·zo·an, pro·to·zo·ic** *adj.*

pro·tract (proh-*trakt*) *v.* To prolong; lengthen out.—**pro·tract·ed** *adj.*—**pro·trac·tion** *n.*

pro·trac·tor *n.* An instrument for laying out or measuring angles.

pro·trude (proh-trood) *v.* [pro·trud·ed; pro·trud·ing] To stick out; bulge; project. —**pro·tru·sion** *n.* —**pro·tru·sive** *adj.* —-sive·ly *adv.*

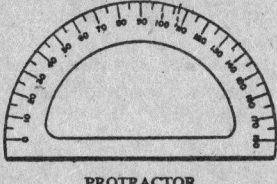

PROTRACTOR

pro·tu·ber·ance (proh-*toob*-er-enss) *n.* A swelling; bulge; prominence.—**pro·tu·ber·an·cy** *n.* [*pl.* -cies].—**pro·tu·ber·ant** *adj.*—**pro·tu·ber·ant·ly** *adv.*—**pro·tu·ber·ate** *v.* [-at·ed; -at·ing].

proud (prowd) *adj.* 1. Vain; haughty; arrogant. 2. Pleased; exultant. 3. Self-respecting. 4. Exalted; mighty; lofty.—**proud·ly** *adv.*

proud-blooded proud-hearted proud-pillared
proud-crested proud-minded proud-spirited

proud flesh. *Medicine.* An abnormal growth of tissue about a wound.

prove (*proov*) *v.* [proved; prov·en; prov·ing] 1. To establish through evidence; confirm. 2. To test; try.—**prov·a·ble** *adj.*—**prov·er** *n.*

Pro·vence (proh-*vahnss*). A region of southern France.—**Pro·ven·çal** *n.* 1. The Romance language of this region. 2. A native of Provence.—**Pro·ven·çal** *adj.*

prov·en·der (*prov*-en-der) *n.* Feed; fodder.

prov·erb *n.* 1. A wise or pithy saying; adage. 2. A byword; symbol.—**Prov·erbs** *n.* A book of the Old Testament containing a store of practical wisdom.—**pro·ver·bi·al** *adj.* 1. Like or pertaining to a proverb. 2. Well known. —**pro·ver·bi·al·ly** *adv.*

pro·vide (proh-*vyde*) *v.* [pro·vid·ed; pro·vid·ing] 1. To furnish; supply; prepare. 2. To stipulate; guarantee.—**pro·vid·er** *n.*

pro·vid·ed *conj.* On condition; in case.

prov·i·dence (*prov*-ih-denss) *n.* 1. Divine power or care. 2. Frugality; economy. 3. [*cap.*] God.

prov·i·dent (*prov*-ih-d'nt) *adj.* Prudent in preparing for the future; foreseeing.—**prov·i·dent·ly** *adv.*

prov·i·den·tial (prov-ih-*den*-shul) *adj.* Denoting God's power or beneficence.—**prov·i·den·tial·ly** *adv.*

pro·vid·ing (proh-*vyde*-ing) *conj.* In the event that.

prov·ince (*prov*-inss) *n.* 1. A region; subdivision of a national area. 2. Sphere of activity; department of knowledge. 3. [*pl.*] Region distant from a center of culture.

pro·vin·cial (proh-*vin*-shul) *adj.* 1. Countrified; rustic. 2. Relating to a province or local area.—*n.* Native of the provinces.—**pro·vin·cial·ism** *n.*—**pro·vin·cial·ly** *adv.*

pro·vi·sion (proh-*vizh*-un) *n.* 1. Stock, esp. of food. 2. A stipulating clause; proviso. 3. A measure taken beforehand.—*v.* To provide with stores.—**pro·vi·sion·al** *adj.*—**pro·vi·sion·al·ly** *adv.*—**pro·vi·sion·er** *n.*

pro·vi·so (proh-*vy*-zoh) *n.* [*pl.* pro·vi·sos, pro·vi·soes] A conditional clause in a document; stipulation.—**pro·vi·so·ry** *adj.*

prov·o·ca·tion (prov-uh-*kay*-shun) *n.* 1. A cause of anger. 2. An aggressive or provoking act.

pro·voc·a·tive (proh-*vok*-uh-tiv) *adj.* Stimulating; exciting anger.—**pro·voc·a·tive** *n.*—**pro·voc·a·tive·ly** *adv.*—**pro·voc·a·tive·ness** *n.*

pro·voke (proh-*vohk*) *v.* [pro·voked; pro·vok·ing] 1. To excite; arouse. 2. To anger. 3. To instigate; cause.—**pro·vok·er** *n.*—**pro·vok·ing** *adj.*—**pro·vok·ing·ly** *adv.*

prov·ost (*prov*-ust) *n.* 1. The superintendent or head of certain organizations. 2. (proh-voh) *Military.* An officer of the military police.

provost marshal (*proh*-voh). *Military.* Officer in charge of military police.

prow *n.* The forward end of a ship; bow.

prow·ess *n.* 1. Courage; valor. 2. Skill.

prowl *v.* To wander about stealthily as in search

of prey.—**prowl** *n.*—**prowl·er** *n.*— -**ing·ly** *adv.*

prowl car. A police-patrol car.

prox·i·mal (*proks*-ih-m'l) *adj.* Nearest to a specified point; opposite of *distal.*

prox·im·i·ty (proks-*im*-ih-tee) *n.* Nearness; propinquity.

prox·y *n.* [*pl.* prox·ies] 1. The authorization to act for another. 2. A person granted such authority.—*v.* [prox·ied; prox·y·ing].—**prox·y·ship** *n.*

prude (*prood*) *n.* A prim, stiffly nice person.

pru·dence (*proo*-denss) *n.* Wise caution and discipline in conduct.—**pru·dent** *adj.*—**pru·dent·ly** *adv.*

pru·den·tial (proo-*den*-sh'l) *adj.* Exercising prudence; showing caution.—**pru·den·tial·ly** *adv.*

prud·er·y (*prood*-er-ee) *n.* [*pl.* prud·er·ies] Excessive nicety of conduct.—**prud·ish** *adj.*—**prud·ish·ly** *adv.*—**prud·ish·ness** *n.*

prune (*proon*) *n.* A dried plum.

prune (*proon*) *v.* To trim; cut off useless parts.

pru·ri·ent (*proor*-ee-ent) *adj.* Eagerly lustful; lascivious.—**pru·ri·ence, pru·ri·en·cy** *n.*—**pru·ri·ent·ly** *adv.*

Prus·sia (*prush*-uh). The largest state in Germany.—**Prus·sian** *adj.* 1. Pertaining to Prussia. 2. Warlike; military.—**Prus·sian** *n.*

Prussian blue. A strong pigment developed from a cyanide of iron.

pry *v.* [pried; pry·ing] 1. To investigate inquisitively. 2. To wedge open or apart with a lever. 3. To pull out; extricate.—**pry** *n.* [*pl.* pries].—**pry·ing·ly** *adv.*

psalm (*sahm*) *n.* 1. Sacred song or hymn. 2. [*pl. cap.*] The hymns collected in the Old Testament.—**psalm** *v.*—**psalm·ist** *n.*

psal·mo·dy (*sal*-muh-dee, *sahm*-) *n.* [*pl.* psal·mo·dies] 1. The singing of psalms. 2. Psalms collectively.—**psal·mo·dist** *n.*

psal·ter (*sawl*-ter) *n.* A book of psalms.

pseu·do (*syoo*-doh, *soo*-) *adj.* False; imitation.

pseu·do- *prefix.* False; spurious; apparent; near.

pseu·do·nym (*soo*-duh-nim) *n.* An assumed name; pen name.—**pseu·do·nym·i·ty** *n.*

pshaw (*shaw*) *interj.* An expression of disbelief, disgust, etc.

psit·ta·co·sis (sit-uh-*koh*-siss) *n.* The virus disease of parrot fever.

pso·ri·a·sis (soh-*ry*-uh-siss) *n.* Chronic skin disease producing inflamed eruptions.

Psy·che (*sy*-kee) *n.* 1. *Greek Mythology.* A human princess loved and immortalized by Cupid. 2. [*not cap.*] The human soul; mind.

psy·chi·a·try (sy-*ky*-uh-tree) *n.* Branch of medicine dealing with mental illness.—**psy·chi·at·ric, psy·chi·at·ri·cal** *adj.*—**psy·chi·a·trist** *n.*

psy·chic (*sy*-kik) *adj.* Also **psy·chi·cal.** 1. Clairvoyant; spiritualistic. 2. Pertaining to the soul or mind.—**psy·chic** *n.* A spiritualistic medium.—**psy·chi·cal·ly** *adv.*

psy·cho·a·nal·y·sis *n.* The branch of psychotherapy which prescribes treatment in the light of experiences elicited from the patient.—**psy·cho·an·a·lyt·ic, -i·cal** *adj.*— -**i·cal·ly** *adv.*

psy·cho·an·a·lyze (sy-koh-*an*-uh-lyze) *v.* [psy·cho·an·a·lyzed; -lyz·ing] To make a mental examination by comparative study of a patient's voluntary communications and outward symptoms.—**psy·cho·an·a·lyst, -a·lyz·er** *n.*

psy·chol·o·gy (sy-*kol*-uh-jee) *n.* [*pl.* -gies] Science of mind and its activities as reflected in behavior.—**psy·cho·log·ic, psy·cho·log·i·cal** *adj.* —**psy·cho·log·i·cal·ly** *adv.*—**psy·chol·o·gist** *n.*

psy·cho·neu·ro·sis (sy-koh-nuh-*roh*-siss) *n.* [*pl.* -ses] Minor mental disorder producing physical manifestations.— -**neu·rot·ic** *adj. & n.*

psy·cho·path·ic (sy-koh-*path*-ik) *adj.* Pertaining to mental diseases or their treatment.—**psy·cho·path·ic** *n.* An insane person.

psy·cho·pa·thol·o·gy (sy-koh-puh-*thol*-uh-jee) *n.* Branch of medicine dealing with diseases of the mind.—**psy·cho·pa·thol·o·gist** *n.*

psy·chop·a·thy (sy-*kop*-uh-thee) *n.* [*pl.* -thies] Mental illness.—**psy·chop·a·thist** *n.* A doctor specializing in mental diseases.

psy·cho·sis (sy-*koh*-siss) *n.* [*pl.* -ses] A serious mental disturbance.—**psy·chot·ic** *adj.*

psy·cho·ther·a·py (sy-koh-*thehr*-uh-pee) *n.* Also **psy·cho·ther·a·peu·tics.** Branch of medicine treating disease by mental suggestion.—**psy·cho·ther·a·peu·tic** *adj.*—**psy·cho·ther·a·pist** *n.* Also **psy·cho·ther·a·peu·tist** *n.*

ptar·mi·gan (*tahr*-mih-gan) *n.* A family of northern grouse having feathered feet.

pter·o·dac·tyl (ter-uh-*dak*-til) *n.* Prehistoric winged reptile of the dinosaur family.

Ptol·e·my (*tol*-eh-mee) Greek astronomer and mathematician who taught that the earth formed the center of the universe.—**Ptol·e·ma·ic** *adj.*

PTARMIGAN (1/10 life-size)

pto·maine, pto·main (toh-*mayn*) *n.* A class of alkaloid food poisons present in decaying matter.

pub *n. British Slang.* A tavern; inn; bar.

pu·ber·ty (*pyoo*-ber-tee) *n.* Attainment of sexual maturity; legally, age 14 for boys and 12 for girls.

pu·bes (*pyoo*-beez) *n.* 1. *Anatomy.* The hair appearing on the lower portion of the abdomen at sexual maturity. 2. *Botany.* The downy covering of plants.—**pu·bic** *adj.*

pu·bes·cent (pyoo-*bess*-ent) *adj.* 1. Reaching sexual maturity. 2. Downy; covered with fine, short hairs.—**pu·bes·cence** *n.*

pub·lic (*pub*-lik) *adj.* 1. Pertaining to people as a whole; relating to a nation or community. 2. Belonging to people at large; common.

3. Open to the knowledge of all; generally known.—*n.* **1.** The people; mankind. **2.** A group of people; audience.—**pub·lic·ly** *adv.* —**pub·lic·ness** *n.*

pub·li·can (*pub*-lih-kan) *n.* **1.** *England.* The keeper of a public house. **2.** *Roman History.* A tax-collector.

pub·li·ca·tion (pub-lih-*kay*-shun) *n.* **1.** Printing and issuing for public sale. **2.** Any book, pamphlet, periodical.

public house. An inn or tavern; in England, a place in which liquor is sold and consumed.

pub·li·cist (*pub*-lih-sist) *n.* A writer on international law or affairs; political journalist.

pub·lic·i·ty (pub-*liss*-ih-tee) *n.* **1.** Notoriety; public attention. **2.** Advertising.—**pub·li·cize** *v.* [pub·li·cized; pub·li·ciz·ing].

public school. 1. An elementary or secondary school maintained at public expense under local governmental authority. **2.** *England.* A privately endowed secondary school.

pub·lic-spir·it·ed *adj.* Interested in and zealous for the community welfare.

public utility. An industry related to public welfare and subject to certain governmental control.

pub·lish *v.* **1.** To print and offer for sale, as a book or periodical. **2.** To make known; divulge. **3.** To put into circulation.—**pub·lish·a·ble** *adj.*—**pub·lish·er** *n.*

puce *adj.* Reddish brown.—**puce** *n.*

puck *n.* **1.** A mischievous fairy; elf. **2.** [*cap.*] Robin Goodfellow. **3.** A thick vulcanized rubber disk used in ice hockey.—**puck·ish** *adj.*

puck·er *v.* To wrinkle; gather into folds.—*n.* A fold or wrinkle.—**puck·er·y** *adj.*

pud·ding (*pood*-ing) *n.* A food of soft consistency, usually a milk dessert.

pud·dle *n.* **1.** A small muddy pool. **2.** A kneaded mixture of wet clay which resists water.—*v.* [pud·dled; pud·dling] **1.** To make muddy. **2.** To make watertight by means of puddle. **3.** To produce wrought iron by the puddling process.—**pud·dler** *n.*

pud·dling *n.* The process of converting pig iron into wrought iron in a reverberatory furnace under gaseous heat.

pudg·y *adj.* [pudg·i·er; pudg·i·est] Short and fat; stumpy.—**pudg·i·ly** *adv.*—**pudg·i·ness** *n.*

pueb·lo (*pweb*-loh) *n.* **1.** An Indian dwelling of Arizona, New Mexico, etc., built of adobe or stone, housing the entire community. **2.** [*cap.*] A member of a pueblo-dwelling Indian tribe. **3.** An Indian village in Southwest U.S.

PUEBLO

pu·er·ile (*pyoo*-er-il) *adj.* Childish; trifling; foolish.—**pu·er·ile·ly** *adv.*—**pu·er·il·i·ty** *n.*

pu·er·per·al (pyoo-*er*-per-al) *adj.* Pertaining to childbirth.

puff *n.* **1.** A sudden single emission of breath; short blast of wind; whiff. **2.** A soft pad, as a powder puff. **3.** A light pastry shell. **4.** A bed quilt filled with down. **5.** Dress material gathered on two sides with the center left loose. **6.** Exaggerated praise, esp. a written commendation. **7.** A protuberance; swelling. —*v.* **1.** To blow with quick blasts; emit puffs. **2.** To swell; become inflated. **3.** To breathe quickly. **4.** To praise excessively. **5.** To swell with pride or importance. **6.** To arrange in puffs, as a coiffure, dress material, etc.—**puff paste.** A rich dough used for flaky pastry.

puff·ball *n.* A spherical mushroomlike fungus.

puff·er *n.* **1.** One who puffs. **2.** A globefish.

puf·fin *n.* A North Atlantic sea bird of the auk family.

puff·y *adj.* [puff·i·er; puff·i·est] **1.** Swollen; inflated. **2.** Soft; fluffy. **3.** Breathing hard; gusty.—**puff·i·ly** *adv.*—**puff·i·ness** *n.*

PUFFIN (1/9 life-size)

pug *n.* **1.** A small short-haired dog related to the Pekingese. **2.** *Slang.* A prize fighter. —*adj.* Snug; turned up.—*v.* [pug·ged; pug·ging] To mix or fill with clay.

pu·gil·ism (*pyoo*-jil-izm) *n.* The sport of boxing; prize fighting.—**pu·gil·ist** *n.* A professional boxer. —**pu·gi·list·ic** *adj.*

pug·na·cious (pug-*nay*-shus) *adj.* Belligerent; combative.— **pug·na·cious·ly** *adv.* —**pug·na·cious·ness** *n.*—**pug·nac·i·ty** *n.* [*pl.* -ties].

PUG (1/12 life-size)

pug nose. A short broad nose turned up at the tip.—**pug-nosed** *adj.*

pu·is·sance (*pyoo*-ih-sanss, *pwis*-sanss) *n.* Power; force.—**pu·is·sant** *adj.*—**pu·is·sant·ly** *adv.*

puke (*pyook*) *v.* [puked; puk·ing] To vomit.—*n.* A vomit.—**puk·er** *n.*

pul·chri·tude (*pul*-krih-tood) *n.* Beauty; comeliness.—**pul·chri·tu·di·nous** *adj.*

pule *v.* [puled; pul·ing] To whimper; whine; cry feebly.—**pul·er** *n.*—**pul·ing** *adj.*—**ing·ly** *adv.*

pull *v.* **1.** To tug; haul. **2.** To draw out; extract. **3.** To draw apart; tear. **4.** To pluck up; gather. **5.** To stretch out. 'To pull candy.' **6.** *Printing.* To run a proof. **7.** To move; get under way. **8.** To take a long drink; puff hard in smoking. **9.** To use the oars of a rowboat.—*n.* **1.** Act of drawing with force; tug. **2.** A difficult ascent, as a pull uphill. **3.** A

P

knob, cord, etc., used for pulling. 4. The rowing of a boat. 5. *Slang*. Advantage; influence.

pul·let *n.* A young hen.

pul·ley *n.* [*pl.* pul·leys] A wheel with a grooved rim on which a rope runs for lifting weights or transmitting power.

Pullman car, Pull·man. 1. A sleeping car. 2. A chair car.

pul·mo·na·ry (*pul*-muh-nehr-ee) *adj.* Pertaining to the lungs.

PULLEY

Pul·mo·tor. Trade-mark name for a machine which produces artificial respiration by forcing oxygen into the lungs.

pulp *n.* 1. Any soft moist mass of organic matter. 2. The flesh of a fruit. 3. The soft sensitive inner portion of a tooth. 4. Soaked ground rags, wool fibers, etc., from which paper is made. 5. Cheap fiction.—*v.* 1. To make into pulp. 2. To remove the pulp.

pul·pit *n.* 1. An elevated, enclosed platform in a church for delivery of sermons. 2. Clergymen collectively.—**pul·pit·eer** *n.* A preacher.

pulp·wood *n.* Soft wood, esp. from spruce and aspen, used in making paper.

pulp·y *adj.* [pulp·i·er; -i·est] Soft; fleshy.—**pulp·i·ness** *n.*

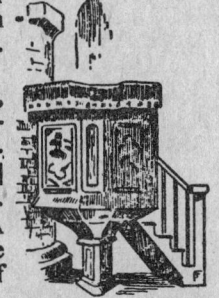

PULPIT

pul·que (*pool*-kay) *n.* A Mexican beverage made from fermented juice of the agave tree.

pul·sate (*pul*-sayt) *v.* [pul·sat·ed; pul·sat·ing] To beat; throb; vibrate.

pul·sa·tion (pul-*say*-shun) *n.* 1. The beating of the heart or an artery. 2. A throb or beat.

pulse *n.* 1. The rhythmical throb of an artery caused by the contractions of the heart. 2. Any measured and repeated motion; pulsation. 3. General trend of feeling; sentiment.—*v.* [pulsed; puls·ing] To beat rhythmically; throb.

pulse *n.* Leguminous plants, as beans, peas, and lentils, or their edible seeds.

pul·ver·ize (*pul*-ver-yze) *v.* [pul·ver·ized; pul·ver·iz·ing] 1. To grind to powder. 2. To disintegrate; destroy utterly. 3. *Slang*. To defeat overwhelmingly.—**pul·ver·iz·a·ble, pul·ver·i·za·tion** *n.*—**pul·ver·iz·er** *n.*

pu·ma (*pyoo*-muh) *n.* The largest of the North American cat family; mountain lion or cougar.

pum·ice (*pum*-iss) *n.* A hard, spongelike variety of lava used for polishing or smoothing.—*v.* [pum·iced; pum·ic·ing] To smooth with pumice.

PUMA (1/60 life-size)

pump *n.* A machine for raising a fluid to a higher level or transferring a gas, by means of suction or pressure. —*v.* 1. To draw or raise with a pump. 2. To remove fluid by a pump. 3. To extract; draw out. 4. To eject; emit. 5. To draw out by artful questions.—**pump·er** *n.*

pump·er·nick·el (*pump*-er-nik-'l) *n.* A coarse bread made from unsifted rye.

PUMP

pump·kin *n.* The large squashlike yellow fruit of a tendril-bearing vine used for food, esp. in pies.

pun *n.* A play on words which are similar in sound but different in meaning.—*v.* [punned; pun·ning] To make a pun.

punch *n.* A drink made of rum or other spirits, sugar, lemon, and water.—**punch bowl.** A large bowl for mixing and serving punch.

PUMPKIN

Punch *n.* 1. The hunchbacked, hooked-nose leading character in the puppet show **Punch and Judy**, who quarrels heartily with his wife, Judy. 2. A satirical English periodical.

punch *n.* 1. A blow with the fist. 2. A tapering tool for making holes, cutting blanks, stamping dies, etc. 3. *Slang*. Emotional impact; forcefulness.—*v.* 1. To perforate; puncture. 2. To strike, as with the fist. 3. To herd cattle.—**punch·er** *n.*—**punch drunk.** Concussion of the brain from prizefighting.

pun·che·on (*pun*-chun) *n.* 1. A perforating tool. 2. A short upright piece of framing timber. 3. A cask containing 84 to 120 gallons.

pun·chi·nel·lo (pun-chih-*nel*-oh) *n.* A buffoon; Punch.

punc·til·i·o (punk-*til*-ee-oh) *n.* Meticulous formality; ceremony.

punc·til·i·ous (punk-*til*-ee-us) *adj.* Precise in conduct; scrupulous.—**punc·til·i·ous·ly** *adv.*—**punc·til·i·ous·ness** *n.*

punc·tu·al (*punk*-choo-al) *adj.* Prompt; on time.—**punc·tu·al·ly** *adv.*—**punc·tu·al·ness** *n.*

punc·tu·al·i·ty (punk-choo-*al*-ih-tee) *n.* [*pl.* -ties] Promptness; exactitude in keeping appointments.

punc·tu·ate (*punk*-choo-ayt) *v.* [punc·tu·at·ed; punc·tu·at·ing] 1. To separate into sentences, clauses, etc., by marking with points. 2. To space; emphasize. 3. To interrupt at intervals.—**punc·tu·a·tor** *n.*

punc·tu·a·tion (punk-choo-*ay*-shun) *n.* The

points used in marking the divisions of sentences or their clauses: period [.], colon [:], semicolon [;], comma [,], interrogation point or question mark [?], exclamation point [!], parentheses [( )], dash [—], brackets [[ ]], apostrophe ['], hyphen [-], quotation marks [" "], etc.

punc·ture (*punk*-cher) *n.* A small hole or wound made by a pointed instrument.—*v.* [punc·tured; punc·tur·ing] 1. To pierce; prick; to make a hole in. 2. To deflate; suffer piercing.

pun·dit *n.* A learned person.

pung *n. New England.* A box-shaped sleigh.

pun·gent (*pun*-jent) *adj.* 1. Tart; acrid; sharp. 2. Painful; poignant. 3. Caustic; biting; penetrating.—**pun·gen·cy** *n.*—**pun·gent·ly** *adv.*

Pun·ic (*pyoo*-nik) *adj.* 1. Pertaining to the ancient Carthaginians. 2. Faithless; treacherous.—*n.* The Carthaginian language.

pun·ish *v.* 1. To inflict a penalty; chastise; discipline. 2. To treat roughly.—**pun·ish·a·ble** *adj.*—**pun·ish·a·bil·i·ty** *n.*—**pun·ish·er** *n.*

pun·ish·ment *n.* 1. Penalty inflicted for a crime or offense. 2. The act of punishing. 3. Severe or rough treatment.

pu·ni·tive (*pyoo*-nih-tiv) *adj.* Also **pun·i·to·ry.** Pertaining to punishment.

punk *n.* 1. Tinder made from decayed wood; touchwood. 2. A worthless person.—*adj. Slang.* Bad; worthless.

pun·kie *n.* A small biting midge; sandfly.

pun·ning·ly *adv.* In a word-playing manner.

pun·ster *n.* One who makes plays on words.

punt *n.* A flat-bottomed boat with square ends, propelled by poles. —*v.* 1. To propel by pushing with a pole; carry in a punt. 2. *Football.* To kick the ball when dropped from the hands and before it touches the ground.—**punt·er** *n.*

PUNT

pu·ny (*pyoo*-nee) *adj.* [pu·ni·er; pu·ni·est] 1. Small and weak; undersized; feeble. 2. Petty; insignificant.

pup *n.* 1. A young dog. 2. A young seal.—*v.* [pupped; pup·ping] To bring forth whelps.

pu·pa (*pyoo*-puh) *n.* The second stage in an insect's development from larva to adult form; chrysalis.—**pu·pal** *adj.*

pu·pil (*pyoo*-p'l) *n.* A youth under the care of a teacher; student in a primary or secondary school.—**pu·pil·age** *n.*—**pu·pil·lar·y** *adj.*

pu·pil *n.* The opening in the iris of the eye through which light rays pass to the retina.

pup·pet *n.* 1. A marionette. 2. A small image in human form; doll. 3. A person acting at another's will; tool.—**pup·pet·ry** *n.*

pup·py *n.* [*pl.* pup·pies] 1. A young dog. 2. A conceited fellow; fop.—**pup·py·ish** *adj.*

pup tent. A small light canvas tent.

pur·blind *adj.* Almost blind; obtuse.—**pur·blind·ly** *adv.*—**pur·blind·ness** *n.*

pur·chase (*per*-chiss) *v.* [pur·chased; pur·chas·ing] 1. To buy; obtain by paying a price. 2. To obtain by means of labor, sacrifice, or danger. 3. To raise or move by mechanical power.—*n.* 1. Buying; acquisition at a price. 2. An object bought at a price. 3. Any hold, power, or force applied to raising or moving heavy objects.—**pur·chas·a·ble** *adj.*—**chas·er** *n.*

pure *adj.* 1. Unmixed; clear; clean; free from foreign matter. 2. Faultless; innocent; guiltless. 3. Absolute; sheer; mere. 4. Chaste. 5. Abstract; theoretic.—**pure·ly** *adv.*

pur·ée (pyoor-*ay*) *n.* 1. A mashed, strained food. 2. A creamed soup.

pur·ga·tive (*per*-guh-tiv) *adj.* Cleansing; cathartic.—*n.* A cathartic or physic.

pur·ga·to·ry (*per*-guh-tor-ee) *n.* 1. Region between heaven and hell. 2. A state of temporary suffering.—**pur·ga·to·ri·al** *adj.*

purge (*perj*) *v.* [purged; purg·ing] 1. To cleanse; purify. 2. To clear of foreign matter or sediment; clarify. 3. *Medicine.* To cleanse by use of a cathartic. 4. To rid oneself of political enemies by drastic measures.—*n.* 1. The act or process of purging. 2. A purgative.—**pur·ga·tion** *n.*—**purg·er** *n.*

pur·i·fy (*pyoor*-ih-fy) *v.* [pur·i·fied; pur·i·fy·ing] 1. To free from admixture; make clean. 2. To free from guilt or sin; cleanse. 3. To free of barbarisms.—**pu·ri·fi·ca·tion** *n.*—**pu·ri·fi·er** *n.*

pur·ist (*pyoor*-ist) *n.* One meticulous and orthodox, esp. in the use of words.—**pur·ism** *n.*

pu·ri·tan (*pyoo*-rih-tan) *n.* 1. A person insistent on a rigorous code of morals. 2. [*cap.*] A dissenter in Tudor England who advocated simpler forms of worship.—**Pu·ri·tan** *adj.*—**Pu·ri·tan·ism** *n.*

pu·ri·tan·i·cal (pyoo-rih-*tan*-ih-k'l) *adj.* Also **pu·ri·tan·ic.** 1. Strict; austere; precise in religious or moral matters. 2. [*cap.*] Pertaining to the Puritans.—**pu·ri·tan·i·cal·ly** *adv.*

pu·ri·ty *n.* [*pl.* pu·ri·ties] 1. Freedom from foreign matter. 2. Cleanness. 3. Innocence; guiltlessness. 4. Chastity. 5. Accuracy; precision in style or language.

purl *n.* An inversion of the stitches in knitting. —*v.* To invert a stitch.

purl *v.* 1. To flow with a gentle murmur. 2. To ripple; swirl; eddy.—*n.* 1. A swirling stream. 2. A murmuring sound.

pur·lieu (*per*-lyoo, -loo) *n.* 1. A bordering district. 2. [*pl.*] Surroundings; environs.

pur·loin (per-*loyn*) *v.* To steal.—**pur·loin·er** *n.*

pur·ple *n.* 1. A color derived from red and blue pigments. 2. A symbol of royalty or other high station. 'Born to the purple.'—**pur·ple** *adj.*—*v.* [pur·pled; pur·pling]—**pur·plish, pur·ply** *adj.*

purple-berried	purple-headed	purple-spiked
purple-clad	purple-hued	purple-tipped
purple-coated	purple-leaved	purple-veined
purple-colored	purple-robed	purplewood

P

Purple Heart. An order of honor awarded to U.S. military men wounded in enemy action.

pur·port (*per*-port) *n.* Meaning; import; significance.

pur·port (per-*port*) *v.* To intend; profess; mean.

pur·pose (*per*-pus) *n.* End; aim; objective; intention.—*v.* [pur·posed; pur·pos·ing]. To intend; design.—**pur·pose·ful** *adj.*—**pur·pose·less** *adj.*— -**pose·ly** *adv.*—**on purpose.** Intentionally.

purr, pur *n.* A low murmur, as made by a cat when pleased or by a smooth-running motor. —**purr** *v.*

purse *n.* 1. A money bag; pocketbook. 2. A sum of money offered as a prize. 3. A treasury; money or finances.—*v.* [pursed; pur·sing] To pucker; contract into folds.

pur·ser (*per*-ser) *n.* Ship's officer in charge of accounts and clerical work.

purs·lane (*perss*-lin, -layn) *n.* A weed with fleshy, succulent leaves, used in salads.

pur·su·ance (per-*syoo*-unss, -*soo*-) *n.* 1. Act of following or carrying out. 2. Consequence; result.—**pur·su·ant** *adj.* Conforming; consequent; according. —**pur·su·ant, pur·su·ant·ly** *adv.*

PURSLANE

pur·sue (per-*syoo*, -*soo*) *v.* [pur·sued; pur·su·ing] 1. To chase; seek; follow. 2. To carry on. 'To pursue studies.'—**pur·suit** *n.* & *adj.*

pur·sy *adj.* [pur·si·er; pur·si·est] Fat and short-winded.—**pur·si·ness** *n.*

pu·ru·lent (*pyoor*-uh-lent) *adj.* Generating pus. —**pu·ru·lence, pu·ru·len·cv** *n.*—**pu·ru·lent·ly** *adv.*

pur·vey (per-*vay*) *v.* To provide; supply; provision.—**pur·vey·ance** *n.*—**pur·vey·or** *n.*

pur·view (*per*-vyoo) *n.* 1. *Law.* Body of a statute; limit or scope of a statute. 2. Scope; extent; limit.

pus *n.* A yellowish fluid formed in a wound, consisting of cells and tissue matter.—**pus·sy** *adj.* [pus·si·er; pus·si·est]

push *v.* 1. To shove; impel; press forcefully; urge. 2. To exert effort. 'To push sales.' —*n.* 1. An impelling; shoving. 2. A heavy assault or offensive. 3. Persevering energy. —**push·er** *n.*—**push·ing** *adj.*—**push·ing·ly** *adv.*

push button. A knob or plug which turns electricity on or off.

push-over *n. Colloquial.* A sinecure; simple task; person easily persuaded.

push·y *adj.* Forward; socially ambitious.

pu·sil·lan·i·mous (pyoo-sil-*lan*-ih-mus) *adj.* Cowardly; timid.—**pu·sil·la·nim·i·ty** *n.*—**pu·sil·la·ni·mous·ly** *adv.*

puss·y·foot *v.* To tread softly; reserve one's opinion.—**puss·y·foot·ed** *adj.*

puss·y·wil·low *n.* A small tree of the willow family bearing round velvety, podlike flowers.

pus·tule *n.* A pus-filled eruption on the skin. —**pus·tu·lant, pus·tu·lar** *adj.*

put *v.* [put; put·ting] 1. To place; set. 2. To express in language. 3. To throw a heavy object with a pushing motion. 4. To go; move. 5. To steer. 6. To incite; urge. 7. To apply.—**put about.** To face around.—**put across.** To convey; deliver effectively.—**put off.** To postpone.—**put over.** 1. To make successful. 2. To deceive.—**put up to.** To request a decision.—**put up with.** To endure.

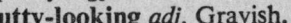

put-and-take	putlog	put-out
put-back	put-off	put-up
put-in	put-on	put-upon

pu·ta·tive (*pyoo*-tuh-tiv) *adj.* Supposed; reputed; commonly believed.—**pu·ta·tive·ly** *adv.*

pu·tre·fac·tion (pyoo-treh-*fak*-shun) *n.* 1. Decomposition of organic matter; rotting. 2. Decayed matter.—**pu·tre·fac·tive** *adj.*

pu·tre·fy (*pyoo*-treh-fy) *v.* [pu·tre·fied; -fy·ing] To rot; decay.—**pu·tre·fi·er** *n.*

pu·trid (*pyoo*-trid) *adj.* Foul; odorously rotten; corrupt.—**pu·trid·i·ty, pu·trid·ness** *n.*

putsch (*putch*) *n.* Sudden forceful drive by a minority group to overthrow a government.

putt *v. Golf.* To hit the ball a short distance to sink it in the hole.—**putt** *n.*

put·tee *n.* A gaiter; legging made of leather, or wool strips spiraled.

put·ter (*puht*-er) *v.* To potter; dawdle. —**put·ter·er** *n.*

put·ter *n. Golf.* 1. A club used for short strokes in putting. 2. One who putts.

put·ter *n.* One who puts or places.

put·ty *n.* 1. An oil-and-lime preparation for retaining panes of glass, etc. 2. Any cement or mortar resembling putty.—*v.* [put·tied; put·ty·ing]

PUTTEE

putty-looking *adj.* Grayish.

puz·zle (*puz*-'l) *v.* [puz·zled; puz·zling] 1. To perplex; bewilder. 2. To wonder; think.—*n.* 1. A perplexity; problem. 2. A device which tries the ingenuity.—**puz·zle·ment** *n.*—**puz·zler** *n.*—**puz·zling** *adj.*

PX *n. Military. Abbreviation* for **post exchange,** a commissary selling small supplies to soldiers.

pyg·my *n.* [*pl.* pyg·mies]. Also **pig·my.** 1. A dwarf. 2. [*cap.*] An undersized race of Central Africa.—**pyg·my** *adj.*

py·ja·ma (puh-*jam*-muh, -*jah*-) Pajama.

py·lon (*py*-lun) *n.* 1. A pyramid cut off at the point. 2. A monumental gateway through a truncated pyramid. 3. A stake marking the course of airplanes.

PYLON

py·lo·rus (py-*loh*-rus) *n.* The muscle-walled opening between the stomach and the small intestine. —**py·lor·ic** *adj.*

py·or·rhe·a (py-uh-*ree*-uh) *n.* Also **py·or·rhoe·a.** Discharge of pus, esp. from the gums.—**py·or·rhe·al** *adj.*

pyr·a·mid (*pihr*-uh-mid) *n.* 1. *Geometry.* A solid body having triangular sides meeting in a point. 2. [*cap.*] Structures in this shape built as tombs by ancient Egyptians.—**pyr·a·mid** *v.* To pile up. —**py·ram·i·dal** *adj.* —**py·ram·i·dal·ly** *adv.*

PYRAMID

pyre *n.* A heap of combustible material for cremating a body.

Pyr·e·nees (*pihr*-eh-neez). A range of high mountains between France and Spain.—**Pyr·e·ne·an** *adj.*

py·rite *n.* (*py*-ryte) [*pl.* py·rites] Iron chemically united with sulphur; fool's gold.

py·ri·tes (py-*ry*-teez) *n.* Any metal compounded with sulphur.

py·ro-, pyr- *prefix.* Fire; heat.

pyrocatechol	pyroelectric	pyrophyllite
pyrochemical	pyrogallate	pyrosis
pyroclastic	pyroligneous	pyrostat
pyroconductivity	pyrolusite	pyrosulphate
pyrocrystalline	pyromorphite	pyrotoxin

py·rog·ra·phy (py-*rog*-ruh-fee) *n.* Inscription of leather or wood with hot tools.—**py·rog·ra·pher** *n.*—**py·ro·graph·ic** *adj.*

py·ro·ma·ni·a (py-roh-*may*-nee-uh) *n.* Urge to start fires.—**py·ro·ma·ni·ac** *adj.* & *n.*

py·rom·e·ter (py-*rom*-eh-ter) *n.* A thermometer for measuring high temperatures.—**py·ro·met·ric** *adj.*

py·ro·tech·nics (py-roh-*tek*-niks). Also **py·ro·tech·ny** *n. sing.* 1. Art of making fireworks. 2. Any brilliant display resembling fireworks. —**py·ro·tech·nic, -ni·cal** *adj.*—**py·ro·tech·nist** *n.*

py·rox·y·lin (py-*roks*-ih-lin) *n.* Soluble guncotton used in the manufacture of collodion.

Pyrrhic victory. A victory gained at great cost.

Pythagorean Theorem (pih-thag-uh-*ree*-un *thee*-uh-rum). *Mathematics.* Principle set forth by the Greek philosopher Pythagoras stating that the square of the hypotenuse of a right triangle equals the sum of the squares on the other two sides.

py·thon (*py*-thon) *n.* 1. Large nonvenomous snake of the boa family. 2. [*cap.*] *Greek Mythology.* A huge serpent slain by Apollo.

PYTHON (1/90 life-size)

Q

quack (kwak) *n.* 1. The cry of a duck. 2. A charlatan, esp. a pretended physician.—*v.* To cry like a duck.— **quack** *adj.*—**quack·er·y** [*pl.* -er·ies] *n.*—**quack·ish** *adj.*

quad·ran·gle (*kwahd*-rang-g'l) *n.* 1. A four-sided plane figure. 2. A four-sided court surrounded by buildings.—**quad·ran·gu·lar** *adj.*

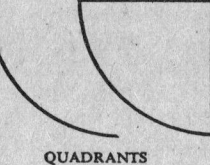

QUADRANGLE

quad·rant (*kwahd*-r'nt) *n.* 1. One-fourth of a circle; a 90° arc. 2. An obsolete navigational instrument for measuring altitudes of heavenly bodies.

quad·rate (*kwahd*-rit) *adj.* Square.—*n.* A square or right-angled figure.—*v.* (kwod-*rayt*) To square.

QUADRANTS

quad·rat·ic (kwah-*drat*-ik) *adj.* 1. Square. 2. *Mathematics.* Raised to the second power; involving terms with the exponent two.—*n.* An equation whose unknown quantity is squared.—**quad·rat·ics** *n.* The algebra of quadratic equations.

quad·ra·ture (*kwahd*-ruh-tyoor) *n.* 1. Act of squaring. 2. *Astronomy.* Position of two heavenly bodies 90° apart.

quad·ren·ni·al (kwah-*dren*-ee-al) *adj.* 1. Comprising four years. 2. Occurring once in four years.—**quad·ren·ni·al·ly** *adv.*

quad·ri·lat·er·al (kwahd-rih-*lat*-er-al) *n.* A four-sided figure.—**quad·ri·lat·er·al** *adj.*

quad·ra·ge·nar·i·an (kwad-ruh-jeh-*nair*-ee-an) *n.* A person between forty and fifty years old. —**quad·ra·ge·nar·i·an** *adj.*

qua·drille (kwah-*dril*) *n.* 1. A dance performed by four sets of couples each forming the side of a square. 2. The music for such a dance.

QUADRILATERALS

quad·ril·lion (kwahd-*ril*-yun) *n.* The number one followed by 15 zeros.—**quad·ril·lion** *adj.* —**quad·ril·lionth** *n.* & *adj.*

quad·ru·ped (*kwad*-ruh-ped) *n.* A four-footed mammal.—**quad·ru·ped** *adj.*—**quad·ru·pe·dal** *adj.*

quad·ru·ple (*kwahd*-roo-p'l) *adj.* Fourfold.—*v.* To multiply by four.—**quad·ru·ple** *n.*

quad·ru·pli·cate (kwahd-*roo*-plih-kayt) *v.* [quad·ru·pli·cat·ed; quad·ru·pli·cat·ing] To make fourfold.—**quad·ru·pli·cate** (kwahd-*roo*-pli-kit) *n.*—**quad·ru·pli·ca·tion** *n.*

quaff (*kwaf, kwahf, kwawf*) *v.* To drink.—**quaff** *n.*—**quaff·er** *n.*

quag·gy *adj.* Spongy; boggy.

quag·mire (*kwag*-myre) *n.* A bog; marsh.

qua·hog, qua·haug (*kwaw*-hog) *n. New England.* A species of large clams.

quail (*kwayl*) *n.* A migratory game bird related to the partridge.

quail *v.* To shrink; lose heart.

quaint *adj.* Odd; charmingly strange or old-fashioned.—**quaint·ly** *adv.*—**quaint·ness** *n.*

QUAIL (1/10 life size)

quake *v.* [quaked; quak·ing] To shake; tremble; shudder.—*n.* 1. A shudder. 2. An earthquake.

Quak·er (*kwayk*-er) *n.* A member of the religious group, the Society of Friends.—**Quak·er·ess** *n.*—**Quak·er·ish** *adj.*

qual·i·fi·ca·tion (kwahl-ih-fih-*kay*-shun) *n.* 1. Ability; possession of requisites; fulfillment of specifications; competence. 2. Limitation; modification; condition.

qual·i·fied (*kwahl*-ih-fyde) *adj.* 1. Capable, competent. 2. Modified; conditional.—**qual·i·fied·ly** *adv.*

qual·i·fy (*kwahl*-ih-fy) *v.* [qual·i·fied; qual·i·fy·ing] 1. To modify; temper. 2. To make fit, as for an office or occupation; vest with power.

qual·i·ta·tive (*kwahl*-ih-tay-tiv) *adj.* Pertaining to quality.—**qual·i·ta·tive·ly** *adv.*

qual·i·ty (*kwahl*-ih-tee) *n.* 1. Nature; property; characteristic. 2. Type; grade. 3. Excellence; fineness. 4. Shade; tone; resonance; feel. 5. *Colloquial.* Aristocracy. 'The quality.'

qualm (*kwahm*) *n.* Scruple; compunction; misgiving.—**qualm·ish** *adj.*—**qualm·ish·ly** *adv.*

quan·da·ry (*kwahn*-der-ee) *n.* Puzzle; dilemma.

quan·ti·ta·tive (*kwahn*-ti-tay-tiv) *adj.* Pertaining to quantity.—**quan·ti·ta·tive·ly** *adv.*

quan·ti·ty (*kwahn*-tih-tee) *n.* 1. Amount; size or number; measure. 2. A large amount; great number.

quan·tum *n.* [*pl.* quan·ta] 1. An amount; quantity. 2. *Physics.* Basic unit of energy emitted in a single wave motion of radiation.

quar·rel (*kwor*-'l) *n.* 1. Altercation; angry dispute. 2. Subject of dispute.—*v.* [quar·reled; quar·relled; quar·rel·ing, quar·rel·ling] To wrangle; bicker.—**quar·rel·er, quar·rel·ler** *n.*

quar·an·tine (*kwahr*-en-teen) *v.* [quar·an·tined; quar·an·tin·ing] To isolate, esp. for illness. —*n.* 1. Isolation of persons infected with contagious diseases. 2. An isolation area. —**quar·an·tine** *adj.*

quar·rel·some *adj.* Pugnacious; contentious. —**quar·rel·some·ly** *adv.*—**quar·rel·some·ness** *n.*

quar·ry (*kwah*-ree, *kwaw*-) *n.* [*pl.* -ries] Marble, slate, or stone pit; area excavated.—*v.* [quar·ried; quar·ry·ing] To dig.—**quar·ri·er** *n.*

quar·ry *n.* [*pl.* -ries] 1. Game, esp. in falconry. 2. A victim; captured prisoner; prey.

quart *n.* One-fourth of a gallon; thirty-two fluid ounces.

quar·tan (*kwor*-t'n) *adj.* Occurring every fourth day.—*n. Medicine.* A type of undulant fever.

quar·ter (*kwor*-ter) *n.* 1. A fourth part or portion. 2. *Astronomy.* A phase of the moon. 3. One of the four figurative divisions of the horizon. 4. A locality; district. 5. A fourth part of the carcass of a quadruped. 6. A 25-cent piece. 7. [*pl.*] Residence; lodgings. 8. Merciful treatment of a vanquished enemy. —*v.* 1. To divide into four equal parts. 2. To furnish with lodgings.—**quar·ter** *adj.*—**quar·tered** *adj.*—**quar·ter·ing** *n. & adj.*

quarter-angled	quarter-cut	quarterpace
quarter boards	quarter-final	quarter-pointed
quarter-breed	quarterland	quarter-sheet
quarter cast	quarter-miler	quarterstretch

quar·ter·back *n. Football.* 1. A backfield position. 2. The backfield player.

quar·ter·deck *n. Navy.* After part of the upper deck set aside for the use of officers and for certain ceremonies.

quar·ter·ly *n.* A publication issued every three months.—*adj.* 1. Occurring four times a year. 2. Consisting of four parts.—**quar·ter·ly** *adv.*

quar·ter·mas·ter *n.* 1. *Army.* An army officer commissioned to superintend distribution of food, clothing, and equipment. 2. *Nautical.* A petty officer or unlicensed seaman who attends the helm and assists the watch officer on the bridge.

quarter section. A tract of 160 acres in the U.S. government surveying system.

quar·ter·staff *n.* [*pl.* -staves] An early English weapon formed of a stout pole, sometimes iron-tipped.

quar·tet, quar·tette (kwor-*tet*) *n.* 1. *Music.* A composition for four voices or four instruments. 2. The performers of a quartet. 3. A group of four.

quar·to (*kwor*-toh) *n.* A book the size of a fourth of a printer's sheet.—**quar·to** *adj.*

quartz (*kworts*) *n.* A common mineral composed of silicon dioxide. (*Symbol:* S_1O_2).

quash (*kwosh*) *v.* 1. To quell; extinguish. 2. To annul; void.

qua·si (*kway*-sy, *kway*-zy) *adv.* As if; in a manner of.—**qua·si** *adj.*

qua·si- *prefix.* Resembling; similar to.

quas·si·a (*kwah*-shee-uh) *n.* A bitter drug, made from the wood of a tropical American tree, used as a tonic and a remedy for threadworms.

qua·ter·na·ry (kwah-*ter*-ner-ee) *adj.* Consisting of four.—**qua·ter·na·ry** *n.*

quat·rain (*kwah*-trayn) *n.* A four-line stanza.

quat·tro·cen·to (kwaht-roh-*chen*-toh) *adj.* Pertaining to the Italian Renaissance of the 15th century.—**quat·tro·cen·to** *n.*

qua·ver (*kway*-ver) *v.* To tremble; pronounce falteringly; trill.—**qua·ver** *n.*—**qua·ver·y** *adj.* Trembling; shaky.

quay (*kee*) *n.* A wharf; dock.

quea·sy (*kwee*-zee) *adj.* 1. Squeamish; sickish; uneasy. 2. Difficult; precarious.—**quea·si·ly** *adv.*—**quea·si·ness** *n.*

queen *n.* 1. The consort of a king. 2. A female sovereign. 3. Sovereign of a swarm of bees. 4. A playing card upon which a queen is pictured. 5. *Chess.* The most powerful piece in a set of chessmen.—*v.* 1. To play the queen. 2. *Chess.* To make into a queen, as a pawn when moved to the eighth square.

Queen Anne's lace. A wild carrot with delicate white flower clusters.

queen·ly *adj.* [queen·li·er, queen·li·est] Becoming a queen; regal.—**queen·li·ness** *n.*

queer *adj.* Strange; peculiar; curious.—*v. Slang.* To spoil; ruin.—**queer·ly** *adv.*—**queer·ness** *n.*

quell *v.* To subdue; quiet; crush.—**quell·er** *n.*

quench *v.* 1. To extinguish; put out. 2. To allay; slake.—**quench·a·ble** *adj.*—**quench·er** *n.*—**quench·less** *adj.*

quer·u·lous (*kwehr*-yoo-lus) *adj.* Petulant; complaining; irritable.—**quer·u·lous·ly** *adv.*—**quer·u·lous·ness** *n.*

que·ry (*kwee*-ree) *n.* [*pl.* que·ries] Question; inquiry.—*v.* [que·ried; que·ry·ing]. To ask.

quest *n.* 1. Search. 2. Expedition; adventure. —**quest** *v.*—**quest·er** *n.*

ques·tion (*kwess*-chun) *n.* 1. Query; interrogation. 2. Subject of discussion. 3. Dispute; controversy; doubt.—*v.* To ask; query.—**ques·tion·er** *n.*—**ques·tion·ing·ly** *adv.*

ques·tion·a·ble (*kwess*-chun-uh-b'l) *adj.* Of doubtful acceptability; dubious.—**ques·tion·a·ble·ness** *n.*—**ques·tion·a·bly** *adv.*

ques·tion·naire (kwess-chun-*air*) *n.* A series of questions designed for a group survey.

quet·zal (ket-*sahl*) *n.* A brilliantly colored bird of Central America.

queue (*kyoo*) *n.* 1. A pigtail; single back braid. 2. A line of people. —**queue** *v.* [queued; queu·ing]. To stand in line.

quib·ble (*kwib*-b'l) *v.* [quib·bled; quib·bling] To equivocate; prevaricate; haggle over details.—**quib·ble** *n.* —**quib·bler** *n.*

quick *adj.* 1. Speedy; swift. 2. Living; animate. 3. Apt; ready. —*adv.* Speedily; with haste.—*n.* 1. The core; the vital living part. 2. The living.—**quick·ly** *adv.*—**quick·ness** *n.*

QUEUE

quick·en *v.* 1. To excite; stimulate. 2. To revive; bring to life. 3. To speed.—**quick·en·er** *n.*

quick·ie *n. Slang.* 1. A low-budget motion picture. 2. A short drink.

quick·lime *n.* Calcium oxide prepared by burning limestone. (*Symbol:* CaO).

quick·sand *n.* An area of loose or moving sand which yields beneath a weight.

quick·set *n.* A plant, usually hawthorne, set to grow as a hedge.

quick·sil·ver (*kwik*-sil-ver) *n.* Common name for mercury.—**quick·sil·vered** *adj.*

quid *n.* A piece of chewing tobacco.

quid·di·ty (*kwid*-it-ee) *n.* [*pl.* -ties] 1. Essence. 2. A quibble.

qui·es·cent (kwee-*ess*-ent, kwy-) *adj.* Latent; still; inactive.—**qui·es·cence** *n.*— -cent·ly *adv.*

qui·et (*kwy*-et) *adj.* 1. Silent; noiseless. 2. Calm; tranquil. 3. Secluded; retired. 4. Restrained; in good taste.—*n.* Stillness; tranquillity.—*v.* To calm; pacify; tranquilize. —**qui·et** *adv.*—**qui·et·ly** *adv.*—**qui·et·ness** *n.*

qui·e·tude (*kwy*-eh-tyood) *n.* Rest; tranquillity.

qui·e·tus (kwy-*ee*-tus) *n.* 1. Death; release. 2. Death blow; finishing stroke.

quill *n.* 1. A large strong feather. 2. A porcupine spine. 3. A pen made from a feather.

quilt *n.* A stuffed coverlet. —**quilt** *v.*—**quilt·er** *n.*—**quilt·ing** *n.*

quince *n.* 1. A hard tart yellow fruit, resembling an apple, used for jellies and preserves. 2. The quince tree.

qui·nine (*kwy*-nyne) *n.* Also **quin·in, quin·i·a, qui·ni·na.** An alkaloid of the cinchona bark acting as a prophylactic and antidote for malaria.

QUILL

quin·qua·ge·nar·i·an (kwin-kwuh-jeh-*nair*-ee-an) *n.* A person between 50 and 60 years old. —**quin·qua·ge·nar·i·an** *adj.*

quin·quen·ni·al (kwin-*kwen*-ee-al) *adj.* Occurring once in five years; lasting for five years. —**quin·quen·ni·al·ly** *adv.*—**quin·quen·ni·um** *n.*

quin·sy (*kwin*-zee) *n. Medicine.* Severe inflammation of the throat and tonsils.

quin·tes·sence (kwin-*tess*-enss) *n.* 1. Primary example; most crucial or characteristic property. 2. The core; intrinsic being.—**quin·tes·sen·tial** *adj.*

quin·tet, quin·tette (kwin-*tet*) *n. Music.* 1. A vocal or instrumental composition in five parts. 2. The performers of a quintet.

quin·til·lion (kwin-*til*-yun) *n.* One followed by 18 zeros.—**quin·til·lion** *adj.*—**quin·til·lionth** *adj.*

quin·tu·ple (kwin-*tuh*-p'l) *adj.* Fivefold.—*v.* [quin·tu·pled; quin·tu·pling] To multiply by five.—**quin·tu·plet** (*kwin*-tuh-plet) *n.* One of five children born together.

quip *n.* A joke; witticism.—*v.* [quipped; quip·ping]—**quip·ster** *n.*

quire *n.* Twenty-four sheets of paper of equal size.

Quir·i·nal (*kweer*-ih-n'l) *n.* 1. Hill in Rome on which the King's palace is located. 2. The Italian monarchy.—**Quir·i·nal** *adj.*

Q

quirk *n.* 1. A vagary; idiosyncrasy. 2. A curlicue; flourish. 3. An evasive or light remark. —**quirk·y** *adj.*

quirt *n.* A short-handled riding whip.—**quirt** *v.*

QUIRT

quis·ling (*kwiz*-ling) *n.* A civilian traitor; collaborator, esp. in World War II.

quit (*kwit*) *v.* [quit; quit·ted; quit·ting] 1. To depart; leave. 2. To stop; cease.—*adj.* Discharged from debt or obligation; free.

quit·claim *n.* *Law.* A deed of release.—**quit·claim** *v.* To renounce legal claim to.

quite (*kwyte*) *adv.* 1. Completely; entirely. 2. Considerably; to an extent.

quits *adj.* On even terms; discharged from obligation.

quit·tance (*kwit*-enss) *n.* Discharge from debt; evening of scores.

quit·ter *n.* One who gives up easily.

quiv·er *v.* To shake; tremble.—**quiv·er** *n.*

quiv·er *n.* A sheath for arrows.

quix·ot·ic (kwiks-*ot*-ik) *adj.* Also **quix·ot·i·cal.** Unrealistically scrupulous; unworldly; —**quix·ot·i·cal·ly** *adv.*—**quix·ot·ism** *n.*

QUIVER

quiz *n.* An examination; test.—*v.* [quizzed; quiz·zing] To interrogate; question.—**quiz·zer** *n.*

quiz·zi·cal *adj.* Teasing; chaffing.—**quiz·zi·cal·ly** *adv.*

quoin *n.* 1. *Architecture.* Stone forming an external angle of a building. 2. *Printing.* A wooden or metal wedge for tightening a galley or page of type.

QUOINS (def. 1)

quoit *n.* 1. A ring tossed at a target. 2. [*pl.*] A game of ring-pitching.—**quoit** *v.*

quon·dam (*kwon*-d'm) *adj.* Former.

quo·rum (*kwoh*-rum) *n.* Number of members of an assembly that must be present to make a meeting official.

QUOIT

quo·ta (*kwoh*-tuh) *n.* [*pl.* quo·tas]. A proportional part or share.

quo·ta·tion (kwoh-*tay*-shun) *n.* 1. The act of quoting. 2. A passage repeated. 3. Current price of commodities or stocks.

quote *v.* [quot·ed; quot·ing] 1. To cite; repeat the words of another. 2. To name a price. —**quote** *n.*—**quot·a·ble** *adj.*—**quot·er** *n.*

quoth *v.* *Archaic.* Said; spoke.

quo·tid·i·an (kwoh-*tid*-ee-an) *adj.* Daily.—*n.* A daily recurrent fever.

quo·tient (*kwoh*-sh'nt) *n.* *Arithmetic.* Number which results from the division of one number by another.

R

Ra (rah) *n.* The sun god of the ancient Egyptians.

rab·bet *v.* [rab·bet·ted; rab·bet·ting] To cut two boards in such a way that they lap or fit together.—**rab·bet** *n.*

rab·bi (*rab*-eye) *n.* [*pl.* rab·bis, rab·bies] A Jewish priest or scholar. —**rab·bin·ic, rab·bin·i·cal** *adj.*

rab·bit *n.* A fleet-footed herb-eating rodent which lives in burrows in the ground.—**rab·bit·ry** [*pl.* -ries] *n.* Area for rabbit hutches.

RABBIT (1/15 life size)

rabbit fever. An undulant fever carried by rodents and communicable to man; tularemia.

rabbit punch. *Boxing.* A short, quick blow aimed at the back of the neck.

rab·ble (*rab*-'l) *n.* 1. A noisy crowd; a mob. 2. The great mass of the people, used contemptuously.

Ra·be·lais (*rab*-eh-lay) *n.* A classic French humorist.—**Rab·e·lai·si·an** *adj.* 1. Pertaining to Rabelais. 2. Exaggeratedly or lewdly funny.

rab·id (*rab*-id) *adj.* 1. Mad; raging; hydrophobic. 2. Intolerant; fanatical.—**ra·bid·i·ty** *n.*—**ra·bid·ly** *adv.*—**ra·bid·ness** *n.*

ra·bies (*ray*-beez) *n. sing.* An acute disease of the central nervous system attacking dogs and other carnivorous animals; in man, called hydrophobia.

rac·coon *n.* Also **ra·coon.** 1. A badger-like American animal with striped fur. 2. Fur of the raccoon.—**rac·coon** *adj.*

RACCOON (1/15 life size)

race (*rayss*) *n.* 1. A speed contest. 2. A rapid course; a swift stream.—*v.* [raced; rac·ing] 1. To speed. 2. To engage in a speed contest.—**rac·er** *n.*

race *n.* **1.** A people descended from a common ancestry. **2.** A strong or distinguished flavor, as of wine.

ra·ceme (ruh-*seem*) *n.* Flowers clustered on a single stem.—**rac·e·mose** *adj.*

race riot. A riot caused by racial prejudice.

ra·cial (ray-sh'l) *adj.* Pertaining to a classification of people according to general physical and linguistic characteristics.—**ra·cial·ly** *adv.*

rac·ism (rayss-izm) *n.* Also **rac·ial·ism. 1.** Discrimination against members of any race because of presumed racial inferiority. **2.** The assumption that any race is superior to another.

rack *n.* **1.** A framework on which articles are deposited. **2.** *Machinery.* A notched bar used with a notched wheel to convert circular motion into straight motion. **3.** A medieval torture instrument. **4.** Utter ruin.—*v.* **1.** To strain; to stretch. **2.** To pain; to torture. **3.** To place on a framework.—**rack·er** *n.*

RACK (def. 2)

rack·et *n.* A loud noise; din.

rack·et *n.* *Colloquial.* **1.** A confidence game; an illegal business. **2.** Any business or calling.—**rack·e·teer** *n.* An operator of a racket; a gangster.—**rack·e·teer·ing** *n.*

rack·et, rac·quet *n.* An instrument for hitting a ball, as in tennis.

rac·on·teur (rak-on-*ter*) *n.* A clever story teller; a narrator.

RACKET

rac·y (ray-see) *adj.* [rac·i·er; rac·i·est] **1.** Strongly flavored; spirited; piquant. **2.** Risqué.—**ra·ci·ly** *adv.*—**rac·i·ness** *n.*

ra·dar (ray-dahr) *n.* A principle of direction- and range-finding by ultrahigh frequency, point-to-point radio wave which is reflected back from any object within its range.

ra·di·al (ray-dee-ul) *adj.* **1.** Referring to a radius. **2.** Extending out like rays or radii. —**ra·di·al·ly** *adv.*

ra·di·ant (ray-dee-unt) *adj.* **1.** Giving off rays; radiating. **2.** Brilliant; sparkling.—**ra·di·ance, ra·di·an·cy** *n.*—**ra·di·ant·ly** *adv.*

ra·di·ate (ray-dee-ayt) *v.* [ra·di·at·ed; -at·ing] **1.** To give out rays. **2.** To spread out from a center, as rays of light. **3.** To treat by exposure to radiation.—*adj.* Having parts extending out from a center.

ra·di·a·tion (ray-dee-ay-shun) *n.* **1.** Emission of radiant energy. **2.** Energy such as light, heat, or electricity emitted in wave patterns. —**ra·di·a·tive** *adj.*

ra·di·a·tor (ray-dee-ay-ter) *n.* A system of pipes for radiating heat or cooling the substance contained in it.

rad·i·cal (rad-ik-'l) *adj.* **1.** Fundamental;

complete; thorough; extreme. **2.** *Politics.* Revolutionary; abrupt.—*n.* **1.** A root; a basic element. **2.** *Politics.* One who favors basic and rapid change in the organization of society. **3.** *Mathematics.* The sign [√] indicating extraction of a root. **4.** *Chemistry.* A group of elements which undergo changes as a single element. **5.** *Philology.* A root word. —**rad·i·cal·ly** *adv.*

ra·di·i (ray-dee-eye). *Plural* of **radius.**

ra·di·o (ray-dee-oh) *n.* [*pl.* ra·di·os] **1.** A system of communication by radiated electromagnetic waves vibrating at a high frequency. **2.** The entertainment or engineering industry grown up about this principle. **3.** A device for converting electric waves to sound waves; a radio receiver.—*v.* To communicate by radio.

ra·di·o (ray-dee-oh) *adj. & combining prefix.* **1.** Referring to a radius. **2.** Pertaining to radioactivity. **3.** Denoting radiated energy.

radioacoustics	radiomovies
radio amplifier	radiomuscular
radio antenna	radionecrosis
radio bearing	radio observer
radio broadcast	radiophare
radiocarpal	radiophotograph
radiocast	radio range
radio channel	radio receiver
radiochemistry	radiosensibility
radiochrometer	radiosensitive
radio communication	radio set
radio compass	radio spectator
radiodetector	radiostereoscopy
radiodiagnosis	radiosurgery
radiodynamic	radiosymmetrical
radio engineer	radiotechnology
radio field	radio transmitter
radiogoniometer	radiotransparent
radiolead	radiotron
radio link	radiotropic
radioman	radiovision
radiometallography	radio wave

ra·di·o·ac·tin·i·um (ray-dee-oh-ak-*tin*-ee-um) *n.* An element formed by the radioactive disintegration of actinium. (*Symbol:* RdAc).

ra·di·o·ac·tiv·i·ty (ray-dee-oh-ak-*tiv*-ih-tee) *n.* Spontaneous decomposition of an atom resulting in radiation of rays of three types and the formation of new substances.—**ra·di·o·ac·tive** *adj.*

radio beacon. A radio transmitter which sends signals for navigation by direction finder.

radio frequency. Any vibration of electric waves above fifteen kilocycles.

ra·di·o·gram (ray-dee-oh-gram) *n.* A message sent by radiotelegraphy.

ra·di·og·raph·y (ray-dee-*og*-ruh-fee) *n.* Practice of producing an image on a sensitive plate by X-rays.—**ra·di·o·graph** *n.* A picture so made.

ra·di·o·me·te·or·o·graph (ray-dee-oh-mee-tee-or-oh-graph) *n.* An apparatus sent into the atmosphere which records and transmits weather data to a receiving station below.

ra·di·om·e·ter (ray-dee-*om*-uh-ter) *n.* An apparatus for measuring the penetrating power of radiation.—**ra·di·o·met·ric** (-*met*-rik) *adj.*—**ra·di·o·met·ri·cal·ly** *adv.*—**ra·di·om·e·try** *n.*

R

ra·di·on·ics (ray-dee-*on*-iks) *n.* The branch of electronics concerned with radio.

ra·di·o·phone (*ray*-dee-oh-fohn) *n.* A radiotelephone.

ra·di·o·scope (*ray*-dee-oh-skohp) *n.* An instrument for the detection and analysis of radioactive rays.—**ra·di·os·co·py** (ray-dee-*oss*-kuh-pee) *n.* Examination of the internal structure of opaque bodies by penetrating radiation. —**ra·di·o·scop·ic, -scop·i·cal** *adj.*— **-scop·i·cal·ly** *adv.*

ra·di·o·te·leg·ra·phy (ray-dee-oh-teh-*leg*-ruh-fee) *n.* Radio transmission of messages by code.—**ra·di·o·tel·e·gram** (-*tel*-uh-gram) *n.* A message so transmitted.—**ra·di·o·tel·e·graph** *v.*

ra·di·o·te·leph·o·ny (ray-dee-oh-teh-*lef*-oh-nee) *n.* Transmission of sound by modulated radio waves.—**ra·di·o·tel·e·phone** *n.* Apparatus for transmitting or receiving sound by radio.—**ra·di·o·tel·e·phon·ic** *adj.*

ra·di·o·tel·lu·ri·um (ray-dee-oh-tel-*oor*-ee-um) *n.* A radioactive element, polonium.

ra·di·o·thal·li·um (ray-dee-oh-*thal*-ee-um) *n.* A radioactive product of the thallium disintegration. (*Symbol:* RdTl).

ra·di·o·ther·a·py (ray-dee-oh-*theh*-ruh-pee) *n.* [*pl.* -pies]. Also **ra·di·o·ther·a·peu·tics** (-*pyoo*-tiks). Treatment of diseases by high-frequency radiation.—**ra·di·o·ther·a·pist** *n.*

ra·di·o·ther·my *n.* [*pl.* -mies] Treatment of disorders by localized fever induced by ultrahigh-frequency radiation.

ra·di·o·thor·i·um *n.* A radioactive element formed by the atomic disintegration of thorium. (*Symbol:* RdTh).

radio tube. An electron tube for picking up or amplifying a radio signal; a vacuum tube.

rad·ish (*rad*-ish) *n.* An annual vegetable with a crisp, pungent root, eaten raw in salads.

ra·di·um (*ray*-dee-um) *n.* A metallic, intensely radioactive element used in treating cancer and in producing luminous paint.

ra·di·us (*ray*-dee-us) *n.* [*pl.* ra·di·i, ra·di·us·es] 1. *Geometry.* A straight line drawn from the center of a circle to its circumference. 2. *Anatomy.* A bone of the forearm.

ra·don (*ray*-don) *n.* A radioactive, gaseous element formed by the decomposition of radium. (*Symbol:* Rn).

RADIUS

raf·fi·a (*raf*-ee-uh) *n.* Rope fiber derived from the bark of the raffia palm tree.

raf·fish *adj.* Rowdy; low; vulgar.—**raf·fish·ly** *adv.*—**raf·fish·ness** *n.*

raf·fle (*raf*-'l) *n.* A drawing; lottery; game of chance.—*v.* [raf·fled; raf·fling] To put up at a raffle.—**raf·fler** *n.*

raft *n.* A platform float formed of timbers or other buoyant materials.—**raft** *v.*—**rafts·man** *n.*

raft·er *n. Construction.* A timber extending from the eaves to the roofpeak to which the lath is secured. —**raft·er** *v.* To make into rafters; to install rafters.

RAFTERS

rag *n.* 1. A tatter; a torn piece of cloth. 2. A musical piece in ragtime tempo. 3. *Slang.* A newspaper, esp. a poor one. 4. [*pl.*] Tattered clothing or garments.—*v.* [ragged; rag·ging] *Colloquial.* To tease; to taunt.

rag·a·muf·fin *n.* A ragged fellow.

rage (*rayj*) *n.* 1. Violent anger; fury. 2. *Fashion*; vogue.—*v.* [raged; rag·ing] 1. To be furious. 2. To act or talk violently. 3. To be out of control; run riot.

rag·ged (*rag*-ed) *adj.* 1. Tattered; torn. 2. Jagged; rough-edged. 3. Unfinished; uneven; crude; raw.—**rag·ged·ly** *adv.*—**rag·ged·ness** *n.*

rag·lan (*rag*-lan) *n.* A coat sleeve having a continuous seam to the collar, giving a sloping shoulderline.—**rag·lan** *adj.*

ra·gout (ruh-*goo*) *n.* Highly seasoned meat stew.

rag·time *n.* A dance music of the early twentieth century having a strongly syncopated one-step rhythm in quick tempo.—**rag·time** *adj.*

rag·weed *n.* A low-growing, bushy weed, pollen of which is one of the chief causes of hay fever.

raid (*rayd*) *v.* 1. To invade or attack without warning, esp. in an isolated detachment. 2. To make a sudden police invasion of an illegal establishment.—**raid** *n.*—**raid·er** *n.*

rail (*rayl*) *v.* To speak bitterly; to rage.—**rail·er** *n.*—**rail·ing** *n.*—**rail·ing** *adj.*

rail *n.* 1. A steel track for trains. 2. A horizontal timber or bar on upright supports. 3. A fence or balustrade. 4. Railroad transportation.—**rail** *v.*—**rail** *adj.*

rail·ing *n.* A fence; a barrier of rails.

rail·ler·y (*rayl*-er-ee) *n.* [*pl.* rail·ler·ies] Banter; jest.

rail·road *n.* 1. A line of rails for trains. 2. A train transportation company with all its assets and properties.—*v.* 1. To send by rail. 2. *Colloquial.* To put through pell-mell. 3. *Colloquial.* To imprison on trumped-up charges. 4. *Printing.* To insert uncorrected matter in a newspaper.

rail·way *n.* 1. A line of train tracks. 2. A railroad company or system.

rai·ment (*ray*-m'nt) *n.* Clothing; garments.

rain *n.* 1. Atmospheric vapor condensed to water and falling toward the earth. 2. A shower; a profuse simultaneous descent.—**rain** *v.*—**rain·less** *adj.*

rain-beaten	rain-drenched	rain-soaked
rainbird	rain-driven	rain-sodden
rain-bitten	raindrop	rainstorm
rain-bleared	rainfall	rain-streaked
rain-bound	rainfowl	rain-swept
rainburst	rain-gutted	raintight
rain-damped	rainproof	rain-worn

rain·bow *n.* A varicolored arch formed on the horizon opposite the sun by refraction of light rays on water particles in the air.—**rain·bowed** *adj.*

rain·coat *n.* An overcoat of waterproof or water-repellent fabric.

rain·y *adj.* [rain·i·er; rain·i·est] Characterized by frequent or heavy rain.—**rain·i·ness** *n.*

raise (*rayz*) *v.* [raised; rais·ing] 1. To elevate; to lift up. 2. To promote. 3. To increase; to intensify. 4. To cause to rise; erect. 5. To present; to bring up. 6. To rouse to action. 7. To collect; to bring together. 8. To rear; to grow; to produce. 9. To evoke; to cause to appear. 10. To create; to originate.—**raise** *n.*—**rais·er** *n.*

rais·in (*rayz*-in) *n.* A dried grape.

ra·ja, ra·jah (*rah*-zhah) *n.* An Indian prince; a Hindu ruler.

rake *n.* A long-handled, toothed tool used for collecting leaves, stirring the soil, etc. —*v.* [raked; rak·ing]. 1. To go over with a rake; to scrape; to scar as with a rake. 2. To strafe; to fire upon from end to end.—**rak·er** *n.*

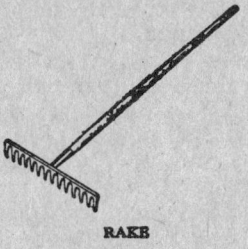

RAKE

rake *n.* A loose-living person; a roué.—*v.* [raked; rak·ing].

rake·hell *n.* A lewd, immoral person; a libertine.—**rake·hell, rake·hell·ish** *adj.*

rak·ish *adj.* 1. Informal; debonair; jaunty. 2. Profligate; like a rake.—**rak·ish·ly** *adv.*

ral·ly *v.* [ral·lied; ral·ly·ing] 1. To assemble for a public demonstration or meeting. 2. To recover from a temporary setback; to reorganize lines of resistance.—*n.* [*pl.* ral·lies].

ram *n.* 1. A male sheep. 2. An instrument for butting or thrusting; a battering-ram.—*v.* [rammed; ram·ming].—**ram·mer** *n.*

ram·ble (*ram*-b'l) *v.* [ram·bled; ram·bling] 1. To rove; to wander; to meander. 2. To talk incoherently; to digress.—**ram·ble** *n.*—**ram·bler** *n.*—**-bling·ly** *adv.*

RAM

ram·e·kin (*ram*-eh-kin) *n.* Also **ram·e·quin**. *Cookery.* 1. Any of several mixtures baked in a small mold. 2. An individual casserole.

ram·i·fy (*ram*-ih-fye) *v.* [ram·i·fied; -fy·ing] To branch out; to extend into many divisions.—**ram·i·fi·ca·tion** *n.*

ramp *n.* An incline leading from one level to another.

ram·page (*ram*-payj) *v.* [ram·paged; ram·pag·ing] To rage and storm; to behave violently. —**ram·page** *n.*—**ram·pa·geous** *adj.*

ramp·ant (*ram*-p'nt) *adj.* 1. Rising on the hind legs and extending the forelegs. 2. Overleaping restraint or bounds; unchecked; predominant.—**ramp·an·cy** *n.*—**ramp·ant·ly** *adv.*

ram·part (*ram*-pahrt) *n.* A bulwark; an elevation for defense.

ram·rod (*ram*-rod) *n.* A rod for cleaning small firearms.

ram·shack·le (*ram*-shak-'l) *adj.* Decrepit; loose; falling apart.

ranch, ranche *n.* A large farm for raising beef cattle.—*v.* To run a ranch.—**ranch·er, ranch·man** *n.*

ran·cid (*ran*-sid) *adj.* Offensively strong-flavored; rank.—**ran·cid·i·ty, ran·cid·ness** *n.*

ran·cor, ran·cour (*rank*-er) *n.* Enmity; spite; bitter hatred.—**ran·cor·ous** *adj.*—**ran·cor·ous·ly** *adv.*—**ran·cor·ous·ness** *n.*

ran·dom (*ran*-dum) *adj.* Chance; haphazard; casual.—**ran·dom** *n.*—**ran·dom·ly** *adv.*

range (*raynj*) *n.* 1. A series; a row. 2. A mountain chain. 3. Scope; extent; compass distance. 4. *Gunnery.* **a.** The proper distance **b.** A shooting practice area. 5. A kitchen stove. 6. Open grazing lands.—*v.* [ranged; rang·ing] 1. To wander over. 2. To set in rows; to arrange. 3. To vary.

range finder. An instrument for determining distance.

rang·er (*rayn*-jer) *n.* 1. An infantryman trained as a commando. 2. A forester. 3. A law-enforcing official. 4. A wanderer.

rang·y (*rayn*-jee) *adj.* [rang·i·er; rang·i·est]. Tall and lanky; long-legged.

rank *adj.* 1. Foul; ill smelling; vile tasting. 2. Luxuriant; overgrown. 3. Extreme; sheer. —**rank·ly** *adv.*—**rank·ness** *n.*

rank *n.* 1. A row; a line. 2. Position; station. 3. Official grade or title. 4. [*pl.*] A body of soldiers. 5. [*pl.*] Enlisted soldiers distinguished from officers.—*v.* 1. To arrange in lines or in the order of quality. 2. *Military.* To outrank; to have priority because of higher rank.

rank and file. Body of members of an organization, excluding officers.

ran·kle *v.* [ran·kled; ran·kling] 1. To fester; to become inflamed. 2. To produce a painful or irritating sensation.

ran·sack (*ran*-sak) *v.* 1. To search through feverishly. 2. To plunder; to pillage.—**ran·sack·er** *n.*

ran·som (*ran*-sum) *n.* Money paid to free a prisoner or kidnapped person.—**ran·som** *v.*

rant *v.* To rave; to speak loudly or extravagantly.—**rant** *n.*—**rant·er** *n.*—**rant·ing·ly** *adv.*

rap *v.* [rapped; rap·ping] To knock sharply. —*n.* *Slang.* Imprisonment; blame; punishment.—**rap** *n.*—**rap·per** *n.*

ra·pa·cious (ruh-*pay*-shus) *adj.* Violent; plundering; greedy.—**ra·pa·cious·ly** *adv.*—**ra·pa·cious·ness** *n.*—**ra·pac·i·ty** (ruh-*pas*-it-tee) *n.*

rape (*rayp*) *v.* [raped; rap·ing] 1. To sack; to

R

plunder. 2. To force sexual intercourse upon. —**rape** *n.*

rape *n.* A hardy annual plant of the mustard family grown for fodder and oil.

rap·id *adj.* Fast; quick; swift.—*n.* [*pl.*] A shallow, swiftly flowing part of a river.—**rap·id·ly** *adv.*—**ra·pid·i·ty** *n.*

ra·pi·er (*ray*-pee-er) *n.* A straight, slender sword wielded by thrusting.

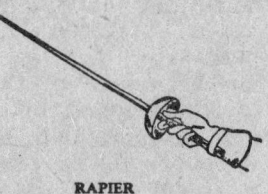

RAPIER

rap·ine (*rap*-in) *n.* Plundering; violent pillage.

rap·port (ruh-*port*) *n.* Harmony; agreement; understanding.

rap·scal·lion (rap-*skal*-yun) *n.* A rascal; a scoundrel.

rapt *adj.* 1. Transported; enraptured; ecstatic. 2. Absorbed in thought.

rap·ture (*rap*-cher) *n.* Ecstasy; transport of delight.—**rap·tur·ous** *adj.*—**rap·tur·ous·ly** *adv.* —**rap·tur·ous·ness** *n.*

rare *adj.* Nearly raw; slightly cooked.—**rare·ness** *n.*

rare *adj.* 1. Scarce; infrequently encountered. 2. Not dense. 'A rare gas.'—**rare·ly** *adv.*

rare·bit (*rair*-bit) *n. Cookery.* A Welsh rabbit; a melted-cheese dish, often made with beer or ale, and served over crackers.

rare earth. One of a series of metallic elements all of which occur naturally as oxides.

rar·e·fy (*rair*-ih-fy) *v.* [ra·re·fied; -fy·ing] To make less dense; to make thin or porous.—**ra·re·fac·tion** *n.*—**ra·re·fac·tive** *adj.*

rar·i·ty (*rair*-ih-tee) *n.* [*pl.* rar·i·ties] 1. That which is encountered infrequently. 2. Thinness; lack of density. 3. Uncommonness; infrequency.

ras·cal (*rass*-k'l) *n.* A dishonest person; a scoundrel.—**ras·cal·i·ty** *n.* [*pl.* -ties].—**ras·cal·ly** *adj.*—**ras·cal·ly** *adv.*

rash *n.* A skin eruption.

rash *adj.* Hasty; foolhardy; reckless.—**rash·ly** *adv.*—**rash·ness** *n.*

rashbrain	rash-hearted
rash-conceived	rash-minded
rash-headed	rash-spoken

rash·er *n.* A slice of bacon.

rasp *n.* 1. A file for use on wood. 2. A harsh, grating sound.—*v.*

1. To file with a rasp.

RASP

2. To make a harsh, grating sound; irritate; offend.—**rasp·ing** *adj.*—**rasp·ing·ly** *adv.*

rasp·ber·ry (*raz*-beh-ree) *n.* An edible berry with seeds embedded in its flesh, grown on a woody biennial bush of the bramble family. 2. *Slang.* Contemptuous sound made with the lips and tongue.

rat *n.* 1. A destructive, vicious pest of the rodent family. 2. *Slang.* Any mean or despicable person. 3. *Colloquial.* Pad supporting a roll of hair in a woman's coiffure.—*v.* [rat·ted; rat·ting] 1. To kill rats. 2. *Slang.* To betray one's associates for personal gain.—**rat·ter** *n.*

RAT (1/12 life-size)

rat bite	ratfish	ratproof
rat catcher	rat-gnawn	rat-ridden
rat-colored	rat-infested	rat-tailed
rat-deserted	rat-inhabited	rattight
rat-eyed	ratlike	rat trap

rat·a·ble (*rayt*-uh-b'l) *adj.* Also **rate·a·ble.** 1. Capable of being evaluated or reckoned. 2. *British.* Taxable.—**rat·a·bil·i·ty, rate·a·bil·i·ty** *n.*—**rat·a·bly, rate·a·bly** *adv.*

ratch·et (*rach*-et) *n. Machinery.* A catch or pawl which fits into a notched wheel or bar to allow motion in only one direction.

rate *n.* 1. A standard value or proportion. 2. Degree; rank; estimate. 3. Degree of speed. 4. Price or unit charge.—*v.* [rat·ed; rat·ing].—**rat·er** *n.*

RATCHET

rath·er (*rath*-er) *adv.* 1. Somewhat; quite. 2. Preferably; more readily or willingly. 3. To the contrary.

raths·kel·ler (*rahts*-kel-er) *n.* A restaurant or beer hall below street level.

rat·i·fy (*rat*-ih-fy) *v.* [rat·i·fied; -fy·ing] To approve; confirm; make valid.—**rat·i·fi·ca·tion** *n.*—**rat·i·fi·er** *n.*

rat·ing (*rayt*-ing) *n.* 1. Determination of rank or value. 2. Rank; grade.

ra·tio (*ray*-shoh) *n.* A proportion; relation which one value bears to another.

ra·ti·oc·i·na·tion (rash-ee-oss-ee-*nay*-shun) *n.* Reasoning, esp. deductive.—**ra·ti·oc·i·nate** *v.* [-nat·ed; -nat·ing].— **-na·tive** *adj.*— **-na·tor** *n.*

ra·tion (*ray*-shun, *rash*-un) *n.* Allowance; a fixed amount dealt or doled out.—*v.* To apportion in equable shares.

ra·tion·al (*rash*-un-'l) *adj.* 1. Endowed with reason. 2. Reasonable; logical. 3. *Mathematics.* Referring to a quantity which can be expressed in whole numbers.—**ra·tion·al** *n.* —**ra·tion·al·ly** *adv.*—**ra·tion·al·i·ty** *n.*

ra·tion·al·ism (*rash*-un-ul-izm) *n.* Any philosophical doctrine holding that reason is the source of knowledge or the arbiter of truth. —**ra·tion·al·is·tic** *adj.*—**ra·tion·al·is·ti·cal·ly** *adv.*

ra·tion·al·ize (*rash*-un-ul-yze) *v.* [ra·tion·al·ized; -iz·ing] 1. To justify one's behavior to oneself or others. 2. To make reasonable or logical. —**ra·tion·al·i·za·tion** *n.*—**ra·tion·al·i·zer** *n.*

ra·tion·ing (*ray*-shun-ing, *rash*-un-ing) *n.* Practice of equably apportioning scarce commodities among consumers.

rat·line (*rat*-lin) *n.* One of a series of lines secured to the shrouds of a ship forming a ladder for climbing aloft.

rats·bane (*rats*-bayn) *n.* An arsenic rat poison.

rat·tan (rat-*tan*). Also **ra· tan.** A family of palms which yield tough, pliable canes used for wickerwork, walking sticks, etc.

rat·tle (*rat*-'l) *v.* [rat·tled; rat·tling] 1. To make a sharp, rapidly repeated noise; clatter; chatter. 2. To make nervous; unnerve.—**rat·tle** *n.* 1. A clattering sound. 2. A rattling toy for babies.—**rat·tler** *n.* 1. One who rattles. 2. A rattlesnake.—**rat· tly** *adj.*

RATLINE

rat·tle·brain *n.* A scatterbrain; a chatterbox. —**rat·tle·brained** *adj.*

rat·tle·head *n.* A madcap; a giddy, undependable person.—**rat·tle·head·ed** *adj.*

rat·tle·snake *n.* One of a group of poisonous snakes having horny rings on the tail which rattle when shaken.

rat·tle·trap *n.* A ramshackle, rattling object, esp. a vehicle.—**rat·tle· trap** *adj.*

rat·ty *adj.* [rat·ti·er; rat· ti·est] 1. Overrun with rats. 2. Despicable; disgusting.

RATTLESNAKE

rau·cous (*raw*-kus) *adj.* Hoarse; harsh; grating. —**rau·ci·ty** *n.*—**rau·cous·ly** *adv.,*—**cous·ness** *n.*

rav·age (*rav*-ij) *v.* [rav·aged; rav·ag·ing] To devastate; ruin; rape.—**rav·age** *n.*—**rav·ag·er** *n.*

rave *v.* [raved; rav·ing] 1. To rage; to talk deliriously. 2. To talk with enthusiasm.

rav·el (*rav*-'l) *v.* [rav·eled, rav·elled; rav·el·ing, rav·el·ling] 1. To unweave; disentangle; untwist. 2. To entangle; twist together; make intricate.—**rav·el** *n.* A thread detached in unweaving; tangle.—**rav·el·ing, rav·el·ling** *n.* 1. Tangling or unweaving. 2. A detached thread.—**rav·el·er, rav·el·ler** *n.*

ra·ven (*ray*-v'n) *n.* Large black bird of the crow family having a powerful beak.—*adj.* Jet-black.—(*rav*-'n) *v.* To prey upon; devour rapaciously.—**rav·en·ing** *adj.* Plundering; greedy. —**ra·ven·er** *n.*

rav·en·ous (*rav*-en-us) *adj.* Voraciously hungry; famished.—**rav·en· ous·ly** *adv.*—**rav·en·ous·ness** *n.*

RAVEN (1/15 life-size)

ra·vine (ruh-*veen*) *n.* A gully; a canyon.

rav·ing (*rayv*-ing) *n.* 1. Furious or irrational talk. 2. Exuberant enthusiasm.—**rav·ing** *adj.*

ra·vi·o·li (rah-vee-*oh*-lee) *n.* A spaghetti paste rolled flat and filled with highly seasoned ground meat.

rav·ish (*rav*-ish) *v.* 1. To enrapture; to transport with joy. 2. To rape.—**rav·ish·er** *n.* —**rav·ish·ing** *adj.*—**rav·ish·ment** *n.*

raw *adj.* 1. Uncooked; unprocessed; in a natural state. 2. Sore. 3. Inexperienced; untried. 4. Chilly and damp; bitterly cold. 5. *Colloquial.* Risqué; vulgar; nude.—**raw·ly** *adv.*—**raw·ness** *n.*

raw-colored	rawhead	raw-nosed
raw-edged	rawheaded	raw-ribbed
raw-faced	raw looking	raw-striped
raw-handed	raw-mouthed	raw wool

raw·boned *adj.* Gaunt; lean and large-boned.

raw·hide *n.* 1. The untanned skin of cattle. 2. A whip made of hide strips.—**raw·hide** *adj.*

raw material. Substances or produce to be manufactured into usable goods.

ray *n.* Any of several broad, flat, gristly-textured fish related to the sharks.

ray *n.* 1. A pencil or beam of light. 2. Any light wave emitted from a heated substance.

ray·on (*ray*-on) *n.* A synthetic silklike fabric produced from a cellulose base.—**ray·on** *adj.*

RAY

raze *v.* [razed; raz· ing] To destroy from the foundation; reduce to the ground.

ra·zor (*ray*-zer) *n.* A sharp-edged instrument used for shaving.

RAZOR

razorback	razor edge	razor making
razor-backed	razor-edged	razor-shaped
razorbill	razor grinder	razor sharp
razor-billed	razor keen	razor strop
razor-bladed	razor-leaved	razor-tongued
razor-bowed	razor maker	razor-witted

razz *v. Slang.* To taunt; tease.—**raz·zer** *n.*—**raz· zing** *n.*

re- *Prefix.* Again; back.
Note: For spelling and hyphenation of compounds see list beginning below.

reabsorb	reassort
reabsorption	reassign
readmission	reassignment
readmit	reassume
readmittance	reawaken
reaffirm	rebaptism
reaffirmance	rebaptize
reappear	rebill
reappearance	rebind
reappoint	reborn
reappointment	rebuild
rearm	recapitalization
rearmament	recapitalize
reascend	recharge
reassemble	recharter
reassembly	recoin
reassert	recoinage

R

re (*ray*) *n. Music.* The second note of the scale.

reach *v.* 1. To stretch; extend. 2. To put out the hand. 3. To achieve; gain. 4. To arrive at; get to.—**reach** *n.*—**reach·er** *n.*

re·act (ree-*akt*) *v.* 1. To respond; behave in a given circumstance. 2. To act reciprocally, each upon the other. 3. To turn back; revert.—**re·ac·tive** *adj.*—**re·ac·tor** *n.*

re·ac·tion (ree-*ak*-shun) *n.* 1. Response; feeling or conduct aroused by a stimulus. 2. *Chemistry.* The reciprocal action of chemical agents upon each other. 3. *Politics.* Reversion to previous and usually more conservative policies. 4. Group in society which favors reactionary policies.

re·ac·tion·ar·y (ree-*ak*-shun-er-ee) *n.* One who favors a reversal of social and political progress.—**re·ac·tion·ar·y** *adj.*—**re·ac·tion·ist** *n.*

read (*reed*) *v.* [read; read·ing] 1. To peruse; take in the sense of written language. 2. To pronounce a writing aloud. 3. To interpret from observation; deduce. 4. To study.

read·a·ble *adj.* 1. Legible. 2. Understandable; easy or pleasant to read.—**read·a·bil·i·ty** *n.*—**read·a·ble·ness** *n.*—**read·a·bly** *adv.*

read·er *n.* 1. One who reads. 2. *Universities.* A teaching assistant who reads and grades papers and examinations. 3. A proofreader. 4. One who considers manuscripts for publication. 5. A school book containing reading exercises.

read·ing *n.* 1. Perusal. 2. Public recitation. 3. A version of a literary work. 4. Interpretation; analysis.—**read·ing** *adj.*

re·ad·just (ree-uh-*just*) *v.* To become settled again; to reorient.—**re·ad·just·ment** *n.*

read·y (*red*-ee) *adj.* 1. Prepared; fit for immediate use. 2. Quick; apt. 3. Available; accessible; at hand. 4. Willing; inclined.—*v.* [read·ied; read·y·ing] To prepare.—**read·i·ly** *adv.*—**read·i·ness** *n.*

ready-built	ready-furnished	ready-typed
ready-coined	ready-grown	ready-witted
ready-cooked	ready-handed	ready-worded
ready-dressed	ready reference	ready-written

re·a·gent (ree-*ay*-jent) *n. Chemistry.* A substance of known strength and reaction used in analyzing an unknown solution.

re·al (ree-'l) *adj.* 1. Actual; true; genuine. 2. *Law.* Pertaining to fixed and immovable property. 3. *Mathematics.* Positive; not imaginary. 4. *Philosophy.* Existing, as opposed to ideal.—**re·al·ness** *n.*

re·al (*ray*-al) *n.* [*pl.* re·ales (ray-*ah*-less)] Former Spanish silver coin worth about five cents.

real estate. Land and buildings; immovable property.

re·al·ism *n.* 1. *Philosophy.* Doctrine holding that the objective world perceived through the senses exists independently of our knowledge of it. 2. *Fine Arts.* The representation of nature as it actually appears. 3. Cognizance of the practical aspects of a situation.—**re·al·ist** *n.* & *adj.*—**re·al·is·tic** *adj.*— -ist·i·cal·ly *adv.*

re·al·i·ty (ree-*al*-ih-tee) *n.* Truth; actuality; concrete being or existence.

re·al·ize (ree-al-yze) *v.* [re·al·ized; re·al·iz·ing] 1. To understand; grasp; comprehend. 2. To actualize; bring into being. 3. To gain; make.—**re·al·i·za·tion** *n.*—**re·al·iz·a·ble** *adj.*

re·al·ly *adv.* In truth; actually.

realm (*relm*) *n.* 1. Kingdom; royal jurisdiction. 2. Domain; sphere.

real wages. The value of wages in terms of purchasable commodities.

ream (*reem*) *n.* 1. A package of 500 sheets of

recombine	re-educate	reinstalment	rerun
recommence	re-education	reintegrate	resail
recommencement	re-election	reintegration	resalable
recompose	re-embark	reinter	resale
recomposition	re-embarkation	reinterment	reseal
reconcentrate	re-emerge	reintroduce	resell
reconcentration	re-emergence	reintroduction	resend
reconquer	re-emphasize	reinvigorate	resettle
reconquest	re-enact	reinvigoration	resettlement
reconsign	re-enactment	relet	reshape
reconsignment	re-engage	relight	resharpen
reconstitute	re-engrave	relive	resole
reconstitution	re-enumerate	reload	respell
reconvene	re-entrance	relocate	restart
reconvey	re-establish	remake	restate
reconveyance	re-establishment	remarry	restatement
recross	re-exchange	remold	restock
recrystallization	re-export	remould	restring
recrystallize	reface	rename	resummon
recurve	refashion	renominate	resurface
redeliver	refasten	renomination	resurvey
redemand	reflow	renumber	retell
redemandable	reforge	reoccupy	retransfer
redeposit	regild	reopen	retype
redetermine	re-ice	repack	revaluate
redirect	reimport	repaint	revaluation
rediscount	reimportation	repave	revalue
rediscover	reimpose	repeople	revictual
rediscovery	reinflate	rephrase	revisit
redistribute	reinflation	replant	revisitation
redistribution	reinsert	replay	revoice
redistrict	reinstall	repurchase	rewind
redraw	reinstallation	reread	rewire
re-edify	reinstallment	reroll	rework

paper. 2. [*pl.*] *Colloquial.* A tremendous quantity.

ream *v.* To enlarge, as the bore of a cannon.

ream·er *n.* An instrument for enlarging a hole.

re·an·i·mate (ree-*an*-ih-mayt) *v.* [re·an·i·mat·ed; re·an·i·mat·ing] To revive; resuscitate.—**re·an·i·ma·tion** *n.*

reap (*reep*) *v.* 1. To cut down and gather a crop. 2. To obtain; receive as a reward.—**reap·a·ble** *adj.*

reap·er (*reep*-er) *n.* 1. One who reaps. 2. A machine for cutting grain.

REAMER

rear (*rihr*) *n.* 1. The back; hind part; posterior. 2. *Military.* Area behind the front battle lines. —**rear** *adj.*—**rear·most** *adj.*

rear *v.* 1. To raise; elevate. 2. To bring up; foster. 3. To rise on the hind legs.—**rear·er** *n.*

rear admiral. An officer of the navy ranking next below vice admiral, above commodore.

rear·ward (*rihr*-werd) *adj.* At or toward the rear. —**rear·ward, rear·wards** *adv.*

rea·son (*ree*-zun) *n.* 1. Grounds; explanation; cause; basis. 2. Thought; intellect; logic. 3. Sanity; rationality. 4. Moderation.—**rea·son** *v.* 1. To reflect; deliberate. 2. To try to persuade.—**rea·son·er** *n.*

rea·son·a·ble (*ree*-zun-uh-b'l) *adj.* 1. Fair; moderate; sane. 2. Rational; having the power of logical thought. 3. Inexpensively priced.—**rea·son·a·bil·i·ty** *n.*—**rea·son·a·ble·ness** *n.*—**rea·son·a·bly** *adv.*—**rea·son·less** *adj.*

rea·son·ing *n.* 1. Thought; cogitation; argumentation. 2. Arguments presented.

re·as·sure (ree-uh-*shoor*) *v.* [re·as·sured; re·as·sur·ing] To relieve of fear; restore courage. —**re·as·sur·ance** *n.*—**re·as·sur·ing·ly** *adv.*

re·bate (*ree*-bayt) *n.* [re·bat·ed; re·bat·ing] Part of a payment returned.—**re·bate** *v.*—**re·bat·er** *n.*

re·bec, re·beck (*ree*-bek) *n.* An ancient three-stringed instrument similar to the violin.

re·bel (rih-*bel*) *v.* [re·belled; re·bel·ling] 1. To defy; rise against; resist. 2. To take up arms against the constituted government; revolt. —**re·bel** (*reb*-'l) *n.* Insurgent; iconoclast.

re·bel·lion (rih-*bel*-yun) *n.* 1. Uprising; revolt. 2. Resistance of authority; defiance.—**re·bel·lious** *adj.* Mutinous; disobedient.—**re·bel·lious·ly** *adv.*—**re·bel·lious·ness** *n.*

re·birth (rih-*berth*) *n.* Renascence; new birth.

re·bound (rih-*bownd*) *v.* To bounce back after an impact.—**re·bound** (*ree*-bownd) *n.*

re·buff (rih-*buf*) *n.* A rejection; a slight.—**re·buff** *v.*

re·buke (rih-*byook*) *v.* [re·buked; re·buk·ing] To reprove; to scold.—**re·buke** *n.*—**re·buk·er** *n.*

re·bus (*ree*-bus) *n.* Writing in which pictures of objects are employed to represent the sounds of the words.

re·but (rih-*but*) *v.* [-ted; -ting] To refute; disprove.—**re·but·tal** *n.* Answer; refutation.

re·cal·ci·trant (rih-*kal*-sih-tr'nt) *adj.* Willful; unruly; refractory.—**re·cal·ci·trant** *n.*—**re·cal·ci·trance** *n.*—**re·cal·ci·tran·cy** *n.*—**re·cal·ci·trate** *v.*

re·call (rih-*kawl*) *v.* 1. To call back; take back. 2. To recollect; remember. 3. *Politics.* To unseat a legislator by popular vote during his term of office.—**re·call** *n.*—**re·call·a·ble** *adj.*

re·cant (rih-*kant*) *v.* To retract; renounce.—**re·can·ta·tion** *n.*—**re·cant·er** *n.*

re·ca·pit·u·late (ree-kuh-*pit*-choo-layt) *v.* [re·ca·pit·u·lat·ed; re·ca·pit·u·lat·ing] To sum up; review.—**re·ca·pit·u·la·tion** *n.* — **-la·tive** *adj.*

re·cap·ture (rih-*kap*-cher) *v.* [re·cap·tured; re·cap·tur·ing] To retake; recall.—**re·cap·ture** *n.*

re·cast *v.* To remold.—**re·cast** *n.*

re·cede (rih-*seed*) *v.* [re·ced·ed; re·ced·ing] To withdraw; retreat.

re·ceipt (rih-*seet*) *n.* 1. The act of receiving. 2. A written acknowledgment of something received. 3. [*pl.*] Money taken in. 4. A cooking recipe.—*v.* To mark as paid.

re·ceive (rih-*seev*) *v.* [re·ceived; re·ceiv·ing] 1. To take; accept. 2. To welcome; greet. 3. To bear; sustain; undergo. 4. *Radio.* To pick up radio waves and convert them to sound through a receiver.

re·ceiv·er (rih-*seev*-er) *n.* 1. One who receives. 2. A receptacle. 3. *Law.* A court-appointed administrator of businesses or estates under litigation.—**re·ceiv·er·ship** *n.*

re·ceiv·er *n.* The part of a communication apparatus which converts electric impulses into auditory or visual signals, as a radio set.

re·cent (*ree*-s'nt) *adj.* Briefly previous; occurring a short time ago.—**re·cen·cy** *n.*—**re·cent·ly** *adv.*—**re·cent·ness** *n.*

re·cept (*ree*-sept) *n. Psychology.* An image retained from a series of related sensations.

re·cep·ta·cle (rih-*sep*-tuh-k'l) *n.* A vessel; a container.

re·cep·tion (rih-*sep*-shun) *n.* 1. Act or manner of receiving; admission. 2. A ceremonious entertainment. 3. *Radio.* Conversion of incoming radio waves to sound by a receiver.

re·cep·tive (rih-*sep*-tiv) *adj.* Amenable; favorably disposed.—**re·cep·tive·ly** *adv.*—**re·cep·tive·ness** *n.*—**re·cep·tiv·i·ty** *n.*—**re·cep·tor** *n.*

re·cess (*ree*-sess, ree-*sess*) *n.* 1. Adjournment; suspension of work. 2. An alcove; niche. 3. A place of withdrawal.—**re·cess** *v.*

re·ces·sion (rih-*sesh*-un) *n.* 1. Withdrawal; retirement; retrogression. 2. The closing procession, esp. of a religious service.

re·ces·sion·al (reh-*sesh*-un-'l) *n.* A hymn sung during a closing procession.—**re·ces·sion·al** *adj.*

re·ces·sive (reh-*sess*-iv) *adj.* 1. Receding. 2. *Biology.* Latent; tending to disappear in successive generations.

rec·i·pe (*ress*-ih-pee) *n.* 1. A formula for preparing a dish. 2. A procedure for achieving an end.

re·cip·i·ent (reh-*sip*-ee-ent) *n.* A receiver.—**re·cip·i·ent** *adj.*—**re·cip·i·ence, re·cip·i·en·cy** *n.*

R

re·cip·ro·cal (reh-*sip*-ruh-k'l) *adj.* Mutual.—**re·cip·ro·cal** *n.* Converse.—**re·cip·ro·cal·ly** *adv.*

re·cip·ro·cate (reh-*sip*-ruh-kayt) *v.* [re·cip·ro·cat·ed; re·cip·ro·cat·ing] 1. To give in return. 2. *Machinery.* To move backward.—**re·cip·ro·ca·tion** *n.*—**re·cip·ro·ca·tive** *adj.*

rec·i·proc·i·ty (ress-ih-*pross*-ih-tee) *n.* 1. Interdependence; co-operation. 2. Corresponding rights or benefits mutually accorded in international trade.

re·cit·al (reh-*syte*-'l) *n.* 1. Narration; account. 2. A musical or dance program often presented by a single artist.

rec·i·ta·tion (ress-ih-*tay*-shun) *n.* 1. The delivery of memorized passages before an audience. 2. An oral exercise given by a student in class.—**rec·i·ta·tive** *n. Music.* A declamatory vocal composition.—**rec·i·ta·tive** *adj.*

re·cite (reh-*syte*) *v.* [re·cit·ed; re·cit·ing] 1. To repeat from memory. 2. To speak in class. 3. To narrate; relate.—**re·cit·er** *n.*

reck·less *adj.* Rash; foolhardy; violently heedless.—**reck·less·ly** *adv.*—**reck·less·ness** *n.*

reck·on (*rek*-un) *v.* 1. To calculate; estimate. 2. To regard; consider. 3. To count; rely. 4. *Colloquial.* To guess; suppose.—**reck·on·er** *n.*—**reck·on·ing** *n.*

re·claim (reh-*klaym*) *v.* 1. To recover possession; to call back. 2. To save; redeem. 3. To restore; reinstate.—**re·claim** *n.*—**re·claim·a·ble** *adj.*—**re·claim·ant** *n.*—**re·claim·er** *n.*

rec·la·ma·tion (rek-luh-*may*-shun) *n.* Restoration; restoration to usefulness of waste products or land.

re·cline (reh-*klyne*) *v.* [re·clined; re·clin·ing] To lean back; rest; lie down.—**re·clin·er** *n.*—**re·clin·ing** *adj.*

re·cluse (reh-*klooss*) *n.* A hermit; one who lives in seclusion.—**re·cluse** *adj.*—**re·clu·sion** *n.*

rec·og·ni·tion (rek-ug-*nish*-un) *n.* 1. Realization; identification by recollection; notice; perception. 2. Acknowledgment of the official status of a nation.—**re·cog·ni·to·ry** *adj.*

re·cog·ni·zance (reh-*kog*-nih-z'nss, re-*kon*-) *n.* A legal obligation to be fulfilled on pain of forfeiture.—**re·cog·ni·zor** (reh-kog-nih-*zawr*) *n.*

rec·og·nize (*rek*-ug-nyze) *v.* [rec·og·nized; rec·og·niz·ing] 1. To identify by recollection; remember. 2. To acknowledge acquaintance; greet. 3. To approve; authorize; sanction. 4. To acknowledge the official status of a nation.—**rec·og·niz·a·ble** *adj.*—**-bly** *adv.*

re·coil (reh-*koyl*) *v.* 1. To shrink; to draw away. 2. To rebound.—**re·coil** *n.*

re·col·lect *v.* To gather together again.

rec·ol·lect (rek-uh-*lekt*) *v.* To recall; remember.—**rec·ol·lect·ed** *adj.*—**rec·ol·lec·tion** *n.*

rec·om·mend (rek-uh-*mend*) *v.* 1. To endorse; commend; support. 2. To advise.—**rec·om·men·da·tion** *n.*—**rec·om·mend·a·to·ry** *adj.*

re·com·mit (ree-kuh-*mit*) *v.* [re·com·mit·ted; re·com·mit·ing] 1. To confine again. 2. To refer again to a committee.—**re·com·mit·ment** *n.*

rec·om·pense (*rek*-um-penss) *v.* [rec·om·pensed; rec·om·pens·ing] To reimburse; repay; compensate.—**rec·om·pense** *n.*

rec·on·cile (*rek*-un-syle) *v.* [rec·on·ciled; rec·on·cil·ing] 1. To resign oneself; adjust. 2. To reunite; bring together. 3. To harmonize; make consistent.—**re·con·cil·a·ble** *adj.*—**re·con·cil·a·bil·i·ty** *n.*—**re·con·cil·a·bly** *adv.*

rec·on·cil·i·a·tion (rek-un-sil-ee-*ay*-shun) *n.* Restoring of harmony; adjustment of differences.—**rec·on·cil·i·a·to·ry** *adj.*

rec·on·dite (*rek*-un-dyte) *adj.* Abstruse; profound.—**rec·on·dite·ly** *adv.*—**rec·on·dite·ness** *n.*

re·con·nais·sance (reh-*kon*-ih-sanss) *n.* A preliminary survey; scouting expedition; reconnoitering.—**re·con·nais·sance** *adj.*

rec·on·noi·ter (rek-uh-*noy*-ter) *v.* Also **rec·on·noi·tre** [rec·on·noi·tered, -noi·tred; rec·on·noi·ter·ing, -noi·tring] To examine; make a preliminary survey; scout.—**rec·on·noi·ter·er, rec·on·noi·trer** *n.*

re·con·sid·er (ree-kun-*sid*-er) *v.* To think again; change one's mind.—**re·con·sid·er·a·tion** *n.*

re·con·struct (ree-kon-*strukt*) *v.* To rebuild; renovate; reform.—**re·con·struct·ed** *adj.*—**re·con·struc·tive** *adj.*

re·con·struc·tion (ree-kon-*struk*-shun) *n.* 1. Rebuilding. 2. That which is re-created. 3. [*cap.*] The period of political and social reorganization of the South following the U.S. Civil War.

re·cord (reh-*kord*) *v.* To chronicle; note; preserve by writing down, photographing, impressing on a phonograph record, etc.

rec·ord (*rek*-erd) *n.* 1. A report; register; entry. 2. Official files; documents. 3. Public facts; known information. 4. Highest achievement made in a particular field. 5. A phonograph disk.

re·cord·er *n.* 1. One employed to register writings or transactions. 2. A kind of flute.

re·count (reh-*kownt*) *v.* To narrate; relate.—**re·count·al** *n.*

re·count (ree-*kownt*) *v.* To count again.—**re·count** (*ree*-kownt) *n.*

re·coup (reh-*koop*) *v.* To retrieve; to regain.—**re·coup·a·ble** *adj.*—**re·coup·ment** *n.*

re·course (*ree*-korss) *n.* Resort; refuge.

re·cov·er (reh-*kuv*-er) *v.* 1. To regain; retrieve. 2. To become well.—**-er·a·ble** *adj.*

re·cov·er (ree-*kuv*-er) *v.* To cover again.

re·cov·er·y (reh-*kuv*-er-ee) *n.* 1. Regaining; retrieval. 2. Restoration of health.

rec·re·ant (*rek*-ree-ent) *adj.* Cowardly; craven.—*n.* Traitor; coward.—**rec·re·an·cy** *n.*

re·cre·ate (ree-kree-*ayt*) *v.* [re·cre·at·ed; re·cre·at·ing] To create or form anew.—**-a·tion** *n.*

rec·re·a·tion (rek-ree-*ay*-shun) *n.* Diversion; amusement.—**rec·re·ate** *v.* [rec·re·at·ed; rec·re·at·ing]—**rec·re·a·tion·al** *adj.*—**rec·re·a·tive** *adj.*

re·crim·i·nate (reh-*krim*-ih-nayt) *v.* [re·crim·i·nat·ed; re·crim·i·nat·ing] To accuse in return.—**re·crim·i·na·tion** *n.*—**re·crim·i·na·tive** *adj.*

re·cruit *n.* A recently enlisted soldier.—*v.* To

muster new soldiers; enroll members in an organization.—**re·cruit·er** *n.*—**re·cruit·ment** *n.*

rec·tan·gle (*rek*-tang-g'l) *n.* A four-sided figure having four right angles.
—**rec·tan·gu·lar** *adj.*
—**rec·tan·gu·lar·i·ty** *n.*
—**rec·tan·gu·lar·ly** *adv.*

rec·ti·fy (*rek*-tih-fy) *v.* rec·ti·fied; rec·ti·fy·ing]
1. To make right; correct; improve. 2. *Chemistry.* To purify by distillation. 3. *Electricity.* To convert alternating current to direct current.—**rec·ti·fi·a·ble** *adj.*—**rec·ti·fi·ca·tion** *n.*—**rec·ti·fi·er** *n.*

RECTANGLE

rec·ti·lin·e·ar (rek-tih-*lin*-ee-er) *adj.* Straight; consisting of or bounded by straight lines.—**rec·ti·lin·e·ar·ly** *adv.*

rec·ti·tude (*rek*-tih-tood) *n.* 1. Rightness. 2. Integrity; uprightness.

rec·tor *n.* 1. A parish minister of the Episcopal Church. 2. Headmaster of certain schools or universities.—**rec·tor·ate** *n.* Office or authority of a rector.—**rec·tor·y** *n.* [*pl.* rec·tor·ies] A rector's house.—**rec·tor·i·al** *adj.*

rec·tum (*rek*-tum) *n.* [*pl.* rec·ta] The terminal part of the digestive tract, ending at the anus.—**rec·tal** *adj.*

re·cum·bent (reh-*kum*-bent) *adj.* 1. Leaning; reclining. 2. Inactive; reposing.—**re·cum·ben·cy** *n.*—**re·cum·bent·ly** *adv.*

re·cu·per·ate (reh-*kyoo*-per-ayt) *v.* [re·cu·per·at·ed; -at·ing] To recover; convalesce.—**re·cu·per·a·tion** *n.*—**re·cu·per·a·tive** *adj.*—**re·cu·per·a·tor** *n.*—**re·cu·per·a·to·ry** *adj.*

re·cur *v.* [re·curred; re·cur·ring] 1. To reappear; come to the fore again. 2. To retrace one's thoughts; revert.—**re·cur·rence** *n.*—**re·cur·rent** *adj.*—**re·cur·rent·ly** *adv.*

red *n.* 1. The primary color between violet and orange in the physical spectrum. 2. [*often cap.*] A political radical. 3. Deficit. 'To be in the red.'—**red** *adj.*—**red·dish** *adj.*

re·dact (reh-*dakt*) *v.* To edit; prepare for publication.—**re·dac·tion** *n.*—**re·dac·tor** *n.*

red·bait·ing *n. Politics.* Indiscriminate application of the label "Communist" to discredit opponents and confuse issues.—**red·bait** *v.*—**red·bait·er** *n.*

red·breast *n.* A robin.

red·bud *n.* A showy, flowering tree or shrub of the pea family.

red·cap *n. Local.* A porter; baggage attendant.

Red Cross. An international charitable organization.

red deer. The common white-tailed deer in its summer pelt.

red·den *v.* To make red; blush.

re·deem (reh-*deem*) *v.* 1. To buy back; regain unrestricted ownership. 2. To rescue; ransom. 3. To expiate; atone. 4. To meet obligations; fulfill. 5. *Theology.* To save from damnation.—**re·deem·a·ble** *adj.*—**re·deem·er** *n.*

re·demp·tion (reh-*demp*-shun) *n.* Deliverance;

ransom; liberation.—**re·demp·tive, re·demp·to·ry** *adj.*

re·de·vel·op (ree-duh-*vel*-up) *v.* 1. To develop again. 2. *Photography.* To intensify the image; put through a second developing process.—**re·de·vel·op·er** *n.* The intensifying chemical.—**re·de·vel·op·ment** *n.*

red-hand·ed *adj.* In the act; undeniably guilty.—**red-hand·ed·ly** *adv.*—**red-hand·ed·ness** *n.*

red·head *n.* 1. A red-haired person. 2. A wild game duck closely related to the canvasback.—**red·head·ed** *adj.*

red herring. An irrelevant matter brought into a controversy to confuse the issue.

red·in·te·gra·tion *n.* 1. *Psychology.* Reaction to an experience conditioned by a similar former experience. 2. Restoration to health or wholeness.—**red·in·te·grate** *v.* [red·in·te·grat·ed; -grat·ing]—**red·in·te·gra·tive** *adj.*

red-let·ter *adj.* Very important; outstanding.

red-light district. A section of a city in which prostitution flourishes.

red·ness *n.* Quality of being red.

red·o·lent (*red*-uh-lent) *adj.* Scented; exuding fragrance.—**red·o·lence** *n.*—**red·o·lent·ly** *adv.*

re·dou·ble (ree-*dub*-'l) *v.* [re·dou·bled; re·dou·bling] To double again or repeatedly; increase.

re·doubt (reh-*dowt*) *n.* A temporary fortification.

re·doubt·a·ble (reh-*dowt*-uh-b'l) *adj.* Formidable; valiant.—**re·doubt·a·ble·ness** *n.*—**re·doubt·a·bly** *adv.*

re·dound (reh-*downd*) *v.* To contribute; accrue.

red pepper. Cayenne pepper; a pungent seasoning derived from the fruit of pepper plants.

re·draft *n.* 1. Additional draft or copy. 2. *Finance.* A bill of exchange replacing a protested bill and including the charges of collection.—**re·draft** *v.*

re·dress (ree-*dres*) *v.* To remedy; to make right; to compensate.—**re·dress** *n.*—**re·dress·er, re·dress·or** *n.*

Red Sea. A long, narrow strip of water between the Arabian peninsula and Africa.

red·skin *n. & adj.* A North American Indian.

red·start *n.* A songbird of the flycatcher family.

red tape. Official formality or routine causing delay or obstruction.—**red·tape** *adj.*—**red·tap·er, red·tap·ist** *n.*

re·duce *v.* [re·duced; re·duc·ing] 1. To make smaller; to degrade. 2. To bring. 'Reduce to order.' 3. To subdue; to render submissive.

REDSTART (1/15 life size)

4. *Chemistry.* To bring a compound to an elemental state or to a lower valence by adding electrons or removing positive charges. 5. *Mathematics.* To change an expression to its simplest form.—**re·duc·er** *n.*—**re·duc·i·bil·i·ty** *n.*—**re·duc·i·ble** *adj.*—**re·duc·tion** *n.*

R

re·dun·dant (reh-*dun*-dent) *adj.* 1. Wordy. 2. Superabundant; superfluous.—**re·dun·dance, re·dun·dan·cy** *n.*—**re·dun·dant·ly** *adv.*

re·du·pli·cate (ree-*doo*-plih-kayt) *v.* [re·du·pli·cat·ed; -cat·ing] 1. To repeat; to multiply. 2. *Philology.* To repeat the root or initial syllable of a word.—**re·du·pli·cate** *adj.*—**re·du·pli·ca·tion** *n.*—**re·du·pli·ca·tive** *adj.*

red·wood *n.* A gigantic, cone-bearing tree of the sequoia family.

re·ech·o *v.* To echo back or again.—*n.* [*pl.* re·ech·oes].

reed *n.* 1. Any of various tall, broad-leaved grasses which grow in marshland. 2. *Music.* **a.** A simple pipe of hollowed cane. **b.** The flat sliver of cane or plastic which produces the tone in instruments such as the clarinet. **c.** Thin plate of metal which produces tone in a reed organ. 3. *Weaving.* The part of a loom which keeps the threads of the warp spaced.

REED

reed·y *adj.* [reed·i·er; reed·i·est] 1. Like or abounding in reeds. 2. Having a tone like a reed instrument.—**reed·i·ness** *n.*

reef *n.* Chain of rocks lying at or near the surface of the ocean.

reef *n.* The part of a sail that may be taken in to reduce its size.—*v.* To reduce the size of a sail by tying up the foot.

reef·er *n. Slang.* 1. A marijuana cigarette. 2. A short, double-breasted overcoat.

reek *n.* A fume; foul vapor.—**reek** *v.*—**reek·y** *adj.* [reek·i·er; reek·i·est].

reel *n.* A revolvable spool used for winding thread, line, etc.—**reel** *v.*—**reel·er** *n.*

reel *n.* 1. A lively country dance. 2. The sprightly music for this dance. —**reel** *v.*

REEL

reel *v.* 1. To stagger; to weave from side to side. 2. To whirl; to feel dizzy.—**reel** *n.*

re·en·force. *Variant spelling* of reinforce.

re·en·try (ree-*en*-tree) *n.* 1. A new or second entry. 2. *Bridge.* A card played to regain the lead.

reeve *v.* [rove; reeved; reev·ing] *Nautical.* To run a rope through a block, cleat, etc.

re·ex·am·i·na·tion (ree-ig-zam-ih-*nay*-shun) *n.* 1. A renewed or repeated examining. 2. *Law.* The questioning of a witness after cross-examination.—**re·ex·am·ine** *v.* [-ined; -in·ing].

re·fec·tion (ree-*fek*-shun) *n.* A meal; a repast. —**re·fec·to·ry** *n.* [*pl.* -ries] A dining hall.

re·fer (reh-*fer*) *v.* [re·ferred; re·fer·ring] 1. To attribute to; trace back. 2. To hand over; assign to. 3. To have bearing on. 4. To have recourse.—**re·fer·a·ble** *adj.*—**re·fer·rer** *n.*

ref·er·ee (ref-er-*ee*) *n.* 1. A moderator; an arbitrator. 2. An umpire; one who governs play in certain sports.—**ref·er·ee** *v.*

ref·er·ence (*ref*-er-uhnss) *n.* 1. Act of referring, alluding, or assigning. 2. Relation; regard. 3. A remark referring to something; allusion. 4. Statement of qualifications of one desiring employment.—*adj.* Used for obtaining specific information.

ref·er·en·dum (ref-er-*en*-dum) *n.* [*pl.* ref·er·en·dums, ref·er·en·da] Practice of submitting a legislative act to popular vote for ratification.

re·fill (ree-fil) *n.* A commodity designed to fit into a container emptied of its original contents.—*v.* (ree-*fil*) To fill again.—**re·fill·a·ble** *adj.*

re·fine (ree-*fyne*) *v.* [re·fined; re·fin·ing] 1. To free of impurities; to purify. 2. To educate; remove coarseness or vulgarity.—**re·fin·er** *n.* —**re·fine·ment** *n.*

re·fin·er·y (ree-*fyne*-er-ee) *n.* [*pl.* re·fin·er·ies] An establishment where raw materials are purified.

re·fit (ree-*fit*) *v.* [re·fit·ted; re·fit·ting] 1. To repair, esp. damaged ships. 2. To fit or provide again.

re·flect (ree-*flekt*) *v.* 1. To bend or cast back, as rays of light, heat, etc. 'A polished surface reflects light.' 2. To mirror. 3. To ponder; to consider seriously. 4. To lay upon by implication. 'To reflect blame.'—**re·flec·tion** *n.*

re·flec·tive (ree-*flek*-tiv) *adj.* 1. Thoughtful; meditative. 2. Throwing back rays or images. —**re·flec·tive·ly** *adv.*—**re·flec·tive·ness, re·flec·tiv·i·ty** *n.*

re·flec·tor (ree-*flek*-ter) *n.* An instrument which reflects light rays or other radiant energy.

re·flex (*ree*-fleks) *n.* 1. An involuntary nervous and muscular reaction. 2. A reflected image.—**re·flex** *adj.*

re·flex·ive (reh-*flek*-siv) *adj.* 1. Reflective; bending or turning backward. 2. *Grammar.* Denoting **a.**

REFLECTOR

a verb whose action reflects back upon the subject; **b.** a pronoun ending in -*self* or -*selves*. —**re·flex·ive** *n.*—**re·flex·ive·ly** *adv.*—**re·flex·ive·ness, re·flex·iv·i·ty** *n.*

re·flux (*ree*-fluks) *n.* A flowing back.

re·for·est (ree-*for*-est) *v.* To plant trees on lumbered-off land.—**re·for·est·a·tion** *n. & adj.*

re·form (reh-*form*) *v.* To change for the better; to abolish abuses and institute improvements; to reclaim.—**re·form** *n. & adj.*—**re·form·a·ble** *adj.*—**re·form·a·tive** *adj.*—**re·form·er** *n.*

reform school. A corrective school for young delinquents.

ref·or·ma·tion (ref-or-*may*-shun) *n.* 1. Correction; amendment. 2. [*cap.*] The religious revolution of the sixteenth century from which the Protestant Churches stem.

re·form·a·to·ry (ruh-*for*-muh-tor-ee) *n.* [*pl.* re·form·a·to·ries] An institution devoted to the correction of juvenile delinquents or less serious offenders.—re·form·a·to·ry *adj.*

re·formed *adj.* 1. Corrected; amended. 2. [*cap.*] Denoting Protestant Churches which rejected the doctrines and discipline of Luther.

re·fract (ree-*frakt*) *v.* To bend; to deflect, as a ray of light.—re·frac·tor *n.*

re·frac·tion (ree-*frak*-shun) *n. Physics.* A change in direction of rays of light, heat, etc., when passing obliquely through substances of different densities.

re·frac·tive (reh-*frak*-tiv) *adj.* Turning or deflecting from a direct course.—re·frac·tive·ly *adv.*—re·frac·tive·ness, re·frac·tiv·i·ty *n.*

REFRACTION

re·frac·to·ry (reh-*frak*-tuh-ree) *adj.* 1. Perversely obstinate; unmanageable. 2. Difficult to process.—re·frac·to·ri·ly *adv.*—re·frac·to·ri·ness *n.*

re·frain (reh-*frayn*) *v.* To abstain; forbear.

re·frain (reh-*frayn*) *n.* Part of a song or poem which is repeated at the end of each stanza.

re·fran·gi·ble (reh-*fran*-jih-b'l) *adj.* Capable of being turned away from a direct course in passage from one medium to another.—re·fran·gi·bil·i·ty *n.*—re·fran·gi·ble·ness *n.*

re·fresh (reh-*fresh*) *v.* To reanimate; reinvigorate; renew.—re·fresh·er *n. & adj.*—re·fresh·ing *adj.*—-ing·ly *adv.*

re·fresh·ment (reh-*fresh*-ment) *n.* 1. The act of refreshing. 2. [*often pl.*] Food and drink; a light or festive repast.

re·frig·er·ate (reh-*frij*-er-ayt) *v.* [re·frig·er·a·ted; re·frig·er·a·ting] To cool or chill artificially for preservation.—re·frig·er·ant *n.*—re·frig·er·a·tion *n.*—re·frig·er·a·tive *adj.*

re·frig·er·a·tor (reh-*frij*-er-ay-ter) *n.* 1. A refrigerated cabinet for preserving food. 2. A mechanical device by which temperature is lowered below that of the surrounding atmosphere.—re·frig·er·a·to·ry *adj.*

ref·uge (*ref*-yooj) *n.* Shelter; asylum; sanctuary.

ref·u·gee (*ref*-yoo-jee) *n.* One who flees from his native country to escape persecution.

re·ful·gent (reh-*fuhl*-jent) *adj.* Luminous; radiant; brilliant.—re·ful·gence *n.*—re·ful·gen·cy *n.*

re·fund (*ree*-fund) *n.* Money paid back; repayment.—re·fund (rih-*fund*) *v.*—re·fund·er *n.*

re·fur·bish (ree-*fer*-bish) *v.* To renovate.

re·fus·al (reh-*fyooz*-'l) *n.* Rejection; denial.

re·fuse (reh-*fyooz*) *v.* [re·fused; re·fus·ing] To deny a request or demand; reject.—re·fus·er *n.*

ref·use (*ref*-yooss) *n.* Waste matter; garbage.

re·fute (reh-*fyoot*) *v.* [re·fut·ed; re·fut·ing] To disprove; to controvert.—ref·u·ta·ble (*ref*-yoo-tuh-b'l) *adj.*—ref·u·ta·bly *adv.*—ref·u·ta·tion *n.*

re·gain (ree-*gayn*) *v.* 1. To recover; to retrieve. 2. To get back to.—re·gain·er *n.*

re·gal (*ree*-g'l) *adj.* Royal; imperial; stately. —re·gal·ly *adv.*

re·gale (ree-*gayl*) *v.* [re·galed; re·gal·ing] To entertain; to delight; to please with festivity.

re·ga·li·a (ree-*gay*-lee-uh) *n. pl.* Trappings; decorations of an order or office.

re·gal·i·ty (ree-*gal*-ih-tee) *n.* [*pl.* re·gal·i·ties] Royalty; sovereignty.

re·gard (ree-*gahrd*) *v.* 1. To look at carefully. 2. To esteem; respect. 3. To consider; evaluate.—*n.* 1. Respect; esteem. 2. [*pl.*] Good wishes; respects. 'Give my regards to him.'

re·gard·ful *adj.* Heedful; attentive.—re·gard·ful·ly *adv.*—re·gard·ful·ness *n.*

re·gard·ing *prep.* Concerning; about.

re·gard·less *adj.* Heedless; unconcerned.—re·gard·less·ly *adv.*—re·gard·less·ness *n.*

re·gat·ta (reh-*gat*-uh) *n.* An important sailing or rowing race.

re·gen·cy (*ree*-jen-see) *n.* The office, government, or jurisdiction of a regent.

re·gen·er·ate (reh-*jen*-er-ayt) *v.* [re·gen·er·at·ed; re·gen·er·at·ing] 1. To reform; to make new. 2. To revive.— -a·tive *adj.*— -a·tive·ly *adv.*

re·gen·er·a·tion (reh-jen-er-*ay*-shun) *n.* 1. Rebirth; reformation. 2. Revival. 3. *Radio.* Feedback of electrical energy from the output circuit to amplify an incoming signal.

re·gen·er·a·tor (reh-*jen*-er-ay-ter) *n.* 1. Regenerating agent. 2. *Machinery.* A device for heating air or gas entering an engine or oven.

re·gent (*ree*-jent) *n.* 1. One who governs a kingdom in the minority, absence, or disability of the king. 2. In New York State, a member of the corporate body superintending all educational institutions in the state.—re·gent *adj.*—re·gent·ship *n.*

reg·i·cide (*rej*-ih-syde) *n.* 1. A murderer of a king. 2. The murder of a king.— -cid·al *adj.*

re·gime (reh-*zheem*) *n.* Also ré·gime. Administration; rule; government.

reg·i·men (*rej*-ih-men) *n. Medicine.* The regulation of diet, exercise, etc., for the preservation or recovery of health.

reg·i·ment (*rej*-ih-ment) *n. Military.* A unit consisting of two or more battalions of troops and commanded by a colonel.—*v.* 1. To form into regiments. 2. To organize into disciplined groups under a single authority.—reg·i·men·tal *adj.*

reg·i·men·tals (rej-ih-*men*-t'lz) *n. pl.* The uniform worn by the troops of a regiment.

reg·i·men·ta·tion (rej-ih-men-*tay*-shun) *n.* 1. The formation of regiments. 2. Arbitrary organization of persons into a disciplined body under a single authority.

re·gion (*ree*-jun) *n.* Area; country; district; zone.—re·gion·al *adj.*—re·gion·al·ly *adv.*

reg·is·ter (*rej*-iss-ter) *n.* 1. List; catalogue; roll. 2. A perforated plate governing the opening into a duct admitting artificial heat into a room. 3. *Printing.* The correspondence in position of two plates to be applied to the same sheet. 4. *Music.* The range of a voice or instrument.—*v.* 1. To record; to enter in a

R

register. 2. *Printing.* To correspond exactly, as columns or lines of printed matter on opposite sheets.—**reg·is·ter·er** *n.*

reg·is·tered *adj.* Recorded; enrolled.

reg·is·trar (*rej*-iss-trahr) *n.* A record-keeper.

reg·is·tra·tion (rej-iss-*tray*-shun) *n.* 1. The entering of data into an official record. 2. The enrollment of the names of those persons who are entitled to vote at an election.

reg·is·try (*rej*-iss-tree) *n.* 1. Enrollment; registration. 2. Place where a register is kept.

reg·nant (*reg*-nent) *adj.* 1. Reigning. 2. Ruling; predominant.—**reg·nal** *adj.*—**reg·nan·cy** *n.*

re·gorge (reh-*gorj*) *v.* [re·gorged; re·gorg·ing] To vomit.

re·gress (reh-*gress*) *v.* To go backward.—**regress** (*ree*-gress) *n.*—**re·gres·sion** *n.*

re·gret (reh-*gret*) *v.* [re·gret·ted; re·gret·ting] To grieve at; be sorry for.—**re·gret** *n.* 1. Sorrow; remorse. 2. [*pl.*] Message declining an invitation.—**re·gret·ta·ble** *adj.*—**re·gret·ta·bly** *adv.*—**re·gret·ter** *n.*

re·gret·ful *adj.* Sorrowful; repentant.—**re·gret·ful·ly** *adv.*—**re·gret·ful·ness** *n.*

reg·u·lar (*reg*-yoo-ler) *adj.* 1. Normal; typical. 2. Orderly; systematic. 3. *Geometry.* Denoting a figure having equal sides and angles, as a square, a cube. 4. *Grammar.* Adhering to the common form in respect to inflectional terminations. 5. Instituted according to established rules or discipline. 6. Belonging to a monastic order and bound to certain rules.—**reg·u·lar** *n.*—**reg·u·lar·i·ty** *n.*

reg·u·late (*reg*-yoo-layt) *v.* [reg·u·la·ted; reg·u·la·ting] To adjust; arrange; order; correct.—**reg·u·la·tion** *n.* 1. Act of regulating. 2. Law; rule.—**reg·u·la·tive** *adj.*—**la·to·ry** *adj.*

reg·u·la·tor (*reg*-yoo-lay-ter) *n.* 1. One who regulates. 2. Any contrivance for producing uniformity of motion. 3. [*pl.*] Committees who maintain law in newly settled regions.

re·gur·gi·tate (reh-*ger*-jih-tayt) *v.* [re·gur·gi·tat·ted; re·gur·gi·tat·ing] To vomit; to pour or throw back.—**re·gur·gi·ta·tion** *n.*

re·ha·bil·i·tate (ree-huh-*bil*-ih-tayt) *v.* [re·ha·bil·i·tat·ed; re·ha·bil·i·tat·ing] To reinstate; to adapt again to a former state.—**-ta·tion** *n.*

re·hash (ree-*hash*) *v.* To work up old material in a new form.—**re·hash** (*ree*-hash) *n.*

re·hearse (ree-*herss*) *v.* [re·hearsed; re·hears·ing] 1. To practice before publicly performing. 2. To prepare by private performances. 'The cast was well rehearsed.' 3. To repeat.—**re·hears·al** *n.*—**re·hears·er** *n.*

Reich (*ryke*) *n.* The German state.

Reichs·bank (*rykse*-bahnk) *n.* The national bank of Germany.

Reichs·füh·rer (*rykse*-feer-er) *n.* The leader of the Third Reich, a title of Adolf Hitler.

Reichs·mark (*rykse*-mahrk) *n.* The basic German monetary unit.

Reichs·kanz·ler (*rykse*-kontz-ler) *n.* The chancellor of Germany.

Reichs·tag (*rykse*-tahk) *n.* The German parliament.

reign (*rayn*) *v.* To rule; govern.—**reign** *n.*

re·im·burse (ree-im-*berss*) *v.* [re·im·bursed; re·im·burs·ing] To repay; to restore a loss; recompense.—**re·im·burse·ment** *n.*

rein (*rayn*) *n.* 1. The strap of a bridle. 2. A curb; a restraint.—**rein** *v.*—**give rein to.** To give free play.

re·in·car·na·tion (ree-in-kahr-*nay*-shun) *n.* The belief that the soul passes to another body after death.—**re·in·car·nate** *v.* [-nat·ed; -nat·ing].

rein·deer *n.* A species of deer characterized by branched antlers, native to northern Europe and Asia.

REINDEER (1/70 life-size)

re·in·force (ree-in-*forss*) *v.* [re·in·forced; re·in·forc·ing] To strengthen; fortify.—**re·in·forc·er** *n.*

re·in·force·ment (ree-in-*forss*-ment) *n.* 1. The act of strengthening. 2. Fresh assistance, esp. additional troops or forces to augment the strength of an army or fleet.

re·in·state (ree-in-*stayt*) *v.* [re·in·stat·ed; re·in·stat·ing] To restore; to reinstall.

re·in·sure (ree-in-*shoor*) *v.* [re·in·sured; re·in·sur·ing] To insure a second time and assume risks in order to relieve another insurer.

re·in·vest (ree-in-*vest*) *v.* To invest anew.—**re·in·vest·ment** *n.*

re·is·sue (ree-*ish*-yoo) *v.* [re·is·sued; re·is·su·ing] To put out a second time.—**re·is·sue** *n.*

re·it·er·ate (ree-*it*-er-ayt) *v.* [re·it·er·a·ted; re·it·er·at·ing] To repeat; to say repeatedly.—**re·it·er·a·tion** *n.*—**re·it·er·a·tive** *adj.*

re·ject (ree-*jekt*) *v.* 1. To refuse; to spurn; to repudiate. 2. To discard; to cast off.—**re·ject** (*ree*-jekt) *n.*—**re·jec·tion** *n.*

re·joice (reh-*joyss*) *v.* [re·joiced; re·joic·ing] To exult; to be elated.—**re·joic·er** *n.*—**re·joic·ing** *n.*

re·join (reh-*joyn*) *v.* 1. To join again. 2. To respond; to reply.

re·join·der (reh-*joyn*-der) *n.* Reply; answer.

re·ju·ve·nate (reh-*joo*-veh-nayt) *v.* [re·ju·ve·nat·ed; re·ju·ve·nat·ing] To make young again; to restore.—**re·ju·ve·na·tion** *n.*—**-na·tor** *n.*

re·ju·ve·nes·cence (ree-joo-vuh-*ness*-uhnss) *n.* 1. A renewing of youth; the state of being young again. 2. *Biology.* Renewal of vigor in a cell.—**re·ju·ve·nes·cent** *adj.*

re·kin·dle (ree-*kin*-d'l) *v.* [re·kin·dled; re·kin·dling] 1. To set on fire anew. 2. To set in action again.

re·lapse (ree-*lapss*) *v.* [re·lapsed; re·laps·ing] 1. To backslide; to return to a former bad state or practice. 2. To become ill again after being convalescent.—**re·lapse** *n.*

re·late (ree-*layt*) *v.* [re·lat·ed; re·lat·ing] 1. To narrate; recite. 2. To associate; connect. 3. To pertain; have reference to.—**re·lat·ed** *adj.*

re·la·tion (ree-*lay*-shun) *n.* 1. Recital; narration. 2. Connection; association. 3. Relative; kin.—**re·la·tion·al** *adj.*—**re·la·tion·ship** *n.*

rel·a·tive (*rel*-uh-tiv) *adj.* 1. Pertinent; relevant. 2. Conditional; not absolute. 3. Referring; pertaining. 4. Comparative. 5. *Grammar.* Denoting a word or clause which refers to an antecedent.—*n.* A relation; a person allied by blood.—**rel·a·tive·ly** *adv.*— **-tive·ness** *n.*

rel·a·tiv·i·ty (rel-uh-*tiv*-ih-tee) *n.* 1. Interdependence; mutual relationship; comparison. 2. *Physics.* Mathematical theory developed by Albert Einstein and others, holding that space, time, mass, and velocity exist only relative to one another, and that physical phenomena appear the same only to two observers moving with uniform velocity relative to each other. One of the basic new concepts derived from this theory is the substitution of a four-dimensional space-time for the traditional three-dimensional space.

re·lax (ree-*laks*) *v.* 1. To loosen; to make less tense or rigid. 2. To abate; to slacken. 3. To divert; to relieve from attention or effort.—**re·lax·a·tion** *n.*—**re·lax·er** *n.*

re·lay (ree-*lay*, *ree*-lay) *v.* To transmit by stages. —*n.* 1. A transmission by stages. 2. Also **relay race.** A track race of four-man teams in which each runner covers only part of the distance.—**re·lay** *adj.*

re·lease (ree-*leess*) *v.* [re·leased; re·leas·ing] 1. To liberate; to free; to let go. 2. To relinquish. 3. To issue; make public.—*n.* 1. Liberation. 2. *Law.* A discharge of a right. 3. A statement handed out for publication.—**re·leas·er** *n.*

rel·e·gate (*rel*-uh-gayt) *v.* [rel·e·gat·ed; rel·e·gat·ing] 1. To consign; banish. 2. To delegate; to hand over.—**rel·e·ga·tion** *n.*

re·lent (ree-*lent*) *v.* To feel compassion; to yield; to soften in temper.

re·lent·less *adj.* Implacable; merciless.—**re·lent·less·ly** *adv.*—**re·lent·less·ness** *n.*

rel·e·vant (*rel*-eh-vent) *adj.* Pertinent; applicable.—**rel·e·vance, rel·e·van·cy** *n.*—**vant·ly** *adv.*

re·li·a·ble (reh-*ly*-uh-b'l) *adj.* Trustworthy; dependable.—**re·li·a·bil·i·ty** *n.*—**re·li·a·ble·ness** *n.*

re·li·ance (reh-*ly*-enss) *n.* Trust; confidence. —**re·li·ant** *adj.* Dependent.

rel·ic (*rel*-ik) *n.* 1. Remain; souvenir. 2. [*pl.*] Religious objects supposed to possess miraculous healing powers.

rel·ict (*rel*-ikt) *n.* A widow.

re·lief (reh-*leef*) *n.* 1. Alleviation; consolation. 2. Government aid given to the poor. 3. Release from a post or duty by a substitute. 4. *Sculpture.* Figures projecting from a two-dimensional background. 5. Conspicuousness by contrast. 6. *Physical Geography.* The undulations or surface elevations of a country.

RELIEF (def. 4)

re·lieve (reh-*leev*) *v.* [re·lieved; re·liev·ing] 1. To mitigate; to alleviate. 2. To take another's post. 3. To break monotony.—**re·liev·a·ble** *adj.*—**re·liev·er** *n.*

re·li·gion (reh-*lij*-un) *n.* 1. The worship of God or gods. 2. A belief; a system of doctrines of faith and worship.

re·li·gious (reh-*lij*-us) *adj.* 1. Devout; pious. 2. Pertaining to religion. 3. Meticulous; careful.—*n.* A person devoted to a life of piety; a monastic.—**re·li·gious·ly** *adv.*

re·lin·quish (reh-*ling*-kwish) *v.* To yield; to abandon; to let go.—**re·lin·quish·er** *n.*—**re·lin·quish·ment** *n.*

rel·i·quar·y (*rel*-ih-kwer-ee) *n.* A depository for relics.

rel·ish (*rel*-ish) *v.* To enjoy; to like.—*n.* 1. Flavor; tang. 2. Liking; zest. 3. A spicy vegetable preparation used as a condiment.

re·luc·tant (reh-*luk*-tent) *adj.* Loath; disinclined.—**re·luc·tance** *n.*—**re·luc·tant·ly** *adv.*

re·ly (reh-*lye*) *v.* [re·lied; re·ly·ing] To count; to trust; to depend.—**re·li·er** *n.*

re·main (reh-*mayn*) *v.* To stay; be left; abide; continue.—*n.* [*pl.*] 1. Relics; remainders. 2. A corpse; dead body.

re·main·der (reh-*mayn*-der) *n.* 1. Residue; rest. 2. *Arithmetic.* The sum which is left after subtraction.—**re·main·der** *adj.*

re·man (ree-*man*) *v.* [re·manned; re·man·ning] To man again.

re·mand (reh-*mand*) *v.* To remit in custody to a future time.—**re·mand** *n.*

re·mark *v.* 1. To comment; to say. 2. To notice; to observe.—**re·mark** *n.*

re·mark·a·ble *adj.* Extraordinary; outstanding; striking.—**-a·ble·ness** *n.*— **-a·bly** *adv.*

re·me·di·a·ble (reh-*mee*-dee-uh-b'l) *adj.* Curable.—**re·me·di·a·bly** *adv.*

re·me·di·al (reh-*mee*-dee-ul) *adj.* Curative; serving as a remedy.

rem·e·dy (*rem*-uh-dee) *n.* 1. A cure; a medicine. 2. Relief; corrective.—*v.* [rem·e·died; rem·e·dy·ing] 1. To cure; heal. 2. To rectify. —**rem·e·di·less** *adj.* Without cure.

re·mem·ber (reh-*mem*-ber) *v.* To recollect; to recall.—**re·mem·ber·er** *n.*

re·mem·brance (reh-*mem*-brenss) *n.* 1. Recollection; memory. 2. A memento; a memorial. 3. A gift; a greeting.— **-branc·er** *n.*

re·mil·i·ta·rize (ree-*mil*-ih-tuh-ryze) *v.* [-ta·rized; -ta·riz·ing] To arm again.— **-ri·za·tion** *n.*

re·mind *v.* To recollect; to call to attention. —**re·mind·er** *n.*—**re·mind·ful** *adj.*

rem·i·nis·cence (rem-ih-*niss*-enss) *n.* Memory; recollection.—**rem·i·nisce** *v.* [rem·i·nisced; rem·i·nisc·ing] To call to mind; to narrate past experiences.—**rem·i·nis·cent** *adj.*

re·miss (reh-*miss*) *adj.* Negligent; lax.

re·mis·si·ble *adj.* Forgivable.

re·mis·sion (reh-*mish*-un) *n.* 1. Pardon; forgiveness. 2. Cancellation of debt. 3. Lessening of intensity.

R

re·mit (reh-*mit*) *v.* [re·mit·ted; re·mit·ting]
1. To return to a lower authority for dealing
with. 2. To pardon; to forgive. 3. To waive;
to suspend. 4. To send.—**re·mit** *n.*—**re·mit·
ta·ble** *adj.*—**re·mit·ter** *n.*

re·mit·tance *n.* 1. Sending of money in payment. 2. Money remitted.—**re·mit·tor** *n.*

re·mit·tent *adj.* Temporarily ceasing; having
remissions from time to time.—*n.* A fever
characterized by remissions.—**re·mit·tence** *n.*

rem·nant (*rem*-nent) *n.* Remainder; piece.

re·mod·el (reh-*mod*-'l) *v.* [re·mod·eled, re·mod·
elled; re·mod·el·ing, re·mod·el·ling] To reconstruct; to make modern or new.

re·mon·e·tize (ree-*mon*-eh-tyze) *v.* [re·mon·e·
tized; -tiz·ing] To reinstate as legal tender.
—**re·mon·e·ti·za·tion** *n.*

re·mon·strance (reh-*mon*-str'nss) *n.* Protest;
objection; attempt at persuasion to another
viewpoint.—**re·mon·strant** *adj.*

re·mon·strate (reh-*mon*-strayt) *v.* [re·mon·strat·
ed; -strat·ing] To protest; argue against; attempt to persuade otherwise.—**re·mon·stra·
tion** *n.*—**re·mon·stra·tive** *adj.*—**re·mon·stra·tor** *n.*

re·morse *n.* Sorrowful repentance; compunction.—**re·morse·ful** *adj.*—**re·morse·ful·ly** *adv.*
—**re·morse·ness** *n.*—**re·morse·less** *adj.*

re·mote (reh-*moht*) *adj.* 1. Far distant; far removed. 2. Operating from a point outside.
'To pilot a plane by remote control.'—**re·
mote·ly** *adv.*—**re·mote·ness** *n.*

re·mount (ree-*mownt*) *v.* To mount again.—*n.*
A new setting, as for a jewel.—**re·mount** *adj.*

re·mov·a·ble (reh-*moov*-uh-b'l) *adj.* Capable of
being displaced or taken out.—**re·mov·a·bil·
i·ty, re·mov·a·ble·ness** *n.*—**re·mov·a·bly** *adv.*

re·move (reh-*moov*) *v.* [re·moved; re·mov·ing]
1. To displace; to take away; to do away with.
2. To change residence.—*n.* 1. Act of dis-
placing. 2. Distance from an object; interval.
—**re·mov·al** *n.*—**re·mov·er** *n.*

re·mun·er·ate (reh-*myoo*-ner-ayt) *v.* [re·mu·ner·
at·ed; -at·ing] To reward; to pay.—**re·mu·ner·
a·tion** *n.*—**re·mu·ner·a·tive** *adj.*— **·tive·ly** *adv.*

ren·ais·sance (ren-uh-*sahnss*) *n.* 1. [*cap.*] Great
period of humanistic revival in Europe from
the 14th to 16th century. 2. An age of widespread artistic productivity. 3. A rebirth; a
restoring to life.

Renaissance architecture. A style of building
marked by a return to the massive grandeur of
the Roman tradition.

re·nal (*ree*-n'l) *adj.* Pertaining to the kidneys.

re·nas·cence (reh-*nass*-enss) *n.* Rebirth; reap-
pearance; rejuvenation.—**re·nas·cent** *adj.*

rend *v.* [rent; rend·ing] To rip; tear; split.

ren·der *v.* 1. To give; give back. 2. To cause
to be; make. 3. To translate. 4. To interpret; convey. 5. To boil down and clarify.
'To render fats.'— **ren·der·a·ble** *adj.*

ren·dez·vous (*rahn*-duh-voo) *n.* [*pl.* ren·dez·
vous] 1. An appointment. 2. A meeting
place.—**ren·dez·vous** *v.*

ren·di·tion (ren-*dish*-un) *n.* A rendering; an
artistic treatment or reproduction.

ren·e·gade (*ren*-uh-gayd) *n.* One who deserts a
belief or party to join the opposition.—**ren·e·
gade** *adj.*

re·nege (ree-*nig*) *v.* [re·neged; re·neg·ing]
1. *Cards.* To violate the rules by failing to
follow suit. 2. To withdraw an offer.

re·new (ree-*noo*) *v.* 1. To make new, fresh, or
vigorous again. 2. To resume; begin again.
3. To renovate; restore.—**re·new·a·ble** *adj.*
—**re·new·al** *n.*

ren·net (*ren*-it) *n.* An extract of calves' stomachs
used to curdle milk.

re·nounce (ree-*nownss*) *v.* [re·nounced; re·noun·
cing] 1. To disown; disclaim; forsake. 2. To
abandon; give up.—**re·nounce·ment** *n.*

ren·o·vate (*ren*-uh-vayt) *v.* [ren·o·vat·ed; -vat·
ing] To renew; restore to a good condition.
—**ren·o·va·tion** *n.*—**ren·o·va·tor** *n.*

re·nown (ree-*nown*) *n.* Fame; reputation.—**re·
nowned** *adj.*

rent *n.* 1. A rip; a slit. 2. A schism; a split in
an organization.

rent *n.* Money paid for the right of occupying
real estate.—*v.* 1. To let out to use for money.
2. To lease; to purchase the right to use.
—**rent·a·ble** *adj.*—**rent·er** *n.*

rent·al (*rent*-'l) *n.* Money paid for use of a property.—**rent·al** *adj.*

re·nun·ci·a·tion (ree-nun-see-*ay*-shun) *n.* 1. A
disavowal or rejection. 2. *Law.* Forswearing
or abandoning a right.—**re·nun·ci·a·tive, re·
nun·ci·a·to·ry** *adj.*

re·or·der (ree-*or*-der) *v.* 1. To place another
order with the same dealer. 2. To rearrange.
—**re·or·der** (*ree*-or-der) *n.*

re·or·gan·ize (ree-*or*-g'n-yze) *v.* [re·or·gan·ized;
-iz·ing] 1. To institute a new system or order.
2. To organize again.—**re·or·gan·i·za·tion** *n.*

re·or·i·en·ta·tion (ree-or-ee-en-*tay*-shun) *n.*
1. Process of regaining direction or comprehension. 2. Process of promoting readjust-
ment to an environment.

rep, repp *n.* A finely ribbed or corded fabric.

re·pair (reh-*pair*) *v.* 1. To fix; to restore to
workable condition. 2. To mend; to heal.
—**re·pair** *n.*—**re·pair·a·ble** *adj.*—**re·pair·man** *n.*

rep·a·ra·ble (*rep*-er-uh-b'l) *adj.* Capable of being restored or mended.—**rep·ar·a·bil·i·ty** *n.*

rep·ar·a·tion (rep-er-*ay*-shun) *n.* 1. Indemnity
paid for loss or damage. 2. A repair; act of
repairing.

rep·ar·tee (rep-er-*tee*) *n.* 1. A ready, witty
reply. 2. Skill in or practice of clever retorts.

re·pass (ree-*pass*) *v.* To pass again; to go back.

re·past (ree-*past*) *n.* A meal; feast.

re·pa·tri·ate (ree-*pay*-tree-ayt) *v.* [re·pa·tri·at·
ed; -at·ing] 1. To restore to one's own country.—**re·pa·tri·a·tion** *n.*

re·pay (ree-*pay*) *v.* [re·paid; re·pay·ing] 1. To
pay back; to pay again. 2. To make a return
in kind; to requite.—**re·pay·a·ble** *adj.*

re·peal (ree-*peel*) *v.* To revoke; cancel; annul. —**re·peal** *n.*—**re·peal·a·ble** *adj.*—**re·peal·er** *n.*

re·peat (ree-*peet*) *v.* 1. To do or say again. 2. To recite; to say over.—*n.* 1. A reiteration; repetition. 2. *Music.* **a.** A sign indicating a section to be performed twice. **b.** The section indicated.—**re·peat** *adj.*—**re·peat·ed** *adj.*

re·peat·er (reh-*peet*-er) *n.* 1. One who repeats or recites. 2. A firearm which fires repeatedly without reloading. 3. A ship in a convoy which relays signals sent out by the commodore.

re·pel (reh-*pel*) *v.* [re·pelled; re·pel·ling] 1. To repulse; to drive back; to oppose. 2. To disgust; cause aversion.—**re·pel·ler** *n.*

re·pel·lent (reh-*pel*-unt) *adj.* 1. Resistant; opposing. 2. Disgusting; causing aversion.—**re·pel·len·cy, re·pel·lence** *n.*

re·pent (reh-*pent*) *v.* 1. To regret past sins or actions. 2. To change one's actions because of regretted past acts.—**re·pent·ance** *n.*—**re·pent·ant** *adj.*—**re·pent·ant·ly** *adv.*—**re·pent·er** *n.*

re·per·cus·sion (reh-per-*kush*-un) *n.* 1. A recoil; reverberation. 2. Reactions or effects of an event.—**re·per·cus·sive** *adj.*

rep·er·toire (*rep*-er-twahr) *n.* The list of works a performer or company is prepared to act.

rep·er·to·ry *n.* [*pl.* -ries] 1. A repository; a storehouse; a treasury. 2. A repertoire.

rep·e·ti·tion (rep-ih-*tish*-un) *n.* 1. Iteration; doing or saying again. 2. Something done or said again.—**rep·e·ti·tious** *adj.*—**rep·e·ti·tious·ly** *adv.*—**rep·e·ti·tious·ness** *n.*

re·pine (reh-*pyne*) *v.* [re·pined; re·pin·ing] To fret; to complain.

re·place (reh-*playss*) *v.* [re·placed; re·plac·ing] 1. To put back; to restore. 2. To supplant; to supersede. 3. To substitute; to supply an equivalent.—**re·place·a·ble** *adj.*—**re·plac·er** *n.*

re·place·ment (reh-*playss*-m'nt) *n.* 1. A substitute. 2. Act of replacing.

re·plen·ish (reh-*plen*-ish) *v.* 1. To fill again; to supply what was removed.— **-ment** *n.*

re·plete (reh-*pleet*) *adj.* Complete; abundant; fully supplied.—**re·ple·tion** *n.*

rep·li·ca (*rep*-lih-kuh) *n.* A copy; a facsimile.

re·ply (reh-*ply*) *v.* [re·plied; re·ply·ing] To answer; respond.—*n.* [*pl.* re·plies]—**re·pli·er** *n.*

re·port (reh-*port*) *n.* 1. A statement or account of an event, investigation, etc. 2. A tale of gossip; rumor. 3. Loud, explosive noise.—*v.* 1. To put in an appearance. 2. To relate; to give a formal account of. 3. To record the proceedings of a court or other assembled body. 4. To write news stories. 5. To indict; to bring a charge of misconduct against.—**re·port·a·ble** *adj.*

re·port·er (reh-*port*-er) *n.* 1. One who records court or legislative proceedings. 2. One who gathers news for a newspaper.

re·pose (reh-*pohz*) *v.* [re·posed; re·pos·ing] 1. To rest; to sleep. 2. To trust; to rely.—**re·pose** *n.*—**re·pose·ful** *adj.*

re·pos·i·to·ry (reh-*poz*-ih-taw-ree) *n.* [*pl.* -ries] A storehouse for treasures.

re·pos·sess (ree-puh-*zess*) *v.* To regain possession of; to retake.—**re·pos·ses·sion** *n.*

rep·re·hend (rep-ree-*hend*) *v.* To reprove; censure; blame.

rep·re·hen·si·ble (rep-ree-*hen*-sih-b'l) *adj.* Blameworthy; censurable; guilty.—**rep·re·hen·si·ble·ness, rep·re·hen·si·bil·i·ty** *n.*— **-si·bly** *adv.*

rep·re·hen·sion (rep-ree-*hen*-shun) *n.* Blame; reproof.—**rep·re·hen·sive** *adj.*— **-sive·ly** *adv.*

rep·re·sent (rep-reh-*zent*) *v.* 1. To portray; to picture; to act the part of. 2. To give one's impressions of. 3. To be an agent for; to act in behalf of. 4. To be a symbol or equivalent of.—**rep·re·sent·a·ble** *adj.*—**rep·re·sen·ta·tion** *n.*

rep·re·sent·a·tive (rep-reh-*zent*-uh-tiv) *adj.* 1. Typical; characteristic. 2. Acting as agent for another. 3. Pertaining to delegated authority.—*n.* A delegate; an elected legislator. —**rep·re·sent·a·tive·ly** *adv.*— **-tive·ness** *n.*

re·press (reh-*press*) *v.* 1. To hold back or down; to curb. 2. To prevent normal expression of. —**re·pressed** *adj.*—**re·press·i·ble** *adj.*—**re·press·ive** *adj.*—**re·press·ive·ly** *adv.*

re·pres·sion (reh-*presh*-un) *n.* 1. A check; a curb; restraint. 2. *Psychology.* The withholding of an objectionable desire from conscious thought or expression.

re·prieve (reh-*preev*) *n.* 1. Respite; interval of relief. 2. *Law.* A staying or postponement of execution.—*v.* [re·prieved; re·priev·ing].

rep·ri·mand (*rep*-rih-mand) *v.* To reproach severely; to reprove officially.—**rep·ri·mand** *n.*

re·print (*ree*-print) *n.* 1. A second or later edition of a printed work. 2. Printed matter used for copy in typesetting, as distinguished from longhand or typewritten manuscript.—*v.* (ree-*print*) 1. To print a new edition of. 2. To print again.—**re·print·er** *n.*

re·pris·al (reh-*pryze*-'l) *n.* Retaliation; a deed done in revenge for a wrong suffered.

re·prise (ree-*pryze*, reh-*preez*) *n.* *Music.* A phrase or part of a composition played over again.

re·proach (reh-*prohch*) *v.* To scold; to censure; to condemn.—*n.* 1. Rebuking. 2. Insult; contempt. 3. Shame; disgrace.—**re·proach·a·ble** *adj.*—**re·proach·a·bly** *adv.*

re·proach·ful (reh-*prohch*-f'l) *adj.* Scolding; rebuking.—**re·proach·ful·ly** *adv.*— **-ful·ness** *n.*

rep·ro·bate (*rep*-roh-bayt) *adj.* Depraved; morally abandoned.—*n.* A profligate person.—*v.* [rep·ro·bat·ed; -bat·ing] To detest; condemn.

rep·ro·ba·tion (rep-roh-*bay*-shun) *n.* Strict disapproval.—**rep·ro·ba·tive** *adj.*— **-tive·ly** *adv.*

re·pro·duce (ree-proh-*dooss*) *v.* [re·pro·duced; -duc·ing] 1. To generate; to produce offspring. 2. To make a copy of. 3. To present again, as a play.— **-duc·er** *n.*— **-duc·i·ble** *adj.*

re·pro·duc·tion (ree-proh-*duk*-shun) *n.* 1. Propagation; bearing of offspring. 2. That which is presented again. 3. A copy.—**re·pro·duc·tive** *adj.*—**re·pro·duc·tive·ly** *adv.*— **-tive·ness** *n.*

R

re·proof (reh-*proof*) *n.* A rebuke; censure.

re·prove (reh-*proov*) *v.* [re·proved; re·prov·ing] To scold; to blame; to reprimand.—**re·prov·a·ble** *adj.*—**re·prov·ing·ly** *adv.*

rep·tile (*rep*-til) *n.* 1. A cold-blooded animal that moves about on its belly or on short legs. 2. A groveling or a sneaky person.—**rep·tile, rep·til·i·an** *adj.*

re·pub·lic (reh-*pub*-lik) *n.* A nation wherein the power is invested in representatives elected by popular vote.

re·pub·li·can (reh-*pub*-lih-k'n) *adj.* Pertaining to a republic.—*n.* 1. One who believes in a republican form of government. 2. [*cap.*] A member of the Republican party.— -**can·ism** *n.*

re·pub·lish (ree-*pub*-lish) *n.* To print again.—**re·pub·li·ca·tion** (ree-pub-lih-*kay*-shun) *n.*

re·pu·di·ate (reh-*pyoo*-dee-ayt) *v.* [re·pu·di·at·ed; -at·ing] To renounce; to reject; to refuse to acknowledge.—**re·pu·di·a·tion** (ree-pyoo-dee-*ay*-shun) *n.*—**re·pu·di·a·tor** *n.*

re·pug·nant (reh-*pug*-nunt) *adj.* 1. Distasteful; disgusting. 2. Repelling; at variance; contrary.—**re·pug·nant·ly** *adv.*

re·pulse (reh-*pulss*) *v.* [re·pulsed; re·puls·ing] 1. To repel; to beat back. 2. To reject; to refuse.—**re·pulse** *n.*—**re·puls·er** *n.*

re·pul·sion (reh-*pul*-shun) *n.* 1. A repelling or driving back. 2. An aversion; repugnance.

re·pul·sive (reh-*pul*-siv) *adj.* 1. Repelling; serving to push back. 2. Repugnant; revolting.—**re·pul·sive·ly** *adv.*—**re·pul·sive·ness** *n.*

rep·u·ta·ble (*rep*-yoo-tuh-b'l) *adj.* Estimable; respected; honorable.—**rep·u·ta·bil·i·ty** *n.*—**rep·u·ta·bly** *adv.*

rep·u·ta·tion (rep-yoo-*tay*-shun) *n.* 1. Opinion of one's character held by others. 2. Fame; distinction. 3. Honor; good name.

re·pute (reh-*pyoot*) *v.* [re·put·ed; re·put·ing] To suppose; to deem.—*n.* Reputation; renown. —**re·put·ed** *adj.*—**re·put·ed·ly** *adv.*

re·quest (reh-*kwest*) *v.* To ask; solicit.— *n.* A petition; asking.

re·qui·em (*ree*-kwee-um, *rek*-wee-um) *n.* 1. In the Catholic Church, a mass for the dead. 2. A funeral hymn or musical setting.

re·quire (reh-*kwyre*) *v.* [re·quired; re·quir·ing] 1. To demand; exact. 2. To need; want. —**re·quire·ment** *n.*

req·ui·site (*rek*-wih-zit) *adj.* Necessary; indispensable.—**req·ui·site** *n.*—**req·ui·site·ly** *adv.*

req·ui·si·tion (rek-wih-*zish*-'n) *n.* Demand; requirement; pressure into service.—**req·ui·si·tion** *v.* To force into service.

re·quite (reh-*kwyte*) *v.* [re·quit·ed; re·quit·ing] To recompense; repay.—**re·quit·al** *n.*—**re·quit·er** *n.*

rere·dos (*reer*-dus) *n.* An altar screen.

re·scind (reh-*sind*) *v.* To revoke; repeal; abrogate.—**re·scind·er** *n.*—**re·scis·sion** *n.*

re·script (*ree*-skript) *n.* 1. An edict; a decree; 2. A second writing.

res·cue (*ress*-kyoo) *v.* [res·cued; res·cu·ing] To save; deliver.—**res·cue** *n.*—**res·cu·er** *n.*

re·search (reh-*serch*) *n.* Investigation; scholarly inquiry.—**re·search** *v.*—**re·search·er** *n.*

re·seat *v.* 1. To seat again. 2. To equip with new seats.

re·sect (ree-*sekt*) *v. Surgery.* To cut away a large part of an organ.—**re·sec·tion** *n.*

re·sem·blance (reh-*zem*-blenss) *n.* Likeness.

re·sem·ble (reh-*zem*-b'l) *v.* [re·sem·bled; re·sem·bling] To look like; be similar to.

re·sent (reh-*zent*) *v.* To take offense or feel bitter at.—**re·sent·ful** *adj.*—**re·sent·ful·ly** *adv.*

re·sent·ment (reh-*zent*-ment) *n.* Anger; irritation; bitterness.

res·er·va·tion (rez-er-*vay*-shun) *n.* 1. The act of reserving. 2. Accommodations arranged for in advance. 3. Doubt; uncertainty; qualification; misgiving. 4. *U.S.* **a.** A tract of land on which American Indians live. **b.** An area set aside for public use, as a park or forest.

re·serve (reh-*zerv*) *v.* [re·served; re·serv·ing] To retain; keep; set aside.—*n.* 1. Stores or assets kept for future or emergency use, or for a special purpose. 2. Reticence; undemonstrativeness. 3. An organized military body not yet called to active duty. 4. [*pl.*] A body of troops kept for an emergency.—**re·serve** *adj.*

re·served *adj.* 1. Saved; kept for other or future use. 2. Reticent; unbending; restrained.—**re·ser·ved·ly** *adv.*—**re·ser·ved·ness** *n.*

re·serv·ist *n.* A member of a military reserve.

res·er·voir (*rez*-er-vwor) *n.* Large tank or natural reserve of public water.

re·set (ree-*set*) *v.* [re·set; re·set·ting] 1. To give a new setting to, as a diamond. 2. *Printing.* To set again, as type.—**re·set** (*ree*-set) *n.*

re·ship (ree-*ship*) *v.* [re·shipped; re·ship·ping] To transport again.—**re·ship·ment** *n.*

re·side (reh-*zyde*) *v.* [re·sid·ed; re·sid·ing] To dwell; live.

res·i·dence (*rez*-ih-denss) *n.* 1. Abode; home; dwelling. 2. Act of residing.—**res·i·den·cy** *n.*

res·i·dent (*rez*-ih-dent) *n.* Inhabitant; dweller. —**res·i·dent** *adj.*—**res·i·den·tial** *adj.*

re·sid·u·al (reh-*zid*-yoo-ul) *adj.* Remaining after removal of another part.—*n.* 1. A remainder. 2. *Mathematics.* An expression which gives the remainder of a subtraction, as $a - b$. 3. *Psychology.* Subconscious memory which conditions future reactions.—**re·sid·u·ar·y** *adj.*

res·i·due (*rez*-ih-dyoo) *n.* Remainder; balance.

re·sid·u·um (reh-*zid*-yoo-um) *n.* [*pl.* re·sid·u·a] Residue; remainder; rest.

re·sign (reh-*zyne*) *v.* [re·signed; re·sign·ing] 1. To yield; relinquish. 2. To submit; acquiesce.

res·ig·na·tion (rez-ig-*nay*-shun) *n.* 1. Act of quitting or giving up, as an office. 2. Submission; acquiescence; patient endurance.

re·signed *adj.* Reconciled; submissive.—**re·sign·ed·ly** *adv.*—**re·sign·ed·ness** *n.*

re·sil·i·ent (reh-*zil*-yent) *adj.* Elastic; springy; buoyant.—**re·sil·i·ence, re·sil·i·en·cy** *n.*

res·in (*rez*-in) *n.* A gummy substance obtained from trees, having great industrial value.—*v.*

To rub with resin.—**res·in·ous, res·in·y** *adj.*

re·sist (reh-*zist*) *v.* To withstand; oppose; strive against.—**re·sist·er** *n.*—**re·sist·i·ble** *adj.*

re·sist·ance (reh-*ziss*-tenss) *n.* 1. Opposition. 2. *Electricity.* Non-conductance of a body or matter. 3. [*cap.*] The underground movement in Nazi-occupied countries during World War II.—**re·sist·ant** *n. & adj.*

re·sist·less *adj.* Irresistible; incapable of being withstood.— -**less·ly** *adv.*— -**less·ness** *n.*

re·sist·or *n. Electricity.* A device for impeding the flow of current in a circuit.

res·o·lute (*rez*-uh-loot) *adj.* Steadfast; determined.—**res·o·lute·ly** *adv.*—**res·o·lute·ness** *n.*

res·o·lu·tion (rez-uh-*loo*-shun) *n.* 1. Mettle; determination. 2. A resolve; decision. 3. A formal proposition brought before a public body for discussion and adoption.

re·solve (reh-*zolv*) *v.* [re·solved; re·solv·ing] 1. To determine; decide. 2. To analyze. 3. To solve; clear of difficulties.—*n.* Fixed purpose; determination.—**re·solv·er** *n.*

re·solved *adj.* 1. Determined; decided. 2. Solved.—**re·solv·ed·ly** *adv.*

res·o·nance (*rez*-uh-nenss) *n.* Vibration; intensification of sound by reflection.—**res·o·nant** *adj.*—**res·o·nant·ly** *adv.*

res·o·na·tor (*rez*-uh-nay-ter) *n.* Any instrument for amplifying, prolonging, or intensifying sound by resonance.

re·sort (reh-*zort*) *v.* To have recourse; to apply. —*n.* 1. A vacationing place. 2. Resource.

re·sound (reh-*zownd*) *v.* To reverberate; echo. —**re·sound·ing** *adj.*—**re·sound·ing·ly** *adv.*

re·source (reh-*sorss, ree*-sorss) *n.* 1. Expedient; device; resort. 2. [*pl.*] Money; funds; means. 3. Natural wealth.—**re·source·ful** *adj.* Ingenious; apt; handy.—**re·source·ful·ness** *n.*

re·spect (reh-*spekt*) *v.* 1. To esteem; regard with deference. 2. To concern; have to do with.—*n.* Regard; esteem.—**re·spect·er** *n.*

re·spect·a·ble (reh-*spek*-tuh-b'l) *adj.* 1. Reputable; conventional; refined. 2. Moderate; fair.—**re·spect·a·bil·i·ty** *n.*—**re·spect·a·bly** *adv.*

re·spect·ful *adj.* Dutiful; civil; obedient.—**re·spect·ful·ly** *adv.*—**re·spect·ful·ness** *n.*

re·spec·tive *adj.* Particular; individual.—**re·spec·tive·ly** *adv.*

re·spect·ing *adj.* About; concerning.

res·pi·ra·tion (ress-per-*ay*-shun) *n.* Breathing; inhalation of oxygen and exhalation of carbon dioxide.—**res·pi·ra·tor** *n.* A device fitted over the nose and mouth for artificial respiration or to permit breathing without the intake of noxious substances.—**re·spir·a·to·ry** *adj.*

re·spire (reh-*spyre*) *v.* [re·spired; re·spir·ing] To breathe.—**re·spir·a·ble** *adj.*

res·pite (*ress*-pit) *n.* Pause; intermission; reprieve.—*v.* [res·pit·ed; res·pit·ing].

re·splend·ent (reh-*splen*-dent) *adj.* Splendid; brilliant; glorious.—**res·plend·ence, res·plend·en·cy** *n.*—**res·plend·ent·ly** *adv.*

re·spond (reh-*spond*) *v.* 1. To answer; rejoin.

2. To react.—**re·spond·ence, re·spond·en·cy** *n.* —**re·spond·ent** *n. & adj.*

re·sponse *n.* 1. Answer; reply. 2. Reaction.

re·spon·si·bil·i·ty (reh-spon-sih-*bil*-ih-tee) *n.* [*pl.* -ies] 1. State of being responsible or accountable. 2. Duty entrusted; charge.

re·spon·si·ble (reh-*spon*-sih-b'l) *adj.* 1. Answerable; accountable. 2. Dependable; trustworthy.—**re·spon·si·ble·ness** *n.*— -**si·bly** *adv.*

res·pon·sive (reh-*spon*-siv) *adj.* Sympathetic; answering.—**re·spon·sive·ly** *adv.*— -**sive·ness** *n.*

rest *n.* 1. Repose; relaxation; release from exertion or action. 2. A support. 3. *Music.* An interval of silence occur-

whole   half   quarter   8th   16th   32nd
RESTS (def. 3)

ring in the course of a movement between sounds; also the mark denoting the interval. —*v.* 1. To relax; repose. 2. To stop; cease action. 3. To lean; recline. 4. To sleep; slumber. 5. To be supported. 6. To stand.

rest *n.* Remainder; balance.

res·tau·rant (*ress*-tuh-r'nt, -rant) *n.* A public establishment serving meals.

res·tau·ra·teur (ress-tuh-ruh-*ter*) *n.* The owner of a restaurant.

rest·ful *adj.* Comfortable; peaceful.—**rest·ful·ly** *adv.*—**rest·ful·ness** *n.*

res·ti·tu·tion (ress-tih-*too*-shun) *n.* Reparation; amends; reimbursement.

res·tive *adj.* 1. Nervous; restless; jumpy. 2. Contrary; balky.—**res·tive·ly** *adv.*

rest·less *adj.* Impatient; fidgety; nervous. —**rest·less·ly** *adv.*—**rest·less·ness** *n.*

res·to·ra·tion (ress-tor-*ay*-shun) *n.* 1. Replacement; renewal; re-establishment; renovation. 2. [*cap.*] The re-establishment of the English monarchy, 1660, after Cromwell Protectorate.

re·stor·a·tive (reh-*stor*-uh-tiv) *adj.* Renewing strength or vigor; reviving to consciousness. —**re·stor·a·tive** *n.*

re·store *v.* [re·stored; re·stor·ing] 1. To renovate; heal; revive. 2. To renew; re-establish; reinstate.—**re·stor·er** *n.*

re·strain *v.* To curb; hold back; check.—**re·strain·a·ble** *adj.*—**strain·ed·ly** *adv.*—**strainer** *n.*

re·straint (reh-*straynt*) *n.* 1. Coercion; repression; restriction. 2. Reserve; inhibition.

re·strict (reh-*strikt*) *v.* To limit; confine.—**re·strict·ed** *adj.*—**re·strict·ed·ly** *adv.*

re·stric·tion (reh-*strik*-shun) *n.* Limitation; confinement; restraint.—**re·stric·tive** *adj.*

re·sult (reh-*zult*) *n.* Consequence; outcome; effect; product.—**re·sult** *v.*

re·sult·ant (reh-*zult*-ent) *adj.* Following as a consequence.—*n.* 1. *Physics.* The composite force resulting from two or more forces acting upon a body. 2. Result.

re·sume (reh-*zyoom*) *v.* [re·sumed; re·sum·ing] To begin again; recommence.—**re·sum·a·ble** *adj.*—**re·sum·er** *n.*—**re·sump·tion** *n.*

R

ré·su·mé (ray-zoo-*may*) *n.* Summary; abridgment.

re·surge (reh-*serj*) *v.* To rise again.—**re·sur·gence** *n.*—**re·sur·gent** *adj.*

res·ur·rec·tion (rez-uh-*rek*-shun) *n.* 1. A rising from the dead. 2. [*cap.*] The rising of Christ from death. 3. Revival; renascence.

re·sus·ci·tate (reh-*sus*-ih-tayt) *v.* [re·sus·ci·tated; -tat·ing] To revive; to arouse from unconsciousness.— -ta·tion *n.*— -ta·tor *n.*

ret *v.* [ret·ted; ret·ting] To soak; steep.

re·tail (*ree*-tayl) *v.* To sell commodities directly to the consumer.—**re·tail** *n. & adj.*—**re·tail·er** *n.*

re·tain *v.* 1. To keep; hold. 2. To hire; engage by paying a preliminary fee. 3. To remember; keep in mind.—**re·tain·a·ble** *adj.*

re·tain·er *n. Law.* A preliminary fee given to a counsel to secure his services.

re·take (ree-*tayk*) *v.* [re·took; re·taken; re·tak·ing] To recapture; take again.—**re·take** (*ree*-tayk) *n.*—**re·tak·er** *n.*

re·tal·i·ate (reh-*tal*-ee-ayt) *v.* [-at·ed; -at·ing] To strike back; to return an injury.—**re·tal·i·a·tive** *adj.*—**re·tal·i·a·tion** *n.*—**re·tal·i·a·to·ry** *adj.*

re·tard (reh-*tahrd*) *v.* To slow down; delay; detain.—**re·tar·da·tion** *n.*—**re·tard·er** *n.*

retch *v.* To vomit or attempt to vomit.

re·ten·tion (reh-*ten*-shun) *n.* Keeping; retaining.

re·ten·tive (reh-*ten*-tiv) *adj.* Having the power to retain.—**re·ten·tive·ness** *n.*

ret·i·cent (*ret*-ih-sent) *adj.* Reserved; uncommunicative; taciturn.—**ret·i·cence, -cen·cy** *n.*

ret·i·cule (*ret*-ih-kyool) *n.* A bag for needlework formerly carried by women.

ret·i·na (*ret*-ih-nuh) *n.* [*pl.* ret·i·nas; ret·i·nae] *Anatomy.* The innermost tissue of the eye which receives and communicates to the brain the visual impression.—**ret·i·nal** *adj.*

ret·i·nue (*ret*-ih-nyoo) *n.* The attendants of a distinguished personage.

re·tire *v.* [re·tired; re·tir·ing] 1. To withdraw; leave. 2. To give up business or a public office. 3. To go to bed.

re·tired *adj.* 1. Secluded. 2. Withdrawn from business or active life. 3. Accruing to a retired person.

re·tire·ment *n.* 1. Withdrawal from public or business life. 2. Retreat; departure. 3. Seclusion; privacy.

re·tir·ing *adj.* Reserved; modest.

re·tort (reh-*tort*) *n.* A sharp answer; rejoinder. —**re·tort** *v.*

re·tort (reh-*tort*) *n. Chemistry.* A glass vessel for distilling or decomposing by heat.

re·touch (ree-*tuch*) *v.* To revise; improve by new touches, as a photographic negative or plate.—**re·touch** *n.* —**re·touch·er** *n.*

RETORT

re·trace *v.* [re·traced; re·trac·ing] To trace back; to go back over.—**re·trace·a·ble** *adj.*

re·tract *v.* 1. To recant; renounce. 2. To draw back; retreat.—**re·tract·a·ble** *adj.*

re·trac·tion *n.* Recantation; renouncement; withdrawal.—**re·trac·tive** *adj.*—**re·trac·tor** *n.*

re·tread (ree-*tred*) *v.* To vulcanize a new rolling surface on a worn automobile tire.—*n.* (ree-tred) A retreaded tire.

re·treat *n.* 1. Withdrawal; retirement; escape. 2. *Military.* Retirement of an army before the enemy. 3. Refuge; shelter; sanctuary. 4. A military signal sounded by trumpets at sunset. —*v.* To retire; withdraw.

re·trench *v.* To curtail; reduce; decrease; economize.—**re·trench·ment** *n.*

re·tri·al (ree-*try*-al) *n.* A second trial.

ret·ri·bu·tion (ret-trih-*byoo*-shun) *n.* Retaliation; revenge.—**re·trib·u·tive** *adj.*

re·trieve (reh-*treev*) *v.* [re·trieved; re·triev·ing] To regain; recover; recoup.—**re·trieve** *n.*—**re·triev·a·ble** *adj.*—**re·triev·al** *n.*

re·triev·er *n.* 1. One who retrieves. 2. A breed of dog trained to locate and bring in game which has been shot.

ret·ro·ac·tive (ret-roh-*ak*-tiv) *adj.* Covering a previous period of time.—**ret·ro·ac·tion** *n.* —**ret·ro·ac·tive·ly** *adv.*—**ret·ro·ac·tiv·i·ty** *n.*

ret·ro·cede (reh-troh-*seed*) *v.* [ret·ro·ced·ed; ret·ro·ced·ing] To retire; go back.— -ces·sion *n.*

ret·ro·grade (*ret*-ruh-grayd) *adj.* Regressive; backward; declining.—*v.* [-grad·ed; -grad·ing].

ret·ro·gres·sion (ret-ruh-*gresh*-un) *n.* Act of going backward.—**ret·ro·gres·sive** *adj.*

ret·ro·spect *n.* Consideration of past events; reflection; mental review.—*v.* To look back. —**ret·ro·spec·tion** *n.*—**ret·ro·spec·tive** *adj.*

ret·rous·sé (reh-troo-*say*) *adj.* Turned up.

ret·ro·ver·sion (reh-troh-*ver*-zhun) *n.* A turning or falling backward.

re·try (ree-*try*) *v.* [re·tried; re·try·ing] To try again. 'They retried the case.'

re·turn *v.* 1. To come back; go back; revert; recur. 2. To give or send back. 3. To repay. 4. To answer; reply.—*n.* 1. Act of coming or going back; recurrence. 2. Repayment; act of giving back; restitution. 3. Profit; advantage. 4. [*pl.*] A set of tabulated statistics; as, census returns, election returns.—**re·turn** *adj.*—**re·turn·a·ble** *adj.*

re·un·ion (ree-*yoon*-yun) *n.* A gathering of persons who have been separated.

re·u·nite (ree-yoo-*nyte*) *v.* [re·u·nit·ed; re·u·nit·ing] To join together again.—**re·u·nit·a·ble** *adj.*

rev *v.* [revved; rev·ving] *Aviation Slang.* To speed up, as a motor.

re·vamp (ree-*vamp*) *v.* To change; reconstruct.

re·veal (reh-*veel*) *v.* To disclose; divulge; impart.—**re·veal·a·ble** *adj.*—**re·veal·ment** *n.*

re·veil·le (*rev*-uh-lee) *n. Military.* A musical signal given at sunrise to awaken soldiers.

rev·el (*rev*-'l) *v.* [rev·eled, rev·elled; rev·el·ing, rev·el·ling] To carouse; disport; make merry. —*n.* Party; orgy.—**rev·el·er, rev·el·ler** *n.*

rev·e·la·tion (rev-uh-*lay*-shun) *n.* 1. The act

of disclosing or divulging. 2. The revealing of divine truth. 3. A disclosure. 4. [*cap.*] The Apocalypse; the last book of the sacred canon, containing the prophesies of St. John.

rev·el·ry (*rev*-'l-ree) *n.* [*pl.* rev·el·ries] Noisy festivity; merrymaking.

rev·e·nant (*rev*-uh-n'nt) *n.* Apparition; phantom; ghost.

re·venge (reh-*venj*) *v.* [re·venged; re·veng·ing] To repay injury; to exact retribution.—*n.* Reprisal; vengeance; retaliation.—**re·veng·er** *n.*

re·venge·ful *adj.* Vindictive.—**re·venge·ful·ly** *adv.*—**re·venge·ful·ness** *n.*

rev·e·nue (*rev*-uh-nyoo) *n.* 1. Income; returns. 2. Total government taxes, customs, etc.

re·ver·ber·ate (reh-*verb*-er-ayt) *v.* [re·ver·ber·at·ed; re·ver·ber·at·ing] To resound; to echo. —**re·ver·ber·ant** *adj.*—**re·ver·ber·a·tion** *n.*

re·vere (reh-*veer*) *v.* [re·vered; re·ver·ing] To venerate; worship; respect.

rev·er·ence (*rev*-er-enss) *n.* Veneration; homage; awe.—*v.* [rev·er·enced; rev·er·enc·ing].

rev·er·end (*rev*-er-end) *adj.* Entitled to respect and homage;—esp. as a title of respect given to clergymen.—**rev·er·end** *n.*

rev·er·ent (*rev*-er-ent) *adj.* Deeply respectful; devout; filled with veneration.— -ent·ly *adv.* — -ent·ness *n.*— -en·tial *adj.*— -en·tial·ly *adv.*

rev·er·ie, rev·er·y (*rev*-er-ee) *n.* [*pl.* rev·er·ies] 1. A daydream; a fancy. 2. Relaxed musing.

re·ver·sal (reh-*verss*-'l) *n.* A complete change; an about-face; a turning in an opposite direction.

re·verse (reh-*verss*) *v.* [re·verse; re·vers·ing] 1. To turn around; invert; put in an opposite direction. 2. *Machinery.* To cause to revolve in a contrary direction.—*n.* 1. The contrary; the opposite. 2. A misfortune; defeat. 3. The back surface; the other side.—**re·verse** *adj.* —**re·verse·ly** *adv.*—**re·vers·er** *n.*

re·vers·i·ble (reh-*verss*-ih-b'l) *adj.* Capable of being turned backward.—*n.* A coat which may be worn with the lining on the outside.—**re·vers·i·bil·i·ty, re·vers·i·ble·ness** *n.*—**re·vers·i·bly** *adv.*

re·ver·sion (reh-*ver*-zhun) *n.* 1. Return; going back. 2. Atavism; throw-back.

re·vert (re-*vert*) *v.* To return; to go back.—**re·vert** *n.*—**re·vert·i·ble** *adj.*

re·view (reh-*vyoo*) *n.* 1. A resurvey; a re-examination. 2. Criticism; critique. 3. Magazine; periodical. 4. A military or naval inspection.— -view *v.*— -view·al *n.*— -view·er *n.*

re·vile *v.* [re·viled; re·vil·ing] To berate; vituperate; excoriate.— -vile·ment *n.*— -vil·ing·ly *adv.*

re·vise (reh-*vyze*) *v.* [re·vised; re·vis·ing] To amend; alter; correct.—**re·vis·er, re·vis·or** *n.*

re·vi·sion (reh-*vizh*-un) *n.* Correction; alteration.—**re·vi·sion·al** *adj.*—**re·vi·sion·ar·y** *n.*

re·vi·sor·y (reh-*vy*-zer-ee) *adj.* Having power to revise; effecting revision.

re·vi·tal·ize (ree-*vy*-t'l-yz) *v.* [re·vi·tal·ized; re·vi·tal·iz·ing] To restore life and vigor.—**re·vi·tal·i·za·tion** *n.*

re·viv·al (reh-*vyve*-'l) *n.* 1. Rebirth; reanima-

tion; recovery. 2. A new presentation of an old theatrical production. 3. A meeting for the purpose of stimulating strong religious feelings.

re·viv·al·ist (reh-*vyve*-'l-ist) *n.* A preacher who conducts revival meetings.

re·vive (reh-*vyve*) *v.* [re·vived; re·viv·ing] 1. To bring back to life. 2. To reanimate; refresh; quicken. 3. To reproduce an old play or motion picture.—**re·viv·er** *n.*

re·viv·i·fy (ree-*viv*-uh-fye) *v.* [re·viv·i·fied; re·viv·i·fy·ing] To reanimate; give new life to.

rev·o·ca·ble (*rev*-uh-kuh-b'l) *adj.* Capable of being repealed or annulled.—**rev·o·ca·bil·i·ty** *n.*—**rev·o·ca·bly** *adv.*

rev·o·ca·tion (rev-oh-*kay*-shun) *n.* Repeal; annulment.

re·voke *v.* [re·voked; re·vok·ing] 1. To take back; repeal; rescind. 2. *Cards.* To renege. —*n.* Violation of the rules by failure to follow suit.—**re·vok·er** *n.*

re·volt (reh-*vohlt*) *n.* Uprising; insurrection.—*v.* 1. To rebel; rise up against a government. 2. To repel; disgust.—**re·volt·er** *n.*

re·volt·ing (reh-*vohlt*-ing) *adj.* Disgusting; shocking.—**re·volt·ing·ly** *adv.*

rev·o·lu·tion (rev-uh-*loo*-shun) *n.* 1. Rotation; the motion of a body around a center. 2. Cycle; complete series of events. 3. Rebellion; insurrection; change of government by an uprising of the people.

rev·o·lu·tion·ar·y (rev-uh-*loo*-shun-ehr-ee) *adj.* Pertaining to a revolution.—*n.* Person who favors a revolution.

rev·o·lu·tion·ist (rev-uh-*loo*-shun-ist) *n.* Person favoring or engaged in a revolution.

rev·o·lu·tion·ize (rev-uh-*loo*-shun-yze) *v.* [rev·o·lu·tion·ized; -iz·ing] 1. To change radically. 2. To engage in revolt against a government.

re·volve (reh-*rolv*) *v.* [re·volved; re·volv·ing] 1. To gyrate; turn; rotate. 2. To consider; weigh.—**re·volv·a·ble** *adj.*—**re·volv·ing** *adj.*

re·volv·er (reh-*vol*-ver) *n.* A small portable firearm having a revolving breech cylinder designed to fire several shots without reloading.

re·vue (reh-*vyoo*) *n.* A musical variety show of songs, dances, and burlesques.

re·vul·sion (reh-*vul*-shun) *n.* 1. Reaction; a sudden violent change. 2. Disgust.—**re·vul·sive** *adj.*

REVOLVER

re·ward (reh-*wawrd*) *v.* To pay; bestow a prize. —*n.* Prize; award; premium.—**re·ward·er** *n.*

re·write (ree-*ryte*) *v.* [re·wrote; re·writ·ing] 1. To write again; to edit by extensive changes. 2. *Journalism.* To write up news which has been sent in orally.—**re·write** (*ree*-ryte) *n.*

rey·nard (*ray*-nahrd) *n.* 1. A fox. 2. [*cap.*] The hero of a medieval animal story, *Reynard the Fox.*

rhap·sod·i·cal (rap-*sod*-ih-k'l) *adj.* Also **rhap·**

sod·ic. Pertaining to a rhapsody; ecstatic; highly emotional.—**rhap·sod·i·cal·ly** *adv*.

rhap·so·dize (*rap*-suh-dyze) *v*. [rhap·so·dized; -diz·ing] To utter ecstatically; speak with intense feeling.

rhap·so·dy (*rap*-suh-dee) *n*. [*pl*. rhap·so·dies] 1. A literary or oral work composed under the influence of strong emotions. 2. *Music*. A composition of irregular form.—**rhap·so·dist** *n*.

rhe·a (*ree*-uh) 1. *Zoology*. The three-toed ostrich of South America. 2. [*cap*.] *Greek Mythology*. The mother of Zeus.

Rhen·ish (*ren*-ish) *adj*. Pertaining to the Rhine River.—*n*. Rhine wine.

rhe·ni·um (*ree*-nee-um) *n*. A very rare chemical element occurring in manganese salts. (*Symbol*: Re).

rhe·o·stat (*ree*-oh-stat) *n*. *Electricity*. An instrument for regulating a circuit so that any required voltage may be maintained.

rhe·sus (*ree*-sus) *n*. A type of monkey inhabiting the Malay Peninsula and the islands of the Indian Archipelago.

rhet·o·ric (*ret*-er-ik) *n*. 1. The art of speaking with elegance and force. 2. Artificial eloquence; declamation.—**rhe·tor·i·cal** (reh-*tawr*-ik-'l) *adj*. Pertaining to rhetoric; figurative; oratorical.—**rhe·tor·i·cal·ly** *adv*.

rhetorical question. A question asked by the speaker for effect and not to evoke an answer.

rhet·o·ri·cian (ret-oh-*rish*-an) *n*. 1. A public speaker; an orator. 2. A teacher of rhetoric.

rheum (*room*) *n*. Mucus; phlegm.

rheu·mat·ic (roo-*mat*-ik) *adj*. Pertaining to or affected by rheumatism.—*n*. One afflicted with rheumatism.

rheumatic fever. An acute disease marked by fever and painful inflammation of the joints, often causing damage to the heart.

rheu·ma·tism *n*. A painful inflammation affecting muscles and joints of the human body.

rheum·y (*room*-ee) *adj*. Watery with mucus.

Rhine (*ryne*). An important river in Europe, coming from SE Switzerland to the North Sea. —**Rhine wine.** A white wine originally produced in the Rhine valley of Germany.

rhine·stone (*ryne*-stohn) *n*. A cut-glass ornament.

rhi·ni·tis (ry-*ny*-tiss) *n*. Inflammation of the mucous membrane of the nose.

rhi·noc·er·os (ry-*noss*-er-us) *n*. [*pl*. -er·os·es] A large, thick-skinned animal of Africa and India having one or two horns jutting out of its snout.

RHINOCEROS (1/100 life-size)

rhi·zome (*ry*-zohm) *n*. *Botany*. A thick stem running along or under the ground, sending forth shoots from its upper side and roots from the lower side.

Rhodes. An island in the Aegean Sea. Area: 545 sq. mi.—**Rho·di·an** *adj*. & *n*.

rho·di·um *n*. A metallic element found in small quantities in platinum ores. (*Symbol*: Rh).

rho·do·den·dron (roh-duh-*den*-drun) *n*. A hardy shrub, usually evergreen, bearing clusters of pink, white, or rosy lilac flowers.

RHODODENDRON

rhom·boid (*rom*-boyd) *n*. *Geometry*. A four-sided figure in which the opposite sides are equal, the angles oblique, and the adjacent sides unequal.

rhom·bus (*rom*-b'ss) *n*. [*pl*. rhom·bus·es, rhom·bi] *n*. *Geometry*. An equilateral parallelogram whose angles are not right angles.

Rhône (*rohn*). An important French river flowing into the Mediterranean.

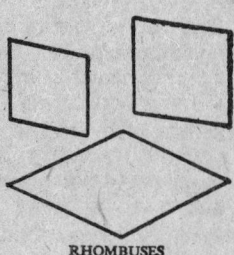
RHOMBUSES

rhu·barb (*roo*-bahrb) *n*. 1. A hardy perennial herb having thick leaf stalks, used in pies, sauces, and preserves. 2. A purgative medicine made from the roots of one type of rhubarb.

rhum·ba (*rum*-buh) *n*. A Latin-American dance.

rhyme, rime *n*. 1. The correspondence in sound of the terminating word, phrase, or syllable of one line of poetry with that of another. 2. Poetry; verse.—*v*. [rhymed; rhym·ing]—**rhym·er, rim·er** *n*.

rhyme·ster, rime·ster *n*. A trivial poet.

rhythm (*rith*-'m) *n*. 1. Cadence; regularity of movement; predictable recurrence. 2. *Prosody*. a. Regular alternation of stress or quantity. b. A poetic form created by use of a particular metrical foot. 3. *Music*. a. Pattern of regularly recurring accent in beats. b. The pattern of tones with regard to their relative time value.—**rhyth·mic, rhyth·mi·cal** *adj*. —**rhyth·mi·cal·ly** *adv*.—**rhyth·mics** *n*.

ri·al (*ry*-ul) *n*. Iranian monetary unit.

Ri·al·to (ree-*ahl*-toh) *n*. 1. In Venice, a bridge over the Grand Canal; a business center. 2. [*not cap*.] (rih-*al*-toh) Theatrical district.

rib *n*. 1. *Anatomy*. One of the curved bones springing from the vertebral column, enclosing the viscera in most vertebrates. 2. *Shipbuilding*. One of the bent timbers or metallic bars springing from the keel, strengthening the side of a ship. 3. *Architecture*. A masonry arch constituting the framework of a vault or dome. 4. A raised stripe on textiles. 5. One of the extension rods over which the cover of an umbrella is stretched.—*v*. [ribbed; rib·bing] 1. To furnish with ribs. 2. *Slang*. To josh; chaff.—**ribbed** *adj*.—**rib·bing** *n*.

rib·ald (*rib*-'ld) *adj*. Obscene; improper; vulgar. —*n*. A gross person.—**rib·ald·ry** *n*.

rib·and (*rib*-and) *n*. A ribbon.

rib·bon (rib-'n) *n.* 1. A narrow strip of fabric used decoratively. 2. A band; a strip. 3. A revolving inked tape on which letters are impressed, as in typewriters.—**rib·bon** *v.*

ri·bo·fla·vin (ry-boh-*flay*-vin) *n.* One of the heat-stable factors in the vitamin B complex, occurring in milk, liver, eggs, etc.

rice (*rysse*) *n.* 1. An annual plant with large, pointed leaves, cultivated on low, moist ground in warm climates. 2. The grain of the rice plant, a food staple in the Far East.

rice paper. A thin delicate paper.

ric·er *n.* A utensil for pressing food into ricelike forms.

rich *adj.* 1. Wealthy. 2. Full; opulent; abundant; having body. 3. Productive; fertile. 4. Containing sweet or heavy ingredients. 5. Mellow; harmonious; deep; resonant. 6. Funny; amusing.—**rich·ly** *adv.*— -**ness** *n.*

rich·es *n.* [*sing.* & *pl.*] Wealth; opulence; abundance.

rick *n.* A stack of corn or hay.—**rick** *v.*

rick·ets *n.* A children's disease caused by vitamin D deficiency and characterized by distortion of the bones.

rick·et·y *adj.* 1. Affected with rickets. 2. Shaky; weak.

rick·ey *n.* A mixed drink made of spirits, a citrous juice, and carbonated water.

rick·rack *n.* A scalloped ribbon edging.

rick·sha, rick·shaw *n.* Also **jin·rik·i·sha.** Man-drawn two-wheeled carriage used in the Orient.

ric·o·chet (rik-oh-*shay*, -uh-*shet*) *n.* A rebounding from or along a flat surface.—*v.* [ric·o·chet·ed; ric·o·chet·ing]. To skip; bounce.

rid *v.* [rid; rid·ding] To free; deliver.

rid·a·ble (*ryde*-uh-b'l) *adj.* 1. Capable of being ridden. 2. Capable of being traversed.

rid·dance *n.* Escape; deliverance.

rid·dle *n.* A puzzle, an enigma.—*v.* [rid·dled; rid·dling] To solve; explain.

rid·dle *n.* A large coarse-meshed sieve.—*v.* [rid·dled; rid·dling] 1. To separate with a riddle. 2. To fill with holes.

ride *v.* [rode; rid·den; rid·ing] 1. To be carried by an animal or vehicle. 2. To be borne along. 'To ride into office.'—*n.* Journey; trip.

rid·er *n.* 1. One who rides, esp. a horseman. 2. An amendment, usually extraneous, to a legislative measure.—**rid·er·less** *adj.*

ridge *n.* 1. A long and narrow elevation; a long summit. 2. A strip of ground between furrows. 3. The meeting of the upper end of the rafters of a building.—*v.* [ridged; ridg·ing].

ridge·pole *n.* The timber forming the ridge of a roof, into which the rafters are fastened.

RIDGEPOLE

rid·i·cule (*rid*-ih-kyool) *n.* Derision; mockery.—*v.* [rid·i·culed; rid·i·cul·ing] To deride; mock.—**rid·i·cul·er** *n.*

ri·dic·u·lous (rih-*dik*-yoo-lus) *adj.* Ludicrous; farcical; preposterous.—**ri·dic·u·lous·ly** *adv.* Absurdly.

rid·ing *adj.* Employed for riding.

rife (*ryfe*) *adj.* Prevalent; abounding.

rif·fle *v.* [rif·fled; rif·fling] To flip through. —**rif·fle** *n.* 1. A way of shuffling cards. 2. A mesh fitted into a gold-washing trough.

riff·raff *n.* The rabble.

ri·fle (*ry*-f'l) *n.* 1. A gun with a spirally grooved inner barrel. 2. [*pl.*] A body of troops

RIFLE

armed with rifles.—*v.* [ri·fled; ri·fling] To groove.—**ri·fle·man** *n.*—**ri·fling** *adj.*

ri·fle *v.* [ri·fled; ri·fling] To ransack; plunder.

rift *n.* Breach; cleavage.—*v.* To split.

rig *v.* [rigged; rig·ging] 1. To fit (a ship) with rigging. 2. To equip; supply with apparatus. 3. To assemble apparatus. 4. To dress; clothe.—*n.* 1. *Nautical.* The arrangement of masts, sails, and tackle of a ship. 2. A carriage with horses. 3. *Colloquial.* Dress; clothing. 4. Apparatus designed for a specific job. 'An oil-well rig.'—**rig·ger** *n.*

rig·ging *n.* 1. The cables, ropes, etc., which support the masts and handle the sails of a vessel. 2. Tackle; gear for any purpose.

right (*ryte*) *adj.* 1. Straight; direct. 2. Perpendicular; encompassing 90°. 'A right angle.' 3. Just; equitable. 4. Fit; suitable; becoming. 5. Correct; accurate; exact; true. 6. On the right-hand side; opposite the left. 7. Politically conservative.—*n.* 1. Justice; uprightness; integrity. 2. Prerogative; privilege; just claim. 3. The side opposite to the left. 4. *Politics.* Conservative organizations and forces collectively.—*v.* 1. To resume a vertical position. 2. To set upright. 3. To relieve from wrong.—**right** *adv.*—**right away.** Immediately; instantly.—**by rights.** Justly; in all fairness.

right-brained	right-minded	right turn
right-eyed	right-principled	rightward

right angle. A 90° angle, formed by perpendicular lines.—**right-an·gled** *adj.*

right·eous (*ry*-chus) *adj.* Virtuous; moral. —**right·eous·ly** *adv.*—**right·eous·ness** *n.*

right·ful (*ryte*-ful) *adj.* 1. Due; just; legal. 2. Supported by a legally right claim.—**right·ful·ly** *adv.*—**right·ful·ness** *n.*

right-hand *adj.* 1. Situated on the right hand; leading to the right. 2. Most dependable or essential. 'The president's right-hand man.' —**right-hand·ed** *adj.* Using the right hand more easily and readily than the left.

right·ist *n.* A political conservative; a reactionary.—**right·ist** *adj.*

right·ly *adv.* 1. Properly; suitably. 2. Correctly.

right·ness *n.* Correctness; rectitude.

right-of-way *n.* Also **right of way.** 1. *Law.*

R

The right of passage across the property of another. 2. A strip of land along which railroad tracks are laid. 3. The right of traffic from one direction to take precedence over that from another.

right triangle. A triangle having one right angle.

right whale. The Greenland whale, often attaining a length of 60–70 feet, now almost extinct.

right wing. The conservative element of an organization, nation, etc.—**right-wing** *adj.*

rig·id (*rij*-id) *adj.* 1. Stiff; not flexible. 2. Strict; uncompromising.—**ri·gid·i·ty** (ri-*jid*-ih-tee) *n.*—**rig·id·ly** *adv.*—**rig·id·ness** *n.*

rig·ma·role (*rig*-muh-rohl) *n.* Complicated and confused talk or writing.

rig·or (*rig*-er) *n.* 1. Difficulty; hardship. 2. Severity; rigidity. 3. Strictness; harshness.

rigor mortis (*ry*-gor-*mor*-tiss; *rih*-ger). Stiffening of the muscles in death.

rig·or·ous (*rig*-er-us) *adj.* Rigid; strict; harsh. —**rig·or·ous·ly** *adv.*—**rig·or·ous·ness** *n.*

rile (*ryle*) *v.* [riled; ril·ing] *Colloquial.* To irritate; exasperate.

rill *n.* A small brook; rivulet.

rim *n.* Edge; border.—*v.* [rimmed; rim·ming] To put a rim around.

rime *n.* Hoarfrost; white frost.—*v.* [rimed; rim·ing] To freeze into hoarfrost.—**rim·y** *adj.*

rind (*rynde*) *n.* The peel; crust; skin of a fruit.

ring *n.* 1. A circular ornament worn on the finger. 2. A metal hoop, as a key ring, napkin ring, etc. 3. The arena of a circus. 4. The enclosed space in which a boxing match is held. 5. A circular group of people. 6. A combination of persons for private and often illegal purposes. 7. One of the annual circular layers in trees.—*v.* To encircle.—**ringed** *adj.*

ring-adorned	ringcraft	ring-shaped
ringbill	ringeye	ring-streaked
ring-billed	ring-eyed	ringtail
ringbird	ring maker	ring-tailed
ring-bound	ringman	ringwalk

ring *v.* [rang, rung; rung; ring·ing] 1. To sound, as a bell. 2. To reverberate; be filled with a vibrating sound; resound. 3. To convey a certain quality. 'To ring true.' 4. To summon, usher in, or celebrate by ringing.—*n.* 1. The sound of a bell. 2. A quality; a note. 'A ring of anger.' 3. A telephone call.

ring·dove *n.* A species of pigeon so named because of a circular marking on the neck.

ring·lead·er *n.* Instigator; captain of a group, esp. one engaged in illegal or unruly activities.

ring·let *n.* A curl of hair.

ring·mas·ter *n.* One who introduces and directs the performances at a circus.

ring·side *n.* The area around a boxing ring.

ring·worm *n.* A contagious skin disease characterized by circular patches covered with scales.

rink *n.* A skating arena.

rinse *v.* [rinsed; rins·ing] 1. To wash lightly.

2. To wash in clear water to remove soap. —**rinse** *n.*—**rins·er** *n.*—**rins·ing** *n.*

Rio Grande (ree-oh-*grand*). A North American river forming part of the boundary between the U.S. and Mexico, and emptying into the Gulf of Mexico.

ri·ot (*ry*-ut) *n.* 1. Mass disorders; illegal disturbance created by a crowd. 2. Tumult; chaos; confusion.—**ri·ot** *v.*—**ri·ot·er** *n.*

ri·ot·ous *adj.* 1. Tumultuous; noisy; clamorous. 2. *Colloquial.* Hilarious.—**ri·ot·ous·ly** *adv.*—**ri·ot·ous·ness** *n.*

rip *v.* [ripped; rip·ping] To tear; rend.—*n.* A tear; a rent.

ri·par·i·an (rih-*pair*-ee-un) *adj.* Pertaining to the banks of a river. 'Riparian rights.'

rip cord. The cord by which a parachute is opened.

ripe (*rype*) *adj.* 1. Ready for reaping or picking; mature; mellow; full-blown. 2. Ready; prepared.—**ripe·ly** *adv.*—**ripe·ness** *n.*

rip·en *v.* To mature; to reach full development.

rip·ple *v.* [rip·pled; rip·pling] To become ruffled, as water.—**rip·ple** *n.*—**rip·plet** *n.*—**rip·pling** *adj.*—**rip·pling·ly** *adv.*

rip-roar·ing *adj. Slang.* Noisy; boisterous.

rip·saw *n.* A saw used for cutting wood with the grain.

rise (*ryze*) *v.* [rose; ris·en; ris·ing] 1. To ascend; move upward. 2. To get out of bed. 3. To stand up. 4. To attain a height. 5. To swell; puff up. 6. To slope upward. 7. To appear; become apparent. 8. To originate; spring. 9. To increase in intensity. 10. To increase in price. 11. To revolt; rebel. 12. To return to life. 13. To appear above the horizon.—*n.* 1. Ascent; upward movement. 2. Gradual elevation. 3. Increase; advance.

ris·er (*ryze*-er) *n.* 1. One who rises. 2. The vertical face of a stair.

ris·i·bil·i·ty (riz-ih-*bil*-ih-tee) *n.* [*pl.* -i·ties] Ability to laugh.—**ris·i·ble** *adj.* Droll; laughable.

RISER (def. 2)

ris·ing *adj.* 1. Ascending; climbing; advancing; growing. 2. Increasing in wealth, importance, or prosperity. 3. Increasing in intensity or strength.—*n.* 1. The appearance of the sun or a star above the horizon. 2. Resurrection. 3. Insurrection; revolt; uprising.

risk *n.* Hazard; danger.—**risk** *v.*—**risk·y** *adj.*

ris·qué (riss-*kay*) *adj.* Suggestive; indelicate.

rite (*ryte*) *n.* A religious ceremony; a ritual.

rit·u·al *n.* Liturgy; rite; ceremonial.—**rit·u·al** *adj.*—**rit·u·al·ism** *n.*—**rit·u·al·ist** *n.*—**rit·u·al·is·tic** *adj.*— **-ti·cal·ly** *adv.*—**rit·u·al·ly** *adv.*

ri·val (*ry*-v'l) *n.* Competitor; antagonist.—*v.* [ri·valed, ri·valled; ri·val·ing, ri·val·ling] 1. To compete with; vie with. 2. To match equal.—**ri·val** *adj.*

ri·val·ry (*ry*-v'l-ree) *n.* Competition.

rive (*ryve*) *v.* [rived; rived or riv·en; riv·ing] To split; cleave.

riv·er *n.* 1. A large stream of water flowing through a well-defined channel into a sea, a lake, or another river. 2. A great flow; abundance.

riverbank	river god	riverwash
river-borne	riverman	river-watered
river-formed	riverside	river-worn

riv·et *n.* A short metallic bolt for fastening two pieces of metal together by hammering the pointed end broad after insertion.—*v.* [riv·et·ed; riv·et·ing] 1. To fasten with a rivet. 2. To anchor; fasten firmly.—**riv·et·er** *n.*

RIVET

riv·u·let (*riv*-yoo-let) *n.* A small stream; a brook.

roach (*rohch*) *n.* A cockroach; troublesome household insect.

roach *n.* A grayish-green fish of the carp family found in temperate waters.

road *n.* 1. A highway; a path for vehicles. 2. Way. 'The road to success.' 3. An extension of a harbor in which ships may anchor; a roadstead.—**road·way** *n.*

road·bed *n.* 1. The foundation on which the superstructure of a railway rests. 2. The material laid for a road.

road·house *n.* A roadside tavern.

road·side *adj.* At the side of a road.

road·stead *n.* An approach to a harbor where ships may ride at anchor at a distance from the shore.

road·ster *n.* A small, open automobile.

roam *v.* To wander; rove.—**roam** *n.*—**roam·er** *n.*

roan *adj.* Reddish or bay mottled with white. —*n.* A roan-colored horse.

roar *v.* 1. To bellow; howl; cry out with a loud resounding noise. 2. To make a loud tumultuous sound. 3. To laugh boisterously. —*n.* A deep, bellowing sound.—**roar·er** *n.* 1. A horse subject to noisy respiration. 2. Anyone making loud noises by voice.

roar·ing *adj.* Noisy; resounding; like a roar. —*n.* A loud continued sound.

roast *v.* 1. To cook meat over a direct fire or, more commonly, in an oven. 2. To heat to excess. 3. To dry and parch by exposure to heat. 4. *Colloquial*. To criticize severely. —**roast** *n. & adj.*

roast·er (*rohst*-er) *n.* 1. A covered pan for roasting. 2. A young animal or bird suitable for roasting.

rob *v.* [robbed; rob·bing] 1. To steal; burglarize. 2. To commit the felony of robbery. —**rob·ber** *n.* Thief; burglar.

rob·ber·y (*rob*-er-ee) *n.* [*pl.* rob·ber·ies] 1. Theft; burglary. 2. *Law.* Larceny of property in the presence of the victim, accompanied by violence or coercion.

robe (*rohb*) *n.* 1. A long loose garment. 2. [*pl.*] The attire of a rank or high position.—*v.* To dress; clothe.

rob·in (*rob*-in) *n.* A migratory, red-breasted bird.

ro·bot (*rob*-ut, *roh*-b't) *n.* 1. Any machine which performs functions so complex that it appears to possess intelligence. 2. An efficient but insensitive and uncreative person.

ro·bust (roh-*bust*) *adj.* Sturdy; healthy; lusty. **ro·bust·ly** *adv.*—**ro·bust·ness** *n.*

ROBIN (1/7 life-size)

roc *n.* A monstrous bird in Arabian mythology.

rock *v.* To tilt backward and forward.—**rock** *n.*

rock *n.* 1. A large mass of stony matter. 2. A stone of any size. 3. A source of disaster. 4. Asylum; refuge; strength.—**rock** *adj.*

rock asphalt	rock-cut	rock-piled
rock-based	rockfall	rock-ribbed
rock-bound	rock firm	rock shaft
rock-built	rock-free	rock slide
rock-cleft	rock-hearted	rock-strewn
rock climber	rock-hewn	rock-torn

rock candy. Large hard crystals of sugar.

rock crystal. Colorless, transparent quartz.

rock·er (*rok*-er) *n.* 1. The curved piece on which a cradle or rocking chair rocks. 2. A chair or toy horse mounted on rockers.

rock·et (*rok*-it) *n.* 1. A projectile or plane propelled by the force of expanding gases produced by combustion of material within. 2. A skyrocket.—*v.* To rise suddenly.

ROCKET (def. 2)

rocking chair. An armchair mounted on rockers.

rocking horse. A wooden horse mounted on rockers for the recreation of children.

rock salt. Large crystals of common salt.

rock wool. A fibrous insulating material.

rock·y (*rok*-ee) *adj.* [rock·i·er; rock·i·est] 1. Stony; full of rocks. 2. Hard as a rock.

Rocky Mountains. Mountain range in western North America, extending from British Columbia to Nevada.

ro·co·co (ruh-*koh*-koh) *n.* French interpretation of baroque decoration in the time of Louis XV, combining curved design, fragile proportions, and florid color. —**ro·co·co** *adj.*

rod *n.* 1. A stick; a wand. 2. A fishing pole. 3. *Slang.* A gun.

ro·dent (*roh*-d'nt) *n.* One of a family of animals including the rat, rabbit, squirrel, and others which nibble or gnaw.—**ro·dent** *adj.*

ROCOCO

R

ro-de-o (roh-dee-oh, roh-*day*-oh) *n*. A tournament, popular in the western U.S., featuring contests in riding, shooting, etc.

roe *n*. The sperm or spawn of fish.

roe *n*. The female of the hart.

roe-buck *n*. A small, agile deer having cylindrical branched horns, forked at the top.

Roentgen ray (*rent*-g'n). X ray; high frequency radiation capable of penetrating a solid, discovered by W. K. Roentgen, German physicist.

rogue (*rohg*) *n*. A knave; rascal.

ro-guer-y (*roh*-ger-ee) *n*. Cheating; fraud.

ro-guish (*roh*-gish) *adj*. Mischievous; playful; waggish.—**ro-guish-ly** *adv*.—**ro-guish-ness** *n*.

roil *v*. 1. To cloud a liquid by stirring up sediment. 2. To irritate; annoy.—**roil-y** *adj*. 1. Turbid; muddy. 2. Angered; exasperated.

roist-er *v*. To bluster; swagger.—**roist-er-er** *n*.

role, rôle *n*. 1. A dramatic part; a character. 2. A function; a duty.

roll (*rohl*) *v*. [rolled; roll-ing] 1. To move along a surface by revolving. 2. To rotate; revolve. 3. To form into a spherical or cylindrical body. 4. To press; smooth out. 5. To surge. 6. To move with or lie in alternate swells and depressions, as waves or rolling land. 7. To sway; rock. 'The ship rolled in the heavy seas.' 8. To rumble; to sound or utter in a deep tone.—*n*. 1. Rotary movement. 2. A cylindrical or round form of material. 3. List; roster; catalog. 4. Bread dough baked in individual servings. 5. Continued deep sound as of a drum beaten.

roll call. The taking of attendance by calling out a list of names.

roll-er (*rohl*-er) *n*. 1. A rotating cylindrical device used for smoothing, crushing, spreading out, etc. 2. A small wheel, as on a roller skate or piece of furniture. 3. A heavy wave rolling onto the shore.

roller skate. A skate mounted on small wheels, enabling one to glide over any smooth surface.—**roll-er-skate** *v*. [roll-er-skat-ed; -skat-ing].

rol-lick (*rol*-ik) *v*. To frolic; romp; be jovial in behavior.—**rol-lick-ing** *adj*.—**rol-lick-some** *adj*.

roll-ing (*rohl*-ing) *adj*. 1. Moving on wheels. 2. Wavy; undulant. 3. Making a continuous noise resembling the roll of a drum.

rolling pin. A round piece of wood having a projecting handle at each end, with which dough is flattened.

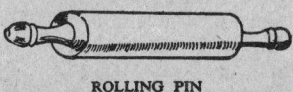

ROLLING PIN

rolling stock. *Railways*. All wheeled vehicles designed to run on the rails.

ro-ly-po-ly (*roh*-lee-*poh*-lee) *adj*. Round; pudgy. —*n*. A rolled, baked pudding.

ro-maine (roh-*mayn*) *n*. Also **romaine lettuce**. A lettuce with long, narrow leaves.

Ro-man (*roh*-m'n) *n*. 1. A native of Rome. 2. *Printing*. [*not cap*.] Any ordinary text type, as distinguished from *italic*. 3. *Typography*. Any of a group of type faces originated in fifteenth-century Italy and characterized by tapered strokes, serifs, and narrow upright body. This book is set in Times New Roman. —**Ro-man** or **ro-man** *adj*.

Roman candle. A kind of firework, which discharges a stream of fiery, colored balls.

Roman Catholic. Adhering to or pertaining to the Roman Catholic Church, of which the Pope in Rome is the head.

ro-mance (roh-*manss*, roh-manss) *n*. 1. A long story of love and adventure in prose or verse. 2. Colorfulness; picturesqueness; idyllic or exotic quality. 3. A love affair.—*v*. [romanced; romanc-ing] 1. To daydream. 2. To make love.—**ro-manc-er** *n*.

Romance languages. The group of languages, including Italian, French, Spanish, and Portuguese, based on the Latin spoken in the western Roman provinces.

Ro-man-esque (roh-m'n-*esk*) *n*. Early medieval style of architecture developed in Italy, characterized by the round arch, arcades, and, sometimes, richly ornamented exterior surface, using highly stylized relief sculpture. —**Ro-man-esque** *adj*.

ROMANESQUE

Roman nose. An aquiline or hooked nose.

Roman numerals. Numerals expressed in letters rather than by the Arabic characters.

Ro-mans *n*. *sing*. *Bible*. St. Paul's Epistle to the Christians in Rome.

ro-man-tic (roh-*man*-tik) *adj*. 1. Fanciful; unworldly; exotic; fabulous. 2. Imaginative; dreamy; impractically or frivolously idealistic. 3. Pertaining to the theories of romanticism. —**ro-man-tic** *n*.—**ro-man-ti-cal-ly** *adv*.

ro-man-ti-cism (roh-*man*-tuh-sizm) *n*. Also **romantic movement**. Trend in 19th-century thought, particularly expressed in literature and painting, rebelling against the cold arbitrariness of classicism, and reasserting human individuality and the power of the imagination.

Rom-a-ny (*rom*-uh-nee) *n*. Also **Rom-ma-ny**. 1. A gypsy. 2. The language spoken by the gypsies.—**Rom-a-ny** *adj*.

Rome-Berlin Axis. The alliance between Nazi Germany and Fascist Italy.

Ro-me-o (*roh*-mee-oh) *n*. 1. Title character in Shakespeare's *Romeo and Juliet*. 2. Hence, any romantic youth.

Rom-u-lus (*rom*-yoo-lus) *n*. Twin brother of Remus, both the legendary founders of Rome.

romp *v*. To frolic; gambol.—*n*. 1. Gambol; sport. 2. A lively, sportive girl.

romp-er *n*. 1. One who gambols. 2. [*pl*.] Combination bloomers and waist for young children.—**romp-ish** *adj*.—**romp-ish-ness** *n*.

rood *n*. A crucifix, esp. one erected on the cross-beam between the crossing and the chancel.

roof *n.* 1. The top of a house or building. 2. Covering or shelter.—*v.* To cover with a roof.—**roof·er** *n.* A mechanic who builds or repairs roofs.—**roof·ing** *n.* Material for building a roof.—**roof·less** *adj.*

rook *n.* 1. A gregarious bird of the crow family which feeds on insects. 2. A cheat; a knave. 3. A castle in chess.—*v.* To cheat; defraud.

rook·er·y *n.* [*pl.* rook·er·ies] 1. A group of nests inhabited by rooks or similar birds. 2. A breeding place for seals.

ROOK (1/14 life-size)

room *n.* 1. Space; compass. 2. A space in a building enclosed by partitions; a chamber. 3. Opportunity; occasion.—*v.* To lodge; reside.—**room·er** *n.* One who rents a room without board.—**room·ful** *n.*—**room·mate** *n.*

room·ette *n. Railroads.* Sleeping compartment designed for single occupancy.

rooming house. A lodging place where rooms are rented without meals.

room·y *adj.* Spacious; large.—**room·i·ly** *adv.* —**room·i·ness** *n.*

roost *n.* A beam upon which fowls perch.—*v.* To occupy a roost; perch; alight.

roos·ter *n.* A male domestic fowl; a cock.

root *n.* 1. The part of a plant fixed in the earth, which absorbs the nutriment. 2. The attaching termination of any living part or organism, as the root of a tooth. 3. Cause; origin. 4. The part of a word which conveys its essential meaning. 5. *Mathematics.* That quantity which multiplied

ROOSTER (1/20 life-size)

by itself produces a given quantity. 6. *Music.* The basic tone of a chord.—*v.* 1. To fix; anchor. 2. To cheer; shout encouragingly. —**root** *adj.*—**root out.** To eradicate.

root beer. A soft drink prepared from various root extracts.

root·er *n.* 1. One who cheers enthusiastically for one side in a sports contest. 2. Anything which pulls up roots.

root·less *adj.* Having no roots; shifting; unstable.

root·let *n.* A little root.

root·y *adj.* Full of roots.—**root·i·ness** *n.*

rope (*rohp*) *n.* 1. A thick cord; a small cable. 2. A string of connected objects.—*v.* [roped; rop·ing] To lasso; to catch with a rope.

rope dancer. Acrobat who performs on a rope extended above the ground.

rop·er·y *n.* A rope-making establishment.

rop·y *adj.* Stringy; viscous; glutinous. —**rop·i·ly** *adv.* —**rop·i·ness** *n.*

Roquefort cheese. Strong white cheese with a blue mold, originally made in France.

ROSARY

ro·sa·ry (*roh*-zuh-ree) *n.* [*pl.* ro·sa·ries] 1. A string of beads on which prayers to the Virgin Mary are counted. 2. A chaplet; a garland.

rose (*rohz*) *n.* 1. A bedding, climbing, or erect shrub with thorny stems; also its fragrant flowers. 2. A rosette; a rose design. 3. A deep pink color.—*v.* [rosed; ros·ing] To redden; flush.

ro·se·ate (*roh*-zee-it) *adj.* 1. Abounding in roses. 2. Rose-colored. 3. Hence, optimistic, hopeful.—**ate·ly** *adv.*

ROSE

rose·bud *n.* A rose blossom just opening.

rose·mar·y (*rohz*-mehr-ee) *n.* [*pl.* rose·mar·ies] A fragrant evergreen shrub with pale blue flowers.

ro·sette (roh-*zet*) *n.* 1. A ribbon ornament formed to resemble a rose. 2. A design representing rose petals.

rose water. Water tinctured with rose fragrance by distillation.

rose·wood (*rohz*-wood) *n.* The wood of various South American trees which has a faint smell of roses and is used for cabinet work.

ros·in (*roz*-'n) *n.* A solid form of resin obtained by the distillation of turpentine.—**ros·in** *v.*

ros·ter (*ross*-ter) *n.* List; register.

ros·trum (*ross*-tr'm) *n.* [*pl.* ros·tra] A speaker's platform; pulpit.

ros·y (*rohz*-ee) *adj.* 1. Red; blooming; blushing. 2. Hopeful; optimistic.—**ros·i·ly** *adv.*

rot *v.* [rot·ted; rot·ting] To decay; putrefy.—*n.* 1. Putrefaction; decomposition. 2. Any of several plant and animal diseases characterized by wastage.—*interj. Slang.* Nonsense; trash.

ro·ta·ry (*roh*-tuh-ree) *adj.* 1. Turning; revolving. 2. Having rotating parts.

rotary engine. An engine deriving power from a rotating part, as a turbine.

rotary press. A large printing press, which prints from curved electrotype or stereotype plates fixed to cylinders, from which the paper is printed in a continuous sheet.

ro·tate (*roh*-tayt) *v.* [ro·tat·ed; ro·tat·ing] 1. To turn; revolve. 2. To alternate.—**ro-**

R

tate *adj.*—**ro·ta·tion** (roh-*tay*-shun) *n.*—**ro·ta·tion·al** *adj.*—**ro·ta·tor** *n.*

ro·ta·to·ry (*roh*-tuh-toh-ree) *adj.* Rotary; turning; revolving; alternating.

rote (roht) *n.* Mechanical repetition of words; automatic routine.

ro·to·gra·vure (roh-tuh-grah-*vyoor*) *n.* 1. A photo-mechanical reproduction process in which prints are obtained from a cylinder mechanically etched by a photographic screen method. 2. An illustrated newspaper supplement printed by rotogravure.

ro·tor (*roh*-ter) *n.* The part of a generator which rotates and cuts lines of force to generate voltage.

rot·ten (*rot*-'n) *adj.* 1. Putrid; decaying. 2. Unsound; treacherous. 3. Corrupt.—**rot·ten·ly** *adv.*—**rot·ten·ness** *n.*

rotten dry	rotten-planked	rotten ripe
rotten-hearted	rotten red	rotten-throated
rotten-minded	rotten rich	rotten-timbered

rot·ten·stone *n.* A soft stone used for polishing certain metals.

rot·ter *n. Slang.* A worthless person.

ro·tund (roh-*tund*) *adj.* 1. Plump; chubby. 2. Spherical; round.—**ro·tun·di·ty** *n.*—**ro·tund·ly** *adv.*—**ro·tund·ness** *n.*

ro·tun·da (roh-*tun*-duh) *n.* A round building or auditorium.

rou·ble (roo-b'l) *n.* Also **rub·le.** Basic unit of the Russian monetary system.

rou·é (rooh-*ay*) *n.* A rake; a sensualist.

rouge (*roozh*) *n.* 1. A cosmetic prepared to give color to the cheeks. 2. A polishing powder made of ground ferric oxide.—**rouge** *v.* [rouged; roug·ing].

rough (*ruf*) *adj.* 1. Uneven; not level; rugged. 2. Unpolished; unworked; crude. 3. Wild; boisterous; untamed. 4. Harsh; gruff.—*n.* 1. State of being coarse or unfinished. 2. *Golf.* The area outside of the fairways.—*v.* To make rough.—**rough** *adv.*—**rough·er** *adj.*—**rough·ly** *adv.*—**rough·ness** *n.*

rough-and-ready. 1. Crude; serviceable. 2. Bluff; unpolished but straightforward.

rough-and-tumble. Unruly; rowdy; unrestrained.

rough·age (*ruf*-ij) *n.* Coarse food which adds bulk to the diet.

rough·cast *v.* 1. To form a first model without correction or polishing. 2. To cover with a coarse plaster of lime and gravel.—**rough·cast** *n.*—**rough·cast·er** *n.*

rough·dry *v.* [rough·dried; rough·dry·ing] To dry laundry without ironing.

rough·en (*ruf*-en) *v.* To make rough.

rough·hew *v.* To chop or shape without finishing.—**rough·hew·er** *n.*

rough·hewn *adj.* 1. Cut or shaped coarsely. 2. Rugged; unpolished.

rough·house *n.* Riotous behavior; disturbance; row.—*v.* [rough·housed; rough·hous·ing] —**rough·hous·er** *n.*—**rough·hous·ing** *n.*

rough·neck *n.* A rowdy; a tough.

Rough Rider. Member of a volunteer cavalry regiment organized by Theodore Roosevelt during the Spanish-American War.

rough·shod *adj.* Wearing spiked shoes.—**ride roughshod over.** To pursue a course regardless of injury to others.

rou·lette (roo-*let*) *n.* A game of chance based on the revolution of a wheel.

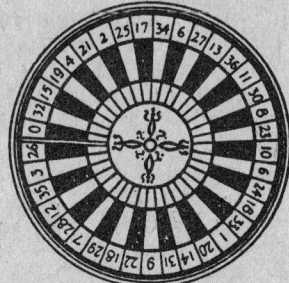
ROULETTE WHEEL

round *adj.* 1. Spherical; globular; circular. 2. Even; having no fraction left over; hence, approximate. 3. Full; open. 4. Including both ways. 'A round trip.'—*n.* 1. The act of going or passing around a circle or company. 2. A circuit of events or actions following a regular course and returning to the same point. 3. Ammunition for one firing. 4. One of a number of equal periods in a game or match. 5. *Music.* A chorus in which different voices successively join in, each beginning the song afresh. 6. A cut of beef.—*v.* 1. To make circular. 2. To move or pass around. 3. To make full.—*adv.* 1. Circularly. 2. In another direction; about. 3. Everywhere; in all directions.—*prep.* 1. On all sides; enclosing. 2. About in a circular course. —**round·ly** *adv.*—Completely; vigorously; boldly.—**round·ness** *n.*

round-arched	roundhead	round seam
round-armed	roundheaded	round-shapen
round-backed	round-heart	round-sided
round-bellied	round-horned	round-spun
round-billed	round-leaved	roundtail
round-bodied	round-limbed	round-toed
round-cornered	roundline	round top
round-crested	round-lipped	round-topped
round-eyed	round-lobed	round-trussed
round-faced	round-mouthed	round-visaged
roundfish	round-nosed	round-winged
round-fruited	round-ribbed	round-wombed
round-furrowed	round ridge	roundworm

round·a·bout *adj.* Circuitous; indirect.—*n.* 1. A merry-go-round. 2. A man's short coat. **round·a·bout·ly** *adv.*—**round·a·bout·ness** *n.*

round·ed *adj.* 1. Full; complete; balanced. 2. Spherical. 3. *Phonetics.* Pronounced with the lips.

roun·de·lay (*rown*-duh-lay) *n.* A song or poem having a frequent refrain.

round·house *n.* 1. A building in which locomotives are repaired. 2. *Slang.* A blow in which the arm describes a wide arc before striking. 3. *Baseball Slang.* A curve ball which breaks widely.

ROUNDHOUSE

round·ish *adj.* Somewhat circular.— **-ish·ness** *n.*

round robin. 1. A signed petition bearing the signatures in a circle. 2. *Sports.* A tournament in which each contestant plays every other contestant.

round-shoul·dered *adj.* Stooped; having sloping shoulders; hunched.

rounds·man *n.* A police officer who visits patrolmen on their beats.

round table. A formal discussion group or conference.—**round-table** *adj.*

round trip. A journey and return.—**round-trip** *adj.*—**round-trip·per** *n.*

round-up *n.* A herding together, esp. of cattle.

rouse (*rowz*) *v.* To stir; awaken.—**rouse** *n.* —**rous·er** *n.*—**rous·ing** *adj.*

roust·a·bout (*rowst*-uh-bowt) *n.* A dock laborer; stevedore.

rout (*rowt*) *n.* Defeat and disorderly retreat of an army.—**rout** *v.*—**rout·er** *n.*

route (*root; rowt*) *n.* Way; course.—*v.* [rout·ed; rout·ing] To direct.—**rout·er** *n.*

rou·tine (roo-*teen*) *n.* A regular course of business; habitual procedure.—**rou·tine** *adj.*

rove *v.* [roved; rov·ing] To wander; roam.

rov·er *n.* 1. A wanderer; rambler. 2. A pirate; freebooter.

row *n.* A brawl; fight.—**row** *v.*

row (*roh*) *n.* A series; an arrangement in a continued line; a file.—**row** *v.*

row (*roh*) *v.* To drive along the surface of water by means of oars.—**row** *n.*—**row·er** *n.*

row·boat *n.* A boat propelled by oars.

row·dy *n.* A hoodlum; a rough, noisy person. —**row·dy** *adj.*—**row·di·ly** *adv.*—**row·di·ness** *n.*

row·el *n.* The small sharp-pointed wheel of a rider's spur.—*v.* [row·eled; row·el·ing].

ROWEL

row·en *n.* A second cutting of hay; an aftermath.

row·lock (*roh*-lok) *n.* A hook on a boat's gunwhale in which the oar rests in rowing.

roy·al *adj.* 1. Regal; imperial; pertaining to or belonging to the crown. 2. Sumptuous; splendid.—*n. Nautical.* A square sail spread immediately above the topgallant sail. —**roy·al·ly** *adv.*

ROWLOCK

roy·al·ism *n.* Belief in monarchical government. —**roy·al·ist** *n.*—**roy·al·ist, roy·al·is·tic** *adj.*

roy·al·ty (*roy*-ul-tee) *n.* [*pl.* roy·al·ties] 1. Members of the royal house. 2. Station or quality of a monarch. 3. A percentage paid to the owner of an article, patent, or copyright for its use.

rub *v.* [rubbed; rub·bing] 1. To apply friction to; scour; polish. 2. To smear all over; spread over.—*n.* 1. Friction. 2. Difficulty; cause of uneasiness.—**rub out.** 1. To erase. 2. *Slang.* To kill.

rub·ber (*rub*-er) *n.* 1. One that rubs. 2. An elastic substance obtained from the milky fluid of various tropical trees. 3. A similar product synthesized from various organic substances. 4. An eraser. 5. *Card Playing.* A contest completed when one side wins two games out of a possible three. 6. [*pl.*] Overshoes used for protection against rain, snow, etc.—**rub·ber** *adj.*—**rub·ber·y** *adj.*

rubber-coated	rubber-lined	rubberproofed
rubber-covered	rubberneck	rubber-soled
rubber-faced	rubbernose	rubber-tired

rub·ber·ize *v.* [rub·ber·ized; -iz·ing] To impregnate with rubber for waterproofing, etc.

rubber plant. A house plant of the fig family with oblong, glossy leaves.

rubber stamp. 1. A rubber form by which an impression may be repeatedly made. 2. One who slavishly accepts and transmits the orders of another.—**rubber-stamp** *v.*

rub·bish (*rub*-ish) *n.* Garbage; refuse.

rub·ble *n.* Broken bricks, stones, etc., of irregular shapes.—**rub·ble** *adj.*—**rub·bly** *adj.*

rub·ble·work *n.* Walls or masonry built of rubble.

rub-down *n. Colloquial.* A massage.

rube (*roob*) *n. Slang.* A person living in a rural section; a provincial person; hayseed.

Ru·bi·con *n.* A small river between Italy and Cisalpine Gaul, which Julius Caesar crossed in defiance of orders, thus precipitating the war which brought him to power.—**cross the Rubicon.** To take an irrevocable step.

ru·bi·cund (*roo*-bih-kund) *adj.* Ruddy; blood-red.—**ru·bi·cun·di·ty** *n.*

ru·bid·i·um (roo-*bid*-ee-um) *n.* A metallic element belonging to the group of alkali metals. (*Symbol:* Rb).

ru·bric (*roo*-brik) *n.* 1. The directions and rules for the conduct of service in prayer books, formerly printed in red. 2. A prescribed formula.—**ru·bri·cal** *adj.*—**-cal·ly** *adv.*

ru·by (*roo*-bee) *n.* [*pl.* ru·bies] A crystallized gem of various shades of red, second to the diamond in hardness and, usually, value.

ruche (*roosh*) *n.* Fluted net, lace, silk, etc., used as trimming for dresses.—**ruch·ing** *n.*

ruck *v.* To wrinkle; crease.

rud·der *n.* The instrument by which a ship is steered. —**rud·der·less** *adj.*

rud·dy *adj.* Reddish; of a healthy flesh color.

rude (*rood*) *adj.* 1. Discourteous; impolite. 2. Rough; crude.—**rude·ly** *adv.*—**rude·ness** *n.*

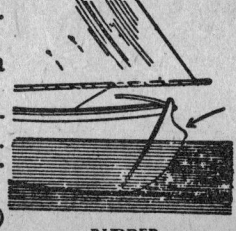

RUDDER

ru·di·ment (*roo*-dih-m'nt) *n.* Elementary notion; first step to any branch of knowledge.—**ru·di·ment·al** *adj.*

R

ru·di·men·ta·ry (roo-dih-*men*-tuh-ree) *adj.* Embryonic; undeveloped; basic.—**ru·di·men·ta·ri·ly** *adv.*—**ru·di·men·ta·ri·ness** *n.*

rue (*roo*) *v.* [rued; ru·ing] To regret; repent.

rue·ful (*roo*-ful) *adj.* 1. Sorrowful; regretful. 2. Woeful; pitiable.—**-ful·ly** *adv.*—**-ful·ness** *n.*

ruff *n.* 1. A stiff disk-shaped collar fashionable in Elizabethan times. 2. A ruffle; anything plaited or crimped. 3. Any of several birds having their neck feathers in the shape of a ruff. 4. *Machinery.* A ridge on a shaft to prevent endwise play or motion.

RUFF

ruf·fi·an (*ruf*-ee-un) *n.* A brutal thug; a tough. —**ruf·fi·an** *adj.*—**ruf·fi·an·ism** *n.*— **-an·ly** *adv.*

ruf·fle (*ruf*-'l) *n.* 1. A frilly pleat or crimp. 2. A soft roll of drums.—*v.* [ruf·fled; ruf·fling] 1. To disorder; disturb; ripple; agitate. 2. To adorn with ruffles; plait.—**ruf·fly** *adj.*

ru·fous (*roo*-fus) *adj.* Reddish; yellowish red.

rug *n.* A floor covering, usually of heavy fabric.

Rug·by (*rug*-bee) *n.* A type of British football game similar to soccer.

rug·ged (*rug*-id) *adj.* 1. Craggy; uneven; rough; wrinkled. 2. Harsh; austere. 3. Violent; rude. 4. Powerful; sturdy; robust. 5. *Colloquial.* Difficult; trying.—**rug·ged·ly** *adv.*—**rug·ged·ness** *n.*

ru·in (*roo*-in) *n.* 1. Destruction; downfall; decay; financial disaster. 2. Moral degradation. 3. [*pl.*] Relics and remains of ancient or destroyed buildings, etc.—**ru·in** *v.*—**ru·in·a·ble** *adj.*—**ru·in·a·tion** *n.*—**ru·in·er** *n.*

ru·in·ous (*roo*-in-us) *adj.* Promoting ruin; disastrous; pernicious.—**ru·in·ous·ly** *adv.*—**ru·in·ous·ness** *n.*

rule (*rool*) *n.* 1. Control; government; authority. 2. An established working principle; precept; law. 3. A ruler; a tool for measuring or drawing straight lines. 4. *Printing.* A line used to separate headings, columns, etc.—*v.* 1. To govern. 2. To mark with straight lines. 3. To lay down an order. 'The chairman ruled the delegate out of order.'

rule of thumb. A principle arrived at practically, rather than scientifically.

rul·er *n.* 1. One that rules. 2. A straight-edge tool for measuring.

rules of the road. *Nautical.* The body of laws governing maritime traffic.

rul·ing (*rool*-ing) *n.* 1. A decision or law handed down by authority. 2. A marking with lines.—*adj.* Having control.

rum *n.* 1. An alcoholic spirit made from sugar cane products. 2. Any intoxicating liquor.

rum·ba, rhum·ba (*rum*-buh) *n.* 1. A popular Latin-American dance. 2. The distinctively syncopated music for the rumba.

rum·ble (*rum*-b'l) *v.* [rum·bled; rum·bling] To make a heavy, protracted noise, as of a roll of thunder.—**rum·ble** *n.*—**rum·bler** *n.*

rumble seat. An outside seat which opens at the rear of an automobile.

ru·mi·nant (*roo*-mih-n'nt) *n.* An animal which chews its cud.—**ru·mi·nant** *adj.*

ru·mi·nate (*roo*-mih-nayt) *v.* [ru·mi·nat·ed; -nat·ing] 1. To chew the cud. 2. To muse; be contemplative.—**ru·mi·na·tion** *n.*—**ru·mi·na·tive** *adj.*—**ru·mi·na·tive·ly** *adj.*—**ru·mi·na·tor** *n.*

rum·mage (*rum*-ij) *v.* [rum·maged; rum·mag·ing] To ransack; to search or explore feverishly.—**rum·mage** *n.*—**rum·mag·er** *n.*

rummage sale. A sale of miscellaneous odds and ends, contributed articles, etc.

rum·my *n.* [*pl.* rum·mies] 1. A kind of card game played by two or more persons. 2. *Slang.* A drunkard.

ru·mor (*roo*-mer) *n.* 1. A report or story circulated with no proof of authenticity. 2. Popular talk.—**ru·mor** *v.*

rump *n.* 1. Of an animal, the end of the backbone and the adjacent parts. 2. The buttocks. 3. The fag end of anything.

rum·ple (*rum*-p'l) *v.* [rum·pled; rum·pling] To wrinkle; disarrange; tousle.—**rum·ple** *n.*

rum·pus (*rum*-p'ss) *n.* A fuss; disturbance.

rum-run·ner (*rum*-run-er) One who smuggles liquor into a country.—**rum-run·ning** *n.*

run *v.* [ran; run·ning] 1. To move swiftly; rush. 2. To function, as a watch or motor. 3. To contend for a public office. 4. To chase; pursue; trace. 5. To flow; to become fluid. 6. To discharge a fluid. 7. To extend. 'The track does not run that far.' 8. To thrust; to stab. 9. To continue in any specified fashion. 10. To occur or recur in a specified quality. 'The class grades run higher this year.' 11. To smuggle. 12. *Colloquial.* To manage; to control.—*n.* 1. Act or instance of running; distance run. 2. A course; progress; flow; passage. 3. A continuous series. 4. The general or usual type. 'The common run of authors.' 5. A section of land where animals are allowed to run. 6. A raveled streak in cloth, as in silk stockings. 7. A pressing demand. 'A run on a bank.' 8. Period of operation, as of a mill.

run·a·bout *n.* 1. An habitual gadabout. 2. A light, sporty roadster.

run·a·gate *n.* 1. A fugitive, esp. a renegade. 2. A vagabond.

run·a·round *n.* Evasion; avoidance of coming to the point.

run·a·way *n.* A fugitive.—**run·a·way** *adj.*

run-down *adj.* 1. Dilapidated; depreciated in value. 2. Stopped, as a clock or a machine. 3. Physically depleted; out of health.—**run down.** 1. *Slang.* To deprecate; find fault with. 2. To knock down and drive over.

run in. *Slang.* To arrest; take into custody. —**run-in** *n.* 1. A quarrel; altercation. 2. A secondary entry.

run on. 1. To chatter incessantly. 2. *Printing.* To continue without a paragraph break. —**run-on** *n. & adj.*

rune (*roon*) *n.* A letter of the ancient Scandinavian, German, or Anglo-Saxon alphabet.—**runic** *adj.*

rung *n.* A round of a chair; a horizontal step of a ladder.

run·let (*run*-lit) *n.* Also **run·nel** (*run*-'l). A rivulet; streamlet.

run·ner (*run*-er) *n.* 1. A competitor in a race. 2. A messenger or errand boy. 3. A support or groove on which a thing runs or slides. 4. A speedy ship for hauling contraband.

RUNGS

run·ner-up *n.* A second-place winner in a race or contest.—**run·ner-up** *adj.*

run·ning (*run*-ing) *n.* 1. Act of rushing. 2. Competition; contest.—*adj.* 1. Continuous; successive. 2. Discharging liquid. 3. Relating to a run.

running board. The low platform on the side of an automobile serving as fender and step.

running gear. *Nautical.* All lines and tackle of a ship that are not permanently fixed.

runt *n.* 1. A small or underdeveloped animal. 2. A dwarf.—**runt·i·ness** *n.*—**runt·y** *adj.* [runt·i·er; runt·i·est].

run·way (*run*-way) *n.* 1. A track beaten down by animals. 2. An area smoothed off to accommodate vehicles, esp. a roadway for airplanes in taking off.

ru·pee (roo-*pee*) *n.* A silver coin current in India and some East Indian islands.

rup·ture (*rup*-cher) *v.* [rup·tured; rup·tur·ing] 1. To break; breach; part. 2. To cause hernia.—**rup·ture** *n.* Hernia.—**rup·tur·a·ble** *adj.*

ru·ral (*roor*-ul) *adj.* Rustic; distinguished from urban.—**ru·ral·ism** *n.* 1. Being rural. 2. A countrified idiom.—**ru·ral·ist** *n.*—**ru·ral·ly** *adv.*

Rural Free Delivery. The division of the Federal postal system handling rural mail.

ruse (*rooz*) *n.* A trick; artifice; stratagem.

rush *v.* 1. To hurry; move with undue eagerness; lunge; drive forward. 2. *Slang.* To court ardently.—**rush** *n.*—**rush·er** *n.*

rush *n.* 1. A family of grasslike plants abundant on moist ground in temperate zones.

2. [*pl.*] *Motion Picture Slang.* A series of recent shots run off for appraisal, cutting, etc.

rush-bordered	rushland	rush-seated
rush-bottomed	rush-leaved	rush-stemmed
rush-floored	rushlight	rush-strewn
rush-ringed	rush-margined	rush-woven

rush·y *adj.* [rush·i·er; rush·i·est] Like, made of, or covered with rushes.—**rush·i·ness** *n.*

rusk *n.* A sweetish, dry kind of toasted biscuit.

rus·set *adj.* Reddish brown.—*n.* 1. A roughskinned, brownish apple. 2. A rich brown color.

Russian dressing. A salad dressing of mayonnaise and chili sauce.

rust *n.* 1. The oxide coating formed on iron surfaces. 2. A parasitic fungus which attacks grains, pine trees, etc.—**rust** *v.*—**rust·a·ble** *adj.*

rust-cankered	rust fungus	rust-resistant
rust-complexioned	rustlike	rust-stained
rust-eaten	rustproof	rust-worn

rus·tic (*rus*-tik) *adj.* Also **rus·ti·cal.** Countrified; rural; bucolic.—**rus·tic** *n.*— **-cal·ly** *adj.*

rus·ti·cate (*rus*-tih-kayt) *v.* [rus·ti·cat·ed; -cat·ing] To reside in the country; to make countrified.—**rus·ti·ca·tion** *n.*—**rus·ti·ca·tor** *n.*

rus·tic·i·ty (rus-*tih*-sih-tee) *n.* [*pl.* -ties] 1. Being rustic. 2. Crudeness; naïveness; simplicity.

rus·tle (*rus*-'l) *v.* [rus·tled; rus·tling] 1. To make a soft rattling or whispering sound. 2. To steal livestock.—*n.* A continuous sibilant sound.—**rus·tler** *n.*

rus·tling *n.* 1. The crime of stealing livestock. 2. Murmuring; crackling.—**rus·tling·ly** *adv.*

rust·y *adj.* [rust·i·er; rust·i·est] 1. Encrusted with or resembling rust. 2. *Colloquial.* Impaired through inaction or disuse; out of practice.—**rust·i·ly** *adv.*—**rust·i·ness** *n.*

rusty-branched	rusty-colored	rusty looking
rusty-coated	rusty-crowned	rusty-spotted
rusty-collared	rusty-leaved	rusty-throated

rut *n.* 1. A track or furrow cut into the soil. 2. Deeply-rooted habit; long-established routine. 3. Period of heightened sexual desire in animals.—*v.* [rut·ted; rut·ting].

ru·ta·ba·ga (roo-tuh-*bay*-guh) *n.* A large yellow turnip having a long fibrous root.

ru·the·ni·um (roo-*thee*-nee-um) *n.* A grayishwhite metal similar to, and usually associated with, platinum. (*Symbol:* Ru).

ruth·less (*rooth*-less) *adj.* Pitiless; cruel; barbarous.—**ruth·less·ly** *adv.*—**ruth·less·ness** *n.*

rut·ty *adj.* [rut·ti·er; rut·ti·est] Full of ruts or deep wheel tracks.—**rut·ti·ness** *n.*

rye *n.* 1. A grain similar to wheat. 2. The hardy annual grasslike plant producing **rye.** 3. A whisky distilled from rye.—**rye** *adj.*

R

S

Sab·bath (*sab*-uth) *n.* Weekly day of rest and worship.

sab·bat·i·cal (suh-*bat*-ih-kal) *n.* Leave of absence for rest, study, or travel, usually every seventh year.—**sab·bat·i·cal** *adj.*—**sab·bat·i·cal·ly** *adv.*

sa·ber, sa·bre (*say*-ber) *n.* Sword with broad and heavy blade, curved toward the point, especially adapted for cutting.—*v.* [sa·bered, sa·bred; sa·ber·ing, sa·bring] To strike, cut, or kill with a saber.

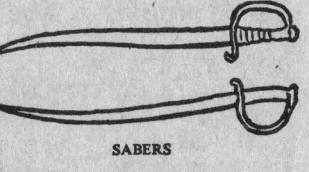

SABERS

Sa·bine (*say*-byne) *n.* One of the ancient peoples of Italy.—**Sa·bine** *adj.*

sa·ble (*say*-b'l) *n.* 1. Small fur-bearing animal found chiefly in the northern regions of Asia. 2. The lustrous, commercially valuable fur of the sable.—*adj.* Black; dark.

sa·bot (*sab*-oh) *n.* A shoe, hollowed out of wood worn by European peasants.

sab·o·tage (*sab*-uh-tahzh) *n.* Deliberate destruction or interference, especially in wartime.—*v.* [sab·o·taged; sab·o·tag·ing] To destroy maliciously.—**sab·o·teur** *n.* (sab-uh-*ter*).

SABOT

sac (*sak*) *n.* A bag or cyst in an animal or plant.

sac·cha·rin (*sak*-uh-rin) *n.* Also **sac·cha·rine.** A coal-tar derivative used as sugar substitute.—**sac·cha·rin; -rine** *adj.* Sugary; oversweet.—**sac·cha·rin·i·ty** (sak-uh-*rin*-it-tee) *n.*

sac·er·do·tal (sass-er-*doh*-tal) *adj.* Pertaining to priests or the priesthood; priestly.—**sac·er·do·tal·ism** *n.* The spirit of the priesthood.—**sac·er·do·tal·ly** *adv.*

sa·chem (*say*-chem) *n.* A chief in some North American Indian tribes.

sa·chet (sash-*ay*) *n.* A bag of powdered scent.

sack *v.* 1. To pack in a bag. 2. To loot or strip a captured place; plunder. 3. To dismiss.—*n.* 1. A large bag. 2. *Slang.* Dismissal of an employee. 'To get the sack.' 3. The plundering of a captured place. 4. A type of white wine.—*adj.* Loose-fitting. 'A sack suit.'

sack·but *n.* An ancient musical instrument much like the present-day trombone.

sack·cloth *n.* A coarse cloth or garment worn in penitential mourning.

sack·ing *n.* A coarse fabric used for bags.

sac·ra·ment (*sak*-ruh-m'nt) *n.* 1. *Theology.* Any of several solemn religious ceremonies enjoined by Christ on his followers. 2. An oath or ceremony symbolizing a covenant.—**sac·ra·men·tal** (sak-ruh-*men*-t'l) *adj.*

sa·cred (*say*-kred) *adj.* 1. Dedicated to religious use; holy; consecrated. 2. Worthy of veneration. 3. Not to be profaned or violated.—**sa·cred·ly** *adv.*—**sa·cred·ness** *n.*

sac·ri·fice (*sak*-rih-fysse) *n.* 1. Anything consecrated and offered to a god. 2. Destruction, renunciation, or loss for a definite purpose. 3. Selling of goods at a price below cost. 4. *Baseball.* A play in which, with a runner on base, the batter hits a ball, advancing the runner, while he himself is put out.—*v.* [sac·ri·ficed; sac·ri·fic·ing]—**sac·ri·fi·cial** (sak-rih-*fish*-'l) *adj.*—**sac·ri·fi·cial·ly** *adv.*

sac·ri·lege (*sak*-rih-lej) *n.* The violation or profanation of sacred things.—**sac·ri·le·gious** (sak-rih-*lih*-jus) *adj.*—**sac·ri·le·gious·ly** *adv.*

sac·ris·tan (*sak*-riss-tan) *n.* An officer of the church in charge of the sacristy.

sac·ris·ty (*sak*-riss-tee) *n.* The vestry; a church room where sacred vessels, altar cloths, vestments, etc., are kept.

sac·ro·sanct *adj.* Most holy; untouchable.—**sac·ro·sanc·ti·ty, sac·ro·sanct·ness** *n.*

sad *adj.* 1. Sorrowful; melancholy. 2. Downcast; gloomy. 3. *Slang.* Second-rate.—**sad·ly** *adv.*—**sad·ness** *n.*

sad·den *v.* To make melancholy or depressed.

sad·dle (*sad*-'l) *n.* 1. A seat, usually leather-covered, used on horses, bicycles, etc. 2. A ridge connecting two hills. 3. *Cooking.* The entire upper back, including both loins, of mutton, venison, hare, etc.—*v.* [sad·dled; sad·dling] 1. To put a saddle on. 2. To burden.

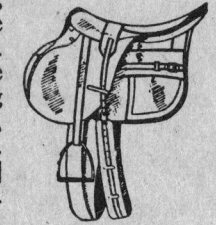

SADDLE

sad·dle·bag *n.* A leather bag strapped on either side of a saddle.

sad·dle·bow *n.* The pommel or peak of a saddle.

sad·dler *n.* Maker or vender of saddles or other equestrian equipment.

Sad·du·cee (*sad*-yoo-see) *n.* One of a sect or party among the ancient Hebrews.

sad·ism (*sad*-izm; *sayd*-izm) *n.* 1. *Psychology.* Inflicting pain or torture on the object of one's love to obtain sexual gratification. 2. Extreme cruelty.—**sad·ist** *n.* & *adj.*—**sa·dis·tic** (suh-*diss*-tik) *adj.*—**sa·dis·ti·cal·ly** *adv.*

sa·fa·ri (suh-*fah*-ree) *n.* An expedition, usually a hunting trip in Africa.—**sa·fa·ri** *v.*

safe *adj.* 1. Secure; protected; without hazard. 2. Trustworthy.—*n.* A strong metal receptacle for valuables.—**safe·ly** *adv.*—**safe·ness** *n.*

safe conduct. Also **safe-conduct** *n.* A pass; a warrant permitting unmolested procedure, especially through enemy areas in wartime.

safe·guard *n.* A protection; a precautionary measure.—*v.* To protect; to care for.

safe·keep·ing *n.* Care; protective holding.

safe·ty *n.* 1. Protection; defense; security. 2. Device on a firearm to prevent firing.

safety belt	safety lamp	safety valve
safety bicycle	safetypin	safety vault
safety glass	safety razor	safety zone

saf·fron (*saf*-ron) *n.* 1. A type of purple-flowered crocus. 2. *Cooking.* A yellow coloring and flavoring agent made from the dried stigmas of this plant.—*adj.* Yellow.

sag *v.* [sagged; sag·ging] 1. To sink or droop. 2. To become depressed.—*n.* A drooping; a sunken place.

sa·ga (*sah*-guh) *n.* 1. An ancient heroic Norse legend. 2. A family chronicle of several generations, as *Forsyte Saga.*

sa·ga·cious (suh-*gay*-shus) *adj.* Wise; shrewd; acute.—**sa·ga·cious·ly** *adv.*—**sa·ga·cious·ness, sa·gac·i·ty** (suh-*gas*-ih-tee) *n.*

sag·a·more (*sag*-uh-mohr) *n.* A chief or leader among some North American Indian tribes.

sage (*sayj*) *n.* 1. A shrublike herb of the salvia family, used for flavoring meats, etc. 2. Sage-brush.

sage *adj.* Wise; prudent; judicious.—*n.* A wise man.—**sage·ly** *adv.*—**sage·ness** *n.*

sage·brush *n.* A low shrub which grows in the dry soil of western U.S. plains.

Sag·it·ta·ri·us (saj-ih-*tair*-ee-us) *n. Astronomy.* "The Archer," a constellation usually depicted as a centaur with bow and arrow.

sa·go (*say*-go) *n.* 1. A palm tree native to the East Indian archipelago. 2. Starch produced from the sago palm.

Sa·ha·ra (suh-*hah*-ruh). Desert in North Africa. Area: 3½ million sq. mi.

sa·hib (*sah*-ib) *n.* 1. A title used by natives of India addressing Europeans. 2. [*cap.*] Master.

said *adj.* Previously mentioned; heretofore stated. 'The said defendant.'

sail *n.* 1. A large cloth, usually canvas, spread to the wind to propel a vessel though water. 2. The arm of a windmill. 3. A voyage.—*v.* 1. To propel a ship by sails, steam, etc. 2. To travel. 3. To begin a voyage. 4. To soar; to fly easily through air. —**sail·a·ble** *adj.*

SAILS

sailboat	sail-drill	sail-propelled
sail-borne	sail flying	sailroom
sailcloth	sailmaker	sail-stretched
sail-dotted	sailplane	sail-winged

sail·fish *n.* A large salt-water fish, with a high dorsal fin.

sail·or (*sayl*-er) *n.* 1. A seaman, either merchant or naval. 2. A round, stiff straw hat with a flat crown.—**sail·or·ly** *adv. & adj.*

saint *n.* A holy or godlike person. —**saint·ed** *adj.* 1. Canonized. 2. Pious; holy.—**saint·hood** *n.*—**saint·li·ness** *n.*—**saint·ly** *adj.* [saint·li·er; saint·li·est].

SAILFISH (1/40 life-size)

Saint Bernard. A large, long-haired dog originally bred at Saint Bernard's Hospice for rescuing travelers lost in the Alps.

Saint Elmo's Fire. A discharge of static electricity appearing as a flame on ships' mastheads during stormy weather.

SAINT BERNARD (1/60 life-size)

Saint Nicholas. The patron saint of children, represented as the bearer of gifts at Christmas; Santa Claus.

Saint Valentine's Day. A day (February 14) devoted to the exchange of love tokens.

Saint Vitus's dance. Chorea; a nervous disease, usually in childhood, characterized by involuntary muscular spasms.

sake (sayk) *n.* 1. Purpose; motive. 2. Benefit; welfare. 'For my sake.'

sa·ke (*sah*-kee) *n.* Japanese fermented drink made from rice.

sal *n.* 1. *Chemistry.* Salt. 2. A tree of India, valuable for its close-grained wood.

sa·laam (suh-*lahm*) *n.* A ceremonious salutation common in the Far East.—*v.* To bow low.

sal·a·ble (*sayl*-uh-b'l) *adj.* Able to be sold.

sa·la·cious (suh-*lay*-shus) *adj.* Indecent; lustful; lewd.— **-cious·ly** *adv.*— **-cious·ness** *n.*

sal·ad (*sal*-ud) *n.* 1. A variety of cold vegetables and lettuce with a dressing, sometimes with fish or meat added. 2. Any of several salad herbs, esp. lettuce.

sal·a·man·der (*sal*-uh-man-der) *n.* 1. An amphibious reptile, with lizard-like form. 2. *Mythology.* An animal capable of living in fire. 3. An old-fashioned cooking utensil.

sa·la·mi (suh-*lah*-mee) *n.* Highly seasoned, sausage-shaped meat delicacy.

SALAMANDER (1/4 life-size)

sal·a·ry (*sal*-uh-ree) *n.* Payment for services fig-

S

ured on weekly periods or longer, as differentiated from wages, which are reckoned on an hourly basis.—**sal·a·ried** *adj*.

sale *n*. 1. Exchange of property for a sum of money. 2. Opportunity to sell. 3. The offering of goods at reduced prices.

sales basement	salespeople	sales tax
salescheck	salesperson	saleswoman
sales clerk	sales resistance	sales work
saleslady	salesroom	sales yard

sale·a·ble, saleability. *Variant spelling* of **sal·able, salability.**

sales·man *n*. [*pl*. -men] A vender; one whose work is selling a commodity, usually in a specified territory or store.—**sales·man·ship** *n*. The technique and skills employed in selling.

sal·i·cyl·ate (suh-*liss*-ih-layt) *n*. Any of various salts used as sedatives.—**salicylic acid.** A compound used to relieve pains and reduce fever, as well as in the manufacture of dyes.

sa·li·ent (*say*-lee-ent) *adj*. 1. Conspicuous; prominent. 2. Projecting outward.—*n. Military*. A projection or bulge of an army's position toward the enemy lines.—**sa·li·ent·ly** *adv*.

sa·line (*say*-lyne) *adj*. Salty; consisting of or containing salt.—**sa·lin·i·ty** (suh-*lin*-ih-tee) *n*.

sa·li·va (suh-*ly*-vuh) *n*. Spit; spittle; the mildly alkaline fluid secreted in the mouth.—**sa·li·va·ry** *adj*.—**sa·li·vate** *v*.—**sa·li·va·tion** *n*.

sal·low (*sal*-oh) *adj*. Yellowish; or a pale, sickish color.—**sal·low·ish** *adj*.—**sal·low·ness** *n*.

sal·ly *v*. [sal·lied; sal·ly·ing] To rush out; to dart or burst forth.—*n*. 1. A sudden eruption. 2. A burst of intellectual fancy or wit.

sal·ma·gun·di *n*. A hodgepodge; a miscellany.

sal·mi *n*. A stew or ragout, esp. of game.

sal·mon (*sam*-un) *n*. A pink-fleshed fish, large and gamy, which abounds in the North Atlantic and Pacific oceans.—**salmon trout.** A freshwater fish resembling the salmon in size.

sa·lon (sal-*on*) *n*. 1. A drawing room. 2. A fashionable assemblage. 3. A room where works of art are exhibited.

sa·loon (suh-*loon*) *n*. 1. A barroom; a tavern. 2. A dining and recreation room aboard ship.

sal·si·fy (*sal*-sih-fee) *n*. An edible chicorylike herb.

salt *n*. 1. Sodium chloride, a white crystalline substance used to season and preserve food. (*Symbol*: NaCl). 2. *Chemistry*. A compound formed by substituting a metallic element for hydrogen in an acid. 3. Savor; flavor. 4. *Colloquial*. A sailor, esp. an old seadog.—*v*. To season or preserve with salt.—**salt away.** To save or invest.—**salt·cellar** *n*. A vessel for holding table salt.—**salt down.** To preserve.—**salt·er** *n*.—**salt·i·ness** *n*.—**salt·ish** *adj*.—**salt·y** *adj*.

salt box	salt house	salt pit
salt-cured	saltmaster	salt shaker
salt-edged	saltmouth	salt works

salt·pe·ter, salt·pe·tre *n*. Potassium nitrate, used in gunpowder and for preserving foods.

sa·lu·bri·ous (suh-*lyoo*-bree-us) *adj*. Healthful; wholesome.—**sa·lu·bri·ous·ly** *adv*.

sal·u·tar·y (*sal*-yoo-tehr-ee) *adj*. Beneficial; curative.—**sal·u·tar·i·ly** *adv*.—**sal·u·tar·i·ness** *n*.

sal·u·ta·tion (sal-yoo-*tay*-sh'n) *n*. 1. A greeting by gesture or word. 2. The opening words of a letter, as "Dear Sir."

sa·lu·ta·to·ri·an (sal-yoo-tuh-*toh*-ree-un) *n*. The student who gives the opening oration at commencement.—**sa·lu·ta·to·ry** *n*. & *adj*.

sa·lute (suh-*loot*) *n*. 1. Greeting. 2. A symbolic gesture made with the arm or by a bow. 3. *Military*. **a.** A mark of respect paid to a superior by raising the hand, rifle, etc., in a prescribed manner. **b.** The ceremonial firing of guns, presenting of arms, dipping of colors, etc.—*v*. [sa·lut·ed; sa·lut·ing].

sal·vage (*sal*-vidj) *v*. [sal·vaged; sal·vag·ing] 1. To save a portion of goods or investments from loss or failure. 2. *Nautical*. To return a damaged ship or its cargo to port for a reconditioning or sale.—*n*. 1. Insurance payment for loss or destruction, esp. of ships. 2. Wreckage reclaimed after a disaster.—**sal·vag·er** *n*.

sal·va·tion (sal-*vay*-sh'n) *n*. 1. Preservation; deliverance. 2. *Theology*. Redemption from sin.

salve (*sav, sahv*) *n*. 1. An ointment. 2. A balm.—*v*. [salved; salv·ing] 1. To apply balm to. 2. To soothe; ease.

sal·ver (*sal*-ver) *n*. A small tray.

sal·vi·a (*sal*-vee-uh) *n*. A family of plants, some bearing scarlet flowers; sage.

sal·vo (*sal*-voh) *n*. 1. Concentrated artillery fire. 2. Cheers or applause of a crowd.

sa·mar·i·tan (suh-*mair*-ih-t'n) *n*. 1. A charitable person. 2. [*cap*.] Native of Samaria, ancient holy city.—**sa·mar·i·tan, Sa·mar·i·tan** *adj*.

Sam·ar·kand (sam-er-*kand*). City of central Asiatic Russia, noted for its silk, cotton, etc.

same *adj*. Identical; equivalent.—**same·ness** *n*. 1. Identity. 2. Monotony.

sam·i·sen *n. Music*. A Japanese stringed instrument.

sam·ite (*sam*-yte) *n*. A rich silk material interwoven or embroidered with gold.

SAMISEN

Sa·mo·a (suh-*moh*-uh). Archipelago of 14 islands in the southern Pacific.—**Sa·mo·an** *n*. Inhabitant of Samoa.—**Sa·mo·an** *adj*.

Sa·mos (*say*-mus). Greek island in the Aegean Sea.

Sam·o·thrace (*sam*-uh-thrayss). Island in northern Aegean Sea.—**Sam·o·thra·cian** *adj*.

sam·o·var (*sam*-uh-vahr) *n*. Russian tea urn.

SAMOVAR

samp *n*. Hominy; grits.

sam·pan (*sam*-pan) *n*. A light boat used in the Far East, often as a dwelling.

sam·ple (*sam*-p'l) *n.* 1. An example. 2. Specimen.—*v.* [sam·pled; sam·pling] To test by examination of a small portion.—**sam·pler** *n.*

sam·pler *n.* A piece of embroidery designed to demonstrate skill in needlework.

sam·u·rai (*sam*-uh-rye) *n.* Hereditary class of Japanese warriors and minor nobles.—**sam·u·rai** *adj.*

san·a·tive (*san*-uh-tiv) *adj.* Healing; curing.

san·a·to·ri·um (san-uh-*tor*-ee-um) *n.* [*pl.* san·a·to·ri·ums, -ia] A hospital or rest home offering special treatment.

Sancho Panza. A character in Cervantes' *Don Quixote;* a shrewd, robust peasant.

sanc·ti·fy (*sank*-tih-fy) *v.* [sant·ti·fied; sanc·ti·fy·ing] 1. To hallow; to consecrate. 2. To purify; to absolve. 3. To make valid.—**sanc·ti·fi·ca·tion** *n.*—**sanc·ti·fied** *adj.*—**sanc·ti·fi·er** *n.*

sanc·ti·mo·ni·ous (sank-tih-*moh*-nee-us) *adj.* Pretending holiness; falsely pious.—**sanc·ti·mon·i·ous·ly** *adv.*— -**ous·ness** *n.*—**sanc·ti·mo·ny** *n.*

sanc·tion (*sank*-sh'n) *n.* 1. Formal approval or ratification. 2. Enforcement of international obligations solemnly undertaken by different nations.—*v.* To ratify; to approve.

sanc·ti·ty (*sank*-tih-tee) *n.* [*pl.* -ties] Sacredness.

sanc·tu·ar·y (*sank*-tyoo-ehr-ee) *n.* [*pl.* -ies] A consecrated place; a refuge.

sanc·tum (*sank*-tum) *n.* A private retreat; a sacred place.

sand *n.* 1. Fine particles of stone. 2. [*pl.*] A beach. 3. [*pl.*] Duration of life, as the sands of time. 4. *Slang.* Pluck; courage.—*v.* 1. To sprinkle. 2. To rub smooth with sand; to sandpaper.—**sand·er** *n.*—**sand·i·ness** *n.*

san·dal (*san*-d'l) *n.* 1. A shoe consisting of a sole laced to the foot; a light slipper. 2. A half rubber overshoe.

san·dal·wood *n.* A strong-scented East Indian wood, used in cabinets.

SANDAL (def. 1)

sand·bag *n.* A sack filled with sand, used in fortification, as ballast, etc.—*v.* [-bagged; -bag·ging] To strike or cover with sandbags.—**sand·bag·ger** *n.*

sand·man *n.* Folklore figure who sprinkles sand on children's eyes to make them sleep.

sand·pa·per *n.* A heavy paper with an abrasive surface.—*v.* To smooth with sandpaper.

sand·piper *n.* Small bird living near streams.

sand·wich (*sand*-wich) *n.* Sliced bread spread with filling.—*v.* To squeeze in.

sandwich man. One who carries a double advertising board in front and back.

sand·y *adj.* [sand·i·er; sand·i·est] 1. Covered with sand. 2. Unstable; shifting. 3. Yellowish; blond.

SANDPIPER

sane *adj.* 1. Mentally sound. 2. Reasonable; level-headed.—**sane·ly** *adv.*—**sane·ness** *n.*

San·for·ize *v.* To preshrink fabric by a trade-marked process.—**san·for·ized** *adj.*

sang-froid (sang-*frwah*) *n.* Coolness; composure.

san·gui·nar·y (*sang*-guih-nehr-ee) *adj.* 1. Bloody; murderous. 2. Bloodthirsty.—**san·gui·nar·i·ly** *adv.*—**san·gui·nar·i·ness** *n.*

san·guine (*sang*-gwin) *adj.* 1. Confident; optimistic. 2. Cheerful; warm; ardent. 3. Blood red.—**san·guine·ly** *adv.*—**san·guine·ness** *n.*—**san·guin·e·ous** *adv.*

san·i·tar·i·an (san-ih-*tayr*-ee-an) *n.* A supporter of health measures.—*adj.* Pertaining to health.

san·i·tar·i·um (san-ih-*tayr*-ee-um) *n.* [*pl.* -i·a; -i·ums]. An institution for patients suffering from mental or physical ailments.

san·i·tar·y (*san*-ih-tehr-ee) *adj.* Hygienic; clean; pertaining to health.—*n.* [*pl.* -ies] A water closet.—**san·i·ta·ri·ly** *adv.*

san·i·ta·tion *n.* The adoption of hygienic measures to promote the health of the community.

san·i·ty (*san*-ih-tee) *n.* Mental normality.

San Juan (san-*wahn*). Capital of Puerto Rico.

sank. *Past tense* of **sink.**

sans (*sanz*) *prep. Archaic.* Without.

sans·culotte (sanz-kuh-*lot*) *n.* A radical; a revolutionist, originally in the French Revolution.—**sans·cu·lot·tic, -lot·tish** *adj.*—**sans·cu·lot·tism** *n.*

san·se·vi·e·ri·a (san-seh-vee-*ee*-ree-uh) *n.* Plant of the lily family with sword-shaped leaves.

San·skrit (*san*-skrit) *n.* Ancient Aryan language of the Hindus, believed to be the source of the Indo-European languages.

sans-ser·if (san-*sehr*-if) *n.* A form of printing type without ornamentation or serifs.

San·ta Claus (*san*-tuh klawz) *n.* A legendary, kindly old man in red costume and white beard who distributes gifts at Christmas.

sap *n.* 1. The juice of a plant. 2. Any life-fluid. 3. *Slang.* A fool; a simpleton.—*v.* [sapped; sap·ping] To drain; to suck dry.

sap *v.* 1. *Military.* To dig underground toward the enemy. 2. To weaken or wear away.—*n.* An underground digging beyond a trench, usually toward the enemy.

sap·head *n. Colloquial.* A slow-witted person; a fool.—**sap·head·ed** *adj.*

sa·pi·ent (*say*-pee-ent) *adj.* Wise; discerning.—**sa·pi·ence, sa·pi·en·cy** *n.*—**sa·pi·ent·ly** *adv.*

sap·ling *n.* 1. A young tree. 2. A young person.

sa·pon·i·fy (suh-*pon*-ih-fy) *v.* [sa·pon·i·fied; sa·pon·i·fy·ing] To make into soap.—**sa·pon·i·fi·ca·tion** *n.*

sap·per *n. Military.* A soldier trained in the methods of underground infiltration.

sap·phire (*saf*-yre) *n.* A precious stone of a brilliant blue.—*adj.* Deep blue.

sap·py *adj.* [sap·pi·er; sap·pi·est] 1. Copiously fluid. 2. *Slang.* Foolish.

S

sap·suck·er *n.* A type of small woodpecker.

Sar·a·cen (*sair*-uh-s'n) *n.* Name given to Mohammedans during the medieval period.—**Sar·a·cen·ic, Sar·a·cen·i·cal** *adj.*

sar·casm (*sahr*-kazm) *n.* 1. Irony; satire. 2. Caustic criticism.—**sar·cas·tic** *adj.*—**sar·cas·ti·cal·ly** *adv.*

sar·coph·a·gus (sahr-*kof*-uh-guhss) *n.* [*pl.* -gi, -gus·es] A stone coffin or tomb.

sar·dine (sahr-*deen*) *n.* A small edible fish of the herring family.

sar·don·ic (sahr-*don*-ik) *adj.* Derisive; mocking. —**sar·don·i·cal·ly** *adv.*—**sar·don·i·cism** *n.*

sar·do·nyx (*sahr*-duh-niks) *n.* A semiprecious variety of onyx.

sa·rong (suh-*rong*) *n.* A draped garment worn by both sexes in the Malay Archipelago.

sar·sa·pa·ril·la (sahrss-puh-*ril*-uh) *n.* 1. A tonic prepared from the roots of the tropical greenbriars. 2. A soft drink.

sar·to·ri·al (sahr-*tor*-ee-ul) *adj.* Pertaining to dress; tailored.—**sar·to·ri·al·ly** *adv.*

sash *n.* 1. A band or ribbon usually worn around the waist. 2. A window frame; the movable portion of a window.

sas·sa·fras (*sass*-uh-frass) *n.* 1. An aromatic North American tree. 2. The root bark used in commercial preparations.

sat. *Past tense* of **sit.**

Sa·tan (*say*-t'n) *n.* The devil; the spirit or symbol of evil. —**sa·tan·ic, sa·tan·i·cal** *adj.* —**sa·tan·i·cal·ly** *adv.*

sat·chel *n.* A small handbag.

SASSAFRAS

sate (sayt) *v.* [sat·ed; sat·ing] 1. To surfeit; to glut. 2. To satisfy fully.

sa·teen (sat-*teen*) *n.* A glossy cotton fabric resembling satin.

sat·el·lite (*sat*-uh-lyte) *n.* 1. A small planet revolving around a larger one; a moon. 2. A subservient follower.—*adj.* Subordinate.

sa·ti·a·ble (*say*-shuh-b'l) *adj.* Capable of satisfaction.—**sa·ti·a·bil·ity, -ble·ness** *n.*— **-a·bly** *adv.*

sa·ti·ate (*say*-shee-ayt) *v.* [sa·ti·at·ed; sa·ti·at·ing] To satisfy beyond desire; to surfeit.—**sa·ti·ate** *adj.* Glutted.—**sa·ti·a·tion** (say-shi-*ay*-shun) *n.*

sat·in (*sat*-in) *n. & adj.* A glossy, close-textured silk or rayon cloth.—**sat·in·y** *adj.*

sat·in·wood *n.* A heavy, durable wood of deep yellow color, native to the East Indies.

sat·ire (*sat*-yre) *n.* 1. An ironic literary work; caricature; parody. 2. Caustic wit; sarcasm. —**sa·tir·ic, sa·tir·i·cal** *adj.*—**sa·tir·i·cal·ly** *adv.* —**sat·i·rist** *n.*—**sat·i·rize** *v.* [sat·i·rized; sat·i·riz·ing] To mock, parody.

sat·is·fac·tion (sat-iss-*fak*-sh'n) *n.* 1. Gratification; contentment. 2. Settlement of a claim; payment; compensation.

sat·is·fac·to·ry *adj.* 1. Fulfilling necessary or desirable conditions. 2. Yielding gratification.—**sat·is·fac·to·ri·ly** *adv.*— **-ri·ness** *n.*

sat·is·fy (*sat*-iss-fy) *v.* [sat·is·fied; sat·is·fy·ing] 1. To gratify fully; to content. 2. To discharge a claim or debt; liquidate. 3. To convince; free from doubt. 4. To fulfill conditions.—**sat·is·fy·ing** *adj.*— **-ing·ly** *adv.*

sa·trap (*say*-trap) *n.* 1. A provincial governor under the ancient Persian monarchy. 2. A prince. 3. A petty despot.—**sa·trap·y** *n.*

sat·u·rate (*sach*-er-ayt) *v.* [sat·u·rat·ed; sat·u·rat·ing] To soak; to impregnate; to steep thoroughly.—**sat·u·ra·tion** (sach-er-*ay*-shun) *n.* 1. Complete soaking. 2. *Chemistry.* The condition of a solution wherein no more of a given substance can be dissolved.

Sat·ur·day *n.* The seventh day of the week.

Sat·urn (*sat*-ern) *n.* 1. A planet of the solar system. 2. Roman god of agriculture.—**sa·tur·ni·an** (suh-*ter*-nee-un) *adj.*

sat·ur·na·li·a (sat-er-*nayl*-yuh) *n.* 1. Unconstrained revelry; a joyous festival. 2. [*cap.*] The week-long festival of the god Saturn in ancient Rome.—**sat·ur·na·li·an** *adj.*

sat·ur·nine (*sat*-er-nyne) *adj.* Morose; gloomy; dull; leaden.—**sat·ur·nine·ly** *adv.*

sat·yr (*sat*-'r; *sayt*-'r) *n.* 1. A mythical Greek demigod, half man and half beast. 2. A man devoted to sensual pleasure.—**sa·tyr·ic, sa·tyr·i·cal** *adj.*

sat·y·ri·a·sis (sat-ih-*rye*-uh-siss) *n.* Unrestrained sexual appetite in a male.

sauce (sawss) *n.* 1. A thick liquid dressing for food. 2. Pertness; impudence; insolence.—*v.* [sauced; sauc·ing] 1. To season; to cover with sauce. 2. To speak to in an impudent manner.

SATYR

sauce·pan (*sawss*-pan) *n.* A small open vessel for boiling or stewing, usually with a handle.

sau·cer (*saw*-s'r) *n.* A piece of china or other ware on which a cup is set.

sau·cy *adj.* [sau·ci·er; sau·ci·est] Impudent; rude.—**sau·ci·ly** *adv.*—**sau·ci·ness** *n.*

sauer·kraut (*sour*-krowt) *n.* Finely cut cabbage steeped in salt and fermented.

saun·ter (*sawn*-t'r) *v.* To stroll idly.—**saun·ter** *n.*

sau·ri·an (*saw*-ree-un) *adj.* Lizardlike.—**-ri·an** *n.*

sau·sage (*saw*-sij) *n.* Chopped seasoned meat, usually pork in a cellulose or other casing.

sau·té (soh-*tay*) *v.* [-téed; -té·ing] To brown by frying lightly in a little fat.—**sau·té** *n.*

sau·terne (soh-*tern*) *n.* Also **sau·ternes.** A white Bordeaux wine.

sav·age (*sav*-ij) *adj.* 1. Wild; untamed. 2. Ferocious; cruel. 3. Uncivilized; primitive.—*n.* 1. A human being in an uncivilized state. 2. A cruel, barbarous person.—**sav·age·ly** *adv.* —**sav·age·ness, sav·age·ry** *n.*

sa·van·na (suh-*van*-uh) *n.* Also **sa·van·nah.** An open plain or meadow in a tropical region.

sa·vant (suh-*vahn; sav*-'nt) *n.* A man of learning; a scholar.

save (*sayv*) *v.* [saved; sav·ing] 1. To rescue; recover. 2. *Theology.* To redeem; deliver from sin. 3. To avoid, as to save trouble. 4. To preserve. 5. To store up; to lay by. —*prep.* Except; but.—*conj.* Unless.

sav·ing *adj.* 1. Economical. 2. Rescuing. 3. Compensating.—*n.* 1. Economy. 2. [*pl.*] Money which is laid by. 3. The act of rescuing.—*conj. & prep.* Except.—**sav·ing·ly** *adv.*

sav·ior (*sayv*-yer) *n.* 1. Deliverer; preserver. 2. [*cap.*] Jesus Christ.

sav·or (*sayv*-er) *n.* 1. Flavor; taste; odor. 2. Characteristic; quality.—*v.* 1. To have a particular smell or taste. 2. To taste or smell with pleasure. 3. To perceive; to discern. —**sav·or·er** *n.*—**sav·or·less** *adj.*

sa·vor·y (*sayv*-er-ee) *n.* [*pl.* -ies] A family of culinary herbs used for flavoring.—*adj.* [sa·vor·i·er; -i·est] Pleasing to smell and taste.

sa·voy (suh-*voy*) *n.* A variety of cabbage having a very compact crinkled head.

Sa·voy·ard (suh-*voy*-erd) *n.* A devotee of the operas of Gilbert and Sullivan, so called from the Savoy Theatre, London, where several of the operas were first performed.

saw. Past tense of see.

saw *n.* A maxim; a proverb.

saw *n.* A cutting instrument consisting of a blade, band, or disk of thin metal with a toothed edge.—*v.* [sawed; sawn; saw·ing] To cut out with a saw. —**saw·yer** *n.*

SAWS

saw·buck *n.* 1. *Slang.* A ten-dollar bill. 2. A sawhorse.

saw·horse *n.* A support upon which wood is placed for cutting by hand.

sax·i·frage (*sak*-sih-frij) *n.* A genus of very hardy perennial plants with white or yellow flowers, often grown in rock gardens.

Sax·on (*sak*-s'n) *n.* 1. One of a people of northern Germany who invaded and conquered England in the 5th and 6th centuries. 2. The language of the Saxons. 3. A native of modern Saxony.—**Sax·on·ism** *n.*

sax·o·phone (*sak*-suh-fohn) *n.* A single-reed musical wind instrument. —**sax·o·phon·ist** *n.*

say *v.* [said; say·ing] 1. To speak; to utter. 2. To express; to convey thought. 3. To recite.—*n.* 1. A statement; a declaration. 2. An opinion. 3. Authority.

say·ing *n.* A maxim; a proverbial expression.

Sb. Symbol for the chemical element antimony.

scab *n.* 1. A dry encrusted substance, formed over a healing sore.

SAXOPHONE

2. *Slang.* One who takes the job of a worker who is out on strike.—*v.* [scabbed; scab·bing].

scab·bard (*skab*-erd) *n.* A sheath or covering for a sword.—*v.* To sheathe.

scab·by *adj.* [scab·bi·er; scab·bi·est] Covered with or made up of scabs.—**scab·bi·ly** *adv.* —**scab·bi·ness** *n.*

scaf·fold (*skaf*-'ld) *n.* 1. A temporary platform or frame used chiefly to support workmen in building, painting, masonry, etc. 2. A platform for execution by hanging.—**scaf·fold·ing** *n.*

SCAFFOLD

scal·a·wag (*skal*-uh-wag) *n.* A rascal; an irresponsible or mischievous person.

scald (*skawld*) *v.* 1. To burn with or to place in a hot liquid. 2. To heat just below boiling. —*n.* An injury resulting from moist heat.

scale (*skayl*) *n.* 1. A thin layer protecting the skin of many fishes. 2 Any small thin incrustation.—*v.* To strip or clear of scales; to shed. —**scal·i·ness** *n.*

scale *n.* 1. An aid to ascent, as a ladder, steps, etc. 2. Anything graduated, esp. when applied to degrees or lines of measurement. 3. An instrument for measuring weight. 4. *Music.* A succession of notes arranged in the order of pitch. 5. A system of graduations, as a wage scale.—*v.* [scaled; scal·ing] 1. To climb. 2. To grade. 3. To diminish in ratio.

scal·lion *n.* 1. A young onion. 2. A shallot.

scal·lop (*skol*-up) *n.* 1. An edible ribbed shellfish. 2. A decorative semicircular border design.—*v.* 1. To make a border line like the edge of a scallop shell. 2. *Cooking.* To bake with sauce and bread crumbs in a casserole or a shell.—**scal·loped** *adj.*—**scal·lop·ing** *n.*

scalp (*skalp*) *n.* The skin and hair covering the skull.—*v.* 1. To tear or cut off the scalp. 2. To make a quick profit. 3. To deal in theater and sports tickets.—**scalp·er** *n.*

scal·pel (*skal*-p'l) *n.* A small knife used in anatomical dissections and surgery.

scal·y (*skayl*-ee) *adj.* [scal·i·er; scal·i·est] Having or covered with scales.

scamp *n.* An irresponsible or worthless person; a rogue.—*v.* To do quickly and poorly; to skimp.—**scam·per** *v.* To run quickly; to dash. —*n.* A scurry; a quick trot.

scamp·ish *adj.* Knavish; rascally.

scan *v.* [scanned; scan·ning] 1. To examine minutely. 2. *Poetry.* To examine by counting the metrical feet or syllables. 3. *Colloquial.* To give a cursory glance.—**scan·na·ble** *adj.* —**scan·ner** *n.*

scan·dal (*skan*-d'l) *n.* 1. Disgrace; shame. 2. Defamatory remarks; slander. 3. Gossip.

scan·dal·ize *v.* [-ized; -iz·ing] To shock; to give offense to.

S

scan·dal·mon·ger *n.* (-mung-ger) One who circulates scandalous gossip.

scan·dal·ous *adj.* Disgraceful; libelous.—**scandal·ous·ly** *adv.*

Scan·di·na·vi·a (skan-dih-*nay*-vee-uh) *n.* Region comprising Norway, Sweden, Denmark, and Iceland.—**Scan·di·na·vi·an** *adj. & n.*

scan·di·um (*skan*-dee-um) *n.* A rare metallic element, atomic number 21. (*Symbol:* Sc).

scan·sion (*skan*-shun) *n.* Dividing verse into metrical feet.

scant *adj.* 1. Scarcely sufficient; meager; skimpy. 2. Just below full measure. 3. Insufficient.—*v.* To stint; furnish in short measure.—**scan·ti·ly** *adv.*—**scan·ti·ness** *n.*—**scan·ty** *adj.* [scant·i·er; scant·i·est].

scant·ling *n.* A small piece of timber; a stud.

scape·goat (*skayp*-goht) *n.* One made to bear the blame for the misdeeds of others.

scape·grace *n.* A rogue; a mean trickster.

scap·u·la (*skap*-yoo-luh) *n.* [*pl.* -lae, -las] Shoulder blade.

scap·u·lar (*skap*-yoo-l'r) *n.* 1. An outer garment worn by monks consisting of two woolen bands which hang from the shoulder. 2. A religious badge, usually cloth, worn under clothing.—*adj.* Pertaining to the shoulder or shoulder blade.—**scap·u·la·ry** *n. & adj.*

scar (*skahr*) *n.* 1. A mark remaining on the skin after a wound has healed. 2. A blemish. 3. A lasting injury to mind or spirit.—*v.* [scarred; scar·ring] To mark; wound; hurt.

scar·ab (*skair*-ub) *n.* 1. A beetle. 2. An Egyptian symbol in the shape of a beetle. 3. A charm cut to resemble a beetle.

scar·a·mouch (*skair*-uh-mowch) *n.* 1. A clown. 2. A ne'er-do-well.

scarce (*skairss*) *adj.* 1. Not abundant; deficient; wanting. 2. Rare; uncommon.—**scarce, scarce·ly** *adv.*—**scarce·ness, scar·ci·ty** *n.* [*pl.* -ties].

scare (*skair*) *v.* [scared; scar·ing] 1. To frighten. 2. To take alarm.—*n.* A sudden fear; a start.—**scar·er** *n.*

SCARABS

scare·crow *n.* 1. A form, usually of a man, set up to frighten crows, etc., from crops. 2. A shabby person.

scare·head *n.* A newspaper headline in very large type.

scarf (*skahrf*) [*pl.* scarves, scarfs] *n.* 1. A band of cloth worn around the neck, waist, shoulders, or head. 2. A runner for a table.

scar·i·fy *v.* [scar·i·fied; -fy·ing] 1. To scratch the skin, especially without drawing blood. 2. To injure the feelings

SCARECROW

by criticism. 3. *Agriculture.* To scratch seed-coats to speed germination.—**scar·i·fi·ca·tion** *n.*—**scar·i·fi·er** *n.*

scar·la·ti·na (skahr-luh-*tee*-nuh) *n.* Scarlet fever.

scar·let *n.* A bright red color, brighter than crimson.—**scar·let** *adj.*

scarlet fever. A disease characterized by fever and red rash.

scarlet letter. The letter A in red used as a symbol for adultery in Colonial times.

scarlet runner. A high climbing bean grown for its brilliant flowers and edible seeds.

scar·y (*skair*-ee) *adj.* [scar·i·er; scar·i·est] 1. Timid; easily frightened. 2. *Colloquial.* Frightening.—**scar·i·ly** *adv.*

scathe (*skayth*) *v.* [scathed; scath·ing] 1. To speak insultingly or heatedly to. 2. *Archaic.* To injure; scorch or blister.—**scathe·less** *adj.* —**scath·ing** *adj.*—**scath·ing·ly** *adv.*

scat·ter *v.* 1. To throw loosely about; to strew. 2. To disperse; separate from each other.—**scat·ter·er** *n.*—**scat·ter·ing** *n. & adj.* —**scat·ter·ing·ly** *adv.*

scat·ter·brain *n.* A giddy or thoughtless person. —**scat·ter·brained** *adj.*

scav·enge *v.* [scav·enged; scav·eng·ing] 1. To clean up filth. 2. To eat carrion, refuse, etc. —**scav·en·ger** *n.* One who collects refuse for personal use or gain.

sce·na·ri·o (sih-*nair*-ee-oh) *n.* The script or synopsis of a motion picture.—**sce·na·rist** *n.*

scene (*seen*) *n.* 1. A view; a landscape; a place and objects seen together. 2. A setting; the place in which the action of a play occurs. 3. A division of an act in a play; an episode. 4. [*pl.*] Stage setting. 5. A place where something occurs. 6. An exhibition of strong feeling, sometimes artificial.—**scen·ic** *adj.*

scen·er·y *n.* 1. The general appearance of a place, regarded pictorially. 2. Devices used on the stage to lend an appearance of reality.

scent (*sent*) *n.* 1. Smell; odor. 2. The power of smell. 3. Trail left by an animal's odor; also simulation of such a trail for sport. 4. A perfume.—*v.* 1. To smell. 2. To perfume.

scep·ter, scep·tre (*sep*-t'r) *n.* A staff carried by a ruler as a symbol of authority.—*v.* [scep·tered; scep·ter·ing]. —**scep·tered** *adj.*

scep·tic (*skep*-tik) *n.* See **skep·tic.** One who doubts the truth of anything. —**scep·ti·cal** *adj.*—**scep·ti·cal·ly** *adv.* —**scep·ti·cism** *n.*

sched·ule (*sked*-yool) *n.* 1. A timetable; a program; an agenda. 2. A list, table, or inventory.—*v.* [-uled; -ul·ing].

SCEPTER

Scheldt (*skelt*) *n.* A river in Belgium, Holland and northern France.

sche·mat·ic (skeh-*mat*-ik) *n. Electronics.* A diagram illustrating the connections and compo-

scheme 507 **scoot**

nent parts of a radio circuit. Also called **sche·matic diagram.**—**sche·mat·ic** *adj.*

scheme (*skeem*) *n.* 1. A system; a plan. 2. A plot. 3. A project; an outline.—*v.* [schemed; schem·ing] To contrive; to plot.—**schem·er** *n.*

Schick test. A test for immunity to diphtheria by injecting diphtheria toxin into the blood.

schip·per·ke (*skip*-er-kih) *n.* A small thickset breed of dog of Belgian origin.

schism (*siz*-'m) *n.* A split or division within a group.—**schis·mat·ic** (*siz-mat*-ik) *adj.* & *n.* —**schis·mat·i·cal** *adj.*—**schis·mat·i·cal·ly** *adv.*

schist (*shist*) *n.* Geology. A form of rock recrystallized in many layers which split easily into sheets.—**schist·ose, schist·ous** *adj.*

schiz·oid (*skiz*-oyd) *n.* A victim of schizophrenia.—**schiz·oid** *adj.*

schiz·o·phre·nia (skiz-uh-*free*-nee-uh) *n.* A mental disease characterized by delusions, hallucinations, and general mental deterioration, formerly regarded as a state of split personality; dementia praecox.—**schiz·o·phrene** *n.* —**shiz·o·phren·ic** *adj.*

schnapps (*shnaps*) *n.* A strong gin, esp. Holland gin.

schnau·zer (*shnow*-zer) *n.* A German breed of wire-haired terrier.

schol·ar (*skol*-er) *n.* 1. A student. 2. A learned person.—**schol·ar·ly** *adj.* & *adv.*

schol·ar·ship *n.* 1. The characteristics and qualities of a student. 2. A grant of money to aid a scholar in his studies.

scho·las·tic (skuh-*lass*-tik) *adj.* Relating to education or learning.—*n.* [*often cap.*] One of a school of medieval philosophy occupied with deductive reasoning based on the Bible.

school (*skool*) *n.* 1. Any place of instruction or training; an educational establishment. 2. The collective body of pupils in a place of instruction. 3. A session of an educational establishment. 4. A group of people with a common doctrine or under the same influence. 5. A group of fishes of the same species.—*v.* To educate; to train.—**school** *adj.* —**school·ing** *n.*

school age	school child	schoolman
school board	schoolfellow	schoolmaster
schoolbook	schoolhouse	schoolroom
schoolboy	school-made	school teacher

schoon·er (*skoon*-er) *n.* 1. A fast type of sailing ship with fore-and-aft sails. 2. A tall beer glass. —**schooner-rigged** *adj.*

Schuyl·kill (*skool*-kil) A river in eastern Pennsylvania. Length: 126 miles.

sci·at·i·ca (sy-*at*-ik-uh) *n.* Inflammation of the sciatic nerve, causing pain in the hip and thigh.—**sci·at·ic** *adj.* Pertaining to the hip.

SCHOONER

sci·ence (*sy*-enss) *n.* 1. Ordered and systematized knowledge of natural phenomena gained by observation, experiment, and induction. 2. Knowledge and learning in general. 3. Technique or art, as the science of bridge. —**sci·en·tif·ic** *adj.*—**sci·en·tif·ic·al·ly** *adv.*—**sci·en·tif·i·cal·ness** *n.*

sci·en·tist *n.* 1. A person skilled in science. 2. [*cap.*] A Christian Scientist.

scim·i·tar, scim·i·ter (*sim*-ih-t'r) *n.* A short, curved oriental sword.

scin·til·la (sin-*til*-uh) *n.* A trace; the least particle.

SCIMITAR

scin·til·late (*sin*-tih-layt) *v.* [-lat·ed; -lat·ing] 1. To sparkle; to glitter. 2. To be lively. —**scin·til·lat·ing** *adj.*— -lat·ing·ly *adv.*— -la·tion *n.*

sci·on (*sy*-un) *n.* 1. Descendant; heir. 2. A shoot or bud of a plant.

scis·sion (*sish*-un) *n.* A division; a cutting; dissension.

scis·sor·bill *n.* Labor Slang. A non-militant, non-union worker.

scis·sors (*siz*-erz) *n. pl.* 1. A cutting instrument consisting of two movable blades fastened with a pin; also called 'a pair of scissors.' 2. *Wrestling.* A leghold. 3. *Gymnastics.* A motion of the legs as in vaulting similar to the opening and closing of scissors.—**scis·sor** *v.* To cut. —**scis·sor·er** *n.*—**scis·sor-kick** *n.* Leg motion in swimming.

scle·ro·sis (skler-*oh*-siss) *n.* [*pl.* scle·ro·ses] Medicine. Hardening of the tissue of any organ.—**scle·rot·ic** (skler-*ot*-ik) *adj.*

SCISSORS

scle·rot·ic *n.* The white outer coating of the eye.

scoff (*skof*) *v.* To treat with derision or scorn; to ridicule.—**scoff·er** *n.*—**scoff·ing·ly** *adv.*

scold (*skohld*) *v.* To reprimand severely; to chide.—**scold, scold·er** *n.*—**scold·ing** *n.* & *adj.* —**scold·ing·ly** *adv.*

sconce (*skonss*) *n.* 1. A wall-bracket holder for candles. 2. *Slang.* The head or skull.

scone (*skohn, skahn*) *n.* A rich baking-powder biscuit.

scoop *n.* 1. An instrument for hollowing out or for ladling materials. 2. The motion of such an instrument. 3. A hollow or cavity. 4. The publishing of a news story which rival newspapers have failed to obtain; the story itself. 5. *Colloquial.* A large quantity, esp. of profits.—*v.* 1. To hollow out or ladle; to dig out. 2. To gather in. 3. To publish a news item before a rival newspaper. —**scoop·er** *n.*—**scoop·ful** *n.*

SCONCE

scoot *v.* To run quickly; to scurry.—*interjection.* Run away!

S

scoot·er *n.* **1.** A child's two-wheeled vehicle pushed with one foot. **2.** Flat-bottomed sailboat with steel skids for use on ice.

scope *n.* **1.** Dimensions of vision or mental activity. **2.** Freedom. **3.** Range; extent.

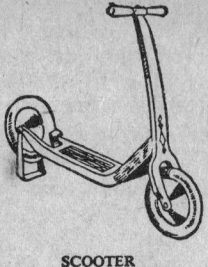

SCOOTER

sco·pol·a·mine (skoh-*pol*-uh-meen) *n.* A sedative which has a hypnotic and narcotic effect on the nerves.

scorch *v.* **1.** To burn superficially; to singe. **2.** To criticize; to rebuke.—**scorch·er** *n. Colloquial.* **1.** Something very hot, exciting, etc. **2.** A very hot summer's day.—**scorched** *adj.* —**scorch·ing·ly** *adv.*

score *n.* **1.** A tally; the number of points made by participants in competitive events. **2.** Twenty. **3.** An account; a reason. **4.** A grudge to be settled. **5.** *Music.* The structure of a composition. **6.** A notch; an incision. —*v.* [scored; scor·ing] **1.** To keep account; to reckon. **2.** To criticize sharply. **3.** To cut notches in; to incise. **4.** *Music.* To arrange a composition. **5.** To achieve success. **6.** To add points to.—**scor·er** *n.*

scorn *v.* **1.** To regard with contempt; to despise. **2.** To reject contemptuously.—*n.* Disdain; contempt.—**scorn·er** *n.*—**scorn·ful** *adj.*

Scor·pi·o *n.* **1.** *Astronomy.* A southern constellation, represented as a scorpion. **2.** *Astrology.* The eighth sign of the Zodiac.

scor·pi·on (*skawr*-pee-'n) *n.* A small segmented animal with a poisonous stinger in its tail.

Scot *n.* A native of Scotland.

Scotch *adj.* Pertaining to Scotland or its inhabitants.—*n.* A whisky distilled in Scotland. —*v.* To put an end to; to squelch.

Scotch·man *n.* An inhabitant or native of Scotland.

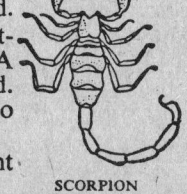

SCORPION

Scotch terrier. A stubby-legged dark-haired terrier with sharply pointed ears and a wiry coat.

scot·free *adj.* Unhurt; safe; unpunished.

Scot·land. The northern division of Great Britain.

Scotland Yard. Headquarters of the London Metropolitan Police Force.

SCOTCH TERRIER

Scots·man *n.* [*pl.* -men] A native or inhabitant of Scotland.

Scot·tish *adj. Variant of* Scotch.

scoun·drel (*skown*-dr'l) *n.* A rascal; a base, unprincipled person.—**scoun·drel·ly** *adj.*

scour (skow-'r) *v.* **1.** To cleanse; rub clean with a rough material. **2.** To search.—**scour·er** *n.*

scourge (*skerj*) *v.* [scourged; scourg·ing] To lash; to torment.—*n.* **1.** A whip. **2.** A punishment; vindictive affliction. **3.** One who destroys.—**scourg·er** *n.*

scour·ings *n. pl.* Waste or refuse removed by scouring.

scout (*skowt*) *n.* **1.** A person sent out to obtain information. **2.** [*cap.*] Member of the Boy Scouts or Girl Scouts of America.—*v.* **1.** To seek information; to reconnoiter. **2.** To reject scornfully; to scoff.

scout·mas·ter *n.* Adult adviser of Boy Scouts.

scow (*skow*) *n.* A large flat-bottomed boat.

scowl *v.* To frown; be displeased.—*n.* A frown; an angry or sullen look.—**scowl·er** *n.*—**scowl·ing** *adj.* —**scowl·ing·ly** *adv.*

SCOW

scrab·ble *v.* [scrab·bled; scrab·bling] **1.** To scrawl; to scribble. **2.** To scrape or scratch.—*n.* **1.** A scribble. **2.** A scramble.

scrag *n.* **1.** A stringy, lean, or leathery person or animal. **2.** A scrawny, tough object. **3.** *Slang.* Neck.—*v.* [scragged; scrag·ging] *Colloquial.* To strangle; to hang.—**scrag·gi·ness** *n.*—**scrag·gly, scrag·gy** *adj.* [scrag·gi·er; scrag·gi·est].

scram *interj. Slang.* Go away! Get out!—*v.* [scrammed; scram·ming] To leave hurriedly.

scram·ble *v.* [scram·bled; scram·bling] **1.** To move or climb quickly in a crouching position. **2.** To struggle for a desired object. **3.** To mix together, esp. for cooking purposes. 'Scrambled eggs.'—*n.* A rough and tumble effort.—**scram·bler** *n.*

scrap *n.* **1.** A small piece; a fragment. **2.** Junk. **3.** *Slang.* A minor quarrel.—*v.* [scrapped; scrap·ping] **1.** To discard; to get rid of. **2.** *Slang.* To fight.—**scrap·per** *n.* —**scrap·py** *adj.* [-pi·er; -pi·est].— -**pi·ly** *adv.*

scrap·book *n.* A book in which newspaper clippings and other mementos are kept.

scrape (*skrayp*) *v.* [scraped; scrap·ing] **1.** To smooth or clean a surface with a rough or sharp instrument. **2.** To collect laboriously; to save. **3.** To manage with difficulty. **4.** To bow low.—*n.* **1** The cleaning of a surface. **2.** A grating sound. **3.** An unpleasant situation.—**scrap·er** *n.*—**scrap·ing** *n.*- -ing·ly *adv.*

scrap·ple *n.* A food made by combining scraps of pork with cornmeal in loaf form.

scratch *v.* **1.** To tear or mark a surface with a sharp object. **2.** To relieve irritation of the skin by rubbing. **3.** To scrape across a rough surface. **4.** To dig with claws or nails.—*n.* **1.** A mark or tear produced by a pointed object. **2.** The noise of scraping. **3.** The starting point in a contest. **4.** *Billiards.* A chance shot; also a penalized shot.—*adj.* **1.** Tentative. **2.** Haphazard.—**scratch·er** *n.* —**scratch·y** *adj.* [scratch·i·er; scratch·i·est]. —**start from scratch.** To start with nothing. —**up to scratch.** Up to a standard.

scrawl *v.* To write carelessly or imperfectly; to scribble.—*n.* Poor, sometimes illegible, handwriting.—**scrawl·er** *n.*—**scrawl·y** *adj.* [scrawl·i·er; scrawl·i·est].

scrawn·y *adj.* [scrawn·i·er; scrawn·i·est] Rawboned; thin.

scream *v.* To make a shrill vocal sound as in fright or pain; to shriek.—*n.* **1.** A sharp, shrill cry. **2.** *Slang.* Anything hilariously amusing.—**scream·er** *n.*—**scream·ing** *adj.*

screech *v.* **1.** To cry out with a shrill voice; to scream. **2.** To make a sharp, high-pitched sound.—*n.* A shrill sound.—**screech·er** *n.* —**screech·ing·ly** *adv.*—**screech·y** *adj.* [screech·i·er; screech·i·est].

screen *n.* **1.** A surface that shelters and conceals. **2.** That which hides or protects. **3.** A wire network or sieve for separating particles of different sizes. **4.** *Motion Pictures.* **a.** Motion pictures in general. **b.** The surface on which pictures are projected. **5.** *Military & Naval.* An advance group out to protect a larger force. **6.** *Photoengraving.* Double sheets of glass having lines at right angles, through which an image is projected on a photographic plate.—*v.* **1.** To shelter; protect; conceal. **2.** To sift; to separate objects of different size or quality. **3.** To project a film on a screen.—**screen·er** *n.*—**screen·ing** *n.*

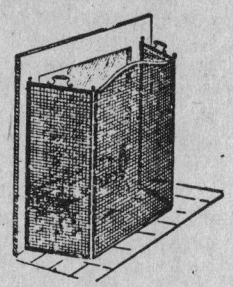

SCREEN

screw (*skroo*) *n.* **1.** A metal cylinder or cone having a spiral ridge (thread) winding around it uniformly, used to fasten objects together, make fine adjustments, etc. **2.** *Nautical.* A ship's propeller.—*v.* **1.** To twist. **2.** To fasten with a screw. **3.** To distort, as to screw up one's face. **4.** To force up or out, as to screw up one's courage.—**screwed** *adj.* **1.** Twisted. **2.** *Slang.* Inebriated.

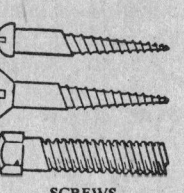

SCREWS

screw·ball (*skroo*-ball) *n. Slang.* An eccentric, irrational person.

screw·driv·er *n.* Instrument for tightening or withdrawing screws.

screw eye. A screw with a loop-shaped head.

SCREWDRIVER

scrib·ble (*skrib*-'l) *v.* [scrib·bled; scrib·bling] To write with haste and carelessness; to scrawl. —**scrib·bler** *n.* An inferior writer or author.

scribe *n.* **1.** A writer. **2.** A copyist; a public or official writer. **3.** *Bible.* A Jewish official who read and explained the law to the people. —**scrib·al** *adj.*—**scribe** *v.* [scribed; scrib·ing].

scrib·er *n.* Tool for embossing leather, etc.

scrim *n.* **1.** A light gauzy fabric used for window curtains. **2.** *Theater.* A translucent curtain hung in front of the stage to give a shadowy appearance to the actors.

scrim·mage (*skrim*-ij) *n.* **1.** A confused row; a tussle. **2.** *Football.* **a.** A close struggle around the ball. **b.** A practice session consisting of actual play.—*v.* [scrim·maged; scrim·mag·ing] To tussle.—**scrim·mag·er** *n.*

scrimp *v.* To live or act very economically.

scrip *n.* **1.** A slip or scrap of paper. **2.** A certificate of stock, subscription to a loan, etc. **3.** Certificate of debt used as substitute for currency; unofficial currency.

script *n.* **1.** Handwriting. **2.** An original document; a manuscript. **3.** *Printing.* A type face resembling handwriting. **4.** *Theater* or *Motion Pictures.* Typescript or scenario.

scrip·tur·al (*skrip*-cher-'l) *adj.* Contained in or according to the Bible.—**scrip·tur·al·ly** *adv.*

scrip·ture (*skrip*-cher) *n.* **1.** [*cap.*] The Bible. **2.** Any sacred writing.

scriv·en·er (*skriv*-ner) *n.* An official recorder; a scribe.

scrod *n.* A young codfish.

scrof·u·la (*skrof*-yoo-luh) *n.* A glandular disease usually of the neck; a kind of tuberculosis. —**scrof·u·lous** *adj.*—**scrof·u·lous·ly** *adv.*—**scrof·u·lous·ness** *n.*

scroll (*skrohl*) *n.* **1.** A rolled sheet of paper or other thin material. **2.** A spiral-shaped ornament resembling a roll of paper.

SCROLL

scroll saw. A thin saw used to cut ornamental patterns in thin wood, etc.

Scrooge. The miser in Dickens' *A Christmas Carol.*

scro·tum (*skroh*-t'm) *n.* [*pl.* scro·ta; scro·tums] An external sac containing the testicles of a male animal.—**scro·tal** *adj.*

scrouge (*skrooj*; *skrowj*) *v.* [scrouged; scroug·ing] *Slang.* To grub around; beg.—**scroug·er** *n.*

scrub *v.* [scrubbed; scrub·bing] **1.** To rub hard, esp. with a damp brush. **2.** To clean. —*n.* **1.** An undersized tree or brush. **2.** *Sports.* A substitute or inferior player. —**scrub·ber** *n.*

scrub·by *adj.* [-bi·er; -bi·est] Small; inferior.

scruff *n.* The back of the neck.

scrump·tious (*skrump*-chus) *adj. Slang.* Delightful; fine; elegant.

S

scrunch *v.* To crunch noisily.—**scrunch** *n.*

scru·ple (*skroo*-p'l) *n.* 1. An idea of rightness; a moral. 2. A conscientious doubt; a hesitation. 3. A very small quantity.—*v.* [scrupled; scru·pling]. To hesitate for moral reasons; to doubt.

scru·pu·lous (*skroop*-yoo-lus) *adj.* 1. Highly moral; strong of conscience. 2. Precise; meticulous; thorough.—**scru·pu·lous·ly** *adv.* —**scru·pu·lous·ness** *n.*

scru·ti·nize (*skroo*-tih-nyze) *v.* To investigate or examine minutely.—**scru·ti·niz·er** *n.*—**scru·ti·niz·ing·ly** *adv.*—**scru·ti·ny** *n.*

scud *v.* [scud·ded; scud·ding] 1. To move lightly and swiftly. 2. *Nautical.* To sail with a driving wind.—*n.* Spray or small clouds blown up by wind.

scuff *v.* 1. To scrape; to scar by scraping. 2. To shuffle.—*n.* 1. A scar made by abrasion, esp. on shoes. 2. A heelless house slipper.

scuf·fle *v.* [scuf·fled; scuf·fling] 1. To struggle closely; to fight confusedly or blindly. 2. To walk with dragging feet.—*n.* A confused struggle.—**scuf·fler** *n.*

scull *n.* 1. A narrow rowboat used for racing. 2. An oar used to propel a boat by working from side to side over the stern.—*v.* To propel a boat by a scull or sculls.

scul·ler·y (*skul*-er-ee) *n.* [*pl.* -ies] A place near the kitchen where household utensils are kept and cleaned.—**scul·ler·y** *adj.*

sculp·tor (*skulp*-ter) *n.* An artist who carves or molds in stone, clay, etc.

sculp·ture (*skulp*-cher) *n.* 1. A piece of art carved in stone, metal, wood, etc. 2. The art of modeling in clay or other material.—*v.* To carve figures.—**sculp·tur·al** *adj.*—**sculp·tur·al·ly** *adv.*—**sculp·tur·esque** *adj.*

scum *n.* 1. Impurities that rise to the surface of boiling liquids, molten metals, stagnant water, etc. 2. Anything vile or worthless; refuse.—*v.* [scum·med; scum·ming] To skim. —**scum·my** *adj.* [scum·mi·er; scum·mi·est].

scup·per *n.* An opening at the base of a ship's railing to allow water to drain overboard; any drain aboard ship.

scup·per·nong *n.* A wine made from a yellow-green grape native to southeastern U.S.

scurf *n.* Dry scales of skin, as in dandruff. —**scurf·y** *adj.*

scur·ril·ous (*skur*-ih-lus) *adj.* Using vile language; indecent; coarse; vulgar.—**scur·ril·i·ty** *n.* [*pl.* -ties].—**scur·ril·ous·ly** *adv.*—**scur·ril·ous·ness** *n.*

scur·ry *v.* [scur·ried; scur·ry·ing] To move rapidly; to hurry.—*n.* Hurry; haste.

scur·vy (*sker*-vee) *n.* A disease causing blemishes on the skin due to vitamin C deficiency.—*adj.* [scur·vi·er; scur·vi·est] 1. Shabby; covered with blemishes. 2. Vile; worthless; despicable.—**scur·vi·ly** *adv.*—**scur·vi·ness** *n.*

scut·ter *v.* To run swiftly a short distance.

scut·tle *n.* 1. A wide-mouthed metal pail for carrying coal. 2. A broad, shallow basket. 3. A small lidded opening. 4. *Nautical.* An opening in a ship's deck covered by a hood.—*v.* [scut·tled; scut·tling] 1. To run briskly. 2. To sink a ship, esp. one's own, by cutting a hole in its side or bottom.

SCUTTLE

scut·tle·butt *n. Nautical.* 1. A drinking fountain. 2. Gossip; rumor.

scythe (*sythe*) *n.* A hand tool for mowing grass, hay, etc.—*v.* [scythed; scyth·ing] To cut with a scythe.

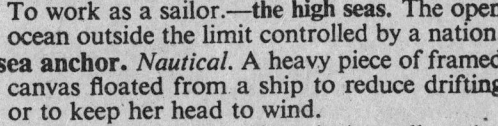

sea (*see*) *n.* 1. Any large body of salt water smaller than an ocean. 2. Any mass of water bounded by land in such a way as to be considered a body. 3. The motion of the sea. 4. Any large body, as a sea of people.—**at sea.** 1. On the sea. 2. Confused; bewildered.—**follow the sea.** To work as a sailor.—**the high seas.** The open ocean outside the limit controlled by a nation.

SCYTHE

sea anchor. *Nautical.* A heavy piece of framed canvas floated from a ship to reduce drifting or to keep her head to wind.

sea anemone (uh-*nem*-oh-nee). A small marine animal whose brightly colored tentacles give it the appearance of a flower.

sea·bee *n.* A member of a U.S. Navy Construction Battalion.

sea·board *n.* The coast line; the country bordering the ocean.—**sea·board** *adj.*

SEA ANEMONE

sea·dog *n.* 1. *Colloquial.* An old sailor; one who has been to sea many years. 2. A dogfish.

sea·far·er (*see*-fair-er) *n.* A seaman.

sea·far·ing *n.* Traveling at sea, usually as an occupation.—**sea·far·ing** *adj.*

sea·girt (*see*-gert) *adj.* Encircled by the sea.

sea horse. 1. A mythical marine monster having the appearance of a horse. 2. A small fish with a spiny covering found mostly in tropical seas.

seal (*seel*) *n.* 1. That which holds a thing closed. 2. An emblem affixed to official papers as a mark of validity.—*v.* 1. To place a seal upon; to validate. 2. To fasten or close. 3. To confirm, as to seal a bargain. 4. To decide or conclude.—**seal·a·ble** *adj.*—**seal·er** *n.*

SEA HORSE
(1/3 life-size)

seal *n.* 1. An amphibious mammal having a long tapering body and broad flippers which serve as a means of propulsion on both water and land. 2. The fur of the seal.—**seal·er** *n.* 1. A hunter of seals. 2. A ship used for hunting seals.—**seal·er·y** *n.*

sea lawyer. Talkative seaman, posing as an authority on many subjects.

sea legs. Ability to maintain one's balance aboard a tossing ship.

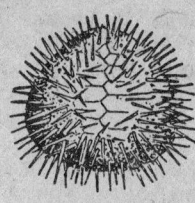

SEAL (1/50 life-size)

sea level. The level of the sea's surface half-way between high and low tides.

sealing wax. A sticking substance used to fasten papers and to carry the imprint of a seal.

sea lion. A large seal of the Pacific Ocean.

seal ring. A finger ring having an engraved design for stamping letters, etc.; a signet ring.

seal·skin *n.* The hide of the fur-bearing seal, used extensively for women's coats.

seam (*seem*) *n.* 1. The line made by two pieces of material joined by sewing; any line formed by the junction of two edges. 2. *Geology.* A sedimentary vein. 3. A scar; a crease.—*v.* 1. To sew together in a line. 2. To wrinkle; to furrow.—**seam·er** *n.*

sea·man *n.* [*pl.* sea·men] Man employed on a ship, esp. one not licensed as an officer.

sea·man·like *adj.* Following the best practice of the sea; competent.

sea·man·ship *n.* The skill and practice of managing a ship.

seam·less *adj.* Made in one piece; invisibly joined.

seam·stress (*seam*-striss) *n.* A woman adept at sewing.

seam·y *adj.* [seam·i·er; seam·i·est] 1. Showing seams. 2. Unpleasant; ugly. 3. Sordid.

se·ance (*say*-ahnss) *n.* 1. A gathering for the purpose of attempting communication with ghostly spirits. 2. A session of any sort.

sea·plane *n.* An airplane fitted with floats to operate from water.

sea·port *n.* A coastal harbor; a city or town with access to the sea.

sea power. 1. The strength and size of a nation's navy. 2. A nation with a large navy.

sear (*seer*) *v.* 1. To burn the surface of; to scorch or singe; to make or become dry. 2. *Cooking.* To brown the surface, as of meat, by exposing briefly to a high temperature. 3. To cauterize; brand.—*n.* A scar made by scorching.

sear, sere (*seer*) *adj.* Withered; dried up.

search (*serch*) *v.* 1. To seek; to look for. 2. To probe; to examine by inspection.—*n.* Investigation; inquiry.—**search·a·ble** *adj.*—**search·er** *n.*—**search·ing** *adj.*—**search·ing·ly** *adv.*

search·light *n.* A powerful electric lamp focused to a small beam, so mounted that it may be turned in almost any direction.

search warrant. A legal document empowering the bearer to search a particular premises for fugitives, contraband, etc.

sea·scape *n.* A view or picture of the ocean or seashore.—**sea·scap·ist** *n.*

sea·scout *n.* A member of the Boy Scouts specializing in seamanship.—**sea·scout·ing** *n.*

sea serpent. A mythical marine monster.

sea·sick *adj.* Ill because of ship's rolling motion.—**sea·sick·ness** *n.*

sea·son (*see*-z'n) *n.* 1. One of the four periods (spring, summer, autumn, winter) into which the year is divided. 2. A suitable time for certain activities, as the music season. 3. The proper or suitable time.—*v.* 1. To fit for any use by time or habit; to accustom or inure. 2. To render more palatable or make spicy. 3. To become fit or accustomed.—**sea·son·er** *n.*

sea·son·a·ble *adj.* Suitable as to time or season; opportune.— **-a·ble·ness** *n.*— **-a·bly** *adv.*

sea·son·al *adj.* Pertaining to or existing during a certain time of the year.—**sea·son·al·ly** *adv.*

sea·son·ing *n.* That which is added to food to give it flavor, as salt, spices, etc.

seat (*seet*) *n.* 1. Place or piece of furniture on which one sits. 2. Place where a government center is situated, as county seat. 3. Manner in which one sits, esp. on horseback. 4. Office or membership in an assembly or body. 5. The buttocks.—*v.* 1. To place on a seat. 2. To settle; to locate or situate. 3. To repair the seat of a chair.—**seat·er** *n.*

sea urchin. Small spiny marine animal.

sea wall. An embankment protecting a low shore from high waves or tides.

sea·ward *n.* The direction toward the sea.—*adj.* Away from the land; closer to the sea.—*adv.* Also **sea·wards** *adv.*

SEA URCHIN (1/6 life-size)

sea·way *n.* 1. *Nautical.* The direction and force of wave motions of the sea. 2. The headway of a ship. 3. An ocean travel lane.

sea·wor·thy *adj.* Capable of floating; strong enough to withstand ordinary weather conditions at sea.—**sea·wor·thi·ness** *n.*

se·ba·ceous (suh-*bay*-shus) *adj.* Secreting fat.

se·cant (*see*-k'nt) *n.* A radius of a circle extended through the circumference to meet a line drawn tangent to the circle.

se·cede (see-*seed*, sih-) *v.* [-ced·ed; -ced·ing] To withdraw from any organization.—**se·ced·er** *n.*

se·ces·sion (see-*sesh*-un, sih-) *n.* 1. Act of withdrawing. 2. *U.S. History.* The separation of eleven states from the U.S. in 1861 to form the Confederate States of America.—**se·ces·sion·al** *adj.*—**se·ces·sion·ism** *n.*—**se·ces·sion·ist** *n.*

se·clude (sih-*klood*) *v.* [se·clud·ed; se·clud·ing] 1. To isolate; to separate from others. 2. To screen protectively.—**se·clud·ed·ly** *adv.*—**se·clud·ed·ness** *n.*

S

se·clu·sion (sih-*kloo*-zhun) *n.* 1. Isolation. 2. Place of retirement.

se·clu·sive *adj.* Tending to exclude others; private.—**se·clu·sive·ly** *adv.*—**se·clu·sive·ness** *n.*

sec·ond (*sek*-'nd) *adj.* Immediately following the first in position, time, value, or rank.—*n.* 1. That which comes after the first; latter of two. 2. The sixtieth part of a minute of time or of angular measurement. 3. An instant; a moment. 4. One who assists or supports another, as in a duel. 5. An article of inferior quality.—*v.* 1. To support; to assist; to promote. 2. In parliamentary procedure, to agree to a motion orally.—**sec·ond** *adv.*—**sec·on·der** *n.* One who seconds a motion.

sec·ond·ar·y (*sek*-un-dehr-ee) *adj.* 1. Following next in order after the first or primary. 2. Subordinate in rank, importance, etc. 3. Derived.—*n.* 1. One who occupies a subordinate position. 2. *Electricity.* Coil in which the induced current flows.—**sec·ond·ar·i·ly** *adv.*

sec·ond-class *adj.* 1. Of an inferior or subordinate nature; next below the first, best, or highest, as in railway or steamship accommodations. 2. Mediocre.

sec·ond·hand *adj.* 1. Not new; used or worn. 2. Not original. 'Second hand knowledge.'

sec·ond·ly *adv.* In the second place.

second nature. Habit which has become almost instinctive.

sec·ond-rate *adj.* Inferior; subordinate.—**sec·ond-rat·er** *n.*

se·cre·cy (*see*-kreh-see) *n.* Concealment; reticence; a state of being hidden.

se·cret (*see*-krit) *adj.* 1. Concealed from the knowledge or sight of others; kept from general observation. 2. Esoteric; mysterious. 3. Secluded.—*n.* 1. Something which is not or should not be revealed. 2. A hidden meaning or explanation.—**se·cret·ly** *adv.*

sec·re·tar·i·at (sek-ruh-*tair*-ee-at) *n.* A governmental subdivision headed by a secretary.

sec·re·tar·y (*sek*-ruh-tehr-ee) *n.* [*pl.* -ies]. 1. One employed to care for and write letters, reports, records, etc. 2. Official appointed, elected, or employed officially to manage or supervise a particular department of government. 3. A writing desk with bookshelves above.—**sec·re·tar·i·al** *adj.*— -**tar·y·ship** *n.*

se·crete (sih-*kreet*) *v.* [se·cret·ed; se·cret·ing] 1. To hide; to conceal. 2. *Biology.* To form and emit a fluid, especially from tissue and glands.—**se·cre·tion** (seh-*kree*-sh'n) *n.* Fluid emitted from glands.—**se·cre·tor** *n.*— -**to·ry** *adj.*

SECRETARY (def. 3)

se·cre·tive (sih-*kree*-tiv) *adj.* Reticent; given to concealment or hiding.—**se·cre·tive·ly** *adv.*

secret service. 1. [*cap.*] A branch of the U.S. Treasury Department chiefly concerned with detection and arrest of counterfeiters. 2. Any espionage service.—**se·cret-serv·ice** *adj.*

sect *n.* A number of people united in ideas; constituting a distinct group; a denomination.

sec·tar·i·an (sek-*tehr*-ee-un) *n.* One who breaks away from an established church.—**sec·tar·i·an** *adj.*— -**an·ism** *n.* Devotion to the interest of a group; partisan zeal.— -**an·ize** *v.* [-ized; -iz·ing].

sec·ta·ry (*sek*-ter-ee) *n.* [*pl.* -ries] 1. A dissenter. 2. Member of a sect.

sec·tion (*sek*-sh'n) *n.* 1. A part cut or separated from the whole; a division; a portion. 2. That part of a country set apart by economic or cultural differences. 3. *Railroads.* Combined upper and lower berths in a sleeping car.—*v.* To cut into parts; to divide.

sec·tion·al (*sek*-sh'n-ul) *adj.* 1. Pertaining to a distinct part of a larger body or territory. 2. Composed of several independent parts.

sec·tion·al·ism (-iz-'m) *n.* Expression of the peculiar interests and ideals of a distinct part of a country.—**sec·tion·al·ize** *v.* [-ized; -iz·ing].

sec·tor (*sek*-ter) *n.* 1. That portion of a circle between the arc and two radii. 2. *Military.* An area of military operations. 3. A plotting instrument made of two rulers linked together at one end.

sec·u·lar (*sek*-yuh-ler) *adj.* Worldly; lay; pertaining to things not sacred or spiritual.—**sec·u·lar·ism** *n.*—**sec·u·lar·ist** *n.*—**sec·u·lar·is·tic** *adj.*

SECTOR

sec·u·lar·ize *v.* [-ized; -iz·ing] 1. To strip of religious control. 2. To make worldly.—**sec·u·lar·i·za·tion** *n.*—**sec·u·lar·iz·er** *n.*

se·cure (sih-*kyoor*) *adj.* 1. Free from danger; safe. 2. In a stable condition; firmly held. 3. Certain; undisputed.—*v.* [se·cured; se·cur·ing] 1. To make safe; to protect; to guard. 2. To fasten firmly. 3. To guarantee payment of, as a loan. 4. To obtain.—**se·cure·ly** *adv.*—**se·cure·ness** *n.*—**se·cur·er** *n.*

se·cu·ri·ty (sih-*kyoor*-ih-tee) *n.* [*pl.* -ties] 1. Safety; freedom from risk or uncertainty. 2. That which makes safe; defense. 3. A guarantee to fulfill a debt or promise; a surety. 4. [*pl.*] An evidence of debt or of property, as a certificate of stock.

se·dan (sih-*dan*) *n.* 1. An enclosed automobile seating four or more people. 2. A covered chair slung between poles carried by two men.

se·date (sih-*dayt*) *adj.* 1. Calm; serene. 2. Dignified; sober. — **se·date·ly** *adv.* — **se·date·ness** *n.*

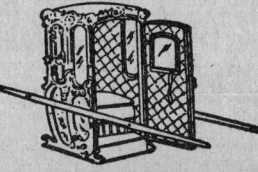

SEDAN (def. 2)

sed·a·tive (*sed*-uh-tiv) *adj.* Tending to calm;

relieving pain.—*n*. Medicine which assuages pain or soothes irritation.

sed·en·tar·y (*sed*-'n-tehr-ee) *adj*. **1.** Spending much time in a sitting posture; requiring much sitting. **2.** Inactive; sluggish.— **-tar·i·ly** *adv*.

sedge (*sej*) *n*. A grasslike plant growing mostly in marshes and along rivers.—**sedg·y** *adj*.

sed·i·ment (*sed*-uh-m'nt) *n*. **1.** Foreign matter which settles to the bottom of a liquid. **2.** *Geology*. A complex mass of material disintegrated, moved, and redeposited by the action of water, wind, or chemical change. —**sed·i·men·ta·ry** *adj*.—**sed·i·men·ta·ri·ly** *adv*.

se·di·tion (sih-*dish*-'n) *n*. Illegal stirring up of discontent against government; acts or language disturbing the public peace or unity. —**se·di·tion·ar·y** *n*. One who incites discontent against the government.—**se·di·tion·ist** *n*.—**se·di·tious** *adj*.— **-tious·ly** *adv*.— **-tious·ness** *n*.

se·duce (sih-*doos*) *v*. [se·duced; se·duc·ing] **1.** To tempt; to corrupt; to lead away from morality or duty. **2.** To entice to sexual acts. —**se·duc·er** *n*.—**se·duc·i·ble** *adj*.—**se·duc·tion** (seh-*duk*-shun) *n*.

se·duc·tive *adj*. Alluring; tempting.—**se·duc·tive·ly** *adv*.—**se·duc·tive·ness** *n*.—**se·duc·tress** *n*.

se·du·li·ty (sih-*dyoo*-lih-tee) *n*. Diligence; persevering activity.

sed·u·lous (*sed*-yuh-lus) *adj*. Painstaking; persevering; zealous.— **-lous·ly** *adv*.— **-lous·ness** *n*.

se·dum (*see*-dum) *n*. A succulent-leaved creeping herb, commonly called stonecrop.

see *v*. [saw; seen; see·ing] **1.** To perceive through the eyes. **2.** To grasp mentally; to comprehend. **3.** To undergo; to experience. **4.** To observe; to scrutinize. **5.** To give attention; to take care. **6.** To escort. **7.** To visit; to deal with. **8.** *Poker*. To match a bet. —*interj*. Behold! look!

see *n*. The territory under ecclesiastical supervision of a bishop.

seed *n*. [*pl*. seed, seeds] **1.** The embryo from which a plant grows. **2.** The origin or principle from which anything arises. **3.** The fertilizing fluid or sperm of male animals; semen. **4.** Progeny; offspring.—*v*. **1.** To plant seeds; to sow. **2.** To produce from fruit. **3.** To remove seeds from. **4.** To select opponents in a tournament so that the top-ranking athletes do not meet in the early matches. —**seed·er** *n*. **1.** A tool used for planting. **2.** Implement for seeding (sense 3) fruit.

seed·ling *n*. A plant reared from seed.

seed·y *adj*. [seed·i·er; -i·est] **1.** Full of seeds; bearing seeds. **2.** *Colloquial*. Shabby; worn out; miserable.—**seed·i·ly** *adv*.— **-i·ness** *n*.

see·ing *n*. Sight; the ability to perceive or act of perceiving through the eyes.—*adj*. Having the ability to see.—*conj*. Considering; because.

seek *v*. [sought; seek·ing] **1.** To look for; search for. **2.** To attempt; strive after.—**seek·er** *n*.

seem *v*. **1.** To present the appearance of being; to look like. **2.** To pretend; to assume an air.

3. To appear to one's own judgment. 'It seems to me.'—**seem·er** *n*.

seem·ing *adj*. Apparent; having the semblance of.—**seem·ing·ly** *adv*.

seem·ly *adj*. [seem·li·er; seem·li·est] **1.** In good taste; pleasing. **2.** Attractively neat and decorous.—**seem·li·ness** *n*.

seen. *Past participle* of see.

seep *v*. To flow through pores; to ooze gently. —*n*. A place through which water or oil flows slowly.—**seep·age** *n*. **1.** A process of oozing. **2.** Fluid which oozes through material.

seer (*seer*) *n*. A prophet; one who predicts future events.—**seer·ess** *n*.

seer·suck·er *n*. A light fabric with a slightly crinkled weave, used mostly for summer clothing.

see·saw (*see*-saw) *n*. **1.** A children's game of riding alternately up and down on either end of a center-supported board. **2.** The board used in this game. **3.** Any alternating motion.—*v*. To move up and down or back and forth.

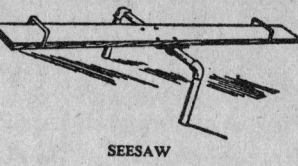

SEESAW

seethe *v*. [seethed; seeth·ing] **1.** To boil; to make or be hot. **2.** To become violently agitated.—**seethe** *n*. A turmoil.

segment (*seg*-m'nt) *n*. **1.** A part cut off or separated from others; one of the parts into which a body naturally divides; a section. **2.** *Geometry*. Part cut off from any figure by a line or plane.—*v*. To divide sectionally.—**seg·men·tal** *adj*. —**seg·men·tal·ly** *adv*.—**seg·men·tar·y** *adj*.

SEGMENT

seg·men·ta·tion (seg-m'n-*tay*-sh'n) *n*. **1.** The act of dividing. **2.** *Biology*. The development of numerous cells from one cell.

seg·re·gate (*seg*-rih-gayt) *v*. To separate from others; to set apart.—*adj*. Set apart.—**seg·re·ga·tion** *n*. The act of separating or state of being part.—**seg·re·ga·tive** *adj*.— **-ga·tor** *n*.

seidlitz powders (*sed*-litss). Two powders which, on mixing with water, effervesce violently and are taken orally as a purgative.

Seine (*sayn*). **1.** A river in France running NW into the English Channel. **2.** A department of northern France. Area: 185 sq. mi.

seine (*sayn*) *n*. A large net for catching fish.—*v*. To fish with this net.

seis·mic (*syze*-mik) *adj*. Of or resembling an earthquake.

seis·mo·graph (*syze*-muh-graf, *sysse*-) *n*. An instrument for detecting and recording earthquakes.—**seis·mo·graph·ic** *adj*.—**seis·mog·ra·phy** (syze-*mog*-raf-ee, *sysse*-) *n*.

seize (*seez*) *v*. [seized; seiz·ing] **1.** To grasp suddenly; to lay hold of. **2.** To take possession by force. **3.** To take prisoner; to arrest.

S

4. To have a sudden and powerful effect upon. **5.** To fasten; to fix. **6.** To comprehend. —**seiz·a·ble** *adj.*—**seiz·er** *n.*

seiz·ing *n.* **1.** Act of laying hold. **2.** *Nautical.* **a.** Act of lashing together with cord or marline. **b.** Small cord used for lashing.

sei·zure (*see*-zher) *n.* **1.** Act of taking sudden hold; a taking possession by force or by law. **2.** A sudden attack of illness.

sel·dom (*sel*-d'm) *adv.* Rarely; infrequently.

se·lect (seh-*lekt*) *v.* To choose with discrimination; to take by preference from a group. —*adj.* Preferred above all others; choice; excellent.—**se·lec·tion** *n.*—**se·lec·tive** *adj.*—**se·lect·ness** *n.*—**se·lec·tor** *n.*

se·lec·tee (seh-lek-*tee*) *n.* A man chosen to serve in the U.S. armed forces under the Selective Service Act.

Selective Service Act. Law passed in 1940 by U.S. Congress providing that men be chosen for compulsory military service by local boards of unpaid volunteers.

se·lec·tiv·i·ty *n. Radio.* Sharpness and accuracy of tuning to a particular frequency desired.

se·lect·man *n.* [*pl.* -men] A New England town officer.

sel·e·nite (*sel*-uh-nyte) *n.* A crystalline mineral.

se·le·ni·um (seh-*lee*-nee-um) *n.* A nonmetallic element used in photoelectric equipment. (*Symbol:* Se).

sel·e·nog·ra·phy (sel-uh-*nog*-ruh-fee) *n.* The study of the geography of the moon.—**sel·e·nog·ra·pher, sel·e·nog·ra·phist** *n.*— **-no·graph·ic** *adj.*

self *n.* [*pl.* selves] **1.** The individual identity. **2.** Personal welfare or interests.

self *adj.* Identical; of the same.

self. *Reflexive prefix*, usually with hyphen, as:

self-aid	self-evident	self-reproach
self-angry	self-expression	self-respect
self-applause	self-fed	self-respecting
self-assurance	self-help	self-restraint
self-centered	selfhood	self-righteous
self-command	self-governing	self-sacrifice
self-complacent	self-importance	self-sacrificing
self-conceit	self-important	selfsame
self-confessed	self-imposed	self-satisfaction
self-confidence	self-interest	self-satisfied
self-control	self-love	self-seeking
self-defense	self-made	self-sufficient
self-denial	selfness	self-sufficiency
self-destruction	self-pity	self-sufficing
self-devotion	self-possessed	self-supporting
self-discipline	self-possession	self-sustaining
self-educated	self-reliance	self-will
self-esteem	self-reliant	self-willed

self-con·scious (self-*kon*-shus) *adj.* Embarrassed; awkward; overly aware of the reactions of others.— **-scious·ly** *adv.*— **-scious·ness** *n.*

self·ish *adj.* Intent upon personal advantage; greedy at expense of others.—**self·ish·ly** *adv.* —**self·ish·ness** *n.*

self-con·tained *adj.* **1.** Reserved; uncommunicative. **2.** Complete within itself.

self-de·ter·mi·na·tion *n.* **1.** Ability to make one's own decisions. **2.** *Law.* Right of a colonial people to determine its government.

self-gov·ern·ment *n.* Democracy; government of, by, and for the people.

self·less *adj.* Without regard to self; unselfish. —**self·less·ly** *adv.*—**self·less·ness** *n.*

self·same *adj.* Identical.—**self·same·ness** *n.*

sell *v.* [sold; sell·ing] **1.** To transfer property for payment. **2.** To persuade another to buy or accept; to find a buyer. **3.** To take a bribe for; to betray.—**sell·er** *n.*—**sell·ing** *adj.*

selling race. A horse race in which the entries are for sale and are handicapped.

sell·out *n.* **1.** *Slang.* Betrayal. **2.** *Theater.* Performance for which all seats are sold.

selt·zer *n.* Charged or carbonated water.

sel·vage (*sel*-vij) *n.* Edge of a fabric, bound to resist ravelling.

selves. *Plural* of self.

se·man·tics (seh-*man*-tiks) *n. sing.* The study and classification of changes in word meanings.

sem·a·phore (*sem*-uh-for) *n.* **1.** A device for signaling by means of flags, movable arrows, etc. **2.** A system of communication by manipulating two hand flags.

sem·blance (*sem*-bl'nss) *n.* **1.** Effect; appearance. **2.** Similarity; resemblance.

SEMAPHORE

se·men (*see*-m'n) *n.* [*pl.* sem·i·na] The fertilizing fluid of the male animal.

se·mes·ter (suh-*mess*-ter) *n.* Half a school year.

sem·i- *prefix.* Half; part; incomplete.

semiacid	semideveloped	seminarcosis
semiannual	semidiameter	semiofficial
semiaquatic	semidiurnal	semiopaque
semiarc	semidivine	semiorganized
semiarid	semieducated	semipolitical
semiarranged	semiellipse	semipublic
semiattached	semienclosed	semirigid
semiautomatic	semifeudal	semi-Romanized
semibarbaric	semifluid	semi-Russian
semibarbarous	semiformal	semiserious
semi-Christian	semiglobe	semiskilled
semicivilized	semiglobular	semi-Slav
semicomatose	semi-Gothic	semisolid
semicone	semihexagon	semiterrestrial
semiconic	semi-imperial	semitransparent
semiconical	semi-invalid	semitropical
semiconscious	semiliquid	semitubular
semidaily	semiliterate	semiurban
semidarkness	semilunar	semiweekly
semidesert	semimonopoly	semiyearly
semidetached	semimute	semi-Zion

sem·i·cir·cle (*sem*-ih-ser-k'l) *n.* Half of a circle; that portion between the diameter and circumference.—**sem·i·cir·cu·lar** *adj.*

sem·i·co·lon (*sem*-ih-koh-l'n) *n.* A mark of punctuation [;] separating complete thoughts within a sentence.

sem·i·fi·nal (sem-ih-*fy*-n'l) *n. Sports.* [*often pl.*]. First of the last two rounds in a contest.—**sem·i·fi·nal** *adj.*—**sem·i·fi·nal·ist** *n.*

sem·i·nal (*sem*-ih-n'l) *adj.* Relating to seeds or

semen; relating to elements of reproduction. —sem·i·nal·ly *adv.*

sem·i·nar (*sem*-ih-nahr) *n.* A class pursuing original or advanced study.

sem·i·nar·y (*sem*-ih-nehr-ee) *n.* [*pl.* -ies]. A school, esp. of religion; an academy.

Sem·i·nole (*sem*-ih-nohl) *n.* Tribe of American Indians formerly inhabiting Florida and southern Georgia.—Sem·i·nole *adj.*

sem·i·pro *n.* Short for sem·i·pro·fes·sion·al. *Slang.* An athlete who performs for pay, but whose income is not chiefly derived from athletics.—sem·i·pro *adj.*

Se·mir·a·mis (seh-*mihr*-uh-miss) Legendary Assyrian queen, known for wisdom and beauty.

Sem·ite (*sem*-yte, *see*-myte) *n.* An ancient Caucasian people now chiefly comprising Arabs, Jews, and Ethiopians.—Se·mit·ic *adj.*—Se·mit·ics *n.* Study of Semitic culture.—Se·mit·ism *n.*

sem·o·lin·a (sem-oh-*leen*-uh) *n.* Wheat product used in macaroni, spaghetti, etc.

sem·pi·ter·nal (sem-pih-*ter*-n'l) *adj.* Everlasting —sem·pi·ter·ni·ty *n.*

sen·ate (*sen*-it) *n.* 1. A government assembly or council. 2. [*cap.*] *U.S.* The upper house of Congress, consisting of two persons from each state elected for a period of six years; a comparable body in certain other countries.—sen·a·tor *n.* One elected to a senate.— -to·ri·al *adj.*

send *v.* [sent; send·ing] 1. To direct from one place to another; dispatch. 2. To emit. 3. *Music Slang.* To excite, esp. by jazz music. 4. To transmit.—send-off *n.* Farewell ceremony.

Sen·e·ca (*sen*-ih-kuh) *n.* A tribe of Iroquois Indians originating in New York State.

se·nes·cent (seh-*ness*-'nt) *adj.* Aging; becoming senile.—se·nes·cence *n.*

sen·es·chal (*sen*-uh-sh'l) *n.* An officer in the household of a feudal dignitary.

se·nile (*see*-nyle, *see*-nil) *adj.* Aged; feeble.—se·nil·i·ty *n.* Old age; mental and physical debility.

sen·ior (*seen*-yer) *adj.* 1. The older. 2. Superior in rank, length of service, or office. 3. Pertaining to the last year of study in college, high school, etc.—sen·ior *n.*

sen·ior·i·ty (sen-*yawr*-ih-tee) *n.* *Labor Relations.* Length of continuous employment, used as a factor in promotion, pay, and job classification and security.

se·ñor (say-*nyawr*) [*pl.* se·ño·res] *n.* A Spanish title corresponding to Mr. or Sir.—se·ño·ra *n.* Spanish title for a married or elderly woman, corresponding to Madam or Mrs.—se·ño·ri·ta (say-nyaw-*ree*-tah) *n.* Spanish title for a young unmarried woman, corresponding to Miss.

sen·sa·tion (sen-*say*-sh'n) *n.* 1. Impression made upon the mind through the organs of sense. 2. The power of receiving impressions through the senses. 3. Feelings; emotional qualities. 4. The state of excited interest.

sen·sa·tion·al *adj.* Exciting; emotional; melodramatic.—sen·sa·tion·al·ly *adv.*

sen·sa·tion·al·ism *n.* 1. An effort to stir up

emotional public interest. 2. *Philosophy.* The doctrine that all knowledge derives from impressions made on the senses.—sen·sa·tion·al·ist *n.*—sen·sa·tion·al·is·tic *adj.*

sen·sa·tion·ism *n.* *Psychology.* A system maintaining that sensations are the chief components of conscious experience.—sen·sa·tion·ist *n.*

sense (senss) *n.* 1. Perception; awareness. 2. One of the five faculties: touch, sight, hearing, taste, and smell. 3. A vague consciousness. 4. Understanding; feeling; appreciation. 5. Correct reasoning; sound judgment. 6. Meaning; import. 'The true sense of a word.'—*v.* [sensed; sens·ing] 1. To perceive. 2. To notice without fully comprehending.

sense·less *adj.* 1. Meaningless; irrational; nonsensical. 2. Incapable of sensation or feeling; unconscious.—sense·less·ly *adv.*— -less·ness *n.*

sen·si·bil·i·ty (sen-sih-*bil*-ih-tee) *adj.* [*pl.* -ties] 1. Awareness of mental or physical sensations. 2. Ability to feel keenly; susceptibility. 3. Mental discernment; receptivity.

sen·si·ble (*sen*-sih-b'l) *adj.* 1. Possessing or containing judgment; cognizant. 2. Reasonable. 3. Capable of receiving external impressions. —sen·si·ble·ness *n.*—sen·si·bly *adv.*

sen·si·tive (*sen*-sih-tiv) *adj.* 1. Impressionable; readily moved; responsive. 2. Able to receive internal or external impressions. 3. Easily affected by an external agent. 'A sensitive scale.'—sen·si·tive·ly *adv.*—sen·si·tive·ness *n.*

sen·si·tiv·i·ty (sen-sih-*tiv*-ih-tee) *n.* 1. Responsiveness; fineness of perception; excitability. 2. *Radio.* The accuracy and range of response of a receiving set to a modulated wave.

sen·si·tize (*sen*-sih-tyze) *v.* [-tized; -tiz·ing] 1. *Chemistry & Photography.* 1. To cause to react readily. 2. *Medicine.* To make highly susceptible, as with an injection.—sen·si·ti·za·tion *n.*—sen·si·tiz·er *n.*

sen·si·tom·e·ter (sen-sih-*tom*-eh-ter) *n.* *Optics.* An instrument which measures the sensitivity of ocular perception.

sen·so·ri·um (sen-*sor*-ee-um) *n.* [*pl.* -ri·ums; -ri·a] *Medicine.* The brain, as the center of sensations; the sensory system.— -ri·al *adj.*

sen·so·ry (*sen*-ser-ee) *adj.* Pertaining to the senses.

sen·su·al (*sen*-shoo-ul) *adj.* 1. Pertaining to the body as distinct from the spirit. 2. Voluptuous; lewd.—sen·su·al·ism *n.*—sen·su·al·ist *n.* — -al·is·tic *adj.*— -al·i·ty *n.*— -al·ly *adv.*

sen·su·al·ize *v.* [-ized; -iz·ing] To make sensual; to debauch.—sen·su·al·i·za·tion *n.*

sen·su·ous (*sen*-shoo-us) *adj.* 1. Luxuriant; pleasurable; inviting to the senses. 2. Readily affected through the senses.—sen·su·ous·ly *adv.* —sen·su·ous·ness *n.*

sen·tence (*sen*-t'nss) *n.* 1. An opinion or judgment expressed. 2. *Law.* Judgment pronounced by the court upon a defendant found guilty. 3. *Grammar.* An order of words expressing a complete thought, followed by a period, exclamation point, or question mark.

S

—*v.* [sen·tenced; sen·tenc·ing] To pronounce judgment upon; to condemn.—**sen·tenc·er** *n.*

sen·ten·tious (sen-*ten*-shus) *adj.* 1. Pithy; aphoristic; curt. 2. Given to using axioms; pompous.— **-tious·ly** *adv.* **-tious·ness** *n.*

sen·ti·ence (*sen*-shunss) *n.* Also **sen·ti·ency.** Consciousness; capacity for feelings and sensations.—**sen·ti·ent** *adj.* Experiencing feelings and sensations.—**sen·ti·ent·ly** *adv.*

sen·ti·ment (*sen*-tih-m'nt) *n.* 1. Feeling; opinion. 2. A mental judgment or view, influenced by emotional factors. 3. A delicately phrased tribute.

sen·ti·men·tal (-*men*-t'l) *adj.* 1. Tender; emotional; inspired by delicate feelings. 2. Appealing to emotion; overly sweet.—**sen·ti·men·tal·ism** *n.*— **-tal·ist** *n.*— **-tal·i·ty** *n.* [*pl.* -ties] — **-tal·ize** *v.* [-ized; -iz·ing]— **-tal·ly** *adv.*

sen·ti·nel (*sen*-tih-n'l) *n.* A guard; a soldier on guard duty.—*v.* [-neled, -nelled; -nel·ling, -nel·ling] To watch over; to furnish sentries.

sen·try (*sen*-tree) *n.* [*pl.* -ies] A soldier placed on guard; a sentinel.—**sentry box.** A booth affording shelter to a guard.

se·pal (*see*-p'l, *sep*-'l) *n.* The leafy part of a blossom.

sep·a·ra·ble (*sep*-er-uh-b'l) *adj.* Divisible; able to be disjoined. —**sep·a·ra·bil·i·ty** *n.*—**sep·a·ra·ble·ness** *n.*—**sep·a·ra·bly** *adv.*

SEPAL

sep·a·rate (*sep*-er-ayt) *v.* [sep·a·rat·ed; -rat·ing] To disunite; to divide; to part.—**sep·a·rate** (*sep*-uh-rit) *adj.*—**sep·a·rate·ly** *adv.*—**sep·a·rate·ness** *n.*

sep·a·ra·tion *n.* 1. State of being parted from. 2. *Law.* Agreement between husband and wife to live apart, usually without a formal divorce.

sep·a·ra·tist *n.* A dissenter; one favoring separation, esp. from an established church.—**sep·a·ra·tism** *n.*—**sep·a·ra·tive** *adj.*

sep·a·ra·tor (-ter) *n.* A mechanical device which divides the components of a mixture.

se·pi·a (*see*-pee-uh) *n.* [*pl.* se·pi·as; se·pi·ae] 1. A cuttlefish. 2. A dark brown pigment used in painting, the secretion of cuttlefish. 3. A rich shade of brown.—**se·pi·a** *adj.*

sep·sis (*sep*-siss) *n. Medicine.* An infection caused by the admission of certain bacteria to the blood stream.

Sep·tem·ber (sep-*tem*-ber) *n.* The ninth month of the year. *Abbreviation:* Sept.

sep·ten·ni·al (scp-*ten*-ee-ul) *adj.* Lasting seven years.—**sep·ten·ni·al·ly** *adv.*

sep·tet *n.* 1. *Music.* A composition for seven voices or instruments. 2. A group of seven.

sep·tic *adj.* Decomposed; poisonous through putrefaction.—**sep·tic** *n.*

sep·ti·ce·mi·a (sep-tuh-*see*-mee-uh) *n.* Blood poisoning.—**sep·ti·ce·mic** *adj.*

septic sore throat. *Medicine.* Throat ailment characterized by high fever, inflamed tonsils, and other symptoms of poisoning.

septic tank. A container which chemically purifies and disposes of sewage.

sep·til·lion (sep-*til*-yun) *n.* Any numeral followed by twenty-four zeros.—**sep·til·lion, sep·til·lionth** *adj.*

sep·tu·a·ge·nar·i·an (sep-choo-uh-juh-*nair*-ee-un) *n.* A person between the ages of seventy and eighty.— **-ge·nar·i·an** *adj.*— **-nar·y** *adj. & n.*

sep·tu·ple (*sep*-tuh-p'l) *adj.* Sevenfold; made up of seven.—*v.* [sep·tu·pled; sep·tu·pling]. To increase sevenfold.

sep·ul·cher, sep·ul·chre (*sep*-'l-ker) *n.* A tomb; a vault.—*v.* To bury.

se·pul·chral (sep-*puhl*-kr'l) *adj.* 1. Pertaining to burial or the grave. 2. Deep, hollow in tone; gloomy.—**se·pul·chral·ly** *adv.*

se·quel (*see*-kw'l) *n.* 1. Continuation. 2. Consequence; result; upshot.

se·quence (*see*-kwenss) *n.* 1. Uniform succession; order. 2. A result. 3. *Motion Pictures.* A single episode in a screen play.—**se·quent** *n. & adj.*—**se·quen·tial** *adj.*—**se·quen·tial·ly** *adv.*

se·ques·ter (seh-*kwess*-ter) *v.* 1. To set aside for safekeeping. 2. *Law.* To appropriate until certain conditions are met.—**se·ques·tered** *adj.* Secluded.

se·ques·tra·ter *v.* [-trat·ed; -trat·ing] To confiscate; to appropriate by law.—**se·ques·tra·tor** *n.*—**se·ques·tra·tion** *n.*

se·quin (*see*-kw'n) *n.* Small glittering disk used for trimming costumes, evening gowns, etc.

se·quoi·a (sih-*kwoy*-uh) *n.* A species of giant pinetree, native to California.

se·ragl·io (sih-*rahl*-yo) *n.* [*pl.* se·ragl·i; seragl·i·os]. A harem.

se·ra·pe (seh-*rah*-pay) *n.* A blanket cloak worn in Latin America.

ser·aph (*sehr*-uf) *n.* [*pl.* ser·a·phim, ser·aphs] A heavenly being; an angel.—**se·raph·ic, -i·cal** *adj.* Angelic; sublime; perfect.— **-i·cal·ly** *adv.*

Ser·bi·a (*ser*-bee-uh) *n.* Southeastern section of Yugoslavia.—**Ser·bi·an** *adj. & n.*

sere (*seer*) *adj.* Dry; shriveled.

ser·e·nade (sehr-uh-*nayd*) *n.* 1. A love song. 2. Music performed out-of-doors, especially at night. 3. A short piece of music, tranquil in mood.—**ser·e·nade** *v.* [-nad·ed; -nad·ing] —**ser·e·nad·er** *n.*

se·rene (suh-*reen*) *adj.* Calm; placid; clear. —**se·rene·ly** *adv.*—**se·ren·i·ty** *n.*

serf *n.* 1. Lowest member of feudal society. 2. Laborer bound to the land.—**serf·dom** *n.*

serge *n.* A worsted twill, usually woolen.

ser·geant (*sahr*-j'nt) *n.* 1. *Military.* A noncommissioned officer of the rank above corporal. 2. A police officer next below captain or lieutenant in rank.—**sergeant-at-arms.** One appointed to keep order.

se·ri·al (*seer*-ee-ul) *n.* A story or article appearing in successive issues of a periodical.—*adj.* Pertaining to a series or sequence.— **-al·ly** *adv.*

serial number. Number providing identification or indicating time of manufacture, etc.

se·ries (*seer*-eez) *n.* 1. A sequence; successive arrangement or occurrence. 2. *Mathematics.*

A succession of terms increasing or diminishing according to a definite law. 3. *Electricity*. Arrangement of sections of a circuit to form a single uninterrupted path of current.

ser·if (*sehr*-if) *n. Printing.* Ornamental and connective hook or line at top and bottom of letter.—**ser·ifed** *adj.*

se·ri·o·com·ic, se·ri·o·com·i·cal (seer-ee-oh-*kom*-ik, -ik-'l) *adj.* Half-serious, half-humorous.

se·ri·ous (*seer*-ee-us) *adj.* 1. Grave; solemn. 2. Important; critical.—**se·ri·ous·ly** *adv.*—**se·ri·ous·ness** *n.*

ser·mon (*ser*-m'n) *n.* Moral discourse or lecture, esp. religious.—**ser·mon·ic** *adj.*—**ser·mon·ize** *v.* [-ized; -iz·ing]— **-iz·er** *n.*— **-iz·ing** *adj.*

se·rous (*sihr*-us) *adj.* Watery; thin; serumlike.

ser·pent (*ser*-p'nt) *n.* 1. Large snake. 2. A malicious person.

ser·pen·tine (*ser*-p'n-teen) *adj.* 1. Resembling a snake; treacherous. 2. Winding; circuitous.

ser·rate *adj.* Notched; toothed.—**ser·rat·ed** *adj.* —**ser·ra·tion** *n.*

ser·ried (*sehr*-eed) *adj.* Crowded; wedged.

ser·ry *v.* [-ried; -ry·ing] To squeeze together.

se·rum (*seer*-'m) [*pl.* se·rums, se·ra] *n.* Antitoxin produced from the watery residue of animal blood after coagulation.

ser·vant (*ser*-v'nt) *n.* 1. Household employee. 2. Agent; delegate. 3. Disciple.

serve *v.* [served; serv·ing] 1. To work for; to represent; to render obedience or worship. 2. To fulfill a duty or term. 3. To suffice; to do. 4. To wait on table; to help others to food. 5. *Law.* To deliver; as, serve a writ. 6. *Tennis.* To put the ball in play.

serv·er *n.* 1. One who performs tasks. 2. A small tray or salver.

Ser·vi·a (*ser*-vee-uh) *n. Variant* of **Serbia.**

serv·ice (*ser*-viss) *n.* 1. The performance of labor for another. 2. Employment. 3. Military or naval duty. 4. [*often pl.*] All military and naval organization. 5. Fulfillment of public office. 6. Religious ritual or meeting. 7. A set of silverware or china.—*v.* [serv·iced; serv·ic·ing] To examine and repair. 'Service an automobile.'—**serv·ice** *adj.*

serv·ice·a·ble *adj.* 1. Practical; useful. 2. Durable; strong.—**serv·ice·a·bil·i·ty, -a·ble·ness** *n.*

ser·vi·ette (ser-vee-*et*) *n.* A table napkin.

ser·vile (*ser*-vil) *adj.* 1. Slavish. 2. Obsequious; toadying.—**ser·vile·ly** *adv.*—**ser·vile·ness, ser·vil·i·ty** *n.*

ser·vi·tor (*ser*-vih-ter) *n.* An attendant.

ser·vi·tude (*ser*-vih-tyood) *n.* 1. Slavery; bondage. 2. *Law.* Punitive labor.

se·sam·e (*seh*-suh-mee) *n.* 1. An East Indian herb whose seeds are used for flavoring. 2. Also **open sesame.** A magic key giving easy entry.

ses·qui- (*sess*-kwee) *prefix.* One and a half times.

ses·qui·cen·ten·ni·al *n.* A one hundred and fiftieth anniversary.—**ses·qui·cen·ten·ni·al** *adj.*

ses·sion (*sesh*-'n) *n.* 1. A meeting; an assembly. 2. Duration of a conference or interview. 3. *Education.* Period of day or year when instruction is in progress.—**ses·sion·al** *adj.*

set *adj.* 1. Located; placed. 2. Fixed in opinion; determined. 3. Established; prescribed; appointed. 4. Prepared; ready. 5. Predetermined; settled beforehand. 6. Immovable; fixed. 7. Permanent; persistent.

set *v.* [set; set·ting] 1. To place; put. 2. To sink before the horizon; decline. 3. To congeal or solidify. 4. To arrange; dispose; post. 5. To establish or appoint. 6. To fasten; fix determinedly, as to set one's jaw. 7. To estimate; value. 8. To adjust or regulate. 9. To adapt, as to set to music. 10. To move in a specific direction, as the current sets to the east. 11. *Printing.* To arrange type.—**set about.** To begin; to start.—**set against.** 1. To compare. 2. To oppose.—**set aside.** To dismiss; reserve; reject.—**set a trap** or snare. To deceive; ambush.—**to set back.** To check; obstruct.—**set down.** 1. To place. 2. To enter in writing. 3. To register.—**set fire.** To cause to burn.—**set forth.** 1. To demonstrate; expound. 2. To start out.—**set off.** 1. To start. 2. To enter upon a journey. 3. To show to the best advantage.—**set on** or **upon.** 1. To attack. 2. To begin or start; incite. —**set sail.** *Nautical.* To start on a voyage.—**set the stage.** To prepare for action.—**set up.** 1. To erect. 2. To establish; found. 3. To exalt; put in power. 4. To raise, as to set up a howl. 5. To buy for one or give free, esp. drinks in a barroom.

set *n.* 1. A matching group. 2. A clique; an associated group. 3. Position or posture. 4. Hardening; solidification. 5. The direction of a current. 6. Fit; drape. 7. A small plant or slip ready to be placed in the ground; a bulb or tuber. 8. *Radio.* An instrument for receiving and reconverting radio waves into sound. 9. *Theater.* Stage scenery. 10. The stage in a motion-picture studio. 11. *Tennis.* A series of games. 12. *Psychology.* An established pattern of reaction. 13. Artificial waving of the hair.

set·back *n.* 1. A kind of card game. 2. An adverse event; a reversal.

set·tee (seh-*tee*) *n.* A long, high-backed bench; a sofa.

set·ter (*set*-er) *n.* 1. One who sets. 2. A long-haired dog used by sportsmen to discover and "point" game.

SETTER (1/35 life-size)

set·ting (*set*-ing) *n.* 1. Mounting; frame. 2. Surroundings; scenery. 3. The solidifying of a soft substance. 4. Music written to accompany a poem.—**set·ting** *adj.*—**setting-up exercise.** Gymnastic exercises for special health purposes.

set·tle (*set*-'l) *n.* A heavy, high-backed bench.

S

set·tle v. [set·tled; set·tling] 1. To fix or make permanent. 2. To grow calm; quiet down. 3. To arrange; bring to conclusion; agree upon. 4. To establish residence; colonize. 5. To become established in a regular mode of life; establish or place in a certain life or occupation. 6. To sink; become clear by the sinking of sediment. 7. To adjust, as by payment. 8. To descend and remain.—**set·tled** adj.—**set·tle·ment** n.—**set·tler** n.

sev·en (sev-'n) n. Number represented by the symbol 7.—adj. Consisting of seven.

sev·en·fold adj. & adv. Seven times over.

sev·en·teen n. The number represented by the symbol 17.—adj. Consisting of seventeen. —**sev·en·teenth** adj. & n.

seventeen-year locust. A type of locust, in the northern U.S., which spends seventeen years underground before reaching maturity.

sev·enth n. 1. Coming in order as 7. 2. Music. a. An interval including ten semitones. b. The seventh tone of the diatonic scale. —**sev·enth** adj.

sev·en·ty (sev-'n-tee) n. [pl. -ies] Seven times ten; number represented by the symbol 70. —adj. Consisting of seventy.— **-ti·eth** adj. & n.

sev·en·ty-five n. 1. The number represented by the symbol 75. 2. A 75mm. artillery piece. —adj. Consisting of seventy-five.

sev·er (sev-er) v. To separate; cut; divide.—**sev·er·a·ble** adj. Capable of being separated.

sev·er·al (sev-er-'l) 1. A few; more than two. 2. Different; various. 3. Individual; particular.—**sev·er·al·ly** adv.

sev·er·ance (sev-er-'nss) n. Parting; separation. —**severance pay.** Extra pay according to length of service given an employee leaving a job.

se·vere (suh-veer) adj. 1. Grave; austere. 2. Stern; unsparing; strict. 3. Plain; unadorned. 4. Cruel; harsh; extreme; arduous. —**se·vere·ly** adv.—**se·vere·ness, se·ver·i·ty** n.

sew (soh) v. [sewed; sewn; sew·ing] To fasten or work with needle and thread.—**sew·a·ble** adj. —**sew·er** (soh-er) n.

sew·age (soo-ij) n. Waste matter passing through drains.

sew·er (soo-er) n. An underground canal for carrying off waste.

sew·er·age n. The removal of surface water and waste, especially in a city, by sewers.

sew·ing (soh-ing) n. 1. A mending; fastening with needle and thread. 2. Articles to be sewed.—**sewing machine.** A mechanical device for stitching, worked either by foot treadle or electricity.

sex n. 1. The two animal classifications, male and female. 2. Their characteristic reproductive attributes.—**sex appeal.** Great attraction for the opposite sex.—**sex hygiene.** Health care in matters of sex and sexual behavior. —**sex·less** adj. Without sex and its characteristics.—**sex·less·ness** n.—**sex·y** adj. Slang. Sexually attractive.

sex·a·ge·nar·i·an (sekss-uh-juh-nehr-ee-'n) n. One between the ages of sixty and seventy years.—**sex·a·ge·na·ry** adj. & n.

sex·tant (sekss-t'nt) n. An instrument for measuring angles, especially in celestial navigation.

sex·tet (sekss-tet) n. 1. A group of six, esp. musicians. 2. A piece scored for six voices or instruments.

sex·til·lion (sekss-til-yun) n. A number consisting of a unit followed by twenty-one ciphers or zeros.—**sex·til·lion** adj.—**sex·til·lionth** adj.

SEXTANT

sex·to·de·ci·mo n. [pl. -mos] Printing. A book or book page size not larger than 4½ x 6¾ inches; written as 16mo; sixteenmo.—adj. Having a sheet folded into sixteen leaves.

sex·ton (sekss-t'n) n. A church employee, usually the caretaker and bellringer.

sex·tu·ple (sekss-tuh-p'l) adj. Sixfold; consisting of or multiplied by six.—v. [sex·tu·pled; -pling] To increase sixfold.—**sex·tu·plet** n. 1. A group of six similar objects. 2. One of six offspring born together.

sex·u·al (sek-shoo-ul) adj. 1. Pertaining to the characteristic distinctions of male and female. 2. Pertaining to intercourse between male and female.—**sex·u·al·i·ty** n. Possession of sexual qualities and desires.—**sex·u·al·ly** adv.

shab·by (shab-ee) adj. [shab·bi·er; shab·bi·est] 1. Well-worn; seedy. 2. Mean; paltry; malicious.—**shab·bi·ly** adv.—**shab·bi·ness** n.

shack n. A shed; a small, flimsy hut.

shack·le (shak-'l) n. 1. A chain or fetter. 2. Nautical. a. A detachable link joining two lengths of chain. b. A bow of metal with a removable pin closing the open end.—v. [shack·led; shack·ling]—**shack·ler** n.

shad n. An important food fish similar to but larger than herring.—**shad roe.** Eggs of the shad, regarded as a food delicacy.

shad·ber·ry (shad-ber-ee) n. Fruit of the shadbush.

shad·bush n. A white-flowered bush with small berry-like fruit.

shade n. 1. Comparative darkness caused by obstruction of direct light. 2. An adjustable window covering. 3. A cylindrical screen for an electric bulb. 4. Protection; shelter; a secluded spot. 5. A small degree; graduation; nuance. 6. A ghost or spirit.—v. [shad·ed; shad·ing] 1. To provide shelter from light; to shelter. 2. To apply gradations of color.

shad·ing (shayd-ing) n. Representation of degrees of light on a drawing or painting.

shad·ow (shad-oh) n. 1. Silhouette projected by an object intercepting light. 2. Dimmer position of a surface. 3. Darkness; obscurity; shade. 4. Shelter. 5. Darker portions of a picture. 6. A spirit; a ghost. 7. Trace; vestige. 8. An inseparable associate.—v. 1. To obscure; to shade. 2. To follow closely, esp. surreptitiously. 3. To mark with grada-tions of tone; to shade.—**shad·ow·er** *n.*—**shad·ow·less** *adj.*—**shad·ow·y** *adj.* [-i·er; -i·est].

shad·y (*shayd*-ee) *adj.* [shad·i·er; shad·i·est] 1. Sheltered from bright light or heat. 2. Of doubtful character or morality.—**shad·i·ly** *adv.* —**shad·i·ness** *n.*

shaft *n.* 1. A rod; a long slender cylinder. 2. An arrow; a spear. 3. A vertical opening; as, an elevator shaft; deep narrow pit; as, a mine shaft. 4. *Machinery.* An axle; a revolv-ing bar serving to convey motion from the source of power to other machines or wheels. 5. [*pl.*] The bars between which a horse is harnessed to a vehicle. 6. The handle of certain instruments or tools, such as golf clubs.

shag *n.* 1. Coarse hair or nap. 2. A kind of cloth having long coarse nap. 3. A bird of the cormorant family. 4. Coarse shredded tobacco. 5. A popular dance step.—*v.* [shagged; shag·ging] 1. To make rough or hairy. 2. To dance the shag.

shag·gy (*shag*-ee) *adj.* [shag·gi·er; shag·gi·est] Rough; hairy; unkempt.—**shag·gi·ness** *n.*

shah *n.* Title of the monarch of Iran.

shake *v.* [shook; shak·en; shak·ing] 1. To vibrate; tremble. 2. To remove; dislodge. 3. To agitate; undermine; implant doubt. 4. To rouse suddenly and forcibly. 5. *Music.* To trill. 6. *Slang.* To rid oneself of.

shake *n.* 1. A vibration; a jerking. 2. *Slang.* An instant. 3. *Music.* A trill. 4. [*pl.*] A fit of trembling.

shake·down *n.* 1. *Slang.* Extortion of money by force, deception, or blackmail. 2. A hast-ily thrown together bedsack.

shakedown cruise. *Nautical.* The trial run of a newly built ship.

shak·en (*shayk*-'n) *adj.* Agitated; jarred; upset.

shak·er *n.* 1. A device for mixing or sprinkling. 2. [*cap.*] One of a small religious sect whose worship involves dancing.—**Shak·er·ism** *n.*

Shake·spear·e·an (shayk-*spihr*-ee-un) *adj.* Also **Shak·sper·i·an.** Pertaining to or in the style of William Shakespeare, noted English play-wright and poet.—**Shake·spear·e·an·ism, Shak·sper·i·an·ism** *n.*

shak·o (*shak*-oh) *n.* [*pl.* shak·os] A tall military cap, usually with a plume.

shak·y (*shayk*-ee) *adj.* [shak·i·er; shak·i·est] 1. Unsub-stantial; poorly put to-gether. 2. Nervous; appre-hensive. 3. Of doubtful integrity.—**shak·i·ly** *adv.* —**shak·i·ness** *n.*

shale *n.* Slate which splits readily into layers.

shall *v.* auxiliary [participles and *infinitive* lacking] 1. Used to express simple futurity with the first person singular and plural of the future tense followed by the infinitive without

SHAKO

"to," as I or we shall go. 2. Used with second or third person to imply command or inevita-bility, as they shall be killed.

shal·lot *n.* 1. A small onion or scallion. 2. A vegetable similar to garlic but milder.

shal·low (*shal*-oh) *adj.* 1. Slight in depth. 2. Superficial.—*n.* A shoal; a place where water is less deep.—**shal·low·ly** *adv.*—**shal·low·ness** *n.*

shalt *Archaic form* of the second person singu-lar of **shall.**

shal·y (*shayl*-ee) *adj.* Flaky; like shale.

sham *n.* A fraud; deception; imitation.—*adj.* False; pretended.—*v.* [shammed; -ming].

sham·ble (*sham*-b'l) *v.* [sham·bled; -bling] To shuffle; to move clumsily along.— -**bling** *adj.*

shambles *n.* [*pl.* but often regarded as *singular*] 1. Ruin; wreckage. 2. Scene of destruction. 3. A slaughterhouse.

shame *n.* 1. Embarrassment; sense of guilt or inferiority. 2. Disgrace; dishonor.—*v.* [shamed; sham·ing] 1. To make conscious of shortcoming; embarrass. 2. To disgrace; mock; deride.—**put to shame.** 1. To inflict disgrace upon. 2. To make appear worthless by comparison.

shame·faced *adj.* 1. Bashful; easily embar-rassed. 2. Guilty looking.—**shame·fac·ed·ly** *adv.*—**shame·fac·ed·ness** *n.*

shame·ful *adj.* 1. Disgraceful; humiliating. 2. Indecent; shocking.—**shame·ful·ly** *adv.* —**shame·ful·ness** *n.*

shame·less *adj.* Immodest; brazen.—**shame·less·ly** *adv.*—**shame·less·ness** *n.*

sham·mer *n.* A deceiver; a pretender.

sham·poo (sham-*poo*) *v.* To wash the hair.—*n.* A liquid soap for the hair.—**sham·poo·er** *n.*

sham·rock *n.* Any of several three-leaved plants of the clover family; now the national flower of the Irish.

Shang·hai (*shang*-hy) *n.* Port city, eastern China.

shang·hai (*shang*-hy) *v.* [shang·haied; shang·hai·ing] 1. To im-press seamen into service by force or treachery. 2. To kid-nap by force.

SHAMROCK

S

shank *n.* 1. The leg; the shin. 2. In horses, the part of the foreleg between knee and the fetlock. 3. The straight shaft of an instru-ment. 4. *Architecture.* Shaft of a column.

shan·tung (shan-*tung*) *n.* Light, rough-textured material, usually silk.

Shan·tung (*shan-tung; shan-dung*) Province in eastern China. Area: 69,198 sq. mi.

shan·ty (*shan*-tee) *n.* [*pl.* shan·ties] A hut; a small and poor dwelling.

shape *n.* 1. Form; dimensions; proportions; outline. 2. A phantom; a dimly-defined form. 3. Pattern or model.—*v.* [shaped; shap·ing] 1. To mold or cut to a certain form. 2. To create; to make. 3. To adapt, adjust, or direct. 4. To imagine.—**shap·er** *n.*

shape·less *adj.* Formless; without symmetry; amorphous.—**shape·less·ly** *adj.*—**shape·less·ness** *n.*

shape·ly *adj.* [shape·li·er; shape·li·est] Well-formed; of pleasing proportions.

shape-up *n.* Technique of hiring whereby all candidates must report daily and wait until foremen give jobs to those from whom they may expect a kickback.

share *v.* [shared; shar·ing] 1. To divide into portions. 2. To partake or experience with others. 3. To possess jointly.—*n.* 1. Allotted quantity. 2. Partial ownership of a firm, as a share of stock.

share cropper (*shair krop-*'r). *U.S.* Tenant farmer who tills a plot of land for its owner in return for a share of the produce.

share·hold·er *n.* A part owner, as one who owns stock in a corporation.

shark *n.* 1. A large and voracious fish. 2. A greedy, deceptive person; a cheat. 3. *Slang.* An expert.

shark·skin *n.* 1. A loosely-woven long-wearing fabric, widely used in men's suitings. 2. A women's dress material, similarly woven, but usually of rayon.

SHARK (1/90 life-size)

sharp *adj.* 1. Keen, thin-edged, or pointed. 2. Abrupt. 3. Distinct; clear. 4. Shrewd; quick of mind; clever. 5. Severe; harsh; biting. 6. *Music.* **a.** Raised a half-tone in pitch. **b.** Slightly above correct pitch.—*n. Music.* 1. A note raised one semitone in pitch. 2. The indicating symbol [#].—**sharp·ly** *adv.*—**sharp·ness** *n.*

sharp-angled	sharp-cornered	sharp looking
sharp-beaked	sharp-cut	sharp-sighted
sharp-billed	sharp-edged	sharp-toothed
sharp-clawed	sharp-faced	sharp-witted

sharp·en *v.* To make keen or pointed.—**sharp·en·er** *n.*

sharp·er *n. Slang.* A cheater; a swindler.

sharp·ie *n.* A light flat-bottomed sailboat.

sharp·shoot·er *n.* Highly skilled marksman.— **-shoot·ing** *n.*

shat·ter *v.* 1. To wreck; splinter; break to pieces. 2. To derange; stun.

SHARPIE

shave *v.* [shaved; shaved, shav·en; shav·ing] 1. To cut off with a sharp-edged instrument, esp. to cut hair with a razor. 2. To cut very thin.—*n.* 1. Removal of the beard. 2. *Colloquial.* A narrow miss or escape.—**shav·er** *n.* 1. One who or that which shaves. 2. *Colloquial.* Humorous term for *boy.*

shave·tail *n. Military Slang.* Humorous term for **Second Lieutenant.**

Sha·vi·an (*shay-*vee-un) *n.* A follower of George Bernard Shaw, British author and critic. —**Sha·vi·an** *adj.*

shav·ing (*shayv-*ing) *n.* A sliver pared off by a plane or other blade.

shawl *n.* A long piece of cloth or knitted material worn loosely over the shoulders or head.

Shaw·nee *n.* [*pl.* Shaw·nee or Shaw·nees] A member of a tribe of Algonquian Indians originating in Georgia and S. Carolina.

shay *n. Colloquial.* A high-wheeled horse-drawn carriage.

she *pronoun.* The nominative case third person pronoun, used in place of the name of a feminine subject.

SHAWL

sheaf (*sheef*) *n.* [*pl.* sheaves] 1. A bundle of stalks or straw. 2. A bundle of light objects, as a sheaf of papers.—*v.* To collect and bind.

shear (*shihr*) *v.* [sheared; sheared, shorn; shear·ing] 1. To cut or clip; separate with scissors. 2. *Mechanics.* To become separated as if cut.—**shear·er** *n.*

shears *n. pl.* A cutting instrument consisting of two cutting edges, operated scissors-fashion.

sheath (*sheeth*) *n.* [*pl.* sheaths (*sheethz*)] A case or covering, esp. for a sword or knife. —**sheathe** *v.* [sheathed; sheathing] To put into a case; enclose.

sheave *n.* A grooved pulley wheel.

SHEARS

shed *v.* [shed; shed·ding] 1. To cast off, as a covering. 2. To spill; make flow; pour.

shed *n.* 1. A small temporary building. 2. A shelter; a lean-to.

sheen *n.* Luster; shine; sleekness. —*v.* To glisten.

sheep *n.* [*pl.* sheep] 1. A grass-eating domestic animal raised for its wool and as food. 2. A bashful fellow. 3. The leather (sheepskin) used in bookbinding.

SHEAVE

sheep·ish *adj.* Embarrassed; clumsy; self-conscious.—**sheep·ish·ly** *adv.*— **-ish·ness** *n.*

sheep·skin *n.* 1. The skin of a sheep, or the leather or parchment prepared from it. 2. *Slang.* A diploma or certificate of graduation from school.

sheer *v. Nautical.* To alter course abruptly; veer.—*n.* 1. A change in a vessel's course. 2. The slope upward from midships to bow and stern of a vessel.

SHEEP (1/35 life-size)

sheer *adj.* 1. Pure; clear; unmixed. 2. Absolute; simple; utter. 3. Perpendicular; precipitously steep. 4. Transparent; filmy. —sheer·ly *adv.*—sheer·ness *n.*

sheet *n.* 1. A page; a thin smooth section or surface of paper, esp. [*pl.*] the pages of a book before binding. 2. Bed linen; the cloth laid between mattress and blankets.—sheet·ing *n.*

sheik, sheikh (*sheek*) *n.* 1. Chief of an Arabic tribe or clan. 2. Title of certain Mohammedan religious leaders. 3. *Slang.* A romantic-looking young man.

shek·el *n.* 1. An ancient coin of Babylon. 2. *Slang.* Money; cash.

shel·drake *n.* A type of European duck.

shelf *n.* [*pl.* shelves] 1. A flat piece fixed horizontally to a wall or frame to hold various objects. 2. A projecting rock.

SHELDRAKE (1/15 life-size)

shell *n.* 1. A hard protective outer covering, as of an animal, egg, or nest. 2. A retreat. 3. An empty structure; a casing. 4. An explosive projectile fired from a gun. 5. A light racing rowboat.—*v.* 1. To remove shells from. 2. *Military.* To bombard.

shel·lac, shel·lak (shuh-*lak*) *n.* A lacquer, having an alcohol base, transparent, waterproof. —shel·lack *v.* [shel·lacked; shel·lack·ing] 1. To coat with shellac. 2. *Slang.* To beat; trounce. —shel·lack·er *n.*

shell·fish *n.* [*pl.* shell·fish] Marine animal having a hard outer covering, as oysters, clams, and mussels.

shell game. A swindling game; originally one wherein the dupe attempted to guess under which of three walnut shells the deft trickster had concealed a pellet.

shel·ter (*shel*-ter) *n.* Lodging; refuge; place of protection.—*v.* To cover; protect.—shel·ter·er *n.*—shel·ter·less *adj.*

shelve *v.* [shelved; shelv·ing] 1. To place on a shelf. 2. To put aside; dismiss. 3. To slope as a sandbank; incline.

shelves. *Plural of* shelf.

shep·herd (*shep*-erd) *n.* 1. One employed to tend and guard sheep. 2. A spiritual leader; pastor.–shep·herd *v.*–shep·herd·ess *n.*

Sher·a·ton *adj.* Designating an elegant but clean style of furniture design formulated by Thomas Sheraton in the late 18th century.

SHEPHERD

sher·bet (*sher*-bit) *n.* A flavored, sweetened ice.

sher·iff (*shehr*-if) *n.* An elected county officer charged with maintaining law and order.— sher·iff·dom *n.*

sher·ry (*shehr*-ee) *n.* A fine grape wine originally made in Spain.

Sherwood *n.* Forest in Nottinghamshire, England, famous in Robin Hood legends.

Shet·land (*shet*-l'nd) *n.* 1. Group of islands north of Scotland comprising two counties of Scotland. Area: 550 sq. mi. 2. A breed of ponies native to these islands. 3. A soft wool derived from the Shetland Islands sheep.

shib·bo·leth (*shib*-uh-leth) *n.* 1. *Bible.* Password used by the Gileadites (*Judges* 12). 2. Test; slogan; countersign.

shield (*sheeld*) *n.* 1. A piece of defensive armor formerly carried on the arm. 2. A protection; a defense.—*v.* To cover; protect from danger; ward off.

SHIELD

shift *v.* 1. To move; transfer; change. 2. To resort to expedients; adopt a course under difficulty. —*n.* 1. A substitution; a switch. 2. An expedient; a device; a last resort. 3. A group of workers having the same hours; working time.—shift·er *n.*

shift·less *adj.* Lazy; unresourceful; inefficient. —shift·less·ly *adv.*—shift·less·ness *n.*

shift·y *adj.* [shift·i·er; shift·i·est] 1. Evasive; unsteady. 2. Alert; tricky.—shift·i·ly *adv.*

shil·le·lagh, shil·la·lah (shil-*lay*-lee, shil-*lay*-luh) *n.* An Irish cudgel or club, often a stout walking-stick.

shil·ling (*shil*-ing) *n.* A British coin equal to twelve pence or one-twentieth of a pound sterling; about twenty cents American.

shil·ly-shal·ly *v.* To vacillate; to waste effort and time.

Shi·loh (*shy*-loh) *n.* 1. Civil War battlefield (1862) SW Tennessee; now military park. 2. Town in ancient Palestine.

shim·mer *v.* To shine tremulously; glisten.—*n.* A glimmer; a sheen.—shim·mer·y *adj.*

shim·my (*shim*-ee) *n.* 1. A dance characterized by shaking of the body. 2. Unusual vibration, esp. of automobile wheels.—*v.* [-mied; -my·ing].

shin *n.* The forepart of the leg between ankle and knee.—*v.* [shinned; shin·ning] To climb a pole by grasping it alternately with arms and legs.

shin·dig *n.* *Slang.* A celebration or party, esp. a noisy one.

shin·dy (*shin*-dee) *n.* [*pl.* shin·dies] *Slang.* 1. A row; rumpus. 2. A party.

shine *v.* [shone; shin·ing] 1. To emit light; gleam; glow. 2. To be conspicuous or eminent; to excel. 3. [shined; shin·ing] To polish.—*n.* 1. Illumination; light. 2. Brightness; luster; gloss. 3. Fair weather. 4. *Slang.* A liking; fancy.—shin·er *n.* 1. *Slang.* A bruise around the eye. 2. A small silvery fish.—shin·ing *adj.* Gleaming; sparkling; splendid.—shin·ing·ly *adv.*

S

shin·gle (*shing*-g'l) *n.* 1. A segment of roofing inserted under another to form tiers. 2. A short hair bob. 3. *Colloquial.* A signboard. 4. *Medicine.* [*pl.*] Inflammatory virus disease of the skin accompanied by blisters and severe neuralgic pain.—*v.* [shin·gled; shin·gling] 1. To cover with shingles. 2. To cut hair in a bob.—**shin·gler** *n.*

shin·ny (*shin*-ee) *v.* [shin·nied; shin·ny·ing] 1. *Colloquial.* To climb a pole or tree; to shin. 2. To play a schoolboy type of hockey.—*n.* [*pl.* shin·nies] Also **shin·ney.** 1. Hockey. 2. A hockey stick.

Shin·to (*shin*-toh) *n.* A Japanese religion, until recently national, revering the spirits of imperial ancestors, historical heroes, and deities of nature.—**Shin·to·ism** *n.*—**Shin·to·ist** *n. & adj.*

shin·y (*shyne*-ee) *adj.* [shin·i·er; shin·i·est] Bright; glossy; glittering.

ship *n.* Any large floating structure with means of propulsion; also, its officers and crew.—*v.* [shipped; ship·ping] 1. To put on board a vessel. 2. To transport by any means. 3. To engage for service on a vessel. 4. To embark or go aboard a vessel.—**ship off.** To send away.—**ship a sea.** To have the deck covered by a wave.—**ship·pa·ble** *adj.*

shipboard	shipload	shipshape
ship-bound	shipman	shipside
shipboy	shipmaster	shipsmith
ship breaker	shipmate	shipway
ship-broken	shipowner	ship work
shipbuilder	shipowning	shipworm
shipbuilding	ship-rigged	shipwright

-ship *suffix.* 1. State or quality. 2. Office, dignity, or profession. 3. Art or skill. 4. Rank or title.

ship·ment *n.* 1. Transportation of goods. 2. A number of articles to be transported.

ship·per *n.* One who transports goods or commits them to transport.

ship·ping *n.* 1. Transporting goods. 2. Ships collectively; tonnage.—**ship·ping** *adj.*

ship·shape *adj. & adv.* Tidy; orderly.

ship·wreck (-rek) *n.* 1. Destruction or sinking of a vessel. 2. A wrecked vessel. 3. An irreparable loss.—**ship·wreck** *v.*

ship·yard *n.* An area for construction or repair of seagoing vessels.

shire (*shyre*- as suffix *sh'r*) *n.* In England, a division corresponding to a county.

shirk *v.* To dodge a duty; side-step.—**shirk·er** *n.*

shirr *n.* *Sewing.* A number of parallel gathers. —*v.* 1. To gather in parallel seams. 2. *Cooking.* To bake eggs in a buttered dish.

shirt *n.* 1. A garment worn on the upper part of the body under the coat or jacket. 2. A close-fitting undergarment.

shirt·ing *n.* Material used for making shirts.

shirtsleeve *n.* Part of the shirt which covers the arms.

shirt·tail *n.* *Journalism.* A brief additional story, esp. a local item, added at the end of a main news item.

shirt·waist *n.* A woman's tailored blouse, worn tucked into a skirt or slacks.

Shi·va (*shee*-vuh) *Variant spelling of* **Siva.**

shiv·er (*shiv*-er) *v.* To tremble; shudder; shake as from cold or excitement.—**shiv·er** *n.*—**shiv·er·y** *adj.*

shiv·er *v.* To shatter; to break into splinters. —*n.* A small piece; a sliver.

shoal (*shohl*) *n.* 1. A sand bank or bar making the water shallow. 2. A shallow area.—*v.* To become more shallow.—**shoal** *adj.*—**shoal·y** *adj.*

shoal *n.* A crowd; a large number.—*v.* To crowd together; to throng.

shoat (*shoht*) *n.* Also **shote.** A young hog.

shock *n.* 1. A blow; a sudden collision; an impact. 2. A horrifying event; sudden calamitous news. 3. Daze; stunned reaction. 4. The effect of electricity passing into the body. 5. *Medicine.* A depressed condition of the body resulting from severe injury or violent mental excitement.—*v.* 1. To jolt; shake; upset. 2. To offend; disgust; terrify.

shock *n.* 1. A pile of sheaves of grain stacked upright. 2. A mass of close matted hair.—*v.* To gather sheaves into a pile.—**shock·er** *n.*

shock absorber. Device for taking up the energy of sudden jolts in instruments, machinery, or structures.

shock·er *n.* *Slang.* A sensational story.

shock·head·ed, shock·head *adj.* Having a mass of thick hair.

shock·ing *adj.* Appalling; horrifying; scandalous.—**shock·ing·ly** *adv.*

shod. *Past tense & past participle of* **shoe.**

shod·dy (*shod*-ee) *n.* [*pl.* shoddies] 1. Coarse inferior woolen cloth. 2. An inferior person or thing.—*adj.* [shod·di·er; shod·di·est] 1. Inferior; of poor quality. 2. Sham; pretentious.

shoe (*shoo*) *n.* 1. A covering for the foot, usually of leather. 2. An iron rim nailed to the hoof of a horse or other hooved animal. 3. A socket; a base; the part of a brake which presses on the brake drum. 4. The outer casing of a tire.—*v.* [shod; shoe·ing] 1. To furnish with covering for the feet. 2. To cover at the bottom to protect.—**sho·er** *n.*

SHOE

shoebill	shoelace	shoeshine
shoeblack	shoemaker	shoe shop
shoe box	shoemaking	shoesmith
shoeboy	shoeman	shoe store
shoe brush	shoe pack	shoestring
shoehorn	shoe scraper	shoe tree

shone. *Past tense & past participle of* **shine.**

shook. *Past tense of* **shake.**

shoon. *Archaic form of* **shoes.**

shoot *v.* [shot; shoot·ing] 1. To fire; let fly or propel. 2. To fly; rush; dart. 3. To wound or kill with a bullet. 4. To push forward; rush. 5. To sprout; grow rapidly. 6. *Mo-*

tion Pictures. To photograph; film. 7. To streak with different colors.—*n.* 1. A shooting match; also, a hunting trip. 2. A young plant stem. 3. A rapid motion or thrust. 4. A chute.—**shoot·er** *n.*

shooting star. A meteor; a body which enters the earth's atmosphere from outer space, appearing as a glowing streak across the sky.

shop *n.* 1. An establishment where goods are sold at retail. 2. A building or room designed for a particular trade; a small factory.—*v.* [shopped; shop·ping] To visit retail stores to purchase goods.—**shop·per** *n.*—**talk shop.** To discuss one's occupation.

shopboard	shopkeeper	shop talk
shopbook	shopman	shop wear
shopboy	shop mark	shop window
shop breaker	shopmate	shopwoman
shopgirl	shop-soiled	shopworn

shop·lift·er *n.* One who steals articles from stores.—**shop·lift·ing** *n.*

shop·walk·er *n.* A supervisor who walks about in a store as overseer and director.

shore *n.* Coast land adjoining a body of water. —**shore·less** *adj.* Having no shore.

shore *n.* A prop; a support used to brace or hold an object.—*v.* To brace with a post or strut.—**shor·ing** *n.* System of braces.

shore·line *n.* Land bordering water.

shore·ward *n.* Toward shore.

shorn. *Past participle* of **shear.** —*adj.* 1. Cropped or shaved. 2. Deprived; removed.

short *adj.* 1. Brief; small; of little height, length, distance, or duration. 2. Below standard; inadequate. 3. Curt; brusque. 4. Rich and crisp, as short pastry.—*adv.* Briefly; abruptly; suddenly.—*n.* 1. *Electricity.* A short circuit. 2. *Motion Pictures.* A brief film shown on the same program with a full length feature. 3. [*pl.*] Trousers or underwear not reaching to the knee.—**short·ish** *adj.* —**short·ness** *n.*—**in short.** Briefly.

SHORING

short-armed	short-fed	short-necked
short-billed	short-haired	shortstaff
shortbread	shorthead	shorttail (*n.*)
short-eared	shorthorn (*n.*)	short-winded
short-faced	short-horned (*adj.*)	short-winged

short·age (*shor*-tij) *n.* Amount deficient or lacking; insufficient quantity.

short·cake *n.* 1. A pastry made rich with shortening. 2. A dessert of sweet biscuits or cake split and covered with fruit.

short·change *v.* [-changed; -chang·ing] To cheat, esp. in changing money.— -chang·er *n.*

short circuit. A sudden drop of normal resistance in a circuit, usually caused by contact between the two sides.—**short-circuit·ed** *adj.*

short·com·ing *n.* A fault; a defect.

short·en *v.* 1. To abbreviate; cut; reduce in length. 2. To enrich pastry with butter, lard, etc.—**short·en·er** *n.*

short·en·ing (*short*-'n-ing) *n.* 1. Abbreviation; reduction of length. 2. Any fat used in baking.

short·hand *n.* A system of writing rapidly by substituting special symbols for words or phrases.—**short·hand** *adj.*

short·hand·ed *adj.* Lacking sufficient workers or helpers.

short·horn *n.* A breed of heavy beef cattle.

short·lived (-*lyvde*) *adj.* Brief; dying early.

short·ly *adv.* 1. Soon; before long. 2. Curtly.

short sale. Sale of property not yet possessed. —**short seller.**

short·sight·ed *adj.* 1. Myopic; seeing poorly at a distance. 2. Blind to consequences; unperceptive; without vision.—**short·sight·ed·ly** *adv.*—**short·sight·ed·ness** *n.*

short·spok·en *adj.* Curt; abrupt.

short·stop *n.* 1. *Baseball.* A player located between second and third base to catch short hits, etc. 2. *Photography.* A chemical stopping action of film developer.

short·tem·pered *adj.* Irritable; easily angered.

short·term *adj.* Of brief validity, esp. of financial negotiations.

short ton. A weight of 2000 pounds.

short wave. A radio wave of high frequency, out of the range of the normal broadcast band. —**short·wave** *adj.*

Sho·sho·ne (shoh-*shoh*-nee) *n.* Tribe of Indians originating in western U. S.—**Sho·sho·ne·an** *adj.*

shot *n.* [*pl.* shots, shot] 1. Discharge from a firearm or other weapon. 2. Any discharged missile; a bullet; a cannon ball. 3. A small sphere of lead for loading cartridges. 4. A marksman. 5. A guess; an attempt. 6. *Slang.* An injection; a drink. 7. Range; flight. 8. *Sports.* **a.** A stroke. **b.** A heavy weight thrown for distance. 9. *Nautical.* A 15-fathom length of chain. 10. A photograph. —*adj.* 1. Exhausted. 2. Streaked; flecked.

shote *n. Variant spelling* of **shoat.**

shot·gun *n.* A gun adapted to firing in volleys.

SHOTGUN

should (*shood*) *v. auxiliary.* 1. *Past tense* of **shall.** 2. Expressing obligation. 'He should go.' 'He should have gone.' 3. Expressing a hypothetical or dubious event. 'If it should rain, I cannot come.'

shoul·der (*shohl*-der) *n.* 1. The projecting portion of the body joining the human arm, or animal foreleg, to the trunk. 2. A cut of meat consisting of the upper foreleg and adjoining parts. 3. A ledge. 'The shoulder of a hill.' 4. The edge of a road. 5. A support.—*v.* 1. To take upon the shoulder; to support.

S

2. To push or thrust with the shoulders.—**cold shoulder.** An uncordial reception.—**shoulder to shoulder.** United; mutually cooperative.

shouldst. *Archaic form* of second person sing. of **should.**

shout (*showt*) *v.* To cry out; to yell. —*n.* An outcry; a loud burst of voices.—**shout·er** *n.*—**shout down.** 1. To drown out another by shouting. 2. To defeat.

shove (*shuv*) *v.* [shoved; shov·ing] To push; jostle.—**shove** *n.*—**shov·er** *n.*

shov·el (*shuv*-'l) *n.* A long-handled tool with a broad scoop used for digging and lifting; also its capacity.—*v.* [shov·eled; shov·elled; shov·el·ing; shov·el·ling].—**shov·el·er, shov·el·ler** *n.*

shovel-beaked	shovel hat
shovel-bladed	shovelhead (*n.*)
shovelboard	shovel-headed (*adj.*)
shovelfish	shovel maker
shovel-footed	shovel making
shovel-handled	shovel-shaped

SHOVEL

shov·el·bill *n.* A broad-billed river duck.

show (*shoh*) *v.* [showed; shown, showed; show·ing] 1. To display; exhibit; present. 2. To demonstrate; explain. 3. To reveal; disclose. 4. To conduct; guide. 5. To become visible. —*n.* 1. An exhibition; a display. 2. Ostentatious display. 3. Appearance. 4. A pretense. 5. *Colloquial.* A theatrical production. —**show off.** To make an exhibition of oneself. —**show up.** 1. To expose; ridicule. 2. To arrive; appear.

show bill	showboat	showpiece
showbird	show card	showroom
showboard	showcase	showyard

show-down *n.* A thrashing out; presentation of conclusive data.

show·er (*shou*-er) *n.* 1. A brief rainfall. 2. Anything like a rainfall; an outburst. 3. A party at which gifts are presented to a bride. 4. A shower bath.—*v.* 1. To rain; to pour down briefly. 2. To give liberally. —**show·er·y** *adj.*

shower bath. A bath taken under a stream or spray of water.

show·man (*shoh*-m'n) *n.* [*pl.* show-men]. 1. The proprietor of an exhibition. 2. A vivid public personality; a dramatizer.—**show·man·ship** *n.*

shown. *Past participle* of **show.**

show-off *n.* One who tries to impress others.

show·y (*shoh*-ee) *adj.* [show·i·er; show·i·est] Attracting attention; gaudy; ostentatious. —**show·i·ly** *adv.*—**show·i·ness** *n.*

shrank. *Past tense* of **shrink.**

shrap·nel (*shrap*-n'l) *n.* The fragments of a bursting shell.

shred *v.* [shred; shred·ded; shred·ding] To tear or cut into strips.—*n.* A scrap; a fragment. —**shred·der** *n.*

shrew (*shroo*) *n.* 1. A vile-tempered woman. 2. A small rodent. —**shrew·ish** *adj.*—**shrew·ish·ly** *adv.*— **-ish·ness** *n.*

shrewd *adj.* Astute; discerning; clever.—**shrewd·ly** *adv.*—**shrewd·ness** *n.*

shriek (*shreek*) *v.* To scream; to utter a sharp, shrill cry.—**shriek·er** *n.*

SHREW (1/7 life-size)

shriev·al (*shreev*-ul) *adj.* Pertaining to a sheriff.—**shriev·al·ty** *n.* [*pl.* shriev·al·ties].

shrift *n.* Confession of sins; acknowledgment.

shrike (*shryke*) *n.* A bird noted for its habit of impaling its prey upon thorns before eating.

shrill *adj.* High-pitched; piercing.—*v.* To make a sharp, high sound.—**shril·ly** *adv.*—**shrill·ness** *n.*

shrimp *n.* 1. A small edible shellfish. 2. *Slang.* A small, unimpressive person.

SHRIKE (1/6 life-size)

shrine (*shryne*) *n.* A sacred place, esp. the tomb of a saint.—*v.* [shrined; shrin·ing] To place in a sacred or hallowed place; to entomb.

shrink *v.* [shrank *or* shrunk; shrunk *or* shrunk·en; shrink·ing] 1. To contract; grow smaller. 2. To recoil; cringe.—**shrink·a·ble** *adj.* —**shrink·age** *n.*—**shrink·er** *n.*— **-ing·ly** *adv.*

shriv·el (*shriv*-'l) *v.* [shriv·eled, shriv·elled; shriv·el·ing, shriv·el·ling] 1. To wither; wrinkle; dry up. 2. To become worthless.

shroud (*shrowd*) *n.* 1. The covering of the dead; a winding sheet. 2. Any covering or disguise. 3. *Nautical.* A rope running from the crosstree of a mast to the side of the ship, supporting the mast.—*v.* To shelter or conceal with a covering.—**shroud·less** *adj.*

shrub *n.* A bush; a woody plant smaller than a tree.

shrub·ber·y *n.* Close-set bushes; low foliage.

shrub·by *adj.* [shrub·bi·er; shrub·bi·est] 1. Covered with small coarse plants. 2. Stunted; short and rough.—**shrub·bi·ness** *n.*

shrug *v.* [shrugged; shrug·ging] To raise one's shoulders in gesture of indifference or distaste. —**shrug** *n.*—**shrug·ging·ly** *adv.*

shrunk·en *adj.* Shriveled; contracted.

shuck *n.* 1. A shell or covering; a husk; a pod. 2. A clam or oyster shell.—*v.* 1. To remove the husks from. 2. To shell.—**shuck·er** *n.*

shud·der (*shud*-er) *v.* To tremble violently; to shiver.—**shud·der** *n.*—**shud·der·ing·ly** *adv.*

shuf·fle (*shuf*-'l) *v.* [shuf·fled; shuf·fling] 1. To mix the order of, as a pack of cards. 2. To move or dance with a dragging, scraping step. —**shuf·fle** *n.*—**shuf·fle off.** 1. To move away with a dragging gait. 2. To rid oneself of.

shuf·fle·board *n.* A game played by shoving disks along a runway at numbered marks.

shun *v.* [shunned; shun·ning] To avoid; elude. —**shun·ner** *n.*

shunt *v.* 1. To move; turn aside; shift. 2. *Electricity.* To equip with a parallel circuit.—*n.* 1. *Railroads.* A diversion switch. 2. *Electricity.* A parallel circuit used to measure or regulate current in a main circuit.—*adj.* Characterized by a turnoff or by-pass as, shunt circuit, shunt meter, etc.—**shun·ter** *n.*

shut *v.* [shut; shut·ting] 1. To close. 2. To enclose; confine. 3. To prohibit; prevent entrance.

shut-down *v.* To stop operation of; to close.

shut·down *n.* Closing, as of a factory.

shut-in *n.* An invalid.—*adj.* Confined indoors, esp. through illness.

shut·out *n. Baseball.* A game in which the losing team scores no runs.

shut·ter *n.* 1. A hinged outer window-covering. 2. *Photography.* Mechanical device for admitting light for a regulated period onto a sensitized surface.—**shut·ter** *v.*

shut·tle (*shut-'l*) *n.* 1. An instrument used in weaving to pass the woof threads across the web between the threads of the warp. 2. Oscillating thread holder of a sewing machine.—*v.* [shut·tled; shut·tling] To move back and forth.

SHUTTER (def. 1)

shut·tle·cock *n.* A small piece of cork or rubber stuck with feathers, used in badminton.—*v.* To throw back and forth.

SHUTTLECOCK

shuttle train. A train running regularly between two nearby points.

shut up. 1. To confine. 2. *Colquial.* To stop speaking.

shy *adj.* [shi·er, shy·er; shi·est, shy·est] 1. Timid; diffident; readily frightened. 2. Cautious; wary; suspicious. 3. *Slang.* Lacking; scant.—*v.* [shied; shy·ing] 1. To start aside in sudden fear. 2. To throw sideways.—*n.* A quick throw or jerk to one's side. —**shy·er** *n.*—**shy·ly** *adv.*—**shy·ness** *n.*

Shy·lock *n.* 1. Money-lender in Shakespeare's *Merchant of Venice.* 2. A usurer.

shy·ster (*shy-ster*) *n.* Dishonest lawyer.

Siamese twins. Twins born with their bodies joined by a fleshy ligament.

Si·be·ri·an *n.* Native or resident of Siberia.

sib·i·lant (*sib-'l-unt*) *adj.* Hissing.—*n.* A speech sound as *s, z, ch, sh, zh, j.*—**sib·i·lance, sib·i·lan·cy** *n.*—**sib·i·lant·ly** *adv.*

sib·ling *n.* A brother or sister.

sib·yl (*sib-'l*) *n.* A woman endowed with magical or prophetic powers; sorceress.—**sib·yl·ic, sib·yl·lic, sib·yl·line** *adj.*

sic *adv.* Thus; usually inserted within brackets in text [*sic*] to show that word or phrase preceding is quoted exactly.

sic, sick *v.* To incite to action against. 'Sick the dog on him.'

sic·ca·tive (*sik-uh-tiv*) *adj.* Drying.—*n.* A drier or drying agent.

Si·cil·i·an (*sih-sil-yun*) *n.* A native of Sicily. —**Si·cil·i·an** *adj.*

sick *adj.* 1. Affected with nausea or vomiting; ill. 2. Disgusted; having a strong dislike for. 3. Sad, depressed.—*n.* [*pl.* sick] An ill person.

sick bay. Cabin aboard ship used as hospital and dispensary.

sick·en (*sik-un*) *v.* 1. To make or become ill or diseased. 2. To disgust or become disgusted. —**sick·en·ing** *adj.* Causing illness or disgust. —**sick·en·ing·ly** *adv.*

sick·ish *adj.* Slightly nauseated or ill.—**sick·ish·ly** *adv.*—**sick·ish·ness** *n.*

sick·le (*sik-'l*) *n.* An implement having a curved blade for cutting grain, grass, etc.—*v.* [sick·led; sick·ling] To cut with a sickle.

Sickle and Hammer. Emblem first used as a symbol of unity between peasant and worker, now (since 1923) part of the national flag of U.S.S.R.

sick·ly *adj.* [sick·li·er; sick·li·est] Somewhat ill or diseased; weak; overly thin and pale.—*v.* [sick·lied; sick·ly·ing] To make ill or wan.—**sick·li·ness** *n.*—**sick·ly** *adv.*

SICKLE

sick·ness (*sik-niss*) *n.* 1. A state of being ill or nauseated. 2. Disease; malady.

side (*syde*) *n.* 1. The long or broad surface of a solid body. 2. Margin; edge; border. 3. One of two opposed surfaces, not the front or back; a lateral surface. 4. Proximity; vicinity. 5. The area between the top and bottom of a hill or mountain. 6. *Theater.* A sheet containing an actor's cues and lines. 'He has twenty sides of dialog.' 7. A group of contestants in a battle or game; any interest or opinion opposed to another. 8. A part with respect to its direction or situation. 9. Branch of a family. 10. *Geometry.* A line forming one of the boundaries of a straight-lined figure. 11. *Slang.* Swagger; ostentation.—*adj.* 1. Lateral; from or toward the side as distinguished from the front or back. 2. Oblique.—*v.* [sided; sid·ing] To uphold the opinions of one party as opposed to another.

sidearms	sideflash	sidepiece
side-cast	side light	sidesway
sidecheck	side line	side-whiskered
side-cut	side-liner	sidewise

side·board (*syde*-bord) *n.* A cabinet holding dining utensils and linens.

side·burns *n. pl.* Whiskers growing down the upper part of the cheeks.

side·car *n.* 1. A small-wheeled vehicle attached at the side of a motorcycle. 2. [*often cap.*] Cocktail containing brandy, Cointreau, lemon juice, and sugar.

S

side·kick *n. Slang.* 1. A constant companion; a friend. 2. A fellow worker.

side·long *adj.* Indirect; oblique.—**side·long** *adv.*

si·de·re·al (sy-*deer*-ee-ul) *adj.* Pertaining to the motion of stars; astronomical.

side·sad·dle (*syde*-sad-'l) *n.* A woman's saddle designed to carry the right leg over the pommel rather than astride.

side·show *n.* 1. A small entertainment outside the main tent of a circus. 2. A diversion.

side·slip *v.* To slide off the intended track or course, as in aviation or skiing.—*n.* A skidding motion.

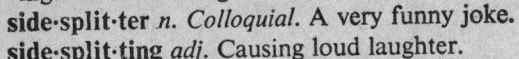

SIDESADDLE

side·split·ter *n. Colloquial.* A very funny joke.

side·split·ting *adj.* Causing loud laughter.

side-step *v.* To avoid; shrink.—*n.* An evasion.

side·swipe *v.* [-swiped; -swip·ing] To hit at an angle or obliquely.—*n.* An oblique blow.

side·track *n. Railroads.* A siding.—*v.* 1. To put railway cars on a sidetrack. 2. To put aside; shift; divert.

side·walk *n.* A raised pavement for foot travel.

side·way, side·ways, or **side·wise** *adv. & adj.* 1. Laterally. 2. Inclined; obliquely.

side·wheel·er *n.* A steamboat driven by a paddle wheel on each side.

side·wind·er *n.* 1. A rattlesnake. 2. A vicious round-arm blow with the fist.

sid·ing *n.* 1. *Railroad.* A short track extending from a main line to a loading platform, etc. 2. Boards used to cover outside walls.

si·dle (*sy*-d'l) *v.* [si·dled; si·dling] To move or glide with one side advanced.

siege (seej) *n.* 1. Encompassment by an army to force surrender. 2. A continued endeavor to obtain control.—*v.* [sieged; sicg·ing].

si·en·na (see-*en*-uh) *n.* A reddish-brown color.

si·er·ra (see-*ehr*-uh) *n.* A chain of jagged hills or mountains.

si·es·ta (see-*ess*-tuh) *n.* A midday nap; a period of sleep or rest.

sieve (siv) *n.* A screened utensil used to separate small particles from larger ones. —*v.* [sieved; siev·ing] To sift; to separate.

sift *v.* 1. To separate fine particles from larger ones. 2. To examine minutely; to analyze. 3. To sprinkle.—**sift·er** *n.*

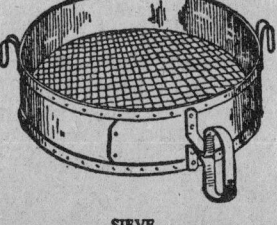

SIEVE

sigh (sy) *v.* 1. To make a deep exhalation of breath, as an expression of sorrow, weariness, etc. 2. To grieve.—*n.* A deep inhalation or exhalation indicating pain, sorrow, etc.—**sigh·er** *n.*

sight (*syte*) *n.* 1. Vision; ability to see. 2. Range of vision; visibility. 3. Notice; estimation; knowledge. 4. Inspection; examination. 5. A spectacle. 6. A small device having an aperture or notch by which an instrument is aimed.—*v.* 1. To come into range of visibility; perceive. 2. To aim, as a firearm.

sight draft. A note payable on presentation.

sight·less *adj.* Blind; incapable of seeing. —**sight·less·ness** *n.*

sight·ly *adj.* [sight·li·er; sight·li·est] Pleasing to the eye; striking.—**sight·li·ness** *n.*

sight·see·ing *n. & adj.* Touring; traveling to places of interest.—**sight·se·er** *n.*

sig·ma (*sig*-muh) *n.* Greek letter corresponding to S.—**sig·mate** *adj.*

sign (*syne*) *n.* 1. A gesture; symbol; indication; mark. 2. A lettered or painted surface giving public information. 3. An omen; a miracle. 4. *Astronomy & Astrology.* A section of the ecliptic or zodiac. 5. *Mathematics.* A symbol indicating a relation between quantities. 6. *Medicine.* A symptom.—*v.* 1. To affix one's handwritten name or mark. 2. To hire. —**sign·er** *n.*—**sign away.** To hand over.—**sign off.** *Radio.* To stop transmission.—**sign on.** To agree to undertake.

sig·nal (*sig*-n'l) *n.* An understandable gesture. —*adj.* Remarkable; notable.—*v.* [sig·naled, -nalled; -nal·ing, -nal·ling].—**-nal·er, -nal·ler** *n.*

sig·nal·ize (*sig*-nul-yze) *v.* [sig·nal·ized; sig·nal·iz·ing] To make remarkable or eminent; to mark.—**sig·nal·ly** *adv.* Notably.

sig·na·to·ry (*sig*-nuh-tor-ee) *n.* [*pl.* sig·na·to·ries] A signer.—*adj.* Bound by a signed agreement.

sig·na·ture (*sig*-nuh-cher) *n.* 1. A person's name written by his own hand. 2. A mark or stamp. 3. *Printing.* **a.** Figure at the foot of the first page of each form to indicate the order in which it is to be bound. **b.** A printed form of four or more pages folded and bound as a unit. 4. *Music.* Marks at the beginning of a piece to indicate the tempo and key of the music. 5. *Radio.* A brief theme in music or words identifying a program.

sign·board (*syne*-bord) *n.* A lettered or painted board giving information.

sig·net (*sig*-nit) *n.* A seal affixed to a document to prove its authority.

sig·nif·i·cance (sig-*nif*-ih-k'nss) *n.* Also **sig·nif·i·can·cy.** 1. Meaning; import. 2. Expressiveness. 3. Importance; weight; consequence.

sig·nif·i·cant *adj.* 1. Meaningful; expressive; full of implication. 2. Indicative; symptomatic; having concealed meaning. 3. Important; crucial.—**sig·nif·i·cant·ly** *adv.*

sig·ni·fi·ca·tion (sig-nif-ih-*kay*-shun) *n.* 1. Communication; expression. 2. Meaning.—**sig·ni·fi·ca·tive** (sig-*nif*-ih-kuh-tiv) *adj.*

sig·ni·fy (*sig*-nih-fy) *v.* [sig·ni·fied; sig·ni·fy·ing] 1. To express; communicate. 2. To mean; show. 3. To matter; be of importance.

si·gnor (*see*-nyor) *n.* 1. An Italian lord or gentleman. 2. Italian title corresponding to Mr.—**si·gno·ra** (see-*nyoh*-rah) *n.* [*pl.* -re] 1. Italian title for a married or elderly woman, corresponding to Madam or Mrs.—**si·gno·re** *n.* (see-*nyoh*-reh) [*pl.* si·gno·ri] Italian term of respect; sir; used without a person's name.—**si·gno·ri·na** (see-nyoh-*ree*-nah) *n.* [*pl.* si·gno·ri·ne] Italian title for a young unmarried woman, corresponding to Miss.

si·lage (*sy*-lij) *n.* Roughage; cured fodder.

si·lence (*sy*-l'nss) *n.* 1. Stillness; absence of any sound. 2. Taciturnity; muteness. 3. Secrecy; failure to communicate.—*v.* [si·lenced; si·lenc·ing] To make quiet; to still.—*interj.* Stop speaking! Be quiet!—**si·lenc·er** *n.*

si·lent (*sy*-l'nt) *adj.* 1. Noiseless; still. 2. Habitually, taciturn. 3. Dumb; speechless.—**si·lent·ly** *adv.*—**si·lent·ness** *n.*

silent butler. A portable receptacle into which ashtrays are emptied.

silent partner. An inactive business partner.

Si·lex (*sy*-lekss) *n.* 1. A trade-marked glass coffee maker. 2. [*not cap.*] Silica.

sil·hou·ette (sil-oo-*et*) *n.* A picture showing outline only, filled in with solid shadow.—*v.* [sil·hou·et·ted; sil·hou·et·ting] 1. To represent in outline. 2. To appear in profile.

sil·i·ca (*sil*-ih-kuh) *n.* A chemical compound found in quartz, flint, sand, etc., and used in making glass. (*Formula:* SiO_2).—**si·lic·ic** *adj.*

SILHOUETTE

sil·i·cate *n.* Any compound of silicon salts, found as mica, feldspar, topaz, etc.

sil·i·con (*sil*-ih-kon) *n.* A nonmetallic chemical element, next in abundance to oxygen. (*Symbol:* Si).

sil·i·co·sis (sil-ih-*koh*-siss) *n.* A lung disease caused by inhaling sand or quartz dust.

silk *n.* 1. A fabric woven of the fine soft thread produced by certain insect larvae. 2. Any similar filament.—**silk, silk·en** *adj.*

silk·screen *n.* Process of reproducing a design by means of a pattern on a screen of silk or nylon.—**silk·screen** *v.*

silk·worm *n.* A larva which spins silk threads to form a cocoon.

silk·y *adj.* [silk·i·er; silk·i·est] Soft and smooth to the touch; delicate.—**silk·i·ly** *adv.*—**silk·i·ness** *n.*

SILKWORM (life-size)

sill *n.* 1. A block forming a base or founda-

tion. 2. The horizontal lower part of a frame, as in a door or window.

sil·ly *adj.* [sil·li·er; sil·li·est] Foolish; lacking in judgment; absurd.—**sil·li·ly** *adv.*— **-li·ness** *n.*

si·lo (*sy*-loh) *n.* [*pl.* si·los] An airtight cylindrical building in which fodder is stored.

silt *n.* A fine sedimentary suspension or deposit of soil, esp. by a river.—*v.* To fill with fine sediment.—**silt·y** *adj.* [silt·i·er; silt·i·est].

sil·va, syl·va (*sil*-vuh) *n.* [*pl.* sil·vas, sil·vae] Woodlands; forested regions.—**sil·van, syl·van** *adj.*

SILO

sil·ver *n.* 1. A malleable, white metallic element. 2. Coins made from silver; money. 3. Domestic utensils made of or plated with silver. (*Symbol:* Ag).—*adj.* 1. Made of silver. 2. Resembling silver, esp. in brilliance. 3. Having a soft clear tone; eloquent.—*v.* To cover with silver or something resembling silver.—**sil·ver·er** *n.*—**sil·ver·ing** *n.*—**sil·ver·ly** *adv.*—**sil·vern** *adj.*

silverback (*n.*)	silverfish	silversmith
silver-backed	silver-haired	silvertip
silver-barked	silver-leaved	silvertop
silverbelly	silversides	silverworker

sil·ver·ware *n.* Articles made of or plated with silver, esp. utensils, vases, tableware, etc.

sil·ver·y (*sil*-ver-ee) *adj.* 1. Resembling silver; of a glistening grayish white. 2. Musical; tinkling.—**sil·ver·i·ness** *n.*

sim·i·an (*sim*-ee-'n) *adj.* Pertaining to an ape or monkey; apelike.—*n.* An ape.—**sim·i·ous** *adj.*

sim·i·lar (*sim*-ih-ler) *adj.* 1. Like; resembling. 2. *Geometry.* Having equal angles and proportional sides.—**sim·i·lar·i·ty** (sim-ih-*lair*-ih-tee) *n.* [*pl.* -i·ties] Likeness.—**sim·i·lar·ly** *adv.*

sim·i·le (*sim*-ih-lee) *n.* A figure of speech in which one thing is explicitly compared with another, using *like* or *as.*

si·mil·i·tude (sih-*mil*-ih-tood) *n.* 1. Likeness; resemblance. 2. A comparison; a simile.

sim·mer *v.* 1. To bubble without boiling. 2. To be close to the boiling point.

si·mon-pure (*sy*-mun-pyoor) *adj.* Completely untainted; genuine.—*n.* An amateur athlete.

sim·o·ny (*syme*-uh-nee; sim-) *n.* The sin of buying or selling church preferment.

si·moom (sih-*moom;* sy-) *n.* Also **si·moon.** A hot, dry, dusty wind that blows over the Sahara and Arabian deserts.

sim·per *v.* To smile in a coy or silly manner. —*n.* A smirk.— **-per·er** *n.*— **-per·ing·ly** *adv.*

sim·ple (*sim*-p'l) *adj.* [sim·pler; sim·plest] 1. Single; uncombined; basic. 2. Plain; unadorned; uncomplicated. 3. Sincere; innocent. 4. Mere; no more than. 5. Feebleminded; silly.—*n.* 1. A humble or ignorant person. 2. A plant used medicinally.—**sim·ple·ness** *n.*

S

sim·ple·ton n. A foolish person.

sim·plic·i·ty (sim-*pliss*-ih-tee) n. [*pl.* sim·plic·i·ties] 1. Clearness; plainness. 2. Sincerity; artlessness. 3. Folly; dullness.

sim·pli·fy v. [sim·pli·fied; sim·pli·fy·ing] To make easier; to eliminate difficulty.—**sim·pli·fi·ca·tion** n.—**sim·pli·fi·er** n.

sim·ply adv. 1. Merely; solely. 2. Without subtlety or complexity. 3. Absolutely; really.

sim·u·late (*sim*-yoo-layt) v. [sim·u·lat·ed; sim·u·lat·ing] To feign; to pretend; to imitate.—**sim·u·late** adj.—**-la·tion** n.—**-la·tive** adj.—**-la·tor** n.

si·mul·ta·ne·ous (sy-mul-*tay*-nee-us) adj. Coincident; occurring at the same time.—**si·mul·ta·ne·ous·ly** adv.—**si·mul·ta·ne·ous·ness, si·mul·ta·ne·i·ty** (sy-mul-tuh-*nee*-ih-tee) n.

sin n. A violation of an accepted moral, religious, or social code.—v. [sinned; sin·ning] To transgress; to commit evil.

since (sinss) adv. 1. Ever afterward; following; from which time. 2. Ago; previously.—prep. After; subsequent.—conj. 1. After which. 2. Because; inasmuch as.

sin·cere (sin-*seer*) adj. [sin·cer·er; sin·cer·est] Unfeigned; earnest; true.—**sin·cere·ly** adv.—**sin·cere·ness, sin·cer·i·ty** (sin-*sehr*-ih-tee) n.

sine n. Mathematics. In a right triangle, the ratio of a side opposite an acute angle to the hypotenuse.

si·ne·cure (sy-neh-kyoor; sih-) n. An office providing revenue without work; an easy job.—**si·ne·cur·ism** n.—**si·ne·cur·ist** n.

sin·ew (*sin*-yoo) n. 1. A tough fibrous tissue joining muscle to bone; a tendon. 2. Source of strength. 3. Energy; power.—**sin·ew·y** adj. 1. Composed of, or resembling, sinews. 2. Strong; vigorous.—**sin·ew·less** adj.

sin·ful adj. Evil; iniquitous.—**sin·ful·ly** adv.

sing v. [sang or sung; sung; sing·ing] 1. To render a melody vocally. 2. To whir; hum. 3. To celebrate in verse or song.—n. Colloquial. 1. A community gathering for singing. 2. A ringing sound.—**sing·a·ble** adj.—**sing·er** n.

singe (sinj) v. [singed; singe·ing] To burn slightly; to scorch.—n. A surface burn.

sin·gle (*sing*-g'l) adj. 1. One; separate. 2. Unmarried. 3. Sincere; pure.—v. [sin·gled; sin·gling] To select.—n. 1. Baseball. A hit allowing the batter to reach first base. 2. [pl.] Tennis. A match played with one player on each side.—**sin·gle·ness** n.

single-banked	single-decker	single-seater
single-barreled	single-edged	singlestick
single-bodied	single-eyed	single-surfaced
single-breasted	single-foot	singletree
single-celled	single-loader	single-valued

sin·gle·hand·ed adj. Unassisted.— **-ed·ly** adv.

sin·gly adv. Individually; separately.

sing·song n. Monotonous tone.—adj. Monotonous in rhythm.

sin·gu·lar (*sing*-gyoo-ler) adj. 1. Unique; remarkable; extraordinary. 2. Strange; odd. 3. Grammar. Denoting one person or thing.—**sin·gu·lar·ly** adv.—**sin·gu·lar·ness** n.

sin·is·ter (*sin*-iss-t'r) adj. 1. Malevolent; ominous. 2. Evil; dishonest. 3. On the left; left.—**sin·is·ter·ly** adv.—**sin·is·ter·ness** n.

sink v. [sank or sunk; sunk; sink·ing] 1. To submerge; fall; descend. 2. To penetrate; dig downward. 3. To invest unprofitably.—n. 1. Basin connected to a drain. 2. A place of vice, corruption, etc.

sin·less n. Pure; without guilt.—**sin·less·ly** adv.

sin·ner n. An evil-doer; an offender against accepted codes.

Sin·o- (sy-noh) prefix. Chinese. 'Sino-American.'

sin·u·ous (*sin*-yoo-us) adj. Undulating; twisting.—**sin·u·ous·ly** adv.—**sin·u·ous·ness, -os·i·ty** n.

si·nus (sy-nus) n. 1. A cavity in the skull or other bony structure. 2. An elongated abscess. 3. Colloquial. Sinusitis; an inflammation of a nasal sinus cavity.

Sioux (soo) n. [pl. Sioux] A North American Indian tribe.—**Siou·an** (*soo*-an) adj.

sip v. [sipped; sip·ping] To drink slowly.—n. A small mouthful.

si·phon (sy-fun) n. 1. A U-shaped tube through which liquid may be forced upward by air pressure and carried across to a lower level. 2. A bottle fitted with a siphon.—v. To convey or draw off by a siphon.

SIPHON

sir n. 1. Masculine term of respect. 2. [cap.] Prefix to the Christian name of a knight or baronet.

sire n. 1. Father; progenitor. 2. Male parent of some animals. 3. Respectful form of address.—v. [sired; sir·ing] To beget; breed.

si·ren (sy-r'n) n. 1. Mythology. A sea nymph whose singing lured sailors to their death. 2. A beautiful and seductive woman. 3. An apparatus producing a pure tone by forcing air jets through rotating, perforated disks.—adj. Bewitching; alluring.

Sir·i·us (*sir*-ee-us) n. The Dog Star; the brightest star in the sky.

sir·loin (*ser*-loyn) n. The upper part of a loin of beef.

si·roc·co (sih-*rok*-oh) n. A sultry dust-bearing Mediterranean wind.

sir·up, syr·up n. A thick viscous solution of sugar.—**sir·up·y, syr·up·y** adj.

sis n. A familiar and affectionate term for sister.

si·sal (sy-s'l) n. A tough plant fiber used for making rope; also the West Indian plant.

sis·sy n. [pl. sis·sies] 1. Term of contempt, esp. among children, for a weak or timid person. 2. An effeminate male.—**sis·sy, sis·sy·ish** adj.

sis·ter n. 1. A female of the same parentage as another person. 2. A nun; a fellow member of any female religious order, society, etc.—adj. Of the same type or family.—**sis·ter·hood** n.—**sis·ter·ly** adj.

sis·ter-in-law *n.* [*pl.* sisters-in-law] The sister of one's wife or husband; the wife of one's brother.

Sis·tine (*siss*-teen) *n.* Pertaining to any of the popes named Sixtus.

Sistine chapel. The Pope's private chapel, containing the frescoes of Michelangelo.

Sistine Madonna. Well-known painting of the Virgin and Child, executed by Raphael for Pope Sixtus, and now in Dresden.

Sis·y·phus (*siss*-ih-fus) *n. Mythology.* Wicked and vengeful Corinthian king, condemned in Hades to roll a rock repeatedly up a hill.—**Sis·y·phe·an** *adj.*

sit *v.* [sat; sit·ting] 1. To settle upon the haunches; to be seated. 2. To have place or position; to be located. 3. To pose for a portrait. 4. To occupy a position in an official assembly. 5. To convene. 6. To cover eggs for hatching; to brood.—**sit·ter** *n.*—**sit-down strike.** A protest strike in which the workers remain idle at their jobs.—**sit in.** To join unofficially in a meeting or activity.—**sit out.** 1. To remain until the end. 2. To fail to participate, as in a dance or game.—**sit tight.** To wait.

site *n.* 1. Location. 2. Scene of an event.

sit·ting *adj.* 1. Resting upon the haunches. 2. Occupying a place in an official capacity. —*n.* 1. An allotted period. 2. A session; meeting of an assembly.

sitting room. Parlor; living room.

sit·u·ate (*sih*-choo-ayt) *v.* [sit·u·at·ed; sit·u·at·ing] To place; to locate.—**sit·u·at·ed** *adj.*

sit·u·a·tion (sih-choo-*ay*-sh'n) *n.* 1. Position; location. 2. Circumstances; condition; state. 3. A job; place of employment.

Si·va, Shi·va (*see*-vuh, *shee*-vuh) *n.* Hindu god of destruction and rebirth.—**Si·va·ism, Shi·va·ism** *n.*—**Si·va·ist, Shi·va·ist** *n.*

six (*sikss*) *n.* Number represented by the symbol 6.—*adj.* Consisting of six.

six·fold *adj. & adv.* Six times over.

six·pence (*sikss*-p'nss) *n.* An English silver coin worth six British pennies; one-half shilling. —**six·pen·ny** *adj.*

six·teen *n.* The number represented by the symbol 16.—*adj.* Consisting of sixteen.—**six·teenth** *adj. & n.*

sixth *n.* 1. One of six equal parts. 2. *Music.* Interval including 6 diatonic degrees.—**sixth** *adj.*

six·ty *n.* [*pl.* six·ties] The number represented by the symbol 60.—*adj.* Consisting of sixty. —**six·ti·eth** *adj. & n.*

siz·a·ble (*syze*-uh-b'l) *adj.* Large; considerable. —**siz·a·ble·ness** *n.*—**siz·a·bly** *adv.*

size *n.* 1. Volume; dimensions; bulk. 2. A relative measure of dimensions, as in clothing. 3. A glue preparation applied to a surface.—*v.* [sized; siz·ing] 1. To arrange according to dimensions. 2. To cover a surface with size. —**size up.** To appraise; form a judgment of.

siz·ing (*syze*-ing) *n.* 1. Glue-like base preparation; size. 2. The application of size.

siz·zle *v.* [siz·zled; siz·zling] To make a hissing sound; to fry.—*n.* A hissing, frying sound. —**siz·zling** *adj.* Very hot.—**siz·zling·ly** *adv.*

skate (*skayt*) *n.* A broad, flat fish; a ray.

skate *n.* 1. A steel blade fixed to the sole of a shoe for gliding over ice. 2. A four-wheeled platform strapped to the foot; a roller skate.—*v.* [skat·ed; skat·ing] To glide or roll on skates. —**skat·er** *n.*

SKATE (1/25 life-size)

skean (*shkeen*) *n.* A dagger.

ske·dad·dle (skeh-*dad*-'l) *v.* [ske·dad·dled; ske·dad·dling] To take flight; to run off.

skeg *n.* Section of the keel of a ship connecting it to the sternpost.

skein (*skayn*) *n.* A bundle of yarn or thread looped together.

skel·e·tal (*skel*-eh-t'l) *adj.* Pertaining to the bony framework.

skel·e·ton (*skel*-eh-t'n) *n.* 1. Framework, esp. the bony structure of the body. 2. An emaciated person or animal.—*adj.* 1. Of or resembling a skeleton. 2. Preliminary; outline. 3. Reduced in numbers; meager.—**skel·e·ton·ize** [-ized; -iz·ing] *v.*

skep·tic, scep·tic (*skep*-tik) *n.* 1. A doubter; a disbeliever. 2. [*cap.*] Follower of a doctrine denying the validity of all knowledge.—**skep·tic·al, scep·ti·cal** *adj.* Incredulous; not easily convinced.—**skep·ti·cism, scep·ti·cism** *n.*

sketch *n.* 1. An outline; a rough draft. 2. A quick or preliminary drawing. 3. Short theatrical feature.—*v.* To draw quickly.—**sketch·er** *n.*

sketch·y *adj.* [sketch·i·er; -i·est] Unfinished; vague; rough.—**sketch·i·ly** *adv.*— **-i·ness** *n.*

skew (*skyoo*) *adj.* Oblique; asymmetrical.—*n.* A slant.—*v.* To twist; to swerve; to distort.

skew·er (*skyoo*-er) *n.* A metal pin for fastening meat during roasting.—**skew·er** *v.*

SKEWERS

ski (*skee*; *shee*) *n.* [*pl.* skis; ski] A long narrow wooden runner strapped to the foot for gliding over snow.—*v.* [skied; ski·ing] To glide on skis.—**ski·er** *n.*

SKIS

skid *n.* 1. A slideway. 2. A clog used to check a wheel's turning; a drag. 3. A sliding. —*v.* [skid·ded; skid·ding] 1. To slide; slip sideways. 2. To check slipping; move on skids.

skies. *Plural* of sky.

skiff *n.* A small, light rowboat, esp. one with a centerboard for sailing.

S

skill *n.* 1. Expertness; dexterity. 2. A specialized ability.—**skilled** *adj.* Trained.

skil·let *n.* A frying pan.

skill·ful, skil·ful *adj.* Adroit; deft.—**skill·ful·ness, skil·ful·ness** *n.*

SKILLET

skim *v.* [skimmed; skim·ming] 1. To remove floating substances from a liquid. 2. To pass quickly over; to read superficially. 3. To glide swiftly.—**skim·mer** *n.*—**skim·ming** *n.*

skimp *v.* To use frugally; to save.

skimp·y [skimp·i·er; skimp·i·est] *adj.* Scanty; insufficient.—**skimp·i·ly** *adv.*—**skimp·i·ness** *n.*

skin *n.* 1. The outer tissue covering the body. 2. The pelt or hide of an animal. 3. Any external covering, as a fruit rind or peel.—*v.* [skinned; skin·ning] 1. To strip off the hide. 2. *Slang.* To cheat. 3. To become covered with skin.—**skin·ner** *n.*

skin-deep *adj.* Superficial; slight.—**skin-deep** *adv.*

skin·flint *n.* A miser; a shrewd dealer.

skin·ny *adj.* [skin·ni·er; skin·ni·est] 1. Thin; scrawny. 2. Like skin.—**skin·ni·ness** *n.*

skip *v.* [skipped; skip·ping] 1. To leap lightly; to jump. 2. To omit.—*n.* 1. A small leap. 2. An omission.

skip·per *n. Nautical.* Familiar term for the master or captain of a vessel.

skirl (*skerl*) *n.* The high-pitched, wavering sound made by a bagpipe.—**skirl** *v.*

skir·mish *n.* A minor battle, often preliminary. —*v.* To fight in small groups.—**skir·mish·er** *n.*

skirt (*skert*) *n.* 1. Article of women's clothing covering the body from the waist down; the loose lower part of a garment. 2. [*usually pl.*] Environs; suburbs. 3. Margin; edge. 4. *Slang.* A female.—*v.* To border; to outly.

skit *n.* A short comic sketch; an act.

skit·tish *adj.* 1. Nervous; scary. 2. Coy; lively.—**skit·tish·ly** *adv.*—**skit·tish·ness** *n.*

skit·tle (*skit-'l*) *n.* 1. [*pl.* used as *sing.*] An English game corresponding to ninepins. 2. A ninepin. 3. [*pl.*] Enjoyment. 'Not all beer and skittles.'

skoal (*skohl*) *interj.* A drinking toast; a health.

skul·dug·ger·y (skul-*dug*-er-ee) *n.* Sinister activity; plotting.

skulk *v.* To lurk; to sneak furtively about.— **skulk·er** *n.*— **skulk·ing·ly** *adv.*

SKUNK (1/15 life-size)

skull *n.* The bony framework of the head.

skull·cap *n.* A close-fitting brimless cap.

skunk *n.* 1. A small, striped animal of North America, noted for the offensive odor of its defense secretion. 2. The fur of this animal. 3. *Slang.* A contemptible person; a bounder. —**skunk** *adj.*

skunk cabbage. A plant, common in swamps, which emits an offensive odor.

sky *n.* [*pl.* skies] 1. The heavens; the upper atmosphere. 2. Heaven.

sky-blasted sky-gazer skyscape
sky blue sky high skyshine
sky-born skyman skyward
sky-capped skysail skyway

sky·lark *n.* A swift small bird noted for its song.—*v.* To cut capers; to play.

SKYLARK (1/5 life-size)

sky·light *n.* A window in a ceiling or roof.

sky line. 1. The outline of buildings, trees, etc., against the sky. 2. The horizon.

sky pilot. *Slang.* A chaplain; a clergyman.

sky·rock·et *n.* A firework that rises and bursts high in the air. —*v. Colloquial.* To rise quickly and vanish.

SKYLIGHT

sky·scrap·er *n.* A tall steel-framed building.

sky·writ·ing (*sky-ryte-ing*) *n.* Words formed by smoke from an airplane. —**sky·write** *v.*—**sky·writ·er** *n.*

slab *n.* 1. A thick flat piece. 2. The outer strip of sawn timber. —*v.* [slabbed; slab·bing] To square a log.

SKYSCRAPER

slack *adj.* 1. Without tautness; relaxed. 2. Lazy; careless. 3. Dull; slow; inactive.—*n.* 1. The dangling end of a rope. 2. A dull season; a lull. 3. Lumps of coal.—**slack off.** *Nautical.* To loosen a line.— **slack·ly** *adv.*—**slack·ness** *n.*

slack·en (*slak-'n*) *v.* 1. To loosen; relax. 2. To abate; calm down. 3. To make slower; retard.—**slack·er** *n.* A shirker.

slacks *n.* 1. Sport trousers. 2. Women's trousers.

slag *n.* The impurities remaining after refinement of ore; dross.—**slag·gy** *adj.*

slain. *Past participle* of **slay.**

slake (*slayk*) *v.* [slaked; slak·ing] 1. To quench; to abate. 2. *Chemistry.* To mix with water.

sla·lom (*slah-lum*) *n.* Zigzagging, downhill skiing, usually timed.

slam *v.* [slammed; slam·ming] To bang; to close or move noisily.—*n.* 1. A bang; the sound of a blow. 2. *Colloquial.* An insult. —**grand slam.** *Bridge.* Taking all the tricks in a hand.—**little** or **small slam.** *Bridge.* Taking all but one of the tricks in a hand.

slan·der (*slan*-der) *n.* 1. Libel; malicious lies; calumny. 2. *Law.* Oral defamation.—*v.* To utter maliciously a false report concerning someone.—**slan·der·er** *n.*—**slan·der·ous** *adj.* —**slan·der·ous·ly** *adv.*—**slan·der·ous·ness** *n.*

slang *n.* 1. Current expressions used in informal speech, but not acceptable in formal writing. 2. Jargon of a trade or group.—*v.* To use slang.—**slang·i·ly** *adv.*—**slang·i·ness** *n.* —**slang·y** *adj.*

slant *n.* 1. A slope; an angle; an oblique. 2. *Colloquial.* A way of viewing a subject, as a new slant.—*v.* To put at a slant.—**slant·ing** *adj.*—**slant·ing·ly** *adv.*—**slant·wise** *adj. & adv.*

slap *v.* [slapped; slap·ping] To strike, esp. with the open hand.—*n.* 1. A blow. 2. An insult.

slap-bang *adv.* Suddenly; sharply.

slap-dash *adv.* Carelessly; at random.

slap·jack *n.* 1. A pancake. 2. A card game.

slap·stick *n.* Comedy involving farcical antics.

slash *v.* 1. To cut in a sweeping random blow. 2. To cut decorative slits in a garment. 3. To lash; to criticize.—*n.* A long cut or slit. —**slash·er** *n.*—**slash·ing·ly** *adv.*

slash pine. A hard Florida pine.

slat *n.* 1. A long, narrow strip of wood; a lath.—*v.* [slat·ted; slat·ting] To flap noisily.

slate (*slayt*) *n.* 1. A bluish stone readily split into thin layers. 2. A small erasable tablet for writing with chalk. 3. A list of candidates for nomination or election.—*v.* 1. To cover with slate. 2. To put on a list; schedule. —**slat·er** *n.*—**slat·ing** *n.*—**clean slate.** A new start.

slath·er *v.* To smear thickly.

slat·tern *n.* A slovenly, lazy, slipshod woman. —**slat·tern·ly** *adj. & adv.*

slat·y (*slayt*-ee) *adj.* [slat·i·er; slat·i·est] 1. Of a bluish-gray color. 2. Pertaining to slate.

slaugh·ter (*slaw*-ter) *v.* 1. To kill brutally, esp. in great numbers. 2. To butcher; to kill animals for meat.—*n.* Killing; carnage. —**slaugh·ter·er** *n.*—**slaugh·ter·house** *n.* Building in which animals are butchered.

Slav (*slahv*) *n.* One of a racial and language group in eastern Europe.—**Slav·ic** *adj. & n.*

slave (*slayv*) *n.* 1. A person legally possessed by another; one having no personal freedom. 2. An addict; devotee.—*v.* [slaved; slav·ing] To toil; drudge.—**slave** *adj.*

slave-born	slaveholder	slave owner
slavebreeder	slave market	slave ship
slavedriver	slave merchant	slave trader

slav·er·y (*slayv*-er-ee) *n.* [*pl.* -ies] 1. Bondage; subjection of human beings. 2. Drudgery.

slav·ish (*slayv*-ish) *adj.* Servile; dependent; fanatical.—**slav·ish·ly** *adv.*—**slav·ish·ness** *n.*

Slav·o·phile, Slav·o·phil (*slahv*-oh-fyle; -fil) *n.* An admirer of Slavic people, culture, etc. —**Sla·voph·i·lism** (sluh-*vof*-ih-lizm).

slaw *n.* A salad of shredded cabbage.

slay *v.* [slew; slain; slay·ing] To kill; put to death.—**slay·er** *n.*

slea·zy (*slay*-zee; *slee*-) *adj.* [slea·zi·er; sleaz·i·est] Unsubstantial; flimsy.

sled *n.* A vehicle mounted on runners or skids for traveling over snow or ice.—*v.* [sled·ded; sled·ding] To travel on a sled.—**sled·der** *n.* —**sled·ding** *n.*

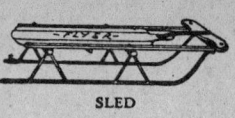

SLED

sledge *n.* (*slej*) 1. A heavy hammer. 2. A carriage mounted on runners; a sleigh.—*v.* [sledged; sledg·ing] To travel by sleigh.

sleek *adj.* Smooth; glossy.—*v.* To smooth; to tidy.—**sleek·ly** *adj.*—**sleek·ness** *n.*

sleep *v.* [slept; sleep·ing] 1. To rest in a state of normal unconsciousness. 2. To be inactive, or at repose. 3. To be dead.—*n.* Slumber; periodical and normal unconsciousness. —*n.* Slumber; state of inactivity.—**sleep·er** *n.* 1. One asleep. 2. A railroad car equipped with beds. 3. *Motion Pictures.* A highly successful low-budget film.—**sleep·less** *adj.*—**sleep·less·ly** *adv.*—**sleep·less·ness** *n.*—**sleep off.** To overcome by sleeping, as intoxication.

sleeping sickness. *Medicine.* 1. A serious disease causing a state of stupor. 2. Epidemic encephalitis.

sleep walker. One who rises and moves about in his sleep; a somnambulist.—**sleep walking.**

sleep·y *adj.* [sleep·i·er; sleep·i·est] 1. Drowsy; ready for slumber. 2. Inactive; quiet.—**sleep·i·ly** *adv.*—**sleep·i·ness** *n.*

sleet *n.* Rain mingled with snow; hail.—**sleet** *v.*—**sleet·y** *adj.* [sleet·i·er; sleet·i·est].

sleeve *n.* 1. The part of a garment covering the arm. 2. A tube into which a rod or another tube is fitted. 3. Cloth tube towed in airplane gunnery practice.—**sleeve·less** *adj.*

sleeve valve. *Mechanics.* A cylindrical inlet and exhaust valve on an internal combustion machine.

sleigh (*slay*) *n.* A vehicle mounted on runners for traveling on snow or ice.—*v.* To travel in a sleigh.

sleight (*slyte*) *n.* 1. A trick. 2. Skill; dexterity.

sleight of hand. A magician's trick.

slen·der *adj.* 1. Thin; small in circumference or width; narrow. 2. Meager; inadequate; feeble.—**slen·der·ize** *v.* [slen·der·ized; slen·der·iz·ing]—**slen·der·ly** *adv.*—**slen·der·ness** *n.*

slept. *Past tense & past participle* of **sleep.**

sleuth (*slooth*) *n.* A detective.

sleuth·hound *n.* A bloodhound.

slew. *Past tense* of **slay.**

slew *n.* A marshy place; a river inlet.

slice (*slysse*) *v.* [sliced; slic·ing] 1. To cut; to carve into thin pieces. 2. *Golf.* To hit the ball so that it curves to the right.—*n.* A strip; a thin section.—**slic·er** *n.*

S

SLEIGH

slick *adj.* 1. Smooth; sleek. 2. Slippery. 3. Clever; shrewd; tricky.—*v.* To make smooth or slippery.—*n.* A smooth area of water, as when covered by oil.

slick·er *n.* 1. A raincoat; a waterproof. 2. *Slang.* A shrewd, designing individual.

slide (*slyde*) *v.* [slid; slid or slid·den; slid·ing]. 1. To move smoothly; glide. 2. To slip; move quietly.—*n.* 1. A gliding motion; a mass of earth moving downhill. 2. A thin plate of glass. 3. *Music.* The U-shaped tubular section of a trombone or trumpet. —**slid·er** *n.*

slide fastener (*fass*-ner). A zipper; opposite rows of small teeth locked by a sliding key.

slide rule. A calculating device in ruler form with logarithmic scales.

slid·ing (*slyde*-ing) *adj.* Changing; varying.

sliding scale. Flexible or relative calculation; an adjustable rate, as of wages.

slight (*slyte*) *adj.* 1. Small; insignificant; meager. 2. Slender; fragile.—*n.* Deliberate neglect; snub.—*v.* To overlook; treat carelessly. —**slight·ly** *adv.*—**slight·ness** *n.*

slight·ing *adj.* Contemptuous.— **-ing·ly** *adv.*

slim *adj.* [slim·mer; slim·mest] 1. Slender; narrow. 2. Slight; scant.—*v.* [slimmed; slim·ming] To make or become slender.—**slim·ly** *adv.*—**slim·ness** *n.*

slime (*slyme*) *n.* A viscous, offensively slippery and clinging substance.—*v.* [slimed; slim·ing] To cover with slime.

slim·sy (*slim*-zee) *adj. Colloquial.* Sleazy.

slim·y (*slyme*-ee) *adj.* [slim·i·er; slim·i·est] Sticky; gluey; covered with muck.—**slim·i·ly** *adv.*— **-i·ness** *n.*

sling *n.* 1. A weapon for throwing missiles. 2. Drink made of sugar, water, and spirits. 3. A loop for supporting a weakened or broken part. 4. Cord network for moving heavy objects. 5. Strap on a rifle.—*v.* [slung; sling·ing] 1. To hurl; to throw. 2. To hang loosely; to place in a sling.—**sling·er** *n.*

sling·shot *n.* A small, forked, missile-hurling weapon.

slink *v.* [slunk; slink·ing] To sneak; move stealthily.—**slink·ing·ly** *adv.* —**slink·y** *adj.* Seductive.

slip *v.* [slipped; slip·ping] 1. To slide; move easily. 2. To skid; fall. 3. To convey inconspicuously. 4. To err. 5. To move suddenly. 6. To lose; escape from. 7. To pass imperceptibly.—*n.* 1. An error; an intentional mistake. 2. A sprig cut for planting. 3. A small piece of paper. 4. A strip. 5. Any easily moved covering, as a pillow case, a woman's undergarment. 6. An opening for a ship between wharves.—**slip off.** To steal away; remove hastily.—**slip the leash.** To free oneself from restraint.—**slip up.** To make an error.—**slip-up** *n.* An error.

SLINGSHOT

slip·knot (*slip*-not) *n.* Knot designed to slide or pull free under strain.

slip·per *n.* A thin, light shoe.—**slip·pered** *adj.*

slip·per·y (*slip*-er-ee) *adj.* [slip·per·i·er; slip·per·i·est]. 1. Smooth; slick; affording little friction. 2. Cunning; evasive; sly.

slip ring. *Electricity.* One of several conducting rings in a dynamo or motor.

slip·shod *adj.* Careless; slovenly.

slip stream. Air driven back by an airplane propeller; backwash of air.

slit *v.* [slit; slit·ting] To cut into long strips.—*n.* A long, narrow cut or opening.—**slit·ter** *n.*

slith·er *v.* To slip; to slide, esp. in a writhing movement.—**slith·er·y** *adj.*

sliv·er (*sliv*-er) *v.* To cut or break into long, thin slices.—*n.* 1. A long fragment; splinter. 2. Strand of loose fiber.

slob·ber *v.* 1. To drool; smear with saliva. 2. To speak gushingly.—*n.* 1. Saliva. 2. Sentimental drivel.—**slob·ber·er** *n.*—**slob·ber·y** *adj.*

sloe (*sloh*) *n.* A plumlike fruit.—**sloe gin.** A liquor flavored with sloes.

slog *v.* [slogged; slog·ging] 1. To box; to beat. 2. To trudge.—*n.* A hard blow.—**slog·ger** *n.*

slo·gan (*sloh*-gun) *n.* A catch-phrase; an expression coined to stimulate public enthusiasm.

sloop *n.* A sailing vessel with one mast and fore-and-aft sails.

slop *v.* [slopped; slopping] To spill a liquid; to soil with liquid.—*n.* 1. Liquid wastes of a household. 2. Slush; soft mud. 3. [*pl.*] Sailors' clothing and other equipment. 4. Liquid food.

slop chest. Small stores aboard ship for sale to seamen.

SLOOP

slope (*slohp*) *n.* An incline; a slant; an oblique surface.—*v.* [sloped; slop·ing]—**slop·ing** *adj.* —**slop·ing·ly** *adv.*—**slop·ing·ness** *n.*

slop·py *adj.* [-pi·er; -pi·est] 1. Slushy. 2. Slovenly; careless.—**slop·pi·ly** *adv.*— **-pi·ness** *n.*

slosh *v.* To flounder in mire; splash.—*n.* Slush.

slot *n.* An aperture; a narrow opening or groove.—*v.* [slot·ted; slot·ting] To cut a slot. —**slot machine.** A device which operates on the insertion of a coin.

sloth (*slohth*) *n.* 1. Sluggishness; laziness; indolence. 2. A small, slow-moving tree-dwelling animal. —**sloth·ful** *adj.*—**sloth·ful·ly** *adv.*—**sloth·ful·ness** *n.*

SLOTH (1/25 life-size)

slouch *n.* 1. A drooping posture; slump. 2. A lazy, ungainly person.—*v.* 1. To slump. 2. To walk with a loose gait.—**slouch·i·ly** *adv.*— **-i·ness** *n.*—**slouch·y** *adj.*

slough (*slou*) *n.* 1. A mire; a muddy ditch. 2. A depressed mental state, as slough of despair.—**slough·y** *adj.*

slough (*sloo*) *n.* Also **slew, slue.** A swamp; a river inlet or tide flat.

slough (*sluf*) *v.* To shed, as to slough off dead tissue.—*n.* Dead, cast-off matter.

Slo·vak (*sloh*-vak) *n.* 1. A native of central Czechoslovakia of northern Slavic descent. 2. The language of the Slovaks.—**Slo·vak** *adj.*

slov·en (*sluv*-'n) *n.* A lazy, unclean person.

Slo·vene (sloh-*veen*) *n.* 1. Native of a southern Slavic group in Yugoslavia. 2. The language of Slovenes, Serbs, and Croats.—**Slo·vene** *adj.*

slov·en·ly (*sluh*-v'n-lee) *adj.* [-li·er; -li·est] Careless; untidy; lazy.—**slov·en·ly** *adv.*— -li·ness *n.*

slow (*sloh*) *adj.* 1. Moving a small distance in a long time. 2. Gradual; occurring over a long period. 3. Late; behind time. 4. Dull; inert.—*v.* To retard; to hinder.—**slow·ly** *adv.* —**slow·ness** *n.*—**slow-down** or **slow-up.** A slackening of speed of workers to force employer's consideration of their demands.

sloyd *n.* Theory, originally Swedish, of teaching the manual arts through woodcarving.

slub *v.* [slubbed; slub·bing] To pull and twist, as yarn.—*n.* 1. A slubbed spool. 2. [*pl.*] Thick spots on a thread.

sludge (*sluj*) *n.* 1. Mud. 2. Thin melting ice. 3. Solid sediment.—**sludg·y** *adj.*

slue (*sloo*) *v.* [slued; slu·ing] Also **slew.** To swing or turn; to twist.—*n.* 1. A sudden turn. 2. *Colloquial.* A sizable quantity.

slug *n.* 1. A type of snail having no shell. 2. A small bullet. 3. *Slang.* A swallow of liquor. 4. A counterfeit coin. 5. *Printing.* A piece of type metal inserted to give space between lines. 6. A hard blow with the fist. —*v.* [slugged; slug·ging] *Colloquial.* To strike hard with fist, bat, etc.—**slug·ger** *n.*

SLUG (1/2 life-size)

slug·gard *n.* A lazy, indolent person; an idler.

slug·gish (*slug*-ish) *adj.* 1. Indolent; dull; idle. 2. Slow; having little motion; inactive.

sluice (*slooss*) *n.* 1. A waterway equipped with a gate or valve to regulate the flow of water. 2. The stream of water issuing through a floodgate. 3. Any opening for the passage of fluid.—*v.* [sluiced; sluic·ing] 1. To direct a stream of liquid upon; to flush. 2. To draw off by a channel.

SLUICE

sluice·way *n.* An artificial channel controlling the flow of water.

slum *n.* A crowded, poverty-stricken neighborhood.—*v.* [slummed; slum·ming] 1. To investigate a slum. 2. *Slang.* To sample a squalid district for amusement.—**slum·mer** *n.*

slum·ber *v.* 1. To sleep. 2. To be in a state of inactivity.—*n.* Sleep; repose.—**slum·ber·er** *n.*—**slum·ber·ous** *adj.*— -ber·y *adj.*

slump *v.* 1. To sink down suddenly; to fall into a drooping posture. 2. To decline in value.—*n.* 1. A slouch; a sagging attitude. 2. A period of economic depression.

slung. *Past tense & past participle* of **sling.**

slunk. *Past tense & past participle* of **slink.**

slur *v.* [slurred; slur·ring] 1. To disparage by insinuation; insult. 2. To utter indistinctly. 3. *Music.* To blend successive tones without interruption.—*n.* 1. A reproach; a slight; a stigma. 2. *Music.* A mark [‿ ⁀] connecting notes to be performed without a break.

slur·ry *n.* [*pl.* -ries] A thin, wet mixture.

slush *n.* 1. Partially melted snow; mire. 2. Grease applied to metal parts to prevent rust. 3. *Slang.* Sentimental drivel.—*v.* To rustproof with slush.—**slush·y** *adj.*—**slush·i·ly** *adv.*—**slush·i·ness** *n.*

slush fund. *Politics.* Money for bribes.

slut *n.* 1. An untidy woman; a slattern. 2. A harlot.—**slut·tish** *adj.*—**slut·tish·ness** *n.*

sly *adj.* [sli·er, sly·er; sli·est, sly·est] 1. Insidious; crafty; underhanded. 2. Mischievous; arch.—**sly·ly, sli·ly** *adv.*—**sly·ness** *n.*—**on the sly.** Secretly.

smack *v.* 1. To slap; to strike loudly, as with the open hand. 2. To make a noise with the lips. 3. To have a trace; to suggest. 4. To kiss noisily.—*n.* 1. A slap; a sharp blow. 2. A sharp noise, esp. made with the lips. 3. A flavor or quality; a tinge. 4. A noisy kiss. 5. *Nautical.* A fishing vessel, usually a sloop.—*adv.* Suddenly; directly.

small (*smawl*) *adj.* 1. Little; diminutive; minor; brief. 2. Trivial; insignificant. 3. Narrow-minded; selfish.—*n.* 1. The slender part; as, the small of the back. 2. [*pl.*] Knee breeches.—*adv.* In little degree; fine.—**small·ish** *adj.*—**small·ness** *n.*

small-acred	small arms	smallsword
small-ankled	small-hearted	small talk
small-armed	small-mouthed	smallware

small fry. 1. Young children. 2. Persons of no importance.

small·pox *n.* An acute contagious disease characterized by fever and skin eruptions.

small·time *adj.* Unimportant; unsuccessful; picayune.

smart (*smahrt*) *n.* A sting; a burning sensation. —*v.* 1. To sting; to burn. 2. To feel pain or resentment.—*adj.* 1. Sharp; keen; severe. 2. Clever; intelligent; witty. 3. Showily dressed; fashionable.—**smart·ly** *adv.* Briskly; sharply.—**smart·ness** *n.*

smart·en *v.* To brighten; spruce.

S

smash v. 1. To shatter; break; crush. 2. To fall to pieces; to be ruined.—n. Ruin; destruction.—**smash·er** n.

smash-up n. A destructive accident.

smat·ter·ing n. 1. A slight and superficial knowledge. 2. An insignificant amount. —**smat·ter** n. & v.— -ter·er n.— -ter·ing·ly adv.

smear (smeer) v. 1. To daub; grease; spread with a wet substance. 2. To slander.—n. 1. A spread; a blotch. 2. An insult; a stain on the reputation.—**smear·y** adj. [smear·i·er; smear·i·est]—**smear·i·ness** n.

smell n. 1. One of the five senses; perception of certain properties received by the nostrils. 2. Odor; scent; fragrance.—v. [smelled, smelt; smell·ing] 1. To detect a scent; perceive by the olfactory nerves. 2. To emit odor or fragrance. 3. To detect by cunning or sagacity. —**smell·er** n.—**smell·y** adj. [smell·i·er; smell·i·est.—**smell a rat.** To suspect something amiss.

smelling salts. A volatile substance which acts as a stimulant when inhaled.

smelt v. To melt ore; to refine its metal.—**smelt·er** n. A furnace where ore is melted down.

smelt n. A small edible fish similar to a trout.

smelt. Past tense & past participle of **smell.**

smi·lax (smy-lakss) n. A trailing vine with rich green foliage.

smile n. A facial expression indicating pleasure, affection, irony, etc.—v. [smiled; smil·ing] 1. To look amused, pleased, etc.; to alter the expression by lifting the corners of the mouth. 2. To be favorable; to augur well.—**smil·er** n. —**smil·ing** adj.—**smil·ing·ly** adv.

smirch v. To sully; to smear.—n. A blotch.

smirk (smerk) v. To smile smugly.—n. A silly smile.

smite v. [smote; smit·ten, smit, smote; smit·ing] 1. To strike forcefully; hit. 2. To punish; destroy. 3. To impress; dazzle.—**smit·er** n.

smith n. One who beats and shapes metals.

smith·er·eens n. pl. Colloquial. Fragments.

smith·y n. [pl. -ies] A blacksmith's workshop.

smit·ten (smit-'n) adj. 1. Distressed. 2. Colloquial. Fascinated.

smock (smok) n. A loose overgarment protecting the clothes.—v. To embroider with shirring.—**smock·ing** n.

smoke n. The visible gaseous vapor rising from a burning substance.—v. [smoked; smok·ing] 1. To emit smoke; fume. 2. To use tobacco by inhaling and exhaling its fumes. 3. To treat with smoke, as to cure meat. 4. To make opaque, as glass.—**smoke out.** To force out of hiding.

SMOCK

smok·er (smoh-ker) n. 1. One who uses tobacco. 2. A railroad car in which smoking is permitted. 3. An informal gathering, usually stag, for smoking and relaxation.

smok·y (smoh-kee) adj. [smok·i·er; smok·i·est] 1. Full of smoke; sending out smoke. 2. Like smoke.—**smok·i·ly** adv.—**smok·i·ness** n.

smol·der, smoul·der (smohl-der) v. 1. To burn and smoke without visible flame. 2. To suppress emotion.—n. A slow, flameless fire.

smooth adj. 1. Even; uninterrupted; without roughness. 2. Steady; without jolts or sudden variations. 3. Serene; bland; soothing. 4. Beardless.—v. 1. To stroke. 2. To make even; polish. 3. To allay; ease.—adv. In an even manner.—**smooth·er** n.—**smooth·ly** adv. —**smooth·ness** n.

smoothbore (n.)	smooth-chinned
smooth-bore (v.)	smooth-combed
smooth-bored	smooth-faced
smooth-browed	smoothpate
smooth-cast	smooth-spoken
smooth-cheeked	smooth-tongued

smör·gas·bord (smur-guhss-bord) n. Table set with Swedish appetizers; hors d'oeuvres.

smote. Past tense of **smite.**

smoth·er (smuth-er) v. 1. To suffocate; to destroy by excluding air. 2. To cover up; suppress; extinguish.—n. A dense cloud.

smoul·der. Variant spelling of **smolder.**

smudge (smuj) v. [smudged; smudg·ing] To smear with dirt or smoke.—n. 1. A smear or stain. 2. A smoky fire made to drive away insects, etc.—**smudg·i·ly** adv.—**smudg·i·ness** n. —**smudg·y** adj.—**smudge pot.** A small device producing smoke to protect fruit from frost.

smug adj. [smug·ger; smug·gest] 1. Blandly self-satisfied. 2. Tidy; neat.—**smug·ly** adv. —**smug·ness** n.

smug·gle v. [smug·gled; smug·gling] 1. To move goods into or out of a country illegally. 2. To convey illicitly.—**smug·gler** n.

smut n. 1. Soot; dirt. 2. Obscenity; filthy language. 3. Botany. Plant diseases caused by fungus.—v. [smut·ted; smut·ting] To soil.

smutch v. To begrime; smudge.—n. A spot.

smut·ty adj. [smut·ti·er; -ti·est] 1. Dirty; sooty. 2. Indecent; lewd.— -ti·ly adv.— -ti·ness n.

snack n. A bit of food; a hurried meal.

snaf·fle n. The curbless bit of a horse's bridle. —v. [snaf·fled; snaf·fling] To control by means of a snaffle bit.

sna·fu (snaf-foo) adj. Military Slang. Muddled; disordered; from Situation Normal, All Fuddled Up.—v. [sna·fued; sna·fu·ing] To foul up.

SNAFFLE

snag n. 1. A sharp projecting branch or stump. 2. An unexpected difficulty; a catch. —v. [snagged; snag·ging] To hook or catch upon.—**snagged** adj.—**snag·gy** adj.

snag·gle-toothed adj. Having irregular teeth.

snail n. 1. A slimy, slow-moving mollusk with a spiral shell. 2. A sluggish person.

snake (*snayk*) *n.* 1. A long, slim, limbless reptile moving by muscular contractions. 2. A sly and treacherous person.—*v.* [snaked; snak·ing] 1. To haul; jerk; drag out. 2. To crawl like a snake.

SNAKE

snake-in-the-grass *n.* A treacherous enemy.

snak·y *adj.* [snak·i·er; snak·i·est] 1. Serpentine; winding. 2. Sly; spiteful; poisonous.

snap *v.* [snapped; snap·ping] 1. To break; sever abruptly. 2. To bite suddenly; snatch. 3. To make a sharp, cracking sound. 4. To retort; speak crossly.—*n.* 1. A split; a sudden break. 2. A bite; a pounce. 3. A click; a small, sharp sound. 4. A small catch or lock; a fastener. 5. A sudden brief interval. 'A cold snap.' 6. *Slang.* An easy task. 7. A thin cookie.—*adj.* 1. Sudden. 'Snap judgment.' 2. *Slang.* Easy. 'A snap assignment.'

snap·drag·on *n.* A garden plant having saclike flowers of many colors likened to dragons' heads.

snap·per *n.* 1. A water turtle which captures prey in its jaws; snapping turtle. 2. Any of several tropical species of edible fish.

snap·pish *adj.* 1. Likely to bite. 2. Peevish; irritable.—**snap·pish·ly** *adv.*—**snap·pish·ness** *n.*

snap·py (*snap-ee*) *adj.* [snap·pi·er; snap·pi·est] 1. Sharp; curt. 2. Quick; brisk. 3. Chilly. —**snap·pi·ly** *adv.*—**snap·pi·ness** *n.*

SNAPDRAGON

snap·shot *n.* A photograph taken instantaneously.—*v.* [snap·shot·ted; snap·shot·ting].

snare (*snair*) *n.* 1. A trap; a noose designed to capture small animals. 2. A string on the lower head of a drum.—*v.* [snared; snar·ing] 1. To catch or entangle; trap. 2. To entice; inveigle.—**snar·er** *n.*

snare drum. A small drum with catgut strings across the lower head to sharpen the sound.

snarl *n.* 1. A tangled mass. 2. A state of confusion.—*v.* To entangle; complicate.

snarl *v.* 1. To growl; bare the teeth menacingly. 2. To speak angrily and roughly.—*n.* An angry growl.—**snarl·er** *n.*—**snarl·ing·ly** *adv.*

snarl·y (*snahr-lee*) *adj.* [snarl·i·er; snarl·i·est] 1. Tangled. 2. Bad-tempered.

snatch *v.* To grab; clutch at; seize abruptly.—*n.* 1. A sudden catching or grasping. 2. A fragment. 3. A brief period. 4. *Slang.* A kidnaping.—**snatch·er** *n.*—**snatch·y** *adj.*

snatch block. A pulley or block having an opening in the side to admit the rope.

sneak (*sneek*) *v.* 1. To creep furtively; slink. 2. To act cowardly.—*n.* A sly, mean person. —**sneak·ing** *adj.*—**sneak·ing·ly** *adv.*

sneak·er *n.* 1. A furtive person. 2. [*pl.*] Rubber-soled canvas shoes.

sneak·y *adj.* [sneak·i·er; -i·est] Stealthy; furtive; contemptible.—**sneak·i·ly** *adv.*— **-i·ness** *n.*

sneer *v.* To scoff; be contemptuous or derisive.—*n.* A look of scorn.—**sneer·er** *n.*—**sneering** *adj.*—**sneer·ing·ly** *adv.*

sneeze *v.* [sneezed; sneez·ing] To exhale violently with an involuntary convulsive motion. —*n.* An audible exhalation.—**sneez·er** *n.* —**sneeze at.** To treat with contempt.

snick·er *v.* Also **snig·ger.** To giggle; to laugh covertly.—*n.* A suppressed laugh.

sniff *v.* 1. To inhale audibly; snuff. 2. To detect; scent.—**sniff** *n.*

snif·fle *v.* [snif·fled; snif·fling] To sniff repeatedly.—**snif·fle** *n.*

snip *v.* [snipped; snip·ping] To cut; to clip with scissors.—*n.* 1. A cut. 2. A severed fragment; bit. 3. [*pl.*] Small shears to cut metal.

snipe (*snype*) *v.* [sniped; snip·ing] 1. To shoot from a hidden place. 2. To criticize deviously. —**snip·er** *n.*

snipe *n.* A large, long-billed game bird inhabiting marshes.—*v.* To hunt snipe.

snip·pet *n.* A small bit; fragment.

snip·py *adj.* [snip·pi·er; snip·pi·est] 1. Very brief; curt. 2. Haughty; supercilious. —**snip·pi·ness** *n.*

SNIPE (1/8 life-size)

snitch *v. Slang.* 1. To steal. 2. To betray.

sniv·el (*sniv-'l*) *v.* [sniv·eled; sniv·el·ing, sniv·el·ling] 1. To have a running nose. 2. To whine; cry snufflingly.—**sniv·el·er** *n.*

snob *n.* A person who apes his superiors and spurns his inferiors; a haughty person.—**snob·ber·y** *n.* Haughtiness.—**snob·bish** *adj.*—**snob·bish·ly** *adv.*—**snob·bish·ness** *n.*

snood *n.* An ornamental head band or net.

snoop *v.* To pry; to investigate.—*n.* A prying person.—**snoop·er** *n.*—**snoop·y** *adj.*

snoot·y *adj.* [snoot·i·er; -i·est] *Slang.* Haughty.

snooze *v.* [snoozed; snooz·ing] To nap; doze.

snore *v.* [snored; snor·ing] To breathe hoarsely while asleep.—*n.* Rasping noise made by a sleeper.—**snor·er** *n.*

snor·kel (*snor-k'l*) *n.* New type of small submarine capable of remaining submerged for long periods.

snort *v.* To exhale loudly through the nose, esp. in scorn.—**snort** *n.*—**snort·er** *n.*

snout (*snowt*) *n.* 1. The projecting muzzle of an animal, as a pig. 2. A large nose.

snow (*snoh*) *n.* White flakes of crystallized water vapor; a fall of frozen flakes.—*v.* To fall in flakes from the sky; cover with snow.—**snow·i·ly** *adv.*—**snow·i·ness** *n.*

snowball	snowcap	snow shed
snowbank	snowfall	snowslide
snowbird	snowflake	snowslip
snow broth	snow plow	snowstorm

S

snow blindness. A temporary blindness caused by the glittering reflection of sunlight on snow. —snow-blind *adj.*

snow·drift *n.* A bank of wind-heaped snow.

snow·scape *n.* A panorama or picture of snow-covered country.

snow·shoe *n.* Wooden frame for the feet, supporting the wearer on soft snow. —snow·sho·er *n.* —snow·shoe·ing *n.*

SNOWSHOE

Snow White. Title of the heroine of one of the Grimms' fairy tales.

snow·y (*snoh*-ee) *adj.* [snow·i·er; snow·i·est] 1. White; pure; clean. 2. Covered with snow. —snow·i·ly *adv.*—snow·i·ness *n.*

snub *v.* [snubbed; snub·bing] 1. To slight; rebuff. 2. To check.—*n.* 1. A rebuff. 2. A quick stop.—*adj.* Stubby; turned up.—snub·ber *n.*—snub·by *adj.*

snub·nosed *adj.* Having a short turned-up nose.

snuff *n.* The burned wick of a candle.—*v.* To put out a flame by pinching; extinguish.

snuff *v.* To inhale; to smell; to sniff.—*n.* Powdered tobacco inhaled through the nose. —snuff·er *n.*

snuff·box *n.* A small, usually decorative, container for powdered tobacco.

snuff·ers *n. pl.* Small tongs for pinching off the wick or light of a candle.

snuf·fle (*snuf*-'l) *v.* [snuf·fled; snuf·fling] To breathe hoarsely; to sniff repeatedly.—*n.* 1. The sound of clogged breathing. 2. [*pl.*] A nasal catarrh.—snuf·fler *n.*

snuf·fy *adj.* [snuf·fi·er; -fi·est] 1. Like tobacco snuff. 2. Cross; irritated.—snuf·fi·ness *n.*

snug *adj.* [snug·ger; snug·gest] 1. Cozy; comfortable; secure. 2. Closely-fitting; compact; tight.—*v.* 1. To make trim and tidy. 2. *Nautical.* To prepare for a gale.—snug·ly *adv.* —snug·ness *n.*

snug·gle (*snug*-g'l) *v.* [snug·gled; snug·gling] To nestle; cuddle; hold closely.

so (*soh*) *adv.* 1. In such a degree or manner, as things turned out so well. 2. As previously stated, as I think so. 3. With equal reason; similarly.—*conj.* Therefore; in order that.

soak *v.* 1. To immerse; to saturate. 2. To absorb. 3. To penetrate. 4. *Slang.* a. To hit hard. b. To overcharge.—*n.* 1. Absorption of liquid. 2. A hard drinker.—soak·er *n.*

so-and-so *n.* A person or thing not named; an unmentionable person.

soap (*sohp*) *n.* 1. A chemical cleansing compound. 2. *Slang.* Bribe money.—*v.* To cover with soapy lather.

soap opera. Sentimental serialized daytime radio drama.

soap·suds *n. pl.* Lather; soapy foam.

soap·y (*sohp*-ee) *adj.* [soap·i·er; soap·i·est] 1. Frothy; covered with soap. 2. Soft; smooth. 3. Unctuous; oily.—soap·i·ly *adv.* —soap·i·ness *n.*

soar (*sohr*; *sawr*) *v.* 1. To fly; to rise high into the air. 2. To rise above the usual course of events; aspire.—soar *n.*—soar·er *n.*

sob *v.* [sobbed; sob·bing] To weep convulsively; gasp.—*n.* A breath-catching sigh.—sob·bing·ly *adv.*—sob sister. *Slang.* A woman reporter.

so·ber (*soh*-ber) *adj.* 1. Serious; solemn; grave. 2. Temperate in the use of intoxicating liquors; abstemious. 3. Calm; dispassionate. 4. Subdued; somber.—*v.* To cure of intoxication.—so·ber·ly *adv.*—so·ber·ness, so·bri·e·ty (soh-*bry*-eh-tee) *n.*

so·bri·quet (*soh*-brih-kay) *n.* A nickname.

so-called *adj.* Commonly termed, usually implying doubt. 'The so-called statesman.'

soc·cer (*sok*-er) *n.* A type of football in which feet, head, shoulders, etc. may be used to strike the ball.

so·cia·ble (*soh*-shuh-b'l) *adj.* Companionable; friendly.—so·cia·ble·ness *n.*—so·cia·bil·i·ty (soh-shuh-*bil*-ih-tee) *n.*—so·cia·bly *adv.*

so·cial (*soh*-sh'l) *adj.* 1. Pertaining to human welfare and relationship. 2. Concerned with fashionable society. 3. Sociable.—*n. Colloquial.* A festive gathering.—so·cial·ly *adv.*—so·cial·ness *n.*

so·cial·ism (*soh*-sh'l-izm) *n.* A theory of social organization aiming at a more equable distribution of income through a regulated system of community or government ownership of land and the means of production and distribution.—so·cial·ist *n.*—so·cial·ist, -is·tic *adj.*

so·cial·ite (*soh*-sh'l-yte) *n.* A member of the wealthy group of a community.

so·cial·ize (*soh*-sh'l-yze) *v.* [-ized; -iz·ing]. 1. To transfer from private to public ownership or operation. 2. To make more sociable.

social science. The study of human communal existence.

Social Security Act. U. S. law passed 1935, providing for compulsory federal old-age insurance and other aid to the socially dependent.—**Social Security Board.** Board appointed by the President to administer the Act.

so·ci·e·ty (suh-*sy*-eh-tee) *n.* [*pl.* -ties] 1. The members of a civilization; the public. 2. Fellowship; company. 3. An association; a club. 4. The wealthy and fashionable class.

so·ci·ol·o·gy (soh-shee-*ol*-eh-jee) *n.* The science of the development of human society.—so·ci·o·log·ic, so·ci·o·log·i·cal (soh-shee-uh-*loj*-ik, -*loj*-ih-k'l) *adj.*—so·ci·o·log·ic·al·ly *adv.*—so·ci·ol·o·gist (soh-shee-*ol*-eh-jist) *n.*

sock *n.* 1. A short stocking. 2. The light, low-heeled shoe worn by the actors of classic comedy. 3. *Slang.* A punch; hard blow of the fist.—*v.* To punch.

sock·dol·a·ger *n. Slang.* A powerful blow.

sock·et *n.* 1. A hollow opening shaped to hold

a corresponding part. 2. *Electricity*. A current outlet to which appliances may be connected.—*v*. To fit in a socket.

Socratic method. Inductive system of teaching and reasoning originated by the Greek philosopher Socrates, and recorded by Plato in his *Dialogues*.—**So·crat·i·cal·ly** *adv*.—**Soc·ra·tism** *n*.—**Soc·ra·tist** *n*.

sod *n*. Turf; the surface layer of earth containing the grass roots.—*v*. [sod·ded; sod·ding] To cover with turf.

so·da (*soh*-duh) *n*. 1. Any of a number of compounds of the metallic element sodium, as **sodium carbonate** or **washing soda**, **sodium bicarbonate** or **baking soda**, or **sodium nitrate**, a fertilizer. 2. A drink consisting of water, usually flavored, into which carbonic acid has been forced under pressure; soda water.

so·dal·i·ty (soh-*dal*-ih-tee) *n*. A charitable or devotional lay association of the Roman Catholic Church.

sod·den (sod-'n) *adj*. Soaked; softened with liquid; soggy; dull; listless.—**sod·den·ly** *adv*.—**sod·den·ness** *n*.

so·di·um (*soh*-dee-um) *n*. A soft white metallic element of extreme instability, found only in compounds. (*Symbol*: Na).

Sod·om (sod-'m) *n*. *Bible*. A city of ancient Palestine whose destruction is recounted in Genesis XVIII and XIX.—**Sod·om·ite** *n*.

sod·om·y *n*. Unnatural sexual relationship between members of the same sex.—**sod·om·ite** *n*.—**sod·o·mit·i·cal** *adj*.—**sod·o·mit·i·cal·ly** *adv*.

so·fa (*soh*-fuh) *n*. A long upholstered seat with raised back and arm.

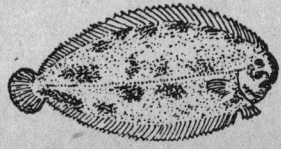
SOFA

soft *adj*. 1. Yielding; easily penetrated; malleable. 2. Mild; kind; easily moved. 3. Affecting the senses in a bland or soothing manner. 4. Effeminate; timid. 5. *Slang*. Foolish; simple; silly; of feeble intellect. 6. Tranquil; undisturbed. 7. *Speech*. Pronounced with a sibilant sound, as *c* in cinder, as opposed to the hard *c* in candle.—*adv*. Gently; quietly.—**soft·ly** *adv*.—**soft·ness** *n*.

soft-armed	soft-brained	soft-hearted
soft-backed	soft coal	softlike
softball	soft-coated	soft-rayed
soft-bedded	soft-eyed	soft-shelled
soft-bellied	soft-finned	softtack
soft-boiled	soft-headed	softwood

soft drink. A non-alcoholic beverage.

soft·en (*sof*-'n) *v*. 1. To make pliant; make more yielding. 2. To mollify. 3. To lessen; ease; mitigate. 4. To tone down; reduce. 5. To enervate.—**sof·ten·er** *n*.—**sof·ten up.** 1. *Slang*. To prepare by persuasion or flattery, in order to obtain a favor or profit. 2. *Military*. To prepare a target for attack by heavy bombardment.

soft soap. 1. A semi-liquid soap. 2. *Slang*. Flatter; blarney.—**soft-soap** *v*. To flatter.

soft-spoken *adj*. Gentle or mild in speech.

soft·y *n*. [*pl*. -ties] *Slang*. A person who can easily be swayed or persuaded.

sog·gy (*sog*-ee) *adj*. [-gi·er; -gi·est] Soaked; heavy with moisture.—**sog·gi·ly** *adv*.—**sog·gi·ness** *n*.

soil (soyl) *n*. 1. The loose, fertile top layer of earth. 2. Ground; earth. 3. Land; the country.

soil *v*. 1. To dirty; stain. 2. To disgrace; defile.—*n*. 1. A spot; stain. 2. Filth, esp. manure.

soi·ree (swah-ray) *n*. A formal evening party.

so·journ (soh-*jern*) *v*. To dwell temporarily.—*n*. A brief stay or visit.—**so·journ·er** *n*.

sol *n*. 1. [*cap*.] The sun or sun-god. 2. *Music*. The syllable for the fifth tone of the scale.

sol·ace (*sol*-iss) *n*. 1. Consolation; alleviation; comfort.—*v*. [sol·aced; sol·ac·ing] To soothe; console.—**sol·ace·ment** *n*.—**sol·ac·er** *n*.

so·lar (*soh*-ler) *adj*. 1. Pertaining to the sun. 2. Measured by the motion of the earth in relation to the sun, as, the solar year.

so·lar·i·um (soh-*lair*-ee-um) *n*. Glass-enclosed room for sun bathing or sunray treatments.

so·lar·ize (*soh*-ler-yze) *v*. [so·lar·ized; so·lar·iz·ing] 1. To subject to the action of sunlight. 2. *Photography*. To injure by overexposure to the sun's rays.—**so·lar·i·za·tion** *n*.

solar plexus. 1. A nerve center in back of the abdomen. 2. The pit of the stomach.

solar system. *Astronomy*. The system of planets which revolve about the sun.

sold. *Past tense & past participle* of **sell**.

sol·der (*sod*-er) *v*. 1. To cement metals together. 2. To unite; to make solid.—*n*. A metal or composition used to unite metallic surfaces.—**sol·der·er** *n*.—**soldering iron.** The tool with which solder is melted and applied.

sol·dier (*sohl*-jer) *n*. 1. An army man; one employed in military service. 2. An enlisted soldier; not an officer. 3. A man of military experience, ability, and daring.—*v*. [sol·diered; sol·dier·ing] 1. To pretend to work; shirk. 2. To do military service.—**sol·dier·like, sol·dier·ly** *adj*.—**sol·dier·ship** *n*.—**soldier of fortune.** An adventurer; a professional soldier.

sol·dier·y *n*. [*pl*. -ies] 1. Soldiers collectively; troops. 2. Military service.

sole *n*. 1. The under surface of the foot. 2. The bottom of a shoe.—*v*. [soled; sol·ing] To provide with a sole.

sole *n*. An edible flatfish.

sole *adj*. Single; solitary; one and only.—**sole·ly** *adv*.

SOLE (1/8 life size)

sol·e·cism (*sol*-eh-sizm) *n*. 1. A grammatical error. 2. An impropriety.—**sol·e·cist** *n*.—**-cis·tic** *adj*.

S

sol·emn (*sol*-um) *adj.* 1. Serious; grave; devout. 2. Sacred; ceremonial; awe-inspiring. —**sol·emn·ly** *adv.*—**sol·emn·ness** *n.*

so·lem·ni·ty (suh-*lem*-nih-tee) *n.* [*pl.* -ties] 1. A sacred rite. 2. Gravity; devoutness.

sol·em·nize (*sol*-um-nyze) *v.* [sol·em·nized; sol·em·niz·ing] To celebrate, as a ritual; perform. —**sol·em·ni·za·tion, sol·em·niz·er** *n.*

sol·en·oid (*soh*-luh-noyd) *n.* A wire coil which, when energized by electric current, acts as a magnet.

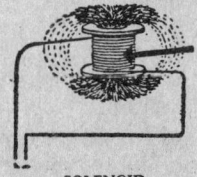
SOLENOID

so·lic·it (suh-*liss*-it) *v.* To plead; to beg; to seek by petition.—**so·lic·it·a·tion** *n.*

so·lic·i·tor (suh-*liss*-ih-ter) *n.* 1. One who requests donations. 2. *England.* An attorney; a court lawyer.—**solicitor general.** [*pl.* solicitors general.] 1. *England.* Second most important law officer. 2. *U.S.* Assistant to the attorney general.

so·lic·it·ous (suh-*liss*-ih-tus) *adj.* Anxious; eager; deeply concerned.— **-ous·ly** *adv.*

so·lic·i·tude (-tyood) *n.* Concern; care.

sol·id (*sol*-id) *adj.* 1. Dense; filled; not hollow. 2. Hard; firm; compact. 3. Unbroken; as, a solid color. 4. Strong; sound; substantial. 5. Financially sound or safe; reliable; as, solid citizen. 6. *Mathematics.* Three dimensional. 7. *Music Slang.* Excellent; satisfying; well performed.—*n.* 1. A mass; a firm, compact body. 2. *Mathematics.* A figure having three dimensions.—**sol·id·ly** *adv.*— **-id·ness** *n.*

sol·i·dar·i·ty (sol-ih-*dair*-ih-tee) *n.* [*pl.* -ties] Unity in mutual interest, responsibility, and trust.

so·lid·i·fy (suh-*lid*-ih-fye) *v.* [so·lid·i·fied; so·lid·i·fy·ing] To harden.—**so·lid·i·fi·ca·tion** *n.*

so·lid·i·ty *n.* [*pl.* -ties] Firmness; soundness.

so·lil·o·quy (suh-*lil*-uh-kwee) *n.* [*pl.* -quies] A monolog; a conversation with oneself.—**so·lil·o·quize** (-kwyze) *v.* [-quized; -quiz·ing].

sol·i·taire (sol-ih-*tair*) *n.* 1. A gem, esp. a diamond, mounted singly. 2. Any card game played by one person.

sol·i·tar·y (*sol*-ih-tehr-ee) *adj.* Isolated; alone; apart; single.—*n.* [*pl.* -ies] One who lives alone; hermit; recluse.— **-tar·i·ly** *adv.*— **-tar·i·ness** *n.*

sol·i·tude (*sol*-ih-tyood) *n.* 1. Seclusion; isolation; withdrawal. 2. An unfrequented place.

so·lo (*soh*-loh) *n.* [*pl.* solos, soli] 1. A melody performed by a single voice or instrument. 2. Anything done by one person.—*adj.* Alone. —*v.* To act or fly singly.—**so·lo·ist** *n.*

Solomon's seal. A symbol in the shape of a six-pointed star.

Sol·o·mon's-seal *n.* A plant having small flowers and creeping roots marked with circular scars.

<!-- SOLOMON'S SEAL illustration -->
SOLOMON'S
SEAL

so·lon (*soh*-lun) *n.* 1. A very wise man. 2. [*cap.*] A legislator.

so long. *Slang.* Goodbye; farewell.

sol·stice (*sol*-stiss) *n. Astronomy.* The time when the sun is farthest from the earth's equator: the beginning of summer, June 21, and of winter, December 21.

sol·u·ble (*sol*-yoo-b'l) *adj.* 1. Capable of being dissolved in a liquid. 2. Explicable.—**sol·u·bil·i·ty** *n.* [*pl.* -ties)— **-ble·ness** *n.*— **-bly** *adv.*

so·lu·tion (suh-*loo*-sh'n) *n.* 1. Answer; result. 2. The transformation of matter from solid or gas to liquid. 3. The preparation produced by dissolving a solid in a liquid.

solve (solv) *v.* [solved; solv·ing] To clear up; unravel; determine the answer.—**solv·a·ble** *adj.*—**solv·a·bil·i·ty, -a·ble·ness** *n.*—**solv·er** *n.*

sol·vent (*sol*-v'nt) *adj.* 1. Having the power of dissolving. 2. Able to pay all debts.—*n.* A dissolving agent.—**solv·en·cy** *n.* [*pl.* -cies]

so·mat·ic *adj.* Pertaining to the body.

som·ber, som·bre (*som*-ber) *adj.* 1. Dark; dull; gloomy. 2. Dismal; melancholy.—**som·ber·ly, som·bre·ly** *adv.*— **-ber·ness, -bre·ness** *n.*

som·bre·ro (som-*brair*-oh) *n.* [*pl.* -ros] Broadbrimmed hat popular in South and Central America and in western U.S.

some (*sum*) *adj.* 1. Indicating an indeterminate person, thing, portion, etc. 2. Applied to those of one group as opposed to others. 'Some men believe one thing, and some another.' —*adv.* About; more or less, as some fifty miles away. —*pron.* An indefinite or unnamed quantity, portion, or number.

<!-- SOMBRERO illustration -->
SOMBRERO

someday	sometime (*adv.*)	somewhen
somehow	sometimes	somewhere
someone	someway	somewhy
something	somewhat	somewise

-some. *suffix.* Indicating a considerable degree of whatever is denoted, as mettlesome, worrisome, lonesome, blithesome; also, a numerical group, as twosome.

some·body *pronoun.* An unnamed person.—*n.* [*pl.* -ies] An important person.

som·er·sault (*sum*-er-sawlt) *n.* Also **som·er·set.** A leap by which one turns heels over head and lands on his feet.—**som·er·sault** *v.*

Somme (*sum*). 1. Department of France. Area: 2,424 sq. mi. 2. River in northern France flowing into the English Channel.

som·nam·bu·late (som-*nam*-byoo-layt) *v.* To walk while asleep.—**som·nam·bu·lant** *adj.* —**som·nam·bu·la·tion, som·nam·bu·lat·or** *n.*

som·nam·bu·lism (som-*nam*-byoo-lizm) *n.* 1. Habitual walking in sleep. 2. Automatic action while asleep or in a trance.—**som·nam·bu·list** *n.*—**som·nam·bu·lis·tic** *adj.*

som·nif·er·ous, som·nif·ic (som-*nif*-er-us, som-*nif*-ik) *adj.* Inducing sleep.

som·no·lent (*som*-nuh-lent) *adj.* Ready to sleep; drowsy; sluggish.—**som·no·lence, som·no·len·cy** *n.*—**som·no·lent·ly** *adv.*

son (*sun*) *n.* 1. A male child; a male descendant. 2. Term of affection for a young man.

3. A native or inhabitant of a country.
4. Member of a faith or sect. 5. [*cap.*] Jesus Christ.

so·nant (*soh*-n'nt) *adj.* 1. Relating to or producing sound. 2. *Phonetics.* Sounded; voiced. —**so·nance** *n.*

so·na·ta (suh-*nah*-tuh) *n.* A musical composition in several movements for one or two instruments.

song *n.* 1. A musical piece composed for the voice. 2. A brief lyrical poem. 3. Poetry or vocal melody in general. 4. A trifle; a small price.—**song·ful** *adj.*—**song·less** *adj.*

song·bird *n.* 1. A melodious bird. 2. *Colloquial.* A female singer.

song·ster *n.* 1. A singer. 2. A songbird. —**song·stress** *n.*

son-in-law *n.* [*pl.* sons-in-law] The husband of one's daughter.

son·net (*sahn*-it) *n.* A fourteen line poem of iambic pentameter with varying but restricted rhyme scheme.—**son·net·eer** (sahn-eh-*teer*) *n.*

son·ny *n.* [*pl.* -nies] Affectionate or condescending form of address for a youth.

so·no·rous (suh-*noh*-russ) *adj.* Resonant; vibrating; full-toned.—**son·o·rous·ly** *adv.*—**so·nor·i·ty, so·no·rous·ness** *n.*

soon *adv.* 1. In a short time; presently. 2. Early; ahead of time. 3. Quickly. 4. Readily; willingly.—**as soon as.** Immediately upon or after another event.

soot *n.* Smoky black substance arising from the burning of organic matter.—*v.* To blacken with soot.—**soot·i·ly** *adv.*— **-i·ness** *n.*

soothe (*sooth*) *v.* [soothed; sooth·ing] 1. To assuage. 2. To calm; pacify.—**sooth·er** *n.* —**sooth·ing** *adj.*—**sooth·ing·ly** *adv.*

sooth·say·er *n.* A prophesier; foreteller.—**sooth·say·ing** *n.*

sop *n.* 1. A morsel soaked in liquid. 2. Something given to pacify; a bribe.—*v.* [sopped; sop·ping] 1. To soak or saturate. 2. To mop.

soph·ism (*sof*-izm) *n.* An argument which deceives, or which contains a hidden fallacy.

soph·ist (*sof*-ist) *n.* 1. [*cap.*] A teacher of philosophy in ancient Greece held in disrepute for clever but shallow reasoning, and for the acceptance of pay. 2. A misleading reasoner; a quibbler.—**soph·is·tic, soph·is·ti·cal** *adj.*—**soph·is·ti·cal·ly** *adv.*—**soph·is·ti·cal·ness** *n.*

so·phis·ti·cate (suh-*fiss*-tih-kayt) *v.* [-cat·ed; -cat·ing] To disillusion; deprive of simplicity; make artificial.—**so·phis·ti·cate** (suh-*fiss*-tih-k't) *n.* A worldly person.—**so·phis·ti·cat·ed** *adj.* —**so·phis·ti·ca·tion** *n.*

soph·ist·ry (*sof*-iss-tree) *n.* [*pl.* -ries] A deceptive argument based on clever subtlety.

soph·o·more (*sof*-uh-mor) *n.* A student in the second year of high school or college.

soph·o·mor·ic *adj.* 1. Pertaining to a sophomore. 2. Immaturely pretentious; high-flown.—**soph·o·mor·i·cal** *adj.*—**soph·o·mor·i·cal·ly** *adv.*

so·po·rif·er·ous (soh-puh-*rif*-er-us) *adj.* Soporific.—**so·po·rif·er·ous·ly** *adv.*—**so·po·rif·er·ous·ness** *n.*

so·po·rif·ic (soh-puh-*rif*-ik) *adj.* 1. Inducing deep sleep. 2. Drowsy; lethargic.—*n.* A narcotic or drug producing slumber.

sop·ping *adj.* Wet; soaked; drenched.

sop·py *adj.* [sop·pi·er; sop·pi·est] Sopping.

so·pra·no (suh-*prah*-noh; -*pran*-oh) *n.* [*pl.* -nos, -ni] 1. The highest singing range of the female voice. 2. A singer of soprano range. —*adj.* Highest in musical voice.

Sor·bonne (sor-*bun*) *n.* The University of Paris, famous for liberal arts and law colleges.

sor·cer·er (*sor*-ser-er) *n.* Magician; one controlling evil spirits.—**sor·cer·ess** *n.*

sor·cer·y *n.* [*pl.* -ies] Witchcraft.

sor·did (*sor*-did) *adj.* 1. Filthy; dirty. 2. Vile; base. 3. Avaricious; mean.—**sor·did·ly** *adv.* —**sor·did·ness** *n.*

sore *adj.* 1. Painful; sensitive; causing discomfort. 2. Easily annoyed or upset. 3. Distressed; vexed. 4. *Slang.* Angry; annoyed. —*n.* 1. A bruised or tender spot on the flesh; a wound or ulcer. 2. A cause of mental grief or trouble.—**sore·ly** *adv.*—**sore·ness** *n.*

sore·head *n.* *Slang.* One easily made angry. — **sore·head·ed** *adj.*

sor·ghum (*sor*-gum) *n.* 1. A family of cane-like cereal grasses. 2. Thick sirup derived from the juice of one species of sorghum.

so·ror·i·ty (suh-*ror*-ih-tee) *n.* [*pl.* -ties] A club of girls or women, usually in a school or college.

sor·rel *n.* A perennial herb with sour tasting leaves.

sor·rel *n.* 1. A reddish-brown color. 2. An animal of that color, esp. a horse.—**sor·rel** *adj.*

sor·row (*sor*-oh) *n.* 1. Sadness; grief. 2. Regret; contrition. 3. A cause of grief; affliction.—*v.* To mourn; grieve.—**sor·row·er** *n.*

sorrow-beaten   sorrow-melted   sorrow-torn
sorrow-blinded sorrowsick   sorrow-wasted
sorrow-laden   sorrow-stricken sorrow-worn

sor·row·ful *adj.* Unhappy; mournful.—**sor·row·ful·ly** *adv.*—**sor·row·ful·ness** *n.*

sor·ry *adj.* [sor·ri·er; sor·ri·est] 1. Regretful; contrite; now used as a minor apology. 2. Dismal; miserable. 3. Pitiable; sordid; worthless.—**sor·ri·ly** *adv.*—**sor·ri·ness** *n.*

sort *n.* 1. Variety; kind; class; species. 2. Manner; fashion. 3. Character; type.—*v.* To segregate; classify; arrange.—**sort·a·ble** *adj.*—**sort·er** *n.*—**of sorts.** Poor; such as it is. —**out of sorts.** Ill; vexed.

sor·tie (*sor*-tee) *n.* Sudden attack by besieged troops; a sallying forth.

SOS. International Morse code symbol used in radio-telegraphic transmission by ships at sea to signify distress.

so-so *adj.* Also **so so.** Passable; mediocre. —*adv.* Fairly; tolerably.

sot *n.* A drunkard.—**sot·tish** *adj.*—**sot·tish·ly** *adv.*—**sot·tish·ness** *n.*

S

sou (*soo*) *n.* **1.** A prewar French five-centime piece; $\frac{1}{20}$ of a franc. **2.** A worthless thing.

sou·brette (*soo-bret*) *n.* **1.** Comedienne; actress of light comedy. **2.** An arch and playful woman; coquette.—**sou·bret·tish** *adj.*

souf·flé (*soo-flay*) *n.* Spongy, fluffy baked dish made light with stiffly beaten egg whites.—*adj.* Fluffy; puffed.

sough (*suf; sow*) *n.* A rustling or murmuring sound.—*v.* To sigh.

soul (*sohl*) *n.* **1.** The spirit; the immaterial entity of life of man believed to survive after death. **2.** The moral and emotional side of man's nature. **3.** The vital part; the source; essence. **4.** Fervor; depth of feeling. **5.** A human being; a person.

soul·ful *adj.* Deeply emotional.—**soul·ful·ly** *adv.*—**soul·ful·ness** *n.*

soul·less *adj.* Lacking in soul; spiritless.—**soul·less·ly** *adv.*—**soul·less·ness** *n.*

sound (*sownd*) *adj.* **1.** Healthy; whole; uninjured; perfect. **2.** Firm; solid; reliable. **3.** True; valid. **4.** Profound; deep. **5.** Thorough.—**sound·ly** *adv.*—**sound·ness** *n.*

sound *n.* **1.** Sensation received through the organs of hearing from vibration transmitted by the air or other medium. **2.** Noise of a specified quality. 'The sound of voices.' **3.** Empty noise without significance. **4.** Meaning; implication. **5.** Hearing distance; earshot.—*v.* **1.** To make a noise. **2.** To indicate; make an impression.—**sound·er** *n.*

sound *n.* **1.** A narrow body of water connecting two large bodies, or between an island and mainland. **2.** The air bladder of a fish.

sound *v.* **1.** To measure depth; to fathom. **2.** To probe; to examine.—**sound·a·ble** *adj.*

sound·er *n.* An instrument for recording telegraphic messages.

sound·ing *adj.* Resonant.—**sound·ing·ly** *adv.*

sound·ing *n.* **1.** Measurement of the depth of water by weighted line. **2.** [*pl.*] Any water whose bottom can be reached by a hand line.

sound·less *adj.* Noiseless; silent.—**sound·less·ly** *adv.*—**sound·less·ness** *n.*

soup (*soop*) *n.* **1.** Broth; liquid food made by simmering meat or vegetables in broth or water. **2.** *Slang.* Electricity. **3.** *Slang.* Nitroglycerin used to blow open a safe.

soup·y *adj.* [soup·i·er; soup·i·est] **1.** Like soup. **2.** *Colloquial.* Drippingly foggy.

sour (*sow-'r*) *adj.* **1.** Acid; tart; without sweetness. **2.** Rancid; changed by fermentation. **3.** Disagreeable; morose. **4.** Bitter; hard to bear.—*v.* **1.** To make or become rancid. **2.** To be tart, bitter, etc.—*n.* A food or beverage sharply acid in taste.—**sour·ish** *adj.*—**sour·ly** *adv.*—**sour·ness** *n.*

sourberry	sour-eyed	sour-natured
sour-blooded	sour-faced	sour-tempered
sour-breathed	sour-hearted	sour-tongued

source (*sorss*) *n.* **1.** Cause; origin. **2.** Fountainhead; wellspring; supplier. **3.** Document, book, etc., with original information.

sour·dough (*sow-'r-doh*) *n.* Alaskan gold prospector.

sour grapes. Things disliked because they cannot be obtained.

sour·puss *n.* *Slang.* A very gloomy person.

souse (*sowss*) *n.* **1.** Food steeped in vinegar, esp. pickled meat. **2.** A plunge in water. **3.** A drunkard.—*v.* [soused; sous·ing] **1.** To plunge into liquid; drench. **2.** To pickle.

south (*sowth*) *n.* **1.** One of the four cardinal points of the compass, directly opposite north. **2.** Territory lying toward the south. **3.** [*cap.*] Southeastern section of the U.S. in Civil War (1861–1865).—*adj.* At, toward, from, in, or of the south.—*adv.* To or in the south.

South Africa, Union of. One of the British Commonwealth of Nations, including Transvaal, Cape of Good Hope, Natal, and Orange Free State. Area: 472,550 sq. mi. Capitals: Pretoria and Capetown.

South African. Native of the Union of South Africa.—**South African** *adj.*

South America. Southern continent of the Western Hemisphere. Area: 7,045,047 sq. mi. —**South American** *adj. & n.*

south by east, south by west. See **compass.**

South·down *n.* A breed of English sheep.

south·east (*sowth-eest*) *n.* A compass point halfway between south and east.—*adj.* At, toward, from, in, or of the southeast.—*adv.* Toward the southeast.—**south·east·ern, south·east·ern·most** *adj.*—**south·east·ward** *adj., adv. & n.*—**south·east·ward·ly** *adj. & adv.*—**south·east·wards** *adv.*

southeast by east, southeast by south. See **compass.**

south·east·er (*sowth-eest-er*) *n.* A windstorm coming from the southeast.

south·east·er·ly *adj. & adv.* Toward or from the southeast.

south·er (*sowth-er*) *n.* A wind from the south.

south·er·ly (*suh-ther-lee*) *adj. & adv.* To, toward, from, or of the south.—**south·er·li·ness** *n.*

south·ern (*suh-thern*) *adj.* **1.** Of, to, in, toward, or from the south. **2.** [*cap.*] Pertaining to the south of the U.S.—**south·ern·ly** *adv.*

south·ern·er (*suh-thern-er*) *n.* **1.** A dweller in the south. **2.** [*cap.*] A native of the southern states of the U.S.

south·land *n.* The southeastern part of the United States; Dixie.

south·paw *n.* *Sports.* A left-handed athlete, esp. a baseball pitcher.—*adj. Slang.* Left-handed.

South Pole. The southern end of the earth's axis of rotation.

south-south·east, south-south·west. See **compass.**

south·ward (*sowth-werd, suh-therd*) *adj. & adv.* Toward the south.—*n.* A place or direction toward the south.—**south·ward·ly** *adj. & adv.* —**south·wards** *adv.*

south·west (*sowth-west*) *n.* A compass point halfway between south and west.—*adj.* At, toward, from, in, or of the southwest.—*adv.* Toward, from, or in the southwest.—**south·west·ern, south·west·ern·most** *adj.*—**south·west·ward** *adj., adv. & n.*—**south·west·ward·ly** *adj. & adv.*—**south·west·wards** *adv.*

southwest by south, southwest by west. See **compass.**

south·west·er *n.* Also **sou'west·er.** A windstorm from the southwest.

south·west·er·ly *adj. & adv.* Toward or from the southwest.

sou·ve·nir (soo-veh-*neer*) *n.* A memento; remembrance; keepsake.

sou'west·er (sou-*wes*-ter) *n.* 1. Gale from the southwest. 2. Waterproof hat, used by fishermen.

sov·er·eign (*sov*-rin) *adj.* 1. Supreme; royal; princely. 2. Autonomous; independent. 3. Excellent; effective. —*n.* 1. Ruler; monarch. 2. English gold coin worth one pound.—**sov·er·eign·ly** *adv.*—**sov·er·eign·ty** *n.* [*pl.* -ties].

SOU'WESTER

so·vi·et (*soh*-vee-et) *n.* 1. Council. 2. A local governing body in the U.S.S.R., composed of peasants, soldiers, and workers, which sends deputies to the higher congresses.—*adj.* Of or pertaining to government by soviets; communistic.—**so·vi·et·ism** *n.*—**so·vi·et·ist** *n.*—**so·vi·et·i·za·tion** (soh-vee-et-uh-*zay*-sh'n) *n.*—**so·vi·et·ize** *v.* [-ized; -iz·ing].

Soviet Russia. The Russian Soviet Federated Socialist Republic (R.S.F.S.R.), Country E. Europe, NW Asia. Capital: Moscow. Area: 6,612,601 sq. mi.

Soviet Union. Union of Soviet Socialist Republic (U.S.S.R.) Capital: Moscow. Area: 8,701,491 sq. mi.

sow (soh) *v.* [sowed; sown] 1. To plant by scattering seeds on the earth; to stock with seed. 2. To spread abroad; to propagate.

sow (sow) *n.* Female of the hog.

soy *n.* Also **soya, soja.** 1. Easily grown, nutritious bean used for food, fodder, and in certain plastics. 2. Sauce made from soybeans.

spa (spah) *n.* Mineral spring resort.

space (spayss) *n.* 1. Expanse; extension. 2. Any quantity or portion of extension; interval; area between objects. 3. Amount of time; duration.—*v.* [spaced; spac·ing] To arrange at proper intervals.—**spac·ing** *n.* Interval between objects; arrangement of objects.—**space out.** To widen the intervals.

space·bar *n.* Lever on a typewriter for spacing.

spa·cious (*spay*-shus) *adj.* Vast; extensive; wide; ample.— **-cious·ly** *adv.*— **-cious·ness** *n.*

spade *n.* 1. Digging tool, consisting of a broad iron blade with a cutting edge, joined

to a long handle. 2. [*pl.*] One of the four suits in cards.—*v.* [spad·ed; spad·ing] To dig with a spade; to delve.—**call a spade a spade.** *Slang.* To speak frankly.

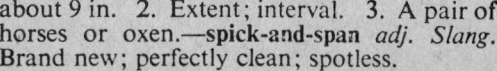

| spadebone | spade-dug | spade-shaped |
| spade-cut | spademan | spadework |

spa·dix (*spay*-dikss) *n.* [*pl.* spa·di·ces] *Botany.* Spike of a flower.

spa·ghet·ti (spuh-*get*-tee) *n.* Thin tubes of hardened dough used in Italian dishes.

span *v.* [spanned; span·ning] 1. To measure with the width of the extended five fingers. 2. To extend from one side to the other.—*n.* 1. Distance from the end of the thumb to the tip of the little finger when extended; about 9 in. 2. Extent; interval. 3. A pair of horses or oxen.—**spick-and-span** *adj. Slang.* Brand new; perfectly clean; spotless.

SPADIX

span·drel (*span*-dr'l) *n. Architecture.* The space between an arch and the enclosing right angle.

span·gle *n.* 1. Small, shiny disk, used as a dress ornament. 2. Any bright, sparkling object.—*v.* [spangled; span·gling] To set or sprinkle with spangles; to glitter.—**span·gly** *adj.*

SPANDREL

Span·iard (*span*-yerd) *n.* Native of Spain.

span·iel (*span*-yul) *n.* Small or medium-sized dog with broad muzzle, long, floppy ears, and a full, sleek coat.

Span·ish *adj.* 1. Pertaining to Spain. 2. The language of Spain and certain Latin American countries.— **-ish·ness** *n.*

SPANIEL (1/15 life-size)

spank *v.* 1. To strike with the open hand, usually across the buttocks; to slap. 2. To move dashingly.—**spank·ing** *n.* Series of sounding blows delivered by the palm of the hand.

spank·er *n.* Longitudinal sail on the mainmast of a square-rigged ship.

spank·ing *adj.* 1. Quick; lively; dashing. 2. *Slang.* Large; considerable; solid.

span·ner *n.* A wrench, esp. a monkey-wrench.

spar (spahr) *n.* 1. A mast; boom; wooden rod. 2. A crystallized mineral found in the earth.—*v.* [sparred; spar·ring] 1. *Boxing.*

SPANKER

S

a. To maneuver with the fists in preparation for a blow. **b.** To train by boxing. 2. To parry cleverly, esp. in debate.—**sparring partner.** A fighter's training opponent.

spare (*spair*) *v.* [spared; spar·ing] 1. To afford; do ·without. 2. To use frugally; dispense carefully. 3. To omit; refrain from; withhold. 4. To show mercy; withhold punishment or destruction.—*adj.* 1. More than is necessary; superfluous; held in reserve. 2. Lean; meager; thin.—*n.* An extra; a thing held in reserve.—**spare·ly** *adv.*—**spare·ness** *n.*

spar·ing *adj.* 1. Saving; frugal. 2. Lenient; merciful.—**spar·ing·ly** *adv.*—**spar·ing·ness** *n.*

spark *n.* 1. Flash; glint; gleam. 2. Small particle of fire. 3. A germ; a particle capable of development. 4. The light caused by a current of electricity passing between two conductors.—**spark** *v.*

spark plug. 1. Device for producing an electric spark to set off combustion in the cylinder of a gasoline engine. 2. *Slang.* A good leader; a pace setter.

spar·kle (*spahr*-k'l) *v.* [spar·kled; spar·kling] 1. To glitter; twinkle; send off sparks. 2. To effervesce.—**spar·kle, spar·kler** *n.*—**spar·kling** *adj.*—**spar·kling·ly** *adv.*—**spar·kling·ness** *n.*

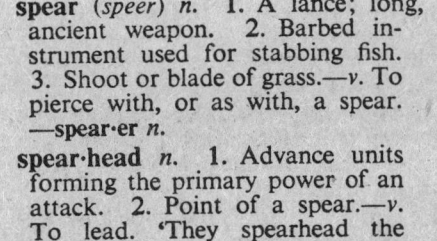

SPARK PLUG

spar·row (*spair*-oh) *n.* Small gray-brown bird numerous in America and the British Isles.

sparrow hawk. Small falcon preying upon pigeons and smaller birds.

SPARROW (1/3 life-size)

sparse *adj.* Few; meager; scattered; far apart.—**sparse·ly** *adv.*—**sparse·ness, spar·si·ty** *n.*

Spar·ta. Ancient city in Greece famous for its military might.—**spar·tan** *adj.* 1. [*cap.*] Pertaining to Sparta. 2. Courageous; enduring; hardy. 3. Simple; rigorous; severe.—**spar·tan·ism** *n.*

spasm (*spazm*) *n.* 1. An involuntary contraction of a muscle or group of muscles. 2. A sudden, violent, and usually fruitless effort.

spas·mod·ic, spas·mod·i·cal (spaz-*mod*-ik, -'l) *adj.* 1. Convulsive. 2. Occasional; fitful.—**spas·mod·i·cal·ly.**

spat *n.* 1. Petty, brief quarrel. 2. [*pl.*] Short covering worn over the shoe.—*v.* [spat·ted; spat·ting] To bicker; to dispute.

spat. *Past tense of* **spit.**

spate (*spayt*) *n.* 1. Sudden heavy flood. 2. A torrent.

spat·ter *v.* 1. To spray; to splash; to sprinkle. 2. To dishonor; to defame.—*n.* A soiled spot.

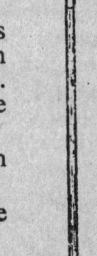

SPAT

—**spat·ter·ing·ly** *adv.*—**spat·ter·dash** *n.* A covering for the leg; legging.—**spatter work.** A finish made by sprinkling paint or dye upon a surface.

spat·u·la (*spat*-choo-luh) *n.* 1. Knifelike utensil with a broad, flexible blade. 2. *Medicine.* Flat instrument used for depressing the tongue.—**spat·u·lar, spat·u·late** *adj.*

spav·in (*spav*-in) *n.* Disease of horses causing enlargement of the hockjoint.—**spav·ined** *adj.*

spawn *n.* 1. The eggs of fishes, frogs, etc. 2. Any product or offspring, used contemptuously.—**spawn** *v.*

spay *v.* To remove the ovaries of an animal.

speak (*speek*) *v.* [spoke; spok·en; speak·ing] 1. To utter; to talk. 2. To discourse; to make a speech. 3. To make mention; to tell. 4. To communicate ideas; to be expressive. 5. To use orally. 'He speaks French.' 6. To ask for; to demand.—**speak·a·ble** *adj.*—**speak·er** *n.*—**speak·er·ship** *n.*—**Speak·er of the House.** The presiding officer of U.S. House of Representatives.—**speak one's mind.** To give a candid opinion.—**speak out.** To speak loudly; to express one's thoughts.—**speak well for.** To give a favorable indication of.

speak·eas·y (*speek*-eez-ee) *n.* A place where liquor is sold illegally, esp. during Prohibition.

speak·ing *adj.* Animated; lifelike; eloquent. 'A speaking likeness.'—*n.* Utterance; oratory. —**speaking acquaintance.** A slight and formal acquaintance.

spear (*speer*) *n.* 1. A lance; long, pointed, ancient weapon. 2. Barbed instrument used for stabbing fish. 3. Shoot or blade of grass.—*v.* To pierce with, or as with, a spear. —**spear·er** *n.*

spear·head *n.* 1. Advance units forming the primary power of an attack. 2. Point of a spear.—*v.* To lead. 'They spearhead the attack.'

spear·man *n.* A soldier armed with a spear.

spear·mint *n.* Aromatic herb of the mint family used for flavoring.

spe·cial (*spesh*-'l) *adj.* 1. Different; extraordinary; unique. 2. Particular; limited.—*n.* 1. Person or thing designated for a purpose. 2. An extra train run for a particular occasion.—**spe·cial·ly** *adv.*

spe·cial·ize (*spesh*-'l-yze) *v.* [-ized; -iz·ing] 1. To devote or apply to a specific function. 2. To concentrate upon a particular field. —**spe·cial·ism** *n.*—**spe·cial·ist** *n.*—**spe·cial·ist, -is·tic** *adj.*—**-i·za·tion** (-ih-*zay*-sh'n) *n.*

spe·cial·ty (*spesh*-'l-tee) *n.* 1. Subject in which one is particularly well versed. 2. A creation of peculiar skill.

spe·cie (*spee*-shee) *n.* Coin, in contrast to paper money.—**specie payment.** Payment in coin.

SPEAR

spe·cies (*spee*-sheez) *n*. Breed; genus; type; a similar group of plants or animals.

spe·cif·ic (speh-*sif*-ik) *adj*. 1. Pertaining to a species. 2. Particular; designated. 3. Definite; precise.—*n. Medicine*. Remedy designed for a particular disease.—**spe·cif·i·cal·ly** *adv*. —**spec·i·fic·i·ty** (speh-sih-*fiss*-uh-tee) *n*.

spe·cif·i·ca·tion (speh-sif-ih-*kay*-sh'n) *n*. Designation; requirement; restriction; limit.

spe·ci·fy (*speh*-sih-fy) *v*. To mention; name; designate.—**spec·i·fi·a·ble** *adj*.

spec·i·men (*spess*-ih-m'n) *n*. 1. A sample; a representative. 2. *Slang*. Person of the type described. 'He was a fine specimen.'

spe·cious (*spee*-shus) *adj*. Deceptive; superficially plausible.—**spe·ci·os·i·ty** (spee-shee-*oss*-uh-tee) *n*.—**spe·cious·ly** *adv*.—**spe·cious·ness** *n*.

speck *n*. Particle; spot.—*v*. To dot; mark.

speck·le *v*. [speck·led; speck·ling] To dot; sprinkle.—*n*. A spot.—**speck·led** *adj*.

spec·ta·cle (*spek*-tuh-k'l) *n*. 1. Exhibition; show; pageant. 2. A sight; an unseemly display. 3. [*pl*.] Eye-glasses; pair of ground lenses worn to assist or correct poor vision. —**spec·ta·cled** *adj*. 1. Wearing spectacles. 2. *Zoology*. Having marks around the eyes resembling spectacles.

spec·tac·u·lar (spek-*tak*-yoo-ler) *adj*. 1. Pertaining to a show or spectacle. 2. Magnificent; unusual; showy.—**spec·tac·u·lar·ly** *adv*.

spec·ta·tor (*spek*-tay-ter; spek-*tay*-ter) *n*. 1. An observer; onlooker. 2. [*pl*.] Women's sport pumps.—*adj*. 1. Designed to be observed rather than participated in. 2. Designed for wear at sporting events; tailored; sporty.

spec·ter, spec·tre (*spek*-ter) *n*. An apparition; ghost; phantom.

spec·tral (*spek*-tr'l) *adj*. 1. Ghostly. 2. Pertaining to the spectrum.—**spec·tral·i·ty** *n*. —**spec·tral·ly** *adv*.

spec·tro·scope (*spek*-truh-skohp) *n*. Optical instrument used in spectrum analysis.—**spec·tro·scop·ic** (spek-truh-*skop*-ik), **spec·tro·scop·i·cal** *adj*.—**spec·tro·scop·i·cal·ly** *adv*.—**spec·tros·co·pist** (spek-*tross*-koh-pist) *n*.—**spec·tros·co·py** *n*.

spec·trum (*spek*-tr'm) *n*. [*pl*. spec·tra] Bands of colored light rays in order of their wave lengths, produced by refraction of white light.

spec·u·late (*spek*-yoo-layt) *v*. 1. To theorize; consider; debate. 2. To buy goods or stocks expecting to sell them at an abnormal profit. —**spec·u·la·tive** *adj*.—**spec·u·la·tive·ly** *adv*. —**spec·u·la·tive·ness** *n*.

spec·u·la·tion (spek-yoo-*lay*-sh'n) *n*. 1. Theory; reasoning. 2. Guesswork. 3. Hazardous business transacted with hope of large returns.—**spec·u·la·tor** *n*.—**spec·u·la·to·ry** (*spek*-yoo-luh-toh-ree) *adj*.

speech *n*. 1. Utterance; articulateness. 2. Language; dialect; parlance. 3. Conversation. 4. Oration; address.—**speech·i·fy** *v*. [speech·i·fied; speech·i·fy·ing] To harangue, used hu-morously or contemptuously.—**speech·i·fier** *n*. —**speech·less** *adj*.—**speech·less·ly** *adv*.—**speech·less·ness** *n*.

speech-bereft   speechcraft   speech-flooded
speech-bound   speech-famed   speechmaker

speed *n*. 1. Swiftness; haste. 2. Rate of movement or progress.—*v*. [sped, speed·ed; speed·ing] 1. To hasten; to hurry. 2. To expedite. 3. To dispatch. 4. To drive too fast; to exceed the speed limit.—**speed·i·ly** *adv*. —**speed·i·ness** *n*.—**speedy** *adj*. [speed·i·er; speed·i·est].

speedboat   speed indicator
speedboatman   speed limit
speed clock   speed reducer
speed controller   speed trap
speed counter   speed-up
speed gear   speedway

speed·om·e·ter (spee-*dom*-eh-ter) *n*. Instrument showing the rate of speed of a vehicle.

speed-up *n*. A technique used to accelerate industrial output.

speed·well *n*. Veronica; a plant with small flowers, usually blue or white.

spell *v*. To take the turn or place of; relieve. —*n*. 1. A piece of work done in relief of another. 2. A turn at work; single period of labor. 3. A short period.

spell *v*. [spelled, spelt; spell·ing] 1. To write the proper letters in correct order. 2. To constitute; indicate; mean. 3. To read slowly; study. 4. To bewitch; charm.—*n*. 1. A charm; an enchantment. 2. A fit; an attack. —**spell·er** *n*.—**spell·ing** *n*. System of forming words with letters; orthography.—**spelling bee**. A contest of spelling skill.—**spelling book**. A book for teaching children to spell.

spell·bind *v*. To captivate with words.—**spell·bind·er** *n*.—**spell·bind·ing** *adj*.

spell·bound *adj*. Entranced; fascinated.

spell·er *n*. 1. One who spells. 2. A book of instructions and exercises in spelling.

spen·cer *n*. 1. A short jacket. 2. A fore-and-aft sail set behind the fore-and main-masts.

Spen·cer·i·an (spen-*sihr*-ee-un) *adj*. Pertaining to Herbert Spencer.—*n*. 1. Follower of Herbert Spencer. 2. *Penmanship*. A sloping style of handwriting designed by R. Spencer.— **Spen·cer·i·an·ism** *n*.

spend *v*. [spent; spend·ing] 1. To lay out money; to use; to devote. 2. To exhaust; to waste. 3. To wear away.—**spend·er** *n*.

spend·thrift *n*. An extravagant person.—*adj*. Improvident; prodigal.—**spend·thrift·y** *adj*.

Spen·ser·i·an (spen-*sihr*-ee-un) *adj*. Relating to the poet Edmund Spenser, esp. the stanza style in his *Faerie Queene*.

Spenserian stanza. Eight ten-syllable lines followed by one of twelve syllables.

spent. *Past tense & past participle* of **spend**. —*adj*. Worn out; exhausted.

sperm *n*. Male generative fluid; semen.—**sper·ma·ry** *n*. Testis.—**sper·mat·ic, sper·mous** *adj*.

S

sper·ma·ce·ti (sper-muh-*set*-tee) *n.* A waxy substance found in sperm whales and dolphins, used in cosmetics and ointments.

sper·ma·ry (*sper*-muh-ree) *n.* [*pl.* -ries] Sperm gland; testis.—**sper·mat·ic** *adj.*

sper·mat·ic cord. The cord within the scrotum which suspends the testicle.

sper·ma·to·zo·on (sper-muh-tuh-*zoh*-un) *n.* [*pl.* sper·ma·to·zo·a] Male germ cell contained in the semen which impregnates the ovum. —**sper·ma·to·zo·al, -zo·an, -zo·ic** *adj.*

sperm oil. A lubricant oil obtained from the head cavity and blubber of the sperm whale.

sperm whale. A large whale, valued for its spermaceti, sperm oil, and ambergris.

spew (spyoo) *v.* 1. To cast forth. 2. To eject from the stomach; vomit; puke.—*n.* A vomit. —**spew·er** *n.*

sphag·num (*sfag*-num) *n.* A mosslike spongy plant used for potting, mulching, packings, etc.—**sphag·nous** *adj.*

sphere (sfihr) *n.* 1. *Geometry.* A solid body which in every part is equally distant from its center. 2. An orb; a globe; a round body. 3. Range; compass; province. 4. The heavens.—*v.* [sphered; spher·ing] To give complete and perfect form.—**spher·al** (*sfehr*-ul), **spher·ic** (*sfehr*-ik), **spher·i·cal** *adj.*—**spher·i·cal·ly** *adv.*—**sphe·ric·i·ty** *n.*—**spher·y** *adj.*

SPHERE

spher·ics (*sfehr*-iks) *n.* Branch of meteorology dealing with long-range electronic detection of atmospheric conditions.

sphere of influence. A region, usually undeveloped politically, under the determinative power of a foreign nation.

sphe·roid (*sfihr*-oyd) *n.* A spherelike body not perfectly round.—**sphe·roi·dal, sphe·roi·dic, sphe·roi·di·cal** *adj.*—**sphe·roi·dic·i·ty, -di·ty** *n.*

sphinc·ter (*sfink*-ter) *n.* A ringlike muscle which opens, closes, or contracts a natural opening. —**sphinc·ter·al** *adj.*

SPHEROID

sphinx (sfinks) *n.* 1. *Greek Myth.* She-monster who proposed riddles and killed all who could not answer them. 2. Egyptian figure with the body of a lion and a human head. 3. A silent or inscrutable person.—**sphinx·like** *adj.*

SPHINX

spice (spyse) *n.* 1. A condiment; a seasoning;

a pungent dried vegetable product. 2. A flavor; a piquancy.—*v.* [spiced; spic·ing] To season.—**spic·er** *n.*—**spic·er·y** *n.*

spiceberry	spicecake	spice-laden
spice-burnt	spice house	spiceland

spick-and-span *adj.* Tidy; neat.

spic·ule (*spik*-yool) *n.* 1. Small slim pointed body. 2. *Zoology.* Minute flinty particles found in sponges.—**spic·u·lar, spic·u·late** *adj.*

spic·y (*spyss*-ee) *adj.* 1. Tangy; keen to taste. 2. Racy; scandalous.—**spic·i·ly** *adv.*—**spic·i·ness** *n.*

spi·der (*spy*-der) *n.* A small animal with four pairs of long slender limbs and silk-producing organs (spinnerets) used to spin webs as nests and snares for prey. —**spi·der·y** *adj.* Delicate; intricate.

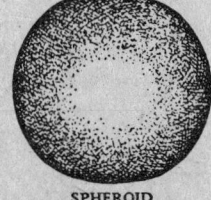
SPIDER (life-size)

spider-fingered	spider-spun
spider-legged	spider web
spider-limbed	spiderwork

spiel (speel) *n. Slang.* A talk; a long story.

spif·fy *adj. Slang.* Well groomed; elegant.

spig·ot (*spig*-it) *n.* 1. Peg used to stop a small opening in a cask of liquid. 2. A faucet.

spike *n.* 1. A slender pointed projection. 2. A large nail. 3. Nail or instrument used to close the vent of a cannon or gun.—*v.* [spiked; spik·ing] 1. To fasten with long nails. 2. To pierce; to impede. 3. To close up; to block. 4. To add liquor to a beverage.—**spiky** *adj.*

spile *n.* 1. A large stake driven into the ground to support a building, pier, etc. 2. A small plug. 3. A spout used in collecting tree sap. —*v.* [spiled; spil·ing]—**spil·ing** *n.*

spill *v.* [spilled, spilt; spil·ling] 1. To lose; let leak; shed; overturn. 2. *Nautical.* To release the sail from wind pressure.—*n.* 1. A little piece; splinter. 2. *Colloquial.* An upset; fall.—**spil·lage, spil·ler** *n.*

spill·way *n.* Concrete passageway in a reservoir or dam through which excess water flows.

SPILLWAY

spin *v.* [spun; spin·ning] 1. To draw and twist into threads. 2. To whirl; twirl. 3. To move rapidly, as in an automobile. —*n.* 1. Whirling motion. 2. Maneuver of an airplane.—**spin a yarn.** To tell a tale.—**spin out.** To protract.

spin·ach (*spin*-ich) *n.* A leafy green vegetable. —**spi·na·ceous** (spih-*nay*-shus) *adj.*

spi·nal (*spy*-n'l) *adj.* Pertaining to the backbone. 'Spinal anaesthetic; spinal canal.'

spin·dle (*spin*-d'l) *n.* 1. Tapered stick on spinning wheels for holding, twisting, and winding thread. 2. Small axle; turning rod or pin. —*v.* [spin·dled; spin·dling] To grow long and thin.—**spin·dling** *adj.* Thin, worthless.

spin·drift *n.* Spray blown from sea waves.

spine *n.* 1. Backbone of a vertebrate animal. 2. *Zoology.* Sharp point of bone; horny tissue. 3. *Botany.* Sharp-pointed growth on a plant. 4. Courage; spirit. 5. Back of a book. —**spine·less** *adj.*—**spine·less·ly** *adv.*—**spine·less·ness** *n.*

spine ache   spine-clad   spine-pointed
spinebill   spine-covered   spine-rayed
spine bone   spine-finned   spinetail
spine-broken   spine-headed   spine-tipped

spin·et (*spin-it*) *n.* Old form of harpsichord. —**spinet piano.** A small upright piano.

spin·naker (*spin-uh-ker*) *n. Nautical.* A large triangular sail, used when sailing before the wind.

spin·ner *n.* 1. One who spins. 2. A revolving fish lure, used by fly fishermen.

SPINET

spin·ning *n.* 1. Operation of making thread. 2. Material processed by this operation.—*adj.* Whirling; revolving.—**spinning jenny.** A spinning machine.—**spin·ning wheel.** Manual spinning machine with single spindle.

spin·ster *n.* 1. Unmarried woman. 2. Woman who spins.—*adj.* Unmarried.—**spin·ster·hood** *n.* —**spin·ster·ish** *adj.*

SPINNAKER

spin·y (*spyn-ee*) *adj.* [spin·i·er; spin·i·est] 1. Full of spines; thorny. 2. Difficult. —**spin·i·ness** *n.*

spiny-backed
spiny-coated
spiny-crested
spiny-finned
spiny-legged
spiny-pointed
spiny-rayed
spiny-skinned

SPINNING WHEEL

spi·ral (*spy-r'l*) *adj.* 1. Circling about and receding from a point. 2. Helical, as the thread of a screw. —*v.* [spi·raled, spi·ralled; spi·ral·ing, spi·ral·ling] To move in a spiral curve. —**spi·ral** *n.*—**spi·ral·ly** *adv.*

spiral-coated   spiral-pointed
spiral-grooved   spiral-shaped
spiral-haired   spiraltail

SPIRALS

spire (*spyre*) *n.* 1. A steeple. 2. A tall, slender cone. 3. Summit.

spir·it *n.* 1. Soul; life force regarded as a mystical entity. 2. Supernatural being; a ghost. 3. Animation; vivacity. 4. Courage; spunk. 5. [*often pl.*] Mental condition. 6. Essence; true meaning. 7. [*pl.*] Distilled alcoholic liquors.—*v.* 1. To animate; to encourage. 2. To convey secretly or stealthily. —**spir·it·ed** *adj.* Lively; bright; active.—**spir·it·ed·ly** *adv.*—**spir·it·ed·ness** *n.*—**spir·it·less** *adj.*—**spir·it·less·ly** *adv.*—**spir·it·less·ness** *n.*

spirit-born   spirit-fallen   spirit-torn
spirit-broken   spiritland   spirit-wise

spir·i·tu·al (*spihr-ih-choo-ul*) *adj.* 1. Not material. 2. Relating to the moral feelings. 3. Pure; holy; sacred. 4. Ecclesiastical; belonging to the church.—**spir·it·u·al·i·ty** *n.*

spir·it·u·al·ism (*spihr-ih-choo-ul-izm*) *n.* 1. *Philosophy.* Doctrine of the existence of spirit as distinct from matter. 2. Belief in communication with departed spirits.—**spir·it·u·al·ist** *n.*

spir·it·u·al·ize (*spihr-ih-choo-ul-yze*) *v.* [-ized; -iz·ing] 1. To purify. 2. To put life into. 3. To convert to a religious meaning.

spir·it·u·ous *adj.* Alcoholic.— **-ous·ness** *n.*

spit *v.* [spat, spit; spit·ting] 1. To eject from the mouth. 2. To expel or throw out with violence.—*n.* 1. Saliva ejected from the mouth; sputum. 2. *Colloquial.* Image; likeness. 'He's the spit of his dad.'

spit *n.* 1. Long, pointed spike on which meat is roasted. 2. Small point of land extending into the sea.—*v.* [spit·ted; spit·ting] To pierce with a spit.

spite (*spyte*) *n.* Malice; ill will; malevolence.—*v.* [spit·ed; spit·ting] To thwart maliciously; to shame; to vex.—**in spite of.** Notwithstanding; regardless of.—**spite·ful** *adj.*—**spite·ful·ly** *adv.*

spit·fire *n.* 1. A fiery, hot-tempered person. 2. [*cap.*] a British fighter plane used in World War II.

spit·tle *n.* Saliva; spit.

spit·toon (*spih-toon*) *n.* Receptacle for spittle or tobacco juice; cuspidor.

spitz *n.* Long-haired breed of dog.

SPIRE

SPITZ

S

splash *v.* To dash water about; spatter with liquid.—*n.* 1. Liquid spattered about. 2. The sound of striking water.—**splash·er** *n.* —**splash·y** *adj.*

splash·board *n.* Dashboard; board to shield from spattered mud, etc.

splat *n.* Flat center support of a chair back.

splat·ter *v.* 1. To splash; spatter. 2. To spray.

splay *adj.* Spread out; turned outward.—*v.* To expand.—*n. Arch.* A slope.

SPLAT

spleen *n.* 1. Large glandular organ in the upper left part of the abdomen. 2. Anger; ill humor.—**spleen·ful** *adj.*—**spleen·ful·ly** *adv.* —**spleen·ish** *adj.*— **-ish·ly** *adv.*— **-ish·ness** *n.*

splen·did (*splen*-did) *adj.* 1. Magnificent; showy. 2. Grand; heroic; noble.—**splen·did· ly** *adv.*—**splen·did·ness** *n.*

splen·dif·er·ous (splen-*dif*-er-us) *adj. Slang.* Magnificent; gorgeous.

splen·dor (*splen*-der) *n.* 1. Brightness; brilliant luster. 2. Magnificence; pomp. 3. Glory; grandeur.—**splen·dor·ous, splen·drous** *adj.*

sple·net·ic (spleh-*net*-ik) *adj.* Fretful; ill-tempered; malicious.

splice *v.* [spliced; splic·ing] 1. To unite; join together by overlapping. 2. *Colloquial.* To join in marriage.—*n.* A union; junction.

splint *n.* 1. Piece of wood or other substance split off; splinter. 2. *Medicine.* Straight piece of apparatus used to hold a broken bone in place when set.—*v.* To hold or support by means of splints.

splin·ter *n.* Fragment split off lengthwise; thin sliver.—*v.* To split or shatter.—**splin·ter·y** *adj.* —**splin·ter·proof** *adj.*

split *v.* [split; split·ting] 1. To divide lengthwise. 2. To tear apart; to burst. 3. To divide into parts, as an organization.—*n.* 1. A crack. 2. A separation; breach.—*adj.* Separated; cleft.—**split hairs.** To make fine distinctions.—**split one's sides.** To laugh vigorously.—**split a vote or ticket.** To vote for candidates of several parties.

split·ting *adj.* Aching or throbbing painfully.

splotch *n.* Large spot; stain; smear.—*v.* To mark with blotches.—**splotch·y** *adj.*

splurge (splerj) *n.* 1. A lavish display. 2. Spending spree.—*v.* [splurged; splurg·ing].

splut·ter *v.* To stammer; speak confusedly. —*n.* A confused noise.—**splut·ter·er** *n.*

spoil *v.* [spoiled, spoilt; spoil·ing] 1. To plunder; strip by violence. 2. To corrupt by indulgence. 3. To destroy; ruin. 4. To rot; decay.—*n.* 1. Plunder; booty. 2. [*pl.*] Fruits of victory.—**spoil·a·ble** *adj.*—**spoil·er** *n.*—**spoils· man** *n.*

spoke. *Past tense* of **speak.**

spoke *n.* Radius of a wheel; bar extending from hub to rim.—*v.* To furnish with spokes.

spo·ken. *Past participle* of **speak.**—*adj.* Oral, as opposed to written.

spokes·man *n.* Representative; one who appears in behalf of others.—**spokes·wom· an** *n.*

spo·li·a·tion (spoh-lee-ay-shun) *n.* 1. Robbery; plundering; despoiling. 2. Decay; rot.—**spo·li·a·tive** (*spoh*-lee-uh-tiv) *adj.*—**spo·li·a·tor** (*spoh*-lee-ay-tor) *n.*

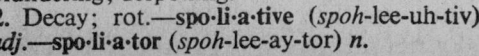
SPOKES

sponge (spunj) *n.* 1. The porous, absorbent framework of certain marine animals, used for washing, wiping, etc. 2. *Colloquial.* Parasite; one who lives upon others.—*v.* [sponged; spong·ing]—**spong·er** *n. Slang.* Parasite.—**spon· gi·ly** *adv.*—**spon·gi·ness** *n.*—**spon·gy** *adj.*

spon·sor *n.* 1. One responsible for another; guarantor. 2. Patron; backer; promoter. 3. Firm that buys radio time for advertising.

spon·ta·ne·i·ty (spon-tuh-*nee*-ih-tee) *n.* Impulsiveness; unforced or unconstrained quality.

spon·ta·ne·ous (spon-*tay*-nee-us) *adj.* Unforced; done without compulsion or restraint; unpremeditated.— **-ous·ly** *adv.*— **-ous·ness** *n.*

spoof *v.* To deceive; to fool.

spook *n.* Ghost; hobgoblin.—**spook·ish** *adj.* —**spook·ish·ly** *adv.*—**spook·y** *adj.*

spool *n.* Hollow cylinder wound with thread, wire, etc.—*v.* To wind on spools.

spoon *n.* Utensil for eating soft foods or liquids.—*v.* 1. To dish out with a spoon; to ladle. 2. *Slang.* To woo.—**spoon·ful** *n.* Amount contained in a spoon.

spoon-backed	spoondrift	spoon maker
spoon-beaked	spoon-fed	spoon-shaped
spoon-billed	spoon-formed	spoonwise

spoon·bill *n.* A wading bird similar to the ibis.

spoor *n.* Trail of a wild animal.—*v.* To follow a spoor.

spo·rad·ic (spoh-*rad*-ik) *adj.* Separate; occurring at uneven intervals; scattered. —**spo·rad·i·cal·ly** *adv.*

spo·ran·gi·um (spor-*ran*-jee-um) *n.* [*pl.* spo·ran·gi·a] *Botany.* Case enclosing spores.—**spo·ran·gi·al** *adj.*

spore *n. Botany.* Reproductive cell more primitive than the seed.—*v.* [spored; spor· ing] To develop spores.

SPOONBILL
(1/20 life-size)

spor·ran *n.* Pouch worn in front of a Scottish kilt.

sport *n.* 1. Diversion; recreation; amusement. 2. [*pl.*] Athletics. 3. Ridicule; mockery. 4. *Colloquial.* **a.** A gambler. **b.** A flashy, gay person. 5. *Biology.* Deviation from a type; mutation.—*v.* 1. To play. 2. To jest; to ridicule. 3. *Slang.* To display in public. —*adj.* Designed for sports.—**sport·ing** *adj.* Generous; fair. —**sport·ing·ly** *adv.* —**sport·ful** *adj.* —**sport·ful·ly** *adv.*—**sport·ful·ness** *n.*

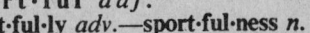
SPORRAN

spor·tive (*spor*-tiv) *adj.* Playful; gay; frolicsome.—**spor·tive·ly** *adv.*—**spor·tive·ness** *n.*

sports·man n. 1. Participant or devotee of sports. 2. A gracious loser; honest rival. —**sports·man·ly** adj.—**sports·man·ship** n. —**sports·wo·man** n.

sport·y adj. [sport·i·er; sport·i·est] Colloquial. Flashy; showy.—**sport·i·ness** n.

spot n. 1. Blot; stain; discolored area. 2. Fault; blemish on character. 3. Site; specific locality.—v. [spot·ted; spot·ting] 1. To stain; to blotch. 2. To disgrace; to stain one's character. 3. Military. To discover the position of; to locate.—adj. Ready at hand. —**on the spot.** 1. Immediately. 2. Slang. In a dangerous position.—**in a spot.** In a predicament.—**spot·ta·ble** adj.

spot-barred spot-eared spot weld n.
spot-billed spot-face spot-weld v.

spot·less adj. 1. Clean; free from stain. 2. Pure; free from blemish; irreproachable. —**spot·less·ly** adv.—**spot·less·ness** n.

spot·light n. 1. Powerful electric lamp focused to a small beam. 2. Circle of light projected by a spotlight. 3. Public notice.—v. 1. To focus a light upon. 2. To make noticeable.

spot·ted adj. 1. Marked with stains or dots. 2. Blemished; tarnished.—**spot·ted·ness** n.

spotted fever. 1. Typhus. 2. Spinal meningitis. 3. Rocky Mountain tick fever.

spot·ter n. 1. A detective. 2. Military. An artillery man who locates the position of an enemy target.

spot·ty adj. [spot·tier; -ti·est] 1. Marked with discolorations. 2. Irregular; uneven.—**spot·ti·ly** adv.—**spot·ti·ness** n.

spous·al (spowz·'l) adj. Matrimonial; bridal.—n. [pl.] The marriage ceremony; nuptials.

spouse (spowz; spowss) n. Married person; husband or wife.

spout (spowt) n. 1. Tube, orifice, or projecting lip, directing the stream of a liquid. 2. Forceful stream of liquid.—v. 1. To stream forth forcefully. 2. To orate; to declaim.—**spout·er** n.

sprain (sprayn) v. To wrench; to strain violently, as a muscle or joint.—n. Injury from stretching muscles or tendons.

SPOUT

sprang. Past tense of spring.

sprat n. Small fish of the herring family.

sprawl v. 1. To stretch the body carelessly in a horizontal position. 2. To spread irregularly or ungracefully, as handwriting.—n. A slovenly posture.—**sprawl·er** n.—**sprawl·ing** adj.

spray n. 1. Water flying in minute drops. 2. Small bunch of twigs and leaves. 3. An atomizer.—v. To cover with a spray of liquid. —**spray·er** n.

sprayboard spraygun spray-topped
spray-decked spray-shaped spray-washed

spread (spred) v. [spread; spread·ing] 1. To distribute over a surface. 2. To stretch; to expand. 3. To open; to unfurl. 4. To disseminate, as news. 5. To set with provisions, as a table.—n. 1. Expansion; diffusion. 2. Extent; compass. 3. Cover for table or bed. 4. Colloquial. Feast; banquet. 5. Food product designed for spreading on bread. —**spread·er** n.—**spread·ing·ly** adv.

spread eagle. A figure of an eagle with raised wings and outthrust legs; national symbol of the U.S.

spread-ea·gle adj. Colloquial. Bombastic; ostentatious.—v. To dive, fall, or lie with limbs outstretched.

spree n. A merry frolic, esp. a drinking bout. —v. [spreed; spree·ing] To carouse.

sprig n. 1. A small shoot or twig. 2. Decorative pattern resembling a twig.—v. [sprigged; sprig·ging] To decorate with sprigs.—**sprig·ged, sprig·gy** adj.

spright·ly (spryte-lee) adj. [spright·li·er; spright·li·est] Lively; animated.—**spright·ly** adv. —**spright·li·ness** n.

spring v. [sprang or sprung; sprung; spring·ing] 1. To jump; to leap. 2. To rise or shoot up. 3. To derive; to result, as from a principle. 4. To announce suddenly; to reveal.

spring n. 1. A leap. 2. Elastic body which recovers its natural position upon release after being compressed. 'Bedspring; mainspring.' 3. Source of water rising from the earth. 4. Resiliency. 5. Season of the year from March 21 to June 21. —adj. 1. Resilient. 2. Vernal. —**spring·er** n.

SPRING

spring-born spring-planted
spring-clean v. spring-plan v.
spring-gathered spring-plowed
spring-grown spring-raised
springhead spring-sowed
springhouse springtail
spring-made spring-touched

spring·board n. 1. Resilient board to aid in performing athletic feats, as diving and vaulting. 2. An aid to advancement; a boost.

'SPRINGBOARD'

spring·tide n. Tide of greatest rise and fall occurring at new and full moon.

spring·time, spring·tide n. The spring season.

spring·y adj. [spring·i·er; -i·est] 1. Elastic; resilient; supple; light. 2. Spongy; sodden. —**spring·i·ly** adv.—**spring·i·ness** n.

sprin·kle (spring-k'l) v. [sprin·kled; sprin·kling] 1. To scatter in fine particles or drops; to strew. 2. To rain moderately and briefly. 3. To dampen.—**sprin·kle** n.—**sprin·kling** n.

sprint v. To run at full speed.—n. 1. A short foot race. 2. A brief period of intense activity.—**sprint·er** n.

sprit n. Naut. Spar fixed diagonally to a longitudinal sail.

S

sprite (*spryte*) *n.* 1. Fairy; elf. 2. Ghost.

sprock·et (*sprok*-it) *n.* 1. Projection on the rim of a wheel designed to fit the link of a chain. 2. Wheel having such projections.—**sprocket wheel.**

SPROCKET

sprout *v.* 1. To begin to grow; to push out shoots. 2. To grow quickly.—*n.* 1. Sprig or bud of a plant. 2. *Slang.* Callow youth; youngster. 3. [*pl.*] Brussels sprouts, leafy vegetable of the cabbage family.

spruce (*sprooss*) *n.* Evergreen tree, used for ornamentation, wood pulp, etc.—*adj.* Neat; smart; dapper.—*v.* [spruced; spruc·ing] To primp; to dress neatly.—**spruce·ly** *adv.*—**spruce·ness** *n.*

spry *adj.* [spri·er; spri·est] Nimble; active; lively.—**spry·ly** *adv.*—**spry·ness** *n.*

spud *n.* 1. A sharp spade. 2. *Slang.* A potato.—*v.* [spud·ded; spud·ding] To dig with a spade.

spume (*spyoom*) *n.* Froth; foam; scum; lather. —*v.* [spumed; spum·ing].—**spu·mes·cence** *n.* —**spu·mous** *adj.*—**spum·y** *adj.* [spum·i·er; spum·i·est].

spun. *Past tense* and *past participle* of **spin.**

spunk *n.* 1. Tinder made from fungus. 2. Spirit; pluck; boldness.—*v.* To ignite. —**spunk·y** *adj.* [spunk·i·er; spunk·i·est].—**spunk·i·ly** *adv.* —**spunk·i·ness** *n.*

spur (*sper*) *n.* 1. A goad on the heel of a rider's boot. 2. A stimulus; incentive. 3. Projection resembling a spur. 4. Ridge extending from the face of a mountain. —*v.* [spurred; spurring] 1. To goad with spurs. 2. To incite to action; to impel. 3. To equip with spurs.—**spur·rer** *n.*

SPURS

spur-clad	spur-geared	spur track
spur-driven	spurgull	spurway
spur-finned	spur-heeled	spur wheel
spurgalled	spurlike	spur-winged

spur·i·ous (*spyoor*-ee-us) *adj.* False; illegitimate; counterfeit.— -**ous·ly** *adv.*— -**ous·ness** *n.*

spurn (*spern*) *v.* 1. To kick; to knock aside, as with the foot. 2. To scorn; to reject with contempt.—**spurn** *n.*—**spurn·er** *n.*

spurt (*spert*) *v.* 1. To gush forth in a small stream; to squirt. 2. To display brief, vigorous activity.—**spurt** *n.*

sput·ter *v.* 1. To speak confusedly and ineffectually; to jabber. 2. To make a spitting noise; to emit in small particles.—*n.* An uproar; bustle.—**sput·ter·er** *n.*

spu·tum (*spyoo*-tum) *n.* 1. Spittle. 2. Mucus or other expectorated matter.

spy *n.* [*pl.* spies] 1. One who keeps a secret watch on the actions of others. 2. A secret agent sent into enemy territory to gain information.—*v.* [spied; spy·ing] 1. To catch sight of; to see. 2. To watch secretly. 3. To act as a secret agent.

spy·glass *n.* A portable telescope.

sq. *Abbreviation* of **square.**

squab (*skwob*) *n.* 1. Young pigeon or dove. 2. Short, plump person.—**squab·bish, squab·by** *adj.* [squab·bi·er; squab·bi·est] Plump; fat.

squab·ble (*skwob*-'l) *v.* [squab·bled; squab·bling] To quarrel noisily and peevishly; to wrangle.—*n.* A petty quarrel; row.—**squab·bler** *n.*

squad (*skwod*) *n.* 1. The basic infantry unit, composed of six to eleven men. 2. Small group assembled for a specific purpose. —**squad car.** Police car.—**squads·left, squads·right.** *Military.* Drill orders.

squad·ron (*skwod*-run) *n.* 1. Small unit of airplanes; basic U. S. airforce unit. 2. Division of a fleet; detachment of warships. 3. Subdivision of a cavalry regiment.

squal·id (*skwol*-id) *adj.* Filthy; foul; dirty and unkempt.—**squal·id·ly** *adv.*

squall (*skwawl*) *v.* To cry out; to scream violently; to yell.—*n.* 1. Loud scream; shrill cry. 2. Small storm accompanied by wind.—**squaller** *n.*—**squal·ly** *adj.* [squal·li·er; -li·est].

squal·or (*skwol*-er, *skway*-ler) *n.* Foulness; filth; slovenliness.

squan·der (*skwon*-der) *v.* To waste; to spend lavishly or prodigally; to dissipate.—**squan·der·er** *n.*—**squan·der·ing·ly** *adv.*

square *n.* 1. *Geometry.* Plane figure having four equal sides and four right angles. 2. Group of buildings facing four sides. 3. Area bounded by four streets. 4. Instrument for making and trying right angles. 5. *Mathematics.* The product of a number multiplied by itself.—*v.* [squared; squar·ing] 1. To form with straight sides and right angles. 2. To reduce to a standard; correct. 3. To settle; come to agreement. 4. *Mathematics.* To multiply by itself.—*adj.* 1. *Geometry.* Having four equal sides and four right angles. 2. Perpendicular. 3. Broad for one's height. 4. Honest; fair. 5. Settled; adjusted, as accounts. 6. Hearty; satisfying, as a meal.—**squar·ish** *adj.* Nearly square. —**square off.** To prepare to fight.—**square·ly** *adv.*—**square·ness** *n.*—**squar·er** *n.*

SQUARE

square dance. Any of several social folk dances.

square deal. Honest transaction; fair treatment.

square root. *Mathematics.* Number which, multiplied by itself, produces a given product.

square shooter. Fair and honest person.

squash (*skwosh*) *n.* Any of several vegetables of the gourd family.

squash *v.* To crush; to press into pulp.—*n.* Game played in an enclosed court with a racket and a small rubber ball.—**squash·er** *n.* —**squash·i·ly** *adv.*—**squash·i·ness** *n.*—**squash·y** *adj.* [squash·i·er; squash·i·est] Soft; pulpy.

squat *v.* (*skwot*) [squat·ted; squat·ting] 1. To sit back on one's heels; to sit close to the ground. 2. To settle on land without any title or legal right.—*n.* Posture of sitting on one's haunches.—*adj.* Short and thick; chunky.—**squat·ter** *n.*—**squatter's rights.** Priority of ownership given to one in possession, esp. of unoccupied land.

squaw (*skwaw*) *n.* 1. North American Indian woman or wife. 2. *Slang.* Woman or wife.

squawk *v.* 1. To yell; to cry out in a loud, harsh voice. 2. *Slang.* To complain; to protest. 3. *Slang.* To reveal a secret; to carry tales.—**squawk** *n.*—**squawk·er** *n.*

squeak (*skweek*) *v.* To utter a sharp, shrill sound; to make a sharp, grating noise.—**squeak** *n.* —**squeak·er** *n.*—**squeak·i·ly** *adv.*—**squeak·i·ness** *n.*—**squeak·y** *adj.* [squeak·i·er; -i·est]. —**tight squeak.** Close fit; narrow escape.

squeal (*skweel*) *n.* A shrill, sharp cry, usually expressing pain or fright.—*v.* 1. To utter shrill noises. 2. *Slang.* To inform; to betray a secret.—**squeal·er** *n.*

squeam·ish (*skweem*-ish) *adj.* 1. Fastidious; easily disgusted or offended. 2. Easy to nauseate.—**squeam·ish·ly** *adv.*—**-ish·ness** *n.*

squee·gee *n.* Also **squil·gee.** Blade of rubber or some soft material for scraping surfaces dry. —**squee·gee** *v.* [squee·geed; -gee·ing].

squeeze *v.* [squeezed; squeez·ing]. 1. To crush; press; pack into an inadequate space. 2. To clasp lovingly; hug. 3. To extort from; oppress by demanding payment from.—**squeeze** *n.*—**squeez·er** *n.*—**squeez·ing** *n.*—**tight squeeze.** Difficult situation; close place.

squelch (*skwelch*) *v.* 1. To crush; destroy. 2. *Colloquial.* To quell; discomfit.—**squelch·er** *n.*

squib (*skwib*) *n.* 1. A firecracker. 2. Brief, sarcastic literary work; petty satire; lampoon. —*v.* [squibbed; squib·bing].

squid (*skwid*) *n.* Marine animal having an elongated head and ten tenacles.

squint (*skwint*) *v.* To stare with the eyes half shut.—*n.* Act of looking with half-closed

SQUID (1/4 life-size)

eyes.—*adj.* Cross-eyed.—**squint·ing** *n.* & *adj.* —**squint·ing·ly** *adv.*—**squint·y** *adj.* [squint·i·er; squint·i·est].

squire (*skwyre*) *n.* 1. English title next in rank to knight. 2. An elective county official. 3. Country gentleman; gentleman farmer. 4. An attendant; male companion or lover. 5. Term of respect.—*v.* [squired; squir·ing] To escort; attend upon.—**squire·hood** *n.*

squirm (*skwerm*) *v.* To writhe; to move with a wriggling motion. —*n.* Wriggling motion.—**squirm·er** *n.* —**squirm·y** *adj.* [squirm·i·er; -i·est].

squir·rel (*skwer*-r'l) *n.* 1. Small, nimble rodent with a long bushy tail. 2. Fur from this animal.

SQUIRREL (1/10 life-size)

squirt (*skwert*) *v.* To eject in a thin, forceful stream.—*n.* 1. A small jet. 2. *Colloquial.* Impertinent young fellow.—**squirt·er** *n.*

st. *Abbreviation* of **street** or [*cap.*] **Saint.**

stab *v.* [stabbed; stab·bing] 1. To pierce or wound with a pointed weapon. 2. To drive; to thrust; to plunge. 3. To inflict unkindness or keen mental anguish.—*n.* 1. Wound made by a pointed weapon. 2. Sudden sharp pain or feeling.—**stab·ber** *n.*—**stab·bing** *adj.* —**stab·bing·ly** *adv.*

sta·bil·i·ty (stuh-*bil*-ih-tee) *n.* 1. Firmness; steadiness; constancy. 2. Firmness of character; steadiness of purpose.

sta·bi·lize (*stay*-bih-lyze) *v.* [sta·bi·lized; -iz·ing] To fix; to make balanced or firm; to establish. —**sta·bi·li·za·tion** *n.*

sta·bi·liz·er *n.* 1. Person or mechanism which renders stable. 2. Horizontal surface of the tail assembly of an airplane. 3. Chemical added to an explosive to reduce spontaneous detonation.

sta·ble (*stay*-b'l) *adj.* 1. Firmly established; well-balanced; steady. 2. Resolute; steady in purpose.

sta·ble *n.* Building containing stalls for horses. —*v.* [sta·bled; sta·bling] To place or keep in a stable.—**sta·bling** *n.*

stableboy	stablekeeper	stableman
stablefly	stable-kept	stableowner

stac·ca·to (stuh-*kah*-toh) *adj. Music.* Disconnected; having each note distinct and separate.

stack *n.* 1. Orderly, compact heap; pile. 2. Chimney or funnel of a ship or locomotive. 3. Structure or compact arrangement of bookcases.—*v.* To pile up in an orderly fashion. —**stack arms.** *Military.* To set up rifles, usually three, in a conical arrangement.—**stack the cards.** 1. To arrange playing cards for cheating. 2. To prearrange the odds.—**stack·er** *n.*

sta·di·um (*stay*-dee-um) *n.* [*pl.* sta·di·ums, sta·di·a] Outdoor amphitheater, used chiefly for athletic events.

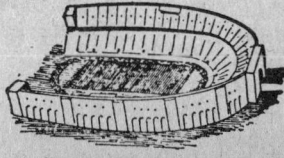

STADIUM

staff *n.* [*pl.* staffs, staves] 1. Heavy stick carried for support; a support; prop. 2. A stick used as a weapon; club; cudgel. 3. *Music.*

S

The five lines on which music is scored. **4.** A flagpole.

staff *n.* [*pl.* staffs] **1.** The personnel charged with an undertaking. **2.** *Military.* Body of officers with administrative duties.—*v.* To furnish with persons capable of doing a given job.—**staff officer.** Officer on the staff of an army or regiment.—**staff sergeant.** Noncommissioned officer one rank above sergeant. —**staff·man** *n.*

stag *n.* **1.** The adult male deer. **2.** *Slang.* Man engaging in social activity unaccompanied by a woman.—*adj.* Purely male; unattended by women.

STAG (1/65 life-size)

stag-eyed	stag-headed	stag hunt
stag-handled	stag-horned	stag-necked
staghead	stag hound	stag skin

stage (*stayj*) *n.* **1.** Platform; floor elevated above the ground, esp. raised platform on which theatrical performances are given. **2.** The theatrical profession; the drama. **3.** Field of action; scene of an event. **4.** Period of development; degree of advance. **5.** A stagecoach.—*v.* [staged; stag·ing] To produce a play; exhibit on the stage.—**stag·ey, stag·y** *adj.* [stag·i·er; stag·i·est] Theatrical; artificial.—**stag·ing** *n.* **1.** Act of putting on the stage. **2.** A scaffolding.—**stag·er** *n.* —**stag·i·ness** *n.*

stage box	stage hand	stageman
stagecraft	stage house	stage-struck
stage door *n.*	stageland	stage whisper
stage-door *adj.*	stagelike	stage-worn

stage·coach (*stayj*-kohch) *n.* A horse-drawn vehicle carrying paying passengers on a regular route.

stag·ger (*stag*-er) *v.* **1.** To reel; to totter. **2.** To hesitate; to waver. **3.** To amaze profoundly. **4.** To arrange in alternate intervals. —*n.* **1.** A sudden reeling of the body. **2.** [*pl.*] A disease of horses and cattle.—**stag·gered** *adj.* Arranged in alternate intervals.—**stag·ger·er** *n.* —**stag·ger·ing·ly** *adv.*

stag·nant (*stag*-nunt) *adj.* **1.** Motionless; impure from lack of motion, as a pond. **2.** Inactive; sluggish.—**stag·nant·ly** *adv.*—**stag·nate** (*stag*-nayt) *v.* [-nat·ed; -nat·ing]—**stag·na·tion** *n.*

staid (*stayd*) *adj.* Sedate; sober; grave.—**staid·ly** *adv.*—**staid·ness** *n.*

stain *v.* **1.** To spot; discolor. **2.** To dye; color. **3.** To dishonor; disgrace; to taint or corrupt morally.—**stain** *n.*—**stained** *adj.*—**stain·er** *n.*—**stain·less** *adj.*— -**less·ly** *adv.*

stainless steel. Chrome steel highly resistant to corrosion.

stair *n.* **1.** Single step in a flight of steps. **2.** [*pl.*] Series of steps one above the other.

stairbreak	staircase	stairstepper
stair builder	stairhead	stairway
stair building	stairstep	stairwork

stake (*stayk*) *n.* **1.** Piece of wood sharpened at one end, to be set into the ground. **2.** That which is pledged or hazarded; interest. **3.** Post to which one is tied to be burned to death. **4.** Financial backing or support. **5.** [*pl.*] The prize in a game or wager.—*v.* [staked; stak·ing] **1.** To support or fasten by stakes. **2.** To mark as one's own. 'Stake a claim.' **3.** To hazard; to pledge.—**at stake.** Involved; jeopardized.—**stake out.** To mark the limits of; measure out.—**stake·hold·er** *n.* One who holds a wager.

Sta·khan·ov·ism (stah-*kahn*-ov-izm) *n.* System developed in U.S.S.R. for increasing production through stimulating the worker's initiative.—**Sta·khan·ov·ite** *n.* Member of an honorary organization of workers in U.S.S.R.

sta·lac·tite (stuh-*lak*-tyte, *stal*-lak-tyte) *n.* Conical mass of calcium carbonate, developing from the roofs of limestone caverns.

sta·lag·mite (stuh-*lag*-myte) *n.* Columnar structure of calcium carbonate developing from the floor of a limestone cavern.

STALACTITES AND STALAGMITES

stale (*stayl*) *adj.* **1.** Old; not freshly made. **2.** Flat; lifeless or tasteless through aging. **3.** Trite; common. **4.** Inefficient from overexercise.—*v.* [staled; stal·ing]—**stale·ly** *adv.*

stale·mate *n.* **1.** Standstill; deadlock; a draw or tie. **2.** *Chess.* Position wherein the king is not in check but no legal move can be made. —*v.* [stale·mat·ed; -mat·ing].

Sta·lin·grad (stah-lin-*graht*) *n.* City SE Russia where the Red Army launched its counteroffensive in November, 1942, turning point in Russo-German phase of World War II.

stalk (*stawk*) *n.* **1.** Stem; main axis of a plant. **2.** That which is long and slender.—**stalk·less** *adj.*—**stalk·y** [stalk·i·er; -i·est].

stalk *v.* **1.** To walk softly and warily. **2.** To pursue stealthily, esp. game. **3.** To walk with dignity and pomp.—*n.* A stately walk.—**stalk·er** *n.*—**stalking horse.** Pretense or device concealing true aims.

stall (*stawl*) *n.* **1.** Compartment in a barn or stable in which one horse or cow is kept. **2.** Small outdoor shed where merchandise is offered for sale. **3.** Partially enclosed seat in a church. **4.** *Aeronautics.* Condition of a plane having insufficient air speed for control. **5.** Ruse or excuse delaying action.—*v.* **1.** To put into a stall. **2.** To render or become unable to proceed, esp. of a vehicle. **3.** *Aeronautics.* To lose air speed necessary for control of a plane. 4. *Colloquial.* To stave off; to play for time.

stal·lion (*stal*-y'n) *n.* A male horse kept for breeding purposes; a stud.

stal·wart (*stawl*-wert) *adj.* 1. Brave; bold; daring. 2. Tall and strong; of large frame. —*n.* 1. Brave or strong person. 2. Unswerving ally or supporter.

sta·men (*stay*-men) *n. Botany.* Male fertilizing organ in plants, composed of a slender filament topped by a pollen-bearing tip.

stam·i·na (*stam*-ih-nuh) *n.* Strength; endurance; staying power; vigor.

stam·mer *v.* To hesitate or repeat sounds in speaking; pronounce imperfectly from emotional strain.—*n.* Defective, faltering speech.—**stam·mer·er** *n.*—**stam·mer·ing** *n.* Speech disorder characterized by hesitation or repetition of sounds.—**stam·mer·ing·ly** *adv.*

STAMEN

stamp *v.* 1. To strike, beat, or press down forcibly with the sole of the foot. 2. To impress with a mark or figure; to imprint. 3. To fix deeply or strongly. 4. To affix a stamp to. —*n.* 1. Act of striking downward. 2. Instrument for making impressions on surfaces. 3. Impression marked or imprinted. 4. Official mark or seal that denotes payment of duty, tax, or fee on that to which it is affixed. 5. Make; cast; mold; character.—**stamp·er** *n.* —**stamp out.** To extinguish; to eliminate.

stam·pede (stam-*peed*) *n.* 1. Panic-stricken herd of animals in violent flight. 2. Any sudden, concerted rush.—*v.* [stam·ped·ed; -ped·ing].

stance *n.* Position of the body; posture.

stanch, staunch (*stanch, stahnch*) *v.* To stop; to prevent the flow of; to dry up.—*adj.* 1. Strong and tight; not leaky; firm. 2. Firm in principle; loyal; steadfast.—**stanch·er** *n.* —**stanch·ly, staunch·ly** *adv.*—**stanch·ness, staunch·ness** *n.*

stan·chion (*stan*-shun) *n.* 1. Prop or support; post used for support; traffic marker. 2. Upright beam supporting a ship's deck.

STANCHION

stand *v.* [stood; stand·ing] 1. To be stationary in an erect position; rest upright on the feet; set in an upright position. 2. To occupy a permanent place; be situated. 3. To stop; pause. 4. To be permanent; endure. 5. To maintain a firm and steady attitude. 6. To rank; be placed with regard to relative position. 7. To bear; sustain; endure. 8. To pay for; bear the expense of.

stand *n.* 1. Cessation of progress or activity; halt. 2. Post; station; place where one remains for a purpose. 3. Act of opposing or resisting. 4. Fixed position; firm attitude.

5. Small table or frame used to support an object. 6. Place where taxicabs wait for hire. 7. Box or seat where a witness testifies in court. 8. Stall or small shop for vending. 9. Growth of timber.

stand-by *n.*	stand-off *n.*	stand-patter
stand-down	stand-offish	stand-pattism
stand-easy	stand-out	standpipe
standfast	stand-pat *adj.*	stand-up *adj.*

stand by. 1. To be near or next to. 2. To support; to defend. 3. To await; be prepared to answer a sudden command.

stand for. 1. To represent; be equivalent to. 2. To become a candidate for. 3. To believe in; support. 4. *Nautical.* To direct a course toward. 5. To suffer; tolerate.

stand up. 1. To rise to one's feet. 2. To rise in opposition or revolt. 3. With *for,* to defend; justify. 4. *Slang.* To break an appointment with.

stand trial. To be examined and judged in a court of law.

stand one's ground. To maintain position.

stand·ard (*stand*-erd) *n.* 1. Flag; banner bearing a coat-of-arms or symbol. 2. Criterion; measure.—*adj.* Fixed; authoritative; much-used.—**standard bearer.**

stand·ard·ize *v.* [stand·ard·ized; stand·ard·iz·ing] To make uniform; to fix by rule.—**stand·ard·i·za·tion** (stand-er-dih-*zay*-sh'n) *n.*—**stand·ard·iz·er** *n.*

stand·ee *n.* One paying fare or admission for standing room.

stand-in *n.* Substitute; understudy.

stand·ing *n.* 1. Establishment; existence; tradition. 2. Position; rank.—*adj.* 1. Permanent; lasting. 2. Fixed. 3. Erect.

stand·point *n.* Point of view.

stand·still *n.* A stop; arrestment.

stank. *Past tense* of **stink.**

stan·za (*stan*-zuh) *n.* A verse; a group of lines forming a division of a poem.—**stan·za·ic** (stan-*zay*-ik) *adj.*

sta·ple (*stay*-p'l) *n.* 1. Basic item or ingredient. 2. Principal product. 3. Unprocessed material.—*adj.* 1. Basic; most important. 2. Established in commerce.

sta·ple *n.* 1. A rounded, two-pointed nail. 2. A wire paper fastener.—*v.* [sta·pled; sta·pling] To attach with staples. —**sta·pler** *n.* Machine for fastening with staples.

star (*star*) *n.* 1. Heavenly body emitting its own heat and light. 2. Figure or design, esp. five-pointed, resembling a star. 3. *Printing.* Asterisk. 4. A leading actor or actress.—*v.* [starred; star·ring] 1. To bespangle; to set with stars. 2. *Printing.* To mark with an asterisk. 3. *Theater.* To enact a leading role.—**Stars and Stripes.** Flag of U.S.A. —**Star-Spangled Banner.** National anthem of U.S.A.—**shooting star.** A small meteor.

STAPLE

S

star·board (*star*-b'd) *n. Nautical.* The right hand side of a vessel.—**star·board** *adj.* On or toward the right.

starch *n.* 1. White powdery carbohydrate forming an important food element. 2. Powder used in solution to stiffen cloth or clothes. 3. Stiffness; formality of manner.—*v.* To stiffen with starch.—**starched** *adj.* Stiffened. —**starch·i·ly** *adv.* —**starch·i·ness** *n.* —**starch·y** *adj.*

stare (*stayr*) *v.* [stared; star·ing] 1. To gaze; look fixedly. 2. To look vacantly. —*n.* A fixed gaze. —**star·er** *n.*—**star·ing** *adj.*—**star·ing·ly** *adv.*

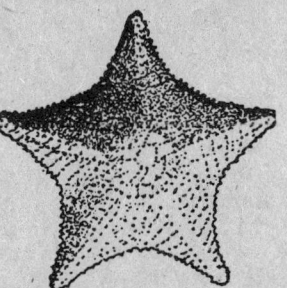

STARFISH (1/3 life-size)

star·fish *n.* A prickly star-shaped marine animal.

stark *adj.* 1. Stiff; rigid. 2. Utter; unrelieved; bare.—**stark·ly** *adv.*

star·ling *n.* A common small black bird introduced into U.S. from Europe.

star·ry *adj.* 1. Stellar; adorned with stars. 2. Bright; starlike. — **star·ri·ness** *n.*

STARLING (1/8 life-size)

start *v.* 1. To begin; commence; set out. 2. To jump; jerk involuntarily.—*n.* 1. A sudden, involuntary movement usually caused by surprise, fear, or pain. 2. Commencement; outset; beginning. 3. Lead or handicap given, as in a race.—**start·er** *n.*

start up. 1. To arise suddenly. 2. To pick a quarrel.—**start-up** *n.*

star·tle *v.* [star·tled; star·tling] To take by surprise.—*n.* Sudden movement of surprise. —**star·tling** *adj.*—**star·tling·ly** *adv.*

star·va·tion (stahr-*vay*-sh'n) *n.* 1. Extreme hunger. 2. Death from hunger.—*adj.* Causing hunger or lack of proper nutrition. 'A starvation diet.'

starve *v.* [starved; starv·ing] To suffer or perish from hunger; to subject to hunger or need.

starve·ling (*stahrv*-ling) *n.* Sufferer from extreme undernourishment.—*adj.* Hungry; lean; suffering from want.—**starv·er** *n.*

state (*stayt*) *n.* 1. Condition; 2. Grandeur; pomp; eminence. 3. A nation. 4. One of the governmental units of a nation. 'The fiftieth state of the United States.' 5. Rank; position; office.—*adj.* Relating to government; public—*v.* [stat·ed; stat·ing] To declare.—**stat·ed** *adj.*—**stat·ed·ly** *adv.*—**stat·er** *n.*

state-aided	statehood	state-owned
state-caused	stateless	state-taxed
statecraft	state line	state-wide

state·house *n.* The capitol building of a state, in which the legislature meets.

state·ly *adj.* [state·li·er; state·li·est] Magnificent; imposing; majestic.—**state·li·ness** *n.*

state·ment *n.* 1. A declaration; report. 2. A bill; a reckoning of charges. 3. A record of debits and credits for a certain period.

state·room *n.* 1. A ship's cabin. 2. A private room on a railroad car; compartment.

states·man *n.* A politician; national leader. —**states·man·like** *adj.*—**states·man·ly** *adj.* —**states·man·ship** *n.*—**states·wo·man** *n.*

stat·ic (*stat*-ik) *adj.* Immobile; at rest; passive. —*n.* Electrical atmospheric disturbance causing interruption of normal radio reception; atmospherics.—**stat·i·cal·ly** *adv.*

stat·ics *n.* The branch of physics dealing with bodies at rest.

sta·tion (*stay*-sh'n) *n.* 1. Post; place of duty. 2. Social position; rank. 3. A depot; a transport junction.—*v.* To appoint to a post.

station wagon (*stay*-sh'n wag-'n). Automobile with a spacious wooden body used as either a passenger car or a light truck.

sta·tion·ar·y *adj.* 1. Fixed; at rest. 2. Immovable.

sta·tion·er *n.* One who sells writing materials. —**sta·tion·er·y** *n.* Writing materials, esp. writing paper.

stat·ist (*stayt*-ist) *n.* One who collects and arranges facts; a statistician.

sta·tis·tics (stuh-*tiss*-tikss) *n.* 1. A numerical collection of facts arranged to indicate general trends or theories. 2. The science of dealing with the arrangement of numerical data. —**sta·tis·ti·cal** *adj.*—**sta·tis·ti·cal·ly** *adv.*—**stat·is·ti·cian** (stat-iss-*tih*-sh'n) *n.*

stat·u·ar·y (*stat*-choo-ehr-ee) *n.* 1. Statues. 2. The art of sculpture.—**stat·u·ar·y** *adj.*

stat·ue (*stat*-choo) *n.* Sculptured representation of a human or animal form carved or cast in a solid material.—**stat·u·esque** *adj.* Tall; majestic. —**stat·u·esque·ly** *adv.* **stat·u·esque·ness** *n.*

stat·u·ette *n.* A figurine; a small statue.

stat·ure (*stat*-choor) *n.* 1. Height. 2. Ability.

sta·tus (*stay*-tus) *n.* 1. Standing; position. 2. Situation; state.

status quo (*stay*-tus kwoh). The present situation; the existing conditions.

STATUE

stat·ute (*stat*-choot) *n.* 1. A written law; a legislative enactment. 2. A corporate act.—**stat·u·to·ry** *adj.*—**statute law.** Written law, as opposed to common law.

staunch (*stawnch*) *adj.* Strong; loyal; faithful. See **stanch.**—**staunch·ly** *adv.*—**staunch·ness** *n.*

stave (*stayv*) *n.* 1. A pole; a staff. 2. One of the narrow strips forming the sides of a barrel, cask, etc. —**stave** *v.* [stove, staved; stav·ing] 1. To break in; to burst. 2. To furnish with staves. 3. To fend off.—**stave off.** To delay; to put off.

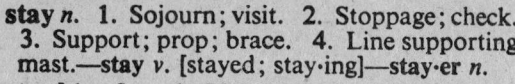

STAVES

staves. *Plural of* **staff, stave.**

stay *n.* 1. Sojourn; visit. 2. Stoppage; check. 3. Support; prop; brace. 4. Line supporting mast.—**stay** *v.* [stayed; stay·ing]—**stay·er** *n.*

stead (*sted*) *n.* 1. Place; substitution. 2. Service; aid. 'Stand in good stead.'

stead·fast *adj.* Constant; loyal; resolute. —**stead·fast·ly** *adv.*—**stead·fast·ness** *n.*

stead·y *adj.* [stead·i·er; stead·i·est] 1. Stable; firm. 2. Unwavering; resolute; unfaltering. 3. Regular; uniform; uninterrupted.—*v.* [stead·ied; stead·y·ing] To stabilize; to balance.—**stead·i·er** *n.*— -i·ly *adv.*— -i·ness *n.*

steak (*stayk*) *n.* A slice of meat, esp. beef, for broiling or frying.

steal (*steel*) *v.* [stole; sto·len; steal·ing] 1. To carry away illegally; to pilfer. 2. To creep furtively or noiselessly. 3. To perform secretly; to gain by imperceptible means.—**steal·er** *n.*—**steal·ing** *n.* & *adj.*

steal a base. *Baseball.* To gain a base without a batter hitting the ball.—**steal a march.** To gain an advantage secretly.

stealth (*stelth*) *n.* Covertness; furtiveness. —**stealth·i·ly** *adv.*—**stealth·y** *adj.*

steam (*steem*) *n.* 1. Water vapor produced by heat. 2. Any visible vapor; exhalation.—*v.* 1. To give off steam or vapor; to rise in gaseous form. 2. To travel or move by steam power. 3. To expose to steam.—**steam·i·ly** *adv.*—**steam·i·ness** *n.*—**steam·ing** *n.*

steamboat	steam-fitter	steam-propelled
steam-cleaned	steam-laundered	steamship
steam-cooked	steam pipe	steam-treated

steam engine. A powerful machine run by steam power.

steam·er *n.* 1. A large steam-driven passenger ship; a steamship. 2. A utensil for cooking, laundering, etc., by steam.

steam roller. Road roller driven by steam.

steam shovel. A steam-driven excavating machine operating a shovel attached to a long swinging arm.

ste·a·rin, ste·a·rine (*stee-uh-rin*) *n.* Chief ingredient of animal and vegetable fats; solid portion of animal fat.—**ste·a·ric** (*stee-air-ik*) *adj.*

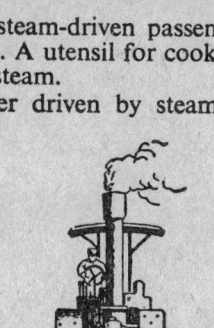

STEAMROLLER

steed *n.* A horse; esp. a spirited mount.

steel *n.* 1. A hard malleable alloy of iron and a small portion of carbon. 2. Hardness; rigor;

might. 3. A weapon; a sword.—*adj.* 1. Made of steel. 2. Hard; rigorous; unfeeling.—*v.* 1. To overlay, or edge with steel. 2. To fortify; to make hard or stubborn.—**steel·i·ness** *n.*—**steel·y** *adj.*

steel blue	steel engraving	steelmaster
steel-bound	steel-faced	steel-mounted
steel-cased	steel-framed	steelware
steel-clad	steel-hearted	steelworker
steel-colored	steel maker	steel works

steel·yard *n.* A type of balance.

steen·bok *n.* A species of antelope native to South Africa.

steep *adj.* 1. Precipitous; having a sharp slope; sheer. 2. *Slang.* Expensive. —*v.* To soak in a liquid; to saturate.—**steep** *n.* —**steep·en** *v.*—**steep·er** *n.*—**steep·ness** *n.*

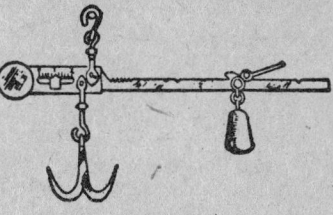

STEELYARD

stee·ple *n.* 1. A lofty structure erected over a tower, often capped with a spire. 2. A church tower.

stee·ple·chase *n.* 1. A horse race across country. 2. A difficult race course complicated by obstacles.—**stee·ple·chas·er** *n.*

steer *n.* 1. Young male bovine animal castrated before maturity. 2. Any young cattle raised for beef.

steer *v.* 1. To direct a course; guide.—**steer·a·ble** *adj.*—**steer·er** *n.* —**steers·man** *n.*

STEEPLE

steer·age (*stihr-ij*) *n.* 1. Guidance; course. 2. Third-class passenger accommodations on a ship.—**steer·age·way** *n. Nautical.* Degree of motion which makes a ship answer the helm.

stein (*styne*) *n.* A heavy mug, esp. for beer.

stein·bok (*styne-bok*) *n. See* **steenbok.**

stel·lar *adj.* Starlike; astral.

stel·late (*stel-it*), **stel·lat·ed** *adj.* Resembling a star.—**stel·late·ly** *adv.*

stem *n.* 1. Stalk; the rising axis of a plant supporting the leaves, flowers, and fruits. 2. Long, slender support. 3. Lineage; family stock. 4. The bow of a vessel.—*v.* [stemmed; stem·ming] 1. To make progress against; to overcome an obstruction. 2. To dam up; stop. 3. To proceed; derive

STEIN

S

from. **4.** To remove stems from. 'Stem a cherry.'—**stem·less** *adj.*—**stem·mer** *n.*

stench *n.* Offensive odor; sickening smell.

sten·cil (*sten*-s'l) *n.* A thin sheet with a pattern cut or pricked through it. —*v.* [sten·ciled, sten·cil·led; sten·cil·ing, sten·cil·ling] To reproduce by inking or painting over a stencil laid on the surface to be marked.—**sten·cil·er, sten·cil·ler** *n.*

STENCIL

sten·o·graph (*sten*-uh-graf) *v.* To write in shorthand characters.—**sten·o·graph** *n.*

ste·nog·ra·pher (steh-*nog*-ruh-fer) *n.* One who takes dictation in shorthand and transcribes it on the typewriter.—**sten·og·ra·phist** *n.*

ste·nog·ra·phy (steh-*nog*-ruh-fee) *n.* Shorthand writing; the taking of dictation in shorthand. —**sten·o·graph·ic, -i·cal** *adj.*— **-i·cal·ly** *adv.*

sten·to·ri·an (sten-*toh*-ree-un) *adj.* Loud and powerful; resounding.—**sten·tor** *n.*

step *v.* [stepped; step·ping] **1.** To walk; to take a step. **2.** To go, esp. a short distance. **3.** To come upon suddenly or by chance. **4.** To walk briskly; trot. **5.** To press down. —*n.* **1.** A pace; an advance or retreat by a movement of the foot. **2.** [*pl.*] Walk; passage. **3.** A gait; footfall. **4.** The space measured by each movement of the foot in walking; short distance. **5.** A degree of progress; action. **6.** The round of a ladder; stair. **7.** *Dancing.* A patterned motion of the feet and body.—**step·per** *n.* **1.** One who has a good gait. **2.** *Slang.* A good dancer.—**step·in** *n.* A woman's undergarment.

step *adj.* Used in combining form to indicate relationship by remarriage, esp. of a parent.

stepbrother	stepgrandchild	steprelation
stepchild	stepmother	stepsister
stepdaughter	stepnephew	stepson
stepfather	stepparent	stepuncle

step·lad·der *n.* A portable, self-supporting ladder with flat steps.

steppe (*step*) *n.* An extensive barren plain, esp. in southeastern Europe, and the lowlands of Siberia.

step·ping·stone *n.* **1.** A stone in a stream or marsh serving as a natural footbridge. **2.** Any aid to progress.

STEPLADDER

ster·e·o·scope (*stehr*-ee-oh-skohp) *n.* An optical instrument in which two images appear as one projected in relief.—**ster·e·o·scop·ic** (stehr-ee-oh-*skop*-ik), **-scop·i·cal** *adj.* **-scop·i·cal·ly** *adv.*— **ster·e·os·cop·ist** (stehr-ee-*oss*-koh-pist) *n.*

STEREOSCOPE

ster·e·o·type (*stehr*-ee-oh-type) *n.* **1.** *Printing.* A plate cast usually from a papier-mâché mold.

2. A facsimile; a duplicate.—*adj.* Pertaining to the method of stereotyping.—*v.* [ster·e·o·typed; ster·e·o·typ·ing] **1.** To cast from a mold as a stereotype plate. **2.** To repeat; to deprive of originality.—**ster·e·o·typed** *adj.* **1.** Made from stereotype plates. **2.** Trite; hackneyed.— **ster·e·o·typ·y** (stehr-ee-oh-type-ee) *n.* **1.** The making of stereotypes. **2.** *Psychology.* Repetition of motion, posture, or speech, as in dementia praecox.—**ster·e·o·typ·ic** (stehr-ee-oh-*tip*-ik), **-typ·i·cal** *adj.*

ster·ile (*stehr*-il) *adj.* **1.** Barren; impotent. **2.** Producing no crop; infertile. **3.** Unimaginative. **4.** Free from bacteria; antiseptic. —**ste·ril·i·ty** (steh-*ril*-ih-tee) *n.*

ster·i·lize (*stehr*-uh-lyze) *v.* [ster·i·lized; -liz·ing] **1.** To deprive of reproductive power; to make infertile. **2.** To disinfect.—**ster·i·li·za·tion** (stehr-il-uh-*zay*-shun) *n.*— **-liz·er** *n.*

ster·ling (*sterl*-ing) *adj.* **1.** Of standard purity or value. **2.** Genuine; pure.—**sterling silver.** Silver meeting the legal standard of purity.

stern *n.* **1.** The after end of a vessel. **2.** Rear; hind part.—**stern** *adj.* Hindmost.

stern *adj.* **1.** Severe; austere; forbidding. **2.** Strict; unrelenting; inflexible.—**stern·ly** *adv.* —**stern·ness** *n.*

ster·num (*stern*-um) *n.* The breastbone.

stet *v.* [stet·ted; stet·ting] *Printing.* **1.** To let stand. **2.** To re-enter a deletion; to allow to remain as originally written.

steth·o·scope (*steth*-uh-skohp) *n.* An instrument used to amplify sounds made by organs of the body.—**steth·o·scop·ic** (steth-uh-*skop*-ik), **-scop·i·cal** *adj.*—**scop·i·cal·ly** *adv.*—**ste·thos·co·pist** (steh-*thoss*-kuh-pist) *n.*—**ste·thos·co·py** *n.*

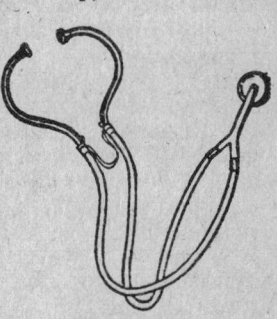
STETHOSCOPE

ste·ve·dore (*stee*-vuh-dor) *n.* One who loads and unloads ships.—**ste·ve·dore** *v.*

stew (*styoo*) *v.* **1.** To boil slowly; cook by simmering. **2.** *Slang.* To worry aimlessly; to fret. —*n.* **1.** A dish of meat and vegetables simmered in a liquid. **2.** A state of agitation. —**stewed** *adj.* **1.** Cooked by simmering. **2.** *Slang.* Intoxicated.—**stew·bum** *n.* A drunkard.

stew·ard (*stoo*-erd) *n.* **1.** An employee on shipboard who superintends provisions; also, a waiter and general attendant. **2.** Royal household officer in England. **3.** A supervisor; an administrator.—**stew·ard·ess** *n.* —**stew·ard·ship** *n.*

stick *n.* **1.** A long, slender piece of wood; a lopped branch. **2.** Any long, slender object. **3.** *Slang.* A dull, awkward person. **4.** *Printing.* A tray for holding type. **5.** [*pl.*] *Slang.* Open, uninhabited country.—*v.* [stuck;

stick·ing] **1.** To pierce; to stab. **2.** To implant; set; fasten by piercing. **3.** To affix; adhere; glue. **4.** *Slang*. To cheat; hold up. **5.** To cling; stay close. **6.** To be brought to a standstill. **7.** To hesitate; balk. **8.** *Printing*. To set type in a tray; compose.

stick-fast	stickpin	sticktight
stickful	stickseed	stick-up
stick-in-the-mud	sticktail	stickweed

stick·er *n.* **1.** A pointed instrument. **2.** A gummed label; an adhering object. **3.** *Slang*. A difficult problem. **4.** *Slang*. An article of merchandise not easily sold.

stick·i·ness *n.* Adhesiveness.

stick·y [stick·i·er; stick·i·est] *adj.* **1.** Gluey. **2.** *Slang*. Difficult; dull. **3.** Hot; muggy. —**stick·i·ly** *adv.*

sticking plaster. An adhesive covering for cuts.

stick·le (*stik-'l*) *v.* [stick·led; stick·ling] **1.** To quibble. **2.** To demur; scruple.—**stick·ler** *n.*

stick·le·back (*stik-'l-bak*) *n.* A small fish having several pointed spines.

stiff *adj.* **1.** Rigid; inflexible. **2.** Tightly drawn; tense. **3.** Cramped; constrained; awkward. **4.** Unbending; formal. **5.** Stubborn; difficult. **6.** Harsh; severe.—*n. Slang.* **1.** A corpse; cadaver. **2.** A bully.—**stif·fish** *adj.*—**stiff·ly** *adv.*—**stiff·ness** *n.*

stif·fen (*stif-'n*) *v.* **1.** To make or become rigid or inflexible. **2.** To become stronger. **3.** To become more constrained.—**stif·fened** *adj.* —**stif·fen·er** *n.*

stif·fen·ing *n.* **1.** The act of making rigid. **2.** The means used to make an article more stiff.—*adj.* Growing harder; strengthening.

sti·fle (*sty-f'l*) *v.* [sti·fled; sti·fling] **1.** To kill by stopping the breath; to suffocate. **2.** To smother; to quench; to extinguish. **3.** To suppress; to choke back; to conceal.—*n.* The knee joint in the hind leg of a quadruped. —**sti·fling** *adj. Slang*. Oppressively warm. —**sti·fler** *n.*—**sti·fling·ly** *adv.*

stig·ma (*stig-muh*) *n.* [*pl.* stig·mas, stig·mata (*stig-muh-tuh*)] **1.** A mark made with a searing iron; brand. **2.** Any mark of infamy or disgrace; blemish. **3.** *Botany*. The part of a flower's pistil which receives the pollen. **4.** A spot, esp. on the skin.—**stig·mat·ic** (*stig-mat-ik*) *adj.* Marked with stigmata.—*n.* A notorious or deformed person.— **-i·cal** *adj.*— **-i·cal·ly** *adv.*—**stig·ma·tism** (*stig-muh-tizm*) *n.*

stig·ma·tize (*stig-muh-tyze*) *v.* [stig·ma·tized; stig·ma·tiz·ing] **1.** To mark with a searing iron; brand. **2.** To mark with shame.—**stig·ma· tized** *adj.*—**stig·ma· ti·za·tion** (stig-muh-tih-*zay*-shun) *n.*— **stig·ma·tiz·er** *n.*

STILE

stile *n.* **1.** A step, or series of steps, for climbing a wall. **2.** A turnstile.

sti·let·to (stih-*let*-oh) *n.* A small dagger with a pointed blade about six inches long.—*v.* To stab.

STILETTO

still *adj.* **1.** Silent; noiseless. **2.** Calm; undisturbed. **3.** Gentle; subdued; low. **4.** Motionless; at rest. **5.** Not effervescent, esp. of wines.—*v.* **1.** To silence. **2.** To check or restrain; to lull. **3.** To appease; to calm.—*adv.* **1.** Till now; yet. **2.** In an increasing degree; even more. 'Still great.' **3.** Always; continually. **4.** After that.—*conj.* Nevertheless; all the same.—*n.* An apparatus for separating volatile matters and re-condensing them into liquid form, especially for distilling spirituous liquors.—**still·ly** *adj. Poetic.* Quiet; tranquil. —**still·ly** *adv.*

still-admired	still-fish (*v.*)	still life (*n.*)
stillbirth	still hunt (*n.*)	still-life (*adj.*)
still-born	still-hunt (*v.*)	stillroom

stilt *n.* **1.** A long stick with a footrest used in pairs for walking high above the ground. **2.** A wading bird with long, slender legs. **3.** A tall pile used to support a pier, boathouse, etc., over water.—*v.* To elevate on stilts.—**stilt·ed** *adj.* Pompous; affected.—**stilt·ed·ness** *n.*

stim·u·lant (*stim*-yoo-l'nt) *n.* **1.** *Medical*. An agent which increases the activity of an organ. **2.** A spur; an excitant.

stim·u·late (*stim*-yoo-layt) *v.* [stim·u·lat·ed; stim·u·lat·ing] **1.** To stir; to excite; to spur on. **2.** To arouse physically, as by a stimulant.—**stim·u·lat·ing** *adj.*—**stim·u·la·tion** (stim-yoo-*lay*-shun) *n.* —**stim·u·la·tive** (*stim*-yoo-luh-tiv) *n. & adj.*

STILTS

stim·u·lus (*stim*-yoo-lus) *n.* [*pl.* stim·u·li] **1.** A goad; incitement; arousing influence. **2.** An agent which stirs or changes muscular, nervous, or glandular activity.

sting *v.* [stang or stung; stung; sting·ing] **1.** To pierce, esp. with the defense organ of an insect; prick sharply. **2.** To smart; pain keenly. **3.** To stimulate; incite.—*n.* **1.** *Zoology*. A sharp-pointed defense organ of certain insects which wounds by injecting a poison into the flesh. **2.** The wound or pain caused by a sting. **3.** A stimulus; spur.–**sting·er** *n.*—**sting· ing** *adj.*—**sting·ing·ly** *adv.*—**sting·y** *adj.*

sting·ray. A flat-bodied tropical fish, noted for the sting of its spiny tail which can produce a painful wound.

stin·gy (*stin*-jee) *adj.* **1.** Avaricious; niggardly; miserly. **2.** Scanty; wanting.—**stin· gi·ly** *adv.*—**stin·gi·ness** *n.*

stink *v.* [stank or stunk; stunk; stink·ing] **1.** To emit an offensive smell. **2.** To be in bad odor or repute.—*n.* **1.** A disgusting odor. **2.** *Slang*.

S

A scandal.—**stink·er** *n. Slang.* An unpleasant person.—**stink·ing** *adj.*—**stink·ing·ly** *adv.*

stinkball	stinkdamp	stinkstone
stinkbird	stinkhorn	stinkweed
stinkbug	stinkpot	stinkwood

stint *v.* 1. To restrict; to confine; to share frugally. 2. To assign a task.—*n.* 1. Limit; bound. 2. A quantity assigned; a task allotted.—**stint·er** *n.*

sti·pend (*sty*-pend) *n.* Fixed payment for service. 'A clerk's stipend.'—**sti·pen·di·a·ry** (sty-*pen*-dee-er-ee) *adj. & n.* [*pl.* -ies].

stip·ple (*stip*-'l) *v.* [stip·pled; stip·pling] 1. To apply small dots to a surface, usually for gradation of tone. 2. *Engraving.* To indicate contours by a series of dots, rather than lines. —**stip·ple, stip·pling** *n.*—**stip·pler** *n.*

stip·u·late (*stip*-yoo-layt) *v.* 1. To impose a specified condition upon an agreement. 2. To contract; specify.—**stip·u·la·tion** (stip-yoo-*lay*-shun) *n.*—**stip·u·la·tor** *n.*—**stip·u·la·to·ry** (*stip*-yoo-luh-toh-ree) *adj.*

stip·ule (*stip*-yool) *n.* Leafy shoot proceeding from the stem of another leaf. —**stip·u·lar, stip·u·late** (*stip*-yoo-lit), **stip·u·lat·ed** *adj.*

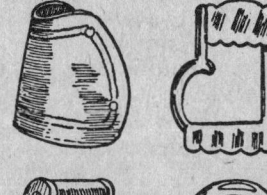

STIPULE

stir *v.* [stirred; stir·ring] 1. To move. 2. To agitate; to mix by rapid motion. 3. To inspire; to affect with strong emotion. 4. To precipitate or incite, as, to stir up trouble. 5. To awaken.—*n.* 1. Widespread excitement; commotion. 2. *Slang.* A jail.—**stir·rer** *n.*

stir·ring *adj.* Inspiring; exciting.— **-ring·ly** *adv.*

stir·rup (*stih*-rup) *n.* 1. Support for the foot in horseback riding. 2. A strap or clamp used as a support.

STIRRUPS

stitch *v.* To sew; to mend—*n.* 1. A single passing of a needle through material, or the amount of thread thus fastened. 2. A single loop of yarn on a knitting needle. 3. A stabbing, momentary pain. —**stitch·ing** *n.* A line of sewing, often decorative.—**stitch·er** *n.*

sti·ver (*sty*-ver) *n.* 1. A Dutch coin worth about two cents. 2. A thing of little value.

stoat (*stoht*) *n.* European weasel or ermine.

stock (*stok*) *n.* 1. A post; stump. 2. Lineage; family background. 3. Supply of goods on hand. 4. Total capital of a business sold in shares; investment in a corporation represented by certificates. 5. Domestic animals; livestock. 6. Meat juices used as a base for soup. 7. A structure with apertures for hands and feet formerly used for public punishment. 8. A broad necktie. 9. The wooden part of a rifle to which the barrel is secured. 10. Raw material, esp. unprinted paper. —*v.* To lay in goods; supply.—*adj.* 1. Standard; regular. 2. Common; trite; banal. 3. Devoted to breeding livestock.—**stock up on.** To lay in a supply of.

STOCK (def. 7)

stockbroker	stockhouse	stock owner
stockbroking	stock-in-trade	stockproof
stockholder	stockkeeper	stockroom

stock·ade (stok-*ayd*) *n.* A tall fence consisting of posts securely planted in the ground, usually for defense.—*v.* To surround with a stockade; to fortify.

stock·bro·ker *n.* A dealer in stocks and bonds.

stock company. A semi-permanent theatrical troupe.

stock exchange. A bourse; trading place for stockbrokers.

stock·i·net (stok-ih-*net*) *n.* Close-ribbed, elastic fabric used for stockings and underwear.

stock·ing *n.* Tight-fitting garment covering the foot and leg.—**stock·ing·less** *adj.*

stock market. 1. A stock exchange. 2. A development in securities prices. 'The stock market is collapsing.'

stock·still *adj.* Motionless, as if petrified.

stock·y *adj.* [stock·i·er; stock·i·est] Heavy; compactly built.—**stock·i·ly** *adv.*— **-i·ness** *n.*

stock·yard *n.* Place where cattle are herded before slaughter.

stodg·y (*stoj*-ee) *adj.* [stodg·i·er; stodg·i·est] Heavy-witted; dull; conventional.—**stodg·i·ly** *adv.*—**stodg·i·ness** *n.*

sto·gie, sto·gy (*stoh*-gee) *n.* A long, slender, and inexpensive cigar.

sto·ic (*stoh*-ik) *n.* 1. One not easily disturbed by events; one indifferent to pain or pleasure. 2. [*cap.*] Follower of an ancient Greek doctrine holding that men should submit their wills to the laws of nature.—**sto·ic, sto·i·cal** *adj.* —**sto·i·cal·ly** *adv.*— **-cal·ness** *n.*—**sto·i·cism** *n.*

stoke (*stohk*) *v.* [stoked; stok·ing] To tend a furnace, esp. to fuel it.—**stok·er** *n.*

stoke·hole *n.* A ship's boiler room.

stole. *Past tense* of steal.

stole *n.* 1. A long heavy band worn over the shoulders by the Roman Catholic clergy. 2. A narrow scarf; a fur-piece.

sto·len. *Past participle* of steal.

stol·id (*stol*-id) *adj.* Slow-witted; lethargic;

without vigorous reactions.—**sto·lid·i·ty** (stuh-*lid*-ih-tee), **stol·id·ness** *n.*—**stol·id·ly** *adv.*

stol·len (*stohl*-'n) *n.* Sweet bread containing fruit and nuts; German coffee cake.

sto·ma (*stoh*-muh) *n.* [*pl.* **sto·ma·ta** (*stoh*-muh-tuh)]. A minute surface opening, esp. in the epidermis of leaves and insects.—**stom·a·tal** *adj.*—**sto·mat·ic** (stuh-*mat*-ik) *adj.*

stom·ach (*stum*-uk) *n.* 1. Organ of the body which receives food and commences digestion. 2. The area within which the stomach is located; the abdomen. 3. Appetite; wish. —*v.* To endure; to accept.—**sto·mach·ic** (stuh-*mak*-ik), **sto·mach·i·cal** *adj.*—**stom·ach·y** *adj.*

stomach ache　　stomach-shaped　stomach-weary
stomach-formed　stomach-sick　　stomach ulcer
stomach pump　　stomach tooth　stomach-worn

stom·ach·er *n.* An ornamental covering worn on the bosom.

stone (*stohn*) *n.* 1. A hard mineral substance. 2. A small piece of rock; a pebble. 3. A gem. 4. A tablet, esp. to mark a grave. 5. A concretion in the bladder or kidneys. 6. The pit of a fruit.—*v.* 1. To attack or kill with stones. 2. To remove seeds or pits.—*adj.* Composed of stone.—**stone-deaf.** Without the faculty of hearing.—**ston·er** *n.*

stone-arched　　stone-covered　stone-hearted
stonebird　　　stonecutter　　stonemason
stone blind　　stone dead　　stoneshot
stoneboat　　　stone-eyed　　stone wall
stone-bruise　　stonefish　　stoneware
stonecast　　　stonegall　　stonework
stone cold　　　stonehead　　stoneyard

stone·crop *n.* A common name for the sedum family, a mosslike succulent perennial, widely used in rock gardens.

Stone·henge (*stohn*-henj) *n.* A circular arrangement of upright stones on Salisbury Plain, England, probably erected in the Bronze Age, either for sun-worship, or as sepulchers.

ston·y *adj.* [ston·i·er; ston·i·est] 1. Abounding in stones. 2. Hard; inflexible; petrifying. —**ston·i·ly** *adv.*—**ston·i·ness** *n.*

stood. *Past tense & past participle* of **stand.**

stooge (*stooj*) *n.* 1. *Slang.* Scapegoat; butt; one who is tolerated only to inflate another's pride or position. 2. *Theater.* The butt of another's jokes.—*v.* [stooged; stoog·ing].

stool *n.* 1. A small seat having no back. 2. An intestinal evacuation. 3. A commode. 4. A living tree-stump or root.—*v.* 1. To evacuate the bowels. 2. *Slang.* To spy upon.

stool pigeon (*stool*-pij-un) *Slang.* A spy; informer. Also **stool·ie.**

stoop *v.* 1. To lean or bend forward; to incline the head and shoulders. 2. To condescend; to degrade oneself. —*n.* 1. A short flight of steps at an entrance, often leading to a small porch with seats. 2. A curvature

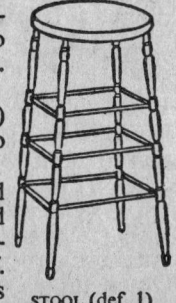

STOOL (def. 1)

of the shoulders. 3. A submission; a moral debasement. 4. *Variant spelling* of **stoup.**

stop *v.* [stopped; stop·ping] 1. To close by plugging or covering. 2. To cease; to put to an end; to check. 3. To visit; to stay.—*n.* 1. A pause; a break; a termination. 2. The part of an organ regulating its tone quality. 3. An obstruction; a hindrance.—**stop·page** *n.*—**stopped** *adj.*

stopback　　stop hound　　stop-over *n.*
stopblock　　stop-loss *adj.*　stop payment
stopboard　　stop-off *n.*　　stop watch
stopgap　　　stop order　　stopwork

stop·per *n.* Device for closing an aperture; a plug, cork, bung, etc.—*v.* To plug.

stop·ple (*stop*-'l) *n.* A stopper.—*v.* [stop·pled; stop·pling] To close with a stopper.

stor·age (*stor*-ij) *n.* 1. Consignment of articles not in use to a rented space for safe-keeping. 2. The cost of space for storing articles.—**storage battery.** A device for generating and storing electrical energy, which can be released by contact.

store *n.* 1. A shop; selling place; market. 2. A hoard; an abundance. 3. [*pl.*] Supplies. —*v.* 1. To stock; to lay up. 2. To deposit for safekeeping.—**in store for.** 1. Reserved. 2. Awaiting.—**store up.** To collect; to keep in mind.—**to set store by.** Have confidence in.

storehouse　　storeman　　storeroom
storekeeper　　storemaster　store ship

sto·rey (*sto*-ree) *n.* Floor of a building; a tier of rooms. *See* **story.**

sto·ried (*sto*-reed) *adj.* 1. Forming the theme of many narratives often mentioned in tales and legends. 2. Decorated with narrative illustrations or historical paintings. 3. Having several floors. 'A five-storied house.'

stork *n.* 1. Tall, long-legged and long-billed European wading bird, usually white. 2. The fabled bearer of newborn children; the emblem of birth.

STORK (1/25 life-size)

storm *n.* 1. A violent rain or snowfall, usually accompanied by a high wind. 2. A crisis; an upheaval of human life. 3. *Military.* An assault.—*v.* 1. To attack; to force entrance to, as to storm the city. 2. To rain or snow, esp. in a gale. 3. To give vent to rage. —**storm·i·ly** *adv.*—**storm·i·ness** *n.*—**storm·y** *adj.* [storm·i·er; storm·i·est].

storm-armed　storm-door　　stormtight
storm-beaten　storm-laden　　storm-tossed
stormbird　　stormproof　　stormwind
storm-bound　storm-swept　　storm-worn

storm trooper. Member of the Elite Guard of the German Nazi party.

S

Stor·thing, Stor·ting (*stor*-ting) *n.* Parliament of Norway.

sto·ry [*pl.* sto·ries] *n.* 1. A narrative; a tale; a brief piece of fiction. 2. Description of an event; an account. 3. *Colloquial.* Situation; set-up. 4. *Colloquial.* A fib. 5. Also **storey.** Floor of a building.

storybook storymonger story work
story maker storyteller story writer

stoup (*stoop*) *n.* 1. Small cask; drinking vessel. 2. *Ecclesiastical.* Basin for holy water at the entrance of a Roman Catholic church.

stout (*stowt*) *adj.* 1. Heavily built; thickset; plump. 2. Strong; robust. 3. Firm; loyal; resolute. 4. Forcible; violent.—*n.* 1. A strong malt liquor. 2. Plump person. 3. A garment designed to fit a large figure.

stout-armed stout-heartedly stout-ribbed
stout-bodied stout-limbed stout-sided
stout-hearted stout-minded stout-soled

stove. *Past tense & past participle* of **stave.**

stove *n.* Apparatus, usually of metal, containing a heating unit for cooking purposes or to supply warmth; an oven.

stove brush stove maker
stove-heated stovepipe
stove house stovewood

STOVE

stow (*stoh*) *v.* [stowed; stowing] 1. To put away compactly in an allotted space or container. 2. To conceal; to hoard. 3. *Slang.* To stop; to cease.—**stow·age** *n.*

stow·a·way *n.* One who conceals himself, as on a ship, to obtain unofficial passage.

strad·dle (*strad*-'l) *v.* [strad·dled; strad·dling] 1. To stand or sit with the legs on opposite sides, as, on a horse. 2. To be on both sides of an issue. 3. *Finance.* To buy in one market and sell short in another.—**strad·dle** *n.*—**strad·dler** *n.*—**strad·dling·ly** *adv.*

strafe (*strayf*) *v.* 1. To machine-gun troops, vehicles, etc., from an airplane. 2. To shell heavily for retribution.—**strafe** *n.*—**straf·er** *n.*

strag·gle (*strag*-'l) *v.* [strag·gled; strag·gling] To disperse or wander with an undisciplined appearance; to look sparse and disorderly. —**strag·gler** *n.*—**strag·gling·ly** *adv.*—**strag·gly** *adj.* [strag·gli·er; strag·gli·est].

straight (*strayt*) *adj.* 1. Direct; undeviating; following the shortest line from one point to another. 2. Honest; upright. 3. *Slang.* Serious; without humor. 'A straight face.' 4. Correct; orderly. 5. Unmixed; pure, as straight whisky.—*n. Poker.* Five consecutive cards in a hand.—**straight·ly** *adv.*—**straight·ness** *n.*—**get straight.** To comprehend or execute correctly.—**go straight.** To reform; to lead an honorable life.

straightarm *v.* straightforwardness
straightaway straight-grained

straight·en (*strayt*-'n) *v.* [-ened; -en·ing] To remove or repair deviations or irregularities. —**straight·en·er** *n.*—**straighten out.** To disentangle; to solve.—**straighten up.** 1. To assume a more erect posture. 2. To make neat.

straight·for·ward *adj.* Honest; candid; simple.

straight·way *adv.* At once; without delay.

strain (*strayn*) *n.* 1. Breed; physical heritage. 2. Trace; a slight amount. 3. Melody; theme; subject. 4. Severe exertion. 5. Minor muscular injury.

strain *v.* 1. To injure by overexerting or pulling; to wrench. 2. To struggle; to make a desperate effort. 3. To interpret loosely; to enlarge a meaning. 4. To hug; to press. 5. To filter through a mesh; to separate liquid from solid.—**strained** *adj.* 1. Stretched. 2. Taut; embarrassed; tense.—**strain·er** *n.* Mesh cup for filtering.

strait (*strayt*) *n.* 1. Narrow passage of water connecting two seas. 2. [*pl.*] Crisis; need, esp. financial.—**strait·ened** *adj.* Impoverished; reduced.—**strait·laced** *adj.* Prudish; narrow-minded.

strait jacket. A kind of coat used to restrain violently insane patients.

strand *n.* 1. A thread of rope or hair; a wisp. 2. Shore; beach.—*v.* 1. To isolate; to leave helpless. 2. To be driven ashore.

STRAIT JACKET

strange (*straynj*) *adj.* 1. Extraordinary; rare; unparalleled. 2. New; unfamiliar. 3. Queer; eccentric. —**strang·er** *n.* 1. One not known or without acquaintance. 2. A foreigner; a traveler.—**strange·ly** *adv.* —**strange·ness** *n.*

strange acting strange-colored strange-mannered
strange-built strange-garbed strange-wayed

stran·gle (*strang*-g'l) *v.* [stran·gled; stran·gling] 1. To choke; to kill by closing the windpipe. 2. To keep down; to repress.—**strangle hold.** 1. A wrestling hold. 2. Power which suppresses one's freedom.—**strang·ler** *n.*—**stran·gu·la·tion** (strang-gyoo-*lay*-shun) *n.*

strap *n.* Narrow band, often of leather, used to fasten, support, or bind.—*v.* [strapped; strapping] 1. To fasten or secure. 2. To beat.

straphanger strap-held strap-shaped
straphead strap-laid strapwork

strap·ping *adj. Colloquial.* Husky; vigorous.

stra·ta. *Plural* of **stratum.**

strat·a·gem (*strat*-uh-j'm) *n.* A deception; an artifice, esp. in warfare.

strat·e·gy (*strat*-uh-jee) *n.* Method of achievement; tactics; a planned operation in the execution of a project.—**strat·e·gic** (struh-*teej*-ik), **strat·e·gi·cal** *adj.* 1. Artful; foresighted. 2. Crucial; focal; advantageous.—**strat·e·gi·cal·ly** *adv.*—**strat·e·gist** (*strat*-uh-jist) *n.*

stra·to·sphere (*strat*-uh-sfihr, *stray*-tuh-sfihr) *n.* Outer layer of the earth's atmosphere.

stra·tum (*stray*-t'm, *strat*-'m) *n.* [*pl.* stra·ta] 1. A layer; one of successive divisions, usually horizontal and parallel and of distinct substances. 2. A level of development or organization, as a social stratum.

STRATA

straw *n.* A brittle, dried stem of grain; also collective.—**last straw.** The final blow.—**straw man.** 1. A figure set up in fields or gardens to guard seeds and plants against birds; a scarecrow. 2. Device or person that diverts attention from a real issue to itself.—**straw boss.** A petty foreman. —**straw vote.** Unofficial polling of public opinion.

straw·ber·ry *n.* Large, edible, red berry containing many seeds.—*adj.* Flavored or colored like a strawberry.—**strawberry blonde.** *Slang.* A redhead.

stray *v.* 1. To leave accustomed surroundings; wander; become lost. 2. To do wrong; err.—*n.* An animal having no owner. —*adj.* Lost; misplaced.

STRAWBERRIES

streak (*streek*) *n.* 1. Long, irregular dash of color or light; a stripe. 2. A trace.—*v.* 1. To apply long, uneven strokes. 2. To become uneven in hue. 3. To dart; to rush.—**streak·i·ly** *adv.*— **-i·ness** *n.*—**streak·y** *adj.* [streak·i·er; -i·est]

stream *n.* 1. Quiet, shallow river; a creek. 2. Continuous course or rhythm; an outpouring; a flow.—*v.* 1. To move swiftly and urgently in a fixed direction. 2. To flow copiously. 3. To shine brightly and beneficently. —**stream·er** *n.* 1. A pennant or ribbon hung in celebration. 2. *Journalism.* A headline running the width of the page.—**stream·let** *n.*

stream·line *v.* 1. To shape so as to offer the least air resistance; to form in a smoothly curved shape. 2. To bring up to date; to make more efficient.—**stream·lined** *adj.*—**stream·lin·ing** *n.*

STREAMLINING

stream·lin·er *n.* A streamlined train or plane.

street *n.* A thoroughfare, esp. in a city, together with its buildings.

street-bred	street door	street peddler
streetcar	street-grown	streetsweeper
street cleaner	streetlamp	streetward
streetcorner	streetlight	streetway

street walker. A harlot; prostitute.

strength *n.* 1. Ability to carry out an action of the body; capability of exertion. 2. Resistance; endurance. 3. Power. 4. Intensity; depth; forcefulness. 5. Degree of the basic element contained.—**strength·en** *v.* —**strength·en·er** *n.*—**strength·en·ing** *adj.* —**strength·less** *adj.*

stren·u·ous (*stren*-yoo-us) *adj.* 1. Laborious; requiring exertion. 2. Vigorous; zealous; active.—**stren·u·ous·ly** *adv.*—**stren·u·ous·ness** *n.*

strep·to·coc·cus (strep-tuh-*kok*-us) *n.* [*pl.* strep·to·coc·ci (-*kok*-ee)] Microorganism of a specific family of bacteria which cause serious diseases.—**strep·to·coc·cal, -coc·cic** *adj.*

stress *v.* 1. To subject to strain. 2. To emphasize; accent.—*n.* 1. Tension; strain. 2. Accent; concentration of attention; focus. —**stressed** *adj.*

stretch (*strech*) *v.* 1. To spread; to extend. 2. To pull to an increased length. 3. To yield to pulling. 4. To become larger; to lose original shape. 5. To exaggerate.—*n.* 1. Broad expanse; a vista. 2. Extent; range of possibility. 3. Allotted period or effort; a stage of progress.—**at a stretch.** At one time; in one endeavor.—**stretch a point.** To exceed limitations; to interpret loosely.

stretch·er *n.* 1. Canvas-covered frame for carrying the sick or wounded. 2. Framework for expanding or retaining original shape, as after laundering. 3. *Masonry.* A brick laid horizontally.

STRETCHER

strew (*stroo*) *v.* To scatter; to cover irregularly by dropping or tossing.

stri·ate (*stry*-ayt) *v.* [stri·at·ed; stri·at·ing] To mark with slender lines; to stripe.—**stri·at·ed** *adj.*—**stri·a·tion** (stry-*ay*-shun) *n.*

strick·en. *Past participle* of **strike.**

strick·en *adj.* Wounded; smitten.

strict *adj.* 1. Severe; exacting; rigorous. 2. Precise; limited.—**strict·ly** *adv.*— **-ness** *n.*

stric·ture (*strik*-cher) *n.* 1. Critical remark; severe criticism. 2. A contraction.

stride (*stryde*) *v.* [strode; strid·den (*strid*-'n); strid·ing] 1. To walk with long steps. 2. To straddle.—*n.* 1. A long or measured step. 2. An advance; progress.—**strid·er** *n.*

stri·dent (*stry*-d'nt) *adj.* Loud; vibrating; grating.—**stri·dence, stri·den·cy** *n.*—**stri·dent·ly** *adv.*

strife *n.* Conflict; struggle.

strike *v.* [struck; strik·ing] 1. To hit; to deal a blow. 2. To ignite. 3. To impress; to affect. 4. To confirm; to ratify. 5. To pierce; to penetrate. 6. To sound. 7. To impress with dies; to stamp. 8. *Colloquial.* To discover, as, to strike gold. 9. To lower, as a flag.—*n.* 1. *Baseball.* A penalty against the batter. 2. Discovery of a source of minerals. 3. A blow. 4. A sudden success. 5. *Bowling.* The act of knocking over all ten pins with the first ball bowled.—**strike a bal-**

S

ance. Weigh both sides equally.—**strike off.**
1. To erase. 2. To print.—**strike oil.** To make
a lucky discovery or investment.—**strike out.**
1. To start off. 2. *Baseball.* To put out on
three strikes.—**strike up.** To commence; begin
suddenly.—**strik·er** *n.*

strike *n.* A work stoppage by organized employees to enforce demands for improved wage
and working conditions.—**strike** *v.*

strike·break·er *n.* A scab; one hired to replace
a striking employee.

strik·ing *adj.* Remarkable; impressive.—**strik·
ing·ly** *adv.*

string *n.* 1. A cord; a small line. 2. A series;
a connected succession. 3. The cord of a
musical instrument. 4. [*pl.*] A group of
stringed instruments. 5. [*pl.*] *Colloquial.* Conditions; terms. 'There are strings to his offer.'
—*v.* [strung; string·ing] 1. To furnish with
strings; to brace. 2. To place on a string; to
tie or fasten. 3. To deprive of strings. 4. To
tune by tightening the strings of a musical
instrument.—**stringed** *adj.*—**string·er** *n.*—**string
along.** *Colloquial.* 1. To lead on. 2. To remain with.

string bean	string maker	string-soled
stringboard	string orchestra	string tie
stringcourse	stringpiece	stringways
stringhalt	string plate	stringwood

strin·gent (*strin*-j'nt) *adj.* Severe; restricted.
—**strin·gen·cy** *n.*—**strin·gent·ly** *adv.*

string·y (*string*-ee) *adj.* [string·i·er; string·i·est]
1. Fibrous. 2. Gluey; ropy. 3. Long and
thin; wiry.—**string·i·ness** *n.*

strip *v.* [stripped; strip·ping] 1. To skin; uncover; undress. 2. To plunder; deprive. 3. To
tear the thread from a screw or bolt.—*n.* A
long narrow segment.—**strip·per** *n.*

stripe (*strype*) *n.* 1. A band differing in color
from its background. 2. The mark made by a
whip; a welt. 3. Character; type. 'Characters
of the same stripe.' 4. *Military & Naval.* An
insignia of rank or length of service.—*v.*
[striped; strip·ing]—**striped** *adj.*

strip·ling (*strip*-ling) *n.* An adolescent youth.

strip tease. A performance of a dance or song
during which the performer, usually female,
disrobes.—**strip·teaser** *n.*

strive (*stryve*) *v.* [strove; striv·en; striv·ing]
1. To try earnestly; labor. 2. To fight; contend.—**striv·er** *n.*

strode. *Past tense* of **stride.**

stroke *n.* 1. A blow; knock. 2. A sudden
affliction or illness. 3. The chiming of a
clock. 4. A light touch; a dash. 'A stroke of
the pen.' 5. A sudden or brilliant move.
6. One of a series of movements. 'The stroke
of an oar.' 7. *Rowing.* The oarsman who
sets the pace. 8. A caress.—*v.* [stroked; strok·
ing] To rub gently; to soothe.—**strok·er** *n.*

stroll (*strohl*) *v.* To saunter; wander.—*n.* A
leisurely walk.—**stroll·er** *n.* 1. One who saun-
ters. 2. A kind of baby carriage.

strong *adj.* 1. Robust; powerful. 2. Re-

sourceful; enduring; firm. 3. Cogent; forceful; valid. 4. Ardent; eager. 5. Potent; concentrated. 6. Affecting the senses forcibly.
'Strong light, strong smell.' 7. Rising in
price. 'A strong market.' 8. *Grammar.* Applied to the conjugation of certain irregular
verbs that inflect by changing the main vowel.
'Sing, sang, sung.'—**strong·ly** *adv.*

strongbacked	strong drink	stronghold
strongbark	strong-headed	strong-minded
strongbox	strong-hearted	strong-willed

strong-arm *v.* *Slang.* To beat up; get rough
with.—*adj.* Unduly forceful.

stron·ti·um (*stron*-shee-um) *n.* A metallic chemical element of the alkaline-earth group.
(*Symbol:* Sr).

strop *n.* A strip of leather used for sharpening
razors.—*v.* [stropped; strop·ping].

stro·phe (*stroh*-fee) *n.* One of two rhymed stanzas, the latter being the antistrophe.—**stroph·
ic, stroph·i·cal** *adj.*

strove. *Past tense* of **strive.**

struck. *Past tense* of **strike.**

struc·ture (*struk*-cher) *n.* 1. A building.
2. Arrangement of parts in a whole; organization.—**struc·tur·al** *adj.*—**struc·tur·al·ly** *adv.*

strug·gle (*strug*-'l) *n.* 1. Violent effort. 2. A
contest; a battle.—*v.* [strug·gled; strug·gling].
To strive; to labor.—**strug·gler** *n.*—**strug·gling**
adv. & adj.—**strug·gling·ly** *adv.*

strum *v.* [strummed; strum·ming] To pluck out
a tune on a stringed instrument.—*n.* The act of
strumming.—**strum·mer** *n.*

strum·pet (*strump*-it) *n.* A prostitute; whore.

strung. *Past tense & past participle* of **string.**

strut *n.* Brace;
supporting
member.

strut *v.* [strut-
ted; strut·ting]
To stride pom-
pously; swag-
ger.—*n.* A pre-
tentious gait.—**strut·ter** *n.*—**strut·ting** *adj.*
—**strut·ting·ly** *adv.*

STRUT

strych·nine, strych·nin (*strik*-nin) *n.* A white,
odorless, crystalline, poisonous alkaloid.
—**strych·nic** *adj.*

stub *v.* [stubbed; stub·bing] 1. To strike with
the toes. 2. To grub up; dig out.—*n.* 1. A
small blunt remnant; remaining section. 2. A
receipt. 3. A stump.—**stubbed** *adj.*—**stub·bed·
ness** *n.*

stub·ble (*stub*-'l) *n.* 1. Stubs of grain left in the
ground. 2. Beard.—**stub·bled** *adj.*— **-bly** *adj.*

stub·born (*stub*-ern) *adj.* 1. Obstinate; refractory. 2. Steady; persistent.—**stub·born·ly**
adv.—**stub·born·ness** *n.*

stub·by *adj.* [stub·bi·er; stub·bi·est] Short and
thick; stocky.–**stub·bi·ly** *adv.*—**stub·bi·ness** *n.*

stuc·co (*stuk*-oh) *n.* A fine plaster, used to coat
walls.—**stuc·co** *v.*—**stuc·co·er** *n.*— **-co·work** *n.*

stuck. *Past tense & past participle* of **stick.**

stuck-up *adj. Slang.* Snobbish; conceited. —**stuck-up·ness** *n.*

stud *n.* 1. A detachable button for a shirt. 2. A large-headed ornamental nail. 3. A collection of stallions and mares for breeding. 4. A game of poker. 5. A scantling; upright interspacing support of a wall. 6. A short, projecting pin.—*v.* [stud·ded; -ding] 1. To set thickly with ornaments or prominent objects. 2. To support with props.—**stud·ding** *n.*

stu·dent (*stoo*-d'nt; *styoo*-) *n.* 1. A scholar; one under instruction. 2. An earnest observer.—**stu·dent·ship** *n.*

stud·ied (*stud*-eed) *adj.* Deliberate; premeditated.—**stud·ied·ly** *adv.*—**stud·ied·ness** *n.*

stu·di·o (*stoo*-dee-oh; *styoo*-) *n.* 1. The working room of an artist. 2. Production center of a motion picture company. 3. Room in which a radio broadcast originates.—**stu·di·o** *adj.*

stu·di·ous (*stoo*-dee-us) *adj.* Diligent; devoted to study; contemplative.—**stu·di·ous·ly** *adv.* —**stu·di·ous·ness** *n.*

stud·y (*stud*-ee) *v.* [stud·ied; stud·y·ing] 1. To apply the mind to learning. 2. To examine closely; ponder.—*n.* [*pl.* stud·ies] 1. Application of the mind to a subject. 2. Any object of study. 3. A room for reading or study, etc. 4. *Art.* A preparatory sketch.

stuff *v.* 1. To cram; pack. 2. To fill a cavity. 3. To eat gluttonously. 4. To vote fraudulently.—*n.* 1. Matter or substance; raw material. 2. Essence; a fundamental part. 3. [*pl.*] General name for fabrics. 'Woolen stuffs, silk stuffs.' 4. Rubbish; trash.

stuffed shirt. *Slang.* A pompous person.

stuff·ing *n.* 1. Filling; material packed into a covering. 2. Dressing; a mixture of foods and seasonings for filling meats, poultry, etc.

stuff·y *adj.* [stuff·i·er; stuff·i·est] 1. Poorly ventilated; close; choked-up. 2. Pompous; stodgy.—**stuff·i·ly** *adv.*—**stuff·i·ness** *n.*

stult·i·fy (*stult*-ih-fy) *v.* [stult·i·fied; stult·i·fy·ing] 1. To make a fool of; appear stupid. 2. To become untrustworthy; disgrace. 3. To restrict; repress.—**stult·i·fied** *adj.*— -**ti·fier** *n.*

stum·ble (*stum*-b'l) *v.* [stum·bled; stum·bling] 1. To trip; stagger after a false step. 2. To act or speak unsteadily. 3. To blunder.—*n.* A trip; fall.—**stumble on.** To come upon by chance.—**stum·bler** *n.*—**stum·bling·ly** *adv.*

stumbling block. An obstacle; difficulty.

stump *n.* 1. The fixed or rooted base remaining after removal of the main part. 2. [*pl.*] The legs. 3. A platform for speechmaking. 4. *Colloquial.* A challenge.—*v.* 1. To puzzle; confound. 2. To make speeches for political purposes; canvass.—**stump·y** [stump·i·er; stump·i·est] *adj.* Short; abbreviated.

stump-bred   stump-legged   stump-rooted
stump-fingered stumpnose (*n.*) stump-tailored
stump-footed   stump-nosed (*adj.*) stumpwork

stun *v.* [stunned; stun·ning] 1. To strike insensible. 2. To overwhelm; shock.—*n.* A

shock.—**stun·ner** *n. Slang.* A person or thing with extraordinary qualities, esp. of beauty.

stung. *Past tense & past participle* of **sting.**

stunk. *Past tense & past participle* of **stink.**

stun·ning *adj.* Strikingly beautiful; of unusual quality.—**stun·ning·ly** *adv.*

stunt *v.* 1. To check normal growth; dwarf. 2. To perform stunts.—*n.* 1. An astonishingly difficult or absurd feat, esp. for public notice. 2. An arrested development.

stu·pe·fac·tion (*stoo*-puh-*fak*-sh'n; *styoo*-) *n.* Daze; insensibility; astonishment.

stu·pe·fy (*stoo*-puh-fy; *styoo*-) *v.* [stu·pe·fied; stu·pe·fy·ing] 1. To deaden; daze. 2. To astonish.—**stu·pe·fi·er** *n.*

stu·pen·dous (*stoo*-*pen*-d'ss; *styoo*-) *adj.* 1. Magnificent; astounding. 2. Enormous. —**stu·pen·dous·ly** *adv.*—**stu·pen·dous·ness** *n.*

stu·pid (*stoo*-pid; *styoo*-) *adj.* 1. Dull-witted; lacking in ability to reason or think. 2. Senseless; stupefied.—**stu·pid·i·ty** (*stoo*-*pid*-i-tee) [*pl.* -ties] *n.* Mental dullness; lack of understanding.—**stu·pid·ly** *adv.*—**stu·pid·ness** *n.*

stu·por (*stoo*-per) *n.* Semi-consciousness; lethargy.—**stu·por·ous** *adj.*

stur·dy (*ster*-dee) *adj.* [stur·di·er; stur·di·est] 1. Strong; robust; hardy. 2. Resolute; unyielding.—**stur·di·ly** *adv.*—**stur·di·ness** *n.*

stur·geon (*ster*-jun) *n.* A large edible fish inhabiting the rivers and seas of the North Temperate regions.

STURGEON (1/60 life size)

stut·ter *v.* To stammer; hesitate in speech.—**stut·ter·er** *n.*— -**ter·ing·ly** *adv.*

sty *n.* 1. A pen for swine. 2. A filthy place. 3. An inflamed swelling of the eyelid.—*v.* [stied; sty·ing] To pen in.

Styg·i·an (*stij*-ee-un) *adj.* 1. *Greek Mythology.* Relating to the River Styx. 2. Hellish; infernal. 3. Dark and gloomy.

style *n.* 1. Mode; fashion. 2. Distinctive manner of performance or conduct. 3. *Botany.* The prolongation of the top of the ovary which supports the stigma of a flower. 4. A pointed instrument.—*v.* [styled; styl·ing] 1. To name; to term. 2. To bring into accord with fashion. 3. To copy-edit.—**styl·ist** *n.* —**sty·lis·tic** (sty-*liss*-tik), -**i·cal** *adj.*—**sty·lis·ti·cal·ly** *adv.*

styl·ish (*style*-ish) *adj.* Modish; fashionable; smart.—**styl·ish·ly** *adv.*—**styl·ish·ness** *n.*

styl·ize (*style*-yze) *v.* To conventionalize; to follow a pattern rather than nature.—**styl·i·za·tion** (style-iz-*ay*-shun) *n.*—**styl·iz·er** *n.*

sty·lus (*sty*-l'ss) *n.* 1. A pointed metal instrument used for drawing, cutting stencils, etc. 2. Phonograph needle for cutting records.

sty·mie, sti·my (*sty*-mee) *n.* 1. Obstruction.

S

2. *Golf.* Situation created by one ball in the line of play of the other.—*v.* [sty·mied; sty·my·ing] To hinder; obstruct.

styp·tic (*stip*-tik) *adj.* Causing contraction; astringent.—*n.* A substance which stops bleeding.—**styptic pencil.** A stick tipped with an astringent, used to stop external bleeding. —**styp·ti·cal** *adj.*—**styp·ti·ci·ty** (-*tiss*-ih-tee) *n.*

Styx (*stikss*) *n. Mythology.* The river which dead souls had to cross to reach Hades.

sua·sion (*sway*-zh'n) *n.* Act of persuading or convincing.—**sua·sive** (*sway*-siv) *adj.*

suave (*swahv*) *adj.* Smooth; bland; urbane. —**suave·ly** *adv.*—**suave·ness, suav·i·ty** *n.*

sub *prefix* 1. Under; lower. 2. Subordinate; inferior; forming a further division. 3. Bordering upon.

subacute	subplot
sub-Alpine	subsection
sub-basement	substation
sub-bituminous	sub-subcommittee
sub-machine gun	subtitle
submarginal	subtreasury

sub·al·tern (sub-*awl*-tern) *n.* 1. *Military.* Commissioned officer below the rank of captain. 2. One who holds a subordinate position.—**sub·or·din·ate** *adj.*

sub·cla·vi·an (sub-*klay*-vee-un) *adj.* Situated under the collar-bone.

sub·com·mit·tee *n.* Small group within a committee delegated to a special task.

sub·con·scious (sub-*kon*-shus) *n. Psychology.* Mental activity below the margin of average awareness.—**sub·con·scious·ly** *adv.*—**sub·con·scious·ness** *n.*

sub·cu·ta·ne·ous (sub-kyoo-*tay*-nee-us) *adj.* Beneath the skin.—**sub·cu·ta·ne·ous·ly** *adv.*

sub·deb *n.* Young woman before making her social debut; teen-age girl.—**sub·deb** *adj.*

sub·di·vide (sub-dih-*vyde*) *v.* [sub·di·vid·ed; sub·di·vid·ing] To break up a unit into smaller parts.—**sub·di·vi·sion** (sub-dih-*vizh*-un) *n.*

sub·due (sub-*dyoo*) *v.* [sub·dued; sub·du·ing] 1. To conquer; subjugate. 2. To overcome by kindness or persuasion. 3. To tone down; soften.—**sub·du·a·ble** *adj.*—**sub·dued** *adj.*— **-du·er** *n.*

sub·ja·cent (sub-*jay*-s'nt) *adj.* Directly below.

sub·ject (*sub*-jekt) *n.* 1. One owing allegiance to a sovereign or government. 2. Recipient; one receiving specified treatment. 3. Topic; material under examination. 4. *Grammar.* Word or phrase predicated, described, or affirmed by the verb. 5. *Music.* Basic theme of a composition or movement. 6. *Art.* Topic chosen for reproduction.—*adj.* 1. Under control of another. 2. Liable; exposed.—*v.* (sub-*jekt*) 1. To expose; cause to undergo. 2. To subdue; bring under control.—**sub·jec·tion** (sub-*jek*-shun) *n.*

sub·jec·tive (sub-*jek*-tiv) *adj.* 1. Personal; affected by peculiar emotions, bias, etc. 2. *Philosophy.* Of or derived from the ego; belonging to personal consciousness. 3. *Psy-*

chology. **a.** Introspective. **b.** Caused by internal stimuli.—**sub·jec·tive·ly** *adv.*— **-tive·ness; -tiv·i·ty** (sub-jek-*tiv*-ih-tee) *n.*—**sub·jec·tiv·ism** *n.*

sub·join *v.* To add; attach.—**sub·junc·tion** (sub-*junk*-shun) *n.*

sub·ju·gate (*sub*-juh-gayt) *v.* [sub·ju·gat·ed; sub·ju·gat·ing] To subdue; bring under control.—**sub·ju·ga·tion** (sub-juh-*gay*-shun) *n.* —**sub·ju·ga·tor** *n.*

sub·junc·tive (sub-*junk*-tiv) *n. & adj.* A verbform expressing condition, hypothesis, or contingency.

sub·lease (sub-*leess*) *v.* To rent property from a person who in turn rents it from the owner.

sub·let (sub-*let*) *v.* [sub·let; sub·let·ting] To let or rent leased property.—**sub·les·see** *n.*—**sub·les·sor** *n.*

sub·li·mate (*sub*-lih-mayt) *v.* [-mat·ed; -mat·ing] 1. To elevate; exalt. 2. *Psychology.* To transfer the energy of an instinctive urge to activities more socially acceptable. 3. *Chemistry.* To change directly from the solid to the gaseous state and back to a solid, without apparent liquefaction.—*n. Chemistry.* Product of sublimation.—**sub·li·ma·tion** (sub-lih-*may*-shun) *n.*

sub·lime (suh-*blyme*) *adj.* Exalted; grand; noble.—*n.* Grandeur; exalted state.—*v.* [sub·limed; sub·lim·ing] 1. To elevate; purify. 2. *Chemistry.* To sublimate.—**sub·lime·ly** *adv* —**sub·lime·ness** *n.*—**sub·lim·er** *n.*—**sub·lim·i·ty** (suh-*blim*-ih-tee) *n.* [*pl.* -ties].

sub·lu·na·ry (sub-*loo*-ner-ee) *adj.* Also **sub·lun·ar.** Earthly; worldly.

sub·ma·rine (sub-muh-*reen*) *n.* An underwater warship armed with torpedoes, used for surprise attacks. —*adj.* Underwater.

sub·max·il·lar·y (sub-*mak*-sih-ler-ee) *adj.* Situated under the lower jaw.

sub·merge (sub-*merj*) *v.* [sub·merged; sub·merg·ing] 1. To plunge under water; sink. 2. To inundate.—**sub·mer·gence** *n.*—**sub·mer·gi·bil·i·ty** (sub-merj-ih-*bil*-ih-tee) *n.*—**sub·mer·gi·ble** *n. & adj.*

SUBMARINE

sub·merse *v.* [sub·mersed; sub·mers·ing] To submerge.—**sub·mersed** *adj.*—**sub·mers·i·ble** *n. & adj.*—**sub·mer·sion** (sub-*mer*-zhun) *n.*

sub·mit (sub-*mit*) *v.* [sub·mit·ted; sub·mit·ting] 1. To yield; surrender. 2. To leave to the judgment of another. 3. To present.—**sub·mis·sion** (sub-*mish*-'n) *n.*—**sub·mis·sive** *adj.* — **-sive·ly** *adv.*— **-sive·ness** *n.*

sub·nor·mal (sub-*nor*-m'l) *adj.* Lower than average.—*n.* A person below normal.—**sub·nor·mal·i·ty** (sub-nor-*mal*-ih-tee) *n.*

sub·or·di·nate (suh-*bor*-dih-nayt) *v.* [sub·or·di·nat·ed; sub·or·di·nat·ing] 1. To place in lower order or rank. 2. To lessen the importance of; bring under control.—*n.* (suh-*bor*-dih-nit) One ranking below another.—*adj.* 1. Of lower order or rank. 2. Submissive; inferior; dependent.—**sub·or·di·na·tion** (suh-bor-dih-*nay*-sh'n) *n.*

sub·orn (sub-*orn*) *n.* 1. To bribe; induce to a criminal act. 2. *Law.* To employ another to commit perjury.—**sub·orn·er** *n.*

sub·poe·na (suh-*pee*-nuh) *n. Law.* A writ demanding appearance in court.—*v.* [sub·poe·naed; sub·poe·na·ing].

sub·scribe (sub-*skrybe*) *v.* [sub·scribed; sub·scrib·ing] 1. To endorse; to sanction. 2. To pay in advance for regular receipt of a periodical or newspaper. 3. To endorse with written signature.—**sub·scrib·er** *n.*—**sub·scrip·tion** (sub-*skrip*-shun) *n.*

sub·se·quent (*sub*-suh-kwent) *adj.* Following; succeeding.—**sub·se·quent·ly** *adv.*—**sub·se·quence, sub·se·quen·cy** *n.*—**sub·se·quent·ness** *n.*

sub·serve (sub-*serv*) *v.* [sub·served; sub·serv·ing] To serve in a subordinate capacity; aid.

sub·ser·vi·ent (sub-*ser*-vee-'nt) *adj.* 1. Obsequious; servile. 2. Instrumental.—**sub·ser·vi·ence, sub·ser·vi·en·cy** *n.*—**sub·ser·vi·ent·ly** *adv.*

sub·side (sub-*syde*) *v.* [sub·sid·ed; sub·sid·ing] To abate; calm down.—**sub·sid·ence** *n.*

sub·sid·i·ar·y (sub-*sid*-ee-er-ee) *adj.* Auxiliary; subordinate.—*n.* [*pl.* -ries] A business concern owned or controlled by another firm.

sub·si·dize (*sub*-suh-dyze) *v.* [sub·si·dized; sub·si·diz·ing] To support by monetary contribution.—**sub·si·dy** *n.*

sub·sist (sub-*sist*) *v.* To exist; be maintained with bare necessities.—**sub·sist·ence** *n.*—**sub·sist·ent** *adj.*

sub·soil (*sub*-soyl) *n.* The earth immediately underlying the surface soil.—*v.* To turn up the under soil.—**sub·soil·er** *n.*

sub·stance (*sub*-st'nss) *n.* 1. Matter; body; material. 2. The essential constituent; purport; theme. 3. Solidity; firmness. 4. Goods; riches.

sub·stan·tial (sub-*stan*-sh'l) *adj.* 1. Solid; large. 2. Of moderate wealth; responsible. 3. Real; permanent.—**sub·stan·ti·al·i·ty** (sub-stan-shee-*al*-ih-tee) *n.*— **-tial·ly** *adv.*— **-tial·ness** *n.*

sub·stan·ti·ate (sub-*stan*-shee-ayt) *v.* [sub·stan·ti·at·ed; sub·stan·ti·at·ing] 1. To verify; prove. 2. To express concretely.—**sub·stan·ti·a·tion** (sub-stan-shee-*ay*-shun) *n.*—**sub·stan·ti·a·tive** (sub-*stan*-shuh-tiv) *adj.*

sub·stan·tive (*sub*-st'n-tiv) *adj.* 1. Expressing truth or existence. 2. Essential; lasting.—*n. Grammar.* A noun, or any part of speech used as a noun.— **-ti·val** *adj.*— **-tive·ness** *n.*

sub·sti·tute (*sub*-stih-toot; -tyoot) *v.* [sub·sti·tut·ed; sub·sti·tut·ing] To exchange; replace.—*n.* A replacement; one filling another's place.

sub·sti·tu·tion (sub-stih-*too*-shun; -tyoo-) *n.* 1. A replacement. 2. The act or process of putting one thing in another's place.

sub·stra·tum (sub-*stray*-tum) *n.* An underlying layer, esp. the subsoil; a base.—**sub·stra·tal, sub·stra·tive** *adj.*

sub·struc·ture (sub-*struk*-cher) *n.* A foundation —**sub·struc·tur·al** *adj.*

sub·sume (sub-*soom*) *v.* [-sumed; -sum·ing] To classify; include the particular in the general.

sub·tend (sub-*tend*) *v.* To be opposite to; extend under. 'The chord subtends the arc.'

sub·ter·fuge (*sub*-ter-fyooj) *n.* An evasion; artifice; a feigned motive concealing another.

sub·ter·ra·ne·an (sub-ter-*ray*-nee-an) *adj.* Also **sub·ter·ra·ne·ous.** Situated underground; secret.

sub·tile (*sut*-'l; *sub*-tyle) *adj.* 1. Delicate. 2. Crafty; cunning.—**sub·tile·ly** *adv.*—**sub·tile·ness, sub·til·i·ty** *n.*

sub·tit·le (*sub*-ty-t'l) *n.* 1. A second explanatory title. 2. *Motion Pictures.* A caption; an explanatory printed note.

sub·tle (*sut*-'l) *adj.* 1. Fine; delicate. 2. Discerning; penetrating; keen. 3. Cunning; ingenious; clever.—**sub·tle·ness, sub·tle·ty** *n.* —**sub·tly** *adv.*

sub·tract (sub-*trakt*) *v.* To deduct; to take one quantity from another.—**sub·trac·ter** *n.*—**sub·trac·tion** (sub-*trak*-shun) *n.*—**sub·trac·tive** *adj.*

sub·tra·hend (*sub*-truh-hend) *n. Mathematics.* The quantity to be subtracted from another.

sub·trop·i·cal (sub-*trop*-ih-k'l) *adj.* Characteristic of regions near the tropical zone.—**sub·trop·ics** *n.*

sub·urb (*sub*-erb) *n.* An outlying residential section of a city.—**sub·ur·ban** *adj.*— **-ban·ite** *n.*

sub·ven·tion (sub-*ven*-sh'n) *n.* Financial aid, esp. a governmental grant.

sub·vert (sub-*vert*) *v.* To overthrow; to corrupt. —**sub·ver·sion** *n.*—**sub·ver·sive** *adj.*— **-vert·er** *n.*

sub·way (*sub*-way) *n.* An underground passage.

suc·ceed (suk-*seed*) *v.* 1. To follow in order; to inherit. 2. To accomplish an end; to achieve success.—**suc·ceed·er** *n.*

suc·cess (suk-*sess*) *n.* A prosperous outcome; achievement.—**suc·cess·ful** *adj.*— **-ful·ly** *adv.*

suc·ces·sion (suk-*sesh*-'n) *n.* 1. A series; a sequence. 2. The assuming of another's place. 3. The order of descendants; lineage.

suc·ces·sive (suk-*sess*-iv) *adj.* Consecutive; following in order.— **-sive·ly** *adv.*— **-sive·ness** *n.*

suc·ces·sor *n.* One who follows; assumes another's place.

suc·cinct (suk-*sinkt*) *adj.* Concise; condensed; pithy.—**suc·cinct·ly** *adv.*—**suc·cinct·ness** *n.*

suc·cor (*suk*-'r) *n.* Relief, help, assistance.—*v.* To aid; rescue.—**suc·cor·able** *adj.*— **-cor·er** *n.*

suc·co·tash (*suk*-uh-tash) *n.* A dish of corn and lima beans cooked together.

suc·cu·lence (*suk*-yoo-lunss) *n.* Juiciness; freshness.—**suc·cu·len·cy** *n.*—**suc·cu·lent** *adj.*—**suc·cu·lent·ly** *adv.*

suc·cumb (suh-*kum*) *v.* 1. To yield; to submit. 2. To die.

S

such *adj.* **1.** Similar; like. **2.** Of the same class. **3.** Extraordinary; extreme.—*pronoun* Object previously mentioned. 'Such was his wish.'

suck *v.* **1.** To draw into the mouth. **2.** To absorb; to inhale.—*n.* The act or object of sucking.

suck·er *n.* **1.** *Slang.* An easily fooled or misled person. **2.** A common fresh-water fish. **3.** *Horticulture.* A shoot springing from buds along a plant's stem. **4.** A suction pipe, valve, etc. **5.** A lollipop.

suck·le (*suk*-'l) *v.* [suck·led; suck·ling] To nurse at the breast.—**suck·ler** *n.*—**suck·ling** *n.* An unweaned child or animal. 'Suckling pig.'

suc·tion (*suk*-shun) *n.* Absorption by creation of a partial vacuum.

sud·den (*sud*-'n) *adj.* Abrupt; instantaneous; unexpected.—**sud·den·ly** *adv.*—**sud·den·ness** *n.*

su·dor·if·er·ous (soo-der-*if*-er-us) *adj.* Secreting or producing sweat.— **-ous·ness** *n.*—**su·dor·if·ic** (soo-der-*if*-ik) *adj. & n.*

suds (*sudz*) *n. pl.* A froth of soap and water; foam.—**suds·y** (*sud*-zee) *adj.*

sue (*soo*) *v.* [sued; su·ing] **1.** To seek reparation by legal process. **2.** To entreat; plead. —**su·er** *n.*

suède (*swayd*) *n.* The treated underside of tanned leather.—*adj.* Made of suède material.

su·et (*soo*-it) *n.* The fatty tissue about the loins and kidneys of certain animals, used in cooking.—**su·et·y** *adj.*

Suez Canal (*soo*-ez). An artificial waterway connecting the Mediterranean and Red Seas.

suf·fer *v.* **1.** To undergo pain; endure. **2.** To allow. **3.** To sustain loss or damage.—**suf·fer·a·ble** *adj.*—**suf·fer·a·ble·ness** *n.*—**suf·fer·a·bly** *adv.*—**suf·fer·er** *n.*—**suf·fer·ing** *adj. & n.* —**suf·fer·ing·ly** *adv.*

suf·fice (suh-*fysse*) *v.* [suf·ficed; suf·fic·ing] **1.** To be enough. **2.** To satisfy; to content. —**suf·fic·er** *n.*

suf·fi·cient (suh-*fish*-'nt) *adj.* Adequate; enough. —**suf·fi·cien·cy** *n.*—**suf·fi·cient·ly** *adv.*

suf·fix (*suf*-ikss) *n.* A modifying syllable at the end of a word.

suf·fo·cate (*suf*-uh-kayt) *v.* [-cat·ed; -cat·ing] To choke; smother; kill by stopping respiration.—**suf·fo·cat·ing·ly** *adv.*—**suf·fo·ca·tion** (suf-uh-*kay*-shun) *n.*—**suf·fo·ca·tive** (*suf*-uh-kuh-tiv) *adj.*

suf·fra·gan (*suf*-ruh-gun) *adj.* Assisting a bishop.—**suf·fra·gan** *n.*

suf·frage (*suf*-rij) *n.* The right to vote.

sug·ar (*shoog*-er) *n.* A white crystalline substance made from the sugar cane or the sugar beet, used for sweetening.—*v.* To add sugar. —**sug·ar-coat** *v.* To disguise; make more palatable.—**sug·ared, sug·ar·y** *adj.*— **-ar·i·ness** *n.*

sugarbird	sugar-coated	sugar-loaf
sugarbush	sugar-colored	sugar maker
sugar cake	sugar-cured	sugarplum
sugar-chopped	sugar-laden	sugar works

sugar cane. A sturdy semi-tropical grass from whose juice sugar is obtained.

sug·gest (sug-*jest*) *v.* **1.** To propose; intimate. **2.** To express through association; call to mind.—**sug·gest·er** *n.* —**sug·gest·i·ble**, *adj.* — **-gest·i·bil·i·ty** (sug-jest-uh-*bil*-ih-tee) *n.*—**sug·ges·tion** (sug-*jess*-chun) *n.* A hint; trace.

SUGAR CANE

sug·gest·ive *adj.* Tending or attempting to arouse lewd or improper thoughts.

su·i·cide (*soo*-ih-syde) *n.* **1.** Self-murder. **2.** One who has killed himself. **3.** Self-inflicted ruin.—**su·i·cid·al** (soo-ih-*syde*-'l) *adj.*

suit (*soot*) *n.* **1.** A set, esp. of clothes. **2.** *Law.* A legal action. **3.** Man's outer garments, consisting usually of jacket, vest, and trousers; tailored woman's garment with jacket. **4.** A petition. **5.** A courtship.—*v.* **1.** To adapt or be adapted to; to accommodate. **2.** To be agreeable to; to please.

suit·a·ble (*soot*-uh-b'l) *adj.* Appropriate; fitting; proper.—**suit·a·bil·i·ty** (soot-uh-*bil*-ih-tee), **suit·a·ble·ness** *n.*—**suit·a·bly** *adv.*

suit·case *n.* A valise; a rectangular traveling bag.

suite (*sweet*) *n.* **1.** A series or set, esp. a chain of connected rooms, or a set of furniture. **2.** *Music.* A series of dance tunes in four movements. **3.** A retinue.

SUITCASE

suit·ing (*soot*-ing) *n.* Cloth for making suits.

suit·or (*soot*-er) *n.* **1.** Man who courts the woman he wishes to marry. **2.** A petitioner.

su·ki·ya·ki (soo-kee-*yah*-kee) *n.* Japanese dish of beef and vegetables served with rice.

sul·fa, sul·pha (*sul*-fuh). *Medicine.* Prefix denoting a class of chemical compounds, recently developed and valuable in treating certain infectious diseases. The sulfa drugs in common use are: **sul·fa·di·a·zine** (-*dy*-uh-zeen), **sul·fa·nil·a·mide** (-*nil*-uh-myde), **sul·fa·pyr·i·dine**, (-*pihr*-ih-din), **sul·fa·thi·a·zole**, (-*thy*-uh-zohl).

sulfonamide drugs (sul-*fon*-uh-mid). Medical term for the class of pharmaceuticals popularly called **sulfa drugs.**

sulk *v.* To become sullen from resentment.—*n.* A morose mood.

sulk·y *n.* [*pl.* sulk·ies] Light two-wheeled vehicle used in trotting races.

sulk·y *adj.* Morose; sullen; surly.—**sulk·i·ly** *adv.*—**sulk·i·ness** *n.*

sul·len *adj.* Surly; dour; morose.—**sul·len·ly** *adv.*—**sul·len·ness** *n.*

sul·ly *v.* [sul·lied; sul·ly·ing] To soil; to tarnish.

sul·phate (*sul*-fayt) *n.* Also **sul·fate.** A salt of sulphuric acid.

sul·phide, sul·fide (*sul*-fyde) *n.* A combination of sulfur with any other element.

sul·phur (*sul*-fer) *n.* Also **sul·fur.** A yellow, nonmetallic, combustible element. (*Symbol:* S).—**sul·phu·reous** *adj.*—**sul·phu·reous·ness** *n.*

sul·phu·ric (sul-*fyoor*-ik) *adj.* Containing sulphur or obtained from it.—**sulphuric acid.** A heavy, almost colorless, highly corrosive liquid.

sul·phur·ous (*sul*-fer-us) *adj.* 1. Containing sulphur. 2. Fiery; heated.

sul·tan (*sul*-t'n) *n.* The title of Mohammedan sovereigns.—**sul·tan·a** *n.* The wife of a sultan. —**sul·tan·ate** *n.* The dominion of a sultan.

sul·try (*sul*-tree) *adj.* [sul·tri·er; sul·tri·est] 1. Hot and humid. 2. Passionate; burning.

sum *n.* 1. Total; full amount. 2. A quantity of money. 3. Substance; gist; summary.—*v.* [summed; sum·ming].

su·mac, su·mach (*soo*-mak) *n.* Common shrub bearing red berries.

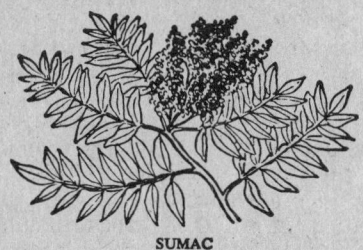

SUMAC

sum·mar·ize (*sum*-uh-ryze) *v.* [sum·marized; sum·mar·iz·ing] To reduce to a concise statement of important points.—**sum·ma·ri·za·tion** (sum-uh-riz-*ay*-shun) *n.*—**sum·ma·ri·zer** *n.*

sum·ma·ry (*sum*-uh-ree) *n.* A condensation; a brief restatement.—*adj.* 1. Concise; succinct. 2. Rapidly performed.—**sum·mar·il·y** *adv.* —**sum·ma·ri·ness** *n.*

sum·ma·tion (sum-*ay*-sh'n) *n.* 1. Aggregate; total. 2. *Law.* Review of points made.

sum·mer *n.* The warmest season of the year, when the sun shines most directly.—*v.* To pass the summer.—**sum·mer·y** *adj.*

summer-grown summer house summertide
summer-hot summerlike summertime

sum·mit *n.* Top; peak; The highest point.

sum·mon (*sum*-un) *v.* 1. To call; send for. 2. To demand appearance in court.—**sum·mons** *n.* [*pl.* sum·mons·es] A written notification to appear in court.—**summon up.** 1. To rouse; excite into action. 2. To call; command to appear.

sump *n.* A marshy spot; lowest point in a drainage system.

sump·ter *n.* A pack-horse.

sump·tu·ar·y (*sump*-choo-er-ee) *adj.* Pertaining to or adjusting expenditures.

sump·tu·ous (*sump*-choo-us) *adj.* Magnificent; costly; lavish.— -ous·ly *adv.*— -ous·ness *n.*

sun *n.* 1. The central body of the solar system, which furnishes light and heat to the earth. 2. Sunshine; the light of the sun. 3. The chief source of honor, glory, or prosperity.

—[sunned; sun·ning] To warm or dry in the light of the sun.—**sun·ny** *adj.*

sunbeam	sun-dried	sunroom
sun-blackened	sunglass	sunset
sun-blind	sunglow	sunshade
sunbonnet	sun god	sunshine
sun-bright	sunkist	sunshiny
sunburn	sunless	sunspot
sunburst	sunlight	sunstone
sun-cured	sunlit	sunup
sundown	sunrise	sunward

sun·dae (*sun*-dee) *n.* A dish of ice-cream served with syrup, fruit, nuts, etc.

Sun·day (*sun*-dee) *n.* The first day of the week; the Christian Sabbath.

sun·der *v.* To separate; to divide; to break.—**i sunder.** In pieces; apart.—**sun·der·ance** *n.*

sun·dial (*sun*-dyle) *n.* An instrument telling approximate time by the sun's shadow cast upon a dial marked off in hours.

SUNDIAL

sun·dry (*sun*-dree) *adj.* Various; assorted; miscellaneous.

sun·fish *n.* A fresh-water fish of the perch family.

sun·flow·er *n.* A large flower with yellow petals and a brown center.

sung. *Past tense & past participle* of sing.

sunk. *Past tense & past participle* of sink.

sunk·en *adj.* Fallen; low; under water.

sun·stroke *n.* Heat prostration.—**sun·struck** *adj.*

sup *v.* [supped; sup·ping] To eat the evening meal.

su·per (*soo*-per) *adj. Slang.* Excellent; fine;—*n.* 1. *Theater Slang.* Supernumerary; an extra. 2. *Slang.* Superintendent.

su·per- Prefix expressing: 1. Over or above in position. 2. Above or beyond in degree or measure, as:

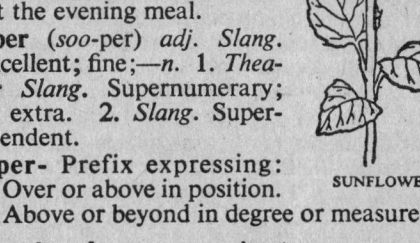

SUNFLOWER

superabound	supereminent	superman
superabundance	superfine	superphysical
superabundant	superheat	superscribe
superabundantly	superhuman	superscription
superadd	superimpose	superstructure
superaddition	superinduce	supersubtle
supercool	superintending	supertax

su·per·a·ble (*soo*-per-uh-b'l) *adj.* Capable of being overcome.

su·per·an·nu·at·ed (soo-per-*an*-yoo-ayt-id) *adj.* Senile; retired and pensioned.—**su·per·an·nu·a·tion** *n.*

su·perb (soo-*perb*) *adj.* Wonderful; magnificent; excellent.—**su·perb·ly** *adv.*—**su·perb·ness** *n.*

su·per·car·go (soo-per-*kahr*-goh) *n.* Employee aboard a merchant ship who manages the commercial affairs of a voyage.

su·per·charg·er *n.* Device for increasing amount of air taken into a gasoline engine.

S

su·per·cil·i·ous (soo-per-*sil*-ee-us) *adj.* Disdainful; contemptuous; arrogant.— -**i·ous·ness** *n.*

su·per·e·go (soo-per-*ee*-goh) *n. Psychoanalysis.* The moral conscience.

su·per·fi·cial (soo-per-*fish*-'l) *adj.* 1. Shallow; unimportant; without profundity. 2. External; on the surface.—**su·per·fi·cial·ly** *adv.*—**su·per·fi·ci·al·i·ty** (soo-per-fish-ee-*al*-ih-tee) *n.*

su·per·flu·i·ty (soo-per-*floo*-ih-tee) *n.* Unnecessary abundance; excess.

su·per·flu·ous (soo-*per*-floo-us) *adj.* Unnecessary; extra.—**su·per·flu·ous·ly** *adv.*

su·per·fort, su·per·for·tress (*soo*-per-fort) *n.* Largest long-range bombing plane developed in World War II, the B-29.

su·per·im·pose (soo-per-im-*pohz*) *v.* To place on or over something else.

su·per·in·tend (soo-prin-*tend*) *v.* To have charge of; take care of.—**su·per·in·tend·ence** *n.* —**su·per·in·tend·en·cy** *n.*—**su·per·in·tend·ent** *n.*

su·pe·ri·or (soo-*peer*-ee-er) *adj.* 1. Higher; above; more elevated. 2. Better; most excellent.—*n.* 1. One higher in rank, office, dignity, etc. 2. [*cap.*] The head of a monastery or convent.

su·per·i·or·i·ty (soo-peer-ee-*or*-ih-tee) *n.* State or quality of excelling.

su·per·la·tive (soo-*per*-luh-tiv) *adj.* Supreme; of utmost degree; surpassingly fine.—*n.* 1. The highest or most eminent. 2. *Grammar.* Degree of adjectives or adverbs expressing the greatest intensity of meaning.—**su·per·la·tive·ly** *adv.*—**su·per·la·tive·ness** *n.*

su·per·nal (soo-*per*-nal) *adj.* Heavenly; celestial.—**su·per·nal·ly** *adv.*

su·per·nat·u·ral (soo-per-*nat*-cher-ul) *adj.* Miraculous; exceeding the powers or laws of nature.—**su·per·nat·u·ral·ism** *n.*—**su·per·nat·u·ral·ist** *n.*—**su·per·nat·u·ral·is·tic** (soo-per-nat-cher-ul-*liss*-tik) *adj.*—**su·per·nat·u·ral·ly** *adv.*

su·per·nu·mer·ar·y (soo-per-*noo*-mer-ehr-ee) *adj.* Exceeding the necessary or usual number. —*n.* [*pl.* -ies] 1. Person added temporarily to a staff. 2. *Theater.* Actor appearing in a special scene, usually without a speaking role.

su·per·pose (-*pohz*) *v.* [-posed; -pos·ing] To lay over or upon.

su·per·scrip·tion (-*skrip*-sh'n) *n.* 1. Address on a letter. 2. Writing at the top of a letter.

su·per·sede (soo-per-*seed*) *v.* [-sed·ed; -sed·ing] To replace; to supplant.—**su·per·sed·ure** *n.*

su·per·son·ic (soo-per-*son*-ik) *adj.* Operating by means of high-frequency vibrations above the range of human hearing.

su·per·sti·tion (soo-per-*stish*-un) *n.* Belief in symbolic or supernatural meanings of chance events.—**su·per·sti·tious** *adj.*—**su·per·sti·tious·ly** *adv.*—**su·per·sti·tious·ness** *n.*

su·per·struc·ture (*soo*-per-struk-cher) *n.* Any structure built on another.

su·per·vene (soo-per-*veen*) *v.* [-vened; -ven·ing] To ensue; follow; succeed.—**su·per·ven·tion** (soo-per-*ven*-shun) *n.*

su·per·vise (*soo*-per-vyze) *v.* [-vised; -vis·ing] To direct; to be in charge;—**su·per·vi·sion** (soo-per-*vizh*-un) *n.*—**su·per·vi·sor** *n.*—**su·per·vi·so·ry** (soo-per-*vy*-zuh-ree) *adj.*

su·pine (soo-*pyne*) *adj.* 1. Lying on the back; reclining. 2. Inert; listless.—**su·pine·ly** *adv.* —**su·pine·ness** *n.*

sup·per *n.* The evening meal.—**sup·per·less** *adj.* —**sup·per·time** *n.*

sup·plant (suh-*plant*) *v.* To replace; supersede. —**sup·plan·ta·tion** (suh-plan-*tay*-shun) *n.*—**sup·plant·er** *n.*

sup·ple (*sup*-'l) *adj.* Pliant, flexible.—**sup·ple·ness** *n.*—**sup·ple·ly** *adv.*

sup·ple·ment (*sup*-lih-m'nt) *n.* 1. An added section; appendix. 2. *Mathematics.* Angle or arc added to another to total 180°.—*v.* To make an addition; to complete.—**sup·ple·men·tal** (sup-lih-*men*-t'l), **sup·ple·men·ta·ry** *adj.*

sup·pli·ance (*sup*-lee-unss) *n.* Entreaty; pleading.—**sup·pli·ant** *n.* & *adj.*—**sup·pli·ant·ly** *adv.* —**sup·pli·ant·ness** *n.*

sup·pli·cate (*sup*-lih-kayt) *v.* [-cat·ed; -cat·ing] To implore; beseech; entreat.—**sup·pli·cant** *n.*—**sup·pli·ca·tion** (sup-lih-*kay*-shun) *n.*—**sup·pli·ca·to·ry** (*sup*-lih-kuh-tor-ee) *adj.*

sup·ply *v.* [sup·plied; sup·ply·ing] To furnish; provide.—*n.* [*pl.* -lies] A stock; store; quantity.—**sup·pli·er** *n.*

sup·port *v.* 1. To sustain; hold up. 2. To provide for; pay living expense. 3. To substantiate; verify. 4. To champion; advocate. 5. To endure; bear.—*n.* 1. A prop; foundation. 2. Sustenance. 3. Aid; support. —**sup·port·a·bil·i·ty** (suh-port-uh-*bil*-ih-tee) *n.* —**sup·port·a·ble** *adj.*—**sup·port·a·ble·ness** *n.* —**sup·port·a·bly** *adv.*—**sup·port·er** *n.*

sup·pose (suh-*pohz*) *v.* [sup·posed; sup·pos·ing] 1. To assume; pretend; accept for the sake of argument. 2. To imagine; presume.—**sup·pos·a·ble** *n.*—**sup·pos·a·bly** *adv.*—**sup·posed** *adj.* —**sup·pos·ed·ly** *adv.*—**sup·pos·ing** *conj.*

sup·po·si·tion (sup-uh-*zish*-un). *n.* An assumption; guess; conjecture.—**sup·po·si·tion·al** *adj.* —**sup·po·si·tion·al·ly** *adv.*

sup·press (suh-*press*) *v.* 1. To subdue; put down. 2. To conceal; repress. 3. To hinder from circulation.—**sup·press·i·ble** *adj.*—**sup·pres·sion** (suh-*presh*-un) *n.*—**sup·pres·sor** *n.* —**sup·pres·sive** *adj.*

sup·pu·rate (*sup*-yer-ayt) *v.* To form pus. —**sup·pu·ra·tion** *n.*

su·pra (*soo*-pruh) *prefix.* Above; over.

supra-abdominal supramolecular suprarenal
supra-auditory supranasal suprasensible
suprabranchial supra-orbital supraterrestrial
suprailiac suprarational supravisual

su·preme (soo-*preem*) *adj.* Highest; greatest; pre-eminent.—**Supreme Being,** God.—**Supreme Court,** Highest judicial body in U.S. —**su·prem·a·cy** (soo-*prem*-uh-see) *n.*—**su·preme·ly** *adv.*—**su·preme·ness** *n.*

sur·cease (ser-*seess*) *n.* Cessation; release.

sur·charge (*ser*-charj) *v.* [sur·charged; sur·charg·ing] 1. To overload; to overburden. 2. To overcharge.—*n.* An excessive load or burden.—sur·charg·er *n.*

sur·cin·gle (*ser*-sing-g'l) *n.* A band holding a saddle on a horse.

sure (*shoor*) *adj.* 1. Certain; positive; confident. 2. Safe; infallible; steady.—sure·fire. Certain; bound to occur.—sure-footed. Unlikely to slip or stumble.—to be sure. Certainly; indeed.—sure·ly *adv.*—sure·ness *n.*

sur·e·ty (*shoor*-uh-tee) *n.* 1. Certainty. 2. Security against loss or damage.—sure·ty·ship *n.*

surf (*serf*) *n.* The breaking of the sea upon the shore.—surf·y *adj.*

surf-battered   surfboat   surf-torn
surfbird   surf-bound   surf-washed
surfboard   surfman   surf-worn

sur·face (*ser*-fiss) *n.* 1. The outside; the extreme part. 2. Superficial appearance.—*v.* [sur·faced; sur·fac·ing] 1. To make smooth. 2. To come to the top of a liquid.—sur·fac·er *n.*

sur·feit (*ser*-fit) *v.* To satiate; glut.—*n.* 1. Disgust caused by excess; satiety. 2. Overabundance.

surge (*serj*) *v.* [surged; surg·ing] To swell; rise and fall.—*n.* 1. A wave. 2. A sudden increase, as of an electric current.

sur·geon (*ser*-jun) *n.* A physician who treats disorders by operation.—sur·geon·cy *n.*

sur·ger·y (*ser*-jer-ee) *n.* 1. Branch of medicine which treats disorders by operation. 2. Room for performance of surgical operations.—sur·gi·cal *adj.*—sur·gi·cal·ly *adv.*

sur·ly (*ser*-lee) *adj.* Sullen; morose.—sur·li·ly *adv.*—sur·li·ness *n.*

sur·mise (ser-*myze*) *v.* [-mised; -mis·ing] To guess; conjecture.—*n.* Speculation; guess.

sur·mount (ser-*mownt*) *v.* 1. To conquer; to overcome. 2. To top; to be at the top.—sur·mount·able *adj.*—sur·mount·er *n.*

sur·name (*ser*-naym) *n.* Family name; the last name.—*v.* [sur·named; sur·nam·ing].

sur·pass (ser-*pass*) *v.* To exceed; transcend; outstrip.—sur·pas·sa·ble *adj.*—sur·pass·ing *adj.* —sur·pas·sing·ly *adv.*—sur·pass·ing·ness *n.*

sur·plice (*ser*-pliss) *n.* A white linen vestment worn by priests, deacons, and choristers in the Anglican and Roman Catholic churches.

sur·plus (*ser*-plus) *n.* Excess; unnecessary abundance.—*adj.* Extra; superfluous.—sur·plus·age *n.*

sur·prise (ser-*pryze*) *v.* [sur·prised; sur·pris·ing] 1. To discover unexpectedly. 2. To astonish; amaze.—*n.* 1. Act of surprising. 2. Wonder; astonishment. 3. Unexpected occurrence. —sur·pris·ing *adj.*— -ing·ly *adv.* —sur·pris·al *n.*—sur·priser *n.*

sur·re·al·ism (suh-*ree*-ul-izm) *n.* A school of modern painting which seeks to express the subconscious imagination, usually by an irrational combination of real objects.—sur·re·al·ist *n.*—sur·re·al·ist·ic (suh-ree-uh-*liss*-tik) *adj.* —sur·re·al·ist·ic·al·ly *adv.*

sur·ren·der (suh-*ren*-der) *v.* To submit; yield. —*n.* Submission.

sur·rep·ti·tious (ser-úp-*tish*-us) *adj.* Furtive; secret; stealthy.—sur·rep·ti·tious·ly *adv.*—sur·rep·ti·tious·ness *n.*

sur·rey (*suh*-ree) *n.* A light, fourwheeled, horse-drawn carriage.

sur·ro·gate (*suh*-ruh-gayt) *n.* 1. A deputy; substitute. 2. *Law.* An official presiding over the probate of wills and settlement of estates.—*v.* To put in place of another; substitute.

SURREY

sur·round (suh-*rownd*) *v.* To encircle; encompass.—sur·round·ings *n. pl.* Environment.

sur·tax (*ser*-takss) *n.* An extra tax levied, in addition to basic income tax, upon incomes exceeding a specific figure.

sur·veil·lance (ser-*vayl*-unss) *n.* Supervision; careful watch.—sur·veil·lant *n. & adj.*

sur·vey (ser-*vay*) *v.* 1. To view; to inspect as a whole. 2. To measure a piece of land scientifically. 3. To examine with a view to disposal; to discard.—*n.* (*ser*-vay) 1. A view. 2. Acquisition and arrangement of facts or statistics; a digest of facts. 3. Mathematical measurement of a piece of land.—sur·vey·ing *n.*—sur·vey·or *n.*—sur·vey·or·ship *n.*

sur·vive *v.* [-vived; -viv·ing] 1. To outlive; endure. 2. To live; exist.—sur·viv·al, sur·viv·ance *n.*—sur·vi·vor *n.*—sur·vi·vor·ship *n.*

sus·cep·ti·ble (suh-*sep*-tuh-b'l) *adj.* Vulnerable; subject; exposed.—sus·cep·ti·bil·i·ty (suh-sep-tuh-*bil*-ih-tee)— -ble·ness *n.*— -bly *adv.*

sus·cep·tive (suh-*sep*-tiv) *adj.* 1. Responsive; receptive. 2. Susceptible.—sus·cep·tive·ness *n.* —sus·cep·tiv·i·ty (suh-sep-*tiv*-ih-tee) *n.*

sus·pect (suh-*spekt*) *v.* 1. To surmise; imagine. 2. To distrust; believe guilty.—*adj.* (*sus*-pekt, suh-*spekt*) Distrusted; thought guilty.—*n.* (*sus*-pekt) One believed guilty.

sus·pend (suh-*spend*) *v.* 1. To hang. 2. To stop temporarily; withhold. 3. To debar temporarily from a position.—sus·pend·ed *adj.*

suspended animation. A trancelike arresting of the vital functions, as in persons suffering from severe shock; comatose condition.

sus·pend·ers (suh-*spend*-ers) *n. pl.* Straps worn over the shoulders to hold up trousers.

sus·pense (suh-*spenss*) *n.* Anxiousness; uncertainty.

sus·pen·sion (suh-*spen*-shun) *n.* 1. System by which a device is held suspended. 2. *Music.* The withholding of an expected resolution of

SURPLICE

S

a chord. 3. *Chemistry & Physics*. Small particles of a solid thoroughly mixed but undissolved in a liquid. 4. Delay; interruption. —**suspension bridge**. Bridge held up by a system of cables anchored on either bank.—**sus·pen·sor** *n.*—**sus·pen·so·ry** *adj.*

sus·pi·cion (suh-*spish*-'n) *n.* Mistrust; foreboding; misgiving.—**sus·pi·cious** *adj.*—**sus·pi·cious·ly** *adv.*—**sus·pi·cious·ness** *n.*

sus·tain (sus-*tayn*) *v.* 1. To support; uphold. 2. To hold up; keep supported. 3. To nourish; maintain. 4. To endure; undergo. 5. *Law*. To confirm; establish by evidence. —**sus·tain·a·ble** *adj.*— -**tained** *adj.*— -**tain·er** *n.*

sustaining program. Also **sus·tain·er**. *Radio*. A program not commercially sponsored.

sus·te·nance (*sus*-tuh-n'nss) *n.* 1. Maintenance; means of support. 2. Food; nourishment.

su·ture (*soo*-cher) *n.* 1. A surgical stitch. 2. *Anatomy*. The seam which unites the bones of the skull.—*v.* [su·tured; su·tur·ing] To sew up a wound.

su·ze·rain (*soo*-zuh-rin) *n.* 1. A feudal lord. 2. A nation controlling the political life of another.—*adj.* Most important; sovereign.

su·ze·rain·ty (*soo*-zuh-rin-tee) *n.* Control, esp. political, of one nation over another.

SW *Abbreviation* for **southwest**.

svelte (*svelt*) *adj.* Youthfully slender; supple.

swab (*swob*) *v.* [swabbed; swab·bing] To clean with a swab.—*n.* 1. A mop. 2. *Medical*. A piece of cotton wrapped on a stick for cleansing, or applying medicament.

swad·dle (*swod*-'l) *v.* [swad·dled; swad·dling] To wrap with cloth or clothes, esp. an infant. —**swaddling clothes**.

swag *n.* 1. *Colloquial*. Stolen property; booty. 2. Bundle of belongings carried by an Australian bushman.—**swag·man** *n.*

swag·ger *v.* To walk with a defiant or insolent strut.—**swag·ger·er** *n.*—**swag·ger·ing·ly** *adv.*

swain (*swayn*) *n.* A country boy; esp. one in love.—**swain·ish** *adj.*—**swain·ish·ness** *n.*—**swain** *v.* To court.

swale (*swayl*) *n.* Marshland; meadow.

swal·low (*swol*-oh) *v.* 1. To receive through the throat. 2. To engulf; to absorb. 3. *Colloquial*. To accept without question. 4. To put up with; to bear.—*n.* The amount taken into the gullet at once; a gulp.—**swal·low·er** *n.*

swal·low *n.* A small bird with long wings and deeply forked tail.

swal·low·tail *n.* Man's formal, long-tailed dress suit.

swam. *Past tense of* **swim**.

swamp (*swahmp*) *n.* Low, boggy ground.—*v.* 1. To deluge; to overwhelm. 2. To sink a boat by filling with water.—**swamp·y** *adj.*—**swamp·ish** *adj.*—**swamp·land** *n.*

SWALLOW (1/6 life-size)

swan (*swahn*) *n.* A large, graceful water-bird with white plumage.

swank *n.* Display of wealth or sophistication. —**swank, swank·y** *adj.*—**swank·i·ly** *adv.*—**swank·i·ness** *n.*

SWAN (1/35 life-size)

swans·down *n.* 1. The smaller feathers of a swan, used in quilts and pillows and as trimming. 2. A thick fleecy fabric.

swan song. A final work completed just before death.

swap (*swop*) *v.* [swapped; swap·ping] *Colloquial*. To trade; barter.—*n. Colloquial*. An exchange, esp. of items of equal value.

sward (*swawrd*) *n.* Turf; grass-covered land.—*v.* To cover with grass.

swarm *v.* 1. To teem; to crowd; to abound. 2. To move in a body.—*v.* 1. A large number of insects. 2. A multitude.—**swarm·er** *n.*

swart, swarth *adj.* Dark-colored; swarthy.

swarth·y *adj.* [swarth·i·er; -i·est] Dark-complexioned.—**swarth·i·ly** *adv.*—**swarth·i·ness** *n.*

swash·buck·ler (*swosh*-buk·ler) *n.* A swaggering, boastful adventurer.—**swash·buck·ling** *adj.*

swas·ti·ka (*swoss*-tih·kuh) *n.* An ancient symbol adopted by the German National Socialist Party as its emblem.

swat (*swot*) *v.* [swat·ted; swat·ting] *Colloquial*. To hit; to strike. —*n. Colloquial*. A blow.—**swat·ter** *n.*

SWASTIKA

swath (*swahth*) *n.* An area cleared by the sweep of a blade of a sickle or scythe.

swathe (*swayth*) *v.* [swathed; swath·ing] 1. To envelop; cover heavily. 2. To bind with a band or bandage.—**swath·er** *n.*

sway *v.* 1. To weave or swing from side to side. 2. To oscillate; to fluctuate. 3. To lean. 4. To influence; to prejudice.—*n.* 1. A swinging motion. 2. Rule; dominion. 3. Influence; authority.

swear (*swair*) *v.* [swore; sworn; swear·ing] 1. To affirm solemnly; vow. 2. To make a statement under oath. 3. To administer an oath. 4. To use profane language.—**swear off**. To renounce.—**swear·er** *n.*

sweat (*swet*) *v.* [sweat, sweat·ed; sweat·ing] 1. To perspire; excrete moisture through the skin. 2. To collect moisture in beads on the surface. 3. To labor; drudge. 4. To overwork another. 5. *Slang*. To persecute with questions; use the third degree.—*n.* Perspiration.—**sweat blood**. To endure extreme tension. —**sweat·y** *adj.*—**sweat·i·ly** *adv.*—**sweat·i·ness** *n.*

sweat·er (*swet*-er) *n.* A woolen knit garment for the upper part of the body.

sweat·shop *n.* Shop or factory where employees

work long hours, under hazardous conditions, for substandard pay.

Swede *n.* A native of Sweden.

sweep *v.* [swept; sweep·ing] 1. To brush clean, as with a broom. 2. To move swiftly over. 3. To extend; to encompass.—*n.* 1. A large free motion. 2. Compass; range; expanse. 3. A chimney cleaner. 4. *Nautical.* A steering oar.—**sweep·er** *n.*

sweep·ing *adj.* Broad; all-inclusive.—**sweep·ing·ly** *adv.*—**sweep·ing·ness** *n.*

sweep·ings *n. pl.* Refuse gathered together by a broom.

sweep·stakes *n.* 1. Lottery offering a few large prizes for money received from many participants. 2. [*sing.*] The total wager placed on an event.

sweet *adj.* 1. Agreeable to the taste, as sugar. 2. Pleasing to the senses. 3. Gentle; kind. 4. Beloved. 5. *Music Slang.* Played in simple harmonic and melodic style, esp. in slow tempo.—*n.* 1. A confection. 2. [*pl.*] Candy; confectionery. 3. A beloved person.—**sweet tooth.** Fondness for sweets.—**sweet·en** *v.* —**sweet·en·er** *n.*—**sweet·en·ing** *n.*—**sweet·ish** *adj.*—**sweet·ly** *adv.*—**sweet·ness** *n.*

sweet-eyed	sweet maker	sweet-scented
sweet-faced	sweet-mouthed	sweet shop
sweetfish	sweet-pickled	sweet-tempered

sweet·bread *n.* The pancreas or thymus of a calf or sheep used as food.

sweet·bri·er, sweet·bri·ar (*sweet*-bry-er) *n.* Eglantine; a semi-climbing prickly rose with pale pink flowers and fragrant leaves.

sweet·heart *n.* A beloved person; lover.

sweet marjoram (*mahr*-jer-'m). An aromatic herb used in cooking as seasoning.

sweet·meats *n.* Candy; fruits preserved with sugar.

sweet·pea *n.* A climbing plant carrying sweet scented, beautifully colored flowers.

sweet potato. 1. A vine grown for its sweet-tasting tuberous root, of yellow or orange color. 2. An ocarina.

sweet william. An old-fashioned perennial of the dianthus family of hardy pinks, with clustered flowers of many colors.

SWEET PEA

swell *v.* [swelled; swelled or swol·len; swell·ing] 1. To expand; increase; inflate. 2. To inflate with pride.—*n.* 1. An expansion; rising; surge. 2. *Slang.* A wealthy, fashionable person. 3. A bulge; protuberance.—*adj. Slang.* 1. Wonderful. 2. Stylish. —**swell·ing** *adj. & n.*

swel·ter *v.* To affect or be affected by great heat; sweat.—*n.* An oppressive heat.—**swel·ter·ing** *adj.*—**swel·ter·ing·ly** *adv.*

swept. *Past tense & past participle* of **sweep.**

swerve *v.* [swerved; swerv·ing] 1. To turn aside sharply. 2. To deviate; deflect.—*n.* A rapid turn.

swift *adj.* 1. Rapid; fleet. 2. Prompt; quick. —*n.* A swallowlike bird, very rapid in flight.—**swift·ly** *adv.*—**swift·ness** *n.*

swig *v.* [swigged; swig·ging] To take a long, quick drink.—*n.* A long swallow —**swig·ger** *n.*

swill *v.* 1. To drink greedily; guzzle. 2. To drench in washing. 'To swill a deck.'—*n.* 1. The mixture of liquids and refuse fed to swine. 2. Garbage. 3. A swig of liquor.

SWIFT (1/5 life-size)

swim *v.* [swam; swum; swim·ming] 1. To move in water by means of the limbs or fins. 2. To be immersed or flooded. 3. To float; be buoyed up. 4. To be dizzy; reel.—*n.* The act of moving through the water; a dip.—**swim·mer** *n.*—**swim·ming** *n. & adj.*—**swim·ming·ly** *adv.* Easily; with rapid progress.—**in the swim.** In style; popular.

swin·dle (*swin*-d'l) *v.* [swin·dled; swin·dling] To defraud; cheat deliberately.—*n.* Act of cheating.—**swin·dler** *n.*—**swin·dling** *n.*

swine (*swyne*) *n.* [*sing. & pl.*] 1. A domestic hog. 2. A scoundrel.—**swine·herd** *n.*—**swin·ish** *adj.*—**swin·ish·ly** *adv.*—**swin·ish·ness** *n.*

swing *v.* [swung; swing·ing] 1. To move to and fro; sway. 2. *Nautical.* To move around with the wind or tide. 3. To manage successfully. 4. *Colloquial.* To be hanged. 5. To brandish.—*n.* 1. Swaying; oscillation. 2. A seat suspended from ropes, on which children may ride. 3. *Music Slang.* Modern dance music played in fast tempo with variations. —**swing at** or **take a swing at.** To aim a blow at.—**swing·er** *n.*—**swing·ing** *adj.*—**swing shift.** Shift working in factories and plants from 3 p.m. to midnight.

swipe (*swype*) *v.* [swiped; swip·ing] 1. *Slang* To steal. 2. To give a blow to.—*n.* A blow.

swirl (*swerl*) *v.* To whirl, as in eddies.—*n.* A twisting motion; a whirl.

swish *n.* 1. A swift hissing noise. 2. *Slang.* A homosexual.—*v.* To move sweepingly.

Swiss *n.* 1. A native of Switzerland. 2. The language of Switzerland.—*adj.* Pertaining to Switzerland.—**swiss cheese.** A hard yellow cheese with large holes.

switch *n.* 1. A small flexible rod; a whip. 2. A contrivance for transferring a train from one line of rails to another. 3. A device for turning electric current and lights on and off. 4. A removable tress of hair.—*v.* 1. To whip. 2. To change; shift. 3. To transfer from one track to another. 4. To turn current and lights on and off.—**switch·er** *n.*

switch-back (*n.*)	switchkeeper	switch tender
switchboard	switchman	switchyard

S

Switz·er·land. A country in central Europe. Area: 15,944 sq. mi.

swiv·el (*swiv-'l*) *n.* A coupling which allows the attached object to rotate freely on its axis.—*v.* [swiv·eled, swiv·elled; swiv·el·ing, swiv·el·ling] To turn on a pin or pivot.

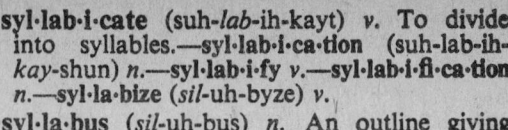

SWIVEL

swivel chain   swivel-hooked
swivel chair   swivellike
swivel gun   swivel lock

swiz·zle (*swiz-'l*) *n.* A drink made of rum or other spirits, sugar, and bitters, poured over crushed ice.—**swizzle stick.** A glass rod for mixing alcoholic drinks.

swob, swob·ber. *Variant spelling* of swab.

swol·len. *Past participle* of swell.

swol·len (*swoh-*len) *adj.* Puffed up; enlarged; inflated.

swoon *v.* To faint; to be overcome.—*n.* A fainting fit.—**swoon·ing·ly** *adv.*

swop. *Variant* of swap.

swoop *v.* To dive sweepingly; pounce down upon.—*n.* A sudden pounce.—**swoop·ing** *adj.*

sword (*sawrd*) *n.* 1. A weapon with a long strong blade fixed into a handle or hilt. 2. War; dissension. 3. A symbol of power and destruction.

SWORDS

sword-armed   swordfishing   sword-shaped
sword bearer   sword grass   swordsman
swordbill   sword knot   swordsmith
swordcraft   swordplay   swordtail

sword·fish *n.* A large, edible salt-water fish.

swore, sworn. *Past tense & past participle* of swear.

sworn *adj.* Avowed; pledged to.

SWORDFISH (1/80 life-size)

swum. *Past participle* of swim.

swung. *Past tense & past participle* of swing.

syb·a·rite (*sib-uh-ryte*) *n.* A voluptuary; one devoted to luxury and pleasure.—**syb·a·rit·ic** (*sib-uh-rit-ik*), **syb·a·rit·i·cal** *adj.*—**syb·a·rit·i·cal·ly** *adv.*—**syb·a·rit·ism** *n.*

syc·a·more (*sik-uh-mor*) *n.* 1. The wide-spreading plane tree or buttonwood often used for street planting. 2. A small fig tree of Egypt and Syria.

syc·o·phant (*sik-uh-f'nt*) *n.* Servile flatterer; fawner.—**syc·o·phan·cy** *n.*—**syc·o·phan·tic** (*sik-uh-fant-ik*), **syc·o·phan·ti·cal** *adj.*—**syc·o·phan·ti·cal·ly** *adv.*

syl·la·ble (*sil-uh-b'l*) *n.* 1. A sound or combination of sounds spoken in one unit. 2. A small detail.—**syl·lab·ic** (*suh-lab-ik*) *adj.*—**syl·lab·i·cal·ly** *adv.*

syl·lab·i·cate (*suh-lab-ih-kayt*) *v.* To divide into syllables.—**syl·lab·i·ca·tion** (*suh-lab-ih-kay-shun*) *n.*—**syl·lab·i·fy** *v.*—**syl·lab·i·fi·ca·tion** *n.*—**syl·la·bize** (*sil-uh-byze*) *v.*

syl·la·bus (*sil-uh-bus*) *n.* An outline giving main headings of a treatise.

syl·lo·gism (*sil-uh-jizm*) *n. Logic.* A form of reasoning consisting of three propositions, of which two are called premises, and the third the conclusion.—**syl·lo·gis·tic** (*sil-uh-jiss-tik*), **syl·lo·gis·ti·cal** *adj.*—**syl·lo·gis·ti·cal·ly** *adv.*

sylph (*silf*) *n.* A graceful and slender woman.—**sylph·id** *n.*—**sylph·ish** *adj.*—**sylph·like** *adj.*

syl·van (*sil-v'n*) *adj.* Forest-like; rustic; rural.—*n.* A rustic.

sym·bol (*sim-b'l*) *n.* 1. An emblem; a token; a mark or sign. 2. *Chemistry & Mathematics.* A sign, letter, or abbreviation, used to replace a word or words.—**sym·bol·ic** (*sim-bol-ik*), **sym·bol·i·cal** *adj.*—**sym·bol·i·cal·ly** *adv.*

sym·bol·ism *n.* Use of symbols to represent things or ideas.—**sym·bol·ist** *n. & adj.*

sym·bol·ize *v.* [sym·bol·ized; sym·bol·iz·ing] To represent by a symbol. 'The stork symbolizes birth.'—**sym·bol·i·za·tion** (*sym-buh-liz-ay-shun*) *n.*

sym·me·try (*sim-uh-tree*) *n.* Balance; proportion; harmony.—**sym·met·ric** (*suh-met-rik*), **sym·met·ri·cal** *adj.*—**sym·met·ri·cal·ly** *adv.*—**sym·met·ri·cal·ness** *n.*

sym·pa·thet·ic (*sim-puh-thet-ik*) *adj.* Agreeable; understanding; favorable.

sym·pa·thize (*sim-puh-thyze*) *v.* [sym·pa·thized; sym·pa·thiz·ing] 1. To commiserate; share another's emotion. 2. To be in harmony; agree.—**sym·pa·thiz·er** *n.*—**sym·pa·thiz·ing** *adj.* — -**thiz·ing·ly** *adv.*

sym·pa·thy (*sim-puh-thee*) *n.* 1. Affinity; congeniality. 2. Compassion; harmony.

sympathy strike. A strike called by a union to support striking workers of another union.

sym·phon·y (*sim-fuh-nee*) *n.* 1. A harmony of sounds; consonance. 2. *Music.* An elaborate composition for full orchestra, usually consisting of three or four movements.—**sym·phon·ic** (*sim-fon-ik*) *adj.*—**sym·pho·ni·ous** (*sim-foh-nee-us*) *adj.*—**sym·pho·ni·ous·ly** *adv.*

sym·po·si·um (*sim-poh-zee-um*) *n.* [*pl.* -sia] 1. A group discussion on a specified subject. 2. A published collection of opinions on a subject.

symp·tom (*simp-tum*) *n.* 1. Sign; mark. 2. *Medical.* An indication of a disease.—**symp·to·mat·ic** (*simp-tuh-mat-ik*), **symp·to·mat·i·cal** *adj.*—**symp·to·mat·i·cal·ly** *adv.*

syn·a·gogue (*sin-uh-gog*) *n.* A Jewish house of worship.—**syn·a·gog·i·cal** (*sin-uh-goj-ih-k'l*) *adj.*

syn·chro·nize (*sing-kruh-nyze*) *v.* [syn·chro·nized; syn·chro·niz·ing] To co-ordinate; coincide in action.—**syn·chro·nism** *n.*—**syn·chro·nis·tic** (*sing-kruh-niss-tik*), **syn·chro·nis·ti·cal** *adj.*—**syn·chro·ni·za·tion** (*sing-kruh-niz-ay-shun*) *n.*—**syn·chro·niz·er** *n.*

syn·chro·nous (*sing*-kruh-nus) *adj.* 1. Concurrent; simultaneous. 2. *Physics.* Having the same period and phase.—**syn·chro·nous·ly** *adv.*—**syn·chro·nous·ness** *n.*

syn·co·pate (*sing*-kuh-payt) *v.* [syn·co·pat·ed; syn·co·pat·ing]. 1. *Music.* To alter rhythm by shifting the accent. 2. To shorten a word by omitting a syllable from the middle.—**syn·co·pa·tion** (sing-kuh-*pay*-shun) *n.*—**syn·co·pa·tor** *n.*

syn·di·cal·ism (*sin*-duh-k'l-izm) *n.* A political doctrine based on establishing communal control of production and a government by trade unions through a revolutionary general strike.—**syn·di·cal·ist** *n. & adj.*—**syn·di·cal·is·tic** (sin-duh-k'l-*iss*-tik) *adj.*

syn·di·cate (*sin*-dih-k't) *n.* An association formed for the promotion of a particular enterprise.—*v.* (*sin*-dih-kayt) [syn·di·cat·ed; syn·di·cat·ing] To release simultaneously copyrighted stories, photographs, etc., on a contract basis to a number of periodicals.—**syn·di·cat·ed** *adj.*

syn·od (*sin*-ud) *n.* 1. A council of churchmen. 2. An assembly; convention.—**syn·od·ic** (sin-*od*-ik), **syn·od·i·cal** *adj.*

syn·o·nym (*sin*-uh-nim) *n.* A word having the same, or nearly the same, meaning as another.—**syn·on·y·mous** (sih-*non*-ih-mus) *adj.* Conveying the same idea; closely related.—**syn·on·y·mous·ly** *adv.*

syn·op·sis (sih-*nop*-siss) *n.* A summary; general abridgment.

syn·tax (*sin*-takss) *n.* The grammatical arrangement of the parts of a sentence.

syn·the·sis (*sin*-thuh-siss) *n.* The combination of separate parts into a whole.—**syn·the·sist** *n.*—**syn·the·size** *v.* [syn·the·sized; syn·the·siz·ing].

syn·thet·ic (sin-*thet*-ik) *adj.* Artificial.—*n.* An artificial product, usually derived from chemical compounds similar to the original natural product.—**syn·thet·i·cal** *adj.*— **-cal·ly** *adv.*

syph·i·lis (*sif*-ih-liss) *n.* A contagious, sometimes hereditary, chronic venereal disease.—**syph·i·lit·ic** *n. & adj.*—**syph·i·lol·o·gist** (sif-ih-*lol*-uh-jist) *n.*—**syph·i·lol·o·gy** *n.*—**syph·i·loid** *adj.*

Syr·a·cuse. 1. An ancient city of Sicily. 2. A city in New York State.— **-cus·an** *adj.*

Syr·i·ac (*sihr*-ee-ak) *n. & adj.* A language formerly used by Christians in the Near East.

sy·rin·ga (sih-*ring*-guh) *n.* 1. The botanical name of the lilac family. 2. An ornamental shrub with fragrant cream-colored flowers; the mock orange.

syr·inge (sih-*rinj*) *n.* An instrument used to draw in a fluid and to eject it with force.—*v.* [syr·inged; syr·ing·ing] To inject with a syringe.

syr·inx (*sihr*-inks) *n.* [*pl.* syr·ing·es] 1. The vocal organ of a bird. 2. A wind instrument composed of reeds of different lengths tied together; the Pipes of Pan.—**sy·rin·ge·al** (sih-*rin*-jee-ul) *adj.*

syr·up, sir·up (*sihr*-up) *n.* A thick viscous solution of sugar.—**syr·up·y, sir·up·y** *adj.*

sys·tem (*siss*-t'm) *n.* 1. A number of parts forming one complex whole. 2. Way; method; series of principles. 3. Regularity; orderliness.—**sys·te·mat·ic** (siss-tuh-*mat*-ik) *adj.*—**sys·tem·at·i·cal** *adj.*— **-mat·ic·al·ly** *adv.*

sys·tem·a·tize (*siss*-t'm-uh-tyze) *v.* [-tized; -tizing] To arrange methodically; present coherently.—**sys·tem·a·tiz·a·tion** (siss-tuh-muh-tiz-*ay*-shun) *n.*—**sys·tem·a·tiz·er** *n.*—**sys·tem·ize** *v.*

sys·to·le (*siss*-tuh-lee) *n.* The contraction of the heart, esp. of the ventricles, which drives the blood into the aorta. See **diastole.**—**sys·tol·ic** (siss-*tol*-ik) *adj.*

T

tab *n.* 1. A small flap or marker. 2. *Colloquial.* A bill, esp. a bar bill.

Ta·bas·co (tuh-*bass*-koh) *n.* Trade-mark for a sharp-tasting sauce for sea food, meat, etc.

tab·by *n.* 1. A striped cat. 2. Watered silk; moiré.—*adj.* Marked with irregular stripes.

tab·er·na·cle (*tab*-er-nak-'l) *n.* A temple; place of worship.

ta·ble (*tay*-b'l) *n.* 1. Article of furniture consisting of a flat surface supported on legs. 2. Food; fare. 'A good table.' 3. A group seated at a table. 4. Condensed arrangement of data; list; index.—*v.* [ta·bled; ta·bling] 1. To arrange in a list; catalogue. 2. To defer discussion of a subject at a meeting.

tab·leau (*tab*-loh) *n.* [*pl.* -leaux] Scene; representation; posed group.

table d'hote (*tab*-luh-*doht*) A restaurant meal served at a fixed price.

ta·ble·land *n.* A plateau; mesa.

ta·ble·spoon *n.* A large spoon; 3 teaspoons.

tab·let *n.* 1. A pad of paper used for writing or drawing. 2. A slab bearing engraved inscriptions. 3. A small medicinal pill.

tab·loid (*tab*-loyd) *n.* A small-sized illustrated newspaper.—*adj.* Of flamboyant journalistic style, featuring photographs and headlines.

ta·boo, ta·bu (tuh-*boo*) *n.* 1. System of religious prohibitions common to certain primitive cultures. 2. A restriction imposed by moral convention.—*adj.* Forbidden.—*v.* To prohibit by social or religious code.

ta·bor (*tay*-ber) *n.* A small drum accompanying a fife, played by the same musician.

tab·u·lar (*tab*-yuh-ler) *adj.* 1. Arranged in a concise form or list. 2. Computed with tables.—**tab·u·lar·ly** *adv.*

tab·u·late (*tab*-yuh-layt) *v.* [-lat·ed; -lat·ing] 1. To list; to arrange in a table. 2. To add; to compute.—**tab·u·la·tion** *n.*—**tab·u·la·tor** *n.*

T

ta·chom·e·ter (tuh-*kom*-uh-ter) *n*. An instrument for gauging the speed of a machine by computing its revolutions per minute.

tac·it (*tass*-it) *adj*. Implied; unspoken.—**tac·it·ly** *adv*.—**tac·it·ness** *n*.

tac·i·turn (*tass*-ih-tern) *adj*. Reserved; habitually silent.—**tac·i·turn·i·ty** *n*.—**tac·i·turn·ly** *adv*.

tack *n*. 1. Small sharp-pointed nail. 2. Course of a sailing ship when close-hauled in the wind. —**a new tack**. A different course of action.—*v*. 1. To fasten; to attach. 2. To sail a vessel into the wind by a zigzag course.

tack·le (*tak*-'l; *Nautical*: *tay*-k'l) *n*. 1. Equipment; gear. 2. System of pulleys and lines for handling heavy weights.

tack·le *v*. [tack·led; tack·ling] 1. To set to work upon, as a task. 2. *Football*. To seize and stop the opposing player having the ball. —*n*. *Football*. 1. One of two players in the line. 2. Act of stopping the player with the ball. —**tack·ler** *n*.

tact *n*. Fine perception; social skill; diplomacy.—**tact·ful** *adj*.—**tact·ful·ness** *n*.—**tact·less** *adj*.—**tact·less·ly** *adv*.—**tact·less·ness** *n*.

TACKLE

tac·tics (*tak*-tikss) *n*. 1. The science and art of disposing and employing military and naval forces in battle. 2. Plan of action.—**tac·tic** *n*. & *adj*.—**tac·ti·cal** *adj*.— -**cal·ly** *adv*.—**tac·ti·cian** *n*.

tac·tile (*tak*-t'l) *adj*. 1. Perceptible by touch. 2. Pertaining to the sense of touch.

tad·pole *n*. The water-breathing larva of certain amphibian animals, esp. the frog.

taf·fe·ta (*taf*-ih-tuh) *n*. Stiff glossy silk or rayon fabric.—**taf·fe·ta** *adj*.

TADPOLE (1/2 life-size)

taff·rail *n*. The rail around a ship's stern.—**taff·rail log**. Instrument for measuring distance traveled by a ship.

taf·fy *n*. A candy made of boiled sugar or molasses.

tag *n*. 1. Tab; strip; tatter. 2. A card or label. 3. A children's game. 4. *Theater*. Final catchword or phrase of a speech or act. —*v*. [tagged; tag·ging] 1. To fasten a card or label upon. 2. To touch, as in the game of tag. 3. *Colloquial*. To follow; to trail after.

tail (*tayl*) *n*. 1. The external termination of the spinal column in animals. 2. Lower or final part; end; rear. 3. *Astronomy*. The luminous train of a comet. 4. Assembly of rudder and stabilizers at the rear of an airplane.—*v*. *Colloquial*. To follow closely; to trail.—*adj*. 1. Last; final. 2. Coming from the rear.

tailband	tailfirst	tailstock
tail-cropped	tailforemost	tail-tied
tail end *n*.	taillight	tailward
tail-end *adj*.	tailpiece	tail wind
tail-ender	tailrace	tailwise

tai·lor *n*. One who makes and repairs outer garments.—*v*. 1. To make clothing. 2. To fit; to shape.—**tai·lored** *adj*. Plain; severe. —**tai·lor·ing** *n*.

tail skid. Skid under an airplane's tail.

tail·spin *n*. Whirling, downward plummeting of an airplane.

taint *v*. To contaminate; to pollute.—*n*. 1. Corruption; pollution. 2. A blemish; a stain. 3. Disgrace.—**taint·ed** *adj*.—**taint·less** *adj*.

Taj Mahal (*tahzh* muh-*hahl*). Famous white marble tomb in India.

take *v*. [took; tak·ing] 1. To seize; grasp. 2. To obtain; win; capture; rent or purchase. 3. To accept; receive; endure. 4. To infer; suppose. 5. To select; choose. 6. To employ; use. 7. To remove; subtract. 8. To perform; undertake. 9. To lead; conduct. 10. To admit of; be adapted to. 11. To occupy; sit or stand in. 12. To act; operate; have effect. 13. *Photography*. To make a photograph of.—*n*. 1. *Colloquial*. Receipts; amount collected. 2. *Motion Pictures*. A scene. 3. *Printing*. Portion of manuscript alloted to a typesetter.—**take aback**. To astonish.—**take after**. To resemble.—**take breath**. To pause; to rest.—**take down**. To write down. —**take heart**. To gain confidence.—**take in**. 1. To observe. 2. To deceive.—**take off**. 1. To rise in flight. 2. *Colloquial*. To burlesque; mimic.—**take on**. 1. To assume, as an appearance or responsibility. 2. *Colloquial*. To make a show of emotion.—**take place**. To occur.—**take to heart**. To feel strongly.—**take to task**. To reprimand.—**take up**. 1. To begin or resume. 2. To tighten up.

take-off *n*. 1. Humorous mimicry. 2. *Aviation*. Act of leaving the ground at the start of a flight.

talc *n*. A very soft mineral used in toilet powder, French chalk, etc.—**talcum powder**. Toilet powder made from talc.

tale *n*. 1. A story; narrative. 2. A rumor; falsehood.—**tale·bear·er** *n*. A gossip.

tal·ent (*tal*-'nt) *n*. Innate skill; endowment; aptitude.—**tal·ent·ed** *adj*.

tales·man (*taylz*-min) *n*. One summoned to jury duty.

tale·tel·ler *n*. 1. A narrator. 2. A gossip. —**tale·tel·ling** *adj*. & *n*.

tal·is·man (*tal*-iss-m'n) *n*. A good-luck charm. —**tal·is·man·ic**, **tal·is·man·i·cal** *adj*.

talk (*tawk*) *v*. 1. To speak; to converse. 2. To gossip. 3. To consult; to confer.—*n*. 1. Conversation; discourse. 2. Report; rumor. 3. Subject of discussion. 4. A conference; discussion.—**talk·a·tive** *adj*.—**talk·a·tive·ly** *adv*. —**talk·a·tive·ness** *n*.

talk·ie *n*. *Colloquial*. A motion picture with sound.

tall (*tawl*) *adj*. 1. High in stature. 2. *Colloquial*. Exaggerated; extravagant.

tal·low (*tal*-oh) *n*. A hard animal fat used for candles, soap, etc.

tal·ly *n.* 1. A count. 2. Mark used in counting. 3. Record; score.—*v.* [tal·lied; tal·ly·ing] 1. To score; to count. 2. To correspond; to agree.—**tal·li·er** *n.*

tal·ly·ho *interj.* A cry of encouragement to hounds on sighting the prey.

Tal·mud *n.* The body of Jewish secular and religious laws.—**Tal·mud·ic** *adj.*

tal·on *n.* Claw, esp. of a bird of prey.

ta·ma·le (tuh-*mah*-lee) *n.* A Mexican food of corn meal and chopped meat, highly seasoned.

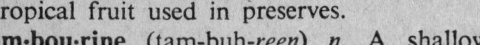
TALONS

tam·a·rind (*tam*-uh-rind) *n.* Acid-tasting tropical fruit used in preserves.

tam·bou·rine (tam-buh-*reen*) *n.* A shallow drum with one head and jingling metal disks set in the side.

tame *adj.* 1. Domesticated; harmless; subdued. 2. Unanimated; flat; dull. —*v.* [tamed; taming] To domesticate; to subdue.—**tame·ly** *adv.* —**tame·ness** *n.*—**tam·er** *n.*

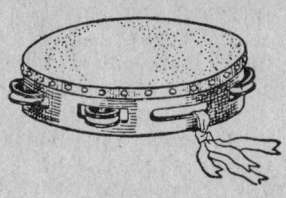
TAMBOURINE

Tam·ma·ny (*tam*-uh-nee). The Democratic organization in Manhattan.

tam·o·shan·ter (tam-uh-*shan*-ter) *n.* A round Scottish cap, usually knitted.

tamp *v.* To drive in or pack down by stamping. —**tam·per** *n.*

tam·per *v.* To meddle; alter; interfere with. —**tam·per·er** *n.*

tan *v.* [tanned; tan·ning] 1. To convert animal skins into leather. 2. To sunburn. 3. To thrash; spank.—*n.* 1. A pale shade of brown. 2. Sunburn. 3. The bark of trees with high tannin content.

tan·a·ger (*tan*-uh-jer) *n.* Bright-colored American songbird.

tan·dem *adj. & adv.* Arranged in a line one behind another.

tang *n.* 1. Flavor; tinge. 2. Invigorating sharpness.

tan·gent (*tan*-j'nt) *n.* 1. *Geometry.* A straight line touching a curve at one point. 2. *Trigonometry.* The sine of an angle divided by the cosine. 3. Abrupt change in course or aim. —*adj.* 1. Touching. 2. *Geometry.* Touching at one point.—**tan·gen·cy** *n.*—**tan·gen·tal, tan·gen·tial** *adj.*—**tan·gen·tal·ly, tan·gen·tial·ly** *adv.*

tan·ge·rine (tan-juh-*reen*) *n.* A small type of orange, with readily-peeling rind; Mandarin orange.

tan·gi·ble (*tan*-juh-b'l) *adj.* 1. Real; material; solid. 2. Able to be accurately valued.—**tan·gi·bil·i·ty** *n.*—**tan·gi·ble·ness** *n.*—**tan·gi·bly** *adv.*

tan·gle (*tang*-g'l) *v.* [tan·gled; tan·gling] 1. To make or become confused, interwoven, knotted. 2. To ensnare; involve.—*n.* 1. A complex knot. 2. Confusion; muddle.—**tan·gler** *n.*

tan·go *n.* A popular Spanish ballroom dance in 2/4 time.

tank *n.* 1. A large vessel for liquids. 2. A swimming pool. 3. An armored military vehicle carrying guns and moving on caterpillar tracks.—*v.* To store or keep in a tank.

tank·ard *n.* A large, lidded drinking vessel with a handle.

tank·er *n.* Cargo ship whose hold is divided into tanklike compartments for liquids.

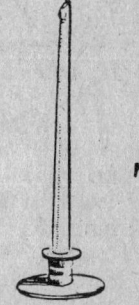
TANKER

tan·ner *n.* One who tans hides.—**tan·ner·y** *n.* [*pl.* -ies] Establishment where hides are tanned.

tan·nin *n.* Substance obtained from the bark of certain trees and used to tan hides.

tan·ta·lize (*tan*-tuh-lyze) *v.* [tan·ta·lized; tan·ta·liz·ing] To tease; to torment.—**tan·ta·li·za·tion** *n.*—**tan·ta·liz·er** *n.*— -liz·ing *adj.*— -liz·ing·ly *adv.*

tan·ta·lum *n.* (*tan*-tuh-l'm) A grayish, acid-resisting metallic element. (*Symbol:* Ta).

tan·ta·mount *adj.* Equivalent; identical.

tan·trum (*tan*-trum) *n.* A fit of temper.

tap *v.* 1. To strike lightly. 2. To pierce in order to let out a liquid. 3. To eavesdrop on a telephone wire.—*n.* 1. A light blow. 2. Plug in a cask, etc. 3. Faucet; small valve on a water pipe. 4. Metal placed on the sole of a shoe.—**on tap.** Ready; at hand for use.—**tap dance.** Dance step performed by rhythmically tapping the feet. —**tap-dance** *v.*

tape *n.* 1. A narrow ribbon, band, strip, etc. 2. *Sports.* Cord stretched across the finish line of a race. —*v.* [taped; tap·ing] 1. To bind with tape. 2. To measure.—**tape·line, tape measure.** Strip marked with linear units for measuring.

ta·per (*tay*-per) *n.* A small wax candle.—*v.* To grow narrow.—**ta·per·ing** *adj.*—**ta·per·ing·ly** *adv.*

TAPER

tap·es·try (*tap*-iss-tree) *n.* Ornamental hangings woven in designs or illustrations.—*v.* [tap·es·tried; -try·ing] To cover or decorate with tapestry.

tape·worm *n.* An intestinal parasite found in man and other animals.

tap·i·o·ca (tap-ee-*oh*-kuh) *n.* A granular starch made from the cassava plant, used for puddings.

T

ta·pir (*tay*-per) *n.* A large, gentle, grass-eating animal common to South America and Malaya.

tap·room *n.* A barroom; a saloon.

tap·root *n.* The deep main plant root.

taps *n.* 1. Military bugle call for "lights out." 2. The same call used in funeral ceremonies.

TAPIR (1/50 life-size)

tar (*tahr*) *n.* 1. A thick black liquid product of wood, coal, peat, etc. 2. A sailor; seaman. —*v.* [tarred; tar·ring].

tar-bedaubed   tarbush   tarpot
tar-bind   tar-dipped   tar-soaked
tar-brand   tar-paved   taryard

tar·an·tel·la (*tair*-'n-tel-uh) *n.* Italian folk dance.

ta·ran·tu·la (tuh-*ran*-choo-luh) *n.* Large poisonous spider.

tar·dy *adj.* 1. Late; overdue. 2. Slow-moving.—**tard·i·ly** *adv.*—**tard·i·ness** *n.*

tare (*tair*) *n. Bible.* A noxious weed.

tar·get *n.* 1. A mark to aim at in shooting. 2. Objective; goal. 3. Butt of ridicule, abuse, etc.

TARANTULA (1/3 life-size)

tar·iff (*tair*-if) *n.* 1. A tax on imports and exports. 2. Tax regulations on imported and exported goods.

tarn (*tahrn*) *n.* Small mountain lake.

tar·nish (*tahr*-nish) *v.* To discolor, esp. metal; to stain; to lose luster.—*n.* Discoloration; stain.—**tar·nish·a·ble** *adj.*—**tar·nished** *adj.*

tar·pau·lin (tahr-*paw*-lin) *n.* Waterproof canvas cover for protection from weather.

tar·pon (*tahr*-p'n) *n.* Large game fish, common in semitropical waters.

tar·ry (*tair*-ee) *v.* [tar·ried; tar·ry·ing] 1. To stay; to remain. 2. To delay.

tart *adj.* 1. Sour; acid. 2. Sharp; sarcastic; cutting.—**tart·ly** *adv.*—**tart·ness** *n.*

tart *n.* 1. A small pie. 2. *Slang.* A harlot.

tar·tan (*tahr*-t'n) *n.* A plaid cloth cross-woven with threads of various colors.

tar·tar (*tahr*-ter) *n.* 1. Acid potassium tartrate used in baking powder, etc. 2. Stain formed on teeth.—**tar·tar·ic** *adj.*

tar·tar *n.* 1. An irascible person. 2. [*cap.*] Member of any of a group of central Asiatic tribes.

task *n.* Job; labor imposed; an undertaking. —*v.* To impose labor upon; to burden.—**task·master** *n.*—**take to task.** To reprimand; to criticize.

task force. Temporary naval unit organized for a specific assignment.

Tass. Official Soviet Russian news agency.

tas·sel (*tass*-'l) *n.* Round, fringed ornament of twisted threads.

taste (*tayst*) *v.* [tast·ed; tast·ing] 1. To perceive flavor through the mouth. 2. To eat a small quantity. 3. To experience; to undergo. 4. To have a certain flavor. —*n.* 1. The sense by which flavor is perceived. 2. Savor; flavor. 3. Discrimination; social or aesthetic discernment. 4. A sample; small portion.—**taste·ful** *adj.*—**taste·ful·ly** *adv.*—**taste·ful·ness** *n.*—**taste·less** *adj.*—**taste·less·ly** *adv.*—**taste·less·ness** *n.*

tast·y (*tayst*-ee) *adj.* [tast·i·er; tast·i·est] Savory.—**tast·i·ly** *adv.*—**tast·i·ness** *n.*

TASSEL

tat *v.* To make lace by looping thread wound on a hand shuttle.—**tat·ting** *n.*

tat·ter *n.* 1. Shred; torn and hanging edge. 2. [*pl.*] Ragged clothing.—**tat·tered** *adj.*

tat·tle (*tat*-'l) *v.* [tat·tled; tat·tling] To tell tales; to betray secrets.—**tat·tler, tat·tle·tale** *n.*

tat·too (tat-*too*) *n.* 1. Indelible design pricked into the skin with dye. 2. *Military.* Call preceding taps.—**tat·too** *v.*—**tat·too·er** *n.* A specialist in the art of tattooing the skin.

taught (*tawt*). *Past tense & past participle* of **teach.**

taunt (*tawnt*) *v.* To mock; torment.—*n.* Scornful remark; insult.—**taunt·ing·ly** *adv.*

taupe (*tohp*) *n.* A grayish-brown color.

Tau·rus (*taw*-rus) *n.* The Bull; the second sign of the Zodiac.

taut (*tawt*) *adj.* Tight; tense.—**taut·en** *v.* To tighten.—**taut·ly** *adv.*—**taut·ness** *n.*

tau·tol·o·gy (taw-*tol*-uh-jee) *n.* [*pl.* tau·tol·o·gies] Redundancy; useless repetition of meaning.—**tau·to·log·i·cal** *adj.*—**tau·to·log·i·cal·ly** *adv.*—**tau·tol·o·gize** (tau-*tol*-uh-jyze) *v.* [-gized; -giz·ing]—**tau·tol·o·gism** *n.*—**tau·tol·o·gist** *n.*

tav·ern (*tav*-ern) *n.* 1. An establishment serving liquor and food. 2. An inn.

taw *n.* 1. A marble used for a shooter. 2. A game of marbles.

taw·dry (*taw*-dree) *adj.* [taw·dri·er; taw·dri·est] Gaudy; flashy; cheap.

taw·ny *adj.* Of a dark golden color; brownish; the color of a lion.

tax *n.* 1. An assessment; a charge levied by law for government expenses. 2. An exaction; an oppressive demand.—*v.* 1. To require payment from. 2. To make demands upon; to strain. 3. To censure; to accuse. —**tax·a·bil·i·ty** *n.*—**tax·a·ble** *adj.*—**tax·a·tion** *n.*

tax-bought   tax-free   tax-paid
tax-burden   tax gatherer   taxpayer
taxeater   tax gathering   taxpaying
taxeating   tax-laden   tax-ridden
tax-exempt   taxman   tax-supported

tax·i (*tak*-see) *n.* An automobile which carries passengers for a fee.—*v.* 1. To travel in a taxi. 2. *Aviation.* To move along the ground before taking off or after landing.

taxiauto	taxicab	taximeter
taxibus	taximan	taxiplane

tax·i·der·my (*tak*-sih-der-mee) *n.* Art of mounting skins of animals or birds to give a lifelike appearance.—**tax·i·der·mist** *n.*

t.b. *Slang.* Tuberculosis.

tea (*tee*) *n.* 1. Small shrub grown in the Far East. 2. The dried leaves of the tea plant. 3. Beverage prepared from tea leaves. 4. An afternoon reception. 5. *Slang.* Marihuana.

tea cake	teacupful	tea shop
tea cart	teakettle	teaspoonful
tea-colored	teapot	teatime

teach (*teech*) *v.* [taught; teach·ing] 1. To instruct; to educate; to impart knowledge or skill.—**teach·a·ble** *adj.*—**teach·er** *n.*—**teach·ing** *n.*

teak (*teek*) *n.* Valuable East Indian wood used for furniture.

teal (*teel*) *n.* A short-necked inland duck.

team *n.* 1. Group engaged in a common activity, as one side in a game. 2. Two or more draft animals harnessed together. —**team·ster** *n.* Driver; one engaged in hauling. —**team up.** To join with others for an activity.

team·work *n.* Close cooperation within a group in accomplishing a common aim.

TEAL (1/15 life-size)

tear (*teer*) *n.* Drop of fluid secreted in the eye by the lachrymal gland.—**tear·drop** *n.*—**tear·ful** *adj.*—**tear·ful·ly** *adv.*

tear-affected	tear-imaged	tear-plagued
tear-bright	tear-kissed	tear-shaped
tear-damped	tear-marked	tearstained
tear-dewed	tear-moist	tear-wet
tear-dimmed	tear-mourned	tear-worn

tear (*tair*) *v.* [tore; torn; tear·ing] 1. To rend; to rip apart. 2. To disrupt by conflict. 3. To rush; to move violently.

tease (*teez*) *v.* [teased; teas·ing] To tantalize; vex; make fun of.—*n.* One who tantalizes or annoys another.—**teas·ing** *adj.*— -**ing·ly** *adv.*

tea·spoon *n.* A small eating spoon.

teat (*teet*) *n.* The nipple; protuberance through which milk is drawn from the breasts or udders of female mammals.

tech·ni·cal (*tek*-nih-kul) *adj.* 1. Pertaining to a specific knowledge, or field of study; highly skilled or trained. 2. *Colloquial.* External; superficial.—**tech·ni·cal·i·ty** (tek-nik-*kal*-uh-tee) *n.*—**tech·ni·cal·ly** *adv.*

Tech·ni·color (*tek*-nih-kul-er) *n.* Patented process of color photography used in motion pictures.

tech·nique (tek-*neek*) *n.* Method or style of execution.—**tech·ni·cian** (tek-*nih*-shun) *n.* 1. A professional worker in a scientific or industrial field. 2. A skilled performer.

tech·noc·ra·cy *n.* A theory of government in which administration would be by scientists and technicians.

tech·nol·o·gy (tek-*nol*-uh-jee) *n.* Knowledge which deals with industrial arts and science. —**tech·no·log·ic, tech·no·log·i·cal** *adj.*—**tech·no·log·i·cal·ly** *adv.*—**tech·nol·o·gist** *n.*

Te Deum (tee *dee*-um). Hymn of praise to God.

te·di·ous (*tee*-dee-us) *adj.* Monotonous; dull; tiresome.—**ted·i·ous·ly** *adv.*—**ted·i·ous·ness** *n.*

te·di·um (*tee*-dee-um) *n.* Monotony.

tee *n.* A small mound of earth from which the ball is struck in playing golf.

teem *v.* To swarm; to abound.—**teem·er** *n.* —**teem·ing** *adj.*

teens *n. pl.* The adolescent years from thirteen to nineteen.—**teen-age** *adj.*—**teen-ager** *n. Slang.* An adolescent.

tee·pee *n.* A type of North American Indian tent.

tee·ter *v.* To totter; to wobble.—*n.* An oscillation.

teeth. *Plural of* tooth.

tee·to·tal·er (tee-*toh*-t'l-er) *n.* One who abstains from all alcoholic drink.—**tee·to·tal** *adj.* 1. *Colloquial.* Total. 2. Abstemious.—**tee·to·tal·ly** *adv.*—**tee·to·tal·ism** *n.* —**tee·to·tal·ist** *n.*

TEEPEE

teg·u·ment (*teg*-yuh-m'nt) *n.* Covering; skin; shell.

tel·e·cast *n.* A television broadcast.

tel·e·gram (*tel*-eh-gram) *n.* A communication sent by telegraph; a wire.

tel·e·graph (*tel*-eh-graf) *n.* An electric transmission by which messages are sent by wires across distances.—**tel·e·graph·ic, -i·cal** *adj.* —**i·cal·ly** *adv.*—**te·leg·ra·phist, te·leg·ra·phy** *n.*

te·lep·a·thy (teh-*lep*-uh-thee) *n.* Belief that thoughts and feelings can be transmitted from one person to another without physical communication.—**tel·e·path·ic** *adj.*—**tel·e·path·i·cal·ly** *adv.*—**te·lep·a·thist** *n.*

tel·e·phone (*tel*-eh-fohn) *n.* An instrument for transmitting speech over distances by means of electric currents through a wire.—*v.* [tel·e·phoned; tel·e·phon·ing] To communicate by telephone.—**te·leph·o·ny** (teh-*lef*-uh-nee) *n.* Art and science of such transmission.—**tel·e·phon·er** *n.*—**tel·e·phon·ic** *adj.*—**tel·e·phon·i·cal·ly** *adv.*

tel·e·pho·to (-*foh*-toh) *adj.* 1. Relating to transmission of photographs by a system of telegraphy. 2. Pertaining to telescopic lenses used for photography.—**tele·pho·to·graph** *n.* 1. Photograph transmitted by telegraphy. 2. Photograph taken through a telescopic lens.—**tel·e·pho·tog·ra·phy** *n.*—**tel·e·pho·to·graph·ic** *adj.*

T

tel·e·scope (*tel*-eh-skohp) *n.* An optical instrument by which distant objects are made more distinct.—*v.* [-scoped;-scop·ing] To drive one object partially into another.—**tel·e·scop·ic**, **-scop·i·cal** *adj.*— **-scop·i·cal·ly** *adv.*—**te·les·co·pist** *n.*—**te·les·cop·y** *n.*

TELESCOPE

tel·e·type·writ·er *n.* Machine, operated as a typewriter, for transmitting and reproducing text by telegraphy.—**Tel·e·type** *n.* Trade-mark name for such a machine.

tel·e·vise *v.* To project a scene or event via television.

tel·e·vi·sion (*tel*-eh-vizh-'n) *n.* The instantaneous transmission and reproduction of scenes and images through the medium of electrical impulses or radio waves.—**tel·e·vi·sion·al**, **tel·e·vi·sion·ar·y** *adj.*—**tel·e·vi·sor** *n.*

tell *v.* [told; tell·ing] 1. To utter; say. 2. To relate; narrate. 3. To report; disclose. 4. To recognize; determine. 5. To count; number. 6. To bid; order.—**tell off**. *Colloquial.* To give somebody a piece of one's mind.

tell·er *n.* 1. A bank employee who receives and disburses money. 2. One appointed to collect and count ballots. 3. A narrator.

tell·ing *adj.* Effective; striking.—**tel·ling** *adv.*

tell·tale *n.* 1. A tattler. 2. A sign; an indication.—*adj.* Betraying.

te·mer·i·ty (tuh-*mehr*-uh-tee) *n.* Audacity; effrontery.

tem·per *v.* 1. To moderate; to qualify. 2. To change in hardness or consistency. 'To temper steel.'—*n.* 1. Anger; passion. 2. Disposition; state of mind. 3. The condition of hardness, esp. of a metal.—**tem·per·a·ble** *adj.* —**tem·pered** *adj.*—**tem·per·er** *n.*—**tem·per·ing** *n.*

tem·per·a (*tem*-per-uh) *n.* Painting technique using water-soluble paints with an egg white solution as the binder.

tem·per·a·ment (*tem*-pruh-m'nt) *n.* Disposition; personality; character.—**tem·per·a·ment·al** *adj.* Given to sudden changes in mood. —**tem·per·a·men·tal·ly** *adv.*

tem·per·ance (*tem*-per-unss) *n.* Moderation; sobriety.

tem·per·ate (*tem*-per-it) *adj.* 1. Moderate. 2. Sober; unimpassioned.—**tem·per·ate·ly** *adv.* —**tem·per·ate·ness** *n.*

tem·per·a·ture (*tem*-pruh-cher) *n.* The degree of heat or cold in a body or place.

tem·pest (*tem*-p'st) *n.* 1. A violent windstorm. 2. A tumult; commotion.—**tem·pest·u·ous** *adj.*—**tem·pest·u·ous·ly** *adv.*—**tem·pest·u·ous·ness** *n.*

tempest-beaten	tempest-scattered
tempest-blown	tempest-sundered
tempest-driven	tempest-swept
tempest-flung	tempest-torn
tempest-gripped	tempest-tossed
tempestproof	tempest-winged
tempest-rocked	tempest-worn

tem·ple (*tem*-p'l) *n.* 1. A house of worship. 2. Either side of the forehead.—**tem·pled** *adj.*

tem·po (*tem*-poh) *n.* [*pl.* tem·pi; tem·pos] 1. The rate of speed of a piece of music. 2. Rhythm; measured motion.

tem·por·al (*tem*-puh-r'l) *adj.* 1. Transitory; short-lived; mortal. 2. Secular; lay. 3. *Anatomy.* Pertaining to the temple.—**tem·por·al·i·ty** *n.*—**tem·por·al·ly** *adv.*—**tem·por·al·ness** *n.*

tem·po·rar·y (*tem*-peh-rair-ee) *adj.* Transitory; brief.—**tem·po·rar·i·ly** *adv.*— **-rar·i·ness** *n.*

tem·po·rize (*tem*-per-yze) *v.* [tem·po·rized; tem·po·riz·ing] To compromise; appear to yield.—**tem·po·ri·za·tion** *n.*—**tem·po·riz·er** *n.*

tempt *v.* 1. To entice; lure. 2. To provoke; incite.—**temp·ta·tion** *n.*—**tempt·er** *n.*—**tempt·ress** *n.*—**tempt·ing** *adj.*— **-ing·ly** *adv.*— **-ing·ness** *n.*

ten *n.* The number represented by the symbol 10.—*adj.* Consisting of 10.—**tenth** *adj.* & *n.* **tenth·ly** *adv.*

ten·a·ble (*ten*-uh-b'l) *adj.* Defensible.

te·na·cious (teh-*nay*-shuss) *adj.* 1. Sturdy; stalwart. 2. Dogged; stubborn. 3. Adhesive; sticky.—**te·na·cious·ly** *adv.*—**te·na·cious·ness** *n.* —**te·nac·i·ty** (teh-*nass*-ih-tee) *n.*

ten·ant (*ten*-'nt) *n.* One who rents land or a dwelling place from an owner; a lessee.—*v.* To occupy.—**ten·an·cy** *n.*—**ten·ant·a·ble** *adj.* —**ten·ant·less** *adj.*—**ten·ant·ry** *n.*

tend *v.* 1. To serve; take care of; look after. 2. To move in a certain direction; incline.

tend·en·cy (*tend*-en-see) *n.* [*pl.* -cies] Inclination; trend; propensity.

ten·der *v.* To offer; proffer.—*n.* 1. *Law.* An offer of money or service in payment of a debt or liability. 2. An offer in writing to execute some task or to supply materials at a certain price. 3. Any bid.—**ten·der·er** *n.*

tend·er *n.* 1. *Nautical.* Small boat for transportation to and from a ship. 2. *Railroad.* A car hooked to a locomotive to carry fuel and water. 3. A caretaker.

ten·der *adj.* [ten·der·er; ten·der·est] 1. Compassionate; humane. 2. Warm; affectionate. 3. Delicate; soft; fragile. 4. Immature. 5. Susceptible, esp. to pain. 6. Careful; considerate.—**ten·der·ly** *adv.*—**ten·der·ness** *n.*

tender-bearded	tender looking
tender-bladed	tender-natured
tender-colored	tender-rooted
tender-conscienced	tender-shelled
tender-eyed	tender-skinned
tender-handed	tender-souled
tender heart	tender-tempered
tender-hearted	tender-witted

ten·der·foot *n.* One unused to hardships.

ten·der·loin *n.* 1. A tender cut of beef or pork from either side of the backbone. 2. *Slang.* A vice-ridden section in a large city.

ten·don (*ten*-d'n) *n.* *Anatomy.* A hard bundle of fibers attaching muscles to other structures; a sinew.

ten·dril (*ten*-dril) *n.* Vinelike clinging shoot of a climbing plant.

ten·e·ment (*ten*-eh-m'nt) *n.* 1. A dwelling. 2. A room or apartment, usually of inferior grade, for rental occupancy.—tenement house. An old rundown apartment building.

ten·et (*ten*-et) *n.* A doctrine; a dogma.

ten·fold *adj.* Ten times.

ten·nis *n.* A ball game played with rackets on a marked court divided by a net.

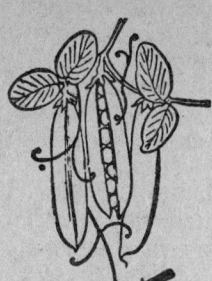

TENDRILS

ten·or (*ten*-er) *n.* 1. Drift; trend. 2. Substance; import. 3. *Music.* The highest of the adult male voices; singer with a tenor voice.

ten·pin *n.* A pin used in the bowling game of ten·pins.

tense (*tenss*) *adj.* 1. Tight; taut; strained. 2. Stiff; inflexible.—*n.* *Grammar.* Inflection of a verb expressing time of action.—tense·ly *adv.*—tense·ness *n.*

ten·sile (*ten*-sil) *adj.* Capable of strain.

ten·sion (*ten*-sh'n) *n.* 1. Strain; stress. 2. Tautness; stretching. —ten·si·ty (*ten*-sih-tee) *n.*

tent *n.* A portable shelter, usually made of canvas stretched over supporting poles and pegged to the ground.—*v.* To camp out.—tent·ed *adj.*

TENPIN

ten·ta·cle (*ten*-tuh-k'l) *n.* An elongated organ of animals and insects used for exploration; a feeler.—ten·tac·u·lar *adj.*

ten·ta·tive (*ten*-tuh-tiv) *adj.* Provisional; experimental.—ten·ta·tive·ly *adv.*—ten·ta·tive·ness *n.*

ten·ter·hook *n.* A sharp, hooked nail for stretching cloth on a frame.

ten·u·ous (*ten*-yoo-us) *adj.* 1. Thin; slender. 2. Diluted; rare. 3. Vague; unconvincing. —ten·u·ous·ly *adv.*—-ous·ness *n.*—ten·u·i·ty *n.*

ten·ure (*ten*-yoor) *n.* 1. The act or right of holding, esp. land. 2. Terms or period of holding.—ten·u·ri·al *adj.*—ten·u·ri·al·ly *adv.*

tep·ee (*tep*-ee) *n.* A teepee.

tep·id (*tep*-id) *adj.* Lukewarm.—tep·id·ness *n.* —te·pid·i·ty *n.*—tep·id·ly *adj.*

term *n.* 1. A fixed period. 2. A division of the school year; semester. 3. Time during which a law court is open for trials. 4. A precise expression; designative word. 5. [*pl.*] Language. 6. [*pl.*] Conditions; stipulations. 'Terms of the contract.' 7. [*pl.*] Relationship; agreement. 'My employees are on good terms with me.' 8. *Mathematics.* A component. —*v.* To name; call.—term·er *n.*

ter·ma·gant (*ter*-muh-g'nt) *n.* A shrew; virago.

ter·mi·nal (*ter*-mih-n'l) *adj.* Final; concluding. —*n.* A final point, location, or junction.

'Grand Central Terminal.'—ter·mi·nal·ly *adv.*

ter·mi·nate (*ter*-mih-nayt) *v.* [ter·mi·nat·ed; ter·mi·nat·ing] To finish; conclude; end.—ter·mi·na·tion *n.*— -tion·al *adj.*—ter·mi·na·tive (*ter*-min-ay-tiv) *n.*—ter·mi·na·tive·ly *adv.*—ter·mi·na·tor *n.*

ter·mi·nol·o·gy (ter-mih-*nol*-uh-jee) *n.* Nomenclature; special vocabulary; cant; jargon. —ter·mi·no·log·i·cal *adj.*—ter·mi·no·log·i·cal·ly *adv.*

ter·mi·nus (*ter*-mih-nus) [*pl.* -ni, -nus·es] *n.* 1. End; limit. 2. Station at the end of a transportation line.

ter·mite (*ter*-myte) *n.* A pale-colored, wood-eating insect with antlike habits.

tern *n.* A small gull-like sea bird, common on the Atlantic coast.

terp·si·cho·re·an (terp-sih-kuh-*ree* un) *adj.* Pertaining to dancing.

ter·race (*tehr*-iss) *n.* 1. An embankment; a raised platform or level of earth. 2. A flat roof of a house.—*v.* [ter·raced; ter·rac·ing].

TERN (1/12 life-size)

ter·ra cot·ta (*tehr*-uh *kot*-uh) 1. A mixture of clay and sand glazed and baked to the hardness of stone, used for statues, vases, etc. 2. The reddish-brown color of baked clay. —ter·ra-cot·ta *adj.*

ter·ra·pin (*tehr*-uh-pin) *n.* Edible fresh-water turtle.

ter·rain (teh-*rayn*) *n.* Surrounding landscape.

ter·rar·i·um (teh-*rair*-ee-um) *n.* Glass tank in which non-aquatic plants or animals are raised.

ter·res·tri·al (teh-*ress*-tree-ul) *adj.* Earthly; mundane.—*n.* A being who lives on the earth. —ter·res·tri·al·ly *adv.*

terre-verte (*tair*-vairt) *n.* A dull green pigment.

ter·ri·ble (*tehr*-uh-b'l) *adj.* Frightful; fearful; awful.—ter·ri·ble·ness *n.*—ter·ri·bly *adv.*

ter·ri·er (*tehr*-ee-er) *n.* A small, usually short-haired dog, formerly used to hunt small game.

ter·rif·ic (teh-*rif*-ik) *adj.* 1. Terrible; dreadful. 2. *Colloquial.* Sensational; tremendous. *n.*—ter·rif·i·cal·ly, ter·rif·ic·ly *adv.*

ter·ri·fy (*tehr*-ih-fy) *v.* [ter·ri·fied; ter·ri·fy·ing] To frighten; horrify; fill with alarm.

TERRIER (1/15 life-size)

ter·ri·to·ry (*tehr*-ih-toh-ree) *n.* 1. Land under the jurisdiction of any nation, state, or city. 2. [*cap.*]. In U.S., a region with autonomous legislature under a federally appointed executive. 3. Region; large tract of land. 4. An

T

assigned area.—ter·ri·to·ri·al *adj.*—-al·ly *adv.*

ter·ror (*tehr*-er) *n.* 1. Desperate fear. 2. Cause of fright and apprehension. 3. *Colloquial.* A rascal.—ter·ror·ism *n.* Systematic intimidation. —ter·ror·ist *n.*— -is·tic *adj.*—ter·ror·ize *v.* [-ized; -iz·ing]—ter·ror·i·za·tion *n.*—-ror·iz·er *n.*

terse (*terss*) *adj.* Concise; pithy; brief.—terse·ly *adv.*—terse·ness *n.*

ter·ti·ar·y (*ter*-shee-er-ee) *adj.* Third in number, rank, or degree.—*n.* [*cap.*] *Geology.* The cenozoic period, or age of mammals.

ter·za ri·ma (*tert*-sah *ree*-mah). Verse form, usually in iambic pentameter, grouping every three stanzas by a continuous rhyme scheme.

tes·sel·late (*tess*-eh-layt) *v.* To inlay, esp. with square tiles.—tes·sel·la·tion *n.*

test 1. A series of questions or problems; an examination; trial of ability or character. 2. Criterion or standard.—*v.* 1. To subject to an examination. 2. To prove by experiment.—test·a·ble *adj.*—test·er *n.*

tes·ta·ment *n.* 1. *Law.* A last will. 2. [*cap.*] Each of the two large divisions of the Bible. 'The Old and the New Testaments.'—tes·ta·ment·al *adj.*—tes·ta·men·ta·ry *adj.*

tes·ti·cle (*tess*-tih-k'l) *n.* A testis.

tes·ti·fy *v.* [tes·ti·fied; tes·ti·fy·ing] 1. *Law.* To assert as a sworn witness. 2. To affirm; support.—tes·ti·fi·ca·tion *n.*—test·i·fi·er *n.*

tes·ti·mo·ni·al (tess-tih-*moh*-nee-ul) *n.* A proof of character or worth.—test·i·mo·ni·al *adj.*

tes·ti·mo·ny (*tess*-tih-moh-nee) *n.* 1. *Law.* Sworn evidence. 2. Presentation of findings; affirmation. 3. Proof.

tes·tis *n.* [*pl.* tes·tes] Male reproductive gland, homologous to the ovary in the female.

test tube. A cylindrical glass container used in scientific experiments.

tes·ty (*tess*-tee) *adj.* [-ti·er; -ti·est] Short-tempered; irascible.—tes·ti·ly *adv.*—tes·ti·ness *n.*

tet·a·nus (*tet*-uh-nus) *n.* Infectious disease causing muscular spasm; lockjaw.

teth·er *n.* A leash confining an animal to a limited area.—*v.* To tie up; confine on a leash.

tet·ra·chlo·ride *n.* A chemical compound containing four atoms of chlorine.

tet·rad (*tet*-r'd) *n.* A group of four.

tet·ra·gon (*tet*-ruh-gon) *n.* Plane four-sided figure.

tet·ra·he·dron (tet-ruh-*hee*-drun) *n. Geometry.* Four-sided solid figure, as a pyramid.—tet·ra·he·dral *adj.*

te·tram·e·ter (teh-*tram*-eh-ter) *n.* Verse form having four beats to the line.

tet·ra·syl·la·ble (tet-ruh-*sil*-uh-b'l) *n.* Word of four syllables.—tet·ra·syl·lab·ic *adj.*

Teu·ton (*too*-t'n; *tyoo*-) *n.* A German; one of Germanic descent.—Teu·ton·ic (too-*ton*-ik) *adj.*

TETRAHEDRON

text *n.* 1. Word-for-word content; original version. 2. Printed matter; literary contents. 3. A short passage, esp. from the Bible, chosen as a theme.

text·book *n.* A standard student's manual on a particular subject.

tex·tile (*tekss*-til, -tyle) *n.* Fabric; woven goods. —tex·tile *adj.*

tex·tu·al (*tekss*-choo-ul) *adj.* Pertaining to original content or wording.—tex·tu·al·ly *adv.*

tex·ture (*tekss*-cher) *n.* Quality of surface; visible or tactile organic pattern.—tex·tur·al *adj.*—tex·tur·al·ly *adv.*

thal·li·um (*thal*-ee-um) *n.* Malleable grayish metallic element. (*Symbol:* Te).

than *conj.* In comparison with or to. 'More than ever; greater than he.'

thane (*thayn*) *n.* Ancient Anglo-Saxon title.

thank *v.* 1. To express appreciation; feel gratitude. 2. To hold responsible; attribute to.—*n.* [*pl.*] 1. Gratitude; recognition. 2. *Colloquial.* Thank you.—thank·ful *adj.*—thank·ful·ly *adv.*—thank·ful·ness *n.*—thank·less *adj.* —thank·less·ly *adv.*—thank·less·ness *n.*

that *adj.* The one mentioned; the one over there. 'Sit in that chair.'—*adv.* Such; in so great degree.—*pronoun.* 1. The one mentioned previously; the one farthest away. 'Give me that.' 2. Used to express approbation or emphasis. 'That's a boy!' 3. Who; which. —*conj.* 1. Because; it being. 2. So; for which; as a result of which. 3. If only; how can.

thatch *n.* Straw used to cover a roof.—*v.* To cover with thatch. —thatch·er *n.* —thatch·ing *n.*—thatch·y *adj.*

THATCH ROOF

thaw *v.* To melt or cause to melt; grow milder. —*n.* A warm spell causing snow to melt. —thaw·er *n.*

the (*thuh*; *thee*) *Definite article* or *adj.* 1. One in particular; one specifically mentioned. 'There is the girl.' 2. Any one of a species. 'As sweet as the rose.'—*adv.* By so much. 'The greater the man.'

the·a·ter, the·a·tre (*thee*-uh-ter) *n.* 1. Building or auditorium designed for presentation of plays, recitals, motion pictures, etc. 2. Drama; the stage. 3. Dramatic effectiveness. 'A sense of theater.' 4. Location of activity; sphere of operation.

the·at·ri·cal (thee-*at*-rih-k'l) *adj.* 1. Of the theater. 2. Also the·at·ric. Artificial; showy. —*n.* [*pl.*] Dramatic presentations.—the·at·ri·cal·ism *n.*—the·at·ri·cal·ly *adv.*—the·at·rics *n.* dramatic art.

thee. *Archaic* and *liturgical form* of you.

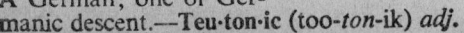

theft n. Robbery; illegal seizure; stealing.

their (thair) adj. Belonging or pertaining to them.—**their, theirs** pron. Possessive case of they.

the·ism (thee-izm) n. Belief in the existence of one God, active in the control of nature, as opposed to **pantheism** or **deism**.—**the·ist** n. —**the·is·tic, the·is·ti·cal** adj.—**the·is·ti·cal·ly** adv.

them pron. Objective case of they.

theme (theem) n. 1. Topic; primary idea. 2. A student's essay. 3. The basic melody in a musical composition.—**theme song**. 1. Radio. Tune identified with a particular program or featured player; signature. 2. Slang. Obsession.—**the·mat·ic, the·mat·i·cal** adj.—**the·mat·i·cal·ly** adv.—**the·ma·tist** n.

them·selves pron. 1. Intensive form of they. 2. Plural of himself, herself, itself.

then adv. 1. At the time in question. 2. Directly following. 3. In that case. 4. At another time, as opposed to now.—**but then**. On the other hand; however.—**by then**. At a specified time.—**now and then**. Occasionally. —**till then**. Previous to an anticipated time or condition.

thence (thenss) adv. 1. From which. 2. As an outcome; therefore. 3. Away.

the·oc·ra·cy (thee-ok-ruh-see) n. [pl. -cies]. State governed by God or his priests.

the·ol·ogy (thee-ol-uh-jee) n. Study of religious philosophy and doctrine.—**the·o·lo·gi·an** n. 1. A clergyman. 2. A religious scholar. —**the·o·log·i·cal** adj.—**the·o·log·i·cal·ly** adv.

the·o·rem (thee-uh-rum) n. 1. Mathematics. A rule which must be proved; a proposition. 2. A statement accepted as established truth. —**the·o·re·mat·ic, the·o·re·mat·i·cal** adj.

the·o·ry (thee-uh-ree) n. 1. A proposed explanation or conclusion; an analysis. 2. An underlying purpose or plan; a guide to action. 3. The principles of an art or science. 4. Science. A philosophical presentation of a natural law.—**the·o·ret·ic, the·o·ret·i·cal** adj.—**the·o·ret·i·cal·ly** adv.—**the·o·rist** n.—**the·o·ri·za·tion** n.—**the·o·rize** v. [-ized; -iz·ing]—**the·o·riz·er** n.

ther·a·peu·tic, ther·a·peu·ti·cal (thehr-uh-pyoo-tik, -tih-k'l) adj. Curative; pertaining to treatment of disease.—n. [pl.] Branch of medicine dealing with treatment of disease.—**ther·a·peu·ti·cal·ly** adv.—**ther·a·peu·tist** n. One skilled in the practice of therapeutics.

ther·a·py (thehr-uh-pee) n. Curative treatment.

there (thair) adv. 1. In or to a specified farther place. 'Here or there.' 2. In that respect; at that.—**there·a·bouts** adv. Approximately; in that neighborhood.—**there·aft·er** adv. From that time on.—**there·at** adv. At which.—**there·by** adv. By means of; through.—**there·fore** conj. Consequently; hence.

thereabout	therein	thereto
thereabove	thereinafter	theretofore
thereafterward	thereinbefore	thereunto
thereagainst	thereinto	thereupon
thereamong	thereof	therewith
therefrom	thereon	therewithal

ther·mal (ther-m'l), **ther·mic** (-mik) adj. 1. Pertaining to heat. 2. Hot.—**ther·mal·ly** adv.

thermo- prefix. Heat; heat-conveying; heat-projecting, etc.

thermoanesthesia	thermogeography
thermobarometer	thermograph
thermobattery	thermo-inhibitory
thermocautery	thermokinematic
thermochemical	thermokinematics
thermochemistry	thermomotive
thermocurrent	thermostatics
thermodiffusion	thermotank
thermogalvanometer	thermotensile
thermogenerator	thermotherapy
thermogenerative	thermotropic
thermogenesis	thermotropism

ther·mo·dy·nam·ics (ther-moh-dy-nam-ikss) n. sing. Science of the mechanics of heat.—**ther·mo·dy·nam·ic, -nam·i·cal** adj.

ther·mo·e·lec·tric·i·ty (ther-moh-ee-lek-trih-sih-tee) n. Electricity produced by the action of heat on various conductors.—**ther·mo·e·lec·tric, -e·lec·tri·cal** adj.—**ther·mo·e·lec·tric·al·ly** adv.

ther·mom·e·ter (ther-mom-eh-ter) n. An instrument which registers degrees of temperature, usually a thin glass tube containing a liquid which varies in level according to temperature.—**ther·mo·met·ric, ther·mo·met·ri·cal** adj.—**ther·mo·met·ri·cal·ly** adv.—**ther·mom·e·try** n.

Ther·mos (ther-mus) n. Trade-mark name of a vacuum bottle designed to keep liquids hot or cold.

ther·mo·stat (ther-muh-stat) n. Device to regulate automatically the temperature of a furnace, motor, etc.—**ther·mo·stat·ic** adj.—**ther·mo·stat·i·cal·ly** adv.—**ther·mo·stat·ics** n.

THERMOM-
ETER

the·sau·rus (theh-saw-rus) n. A treasury; hence, a collection, esp. of words; a lexicon.

these. Plural of this.

The·seus (thee-sooss) Mythology. Main legendary hero of Athens.—**The·se·an** (theh-see-un) adj.

the·sis (thee-siss) n. [pl. the·ses] 1. Argument; position; formulated viewpoint. 2. An essay. 3. Logic. The primary statement. 4. Music. An accented beat. 5. Prosody. An unstressed syllable; a dropping of the voice.

Thes·pi·an (thess-pee-un) adj. 1. Pertaining to Thespis, the creator of Greek drama. 2. Tragic; dramatic.—n. An actor.

The·tis (thee-tiss) n. 1. Greek Mythology. A Nereid; the mother of Achilles and a symbol of water. 2. Astronomy. A minor planet between Mars and Jupiter.

they. Pron. Plural of all third person pronouns.

thiamin chloride. Also **thiamine chloride**. n. Vitamin B_1.

thick adj. 1. Deep; third-dimensional. 2. Heavy; solid. 3. Dense; close-set; compact. 4. Indistinct; mumbled; hoarse. 5. Stupid; dull. 6. Turbid; soggy. 7. Slang. In-

T

timate; on confidential terms.—**thick·ness** *n.*
—Denseness; impenetrability.—*adv.* Densely.

thick-ankled	thick-jawed	thick-rinded
thick-barked	thick-jeweled	thick-rooted
thick-barred	thick-laid	thick-set
thick-bedded	thick-leaved	thick-shadowed
thick-billed	thick-legged	thick-shafted
thick-blooded	thick-lined	thick-shelled
thick-bodied	thick-lipped	thick-sided
thick-bottomed	thick looking	thick skin
thick-eared	thick-maned	thick-skinned
thick-fingered	thick-necked	thickskull
thick-flanked	thick-packed	thick-walled
thick-haired	thickpated	thickwit
thickhead	thick-peopled	thick-wooded
thickheaded	thick-piled	thick-woven
thick-hided	thick-ribbed	thick-wrought

thick·en *v.* 1. To make heavier; to grow denser; to congeal. 2. To complicate; to intensify.—**thick·en·er** *n.*—**thick·en·ing** *adj. & n.*

thick·et *n.* A clump of shrubbery; a thick grove.

thief (*theef*) *n.* [*pl.* thieves] One who steals without open violence.

thieve *v.* [thieved; thiev·ing] To steal; to take by theft.—**thiev·er·y** *n.*—**thiev·ish** *adj.*—**thiev·ish·ly** *adv.*—**thiev·ish·ness** *n.*

thigh (*thy*) *n.* Portion of the leg between the knee and trunk.

thim·ble (*thim·b'l*) *n.* Metal cap for the finger worn while sewing.

thimble-crowned	thimble making	thimblerigger
thimble-eye	thimbleman	thimblerigging
thimble-eyed	thimble-pie	thimble-shaped
thimble maker	thimblerig	thimble-sized

thin *adj.* 1. Slim; of slight thickness or depth. 2. Flimsy; transparent; insubstantial. 3. Rarefied; attenuated. 4. Sparse; meager. 5. High-keyed; without resonance.—*v.* 1. To become or make slender. 2. To space out; diminish.

thine *pron. & adj. Archaic & liturgical form of yours*:—used instead of thy before a vowel or h.

thing *n.* 1. An object; entity; article. 2. An inanimate object. 3. An event; circumstance; matter. 4. A detail; an iota. 'He doesn't know a thing.' 5. [*pl.*] Belongings; personal effects.—**the thing.** Proper; according to convention.

think *v.* [thought; think·ing] 1. To meditate; reflect; engage the mind. 2. To believe; consider; hold an opinion. 3. To intend; to plan. 4. To recollect; call to mind. 5. To venture; to dare.—**think·a·ble** *adj.* Conceivable; to be considered.—**think·er** *n.* A meditative person; a philosopher.

think·ing *adj.* Rational.—**think·ing·ly** *adv.* Intentionally.

third (*therd*) *adj.* Next in order to the second in position, time, value, or rank.—*n.* 1. One of three equal parts of a whole. 2. *Music.* An interval of a major and a minor tone, sometimes including a semitone; the higher note of the interval. 3. The sixtieth part of a second of time or an arc.—**third·ly** *adv.*

third degree. Brutal police extortion of a confession.

Third Reich (*therd-ryke*). The German fascist dictatorship formed in 1933, and dissolved in 1945 after World War II.

thirst (*therst*) *n.* 1. Desire for liquid; sensation aroused by need of drink. 2. Longing; strong desire.—**thirst** *v.*—**thirst·er** *n.*—**thirst·less** *adj.*

thirst·y *adj.* [thirst·i·er; thirst·i·est] 1. Avid; desiring. 2. Parched; dry. 3. Provoking thirst.—**thirst·i·ly** *adv.*— **-i·ness** *n.*

thir·teen *n.* The number represented by the symbol 13.—*adj.* Consisting of 13.—**thir·teenth** *adj. & n.*

thir·ty *n.* The number represented by the symbol 30.—*adj.* Consisting of 30.—**thir·ti·eth** *adj. & n.* —**thir·ty·fold** *adj. & adv.* Thirty times over.

this (*thiss*) [*pl.* these] The present or nearer object; that just mentioned.

this·tle (*thiss-'l*) *n.* 1. A prickly-leaved plant of many varieties, some bearing white or purple flowers. 2. The emblem of Scotand.—**this·tly** *adj.*—**this·tle·down** *n.*

THISTLE

thith·er (*thith-*er) *adv.* There; to that place. —**thith·er·to** *adv.* Till that time.—**thith·er·ward** *adv.*

thole *n.* Wooden pin set in gunwale of a boat as a brace for the oar.—**thole·pin** *n.*

THOLE

thong *n.* A leather strap used for fastening.

Thor (*thawr*) *n.* Ancient Scandinavian god of thunder, represented as bearing a hammer.

tho·rax (*thoh*-rakss) *n.* The chest cavity.—**tho·rac·ic** (thor-*ass*-ik) *adj.* Pertaining to the chest. —*n.* 1. A thoracic artery. 2. Fish such as mackerel or flounder having the ventral fins under the thorax.

tho·ri·um (*thoh*-ree-um) *n.* A rare radioactive metallic element. (*Symbol:* Th).

thorn *n.* 1. Any of a variety of spiny shrubs and trees. 2. A sharp, woody plant; a prickle. 3. An irritation; annoyance.—**thorn·y** *adj.*

thornback	thorn-headed	thorn-set
thornbill	thorn-hedged	thornstone
thorn-bound	thorn-marked	thorntail
thorn-covered	thorn-pricked	thorn-wreathed

tho·ron (*thoh*-ron) *n.* Radioactive gaseous element of the thorium series of radioactive changes. (*Symbol:* Tn).

thor·ough (*ther*-oh) *adj.* 1. Complete; fully realized. 2. Meticulous; careful.—**thor·ough·ly** *adv.*—**thor·ough·ness** *n.*

thor·ough·bred *n.* One of a pure-blooded breed of horses or dogs.

thor·ough·fare *n.* A through road.

thor·ough·go·ing *adj.* Extremely thorough.

those. *Plural* of *that.*

Thoth (*thawth*) *n.* Ancient Egyptian god of wisdom and magic.

thou (*thow*). *Archaic form* of you; *nominative case* of thee.

though (*thoh*) *conj.* 1. Notwithstanding; while. 2. *Colloquial.* However; nevertheless.

thought (*thawt*) *n.* 1. Occupation of the mind; mental activity. 2. An idea; notion; view. 3. Reflection; meditation.—**thought·ful** *adj.* —**thought·ful·ly** *adv.*— -**ful·ness** *n.*—**thought·less** *adj.*— -**less·ly** *adv.*— -**less·ness** *n.*

thou·sand (*thow-z'nd*) *n.* The number represented by the symbol 1,000; ten hundred. —**thou·sand** *adj.*—**thou·sand·fold** *adj.*—**thou·sandth** *n.* & *adj.*

thrall (*thrawl*) *n.* 1. Slave; vassal. 2. Bondage; slavery.—**thrall·dom** *n.*

thrash *v.* 1. To crush out the kernels from grain. 2. To pitch about; to toss. 3. To beat.—**thrash out.** To settle through argument. —**thrash·er** *n.*—**thrash·ing** *n.* & *adj.*

thread (*thred*) *n.* 1. A fibrous, spun filament. 2. A thin strip; a strand. 3. *Mining.* A vein of ore. 4. Central theme; direction.—*v.* 1. To pass a thread through, as the eye of a needle. 2. To string together. 3. To penetrate deviously. 'To thread one's way.' —**thread·bare** *adj.* 1. Shabby. 2. Trite; hackneyed.

threat (*thret*) *n.* Expression of evil intention; portent; menace.

threat·en *v.* 1. To warn; to inform beforehand of evil consequences. 2. To menace; to appear foreboding.—**threat·en·er** *n.*—**threat·en·ing** *adj.*—**threat·en·ing·ly** *adv.*

three *n.* The number represented by the symbol 3.—*adj.* Consisting of three.—**three·fold** *adj.*

three-angled	three-faced	threepence
three-armed	three-fibered	threepenny
three-bagger	three-fingered	three-ply
three-cornered	three-handed	threescore
three-decker	three-in-hand	threesome
three-edged	three-master	three-spot
three-eyed	three-necked	three-square

thre·no·dy, thre·node (*thren-uh-dee, thren-ohd*) *n.* A dirge; a funeral poem.—**thre·no·di·al, thre·nod·ic** *adj.*—**thren·o·dist** *n.*

thresh *v.* To pound out the grain from the stalk.—**thresh·er** *n.*

thresh·old *n.* 1. Doorsill. 2. Entrance; doorway; beginning. 3. *Psychology.* Point of sensitivity at which a given stimulus begins to produce a conscious effect.

thrice *adv.* Three times.

thrift *n.* Economy; careful management; providence.—**thrift·less** *adj.*— -**less·ly** *adv.*— -**less·ness** *n.*

thrift·y *adj.*—Economical.—**thrift·i·ly** *adv.* —**thrift·i·ness** *n.*

thrill *v.* 1. To strike, or be struck, with emotion; transport; enrapture. 2. To vibrate; quiver.—*n.* 1. An exciting experience. 2. A tremor.—**thrill·er** *n.* Entertainment exciting horror.—**thrill·ing** *adj.*— -**ing·ly** *adv.*— -**ing·ness** *n.*

thrive (*thryve*) *v.* [thrived or throve; thrived or thriv·en; thriv·ing] To grow; to flourish. —**thriv·ing** *adj.* Successful; prosperous.

throat (*throht*) *n.* Anterior part of the neck, containing the respiratory and food passages. —**throat·y** *adj.* Husky; resonant.

throb *v.* [throbbed; throb·bing] To palpitate; to vibrate.—*n.* A violent pulsation.—**throb·bing** *adj.*—Tremendous; pounding; painful.

throe (*throh*) *n.* [usually *pl.*] Pang; agony.

throm·bo·sis (*throm-boh-siss*) *n. Medicine.* Formation of a clot in a blood vessel.—**throm·bot·ic** *adj.*

throne (*throhn*) *n.* 1. Official chair of state of a sovereign or dignitary. 2. Royal authority. —*v.* To put on a throne; to elevate.

throng *n.* A crowd; a multitude.—*v.* To crowd.

thros·tle (*thross-'l*) *n.* A spinning machine.

throt·tle (*throt-'l*) *v.* [throt·tled; throt·tling] 1. To choke; to strangle. 2. To slow an engine by closing the throttle valve.—*n.* 1. A threat. 2. A valve regulating supply of fuel to an internal combustion engine.

through (*throo*) *prep.* 1. From one end to another; all over. 2. By means of. 3. Because of; on account of. 4. Amid; among. —*adj.* 1. Uninterrupted. 'A through trip.' 2. *Colloquial.* Completed; finished.

throw (*throh*) *v.* [threw; thrown; throw·ing] 1. To hurl; propel; cast. 2. To cast to the ground. 3. *Sports.* To lose intentionally. 4. *Machinery.* To engage or disengage, as a switch, clutch, etc.—**throw** *n.*—**throw·er** *n.* —**throw away.** To discard.—**throw-away** *n.* 1. Uncompetitive contest. 2. A free leaflet, magazine, etc.—**throw back.** To revert to an earlier stage.—**throw-back** *n.* Recurrence; reversion to an earlier stage.—**throw off.** 1. To rid oneself of. 2. To mislead.—**throw over.** *Colloquial.* To jilt; to reject.—**throw up.** 1. To construct hastily. 2. To vomit.

thrum *v.* [thrummed; thrum·ming] 1. To strum, as a stringed instrument. 2. To drum with the fingers.—*n.* 1. The end of a weaver's thread. 2. Coarse yarn.

thrush *n.* A small sweet-singing bird, common to North America and Europe.

thrust *v.* [thrust; thrust·ing] To push; force; drive; stab.—*n.* 1. A push. 2. *Mechanics.* Force exerted by one member of a structure against another.—**thrust·er** *n.*

thud *n.* The dull sound of a heavy impact.—*v.* [thud·ded; thud·ding].

thug *n.* A hired killer; a gangster; a tough. —**thug·ger·y** *n.*—**thug·gish** *adj.*

thu·li·um (*thyoo-lee-um*) *n.* A rare metallic element. (*Symbol:* Tm).

thumb (*thum*) *n.* The short, thick first finger of the human hand.—*v.* [thumbed; thumb·ing] To handle clumsily; to soil or wear with the fingers.—**thumb a ride.** To hitch-hike.—**thumb one's nose.** To make an impolite gesture.

thumb-fingered	thumbnail	thumbscrew
thumb-made	thumbpiece	thumbtack
thumb mark	thumbprint	thumb-worn

T

thump *n.* **1.** A heavy blow; thud. **2.** A palpitation.—*v.* **1.** To drum; strike; thud. **2.** To palpitate, as the heart.—**thump·ing** *adj.* & *n.*

thun·der *n.* **1.** Noise made by the sudden expansion of the air caused by lightning. **2.** A roar; an outburst.—**thun·der** *v.*—**thun·der·er** *n.* —**thun·der·ing** *n.*—**thun·der·ing·ly** *adv.*

thunderbolt	thunder god	thundersquall
thunderburst	thunderhead	thunderstone
thunderclap	thunderlight	thunderstorm
thundercloud	thunderproof	thunderstroke
thundercrack	thundershower	thunderstruck

thu·ri·ble (*thyoor*-uh-b'l) *n. Ecclesiastical.* A censer; incense burner.

Thurs·day (*therz*-dee, *therz*-day) *n.* The fifth day of the week.

thus *adv.* **1.** In this way. **2.** Hence; accordingly.—**thus far.** Up to now; to this point.

thwack *v.* To bang; to thump.—*n.* A blow with a flat object.—**thwack·er** *n.*

thwart (*thwawrt*) *v.* To disappoint; frustrate; foil.—*n. Nautical.* Seat extending across a rowboat.—**thwart·er** *n.*

thwart·ships *adv.* & *adj.* Across a ship.

thy *pron. Archaic & liturgical form* of **your.**

thyme (*time*) *n.* Aromatic plant of the mint family, used in cooking.

thy·roid, thyroid gland (*thy*-royd) *n.* Throat gland which influences metabolism and growth.—**thy·roid** *adj.*—**thy·roid·ec·to·my** (thy-royd-*ek*-toh-mee) *n.* Removal of the thyroid gland by surgery.—**thy·roid·i·tis** (thy-royd-*eye*-tiss) *n.* Inflammation of the thyroid gland.

thy·rox·ine, thy·rox·in (thy-*rokss*-in) *n.* The hormone secreted by the thyroid gland used to treat many disorders.

ti·ar·a (ty-*air*-uh; tee-*ahr*-uh) *n.* A head ornament; a coronet.

tib·ia (*tib*-ee-uh) *n.* [*pl.* tib·i·ae or tib·i·as] Larger of the two bones of the leg, below the knee. —**tib·i·al** *adj.*

tick *n.* **1.** A small, blood-sucking parasite. **2.** A light, distinct noise, as made by a clock. **3.** A small mark, used as a check. **4.** The stout outer covering of a pillow or mattress. —*v.* **1.** To make a small, distinct, steady noise. **2.** To note or mark, as the passing of time.—**tick off.** To check off as listed items.

tick·er *n.* A telegraphic machine which automatically records stock reports on a continuous tape.—**ticker tape.**

tick·et *n.* **1.** A printed card serving as admission permit, receipt, etc. **2.** List of candidates running for office; a ballot. **3.** A label; tag.—*v.* To label; put a ticket on.

TICKER

tick·ing *n.* A strong cotton fabric used to cover mattresses and pillows.

tick·le (*tik*-'l) *v.* [tick·led; tick·ling] **1.** To touch lightly and cause a nervous reflex result-ing usually in laughter; titillate. **2.** To please; to gratify.—*n.* A tingling sensation.—**tick·ler** *n.*—**tick·ling** *n.* & *adj.*

tick·lish *adj.* Sensitive to tickling.—**tick·lish·ly** *adv.*—**tick·lish·ness** *n.*

Ti·con·der·o·ga (ty-kon-der-*oh*-guh). Fort NE of Albany, captured by Ethan Allen from the British during the Revolutionary War.

tid·al (*ty*-d'l) *adj.* **1.** Periodically rising and falling or flowing and ebbing. **2.** Regulated by tide.—**tidal wave.** A broad, engulfing wave.

tid·bit *n.* **1.** Morsel; delicacy. **2.** Bit of gossip.

tid·dly·winks (*tid*-lee-winkss) *n. pl.* A game played among children by snapping small chips into a cup.

tide (*tyde*) *n.* **1.** Alternate rising and ebbing of the sea. **2.** Time or season. **3.** A stream; flood. **4.** Current; tendency; course.—*v.* [tid·ed; tid·ing] **1.** To move with the tide. **2.** To aid or support. **3.** To surmount. 'To tide over the lean years.'

tide-beaten	tide-free	tide-swept
tide-beset	tideland	tide-tossed
tide-bound	tide-locked	tide-trapped
tide-covered	tide mark	tide-washed
tide-driven	tide-marked	tidewater
tide-flooded	tiderace	tide-worn

tid·ings (*tyde*-ingz) *n.pl.* News; information.

ti·dy (*ty*-dee) *adj.* [ti·di·er; ti·di·est] **1.** Neat; trim; orderly. **2.** *Slang.* Considerable; moderately large.—*v.* [ti·died; ti·dy·ing] To arrange in good order; to make neat.—*n.* [*pl.* ti·dies] Doily.—**ti·di·ly** *adv.*—**ti·di·ness** *n.*

tie (*ty*) *v.* [tied; ty·ing] **1.** To fasten with a knot. **2.** To restrain; confine. **3.** To score equally in a contest. **4.** *Colloquial.* To match; equal. 'Can you tie that?'—*n.* **1.** A fastening. **2.** A necktie. **3.** A bond; an obligation. **4.** A wooden support for the rails of a railroad track. **5.** A contest in which the score is even. —**ti·er** (ty-er) *n.*—**tie·in** *n.* Relationship; connection.—**tie-in sale.** Selling of goods on condition that additional unwanted purchases are made.

tier (*teer*) *n.* A layer; a level.—*v.* To place in layers.—**tiered** *adj.*

tiff *v.* To spat; squabble.—*n.* A minor quarrel —**tif·fish** *adj.* Peevish; petulant.

ti·ger (*ty*-ger) *n.* A large powerful beast of prey of the cat family, having tawny skin striped with black.—**ti·gress** *n.*—**ti·grish** *adj.* Ferocious.

TIGER (1/60 life-size)

ti·ger·eye, tiger's eye *n.* An opalescent yellowish-black stone, used for ornament.

tiger lily. A tall garden lily bearing orange flowers spotted with black.

tight (*tyte*) *adj.* 1. Impenetrable; secure; well closed. 2. Firmly constructed; sound; strong. 3. Firmly packed; fixed. 4. Close fitting. 5. Taut; stretched; tense. 6. *Slang.* Stingy; close-fisted. 7. *Commercial.* Not to be had on ordinary terms, esp. of money when investors are disinclined to speculate. 8. *Slang.* Intoxicated.—*n.* [*pl.*] Tight fitting breeches worn by acrobats, dancers, etc.—**tight·ly** *adv.*— **-ness** *n.*

tight-ankled	tight-hosed	tight-skinned
tight-belted	tight-limbed	tight-skirted
tight-bodied	tight-lipped	tight-sleeved
tight-booted	tight looking	tight-stretched
tight-bound	tight-made	tight-tie
tight-clad	tight-necked	tight-valved
tight-clenched	tight-packed	tight-waisted
tight-closed	tight-pressed	tightwire
tight-draped	tight-rooted	tight-wound
tight-drawn	tight-set	tight-woven

tight·en (*tyte*-'n) *v.* To make taut; draw tighter. —**tight·en·er** *n.*—**tight·en·ing** *n.*

tight-fist·ed *adj.* Stingy; miserly.

tight·rope *n.* A horizontal rope, tightly drawn, on which acrobats walk or perform.

tight·wad (*tyte*-wod) *n.* A miser; a skinflint.

til·de (*til*-deh; -dee) *n.* A diacritical mark [~], used esp. over the Spanish ñ.

tile *n.* 1. Thin small flat plate of baked clay. 2. A short earthenware drain pipe.—*v.* [tiled; til·ing] To set or cover with tiles.—**til·er** *n.* —**til·ing** *n.* 1. The operation of setting with tiles. 2. Tiles collectively.

till *n.* 1. Money box in a shop; cash drawer. 2. Coarse, obdurate land.—*prep.* To the time of; until.—*conj.* To the time when; until.—*v.* To plow and prepare for seed; to cultivate. —**till·a·ble** *adj.* Capable of cultivation; arable. —**till·age** *n.*—Cultivation; husbandry.

til·ler *n.* 1. A cultivator; a plowman. 2. *Nautical.* The lever which turns the rudder of a boat.

tilt *v.* 1. To incline; tip; lean. 2. To thrust with a lance; joust; engage in combat.—*n.* 1. A slant; slope. 2. A knightly combat with lances. 3. A thrust; dispute; match of wits. 4. Speed, as in full tilt.—**tilt·er** *n.* —**tilt·ing** *n.*

TILLER (def. 2.)

tim·bale (*tim*-b'l) *n. Cooking.* 1. A pastry shell filled with seasoned food. 2. A drum-like mold used for making timbale shells.

tim·ber *n.* 1. Material, esp. wood, used in building and carpentry. 2. Trees yielding wood for construction. 3. A single piece of a main beam. 4. *Nautical.* A curving piece forming the rib of a ship.—*v.* To furnish with timber; build.—**tim·bered** *adj.*— **-ber·ing** *n.*

tim·bre (*tam*-ber) *n.* 1. The character of a sound. 2. *Music.* Tone, distinguished from intensity and pitch.

tim·brel (*tim*-brel) *n.* A tambourine.—**tim·breled, tim·brelled** *adj.*

time *n.* 1. Duration; the idea or measure of successive existence. 2. A period; occasion. 3. A fixed moment; an appointed season; opportunity. 4. An age; era. 5. The length of life; allotted period. 6. [*pl.*] Prevailing state of circumstances. 7. Occurrence of an event with reference to repetition; being multiplied by. 'Five times five.' 8. Leisure; convenience. 9. Experience. 10. Hour of death. 11. *Music.* Style or rate of movement or peculiarity of accent in a composition.—*v.* [timed; tim·ing] 1. To adapt to the occasion; schedule. 2. To regulate as to time; set the tempo. 3. To ascertain duration or rate. —**tim·er** *n.*—**tim·ing** *n.*

time card	timesaving	time work
timekeeper	timetable	time-worn

time·less *adj.* Eternal; ageless; lasting.—**time·less·ly** *adv.*—**time·less·ness** *n.*

time·ly *adj.* [time·li·er; tim·li·est] Seasonable; opportune.—**time·li·ness** *n.*

time·piece *n.* Instrument to measure time; watch; clock; sundial.

tim·id *adj.* Easily frightened; shy.—**tim·id·i·ty, tim·id·ness** *n.*—**tim·id·ly** *adj.*

tim·ing (*tyme*-ing) *n.* 1. Determination of the most effective moment for presentation; perceptive regulation of dramatic tempo. 2. Regulation of speed of action to assure the greatest speed when desired.

tim·or·ous (*tim*-er-us) *adj.* Fearful; apprehensive.—**tim·or·ous·ly** *adv.*— **-ous·ness** *n.*

tim·o·thy (*tim*-eh-thee) *n.* A fodder grass.

tim·pan·i *n. pl.* The tympani.

tin *n.* 1. Extremely malleable crystalline metal of bluish-white color. (*Symbol:* Sn). 2. A tin can; a can containing processed food.—*v.* [tinned; tin·ning] 1. To cover or overlay with tin. 2. To seal in a can.—**tinned** *adj.* Canned.—**tin·ner** *n.*—**tin·ning** *n.*

tin can. *Navy Slang.* A destroyer.

tinc·ture (*tink*-cher) *n.* 1. Medicinal solution of a substance in alcohol. 2. A dash; a trace.—*v.* [tinc·tured; tinc·tur·ing] To imbue; to tinge.

tin·der *n.* A highly inflammable substance used for kindling fire; hence any inflammable material.—**tin·der·box** *n.*

tine (*tyne*) *n.* A prong, as of a fork; a spike.

tin fish. *Nautical Slang.* A torpedo.

TINES

ting *v.* [tinged; ting·ing] To make a light, high-pitched sound, esp. by tapping on glass.—*n.* A tap.

T

tinge (*tinj*) *n.* Trace; tint; flavor; suggestion. —*v.* [tinged; ting·ing, tinge·ing] To mix or imbue with a foreign substance; to change or modify slightly.

tin·gle (*ting*-g'l) *n.* 1. A thrilling sensation; a prickly feeling. 2. A tinkle.—*v.* [tin·gled; tin·gling] 1. To feel a sharp stinging sensation. 2. To ring lightly.—**tin·gling** *n.*

tin·horn *adj.* Cheap; flashy; pretentious.

tink·er *n.* A mender of pots and pans.—*v.* 1. To work as a tinker. 2. To patch clumsily; to putter uselessly.—**tink·er·er** *n.*—**tinker's damn.** A worthless thing.

tin·kle *v.* [tin·kled; tin·kling] To make a series of small jingling sounds; to ring.—*n.* A thin ringing sound.—**tin·kler** *n.*—**tin·kling** *n.*

tin·ny *adj.* [tin·ni·er; tin·ni·est] Of tin; resembling tin.—**tin·ni·ly** *adv.*—**tin·ni·ness** *n.*

tin·sel (*tin*-s'l) *n.* 1. A thin, shining metallic plate; foil. 2. Material made of silk interwoven with silver or gold threads; cloth overlaid with foil. 3. Artificial display; false glitter.—*adj.* 1. Of tinsel. 2. Gaudy; superficial; tawdry.—*v.* [tin·seled, tin·selled; tin·seling, tin·sel·ling] 1. To adorn with tinsel or with glittering ornament. 2. To make gaudy.

tinsel bright   tinsel-embroidered   tinsel-slippered
tinsel-covered   tinsel making   tinsel weaver

tint *n.* 1. A delicate color. 2. Tinge; hue. 3. A dye.—*v.* 1. To color lightly. 2. To change color; to dye.—**tint·ed** *adj.*—**tint·er** *n.*

tin·tin·nab·u·la·tion *n.* A bell-like tinkling. —**tin·tin·nab·u·lar, -u·lar·y, -u·lous** *adj.*

ti·ny (*ty*-nee) *adj.* [ti·ni·er; ti·ni·est] Very small; minute.—**tin·i·ness** *n.*

tip *n.* 1. The top; a small-pointed end or extremity. 2. A small present of money; a gratuity. 3. A useful piece of advice. 4. A tap; a light blow. 5. Private information given for betting purposes.—*v.* [tipped; tip·ping]—**tip·ster** *n.*

tipcart	tip-off	tiptilt
tipcat	tipstaff	tiptilted
tip-curled	tiptail	tiptoe
tipman	tip-tap	tiptop

tip·pet *n.* A short scarf of fur or cloth.

tip·ple (*tip*-'l) *v.* [tip·pled; tip·pling] To drink strong liquor regularly in small quantities.—*n.* 1. A small portion of liquor. 2. An apparatus for emptying loaded cars.—**tip·pler** *n.* Habitual drinker; sot.

tip·sy *adj.* [-si·er; -si·est] Mildly intoxicated; befuddled.—**tip·si·ly** *adv.*—**tip·si·ness** *n.*

ti·rade (*ty*-rayd) *n.* A long and violent oration.

tire *n.* A cushioned rubber rim on the wheel of a vehicle.—*v.* [tired; tir·ing] 1. To exhaust; to fail in strength. 2. To satiate; bore; sicken. —**tir·ing** *adj.* Exhausting; fatiguing.

tired *adj.* Exhausted; fatigued.—**tired·ly** *adv.* —**tired·ness** *n.*

tire·less *adj.* Indefatigable; diligent.—**tire·less·ly** *adv.*—**tire·less·ness** *n.*

tire·some *adj.* Fatiguing; wearisome; irksome; dull.—**tire·some·ly** *adv.*—**tire·some·ness** *n.*

tis·sue (*tish*-oo) *n.* 1. *Anatomy.* A collection of specialized cells. 2. A thin, gauzy material. 3. A web; a chain; a connected series. 4. Soft paper sheets or toweling used to remove cosmetics, etc.—*v.* [tis·sued; tis·su·ing] To form tissue of; to interweave.—**tis·sued** *adj.*

tissue paper. Thin, soft paper.

tit *n.* 1. A small bit; a morsel. 2. A tap; a light blow. 3. A nipple; teat. 4. A titmouse. 5. A small horse.—**tit for tat.** An equivalent return.

ti·tan (*ty*-t'n) *n.* 1. [*cap.*] *Greek Mythology.* Ancient deity. 2. A giant; a huge and powerful person.—**ti·tan, ti·tan·ic** *adj.* Enormous; superhuman.—**ti·tan·esque** *adj.*

ti·ta·ni·um (ty-*tay*-nee-um) *n.* A metallic element resembling silicon, found only in combination (*Symbol:* Ti).—**ti·tan·ic** *adj.*—**ti·tan·ous** *adj.*

tithe (*tythe*) *n.* 1. A tenth; ten per cent of the income, formerly an ecclesiastical tax. 2. A small portion.—*v.* [tithed; tith·ing] To levy or pay a tenth part.—**tith·ing** *n.* 1. The levying of tithes. 2. A tenth.

ti·tian (*tih*-sh'n) *n.* An auburn color used by the painter Titian.—**titian-haired** *adj.* Redhaired.

tit·il·late (*tit*-uh-layt) *v.* [tit·il·lat·ed; tit·il·lat·ing] To tickle; to excite pleasurably.—**tit·il·la·tion** *n.*—**tit·il·la·tive** *adj.*

tit·i·vate (*tit*-uh-vayt) *v.* [-vat·ed; -vat·ing] To smarten up; dress sprucely.—**ti·ti·va·tion** *n.*

ti·tle (*ty*-t'l) *n.* 1. A name; appellation of dignity inherited by, or bestowed upon, an individual. 2. A claim; right. 3. *Sports.* Championship.—*v.* [ti·tled; ti·tling] 1. To name; entitle. 2. To ennoble.—**ti·tled** *adj.* —**ti·tle·less** *adj.*

tit·mouse (*tit*-mowss) *n.* A small songbird common in North America and Europe.

tit·ter *v.* To giggle; to laugh with restraint. —*n.* A snicker. —**tit·ter·er** *n.* —**tit·ter·ing·ly** *adv.*

TITMOUSE (1/8 life-size.)

tit·tle *n.* An iota; jot.

tit·tle-tat·tle *n.* 1. Gossip. 2. A tattler.—*v.* [tit·tle-tat·tled; tit·tle-tat·ling] To gossip idly.

tit·tup *v.* [tit·tuped, tit·tupped; tit·tup·ing, tit·tup·ping] To frisk; to act in a lively way.—*n.* A caper; cheery behavior.

tit·u·lar (*tit*-choo-ler) *adj.* 1. In name only; nominal. 2. Pertaining to a title.—*n.* Possessor of a title without authority.—**tit·u·lar·i·ty** *n.*—**tit·u·lar·ly** *adv.*—**tit·u·lar·y** *adj.*

tiz·zy *n. Colloquial.* An hysterical state; nervous or emotional upset.

TNT. *Abbreviation* for **trinitrotoluene**, a high explosive.

to *prep* 1. Toward; in the direction of. 2. As far as; without exception. 3. A result, end, or consequence. 'They came, to his disappointment.' 4. In addition or possession. 5. In junction or union with. 'Tied to a tree.' 6. In comparison, proportion, or ratio. 7. In opposition or contest. 'Ten to one.' 8. Accompaning or corresponding. 'Dance to music.' 9. A sign of the infinitive of a verb. —*adv.* 1. Forward; on. 2. In a certain direction. 3. Toward; at hand.—**to and fro.** Forward and backward.

toad (*tohd*) *n.* Small tailless amphibian vertebrate with a thick, warty skin. —**toad·y** *n.* Truckler; flatterer.—*v.* [toad·ied; toad·y·ing] To fawn upon; to truckle.—**toad·y·ish** *adj.* —**toad·y·ism** *n.*

TOAD (1/4 life-size)

toadback	toadeater	toad-spotted
toad-bellied	toadfish	toadstone
toad blind	toad-legged	toadstool
toadbug	toad-shaped	toad-swollen

toad·stabber *n. U.S.* A knife; a jackknife.

toast *v.* 1. To brown by heat; warm thoroughly. 2. To drink a health; honor by proposing a drink.—*n.* 1. Sliced bread browned by fire or heat. 2. Person or sentiment honored in drinking.—**toast·er** *n.* 1. Person who toasts. 2. A device which toasts bread.—**toast·mas·ter** *n.* Master of ceremonies at a banquet.

to·bac·co (tuh-*bak*-oh) *n.* 1. A tall, erect plant of the nightshade family, with large leaves containing alkaloid nicotine. 2. The dried tobacco leaf used for smoking, chewing, or as snuff. —**to·bac·co·nist** *n.* A dealer in tobacco.

to·bog·gan (tuh-*bog*-un) *n.* A sled made of a long, pliant board curved up at one end.—*v.* 1. To slide down a snow-covered hill on a toboggan. 2. To decline suddenly. —**to·bog·gan·er,** **to·bog·gan·ist** *n.*

TOBACCO

toc·ca·ta (tuh-*kah*-tuh) *n. Music.* A fantasia, usually for the organ.

to·col·o·gy (tuh-*kol*-uh-jee) *n.* Obstetrics; midwifery.

toc·sin (*tok*-sin) *n.* A bell rung to warn of danger; an alarm.

to·day (tuh-*day*) *n.* 1. The present day. 2. The present time; the age in which we live.—*adv.* 1. On this day. 2. At this time; now.

tod·dle (*tod*-'l) *v.* [tod·dled; tod·dling]. To walk with short unsteady steps; to totter.—*n.* A tottering gait.—**tod·dler** *n.* An infant.

tod·dy (*tod*-ee) *n.* [*pl.* -dies] A hot sweetened mixture of liquor, esp. rum, spices, sugar, and water.

toe (toh) *n.* 1. One of the five digits of the foot; the foremost part of a foot. 2. The front of a shoe or boot; tip.—*v.* [toed; toe·ing] To touch or reach with the toes.—**toed** *adj.*—**toe·less** *adj.* —**toe dance.** Dance done on the tip of the toes.—**toe·dance** *v.*—**toe dancer.**

tof·fee, tof·fy *n.* A chewy molasses candy.

tog *v.* [togged; tog·ging] To dress in one's best. —*n.* [*usually pl.*] Clothes.—**tog·ger·y** *n.*

to·ga (*toh*-guh) *n.* Flowing outer garment worn by the Roman citizen.—**to·gaed** *adj.*

to·geth·er (too-*geth*-er) *adv.* 1. In concert; in union; with one another; mutually. 2. At the same time or place; coincidentally. 3. In contact. 4. Without intermission.

toil (*toyl*) *n.* Painful, heavy labor; drudgery.—*v.* 1. To work hard. 2. To struggle.—**toil·er** *n.* —**toil·ful** *adj.*—**toil·ful·ly** *adv.*

toi·let (*toy*-lit) *n.* 1. A bathroom; a water closet. 2. Personal grooming.—**toi·let·ry** *n.* [*pl.* toi·let·ries] An article used in personal grooming.

toilet paper, toilet tissue. Thin tissue paper used to wipe dry the urinary or rectal area.

toi·lette (toy-*let*) *n.* 1. The process or mode of dressing, arranging the hair, etc. 2. Dress; attire.

toilet water. Cologne.

toil·some *adj.* Laborious; wearisome.—**toil·somely** *adv.*—**toil·some·ness,** *n.*

To·kay (toh-*kay*) *n.* 1. A sweet table grape, green or purple in color. 2. Wine originally made in Tokay, Hungary.

to·ken (*toh*-ken) *n.* 1. An evidence; symbol; sign. 2. A souvenir; keepsake. 3. Coin issued as special currency.

told. *Past tense & past participle* of tell.

tol·er·a·ble (*tol*-er-uh-b'l) *adj.* 1. Bearable; endurable. 2. Moderately good; passable. —**tol·er·a·bly** *adv.*—**tol·er·a·ble·ness** *n.*

tol·er·ant (*tol*-er-'nt) *adj.* 1. Forbearing; lenient. 2. Liberal; respectful of others' beliefs. —**tol·er·ance** *n.*—**tol·er·ant·ly** *adv.*

tol·er·ate (*tol*-er-ayt) *v.* [tol·er·at·ed; tol·er·at·ing] 1. To allow; suffer; abide; forbear. 2. To evidence; to bear.—**tol·er·a·tion** *n.* —**tol·er·a·tive** *adj.*—**tol·er·a·tor** *n.*

toll (*tohl*) *v.* 1. To ring slowly and uniformly; ring mournfully. 2. To strike the hour. 3. To exact or levy a tax; to take as toll.—*n.* 1. The ringing of a bell with slow, measured strokes. 2. A tax paid, or fee imposed, for some right, privilege, or service; levy; duty.—**toll·a·ble** *adj.* —**toll·age** *n.*—**toll·er** *n.*

tom *n.* 1. The male of certain animals; a male cat. 2. [*cap.*] Popular contraction of Thomas. —**Tom and Jerry.** A hot rum and water drink made with beaten eggs, sweetened, and spiced. —**Tom Collins.** A mixed drink of gin, lime or lemon juice, sugar, and soda water.

tom·a·hawk (*tom*-uh-hawk) *n.* A lightweight North American Indian hatchet.—*v.* To strike or kill with a tomahawk.

T

to·ma·to (tuh-*may*-toh, tuh-*mah*-toh) *n.* 1. [*pl.* to·ma·toes] The fleshy, edible fruit, usually red or yellow-red, of a plant of the nightshade family. 2. *Slang.* A woman, esp. one of easy virtue.—*adj.* Colored like a tomato.

tomb (toom) *n.* A grave; a place for burial; sepulcher.—*v.* To bury; inter.—**tomb·stone** *n.* Memorial stone marking a grave.

tom·boy *n.* A girl who acts like a boy.

tome (tohm) *n.* A volume; part of a large work; a large book.

tom·my (*tom*-ee) *n.* Slang term for British Army private, comparable to *doughboy* or *G.I.*—**Tommy Atkins.** Name for British enlisted man comparable to *G.I. Joe.*

tom·my·gun *n. Slang.* Light machine gun.

tom·my·rot *n. Slang.* Nonsense; foolishness.

to·mor·row (tuh-*mor*-oh; -*mahr*-) *n.* The day following the present day.—*adv.* On the day next after today.

tom-tom *n.* 1. A primitive drum of oriental origin, beaten with the hands. 2. A monotonous rhythm.

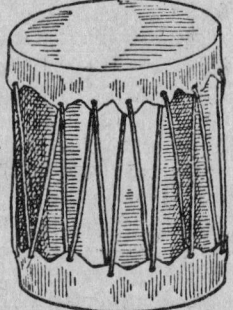

TOM-TOM

ton (tun) *n.* 1. In the U.S., a weight of 2000 pounds commonly called the short ton. 2. In England, a weight of 2240 pounds called the long ton. 3. *Nautical.* A unit of ships' capacity or weight.

tone (tohn) *n.* 1. Sound in relation to pitch, volume, and regularity of vibration. 2. Inflection; modulation; accent. 3. Normal functioning of the bodily organs; strength. 4. Mood; temper. 5. Character; trend. 6. *Painting.* **a.** Relationship of light and dark areas. **b.** Shade of color. 7. *Music.* A full step of the diatonic scale.—*v.* [toned; ton·ing] 1. To harmonize; to blend. 2. To change in color or sound; to modify.—**ton·al** *adj.*—**ton·al·ly** *adv.*—**to·nal·i·ty** *n.*—**tone·less** *adj.*—**tone·less·ly** *adv.*—**tone·less·ness** *n.*—**ton·er** *n.*—**tone down.** To lower in tone; soften. —**tone up.** To give a higher tone to; strengthen.

tongs *n. pl.* Pincer-like instrument used for lifting or handling, as hot coals or ice.

tongue (tung) *n.* 1. Organ of taste and speech, attached to the floor of the mouth. 2. Power of speech; way of speaking. 3. Language. 4. Beef or lamb tongue used as food. 5. Tonguelike appendage. 'The tongue of a shoe.' —*v.* [tongued; tongu·ing] 1. To lick; touch with the tongue. 2. *Music.* To start a tone on an instrument.—**tongued** *adj.*

ICE TONGS

tongue-tie *n.* Difficulty in speech or articulation.—*v.* [tongue-tied; -ty·ing] To lose power of speech or clear articulation.—**tongue-tied** *adj.*

ton·ic (*ton*-ik) *n.* 1. *Medicine.* A compound promoting energy or appetite; an invigorating agent. 2. *Music.* The keynote.—*adj.* 1. Bracing; invigorating. 2. *Music.* Pertaining to the keynote. 3. Pertaining to sounds. 4. *Medicine.* Producing health.—**to·nic·i·ty** (ton-*iss*-uh-tee) *n.* Vitality; health.

to·night (tuh-*nyte*) *n.* The present night.—*adv.* On this night.

ton·nage (*tun*-ij) *n.* 1. Total weight in tons. 2. The cubical content of a ship in tons. 3. A duty on ships. 4. Ships collectively.

ton·neau (*tun*-oh) *n.* Enclosed part of an automobile, behind the driver's seat.

ton·sil (*ton*-sil) *n.* One of two masses of lymphoid tissue on either side of the pharynx in the throat.—**ton·sil·lec·to·my** (ton-sil-*ek*-toh-mee) *n.* Surgical removal of the tonsils.—**ton·sil·lar** *adj.*—**ton·sil·lit·ic** *adj.*—**ton·sil·li·tis** *n.* Inflammation of the tonsils.

ton·so·ri·al *adv.* Pertaining to a barber.

ton·sure *n.* The shaven crown of the head, esp. of a priest.—**ton·sured** *adj.*

too *adv.* 1. Over; excessively. 2. Also; likewise. 3. In addition; besides.

took. *Past tense of* **take.**

tool *n.* 1. Implement; manual instrument. 2. A person used as a means; a dupe.—*v.* 1. To indent with a design. 2. To drive. —**tooled** *adj.*—**tool·ing** *n.*

tool box	tool holding	toolroom
tool builder	tool maker	tool setter
tool dresser	toolman	toolsmith
tool head	toolmark	tool stock
tool holder	toolmarking	toolstone

toot *v.* To blow, as a horn, in rapid blasts.—*n.* A short note; a blast.—**toot·er** *n.*

toot·le *v.* [toot·led; toot·ling] To toot musically. —*n.* A continuous sound.

tooth *n.* [*pl.* teeth] 1. One of the hard, conical structures in the jaws of vertebrate animals, used for chewing, defense, etc. 2. A toothlike projection, as on the cutting edge of a saw. 3. A sharp, piercing section. 4. Taste; palate; fondness. 'A sweet tooth.'—*v.* 1. To furnish with teeth. 2. To indent; serrate. —**toothed** *adj.*—**tooth·less** *adj.*—**tooth·some** *adj.* Palatable; delicious.—**tooth·some·ness** *n.* —**tooth·y** *adj.* Showing the teeth, as in a smile. —**tooth·i·ly** *adv.*—**tooth·i·ness** *n.*

toothache	tooth-leaved	tooth-set
toothachy	tooth-marked	tooth-shaped
tooth brush	toothpick	toothwash
tooth-chiseled	toothproof	toothwork

top *n.* 1. The summit; highest point. 2. Surface; upper side. 3. The choicest part; best. 4. The highest authority; head. 5. The utmost degree; acme; pinnacle. 6. The crown; head. 7. A fitted covering; lid. 8. A child's toy designed to spin on a tapering point. 9. *Nautical.* A platform at the head of the lower mast.—*v.* [topped; top·ping] 1. To cover; cap. 2. To remove the top; trim. 3. To exceed. 4. To excel; surpass. 5. To finish; conclude.—*adj.* Highest; foremost. —**top·per** *n.* 1. A superior person or object. 2. *Slang.* A high silk hat.—**top·ping** *adj.* 1. Rising aloft; eminent. 2. *Slang.* Fine; excellent; splendid.—*n.* The upper part. 'Marshmallow topping for a sundae.'—**top·ping·ly** *adv.*—**tops** *adj. & n. Slang.* Perfect; the best.

top armor	top-heavy	top-notcher
topcap	top-heaviness	toppiece
topcoat	topknot	top rail
topcoating	topknotted	top rope
top cutter	top line	topsail
top drain	toploftiness	top-shaped
top-dress (*v.*)	toplofty	top side
top dressing	top maker	topsoil
topgallant	topman	top stone
top-graft	top mark	toptail
top-hampered	topmast	top timber
top-hatted	topmost	top work

to·paz (*toh*-paz) *n.* Yellow mineral valued as a semi-precious gem in crystalline formation.

tope (*tohp*) *v.* [toped; top·ing] To drink hard liquors to excess.—**top·er** *n.* A drunkard; sot.

to·pee (*tuh-pee*) *n.* Pith sun-helmet commonly worn by Europeans in the tropics.

top hat. A tall-crowned man's hat, worn on formal occasions.

to·pi·ar·y (*toh*-pee-er-ee) *n.* [*pl.* -ar·ies] The art of training shrubbery into decorative or representational forms.—**to·pi·ar·y** *adj.*

TOP HAT

top·ic (*top*-ik) *n.* 1. Subject matter; theme. 2. *Rhetoric.* A form of argument used in reasoning.—**top·i·cal** *adj.* 1. Pertaining to a particular subject. 2. Local. 3. Having contemporary reference.—**top·i·cal·ly** *adv.*

top kick. *Army Slang.* First sergeant; highest ranking sergeant of a platoon.

top·loft·y *adj.* Haughty; contemptuous.—**top·loft·i·ness** *n.*

top-notch *adj. Slang.* Excellent; first-rate.

to·pog·ra·phy (*tuh-pog*-ruh-fee) *n.* 1. The physical pattern of a place or region. 2. Graphic delineation of the physical contours of a region.—**to·pog·ra·pher** *n.*—**top·o·graph·ic, top·o·graph·i·cal** *adj.*— -i·cal·ly *adv.*

top·ple *v.* [top·pled; -pling] 1. To fall; pitch over. 2. To push over.—**top·pling** *n. & adj.*

top·sail (*top*-s'l) *n.* Second lowermost sail, on a square-rigged vessel.

top·sy-tur·vy (*top*-see-*ter*-vee) *adj. & adv.* Inverted; upside-down; confused.—**top·sy-tur·vi·ly** *adv.*—**top·sy-tur·vi·ness** *n.*

toque (*tohk*) *n.* A small brimless hat.

To·rah, To·ra (*toh*-ruh) *n. Hebrew Literature.* Divine law; the first five books of the Old Testament.

torch *n.* 1. A flaming stick. 2. A hoselike device producing an intense flame for mechanical purposes. 3. A flashlight. 4. A guiding symbol.—**put to the torch.** To burn; set afire. —**carry a torch.** To be smitten with an unrequited love.

torch song. *Slang.* Slow, mournful lament for an unfaithful lover.

tore. *Past tense* of **tear.**

tor·e·a·dor (*tor*-ee-uh-dor) *n.* A bullfighter.

tor·ment (*tor*-ment) *n.* 1. Anguish; torture. 2. A cause of suffering.—*v.* (tor-*ment*) 1. To inflict extreme pain or anguish; to torture. 2. To vex; to harass.—**tor·ment·ed** *adj.*—**tor·ment·ing** *adj.*—**tor·ment·ing·ly** *adv.*—**tor·men·tor, tor·men·ter** *n.*—**tor·men·tress** *n.*

torn. *Past participle* of **tear.**

tor·na·do (tor-*nay*-doh) *n.* [*pl.* tor·na·does] Violent, whirling wind moving in a narrow path at high speed; cyclone.—**tor·nad·ic** *adj.*

tor·pe·do (tor-*pee*-doh) *n.* [*pl.* tor·pe·does] 1. An explosive, self-propelled weapon, designed to

TORPEDO

damage ships from under water. 2. Small explosive charge set to warn trains of danger. 3. An explosive firecracker. 4. An electric ray fish; crampfish.—*v.* [tor·pe·doed; tor·pe·do·ing] 1. To destroy with a torpedo. 2. To shatter; ruin.—**tor·pe·do·man** *n.* Navy petty officer rating.—**tor·pe·do·plane** *n.* Airplane designed to launch torpedoes.

tor·pid (*tor*-pid) *adj.* 1. Without power of feeling or exertion; numb. 2. Dull; inert; sluggish.—**tor·pid·ly** *adv.*—**tor·pid·i·ty, tor·pid·ness** *n.*

tor·por *n.* Sluggishness; stupor; lethargy.

torque (*tork*) *n. Mechanical.* A force tending to produce rotation.

tor·rent (*tor*-ent) *n.* A violent downpour; a strong current; flood.—**tor·ren·tial** *adj.*—**tor·ren·tial·ly** *adv.*

tor·rid (*tor*-id) *adj.* 1. Parched; dried with heat. 2. Intensely hot; burning; scorching. —**tor·rid·i·ty, tor·rid·ness** *n.*—**tor·rid·ly** *adv.* —**Tor·rid Zone.** Hottest zone lying on either side of the equator between the tropic lines.

tor·sion (*tor*-sh'n) *n.* 1. A twisting or turning force. 2. *Mechanical.* Internal stress caused by twisting.—**tor·sion·al** *adj.*— -al·ly *adv.*

tor·so (*tor*-soh) *n.* Trunk; body without head and limbs.—**tor·soed** *adj.*

tort. *n. Law.* Any wrong or damage, except breach of contract, for which civil action may be brought.

tor·til·la (tor-*tee*-yuh) *n.* Thin, unleavened Mexican corn cake.

tor·toise (*tor*-tus) *n.* 1. A turtle, esp. a land turtle. 2. Any creature that moves slowly.

tor·to·ni (tor-*toh*-nee) *n.* Also **biscuit tortoni.** Sherry-flavored Italian ice cream, packed in a

T

paper cup and sprinkled with macaroon crumbs.

tor·tu·ous (*tor*-choo-us) *adj.* 1. Twisted; winding; serpentine. 2. Underhanded; devious.—**tor·tu·os·i·ty** (tor-choo-*oss*-uh-tee) *n.* [*pl.* tor·tu·os·i·ties]—**tor·tu·ous·ly** *adv.* — **-ous·ness** *n.*

tor·ture (*tor*-cher) *n.* Excruciating pain; agony; torment.—*v.* [tor·tured; tor·tur·ing] To inflict severe pain.—**tor·ture** *adj.*—**tor·tured·ly, tor·tur·ing·ly** *adv.*—**tor·tur·er** *n.*

To·ry (*tor*-ee) *n.* 1. Member of the Conservative party in England. 2. An American loyal to England during the Revolutionary War. 3. [*not cap.*] A reactionary; conservative.—**to·ry** *adj.*—**to·ry·ism** *n.*

toss *v.* 1. To pitch; fling; throw. 2. To turn restlessly; thrash about.—*n.* 1. A pitch. 2. A sudden upward motion; jerk. 3. *Basketball.* Act of setting the ball in play.—**toss·er** *n.*—**toss·ing** *n.*—**toss·pot** *n.* An habitual drunkard; sot.—**toss-up** *n.* The throwing up of a coin; an even chance.—**toss off.** To gulp.

tot *n.* 1. Small quantity, esp. applied to liquor. 2. Small child; toddler.—*v.* [tot·ted; tot·ting] To add; to total.

to·tal (*toh*-t'l) *n.* Sum; aggregate; entirety.—*adj.* 1. Complete; entire. 2. Absolute; utter.—*v.* [to·taled, to·talled; to·tal·ing, to·tal·ling] To add; sum.—**to·tal·i·ty** *n.*—**to·tal·ly** *adv.*

to·tal·i·tar·i·an (toh-tal-ih-*tair*-ee-un) *n.* A believer in the complete centralization of government control under one political group and the suppression of all other parties.—*adj.* Resembling the Fascist and Nazi movements.

to·tal·i·tar·i·an·ism *n.* Subordination of all ideological and educational trends to the political aims of an authoritarian dictatorship.

to·tal·i·za·tor (*toh*-t'l-ih-zay-ter) *n.* Also **tote.** A machine for registering the total betting on a horse race.

total·ize (*toh*-t'l-yze) *v.* [to·tal·ized; to·tal·iz·ing] To combine into a whole; ascertain a total.—**to·tal·i·za·tion** *n.*—**to·tal·iz·er** *n.*

tote (*toht*) *v.* [tot·ed; tot·ing] To carry.—*n.* 1. A load; haul. 2. A totalizator.—**tot·er** *n.*

to·tem (*toh*-t'm) *n.* An emblem of relationship between an animal and a group, family, or tribe of people.—**to·tem·ic** *adj.*—**to·tem·ism** *n.*—**to·tem·is·tic** *adj.*

totem pole. A pole, carved and painted to represent totemic symbols, set before the houses of certain Indian tribes of the northwest coast of North America.

tot·ter *v.* To wobble; teeter.—**tot·ter·ing** *adj.*—**tot·ter·ing·ly** *adv.*—**tot·ter·y** *adj.*

tou·can (*too-kan*) *n.* Tropical American bird with brilliant plumage and tremendous beak.

touch (*tuch*) *n.* 1. Light physical contact. 2. The sense of feeling. 3. Trait; quality. 4. A trace; suggestion. 5. *Slang.* Request for a

TOTEM POLE

loan.—*v.* 1. To be in contact with. 2. To perceive through the sense of touch. 3. To arouse sympathy; move. 4. To approach; reach. 5. To treat lightly. 6. To concern; pertain. 7. *Slang.* To borrow.—**touch·a·ble** *adj.*—**touched** *adj.* Mentally unbalanced.—**touch·er** *n.*—**touch and go.** A precarious situation.—**touch off.** To start.—**touch up.** To improve; add finish to.

touchback	touch-in-goal	touchpiece
touch bell	touch line	touchstone
touch box	touch-me-not	touch-up (*n.*)
touchhole	touchpan	touchwood

touch·down (*tuch*-down) *n. Football.* Crossing the opposition's goal line to score.

touch·ing *adj.* Pathetic; affecting.—*prep.* Concerning.—**touch·ing·ly** *adv.*—**touch·ing·ness** *n.*

touch·y *adj.* [touch·i·er; touch·i·est] 1. Irritable; hypersensitive; cranky. 2. Delicate; critical; difficult to approach.—**touch·i·ly** *adv.* —**touch·i·ness** *n.*

tough (*tuf*) *adj.* 1. Firm in texture; not brittle. 2. Tenacious; stiff. 3. Sturdy; robust. 4. Stubborn; unruly; difficult.—*n.* A strong, rough person; a rowdy.—**tough·en** *n.*—**tough·ly** *adv.*—**tough·ness** *n.*

tough-backed	tough-headed	tough-muscled
tough-fibered	tough-hearted	tough-shelled
tough-fisted	tough-lived	tough-sinewed
tough-handed	tough-minded	tough-skinned

tou·pee (too-*pay*) *n.* A small wig; a patch of false hair.

tour (*toor*) *n.* 1. A journey; a sightseeing trip. 2. A change or shift.—*v.* 1. To travel around. —**tour·ing** *adj.*—**tour·ist** *n. & adj.*

tour de force (toor d'-*fohrss*) *n.* Resourcefulness; inventive technique; a clever feat.

tourist class. Special class of inexpensive accommodations on ship or train.

tour·na·ment (*ter*-nuh-m'nt) *n.* 1. A medieval knightly contest. 2. Any contest of skill.

tour·ney (*ter*-nee) *n.* A tournament.—*v.* To exhibit one's skill at a contest.

tour·ni·quet (*toor*-nih-ket) *n.* A device used to check bleeding by compression.

tou·sle (*tow*-z'l) *v.* [tou·sled; tou·sling] To rumple; dishevel.—*n.* Rumpled mass of hair.

tout (*towt*) *n.* 1. A solicitor. 2. A peddler of horse-racing tips.—*v.* 1. To canvass; solicit. 2. To give a tip on a horse race.—**tout·er** *n.*

tow (*toh*) *v.* To drag, esp. through water, with a rope.—*n.* 1. The act of dragging. 2. A vessel in tow; a barge.—**tow·age** *n.*—**tow·head** *n.* A light-haired person.—**take in tow.** To drag along.

towboat	towline	townet
tow-colored	tow-made	towpath
tow-haired	towmast	towrope

tow (*toh*) *n.* A rough unfinished piece of flax or hemp ready for spinning.—**tow·y** *adj.*

to·ward (*tohrd*) *prep.* Also **towards.** 1. In the direction of. 2. For; in relation to. 3. Approaching; about.—*adj.* Imminent.—**to·ward·ly** *adj.* 1. Docile. 2. Timely.— **-li·ness** *n.*

tow·el (*tow*-'l) *n.* A cloth for wiping and drying. —*v.* [tow·eled, tow·elled; tow·eling, towel·ling] —tow·el·ing, tow·el·ling *n.*

tow·er (*tow*-er) *n.* 1. A lofty, slender building. 2. A narrow, tapering superstructure. 3. A citadel; a fortress.—*v.* To rise aloft.—**tow·ered** *adj.*—**tow·er·ing** *adj.* 1. Lofty. 2. Intense; violent.—**tow·er·ing·ly** *adv.*—**tow·er·y** *adj.*

tower-capped	tower-encircled	towerproof
tower chime	tower-flanked	tower-shaped
tower-created	tower high	tower-studded
tower-crowned	towerman	tower work

town *n.* 1. *U.S.* A community larger than a village and smaller than a city. 2. *Britain.* Any well-populated place. 3. The inhabitants of a town. 4. A township.—*adj.* Urban.

town-born	town-girdled	town site
town-bred	town goer	town-tied
town-dotted	town hall	town-trained
town faring	town-imprisoned	townward
town-flanked	town-made	town wear
townfolk	townman	town-weary
town gate	townsick	town yard

town·ship *n.* A unit of local government; subdivision of a county.

towns·man *n.* 1. In New England, a selectman. 2. A town resident.—**towns·peo·ple** *n. pl.*

tox·in (*tok*-sin) *n.* A poisonous substance of animal, vegetable, or microbic origin.—**tox·ic** *adj.*—**tox·i·cant** *adj. & n.*—**tox·i·ca·tion** *n.* Poisoning.—**tox·ic·i·ty** *n.* Poisonousness.

tox·i·col·o·gy (tok-sih-*kol*-uh-jee) *n.* The science of poisons, their actions, antidotes, etc.—**tox·i·co·log·i·cal** (tok-sik-uh-*loj*-ih-kul) *adj.*— **-i·cal·ly** *adv.*—**tox·i·col·o·gist** (tok-sih-*kol*-uh-jist) *n.*

toy *n.* 1. A plaything. 2. Any diminutive object, as a very small breed of dogs.—*v.* To play with; finger; consider lightly.—*adj.* Miniature in size.—**toy·er** *n.*

toy house	toy maker	toy-sized
toyland	toy shop	toy town

trace (*trayss*) *n.* 1. Imprint; track. 2. Vestige; sign. 3. Harness strap.—*v.* [traced; trac·ing] 1. To draw; delineate. 2. To reproduce a design on a superimposed, transparent sheet. 3. To track; deduce; follow.—**trace·a·ble** *adj.*—**trac·ing** *n.*

trac·er (*trayss*-er) *n.* 1. One employed to trace missing articles. 2. An inquiry for a lost article. 3. *Ordnance.* A projectile designed to produce a streak of light to indicate its line of flight.

trac·er·y (*trayss*-er-ee) *n. Architecture* 1. The ornamentation in the head of a Gothic window. 2. A design of interlacing lines.

tra·che·a (*tray*-kee-uh) *n.* [*pl.* tra·che·ae (-ee)] The windpipe.—**tra·che·al** *adj.*

track (*trak*) *n.* 1. Mark, as of a wheel. 2. Trace; vestige. 3. Path; trail; course. 4. Sequence of events or ideas. 5. Set of rails for trains.—*v.* 1. To trace; follow. 2. To make footprints.—**track·less** *adj.*

tract (*trakt*) *n.* 1. Area; region. 2. A treatise; a dissertation. 3. *Anatomy.* Group of organs forming a system.

trac·ta·ble (*trak*-tuh-b'l) *adj.* Docile; amenable. —**tract·a·bil·i·ty** *n.*—**tract·a·bly** *adv.*

trac·tion (*trak*-sh'n) *n.* 1. Act of drawing or pulling. 2. Contraction; a tightening. 3. Adhesive friction, as of a wheel on a roadway. 4. Motive power; the moving of a vehicle.—**trac·tion·al** *adj.*

trac·tor *n.* 1. Tightening or drawing device. 2. Motor-driven vehicle for drawing heavy implements or loads.

TRACTOR

trade (*trayd*) *n.* 1. Commerce; business. 2. Occupation; handicraft. —*v.* [trad·ed; trad·ing] 1. To barter; buy and sell. 2. To transact; deal.—**trad·er** *n.*

trade-in *n. & adj.*	trademaster	tradesman
trade-made	trade name	tradespeople
trade-mark	tradesfolk	tradeswoman

trade union. Also **trade-un·ion** *n.* Organization on a craft rather than industry-wide basis of workers for collective bargaining with employers.—**trade un·ion·ism, trade-un·ion·ism** *n.* —**trade un·ion·ist, trade-un·ion·ist** *n.*

tra·di·tion (truh-*dish*-'n) *n.* 1. Established custom; historic practice; mores. 2. Style; school of thought.—**tra·di·tion·al** *adj.*—**tra·di·tion·al·ism, tra·di·tion·al·ist** *n.*— **-al·ly** *adv.*

tra·duce (truh-*dyooss*) *v.* [-duced; -duc·ing] To slander; vilify.

traf·fic (*traf*-ik) *n.* 1. Transportation. 2. Dealings; intercourse. 3. Movement of vehicles and pedestrians. 4. Articles transported.—*v.* [traf·ficked; traf·fick·ing] To deal; have to do with.—**traf·fick·er** *n.*

trag·e·dy (*traj*-eh-dee) *n.* 1. A heroic drama presenting a catastrophe, stimulating compassion and awe. 2. A calamity; catastrophe. —**tra·ge·di·an** (truh-*jee*-dee-un) *n.*

trag·ic (*traj*-ik) *adj.* 1. Of the art of tragedy. 2. Lamentable; calamitous; sad.—**trag·ic** *n.* —**trag·i·cal·ly** *adv.*

trail *v.* 1. To drag; draw along. 2. To lag behind. 3. To follow surreptitiously.—*n.* 1. Track of game; spoor. 2. Footpath.

trail·er *n.* 1. A vehicle drawn behind an automobile; a portable home connected to an automobile. 2. A vinelike plant. 3. A movie preview.

TRAILER

train *v.* 1. To teach; rear; educate. 2. To

T

aim; point. 3. To drill; prepare. 'I am training for the race.'—*n.* 1. A vehicle composed of linked cars. 'A railroad train.' 2. A series; a connected succession. 3. A body of attendants.—**train·er** *n.*—**train·ing** *n.* & *adj.*

train bearer	trainload	train-mile
trainboy	trainman	traintime
train-giddy	trainmaster	trainway

train·ee *n.* One undergoing training, esp. army training under Selective Service.

trait *n.* Distinguishing feature; characteristic.

trai·tor (*tray*-ter) *n.* 1. A betrayer; one who breaks faith. 2. One guilty of treason.—**trai·tor·ous** *adj.*—**trai·tor·ous·ly** *adv.*

tra·jec·to·ry (truh-*jek*-tor-ee) *n.* [*pl.* -ries] The curve made by a body passing through space.

tram *n.* A trolley car.—**tram·way** *n.*

tram·mel (*tram*-'l) *n.* 1. A three-layered fishnet. 2. A shackle restricting a horse's gait. 3. Restraint; check. 4. Compass for drawing ellipses; a measuring instrument.—*v.* [trammeled, tram·melled; tram·mel·ing, tram·mel·ling] 1. To intercept; enmesh. 2. To interfere with; cramp.—**tram·mel·er, tram·mel·ler** *n.*

tramp *n.* 1. A hobo; vagrant. 2. Thud of footsteps. 3. A hike.—*v.* To travel on foot.

tram·ple (*tram*-p'l) *v.* [tram·pled; tram·pling] To tread under foot.

trance (*transs*) *n.* 1. Oblivion to surroundings; stupor. 2. A hypnotic state.—**trance·like** *adj.*

tran·quil (*tran*-kwil) *adj.* Quiet; calm.—**tran·quil·li·ty** *n.* Calmness.—**tran·quil·ly** *adv.*—**tran·quil·ize** *v.* [-ized; -iz·ing]—**tran·quil·iz·er** *n.*

trans·act (transs-*akt*) *v.* To perform; negotiate.—**trans·ac·tion** *n.* 1. A deal. 2. [*pl.*] The published reports of an association.

trans- *Prefix.* Over; across; beyond; through.

trans-Arctic	transcontinental	trans-European
trans-Atlantic	trans-Equatorial	transoceanic

tran·scend (tran-*send*) *v.* To surpass; to rise above.—**tran·scend·ent** *adj.* 1. Incomparable; peerless. 2. Ideal; abstract.—**tran·scen·den·tal** *adj.*—**tran·scen·den·tal·ly** *adv.*

tran·scen·den·tal·ism (tran-sen-*den*-t'l-izm) *n. Philosophy.* System which seeks to unify experience under universal concepts.

tran·scribe *v.* [tran·scribed; tran·scrib·ing] To copy.—**tran·script** *n.* A copy.

tran·scrip·tion (tran-*skrip*-sh'n) *n.* 1. A copy. 2. The recording of a radio program or announcement.

tran·sept (*tran*-sept) *n.* Projecting arms of a church, forming the shorter part of a cross.—**tran·sep·tal** *adj.*—**tran·sep·tal·ly** *adv.*

trans·fer (transs-*fer*) *v.* [trans·ferred; trans·fer·ring] 1. To move; shift; change. 2. *Law.* To convey from one person to another.—*n.* (*transs*-fer) 1. A change; conveyance of title, right, or property from one person to another. 2. A ticket permitting a change from one public vehicle to another.—**trans·fer·a·bil·i·ty** *n.*—**trans·fer·a·ble** *adj.*—**trans·fer·ence, trans·fer·ral** *n.*—**trans·fer·rer** *n.*

trans·fig·u·ra·tion (transs-fig-yuh-*ray*-sh'n) *n.* 1. Change of form. 2. [*cap.*] *Theology.* The miraculously glorified appearance of Christ with Moses and Elias, upon a mountain.

trans·fig·ure (transs-*fig*-yoor) *v.* [trans·fig·ured; trans·fig·ur·ing] 1. To transform; alter appearance. 2. To exalt.—**trans·fig·ured** *adj.*

trans·fix *v.* To impale; fasten by piercing.—**trans·fixed, trans·fix·ing** *adj.*

trans·form *v.* To change; convert.—**trans·formed** *adj.*

trans·for·ma·tion (transs-for-*may*-sh'n) *n.* 1. A metamorphosis. 2. A woman's wig.

trans·form·er *n.* 1. A converting agent. 2. *Electricity.* Device for changing the voltage or potential of a current without altering the total current energy.

trans·fuse (transs-*fyooz*) *v.* 1. To pass through; to mix thoroughly. 2. *Medicine.* To transfer blood from one individual to another.—**trans·fus·er** *n.*—**trans·fus·i·ble** *adj.*—**trans·fu·sive** *adj.*

trans·fu·sion (transs-*fyoo*-zh'n) *n. Medicine.* Transfer of blood of one person into the veins of another.

trans·gress (transs-*gress*) *v.* To violate; trespass; sin.—**trans·gres·sive** *adj.*—**trans·gres·sive·ly** *adv.*—**trans·gres·sion** *n.*—**trans·gres·sor** *n.*

tran·sient (*tran*-sh'nt) *adj.* Temporary; short-lived; fugitive.—*n.* A temporary inhabitant.—**tran·sient·ly** *adv.*—**tran·sient·ness** *n.*

tran·si·gent (*tran*-sih-jent) *n.* A compromiser.—*adj.* Vacillating; compromising.

trans·it *n.* 1. Travel; passage; conveyance. 2. Means of conveyance; transportation.

tran·si·tion (tran-*zish*-'n) *n.* Change; movement.—**tran·si·tion·al** *adj.*— -**tion·al·ly** *adv.*

tran·si·tive (*tran*-sih-tiv) *adj. Grammar.* Denoting a class of verbs requiring a direct object.

tran·si·to·ry (*tran*-sih-tor-ee) *adj.* Brief; ephemeral; fleeting.—**tran·si·to·ri·ly** *adv.*— -**ri·ness** *n.*

trans·late (transs-*layt*) *v.* [trans·lat·ed; trans·lat·ing] To reproduce in another language; interpret; transfer; remove.—**trans·lat·a·ble** *adj.*—**trans·la·tion** *n.*—**trans·la·tor** *n.*

trans·lit·er·ate (transs-*lit*-er-ayt) *v.* To write in another alphabet.—**trans·lit·er·a·tion** *n.*

trans·lu·cent (transs-*loo*-s'nt) *adj.* 1. Penetrating; gleaming through. 2. Semi-transparent; admitting light.—**trans·lu·cence, trans·lu·cen·cy** *n.*—**trans·lu·cent·ly** *adv.*

trans·mis·sion (transs-*mish*-'n) *n.* 1. Gear transmitting power from an engine to the axle. 2. *Radio.* Travel of radio waves between transmitter and receiver.

trans·mit (transs-*mit*) *v.* [trans·mit·ted; trans·mit·ting] To convey; carry; send.—**trans·mit·ta·ble** *adj.*—**trans·mit·tal, trans·mit·tance** *n.*

trans·mit·ter *n.* Mechanism for sending out electrical waves of supersonic frequency.

trans·mute *v.* [trans·mut·ed; trans·mut·ing] To change in form; convert.—**trans·mut·a·bil·i·ty** *n.*—**trans·mut·a·ble** *adj.*—**trans·mut·a·ble·ness** *n.*—**trans·mut·a·bly** *adv.*—**trans·mu·ta·tion** *n.*

tran·som (*tran*-sum) *n.* Crossbar or window, usually hinged, above a door.

trans·par·en·cy *n.* [*pl.* -ies] A gelatine positive plate used in still color photography.

TRANSOM

trans·par·ent (transs-*pair*-'nt) *adj.* 1. Clean; sheer. 2. Readily detected; guileless.—**trans·par·ent·ly** *adv.*

tran·spire *v.* [-spired; -spir·ing] 1. To happen; occur. 2. To breathe across; perspire; give off.—**tran·spi·ra·tion** *n.*

trans·plant *v.* 1. To uproot and set in other soil. 2. To transfer to another environment. —**trans·plan·ta·tion** *n.*—**trans·plant·er** *n.*

trans·port (transs-*port*) *v.* 1. To convey; ship. 2. To inspire; possess with rapture. 3. To deport to a prison colony.—*n.* (*transs*-port) 1. Conveyance. 2. Troopship.

trans·por·ta·tion (-*tay*-sh'n) *n.* 1. Modes of conveyance. 2. The charge for conveyance or travel.

trans·pose (transs-*pohz*) *v.* [trans·posed; trans·pos·ing] 1. To shift; to place in different order. 2. *Music.* To change the key. 3. *Algebra.* To move from one side of an equation to the other by inverting the sign.—**trans·po·si·tion** (transs-puh-*zih*-sh'n) *n.*— -**po·si·tional** *adj.*

tran·sub·stan·ti·a·tion (tran-sub-stan-shee-*ay*-sh'n) *n. Theology.* The changing of the elements of Holy Communion to the body and blood of Christ.—**trans·sub·stan·ti·ate** *v.*

trans·verse (transs-*verss*) *adj.* Crosswise.—**trans·ver·sal** *adj. & n.*— -**ver·sal·ly**, -**verse·ly** *adv.*

trap *n.* 1. A device used to catch and hold an animal. 2. A snare; trick; ambush. 3. A carriage.—*v.* [trapped; trap·ping]—**trap·ping** *n.*

tra·peze (truh-*peez*) *n.* A swing hung at considerable height for acrobatic stunts.

tra·pe·zi·um (truh-*pee*-zee-'m) *n.* A four-sided plane figure, no two sides of which are parallel.

trap·e·zoid (*trap*-eh-zoyd) *n. Geometry.* A quadrilateral having two parallel sides.—**trap·e·zoid, trap·e·zoi·dal** *adj.*

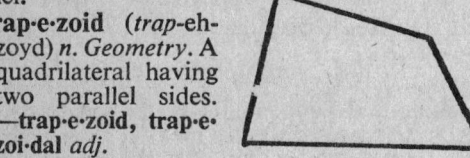
TRAPEZIUM

TRAPEZOID

trap·pings *n.* Paraphernalia; trimmings.

Trap·pist *n.* A monk of the Cistercian Order.

trash *n.* Rubbish; refuse. —**trash·i·ly** *adv.*—**trash·y** *adj.* [trash·i·er; trash·i·est].

trau·ma (*traw*-muh) *n.* A sudden injury.—**psychic trauma.** An emotional shock.—**trau·mat·ic** (traw-*mat*-ik) *adj.*

tra·vail (trav-*ayl*) *n.* 1. Toil; drudgery. 2. Childbirth; labor.

trav·el *v.* [trav·eled, trav·elled; trav·el·ing, trav·el·ling] 1. To journey; visit distant places. 2. To move; pass.—*n.* [*pl.*] Journeys; trips. —**trav·el·ed, trav·elled** *adj.*—**trav·el·er, trav·el·ler** *n.*—**trav·el·ing, trav·el·ling** *adj.*

travel-bent
travel-broken
travel-changed
travel-famous
travel-gifted

travel-infested
travel-jaded
travel-mad
travel-parted
travel-sated

travel-spent
travel-stained
traveltime
travel-tired
travel-weary

trav·e·log. Also **trav·e·logue** (*trav*-eh-log) *n.* An illustrated description of a tour.

trav·erse (*trav*-erss) *v.* [trav·ersed; trav·ers·ing] 1. To cross. 2. *Law.* To deny a contention of the opposition.—**trav·erse** *n. & adj.*—**trav·ers·a·ble** *adj.*—**trav·ers·al** *n.*—**trav·ers·er** *n.*

trav·es·ty (*trav*-ess-tee) *n.* An incongruous copy; caricature.—*v.* [trav·es·tied; -ty·ing].

trawl *n.* 1. A long fishing line holding shorter lines with baited hooks. 2. A triangular purse-shaped fishing net for deep-water fishing. —**trawl** *v.*—**trawl·er** *n.*

tray *n.* 1. A salver; a flat or shallow receptacle. 2. A meal set on a tray.

treach·er·y (*trech*-er-ee) *n.* Perfidy; betrayal; treason.—**treach·er·ous** *adj.*—**treach·er·ous·ly** *adv.*—**treach·er·ous·ness** *n.*

trea·cle (*tree*-k'l) *n.* Molasses; drippings from sugar vats.—**trea·cly** *adj.*

tread (*tred*) *v.* [trod; trod or trod·den; tread·ing] 1. To step; walk. 2. To dance. 3. To trample; crush.—*n.* 1. Footprint; track. 2. Manner of walking. 3. Horizontal surface of a step in a staircase. 4. Part of the sole which touches the ground. 5. The face of a tire.—**tread·er** *n.*

trea·dle (*tred*-'l) *n.* Foot-lever by which a machine is operated.—*v.* [trea·dled; trea·dling].

tread·mill (*tred*-mil) *n.* A mill operated by continuous climbing of steps forming the rim of a large wheel.

trea·son (*tree*-z'n) *n.* 1. Sedition. 2. Treachery; betrayal. —**trea·son·a·ble** *adj.*—**trea·son·a·ble·ness** *n.* —**trea·son·a·bly** *adv.*—**trea·son·ous** *adj.*—**trea·son·ous·ly** *adv.*

TREADMILL

treas·ure (*trezh*-er) *v.* [treas·ured; treas·ur·ing] To value; cherish.—*n.* 1. Accumulated wealth; riches. 2. A cherished possession.

treas·ur·er *n.* One having charge of funds or valuables; an official in charge of finance.

treas·ur·y *n.* [*pl.* -ies]. 1. Depository for funds and valuables. 2. [*cap.*] Government department in charge of national finance.

T

treat (*treet*) *v.* **1.** To handle; deal with. **2.** To discuss. **3.** To pay another's way; devise pleasure for another. **4.** To process. **5.** To apply remedies.—*n.* An unusual pleasure; enjoyment provided by another.—**treat·a·ble** *adj.* —**treat·a·ble·ness** *n.*

trea·tise (*tree*-tiss) *n.* A detailed study; a scholarly monograph.

treat·ment (*treet*-m'nt) *n.* **1.** Manner of dealing; use. **2.** Medical remedy.

treat·y (*tree*-tee) *n.* A formal agreement between nations; a pact.

tre·ble (*treh*-b'l) *v.* [tre·bled; tre·bling] To multiply by three.—*n.* **1.** *Music.* The highest vocal or instrumental part. **2.** A high-pitched voice.—**tre·ble** *adj.*—**tre·bly** *adv.*

tre·cen·to (treh-*chen*-toh) *n.* The 14th century. —*adj.* Of the early Italian Renaissance.

tree *n.* **1.** A massive perennial plant with woody trunk and branches. **2.** A device for keeping a shoe in shape.—*v.* [treed; tree·ing] **1.** To drive up a tree. **2.** To put in a fix. —**tree·less** *adj.*

tree-clad	tree-girt	treeman
tree-covered	tree god	tree-marked
tree-crowned	tree goddess	tree-shaded
tree-dotted	tree-lined	tree surgery
tree-fringed	tree maker	treetop

tre·foil (*tree*-foyl) *n.* **1.** Three-leafed clover. **2.** *Architecture.* An ornamental design with three sections.

trek *v.* [trekked; trek·king] To tramp a long distance. —*n.* A march.

trel·lis *n.* A lattice supporting climbing plants. —**trel·lis** *v.*

TREFOIL

trem·ble *v.* [trem·bled; trem·bling] To quiver; shudder. —**trem·ble** *n.*—**trem·bler** *n.*—**trem·bling** *n.* & *adj.*— -bling·ly *adv.*

tre·men·dous (trih-*men*-d'ss) *adj.* Immense; enormous; extraordinary; overwhelming.—**tre·men·dous·ly** *adv.*— -dous·ness *n.*

TRELLIS

trem·o·lo (*trem*-uh-loh) *n. Music.* **1.** Staccato repetition of a chord or note. **2.** A device in an organ producing a tremulous sound.

trem·or (*trem*-er; *tree*-mer) *n.* A shiver; vibration.

trem·u·lous (trem-*yuh*-lus) *adj.* **1.** Timid; apprehensive. **2.** Shaking; quivering.—**trem·u·lous·ly** *adv.*—**trem·u·lous·ness** *n.*

trench *n.* **1.** A ditch. **2.** *Military.* A long deep ditch for defense.—*v.* To cut a ditch.

trench·ant (*tren*-chunt) *adj.* Incisive; biting. —**trench·an·cy** *n.*—**trench·ant·ly** *adv.*

trend *n.* Tendency; direction.—*v.* To tend.

trep·i·da·tion (trep-ih-*day*-sh'n) *n.* Fear; apprehension; alarm.

tres·pass (*tress*-p'ss) *v.* **1.** To encroach; to enter property unlawfully. **2.** To violate; transgress; do wrong.—**tres·pass** *n.*—**tres·pas·ser** *n.*

tress *n.* A lock of hair.

tres·tle (*tress*-'l) *n.* **1.** A horizontal prop or frame supported on legs. **2.** A sturdy framework, usually of steel, carrying a road or railroad tracks across a deep ravine.

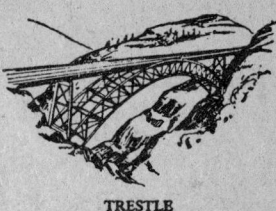

TRESTLE

tri- *prefix.* Three or thrice.

triacid	triazole	trifoliate
triagonal	tribasic	triform
triapsidal	tribrach	trilateral
triarchy	tricentennial	trilinear
triatic	tricornered	trilingual
triatomic	tricuspid	trinomial
triaxial	tridimensional	trioxide
triazine	triennial	trisyllable
triazoic	trierarchy	triweekly

tri·ad (*try*-ad) *n.* **1.** Group of three. **2.** *Music.* Simplest consonant chord composed of a given tone with the third above (major or minor) and its perfect fifth.

tri·al (*try*-'l) *n.* **1.** A test. **2.** Affliction; ordeal. **3.** *Law.* Examination of a controversial cause between parties before a proper tribunal. —**trial** *adj.*—**trial lawyer.**

tri·an·gle (*try*-ang-'l) *n.* **1.** *Geometry.* A three-sided figure having three angles. **2.** A love affair involving three people. **3.** *Music.* A three-sided percussion instrument. —**tri·an·gu·lar** *adj.*—**tri·an·gu·late** *v.* [tri·an·gul·ated; tri·an·gu·lat·ing]—**tri·an·gu·la·tion** *n.*

tribe (*trybe*) *n.* **1.** A simple social group with a common ancestry and language. **2.** Any group.—**trib·al** *adj.*— -al·ly *adv.*—**tribes·man** *n.*

TRIANGLES

trib·u·la·tion (trib-yuh-*lay*-sh'n) *n.* Affliction; sorrow.

tri·bu·nal (try-*byoo*-n'l) *n.* A court of justice.

trib·une (*trib*-yoon) *n.* **1.** In ancient times, a representative of the people. **2.** A speaker's platform.—**trib·une·ship** *n.*—**trib·u·ni·cial** *adj.*

trib·u·tar·y (*trib*-yuh-tair-ee) *n.* **1.** A nation or state paying tax. **2.** A stream flowing into river or lake.—**trib·u·tar·y** *adj.*— -tar·i·ly *adv.*

trib·ute (*trib*-yoot) *n.* **1.** Praise; homage. **2.** Tax; obligation to contribute.

trice (*trysse*) *n.* An instant; a moment.—*v.* [triced; tric·ing] To tie; bind securely.

tri·ceps (*try*-sepss) *n.* Muscle at the back of the upper arm.

tri·chi·na (trih-*ky*-nuh) *n.* [*pl.* tri·chi·nae] Parasitic worm infecting man and many animals, particularly swine.—**trich·i·nize** *v.* [-nized; niz·ing]—**trich·i·ni·za·tion** *n.*

trich·i·no·sis (trik-ih-*noh*-siss) *n. Medicine.* Disease caused by the presence of the trichina parasite in the intestines and in the muscles, usually resulting from eating improperly prepared pork.—**trich·i·nous, trich·i·nosed** *adj.*

trick *n.* 1. An artifice; ruse; deception; prank. 2. A sleight of hand; piece of magic. 3. A personal peculiarity. 4. A single play in certain card games.—*v.* To deceive; dupe.—**trick·er** *n.*—**trick·er·y** *n.*—**trick·ish, trick·sy** *adj.*

trick·y *adj.* [-i·er; -i·est] 1. *Colloquial.* Seemingly safe but actually precarious. 'A tricky predicament.' 2. Given to tricks and pranks.

trick·le (*trik*-'l) *v.* [trick·led; trick·ling] To flow in a small stream; drip.—**trick·le** *n.*

tri·col·or (*try*-kul-er) *n.* 1. The French flag. 2. A flag of three colors in almost equal proportions.—**tri·col·ored** *adj.*

tri·cy·cle (*try*-sih-k'l) *n.* Three-wheeled velocipede.

tri·dent (*try*-d'nt) *n.* 1. *Mythology.* Three-pronged spear carried by the sea god Poseidon (Neptune). 2. A three-pronged fish spear.—**tri·dent, tri·den·tate** *adj.*

tried. *Past tense* of **try.** —*adj.* Trustworthy; proven.

TRICYCLE

tri·fle (*try*-f'l) *n.* 1. A small, insignificant thing. 2. A wine-soaked spongy cake covered with whipped cream.—*v.* [tri·fled; tri·fling] To act frivolously or thoughtlessly.—**tri·fler** *n.*

tri·fo·cal *adj. Optics.* Having lenses in three sections for seeing at various distances.

trig·ger *n.* Releasing catch or lever, esp. the part of a gun lock releasing the hammer.

trig·o·nom·e·try *n.* Science of studying relations between sides and angles of triangles.

trill *n.* 1. A warbling, quavering sound. 2. A consonant produced with a trilling sound, as *l* or *r.*—*v.* To sing with tremulous vibrations.

tril·li·um (*tril*-ee-um) *n.* Three-leaved plant of the lily family.

tril·o·gy (*tril*-uh-jee) *n.* A group of three novels, plays, poems, or pieces of music on one theme.

trim *adj.* [trim·mer; trim·mest] Neat; tidy; well-ordered. —*v.* [trimmed; trim·ming] 1. To put in order; adjust. 2. To ornament; embellish. 3. To clip. 4. *Nautical.* To balance cargo before sailing. 5. *Slang.* To chastise;

TRILLIUM

to defeat.—*n.* 1. Order; condition. 'The swimmer was in good trim.' 2. *Nautical.* Balance of a ship.—**trim·ly** *adv.*—**trim·mer** *n.* —**trim·ness** *n.*

trim·ming *n.* 1. Accessories. 2. A beating.

trim-ankled	trim-cut	trim looking
trim-bearded	trim-dressed	trim-suited
trim-bodiced	trim-hedged	trim-swept
trim-bodied	trim-kept	trim-waisted

trim·e·ter (*trim*-eh-ter) *n.* A verse form having three beats to the line.—**trim·e·ter, tri·met·ric, tri·met·ri·cal** *adj.*

tri·ni·tro·tol·u·ene (try-ny-troh-*tol*-yoo-een) *n.* Also TNT. High explosive derived from toluene, a coal-tar product which has been acted upon by nitric acid.

trin·i·ty (*trin*-uh-tee) *n.* [*pl.* -ties] 1. [*cap.*] *Theology.* The Father, the Son, and the Holy Ghost united in one Godhead. 2. A triad. —**trin·i·tar·ian** (trin-uh-*tair*-ee-un) *adj.* Pertaining to the Trinity.—*n.* [*cap.*] Believer in the doctrine of the Trinity.—**Trin·i·tar·i·an·ism** *n.*

trin·ket (*tring*-kit) *n.* 1. A small ornament. 2. A trifle; a toy.

tri·o (*tree*-oh) *n.* [*pl.* tri·os] 1. Group of three. 2. *Music.* A composition for three voices or instruments. 3. Performers of a three-part composition.

tri·o·let (*try*-uh-let) *n.* An eight-line poem in which the first, fourth, and seventh lines are the same, and so are the second and eighth lines.

trip *n.* 1. A journey or voyage; excursion. 2. A light, short step. 3. A stumble; misstep; mistake. 4. A sudden catch by which a wrestler throws his opponent.—*v.* [tripped; trip·ping] 1. To move the feet nimbly. 2. To stumble; lose footing. 3. To err. 4. To cause to fall. 5. To obstruct.—**trip·per** *n.* A mechanism to release a catch.

tri·par·tite (try-*pahr*-tyte) *adj.* Divided in three; involving three parties.

tripe *n.* 1. Stomach walls of sheep or oxen used as food. 2. *Slang.* Something worthless.

tri·ple *n. Baseball.* A three-base hit.

tri·ple *adj.* Threefold; three times repeated; treble.—*v.* [tri·pled; tri·pling].—**tri·ply** *adv.*

triple-aisled	triple-decked	triple-roofed
triple-arched	triple-dyed	triple-stranded
triple-awned	triple-edged	tripletail
tripleback	triplefold	triple-tailed
triple-barbed	triple-formed	triple-terraced
triple-barred	triple-gemmed	triple-throated
triple-bodied	triple-hatted	triple-tiered
triple-bolted	triple-headed	triple-tongued
triple-branched	triple-lived	triple-toothed
triple-chorded	triple-piled	triple-towered
triple-colored	triple-rayed	tripletree
triple-crested	triple-ribbed	triple-turreted

triple play. *Baseball.* A play in which three men are put out.

tri·plet (*trip*-let) *n.* 1. A group of three. 2. [*pl.*] Three offspring born together. 3. *Music.* Three notes performed in the time of two.

T

trip·li·cate (*trip*-lih-kit) *n.* A third copy.—**trip·li·cate** (*trip*-lih-kayt) *v.* To triple.—**trip·li·cate** *adj.*

tri·pod (*try*-pod) *n.* A three-legged stand, supporting a camera or surveying instrument.

trip·tych (*trip*-tik) *n.* 1. A three-paneled altarpiece. 2. Three related pictures grouped together.

Tris·tan, Tris·tram *n.* A favorite hero of British, Scandinavian, and German knightly remances of the Middle Ages.

trite (*tryte*) *adj.* Hackneyed; commonplace; over-used.—**trite·ly** *adv.*—**trite·ness** *n.*

Tri·ton (*tryte*-'n) *n. Greek Mythology.* Sea deity, half man and half fish, with power to raise and compose storms.—**Tri·ton·ess** *n.*

TRIPOD

trit·u·rate (*trih*-chuh-rayt) *v.* To grind; crush to powder.—**trit·u·ra·tion** *n.* 1. Grinding process. 2. *Pharmacy.* A ground powder. ·

tri·umph (*try*-umf) *n.* 1. Victory; achievement; conquest. 2. Exultation; glory.—*v.* 1. To celebrate victory. 2. To obtain victory; conquer. 3. To boast.—**tri·um·phant** *adj.*—**tri·um·phant·ly** *adv.*—**tri·um·pher** *n.*

tri·um·phal *adj.* For victory.—**triumphal arch.** Massive, ornamental archway commemorating a great victory.

triv·et (*triv*-et) *n.* 1. A tripod. 2. A metal three-legged stand for resting hot dishes.

triv·i·a (*triv*-ee-uh) *n. pl.* Trifles.

triv·i·al (*triv*-ee-ul) *adj.* Petty; insignificant.—**triv·i·al·i·ty, triv·i·al·ness** *n.*—**triv·i·al·ly** *adv.*

tro·cha·ic (troh-*kay*-ik) *adj.* Consisting of verse feet (trochees) of two syllables, the accent falling on the first.—**tro·cha·ic** *n.*

tro·che (*troh*-kee) *n.* A soothing lozenge, as a cough drop.

tro·chee (*troh*-kee) *n.* A verse foot of two syllables, accented on the first.

trog·lo·dyte (*trog*-luh-dyte) *n.* 1. A cave-dweller. 2. One who lives in an uncivilized fashion. 3. An ape.—**trog·lo·dyt·ic** (trog-luh-*dit*-ik), **trog·lo·dyt·i·cal** *adj.*

Tro·jan (*troh*-jun) *adj.* 1. Pertaining to ancient Troy. 2. Hard-working; heroic.—*n.* 1. Inhabitant of ancient Troy. 2. One having great power of endurance.

Trojan horse. 1. *Mythology.* Wooden horse concealing armed men by which the Greeks gained entrance into Troy during the Trojan War. 2. Group within a nation seeking to sabotage its defense.

troll (*trohl*) *v.* 1. To sing in parts, as a round; sing heartily. 2. To angle for; entice. 3. To fish by trailing a hook and line from a boat. —*n.* 1. A gnome; elf. 2. A song sung in parts; a round.—**trol·ler** *n.*—**trol·ling** *n.*

trol·ley (*trol*-ee) *n.* [*pl.* **trol·leys, trol·lies**] 1. Electric street car running on rails. 2. Cable car.—**trol·ley** *v.*—**trol·ley·man** *n.*

trol·lop (*trol*-up) *n.* A loose woman; a harlot. —**trol·lop·y** *adj.*

trom·bone (*trom*-bohn) *n. Music.* Deep-toned instrument of the trumpet family, consisting of one sliding and two stationary tubes.—**trom·bon·ist** *n.*

TROMBONE

troop *n.* 1. A body of soldiers, esp. a cavalry unit corresponding to an infantry company. 2. [*pl.*] Soldiers collectively. 3. A crowd; company; multitude.—*v.* 1. To march in a body. 2. To collect in numbers; assemble. —**troop·er** *n.* A private cavalry soldier.—**troop·ship** *n.* A ship carrying soldiers; transport.

tro·phy (*troh*-fee) *n.* [*pl.* **tro·phies**] 1. An article taken from an enemy. 2. Prize awarded the winner of a contest. 3. A relic; remains.

trop·ic (*trop*-ik) *n.* 1. One of the two parallels of latitude equally distant from the equator: The *Tropic of Cancer* and the *Tropic of Capricorn.* 2. [*pl.*] The regions between the two tropics.—*adj.* Pertaining to the tropics.—**trop·i·cal** *adj.*—**trop·i·cal·ly** *adv.*

tro·pism (*troh*-pizm) *n. Biology.* Tendency to turn; consistent instinctive reaction to stimuli. —**tro·pis·tic** *adj.*

trot *v.* [trot·ted; trot·ting] 1. To move between a walk and a run, as a horse. 2. To walk rapidly; to run. 3. To ride at a trot.—**trot** *n.* —**trot·ter** *n.*—**trot out.** To show off; to exhibit.

troth (*trohth*) *n.* 1. Pledge; vowed faith. 2. Truth.—**troth·less** *adj.* Faithless.

Trot·sky·ite *n.* A follower of the late Leon Trotsky, exiled Russian revolutionist.

trou·ba·dour (*troo*-buh-door) *n.* Romantic lyrical poet of the Middle Ages; minstrel.

trou·ble (*trub*-'l) *v.* [trou·bled; trou·bling] 1. To agitate; disturb. 2. To annoy. 3. To afflict; grieve. 4. To put to labor or exertion; bother.—**trou·ble** *n.*—**trou·bled** *adj.*—**trou·bled·ly** *adv.*—**trou·bler** *n.*

trouble-free	troublemaker	troublesmith
trouble-haunted	trouble-shoot	trouble-tossed
trouble house	trouble-shooter	trouble-worn

trou·ble·some *adj.* Disturbing; annoying. —**trou·ble·some·ly** *adv.*—**trou·ble·some·ness** *n.*

trou·blous *adj.* Unsettled; tumultuous.

trough (*trawf*) *n.* 1. Long oblong vessel for water or animal feed. 2. Gutter along a roof for draining off rain. 3. Depression or hollow.

trounce (*trownss*) *v.* To beat.—**trounc·ing** *n.*

troupe (*troop*) *n.* A company or band, esp. of actors or performers.—**troup·er** *n.* Experienced, seasoned actor.

trou·sers (*trow*-zerz) *n. pl.* Man's outer garment covering the body from waist to ankle and the legs separately from thigh to ankle.

trous·seau (*troo*-soh) *n.* [*pl.* **trous·seaux; trous·seaus**] A bride's wardrobe.

trout (*trowt*) *n.* Species of game fish related to the salmon, found in both fresh and salt water.

trow·el *n.* 1. Tool for spreading cement or plaster. 2. Scooped, short-handled gardener's tool.—*v.* [trow·elled; trow·el·ling] To spread or dig up with a trowel.

TROWEL

Troy. Ancient city near the Dardenelles.

troy weight. System of weights used for precious metals and jewelry.

tru·ant (*troo*-unt) *n.* Shirker; one absent without permission.—*adj.* Wilfully absent; idle. —**tru·an·cy** *n.*—**tru·ant·ly** *adv.*

truce (*trooss*) *n.* 1. *Military.* Armistice; temporary cessation of hostilities by agreement. 2. Respite; brief cessation.

truck *n.* 1. Large motor vehicle for transporting goods. 2. Small hand-propelled carriage. —*v.* To convey by truck.—**truck·age** *n.* Truck transportation.—**truck·er** *n.*

truck *n.* 1. Barter; small trade. 2. Small commodities; produce. 3. *Colloquial.* Worthless articles.—*v.* To exchange; to barter.

truck·le *v.* [truck·led; truck·ling] To yield obsequiously.—**truck·ler** *n.*—**truck·ling·ly** *adv.*

truckle bed. A low bed on casters which fits under a full-sized bed; a trundle bed.

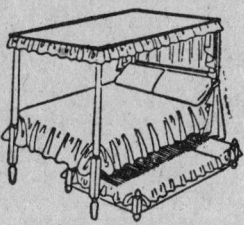

TRUCKLE BED

truc·u·lent (*truk*-yoo-l'nt) *adj.* Ferocious; savage.—**truc·u·lence** *n.*—**truc·u·lent·ly** *adv.*

trudge(*truj*)*v.*[trudged; trudg·ing] To tramp laboriously.—*n.* An exhausting hike. —**trudg·er** *n.*

true (*troo*) *adj.* 1. Correct; precise; according to fact. 2. Genuine; authentic. 3. Faithful; constant; loyal.—*v.* [trued; tru·ing] To adjust nicely; make exact.—**true·ness** *n.*

true-aimed	true-grained	true-spoken
true-born	true-hearted	true-toned
true-bred	true-paced	true-tongued

tru·ism (*troo*-izm) *n.* Platitude; self-evident statement.

trull *n.* A prostitute; a trollop.

tru·ly *adv.* Honestly; accurately; in fact.

trump *n.* 1. *Cards.* One of a suit of cards which defeats any of the other suits. 2. *Colloquial.* A fine fellow; dependable person.—*v.* To take with a trump card.—**trump up.** To plot; fabricate.

trum·pet *n.* 1. *Music.* Brass wind instrument with three valves. 2. Trumpet-shaped device for intensifying and directing sound. —*v.* 1. To make a trumpetlike sound. 2. To proclaim; noise abroad.—**trum·pet·er** *n.* 1. Trumpet player. 2. A herald.

TRUMPET

trun·cate (*trung*-kayt) *v.* [trun·cat·ed; trun·cat·ing] To cut short; lop. —*adj.* Cut off square; having no point.—**trun·cat·ed** *adj.* Cut off; abruptly lopped.—**trun·ca·tion** *n.*

trun·cheon (*trun*-chun) *n.* A stick or club, esp. a policeman's club.—*v.* To beat with a club; cudgel. —**trun·cheoned** *adj.*

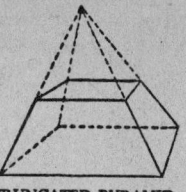

TRUNCATED PYRAMID

trun·dle *n.* 1. Small, low-wheeled carriage or truck. 2. Small roller or caster.—*v.* [trun·dled; trun·dling] To roll along on rollers. —**trundle bed.** Low bed on wheels, which fits under a higher bed.—**trun·dler** *n.*

trunk *n.* 1. The woody stem of a tree. 2. The human body without head and limbs. 3. A main body. 4. Box or chest, esp. for holding clothes. 5. The snout of an animal, esp. an elephant. 6. [*pl.*] Men's swimming shorts. —*adj.* Designating the main section. 'A railway trunk line.'

truss *n.* 1. Bundle; package. 2. *Surgery.* Supporting apparatus worn for hernia. 3. *Architecture.* Bracket; supporting frame. 4. *Engineering.* Rigid framework of beams.—*v.* 1. To tie in a bundle, often with *up.* 2. To bind; fasten. 3. To support by a truss. —**trussed** *adj.*—**truss·er** *n.*—**truss·ing** *n.* *Engineering.* Bracing; supporting members.

trust *n.* 1. Reliance; confidence. 2. Confident anticipation; belief. 3. Responsibility; custody. 4. Credit; property committed to trust. 5. Organization of corporations managed by trustees. 6. Monopoly; cartel.—*adj.* Held in trust.—*v.* To believe; rely on; entrust. —**trust·ing** *adj.*—**trust·ing·ly** *adv.*

trus·tee (trus-*tee*) *n.* Person holding or administrating property in trust.—**trus·tee·ship** *n.*

trust·ful *adj.* Unquestioning; confiding.—**trust·ful·ly** *adv.*—**trust·ful·ness** *n.*

trust·wor·thy (*trust*-wer-thee) *adj.* Reliable; dependable.— -**thi·ly** *adv.*— -**thi·ness** *n.*

trust·y *adj.* 1. Reliable; deserving of confidence. 2. Strong; firm; unfailing.—*n.* A prisoner allowed certain privileges for good conduct.—**trust·i·ly** *adv.*—**trust·i·ness** *n.*

truth (*trooth*) *n.* 1. Honesty; veracity; sincerity. 2. A fact, proposition, or principle representing the convergence of evidence.—**truth·ful** *adj.*—**truth·ful·ly** *adv.*—**truth·ful·ness** *n.*

truth-armed	truth-instructed	truthteller
truth-dictated	truth-led	truth-tired
truth-filled	truth-shod	truth-writ

try *v.* [tried; try·ing] 1. To attempt; endeavor. 2. To test; examine. 3. To torment; harass. 4. To judge. 5. To strain; overwork.—*n.* An endeavor.—**try·a·ble** *adj.*—**try·er** *n.*

try·ing *adj.* Vexing; severe; harassing.

try·out *n.* Audition; test; demonstration to determine fitness.

try·sail (*try*-s'l) *n. Nautical.* Small longitudinal triangular sail hoisted on a lower mast.

T

tryst (*trist, tryste*) *n.* 1. An appointed meeting, esp. a secret meeting. 2. Designated meeting place.—*v.* To meet secretly.—**tryst·er** *n.*

tsar. *Variant spelling* of **Czar.**—**tsar·e·vitch** *n.*

tset·se (*tset*-suh) *n.* African fly which carries sleeping sickness.

T-square *n.* A ruler with a perpendicular head, used in drafting.

tub *n.* 1. Large shallow vessel for laundering, etc. 2. Cask; keg. 3. *Slang*. An old ship. —*v.* [tubbed; tub·bing] To wash or bathe in a tub.

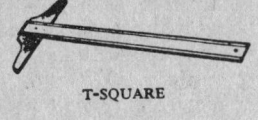

T-SQUARE

tu·ba (*too*-buh) *n. Music*. Large bass-voiced brass instrument.

tube (*tyoob, toob*) *n.* 1. Long hollow cylinder; small pipe. 2. Collapsible container for pastes. 3. Tunnel; subway. 4. *Electronics*. A vacuum tube.

tube-fed	tube maker	tube-shaped
tube-form	tubeman	tubesmith

tu·ber (*too*-ber; *tyoo*-) *n. Botany*. An underground fleshy stem; a modification of the root.

tu·ber·cle (*too*-ber-k'l; *tyoo*-) *n.* 1. Small rounded knob; pimple; nodule. 2. *Pathology*. Mass of nodules produced by the bacillus of tuberculosis.—**tu·ber·cu·late, tu·ber·cu·lat·ed** *adj. Botany.* Having small knobs.

tu·ber·cu·lar (too-*ber*-kyoo-ler) *adj.* 1. Having or resembling tubercles. 2. Tuberculous; infected with tuberculosis.

tu·ber·cu·lo·sis (too-ber-kyoo-*loh*-siss) *n.* Infectious disease, usually of the lungs, characterized by the formation of tubercles in the tissues.—**tu·ber·cu·lous** *adj.*

tube·rose (*tyoob*-rohz; *toob*-) *n.* A bulbous herb bearing white flowers.

tu·ber·ous *adj.* Covered with tubers or tubercles.

tub·ing (*toob*-ing) *n.* 1. Series of network of tubes. 2. Material for tubes.

tub·u·lar (*too*-byoo-ler) *adj.* Formed as a tube.

tuck *n.* 1. Ornamental fold stitched in a garment. 2. Horizontal fold for shortening.—*v.* 1. To press together; gather up. 2. To enclose; enfold. —**tucked** *adj.*—**tuck·er** *n.* —**tuck·ing** *n.*

tuck·er *v. Colloquial*. To fatigue; exhaust; tire. —**tuck·ered** *adj.*

Tues·day (*tyooz*-dee; *tooz*-) *n.* Third day of the week; day after Monday.

tuft *n.* 1. A knot of small soft fibers; bunch. 2. A cluster; clump.—*v.* To separate into or adorn with tufts.—**tuft·ed** *adj.*

TUBEROSE

tug *v.* [tugged; tug·ging] To pull with great effort; haul; struggle.—*n.* 1. A supreme effort. 2. A tugboat.—**tug·ger** *n.*—**tug·ging·ly** *adv.*

tug·boat *n.* A powerful steamboat used for towing.—**tug·boat·man** *n.*

Tui·ler·ies (*twee*-ler-eez) Famous gardens of a former royal palace in Paris.

tu·i·tion (too-*ish*-'n) *n.* 1. Instruction; business of teaching. 2. Fee for instruction or schooling.—**tu·i·tion·ar·y** *adj.*

tu·lip (*too*-lip; *tyoo*-) *n.* A bulbous plant cultivated for its beautiful flowers. —**tu·lip·o·man·i·a** *n.* Violent passion for the cultivation or acquisition of tulips occurring in Holland about 1634.—**tu·lip·o·man·i·ac** *n.*

tulle (*tool*) *n.* Fine silk net used for women's garments.

tum·ble (*tum*-b'l) *v.* [tum·bled; tum·bling] 1. To lose support and fall. 2. To perform acrobatic stunts. 3. To disorder; rumple; pitch about.—*n.* A fall; a rolling over.—**tum·ble·down** *adj.* Dilapidated; ruined.

tum·bler *n.* 1. Acrobat. 2. Large cylindrical drinking glass.—**tumbler·ful** *n.* [*pl.* tum·bler·fuls].

tum·ble·weed *n.* A plant common in the U.S. which breaks loose from its roots in autumn and is blown about the countryside by wind.

TULIP

tu·mid (*too*-mid) *adj.* Bulbous; swollen.—**tu·mid·i·ty** *n.*—**tu·mid·ly** *adv.*—**tu·mid·ness** *n.*

tu·mor (*too*-mer; *tyoo*-) *n.* A permanent localized swelling caused by a new growth of tissue. —**tu·mor·ous** *adj.*

tu·mult (*too*-mult; *tyoo*-) *n.* 1. Uproar; commotion. 2. Extreme agitation; confused motion.—**tu·mul·tu·ous** *adj.*— **-ous·ly** *adv.*— **-ous·ness** *n.*

tun *n.* A large wine cask.

tu·na (*too*-nah) *n.* Game and food fish; a species of tunny.

tune *n.* 1. A sound or tone. 2. An air; melody. 3. Correct intonation in singing or playing. 4 Frame of mind; mood; temper. —*v.* [tuned; tun·ing] 1. To adjust; regulate. 2. To imbue with a special tone; attune.—**tun·a·ble** *adj.*—**tun·a·bly** *adv.*—**tune·ful** *adj.* Harmonious; melodious. —**tune·ful·ly** *adv.*—**tune·ful·ness** *n.*—**tune·less** *adj.*—**tun·er** *n.* Adjuster of musical instruments. —**tun·ing** *n.*

tung·sten (*tung*-sten) *n.* Grayish white, brittle, hard metallic element used to produce special alloy steels. (*Symbol*: W).

tu·nic (*too*-nik; *tyoo*-)*n.* 1. Sleeveless undergarment worn by ancient Romans. 2. Hip-length blouse girdled at the waist.

TUNIC

tuning fork. *Music.* Two-pronged instrument which produces a pure tone when struck.

tun·nel *n.* 1. An underground passage. 2. *Mining.* Level passage cut at right angles to the veins.—*v.*

TUNING FORK

[tun·neled; tun·nel·ing] 1. To cut a tunnel. 2. To hollow out in length.

tun·ny (*tun*-ee) *n.* Large edible fish of the mackerel family.

tur·ban (*ter*-b'n) *n.* 1 Oriental headdress consisting of cap wound with sash. 2. Woman's hat of similar style.

tur·bid (*ter*-bid) *adj.* 1. Muddy; foul with sediment. 2. Vexed; disturbed.—**turbid·i·ty** *n.*—**tur·bid·ness** *n.*—**tur·bid·ly** *adv.*

tur·bine (*ter*-bin) *n.* An engine driven by pressure of a liquid or gas upon curved blades arranged about a rotating axis.

TURBAN

tur·bo- *prefix.* Turbine.

turboelectric	turbogenerative	turbojar
turbofan	turbogenerator	turboprop

tur·bu·lent (*ter*-byoo-l'nt) *adj.* 1. Disturbed; agitated; in violent commotion. 2. Restless; riotous.—**tur·bu·lence** *n.*—**tur·bu·lent·ly** *adv.*

tu·reen (tuh-*reen*) *n.* Large, deep vessel for holding soup at the table.

turf *n.* 1. Sod; top layer of earth containing grass roots. 2. Blackish fibrous substances used as fuel. 3. The sport of horse racing.—*v.* To cover with turf.—**turf·i·ness** *n.*—**turf·y** *adj.*

turf-bound	turf-grown	turf-roofed
turf-built	turf-laid	turf-spread
turf-covered	turfman	turf-walled

tur·gid (*ter*-jid) *adj.* Swollen; bloated; inflated. —**tur·gid·i·ty** (ter-*jid*-uh-tee) *n.*—**tur·gid·ly** *adv.*

Turk *n.* Native or inhabitant of Turkey.

Tur·ke·stan (ter-keh-*stan*). Large plain in SW Russia, bounded on the west by the Caspian Sea.

tur·key (*ter*-kee) *n.* 1. Large game bird of North and Central America, raised for its excellent meat. 2. *Theater Slang.* An unsuccessful production.

Turk·ish *adj.* Of or pertaining to Turkey.—*n.* The language of the Turks.

TURKEY (1/22 life-size)

Turk·man *n.* [*pl.* Turk·men] Native of the Turkmen S.S.R.

Turk·o·man *n.* [*pl.* Turk·o·mans] Member of a racial group of SW U.S.S.R.

tur·moil (*ter*-moyl) *n.* Commotion; harassing disturbance; tumult.—*v.* To agitate.

turn (*tern*) *v.* 1. To revolve; rotate. 2. To change direction or position; reverse. 3. To apply; use; employ. 4. To shape on a lathe; to form. 5. To alter the purpose or opinions of another. 6. To transform; translate; transfer. 7. To cause to ferment; become sour. 8. To place in or bring to a stated condition. —*n.* 1. Revolution; rotation. 2. Winding; curve; bend. 3. Short walk or drive. 4. Opportune act or deed. 5. Form; character; temper. 6. Short spell; little task. 7. Nervous shock or start. 8. Particular aptitude or bent.—**turn·er** *n.*—**turn·er·y** *n.*—**turn·ing** *n.* **by turns.** In alternate succession.—**in turn.** In established order.—**to a turn.** Nicely; precisely.—**turn down.** To reject.—**turn out.** 1. To produce. 2. To become. 3. To come out. —**turn tail.** To flee.—**turn to.** To go to work. —**turn up.** To appear suddenly.

turn-about	turnpiker	turnskin
turn-away	turnpin	turnsole
turn-back	turnplate	turnspit
turnbout	turnplow	turnstone
turncap	turn-round	turntable
turncoat	turnrow	turn-to
turncock	turnscrew	turn-under
turn-down	turn server	turn-up
turn-off	turnsheet	turnwrest

turn·back *n.* 1. A coward; craven. 2. Something turned back; a cuff.

turn·buck·le *n.* A metal sleeve with ends threaded in opposite directions, used between rods or stays to maintain or increase tension.

TURNBUCKLE

turn·ip (*ter*-nip) *n.* Yellow or white fleshy vegetable of the mustard family, frequently used in stews, ragouts, etc.

turnip-fed	turnip-pointed	turnip-shaped
turnip-headed	turnip-rooted	turnip-tailed
turnip-leaved	turnip seed	turnipwood

turn·key (*tern*-kee) *n.* Person in charge of the keys of a prison.

turn·out *n.* Also **turn-out.** 1. A quitting of work; strike. 2. A purposeful gathering of people; party. 3. An equipage. 4. Net quantity yielded; output.

turn·o·ver (*tern*-oh-ver) *n.* 1. Pie or tart with the circular crust folded over. 2. Amount of business done in a given time. —**turn·o·ver** *adj.*

turn·pike *n.* Tollgate; gate set across a road. —**turnpike road.** A road with tollgates established by law.

turn·stile *n.* A gate equipped with four arms pivoting counterclockwise to allow entrance of one person at a time.

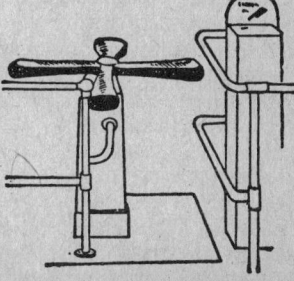

TURNSTILE

T

tur·pen·tine (*ter*-pen-tyne) *n.* 1. A resinous substance obtained from certain evergreen trees. 2. Spirits of turpentine distilled from this resin.—*v.* [tur-pen-tined; tur-pen-tin-ing] To apply or rub with turpentine.

tur·pi·tude (*ter*-pih-tyood) *n.* Moral baseness; depravity.

tur·quoise (*ter*-kwoyz) *n.* 1. A greenish-blue, opaque precious stone. 2. A greenish-blue color.

tur·ret *n.* 1. Small tower. 2. *Military.* A heavily armored tower, often rotating, mounted with large guns.—**tur·ret·ed** *adj.*

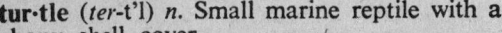

TURRET

tur·tle (*ter*-t'l) *n.* Small marine reptile with a bony shell covering.

turtle dove. 1. Pigeonlike bird noted for its affectionate nature. 2. *Slang.* Lover.

TURTLE (1/6 life-size)

tush *interj.* Be silent; hush.

tusk *n.* 1. Long pointed tooth of certain animals, as the elephant. 2. Any long projecting tooth.—**tusked** *adj.*—**tusk·er** *n.* Elephant with fully developed tusks.

tussah, tussore *n.* Also **tusseh.** 1. A silkworm in the Far East which produces a brown silk. 2. The silk itself.

tus·sle *v.* [tus·sled; tus·sling] To struggle; scuffle.—*n.* A disorderly conflict.

tut *interj.* Exclamation of mild rebuke or impatience.

tu·te·lage (*too*-teh-lij) *n.* 1. Guardianship; protection. 2. Instruction; teaching.—**tu·te·lar, tu·te·lar·y** *adj.*

tu·tor (*too*-ter) *n.* 1. Private teacher or instructor. 2. College teacher subordinate to an instructor.—*v.* 1. To instruct; teach, esp. privately. 2. To train; discipline; drill.—**tu·tor·age, tu·tor·ship** *n.*—**tu·tor·i·al** *adj.*

tu·tu (*too*-too) *n. Ballet.* Traditional costume of the danseuse, consisting of a tight bodice with short extended skirt.

tux·e·do (tuk-*see*-doh) *n.* Man's semi-formal dinner suit.

twad·dle (*twod*-'l) *v.* [twad·dled; twad·dling] To prattle; make silly, meaningless conversation.—*n.* Gabble; pretentious, high-flown balderdash.

twain *adj. & n. Poetic.* Two.

twang *n.* 1. Sharp, quick, ringing sound. 2. Harsh nasal vocal sound.—**twang** *v.* —**twang·y** *adj.*

tweak (*tweek*) *v.* To pinch; twitch.—**tweak** *n.*

tweed *n.* Soft woolen fabric with a rough unfinished surface.

tweez·ers *n. pl.* Small pincers; two-pronged instrument for grasping tiny objects.

twelfth *adj.* In consecutive order as twelve. —*n.* One of twelve equal parts.

Twelfth·night *n.* Evening of January 6; Epiphany.

TWEEZERS

twelve (*twelv*) *n.* The number represented by the symbol 12; a dozen.—*adj.* Consisting of twelve.

twen·ty (*twen*-tee) *n.* The number represented by the symbol 20; twice ten.—*adj.* Consisting of twenty.—**twen·ti·eth** *adj.* In consecutive order as twenty.—*n.* One of twenty equal parts.

twice (*twysse*) *adv.* 1. Two times. 2. Doubly; two-fold.

twid·dle (*twid*-'l) *v.* [twid·dle; twid·dling] To twirl idly; fidget with.—**twid·dler** *n.*

twig *n.* Small shoot; slender branch.—*v.* [twigged; twig·ging] To observe keenly; detect.—**twig·gy** *adj.*

twi·light (*twy*-lyte) *n.* 1. The faint light after sunset. 2. The time between sunset and dark; evening. 3. Faint light.—*adj.* Obscure; imperfectly illuminated.

twilight sleep. Somnolent condition induced by scopolamine-morphine, deadening pain; often used in childbirth.

twill *n.* 1. Diagonally ribbed textile fabric. 2. The raised line or rib made by twilling.—*v.* To weave so as to form a diagonal ribbing. —**twilled** *adj.*

twin *n.* 1. One of two young produced at a single birth. 2. One resembling another; duplicate.—*adj.* 1. Born at a single birth. 2. Resembling one other.—*v.* [twinned; twin·ning] 1. To be born at the same birth. 2. To bring forth two at one birth.—**twinned** *adj.*

twin-balled	twin-headed	twin-spiked
twin-begot	twin-hued	twin-spired
twin-blossomed	twin-leaved	twin-striped
twin-engined	twin-named	twin-towered
twin-forked	twin-peaked	twin-wheeled

twine (*twyne*) *n.* 1. Cord; strong thread consisting of twisted strands. 2. A winding; convolution.—*v.* [twined; twin·ing] 1. To twist; form by twisting of threads or fibers. 2. To wind round; encircle. 3. To bend; make turns.—**twin·ing** *adj.*—**twin·ing·ly** *adv.*

twinge (*twinj*) *v.* [twinged; twing·ing] 1. To affect with a sudden local pain. 2. To pinch; tweak.—*n.* 1. A momentary sharp pain; pang. 2. A pinch; a tweak.

twin·kle (*twing*-k'l) *v.* [twin·kled; twin·kling] 1. To wink; to blink. 2. To gleam; to sparkle. 3. To flash rapidly; to shine with a quivering light.—*n.* 1. A wink. 2. Twinkling. 3. Gleam; sparkle, esp. of the eye.—**twin·kler** *n.*—**twin·kling** *n.* Brief time; moment; instant.—*adj.* Gleaming; flashing.

twirl (*twerl*) *v.* To spin; rotate, esp. with the fingers.—*n.* Rapid rotating; whirl; spin.

twist *v.* **1.** To form by winding one strand round another. **2.** To contort; deform; pervert. **3.** To wreathe; wind; encircle. **4.** To wrench; turn painfully.—*n.* **1.** A bending; contortion; convolution. **2.** Manner of twisting. **3.** Something formed by twisting. 'Twist of tobacco.' **4.** *Slang.* A young woman.

twist·er *n.* **1.** Twisting agent. **2.** Violent, whirling wind; tornado.

twit *v.* [twit·ted; twit·ting] To taunt.—*n.* A jeer.

twitch *v.* **1.** To jerk; pluck; snatch. **2.** To contract suddenly, as a muscle.—*n.* **1.** A short, sudden pull; jerk. **2.** Sudden, spastic muscle contraction.—**twitch·er** *n.*—**twitch·y** *adj.*—**twitch·i·ness** *n.*

twit·ter *v.* **1.** To make tremulous, intermittent sounds; chirp. **2.** To be flurried; be agitated or excited.—*n.* **1.** Series of chirpings. **2.** Slight nervous excitement.—**twit·ter·ing** *n.*

two (*too*) *n.* The number represented by the symbol 2.—*adj.* Consisting of two.—**in two.** In two parts; asunder.—**two·some** *n.* A pair.

ty·coon (ty-*koon*) *n.* **1.** Generalissimo of Japanese army; shogun. **2.** *Colloquial.* Powerful business leader; wealthy industrialist.

tyke *n.* **1.** *Slang.* Small boy; child. **2.** A dog.

tym·pa·ni *n. pl.* Pair of tunable kettledrums used chiefly in symphony orchestras.—**tym·pa·nist** *n.*

tym·pa·num *n.* [*pl.* -nums; na] The eardrum.

type *n.* **1.** Class or category; kind; sort; nature. **2.** *Printing.* Block of wood or metal having a raised character on one side which can be reproduced by printing. **3.** A body of type characters set together. **4.** Printed matter.—*v.* [typed; typ·ing] **1.** To exhibit an example of; typify. **2.** *Slang.* To cast in the same pattern or mold; to stereotype. **3.** To typewrite.—**in type.** Printed; set up for printing.

typecasting	type holder	typesetter
type high	typescript	typesetting

type·write *v.* To write with a typewriter.—**type·writ·ing** *n.*—**type·writ·ten** *adj.*

type·writ·er *n.* **1.** Manually-operated machine for writing in characters similar to printing types. **2.** One who operates a typewriter.

ty·phoid (*ty*-foyd) *adj.* Pertaining to or resembling typhus.—**typhoid fever.** Abdominal typhus; enteric fever.

ty·phoon (ty-*foon*) *n.* Violent windstorm common off the coast of China; hurricane.

ty·phus (*ty*-fus) *n.* Typhus fever; an acute infectious and contagious disease, transmitted by body lice.

typ·i·cal (*tip*-ih-k'l) *adj.* **1.** Conforming to a type. **2.** Normal; universal; regular; expected.—**typ·i·cal·ly** *adv.*—**typ·i·cal·ness** *n.*

typ·i·fy (*tip*-ih-fy) *v.* [typ·i·fied; typ·i·fy·ing] **1.** To represent by an image or model. **2.** To exemplify; to be typical of.—**typ·i·fi·ca·tion** *n.* (tip-ih-fih-*kay*-sh'n)—**typ·i·fi·er** *n.*

typ·ist *n.* One skilled in operating a typewriter.

ty·pog·ra·phy (ty-*pog*-ruh-fee) *n.* **1.** Art of printing by type. **2.** Style of printed matter.

ty·ran·ni·cal (tih-*ran*-ih-k'l) *adj.* Despotic; cruelly imperious; unjustly severe.—**ty·ran·ni·cal·ly** *adv.*—**ty·ran·ni·cal·ness** *n.*

tyr·an·nize (*tihr*-uh-nyze) *v.* [tyr·an·nized; tyr·an·niz·ing] To rule with unjust and oppressive severity.—**tyr·an·nous** *adj.*

tyr·an·ny (*tihr*-uh-nee) *n.* [*pl.* ty·ran·nies] **1.** Government by a tyrant. **2.** Arbitrary exercise of power; despotism.

ty·rant (*ty*-runt) *n.* An oppressive or arbitrary ruler; despot; autocrat; cruel master or disciplinarian.

ty·ro (*ty*-roh) *n.* An amateur.

TYMPANI

U

u·biq·ui·tous (yoo-*bik*-wih-tus) *adj.* Being everywhere; omnipresent.—**u·biq·ui·tous·ly** *adv.*

u·biq·ui·ty *n.* The quality of being or seeming to be in more than one place at the same time; omnipresence.

U-boat *n.* A German submarine first used in World War I.

ud·der *n.* The milk gland of cows and other quadrupeds.

u·do (*oo*-doh) *n.* An edible herb common in Japan.

u·dom·e·ter (yoo-*dom*-eh-ter) *n.* A gauge for measuring rainfall.—**u·do·met·ric** (yoo-duh-*met*-rik) *adj.*—**u·dom·e·try** *n.*

ugh *interj.* An exclamation of disgust.

ug·ly *adj.* **1.** Offensive; hideous; loathsome; deformed. **2.** Ill-natured; nasty.—**ug·li·ness** *n.*

u·kase (yoo-*kayss*, *yoo*-kayss) *n.* Official order or decree.

u·ku·le·le (yoo-kuh-*lay*-lee) *n.* A small four-stringed Hawaiian musical instrument.

ul·cer (*ul*-ser) *n.* A surface sore on the skin or mucous membrane.—**ul·cer·a·tive** (*ul*-ser-ay-tiv) *adj.*—**ul·cer·ous** *adj.*

UKULELE

ul·na (*ul*-nuh) *n.* [*pl.* ul·nae, -nas] The inner bone of the forearm.—**ul·nar** *adj.*

U

ul·ster *n.* Long, loose overcoat.

ul·te·ri·or (ul-*teer*-ee-er) *adj.* 1. Lying beyond; distant. 2. Undisclosed; secret.

ul·ti·mate (*ul*-tih-mit) *adj.* Final; extreme; last. —**ul·ti·mate·ly** *adv.*

ul·ti·ma·tum (ul-tih-*may*-tum) *n.* [*pl.* -tums, -ta] A last offer; final terms offered in a negotiation.

ul·tra- (*ul*-truh) *prefix.* 1. Beyond; on the further side of. 2. Exceedingly; excessively.

ultra-ambitious	ultramodernism
ultra-agnostic	ultramodernist
ultra-atomic	ultramodernistic
ultraconfident	ultramodest
ultraconservative	ultramolecular
ultracredulous	ultranational
ultracritical	ultranationalism
ultraexclusive	ultranationalist
ultrafashionable	ultranationalistic
ultrafiltration	ultra-Puritan
ultragaseous	ultrarefined
ultraliberal	ultrareligious
ultraloyal	ultraroyalist
ultramicroscopic	ultrasterile
ultramodern	ultratropical

ul·tra·ma·rine *n.* 1. Blue pigment made from lapis lazuli. 2. A deep greenish-blue color. —**ul·tra·ma·rine** *adj.*

ul·tra·vi·o·let *adj. Physics.* Pertaining to invisible rays shorter than the violet rays of visible light, useful as a source of vitamin D.

ul·u·late (*yool*-yoo-layt) *v.* [-lat·ed; -lat·ing] To howl; wail.—**ul·u·lant, ul·u·la·tory** *adj.*—**ul·u·la·tion** *n.*

U·lys·ses (yoo-*liss*-eez) *n.* Odysseus, legendary Greek hero of the *Odyssey*.

um·bel *n.* Cluster of flowers whose stems seem to grow from a common center. —**um·bel·late, um·bel·la·ted** *adj.*—**um·bel·lif·er·ous** *adj.*

um·ber *n.* 1. Brown pigment which becomes reddish when heated. 2. Dull reddish-brown color (raw umber). 3. Orange-brown color (burnt umber).

UMBEL

um·bil·i·cal (um-*bil*-ih-k'l) *adj.* Of or pertaining to the navel.—**umbilical cord.** Cord connect-ed at the navel through which the fetus of a mammal receives nourishment.

um·bil·i·cus (um-*bil*-ih-kus) *n.* The navel; abdominal scar where the umbilical cord was attached.

um·bra *n.* A complete shadow.

um·brage (*um*-brij) *n.* Resentment; anger.—**um·bra·geous** *adj.*—**um·bra·geous·ly** *adv.*

um·brel·la (um-*brel*-uh) *n.* Portable, collapsible cloth shield for protection from the weather.

u·mi·ak (*oo*-mee-ak) *n.* Eskimo open boat.

um·laut (*oom*-lowt) *n. German.* The two dots indicating a change in vowel sound.

um·pire (*um*-pyre) *n.* Arbiter; referee, esp. in baseball.—*v.* [um·pired; um·pir·ing] 1. To supervise a game. 2. To render decision in a dispute.

un- *prefix.* 1. Not. 2. The opposite; reversal of. *Note-* Many compounds in sense 1 do not need defining because they represent a simple negation of the idea expressed in the root word. These are listed for spelling purposes beginning at the foot of this page.

un·a·bat·ed *adj.* Undiminished; not lessened.

un·a·ble *adj.* Incapable; powerless.

un·a·bridged *adj.* Complete; not shortened.

un·ac·count·a·ble *adj.* 1. Strange; inexplicable. 2. Irresponsible.—**un·ac·count·a·bly** *adv.*

unaccounted for. 1. Not found. 2. Not understood or explained.

un·a·dul·ter·at·ed *adj.* Pure; genuine; unmixed.

un·ad·vised *adj.* 1. Without warning or counsel. 2. Foolish; indiscreet; rash.—**un·ad·vis·ed·ly** *adv.*—**un·ad·vis·ed·ness** *n.*

un·af·fect·ed *adj.* Plain; natural; simple.—**un·af·fect·ed·ly** *adv.*—**un·af·fect·ed·ness** *n.*

un·al·loyed *adj.* Pure; unqualified.

un·al·ter·a·ble *adj.* Unchangeable; fixed.—**un·al·ter·a·bly** *adv.*—**un·al·tered** *adj.*

un-American *adj.* Not in accordance with the democratic traditions of America.

u·nan·i·mous (yoo-*nan*-ih-mus) *adj.* In complete accord; agreeing in opinion.—**u·nan·i·mous·ly** *adv.*—**u·na·nim·i·ty** (yoo-nun-*im*-uh-tee), **u·nan·i·mous·ness** (yoo-*nan*-ih-mus-nus) *n.*

un·an·swer·a·ble *adj.* Conclusive; irrefutable.

un·ap·proach·a·ble *adj.* Remote; inaccessible; forbidding.

unabashed	unadjusted	unappetizing	unauspicious
unabetted	unadorned	unapproached	unauthentic
unabsolved	unafraid	unappropriated	unauthenticated
unacademic	unaided	unapproved	unavailable
unaccented	unalleviated	unapt	unavenged
unacceptable	unallied	unaptly	unavowed
unacclimatized	unallowable	unaptness	unbacked
unaccommodated	unaltering	unargued	unbaked
unaccommodating	unambiguous	unarmored	unballasted
unaccompanied	unambiguously	unarrested	unbaptized
unaccomplished	unambitious	unartistic	unbarbed
unaccredited	unamiable	unasked	unbated
unaccustomed	unanimated	unaspirated	unbeaten
unacknowledged	unannounced	unassignable	unbefitting
unacquainted	unapparent	unassisted	unbeneficed
unacquitted	unappealable	unattached	unbeseeming
unadaptable	unappeasable	unattempted	unbeseemingly
unadjustable	unappeased	unattended	unbeseemingness

un·arm v. To strip of arms.—**un·armed** adj.

un·a·shamed adj. Not reluctant or embarrassed. —**un·a·sham·ed·ly** adv.

un·as·sail·a·ble adj. Impregnable; invulnerable.

un·as·sum·ing adj. Modest.— -**ing·ly** adv.

un·at·tain·a·ble adj. Out of reach.

un·at·trac·tive adj. Ugly; not pleasing to the senses.—**un·at·trac·tive·ly** adv.

un·au·thor·ized adj. Illegal; not sanctioned.

un·a·vail·ing adj. Vain; useless; futile.

un·a·void·a·ble adj. Inevitable; inescapable. —**un·a·void·a·bly** adv.

un·a·ware adj. Unconscious of; not cognizant; ignorant.

un·a·wares adv. Unexpectedly; by surprise.

un·bal·anced adj. 1. Not poised; unsteady. 2. Mentally unstable.—**un·bal·ance** v. [un·bal·anced; un·bal·anc·ing].

un·bar v. [un·barred; un·bar·ring] To unfasten; open.

un·bear v. To remove a horse's bearing rein.

un·bear·a·ble adj. Intolerable.— -**a·bly** adv.

un·be·com·ing adj. Improper; unsuitable.—**un·be·com·ing·ly** adv.—**un·be·com·ing·ness** n.

un·be·known adj. Not known.—**un·be·knownst** adv.

un·be·liev·a·ble adj. Incredible.—**un·be·liev·a·bly** adv.

un·be·liev·er n. 1. Agnostic; infidel. 2. Doubter.—**un·be·lief** n.

un·be·liev·ing adj. 1. Lacking religious faith. 2. Doubting; incredulous.—**un·be·liev·ing·ly** adv.—**un·be·liev·ing·ness** n.

un·belt v. To loose from a belt or support.

un·bend v. [un·bent; un·bend·ing] 1. To straighten. 2. To relax; loosen.—**un·bend·ing** adj.—**un·bend·ing·ly** adv.—**un·bend·ing·ness** n.

un·bi·ased adj. Also **un·bi·assed**. Impartial; objective; unprejudiced.

un·bind v. To loose; untie.

un·blem·ished adj. Pure; spotless.

un·blush·ing adj. Shameless; unabashed.—**un·blush·ing·ly** adv.

un·bolt v. To unlock; open.—**un·bolt·ed** adj.

un·born adj. Not yet created; future.

un·bos·om v. To confess; lay bare; disclose.

un·bound·ed adj. Limitless; inexhaustible; unrestricted.

un·brace v. To free from tension; loose.—**un·braced** adj.

un·bred adj. Crude; vulgar.

un·bri·dle v. [un·bri·dled; un·bri·dling] To release from a bridle.

un·bri·dled adj. Uncontrolled; wild; rampant.

un·buck·le v. [un·buck·led; un·buck·ling] To uncouple; detach.

un·build v. To destroy; tear down.—**un·built** adj. Not yet erected.

un·bur·den v. 1. To rid of a load. 2. To confess.

un·but·ton v. To open by undoing buttons.

un·cage v. To free from confinement.

un·called-for adj. Gratuitous; not merited.

un·can·ny adj. Weird; mysterious.—**un·can·ni·ly** adv.—**un·can·ni·ness** n.

un·cap v. [un·capped; un·cap·ping] To uncover; open by removing the top.

un·cared-for adj. Neglected; disliked.

un·ceas·ing adj. Everlasting; endless.

un·cer·e·mo·ni·ous adj. Abrupt; informal. —**un·cer·e·mo·ni·ous·ly** adv.—**un·cer·e·mo·ni·ous·ness** n.

un·cer·tain adj. 1. Undecided; insecure. 2. Doubtful; wavering.—**un·cer·tain·ness** n. —**un·cer·tain·ly** adv.—**un·cer·tain·ty** n.

un·chain v. To free; loose from chains.—**un·chained** adj.

un·change·a·ble adj. Fixed; immutable.—**un·change·a·bil·i·ty** n.—**un·change·a·bly** adv.

un·chang·ing adj. Constant; undeviating.

un·charge v. [un·charged; un·charg·ing] To unload.—**un·charged** adj.

un·char·i·ta·ble adj. 1. Stingy; illiberal. 2. Harsh; severe.—**un·char·i·ta·ble·ness** n.—**un·char·i·ta·bly** adv.

un·chris·tian adj. 1. Pagan; uncivilized. 2. Unkind; not generous.

un·church v. To expel from a church.—**un·churched** adj.

unbesought	unbrotherly	unchaste	uncollectible
unbetrayed	unbruised	unchastely	uncolored
unbetrothed	unburied	unchastened	uncombined
unbewailed	unburned	unchastised	uncomely
unbid	unburnt	unchastity	uncomforted
unbidden	unbusinesslike	unchecked	uncommitted
unbitted	uncalendered	unchewed	uncommunicative
unblamable	uncanceled	unchivalrous	uncompanionable
unblamed	uncancelled	unchristened	uncomplaining
unbleached	uncanonical	uncircumcised	uncomplaisant
unblenched	uncapable	unclad	uncompleted
unblessed	uncarbureted	unclaimed	uncomplimentary
unboned	uncastrated	unclassified	uncompounded
unbonneted	uncaught	uncleaned	uncomprehended
unbookish	uncaused	uncleanliness	uncomprehending
unbought	uncensured	uncleanly	uncompromised
unbound	unchallenged	uncleared	uncomputed
unbowed	unchancy	unclouded	unconcealed
unbranched	unchanged	uncloyed	unconcerted
unbranded	unchaperoned	uncocked	unconcertedly
unbreakable	uncharged	uncoerced	unconditioned
unbreathed	uncharted	uncollected	unconfined

U

un·civ·il *adj.* Ill-mannered; discourteous; rude. —**un·civ·il·ly** *adv.*

un·civ·i·lized *adj.* Barbarous; savage.

un·clasp *v.* To open; release.

un·cle *n.* The brother of one's father or mother; the husband of one's aunt.

un·clean *adj.* 1. Dirty; filthy. 2. Morally impure; defiled; obscene.

un·clench *v.* To open, as a hand.

Uncle Sam. *Colloquial.* The government of the United States, often personified as a thin, hawk-nosed gentleman with white hair and goatee.

un·clinch *v.* To release.

un·cloak *v.* To remove a cloak from; uncover.

un·close *v.* [un·closed; un·clos·ing] To open; reveal.

un·clothe (un-*klohth*) *v.* [un·clothed; un·cloth·ing] To undress; strip of clothes.—**un·clothed** *adj.* Naked.

un·coil *v.* To unwind; unroll.

un·com·fort·a·ble *adj.* 1. Awkward; cramped; unpleasant. 2. Uneasy; ill at ease.—**un·com·fort·a·bly** *adv.*

un·com·mon *adj.* Rare; infrequent; unusual. —**un·com·mon·ly** *adv.*—**un·com·mon·ness** *n.*

un·com·mu·ni·ca·tive (un-kuh-*myoo*-nih-kay-tiv) *adj.* Reticent; not talkative; close-mouthed.

un·com·pro·mis·ing *adj.* Inflexible; obstinate. —**un·com·pro·mis·ing·ly** *adv.*

un·con·cern *n.* Indifference; lack of interest. —**un·con·cerned** *adj.*—**un·con·cern·ed·ly** *adv.* —**un·con·cern·ed·ness** *n.*

un·con·di·tion·al (un-k'n-*dish*-un-'l) *adj.* Absolute; unlimited; unequivocal.— **-al·ly** *adv.*

un·con·quer·a·ble (un-*kong*-ker-uh-b'l) *adj.* Invincible; indomitable.—**un·con·quered** *adj.* Unsubdued.

un·con·scion·a·ble (un-*kon*-shun-uh-b'l) *adj.* 1. Unreasonable; excessive. 2. Evil; unprincipled.—**un·con·scion·a·bly** *adv.*

un·con·scious (un-*kon*-shus) *adj.* 1. Insensible. 2. Oblivious; unknowing. 3. Not deliberate.— **-scious·ly** *adv.*— **-scious·ness** *n.*

un·con·stant *adj.* Unfaithful; fickle; inconstant. —**un·con·stant·ly** *adv.*

un·con·sti·tu·tion·al *adj.* Contrary to or not authorized by a constitution.—**un·con·sti·tu·tion·al·i·ty** *n.*—**un·con·sti·tu·tion·al·ly** *adv.*

un·con·ven·tion·al *adj.* Not conforming to the usual pattern.—**un·con·ven·tion·al·i·ty** *n.*

un·cork *v.* To pull out the cork; unleash; let loose.—**un·corked** *adj.*

un·count·ed *adj.* Untold; innumerable.

un·cou·ple *v.* [un·cou·pled; -pling] To break apart; disjoin.

un·couth (un-*kooth*) *adj.* Rude; boorish; ill-mannered.—**un·couth·ly** *adv.*—**un·couth·ness** *n.*

un·cov·er *v.* 1. To divest of covering; disclose; lay bare. 2. To bare the head.

un·crown *v.* To dethrone; depose.—**un·crowned** *adj.* Having the power but not the title.

unc·tion (*unk*-shun) *n.* 1. Sacred anointment. 2. Ointment; salve. 3. Suavity; fervor.

unc·tu·ous (*unk*-choo-us) *adj.* 1. Oily; greasy. 2. Suave; smooth-tongued; gushing.—**unc·tu·os·i·ty** *n.*—**unc·tu·ous·ly** *adv.*— **-ous·ness** *n.*

un·cul·ti·vat·ed *adj.* 1. Not tilled; fallow. 2. Ignorant; ill-educated.

un·curl *v.* To straighten out.

un·cut *adj.* 1. Unabridged; complete. 2. Not shaped or divided.

un·daunt·ed (un-*dawnt*-ed) *adj.* Bold; resolute; intrepid.—**undaunted·ly** *adv.*— **-ed·ness** *n.*

un·de·ceive (un-dee-*seev*) *v.* [un·de·ceived; un·de·ceiv·ing] To set right; correct.—**un·de·ceived** *adj.*

un·de·cid·ed *adj.* 1. Irresolute; hesitating. 2. Unsettled; not resolved.—**un·de·cid·ed·ly** *adv.*—**un·de·cid·ed·ness** *n.*

un·dem·o·crat·ic (un-dem-uh-*krat*-ik) *adj.* 1. Snobbish; haughty. 2. Totalitarian; reactionary.

un·de·mon·stra·tive (un-duh-*mon*-struh-tiv) *adj.* Reserved; restrained.

un·de·ni·a·ble (un-duh-*ny*-uh-b'l) *adj.* Indisputable; beyond question.—**un·de·ni·a·bly** *adv.*

un·de·nom·i·na·tion·al (un-duh-nom-ih-*nay*-shun-ul) *adj.* Embracing all religious faiths.

unconfirmed	uncorroborated	undeceivable	undeserved
unconformity	uncorrupted	undecipherable	undeserving
unconfused	uncountable	undeciphered	undesignated
uncongealable	uncourteous	undecked	undesigned
uncongenial	uncovenanted	undeclared	undesigning
unconnected	uncreated	undeclinable	undesired
unconscious	uncredited	undecorated	undespairing
unconsecrated	uncrippled	undefaceable	undetachable
unconsidered	uncritical	undefeated	undetected
unconstrained	uncriticizable	undefended	undeterminable
unconsumed	uncultivable	undefensible	undeterred
uncontaminated	uncultured	undefiled	undeveloped
uncontested	uncurbed	undefinable	undeviating
uncontradictable	uncurdled	undefined	undifferentiated
uncontradicted	uncured	undelayed	undigested
uncontrollable	uncurious	undeliverable	undignified
uncontrolled	uncurrent	undelivered	undiluted
unconverted	uncurtained	undemonstrable	undiminished
unconvinced	undamaged	undenominational	undimmed
unconvincing	undamped	undependable	undiplomatic
uncooked	undated	undeposed	undirected
uncoordinated	undaughterly	undepreciated	undiscernible
uncorrected	undazzled	underived	undiscerning

un·der *prep.* 1. Below; beneath. 2. Less than; short of. 3. Subordinate or subject to. 4. Included in; comprehended by. 5. During the time or existence of.—*adv.* Beneath; in a lower or subject condition.—*adj.* 1. Subordinate; lower in degree. 2. Lying below; less.

un·der- *prefix.* Below; beneath; lower; inside.

underbodice	underdrain	under lip
undercasing	undergarb	undersea
under class	under jaw	undershirt
underclassman	underlay	underskirt
undercloth	underlinen	undersurface

un·der *prefix.* Lower in rank; assistant; subordinate.

under agent	under janitor
under bailiff	under man (*n.*)
under chief	under officer (*n.*)
under clerk	under secretary
under deacon	under-secretaryship
under farmer	under servant

un·der- *prefix.* Poorly; insufficiently; below standard or normal.

underclad	underofficered
undercultivation	underpaid
underdress (*v.*)	underpressure (*v.*)
underman (*v.*)	understaff (*v.*)
undermanned	understaffed
underofficer (*v.*)	undertax (*v.*)

un·der·brush *n.* Low, tangled shrubs and bushes.

un·der·charge *v.* [un·der·charge; un·der·charg·ing] To charge less than the normal price.

un·der·clothes *n. pl.* Underwear; lingerie.

un·der·cur·rent *n.* 1. Eddy; current below the surface. 2. Concealed feeling or movement.

un·der·cut *v.* [un·der·cut; un·der·cut·ting] 1. To sell goods or services at a lower rate. 2. To cut away underneath, esp. so as to leave an overhanging part. 3. *Golf.* To hit the ball so as to give it a back spin.—**un·der·cut** *n.*

un·der·dog *n.* A losing or weaker contestant.

un·der·es·ti·mate *v.* [un·der·es·ti·mat·ed; -ti·mat·ing] To value below its worth; belittle.

un·der·foot *adj.* On the ground; in the way.

un·der·go *v.* [un·der·went; un·der·gone; un·der·go·ing] To suffer; endure; sustain.

un·der·grad·u·ate (un-der-*grad*-joo-it) *n.* A student who has not taken his first degree or diploma.

un·der·ground *n.* 1. Any organized, secret opposition to the government in power, esp. in fascist-controlled countries during World War II. 2. A subway.—*adj.* 1. Subterranean. 2. Hidden; pertaining to the antifascist-resistance movements.—*adv.* 1. Beneath the earth's surface. 2. Into hiding.

un·der·growth *n.* Low shrubbery growing beneath large trees.

un·der·hand, un·der·hand·ed *adj.* 1. Stealthy; covert; dishonest. 2. With the arm swinging forward and upward.—**un·der·hand·ed·ly** *adv.* —**un·der·hand·ed·ness** *n.*

un·der·line *v.* [un·der·lined; un·der·lin·ing] To mark beneath with a line; emphasize.

un·der·ling *n.* Petty official; subordinate.

un·der·ly·ing *adj.* 1. Situated beneath. 2. Basic; fundamental.

un·der·mine *v.* [un·der·mined; un·der·min·ing] 1. To burrow; excavate. 2. To weaken; sap; impair secretly and gradually.— **-min·er** *n.*

un·der·neath *prep. & adv.* Below; beneath; under.

un·der·nour·ished (un-der-*ner*-isht) *adj.* Ill-fed; starved.

un·der·pass *n.* A short tunnel; passage beneath a bridge or railway.

un·der·pin·ning *n.* Props or supports, esp. beneath a wall or building.

un·der·priv·i·leged (un-der-*priv*-ih-lijd) *n. pl.* That class of society which is denied basic social and economic benefits.—**un·der·priv·i·leged** *adj.*

un·der·score *v.* [un·der·scored; un·der·scor·ing] To draw a line beneath; underline.

un·der·sell *v.* [un·der·sold; un·der·sel·ling] To sell at a price lower than standard, esp. to best a competitor.

un·der·side *n.* The under surface; belly.

un·der·stand *v.* [un·der·stood; un·der·stand·ing] 1. To comprehend; appreciate. 2. To learn; be informed. 3. To suppose to mean; interpret.—**un·der·stand·ing** *adj.* Knowing; sym-

undischarged	undrained	unemphatic	uneventful
undisciplined	undramatic	unemployable	unexaggerated
undiscovered	undraped	unenclosed	unexcelled
undiscriminating	undreamed	unencumbered	unexchangeable
undisguised	undreamt	unendangered	unexciting
undisheartened	undressed	unendorsed	unexecuted
undismayed	undrilled	unenduring	unexhausted
undismembered	undrinkable	unenforceable	unexpended
undisposed	undutiful	unenforced	unexperienced
undisputed	undyed	unengaged	unexpired
undissolved	unearned	unenjoyable	unexplainable
undistilled	uneatable	unenlightened	unexplained
undistinguishable	uneaten	unenrolled	unexploded
undistributed	uneclipsed	unenterprising	unexplored
undisturbed	uneconomical	unentertaining	unexpressed
undiverted	unedifying	unenthusiastic	unexpressive
undivided	uneducable	unenviable	unextinguished
undivulged	uneducated	unenvied	unfadable
undomestic	uneffaced	unenvious	unfading
undomesticated	uneliminated	unequipped	unfaltering
undoubled	unembarrassed	unescapable	unfashionable
undoubted	unembellished	unestimated	unfinished
undoubting	unemotional	unethical	unfitting

U

pathetic.—*n.* 1. Comprehension; wisdom. 2. Agreement; accord.— -**stand·ing·ly** *adv.*

un·der·state *v.* [un·der·stat·ed; un·der·stat·ing] To play down; minimize.—**un·der·state·ment** *n.*

un·der·stood. *Past tense & past participle* of understand.—*adj.* Implicit; inferential; tacitly agreed upon.

un·der·stud·y *n.* Substitute, esp. in the theater; pinch hitter.—*v.* [-stud·ied; -stud·y·ing].

un·der·take *v.* [un·der·took; un·der·tak·en] 1. To assume; attempt. 2. To promise; engage; contract.—**un·der·tak·ing** *n.*

un·der·tak·er *n.* A mortician; funeral director.

un·der·tone *n.* 1. A murmur; whisper. 2. Undercurrent. 3. Subdued shade or color.

un·der·took. *Past tense* of **un·der·take.**

un·der·tow *n.* A strong current of water below and opposed to the surface current.

un·der·wear *n.* Garments worn next to the skin.

un·der·went. *Past tense* of **undergo.**

un·der·wood *n.* Undergrowth; underbrush.

un·der·world *n.* 1. *Mythology.* Hades. 2. The criminal element.—**un·der·world** *adj.*

un·der·write *v.* [un·der·wrote; un·der·writ·ten] To insure; guarantee.—**un·der·writ·er** *n.*

un·de·sir·a·ble *adj.* Not wanted; objectionable. —**un·de·sir·a·ble** *n.*

un·did. *Past tense* of **undo.**

un·dis·tin·guished *adj.* Mediocre; commonplace; ordinary.

un·do *v.* [un·did; un·done; un·do·ing] 1. To annul; render void. 2. To unfasten; untie; take apart. 3. To destroy; ruin.—**un·do·ing** *n.*

un·doubt·ed (un-*dowt*-ed) *adj.* Accepted without question; indisputable.—**un·doubt·ed·ly** *adv.*

un·drape *v.* [un·draped; un·drap·ing] To uncover; bare.—**un·draped** *adj.*

un·draw *v.* [un·drew; un·drawn; un·draw·ing] To draw back; pull aside.

un·dress *v.* To take off clothing; disrobe.—*adj.* Not formal; worn on duty. 'Undress uniform.'

un·due *adj.* 1. Excessive; inordinate. 2. Illegal; improper.—**un·du·ly** *adv.*

un·du·late (*un*-dyoo-layt) *v.* [un·du·lat·ed; un·du·lat·ing] To move in waves; sway; oscillate. —*adj.* Wavy.—**un·du·lant, un·du·la·tive** *adj.* —**un·du·la·tion** *n.*—**un·du·la·to·ry** *adj.*

un·dy·ing *adj.* Eternal; deathless.

un·earth *v.* To disinter; discover; bring to light.

un·earth·ly *adj.* 1. Spiritual; supernatural. 2. Weird; eerie. 3. Outlandish.—**un·earth·li·ness** *n.*

un·eas·y *adj.* Disturbed; troubled.—**un·eas·i·ly** *adv.*—**un·eas·i·ness** *n.*

un·em·ployed *adj.* 1. Jobless; without work. 2. Not in use.—**un·em·ployed** *n.*—**un·em·ploy·ment** *n.*

un·end·ing *adj.* Interminable; everlasting.

un·en·dur·a·ble *adj.* Intolerable; unbearable.

un·e·qual (un-*ee*-kwal) *adj.* 1. Not the same; disparate; uneven. 2. Erratic; uncertain; variable. 3. Inequitable; one-sided. 4. Inadequate; not competent.—**un·e·qual·ly** *adv.*

un·e·qualed, un·e·qualled *adj.* Having no match or rival; peerless.

un·e·quiv·o·cal (un-eh-*kwiv*-uh-k'l) *adj.* Clear; evident; unmistakable.—**un·e·quiv·o·cal·ly** *adv.*

un·err·ing *adj.* 1. Infallible. 2. Exact; precise.—**un·err·ing·ly** *adv.*

un·e·ven *adj.* 1. Rough; rugged. 2. Not uniform; irregular. 3. *Arithmetic.* Odd; not divisible by 2.— -**ven·ly** *adv.*— -**ven·ness** *n.*

uneven-aged	uneven-numbered
uneven-carriaged	uneven-priced
uneven-handed	uneven-roofed

un·ex·am·pled *adj.* Unprecedented; exceptional.

un·ex·cep·tion·a·ble *adj.* Excellent; faultless. —**un·ex·cep·tion·a·bly** *adv.*

un·ex·pect·ed *adj.* Unforeseen; sudden.—**un·ex·pect·ed·ly** *adv.*—**un·ex·pect·ed·ness** *n.*

un·ex·pur·gat·ed (un-*ekss*-per-gayt-ed) *adj.* Complete; uncensored.

un·fail·ing *adj.* Inexhaustible; constant.—**un·fail·ing·ly** *adv.*

un·fair *adj.* Dishonest; not right or just; inequitable.—**un·fair·ly** *adv.*—**un·fair·ness** *n.*

un·faith·ful *adj.* 1. Disloyal; false; perfidious. 2. Adulterous.—**un·faith·ful·ly** *adv.*—**un·faith·ful·ness** *n.*

un·fa·mil·iar *adj.* Strange; not well known; unacquainted.—**un·fa·mil·i·ar·i·ty** (un-fuh-mil-*yair*-ih-tee) *n.*—**un·fa·mil·iar·ly** *adv.*

un·fas·ten (un-*fass*-'n) *v.* To open; loose.—**un·fas·tened** *adj.*

un·fathered (un-*fah*-therd) *adj.* Illegitimate.

unflattering	unfree	ungotten	unhampered
unflavored	unfrequent	ungraceful	unhandicapped
unfleshly	unfulfilled	ungracefully	unhandsome
unforbidden	unfunded	ungracefulness	unhanged
unforced	unfurnished	ungracious	unharassed
unforeknown	ungallant	ungraded	unhardened
unforeseeable	ungalled	ungrained	unharmonious
unforeseen	ungarnished	ungrammatical	unhatched
unforgettable	ungathered	ungrammatically	unhealthful
unforgetting	ungenerous	ungrateful	unheard
unforgivable	ungenerously	ungratefully	unheeded
unforgiven	ungentle	ungratefulness	unheedful
unforgiving	ungentlemanly	ungrounded	unheeding
unforgotten	ungifted	ungrudging	unheralded
unformed	unglazed	unguided	unheroic
unformulated	unglossed	unhabitable	unhindered
unfortified	ungloved	unhackneyed	unhonored
unframed	ungoverned	unhallowed	unhoped

un·fath·om·a·ble *adj.* 1. Immeasurable; infinite; bottomless. 2. Inscrutable; impenetrable.—**un·fath·omed** *adj.*

un·fa·vor·a·ble (un-*fayv*-ruh-b'l) *adj.* Adverse; opposed; obstructive.—**un·fa·vor·a·ble·ness** *n.* —**un·fa·vor·a·bly** *adv.*

un·feas·i·ble (un-*feez*-ih-b'l) *adj.* Impracticable.

un·fed *adj.* Hungry; starving.

un·feel·ing *adj.* Insensible; callous; hardhearted.—**un·feel·ing·ly** *adv.*— **-ing·ness** *n.*

un·feigned (un-*faynd*) *adj.* Sincere; genuine. —**un·feign·ed·ly** *adv.*—**un·feign·ed·ness** *n.*

un·fem·i·nine (un-*fem*-ih-nin) *adj.* Mannish; unwomanly.

un·fenced *adj.* Open; not enclosed.

un·fet·ter *v.* To free; liberate.—**un·fet·tered** *adj.*

un·fil·i·al *adj.* Unbecoming or disrespectful, as a son to his parents.

un·filled *adj.* Empty; barren.

un·fired *adj.* Undischarged, as a gun.

un·fit *adj.* 1. Incompetent; unhealthy. 2. Improper; unsuitable.—*v.* [un·fit·ted; un·fit·ting] To disable.—**un·fit·ly** *adv.*—**un·fit·ness** *n.*—**un·fit·ting** *adj.*

un·fix *v.* To loosen; detach.—**un·fixed** *adj.*

un·flag·ging *adj.* Tireless; persevering; constant.

un·fledged *adj.* Immature; callow; untried.

un·flinch·ing *adj.* Stalwart; firm.—**un·flinch·ing·ly** *adv.*

un·fold *v.* 1. To expand; spread out. 2. To disclose; reveal.

un·fore·seen *adj.* Not anticipated.

un·for·get·ta·ble *adj.* Memorable.—**un·for·get·ta·bly** *adv.*

un·for·tu·nate (un-*for*-choo-nit) *adj.* Unlucky; unhappy.—**un·for·tu·nate·ly** *adv.*

un·found·ed *adj.* Baseless; without foundation.

un·fre·quent·ed (un-free-*kwent*-ed) *adj.* Solitary; seldom visited.

un·friend·ly *adj.* Antagonistic; hostile; inimical. —**un·friend·ly** *adv.*—**un·friend·li·ness** *n.*

un·frock *v.* To deprive of the character and privileges of a clergyman.

un·fruit·ful (un-*froot*-f'l) *adj.* Barren; sterile; unprofitable.—**un·fruit·ful·ly** *adv.*—**un·fruit·ful·ness** *n.*

un·furl *v.* To unfold; spread to the wind.

un·gain·ly *adj.* Clumsy; awkward.—**un·gain·ly** *adv.*—**un·gain·li·ness** *n.*

un·gird *v.* [un·girt; un·gird·ing] To unbind. —**un·girt** *adj.*

un·glue *v.* [un·glued; un·glu·ing] To separate, as objects glued together.

un·god·ly *adj.* 1. Irreligious; wicked; sinful. 2. Outlandish; fantastic.—**un·god·li·ness** *n.*

un·gov·ern·a·ble *adj.* Unruly; willful.—**un·gov·ern·a·ble·ness** *n.*—**un·gov·ern·a·bly** *adv.*

un·guard (un-*gahrd*) *v.* To render defenseless. —**un·guarded** *adj.* 1. Undefended; unwatched. 2. Careless; negligent.—**un·guard·ed·ly** *adv.*—**un·guard·ed·ness** *n.*

un·guent (*ung*-gwent) *n.* An ointment; healing or lubricating substance.

un·gu·la (*ung*-gyoo-luh) *n.* [*pl.* -lae (-lee)] A hoof, nail, or claw.—**un·gu·lar** *adj.*

un·gu·late (*ung*-gyoo-lit) *adj.* Having or resembling hoofs.—*n.* Any hoofed animal, as a horse, sheep, elephant, cow, or swine.

un·hal·low *v.* To profane; desecrate.—**un·hallowed** *adj.* 1. Not consecrated; unsanctified. 2. Profane; impious.

un·hand *v.* To release from a grasp.

un·hand·y *adj.* 1. Out of reach; inconvenient. 2. Awkward; unmanageable.— **-hand·i·ly** *adv.*

un·hap·py *adj.* 1. Unfortunate; ill-fated. 2. Sad; miserable; sorrowful. 3. Unsuitable; improper; deplorable.—**un·hap·pi·ly** *adv.*—**un·hap·pi·ness** *n.*

un·harmed *adj.* Unimpaired; not injured.

un·har·ness *v.* To remove a harness or gear. —**un·har·nessed** *adj.*

un·hat *v.* [un·hat·ted; un·hat·ting] To bare the head.

un·health·ful *adj.* Injurious to health.

un·health·y *adj.* 1. Not well; sickly; diseased. 2. Injurious to health or morals; unwholesome.—**un·health·i·ly** *adv.*—**un·health·i·ness** *n.*

un·heard-of *adj.* Fantastic; unprecedented.

un·helm *v.* To deprive of the helm.

un·hes·i·tat·ing *adj.* Prompt; unfaltering.—**un·hes·i·tat·ing·ly** *adv.*

un·hinge *v.* [un·hinged; un·hing·ing] 1. To remove from the hinges; dislocate. 2. To disorder; derange.

un·hitch *v.* To release; disengage.

un·ho·ly *adj.* 1. Ungodly; wicked; profane.

U

unhoped-for	unimportance	uninspired	unkindness
unhoused	unimportant	uninstructive	unknowable
unhurried	unimposing	unintended	unknowing
unhurt	unimpressible	unintentional	unlabeled
unhurtful	unimpressionable	unintentionally	unlabelled
unhygienic	unimpressive	uninteresting	unlabored
unhyphenated	uninclosed	unintermitted	unladylike
unhyphened	unincorporated	unintermittent	unlaid
unideal	unincumbered	unintermitting	unlamented
unidentified	uninfected	uninterrupted	unleaded
unidiomatic	uninflammable	uninventive	unleavened
unilluminated	uninflected	uninvited	unlettered
unimaginable	uninfluenced	uninviting	unlicensed
unimaginative	uninformed	unissued	unlighted
unimpaired	uninhabited	unjustifiable	unlikable
unimpassioned	uninitiated	unkept	unlikeable
unimpeded	uninjured	unkindly	unlimited

2. *Colloquial.* Awful; terrible.—**un·hol·i·ly** *adv.* —**un·ho·li·ness** *n.*

un·hood *v.* To uncover.

un·hook *v.* To detach; remove from a hook.

un·horse *v.* [un·horsed; un·hors·ing] To throw from a horse.

un·husk *v.* To husk; strip of the husk.

uni- *prefix.* Single; having or characterized by one.

unicameral	unilateral	unipolar
unicellular	unilingual	unisexual
unicycle	uniocular	unisonous
unifilar	uniparous	univalve
unifoliate	uniplanar	univalvular

u·ni·corn (*yoo*-nih-korn) *n.* Legendary one-horned animal.

u·ni·fi·ca·tion (yoo-nih-fih-*kay*-shun) *n.* State or process of being unified; amalgamation.

u·ni·form (*yoo*-nih-form) *adj.* **1.** Similar; alike. **2.** Even; constant; regular. —*n.* A prescribed or regulation outfit worn by members of the same organ-

UNICORN

ization.—**u·ni·formed** *adj.* Wearing a uniform. —**u·ni·form·i·ty** *n.*—**u·ni·form·ly** *adv.*

u·ni·fy *v.* [u·ni·fied; u·ni·fy·ing] To consolidate; unite; integrate.—**u·ni·fi·a·ble** *adj.*—**u·ni·fi·er** *n.*

un·im·peach·a·ble *adj.* Blameless; irreproachable.—**un·im·peach·a·bly** *adv.*

un·in·tel·li·gi·ble (un-in-*tel*-ih-jih-b'l) *adj.* Incomprehensible; not understandable.—**un·in·tel·li·gi·bil·i·ty** *n.*

un·ion (*yoon*-yun) *n.* **1.** Act of combining or uniting. **2.** Junction; solidarity. **3.** A confederation or coalition. **4.** Organization of workers formed for collective bargaining with employers. **5.** A marriage. **6.** A coupling for connecting pipes.

un·ion·ize *v.* [un·ion·ized; un·ion·iz·ing] To organize into a trade or industrial union.—**un·ion·ism** *n.*—**un·ion·ist** *n.*—**un·ion·i·za·tion** *n.*

Union Jack. National flag of Great Britain.

u·nique (yoo-*neek*) *adj.* **1.** Single; lone. **2.** Singular; peculiar.—**u·nique·ly** *adv.*—**u·nique·ness** *n.*

u·ni·son *n.* **1.** Concord; harmony. **2.** *Music.* Performance of the same tones simultaneously. —**in unison.** Together; as one.

u·nit *n.* **1.** A whole; single entity. **2.** Designated quantity used as a standard of measurement. **3.** *Arithmetic.* **a.** The smallest whole number; one (1). **b.** An undivided number or amount.—**u·nit** *adj.*

U·ni·tar·i·an *n.* Member of a Christian sect which does not accept the doctrine of the Trinity.— -**tar·i·an** *adj.*— -**tar·i·an·ism** *n.*

u·nite (yoo-*nyte*) *v.* [u·nit·ed; u·nit·ing] To combine; coalesce; join.—**u·nit·ed** *adj.*—**u·nit·ed·ly** *adv.*

United Nations. **1.** Group of 32 nations which declared war on one or more of the Axis nations during World War II. **2.** [*Abbreviation:* U.N.] Permanent organization set up in 1945 to establish and preserve world peace, security, and democracy.

u·ni·ty (*yoo*-nih-tee) *n.* [*pl.* -ties] **1.** Oneness; singleness; identity. **2.** A whole composed of related individual parts. **3.** Harmony; uniformity. **4.** *Drama.* Any one of Aristotle's three fundamental laws governing the structure of a play, called the unities of time, place, and action.

u·ni·ver·sal (yoo-nih-*ver*-s'l) *adj.* **1.** Worldwide; cosmopolitan; general; unlimited. **2.** Whole; entire. **3.** *Logic.* Applicable to all cases.—*n. Logic.* A general proposition or concept.—**u·ni·ver·sal·i·ty** *n.* [*pl.* -ties]—**u·ni·ver·sal·ly** *adv.*—**u·ni·ver·sal·ness** *n.*

universal joint. A coupling designed to allow two joined pieces to turn at any angle within certain limits.

u·ni·verse *n.* The cosmos; creation.

UNIVERSAL JOINT

u·ni·ver·si·ty *n.* [*pl.* -ties] An institution of higher learning, empowered to confer degrees in its various branches of study.

un·just *adj.* Unfair; inequitable.—**un·just·ly** *adv.* —**un·just·ness** *n.*

un·kempt *adj.* Slovenly; disheveled.—**un·kempt·ness** *n.*

un·ken·nel *v.* [un·ken·neled; un·ken·nelled; un·ken·nel·ing; un·ken·nel·ling] To release from a kennel.—**un·ken·neled, un·ken·nelled** *adj.*

un·kind *adj.* Unsympathetic; harsh; cruel.—**un·kind·ly** *adv.*—**un·kind·ness** *n.*

un·knit (un-*nit*) *v.* [un·knit·ted; un·knit·ting] To unravel.

un·known (un-*nohn*) *adj.* Strange; unfamiliar; unidentified.

un·lace *v.* [un·laced; un·lac·ing] To untie the laces; loose.

unlined	unmagnified	unmeant	unmilitary
unliquefiable	unmailable	unmeasurable	unmilled
unliquefied	unmeasured	unmeasured	unmindful
unliquidated	unmanageable	unmechanical	unmingled
unlisted	unmanufactured	unmedita	unmirthful
unlit	unmarked	unmelodious	unmistaken
unlooked	unmarketable	unmelted	unmitigable
unlooked-for	unmarriageable	unmensurable	unmitigated
unlovable	unmarried	unmentioned	unmixed
unloved	unmastered	unmerchantable	unmodified
unlovely	unmatched	unmerited	unmodulated
unloving	unmeaning	unmethodical	unmolested

un·lade v. [un·lad·ed; un·lad·en; un·lad·ing] To discharge cargo; unload.

un·lash v. *Nautical.* To loose or unfasten objects which are tied down.

un·latch v. To open by lifting the latch.

un·law·ful adj. 1. Illegal; prohibited; against the law. 2. Illegitimate.—**un·law·ful·ly** adv. —**un·law·ful·ness** n.

un·lay v. *Nautical.* To unravel; untwist.

un·learn v. To forget; strip of or lose knowledge or skill.—**un·learn·ed** adj. Ignorant; uneducated.

un·leash v. To free; let loose.

un·less conj. If not; except; without.

un·like adj. Dissimilar; having no resemblance. —**un·like·ness** n.

un·like·ly adj. Improbable.—**un·like·li·hood** n. —**un·like·li·ness** n.

un·lim·ber v. To prepare for action.

un·link v. To disjoin; break apart.

un·live v. [un·lived; un·liv·ing] To undo; nullify; live down.

un·load v. 1. To discharge a cargo or a burden; disencumber. 2. *Colloquial.* To sell or get rid of in great quantities.—**un·load ed** adj. —**un·load·er** n.

un·lock v. To unfasten; open; reveal.

un·looked-for adj. Not expected; unforeseen.

un·loose v. [un·loosed; un·loos·ing] To unfasten; free; liberate.

un·loos·en v. To loosen.

un·luck·y adj. 1. Ill-fated; luckless. 2. Having or causing bad luck; ill-starred.—**un·luck·i·ly** adv.—**un·luck·i·ness** n.

un·make v. [un·made; un·mak·ing] 1. To destroy. 2. To take apart.—**un·made** adj.

un·man v. [un·manned; un·man·ning] 1. To unnerve; dishearten. 2. To emasculate; weaken. 3. To deprive of men; deplete.—**un·manned** adj.

un·man·ly adj. 1. Womanish; effeminate. 2. Cowardly; soft.—**un·man·li·ness** n.

un·man·nered adj. 1. Rude; uncivil. 2. Simple; unaffected.

un·man·ner·ly adj. Rude; discourteous.—adv. Uncivilly.—**un·man·ner·li·ness** n.

un·mask v. To strip of a mask or disguise; reveal; expose.

un·meet adj. Unfit; inappropriate.

un·men·tion·a·ble adj. Infamous; scandalous; not to be discussed.—**un·men·tion·a·bles** n. pl. Undergarments.—**un·men·tion·a·ble·ness** n.

un·mer·ci·ful (un-*mer*-sih-f'l) adj. Cruel; pitiless; unrelenting.—**un·mer·ci·ful·ly** adv.—**un·mer·ci·ful·ness** n.

un·mis·tak·a·ble adj. Clear; evident.—**un·mis·tak·a·bly** adv.

un·mi·ter, un·mi·tre (un-*my*-ter) v. To strip of the rank and dignity of a bishop.

un·moor v. To loose from anchorage.

un·mor·al adj. Amoral; devoid of moral sense. —**un·mor·al·i·ty** n.—**un·mor·al·ly** adv.

un·mor·tise (un-*mawr*-tyze) v. [un·mor·tised; un·mor·tis·ing] To separate, as a joint from a socket.

un·muf·fle v. [un·muf·fled; un·muf·fling] To uncover; remove obstruction to sound.

un·muz·zle v. [un·muz·zled; un·muz·zling] 1. To free from a muzzle. 2. To free from censorship.—**un·muz·zled** adj.

un·nail v. To unfasten by removing nails.

un·nat·u·ral adj. Abnormal; inhuman; artificial. —**un·nat·u·ral·ly** adv.—**un·nat·u·ral·ness** n.

un·nerve v. [un·nerved; un·nerv·ing] To perturb; shock into unsteadiness.

un·num·bered adj. Numberless.

un·ob·serv·ant adj. Heedless; inattentive.—**un·ob·serv·ing** adj.

un·ob·served adj. Unseen; not obeyed.

un·ob·tru·sive (un-ub-*troo*-siv) adj. Shy; not forward.—**un·ob·tru·sive·ly** adv.

un·of·fi·cial (un-uh-*fish*-'l) adj. Not authorized. —**un·of·fi·cial·ly** adv.

un·pack v. To empty; remove the contents in order, as from a suitcase.—**un·packed** adj.

un·par·al·leled adj. Exceptional; unequaled; without match.

un·peg v. [un·pegged; un·peg·ging] To open by removing a peg.

un·peo·ple v. [un·peo·pled; un·peo·pling] To depopulate.—**un·peo·pled** adj.

un·pile v. [un·piled; un·pil·ing] To separate from a pile.

un·pin v. [un·pinned; un·pin·ning] To unfasten by removing the pins.

un·plait v. To unbraid; undo.

un·pleas·ant adj. Disagreeable; objectionable. —**un·pleas·ant·ly** adv.—**un·pleas·ant·ness** n.

un·pop·u·lar adj. Disliked; not favored or approved generally.—**un·pop·u·lar·i·ty** n.— **-lar·ly** adv.

un·prec·e·dent·ed (un-*press*-eh-dent-ed) adj. Extraordinary; unexampled. —**-dent·ed·ly** adv.

un·pre·med·i·tat·ed adj. Unplanned; impromptu; not deliberate.—**un·pre·med·i·tat·ed·ly** adv.

U

unmortgaged	unnecessary	unoccasioned	unowned
unmotivated	unneedful	unoccupied	unpaid
unmounted	unnegotiable	unoffending	unpaired
unmovable	unneighborly	unoffered	unpalatable
unmoved	unnoted	unofficious	unpardonable
unmusical	unnoticeable	unopened	unpardoned
unnamable	unnoticed	unopposed	unparliamentary
unnameable	unobjectionable	unordained	unpartisan
unnamed	unobliging	unorganized	unpasteurized
unnaturalized	unobscured	unoriginal	unpatriotic
unnavigable	unobstructed	unorthodox	unpaved
unnecessarily	unobtainable	unostentatious	unpeaceable

un·prin·ci·pled *adj.* Lacking moral principles; unethical.

un·print·a·ble *adj.* Unfit for printing; obscene.

un·pro·duc·tive *adj.* Barren; unfruitful.—**un·pro·duc·tive·ness** *n.*

un·qual·i·fied *adj.* 1. Incompetent; incapable. 2. Not modified or restricted.—**un·qual·i·fied·ly** *adv.*

un·quench·a·ble *adj.* Insatiable.

un·ques·tion·a·ble *adj.* Certain; undeniable; beyond doubt.—**un·ques·tion·a·bly** *adv.*—**un·ques·tion·ed** *adj.*

un·qui·et *adj.* Restless; fidgety; disturbed.

un·quote *v.* [un·quot·ed; un·quot·ing] To close a quotation.

un·ravel *v.* [un·rav·eled, un·rav·elled; un·rav·el·ing, un·rav·el·ling] 1. To disentangle; separate. 2. To clear up; solve.

un·real *adj.* Imaginary; illusory.—**un·re·al·i·ty** *n.* [*pl.* -ties].

un·rea·son·a·ble *adj.* 1. Irrational. 2. Exorbitant; immoderate.—**un·rea·son·a·ble·ness** *n.*—**un·rea·son·a·bly** *adv.*

un·reel *v.* To unwind.—**un·reel·a·ble** *adj.*

un·reeve *v.* [un·reeved; un·reev·ing] *Nautical.* To withdraw a rope, as from a pulley.

un·re·gen·er·ate, un·re·gen·er·at·ed (un·ree·jen·er·it) *adj.* Hardened; beyond redemption. —**un·re·gen·er·a·cy** *n.*—**un·re·gen·er·ate·ly** *adv.*

un·re·lent·ing *adj.* Implacable; merciless.—**un·re·lent·ing·ly** *adv.*

un·re·li·a·ble *adj.* Not dependable; untrustworthy.—**un·re·li·a·bil·i·ty** *n.*

un·re·li·gious *adj.* Not religious; ungodly.

un·re·mit·ting *adj.* Incessant; continuous.—**un·re·mit·ting·ly** *adv.*—**un·re·mit·ting·ness** *n.*

un·re·served *adj.* 1. Not restricted. 2. Open; frank.—**un·re·serv·ed·ly** *adv.*—**un·re·serv·ed·ness** *n.*

un·re·spon·sive *adj.* Not responding easily; insensible.—**un·re·spon·sive·ly** *adv.*—**un·re·spon·sive·ness** *n.*

un·rest *n.* Disquiet; disturbance; uneasiness. —**un·rest·ful** *adj.*

un·re·strained *adj.* Unchecked; uncontrolled; not limited.—**un·re·strain·ed·ly** *adv.*

un·rid·dle *v* [un·rid·dled; un·rid·dling] To solve; interpret.

un·rig *v.* [un·rigged; un·rig·ging] *Nautical.* To strip of rigging, as a ship.

un·rip *v.* [un·ripped; un·rip·ping] To slit open.

un·ripe *adj.* Immature; callow; green.—**un·ripe·ness** *n.*

un·robe *v.* [un·robed; un·rob·ing] To undress.

un·roll *v.* To unfold; reveal.

un·root *v.* To uproot; extirpate; eradicate.

un·ruf·fled *adj.* Calm; composed; serene.

un·rul·y *adj.* Turbulent; disorderly; ungovernable.—**un·rul·i·ness** *n.*

un·sat·is·fac·to·ry *adj.* Poor; unsuitable; inexpedient.—**un·sat·is·fac·to·ri·ly** *adv.*—**un·sat·is·fac·to·ri·ness** *n.*

un·sat·is·fied *adj.* 1. Unquenched; not gratified. 2. Unhappy; discontented. 3. Unconvinced; not persuaded.—**un·sat·is·fy·ing** *adj.*

un·sa·vor·y (un-*say*-ver-ee) *adj.* 1. Tasteless; unappetizing. 2. Disagreeable; nasty.—**un·sa·vor·i·ness** *n.*

un·say *v.* [un·said; un·say·ing] To retract; recant.

un·scathed (un-*skaythd*) *adj.* Unharmed; uninjured.

unpolished	unpropitious	unrecognized	unrepresentative
unpolitic	unrecompensed	unrepresented
unpolled	unproportionate	unreconcilable	unrepressed
unpractical	unproportioned	unreconciled	unreproved
unpracticed	unprosperous	unrecorded	unrequited
unpredictable	unprotected	unredeemed	unreserve
unprejudiced	unproved	unrefined	unresigned
unpreoccupied	unproven	unreflecting	unresistant
unprepared	unprovided	unreflectingly	unresisted
unpreparedness	unprovoked	unreflective	unresisting
unprepossessing	unprovoking	unreflectively	unrespited
unprescribed	unpruned	unreformable	unrestraint
unpresentable	unpublished	unreformed	unrestricted
unpressed	unpunctual	unregarded	unretentive
unpretending	unpunished	unregistered	unretracted
unpretentious	unpurchasable	unregulated	unretrieved
unprevailing	unpure	unrelated	unrevealed
unpreventable	unpurposed	unrelatedness	unrevenged
unpriced	unpursuing	unrelaxed	unrevoked
unprinted	unquailing	unrelaxing	unrewarded
unprivileged	unqualifying	unrelievable	unrhymed
unprizable	unquenched	unrelieved	unrighteous
unprized	unquestioning	unremembered	unrighteously
unprocessed	unquotable	unremitted	unrighteousness
unprocurable	unraised	unremovable	unrightful
unprofaned	unransomed	unremoved	unrimed
unprofessional	unratified	unremunerated	unripened
unprofitable	unread	unremunerative	unrivaled
unprofitableness	unreadable	unrenowned	unrivalled
unprogressive	unready	unrented	unromantic
unprohibited	unrealized	unrepaid	unruled
unpromising	unreasoned	unrepaired	unsafe
unprompted	unreasoning	unrepealed	unsafely
unpronounceable	unrebuked	unrepentant	unsaid
unpronounced	unreceived	unrepenting	unsaintly
unpropitiable	unreclaimed	unreported	unsalable
	unrecognizable		

un·scram·ble v. [un·scram·bled; un·scram·bling] To separate into its component parts; put in proper order.

un·screw v. To unfasten by turning or removing the screws.

un·scru·pu·lous (un-*skroo*-pyuh-lus) adj. Dishonest; unprincipled.—**un·scru·pu·lous·ly** adv.

un·seal v. To open, esp. by breaking or removing the seal.

un·seam v. To rip; cut open.

un·sea·son·a·ble adj. Unusual; inappropriate; untimely.—**un·sea·son·a·ble·ness** n.—**un·sea·son·a·bly** adv.

un·seat v. To displace or remove, esp. from a legislative body.

un·seem·ly adj. Improper; unbecoming.—**un·seem·li·ness** n.

un·set·tle v. [un·set·tled; un·set·tling] To disturb; disorder; disorganize.—**un·set·tled** adj.

un·sew v. To rip out.

un·sex v. To deprive of sexual characteristics.

un·shack·le v. [un·shack·led; un·shack·ling] To set free; unfetter.—**un·shack·led** adj.

un·sheathe v. [un·sheathed; un·sheath·ing] To draw from a sheath, as a weapon.

un·ship v. [un·shipped; un·ship·ping] 1. To take off a ship. 2. *Nautical.* To remove from its fixed place, as an oar.

un·sight·ly adj. Ugly; deformed.—**un·sight·li·ness** n.

un·skilled adj. 1. Untrained; inexperienced. 2. Not requiring any special training.

un·sling v. [un·slung; un·sling·ing] To take or release from a sling or supporting strap.

un·snap v. [un·snapped; un·snap·ping] To open, as by undoing a snap.

un·snarl v. To disentangle; unravel.

un·so·cia·ble adj. Retiring; not desirous of company or conversation; inhospitable.—**un·so·cia·bil·i·ty, un·so·cia·ble·ness** n.—**un·so·cia·bly** adv.

un·sol·der (un-*sod*-er) v. To sunder; disunite.

un·so·phis·ti·cat·ed (un-suh-*fiss*-tih-kayt-id) adj. 1. Ingenuous; naïve; artless. 2. Simple; natural.—**un·so·phis·ti·cat·ed·ness** n.

un·sound adj. 1. Diseased; defective; imperfect. 2. Not firm; shaky. 3. Deceptive; illogical. 4. Light; disturbed, as of sleep. —**un·sound·ly** adv.—**un·sound·ness** n.

un·speak v. [un·spo·ken; un·speak·ing] To retract; unsay.

un·speak·a·ble adj. Indescribable; unutterable; ineffable.—**un·speak·a·bly** adv.

un·sphere (un-*sfihr*) v. [un·sphered; un·spher·ing] To remove from its sphere.

un·sprung adj. Lacking springs.

un·sta·ble adj. 1. Wavering; irregular. 2. Inconstant; changeable.—**un·sta·ble·ness** n.—**un·sta·bly** adj.

un·state v. [un·stat·ed; un·stat·ing] To degrade; deprive of dignity.

un·stead·y adj. Insecure; fluctuating; unsettled. —**un·stead·i·ly** adv.—**un·stead·i·ness** n.

un·steel v. To propitiate; soften.

un·step v. *Nautical.* To remove (a mast) from its seat or step.

un·stick v. [un·stuck; un·stick·ing] To unglue; separate.

un·stop v. [un·stopped; un·stop·ping] To uncork; open.—**un·stopped** adj.

un·strap v. [un·strapped; un·strap·ping] To untie; unfasten.

unsalaried	unset	unsorted	unsuggestive
unsaleable	unsettled	unsought	unsuited
unsalted	unshaded	unsounded	unsullied
unsanctified	unshakable	unsowed	unsupportable
unsanctioned	unshakeable	unsown	unsupported
unsanitary	unshaken	unsparing	unsuppressed
unsatiated	unshaped	unsparingly	unsure
unsatisfying	unshapely	unspecialized	unsusceptible
unsaturated	unshapen	unspecified	unsuspicious
unscaled	unshaven	unspeculative	unsustained
unscarred	unshed	unspent	unswayed
unscented	unsheltered	unspiritual	unsweetened
unscholarly	unshod	unspoiled	unswept
unschooled	unshorn	unspoilt	unswerving
unscientific	unshrinkable	unspoken	unsymmetrical
unscorched	unshrinking	unsportsmanlike	unsympathetic
unscoured	unsifted	unspotted	unsympathizing
unscreened	unsighted	unsquared	unsystematic
unscriptural	unsigned	unstainable	untactful
unsculptured	unsinkable	unstained	untainted
unsearchable	unsisterly	unstigmatized	untaken
unsearchably	unsized	unstinted	untalented
unseasoned	unskilful	unstitched	untamable
unseaworthy	unskillful	unstrained	untamed
unseconded	unskillfully	unstratified	untanned
unsectarian	unskillfulness	unstressed	untarnished
unsecured	unslacked	unstriated	untaught
unseeing	unslaked	unstriped	untaxable
unseen	unsocial	unstudied	untaxed
unsegmented	unsoiled	unstuffed	untechnical
unselective	unsold	unsubdued	untempered
unselfish	unsoldierly	unsubmissive	untenable
unselfishly	unsolicited	unsubstantial	untenanted
unselfishness	unsolicitous	unsubstantiality	untended
unsentimental	unsoluble	unsubstantially	untented
unserviceable	unsolvable	unsubstantiated	unterrified

U

un·string v. [un·strung; un·string·ing] 1. To remove from a string. 2. To untie; release; loosen. 3. To unnerve.—**un·strung** adj.

un·suc·cess·ful adj. Not producing the desired result; not triumphant.—**un·suc·cess** n.—**un·suc·cess·ful·ly** adv.

un·suit·a·ble adj. Inappropriate; unbecoming; improper.—**un·suit·a·bil·i·ty** n.—**un·suit·a·ble·ness** n.—**un·suit·a·bly** adv.

un·sur·passed adj. Unexcelled.

un·sus·pect·ing adj. Trusting; not suspicious.

un·swathe (un-*swayth*) v. [un·swathed; un·swath·ing] To remove bandages or wrapping.

un·swear v. [un·swore; un·swear·ing] To retract an oath; recant.

un·tan·gle v. [un·tan·gled; un·tan·gling] To extricate; clear up.

un·teach v. [un·taught; un·teach·ing] To cause to forget or disbelieve.

un·teach·a·ble adj. Obtuse.

un·think v. [un·thought; un·think·ing] To retract mentally; remove from the mind.

un·think·a·ble adj. Inconceivable; impossible.

un·think·ing adj. Heedless; inconsiderate.—**un·think·ing·ly** adv. Without thought.

un·thread v. To draw a thread from. 'Unthread a needle.'

un·throne v. [un·throned; un·thron·ing] To depose; dethrone.

un·tidy adj. Slovenly; disorderly.—**un·ti·di·ly** adv.—**un·ti·di·ness** n.

un·tie v. [un·tied; un·ty·ing] To free from a tie or fastening; loosen.—**un·tied** adj.

un·til prep. To; up to; till.—conj. Up to the time or point that.

un·tir·ing adj. Indefatigable; unflagging; unwearying.

un·to prep. Archaic. To.

un·told adj. 1. Not related or revealed. 2. Countless; innumerable.

un·touch·a·ble n. Member of the lowest social caste in India, whose touch is considered defiling.—adj. 1. Out of reach. 2. Offensive or forbidden to the touch.—**un·touch·a·bil·i·ty** n.

un·touched adj. 1. Fresh; unused; uninjured. 2. Not affected; unmoved.

un·to·ward (un-*tord*) adj. Awkward; inconvenient; inappropriate.— -ward·ly adv.— -ward·ness n.

un·tram·meled, un·tram·melled adj. Unimpeded; unconfined.

un·tread v. To retrace; tread back.

un·trod, un·trod·den adj. Not passed over; unfrequented.

un·truss v. To free from a truss; untie; loosen.—**un·trussed** adj.

un·truth n. 1. Lack of truthfulness; falsity. 2. A lie; fabrication; falsehood.

un·tuck v. To let out; unfold.

un·twine v. [un·twined; un·twin·ing] To untwist; unwind.

un·twist v. To separate and open, as the strands of a rope.—**un·twist·ed** adj.

un·u·su·al adj. Strange; uncommon; rare.—**un·u·su·al·ly** adv.—**un·u·su·al·ness** n.

un·ut·ter·a·ble adj. Inexpressible; unspeakable.—**un·ut·ter·a·bly** adv.

un·var·y·ing adj. Uniform; unchanging.

un·veil v. 1. To uncover; disclose; reveal. 2. To dedicate, as a monument.—**un·veiled** adj.—**un·veil·ing** n.

un·war·rant·a·ble adj. Indefensible; unjustifiable.—**un·war·rant·a·bly** adv.

un·war·y adj. Unguarded; incautious.—**un·war·i·ly** adv.—**un·war·i·ness** n.

un·weave v. [un·weaved; un·weav·ing] To ravel; disentangle.

un·well adj. 1. Ill; ailing. 2. Menstruous.

un·whole·some adj. Pernicious; unsound; diseased.—**un·whole·some·ly** adv.—**un·whole·some·ness** n.

un·wield·y adj. Cumbersome; unmanageable.—**un·wield·i·ness** n.

un·wind v. [un·wound; un·wind·ing] To let out; wind off.

un·wise adj. Foolish; injudicious.—**un·wise·ly** adv.

un·wish v. To wish undone.

un·wit·ting·ly adv. Inadvertently; unconsciously.

un·wont·ed (un-*wohnt*-ed) adj. Rare; unusual.—**un·wont·ed·ly** adv.—**un·wont·ed·ness** n.

un·wor·thy adj. 1. Bad; wanting merit. 2. Undeserving. 3. Unbecoming.—**un·wor·thi·ly** adv.—**un·wor·thi·ness** n.

un·wrap v. [un·wrapped; un·wrap·ping] To open; undo, as a package.

un·wreathe v. [un·wreathed; un·wreath·ing] To uncoil; untwine.

un·wrin·kle v. [-kled; -kling] To smooth out; free of wrinkles.

un·writ·ten adj. Not in writing; oral; customary.—**unwritten law.** Custom; rule established by long and general usage.

untested	untitled	untraversable	untufted
unthanked	untraceable	untraversed	untunable
unthankful	untraced	untried	untutored
unthought	untracked	untrimmed	untwilled
unthoughtful	untractable	untroubled	unusable
unthought-of	untrained	untrue	unused
unthrifty	untransferable	untruly	unutilizable
untillable	untranslatable	untrustful	unuttered
untilled	untranslated	untrustworthy	unvaccinated
untimeliness	untransmitted	untruthful	unvacillating
untimely	untraveled	untruthfully	unvalidated
untired	untravelled	untruthfulness	unvalued

un·yield·ing *adj.* Obstinate; firm.

un·yoke *v.* [un·yoked; un·yok·ing] To free from a yoke.—**un·yoked** *adj.*

up *adj.* 1. Higher in place or condition. 2. Raised; elevated. 3. Risen from bed. 4. In a state of action. 5. Higher or more advanced in degree. 6. Expired; finished. 7. *Sports.* **a.** Ahead or in advance of one's opponent. **b.** Needed for winning.—*adv.* 1. To a higher or more advanced place or condition. 2. Denoting approach or arrival. 3. Into a final state; completely; thoroughly. 4. *Baseball.* In a position to bat. 5. *Games. Colloquial.* **a.** Apiece; each. **b.** Ahead.—*prep.* 1. Along; through. 2. Toward the source, center, or top of.—*v.* [upped; up·ping] To raise.—**up to.** 1. As far as. 2. Acquainted with; capable of. 3. Equal to.

up-anchor	upraise	upswing
upbeat	uprose	up-to-date
upbuild	upside	uptrend
upgrade	up-state	upturn

up·braid *v.* To accuse; berate; scold.—**up·braid·ing** *n. & adj.*

up·bring·ing (*up*-bring-ing) *n.* Training; breeding; rearing.

up·cast *n.* That which is thrown or cast up. —*adj.* Turned or directed upward.

up·coun·try *Colloquial. n.* The interior of a country.—*adj.* Interior; inland.—**up·coun·try** *adv.*

up·heav·al (up-*heev*-'l) *n.* Turmoil; violent over-turning.—**up·heave** *v.* [up·heaved; up·hove; up·heav·ing] To lift from below.

up·hill *adj.* 1. Ascending; rising. 2. Difficult; fatiguing.—*adv.* Upward.—*n.* Rising ground.

up·hold *v.* [up·held; up·hold·ing] 1. To support; hold erect. 2. To champion.—**up·hold·er** *n.*

up·hol·ster *v.* To stuff and cover furniture. —**up·hol·ster·er** *n.*—**up·hol·ster·y** *n.*

up·keep *n.* Expenses of repair and maintenance.

up·land *n.* Elevated ground; slopes; plateaus. —**up·land** *adj.*—**up·land·er** *n.*

up·lift *v.* 1. To raise; elevate. 2. To improve in condition.—*n.* An elevation of condition or spirit; boost.

up·most *adj.* Highest; topmost.

up·on (uh-*pon*) *prep.* On.

up·per *adj.* Above; higher; superior.—*n.* 1. Part of a shoe or boot attached to the sole. 2. *Colloquial.* Upper berth.—**upper case.** *Printing.* Capital letters.—**upper-case** *adj.*—**upper**

house. [*often cap.*] That part of a legislature with a smaller or more restricted membership, esp. the U.S. Senate.

up·per·most *adj.* Highest; upmost; predominant.

up·pish *adj.* Also **up·pi·ty.** *Colloquial.* Snobbish; arrogant.—**up·pish·ly** *adv.*—**up·pish·ness** *n.*

up·right *adj.* 1. Erect. 2. Honest; scrupulous.—**up·right·ness** *n.*

up·ris·ing *n.* 1. A rebellion; insurrection. 2. A steep slope.

up·roar *n.* Tumult; noisy disturbance; racket.

up·roar·i·ous *adj.* 1. Tumultuous. 2. Hilarious.—**up·roar·i·ous·ly** *adv.*—**up·roar·i·ous·ness** *n.*

up·root *v.* 1. To tear up by the roots. 2. To destroy; eradicate.—**up·root·ed** *adj.*

up·set *v.* [up·set; up·set·ting] 1. To overthrow; overturn. 2. To disturb or distress. —**up·set** *n.*—**up·set·ting** *adj.*

up·shot *n.* Result; outcome.

up·side-down *adj.* Inverted; with the bottom side up; in confusion.

up·stage *adj.* 1. Pertaining to the rear of the stage. 2. *Colloquial.* Supercilious; haughty; disdainful.—**up·stage** *adv.*

up·stairs *n.* Upper story or portion of a building.—*adv.* To a higher story or position.—**up·stairs** *adj.*

up·stand·ing *adj.* 1. Upright; erect. 2. Honest; trustworthy; dependable.

up·start *n.* One who suddenly makes himself conspicuous; parvenu.—**up·start** *adj.*

up·stream *adv.* Toward the source of a stream.

up·take *n.* 1. A raising or lifting. 2. Comprehension; grasp.

up·town *adj.* In or relating to the upper part of a city.—**up·town** *adv.*

up·ward, up·wards *adv.* In or toward a higher position or degree.—*adj.* Rising.—**up·ward·ly** *adv.*

U·rals (*yoo*-ralz) *n. pl.* A mountain range in the U.S.S.R. separating Europe from Asia.

u·ra·nal·y·sis, ur·in·al·y·sis (yoo-ruh-*nal*-ih-siss) *n. Medicine.* Chemical or microscopic analysis of urine.

U·ra·ni·a (yoo-*ray*-nee-uh) *n. Mythology.* A daughter of Zeus; the muse of astronomy.

u·ran·i·nite *n.* Pitchblende; an ore yielding uranium and other valuable radioactive elements.

u·ra·nite *n.* General term for a number of uranium phosphate ores.

U

unvaried	unwanted	unwelcome	unwomanly
unvarnished	unwarlike	unwept	unworkable
unventilated	unwashed	unwifelike	unworkmanlike
unveracious	unwatched	unwifely	unworldliness
unverifiable	unwavering	unwilled	unworldly
unverified	unweaned	unwilling	unworshiped
unversed	unwearied	unwillingly	unworshipped
unvexed	unwearying	unwillingness	unwound
unvisited	unweathered	unwincing	unwounded
unvitrified	unwed	unwinking	unwoven
unvocal	unwedded	unwitnessed	unwrought
unvoiced	unweeded	unwitting	unzealous

u·ra·ni·um (yoo-*ray*-nee-um) *n.* Metallic radioactive element of many forms, found in pitchblende ore. The isolation of certain of its isotopic forms, especially U235, led to the achievement of atomic fissure as employed in the atom bomb. (*Symbol:* U).—**u·ran·ic** *adj.* —**u·ran·ous** *adj.*

U·ra·nus (*yoo*-ruh-nus) *n.* 1. Seventh planet in order of distance from the sun. 2. *Mythology.* Heaven; the father of the Titans.

ur·ban (er-b'n) *adj.* Metropolitan; pertaining to cities or towns.—**ur·ban·i·za·tion** *n.*—**ur·ban·ize** *v.* [-ized; -iz·ing].

ur·bane (er-*bayn*) *adj.* Suave; courteous.—**ur·ban·i·ty** (er-*ban*-uh-tee) *n.*

ur·chin (er-chin) *n.* 1. A mischievous child; ragamuffin. 2. A hedgehog.

Ur·du (*oor*-doo) *n.* Language of the Mohammedans in India; form of Hindustani.

u·re·a (yoo-*ree*-uh) *n. Biochemistry.* The white crystallizable substance forming the chief solid present in urine.—**u·re·al** *adj.*

u·re·mi·a, u·rae·mi·a (yoo-*ree*-mee-uh) *n. Medicine.* Poisoned condition caused by the presence in the blood of matter normally carried off by the urine.—**u·re·mic, u·rae·mic** *adj.*

u·re·ter (yoo-*ree*-ter) *n.* The tube carrying the urine from the kidney to the bladder.—**u·re·ter·al, u·re·ter·ic** *adj.*

u·re·thra (yoo-*ree*-thruh) *n.* [*pl.* -thrae; -thras] The canal conveying the urine from the bladder and also serving, in the male, as a genital duct.—**u·re·thral** *adj.*

urge *v.* [urged; urg·ing] 1. To press; importune. 2. To encourage; press forward; drive. —*n.* Craving; impulse.

ur·gent (er-j'nt) *adj.* Pressing; demanding immediate attention.—**ur·gent·ly** *adv.*—**ur·gen·cy** *n.*

u·ric (*yoo*-rik) *adj.* Pertaining to urine.—**uric acid.** *Chemistry.* A white, nearly insoluble substance found in urine.

u·ri·nal (*yoo*-rih-n'l) *n.* 1. A receptacle for urine. 2. An enclosure for urinating.

u·ri·nal·y·sis (yoo-rih-*nal*-ih-siss) *n.* Chemical or microscopic analysis of the urine.

u·ri·nar·y (*yoo*-rih-nehr-ee) *adj.* Pertaining to the urine; secreting urine.

u·rine (*yoo*-rin) *n.* Amber-colored waste fluid excreted by the kidneys.—**u·ri·nate** *v.* [u-ri·nat·ing; u·ri·nat·ed]—**u·ri·na·tion** *n.*

u·ri·nous, u·ri·nose (*yoo*-rih-nus) *adj.* Pertaining to or containing urine.

urn *n.* 1. A tall, curving vase, esp. for holding ashes of the dead. 2. Covered vessel with a handle and spout for serving hot beverages.

URNS

Ur·sa Ma·jor. Northern constellation, often called the Great Bear, which contains the stars forming the Big Dipper.

Ursa Minor. Constellation, sometimes called the Little Bear or Little Dipper, which contains the North Star or polestar (Polaris).

us *pron.* The objective case of **we.**

us·age (*yooss*-ij, *yooz*-) *n.* 1. Practice; custom. 2. Treatment. 3. *Grammar.* Normal or correct use.

use (*yooz*) *v.* [used; us·ing] 1. To employ; utilize. 2. To treat; behave toward. 3. To accustom; inure.—(*yooss*) *n.* 1. Employment; service; function; utility. 2. Wear. 3. Need; requirement.—**us·a·ble** *adj.*—**use·ful** *adj.*—**use·ful·ly** *adv.*—**use·ful·ness** *n.*—**us·er** *n.*

use·less *adj.* Unserviceable; worthless.—**use·less·ly** *adv.*—**use·less·ness** *n.*

ush·er *v.* To lead; introduce.—*n.* 1. One who seats people in a theater, church, etc. 2. One of the bridegroom's attendants at a wedding.

U.S.P. United States Pharmacoepia.

us·que·baugh (*us*-kweh-bah) *n.* Irish whisky.

u·su·al (*yoo*-zhoo-ul) *adj.* Customary; habitual; ordinary.—**u·su·al·ly** *adv.*—**u·su·al·ness** *n.*

u·surp (yoo-*zerp*, -*serp*) *v.* To pre-empt; seize and hold forcibly or unrightfully.—**u·sur·pa·tion** *n.*—**u·surp·er** *n.*

u·su·ry (*yoo*-zhoo-ree) *n.* [*pl.* -ies] Supplying loans at an exorbitant rate of interest.—**u·su·rer** *n.*—**u·su·ri·ous** *adj.*

u·ten·sil (yoo-*ten*-s'l) *n.* An implement; tool.

u·ter·us (*yoo*-ter-us) *n.* The womb.

u·til·i·tar·i·an *adj.* Useful; functional.—*n.* Adherent of the doctrine that the aim of all action should be the happiness of the greatest number.—**u·til·i·tar·i·an·ism** *n.*

u·ti·lize *v.* To use; employ.—**u·til·i·ty** *n.*

ut·most *adj.* Extreme; greatest.

U·to·pi·a (yoo-*toh*-pee-uh) *n.* A land of ideal perfection.—**U·to·pi·an** *adj.*

ut·ter *v.* To speak; express; pronounce.—*adj.* Complete; total.—**ut·ter·ance** *n.*—**ut·ter·ly** *adv.*

ut·ter·most *adj.* Extreme; farthest.

V

va·can·cy (*vay*-k'n-see) *n.* [*pl.* -cies] 1. State of being empty. 2. Unoccupied place.

va·cant (*vay*-k'nt) *adj.* 1. Empty; blank; unoccupied. 2. Free from thought or expression. 3. *Law.* Unused; abandoned.—**va·cant·ly** *adv.*

va·cate (*vay*-kayt) *v.* [va·cat·ed; va·cat·ing] 1. To quit; leave empty. 2. To void.

va·ca·tion (vay-*kay*-shun) *n.* Holiday; break in the routine of work; recess.—**va·ca·tion·ist** *n.*

vac·ci·nate (*vak*-sih-nayt) *v.* [-nat·ed; -nat·ing] 1. To immunize against smallpox by inoculation with cowpox virus. 2. To inoculate with any toxic serum for protective purpose.—**vac·ci·na·tion** *n.*—**vac·ci·na·tion·ist**, **vac·ci·na·tor** *n.*

vac·cine (*vak*-seen) *n.* 1. Substance containing the virus of cowpox. 2. Any serum for preventive inoculation.—*adj.* Pertaining to cows or to vaccination.

vac·il·late (*vass*-ih-layt) *v.* [vac·il·lated; vac·il·lat·ing] 1. To waver; fluctuate; sway. 2. To hesitate; falter, esp. in mind or opinion.—**vac·il·lat·ing** *adj.*—**vac·il·la·tion** *n.*

va·cu·i·ty (vuh-*kyoo*-ih-tee) *n.* [*pl.* -ties] 1. Emptiness; vacancy. 2. Mental listlessness or deficiency. 3. An inanity; foolish act.

vac·u·ous (*vak*-yoo-us) *adj.* 1. Empty; vacant. 2. Devoid of intelligence; stupid.—**vac·u·ous·ly** *adv.*—**vac·u·ous·ness** *n.*

vac·u·um (*vak*-yoo-um) *n.* [*pl.* vac·u·ums, vac·u·a] 1. A space empty of all matter, including air; void. 2. Any enclosed area where the pressure is less than normal atmospheric pressure.—*v.* To remove dirt with a vacuum cleaner.—**vac·u·um** *adj.*

vacuum cleaner. Machine, usually electric, that sucks up dirt by creating a vacuum.

vacuum tube. *Electronics.* Sealed tube with air exhausted which secures a flow of electrons from a negative to a positive plate.

vag·a·bond (*vag*-uh-bond) *n.* 1. Wanderer; person with no fixed home. 2. Tramp; vagrant.—*adj.* Wandering; roaming.—**vag·a·bond·age** *n.*

va·gar·y (vuh-*gair*-ee) *n.* [*pl.* -ies] Whim; caprice.

va·gi·na (vuh-*jy*-nuh) *n.* [*pl.* -nae, -nas] 1. A sheath. 2. *Anatomy.* Cylindrical canal in the female pelvis leading to the uterus.—**va·gi·nal**, **va·gi·nate** (vaj-ih-nit) *adj.*

va·grant (*vay*-gr'nt) *n.* Idle wanderer; vagabond; tramp.—*adj.* Wandering; itinerant; unsettled.—**va·gran·cy** *n.*—**va·grant·ly** *adv.*

vague (*vayg*) *adj.* Not distinct or certain; indefinite; hazy.—**vague·ly** *adv.*—**vague·ness** *n.*

vain *adj.* 1. Empty; idle; useless. 2. Ineffectual; futile. 3. Conceited.—**vain·ly** *adv.*—**vain·ness** *n.*—**in vain.** To no avail.

vain·glo·ry *n.* Undue pride; boastfulness; bombast.—**vain·glo·ri·ous** *adj.*— -**glo·ri·ous·ly** *adv.*

val·ance (*val*-unss) *n.* Horizontal band of drapery, esp. over the top of a window.

VALANCE

vale (*vayl*) *n. Poetic.* A valley.

val·e·dic·tion (val-uh-*dik*-shun) *n.* A bidding farewell.

val·e·dic·to·ri·an (val-uh-dik-*tor*-ee-un) *n.* Honor student who delivers the farewell address at a graduation ceremony.—**val·e·dic·to·ry** *n.* [*pl.* -ries] Commencement oration. —*adj.* Bidding farewell.

va·lence (*vay*-lunss) *n.* Also **va·len·cy** [*pl.* -cies] *Chemistry.* The measure of an element's ability to combine with other elements.

val·en·tine (*val*-un-tyne) *n.* 1. A greeting card or gift sent on St. Valentine's Day (February 14). 2. Sweetheart chosen on this day.

val·et (*val*-it) *n.* 1. Gentleman's personal attendant; manservant. 2. Hotel attendant performing like services for guests.—**val·et** *v.*

Val·hal·la (val-*hal*-uh) *n. Norse Mythology.* The heaven for heroes slain in battle.

val·iant (*val*-yunt) *adj.* 1. Heroic; courageous; brave. 2. Strong; stalwart.—**val·iant·ly** *adv.*

val·id (*val*-id) *adj.* 1. Sound; convincing; supported by fact. 2. Binding; having legal force.—**va·lid·i·ty**, **val·id·ness** *n.*—**val·id·ly** *adv.*

val·i·date (*val*-ih-dayt) *v.* [val·i·dat·ed; val·i·dat·ing] 1. To make valid. 2. To confirm; verify.—**val·i·da·tion** *n.*

va·lise (vuh-*leess*) *n.* Small suitcase; traveling bag.

Val·kyr·ie (val-*kihr*-ee) *n. Norse Mythology.* One of Odin's maidens who hovered over battlefields selecting the heroes to die and afterward guiding them to Valhalla.—**Val·kyr·i·an** *adj.*

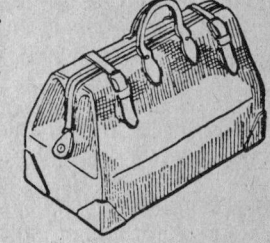
VALISE

val·ley *n.* Long hollow or depression between hills; lowland.

Valley Forge. Encampment in SE Pennsylvania where George Washington spent the difficult winter of 1777–78.

val·or (*val*-er) *n.* Courage; bravery; gallantry. —**val·or·ous** *adj.*— -**ous·ly** *adv.*— -**ous·ness** *n.*

val·u·a·ble (*val*-yoo-uh-b'l, -yuh-) *adj.* 1. Useful; having worth or desirability; precious.

V

2. Costly; high-priced.—*n.* [*pl.*] Articles of small bulk and great value.—**val·u·a·ble·ness** *n.*—**val·u·a·bly** *adv.*

val·u·a·tion (val-yoo-*ay*-shun) *n.* Price; estimate of worth.

val·ue (*val*-yoo) *n.* 1. Worth; usefulness. 2. Price; cost; monetary equivalent. 3. Importance; significance. 4. *Painting.* Tonal quality. 5. *Music.* Relative length of a note. —*v.* [val·ued; val·u·ing] 1. To appraise; estimate; evaluate. 2. To esteem; appreciate. —**val·ued** *adj.* Prized; esteemed.

valve *n.* 1. A device to control or regulate a flow or current. 2. *Anatomy.* Membrane fold which retards or prevents the flow of a fluid. 3. *Music.* Device for changing the tone of a wind instrument by varying the tube length. 4. Division of the shell of a mollusk.—**val·vu·lar** *adj.*

va·moose (vuh-*mooss*, vam-) *v. Slang.* To leave hurriedly.

vamp *n.* 1. Upper leather of a boot or shoe. 2. *Slang.* Volunteer fireman.—*v.* 1. To mend; furbish. 2. *Music.* To improvise.

vam·pire (*vam*-pyre) *n.* 1. Bloodsucking ghost or demon who wanders by night. 2. Extortioner; leech. 3. *Slang.* Also **vamp.** Woman who preys on men. 4. Also **vampire bat.** A species of bloodsucking bat.—**vam·pir·ism** *n.*

van *n.* Foremost part, esp. of an army or fleet. —**van·ward** *adj. & adv.*

van *n.* 1. Large covered truck for moving furniture, etc. 2. Railway baggage car.

va·na·di·um (vuh-*nay*-dee-um) *n.* Silvery-white metallic element. (*Symbol:* V).—**vanadium steel.** Steel strengthened by being alloyed with vanadium.

van·dal (*van*-d'l) *n.* 1. Wanton destroyer of cultural objects. 2. [*cap.*] Member of a Teutonic race which conquered and sacked Rome in the 5th century.—*adj.* Barbarous; wantonly destructive.—**van·dal·ism** *n.*—**van·dal·ize** *v.* [van·dal·ized; van·dal·iz·ing].

Van·dyke *adj.* Pertaining to the style of Anthony Van Dyke, or Vandyke, Flemish painter. —*n.* A short pointed beard.

vane *n.* 1. Weathercock; device which indicates wind direction. 2. Any bladelike, revolving surface. 3. *Surveying.* The sight of a quadrant for measurement of angles.

van·guard (*van*-gahrd) *n.* 1. Van; leading position, esp. in an army. 2. Those in the forefront; leaders.

va·nil·la (vuh-*nil*-uh, often vuh-*nel*-uh) *n.* 1. A tropical climbing plant. 2. The sweet, aromatic flavoring extracted from its fruit.

van·ish (*van*-ish) *v.* To become invisible; disappear suddenly or completely.—**van·ish·er** *n.*

van·i·ty (*van*-ih-tee) *n.* [*pl.* -ties] 1. Empty pride; conceit; idle show. 2. Also **vanity table.** A mirrored dressing table. 3. Also **vanity case.** Make-up case; compact.

van·quish (*van*-kwish, *vang*-) *v.* 1. To defeat;

conquer; overcome. 2. To refute; prove wrong.—**van·quish·a·ble** *adj.*—**van·quish·er** *n.*

van·tage (*van*-tij) *n.* Advantage; opportunity. —**vantage point.** Superior position.

vap·id (*vap*-id) *adj.* 1. Insipid; flat; stale. 2. Stupid; dull.—**va·pid·i·ty, vap·id·ness** *n.*

va·por (*vay*-per) *n.* 1. *Physics.* Matter in a gaseous state. 2. Any fine substance clouding the air, as fog or steam. 3. Transitory feeling; fancy.—**va·por** *v.*—**va·por·ous** *adj.*

va·por·ize (*vay*-per-yze) *v.* [va·por·ized; va·por·iz·ing] To form into vapor.—**va·por·iz·a·ble** *adj.*—**va·por·i·za·tion** *n.*

va·que·ro (vah-*kay*-roh) *n.* A cowboy, esp. in southwestern U.S.

var·i·a·ble (*vair*-ee-uh-b'l) *adj.* 1. Changeable; unstable. 2. Fickle; inconstant. 3. *Biology.* Deviating from type; abnormal.—*n.* 1. That which varies. 2. *Mathematics.* Quantity whose value may fluctuate. 3. A shifting wind.—**var·i·a·bil·i·ty, var·i·a·ble·ness** *n.*—**var·i·a·bly** *adv.*

var·i·ance (*vair*-ee-unss) *n.* 1. Difference; divergency. 2. Discord; contention; strife.

var·i·ant (*vair*-ee-unt) *adj.* Different; deviating from the standard.—*n.* Different form or version.

var·i·a·tion (vair-ee-*ay*-shun) *n.* 1. Change; deviation; modification. 2. Degree or rate of change. 3. *Music.* Ornamental change in the treatment of a tune or theme.— -**tion·al** *adj.*

var·i·col·ored (*vair*-ih-kul-erd) *adj.* Having various colors.

var·i·cose (*vair*-ih-kohss) *adj.* Swollen; enlarged.—**var·i·cos·i·ty** *n.* [*pl.* -ties].

var·ied (*vair*-eed) *adj.* Changed; diverse; divergent.

var·i·e·gate (*vair*-ee-uh-gayt) *v.* [var·i·e·gat·ed; var·i·e·gat·ing] To diversify; dapple or streak. —**var·i·e·gat·ed** *adj.*—**var·i·e·ga·tion** *n.*

va·ri·e·ty (vuh-*ry*-uh-tee) *n.* [*pl.* -ties] 1. Medley; mixture or succession of different things. 2. Change; diversity. 3. Sort; kind; subdivision of a species. 4. A show consisting of several different, unrelated performances.

var·i·o·rum (vair-ee-*or*-um) *n.* 1. An edition, esp. of a classic, containing various versions of the text. 2. Edition with notes by several critics or editors.—**var·i·or·um** *adj.*

var·i·ous (*vair*-ee-us) *adj.* 1. Different; assorted; not uniform. 2. Several; numerous. 3. Changeable.

var·let (*vahr*-let) *n.* Menial person; scoundrel.

var·nish (*vahr*-nish) *n.* 1. Liquid, resinous compound giving a hard, glossy finish to a surface. 2. Shiny, lustrous coating or appearance. 3. Outer show or pretense.—*v.* 1. To cover with varnish. 2. To gloss over; cover up.—**var·nish·er** *n.*

var·si·ty (*vahr*-sih-tee) *adj.* Pertaining to a college or university.—*n. Sports.* The first-string team in interscholastic sporting events.

var·y (*vair*-ee) *v.* [var·ied; var·y·ing] 1. To

change; alter; modify. 2. To differ; diverge; deviate. 3. *Mathematics.* To fluctuate in value.

vas·cu·lar (*vass*-kyoo-ler) *adj.* Pertaining to the vessels of plant and animal circulatory systems.—**vas·cu·lar·i·ty** (vas-kyoo-*lair*-ih-tee) *n.*

vase (*vayss, vayz, vahz*) *n.* Ornamental vessel for holding flowers, decorations, etc.

Vas·e·line (*vass*-uh-leen) *n.* Trade-mark for various ointments made from petroleum.

vas·sal (*vass*-'l) *n.* 1. Feudal tenant; subject. 2. Dependent; slave.—*adj.* Servile; subservient.—**vas·sal·age** *n.*

vast *adj.* Immense; enormous; of great range or quantity.—**vast·ly** *adv.*—**vast·ness** *n.*

vat *n.* Large tank or tub, esp. for holding or storing fluids.—*v.* [vat·ted; vat·ting].

vat-dyed *adj. Textiles.* Dyed before weaving; colorfast.

Vat·i·can (*vat*-ih-k'n) *n.* 1. Pope's palace at Rome. 2. Papal authority.

vaude·ville (*vohd*-vil) *n.* Series of disconnected acts performed on a public stage; variety.

vault (*vawlt*) *n.* 1. Arched roof or ceiling. 2. Large underground room for storing valuables, wines, etc. 3. Tomb; sepulcher. 4. Leap; jump; buck.—*v.* 1. To shape like or cover with an arch. 2. To leap; jump.—**vault·ed** *adj.*—**pole vault.** To leap for height with the aid of a pole.—**pole vaulter.**

vaunt (*vawnt*) *v.* To brag; boast; exhibit ostentatiously.—*n.* Vain display; boast.—**vaunt·er** *n.*—**vaunt·ing·ly** *adv.*

veal (*veel*) *n.* Calf's flesh.

vec·tor (*vek*-ter) *n. Mathematics.* A straight line representing a force having both magnitude and direction.

Ve·da (*vay*-duh, *vee*-duh) *n.* Body of ancient Sanskrit books, the basis of the Hindu religion.—**Ve·da·ic, Ve·dic,** *adj.*—**Ve·da·ism** *n.*

veer *v.* To change direction; swerve; shift.—*n.* A change of direction or position.

Ve·ga (*vee*-guh) *n.* Brightest star in Lyra.

veg·e·ta·ble (*vej*-uh-tuh-b'l) *n.* 1. Any plant deriving its nourishment from the soil. 2. Fleshy or leafy plant cultivated for food. —**veg·e·ta·ble** *adj.*

veg·e·tal (*vej*-uh-t'l) *adj.* Pertaining to plants.

veg·e·tar·i·an (vej-uh-*tair*-ee-un) *n.* Person who abstains from meats, living on vegetables and cereals.—**veg·e·tar·i·an** *adj.*—**veg·e·tar·i·an·ism** *n.*

veg·e·tate (*vej*-uh-tayt) *v.* [veg·e·tat·ed; veg·e·tat·ing] 1. To grow like a plant. 2. To live an idle, passive life.—**veg·e·ta·tion** *n.* 1. Plant growth. 2. Stagnant existence. 3. Plant life in general.

veg·e·ta·tive (*vej*-uh-tay-tiv) *adj.* 1. Growing, as a plant; passive; inactive. 2. Causing growth; productive. 3. Relating to plant life. —**veg·e·ta·tive·ly** *adv.*—**veg·e·ta·tive·ness** *n.*

ve·he·ment (*vee*-uh-m'nt) *adj.* 1. Intense; forceful. 2. Fervent; ardent.—**ve·he·mence, ve·he·men·cy** *n.*—**ve·he·ment·ly** *adv.*

ve·hi·cle (*vee*-uh-k'l) *n.* 1. Any land conveyance for persons or goods. 2. Means of expression; instrument; medium.—**ve·hic·u·lar** (vee-*hik*-yoo-ler, -yuh-) *adj.*

veil (*vayl*) *n.* 1. A covering for concealment; curtain; mask. 2. Transparent, usually ornamental, face covering.—*v.* 1. To cover. 2. To conceal; disguise.—**veiled** *adj.*—**veil·ing** *n.* Filmy material for veils.

vein *n.* 1. Vessel conveying blood to the heart. 2. *Botany.* Vascular framework supporting a leaf. 3. Contrasting streak; strain. 4. *Mining.* Deposit of useful mineral or ore. 5. Temper; mood; manner.—*v.* To mark with veins; streak.—**veined** *adj.*—**vein·y** [-i·er; -i·est] *adj.*

veld, veldt *n.* Grassy plain in South Africa.

vel·lum (*vel*-um) *n.* Fine parchment; any smooth, fine writing paper.

vel·oc·i·pede (vuh-*loss*-ih-peed) *n.* Any light pedal-operated vehicle, as a bicycle or tricycle.

vel·oc·i·ty (vuh-*loss*-ih-tee) *n.* [*pl.*-ties] 1. Speed; rapidity. 2. *Physics.* Rate of motion.

ve·lours (vuh-*loor*) *n.* A heavy, velvetlike fabric.

vel·vet (*vel*-vit) *n.* 1. Rich silk or rayon cloth with a thick soft nap or pile. 2. Fine down covering a young deer's antlers. 3. *Slang.* Clear profit; surplus.—*adj.* Made of or resembling velvet.—**vel·vet·y** *adj.* Soft; sleek.

velvet-banded	velvet-eared	velvet-lined
velvet black	velvet-edged	velvet-soled
velvet-clad	velvet-faced	velvet-tipped
velvet-covered	velvet-hooded	velvetwork

vel·ve·teen (vel-vuh-*teen*) *n.* Cotton cloth resembling velvet.

ve·nal (*vee*-n'l) *adj.* Mercenary; corrupt; easily bribed.—**ve·nal·i·ty** *n.* [-ties].—**ve·nal·ly** *adv.*

vend *v.* To sell; peddle.—**vend·er** *n.* Seller.

vend·ee (ven-*dee*) *n.* Buyer; person to whom a thing is sold, as opposed to **vendor.**

ven·det·ta (ven-*det*-uh) *n.* Blood feud to avenge the killing of a relative.—**ven·det·tist** *n.*

vend·i·ble (*vend*-uh-b'l) *adj.* Salable; marketable.—*n.* Article capable of being sold.—**vend·i·bil·i·ty** *adv.*

ven·dor (*ven*-der) *n.* Seller; as opposed to **vendee.**

ve·neer (vuh-*neer*) *n.* 1. Thin strips of choice wood laid on a cheaper base. 2. Surface fineness; superficial show.—*v.* 1. To overlay with fine wood. 2. To gild; gloss.

ven·er·a·ble (*ven*-er-uh-b'l) *adj.* Deserving of respect or reverence, esp. because of age, dignity, or religious association.—**ven·er·ate** *v.* To revere; admire.

ve·ne·re·al (veh-*neer*-ee-ul) *adj.* Pertaining to or arising from sexual intercourse.

ven·er·y (*ven*-er-ee) *n.* 1. Quest for sexual pleasure. 2. Hunting.

Ve·ne·tian (veh-*nee*-shun) *adj.* Pertaining to Venice.—*n.* Inhabitant of Venice.

Venetian blind. Window blind of thin horizontal slats which can be regulated to admit light and air.

venge·ance (*ven*-junss) *n.* Revenge; punishment

V

inflicted in return for an injury.—**with a vengeance.** 1. Vehemently; forcefully. 2. Extremely. 3. In great quantity.

venge·ful *adj.* Vindictive; desiring revenge.
—**venge·ful·ly** *adv.*—**venge·ful·ness** *n.*

ve·ni·al (*veen*-yul) *adj.* Forgivable; trifling; excusable.—**ve·ni·al·i·ty, ve·ni·al·ness** *n.*— -**al·ly** *adv.*

ven·i·son (*ven*-uh-zun) *n.* Deer flesh.

ven·om (*ven*-um) *n.* 1. Poison, esp. that in-
jected by a bite or sting. 2. Spite; malice.
—**ven·o·mous** *adj.*— -**ous·ly** *adv.*— -**ous·ness** *n.*

vent *n.* 1. Small hole or opening; flue. 2. Escape; outlet; utterance; expression.—*v.* 1. To
let out. 2. To express; utter.—**vent·er** *n.*

ven·ti·late (*ven*-tuh-layt) *v.* 1. To open to the
passage of fresh air. 2. To air; expose to free
discussion.—**ven·ti·la·tion** *n.*—**ven·ti·la·tor** *n.*
Mechanism for supplying fresh air.

ven·tral (*ven*-tr'l) *adj.* On or pertaining to the
belly or undersurface.—**ven·tral·ly** *adv.*

ven·tri·cle (*ven*-trih-k'l) *n.* Small cavity in an
animal organ, esp. a heart chamber pumping
blood into the arteries.—**ven·tric·u·lar** *adj.*

ven·tril·o·quism (ven-*tril*-uh-kwizm). Also **ven-
tril·o·quy** *n.* Art of making voice sounds seem
to come from a source other than the speaker.
—**ven·tril·o·quist** *n.*—**ven·tril·o·quize** *v.* [ven-
tril·o·quized; ven·tril·o·quiz·ing].

ven·ture (*ven*-cher) *n.* 1. Hazardous undertaking; risk; speculation. 2. That which is
risked; stake.—*v.* [ven·tured; ven·tur·ing].
1. To risk; dare; chance. 2. To put forth, as
an opinion.

ven·ture·some (*ven*-cher-sum) *adj.* 1. Bold;
daring; willing to take risks. 2. Hazardous;
risky.—**ven·ture·some·ly** *adv.*— -**some·ness** *n.*

ven·tur·ous (*ven*-cher-us) *adj.* 1. Rash; daring.
2. Perilous; involving risk.—**ven·tur·ous·ly**
adv.—**ven·tur·ous·ness** *n.*

ven·ue (*ven*-yoo) *n. Law.* Place where the events
leading to the trial occurred or where the jury
is selected and the trial is held.

ve·nus (*vee*-nus) *n.* 1. [*cap.*] Roman goddess of
love and beauty. 2. Beautiful woman.
3. [*cap.*] Planet nearest the earth.

Ve·nus's-fly·trap *n.* Plant whose leaves close
when irritated, thereby trapping insects.

ven·er·ate (*ven*-er-ayt) *v.* [ven·er·at·ed; ven·er-
at·ing] To revere; hold in awe or respect.
—**ven·er·a·tion** *n.*

ve·rac·i·ty (vuh-*rass*-ih-tee) *n.* [*pl.* -ties]
1. Truthfulness; verity; correctness; precision.
2. Truth.—**ve·ra·cious** (vuh-*ray*-shus) *adj.*—**ve-
ra·cious·ly** *adv.*—**ve·ra·cious·ness** *n.*

ve·ran·da, ve·ran·dah (ver-*an*-duh) *n.* Large,
usually roofed, front porch.

verb *n. Grammar.* Part of speech showing action
or state of being.

ver·bal (*ver*-b'l) *adj.* 1. Concerning words
rather than ideas. 2. Spoken; oral. 3. Literal; word for word. 4. *Grammar.* Like or
pertaining to a verb.—**ver·bal·ism** *n.*—**ver·bal·
ist** *n.*—**ver·bal·ly** *adv.*

ver·ba·tim (ver-*bay*-tim) *adv.* Word for word.

ver·be·na (ver-*bee*-nuh) *n.* Weedy plant having
clusters of large varicol-
ored flowers.

ver·bi·age (*ver*-bee-ij) *n.*
Wordiness; verbosity.

ver·bose (ver-*bohss*) *adj.*
Wordy; using many un-
necessary or meaningless
words.—**ver·bose·ly** *adv.*
—**ver·bos·i·ty, ver·bose·
ness** *n.*

ver·dant (*ver*-d'nt) *adj.*
Green; flourishing.—**ver·
dan·cy** *n.*—**ver·dant·ly** *adv.*

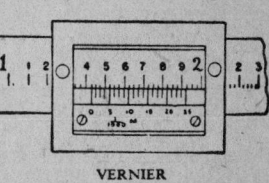
VERBENA

ver·dict (*ver*-dikt) *n.* 1. *Law.* Decision of a
jury. 2. Judgment; opinion.

ver·dure (*ver*-jer) *n.* Greenness; fresh vegetation.—**ver·dur·ous** *adj.*—**ver·dur·ous·ness** *n.*

verge *n.* Edge; border; brink.—*v.* [verged;
verg·ing] To border; incline; approach.

ver·i·fy (*vehr*-ih-fy) *v.* [ver·i·fied; ver·i·fy·ing]
1. To confirm; prove true. 2. To check for
accuracy. 3. To vouch for; authenticate.
—**ver·i·fi·ca·tion** *n.*—**ver·i·fi·er** *n.*

ver·i·ly (*vehr*-ih-lee) *adv.* Truly; in truth.

ver·i·si·mil·i·tude (vehr-ih-sih-*mil*-ih-tyood,
-tood) *n.* Appearance of truth; probability.

ver·i·ta·ble (*vehr*-ih-tuh-b'l) *adj.* Real; actual;
genuine.—**ver·i·ta·ble·ness** *n.*—**ver·i·ta·bly** *adv.*

ver·i·ty (*vehr*-ih-tee) *n.* [*pl.* -ties] 1. Truth; honesty; reality. 2. A truth.

ver·mi·cel·li (ver-mih-*sel*-ee) *n.* Thin spaghetti.

ver·mic·u·lar (ver-*mik*-yoo-ler) *adj.* 1. Like,
or pertaining to, a worm. 2. Worm-eaten.

ver·mi·form (*ver*-mih-form) *adj.* Shaped like a
worm.—**vermiform appendix.** Small tubelike
extension of the large intestine.

ver·mi·fuge (*ver*-mih-fyooj) *n.* Medicine for destroying intestinal worms.

ver·mil·ion (ver-*mil*-yun) *n.* 1. Mercury compound producing a clear red dye. 2. A bright
red color.—**ver·mil·ion** *adj.*

ver·min (*ver*-min) *n. sing. & pl.* 1. Offensive or
destructive animal or animals. 2. Obnoxious,
despicable person.—**ver·min·ous** *adj.*

ver·mouth (ver-*mooth*) *n.* A blended white
wine, often sweet, used esp. in mixed drinks.

ver·nac·u·lar (ver-*nak*-yuh-ler) *n.* 1. Everyday, idiomatic speech. 2. Jargon; slang.
—*adj.* Native; indigenous.

ver·nal (*ver*-n'l) *adj.* Belonging to or appearing
in the spring; youthful.

ver·ni·er (*ver*-nee-er) *n.* Graduated sliding scale
for precision meas-
uring.

Ver·o·nal (*vehr*-uh-
n'l) *n.* Trade-mark
for a sleep-induc-
ing drug.

ve·ron·i·ca (vuh-
ron-ih-kuh) *n.*
Plant with small, colored flowers; the speed-
well.

VERNIER

Ver·sailles (ver-*sy*) *n.* Suburb of Paris, site of signing of the World War I peace treaty.

ver·sa·tile (*ver*-suh-t'l) *adj.* 1. Many-sided; having facility in many lines. 2. Capable of turning freely.—**ver·sa·til·i·ty** *n.*—**ver·sa·tile·ly** *adv.*

verse *n.* 1. A rhymed or metric line of poetry. 2. A stanza. 3. Metrical form; versification. 4. Poetry in general.—**versed** *adj.* Thoroughly familiar; skilled.

ver·si·cle (*ver*-sih-k'l) *n.* Line or verse said or sung by a clergyman and replied to by the congregation.

ver·si·fy (*ver*-sih-fy) *v.* [ver·si·fied; ver·si·fy·ing] 1. To write poetry; rhyme. 2. To convert prose into verse.—**ver·si·fi·ca·tion** *n.*

ver·sion (*ver*-zhun) *n.* 1. Translation, esp. from another language; paraphrase. 2. Particular account; description; interpretation.

vers libre (vair *lee*-br'). Free verse; verse having no fixed meter or rhyme.

ver·sus (*ver*-sus) *prep.* Against; opposed to.

vert emeraude (vert *em*-er-ohd). A dull green earth pigment.

ver·te·bra (*ver*-tuh-bruh) *n.* [*pl.* -brae (-bree), -bras] Single bone of the spinal column.—**ver·te·bral** *adj.*

ver·te·brate (*ver*-tuh-brayt) *adj.* Having vertebrae.—*n.* Any animal having a spinal column or backbone.

ver·tex (*ver*-teks) *n.* [*pl.* -tex·es; -ti·ces] 1. Apex; top; summit. 2. *Mathematics.* Point in any figure opposite to and farthest from the base.

ver·ti·cal (*ver*-tuh-k'l) *adj.* 1. Pertaining to the vertex. 2. Upright; perpendicular to the horizon.—**ver·ti·cal** *n.*—**ver·ti·cal·ly** *adv.*

vertical union. Industrial union; organization of workers engaged in various stages of the same industry, as opposed to craft or horizontal unions.

ver·ti·go (*ver*-tih-goh) *n.* [*pl.* -goes, ver·tig·i·nes] Dizziness; giddiness.—**ver·tig·i·nous** (-*tij*-) *adj.*

verve *n.* Spirit; liveliness; enthusiasm.

ver·y (*vehr*-ee) *adv.* Extremely; to a great extent.—*adj.* [-ier; -iest] 1. Identical; same. 2. Sheer; utter; actual.

ves·i·ca·to·ry (*vess*-ih-kuh-tor-ee) *adj.* Tending to blister.—*n.* [*pl.* -ries] A blistering agent.

ves·i·cle (*vess*-ih-k'l) *n.* 1. Small bladder filled with liquid. 2. Small blister.—**ve·sic·u·lar, ve·sic·u·late** *adj.*—**ve·sic·u·lar·ly** *adv.*

ves·per (*vess*-per) *n.* 1. [*cap.*] Venus; the evening star. 2. [*pl.*] Evening worship or prayers.

ves·sel (*vess*-'l) *n.* 1. Hollow utensil for holding any substance or object. 2. Ship; boat. 3. *Anatomy.* Canal or tube in which fluids are circulated.

vest *n.* Men's short, sleeveless garment; waistcoat.—*v.* 1. To clothe; garb. 2. To bestow; commit; invest as with authority.

Ves·ta *n.* Roman goddess of the hearth.

ves·tal (*vess*-t'l) *adj.* 1. Pertaining to Vesta.

2. Like a vestal virgin; chaste; virginal.—*n.* 1. Also **vestal virgin.** Young girl serving in the temple of Vesta. 2. Virgin; nun.

vest·ed *adj.* 1. *Law.* Fixed; inalienable. 'A vested interest.' 2. Clothed; arrayed.

vest·ee (vess-*tee*) *n.* Ornamental yoke or sleeveless blouse; dickey.

ves·ti·bule (*vess*-tih-byool) *n.* Passage between the outer door and inside of a building; hall; antechamber.—**ves·tib·u·lar** *adj.*

ves·tige (*vess*-tij) *n.* 1. Mark of something no longer present; trace. 2. *Biology.* Useless remains of an organ or part which was fully developed in ancestral types.—**ves·tig·i·al** *adj.* —**ves·tig·i·al·ly** *adv.*

vest·ment *n.* 1. Garment; apparel. 2. Article of attire worn by clergyman conducting services.

ves·try (*vess*-tree) *n.* 1. Church room for keeping vestments and holding parish meetings. 2. Administrative committee meeting of parishioners.—**ves·try·man** *n.*

ves·ture (*vess*-cher) *n.* 1. Attire; clothing; covering.—*v.* [ves·tured; ves·tur·ing] To clothe.

vetch *n.* Weedlike plant often used for fodder.

vet·er·an (*vet*-er-un) *n.* One long experienced in some field, esp. military service; an ex-serviceman.—**vet·er·an** *adj.*

vet·er·i·nar·i·an (vet-er-ih-*nair*-ee-un) *n.* One trained to treat animal diseases and injuries.

vet·er·i·nar·y (*vet*-er-ih-nair-ee) *n.* [*pl.* -ies] A veterinarian.—*adj.* Pertaining to the medical care and treatment of domestic animals.

ve·to (*vee*-toh) *n.* [*pl.* ve·toes]. 1. Power of the executive to reject bills passed by the legislature or the exercise of this power. 2. Authoritative prohibition; refusal of consent.—*v.* [ve·toed; ve·to·ing]—**ve·to·er** *n.*

vex *v.* 1. To irritate; annoy; harass. 2. To agitate; disturb.—**vex·a·tion** *n.*—**vex·a·tious** *adj.*—**vex·a·tious·ly** *adv.*

vi·a (*vy*-uh) *prep.* By way of.

vi·a·duct (*vy*-uh-dukt) *n.* Elevated roadway or long bridge across low ground.

vi·al (*vy*-ul) *n.* Also **phi·al.** Small, narrow glass bottle.

vi·ands (*vy*-'ndz) *n. pl.* Food; provisions; victuals.

vi·at·i·cum (vy-*at*-ih-kum) *n.* 1. Supplies or money for traveling. 2. Communion given to a dying person.

vi·brant (*vy*-brunt) *adj.* 1. Resonant; resounding. 2. Vibrating.—**vi·bran·cy** *n.*

vi·brate (*vy*-brayt) *v.* [vi·brat·ed; vi·brat·ing] 1. To swing; oscillate. 2. To sound; quiver; thrill.—**vi·bra·tion** *n.*—**vi·bra·tion·al** *adj.*—**vi·bra·to·ry** *adj.*

VIADUCT

V

vi·bra·tor (*vy*-bray-ter) *n*. 1. Electrical machine for massage, etc. 2. *Electricity*. Device converting direct current to alternating current; oscillator.

vic·ar (*vik*-er) *n*. 1. Deputy; substitute. 2. Parish priest; curate.—**vic·ar·age** *n*. Residence or salary of a vicar.—**vic·ar·ship** *n*.

vi·car·i·ous (vy-, vih-*kair*-ee-us) *adj*. 1. Delegated; performed by or for another. 2. Substituted, esp. indicating substitution of mental for actual experiences.—**vi·car·i·ous·ly** *adv*. —**vi·car·i·ous·ness** *n*.

vice (*vysse*) *n*. 1. Fault; blemish; evil habit. 2. Immorality; depravity. 3. A vise.

vice *prep*. In the place or stead of.

vice *prefix*. Deputy or substituting for another.

vice admiral	vice president
vice-admiralty	vice-presidential
vice consul	vice rector
vice-consulate	vice-rectorship
vice governor	vice regent
vice-governorship	vice-regency
vice minister	viceroy
vice-ministry	viceroyalty
vice-presidency	vice warden

vice-ver·sa (*vy*-suh-*ver*-suh) *adv*. The conditions being reversed; conversely.

vi·cin·i·ty (vih-*sin*-ih-tee) *n*. [*pl*. -ties] 1. Proximity; nearness. 2. Neighborhood.

vi·cious (*vish*-us) *adj*. 1. Depraved; evil; corrupt. 2. Cruel; savage; malignant. 3. Faulty; impure.—**vi·cious·ly** *adv*.—**vi·cious·ness** *n*. —**vicious circle.** 1. Constantly repeating chain of undesirable events each of which causes or exaggerates the next. 2. Defective reasoning which bases a statement on a premise not yet proved.

vi·cis·si·tude (vih-*siss*-ih-tyood, -tood) *n*. Constantly occurring change, esp. in fortune or condition.

Vicks·burg. City in Mississippi, site of an important Civil War battle.

vic·tim (*vik*-tim, -tum) *n*. 1. Person or animal destroyed or injured. 2. Prey; dupe. 3. Living creature sacrificed to a deity.—**vic·tim·ize** *v*. [vic·tim·ized; vic·tim·iz·ing].

vic·tor (*vik*-ter) *n*. Winner; conqueror.—**vic·tor** *adj*.

vic·to·ri·a (vik-*tor*-ee-uh) *n*. Low, four-wheeled carriage seating two persons.

Vic·to·ri·an (vik-*tor*-ee-un) *adj*. Pertaining to reign of Queen Victoria of England.—*n*. Person, esp. author, of that time.

vic·to·ry (*vik*-tree) *n*. [*pl*. -ries] *n*. Conquest; defeat of an opponent.—**vic·to·ri·ous** *adj*. —**vic·to·ri·ous·ly** *adv*.

Vic·tro·la (vik-*troh*-luh) *n*. Trade-mark name for a type of phonograph.

vict·ual (*vit*-'l) *v*. To supply with food.—*n*. [*pl*.] Food, esp. when prepared for the table.

vi·cu·ña (vih-*koon*-yuh) *n*. Animal of the Andes mountains, having valuable wool.

vi·de·li·cet (vih-*del*-ih-sit) *adv*. Namely; to wit.

vid·e·o (*vid*-ee-oh) *n*. *Television*. The process of transmitting a picture through the air.

vie (*vy*) *v*. To contend; strive for superiority.

view (*vyoo*) *n*. 1. Act of seeing; look; survey. 2. Power of seeing; sight. 3. Mental examination; scrutiny. 4. Scene; prospect. 5. Opinion; belief. 6. Aim; intention.—**view** *v*. —**view·er** *n*.

view·point (*vyoo*-poynt) *n*. Mental attitude or position; point from which something is viewed.

vig·il (*vij*-'l) *n*. 1. Watch; wakefulness. 2. [*pl*.] Evening prayers, esp. on the eve of a religious holiday.

vig·i·lance (*vij*-ih-l'nss) *n*. Watchfulness; care.

vigilance committee. A volunteer and illegal committee of citizens to wipe out criminal activity, now often used as a cloak for the protection of selfish interests.—**vig·i·lan·te** (vih-jih- *lan*-tee) *n*.—**vig·i·lan·tism** *n*.

vig·i·lant (*vij*-ih-l'nt) *adj*. Watchful; alert.

vi·gnette (vin-*yet*) *n*. 1. Small decorative design on a page of a book. 2. Picture gradually shading off into the background. 3. Short description; thumbnail sketch.—*v*. [vi·gnet·ted; vi·gnet·ting].

vig·or (*vig*-er) *n*. Strength; energy; potency. —**vig·or·ous** *adj*.—**vig·or·ous·ly** *adv*.—**vig·or· ous·ness** *n*.

vi·king (*vy*-king) *n*. One of the Scandinavian sea rovers who ravaged the European coasts from the eighth to the tenth century.

vile *adj*. Depraved; base; extremely bad.—**vile ly** *adv*.—**vile·ness** *n*.

vil·i·fy (*vil*-ih-fy) *v*. [vil·i·fied; vil·i·fy·ing] To defame; slander.—**vil·i·fi·ca·tion** *n*.— **-fi·er** *n*.

vil·la (*vil*-uh) *n*. Rural or suburban mansion.

vil·lage (*vil*-ij) *n*. Rural assemblage of houses, smaller than a town.—**vil·lage** *adj*.— **-lag·er** *n*.

vil·lain (*vil*-in) *n*. Scoundrel; rogue.—**vil·lain· ous** *adj*.—**vil·lain·ous·ly** *adv*.—**vil·lain·y** *n*. [*pl*. -ies] Wicked act or nature.

vil·lein (*vil*-in) *n*. Serf; feudal tenant of the lowest class.

vim *n*. Energy; vitality.

vin·di·cate (*vin*-dih-kayt) *v*. [vin·di·cat·ed; vin· di·cat·ing] 1. To defend; justify. 2. To exonerate; absolve.—**vin·di·ca·tion** *n*.— **-ca·tor** *n*.

vin·dic·tive (vin-*dik*-tiv) *adj*. Revengeful; spiteful.—**vin·dic·tive·ly** *adv*.—**vin·dic·tive·ness** *n*.

vine *n*. Woody, climbing or trailing plant, esp. the common grapevine.

vine-bordered	vine-encircled	vine-leafed
vine-clad	vine grower	vine-mantled
vine-covered	vine-hung	vine-robed
vine-decked	vine-laced	vine-wreathed
vine dresser	vineland	vineyard

vin·e·gar (*vin*-uh-ger) *n*. A sour liquid; dilute acetic acid produced by the fermentation of wine, cider, etc.—**vin·e·gar·ish, vin·e·gar·y** *adj*.

vin·tage (*vin*-tij) *n*. 1. The wine produced in any one season. 2. Properly aged wine, esp. of a certain locality or year. 3. Quality or style of any particular time.

vint·ner (*vint*-ner) *n*. Wine merchant.

vi·ol (*vy*-ul) *n. Music.* Any stringed instrument played with a bow, including the viola, violin, and contrabass.

vi·o·la (vee-oh-luh) *n. Music.* Instrument of the viol class pitched a fifth lower than the violin.

vi·o·late (*vy*-uh-layt) *v.* [vi·o·lat·ed; vi·o·lat·ing] 1. To infringe or trespass on; break, as the law. 2. To desecrate; outrage; rape. 3. To disturb.—**vi·o·la·ble** *adj.*—**vi·o·la·tion** *n.*—**vi·o·la·tor** *n.*

vi·o·lence (*vy*-uh-lunss) *n.* 1. Active force; intensity of action or emotion. 2. Lawless force; assault; attack.

vi·o·lent (*vy*-uh-lunt) *adj.* 1. Caused, acting, or produced by active force; fierce; unnatural. 2. Sharp; extreme.—**vi·o·lent·ly** *adv.*

VIOLET

vi·o·let (*vy*-uh-lit) *n.* 1. Plant having a small, usually purple flower and a sweet perfume. 2. A bluish red color; purple.

violet black	violet-hooded
violet blue	violet-hued
violet-colored	violet-rayed
violet-crowned	violet-scented
violet-dyed	violet-shrouded
violet-embroidered	violet-striped
violet-flowered	violet sweet

vi·o·lin (vy-uh-*lin*) *n. Music.* Four-stringed instrument played with a bow.—**vi·o·lin·ist** *n.*

vi·o·lon·cel·lo (vee-uh-lun-*chel*-oh) *n. Music.* Large bass violin, commonly called **cel·lo.**—**vi·o·lon·cel·list** *n.*

VIOLIN

vi·per (*vy*-per) *n.* 1. Any of a family of poisonous snakes, including the rattlesnake. 2. Malignant person.—**vi·per·ous** *adj.*

vi·ra·go (vih-*ray*-goh) *n.* [*pl.* -goes]. Shrew; vixen.

vir·e·o (*vihr*-ee-oh) *n.* Small insect-eating American songbird.

vir·gin (*ver*-jin) *n.* 1. [*cap.*] The Virgin Mary. 2. Maiden; a person, usually a woman, who has never had sexual intercourse.—*adj.* 1. Maidenly; modest. 2. Pure; untouched.—**vir·gi·nal** *adj.*—**vir·gin·i·ty** (ver-*jin*-ih-tee) *n.*

VIREO (1/4 life-size)

vir·go (*ver*-goh) *n. Astronomy.* 1. Constellation south of the Big Dipper. 2. The sixth sign of the Zodiac.

vir·ile (*vihr*-il) *adj.* 1. Manly; masculine. 2. Sexually potent.—**vi·ril·i·ty** (vih-*ril*-ih-tee) *n.*

vir·tu·al (*ver*-choo-ul) *adj.* Implicit; in fact but not in name.—**vir·tu·al·i·ty** *n.*—**vir·tu·al·ly** *adv.*

vir·tue (*ver*-choo) *n.* 1. Goodness; morality; chastity. 2. A good moral quality, as justice. 3. Excellence; merit; efficacy.—**vir·tu·ous** *adj.*—**vir·tu·ous·ly** *adv.*—**vir·tu·ous·ness** *n.*

vir·tu·o·so (ver-choo-*oh*-soh) *n.* 1. One skilled in an art, esp. in playing a musical instrument. 2. Person having cultivated a taste for the fine arts.—**vir·tu·os·i·ty** (ver-choo-*oss*-ih-tee) *n.* Very great skill.

vir·u·lent (*vihr*-yuh-lunt) *adj.* Malignant; poisonous; deadly.—**vir·u·lence, vir·u·lency** *n.*—**vir·u·lent·ly** *adv.*

vi·rus (*vy*-rus) *n.* 1. Poison or bacteria of an infectious disease. 2. That which poisons or corrupts the mind.

vi·sa, vi·sé (*vee*-zuh) *n.* Official approval stamped or written on a passport or document.—*v.* [vi·saed, vi·séed; vi·sa·ing, visé·ing].

vis·age (*viz*-ij) *n.* Face; countenance.

vis·cer·a (*viss*-er-uh) *n. pl.* Internal organs of the body.—**vis·cer·al** *adj.*

vis·cid (*viss*-id) *adj.* Sticky; viscous.

vis·count (*vy*-kownt) *n.* Title of nobility just below earl and above baron.—**vis·count·ess** *n.*—**vis·count·cy** *n.*

vis·cous (*viss*-kus) *adj.* Thick and sticky, as glue.—**vis·cos·i·ty, vis·cous·ness** *n.*—**vis·cous·ly** *adv.*

vise, vice (*vysse*) *n.* 1. Two-jawed instrument for holding objects in work. 2. Clasp; grip.

vi·sé (*vee*-zuh, *vee*-zay) *n.* A visa.

Vish·nu *n.* Second god in the Hindu trinity.

vis·i·ble (*viz*-uh-b'l) *adj.* Open to view; perceptible; apparent.—**vis·i·bil·i·ty** (viz-uh-*bil*-ih-tee) *n.*—**vis·i·bly** *adv.*

vi·sion (*vizh*-un) *n.* 1. Sight; ability to see. 2. Foresight; active imagination. 3. Sense of sight. 4. Dream; revelation; apparition.—**vi·sion·ar·y** *n.* [*pl.* -ies] Dreamer; impractical planner.—**vi·sion·ar·y** *adj.*

vis·it (*viz*-it) *v.* 1. To pay a call upon, either officially or as a guest; go to see. 2. To enter; go to, esp. regularly. 3. To afflict; overtake.—*n.* A call; short stay.—**vis·i·tor** *n.*

vis·it·a·tion (viz-ih-*tay*-shun) *n.* 1. A formal or official call. 2. Affliction; divine retribution. 3. [*cap.*] Feast in honor of the Virgin Mary's visit to Elizabeth, mother of John the Baptist.

vis·or (*vy*-zer) *n.* Projecting forepiece of a helmet or cap.—**vis·ored** *adj.*

vis·ta (*viss*-tuh) *n.* 1. Long view; prospect. 2. Long-range mental view.

vis·u·al (*vih*-zhoo-ul) *adj.* Pertaining to or achieved by sight.—**vis·u·al·ize** *v.* [vis·u·al·ized; vis·u·al·iz·ing] To see in the mind; image.—**vis·u·al·i·za·tion** *n.*

VISOR

V

vi·tal (*vy*-t'l) *adj.* 1. Pertaining to or necessary to life. 2. Essential; most important. 3. Fatal; causing death. 4. Lively; animated.—**vi·tal·i·ty** *n.* [*pl.* -ies]—**vi·tal·ly** *adv.*

vi·tal·ize (*vy*-t'l-yze) *v.* [-ized; -iz·ing] Give life to; animate.—**vi·tal·i·za·tion** *n.*—**vi·tal·iz·er** *n.*

vi·ta·min (*vy*-tuh-min) *n.* One of a group of complex organic compounds necessary to nutrition and growth, and classified by an alphabetical system, according to the effects of their deficiency in the diet.—**vi·ta·min** *adj.*

vi·ti·ate (*vish*-ee-ayt) *v.* [vi·ti·at·ed; vi·ti·at·ing] 1. To impair; pollute; corrupt. 2. To invalidate; nullify.—**vi·ti·at·ed** *adj.*— -a·tion *n.*

vit·re·ous (*vih*-tree-us) *adj.* Like or pertaining to glass.—**vit·re·ous·ness** *n.*

vit·ri·fy (*vit*-rih-fy) *v.* [vit·ri·fied; vit·ri·fy·ing] To convert into glass by fusion or the action of heat.—**vit·ri·fi·a·ble** *adj.*—**vit·ri·fi·ca·tion** *n.*

vit·ri·ol (*vit*-ree-ul) *n.* 1. Sulphuric acid. 2. That which is acid, bitter, or caustic.—**vit·ri·ol·ic** (vit-ree-*ol*-ik) *adj.*

vi·tu·per·ate (vy-*too*-per-ayt, vih-, -*tyoo*-) *v.* [vi·tu·per·at·ed; vi·tu·per·at·ing] To abuse; revile; berate.—**vi·tu·per·a·tion** *n.*—**vi·tu·per·a·tive** *adj.* —**vi·tu·per·a·tive·ly** *adv.*

vi·va·cious (vy-*vay*-shus, vih-) *adj.* Lively; spirited; animated.—**vi·va·cious·ly** *adv.*—**vi·va·cious·ness, vi·vac·i·ty** (vih-*vass*-ih-tee) *n.*

viv·id (*viv*-id) *adj.* 1. Bright; intense. 2. Lively. 3. Clear; graphic.—**viv·id·ly** *adv.*— -ness *n.*

viv·i·sec·tion (viv-ih-*sek*-shun) *n.* Dissection of living animals for scientific research.—**viv·i·sect** *v.*—**viv·i·sec·tion·ist, viv·i·sec·tor** *n.*

vix·en (*vik*-s'n) *n.* 1. Female fox. 2. An ill-tempered, shrewish woman.—**vix·en·ish** *adj.*

viz. *adv.* Namely; to wit; videlicet.

vi·zier (vih-*zeer*) *n.* High political officer in many Mohammedan states.

V-mail (*vee*-mayl) *n.* A postal system developed in World War II by which a letter is photographed on microfilm, transmitted, then reprinted and enlarged at its destination.

vo·cab·u·lar·y (vuh-*kab*-yuh-ler-ee) *n.* [*pl.* -ries] 1. Stock of words; range of language. 2. List of words.

vo·cal (*voh*-k'l) *adj.* 1. Oral; pertaining to the voice. 2. Articulate; voluble.—**vo·cal·ist** *n.* —**vo·cal·i·za·tion** *n.*—**vo·cal·ly** *adv.*—**vo·cal·ize** *v.* [vo·cal·ized; vo·cal·iz·ing] To sing; utter.

vo·ca·tion (voh-*kay*-shun) *n.* 1. Employment; occupation; profession. 2. *Theology.* Divine summons to do religious work.—**vo·ca·tion·al·ly** *adv.*—**vo·ca·tion·al** *adj.*

vo·cif·er·ate (voh-*sif*-er-ayt) *v.* [-at·ed; -at·ing] To cry out noisily.—**vo·cif·er·ant** *n.* & *adj.*—**vo·cif·er·a·tion** *n.*

vo·cif·er·ous (voh-*sif*-er-us) *adj.* Noisy; clamorous.—**vo·cif·er·ous·ly** *adv.*—**vo·cif·er·ous·ness** *n.*

vod·ka (*vod*-kuh) *n.* Russian alcoholic rye or potato liquor.

vogue (*vohg*) *n.* Fashion; mode.

voice (*voyss*) *n.* 1. Sound uttered by the mouth, esp. utterance. 2. Sound compared to human speech. 'The voice of the forest.' 3. Faculty or mode of speaking; language. 4. Vote; expressed opinion; will.—*v.* [voiced; voic·ing]. —**voiced** *adj.*—**voice·less** *adj.*

void (*voyd*) *n.* Empty space; vacuum.—*adj.* 1. Empty; vacant. 2. Devoid; destitute. 3. *Law.* Null; having no legal force.—*v.* 1. To nullify; invalidate. 2. To empty; vacate. —**void·a·ble** *adj.*—**void·ance** *n.*

voile (*voyl*) *n.* Thin, fine cotton material.

vol·a·tile (*vol*-uh-t'l) *adj.* 1. Evaporating rapidly. 2. Lively; buoyant. 3. Fickle; unstable.—**vol·a·til·i·ty** *n.* [*pl.* -ties].

vol·ca·no (vol-*kay*-noh) *n.* [*pl.* -noes, -nos] Conical mountain topped by a crater which periodically emits hot vapor, ashes, or lava. —**vol·can·ic** *adj.*—**vol·can·i·cal·ly** *adv.*—**vol·can·ism** *n.*—**vol·can·ize** *v.* [-ized; -iz·ing].

Vol·ga (*vol*-guh) *n.* Great river in east Russia.

vo·li·tion (voh-*lish*-un) *n.* Will; determination. —**vo·li·tion·al** *adj.*—**vo·li·tion·al·ly** *adv.*

vol·ley (*vol*-ee) *n.* 1. A simultaneous discharge of several weapons. 2. Explosive burst. 3. Succession of shots in tennis, ping-pong, etc.—**vol·ley** *v.*—**volley ball.** Game played by hitting a large ball back and forth over a high net without letting the ball touch the ground.

volt *n.* Unit of electromotive force.—**volt·age** *n.*

vol·u·ble (*vol*-yuh-b'l) *adj.* Talkative; eloquent; fluent.—**vol·u·ble·ness, vol·u·bil·i·ty** *n.*—**vol·u·bly** *adv.*

vol·ume (*vol*-yoom, -yum) *n.* 1. A single bound book. 2. Mass; bulk; dimensions. 3. *Music.* Fullness and power of tone.

vo·lu·mi·nous (vuh-*loo*-mih-nus) *adj.* Bulky; extensive; copious.—**vo·lu·mi·nous·ly** *adv.*—**vo·lu·mi·nous·ness** *n.*

vol·un·tar·y (*vol*-un-ter-ee) *adj.* 1. Proceeding from or regulated by the will. 2. Freely chosen; spontaneous. 3. Deliberate; intended.—**vol·un·tar·y** *n.* [*pl.* -ries] *n. Music.* A prelude or solo on the organ.— -tar·i·ly *adv.*

vol·un·teer (vol-un-*teer*) *n.* A person who freely offers to do service, esp. military service. —*v.* To offer, or enter into, by choice.—**vol·un·teer** *adj.*

vo·lup·tu·ar·y (vuh-*lup*-choo-er-ee) *n.* [*pl.* -ries]. Sensualist.

vo·lup·tu·ous (vuh-*lup*-choo-us) *adj.* Sensual; luxurious.—**vo·lup·tu·ous·ly** *adv.*— -ous·ness *n.*

vom·it (*vom*-it) *v.* 1. To discharge from the stomach through the mouth; throw up. 2. To eject with violence.—*n.* Matter ejected from the stomach.

voo·doo *n.* 1. Form of magic or sorcery practiced by Negroes in the West Indies and southern U.S. 2. Negro sorcerer.—**voo·doo** *v.* & *adj.*—**voo·doo·ism** *n.*

vo·ra·cious (voh-*ray*-shus) *adj.* Greedy; gluttonous; rapacious.—**vo·ra·cious·ly** *adv.*—**vo·ra·cious·ness, vo·rac·i·ty** (voh-*rass*-ih-tee) *n.*

vor·tex *n.* [*pl.* -tex·es, -tic·es] Whirlpool; circular cavity formed by a liquid in rotation.—**vor·ti·cal** *adj.*

vo·tar·y (*voh*-ter-ee) *n.* [*pl.* -ries] Devotee; fan.

vote *n.* 1. Expressed will; the legal expression of a wish or choice. 2. Franchise; the right to legal expression of a wish.—*v.* [vot·ed; vot·ing] To express a choice; voice one's will.—**vot·er** *n.*

vo·tive (*voh*-tiv) *adj.* Consecrated; promised by vow.—**vo·tive·ly** *adv.* —**vo·tive·ness** *n.*

vouch (*vowch*) *v.* To attest; certify; authenticate.—**vouch·er** *n.* 1. Witness. 2. Document guaranteeing accuracy.

vouch·safe (vowch-*sayf*) *v.* [-safed; -saf·ing] To grant; concede.

vow *n.* Pledge; solemn promise.—**vow** *v.*

vow·el (*vow*-'l) *n.* 1. Unbroken speech sound produced with open mouth. 2. Letter representing such a sound.—**vow·el** *adj.*

VORTEX
(diagrammatic representation)

voy·age (*voy*-ij) *n.* Long journey by water; cruise.—*v.* [voy·aged; voy·ag·ing]—**voy·ag·er** *n.*

Vul·can (*vul*-kun) *n.* Roman god of fire and metal work.

vul·can·ite (*vul*-kun-yte) *n.* Hard, vulcanized rubber.—**vul·can·i·za·tion** *n.* Process of strengthening rubber by treating it with some form of sulphur.—**vul·can·ize** *v.* [-ized; -iz·ing].

vul·gar (*vul*-ger) *adj.* 1. Common; ordinary; plebeian. 2. Rude; coarse; obscene.—**vul·gar·i·an** *n.*—**vul·gar·ism** *n.*—**vul·gar·i·ty** *n.* [*pl.* -ties].

vul·ner·a·ble (*vul*-ner-uh-b'l) *adj.* Liable to injury; open to attack. —**vul·ner·a·bil·i·ty** *n.*

vul·ture (*vul*-cher) *n.* Large bird of prey, commonly feeding on carcasses.

VULTURE (1/24 life-size)

W

wad (*wod*, *wahd*) *n.* Soft mass of fibrous material for plugging an opening.—*v.* [wad·ded; wad·ding] 1. To form into a wad. 2. To plug; stuff; pad.—**wad·ding** *n.* Soft material for wads; stuffing.

wad·dle (*wod*-'l) *v.* [wad·dled; wad·dling] To toddle; rock clumsily from side to side in walking.—*n.* A swaying gait.—**wad·dler** *n.* —**wad·dling·ly** *adv.*

wade *v.* [wad·ed; wad·ing] 1. To walk through water, snow, or other resistant substance. 2. To proceed with difficulty. 'He waded through the book.'—**wade into.** *Colloquial.* To set about vigorously.—**wad·er** *n.*

wa·fer (*way*-fer) *n.* 1. Thin, disk-shaped cake, cracker, or candy. 2. Flat disk of dried paste or wax for sealing.

waf·fle (*wof*-'l, *wah*-'l) *n.* Crisply baked, pressed batter cake.

waffle iron. Cooking appliance having two studded hinged plates between which a waffle is baked.

waft *v.* 1. To convey through a fluid or air. 2. To buoy up; float.—*n.* A whiff; current of air.—**waft·age** *n.* —**waft·er** *n.*

wag *v.* [wagged; wag·ging] To move back and forth with short, jerky movements; oscillate.—**wag** *n.* A prankster.

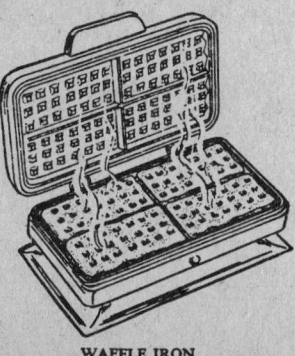

WAFFLE IRON

wage (*wayj*) *v.* [waged; wag·ing] To undertake; carry on.

wa·ger (*way*-jer) *n.* 1. A stake; that which is hazarded in gambling. 2. Act of betting. —*v.* To gamble; bet.—**wa·ger·er** *n.*

wages *n. pl.* Also **wage** *n.* Pay; remuneration for services computed on an hourly basis.

wag·gle (*wag*-'l) *v.* [wag·gled; wag·gling] To move quickly from side to side.—*n.* Short swaying motion; nod.

wag·on (*wag*-'n) *n.* 1. Four-wheeled vehicle for transporting heavy loads. 2. *Colloquial.* Police van. —*v.* To convey by wagon.—**wag·on·er** *n.*

WAGON

waif (*wayf*) *n.* 1. Neglected, homeless person, esp. a child. 2. Unclaimed or stray article.

wail (*wayl*) *v.* To lament; moan.—*n.* Long cry of sorrow.—**wail·er** *n.*—**wail·ing·ly** *adv.*

wain·scot (*wayn*-sk't, -skoht, -skaht) *n.* Wooden wall lining; paneling. —*v.* [wain·scot·ed, wain·scot·ted; wain·scot·ing, wain·scot·ting] To line with panels.—**wain·scot·ing, wain·scot·ting** *n.* Material for wainscot.

waist *n.* 1. Part of the human body between the ribs and hips. 2. Middle part, esp. of a ship. 3. Blouse; shirtwaist.

waist·coat (*wayst*-koht, *wes*-k't) *n.* Man's vest;

WAINSCOT

W

sleeveless garment worn, esp. one under a coat.

wait (*wayt*) *v.* **1.** To remain in expectation; stay. **2.** To serve at the table; attend.—*n.* Delay; period of waiting.

wait·er *n.* Table attendant.—**wait·ress** *n.*

wait·ing *n.* Attendance; personal service. 'Lady in waiting.'

waive (*wayv*) *v.* [waived; waiv·ing] To relinquish; forego; cede.

waiv·er *n. Law.* **a.** Legal act of relinquishing a claim, right, etc. **b.** Document containing the declaration of such act.

wake *v.* [woke or waked; woken; wak·ing] **1.** To rouse from sleep; awake. **2.** To excite; put in motion.—*n.* **1.** Vigil. **2.** Ceremony of watching over a dead body prior to burial. —**wak·er** *n.*—**wake·ful** *adj.*—**wake·ful·ly** *adv.* —**wake·ful·ness** *n.*

wak·en (*way*-k'n) *v.* **1.** To awake; cease to sleep. **2.** To rouse; call forth.—**wak·en·er** *n.*

walk (*wawk*) *v.* **1.** To advance by alternate steps; step along. **2.** To travel slowly; stroll. **3.** To go restlessly about, as a ghost. **4.** *Baseball.* To advance to first base on balls.—*n.* **1.** Act of walking. **2.** Pace; gait; carriage. **3.** Promenade; path. **4.** Sphere; station; social rank.—**walk·er** *n.*

walk·a·thon *n.* A walking endurance contest.

walk·a·way, walk·o·ver *n.* An easy victory.

walk-out *n.* A labor strike.

walk·ie-talk·ie *n.* Portable two-way short-wave radio, light enough to be carried in the hand.

wall (*wawl*) *n.* **1.** High, solid structure raised to enclose a space. **2.** Rampart; fortified barrier. **3.** Solid surface enclosing a cavity or vessel.—*v.* **1.** To enclose; surround. **2.** To fortify; protect. **3.** To obstruct; block off. —**walled** *adj.*

wallbird	walleye *n.*	wall-like
wallboard	wall-eyed	wallpaper
wall-bound	wall-fed	wallpiece
wall-defended	wall-girt	wall-sided

wal·la·by (*wol*-uh-bee) *n.* A small kangaroo.

wall·flow·er *n.* **1.** A kind of flower. **2.** *Colloquial.* A person who watches a dance without taking part.

wal·let (*wol*-lit, *waw*-) *n.* Flat pocketbook for paper money, etc.

wal·lop (*wol*-up, *wahl*-) *v.* [wal·loped; wal·loping] To beat soundly; thrash.—*n.* A severe blow.—**wal·lop·er** *n.*

wal·low (*wol*-oh, *wahl*-) *v.* **1.** To roll to and fro in a soft substance. **2.** To revel or be immersed in. 'He wallows in vice.'—*n.* A muddy spot where animals wallow.—**wal·low·er** *n.*

wall·pa·per *n.* Paper covering for room walls.

Wall Street. 1. In downtown New York City, a street where the Stock Exchange is located. **2.** U.S. financial leaders and their interests, collectively.

wal·nut (*wawl*-nut) *n.* **1.** Species of edible nut. **2.** Nut-bearing tree valued for its fine, durable wood.

wal·rus (*wawl*-rus) *n.* Large Arctic marine mammal, with protruding ivory tusks.

waltz (*wawltz*) *n.* **1.** Graceful, whirling dance step in triple time. **2.** Music written in $\frac{3}{4}$ time. —**waltz** *v.*—**waltz·er** *n.*

WALRUS (1/120 life-size)

wam·pum (*wom*-pum, *wahm*-) *n.* **1.** Shell beads used by American Indians as ornaments and money. **2.** *Slang.* Money.

wan (*wahn*) *adj.* Pallid; pale and sickly; languid.—**wan·ness** *n.*—**wan·ly** *adv.*

wand (*wond, wahnd*) *n.* **1.** Small stick or twig. **2.** Staff of authority. **3.** Small rod used by magicians, etc.

wan·der (*wahn*-der) *v.* **1.** To roam; travel without purpose or destination. **2.** To deviate; stray. **3.** To be delirious; lose reason.—**wan·der·er** *n.*—**wan·der·ing** *n.*—**wan·der·ing·ly** *adv.*

wan·der·lust *n.* A longing to travel.

wane (*wayn*) *v.* [waned; wan·ing] **1.** To diminish; subside; ebb. **2.** To decline; sink. —*n.* **1.** A decrease, esp. of the visible portion of the moon. **2.** Decline; failure.

wan·gle (*wang*-g'l) *v. Colloquial.* To contrive; obtain by trickery.

want (*wahnt, wawnt*) *n.* **1.** State of being without; absence; deficiency. **2.** Need; exigency; craving. **3.** Poverty; indigence; destitution. —*v.* **1.** To lack; be without. **2.** To need; require; covet; desire. **3.** To miss; have need. —**want·er** *n.*—**want·ing** *adj.*—**want·less** *adj.*

wan·ton (*wahn*-t'n) *adj.* **1.** Licentious; dissolute; lewd. **2.** Playful; unrestrained. **3.** Excess; overabundant; uncalled for; gratuitous. —*n.* A dissolute trifler.—*v.* To revel; sport; dally in lewdness.— -**ton·ly** *adv.*— -**ton·ness** *n.*

war (*wor*) *n.* **1.** A contest between nations or states carried on by force of arms. **2.** Violent opposition; hostility; enmity.—*v.* [warred; war·ring]—**war·like** *adj.* Martial; belligerent.

war-blasted	warplane	war-weary
war maker	warship	war worker
warpath	wartime	war-worn

War between the States. *U.S.* The Civil War.

war·ble (*wor*-b'l) *v.* [war·bled; war·bling] **1.** To trill; sing in a tremulous tone. **2.** To sing; carol.—*n.* A trilling melody.—**war·bling** *adj.*

war·bler *n.* **1.** A singer. **2.** Small bright-plumaged bird with a trilling, melodious song.

ward (*wawrd*) *v.* To defend; protect; guard.—*n.* **1.** Defense; protection. **2.** Confinement; custody; guardianship. **3.** A minor or person under guardianship. **4.** Division, esp. politi-

WARBLER (1/5 life-size)

cal, of a town or city. 5. Hospital department.—**ward·er** n.—**ward off.** To repel; turn aside; avert.

wardmaid	wardroom	ward walk
wardman	wardship	wardwoman

war·den (*wor*-den) n. 1. Watchman; keeper; guardian. 2. Chief officer in a prison. 3. An officer of certain colleges and churches.—**war·den·ship** n.

ward·robe (*wawrd*-rohb) n. 1. Clothes closet. 2. Wearing apparel; clothes.

wares n. pl. Merchandise; goods; commodities.

ware·house (*wair*-hows) n. Building for storing goods.—v. (*wair*-howz) To store in a warehouse.—**ware·house·man** n.

war·fare (*wor*-fair) n. 1. Armed conflict between nations. 2. Struggle; conflict.

warm (*wahrm*) adj. 1. Having or feeling heat in a moderate degree; not cold. 2. Zealous; tender; ardent. 3. Furious; violent; animated. 4. *Painting.* Glowing; colored with reds and yellows. 5. *Colloquial.* Close on discovery.—**warm** v.—**warm·ing** n.—**warm·ly** adv.—**warm·ness** n.—**warmth** n.

warm-backed	warm-hearted
warm-blooded	warm-heartedly
warm-breathed	warm-heartedness
warm-clad	warm-tempered
warm-colored	warm-tinted
warm-contested	warm-wrapped

warn (*worn*) v. 1. To caution; give notice of approaching danger. 2. To inform previously; notify. 3. To admonish; advise.—**warn·er** n.—**warn·ing** n. Notice; summons.—**warn·ing·ly** adv.

warp (*worp*) v. 1. To twist; turn out of shape; distort; pervert. 2. *Nautical.* To haul along on a line secured to a stationary object. 3. *Aeronautics.* To fly with a twisting motion.—n. 1. *Weaving.* Lengthwise threads. 2. *Nautical.* Line used for warping a vessel. 3. Warped or twisted condition.—**warped** adj.—**warp·er** n.

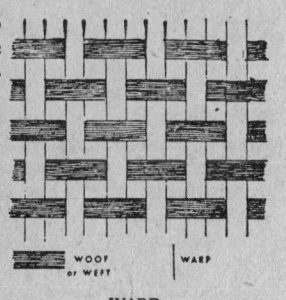

WARP

war·rant (*wor*-'nt) v. 1. To secure; guarantee against harm. 2. To sanction; justify. 3. *Colloquial.* To declare; assert. 4. *Law.* To assure title to.—n. 1. Authorization; sanction. 2. Guarantee; voucher.—**war·ran·ta·ble** adj.—**war·ran·ta·bly** adv.—**war·ran·tee** n. *Law.* Receiver of a warrant.—**war·ran·tor** n. *Law.* One who guarantees.—**war·ran·ty** n. [pl. -ties].

warrant officer. Army or navy officer ranking just below a commissioned officer.

war·ren (*wor*-in) n. Piece of ground for the breeding of rabbits.—**war·ren·er** n.

war·rior (*wor*-ee-er) n. A soldier, esp. a brave or expert fighter.

wart (*wort*) n. Small hard growth on the skin.—**wart·y** adj. [wart·i·er; wart·i·est].

wart·hog n. A wild hog of South Africa.

war·y adj. [war·i·er; war·i·est] Careful; cautious; prudent.—**war·i·ly** adv.—**war·i·ness** n.

WARTHOG (1/30 life-size)

was. *First* and *third person singular past tense* of the verb **be.**

wash (*wahsh, wawsh*) v. 1. To cleanse; remove dirt with water; purify. 2. To cover with water; lave. 3. To wear down by water pressure; sweep away with water. 4. To overlay with a thin coat, as of paint or metal. 5. *Mining.* To separate metal from other matter. 6. To withstand washing without injury.—n. 1. Cleansing. 2. Material to be washed. 3. Bog; fen; marsh. 4. Debris; drift. 5. Waste liquid; swill. 6. Thin coating.—**wash·a·ble** adj. Capable of being washed without injury.—**wash·er** n. 1. Person or machine that washes. 2. Disk of metal for reducing friction.—**wash·ing** n.—**wash·y** adj. Watery; diluted.—**wash·i·ness** n.

washbasin	washland	wash shed
washbasket	washmaid	washstand
washbowl	wash-off	washtray
washcloth	wash-out	washtub
washday	washpot	wash-up
wash-down	washrag	washwoman
wash house	washroom	wash work

wasp (*wahsp*) n. Four-winged insect able to inflict a painful sting.

wasp·ish adj. 1. Slender. 2. Snappish; petulant; irritable.—**wasp·ish·ly** adv.—**wasp·ish·ness** n.

WASP (2/3 life-size)

was·sail (*woss*-'l) n. 1. A toast; drinking bout. 2. A sweet, spicy ale.

Wassermann test. Blood test for syphilis.

wast (*wahst, wost*). *Poetic second-person singular past tense of* **be.**

waste v. [wast·ed; wast·ing] 1. To devastate; destroy. 2. To use up; consume. 3. To spend extravagantly; squander. 4. To grow feeble.—adj. 1. Desolate; bare. 2. Spoiled; useless; worthless.—n. 1. Wild uncultivated land. 2. Useless expenditure. 3. Refuse.—**waste·ful** adj.—**waste·ful·ly** adv.—**waste·ful·ness** n.—**wast·er** n.—**wast·ing** adj.

wastebasket	wasteland	wasteway
wasteboard	waste paper	wastewood
	waste-paper basket	

wast·rel (*wayst*-r'l) n. A spendthrift; profligate.

watch (*wahch, woch*) n. 1. Vigil; attendance without sleep. 2. Close observation; vigilance; supervision. 3. A sentinel; guard. 4. Period of watch duty. 5. *Nautical.* Period of duty. 6. A small timepiece carried on the

W

person.—*v.* **1.** To keep vigil or guard. **2.** To observe closely; notice carefully. **3.** To wait; expect.—**watch·er** *n.*—**watch·ful** *adj.*—**watch·ful·ly** *adv.*—**watch·ful·ness** *n.*

watch boat	watch house	watchmate
watchcase	watchkeeper	watchtower
watchcry	watchmaker	watchwoman
watchdog	watchmaking	watchword
watch-free	watchman	watch work

wa·ter (*waw*-ter, *wah*-ter) *n.* **1.** A colorless, odorless, tasteless fluid. (*Symbol:* H_2O). **2.** Any form of this liquid, as rain. **3.** A natural body of water. **4.** Liquid resembling water, as tears or saliva. **5.** Luster of a precious stone.—*v.* **1.** To irrigate; wet. **2.** To pattern with wavy lines, as silk. **3.** *Finance.* To increase by the unwarranted issue of new shares. **4.** To shed or gather water or liquid. **5.** To dilute; weaken; adulterate.—**wa·ter·er** *n.*

water closet. A toilet. *Abbreviation* w.c.

water color. 1. Pigment dissolved in water for art work. **2.** The art of painting in water color. —**wa·ter·col·or, wa·ter·col·or·ed** *adj.*

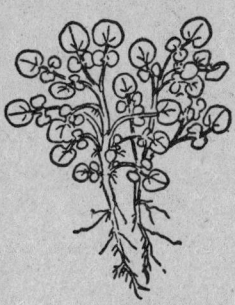
WATER CRESS

water cress. Edible water plant with small, round, sharp-tasting leaves.

water·fall *n.* A cataract; precipice over which a stream runs.

water front. Section of a city along a harbor.

water gap. In a mountain range, a depression through which a stream flows.

WATER GAP

water lily. A flowering plant which grows in still water.

Wa·ter·loo *n.* **1.** Site of Napoleon's final defeat, July 14, 1815, by Wellington. **2.** Any defeat or insurmountable obstacle.

wa·ter·mark *n.* **1.** Mark indicating the depth of water. **2.** A faint design or wording made in paper and best seen when held between a light and the eye.—*v.* To impress with a watermark.

WATER LILY

wa·ter·mel·on (*waw*-ter-mel-'n) *n.* Large edible fruit of the gourd family, having juicy red pulp.

water moccasin. A poisonous, usually aquatic snake found in southern U.S.

WATER MOCCASIN

wa·ter·y *adj.* **1.** Resembling water. **2.** Wet. **3.** Insipid; diluted.

watt (*waht, wot*) *n.* metric unit of power.—**watt·age** *n.*

wat·tle (*waht*-'l, *wot*-) *n.* **1.** A flexible twig or rod. **2.** A type of acacia tree or shrub. **3.** Loose, usually red, flap of skin on the throat of certain birds.—*v.* [wat·tled; wat·tling] To plait or bind with wattles.—**wat·tle** *adj.*

wave *n.* **1.** Billow; breaker; swell on the water's surface. **2.** *Physics.* A vibratory motion of regular frequency. **3.** Surge; widespread movement; effervescence. **4.** Flourish; signal made by waving. **5.** A curl of hair; a waved coiffure. **6.** A tilde.—*v.* [waved; wav·ing] **1.** To undulate; sway. **2.** To swing; brandish. **3.** To greet or signal by a swinging gesture.—**wave·less** *adj.*—**wave·let** *n.* Small wave; ripple.—**wav·er** *n.*

wave-beaten	wave length (*dimens.*)
wave-buffeted	wavelength (*energy*)
wave-dashed	wave mark
wave-edged	wavemeter
wave-encircled	wave-swept
wave-haired	wave-tossed
wave-hollowed	wave-washed
wave-lashed	wave-wet
wave-laved	wave-worn

wa·ver (*way*-ver) *v.* **1.** To sway; totter. **2.** To fluctuate; vacillate; falter.—**wa·ver·er** *n.*—**wa·ver·ing** *adj.*—**wa·ver·ing·ly** *adv.*

wav·y *adj.* [wav·i·er; wav·i·est] Swelling in waves; undulating; rippling.—**wav·i·ness** *n.*

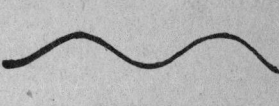
WAVY LINE

wax *n.* **1.** Thick, tenacious substance secreted by bees. **2.** Vegetable or animal substance resembling beeswax.—*v.* [waxed; waxed or wax·en; wax·ing] **1.** To increase in size, as the moon. **2.** To become; grow. **3.** To treat with wax.—**wax·en** *adj.*—**wax·er** *n.* —**wax·y** *adj.* [wax·i·er; wax·i·est] Soft; pliable. —**wax·i·ness** *n.*

wax·wing *n.* A brown songbird with red-tipped feathers.

way *n.* **1.** Path; road; street. **2.** Distance; progression. **3.** Direction; course; route. **4.** Means; method; style. **5.** [*pl.*] *Nautical.* Timbers on which a ship is launched; skids. **6.** Will; determined desire. **7.** *Colloquial.* Situation; condition. **8.** *Colloquial.* Neighborhood; region.

WAXWING
(1/7 life-size)

way back	wayfarer	wayside
waybill	way house	way-weary
waybook	way maker	way-worn

way·lay v. [way·laid; way·lay·ing] To attack from ambush.—**way·lay·er** n.

way·ward (way-werd) adj. Capricious; unruly; headstrong. —**way·ward·ly** adv.—**way·ward·ness** n.

we pron. Plural of I.

weak (week) adj. 1. Feeble; infirm; fragile; having little strength. 2. Having little volume; faint. 3. Diluted; thin. 4. Unable to perform a function; unfit. 5. Lacking mental or moral strength; easily swayed. 6. Unconvincing; ineffective; vacillating. 7. Grammar. Indicating a noun whose plural is formed by adding s or a verb whose past tense or participle is formed by adding ed.—**weak·ling** n. Feeble person.—**weak·ly** adj. [weak·li·er; weak·li·est] In a weak manner.—**weak·ness** n.

weakfish	weak looking	weak-spirited
weak-kneed	weak-minded	weak-sighted

weak·en v. To enfeeble; deprive of strength; enervate.—**weak·en·er** n.—**weak·en·ing** adj.

weak·ling n. A weak person.

weal n. Archaic. Prosperity; welfare.

wealth (welth) n. 1. Abundance; affluence; riches. 2. Economics. **a.** All objects with utility and money value. **b.** Natural resources and labor.—**wealth·i·ly** adv.—**wealth·i·ness** n. —**wealth·y** adj. [wealth·i·er; wealth·i·est].

wean (ween) v. 1. To cease nursing. 2. To disengage from habit or pursuit; detach; alienate.—**wean·er** n.—**wean·ling** n. Recently weaned child.—**wean·ling** adj.

weap·on (wep-un) n. 1. Any instrument used in combat. 2. [pl.] Arms.—**weap·oned** adj. —**weap·on·less** adj.

wear (wehr) v. [wore; worn; wear·ing] 1. To carry on one's person; have on, as clothing. 2. Consume; use up. 3. To waste by friction; destroy gradually. 4. To exhaust; fatigue. 5. To bear; show; carry. 6. To last; be unaffected by time and use.—n. 1. Style of dress; fashion; vogue. 2. Loss or injury sustained in normal use.—**wear·a·ble** adj.—**wear·er** n.—**wear·ing** adj.

wea·ry (wee-ree) adj. [wea·ri·er; wea·ri·est] 1. Tired; fatigued; exhausted. 2. Irksome; tiresome.—v. [wea·ried; wea·ry·ing] 1. To tire; fatigue. 2. To make impatient; harass. —**wea·ri·ly** adv.—**wea·ri·ness** n.—**wea·ri·some** adj.—**wea·ri·some·ly** adv.—**wea·ri·some·ness** n.

wea·ry·ing adj. Tiring.

wea·sel (wee-z'l) n. 1. Small carnivorous animal related to the ferret. 2. Colloquial. Mean, sneaking person.

weath·er (weth-er) n. 1. Atmospheric conditions; state of the atmosphere as to temperature, pressure, humidity, motion, etc. 2. Vicissitude; change of condition. —v. 1. To expose to the air. 2. Nautical. To pass to the windward of. 3. To endure; sustain.—adj. Nautical. Windward.—**weath·**

WEASEL (1/9 life-size)

ered adj.—**weath·er·ing** n.—**weath·er·ly** adj. Nautical. Making little leeway.

weather-beaten	weathercock	weathermost
weather-bitten	weatherfish	weatherproof
weatherboard	weather glass	weathertight
weather-bound	weather man	weather-wise

weather strip. Band of material covering the joint of a window or door to keep out wind, rain, etc.

weave (weev) v. [wove; woven, wove; weav·ing] 1. To interlace; entwine into a fabric. 2. To contrive; fabricate. 3. To unite by intermixture. 4. To wind to and fro.—**weav·er** n.

web n. 1. Whole piece of woven cloth. 2. Membrane uniting the toes of many waterfowl and amphibians. 3. Net of delicate threads spun by a spider. 4. Elaborately woven story; plot.—v. [webbed; web·bing] To envelop.—**webbed** adj.

webeye	web-glazed	web-winged
web-fingered	web maker	web-worked
webfoot	web-toed	webworm

wed v. [wed·ded; wed·ded or wed; wed·ding] 1. To marry; espouse. 2. To join in marriage. 3. To unite closely.

wed·ding n. Marriage ceremony; nuptials.

wedge (wej) n. 1. Piece of wood or metal sloping to a thin edge for splitting logs, etc., or raising heavy weights. 2. Object in the form of a wedge. —v. [wedged; wedg·ing] 1. To cleave; rive. 2. To force; crowd; compress. 3. To fasten with a wedge.—**wedg·y** adj.

WEDGE

wedgebill	wedge-grafted	wedge-spliced
wedge-billed	wedge-shaped	wedge-tailed
wedge-formed	wedge-sided	wedgewise

wed·lock n. Marriage; matrimony.

Wednes·day (wenz-dee, -day) n. The fourth day of the week.

wee adj. Very small; tiny.

weed n. 1. Useless or injurious plant. 2. Worthless animal, esp. a lank horse. 3. Slang. **a.** Tobacco. **b.** Marijuana.—v. 1. To free (a garden) from weeds. 2. To remove what is noxious; extirpate.—**weed·er** n.—**weed·less** adj.—**weed·y** adj. [weed·i·er; weed·i·est].

weed-choked	weed-grown	weed-hung
weed-fringed	weedhook	weed-spoiled

weed killer. Chemical used for exterminating weeds.

week n. Period of seven successive days; time from one Sunday to the next.—**week·ly** adj. —**week·ly** adv. Once a week.—n. [pl. week·lies] A periodical appearing once a week.

week·day n. Any day except Sunday.

week end, week-end n. End of the week, from Friday night to Monday.—**week-end** adj.

week-long adj. That which lasts for a week.

weep v. [wept; weep·ing] 1. To shed tears; cry. 2. To lament; bewail; complain. 3. To shed; let fall in drops.—**weep·er** n.—**weep·ing·ly** adv.

W

wee·vil (*wee*-v'l) *n*. Small beetle, harmful to certain plants.—**wee·vil·y** *adj*.

weft *n*. *Weaving*. 1. Cross threads; woof. 2. The shuttle which carries the cross threads between the threads of the warp.

WEEVIL (7 times life-size)

weigh (*way*) *v*. 1. To determine the heaviness of; balance. 2. To compare; consider. 3. To amount in heaviness. 4. To bear heavily; press hard. 5. *Nautical*. To raise, as an anchor.

weighbar   weigh house   weighmaster
weighbridge   weighlock   weigh-out
weighbridgeman   weighman   weighshaft

weight (*wayt*) *n*. 1. Measure of the force of gravity; amount of heaviness. 2. Heavy object for balancing or holding down. 3. Scale or system of estimating relative heaviness. 4. Pressure; burden. 5. Importance; influence; consequence.—*v*. To make heavy.—**weight·less** *adj*.

weigh·ty (*way*-tee) *adj*. [weight·i·er; weight·i·est] 1. Heavy. 2. Burdensome. 3. Important; serious.

Weimar Republic (*vy*-mahr). The German republic established after World War I and lasting until the establishment of the Third Reich in 1933.

weir (*weer*) *n*. 1. Dam raising the water level. 2. Twig fence put in a stream to catch fish.

weird (*weerd*) *adj*. Supernatural; unearthly; eerie.—**weird·ly** *adv*.—**weird·ness** *n*.

wel·come (*wel*-kum) *adj*. 1. Received gladly; admitted willingly. 2. Causing pleasure; pleasing. 3. Readily permitted or granted.—*n*. Cordial greeting; kind reception.—*v*. [wel·comed; wel·com·ing] To greet with eagerness; receive hospitably.—**wel·com·er** *n*.

weld *v*. 1. To unite, as metal parts, by melting and fusing together. 2. To unite closely; join firmly.—*n*. Junction; joint.—**weld·a·ble** *adj*.—**weld·er** *n*.

wel·fare (*wel*-fair) *n*. Well-being; prosperity; happiness.

wel·kin *n*. *Archaic*. The sky.

well *n*. 1. Spring; fountain. 2. Cylindrical walled pit sunk into the earth to reach a supply of water. 3. Any enclosed space. 4. Source; origin.—*v*. To issue forth; flow.—**wel·ling** *adj*.

well *adj*. 1. Fortunate; just; proper. 2. In good health; sound in body. 3. Comfortable; in satisfactory condition.—*adv*. [bet·ter; best] 1. In a proper manner; rightly; skillfully. 2. Sufficiently; thoroughly; amply. 3. Favorably; with praise; commendably. 4. Far; considerably; greatly.

well-balanced   well-informed   well-read
well-beloved   well-known   wellside
well-born   well-liked   well-spoken
well-bred   well looking   well-timed
welldoer   well maker   well-trained

well·being *n*. Welfare; comfortable, happy, or satisfactory condition.

well·nigh *adv*. Almost; very nearly.

well off, well-off *adj*. Fortunate; prosperous; in good condition.

well·spring *n*. Source; origin; fountainhead.

well-to-do *adj*. Prosperous; wealthy; successful.

Welsh *adj*. Of or pertaining to Wales.—*n*. The language or inhabitants of Wales.—**Welsh·man** *n*. Native of Wales.

Welsh rabbit. Dish of melted cheese poured on toast or crackers.

welt *n*. 1. Border; reinforced seam. 2. Strip of leather between the upper and sole of a shoe. 3. *Colloquial*. Painful ridge made by a blow on the flesh.—**welt** *v*.

wel·ter *v*. 1. To wallow; roll, esp. in foul matter. 2. To rise and fall; toss.—*n*. Confusion; turmoil.

wel·ter·weight (*wel*-ter-wayt) *n*. Boxer of intermediate weight, up to 147 pounds.

wen *n*. Small lump on the skin or scale.

wench *n*. 1. A young woman. 2. Strumpet; girl of loose morals. 3. Maidservant.—*v*. To consort with lewd women.—**wench·er** *n*.

wend *v*. [wend·ed; wend·ing] To go; travel.

were·wolf (*weer*-woolf) *n*. [*pl*. -wolves] *Folklore*. A person able to assume a wolf's form.

west *n*. 1. One of the four cardinal points of the compass, directly opposite east. 2. Territory lying toward the west. 3. [*cap*.] a. The Western Hemisphere; the Americas. b. Area of the U.S. lying west of the Mississippi River.—*adj*. At, toward, from, in, or of the west.—*adv*. To or in the west.

west by north, west by south. See **compass**.

west·er·ly (*west*-er-lee) *n*. [*pl*. -lies] A wind blowing from the west.—*adj. & adv*. To, toward, from, or of the west.—**west·er·li·ness** *n*.

west·ern (*west*-ern) *adj*. 1. Of, to, in, toward, or from the west. 2. [*cap*.] Pertaining to the west; occidental.—*n*. A story or moving picture concerning cowboy or frontier life in the West.—**west·ern·most** *adj*.

West·ern·er *n*. 1. A dweller in the West. 2. A native of any western state of the U.S.

West Indies. Island group bounding the Caribbean Sea on the east.—**West Indian** *adj. & n*.

West·mins·ter. City in the administrative county of London containing most government buildings.—**Westminster Abbey**. Famous London church where England's rulers are crowned and many of her distinguished citizens are buried.

west-northwest, west-southwest *adj. & adv*. See **compass**.

West Point. U.S. Military Academy in N. Y. State, established by the government for the training of army officers.

west·ward *adj. & adv*. Toward the west.—*n*. A place or direction to the west.—**west·ward·ly** *adj. & adv*.—**west·wards** *adv*.

wet *adj.* [wet·ter; wet·test] 1. Containing water or fluid; soaked; drenched. 2. Rainy; damp; humid. 3. Indicating a locality where liquor may be sold legally.—*v.* [wet·ted; wet·ting] To moisten; drench; dip in liquid.—**wet·ness** *n.*—**wet·ting** *n.*—**wet·tish** *adj.* Damp.

whack (*hwak*) *n.* 1. *Colloquial.* A heavy blow. 2. *Slang.* A share; portion. 3. *Slang.* An attempt; try.—*v. Colloquial.* To strike heavily. —**whack·er** *n.*—**whack·ing** *adj. Colloquial.* Large; lusty.

whale (*hwayl*) *n.* Huge marine mammal, valued for its oil and amber-gris.—*v.* [whaled; whal-ing] To hunt whales.

WHALE (1/350 life-size)

whaleback	whalebone	whaleman
whalebird	whalehead	whale-mouthed
whaleboat	whale-headed	whale ship

whale (*hwayl*) *v. Colloquial.* To thrash; beat.

whal·er (*hwayl*-er) *n.* Man or vessel engaged in hunting whales.

wharf (*hworf*) *n.* [*pl.* wharves, wharfs] Dock; quay; water-front structure for loading ships. —**wharf·age** *n.* 1. Loading fee. 2. Wharves collectively.

what (*hwot*) *pron.* 1. Which one of an indefinite number; which kind of thing. 2. That which.—*adj.* Referring to the nature or identity of the object or matter in discussion. 'We know what qualities are essential.'

what·ev·er (*hwot*-*ev*-er) *pron.* 1. Anything that. 'Take whatever is left.' 2. No matter what. 'Whatever you do, don't give up.'—*adj.* At all.

what·not (*hwot*-not) *n.* 1. Light stand with shelves for bric-a-brac. 2. An undescribed article.

what·so·ev·er (hwot-soh-*ev*-er) *pron.* & *adj.* Whatever:—used more forcefully.

wheat (*hweet*) *n.* Plant producing a nutritious cereal grain.—**wheat·en** *adj.*

wheatbird	wheat-fed	wheatland
wheat cake	wheatfield	wheatstack

whee·dle (*hweed*-'l) *v.* [whee·dled; whee·dling] 1. To coax; cajole; flatter. 2. To gain by flattery.—**whee·dler** *n.*—**whee·dling·ly** *adv.*

wheel (*hweel*) *n.* 1. Circular frame or disk turning on an axis. 2. Any wheel-shaped instrument or object. 3. Circular motion; revolution.—*v.* 1. To turn on an axis; revolve; rotate. 2. To convey on wheels. 3. To change direction. 4. To roll forward; progress.—**wheeled** *adj.*—**wheel·er** *n.*—**wheel·ing** *n.*

wheel band	wheelman	wheel-spun
wheelbarrow	wheel-marked	wheel-twined
wheel box	wheelrace	wheelway
wheel chair	wheel road	wheelwork
wheel-cut	wheel-shaped	wheel-worn
wheel maker	wheelsmith	wheelwright

wheeze *v.* [wheezed; wheez·ing] To breathe hard and audibly.—*n.* 1. A whistling breath. 2. *Slang.* An old joke.—**wheez·i·ly** *adv.* —**wheez·y** *adj.* [wheez·i·er; wheez·i·est].

whelp *n.* 1. The young of the canine species; puppy; cub. 2. Son; young man, used in contempt.—*v.* Of dogs, to bring forth young.

when (*hwen*) *adv.* 1. At what or which time: —used interrogatively. 'When will you return?' 2. At or just after the moment that. 'He had just arrived when the accident occurred.' 3. Although; while; on the contrary. 'He failed when he might have succeeded.'—**when·ev·er** *adv.* At whatever time.

whence (*hwenss*) *adv.* From what place; from which source, cause, etc.

where (*hwehr*) *adv.* 1. At, in, or to what place: —used interrogatively. 2. At, in, or to which. 'The room where he worked.'—*conj.* 1. In or at which place. 2. In the respect in which. —*n.* Place; site; scene.—*pron.* What place.

where·a·bouts (*hwehr*-uh-bowtss) *n. sing.* Location.—*adv.* Near what place?

where·as (hwehr-*az*) *conj.* 1. When in fact; while on the contrary. 2. Considering that; since.

where·at (hwehr-*at*) *adv.* 1. To or at which. 2. For which reason.

where·by (hwehr-*by*) *adv.* By or through which.

where·fore (*hwehr*-for) *adv.* 1. For what reason; why? 2. For which reason; so.—*n.* Reason.

where·in (hwehr-*in*) *adv.* 1. In what or which. 2. During which.

where·of (hwehr-*ov*) *adv.* Of what, which, or whom.

where·so·ev·er (hwehr-soh-*ev*-er) *adv.* & *conj.* In whatever place.

where·up·on (hwehr-uh-*pon*) *adv.* Immediately after and in consequence of which.

wher·ev·er *adv.* 1. At whatever place. 2. In every case in which. 3. Regardless of where.

where·with (hwehr-*with*) *adv.* By means of which.

where·with·al (*hwehr*-with-awl) *n.* The necessary means; money.

wher·ry (*hwehr*-ee) *n.* A light shallow river boat which carries passengers.

whet *v.* [whet·ted, whet; whet·ting] 1. To sharpen. 2. To stimulate; excite.—**whet·stone** *n.*

wheth·er (*hweth*-er) *conj.* Which of two or more alternatives:—used to introduce the first of a series of alternative clauses.

whew (*hyoo*) *interj.* Exclamation of fatigue, surprise, etc.

whey (*hway*) *n.* The watery part of milk, separated from the thicker part or curd, particularly in making cheese.

wheybeard	whey-blooded	wheyface
whey-bearded	whey-brained	wheyfaced
wheybird	whey-colored	wheyworm

which (*hwich*) *pron.* 1. What one of several. 'Which is your car?' 2. That:—used to in-

W

troduce a subordinate clause. 'The dog which I bought is brown.'—*adj.* What one of several. 'Which book is yours?'

which·ev·er *pron.* 1. No matter which. 2. Which:—used to indicate emphasis.

whiff (*hwif*) *n.* 1. An odor. 2. A puff; slight gust of air.—*v.* 1. To puff. 2. To smell.

Whig (*hwig*) *n.* 1. A member of an English political party which supported increased power for Parliament, opposing the Tory party. 2. A member of a U.S. political party formed in 1834 to oppose the Democratic party.

while *n.* An indefinite space of time.—*conj.* 1. During the time. 2. At the same time.—*v.* [whiled; whil·ing] To pass time pleasantly.

whilst (*hwylst*) *conj.* While.

whim (*hwim*) *n.* A fancy; capricious notion.

whim·per *v.* To cry with a low, whining voice. —whim·per *n.*— -per·er *n.*— -per·ing·ly *adv.*

whim·sey, whim·sy *n.* 1. A caprice; odd fancy. 2. Quality of delicately fantastic humor.—whim·si·cal *adj.*—whim·si·cal·ly *adv.*

whine (*hwyne*) *v.* [whined; whin·ing] To express distress or complaint by plaintive crying. —whine *n.*—whin·er *n.*—whin·ing·ly *adv.*

whin·ny (*hwin-ee*) *v.* [whin·nied; whin·ny·ing] To neigh softly.—whin·ny *n.* [*pl.* whin·nies].

whip (*hwip*) *v.* [whipped; whip·ping] 1. To lash; flog. 2. To beat; conquer. 3. To take or seize with a sudden motion. 4. To beat into a froth, as eggs, cream, etc. 5. To bind a rope with cord to prevent fraying; finish the edge of cloth with overcast stitches.—*n.* 1. An instrument consisting of a lash attached to a handle and used for driving animals or for punishment. 2. A swift thrashing motion. 3. A member of a legislature who maintains discipline within his own party. 4. *Cooking.* A frothy dish made by beating.—whip·per *n.*

whip hand. Control; mastery.

whip·pet *n.* Small lean dog bred for racing.

whip·poor·will (*hwip-er-wil*) *n.* A nocturnal bird whose call resembles its name.

whir *v.* [whirred; whir·ring] To whiz; move quickly with a buzzing sound. —whir *n.*

whirl (*hwerl*) *v.* 1. To spin; revolve rapidly. 2. To carry away or move swiftly. 3. To feel dizzy or confused. —whirl *n.*—whirl·er *n.*

WHIPPET (1/20 life-size)

WHIPPOORWILL (1/9 life-size)

whirl·i·gig *n.* That which spins rapidly, esp. a merry-go-round.

whirl·pool (*hwerl-pool*) *n.* A circular current or eddy in a body of water.

whirl·wind (*hwerl-wind*) *n.* A violent spiral windstorm.

whisk (*hwisk*) *v.* 1. To move nimbly and with speed. 2. To sweep or brush with a light, rapid motion.—*n.* 1. A swift motion. 2. A small brush.

whisk·ers *n. pl.* 1. The beard; hair growing on the face of a man. 2. The bristly hairs growing on the upper lip of a cat or other animal.—whisk·ered *adj.*

whis·ky, whis·key *n.* [*pl.* -kies; -keys] An alcoholic liquor distilled from grain.

whis·per (*hwiss-per*) *v.* 1. To speak without voicing any sounds. 2. To utter secretly. —whis·per *n.*—whis·per·er *n.*

whist (*hwist*) *n.* A card game, involving bidding and play similar to bridge.

whis·tle (*hwiss-'l*) *v.* [whis·tled; whis·tling] 1. To produce a sound through the lips. 2. To make a shrill sound in motion. 3. To operate a mechanical whistle.—*n.* 1. A shrill sound produced through the lips or teeth. 2. An apparatus designed to produce a loud shrill sound. 3. *Colloquial.* The mouth or throat. —whis·tler *n.*

whit (*hwit*) *n.* A bit; iota; smallest part.

white (*hwyte*) *n.* 1. A color produced by the combination of all the prismatic colors in the same proportions as they exist in the sun's rays. 2. The abumen of an egg. 3. That part of the ball of the eye surrounding the iris or colored part.—*adj.* 1. Reflecting to the eye the combined rays of the spectrum. 2. Pale; bloodless. 3. Pure; stainless.—whit·en *v.* —white·ness *n.*—whit·ish *adj.*

white-acre	white-collared	white hot
whiteback	white-ear	white lead
whitebait	whiteface	white-minded
whitebark	white-faced	whitepot
whitebeard	whitefish	whitethroat
whitebill	whitefoot	whitetip
whitebird	white-haired	whitewood
whiteblaze	whitehead	whitestone
whitecoat	white-headed	whitetail

white·cap *n.* Foaming crest of a wave.

white collar. *Colloquial.* Relating to clerical or professional workers.

white elephant. 1. A pale-colored elephant venerated in India. 2. A burdensome possession.

white feather. A symbol of cowardice.

white flag. Flag of truce.

White·hall *n.* A section of London where government offices are located.

White House. The official residence of the presidents of the U.S.

white slave. A woman forced into prostitution. —white slaver.—white slavery.

white·wash (*hwyte-wahsh*) *v.* 1. To cover with a mixture of lime and water. 2. To exonerate; cover up wrongdoing.—white·wash *n.*

whith·er (*hwih-ther*) *adv.* Where; to what or which place.

whith·er·so·ev·er (*hwih-ther-soh-ev-er*) *adv.* To whatever place.

Whit·sun·day *n.* The seventh Sunday after Easter.—**Whit·sun·tide** *n.*

whit·tle (*hwit*-'l) *v.* [whit·tled; whit·tling] 1. To cut or shape with a knife. 2. To pare or reduce gradually.

whiz, whizz *v.* [whizzed; whiz·zing] To move rapidly with a humming or hissing sound.

who (*hoo*) *pron.* [whose; whom] 1. Which person or persons. 'Who has seen my brother?' 2. A previously mentioned person. 'He is the man who spoke.'

whoa (*woh*) *interj.* Stop; stand still.

who·dun·it (hoo-*dun*-it) *n. Slang.* A mystery story or novel.

who·ev·er (hoo-*ev*-er) *pron.* Any person whatever.

whole (*hohl*) *n.* 1. Entirety; total assemblage of parts. 2. Entire thing; complete system. —*adj.* 1. Entire; complete; undivided. 2. Perfect; intact; unimpaired.—**whole·ness** *n.*

whole-backed   whole-headed   whole-mouthed
whole-bodied   wholehearted   whole-skinned
whole-colored   whole-hogger   whole-soled
whole-eared   whole-hoofed   whole-souled

whole·sale (*hohl*-sayl) *n.* The sale of goods in large quantities to retailers rather than to consumers.—*adj.* 1. Pertaining to wholesale business. 2. Extensive and indiscriminate. —*v.* [-saled; -sal·ing].—**whole·sal·er** *n.*

whole·some (*hohl*-sum) *adj.* 1. Healthful; beneficial. 2. Sound; healthy; robust.—**whole·some·ly** *adv.*—**whole·some·ness** *n.*

whole·wheat *adj.* Of flour containing bran.

whol·ly (*hohl*-ee) *adv.* Entirely; fully; completely.

whom (*hoom*) *pron. Objective case* of **who.** 'For whom are you working?'

whoop (*hoop, hwoop*) *v.* 1. To shout excitedly. 2. To inhale with loud gasps, as after a coughing fit.—**whoop** *n.*

whoo·pee (*hwoo*-pee, *hoo*-pee) *interj.* Exclamation indicating hilarious joy.—*n. Slang.* Hilarity; joyous celebration.

whooping cough. Contagious children's disease, marked by convulsive coughing spasms.

whop·per (*hwop*-er) *n. Colloquial.* 1. Any unusually large object. 2. An enormous lie. —**whop·ping** *adj.*

whore (*hohr*) *n.* A prostitute; woman who has sexual relations for pay.—**whore** *v.* [whored; whor·ing].—**whore·dom** *n.* Prostitution; sinful desire.—**whor·ish** *adj.*—**-ish·ly** *adv.*

whorl (*hwerl*) *n.* 1. Coil; spiral. 2. *Botany.* An arrangement of leaves or flowers around a common center. 3. Single coil of a spiral shell. —**whorled** *adj.*

whose (*hooz*) *pron. Possessive case* of **who** or **which.**

who·so·ev·er (hoo-soh-*ev*-er) *pron.* Whatever person.

WHORL (def. 3)

why (*hwy*) *adv.* 1. For what cause or reason:

—used interrogatively. 2. For which; because of which.—*n.* Reason; cause.—(*wy*) *interj.* Exclamation of surprise, doubt, or hesitation.

wick *n.* In a lamp or candle, a twist of cotton threads which draws up oil or wax for burning.

wick·ed (*wik*-id) *adj.* 1. Evil; sinful. 2. Bad; vicious; roguish.—**wick·ed·ly** *adv.*— **-ness** *n.*

wick·er (*wik*-er) *n.* 1. Small supple twig for weaving or plaiting. 2. Wickerwork.—**wick·er** *adj.*—**wick·er·work** *n.* Objects of plaited wicker.

wick·et (*wik*-it) *n.* 1. A small gate or door. 2. A small window covered by a grating. 3. *Cricket.* **a.** Wooden posts at which the bowler aims. **b.** Playing field between the two wickets. 4. *Croquet.* Wire hoop.

wide *adj.* 1. Broad; having a considerable distance between the sides. 2. Vast; extensive; comprehensive. 3. Of a certain measure between the sides. 4. Fully opened.—*adv.* 1. To a distance; far. 2. To a great extent; fully. 'Spread your arms wide.' 3. Far from the mark; astray.—**wide·ly** *adv.*—**wid·en** *v.*—**wid·en·er** *n.*—**wide·ness** *n.*

WIDGEON (1/15 life-size)

widg·eon, wig·eon (*wij*-un) *n.* [*pl.* widg·eons, -eon] Any of several varieties of fresh-water duck.

wid·ow (*wid*-oh) *n.* A woman whose husband died and who has not remarried.—**wid·ow** *v.*

wid·ow·er (*wid*-uh-wer) *n.* A man whose wife has died and who has not remarried.

width *n.* Breadth; extent from side to side.

wield (*weeld*) *v.* To handle with skill; manipulate; manage.—**wield·er** *n.*—**wield·y** *adj.*

wie·ner (*wee*-ner), **wie·nie** (*wee*-nee) *n.* Small frankfurter.

wife *n.* A woman legally married to a man.

wig *n.* Artificial covering of hair for the head. —**wigged** *adj.*

wig·gle (*wig*-'l) *v.* [wig·gled; wig·gling] To move restlessly from side to side; wriggle.—**wig·gler** *n.*—**wig·gly** *adj.*

wight (*wyte*) *Archaic.* Creature; being.

wig·wag *v.* [wig·wagged; wig·wag·ging] 1. To wag. 2. To signal with flags or lights, according to a code.—*n.* Wigwagged message.—**wig·wag·ger** *n.*

wig·wam (*wig*-wahm) *n.* North American Indian tent of bark or hides covering a framework of poles.

WIGWAM

wild (*wylde*) *adj.* 1. Savage; uncivilized; untamed. 2. Natural; uncultivated. 3. Unrestrained; violent; boisterous; turbulent. 4. Crazy; fantastic; reckless. 5. *Colloquial.*

W

Eager; frantic; distracted. 6. *Colloquial.* Erratic; wide of the mark.—*n.* [*pl.*] Uninhabited or desolate regions.—**wild** *adv.*—**wild·ly** *adv.* —**wild·ness** *n.*

wild-armed	wildgrave	wild-spirited
wildfire	wildlife	wildwood

wild·cat *n.* 1. Any small, untamed member of the cat family. 2. Savage, quick-tempered person. 3. *Colloquial.* Oil well sunk in a spot not known to contain oil. 4. Unsound business or speculation.—*adj.* 1. Unsafe; reckless. 2. Illegitimate.—*v. Colloquial.* To drill oil wells in a region not known to contain oil.—**wild·cat·ter** *n.*

WILDCAT (1/20 life-size)

wil·de·beest (*wil*-duh-beest) *n.* The gnu, an African oxlike antelope.

wil·der·ness (*wil*-der-niss) *n.* Wasteland; uncultivated region; forest.

wile (*wyle*) *n.* 1. A trick; artifice. 2. Slyness; trickery.—*v.* [wiled; wil·ing] To lure.

wil·i·ness (*wyle*-ee-ness) *n.* Cunning; trickery.

will *n.* 1. Power of the mind to determine one's actions. 2. Resolution; determined choice or desire. 3. *Law.* Legal declaration of a person's wishes regarding disposition of his property after death.—*v.* 1. To resolve; determine; command. 2. To influence by power of the will. 3. To bequeath.—**will·a·ble** *adj.*—**willed** *adj.*

will *v. auxiliary.* [participles and infinitive lacking] Followed by the infinitive without "to," denoting: **a.** Futurity. 'She will arrive later.' **b.** Futurity combined with determination or volition. 'I will go if I wish.' **c.** Being accustomed. 'He will read for hours.' **d.** Ability. 'The pie will serve six.'

will·ful, wil·ful *adj.* 1. Stubborn; headstrong. 2. Intentional; deliberate.—**will·ful·ly, wil·ful·ly** *adv.*—**will·full·ness, wil·ful·ness** *n.*

Will·iams·burg. Historic city in SE Virginia, noted for the restoration of many of its streets and houses in the spirit of its Colonial founders.

will·ing *adj.* 1. Favorably disposed; ready; not reluctant. 2. Voluntary.—**will·ing·ly** *adv.* —**will·ing·ness** *n.*

will-o'-the-wisp *n.* 1. Light seen at night over marshes. 2. Elusive or misleading thing.

wil·low (*wil*-oh) *n.* 1. A tree or shrub with slender pliable shoots used in basketry. 2. The wood of a willow.—**wil·low** *adj.*—**wil·low·y** *adj.* 1. Abounding in willows. 2. Slender and graceful; pliant.

wilt *v.* 1. To droop; become limp. 2. To weaken; lose strength or spirit.—**wilt·ed** *adj.* Limp; soggy.

wil·ly-nil·ly *adv.* Having no choice.

wil·y (*wy*-lee) *adj.* [wil·i·er; wil·i·est] Crafty; cunning.

wim·ple *n.* Medieval woman's head covering, retained in the dress of some nuns.—*v.* [wim·pled; wim·pling] 1. To lie in folds. 2. To cover with a wimple; veil.

WIMPLE

win *v.* [won; win·ning] 1. To be victorious; succeed; triumph. 2. To gain; secure; acquire. 3. To induce; persuade.

wince (*winss*) *v.* [winced; winc·ing] To flinch; draw back.—**wince** *n.*

winch *n.* A machine for hoisting or pulling by means of a cable wound about a drum.

wind *n.* 1. Air in motion. 2. Breath; respiratory power. 3. Air or gas produced in the stomach or bowels. 4. Air carrying a scent; scent; hint. 5. Idle talk.—**wind·ed** *adj.* Out of breath.

WINCH

windball	windfish	windproof
wind-blown	wind force	wind puff
wind-borne	wind god	wind screen
wind-broken	wind-hungry	wind-shaken
wind cloud	wind-pollination	wind-swept

wind (*wynde*) *v.* [wound; wind·ing] 1. To twist; coil, esp. around a fixed object. 2. To curve. 3. To fold or wrap. 4. To put or keep in motion, as a watch, by tightening the spring. —**wind up.** 1. To conclude; finish. 2. *Baseball.* To rotate the arm before pitching.—**wind-up** *n.*

wind·bag (*wind*-bag) *n.* 1. Bag of wind; bellows. 2. One who talks too much, saying little.

wind·break *n.* Object, as a fence or wall, serving as a shelter from the wind.

wind·break·er *n.* Lightweight, wind-resistant sports jacket.

wind·er (*wynde*-er) *n.* Person, plant, or device that winds.

wind·fall *n.* 1. Object blown down by the wind. 2. Unexpected fortune or gain.

wind·i·ly *adv.* In a windy manner.

wind·i·ness *n.* Quality or condition of being windy.

wind·ing (*wynde*-ing) *n.* 1. Act of coiling, esp. around some fixed object. 2. The material coiled in this manner. 3. A bend or curve, as in a road.—**wind·ing** *adj.*—**wind·ing·ly** *adv.*

winding sheet. Burial garment; shroud.

wind instrument. Musical instrument sounded by the breath.

wind·jam·mer (*wind*-jam-er) *n. Nautical.* A sailing vessel or member of its crew.

wind·lass (*wind*-l'ss) *n.* Machine for pulling or hoisting; winch.

wind·mill *n.* Machine deriving power from the force of wind against its broad, revolving blades.

WINDMILL

win·dow (*win*-doh) *n.* 1: Opening in a wall to admit light and air, usually containing glass panes capable of being opened or shut. 2. Any opening suggestive of a window.—*v.* To provide with windows.—**win·dow** *adj.*

window dressing. Display of goods in a store window; outward show or appearance.—**window dresser.**—**win·dow-dress·ing** *adv.*

window envelope. Envelope having a transparent space displaying the enclosed address.

window·pane (*win*-doh-payn) *n.* Section of glass set in a window.

window seat. Seat built into the ledge beneath a window.

window shade. Adjustable shade covering a window.

win·dow-shop *v.* [-shopped; -shop·ping] To look at the goods in shop windows with no intention of buying.—**window shopper** *n.*—**window shopping** *n.*

window sill. Ledge across the bottom of a window.

wind·pipe *n.* The breath passage from the larynx to the lungs; trachea.

wind·row (*win*-roh) *n.* 1. Row of hay or grain raked up to dry. 2. Line, as of leaves or foam, swept together by the wind.—**wind·row** *v.*—**wind·row·er** *n.*

wind scale. Numerical system for indicating wind force or velocity.

wind·shield (*wind*-sheeld) *n.* Protective pane of glass in the front of a vehicle.

wind·sock. Cloth tube determining wind direction.

Windsor chair. Wooden chair with a fan-shaped back.

wind·storm *n.* Storm marked by high wind and little or no rain.

wind·ward (*wind*-werd) *n.* The point from which the wind blows.—*adv.* Toward the wind.—*adj.* On the side near the wind.—**wind·ward·ly** *adv.*—**wind·ward·ness** *n.*

wind·y *adj.* [-i·er; -i·est] 1. Of or accompanied by wind. 2. Exposed to wind; stormy. 3. Flatulent. 4. Empty; boastful, as talk.

wine *n.* The fermented juice of various fruits, usually grapes.—**wine** *v.* [wined; win·ing].

wineball	winegrower	wineskin
wine-colored	winegrowing	wine-stained
wineglass	wine house	wine taster

wine·bib·ber *n.* Habitual drinker; tippler.—**wine·bib·bing** *n. & adj.*

wine cellar. Cellar for storing wine; the wine stored there.

wine·glass·ful *n.* [*pl.* -glass·fuls] Amount held by a wineglass, usually four fluid ounces.

wine press. A vat or machine for extracting the juice from grapes.—**wine presser.**

win·er·y (*wyne*-er-ee) *n.* [*pl.* win·er·ies] Establishment where wine is made.

wine·sap *n.* A variety of red winter apple.

wing *n.* 1. One of the paired anterior limbs of birds and insects, usually serving as an organ of flight. 2. Broad plane structure of an airplane, providing lifting power. 3. Part

WING

of a building projecting from the main portion. 4. *Military.* **a.** Extreme division of an army, etc. **b.** Unit of aircraft. 5. Faction; group within an organization. 6. *Theater.* Space on either side of the stage. 7. *Sports.* Team position on either side of center. 8. [*Pl.*] Emblem worn by airmen.—*v.* 1. To furnish with wings. 2. To fly. 3. To make fly; send off. 4. *Colloquial.* To wound, esp. in the wing or arm.—**winged** *adj.*—**wing·less** *adj.*

wing chair, winged chair. Upholstered chair with narrow side pieces as high as the back.

wing·spread (*wing*-spred) *n.* Measurement between the tips of the wings when spread.

wink *v.* 1. To close and open the eyes rapidly. 2. To twinkle. 3. To overlook; tolerate.—*n.* 1. Act of winking, esp. as a signal. 2. Time taken in shutting the eye; instant.—**wink·er** *n.* —**forty winks.** A short nap.

win·kle (*wink*-'l) *n.* 1. A periwinkle. 2. Large sea snail.

win·ner *n.* One that wins.

win·ning *adj.* 1. Having won, or capable of winning. 2. Charming.—*n.* 1. Act of winning; victory. 2. [*pl.*] Gains, esp. from success in a contest or gambling.—**win·ning·ly** *adv.*

win·now (*win*-oh) *v.* 1. To blow the chaff from, as grain. 2. To sift; sort; separate or eliminate. 3. To blow away; disperse.—**win·now** *n.* —**win·now·er** *n.*

win, place, and show. Term used by bettors when wagering on a horse to finish first, second, or third.

win·some (*win*-sum) *adj.* Engaging; agreeable; winning.—**win·some·ly** *adv.*—**win·some·ness** *n.*

win·ter *n.* 1. The coldest season of the year, in U.S. from Dec. 21 to March 21. 2. Last period, as of life; time of decline or decay.—*v.* To manage during or pass the winter.

win·ter·green (*win*-ter-green) *n.* 1. Small evergreen plant yielding an oil used in flavoring and medicine. 2. This oil or its flavor.

winter wheat. Wheat planted in autumn and ripening the following spring or summer.

win·try (*win*-tree) *adj.* [win·tri·er; win·tri·est] Of or resembling winter; cold; hoary.—**wint·ri·ly** *adv.*—**wint·ri·ness** *n.*

win·y (*wyne*-ee) *adj.* Like wine.

wipe *v.* [wiped; wip·ing] 1. To clean, dry, or remove by rubbing. 2. To efface; obliterate. 3. To pass over a surface, as for cleansing.

W

wire *n.* 1. Metal drawn into a flexible, cylindrical thread. 2. The telegraph system; telegraph message; telegram. 3. *Racing*. The finish line.—*v.* [wired; wir·ing] 1. To connect or furnish with wire. 2. To send a telegram.

wire·hair *n.* A wire-haired fox terrier.—**wire-haired** *adj.* Having short, stiff hair.

wire·less *adj.* Having no wires.—*n.* Short for **wireless telegraphy.**

wireless telegraphy. Code communication by means of emission and reception of high-frequency electrical waves.

wire photo. A photograph transmitted by tele-photography; telephotograph.

wire·pul·ling *n. Colloquial.* Use of political or social influence to accomplish an aim.— -**pul·ler** *n.*

wir·ing (*wyre*-ing) *n.* 1. Act of connecting with wires. 2. System of wires to provide electric current.—**wir·ing** *adj.*

wir·y (*wyre*-ee) *adj.* [wir·i·er; wir·i·est] 1. Like wire. 2. Sinewy; lean and tough.—**wir·i·ly** *adv.*—**wir·i·ness** *n.*

wis·dom (*wiz*-dum) *n.* Learning; judgment.

wisdom tooth. The last tooth on either side of each jaw, usually appearing between the eighteenth and twenty-fifth year.

wise (*wyze*) *n.* Manner; way.

wise *adj.* 1. Sage; judicious. 2. Learned; erudite. 3. *Slang*. Having information; aware.—**wise·ly** *adv.*

wise·a·cre (*wyze*-ay-ker) *n.* Person who thinks he is very wise; know-it-all.

wise·crack (*wyze*-krak) *n. Slang*. A joke; witty remark.—**wise·crack** *v.*—**wise·crack·er** *n.*

wish *v.* 1. To desire; crave. 2. To express a hope or inclination.—**wish** *n.*—**wish·er** *n.*

wish·bone (*wish*-bohn) *n.* The forked bone in front of a bird's breastbone.

wish·ful *adj.* Having or expressing a hope or desire.—**wish·ful·ly** *adv.*—**wish·ful·ness** *n.* —**wishful thinking.** Subconsciously expressing one's desires in one's judgment or opinion.

wish·y-wash·y *adj.* 1. Weak; dilute. 2. Feeble; unsubstantial.

wisp *n.* A small handful, as of hay; small portion, bit, or shred.—**wisp·y** *adj.*

wis·ta·ri·a, wis·te·ri·a (wiss-*tehr*-ee-uh, wiss-*tihr*-ee-uh) *n.* Climbing plant with clusters of purple, blue, or white flowers.

wist·ful *adj.* Yearning; feeling desire with little possibility of satisfaction.—**wist·ful·ly** *adv.* —**wist·ful·ness** *n.*

wit *n.* 1. Humor; power to express ideas cleverly and amusingly. 2. [*pl.*] Mental balance or soundness; power of understanding. 3. Person with a clever and

WISTARIA

lively sense of humor; one noted for bright, amusing repartee.

witch *n.* 1. Sorceress; woman supposed to have evil magic power. 2. An ugly old woman. 3. *Colloquial*. A fascinating or bewitching woman.—**witch·er·y** *n.* [*pl.* -ies] 1. Magic sorcery. 2. Fascination.

witch hazel. 1. A kind of flowering shrub. 2. A soothing solution made from the bark of this plant.

with *prep.* 1. In the company of; among. 2. Against. 'He argued with us.' 3. In the sphere or opinion of. 'Tea is popular with Englishmen.' 4. Using; by means of; because of. 'They shivered with cold.' 5. Having; characterized by; showing. 'An artist with talent.' 6. Toward; in relation or regard to. 'We must be friendly with him.' 7. Compared, equal, or in proportion to. 'It changes with the weather.' 8. On the side of; in the same direction as. 9. In keeping or charge of. 'Leave it with me.' 10. In spite of. 11. At the time of. 12. From. 'She parted with it willingly.'

with·al (-*awl*) *adv. Archaic*. Besides; still.

with·draw (with-*draw*) *v.* [-drew; -drawn; -draw·ing] 1. To retire; depart. 2. To remove; draw back. 3. To recall; retract. —**with·draw·al** *n.*—**with·drawn** *adj.* Reserved; inhibited.

with·er (*with*-er) *v.* 1. To shrivel; dry up. 2. To lose or cause to lose freshness, confidence, etc.—**with·er·ing** *adj.*—**with·er·ing·ly** *adv.*

with·ers *n. pl.* Ridge between a horse's shoulder blades.

with·hold (with-*hohld*) *v.* [with·held; with·hold·ing] 1. To detain; hold back. 2. To refuse to grant.

withholding tax. Income tax which is taken out of an employee's salary or wages before payment.

with·in (with-*in*) *prep.* 1. Inside; in or to the inner part of. 2. Inside the limits or range of. —*adv.* On the inside; in the interior; indoors.

with·out (with-*owt*) *prep.* 1. Lacking; free from. 2. Omitting the act of. 'He left without saying goodby.'—*adv.* On the outside; outdoors.

with·stand (with-*stand*) *v.* [with·stood; with·stand·ing] To resist; oppose.

wit·less (*wit*-liss) *adj.* Senseless; foolish.—**wit·less·ly** *adv.*—**wit·less·ness** *n.*

wit·ness (*wit*-niss) *n.* 1. Testimony; evidence. 2. Observer; person who saw an event. 3. *Law*. **a.** A person who gives evidence or testimony under oath. **b.** A person present at a proceeding and able to testify that it occurred.—*v.* 1. To observe; see or hear. 2. To give evidence of; attest to. 3. *Law*. To be a witness (sense 3 b).

wit·ti·cism (*wit*-ih-sizm) *n.* A witty remark; clever jest.

wit·ting·ly (*wit*-ing-lee) *adv.* Knowingly; intentionally.

wit·ty adj. [-ti·er; -ti·est] 1. Possessing wit; clever and amusing. 2. Intelligent; perceptive.—**wit·ti·ly** adv.—**wit·ti·ness** n.

wives. Plural of wife.

wiz·ard (wiz-erd) n. 1. A sorcerer; magician. 2. An expert; skilled performer.—**wiz·ard** adj.—**wiz·ard·ry** n.

wiz·ened (wiz-'nd) adj. Shriveled; dried up.

wob·ble v. [wob·bled; wob·bling] 1. To teeter; move unsteadily. 2. To waver; vacillate.—**wob·ble** n.—**wob·bler** n.—**wob·bly** adj.

woe (woh) n. 1. Grief; misery. 2. A sorrow or affliction.

woe·be·gone ((woh-bee-gon) adj. Miserable; showing woe.

woe·ful, wo·ful (woh-f'l) adj. Sad; wretched.—**woe·ful·ly, wo·ful·ly** adv.—**woe·ful·ness, wo·ful·ness** n.

woke (wohk). Past tense of wake.

wold (wohld) n. A plain; high, open country.

WOLF (1/35 life-size)

wolf (woolf) n. [pl. wolves] 1. A large, wild, doglike animal noted for its craft and ferocity. 2. Slang. One, esp. a man, who pursues the opposite sex.—**wolf·ish** adj.—**wolf·ish·ly** adv.—**wolf·ish·ness** n.

wolf pack. A small fleet of German submarines in World War II, used for surprise attacks on convoys.

wolf·ram (woolf-rum) n. Tungsten, an element of the chromium family, used in electric-light filaments because it has the highest melting point of any metal.

wol·ver·ine, wol·ver·ene (wool-ver-een) n. 1. A thickset meat-eating mammal of North America. 2. [cap.] Colloquial. A native of Michigan, the Wolverine state.

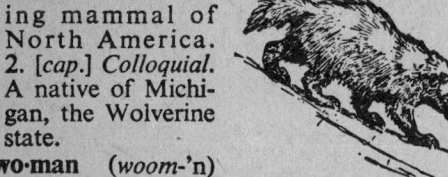
WOLVERINE (1/30 life-size)

wo·man (woom-'n) n. [pl. wo·men (wih-min)] 1. An adult human female. 2. Women collectively.—adj. Feminine.—**wo·man·li·ness** n.—**wo·man·ly** adj.

wo·man·hood n. 1. State or character of being a woman. 2. Women in general.

wo·man·ish adj. Like or suitable to a woman; unmanly.—**wo·man·ish·ly** adv. -**ish·ness** n.

wo·man·kind n. Women in general.

woman suffrage. The right of women to vote; the exercise of this right.—**wo·man·suff·rage** adj.—**woman suffragist.**

womb (woom) n. The uterus; female organ for containing and nourishing the young until birth.

wom·bat n. Australian burrowing animal which resembles a small bear.

wo·men (wih-min) Plural of woman.—**wo·men·folk, wo·men·folks** n. pl. Women in general.

WOMBAT (1/36 life-size)

won (wun). Past tense and past participle of win.

won·der (wun-der) n. 1. Astonishment; feeling aroused by that which is strange or marvelous. 2. A marvel; source of astonishment.—v. 1. To marvel; be surprised. 2. To be curious or doubtful.—**won·der·er** n.—**won·der·ing** adj.—**won·der·ing·ly** adv.—**won·der·ment** n.—**won·der·work** n.

won·der·ful (wun-der-f'l) adj. Arousing wonder or joy; marvelous.—**won·der·ful·ly** adv.—**won·der·ful·ness** n.

won·der·land (wun-der-land) n. A land of great wonders; magic land.

won·drous (wun-drus) adj. Wonderful.—adv. Marvelously; wonderfully.—**won·drous·ly** adv.—**won·drous·ness** n.

wont (wohnt, wunt) n. Habit; custom.—adj. Accustomed.

wont·ed adj. Accustomed.

woo v. 1. To court; make love to. 2. To urge; entreat. 3. To seek.—**woo·er** n.

wood n. 1. The hard, fibrous substance under the bark of trees and shrubs. 2. [often woods] Forest. 3. Trees cut for use, as lumber or firewood.—**wood·ed** adj.

wood bark	woodhouse	wood ranger
wood box	woodland	woodshed
woodcock	woodman	wood-shop
woodcraft	wood pile	woodworm
wood cutter	wood print	woodyard

wood·chuck n. Short-legged North American rodent with coarse fur.

wood·en adj. 1. Made of wood. 2. Stiff; awkward; stupid.—**wood·en·ly** adv.—**wood·en·ness** n.

WOODCHUCK (1/20 life-size)

wood·peck·er (wood-pek-er) n. Any of several birds with a long, hard bill for boring into trees to get insects.

wood wind. A wooden musical instrument sounded by the breath.—**wood-wind** adj.

WOODPECKER (1/10 life-size)

wood·work (wood-werk) n. Work made of wood, esp. paneling and mouldings.—**wood·work·er** n.—**wood·work·ing** n. & adj.

wood·y (wood-ee) adj. [-i·er; -i·est] 1. Like or consisting of wood. 2. Abounding in wood; having many trees.—**wood·i·ness** n.

woof n. 1. Horizontal threads in weaving. 2. Cloth; texture.

W

wool n. 1. The soft, curly coat of certain animals, esp. sheep; yarn or fabric made of this material. 2. Short, kinky hair.—**wool** adj. —**wool·en, wool·len** n. & adj.

wool-backed	woolman	woolskin
wool-dyed	woolpack	wool sorter
woolfell	wool press	wool stock
wool flock	woolsack	wool washer
wool-laden	wool shearer	wool winder
wool-lined	wool shears	woolwork

wool·gath·er·ing n. Day dreaming; absent-mindedness.—**wool·gath·er·ing** adj.

wool·ly (wool-ee) adj. [wool·li·er; -li·est] Also **wool·y**. 1. Of or like wool. 2. Covered or clothed with wool.—n. pl. Slang. Woolen undergarments.—**wool·li·ness, wool·i·ness** n.

word (werd) n. 1. An articulate sound or combination of sounds expressing an idea; the smallest independent unit of speech. 2. The letter or letters representing such a unit. 3. Promise. 4. Command; signal. 5. Speech, esp. a short remark or discussion. 6. News; information. 7. [pl.] Angry discussion; dispute.—v. To phrase; put in words.—**word·less** adj.—**word for word**. In the exact words.

wordbook	word-deaf	wordmongering
word building	word maker	wordplay
word catcher	wordman	word slinger
wordcraftsman	wordmonger	word slinging

word·age (werd-ij) n. 1. Word count. 2. Wordiness.

word·ing (werd-ing) n. Use of words; phrasing.

word·y (werd-ee) adj. [-i·er; -i·est] Abounding in words; verbose.—**word·i·ly** adv.— **-i·ness** n.

wore. Past tense of **wear**.

work (werk) v. [worked, wrought; work·ing] 1. To labor; toil. 2. To perform; operate; function; go. 3. To manage; keep busy or employed. 4. To attain by continuous and severe labor; force gradually. 5. To form; fashion. 6. To excite by degrees.—n. 1. Effort; toil; labor. 2. An undertaking; enterprise. 3. Performance; deed; achievement. 4. An article, fabric, or structure; product of nature or art. 5. [pl.] An industrial establishment. 6. [pl.] Theology. Moral duties or acts, as distinct from faith.—**work·a·ble** adj.—**work·er** n.—**work·ing** adj. & n.

workaday	work-hardened	work-stained
workbasket	work horse	workstand
workbench	workmaster	work table
workbook	workpeople	worktime
workbox	workplace	work-up
work cure	workroom	workweek
work-driven	work sheet	workwoman
workfellow	workshop	work-worn

work·day n. 1. A day on which business is open and work is performed; a weekday, as distinguished from Sunday. 2. The sum of hours worked in a day.

work·house n. 1. A house of detention for petty offenders. 2. In England, a poorhouse.

work·man n. A laborer.

work·man·like adj. Well executed; technically skillful.

work·man·ship n. Manner of execution; craftsmanship.

work·out n. A vigorous preparatory test of strength or ability.

work·shop n. Manufacturing place.

world n. 1. All creation; the universe. 2. Any celestial body believed to be peopled. 3. The earth; the globe. 4. A large division of the globe, as the old world, the new world. 5. Any state or sphere of existence. 6. Humanity; mankind. 7. The public; society. 8. A body of people united by a common faith, object, or pursuit. 9. Social life. 10. Secular affairs or interests. 11. The ways and manners of men; the habits and customs of society. 12. Any complex and ordered system; microcosm. 13. Sphere; realm. 14. A great multitude or quantity.—**world·li·ness** n.—**world·ly** adj.

world-beater	world-weariness
world-consciousness	world-weary
world maker	world-wide

World War I. Conflict (1914–1918) involving most of the principal countries of the world.

World War II. Total war (1939–1945) in which nearly all of the nations of the world were engaged.

WORM

worm (werm) n. 1. Any small, elongated, limbless, creeping animal. 2. An earthworm. 3. A division of parasitic animals chiefly present in the intestines. 4. A groveling, despicable person.—v. To move slowly and insidiously.—**worm·y** adj.

worm-cankered	worm hole	worm-shaped
worm-eaten	wormholed	worm-tongued
worm-gnawed	worm-riddled	worm-worn

worm gear. Machinery. A revolving screw which gears with a toothed wheel.

worm·wood n. 1. A perennial herb, aromatic and bitter, used in making absinthe and ointment. 2. Bitterness; sadness.

worm·y adj. [-i·er: -i·est] Of, or eaten by, worms.

WORM GEAR

worn. Past participle of **wear**.

worn·out adj. 1. Impaired by long use. 2. Wearied; exhausted.

worry (wer-ee) v. [wor·ried; wor·ry·ing] 1. To annoy; plague; trouble; make anxious or disturbed. 2. To tear with the teeth; gnaw. —**wor·ry** n.—**wor·ry·ing** adj.

worse (werss) adj. 1. Bad, ill, or corrupt in a greater degree. 2. In poorer health. 3. In a less favorable situation.—**wors·en** v.

wor·ship (wer-ship) v. [wor·shipped; wor·shipping] 1. To adore; offer religious devotions. 2. To idolize; love or admire inordinately.—n. 1. Veneration; the act of paying homage to divinities. 2. A title of honor used in addressing certain high-ranking officials.—**wor·ship·ful** *adj.*—**wor·ship·ful·ly** *adv.*—**wor·ship·per** *n.*

worst (*werst*) *adj.* Bad in the highest degree. —**worst** *n.*

worst *v.* To beat; defeat.

wor·sted (*wus*-ted) *n.* A variety of woolen yarn or thread, spun from long-staple combed wool, twisted tighter than ordinarily.—**wor·sted** *adj.*

worth (*werth*) *n.* 1. Value; price. 2. Merit; virtue.—*adj.* 1. Equal in value to; valued at. 2. Deserving; meriting. 3. Possessing; equal in possessions to.—**worth·less** *adj.*—**worth·less·ly** *adv.*—**worth·less·ness** *n.*

worth-while *adj.* Fruitful; satisfying.

wor·thy (*wer*-thee) *adj.* 1. Deserving; fit; suitable. 2. Excellent; noble; virtuous.—*n.* 1. A distinguished person. 2. *Now Humorous.* A local celebrity.—**wor·thi·ly** *adv.*— **-thi·ness** *n.*

would-be *adj.* Wishing to be; vainly pretending.

wound (*woond*) *n.* 1. An injury; breach of the skin and flesh caused by violence. 2. A grief; hurt.—*v.* To inflict hurt or injury.

wow *interj.* An exclamation of surprise, etc.—*n. Slang.* A spectacular or sensational success. —**wow** *v.* To score a success.

wrack (*rak*) *n.* 1. Destruction; ruin. 2. Seaweed cast on the shore.—*v.* To wreck.

wraith *n.* Ghost; apparition.

wran·gle (*rang*-g'l) *v.* [wran·gled; wran·gling] 1. To squabble; quarrel; argue noisily. 2. To herd cattle.—*n.* Quarrel.—**wran·gler** *n.* 1. A quarrelsome person. 2. A herdsman.

wrap *v.* [wrapped; wrap·ping] To cover; envelop.—**wrap** [*Also pl.*] *n.* Outer garment; coat. —**wrap·per** *n.* 1. One who makes packages. 2. A woman's dressing gown.—**wrap·ping** *n.*

wrath *n.* Indignation; anger; fury.—**wrath·ful** *adj.*—**wrath·ful·ly** *adv.*—**wrath·ful·ness** *n.*

wreak (*reek*) *v.* To inflict; execute. 'He was swift to wreak vengeance.'

wreath (*reeth*) *n.* 1. A garland. 2. A circular form.

WREATH

wreathe *v.* [wreathed; wreath·ing] 1. To intertwine. 2. To surround; encircle.

wreck (*rek*) *v.* To destroy; ruin.—*n.* 1. The broken hulk of a ship. 2. Damaged or broken remains. 3. Ruin; destruction.—**wreck·age** *n.* —**wreck·er** *n.*

wren (*ren*) *n.* A small singing bird closely allied to the warbler, distinguished by its slender beak, short, rounded wings, and mottled plumage.

WREN (1/5 life-size)

wrench *n.* 1. A violent twist. 2. A sprain. 3. A tool having jaws adapted to catch upon the head of a bolt or nut to turn it.—*v.* 1. To wrest or twist by violence. 2. To sprain; strain.

wrest (*rest*) *v.* To seize; obtain forcibly.

wres·tle (*ress*-'l) *v.* [wres·tled; wres·tling] 1. To fight by grappling and trying to throw down one's opponent. 2. To struggle; strive. —**wres·tler** *n.*

wretch (*rech*) *n.* 1. A miserable person. 2. A base or vile person.—**wretch·ed** (*rech*-id) *adj.* —**wretch·ed·ly** *adv.*—**wretch·ed·ness** *n.*

wrig·gle (*rig*-'l) *v.* [wrig·gled; wrig·gling] 1. To wiggle; squirm; move with writhings and contortions of the body. 2. To escape trickily. —**wrig·gle** *n.*—**wrig·gler** *n.*—**wrig·gly** *adj.*

wright (*ryte*) *n.* A craftsman; workman, as a wheelwright, playwright, millwright.

wring (*ring*) *v.* [wrung; wring·ing] 1. To twist and squeeze. 2. To torture; torment. 3. To squeeze or press out; extort.

wring·er *n.* Device for pressing water from wet clothes.

wrin·kle (*rink*-'l) *v.* [wrin·kled; wrin·kling] To furrow; crease.—*n.* 1. A crease; fold. 2. *Colloquial.* A notion; new idea or device.—**wrin·kled** *adj.*

WRINGER

wrist (*rist*) *n.* The joint between the hand and the forearm.

writ (*rit*) *n.* 1. [*cap.*] The Scriptures; the Old and New Testaments. 2. *Law.* A document directed to some public officer or private person, commanding him to do a certain act therein specified.

write (*ryte*) *v.* [wrote; writ·ten; writ·ing] 1. To form (characters or words) on a surface. 2. To communicate; disclose in written or printed form. 3. To compose; be the author of. 4. To communicate with in writing. 'Write your Senator.'—**writ·er** *n.*—**writ·ing** *n. & adj.* —**write up.** 1. To write an account of. 2. To publicize favorably. 3. *Accounting.* To enter too large a figure.

writhe (*rythe*) *v.* [writhed; writh·ing] To twist about, as in pain.—*n.* A contortion.

wrong (*rawng*) *adj.* 1. Violating moral or divine standard; sinful. 2. False; erroneous. 3. In error; mistaken.—*n.* 1. Departure from right. 2. An injustice; injury.—*v.* To injure; oppress.—**wrong·ful** *adj.*

wrong·do·er (*rawng*-doo-er) *n.* A sinner; one who violates law or convention.— **-do·ing** *n.*

wrote (*roht*). *Past tense* of write.

wroth *adj.* Angry; vexed; irate.

wrought (*rawt*) *adj.* 1. Fashioned; formed. 2. Processed; manufactured. 3. Ornamented; decorated.

wry (*ry*) *adj.* Twisted; contorted; warped.

Wy·an·dot (*wy*-un-dot) *n.* An Iroquois Indian tribe of midwestern U.S.

wy·an·dotte *n.* A variety of medium-sized American domestic fowl.

W

X

xan·thate (zan-thayt) n. Chemistry. A yellow salt used in processing silk.

xan·the·in (zan-thee-in) n. Yellow, water-soluble coloring matter derived from plant blossoms.

xan·thic (zan-thik) adj. 1. Yellow. 2. Chemistry. Containing xanthine.

xan·thin (zan-thin) n. Insoluble yellow coloring matter found in blossoms.

xan·thine (zan-thin) n. A carbonic-acid derivative secreted in the human body.

Xan·thip·pe, Xan·tip·pe (zan-tip-ee) n. 1. Socrates' wife, noted as a shrewish woman. 2. A nagging shrewish woman.

xan·tho·phyll (zan-thoh-fil) n. The yellow coloring matter found in dead leaves.

xan·thous (zan-thus) adj. Relating to the Mongoloid and other yellow-skinned racial groups.

xat (zaht) n. Elaborately carved ceremonial post erected in front of the huts of some North American tribes.

X chromosome. Biology. Factor determining the sex of an offspring. When two X chromosomes are present in the germ cell, the offspring is female; if one X and one Y chromosome are present, the offspring is male.

xe·bec (zee-bek) n. Nautical. A small ship used in the Mediterranean Sea.

xe·non (zee-non) n. A chemically inactive gaseous element occurring in air. (Symbol: Xe).

xen·o·pho·bi·a (zen-oh-foh-bee-uh) n. Hatred of foreigners or strangers.

xe·roph·i·lous (zee-rof-uh-lus) adj. Botany. Able to grow with very little water.

xe·rus (zee-rus) n. A bristly-haired African ground squirrel.

Xmas. Abbreviation of Christmas.

X-ray n. 1. Physics. Radiation similar to rays of light but of extremely high frequency, having the property of passing through a solid. X-rays are used in medicine for photographing internal tissues and treating cancer; Roentgen ray. 2. Photograph taken by X-rays.—v. To view or photograph by means of X-rays. —X-ray adj.

xy·lem (zy-l'm) n. Botany. In a plant stem, the layer of wood which surrounds the central core and conveys water upward from the roots.

xy·lene (zy-leen) n. Chemistry. A hydrocarbon of the benzene group obtained from tar and used in the manufacture of dyestuffs.

xy·loid (zy-loyd) adj. Resembling wood.

xy·loph·a·gous (zy-lof-uh-gus) adj. Living on a diet of wood. 'Termites are xylophagous.'

xyl·o·phone (zyle-uh-fohn) n. A musical instrument having wooden bars of graduated length which are struck with mallets.

XYLOPHONE

xy·lose (zy-lohss) n. Wood sugar; a white crystalline substance prepared from wood pulp.

xys·ter (ziss-ter) n. A surgical instrument used for scraping bones.

Y

yacht (yot) n. A small vessel used for pleasure trips and racing.—yacht v.—yachts·man n. —yachts·man·ship.

ya·hoo (yah-hoo, yay-hoo) n. 1. [cap.] A race of brutes in Swift's Gulliver's Travels. 2. Slang. A stupid person; lout.

Yah·weh (yah-weh) n. Jehovah.

yak n. Large, black, shaggy ox of Tibet.

yam n. 1. The sweet potato. 2. Tropical vine bearing edible tubers similar to the sweet potato.

YAK (1/65 life-size)

Yang·tze (yahng-tsee) The most important Chinese river, some 3,000 miles long, from Tibet to the China Sea.

yank v. To pull; jerk.—n. 1. A sharp tug. 2. [cap.] Yankee.

Yan·kee (yang-kee) n. 1. A native of northern U.S., esp. New England. 2. Among foreigners, any American.

yap v. [yapped; yap·ping] 1. To yelp. 2. Slang. To talk inanely.—n. 1. A bark. 2. Slang. Talk. 3. Slang. The mouth.

yard (yahrd) n. 1. The American standard measure of length equal to three feet or 36 inches. 2. A long piece of timber secured thwartships to the mast of a square-rigged ship.

yard n. 1. A small piece of ground adjoining a house. 2. An enclosure within which any work or business is carried on; as a brickyard or dockyard.

yard·age (yahrd-ij) n. Length measured in yards.

yard·arm *n.* Either end of a ship's yard extending thwartships from the mast.

yard·stick *n.* 1. A three-foot measure. 2. A criterion; standard.

yarn *n.* 1. Any textile fiber prepared for weaving into cloth. 2. *Colloquial.* A story; tale.

yaw *n.* A vessel's sudden veering from the course.—**yaw** *v.*

yawl *n.* Small two-masted sailing vessel with longitudinal sails, having the mizzenmast aft of the helm.

YAWL

yawn *v.* 1. To stretch the mouth open involuntarily through drowsiness. 2. To gape; open wide. —**yawn** *n.*

y·clept (ee-*klept*) *adj. Archaic.* Called.

ye (*yee*). *Archaic form* of the *plural* of **you.**

ye (*thee*; also, popularly, *yee*). *Archaic spelling* of **the.** The *y* represents an Anglo-Saxon character pronounced *th*, as in *thorn.*

yea (*yay*) *adv. Archaic.* Indeed; yes; certainly.

year (*yeer*) *n.* 1. The twelve-month period during which the earth makes one complete revolution around the sun. 2. Fixed annual period. 'A work year.'—**year·ly** *adj.* Annual.

year·ling (*yeer*-ling, *yer*-) *n.* A one-year old animal.

yearn (*yern*) *v.* To long; pine; thirst.—**yearn·ing** *n.*

yeast (*yeest*) *n.* A fungus plant which can decompose sugar into alcohol and carbon dioxide.

yell *v.* To shout; scream.—**yell** *n.*

yel·low (*yel*-oh) *n.* 1. A bright golden color; the color in the solar spectrum between red and green. 2. The yolk of an egg. 3. *pl.* A disease which turns plants yellow.—*adj.* 1. Of the color yellow. 2. Cowardly. 3. Designating a style of journalism devoted to sensationalism at the expense of social responsibility.—**yel·low·ish** *adj.*

yellowback	yellow-breasted	yellow-headed
yellow-bellied	yellow-covered	yellow-legger
yellowbill	yellow-eyed	yellow-shafted
yellow-billed	yellowfish	yellow-tailed
yellowbird	yellowhammer	yellow-throated

yellow fever. A malignant tropical fever transmitted by the bite of a mosquito.

yellow jack. 1. Yellow fever. 2. The flag indicating quarantine.

yellow jacket. A yellow-colored wasp.

Yel·low·stone. A national park located in Wyoming and Montana.

yelp *v.* To give a sharp cry; bark.—**yelp** *n.*

yen *n.* The Japanese monetary unit.

yen *n. Slang.* A desire; longing.

yeo·man (*yoh*-m'n) *n.* 1. *English History.* A small landholder; freeman farmer. 2. *Navy.* A clerical petty officer.—**yeo·man·ry** *n.*

yes *adv.* Aye; it is so; right; agreed.

yes·ter·day (*yes*-ter-day) *n.* The day before today.

yet *adv.* 1. So far; up till now. 2. But; nevertheless; still. 3. Ultimately; eventually.

yew *n.* A family of broad-needled evergreens ranging from dwarf bushes to trees 60 feet tall.

Yid·dish (*yid*-ish) *n.* A German dialect originating in the Middle Rhine region, written in Hebrew characters.

yield (*yeeld*) *v.* 1. To produce; bear. 2. To relinquish; give; abandon. 3. To submit; capitulate.—**yield** *n.*—**yield·ing** *adj.*

yo·del (*yoh*-d'l) *v.* Also **yo·dle.** [yo-deled, yo·delled, yo·dled] yo·deling, yo·del·ling] To warble; sing with abrupt variations in key. —**yo·del, yo·dle** *n.*—**-del·er, -del·ler, -dler** *n.*

Yo·ga (*yoh*-guh) *n.* An oriental philosophy advocating withdrawal from worldly matters in favor of spiritual contemplation directed toward attainment of perfect peace.

yo·gi (*yoh*-gee) *n.* Also **yo·gin.** Devotee of Yoga.

yoke *n.* 1. A contrivance by which pairs of draught animals are hitched together, usually consisting of a piece of timber curved near each end and fitted with bows into which the animals' necks are placed. 2. A frame to fit the shoulders and neck of a person, and support a pair of pails, etc. 3. A mark of servitude or suffering. 4. A pair of draught animals tied together. 5. Ornamental dress or shirt front. —*v.* [yoked; yok·ing].

YOKE

yo·kel (*yoh*-k'l) *n.* A country fellow:—used contemptuously.

yolk (*yohk*) *n.* The yellow spherical part of an egg, comprising the nourishment of the young organism.

Yom Kippur. The Jewish Day of Atonement.

yon *adj.* That; those; yonder.

yon·der *adj.* That or those, referring to persons or objects at a distance.—*adv.* At or in that place.

yore *n.* Times past; long ago.

York·town. A city in Virginia, the site of the surrender of the British forces to the Americans in 1781.

Yo·sem·i·te (yoh-*sem*-ih-tee). A great valley and national park in central California.

you (*yoo*) *pron.* [*pl.* you] 1. Person being addressed. 2. *Colloquial.* One; anyone.

young (*yung*) *adj.* Immature; not old; in an early stage of development; new.—*n. pl.* 1. The offspring of an animal. 2. Young people, collectively.

young-bladed	young-ladyish
young-eyed	young-ladylike
young-headed	young-manhood
young-hearted	young-manliness
young-ladyhood	young-womanhood

Y

young blood. Youth; also, the vigor of youth.

youngish *adj.* Rather young.

youngling *n.* A young person; also a young animal or plant; anything immature.

young one. Also **young'un** *n. Colloquial.* A child; also, a young animal, esp. a colt; stripling.

youn·ker (*yung-ker*) *n. Colloquial.* Young fellow; youngster.

your (*yor, yoor*) *adj.* Pertaining or belonging to you.

yours *pron.* That or those belonging to you.

your·self *pron.* [*pl.* your·selves] You; not another or others; used reflexively and emphatically.

youth (*yooth*) *n.* 1. The adolescent period; early adulthood. 2. A young man. 3. Young people.—**youth·ful** *adj.*—**youth·ful·ness** *n.*

yowl *n.* A loud, mournful cry, as of a cat.—*v.* To cry loudly.

yuc·ca (*yuk-uh*) *n.* A subtropical family of tree-like plants with stiff sword-shaped leaves and white bell-shaped flower clusters.

YUCCA

Yu·kon (*yoo-*kon) 1. A large Alaskan river. 2. A NW territory of Canada, bordering on Alaska.

Yule (*yool*) *n.* Christmas. —**Yule·tide** *n.* Christmas season.

Z

za·ny (*zay-*nee) *n.* A fool; clown.

zeal (*zeel*) *n.* Fervor; ardor; enthusiasm. —**zeal·ot** (*zel-*ut) *n.* A fanatical partisan.—**zeal·ous** (*zel-*us) *adj.*—**zeal·ous·ly** *adv.* — **zeal·ous·ness** *n.*

ze·bra (*zee-*bruh) *n.* African animal related to the horse, having vivid brownish-black stripes on a white body.

ZEBRA (1/45 life-size)

ze·bu (*zee-*byoo) *n.* A kind of Indian ox, widely used as a beast of burden in the Orient.

ze·nith (*zee-*nith) *n.* 1. The point in the heavens directly above the observer's head. 2. Culmination; peak; summit.

ZEBU (1/45 life-size)

zeph·yr (*zef-*er) *n.* 1. The west wind; a mild, gentle breeze. 2. A soft, light fabric.

zep·pe·lin (*zep-*uh-lin, *zep-*lin) *n.* Airship; dirigible.

ze·ro (*zeer-*oh) *n.* 1. *Mathematics.* The character representing no quantity; naught. 2. Nothing; absence of number or quantity. 3. The starting-point on a scale; the level from which measurement commences. 4. [*cap.*] Japanese fighter airplane of World War II; the Mitsubishi 00.

zest *n.* Relish; gusto; enthusiasm.—**zest·ful** *adj.*

Zeus (*zooss*) *n. Greek Mythology.* The supreme divinity among the gods of Olympus; Jupiter.

zig·zag *v.* [zig·zagged; zig·zag·ging] To move alternately right and left with sudden, sharp right-angled turns.—**zig·zag** *adj.*

zinc *n.* White metallic element used in alloys, galvanizing, and electrical work. (*Symbol:* Zn).

zin·ni·a (*zin-*ee-uh) *n.* Small American shrub related to the aster and bearing richly colored double flowers.

Zi·on (*zy-*un) *n.* 1. Ancient sacred hill in Jerusalem, forming the center of Hebrew religious and national life. 2. The celestial city. 3. The church.—**Zi·on·ism** *n.* A movement seeking to make Palestine the Jewish homeland.—**Zi·on·ist** *n.*

zip *v.* (zipped; zip·ping) To whizz; flash past.—*n.* 1. *Slang.* Vigor; energy. 2. A swift, shooting movement.

ZINNIA

zip·per *n.* A slide fastener.—**zip·per** *v.*

zir·con (*zer-*kon) *n.* A mineral ore of zirconium, used, when transparent, as a gem.

zir·co·ni·um (*zer-koh-*nee-um) *n.* A common heat- and acid-resisting metallic element used in alloys. (*Symbol:* Zr).

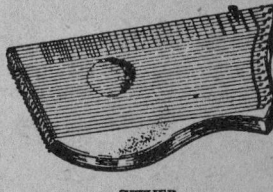

zith·er (*zith-*er) *n.* Also **zith·ern.**

ZITHER

Stringed lyre-like musical instrument.

Zo·di·ac (*zoh*-dee-ak) *n. Astronomy.* An imaginary zone in the heavens, divided into twelve equal parts, called signs, and encompassing the paths of the sun, moon, and major planets.

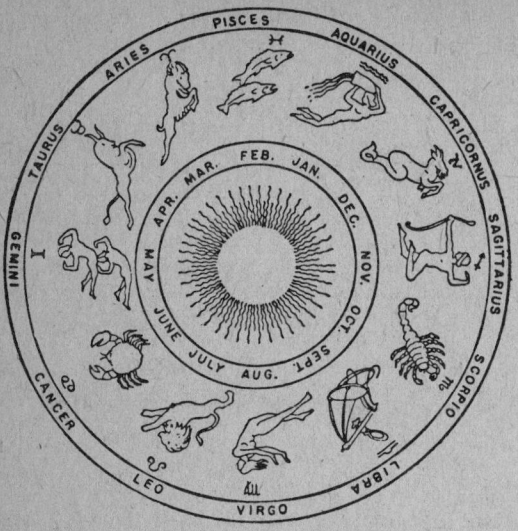

SIGNS OF THE ZODIAC

zom·bi (*zom*-bee) *n.* Also **Zom·bie. 1.** A corpse physically reanimated by a supernatural spirit. **2.** In voodoo, the snake god. **3.** A large, strongly alcoholic drink concocted of four or five types of rum and small amounts of fruit juices and brandy.

zone *n.* **1.** A region; area. **2.** *Geography.* One of the five latitudinal and climatic divisions of the earth's surface: the Torrid Zone, bisected by the equator, and the two Temperate and Frigid zones approaching either pole. **3.** A transport or postal region marked off for de-termination of fare or postage rates.—*v.* [zoned; zon·ing] **1.** To regulate building construction by law. **2.** To divide into zones.

zoo *n.* A park for exhibiting animals in captivity.

zo·ol·o·gy (zoh-*ol*-uh-jee) *n.* The natural science studying the physiology, classification, and habits of animals.—**zo·o·log·i·cal** *adj.*—**zo·ol·o·gist** *n.*

zoom *v.* **1.** To move with a heavy humming sound. **2.** *Aeronautics.* To climb at a steeper angle than may be maintained in continuous flight.—**zoom** *n.*

Zo·ro·as·tri·an (zor-oh-*ass*-tree-un) *adj.* Pertaining to the ancient Iranian religion developed by Zoroaster from the early Aryan folk-beliefs, teaching that there exists a permanent warfare between a good and an evil being, manifested by human history.—**Zo·ro·as·tri·an·ism** *n.*

Zou·ave (zoo-*ahv*) *n.* Infantryman, originally Algerian, in the French Army, characterized by a spectacular uniform.

Zu·lu (*zoo*-loo) *n.* A member of a southeastern-African tribe.—**Zu·lu** *adj.*

Zu·ñi (*zoo*-nyee) *n.* Member of a tribe of New Mexican pueblo Indians.

zwie·back (*swee*-bok; *zwy*-bak) *n.* A hard, slightly sweet toasted bread.

Zwing·li·an (*zwing*-glee-un) *n.* A follower of the Swiss reformer, Zwingli, who diverged from Luther in seeking broad reforms in church administration as well as theology, and in recognizing a symbolical experience alone in Holy Communion.—**Zwing·li·an** *adj.*—**Zwing·li·an·ism** *n.*—**Zwing·li·an·ist** *n.*

zy·gote (*zy*-goht) *n.* A cell formed by the conjugation of two similar sex cells.

Z

GAZETTEER

NOTE: All population figures for cities are for the city proper, unless marked by a dagger [†], in which case they include either suburbs or metropolitan districts.

Abbreviations:

dept. — department
Is. — Island
SFSR — Soviet Federated Socialist Republic
SSR — Soviet Socialist Republic
U.S. — United States
USSR — Union of Soviet Socialist Republics

□ — square miles
* — capital
P. — population
N,S,E,W — North, South, East, West (when followed by period, word is part of proper place name).

A

Adelaide (ad-uh-layd) City * of S. Australia. P. 770,628.
Aegean Islands (uh-jee-un) Islands, Aegean Sea SW of Turkey.
Afghanistan (af-gan-is-tan) Kingdom in S central Asia. □ 253,861. P. 15,909,000 * Kabul.
Africa (af-rih-kuh) Continent. □ 11,626,283. P. 318,290,000.
Agra (ahg-rah) City, N central India. P. 517,699.
Ahmedabad (ah-med-ah-bahd) City, W India. P. 1,285,447.
Ajmer (aj-meer) City, central India. P. 242,777.
Akron (ak-r'n) City, Ohio. P. 290,351.
Alabama (al-uh-bam-uh) State, southern U.S. □ 51,609. P. 3,266,740 * Montgomery.
Alaska (uh-lass-kuh) State, NW N. America. □ 586,400. P. 226,167 * Juneau.
Albania (al-bay-nee-uh) Mountainous country in S Europe. □ 11,100. P. 1,914,000 * Tirana.
Albany (awl-buh-nee) City * New York. P. 128,011.
Alberta (al-ber-tuh) Province, SW Canada. □ 255,285. P. 1,331,944 * Edmonton.
Alexandria (al-ig-zan-dree-uh) Port city, N Egypt. P. 1,587,700.
Algeria (al-jeer-ee-uh) Republic, formerly in French Union, N. Africa. □ 919,591. P. 12,102,000 * Algiers.
Algiers (al-jeerz) Port city * of Algeria. P. 883,879.
Allahabad (al-uh-hah-bahd) City * of United Provinces. P. 455,158.
Allentown (al-'n town) City, Pennsylvania. P. 108,347.
Alma-Ata (ahl-mah-ah-tah) City * of Kazakh SSR. P. 653,000.
America (uh-mehr-uh-kuh). See North, South, and Central America.
Amoy (ah-moy) Port city. SE China. P. 240,000.
Amsterdam (am-ster-dam) City * Netherlands. P. 868,159.
Andaman and Nicobar Islands (an-duh-man, nik-oh-bahr) Islands, Indian Ocean, province of India. □ 3,143. P. 63,548.
Andorra (ahn-doh-ruh) Republic in Pyrenees under French protection. □ 179. P. 14,408.
Angola (an-goh-luh) Overseas province of Portugal, SW Africa. □ 481,351. P. 5,084,000 * Luanda.
Annapolis (uh-nap-uh-lus) City * Maryland. P. 23,385.
Antigua (an-teeg-wah) One of the British Leeward islands. □ 108. P. 54,304 * St. John.
Antwerp (ant-werp) City, N Belgium, P. 657,485.
Archangel (ahrk-ayn-jul) Port city, NW USSR. P. 298,000.
Argentina (ahr-j'n-tee-nuh) Republic, S. America. □ 1,072,068. P. 22,700,000 * Buenos Aires.
Arizona (air-uh-zoh-nuh) State, SW U.S. □ 113,909. P. 1,302,161 * Phoenix.
Arkansas (ahr-k'n saw) State, S central U.S. □ 53,102. P. 1,786,272 * Little Rock.
Armenian SSR (ahr-mee-nee-un) Republic, SW USSR. □11,661. P. 2,253,000 * Yerevan.
Ascension Island (uh-sen-sh'n) British island colony, S. Atlantic. □ 34. P. 600 * Georgetown.
Asia (ay-zhuh) Largest continent of earth. □ 18,519,568 P. 1,868,979,000.

Astrakhan (ass-truh-kan) City, SW USSR. P. 361,000.
Athens (ath-inz) City * of Greece. P. 1,852,709.
Atlanta (at-lan-tuh) City * of Georgia. P. 487,455.
Auckland (awk-l'nd) Port city, N New Zealand. P. 548,300.
Augusta (aw-guss-tuh) City * of Maine. P. 21,680.
Austin (awss-tin) City * of Texas. P. 186,545.
Australia (aw-strayl-yuh) Continent, S Pacific. □ 2,967,902. P. 11,651,340 * Canberra.
Austria (awss-tree-uh) Republic, central Europe. □ 32,374. P. 7,290,000 * Vienna.
Azerbaidzhan SSR (ah-zer-by-jahn) Republic, southern USSR. □ 33,345. P. 4,802,000 * Baku.
Azores (uh-zohrz, ay-zohrz) Portuguese Islands, N. Atlantic. □ 922. P. 327,480 * Ponta Delgada.

B

Baghdad (bag-dad) City * of Iraq. P. 2,124,323.
Bahamas (buh-hay-muz) British Islands, West Indies. □ 4,404. P. 138,700 * Nassau.
Bahia (buh-hee-uh, bah-ee-uh) Port city (also called Salvador), E. Brazil. P. 630,878.
Bahrein Islands (bah-hrayn) British Islands, Persian Gulf. □ 213. P 193,000 * Manamah.
Baku (bah-koo) City * Azerbaidzhan SSR. P. 1,175,000.
Balearic Islands (bal-ee-air-ik) Islands, Mediterranean Sea, forming province of Spain. □ 1,936. P. 443,327 * Palma.
Bali and Lombok (bah-lee, lom-bok) Islands, U.S. of Indonesia. □ 3,973. P. 2,200,000.
Baltimore (bawl-tih-mohr) City, Maryland. P. 939,024.
Bangalore (bang-uh-lohr) City, S India. P. 959,803.
Bangkok (bang-kok) City * of Thailand. P. 2,318,000.
Barbados (bahr-bay-dohz) Independent island nation in West Indies. □ 166. P. 245,000 * Bridgetown.
Barcelona (bahr-s'l-oh-nuh) Port city, NE Spain. P. 1,696,756.
Batavia. See Jakarta.
Baton Rouge (bat-'n-roozh) City * Louisiana. P. 152,419.
Bavaria (buh-vehr-ee-uh) State, S Germany. □ 32,369. P. 9,514,000 * Munich.
Belém [Para] (bel-enh) Port city, N Brazil. P. 516,000.
Belfast (bel-fast) City * Northern Ireland. P. 406,800.
Belgium (bel-j'm) Kingdom, western Europe. □ 11,781. P. 9,528,000 * Brussels.
Belgrade (bel-grayd) City * of Yugoslavia. P. 700,000.
Benares (buh-nah-reez) City, E central India. P. 573,558.
Bengal, Eastern (ben-gawl) Province, E Pakistan. □ 42,192. P. 42,062,610.
Bengal, West Province, NE India. □ 33,928. P. 34,967,634 * Calcutta.
Berlin (ber-lin) Divided city, Germany. P. 3,256,800.
Bermuda (ber-myoo-duh) British Islands, N. Atlantic. □ 19. P. 48,355 * Hamilton.
Bhutan (boo-tahn) Semi-independent kingdom, S central Asia. □ 18,000. P. 750,000 * Thimbu.
Bihar (bee-hahr) Province, NE India. □ 67,198. P. 46,457,042 * Patna.

Birmingham (*ber*-meen-'m) City, central England. P. 1,102,570.
Birmingham (*ber*-meen-ham) City, Alabama. P. 340,887.
Bismarck (*biz*-mahrk) City * of N. Dakota. P. 27,670.
Bismarck Archipelago. British mandated islands E of New Guinea. □ 19,200.
Bochum (*boh*-k'm, *bok*-um) City, W Germany. P. 356,900.
Bogotà (boh-guh-*tah*) City * of Colombia. P. 1,980,000.
Boise (*boy*-zee) City * of Idaho. P. 34,481.
Bolivia (buh-*liv*-ee-uh) Republic, W central S. America. □ 424,163. P. 4,136,400 * LaPaz.
Bologna (buh-*lon*-yuh) City, N Italy. P. 483,000.
Bombay. Port city, W India. P. 4,563,687.
Bordeaux (bawr-*doh*) Port city, SW France. P. 254,122.
Borneo (*bohr*-nee-oh, *bawr*-) Large island, Indonesia, divided into Kalimantan, Sarawak, Brunei, and N. Borneo.
Boston (*bawss*-t'n) City * of Massachusetts. P. 697,197.
Botswana (bahtz-*wah*-nuh) Republic [former Bechuanaland], S Africa. □ 275,000. P. 576,000 * Gaberones.
Bradford (*brad*-ferd) City, N England. P. 297,100.
Brazil (bruh-*zil*) Republic, eastern S. America. □ 3,286,-473. P. 84,679,000 * Brasilia.
Bremen (*bray*-m'n) State, NW Germany. □ 99. P. 724,800.
Bremen. Port city, NW Germany. P. 592,400.
Bridgeport (*brij*-pawrt) City, Conn. P. 156,748.
Brisbane (*briz*-bayn, -b'n) Port city * Queensland. P. 777,935.
Bristol (*briss*-t'l) City, S England. P. 429,370.
British Columbia. Province, SW Canada. □ 366,255. P. 1,629,082 * Victoria.
British Empire. A term used to designate the United Kingdom of Great Britain and Northern Ireland, the Indian Empire, the colonial or dependent empire, and the self-governing Dominions.
British Guiana (gee-*an*-uh) Former British colony, NE S. America. Now Guyana.
British Honduras (hon-*door*-uss) British colony, NE Central America. □ 8,867. P. 103,000 * Belize.
British Isles. See United Kingdom.
British N. Borneo. See Sabah.
Brno (*ber*-noh) City, SW Czechoslovakia. P. 325,332.
Bronx, The. Borough, New York City. P. 1,424,815.
Brooklyn. Borough, New York City. P. 2,627,319.
Brunei (broo-*nye*) British protectorate, island of Borneo. □ 2,226. P. 104,000 * Brunei.
Brunswick. City, N central Germany. P. 236,200.
†**Brussels** (*bruss*-'lz) City * of Belgium. P. 1,065,921.
Bucharest (byoo-ker-*est*, boo-) City * of Rumania. P. 1,372,130.
†**Budapest** (byoo-duh-*pest*, boo-) City * of Hungary. P. 1,928,000.
Buenos Aires (*boh*-nuss-*ehr*-eez, *bwayn*-uss-*eye*-reez) City *of Argentina. P. 2,966,816.
Buffalo (*buf*-uh-loh) City, New York. P. 532,759.
Bulgaria (bul-*gehr*-ee-uh) Republic, S central Europe. □ 42,729. P. 8,258,000 * Sofia.
Burma (*ber*-muh) Republic, S central Asia. □ 261,789. P. 25,246,000 * Rangoon.
Burundi (ber-*roon*-dee) Country, E central Africa. □ 10,747. P. 3,274,000 * Bujumbura.
Byelorussian SSR. Republic, western USSR. □ 82,131. P. 8,744,000 * Minsk.

C

Cairo (*ky*-roh) City * of Egypt. P. 3,518,000.
Calcutta (kal-*kut*-uh) City, E India. P. 3,026,436.
California (kal-uh-*fawrn*-yuh) State, W coast U.S. □ 158,693. P. 18,084,000 * Sacramento.
Cambodia (kam-*boh*-dee-uh) Kingdom, SE Asia. □ 69,898. P. 6,250,000 * Pnom-Penh.
Cambridge (*kaym*-brij) City, Massachusetts. P. 107,716.
Camden (*kam*-d'n) City, New Jersey. P. 117,759.
Cameroon (kam-er-*oon*) Federal republic in W Africa. □183,569. P. 5,229,000 * Yaoundé.
Canada (*kan*-uh-duh) N. American Dominion, British Commonwealth of Nations. □ 3,851,809. P. 20,014,880 * Ottawa.
Canary Islands, Islands, Atlantic Ocean, province of Spain. □ 2,807. P. 944,448 * Santa Cruz.
Canton (*kan*-tahn) Port city, SE China. P. 1,867,000.
Canton (*kan*-t'n) City, Ohio. P. 113,631.
Cape of Good Hope. Province, Republic of South Africa. □ 277,169. P. 3,926,931 * Capetown.

Capetown. City, legislative * of Republic of S. Africa. P. 807,211.
Cape Verde Islands (kayp-*verd*) Portuguese islands, Atlantic Ocean. □ 1,557. P. 201,500 * Praia.
Caracas (kuh-*rak*-us) City * of Venezuela. P. 1,638,860.
Cardiff (*kahr*-dif) Port city, Wales. P. 259,705.
Carson City. City * of Nevada. P. 5,163.
Casablanca (*kahss*-uh-*blahn*-kuh, *kass*-uh-*blan*-kuh) Port city, W Morocco. P. 965,277.
Catania (kuh-*tahn*-yuh) City, E Sicily. P. 383,739.
Cayman Islands (*kye*-m'n) British islands, West Indies. □ 104. P. 7,662.
Celebes (*sel*-uh-beez) Islands, Republic of Indonesia. □ 72,886. P. 6,000,000.
Central African Republic. Former French territory of Ubangi-Shari, central Africa. □ 236,293. P. 2,088,000 * Bangui.
Central America. Narrow neck of land connecting N. and S. America.
Ceylon (see-*lahn*) Island, member of British Commonwealth, S of India. □ 25,332. P. 11,500,000 * Colombo.
Chad. African republic. □ 495,753. P. 3,500,000 * Fort Lamy.
Changsha (*chahng*-shah) City, SE China. P. 709,000.
Channel Islands. British islands. English channel. □ 75. P. 110,500 * St. Helier, St. Peter Port.
Charleston (*chahrlz*-t'n) City * W. Virginia. P. 85,796.
Charlotte (*shahr*-l't) City, N. Carolina. P. 201,564.
Chattanooga (chat-'n-*oo*-guh) City, Tennessee. P. 130,009.
Chelyabinsk (chel-*yah*-binsk) City, central USSR. P. 820,000.
Cheyenne (shy-*en*) City * of Wyoming. P. 43,505.
Chicago (shuh-*kah*-goh) City, Illinois. P. 3,550,404.
Chile (*chil*-ee) Republic along SW coast S. America. □ 286,322. P. 9,200,000 * Santiago.
China (*chy*-nuh) Republic, E. central Asia. □ 3,760,339. P. 760,300,000 * Peking.
Chungking (*chung-king*) City, S central China. P. 2,165,000.
Cincinnati (sin-suh-*nat*-ee) City, Ohio. P. 502,550.
Cleveland (*kleev*-l'nd) City, Ohio. P. 876,050.
Cologne (kuh-*lohn*) City, W Germany. P. 854,500.
Colombia (kuh-*lum*-bee-uh) Republic, NW S. America. □ 455,335. P. 18,700,000 * Bogota.
Colombo (kuh-*lum*-boh) Port city * Ceylon. P. 510,947.
Colorado (kol-er-*ad*-oh, -*od*-oh) State, western U.S. □ 104,247. P. 1,753,947 * Denver.
Columbia (kuh-*lum*-be-uh) City * S. Carolina. P. 97,433.
Columbus (kuh-*lum*-b'ss) City * Ohio. P. 471,316.
Concord (*kon*-kawrd) City * New Hampshire. P. 28,991.
Congo (*kon*-goh) Republic, central Africa. Former French Congo. □ 132,046. P. 840,000 * Brazzaville.
Congo Republic of the, central Africa. Former Belgian Congo. □ 905,563. P. 15,986,000 * Kinshasa.
Connecticut (kuh-*net*-ih-kut) State, NE U.S. □ 5,009. P. 2,535,234 * Hartford.
Copenhagen (kohp-'n-*hay*-g'n) Port city * of Denmark. P. 1,342,878.
Córdoba (*kawr*-doh-vuh) City, central Argentina. P. 635,000.
Corsica (*kawr*-sih-kuh) Island, Mediterranean Sea, forming department of France. □ 3,367. P. 275,465 * Ajaccio.
Costa Rica (*koss*-tuh-*ree*-kuh) Republic, Central America. □ 19,575. P. 1,486,000 * San José.
Cracow (*kray*-koh, *krak*-ow) City, SW Poland. P. 509,000.
Crete (*kreet*) Island S of, and forming district of, Greece. □ 3,330. P. 483,258 * Candia.
Croydon (*kroy*-d'n) City, SE England. P. 253,430.
Cuba (*kyoo*-buh) Island republic, Caribbean Sea. □ 44,217. P. 7,833,000 * Havana.
Curaçao (kyoor-uh-*soh*) Dutch island territory N of Venezuela. □ 403. P. 125,100 * Willemstad.
Cyprus (*sy*-pruss) Island republic, Mediterranean Sea. □ 3,572. P. 603,000 * Nicosia.
Czechoslovakia (chek-uh-sloh-*vak*-ee-uh) Republic, Central Europe. □ 49,321. P. 14,240,000 * Prague.

D

Dacca (*dak*-uh) City, Pakistan. P. 556,712.
Dahomey (duh-*hoh*-mee, -may) Republic, W Africa. □ 43,483. P. 2,410,000 * Porto Novo.
Dairen (*dy*-ren) Port city, S Manchuria. P. 1,590,000.
Dakar (dah-*kahr*) Capital and chief city of the Republic of Senegal, W Africa. P. 374,700.
Dallas (*dal*-iss) City, Texas. P. 679,684.

Danzig (*dant*-sig) Port city and territory (also called Gdansk), N Poland, formerly free city. P. 313,500.
Dayton (*day*-t'n) City, Ohio. P. 262,332.
Delaware (*del*-uh-wehr) State, E coast U.S. ☐ 2,057. P. 446,292 * Dover.
Delhi (*del*-ee) Territory, N central India. ☐ 9,573. P. 2,658,612 * Delhi.
Delhi. City * Delhi Territory. P. 2,369,464.
Denmark (*den*-mahrk) Kingdom, northern Europe. ☐ 16,619. P. 4,797,000 * Copenhagen.
Denver. City * of Colorado. P. 493,887.
Des Moines (dih-*moyn*, -*moynz*) City * of Iowa. P. 208,982.
Detroit (dih-*troyt*) City, Michigan. P. 1,670,144.
District of Columbia. Federal district co-extensive with city of Washington.
Djakarta (juh-*kahr*-tuh) City, NW Java * of Indonesia. P. 2,906,533.
Dnepropetrovsk (dyneh-proh-pyeh-*trawfsk*) City, SE Ukranian SSR. P. 790,000.
Dominican Republic (duh-*min*-ih-kun) Republic, E half Hispaniola Is., Caribbean Sea. ☐ 18,816. P. 3,452,000 * Ciudad Trujillo.
Donetsk (duh-*netsk*) City [formerly Stalino], SW European USSR. P. 823,000.
Dortmund (*dawrt*-m'nd) City, NW Germany. P. 656,000.
Dover (*doh*-ver) City * of Delaware. P. 7,250.
Dresden (*drez*-d'n) City, E Germany. P. 503,859.
Dublin (*dub*-lin) City * of Eire. P. 537,448.
Duisburg-Hamborn (*dyooz*-berg-*ham*-bawrn) City, western Germany. P. 501,123.
Duluth (duh-*looth*) City, Minnesota. P. 106,884.
Dusseldorf (doo-s'l-dawrf) City, western Germany. P. 703,989.
Dutch Guiana. See Surinam.
Dutch New Guinea. See New Guinea, West; Indonesia.

E

Ecuador (*ek*-wuh-dawr) Republic, NW S. America. ☐ 116,270. P. 5,326,000 * Quito.
Edinburgh (*ed*'-n-ber-oh) City * of Scotland. P. 468,765.
Egypt (*ee*-j'pt) United Arab Republic, NE Africa, ☐ 386,000. P. 30,147,000 * Cairo.
Eire [Ireland] (*eh*-ruh, *ehr*-uh) Southern part, island W of Great Britain. ☐ 26,601. P. 2,849,000 * Dublin.
Elizabeth (ih-*liz*-uh-b'th) City, New Jersey, P. 107,698.
El Paso (*pas*-oh) City, Texas. P. 276,687.
El Salvador (*sal*-vuh-dawr) Republic, Central America. ☐ 8,260. P. 3,037,000 * San Salvador.
England (*ing*-l'nd) Country, United Kingdom. ☐ 50,870. P. 43,431,000 * London.
Equatorial Guinea. Republic, W Africa. Former Portuguese Guinea. ☐ 13,948. P. 544,184 * Bissau.
Erie (*ih*-ree) City, Pennsylvania. P. 138,440.
Eritrea (*ehr*-ih-tree-uh) Province of Ethiopia, NE Africa. ☐ 45,783. P. 2,000,000 * Asmara.
Essen. City, western Germany. P. 726,800.
Estonian SSR (es-*toh*-nee-'n) Republic, NW USSR. ☐ 18,525. P. 1,244,000 * Tallinn.
Ethiopia (ee-thee-*oh*-pee-uh) Country, E central Africa. ☐ 398,350. P. 23,000,000 * Addis Ababa.
Europe (*yoor*-up) Continent. ☐ 2,116,589. P. 675,000,000.
Evansville. City, Indiana. P. 141,543.

F

Faeroe Islands (*fehr*-oh) Danish Islands, N. Atlantic. ☐ 540. P. 34,596 * Thornshavn.
Falkland Islands (*fawk*-l'nd) British islands off Argentina. ☐ 4,618. P. 2,172 * Port Stanley.
Fiji Islands (*fee*-jee) British islands, S. Pacific. ☐ 7,083. P. 413,000 * Suva.
Finland. Republic, NE Europe. ☐ 130,119. P. 4,650,000 * Helsinki.
Flint. City, Michigan. P. 196,940.
Florence (*flaw*-r'ns, *flah*-r'ns) City, N central Italy. P. 455,000.
Florida (*flaw*-ruh-duh, *flah*-) Southernmost state U.S. ☐ 58,560. P. 4,951,560 * Tallahassee.
Foochow. Port city, SE China. P. 400,000.
Formosa [Taiwan] (fawr-*moh*-suh) Large Chinese island SE of China. ☐ 13,880. P. 12,070,000 * Taihoku.
Fort Wayne. City, Indiana. P. 144,897.

Fort Worth. City, Texas. P. 356,268.
France (*franss*) Republic, western Europe. ☐ 212,918. P. 49,610,000 * Paris.
Frankfort (*frank*-f'rt) City, W central Germany. P. 690,900.
Frankfort. City * of Kentucky. P. 18,365.
French Guiana (gee-*an*-uh) Department, French Union, NE S. America. ☐ 34,740. P. 36,000 * Cayenne.
French India. Name given to French territories in India prior to their transfer to India.
French Indo-China. See Indo-China.
French Union. France and associated states, replaced by the French Community in 1958.
French West Africa. Former federation of eight French overseas territories, NW Africa.
Friendly Islands. See Tonga Islands.
Fukuoka (foo-koo-*oh*-kah) City, SW Japan. P. 771,679.
Fushun (foo-*shun*) City, S Manchuria. P. 985,000.

G

Gabon [Gabun] (guh-*bohn*) Republic, W central Africa. ☐ 102,089. P. 468,000 * Libreville.
Gambia (*gam*-bee-uh) Nation, British Commonwealth, W Africa. ☐ 4,068. P. 316,000 * Bathurst.
Gary (*gehr*-ee) City, Indiana. P. 178,320.
Gelsenkirchen (*gel*-z'n-kihr-k'n) City, western Germany. P. 373,600.
Geneva (juh-*nee*-vuh) City, Switzerland, seat of former League of Nations. P. 174,700.
Genoa (*jen*-uh-wuh) Port city, NW Italy. P. 848,000.
Georgia (*jawr*-juh) State, SE U.S. ☐ 58,876. P. 3,943,116 * Atlanta.
Georgian SSR (*jawr*-j'n) Republic, SW USSR. ☐ 26,911. P. 4,611,000 * Tbilisi.
Germany, Democratic Republic. E Germany. ☐ 41,659. P. 17,067,000 * East Berlin.
Germany, Federal Republic. W Germany. ☐ 95,742. P. 59,676,000 * Bonn.
Ghana (*gah*-nuh) Republic, W Africa, formed from Gold Coast and Togoland. ☐ 91,843. P. 7,945,000 * Accra.
Gibraltar (jih-*brawl*-ter) British colony, southern tip Spain. ☐ 2. P. 24,000.
Gilbert and Ellice Islands. British islands, S Pacific. ☐ 180. P. 50,000.
Glasgow (*glass*-goh) City, SW Scotland. P. 979,798.
Goa (*goh*-uh) Former Portuguese colony, SW India. ☐ 1,426. P. 626,978 * Nova Goa.
Gold Coast. Former British colony now comprising with Togoland the republic of Ghana.
Gorki (*gawr*-kee) City, W central USSR. P. 1,042,000.
Göteborg (*yeh*-tuh-bawrg) Port city, SW Sweden. P. 442,799.
Grand Rapids. City, Michigan. P. 177,313.
Graz (*grahtss*) City, SE Austria. P. 248,620.
Great Britain (*brih*-t'n). See United Kingdom.
Greece (*greess*) Kingdom, SE Europe. ☐ 50,269. P. 8,612,000 * Athens.
Greenland. Large Danish island, N. Atlantic. ☐ 839,782. P. 39,500 * Godthaab.
Guadeloupe (gaw-d'l-*oop*, gwah-) Department in French Union, W. Indies. ☐ 690. P. 306,000 * Basse-Terre.
Guam (*gwahm*) U.S. island. N. Pacific. ☐ 206. P. 67,044 * Agaña.
Guatemala (gwat-uh-*mahl*-uh) Republic, NW Central America. ☐ 42,042. P. 4,575,000 * Guatemala.
Guinea (*gin*-ee) Republic, W Africa. ☐ 94,925. P. 3,608,000 * Conakry.
Guyana (gee-*an*-uh) Country in NE S. America. ☐ 83,000. P. 662,000 * Georgetown.

H

Hague, The (*hayg*) City, seat of government of The Netherlands. P. 604,818.
Haiti (*hay*-tee) Republic, W half Hispaniola Is., Caribbean Sea. ☐ 10,695. P. 4,551,000 * Port-au-Prince.
Hakodate (*hah*-koh-dah-tuh) Port city, N Japan. P. 251,000.
Halle (*hah*-luh) City, central Germany. P. 274,402.
Hamburg (*ham*-berg) State, N Germany. ☐ 288. P. 1,854,000 * Hamburg.
Hamburg. Port city, N Germany. P. 1,854,000.

Hangchow. Port city, SE China. P. 784,000.
Hankow. City, SE China. P. 1,000,000.
Hanover (han-oh-ver) City, NW Germany. P. 559,000.
Harbin (hahr-bin) City, central Manchuria. P. 1,552,000.
Harrisburg. City * of Pennsylvania. P. 79,697.
Hartford (hahrt-ferd) City * of Connecticut. P. 162,178.
†Havana (huh-van-uh) City * of Cuba. P. 1,517,700.
Hawaii (huh-wy-uh) Fiftieth state of the U.S., Pacific Ocean. ☐ 6,454. P. 632,772 * Honolulu.
Hejaz (hej-ahz) State, W Saudi Arabia. ☐ 182,192. P. 2,000,000.
Helena (hel-in-uh) City * of Montana. P. 20,227.
Helsinki (hel-sin-kee) City * of Finland. P. 518,000.
Hesse (hess) State, W central Germany. ☐ 2,969. P. 4,814,400 * Darmstadt.
Hiroshima (hihr-oh-shee-muh) City, SW Japan. P. 791,000.
Holland (hol-'nd). See Netherlands.
Honduras (hon-door-us) Republic, Central America. ☐ 43,277. P. 2,363,000 * Tegucigalpa.
Hong Kong. British colony, SE China. ☐ 391. P. 3,739,900. * Victoria.
Honolulu (hon-uh-loo-loo) City * of Hawaii. P. 294,179.
Houston (hyooss-t'n) City, Texas. P. 938,219.
Howrah (how-rah) City, eastern India. P. 1,611,373.
Hsinking (sheen-jeeng) City [now called Changchun] S central Manchuria. P. 975,000.
Hull [Kingston upon Hull] Port city, NE England. P. 298,000.
Hungary (hun-ger-ee) Republic, central Europe. ☐ 35,911. P. 10,119,000 * Budapest.
Hyderabad (hy-der-uh-bad) Former state, now partitioned, S central India.
Hyderabad. City * of Andhra Pradesh state. P. 2,062,995.

I

Iceland (eyess-l'nd) Island republic, N. Atlantic. ☐ 39,768. P. 196,549 * Reykjavik.
Idaho (eye-duh-hoh) State, NW U.S. ☐ 83,557. P. 667,191 * Boise.
Illinois (il-uh-noy) State, midwestern U.S. ☐ 56,400. P. 10,081,158 * Springfield.
India (in-dee-uh) Republic, British Commonwealth of Nations, S central Asia. ☐ 1,261,597. P. 483,000,000 * New Delhi.
Indiana (in-dee-an-uh) State, central U.S. ☐ 36,291. P. 4,662,498 * Indianapolis.
Indianapolis (in-dee-'n-ap-'l-iss) City * Indiana. P. 476,258.
Indo-China. Former federation of states consisting of Cambodia, Laos, and Viet Nam.
Indonesia. Islands and archipelago N of Australia (formerly Netherlands Indies).
Indonesia, Republic of. ☐ 735,865. P. 110,000,000 * Djakarta.
Indore (in-dohr) City, W central India. P. 395,000.
Iowa (eye-uh-wuh) State, central U.S. ☐ 56,280. P. 2,757,537 * Des Moines.
Iran (eye-ran, ee-rahn) Kingdom, western Asia. ☐ 636,293. P. 25,780,000 * Tehran.
Iraq (ee-rahk) Kingdom, western Asia. ☐ 173,259. P. 8,261,521 * Baghdad.
Ireland (eyre-l'nd). See Eire.
Irkutsk (ihr-kootsk) City, S central Russian SFSR. P. 409,000.
Isfahan (iss-fuh-hahn, -han) City, W central Iran. P. 339,909.
Isle of Man. Island, Irish Sea, part of United Kingdom. ☐ 227. P. 48,200 * Douglas.
Israel (iz-ray-el) Republic, Western Asia. ☐ c.7,800. P. 2,643,000 * Tel Aviv.
Istanbul (iss-tahn-bool) City, NW Turkey. P. 2,302,438.
Italy (it-'l-ee) Republic, southern Europe. ☐ 116,303. P. 52,736,000 * Rome.
Ivory Coast, Republic of the, W Africa. ☐ 127,520. P. 3,835,000 * Abidjan.

J

Jackson. City * of Mississippi. P. 144,420.
Jacksonville. City, Florida. P. 201,030.
Jamaica (juh-may-kuh) Island nation, West Indies. ☐ 4,411. P. 1,859,800 * Kingston.
Japan (juh-pan) Island nation, western Pacific. ☐ 142,741. P. 98,865,955 * Tokyo.

Java and Madura (jah-vuh, mah-doo-rah) Islands, Republic of Indonesia. ☐ 51,032. P. 63,059,575.
Jefferson City. City * of Missouri. P. 28,228.
Jersey City (jer-zee) City, New Jersey. P. 276,101.
Johannesburg (joh-han-iss-berg) City, S Transvaal. P. 1,152,525.
Johore (juh-hohr) State, Malaysia. ☐ 7,670. P. 1,126,000.
Jordan [Trans-Jordan] Kingdom, W Asia. ☐ 34,820. P. 1,976,000 * Amman.

K

Kalinin (kah-leen-in) City, NW European USSR. P. 299,000.
Kanpur (kawn-poor) City, central India. P. 987,227.
Kansas (kan-zuss) State, central U.S. ☐ 82,276. P. 2,178,-611 * Topeka.
Kansas City. City, Missouri. P. 475,539.
Kansas City. City, Kansas. P. 121,901.
Karachi (kuh-rach-ee) Port city * of Pakistan. P. 1,912,598.
Karelo-Finnish SSR (kuh-reel-oh-fin-ish) Republic, NW USSR. ☐ 76,440. P. 649,000 * Petrozavodsk.
Kashmir (kash-meer) State, N India. ☐ 84,516. P. 3,560,976 * Srinagar.
Kassel (kahss-'l) City, W central Germany. P. 214,700.
Kazakh SSR (kah-zahk) Republic, central Asiatic USSR. ☐ 1,066,533. P. 12,413,000 * Alma-Ata.
Kazan (kah-zahn) City, E central European USSR. P. 743,000.
Kedah (kay-dah) State, Malaysia. ☐ 3,648. P. 817,000.
Kelantan (kuh-lahn-tahn) State, Malaysia. ☐ 5,713. P. 596,000.
Kentucky (k'n-tuk-ee) State, E central U.S. ☐ 40,395. P. 3,038,156 * Frankfort.
Kenya (ken-yuh) Republic, E central Africa. ☐ 224,960. P. 9,643,000 * Nairobi.
Kharkov (khar-kawf, -kof) City, S central European USSR. P.1,092,000.
Kiel (keel) Port city, N Germany. P. 270,803.
Kiev (kee-ev, -ef) City, SW European USSR. P. 1,383,000.
Kirghiz SSR (keer-geez) Republic, central Asiatic USSR. ☐76,642. P. 2,740,000 * Frunze.
Knoxville (nokss-vil) City, Tennessee. P. 172,734.
Kobe (koh-bee) Port city, SE Japan. P. 1,216,579.
Korea, North (koh-ree-uh) NE Asia. ☐ 46,768. P. 12,100,000 * Pyongyang.
Korea, South, NE Asia. ☐ 38,031. P. 29,194,379 * Seoul.
Krasnodar (krahss-noh-dahr) City, S European USSR. P. 395,000.
Kuibyshev (kwee-bih-shef) City, E central European USSR. P. 969,000.
Kure (koo-ray) City, SE Japan. P. 224,000.
Kuwait (koo-wyte) Sheikhdom, NE of Saudi Arabia. ☐ 6,178. P. 468,000 * Al Kuwait.
Kwantung (kwan-tung) Province, S China, on the South China Sea. ☐ 89,400. P. 35,900,000.
Kyoto (kyoh-toh) City, S central Japan. P. 1,364,000.

L

Labrador. See Newfoundland and Labrador.
Lahore (luh-hohr) City * of Punjab Province, Pakistan. P. 1,296,477.
Lansing. City * of Michigan. P. 107,807.
Laos (lay-ohss) Kingdom, SE Asia. ☐ 91,428. P. 3,000,000 * Vientiane.
LaPaz (luh-pahss) City * of Bolivia. P. 420,000.
La Plata (luh-plah-tuh) City, eastern Argentina. P. 410,000.
Latvian SSR (lat-vee-'n) Republic, NW USSR. ☐ 24,695. P. 2,285,000 * Riga.
Lebanon (leb-uh-n'n) Republic, W central Asia, on Mediterranean Sea. ☐ 4,015. P. 2,405,000 * Beirut.
Leeds. City, N central England. P. 508,790.
Leicester (less-ter) City, central England. P. 283,540.
Leipzig (lype-sig) City, central Germany. P. 595,203.
Leningrad (len-in-grad, -grahd) City, NW European USSR P. 3,665,000.
Lesotho (luh-soh-thoh) Kingdom, SE Africa. Former Basutoland. ☐ 11,716. P. 859,000 * Maseru.
Liberia (ly-beer-ee-uh) Republic, W Africa. ☐ 43,000. P. 1,090,000 * Monrovia.
Libya (lib-ee-uh) Kingdom, N. Africa. ☐ 679,358. P. 1,677,000 * Tripoli.

Liechtenstein (*lik*-t'n-styne) Independent principality, W central Europe. □ 62. P. 19,917 * Vaduz.

Lille (*leel*) City, NE France. P. 199,033.

Lima (*leem*-uh) City * of Peru. P. 2,093,435.

Lincoln (*lin*-k'n) City * of Nebraska. P. 128,521.

Lisbon (*liz*-b'n) City * of Portugal. P. 817,326.

Lithuanian SSR (lith-oo-*ayn*-ee'n) Republic, NW USSR. □ 26,173. P. 3,026,000 * Vilnius.

Little Rock. City * of Arkansas. P. 107,813.

Liverpool. Port city, NW England. P. 712,040.

Lodz (*ludzh*) City, W Poland. P. 737,400.

†London (*lun*-d'n) City * of England, the United Kingdom, and the British Empire. P. 10,975,000.

Long Beach. City, California. P. 344,168.

Los Angeles (lawss-*an*-guh-luss, -juh-luss) City, California. P. 2,479,015.

Louisiana (loo-eez-ee-*an*-uh) State, southern U.S. □ 48,523. P. 3,257,022 * Baton Rouge.

Louisville (*loo*-ee-vil) City, Kentucky. P. 389,044.

Lowell (*loh*-ul) City, Massachusetts. P. 92,107.

Lucknow (*luk*-now) City, N central India. P. 662,196.

Luxemburg (*luk*-s'm-berg) Independent Grand Duchy, NW Europe. □ 999. P. 335,000 * Luxemburg.

Lwow (*lvoof*) City, W Ukraine SSR. P. 502,000.

Lyon (lee-*ohn*) City, SE France. P. 535,784.

M

Macao (muh-*kow*) Portuguese colony, SE China. □ 6. P. 280,000.

Madagascar (mad-ug-*gass*-ker) Republic, French Community, Indian Ocean. □ 228,000. P. 6,336,000 * Antananarivo.

Madeira (muh-*deer*-uh) Islands. N. Atlantic, district of Portugal. □ 314. P. 268,900 * Funchal.

Madison (*mad*-uh-s'n) City * of Wisconsin. P. 157,844.

Madras (muh-*drass*, -*drahss*) State, SE India. □ 126,166. P. 33,686,953 * Madras.

Madras. Port city, SE India. P. 1,864,813.

Madrid (muh-*drid*) City * of Spain. P. 2,599,330.

Madura (*mad*-joo-ruh) City, SE India. P. 452,123.

Magdeburg (*mag*-duh-berg) City, E central Germany. P. 265,141.

Maine (*mayn*) State, NE U.S. □ 33,215. P. 969,265 * Augusta.

Makeevka (mah-*kay*-ef-kuh) City, SW European USSR. P. 410,000.

Málaga (*mal*-uh-guh) Port city, S Spain. P. 324,949.

Malagasy (mal-uh-*gass*-ee). See Madagascar.

Malawi (muh-*law*-wee) Nation, British Commonwealth, SE Africa. Former Nyasaland. □ 36,100. P. 4,042,000 * Zomba.

Malaya (muh-*lay*, *may*-lay) region SE Asia, S Malay Peninsula.

Malaysia. Federation, SE Asia, comprising Malaya, Sabah, and Sarawak. □ 128,430. P. 9,661,000 * Kuala Lumpur.

Maldive Islands (*mal*-dyve) Sultanate. Islands off Ceylon, Indian Ocean. □ 112. P. 97,000 * Malé.

Mali. Republic of, W Africa. □ 464,874. P. 4,576,000 * Bamako.

Malta (*mawl*-tuh) Island nation, Mediterranean Sea. □ 122. P. 325,000 * Valletta.

Manchester (*man*-ches-ter) City, NW England. P. 625,250.

Manchuria (man-*choo*-ree-uh) Area comprising three NE provinces of China. □ 404,428. P. 60,000,000.

Manhattan (man-*hat*-'n) Borough, New York City. P. 1,698,281.

Manitoba (man-uh-*toh*-buh) Province, central Canada. □ 246,512. P. 921,686 * Winnipeg.

Mannheim (*man*-hyme) City, W Germany. P. 326,900.

Mariupol (mah-ree-*oo*-pohl) City [now called Zhdanov], SW European USSR. P. 373,000.

Marseilles (mahr-*saylz*, -*say*) Port city, SE France. P. 783,738.

Martinique (mahr-t'n-*eek*) Department, French Community, West Indies. □ 386. P. 303,000 * Fort-de-France.

Maryland (*mer*-uh-l'nd) State, eastern U.S. □ 10,577. P. 3,100,689 * Annapolis.

Massachusetts (mass-uh-*choo*-sitss) State, NE U.S. □ 8,257. P. 5,148,578 * Boston.

Mauritania (mawr-ih-*tayn*-ee-uh) Republic, W Africa. □ 419,230. P. 1,070,000 * Nouakchott.

Mauritius (moh-*rish*-uss) Republic, Indian Ocean □ 720. P. 759,000 * Port Louis.

Melbourne (*mel*-bern) City * of Victoria. P. 2,228,511.

Memphis (*mem*-fiss) City, Tennessee. P. 497,524.

Mexico (*mek*-sih-koh) Republic, southern N. America. □ 758,259. P. 44,100,000 * Mexico City.

Mexico City. City * of Mexico. P. 3,118,059.

Miami (my-*am*-uh, -ee) City, Florida. P. 291,688.

Michigan (*mish*-uh-g'n) State, N central U.S. □ 58,216. P. 7,823,194 * Lansing.

Milan (mih-*lan*) City, N Italy. P. 1,672,000.

Milwaukee (mil-*waw*-kee) City, Wisconsin. P. 741,324.

Minneapolis (min-ee-*ap*-'l-is) City, Minnesota. P. 482,872.

Minnesota (min-ih-*soh*-tuh) State, N central U.S. □ 84,068. P. 3,413,864 * St. Paul.

Minsk (*meensk*) City * of Byelorussian SSR. P. 749,000.

Miquelon. See St. Pierre and Miquelon.

Mississippi (miss-uh-*sip*-ee) State, southern U.S. □ 47,716. P. 2,178,141 * Jackson.

Missouri (muh-*zoo*-ree) State, central U.S. □ 69,674. P. 4,318,813 * Jefferson City.

Moldavian SSR (mol-*day*-vee-'n) Republic, SW USSR. □ 13,012. P. 3,425,000 * Kishev.

Molucca Islands (moh-*luk*-uh) Islands, Republic of Indonesia. □ 25,000 P. 700,000.

Monaco (*mon*-uh-koh) Principality, Mediterranean coast of France. □ 0.6 P. 22,297 * Monaco.

Mongolian Peoples Republic (formerly Outer Mongolia) Republic NE Asia. □ 592,664. P. 1,104,000 * Ulan Bator.

Mongolia, Inner (mon-*goh*-lee-uh) Republic, comprising three northern provinces of China.

Montana (mon-*tan*-uh) State, western U.S. □ 147,138. P. 674,767 * Helena.

Montevideo (mon-tuh-*vid*-ee-oh, mon-tuh-vi-*day*-oh) City *of Uruguay. P. 1,173,114.

Montgomery (mont-*gum*-ree) City * of Alabama. P. 134,393.

Montpelier (mont-*peel*-yer) City * of Vermont. P. 8,782.

Montreal (mont-ree-*awl*) City, SE Canada. P. 2,553,000.

Morocco (muh-*rok*-oh) Kingdom, NW Africa. □ 172,834. P. 13,451,000 * Rabat.

Moscow (*mos*-kow, -koh) City * of USSR. P. 6,412,000.

Mozambique (mohz-'m-*beek*) Portuguese province, SE Africa. □ 297,731. P. 6,956,000 * Lourenco-Marques.

Mukden (muk-*den*) City, S Manchuria. P. 2,411,000.

Munich (*myoon*-ik) City, S Germany. P. 1,210,500.

Muscat and Oman (*muhss*-kat, oh-*mahn*) Sultanate, SE Arabia. □ 82,000. P. 750,000 * Muscat.

Mysore (my-*soh*, -*sawr*) State, S India. □ 74,210. P. 23,586,772 * Bangalore.

N

Nagasaki (nag-uh-*sah*-kee) Port city, SW Japan. P. 404,000.

Nagoya (nuh-*goy*-uh) City, SE Japan. P. 1,935,430.

Nagpur (nag-*poor*) City, central India. P. 713,577.

Nanking (*nan*-king) City, S. China. P. 1,419,000.

Naples (*nay*-pl'z) City, SW Italy. P. 1,240,000.

Nashville. City * of Tennessee. P. 170,874.

Natal (nuh-*tal*) Province, Republic of S. Africa. □ 35,284. P. 2,979,200 * Pietermaritzburg.

Nauru (nah-*oo*-roo) Island under U.N. trusteeship, S. Pacific. □ 8. P. 5,561.

Nebraska (nuh-*brass*-kuh) State, central U.S. □ 77,237. P. 1,411,330 * Lincoln.

Nejd (*nezhd*, *nayd*) State, central Saudi Arabia. □ 413,792. P. 5,000,000.

Nepal (nih-*pawl*) Kingdom, S central Asia. □ 54,362. P. 10,294,000 * Katmandu.

Netherlands (*neth*-er-l'ndz) Kingdom, western Europe. □ 15,800. P. 12,455,000 * Amsterdam; seat of gov't: The Hague.

Nevada (nuh-*vad*-uh, nuh-*vah*-duh) State, western U.S. □ 110,540. P. 285,278 * Carson City.

Newark (*nyoo*-erk, *noo*-) City, New Jersey. P. 405,220.

New Bedford. City, Massachusetts. P. 102,477.

New Brunswick (*brunz*-wik) Province, SE Canada. □ 27,985. P. 597,936 * Fredericton.

New Caledonia (kal-uh-*dohn*-yuh) Islands, French Community, S. Pacific. □ 7,335. P. 86,500 * Nouméa.

Newcastle (*nyoo*-kass-'l, *noo*-) City, NE England. P. 253,780.

New Delhi. City * of India, central India. P. 294,565.

Newfoundland and Labrador (*nyoo*-f'nd-land, *lab*-ruh-dawr) Canadian Province, NE coast N. America. □ 152,734. P. 457,853.

New Guinea (*gin*-ee) Large island S. Pacific, comprising West New Guinea, N.E. New Guinea, and Papua.

New Guinea, N.E. Australian Trust Territory, New Guinea Island. □ 93,000. P. 1,576,000.

New Guinea, West [also called West Irian], Territory under control of Indonesia. □ 159,375. P. 750,000 * Kotabaru.

New Hampshire (*hamp*-sher) State, NE U.S. □ 9,304. P. 606,921 * Concord.

New Haven (*hay*-v'n) City, Connecticut. P. 152,048.

New Hebrides (*heb*-ruh-deez) Fr.-Brit. protectorate, S. Pacific. □ 5,790. P. 65,000 * Vila.

New Jersey (*jer*-zee) State, Eastern U.S. □ 7,836. P. 6,066,782. * Trenton.

New Mexico (*mek*-sih-koh) State, SW U.S. □ 121,666. P. 951,023 * Santa Fe.

New Orleans (*awr*-lee-'nz) City, Louisiana. P. 640,000.

New South Wales. State, SE Australia. □ 409,432. P. 4,965,400 * Sydney.

New York. State, eastern U.S. □ 49,576. P. 17,915,000 * Albany.

New York. City, New York. P. 8,086,000.

New Zealand (*zee*-l'nd) Dominion, British Commonwealth of Nations, S. Pacific. □ 103,415. P. 2,712,251 * Wellington.

Nicaragua (nik-uh-*rahg*-wuh) Republic, Central America. □ 53,938. P. 1,655,000 * Managua.

Nice (*neess*) Port city, SE France. P. 294,976.

Niger (*ny*-jer, -ger) Republic of the, W Africa. □ 489,190. P. 3,433,000 * Niamey.

Nigeria (ny-*jeer*-ee-uh) Republic, member of British Commonwealth of Nations, W Africa. □ 356,669. P. 57,500,-000 * Lagos.

Ningpo (*ning*-poh) Port city, E China. P. 237,500.

Norfolk (*nawr*-f'k) City, Virginia. P. 304,869.

North America (uh-*mehr*-uh-kuh) Continent, W. Hemisphere. □ 8,780,661. P. 299,022,000.

North Carolina (kair-uh-*ly*-nuh) State, SE U.S. □ 52,712. P. 4,556,155 * Raleigh.

North Dakota (duh-*koh*-tuh) State, N central U.S. □ 70;665. P. 632,446 * Bismarck.

Northern Ireland (*eyre*-l'nd) Country of United Kingdom, N of Eire. □ 5,451. P. 1,478,000 * Belfast.

Northern Territory. Territory, N Australia. □ 523,620. P. 47,500.

N.W. Frontier Region, West Pakistan. □ 39,259. P. 7,563,000 * Peshawar.

N.W. Territories. Territory, NW Canada. □ 1,309,682. P. 22,928.

Norway (*nawr*-way) Kingdom, northern Europe. □ 125,181. P. 3,753,000 * Oslo.

Nottingham (*not*-ing-'m) City, central England. P. 311,850.

Nova Scotia (noh-vuh-*skoh*-shuh) Province, SE Canada. □ 21,428. P. 737,007 * Halifax.

Novosibirsk (noh-voh-sih-*beersk*) City, W Asiatic USSR. P. 1,013,000.

Nuremberg (*nyoo*-r'm-berg, *noo*-) City, S Germany. P. 472,000.

Nyasaland (ny-*ass*-uh-land) Former British protectorate, now the independent nation of **Malawi.**

O

Oakland. City, California. P. 367,548.

Odessa (oh-*dess*-uh) Port city, SW European USSR. P. 753,000.

Ohio (oh-*hy*-oh) State, central U.S. □ 41,222. P. 9,706,397 * Columbus.

Oklahoma (ohk-luh-*hoh*-muh) State, S central U.S. 69,919. P. 2,328,284 * Oklahoma City.

Oklahoma City. City * of Oklahoma. P. 324,253.

Olympia (oh-*lim*-pee-uh) City * of Washington. P. 18,273.

Omaha (*oh*-muh-haw, -hah) City, Nebraska. P. 301,579.

Oman. See Muscat and Oman.

Omsk. City, W Asiatic USSR. P. 746,000.

Ontario (on-*tehr*-ee-oh) Province, S central Canada. □ 412,582. P. 6,236,092 * Toronto.

Oporto (oh-*pohr*-toh, oh-*pawr*-toh) Port City, NW Portugal. P. 305,445.

Orange Free State. Province, Republic of S. Africa. □ 49,647. P. 1,386,547 * Bloemfontein.

Oregon (*aw*-rih-gon) State, W coast U.S. □ 96,981. P. 1,768,687 * Salem.

Orissa (uh-*riss*-uh) State, E India on the Bay of Bengal. □ 60,164. P. 17,548,846.

Orkney Islands (*awrk*-nee) Islands N of, and forming county of, Scotland. □ 392. P. 18,700 * Kirkwall.

†**Osaka** (oh-*sah*-kuh) Port city, SE Japan. P. 3,214,330.

Oslo (*oz*-loh, *oss*-loh) City * of Norway. P. 484,747.

Ottawa (*ah*-tuh-wah) City * of Canada. P. 494,535.

P

Pakistan (pak-iss-*tan*) Moslem republic, S Asia. □ 365,529. P. 105,044,000 * Islamabad.

Palermo (puh-*ler*-moh) City * of Sicily. P. 618,327.

Panama (*pan*-uh-mah) Republic, S Central America. □ 29,208. P. 1,287,000 * Panama City.

Panama Canal Zone. U.S. area surrounding Panama Canal, Panama. □ 553. P. 54,000.

Papua (*pap*-yoo-uh) Australian Territory, SE New Guinea. □ 90,540. P. 573,000 * Port Moresby.

Paraguay (*par*-uh-gway, -gwye) Republic, S central S. America. □ 157,047. P. 2,094,000 * Asuncion.

Paris (*par*-iss) City * of France. P. 2,811,171.

Paterson. City, New Jersey. P. 143,663.

Peking (*pee*-*king*) City * China. P. 4,010,000.

Pemba. See Tanganyika.

Pennsylvania (pen-s'l-*vayn*-yuh) State, eastern U.S. □ 45,333. P. 11,319, 366 * Harrisburg.

Peoria (pee-*oh*-ree-uh) City, Illinois. P. 103,162.

Perak (*pay*-rak) State, Malaysia. □ 7,980. P. 1,449,200.

Perlis (*per*-liss) State, Malaysia. □ 316. P. 106,000.

Perm. City, W Asiatic USSR. P. 785,000.

Pernambuco (per-n'm-*byoo*-koh). See Recife.

Persia (*per*-zhuh). See Iran.

Perth. City * of Western Australia. P. 558,297.

Peru (puh-*roo*) Republic, western S. America. □ 496,222. P. 12,012,000 * Lima.

Philadelphia (fil-uh-*delf*-yuh) City, Pennsylvania. P. 2,050,000.

Philippines, Republic of the (*fil*-uh-peenz) Islands off SE coast Asia. □ 115,707. P. 33,477,000 * Manila.

Phoenix (*fee*-nikss) City * of Arizona. P. 439,170.

Pierre (*pir*) City * of S. Dakota. P. 10,088.

Piraeus (py-*ree*-uss) Port city, E Greece. P. 183,957.

Pitcairn Island (*pit*-kehrn) British island, S. Pacific. □ 2. P. 90.

Pittsburgh (*pitss*-berg) City, Pennsylvania. P. 604,332.

Plymouth (*plim*-uth) Port city, SW England. P. 213,800.

Poland (*poh*-l'nd) Republic, NE Europe. □ 120,664. P. 31,698,000 * Warsaw.

Poona (*poo*-nuh) City, W India. P. 721,134.

Portland. City, Maine. P. 72,566.

Portland. City, Oregon. P. 372,676.

Porto Alegre (*por*-toh-ah-*leg*-ree) Port city, S Brazil. P. 840,000.

Portsmouth (*pawrtss*-muth) Port city, S England. P. 213,980.

Portugal (*pohr*-chuh-g'l, *pawr*-) Republic, western Europe. □ 35,582. P. 9,107,000 * Lisbon.

Potsdam. City, N central Germany. P. 109,867.

Poznan (poz-*nahn*) City, W Poland. P. 431,700.

Prague (*prayg*, *prahg*) City * of Czechoslovakia. P. 1,017,156.

Prince Edward Island, Island province, SE Canada. □ 2,184. P. 104,629 * Charlottetown.

Providence (*prov*-uh-d'nss) City * of Rhode Island, P. 207,498.

Puerto Rico (pwehr-tuh-*ree*-koh) Island commonwealth in association with U.S., Caribbean Sea. □ 3,435. P. 2,572,000 * San Juan.

Punjab (pun-*jahb*) State of India. □ 47,205. P. 20,306,812 * Chandigarh.

Q

Quebec (kwih-*bek*) Province, eastern Canada. □ 594,534. P. 5,259,211 * Quebec.

Quebec. City * of Quebec province, Canada. P. 166,984.

Queens (*kweenz*) Borough, New York City. P. 1,809,578.

Queensland. State, NE Australia. □ 670,500. P. 1,518,528 * Brisbane.

R

Raleigh (*raw*-lee) City * of North Carolina. P. 93,931.

Rangoon (ran-*goon*) City * of Burma. P. 821,800.

Recife [Pernambuco] (reh-*see*-fuh) Port city, E Brazil. P. 1,006,000.

Reading (*red*-ing) City, Pennsylvania. P. 98,177.

Réunion (ree-*oon*-yun) Dept. in French Union, Indian Ocean. □ 970. P. 382,000 * St. Denis.

Rhode Island (*rohd*) State, NE U.S. □ 1,214, P. 859,848 * Providence.

Rhodesia (roh-*dee*-zhuh) Nation, S. Africa. □ 150,333. P. 4,400,000 * Salisbury.

Riau-Lingga Archipelago (*ree*-ow-*lin*-gah) Islands, Indonesia. □ 12,225. P. 278,966.

Richmond. City * of Virginia. P. 219,958.

Richmond. Borough, New York City. P. 221,991.

Riga (*ree*-guh) City * of Latvian SSR. P. 669,000.

Rio de Janeiro (*ree*-oh-duh-juh-*neer*-oh, -*nayr*-oh) City * of Brazil. P. 3,977,000.

Rochester (*rah*-chess-ter) City, New York. P. 305,849.

Romania (roo-*may*-nee-ah) Republic, SE Europe. □ 91,700. P. 19,150,000 * Bucharest.

Rome (*rohm*) City * of Italy. P. 2,328,930.

Rosario (roh-*sah*-ree-oh) City, E Argentina. P. 761,300.

Rostov (*ross*-tof) Port city, S European USSR. P. 737,000.

Rotterdam (*rot*-er-dam) Port city, SW Netherlands. P. 732,232.

Ruanda-Urundi (roo-*ahn*-dah-oo-*run*-dee) Former Belgian mandate, central Africa, now two independent states of Rwanda and Burundi.

Russian SFSR. Largest of the Soviet Socialist Republics, NE Europe and N Asia. □ 6,612,601. P. 127,312,000 * Moscow.

Rwanda (roo-*ahn*-dah) Republic, E central Africa. □ 10,166. P. 3,000,000 * Kigali.

S

Saarland (*sahr*-land) Industrial state, W Germany. □ 900. P. 1,072,600 * Saarbrucken.

Sabah (*sah*-bah) State, Federation of Malaysia. □ 29,388. P. 498,031 * Sandakan.

Sacramento (sak-ruh-*men*-toh) City * of California. P. 237,712.

St. Helena (huh-*lee*-nuh) British island colony, S. Atlantic. □ 47. P. 5,000 * Jamestown.

St. Louis (*loo*-is) City, Missouri. P. 711,000.

St. Paul (*pawl*) City * of Minnesota. P. 313,411.

St. Pierre and Miquelon Islands (pee-*ehr*, mik-uh-*lon*) Territory, French Community, S of Newfoundland. □ 93. P. 4,606 * St. Pierre.

Salem (*say*-l'm) City * of Oregon. P. 49,142.

Salonika (sal-uh-*neek*-uh, suh-*lon*-ik-uh) Port city, NE Greece. P. 309,205.

Salt Lake City. City * of Utah. P. 189,454.

Samoa, American (suh-*moh*-uh) U.S. islands, S. Pacific. □ 76. P. 24,000 * Pago Pago.

Samoa, Western. Former U.N. trusteeship, [now independent] New Zealand, S. Pacific. □ 1,133. P. 131,000 * Apia.

San Antonio (san-'n-*toh*-nee-oh) City, Texas. P. 587,718.

San Diego (dee-*ay*-goh) City, California. P. 573,224.

San Francisco (fr'n-*siss*-koh) City, California. P. 741,000.

San Marino (muh-*ree*-noh) Republic, N Italy. □ 38. P. 17,000 * San Marino.

Santa Fe (*san*-tuh-fay) City * of New Mexico. P. 34,676.

Santiago (san-tee-*ay*-goh, -*ah*-goh) City * of Chile. P. 2,550,000.

São Paulo (sow-*pow*-loo) City, SE Brazil. P. 5,251,000.

São Tomé and Principe Islands (sow-toh-*may*, princ-*see*-pay) Portuguese islands off W Africa. □ 372. P. 63,676 * São Tomé.

Saratov (sah-*rah*-tof) City, E European USSR. P. 669,000.

Sarawak (suh-*rah*-wahk) State, Malaysia, island of Borneo. □ 48,250. P. 809,737.

Sardinia (sahr-*din*-ee-uh) Island SW of, and forming dept. of, Italy. □ 9,301. P. 1,419,362 * Cagliari.

Saskatchewan (sass-*kach*-uh-wahn) Province, central Canada. □ 251,700. P. 925,181 * Regina.

Saudi Arabia (sah-oo-dee-uh-*ray*-bee-uh) Kingdom, SW Asia. □ 870,000. P. 8,000,000 * Riyadh.

Savannah (suh-*van*-uh) City, Georgia. P. 149,245.

Schaumburg-Lippe (*shown*-berg-*lip*-uh) Former state [now part of Lower Saxony] in (West) German Federal Republic.

Scotland (*skot*-l'nd) Country, United Kingdom. □ 30,405. P. 5,240,000 * Edinburgh.

Scranton (*skran*-t'n) City, Pennsylvania. P. 111.443.

Seattle (see-*at*-l) City, Washington. P. 557,087.

Selangor (say-*lahn*-gawr) State, Malaysia. □ 3,160. P. 1,159,900.

Sendai (*sen*-dye) City, NE Japan. P. 486,000.

Senegal (sen-ih-*gawl*) Republic, W Africa. □ 76,124. P. 3,400,000 * Dakar.

Seoul (say-*ool*, say-ul, *sohl*) City * of South Korea. P. 3,470,880.

Seville (suh-*vil*) City, S Spain. P. 531,571.

Seychelles Islands (say-*shelz*) British colony, Indian Ocean. □ 69. P. 45,000 * Victoria.

Shanghai (*shang*-hye) Port city, E China. P. 6,900,000.

Sheffield (*shef*-eeld) City, N central England. P. 486,490.

Shetland Islands. Islands NE of, and forming county of, Scotland. □ 550. P. 17,800 * Lerwick.

Shizuoka (shee-zoo-*oh*-kah) City, E central Japan. P. 363,000.

Sholapur (shoh-luh-*poor*) City, SW India. P. 357,750.

Shreveport (*shreev*-pawrt) City, Louisiana. P. 164,372.

Siam (sy-am, sy-am) See Thailand.

Sicily (*siss*-'l-ee) Island S of, and forming dept. of Italy. □ 9,926. P. 4,721,001 * Palermo.

Sierra Leone (see-*ehr*-uh-lee-*oh*-nee) Independent state, W Africa □ 27,699. P. 2,403,000 * Freetown.

Sikkim (*sik*-im) Protectorate, NE India. □ 2,818. P. 162,189 * Gangtok.

Sind. Former province, now merged into province of West Pakistan.

Singapore (*sing*-up-pohr, -pawr) Island republic, off Malay Peninsula. □ 225. P. 1,913,500 * Singapore.

Singapore. City * of Singapore. P. 1,820,000.

Sinkiang (*sin*-kyang) Autonomous region, NW China. □ 705,769. P. 6,500,000 * Urumchi.

Society Islands. Territory, French Community, S. Pacific (including Tahiti). □ 1,520. P. 54,450 * Papeete.

Socotra (soh-*koh*-truh) Island, South Arabia protectorate. □ 1,400. P. 12,000.

Soerabaya (soo-ruh-*bah*-yah) Port city, NE Java. P. 1,310,631.

Sofia (*soh*-fee-uh, soh-*fee*-uh) City * of Bulgaria. P. 800,953.

Solomon Islands (*sol*-uh-m'n) British islands, S. Pacific. □ 11,700. P. 133,000.

Somalia (soh-*mah*-lee-uh) Independent republic, E Africa. □ 246,202. P. 2,500,000 * Mogadishu.

Somerville (*sum*-er-vil) City, Massachusetts. P. 94,697.

Soochow (*soo*-chow) City, E China. P. 633,000.

South Africa, Republic of. □ 471,445. P. 18,298,000 * Pretoria.

South America (uh-*mehr*-uh-kuh) Continent, W. Hemisphere. □ 7,045,047. P. 180,000,000.

South Australia (awss-*trayl*-yuh) State, S Australia. □ 380,070. P. 1,025,000 * Adelaide.

South Bend. City, Indiana. P. 132,445.

South Carolina (kair-uh-*ly*-nuh) State, SE U.S. □ 31,055. P. 2,382,594 * Columbia.

South Dakota (duh-*koh*-tuh) State, central U.S. □ 77,047. P. 680,514 * Pierre.

Southern Yemen. Nation, S Arabia, comprising Aden and other former British states. □ 112,000. P. 1,500,000 * Medina as-Shaab.

S.W. Africa (*af*-ruh-kuh) Mandate, Republic of S. Africa. □ 317,725. P. 554,000 * Windhoek.

Spain (*spayn*) Country, SW Europe. □ 196,607. P. 31,871,000 * Madrid.

Spitzbergen (*spitts*-berg-'n) Norwegian islands, Arctic Ocean. □ 24,290. P. 4,000.

Spokane (spoh-*kan*) City, Washington. P. 181,608.

Springfield. City, Massachusetts. P. 174,463.

Springfield. City * of Illinois. P. 83,271.

Srinagar (sree-*nug*-er) City, N India. P. 295,084.

Stalingrad. See Volgograd.

Stalino. See Donetsk.

Stettin (shteh-*teen*) Port city, Poland. P. 302,900.

Stockholm (*stok*-hohm) City * of Sweden. P. 779,000.

Stoke-on-Trent (*stohk*) City, W central England. P. 276,300.

Stuttgart (*stut*-gert, -gahrt) City, SW Germany. P. 632,700.

Sudan, Republic of the, E central Africa. □ 967,500. P. 13,940,000 * Khartoum.

Sumatra (soo-*mah*-truh) Island, Indonesia. □ 182,900. P. 15,739,000.

Surinam (*soor*-ih-nahm, -nam) Autonomous region of the Netherlands [formerly Dutch Guiana], NE S. America. □ 55,400. P. 325,000 * Paramaribo.

Sverdlovsk (svehrd-*lofsk*) City, NW Asiatic USSR. P. 940,000.

Swaziland (*swah*-zee-land) Kingdom, S Africa. □ 6,705. P. 385,000 * Mbabane.

Sweden (*swee*-d'n) Kingdom, N Europe. □ 173,347. P. 7,847,395 * Stockholm.

Switzerland (*swit*-ser-l'nd) Republic, W central Europe. □ 15,944. P. 5,999,000 * Berne.
Sydney (*sid*-nee) City * of New South Wales. P. 2,539,627.
Syracuse (*sihr*-uh-kyooss) City, New York. P. 216,038.
Syria (*sihr*-ee-uh) Republic, western Asia. □ 72,234. P. 5,300,000 * Damascus.

T

Tabriz (tah-*breez*) City, NW Iran. P. 387,803.
Tacoma (tuh-*koh*-muh) City, Washington. P. 147,979.
Tadzhik SSR (tahd-*zeek*) Republic, N central Asia. □ 54,019. P. 2,654,000 * Stalinabad.
Taihoku (ty-*hoh*-koo) City * of Formosa [also called Taipei]. P. 979,100.
Tallahassee (tal-uh-*hass*-ee) City * of Florida. P. 48,174.
Tampa (*tam*-puh) City, Florida. P. 274,970.
Tanganyika. Former British territory now merged with Zanzibar and Pemba to form Tanzania.
Tangier (tan-*jeer*) Former internationalized zone, N. Morocco. □ 232. P. 141,714.
Tanzania (tan-*zay*-nee-uh) Republic, E Africa. □ 363,700. P. 10,578,000 * Dar es Salaam.
Tashkent (tahsh-*kent*) City * of Uzbek SSR. P. 1,140,000.
Tasmania (taz-*may*-nee-uh, -nyuh) Island S of, and forming state of, Australia. □ 26,215. P. 361,300 * Hobart.
Tbilisi (tbee-lee-*see*) City * of Georgian SSR. P. 830,000.
Tehran [Teheran] (teh-*rahn*) City * of Iran. P. 2,317,116.
Tennessee (ten-uh-*see*) State, southern U.S. □ 42,246. P. 3,567,089 * Nashville.
Texas (*tek*-suss) State, southern and SW U.S. □ 267,339. P. 9,579,677 * Austin.
Thailand [Siam] Kingdom SE Asia. □ 200,148. P. 31,508,000 * Bangkok.
Thuringia (thuh-*rin*-jee-uh) Former state, central Germany, now a region of East German Republic.
Tibet (tih-*bet*, *tib*-it) Chinese region, central Asia. □ 450,000. P. 1,300,000 * Lhasa.
Tientsin (*tyen-tsin*, tin-) Port city, NE China. P. 3,220,000.
Tiflis (*tif*-liss) See Tbilisi.
Timor (*tee*-mohr, -mawr) Island, Republic of Indonesia.
Timor, Portuguese. Colony, E half Timor island. □ 7,332. P. 536,000 * Dilly.
Tobago (tuh-*bay*-goh) Island, W. Indies, part of the state of Trinidad and Tobago. □ 116. P. 33,200 * Port of Spain.
Togo. Republic, W Africa. □ 20,400. P. 1,680,000 * Lomé.
†Tokyo (*toh*-kee-oh, -kyoh) City * of Japan. P. 11,021,579.
Toledo (tuh-*lee*-doh) City, Ohio. P. 318,003.
Tonga [Friendly] Islands (*ton*-guh) British protectorate, S. Pacific. □ 256. P. 70,000 * Nukualofa.
Tonkin (*ton-kin*) [Bac-Ky] Territory, North Vietnam. □ 43,800.
Topeka (tuh-*pee*-kuh) City * of Kansas. P. 119,484.
Toronto (tuh-*ron*-toh) City * of Ontario. P. 2,316,000.
Toulouse (too-*looz*) City, S France. P. 330,570.
Transvaal (transs-*vahl*, tranz-) Province, Republic of S. Africa. □ 110,450. P. 6,273,477 * Pretoria.
Trengganu (tren-*gah*-noo) State, Malaysia. □ 5,050. P. 331,000.
Trenton (*tren*-t'n) City * of New Jersey. P. 114,167.
Trieste, Free Territory of (tree-*est*) Port city, N Italy. P. 385,000.
Trinidad (*trin*-uh-dad) Island, West Indies, comprising with Tobago the independent state of Trinidad and Tobago. □ 1,979. P. 1,000,000 * Port of Spain.
Tristan de Cunha (triss-*tahn*-duh-*koon*-yah) Islands included in St. Helena.
Tsingtao (*tsing-tow*) Port city, E China. P. 1,121,000.
Tula (*too*-lah) City, W central European USSR. P. 371,000.
Tulsa (*tul*-suh) City, Oklahoma. P. 261,685.
Tunis (*tyoon*-iss, *toon*-) City * of Tunisia. P. 680,000.
Tunisia (tyoo-*nish*-ee-uh, too-) Republic, N. Africa. □ 58,000. P. 4,458,000 * Tunis.
Turin (*tyoor*-in, *toor*-) City, NW Italy. P. 1,114,300.
Turkey (*ter*-kee) Republic, SE Europe and N Asia. □ 296,500. P. 32,901,000 * Ankara.
Turkmen SSR (*terk*-men) Republic, N central Asia. □ 188,417. P. 1,971,000 * Ashkhabad.
Turks and Caicos Islands (*terkss*, *ky*-koss) Included in Jamaica.

U

Ufa (oo-*fah*) City, E European USSR. P. 683,000.

Uganda (yoo-*gan*-duh, yoo-*gahn*-duh) Independent state, E Africa. □ 91,134. P. 7,740,000 * Kampala.
Ukrainian SSR (yoo-*kray*-nee-'n) Republic, SW European USSR. □ 232,046. P. 45,966,000 * Kiev.
Ulster. Nine counties of Ireland, six of which are comprised in Northern Ireland.
Union of Soviet Socialist Republics. Federation of Soviet Socialist Republics, E Europe and N and central Asia. □ 8,647,172. P. 235,000,000 * Moscow.
United Arab Republic. See Egypt.
United Kingdom. Kingdom comprising Great Britain (England, Scotland, Wales, Channel Islands, Isle of Man) and Northern Ireland, off NW coast of Europe. □ 94,209. P. 54,744,000 * London.
United States of America (uh-*mer*-uh-kuh) Federal republic, N. America. □ 3,615,211. P. 204,300,000 * Washington, D.C.
Upper Volta. Republic, NW Africa. □ 105,869. P. 4,955,000 * Ouagadougou.
Uruguay (*yoor*-uh-gway, -gwye) Republic, SE S. America. □ 72,172. P. 2,845,734 * Montevideo.
Utah (*yoo*-taw, -tah) State, western U.S. □ 84,916. P. 890,627 * Salt Lake City.
Utica (*yoo*-tih-kuh) City, New York. P. 100,410.
Uttar Pradesh. State, N central India. □ 113,654. P. 73,746,401 * Lucknow.
Uzbek SSR (*uz*-bek) Republic, central Asia. □ 158,069. P. 10,896,000 * Tashkent.

V

Valencia (vuh-*len*-shee-uh, -shuh) City, E Spain. P. 583,151.
Valparaiso (val-puh-*ray*-soh, -ry-zoh) Port city, central Chile. P. 300,000.
Vancouver (van-*koo*-ver) City, SW British Columbia. P. 410,375.
Vatican City State (*vat*-ih-k'n) Independent Papal state, W central Italy. □ .50. P. 1,500.
Venezuela (ven-uh-*zweel*-uh) Republic, N coast S. America. □ 352,170. P. 9,189,282 * Caracas.
Venice (*ven*-iss) City, NE Italy. P. 363,000.
Vermont. State, NE U.S. □ 9,609. P. 389,881 * Montpelier.
Victoria (vik-*toh*-ree-uh, vik-*taw*-ree-uh) State, SE Australia. □ 87,884. P. 2,930,366 * Melbourne.
Vienna (vee-*en*-uh) City * of Austria. P. 1,634,253.
Vietnam, North. Republic. □ 61,293. P. 19,000,000 * Hanoi.
Vietnam, South. Republic. □ 65,948. P. 16,543,000 * Saigon.
Vilnius (*vil*-nee-us) City * of Lithuanian SSR. P. 282,000.
Virginia (ver-*jin*-yuh) State, SE U.S. □ 40,815. P. 3,966,949 * Richmond.
Virgin Islands. U.S. Islands, Caribbean Sea. □ 133. P. 32,099 * Charlotte Amalie.
Vladivostok (vlad-ih-*vahss*-tahk) Port city, SE Asiatic USSR. P. 379,000.
Volgograd (*vohl*-guh-grad) City [formerly Stalingrad], SE European USSR. P. 703,000.
Voronezh (voh-*roh*-nesh) City, S central European USSR. P. 592,000.

W

Wake Island. U.S. island N. Pacific. □ 4.
Wales (*waylz*) Country of United Kingdom. □ 7,469. P. 2,640,600 * Cardiff.
Warsaw (*wawr*-saw) City * of Poland. P. 1,232,000.
Washington (*wahsh*-ing-t'n) State, NW U.S. □ 68,192. P. 2,853,214 * Olympia.
Washington. City, District of Columbia, * of U.S. P. 798,000.
Waterbury (*waw*-ter-ber-ee) City, Connecticut. P. 107,130.
Wenchow (*wen-chow*) Port city, SE China. P. 631,276.
Western Australia (awss-*trayl*-yuh) State, W Australia. □ 975,920. P. 784,000 * Perth.
West Virginia (ver-*jin*-yuh) State, E central U.S. □ 24,181. P. 1,860,421 * Charleston.
Wichita (*wich*-uh-taw) City, Kansas. P. 254,698.
Wilmington (*wil*-ming-t'n) City, Delaware. P. 95,827.
Windward Islands. Former British colony, Caribbean Sea. □ 825. P. 546,700 * St. George's.
Winnipeg (*win*-uh-peg) City * of Manitoba. P. 257,005.
Wisconsin (wiss-*kon*-s'n) State, N central U.S. □ 56,154. P. 3,951,777 * Madison.

Worcester (*wuss*-ter) City, Massachusetts. P. 186,587.

Wroclaw (vrawt-*slahf*) City, W Poland. P. 465,600.

Wuppertal (*vup*-er-tahl) City, W Germany. P. 422,870.

Wyoming (wy-*oh*-ming) State, western U.S. ☐ 97,914. P. 330,066 * Cheyenne.

Yonkers. City, New York. P. 190,634.

Youngstown. City, Ohio. P. 166,689.

Yugoslavia (yoo-goh-*slahv*-ee-uh, -yuh) Republic, SE Europe. ☐ 98,766. P. 19,756,000 * Belgrade.

Yukon (*yoo*-kon) Territory, NW Canada. ☐ 207,076. P. 14,628 * Dawson.

Y

Yalta (*yahl*-tah) Port city, SW European USSR. P. 47,100.

Yaroslavl (yah-roh-*slahfl*) City, N central European USSR. P. 486,000.

Yemen (*yeh*-m'n, *yay*-) Arab Republic, SW Asia. ☐ 75,300. P. 5,000,000 * Sanaa.

Yerevan (yeh-reh-*vahn*) City * Armenian SSR. P. 601,000.

Yokohama (yoh-koh-*hah*-muh) Port city, E central Japan. P. 1,788,796.

Z

Zambia (*zam*-bee-uh) Republic, S central Africa. ☐ 288,130. P. 3,837,000 * Lusaka.

Zanzibar and Pemba. See Tanganyika.

Zaporozhe (zah-poh-*rozh*-yuh) City, SW European USSR. P. 571,000.

Zaragoza (thah-rah-*goh*-thah) City, NE Spain. P. 377,412.

Zurich (*zoor*-ik, *zyoor*-ik) City, N Switzerland. P. 434,000.